oscar

OSCAR® a to Z

A COMPLETE GUIDE TO MORE THAN 2,400 MOVIES NOMINATED FOR ACADEMY AWARDS®

Charles Matthews

MAIN STREET BOOKS

DOUBLEDAY

NEW YORK LONDON TORONTO SYDNEY AUCKLAND

A MAIN STREET BOOK

PUBLISHED BY DOUBLEDAY

A DIVISION OF BANTAM DOUBLEDAY DELL PUBLISHING GROUP, INC.

1540 BROADWAY, NEW YORK, NEW YORK 10036

MAIN STREET BOOKS, DOUBLEDAY, AND THE PORTRAYAL OF A BUILDING
WITH A TREE ARE TRADEMARKS OF DOUBLEDAY,
A DIVISION OF BANTAM DOUBLEDAY DELL PUBLISHING GROUP, INC.

BOOK DESIGN BY JULIE DUQUET

"OSCAR" AND "ACADEMY AWARDS" ARE REGISTERED TRADEMARKS OF THE
ACADEMY OF MOTION PICTURE ARTS AND SCIENCES. THIS BOOK IS NEITHER
AUTHORIZED NOR ENDORSED BY THE ACADEMY OF MOTION PICTURE ARTS AND SCIENCES.

LIBRARY OF CONGRESS CATALOGING-IN-PUBLICATION DATA

MATTHEWS, CHARLES.
    OSCAR A TO Z: A COMPLETE GUIDE TO MORE THAN 2,400 MOVIES NOMINATED FOR
ACADEMY AWARDS / CHARLES MATTHEWS.—1ST ED.
        P.   CM.
    "A MAIN STREET BOOK."
    1. ACADEMY AWARDS (MOTION PICTURES)—ENCYCLOPEDIAS.   2. MOTION PICTURES—
PLOTS, THEMES, ETC.—ENCYCLOPEDIAS.   I. TITLE.
    PN1993.92.M38   1995
    791.43'75—DC20   94-47288
                                                            CIP

ISBN 0-385-47364-8
COPYRIGHT © 1995 BY CHARLES MATTHEWS
ALL RIGHTS RESERVED
PRINTED IN THE UNITED STATES OF AMERICA
OCTOBER 1995

10 9 8 7 6 5 4 3 2 1

FIRST EDITION

contents

introduction

Every year in March, the world turns its attention to a ceremony at which overdressed and overpaid people gather to honor themselves: the Academy Awards.

As participants in the Oscar ceremonies never tire of reminding us, more than a billion people around the world watch this event, making it the World Series of glitz. We gather at our TV sets to gawk at improbable dresses and impractical hairstyles, to laugh at bad jokes and worse production numbers, to cheer our favorites and fume at undeserving winners —of which, over the years, there have been more than a few.

But for all their shortcomings, the Oscars actually mean something. The Academy's choice of the people and films it honors tells us a lot about how the American film industry sees itself, its political and social biases, and its pretensions—however lame—to art. And while there may be film awards that are more reliable indicators of a movie's lasting artistic value, only the label ''Oscar winner'' or ''Oscar nominee'' truly gives a picture cachet with most people.

This book is a guide to the more than 2,400 feature films that have competed for Oscars, from best picture nominees to contenders for best sound effects editing. Each entry provides—in addition to the film's title, the studio that produced or released it, and the year of release—the following information:

- The Academy Awards and nominations received by the film.
- A brief summary of the plot of the movie.
- A concise critical evaluation of the movie, reflecting the current critical consensus as well as my opinion.
- The stars and significant supporting players, the director, and other well-known behind-the-camera personnel, plus information on the production of the film.
- An assessment of the film's significance in the context of Oscar history: why it received the

sort of attention it did from the Academy and whether, from the lofty point of view of posterity, it deserved it.

- Biographical information on the winners or nominees, with a discussion of the Oscar's effect on their careers.
- In the case of losing nominees, who won the awards for which they were contenders.
- Cross-referencing of each winner or nominee to the other films for which he or she was nominated.

In addition to the entries for each film, the book also contains an index alphabetically listing all the people who were nominees, and an annotated list of the awards and nominations by year.

A Note on Numbering

Each film in this book has been given a number for convenient cross-referencing. But obviously, every year more films will have to be added, so to allow room for expansion I've used a decimal system. Otherwise, all the entries—as well as the cross-references —would have to be renumbered each year. I began work on the book after the 1991 awards, and the films that have received nominations and awards since then (plus a few accidental omissions from the original list) have decimal points in their numbers. So, for example, *Age of Innocence, The,* which had to be added between *Agatha,* no. 27, and *Agnes of God,* no. 28, is no. 27.5.

Within individual entries, there are also cross-references for people connected with the film who were not nominated for their work on it, but who received nominations at other times in their careers. E.g., ''Mark Rydell [1473] directed from a script by Irving Ravetch [956 . . .].'' Ellipsis dots indicate that the person was a multiple nominee; the number given is for the first entry listed in this book.

Entries are alphabetical by word: e.g., *I Dream Too Much* comes between *I Am a Fugitive From a Chain Gang* and *I Even Met Happy Gypsies,* and not between *Ice Station Zebra* and *If I Were King.* In the case of foreign-language titles beginning with a definite or indefinite article, these are alphabetized by the second word in the title: e.g., *Das Boot* as *Boot, Das, La Dolce Vita* as *Dolce Vita, La, I Vitelloni* as *Vitelloni, I,* and so on. (There are two exceptions to this rule: *El Cid,* because the title is the name of the film's leading character, and *Les Girls,* because the title is a macaronic joke and not a real French phrase.)

In a few instances—e.g., *À Nous la Liberté, B.F.'s Daughter,* and *G.I. Honeymoon*—data-entry errors caused the films to appear out of proper alphabetical sequence. *B.F.'s Daughter,* for example, should be the first entry in the *B*s, as *E.T. The Extra-Terrestrial* is the first entry in the *E*s. By the time these errors were discovered, correcting the order would have caused a monumental renumbering of the cross-references, so they were allowed to remain out of their proper sequence. Instead, references were inserted where they belong to direct readers to the full entries.

For Susan and Maggie
"The fundamental things apply . . ."

acknowledgments

Like Maureen Stapleton accepting her Oscar for *Reds,* I want to thank everyone I ever met in my whole life. But I won't.

I have to thank the Academy of Motion Picture Arts and Sciences and the staff of the National Film Information Service who were more than helpful in answering my questions and helping me track down information on some of the more obscure films in this book. Thanks, too, to the reference desk at the Palo Alto Public Library for pointing me in the right direction numerous times. I'm also grateful to Don Devich, sysop of the CompuServe Show Biz Forum, for pointing the way to some online sources.

I have owed a debt for many years to Russell Merritt, who first showed me how movies were made, and who taught me that they were a subject worthy of study. Over the years, Russell and his wife, Karen, have instructed, informed, and debated with me about movies, and their opinions and insights show up in one form or another throughout this book.

I'm also grateful to my editors at the *San Jose Mercury News' West* magazine, Patrick Dillon and Fran Smith, for their patience, encouragement, and enthusiasm as I went through the process of working on this project while also working for them. Fortunately, my fellow managing editor at *West,* Sheila Himmel, was there to take up the slack, and she can't know how glad I am that she was. I'm also indebted to the following colleagues at *West* for their observations on movies and the Oscars and their support of this project: Sue Chenoweth, Tracie Cone, Tracy Cox, Bob Frost, David E. Early, and Mike Weiss. And I feel obligated to mention some friends and former colleagues who over the years have either encouraged me as a writer or provided insights into the subject of this book: Wick Allison, Jim Atkinson, David Bauer, Betty Blaylock, David Blaylock, Jo Brans, Willem Brans, Steve Daniels, David Dillon, Susan Faludi, Jan Freeman, Elyse M. Friedman, Kathy Holub, Jeffrey Klein, Carol Doup Muller, David Riggs, Sue Riggs, Paul Solman, and Nancy Spiller.

That great enthusiast John Hubner has my undying gratitude for persuading me that this project made sense as a book, and for putting me in the hands of Joel E. Fishman, whom I thank for teaching me how to make it one. I'm fortunate, too, that at Doubleday I had the diligent and generous Bruce Tracy as an editor, and that the manuscript came under the sharp copy-editing gaze of Bill Betts.

But my greatest good fortune is that I have been nurtured and supported by two movie lovers, my wife, Susan, and my daughter, Maggie. They won't agree with everything they read in this book, but maybe they'll find some of their own observations here and there.

oscar

~ a to z ~

À NOUS LA LIBERTÉ
See 89.

1 • ABE LINCOLN IN ILLINOIS
MAX GORDON PLAYS AND PICTURES; RKO RADIO. 1940.
NOMINATIONS *Actor:* Raymond Massey. *Black-and-White Cinematography:* James Wong Howe.

Young Abe (Massey) comes out of the backwoods and falls in love with Ann Rutledge (Mary Howard), who dies. The ambitious Mary Todd, played by Ruth Gordon [11 . . .], sets her cap for him and finally lands him. The movie ends with the newly elected president leaving for Washington. Massey's fine performance captures Lincoln's wit and charisma but also his melancholia. The film is marred by lapses into historical pageantry, and director John Cromwell lets Gene Lockhart [36] ham away as Stephen A. Douglas. Although Gordon begins badly as the young Mary Todd, flouncing around almost campily, she becomes quite effective in her later scenes as the pushy but doom-haunted Mrs. Lincoln. The screenplay, based on the 1939 Pulitzer Prize–winning play by Robert E. Sherwood [184 . . .], is by Grover Jones [1116 . . .].

Massey had appeared in the play on Broadway, and it became his signature role. He played Lincoln again briefly in *How the West Was Won.* He also played abolitionist John Brown in *Santa Fe Trail* (1940) and *Seven Angry Men* (1955) as well as Junius Brutus Booth, the father of Lincoln's assassin, in *Prince of Players* (1955). Massey, who was born in Toronto, began his acting career on stage in England and moved into films with the arrival of sound. An important character player for nearly forty years, he died in 1983. His son, Daniel [1907], and daughter, Anna, have both had distinguished stage careers, primarily in Britain. The acting Oscar went to James Stewart for *The Philadelphia Story.* George Barnes won the cinematography award for *Rebecca.*

Howe: 30, 36, 738, 956, 1095, 1451, 1470, 1727, 1774.

2 • ABOVE AND BEYOND
MGM. 1953.
NOMINATIONS *Motion Picture Story:* Beirne Lay, Jr. *Scoring of a Dramatic or Comedy Picture:* Hugo Friedhofer.

Robert Taylor plays Col. Paul Tibbetts, the pilot of the plane that dropped the bomb on Hiroshima. The film's dramatic potential is watered down by too many domestic interludes between Tibbetts and his wife, played by Eleanor Parker [328 . . .], who keeps going into fits of pique because he's so secretive about his mission. Directed by Melvin Frank [636 . . .], Taylor gives his typically earnest but wooden performance. Contemporary audiences tend to giggle at the casting of Jim Backus as Gen. Curtis LeMay.

Frank and his frequent partner Norman Panama [636 . . .] coproduced the film and also wrote the screenplay based on Lay's story. The writing Oscar went to Dalton Trumbo (or actually to his front, Ian McLellan Hunter, because Trumbo was blacklisted) for *Roman Holiday.* Bronislau Kaper's score for *Lili,* oddly placed in the dramatic rather than the musical category, took the music award.

Lay: 1942. Friedhofer: 21, 184, 187, 214, 267, 1048, 2303, 2336.

3 • ABSENCE OF MALICE
MIRAGE ENTERPRISES PRODUCTION; COLUMBIA. 1981.
NOMINATIONS *Actor:* Paul Newman. *Supporting Actress:* Melinda Dillon. *Screenplay Written Directly for the Screen:* Kurt Luedtke.

Aggressive but unscrupulous newspaper reporter Sally Field [1448 . . .] writes a story that damages Newman's reputation and leads to Dillon's suicide. Effective press-bashing drama, directed by Sydney Pollack [1512 . . .], but screenwriter Luedtke, a former newspaperman, surely knows that Field wouldn't last long in the newsroom of any major urban daily. Pollack and Luedtke would later collaborate with greater success on *Out of Africa.* Newman lost to the sentimental favorite, Henry Fonda in *On Golden Pond,* and the supporting actress award went to Maureen Stapleton for *Reds.* The writing Oscar was won by Colin Welland for *Chariots of Fire.*

Newman: 372, 422, 443, 956, 964, 1444.5, 1645, 2198. Dillon: 416. Luedtke: 1512.

4 • ABSENT MINDED PROFESSOR, THE

WALT DISNEY PRODUCTIONS; BUENA VISTA. 1961.
NOMINATIONS *Black-and-White Cinematography:* Edward Colman. *Black-and-White Art Direction—Set Decoration:* Carroll Clark; Emile Kuri and Hal Gausman. *Special Effects:* Robert A. Mattey and Eustace Lycett.

Fred MacMurray plays a professor who discovers a substance called flubber—short for ''flying rubber'' —that makes cars and basketball teams fly. Likable family comedy, directed by Robert Stevenson [1284] from a screenplay by Bill Walsh [1284]. The cast includes Tommy Kirk, Keenan Wynn, Nancy Olson [1975], Leon Ames, and Ed Wynn [542]. Unlike most Disney live-action comedies of the period, this one was shot in black and white to control the costs of the special effects. The cost-cutting may have contributed to the loss to the more extravagant *The Guns of Navarone* in the effects category. The cinematography award went to Eugen Shuftan for *The Hustler,* which also took home the art direction Oscar.

Colman: 1284. Clark: 481, 686, 754, 1284, 1924, 2115. Kuri: 166, 363, 629, 894, 1284, 1823, 2155. Gausman: 166, 1022, 1284, 2185. Lycett: 166, 219, 1284.

5 • ABYSS, THE

20TH CENTURY FOX FILM PRODUCTION; 20TH CENTURY FOX. 1989.
AWARD *Visual Effects:* John Bruno, Dennis Muren, Hoyt Yeatman, and Dennis Skotak.
NOMINATIONS *Cinematography:* Mikael Salomon. *Art Direction—Set Decoration:* Leslie Dilley; Anne Kuljian. *Sound:* Don Bassman, Kevin F. Cleary, Richard Overton, and Lee Orloff.

A rescue crew from an offshore oil rig is sent out in futuristic underwater gear to a distressed nuclear submarine. In the deep they encounter watery aliens. For the most part it's exciting, but the movie lasts about half an hour too long and grows somewhat incoherent toward the end. Much of it was filmed in an abandoned nuclear power plant whose contain-

ment tanks were flooded with water. Director James Cameron and his cast, including Mary Elizabeth Mastrantonio [422], Ed Harris, and Michael Biehn, spent a large part of the grueling shoot in specially designed underwater gear. The movie was an expensive box-office flop, but the visual effects, particularly the computer-generated images of the aliens, provided a step toward Cameron's commercially more successful *Terminator 2.*

Freddie Francis won the cinematography Oscar for *Glory,* which also took the award for sound. The art direction award went to Anton Furst and Peter Young for *Batman.*

Bruno: 153.5, 413.5, 766, 1590, 2147.5. Muren: 577, 588, 614, 997, 1002, 1071.5, 1684, 2019, 2284, 2339. Skotak: 153.5. Salomon: 129. Dilley: 44, 614, 1652, 1916. Bassman: 544, 961, 1541. Cleary: 544, 961. Overton: 544, 961. Orloff: 761.5, 2019.

6 • ACCIDENTAL TOURIST, THE

WARNER BROS. PRODUCTION; WARNER BROS. 1988.
AWARD *Supporting Actress:* Geena Davis.
NOMINATIONS *Picture:* Lawrence Kasdan, Charles Okun, and Michael Grillo, producers. *Screenplay Based on Material From Another Medium:* Frank Galati and Lawrence Kasdan. *Original Score:* John Williams.

After the senseless death of their twelve-year-old son, William Hurt [293 . . .] and Kathleen Turner [1545] find their marriage falling apart, and they separate. He falls in love with an eccentric young woman (Davis) who trains dogs, but his emotional numbness puts a limitation on their relationship. Although faithful in literal ways to the novel by Anne Tyler on which it is based, the movie entirely misses the spirit of the book. Director Kasdan swamps the novel's affectionately humorous treatment of its characters with slow-paced storytelling and a melancholy tone, unfortunately reinforced by Williams' lugubrious score. Admirers of the novel find the movie frustratingly sketchy, and people who haven't read the book often find the movie's action and motivation baffling. Amy Wright, David Ogden Stiers, and Ed Begley, Jr., do amusing work as Hurt's eccentric siblings.

Critical reception was lukewarm and the box office only fair, which makes the film's inclusion among the best picture nominees something of a puzzle. The other nominees were an offbeat costume picture, *Dangerous Liaisons;* the controversial social drama *Mississippi Burning;* Mike Nichols' comic treatment of eighties corporate-ladder-climbing, *Working Girl;* and the winner, a buddy film with a twist, *Rain Man.* *Tourist* is the only heavy-duty psychological drama in this company, but the failure to nominate Kasdan as director indicates that the Academy probably never took it seriously as a contender. Among the films that perhaps deserved nominations instead are *Big, Pelle the Conqueror, A Fish Called Wanda, Married to the Mob, A Cry in the Dark, Gorillas in the Mist, The Unbearable Lightness of Being, The Last Temptation of Christ,* and *Who Framed Roger Rabbit.*

Davis is unquestionably the best thing about *Tourist,* though her nomination as supporting actress is questionable—the role is central to the film. She made her film debut in *Tootsie* as a soap-opera actress who, wearing next to nothing, embarrasses Dustin Hoffman in the dressing room. She also gave a fine performance opposite then-husband Jeff Goldblum in *The Fly* in 1986. *The Accidental Tourist* and the Oscar helped establish her as a major star, and she has developed a strong, wry screen presence in such films as *Thelma & Louise* and *A League of Their Own* (1992).

The writing award went to Christopher Hampton for *Dangerous Liaisons,* and Williams' score lost to Dave Grusin's for *The Milagro Beanfield War.*

Davis: 2039. Kasdan: 199, 811. Williams: 260, 403, 416, 588, 613, 614, 659, 805, 933, 937, 982, 996, 997, 1041, 1047, 1596, 1652, 1679, 1684, 1701, 1764.65, 1916, 1977, 2107, 2126, 2194, 2293, 2322.

7 • ACCUSED, THE
JAFFE/LANSING PRODUCTION; PARAMOUNT. 1988.
AWARD *Actress:* Jodie Foster.

Foster plays Sarah Tobias, a tough young blue-collar woman who is gang-raped in a bar. Kelly McGillis is the lawyer who reluctantly prosecutes the case, knowing that victims of rape often end up as the accused in such trials, especially when they're as uncompromising as Sarah. The story is loosely based on a notorious incident in New Bedford, Massachusetts, where patrons of a bar stood by and cheered as a young woman was raped on a pool table. Foster's powerful performance and Jonathan Kaplan's intelligent direction raise this film above its rather predictable courtroom histrionics.

Foster, who made her feature film debut at the age of ten in 1972, is one of the few child stars to make the transition to adult performer. Even as a child, she often specialized in tough, wise-beyond-their-years characters, as in *Taxi Driver* and *Alice Doesn't Live Here Anymore.* Her own ordeal by press, after an obsessed fan, John Hinckley, attempted to get her attention by trying to assassinate Ronald Reagan in 1981, may have provided some of the emotional subtext for her performance in *The Accused* as the unwilling object of media attention. The Oscar established her as the leading screen actress of her generation.

Foster: 1421.5, 1820, 2005.

8 • ACTION IN THE NORTH ATLANTIC
WARNER BROS. 1943.
NOMINATION *Original Story:* Guy Gilpatric.

Humphrey Bogart [24 . . .] is first mate and Raymond Massey [1] captain of a ship in the merchant marine whose convoy is attacked by German submarines. As in most such wartime dramas, the propaganda sometimes gets in the way, and too much of it is clearly taking place on a soundstage, but there's plenty of action. Ruth Gordon [11 . . .] plays Massey's wife. Directed by Lloyd Bacon. The screenplay, by John Howard Lawson [233], was based on a novel by Gilpatric, who lost to William Saroyan for *The Human Comedy.*

9 • ACTRESS, THE
MGM. 1953.
NOMINATION *Black-and-White Costume Design:* Walter Plunkett.

Stagestruck Jean Simmons [858 . . .] has to overcome the objections of her father, Spencer Tracy [131 . . .], when she decides to become an actress.

Teresa Wright [1182 . . .] plays her mother. A cast as strong as that can't help being watchable, but it's a rather thin little movie. Since it's based on the highly readable memoirs of Ruth Gordon [11 . . .] and directed by George Cukor [262 . . .], one expects more. Anthony Perkins [730] makes his screen debut in the film as the suitor that Tracy and Wright wish she'd give up her stage career for. The costuming Oscar went to Edith Head for *Roman Holiday*.

Plunkett: 66, 953, 1087, 1243, 1587, 1657, 1859, 2029, 2330.

10 • ADALEN '31
A.B. SVENSK FILMINDUSTRI PRODUCTION (SWEDEN). 1969.
NOMINATION *Foreign Language Film*.

A prolonged strike in a Swedish paper mill ends in violence; there is also a Romeo and Juliet–style romance between a worker's son and a manager's daughter. Bo Widerberg, who directed the 1967 sentimental romance *Elvira Madigan,* contrasts the sociopolitical struggle with the beauty of the setting, not entirely successfully. The Oscar went to *Z*.

11 • ADAM'S RIB
MGM. 1950.
NOMINATION *Story and Screenplay:* Ruth Gordon and Garson Kanin.

Lawyer Katharine Hepburn [24 . . .] goes up in court against her husband, lawyer Spencer Tracy [131 . . .]. Hepburn is defending Judy Holliday [262], accused of shooting her philandering husband, Tom Ewell. (She just wounded him.) Wonderful in all respects. Tracy and Hepburn are finely supported by Holliday, Jean Hagen [1831] as the other woman, and David Wayne as a songwriting neighbor modeled on Cole Porter [261 . . .] (he also sings a bottom-drawer Porter song, ''Farewell, Amanda''). This was the second collaboration of director George Cukor [262 . . .] with Gordon and Kanin—their first was *A Double Life*—and the good chemistry of director, writers, and stars is evident. So why only one Oscar nomination? Perhaps because this was the year of *All About Eve* and *Sunset Boulevard,* which dominated the nominations; the script by Charles Brackett, Billy Wilder, and D. M. Marshman, Jr., for *Sunset Boulevard* defeated *Adam's Rib* in the story and screenplay category. And that year, Tracy was nominated for *Father of the Bride* and Holliday and Cukor for *Born Yesterday*. The teaming of Tracy, Hepburn, Cukor, Gordon, and Kanin two years later for *Pat and Mike* met a similar fate at Oscar time. But *Adam's Rib* has endured, even spawning a short-lived TV sitcom.

Gordon: 567, 1003, 1536, 1728. Kanin: 567, 1536.

12 • ADDAMS FAMILY, THE
SCOTT RUDIN PRODUCTION; PARAMOUNT. 1991.
NOMINATION *Costume Design:* Ruth Myers.

To con the sweetly ghoulish family out of their property, an unscrupulous lawyer tries to pass off an imposter as their long-lost Uncle Fester (Christopher Lloyd), who disappeared in the Bermuda Triangle. But is he an imposter? Very silly stuff, made tolerable by its performers, especially Anjelica Huston [617 . . .] as Morticia and Raul Julia as Gomez. It was a big hit with baby boomers who grew up with the TV series on which this mildly macabre fantasy is based. The series was, in turn, based on Charles Addams' *New Yorker* cartoons. Barry Sonnenfeld, who was cinematographer for such films as *Big, When Harry Met Sally . . . ,* and *Misery,* makes his directorial debut. Myers' costumes are evocative translations of Addams' drawings, but Academy voters preferred Albert Wolsky's work for *Bugsy*.

12.5 • ADDAMS FAMILY VALUES
SCOTT RUDIN PRODUCTION; PARAMOUNT. 1993.
NOMINATION *Art Direction:* Ken Adam and Marvin March.

When Morticia, played by Anjelica Huston [617 . . .], has a baby, she and Gomez (Raul Julia) hire a nanny, played by Joan Cusack [2313], who plots to lure Uncle Fester (Christopher Lloyd) into marriage so she can get her hands on the Addams family fortune. Meanwhile, Wednesday (Christina Ricci) and Pugsley (Jimmy Workman) exhibit intense—indeed, homicidal—sibling rivalry with the newest Addams, whose name is Pubert. (Reportedly, cartoonist

Charles Addams had suggested the name Pubert for Pugsley when the TV series was being made, but the censors balked.) Endearingly silly sequel to a film that had "moneymaking series" written all over it. This one has a bright string of macabre gags, provided by screenwriter Paul Rudnick, but it's really a slightly overextended skit. Huston is as droll as ever, Cusack makes the most of her role—a predator posing as an airhead—and Ricci has one of the film's most frightening moments, when the deadpan Wednesday is forced into smiling. Carol Kane [908] replaces Judith Malina, who played Granny in the first film. Barry Sonnenfeld directs again. The art direction Oscar went to Allan Starski and Ewa Braun for *Schindler's List.*

Adam: 101, 151, 1234.5, 1898. March: 86, 332, 1976, 2152.

13 • ADDRESS UNKNOWN
COLUMBIA. 1944.

NOMINATIONS *Black-and-White Interior Decoration:* Lionel Banks and Walter Holscher, art direction; Joseph Kish, set decoration. *Scoring of a Dramatic or Comedy Picture:* Morris Stoloff and Ernst Toch.

Paul Lukas [2233] plays a German-born American who returns to his native land and becomes a Nazi in this rather confused and dull melodrama directed by William Cameron Menzies [38 . . .]. The art direction award went to *Gaslight,* and Max Steiner's *Since You Went Away* score won the music Oscar.

Banks: 98, 455, 928, 1115, 1370, 1998. Holscher: 1521. Kish: 1048, 1062, 1812, 1840. Stoloff: 432, 455, 596, 643, 677, 732, 773, 1057, 1058, 1115, 1206, 1862, 1872, 1873, 1998, 2110, 2329. Toch: 1115, 1556.

14 • ADVENTURES OF BARON MUNCHAUSEN, THE
PROMINENT FEATURES & LAURA FILM PRODUCTION; COLUMBIA (UNITED KINGDOM). 1989.

NOMINATIONS *Art Direction—Set Decoration:* Dante Ferretti; Francesca Lo Schiavo. *Costume Design:* Gabriella Pescucci. *Makeup:* Maggie Weston and Fabrizio Sforza. *Visual Effects:* Richard Conway and Kent Houston.

The baron, John Neville, accompanies young Sarah Polley through a series of extravagant fantasy episodes, including an encounter with the man in the moon, played by Robin Williams [511 . . .]. Strictly for those with a high tolerance for whimsy and very expensive special effects, and a willingness to put up with the absence of plot. *Monty Python* alumnus Terry Gilliam [275] is the director and overall creative force behind all this, and fellow *Python* Eric Idle has a role, along with such varied performers as Valentina Cortese [501], Oliver Reed, Uma Thurman [1633.5], and Sting. If the producers hoped Oscars would help them overcome the film's poor box office, they were disappointed: The art direction award went to the similarly over-the-top *Batman.* The costuming Oscar was won by Phyllis Dalton for *Henry V,* and the makeup award went to *Driving Miss Daisy* and the visual effects Oscar to *The Abyss.*

Ferretti: 27.5, 859, 1007.5. Lo Schiavo: 859, 1007.5. Pescucci: 27.5.

15 • ADVENTURES OF DON JUAN
WARNER BROS. 1949.

AWARD *Color Costume Design:* Leah Rhodes, Travilla, and Marjorie Best.

NOMINATION *Color Art Direction—Set Decoration:* Edward Carrere; Lyle Reifsnider.

The great lover Don Juan (Errol Flynn) enters the service of his queen, played by Viveca Lindfors. Directed by Vincent Sherman, with Alan Hale, Ann Rutherford, Una O'Connor, and Raymond Burr. The story doesn't amount to much, though it's one of the films Warner Bros. hired William Faulkner to work on. The writing credits, however, went to George Oppenheimer [2227] and Harry Kurnitz [2250]. Unfortunately Flynn is ten years past his peak as a swashbuckler, and the more daring feats were doubled by stuntman and future Tarzan Jock Mahoney. The art direction Oscar went to MGM's *Little Women* remake.

Travilla: 954, 1952, 2043. Best: 768, 833, 1973. Carrere: 334, 1973.

16 • *ADVENTURES OF MARK TWAIN, THE*

WARNER BROS. 1944.

NOMINATIONS *Black-and-White Interior Decoration:* John J. Hughes, art direction; Fred MacLean, set decoration. *Scoring of a Dramatic or Comedy Picture:* Max Steiner. *Special Effects:* Paul Detlefsen and John Crouse, photographic; Nathan Levinson, sound.

Fredric March [184 . . .] plays Hollywood's idea of Sam Clemens in a routine biopic that mingles fiction—e.g., the Calaveras frog-jumping contest—with fact, along with all the usual clichés of the genre. As usual in such movies, there's more fiction than fact. Alexis Smith plays Mrs. Clemens. Directed by Irving Rapper, with Donald Crisp [952], Alan Hale, C. Aubrey Smith, John Carradine, and Walter Hampden. *Gaslight* won the art direction Oscar, the scoring award went to Max Steiner for *Since You Went Away,* and *Thirty Seconds Over Tokyo* took the effects trophy.

Hughes: 1779, 2058. MacLean: 833, 1779. Steiner: 154, 190, 330, 365, 385, 492, 679, 747, 754, 798, 999, 1043, 1046, 1052, 1162, 1169, 1170, 1207, 1324, 1408, 1430, 1456, 1690, 1779, 1828. Levinson: 30, 343, 385, 531, 689, 710, 712, 790, 930, 965, 1052, 1169, 1621, 1690, 1768, 1769, 1779, 1930, 1949, 2058, 2318.

16.5 • *ADVENTURES OF PRISCILLA, QUEEN OF THE DESERT, THE*

LATENT IMAGES PRODUCTION; GRAMERCY PICTURES (AUSTRALIA). 1994.

AWARD *Costume Design:* Lizzy Gardiner, Tim Chappel.

A trio made up of two drag queens—Tick/Mitzi (Hugo Weaving) and Adam/Felicia (Guy Pearce)—and a transsexual who used to be Ralph but firmly insists on being called Bernadette, played by Terence Stamp [206], sets out across the Australian Outback to make a club date in Alice Springs. (Priscilla is the name of their bus.) Entertaining road movie with music—some high-spirited lip-sync scenes by the drag trio—written and directed by Stephan Elliott. Some of the self-revelations and confrontations with homophobic Aussies are predictable, but it's a very likable movie. The award-winning costumes were achieved on a budget that was a fraction of those for the other nominated films, *Bullets Over Broadway, Little Women, Maverick,* and *Queen Margot.* Australian designer Gardiner and drag performer Chappel said one of the chief challenges was to make convincing breasts that would stand up in the desert heat: The water-filled balloons that were used were constantly exploding. Accepting her Oscar, Gardiner made one of the most amusing appearances of the evening by wearing a dress made out of 254 American Express Gold cards.

17 • *ADVENTURES OF ROBIN HOOD, THE*

WARNER BROS. 1938.

AWARDS *Interior Decoration:* Carl J. Weyl. *Original Score:* Erich Wolfgang Korngold. *Film Editing:* Ralph Dawson.

NOMINATION *Picture:* Hal B. Wallis, with Henry Blanke, producers.

Errol Flynn is the legendary outlaw, who rescues Maid Marian, played by Olivia de Havilland [798 . . .], from the evil Prince John, played by Claude Rains [365 . . .], and Sir Guy of Gisborne, played by Basil Rathbone [979 . . .]. The director was Michael Curtiz [79 . . .], who shows why he was regarded as one of the finest craftsmen of the studio era. This Technicolor swashbuckler is beautifully filmed by Tony Gaudio [90 . . .], Sol Polito [353 . . .], and W. Howard Greene [96 . . .]. The screenplay is by Seton I. Miller [463 . . .] and Norman Reilly Raine [1169]. The supporting cast includes Eugene Pallette as Friar Tuck, Alan Hale as Little John, Melville Cooper as the sheriff of Nottingham, Patric Knowles as Will Scarlett, and Herbert Mundin, Una O'Connor, and Montagu Love. One of the most enjoyable films ever made, it has stood the test of time far better than the one that beat it for best picture, *You Can't Take It With You.*

Korngold's lush Warners scores fell out of favor for a while and were inevitably dismissed as "more corn than gold." But although the Czech-born composer's opera *Die Tote Stadt* is still in the repertory of European opera houses, he will be remembered most for the film scores he composed at Warners in the mid-thirties and early forties, many of which turn routine action sequences into something approaching ballet. He died in 1957.

Weyl: 1332. Korngold: 90, 1621, 1768. Dawson: 90, 911, 1315. Wallis: 55, 85, 164, 343, 365, 676, 689, 712, 965, 1046, 1095, 1162, 1248, 1482, 1727, 1779, 2233, 2318. Blanke: 90, 712, 1046, 1169, 1315, 1457, 1936, 2136.

18 • ADVENTURES OF ROBINSON CRUSOE

Oscar Dancigers-Henry Ehrlich; United Artists (Mexico). 1954.

Nomination *Actor:* Dan O'Herlihy.

O'Herlihy is the legendary castaway who battles nature and loneliness until he discovers Friday, played by Jaime Fernandez. Splendid film of the Daniel Defoe novel, directed by Luis Buñuel [549 . . .], who also wrote the screenplay in collaboration with Philip Roll.

O'Herlihy, born in Ireland, acted in a few British films, including *Odd Man Out,* before coming to America in the late forties. His career in American films was unspectacular. He played Macduff opposite Orson Welles [407 . . .] in Welles' 1948 film of *Macbeth.* In recent years he has been seen in *The Dead* and *Robocop 2* (1990). The Oscar went to Marlon Brando for *On the Waterfront.*

19 • ADVENTURES OF TOM SAWYER, THE

Selznick International Pictures; United Artists. 1938.

Nomination *Interior Decoration:* Lyle Wheeler.

Tommy Kelly is Tom and Jackie Moran is Huckleberry Finn in perhaps the best of the many film versions of Mark Twain's novel. This David O. Selznick [497 . . .] production is especially distinguished in its supporting cast, which features May Robson [1119], Walter Brennan [424 . . .], Spring Byington [2325], and Margaret Hamilton, among others, directed by Norman Taurog [271 . . .]. The fine, pioneering Technicolor cinematography is by James

Wong Howe [1 . . .]. The art direction Oscar went to *The Adventures of Robin Hood.*

Wheeler: 46, 83, 356, 376, 428, 476, 495, 530, 542, 719, 721, 798, 950, 1062, 1088, 1149, 1153, 1213, 1391, 1475, 1601, 1616, 1670, 1706, 1852, 2008, 2093, 2212.

20 • AFFAIR IN TRINIDAD

The Beckworth Corporation; Columbia. 1952.

Nomination *Black-and-White Costume Design:* Jean Louis.

When nightclub singer Rita Hayworth's husband is murdered, she enlists the aid of his brother, Glenn Ford, in tracking down the killers, who are mixed up in international espionage. Alexander Scourby is the chief bad guy. Directed by Vincent Sherman. The teaming of Hayworth and Ford doesn't generate the heat it did in the more famous *Gilda* (1946), but Louis' gowns never had a more glamorous model. The Oscar went to Helen Rose for *The Bad and the Beautiful,* however.

Louis: 126, 170, 262, 732, 744, 1028, 1065, 1521, 1640, 1812, 1858, 1910, 2064.

21 • AFFAIR TO REMEMBER, AN

20th Century-Fox. 1957.

Nominations *Cinematography:* Milton Krasner. *Song:* "An Affair to Remember," music by Harry Warren, lyrics by Harold Adamson and Leo McCarey. *Score:* Hugo Friedhofer. *Costume Design:* Charles LeMaire.

Playboy Cary Grant [1445 . . .] and singer Deborah Kerr [599 . . .] have a shipboard fling, but their planned reunion onshore is aborted when she is struck by a taxi on the way to their tryst atop the Empire State Building. She is paralyzed, and her motive for not telling him of the accident is one of those that exist only in the movies. The accident also sinks a charming romantic comedy up to its neck in suds. Writer-director McCarey's remake of his 1939 best picture nominee, *Love Affair,* has Grant and Kerr in roles originally played by Charles Boyer and Irene Dunne. The original version seems less sticky and lathery, partly because it's about half an hour shorter, but Grant and Kerr are appealing performers. Most of Kerr's songs are dubbed by Marni Nixon, who also sang for her in *The King and I.* The movie enjoyed a video revival in 1993, when it became the focus of a men-vs.-women debate (it was cited as the quintessential ''woman's picture'') in the film *Sleepless in Seattle,* which in turn inspired the 1994 remake, once again titled *Love Affair,* by Warren Beatty [255 . . .].

Krasner's CinemaScope photography lost to Jack Hildyard's work on *Bridge on the River Kwai,* which also won for Malcolm Arnold's score. The title song, Vic-Damoned on the soundtrack and everywhere else in 1957, lost to James Van Heusen and Sammy Cahn's ''All the Way,'' from *The Joker Is Wild.* Orry-Kelly's designs for *Les Girls* won the costume award.

Krasner: 46, 96, 654, 953, 1219, 2072. Warren: 324, 569, 788, 791, 877, 897, 1072, 1367, 1501, 1964. Adamson: 916, 921, 1980, 2028. McCarey: 114, 173, 787, 1212, 1394, 1404. Friedhofer: 2, 184, 187, 214, 267, 1048, 2303, 2336. LeMaire: 46, 376, 495, 530, 542, 954, 1213, 1338, 1391, 1601, 1706, 2008, 2043, 2205, 2294.

22 • AFFAIRS OF CELLINI

20TH CENTURY; UNITED ARTISTS. 1934.
NOMINATIONS *Actor:* Frank Morgan. *Cinematography:* Charles Rosher. *Interior Decoration:* Richard Day. *Sound Recording:* Thomas T. Moulton.

Fredric March [184 . . .] plays the Renaissance artist Benvenuto Cellini and romances Duchess Constance Bennett in this enjoyably fluffy swashbuckler directed by Gregory La Cava [1401 . . .] from a screenplay by Bess Meredyth [2303.5 . . .]. Also on hand are Fay Wray, Jessie Ralph, and, in a bit part, Lucille Ball.

Morgan's role as the duke of Florence was decidedly a supporting one, but Academy records show that he came in a close second to Clark Gable in *It Happened One Night.* The disparity between their roles helped lead to the establishment of the supporting performance Oscars two years later.

Rosher and Day placed third in their respective races. The cinematography award went to Victor Milner for *Cleopatra,* and the art directing Oscar was won by Cedric Gibbons and Frederic Hope for *The Merry Widow. One Night of Love* took the award for sound.

Morgan: 2123. Rosher: 87, 1096, 1818, 1972, 2320. Day: 102, 235, 487, 510, 560, 569, 797, 833, 864, 952, 1048, 1175, 1397, 1477, 1666, 1949, 2056, 2120, 2276. Moulton: 46, 138, 366, 457, 487, 560, 706, 798, 962, 1153, 1200, 1451, 1510, 1607, 1849, 2154, 2294.

23 • AFFAIRS OF SUSAN, THE

HAL WALLIS PRODUCTIONS; PARAMOUNT. 1945.
NOMINATION *Original Story:* Laszlo Gorog and Thomas Monroe.

At a bachelor party before his marriage to Broadway star Joan Fontaine [441 . . .], Walter Abel and his guests, George Brent, Dennis O'Keefe, and Don Defore, tell stories about her that reveal that each sees her as an entirely different kind of woman. A mildly amusing romantic comedy, flawed by the lack of a leading man with Fontaine's star power. Directed by William A. Seiter. The Oscar went to Charles G. Booth for *The House on 92nd Street.*

Monroe: 138.

24 • AFRICAN QUEEN, THE

HORIZON ENTERPRISES INC.; UNITED ARTISTS. 1951.
AWARD *Actor:* Humphrey Bogart.
NOMINATIONS *Actress:* Katharine Hepburn. *Director:* John Huston. *Screenplay:* James Agee and John Huston.

When her missionary brother, Robert Morley [1274], is killed, Hepburn is forced to flee downriver with Bogart, the raffish, alcoholic captain of a supply boat. En route, they encounter rapids, leeches, Germans—the time is World War I—and each other. Entertainment of the highest order and one of the classics of Hollywood film. Based on a novel by C. S. Forester, its filming inspired yet another novel, Peter Viertel's *White Hunter, Black Heart,* which was in turn filmed by Clint Eastwood [2179.5] in 1990. (Viertel was an uncredited, and hence unnominated, collaborator on the *African Queen* screenplay.)

So why was it not a nominee for best picture? The answer lies in the desperate politics that afflicted the

Oscars during the early fifties, when financially troubled studios resorted to publicity campaigns and bloc voting to ensure nominations for pet projects. In this case, Darryl F. Zanuck [34 . . .] pushed for a best picture nod for Fox's *Decision Before Dawn,* a film that received only one other nomination. United Artists was incapable of mounting a competitive campaign for *The African Queen.*

Bogart, however, sponsored his own campaign for the award that he had been known to mock: He once suggested that the only way to make acting awards fair would be to have all candidates perform the same role. Three years earlier, Bogart had been passed over by the Academy, failing to receive a nomination for one of his most memorable roles, as Fred C. Dobbs in *The Treasure of the Sierra Madre.* As good as he is as Charlie Allnut in *The African Queen,* the Oscar was probably at least partly an attempt by the Academy members to make up for that notorious oversight. It was also, of course, a tribute to one of Hollywood's genuine legends, a most unlikely leading man who moved from Broadway to Hollywood in 1930 but failed to make much of an impression on screen until he appeared in *The Petrified Forest* in 1936 as the menacing Duke Mantee. That role led to a series of heavies and gangsters as he worked through his Warners contract, but true stardom eluded him until 1941 and *The Maltese Falcon,* followed two years later by the role that made him one of the screen's great icons, Rick in *Casablanca.* After his death in 1957, the Bogart legend continued to grow, fueled by the *hommage* of Jean-Luc Godard in *Breathless* (1959) and the adoption of his tough, loner persona by college students in the sixties. Bogart's chief competitor for the Oscar was another great screen icon: Marlon Brando's Stanley Kowalski in *A Streetcar Named Desire.*

Hepburn was beaten by Vivien Leigh in *Streetcar,* but *The African Queen* revived her film career. Her rapport with Bogart is virtually a textbook demonstration of what is known as chemistry. Huston lost out to George Stevens for *A Place in the Sun,* but his advice that Hepburn base her character on Eleanor

Roosevelt stands as one of screen directing's greatest inspirations.

Agee was one of the most gifted film critics of the forties, reviewing for *Time* and *The Nation.* He also wrote the screenplay for the film *The Night of the Hunter* (1955). He is best known for his books *Let Us Now Praise Famous Men* and *A Death in the Family.* The latter won the Pulitzer Prize for fiction in 1958, three years after his death. The Oscar went to Michael Wilson and Harry Brown for *A Place in the Sun.*

The African Queen was a breakthrough film for its producer, Sam Spiegel [287 . . .], who would go on to win three best picture Oscars and an Irving G. Thalberg Award. Failure to nominate the fine cinematography of Jack Cardiff [221 . . .] or the supporting performance of Morley can probably also be attributed to studio politics.

Bogart: 330, 365. Hepburn: 40, 843, 1177, 1199, 1357, 1473, 1563, 1654, 1956, 1963, 2305. Huston: 105, 356, 571, 891, 1248, 1263, 1363, 1625, 1779, 2136.

25 • *AFTER THE THIN MAN*
MGM. 1936.

NOMINATION *Screenplay:* Frances Goodrich and Albert Hackett.

Bibulous sleuthing couple Nick and Nora Charles, played by William Powell [1170 . . .] and Myrna Loy, investigate a murder of which her cousin Elissa Landi is accused. The second in the extremely popular series of films based on the Dashiell Hammett [2233] novel, *The Thin Man,* it's beginning to fall victim to the cuteness that ultimately undermined the series: too much Asta, not enough astringency. But it's still entertaining, and worth watching for an early appearance by James Stewart [73 . . .], whose familiar screen persona hadn't yet emerged. Directed by W. S. Van Dyke [1751 . . .]. Goodrich and Hackett lost to Pierre Collings and Sheridan Gibney for *The Story of Louis Pasteur.*

Goodrich: 656, 1782, 2052. Hackett: 656, 1782, 2052.

26 • AGAINST ALL ODDS

NEW VISIONS PRODUCTION; COLUMBIA. 1984.

NOMINATION *Song:* "Against All Odds (Take a Look at Me Now)," music and lyrics by Phil Collins.

James Woods [1746] hires washed-up jock Jeff Bridges [1139 . . .] to find his girlfriend, Rachel Ward. A loose remake of the 1947 film noir *Out of the Past,* which starred Robert Mitchum [1935] and Jane Greer. In this version, directed by Taylor Hackford, Greer plays Ward's mother. Unfortunately, clever casting and solid performances are all this overplotted film has going for it. Collins' song lost to Stevie Wonder's "I Just Called to Say I Love You," from *The Lady in Red.*

Collins: 315.

27 • AGATHA

SWEETWALL PRODUCTION IN ASSOCIATION WITH CASABLANCA FILMWORKS; FIRST ARTISTS PRESENTATION; WARNER BROS. 1979.

NOMINATION *Costume Design:* Shirley Russell.

An American journalist played by Dustin Hoffman [810 . . .] trails mystery writer Agatha Christie, played by Vanessa Redgrave [263 . . .], whose marriage is breaking up. The story is based on the actual disappearance of Christie for eleven days in 1926—an event that doesn't warrant the speculation that has been devoted it, and certainly didn't warrant a movie so lavishly produced and so oddly cast: Has there ever been a more peculiar couple on screen than Redgrave and Hoffman? Directed by Michael Apted, with Timothy Dalton as Christie's husband. Russell's costumes lost to Albert Wolsky's for *All That Jazz.*

Russell: 1678.

27.5 • AGE OF INNOCENCE, THE

CAPPA/DE FINA PRODUCTION; COLUMBIA. 1993.

AWARD *Costume Design:* Gabriella Pescucci.

NOMINATIONS *Supporting Actress:* Winona Ryder. *Screenplay Based on Material Previously Produced or Published:* Jay Cocks and Martin Scorsese. *Art Direction:* Dante Ferretti, Robert J. Franco. *Original Score:* Elmer Bernstein.

Newland Archer, played by Daniel Day-Lewis

[992.5 . . .], an eminently respectable young man in 1870s New York, is engaged to marry dewy young thing May Welland (Ryder), when the beautiful Countess Ellen Olenska, played by Michelle Pfeiffer [485 . . .], arrives in town. The countess causes tongues to wag because she's not *quite* respectable— for one thing, she has separated from her husband. Gradually Archer and the countess realize that they're in love, but he's inescapably trapped into marrying May, who turns out to have a very strong will beneath her facade of innocent girlishness. Extraordinarily beautiful rendering of a novel by Edith Wharton by (in the estimation of some) a very unlikely director— Scorsese, known for films about gangsters and street punks. But working with meticulous designers, cinematographer Michael Ballhaus [293 . . .], and his longtime collaborator, editor Thelma Schoonmaker [806 . . .], Scorsese crafts a film about emotional violence that's as subtle as his films about physical violence are harsh. The three principals, playing at top form, are well supported by Miriam Margolyes as the corpulent Mrs. Mingott and Richard E. Grant and Alec McCowen as a pair of arbiters of social correctness. Moreover, the film is given a drily nuanced off-camera narrative voice by the unseen but superb Joanne Woodward [1365 . . .]. Unfortunately this opulent, expensive production was something of a box-office disappointment. And awareness of that, in turn, may have caused the Academy to pass it over in such categories as picture, actress, director, cinematography, and editing. In a less intensely competitive year than 1993, *The Age of Innocence* might have been a shoo-in for consideration, attracting the same attention that the Academy has lavished on the Merchant Ivory period re-creations—*A Room with a View, Howards End,* and the film that displaced it in the 1993 best picture contest, *The Remains of the Day* (which was also about frustrated passion).

Ryder lost to Anna Paquin in *The Piano. Schindler's List* took the remaining Oscars, for Steven Zaillian's screenplay, Allan Starski and Ewa Braun's art direction, and John Williams' score.

Pescucci: 14. Ryder: 1190.5. Scorsese: 806, 1142, 1650. Ferretti: 14, 859, 1007.5. Bernstein: 789,

882, 1242, 1264, 1685, 1959, 2064, 2101, 2130, 2147, 2223.

28 • AGNES OF GOD

COLUMBIA PICTURES PRODUCTION; COLUMBIA. 1985.
NOMINATIONS *Actress:* Anne Bancroft. *Supporting Actress:* Meg Tilly. *Original Score:* Georges Delerue.

Tilly is a young nun who has apparently given birth and murdered her child, and is of course in the grip of a religious delusion. Mother Superior Bancroft is at odds with the psychiatrist brought into the case, Jane Fonda [394 . . .]. A talky play about the ways of God to woman, and vice versa, becomes a talky movie—both stage and screen versions are by John Pielmeyer. Directed by Norman Jewison [659 . . .], with cinematography by Sven Nykvist [460 . . .].

Bancroft lost to the actress who had played the mother superior in the Broadway production of *Agnes of God:* Geraldine Page, who won for *The Trip to Bountiful.*

Tilly made her screen debut in a bit part in *Fame* and moved into larger roles in *Tex* (1982) and *The Big Chill.* Her career has been dogged by bad luck: She was cast in the major female role in *Amadeus* but broke her ankle just before filming started and was replaced by Elizabeth Berridge. The director of *Amadeus,* Milos Forman, tried to make amends by casting her in *Valmont,* but that movie was beaten to the screen by *Dangerous Liaisons,* based on the same story, and failed at the box office. The Oscar went to Anjelica Huston for *Prizzi's Honor.*

Delerue's score lost to John Barry's for *Out of Africa.*

Bancroft: 810, 1326, 1634, 2152. Delerue: 85, 502, 1066, 1187.

29 • AGONY AND THE ECSTASY, THE

INTERNATIONAL CLASSICS PRODUCTION; 20TH CENTURY-FOX. 1965.
NOMINATIONS *Color Cinematography:* Leon Shamroy. *Color Art Direction—Set Decoration:* John DeCuir and Jack Martin Smith; Dario Simoni. *Sound:* James P. Corcoran. *Music Score—Substantially Original:* Alex North. *Color Costume Design:* Vittorio Nino Novarese.

Pope Julius II, played by Rex Harrison [413 . . .], squabbles with Michelangelo, played by Charlton Heston [175], about the painting of the Sistine Chapel. Critics inevitably had fun with the film's title, which came from the Irving Stone novel on which the film is based, and while it's not really agonizing, it's long and slow. The box-office failure of the film was the near undoing of Fox, coming on the heels of the *Cleopatra* debacle two years earlier. Directed by Carol Reed [639 . . .] from a screenplay by Philip Dunne [495 . . .].

The true stars of the movie were, as the Academy's nominations reflect, the technical staff. Shamroy's eighteen nominations, resulting in four Oscars, is an Academy record for cinematographers, but he lost this one to Freddie Young and *Doctor Zhivago,* which also took the awards for art direction, for Maurice Jarre's score, and for Phyllis Dalton's costumes. The Oscar for sound went to *The Sound of Music.*

Shamroy: 226, 356, 413, 495, 569, 602, 1088, 1153, 1213, 1592, 1610, 1706, 1852, 1883, 2013, 2286, 2334. DeCuir: 201, 376, 413, 476, 896, 950, 1088, 1391, 1852, 2000. Smith: 413, 557, 646, 896, 1230, 2008, 2120, 2247. Simoni: 558, 1151, 2000. Corcoran: 413, 1753, 1881. North: 215, 413, 515, 577, 1654, 1727, 1802, 1814, 1886, 1949, 2174, 2177, 2212, 2277. Novarese: 413, 465, 833, 1610.

30 • AIR FORCE

WARNER BROS. 1943.
AWARD *Film Editing:* George Amy.
NOMINATIONS *Original Screenplay:* Dudley Nichols. *Black-and-White Cinematography:* James Wong Howe, Elmer Dyer, and Charles Marshall. *Special Effects:* Hans Koenekamp and Rex Wimpy, photographic; Nathan Levinson, sound.

Episodic film about the lives and deaths of the members of a bomber crew during the Wake Island and Coral Sea battles. The World War II propaganda is as thick as the flak, but the movie is generally exciting. Produced by Hal Wallis [17 . . .] and directed by Howard Hawks [1779], with the latter's usual fast-paced tough-guy camaraderie, but not as much wit and spontaneity as his best films. The crew is the usual Hollywood wartime ethnic stew—with names like Quincannon and Weinberg and Winocki—and includes John Garfield [251 . . .], Gig Young [427 . . .], and Arthur Kennedy [291 . . .].

Amy began his career as an editor in silent films, worked on many of the Warners Errol Flynn swashbucklers of the thirties, and was a frequent collaborator with director Michael Curtiz [79 . . .]. He also directed several Warners B pictures.

William Faulkner was an uncredited collaborator on the screenplay, which lost to Norman Krasna's *Princess O'Rourke.* The cinematography Oscar went to Arthur Miller for *The Song of Bernadette.* The competition for special effects was dominated by wartime action films, including *Bombardier, Stand By for Action,* and the winner, *Crash Dive.*

Amy: 1459, 2318. Nichols: 999, 1200, 2092. Howe: 1, 36, 738, 956, 1095, 1451, 1470, 1727, 1774. Levinson: 16, 343, 385, 531, 689, 710, 712, 790, 930, 965, 1052, 1169, 1621, 1690, 1768, 1769, 1779, 1930, 1949, 2058, 2318.

31 • *AIRPORT*

Ross Hunter-Universal Production; Universal. 1970.
Award *Supporting Actress:* Helen Hayes.
Nominations *Picture:* Ross Hunter, producer. *Supporting Actress:* Maureen Stapleton. *Screenplay—Based on Material From Another Medium:* George Seaton. *Cinematography:* Ernest Laszlo. *Art Direction—Set Decoration:* Alexander Golitzen and E. Preston Ames; Jack D. Moore and Mickey S. Michaels. *Sound:* Ronald Pierce and David Moriarty. *Original Score:* Alfred Newman. *Film Editing:* Stuart Gilmore. *Costume Design:* Edith Head.

Mad bomber Van Heflin [1055] blasts a hole in a plane, and various pilots, stewardesses, airline personnel, and passengers try to get the thing safely on ground. Enormously popular junk based on a schlock best-seller by Arthur Hailey, with an all-star cast going through their paces. Screenwriter Seaton also directed, with Burt Lancaster [107 . . .], George Kennedy [443], Dean Martin, Jean Seberg, Jacqueline

Bisset, Barry Nelson, Dana Wynter, Lloyd Nolan, and Barbara Hale suffering in various ways.

After winning her first Oscar, for *The Sin of Madelon Claudet,* Hayes found that she was being offered few film roles to her taste, and returned to Broadway, where she became one of the most celebrated American actresses. She was absent from the screen, except for a cameo in *Stage Door Canteen* in 1943, from 1935 to 1952, and played only a handful of character roles in the years up to her death in 1993. In *Airport* her part is that of a cute little old stowaway—and it's done with the audience-pleasing wit and timing developed over a lifetime of performing. But is it really a better performance than that of Stapleton, as Heflin's wife, or the other nominees—Karen Black for *Five Easy Pieces,* Lee Grant for *The Landlord,* or Sally Kellerman for *MASH?* Hayes also entered the Oscar record books as the first performer to win a supporting performance award after a previous win in a leading role, and as the performer who went the longest time between nominations: thirty-eight years, a record that has since been tied by Jack Palance [408 . . .] and beaten only by Henry Fonda [815 . . .], who went forty-one years between acting nominations. (Fonda, however, was nominated as producer of *12 Angry Men* in the interim.)

The best picture Oscar went to *Patton,* which also won for art direction, sound, and Hugh S. Fowler's editing. *MASH* won for Ring Lardner, Jr.'s, screenplay. The Oscar for cinematography went to Freddie Young for *Ryan's Daughter.* Francis Lai won for his *Love Story* score. The best costumes were Nino Novarese's for *Cromwell.*

Hayes: 1827. Stapleton: 1005, 1198, 1678. Seaton: 450, 1325, 1868. Laszlo: 646, 1000, 1032, 1065, 1196, 1812, 1907. Golitzen: 96, 414, 591, 690, 706, 744, 1560, 1886, 1968, 1986, 2035, 2064, 2101. Ames: 66, 290, 591, 769, 1226, 1937, 2184. Moore: 1190, 1662, 1937, 1986, 2112, 2330. Michaels: 32. Pierce: 591, 1927. Newman: 34, 46, 72, 138, 182, 226, 333, 334, 347, 375, 428, 437, 457, 476, 495, 542, 690, 797, 833, 952, 953, 959, 962, 1016, 1082, 1088, 1213, 1278, 1362, 1397, 1475, 1616, 1655, 1849, 1868, 1883, 1921, 2043,

2046, 2091, 2258, 2286, 2294, 2316. Gilmore: 33, 77. Head: 32, 46, 305, 357, 363, 612, 636, 675, 736, 832, 894, 945, 1003, 1219, 1261, 1263, 1398, 1427, 1504, 1550, 1579, 1587, 1631, 1716, 1727, 1738, 1748, 1840, 1927, 1986, 2012, 2098, 2247, 2298.

32 • AIRPORT '77

JENNINGS LANG PRODUCTION; UNIVERSAL. 1977.
NOMINATIONS *Art Direction–Set Decoration:* George C. Webb; Mickey S. Michaels. *Costume Design:* Edith Head and Burton Miller.

The second of the three sequels to *Airport,* this one, about a jet that sinks in the ocean (sort of a cross between *Airport* and *The Poseidon Adventure*) has little to recommend it other than an astonishing cast: Jack Lemmon [91 . . .], Lee Grant [534 . . .], Brenda Vaccaro [1038], George Kennedy [443], James Stewart [73 . . .], and Olivia de Havilland [798 . . .], among others. Directed by Jerry Jameson. *Star Wars* took the Oscars for art direction and John Mollo's costumes. This was the last of Edith Head's thirty-five nominations.

Webb: 744, 1986, 2064. Michaels: 31. Head: 31, 46, 305, 357, 363, 612, 636, 675, 736, 832, 894, 945, 1003, 1219, 1261, 1263, 1398, 1427, 1504, 1550, 1579, 1587, 1631, 1716, 1727, 1738, 1748, 1840, 1927, 1986, 2012, 2098, 2247, 2298.

32.5 • ALADDIN

WALT DISNEY PICTURES PRODUCTION; BUENA VISTA. 1992.
AWARDS *Original Score:* Alan Menken. *Song:* "Whole New World," music by Alan Menken, lyrics by Tim Rice.
NOMINATIONS *Song:* "Friend Like Me," music by Alan Menken, lyrics by Howard Ashman. *Sound:* Terry Porter, Mel Metcalfe, David J. Hudson, Doc Kane. *Sound Effects Editing:* Mark Mangini.

With the help of a big blue genie, voiced by Robin Williams [511 . . .], young Aladdin battles the evil vizier and wins the heart of a princess. Absolutely smashing animated cartoon feature that completes a trio of films—the others are *The Little Mermaid* and *Beauty and the Beast*—centered on the music of

Menken and the lyrics of Ashman. (Rice was brought in to complete the lyrics for this film after Ashman's death.) Lack of competition has prevented the Academy from establishing an award for feature-length cartoons, but a special Oscar should have been granted to the team that brought the imagination of Robin Williams to life. If movies had showstoppers, the performance of "Friend Like Me" would be one. The film has been criticized, it must be noted, by Arab-American groups who point out that it stereotypes Arab culture.

Rice is best known for his frequent collaboration with Andrew Lloyd Webber [1044] on a series of big showy stage musicals starting with *Jesus Christ Superstar.* Menken's lovely melody for "Whole New World" doubtless swayed the Academy in the direction of that song.

The sound award went to *The Last of the Mohicans* and the sound effects editing Oscar to *Bram Stoker's Dracula.*

Menken: 162, 1184, 1188. Rice: 1177.5. Ashman: 162, 1184, 1188. Porter: 162, 1914. Metcalfe: 162, 1914. Hudson: 162, 1914. Kane: 162. Mangini: 1914.

33 • ALAMO, THE

BATJAC PRODUCTION; UNITED ARTISTS. 1960.
AWARD *Sound:* Gordon E. Sawyer, sound director, Samuel Goldwyn Studio Sound Department, and Fred Hynes, sound director, Todd-AO Sound Department.
NOMINATIONS *Picture:* John Wayne, producer. *Supporting Actor:* Chill Wills. *Color Cinematography:* William H. Clothier. *Song:* "The Green Leaves of Summer," music by Dimitri Tiomkin, lyrics by Paul Francis Webster. *Scoring of a Dramatic or Comedy Picture:* Dimitri Tiomkin. *Film Editing:* Stuart Gilmore.

Producer-director Wayne plays Davy Crockett, Richard Widmark [1098] is Jim Bowie, Laurence Harvey [1724] is Colonel Travis, and Richard Boone is Sam Houston in this re-creation of a famous defeat. Other less historical figures are played by Wills, Frankie Avalon, Ken Curtis, Hank Worden, Denver Pyle, and Olive Carey—many of them members of the stock company of director John Ford [815 . . .], who was an adviser of Wayne's on the film. Wayne spent millions, much of it his own money, on this attempt at an American epic. Although it was cut by nearly half an hour after a disastrous premiere, it still goes on and on, for nearly three hours. After the film bombed at the box office, Wayne mounted a heavy campaign in the trade papers to get the picture nominated for as many Oscars as possible.

The hoopla produced a best picture nomination for the film, edging worthier films, particularly *Psycho* and *Spartacus,* out of the competition, but *The Apartment* took the top Oscar as well as one for Daniel Mandell's editing. *The Alamo*'s sole Oscar, the sound award, was the first of two wins in a row for Hynes and Sawyer, who took the award the following year for *West Side Story.*

Wills also hired his own publicist to get a nomination, including an ad in the trade papers that listed all the Academy members and noted: "You're all my cousins, and I love you." Groucho Marx retorted with his own ad: "Dear Mr. Chill Wills, I am delighted to be your cousin, but I voted for Sal Mineo." Wills' cousins chose Peter Ustinov in *Spartacus* instead.

Spartacus also won the cinematography Oscar for Russell Metty. The best song was Manos Hadjidakis' title tune from *Never on Sunday,* and the scoring award went to Ernest Gold for *Exodus.*

Sawyer: 91, 184, 214, 393, 730, 864, 882, 973, 974, 1032, 1511, 1592, 2244, 2297, 2310. Hynes: 413, 1469, 1592, 1881, 1883, 2244. Wayne: 1756, 2147. Clothier: 389. Tiomkin: 286, 380, 446, 638, 663, 730, 768, 850, 911, 912, 1206, 1347, 1370, 1470, 2006, 2127, 2282, 2335. Webster: 64, 95, 331, 376, 604, 663, 730, 856, 1213, 1276, 1322, 1388, 1755, 1925, 2014. Gilmore: 31, 77.

34 • ALEXANDER'S RAGTIME BAND

20TH CENTURY-FOX. 1938.

AWARD *Score:* Alfred Newman.

NOMINATIONS *Picture:* Darryl F. Zanuck, with Harry Joe Brown, producers. *Original Story:* Irving Berlin. *Interior Decoration:* Bernard Herzbrun and Boris Le-

ven. *Song:* "Now It Can Be Told," music and lyrics by Irving Berlin. *Film Editing:* Barbara McLean.

Songwriters Tyrone Power and Don Ameche [419] squabble for years about which one will get Alice Faye. Cliché piles on cliché in this backstage musical, directed by Henry King [1868 . . .], but fortunately Berlin's songs keep coming—and we get a chance to see the young Ethel Merman and wonder why Faye was the bigger movie musical star.

Over the course of his career, Newman received forty-five nominations and won nine Oscars, a record for film composers. It's fitting that this, his first Oscar, was for an Irving Berlin film: Newman had been an orchestra conductor on Broadway since he was seventeen and was brought to Hollywood by Berlin in 1930 to be musical director for the film *Reaching for the Moon,* for which Berlin had written the title song. He was snapped up by Sam Goldwyn [102 . . .], his primary employer until 1939, when he became music director for 20th Century-Fox. Among Newman's many compositions is one of the most familiar: the fanfare that accompanies the searchlights and art deco rooftops of the Fox logo.

Berlin, who had two song nominations—the other one for "Change Partners and Dance With Me" from *Carefree*—as well as the original story nomination, suffered multiple disappointments: The writing award was won by Eleanore Griffin and Dore Schary for *Boys Town,* and the song Oscar went to Ralph Rainger and Leo Robin for "Thanks for the Memory," from *Big Broadcast of 1938.*

The best picture Oscar went to *You Can't Take It With You. The Adventures of Robin Hood* took the awards for art direction and Ralph Dawson's editing.

Newman: 31, 46, 72, 138, 182, 226, 333, 334, 347, 375, 428, 437, 457, 476, 495, 542, 690, 797, 833, 952, 953, 959, 962, 1016, 1082, 1088, 1213, 1278, 1362, 1397, 1475, 1616, 1655, 1849, 1868, 1883, 1921, 2043, 2046, 2091, 2258, 2286, 2294, 2316. Zanuck: 46, 550, 710, 759, 815, 946, 952, 990, 1201, 1327, 1666, 2154, 2286. Brown: 343. Berlin: 244, 358, 929, 1773, 2115, 2268. Leven: 77, 422, 768, 1753, 1801, 1881, 1907, 2244. McLean: 46, 1195, 1327, 1655, 1868, 2286.

35 • ALFIE

SHELDRAKE FILMS LTD.; PARAMOUNT (UNITED KINGDOM). 1966.

NOMINATIONS *Picture:* Lewis Gilbert, producer. *Actor:* Michael Caine. *Supporting Actress:* Vivien Merchant. *Screenplay—Based on Material From Another Medium:* Bill Naughton. *Song:* "Alfie," music by Burt Bacharach, lyrics by Hal David.

Caine plays a Cockney sexual predator whose life is finally set in order when he has to deal with a personal crisis. With its scenes of life in the "swinging London" of the sixties, the movie seems almost as dated as its bouffant hairdos, but it provided a star-making role for Caine. The strong supporting cast includes Shelley Winters [542 . . .] and Denholm Elliott [1725].

Along with fellow best picture nominee *Who's Afraid of Virginia Woolf?, Alfie* was one of the pictures that signaled the demise of the old Production Code, which had been Hollywood's standard for self-censorship for three decades. The Oscar, however, went to *A Man for All Seasons,* which would scarcely have raised an eyebrow in the Breen office of old. Caine lost to that film's star, Paul Scofield, and Robert Bolt's screenplay for *A Man for All Seasons* won over Naughton's.

Merchant, a respected British stage actress, was married to playwright Harold Pinter [185 . . .], who created several good roles for her on stage and screen—most notably the 1973 film of his play *The Homecoming.* Sandy Dennis, in *Who's Afraid of Virginia Woolf?,* took the supporting actress award.

The winner for song was John Barry and Don Black's title tune for *Born Free.*

Caine: 598, 863, 1841. Bacharach: 103, 317, 370, 2251. David: 317, 370, 2251.

36 • ALGIERS

WALTER WANGER; UNITED ARTISTS. 1938.

NOMINATIONS *Actor:* Charles Boyer. *Supporting Actor:* Gene Lockhart. *Cinematography:* James Wong Howe. *Interior Decoration:* Alexander Toluboff.

Gangster Boyer, the king of the Casbah, falls for a beautiful Parisienne, Hedy Lamarr, who is visiting Algiers. Lockhart is the informer who is Boyer's undoing. A famous romance, something of a legend in its time, it now seems poky and overdressed: As a Haunt of Unspeakable Vice, the Casbah looks awfully cozy. And while the teaming of Boyer and Lamarr, in her American debut, made the movie a hit, they don't really seem to connect. In the end we're not certain whether Boyer makes his fateful choice out of passion for Hedy or nostalgia for Paris. The movie spawned a famous catchphrase, "Come with me to the Casbah," which is never spoken in the film—in fact, the plot hinges on the fact that Boyer can't leave the Casbah.

The director of *Algiers,* John Cromwell, says of Boyer, "*Algiers* is the cross he had to bear. . . . It was all the fussing over the love scenes and the come-with-me-to-the-Casbah lunacy. I say the love scenes are strong, but Boyer made high demands on the art of acting, and he was embarrassed by them, he thought they were so bad." Boyer was also embarrassed because *Algiers* was a remake of *Pépé le Moko,* a 1937 French film that starred an actor Boyer admired, Jean Gabin. For the second year in a row, Boyer lost the Oscar to Spencer Tracy, this time for *Boys Town.*

Lockhart was a durable character actor, seen in more than a hundred movies from the silent era up to the year of his death, 1957. His daughter, June, followed him into films and is still seen in character parts on TV. Walter Brennan won the supporting actor award for *Kentucky.*

The cinematography award was won by Joseph Ruttenberg for *The Great Waltz,* and the art direction Oscar went to *The Adventures of Robin Hood.*

Boyer: 440, 643, 749. Howe: 1, 30, 738, 956, 1095, 1451, 1470, 1727, 1774. Toluboff: 1901, 2214.

37 • ALI BABA GOES TO TOWN

20TH CENTURY-FOX. 1937.

NOMINATION *Dance Direction:* Sammy Lee.

Eddie Cantor travels back in time—or thinks he does—and encounters, among others, Louise Hovick, better known as Gypsy Rose Lee, Tony Martin, Roland Young [2117], and a gallery of Fox contract artists, including Shirley Temple. Silly musical vehicle for Cantor, directed by David Butler, with songs by Mack Gordon [428 . . .] and Harry Revel [1291 . . .]. Dance director Lee's nomination was for the production number "Swing Is Here to Stay." The award went to Hermes Pan for *A Damsel in Distress*.

Lee: 1090.

38 • *ALIBI*

ART CINEMA; UNITED ARTISTS. 1928–29.

NOMINATIONS *Production:* Roland West, producer. *Actor:* Chester Morris. *Interior Decoration:* William Cameron Menzies.

Policeman's daughter Eleanor Griffith falls in love with gangster Morris, providing an alibi when he kills a cop during a robbery. Eventually he comes to a bad end. Written and directed by West, *Alibi* was originally shot as a silent but was swiftly refilmed once sound came in. The film provided a second debut for Morris, who had appeared in silent films as a child, before going to Broadway in his teens. His work in *Alibi* established him in Hollywood, but he wound up in B pictures. He is best known for the series of *Boston Blackie* movies. His last screen appearance was in *The Great White Hope* in the year of his death, 1970.

In fact, Morris, Menzies, and the film itself were not official nominees. The Academy announced only the winners of the 1928–29 awards. But the lists of the other films and people under consideration by the Academy branches that chose the winners are on record, and the names on those lists have traditionally been treated as if they were official nominations. The best picture Oscar went to *Broadway Melody*. Warner Baxter was named best actor for *In Old Arizona*. The art direction award went to Cedric Gibbons for *The Bridge of San Luis Rey* "and other pictures."

Menzies: 112.5, 311, 568, 798, 1018, 2010.

39 • *ALICE*

JACK ROLLINS AND CHARLES H. JOFFE PRODUCTION; ORION. 1990.

NOMINATION *Screenplay Written Directly for the Screen:* Woody Allen.

Mia Farrow, unhappily married to William Hurt [293 . . .], goes to an acupuncturist, played by Keye Luke in his last film, who gives her some herbs that have oddly magical consequences. A not-very-satisfying fantasy, but like most of Allen's films, it has a fascinating supporting cast: Joe Mantegna, Alec Baldwin, Blythe Danner, Judy Davis [962.5 . . .], Bernadette Peters, Cybill Shepherd, and many others. The writing Oscar went to Bruce Joel Rubin for *Ghost*.

Allen: 88, 294, 311.5, 461, 863, 962.5, 1005, 1267, 1636, 1647.

40 • *ALICE ADAMS*

RKO RADIO. 1935.

NOMINATIONS *Picture:* Produced by Pandro S. Berman. *Actress:* Katharine Hepburn.

Alice (Hepburn) longs to rise above her hopelessly vulgar family and sees the chance when the socially prominent Fred MacMurray pays court. Booth Tarkington's study of small-town pretensions and snobbery receives an almost perfect treatment, thanks to Hepburn's wonderful performance. The only flaw is an unearned happy ending. The highlight is an awful attempt to impress MacMurray with a dinner party, held in wilting heat by a poorly coached servant, played wonderfully by the valiant Hattie McDaniel [798]. The film is the first major directing triumph of George Stevens [542 . . .]. Also in the cast are Evelyn Venable, Fred Stone, Frank Albertson, and Charley Grapewin.

Berman never won an Oscar, though his films include some of the most memorable RKO productions, including the great Astaire-Rogers series. In 1940 he went to MGM, where he presided over some equally prestigious projects. He received the 1976 Irving G. Thalberg Award from the Academy. *Mutiny on the Bounty* received the best picture award.

Many regard Hepburn's Alice Adams as one of her greatest roles, and she ran a strong race for the Oscar, coming in second to Bette Davis in *Dangerous*.

Berman: 656, 754, 1035, 1899, 2115. Hepburn: 24, 843, 1177, 1199, 1357, 1473, 1563, 1654, 1956, 1963, 2305.

41 • ALICE DOESN'T LIVE HERE ANYMORE

WARNER BROS. 1974.

AWARD *Actress:* Ellen Burstyn.

NOMINATIONS *Supporting Actress:* Diane Ladd. *Original Screenplay:* Robert Getchell.

The sudden death of her husband leaves Alice, played by Burstyn, and her young son, Alfred Lutter, with very little money, but with a freedom she has never known. So they set out to find a new life. After various mishaps, she finds employment in a diner, friendship in the form of foul-mouthed waitress Ladd, and love in the form of rancher Kris Kristofferson [1874]. Strong performances, Getchell's solid script, and excellent direction by comparative newcomer Martin Scorsese [27.5 . . .] transform what could have been routine and soapy into a lively and provocative film, marred only by its rather flat ending. The strong supporting cast includes Jodie Foster [7 . . .] and Harvey Keitel [308].

Burstyn first came to prominence under the name Ellen McRae on Broadway and TV and in her first small film roles in 1964. She took the name Burstyn from her third husband and emerged as a leading film actress in the early seventies. *Alice* was a personal project of Burstyn's; she peddled the script around Hollywood, finally persuading Warners that a film with a strong central role for a woman would attract an audience. She reportedly chose Scorsese as director because he admitted that he didn't know anything about women and looked on the project as a learning experience. The Oscar marked a year of exceptional achievement for Burstyn, who also won the Tony in 1975 for her performance in the Broadway production of *Same Time, Next Year*. In the eighties her screen career began to decline, and she has been seen recently only in occasional supporting roles in films such as *Dying Young* (1991) and *The Cemetery Club* (1993).

The supporting actress Oscar went to Ingrid Bergman for *Murder on the Orient Express*. Robert Towne's *Chinatown* script won the writing award.

Burstyn: 631, 1139, 1682, 1747. Ladd: 1659, 2279. Getchell: 264.

42 • ALICE IN WONDERLAND

WALT DISNEY PRODUCTIONS; RKO RADIO. 1951.

NOMINATION *Scoring of a Musical Picture:* Oliver Wallace.

Alice falls down a rabbit hole and encounters a variety of strange characters. The film's highlight is the Mad Tea Party, with the off-screen voices of Ed Wynn [542] as the Mad Hatter and Jerry Colonna as the March Hare. Alice is voiced by Kathryn Beaumont; Verna Felton is the Queen of Hearts, Richard Haydn the Caterpillar, and Sterling Holloway the Cheshire Cat. This animated adaptation of the Lewis Carroll classic—with interpolations from *Through the Looking Glass*—is generally regarded as one of the lesser products of the Disney studios, a sign of the decline of animated features that began in the fifties and lasted until the resurgence of the genre in the late eighties. The film was a box-office failure, which Walt Disney [645 . . .] later explained as the result of characters that were too weird and a heroine who was unsympathetic. Some others thought it was "too English" for American audiences, although the English critics had complained of the Americanizing of the characters. When *Alice* was revived in the sixties, however, it became a hit with audiences who found precursors of psychedelia in it, as well as in Disney's other famous flop, *Fantasia*.

The failure of *Alice* was somewhat ironic, because an animated feature based on the Alice books had been a pet project of Disney's for many years. He had begun his filmmaking career with a series of silent shorts that combined a live-action little girl named Alice with animated cartoon characters. In the 1940s he hired Aldous Huxley to write a screenplay for an Alice film, but Huxley's script perplexed the studio: It involved live-action sequences in which C. L. Dodgson and the real Alice encounter oddball Victorians who would then have counterparts in the cartoon wonderland Alice would visit. The project was turned over to a team of studio writers, who produced a more workable script.

The scoring Oscar went to Johnny Green and Saul Chaplin for *An American in Paris*.

Wallace: 402, 585, 2202, 2273.5.

43 • ALICE'S RESTAURANT

FLORIN PRODUCTION; UNITED ARTISTS. 1969.

NOMINATION *Director:* Arthur Penn.

Arlo Guthrie plays himself in this episodic exploration of the sixties counterculture, based on his hit record "The Alice's Restaurant Massacree." The center of the film is a group of hippies who live in a deconsecrated church in western Massachusetts under the permissive eye of an older couple, Alice (Pat Quinn) and Ray (James Broderick). Arlo visits the deathbed of his father, Woody, works in a Greenwich Village club, and finally dodges the draft because he has a police record: He was busted for littering after a Thanksgiving dinner at Alice's. This sweet-natured, sometimes funny, but ultimately very sad film can't seem to make up its mind what it wants to be: satire, social commentary, or drama. But it also seems genuine and sincere, unlike a lot of the "youth culture" films of the sixties. *Alice's Restaurant* was Penn's first film after *Bonnie and Clyde* made him a hero of the counterculture. He also cowrote the screenplay, with Venable Herndon. The Oscar went to John Schlesinger for *Midnight Cowboy*.

Penn: 255, 1326.

44 • ALIEN

20TH CENTURY-FOX PRODUCTIONS LTD.; 20TH CENTURY-FOX. 1979.

AWARD *Visual Effects:* H. R. Giger, Carlo Rambaldi, Brian Johnson, Nick Allder, and Denys Ayling.

NOMINATION *Art Direction–Set Decoration:* Michael Seymour, Les Dilley, and Roger Christian; Ian Whittaker.

A spacecraft falls prey to a particularly nasty creature that reproduces by incubating within the bodies of crew members. The crew includes Sigourney Weaver [45 . . .], John Hurt [608 . . .], Tom Skerritt, Ian Holm [386], Harry Dean Stanton, Yaphet Kotto, and Veronica Cartwright. A particularly grisly shocker, *Alien* was a smash hit, spawning not only two sequels but also a flood of inferior derivatives. The production design is almost as memorable as its shock effects. Ridley Scott [2039] directed the film imaginatively. To shoot a notorious scene in which the crea-ture bursts from the chest of a crew member, Scott withheld the details of the script from the rest of the cast until the actual filming. They display genuine shock and horror as the creature pops out in a flux of plastic tubing mixed with offal—one of the award-winning visual effects. Giger and Rambaldi are largely responsible for the appearance of the hideous alien, with the remaining team supervising the spaceflight effects. The art direction Oscar went to *All That Jazz*.

Rambaldi: 588, 1089. Johnson: 577, 614. Dilley: 5, 614, 1652, 1916. Christian: 1916. Whittaker: 954.5, 1679.5.

45 • ALIENS

20TH CENTURY-FOX. 1986.

AWARDS *Visual Effects:* Robert Skotak, Stan Winston, John Richardson, and Suzanne Benson. *Sound Effects Editing:* Don Sharpe.

NOMINATIONS *Actress:* Sigourney Weaver. *Art Direction–Set Decoration:* Peter Lamont; Crispian Sallis. *Sound:* Graham V. Hartstone, Nicolas Le Messurier, Michael A. Carter, and Roy Charman. *Original Score:* James Horner. *Film Editing:* Ray Lovejoy.

After surviving an encounter with creatures that breed in human bodies in *Alien,* Weaver reluctantly allows herself to be sent out with a squadron of marines to investigate the disappearance of colonists on the aliens' home planet. One of the few sequels that actually surpass their originals, this one works in part because of the original: We know how nasty the alien can be, so the film can take more time developing its characters. Director James Cameron keeps things pumping, and he has fun with war-movie clichés—conflicts between individual and authority, the blus-terer (Bill Paxton) who turns out to be a coward but finally redeems himself, the quisling (Paul Reiser) who gets his just deserts. Weaver, who seems to enjoy playing a female Rambo, is well supported by Michael Biehn and Lance Henriksen and by young Carrie Henn as the planet's sole survivor. When Weaver takes on the alien queen, defending Henn just as the queen is trying to defend her brood, it's a battle of real mothers, in every sense of the word.

The Academy's tendency to high seriousness has

caused it to neglect action directors like Cameron, whose work on *Aliens* is at least as impressive as that of the earnest Roland Joffé, who was nominated for *The Mission*. Cameron also cowrote the screenplay with Walter Hill and David Giler. Similarly, Academy voters tend to undervalue performances in action-adventure movies with big special effects. Weaver lost to Marlee Matlin in *Children of a Lesser God*. The art direction Oscar went to *A Room With a View*. *Platoon* took the awards for sound and Claire Simpson's editing. Horner's score lost out to Herbie Hancock's jazz for *'Round Midnight*.

Skotak: 2019. Winston: 153.5, 600, 886, 1071.5, 1600, 2019. Richardson: 413.5. Weaver: 808, 2313. Lamont: 659, 1898. Sallis: 580. Hartstone: 1533, 1977. Le Messurier: 1533, 1977. Carter: 1533. Charman: 1652, 1977, 2287. Horner: 67, 661.

45.5 • *ALIEN*[3]

20TH CENTURY FOX PRODUCTION; 20TH CENTURY FOX. 1992.
NOMINATION *Visual Effects:* Richard Edlund, Alec Gillis, Tom Woodruff, Jr., George Gibbs.

Returning from her mission in *Aliens,* Sigourney Weaver [45 . . .] crash-lands on a penal-colony planet, where she discovers that the horrible creatures she had battled in two previous films have been borne there by the spaceship and are reestablishing themselves. This sequel begins depressingly, with the deaths of all the survivors of the previous film except Weaver, and only gets worse. The action is predictable, and director David Fincher, a comparative novice, stages it poorly. There are a few good performances, notably from Weaver, Charles S. Dutton, and Charles Dance, but the characters are not so well drawn as in the previous films and we cease to care as they are picked off one by one. Even the visual effects have nothing new to show us, and they are sometimes undermined by the choppiness of the film's editing. The Oscar went to *Death Becomes Her.*

Edlund: 544, 614, 766, 1589, 1590, 1652, 1684, 1916, 2165. Woodruff: 513.5. Gibbs: 997, 2274.

46 • *ALL ABOUT EVE*

20TH CENTURY-FOX. 1950.
AWARDS *Picture:* Darryl F. Zanuck, producer. *Supporting Actor:* George Sanders. *Director:* Joseph L. Mankiewicz. *Screenplay:* Joseph L. Mankiewicz. *Sound Recording:* Thomas T. Moulton, 20th Century-Fox Sound Department. *Black-and-White Costume Design:* Edith Head and Charles LeMaire.
NOMINATIONS *Actress:* Bette Davis. *Actress:* Anne Baxter. *Supporting Actress:* Celeste Holm. *Supporting Actress:* Thelma Ritter. *Black-and-White Cinematography:* Milton Krasner. *Black-and-White Art Direction—Set Decoration:* Lyle Wheeler and George Davis; Thomas Little and Walter M. Scott. *Scoring of a Dramatic or Comedy Picture:* Alfred Newman. *Film Editing:* Barbara McLean.

Famous Broadway star Margo Channing (Davis), who is at the peak of her career but beginning to glimpse the downward slope, befriends and employs a young admirer, Eve Harrington (Baxter), only to discover that she's nursed a viper in her bosom. The barbed dialogue in this great backstage comedy of manners would sound phony coming from anyone other than these theatrical types whose job it is to be phony. Everyone in the cast is at his or her best, including a young Marilyn Monroe in a walk-on role. If you ever need proof that Monroe was a natural, watch her hold her own in scenes with Davis and Sanders—there's a glow about her that none of her imitators, from Mansfield to Madonna, has come close to capturing. The film received more nominations (fourteen) than any other picture in Oscar history.

Over the course of his career, Zanuck would accumulate fourteen nominations of his own, plus three Oscars and three Thalberg awards, a record unapproached by any other producer. He had begun his career as a writer at Warner Bros. and moved into producing, reaching his peak at that studio with the coming of sound. In 1933 he left Warners to found his own studio, 20th Century, which merged with Fox the following year, creating one of the great studios of the so-called Hollywood golden age of the thirties and forties. This award, on the cusp of the fifties, found him, like Davis' Margo Channing, at his peak of power in Hollywood, but by middecade he would be on his way out as head of 20th Century-Fox, and his later years were spent in political battles in which he regained control of the studio and lost it again, at one point firing his own son, Richard [580 . . .], whom he had placed at its head—a struggle that makes the backstage squabbling of *All About Eve* seem tame.

Sanders aptly titled his autobiography *Memoirs of a Professional Cad*—the role he played most often in his screen career, and never more skillfully than in this film, as the acerbic, manipulative Addison DeWitt. Sanders began his film career in England in the mid-thirties, and in 1936 came to America, where he played some leading roles but more often was cast as the hero's confidant or foe. He worked steadily in films up until 1972, when he took an overdose of sleeping pills, leaving a suicide note that reportedly said simply, "I'm bored."

Mankiewicz and John Ford [815 . . .] share the distinction of being the only winners of consecutive Oscars for directing. Interestingly both of them received their back-to-back awards for films made for 20th Century-Fox, a suggestion of the kind of power that Zanuck had over the Oscars during his heyday. Markiewicz is also the only person to win both writing and directing Oscars two years in a row. In the fifties, as the studio system that had nurtured him began to fall apart, Mankiewicz attempted independent production with mixed results, as in *The Barefoot Contessa*. He also accepted several challenging but ultimately frustrating directorial assignments under other producers, such as Samuel Goldwyn for *Guys and Dolls* and Walter Wanger for the ill-fated *Cleopatra*. He died in 1993.

Margo Channing is a signature role for Davis, but she was not the first choice for the part. It was originally intended for Claudette Colbert [1025 . . .], who was forced to withdraw after a back injury. It's generally thought that dual nominations for a film are a jinx; if so, *All About Eve* was doubly jinxed, with two nominations in each actress category. The best actress Oscar went to Judy Holliday for *Born Yesterday;* the

supporting award went to Josephine Hull for *Harvey*. Robert Krasker received the cinematography Oscar for *The Third Man. Sunset Boulevard* won for art direction and Franz Waxman's score, and the editing Oscar was won by Ralph E. Winters and Conrad A. Nervig for *King Solomon's Mines*.

Zanuck: 34, 550, 710, 759, 815, 946, 952, 990, 1201, 1327, 1666, 2154, 2286. Mankiewicz: 146, 673, 1163, 1444, 1563, 1836, 1841. Moulton: 22, 138, 366, 457, 487, 560, 706, 798, 962, 1153, 1200, 1451, 1510, 1607, 1849, 2154, 2294. Head: 31, 32, 305, 357, 363, 612, 636, 675, 736, 832, 894, 945, 1003, 1219, 1261, 1263, 1398, 1427, 1504, 1550, 1579, 1587, 1631, 1716, 1727, 1738, 1748, 1840, 1927, 1986, 2012, 2098, 2247, 2298. LeMaire: 21, 376, 495, 530, 542, 954, 1213, 1338, 1391, 1601, 1706, 2008, 2043, 2205, 2294. B. Davis: 484, 492, 1046, 1162, 1182, 1369, 1456, 1462.5, 1908, 2248. Baxter: 1666. Holm: 428, 759. Ritter: 210, 1289, 1564, 1572, 2294. Krasner: 21, 96, 654, 953, 1219, 2072. Wheeler: 19, 83, 356, 376, 428, 476, 495, 530, 542, 719, 721, 798, 950, 1062, 1088, 1149, 1153, 1213, 1391, 1475, 1601, 1616, 1670, 1706, 1852, 2008, 2093, 2212. G. Davis: 69, 401, 495, 542, 736, 953, 1213, 1335, 1388, 1537, 1552, 1706, 1814, 2157, 2184, 2312. Little: 83, 235, 428, 495, 719, 721, 746, 950, 952, 1082, 1149, 1153, 1397, 1475, 1666, 1852, 1868, 2056, 2212, 2286. Scott: 376, 413, 476, 530, 542, 557, 646, 896, 1088, 1213, 1391, 1475, 1706, 1753, 1881, 1907, 2008, 2120, 2247. Newman: 31, 34, 72, 138, 182, 226, 333, 334, 347, 375, 428, 437, 457, 476, 495, 542, 690, 797, 833, 952, 953, 959, 962, 1016, 1082, 1088, 1213, 1278, 1362, 1397, 1475, 1616, 1655, 1849, 1868, 1883, 1921, 2043, 2046, 2091, 2258, 2286, 2294, 2316. McLean: 34, 1195, 1327, 1655, 1868, 2286.

47 • ALL-AMERICAN CO-ED

HAL ROACH; UNITED ARTISTS. 1941.

NOMINATIONS *Song:* "Out of the Silence," music and lyrics by Lloyd B. Norlind. *Scoring of a Musical Picture:* Edward Ward.

To get even with students at a women's college

who have snubbed them, fraternity members at an all-male school enter one of their members in a beauty contest being held at the women's college. This silly *Charley's Aunt* rip-off from the Hal Roach B-movie factory stars big-band singer Frances Langford and features the silent-movie comedian Harry Langdon in a supporting role.

For many years the individual branches of the Academy were allowed to set their own rules for nominations and awards. The music branch, for example, allowed each studio and independent producer to submit a candidate for the Oscars, with the result that at one point more nominations were being generated for music than for any other category. In 1941, for example, there were nine nominations for best song, twenty for scoring of a dramatic picture, and ten for scoring musicals. So a lot of forgotten and forgettable films, such as this one, have entered the record books. Norlind's song was defeated by "The Last Time I Saw Paris," by Jerome Kern and Oscar Hammerstein II, from *Lady Be Good*. Frank Churchill and Oliver Wallace won the scoring award for *Dumbo*.

Ward: 388, 694, 1270, 1560, 2002.

48 • ALL QUIET ON THE WESTERN FRONT

UNIVERSAL. 1929–30.

AWARDS *Production:* Carl Laemmle, Jr., producer. *Director:* Lewis Milestone.

NOMINATIONS *Writing Achievement:* George Abbott, Maxwell Anderson, and Del Andrews. *Cinematography:* Arthur Edeson.

A group of young Germans enthusiastically volunteer for duty in World War I and meet death and disillusionment in the trenches. The central character, played by Lew Ayres [1052], is killed by a sniper as he reaches for a butterfly at the film's end. (In fact, the hand that reaches out is director Milestone's.) This adaptation of Erich Maria Remarque's antiwar novel was the third winner for best picture, but unlike the first two, *Wings* and *Broadway Melody,* it still looks like a classic and not just a transitional effort as Hollywood edged into the sound era. Ben Alexander, of TV's *Dragnet,* is one of the boys, and future Oscar-

winning director Fred Zinnemann [732 . . .] can be glimpsed as an extra. Yet another director, George Cukor [262 . . .], began his Hollywood career as a dialogue director on the film. His services were sorely needed in these early days of sound: The young actors in *All Quiet* still seem to be raising their voices to be heard by the microphones, and few of them have developed a naturalistic style. Milestone himself hasn't fully crossed the bridge from silents to talkies; he still allows actors to telegraph their emotions before they speak their lines. The most assured performance in the film is that of Lewis Wolheim as the gruff soldier Katczinsky. In the end, however, the stunning action sequences and genuine emotion of the film more than compensate for its stagy and preachy moments.

Laemmle was the son of one of Hollywood's pioneers. The elder Laemmle was noted for staffing his studio with relatives, including the young William Wyler [175 . . .], leading to the couplet attributed to Ogden Nash: "Uncle Carl Laemmle/Has a very large faemmle." Carl Jr. was placed at the head of the studio at age twenty-one, and *All Quiet* is one of his first productions. He also launched the series of horror films—*Dracula, Frankenstein, The Invisible Man,* etc.—that were Universal's chief claim to fame for many years. The studio's financial difficulties led to his firing in 1936, and after an unsuccessful attempt at independent production he left the film industry. He died in 1979.

Milestone, born in Russia, emigrated to the United States in 1913. During World War I, he served with the Signal Corps making training films. He was hired as a director by Howard Hughes [734 . . .] in 1925 and made several important films in the twenties and thirties. His later Hollywood career was spotty, and he became a television director in the mid-fifties. He died in 1980.

Abbott worked as a writer and director in Hollywood in the very early thirties, but he found Broadway more congenial and returned to Hollywood only occasionally, most notably for the films of his stage hits *The Pajama Game* and *Damn Yankees*. He was still active as a Broadway director after he turned one hundred. Abbott died in 1995 at one hundred and seven, a year or so after consulting on a hit Broadway revival of *Damn Yankees.* Anderson was a much-admired playwright, though his work is seldom revived today; like many prominent authors, he found the lure of Hollywood money irresistible, but his screenwriting output, except for *All Quiet,* is undistinguished. Andrews began as a film editor at Universal; his skill at shaping a story led him into screenwriting. The writing Oscar went to Frances Marion for *The Big House.*

The award for cinematography went to Joseph T. Rucker and Willard Van Der Meer for the documentary *With Byrd at the South Pole.*

Milestone: 734, 1464, 2159. Edeson: 365, 989.

49 • ALL THAT JAZZ

COLUMBIA/20TH CENTURY-FOX PRODUCTION; 20TH CENTURY-FOX. 1979.

AWARDS *Art Direction–Set Decoration:* Philip Rosenberg and Tony Walton; Edward Stewart and Gary Brink. *Original Song Score and Its Adaptation or Adaptation Score:* Ralph Burns. *Film Editing:* Alan Heim. *Costume Design:* Albert Wolsky.

NOMINATIONS *Picture:* Robert Alan Aurthur, producer. *Actor:* Roy Scheider. *Director:* Bob Fosse. *Screenplay Written Directly for the Screen:* Robert Alan Aurthur and Bob Fosse. *Cinematography:* Giuseppe Rotunno.

Scheider plays a self-destructive Broadway director whose appearance, appetites, and attitude all mirror Fosse's own, and the film includes a chilling forecast of its creator's end: The central character dies of a heart attack. The movie has been compared, by Scheider among others, with *8¹/₂* because of its autobiographical element and its mingling of fantasy sequences with realistic ones. Though something of a mess, it has some moments of musical excitement, mixed with scenes that are hard to take: Name another musical with an extended up-close look at open-heart surgery. Jessica Lange [244.5 . . .] appears as the hero's Muse, and the cast includes Ann Reinking, Cliff Gorman, Ben Vereen, Sandahl Bergman, and John Lithgow [2020 . . .]. Editor Heim, who first worked for Fosse on the TV special *Liza*

With a "Z," and cut the director's *Lenny* and *Star 80* as well, makes an appearance playing himself.

Scheider, who replaced Richard Dreyfuss [803], originally cast in the lead role, lost to Dustin Hoffman for *Kramer vs. Kramer,* which also took the awards for best picture and for director Robert Benton. The writing award went to Steve Tesich for *Breaking Away.* The cinematography Oscar was won by Vittorio Storaro for *Apocalypse Now.*

Rosenberg: 2299. Walton: 1284, 1378, 2299. Stewart: 2299. Burns: 86, 321. Heim: 1424. Wolsky: 308, 1061, 1876, 2127.5. Scheider: 724. Fosse: 321, 1155.

50 • ALL THAT MONEY CAN BUY

RKO RADIO. 1941.

AWARD *Scoring of a Dramatic Picture:* Bernard Herrmann.

NOMINATION *Actor:* Walter Huston.

Huston plays Mr. Scratch, the devil, who tempts a farmer into selling his soul. But the eminent orator Daniel Webster (Edward Arnold) is more than a match for Scratch. Very entertaining adaptation of Stephen Vincent Benét's story "The Devil and Daniel Webster," which was the film's original title. Weak box office led RKO to change the title to the one the Academy recognized, and when that didn't work, the movie was released under at least two other titles: *Daniel and the Devil* and *Here Is a Man.* Today it's hard to see why audiences shunned the film. The fine cast includes James Craig, Anne Shirley [1923], Jane Darwell [815], Gene Lockhart [36], Simone Simon, John Qualen, and H. B. Warner [1206]. William Dieterle [1169] directed, with handsome photography by Joseph August [849 . . .] and special effects supervised by Vernon Walker [253 . . .].

Herrmann began his composing and conducting career in his native New York City, working for CBS radio. He was brought to Hollywood by Orson Welles [407 . . .], with whom he had worked on the celebrated *Mercury Theater* radio shows, and received two nominations in his first year as a film composer—the other one for *Citizen Kane.* Though he was best known for his scores for Alfred Hitchcock

[1171 . . .], especially *Vertigo* and *Psycho,* he never received a nomination for a Hitchcock film, and this is his sole Oscar. He died in 1975 after completing the recording of his score for *Taxi Driver,* which is dedicated to his memory.

The acting Oscar went to Gary Cooper for *Sergeant York.*

Herrmann: 83, 407, 1460, 2005. Huston: 560, 2136, 2318.

51 · ALL THE BROTHERS WERE VALIANT
MGM. 1953.
NOMINATION *Color Cinematography:* George Folsey.

New England whalers Robert Taylor and Stewart Granger battle over Ann Blyth [1319] in this adaptation by Harry Brown [1579 . . .] of a Ben Ames Williams novel. Routine adventure-romance, directed by Richard Thorpe, with Keenan Wynn, James Whitmore [157 . . .], and Lewis Stone [1540].

Folsey was responsible for the rich, glossy look of countless MGM films in the years of the studio's dominance, earning a string of nominations but never receiving an Oscar. This time the cinematography award went to Loyal Griggs for *Shane.*

Folsey: 137, 629, 807, 835, 838, 1124, 1299, 1320, 1500, 1688, 1782, 2068, 2269.

52 · ALL THE KING'S HORSES
PARAMOUNT. 1935.
NOMINATION *Dance Direction:* LeRoy Prinz.

Movie star Carl Brisson goes home to his Ruritanian country and finds that he's the spitting image of the king. No doubt having seen *The Prisoner of Zenda,* the two change places. Conventional musical, directed by Frank Tuttle, and enlivened only by the indispensable Edward Everett Horton and Eugene Pallette. Prinz, nominated for the "Viennese Waltz" number, lost to David Gould's work on *Broadway Melody of 1936* and *Folies Bergère.* Though he continued to work as a film choreographer well into the fifties, Prinz also produced and directed documentaries and educational films. He directed the Oscar-winning short film *A Boy and His Dog* in 1946.

Prinz: 196, 2220.

53 · ALL THE KING'S MEN
ROBERT ROSSEN PRODUCTIONS; COLUMBIA. 1949.
AWARDS *Picture:* Robert Rossen, producer. *Actor:* Broderick Crawford. *Supporting Actress:* Mercedes McCambridge.
NOMINATIONS *Supporting Actor:* John Ireland. *Director:* Robert Rossen. *Screenplay:* Robert Rossen. *Film Editing:* Robert Parrish and Al Clark.

Crawford plays Willie Stark, who begins as an honest man but is corrupted by power into a Huey Long–style demagogue. McCambridge is Stark's hard-boiled assistant who is also, if you know how to decode the Production Code, his mistress. Ireland plays a reporter who begins as an admirer of Stark but grows increasingly, and fatally, disillusioned. Strong performances and good direction make this adaptation of Robert Penn Warren's novel a lively political drama, even if we always know what's going to happen next.

Beginning as a screenwriter, Rossen moved into producing and directing in the forties, specializing in dark-toned dramas such as *Body and Soul.* He lost the directing and writing Oscars to Joseph Mankiewicz for *A Letter to Three Wives,* but Rossen could have been a rival to Mankiewicz as a triple-threat producer-director-writer. Then, at the peak of his career, having just won the Oscar for *All the King's Men,* Rossen was called before the House Un-American Activities Committee. When he refused to testify about his past membership in the Communist Party and to identify others, he was blacklisted. He was removed from the blacklist two years later when he voluntarily gave names to the committee, but he found it hard to live with the guilt and left Hollywood. His later films, most notably *The Hustler,* were made outside of Hollywood. He died in 1966, shortly after the commercial and critical failure of his last film, *Lilith.*

Crawford, the son of actress Helen Broderick, had a measure of success on the stage before going to Hollywood, where much of his career was spent in B pictures. The Oscar seemed to be his big break, landing him the lead in *Born Yesterday* the year after, but he was soon back in mediocre films. In his later career he was best known for the TV series *Highway Patrol*. He died in 1986.

McCambridge, already well known as a Broadway and radio actress, made her screen debut with her Oscar-winning role. Her subsequent career was affected by personal problems and alcoholism, but she made her mark with some strong character roles, most memorably perhaps in the oddball western *Johnny Guitar* (1954) and the Orson Welles [407 . . .] film *Touch of Evil* (1958). She also supplied the voice of the demon that possesses Linda Blair in *The Exorcist*.

Ireland's film career, which began in 1946 and lasted till his death in 1992, was spent mostly in westerns, including *My Darling Clementine* (1946) and *Red River*. The Oscar went to Dean Jagger for *12 O'Clock High*.

The film editing Oscar went to Harry Gerstad for *Champion*.

Rossen: 964. McCambridge: 768. Parrish: 251. Clark: 114, 456, 1370, 1550.

54 • ALL THE PRESIDENT'S MEN

Wildwood Enterprises Inc. Production; Warner Bros. 1976.

Awards *Supporting Actor:* Jason Robards. *Screenplay— Based on Material From Another Medium:* William Goldman. *Art Direction—Set Decoration:* George Jenkins; George Gaines. *Sound:* Arthur Piantadosi, Les Fresholtz, Dick Alexander, and Jim Webb.

Nominations *Picture:* Walter Coblenz, producer. *Supporting Actress:* Jane Alexander. *Director:* Alan J. Pakula. *Film Editing:* Robert L. Wolfe.

Bob Woodward, played by Robert Redford [1502 . . .], and Carl Bernstein, played by Dustin Hoffman [810 . . .], are young *Washington Post* reporters who sense that the whole story behind an attempted burglary at the Democratic Party headquarters in the Watergate complex hasn't been told. So they get the story and bring down an administration. Gripping, fascinating, and very entertaining telling of a story whose ending we know, yet somehow it keeps us on the edge of our seats. Much of the credit goes to Redford, who pushed the project all the way

as an executive producer, and gives one of his best performances. Few actors are as good as Redford at reacting—watch, for example, as his face reveals what he's being told during the film's many phone calls. He is ably partnered by Hoffman; the uneasy relationship of the two reporters is echoed by the conflicting styles of the two actors. That neither was nominated—and that Sylvester Stallone was (for *Rocky*)—has to rank among the Academy's greatest oversights, along with the failure to nominate the moody cinematography of Gordon Willis [786 . . .].

This was the first of two consecutive Oscars for Robards, whose film career was secondary to his stage work for many years. He began acting in movies in 1959, but except for his superb re-creation of his stage role as Jamie in *Long Day's Journey into Night* in the 1962 film, his screen work lacked the intensity that theater audiences know. But his turn as *Washington Post* editor Ben Bradlee certainly deserved the notice the Academy gave it, and was the more impressive because of the fine ensemble that surrounded him, including Jack Warden [890 . . .], Martin Balsam [2067], Ned Beatty [1424], Hal Holbrook, Stephen Collins, Robert Walden, and, for those who keep an eye out, F. Murray Abraham [60] in a small role.

Goldman's second Oscar came for a film that, in his memoir *Adventures in the Screen Trade,* he doesn't have much good to say about. The script was much worked over, including a try at it by Bernstein himself and his then wife, Nora Ephron [1821 . . .]. According to Goldman, the only scene that survives from their contribution is the one in which Bernstein connives his way into Ned Beatty's office—an episode that never happened in real life, despite the film's otherwise careful attempt to maintain a documentarylike accuracy.

The design team carefully re-created the *Washington Post* newsroom on the soundstage, a process that involved, among other things, hauling the contents of reporters' wastebaskets to the set. The sound team likewise captured the clattery ambiance of a pre-electronic newsroom.

The race for the Oscar that year was a tight one, with *All the President's Men* and *Network* dominating the nominations. Only the fierce competition of the two movies, perhaps splitting the vote, can explain the emergence of *Rocky* as best picture. Pakula's loss to John G. Avildsen, who has continued to remake *Rocky* in various guises (e.g., *The Karate Kid*), is equally shocking. *Rocky* also won, somewhat more plausibly, for Richard Halsey and Scott Conrad's editing.

Alexander, who plays a nervous bookkeeper appalled at the underhandedness she has witnessed, lost to Beatrice Straight for *Network*.

Robards: 1066, 1300. Goldman: 317. Jenkins: 394. Gaines: 448, 890, 1798. Piantadosi: 58, 215, 319, 606, 1279, 2113. Fresholtz: 58, 209, 215, 606, 888, 1127, 1158.5, 1279, 1526, 2113, 2179.5. D. Alexander: 209, 519, 888, 1127, 1158.5, 2113, 2179.5. Webb: 1726. J. Alexander: 830, 1111, 2023. Pakula: 1876, 2101. Wolfe: 1473, 1726.

55 • ALL THIS, AND HEAVEN TOO

WARNER BROS. 1940.

NOMINATIONS *Picture:* Jack L. Warner and Hal B. Wallis, with David Lewis, producers. *Supporting Actress:* Barbara O'Neil. *Black-and-White Cinematography:* Ernest Haller.

Nobleman Charles Boyer [36 . . .] bumps off wife O'Neil for love of governess Bette Davis [46 . . .], who is of course the one to suffer the most. Nobody's finest two hours and twenty-three minutes on screen (it only *seems* longer). Warner designed this elaborate production, directed by Anatole Litvak [517 . . .], as a response to the success of *Gone With the Wind,* even instructing the studio to refer to the movie as *ATAHT,* in imitation of the familiar shorthand *GWTW.* Like the latter, *ATAHT* was based on a best-seller, a novel by Rachel Field, adapted by Casey Robinson. Several key personnel, including O'Neil, Haller, and composer Max Steiner [16 . . .], had also worked on *GWTW.* Davis had been one of the key contenders for the role of Scarlett O'Hara, and even *ATAHT*'s second lead, Jeffrey Lynn, had been considered for the role of Ashley Wilkes; he can be seen in some of the existing screen tests made

during the hunt for Scarlett. Even though Warners cut corners, filming in black and white rather than color, for example, it was still an expensive film; publicists claimed that sixty-seven sets were built for it, fourteen more than were built for *GWTW.* But David O. Selznick [497 . . .] had the last laugh. He won the best picture Oscar for *Rebecca,* which is also about a highborn man who is thought to have done in his first wife.

O'Neil had a respectable career in second leads and character roles, most notably as Scarlett O'Hara's mother. The Oscar went to Jane Darwell for *The Grapes of Wrath.* The cinematography award went to George Barnes for *Rebecca.*

Warner: 110, 550, 689, 1393, 2318. Wallis: 17, 85, 164, 343, 365, 676, 689, 712, 965, 1046, 1095, 1162, 1248, 1482, 1727, 1779, 2233, 2318. Lewis: 492. Haller: 679, 798, 1046, 1174, 1319, 2248.

56 • ALOMA OF THE SOUTH SEAS

PARAMOUNT. 1941.

NOMINATIONS *Color Cinematography:* Wilfred M. Cline, Karl Struss, and William Snyder. *Special Effects:* Farciot Edouart and Gordon Jennings, photographic; Louis Mesenkop, sound.

Jon Hall plays an islander who has been sent to the States for an education but has to return to quell a rebellion that erupts, along with a volcano, after his father dies. Dorothy Lamour, of course, is the girl he loves. Lamour and Hall made a strong impression in *Hurricane,* he by baring his chest, she by wrapping hers in a sarong, so this reteaming was inevitable. But the handsome stars, the lurid color, and the volcanic special effects are all the movie has going for it. Directed by Alfred Santell. The cinematography Oscar went to Ernest Palmer and Ray Rennahan for *Blood and Sand.* The effects team of Edouart, Jennings, and Mesenkop defeated themselves; they took home the Oscar for *I Wanted Wings* instead.

Struss: 572, 582, 1819, 1972. Snyder: 1057, 1223. Edouart: 570, 975, 1668, 1855, 1887, 1934, 2168, 2175, 2181. Jennings: 570, 975, 1668, 1855, 1887, 1934, 2168, 2175, 2181. Mesenkop: 975, 1668, 1887.

57 • ALSINO AND THE CONDOR

NICARAGUAN FILM INSTITUTE PRODUCTION (NICARAGUA). 1982.
NOMINATION *Foreign Language Film.*

An American pilot, played by Dean Stockwell [1281], gives Alsino, a twelve-year-old Nicaraguan boy, a ride in his helicopter, fueling the boy's dreams of flying like the birds. Alsino injures himself badly in a fall but becomes a hero when he joins the guerrillas fighting the Somoza dictatorship. The blend of realism and fantasy, well handled by director Miguel Littín, keeps the political allegory from becoming too heavy-handed, though it's never likely to be one of Oliver North's favorite movies. The Oscar went to *Volver a Empezar (To Begin Again).*

58 • ALTERED STATES

WARNER BROS. PRODUCTION; WARNER BROS. 1980.
NOMINATIONS *Sound:* Arthur Piantadosi, Les Fresholtz, Michael Minkler, and Willie D. Burton. *Original Score:* John Corigliano.

In his film debut William Hurt [293 . . .] plays a scientist investigating human evolution who experiments on himself, with disastrous results. This messy intellectual horror movie tries to update *Dr. Jekyll and Mr. Hyde,* but it has fallen into the hands of director Ken Russell [2307], whose excesses have wrecked many a film. Screenwriter Paddy Chayefsky [783 . . .] was so appalled at what Russell had made of the script he adapted from his own novel that he insisted on being billed as Sidney Aaron in the credits, but he still has to take the blame for much of the tedium and pretentiousness of the dialogue. The cast includes Blair Brown, Bob Balaban, Charles Haid, and Drew Barrymore.

The sound Oscar went to *The Empire Strikes Back.* Michael Gore won the music award for *Fame,* but Corigliano has continued to make his name as a composer, particularly with his opera *The Ghosts of Versailles,* which was staged at the Met.

Piantadosi: 54, 215, 319, 606, 1279, 2113. Fresholtz: 54, 209, 215, 606, 888, 1127, 1158.5, 1279, 1526, 2113, 2179.5. Minkler: 260, 398, 413.5, 606, 1047, 2144. Burton: 209, 307, 1802.5, 2231.

59 • ALWAYS IN MY HEART

WARNER BROS. 1942.
NOMINATION *Song:* "Always in My Heart," music by Ernesto Lecuona, lyrics by Kim Gannon.

Walter Huston [50 . . .], released from prison, returns home to find his wife, Kay Francis, about to remarry. Tedious soap opera, directed by Jo Graham, with Gloria Warren, Una O'Connor, and Sidney Blackmer. The Oscar went to Irving Berlin's "White Christmas," from *Holiday Inn.*

Gannon: 589, 1870.

60 • AMADEUS

SAUL ZAENTZ COMPANY PRODUCTION; ORION. 1984.
AWARDS *Picture:* Saul Zaentz, producer. *Actor:* F. Murray Abraham. *Director:* Milos Forman. *Screenplay Based on Material From Another Medium:* Peter Shaffer. *Art Direction—Set Decoration:* Patrizia Von Brandenstein; Karel Cerny. *Sound:* Mark Berger, Tom Scott, Todd Boekelheide, and Chris Newman. *Costume Design:* Theodor Pistek. *Makeup:* Paul LeBlanc and Dick Smith.
NOMINATIONS *Actor:* Tom Hulce. *Cinematography:* Miroslav Ondricek. *Film Editing:* Nena Danevic and Michael Chandler.

Composer Antonio Salieri (Abraham) goes to meet the latest musical sensation, Wolfgang Amadeus Mozart (Hulce), and is appalled to discover that God has lavished genius on a randy buffoon, so he obsessively sets out to engineer Mozart's destruction. The movie is gorgeous to look at, and it supplies us with generous amounts of some of the greatest music ever written, so perhaps we shouldn't complain that Shaffer's screen adaptation of his own stage play is full of false history and pretentious philosophizing. Elizabeth Berridge plays Mozart's wife, and the cast includes Simon Callow, Roy Dotrice, Christine Ebersole, and Jeffrey Jones.

Costume dramas have traditionally been a British specialty, and Forman began his casting search among English actors such as Kenneth Branagh [902], who was a leading contender for the role of Mozart. Instead, he chose Hulce, whose best-known screen performance to this point had been in *National Lampoon's*

Animal House, and Abraham, a Broadway actor. The decision was controversial: British film historian Leslie Halliwell sniffed, "The American accents jar the ear"—as though eighteenth-century Austrians and Italians spoke Oxbridge English. But Forman set a trend that director Stephen Frears would continue four years later in casting *Dangerous Liaisons,* a film that would, ironically, beat Forman's own treatment of the Choderlos de Laclos novel, *Valmont,* to the screen.

Abraham was a veteran performer on stage and TV whose movie appearances had consisted of small supporting roles in such films as *Serpico* and *All the President's Men,* but his face was perhaps most familiar to audiences from his role as a bunch of grapes in a Fruit of the Loom underwear commercial. Although the Oscar boosted his name recognition and put the embarrassment of the commercial to rest, Abraham has still not had much success finding major film roles.

Amadeus was something of a comeback film for director Forman, who had two flops, *Hair* and *Ragtime,* after his first Oscar for *One Flew Over the Cuckoo's Nest.* But he followed with *Valmont,* which, overshadowed by *Dangerous Liaisons,* was a commercial failure. Zaentz's film production record has been similarly jinxed: Most recently he produced the unsuccessful *At Play in the Fields of the Lord* (1991).

The Killing Fields took the Oscars for Chris Menges' cinematography and Jim Clark's editing.

Zaentz: 1481. Forman: 1481. Shaffer: 621. Von Brandenstein: 1651, 2185. Berger: 92, 1698. Scott: 1698. Boekelheide: 1425. Newman: 398, 631, 641, 724, 784, 1820. Pistek: 2195. Smith: 475. Ondricek: 1651.

61 • AMARCORD

F.C. (Rome)-P.E.C.F. (Paris) Production; New World Pictures (Italy). 1975.
Award *Foreign Language Film. (1974)*
Nominations *Director:* Federico Fellini. *Original Screenplay:* Federico Fellini and Tonino Guerra.

Fellini returns to scenes from his childhood in the coastal town of Rimini during the thirties, and the result, though loose and episodic, is one of his warmest films. It qualified for the foreign language film award a year before it met the distribution requirements for the other competitive awards. The directing Oscar went to Milos Forman for *One Flew Over the Cuckoo's Nest.* Frank Pierson's script for *Dog Day Afternoon* won the writing Oscar.

Fellini: 562, 603, 657, 658, 1496, 1519, 1938, 2209. Guerra: 240, 367.

62 • AMAZING MRS. HOLLIDAY, THE

Universal. 1943.
Nomination *Scoring of a Dramatic or Comedy Picture:* Hans J. Salter and Frank Skinner.

American schoolteacher Deanna Durbin tries to smuggle nine Chinese orphans into wartime San Francisco. Edmond O'Brien [146 . . .] is the unlikely leading man, and Barry Fitzgerald [787] plays a ship's steward. Inconsequential and silly movie with Durbin's usual musical numbers interpolated. Much of the film was directed by Jean Renoir [1884], though it's credited to Bruce Manning. Despite Durbin's songs, the film's score competed in the dramatic rather than the musical category. It lost to Alfred Newman's score for *The Song of Bernadette.*

Salter: 340, 399, 1030, 1307, 2060. Skinner: 96, 125, 947, 1229.

63 • AMERICA, AMERICA

Athena Enterprises Production; Warner Bros. 1963.
Award *Black-and-White Art Direction—Set Decoration:* Gene Callahan.
Nominations *Picture:* Elia Kazan, producer. *Director:* Elia Kazan. *Story and Screenplay—Written Directly for the Screen:* Elia Kazan.

A Greek boy longs to escape the second-class status of Greeks living in turn-of-the-century Turkey, and emigrate to America. He succeeds, but only after much suffering. Kazan's screenplay, based on his uncle's experiences, was meant to be the first of a trilogy, but the film's box-office failure doomed that plan. Stathis Giallelis, who plays the main role, simply isn't up to the part, but he is well supported by Frank Wolff, Elena Karam, Lou Antonio, and John Marley [1218]. The cinematography is by Haskell Wexler

[229 . . .] and the score by Manos Hadjidakis [1426].

The film's nomination as best picture is a testimony to the weakness of 1963's offerings. The other competitors included the mammoth disaster *Cleopatra,* the overblown Cinerama epic *How the West Was Won,* the small sentimental drama *Lilies of the Field,* and the easy winner, *Tom Jones.* Some have speculated that *America, America* was nominated to counter the British front-runner with a celebration of America. Whatever the reason, it knocked several more deserving films out of the running, notably *Hud,* and one of the greatest films of the sixties, *8¹/₂.* Interestingly, only two of the directors of the nominated films were candidates for best director; Kazan lost to the other one, *Tom Jones'* Tony Richardson. The writing award went to James R. Webb for *How the West Was Won.*

Callahan: 356, 964, 1143. Kazan: 593, 759, 1477, 1949.

64 • AMERICAN DREAM, AN
WARNER BROS. 1966.

NOMINATION *Song:* ''A Time for Love,'' music by Johnny Mandel, lyrics by Paul Francis Webster.

A TV newsman murders his wife and gets involved with the mob. Stuart Whitman [1277], Janet Leigh [1632], and Eleanor Parker [328 . . .] are wasted in this inept version of Norman Mailer's novel, directed by Robert Gist. Trekkies may want to check it out for a glimpse of George Takei in a minor role. The rather lovely song, which is completely at odds with the sleazy goings-on, lost to John Barry and Don Black's title song from *Born Free.*

Mandel: 1755. Webster: 33, 95, 331, 376, 604, 663, 730, 856, 1213, 1276, 1322, 1388, 1755, 1925, 2014.

65 • AMERICAN GRAFFITI
UNIVERSAL-LUCASFILM LTD.-COPPOLA COMPANY PRODUCTION; UNIVERSAL. 1973.

NOMINATIONS *Picture:* Francis Ford Coppola, producer; Gary Kurtz, coproducer. *Supporting Actress:* Candy Clark. *Director:* George Lucas. *Story and Screenplay— Based on Factual Material or Material Not Previously Pub-* *lished or Produced:* George Lucas, Gloria Katz, and Willard Huyck. *Film Editing:* Verna Fields and Marcia Lucas.

In the summer after their high school graduation, a group of friends bide their time before leaving for college or entering the workforce by cruising the streets of Modesto, California. Richard Dreyfuss [803], who is college-bound, spends an evening trying to find a blonde (Suzanne Somers) he has glimpsed in a passing car. Ron (billed as Ronny) Howard plays his friend who can't quite decide between going off to college or settling down with his girlfriend, played by Cindy Williams. Paul LeMat is the somewhat older drag-racing mentor to the group. Charles Martin Smith is the nerdy Terry the Toad, who hooks up with a ditzy young woman, played by Clark. Mackenzie Phillips is a preteen who tags along, trying to fit in with the older kids. And a then-unknown Harrison Ford [2296] has a very small part as LeMat's drag-racing rival. It's one of the most entertaining movies of its time, artfully achieving a very difficult effect, nostalgia with a bite, though the ending has been rightly faulted by feminists: The titles in the epilogue account for the fates of the male characters, but not the female ones.

Lucas outlined the characters and drafted the episodic story line, and turned it over to fellow USC film-school grad Huyck and Huyck's wife, Katz, for the scenario and dialogue. He then approached Coppola, whom Lucas had met at Warner Bros. while serving an internship. Coppola, who had won enormous clout with the success of *The Godfather,* persuaded the initially reluctant studio to back Lucas' project, although when it was finished, one executive proclaimed that *American Graffiti* was unreleasable. Instead, it became one of the most profitable movies of all time—a classic sleeper. It also launched a much-imitated practice of filling the soundtrack with golden oldies—originally a cost-cutting device because Lucas couldn't afford to commission a score.

Dreyfuss, Howard, and especially Ford went on to substantial careers, but the sole acting nominee, Clark, not only failed to find roles that would make her a star but also lost the Oscar—to Tatum O'Neal in *Paper Moon*. Lucas, of course, went on to the great-est success of all, using the proceeds from this film and the *Star Wars* and *Indiana Jones* trilogies to establish a major special effects studio, Industrial Light and Magic, that has had a major impact on American film. He has never succeeded in winning an Oscar, al-though he received the 1991 Irving G. Thalberg Award. *The Sting* took the awards for picture, director George Roy Hill, screenwriter David S. Ward, and editor William Reynolds.

Coppola: 92, 442, 784, 785, 786, 1541. Kurtz: 1916. G. Lucas: 1916. Fields: 1041. M. Lucas: 1916.

66 • AMERICAN IN PARIS, AN

MGM. 1951.

Awards *Picture:* Arthur Freed, producer. *Story and Screenplay:* Alan Jay Lerner. *Color Cinematography:* Al-fred Gilks and John Alton. *Color Art Direction–Set Dec-oration:* Cedric Gibbons and Preston Ames; Edwin B. Willis and Keogh Gleason. *Scoring of a Musical Picture:* Johnny Green and Saul Chaplin. *Color Costume Design:* Orry-Kelly, Walter Plunkett, and Irene Sharaff.
Nominations *Director:* Vincente Minnelli. *Film Editing:* Adrienne Fazan.

Expatriate artist Gene Kelly [74] falls in love with a Parisian girl, Leslie Caron [1113 . . .], unaware that she's engaged to his friend Georges Guetary. Nina Foch [629] is the rich woman who would like to buy Kelly's affections as well as his paintings. Oscar Le-vant is—what else?—Kelly's acerbic sidekick. All of this musical comedy nonsense is set to wonderful songs by George [1797] and Ira Gershwin [455 . . .] and concludes with a seventeen-minute ballet to the Gershwin tone poem from which the film gets its name.

The Oscar for best picture was seen at the time as a tribute to the Freed Unit—the MGM production unit devoted to making musicals. Freed was present at the dawning of movie musicals, having been hired as a lyricist by Irving Thalberg [150 . . .] in 1929. He graduated to associate producer on *The Wizard of Oz* and for the next two decades was the most celebrated producer of musicals in Hollywood. He also received the Thalberg Award in 1951. *An American in Paris* was

his idea: a film that would showcase the songs of the Gershwins just as his *Easter Parade* had showcased those of Irving Berlin [34 . . .]. The climactic ballet was also Freed's idea.

The producer thought of casting Fred Astaire [2126] in the lead, but Kelly was eager for the part and quickly won him over. The part of Kelly's friend and Caron's fiancé was originally intended for Mau-rice Chevalier [203 . . .], but that fell through for reasons that are still something of a mystery: Some say that Chevalier turned down the part because he didn't like losing the girl, others that MGM got cold feet because of Chevalier's alleged collaboration with the Vichy government during the war. An alternative choice, Yves Montand, was passed over because his leftist leanings were suspect in the era of the blacklist. Guetary, who was appearing on Broadway at the time, was signed, but his American career fizzled af-ter this film. Leslie Caron, still in her teens, made a more successful debut. She was discovered by Kelly, who had seen her dancing in Paris two years earlier.

Lerner, best known for the partnership with com-poser Frederick Loewe [769 . . .] that resulted in *My Fair Lady* and *Gigi,* was under contract to MGM, for which he first wrote the story and screenplay to *Royal Wedding.* The chief challenge of the *American in Paris* screenplay is in finding ways to work into the film Gershwin songs that had existed in other con-texts before, and to provide a pretext for the final ballet.

While art department head Gibbons gets the top credit, the real design work fell to Ames, who had studied architecture in Paris. Minnelli himself had be-gun his career as a set designer, which sometimes led to conflicts between the director and the art directors assigned to him, but the partnership with Ames was fruitful and continued on Minnelli's other MGM musicals. The realistic re-creation of the quai across from Notre Dame that features in the ''Our Love Is Here to Stay'' number is one of the designers' tri-umphs. Kelly had protested that the sequence needed to be shot on location in Paris, to which Ames re-plied, ''Have you ever danced on cobblestones?''

Minnelli was less simpatico with Gilks, not one of

MGM's first-string cameramen, and insisted that Alton, who had shot *Father of the Bride* for him, be assigned to the ballet, for which he wanted someone who could evoke the palette of the painters—Dufy, Lautrec, Utrillo—who are the ballet's inspiration.

MGM music department head Green was a natural choice for the musical, since he had worked with the Gershwins on Broadway in the thirties, but much of the actual work of orchestration was done by Chaplin. The original score for the film included several songs that were cut from the final release print, including a dance for Kelly and Caron to "Somebody Loves Me," Kelly's "I've Got a Crush on You," and two numbers for Guetary, "Love Walked In" and "But Not for Me."

Kelly contributed more than his usual charm to the film: He choreographed all the numbers and even directed the sequence set to "Embraceable You." During the 1951 awards he received an honorary Oscar, which was not specifically for *An American in Paris* but was clearly prompted by it. The film also shows Kelly's weakness: The overlong and too-arty final ballet is the product of a popular artist who wants to be taken seriously—it has the sentimental excess of the clown who wants to play Hamlet.

Minnelli lost to George Stevens for *A Place in the Sun,* revealing the ambivalence that the voters seemed to feel about the best picture winner. Some speculate that the two serious dramas in the running, *A Place in the Sun* and *A Streetcar Named Desire,* may have split the vote, allowing *An American in Paris* to slip through. (The other two nominees, *Decision Before Dawn* and *Quo Vadis?,* were not strong contenders.) *A Place in the Sun* also won for William Hornbeck's editing. *Streetcar* had to content itself with three of the four acting Oscars. *An American in Paris,* incidentally, is among the handful of best picture winners that received no acting nominations whatever.

Freed: 769. Lerner: 769, 1186, 1393, 1731. Gibbons: 87, 130, 217, 227, 239, 285, 290, 440, 629, 749, 831, 980, 1069, 1096, 1173, 1190, 1226, 1230, 1232, 1274, 1308, 1309, 1417, 1567, 1604, 1644, 1662, 1673, 1721, 1861, 1937, 2068, 2112, 2256, 2257, 2300, 2320, 2330. Ames: 31, 290, 591, 769, 1226, 1937, 2184. Willis: 87, 130, 227, 239, 290, 629, 749, 831, 980, 1069, 1096, 1157, 1173, 1190, 1226, 1230, 1232, 1309, 1417, 1567, 1657, 1662, 1673, 1721, 1861, 1937, 2068, 2112, 2257, 2320, 2330. Gleason: 130, 290, 769, 1226, 1861, 1937. Green: 320, 594, 662, 817, 914, 1298, 1471, 1550, 1657, 2047, 2244. Chaplin: 914, 1097, 1782, 2244. Orry-Kelly: 853, 1157, 1860. Plunkett: 9, 953, 1087, 1243, 1587, 1657, 1859, 2029, 2330. Sharaff: 290, 333, 338, 413, 690, 852, 896, 1088, 1507, 1592, 1910, 2000, 2244, 2277. Minnelli: 769. Fazan: 769.

67 • *AMERICAN TAIL, AN*

AMBLIN ENTERTAINMENT PRODUCTION; UNIVERSAL. 1986.

NOMINATION *Song:* "Somewhere Out There," music by James Horner and Barry Mann, lyrics by Cynthia Weil.

Fievel, a young Russian mouse, emigrates with his family to the New World at the turn of the century but is separated from them and has to fend for himself. Well-done but occasionally too sticky feature-length animated cartoon, produced by Steven Spielberg [416 . . .] and executed by a team under the direction of Don Bluth. Voices are supplied by Dom DeLuise, Christopher Plummer, and Madeline Kahn [230 . . .]. The song Oscar went to Giorgio Moroder and Tom Whitlock's "Take My Breath Away," from *Top Gun.*

Horner: 45, 661.

68 • *AMERICAN WEREWOLF IN LONDON, AN*

UNIVERSAL. 1981.

AWARD *Makeup:* Rick Baker.

David Naughton and Griffin Dunne are hitchhiking around England when they make the mistake of walking through the wrong wood at the wrong time—the title gives the rest away. Spoofy horror film that would be a lot better if director John Landis were in more control: The excessive mayhem of the final scenes is particularly unnecessary. Much of it, however, is good scary fun. Dunne spends much of the film in increasing states of decay, while Naughton's transformations, courtesy of Baker, are far more convincing than the old slow dissolves that used to put fur on Lon Chaney, Jr. Baker, who began his career as a monster-makeup specialist in the early seventies, was the first recipient of the newly created competitive award for makeup.

Baker: 431, 595.8, 839, 874.

69 • AMERICANIZATION OF EMILY, THE

MGM. 1964.

NOMINATIONS *Black-and-White Cinematography:* Philip H. Lathrop. *Black-and-White Art Direction–Set Decoration:* George W. Davis, Hans Peters, and Elliot Scott; Henry Grace and Robert R. Benton.

Julie Andrews [1284 . . .] falls in love with naval officer James Garner [1380] during World War II, but Garner is involved in a plot by the navy to make him the first casualty in the Normandy invasion. This muddled comedy-drama, based on a novel by William Bradford Huie, was one of Andrews' attempts to change her image from wholesome nanny to sexy heroine. It didn't work, and neither does the film, despite the efforts of its stars, writer Paddy Chayefsky [783 . . .], director Arthur Hiller [1218], and a cast that includes Melvyn Douglas [169 . . .], James Coburn, Joyce Grenfell, and Keenan Wynn. The cinematography and art direction Oscars went to *Zorba the Greek.*

Lathrop: 591. Davis: 46, 401, 495, 542, 736, 953, 1213, 1335, 1388, 1537, 1552, 1706, 1814, 2157, 2184, 2312. Peters: 1107, 1226, 1567, 1673. Scott: 995, 2274. Grace: 227, 401, 769, 953, 1335, 1388, 1450, 1537, 1552, 2157, 2184, 2312. Benton: 956, 1504, 1840.

70 • AMITYVILLE HORROR, THE

AMERICAN INTERNATIONAL. 1979.

NOMINATION *Original Score:* Lalo Schifrin.

James Brolin and Margot Kidder move their family into a haunted house on Long Island; Rod Steiger [992 . . .] is the priest who tries to help them get rid of the ghoulies. Directed by Stuart Rosenberg, this boring and predictable attempt to recapture the rapture of *The Exorcist* spawned a string of lousy se-

quels. The story is supposedly true, but don't believe everything you read. Schifrin lost to Georges Delerue for *A Little Romance.*

Schifrin: 434, 443, 720, 1928, 2218.

71 • AMOR BRUJO, EL

FILMS R.B. S.A. PRODUCTION (SPAIN). 1967.

NOMINATION *Foreign Language Film.*

The story of a fatal Gypsy love triangle is told in song and dance, set to the music of Manuel de Falla. Directed by Rovira Beleta. The Oscar went to *Closely Watched Trains.*

72 • ANASTASIA

20TH CENTURY-FOX. 1956.

AWARD *Actress:* Ingrid Bergman.

NOMINATION *Scoring of a Dramatic or Comedy Picture:* Alfred Newman.

Russian prince Yul Brynner [1088] schemes to pass off amnesiac Bergman as the youngest daughter of Nicholas II, rumored to have escaped massacre by the Bolsheviks. Can Bergman convince the dowager empress, Helen Hayes [31 . . .]? And is she, perhaps, really Anastasia? Engrossing if somewhat stagy adaptation by Arthur Laurents [2152] of a play by Marcelle Maurette and Guy Bolton.

The Oscar to Bergman ended one of the most famous scandals involving a Hollywood star. It began in 1949, when Bergman left her husband, Petter Lindstrom, for director Roberto Rossellini [1519], with whom she conceived a child before she could receive a divorce from Lindstrom. Americans who were captivated by her chaste and saintly image in films like *The Bells of St. Mary's* and *Joan of Arc* were scandalized. But Bergman's career in European films was less than successful, and when the marriage to Rossellini began to come apart, she signaled her readiness to return to Hollywood. When director Anatole Litvak [517 . . .] first proposed casting Bergman in *Anastasia,* Fox president Spyros Skouras nixed the idea, suggesting Jennifer Jones [584 . . .] for the role instead. But producer Buddy Adler [732 . . .], with the backing of Darryl F. Zanuck [34 . . .], persuaded Skouras that audiences were ready to "forgive" Bergman, which they were. TV impresario Ed Sullivan went so far as to poll his audience on whether he should show a clip from the film on his show. The vote went against Bergman, but the controversy stirred by the poll ironically aroused sympathy for her. The Bergman-Rossellini marriage was annulled, and she resumed the career that earned her three Oscars, more than any actress except Katharine Hepburn [24 . . .].

Newman's score lost to Victor Young's for *Around the World in 80 Days.*

Bergman: 111, 173, 701, 749, 1048, 1378. Newman: 31, 34, 46, 138, 182, 226, 333, 334, 347, 375, 428, 437, 457, 476, 495, 542, 690, 797, 833, 952, 953, 959, 962, 1016, 1082, 1088, 1213, 1278, 1362, 1397, 1475, 1616, 1655, 1849, 1868, 1883, 1921, 2043, 2046, 2091, 2258, 2286, 2294, 2316.

73 • ANATOMY OF A MURDER

COLUMBIA. 1959.

NOMINATIONS *Picture:* Otto Preminger, producer. *Actor:* James Stewart. *Supporting Actor:* Arthur O'Connell. *Supporting Actor:* George C. Scott. *Screenplay— Based on Material From Another Medium:* Wendell Mayes. *Black-and-White Cinematography:* Sam Leavitt. *Film Editing:* Louis R. Loeffler.

Stewart is a small-town attorney who takes on a sensational case, defending Ben Gazzara, a soldier accused of murdering a man who had raped Gazzara's sexy wife, Lee Remick [508]. Stewart is assisted by O'Connell, an alcoholic lawyer, and Eve Arden [1319], his secretary. Scott is the prosecuting attorney, and the judge presiding over the case is played by Joseph N. Welch, a real-life lawyer who became famous on television for his defiance of Senator Joseph McCarthy during the Army-McCarthy hearings of 1953. The movie, directed by Preminger, is based on a best-seller by Robert Traver—the pen name of John D. Voelker, a Michigan judge. Strong characterization and terrific performances help keep this somewhat overextended courtroom melodrama interesting, though its clinical treatment of the rape charges, once considered daring, seems tame compared with the language now routinely used on the evening news.

Preminger gained famed for defying the Production Code in the early fifties with such films as *The Moon Is Blue* and *The Man With the Golden Arm.* His ability to push the censorship envelope is evident in this film as well; *Time*'s reviewer asserted that the film was more about anatomy than about murder. Stewart's father, who displayed his son's Oscar for *The Philadelphia Story* in the window of his hardware store in Indiana, Pennsylvania, was so scandalized he urged people in the actor's hometown not to see the film. But apart from his readiness to shock, Preminger also often brought energy and imagination to his films, evident here in the casting, as well as in hiring the great Duke Ellington [1531] to write the film's score and to appear in a small role.

This was the year of *Ben-Hur,* which won for picture, actor Charlton Heston, supporting actor Hugh Griffith, and editors Ralph E. Winters and John D. Dunning. Neil Paterson's screenplay for *Room at the Top* took the writing Oscar, and William C. Mellor won for his cinematography for *The Diary of Anne Frank.*

Preminger: 356, 1149. Stewart: 876, 1033, 1370, 1563. O'Connell: 1566. Scott: 942, 964, 1541. Leavitt: 522, 630. Loeffler: 356.

74 • ANCHORS AWEIGH

MGM. 1945.

AWARD *Scoring of a Musical Picture:* Georgie Stoll.

NOMINATIONS *Picture:* Joe Pasternak, producer. *Actor:* Gene Kelly. *Color Cinematography:* Robert Planck and Charles Boyle. *Song:* "I Fall in Love Too Easy," music by Jule Styne, lyrics by Sammy Cahn.

Sailors Kelly and Frank Sinatra [732 . . .] both fall for Kathryn Grayson, with predictable consequences for their friendship. Grayson's nephew is played by nine-year-old Dean Stockwell [1281]. The Styne-Cahn tunes are pleasant, and Kelly and Sinatra make an enormously appealing team, but the film, directed by George Sidney, is rather lightweight and predictable, with the usual tedious appearance by MGM's attempt at class, pianist Jose Iturbi. The highlight is the wonderful sequence in which Kelly dances with Jerry, the mouse from MGM's Tom and Jerry cartoons. Today, one wonders why *Anchors Aweigh* was thought worthy of a best picture nomination, when *To Have and Have Not,* the great Howard Hawks [1779] movie that first teamed Humphrey Bogart [24 . . .] and Lauren Bacall, received not a single nomination.

Anchors Aweigh was Kelly's first big hit for MGM. After his 1942 debut in *For Me and My Gal,* the studio seemed unable to find anything suitable to his talents. But in 1944 he was loaned out to Columbia for *Cover Girl,* for which he did his own choreography, displaying his ingratiating athletic style to good advantage for the first time on screen. He was allowed to choreograph *Anchors Aweigh,* too, and helped Sinatra become a surprisingly good dancer. This was Kelly's sole nomination, and he lost to Ray Milland for *The Lost Weekend,* which also took the best picture award. Kelly received an honorary Oscar in 1951.

The cinematography Oscar went to Leon Shamroy for *Leave Her to Heaven.* The best song was Rodgers and Hammerstein's "It Might As Well Be Spring," from *State Fair.*

Stoll: 115, 207, 699, 1216, 1298, 1299, 1950. Pasternak: 1485, 2081. Planck: 1173, 1190, 2079. Styne: 696, 737, 920, 921, 1031, 1719, 2072, 2110, 2343. Cahn: 163, 182, 696, 915, 926, 1031, 1056, 1216, 1524, 1587, 1692, 1708, 1719, 1859, 1907, 2016, 2064, 2072, 2103, 2110, 2125, 2263, 2264, 2315, 2343.

75 • . . . AND JUSTICE FOR ALL

MALTON FILMS LTD. PRODUCTION; COLUMBIA. 1979.
NOMINATIONS *Actor:* Al Pacino. *Screenplay Written Directly for the Screen:* Valerie Curtin and Barry Levinson.

Pacino, a lawyer, goes nuts over the inequities of the judicial system when he is forced to become the defense attorney for a martinet judge, played by John Forsythe, who had earlier stymied Pacino's efforts to free an unjustly imprisoned man. This would-be satire, directed by Norman Jewison [659 . . .], can't quite make up its mind whether to be realistic or outrageous, but Pacino manages to play whatever he's given convincingly. So do Jack Warden [890 . . .], Lee Strasberg [785], and, in her screen debut, Christine Lahti [1989]. Not screenwriter Levinson's finest

hour, but three years later he would come into his own with *Diner,* also set in his native Baltimore. Curtin, his wife, has also been seen on screen as an actress in such films as *Alice Doesn't Live Here Anymore, All the President's Men,* and *Down and Out in Beverly Hills* (1986).

The acting Oscar went to Dustin Hoffman for *Kramer vs. Kramer.* Steve Tesich won for the screenplay for *Breaking Away.*

Pacino: 543, 561, 775.5, 784, 785, 1764.5, 1780. Levinson: 112, 308, 546, 1653.

76 • AND NOW MY LOVE

RIZZOLI FILM-LES FILMS 13 PRODUCTION; AVCO EMBASSY (FRANCE). 1975.
NOMINATION *Original Screenplay:* Claude Lelouch and Pierre Uytterhoeven.

Marthe Keller plays a rich woman who falls for small-time crook Andre Dussollier in this glossy sentimental romance, directed by Lelouch, that spans three generations. Strictly for fans of Lelouch's brand of Gallic schmaltz, the ones who made *A Man and a Woman* the most successful French film of all time. The Oscar went to Frank Pierson for *Dog Day Afternoon.*

Lelouch: 1250. Uytterhoeven: 1250.

77 • ANDROMEDA STRAIN, THE

UNIVERSAL-ROBERT WISE PRODUCTION; UNIVERSAL. 1971.
NOMINATIONS *Art Direction–Set Decoration:* Boris Leven and William Tuntke; Ruby Levitt. *Film Editing:* Stuart Gilmore and John W. Holmes.

A killer virus from outer space hitches a ride on a satellite that falls to Earth in a remote desert village. A team of scientists struggles to zap the bug before it gets out of hand. Michael Crichton's novel would seem to be a natural for the movies, but director Robert Wise [407 . . .] lets the movie drag out much too long, and he chooses a realistic style that avoids sci-fi clichés and phony heroics, but also saps much of the fun from the drama. The cast is full of fine actors—Arthur Hill, David Wayne, James Olson, and Kate Reid—who don't have much film charisma.

The art direction award went to *Nicholas and Alex-*

andra, and the editing Oscar was won by Jerry Greenberg for *The French Connection.*

Leven: 34, 422, 768, 1753, 1801, 1881, 1907, 2244. Tuntke: 1284. Levitt: 395, 1572, 1881. Gilmore: 31, 33.

78 • ANGELS OVER BROADWAY

COLUMBIA. 1940.
NOMINATION *Original Screenplay:* Ben Hecht.

Douglas Fairbanks, Jr., Rita Hayworth, and Thomas Mitchell [962 . . .] play some Runyonesque Manhattan types who team up to rescue mousy John Qualen, who is in trouble because he's embezzled from his business partner. Hecht and cinematographer Lee Garmes [201 . . .] codirected this talky, quirky comedy that still has passionate admirers. It stiffed at the box office, however. The Oscar went to Preston Sturges for *The Great McGinty.*

Hecht: 1455, 1765, 2179, 2211, 2316.

79 • ANGELS WITH DIRTY FACES

WARNER BROS.-FIRST NATIONAL. 1938.
NOMINATIONS *Actor:* James Cagney. *Director:* Michael Curtiz. *Original Story:* Rowland Brown.

Mobster Cagney comes back to the old neighborhood after doing time, determined to get revenge on Humphrey Bogart [24 . . .], a crooked lawyer for whom he has taken the fall. Cagney's boyhood friend Pat O'Brien tries to steer Cagney right and to encourage a romance with Ann Sheridan. O'Brien has become a priest, working with the neighborhood toughs, played by the Dead End Kids—Leo Gorcey, Huntz Hall, et al. Eventually Cagney gets even with Bogart and is arrested for his murder. The film's climax is its most famous moment: Cagney has become a hero to the Kids, so O'Brien asks him to show cowardice on his way to the chair so the Kids will think he's yellow after all. Sheer, wonderful hokum—the Warners studio machine at its most efficient—with what some think is Cagney's finest performance. It is certainly one of them: Only a great star could have pulled off the walk-to-the-chair scene. The role won him the New York Film Critics Award, but

Cagney lost the Oscar to another mentor to the young, Spencer Tracy in *Boys Town.*

Curtiz received two nominations for directing this year—the last time that has happened in Oscar history. The other one was for *Four Daughters,* but he lost to Frank Capra for *You Can't Take It With You.*

Brown's "original story" is hardly original; Arthur Caesar had won an Oscar four years earlier for *Manhattan Melodrama,* a tale about boyhood pals whose paths diverge. This time the Oscar went to Eleanore Griffin and Dore Schary for *Boys Town.*

Cagney: 1216, 2318. Curtiz: 365, 712, 2318. Brown: 564.

80 • ANGRY HARVEST

CCC-FILMKUNST GMBH/ADMIRAL FILM PRODUCTION (FEDERAL REPUBLIC OF GERMANY). 1985.
NOMINATION *Foreign Language Film.*

Armin Mueller-Stahl plays a Polish farmer who shelters a Jewish woman during World War II. Ultimately he abuses the power he has over her. An interesting premise turns into a film that some find moving and provocative, while others see it as heavy-handed and pretentious. Directed by Agnieszka Holland [625]. The Oscar went to *The Official Story.*

81 • ANGRY SILENCE, THE

LION INTERNATIONAL (BRITISH). 1960.
NOMINATION *Story and Screenplay—Written Directly for the Screen:* Richard Gregson and Michael Craig; Bryan Forbes.

Richard Attenborough [745] refuses to join in a wildcat strike and suffers the consequences. Attenborough and Forbes also produced this tidy, moving little film—a far cry from Attenborough's later overproduced epics *Gandhi* and *Chaplin.* Directed by Guy Green [820], with Pier Angeli, Bernard Lee, and Oliver Reed. The Oscar went to Billy Wilder and I. A. L. Diamond for *The Apartment.*

82 • ANNA

MAGNUS FILM PRODUCTION; VESTRON. 1987.
NOMINATION *Actress:* Sally Kirkland.

Kirkland, a Czech expatriate actress in New York

struggling to make ends meet, comes to the aid of Paulina Porizkova, a young woman from her homeland who eventually achieves the success that has always eluded Kirkland. A moderately interesting, very low-budget independent film with good performances by both actresses. Directed by Yurek Bogayevicz.

The flamboyant Kirkland was much better known for her lack of inhibitions—she appeared nude riding a pig in the movie *Futz!* (1969)—than for her acting, but she gives a strong performance here. She also played the publicity channels for everything they were worth to get the nomination. She lost, however, to the slightly less uninhibited Cher in *Moonstruck.*

83 • ANNA AND THE KING OF SIAM

20TH CENTURY-FOX. 1946.

AWARDS *Black-and-White Cinematography:* Arthur Miller. *Black-and-White Interior Decoration:* Lyle Wheeler and William Darling, art direction; Thomas Little and Frank Hughes, set decoration.

NOMINATIONS *Supporting Actress:* Gale Sondergaard. *Screenplay:* Sally Benson and Talbot Jennings. *Scoring of a Dramatic or Comedy Picture:* Bernard Herrmann.

Irene Dunne [114 . . .] is Anna and Rex Harrison [413 . . .] the king in this pre–Rodgers and Hammerstein version of Margaret Landon's book about the experiences of Victorian British governess Anna Leonowens in the royal household of Thailand. Unfortunately the musical is so familiar that one feels let down when the songs don't come. As usual in Hollywood films of the forties, occidental actors play Asians; the cast includes Linda Darnell as Tuptim and Lee J. Cobb [301 . . .] as the Siamese prime minister. John Cromwell directed. Orson Welles [407 . . .] said he was approached to play the king, but declined, suggesting either Alfred Lunt [841] or Harrison. The latter, an established star in England, made his American film debut in the role. Later, Rodgers and Hammerstein considered him when they were casting *The King and I* for Broadway, but according to Harrison, they were dubious of his singing ability, so the part went to Yul Brynner [1088].

This was the last of Miller's three Oscars, all for the black-and-white photography in which he special-

ized. Only a handful of cinematographers received more Oscars than Miller, who retired because of ill health in 1951, but remained active in the industry, serving as president of the American Society of Cinematographers. He died in 1970.

The lavish decor for the film sometimes resembles that of a very expensive Thai restaurant. Wheeler was also the art director in charge of the film musical version ten years later.

Sondergaard, who plays Lady Thiang, would soon be forced into retirement by the McCarthy-era blacklist. The supporting actress Oscar was won by Anne Baxter for *The Razor's Edge.*

Benson was a fiction writer whose stories for the *New Yorker* were collected into several books, including *Meet Me in St. Louis,* on which the MGM musical was based. Her first work in Hollywood was on the screenplay of *Shadow of a Doubt.* Jennings, her collaborator on this film, was a more experienced screenwriter who began his career in Hollywood for Irving Thalberg [150 . . .] in the thirties. Robert E. Sherwood won the screenplay Oscar for *The Best Years of Our Lives,* for which Hugo Friedhofer took the scoring award.

Miller: 241, 952, 1082, 1655, 1868, 2056. Wheeler: 19, 46, 356, 376, 428, 476, 495, 530, 542, 719, 721, 798, 950, 1062, 1088, 1149, 1153, 1213, 1391, 1475, 1601, 1616, 1670, 1706, 1852, 2008, 2093, 2212. Darling: 374, 1082, 1195, 1655, 1868, 2240. Little: 46, 235, 428, 495, 719, 721, 746, 950, 952, 1082, 1149, 1153, 1397, 1475, 1666, 1852, 1868, 2056, 2212, 2286. Hughes: 1082. Sondergaard: 90. Jennings: 1387. Herrmann: 50, 407, 1460, 2005.

84 • ANNA CHRISTIE

MGM. 1929–30.

NOMINATIONS *Actress:* Greta Garbo. *Director:* Clarence Brown. *Cinematography:* William Daniels.

Garbo plays Anna, a down-on-her-luck waterfront shady lady who attempts to find love with a sailor, played by Charles Bickford [651 . . .]. Garbo's first sound film provided MGM with an opportunity to proclaim, in one of the classic ad lines, ''Garbo

Talks!'' So she does, as does everyone else—including Marie Dressler [611 . . .]—in this too-stagy adaptation of Eugene O'Neill's play.

Brown, Garbo's favorite director, worked with her on seven films. Neither would ever receive an Oscar. This time she lost to Norma Shearer in *The Divorcée,* and he lost to Lewis Milestone for *All Quiet on the Western Front.* Daniels, who was Garbo's favorite cameraman, lost to documentary-film makers Joseph T. Rucker and Willard Van Der Veer's work on *With Byrd at the South Pole.*

Garbo: 336, 1440, 1718. Brown: 723, 957, 1417, 1718, 2320. Daniels: 372, 953, 1410.

85 • *ANNE OF THE THOUSAND DAYS*

HAL B. WALLIS-UNIVERSAL PICTURES LTD. PRODUCTION; UNIVERSAL. 1969.

AWARD *Costume Design:* Margaret Furse.
NOMINATIONS *Picture:* Hal B. Wallis, producer. *Actor:* Richard Burton. *Actress:* Genevieve Bujold. *Supporting Actor:* Anthony Quayle. *Screenplay—Based on Material From Another Medium:* John Hale, Bridget Boland, and Richard Sokolove. *Cinematography:* Arthur Ibbetson. *Art Direction-Set Decoration:* Maurice Carter and Lionel Couch; Patrick McLoughlin. *Sound:* John Aldred. *Original Score—for a Motion Picture (Not a Musical):* Georges Delerue.

Burton is Henry VIII and Bujold is his ill-fated second wife, Anne Boleyn, in this handsomely mounted but much too stately adaptation of a play by Maxwell Anderson [48]. It's one of those English historical pageants that were unaccountably in vogue during the sixties, starting with *Becket* and continuing through *A Man for All Seasons* and *The Lion in Winter.* The fad finally ran its course in 1971 with the box-office failure of *Mary, Queen of Scots,* though by that time public television had taken up the task of bringing English history to American audiences. Directed by Charles Jarrott, with Irene Papas as first wife Catharine of Aragon.

Producer Wallis must have felt something like déjà vu: His *Becket* had pulled down a dozen nominations but only one Oscar, and Furse, who had developed a reputation as a historical-drama costumer, was the

sole beneficiary of the multiple nominations for *Anne.* The best picture this year was *Midnight Cowboy,* about as far from intrigue in Renaissance England as one can get.

More Oscar nominations have resulted from playing Henry VIII than any other historical or literary figure; Charles Laughton won for *The Private Life of Henry VIII,* and Robert Shaw was nominated for playing the monarch in *A Man for All Seasons.* This time the role resulted in the sixth of Burton's seven unsuccessful nominations. The Oscar went to the year's sentimental favorite, John Wayne in *True Grit.*

When Burton was cast in the film, Elizabeth Taylor [318 . . .] volunteered her services as Anne Boleyn. Producer Wallis held firm: Taylor was too old for the part. Bujold had made several films in Canada and abroad, including *La Guerre Est Finie* and the cult favorite *King of Hearts* (1966). This was her first mainstream Hollywood movie. Though she's much admired by the critics, her American career has never been spectacular. The Oscar went to Maggie Smith for *The Prime of Miss Jean Brodie.*

Quayle's stage career in England was a notable one. In addition to acting and directing, he managed the Shakespeare Memorial Theatre Company in Stratford-on-Avon for much of the fifties. His screen career, however, was largely spent in character roles in films ranging from *Tarzan's Greatest Adventure* (1959)—a movie that also featured young Sean Connery [2185]—to *Lawrence of Arabia.* He plays Cardinal Wolsey in *Anne of the Thousand Days* and lost to Gig Young for *They Shoot Horses, Don't They?* He received a knighthood in 1985, four years before his death.

The writing award went to Waldo Salt for *Midnight Cowboy. Butch Cassidy and the Sundance Kid* won the Oscars for Conrad Hall's cinematography and Burt Bacharach's score. *Hello, Dolly!* took the art direction and sound awards.

Furse: 164, 1177, 1285, 1374, 1766. Wallis: 17, 55, 164, 343, 365, 676, 689, 712, 965, 1046, 1095, 1162, 1248, 1482, 1727, 1779, 2233, 2318. Burton: 164, 621, 1391, 1706, 1897, 2277. Carter: 164. Couch: 1875. McLoughlin: 164. Aldred: 1285. Delerue: 28, 502, 1066, 1187.

86 • ANNIE

RASTAR FILMS PRODUCTION; COLUMBIA. 1982.

NOMINATIONS *Art Direction—Set Decoration:* Dale Hennesy; Marvin March. *Original Song Score and Its Adaptation or Adaptation Score:* Ralph Burns.

Warbucks, a millionaire, played by Albert Finney [579 . . .], shows an interest in adopting a little orphan named Annie (Aileen Quinn), which in turn arouses the interest of some con artist cronies (Tim Curry and Bernadette Peters) of the head of the orphanage, Miss Hannigan (Carol Burnett). Bloated and blundering version of a Broadway hit. Many stage musicals have come down with elephantiasis on their way to Hollywood, but *Annie* had one of the worst cases on record. The errors began when producer Ray Stark [737 . . .] chose John Huston [24 . . .] to direct. Perhaps Stark recalled his huge success with William Wyler [175 . . .] as director of *Funny Girl*. Choosing one of the most gifted nonmusical directors of all time worked once, so why not again? But anyone familiar with Huston's work—predicated on a very cynical, very adult, very masculine vision of human nature—would have known he was the wrong one to handle a campy whimsy about an orphan's search for a father. Casting performers of wildly varying styles didn't help. Burnett and Finney do their considerable best, but they might be performing in two different films. Although Quinn is appealing as Annie, and Bernadette Peters, Tim Curry, and Geoffrey Holder make solid contributions, Ann Reinking, as the supposed romantic lead, demonstrates that Broadway presence—for which she was known—does not automatically translate to screen personality. The songs, by Martin Charnin and Charles Strouse, are good, but Huston is always putting the camera in the wrong place in the production numbers.

The art direction Oscar went, like almost all others this year, to *Gandhi*. Leslie Bricusse and Henry Mancini won for their scoring of *Victor/Victoria*.

Hennesy: 646, 1196. March: 12.5, 332, 1976, 2152. Burns: 49, 321.

87 • ANNIE GET YOUR GUN

MGM. 1950.

AWARD *Scoring of a Musical Picture:* Adolph Deutsch and Roger Edens.

NOMINATIONS *Color Cinematography:* Charles Rosher. *Color Art Direction—Set Decoration:* Cedric Gibbons and Paul Groesse; Edwin B. Willis and Richard A. Pefferle. *Film Editing:* James E. Newcom.

Sharpshooter Annie Oakley (Betty Hutton) comes out of the backwoods to join Buffalo Bill's Wild West Show and falls in love with rival sharpshooter Frank Butler (Howard Keel). This film of Irving Berlin's [34 . . .] wonderful musical has been out of circulation for many years, owing to legal difficulties. But then, the movie has always seemed to be jinxed. The calamities began when Judy Garland [1065 . . .] bowed out because of the drug and health problems that would shadow her career for the rest of her life. She had filmed several tests for musical numbers, some of which still exist as evidence of what might have been. After considering Betty Garrett as a replacement, producer Arthur Freed [66 . . .] hired Hutton, who gives a strong, energetic performance that her detractors find lacking in charm. Then Frank Morgan [22 . . .], cast as Buffalo Bill, died. Much of his role had already been filmed, so his scenes had to be completely reshot with Louis Calhern [1243] in the role. A succession of directors—Busby Berkeley [791 . . .], Charles Walters [1173], and finally George Sidney—was called in. John Raitt was tested for Frank Butler but was thought not photogenic enough. The part went to Keel, whose only previous film work had been a small role in a British film made while he was performing in the London company of *Oklahoma!* But on the second day of shooting, he fell off a horse, broke his ankle, and was sidelined for three months.

Deutsch began his career as a Broadway music director and moved to Hollywood in the late thirties, working first for Warner Bros. and then for MGM. Though his three Oscars are for adaptations of music by other composers, he also composed many film scores. This was Edens' third Oscar; he turned to producing in the fifties.

The finale of the movie, "There's No Business Like Show Business," was a challenge to Rosher. The number, featuring eight hundred riders circling Hutton and Keel, was filmed from two towers, one five hundred feet high and one two hundred feet high. But the cinematography award went to Robert Surtees for *King Solomon's Mines,* which also won for Ralph E. Winters and Conrad Nervig's editing; the art direction Oscar was won by *Samson and Delilah.*

Deutsch: 141, 1469, 1782, 1818. Edens: 115, 594, 699, 801, 1476, 1950. Rosher: 22, 1096, 1818, 1972, 2320. Gibbons: 66, 130, 217, 227, 239, 285, 290, 440, 629, 749, 831, 980, 1069, 1096, 1173, 1190, 1226, 1230, 1232, 1274, 1308, 1309, 1417, 1567, 1604, 1644, 1662, 1673, 1721, 1861, 1937, 2068, 2112, 2256, 2257, 2300, 2320, 2330. Groesse: 1173, 1190, 1232, 1309, 1335, 1385, 1604, 2112, 2157, 2320. Willis: 66, 130, 227, 239, 290, 629, 749, 831, 980, 1069, 1096, 1157, 1173, 1190, 1226, 1230, 1232, 1309, 1417, 1567, 1657, 1662, 1673, 1721, 1861, 1937, 2068, 2112, 2257, 2320, 2330. Pefferle: 1096, 1157, 1230, 1552, 2312. Newcom: 798, 1828, 2120.

88 • *ANNIE HALL*

Jack Rollins and Charles H. Joffe Production; United Artists. 1977.
Awards *Picture:* Charles H. Joffe, producer. *Actress:* Diane Keaton. *Director:* Woody Allen. *Screenplay— Written Directly for the Screen:* Woody Allen and Marshall Brickman.
Nomination *Actor:* Woody Allen.

A New Yorker (Allen) falls in love with his near antithesis, a midwesterner (Keaton). East is East and West is West, but the twain meet for a while, then go their separate ways. Many think this romantic comedy, based in part on the real-life relationship between Allen and Keaton, is Allen's best film. Certainly it's the most accessible, lacking the self-conscious evocations of European filmmakers such as Ingmar Bergman [111 . . .] that may make his later films more intellectually stimulating but not as much fun. Keaton's giddy insouciance perfectly balances Allen's neurotic introspection. And the film is full of delightful secondary characters: Tony Roberts as Allen's sidekick, Shelley Duvall as a rock groupie, Carol Kane [908] and Janet Margolin as ex-wives, Colleen Dewhurst as Annie's mother, and Christopher Walken [521] as her spooky brother.

The film almost got called *Anhedonia,* which means "an inability to feel pleasure," but wiser heads prevailed. In his book *When the Shooting Stops, the Cutting Begins,* film editor Ralph Rosenblum claims a large share of the credit for whipping the picture into final shape, but the movie is consistent in theme, tone, and style with much of Allen's later work. Its success at the Oscars was something of a surprise, however: Many expected the award to go to the more serious *Julia.* (The other nominees were *The Goodbye Girl, Star Wars,* and *The Turning Point.*)

Keaton, whose real name is Diane Hall, was first teamed with Allen on Broadway in 1969, when she played the lead in his *Play It Again, Sam,* a part she repeated in the 1972 film version. She has alternated between comic and serious roles and has dabbled with directing, most notably her offbeat documentary, *Heaven* (1987).

Brickman was Allen's partner as a comedy writer for many years. After *Manhattan* they split up—some think to Allen's detriment—but reunited again in 1993 for *Manhattan Murder Mystery,* which also reteamed Allen with Keaton for the first time since *Manhattan.*

Like Orson Welles [407 . . .] and Warren Beatty [255 . . .], Allen received nominations for directing, writing, and acting in the same film. He is the only one of them, however, to win two of the three awards for which he was nominated. The acting Oscar went to Richard Dreyfuss for *The Goodbye Girl.*

Keaton: 1678. Allen: 39, 294, 311.5, 461, 863, 962.5, 1005, 1267, 1636, 1647. Brickman: 1267.

89 • *À NOUS LA LIBERTÉ*

Film Sonores-Tobis; Harold Auten (France). 1931–32.
Nomination *Interior Decoration:* Lazare Meerson.

A prison escapee becomes a successful industrialist, but his success is threatened when a fellow former inmate shows up. René Clair's sweetly funny satire has often been compared to Charles Chaplin's [405 . . .] 1936 film, *Modern Times,* a resemblance that didn't escape the French film's producers, who proposed using Chaplin but were deterred by Clair. Meerson's art deco sets are among the film's delights, which also include music by Georges Auric.

The question of including foreign language films in the awards process has dogged the Academy over the years, and the problem has never been fully resolved. In the same year that *À Nous la Liberté* became the first foreign-made nominee, the cinematographers branch voted to exclude foreign-made films from consideration in their category. The next year the art directors followed suit. But while the Academy wanted to promote American films, it also wanted to cement good relationships with distributors in overseas markets. After World War II, this led first to an annual honorary award to a board-chosen "outstanding foreign language film" and eventually to the rather awkwardly handled competitive award for best foreign language film. Over the years, a few foreign language films have entered the lists for best picture, and several have received nominations in other categories. So far, only Sophia Loren has won an Oscar for acting in a foreign language film, *Two Women.* And while directors of the stature of Federico Fellini [61 . . .], Akira Kurosawa [1661], and Ingmar Bergman [111 . . .] have competed for best director, none has won. The movie that beat *À Nous la Liberté* for art direction was called *Transatlantic,* but it was a homegrown product.

90 • *ANTHONY ADVERSE*

WARNER BROS. 1936.

AWARDS *Supporting Actress:* Gale Sondergaard. *Cinematography:* Gaetano Gaudio. *Score:* Warner Bros. Studio Music Department, Leo Forbstein, head; score by Erich Wolfgang Korngold. *Film Editing:* Ralph Dawson.

NOMINATIONS *Picture:* Henry Blanke, producer. *Interior Decoration:* Anton Grot. *Assistant Director:* William Cannon.

Fredric March [184 . . .] goes to seek his fortune in nineteenth-century Europe, Africa, and America,

leaving Olivia de Havilland [798 . . .] behind. He gets rich, she becomes an opera star, but the piper must be paid. Sondergaard and Claude Rains [365 . . .] play villains, of course, and the cast of thousands of Warners extras and supporting players includes Edmund Gwenn [1325 . . .], Akim Tamiroff [701 . . .] and J. Carrol Naish [1294 . . .], directed by Mervyn LeRoy [1662 . . .]. Some of this flamboyant nonsense is fun to watch, but it soon gets tiresome.

Sondergaard was the first winner of the newly introduced supporting actress award, which was designed not only to reward character players but also to get them out of competition for best actor and actress. Two years earlier, Frank Morgan had made a run at best actor with his showy but small part in *Affairs of Cellini,* and the year before, three of the players in *Mutiny on the Bounty* had been nominated, including Franchot Tone, whose role was decidedly secondary. The awards were still considered second-class; until the 1943 ceremonies, supporting players received plaques instead of Oscar statuettes. Sondergaard was the first performer to win an award for a debut role. The Minnesota-born actress had appeared on Broadway but moved to Hollywood in the early thirties with her husband, director Herbert Biberman. The debut role caused her to be typecast as a villain or malicious gossip throughout the thirties and forties. Her career was interrupted in the fifties by blacklisting. Biberman was one of the Hollywood Ten and was jailed for six months for refusing to testify before the House Un-American Activities Committee. Sondergaard returned to film and stage work in the mid-sixties. She died in 1985.

Gaudio, who was often billed as Tony or Antonio Gaudio, was born in Italy and immigrated to the States around the turn of the century. He became a cameraman in 1910 and worked on literally hundreds of movies. He was one of the founders of the American Society of Cinematographers. He died in 1951.

Academy rules gave the Oscar to the head of the studio music department, in this case Forbstein, although anyone who knows Korngold's work for Warners films such as *The Adventures of Robin Hood* and

The Sea Hawk will recognize his sweeping operatic style.

The best picture Oscar went to *The Great Ziegfeld.* *Dodsworth* won the art directing award, and Jack Sullivan won as assistant director for *The Charge of the Light Brigade.*

Sondergaard: 83. Gaudio: 447, 898, 1064, 1162, 1872. Forbstein: 385, 1169. Korngold: 17, 1621, 1768. Dawson: 17, 911, 1315. Blanke: 17, 712, 1046, 1169, 1315, 1457, 1936, 2136. Grot: 1169, 1621, 1768, 1981.

91 • *APARTMENT, THE*

THE MIRISCH COMPANY INC.; UNITED ARTISTS. 1960.
AWARDS *Picture:* Billy Wilder, producer. *Director:* Billy Wilder. *Story and Screenplay—Written Directly for the Screen:* Billy Wilder and I. A. L. Diamond. *Black-and-White Art Direction–Set Decoration:* Alexander Trauner; Edward G. Boyle. *Film Editing:* Daniel Mandell.
NOMINATIONS *Actor:* Jack Lemmon. *Actress:* Shirley MacLaine. *Supporting Actor:* Jack Kruschen. *Black-and-White Cinematography:* Joseph LaShelle. *Sound:* Gordon E. Sawyer, sound director, Samuel Goldwyn Studio Sound Department.

Lonely guy Lemmon, who works for an enormous insurance company, tries to advance his career by letting executives in the company use his apartment for extramarital affairs. But when MacLaine, who is seeing Fred MacMurray there, tries to commit suicide in the apartment, she and Lemmon are drawn together. Bright dialogue and superb performances alleviate the dark cynicism of the story, but the years have not been kind to the movie. At the time, it must have seemed like a sharp riposte to the complacent fifties. Now the shaky construction of the drama shows through, and the failures of tone and lapses of taste are more obvious. It's interesting, however, to see MacMurray, just entering his phase as Disney's Everydad, playing a sleaze—the kind of role he had done with skill in earlier films such as *Double Indemnity* and *The Caine Mutiny.* He was a last-minute replacement for Paul Douglas, who died shortly before filming started. Wilder claimed that the central premise of the film—the man who lends his apartment to others for adulterous affairs—was inspired by, of all films, *Brief Encounter.* In that movie a friend loans Trevor Howard his apartment for an assignation with Celia Johnson. The plot further developed in Wilder's mind when producer Walter Wanger [413 . . .] was arrested for shooting agent Jennings Lang, who was having an affair with Wanger's wife, Joan Bennett, in an apartment Lang had borrowed from a junior executive at MCA. (Tony Curtis [522], on the other hand, has claimed that the germ of *The Apartment* was his own borrowing of actor Nicky Blair's home for liaisons, which columnist Sidney Skolsky learned about and sold as an idea for a film.)

Wilder's triple win, the first since Leo McCarey took Oscars as producer-director and writer for *Going My Way,* put a cap on a career that flourished brilliantly through the forties and fifties but would begin to decline in the sixties, when Wilder's cynicism began to overwhelm his sense of humor in such films as *Kiss Me Stupid* and *The Fortune Cookie.* It's difficult to say whether the shift was in Wilder's own view or in the change in writing partnership from Charles Brackett [705 . . .] to Diamond.

Diamond, born Itek Dommnici in Romania, came to the States as a boy. After graduating from Columbia, he went to Hollywood in the late forties. His career as a screenwriter was undistinguished until he teamed with Wilder in 1956 for the film *Love in the Afternoon.* Diamond also served as an associate producer on many of Wilder's later films. He died in 1988.

Lemmon has been one of Wilder's most frequent performers, appearing in seven of his films, from *Some Like It Hot* to Wilder's last, *Buddy Buddy,* in 1981. Wilder has used Lemmon's likable, average-guy Americanness as counterpoint to his own European jadedness. And more than anyone, Wilder helped establish Lemmon as a leading man, lifting him out of the sidekick roles that fell to the likes of Tony Randall and Gig Young [427 . . .]. Lemmon lost to Burt Lancaster for *Elmer Gantry.*

This was MacLaine's second nomination for playing what used to be called a woman of easy virtue, though there is nothing easy about the lives led by the characters in *Some Came Running* or *The Apartment.* Interestingly she lost to another actress playing a call girl, Elizabeth Taylor in *Butterfield 8*—and their competition included Melina Mercouri's happy hooker in *Never on Sunday.*

Kruschen, a durable character player of the fifties and sixties, lost to Peter Ustinov in *Spartacus.* The cinematography award went to Freddie Francis for *Sons and Lovers.* The award for sound went to *The Alamo.*

Wilder: 138, 198, 566, 705, 709, 925, 1208, 1440, 1738, 1860, 1903, 1975, 2297. Diamond: 709, 1860. Trauner: 1263. Boyle: 393, 709, 743, 1783, 1860, 1866. Mandell: 184, 1182, 1607, 2297. Lemmon: 394, 508, 1330, 1337, 1761, 1860, 2140. MacLaine: 1017, 1859, 2020, 2152. LaShelle: 357, 428, 709, 953, 1017, 1149, 1283, 1391. Sawyer: 33, 184, 214, 393, 730, 864, 882, 973, 974, 1032, 1511, 1592, 2244, 2297, 2310.

92 • APOCALYPSE NOW

OMNI ZOETROPE PRODUCTION; UNITED ARTISTS. 1979.

AWARDS *Cinematography:* Vittorio Storaro. *Sound:* Walter Murch, Mark Berger, Richard Beggs, and Nat Boxer.

NOMINATIONS *Picture:* Francis Coppola, producer; Fred Roos, Gray Frederickson, and Tom Sternberg, coproducers. *Supporting Actor:* Robert Duvall. *Director:* Francis Coppola. *Screenplay Based on Material From Another Medium:* John Milius and Francis Coppola. *Art Direction–Set Decoration:* Dean Tavoularis and Angelo Graham; George R. Nelson. *Film Editing:* Richard Marks, Walter Murch, Gerald B. Greenberg, and Lisa Fruchtman.

Captain Willard (Martin Sheen), a special agent, is sent into Cambodia during the Vietnam War to liquidate Colonel Kurtz, played by Marlon Brando [583 . . .], who has gone mad and is venerated by the natives as a kind of divinity. The tribulations of the production of Coppola's film, based on Joseph Conrad's novella *Heart of Darkness,* have been recorded in the journals published by Coppola's wife, Eleanor, and in the documentary *Hearts of Darkness: A Filmmaker's Apocalypse* (1991). The original Willard,

Harvey Keitel [308], was fired after shooting started. Sheen himself had a heart attack midway through filming, delaying the completion of the film until he had recovered. The Philippine sets were destroyed by a typhoon. Brando showed up grossly overweight. Coppola himself had something like a nervous breakdown, and his marriage barely survived an affair he had during the ordeal. But out of adversity came something of a triumph: Though overlong and incoherent at the end, *Apocalypse Now* is a fascinating, compelling film. The cast includes, among others, Frederic Forrest [1726], Dennis Hopper [595 . . .], Harrison Ford [2296], and a teenage Laurence Fishburne [2250.7]. The best picture Oscar went to the far less ambitious *Kramer vs. Kramer,* for which Robert Benton also won the writing and directing awards.

Duvall's small role, as a marine colonel who loves surfing, was a tour de force for one of the screen's most versatile actors. He lost when the Academy made one of its sentimental gestures, granting a valedictory Oscar to a Hollywood veteran, Melvyn Douglas, for *Being There.*

All That Jazz took the awards for art direction and Alan Heim's editing.

Storaro: 543, 1136, 1678. Murch: 442, 764, 786, 1066. Berger: 60, 1698. Coppola: 65, 442, 784, 785, 786, 1541. Roos: 442, 785. Frederickson: 785. Duvall: 784, 826, 2015. Tavoularis: 292, 785, 786, 2148. Graham: 292, 785, 1418. Nelson: 292, 785, 1698. Marks: 293, 2020. Greenberg: 724, 1111. Fruchtman: 786, 1698.

93 • APPOINTMENT FOR LOVE

UNIVERSAL. 1941.

NOMINATION *Sound Recording:* Bernard B. Brown.

Charles Boyer [36 . . .] and Margaret Sullavan [2073] are so wedded to their careers—he's a playwright, she's a doctor—that they have little time left for their marriage. The stars are the salvation of this amusing little comedy with a predictable ending, directed by William A. Seiter. The sound Oscar went to *That Hamilton Woman.*

Brown: 96, 269, 919, 1010, 1011, 1125, 1560, 1896, 2028, 2260.

94 • APPRENTICESHIP OF DUDDY KRAVITZ, THE

INTERNATIONAL CINEMEDIA CENTRE LTD. PRODUCTION; PARAMOUNT (CANADA). 1974.

NOMINATION *Screenplay Adapted From Other Material:* Mordecai Richler and Lionel Chetwynd.

Richard Dreyfuss [803] is the picaresque antihero of the title, determined to make his way out of the Montreal ghetto by any means possible. The film, set in the 1940s, also features Jack Warden [890 . . .] and Randy Quaid [1135], with Denholm Elliott [1725] as a pretentiously arty film director who makes a hilarious movie about a bar mitzvah. A well-made film, directed by Ted Kotcheff, but some find it unrewarding because of the central figure's unlikableness. Dreyfuss' performance is fine, and the film, coming on the heels of *American Graffiti,* helped establish him as a star. It would take years, however, before he could shed the "Duddy Kravitz" persona and take on roles that were less abrasive.

The screenplay, based on Richler's novel, lost to Francis Ford Coppola and Mario Puzo's *The Godfather, Part II.*

95 • APRIL LOVE

20TH CENTURY-FOX. 1957.

NOMINATION *Song:* "April Love," music by Sammy Fain, lyrics by Paul Francis Webster.

When he gets into trouble, Pat Boone is sent to his uncle's Kentucky horse farm, where he falls for Shirley Jones [609]. They sing a few Fain-Webster songs, of which the title tune is the most memorable. (It lost to James Van Heusen and Sammy Cahn's "All the Way," from *The Joker Is Wild.*) Directed by Henry Levin, with Arthur O'Connell [73 . . .] as the uncle. This forgettable attempt to make Boone as big a film star as Elvis Presley didn't work in the long run but was a modest box-office success.

Fain: 331, 376, 856, 1213, 1276, 1681, 1925, 2014, 2214. Webster: 33, 64, 331, 376, 604, 663, 730, 856, 1213, 1276, 1322, 1388, 1755, 1925, 2014.

96 • ARABIAN NIGHTS

WALTER WANGER; UNIVERSAL. 1942.

NOMINATIONS *Color Cinematography:* Milton Krasner, William V. Skall, and W. Howard Greene. *Color Interior Decoration:* Alexander Golitzen and Jack Otterson, art direction; Russell A. Gausman and Ira S. Webb, set decoration. *Sound Recording:* Bernard Brown. *Scoring of a Dramatic or Comedy Picture:* Frank Skinner.

Jon Hall, Maria Montez (as Scheherazade), and Sabu thwart the efforts of an evil pretender to the throne of Baghdad. The success of this colorful idiocy led to the reteaming of the trio in *White Savage* (1943) and *Cobra Woman* (1944); Montez and Hall, sans Sabu, also made *Ali Baba and the Forty Thieves* in 1944. Nobody thinks any of these jewel-in-the-navel sagas is good, but their profits helped keep Universal afloat. John Rawlins directs, and the cast includes Leif Erickson, Turhan Bey, Billy Gilbert, Shemp Howard, John Qualen, and Thomas Gomez [1695].

The cinematography Oscar was won by Leon Shamroy for *The Black Swan,* and the art direction award went to *My Gal Sal. Yankee Doodle Dandy* won for sound and *Now, Voyager* for Max Steiner's score.

Krasner: 21, 46, 654, 953, 1219, 2072. Skall: 208, 1048, 1170, 1317, 1453, 1644, 1668, 1822, 2102. Greene: 239, 747, 1070, 1452, 1560, 1621, 1909, 2262. Golitzen: 31, 414, 591, 690, 706, 744, 1560, 1886, 1968, 1986, 2035, 2064, 2101. Otterson: 269, 668, 681, 1229, 1240, 1895, 2342. Gausman: 414, 681, 1560, 1572, 1886, 1895. Webb: 414, 1560. Brown: 93, 269, 919, 1010, 1011, 1125, 1560, 1896, 2028, 2260. Skinner: 62, 125, 947, 1229.

97 • ARISE, MY LOVE

PARAMOUNT. 1940.

AWARD *Original Story:* Benjamin Glazer and John S. Toldy.

NOMINATIONS *Black-and-White Cinematography:* Charles B. Lang, Jr. *Black-and-White Interior Decoration:* Hans Dreier and Robert Usher. *Score:* Victor Young.

Reporter Claudette Colbert [1025 . . .] meets soldier of fortune Ray Milland [1208] during the Spanish Civil War. World events keep getting in the way of their love affair, which is treated here almost as an equal to the problems of a world careening toward universal conflict, so the movie seems a little topsy-turvy. But Colbert, Milland, and Walter Abel (as Colbert's exasperated editor) are agreeable performers, and they're smoothly directed by Michell Leisen [587].

That Glazer and Toldy won while the screenplay's authors, Charles Brackett [705 . . .] and Billy Wilder [91 . . .], weren't even nominated illustrates something of the schizoid nature of the writing awards. At the time, there were three awards: original story, original screenplay, and just plain screenplay. Sometimes a script was cited in more than one category, and sometimes it wasn't. Eventually the Academy sorted things out into the current division between "original" and "adapted" screenplays.

Rebecca won for George Barnes' cinematography, *Pride and Prejudice* for art direction, and *Tin Pan Alley* for Alfred Newman's score.

Glazer: 1792. Lang: 250, 319, 636, 649, 705, 765, 953, 1480, 1640, 1699, 1738, 1778, 1855, 1860, 1955, 1968, 2180. Dreier: 161, 649, 674, 701, 726, 925, 979, 1101, 1120, 1194, 1214, 1217, 1358, 1443, 1452, 1540, 1668, 1748, 1880, 1975, 1994, 2190. Usher: 925, 1443. Young: 98, 100, 101, 280, 489, 612, 693, 701, 794, 846, 925, 1214, 1257, 1396, 1452, 1748, 1823, 1994, 2235, 2315.

98 • *ARIZONA*

COLUMBIA. 1940.
NOMINATIONS *Black-and-White Interior Decoration:* Lionel Banks and Robert Peterson. *Original Score:* Victor Young.

Jean Arthur [1353] is an Arizona settler, determined to make it with or without the help of William Holden [1424 . . .]. For all the star power at the top, this is a routine western with pretentions to epic status. Directed by Wesley Ruggles, with Warren William, Porter Hall, Edgar Buchanan, and Paul Harvey.

The art direction Oscar went to *Pride and Prejudice,* the scoring award to Leigh Harline, Paul J. Smith, and Ned Washington for *Pinocchio.*

Banks: 13, 455, 928, 1115, 1370, 1998. Young: 97, 100, 101, 280, 489, 612, 693, 701, 794, 846, 925, 1214, 1257, 1396, 1452, 1748, 1823, 1994, 2235, 2315.

99 • *ARMS AND THE MAN*

H.R. SOKAL-P. GOLDBAUM PRODUCTION; BAVARIA FILMKUNST A.G. (FEDERAL REPUBLIC OF GERMANY). 1958.
NOMINATION *Foreign Language Film.*

A mercenary soldier escapes the enemy by hiding out in the bedroom of a young woman whose fiancé is the officer pursuing him. The play by George Bernard Shaw [1637] loses a bit for English audiences by being translated into German and back out again. Moreover, all that Shavian palaver is uncinematic, and director Franz Peter Wirth finds few ways to "open up" the play. The cast includes, in supporting roles, the opera diva turned character actress Ljuba Welitsch, and Kurt Kasznar, well known for character parts in American films. The Oscar went to Jacques Tati's *My Uncle.*

100 • *ARMY GIRL*

REPUBLIC. 1938.
NOMINATIONS *Cinematography:* Ernest Miller and Harry Wild. *Sound Recording:* Charles Lootens. *Original Score:* Victor Young.

Long-forgotten B picture, starring Madge Evans and Preston Foster, that has to do with conflicts on an army base when tanks replace cavalry troops. Directed by George Nicholls, Jr., with James Gleason [904], H. B. Warner [1206], Billy Gilbert, Heather Angel, and Ralph Morgan—a pretty good cast for Republic. But its presence among more prestigious films results from the Academy's liberalizing of the nomination rules to attract more participants, the legacy of a battle between the Academy and the unions. Members of the industry's guilds and unions as well as Academy members were allowed to participate in the nominations and voting. Every studio and production company could submit nominees for cinematography, art direction, sound, and music awards. Republic, the most successful of the "poverty row" studios, proceeded to do so, though with no real hope of success on Oscar night. The awards went to *The Great Waltz* for Joseph Ruttenberg's cinematography, *The Cowboy and the Lady* for sound, and *The Adventures of Robin Hood* for Erich Wolfgang Korngold's score.

Lootens: 168, 538, 1257. Young: 97, 98, 101, 280, 489, 612, 693, 701, 794, 846, 925, 1214, 1257, 1396, 1452, 1748, 1823, 1994, 2235, 2315.

101 • AROUND THE WORLD IN 80 DAYS

THE MICHAEL TODD CO. INC.; UNITED ARTISTS. 1956.
AWARDS *Picture:* Michael Todd, producer. *Screenplay—Adapted:* James Poe, John Farrow, and S. J. Perelman. *Color Cinematography:* Lionel Lindon. *Scoring of a Dramatic or Comedy Picture:* Victor Young. *Film Editing:* Gene Ruggiero and Paul Weatherwax.
NOMINATIONS *Director:* Michael Anderson. *Color Art Direction–Set Decoration:* James W. Sullivan and Ken Adam; Ross J. Dowd. *Color Costume Design:* Miles White.

David Niven [1778] plays Phileas Fogg, who wagers that he can circumnavigate the globe in eighty days. He is accompanied by his valet, Passepartout, played by the Mexican clown Cantinflas, and pursued by Robert Newton, who thinks Fogg is a bank robber. Along the way, he rescues the Indian princess Aouda —Shirley MacLaine [91 . . .] in one of her earliest films. The travelers encounter scores of stars in cameo roles, including Charles Boyer [36 . . .], Charles Coburn [535 . . .], Ronald Colman [311 . . .], Noël Coward [993], Marlene Dietrich [1358], John Gielgud [103 . . .], Trevor Howard [1875], Glynis Johns [1969], Victor McLaglen [999 . . .], John Mills [1737], Robert Morley [1274], Jack Oakie [818], and Frank Sinatra [732 . . .]. (With all those stars, however, *Around the World* is one of the few best picture winners to receive no acting nominations.) It's all a bit much— almost three hours too much, and the best part, the animated credits by Saul Bass, is at the very end.

Gigantism afflicted the best picture nominees of 1956. *Around the World*'s chief competitors, *Giant* and

The Ten Commandments, were both well over three hours long. The other nominees were an expensive musical, *The King and I,* and *Friendly Persuasion*—even the last, the only comparatively small-scale drama in the lot, was more than two hours long. This was also the first year that all five nominated films were made in color. To compete with TV, movies had become, if not better than ever, at least bigger than ever. This was the perfect milieu for someone like Todd, a larger-than-life self-made man who might well have become a movie mogul if he'd been born a decade or two earlier. As it was, he got into the film business late, after a successful stint as a Broadway producer. He made a gamble that big-screen processes were the best way for films to compete with TV, investing first in Cinerama and then developing his own 65mm process, which he called Todd-AO. The film version of *Oklahoma!* was the first production in the process, but he was forced to relinquish some control over that one, so he vowed that his next movie would be his very own. He wheedled the stars into their cameos and fired Farrow, who was the film's first director, replacing him with the more docile Anderson. He also tried to remove Farrow and Poe from the writing credits, believing Perelman the more prestigious name, but was forced by the Writers Guild to reinstate them. A relative tyro when it came to movie producing, Todd enlisted the aid of William Cameron Menzies [38 . . .], the remarkable designer, director, and producer, who was no stranger to working with megalomaniacs, since he had survived a collaboration with David O. Selznick on *Gone With the Wind.* Todd wanted the movie treated as if it were a Broadway show, with reserved seating and playbills and with no refreshments allowed in the theater. It was a smash hit, but in 1958, at the peak of his fame, having won an Oscar and married Elizabeth Taylor [318 . . .], Todd was killed in a plane crash while on his way to New York to receive a "Showman of the Year" award.

Poe, who had begun his film writing career with *The March of Time,* was noted for adapting literary works, including Tennessee Williams' *Cat on a Hot Tin Roof* and *Summer and Smoke* and the 1961 film of William Faulkner's *Sanctuary*. Farrow was known as much for directing as for screenwriting. Married to Maureen O'Sullivan, he was the father of Mia Farrow. Humorist Perelman was known more for his magazine pieces than for his dramatic writings, although he did a few screenplays, including the Marx Brothers' *Monkey Business* and *Horse Feathers*. *Around the World* was his last screenplay.

Young was one of the most prolific composers in movie history, having come to Hollywood with the advent of sound. He worked for a variety of studios, from Paramount to Republic, and racked up twenty-one nominations before winning an Oscar, which was awarded to him posthumously: He died before the ceremony took place.

Editors Ruggiero and Weatherwax faced the enormous task of not only working with Todd's new film process but also putting together footage shot quite literally around the world. Locations included London, southern France, the Mediterranean, Spain, Egypt, India, Pakistan, Thailand, Hong Kong, Japan, Mexico, California, and Colorado.

Anderson, who took over from Farrow, had worked primarily in Britain, where he was an assistant director on *Pygmalion* and a second unit man on *In Which We Serve*. His work since *Around the World* has been unmemorable, except for the cult sci-fi film *Logan's Run*. The Oscar went to George Stevens for *Giant*.

The King and I won for art direction and Irene Sharaff's costumes.

Poe: 372, 1174, 2047. Farrow: 2222. Lindon: 787, 973. Young: 97, 98, 100, 280, 489, 612, 693, 701, 794, 846, 925, 1214, 1257, 1396, 1452, 1748, 1823, 1994, 2235, 2315. Ruggiero: 1469. Weatherwax: 1410. Adam: 12.5, 151, 1234.5, 1898. Dowd: 636. White: 832, 2043.

102 • ARROWSMITH

SAMUEL GOLDWYN PRODUCTIONS; UNITED ARTISTS. 1931–32.
NOMINATIONS *Picture:* Samuel Goldwyn, producer. *Adaptation:* Sidney Howard. *Cinematography:* Ray June. *Interior Decoration:* Richard Day.

A young doctor, played by Ronald Colman [311 . . .], begins his practice in a small North Dakota town, then moves to a prestigious research institute and finally winds up in the tropics, searching for a plague cure. Along the way he marries Helen Hayes [31 . . .] and has an affair with Myrna Loy. Colman is too old for the role, and the condensation of Sinclair Lewis' novel makes for a choppy script, whose message about self-sacrifice is fortunately not as thick as it might have been. The director is John Ford [815 . . .], who is just beginning to look comfortable with sound films.

As an independent producer, Goldwyn tried to make his mark with prestige projects, which led him to buy the rights to Sinclair Lewis' novel, which had won the Pulitzer Prize, and to hire Pulitzer playwright Howard as a screenwriter. The Oscar would elude Goldwyn for the next fifteen years, however. This time it went to *Grand Hotel*.

Howard's screenplay lost to Edwin Burke's for *Bad Girl*. The cinematography Oscar went to Lee Garmes for *Shanghai Express* and the art direction award to *Transatlantic*.

Goldwyn: 184, 214, 510, 560, 1182, 1607, 2316. Howard: 560, 798. June: 145, 736. Day: 22, 235, 487, 510, 560, 569, 797, 833, 864, 952, 1048, 1175, 1397, 1477, 1666, 1949, 2056, 2120, 2276.

103 • ARTHUR

JOFFE, MORRA AND BREZNER PRODUCTION; ORION. 1981.
AWARDS *Supporting Actor:* John Gielgud. *Original Song:* ''Arthur's Theme (Best That You Can Do),'' music and lyrics by Burt Bacharach, Carole Bayer Sager, Christopher Cross, and Peter Allen.
NOMINATIONS *Actor:* Dudley Moore. *Screenplay Written Directly for the Screen:* Steve Gordon.

Alcoholic millionaire playboy Moore falls in love with a waitress, Liza Minnelli [321 . . .], which complicates things because he is set to marry Jill Eikenberry in order to bring about a big business deal. An attempt to recapture the spirit of thirties screwball comedies, it almost succeeds because of Moore's comic gifts, and especially because of the superb, poised, and perfectly timed performance of Gielgud as Moore's valet and surrogate father. In the end it's a collection of wonderful moments that don't quite hang together, and some find the film's notion of a lovable alcoholic a bit hard to take. Directed by Gordon, with Geraldine Fitzgerald [2316], Stephen Elliott, and Barney Martin.

Gielgud's film stardom was largely confined to the latter half of his acting career. He found himself unwatchable as a young man and has described himself as looking and walking like a camel. The most notable of his early films is the 1936 *Secret Agent,* directed by Alfred Hitchcock [1171 . . .], in which he looks decidedly ill at ease. His avoidance of film roles in his youth may also have been in deference to the screen success of Laurence Olivier [268 . . .], who had the matinee-idol good looks that Gielgud lacked. As a result, we have no screen record of Gielgud's Hamlet, said to be a greater performance than Olivier's. In the 1950s, and increasingly in the sixties and seventies, Gielgud took on more and more character roles, always with wit and style, but seldom in films of much note. He may have entered into *Arthur* thinking of it as just one more way to pay the rent, but he emerged from it covered with glory.

At the Oscars, Bette Midler [700 . . .] wise-cracked her way through the list of nominated songs, citing the Bacharach-Sager-Cross-Allen work as "That song about the moon and New York City." The tune has the hallmarks of Bacharach's work—complex rhythms that make it catchy but not hummable—and Midler's gibe at the oddly unmemorable lyrics is on target. Cross was at the brief peak of his career: After winning multiple Grammys in 1980, he has scarcely been heard of since. Allen, a popular nightclub entertainer, who was briefly married to Minnelli, died of AIDS in 1992.

Moore has had a roller-coaster career in films. He reached fame with the English four-man revue *Beyond the Fringe,* whose remaining members, Peter Cook, Jonathan Miller, and Alan Bennett, went on to varying degrees of success as writers, directors, and performers. Moore was teamed with Cook in his first two films, *The Wrong Box* (1966) and *Bedazzled* (1967). After the success of these films, there was a dry spell, during which Moore worked as a composer as well as

actor, followed by two big hits in a row in 1979 and 1980: *10* and *Arthur.* Though these movies landed Moore a spot on the list of top box-office stars, his stay there was short-lived. His attempt to recapture the *Arthur* magic by producing and starring in a sequel in 1988 was disastrous. The best actor Oscar for 1981 went to Henry Fonda for *On Golden Pond.*

Writer-director Gordon was considered one of the most promising young talents in Hollywood, but he died suddenly of a heart attack in 1982. The writing Oscar went to Colin Welland for *Chariots of Fire.*

Gielgud: 164. Bacharach: 35, 317, 370, 2251. Sager: 166.5, 977, 1071.3, 1898.

104 • ARTISTS & MODELS
PARAMOUNT. 1937.
NOMINATION *Song:* "Whispers in the Dark," music by Frederick Hollander, lyrics by Leo Robin.

Jack Benny is an advertising exec trying to land a silverware account, but the plot doesn't matter. It's an excuse for turns by Benny, Ben Blue, Judy Canova, Martha Raye, Louis Armstrong and his orchestra, and various jugglers and tumblers. The "artists" of the title include cartoonists Peter Arno and Rube Goldberg. Benny's jokes about his lackluster movie career always centered on *The Horn Blows at Midnight* (1945), but that's a better film than this one, which is only a showcase for vaudeville numbers. The director was Raoul Walsh. The song award went to Harry Owens' "Sweet Leilani," from *Waikiki Wedding.*

Hollander: 677, 1998, 2032. Robin: 197, 368, 846, 1072, 1805, 1843, 2032, 2088, 2310.

105 • ASPHALT JUNGLE, THE
MGM. 1950.
NOMINATIONS *Supporting Actor:* Sam Jaffe. *Director:* John Huston. *Screenplay:* Ben Maddow and John Huston. *Black-and-White Cinematography:* Harold Rosson.

Sterling Hayden, Louis Calhern [1243], James Whitmore [157 . . .], and Jaffe plot a jewel robbery. Very noirish and a bit slowly paced, focusing on the characters rather than on the crime. A movie that a lot of people admire but that only Huston's hardcore aficionados really love. Jean Hagen [1831] has a nice tough-girl part—her name is Doll—and Marilyn Monroe gets one of her star-making moments in a small role (she was reportedly Huston's second choice, after Lola Albright).

The previous high points of Jaffe's screen career came in the thirties as the ancient High Lama of *Lost Horizon* and in the title role in *Gunga Din.* He won the best actor award for *The Asphalt Jungle* at the Venice Film Festival but lost the Oscar to George Sanders in *All About Eve.* Though he continued in films up till his death in 1984, in his later career he was best known as Dr. Zorba on the *Ben Casey* TV series.

The late forties and early fifties are sometimes thought of as the high-water mark of Huston's career, with films such as *The Treasure of the Sierra Madre, Key Largo, The Asphalt Jungle,* and *The African Queen* coming in swift succession. This time he lost the Oscars for directing and writing to Joseph L. Mankiewicz for *All About Eve.*

Maddow began his film career in the thirties as a writer and director on documentary films and began working on feature screenplays in the late forties, notably on the fine adaptation of William Faulkner's *Intruder in the Dust* (1949). His flirtation with communism in the thirties and the leftist slant of his earlier documentaries contributed to his blacklisting, but during the fifties he continued his work uncredited on such movies as the kinky antiwestern *Johnny Guitar* (1954). He died in 1992.

The cinematography Oscar went to Robert Krasker for *The Third Man.*

Huston: 24, 356, 571, 891, 1248, 1263, 1363, 1625, 1779, 2136. Rosson: 133, 256, 747, 2055, 2300.

106 • ASSAULT, THE

Fons Rademakers Production B.V. for Cannon Group Holland (the Netherlands). 1986.
Award *Foreign Language Film.*

A twelve-year-old boy witnesses the extermination of his family by the Nazis. Years later, he meets people from that era who bring back the memories he has long repressed. The film, directed by Fons Rade-

makers, works both as a psychological thriller and as a portrait of the political changes in Europe.

107 • ATLANTIC CITY

International Cinema Corporation Production; Paramount (U.S./France/Canada). 1981.
Nominations *Picture:* Denis Heroux and John Kemeny, producers. *Actor:* Burt Lancaster. *Actress:* Susan Sarandon. *Director:* Louis Malle. *Screenplay Written Directly for the Screen:* John Guare.

Lancaster, an elderly small-time hood, supports himself by running numbers and tending to the needs of a mobster's widow (Kate Reid). He also spies on his neighbor, Sarandon, an oyster-bar waitress, as she stands at her kitchen window and scrubs herself with lemon juice to remove the smell of fish. They finally meet when Sarandon's husband, accompanied by her very pregnant sister, shows up carrying a stash of cocaine he has ripped off from the mob. A funny, loopy film about lost souls that never gets sentimental or morbid, and doesn't condescend to either its characters or its audience. As a nominee, the movie never had much chance against its bigger, glossier competitors: the sugary *On Golden Pond,* the rowdy *Raiders of the Lost Ark,* the epic *Reds,* or the surprise winner, the high-toned *Chariots of Fire.* But it won major critics' circle awards if not the crowds who pay money to see movies.

Lancaster had reached the point in his career when most available roles were cameos. The part was tailor-made for him by Malle and Guare, but he lost to another veteran, Henry Fonda in *On Golden Pond.* Before his death in 1994, Lancaster was seen at his best form only once more, in another wonderful offbeat comedy, *Local Hero,* in 1983—a film neglected by the Academy.

Sarandon, who lost to Katharine Hepburn in *On Golden Pond,* made her film debut in 1970 in *Joe.* She had been married to Chris Sarandon [561] and retained his surname after their divorce. Before *Atlantic City,* her most memorable roles had been in the cult phenomenon *The Rocky Horror Picture Show* (1975) and in Malle's *Pretty Baby.* Her career didn't really bloom, however, until the late eighties, with *The Witches of*

Eastwick and a particularly fine (though curiously unnominated) performance in *Bull Durham.*

Malle broke into film when his work as a film
student attracted the attention of underwater explorer Jacques Cousteau, with whom he codirected
the 1956 Oscar-winning documentary *The Silent
World.* His first two nondocumentary features, released in 1958, were *Frantic* and *The Lovers,* both starring Jeanne Moreau. They established both director
and star. Since his first American-made film, *Pretty
Baby,* Malle has alternated between French and American productions. The directing Oscar went to Warren Beatty for *Reds.*

Playwright Guare's forte is crafting offbeat characters like the ones that populate *Atlantic City.* His most
recent success has been the Broadway drama—and
subsequent film—*Six Degrees of Separation.* The writing Oscar went to Colin Welland for *Chariots of Fire.*

Lancaster: 210, 609, 732. Sarandon: 413.3,
1205.5, 2039. Malle: 109, 1379.

108 • ATOMIC CITY, THE

PARAMOUNT. 1952.
NOMINATION *Story and Screenplay:* Sydney Boehm.

When his son is kidnaped by the Soviets, Gene
Barry, a scientist working at Los Alamos, joins forces
with the FBI to rescue him. Okay thriller, directed by
Jerry Hopper, that incorporates documentary footage
of the nuclear research center, with the expected
fifties propaganda overtones. The Oscar went to
T. E. B. Clarke for *The Lavender Hill Mob.*

109 • AU REVOIR, LES ENFANTS

NEF (PARIS) PRODUCTION; ORION CLASSICS (FRANCE). 1987.
NOMINATIONS *Screenplay Written Directly for the Screen:*
Louis Malle. *Foreign Language Film.*

A boy at a boarding school in 1944 discovers that a
classmate he has befriended is Jewish. Eventually an
informer turns in the headmaster, who has conspired
to hide several Jewish boys from the Gestapo. This
superb film never turns mawkish or sensational but
concentrates on the character and the escapades of the
boys while keeping the viewer subtly aware of the
horror that is being held at bay. A critical success that

was also a big hit with the audience that goes to
foreign films, it lost the foreign language film award
to *Babette's Feast.*

Malle, the son of a wealthy industrialist, based the
story on events in his own childhood. The writing
Oscar went to John Patrick Shanley for *Moonstruck.*

Malle: 107, 1379.

110 • AUNTIE MAME

WARNER BROS. 1958.
NOMINATIONS *Picture:* Jack L. Warner, studio head,
producer. *Actress:* Rosalind Russell. *Supporting Actress:*
Peggy Cass. *Color Cinematography:* Harry Stradling, Sr.
Art Direction–Set Decoration: Malcolm Bert; George
James Hopkins. *Film Editing:* William Ziegler.

After the death of his parents, young Patrick Dennis is sent to live with his aunt (Russell), a flamboyant, unconventional woman who becomes in her own
way a very good parent. Something of a phenomenon,
Auntie Mame began as a best-selling novel, became a
hit Broadway play that was turned into a successful
movie, returned to Broadway as a smash hit musical,
Mame, and only ran out of steam with the disastrous
1974 film version of the musical. This incarnation
would have been much better if director Morton
DaCosta had reined in Russell and Cass, who played
the roles on stage and still seem to be pitching their
performances to the back of the balcony. The Oscar
for best picture went to *Gigi,* which also won for
Joseph Ruttenberg's cinematography, for art direction, and for Adrienne Fazan's editing.

This was Russell's fourth try for the Oscar she
never won. But Susan Hayward, making her fifth try,
finally landed the award for *I Want to Live!* Russell's
career after *Auntie Mame* was in a series of not-very-
memorable character roles. Although she landed a
plum part in 1962 as Mama Rose in the film version
of *Gypsy,* the movie was a box-office flop. She received the Jean Hersholt Humanitarian Award at the
1972 ceremony and died four years later.

Cass won a Tony Award for playing Agnes Gooch,
Mame's ugly-duckling secretary who becomes a very
pregnant swan, on Broadway, but her film career after
the Oscar nomination was almost nonexistent. She

has made a career of appearing on TV game shows. The Oscar went to Wendy Hiller for *Separate Tables.*

Warner: 55, 550, 689, 1393, 2318. Russell: 1364, 1403, 1834. Stradling: 149, 596, 737, 852, 853, 864, 896, 957, 1246, 1393, 1567, 1949, 2338. Bert: 1910. Hopkins: 508, 896, 1003, 1170, 1332, 1385, 1393, 1910, 1949, 1973, 2058, 2277. Ziegler: 1385, 1393.

111 • *AUTUMN SONATA*

PERSONAFILM GMBH PRODUCTION; SIR LEW GRADE-MARTIN STARGER-ITC ENTERTAINMENT PRESENTATION; NEW WORLD PICTURES (SWEDEN). 1978.
NOMINATIONS *Actress:* Ingrid Bergman. *Screenplay Written Directly for the Screen:* Ingmar Bergman.

Concert pianist Ingrid Bergman goes to visit her daughter, Liv Ullmann [610 . . .], whom she has not seen for many years. Ullmann berates Bergman for putting her career first and neglecting her and her chronically ill sister when they were children. Ingrid Bergman's last film was made in her native language, although it was actually shot in Norway because of director Bergman's refusal to work in Sweden after a bout with the Swedish tax authorities. It is, like many of the director's films, a harrowing investigation of the characters' psyches, and it takes added resonance from the actress' own life: In 1949, she had left her daughter, Pia Lindstrom, with her first husband when she went to live in Europe with director Roberto Rossellini. Handsomely filmed by Sven Nykvist [460 . . .], it is neither its director's nor its star's best work, but it's not their worst, either.

Jane Fonda won the acting Oscar for *Coming Home,* which also took the award for the story and screenplay by Nancy Dowd, Waldo Salt, and Robert C. Jones.

Ingrid Bergman: 72, 173, 701, 749, 1048, 1378. Ingmar Bergman: 460, 634, 644, 2082, 2283.

112 • *AVALON*

TRI-STAR PICTURES PRODUCTION; TRI-STAR. 1990.
NOMINATIONS *Screenplay Written Directly for the Screen:* Barry Levinson. *Cinematography:* Allen Daviau. *Original Score:* Randy Newman. *Costume Design:* Gloria Gresham.

Armin Mueller-Stahl plays an immigrant who establishes a new life in Baltimore. Joan Plowright [614.5] plays his wife and Aidan Quinn their son in this episodic, somewhat sentimental and slow-moving film. The Oscar for *Rain Man* gave Levinson the clout to make *Avalon,* which with its period sets and costumes and spectacular appliance store fire scene has considerably more elaborate production values than his two previous "Baltimore films," *Diner* and the 1982 *Tin Men.* But despite some fine performances, particularly by Mueller-Stahl, it's the weakest film in the trilogy.

The writing award went to Bruce Joel Rubin for *Ghost.* Dean Semler won the cinematography Oscar and John Barry the scoring award for *Dances With Wolves.* Franca Squarciapino's work on *Cyrano de Bergerac* won the costume Oscar.

Levinson: 75, 308, 546, 1653. Daviau: 308, 423, 588, 613. Newman: 1418, 1524.5, 1530, 1651.

112.5 • *AWAKENING, THE*

SAMUEL GOLDWYN PRODUCTIONS; UNITED ARTISTS. 1928–29.
NOMINATION *Interior Decoration:* William Cameron Menzies.

Vilma Banky stars as a woman living in Alsace-Lorraine during World War I who is engaged to a Frenchman but in love with a German officer. This mostly silent film, produced by Samuel Goldwyn [102 . . .], included a song by Irving Berlin [34 . . .], "Marie"; the screenplay was written by Frances Marion [202 . . .].

Menzies was one of the unofficial nominees of 1928–29, a year in which the Academy announced only the winners of the awards. The names of the runners-up were kept in Academy files, but some confusion has arisen over which of Menzies' films were under consideration. In some lists based on Academy records, he is cited for his work on *Alibi* and *The Awakening;* in others, he is said to have been a contender for his work on *The Iron Mask.* The most recent revision of the nominations and winners list by the Academy says he was under consideration for the first two films, but because of the confusion, this book includes all three. The Oscar went to Cedric Gibbons for *The Bridge of San Luis Rey* "and other pictures."

Menzies: 38, 311, 568, 798, 1018, 2010.

113 • *AWAKENINGS*

COLUMBIA PICTURES PRODUCTION; COLUMBIA. 1990.
NOMINATIONS *Picture:* Walter F. Parkes and Lawrence Lasker, producers. *Actor:* Robert De Niro. *Screenplay Based on Material From Another Medium:* Steven Zaillian.

A shy, eccentric doctor, played by Robin Williams [511 . . .], discovers that certain patients can be brought out of comatose states by administering the drug L-dopa. Among them is De Niro, who has been in a coma for thirty years. On being awakened, he has to learn how to deal with a new life. Ultimately, however, the drug proves only temporarily successful, and De Niro and the others must return to their states of paralyzed half-awareness. Despite a fascinating story, based on the experiences of Dr. Oliver Sacks, the movie often becomes needlessly sentimental and uplifting, with a tiresome thematic stress on Williams' own "awakening" through a budding romance with Julie Kavner. Williams is forced to play second fiddle to De Niro's showier role, but he's funny and touching. Penny Marshall directed, and her failure to receive a nomination touched off charges of sexism against the directors branch of the Academy, which had to that point given a directorial nomination to only one woman—Lina Wertmüller for *Seven Beauties*—and had previously passed over Randa Haines, a woman director whose film *Children of a Lesser God* was also nominated for best picture. The best picture Oscar went to *Dances With Wolves*, which also won for Michael Blake's screenplay.

The two previous best actor Oscars had gone to Dustin Hoffman as an autistic savant in *Rain Main* and Daniel Day-Lewis as a writer with cerebral palsy in *My Left Foot*. De Niro's coma patient would have made it three disabled people in a row, but he lost to Jeremy Irons' performance in *Reversal of Fortune* as Claus Von Bulow—who was at least accused of putting his wife in a coma.

Parkes: 2231. Lasker: 2231. De Niro: 342, 521, 785, 1650, 2005. Zaillian: 1764.65.

114 • *AWFUL TRUTH, THE*

COLUMBIA. 1937.
AWARD *Director:* Leo McCarey.
NOMINATIONS *Picture:* Leo McCarey, with Everett Riskin, producers. *Actress:* Irene Dunne. *Supporting Actor:* Ralph Bellamy. *Screenplay:* Viña Delmar. *Film Editing:* Al Clark.

Dunne and Cary Grant [1445 . . .] have separated, and she plans to marry the very square Bellamy. But Dunne and Grant are, of course, made for each other. One of the best and brightest screwball comedies, marred only by a little aimlessness at the very end. One of the funniest scenes may be the one in which Grant, after a tiff with Dunne, grabs a hat and starts to leave, only to discover, and demonstrate in several bemused moments before a mirror, that the hat isn't his. No actor on earth could do more with a situation like that than Grant, and though he failed to be nominated for the movie, it helped establish him as a major star.

McCarey gave up a law career to go into movies in 1918 and became one of the top writers and directors of comedies for Hal Roach in the twenties. He worked with Laurel and Hardy, Eddie Cantor, the Marx Brothers (he directed the sublime *Duck Soup* in 1933), Mae West, and W. C. Fields. In the year of *The Awful Truth,* McCarey began producing, writing, and directing most of his films, a practice that didn't become common until a decade later, with the emergence of such triple threats as Joseph Mankiewicz [46 . . .] and Billy Wilder [91 . . .]. Though he won for directing *The Awful Truth,* the best picture Oscar went to *The Life of Emile Zola,* the Academy preferring high seriousness to high hilarity.

Dunne stood little chance of capturing the Oscar this time, on her third nomination, in a comedy role that faced such serious dramatic competition as Greta Garbo for *Camille,* Barbara Stanwyck for *Stella Dallas,* and the winner, Luise Rainer's long-suffering Chinese peasant in *The Good Earth.*

Bellamy had come to Hollywood in the early thirties, appearing mostly in B pictures. The nomination for *The Awful Truth* boosted his career, but also led to typecasting as the slightly thick "other man," the one Fred Astaire [2126] takes Ginger Rogers [1102] away from in *Carefree,* and Cary Grant bests again in *His Girl Friday* (1940) by winning Rosalind Russell [110 . . .]. After finding himself stuck back in the Bs and in Universal horror movies in the forties, Bellamy turned his attention to radio, TV, and the stage. He won a Tony in 1958 for *Sunrise at Campobello* and re-created the role of FDR in the screen version in 1960. He also had memorable roles as character villains in *Rosemary's Baby* and *Trading Places.* The Academy gave him an honorary award for "his unique artistry and his distinguished service to the profession of acting" at the 1986 ceremonies.

"Viña Delmar" was actually a husband-and-wife team, working under the wife's name. Their screenplay was based on a 1921 Broadway comedy that starred Ina Claire and had been filmed as a silent in 1925 and, with Claire, as a talkie in 1929. Dwight Taylor did the first draft of the 1937 version, and it was also worked on by Mary McCall, Jr., Sidney Buchman [904 . . .], Dorothy Parker [1845 . . .], and Alan Campbell [1909]. Additional material was also improvised during the shooting. The screenplay award went to Norman Reilly Raine, Heinz Herald, and Geza Herczeg for *The Life of Emile Zola,* and the editing Oscar to Gene Havlick and Gene Milford for *Lost Horizon.*

McCarey: 21, 173, 787, 1212, 1394, 1404. Riskin: 904, 1488. Dunne: 400, 972, 1212, 2041. Clark: 53, 456, 1370, 1550.

B.F.'s DAUGHTER
See 192.

115 • BABES IN ARMS
MGM. 1939.
NOMINATIONS *Actor:* Mickey Rooney. *Score:* Roger Edens and George E. Stoll.

Rooney and Judy Garland [1065 . . .], playing the offspring of vaudevillians, stage a show. Garland and Rooney had appeared together before, in *Thoroughbreds Don't Cry* (1937) and *Love Finds Andy Hardy* (1938), but this adaptation of the Richard Rodgers [1921] and Lorenz Hart stage musical was the one that made Mickey and Judy, for a time, as familiar a team as Dick Powell/Ruby Keeler or Fred Astaire [2126]/Ginger Rogers [1102]. It was also the first film produced by Arthur Freed [66 . . .], whose production unit was responsible for many of the great MGM musicals of the forties and fifties. This is not one of his best, for it jettisoned most of the great Rodgers and Hart songs (interpolating several of Freed's own), and the let's-put-on-a-show plot is silly. But admirers of Garland and Rooney, or of their director, Busby Berkeley [791 . . .], couldn't care less.

The hyperactive Rooney, himself the child of vaudevillians, made a stage debut at fifteen months of age and a film debut at age six. Born Joe Yule, Jr., he picked up his first name from a series of short subjects in which he starred as Mickey McGuire. He was signed by MGM in 1934 and began a climb to stardom that included playing Clark Gable [798 . . .] as a boy in *Manhattan Melodrama* and (on loan-out to Warner Bros.) Puck in *A Midsummer Night's Dream.* In 1937 he appeared in the first Andy Hardy movie, *A Family Affair,* launching a fifteen-film series that by 1939 had made him the top box-office star. He would never win a competitive Oscar but received two honorary awards: for outstanding juvenile in 1938 and "in recognition of his 60 years of versatility" in 1982. He lost the 1939 Oscar to Robert Donat in *Goodbye, Mr. Chips.*

Edens and Stoll had some great songs to work with: "Where or When" and "The Lady Is a Tramp," by Rodgers and Hart, "Good Morning" and "You Are My Lucky Star," by Freed and Nacio Herb Brown, and "I Cried for You," by Freed, Gus Arnheim, and Abe Lyman. The Oscar went to Richard Hageman, Frank Harling, John Leipold, and Leo Shuken for *Stagecoach.*

Rooney: 225, 252, 957. Edens: 87, 594, 699, 801, 1476, 1950. Stoll: 74, 207, 699, 1216, 1298, 1299, 1950.

116 • BABES IN TOYLAND

WALT DISNEY PRODUCTIONS; BUENA VISTA. 1961.

NOMINATIONS *Scoring of a Musical Picture:* George Bruns. *Color Costume Design:* Bill Thomas.

Ray Bolger plays the villain, who kidnaps Tommy Sands, his rival for the affections of Annette Funicello, and miniaturizes his opponents with a ray gun. Sands defeats Bolger with an army of toy soldiers. Directed by Jack Donohue, with Ed Wynn [542] as the toymaker and a collection of moppets that includes the very young Ann Jillian. This rather sticky version of the Victor Herbert operetta aims at too wide an audience—from rug rats to the teenage admirers of Sands and Funicello—resulting in a clash of styles. The special effects, planned by animator Ward Kimball, are the film's highlight. This was the Disney studio's first live-action musical, and it had only modest box-office success. Disney had proposed doing an animated version in the early thirties, but RKO owned the rights and turned him down. A superior version of the operetta was made in 1934, with Laurel and Hardy.

West Side Story won for Saul Chaplin, Johnny Green, Sid Ramin, and Irwin Kostal's scoring and for Irene Sharaff's costumes.

Bruns: 1709, 1839, 1992. Thomas: 166, 254, 866, 883, 1003, 1789, 1812, 1886, 2128.

117 • BABES ON BROADWAY

MGM. 1942.

NOMINATION *Song:* "How About You?," music by Burton Lane, lyrics by Ralph Freed.

Another "hey kids, let's put on a show" musical starring Judy Garland [1065 . . .] and Mickey Rooney [115 . . .]. This one is about staging a benefit for poor children and war refugees. The plot doesn't matter, except when it gets in the way of the musical numbers, which are staged by the film's director, Busby Berkeley [791 . . .]. Along the way, Garland and Rooney do impersonations of famous Broadway performers, with Rooney as George M. Cohan (a year before James Cagney's *Yankee Doodle Dandy*) and Garland essaying Sarah Bernhardt. Rooney also gets to do a drag number parodying Carmen

Miranda. The cast includes Virginia Weidler in a part that MGM tried to get Shirley Temple to play, and four-year-old Margaret O'Brien in her debut. The minstrel show finale, with Rooney and Garland in blackface, is a bit hard to take today, though Garland's singing of "Franklin D. Roosevelt Jones" is terrific. (Because a preview audience failed to recognize the stars in blackface, a sequence was shot that shows them putting on their makeup.)

Like many Tin Pan Alley greats, Lane got his start playing piano for a song publisher, demonstrating sheet music. There he came in contact with George Gershwin [1797], to whose music, as Alec Wilder points out in *American Popular Song*, "How About You?" owes a debt. (Freed partially repaid the debt in the song's lyrics: "I like a Gershwin tune.") Later, Lane would write the songs for two Broadway shows that became flop movies, *Finian's Rainbow* and *On a Clear Day You Can See Forever* (1970). "How About You?" is a bright and memorable song that might have been a winner in any other year, but Irving Berlin's "White Christmas," from *Holiday Inn,* was unbeatable.

Lane: 1731.

118 • BABETTE'S FEAST

PANORAMA FILM INTERNATIONAL PRODUCTION IN COOPERATION WITH NORDISK FILM AND THE DANISH FILM INSTITUTE (DENMARK). 1987.

AWARD *Foreign Language Film.*

In the 1870s two sisters devote themselves to the memory of their father, the minister of an abstemious and devout sect. They take in a Parisian refugee, who cooks and keeps house for them for fourteen years before revealing that she is a superb chef. The feast she prepares for the sisters and their friends opens their eyes to the delights of the senses. Lovely, funny, touching film, directed by Gabriel Axel. It was the first Danish film to win the Oscar.

119 • BABY DOLL

NEWTOWN PRODUCTION; WARNER BROS. 1956.

NOMINATIONS *Actress:* Carroll Baker. *Supporting Actress:* Mildred Dunnock. *Screenplay—Adapted:* Tennessee

Williams. *Black-and-White Cinematography:* Boris Kaufman.

Teenager Baker, who sucks her thumb and sleeps in a crib, has married middle-aged Karl Malden [1477 . . .] on the understanding that they will wait till she turns twenty before consummating the marriage. Meanwhile, Eli Wallach, her husband's business rival, tries to seduce her. This deliciously perverse comedy seems tamer today than it did in the mid-fifties, when it drew the ire of the Catholic Legion of Decency and other guardians of public morality, but Baker's performance still generates heat. Films like *Baby Doll* gradually chipped away at the old Production Code until there was nothing left of it. Directed by Elia Kazan [63 . . .], with a cast that includes Rip Torn [466] and the citizens of Benoit, Mississippi, where the movie was shot.

Baker had come to Hollywood in the early fifties and landed a bit part in the 1953 Esther Williams musical *Easy to Love.* Lack of work sent her to New York, where, after doing some TV and studying at the Actors Studio, she was discovered by Hollywood and cast in *Giant.* It was *Baby Doll,* released the same year, that established her image and led to her being cast as a variety of bad, or not-very-good, girls in *The Big Country, How the West Was Won,* and other films. By the mid-sixties, she found Hollywood roles scarce, so she moved to Europe, where she made numerous Spanish and Italian features. The Oscar went to Ingrid Bergman for *Anastasia.*

Dunnock, who plays Baker's dotty aunt, spent most of her film career in character roles as elderly eccentrics. Dorothy Malone took the Oscar for *Written on the Wind.*

Williams created the screenplay for *Baby Doll* out of two of his one-act plays, *27 Wagons Full of Cotton* and *The Unsatisfactory Supper.* The Oscar went to James Poe, John Farrow, and S. J. Perelman for *Around the World in 80 Days.*

Kaufman lost to Joseph Ruttenberg's cinematography for *Somebody Up There Likes Me.*

Dunnock: 515. Williams: 1949. Kaufman: 1477.

120 • BABY MAKER, THE

ROBERT WISE PRODUCTION; NATIONAL GENERAL PICTURES. 1970.
NOMINATION *Original Song Score:* Fred Karlin and Tylwyth Kymry.

Hippie Barbara Hershey agrees to be a surrogate mother for a childless couple. Dated and slightly pretentious film that was the debut of writer-director James Bridges [394 . . .]. The cast also includes Scott Glenn and Jeannie Berlin [887].

Karlin lost to the Beatles, for *Let It Be,* but he didn't go home empty-handed. At the same ceremony, he received an Oscar for the song ''For All We Know,'' from *Lovers and Other Strangers.*

Karlin: 1178, 1221, 1926.

121 • BACHELOR AND THE BOBBY-SOXER, THE

RKO RADIO. 1947.
AWARD *Original Screenplay:* Sidney Sheldon.

Myrna Loy's teenage kid sister, Shirley Temple, falls for playboy Cary Grant [1445 . . .], so Loy tries to cure her of the infatuation by making Grant take Temple out on dates. It's as silly as it sounds, but Grant and Loy make it tolerable. Unfortunately there's too much Temple, whose career was nearly over, and not enough Loy. Directed by Irving Reis, with Rudy Vallee, Ray Collins, and Harry Davenport.

Sheldon, a screenwriter of no particular distinction apart from this film, also produced and directed a few movies, without much success. Then, in the seventies, he found his métier and began turning out block-buster schlock novels such as *Bloodline* and *The Other Side of Midnight.* The Oscar for *The Bachelor and the Bobby-Soxer* is something of a shocker in the light of the rest of his career—the more so when one realizes that his competition for the award included the screenplays for such distinguished films as *Body and Soul, A Double Life, Monsieur Verdoux,* and *Shoeshine.*

122 • BACHELOR IN PARADISE

TED RICHMOND PRODUCTION; MGM. 1961.
NOMINATION *Song:* ''Bachelor in Paradise,'' music by Henry Mancini, lyrics by Mack David.

Bob Hope plays an advice-to-the-lovelorn columnist in search of material who moves to a wealthy suburb, where he's the only unmarried man. Lame romantic comedy, directed by Jack Arnold, with a good cast: Lana Turner [1558], Janis Paige, Jim Hutton, Paula Prentiss, and Agnes Moorehead [963 . . .].

Mancini lost to himself; the Oscar went to "Moon River," from *Breakfast at Tiffany's,* which he composed with Johnny Mercer. Mack David was not so fortunate. A songwriter since the early forties, he had multiple nominations but never won. Moreover, he had to witness his younger brother, Hal David [35 . . .], go on to greater success, including an Oscar, in collaboration with Burt Bacharach [35 . . .].

Mancini: 278, 384, 494, 508, 512, 776, 825, 1573, 1574, 1864, 1970, 2011, 2037, 2201. David: 371, 402, 861, 882, 963, 1032, 2223.

123 • BACHELOR MOTHER

RKO RADIO. 1939.
NOMINATION *Original Story:* Felix Jackson.

Ginger Rogers [1102] finds an abandoned baby that everyone assumes is hers—the kind of misapprehension that real people can clear up in thirty seconds but movie people take an hour and a half to unravel. At first, her single parenting puts her in Dutch with her employer, Charles Coburn [535 . . .], but eventually she lands his son, David Niven [1778]. This screwball farce is laced with more sentiment than most, but everyone brings it off beautifully. Directed by Garson Kanin [11 . . .].

Though Jackson got the nomination, the real credit probably belongs to Norman Krasna [535 . . .], who wrote the screenplay. It's worth comparing this movie with *The Devil and Miss Jones,* another farce about a shop girl and her boss, also with Coburn and also written by Krasna. The Oscar went to Lewis R. Foster for *Mr. Smith Goes to Washington.*

124 • BACHELOR PARTY, THE

NORMA PRODUCTION; UNITED ARTISTS. 1957.
NOMINATION *Supporting Actress:* Carolyn Jones.

A group of New York office workers, including Don Murray [314], E. G. Marshall, and Jack Warden [890 . . .], throw a party for one of their fellow workers who is about to get married. Alcohol loosens their inhibitions and they start confessing their problems. If this is the sort of thing you like—a look into lives of quiet desperation—this talky melodrama will do the trick. Some of us, however, would rather have a root canal. The film is an attempt by director Delbert Mann [1283] and writer Paddy Chayefsky [783 . . .] to repeat their success with *Marty.*

Jones plays a beatnik known as the Existentialist. Originally from Amarillo, Texas, Jones was dark and slightly exotic-looking, which meant she was typecast as a villain, an oddball, or, as in *The Bachelor Party,* what the fifties called a nympho. She worked steadily in such character roles through the fifties but is probably best known for playing Morticia Addams on the sixties TV series *The Addams Family.* The Oscar went to Miyoshi Umeki for *Sayonara.*

125 • BACK STREET

UNIVERSAL. 1941.
NOMINATION *Scoring of a Dramatic Picture:* Frank Skinner.

Margaret Sullavan [2073] falls in love with Charles Boyer [36 . . .], who just happens to be married and can't divorce his wife because it would ruin his career. Ah, but love will find a way, even if it happens to be one not sanctioned by the Production Code. This means Sullavan must suffer, but she does it sweetly. The Fannie Hurst potboiler had been filmed before, with Irene Dunne [114 . . .] and John Boles in 1932; it would be filmed again, in 1961, with Susan Hayward [973 . . .] and John Gavin. Fortunately Sullavan and Boyer are an appealing team. The director is Robert Stevenson [1284].

The scoring award went to Bernard Herrmann for *All That Money Can Buy.*

Skinner: 62, 96, 947, 1229.

126 • BACK STREET

UNIVERSAL-INTERNATIONAL-ROSS HUNTER PRODUCTIONS INC.-
CARROLLTON INC.; UNIVERSAL-INTERNATIONAL. 1961.
NOMINATION *Color Costume Design:* Jean Louis.

God's—or, anyway, Hollywood's—gift to the
makers of Kleenex returns for a third time (see 125),
directed by David Miller. It's Susan Hayward
[973 . . .] who must suffer this time, because her
lover, John Gavin, is stuck in his marriage to Vera
Miles, who has threatened to commit suicide if he
leaves her. The nomination for costumes says it all:
The life of the Other Woman may be hard, but at
least she gets to wear a few nice things. The Oscar
went to Irene Sharaff for *West Side Story.*

Louis: 20, 170, 262, 732, 744, 1028, 1065, 1521,
1640, 1812, 1858, 1910, 2064.

127 • BACK TO THE FUTURE

AMBLIN ENTERTAINMENT/UNIVERSAL PICTURES PRODUCTION;
UNIVERSAL. 1985.
AWARD *Sound Effects Editing:* Charles L. Campbell and
Robert Rutledge.
NOMINATIONS *Screenplay Written Directly for the Screen:*
Robert Zemeckis and Bob Gale. *Sound:* Bill Varney,
B. Tennyson Sebastian II, Robert Thirlwell, and Wil-
liam B. Kaplan. *Song:* "Power of Love," music by
Chris Hayes and Johnny Colla, lyrics by Huey Lewis.

Teenager Michael J. Fox is transported back to the
fifties by a DeLorean that scientist Christopher Lloyd
has converted into a time machine. His mission, once
he gets there, is to make sure that his parents, Crispin
Glover and Lea Thompson, fall in love and get married. Oh, yes, and then somehow manage to get the
DeLorean powered up so he can return to the eighties. Ingeniously plotted, highly appealing fantasy that
has been much imitated—including by its two sequels
—but never surpassed. The movie made a star of
Fox, who replaced Eric Stoltz after filming had
started.

Zemeckis (who also directed) and Gale had written several previous scripts, including *I Wanna Hold
Your Hand* (1978), *1941,* and *Used Cars* (1980), that
had been filmed without attracting the notice that this
one did. They quickly became the hottest writing

team in Hollywood. The Oscar, however, went to
Earl W. Wallace, William Kelley, and Pamela Wallace
for *Witness.*

Huey Lewis and the News, the band that included
Hayes and Colla among its members, was one of the
hottest groups in the mid-eighties, and the songs they
wrote for *Back to the Future* helped establish them on
top of the charts. Lewis also has a cameo in the film;
he's the teacher who tells Fox his music is too loud.
The Oscar went to Lionel Richie for "Say You, Say
Me," from *White Nights.*

The sound award was won by *Out of Africa.*

Campbell: 588, 684, 2274. Zemeckis: 708.5. Varney: 586, 614, 1652. Thirlwell: 1513, 1701. Kaplan:
708.5, 2114.

128 • BACK TO THE FUTURE PART II

UNIVERSAL/AMBLIN ENTERTAINMENT PRODUCTION; UNIVERSAL.
1989.
NOMINATION *Visual Effects:* Ken Ralston, Michael
Lantieri, John Bell, and Steve Gawley.

Following up on the teaser at the end of *Back to the
Future,* Michael J. Fox, Christopher Lloyd, and Elizabeth Shue (who replaced Claudia Wells in the role of
Fox's girlfriend) head for the future to straighten out
the lives of Fox and Shue's children. As if that weren't
complicated enough, Fox then must make trips back
to the present and then to the fifties to sort out the
mischief being caused by villain Thomas F. Wilson.
The head-spinning plot and the dark and unpleasant
tone—the result of an attempt to make the movie
into a modern version of *It's a Wonderful Life*—cause
this sequel to be unsatisfying, especially since it ends
with a setup for *Part III* (1990), which fortunately is a
more enjoyable movie. Robert Zemeckis [127 . . .]
cowrote the screenplay with Bob Gale [127], and also
directed.

The chief pleasures of the film come from the truly
ingenious special effects, which include a breakthrough use of multiple images. At one point, Fox
plays four roles on screen: young Marty McFly, middle-aged Marty, and Marty's son and daughter. The
seamless visual effect is complemented by seamless

tour de force acting from Fox. The special effects Oscar, however, went to *The Abyss.*

Ralston: 419, 513.5, 577, 708.5, 1684, 2274. Lantieri: 937, 1071.5.

129 • BACKDRAFT

Trilogy Entertainment Group/Brian Grazer Production; Universal. 1991.

Nominations *Sound:* Gary Summers, Randy Thom, Gary Rydstrom, and Glenn Williams. *Visual Effects:* Mikael Salomon, Allen Hall, Clay Pinney, and Scott Farrar. *Sound Effects Editing:* Gary Rydstrom and Richard Hymns.

After their father died fighting a fire, brothers William Baldwin and Kurt Russell went their separate ways. Now Baldwin is back, determined to join his brother as a firefighter, but sibling rivalry may be thicker than blood. The film has a good cast, including Robert De Niro [113 . . .] as an arson inspector, Donald Sutherland as an arsonist, plus Scott Glenn, Jennifer Jason Leigh, and Rebecca De Mornay, but neither they nor director Ron Howard can lift it very far above the clichés and predictable outcome of the script. The task of doing that, naturally, falls to the special effects crew, which created some of the most beautiful fires ever seen on screen. Unfortunately *Terminator 2: Judgment Day* had even more spectacular special effects and swept the awards for which *Backdraft* was nominated.

Summers: 996, 1071.5, 1684, 2019. Thom: 708.5, 1425, 1684, 1698. Rydstrom: 1071.5, 2019. Salomon: 5. Hall: 708.5. Farrar: 419. Hymns: 996, 1071.5, 2284.

130 • BAD AND THE BEAUTIFUL, THE

MGM. 1952.

Awards *Supporting Actress:* Gloria Grahame. *Screenplay:* Charles Schnee. *Black-and-White Cinematography:* Robert Surtees. *Black-and-White Art Direction—Set Decoration:* Cedric Gibbons and Edward Carfagno; Edwin B. Willis and Keogh Gleason. *Black-and-White Costume Design:* Helen Rose.

Nomination *Actor:* Kirk Douglas.

Director Barry Sullivan, actress Lana Turner [1558], and writer Dick Powell gather in the office of studio head Walter Pidgeon [1232 . . .] to contemplate going back to work for Douglas, a ruthless hotshot of a producer who has exiled himself from Hollywood after a career-damaging flop. All have reasons for hating Douglas, and the film tells their stories in flashbacks. A fairly entertaining melodrama, its chief attraction to movie buffs is trying to figure out whom the characters are based on: Is Douglas playing Zanuck [34 . . .] or Selznick [497 . . .]? Is Turner supposed to be John Barrymore's daughter, Diana? Is Leo G. Carroll parodying Alfred Hitchcock [1171 . . .]? It's all handled with MGM's glossy style, but as a satire of Hollywood it has to take a backseat to *Singin' in the Rain,* which the same studio released the same year. John Houseman [1069 . . .] produced and Vincente Minnelli [66 . . .] directed. For the record, *The Bad and the Beautiful* won more Oscars than any other film not nominated for best picture. As to why it wasn't nominated, that probably has to do with the studio's desire to push its extravagant Technicolor version of *Ivanhoe,* which got a best picture nod, but only two other nominations and no awards. Producer Houseman, too, was something of an industry outsider, and *The Bad and the Beautiful* may have been considered a bite on the hand that was currently feeding him.

Grahame plays Powell's wife, a southern belle who thinks she's nurturing his career as a writer but may in fact be retarding it. It's offbeat casting for Grahame, whose sultry poutiness usually got her cast as sluts. Watching her handle this character, which is slightly underdeveloped in the script, one wishes she'd been cast in the Lana Turner role instead— Grahame would have been able to do what Turner is incapable of: play a bad actress who turns into a good one. Hollywood-born Grahame was discovered on Broadway by MGM in 1943 and signed to a contract. Although she'd been noticed by the Academy in 1947 for her work in *Crossfire,* 1952 was her big year, not only for her Oscar-winning role but for her performance in the best picture winner, *The Greatest Show on Earth.* But aside from a delightful turn as Ado Annie in the film of *Oklahoma!,* Grahame's post-Oscar career was pretty much a reversion to type, and she disappeared from the screen at the end of the fifties except for occasional forgettable films and one memorable one, *Melvin and Howard,* in which she played a small role, the year before her death from cancer in 1981.

Schnee had been hired by Dore Schary [157 . . .] as a writer-producer when Schary headed the MGM B-picture division. The story on which *The Bad and the Beautiful* was based had been discovered by Houseman in *Ladies' Home Journal.* It was set on Broadway, and the ambitious producer was thought to be a portrait of Jed Harris [1433]. Houseman suggested that Schnee shift the scene to Hollywood. After the Oscar, Schnee turned to producing for a while but eventually returned to writing. In 1962 he reteamed with Houseman, Minnelli, and Douglas on another movie about moviemaking, *Two Weeks in Another Town.*

Surtees had distinguished himself as a color cinematographer, for which he had already won an Oscar, but his black-and-white work was equally impressive. He had trained as an assistant cameraman with Gregg Toland [407 . . .], and he has that master's way with interior shots—especially notable in this film. But he also excelled at location shooting in black and white, demonstrated in films from the 1949 *Intruder in the Dust,* shot in Mississippi, to *The Last Picture Show,* filmed in West Texas.

The grit and determination that made Douglas a standout in action films also make his monomaniacal producer a character you can't take your eyes off of. His three Oscar nominations came to naught. This time he lost to Gary Cooper for *High Noon.*

Grahame: 467. Surtees: 175, 557, 810, 917, 1094, 1139, 1388, 1469, 1644, 1747, 1911, 1927, 1960, 2055, 2152. Gibbons: 66, 87, 217, 227, 239, 285, 290, 440, 629, 749, 831, 980, 1069, 1096, 1173, 1190, 1226, 1230, 1232, 1274, 1308, 1309, 1417, 1567, 1604, 1644, 1662, 1673, 1721, 1861, 1937, 2068, 2112, 2256, 2257, 2300, 2320, 2330. Carfagno: 175, 629, 917, 1069, 1552, 1644, 1814, 1937, 2312. Willis: 66, 87, 227, 239, 290, 629, 749, 831, 980, 1069, 1096, 1157, 1173, 1190, 1226, 1230, 1232, 1309, 1417, 1567, 1657, 1662, 1673, 1721, 1861, 1937, 2068, 2112, 2257, 2320, 2330.

Gleason: 66, 290, 769, 1226, 1861, 1937. Rose: 578, 629, 755, 817, 980, 1007, 1309, 1335, 1599. Douglas: 380, 1226.

131 • BAD DAY AT BLACK ROCK
MGM. 1955.

NOMINATIONS *Actor:* Spencer Tracy. *Director:* John Sturges. *Screenplay:* Millard Kaufman.

Tracy arrives in a small southwestern town to investigate a wartime atrocity against a Japanese-American and is met with hostility by the locals, who include Robert Ryan [467], Dean Jagger [2154], Walter Brennan [424 . . .], Ernest Borgnine [1283], and Lee Marvin [371]. This suspense melodrama is well staged and superbly paced, and though it was one of the first movies to explore U.S. treatment of Japanese-Americans, it never gets preachy. In many ways, it's superior to some of the best picture nominees, such as the tear-jerking *Love Is a Many-Splendored Thing* or the overproduced *Mister Roberts.* And it has held up in both popular and critical esteem far better than the winner, *Marty,* which was the undoing of *Bad Day* in all of the categories in which it was nominated.

Tracy, who brings his usual forthright everymanness to the role, lost to one of his supporting players, Borgnine, for his role in *Marty.*

The Oscar for directing went to *Marty's* Delbert Mann. Sturges began in a variety of jobs at RKO and worked his way up to film editor. After World War II, he became a director, mostly of westerns and action films. He's best known for *Gunfight at the O.K. Corral, The Magnificent Seven,* and *The Great Escape.*

Kaufman lost to Paddy Chayefsky for *Marty.*

Tracy: 271, 352, 656, 843, 1000, 1065, 1470, 1751. Kaufman: 1995.

132 • BAD GIRL
Fox. 1931–32.

AWARDS *Director:* Frank Borzage. *Adaptation:* Edwin Burke.

NOMINATION *Picture:* Winfield Sheehan, studio head.

Sally Eilers and James Dunn [2137] play a young couple trying to make ends meet when they discover they're expecting a child. Burke's adaptation of a novel by Viña Delmar [114] resulted in a hit, even without major stars, but the movie has vanished from circulation today.

Borzage's career peaked with his second Oscar, and his films are generally too sentimental for contemporary tastes. His best subsequent work is probably the first version of Hemingway's *A Farewell to Arms* and two pictures with Margaret Sullavan [2073], *Three Comrades* and *The Mortal Storm* (1940). He died in 1962.

The Oscar for best picture went to a movie that decidedly did have big stars, *Grand Hotel*.

Borzage: 1792. Sheehan: 374, 592, 989, 1920.

133 • BAD SEED, THE

WARNER BROS. 1956.

NOMINATIONS *Actress:* Nancy Kelly. *Supporting Actress:* Eileen Heckart. *Supporting Actress:* Patty McCormack. *Black-and-White Cinematography:* Hal Rosson.

Sweet little McCormack is actually a killer, as her mother (Kelly) and Heckart learn to their peril. All three actors created their roles on Broadway, in the play by Maxwell Anderson [48], which was tidy melodrama based on a dubious premise: that "evil" is genetically borne. The censors managed to muddle things up in the movie version, forcing the replacement of the shocker stage ending in which McCormack literally gets away with murder with one in which she suffers divine retribution. Warners released the movie with an "adults only" warning that was as much come-on as caveat, and there's a silly "curtain call" in the end credits in which McCormack is administered the classic corrective for misbehavior (if not murder): a good spanking. In short, dated but not unwatchable. Directed by Mervyn LeRoy [1662 . . .] from a screenplay by John Lee Mahin [352 . . .].

Like her costar McCormack, Kelly had started as a child actress. And like McCormack, she had some difficulty restarting her career after adolescence. In the late thirties and early forties she was under contract to Fox and appeared in numerous unremembered films. Like other actresses in that position, she turned to the stage, where she won a Tony

for *The Bad Seed*. After re-creating the role on film, she returned to the theater. The Oscar went to Ingrid Bergman for *Anastasia*.

Heckart and McCormack lost the supporting actress award to Dorothy Malone for *Written on the Wind*. Many of Heckart's film roles have been re-creations of stage performances, such as this one, or her parts in *Bus Stop* and her Oscar winner, *Butterflies Are Free*. She continued her stage career with success but has also been seen from time to time in movie character parts.

What do you do when you've been nominated for an Oscar at the age of eleven for playing a killer kid? In McCormack's case, you go on to play troubled teens in films with tell-all titles like 1968's *The Miniskirt Mob*. In short, you experience what Linda Blair [631] experienced after *The Exorcist*.

Rosson lost to Joseph Ruttenberg for *Somebody Up There Likes Me*.

Heckart: 319. Rosson: 105, 256, 747, 2055, 2300.

134 • BAGDAD CAFE

PELEMELE FILM PRODUCTION; ISLAND PICTURES. 1988.

NOMINATION *Song:* "Calling You," music and lyrics by Bob Telson.

This offbeat comic mood piece by German director Percy Adlon features the zaftig Marianne Sägebrecht as a woman stranded at a café run by CCH Pounder in the California desert, and Jack Palance [408 . . .] as a Hollywood set decorator. An attempt to make a TV series out of the film failed, though it starred Jean Stapleton and Whoopi Goldberg [423 . . .]. The song Oscar went to Carly Simon's "Let the River Run," from *Working Girl*.

135 • BAL, LE

CINEPRODUCTION S.A.-FILMS A2 (PARIS)/MASSFILM (ROME)/O.N.C.I.C. (ALGER) PRODUCTION (ALGERIA). 1983.

NOMINATION *Foreign Language Film*.

Fifty years of French history as seen from the viewpoint of a ballroom. People come, people go, music and fashions change, but there's no dialogue.

Intriguing but certainly not for all tastes. Director Ettore Scola's film lost to *Fanny & Alexander*.

136 • BALALAIKA
MGM. 1939.
NOMINATION *Sound Recording:* Douglas Shearer.

Nelson Eddy, with Ilona Massey subbing for Jeanette MacDonald, stars in a forgettable (and mostly forgotten) operetta about the Russian Revolution and its Parisian exiles. Directed by Reinhold Schunzel, with Charles Ruggles and Frank Morgan [22 . . .]. The Oscar for sound went to *When Tomorrow Comes*.

Shearer: 202, 256, 397, 685, 817, 835, 1096, 1232, 1292, 1371, 1419, 1751, 1950, 1988, 2048, 2055, 2211, 2300.

137 • BALCONY, THE
WALTER READE-STERLING-ALLEN HODGON PRODUCTION; WALTER READE-STERLING-CONTINENTAL · DISTRIBUTING (UNITED KINGDOM). 1963.
NOMINATION *Black-and-White Cinematography:* George Folsey.

Adaptation by Ben Maddow [105] of Jean Genet's surrealist play, which takes place in a brothel during wartime. On stage its poetic allegory can make a strong effect, but the film, directed by Joseph Strick [2170], just seems confused and pretentious, despite a cast that includes Shelley Winters [542 . . .], Peter Falk [1377 . . .], Lee Grant [534 . . .], Ruby Dee, and Leonard Nimoy. This was the last of cinematographer Folsey's fourteen unsuccessful nominations. He lost to James Wong Howe for *Hud*.

Folsey: 51, 629, 807, 835, 838, 1124, 1299, 1320, 1500, 1688, 1782, 2068, 2269.

138 • BALL OF FIRE
SAMUEL GOLDWYN PRODUCTIONS; RKO RADIO. 1941.
NOMINATIONS *Actress:* Barbara Stanwyck. *Original Story:* Thomas Monroe and Billy Wilder. *Sound Recording:* Thomas Moulton. *Scoring of a Dramatic Picture:* Alfred Newman.

Stanwyck plays nightclub entertainer Sugarpuss O'Shea, who hides out from the mob with a houseful of mostly elderly bachelor professors at work on an encyclopedia. The youngest of the lot is linguistics scholar Gary Cooper [701 . . .], who wants to use Stanwyck as a source for his entry on slang, but ends (you guessed it) by falling in love and rescuing Stanwyck from her gangster boyfriend, played by Dana Andrews. Delightful, even if the cuddly little old professors occasionally get cloying. They're played by a gallery of pros: Oscar Homolka [972], Henry Travers [1371], S. Z. Sakall, Tully Marshall, Leonid Kinskey, Richard Haydn, and Aubrey Mather. The idea of Cooper as a professor strikes some as ludicrous, but he handles the role with great charm. Howard Hawks [1779] directed, and if it doesn't seem as lively as some of his films, it's probably because he was under the obsessive eye of producer Samuel Goldwyn [102 . . .].

Stanwyck had earned her first Oscar nomination in a Goldwyn picture, *Stella Dallas,* for which she was not the first choice. She wasn't Goldwyn's first choice to play Sugarpuss, either. Ginger Rogers [1102] was, but she had just won the Oscar for *Kitty Foyle* and was being choosy about her roles. Jean Arthur [1353] and Carole Lombard [1401] also turned it down before Stanwyck was approached. The Oscar went to Joan Fontaine for *Suspicion.*

Goldwyn obtained Wilder's services while on a hunt for a project that would feature Cooper, whom Goldwyn had under contract. Wilder, with his partner Charles Brackett [705 . . .], had had a series of hits—*Midnight* (1939), *Ninotchka,* and *Arise My Love*—and was now under contract with Paramount, which wanted Cooper for *For Whom the Bell Tolls*. Goldwyn struck a deal for the writers in exchange for Cooper's services. While Wilder and Monroe received a nomination for their story, Brackett failed to be nominated for his work with Wilder on the screenplay. The Oscar went to Harry Segall for *Here Comes Mr. Jordan*.

The sound Oscar went to *That Hamilton Woman* and the scoring Oscar to Bernard Herrmann for *All That Money Can Buy*.

Stanwyck: 566, 1879, 1923. Monroe: 23. Wilder: 91, 198, 566, 705, 709, 925, 1208, 1440, 1738, 1860, 1903, 1975, 2297. Moulton: 22, 46, 366, 457, 487, 560, 706, 798, 962, 1153, 1200, 1451, 1510,

1607, 1849, 2154, 2294. Newman: 31, 46, 78, 182, 226, 333, 334, 347, 375, 428, 437, 457, 476, 495, 542, 690, 797, 833, 952, 953, 959, 962, 1016, 1082, 1088, 1213, 1278, 1362, 1397, 1475, 1616, 1655, 1849, 1868, 1883, 1921, 2043, 2046, 2091, 2258, 2286, 2294, 2316.

139 • _BALLAD OF A SOLDIER_

Mosfilm Studios Production; Kingsley International-M.J.P. Enterprises Inc. (USSR). 1961.

Nomination _Story and Screenplay—Written Directly for the Screen:_ Valentin Yoshov and Grigori Chukhrai.

A soldier on leave during World War II meets and falls in love with a young girl while traveling home to see his mother. The film's simplicity and charming sentimentality as well as the pictures of the hardships of life in wartime won over audiences, but it now seems a little too naive. It was the first postwar Soviet film to attract attention in the West, winning awards at the San Francisco and Cannes film festivals. Originally released in 1959, it didn't meet the exhibition requirements for Oscar consideration until two years later. It joined two other foreign-made films, _General Della Rovere_ and _La Dolce Vita,_ along with _Lover Come Back,_ in the Oscar race, but the award went to William Inge for _Splendor in the Grass._ Screenwriter Chukhrai also directed the film.

140 • _BAMBI_

Walt Disney Productions; RKO Radio. 1942.

Nominations _Sound Recording:_ Sam Slyfield. _Song:_ "Love Is a Song," music by Frank Churchill, lyrics by Larry Morey. _Scoring of a Dramatic or Comedy Picture:_ Frank Churchill and Edward Plumb.

A deer grows up in the forest, making friends with a rabbit named Thumper and a skunk named Flower. His mother is killed by hunters and he nearly dies in a forest fire, but he survives to raise a family with the doe Faline. Perhaps the most visually beautiful of all Disney films, with its rich forest and meadow backgrounds, it's also a little sticky because most of the voices are those of small children. It's often asserted that the tots at whom it seems to be aimed are traumatized by the scene of Bambi's mother's death, but

we've never met anyone who was permanently scarred by it. The novel by Felix Salten on which the movie is based is far more graphically violent. And the Disney version has probably done more to discourage deer hunting than any protest movement could.

The Oscar for sound went to _Yankee Doodle Dandy._ The song winner was Irving Berlin's "White Christmas," from _Holiday Inn._ Though _Bambi_ contains several songs, it competed in the dramatic and comedy picture scoring category rather than with the musicals. It lost to Max Steiner for _Now, Voyager._

Slyfield: 402, 1745, 2071. Churchill: 585, 1851. Morey: 1853. Plumb: 1745, 2071, 2202.

141 • _BAND WAGON, THE_

MGM. 1953.

Nominations _Story and Screenplay:_ Betty Comden and Adolph Green. _Scoring of a Musical Picture:_ Adolph Deutsch. _Color Costume Design:_ Mary Ann Nyberg.

Hollywood star Fred Astaire [2126] finds his career on the skids—neatly demonstrated in an opening sequence in which he is met by reporters at Grand Central Station only to be deserted by them when they spot Ava Gardner [1339]. He has come to New York to try a Broadway comeback in a show written by his friends Nanette Fabray and Oscar Levant—characters based on Comden and Green themselves. The show, however, is in the heavy hands of Jack Buchanan, a director with pretensions to art, who has hired classical ballerina Cyd Charisse to be Astaire's dancing partner. Astaire is at first wary of his new partner, but they come together in the film's musical highlight, a duet in Central Park to "Dancing in the Dark." The rest of the plot deals with Astaire's rescue of the show from Buchanan's arty clutches—and, of course, his winning of Charisse after the usual misunderstandings. The movie is one of the most highly regarded MGM musicals, largely because of its screenplay, the direction of Vincente Minnelli [66 . . .], the songs by Arthur Schwartz [2026 . . .] and Howard Dietz, and most of all, the dancing of Astaire and Charisse.

Comden and Green were enlisted by producer Arthur Freed [66 . . .] after the success of *Singin' in the Rain,* for which they also wrote the script. Freed liked to do "songbook" musicals—strings of numbers by a particular composer loosely linked by plot: *An American in Paris* uses the Gershwins' songbook, *Easter Parade* Irving Berlin's, and *Singin' in the Rain* the work of Nacio Herb Brown and Freed himself. *The Band Wagon* does the same thing with the songs of Dietz (who had been head of MGM publicity) and Schwartz. The composers' 1931 Broadway musical called *The Band Wagon,* which was coincidentally the last show in which Fred and Adele Astaire appeared together, bears no relationship to the Comden-Green script, which is an affectionate lampoon of Broadway pretensions, just as their *Singin' in the Rain* was a takeoff on Hollywood vanity. Freed and Minnelli hired Broadway talent, including choreographer Michael Kidd and designer Oliver Smith [852], in an effort to get the ambiance right. They wanted Clifton Webb [1149 . . .], who like Astaire had appeared in the Broadway *Band Wagon,* to play the pretentious director, but Webb thought the role too small. He suggested Buchanan, who had sometimes been called "the British Astaire."

Like *Singin' in the Rain, The Band Wagon* failed to be nominated in several categories where one might have thought it a strong contender. Four of the five nominees for color art direction that year were MGM films, but Smith's designs for *The Band Wagon* were not among them—perhaps because Smith had clashed with studio regular Preston Ames [31 . . .], who did get nominated for *The Story of Three Loves.* More astonishingly, the most durable of the new songs composed by Dietz and Schwartz for the film, "That's Entertainment," was not nominated for best song. The only explanation is that some have thought the song too derivative of Irving Berlin's "There's No Business Like Show Business."

Comden and Green lost to Charles Brackett, Walter Resich, and Richard Breen for the disaster-melodrama *Titanic.* Deutsch's scoring was thought inferior to Alfred Newman's for *Call Me Madam.* And Nyberg's designs were valued less than Charles Lemaire and Emile Santiago's togas and tunics for *The Robe.*

Comden: 1034. Green: 1034. Deutsch: 87, 1469, 1782, 1818. Nyberg: 1910.

142 • *BANG THE DRUM SLOWLY*

ROSENFIELD PRODUCTION; PARAMOUNT. 1973.
NOMINATION *Supporting Actor:* Vincent Gardenia.

Pitcher Michael Moriarty befriends catcher Robert De Niro [113 . . .], who is dying of Hodgkin's disease. Gardenia is the team's manager. Like most movie attempts to mythologize baseball, this one, adapted by Mark Harris from his novel and directed by John Hancock, doesn't quite work. What seems poignant and insightful on paper turns into mush on screen. It did, however, provide De Niro with one of his first important screen roles. The novel had earlier been dramatized on TV, with Paul Newman [3 . . .] in the Moriarty role.

Born in Naples but raised in New York, Gardenia established a solid career as a character actor on TV and stage, and sometimes in the movies, in the late fifties. A year before his Oscar nomination, he received a Tony Award for his role in *The Prisoner of Second Avenue.* The Oscar went to John Houseman for *The Paper Chase.*

Gardenia: 1351.

143 • *BANJO ON MY KNEE*

20TH CENTURY-FOX. 1936.
NOMINATION *Sound Recording:* E. H. Hansen.

Barbara Stanwyck [138 . . .] and Joel McCrea star in this comedy with music (provided by a young Tony Martin) set on a Mississippi riverboat. Directed by John Cromwell, with Walter Brennan [424 . . .] and Buddy Ebsen. The Oscar went to another period music drama, *San Francisco.*

Hansen: 241, 815, 952, 990, 1655, 1868, 1957, 2027, 2056, 2272, 2286, 2317.

144 • *BANNING*

UNIVERSAL. 1967.
NOMINATION *Song:* "The Eyes of Love," music by Quincy Jones, lyrics by Bob Russell.

Robert Wagner is a golf pro at a country club that is the setting for various kinds of soap-operatic intrigue. Passable if you go in for this sort of thing, though like a lot of late-sixties movies, it has a garish look to it. Directed by Ron Winston. Among the mostly low-wattage cast (Jill St. John, James Farentino, Susan Clark) is Gene Hackman [255 . . .], who was getting his big break in another movie that year, *Bonnie and Clyde.*

As producer, composer, and performer, Jones has won more Grammy Awards than any other person, and Russell was a veteran lyricist who had worked with Duke Ellington [1531] and would team again with Jones on *For Love of Ivy.* But their luck at the Oscars has not been good. This time they lost to Leslie Bricusse's ''Talk to the Animals,'' from *Doctor Dolittle.*

Jones: 423, 698, 987, 2299. Russell: 698.

145 • BARBARY COAST

SAMUEL GOLDWYN PRODUCTIONS; UNITED ARTISTS. 1935.
NOMINATION *Cinematography:* Ray June.

A gangster movie set in gold-rush era San Francisco, with gangster par excellence Edward G. Robinson as a club owner and Miriam Hopkins [165] as his main attraction. Joel McCrea is the young prospector who tries to win her away from Robinson, and Walter Brennan [424 . . .], without his false teeth, plays a character known as Old Atrocity. David Niven [1778], who had just signed a contract with producer Samuel Goldwyn [102 . . .], has a one-line bit part. For all the talent involved—direction by Howard Hawks [1779], screenplay by Ben Hecht [78 . . .] and Charles MacArthur [1664 . . .]—it's a fairly routine action flick, with all its raffishness smoothed out by the Production Code.

This was June's second nomination for a Goldwyn film. Shortly afterward, he moved over to MGM, where he spent most of the rest of his career. He lost the Oscar this time to Hal Mohr, who won for *A Midsummer Night's Dream*—the only write-in candidate ever to receive the award.

June: 102, 736.

146 • BAREFOOT CONTESSA, THE

FIGARO INC.; UNITED ARTISTS. 1954.
AWARD *Supporting Actor:* Edmond O'Brien.
NOMINATION *Story and Screenplay:* Joseph Mankiewicz.

Spanish dancer Ava Gardner [1339] is discovered in the slums of Madrid by publicist O'Brien and director Humphrey Bogart [24 . . .]. They turn her into a big star, but she comes to a bad end. Also in the cast are Marius Gorin, Rossano Brazzi, Valentina Cortese [501], and Bessie Love [296]. Entertainingly trashy melodrama, directed by Mankiewicz, but as a satire of Hollywood it can't compare with its near contemporaries *The Bad and the Beautiful, Sunset Boulevard,* or *Singin' in the Rain.* Though Mankiewicz said he based the role on Rita Hayworth, it was custom-made for Gardner, whose origins were as humble as the heroine's, and she was so taken with Madrid that she settled there three years later after her divorce from Frank Sinatra [732 . . .].

O'Brien began his acting career in his native New York and was a member of Orson Welles' [407 . . .] Mercury Players before making his film debut in *The Hunchback of Notre Dame* in 1939. He started as a juvenile lead, but after gaining weight became a much-used character actor. Mankiewicz, who had earlier directed O'Brien as Casca in *Julius Caesar,* recalled that during the rehearsals for that film, O'Brien had often parodied actor Martin Gabel's performance as Casca in the *Mercury Theater* production of *Julius Caesar.* Gabel, it seems, played Casca with New York Jewish mannerisms and inflections, which Mankiewicz had O'Brien adopt for his role in *Contessa.* O'Brien continued his career as a character player into the early seventies; he died of Alzheimer's in 1985.

After his double wins as writer-director for *A Letter to Three Wives* and *All About Eve,* Mankiewicz's career began to decline. The bitterness expressed toward Hollywood in *The Barefoot Contessa* seems prophetic, especially since he was about to tangle with the megalomaniac Samuel Goldwyn [102 . . .] on *Guys and Dolls* and a few years later would be involved in one of the movies' most notorious disasters, *Cleopatra. Contessa* has a few flashes of Mankiewicz's wit, but not enough. He lost to Budd Schulberg for *On the Water-front.*

O'Brien: 1783. Mankiewicz: 46, 673, 1163, 1444, 1563, 1836, 1841.

147 • BAREFOOT IN THE PARK

HAL WALLIS PRODUCTIONS; PARAMOUNT. 1967.
NOMINATION *Supporting Actress:* Mildred Natwick.

Newlyweds Jane Fonda [394 . . .] and Robert Redford [1502 . . .] rent a dreary little flat on the fifth floor of a Greenwich Village building that doesn't have an elevator, and author Neil Simon [332 . . .] proceeds to wring one-liners out of that situation, their postnuptial difficulties (she's a free spirit, he's inhibited), and their relationships with his mother, Natwick, and an eccentric neighbor, Charles Boyer [36 . . .]. It was a Broadway hit, and it's a modestly enjoyable movie, but the staginess and plotlessness show, especially when director Gene Saks tries to open it up toward the end. The four featured performers are all quite good, though Fonda sometimes seems to be trying too hard to be funny. Redford and Natwick had performed the roles on stage, so their comfort with them may have put the other actors at a disadvantage.

Natwick made her screen debut in 1940 in *The Long Voyage Home* and a decade later appeared in three more of director John Ford's films: *Three Godfathers, She Wore a Yellow Ribbon,* and *The Quiet Man.* Her screen appearances were occasional, usually in dowdy, dotty character parts. The Oscar went to Estelle Parsons for *Bonnie and Clyde.*

148 • BARKER, THE

FIRST NATIONAL. 1928–29.
NOMINATION *Actress:* Betty Compson.

Romantic melodrama set in a carnival, with Douglas Fairbanks, Jr. By one estimate, half of all films made before 1950 have disappeared, and less than 20 percent of those made in the twenties still exist. *The Barker* is apparently among the lost. Compson, who started in show business at fifteen as a vaudeville artist, began her film career in short slapstick comedies. She became a star in the early twenties, but when her career slumped, she moved to England, where she had a successful second career. She returned to Hollywood, where, in the middle of another career slump, she was discovered by director George Fitzmaurice and cast in *The Barker.* The success of the film briefly revived her career. She continued to work in supporting roles until the late forties. The only notable film in which she can easily be seen today is the minor Alfred Hitchcock [1171 . . .] comedy *Mr. and Mrs. Smith* (1941). She had previously worked with Hitchcock in 1923 on the British film *Woman to Woman,* for which he was art director. Compson's nomination was not official: The Academy announced only the winners of the Oscars for 1928–29—in this case, Mary Pickford for *Coquette.* However, the records of the actors branch show that she was one of five others who were being considered for the award. Compson died in 1974.

149 • BARKLEYS OF BROADWAY, THE

MGM. 1949.
NOMINATION *Color Cinematography:* Harry Stradling.

Fred Astaire [2126] and Ginger Rogers [1102] play a married dance team who are in perfect sync on stage but bicker endlessly when they're off. Rogers wants to be taken seriously as an actress, while Astaire insists she'd be nothing without him. In the end Rogers has a stage triumph in a serious role but decides she's happier working with Astaire. This reteaming of Astaire and Rogers came about by accident. They had gone their separate ways after nine RKO films in the thirties. Rogers went on to do mostly nonmusical films and by the mid-forties was one of the top box-office stars. Astaire's career had been somewhat less spectacular. After the smash success of *Easter Parade,* however, he seemed to be on top again, just as Rogers' star seemed to be declining. Producer Arthur Freed [66 . . .] was eager to reunite Astaire with his *Easter Parade* costar, Judy Garland [1065 . . .], and a script was prepared for them by the writing team of Betty Comden [141 . . .] and Adolph Green [141 . . .]. But when Garland's physical and mental health collapsed, Rogers stepped into the role. Unfortunately the movie, directed by

Charles Walters [1173], is something of a dud. It has a mediocre song score, the product of a mismatch between composer Harry Warren [21 . . .] and lyricist Ira Gershwin [455 . . .]. Warren resented the adulation lavished by Freed on Gershwin and was especially miffed at Freed's decision to include George Gershwin's [1797] "They Can't Take That Away From Me" in the film. Rogers is unbecomingly coiffed and made up, and her great dramatic triumph —a scene in which she plays the young Sarah Bernhardt and recites "La Marseillaise"—is utterly ridiculous. The film's best number is "Shoes With Wings On," in which Astaire dances with a roomful of disembodied shoes. The movie was a hit, but choreographer Hermes Pan [481 . . .] said Astaire may have thought reuniting with Rogers "a step backwards," for there were never any efforts to do it again.

The cinematography Oscar went to Winton Hoch for *She Wore a Yellow Ribbon*.

Stradling: 110, 596, 737, 852, 853, 864, 896, 957, 1246, 1393, 1567, 1949, 2338.

150 • BARRETTS OF WIMPOLE STREET, THE

MGM. 1934.
NOMINATIONS *Picture:* Irving Thalberg, producer. *Actress:* Norma Shearer.

Fredric March [184 . . .], as Victorian poet Robert Browning, falls in love with Shearer, as fellow poet Elizabeth Barrett, but Charles Laughton [1387 . . .], as her tyrannical father, forbids their marriage. Katharine Cornell had a huge success on Broadway in the Rudolf Besier play on which the movie is based, and it's just the kind of high-toned period drama that MGM came to specialize in. Unfortunately it's rather stiff and stately, though Laughton is, as usual, fun to watch. It was directed by Sidney Franklin [799 . . .], who also directed the inferior remake in 1957 that starred Jennifer Jones [584 . . .] and Bill Travers, with John Gielgud [103 . . .] as the ogre-father.

Barretts was one of the first productions overseen by Thalberg on his return from a leave after suffering a heart attack in 1932. It was in large part a showcase

for Shearer, his wife. They missed their chance to be the first married couple to take home Oscars, however: Both the film and Shearer came in second to *It Happened One Night* and its star, Claudette Colbert.

Thalberg: 202, 799, 812, 1387, 1721, 1846, 2129. Shearer: 555, 723, 1274, 1721, 2038.

151 • BARRY LYNDON

HAWK FILMS LTD. PRODUCTION; WARNER BROS. (UNITED KINGDOM). 1975.
AWARDS *Cinematography:* John Alcott. *Art Direction—Set Decoration:* Ken Adam and Roy Walker; Vernon Dixon. *Scoring—Original Song Score and/or Adaptation:* Leonard Rosenman. *Costume Design:* Ulla-Britt Soderlund and Milena Canonero.
NOMINATIONS *Picture:* Stanley Kubrick, producer. *Director:* Stanley Kubrick. *Screenplay Adapted From Other Material:* Stanley Kubrick.

Irish rogue Lyndon, played by Ryan O'Neal [1218], connives his way to fortune and position in this handsome if somewhat remote film based on a novel by Thackeray—a twentieth-century film of a nineteenth-century novel about eighteenth-century characters. It's been called a coffee-table movie by more than one critic. No one disputes its beauty, but no one cares much about the people in it.

Alcott began his career as a cinematographer with Kubrick, working on *2001: A Space Odyssey* as a second unit cameraman and moving up to director of photography on *A Clockwork Orange*. On *Barry Lyndon* Kubrick demanded that each shot be composed as if it were a painting, and Alcott used new lenses designed by NASA for space photography to capture candlelit interiors shot on various locations in England. The design team, like the costumers, were instructed to copy eighteenth-century drawings and paintings. The music, too, was adapted from works of the period, although Rosenman considered refusing the Oscar because he found Kubrick's use of his orchestrations patchy and vulgar. The Academy's recognition of the film's verisimilitude set a trend toward greater accuracy in period films.

Kubrick had announced after *2001* that his next film would be about Napoleon, a project that never came together. But after two successive ventures into the future with *2001* and *A Clockwork Orange,* he managed in *Barry Lyndon* to deliver a pre-Napoleonic film. Like almost every movie he has made, it divided critics sharply. Its nomination came in one of the most remarkable years in recent Hollywood history: The other nominees for best picture were *Dog Day Afternoon, Jaws, Nashville,* and the winning *One Flew Over the Cuckoo's Nest.* In company that strong, *Barry Lyndon* looks like perhaps the weakest choice, except for its technical brilliance. Many would have preferred to see either *The Man Who Would Be King* or Woody Allen's *Love and Death* among the nominees. Kubrick lost as producer to Saul Zaentz and Michael Douglas, as director to Milos Forman, and as writer to Lawrence Hauben and Bo Goldman, all for *Cuckoo's Nest.*

Adam: 12.5, 101, 1234.5, 1898. Walker: 2321. Dixon: 1429, 1471. Rosenman: 264, 466, 1914. Canonero: 386, 543, 1512, 2148. Kubrick: 415, 574, 735, 2164.

152 • *BARTON FINK*

BARTON CIRCLE PRODUCTION; 20TH CENTURY FOX. 1991.
NOMINATIONS *Supporting Actor:* Michael Lerner. *Art Direction–Set Decoration:* Dennis Gassner; Nancy Haigh. *Costume Design:* Richard Hornung.

In 1941 successful young playwright Fink (John Turturro), hired by Hollywood to write a screenplay, is subjected to the bullying flattery of a studio head, Lerner—a caricature of Louis B. Mayer with dashes of Sam Goldwyn [102 . . .], Harry Cohn [1025 . . .], Darryl Zanuck [34 . . .], et al. At the studio Fink encounters an alcoholic southern writer, played by John Mahoney, and his mistress, played by Judy Davis [962.5 . . .]. To escape what he sees as the phoniness of Hollywood, he holes up in a ratty hotel, where he meets John Goodman, who seems at first to be the only "real person" in town but gradually emerges as very sinister indeed. Brothers Joel and Ethan Coen, the writing-directing team that produced such cultish movies as *Blood Simple* (1985) and *Raising Arizona* (1987), go over the top here, but not without a certain style. As a horror-comedy, *Barton Fink* delivers its share of shocks and laughs. But the Coens seem to be striving for something more satiric, and there the movie simply seems pretentious and anachronistic. The studio-driven Hollywood they portray is long gone, replaced by the artful dealers more successfully satirized by *The Player. Barton Fink* is terrifically acted, however, with Goodman and Mahoney (the latter doing a spot-on impression of William Faulkner) among the standouts.

Lerner was no stranger to playing movie moguls. He had previously played Harry Cohn in the TV movie *Rita Hayworth: The Love Goddess* (1983) and Jack Warner [55 . . .] in the miniseries *Moviola* (1980). The Oscar went to Jack Palance for *City Slickers.*

Gassner and Haigh were called on to create a period Hollywood as well as a hotel with wallpaper and plumbing that seem to have a life of their own. The Academy preferred their work on *Bugsy,* for which they won the Oscar. *Bugsy* also won for Albert Wolsky's costumes.

Gassner: 308. Haigh: 308, 708.5.

152.5 • *BASIC INSTINCT*

CAROLCO PRODUCTION; TRISTAR. 1992.
NOMINATIONS *Film Editing:* Frank J. Urioste. *Original Score:* Jerry Goldsmith.

Self-destructive cop Michael Douglas [1481 . . .] falls for murder suspect Sharon Stone, a thriller writer whose plots seem curiously close to real events. Screenwriter Joe Eszterhas, who was paid something in seven figures for the script, supplies plenty of sex and violence, but also a plot that never really makes sense—especially at the nonending, which seems designed to leave room for a sequel. While it was filming in San Francisco, the movie became a target for protests by gay and lesbian activists, who had learned of its exploitive treatment of lesbian/bisexual characters. Protest groups even mounted billboards that tried to give away the ending, but the released film pulled its punches. Eszterhas tried to distance himself from the film as a result of the protests, charging that director Paul Verhoeven had altered his material. A box-office smash, the movie made Stone one of the hottest stars in Hollywood. But like Eszterhas, the otherwise uninhibited

Stone found herself embarrassed by the film and has blamed director Verhoeven for the famous police interrogation scene in which she demonstrates that she is wearing no underwear. The film features a cameo appearance by Dorothy Malone [2315].

The editing Oscar went to Joel Cox for *Unforgiven* and the scoring award to Alan Menken for *Aladdin*.

Urioste: 544, 1711. Goldsmith: 268, 395, 727, 939, 1472, 1527, 1537, 1541, 1583, 1589, 1753, 1913, 2176, 2287.

153 • *BATMAN*

WARNER BROS. PRODUCTION; WARNER BROS. 1989.

AWARD *Art Direction—Set Decoration:* Anton Furst; Peter Young.

In the nightmarish city of Gotham, Batman, played by Michael Keaton, does battle with the Joker, played by Jack Nicholson [395 . . .]. *Batman* owes its huge box-office success largely to the extravagant overplaying of Nicholson, who really does seem to be having fun. And the design of the film is an extraordinary melding of comic-book art, German expressionism, and Hollywood art deco. But aside from that, and a fine score by Danny Elfman and some songs by Prince [1635], the movie has a jumbled plot, sketchy characterization, and choppy editing. Director Tim Burton clearly has a vision, but he hasn't quite developed the skills to communicate it. Keaton was a controversial choice for the lead. Noted for over-the-top performance in films such as *Night Shift* (1982) and Burton's *Beetlejuice,* he's forced to rein in so tightly here that he sometimes seems to be letting the batsuit do the acting for him. Interesting performers such as Pat Hingle, Billy Dee Williams, Robert Wuhl, Michael Gough, and Jack Palance [408 . . .] get lost in the scenery.

Art director Furst, born in England and educated at the Royal College of Art, had worked on several interesting projects in Great Britain, including *The Company of Wolves* (1985) and Stanley Kubrick's *Full Metal Jacket;* in the latter a major challenge was concealing the fact that a film set in Vietnam was actually shot in England. After the success of *Batman* Furst

formed his own production company, but he died in a fall from a rooftop, an apparent suicide, a year after his most celebrated film earned him the Oscar.

153.5 • *BATMAN RETURNS*

WARNER BROS. PRODUCTION; WARNER BROS. 1992.

NOMINATIONS *Makeup:* Ve Neill, Ronnie Specter, Stan Winston. *Visual Effects:* Michael Fink, Craig Barron, John Bruno, and Dennis Skotak.

Batman (Michael Keaton) faces two new antagonists: the Penguin, played by Danny DeVito, and Catwoman, played by Michelle Pfeiffer [485 . . .]. The movie was not the blockbuster that the first film was; after a record-breaking opening weekend, word got around that the sequel was overelaborate and not very much fun and that it was a bit too violent and grotesque for the very young. But in some ways director Tim Burton succeeds here in doing what he only feinted at in the first film: painting Batman as an eccentric loner who just happens to be on the right side of the law (if, that is, superheroic vigilantism is the right side). Of its star trio, Pfeiffer comes off best, demonstrating once again that she's perhaps the best contemporary screen actress. Who else could have made psychological and dramatic sense of a character who starts as a mousy secretary and is transformed into a whip-wielding acrobatic hyperfeminist after being thrown from a skyscraper by Christopher Walken [521] and nursed back to life by a gang of stray cats? DeVito's performance is buried under tons of makeup, and what emerges is nervy but also too nasty to be enjoyable. Keaton's quietly understated performance just gets lost.

The makeup team received its nomination primarily for DeVito's transformation, but lost to the artists who worked on *Bram Stoker's Dracula.* The visual effects group was, among other things, charged with producing an army of penguins armed with rockets. The body manglings of *Death Becomes Her* were thought superior by the Academy.

Neill: 167, 595.8, 600, 924.5, 1370.5. Winston: 45, 600, 886, 1071.5, 1600, 2019. Bruno: 5, 413.5, 766, 1590, 2147.5. Skotak: 5.

154 • BATTLE CRY

WARNER BROS. 1955.
NOMINATION *Scoring of a Dramatic or Comedy Picture:*
Max Steiner.

A group of marines prepares for action in World
War II. They include Van Heflin [1055], Aldo Ray,
James Whitmore [157 . . .], Raymond Massey [1],
and Tab Hunter. Dorothy Malone [2315] has her usual
role: a woman on the prowl. Fairly routine stuff,
based on a novel by Leon Uris, with all the raunch
and realism removed by the censors, but it's kept
moving by director Raoul Walsh.

Steiner lost to Alfred Newman for *Love Is a Many-
Splendored Thing.*

Steiner: 16, 190, 330, 365, 385, 492, 679, 747,
754, 798, 999, 1043, 1046, 1052, 1162, 1169,
1170, 1207, 1324, 1408, 1430, 1456, 1690, 1779,
1828.

155 • BATTLE OF ALGIERS, THE

IGOR FILM-CASBAH FILM PRODUCTION; ALLIED ARTISTS (ITALY).
1968.
NOMINATIONS *Director:* Gillo Pontecorvo. *Story and
Screenplay—Written Directly for the Screen:* Franco
Solinas and Gillo Pontecorvo.

Docudrama about the guerrilla war to free Algiers
from the French focuses on the struggle from 1954 to
1962. Pontecorvo re-creates events without actually
using newsreel footage, combining actors and actual
participants. The film's dispassionate portrait of terrorism led to its being banned in France until 1971,
and now that the revolutionary ardor of the sixties is a
thing of the past and terrorism is often the tool of
reactionaries, the film may seem naive. It took first
prize at the 1966 Venice Film Festival but didn't receive the distribution that made it eligible for Oscars
until 1968.

In nominating Pontecorvo as director, the Academy passed over others whose pictures had been
nominated for best picture: the veteran William
Wyler (for *Funny Girl*) and the newcomer Paul Newman (for *Rachel, Rachel*). Pontecorvo's earlier film
Kapo had received a foreign language film nomination
in 1960, but his subsequent career, which included

Burn! with Marlon Brando [583 . . .] in 1969,
didn't provide him with many opportunities to repeat
his Oscar attempt. The directing Oscar went to Carol
Reed for *Oliver!* Mel Brooks won the writing award
for *The Producers.*

156 • BATTLE OF NERETVA, THE

UNITED FILM PRODUCERS-IGOR FILM-EICHBERG FILM-COMMON-
WEALTH UNITED PRODUCTION (YUGOSLAVIA). 1969.
NOMINATION *Foreign Language Film.*

An epic about the struggle of Yugoslav partisans
against the Germans, Italians, and local Axis sympathizers during World War II, with an all-star international cast including Yul Brynner [1088] and Orson
Welles [407 . . .], directed by Veljko Bulajic. It ran
almost three hours in its original version but was
slashed by more than an hour for American release in
1971. That incoherent version seems to be the only
one readily available today. The best picture Oscar
went to *Z.*

157 • BATTLEGROUND

MGM. 1949.
AWARDS *Story and Screenplay:* Robert Pirosh. *Black-
and-White Cinematography:* Paul C. Vogel.
NOMINATIONS *Picture:* Dore Schary, producer. *Supporting Actor:* James Whitmore. *Director:* William A. Wellman. *Film Editing:* John Dunning.

This re-creation of the Battle of the Bulge stars Van
Johnson, John Hodiak, Ricardo Montalban, Richard
Jaeckel [1864], and a few score of other MGM contract players, including a young James Arness. Episodic and fairly heavy on war-movie clichés, it hasn't
held up well, but less than a decade after the war's
end, it seemed real and exciting. Perhaps the true
battleground was off the screen: Producer Schary was
at war with studio head Louis B. Mayer, who resisted
Schary's desires to make a war movie but finally gave
in with the idea that it would flop and "teach him a
lesson." Instead, it was a hit, and solidified Schary's
position when Mayer was finally edged out of the
company in 1951.

A Baltimore-born, European-educated former advertising man, Pirosh turned screenwriter in the thir-

ties, contributing to such films as the Marx Brothers' *A Day at the Races.* After the Oscar, he turned to directing for a while, but with not much success. He also worked in TV as a producer and writer.

Vogel worked largely on MGM B pictures, but in 1946 he made an impression by shooting *Lady in the Lake,* a movie directed by and starring Robert Montgomery [904 . . .]. In this version of the Raymond Chandler [242 . . .] whodunit, all the action is seen through the eyes of Philip Marlowe (Montgomery), who is glimpsed only in mirrors.

Schary had moved from screenwriter to head of production on MGM's B-picture unit to a brief stint as production head at RKO under the impossible Howard Hughes [734 . . .] before coming back to MGM in 1948 for the last days of Mayer, whom he succeeded as studio chief in 1951. An earnest liberal, he tried to balance the glossier output of the studio with such serious if leaden message pictures as 1950's *The Next Voice You Hear,* a drama in which God speaks to the nation on the radio. His own ouster from MGM came in 1956, after which Schary moved to New York and wrote the hit play *Sunrise at Campobello,* which was later filmed—at Warner Bros. The best picture Oscar went to *All the King's Men.*

Whitmore had attended Yale and served in the marines in World War II. *Battleground* was only his second film, but his war experience helped him shape the character who earned him his first nomination. His resemblance to Spencer Tracy [131 . . .] was noted by some, and may have helped restrict his career to character parts. The Oscar went to Dean Jagger for *Twelve O'Clock High.*

Wellman, known as Wild Bill, for a roistering and combative personality, had directed the very first Oscar winner, *Wings,* and brought his experiences as a highly decorated World War I soldier to this film. The Oscar, however, went to Joseph L. Mankiewicz for *A Letter to Three Wives,* a movie that is the antithesis of macho.

Dunning had worked as editor under Frank Capra [1025 . . .] on the wartime documentary film series *Why We Fight.* He was chosen to cut *Battleground* because of this experience and helped locate stock docu-

mentary footage to aid the art directors in creating the film's sets. He skillfully blended the real war footage with the film shot by Vogel. The editing Oscar went to Harry Gerstad for *Champion.*

Pirosh: 780. Vogel: 2312. Schary: 271, 597. Whitmore: 774. Wellman: 911, 1909. Dunning: 175.

158 • BEACH RED

THEODORA PRODUCTIONS; UNITED ARTISTS. 1967.
NOMINATION *Film Editing:* Frank P. Keller.

Cornel Wilde [1872] directed and stars in this rather grim and brutal war movie, about the assault on a Japanese-held island in World War II. Its antiwar message comes through loud and clear, but many viewers are not likely to stick around for the full delivery of it. The cast includes Rip Torn [466]. The editing Oscar went to Hal Ashby for *In The Heat of the Night.*

Keller: 313, 944, 1059.

159 • BEACHES

TOUCHSTONE PICTURES IN ASSOCIATION WITH SILVER SCREEN PARTNERS III; BUENA VISTA. 1988.
NOMINATION *Art Direction–Set Decoration:* Albert Brenner; Garrett Lewis.

A poor girl meets a rich girl on the beach at Atlantic City. The former grows up to be Bette Midler [700 . . .], the latter Barbara Hershey. One sings, the other dies. Maybe there's more to this adaptation of a novel by Iris Rainer Dart than that, but not much more. It was very popular, however, apparently tapping a need for the old-fashioned two-hanky romance that contemporary Hollywood hasn't yet figured out how to fill. For those immune to its sentimentality, there are still generous dollops of Midler performing, including her big hit "The Wind Beneath My Wings." Garry Marshall directed, and the cast includes Mayim Bialik, who plays Midler as a girl and went on to star in the TV sitcom *Blossom.*

The sets, which range from period nostalgia to contemporary, and include some stagings for Midler's musical numbers, lost to those for *Dangerous Liaisons.*

Brenner: 332, 1976, 2152, 2165. Lewis: 272.5, 779, 937.

160 • BEAR, THE

RENN PRODUCTIONS; TRI-STAR (FRANCE). 1989.
NOMINATION *Film Editing:* Noëlle Boisson.

The hairiest leading man since King Kong is the star of this film about an orphaned bear cub who joins forces with an adult bear being pursued by hunters. The environmentalist message is strong, and the scenery is handsome, but it still comes across as a slightly hipper version of a Disney True-Life Adventure. It was a big hit in Europe, less successful in the States. Directed by Jean-Jacques Annaud from a screenplay by Gérard Brach. The cinematography is by Philippe Rousselot [900 . . .]. The editing nomination recognizes Boisson's work assembling footage that blends live-action nature film, puppetry, and actors in bear suits. The Oscar went to *Born on the Fourth of July.*

161 • BEAU GESTE

PARAMOUNT. 1939.
NOMINATIONS *Supporting Actor:* Brian Donlevy. *Interior Decoration:* Hans Dreier and Robert Odell.

Brothers Gary Cooper [701 . . .], Ray Milland [1208], and Robert Preston [2201] serve together heroically in the Foreign Legion, where they must battle not only the Arabs but also the sadistic sergeant played by Donlevy. The 1926 silent-film version of the novel by P. C. Wren starred Ronald Colman [311 . . .] in the Cooper role, and was a huge hit. This remake isn't nearly as much fun as the other heroics-in-the-desert classic of 1939, *Gunga Din,* and Cooper is miscast as an Englishman, but it's still entertaining. The cast features Susan Hayward [973 . . .], J. Carrol Naish [1294 . . .], and Broderick Crawford [53], and fourteen-year-old Donald O'Connor plays Cooper as a child.

Like the director of *Beau Geste,* William Wellman [157 . . .], Donlevy had served as a pilot in the Lafayette Escadrille during World War I. He was born in Ireland and came to the States after the war, where he began a stage and screen career in the mid-twenties. Beefy and good-looking, he projected a smooth arrogance that made him a natural for villains. After his Oscar-nominated role, he played the memorable title role in Preston Sturges' *The Great McGinty,* where

his swagger was used to comic effect. Donlevy died in 1972. The Oscar went to Thomas Mitchell for *Stagecoach.*

The art direction award was won by *Gone With the Wind.*

Dreier: 97, 649, 674, 701, 726, 925, 979, 1101, 1120, 1194, 1214, 1217, 1358, 1443, 1452, 1540, 1668, 1748, 1880, 1975, 1994, 2190.

162 • BEAUTY AND THE BEAST

WALT DISNEY PICTURES PRODUCTION; BUENA VISTA. 1991.
AWARDS *Song:* "Beauty and the Beast," music by Alan Menken, lyrics by Howard Ashman. *Original Score:* Alan Menken.
NOMINATIONS *Picture:* Don Hahn, producer. *Sound:* Terry Porter, Mel Metcalfe, David J. Hudson, and Doc Kane. *Song:* "Be Our Guest," music by Alan Menken, lyrics by Howard Ashman. *Song:* "Belle," music by Alan Menken, lyrics by Howard Ashman.

When her inventor father is taken prisoner by a fierce man-beast, who is actually an enchanted prince, Belle offers to take his place. The love that develops between beauty and beast eventually breaks the spell. This lively, well-paced version of the fairy tale is the second in the Menken-Ashman trilogy of animated features begun by *The Little Mermaid* and concluded by *Aladdin.* Its elegant twists of characterization—Belle is the village intellectual, her suitor is an arrogant hunk named Gaston—add to the usual pleasures provided by good Disney animation: a gallery of fantastic creatures, in this case the Beast's household servants, who have been enchanted into furniture. Angela Lansbury [749 . . .] is the voice for a motherly teapot, with Jerry Orbach as a candelabra and David Ogden Stiers as a clock. Nobody claims it's the equal of *Pinocchio* or *Dumbo,* but *Beauty and the Beast* signaled clearly that Disney-style animation wasn't dead, even if the occasional use of computer animation doesn't match up well with the more traditional pen-and-ink style. It was the first animated feature to be nominated for best picture, though it lost to a different kind of beauty-and-beast fable, *The Silence of the Lambs.*

Composer Menken and lyricist Ashman had first teamed up for the stage, developing the off-Broadway hit *Little Shop of Horrors,* which brought them to Hollywood and the fruitful collaboration with Disney. *Beauty and the Beast* was the first film to receive three nominations for best song—though it must be noted that the Academy didn't have much else to choose from.

The sound award went to *Terminator 2: Judgment Day.*

Menken: 32.5, 1184, 1188. Ashman: 32.5, 1184, 1188. Porter: 32.5, 1914. Metcalfe: 32.5, 1914. Hudson: 32.5, 1914. Kane: 32.5.

163 • BECAUSE YOU'RE MINE

MGM. 1952.
NOMINATION *Song:* "Because You're Mine," music by Nicholas Brodszky, lyrics by Sammy Cahn.

Mario Lanza is drafted and falls in love with Doretta Morrow, who turns out to be the sister of James Whitmore [157 . . .], his sergeant. Lanza's meteoric career was beginning to fizzle with this, his fourth film. Directed by Alexander Hall. The inanity of the plot is obvious, and the film has chiefly the handsome title tune to recommend it, but that lost to the Dimitri Tiomkin–Ned Washington title tune for *High Noon.*

Brodszky: 1216, 1692, 1843, 2103. Cahn: 74, 182, 696, 915, 926, 1031, 1056, 1216, 1524, 1587, 1692, 1708, 1719, 1859, 1907, 2016, 2064, 2072, 2103, 2110, 2125, 2263, 2264, 2315, 2343.

164 • BECKET

HAL WALLIS PRODUCTIONS; PARAMOUNT. 1964.
AWARD *Screenplay—Based on Material From Another Medium:* Edward Anhalt.
NOMINATIONS *Picture:* Hal B. Wallis, producer. *Actor:* Richard Burton. *Actor:* Peter O'Toole. *Supporting Actor:* John Gielgud. *Director:* Peter Glenville. *Color Cinematography:* Geoffrey Unsworth. *Color Art Direction—Set Decoration:* John Bryan and Maurice Carter; Patrick McLoughlin and Robert Cartwright. *Sound:* John Cox, sound director, Shepperton Studio Sound Department. *Music Score—Substantially Original:* Laurence Rosenthal. *Film Editing:* Anne Coates. *Color Costume Design:* Margaret Furse.

Lifelong friends King Henry II (O'Toole) and Thomas Becket (Burton) become enemies when Becket is made archbishop of Canterbury and challenges Henry's political authority. The film is handsomely produced, but a firm grounding in English history and a clear head are necessary if you plan to follow the plot closely. Jean Anouilh's play had been a success on Broadway with Laurence Olivier [268 . . .] as Becket and Anthony Quinn [1226 . . .] as Henry. Anhalt's adaptation for the screen adds some action and pageantry, but unfortunately the real drama and conflict are intellectual and uncinematic. Some find the movie rewarding for the acting alone, however. Also in the cast are Martita Hunt, Pamela Brown, Felix Aylmer, and Donald Wolfit, the famous Shakespearean actor who is said to be the model for the character played by Albert Finney in *The Dresser.*

Wallis spent much of the last decade of his career as a producer mounting a trilogy of English historical epics—the others are *Anne of the Thousand Days* and *Mary Queen of Scots.* They gave him a reputation as a prestige producer but won him no Oscars. This time the award went to *My Fair Lady,* produced by his archrival, Jack Warner.

This is the only film teaming of Burton and O'Toole, who are the actors with the most nominations—seven each—that resulted in no Oscars. For Burton, this serious dramatic role was a kind of redemption. His career in films to this point had been marked by little worthy of his talents, including the notorious *Cleopatra.* Burton is said to have wanted O'Toole's part, the more colorful one, but O'Toole had already been cast. In the end Burton's underplaying is more effective than O'Toole's flamboyance. One of their competitors was the Broadway Henry, Quinn, who was nominated for *Zorba the Greek.* The Oscar went to Rex Harrison for *My Fair Lady.* Four years later, O'Toole would play Henry II again, in *The Lion in Winter,* and pick up another nomination.

Gielgud, who plays King Louis VII of France, lost his first nomination to Peter Ustinov in *Topkapi.* During the filming of *Becket,* Burton asked Gielgud to direct him in *Hamlet,* which had a highly successful, though controversial, run on Broadway in 1965.

Glenville had worked primarily as an actor and as a stage director, and his films are usually adaptations of stage plays, such as *Summer and Smoke.* The Oscar went to George Cukor for *My Fair Lady,* which also won for Harry Stradling's cinematography, Cecil Beaton's costuming, and for art direction and sound. *Mary Poppins* won the Oscars for the Sherman brothers' scoring and Cotton Warburton's editing.

Anhalt: 1523, 1850. Wallis: 17, 55, 85, 343, 365, 676, 689, 712, 965, 1046, 1095, 1162, 1248, 1482, 1727, 1779, 2233, 2318. Burton: 85, 621, 1391, 1706, 1897, 2277. O'Toole: 805, 1151, 1177, 1395, 1733, 1953. Gielgud: 103. Unsworth: 321, 1378, 2021. Bryan: 325, 820. Carter: 85. McLoughlin: 85. Cartwright: 608, 1285, 1766. Cox: 850, 1151. Rosenthal: 1259. Coates: 608, 992.3, 1151. Furse: 85, 1177, 1285, 1374, 1766.

165 • BECKY SHARP
PIONEER PICTURES; RKO RADIO. 1935.
NOMINATION *Actress:* Miriam Hopkins.

Hopkins plays the title role, the antiheroine of Thackeray's novel *Vanity Fair,* who intrigues her way around Europe during the Napoleonic wars. The film's chief claim to fame is that it was the first feature made in three-color Technicolor. The untried process surely explains the lack of fluency in the camera work, and the strong lighting unfortunately sometimes makes the sets and costumes look flimsy and cheap. As drama, it's a series of set pieces chopped from the book, with performances that don't come to life. In short, a curiosity worth checking out, but don't expect to like it much. Directed by Rouben Mamoulian, with Frances Dee, Cedric Hardwicke, Billie Burke [1306], and Nigel Bruce.

Hopkins had been a Broadway star in the twenties and came to Hollywood with the advent of sound. She became one of Paramount's biggest stars in the early thirties and later worked for Warner Bros. The latter studio's publicity department invented a feud (or perhaps exaggerated an antipathy) between Hopkins and Bette Davis [46 . . .], with whom she costarred

memorably in *The Old Maid* (1939) and *Old Acquaintance* (1943). Hopkins' career as a leading player declined in the early forties, so she returned to stage work but made occasional film appearances in character parts. The Oscar went to her future ''rival,'' Bette Davis, for *Dangerous.* Hopkins died in 1972.

166 • BEDKNOBS AND BROOMSTICKS
WALT DISNEY PRODUCTIONS; BUENA VISTA. 1971.
AWARD *Special Visual Effects:* Alan Maley, Eustace Lycett, and Danny Lee.
NOMINATIONS *Art Direction—Set Decoration:* John B. Mansbridge and Peter Ellenshaw; Emile Kuri and Hal Gausman. *Song:* ''The Age of Not Believing,'' music and lyrics by Richard M. Sherman and Robert B. Sherman. *Scoring—Adaptation and Original Song Score:* Richard M. Sherman, Robert B. Sherman, and Irwin Kostal. *Costume Design:* Bill Thomas.

Angela Lansbury [749 . . .] plays an amateur witch who, with the aid of magician David Tomlinson and three Cockney children, takes a fantastic journey on an enchanted brass bed and finally thwarts the Nazi invasion of England with a magical army of knights in armor. This rather ungainly fantasy was designed to recapture the appeal of *Mary Poppins,* and it enlists the talents of Tomlinson, director Robert Stevenson, the Sherman brothers, and many of the technicians from that film. An attempt was made, of course, to get Julie Andrews to star, but she was trying to shake the pixie dust from her feet and refused. After considering Lynn Redgrave [761], Leslie Caron [1113 . . .], and even *Laugh-In*'s Judy Carne, the studio signed Lansbury, who had just made a smash hit on Broadway in *Mame.* The first cut of the film was too long, so several songs and a good deal of characterization hit the cutting-room floor, along with much of Roddy McDowall's role as a suitor for Lansbury's hand. After disappointing box-office returns, the movie received another cut that sacrificed virtually all the songs. The first release cut, however, is the one available on video.

The art direction Oscar went to *Nicholas and Alexandra,* which also won for Yvonne Blake and Antonia Castillo's costumes. The Sherman's kiddie-pop song lost to a very different kind of music from a film from another universe: Isaac Hayes' "Theme from *Shaft*." The scoring Oscar was won by John Williams for *Fiddler on the Roof*.

Lycett: 4, 219, 1284. Lee: 219. Mansbridge: 1022. Ellenshaw: 219, 1022, 1284. Kuri: 4, 363, 629, 894, 1284, 1823, 2155. Gausman: 4, 1022, 1284, 2185. R. M. Sherman: 396, 1238, 1284, 1842, 2107. R. B. Sherman: 396, 1238, 1284, 1842, 2107. Kostal: 1284, 1557, 1881, 2244. Thomas: 116, 254, 866, 883, 1003, 1789, 1812, 1886, 2128.

166.5 • *BEETHOVEN'S 2ND*
UNIVERSAL PICTURES PRODUCTION; UNIVERSAL. 1993.
NOMINATION *Song:* "The Day I Fall in Love," music and lyrics by Carole Bayer Sager, James Ingram, and Clif Magness.

Beethoven, a St. Bernard dog owned by a suburban family headed by Charles Grodin, fathers a litter of puppies that then become the focus of a dognaping plot. Saggy sequel to *Beethoven,* a hugely successful family comedy in 1992. Grodin's finely tuned comic work as the reluctant dog owner and the comic villainy of Debi Mazar and Chris Penn are all the movie has to offer—except, of course, countless stupid pet tricks. Directed by Rod Daniel. The nominated song, which accompanies the wooing of Beethoven and another St. Bernard named Missy, lost to Bruce Springsteen's "Streets of Philadelphia," from *Philadelphia*.

Sager: 103, 977, 1071.3, 1898. Ingram: 1071.3.

167 • *BEETLEJUICE*
GEFFEN FILM COMPANY PRODUCTION; GEFFEN/WARNER BROS. 1988.
AWARD *Makeup:* Ve Neill, Steve LaPorte, and Robert Short.

Geena Davis [6 . . .] and Alec Baldwin die in an accident and come back as ghosts, only to discover that the home they loved has been taken over by an arty couple (Catherine O'Hara and Jeffrey Jones) with atrocious taste. To oust them, Davis and Baldwin enlist the aid of Michael Keaton, who plays a malicious ghost named Betelgeuse, but discover that he's more than they can handle. Some very funny special

effects, a hilariously manic performance by Keaton, witty acting by Winona Ryder [27.5 . . .] as the usurping couple's gloom-haunted teenage daughter, and self-mocking cameos by Robert Goulet and Dick Cavett make all this nonsense work. It doesn't amount to much, but it's less pretentious and ultimately more enjoyable than director Tim Burton's more elaborate and expensive *Batman* movies.

Neill: 153.5, 595.8, 600, 924.5, 1370.5.

167.5 • *BEFORE THE RAIN*
AIM PRODUCTION/NOE PRODUCTIONS/VARDAR FILMS PRODUCTION; GRAMERCY PICTURES (THE FORMER YUGOSLAV REPUBLIC OF MACEDONIA). 1994.
NOMINATION *Foreign Language Film.*

Three interrelated episodes—two of them set in Macedonia, the middle one in London—dramatize the cultural conflicts that have torn apart the countries that used to be Yugoslavia, in this case the animosity between Macedonians and Albanians. Writer-director Milcho Manchevski has noted that the wholesale bloodletting seen in Bosnia has not yet come to Macedonia, though the title of his absorbing, well-acted film may be an ironic prediction. The conflicts of the film, in fact, had an echo even at the Oscar ceremony. The Academy, which had first cited *Before the Rain* as an entry from "Macedonia," changed the citation to read "the Former Yugoslav Republic of Macedonia." The government of Greece has protested the name adopted by the country after its separation from Yugoslavia in 1991 on the grounds that Macedonia is a Greek province—one with potentially separatist aims of its own. The U.N. and the U.S. Government have adopted the longer name for the country as a provisional compromise, and the Academy, after protests from Greeks, followed suit. But Manchevski announced that he would boycott the awards ceremony if the longer name were used: "In the larger picture, the name is a small thing," Manchevski said. "But it would be like calling the U.S. 'the former British colony of America.' It's an insult to the people back there." The protest was made moot when the foreign-language film Oscar went to the Russian *Burnt by the Sun.*

168 • BEHIND THE NEWS

REPUBLIC. 1940.

NOMINATION *Sound Recording:* Charles Lootens.

A journalism student helps an alcoholic has-been reporter revive his career by joining him in solving a crime. A long-forgotten programmer starring Lloyd Nolan, it owes its nomination to the Academy's temporary liberalizing of the rules to allow each studio to submit a contender in certain categories. The Oscar went to *Strike Up the Band.*

Lootens: 100, 538, 1257.

169 • BEING THERE

LORIMAR FILM-UND FERNSEHPRODUKTION GMBH PRODUCTION; UNITED ARTISTS (U.S./FEDERAL REPUBLIC OF GERMANY). 1979.

AWARD *Supporting Actor:* Melvyn Douglas.
NOMINATION *Actor:* Peter Sellers.

Sellers plays a simpleminded gardener who has never set foot in the outside world that he knows only from watching television, but when his wealthy and eccentric employer dies, he must venture forth. His innocence is taken for profundity by a variety of sophisticates, and he becomes a celebrity. This film from Jerzy Kosinski's novel, a variation on *Candide,* never quite makes it as satire, and it's about half an hour too long, but the sweetness of Sellers' performance and a few good hits at pop culture make it worthwhile. The excellent cast also includes Shirley MacLaine [91 . . .] and Jack Warden [890 . . .]. Director Hal Ashby [430 . . .] also directed *Harold and Maude* (1972), which like *Being There* and another cult favorite, *King of Hearts* (1966), is based on the dubious premise that misfits and madmen have access to deeper truths—an idea that seems to appeal to a lot of people.

Laurence Olivier [268 . . .] was the first choice for the role of the cantankerous, dying billionaire that won Douglas his second Oscar. According to MacLaine, Olivier turned down the part because he was offended by the scene in which MacLaine masturbates. Douglas was seventy-nine when he won—the second oldest performer to win an Oscar. (George Burns [1976] held the record until Jessica Tandy broke it with her win for *Driving Miss Daisy.*) One of Douglas' competitors was Justin Henry for *Kramer vs. Kramer*—seventy years Douglas' junior, and the youngest performer ever nominated. Douglas died in 1981.

Sellers campaigned hard for his part in *Being There.* He had written Kosinski about his desire to play the role when the novel first appeared, and enlisted Ashby's support in getting it to the screen. The series of *Pink Panther* films had made Sellers bankable, enabling him to get the money to make *Being There* and to play the role of his dreams. It would, sadly, be his last important role before his death in 1980. The Oscar went to Dustin Hoffman for *Kramer vs. Kramer.*

Douglas: 956, 971. Sellers: 574.

170 • BELL, BOOK AND CANDLE

PHOENIX PRODUCTIONS INC.; COLUMBIA. 1958.

NOMINATIONS *Art Direction–Set Decoration:* Cary Odell; Louis Diage. *Costume Design:* Jean Louis.

Book publisher James Stewart [73 . . .] is about to marry Janice Rule when he encounters a glamorous witch, Kim Novak, and her cronies, Jack Lemmon [91 . . .], Elsa Lanchester [428 . . .], and Hermione Gingold. Novak puts a spell on him that alters his marriage plans, but when she finds herself falling in love with Stewart, she loses her powers. Directed by Richard Quine from a screenplay by Daniel Taradash [732] based on a play by John Van Druten [749]. The play wasn't much to start with, and cutely mischievous witches have been done to death by sitcoms such as *Bewitched,* but this is fairly amusing stuff, especially when Lemmon, Lanchester, Gingold, and Ernie Kovacs (as an obtuse investigator of the occult) are on screen. Stewart also has a classic moment of physical comedy when he has to choke down a vile potion brewed by Gingold. Novak is very sexy, but she and Stewart don't make a convincing couple here. They were better teamed that year in *Vertigo,* where the difference in their ages—he was fifty, she was twenty-five—seems to highlight the perversity of their relationship.

Gigi won the Oscars for art direction and Cecil Beaton's costumes.

Odell: 455, 1783. Diage: 1521, 1858. Louis: 20, 126, 262, 732, 744, 1028, 1065, 1521, 1640, 1812, 1858, 1910, 2064.

170.5 • *BELLE EPOQUE*

Fernando Trueba P.C. (Madrid)/Lola Films (Barcelona)/French Production (Paris), (Spain). 1993.
Award *Foreign Language Film.*

A deserter from the Spanish army happens upon the household of an elderly anarchist with four beautiful daughters—who proceed to seduce him. Enjoyably ribald fable that takes place in 1930, just before the Spanish Civil War, giving the comedy a slightly bittersweet tone. Directed by Fernando Trueba, who made perhaps the most charming acceptance speech of the Oscar ceremonies, concluding with the words "I would like to believe in God so that I could thank him, but I just believe in Billy Wilder. So thank you, Billy Wilder." Trueba subsequently explained that he considered Wilder [91 . . .] "the best director ever." *Belle Epoque*'s win took many observers by surprise. Most bets were on *Farewell, My Concubine,* the entry from Hong Kong that might well have won if the foreign language category were not subject to its own peculiar rules and politics. Only those who can certify that they attended the Academy screenings of all five nominees are allowed to vote in the category, which tips the award to a producer who can muster enough supporters who meet the qualifications. But *Belle Epoque* is certainly not an undeserving winner—just a very unexpected one.

171 • *BELLE OF THE YUKON*

International Pictures; RKO Radio. 1945.
Nominations *Song:* "Sleighride in July," music by James Van Heusen, lyrics by Johnny Burke. *Scoring of a Musical Picture:* Arthur Lange.

Randolph Scott runs a saloon that features entertainers Gypsy Rose Lee and Dinah Shore. Minor Technicolor musical, directed by William Seiter, with clowning by Bob Burns and Charles Winninger. The song Oscar went to Richard Rodgers and Oscar Hammerstein II for "It Might As Well Be Spring," from *State Fair. Anchors Aweigh* took the scoring award.

Van Heusen: 173, 787, 915, 926, 1056, 1524, 1587, 1708, 1859, 1907, 2016, 2064, 2263. Burke: 173, 787, 1547, 1691. Lange: 366, 827, 1123, 2303.

172 • *BELLS ARE RINGING*

Arthur Freed Productions Inc.; MGM. 1960.
Nomination *Scoring of a Musical Picture:* André Previn.

Judy Holliday [262], who runs a telephone answering service in New York, keeps getting involved in the lives of her clients, adopting various personae to conceal her identity. When she tries to help a playwright, Dean Martin, who has run up against writer's block, they fall in love. A pleasant version of a Broadway show that was little more than a vehicle for its star, it contains several memorable songs—"Just in Time," "The Party's Over"—with music by Jule Styne [74 . . .] and lyrics by Betty Comden [141 . . .] and Adolph Green [141 . . .], who also wrote the screenplay. (The songs from the Broadway show were ineligible for the Oscars; those written especially for the movie failed to make the cut.) The film has its own poignancy: It was the last movie musical produced by Arthur Freed [66 . . .], who was largely responsible for the golden age of the MGM musical, as well as the last musical directed by Vincente Minnelli [66 . . .] and the last film for Holliday, who died in 1965.

The scoring Oscar went to Morris Stoloff and Harry Sukman for *Song Without End.*

Previn: 609, 769, 1017, 1034, 1044, 1097, 1393, 1550, 1592, 2064, 2077, 2161.

173 • *BELLS OF ST. MARY'S, THE*

Rainbow Productions; RKO Radio. 1945.
Award *Sound Recording:* Stephen Dunn.
Nominations *Picture:* Leo McCarey, producer. *Actor:* Bing Crosby. *Actress:* Ingrid Bergman. *Director:* Leo McCarey. *Song:* "Aren't You Glad You're You," music by James Van Heusen, lyrics by Johnny Burke. *Scoring of a Dramatic or Comedy Picture:* Robert Emmett Dolan. *Film Editing:* Harry Marker.

Priest Crosby is assigned to head a parochial school in financial trouble. Bergman is the school's mother superior. Together, they rescue the school. The film had a lot going for it when it was released: Bergman and Crosby had both just won Oscars, as had *Going My Way,* to which this was a sequel. It was, predictably, a huge hit, though to contemporary viewers it seems like pure treacle. It was also the first sequel to be nominated for best picture, and Crosby the first actor to be nominated for playing the same role in two different films. (He has since been joined by Peter O'Toole, who played Henry II in *Becket* and *The Lion in Winter,* Al Pacino, who played Michael Corleone in the *Godfather* films, and Paul Newman as Fast Eddie Felson in *The Hustler* and *The Color of Money.*)

After honoring the sentimental *Going My Way,* the Academy made something of an about-face, for the film that bested *Bells of St. Mary's* in the picture, acting, and directing categories is the hard-eyed look at alcoholism, *The Lost Weekend.* Ray Milland and Billy Wilder were the actor and director winners. For best actress, Joan Crawford's sufferings in *Mildred Pierce* beat Bergman's saintliness.

The song Oscar went to Rodgers and Hammerstein's "It Might As Well Be Spring," from *State Fair.* The scoring award was won by Miklos Rozsa for *Spellbound,* and the editing award went to Robert J. Kern for *National Velvet.*

Dunn: 1383, 1479, 2059. McCarey: 21, 114, 787, 1212, 1394, 1404. Crosby: 450, 787. Bergman: 72, 111, 701, 749, 1048, 1378. Van Heusen: 171, 787, 915, 926, 1056, 1524, 1587, 1708, 1859, 1907, 2016, 2064, 2263. Burke: 171, 787, 1547, 1691. Dolan: 213, 244, 929, 994, 1120, 1704, 1912.

174 • BEN

BCP PRODUCTIONS; CINERAMA. 1972.
NOMINATION *Song:* "Ben," music by Walter Scharf, lyrics by Don Black.

An invalid boy (Lee Harcourt Montgomery) pals up with the killer king of the rats. A boy's best friend is his rat. That's more or less what this exploitive sequel to the exploitive hit horror-thriller *Willard* (1971) amounts to. Directed by Phil Karlson, with Joseph Campanella, Arthur O'Connell [73 . . .], Rosemary Murphy, and Meredith Baxter. The title song, which was sung by Michael Jackson, lost to Al

Kasha and Joel Hirschhorn's "The Morning After," from *The Poseidon Adventure.*

Scharf: 274, 665; 737, 864, 921, 991, 1054, 1305, 2285. Black: 259, 789, 1574, 2147.

175 • BEN-HUR

MGM. 1959.
AWARDS *Picture:* Sam Zimbalist, producer. *Actor:* Charlton Heston. *Supporting Actor:* Hugh Griffith. *Director:* William Wyler. *Color Cinematography:* Robert L. Surtees. *Color Art Direction–Set Decoration:* William A. Horning and Edward Carfagno; Hugh Hunt. *Sound:* Franklin E. Milton, sound director, MGM Studio Sound Department. *Scoring of a Dramatic or Comedy Picture:* Miklos Rozsa. *Film Editing:* Ralph E. Winters and John D. Dunning. *Color Costume Design:* Elizabeth Haffenden. *Special Effects:* A. Arnold Gillespie and Robert MacDonald, visual; Milo Lory, audible.
NOMINATION *Screenplay—Based on Material From Another Medium:* Karl Tunberg.

The Jewish prince Judah Ben-Hur (Heston) and his best friend, the Roman Messala (Stephen Boyd), quarrel over Ben-Hur's refusal to inform on Jewish opponents of Roman rule. Finally Messala finds a pretext for turning Ben-Hur into a galley slave and sending his mother, Martha Scott [1510], and sister, Cathy O'Donnell, to prison. But in a sea battle, Ben-Hur saves the life of a Roman admiral, Jack Hawkins, who adopts him. Eventually he gets even with Messala in a chariot race, with a team supplied by an Arab horse fancier played by Griffith. Then he must find his family, who have been taken from prison to a leper colony. They are cured of the disease by a miracle during Christ's crucifixion. Long (nearly four hours), hammy, exciting, colorful, and almost endearingly hokey version of the novel by Lew Wallace that had already been filmed by MGM as a silent in 1926. (The original is a classic in its own right, with sea battle and chariot race sequences that spared neither extras nor horses.)

Ben-Hur is the most honored movie in Oscar history, and its record of eleven awards doesn't seem likely to be challenged anytime soon. That doesn't mean that it's the greatest picture ever made, of course, but just that it was in the right place at the right time. None of the contenders for best picture stood a chance against it: *Anatomy of a Murder* was a capable trial drama with a dash of sensationalism, *The Diary of Anne Frank* a somewhat overproduced version of a hit play, *The Nun's Story* a stately account of a novice's life, and *Room at the Top* an imported British working-class drama. The year's real best pictures— *Some Like It Hot, The 400 Blows, Wild Strawberries, North by Northwest*—weren't in contention, but they couldn't have competed against the big-screen, big-money approach taken by MGM in creating *Ben-Hur.* The studio, which had been on the skids, took its lead from Paramount, which had made a bundle on *The Ten Commandments* three years earlier. Zimbalist, a producer who had overseen such big-budget, location-shot spectacles as *Quo Vadis?, King Solomon's Mines,* and *Mogambo,* was a logical choice to produce. He died during the filming.

Heston's heroic physique made him a logical choice to play Ben-Hur, though there was talk of Marlon Brando [583 . . .], Rock Hudson [768], and Burt Lancaster [107 . . .] in the role during preproduction. (Such casting speculation, it must be noted, is often used to hold down the salary demands of the leading candidate.) A capable and intelligent actor, he has probably played more historic figures than any film actor in history: Andrew Jackson (several times), Moses, El Cid, John the Baptist, Buffalo Bill, Michelangelo, Cardinal Richelieu, Henry VIII, Marc Antony, General Gordon, and Thomas More among them. But *Ben-Hur,* though it won him an Oscar, provided his only nomination.

Griffith, a Welsh-born actor and notorious scene-stealer, got his start in British films in the forties. The Oscar, for his first American-made film, created a demand for his agreeable bluster, and he worked steadily up to his death in 1980.

Wyler is the most honored director in Academy history. Only John Ford [815 . . .] won more awards, but Wyler holds the record for nominations as director, with three nominations as producer and a 1965 Irving Thalberg Award to boot. However, the Oscar for directing *Ben-Hur* might have been shared

with several second unit directors, most notably Andrew Marton and Yakima Canutt, who are largely responsible for staging the movie's most famous sequence, the chariot race. Both Boyd and Heston participated in the carefully choreographed stunts for the race, although Canutt's son Joe doubled for Heston in the sequence in which Ben-Hur is thrown from the chariot but hangs on and clambers back in. Joe Canutt was injured in the stunt. At the 1966 awards ceremony the Academy gave Yakima Canutt an honorary award "for achievements as a stunt man and for developing safety devices to protect stunt men."

Surtees, one of the great Hollywood cameramen, received his third Oscar, all of them awarded during the fifties. But he continued to work on some of the most memorable projects of the sixties and seventies, including *The Graduate, The Last Picture Show,* and *The Sting.* His son, Bruce Surtees [1155], has followed in his footsteps.

Dunning recalls that the chariot race was entirely created in the editing room, with Winters in charge of the footage shot by the second unit directors. The cutting of the race alone took three months. Dunning was in charge of cutting the sea battle, which was directed by Richard Thorpe. When Thorpe was pulled off the film for another commitment, Dunning himself directed several of the interior sequences aboard the galley ships. He also worked with writer Christopher Fry in assembling the sea battle footage —Fry providing a narrative continuity for the various bits of film as they were put together.

Fry's work on *Ben-Hur* received no screen credit. Nor did the work by Maxwell Anderson [48], S. N. Behrman, or Gore Vidal—all of whom had a hand in the screenplay. (Vidal claimed that he had conceived of the relationship between Ben-Hur and Messala as homosexual, and that his contribution could still be seen in the film.) In the end, however, the Writers Guild decided that only Tunberg deserved screen credit, eliciting a strong protest from Wyler. At the Academy Awards ceremony, Heston thanked Fry in his acceptance speech, but Tunberg had already gone down in *Ben-Hur*'s sole defeat, to Neil Paterson's adaptation of *Room at the Top.*

Zimbalist: 1094, 1644. Griffith: 2106. Wyler: 184, 420, 534, 560, 730, 894, 1162, 1182, 1371, 1716, 2316. Surtees: 130, 557, 810, 917, 1094, 1139, 1388, 1469, 1644, 1747, 1911, 1927, 1960, 2055, 2152. Horning: 440, 769, 1157, 1450, 1644, 1657, 2300. Carfagno: 130, 629, 917, 1069, 1552, 1644, 1814, 1937, 2312. Hunt: 401, 980, 1069, 1232, 1335, 1388, 1567, 1644, 1657, 1673, 2157, 2184. Milton: 401, 558, 814, 953, 2184. Rozsa: 566, 567, 604, 1035, 1069, 1070, 1085, 1208, 1227, 1644, 1872, 1890, 1968, 2050, 2304. Winters: 825, 1094, 1109, 1644, 1782. Dunning: 157. Haffenden: 1252. Gillespie: 256, 685, 704, 835, 1371, 1388, 1905, 2048, 2055, 2122, 2300. MacDonald: 1201, 2048. Lory: 1388. Tunberg: 1999.

176 • BENEATH THE 12 MILE REEF

20TH CENTURY-FOX. 1953.

NOMINATION *Color Cinematography:* Edward Cronjager.

Robert Wagner, Terry Moore, Gilbert Roland, and Richard Boone play sponge divers off Key West who battle the elements and one another. The watery spectacle, directed by Robert Webb, was designed primarily to show off the new CinemaScope process; the story is secondary. Cronjager lost to Loyal Griggs for *Shane.*

Cronjager: 400, 889, 934, 1569, 1964, 2102.

177 • BENJI

MULBERRY SQUARE. 1974.

NOMINATION *Song:* "Benji's Theme (I Feel Love)," music by Euel Box, lyrics by Betty Box.

A small dog thwarts the kidnaping of two children. This modest sleeper hit from Dallas-based producer-director Joe Camp made tons of money and led to several sequels about the most popular canine star since Lassie. The song by the Boxes, a Texas song-writing couple, lost to Al Kasha and Joel Hirschhorn's "We May Never Love Like This Again," from *The Towering Inferno.*

178 • BERKELEY SQUARE

JESSE L. LASKY; FOX. 1932–33.

NOMINATION *Actor:* Leslie Howard.

Howard, playing an American living in London, finds that the house he's inhabiting has sent him back to the eighteenth century as his own ancestor. Pleasant wisp of a fantasy, directed by Frank Lloyd [374 . . .] from a screenplay by Sonya Levien [1007 . . .] and John Balderston [749 . . .], based on Balderston's play.

Howard was born in England to Hungarian parents and began acting when it was recommended as therapy for the shell shock he suffered during World War I. After stage work and a few films in Britain, he came to the States, where he became a star first on Broadway and then in Hollywood. He lost his first nomination to Charles Laughton in *The Private Life of Henry VIII,* coming in third in the three-man Oscar race, after Paul Muni in *I Am a Fugitive From a Chain Gang.*

Howard: 1637.

179 • BEST FRIENDS

TIMBERLANE FILMS PRODUCTION; WARNER BROS. 1982.

NOMINATION *Song:* "How Do You Keep the Music Playing?," music by Michel Legrand, lyrics by Alan Bergman and Marilyn Bergman.

Burt Reynolds and Goldie Hawn [323 . . .] play cohabiting screenwriters who finally decide that it makes sense to get married. But after experiencing what it involves, they begin to think maybe it doesn't. Agreeable leads and an interesting cast—Jessica Tandy [580 . . .], Keenan Wynn, Ron Silver—can't keep this thin domestic sitcom alive. Norman Jewison [659 . . .] directs from a semiautobiographical screenplay by Valerie Curtin [75] and Barry Levinson [75 . . .].

The Bergmans, another writing couple, had three song nominations this year, for work with three different composers: John Williams for a song from *Yes, Giorgio* and Dave Grusin for a song from *Tootsie,* in addition to Legrand. But they lost to Jack Nitzsche, Buffy Sainte-Marie, and Will Jennings' "Up Where We Belong," from *An Officer and a Gentleman.*

Legrand: 867, 1568, 1960, 2063, 2172, 2321,

2332. A. Bergman: 867, 1168, 1568, 1628, 1747, 1813, 1864, 2063, 2113, 2238, 2321, 2322. M. Bergman: 867, 1168, 1568, 1628, 1747, 1813, 1864, 2063, 2113, 2238, 2321, 2322.

180 • BEST LITTLE WHOREHOUSE IN TEXAS, THE

Universal and RKO Pictures Presentation of a Miller-Milkis-Boyett Production; Universal. 1982.

Nomination *Supporting Actor:* Charles Durning.

The titular establishment, run by Dolly Parton [1438], comes under attack from hypocritical politicians. She and boyfriend Burt Reynolds, who happens to be the sheriff, have to figure out a way to keep it open. The movie is based on an actual incident in Texas, when authorities shut down the Chicken Ranch, a brothel that had been popular with college students and state legislators but had actually been outmoded by the sexual revolution. The original Broadway production was a cheerful, tongue-in-cheek musical with lots of dancing. On screen, under the direction of Colin Higgins, it comes off as loud and lazy, its dances clumsily filmed and its humor smirky and dated. Parton gives her considerable all, and Durning, playing the governor, has a surprising gift for hoofing, but Reynolds keeps doing the good-ol'-boy shtick that eventually wore out his welcome on the big screen.

The corpulent Durning established a steady film career as a character actor during the seventies, usually playing a villain. In 1975 he attracted wide critical acclaim for his performance opposite Maureen Stapleton [31 . . .] in a made-for-TV movie, *Queen of the Stardust Ballroom,* and found more substantial parts coming his way. One of his most memorable performances in 1982 was as Jessica Lange's father in *Tootsie.* The Oscar went to Louis Gossett, Jr., for *An Officer and a Gentleman.*

Durning: 2097.

181 • BEST MAN, THE

Millar-Turman Production; United Artists. 1964.

Nomination *Supporting Actor:* Lee Tracy.

Presidential hopefuls Henry Fonda [815 . . .] and Cliff Robertson [387] square off against each other at a political convention. Fonda is the man of principle, Robertson the Nixon-McCarthy surrogate, but the moral issues, as you might imagine, are not so clear-cut. Gore Vidal's script is based on his stage play, as soon becomes obvious when the big speeches and carefully placed punch lines start coming at you. The political, social, and moral issues are very much of an era—the saddened post-Kennedy period that preceded the era of vehement protest we now think of as the sixties. It's still entertaining, however, thanks to no-nonsense direction by Franklin Schaffner [1541] and a cast that includes Edie Adams, Margaret Leighton [782], Shelley Berman, Ann Sothern [2246], and Richard Arlen.

This was the last screen appearance for Tracy, who created the role of Hildy Johnson in *The Front Page* on Broadway and was often cast as a reporter or similar hotshot type. Aside from *Dinner at Eight* in 1933, he was rarely seen in big-budget features, and by the fifties much of his work was in TV, where he starred in the early series *Martin Kane—Private Eye.* His return to the movies as the pragmatic ex-president in *The Best Man* got him fine reviews, but the Oscar went to Peter Ustinov for *Topkapi.*

182 • BEST OF EVERYTHING, THE

Company of Artists Inc.; 20th Century-Fox. 1959.

Nominations *Song:* "The Best of Everything," music by Alfred Newman, lyrics by Sammy Cahn. *Color Costume Design:* Adele Palmer.

Today it might be called *Having It All,* since the movie deals with the career and personal problems of ambitious young women, played by Hope Lange [1558], Suzy Parker, Martha Hyer [1859], and Diane Baker, in a large New York publishing firm headed by Joan Crawford [1319 . . .]. Glossy trash from a Rona Jaffe novel, with Stephen Boyd as the hunky hero-heel and a cast that includes future Paramount exec Robert Evans [395], Brian Aherne [1064], and Louis Jourdan, directed by Jean Negulesco [1052].

The title song is sung by Johnny Mathis. At the Oscars, Newman went home empty-handed, but not Cahn: He was also nominated this year for "High

Hopes,'' from *A Hole in the Head,* with music by James Van Heusen, and he won.

The costume Oscar went to Elizabeth Haffenden for *Ben-Hur.*

Newman: 31, 34, 46, 72, 138, 226, 333, 334, 347, 375, 428, 437, 457, 476, 495, 542, 690, 797, 833, 952, 953, 959, 962, 1016, 1082, 1088, 1213, 1278, 1362, 1397, 1475, 1616, 1655, 1849, 1868, 1883, 1921, 2043, 2046, 2091, 2258, 2286, 2294, 2316. Cahn: 74, 163, 696, 915, 926, 1031, 1056, 1216, 1524, 1587, 1692, 1708, 1719, 1859, 1907, 2016, 2064, 2072, 2103, 2110, 2125, 2263, 2264, 2315, 2343.

183 • BEST THINGS IN LIFE ARE FREE, THE

20TH CENTURY-FOX. 1956.
NOMINATION *Scoring of a Musical Picture:* Lionel Newman.

Biopic of the songwriting team of DeSylva, Brown, and Henderson, with Gordon MacRae as Buddy De-Sylva [1212], Ernest Borgnine [1283] as Lew Brown [2214], and Dan Dailey [2258] as Ray Henderson. The plot, the usual hokum about the Roaring Twenties, is just there to string songs on. Directed by Michael Curtiz [79 . . .]. Newman lost the Oscar to his brother Alfred's work with Ken Darby on *The King and I.*

Newman: 457, 557, 795, 896, 981, 1160, 1273, 1585, 1762, 2043.

184 • BEST YEARS OF OUR LIVES, THE

SAMUEL GOLDWYN PRODUCTIONS; RKO RADIO. 1946.
AWARDS *Picture:* Samuel Goldwyn, producer. *Actor:* Fredric March. *Supporting Actor:* Harold Russell. *Director:* William Wyler. *Screenplay:* Robert E. Sherwood. *Scoring of a Dramatic or Comedy Picture:* Hugo Friedhofer. *Film Editing:* Daniel Mandell. *Special Award:* Harold Russell for bringing hope and courage to his fellow veterans.
NOMINATION *Sound Recording:* Gordon Sawyer.

Three servicemen—March, Russell, and Dana Andrews—come home from World War II to face a variety of adjustments: March finds his bank job frustrating, Russell has lost his hands and must deal with other people's reactions to the hooks that replaced them, and Andrews and his wife have gone their separate ways. You might expect either tear-jerking sentiment or depressing domestic tragedy from this, but the movie treats its audiences like adults. It manages to be funny and touching and, yes, a little preachy in about the right proportions. It's still very much a film of its time, and to appreciate it fully you have to make an imaginative leap to feel what audiences whose own households were welcoming home servicemen must have felt. The cast is uniformly fine. Others in it include Myrna Loy as March's wife, Teresa Wright [1182 . . .] as their daughter, songwriter Hoagy Carmichael [341 . . .] as a bartender, Gladys George [2192] as Andrews' mother, and Virginia Mayo, giving the best performance of her career, as Andrews' wife.

The germ of *Best Years* was a *Time* magazine article about returning servicemen that Goldwyn's wife, Frances, had brought to his attention in 1944. He passed the idea along to writer MacKinlay Kantor, who wrote it as a novel—in free verse—called *Glory for Me.* Goldwyn hired Sherwood to turn it into a screenplay. He had Andrews, Mayo, Wright, and Cathy O'Donnell (who plays Russell's fiancée) under contract—and first tried to interest Fred MacMurray and Olivia de Havilland [798 . . .] in the roles that March and Loy finally accepted. Goldwyn also stood firm against the Production Code Administration, which had numerous objections to the film, especially to the breakup of the marriage of Andrews and Mayo and what it saw as the film's condoning of an affair between Andrews and Wright. He also gambled on the film's unusual length—almost three hours, which meant that theaters could show it only half as frequently as a normal-length film. He won: It was the biggest moneymaker since *Gone With the Wind.*

This was the only competitive Oscar Goldwyn ever won, though he received the Irving G. Thalberg Memorial Award at the same ceremony. It was, however, the peak of his career. He would receive only one more nomination, plus the Jean Hersholt Humanitarian Award at the 1957 awards. The most successful independent producer of his day, with the possible exception of David O. Selznick [497 . . .], Goldwyn had been present at the creation of Hollywood when he coproduced *The Squaw Man* in 1913. His commitment to quality sometimes led only to a glossy sterility in his films, but at his best—movies like *Dodsworth, Wuthering Heights,* and *Best Years*—his obsessive, niggling attention to detail paid off. He can also be credited with furthering the careers of some of the movies' most skilled technicians: Wyler, cinematographer Gregg Toland [407 . . .], composer Alfred Newman [31 . . .], and art director Richard Day [22 . . .] among them. After *Best Years,* Goldwyn's decline parallels that of the great studios that he had grown up alongside and in competition with. His last film was *Porgy and Bess* in 1959, and he died in 1974.

Fourteen years after his first Oscar, March had entered the final phase of his career. At fifty-one he was a bit too old for the role he played in *Best Years,* but he brings his usual integrity to the part. He is often ranked alongside Spencer Tracy [131 . . .] as one of the screen's most natural actors—for verification of that judgment, see *Inherit the Wind,* in which they're teamed. March died in 1975.

Russell was born in Nova Scotia and grew up in Boston. As an army sergeant, he lost his hands while working with explosives during a training exercise. In the screenplay the Russell character had suffered neurological damage causing spastic paralysis, and Goldwyn thought of casting contract player Farley Granger in the role. But a spastic character would have been hard for Hollywood audiences of that day to accept, so when Wyler remembered Russell from an army documentary about amputees, the role was rewritten for him. Wyler nixed Goldwyn's plan to give Russell acting lessons, preferring to coach him through scenes, letting his genuine nonactorness show through. It worked splendidly, although the Academy may not have taken Russell's nomination seriously. At the same ceremony he received an honorary Oscar that seemed to be designed as a consolation prize in case he lost. Instead, he became the only performer

to take home two Oscars for a single role. He left films after *Best Years* but returned thirty-six years later for a small role in *Inside Moves.* In 1991 he made news by selling one of his Oscars to pay for his wife's medical expenses.

Wyler brought his own wartime experiences to *Best Years.* After directing *Mrs. Miniver,* for which he received his first Oscar, he joined the air force. In addition to flying several missions, he also made documentary films about wartime bombing runs.

Sherwood, who had worked for Goldwyn before on fluff like *Roman Scandals* (1933) and *The Adventures of Marco Polo* (1938), had won three Pulitzer Prizes for the plays *Idiot's Delight, Abe Lincoln in Illinois,* and *There Shall Be No Night.* While he's no longer regarded as a major playwright, his craftsmanship was solid.

Friedhofer's first Hollywood score was for Goldwyn's 1938 *The Adventures of Marco Polo.* He had been recommended for the job by Alfred Newman, who also suggested that Goldwyn hire Friedhofer for *Best Years.*

The only Oscar loss suffered by *Best Years* was the sound award that went to John Livadary for *The Jolson Story.* A conspicuous omission from the nominations was Gregg Toland, whose outstanding work was rewarded by Goldwyn with a solo screen credit; at the time, cinematographers were usually grouped with other technicians in the credits. The various branches of the Academy greatly reduced the number of nominations in many categories for the 1946 awards. Cinematography was cut to only two nominations in each (black-and-white and color) category, and Toland, who received his last nomination for *Citizen Kane,* was not among them. He died of a heart attack in 1948 at the age of forty-four.

Goldwyn: 102, 214, 510, 560, 1182, 1607, 2316. March: 515, 572, 1730, 1909. Wyler: 175, 420, 534, 560, 730, 894, 1162, 1182, 1371, 1716, 2316. Sherwood: 1670. Friedhofer: 2, 21, 187, 214, 267, 1048, 2303, 2336. Mandell: 91, 1182, 1607, 2297. Sawyer: 33, 91, 214, 393, 730, 864, 882, 973, 974, 1032, 1511, 1592, 2244, 2297, 2310.

185 • BETRAYAL

HORIZON FILM PRODUCTION; 20TH CENTURY-FOX INTERNATIONAL CLASSICS. 1983.

NOMINATION *Screenplay Based on Material From Another Medium:* Harold Pinter.

Jeremy Irons [1689] has betrayed his best friend, Ben Kingsley [308 . . .], by having an affair with Kingsley's wife, Patricia Hodge. The gimmick is that the story moves backward in time, from two years after the affair ended to its beginning nine years earlier. Unfortunately what seemed absorbing when Pinter's play was performed on stage seems stiff and verbose on screen, even though it has top-notch actors performing it. The director is David Jones. Pinter's own affair with Lady Antonia Fraser, which was hot stuff in the tabloids before they found royal fish to fry, no doubt contributed to the texture of the play. The Oscar went to James L. Brooks for *Terms of Endearment.*

Pinter: 725.

186 • BETTY BLUE

GAUMONT PRESENTATION OF A CONSTELLATION/CARGO PRODUCTION (FRANCE). 1986.

NOMINATION *Foreign Language Film.*

Betty, a psychologically unstable young waitress, has a destructive affair with a handyman. Character, not plot, dominates this erotic and unsettling film by Jean-Jacques Beineix, better known in this country for the 1981 movie *Diva.* The Oscar went to *The Assault.*

187 • BETWEEN HEAVEN AND HELL

20TH CENTURY-FOX. 1956.

NOMINATION *Scoring of a Dramatic or Comedy Picture:* Hugo Friedhofer.

Southerner Robert Wagner learns racial tolerance during his service in World War II. Mild but unmemorable message film, directed by Richard Fleischer, with Terry Moore [425], Broderick Crawford [53], and Buddy Ebsen. Friedhofer lost to Victor Young for *Around the World in 80 Days.*

Friedhofer: 2, 21, 184, 214, 267, 1048, 2303, 2336.

188 • BEVERLY HILLS COP

DON SIMPSON/JERRY BRUCKHEIMER PRODUCTION IN ASSOCIATION WITH EDDIE MURPHY PRODUCTIONS; PARAMOUNT. 1984.

NOMINATION *Screenplay Written Directly for the Screen:* Daniel Petrie, Jr.; story by Danilo Bach and Daniel Petrie, Jr.

Eddie Murphy plays Axel Foley, a Detroit police detective who goes to Beverly Hills to track down a friend's murderer and winds up exposing a lucrative drug-smuggling operation. The film, directed by Martin Brest [1764.5], derives its great energy from playing off the mouthy, streetwise Murphy against the sleek, smug Beverly Hills police force. Murphy has never been better in the movies. He does a variety of characters as he cons his way around the town, but even he is upstaged by Bronson Pinchot, as an art gallery clerk with a marvelously unplaceable accent. This huge box-office hit was originally planned for Sylvester Stallone [1712]. The screenplay lost to Robert Benton's for *Places in the Heart.*

189 • BEVERLY HILLS COP II

DON SIMPSON/JERRY BRUCKHEIMER PRODUCTION IN ASSOCIATION WITH EDDIE MURPHY PRODUCTIONS; PARAMOUNT. 1987.

NOMINATION *Song:* "Shakedown," music by Harold Faltermeyer and Keith Forsey, lyrics by Harold Faltermeyer, Keith Forsey, and Bob Seger.

Eddie Murphy's Detroit cop Axel Foley returns to the scene of his earlier triumph and does it all again: this time to some arms smugglers, played by Jurgen Prochnow and Brigitte Nielsen. Noisier, nastier, and a lot less funny. Directed by Tony Scott. The song, performed by Detroit rocker Seger, lost to Franke Previte, John DeNicola, and Donald Markowitz's "(I've Had) The Time of My Life," from *Dirty Dancing.*

Forsey: 682.

190 • BEYOND THE FOREST

WARNER BROS. 1949.

NOMINATION *Scoring of a Dramatic or Comedy Picture:* Max Steiner

Bette Davis [46 . . .], restless in her marriage to Joseph Cotten, a small-town doctor, has an affair with

Chicago industrialist David Brian. She fumes and plots and commits murder and flings herself from a car to abort a pregnancy but eventually gets what's coming to her. This is the one in which she utters the immortal line "What a dump!" that was later given a renewed celebrity by Elizabeth Taylor in *Who's Afraid of Virginia Woolf?* It was also Davis' final film on the Warners contract she fought bitter court battles to be released from, so she might be intentionally overplaying—though it's hard to see how this nonsense, a trashed-up version of *Madame Bovary,* could be played otherwise. Director King Vidor [378 . . .] had recently worked on the overheated *Duel in the Sun,* and he repeats some of its fevered melodramatics here. The screenplay, by Lenore Coffee [712], is based on a novel by Stuart Engstrand. Steiner's score is as overstated as everything else about the movie; he lost to Aaron Copland for *The Heiress.*

Steiner: 16, 154, 330, 365, 385, 492, 679, 747, 754, 798, 999, 1043, 1046, 1052, 1162, 1169, 1170, 1207, 1324, 1408, 1430, 1456, 1690, 1779, 1828.

191 • *BEYOND THE WALLS*

April Films Ltd. Production (Israel). 1984.
Nomination *Foreign Language Film.*

Arab and Jewish inmates of an Israeli prison are at each other's throats, their hatred exacerbated by the prison authorities, until an Arab and a Jew come together to lead a prison strike. Uri Barbash's film is perhaps meant as a look at the Arab-Israeli conflict in microcosm, as the title suggests, but the point gets lost in typical prison-movie violence and melodrama. The Oscar went to the Swiss film *Dangerous Moves.*

192 • *B.F.'S DAUGHTER*

MGM. 1948.
Nomination *Black-and-White Costume Design:* Irene.

Barbara Stanwyck [138 . . .], daughter of wealthy Charles Coburn [535 . . .], manipulates the success of her husband, Van Heflin [1055]. Mediocre romantic drama adapted from a novel by J. P. Marquand. Directed by Robert Z. Leonard [555 . . .].

Irene, the head of the costume design department

at MGM, worked under her given name—she was Irene Gibbons, sister-in-law of MGM head art director Cedric Gibbons [66 . . .]—and is sometimes confused with fellow MGM costumer Irene Sharaff [66 . . .]. The costume design category was introduced this year; the winner was Roger K. Furse for *Hamlet.*

Irene: 1314.

193 • *BIBLE, THE*

Thalia, A.G. Production; 20th Century-Fox (U.S./Italy). 1966.
Nomination *Original Music Score:* Toshiro Mayazumi.

Not the whole Bible, of course. Just the first twenty-two chapters of Genesis, with Michael Parks and Ulla Bergryd as Adam and Eve—artfully shadowed and screened by the obliging foliage of Eden. Plus Richard Harris [660 . . .] and Franco Nero as Cain and Abel, George C. Scott [73 . . .] and Ava Gardner [1339] as Abraham and Sarah, Peter O'Toole [164 . . .] as all three archangels, and John Huston [24 . . .] as Noah and the Narrator. Long, slow, ponderous, misguided, but not unwatchable, thanks to beautiful photography by Giuseppe Rotunno [49] and a lively performance by Huston, who also directed. Dino de Laurentiis, the overreaching producer, originally planned for individual segments to be directed by Orson Welles [407 . . .], Federico Fellini [61 . . .], and Robert Bresson, but that fell through for a variety of reasons, one of which is that Bresson insisted that Adam and Eve should be black. Welles claimed to have contributed to the script, but the screen credit goes to Christopher Fry. By the time the film hit the screen, the vogue for biblical epics, an old movie genre that had been revived in the early fifties, had run its course. One of the chief attractions of such movies, especially as practiced by Cecil B. DeMille in *Samson and Delilah* and *The Ten Commandments,* had been their generous servings of sex and violence, allowed by the censors because of the purity of the source and because the on-screen perpetrators were always severely punished. But loosening censorship had made it possible for Hollywood to provide sex and violence without divine retribution, so tales from the Old and New Testaments lost their appeal to producers and audiences alike. *The Bible,* like many later biblical films, tried to be arty—hence de Laurentiis' choice of directors, or his plan to have the score composed by Igor Stravinsky. Japanese composer Mayuzumi lost to John Barry for *Born Free.*

194 • BICYCLE THIEF, THE

VITTORIO DE SICA PRODUCTIONS: MAYER-BURSTYN (ITALY). 1949.
AWARD *Special Award:* Outstanding foreign language film.
NOMINATION *Screenplay:* Cesare Zavattini.

The head of a poverty-stricken Roman family gets a job that requires him to have a bicycle. They scrape together enough to get one from a pawnshop, but it is stolen. The remainder of the film shows the desperate search by the man and his young son for the bicycle. The film, by Vittorio de Sica [650], is one of the most celebrated in history for the skill with which its simple story is treated. Legend has it that David O. Selznick [497 . . .], impressed by de Sica's earlier *Shoeshine,* offered to finance the filming of *The Bicycle Thief* if de Sica would make it with Cary Grant [1445 . . .], though the version given by Selznick's biographer, David Thomson, sounds more probable: that Selznick considered remaking the film with Grant. Fortunately we were spared either attempt. De Sica raised the money from other sources and worked with untrained actors recruited from the streets of Rome.

The Academy's honoring *The Bicycle Thief* is interesting in the light of the film's treatment by the American censors. The Production Code Administration objected to a scene set in a brothel and one in which the small boy urinates against a wall—scenes that would never have been allowed in Hollywood films of the day—and refused to grant it their seal. The controversy greatly damaged the industry-sponsored film censorship board's credibility and authority, which until the very late forties was virtually unchallenged.

Zavattini's screenplay lost to Joseph L. Mankiewicz's for *A Letter to Three Wives.*
Zavattini: 1815, 2171.

195 • BIG

20TH CENTURY FOX PRODUCTION; 20TH CENTURY FOX. 1988.
NOMINATIONS *Actor:* Tom Hanks. *Screenplay Written Directly for the Screen:* Gary Ross and Anne Spielberg.

A boy, frustrated by the restrictions of preadolescent life, makes a wish at a mysterious carnival machine and wakes up with the body of thirty-year-old Hanks. His twelve-year-old sensibility makes him a natural when he wangles a job with a toy company and his naïveté wins the affections of exec Elizabeth Perkins, who finds him a refreshing contrast to the grasping yuppies who surround her. Funny, touching, charming—proof that a flimsy high-concept premise doesn't necessarily result in a flimsy movie. In fact, a similar premise was used in two other films the same year—*Like Father, Like Son,* with Dudley Moore [103], and *Vice Versa,* with Judge Reinhold—and back in 1977 in *Freaky Friday,* with Barbara Harris [2275] and Jodie Foster [7 . . .], and all of them turned out more or less flimsily. The success of this one is due to the inventiveness of the script, the lightness of director Penny Marshall's touch, and the skill of the cast, including Mercedes Ruehl [671] as the boy's mother, Robert Loggia [1039] as the head of the toy company, and young David Moscow and Jared Rushton as the boy and his best friend. Among the film's many highlights is Hanks and Loggia tap-dancing out "Heart and Soul" on a giant keyboard in F. A. O. Schwartz.

Above all, Hanks is absolutely splendid. With a boyish face that dances between handsome and homely, he has a clown's timing and a Chaplinesque gift at shifting from comedy to pathos. After a few mediocre movies and a failed TV sitcom, *Bosom Buddies,* he shot to stardom in *Splash*—another high-concept comedy with transcendent performances. *Big* gave him universal critical acclaim in a role that, of all people, Robert De Niro [113 . . .] was eager to play. The Oscar went to Dustin Hoffman for *Rain*

Man, which also won for the screenplay by Ron Bass and Barry Morrow.

Hanks: 708.5, 1562.5. Ross: 494.5.

196 • *BIG BROADCAST OF 1936, THE*

PARAMOUNT. 1935.
NOMINATION *Dance Direction:* LeRoy Prinz.

Jack Oakie [818] runs a radio station and presides over the inconsequential plot that links a plethora of vaudeville turns from George Burns [1976] and Gracie Allen, Bing Crosby [173 . . .], Ethel Merman, Amos 'n' Andy, Bill "Bojangles" Robinson, the Nicholas Brothers, and (we're not making this up) the Vienna Boys Choir. The movies in the *Broadcast* were forgettable, but they do give contemporary audiences a look at some legendary talents. Directed by Norman Taurog [271 . . .].

Prinz was simultaneously nominated for the "It's the Animal in Me" number in this film and for the "Viennese Waltz" sequence in *All the King's Horses.* He lost to David Gould for *Broadway Melody of 1936* and *Folies Bergère.*

Prinz: 52, 2220.

197 • *BIG BROADCAST OF 1938, THE*

PARAMOUNT. 1938.
AWARD *Song:* "Thanks for the Memory," music by Ralph Rainger, lyrics by Leo Robin.

Bob Hope makes his feature film debut in this musical revue, set on an ocean liner, which also provided him with his theme song. The talent on board ranges from W. C. Fields to Kirsten Flagstad. Mitchell Leisen [587] directed this last in the series of Paramount *Big Broadcast*s, which is worth sitting through only for Fields and the rendition of the award-winning song by Hope and Shirley Ross.

Rainger was a staff composer at Paramount from 1930 to his death in a plane crash in 1942. His songs include "June in January." Robin, also under contract to Paramount, often worked with Rainger, but he supplied the lyrics to other familiar songs: "Hallelujah!" with Vincent Youmans, "Louise" and "Beyond the Blue Horizon" with Richard Whiting, "Love Is Just Around the Corner" with Lewis E.

Gensler, and the songs for the Broadway hit *Gentlemen Prefer Blondes,* including "Diamonds Are a Girl's Best Friend," with Jule Styne. Robin died in 1984.

Rainger: 846, 1805. Robin: 104, 368, 846, 1072, 1805, 1843, 2032, 2088, 2310.

198 • *BIG CARNIVAL, THE*

PARAMOUNT. 1951.
NOMINATION *Story and Screenplay:* Billy Wilder, Lesser Samuels, and Walter Newman.

Cynical hotshot newspaperman Kirk Douglas [130 . . .] milks a big story, about a man trapped in a mining cave-in, for all it's worth, delaying the rescue. Unfortunately the man dies, and Douglas is exposed for the heel that he is. This satire directed by Wilder was a box-office failure, and one can see why. Despite some good lines and vivid location filming by Charles Lang [97 . . .], it's pretty bleak stuff. Still, some think it's a masterpiece. It was originally titled *Ace in the Hole;* the change was apparently designed to make it sound more fun than it is. The writing award went to Alan Jay Lerner for *An American in Paris.*

Wilder: 91, 138, 566, 705, 709, 925, 1208, 1440, 1738, 1860, 1903, 1975, 2297. Samuels: 1444. Newman: 238, 371.

199 • *BIG CHILL, THE*

CARSON PRODUCTIONS GROUP PRODUCTION; COLUMBIA. 1983.
NOMINATIONS *Picture:* Michael Shamberg, producer. *Supporting Actress:* Glenn Close. *Screenplay Written Directly for the Screen:* Lawrence Kasdan and Barbara Benedek.

College classmates gather for the funeral of one of their friends and discover what time has done to them. A terrific ensemble cast, well directed by Kasdan, overcomes the deficiencies of the film, which are that there's no plot and no real surprises in the relationships. The title became a label for a generation, however, and the movie's success clearly inspired the TV series *thirtysomething.* It's often noted that John Sayles [1533.5] had done the same thing three years earlier—and some think better—on a shoestring budget and a mostly no-name cast in *The Return of the Secaucus 7.* Kasdan's stellar company includes, in addition to Close, Tom Berenger [1584], Jeff Goldblum, William Hurt [293 . . .], Kevin Kline [670], Mary Kay Place, Meg Tilly [28], and JoBeth Williams. Kevin Costner [482] was to be seen as the deceased friend in flashbacks, but those were cut. That's his body being dressed in the opening credits. The film's soundtrack album of sixties songs was also a big hit.

Terms of Endearment was the best picture winner from a slate of films that reflected a very soft year in Hollywood. Aside from *Chill,* they included a small-scale British import, *The Dresser,* a small-scale American product, *Tender Mercies,* and a big-scale box-office failure, *The Right Stuff.*

From a cast of almost evenly matched talents, the Academy chose Close, the only one in the group who had previously been nominated—perhaps that was the tiebreaker. She lost to Linda Hunt's cross-dressed performance in *The Year of Living Dangerously.*

Kasdan had begun his rise in Hollywood with work on the screenplays for *The Empire Strikes Back* and *Raiders of the Lost Ark* and made his directing debut with the 1981 fantasia on film noir themes, *Body Heat.* For *Chill* he enlisted the aid of Benedek, his lawyer's wife, a social worker who had never written a screenplay before. They lost to Horton Foote's *Tender Mercies.*

Close: 485, 653, 1418, 2314. Kasdan: 6, 811.

200 • BIG COUNTRY, THE

ANTHONY-WORLDWIDE PRODUCTIONS; UNITED ARTISTS. 1958.
AWARD *Supporting Actor:* Burl Ives.
NOMINATION *Scoring of a Dramatic or Comedy Picture:* Jerome Moross.

Tenderfoot Gregory Peck [759 . . .] wades into the middle of a feud over water rights, with patriarchs Ives and Charles Bickford [651 . . .] as the chief antagonists. Peck plans to marry Bickford's daughter, Carroll Baker [119], who thinks he's a wimp because he believes there might be a peaceable solution to all this feuding. So does surly ranch foreman Charlton Heston [175], with whom Peck is forced to slug it out. Incredibly, given that Heston looks as if he's carved out of granite, Peck wins. Eventually Peck

finds true love with Jean Simmons [858 . . .]. This very watchable western is a little too sprawling, perhaps because it was produced by Peck and director William Wyler [175 . . .], who find little incentive to cut back, even though the film could lose half an hour without suffering.

The Oscar to Ives is specifically for *The Big Country,* but it was clearly a kind of services-rendered award for having brought his big presence to three major roles in the same year. The other two—all were troubled patriarchs—are in *Desire Under the Elms* and *Cat on a Hot Tin Roof.* The latter performance, as Big Daddy, may have been the best of the lot. A former pro football player, Ives was best known as a folksinger before he became a larger-than-life character actor, making his first big impression in *East of Eden.* After the Oscar, he never had a year quite as good as 1958.

Moross lost to Dimitri Tiomkin for *The Old Man and the Sea.*

201 • BIG FISHERMAN, THE

ROWLAND V. LEE PRODUCTIONS; BUENA VISTA. 1959.
NOMINATIONS *Color Cinematography:* Lee Garmes. *Color Art Direction—Set Decoration:* John DeCuir; Julia Heron. *Color Costume Design:* Renie.

Howard Keel plays St. Peter in this adaptation of the novel by Lloyd C. Douglas, a sequel to *The Robe.* Long, earnest, pious, and empty. You know not to expect too much when a movie's big stars are Keel, John Saxon, Susan Kohner [984], Herbert Lom, and Martha Hyer [1859]. The last film of director Frank Borzage [132 . . .], who won the very first Oscar ever given for directing.

This was the year of *Ben-Hur,* which took all the Oscars in the categories in which *The Big Fisherman* was nominated: cinematography (Robert Surtees), art direction, and costumes (Elizabeth Haffenden).

Garmes: 1358, 1800, 1828. DeCuir: 29, 376, 413, 476, 896, 950, 1088, 1391, 1852, 2000. Heron: 366, 1070, 1886, 2031. Renie: 355, 413, 1338, 1601.

202 • BIG HOUSE, THE

COSMOPOLITAN; MGM. 1929–30.

AWARDS *Writing Achievement:* Frances Marion. *Sound Recording:* Douglas Shearer.

NOMINATIONS *Production:* Irving G. Thalberg, producer. *Actor:* Wallace Beery.

Beery and Chester Morris [38] play prison inmates in this behind-the-bars melodrama that practically invented the genre—and its clichés. Still watchable, though it has some of the stiffness of camera and hamminess of acting that afflict early talkies. The cast includes Robert Montgomery [904 . . .] and Lewis Stone [1540].

Marion was the first woman to win an Oscar for something other than acting, but she was no stranger to pioneering: During World War I, she was one of the first female war correspondents. She became an extraordinarily prolific and well-paid screenwriter in the silent era and moved easily into sound. Her career tapered off in the later thirties. She was married to George Hill, who directed *The Big House.* She died in 1973.

Shearer, the brother of actress Norma Shearer [150 . . .], began as an assistant cameraman and became an instant expert in recording when sound came in. Over the years there have been allegations that Shearer used his position as brother-in-law of MGM's head of production, Irving G. Thalberg, to advance his career, and that he was not so technically proficient as his many awards suggest. But he unquestionably helped build MGM into the most prestigious and efficient film factory ever known.

The best picture Oscar went to *All Quiet on the Western Front.* Beery, who took over the role when Lon Chaney died suddenly, lost to George Arliss in *Disraeli.*

Marion: 378, 1624. Shearer: 136, 256, 685, 817, 835, 1096, 1232, 1292, 1371, 1419, 1751, 1950, 1988, 2048, 2055, 2211, 2300. Thalberg: 150, 799, 812, 1387, 1721, 1846, 2129. Beery: 378.

203 • BIG POND, THE

PARAMOUNT PUBLIX. 1929–30.

NOMINATION *Actor:* Maurice Chevalier.

A Frenchman (Chevalier, of course) comes to America, where he makes his fortune in bubble gum and wins the love of Claudette Colbert [1025 . . .]. A lightweight musical romance that was one of the first films on which Preston Sturges [823 . . .] worked as writer. Directed by Hobart Henley. Among other things, Chevalier gets to sing "You Brought a New Kind of Love to Me." Nowhere near as good as the other film for which Chevalier was nominated this year, *The Love Parade,* but easy to watch.

Chevalier, who lost to George Arliss in *Disraeli,* had been recruited by Paramount in the great rush to find musical and dramatic talent after sound came in. The legendary entertainer had begun his career at the Folies-Bergère. During World War I he was wounded and taken prisoner, and returned to the music hall stages as a decorated hero. His early-thirties films were quite popular, but he left Hollywood in a huff in 1935 after a dispute with Irving Thalberg [150 . . .] over screen billing. His later career was dogged with controversy because of charges that he collaborated with the Nazis during World War II, but he made a successful return to American films in the late fifties, particularly in *Gigi,* and was given an honorary award by the Academy in 1958. He died in 1972.

Chevalier: 1217.

204 • BIG SKY, THE

WINCHESTER PICTURES CORPORATION; RKO RADIO. 1952.

NOMINATIONS *Supporting Actor:* Arthur Hunnicutt. *Black-and-White Cinematography:* Russell Harlan.

Kirk Douglas [130 . . .] leads an expedition of fur trappers up the Missouri River in 1830. Howard Hawks [1779] directed from a screenplay by his frequent collaborator Dudley Nichols [30 . . .], and it has their usual humorous male bonding and lively action.

Hunnicutt, a character actor since the early forties, was a kind of second-string Walter Brennan [424 . . .]. He lost to Anthony Quinn in *Viva*

Zapata! Harlan's cinematography lost to Robert Surtees' work on *The Bad and the Beautiful*.

Harlan: 227, 825, 879, 882, 2101.

205 • BILL AND COO

REPUBLIC. 1947.

AWARD *Special Award: Bill and Coo,* in which artistry and patience blended in a novel and entertaining use of the medium of motion pictures.

A cast composed entirely of birds enacts a love story. As Samuel Johnson said, in another context, "It is not done well, but you are surprised to find it done at all." Actually they're pretty good. For birds. This indescribable but not unwatchable oddity was produced and narrated by former vaudevillian and early TV pioneer Ken Murray and directed by Dean Riesner.

206 • BILLY BUDD

HARVEST PRODUCTIONS; ALLIED ARTISTS (UNITED KINGDOM). 1962.

NOMINATION *Supporting Actor:* Terence Stamp.

Stamp plays the title role in this adaptation of Herman Melville's story about a beautiful tongue-tied young sailor who is goaded into killing his tormentor, a sadistic master-at-arms, played by Robert Ryan [467]. Peter Ustinov [943 . . .] plays the captain who is forced to execute the young man; he also directed, coproduced, and cowrote the screenplay. It's too tidy an adaptation of a story that is anything but tidy in its exploration of the characters' motivations and moral dilemmas. If you know Melville's story, you won't be satisfied, and if you don't, you may wonder why it takes two hours to tell it. The cast also includes Melvyn Douglas [169 . . .], Paul Rogers, and David McCallum.

Stamp's rather sinister good looks caused him to be typecast as weird or perverse characters, such as the title role of *The Collector*. His career was spotty throughout the seventies, as he pursued a variety of spiritual quests rather than an acting career, but he returned in the eighties, often as a character villain, as in the first two *Superman* movies, and was critically acclaimed for his performance as a transsexual in *Pris-* *cilla, Queen of the Desert*. He lost to Ed Begley in *Sweet Bird of Youth*.

207 • BILLY ROSE'S JUMBO

EUTERPE-ARWIN PRODUCTION; MGM. 1962.

NOMINATION *Scoring of Music—Adaptation or Treatment:* George Stoll.

Circus musical centering on the attempts of Doris Day [1572], Jimmy Durante, and Martha Raye to thwart an attempt to take over Day's father's circus. Stephen Boyd comes to their aid. Pleasant and colorful, but the real strength of the film is its song score by Richard Rodgers [1921] and Lorenz Hart. Any musical that includes songs like "My Romance" and "Little Girl Blue" has so much going for it that even a tired plot can't drag it down. Day is in her sweetest voice, and Durante has some very endearing moments, particularly when he attempts to hide an elephant. The film is based on a superspectacular production originally staged by showman Rose in 1935 at the Hippodrome in New York, with lots of circus acts and a book by Ben Hecht [78 . . .] and Charles MacArthur [1664 . . .] under the direction of George Abbott [48]. Here, the screenplay is by Sidney Sheldon [121], and Charles Walters [1173] directed, with help from Busby Berkeley [791 . . .]. Stoll lost to Ray Heindorf for *The Music Man*.

Stoll: 74, 115, 699, 1126, 1298, 1299, 1950.

208 • BILLY THE KID

MGM. 1941.

NOMINATION *Color Cinematography:* William V. Skall and Leonard Smith.

Robert Taylor is Billy, with Brian Donlevy [161] as the marshal on his trail. You can guess from the casting that Billy isn't the slimy little punk he was in real life. Rather square and plodding remake of a 1930 movie that starred Johnny Mack Brown and Wallace Beery [202 . . .]. Directed by David Miller, with Gene Lockhart [36] and Lon Chaney, Jr. The cinematography Oscar went to Ray Rennahan and Ernest Palmer for *Blood and Sand*.

Skall: 96, 1048, 1170, 1317, 1453, 1644, 1668, 1822, 2102. Smith: 1132, 1417, 2320.

209 • BIRD

MALPASO PRODUCTION; WARNER BROS. 1988.
AWARD *Sound:* Les Fresholtz, Dick Alexander, Vern Poore, and Willie D. Burton.

Forest Whitaker plays the great jazz sax player Charlie Parker, in a film directed by Clint Eastwood [2179.5] that focuses on the musician's destruction by drug addiction. Gloomy story with great music and fine performances. Whitaker won the best actor award at Cannes, and Diane Venora, as Parker's girlfriend, was the New York Film Critics Circle winner for best supporting actress. American audiences failed to respond to the film, however. The sound award recognizes a remarkable technical feat: Parker's original performances, remastered, were wedded to new recordings of the accompaniment.

Fresholtz: 54, 58, 215, 606, 888, 1127, 1158.5, 1279, 1526, 2113, 2179.5. Alexander: 54, 519, 888, 1127, 1158.5, 2113, 2179.5. Poore: 888, 1127, 1158.5, 2179.5. Burton: 58, 307, 1802.5, 2231.

210 • BIRDMAN OF ALCATRAZ

HAROLD HECHT PRODUCTIONS; UNITED ARTISTS. 1962.
NOMINATIONS *Actor:* Burt Lancaster. *Supporting Actor:* Telly Savalas. *Supporting Actress:* Thelma Ritter. *Black-and-White Cinematography:* Burnett Guffey.

Lancaster is Robert Stroud, who becomes a world-famous ornithologist while imprisoned on the Rock for murder. Unfortunately there's not much inherent drama in the story, so the chief attraction of the film is watching superior performers go through their paces under the direction of John Frankenheimer. The cast includes Karl Malden [1477 . . .], Betty Field, Neville Brand, and Edmond O'Brien [146 . . .]. The screenplay is by Guy Trosper [1605].

Lancaster won the acting award at the Venice Film Festival for his portrayal of Stroud, but the Oscar went to Gregory Peck for *To Kill a Mockingbird*.

After World War II, Savalas went to work first for the State Department and then for ABC News, where he won a Peabody Award for producing a series called *Your Voice of America*. The lure of acting drew him into TV, and then into movies, where he typically played a heavy. To break the mold, he went back to TV as the lollipop-sucking police detective Kojak, his most famous role. The Oscar went to Ed Begley for *Sweet Bird of Youth*. Savalas died in 1994.

This was the last of Ritter's six nominations. The award went to Patty Duke for *The Miracle Worker*. Ritter died in 1969.

Guffey lost to Jean Bourgoin and Walter Wottitz for *The Longest Day*.

Lancaster: 107, 609, 732. Ritter: 46, 1289, 1564, 1572, 2294. Guffey: 255, 732, 870, 1093.

211 • BIRDS, THE

ALFRED J. HITCHCOCK PRODUCTIONS INC.; UNIVERSAL. 1963.
NOMINATION *Special Visual Effects:* Ub Iwerks.

In a coastal community north of San Francisco, birds of all sorts suddenly and inexplicably begin to terrorize people, including Tippi Hedren, Rod Taylor, Jessica Tandy [580 . . .], Suzanne Pleshette, and Veronica Cartwright. There's really not much more to this celebrated thriller by Alfred Hitchcock [1171 . . .] than that. The director's most devoted advocates consider it a masterwork; others find it a display of Hitchcockian tricks put to the service of nothing in particular. This was the first of Hitchcock's two attempts—the other was *Marnie* (1964)—to make Hedren a star in the mold of Grace Kelly [450 . . .]. His treatment of her during the filming of *The Birds* has become part of Hollywood legend: During the filming of one scene she was pelted repeatedly with gulls, finally reducing her to unfeigned hysteria.

Ub Iwerks—his real name; Ub is short for Ubbe —is legendary for his association with Walt Disney [645 . . .], which began in Kansas City long before either man was famous, and continued when the men moved to California and created Mickey Mouse. In 1931 Iwerks left Disney to create his own cartoon series but returned a decade later to concentrate on special effects—live action as well as animation. His efforts led to two citations by the Academy in its technical awards: in 1959 for the design of an improved optical printer for special effects and matte shots, and in 1964 for the conception and perfection of techniques for color traveling matte composite cinematography. His matte techniques—essentially the combining of several different pieces of film in a single frame—are particularly evident in the last scene of *The Birds,* which involves thirty-odd pieces of film joined in a single image. The Oscar, however, went to *Cleopatra.*

212 • BIRDS DO IT, BEES DO IT

WOLPER PICTURES LTD. PRODUCTION; COLUMBIA. 1975.
NOMINATION *Original Score:* Gerald Fried.

Documentary about the sex lives of animals—rather like a dirty Disney True-Life Adventure. What the Academy's music branch was thinking when it nominated this score instead of the one by Maurice Jarre [558 . . .] for *The Man Who Would Be King* is beyond our ken. The Oscar went to one of the most familiar of all film scores: John Williams' for *Jaws.*

213 • BIRTH OF THE BLUES

PARAMOUNT. 1941.
NOMINATION *Scoring of a Musical Picture:* Robert Emmett Dolan.

New Orleans band led by Bing Crosby [173 . . .] becomes a smash success. Enjoyable chiefly for its music, if you can ignore the inconsequential plot and swallow the notion that a bunch of white guys created jazz. The cast, directed by Victor Schertzinger [1488 . . .], includes Mary Martin and Brian Donlevy [161], and among the songs are "St. Louis Blues," "Melancholy Baby," "St. James Infirmary," and "Cuddle Up a Little Closer." The scoring award went to *Dumbo.*

Dolan: 173, 244, 929, 994, 1120, 1704, 1912.

214 • BISHOP'S WIFE, THE

SAMUEL GOLDWYN PRODUCTIONS; RKO RADIO. 1947
AWARD *Sound Recording:* Samuel Goldwyn Studio Sound Department, Gordon Sawyer, sound director.
NOMINATIONS *Picture:* Samuel Goldwyn, producer. *Director:* Henry Koster. *Scoring of a Dramatic or Comedy Picture:* Hugo Friedhofer. *Film Editing:* Monica Collingwood.

Episcopalian bishop David Niven [1778] is so pre-occupied with wooing wealthy contributors to his building fund that he neglects both his flock and his wife, Loretta Young [428 . . .]. An angel, played by Cary Grant [1445 . . .], comes down to earth to set things right, partly by courting Young and arousing Niven's jealousy. Tiresomely sugary fantasy with central miscasting: Grant is nobody's idea of an angel, and the part turns him all stiff and twinkly. The film has a good supporting cast—James Gleason [904], Gladys Cooper [1393 . . .], and Elsa Lanchester [428 . . .], among others—and the usual first-class Goldwyn production values, including cinematography by Gregg Toland [407 . . .]. Based on a novel by Robert Nathan, with a screenplay by Robert E. Sherwood [184 . . .] and Leonardo Bercovici on which Billy Wilder [91 . . .] and Charles Brackett [705 . . .] did some uncredited fixing. This was Goldwyn's first major production after the celebrated *The Best Years of Our Lives,* and it demonstrated clearly what a hard act that film would be to follow. The Oscar went to *Gentleman's Agreement.*

Koster, a German director (under the name Hermann Kosterlitz) who fled to France and eventually America when Hitler came to power, had made his name with a series of popular musicals starring Deanna Durbin. A dependable second-string director, he replaced William Seiter on *The Bishop's Wife* after several weeks of filming. Koster's later career was steady but unmemorable. He is noted only for having directed the first CinemaScope epic, *The Robe.* The Oscar went to Elia Kazan for *Gentleman's Agreement.*

The scoring Oscar was won by Miklos Rozsa for *A Double Life* and the editing award by Francis Lyon and Robert Parrish for *Body and Soul.*

Sawyer: 33, 91, 184, 393, 730, 864, 882, 973, 974, 1032, 1511, 1592, 2244, 2297, 2310. Goldwyn: 102, 184, 510, 560, 1182, 1607, 2316. Friedhofer: 2, 21, 184, 187, 267, 1048, 2303, 2336.

215 • BITE THE BULLET

PAX ENTERPRISES PRODUCTION; COLUMBIA. 1975.
NOMINATIONS *Sound:* Arthur Piantadosi, Les Fresholtz, Richard Tyler, and Al Overton, Jr. *Original Score:* Alex North.

The lure of prize money attracts a variety of contestants to a six-hundred-mile cross-country horse race. Gene Hackman [255 . . .] is an animal-loving loner, Candice Bergen [1919] a prostitute out to rescue her outlaw boyfriend, James Coburn a friendly rival of Hackman's, Ben Johnson [1139] a tubercular cowboy, Ian Bannen [688] an English sportsman, and Jan-Michael Vincent a bigmouthed kid. The script and direction by Richard Brooks [227 . . .] lift the movie high above the clichés in which it might have wallowed and produce an exciting western. Many films of the seventies take an established genre, as *The Godfather* did with the gangster flick, and try to inject new meaning into it. Sometimes that results in muddled tone and pretentiousness; *Bite the Bullet* veers near these pitfalls but manages to avoid them. The performances, particularly by Hackman, Coburn, and Johnson, are excellent. This was the first film in which Bergen made an effort to act, as she admits in her autobiography, *Knock Wood.* Though she says she felt miscast as the voluptuous prostitute, she succeeds in bringing a fresh and lively presence to her role—a step toward the cheeky persona she later honed into Murphy Brown.

Jaws won the Oscars for sound and John Williams' scoring.

Piantadosi: 54, 58, 319, 606, 1279, 2113. Fresholtz: 54, 58, 209, 606, 888, 1127, 1158.5, 1279, 1526, 2113, 2179.5. Tyler: 1548, 1824, 1877. Overton: 540, 544, 606, 1548. North: 29, 413, 515, 577, 1654, 1727, 1802, 1814, 1886, 1949, 2174, 2177, 2212, 2277.

216 • BITTER RICE

Lux Films S.A.; Lux Films (Italy). 1950.
Nomination *Motion Picture Story:* Giuseppe De Santis and Carlo Lizzani.

Silvana Mangano, working in the rice fields of the Po Valley, falls for crook Vittorio Gassman, who plans to steal the rice crop. Though ostensibly intended as an exposé of the conditions under which farm workers labored, the film developed its international celebrity because of the voluptuous nineteen-year-old Mangano and sex scenes that would not have passed the censors in an American film of the era. The writing Oscar went to Edna and Edward Anhalt for *Panic in the Streets.*

217 • BITTER SWEET

MGM. 1940.
Nominations *Color Cinematography:* Oliver T. Marsh and Allen Davey. *Color Interior Decoration:* Cedric Gibbons and John S. Detlie.

Operetta by Noël Coward [993] set in 1870s Vienna, with Jeanette MacDonald and Nelson Eddy, gets a lavish MGM treatment that smothers any charm the original may have had. Only for fans of Jeanette and Nelson. Directed by W. S. Van Dyke [1751 . . .], with George Sanders [46], Felix Bressart, Sig Ruman, and Herman Bing. *The Thief of Bagdad* won for Georges Périnal's cinematography and Vincent Korda's art direction.

Marsh: 1988. Davey: 455, 897, 1872, 1988. Gibbons: 66, 87, 130, 227, 239, 285, 290, 440, 629, 749, 831, 980, 1069, 1096, 1173, 1190, 1226, 1230, 1232, 1274, 1308, 1309, 1417, 1567, 1604, 1644, 1662, 1673, 1721, 1861, 1937, 2068, 2112, 2256, 2257, 2300, 2320, 2330.

218 • BLACK AND WHITE IN COLOR

Arthur Cohn Production/Société Ivoirienne de Cinéma (Ivory Coast). 1976.
Award *Foreign Language Film.*

At the start of World War I, a group of French colonials in West Africa decide to attack a nearby German garrison. Amusing but lightweight satiric film directed by Jean-Jacques Annaud, who later did *The Bear* and *The Name of the Rose* (1986). The film's win was something of an upset, as it was competing against *Seven Beauties,* a widely acclaimed film whose director, Lina Wertmüller, and star, Giancarlo Giannini, were nominated in the directing and acting categories. This served to draw attention once more to the anomalous and often controversial foreign film category, candidates for which are submitted by their countries of origin and trimmed down to five finalists by an Academy committee. This was the first year for a new Academy regulation that limited the voting in this category to only those members of the Academy who can document that they have seen all five nominees.

218.5 • BLACK FURY

First National. 1935.

Nomination *Actor:* Paul Muni. (Write-in candidate.)

Muni is a coal miner fighting union corruption in this tough-minded melodrama directed by Michael Curtiz [79 . . .] from a screenplay by Abem Finkel [1779] and Carl Erickson. The cast includes Karen Morley, William Gargan [2045], Barton MacLane, and J. Carrol Naish [1294 . . .].

Although Muni was not an official nominee, the Academy's opening the competition to write-in votes allowed Warners (of which First National was a subsidiary) to do a substantial amount of logrolling, even winning a write-in campaign for cinematographer Hal Mohr's work on *A Midsummer Night's Dream.* Muni was almost a beneficiary, too, coming in second to Victor McLaglen in *The Informer.*

Muni: 965, 1133, 1169, 1936, 2191.

219 • BLACK HOLE, THE

Walt Disney Productions; Buena Vista. 1979.

Nominations *Cinematography:* Frank Phillips. *Visual Effects:* Peter Ellenshaw, Art Cruickshank, Eustace Lycett, Danny Lee, Harrison Ellenshaw, and Joe Hale.

Mad scientist Maximilian Schell [1065 . . .] is determined to take a spaceship into a black hole—and Anthony Perkins [730], Robert Forster, Yvette Mimieux, Joseph Bottoms, and Ernest Borgnine [1283] along with it. Gary Nelson directed this busy, gimmicky attempt by Disney to cash in on the *Star Wars* phenomenon by remaking *20,000 Leagues Under the Sea* in outer space. Though the studios actually began work on the movie before *Star Wars* revived sci-fi as a film genre, the Disney version looks like a copycat, right down to its cute robots, which have voices by Roddy McDowall and Slim Pickens. Unfortunately the film was pitched to kids more than to general audiences, which flocked instead to *Alien* and *Star Trek—the Motion Picture.* The film's box-office failure added to the woes of the studio, which was several years away from the reorganization and renaissance that made it one of the greatest Hollywood success stories of the eighties.

The special effects are the star of the show, using a computerized camera system designed specifically for the film. The Oscar, however, went to *Alien.* The cinematography award was won by Vittorio Storaro for *Apocalypse Now.*

P. Ellenshaw: 166, 1022, 1284. Cruickshank: 646. Lycett: 4, 166, 1284. Lee: 166.

220 • BLACK LEGION

Warner Bros. 1937.

Nomination *Original Story:* Robert Lord.

Humphrey Bogart [24 . . .] joins a Klan-like organization after a foreigner gets the factory job he sought. Warners' reputation for socially conscious films is bolstered by this solid melodrama, directed by Archie Mayo, though its chief interest today is as an early Bogart movie. Lord, who also produced the film, lost to William Wellman and Robert Carson for *A Star Is Born.*

Lord: 689, 1493.

221 • BLACK NARCISSUS

J. Arthur Rank-Archers; Universal-International (United Kingdom). 1947.

Awards *Color Cinematography:* Jack Cardiff. *Color Art Direction–Set Decoration:* Alfred Junge.

Anglican nun Deborah Kerr [599 . . .] tries to run a hospital and school in the Himalayas, but sex and the mores of the natives keep getting in the way. Jean Simmons [858 . . .] plays a native girl, Sabu is an Indian prince, Flora Robson [1759] the convent horticulturalist, David Farrar the virile British agent, and Kathleen Byron a nun who goes mad with lust for Farrar. Highly entertaining and gorgeously filmed version of a novel by Rumer Godden, with the usual strong production values and good storytelling of the producing-directing-writing team of Michael Powell [1008 . . .] and Emeric Pressburger [1008 . . .]. American censors made hash of the original-release version because of the Production Code's strictures on the portrayal of the sex lives of clerics.

Cardiff, an early color expert, worked primarily in Britain and was a major contributor to the success of the Powell-Pressburger team. He also shot *The African Queen* and in the late fifties turned to directing, with considerable success, particularly on *Sons and Lovers.*

Junge began his career in Germany but in the late twenties moved to Britain, where he worked not only on Powell and Pressburger's films but also on many MGM productions shot in England, such as *The Citadel, Goodbye, Mr. Chips,* and *Gaslight.* He became head of MGM's British studios art department in the late forties, supervising such films as *Ivanhoe* and *Mogambo.* He died in 1964.

Cardiff: 643, 1875, 2228. Junge: 1107.

222 • BLACK ORPHEUS

DISPATFILM & GEMMA CINEMATOGRAFICA (FRANCE). 1959.
AWARD *Foreign Language Film.*

Retelling of the myth of Orpheus and Eurydice, set in Brazil at carnival time, with Eurydice a young woman pursued by a former lover costumed as Death, and Orpheus the young man who brings about her accidental death. A huge art-house hit at the time, it also won the grand prize at Cannes. Its chief virtues are the vivid camera work by Jean Bourgoin [1201] and pulsing music by Luis Bonfa and Antonio Carlos Jobim. Directed by Marcel Camus.

223 • BLACK RAIN

JAFFE/LANSING PRODUCTION IN ASSOCIATION WITH MICHAEL DOUGLAS; PARAMOUNT. 1989.
NOMINATIONS *Sound:* Donald O. Mitchell, Kevin O'Connell, Greg P. Russell, and Keith A. Wester. *Sound Effects Editing:* Milton C. Burrow and William L. Manger.

New York cops Michael Douglas [1481 . . .] and Andy Garcia [786] pursue a murder suspect through Osaka, their American-style methods clashing with those of the Japanese police. Dark, violent thriller directed by Ridley Scott [2039], who manages to make Japan look a lot like the futuristic L.A. he created in *Blade Runner.* Admirers of Scott's style will find much to watch here, and Garcia's performance makes the first half of the movie more entertaining than the second, which is just Douglas going through the hard-bitten loner routine he's developed of late—his role in *Basic Instinct* is essentially the same character. Kate Capshaw has a very curious little role as an American bar girl who caters to Osaka businessmen. The somewhat racist subtext of the film is mitigated by Ken Takakura's very likable performance as an Osaka cop. The sound award went to *Glory* and the one for sound effects editing to *Indiana Jones and the Last Crusade.*

Mitchell: 398, 411.5, 507, 734.5, 779, 1525, 1650, 1824, 1825, 2020, 2114, 2176.5. O'Connell: 507, 586, 658.5, 1825, 2020, 2114.

224 • BLACK ROSE, THE

20TH CENTURY-FOX (UNITED KINGDOM). 1950.
NOMINATION *Color Costume Design:* Michael Whittaker.

Scholar Tyrone Power journeys to the land of the Mongols in this adaptation of a Thomas B. Costain novel set in the Middle Ages. Fine color photography by Jack Cardiff [221 . . .] and a supporting cast that includes Orson Welles [407 . . .], Jack Hawkins, Finlay Curry, Herbert Lom, and a young Laurence Harvey [1724] are the only things that make this Hollywood historical pageant worth watching. Directed by Henry Hathaway [1194]. The costume Oscar went to the team that clad *Samson and Delilah.*

225 • BLACK STALLION, THE

OMNI ZOETROPE PRODUCTION; UNITED ARTISTS. 1979.
AWARD *Special Achievement Award for Sound Editing:* Alan Splet.
NOMINATIONS *Supporting Actor:* Mickey Rooney. *Film Editing:* Robert Dalva.

A young boy (Kelly Reno) and a magnificent horse are the only survivors of a shipwreck. After their rescue the boy, with the aid of Rooney, trains the horse for a championship race. Sort of a cross between *The Blue Lagoon* and *National Velvet,* you might say. Entertaining adaptation of Walter Farley's novel for children that's a bit better in its desert-island half than in the training and racing half. Directed by Carroll Ballard, with extraordinary photography by Caleb Deschanel [1418 . . .] that won several critics' awards but inexplicably failed to make the Oscar slate. Francis Ford Coppola [65 . . .] produced, and his father, Carmine [785 . . .], wrote the score. Teri Garr [2113] plays the boy's mother.

Sound technicians are usually uncelebrated figures, even when they win, but Splet made a name for himself by not being present to pick up his award: "First George C. Scott doesn't show, then Marlon Brando, and now Alan Splet," wisecracked emcee Johnny Carson, who continued to provide updates throughout the show on the putative whereabouts of Alan Splet. More recently, Splet has been noted for his work with director David Lynch [247 . . .].

Rooney's fourth nomination ended, like the others, in defeat—this time to another old pro, Melvyn Douglas for *Being There*. Only a year or so earlier, Rooney had announced his intention to retire but was immediately wooed out again for the hit Broadway revue *Sugar Babies*. He continued his career, winning an Emmy in 1981 for his portrayal of a retarded man in the TV movie *Bill*. He received an honorary Oscar at the 1982 awards "in recognition of his 60 years of versatility" in movies.

The editing award went to Alan Heim for *All That Jazz*.

Splet: 1425. Rooney: 115, 252, 957.

226 • BLACK SWAN, THE

20TH CENTURY-FOX. 1942.

AWARD *Color Cinematography:* Leon Shamroy.
NOMINATIONS *Scoring of a Dramatic or Comedy Picture:* Alfred Newman. *Special Effects:* Fred Sersen, photographic; Roger Heman and George Leverett, sound.

Pirate Tyrone Power swashes and buckles his way into Maureen O'Hara's heart. Enjoyable nonsense from a Rafael Sabatini novel, with a colorful cast of such characters as Thomas Mitchell [962 . . .], George Sanders [46], and Anthony Quinn [1226 . . .], directed by Henry King [1868 . . .].

Shamroy's eighteen nominations give him a tie with Charles B. Lang among cinematographers for most nominations, and he ties with Joseph Rut-

tenberg [318 . . .] for the most Oscars won by a cinematographer. This was the first of his four wins.

Newman lost to Max Steiner for *Now, Voyager*. The special effects Oscar went to *Reap the Wild Wind*.

Shamroy: 29, 356, 413, 495, 569, 602, 1088, 1153, 1213, 1592, 1610, 1706, 1852, 1883, 2013, 2286, 2334. Newman: 31, 34, 46, 72, 138, 182, 333, 334, 347, 375, 428, 437, 457, 476, 495, 542, 690, 797, 833, 952, 953, 959, 962, 1016, 1082, 1088, 1213, 1278, 1362, 1397, 1475, 1616, 1655, 1849, 1868, 1883, 1921, 2043, 2046, 2091, 2258, 2286, 2294, 2316. Sersen: 241, 346, 458, 520, 1655, 2286, 2317. Heman: 346, 418, 458, 520, 1041, 2286.

227 • BLACKBOARD JUNGLE

MGM. 1955.

NOMINATIONS *Screenplay:* Richard Brooks. *Black-and-White Cinematography:* Russell Harlan. *Black-and-White Art Direction–Set Decoration:* Cedric Gibbons and Randall Duell; Edwin B. Willis and Henry Grace. *Film Editing:* Ferris Webster.

Idealistic teacher Glenn Ford comes to what we'd now call an inner-city school whose teachers range from apathetic to terrorized. When he rescues a woman teacher from rape, he provokes the local gang, led by Vic Morrow, who beat him up and harass his pregnant wife, Anne Francis. Ford finally wins over a bright but wary student, Sidney Poitier [522 . . .] and gains control of the classroom. *The Wild One* (1954) and *Rebel Without a Cause* may loom larger in Hollywood's iconography of troubled fifties youth, but *Blackboard Jungle* was in many ways a more powerful and radical film, featuring as it did a multiracial cast and the first important use of rock and roll on a soundtrack. Brando's motorcycle gang and Dean's young rebels seem faintly absurd today when they groove on jazz, but when Bill Haley and the Comets' "Rock Around the Clock" bursts from the soundtrack, you know you're in the latter half of the twentieth century. To be sure, fifties attitudes abound: Francis is certain the teacher Ford rescues from rape must have "provoked" it. And the movie begins with a pre-credits crawl that reassures us that most schools are terrific, most kids well behaved, and most teachers dedicated. The movie was banned in several cities—some because of the multiracial cast, some because of the fear that it might spark violence —and the Eisenhower administration kept it from being shown at the Venice Film Festival. Ford's performance leaves something to be desired: He can't quite project authority through his nice-guy facade, so we don't really believe it when he triumphs over his classroom. But otherwise it's an impressive cast. Poitier, who was twenty-six, makes a credible teenager and gives the film a center that Ford can't provide. Morrow does a brooding, Brandoesque turn that surprisingly failed to make him a major star. Louis Calhern [1243] plays a teacher sunk in cynicism, and Richard Kiley a young teacher whose ideals (along with his beloved rare jazz records) are shattered by the kids. The kids include future writer-director Paul Mazursky [250 . . .] and TV's *M*A*S*H* star Jamie Farr, billed here as Jameel Farah.

Blackboard was a breakthrough film for Brooks, who directed it as well as adapting the novel by Evan Hunter. He had begun his screenwriting career before the war, and his service in the marines led to his first novel, *The Brick Foxhole,* which was adapted as the film *Crossfire.* He began directing in 1950. The screenplay award went to Paddy Chayefsky for *Marty.*

Harlan's second nomination, for a film with a gritty, claustrophobic urban setting, is in sharp contrast to his first, for *The Big Sky,* which had the outdoors western setting of most of his early films. He lost to James Wong Howe for *The Rose Tattoo.*

It's a mark of how MGM was changing in the fifties, after the departure of Louis B. Mayer and during the brief ascension of Dore Schary [157 . . .] to studio head, that the name of Cedric Gibbons, the art department chief who crafted the glossy look of MGM films, should be attached to this down-and-dirty urban melodrama. But Gibbons' name, as well as Willis', appeared on almost all MGM films by virtue of their positions at the head of the art and set decorating departments, so much of the credit for the look of this film probably should go to Duell and Grace—and to director Brooks, who fought to give his film a gritty look. Once, noting that the light switches in the classroom were clean, he had the cast smudge them with their fingerprints, only to be informed that this sort of realistic touch was not acceptable in an MGM movie. The Academy preferred the work of Paramount's design team on *The Rose Tattoo.*

The editing Oscar went to Charles Nelson and William A. Lyon for *Picnic.*

Brooks: 372, 609, 987, 1627. Harlan: 204, 825, 879, 882, 2101. Gibbons: 66, 87, 130, 217, 239, 285, 290, 440, 629, 749, 831, 980, 1069, 1096, 1173, 1190, 1226, 1230, 1232, 1274, 1308, 1309, 1417, 1567, 1604, 1644, 1662, 1673, 1721, 1861, 1937, 2068, 2112, 2256, 2257, 2300, 2320, 2330. Duell: 1662, 2257. Willis: 66, 87, 130, 239, 290, 629, 749, 831, 980, 1069, 1096, 1157, 1173, 1190, 1226, 1230, 1232, 1309, 1417, 1567, 1657, 1662, 1673, 1721, 1861, 1937, 2068, 2112, 2257, 2320, 2330. Grace: 69, 401, 769, 953, 1335, 1388, 1450, 1537, 1552, 2157, 2184, 2312. Webster: 819, 1265.

228 • *BLADE RUNNER*

Michael Deeley-Ridley Scott Production; The Ladd Company/Sir Run Run Shaw. 1982.

Nominations *Art Direction—Set Decoration:* Lawrence G. Paull and David Snyder; Linda DeScenna. *Visual Effects:* Douglas Trumbull, Richard Yuricich, and David Dryer.

Harrison Ford [2296] plays a former "blade runner," a police officer in the year 2019 whose job it is to track down and eliminate renegade "replicants"— genetically engineered androids who do slave labor on other planets and are barred from returning to earth. A group of replicants has come back to force their creator to extend their lives: Replicants have a fixed and inalterable termination date. Ford reluctantly agrees to return to work to track down the group. When he goes to see the head of the corporation that creates the replicants, he meets a beautiful replicant, played by Sean Young, with whom he falls in love. His feelings for her inevitably complicate his mission. This brilliantly imaginative sci-fi film, directed by Ridley Scott [2039] and shot by Jordan Cronenweth [1545], was a flop when it first appeared. Critics found it puzzling and off-putting, and audiences, used to Ford as the heroic Indiana Jones and Han Solo, were not ready to accept him as a weary, troubled futuristic version of a film noir private eye. Since then, however, *Blade Runner*'s reputation has grown steadily, partly because its availability on video has allowed repeat viewings that help unsnarl some of its plot obscurities and enable one to relish not only its visual inventiveness but also some of the film's questioning of what it means to be human. After preview screenings, Scott made cuts in the film, added a voice-over narration by Ford to clarify situations, and provided an unconvincing happy ending. After the later success of the movie, however, Scott released a "director's cut" that is closer to the first version. The excellent cast includes Edward James Olmos [1904], Rutger Hauer, and Daryl Hannah. The screenplay is by Hampton Fancher and David Peoples [2179.5] and the score by Vangelis [386].

In addition to the nominated team, the design for the movie was conceived by conceptual artist Syd Mead, who took his inspiration for twenty-first-century Los Angeles from twentieth-century New York. It's an extraordinary achievement that anticipates the more celebrated but ultimately less convincing designs that won *Batman* an art direction Oscar seven years later. This time the Oscar went to the wholly conventional work of historical re-creation for *Gandhi.*

The visual effects of *Blade Runner* lost to those for *E.T. The Extra-Terrestrial.*

DeScenna: 423, 1653, 1913, 2127.5. Trumbull: 416, 1913. Yuricich: 416, 1913.

229 • BLAZE

TOUCHSTONE PICTURES PRODUCTION IN ASSOCIATION WITH SILVER SCREEN PARTNERS IV; BUENA VISTA. 1989.

NOMINATION *Cinematography:* Haskell Wexler.

Paul Newman [3 . . .] plays Louisiana Governor Earl Long, an uninhibited but lovable weirdo who fell hard for a Bourbon Street stripper, Blaze Starr, played by Lolita Davidovich. Writer-director Ron Shelton [310] provides a colorful set of characters but gives them no particular place to go and lets them take an awful long time going there. The real Earl Long, who was more like Walter Brennan than Paul Newman, must have bribed somebody good up in heaven to rate this kind of casting. Wexler lost to Freddie Francis for *Glory.*

Wexler: 264, 1288, 1481, 2277.

230 • BLAZING SADDLES

WARNER BROS. 1974.

NOMINATIONS *Supporting Actress:* Madeline Kahn. *Song:* "Blazing Saddles," music by John Morris, lyrics by Mel Brooks. *Film Editing:* John C. Howard and Danford Greene.

A western town needs a sheriff, but nobody is fool enough to take the job, so the townspeople press into service a black convict, played by Cleavon Little. With the aid of alcoholic gunfighter Gene Wilder [1626 . . .], he succeeds in thwarting the villains, who include Harvey Korman and Kahn, doing a parody of Marlene Dietrich [1358]. Some good lampooning of western clichés, but except for some smutty playground humor and the racial angle, it's all been done before in spoof westerns from *Ruggles of Red Gap* to *Cat Ballou.* Mostly a collection of a few inspired moments linked by long stretches of less inspired stuff, but it was a huge hit. Brooks directed and wrote, with help on the screenplay from Andrew Bergman, Richard Pryor, Norman Steinberg, and Alan Unger.

Kahn's second nomination in a row marked the peak of her Hollywood career, which also included, the same year as *Blazing Saddles,* a memorable role in Brooks' *Young Frankenstein.* As Brooks' stock went down, so did hers, so she devoted more time to stage work. The Oscar went to Ingrid Bergman for *Murder on the Orient Express.*

The presence of a throwaway parody of movie title songs among the nominees suggests that 1974 was not a great year for movie songs. The other nominees were from such films as *Benji, Gold,* and the flop Lerner and Loewe musical *The Little Prince.* The Oscar went to Al Kasha and Joel Hirschhorn for "We May Never Love Like This Again," from *The Towering In-*

ferno, which also won for Harold F. Kress and Carl Kress' editing.

Kahn: 1526. Morris: 608. Brooks: 1626, 2331. Greene: 1286.

231 • BLESS THE BEASTS AND CHILDREN

COLUMBIA. 1971.

NOMINATION *Song:* "Bless the Beasts and Children," music and lyrics by Barry DeVorzon and Perry Botkin, Jr.

Teenage summer campers try to save a herd of buffalo that have been scheduled for slaughtering. Produced and directed by the always earnest Stanley Kramer [330 . . .], this is about as obvious as its title and as interesting as it sounds. The title song, which lost to Isaac Hayes' "Theme from *Shaft,*" later became the theme music for the TV soap *The Young and the Restless.*

232 • BLITHE SPIRIT

J. ARTHUR RANK-NOËL COWARD-CINEGUILD; UNITED ARTISTS (UNITED KINGDOM). 1946.

AWARD *Special Effects:* Thomas Howard, visual.

Doing research for a book, novelist Rex Harrison [413 . . .] hires medium Margaret Rutherford [2204] to conduct a séance. To everyone's surprise, she conjures up the ghost of Harrison's ex-wife, Kay Hammond, who torments him and his second wife, Constance Cummings. The play, by Noël Coward [993], was a huge hit on both sides of the Atlantic, but as a movie it never quite shakes off the smell of the greasepaint. Howard's special effects, which don't seem very special today, were among the few attempts made to bring the play off the stage and onto the screen. In his memoirs Harrison blamed director David Lean [287 . . .] for the movie's staginess and lack of life. "I was doing my best, such as it is, when David said: 'I don't think that's very funny.' And he turned round to the cameraman, Ronnie Neame [289 . . .], and said: 'Did you think that was funny, Ronnie?' Ronnie said: 'Oh, no, I didn't think it was funny.' So what do you do next, if it isn't funny?"

Apparently no one ever found out, except Rutherford, who is hilarious.

Howard: 2108.

233 • BLOCKADE

WALTER WANGER; UNITED ARTISTS. 1938.

NOMINATIONS *Original Story:* John Howard Lawson. *Original Score:* Werner Janssen.

During the Spanish Civil War, Madeleine Carroll is forced to spy for one side while falling in love with Henry Fonda [815 . . .], who is on the other side. The film was widely criticized at the time for failing to make it clear which of the real sides in the war—Franco's or the Loyalists—any of the characters belonged to. This Hollywood attempt to deal with serious international concerns became a laughingstock instead. Viewed from a nonpolitical standpoint, it's a mildly entertaining romance. Directed by William Dieterle [1169].

Lawson was not successful, however, in steering away from political controversy. A founder of the Screen Writers Guild and its first president, he was also an avowed Marxist. In 1948 he was one of the Hollywood Ten, cited for their failure to cooperate with the House Un-American Activities Committee. He went into exile in Mexico but later returned to the States and taught at several universities before his death in 1977. The writing Oscar went to Eleanore Griffin and Dore Schary for *Boys Town.*

The scoring Oscar was won by Erich Wolfgang Korngold for *The Adventures of Robin Hood.*

Janssen: 349, 624, 757, 844, 1884.

234 • BLOCK-HEADS

HAL ROACH; MGM. 1938.

NOMINATION *Original Score:* Marvin Hatley.

When Stan Laurel is discovered guarding his old trench, twenty years after World War I ended, Oliver Hardy takes him home, where the usual slapstick mayhem ensues. One of the last first-rate Laurel and Hardy features, directed by John G. Blystone. Hatley's score lost to Erich Wolfgang Korngold's for *The Adventures of Robin Hood.*

Hatley: 2042, 2237.

235 • BLOOD AND SAND

20TH CENTURY-FOX. 1941.

AWARD *Color Cinematography:* Ernest Palmer and Ray Rennahan.

NOMINATION *Color Interior Decoration:* Richard Day and Joseph C. Wright, art direction; Thomas Little, set decoration.

Remake of the 1922 Rudolph Valentino melodrama, based on a novel by Vicente Blasco Ibañez about a bullfighter under the spell of two women, with Tyrone Power in the Valentino role, Rita Hayworth and Linda Darnell as the women, Nazimova as Power's mother, and Anthony Quinn [1226 . . .], J. Carrol Naish [1294 . . .], and John Carradine. Heavy-handed and dull, but great-looking. Director Rouben Mamoulian worked with the designers and cameramen in an attempt to capture the look of Spanish painting. Goya or Velazquez it isn't, but much of it is quite handsome. The art direction award went to *Blossoms in the Dust.*

Palmer: 298, 714, 1946. Rennahan: 241, 569, 581, 701, 798, 1120, 1210. Day: 22, 102, 487, 510, 560, 569, 797, 833, 864, 952, 1048, 1175, 1397, 1477, 1666, 1949, 2056, 2120, 2276. Wright: 428, 508, 569, 690, 746, 852, 1175, 1264, 1397, 1475, 2056. Little: 46, 83, 428, 495, 719, 721, 746, 950, 952, 1082, 1149, 1153, 1397, 1475, 1666, 1852, 1868, 2056, 2212, 2286.

236 • BLOOD ON THE LAND

TH. DAMASKINOS & V. MICHAELIDES, A.E.-FINOS FILM (GREECE). 1965.

NOMINATION *Foreign Language Film.*

Disputes over land at the turn of the century form the main plotline of this film by director Vassilis Georgiades. The Oscar went to *The Shop on Main Street.*

237 • BLOOD ON THE SUN

CAGNEY PRODUCTIONS; UNITED ARTISTS. 1945.

AWARD *Black-and-White Interior Decoration:* Wiard Ihnen, art direction; A. Roland Fields, set decoration.

James Cagney [79 . . .] is a newspaper editor in pre–World War II Japan who discovers a secret plan to dominate Asia. Eurasian Sylvia Sidney [1962], enlisted by the Japanese to thwart Cagney's efforts to expose them, turns out to be a counterspy. Thick with propaganda, the movie still manages to be fairly entertaining today. Cagney learned judo for the fight scenes, but he's no Bruce Lee. Ihnen picked up his second Oscar in a row for the film, which was produced by Cagney and his brother William [2318] for their independent production company. Frank Lloyd [374 . . .] directed, and the score is by Miklos Rozsa [175 . . .].

Ihnen: 627, 2286.

238 • BLOODBROTHERS

WARNER BROS. PRODUCTION; WARNER BROS. 1978.

NOMINATION *Screenplay Based on Material From Another Medium:* Walter Newman.

Sensitive young Richard Gere is at odds with the other men in his Italian-American family, particularly his father, Tony LoBianco, and uncle, Paul Sorvino, who expect him to become a hard hat like the rest of them. Lots of noisy and profane talk, but not much here to engage or entertain. Directed by Robert Mulligan. Newman's screenplay, based on a novel by Richard Price [422], lost to Oliver Stone's for *Midnight Express.*

Newman: 198, 371.

239 • BLOSSOMS IN THE DUST

MGM. 1941.

AWARD *Color Interior Decoration:* Cedric Gibbons and Urie McCleary, art direction; Edwin B. Willis, set decoration.

NOMINATIONS *Picture:* Irving Asher, producer. *Actress:* Greer Garson. *Color Cinematography:* Karl Freund and W. Howard Greene.

Garson plays Edna Gladney, founder of an orphanage in Fort Worth, Texas, in this rather icky biopic. Walter Pidgeon [1232 . . .], as usual, plays her husband. Mervyn LeRoy [1662 . . .] directed. The screenplay is by Anita Loos, but it's no *Gentlemen Prefer Blondes,* more's the pity. The best picture Oscar went to *How Green Was My Valley.*

Garson's second nomination solidified her position

as a box-office draw and as the successor at MGM to Norma Shearer [150 . . .] in rather noble, rather weepy roles. She lost to Joan Fontaine in *Suspicion*.

The cinematography award went to Ernest Palmer and Ray Rennahan for *Blood and Sand*.

Gibbons: 66, 87, 130, 217, 227, 285, 290, 440, 629, 749, 831, 980, 1069, 1096, 1173, 1190, 1226, 1230, 1232, 1274, 1308, 1309, 1417, 1567, 1604, 1644, 1662, 1673, 1721, 1861, 1937, 2068, 2112, 2256, 2257, 2300, 2320, 2330. McCleary: 1417, 1537, 1541, 1657, 2330. Willis: 66, 87, 130, 227, 290, 629, 749, 831, 980, 1069, 1096, 1157, 1173, 1190, 1226, 1230, 1232, 1309, 1417, 1567, 1657, 1662, 1673, 1721, 1861, 1937, 2068, 2112, 2257, 2320, 2330. Garson: 804, 1232, 1371, 1372, 1973, 2193. Freund: 397, 799. Greene: 96, 747, 1070, 1452, 1560, 1621, 1909, 2262.

240 • *BLOWUP*

CARLO PONTI PRODUCTION; PREMIER PRODUCTIONS (UNITED KINGDOM/ITALY). 1966.

NOMINATIONS *Director:* Michelangelo Antonioni. *Story and Screenplay—Written Directly for the Screen:* Michelangelo Antonioni, Tonino Guerra, and Edward Bond.

Photographer David Hemmings takes some pictures in a London park, but when he develops and enlarges them, he discovers that he has photographed what appears to be a murder. At the time, the movie seemed creepy, intense, and provocative. A quarter of a century or so later, it has lost its edge, in part because the narrative techniques—the jumpy cutting, the oblique dialogue, the seemingly unrelated incidents—have become old hat, but also because there really isn't enough going on in the movie. The nudity and casual sex caused the Production Code office to withhold its seal, whereupon MGM, which had obtained the distribution rights, released the film through a subsidiary that was not a partner to the Code agreement. Today the sexy parts have lost their power to shock, and the inconclusive ending just seems—well, inconclusive. But it's worth taking a look at for the performance of Vanessa Redgrave [263 . . .] in her first year in films, as well as that of

Sarah Miles [1737]. The fine color cinematography is by Carlo Di Palma.

Antonioni became an international film celebrity with the release of *L'Avventura* in 1960, another unsolved-mystery film that was the first in a trilogy that continued with *La Notte* (1961) and *L'Eclisse* (1962). In the early sixties Antonioni was thought by many to be a master on a par with Fellini [61 . . .], Bergman [111 . . .], and Kurosawa [1661], but his explorations of the tedium of existence don't hold up on repeated viewings. His nadir came with his first American film, *Zabriskie Point* (1970), an incoherent portrait of the rebellious youth culture. *The Passenger* (1975) starred the always watchable Jack Nicholson [395 . . .], but its commercial failure put an end to the vogue for Antonioni, whose later films, such as *The Oberwald Mystery* (1980) and *Identification of a Woman* (1982), received little attention, critical and otherwise, in the States. *Blowup* remains his most popular and accessible film, and it won awards at Cannes and from the National Society of Film Critics. Antonioni received an honorary award from the Academy at the 1994 awards ceremony. He lost the directing Oscar to Fred Zinnemann for *A Man for All Seasons,* and the writing award went to Claude Lelouch and Pierre Uytterhoeven for *A Man and a Woman*.

Guerra: 61, 367.

241 • *BLUE BIRD, THE*

20TH CENTURY-FOX. 1940.

NOMINATIONS *Color Cinematography:* Arthur Miller and Ray Rennahan. *Special Effects:* Fred Sersen, photographic; E. H. Hansen, sound.

Shirley Temple and Johnny Russell set out from their fairy-tale home to find the bluebird of happiness in this version of the story by Maurice Maeterlinck. Directed by Walter Lang, with Gale Sondergaard [83 . . .], Nigel Bruce, Jessie Ralph, and Spring Byington [2325]. Fox mounted this elaborate but leaden production as a vehicle for Temple, who at twelve was beginning to lose her appeal to audiences. It was a box-office failure, however, and hastened the end of her career as a child star. Some believed it to be inspired by MGM's *The Wizard of Oz,* but the productions were conceived almost simultaneously. *The Thief of Bagdad,* a much better film for children, won for Georges Périnal's cinematography and for special effects.

Miller: 83, 952, 1082, 1655, 1868, 2056. Rennahan: 235, 569, 581, 701, 798, 1120, 1210. Sersen: 226, 346, 458, 520, 1655, 2286, 2317. Hansen: 143, 815, 952, 990, 1655, 1868, 1957, 2027, 2056, 2272, 2286, 2317.

242 • BLUE DAHLIA, THE
PARAMOUNT. 1946.
NOMINATION *Original Screenplay:* Raymond Chandler.

Ex-serviceman Alan Ladd and his shell-shocked friend William Bendix [2222] are the chief suspects in the murder of Ladd's faithless wife in this film noir thriller. Like most of Chandler's work, it's full of intrigue and double-crossing and almost impossible to unravel. To keep the audience interested, this sort of thing needs performers like Humphrey Bogart [24 . . .] and Lauren Bacall and directors like Howard Hawks [1779], who gave us the classic but unnominated *The Big Sleep,* based on a Chandler novel, the same year. Here we get Ladd and Veronica Lake and director George Marshall, who just don't cut it. Chandler's screenplay was unfinished when filming started, and its ending still remains something of a muddle. He lost to Muriel and Sydney Box for *The Seventh Veil.*

Chandler: 566.

243 • BLUE LAGOON, THE
COLUMBIA PICTURES PRODUCTION; COLUMBIA. 1980.
NOMINATION *Cinematography:* Nestor Almendros.

Fifteen-year-old Brooke Shields and nineteen-year-old Christopher Atkins are shipwrecked on a desert island. Idiotic romantic adventure, one step from kiddie porn, that was clearly made for an audience the movie's R rating was designed to exclude. Directed by Randal Kleiser. Almendros has beautiful scenery and beautiful people to work with—how hard could it have been? The Academy should have nominated his work on *The Last Metro* or Freddie Francis' for *The Elephant Man* instead. The Oscar went to Geoffrey Unsworth and Ghislain Cloquet for *Tess.*

Almendros: 506, 1111, 1876.

244 • BLUE SKIES
PARAMOUNT. 1946.
NOMINATIONS *Song:* "You Keep Coming Back Like a Song," music and lyrics by Irving Berlin. *Scoring of a Musical Picture:* Robert Emmett Dolan.

Bing Crosby [173 . . .] and Fred Astaire [2126] play entertainers who are rivals for the affections of Joan Caulfield. Crosby marries her, but they squabble and divorce. She becomes engaged to Astaire but breaks it off when she realizes she's still in love with Crosby. Astaire takes to drink and is injured in a fall while performing, ending his dancing career. At the end, Caulfield and Crosby are reconciled with Astaire's blessing. This rather unpleasant plot recalls the Astaire-Crosby teaming in *Holiday Inn,* in which they were also romantic rivals and which also had a song score by Berlin. The Astaire part was originally set for dancer Paul Draper, who was fired after Crosby objected to Draper's stuttering. The film was a big hit, but the tiresome story and mostly uninspired production numbers—of which Crosby has the lion's share—make it slow going. The highlight is Astaire's "Puttin' on the Ritz" number. Astaire had announced that he would retire from performing after the completion of the film; his retirement lasted two years. Director Stuart Heisler took over the production after the original director, Mark Sandrich, died.

Berlin's song lost to Harry Warren and Johnny Mercer's "On the Atchison, Topeka and Santa Fe," from *The Harvey Girls.* The scoring Oscar went to Morris Stoloff for *The Jolson Story.*

Berlin: 34, 358, 929, 1773, 2115, 2268. Dolan: 173, 213, 929, 994, 1120, 1704, 1912.

244.5 • BLUE SKY
ROBERT H. SOLO PRODUCTION; ORION. 1994.
AWARD *Actress:* Jessica Lange.

Tommy Lee Jones [734.5 . . .] plays a career military officer and nuclear scientist who is devoted to his unstable and promiscuous wife, played by Lange.

His commanding officer (Powers Boothe), who has designs on Lange, sends Jones to supervise nuclear tests in Nevada. (The film is set in the early sixties.) The plot—from a story by Rama Laurie Stagner, who wrote the screenplay with Arlene Sarner and Jerry Leichtling—thickens when Jones uncovers evidence that radioactivity from the tests has contaminated civilians. The blend of domestic and political melodrama isn't always a stable one, but the film is greatly helped by a strong cast, which also includes Carrie Snodgress [541], Chris O'Donnell, and Amy Locane. Jones is particularly good in a role that for once calls on him to underplay. It was the last movie directed by Tony Richardson [2106], who completed it in 1991, the year of his death. The film was held up in release by the bankruptcy of its studio, Orion, and despite generally favorable reviews—particularly for Lange and Jones—it was a box-office failure.

Lange won the Golden Globe award for dramatic performance shortly before the Oscar nominations were announced, making her a leading contender for the Academy Award. She became only the second woman to receive an Oscar for a leading role after a prior win for a supporting performance. The first was Meryl Streep, who won for *Sophie's Choice* after an earlier win for *Kramer vs. Kramer.*

Lange: 449, 722, 1381, 1987, 2113.

245 • BLUE THUNDER

Rastar Features Production; Columbia. 1983.
Nomination *Film Editing:* Frank Morriss and Edward Abroms.

Police helicopter pilot Roy Scheider [49 . . .] discovers that the fancy high-tech supercopter he's being trained to fly has actually been designed with nefarious sociopolitical purposes in mind. Malcolm McDowell is the villain. Noisy, mindless thriller, directed by John Badham, that exploits all sorts of angles—post-Vietnam stress, racial antagonisms, corporate greed—to no very good end. The Oscar went to the editing team for *The Right Stuff.*

Morriss: 1720.

246 • BLUE VEIL, THE

Wald-Krasna Productions Inc.; RKO Radio. 1951.
Nominations *Actress:* Jane Wyman. *Supporting Actress:* Joan Blondell.

Nursemaid Wyman sacrifices herself for the families she serves. Very soppy stuff, but fun to watch because of its cast: Charles Laughton [1387 . . .], Agnes Moorehead [963 . . .], Cyril Cusack, Natalie Wood [1219 . . .], and Vivian Vance. Directed by Curtis Bernhardt.

With her third nomination—the first after her Oscar for *Johnny Belinda*—Wyman entered the tearjerker phase of her career, which would continue through such movies as *Magnificent Obsession* and *All That Heaven Allows* (1956). The Oscar went to Vivien Leigh for *A Streetcar Named Desire.*

Blondell's sole nomination honors a performer who was brought up in vaudeville by a performing family, won a beauty contest in Dallas, appeared in the *Ziegfeld Follies* on Broadway, and came to Hollywood at the beginning of the sound era to play brassy sidekicks in Warners musicals, where perhaps her most memorable moment was singing ''Remember My Forgotten Man'' in *Gold Diggers of 1933.* A superb character actress, she spent much of the decade after her nomination—which she lost to Kim Hunter in *A Streetcar Named Desire*—on the Broadway stage, but she appeared in movies, including *Grease,* almost till her death in 1979.

Wyman: 1052, 1241, 2320.

247 • BLUE VELVET

Blue Velvet S.A. Production; Dino de Laurentiis Entertainment Group. 1986.
Nomination *Director:* David Lynch.

Kyle McLachlan discovers a severed ear in a field, and with the encouragement of teenager Laura Dern [1659] sets out to find out whom it belongs to. The trail leads him into the company of sadomasochists Isabella Rossellini, Dennis Hopper [595 . . .], and Dean Stockwell [1281], among others. Lynch's bizarre film about the nightmares that lie just below the surface in an all-American small town was an unexpected hit, both critically and commercially. Woody

Allen said it was better than the film for which he was nominated, *Hannah and Her Sisters,* and the National Society of Film Critics gave it, Lynch, Hopper, and cinematographer Frederick Elmes their top awards. It's not quite the masterpiece that many thought it was, but it certainly gets under your skin.

Since the success of *Blue Velvet,* Lynch has tried to tug the mainstream in his direction with the eccentric TV series *Twin Peaks* and the off-kilter *Wild at Heart.* But ironically he's beginning to lose the ability to shock as his work receives more exposure. Lynch is one of several directors in recent years who have been cited by the Academy with a nomination for best director though their films received no other nominations. Among the other directors are Martin Scorsese for *The Last Temptation of Christ,* Federico Fellini for *Fellini Satyricon,* and Arthur Penn for *Alice's Restaurant* —all filmmakers who made commercially successful movies before turning their hands to controversial or experimental ones. The Academy occasionally likes to admire risks but seldom rewards risk-takers. The directing Oscar this time went to Oliver Stone for *Platoon,* a film on which Stone took a risk—movies about Vietnam were thought to be box-office poison—but also a far more conventional film than Lynch's.

Lynch: 608.

248 • BLUES IN THE NIGHT

WARNER BROS. 1941.
NOMINATION *Song:* "Blues in the Night," music by Harold Arlen, lyrics by Johnny Mercer.

Melodrama about a traveling band and the various personal and romantic entanglements of its members. Aside from the music, it's routine stuff, with a fairly undistinguished cast—Priscilla Lane, Richard Whorf, Betty Field, Lloyd Nolan—though among the band members is a young Elia Kazan [63 . . .]. Directed by Anatole Litvak [517 . . .] from a screenplay by Robert Rossen [53 . . .].

The Arlen-Mercer song was so popular even before the film's release that the title of the movie was changed—it was originally called *Hot Nocturne.* The song's loss in the Oscar race is something of a surprise, though the winning song was a distinguished

competitor: Jerome Kern and Oscar Hammerstein's "The Last Time I Saw Paris," from *Lady Be Good.*

Arlen: 322, 368, 903, 1838, 1910, 1912, 2186, 2300. Mercer: 278, 384, 476, 494, 508, 636, 788, 825, 877, 903, 905, 1109, 1772, 1838, 1912, 2327, 2328.

249 • BOAT IS FULL, THE

LIMBO FILM A.G. PRODUCTION (SWITZERLAND). 1981.
NOMINATION *Foreign Language Film.*

A group of Jews escape from the Nazis into Switzerland but are sent back by the Swiss villagers. Markus Imhoof's film explores the motives, attitudes, and prejudices of the villagers. The Oscar went to a very different kind of film about the Nazi era, *Mephisto.*

250 • BOB & CAROL & TED & ALICE

FRANKOVICH PRODUCTIONS; COLUMBIA. 1969.
NOMINATIONS *Supporting Actor:* Elliott Gould. *Supporting Actress:* Dyan Cannon. *Story and Screenplay—Based on Material Not Previously Published or Produced:* Paul Mazursky and Larry Tucker. *Cinematography:* Charles B. Lang.

Two married couples—Gould and Cannon, Robert Culp and Natalie Wood [1219 . . .]—very nearly get drawn into a spouse-swapping episode. This satire on sixties mores plays with the audience's prurience in ways that outraged many of the obtuser critics of the time, but it's really more sweet-natured than sniggery. It's dated, in that the attitudes and motives of the characters are very much those of the era in which the movie was made, but when viewed as a period piece—as you would watch, say, a thirties gangster movie or a wartime romance or a fifties rebellious-youth melodrama—it's still quite enjoyable.

Few actors have risen and fallen so fast in Hollywood as Gould, who began his acting career in New York as a child, working as a model and occasionally on TV. He landed a lead in a musical, *I Can Get It for You Wholesale,* in the cast of which he met Barbra Streisand [737 . . .], whom he married. As her career rose, his stagnated. But just as their marriage broke up, he landed the role of Ted, which earned him an Oscar nomination (he lost to Gig Young for *They Shoot Horses, Don't They?*) and led to his most famous role, in *MASH*. In 1971 he became the first American to perform in an Ingmar Bergman [111 . . .] film, *The Touch*. But from there it was mostly downhill, his hip urban persona and good comic timing insufficient to keep him a top star. He continues to do character roles in films such as *Bugsy*.

When Cannon was cast in *Bob & Carol*, she was more famous as the ex-wife of Cary Grant [1445 . . .] than as an actress, though she had been a stage, TV, and film performer in small roles. A gifted and likable comedian, she also wrote, produced, and directed a short film, *Number One*, that was nominated for an Oscar in the live-action short film category in 1976. She lost the supporting actress Oscar to Goldie Hawn in *Cactus Flower*.

Mazursky had begun as an actor, including a sizable supporting part in *Blackboard Jungle*, but turned his attention to writing for TV, where he teamed with Tucker. Together, they wrote the screenplay for *I Love You, Alice B. Toklas* (1968), and for the first films Mazursky also directed, *Bob & Carol* and *Alex in Wonderland* (1970). Mazursky has worked steadily as writer and director ever since—often with distinction, as on such films as *An Unmarried Woman* and *Enemies, a Love Story*. The writing Oscar went to William Goldman for *Butch Cassidy and the Sundance Kid*, for which Conrad Hall also won the cinematography award.

Cannon: 890. Mazursky: 617, 875, 2182. Lang: 97, 319, 636, 649, 705, 765, 953, 1480, 1640, 1699, 1738, 1778, 1855, 1860, 1955, 1968, 2180.

251 • BODY AND SOUL

ENTERPRISE PRODUCTIONS; UNITED ARTISTS. 1947.
AWARD *Film Editing:* Francis Lyon and Robert Parrish.
NOMINATIONS *Actor:* John Garfield. *Original Screenplay:* Abraham Polonsky.

Garfield plays an ambitious young boxer who'll do anything to get to the top. Powerful melodrama, well directed by Robert Rossen [53 . . .], with a cast that includes Lilli Palmer, Anne Revere [759 . . .],

and Canada Lee. James Wong Howe [1 . . .] wore roller skates and used a handheld camera—a rarity in those days—to capture some of the fight action.

Both Lyon and Parrish had subsequent careers as directors. Lyon's films were mostly routine B-grade action movies, and TV episodes. Parrish started in films as a child actor and appeared in *All Quiet on the Western Front* and several films of John Ford [815 . . .], with whom he got a start as an editor. He turned to directing in 1951, but for the most part his directorial work was undistinguished.

Garfield's commitment to *Body and Soul* was total. After leaving Warners, he had formed his own production company and financed this film himself. He suffered a heart attack and a severe concussion filming the strenuous boxing scenes. Like many of the people who worked on the film—Rossen, Revere, Lee, and Polonsky among them—he came under attack from the House Un-American Activities Committee. Threatened with blacklisting for refusing to testify about the putative communist activities of his friends, he suffered a fatal heart attack in 1952. The Oscar went to Ronald Colman for *A Double Life*.

After *Body and Soul*, Polonsky was encouraged by Garfield to try directing. The resulting film, *Force of Evil* (1948), which starred Garfield, was a taut film noir that has been hailed by many as a classic, though it was a commercial and critical flop at the time. Polonsky was set to direct another feature for 20th Century-Fox, but before he was able to do so he was summoned before HUAC and, refusing to testify, was blacklisted. He continued to write under pseudonyms but did not direct again until 1970's *Tell Them Willie Boy Is Here*. Polonsky's fellow nominees included Ruth Gordon and Garson Kanin for *A Double Life*, Charles Chaplin for *Monsieur Verdoux*, and the writers of the Italian neorealist classic *Shoeshine*, but the writing Oscar went to Sidney Sheldon's *The Bachelor and the Bobby-Soxer*. What *could* the Academy have been thinking?

Parrish: 53. Garfield: 712.

251.5 • BODYGUARD, THE

WARNER BROS. PRODUCTION; WARNER BROS. 1992.
NOMINATIONS *Song:* "I Have Nothing," music by David Foster, lyrics by Linda Thompson. *Song:* "Run to You," music by Jud Friedman, lyrics by Allan Rich.

Former Secret Service agent Kevin Costner [482] takes a job protecting singer-actress Whitney Houston after she receives death threats. Naturally they fall in love, and naturally there's a big shoot-out—this one at the Academy Awards ceremony at which Houston receives the best actress Oscar. Though it's hardly Oscar caliber, Houston's performance in her film debut isn't bad, but there's no chemistry between her and Costner. The script had been around for some twenty years: Lawrence Kasdan [6 . . .] originally wrote it with Steve McQueen [1753] in mind. Costner even adopts a McQueenish burr-cut hairstyle, but his laid-back boyish manner is all wrong for the role—it needs McQueen's bulldog, streetwise toughness. The movie lacks originality, or the wit to conceal its lack of originality, and Mick Jackson's plodding direction doesn't help. It was a hit despite critical scorn, and the soundtrack album was a best-seller. Neither nominated song was particularly responsible for the album's success; its biggest hit was "I Will Always Love You," written much earlier by Dolly Parton [1438] and therefore ineligible for Oscar contention. The award went to Alan Menken and Tim Rice's "A Whole New World," from *Aladdin.*

Foster: 1078.

252 • BOLD AND THE BRAVE, THE

FILMAKERS RELEASING ORGANIZATION; RKO RADIO. 1956.
NOMINATIONS *Supporting Actor:* Mickey Rooney. *Screenplay—Original:* Robert Lewin.

Rooney, Wendell Corey, and Don Taylor are soldiers fighting in Italy during World War II. Fairly routine and modestly budgeted war film, directed by Lewis R. Foster. Rooney lost to Anthony Quinn in *Lust for Life.* The writing award went to Albert Lamorisse for the short, wordless film *The Red Balloon.*

Rooney: 115, 225, 957.

252.5 • BOLSHOI BALLET, THE

RANK ORGANIZATION PRESENTATION-HARMONY FILM; RANK FILM DISTRIBUTORS OF AMERICA INC. (UNITED KINGDOM). 1958.
NOMINATION *Scoring of a Musical Picture:* Yuri Faier and Gennady Rozhdestvensky.

A handsomely filmed—by F. B. Onions—documentary of the great Soviet ballet company, featuring Galina Ulanova. It includes excerpts from six ballets: *Giselle, Dance of the Tartars, Swan Lake, Spring Water, Polonaise and Gracovienne,* and *The Dying Swan.* Directed by Paul Czinner. The scoring Oscar went to André Previn for *Gigi.*

253 • BOMBARDIER

RKO RADIO. 1943.
NOMINATION *Special Effects:* Vernon L. Walker, photographic; James G. Stewart and Roy Granville, sound.

Bomber cadets learn about war in missions over Japan. Pretty good contribution to the war effort, with Pat O'Brien, Randolph Scott, Anne Shirley [1923], Eddie Albert [887 . . .], and Robert Ryan [467], directed by Richard Wallace. Most of the year's nominees for special effects were for films of this genre, simulating combat situations with what seem today fairly obvious miniatures, process screens, and matte effects. The Oscar was won by *Crash Dive.*

Walker: 505, 1421, 1991. Stewart: 505, 1421, 1595. Granville: 505.

254 • BON VOYAGE!

DISNEY; BUENA VISTA. 1962.
NOMINATIONS *Sound:* Robert O. Cook, sound director, Walt Disney Studio Sound Department. *Color Costume Design:* Bill Thomas.

Disney's favorite dad, Fred MacMurray, takes his family—spouse Jane Wyman [246 . . .] and kids Deborah Walley, Tommy Kirk, and Kevin Corcoran—to Europe. Predictably silly stuff, though a scene of MacMurray being propositioned by a *poule* comes as something of a jolt in the middle of a Disney film. Directed by James Neilson. The sound award went to *Lawrence of Arabia* and the costume Oscar to Mary Wills for *The Wonderful World of the Brothers Grimm.*

Cook: 1284, 1529. Thomas: 116, 166, 866, 883, 1003, 1789, 1812, 1886, 2128.

255 • BONNIE AND CLYDE

TATIRA-HILLER PRODUCTIONS; WARNER BROS.-SEVEN ARTS. 1967.
AWARDS *Supporting Actress:* Estelle Parsons. *Cinematography:* Burnett Guffey.
NOMINATIONS *Picture:* Warren Beatty, producer. *Actor:* Warren Beatty. *Actress:* Faye Dunaway. *Supporting Actor:* Gene Hackman. *Supporting Actor:* Michael J. Pollard. *Director:* Arthur Penn. *Story and Screenplay—Written Directly for the Screen:* David Newman and Robert Benton. *Costume Design:* Theadora Van Runkle.

Drifter Clyde Barrow (Beatty) links up with bored young Bonnie Parker (Dunaway) and the two set out on a bank-robbing spree, joined by Clyde's brother, Buck (Hackman); Buck's wife, Blanche (Parsons); and young C. W. Moss (Pollard). Eventually their life of crime turns from larky into violent, and they are betrayed by C.W.'s father, Dub Taylor, to their Texas Ranger nemesis, Denver Pyle. Enormously popular, enormously influential film that took a lot of contemporary critics off guard. (It may have hastened the retirement of *New York Times* critic Bosley Crowther, who bitterly denounced the movie and was astonished at the vehemence with which readers reacted against his review.) It's hard to recapture the impact that films like *Bonnie and Clyde, The Graduate,* and *Easy Rider* had on young audiences in the sixties. Today *Bonnie and Clyde*'s violence looks rather tame and stylized, and Beatty and Dunaway seem too chic and knowing for the backwoods bandits they're portraying. Curiously omitted in the nominations was editor Dede Allen [561 . . .], whose cutting of the slow-motion shoot-out at the film's end is a textbook classic. Special effects expert Danny Lee [166 . . .] is largely responsible for the realism of the bullets that riddle Bonnie, Clyde, and their car.

Parsons had begun her career in TV, working as a writer and producer on the *Today* show and appearing both off and on Broadway. She has continued to perform in a variety of character roles on both screen and stage, and is most familiar today as Roseanne's mother on the TV sitcom *Roseanne*.

Guffey was a veteran with forty-five years in the business when he received his second Oscar. He died in 1983.

Beatty, the driving force behind *Bonnie and Clyde,* was a modestly successful leading man whose career had been decidedly less impressive than that of his sister, Shirley MacLaine [91 . . .]. The Newman-Benton screenplay originally attracted the attention of Leslie Caron [1113 . . .], Beatty's lover, who wanted to play the part of Bonnie. Beatty bought the script but realized that Caron could hardly play a young Texan, and considered Sue Lyon, Jane Fonda [394 . . .], and Tuesday Weld [1205] for the part before settling on Dunaway. He also approached François Truffaut [501 . . .] and Jean-Luc Godard about directing before hiring Penn, with whom he had worked on the film *Mickey One* in 1965. Though *Bonnie and Clyde* launched Beatty as a major Hollywood player, he lost the best picture Oscar to *In the Heat of the Night,* whose star, Rod Steiger, took the acting award.

Dunaway had worked as a model and been a member of the Lincoln Center Repertory Company before starting in films. Bonnie Parker was her breakthrough role. The Oscar went to Katharine Hepburn for *Guess Who's Coming to Dinner.*

Hackman's career was also launched by the film, and he has since become one of Hollywood's most celebrated and durable actors. He had dropped out of school at sixteen to join the marines and worked odd jobs before entering TV production and finally breaking into acting. His pre–*Bonnie and Clyde* film career was undistinguished, but his work on the 1964 film *Lilith,* in which Beatty starred, formed a connection that would land him his breakthrough role.

Pollard, an eccentric character actor, has also built a durable career, although never with the acclaim he received for this film. The supporting actor Oscar went to George Kennedy for *Cool Hand Luke.*

Penn's second nomination comes for strikingly different work from his first, which was essentially a restaging for the screen of a play he had directed on

Broadway, *The Miracle Worker*. The failure of *Mickey One*, a film he also produced, was a setback to his career, as was the very troubled shoot of *The Chase* in 1966, on which Penn was at odds with star Marlon Brando [583 . . .], producer Sam Spiegel [287 . . .], and writer Lillian Hellman [1182 . . .]. Beatty rescued Penn's career, which has, however, never regained the peak it reached with *Bonnie and Clyde*. The directing Oscar went to Mike Nichols for *The Graduate*.

Benton and Newman had met on the staff of *Esquire* magazine, for which Newman was an editor and Benton art director. The screenplay for *Bonnie and Clyde* was their first. It drew in large part from Benton's Texas background. They continued to collaborate for several years, but eventually Benton's career, as he moved into directing as well as writing, took off on its own. The Oscar went to William Rose for *Guess Who's Coming to Dinner*.

Van Runkle, a former fashion illustrator, made her first major mark with the fashions for *Bonnie and Clyde,* which evoke a period without actually reproducing it, and were quite influential, such as the widely copied beret worn by Dunaway. The Oscar went to John Truscott for *Camelot*.

Parsons: 1645. Guffey: 210, 732, 870, 1093. Beatty: 308, 890, 1678, 1798. Dunaway: 395, 1424. Hackman: 724, 971, 1333, 2179.5. Penn: 43, 1326. Benton: 1111, 1146, 1444.5, 1580. Van Runkle: 785, 1545.

256 • *BOOM TOWN*

MGM. 1940.
NOMINATIONS *Black-and-White Cinematography:* Harold Rosson. *Special Effects:* A. Arnold Gillespie, photographic; Douglas Shearer, sound.

Clark Gable [798 . . .] plays Big John, and Spencer Tracy [131 . . .] is Square John, oil drillers in search of the big score. Nice, brawling nonsense, directed by Jack Conway, with a fun cast: Claudette Colbert [1025 . . .], Hedy Lamarr, Frank Morgan [22 . . .], Chill Wills [33], and others, including Joe Yule, the father of Mickey Rooney [115 . . .]. The Oscars went to George Barnes for the cinematography for *Rebecca* and to Lawrence Butler and Jack Whitney for *The Thief of Bagdad*'s special effects.

Rosson: 105, 133, 747, 2055, 2300. Gillespie: 175, 685, 704, 835, 1371, 1388, 1905, 2048, 2055, 2122, 2300. Shearer: 136, 202, 397, 685, 817, 835, 1096, 1232, 1292, 1371, 1419, 1751, 1950, 1988, 2048, 2055, 2211, 2300.

257 • *BOOMERANG!*

20TH CENTURY-FOX. 1947.
NOMINATION *Screenplay:* Richard Murphy.

District Attorney Dana Andrews realizes that the man he's supposed to prosecute for murder is innocent and winds up gathering evidence to exonerate him. Well-done documentary-style "message drama" with a fine cast: Jane Wyatt, Lee J. Cobb [301 . . .], Arthur Kennedy [291 . . .], Cara Williams [522], Ed Begley [1985], and Karl Malden [1477 . . .] among others. One of the first films directed by Elia Kazan [63 . . .]. Murphy's screenplay is based on a magazine article about an incident that took place in Bridgeport, Connecticut. The film was made on location in Stamford, Connecticut. The Oscar went to George Seaton for *Miracle on 34th Street*.

Murphy: 526.

258 • *BOOT, DAS*

BAVARIA ATELIER GMBH PRODUCTION; COLUMBIA/PSO (FEDERAL REPUBLIC OF GERMANY). 1982.
NOMINATIONS *Director:* Wolfgang Petersen. *Screenplay Based on Material From Another Medium:* Wolfgang Petersen. *Cinematography:* Jost Vacano. *Sound:* Milan Bor, Trevor Pyke, and Mike Le-Mare. *Film Editing:* Hannes Nikel. *Sound Effects Editing:* Mike Le-Mare.

Jürgen Prochnow plays the captain of a German submarine in World War II whose crew undergoes the terrors of undersea combat. This surprise international hit owes much to its fine camera work and to its evocation of the claustrophobic life aboard the boat. Originally a six-hour miniseries for TV, it was edited down to 145 minutes. It received more Oscar nominations than any other foreign language film in history—a record that was tied the following year by *Fanny & Alexander*.

Petersen has since moved into English-language films, such as *The Neverending Story* (1984) and *Enemy Mine* (1985), and scored his biggest hit since *Das Boot* in 1993 with *In the Line of Fire*. The directing Oscar went to Richard Attenborough for *Gandhi,* the writing award to Costa-Gavras and Donald Stewart for *Missing.*

Gandhi won for the cinematography of Billy Williams and Ronnie Taylor and for John Bloom's editing. The awards for sound and for sound effects editing were won by *E.T. The Extra-Terrestrial.*

259 • BORN FREE

OPEN ROAD FILMS LTD.-ATLAS FILMS LTD. PRODUCTION; CO-LUMBIA (UNITED KINGDOM). 1966.

AWARDS *Song:* "Born Free," music by John Barry, lyrics by Don Black. *Original Music Score:* John Barry.

George Adamson (Bill Travers), a game warden in Kenya, and his wife, Joy (Virginia McKenna), raise three orphaned lion cubs—one of which, Elsa, becomes a particular favorite. When Elsa grows too old to be a pet, Joy must teach the lioness how to survive in the wild. This very popular family film, directed by James Hill, now seems naive: The portrayal of wild animals as overgrown house pets sugarcoats the problems of disappearing species. The real story had a violent end: Some years after the film was released, Joy Adamson died mysteriously. First reports were that she had been killed by a lion, but others have suggested that she may have been murdered. *Born Free* should be compared with the story of Dian Fossey presented in *Gorillas in the Mist,* a film that takes a less sentimental look at wildlife and its defenders—and is definitely not "family entertainment."

Barry's first nomination earned him an Oscar and established him as one of the leading film composers. Up to this point, he was known chiefly as the composer for the James Bond films, whose hip, jazzy sound is quite different from the stirring, sweeping melodies that have characterized much of his later work. Black's lyrics are unmemorable—it's clearly Barry's melody that caught the Oscar voters' fancy—and the song has had little life outside of the context of the film.

Barry: 382.5, 482, 1177, 1285, 1512. Black: 174, 789, 1574, 2147.

260 • BORN ON THE FOURTH OF JULY

A. KITMAN HO & IXTLAN PRODUCTION; UNIVERSAL. 1989.

AWARDS *Director:* Oliver Stone. *Film Editing:* David Brenner and Joe Hutshing.

NOMINATIONS *Picture:* A. Kitman Ho and Oliver Stone, producers. *Actor:* Tom Cruise. *Screenplay Based on Material From Another Medium:* Oliver Stone and Ron Kovic. *Cinematography:* Robert Richardson. *Sound:* Michael Minkler, Gregory H. Watkins, Wylie Stateman, and Tod A. Maitland. *Original Score:* John Williams.

Naive teenager Ron Kovic (Cruise) joins the marines and is shipped to Vietnam, where he is wounded. When he discovers that he is paralyzed and will be confined to a wheelchair for the rest of his life, he enters a wildly self-destructive period but finally becomes a leading antiwar activist. Powerful filmmaking, but sometimes sheer power isn't enough. Stone grabs on to this story, from Kovic's autobiography, and almost shakes the life out of it with his relentless exploration—and exploitation—of Kovic's pain. He deprives us of the more thoughtful side of the character, which would have helped explain Kovic's transformation into activist and author—we're apparently expected to take it for granted. That said, the film is splendidly cast, with particularly fine performances by Raymond J. Barry and Caroline Kava as Kovic's parents, Lili Taylor as the young wife of a soldier whose death Kovic causes, and Willem Dafoe [1584] as a fellow paraplegic. Dafoe had a lead role in Stone's *Platoon,* and his costar in that film, Tom Berenger, has a cameo as a marine recruiting sergeant. Abbie Hoffman plays a sixties antiwar activist, Stone himself appears as a reporter, and Kovic is in one of the parade sequences. Stone has said that the film is the second in a trilogy about Vietnam that began with *Platoon* and concluded with *Heaven and Earth* (1993). Like many of Stone's recent films—including *JFK* and *The Doors* (1991)—it is an exploration of the culture of the sixties.

Born was designed to be an "event" film, with its casting of box-office superstar Cruise, its substantial budget, and Stone's personal publicity crusade. But its heavy-handedness became more obvious in the company of such lower-key nominees as the prep-school drama *Dead Poets Society,* the baseball fantasy *Field of Dreams,* the small-scale biopic *My Left Foot,* and the best picture winner, the gentle *Driving Miss Daisy,* all of which use subtler means to make their points. Stone's award is a tribute to his tenacity: Kovic's story had been kicking around Hollywood for years before Stone, boosted by the strength of *Platoon,* finally got it made. His path to the directing Oscar was also smoothed by one of the Academy's more remarkable oversights: Bruce Beresford, the director of *Driving Miss Daisy,* had not been nominated.

Cruise was a strong contender for the acting award, which was seen by many as a three-way race: Cruise, Morgan Freeman for *Driving Miss Daisy,* and Daniel Day-Lewis, who won, for *My Left Foot.* (Neither Kenneth Branagh of *Henry V* nor Robin Williams of *Dead Poets Society* was given much chance.) Cruise made his first big splash in Hollywood in 1983 with *Risky Business,* and he parlayed his cocky grin into the big time with *Top Gun* three years later. Determined to prove himself as an actor, he took secondary parts to Paul Newman in *The Color of Money* and Dustin Hoffman in *Rain Man,* providing support to actors who won Oscars for their roles. Cruise's performance in *Rain Man* is subtler and more convincing than his work in *Born,* where Stone's sledgehammer approach sometimes overwhelms his performers.

The Stone-Kovic screenplay attracted some controversy by its departures from the facts. Many found it odd that Kovic would be a partner to rewriting his own life, especially since he had expressed political ambitions, considering a run for Congress. The Oscar went to Alfred Uhry for *Driving Miss Daisy.*

Richardson, who has been closely associated with Stone, lost to Freddie Francis for *Glory,* which also won the Oscar for sound. The scoring award went to Alan Menken for *The Little Mermaid.*

Stone: 1047, 1313, 1584, 1746. Hutshing: 1047. Ho: 1047. Richardson: 1047, 1584. Minkler: 58, 398, 413.5, 606, 1047, 2144. Watkins: 482. Stateman: 413.5. Maitland: 1047. Williams: 6, 403, 416, 588, 613, 614, 659, 805, 933, 937, 982, 996, 997, 1041, 1047, 1596, 1652, 1679, 1684, 1701, 1764.65, 1916, 1977, 2107, 2126, 2194, 2293, 2322.

261 • BORN TO DANCE
MGM. 1936.
NOMINATIONS *Song:* "I've Got You Under My Skin," music and lyrics by Cole Porter. *Dance Direction:* Dave Gould.

A Broadway musical comedy performer, Eleanor Powell, falls for a sailor, James Stewart [73 . . .]—beyond that, the plot isn't really worth telling. MGM hadn't really got the hang of musicals yet; why else would they have cast Stewart and had him sing (or whatever you call what he's doing) "Easy to Love"? The supporting cast includes Virginia Bruce, Una Merkel [1959], and Sid Silvers. At least it has Frances Langford, who could sing, and Buddy Ebsen and Powell, who could dance. And it has two great Porter songs (plus a bunch of deservedly forgotten ones; anyone remember "Love Me, Love My Pekinese" or "I'm Nuts About You"?). Directed by Roy Del Ruth.

Born to Dance was Porter's first Hollywood score, although adaptations of some of his Broadway shows, notably *The Gay Divorce,* which became *The Gay Divorcée,* had been filmed before. His style was probably too sophisticated for the movies, and certainly his lyrics—which were often bowdlerized in the move from stage to screen—were too risqué. He never won an Oscar, but this time he lost it honorably—to Jerome Kern and Dorothy Fields for "The Way You Look Tonight," from *Swing Time.*

Gould was nominated for the "Swingin' the Jinx Away" number—the film's big finale, which has Powell tapping away on a battleship. The Oscar went to Seymour Felix for the way-over-the-top extravaganza "A Pretty Girl Is Like a Melody," from *The Great Ziegfeld.*

Porter: 914, 1862, 2329. Gould: 297, 500, 695.

262 • BORN YESTERDAY

COLUMBIA. 1950.

AWARD *Actress:* Judy Holliday.

NOMINATIONS *Picture:* S. Sylvan Simon, producer. *Director:* George Cukor. *Screenplay:* Albert Mannheimer. *Black-and-White Costume Design:* Jean Louis.

Holliday plays Billie Dawn, the mistress of a millionaire junk dealer, Broderick Crawford [53]. Trying to become a player in Washington, Crawford hires journalist William Holden [1424 . . .] to give Holliday a smattering of culture to help her get by socially as he entertains VIPs. Naturally Holden and Holliday fall in love, and Crawford gets his comeuppance—*Pygmalion* meets *Mr. Smith Goes to Washington.* This famous comedy of manners, based on a play by Garson Kanin [11 . . .], has not worn well over the years, as demonstrated by a disastrous attempt to update it in 1993 with Melanie Griffith [2313], John Goodman, and Don Johnson. Its politics (in Washington the people rule) seem naive, and its relationships (a blonde's best friend is a hunky intellectual) don't quite rise above sexual stereotypes. Moreover, its best scenes—notably, the famous gin rummy game—are at the beginning. Billie gets less interesting the more couth she becomes.

Holliday's performance is justly celebrated. Paul Douglas, who played the Crawford part opposite Holliday in the Broadway version, turned down the film in part because he was aware that she stole the show. But Holliday won the part on both stage and film by default: Jean Arthur [1353] had been cast in the Broadway production, and Holliday got the role when Arthur withdrew from the play during rehearsals. Columbia head Harry Cohn [1025 . . .] bought the film rights to the play for Rita Hayworth. When Hayworth married Aly Khan and announced her retirement from movies, the role went to Holliday over Cohn's opposition. He reportedly referred to her as "that fat Jewish broad" and was brought round to the idea of casting her only after she received strong reviews for her debut role in *Adam's Rib,* which had been directed by Cukor and written by Kanin. Holliday had first made her stage reputation under her real name, Judith Tuvim, as a cabaret performer partnered with Betty Comden [141 . . .] and Adolph Green [141 . . .]. After playing small roles in three movies in 1944, she returned to Broadway, where *Born Yesterday* made her a star. Her Oscar nomination put her in one of the most hotly contested best actress races in Academy Award history. She was up against Bette Davis and Anne Baxter for *All About Eve* and Gloria Swanson for *Sunset Boulevard.* (Eleanor Parker's nomination for *Caged* looks out of place in this company.) Since Academy voting results are not available, it's tempting to speculate that front-runners Davis and Swanson split the vote, allowing Holliday to emerge with a plurality. The Oscar helped her establish a solid movie career, though she never strayed far from the blond naïveté of Billie Dawn in her characters. She died of cancer at the age of forty-three in 1965.

Although Holliday won out over both actresses nominated for *All About Eve,* that movie was unbeatable in the other categories, winning for best picture, for Joseph L. Mankiewicz's direction and screenplay, and for Edith Head and Charles LeMaire's costumes.

Cukor: 567, 1189, 1393, 1563. Louis: 20, 126, 170, 732, 744, 1028, 1065, 1521, 1640, 1812, 1858, 1910, 2064.

263 • BOSTONIANS, THE

MERCHANT IVORY PRODUCTIONS; ALMI PICTURES (UNITED KINGDOM). 1984.

NOMINATIONS *Actress:* Vanessa Redgrave. *Costume Design:* Jenny Beavan and John Bright.

Madeleine Potter plays Verena Tarrant, a young woman whose supposed spiritual powers attract a group of followers in nineteenth-century Boston, among them Olive Chancellor (Redgrave), whose attraction to Verena has a strong but suppressed sexual undercurrent. Into this group comes a young southerner, Basil Ransom (Christopher Reeve), who is both reactionary and skeptical. Naturally Basil and Olive do battle for Verena. Henry James' novel has been adapted by Ruth Prawer Jhabvala [954.5 . . .] with skill, although the characters have been reinterpreted and the story somewhat rewritten to provide a feminist edge not present in the book. The production is handsomely designed, with the splendid re-creation of the period one has come to expect from the team of producer Ismail Merchant [954.5 . . .], director James Ivory [954.5 . . .], and writer Jhabvala. But the whole thing is somewhat lifeless. One misses the satiric tone James brought to the material, even though we might find different targets for the satire today. Potter and Reeve don't quite hold their own in the company of Redgrave and other cast members such as Jessica Tandy [580 . . .] and Linda Hunt [2319]. Redgrave lost to Sally Field in *Places in the Heart,* and the costume award went to Theodor Pistek for *Amadeus.*

Redgrave: 954.5, 1021, 1066, 1285, 1354. Beavan: 954.5, 1290, 1679.5, 1725. Bright: 954.5, 1290, 1679.5, 1725.

264 • BOUND FOR GLORY

THE BOUND FOR GLORY COMPANY PRODUCTION; UNITED ARTISTS. 1976.

AWARDS *Cinematography:* Haskell Wexler. *Original Song Score and Its Adaptation or Adaptation Score:* Leonard Rosenman.

NOMINATIONS *Picture:* Robert F. Blumofe and Harold Leventhal, producers. *Screenplay Based on Material From Another Medium:* Robert Getchell. *Film Editing:* Robert Jones and Pembroke J. Herring. *Costume Design:* William Theiss.

David Carradine plays Woody Guthrie in this adaptation of parts of Guthrie's autobiography, dealing with his odyssey from dust bowl Oklahoma to his leadership in the left wing of the union movement and his success as a singer-songwriter. The movie gets high marks for its admirable re-creation of a period and mostly unsentimental portrait of the man, but it's a bit too long and loosely constructed for people who need to be persuaded to sit through a film about folksingers and labor activists. Under the direction of Hal Ashby [430 . . .], Carradine gives a strong performance. Before, he was best known for the TV series *Kung Fu* and as a member of the Hollywood clan of Carradines. He got the part only after several others had turned it down, including Dustin Hoffman [810 . . .], Jack Nicholson [395 . . .], Robert De

Niro [113 . . .], and Bob Dylan. The cast also includes Melinda Dillon [3 . . .] as Woody's wife, and Randy Quaid [1135] as a migrant worker.

Wexler's previous win for *Who's Afraid of Virginia Woolf?* boosted his status in Hollywood and enabled him to write, produce, direct, and film *Medium Cool* (1969), one of the most remarkable films of the sixties, a blend of drama and documentary footage shot at the riots during the Democratic Convention in Chicago in 1968. His achievement was overlooked by the Academy, but he continued work that had strong political overtones, including a documentary of the notorious trip to North Vietnam by Jane Fonda [394 . . .], *Introduction to the Enemy* (1974). *Bound for Glory* is of a piece with his politically oriented filmmaking.

Since his start in Hollywood in the mid-fifties on *East of Eden* and *Rebel Without a Cause,* Rosenman had composed many of his own film scores, but his two Oscars are for adaptation scores—the eighteenth-century music of *Barry Lyndon* and the twentieth-century folk songs of *Bound for Glory.*

At the Oscars, *Bound for Glory* was one of the remarkably strong and original best picture nominees—the others are *All the President's Men, Network,* and *Taxi Driver*—that went down in defeat to the most conventional and formulaic of the lot: *Rocky,* which also won for Richard Halsey and Scott Conrad's editing.

Getchell's screenplay—to which director Ashby and editor Jones made uncredited contributions—lost to William Goldman's for *All the President's Men.*

Theiss' drab Depression-era costumes lost to the eighteenth-century finery designed by Danilo Donati for *Fellini's Casanova.*

Wexler: 229, 1288, 1481, 2277. Rosenman: 151, 466, 1914. Getchell: 41. Jones: 430, 843, 1032. Herring: 1512, 2120. Theiss: 316, 885.

265 • BOY FRIEND, THE

RUSSFLIX LTD. PRODUCTION; MGM (UNITED KINGDOM). 1971.

NOMINATION *Scoring—Adaptation and Original Song Score:* Peter Maxwell Davies and Peter Greenwell.

A provincial theater company in 1920s England

puts on a musical whose onstage plot mirrors the offstage romantic intrigues. The stage production of Sandy Wilson's musical comedy was a cheerful trifle that launched Julie Andrews [1284 . . .] to stardom. But as a movie it fell into the hands of director Ken Russell [2307], whose determination to be extravagant and outrageous overwhelms almost every project he undertakes. Here he takes the wisp of a show and adds elaborate "dream sequences" in the manner of the Warners musical fantasias directed by Busby Berkeley [791 . . .]—no matter that the Berkeley musicals came along a decade after the era depicted in *The Boy Friend*. While individual numbers may be entertaining to watch, if taken in the "what'll he think of next?" spirit that Russell encourages, the whole enterprise soon bogs down. In the Julie Andrews part, Russell casts Twiggy, then best known as a fashion model with a waifish look. She can sing a little and dance a little more, but she's clearly chosen mainly for the campiness of the concept. Her appearance in the movie later led to a Broadway appearance with *Boy Friend* costar Tommy Tune in *My One and Only*, by which time she'd matured as a performer. Glenda Jackson [893 . . .] repays a favor to Russell, in whose *Women in Love* she'd won an Oscar, by making a cameo appearance as the star who breaks an ankle, enabling understudy Twiggy to go on in her place—as Ruby Keeler does when Bebe Daniels is incapacitated in *42nd Street*. The Oscar for adaptation scoring went to John Williams for *Fiddler on the Roof*.

266 • BOY NAMED CHARLIE BROWN, A

LEE MENDELSON FILM-MELENDEZ FEATURES PRODUCTION; CINEMA CENTER FILMS PRESENTATION; NATIONAL GENERAL PICTURES. 1970.
NOMINATION *Original Song Score:* Music by Rod McKuen and John Scott Trotter; lyrics by Rod McKuen, Bill Melendez, and Al Shean; adaptation score by Vince Guaraldi.

Charlie Brown makes it to the finals in the National Spelling Bee. Does he win? Will Lucy ever hold the football? Charles Schulz's ubiquitous comic-strip characters make it to the big screen in a modestly successful animated feature marred only by McKuen's

icky songs. (The rest of the score, performed by Guaraldi's jazz trio, is okay.) The Academy gave the Oscar to the Beatles for *Let It Be*, perhaps to make up for ignoring their work on *A Hard Day's Night* and *Help!* (1965).

McKuen: 1608.

267 • BOY ON A DOLPHIN

20TH CENTURY-FOX. 1957.
NOMINATION *Score:* Hugo Friedhofer.

Diver Sophia Loren [1280 . . .] discovers a priceless artifact. Archaeologist Alan Ladd must contend with collector Clifton Webb [1149 . . .] over the item's fate. There's not much to this adventure story besides scenery: the Greek islands, handsomely photographed by Milton Krasner [21 . . .], and the scantily (and often wetly) clad Loren, in her American debut. Directed by Jean Negulesco [1052]. Malcolm Arnold's score for *The Bridge on the River Kwai* won the Oscar.

Friedhofer: 2, 21, 184, 187, 214, 1048, 2303, 2336.

268 • BOYS FROM BRAZIL, THE

ITC ENTERTAINMENT PRODUCTION; 20TH CENTURY-FOX. 1978.
NOMINATIONS *Actor:* Laurence Olivier. *Original Score:* Jerry Goldsmith. *Film Editing:* Robert E. Swink.

Olivier plays a character based on Simon Wiesenthal, determined to hunt down the surviving Nazi war criminals. In this case, his target is a Nazi geneticist, played by Gregory Peck [759 . . .], who wants to populate the world with clones of Adolf Hitler. The Ira Levin novel on which this is based made a good beach read, but the movie exposes its flaws of logic and then compounds them by asking us to accept archetypal good guy Peck as Josef Mengele. Olivier is superb, and the cast includes such pros as James Mason [761 . . .], Lilli Palmer, Uta Hagen, Rosemary Harris [2104.5], Denholm Elliott [1725], and Michael Gough. Directed by Franklin J. Schaffner [1541].

This was Olivier's tenth nomination—a record surpassed only by Katharine Hepburn [24 . . .] and tied only by Bette Davis [46 . . .] and Jack Nicholson [395 . . .]. Though he lost to Jon Voight for *Coming Home,* the Academy presented Olivier with his second honorary award (the first was for *Henry V* thirty-two years earlier) for "the full body of his work, for the unique achievements of his entire career and his lifetime of contribution to the art of film."

The scoring award went to Giorgio Moroder for *Midnight Express.* The editing Oscar was won by Peter Zinner for *The Deer Hunter.*

Olivier: 619, 858, 901, 1272, 1506, 1670, 1693, 1841, 2316. Goldsmith: 152.5, 395, 727, 939, 1472, 1527, 1537, 1541, 1583, 1589, 1753, 1913, 2176, 2287. Swink: 737, 1716.

269 • BOYS FROM SYRACUSE, THE

MAYFAIR; UNIVERSAL. 1940.

NOMINATIONS *Black-and-White Interior Decoration:* John Otterson. *Special Effects:* John P. Fulton, photographic; Bernard B. Brown and Joseph Lapis, sound.

Shakespeare's *Comedy of Errors,* in which both master and slave have identical twins (hence the errors), was turned into a Broadway musical in 1938 with a book by George Abbott [48] and songs by Richard Rodgers [1921] and Lorenz Hart that include "This Can't Be Love" and "Falling in Love With Love." Unfortunately Universal never came up with a screenplay that would satisfy the censors or anyone else, and the whole business, directed by Edward Sutherland, is pretty dull. The art direction Oscar went to *Pride and Prejudice.* The special effects mostly involve duplicating Allan Jones (the masters) and Joe Penner (the slaves)—on stage the twins were played by look-alike actors—and the award went to *The Thief of Bagdad.*

Otterson: 96, 668, 681, 1229, 1240, 1895, 2342. Fulton: 1010, 1011, 1012, 2012, 2310. Brown: 93, 96, 919, 1010, 1011, 1125, 1560, 1896, 2028, 2260.

270 • BOYS OF PAUL STREET, THE

BOHGROS FILMS-MAFILM STUDIO I PRODUCTION (HUNGARY).

NOMINATION *Foreign Language Film, 1968.*

Children in Budapest battle for control of a vacant lot in this antiwar allegory directed by Zoltan Fabri. The Oscar went to the Soviet Union's *War and Peace.*

271 • BOYS TOWN

MGM. 1938.

AWARDS *Actor:* Spencer Tracy. *Original Story:* Eleanore Griffin and Dore Schary.

NOMINATIONS *Picture:* John W. Considine, Jr., producer. *Director:* Norman Taurog. *Screenplay:* John Meehan and Dore Schary.

Tracy plays Father Flanagan, creator of an orphanage and school for what used to be called juvenile delinquents. Mickey Rooney [115 . . .] is Whitey Marsh, Flanagan's toughest challenge. The purest corn syrup, but it was enormously popular in its day. The real Flanagan complained that MGM made Boys Town look so clean and well run that he was having trouble raising money.

Tracy became the first person to receive consecutive best actor Oscars—a distinction that would stand until the 1994 awards, when Tom Hanks was honored for *Forrest Gump* a year after his win for *Philadelphia.* Jason Robards would receive consecutive supporting actor awards for *All the President's Men* and *Julia,* and Katharine Hepburn won two best actress Oscars in a row for *The Lion in Winter* and *Guess Who's Coming to Dinner,* as did Luise Rainer for *The Great Ziegfeld* and *The Good Earth.* But Tracy found that the honor was a bit tarnished. First, the trophy arrived inscribed to "Dick Tracy." Then the studio announced that he was going to donate his Oscar to Boys Town—which Tracy flatly refused to do unless he was given a duplicate statuette. The Academy complied. Although Tracy received six more nominations, including a posthumous one for his work in his last film, *Guess Who's Coming to Dinner,* he never won another Oscar.

Schary had been an actor—he made his Broadway debut in 1930 in a play that starred Tracy—but turned to writing, first for the stage and then for the screen. The *Boys Town* screenplay was a turning point in his career, establishing him at MGM, where he soon became a producer. He was briefly in charge of the B-picture division of the studio in the early forties, but his stubbornness compounded by his liberal political views in a studio headed by staunch Republican Louis B. Mayer soon put him at odds with studio management. After working for David O. Selznick

[497 . . .] and for RKO, he returned to MGM in 1948 as head of production. By 1951, when Mayer was forced out, he was head of the studio, but his tenure in the job lasted only five more years.

Boys Town lost the best picture award to *You Can't Take It With You,* whose director, Frank Capra, beat out Taurog for the Oscar. In the screenplay category the film lost to no less than George Bernard Shaw, and adapters Ian Dalrymple, Cecil Lewis, and W. P. Lipscomb, for *Pygmalion.* (Writer Meehan is sometimes confused with another John Meehan [894 . . .], a three-time winner for art directing.)

Tracy: 131, 352, 656, 843, 1000, 1065, 1470, 1751. Schary: 157, 597. Considine: 297. Taurog: 1836. Meehan: 555.

272 • BOYZ N THE HOOD

COLUMBIA PICTURES PRODUCTION; COLUMBIA. 1991.
NOMINATIONS *Director:* John Singleton. *Screenplay Written Directly for the Screen:* John Singleton.

Divorced father Laurence Fishburne [2250.7] struggles to raise his son, Cuba Gooding, Jr., amid the poverty and gang warfare of South-Central Los Angeles. A timely and powerful "message film," though unlike some message films, it has a story to tell that transcends the message, and performances that stick in the mind. Rapper Ice Cube is particularly fine as Gooding's doomed neighbor, and Fishburne establishes himself as one of the movies' best actors. Angela Bassett [2250.7], Fishburne's costar in *What's Love Got to Do With It,* appears as his ex-wife. The movie's chief flaw is that to deliver its message against violence, it resorts to conventional movie violence, a revenge killing. (The best picture winner of 1992, *Unforgiven,* takes the same course.) Ironically the film became the focus of controversy after violent incidents at several of its first showings. Singleton, the film's twenty-three-year-old writer-director, was the youngest nominee for best director in Oscar history, as well as the first African-American to be nominated in that category. The directing Oscar went to Jonathan Demme for *The Silence of the Lambs.* Callie Khouri won the screenplay award for *Thelma & Louise.*

272.5 • BRAM STOKER'S DRACULA

COLUMBIA PICTURES PRODUCTION; COLUMBIA. 1992.
AWARDS *Costume Design:* Eiko Ishioka. *Makeup:* Greg Cannom, Michele Burke, and Matthew W. Mungle. *Sound Effects Editing:* Tom C. McCarthy and David E. Stone.
NOMINATIONS *Art Direction:* Thomas Sanders and Garrett Lewis.

Jonathan Harker (Keanu Reeves) journeys on business to Transylvania, where he becomes the unwitting means of unleashing Count Dracula (Gary Oldman) on London. Only with the aid of Dr. Van Helsing, played by Anthony Hopkins [1679.5 . . .], does Jonathan succeed in thwarting the near-omnipotent undead and rescuing his fiancée, Mina, played by Winona Ryder [27.5 . . .]. Director Francis Ford Coppola [65 . . .], noting that most previous versions of the story had been based on stage dramatizations of Stoker's thriller, went back to the novel for inspiration—hence the film's title. But he takes many liberties with the story, and the style he imposes on the material is ludicrously at odds with the turn-of-the-century setting. Mina and her friend Lucy (Sadie Frost) behave more like Valley girls than proper English maidens. Stoker's vampirism is, of course, a metaphor for sex, but the tension of his story depends on an unholy threat to virginity. These women never behave virginally, and consequently the threat loses its power to shock. While he fails to give us anything new in his treatment of the story, Coppola does give us a visual phantasmagoria—sometimes fun, but eventually rather tiresome. The art direction award went to *Howards End.*

Cannom: 924.5, 937, 1370.5. Burke: 409, 474, 1641. Mungle: 1764.65. Lewis: 159, 779, 937.

273 • BRAVE ONE, THE

KING BROTHERS; RKO RADIO. 1956.
AWARD *Motion Picture Story:* Dalton Trumbo. (Trumbo, who was blacklisted, was nominated under the name Robert Rich; the award was presented to him on May 2, 1975.)
NOMINATIONS *Sound Recording:* John Myers. *Film Editing:* Merrill G. White.

A small Spanish boy becomes so fond of his pet bull that he saves the animal's life when it's sent to fight in the bull ring. Sentimental little tale, directed by Irving Rapper, that inadvertently became the center of controversy when its screenplay, by a blacklisted writer working under a pseudonym, won the Oscar. In the same year, another blacklisted writer, Michael Wilson, had been ruled ineligible for his nomination for *Friendly Persuasion* because of his refusal to testify before Congress during the investigation into communist activity in Hollywood. Even in Hollywood's darkest hour there was an element of farce.

Trumbo, a former newspaperman who had become a screenwriter in the mid-thirties, was under contract to MGM when he was subpoenaed by the House Un-American Activities Committee. Refusing to testify, he was sentenced to ten months in prison, during which time he smuggled out a screenplay under a pseudonym. In 1960 his name was restored to the screen by both Kirk Douglas, for *Spartacus,* and Otto Preminger, for *Exodus,* although right-wing groups picketed the films. In 1970 he directed a film of his 1939 antiwar novel, *Johnny Got His Gun.* He died in 1976—a year after the twenty-year-old Oscar for *The Brave One* had been officially awarded to him under his real name.

Trumbo: 1102, 1716.

274 • *BRAZIL*

REPUBLIC. 1944.

NOMINATIONS *Sound Recording:* Daniel J. Bloomberg. *Song:* "Rio de Janeiro," music by Ary Barroso, lyrics by Ned Washington. *Scoring of a Musical Picture:* Walter Scharf.

Virginia Bruce goes to Brazil in search of material for her novel and is guided around by a composer, Tito Guizar, who wants to get even with her for her snobbish remarks about his country. Will they fall in love or not? Comic relief Edward Everett Horton and guest star Roy Rogers provide more interest than the leads, though the music is nice. Directed by Joseph Santley.

The sound award went to *Wilson.* "Swinging on a Star," from *Going My Way,* by James Van Heusen and Johnny Burke, won the song Oscar, and Carmen Dragon and Morris Stoloff won for the score for *Cover Girl.*

Bloomberg: 680, 693, 991, 1350, 1642, 1756. Washington: 585, 911, 912, 1329, 1396, 1576, 1745, 2127, 2282, 2335. Scharf: 174, 665, 737, 864, 921, 991, 1054, 1305, 2285.

275 • *BRAZIL*

EMBASSY INTERNATIONAL PICTURES PRODUCTION; UNIVERSAL (UNITED KINGDOM). 1985.

NOMINATIONS *Screenplay Written Directly for the Screen:* Terry Gilliam, Tom Stoppard, and Charles McKeown. *Art Direction—Set Decoration:* Norman Garwood; Maggie Gray.

Futuristic satire about the attempts of a mild-mannered clerk, Jonathan Pryce, to deal with a monstrously bureaucratic society—a mélange of themes from various dystopian works, ranging from *1984* to *A Clockwork Orange* to Kafka's *The Trial.* Intriguing but somewhat rambling and overextended. Universal pressured Gilliam into making cuts before it was released in the United States, but it was an expensive flop at the box office. It won the Los Angeles Film Critics Award for best picture, and Gilliam was named best director. The cast includes Robert De Niro [113 . . .], Bob Hoskins [1343], Ian Holm [386], and Gilliam's old colleague from *Monty Python's Flying Circus,* Michael Palin. The screenplay award went to Earl W. Wallace, William Kelley, and Pamela Wallace for *Witness* and the art direction Oscar to *Out of Africa.*

Garwood: 779, 937.

276 • *BREAD, LOVE AND DREAMS*

TITANUS PRODUCTION; I.F.E. RELEASING CORPORATION (ITALY). 1954.

NOMINATION *Motion Picture Story:* Ettore Margadonna.

Vittorio de Sica [650] plays a new police sergeant in a small Italian village. In search of a wife, he courts Gina Lollobrigida, but she prefers his deputy. This mild little comedy, directed by Luigi Comencini, made Lollobrigida a star, and its success led to some forgettable sequels, starting with *Bread, Love and Jealousy.* The Oscar went to Philip Yordan for *Broken Lance.*

277 • *BREAKER MORANT*

PRODUCED IN ASSOCIATION WITH AUSTRALIAN FILM COMMISSION, THE SOUTH AUSTRALIAN FILM CORPORATION, AND THE SEVEN NETWORK AND PACT PRODUCTIONS; NEW WORLD PICTURES/QUARTET/FILMS INC. (AUSTRALIA). 1980.

NOMINATION *Screenplay Based on Material From Another Medium:* Jonathan Hardy, David Stevens, and Bruce Beresford.

During the Boer War, three Australian soldiers are court-martialed for killing prisoners in retribution for the guerrilla tactics of the Boers that led to the death of one of their comrades. The story is based on an actual case, although the screenplay, based on a stage play, is slanted in favor of the three soldiers to deliver an antiwar and anti-imperialist message. Compelling direction by Beresford, who was immediately wooed by Hollywood, as was Bryan Brown, the showiest performer among the three soldiers. The Oscar went to Alvin Sargent for *Ordinary People.*

Beresford: 2015.

278 • *BREAKFAST AT TIFFANY'S*

JUROW-SHEPHERD PRODUCTION; PARAMOUNT. 1961.

AWARDS *Song:* "Moon River," music by Henry Mancini, lyrics by Johnny Mercer. *Scoring of a Dramatic or Comedy Picture:* Henry Mancini.

NOMINATIONS *Actress:* Audrey Hepburn. *Screenplay—Based on Material From Another Medium:* George Axelrod. *Color Art Direction—Set Decoration:* Hal Pereira and Roland Anderson; Sam Comer and Ray Moyer.

Hepburn plays Holly Golightly, a young woman who claims to live on the money men give her to tip the powder room attendant. She and George Peppard, a writer who's being kept by the wealthy Patricia Neal [956 . . .] in the same apartment building, are drawn together, forcing Holly to reveal some secrets and make some commitments she's not ready for. This candy-box fantasy about various forms of prostitution has great charm if you don't think about what's going on underneath its glossy surface, which is what the Truman Capote story on which it's based made you do. With a performer less commanding than Hepburn at its center, it would fall into shambles. (She lost the Oscar to Sophia Loren in *Two Women.*) Mickey Rooney [115 . . .], with enormous buckteeth, does an unpleasantly racist caricature as Holly's Japanese neighbor. Blake Edwards [2201] directed, and the cast includes Buddy Ebsen, Martin Balsam [2067], and John McGiver.

Mancini had been an arranger for Glenn Miller and other big bands and was brought to Hollywood to work on the score of *The Glenn Miller Story.* He began to work regularly as a film composer but didn't hit the big time until the sixties. Much of his film work has been in association with producer-director Edwards. Mancini was also the last of the major composers who worked with Mercer—joining a line that included Jerome Kern [340 . . .], Hoagy Carmichael [341 . . .], and Harold Arlen [248 . . .].

Axelrod, who had been a prolific radio and TV writer, had a big Broadway hit in 1953 with *The Seven Year Itch* and for the next few years divided his writing career between Broadway and the movies, for which he adapted his own play, as well as the work of others, such as *Bus Stop,* by William Inge [1894]. He moved into producing and directing, though with somewhat less success. The Oscar went to Abby Mann for *Judgment at Nuremberg.*

The art direction award went to *West Side Story.*

Mancini: 122, 384, 494, 508, 512, 776, 825, 1573, 1574, 1864, 1970, 2011, 2037, 2201. Mercer: 248, 384, 476, 494, 508, 636, 788, 825, 877, 903, 905, 1109, 1772, 1838, 1912, 2327, 2328. Hepburn: 1457, 1716, 1738, 2221. Pereira: 357, 363, 426, 450, 736, 956, 1029, 1219, 1504, 1570, 1631, 1674, 1716, 1727, 1738, 1840, 1897, 1959, 2012, 2098, 2200, 2208. Anderson: 363, 426, 450, 649, 1029, 1194, 1214, 1219, 1452, 1570, 1668, 1674, 1880, 1994. Comer: 357, 426, 450, 726, 736, 925, 956, 1029, 1101, 1214, 1219, 1443, 1570, 1631, 1674, 1727, 1738, 1748, 1959, 1975, 1994, 2012, 2098, 2200, 2208. Moyer: 413, 736, 833, 1101, 1120, 1214, 1674, 1738, 1748, 1975, 2012.

279 • BREAKING AWAY

20TH CENTURY-FOX PRODUCTION; 20TH CENTURY-FOX. 1979.
AWARD Screenplay Written Directly for the Screen: Steve Tesich.
NOMINATIONS Picture: Peter Yates, producer. Supporting Actress: Barbara Barrie. Director: Peter Yates. Original Song Score and Its Adaptation or Adaptation Score: Patrick Williams.

Dennis Christopher plays a working-class high school grad in Bloomington, Indiana, a college town with a sharp division between town and gown. He still pals around with his fellow townies—played by Daniel Stern, Jackie Earle Haley, and, in one of his first major film roles, Dennis Quaid—but Christopher's passion for bicycle racing sparks an enthusiasm for Italian culture that eventually has him posing as an Italian exchange student to woo a pretty female student. Brightly original comedy, with fine performances by all, including Barrie and Paul Dooley as Christopher's bemused parents.

Tesich was born in Yugoslavia and after immigrating to the States attended Indiana University. The screenplay for Breaking Away was actually a fusion of two of his unproduced scripts: one about a bicycle race between students and townies, the other about the men who worked in the limestone quarries near Bloomington. Tesich's post-Oscar career has been disappointing. The 1981 thriller Eyewitness, also directed by Yates, was something of a muddle that even a cast including William Hurt [293 . . .], Sigourney Weaver [45 . . .], James Woods [1746], and Morgan Freeman [580 . . .] couldn't save. The autobiographical Four Friends (1981), about a Yugoslavian immigrant in sixties America, was well directed by Arthur Penn [43 . . .], but too low-key and sentimental to make much impact. Only his successful adaptation of the complex John Irving novel The World According to Garp earned him substantial praise from the critics.

The British-born Yates, who worked as an assistant director on The Guns of Navarone before moving into the director's chair, was best known for the action films Bullitt and The Deep, so the comparatively unexplosive Breaking Away was seen as something of a change of pace. Even here, however, his experience on action films helped: The movie's bicycle races, while not on a par with Bullitt's famous and trendsetting car chases, are excitingly filmed. The best picture Oscar went to Kramer vs. Kramer, which also won for its director, Robert Benton.

Barrie, an actress with a long Broadway and TV résumé, lost to Meryl Streep in Kramer vs. Kramer. Williams' scoring work lost to Ralph Burns' for All That Jazz.

Yates: 579.

280 • BREAKING THE ICE

PRINCIPAL PRODUCTIONS; RKO RADIO. 1938.
NOMINATION Original Score: Victor Young.

Believing he can help his mother (Dolores Costello) buy her own farm, a young Mennonite boy (Bobby Breen) runs away to the city. Somehow this plot gets grafted onto one about a big ice-skating show, providing an excuse for musical numbers. Thin ice indeed. Directed by Edward F. Cline, with Charles Ruggles, Billy Gilbert, and Margaret Hamilton. The Oscar went to Erich Wolfgang Korngold for The Adventures of Robin Hood.

Young: 97, 98, 100, 101, 489, 612, 693, 701, 794, 846, 925, 1214, 1257, 1396, 1452, 1748, 1823, 1994, 2235, 2315.

281 • BREAKING THE SOUND BARRIER

LONDON FILMS; UNITED ARTISTS (UNITED KINGDOM). 1952.
AWARD Sound Recording: London Film Sound Department.
NOMINATION Story and Screenplay: Terence Rattigan.

Aircraft manufacturer Ralph Richardson [839 . . .] continues to develop experimental planes even after his son, Denholm Elliott [1725], dies testing one of them. Daughter Ann Todd fears that her husband, Nigel Patrick, an ex–fighter pilot, will also be a victim of Richardson's desire to achieve supersonic flight. The domestic drama in this film directed by David Lean [287 . . .] gets a bit mushy, but the exciting aerial photography supervised by Jack Hildyard [287] is what you came to see. The stiff-upper-lip, stout-fellow tone of this movie still has many Brits convinced that one of their own, and not Chuck Yeager, was the first to fly faster than the speed of sound.

World War II, in which he was an aerial gunner, interrupted Rattigan's successful career as a playwright. He is best known for the plays *The Browning Version,* which was filmed in 1951 and remade in 1994, and *The Sleeping Prince,* which was made into *The Prince and the Showgirl,* with Laurence Olivier [268 . . .] and Marilyn Monroe, in 1957. The Oscar went to T. E. B. Clarke for *The Lavender Hill Mob.*

Rattigan: 1778.

282 • BREWSTER'S MILLIONS

EDWARD SMALL; UNITED ARTISTS. 1945.
NOMINATION *Scoring of a Dramatic or Comedy Picture:* Lou Forbes.

Dennis O'Keefe inherits a fortune on the condition that he spend a million dollars in one month. Likable if dated comedy directed by Allan Dwan and featuring Eddie "Rochester" Anderson, June Havoc, Gail Patrick, and Mischa Auer [1401]. Based on a novel by George Barr McCutcheon first published in 1902, when unloading a million was a lot harder to do, this is by one count the fifth film version of the story, and by no means the last: It was filmed again in 1985 with Richard Pryor in the lead. The Oscar went to Miklos Rozsa for *Spellbound.*

Forbes: 1006, 2057, 2186, 2310.

283 • BRIDE OF FRANKENSTEIN, THE

UNIVERSAL. 1935.
NOMINATION *Sound Recording:* Gilbert Kurland.

Just when he thought it was safe to go back into the laboratory, Baron Frankenstein (Colin Clive) is forced by the creepy Dr. Pretorious (Ernest Thesiger) not only to revive the first monster (Boris Karloff) but also to create its mate, played by Elsa Lanchester [428 . . .]. The first and best of the endless sequels to the 1931 original, this one is both scary and funny——many think it's the greatest horror movie of all. The encounter of the monster and his bride is one of those classic movie moments—often parodied, sometimes imitated, never surpassed. Lanchester also plays Mary Shelley in a prologue that sometimes gets chopped off on TV. Directed by John Whale, with a cast that includes the hysterically fussy Una O'Connor, John Carradine, Billy Barty, and, in a bit part, Walter Brennan [424 . . .]. The Oscar went to Douglas Shearer for *Naughty Marietta.*

284 • BRIDGE, THE

FONO FILM (FEDERAL REPUBLIC OF GERMANY). 1959.
NOMINATION *Foreign Language Film.*

In 1945, a few days before the end of the war, a handful of teenage German boys are sent out to defend a bridge against Allied troops. Moving little anti-war film that echoes *All Quiet on the Western Front* in its portrait of the senselessness of to-the-death patriotism. Directed by Bernhard Wicki, who would later do the German-language sections of *The Longest Day.* The Oscar went to *Black Orpheus.*

285 • BRIDGE OF SAN LUIS REY, THE

MGM. 1928–29.
AWARD *Interior Decoration:* Cedric Gibbons.

Five people meet death when a rope bridge across a Peruvian chasm collapses. Based on a novel by Thornton Wilder, this is a mostly silent film no longer in circulation. Directed by Charles Brabin, with Lily Damita, Raquel Torres, and Henry B. Walthall.

The first of Gibbons' eleven Oscars, as well as the first of thirty-nine nominations, was presented to him in recognition of his work on *The Bridge of San Luis Rey* "and other pictures." Gibbons began his career with the Edison studio in 1915, worked for a few years for Goldwyn, and in 1924 began his long association with MGM that continued almost to his death in 1960. Although as head of the production design department his name went on many films that others designed, his taste was felt in the creations of Hollywood's most powerful studio. His influence was felt off screen, too: He designed the home of studio head Louis B. Mayer and, at Mayer's behest, created one of the most famous of all icons—the Oscar statuette.

Gibbons: 66, 87, 130, 217, 227, 239, 290, 440, 629, 749, 831, 980, 1069, 1096, 1173, 1190, 1226, 1230, 1232, 1274, 1308, 1309, 1417, 1567, 1604,

1644, 1662, 1673, 1721, 1861, 1937, 2068, 2112, 2256, 2257, 2300, 2320, 2330.

286 • BRIDGE OF SAN LUIS REY, THE

BOGEAUS; UNITED ARTISTS. 1944.

NOMINATION *Scoring of a Dramatic or Comedy Picture:* Dimitri Tiomkin.

The second filming of Thornton Wilder's story about a priest's investigation of why five people happened to be on a bridge that collapsed, this version, directed by Rowland V. Lee, is rather slow and dull. It does have an interesting cast, including Nazimova, Louis Calhern [1243], and Akim Tamiroff [701 . . .]. Tiomkin's score lost to Max Steiner's for *Since You Went Away.*

Tiomkin: 33, 380, 446, 638, 663, 730, 768, 850, 911, 912, 1206, 1347, 1370, 1470, 2006, 2127, 2282, 2335.

287 • BRIDGE ON THE RIVER KWAI, THE

A HORIZON PICTURES PRODUCTION; COLUMBIA (UNITED KINGDOM). 1957.

AWARDS *Picture:* Sam Spiegel, producer. *Actor:* Alec Guinness. *Director:* David Lean. *Screenplay—Based on Material From Another Medium:* Pierre Boulle, Michael Wilson, and Carl Foreman. (The award was originally presented to Boulle, who received solo screen credit because Foreman and Wilson had been blacklisted. Oscars were presented to Foreman and Wilson posthumously on December 11, 1984.) *Cinematography:* Jack Hildyard. *Score:* Malcolm Arnold. *Film Editing:* Peter Taylor.

NOMINATION *Supporting Actor:* Sessue Hayakawa.

Colonel Saito (Hayakawa), the commander of a POW camp in Southeast Asia during World War II, orders the construction of a railroad bridge. The leader of the POWs, Colonel Nicholson (Guinness), after a standoff in which he demonstrates his courage and determination to Saito, pushes his men to complete the bridge ahead of schedule, to prove the worth of the British soldier. But an American POW, Shears, played by William Holden [1424 . . .], protests Nicholson's plan, arguing that it will only aid the

Japanese in the war. Shears escapes and destroys the bridge. Terrific action epic with more psychological depth than most, thanks to the superb performances of Guinness and Hayakawa as the chief antagonists. The conclusion is not well handled—perhaps owing to some difficulty in filming the destruction of the bridge—but what leads up to it is classic. As often with movies that have become legendary, there are tales about who might have been cast in it. One version has Cary Grant [1445 . . .] as the first choice for the Holden role and Noël Coward [993] in the Guinness part. Others say that Spiegel, who had produced *The African Queen,* wanted Humphrey Bogart [24 . . .] in the Guinness role, with Laurence Olivier [268 . . .] as his second choice. Charles Laughton [1387 . . .] had also been approached for the role.

Before World War II, Guinness had been a member of the company of the Old Vic, but he became a leading light of the reviving British film industry after his service in the navy during the war. To Americans he was best known as the man of many faces in the superb light comedies that came out of the Ealing studios in the late forties and early fifties, *Kind Hearts and Coronets, The Lavender Hill Mob, The Man in the White Suit,* and *The Ladykillers* chief among them. *Kwai,* a straight dramatic role, was seen as a change of pace for him. It won him numerous awards and doubtless led to his knighthood two years later.

The controversy over the authorship of the screenplay was a further blemish on an already tarnished Academy, struggling to deal with the fear and paranoia of the McCarthy-era blacklist. The year before, the Academy had denied Wilson eligibility for the Oscars, even though it had nominated his screenplay for *Friendly Persuasion.* At the same ceremony, it had presented an award to "Robert Rich," author of the story for *The Brave One.* Rich turned out to be the blacklisted Dalton Trumbo. The Academy shored up its rules, barring anyone from nomination who had admitted membership in the Communist Party and failed to renounce it, as well as anyone who refused to testify before a congressional committee. Wilson had refused to testify, and Foreman had declined to confirm or deny party membership in an appearance before the House Un-American Activities Committee. Columbia pulled their screen credits from *Kwai*, giving sole credit to Boulle, the author of the novel on which it was based. Boulle, however, had written the novel in French, and spoke and wrote very little English. The Academy finally awarded the Oscars to Foreman and Wilson posthumously, at a special ceremony in 1984.

Lean's Oscar, after three previous nominations, marks a turning point in his directing career. Previously he had concentrated on well-mounted productions of intimate dramas such as *Brief Encounter* and *Summertime* or classics such as *Great Expectations* and *Oliver Twist*. But the size and budget of *Kwai* would be the hallmark of his later works—extravaganzas such as *Lawrence of Arabia* and *Doctor Zhivago* that are sometimes referred to as "intelligent epics."

After an apprenticeship as a cameraman on several major British films, including *Henry V*, Hildyard became a director of photography in the late forties, with notable work on Lean's *Breaking the Sound Barrier*. His major work has been in color on such films as *Anastasia* and *The Sundowners*, but he also did fine work in black and white, notably in *Suddenly, Last Summer*.

Hayakawa, who lost to Red Buttons for *Sayonara*, was one of the movies' earliest stars. Born in Japan, but educated at the University of Chicago, he was spotted by Thomas Ince in a company of Japanese players Hayakawa had formed and brought to the States. He starred in Ince's *The Typhoon* in 1914 and *The Cheat*, directed by Cecil B. DeMille [412 . . .], in 1915. He moved to Europe in the 1920s and worked in French films but returned to Hollywood after World War II. His performance as the cultivated Japanese prison camp head in *Three Came Home* (1950) led to his casting in *Kwai*. He died in 1973.

Spiegel: 1151, 1429, 1477. Guinness: 941, 1150, 1181, 1916. Lean: 289, 558, 820, 1151, 1533, 1963. Wilson: 673, 730, 1579. Foreman: 380, 850, 912, 1302, 2340.

288 • BRIDGES AT TOKO-RI, THE

PERLBERG-SEATON PRODUCTION; PARAMOUNT. 1955.
AWARD *Special Effects.* (no individual citation.)
NOMINATION *Film Editing:* Alma Macrorie.

Lawyer William Holden [1424 . . .] gets called up for duty during the Korean War, to the dismay of his wife, Grace Kelly [450 . . .]. Mark Robson [1001 . . .] directed this intelligent adaptation by Valentine Davies [776 . . .] of a novel by James Michener. The film has a rather jaundiced view of the Korean conflict, which is surprising for Hollywood during the fifties, when Cold War jitters made anything but superpatriotism suspect. On the other hand, the action sequences, which earned the film a special effects Oscar, make aerial combat look like fun. And Davies evened things out by working on the propagandistic *Strategic Air Command*. The strong cast includes Fredric March [184 . . .], Mickey Rooney [115 . . .], Robert Strauss [1903], and Earl Holliman. The editing Oscar went to Charles Nelson and William A. Lyon for *Picnic*.

289 • BRIEF ENCOUNTER

J. ARTHUR RANK-CINEGUILD-PRESTIGE; UNIVERSAL-INTERNATIONAL (UNITED KINGDOM). 1946.
NOMINATIONS *Actress:* Celia Johnson. *Director:* David Lean. *Screenplay:* Anthony Havelock-Allan, David Lean, and Ronald Neame.

Johnson and Trevor Howard [1875] are happily married—but not to each other, which makes things very difficult indeed when their chance meeting on a railway platform turns into love. Perhaps second only to *Camille* as the movies' greatest tearjerker, this wonderful little film generates more heat with the longing glances of two ordinary people than many movies do by rubbing together two perfect bodies. The photography by Robert Krasker [2053] is delicate and precisely evocative of mood, and the music track turned Rachmaninoff's Piano Concerto No. 2 into one of the all-time great make-out hits. To understand how important the contributions of Johnson, Howard, Lean, Krasker, et al. were to the success of the movie, you need only turn to the appalling remake for TV in 1974 that starred Richard Burton [85 . . .] and Sophia Loren [1280 . . .] or the lackluster rip-off *Falling in Love* in 1984 that starred Meryl Streep [472 . . .] and Robert De Niro [113 . . .]. Star power alone clearly isn't enough. The cast also includes Stanley Holloway [1393], Cyril Raymond, and Joyce Carey.

Johnson made only a handful of films, concentrating her career primarily on stage in England, where she was a valued and honored player. A few years before her death in 1982, she reteamed with Howard for a touching little film, *Staying On* (1980), based on a Paul Scott novel that's a coda to his quartet of books that was filmed for TV as *The Jewel in the Crown*. The Oscar went to Olivia de Havilland for *To Each His Own*.

This was Lean's first nomination as director, and it stands in sharp contrast to the blockbuster epics, starting with *The Bridge on the River Kwai,* that would later win him Oscars. It's the culmination of a collaboration with Noël Coward [993] that began with *In Which We Serve,* a film that Lean codirected with Coward, and continued on the movies *This Happy Breed* (1944) and *Blithe Spirit,* both of which, like *Brief Encounter,* were adaptations of material written by Coward. *Brief Encounter* is based on Coward's one-act play *Still Life.* The Oscar went to William Wyler for *The Best Years of Our Lives.*

In addition to his screenwriting duties, Havelock-Allan served as producer on this and other films by Lean, turning primarily to producing in the later part of his career. Neame began as a cinematographer, working on such films as *Pygmalion* and *Blithe Spirit,* and produced several films but after 1950 was best known as a director on projects ranging from *The Horse's Mouth* to *The Prime of Miss Jean Brodie* to *The Poseidon Adventure.* The screenplay Oscar went to Robert E. Sherwood for *The Best Years of Our Lives.*

Lean: 287, 558, 820, 1151, 1533, 1963. Havelock-Allan: 820, 1722. Neame: 820, 1489.

290 • *BRIGADOON*
MGM. 1954.
Nominations *Color Art Direction—Set Decoration:* Cedric Gibbons and Preston Ames; Edwin B. Willis and

Keogh Gleason. *Sound Recording:* Wesley C. Miller. *Color Costume Design:* Irene Sharaff.

American tourists Gene Kelly [74] and Van Johnson happen into an idyllic Scottish village that's enchanted: It comes to life only one day every hundred years. Naturally Kelly falls in love with the town's most beautiful woman, Cyd Charisse, presenting a serious problem: He can't exactly wait around for her return. This rather dull filming of a Broadway musical hit by Alan Jay Lerner [66 . . .] and Frederick Loewe [769 . . .] marked a turning point for the MGM musical—it was virtually the end of its greatest period, which began in 1939 with *The Wizard of Oz* and ended in the mid-fifties as one big project after another failed to attract audiences. In the case of *Brigadoon,* budget tightening caused producer Arthur Freed [66 . . .] to scrap plans for location filming in Scotland. Big Sur was proposed as an acceptable substitute, but instead, an enormous replica of the Scottish Highlands was created in an MGM soundstage. Though it earned the design team an Oscar nomination, it was an abject failure. The musical was filmed in CinemaScope, whose enormous images magnified the artificial turf and painted sky, making the whole thing look like the glassed-in dioramas in a natural history museum. Director Vincente Minnelli [66 . . .] was stymied by the artifice. Originally the musical had been bought by MGM as a vehicle for Kelly and Kathryn Grayson, but Grayson's contract with the studio had ended. Ballerina Moira Shearer was considered for the role, which was rewritten for a dancer, but her contract with Sadlers Wells prevented her from taking the part, so Charisse was signed instead. Johnson was cast after several others were considered, including Donald O'Connor and Steve Allen.

The art direction Oscar went to *20,000 Leagues Under the Sea. The Glenn Miller Story* won for sound, and the costuming award went to Sanzo Wada for *Gate of Hell.*

Gibbons: 66, 87, 130, 217, 227, 239, 285, 440, 629, 749, 831, 980, 1069, 1096, 1173, 1190, 1226, 1230, 1232, 1274, 1308, 1309, 1417, 1567, 1604, 1644, 1662, 1673, 1721, 1861, 1937, 2068, 2112,

2256, 2257, 2300, 2320, 2330. Ames: 31, 66, 591, 769, 1226, 1937, 2184. Willis: 66, 87, 130, 227, 239, 629, 749, 831, 980, 1069, 1096, 1157, 1173, 1190, 1226, 1230, 1232, 1309, 1417, 1567, 1657, 1662, 1673, 1721, 1861, 1937, 2068, 2112, 2257, 2320, 2330. Gleason: 66, 130, 769, 1226, 1861, 1937. Miller: 704, 1157, 1216. Sharaff: 66, 333, 338, 413, 690, 852, 896, 1088, 1507, 1592, 1910, 2000, 2244, 2277.

291 • BRIGHT VICTORY

UNIVERSAL-INTERNATIONAL. 1951.

NOMINATIONS *Actor:* Arthur Kennedy. *Sound Recording:* Leslie I. Carey.

Kennedy plays a veteran blinded in combat who has difficulty adjusting to civilian life. As the title suggests, he succeeds. Well-acted inspirational drama, directed by Mark Robson [1001 . . .], with Peggy Dow, Julia Adams, Will Geer, Jim Backus, Murray Hamilton, and young Universal contract player Rock Hudson [768] in a bit part as a soldier.

This was Kennedy's sole nomination in a leading role, though he received four others as a supporting player. His competition was formidable: Humphrey Bogart won for *The African Queen,* and the others nominated were Marlon Brando for *A Streetcar Named Desire* (Kennedy had beaten him in the voting of the New York film critics), Montgomery Clift in *A Place in the Sun,* and Fredric March for *Death of a Salesman.* Kennedy had won a Tony Award for playing Biff in the original Broadway production of *Salesman* but was passed over in favor of Kevin McCarthy for the film version.

The sound award went to Douglas Shearer for *The Great Caruso.*

Kennedy: 380, 1558, 1859, 2139. Carey: 776, 1209, 1334, 1478, 2089.

292 • BRINK'S JOB, THE

WILLIAM FRIEDKIN FILM/UNIVERSAL PRODUCTION; DINO DE LAURENTIIS PRESENTATION; UNIVERSAL. 1978.

NOMINATION *Art Direction—Set Decoration:* Dean Tavoularis and Angelo Graham; George R. Nelson and Bruce Kay.

In 1950 eight masked bandits robbed the Brink's armored-car company of $2.8 million. The case, which looked like the perfect crime, was finally solved eight years later. Screenwriter Walon Green [2280], director William Friedkin [631 . . .], and a cast including Peter Falk [1377 . . .], Peter Boyle, Warren Oates, and Gena Rowlands [777 . . .] play this story for laughs, not with complete success. As the nomination suggests, the re-creation of Boston in the fifties is the most interesting thing about the movie. The art directing Oscar went to *Heaven Can Wait.*

Tavoularis: 92, 785, 786, 2148. Graham: 92, 785, 1418. Nelson: 92, 785, 1698.

293 • BROADCAST NEWS

20TH CENTURY FOX PRODUCTION; 20TH CENTURY FOX. 1987.

NOMINATIONS *Picture:* James L. Brooks, producer. *Actor:* William Hurt. *Actress:* Holly Hunter. *Supporting Actor:* Albert Brooks. *Screenplay Written Directly for the Screen:* James L. Brooks. *Cinematography:* Michael Ballhaus. *Film Editing:* Richard Marks.

Hunter is an intense, ambitious network TV news producer, Hurt a vain, somewhat empty-headed local anchorman bidding for network stardom, and Albert Brooks a solid, professional reporter who thinks he should get the kudos the on-camera newsreaders like Hurt always steal. This nifty triangular relationship is played for satire as well as romance, but in the end the satire keeps getting in the way of our enjoyment of the characters, and the movie unfortunately doesn't have much more to tell us about TV than the earlier *Network* did. Critics loved the movie, but audiences were rather cool to it—a dynamic that often means lots of nominations but few awards (see *Bugsy* for a similar instance). Jack Nicholson [395 . . .] does a cameo as a veteran network anchorman, a wonderful amalgam of Chet Huntley, Walter Cronkite, and John Chancellor. Joan Cusack [2313] has a small but entertaining role as a frantic production assistant.

After his triple play with *Terms of Endearment,* for which he won Oscars as writer, director, and producer, James Brooks had the very real problem of what to do for an encore. *Broadcast News* was at least in part his way of evening old scores. He had worked as a newswriter for CBS before hitting the big time with his classic TV sitcom *The Mary Tyler Moore Show,* set in a Minneapolis TV newsroom. Hunter's character is a reworking of the sitcom's Mary Richards, just as the Hurt character is a more polished Ted Baxter. By failing to nominate Brooks as director for *Broadcast News,* the Academy put the movie all but out of the running for the best picture Oscar, which went to *The Last Emperor.* The writing award went to John Patrick Shanley for *Moonstruck.* After *Broadcast News,* Brooks was long absent from the screen; his comeback vehicle, *I'll Do Anything* (1994), began as a musical but after disastrous test screenings was released without its songs. It flopped anyway, both critically and commercially.

Hurt's third consecutive nomination capped a remarkable series of performances in the films of the eighties. After he lost this time to Michael Douglas in *Wall Street,* Hurt's career began to cool. While he performed strongly in *The Accidental Tourist,* the best notices for that film went to Geena Davis. And his fine work in *The Doctor* (1991) was overlooked by the Academy.

Hunter's role was written for Debra Winger [1465 . . .], who had to withdraw when she became pregnant. It was a star-making part for the Georgia-born actress, who had previously been seen in small roles in a 1983 TV movie, *Svengali,* and such movies as *Swing Shift* and the 1987 cult comedy *Raising Arizona.* However, Cher's win for *Moonstruck* was all but a foregone conclusion at the Oscars.

Albert Brooks, who made his film debut in *Taxi Driver* and appeared in *Private Benjamin,* is a filmmaker in his own right, having written and directed *Real Life* (1979), *Modern Romance* (1981), *Lost in America* (1985), and *Defending Your Life* (1991), as well as some eccentric short films that were seen on *Saturday Night Live.* He lost to Sean Connery in *The Untouchables.*

The irresistible force at the Oscars that year was *The Last Emperor,* whose cinematographer, Vittorio Storaro, took the Oscar away from Ballhaus, who is emerging as one of the leading cinematographers of the nineties. Gabriella Cristiana won the editing Oscar for *The Last Emperor.*

J. Brooks: 2020. Hurt: 390, 1099. Hunter: 667.5, 1563.5. Ballhaus: 633. Marks: 92, 2020.

294 • *BROADWAY DANNY ROSE*

Jack Rollins and Charles H. Joffe Production; Orion. 1984.

Nominations *Director:* Woody Allen. *Screenplay Written Directly for the Screen:* Woody Allen.

A group of showbiz veterans swap stories about Danny Rose (Allen), a down-at-the-heels talent agent whose affection for his less-than-star-quality clients got him into trouble. Critics praised the movie, particularly Mia Farrow's against-type performance as a brassy dame, but audiences were lukewarm. It was the first in a series of period pieces—*The Purple Rose of Cairo, Radio Days, Zelig*—made by Allen in the mid-eighties.

Allen was odd man out in the directing race: All the other nominees were directors of films in the running for best picture. Allen took the slot that might otherwise have gone to Norman Jewison, whose film *A Soldier's Story* was nominated for best picture—one of several instances where the Academy has appeared to slight Jewison. The directing Oscar went to Milos Forman for *Amadeus.* Robert Benton won for the screenplay for *Places in the Heart.*

Allen: 39, 88, 311.5, 461, 863, 962.5, 1005, 1267, 1636, 1647.

295 • *BROADWAY HOSTESS*

Warner Bros.-First National. 1935.

Nomination *Dance Direction:* Bobby Connolly.

Minor musical about the rise to stardom of a small-town girl (Wini Shaw, best known for her performance of ''Lullaby of Broadway'' in *Gold Diggers of 1935*). Directed by Frank McDonald. Connolly was nominated for his work on the ''Playboy From Paree'' number in this film and for the ''Latin From Manhattan'' number in *Go Into Your Dance.* He lost to David Gould's work on *Broadway Melody of 1936* and *Folies Bergère.*

Connolly: 329, 781, 1667.

296 • BROADWAY MELODY

MGM. 1928–29.

AWARD *Production:* Harry Rapf, producer.

NOMINATIONS *Actress:* Bessie Love. *Director:* Harry Beaumont.

Love and Anita Page play sisters in search of stardom. Songs are sung, dances danced, hearts broken, etc. The years have not been kind to the movie, with its chubby, clunky chorus girls and nailed-to-the-floor camera work, but its place in the record books assures it a continued, if sometimes derisive, audience: It was the first sound film and first musical to win an Oscar for best picture. The movie triumphed over lackluster competition: the gangster film *Alibi,* which was hastily refilmed for sound; *Hollywood Revue,* a cobbled-together musical in which MGM contract stars demonstrate that they have voices (sometimes unconvincingly); *In Old Arizona,* a Cisco Kid western; and *The Patriot,* a historical drama that was the last silent movie to receive a best picture nomination. It's one of the weakest years for movies in history, primarily because the industry was in turmoil with the coming of sound. *Broadway Melody* does, however, have some standout songs by Arthur Freed [66 . . .] and Nacio Herb Brown: the title tune, plus "Wedding of the Painted Doll," "You Were Meant for Me," and others. With this movie, lyricist Freed began his long association with MGM; in the forties and fifties he would become the most successful producer of musicals in Hollywood history.

The nominations of Love and Beaumont were not announced by the Academy when it made its awards in April 1930. This time it chose to cite only the winners, and the runners-up were not even given certificates of nomination. The others on record with the Academy as having been considered by the various branches for Oscars have, however, been traditionally treated as if they were official nominees.

Like Mary Pickford, who won the Oscar for *Coquette,* Love was a veteran performer, having made her screen debut as a teenager in 1915 and appeared as the Bride of Cana in D. W. Griffith's *Intolerance* (1916). She made scores of silent films but decided to retire from movies in 1931. She later came out of retirement to play character roles in numerous movies, including *The Barefoot Contessa,* the George Lazenby James Bond movie *On Her Majesty's Secret Service* (1969), *Sunday, Bloody Sunday,* and *Isadora,* in which she plays Vanessa Redgrave's mother. She died in 1986.

Beaumont began as an actor in films in 1912 and directed his first movie in 1915. His work on *Our Dancing Daughters,* starring Joan Crawford [1319 . . .], led to his assignment to *Broadway Melody.* His postnomination career consisted mainly of B pictures, including several of the *Maisie* comedies starring Ann Sothern [2246] in the forties. The Oscar went to Frank Lloyd for *The Divine Lady.*

Rapf: 931.

297 • BROADWAY MELODY OF 1936

MGM. 1935.

AWARD *Dance Direction:* David Gould.

NOMINATIONS *Picture:* John W. Considine, Jr., producer. *Original Story:* Moss Hart.

Newspaper columnist Jack Benny, feuding with Broadway producer Robert Taylor, tries to use Eleanor Powell to frame Taylor. Amusing stuff, though those who grew up with Benny's familiar radio-TV personality sometimes find it hard to accept him in a different persona. Nice songs by Arthur Freed [66 . . .] and Nacio Herb Brown, including "Broadway Rhythm," "You Are My Lucky Star," and "I've Got a Feelin' You're Foolin'," and fun dance numbers by Powell and Buddy Ebsen. Directed by Roy Del Ruth, with Una Merkel [1959] and Sid Silvers.

Gould was cited for both the "I've Got a Feelin' You're Foolin' " number and the "Straw Hat" number from *Folies Bergère.* He won out over some more famous contenders: Busby Berkeley's spectacular "Lullaby of Broadway," from *Gold Diggers of 1935,* and Hermes Pan's staging of the title number from *Top Hat.*

Though MGM all but invented the movie musical with the first *Broadway Melody,* it turned its attention to other genres, letting Warner Bros. and RKO perfect the musical with, respectively, Berkeley's extravaganzas and the classic teaming of Fred Astaire [2126] and Ginger Rogers [1102]. This musical, by picking up on the title of the original film and using that movie's songwriting team of Freed and Brown, signaled the studio's reentry into the film musical game. There were two more in the *Broadway Melody* series, 1938 and 1940, but apart from the performance by Judy Garland [1065 . . .] of "Dear Mr. Gable" in the former and the great "Begin the Beguine" number danced by Astaire and Powell in the latter, they are pretty forgettable. MGM didn't truly become a leader in musicals until the formation of the production unit headed by Arthur Freed in the early forties. The Oscar this time went to a project more in the MGM mainstream, *Mutiny on the Bounty*.

Hart, one of the greatest figures of the American theater, was not at home in Hollywood. He is best known for the plays he wrote in collaboration with George S. Kaufman, including *You Can't Take It With You,* which was adapted into the best picture winner, and *The Man Who Came to Dinner,* which was filmed in 1942. He was also a distinguished director and won a Tony Award for *My Fair Lady* in 1957. His autobiography, *Act One,* was filmed in 1963, with George Hamilton playing Hart. At the Oscars, Hart came in third, behind a write-in candidate, Gregory Rogers for *"G" Men*. The writing award went to Ben Hecht and Charles MacArthur for *The Scoundrel*.

Gould: 261, 500, 695. Considine: 271. Hart: 759.

298 • BROKEN ARROW

20TH CENTURY-FOX. 1950.
NOMINATIONS *Supporting Actor:* Jeff Chandler. *Screenplay:* Michael Blankfort. (Screenplay actually by blacklisted writer Albert Maltz, who received official screenplay credit from the Writers Guild of America in 1991.) *Color Cinematography:* Ernest Palmer.

James Stewart [73 . . .] attempts to make peace between the white settlers and the Apaches, led by Cochise (Chandler). In the process he falls in love with an Indian woman, played by Debra Paget. An entertaining blend of action and earnestness, it's generally recognized as one of the first popular movies to present the Indians' side of the conflict. Although the leads are played by white actors, the cast includes many Native Americans, including Jay Silverheels, best known for playing Tonto on TV's *The Lone Ranger,* and Iron Eyes Cody, who became famous for a TV public service spot in which he shed tears over the pollution of the environment. Directed by Delmer Daves.

Chandler, born Ira Grossel in Brooklyn, was best known for westerns and action films, and played Cochise again in *The Battle at Apache Pass* (1952). He died, aged forty-two, in 1961, of complications following surgery. The Oscar went to George Sanders for *All About Eve.*

Blankfort fronted for Maltz, a practice that became common in the days of the blacklist and was later memorialized in the movie *The Front.* Before his death in 1982, Blankfort served as president of the Writers Guild and as a governor of the Academy. Maltz had done his share of wartime flag-waving with screenplays for *Destination Tokyo* and *Pride of the Marines* and wrote two documentaries that received notice from the Academy: *Moscow Strikes Back,* an English-language version of a Soviet film that won the Oscar for best documentary in 1942, and *The House We Live In,* a short film about tolerance that received an honorary award in 1945. In 1947 he became one of the Hollywood Ten, convicted of contempt of Congress for refusing to testify about their membership in the Communist Party. He served ten months in prison, and though he continued to do uncredited work on movies, after *Naked City* in 1948 his name would not appear on screen again until 1970, for *Two Mules for Sister Sara.* The Oscar went to Joseph L. Mankiewicz for *All About Eve.*

The cinematography award went to Robert Surtees for *King Solomon's Mines.*

Maltz: 1606. Palmer: 235, 714, 1946.

299 • BROKEN LANCE

20TH CENTURY-FOX. 1954.
AWARD *Motion Picture Story:* Philip Yordan.
NOMINATION *Supporting Actress:* Katy Jurado.

Rancher Spencer Tracy [131 . . .] presides over a family and a cattle business that seem likely to self-destruct after his death. Charlemagne on the range,

Lear on the prairie, this excellent western, directed by Edward Dmytryk [467], has moments of pretentiousness, but Tracy, Jurado, Richard Widmark [1098], and Earl Holliman are quite fine, and even Robert Wagner manages to act a little.

The award to Yordan is one of the most controversial in the history of the Oscars. *Broken Lance* is essentially a remake of the 1949 film *House of Strangers,* in which the family is Italian-American and the rancher is a financier. That movie was based on a novel by Jerome Weidman, and Yordan says he did the adaptation that reached the screen—a claim disputed by director Joseph L. Mankiewicz [46 . . .], who asserted that Yordan was fired by producer Sol Siegel [1163 . . .] and that Mankiewicz himself rewrote Yordan's work on *House of Strangers.* Mankiewicz declined the screen credit as coauthor after an arbitration by the Writers Guild. From the beginning of his career, there had been questions about Yordan's work. His first major success was the Broadway play *Anna Lucasta,* hailed by some critics but condemned by others as a blatant recasting of the Eugene O'Neill play *Anna Christie* with a Harlem setting. Over the years, there were also charges that much of the work attributed to Yordan was actually done by writers under his hire—particularly during the era of the blacklist, when many leftist writers were prevented from doing credited work in Hollywood. Chief among these is Ben Maddow [105], to whom quite a few Yordan screenplays have been attributed. "Philip Yordan has never written more than a sentence in his life," Maddow once charged. In the case of *Broken Lance,* Yordan admitted that he did no work on the film for which he won the Oscar. The story, he says, was pulled from the files at Fox; the actual screenplay was by Richard Murphy [257 . . .]. A joke made the rounds that the reason Yordan said only "Thank you" when he accepted the Oscar was that he didn't have time to hire a speechwriter.

Jurado appeared in films in her native Mexico before coming to Hollywood, where she made her first strong screen appearance in *High Noon.* After the nomination, which she lost to Eva Marie Saint in *On*

the Waterfront, she continued a modestly successful career, returning to Mexico for films but also performing character roles in the States.

Yordan: 534, 545.

300 • *BROTHER SUN, SISTER MOON*

EURO INTERNATIONAL FILMS-VIC FILM (PRODUCTIONS) LTD.; PARAMOUNT (ITALY/UNITED KINGDOM). 1973.

NOMINATION *Art Direction—Set Decoration:* Lorenzo Mongiardino and Gianni Quaranta; Carmelo Patrono.

The life of St. Francis of Assisi (Graham Faulkner), whom director Franco Zeffirelli [1722 . . .] views as a proto-hippie—he even uses songs by Donovan on the soundtrack. A critical and commercial flop. Alec Guinness [287 . . .] plays the pope, and the cast includes Judi Bowker, Leigh Lawson, and Valentina Cortese [501]. The screenplay is by Suso Cecchi D'Amico [367], Kenneth Ross, Lina Wertmüller [1781], and Zeffirelli. The art direction award went to *The Sting.*

Mongiardino: 2000. Quaranta: 1725, 2135.

301 • *BROTHERS KARAMAZOV, THE*

AVON PRODUCTIONS INC.; MGM. 1958.

NOMINATION *Supporting Actor:* Lee J. Cobb.

Cobb plays the patriarch of Dostoevsky's dysfunctional family, with Yul Brynner [1088] as the sensualist son Dmitri, Richard Basehart the intellectual Ivan, and William Shatner, in his film debut, as the saintly Alyosha. Albert Salmi is the epileptic Smerdyakov, Maria Schell plays Grushenka, and Claire Bloom is Katya. Marilyn Monroe became the object of sexist derision—how dare a sex object pretend to have a brain?—when she expressed her desire to play the earthy Grushenka, but she might have brought some much-needed life to this outline of a masterpiece. Writer-director Richard Brooks [227 . . .] certainly tries to make it work, but the mélange of acting styles and the Hollywoodenness of the production defeat him. Cobb, a major actor whose theatricality was not always appropriate on screen, lost to Burl Ives in *The Big Country.*

Cobb: 1477.

302 • BROTHERS KARAMAZOV, THE

MOSFILM STUDIOS PRODUCTION (USSR). 1969.
NOMINATION *Foreign Language Film.*

The Soviet version comes closer to the spirit of the Dostoevsky novel than Hollywood's attempt a decade earlier, but it's reverent, slow, and almost four hours long. The film was also released under the title *The Murder of Dmitri Karamazov.* Director Ivan Pyriev died during filming, and the movie was completed by Mikhail Ulianov, who plays Dmitri, and Kirill Lavrov, who plays Ivan. The Oscar went to *Z.*

303 • BRUBAKER

20TH CENTURY-FOX PRODUCTION; 20TH CENTURY-FOX. 1980.
NOMINATION *Screenplay Written Directly for the Screen:* W. D. Richter and Arthur Ross.

Robert Redford [1502 . . .] plays the new warden of a southern prison whose guards are hiring out inmates as slave labor. Based on an actual scandal that was uncovered in Arkansas in the 1960s, this is an honorable contribution to the prison-drama genre, with good work by Yaphet Kotto, Jane Alexander [54 . . .], Morgan Freeman [580 . . .], and others, though Redford seems miscast—you keep wishing he'd lose the frat-boy hairstyle. Stuart Rosenberg directed, after Bob Rafelson [672] withdrew from the project. The writing award went to Bo Goldman for *Melvin and Howard.*

304 • BUCCANEER, THE

PARAMOUNT. 1938.
NOMINATION *Cinematography:* Victor Milner.

The Battle of New Orleans, as restaged by Cecil B. DeMille [412 . . .], with curly-haired Fredric March [184 . . .] doing a lot of eye- and teeth-flashing as the pirate turned patriot Jean Lafitte. The cast of thousands includes Akim Tamiroff [701 . . .], Walter Brennan [424 . . .], Spring Byington [2325], Beulah Bondi [807 . . .], and Anthony Quinn [1226 . . .], who directed the flop remake twenty years later. Big, blustery, silly—in short, strictly for DeMillions. Milner's cinematography lost to Joseph Ruttenberg's for *The Great Waltz.*

Milner: 412, 470, 740, 757, 827, 1217, 1452, 1668.

305 • BUCCANEER, THE

CECIL B. DeMILLE PRODUCTIONS; PARAMOUNT. 1958.
NOMINATION *Costume Design:* Ralph Jester, Edith Head, and John Jensen.

Pirate Jean Lafitte, played by Yul Brynner [1088], joins forces with Andrew Jackson, played by Charlton Heston [175], during the War of 1812. If it seems like déjà vu, it is: It's a remake of the 1938 Cecil B. DeMille [412 . . .] blockbuster, reteaming DeMille's *Ten Commandments* stars, Brynner and Heston, plus Charles Boyer [36 . . .] and Claire Bloom. Heston had played Jackson before, in 1953's *The President's Lady.* The only new thing about the movie is its director, Anthony Quinn [1226 . . .], who after it bombed never tried directing again. Quinn was married to executive producer DeMille's daughter, Katherine, at the time. The son-in-law also flops.

The costuming Oscar went to Cecil Beaton for *Gigi.*

Jester: 2012. Head: 31, 32, 46, 357, 363, 612, 636, 675, 736, 832, 894, 945, 1003, 1219, 1261, 1263, 1398, 1427, 1504, 1550, 1579, 1587, 1631, 1716, 1727, 1738, 1748, 1840, 1927, 1986, 2012, 2098, 2247, 2298. Jensen: 2012.

306 • BUCK PRIVATES

UNIVERSAL. 1941.
NOMINATIONS *Song:* "Boogie Woogie Bugle Boy of Company B," music by Hugh Prince, lyrics by Don Raye. *Scoring of a Musical Picture:* Charles Previn.

Bud Abbott and Lou Costello, on the lam, decide to hide out in the army. The first feature film for the famous team, directed by Arthur Lubin, is strictly for their fans. For the rest of us, it's mostly notable for the nominated song, performed by the Andrews Sisters, but even that has mostly camp charm, as demonstrated by its revival thirty years later by Bette Midler [700 . . .]. The song Oscar went to Jerome Kern and Oscar Hammerstein's "The Last Time I Saw Paris," from *Lady Be Good.* The scoring award went to *Dumbo*'s Frank Churchill and Oliver Wallace.

Raye: 899. Previn: 668, 1030, 1229, 1485, 1870, 1896.

307 • BUDDY HOLLY STORY, THE

INNOVISIONS-ECA PRODUCTION; COLUMBIA. 1978.

AWARD *Original Song Score and Its Adaptation or Adaptation Score:* Joe Renzetti.

NOMINATIONS *Actor:* Gary Busey. *Sound:* Tex Rudloff, Joel Fein, Curly Thirlwell, and Willie Burton.

Busey plays the rock and roll legend from the formation of his group, the Crickets, played by Charles Martin Smith and Don Stroud, to his death in the plane crash that also killed Ritchie Valens and the Big Bopper. Entertaining biopic that wisely concentrates on the music. Busey, Smith, and Stroud do their own versions of Holly's songs, and they're quite good. The movie didn't succeed in reviving the film musical, though it helped pave the way for *La Bamba* (1987), a parallel story. Directed by Steve Rash.

Like Buddy Holly, Busey was born in Texas. He'd been active in the movies since the early seventies, playing sidekicks, tough guys, and villains in films such as *Thunderbolt and Lightfoot* and the 1976 version of *A Star Is Born.* After losing the Oscar to Jon Voight in *Coming Home,* Busey got larger parts, but mostly in second-rate action pictures. His near death in a motorcycle accident in 1988 converted him from an opponent to a supporter of California's mandatory-helmet law.

The sound award went to *The Deer Hunter.*

Thirlwell: 738. Burton: 58, 209, 1802.5, 2231.

308 • BUGSY

TRISTAR PICTURES PRODUCTION; TRISTAR. 1991.

AWARDS *Art Direction—Set Decoration:* Dennis Gassner; Nancy Haigh. *Costume Design:* Albert Wolsky.

NOMINATIONS *Picture:* Mark Johnson, Barry Levinson, and Warren Beatty, producers. *Actor:* Warren Beatty. *Supporting Actor:* Harvey Keitel. *Supporting Actor:* Ben Kingsley. *Director:* Barry Levinson. *Screenplay Written Directly for the Screen:* James Toback. *Cinematography:* Allen Daviau. *Original Score:* Ennio Morricone.

Beatty plays mobster Benjamin ''Bugsy'' Siegel as a madly obsessive dreamer undone both by his passion for starlet Virginia Hill, played by Annette Bening [840], and by his visions of turning a dusty gambling town into the Las Vegas we now know. Wittily written, packaged with a glossiness that suits its subject, and acted by a gallery of pros that includes Kingsley as Meyer Lansky, Keitel as Mickey Cohen, Elliott Gould [250] as a dopey stool pigeon, and Joe Mantegna as George Raft. But unfortunately the total effect is rather chilly: We come away with the feeling that a lot of talent has been expended on a project that didn't deserve it—there's no resonance, no depth to the story. Critics were initially enthusiastic, and the film won numerous end-of-the-year awards from their various circles, but audiences were indifferent. When the Oscar nominations were announced in February, *Bugsy* led the pack, but by ballot time it was clear that the film was a box-office disappointment. Faced with a best picture slate that included the animated cartoon *Beauty and the Beast,* the shrill docudrama *JFK,* and the melodramatic *The Prince of Tides,* the Oscar voters chose *The Silence of the Lambs,* which had been a critical and popular success. The art direction and costuming Oscars that went to *Bugsy* are revealing: The movie's real strengths are mostly on the surface.

Beatty's performance is one of the strongest he's ever given. Bugsy's womanizing clearly evokes Beatty's own reputation, and the character is in some ways a more polished and urbane version of the one he created in *Bonnie and Clyde.* But Beatty also demonstrates a new fierceness, a sense of something coiled within. Bening, cool and sarcastic, is a perfect foil, and their on-screen chemistry turned into an off-screen marriage. The Oscar went to Anthony Hopkins for *The Silence of the Lambs.*

Keitel, a Brooklyn-born ex-marine who studied at the Actors Studio, got his start in films with the help of director Martin Scorsese [27.5 . . .], in whose first movie, *Who's That Knocking at My Door?* (1968), he appeared. Scorsese's 1973 *Mean Streets* established Keitel as a tough, streetwise presence, and roles in other Scorsese films such as *Alice Doesn't Live Here Anymore* and *Taxi Driver* reinforced the image. Interestingly Keitel played Bugsy Siegel in the 1974 TV movie *The Virginia Hill Story.* An uncompromising performer, Keitel has usually been seen in films that call for intense and sometimes daring work, such as the critically praised *Reservoir Dogs* and *The Bad Lieutenant* in 1992.

The Oscar for *Gandhi* had not made Kingsley a star, but at least he wasn't typecast. There aren't many parts, he once observed, that require an actor to wear a diaper. The award did help keep him employed, primarily as a character actor. The supporting actor Oscar went to Jack Palance for *City Slickers*.

The success of *Rain Man* made Levinson a major Hollywood player, able to choose projects that interested him. Sometimes, unfortunately, these didn't interest others. *Bugsy* was a box-office disappointment, and his next film, *Toys,* an expensive disaster. The directing Oscar went to Jonathan Demme for *The Silence of the Lambs.*

Toback's 1978 film *Fingers,* which he wrote and directed, won him critical acclaim. It attracted the attention of Beatty, as well as critic Pauline Kael, who took a leave from her reviewing duties at the *New Yorker* to try to work on a film project with Toback and Beatty. That project evaporated, and so, it seemed for a while, did Toback's talent. The former English professor's subsequent attempts at moviemaking were bombs: the oddball *Exposed* (1983), which starred Rudolf Nureyev, and the dull *The Pick-up Artist* (1987). The latter film also sparked a devastating *Spy* magazine exposé of Toback's own ways with women. However, his *Bugsy* screenplay fell into good hands— both the star, Beatty, and the director, Levinson, are experienced screenwriters—and Toback was thought to be a leading contender for the Oscar. The award went, however, to Callie Khouri for *Thelma & Louise* —a movie involving womanizers who get their comeuppance.

Daviau lost the cinematography award to Robert Richardson's work on *JFK*. The scoring Oscar went to Alan Menken for *Beauty and the Beast.*

Gassner: 152. Haigh: 152, 708.5. Wolsky: 49, 1061, 1876, 2127.5. Johnson: 1653. Levinson: 75, 112, 546, 1653. Beatty: 255, 890, 1678, 1798. Kingsley: 745. Daviau: 112, 423, 588, 613. Morricone: 506, 1331, 2185.

309 • BUGSY MALONE

GOODTIMES ENTERPRISES LTD. PRODUCTION; PARAMOUNT. 1976.
NOMINATION *Original Song Score and Its Adaptation or Adaptation Score:* Paul Williams.

A very peculiar business: a musical gangster-movie spoof in which all the parts are played by children, and all the machine guns shoot whipped cream. Many of the talents involved here went on to projects that made more sense, including writer-director Alan Parker [1313 . . .], cinematographer Peter Biziou [1333], and art director Geoffrey Kirkland [1698], not to mention the twelve-year-old actress playing Tallulah, Jodie Foster [7 . . .]. The scoring award went to Leonard Rosenman for *Bound for Glory.*

Williams: 403, 1375, 1561, 1911.

310 • BULL DURHAM

MOUNT COMPANY PRODUCTION; ORION. 1988.
NOMINATION *Screenplay Written Directly for the Screen:* Ron Shelton.

Susan Sarandon [107 . . .] plays an intellectual baseball groupie who annually selects a rookie from the hometown minor league team for her favors, which include helping him become a better ballplayer. This time her choice is the dense but talented Tim Robbins, but her plans are complicated by the arrival of Kevin Costner [482], a veteran player who not only has a thing or two to tell Robbins but also has his designs on Sarandon. Witty, sexy comedy that established writer-director Shelton as the closest thing we have to Preston Sturges [823 . . .]. The three leads have never been better—particularly Costner, just on the verge of becoming a film icon. The movie gets much of its texture from the supporting cast's infield chatter and locker-room minidramas. Shelton followed with the less successful *Blaze,* then returned to fine form with *White Men Can't Jump* (1992), whose screenplay was unaccountably overlooked by the Academy. His *Bull Durham* screenplay lost to Ronald Bass and Barry Morrow for *Rain Man.*

311 • *BULLDOG DRUMMOND*

Samuel Goldwyn Productions; United Artists. 1929–30.
Nominations *Actor:* Ronald Colman. *Interior Decoration:* William Cameron Menzies.

Colman plays the famous sleuth, a World War I veteran who in this film is hired by Joan Bennett to rescue her uncle from the clutches of a villainous doctor. F. Richard Jones directs this first sound film about Drummond, whose adventures had been presented on stage and in silent movies. It still has a little of the stiffness of early talkies, but it holds up well, thanks to Colman, the screenplay by Sidney Howard [102 . . .], and the cinematography of Gregg Toland [407 . . .] and George Barnes [537 . . .]. *Bulldog Drummond* was so popular that it launched an endless string of sequels, with various actors, including Ray Milland [1208], in the lead. The film made Colman the first major star to move from silents to talkies, but he lost the Oscar to the star of *Disraeli,* George Arliss, one of the many recruits from the theater making their mark in the sound era. Menzies lost the art direction award to Herman Rosse for *King of Jazz.*

Colman: 436, 567, 1662. Menzies: 38, 112.5, 568, 798, 1018, 2010.

311.5 • *BULLETS OVER BROADWAY*

Jean Doumanian Production; Miramax. 1994.
Award *Supporting Actress:* Dianne Wiest.
Nominations *Supporting Actor:* Chazz Palminteri. *Supporting Actress:* Jennifer Tilly. *Director:* Woody Allen. *Screenplay Written Directly for the Screen:* Woody Allen and Douglas McGrath. *Art Direction–Set Decoration:* Santo Loquasto; Susan Bode. *Costume Design:* Jeffrey Kurland.

John Cusack is a young playwright about to make his debut on the twenties Broadway stage with a play whose chief backer is a gangster determined to see that his talentless bimbo mistress (Tilly) gets to act in it. Wiest is an aging alcoholic star determined to use Cusack to reestablish a fading career. Palminteri plays the enforcer hired by the gangster as a bodyguard for Tilly; he turns out to be a better playwright than the play's real author, precipitating the film's black-comedy denouement. Deft backstage comedy, partly a parody of the genre, partly a satire on theatrical conventions and mannerisms, that like many of Allen's movies centers on a philosophical dilemma—in this case the relationship between art and morality. Also in the very enjoyable cast: Jack Warden [890 . . .], Rob Reiner, Mary-Louise Parker, Harvey Fierstein, Jim Broadbent, and Tracey Ullman.

After her Oscar for Allen's *Hannah and Her Sisters,* Wiest somehow found herself typecast as mothers of troubled offspring in *The Lost Boys* (1987), *Parenthood,* and *Edward Scissorhands.* She turned to theater work for more challenging roles, but her performance as the flamboyant egotistical star in *Bullets* won every major film critics' group award, and demonstrated once again that she has a formidable screen talent. Her win made her the only person in Oscar history to take home two awards for films directed by a single person.

Reaching stardom in his forties, Palminteri is one of the movies' most interesting late bloomers: He knocked around theater and film for years, mostly playing bit parts, until he hit the big time by writing a one-man show for himself about growing up in the Bronx. When he turned it into a screenplay, he attracted the interest of Robert De Niro [113 . . .], who produced and directed it in 1993 as *A Bronx Tale,* a substantial critical success. Palminteri played the lead role, catching Allen's attention. The Oscar went to Martin Landau for *Ed Wood.*

Tilly's career was for a time overshadowed by that of her older sister, Meg Tilly [28], and like Wiest she has had to overcome typecasting: A memorable bit as an empty-headed would-be lounge singer in *The Fabulous Baker Boys* led to offers to play more bimbos. Though her role in *Bullets* is very much in that mold, she has said she took it for the chance to work for Allen—and that it would be her last bimbo.

One of Allen's most entertaining movies in years came forth in a period that would seem to be no time for comedy: He had lost a bruising court battle with Mia Farrow over the custody of their children. He had seen the life he had tried to keep private become the stuff of tabloid headlines and made-for-TV movies. And he had even lost the support of his longtime film distributor, Orion, when the studio went bankrupt. The film's seven nominations may have been at least partly an expression of sympathy for one of the industry's most enduring and prolific talents. The directing Oscar went to Robert Zemeckis for *Forrest Gump.*

McGrath's most prominent—or perhaps most notorious—screenwriting credit was for the 1993 remake of *Born Yesterday,* a critical and commercial flop. He had worked as a writer for *Saturday Night Live* and as a regular contributor to *The New Republic.* He was hired by Allen, for whom his girlfriend worked, to collaborate on the screenplay for *Bullets* at the height of the custody battle between Allen and Farrow. The screenplay Oscar went to Quentin Tarantino and Roger Avary for *Pulp Fiction.*

The art direction award went to *The Madness of King George.* Lizzy Gardiner and Tim Chappel won for the costumes for *The Adventures of Priscilla, Queen of the Desert.*

Wiest: 863, 1530. Allen: 39, 88, 294, 461, 863, 962.5, 1005, 1267, 1636, 1647. Loquasto: 1647, 2345.

312 • *BULLFIGHTER AND THE LADY, THE*

REPUBLIC. 1951.
NOMINATION *Motion Picture Story:* Budd Boetticher and Ray Nazarro.

American Robert Stack [2315] becomes fascinated with bullfighting and hires matador Gilbert Roland to teach him the art, inadvertently causing Roland's death. The lady of the title is Joy Page, best known as Annina in *Casablanca.* Well-handled drama, but your interest in the movie will depend largely on your enthusiasm, or tolerance, for bullfighting. John Wayne [33 . . .] produced and Boetticher directed.

The story is based on Boetticher's own experiences. After graduating from Ohio State, where he played football, he went to Mexico in the mid-thirties and became a professional bullfighter. He was hired as a consultant on the film *Blood and Sand* in 1941 and remained in Hollywood, where his work as a director of westerns attracted a cult following. Andrew Sarris calls him "one of the most fascinating unrecognized

talents in the American cinema." In 1988 Boetticher played a small part in the film *Tequila Sunrise.* His collaborator on the story, Nazarro, was best known as a director of low-budget westerns, primarily for Columbia. They lost to Paul Dehn and James Bernard's *Seven Days to Noon.*

313 • *BULLITT*

SOLAR PRODUCTION; WARNER BROS.-SEVEN ARTS. 1968.
AWARD *Film Editing:* Frank P. Keller.
NOMINATION *Sound:* Warner Bros.-Seven Arts Studio Sound Department.

San Francisco cop Steve McQueen [1753] is assigned to protect the key witness in a criminal case, but when the witness is murdered, McQueen figures there's something fishy going on. This exciting action film may look a little old hat today, but that's because it set the pace for many imitations, particularly its car-chase sequence. With his editing, Keller created the model for all subsequent chases over the vertiginous slopes of San Francisco. Peter Yates [279 . . .] directed, and the cast includes Robert Vaughn [2338], Jacqueline Bisset, and Robert Duvall [92 . . .]. The sound award went to *Oliver!*

Keller: 158, 944, 1059.

313.5 • *BURNT BY THE SUN*

CAMERA ONE/STUDIO "TRITE" PRODUCTION; SONY PICTURES CLASSICS (RUSSIA). 1994.
AWARD *Foreign Language Film.*

Director Nikita Mikhalkov and his six-year-old daughter are the stars of this elegiac, Chekhovian film set in the Soviet Union in 1936, just before the Stalinist purges. Mikhalkov's film was something of a surprise winner, because it was the only one of the five nominees that had not yet received American distribution. Voting in the foreign film category, however, is limited to those Academy members who can certify that they have attended special Academy screenings of all five nominees. But there are other anomalies in the foreign film category that have stirred criticism. Mikhalkov's film, which takes a critical look at Russian history, shared a jury prize at the Cannes Festival with Zhang Yimou's *To Live,* which was about China's recent political past. But Zhang's film was not submitted by the Chinese government for Oscar consideration; in fact, the director was disciplined by his government for political incorrectness. The omission of *To Live* once again brought into question the Academy's method of selecting foreign language film nominees by having each country submit a single candidate for the final slate. More controversy arose when Switzerland's entry, *Red,* was declared ineligible because its director, writers, and cinematographer were Polish, not Swiss. Many critics asked how the Academy could justify an award that excluded from consideration two of the most critically acclaimed foreign films of the year.

314 • BUS STOP

20TH CENTURY-FOX. 1956.

NOMINATION *Supporting Actor:* Don Murray.

Rodeo cowboy Murray falls hard for Marilyn Monroe, a cheesy saloon singer, and carries her off to get married much against her will. Adapted by George Axelrod [278] from a play by William Inge [1894], it's a comparative rarity: a Broadway play successfully "opened up" for the movies. The play took place in the roadside café of the title, but Axelrod places the action at a rodeo in Phoenix and a run-down club where Monroe works, too. It's also perhaps the best film directing of Joshua Logan [643 . . .], a hugely successful Broadway director whose work on movies often leaves much to be desired. In particular, Logan elicits one of Monroe's finest performances. It was her first film after working with famous acting teachers Paula and Lee Strasberg [785]. In his memoirs Logan recounts his hesitations about Monroe, who was playing a role that had won Kim Stanley [722 . . .] great acclaim in the theater. But he found that Monroe's notorious insecurity and unprofessional behavior were kept in abeyance during much of the filming. Logan also stipulated that Paula Strasberg, on whom Monroe had come to rely for approbation after every take, be kept off the set. Monroe triumphs particularly in the night-

club scene, with her hilariously inept rendition of "That Old Black Magic." The cast also includes Arthur O'Connell [73 . . .], Eileen Heckart [133 . . .], and Hope Lange [1558].

At Oscar time *Bus Stop* was curiously overlooked. In part, the neglect was caused by Fox's reluctance to promote Monroe as an actress. Despite her huge box-office presence, the studio was concerned that she was hard to discipline. It put its publicity support instead behind its blockbuster musical *The King and I* and in the actress category promoted both that film's star, Deborah Kerr, and the eventual winner, Ingrid Bergman, making a risky comeback in *Anastasia.*

Murray was nominated for his film debut, though his casting was a disappointment to Monroe, who wanted Rock Hudson [768] for the part. The son of stage people, Murray had served in the Korean War and was appearing on Broadway in *The Skin of Our Teeth* when Logan spotted him. Though tall and handsome, Murray was also skinny, a problem the costumers solved by having him wear a sweatshirt underneath his other clothing. After the nomination, which he lost to Anthony Quinn in *Lust for Life,* Murray continued to work steadily, though he never achieved major stardom. In recent years he has been seen largely in made-for-TV movies. In 1974 he directed a documentary, *The Sex Symbol,* about his costar, Monroe.

315 • BUSTER

N.F.H. PRODUCTION; HEMDALE RELEASING. 1988.

NOMINATION *Song:* "Two Hearts," music by Lamont Dozier, lyrics by Phil Collins.

Collins makes his acting debut in the title role, as one of the men who committed a famous train robbery in England in 1963. Julie Walters [598] plays his wife. Very English little film, directed by David Green, with not much to recommend it other than good performances and Collins' songs on the soundtrack. The Oscar went to Carly Simon's "Let the River Run," from *Working Girl.*

Collins: 26.

316 • BUTCH AND SUNDANCE: THE EARLY DAYS

20TH CENTURY-FOX. 1979.

NOMINATION *Costume Design:* William Ware Theiss.

Prequel to the more celebrated *Butch Cassidy and the Sundance Kid,* this one did very little box office and almost nothing for the careers of the people who participated in it. Tom Berenger [1584] as Butch and William Katt as Sundance have the onerous task of trying to establish their own characters while shadowing Paul Newman [3 . . .] and Robert Redford [1502 . . .]. Director Richard Lester, always inventive, has had better material to work with. The cast includes people who would eventually go on to various degrees of success: Brian Dennehy, Jill Eikenberry, and Peter Weller. Theiss lost to Albert Wolsky's work for *All That Jazz.*

Theiss: 264, 885.

317 • BUTCH CASSIDY AND THE SUNDANCE KID

GEORGE ROY HILL-PAUL MONASH PRODUCTION; 20TH CENTURY-FOX. 1969.

AWARDS *Story and Screenplay—Based on Material Not Previously Published or Produced:* William Goldman. *Cinematography:* Conrad Hall. *Song:* ''Raindrops Keep Fallin' on My Head,'' music by Burt Bacharach, lyrics by Hal David. *Original Score—for a Motion Picture (Not a Musical):* Burt Bacharach.

NOMINATIONS *Picture:* John Foreman, producer. *Director:* George Roy Hill. *Sound:* William Edmundson and David Dockendorf.

Train-robbing outlaws Butch, played by Paul Newman [3 . . .], and Sundance, played by Robert Redford [1502 . . .], team up with a schoolteacher played by Katharine Ross [810] but meet a bad end when they go in search of wealth in Bolivia. This larky, loose-jointed western, very much enlivened by the leads, was a whopping hit. Newman insisted on Redford despite the eagerness of Steve McQueen [1753] to play the role and the studio's desire to cast Warren Beatty [255 . . .]. As a result, Redford, up

to that point regarded only as a pleasant light leading man, became a superstar overnight. Also in the cast are Strother Martin, Henry Jones, Jeff Corey, Cloris Leachman [1139], and Kenneth Mars.

Goldman, a novelist turned screenwriter, also became a hot property, though he later said he found the *Butch Cassidy* screenplay too cutesy. His work on the film *Harper* in 1966, which starred Newman, led to this one, and this one to subsequent work for Redford, including *The Great Waldo Pepper* (1975) and *All the President's Men.*

Hall, the son of one of the coauthors of *Mutiny on the Bounty,* studied film at the University of Southern California and began his work on TV films, commercials, and industrial films. Like Goldman, he was a collaborator with Newman, having shot *Harper* and *Cool Hand Luke.*

The Bacharach-David song was a monster hit, though critics scoffed at its use in the film: to cover a comic-lyrical sequence in which Newman and Ross ride a bicycle. The scene furthers the plot not at all, and its sixties pop flavor is at odds with the period in which the movie takes place. It's like a music video (a genre that didn't exist) dropped into the middle of the movie.

Butch Cassidy seems tame and middle-of-the-road for a year that saw such high-impact films as *The Wild Bunch, Easy Rider, Z, They Shoot Horses, Don't They?, Medium Cool, Alice's Restaurant,* and the winner of the best picture Oscar, *Midnight Cowboy.* Hill, a director who was best known for such high-gloss entertainments as *Hawaii* and *Thoroughly Modern Millie,* said he chose to end *Butch Cassidy* with a freeze-frame of the outlaws heading for certain death because he disliked violence. Other films of the year didn't pull their punches, however, and the Academy gave the directing Oscar to John Schlesinger for *Midnight Cowboy.* The sound award, on the other hand, went to one of the year's escapist films, *Hello, Dolly!*

Goldman: 54. Hall: 504, 987, 1355, 1627, 1771.5, 2017. Bacharach: 35, 103, 370, 2251. David: 35, 370, 2251. Foreman: 1625. Hill: 1927.

318 • BUTTERFIELD 8

AFTON-LINEBROOK PRODUCTION; MGM. 1960.
AWARD *Actress:* Elizabeth Taylor.
NOMINATION *Color Cinematography:* Joseph Ruttenberg and Charles Harten.

Taylor plays Gloria Wandrous, a high-class call girl who wants to get out of the business. Trashy stuff based on a novel by John O'Hara, updated and cheapened, though bowdlerized, by adapters Charles Schnee [130] and John Michael Hayes [1558 . . .], and indifferently directed by Daniel Mann. The cast includes Laurence Harvey [1724], Eddie Fisher, Dina Merrill, Mildred Dunnock [119 . . .], and Kay Medford [737].

Taylor hated the film from the start and agreed to do it only because she had one film left on her contract with MGM. She insisted that Fisher, her husband at the time, be included in the cast. Between the film's release and the Oscars, she became seriously ill, and her life was saved by an emergency tracheotomy. This was her fourth consecutive nomination and she had never won, so the sympathy vote may have put her over the top in the Oscar race. By winning, she deprived Deborah Kerr, nominated for *The Sundowners,* of the award, in the last of Kerr's six unsuccessful runs at the Oscar. Afterward, asked about the movie, Taylor replied, "I still say it stinks."

The cinematography Oscar went to Russell Metty for *Spartacus.*

Taylor: 372, 1657, 1956, 2277. Ruttenberg: 573, 749, 769, 828, 1069, 1232, 1371, 1861, 2234.

319 • BUTTERFLIES ARE FREE

FRANKOVICH PRODUCTIONS; COLUMBIA. 1972.
AWARD *Supporting Actress:* Eileen Heckart.
NOMINATIONS *Cinematography:* Charles B. Lang. *Sound:* Arthur Piantadosi and Charles Knight.

Edward Albert, who is blind and trying to make it on his own without the help of his domineering mother, Heckart, falls in love with his neighbor, Goldie Hawn [323 . . .]. Heckart naturally tries to break it up. Leonard Gershe [736] adapted his Broadway play for the screen, but it remains as thin and saccharine as its smiley-face title, despite good performances. Directed by Milton Katselas.

A major Broadway performer, Heckart seldom found screen roles unless she could reprise one she had played on stage, which she did in both of the films for which she was nominated. Often, however, roles she had played on stage were given to established Hollywood actresses, such as her part in *Picnic,* which went to Rosalind Russell [110 . . .]. She has continued to give strong character performances in her infrequent film and more frequent TV appearances.

Though he received more nominations than any cinematographer in Oscar history, Lang won the award only once. This was his last nomination. He lost to Geoffrey Unsworth for *Cabaret.* The sound award also went to *Cabaret.*

Heckart: 133. Lang: 97, 250, 636, 649, 705, 765, 953, 1480, 1640, 1699, 1738, 1778, 1855, 1860, 1955, 1968, 2180. Piantadosi: 54, 58, 215, 606, 1279, 2113.

320 • BYE BYE BIRDIE

KOHLMAR-SIDNEY PRODUCTION; COLUMBIA. 1963.
NOMINATIONS *Sound:* Charles Rice, sound director, Columbia Studio Sound Department. *Scoring of Music —Adaptation or Treatment:* John Green.

Rock and roll star Conrad Birdie (Jesse Pearson) is set for a publicity stunt in which he will deliver a good-bye kiss to a fan, played by Ann-Margret [362 . . .], on *The Ed Sullivan Show,* before being drafted into the army. Songwriter Dick Van Dyke hopes that Birdie's performance of his song on the show will make him enough money to marry his secretary, Janet Leigh [1632], and escape his domineering mother, Maureen Stapleton [31 . . .]. But the plot is complicated by Bobby Rydell as Ann-Margret's jealous boyfriend and Paul Lynde as her father. Despite bright songs by Charles Strouse and Lee Adams, dances choreographed by Onna White [1471], and a high-powered, star-making performance by Ann-Margret, this adaptation of a hit stage musical is a mess, overloaded with dumb gags and unconvincing plot twists and ineptly directed by George Sidney. Van Dyke and Lynde haven't sufficiently toned down for the camera the performances they gave on stage. And Leigh is miscast: Her character, played on stage by Chita Rivera, is Hispanic, so Leigh has to wear an unbecoming black wig, and her approximation of dancing is no substitute for that of the dynamic Rivera.

The Oscar for sound went to *How the West Was Won.* The scoring award was won by André Previn for *Irma la Douce.*

Rice: 1550. Green: 66, 594, 662, 817, 914, 1298, 1471, 1550, 2047, 2244.

321 • *CABARET*

ABC PICTURES PRODUCTION; ALLIED ARTISTS. 1972.

AWARDS *Actress:* Liza Minnelli. *Supporting Actor:* Joel Grey. *Director:* Bob Fosse. *Cinematography:* Geoffrey Unsworth. *Art Direction—Set Decoration:* Rolf Zehetbauer and Jurgen Kiebach; Herbert Strabel. *Sound:* Robert Knudson and David Hildyard. *Scoring —Adaptation and Original Song Score:* Ralph Burns. *Film Editing:* David Bretherton.

NOMINATIONS *Picture:* Cy Feuer, producer. *Screenplay —Based on Material From Another Medium:* Jay Allen.

Brian, a young Englishman played by Michael York, comes to Berlin in the pre-Hitler 1930s, where he meets the free-spirited American expatriate Sally Bowles (Minnelli), a singer in a raffish cabaret presided over by a sinister master of ceremonies, played by Grey. Sally initiates Brian into the decadent delights of Berlin, and both have affairs with a bisexual baron, played by Helmut Griem. But eventually the encroachment of Nazism, affecting the romance of Brian's student, played by Fritz Tepper, and his aristocratic Jewish girlfriend, played by Marisa Berenson, becomes too much for Brian to tolerate. Perhaps the last great movie musical—one of the few film adaptations of a stage musical that actually improve on the original. Fosse learned a hard lesson from the failure of the first film musical he directed, *Sweet Charity,* that characters in highly charged dramatic situations can break into song on stage, but they look silly doing it in the realistic settings of a movie. For *Cabaret* he chose to relegate all the musical numbers to the stage of the cabaret itself, except for "Tomorrow Belongs

to Me," which he turns into a Nazi propaganda anthem by having it sung by a cherubic Hitler Youth in an outdoor beer garden—the most chilling scene in the film. The film's songs are by the team of John Kander [738] and Fred Ebb [738]. Their song "Maybe This Time," which was composed for the film and thus eligible for the song Oscar, was unaccountably overlooked in the nominations.

Minnelli benefited from the film's revision of the stage musical, in which the role of Sally Bowles was smaller and less central to the theme of societal corruption. The daughter of Judy Garland [1065 . . .] and Vincente Minnelli [66 . . .], she became the first child of two Oscar recipients to win the award. (Her mother's Oscar was a miniature statuette that she received as an honorary award for the "outstanding performance by a screen juvenile" in 1939.) Like her mother, Liza began early in show business, winning a Tony Award at nineteen for *Flora, the Red Menace. Cabaret* established her as a star, but with the decline of the movie musical she has ranged from Broadway to TV to Las Vegas, never quite reaching the top again in movies. Only *New York, New York,* the controversial musical directed by Martin Scorsese [27.5 . . .] in 1977, has given her a second chance to demonstrate her full range as a singing actress on screen.

Like Minnelli, Joel Grey was a performer almost from birth. The son of a Borscht Belt comic, Mickey Katz, he was on stage in his teens. The stage version of *Cabaret* won him a Tony Award in 1966, and he was the only member of the original cast to appear in the film. His subsequent film career has also been spotty. His daughter, Jennifer Grey, has had a modest success as a screen actress, best known for her work in *Dirty Dancing.*

Fosse, too, was the child of vaudevillians, beginning his career as a dancer in his teens. He came to Hollywood in the fifties and appeared in several musicals, including *Kiss Me Kate,* but he made his mark chiefly as a Broadway choreographer and later as a director of musicals. *Cabaret* was only his second film as director, and the Oscar for it crowned a year of achievement in which he won a Tony for his direction of *Pippin* and an Emmy for directing Minnelli's TV special *Liza With a "Z"*—Fosse is the only person to win all three awards in a single year. A workaholic, he continued his frantic creativity until slowed by a serious heart attack—and then turned the experience into an autobiographical movie, *All That Jazz*. His bad habits finally caught up with him, and he died of a heart attack in 1987.

The Oscars were a toe-to-toe contest between *Cabaret* and *The Godfather*. (The other contenders for best picture were *Deliverance, The Emigrants,* and *Sounder.*) In the end *Cabaret* won eight awards—more than any other picture that failed to win the best picture award, which went to *The Godfather*. Mario Puzo and Francis Ford Coppola of *The Godfather* took the screenwriting award away from Jay Allen, who had drawn her screenplay not only from the Broadway show but from its ultimate source, the *Berlin Stories* of Christopher Isherwood, which had previously been turned into the nonmusical play *I Am a Camera,* filmed in 1955.

Minnelli: 1926. Fosse: 49, 1155. Unsworth: 164, 1378, 2021. Knudson: 416, 588, 613, 631, 938, 1439, 1877, 1911, 2274. Hildyard: 659. Burns: 49, 86. Feuer: 920, 976, 1305, 1806, 1932. Allen: 1611.

322 • *CABIN IN THE SKY*

MGM. 1943.
NOMINATION *Song:* "Happiness Is a Thing Called Joe," music by Harold Arlen, lyrics by E. Y. Harburg.

Little Joe, played by Eddie "Rochester" Anderson, is torn between his wife, Petunia, played by Ethel Waters [1575], and the glamorous singer Georgia Brown, played by Lena Horne. When he's wounded in a nightclub fight, a battle for his soul begins. He's saved by Waters' devotion. The racial stereotypes may be offensive, but the performances are wonderful. In addition to the principals, the cast includes Louis Armstrong, John Bubbles (the original Sportin' Life of *Porgy and Bess),* and Duke Ellington [1531] and his orchestra. Many of the cast, including Anderson, had been involved in the 1936 film of the stage hit *The Green Pastures,* which had provoked protests from black leaders, so there was some attempt

on the part of producer Arthur Freed [66 . . .] to defuse protests against *Cabin* by consulting with members of the Hollywood black community on the production. Interestingly one of the people called in for uncredited revisions on the script of *Cabin* was Marc Connelly [352], a coauthor of *Green Pastures*. This was the film directing debut of Vincente Minnelli [66 . . .].

The score for the original Broadway version of *Cabin* was by Vernon Duke and John Latouche. Much of it was retained, but Arlen and Harburg—as well as others, including Ellington—contributed several new songs, of which the nominated song is by far the most memorable. Arlen had three songs in the running; "My Shining Hour," from *The Sky's the Limit,* and "That Old Black Magic," from *Star Spangled Rhythm,* are the others. The winner, however, was Harry Warren and Mack Gordon's "You'll Never Know," from *Hello, Frisco, Hello*.

Arlen: 248, 368, 903, 1838, 1910, 1912, 2186, 2300. Harburg: 340, 2300.

323 • *CACTUS FLOWER*

FRANKOVICH PRODUCTIONS; COLUMBIA. 1969.
AWARD *Supporting Actress:* Goldie Hawn.

To deceive his mistress, Hawn, who's trying to push him into matrimony, Walter Matthau [709 . . .] persuades his secretary, Ingrid Bergman [72 . . .], to pose as his wife. When the dour Bergman loosens up, Matthau falls in love with her. I. A. L. Diamond [91 . . .] adapted the Broadway play by Abe Burrows, which was based on a French farce. It was pretty flimsy stuff even on Broadway, where Lauren Bacall's performance in the Bergman role made it work. It's still more flimsy on screen, but excellent casting keeps it alive. Directed by Gene Saks.

Hawn had become a star on TV's *Laugh-In* by playing a giggly ditz. Her role in *Cactus Flower* was only a slight extension of that persona, but she captured the audience, and the Oscar, by displaying real screen presence in her first major role. Her only previous film work had been in a bit part the year before in a Disney movie, *The One and Only, Genuine, Original*

Family Band, which also featured Kurt Russell, with whom she would later establish a long-term relationship. A series of hits made her a major box-office star.

Hawn: 1617.

324 • CADDY, THE

YORK PICTURES CORPORATION; PARAMOUNT. 1953.
NOMINATION *Song:* "That's Amore," music by Harry Warren, lyrics by Jack Brooks.

A series of Dean Martin–Jerry Lewis routines loosely strung on a thread of a plot about golf nut Lewis teaching Martin how to become a champion. For die-hard fans only. Directed by Norman Taurog [271 . . .], with Donna Reed [732] and Fred Clark.

"That's Amore" was Martin's first hit record, and his success as a recording star eventually led to the breakup of the team. This pleasant novelty song, which made its own comeback thirty-four years later on the soundtrack of *Moonstruck,* lost to Sammy Fain and Paul Francis Webster's "Secret Love" from *Calamity Jane.*

Warren: 21, 569, 788, 791, 877, 897, 1072, 1367, 1501, 1964. Brooks: 341, 1867.

325 • CAESAR AND CLEOPATRA

J. ARTHUR RANK-GABRIEL PASCAL UNITED ARTISTS (UNITED KINGDOM). 1946.
NOMINATION *Color Interior Decoration:* John Bryan.

The George Bernard Shaw [1637] play about the political education of the young Cleopatra, played by Vivien Leigh [798 . . .], receives an elaborate but deadeningly faithful production from producer-director Gabriel Pascal [1637]. Claude Rains [365 . . .] is Julius Caesar, and the cast includes Flora Robson [1759], Stewart Granger, Leo Genn [1644], and Jean Simmons [858 . . .]. It was at the time the most expensive British production in history, involving, among other things, four cinematographers of the first rank: Freddie Young [558 . . .], Robert Krasker [2053], Jack Hildyard [287], and Jack Cardiff [221 . . .]. It's handsome to look at, but it keeps going and going and . . .

The art direction Oscar went to *The Yearling.*

Bryan: 164, 820.

326 • CAGE AUX FOLLES, LA

LES PRODUCTIONS ARTISTES ASSOCIÉS/DA MA PRODUZIONE SPA PRODUCTION; UNITED ARTISTS (FRANCE). 1979.
NOMINATIONS *Director:* Edouard Molinaro. *Screenplay Based on Material From Another Medium:* Francis Veber, Edouard Molinaro, Marcello Danon, and Jean Poiret. *Costume Design:* Piero Tosi and Ambra Danon.

A gay couple, Ugo Tognazzi and Michel Serrault, who run a nightclub in which Serrault stars with a drag act, pretends to be a heterosexual husband and wife when Tognazzi's son brings home his fiancée and her parents. Good performances and the general dizziness of the farce made it a huge success for a foreign language film. Some find its attitude toward gays condescending, however. It was turned into a hit Broadway musical and produced two less successful film sequels.

Molinaro, one of the most successful popular filmmakers in Europe, has yet to repeat the intercontinental success he attained with *La Cage.* His nomination as a director was the only one that year for a film not also nominated for best picture. He took the slot that otherwise might have gone to Martin Ritt for *Norma Rae.* The directing Oscar went to Robert Benton for *Kramer vs. Kramer,* for which he also won the screenplay award. Albert Wolsky won for his costumes for *All That Jazz.*

Tosi: 514, 1156, 1225, 2135.

327 • CAGE OF NIGHTINGALES, A

GAUMONT; LOPERT FILMS (FRENCH). 1947.
NOMINATION *Original Story:* Georges Chaperot and Rene Wheeler.

Noël-Noël, who also contributed to the screenplay, plays the author of a novel about his experiences as a boy at a reform school. The story is told from the point of view of his girlfriend as she reads the book. Unassuming little film, directed by Jean Dréville. The Oscar went to Valentine Davies for *Miracle on 34th Street.*

328 • CAGED

WARNER BROS. 1950.

NOMINATIONS *Actress:* Eleanor Parker. *Supporting Actress:* Hope Emerson. *Story and Screenplay:* Virginia Kellogg and Bernard C. Schoenfeld.

As a young woman, Parker is sentenced to prison as accessory to a robbery her husband initiated, in the course of which he was killed. Essentially innocent, she is hardened by the experience of prison, where she is cheated and abused. Pregnant when she was sentenced, she has to give up the child for adoption. Although the prison warden, Agnes Moorehead [963 . . .], wants to improve conditions for the women, she is denied the funds and support she needs. At the film's end, Parker leaves the prison for a life of prostitution—the only trade for which she has been prepared. Better-than-average women-in-prison film, thanks to good direction by John Cromwell and performances by Ellen Corby [972], Jan Sterling [911], Lee Patrick, and Jane Darwell [815], but there's something cheesily exploitive about the genre itself.

Parker never quite made it to superstardom, but she worked steadily as an actress for almost thirty years, from her first appearances in small roles in the early forties until the early seventies, when like most actresses she found roles for women in their fifties few and far between. Undeniably beautiful, she often seemed stiff and somewhat remote on screen, but landed parts that attracted attention and Oscar nominations. This time she was the weakest nominee in a spectacular contest that featured Bette Davis and Anne Baxter from *All About Eve,* Gloria Swanson from *Sunset Boulevard,* and the winner, Judy Holliday from *Born Yesterday.*

Emerson, who plays an evil, sadistic prison matron, was six feet two inches tall and formidable in build, attributes that she used in menacing roles, but also for comedy in vaudeville and on Broadway, as well as in a memorable bit in *Adam's Rib* in which she hoists a nonplussed Spencer Tracy. The Oscar went to tiny Josephine Hull in *Harvey.*

The writing Oscar went to Charles Brackett, Billy Wilder, and D. M. Marshman, Jr., for *Sunset Boulevard.*

Parker: 534, 1007. Kellogg: 2270.

329 • CAIN AND MABEL

WARNER BROS.-COSMOPOLITAN. 1936.

NOMINATION *Dance Direction:* Bobby Connolly.

Prizefighter Clark Gable [798 . . .] and musical comedy star Marion Davies are thrown together by a publicity stunt, so they fall in love, and out of love, and back in again—you know the routine. Directed by Lloyd Bacon, with Roscoe Karnes, Allen Jenkins, Walter Catlett, and Pert Kelton. Connolly was nominated for his choreography on the production number "1000 Love Songs" but lost to Seymour Felix for the "A Pretty Girl Is Like a Melody" extravaganza in *The Great Ziegfeld.*

Connolly: 295, 781, 1667.

330 • CAINE MUTINY, THE

STANLEY KRAMER PRODUCTIONS; COLUMBIA. 1954.

NOMINATIONS *Picture:* Stanley Kramer, producer. *Actor:* Humphrey Bogart. *Supporting Actor:* Tom Tully. *Screenplay:* Stanley Roberts. *Sound Recording:* John P. Livadary. *Scoring of a Dramatic or Comedy Picture:* Max Steiner. *Film Editing:* William A. Lyon and Henry Batista.

Bogart plays Queeg, the captain of a U.S. Navy destroyer who panics during a typhoon and is relieved of duty by Lieutenant Maryk (Van Johnson), with the support of his fellow officers. But the real villain of the piece, according to Herman Wouk in his novel and the play he based on it, *The Caine Mutiny Court-Martial,* is the snide Captain Keefer (Fred MacMurray), who has steadily undermined the crew's confidence in the unlikable captain. Jose Ferrer [473 . . .] plays Lt. Barney Greenwald, appointed to defend Maryk at the court-martial; afterward, he denounces Keefer's cynical undermining of the captain's authority. Like so many films produced by Kramer, this one seems a little pompous and self-important, especially Greenwald's posttrial speech denouncing Keefer and praising Queeg for "standing guard over this fat, dumb, happy country of ours." There's a needless romantic subplot designed to make stars out of Robert Francis and May Wynn. It didn't, though in Francis' case it was because he was killed in a plane crash the year after the movie's release. Wynn, whose real name was Donna Lee Hickey, took her screen name from the character she plays in this film. She used it in three more movies and disappeared. Edward Dmytryk [467] directed.

Columbia was riding high at the Oscars, with two nominees for best picture. Though *Caine* was the bigger moneymaker, the other one, *On the Waterfront,* was the Oscar winner.

Bogart's Queeg is one of his most memorable performances. He longed to play the part from the time he read Wouk's novel, and took a salary cut to do so in the film after Lloyd Nolan won acclaim in the role on stage. Today, Bogart's itchy, paranoid Queeg, rattling his steel ball bearings and babbling about strawberries, resembles no one more than Richard M. Nixon in the final days. The Oscar went to Marlon Brando for *On the Waterfront.*

With several strong supporting performances to choose from—MacMurray is particularly good in one of his infrequent bad-guy roles—it's surprising that the Academy chose the relatively unmemorable performance by Tom Tully as Captain DeVriess. The Oscar went to the more flamboyant performance of Edmond O'Brien in *The Barefoot Contessa.*

George Seaton's screenplay for *The Country Girl* took the writing award. The winner for sound was *The Glenn Miller Story.* Dimitri Tiomkin won for scoring *The High and the Mighty* and Gene Milford for the editing of *On the Waterfront.*

Kramer: 522, 843, 912, 1065, 1812. Bogart: 24, 365. Livadary: 455, 596, 732, 1058, 1206, 1215, 1303, 1366, 1370, 1488, 1521, 1740, 1872, 2111, 2325, 2327. Steiner: 16, 154, 190, 365, 385, 492, 679, 747, 754, 798, 999, 1043, 1046, 1052, 1162, 1169, 1170, 1207, 1324, 1408, 1430, 1456, 1690, 1779, 1828. Lyon: 456, 732, 1058, 1566, 1776.

331 • CALAMITY JANE

WARNER BROS. 1953.
AWARD *Song:* "Secret Love," music by Sammy Fain, lyrics by Paul Francis Webster.
NOMINATIONS *Sound Recording:* William A. Mueller,

sound director, Warner Bros. Sound Department. *Scoring of a Musical Picture:* Ray Heindorf.

Doris Day [1572] plays the title role and Howard Keel is Wild Bill Hickok in this poor man's *Annie Get Your Gun,* directed by David Butler. It's colorful and very pleasant, though its assumption that Jane is a freak until she lands a man is the fifties at its worst. Day and Keel are in very fine voice indeed.

Fain was one of the most prolific Hollywood songwriters, with nominations spread across forty years—from "That Old Feeling," from *Vogues of 1938,* to "Someone's Waiting for You," from *The Rescuers* in 1977. Webster, his frequent lyricist, was still more prolific, though the quality of his output varies—he was often called on to supply title songs for films whose titles (e.g., *Friendly Persuasion, Tender Is the Night)* hardly lend themselves to being used in song lyrics. He rarely achieved the colloquial simplicity of his most memorable lyric, for the Duke Ellington [1531] song "I Got It Bad (and That Ain't Good)." "Secret Love" has a lovely melody by Fain that showed off Doris Day's voice well, but Webster's lyrics are a bit banal: "Highest hill" leads too easily to the rhyme "golden daffodil." Even in Wordsworth that one sounds trite.

The Oscar for sound went to *From Here to Eternity.* The scoring award was won by Alfred Newman for *Call Me Madam.*

Fain: 95, 376, 856, 1213, 1276, 1681, 1925, 2014, 2214. Webster: 33, 64, 95, 376, 604, 663, 730, 856, 1213, 1276, 1322, 1388, 1755, 1925, 2014. Mueller: 1337. Heindorf: 479, 666, 930, 1043, 1204, 1385, 1408, 1430, 1690, 1719, 1750, 1910, 2058, 2186, 2243, 2310, 2318.

332 • CALIFORNIA SUITE

RAY STARK PRODUCTION; COLUMBIA. 1978.
AWARD *Supporting Actress:* Maggie Smith.
NOMINATIONS *Screenplay Based on Material From Another Medium:* Neil Simon. *Art Direction–Set Decoration:* Albert Brenner; Marvin March.

Playwright Simon's version of *Grand Hotel:* four unrelated stories that take place at the Beverly Hills Hotel. Smith stars with Michael Caine [35 . . .] in the best of the four, about a neurotic actress and her husband waiting out Oscar night—she loses, making Smith the only person to win an Oscar for playing an Oscar loser. In descending order of quality, the other stories involve a divorcing couple, played by Jane Fonda [394 . . .] and Alan Alda; a man, played by Walter Matthau [709 . . .], whose wife, played by Elaine May [890], discovers him with a prostitute; and doctors played by Bill Cosby and Richard Pryor, whose vacation at the hotel turns into a slapstick disaster. The mixture of stories and styles keeps the film moving, so that the unfunny Pryor-Cosby sequence doesn't sink the movie completely, but if the whole thing had been on the level of Smith and Caine's delicate performing, it would have been a lot better. Herbert Ross [2152] directed.

Smith made her London stage debut in 1952 and soon became one of the most celebrated actresses of her generation, as renowned for her work in serious drama and the classics as for her performances in contemporary works and comedy. Although a gift for accents and attitudes has caused most of her film work to be in character roles, she has never settled into a small range of mannerisms. She continues to find ways of making each role unique, even in parts where a lesser actress might simply resort to caricature and familiar shtick.

Simon lost to Oliver Stone's screenplay for *Midnight Express*. The art direction Oscar went to *Heaven Can Wait*.

Smith: 1506, 1608, 1725, 2134. Simon: 803, 1461, 1976. Brenner: 159, 1976, 2152, 2165. March: 12.5, 86, 1976, 2152.

333 • CALL ME MADAM

20TH CENTURY-FOX. 1953.
AWARD *Scoring of a Musical Picture:* Alfred Newman.
NOMINATION *Color Costume Design:* Irene Sharaff.

Ethel Merman plays a wealthy Washington party-giver who is rewarded for her fund-raising activities with an ambassadorship to a tiny European principality, where she sets in motion various romantic and political intrigues that come out for the best in the end. Howard Lindsay and Russel Crouse converted

the experiences of actual Washington socialite Perle Mesta, ambassador to Luxembourg under Truman, into the book for a musical by Irving Berlin [34 . . .]. Donald O'Connor and Merman sing the most famous song in the score, the duet "You're Just in Love," and the cast includes George Sanders [46], who does his own singing, and Vera-Ellen, who doesn't (she's dubbed by Carole Richard), as well as Walter Slezak, Billy DeWolfe, and Lilia Skala [1174]. The score's the thing here, and the chance to see Merman in one of the parts she created on Broadway, since some of her most famous roles, in *Annie Get Your Gun* and *Gypsy,* for example, went to other performers. Otherwise, it's a minor effort as far as film musicals go, slackly directed by Walter Lang. Newman's scoring won over that of a more celebrated film musical, *The Band Wagon.*

The costuming Oscar went to Charles LeMaire and Emile Santiago for *The Robe.*

Newman: 31, 34, 46, 72, 138, 182, 226, 334, 347, 375, 428, 437, 457, 476, 495, 542, 690, 797, 833, 952, 953, 959, 962, 1016, 1082, 1088, 1213, 1278, 1362, 1397, 1475, 1616, 1655, 1849, 1868, 1883, 1921, 2043, 2046, 2091, 2258, 2286, 2294, 2316. Sharaff: 66, 290, 338, 413, 690, 852, 896, 1088, 1507, 1592, 1910, 2000, 2244, 2277.

334 • CAMELOT

WARNER BROS.-SEVEN ARTS. 1967.
AWARDS *Art Direction—Set Decoration:* John Truscott and Edward Carrere; John W. Brown. *Scoring of Music —Adaptation or Treatment:* Alfred Newman and Ken Darby. *Costume Design:* John Truscott.
NOMINATIONS *Cinematography:* Richard H. Kline. *Sound:* Warner Bros.-Seven Arts Studio Sound Department.

King Arthur, played by Richard Harris [660 . . .], weds Queen Guinevere, played by Vanessa Redgrave [263 . . .], but she falls in love with Sir Lancelot (Franco Nero). Meanwhile, the evil Mordred (David Hemmings) plots the fall of the Table Round. Big budget, big flop. The chief culprits here are director Joshua Logan [643 . . .] and producer Jack L. Warner [55 . . .]. Logan had been unimpressed with the Broadway production of the musical by Alan Jay Lerner [66 . . .] and Frederick Loewe [769 . . .], which had starred Richard Burton [85 . . .], Julie Andrews [1284 . . .], and Robert Goulet. He found Burton's performance detached and uninvolved, felt that the "cozy and little girlish and adorable" Andrews was miscast as the lusty Guinevere, and decided that Goulet was too American for his part. Logan was determined to do it right in the film version and got, he thought, the complete backing of Warner to bring his visions to the screen. Warner agreed to give Logan a free hand on the production if, like Warner's huge success, *My Fair Lady,* the film could be made entirely at the studio in Burbank. Redgrave was cast after Logan's son saw her in *Morgan!,* one of her first important film roles. Harris, eager to be considered the "next Burton," volunteered to test for the role. And Nero, who up to that point had appeared largely in Italian films, spaghetti westerns, and the epic *The Bible* (in which, interestingly, he played Abel and was slain by Harris as Cain), was chosen largely on the strength of his extraordinary good looks. The problem was that none of these actors could sing very well, and from a box-office standpoint none was a major star. The deficiencies of the cast were reinforced by what was always a major problem with *Camelot,* even on stage: a weak book that relied on its memorable songs and spectacular scenic effects to overcome the monotony of its characters and plot. Based on *The Once and Future King,* by T. H. White, the first part of which had been animated by Disney as *The Sword in the Stone,* the script necessarily dropped much of the book's fantasy and medieval lore and concentrated on the love triangle. The result is that Arthur's weakness, Guinevere's horniness, and Lancelot's conceit become the dominant notes of their characters. Logan persuaded Warner to allow him to shoot on location in Spain while waiting for Redgrave to complete a prior commitment, which gave Warner leverage when the film fell behind schedule and went over budget. Warner took control of the picture, preventing Logan from doing the reshooting and final touches he says the film needed. In Logan's memoirs he implicitly blames

Warner for the movie's failure, though he says it was "the most beautiful picture I ever made."

The credit for the film's beauty goes to its design team, and chiefly to Truscott, a twenty-nine-year-old Australian who had designed the London stage production of *Camelot.* Logan wanted to eliminate pseudo-medieval clichés; together, they agreed that they would avoid the color red in the film's design—"just because it was used so often in medieval pageant pictures," Logan says. Truscott also helped find the principal Spanish locations: the castle of Coca, which is used for Camelot, and the Alcázar in Segovia, which is Lancelot's Joyous Gard. The arid Spanish locations, however, meant that the terrain around the castles had to be replanted, and the grass spray-painted green, to resemble England.

Newman and Darby, who had worked with Logan on *Picnic* and *South Pacific,* arranged Loewe's music, with some changes worked out by Logan and Loewe that included taking Guinevere's "The Lusty Month of May" at a slower, more sensuous tempo, and turning the Arthur-Guinevere duet "What Do the Simple Folk Do?" into a sadder, less comic song.

Kline, who was just beginning his career as director of photography after serving an apprenticeship as cameraman and camera assistant, lost to Burnett Guffey for *Bonnie and Clyde.* The sound award went to *In the Heat of the Night.*

Carrere: 15, 1973. Newman: 31, 34, 46, 72, 138, 182, 226, 333, 347, 375, 428, 437, 457, 476, 495, 542, 690, 797, 833, 952, 953, 959, 962, 1016, 1082, 1088, 1213, 1278, 1362, 1397, 1475, 1616, 1655, 1849, 1868, 1883, 1921, 2043, 2046, 2091, 2258, 2286, 2294, 2316. Darby: 690, 953, 1088, 1592, 1883. Kline: 1089.

335 • CAMILA

GEA CINEMATOGRAPHICA S.R.L PRODUCTION (ARGENTINA). 1984.

NOMINATION *Foreign Language Film.*

Camila, a woman from a well-to-do family, falls in love with a Jesuit priest in mid-nineteenth-century Argentina. The lovers flee from the church and state authorities, but in the end the priest's weakness betrays them. Director and coscreenwriter Maria Luisa Bemberg gives the story a feminist slant that saves it from melodrama. The Oscar went to the Swiss film *Dangerous Moves.*

336 • CAMILLE
MGM. 1937.
NOMINATION *Actress:* Greta Garbo.

Marguerite Gautier (Garbo), a Parisian courtesan who is being supported by the Baron de Varville (Henry Daniell), falls in love with Armand Duval (Robert Taylor), but his father, played by Lionel Barrymore [723 . . .], persuades her to break off the relationship. She returns to Varville and is denounced by Armand for her faithlessness. But when the consumption that has been sapping her strength finally takes its toll, she dies in the arms of Armand, who has learned the truth from his father. The greatest tearjerker of all, given the best that MGM's money could buy: sensitive direction by George Cukor [262 . . .], luminous camera work by William Daniels [84 . . .], a screenplay from the prestigious hands of Frances Marion [202 . . .], James Hilton [1371], and Zoë Akins, and the prime hamming of Laura Hope Crews, Jessie Ralph, and a host of character actors. Above all, it has Garbo, and though you can't quite see what she sees in the pretty, wooden Taylor, you're always convinced she's a woman in love. The only mystery is why the film, one of the classics of the Hollywood golden age, received only a single nomination, especially with a best picture slate whose ten nominees included such nonclassics as *In Old Chicago* and *One Hundred Men and a Girl.* The answer probably lies in the studio's desire to promote the far more expensive *The Good Earth,* which was seen as a memorial to its producer, Irving Thalberg [150 . . .], who had died in 1936 before its completion. Thalberg had also produced *Camille,* but it was considered a less risky venture than the epic about the tribulations of Chinese peasants. *The Good Earth* received five nominations, and its star, Luise Rainer, deprived Garbo of an Oscar for one of the screen's definitive performances.

Garbo: 84, 1440, 1718.

337 • CAMILLE CLAUDEL
FILMS CHRISTIAN FECHNER/LILITH FILMS/GAUMONT/A2 TV FRANCE/FILMS A2/DD PRODUCTION; ORION CLASSICS (FRANCE). 1989.
NOMINATIONS *Actress:* Isabelle Adjani. *Foreign Language Film.*

Adjani plays the title role, a young woman who takes lessons from the sculptor August Rodin, played by Gérard Depardieu [474], and soon becomes his lover. When Rodin refuses to break with the woman who has been his mistress for twenty years, Camille sets out on her own as an artist but is thwarted at every turn by society and her own narrow-minded family. Lavishly produced but somewhat overstated film that was cut by almost half an hour for its American release. Directed by Bruno Nuytten.

Adjani proves once again that she's one of the world's great actresses. She has been deprived of the success she might have achieved in the States by the lack of good roles for women in recent years. As she has noted, the parts for which she might best be suited in American films are immediately picked off by stars such as Meryl Streep [472 . . .] and Jessica Lange [244.5 . . .]. She lost this time to Jessica Tandy in *Driving Miss Daisy.* The foreign language film award went to Italy's *Cinema Paradiso.*

Adjani: 1933.

338 • CAN-CAN
SUFFOLK-CUMMINGS PRODUCTIONS; 20TH CENTURY-FOX. 1960.
NOMINATIONS *Scoring of a Musical Picture:* Nelson Riddle. *Color Costume Design:* Irene Sharaff.

Shirley MacLaine [91 . . .], the proprietor of a nightclub, is brought to court for the crime of presenting the "immoral" dance that gives the film its title. Frank Sinatra [732 . . .] is the lawyer who defends her. There are lots of things wrong with this film version of a Broadway musical by Cole Porter [261 . . .], not the least of which is that MacLaine and Sinatra are two of the most American performers around, as becomes glaringly obvious when they are forced to share the screen with Maurice Chevalier [203 . . .] and Louis Jourdan, who were obviously signed on in hope that some of the charm of *Gigi* would rub off on the project. It didn't. On the other hand, the score is full of wonderful Porter songs, including "I Love Paris" and "C'est Magnifique," as well as some that weren't in the Broadway show but are interpolated from other Porter scores: "Let's Do It," "Just One of Those Things," and "You Do Something to Me." Too bad the whole package isn't up to that standard. The film's chief claim to fame is that Soviet Premier Nikita Khrushchev and his wife visited the set during its filming and were scandalized by the dancing girls. Directed by Walter Lang.

The Oscar for scoring went to Morris Stoloff and Harry Sukman for *Song Without End.* The costume award was won by Valles and Bill Thomas for *Spartacus.*

Riddle: 821, 1172, 1518, 1708. Sharaff: 66, 290, 333, 413, 690, 852, 896, 1088, 1507, 1592, 1910, 2000, 2244, 2277.

339 • CANDIDATE, THE

Redford-Ritchie Production; Warner Bros. 1972.
Award *Story and Screenplay—Based on Factual Material or Material Not Previously Published or Produced:* Jeremy Larner.
Nomination *Sound:* Richard Portman and Gene Cantamessa.

Robert Redford [1502 . . .] is persuaded to run for the Senate because political operative Peter Boyle thinks his sincerity, combined with his extreme good looks, might attract voters. But during the campaign he loses his chief virtue—sincerity. Shrewd look at politics in the media era that still seems relevant, though the film is a bit formulaic and heavy-handed at times. Directed by Michael Ritchie, with a cast that includes Don Porter as the Nixonian opponent, Melvyn Douglas [169], and Michael Lerner [152].

Screenwriter Larner knew the political campaign scene from working as an aide to former Senator Eugene McCarthy. Larner's novel, *Drive, He Said,* was filmed in 1972 under the direction of Jack Nicholson [395 . . .].

The Oscar for sound went to *Cabaret.*

Portman: 418, 502, 521, 738, 784, 1109, 1473, 1526, 1701, 2331. Cantamessa: 416, 588, 1439, 1914, 2165, 2331.

340 • CAN'T HELP SINGING

Universal. 1945.
Nominations *Song:* "More and More," music by Jerome Kern, lyrics by E. Y. Harburg. *Scoring of a Musical Picture:* Jerome Kern and H. J. Salter.

Tenderfoot Deanna Durbin goes West in pursuit of her man. Even the Kern-Harburg songs, which are not up to their highest standards, can't save this snooze of a musical, directed by Frank Ryan and featuring Akim Tamiroff [701 . . .], Leonid Kinskey, Clara Blandick, and Thomas Gomez [1695]. In addition to the nominated song, Durbin sings "Californ-i-ay," "Any Moment Now," and the title tune. Durbin fans will note that it's her only color film.

The song Oscar went to Rodgers and Hammerstein's "It Might As Well Be Spring," from *State Fair.* The scoring award was won by Georgie Stoll for *Anchors Aweigh.*

Kern: 375, 455, 1117, 1707, 1990, 2327. Harburg: 322, 2300. Salter: 62, 399, 1030, 1307, 2060.

341 • CANYON PASSAGE

Walter Wanger: Universal. 1946.
Nomination *Song:* "Ole Buttermilk Sky," music by Hoagy Carmichael, lyrics by Jack Brooks.

Dana Andrews squares off against Brian Donlevy [161] in this entertaining western with handsome Technicolor photography by Edward Cronjager [176 . . .]. The stalwart cast includes Susan Hayward [973 . . .], Ward Bond, Andy Devine, and Lloyd Bridges, directed by Jacques Tourneur. Carmichael sings his song on screen. The Oscar went to Harry Warren and Johnny Mercer for "On the Atchison, Topeka and Santa Fe," from *The Harvey Girls.*

Carmichael: 905. Brooks: 324, 1867.

342 • CAPE FEAR

Amblin Entertainment Production in association with Cappa Films and Tribeca Productions; Universal. 1991.
Nominations *Actor:* Robert De Niro. *Supporting Actress:* Juliette Lewis.

Psychotic ex-con De Niro takes revenge on the lawyer, Nick Nolte [1612], who prosecuted him, by tormenting Nolte and his family—wife Jessica Lange [244.5 . . .] and daughter Lewis. An almost baroque remake of a 1962 thriller that starred Robert Mitchum [1935] and Gregory Peck [759 . . .], who, along with original cast member Martin Balsam [2067], make cameo appearances here. Director Martin Scorsese [27.5 . . .] intended his version as a kind of *hommage* to the original, but there's an unpleasantly show-offy quality to this film—as if Scorsese were trying to show what a truly gifted director can do with a generic thriller plot. The talent involved, in addition to director and actors, is impressive: cinematography by Freddie Francis [779 . . .], editing by Thelma Schoonmaker [806 . . .], and music adapted by Elmer Bernstein [27.5 . . .] from the original Bernard Herrmann [50 . . .] score. But it's used to produce little more than two hours of shock effects and in-jokes for cineastes.

De Niro, like Jack Nicholson [395 . . .], is one of the few actors who can play an over-the-top role like this one and not look foolish. The part gives him a wide range to work in—plausibly sane one moment, raving loon the next. The Academy voters, however, preferred the more understated and cerebral menace of Anthony Hopkins in *The Silence of the Lambs.*

Only the year before, Lewis, still in her teens, was playing in movies such as *National Lampoon's Christmas Vacation* and such barely released items as *The Runnin' Kind* and *Meet the Hollowheads.* Her appearance in *Cape Fear* as the rebellious daughter, particularly in the scene in which De Niro makes teasing overtures to her on the set of a school play, made her the talk of Hollywood. She has developed into a specialist in eccentrics, ranging from the college student who attracts Woody Allen in *Husbands and Wives* to the psychotic thrill killer in *Natural Born Killers* (1994). The Oscar went to Mercedes Ruehl for *The Fisher King.*

De Niro: 113, 521, 785, 1650, 2005.

343 • CAPTAIN BLOOD

COSMOPOLITAN; FIRST NATIONAL. 1935.

NOMINATIONS *Picture:* Hal Wallis, with Harry Joe Brown and Gordon Hollingshead, producers. *Sound Recording:* Nathan Levinson.

Unjustly transported to the colonies for providing medical aid to rebels against James II, Dr. Peter Blood (Errol Flynn) turns pirate, matching swords with French buccaneer Basil Rathbone [979 . . .] and wooing Olivia de Havilland [798 . . .]. The first of Flynn's swashbucklers and one of the best—chock full of action and romance, a popcorn classic. It put Warner Bros. (of which First National was a subsidiary) in the business of finding vehicles for Flynn and de Havilland, who starred together in seven films, although Flynn had been cast in *Captain Blood* only after Robert Donat [406 . . .] became unavailable. Studio head Jack Warner [55 . . .] was furious at the comparatively few nominations for *Captain Blood* and his other best picture candidate, *A Midsummer Night's Dream,* so he mounted write-in campaigns for both films, pushing *Blood*'s director, Michael Curtiz [79 . . .], and *Dream*'s cinematographer, Hal Mohr, in particular. It paid off for Mohr, who became the only person to win an Oscar as a write-in candidate, but Curtiz finished second, after John Ford for *The Informer.* Another *Captain Blood* write-in candidate, the score by Erich Wolfgang Korngold [17 . . .], placed third, behind the officially nominated scores for *Mutiny on the Bounty* and the winner, *The Informer.* And Casey Robinson's screenplay also placed third after those two films. The confusion caused by these write-in campaigns led to a change in Academy rules, eliminating write-ins but expanding the number of nominations in several categories.

The movie itself took third place in the best picture race, after *The Informer* and the winner, *Mutiny on the Bounty.* This was the sole feature film nomination for coproducer Hollingshead, but as the executive in charge of Warners' short subjects he received twenty-one nominations and five Oscars for short films.

The sound award went to Douglas Shearer for *Naughty Marietta.*

Wallis: 17, 55, 85, 164, 365, 676, 689, 712, 965, 1046, 1095, 1162, 1248, 1482, 1727, 1779, 2233, 2318. Brown: 34. Levinson: 16, 30, 385, 531, 689, 710, 712, 790, 930, 965, 1052, 1169, 1621, 1690, 1768, 1769, 1779, 1930, 1949, 2058, 2318.

344 • CAPTAIN CAREY, U.S.A.

PARAMOUNT. 1950.

AWARD *Song:* "Mona Lisa," music and lyrics by Ray Evans and Jay Livingston.

Alan Ladd returns to an Italian village where, during the war, an informer betrayed Ladd's comrades and the villagers who supported them. Moderately interesting melodrama, directed by Mitchell Leisen [587], with Wanda Hendrix, Francis Lederer, and Russ Tamblyn [1558]. The most memorable thing about it is the song, which became a huge hit for Nat King Cole and helped set the vogue for spin-off pop tunes with only tangential relevance to the movies in which they appear.

Evans: 512, 951, 1260, 1522, 2001, 2278. Livingston: 512, 951, 1260, 1522, 2001, 2278.

345 • CAPTAIN CAUTION

HAL ROACH; UNITED ARTISTS. 1940.

NOMINATION *Sound Recording:* Elmer Raguse.

When her father is killed, Louise Platt takes over his ship and fights the British in the War of 1812. Busy little action programmer from producer Hal Roach's film factory, directed by Richard Wallace and featuring Victor Mature, Bruce Cabot, and in a bit part, Alan Ladd. The Oscar went to Douglas Shearer for *Strike Up the Band.*

Raguse: 757.5, 1306, 1464, 1487, 2117, 2118.

346 • CAPTAIN EDDIE

20TH CENTURY-FOX. 1945.

NOMINATION *Special Effects:* Fred Sersen and Sol Halprin, photographic; Roger Heman and Harry Leonard, sound.

Fred MacMurray plays aviator Eddie Rickenbacker, whose life flashes before his eyes as he floats in a raft after his plane has been shot down. This rather plodding biopic, directed by Lloyd Bacon, wastes a good cast—Charles Bickford [651 . . .], Thomas Mitchell [962 . . .], Lloyd Nolan, and James Gleason [904] —not to mention a subject that had real potential. The special effects award was won by *Wonder Man.*

Sersen: 226, 241, 458, 520, 1655, 2286, 2317. Heman: 226, 418, 458, 520, 1041, 2286.

347 • CAPTAIN FROM CASTILE

20TH CENTURY-FOX. 1947.

NOMINATION *Scoring of a Dramatic or Comedy Picture:* Alfred Newman.

When his family is robbed of its fortune, young Pedro de Vargas (Tyrone Power) sets out to recoup the losses and get revenge by finding wealth in the New World with Cortés (Cesar Romero). Big, colorful adventure epic adapted by Lamar Trotti [1516 . . .] from a Samuel Shellabarger best-seller, directed by Henry King [1868 . . .]. There may be less here than meets the eye, but what meets the eye—color cinematography by Charles Clarke [837 . . .] and Arthur Arling [980 . . .], art direction supervised by Richard Day [22 . . .] and James Basevi [746 . . .]—is handsome. Newman's score, which lost to Miklos Rozsa's for *A Double Life,* is one of his best.

Newman: 31, 34, 46, 72, 138, 182, 226, 333, 334, 375, 428, 437, 457, 476, 495, 542, 690, 797, 833, 952, 953, 959, 962, 1016, 1082, 1088, 1213, 1278, 1362, 1397, 1475, 1616, 1655, 1849, 1868, 1883, 1921, 2043, 2046, 2091, 2258, 2286, 2294, 2316.

348 • CAPTAIN FURY

HAL ROACH; UNITED ARTISTS. 1939.

NOMINATION *Interior Decoration:* Charles D. Hall.

Brian Aherne [1064] and Victor McLaglen [999 . . .] tangle with each other in this action drama set in a nineteenth-century Australian penal colony. The cast, directed by Hal Roach, also includes Paul Lukas [2233] and John Carradine. Passable stuff, but it never stood a chance in the Oscar race against Lyle Wheeler's work on *Gone With the Wind.*

Hall: 1306.

349 • CAPTAIN KIDD

BOGEAUS; UNITED ARTISTS. 1945.

NOMINATION *Scoring of a Dramatic or Comedy Picture:* Werner Janssen.

With his career in a slump, Charles Laughton [1387 . . .] signed on to ham his way through a low-budget picture about the famous pirate. The cast, directed by Rowland V. Lee, includes Randolph Scott, John Carradine, and Gilbert Roland. To make matters worse, Laughton reprised the role in 1952 in *Abbott and Costello Meet Captain Kidd*. At least in that one he was *supposed* to be funny.

This was the last year that the Academy allowed each studio or production company to name its own candidate for the music awards. There were twenty-one entries in the category for scoring a dramatic or comedy film alone, and Janssen was responsible for three of them. (The other two were *Guest in the House* and *The Southerner.*) The award was won by Miklos Rozsa for *Spellbound*.

Janssen: 233, 624, 757, 844, 1884.

350 • *CAPTAIN NEWMAN, M.D.*

UNIVERSAL-BRENTWOOD-REYNARD PRODUCTION; UNIVERSAL. 1963.
NOMINATIONS *Supporting Actor:* Bobby Darin. *Screenplay —Based on Material From Another Medium:* Richard L. Breen, Phoebe Ephron, and Henry Ephron. *Sound:* Waldon O. Watson, sound director, Universal City Studio Sound Department.

Gregory Peck [759 . . .] plays the title role in this seriocomic look at an army psychiatrist's battle with the brass during World War II. The film, directed by David Miller, has a few problems with tone, veering from earnest to wacky and back again once too often. Movies like *MASH* and *One Flew Over the Cuckoo's Nest* have only made the inadequacy of this film more glaring, but at least it has a strong cast: Tony Curtis [522], Eddie Albert [887 . . .], James Gregory, Angie Dickinson, Jane Withers, and in his second film role, Robert Duvall [92 . . .].

Darin plays one of Peck's patients who is tormented by cowardice in battle. One of the most talented of the teen pop idols who flourished between Elvis and the Beatles, Darin was able to move from bubblegum novelties like ''Splish, Splash'' and ''Queen of the Hop'' to the more jazz-influenced ''Mack the Knife,'' his 1959 smash hit. The Oscar nomination, for which he lost to Melvyn Douglas in *Hud,* recognized a solid performance but did nothing

for his career as an actor. He died of a heart attack in 1973, at the age of thirty-seven.

The Ephrons worked together as playwrights and screenwriters for many years, and Henry Ephron produced several films as well, including *Carousel* (1956) and *Desk Set* (1957). Writer-director Nora Ephron [1821 . . .] is their daughter. John Osborne won the Oscar for *Tom Jones*.

The sound award went to *How the West Was Won*.

Breen: 705, 2093. Watson: 655, 690, 744, 1810, 2035.

351 • *CAPTAIN OF KOPENICK, THE*

REAL-FILM GMBH (FEDERAL REPUBLIC OF GERMANY). 1956.
NOMINATION *Foreign Language Film*.

An unemployed man impersonates an army officer and leads a military takeover of the city hall in the Berlin suburb of Köpenick. A mildly satiric version of a play by Karl Zuckmayer, directed by Helmut Käutner, this was one of the first nominees for the foreign language film award. It lost to a far more memorable film, *La Strada*.

352 • *CAPTAINS COURAGEOUS*

MGM. 1937.
AWARD *Actor:* Spencer Tracy.
NOMINATIONS *Picture:* Louis D. Lighton, producer. *Screenplay:* Marc Connelly, John Lee Mahin, and Dale Van Every. *Film Editing:* Elmo Vernon.

Tracy, a Portuguese fisherman, rescues Freddie Bartholomew, who has fallen off a cruise ship. With the aid of the captain of the fishing boat, Lionel Barrymore [723 . . .], Tracy educates Bartholomew in the ways of the sea. What with its star turns and prestige MGM production values, this adaptation of Rudyard Kipling's novel seems too hokey by a mile today. The huge cast, directed by Victor Fleming [798], includes Melvyn Douglas [169 . . .], Mickey Rooney [115 . . .], Charley Grapewin, John Carradine, and Leo G. Carroll.

Tracy had fallen into acting while in college and supported himself with odd jobs while waiting for his break on Broadway. Director John Ford [815 . . .] spotted him in a prison drama on Broadway and cast him in a gangster film, *Up the River,* in 1930. After a variety of minor roles, he was signed by MGM in 1935, beginning his long career as a leading man. Tracy, who did his best acting when he didn't seem to be acting, was embarrassed by his performance in *Captains Courageous,* in which he has curly hair (Joan Crawford said he looked like Harpo Marx) and a ''feeshy'' accent. But the Academy has always been more impressed by acting that shows than by acting that convinces, and granted Tracy the first of his two consecutive Oscars.

The Life of Emile Zola won for best picture and for the screenplay by Heinz Herald, Geza Herczeg, and Norman Reilly Raine. The editing Oscar went to Gene Havlick and Gene Milford for *Lost Horizon.*

Tracy: 131, 271, 656, 843, 1000, 1065, 1470, 1751. Lighton: 1194, 2022. Mahin: 891.

353 • CAPTAINS OF THE CLOUDS

WARNER BROS. 1942.
NOMINATIONS *Color Cinematography:* Sol Polito. *Color Interior Decoration:* Ted Smith, art direction; Casey Roberts, set decoration.

Canadian bush pilot James Cagney [79 . . .], an obnoxious loner, joins the Royal Canadian Air Force when World War II starts, but his refusal to follow orders gets him kicked out. Finally he gets a chance to prove his heroism. A routine win-the-war film, directed by Michael Curtiz [79 . . .], with little more than some handsome color photography to distinguish it. Also in the cast are Dennis Morgan, Alan Hale, Brenda Marshall, and George Tobias.

The Oscar went to Leon Shamroy for the cinematography of *The Black Swan. My Gal Sal* won for art direction.

Polito: 1621, 1779. Smith: 1750. Roberts: 760, 1048.

354 • CAPTAIN'S PARADISE, THE

LONDON FILMS; LOPERT FILMS-UNITED ARTISTS (UNITED KINGDOM). 1953.
NOMINATION *Motion Picture Story:* Alec Coppel.

Alec Guinness [287 . . .], captain of a ferry at the Straits of Gibraltar, has a wife in each port: Celia Johnson [289], quiet and proper, waits for him in Gibraltar while he's with passionate Yvonne De Carlo in Tangier, and vice versa. But he's overlooking the fact that Johnson has a passionate side and De Carlo a domestic one. An amusing premise, but the movie never does it justice, despite sterling performances. Directed by Anthony Kimins. Coppel lost to Dalton Trumbo—or to his front, Ian McLellan Hunter—for *Roman Holiday.*

355 • CARAVANS

IBEX FILMS-F.I.D.C.I. PRODUCTION; UNIVERSAL (U.S./IRAN). 1978.
NOMINATION *Costume Design:* Renie Conley.

Michael Sarrazin is sent to the Middle East by the State Department to find Jennifer O'Neill, a senator's daughter who has left her Arab husband and joined a Bedouin caravan. Picturesque piffle from a James Michener novel, directed by James Fargo, with Anthony Quinn [1226 . . .], Christopher Lee, Joseph Cotten, and lots of camels. Anthony Powell won the costuming award for *Death on the Nile.*

Conley: 201, 413, 1338, 1601.

356 • CARDINAL, THE

GAMMA PRODUCTION; COLUMBIA. 1963.
NOMINATIONS *Supporting Actor:* John Huston. *Director:* Otto Preminger. *Color Cinematography:* Leon Shamroy. *Color Art Direction–Set Decoration:* Lyle Wheeler; Gene Callahan. *Film Editing:* Louis R. Loeffler. *Color Costume Design:* Donald Brooks.

Priest Tom Tryon battles Ku Kluxers in the South and Nazis in Austria before becoming a cardinal of the Roman Catholic church in this adaptation of a novel by Henry Morton Robinson. This would-be blockbuster is certainly handsome, but Tryon is a dull actor (he gave it up and became a successful novelist), so the burden of the film falls on its endless roster of supporting players: Huston as the Boston cardinal and Burgess Meredith [504 . . .] as the old priest who serve as Tryon's mentors; Carol Lynley as Tryon's sister, who falls in love with a Jew, John Saxon; Ossie Davis as a black priest attacked by the Klan; and Maggie McNamara [1348], Cecil Kellaway

[843 . . .], Robert Morse, Raf Vallone, Chill Wills [33], Arthur Hunnicutt [204], and Romy Schneider, among many others. But there are better ways to spend three hours.

Huston had begun his Hollywood career as an actor, hired by William Wyler [175 . . .] for several small roles in the early thirties, but he wanted to write, and his success as a screenwriter led to his career as a director. The small role in *The Cardinal*, and the nomination, led to a string of character parts in films and voice-overs for TV commercials, the proceeds from which helped finance his own films. The Oscar went to Melvyn Douglas for *Hud*.

Preminger was one of two directors whose films were not nominated for best picture—the other was Federico Fellini for *8½*—and consequently stood little chance of winning the Oscar. It went to Tony Richardson for *Tom Jones*.

Shamroy had two nominations, and won for the other one, *Cleopatra*. When he reached the stage to accept his award, he whispered to presenter James Stewart [73 . . .], "Which one did I win for?" *Cleopatra* also won the awards for art direction and costumes. The editing Oscar went to Harold F. Kress for *How the West Was Won*.

Huston: 24, 105, 571, 891, 1248, 1263, 1363, 1625, 1779, 2136. Preminger: 73, 1149. Shamroy: 29, 226, 413, 495, 569, 602, 1088, 1153, 1213, 1592, 1610, 1706, 1852, 1883, 2013, 2286, 2334. Wheeler: 19, 46, 83, 376, 428, 476, 495, 530, 542, 719, 721, 798, 950, 1062, 1088, 1149, 1153, 1213, 1391, 1475, 1601, 1616, 1670, 1706, 1852, 2008, 2093, 2212. Callahan: 63, 964, 1143. Loeffler: 73. Brooks: 494, 1907.

357 • CAREER

HAL WALLIS PRODUCTIONS; PARAMOUNT. 1959.

NOMINATIONS *Black-and-White Cinematography:* Joseph LaShelle. *Black-and-White Art Direction–Set Decoration:* Hal Pereira and Walter Tyler; Sam Comer and Arthur Krams. *Black-and-White Costume Design:* Edith Head.

Anthony Franciosa [880] plays a struggling actor trying to make it on Broadway. One of those rat-race melodramas that had a sort of vogue in the fifties, this one, directed by Joseph Anthony, has an interesting cast—Dean Martin as a director, Shirley MacLaine [91 . . .] as Franciosa's wife, and Carolyn Jones [124] as an agent—but it's pretty dated. Location filming gives it a pseudo-documentary quality that helped it in the technical categories. Oscars went to *The Diary of Anne Frank* for William C. Mellor's cinematography and for art direction. Orry-Kelly won for the costumes for *Some Like It Hot*.

LaShelle: 91, 428, 709, 953, 1017, 1149, 1283, 1391. Pereira: 278, 363, 426, 450, 736, 956, 1029, 1219, 1504, 1570, 1631, 1674, 1716, 1727, 1738, 1840, 1897, 1959, 2012, 2098, 2200, 2208. Tyler: 1022, 1101, 1716, 1738, 1748, 1959, 2012, 2208. Comer: 278, 426, 450, 726, 736, 925, 956, 1029, 1101, 1214, 1219, 1443, 1570, 1631, 1674, 1727, 1738, 1748, 1959, 1975, 1994, 2012, 2098, 2200, 2208. Krams: 1173, 1309, 1727, 1937, 1959, 2098, 2208. Head: 31, 32, 46, 305, 363, 612, 636, 675, 736, 832, 894, 945, 1003, 1219, 1261, 1263, 1398, 1427, 1504, 1550, 1579, 1587, 1631, 1716, 1727, 1738, 1748, 1840, 1927, 1986, 2012, 2098, 2247, 2298.

358 • CAREFREE

RKO RADIO. 1938.

NOMINATIONS *Interior Decoration:* Van Nest Polglase. *Song:* "Change Partners and Dance With Me," music and lyrics by Irving Berlin. *Score:* Victor Baravelle.

Wonderful as they are, the Fred Astaire [2126]–Ginger Rogers [1102] musicals were cut from a pattern: Astaire and Rogers meet cute, fall in love, fall out, fall back in. Their romance is abetted or retarded by his fussy sidekicks, Edward Everett Horton and/or Eric Blore, and her acerbic friends, Helen Broderick or Alice Brady [990 . . .]. But after seven such films, everyone was ready to try something different. So in *Carefree*, directed by Mark Sandrich, Astaire plays a psychiatrist instead of a professional musician-dancer. He doesn't pursue Rogers; she pursues him, resorting to the physical comedy that she excelled in but rarely employed in the series. In place of Horton and/or Blore, there's a rival love interest, Ralph Bellamy [114], playing what he played throughout the screwball comedies of the thirties, the guy who doesn't get the girl. It's lively and charming, but audiences weren't ready for the change, and *Carefree* was the first Astaire-Rogers flop. Audiences clearly preferred the unreality of the earlier musicals, with their top hats and slinky feathered dresses, and fantasyland versions of New York, Venice, and Paris. The decor for *Carefree* departs from the art deco splendors that dominated the earlier films supervised by Polglase, RKO's design department head; for *Carefree*, RKO's designers created a suburban country club ambiance. There is also a Disneyesque fantasy setting for the "I Used to Be Color-Blind" dream sequence, which was planned for color but shot in black and white because of financial retrenchment at RKO. The art direction Oscar went to *The Adventures of Robin Hood*, which *was* shot in color.

Berlin found himself in competition with himself this year: "Now It Can Be Told," his song from *Alexander's Ragtime Band*, was also a nominee. He lost to Ralph Rainger and Leo Robin's "Thanks for the Memory," from *The Big Broadcast of 1938*. Baravelle's score, ironically, lost to Alfred Newman's for *Alexander's Ragtime Band*, which was wall-to-wall orchestrations of Berlin melodies.

Polglase: 407, 754, 1212, 1394, 2115. Berlin: 34, 244, 929, 1773, 2115, 2268.

359 • CARETAKERS, THE

HALL BARTLETT PRODUCTIONS; UNITED ARTISTS. 1963.
NOMINATION *Black-and-White Cinematography:* Lucien Ballard.

Miscellaneous goings-on in a mental hospital. You know things are going to get hairy when you discover that Joan Crawford [1319 . . .] is one of the nurses. The cast, directed by Hall Bartlett, includes Polly Bergen, Robert Stack [2315], Barbara Barrie [279], Herbert Marshall, and Robert Vaughn [2338]. Not as bad as it sounds. This was the sole nomination for veteran cinematographer Ballard, a protégé of Josef von Sternberg [1358 . . .] and Lee Garmes [201 . . .]; his films include such visually impressive westerns as *Ride the High Country* (1962) and *The Wild Bunch*. The Oscar went to James Wong Howe for *Hud*.

360 • CARMEN

EMILIANO PIEDRA PRODUCTION (SPAIN). 1983.
NOMINATION *Foreign Language Film.*

An on-stage production of a ballet based on Bizet's opera is mirrored by the off-stage relationship of the choreographer and the lead dancer. Director Carlos Saura's film is full of superb dancing, set to Bizet's music as recorded by Regina Resnik and Mario Del Monaco. The interaction between art and life gets a bit heavy-handed, however. The award went to Ingmar Bergman's *Fanny & Alexander*.

361 • CARMEN JONES

OTTO PREMINGER PRODUCTIONS; 20TH CENTURY-FOX. 1954.
NOMINATIONS *Actress:* Dorothy Dandridge. *Scoring of a Musical Picture:* Herschel Burke Gilbert.

Bizet's opera about the fiery Gypsy who tempts a young soldier but is unfaithful to him with a bullfighter was turned into a stage musical in 1944, with a book and lyrics by Oscar Hammerstein II [375 . . .] that moved the action to the American South. In the film version, Dandridge plays the title role, a factory worker. Bizet's Don José becomes Joe, played by Harry Belafonte, and the bullfighter Escamillo becomes the prizefighter Husky Miller, played by Joe Adams. (The "Toreador" aria now has lyrics like "Stand up and fight until you hear the bell.") Colorful and entertaining, if you can accept a white writer's version of black lives, interpreted by a white director, Otto Preminger [73 . . .], and the "dis" and "dat" of the lyrics. Apart from Dandridge, Pearl Bailey is the standout in the cast, delivering her song "Beat Out Dat Rhythm on a Drum" with gusto—and in her own voice. Cast members Diahann Carroll [411] and Brock Peters also do their own singing, but others are dubbed: Dandridge by Marilyn Horne, Belafonte by La Vern Hutcheson, Adams by Marvin Hayes. Hearing the twenty-year-old Horne sing Bizet's music, even with Hammerstein's words, is one of the film's delights.

Dandridge, the first black woman to be nominated for best actress, began performing as a child, and can be glimpsed in the Marx Brothers' *A Day at the Races* (1937), when she was fourteen. Not until the fifties did she begin to cross over from bit parts and films made exclusively for black audiences into major Hollywood roles, moving from *Tarzan's Peril* (1951) into *Carmen Jones, Island in the Sun* (1957), and *Porgy and Bess*. But she never achieved the stardom she longed for, and after being cheated out of her fortune by an oil-investment scam, she committed suicide in 1965, aged forty-two. The Oscar went to Grace Kelly for *The Country Girl*.

The scoring award went to Adolph Deutsch and Saul Chaplin for *Seven Brides for Seven Brothers*.

Gilbert: 1348, 2049.

362 • *CARNAL KNOWLEDGE*

ICARUS PRODUCTIONS; AVCO EMBASSY. 1971.

NOMINATION *Supporting Actress:* Ann-Margret.

This essentially plotless film, written first for the stage but converted into a screenplay by its author, Jules Feiffer, follows college roommates Jack Nicholson [395 . . .] and Art Garfunkel from the mid-forties to the early seventies. Garfunkel becomes a doctor and marries Candice Bergen [1919] but seeks solace outside the marriage, finally winding up with hippie Carol Kane [908]. Nicholson, a lawyer, takes Ann-Margret as a mistress but becomes impotent. Rita Moreno [2244] plays the prostitute who tries to revive his prowess. Mike Nichols [810 . . .] directs with such ironic detachment that you feel he doesn't really believe the film's about anything, even though the material for a satire on male chauvinism is certainly present in the screenplay. Instead, there's the tonelessness of a lot of late-sixties/early-seventies films: These mixed-up lives are supposed to represent something about America, but the filmmakers don't seem to have anything particular in mind.

Any feeling you have for the people in the film is generated by their performances, which is why Ann-Margret was singled out by both critics and the Academy. The vulnerability beneath her sexy exterior is enormously appealing. *Carnal Knowledge* was a turning point in her career, which up to this point had mostly been variations on the sex-kittenish teenager she played in *Bye Bye Birdie* or the violent vixen of *Kitten*

With a Whip (1964). The Oscar went to Cloris Leachman for *The Last Picture Show*.

Ann-Margret: 2109.

363 • *CARRIE*

PARAMOUNT. 1952.

NOMINATIONS *Black-and-White Art Direction—Set Decoration:* Hal Pereira and Roland Anderson; Emile Kuri. *Black-and-White Costume Design:* Edith Head.

In turn-of-the-century Chicago, well-to-do restaurateur Laurence Olivier [268 . . .] makes a sexual conquest of a naive provincial girl, Jennifer Jones [584 . . .], but soon the tables are turned—she becomes a success as an actress, while he becomes a pathetic bum. Theodore Dreiser's novel *Sister Carrie* is translated from an ironic sociological study into a rather ordinary melodrama, hindered by censorship and conventional Hollywood ideas. (The title, for example, was changed for fear that audiences would think it was about a nun.) *Carrie* was a comparative flop both critically and commercially. But Olivier, greatly aided by his *Wuthering Heights* director, William Wyler, turns in a towering performance—so fine that his long absence from the screen as Jones makes her rise to success leaves a big hole in the picture. He took the role to be near Vivien Leigh while she filmed *A Streetcar Named Desire*. His omission from the actor nominations is something of a surprise, but the nominees reflect a year of extraordinary performances: Marlon Brando in *Viva Zapata!,* Kirk Douglas in *The Bad and the Beautiful,* Jose Ferrer in *Moulin Rouge,* Alec Guinness in *The Lavender Hill Mob,* and the winner, Gary Cooper in *High Noon.* The cast also includes Miriam Hopkins [165] and Eddie Albert [887 . . .].

The Oscars went to *The Bad and the Beautiful* for both art direction and Helen Rose's costumes.

Pereira: 278, 357, 426, 450, 736, 956, 1029, 1219, 1504, 1570, 1631, 1674, 1716, 1727, 1738, 1840, 1897, 1959, 2012, 2098, 2200, 2208. Anderson: 278, 426, 450, 649, 1029, 1194, 1214, 1219, 1452, 1570, 1668, 1674, 1880, 1994. Kuri: 4, 166, 629, 894, 1284, 1823, 2155. Head: 31, 32, 46, 305, 357, 612, 636, 675, 736, 832, 894, 945, 1003, 1219, 1261, 1263, 1398, 1427, 1504, 1550, 1579,

1587, 1631, 1716, 1727, 1738, 1748, 1840, 1927, 1986, 2012, 2098, 2247, 2298.

364 • CARRIE

REDBANK FILMS PRODUCTION; UNITED ARTISTS. 1976.
NOMINATIONS *Actress:* Sissy Spacek. *Supporting Actress:* Piper Laurie.

Carrie (Spacek) has been raised by her spooky religious-fanatic mother (Laurie) in complete denial of her body, so that when she starts to menstruate in the high school showers, she is terrified. The other girls just laugh at her and pelt her with tampons. But with the onset of puberty, a new power is released in Carrie: telekinesis—the ability to move things about with her mind. She holds this power in check until the taunts of other teens—including Amy Irving [2321], John Travolta [1633.5 . . .], and Nancy Allen—release a murderous anger in her, and she brings down a holocaust on the high school prom. Stephen King's thriller is wittily directed by Brian De Palma. It's silly stuff, to be sure, and it led to a lot of very bad imitations, but it's one of the touchstones of the genre.

After *Carrie,* Spacek, who had attracted a lot of critical attention with her performance as a murderous teenager in *Badlands* in 1973, was in real danger of being typecast. Fortunately roles in which she could act her age—she was twenty-seven when she made *Carrie*—were right around the corner, and one of them was *Coal Miner's Daughter.* This time the Oscar went to Faye Dunaway for *Network.*

Carrie was a comeback role for Laurie, who had quit movies after her nomination for *The Hustler* and married Joseph Morgenstern, film critic for *Newsweek.* She was nonplussed by the role of the Bible-thumping mother at first but finally found a way to play it for humor—her ecstatic death scene is one of the movie's highlights. She lost to Beatrice Straight in *Network.*

Spacek: 418, 462, 1330, 1701. Laurie: 390, 964.

365 • CASABLANCA

WARNER BROS. 1943.
AWARDS *Picture:* Hal B. Wallis, producer. *Director:* Michael Curtiz. *Screenplay:* Julius J. Epstein, Philip G. Epstein, and Howard Koch.

NOMINATIONS *Actor:* Humphrey Bogart. *Supporting Actor:* Claude Rains. *Black-and-White Cinematography:* Arthur Edeson. *Scoring of a Dramatic or Comedy Picture:* Max Steiner. *Film Editing:* Owen Marks.

Café owner Bogart is trying to sit out World War II in Casablanca, when Ingrid Bergman [72 . . .], with whom he had an affair in Paris just before the Germans occupied the city, reenters his life. She is accompanied by her husband, Paul Henreid, a hero of the Resistance. Bogart possesses two "letters of transit," documents that would enable them to fly to neutral Lisbon and thence to America. Will Bogart give the letters to Bergman and Henreid, or will Bergman leave Henreid and stay in Casablanca with Bogart? Of such stuff legends were made.

Possibly the most popular movie of all time—its chief rival being *Gone With the Wind*—*Casablanca* was something of a sleeper, though it was never planned as a routine studio potboiler, as some have said. That myth grew up from the first publicity Warners put out on the film, listing its stars as Ronald Reagan, Ann Sheridan, and Dennis Morgan—a decidedly B-team cast. That was either an error committed in the publicity department—the trio was actually assigned to another film—or simply a preliminary announcement intended to get the name of the film into print and incidentally boost some players the studio thought had potential. It's unlikely that Hal Wallis, Warners' foremost producer, would have been attached to a project with so low-profile a cast. Bogart had been his first choice all along, and Wallis claimed that Bergman was, too, though Michele Morgan, Hedy Lamarr, and ballerina Tamara Toumanova (a friend of screenwriter Casey Robinson) were considered. David O. Selznick [497 . . .], who owned Bergman's contract, agreed to loan her to Warners in exchange for Olivia de Havilland [798 . . .]. Curtiz, one of Warners' top directors, was assigned to the film after William Wyler [175 . . .] turned it down, and a gallery of secondary players was assembled: Rains, Conrad Veidt, Sydney Greenstreet [1248], Peter Lorre, S. Z. Sakall, Leonid Kinskey, and Marcel Dalio, among many others. The secondary roles give *Casablanca* its texture and make repeat viewings of the film a delight. Chief among the supporting characters is the piano player, Sam, played by Dooley Wilson. Though racism still taints the script—Bergman is made to refer to Sam as "the boy" at one point—the part is one of the strongest given to a black actor in its day, or for a decade after. Though the role could have been rewritten for a white actor, that was never considered. There was, however, some thought of rewriting it for a woman, and Hazel Scott, Lena Horne, and Ella Fitzgerald were considered for the role. Clarence Muse, who had often played stereotypical blacks in movies, was also tested for the part, but Wilson, a Paramount contract player, was finally cast —though he couldn't play the piano.

The script was based on an unperformed play, *Everybody Comes to Rick's*. Because of the film's enduring success, authorship of the screenplay has been contested over the years. The Epsteins produced the first workable version, and Wally Kline, Aeneas MacKenzie, and Lenore Coffee [712] also contributed to early drafts. Koch then did a rewrite, and Casey Robinson was brought in especially for the romantic scenes. In the end the Writers Guild gave the screen credits to the Epsteins and Koch, excluding Robinson for reasons that have never been entirely clear. Robinson, who had worked closely with Wallis over the years, claimed at one point that he asked to have his name withdrawn because he didn't want to share screen credit with anyone. In her memoirs Bergman says she was disturbed at not knowing whether she would wind up with Henreid or Bogart at the film's end. She was told, she says, to "play it in between," because the writers hadn't decided yet. But there is no evidence that that part of the ending was ever seriously in doubt. The chief difficulty the writers had with the ending centered on the role of Rains and the handling of the fate of Major Strasser, the Veidt character.

The movie was a box-office hit, but that doesn't inevitably translate into Oscars. The favorite for best picture was *The Song of Bernadette,* which had received twelve nominations to *Casablanca*'s eight. The movie's four awards include the only Oscar Wallis ever won, even though he racked up more nominations than any feature film producer in history, as well as two Thalberg awards. His triumph was marred, however, when at the awards ceremony, studio head Jack Warner [55 . . .] raced to the podium to accept the statuette, which was in fact within his rights: Until the 1951 awards, the Oscar went to the production company or the studio, and not to the individual producer. Wallis claimed that a phalanx of Warner family members blocked his way to the stage. The following year Wallis left Warner Bros. to form an independent producing company, which released its films through Paramount. But his post-Warners career was comparatively less successful, ranging from Dean Martin–Jerry Lewis and Elvis Presley films to a trio of arty historical dramas—*Becket, Anne of the Thousand Days,* and *Mary, Queen of Scots*—in the late sixties. Wallis died in 1986.

Curtiz directed more than one hundred films for Warners in the quarter century he spent with the studio, which hired him in 1926. He made Errol Flynn a star with a series of late-thirties swashbucklers and is regarded by some as the epitome of the studio craftsman: a creator of movies that have no particular personal vision but strong production values and solid performances. It is said that actors hated him, but he made them look good. Curtiz died in 1962.

The Epstein twins collaborated on scripts starting in 1939, with Julius continuing on his own after Philip's death in 1952. Of *Casablanca,* Julius told writer Harlan Lebo, "There wasn't a word of truth in the picture. There were no Germans in Casablanca, certainly not in uniform, no letters of transit, there was nothing. And it was slapped together. For example, I don't know what would have happened if my brother and I hadn't come up with 'round up the usual suspects' for the ending. And it wasn't the result of a lot of thought, either; it was just one of those flashes." Cowriter Koch began his career as a writer for radio, winning notoriety as one of the writers for Orson Welles [407 . . .] who produced the script that panicked America, *The War of the Worlds.* He came to Hollywood in 1940 but was blacklisted in 1951. He spent his later screenwriting career in England.

He is sometimes confused with producers Howard W. Koch Sr. and Jr., to whom he is not related.

Though *Casablanca* provided Bogart with his signature role, he lost the Oscar to Paul Lukas for *Watch on the Rhine.* Bergman failed to be nominated for her role but was up for *For Whom the Bell Tolls,* losing to Jennifer Jones in *The Song of Bernadette.*

Rains is one of Oscar's most notorious also-rans. Film after film thrives on his suave presence, and his role in *Casablanca* as the amoral police chief whose heart is really in the right place fits like a glove: No one was better at charming menace or menacing charm. The Academy voters preferred the more unambiguous charm of Charles Coburn in *The More the Merrier.*

Edeson was a double pioneer. He became a movie cameraman in 1911 and had a long working relationship with Douglas Fairbanks, Sr. Then, when sound came in, he was one of the first to use the bulky new equipment on location, in the western *In Old Arizona.* He was not Wallis' first choice as *Casablanca* cameraman; the producer wanted James Wong Howe [1 . . .]. But Edeson produced some of the movies' most durable images, and uses shadows and textures to eloquent effect in the café scenes. He lost to Arthur Miller's work on *The Song of Bernadette.*

There is a famous irony about Steiner's score: He professed to dislike the song "As Time Goes By." Composed by Herman Hupfeld for a 1931 Broadway revue, it was carried over to the film from the play on which *Casablanca* is based. Steiner clearly swallowed his dislike, for the tune is part of the tapestry of his score, though he also managed to work in "Perfidia," the melody he wanted to substitute for Hupfeld's song. Alfred Newman won the scoring Oscar for *The Song of Bernadette.*

The editing Oscar went to George Amy for *Air Force.*

Wallis: 17, 55, 85, 164, 343, 676, 689, 712, 965, 1046, 1095, 1162, 1248, 1482, 1727, 1779, 2233, 2318. Curtiz: 79, 712, 2318. J. Epstein: 712, 1555, 1687. Koch: 1779. Bogart: 24, 330. Rains: 1369, 1370, 1455. Edeson: 48, 989. Steiner: 16, 154, 190, 330, 385, 492, 679, 747, 754, 798, 999, 1043, 1046, 1052, 1162, 1169, 1170, 1207, 1324, 1408, 1430, 1456, 1690, 1779, 1828. Marks: 1040.

366 • *CASANOVA BROWN*

INTERNATIONAL PICTURES; RKO RADIO. 1944.
NOMINATIONS *Black-and-White Interior Decoration:* Perry Ferguson, art direction; Julia Heron, set decoration. *Sound Recording:* Thomas T. Moulton, Goldwyn Sound Department. *Scoring of a Dramatic or Comedy Picture:* Arthur Lange.

Gary Cooper [701 . . .] and Teresa Wright [1182 . . .] decide to divorce, but just as the decree becomes final, they discover she's pregnant. A wispy premise for a comedy became almost nonexistent once the censors got through with it, but for some reason—perhaps the previously successful teaming of Cooper and Wright in *Pride of the Yankees,* which like *Casanova Brown* was directed by Sam Wood [701 . . .]—everyone decided to go through with filming it. Unmemorable in all respects. The cast includes Frank Morgan [22 . . .] and Anita Louise.

The art direction Oscar went to *Gaslight,* the sound award to *Wilson,* and the scoring award to Max Steiner for *Since You Went Away.*

Ferguson: 407, 1451, 1607, 2292. Heron: 201, 1070, 1886, 2031. Moulton: 22, 46, 138, 457, 487, 560, 706, 798, 962, 1153, 1200, 1451, 1510, 1607, 1849, 2154, 2294. Lange: 171, 827, 1123, 2303.

367 • *CASANOVA '70*

C.C. CHAMPION-LES FILMS CONCORDIA PRODUCTION; EMBASSY PICTURES CORPORATION (FRANCE/ITALY). 1965.
NOMINATION *Story and Screenplay—Written Directly for the Screen:* Age, Scarpelli, Mario Monicelli, Tonino Guerra, Giorgio Salvioni, and Suso Cecchi D'Amico.

Marcello Mastroianni [490 . . .] plays a womanizer who finds sex interesting only when his conquests involve danger. This entertaining little comedy directed by Monicelli depends largely on its star's abundant charm. The Oscar went to Frederic Raphael for *Darling.*

Age: 1503. Scarpelli: 1503. Monicelli: 1503. Guerra: 61, 240.

368 • CASBAH

MARSTON PICTURES; UNIVERSAL-INTERNATIONAL. 1948.
NOMINATION *Song:* "For Every Man There's a Woman," music by Harold Arlen, lyrics by Leo Robin.

Musical remake of *Algiers,* with Tony Martin in the Charles Boyer role and Marta Toren in Hedy Lamarr's. Directed by John Berry, with Peter Lorre and Yvonne De Carlo. A bad idea not so badly executed, all things considered, thanks particularly to the Arlen-Robin songs, which also included "Hooray for Love," "It Was Written in the Stars," and "What's Good About Goodbye?" Jay Livingston and Ray Evans won the Oscar for "Buttons and Bows," from *The Paleface.*

Arlen: 248, 322, 903, 1838, 1910, 1912, 2186, 2300. Robin: 104, 197, 846, 1072, 1805, 1843, 2032, 2088, 2310.

369 • CASE OF SERGEANT GRISCHA, THE

RKO RADIO. 1929–30.
NOMINATION *Sound Recording:* John Tribby.

Adventures of a Russian escapee from a German prison camp, starring Chester Morris [38], Betty Compson [148], and Jean Hersholt, directed by Herbert Brenon [1878]. The film is no longer in circulation. The Oscar for sound, the first ever awarded, went to Douglas Shearer for *The Big House.*

370 • CASINO ROYALE

FAMOUS ARTISTS PRODUCTIONS; COLUMBIA (UNITED KINGDOM). 1967.
NOMINATION *Song:* "The Look of Love," music by Burt Bacharach, lyrics by Hal David.

An aging James Bond, played by David Niven [1778], is called out of retirement to fight the forces of SMERSH. He longs to hand over the role of 007 to a successor—perhaps to his nephew Jimmy Bond, played by Woody Allen [39 . . .]? This was one of the few Ian Fleming titles not owned by producer Albert Broccoli. Unfortunately, when producers Charles K. Feldman [1949] and Jerry Bresler decided to bring it to the screen, they thought big—as in elephantine—and wound up with something that had

at least five directors, including John Huston [24 . . .] and Robert Parrish [53 . . .], and a cast including Peter Sellers [169 . . .], Orson Welles [407 . . .], Deborah Kerr [599 . . .], William Holden [1424 . . .], Charles Boyer [36 . . .], and Peter O'Toole [164 . . .]. The result is a leaden spoof with fitful moments of humor: Allen's few scenes are the best.

The Bacharach-David song was beaten by Leslie Bricusse's "Talk to the Animals," from *Doctor Dolittle.* The rest of the world was listening to Beatles and Stones, Dylan and Hendrix, but not Hollywood.

Bacharach: 35, 103, 317, 2251. David: 35, 317, 2251.

371 • CAT BALLOU

HAROLD HECHT PRODUCTIONS: COLUMBIA. 1965.
AWARD *Actor:* Lee Marvin.
NOMINATIONS *Screenplay—Based on Material From Another Medium:* Walter Newman and Frank R. Pierson. *Song:* "The Ballad of Cat Ballou," music by Jerry Livingston, lyrics by Mack David. *Scoring of Music—Adaptation or Treatment:* DeVol. *Film Editing:* Charles Nelson.

Cat, a mild-mannered schoolteacher played by Jane Fonda [394 . . .], turns outlaw by necessity, but eventually she is forced to face her nemesis, the gunfighter Strawn (Marvin). To aid her in the showdown, she calls on Strawn's twin, Kid Shelleen (Marvin), once a crack shot but now a drunk. This light-as-a-feather spoof of westerns is made memorable by Marvin's performance and by Nat King Cole and Stubby Kaye, who stroll through the film singing the Livingston-David songs that comment on the action. Fonda never had the lightest touch for comedy, so she gets a bit grating at times, but there are pleasant performances from Michael Callan, Dwayne Hickman, Tom Nardini, John Marley [1218], and Arthur Hunnicutt [204]. Directed by Elliot Silverstein.

Marvin's roughneck persona belies his origins as the son of an adman and a journalist in New York City. From the beginning of his work in films, he was cast as a heavy, a brawler, or a slob in dozens of movies, including *The Wild One* (1954), *The Caine Mu-*

tiny, *Bad Day at Black Rock, The Man Who Shot Liberty Valance,* and *Donovan's Reef* (1963). The Oscar didn't exactly change that, but it made his roles more prominent. His most notorious off-screen moment was the famous palimony case of 1979, in which he was sued by former live-in lover Michelle Triola and was ordered to pay damages. He died at sixty-three in 1987. His nomination was thought to be at least partly in recognition of a contrasting role he played the same year in *Ship of Fools.* But while his performance in *Cat Ballou* was certainly a wonderful tour de force, and may have surpassed that of nominee Oskar Werner in *Ship of Fools,* it's hard to justify the Academy's choice of Marvin over Richard Burton in *The Spy Who Came in From the Cold,* Laurence Olivier in *Othello,* or Rod Steiger in *The Pawnbroker.* Marvin was himself bemused when he accepted the Oscar. "I think one-half of this belongs to some horse somewhere in the Valley," he said, referring to the steed that posed drunkenly in the film bearing the soused Kid Shelleen.

The screenplay award was won by Robert Bolt for *Doctor Zhivago.* Johnny Mandel and Paul Francis Webster took the Oscar for "The Shadow of Your Smile," from *The Sandpiper.* Irwin Kostal won for scoring *The Sound of Music,* which was also honored for William Reynolds' editing.

Newman: 198, 238. Pierson: 443, 561. Livingston: 402, 861. David: 122, 402, 861, 882, 963, 1032, 2223. DeVol: 843, 963, 1572. Nelson: 1566, 1872.

372 • *CAT ON A HOT TIN ROOF*

AVON PRODUCTIONS INC.; MGM. 1958.

NOMINATIONS *Picture:* Lawrence Weingarten, producer. *Actor:* Paul Newman. *Actress:* Elizabeth Taylor. *Director:* Richard Brooks. *Screenplay—Based on Material From Another Medium:* Richard Brooks and James Poe. *Color Cinematography:* William Daniels.

A southern family gathers for the birthday of the patriarch known as Big Daddy, played by Burl Ives [200] in this adaptation of a celebrated play by Tennessee Williams [119 . . .]. Newman and Taylor play

Brick and Maggie, the younger son and his wife. The handsome, athletic Brick, tormented by the death of a friend, drinks himself into oblivion and refuses to sleep with Maggie. Brick, Maggie, and the older son, Gooper (Jack Carson), and his wife, Mae (Madeleine Sherwood), also know that Big Daddy is dying of cancer but have kept the truth from him and Big Mama, played by Judith Anderson [1670]. The working out of these relationships takes much talking and fighting, and censorship has eliminated a key element from Brick's characterization—homosexuality—so that the last part of the film is muddled. Fine performances and direction don't eliminate the staginess, but they make it tolerable. The best picture Oscar went to *Gigi.*

Newman's first nomination came in a year in which he also won the Cannes Festival award for acting in *The Long Hot Summer.* He was unable to attend the Oscar ceremony because he was appearing on Broadway in Tennessee Williams' *Sweet Bird of Youth.* The trip would have been unnecessary anyway: The award went to David Niven for *Separate Tables.*

Taylor was the object of sympathy because her husband, Mike Todd [101], had died shortly before she began filming *Cat.* But it was not enough to overcome the support for Susan Hayward, a frequent nominee who had never won, for her performance in *I Want to Live!* This was the second of four consecutive nominations for Taylor, who finally won on the fourth try, for *Butterfield 8.* There had been talk of casting Grace Kelly [450 . . .] as Maggie before her marriage to Prince Rainier.

Brooks took over the direction of *Cat* after George Cukor [262 . . .] bowed out, in part because of difficulties with the script. *Gigi*'s director, Vincente Minnelli, and writer, Alan Jay Lerner, won the Oscars. The cinematography award went to *Gigi*'s Joseph Ruttenberg.

Weingarten: 1166. Newman: 3, 422, 443, 956, 964, 1444.5, 1645, 2198. Taylor: 318, 1657, 1956, 2277. Brooks: 227, 609, 987, 1627. Poe: 101, 1174, 2047. Daniels: 84, 953, 1410.

373 • CATS' PLAY

HUNNIA STUDIO PRODUCTION (HUNGARY). 1974.

NOMINATION *Foreign Language Film.*

The orderly pattern of an elderly widow's life is disturbed by the visit of an old friend, who falls in love with the widow's gentleman friend. Very low-key but quietly affecting film directed by Károly Makk. The Oscar went to Federico Fellini's *Amarcord.*

374 • CAVALCADE

FOX. 1932–33.

AWARDS *Picture:* Winfield Sheehan, studio head. *Director:* Frank Lloyd. *Interior Decoration:* William S. Darling.

NOMINATION *Actress:* Diana Wynyard.

Wynyard and Clive Brook head a British household in this drama, based on a play by Noël Coward [993], that spans the years from the turn of the century to the early thirties. It anticipates the TV series *Upstairs, Downstairs* by forty-some years—in both, for example, characters go down on the *Titanic,* are killed in World War I, and so forth. Hollywood Anglophilia of a type not witnessed again until *Mrs. Miniver,* it is a bit loose-jointed and sketchy at points, and its transitional devices—a procession of medieval figures, various musical interludes, and a progressively darker World War I montage—are awkwardly handled. The film casts a nostalgic haze over the British class system, imperialism, and social and political inequities, though it also gets in a few solid hits at the folly of war. Herbert Mundin and Una O'Connor, as the servants who set out to make it on their own as publicans, bring some life to the film, which gets a little too stiff-upper-lip at times. Also in the cast are ten-year-old Bonita Granville [2044] and an extra listed as "Girl on Couch," Betty Grable.

Sheehan, a former journalist, was secretary to the police commissioner of New York in 1911, when movie pioneer William Fox [1792] was fighting an antitrust battle against the Motion Picture Patents Company, which held the right to license anyone making movies in the United States. Fox rewarded Sheehan for siding with him in the successful fight, and by 1916 Sheehan was vice-president and general manager of the studio. He lost his job as production head when the Fox studios merged with 20th Century in 1935. He died in 1945. As the winner of the best picture Oscar, *Cavalcade* is the most memorable production to bear Sheehan's name as producer, though today it seems less impressive than some of the nominees it defeated—*42nd Street, I Was a Fugitive From a Chain Gang, Little Women,* and *She Done Him Wrong*—not to mention several that weren't nominated—*King Kong, Duck Soup,* and *Dinner at Eight.*

Lloyd won his second Oscar over only two competitors: George Cukor for *Little Women* and Frank Capra for *Lady for a Day.* Both nominees, much younger men, would go on to be among the most celebrated of Hollywood directors, while Lloyd's career, though he continued as both director and producer into the fifties, had only one more peak: the best picture winner *Mutiny on the Bounty.*

Hungarian-born designer Darling began his Hollywood career in 1920 and was a key designer for 20th Century-Fox until the mid-forties.

Wynyard was recruited from Broadway and made several films in addition to *Cavalcade* during a brief stay in Hollywood before returning to England, where she concentrated on stage work. She made a few films in England, most notably the first version of *Gaslight* (1940), in the role played by Ingrid Bergman in the remake. Her role in *Cavalcade* is one of those thankless women-must-weep parts—she's forever looking down in mute suffering. In the Oscar voting, Wynyard came in third in a three-person race, after May Robson for *Lady for a Day* and the winner, Katharine Hepburn for *Morning Glory.*

Sheehan: 132, 592, 989, 1920. Lloyd: 552, 575, 1387, 2239. Darling: 83, 1082, 1195, 1655, 1868, 2240.

375 • CENTENNIAL SUMMER

20TH CENTURY-FOX. 1946.

NOMINATIONS *Song:* "All Through the Day," music by Jerome Kern, lyrics by Oscar Hammerstein II. *Scoring of a Musical Picture:* Alfred Newman.

A Philadelphia family eagerly awaits the Centennial Exposition of 1876. Sound familiar? Does the suggestion of studio head Darryl Zanuck [34 . . .] that it be called *See You in Philadelphia* make it sound even more familiar? But this Fox knockoff of *Meet Me in St. Louis* has Jeanne Crain [1575] and Linda Darnell instead of Judy Garland [1065 . . .]. They play sisters fighting over Cornel Wilde [1872]. It also has the last complete score by Kern, who died in November 1945. Unfortunately it doesn't have a cast in which anyone can sing, including Walter Brennan [424 . . .], Constance Bennett, and Dorothy Gish. The director is Otto Preminger [73 . . .]. In addition to the nominated song, the score also features the song ''In Love in Vain.'' Harry Warren and Johnny Mercer won for ''On the Atchison, Topeka and Santa Fe,'' from *The Harvey Girls*. Newman lost to Morris Stoloff for *The Jolson Story*.

Kern: 340, 455, 1117, 1707, 1990, 2327. Hammerstein: 1117, 1122, 1921, 1951. Newman: 31, 34, 46, 72, 138, 182, 226, 333, 334, 347, 428, 437, 457, 476, 495, 542, 690, 797, 833, 952, 953, 959, 962, 1016, 1082, 1088, 1213, 1278, 1362, 1397, 1475, 1616, 1655, 1849, 1868, 1883, 1921, 2043, 2046, 2091, 2258, 2286, 2294, 2316.

376 • CERTAIN SMILE, A

20TH CENTURY-FOX. 1958.

NOMINATIONS *Art Direction–Set Decoration:* Lyle R. Wheeler and John DeCuir; Walter M. Scott and Paul S. Fox. *Song:* ''A Certain Smile,'' music by Sammy Fain, lyrics by Paul Francis Webster. *Costume Design:* Charles LeMaire and Mary Wills.

The romance of students Christine Carere and Bradford Dillman goes awry when she's seduced by Rossano Brazzi. A wisp of a novella by Françoise Sagan becomes a CinemaScope soap, with the life polished out of it by director Jean Negulesco [1052], writers Frances Goodrich [25 . . .] and Albert Hackett [25 . . .], and the Fox production team. Joan Fontaine [441 . . .] can be spotted sinking unhappily into the suds. All of the awards went to an entirely different film about troubled love in Paris— *Gigi*—including Lerner and Loewe's title song and Cecil Beaton's costumes, as well as the work of the MGM art directors.

Wheeler: 19, 46, 83, 356, 428, 476, 495, 530, 542, 719, 721, 798, 950, 1062, 1088, 1149, 1153, 1213, 1391, 1475, 1601, 1616, 1670, 1706, 1852, 2008, 2093, 2212. DeCuir: 29, 201, 413, 476, 896, 950, 1088, 1391, 1852, 2000. Scott: 46, 413, 476, 530, 542, 557, 646, 896, 1062, 1088, 1213, 1391, 1475, 1706, 1753, 1881, 1907, 2008, 2120, 2247. Fox: 413, 428, 476, 495, 530, 721, 950, 1088, 1601, 1666, 1706, 1852. Fain: 95, 331, 856, 1213, 1276, 1681, 1925, 2014, 2214. Webster: 33, 64, 95, 331, 604, 663, 730, 856, 1213, 1276, 1322, 1388, 1755, 1925, 2014. LeMaire: 21, 46, 495, 530, 542, 954, 1213, 1338, 1391, 1601, 1706, 2008, 2043, 2205, 2294. Wills: 542, 864, 1534, 2008, 2205, 2312.

377 • CHALK GARDEN, THE

QUOTA RENTALS LTD.-ROSS HUNTER PRODUCTION; UNIVERSAL (UNITED KINGDOM). 1964.

NOMINATION *Supporting Actress:* Edith Evans.

Evans hires Deborah Kerr [599 . . .] as governess for Hayley Mills [1588.5], Evans' teenage granddaughter, but Kerr's past returns to haunt them. The heavy-handed direction of Ronald Neame [289 . . .] and the too-obvious score by Malcolm Arnold [287] keep trying to turn this adaptation of a play by Enid Bagnold into something more than it is: a modest character study with a fine cast that also includes Hayley's father, John Mills [1737]. Evans, playing one of her formidable matriarchs, is particularly fun to watch, though you keep expecting her to turn into Lady Bracknell. She lost to Lila Kedrova in *Zorba the Greek*.

Evans: 2106, 2265.

378 • CHAMP, THE

MGM. 1931–32.

AWARDS *Actor:* Wallace Beery. *Original Story:* Frances Marion.

NOMINATIONS *Picture:* King Vidor, producer. *Director:* King Vidor.

Beery is an over-the-hill prizefighter who returns to the ring to help support his son, Jackie Cooper [1836], whose faith in his father is unswerving. Only the talents of director and stars keep this from being the appalling mush it became when it was remade forty-eight years later. Very much a period piece, but enjoyable if you're in the mood for this sort of thing. Get out your handkerchiefs.

At the Oscar ceremonies the award for best actor had already been presented to Fredric March for *Dr. Jekyll and Mr. Hyde* when an Academy official noted that the tally for Beery was one vote short of that for March. Under the rules, a three-vote difference constituted a tie, so Beery was called to the podium for his award—the only tie for best actor in Oscar history. (The subsequent tie for best actress between Barbra Streisand for *Funny Girl* and Katharine Hepburn for *The Lion in Winter* was a true one. The Academy rules were changed so that only an equal tally constitutes a tie.) Though the presentation of the award was something of an anticlimax, it recognized how far Beery had come in his career. He had joined the circus as a boy, but his older brother, Noah, soon found jobs for him in the New York theater. In 1913 he started making movies, including a series of one-reel comedies in which he played a drag role: Sweedie, the Swedish maid. Through the silent era, he worked steadily as a comic or a villain, but his true stardom came with sound, particularly when he teamed with Marie Dressler [611 . . .] in *Min and Bill* and *Tugboat Annie* (1933). Beery's turn as a star was brief. By the mid-thirties he was back in supporting roles, which he played steadily until his death in 1949. To some extent, Beery owed his stardom to two women: Dressler and screenwriter Marion, whose previous Oscar for *The Big House* was also for a picture starring Beery.

In the third of his five unsuccessful Oscar nominations, Vidor lost the directing Oscar to Frank Borzage for *Bad Girl*. The best picture was *Grand Hotel*.

Beery: 202. Marion: 202, 1624. Vidor: 406, 468, 857, 2228.

379 • CHAMP, THE

Metro-Goldwyn-Mayer Production; MGM. 1979.
Nomination *Original Score:* Dave Grusin.

Maudlin, unnecessary remake of the 1931 tearjerker about a has-been boxer and his devoted son. Here the boxer is Jon Voight [430 . . .] and the boy Ricky Schroder. Faye Dunaway [255 . . .] is ludicrously miscast as the boy's mother, and the film wastes the talents of Jack Warden [890 . . .], Arthur Hill, Strother Martin, Elisha Cook, and Joan Blondell [246]. The chief culprit here is probably director Franco Zeffirelli [1722 . . .], whose sentimentality and talent for overstatement seem boundless. But why did anyone think this was a good idea? Grusin's score lost to Georges Delerue's for *A Little Romance*.

Grusin: 633, 667.5, 881, 890, 1318, 1473, 2113.

380 • CHAMPION

Screen Plays Corporation; United Artists. 1949.
Award *Film Editing:* Harry Gerstad.
Nominations *Actor:* Kirk Douglas. *Supporting Actor:* Arthur Kennedy. *Screenplay:* Carl Foreman. *Black-and-White Cinematography:* Frank Planer. *Scoring of a Dramatic or Comedy Picture:* Dimitri Tiomkin.

Douglas plays an ambitious prizefighter who will stop at nothing and double-cross anybody to get to the top. Widely acclaimed as the best film about boxing, at least until *Raging Bull,* it made a star of Douglas and made producer Stanley Kramer [330 . . .] into a major player. Mark Robson [1001 . . .] directed, with more than a little help from Kramer. The cast includes Marilyn Maxwell, Paul Stewart, Ruth Roman, and Lola Albright.

The first of Douglas' unsuccessful nominations established his type: intense, charismatic, ruthless but charming. Douglas had been a college wrestler and even did some professional wrestling to pay for his studies at the American Academy of Dramatic Arts, but had never boxed. Most of the fight scenes in *Champion* are done without the use of doubles, and Douglas was knocked unconscious in one of them. His rags-to-riches life has been documented in his memoir *The Ragman's Son*. His stage career, which began in 1941, was interrupted by World War II, but he returned to the theater after the war and used it as a springboard to Hollywood, where he made his debut in 1946 in *The Strange Love of Martha Ivers*. Three years later he was starring in *Champion* and a contrasting role—an acerbic English professor—in *A Letter to Three Wives,* and a film career that has lasted more than forty years had established itself. But as far as the Oscars are concerned, he has had to take a secondary role as both actor and producer to his son Michael Douglas [1481 . . .]. This time the Oscar went to Broderick Crawford for *All the King's Men.*

If Douglas' Oscar fortunes were bad, Kennedy's were even worse. This was the first of five unsuccessful nominations. Kennedy was discovered on stage by James Cagney [79 . . .], who signed him for a role in his 1940 film *City of Conquest.* But Kennedy's film career didn't take off until after he returned to Broadway and won a Tony for creating the role of Biff in *Death of a Salesman.* He came back to Hollywood and a substantial career as a second lead and character actor. The Oscar went to Dean Jagger for *12 O'Clock High.*

Foreman began his screenwriting career just before World War II with work on Bowery Boys movies, but after the war he went to work for Kramer, with whom he would be associated until 1951, when his refusal to testify before the House Un-American Activities Committee caused him to be blacklisted. He moved to England, where he continued to write anonymously or under pseudonyms—a practice that led to his uncredited work on *The Bridge on the River Kwai,* for which novelist Pierre Boulle received the Oscar that belonged in fact to Foreman and Michael Wilson. After the blacklist faded away, he returned as a successful writer, producer, and director. The Oscar went to Joseph L. Mankiewicz for *A Letter to Three Wives.*

This was the first of Planer's unsuccessful nominations, sometimes as Franz Planer. He was born in Czechoslovakia and worked in German films until 1937, when he came to Hollywood. The Oscar went to Paul Vogel for *Battleground.*

Tiomkin lost to Aaron Copland for *The Heiress.*

Gerstad: 912. Douglas: 130, 1226. Kennedy: 291, 1558, 1859, 2139. Foreman: 287, 850, 912, 1302, 2340. Planer: 393, 515, 1457, 1716. Tiomkin: 33,

286, 446, 638, 663, 730, 768, 850, 911, 912, 1206, 1347, 1370, 1470, 2006, 2127, 2282, 2335.

381 • CHANCES ARE

TRI-STAR PICTURES PRODUCTION; TRI-STAR. 1989.
NOMINATION *Song:* "After All," music by Tom Snow, lyrics by Dean Pitchford.

Widow Cybill Shepherd has remained unmarried, but one day her daughter, Mary Stuart Masterson, brings home a new boyfriend, Robert Downey, Jr. [382.5], who begins to realize that he's the reincarnation of Shepherd's husband. This brew of fantasy, farce, and romantic comedy needs a surer hand than that of director Emile Ardolino and a more skillful actress than Shepherd to make it work, but Downey and Masterson are very good. Ryan O'Neal [1218] plays the late husband's best friend who wants Shepherd to forget the past and marry him—a quirky part that O'Neal doesn't quite master. In short, amusing fluff if you don't expect too much. The Oscar went to Alan Menken and Howard Ashman for "Under the Sea," from *The Little Mermaid.*

Snow: 697. Pitchford: 641, 697.

382 • CHANG

PARAMOUNT FAMOUS LASKY. 1927–28.
NOMINATION *Unique and Artistic Picture.*

Documentary about the lives of a rice grower and his family in the jungles of Thailand, focusing on their battle against wild animals, including a herd of elephants. Producer-director-writers Merian C. Cooper [1189 . . .] and Ernest B. Schoedsack later gave us *King Kong* (1933). The Oscar in this category, eliminated after the first year of the awards, went to *Sunrise.*

382.5 • CHAPLIN

CAROLCO PRODUCTION; TRISTAR. 1992.
NOMINATIONS *Actor:* Robert Downey, Jr. *Art Direction:* Stuart Craig, Chris A. Butler. *Original Score:* John Barry.

Downey plays Charles Chaplin [405 . . .], from his impoverished beginnings in London through his music hall years, his rise to stardom in silent films, his exile from the United States on a variety of political and moral grounds, and his triumphant return to receive an honorary Oscar at the 1971 awards show. The movie would seem to have everything going for it: a fascinating subject, a screenplay by William Boyd, Bryan Forbes [81], and William Goldman [54 . . .], cinematography by Sven Nykvist [460 . . .], and an impressive cast—Geraldine Chaplin as her own grandmother, Dan Aykroyd [580] as Mack Sennett, Kevin Kline [670] as Douglas Fairbanks, Marisa Tomei [1391.5] as Mabel Normand, Anthony Hopkins [1679.5 . . .] as the editor of Chaplin's autobiography, Diane Lane as Paulette Goddard [1855], James Woods [1746] as the attorney who prosecutes Chaplin in a paternity suit, and so on. Producer-director Richard Attenborough [745] provides lavish sets, costumes, and music. But *Chaplin* is undermined by too many oversimplifications of fact and psychology and too many biopic clichés. Chaplin's predilection for marrying teenagers is "explained" by a thwarted first love for a sixteen-year-old chorus girl. (Three of his four brides were in their teens. Goddard was the oldest, but because both the year of her birth and the date of their marriage are disputed, we don't know how old she was. The range is from twenty-two to thirty-one.) His brother, Sydney (Paul Rhys), is turned into the conventional worrywart voice of doom, forever warning Charlie against making political statements in his films. His exile from the United States is attributed to a vendetta by J. Edgar Hoover (Kevin Dunn), who seems to have been motivated by Chaplin's upstaging him at a dinner party. Attenborough is far more in tune with Chaplin the sentimentalist—we are treated to a long, gooey clip from *The Kid* at film's end—than with the Chaplin who made people laugh.

Downey, however, is terrific, not simply mimicking Chaplin routines, but making the on-screen persona coherent with the off-screen Chaplin. Best known as a light comedian in films such as *Chances Are*, *Less Than Zero* (1987), and *Soapdish* (1991), Downey is the son of the satiric experimental filmmaker Robert Downey, whose most famous works, *Greaser's Palace* and *Putney Swope*, were made at the end of the sixties.

If the younger Downey had won, he would have been the first to receive the best actor Oscar while still in his twenties, but the contest was almost a foregone conclusion: Al Pacino in *Scent of a Woman*. It's likely that Downey ran a strong third after Denzel Washington in *Malcolm X*.

The art direction Oscar went to *Howards End*. Alan Menken won for the scoring of *Aladdin*.

Craig: 485, 608, 745, 1331. Barry: 259, 482, 1177, 1285, 1512.

383 • CHAPTER TWO

RAY STARK PRODUCTION; COLUMBIA. 1979.
NOMINATION *Actress:* Marsha Mason.

Writer James Caan [784], recovering from the death of his wife, meets divorcée Mason and reluctantly falls in love again. Neil Simon [332 . . .] adapts his own Broadway play for the screen with little success. What was wryly funny when done by live actors seems formulaic and gag-ridden on screen. Caan is miscast, and Robert Moore's uninspired directing doesn't help. The cast also includes Valerie Harper and Joseph Bologna.

For Mason, the role presented a unique challenge: Simon, her husband, had written the play about their own relationship. She had declined to play the part on stage for that reason but changed her mind for the movie. Three of Mason's four Oscar nominations were for Simon roles, and when their marriage lost its magic—they divorced in 1983—so did her career. She makes only occasional screen appearances today. Sally Field won for *Norma Rae*.

Mason: 403, 803, 1495.

384 • CHARADE

UNIVERSAL-STANLEY DONEN PRODUCTION; UNIVERSAL. 1963.
NOMINATION *Song:* "Charade," music by Henry Mancini, lyrics by Johnny Mercer.

When her husband is murdered, Audrey Hepburn [278 . . .] finds herself being harassed by several strange men—James Coburn, Ned Glass, and George Kennedy [443]. Then a handsome stranger, Cary Grant [1445 . . .], comes to her aid, as does a rather bumbling consular official, Walter Matthau

[709 . . .]. But nobody, least of all her dead husband, is what he seems to be. This larky, tongue-in-cheek thriller was undervalued by the critics, who dismissed it with their usual epithet, "Hitchcockian" —meaning not as good as. Actually Stanley Donen is one of the few directors who have played the comedy romantic thriller game in the same league as the master. *Charade* may not be up there with *Rear Window* or *North by Northwest,* but it's better than some of Hitchcock's own efforts in this vein, such as *The Trouble With Harry* (1955) or *The Family Plot* (1976). And it's the only screen teaming of those wizards of charm, Hepburn and Grant. Writer Peter Stone [655] finds countless ways to exploit their nonpareil gifts. In a year so doom-haunted as 1963, it's not surprising that the Academy found few reasons to honor this escapist movie, which has occasional brutal moments, but one suspects that it has a lot more repeat viewers today than the year's best picture contenders—*America, America, Cleopatra, How the West Was Won, Lilies of the Field*—or perhaps even the winner, *Tom Jones.*

The nominated song, not from its melodist's or its lyricist's top drawer, is virtually thrown away in the film, its lyrics inaudible. The Oscar went to James Van Heusen and Sammy Cahn's "Call Me Irresponsible," from *Papa's Delicate Condition.*

Mancini: 122, 278, 494, 508, 512, 776, 825, 1573, 1574, 1864, 1970, 2011, 2037, 2201. Mercer: 248, 278, 476, 494, 508, 636, 788, 825, 877, 903, 905, 1109, 1772, 1838, 1912, 2327, 2328.

385 • CHARGE OF THE LIGHT BRIGADE, THE

WARNER BROS. 1936.

AWARD *Assistant Director:* Jack Sullivan.

NOMINATIONS *Sound Recording:* Nathan Levinson. *Score:* Warner Bros. Studio Music Department, Leo Forbstein, head; score by Max Steiner.

That horrifying moment of imperialist idiocy during the Crimean War, in which the British cavalry rushed headlong at a gun emplacement and were mowed down, was memorialized by Tennyson in a poem whose irony subsequent generations failed to heed. Warners likewise plays the story for heroism,

not folly, with Errol Flynn as the captain who causes the whole thing, disobeying orders and leading the charge because he and his fellow soldiers want revenge for a massacre that took place while they were stationed in India. But Flynn also sacrifices himself for his brother (Patric Knowles)—a rival for the affections of Olivia de Havilland [798 . . .]. The whole thing has only the most tangential relationship with history, but it doesn't really matter: It's one of the best of the Flynn–de Havilland–Michael Curtiz [79 . . .] epics, rousing and spectacular—and not wholly lacking in irony, either, though as with Tennyson's poem, it's easy to ignore it and see only the glory. Second unit director Sullivan's staging of the charge is wonderful, and certainly justifies the existence of the assistant director category, which was discontinued after the 1937 awards. The cast includes such stalwarts of the genre as Nigel Bruce, the young David Niven [1778], Donald Crisp [952], Spring Byington [2325], and J. Carrol Naish [1294 . . .].

The sound award went to Douglas Shearer for *San Francisco.* From its inception through the 1937 awards, the scoring Oscar was presented to the studio music department head, and not to the composer himself, so in this instance Forbstein lost to himself, winning for *Anthony Adverse*—whose score was by Erich Wolfgang Korngold—instead.

Levinson: 16, 30, 343, 531, 689, 710, 712, 790, 930, 965, 1052, 1169, 1621, 1690, 1768, 1769, 1779, 1930, 1949, 2058, 2318. Forbstein: 90, 1169. Steiner: 16, 154, 190, 330, 365, 492, 679, 747, 754, 798, 999, 1043, 1046, 1052, 1162, 1169, 1170, 1207, 1324, 1408, 1430, 1456, 1690, 1779, 1828.

386 • CHARIOTS OF FIRE

ENIGMA PRODUCTIONS LTD.; THE LADD COMPANY/WARNER BROS. (UNITED KINGDOM). 1981.

AWARDS *Picture:* David Puttnam, producer. *Screenplay Written Directly for the Screen:* Colin Welland. *Original Score:* Vangelis. *Costume Design:* Milena Canonero.

NOMINATIONS *Supporting Actor:* Ian Holm. *Director:* Hugh Hudson. *Film Editing:* Terry Rawlings.

At the 1924 Olympics in Paris, the best hope for a British gold medal lies with two Cambridge University students: runners Harold Abrahams (Ben Cross), a Jew, and Eric Liddell (Ian Charleson), a pious Scot. Abrahams is motivated by a desire to spite the anti-Semites, embodied in the film by a pair of Cambridge dons played by John Gielgud [103 . . .] and Lindsay Anderson. Liddell's motives are less vengeful, but his faith prevents him from running a crucial race on Sunday. Good characterization, fine performances, and slick production values make this a highly watchable movie, and it set box-office records for an import. But its triumph at the Oscars is still something of a mystery. It's no surprise that it defeated *On Golden Pond* for best picture: In its way, that thin melodrama is the American equivalent of *Chariots of Fire*—the kind of thing you'd expect to see done, perhaps a little less glossily, on TV. Or that it won out over *Raiders of the Lost Ark*—a hugely entertaining movie that's just not the sort of thing that wins Oscars. But it also defeated *Atlantic City,* a wholly original and satisfying work, and *Reds,* a huge but literate epic—both of them films with a claim to be more than just entertainment, a claim that *Chariots* can hardly make.

Puttnam, youngish, ambitious but abrasive, parlayed his triumph into a disaster: Five years later he became the chairman and CEO of Columbia Pictures. He lasted less than a year, offending some of Hollywood's most powerful men: agent Michael Ovitz, by making caustic comments about the expensive talent Ovitz manages; producer Ray Stark [737 . . .], by rejecting several of Stark's proposed projects; Bill Murray, by an alleged remark that the star of Columbia's moneymaking *Ghostbusters* was the sort of person who took from Hollywood without giving in return; and Bill Cosby, by showing contempt for the comedian's film *Leonard Part 6,* which subsequently became the studio's biggest money-loser of 1987. During his tenure, Puttnam turned his attention to what he considered "quality" projects, such as *Hope and Glory* and *The Last Emperor,* but failed to provide enough profitable films to compensate for less profitable but prestigious ones. When Columbia owner Coca-Cola decided to reorganize the studio, merging Columbia with Tri-Star, Puttnam was not

consulted, and resigned—perhaps under pressure. His subsequent productions, *Memphis Belle* (1990) and *Meeting Venus* (1991), were neither commercially nor critically successful.

Receiving his Oscar, Welland held it aloft and proclaimed, "The British are coming!" But although British actors such as Daniel Day-Lewis [992.5 . . .], Jeremy Irons [1689], Anthony Hopkins [1679.5 . . .], and Emma Thompson [954.5 . . .] have certainly come to accept awards, British producers, with the exception of Richard Attenborough for *Gandhi* the following year, had a hard time of it during the tight budgets of the Thatcher years. Welland has since done the moderately well received *Twice in a Lifetime,* an American production with an American setting and story. He also wrote a draft of the screenplay for *A Dry White Season* with its director, Euzhan Palcy.

Vangelis—born Evangelos Papathanasiou in Greece—is one of the most popular of the so-called New Age composers, producing rich, moody but somewhat repetitious electronic compositions and scores for films such as *Blade Runner* and *1492: The Conquest of Paradise* (1992).

Holm has been a major British actor since the fifties, a superb Shakespearean, but also a valuable character actor. His film roles have ranged from *Alien* to Kenneth Branagh's *Henry V.* In *Chariots* he plays the Italian-Turkish running coach. He lost the Oscar to his *Chariots* costar John Gielgud's performance in *Arthur.*

Hudson, who lost to Warren Beatty for *Reds,* has not fulfilled the promise he showed with *Chariots.* His next film, *Greystoke: The Legend of Tarzan, Lord of the Apes,* was a troubled production, somewhat pretentious in concept and made incoherent by much rewriting of the script. And *Revolution* (1985) was an outright disaster: an attempt to make an epic about the American Revolutionary War with a riot of miscast performers including Al Pacino [75 . . .], Nastassja Kinski, and rocker Annie Lennox.

The editing award went to Michael Kahn for *Raiders of the Lost Ark.*

Puttnam: 1086, 1313, 1331. Canonero: 151, 543, 1512, 2148.

387 • *CHARLY*

AMERICAN BROADCASTING COMPANIES-SELMUR PICTURES PRODUCTION; CINERAMA. 1968.

AWARD *Actor:* Cliff Robertson.

Robertson plays a mentally retarded man who undergoes experimental surgery that turns him into a genius. He falls in love with his teacher, Claire Bloom, but discovers that the effects of the treatment are temporary: He will return to his original state. Sentimental problem drama, directed by Ralph Nelson [1174] with a late-sixties look and sound—music by Ravi Shankar [745]—that hasn't worn well. Adapted by Stirling Silliphant [992] from a novel, *Flowers for Algernon,* that had been dramatized on TV, also with Robertson, in 1961. The movie *Awakenings* takes a similar theme and handles it with more plausibility and finesse.

Robertson had been a light leading man since his debut in a supporting role in *Picnic.* Before *Charly,* he was best known for playing John F. Kennedy in the 1963 movie *PT-109*—with Kennedy's approval, though the president is said to have wanted Warren Beatty [255 . . .] for the part. Robertson bought the rights to the screenplay for *Charly* after his appearance in the role on TV, in part because the film versions of other TV dramas he had done were cast with more established actors: Jack Lemmon had played Robertson's role in the film of *Days of Wine and Roses,* and Paul Newman was cast in *The Hustler.* Robertson won the Oscar against such competitors as Alan Arkin for *The Heart Is a Lonely Hunter,* Alan Bates for *The Fixer,* Ron Moody for *Oliver!,* and Peter O'Toole for *The Lion in Winter.* But though the award increased his name recognition, it failed to make him a major star. His career took another odd turn in 1977, when Robertson discovered that Columbia head David Begelman had been embezzling funds from the studio, forging Robertson's and others' names on checks. Though Begelman fell from power, Robertson suffered the ostracism that sometimes be-

falls whistle-blowers and found roles even harder to come by.

388 • *CHEERS FOR MISS BISHOP*

UNITED ARTISTS. 1941.

NOMINATION *Scoring of a Dramatic Picture:* Edward Ward.

Martha Scott [1510] graduates from college with the usual ambitions, but circumstances keep her in the same small town for the next fifty years; she becomes a beloved schoolteacher—Mr. Chips with a sex change. Pleasant, forgettable, not-too-saccharine stuff from a Bess Streeter Aldrich novel. This is the sort of thing people who talk about "traditional values" mean. The cast, directed by Tay Garnett, includes William Gargan [2045], Edmund Gwenn [1325 . . .], Sterling Holloway, and Sidney Blackmer. The Oscar went to Bernard Herrmann's score for *All That Money Can Buy.*

Ward: 47, 694, 1270, 1560, 2002.

389 • *CHEYENNE AUTUMN*

JOHN FORD-BERNARD SMITH PRODUCTION; WARNER BROS. 1964.

NOMINATION *Color Cinematography:* William H. Clothier.

In 1878 the remnants of the Cheyenne tribe make a trek from Oklahoma, where the government has resettled them, to their ancestral home in Wyoming. The last western directed by John Ford [815 . . .], it's an attempt to make a film sympathetic to the Indians who were the villains in many of his westerns. It's sprawling and unfocused, but frequently quite moving, too. Ford's admirers speak of it with reverence, but one wishes he had chosen to do the film at the peak of his powers, fifteen or twenty years earlier. An odd comic sequence with James Stewart [73 . . .] as Wyatt Earp pointlessly interrupts the film—as if Ford wanted to use it in one of his movies but hadn't got around to it before. The huge cast includes Richard Widmark [1098], Carroll Baker [119], Karl Malden [1477 . . .], Dolores Del Rio, Sal Mineo [630 . . .], Edward G. Robinson, Arthur Kennedy [291 . . .], and such Ford stock company players as Patrick Wayne, Elizabeth Allen, John Car-radine, and John Qualen.

Clothier had been a cameraman since 1923 and worked on the aerial sequences for the first Oscar winner, *Wings,* a specialty he repeated in other films, such as *The High and the Mighty.* He became best known in the sixties as a color cinematographer specializing in location shoots. He lost to Harry Strad-ling's work on *My Fair Lady.*

Clothier: 33.

390 • *CHILDREN OF A LESSER GOD*

Burt Sugarman Production; Paramount. 1986.
Award *Actress:* Marlee Matlin.
Nominations *Picture:* Burt Sugarman and Patrick Palmer, producers. *Actor:* William Hurt. *Supporting Actress:* Piper Laurie. *Screenplay Based on Material From Another Medium:* Hesper Anderson and Mark Medoff.

Hurt goes to teach at a school for the deaf, where he's a hit with his students but a flop with the beautiful, obviously intelligent but surly Matlin, a former student at the school who has chosen to work there as a janitor. Eventually he breaks through and they fall in love, but the relationship falls apart because she resents his manipulating her life and feels that he condescends to her. Splendidly performed, but this adaptation of Medoff's Tony-winning Broadway play seems a little formulaic and calculating—its laughs and tears come like clockwork. Randa Haines, making her feature film debut, was the only director of a movie nominated for best picture who didn't make the slate for best director; in her place, David Lynch was nominated for *Blue Velvet.* She was subsequently joined by Penny Marshall, director of *Awakenings,* and Barbra Streisand, director of *The Prince of Tides,* on the roster of women who have directed best picture nominees but were overlooked in the directing category. The best picture Oscar went to *Platoon.*

Matlin, who was twenty-one, became the youngest winner of the best actress Oscar. After a long search for an actress to play the role, she was spotted in a video made in Chicago, where she had grown up. She had become deaf in infancy. Roles for deaf performers, however talented, are hard to come by, and Mat-lin's subsequent career has been limited. She has appeared in several TV movies and became a regular on the dramatic series *Reasonable Doubts* in 1991, playing a lawyer.

Hurt lost to Paul Newman for *The Color of Money.* Laurie, who plays Matlin's mother, lost to Dianne Wiest in *Hannah and Her Sisters.* The writing award went to Ruth Prawer Jhabvala for *A Room With a View.*

Palmer: 1351, 1857. Hurt: 293, 1099. Laurie: 364, 964.

391 • *CHILDREN OF NATURE*

Icelandic Film Corporation Ltd./Max Film (Berlin)/ Metro Film (Oslo) Production (Iceland). 1991.
Nomination *Foreign Language Film.*

An elderly man goes to the city where he finds his old love in a nursing home. Together they flee to the Icelandic coast. The first film from Iceland to be nominated for the Oscar, this "mystical road movie," as one critic called it, is filled with spectacular scenery. Directed by Fridrik Thor Fridrikkson. The Oscar went to *Mediterraneo.*

392 • *CHILDREN OF PARADISE*

Pathé-Cinema, Tricolore Films (France). 1946.
Nomination *Original Screenplay:* Jacques Prévert.

Arletty plays a courtesan in 1840s Paris loved by several men, including a mime played by Jean-Louis Barrault and an actor played by Pierre Brasseur. Barrault gives up hope and marries another woman but later encounters Arletty again and plots to run away with her. Marcel Carné's brilliant evocation of an era and the life of the theater is regarded as one of the masterpieces of French film. Much of it was made under the harshness and deprivation of the German occupation. (Arletty was later disgraced and imprisoned as a collaborator for her affair with a German officer.) Prévert's witty, romantic screenplay lost to Muriel and Sydney Box's *The Seventh Veil.*

393 • *CHILDREN'S HOUR, THE*

Mirisch-Worldwide Production; United Artists. 1961.
Nominations *Supporting Actress:* Fay Bainter. *Black-and-White Cinematography:* Franz F. Planer. *Black-and-White*

Art Direction—Set Decoration: Fernando Carrere; Edward G. Boyle. *Sound:* Gordon E. Sawyer, sound director, Goldwyn Studio Sound Department. *Black-and-White Costume Design:* Dorothy Jeakins.

A malicious student at a girls' school run by Audrey Hepburn [278 . . .] and Shirley MacLaine [91 . . .] spreads a rumor that the two women are lesbians, setting in motion tragic consequences. The play by Lillian Hellman [1182 . . .] had been filmed in 1936 as *These Three,* with the lesbianism carefully censored out, but oddly, the earlier version is superior—perhaps because it's less eager to shock us with loves that dare not speak their name and more content to concentrate on the characters. Hellman herself had not objected to the earlier version because, she explained, the play was not about lesbianism, it "was about the power of a lie." William Wyler [175 . . .] directed both versions, and Miriam Hopkins [165], who played one of the young women in the first film, is the interfering aunt in this one. The cast also includes James Garner [1380] as Hepburn's fiancé.

This was the last film for Bainter, and it was an interesting change of character for an actress who had spent her career playing sympathetic roles—here she's the grandmother of the girl who tells the fatal lie. The Oscar went to Rita Moreno for *West Side Story.* Bainter died in 1968.

The Hustler took the awards for Eugen Shuftan's cinematography and for art direction. The Oscar for sound went to *West Side Story* and the costuming award to *La Dolce Vita.*

Bainter: 1046, 2266. Planer: 380, 515, 1457, 1716. Boyle: 91, 709, 743, 1783, 1860, 1866. Sawyer: 33, 91, 184, 214, 730, 864, 882, 973, 974, 1032, 1511, 1592, 2244, 2297, 2310. Jeakins: 509, 832, 882, 1048, 1385, 1391, 1432, 1748, 1881, 2012, 2238.

394 • *CHINA SYNDROME, THE*

Michael Douglas/IPC Films Production; Columbia. 1979.
Nominations *Actor:* Jack Lemmon. *Actress:* Jane Fonda. *Screenplay Written Directly for the Screen:* Mike Gray, T. S. Cook, and James Bridges. *Art Direction—Set Decoration:* George Jenkins; Arthur Jeph Parker.

Fonda plays a somewhat vapid TV news reporter who suddenly finds herself covering a major story: an accident at a nuclear power plant. Lemmon, a supervisor at the plant, is shaken by his discovery of the plant's faulty construction, and his resistance to the officials who want to cover it up costs him his life. This excellent thriller found itself at the center of the news when, shortly after it opened, the accident at Three Mile Island embarrassed the power industry spokesmen who had earlier claimed the movie was hysterical and exaggerated. The title refers to the theoretical consequences of a meltdown at a nuclear plant: The heat would be so intense that it might burn through the earth's mantle and blast a hole through to China, or at least, as one character observes, the fallout would contaminate "an area the size of Pennsylvania"—the state in which Three Mile Island is located. (The eerie prescience of some of the movie's dialogue has continued. At one point, before he realizes that the plant has been poorly constructed, Lemmon claims, "We've got a quality control system that's only equaled by NASA.") Produced by Michael Douglas [1481 . . .], who plays Fonda's cameraman. The film was directed by cowriter Bridges. The cast also includes Wilford Brimley, Scott Brady, and Peter Donat.

Both Lemmon and Fonda were social activists, and Lemmon, who had narrated antinuclear documentaries, was eager for the role. Fonda's production company, IPC, was also involved in the project. The Oscars went to Dustin Hoffman for *Kramer vs. Kramer* and Sally Field for *Norma Rae.*

The writing award went to Steve Tesich for *Breaking Away.* The art direction award was won by *All That Jazz.*

Lemmon: 91, 508, 1330, 1337, 1761, 1860, 2140. Fonda: 430, 1066, 1104, 1356, 1473, 2047. Bridges: 1525. Jenkins: 54. Parker: 1816.

395 • *CHINATOWN*

Robert Evans Production; Paramount. 1974.

Award *Original Screenplay:* Robert Towne.

Nominations *Picture:* Robert Evans, producer. *Actor:* Jack Nicholson. *Actress:* Faye Dunaway. *Director:* Roman Polanski. *Cinematography:* John A. Alonzo. *Art Direction–Set Decoration:* Richard Sylbert and W. Stewart Campbell; Ruby Levitt. *Sound:* Bud Grenzbach and Larry Jost. *Original Dramatic Score:* Jerry Goldsmith. *Film Editing:* Sam O'Steen. *Costume Design:* Anthea Sylbert.

Nicholson plays Jake Gittes, a private eye in thirties Los Angeles, who finds himself in the thick of an elaborate plot involving Dunaway and the sinister millionaire Noah Cross, superbly embodied by John Huston [24 . . .]. Rich, witty, intricate thriller that uses its film noir milieu to explore political and moral corruption. (It's partly based on an episode in the early history of L.A., several decades before the time in which the film is set, involving corrupt maneuvering over water rights.) One of the most celebrated and influential films of the Watergate-era seventies, it competed for the Oscars against three films that were similarly dark in tone: *The Conversation, The Godfather, Part II* (which won), and *Lenny*. The only nominee that was purely escapist was *The Towering Inferno*, but even that had corruption and an attempted cover-up as a plot device. The cast also includes Diane Ladd [41 . . .], Burt Young [1712], and director Polanski as a knife-wielding thug.

The Oscar established Towne as one of the most sought-after writers in Hollywood, though he was at odds with director Polanski over the ending of the film. Towne's screenplay was more hopeful. Polanski himself supplied the bleaker ending that was filmed. Towne has subsequently turned to directing his own screenplays, including *Personal Best* (1982) and *Tequila Sunrise*.

Producer Evans began acting as a child but gave it up temporarily because of illness. He returned to the profession in the film *The Man of a Thousand Faces,* playing producer Irving Thalberg [150 . . .] in the biopic of actor Lon Chaney. Thalberg's widow, Norma Shearer [150 . . .], personally approved his

casting. Evans moved into producing and in the late sixties was head of production for Paramount, responsible for such films as *Rosemary's Baby, Love Story,* and *The Godfather*. In the mid-seventies he formed an independent production company, but his career began a steady decline, in part because of his involvement with drugs. In 1980 he was convicted of cocaine possession. He was also involved in a sensational case involving a former girlfriend, who was found guilty of conspiring to murder one of the backers of *The Cotton Club,* a film Evans produced in 1984. Although Evans was not implicated in the murder, the scandal greatly affected his career. He attempted a comeback in 1993 as producer of the film *Sliver,* but it was a box-office failure.

Nicholson's loss to Art Carney for *Harry and Tonto* is the result either of the Academy's making a sentimental gesture toward a veteran or of three extraordinary performances by younger actors splitting the vote, for Nicholson was also competing against Dustin Hoffman for *Lenny* and Al Pacino for *The Godfather, Part II*. (Albert Finney's nomination for *Murder on the Orient Express* is more a tribute to the makeup artist than to his performance.) In 1990 Nicholson directed a sequel to *Chinatown, The Two Jakes,* which was a critical and box-office disaster.

Dunaway, who fought bitterly with Polanski during the filming, lost to Ellen Burstyn for *Alice Doesn't Live Here Anymore*. Polanski lost to Francis Ford Coppola for *The Godfather, Part II,* which also won for art direction and score. *The Towering Inferno* won for Fred Koenekamp and Joseph Biroc's cinematography and Harold F. Kress and Carl Kress' editing. The sound award went to *Earthquake* and the costuming Oscar to Theoni V. Aldredge for *The Great Gatsby*.

Towne: 839, 1135, 1798. Nicholson: 595, 658.5, 672, 1019, 1135, 1481, 1625, 1678, 2020. Dunaway: 255, 1424. Polanski: 1728, 2021. Jost: 502, 1525. R. Sylbert: 448, 543, 1678, 1798, 2277. Campbell: 1698, 1798. Levitt: 77, 1572, 1881. Grenzbach: 784, 1584. Goldsmith: 152.5, 268, 727, 939, 1472, 1527, 1537, 1541, 1583, 1589, 1753, 1913, 2176, 2287. O'Steen: 1821, 2277. A. Sylbert: 1066.

396 • CHITTY CHITTY BANG BANG

WARFIELD PRODUCTIONS LTD.; UNITED ARTISTS. 1968.
NOMINATION *Song:* "Chitty Chitty Bang Bang," music and lyrics by Richard M. Sherman and Robert B. Sherman.

Inventor Dick Van Dyke creates a flying car that transports him and a group of children to a land where children are not wanted. With the help of Sally Ann Howes, they overthrow the bad guys. The success of *Mary Poppins* led to a series of bad musicals for children: *Doctor Dolittle, Bedknobs and Broomsticks,* and this one, which reunites *Poppins* star Van Dyke and that film's songwriters, the Shermans. Unable to get Julie Andrews, the producers cast Howes, who had succeeded Andrews on Broadway in *My Fair Lady.* Even the special effects are cheesy. The story is based on a book by, of all people, James Bond creator Ian Fleming. Directed by Ken Hughes. The song Oscar went to "The Windmills of Your Mind," by Michel Legrand and Marilyn and Alan Bergman, from *The Thomas Crown Affair.*

R. M. Sherman: 166, 1238, 1284, 1842, 2107. R. B. Sherman: 166, 1238, 1284, 1842, 2107.

397 • CHOCOLATE SOLDIER, THE

MGM. 1941.
NOMINATIONS *Black-and-White Cinematography:* Karl Freund. *Sound Recording:* Douglas Shearer. *Scoring of a Musical Picture:* Herbert Stothart and Bronislau Kaper.

Nelson Eddy and Risë Stevens are an opera-singing married couple. He grows jealous and woos her in disguise to test her fidelity. Though it has the title of the operetta based on the George Bernard Shaw [1637] play *Arms and the Man,* this one is based on Ferenc Molnar's play *The Guardsman,* which had been filmed by MGM in 1931. The music is by Oscar Straus, and the screenplay is so talky you keep wishing Eddy and Stevens would shut up and sing. Directed by Roy Del Ruth, with Nigel Bruce, Florence Bates, and Nydia Westman. Arthur Miller's cinematography for *How Green Was My Valley,* Jack Whitney's sound direction for *That Hamilton Woman,* and Frank Churchill and Oliver Wallace's scoring for *Dumbo* took the Oscars.

Freund: 239, 799. Shearer: 136, 202, 256, 685, 817, 835, 1096, 1232, 1292, 1371, 1419, 1751, 1950, 1988, 2048, 2055, 2211, 2300. Stothart: 1096, 1232, 1274, 1292, 1387, 1662, 1988, 2068, 2193, 2234, 2300. Kaper: 1173, 1388.

398 • CHORUS LINE, A

EMBASSY FILMS ASSOCIATES AND POLYGRAM PICTURES PRODUCTION; COLUMBIA. 1985.
NOMINATIONS *Sound:* Donald O. Mitchell, Michael Minkler, Gerry Humphreys, and Chris Newman. *Song:* "Surprise, Surprise," music by Marvin Hamlisch, lyrics by Edward Kleban. *Film Editing:* John Bloom.

Broadway director Michael Douglas [1481 . . .] puts a group of singers and dancers through hell as they audition for a musical. The smash hit stage musical becomes a painful dud in the hands of director Richard Attenborough [745], who has no idea how to convert an essentially theatrical experience into a cinematic one. The cast of unknowns has remained unknown.

The Oscar for sound went to *Out of Africa.* Lionel Richie's "Say You, Say Me," from *White Nights,* won the song award. The editing Oscar went to Thom Noble for *Witness.*

Mitchell: 223, 411.5, 507, 734.5, 779, 1525, 1650, 1824, 1825, 2020, 2114, 2176.5. Minkler: 58, 260, 413.5, 606, 1047, 2144. Humphreys: 745. Newman: 60, 631, 641, 724, 784, 1820. Hamlisch: 977, 1109, 1747, 1813, 1876, 1898, 1927, 2238. Bloom: 725, 745.

399 • CHRISTMAS HOLIDAY

UNIVERSAL. 1944.
NOMINATION *Scoring of a Dramatic or Comedy Picture:* H. J. Salter.

Deanna Durbin marries Gene Kelly [74], who turns out to be a killer. She ruins her life in her attempts to help him. This peculiar career move for both actors was based on a story by Somerset Maugham, adapted by Herman J. Mankiewicz [407 . . .] and atmospherically directed by Robert Siodmak [1085]. Also in the cast are Gladys George

[2192] and Gale Sondergaard [83 . . .]. Despite the rather grim melodrama, Durbin gets to introduce a lovely Frank Loesser [864 . . .] song, "Spring Will Be a Little Late This Year." It was not nominated, however—Universal chose instead to push "I'll Walk Alone," a Jule Styne–Sammy Cahn song from *Follow the Boys.* The Oscar for scoring went to Max Steiner for *Since You Went Away.*

Salter: 62, 340, 1030, 1307, 2060.

400 • *CIMARRON*

RKO RADIO. 1930–31.
AWARDS *Picture:* William LeBaron, producer. *Adaptation:* Howard Estabrook. *Interior Decoration:* Max Ree.
NOMINATIONS *Actor:* Richard Dix. *Actress:* Irene Dunne. *Director:* Wesley Ruggles. *Cinematography:* Edward Cronjager.

Dix and Dunne play Yancey and Sabra Cravat (novelist Edna Ferber had a way with names) in this saga of the settling of the West whose highlight is the great Oklahoma land rush of 1888. One of the weakest films to win the best picture Oscar, it was also the only western to hold that honor for almost sixty years —until *Dances With Wolves.* Its success at the awards is largely due to the industry's still-clumsy adaptation to sound: *Cimarron* had more action than most other early talkies. And the competition was particularly weak: The maudlin *East Lynne* and the kid movie *Skippy* hardly seem like contenders; *Trader Horn* had only the novelty of its location photography in Africa to recommend it; and *The Front Page,* perhaps the best of the nominated pictures, was essentially a filmed play. Some of the year's finest films were not nominated, however: *City Lights, Little Caesar, The Public Enemy,* and *The Blue Angel,* all of which are far more enduring films than *Cimarron.*

LeBaron, chief of production at RKO, had been a playwright and a magazine editor before he entered films as a writer. After winning the Oscar for *Cimarron,* he moved over to Paramount, where he produced several Mae West and W. C. Fields films before becoming head of production. In 1941 he went to 20th Century-Fox, where he produced many of the musi-cals starring Alice Faye and Betty Grable before his retirement in the late forties. He died in 1958.

Estabrook had been an actor, director, and producer in the theater before going to Hollywood in the late twenties, when the call went out for people who could write dialogue rather than just title cards. His career as screenwriter lasted into the fifties and included such films as *David Copperfield, The Human Comedy,* and *The Big Fisherman.* He died in 1978.

Dix had been a very popular actor in the silent era, working primarily at Paramount. But except for *Cimarron,* his work in the sound era was undistinguished, and though his career lasted into the forties, it was mostly in B pictures. He died in 1947, aged fifty-five. The Oscar was won by Lionel Barrymore for *A Free Soul.*

Dunne had trained as a singer and was discovered by the movies in the road company of *Show Boat,* playing the role of Magnolia that she re-created in the 1936 film version. *Cimarron* was her second feature, and its success established her as a star. It also led to the first of her five unsuccessful nominations—Marie Dressler won for *Min and Bill.*

Like his brother, Charles Ruggles, Wesley Ruggles had begun as an actor. He was one of the Keystone Cops and appeared in several Charles Chaplin [405 . . .] shorts. He turned to directing in 1917 and continued in that career until the mid-forties. Other than *Cimarron* and Mae West's *I'm No Angel,* however, his directing work is forgettable. The Oscar went to Norman Taurog for *Skippy.*

Cronjager lost to Floyd Crosby's work on *Tabu.*

LeBaron: 1804. Estabrook: 1947. Dunne: 114, 972, 1212, 2041. Cronjager: 176, 889, 934, 1569, 1964, 2102.

401 • *CIMARRON*

MGM. 1960.
NOMINATIONS *Color Art Direction–Set Decoration:* George W. Davis and Addison Hehr; Henry Grace, Hugh Hunt, and Otto Siegel. *Sound:* Franklin E. Milton, sound director, MGM Studio Sound Department.

Remake of the 1930–31 best picture winner,

based on a novel by Edna Ferber, about a family's struggle in turn-of-the-century Oklahoma Territory. Glenn Ford and Maria Schell play the parts taken by Richard Dix and Irene Dunne in the original. Big, expensive, and dull, despite a cast that includes Anne Baxter [46 . . .], Arthur O'Connell [73 . . .], Russ Tamblyn [1558], Mercedes McCambridge [53 . . .], and Vic Morrow. Directed by Anthony Mann, but without the finesse he brought to such westerns as *Winchester 73* and *The Naked Spur*. The art direction Oscar went to *Spartacus,* the sound award to *The Alamo.*

Davis: 46, 69, 495, 542, 736, 953, 1213, 1335, 1388, 1537, 1552, 1706, 1814, 2157, 2184, 2312. Hehr: 953. Grace: 69, 227, 769, 953, 1335, 1388, 1450, 1537, 1552, 2157, 2184, 2312. Hunt: 175, 980, 1069, 1232, 1335, 1388, 1567, 1644, 1657, 1673, 2157, 2184. Milton: 175, 558, 814, 953, 2184.

402 • CINDERELLA

WALT DISNEY PRODUCTIONS; RKO RADIO. 1950.
NOMINATIONS *Sound Recording:* C. O. Slyfield, Walt Disney Studio Sound Department. *Song:* "Bibbidi-Bobbidi-Boo," music and lyrics by Mack David, Al Hoffman, and Jerry Livingston. *Scoring of a Musical Picture:* Oliver Wallace and Paul J. Smith.

The Disney version of the fairy tale is one of the studio's classics—not perhaps on a par with *Snow White* or *Pinocchio,* but one of the best of the postwar features, coming out before the studio divided its efforts into live-action films, amusement parks, and television. The tale is fleshed out by a gallery of small household animals, chief among them the resourceful mice Gus and Jaq and their nemesis, the cat Lucifer. The voices include Ilene Woods as Cinderella, Eleanor Audley as the wicked stepmother, and Verna Felton as the fairy godmother. Gus and Jaq are voiced by studio sound effects specialist Jimmy Macdonald, who had also taken over from Walt Disney himself the task of speaking for Mickey Mouse.

Though the sound department deserved recognition for its synchronization of speeded-up mice and bird voices with the music score, it lost to *All About*

Eve. The song award went to Ray Evans and Jay Livingston for "Mona Lisa," from *Captain Carey, U.S.A.* Adolph Deutsch and Roger Edens took the scoring Oscar for *Annie Get Your Gun.*

Slyfield: 140, 1745, 2071. David: 122, 371, 861, 882, 963, 1032, 2223. Livingston: 371, 861. Wallace: 42, 585, 2202, 2273.5. Smith: 1553, 1576, 1745, 1851, 1871, 2071, 2202.

403 • CINDERELLA LIBERTY

SANFORD PRODUCTION; 20TH CENTURY-FOX. 1973.
NOMINATIONS *Actress:* Marsha Mason. *Song:* "Nice to Be Around," music by John Williams, lyrics by Paul Williams. *Original Dramatic Score:* John Williams.

Sailor James Caan [784] picks up prostitute Mason and is particularly moved by the plight of her young part-black son (Kirk Calloway). Director Mark Rydell [1473] and writer Darryl Ponicsan want this to be an affecting slice of life but it's too mushy and sticky. Also in the cast are Eli Wallach, Burt Young [1712], Allyn Ann McLerie, Dabney Coleman, Sally Kirkland [82], and Bruno Kirby—billed as Bruce Kirby, Jr.

Mason had made her movie debut in 1966 in a long-forgotten exploitation flick, *Hot Rod Hullabaloo.* Fortunately she got better work in New York on the stage, so she was able to return to Hollywood and start over near the top. The first of her Oscar nominations is the only one for a film not written by the man she married, Neil Simon [332 . . .]. The Oscar went to Glenda Jackson for *A Touch of Class.*

The song Oscar went to Marvin Hamlisch and Marilyn and Alan Bergman for the title song from *The Way We Were,* for which Hamlisch also won the scoring award.

Mason: 383, 803, 1495. J. Williams: 6, 260, 416, 588, 613, 614, 659, 805, 933, 937, 982, 996, 997, 1041, 1047, 1596, 1652, 1679, 1684, 1701, 1764.65, 1916, 1977, 2107, 2126, 2194, 2293, 2322. P. Williams: 309, 1375, 1561, 1911.

404 • CINEMA PARADISO

CRISTALDIFILM/FILMS ARIANE PRODUCTION (ITALY). 1989.
AWARD *Foreign Language Film.*

A small boy in postwar Sicily finds escape from the

grind of poverty and the harshness of the local church by helping the projectionist in the village movie house. He grows up to be a filmmaker himself. Writer-director Giuseppe Tornatore's film also took the special jury prize at Cannes, perhaps because it captures the fascination with movies that the jurors—and Academy voters—must also have experienced. On the other hand, it's too long (even though it was shortened by half an hour after its initial release) and occasionally too sentimental.

405 • CIRCUS, THE

CHAPLIN; UNITED ARTISTS. 1927–28.

AWARD *Special Award:* Charles Chaplin, for versatility and genius in writing, acting, directing, and producing *The Circus.*

NOMINATIONS *Actor:* Charles Chaplin. *Comedy Direction:* Charles Chaplin.

Chaplin joins a circus and falls in love with bareback rider Merna Kennedy, who loves high-wire artist Harry Crocker. Chaplin must choose between her happiness—marriage to another—and his own. Not as highly regarded, or as often shown, as other Chaplin features, *The Circus* gives Chaplin an obvious milieu in which to perform, which he does brilliantly, but the plot betrays him into predictable sentimentality.

The Academy of Motion Picture Arts and Sciences had been formed primarily as a kind of company union, an attempt by Louis B. Mayer and other industry stalwarts to head off attempts to organize film craftspeople. The awards whose presentation later became the Academy's most famous function were something of an afterthought, and granting them a far more casual affair than it is today. So when an internal dispute arose over Chaplin's presence in the competitive categories, the Academy Board of Governors withdrew his name from competition and voted him a special award. His "collective accomplishments," the Academy told Chaplin, "place you in a class by yourself." Chaplin didn't show up to accept the award, which he may have interpreted as a snub. His next two films, *City Lights* (1931) and *Modern Times* (1936), received no notice at all from the Academy. The acting Oscar went to Emil Jannings for *The Last Command*

and *The Way of All Flesh.* The comedy directing award, which was discontinued after this year, went to Lewis Milestone for *Two Arabian Knights.*

Chaplin: 818, 1176, 1345.

406 • CITADEL, THE

MGM (UNITED KINGDOM). 1938.

NOMINATIONS *Picture:* Victor Saville, producer. *Actor:* Robert Donat. *Director:* King Vidor. *Screenplay:* Ian Dalrymple, Elizabeth Hill, and Frank Wead.

Young Dr. Donat begins his career tending to the needs of poor Welsh miners but is seduced into a life of luxury ministering to wealthy Harley Street clients. The course of this doctor drama, from an A. J. Cronin best-seller, is obvious from the outline, but MGM gives it the best that money can buy, including cinematography by Harry Stradling [110 . . .] and performances by Rosalind Russell [110 . . .], Rex Harrison [413 . . .], Ralph Richardson [839 . . .], and Emlyn Williams.

MGM, grown affluent in the late thirties, was inspired by the success of British producers such as Michael Balcon, Alexander Korda [1620], and J. Arthur Rank to enter into an Anglo-American film production arrangement. The Cinematograph Films Act of 1938 severely restricted the percentage of films that could be imported into Britain, providing another incentive for Hollywood to set up production units there. MGM's was the most ambitious, although the coming of World War II made it short-lived. Saville, an established director and producer, was hired to oversee the output of the MGM British studios. The best picture Oscar nominees included another film from this arrangement, *Pygmalion;* the Oscar went to *You Can't Take It With You,* for which Frank Capra took the directing Oscar.

Donat had established himself as one of Britain's top leading men with his performance in the 1935 Alfred Hitchcock [1171 . . .] classic, *The 39 Steps.* His competition for the Oscar was formidable: Charles Boyer in *Algiers,* James Cagney in *Angels With Dirty Faces,* Leslie Howard in *Pygmalion,* and the winner, Spencer Tracy in *Boys Town.*

In addition to the nominated writers, actor Emlyn

Williams and playwright John Van Druten [749] also contributed to the screenplay. Dalrymple didn't go home from the awards empty-handed: He won for his work on the screenplay of *Pygmalion*.

Saville: 804. Donat: 804. Vidor: 378, 468, 857, 2228. Dalrymple: 1637. Wead: 2022.

407 • CITIZEN KANE

MERCURY; RKO RADIO. 1941.

AWARD *Original Screenplay:* Herman J. Mankiewicz and Orson Welles.

NOMINATIONS *Picture:* Orson Welles, producer. *Actor:* Orson Welles. *Director:* Orson Welles. *Black-and-White Cinematography:* Gregg Toland. *Black-and-White Interior Decoration:* Perry Ferguson and Van Nest Polglase, art direction; Al Fields and Darrell Silvera, set decoration. *Sound Recording:* John Aalberg. *Scoring of a Dramatic Picture:* Bernard Herrmann. *Film Editing:* Robert Wise.

Newspaper publisher Charles Foster Kane (Welles) has achieved great power and influence, but on his deathbed he utters a single word, "Rosebud," that sends reporters scurrying to discover its meaning and thereby, they hope, uncover the secrets of his life. This is the most celebrated of all American films, and as Pauline Kael has said, "it may be more fun than any other great movie." Welles' battle with William Randolph Hearst, the newspaper magnate on whose life *Kane* is clearly based, is the stuff of legends, many of which were spun by Welles. He claimed that the negative of his film would have been burned if he had not carried a rosary to a meeting with the chief Hollywood censor, Joseph I. Breen. At a key moment, Welles said, he let the rosary fall from his pocket, giving Breen the impression that Welles was really a nice Catholic boy. True or not, the film survived Hearst's attempts to have it destroyed or banned, though distribution was spotty and the box office disappointing. The Academy, interestingly, didn't shy from the controversy, giving *Kane* a generous share of nominations. But mentions of Welles' name were greeted with catcalls at the Oscar ceremonies, and the film received only one award. The Academy didn't possess our awareness of how influential the cinematic

and narrative techniques developed under Welles' supervision would become over the next half century.

In recent years much controversy has been generated by Kael's 1971 essay "Raising Kane," which first appeared in the *New Yorker* and later in *The Citizen Kane Book*. In it, Kael attempts to extend greater credit for the film's success to Mankiewicz, claiming that the screenplay is largely his. To some extent, Kael's argument is a riposte to the so-called auteur critics, whose chief American spokesman is Andrew Sarris, who see the director as the chief "author" of a film and to whom Welles is one of the great heroes. Welles' defenders point out that nothing else in Mankiewicz's career as a screenwriter is as good as *Kane*. Mankiewicz, the elder brother (by eleven years) of Joseph L. Mankiewicz [46 . . .], was a former journalist who came to Hollywood in 1926. Welles himself has credited Mankiewicz with an "enormous" contribution to the screenplay, including the "Rosebud" device that sets the narrative in motion. Welles says they argued, however, over the name of the central character, Mankiewicz fearing that "Kane" would be seen as a clumsy biblical allusion. John Houseman [1069 . . .], Welles' former Mercury Theater associate, on the other hand, was one of those who gave Mankiewicz chief, if not sole, credit for the screenplay. The controversy will never be resolved, and in the end it's of interest only to partisans and ideologues.

Welles was the first person to receive simultaneous nominations as producer, actor, director, and writer, a feat that has been repeated only by Warren Beatty, for *Heaven Can Wait* and *Reds*. Dubbed the "boy wonder" by the publicity machine, Welles came to Hollywood after a critically successful theatrical career and a famous stint on radio that included the *War of the Worlds* hoax on Halloween 1938 that had much of the nation believing that Martians had landed in New Jersey. Still in his mid-twenties, he was given carte blanche by RKO, a major if troubled studio. Taking on Hearst was seen in Hollywood as proof of Welles' arrogance and untrustworthiness, and though his later film career is full of splendid moments, nothing would ever come together as superbly for him as *Kane* did. The Oscars for picture and direction went to *How Green Was My Valley* and to John Ford's work on it. The acting award was won by Gary Cooper for *Sergeant York.*

As a novice filmmaker, Welles found in Toland both a teacher and a willing experimenter. The visual richness, the dramatic lighting, the deep-focus compositions, are all Toland achievements that Welles used in a fresh and inventive way. The Oscar went to Arthur Miller for *How Green Was My Valley.*

Welles credited Ferguson and Silvera with the major work on *Kane;* Polglase and Fields have their names in the credits because they were studio department heads, not because they did actual work on the film. Among other things, Welles is noted for insisting on sets that have ceilings and for using low-angle shots that require their presence. He did so, he claimed, to break away from the theatrical conventions that had dominated movies. The art direction award also went to *How Green Was My Valley.*

Even the sound in *Kane* broke new ground, with dialogue that overlaps cuts. Aalberg, the head of the RKO sound department, never won an Oscar, though he received the Gordon E. Sawyer Award for technical achievement at the 1982 ceremonies. This time he lost to Jack Whitney for *That Hamilton Woman.*

More than any other Oscar loss, perhaps Herrmann's is the clearest slap at *Kane,* for he won the Oscar for *All That Money Can Buy* instead of *Kane.* Among other things, Herrmann composed the opening scene of an opera, *Salammbo,* for the film. The music for Susan Alexander Kane's disastrous debut vehicle is actually quite good, though it does what no opera ever does: open with the diva singing.

Though Welles never won an Oscar for directing, his editor, Wise, would win two as director of *West Side Story* and *The Sound of Music.* The editing Oscar went to William Holmes for *Sergeant York.*

Mankiewicz: 1607. Welles: 1239. Toland: 510, 1006, 1200, 1327, 2316. Ferguson: 366, 1451, 1607, 2292. Polglase: 358, 754, 1212, 1394, 2115. Fields: 1239. Silvera: 632, 686, 1239, 1264, 1341, 1924. Aalberg: 923, 959, 1033, 1102, 1978, 1991, 2030, 2166, 2213. Herrmann: 50, 83, 1460, 2005. Wise: 973, 1753, 1881, 2244.

408 • CITY SLICKERS

CASTLE ROCK ENTERTAINMENT PRODUCTION; COLUMBIA. 1991.
AWARD *Supporting Actor:* Jack Palance.

Yuppies Billy Crystal, Daniel Stern, and Bruno Kirby, experiencing various forms of midlife malaise, decide to go on a cattle drive for tenderfeet. Palance, the tough and cynical trail boss, dies halfway through the drive, however, and the three protagonists are faced with completing the task entirely on their own. Funny comedy, occasionally schmaltzy and improbable, but held together by Crystal's charm and timing. Also in the cast, directed by Ron Underwood, are Patricia Wettig, Helen Slater, Noble Willingham, David Paymer [1368.5], and Jeffrey Tambor.

Palance went thirty-eight years between nominations—a record tied only by Helen Hayes [31 . . .] and surpassed only by the forty-one years that separated Henry Fonda's two acting nominations. (On the other hand, during those forty-one years, Fonda was nominated as producer of *Twelve Angry Men,* so if it matters, Hayes and Palance can claim the record.) Palance began his career on stage and moved to Hollywood to play heavies and sinister types—the source of his first two nominations. His most sympathetic early role was in the original TV production of *Requiem for a Heavyweight,* which appeared on *Playhouse 90* in 1956. When it was filmed in 1962, however, the part went to Anthony Quinn [1226 . . .]. Palance has never lacked for work, but he has seldom found roles that allow him much range as an actor. Age has softened the gauntness of his face, allowing him to play more sympathetic parts, but Hollywood is also wary about casting older actors—a point the seventy-two-year-old Palance was quick to make by doing one-handed push-ups on stage when he accepted his Oscar. Palance wanted it known that unlike the character he played in *City Slickers,* he wasn't dead yet.

Palance: 1799, 1955.

409 • CLAN OF THE CAVE BEAR, THE

WARNER BROS. AND PSO PRODUCTION; WARNER BROS. 1986.
NOMINATION *Makeup:* Michael G. Westmore and Michele Burke.

Cro-Magnon Daryl Hannah teams up with a band of Neanderthals after the death of her parents. This dud version of the Jean M. Auel best-seller about prehistoric hominids is more pretentious than such schlock classics as the 1966 *One Million Years B.C.,* but Hannah is no more convincing a cavewoman than Raquel Welch was. Directed by Michael Chapman [734.5 . . .] from a screenplay by John Sayles [1533.5]. Chris Walas and Stephan Dupuis won the makeup Oscar for *The Fly.*

Westmore: 1287, 2165. Burke: 272.5, 474, 1641.

410 • CLAUDELLE INGLISH

WARNER BROS. 1961.
NOMINATION *Black-and-White Costume Design:* Howard Shoup.

Diane McBain plays a young woman brought up on a southern farm who thinks there's got to be more to life. You've heard the one about the farmer's daughter? Forgettable flop based on an Erskine Caldwell novel. Directed by Gordon Douglas, with Arthur Kennedy [291 . . .], Will Hutchins, Claude Akins, and Chad Everett. The costume award went to Piero Gherardi for *La Dolce Vita.*

Shoup: 1100, 1649, 1700, 2338.

411 • CLAUDINE

THIRD WORLD CINEMA PRODUCTIONS IN ASSOCIATION WITH JOYCE SELZNICK AND TINA PINE; 20TH CENTURY-FOX. 1974.
NOMINATION *Actress:* Diahann Carroll.

Carroll is trying to raise six children and carry on a romance with garbageman James Earl Jones [830], too. This attempt to make a romantic comedy with a semirealistic ghetto setting doesn't quite work, though it has some charm. Directed by John Berry.

Carroll had starred in the 1969 TV sitcom *Julia,* the first to feature black performers in leading roles, but had been criticized for the show's middle-class setting—"Doris Day in blackface," activists sneered. So she welcomed the chance to play a woman strug-

gling to make ends meet, and to shed the glamorous image that she had developed as a Broadway and nightclub performer. Carroll made her screen debut while still in her teens in *Carmen Jones* but found few movie roles available. She won a Tony Award in 1962 for the musical *No Strings.* She lost the Oscar to Ellen Burstyn for *Alice Doesn't Live Here Anymore*—a movie about a white woman struggling to make ends meet.

411.5 • CLEAR AND PRESENT DANGER

MACE NEUFELD AND ROBERT REHME PRODUCTION; PARAMOUNT. 1994.
NOMINATIONS *Sound:* Donald O. Mitchell, Michael Herbick, Frank A. Montaño, and Arthur Rochester. *Sound Effects Editing:* Bruce Stambler and John Leveque.

Harrison Ford [2296] plays CIA agent Jack Ryan, who gets a top-level White House intelligence job when his boss, Admiral Greer, played by James Earl Jones [830], develops terminal cancer. Unfortunately, Ryan immediately finds himself in the thick of a plot devised by presidential advisers to strike back at the Colombian drug cartel using means not sanctioned by Congress. When the plot goes awry and the presidential advisers decide to cover their asses, Ryan finds himself teaming up with a shadowy freelance operative, Clark, played by Willem Dafoe [1584], to rescue the troops the country has left behind. Entertaining cut-to-the-chase adaptation of Tom Clancy's big, baggy bestseller that benefits greatly from an intelligent script by Donald Stewart [1330], Steven Zaillian [113 . . .], and John Milius [92], and the crispness of the direction by Phillip Noyce and editing by Neil Travis [482]. Ford demonstrates once again what an invaluable property he is as an action hero—stalwart but self-effacing, and hence believable in ways that the more muscle-bound specialists in the genre never are. The fine cast includes Anne Archer [653] in the thankless role of Mrs. Ryan, Henry Czerny and Harris Yulin as the American villains, and Donald Moffat as the president. *Speed* took the awards for sound and sound effects editing.

Mitchell: 223, 398, 507, 734.5, 779, 1525, 1650, 1824, 1825, 2020, 2114, 2176.5. Herbick: 734.5,

1802.5. Montaño: 734.5, 2176.5. Rochester: 442, 2293. Stambler: 734.5, 2176.5. Leveque: 734.5, 2176.5.

412 • *CLEOPATRA*

PARAMOUNT. 1934.

AWARD *Cinematography:* Victor Milner.

NOMINATIONS *Picture:* Cecil B. DeMille, producer. *Sound Recording:* Franklin Hansen. *Assistant Director:* Cullen Tate. *Film Editing:* Anne Bauchens.

Claudette Colbert [1025 . . .] is the legendary Egyptian princess, with Warren William as Julius Caesar and Henry Wilcoxon as Marc Antony. Ludicrous as drama, ridiculous as history, but short enough (one hundred minutes) that you don't have to tolerate much bad acting and foolish dialogue to get to the good parts: the battles, the barge scene, and DeMille's usual sin, sex, and sadism. If the 1963 version had been half this campy, it might have made money.

Cleopatra won Milner his only Oscar in a career that spanned almost forty years, most of it with Paramount. The film lost the best picture Oscar to *It Happened One Night.* The sound award went to *One Night of Love.* Tate came in second to John Waters, who won as assistant director of *Viva Villa!* Bauchens placed third in the race for the editing Oscar, which went to Conrad Nervig for *Eskimo.*

Milner: 304, 470, 740, 757, 827, 1217, 1452, 1668. DeMille: 832, 2012. Hansen: 649, 1194, 1217, 2024. Bauchens: 832, 1452, 2012.

413 • *CLEOPATRA*

20TH CENTURY-FOX LTD.-MCL FILMS S.A.-WALWA FILMS S.A. PRODUCTION; 20TH CENTURY-FOX. 1963.

AWARDS *Color Cinematography:* Leon Shamroy. *Color Art Direction—Set Decoration:* John DeCuir, Jack Martin Smith, Hilyard Brown, Herman Blumenthal, Elven Webb, Maurice Pelling, and Boris Juraga; Walter M. Scott, Paul S. Fox, and Ray Moyer. *Color Costume Design:* Irene Sharaff, Vittorio Nino Novarese, and Renie. *Special Visual Effects:* Emil Kosa, Jr.

NOMINATIONS *Picture:* Walter Wanger, producer. *Actor:* Rex Harrison. *Sound:* James P. Corcoran, sound director, 20th Century-Fox Studio Sound Department, and Fred Hynes, sound director, Todd-AO Sound Department. *Music Score—Substantially Original:* Alex North. *Film Editing:* Dorothy Spencer.

As Cleopatra, Elizabeth Taylor [318 . . .] is wooed by Julius Caesar (Harrison) and Marc Antony (Richard Burton [85 . . .]). Meanwhile, there is much intrigue being conducted by Hume Cronyn [1791], Martin Landau [461 . . .], Roddy McDowall, and even Carroll O'Connor. This egregious epic was a famous disaster for all concerned. It almost bankrupted Fox. It wrecked the respective marriages of Burton and Taylor and made them, as a couple, so notorious that their lives would never again be truly private. It turned Burton, who could have been one of the major actors of the century, into an easy mark for stand-up comics. It put an end to Wanger's career as a producer and seriously damaged that of Joseph Mankiewicz [46 . . .], its writer-director, who said the film "was conceived in emergency, shot in hysteria, and wound up in blind panic." Even McDowall, who got excellent reviews for his performance, was jinxed by it: Considered a strong contender for a supporting actor Oscar, he was deprived of a nomination when he was listed by the studio as candidate for a leading role. This led to a rules change under which Academy members now decide for themselves which category an acting performance belongs in.

Taylor was the Cleopatra of Wanger's dreams, though Fox suggested Brigitte Bardot or Marilyn Monroe for the role. Laurence Olivier [268 . . .] was his first choice for Caesar, though Cary Grant [1445 . . .] was considered, and Burt Lancaster [107 . . .] was mentioned for Antony. But by the time Taylor was signed for the film, Peter Finch [1424 . . .] had been cast as Caesar and Stephen Boyd as Antony. Rouben Mamoulian was to direct, with filming in England. Then Taylor became ill, delaying the picture, which had been started under the insistence of studio head Spyros Skouras, even though a satisfactory script hadn't been completed. Both Taylor and Mamoulian were unhappy with what there was of the script, and when he left the film, she suggested Mankiewicz as writer. Taking over as director as well, Mankiewicz brought in Harrison and Burton, inadvertently sparking the fire that almost reduced the film to ashes. The emotional turmoil and storm of publicity that the Burton-Taylor affair created did little to advance an already troubled production. "A weaker man [than Mankiewicz] would have gone mad," Burton commented. Finally Darryl Zanuck [34 . . .], who had just had a big hit with an unwieldy, expensive production of his own, *The Longest Day,* was brought in to head the studio, and he took the production away from Wanger and eventually from Mankiewicz. The script, in fact, had not been completed by the time Zanuck took over—and there was talk of releasing the film in two parts because of its excessive length. Zanuck edited it down to its current running length, sacrificing characters and dialogue in the process. Until his death in 1993, Mankiewicz talked of rescuing the outtakes from the vaults and issuing a director's cut.

The finished *Cleopatra* is an aimless and often boring movie, brought to life fitfully by an occasional interesting performance or spectacular scene—though its spectacle is lost on video, the only place it's ever seen today. But the awards the film won were deserved. Shamroy's long experience in the industry helped overcome the technical difficulties of the countless false starts and retakes. The sets were completely redone in Rome after a failed attempt to shoot the film in England. Costuming the hundreds of extras was a major undertaking. And the film's visual effects are undeniably splendid.

The best picture Oscar went to a relatively small-scale production released by United Artists: *Tom Jones,* which also won for John Addison's score. The best actor Oscar was won by Sidney Poitier for *Lilies of the Field. How the West Was Won* took the awards for sound and Harold F. Kress' editing.

Shamroy: 29, 226, 356, 495, 569, 602, 1088, 1153, 1213, 1592, 1610, 1706, 1852, 1883, 2013, 2286, 2334. DeCuir: 29, 201, 376, 476, 896, 950, 1088, 1391, 1852, 2000. Smith: 29, 557, 646, 896, 1230, 2008, 2120, 2247. Blumenthal: 896, 1062. Webb: 2000. Scott: 46, 376, 476, 530, 542, 557, 646, 896, 1062, 1088, 1213, 1391, 1475, 1706, 1753, 1881, 1907, 2008, 2120, 2247. Fox: 376, 428, 476, 495, 530, 721, 950, 1088, 1601, 1666, 1706, 1852. Moyer: 278, 736, 833, 1101, 1120, 1214, 1674, 1738, 1748, 1975, 2012. Sharaff: 66, 290, 333, 338, 690, 852, 896, 1088, 1507, 1592, 1910, 2000, 2244, 2277. Novarese: 29, 465, 833, 1610. Renie: 201, 355, 1338, 1601. Wanger: 706, 1048, 1901. Harrison: 1393. Corcoran: 29, 1753, 1881. Hynes: 33, 1469, 1592, 1881, 1883, 2244. North: 29, 215, 515, 577, 1654, 1727, 1802, 1814, 1886, 1949, 2174, 2177, 2212, 2277. Spencer: 517, 591, 1901.

413.3 • CLIENT, THE

CLIENT PRODUCTION; WARNER BROS. 1994.
NOMINATION *Actress:* Susan Sarandon.

A young boy, played by Brad Renfro, witnesses the suicide of a lawyer for the mob and accidentally comes across evidence that the state wants and the mob would kill for. Figuring that he needs a lawyer himself, the boy talks a struggling Memphis attorney, Reggie Love (Sarandon), into acting on his behalf. Reggie's chief adversary is the showboating prosecutor "Reverend" Roy Foltrigg, played by Tommy Lee Jones [734.5 . . .], who doesn't care how much jeopardy he puts the boy in, as long as he gets the evidence he needs to bust the mob. But Reggie and the boy turn out to be more than a match not only for the Reverend but also for the mob. Well-handled adaptation of a blockbuster page-turner by John Grisham. Of the three Grisham-based movies to date, which also include *The Firm* and *The Pelican Brief* (1993), *The Client* is by far the best, thanks to charismatic performances by Sarandon and Jones, good pacing by director Joel Schumacher and editor Robert Brown, atmospheric cinematography by Tony Pierce-Roberts [954.5 . . .], and a script by Akiva Goldsman and Robert Getchell [41 . . .] that keeps things moving fast enough that you almost don't notice the holes in the plot. It also helps that the film has a strong supporting cast. Young Renfro, in his film debut, is terrific, as is Mary-Louise Parker as his tough white-trash mom; Anthony LaPaglia is a suitably slimy Mafioso, and J. T. Walsh once again effectively plays the sort of sleazy numskull he perfected in such movies as *Good Morning, Vietnam* and *Tequila Sunrise*.

Sarandon continued to maintain her career well into her forties by accepting more and more motherly roles, which in 1994 included not only the maternal Reggie Love but also the understanding Marmee in *Little Women* and the mother of a houseful of boys in *Safe Passage*. The Oscar went to Jessica Lange for *Blue Sky*.

Sarandon: 107, 1205.5, 2039.

413.5 • *CLIFFHANGER*

CLIFFHANGER B.V. PRODUCTION; TRISTAR. 1993.

NOMINATIONS *Sound:* Michael Minkler, Bob Beemer, and Tim Cooney. *Sound Effects Editing:* Wylie Stateman and Gregg Baxter. *Visual Effects:* Neil Krepela, John Richardson, John Bruno, and Pamela Easley.

Sylvester Stallone [1712] plays an expert in mountain survival and rescue who has all but given up his career after being involved in the accidental death of a young woman. But he happens to be visiting members of his old team when a plane crashes in the mountains nearby and sends out a distress signal. Along with Janine Turner and Michael Rooker (the boyfriend of the woman whose death Stallone may have caused), Stallone goes to the aid of the crash victims, only to find that they're a vicious gang of hijackers, led by John Lithgow [2020 . . .], whose plot has gone awry. They want the rescue team to help them recover their loot. Stallone has to deal not only with the bad guys but also with Rooker, who mistrusts him. The movie has some truly stunning action sequences —dizzying rock-climbing stunts, amazing aerial work. But it's undermined by cliché-clotted characterization and dialogue, a plot whose turns you can see coming a reel away, and too much overdone violence. Renny Harlin directs from a script by Stallone and Michael France. The movie was a substantial box-office success, reviving Stallone's career, which had stalled after the third *Rambo* and the fifth *Rocky* film. The awards in all the categories for which *Cliffhanger* was nominated went to *Jurassic Park*.

Minkler: 58, 260, 398, 606, 1047, 2144. Beemer: 1888.5. Stateman: 260. Krepela: 2165. Richardson: 45. Bruno: 5, 153.5, 766, 1590, 2147.5.

414 • *CLIMAX, THE*

UNIVERSAL. 1944.

NOMINATION *Color Interior Decoration:* John B. Goodman and Alexander Golitzen, art direction; Russell A. Gausman and Ira S. Webb, set decoration.

Mad doctor Boris Karloff has a young soprano (Susanna Foster) under his spell. A bit of *Phantom of the Opera*, a dash of *Trilby*, and not bad as this sort of claptrap goes. Directed by George Waggner, with Gale Sondergaard [83 . . .] doing her usual witchy part, accompanied by Turhan Bey and Thomas Gomez [1695]. If it looks a little familiar, it's because the sets were left over from *Phantom of the Opera*, in which Foster also appeared, and for which the art direction team had already received an Oscar. The Academy decided once was enough and gave the award to *Wilson*.

Goodman: 979, 1560, 1895. Golitzen: 31, 96, 591, 690, 706, 744, 1560, 1886, 1968, 1986, 2035, 2064, 2101. Gausman: 96, 681, 1560, 1572, 1886, 1895. Webb: 96, 1560.

415 • *CLOCKWORK ORANGE, A*

HAWK FILMS LTD. PRODUCTION; WARNER BROS. (UNITED KINGDOM). 1971.

NOMINATIONS *Picture:* Stanley Kubrick, producer. *Director:* Stanley Kubrick. *Screenplay—Based on Material From Another Medium:* Stanley Kubrick. *Film Editing:* Bill Butler.

Malcolm McDowell plays a futuristic punk who is sent to prison for murder. After being brainwashed into a revulsion against violence, he is returned to society, where he becomes a victim. Kubrick's adaptation of Anthony Burgess' novel was controversial in its day—denounced as a shallowly sensational perversion of a complexly ironic book, praised as a prophetic glimpse of the future. It's a chilly work whose prophesies do seem to have come true; the mindless violence of the film is much like the drive-by shootings and gang warfare of American inner cities. But it has the problem of all films with intellectual under-pinnings: Its ideas get swamped by its images. And Kubrick is a master of images, brilliantly abetted here by cinematographer John Alcott [151] and production designer John Barry [1916]. As often, Kubrick's use of music is noteworthy, although the most often cited examples of it in the film come from other people: The McDowell character's love of Beethoven is from the book, and the use of "Singin' in the Rain" as accompaniment to an act of violence was McDowell's own improvisation. Originally given an X rating, it is now rated R.

A Clockwork Orange was defeated by *The French Connection* in all the categories for which it was nominated: picture, director (William Friedkin), writing (Ernest Tidyman), and editing (Jerry Greenberg).

Kubrick: 151, 574, 735, 2164.

416 • *CLOSE ENCOUNTERS OF THE THIRD KIND*

Julia Phillips/Michael Phillips-Steven Spielberg Film Production; Columbia. 1977.

Awards *Cinematography:* Vilmos Zsigmond. *Special Achievement Award for Sound Effects Editing:* Frank E. Warner.

Nominations *Supporting Actress:* Melinda Dillon. *Director:* Steven Spielberg. *Art Direction–Set Decoration:* Joe Alves and Dan Lomino; Phil Abramson. *Sound:* Robert Knudson, Robert J. Glass, Don MacDougall, and Gene S. Cantamessa. *Original Score:* John Williams. *Film Editing:* Michael Kahn. *Visual Effects:* Roy Arbogast, Douglas Trumbull, Matthew Yuricich, Gregory Jein, and Richard Yuricich.

Dillon's young son is kidnaped by a UFO, and an electric company worker, Richard Dreyfuss [803], encounters one when he goes to check a strange power outage. Both subsequently find themselves mysteriously drawn to the Devil's Tower, a huge extinct volcano in Wyoming, where humankind has its first meeting with extraterrestrial life. Wonderfully silly stuff, made with an awe for the things movies can do —plus an ability to do them. Considering that the actors were asked to respond to things that weren't there until the special effects people added them

much later, the movie is full of good performances, including little Cary Guffey as Dillon's son, Teri Garr [2113] as Dreyfuss' helplessly uncomprehending wife, and François Truffaut [501 . . .] as a French UFOlogist.

Close Encounters was Spielberg's first film after *Jaws,* which made him a hot property in Hollywood. As with virtually all of his work, the Academy has given him mixed messages—in this case a nomination as director but not a best picture nod, the reverse of the situation he faced with *Jaws* and later with *The Color Purple.* The omission of *Close Encounters* from the best picture slate can be explained only by the presence of the year's other blockbuster sci-fi film, *Star Wars,* among the nominees. But *Close Encounters* has held up better in the long run than most of the other nominees, including *The Goodbye Girl, Julia,* and *The Turning Point.* The best picture Oscar went to *Annie Hall.* No director has won the Oscar for a film not nominated for best picture since Frank Lloyd took the award for *The Divine Lady* at the 1928–29 ceremonies, so Spielberg didn't stand a chance. He lost to Woody Allen for *Annie Hall.*

Zsigmond came to Hollywood during the 1956 Hungarian uprising and did his apprenticeship on grade-Z pictures such as *The Name of the Game Is Kill!* (1968) and *Horror of the Blood Monster* (1970), before establishing himself with his work on *McCabe and Mrs. Miller* and Spielberg's first feature, *The Sugarland Express* (1974). He is now one of the industry's most respected cinematographers.

Dillon lost to Vanessa Redgrave for *Julia.* John Williams lost to himself, for the score for *Star Wars,* which also took the remaining awards: art direction, sound, editing (Paul Hirsch, Marcia Lucas, and Richard Chew), and visual effects.

Zsigmond: 521, 1701. Dillon: 3. Spielberg: 423, 588, 1652, 1764.65. Knudson: 321, 588, 613, 631, 938, 1439, 1877, 1911, 2274. Glass: 588, 938, 1439, 1877, 1911. MacDougall: 738, 938, 1439, 1916. Cantamessa: 339, 588, 1439, 1914, 2165, 2331. Williams: 6, 260, 403, 588, 613, 614, 659, 805, 933, 937, 982, 996, 997, 1041, 1047, 1596, 1652, 1679, 1684, 1701, 1764.65, 1916, 1977,

2107, 2126, 2194, 2293, 2322. Kahn: 613, 653, 1652, 1764.65. Trumbull: 228, 1913. M. Yuricich: 1196. Jein: 1439. R. Yuricich: 228, 1913.

416.5 • CLOSE TO EDEN

CAMERA ONE-HACHETTE PREMIÈRE ET COMPAGNIE/UGC IMAGES (FRANCE)/STUDIO TRITE (URSS) PRODUCTION (Russia). 1992.

NOMINATION *Foreign Language Film.*

A Mongolian peasant's idyllic way of life is threatened by the incursions of contemporary life, including television. Good-natured, subtle film from director Nikita Mikhalkov. The Oscar went to the French film *Indochine.*

417 • CLOSELY WATCHED TRAINS

BARRANDOV FILM STUDIOS PRODUCTION (CZECHOSLOVAKIA). 1967.

AWARD *Foreign Language Film.*

A young railway officer tries to lose his virginity during World War II, and finally does so with a member of the Resistance. Jiri Menzel's light comedy suddenly takes a serious turn toward the end—a move that many found pointlessly unsettling.

418 • COAL MINER'S DAUGHTER

BERNARD SCHWARTZ-UNIVERSAL PICTURES PRODUCTION; UNIVERSAL. 1980.

AWARD *Actress:* Sissy Spacek.

NOMINATIONS *Picture:* Bernard Schwartz, producer. *Screenplay Based on Material From Another Medium:* Tom Rickman. *Cinematography:* Ralf D. Bode. *Art Direction—Set Decoration:* John W. Corso; John M. Dwyer. *Sound:* Richard Portman, Roger Heman, and Jim Alexander. *Film Editing:* Arthur Schmidt.

Spacek plays country-music legend Loretta Lynn in a biopic that takes her from poverty in Appalachia to stardom at the *Grand Ole Opry.* Solid entertainment that doesn't sugarcoat its subject—Lynn herself was impressed with the handling of her story. It's well cast, with Levon Helm as Lynn's father, Tommy Lee Jones [734.5 . . .] as her husband, and Beverly D'Angelo as Patsy Cline. Spacek and D'Angelo do their own singing, and while neither is a match for

Lynn or Cline, they're both quite good. Directed by Michael Apted.

Spacek, a Texas-born actress who studied at the Actors Studio in New York, wowed the critics with her performance as the amoral teen killer in *Badlands* (1973) and became a cult star in the title role of *Carrie.* Her win for *Coal Miner's Daughter* can be interpreted as a tribute to her skill or as an expression of surprise at her versatility; this is her first major role in which she doesn't play a creepy teenager (though there's some of that in her portrayal of Lynn as an adolescent). It also has to be noted that she wasn't up against heavyweight competition: Ellen Burstyn and Gena Rowlands were nominated for films that few people saw *(Resurrection* and *Gloria* respectively), and Goldie Hawn was up for the featherweight comedy *Private Benjamin.* Her only serious opponent was Mary Tyler Moore, cast sharply against type in *Ordinary People,* the sort of performance that gets nominations but rarely wins Oscars. The award made Spacek a leading actress of the eighties and led to performances that earned three more nominations. But she's essentially a character type—slightly oddball, usually southern—for whom major roles aren't always easy to find.

Ordinary People won for best picture and Alvin Sargent's screenplay. *Tess* took the awards for the cinematography of Geoffrey Unsworth and Ghislain Cloquet and for art direction. *The Empire Strikes Back* won for sound and *Raging Bull* for Thelma Schoonmaker's editing.

Spacek: 364, 462, 1330, 1701. Portman: 339, 502, 521, 738, 784, 1109, 1473, 1526, 1701, 2331. Heman: 226, 346, 458, 520, 1041, 2286. Alexander: 2020. Schmidt: 708.5, 1763, 1975, 2274.

419 • COCOON

FOX-ZANUCK/BROWN PRODUCTION; 20TH CENTURY FOX. 1985.

AWARDS *Supporting Actor:* Don Ameche. *Visual Effects:* Ken Ralston, Ralph McQuarrie, Scott Farrar, and David Berry.

Retirees Ameche, Wilford Brimley, and Hume Cronyn [1791] go for a swim one day and are so rejuvenated that they think they've found the fountain of youth. Instead, they've discovered where some extraterrestrials have hidden the cocoons in which they incubate. This close encounter leads to an ending that has been seen much too often in the Spielberg era, but a warm, fuzzy script (by Tom Benedek) and terrific performances make the rest of the movie worthwhile. Ron Howard directs a cast that includes such pros as Brian Dennehy, Jack Gilford [1761], Maureen Stapleton [31 . . .], Jessica Tandy [580 . . .], and Gwen Verdon. The aliens include Tyrone Power, Jr., the son of Ameche's frequent costar of the thirties and forties, and Raquel Welch's daughter Tahnee Welch. An unnecessary dud of a sequel followed in 1988.

Ameche was a hugely busy actor for much of the later thirties and early forties, when he was under contract to 20th Century-Fox. His most famous role of the era was the title part in *The Story of Alexander Graham Bell* (1939), which led to so many running jokes by radio comedians that for a time "Ameche" became slang for telephone. A light comedian and pleasant singer, he was in countless Fox musicals starring Alice Faye and/or Betty Grable, but otherwise never achieved what we think of as superstardom. He faded from view in the fifties, with occasional character roles throughout the next few decades. Then he reemerged for a wicked cameo, teamed with Ralph Bellamy [114], in the Eddie Murphy comedy *Trading Places.* Suddenly, in his late seventies, Ameche was a star again. The Oscar was something of a sentimental tribute, but it was also well deserved: Ameche holds the screen in *Cocoon,* and even if we know it's a double in the scene in which he does a break dance, his performance has so much vitality he makes us believe he *could* do it. Ameche died in 1993.

Ralston: 128, 513.5, 577, 708.5, 1684, 2274. Farrar: 129.

420 • COLLECTOR, THE

THE COLLECTOR COMPANY; COLUMBIA (U.S./UNITED KINGDOM). 1965.
NOMINATIONS *Actress:* Samantha Eggar. *Director:* William Wyler. *Screenplay—Based on Material From Another Medium:* Stanley Mann and John Kohn.

Butterfly collector Terence Stamp [206] one day decides to go for larger game: Eggar, whom he stalks, kidnaps, locks in his basement, and woos. When she finally returns his affections, he recoils. If you've seen *The Silence of the Lambs,* you might expect something more shocking from this situation, but you'll be disappointed. It's a creepy, talky adaptation of a novel by John Fowles, which loses the book's intricate language and psychology but doesn't give us much to compensate.

Eggar won the Cannes Festival award for her performance in *The Collector* but lost the Oscar to her compatriot Julie Christie for *Darling.* Overshadowed by other British stars such as Christie, Julie Andrews [1284 . . .], and Vanessa Redgrave [263 . . .], Eggar's career never caught fire. She won the lead in the expensive disaster *Doctor Dolittle* and followed that with another expensive disaster, *The Molly Maguires.* She continues to be seen in occasional supporting roles.

This was the last of Wyler's record twelve nominations for directing. He lost to Robert Wise for *The Sound of Music* but was given the Irving G. Thalberg Memorial Award at the ceremony.

The writing award went to Robert Bolt for *Doctor Zhivago.*

Wyler: 175, 184, 534, 560, 730, 894, 1162, 1182, 1371, 1716, 2316.

421 • COLONEL REDL

MAFILM-OBJEKTIV STUDIO/MANFRED DURNIOK/ORF/ZDF PRODUCTION (HUNGARY). 1985.
NOMINATION *Foreign Language Film.*

Klaus Maria Brandauer [1512] stars in this story of a highly placed officer in the last years of the Austro-Hungarian Empire, who is driven to espionage and treason in order to conceal that he is both Jewish and gay. The second film in a trilogy by director István Szabó that began with *Mephisto* and ends with *Hanussen.* Sweeping, superbly executed film based in part on the John Osborne [2106] play, *A Patriot for Me.* The cast also includes Armin Mueller-Stahl. The Oscar went to Argentina's *The Official Story.*

422 • COLOR OF MONEY, THE

TOUCHSTONE PICTURES PRODUCTION IN ASSOCIATION WITH SIL-
VER SCREEN PARTNERS II; BUENA VISTA. 1986.

AWARD *Actor:* Paul Newman.

NOMINATIONS *Supporting Actress:* Mary Elizabeth Mastrantonio. *Screenplay Based on Material From Another Medium:* Richard Price. *Art Direction—Set Decoration:* Boris
Leven; Karen A. O'Hara.

Newman reprises the role of Fast Eddie Felson, the
pool shark he created in *The Hustler* twenty-five years
earlier. Here he takes a protégé, played by Tom
Cruise [260], whose hotshot ways remind Eddie of his
earlier self. This sequel, adapted by Price from the
novel by Walter Tevis, has a dazzling texture, supplied
by director Martin Scorsese [27.5 . . .], cinematographer Michael Ballhaus [293 . . .], the charismatic
leads, and a fine supporting cast that includes Mastrantonio as Cruise's girlfriend, Helen Shaver, John
Turturro, and Forest Whitaker. It lacks the depth and
poignancy of the first movie, however, and at the end
you may feel that you've been watching an exercise in
moviemaking with no purpose other than to make
Cruise a superstar (which his other film of the year,
Top Gun, also helped do) and to win Newman his
long-denied Oscar. It's certainly one of the least personal of Scorsese's movies.

Newman had seemed a little bemused by the honorary award—"in recognition of his many memorable and compelling screen performances and for his
personal integrity and dedication to his craft"—that
had been presented to him at the awards ceremony a
year earlier. "I'm especially grateful that this does not
come wrapped as a gift certificate to Forest Lawn,"
he said in his acceptance, which was broadcast from
the location shoot of *Color of Money.* Through his career, he had invariably demonstrated skill and professionalism, sometimes in films that didn't deserve it.
He had lost the Oscar to David Niven for *Separate
Tables,* to Maximilian Schell for *Judgment at Nuremberg,*
to Sidney Poitier for *Lilies of the Field,* to Rod Steiger
for *In the Heat of the Night,* to Henry Fonda for *On
Golden Pond,* and to Ben Kingsley for *Gandhi.* But his
win for *The Color of Money* was the closest to a sure
thing that has been seen in an Oscar race. The compe-

tition was weak: Jazz musician Dexter Gordon was a
surprise nominee for *'Round Midnight;* Bob Hoskins'
nomination for *Mona Lisa* was little more than a
"promising newcomer" award; William Hurt's performance in *Children of a Lesser God* was decidedly
secondary to Marlee Matlin's, and Hurt had won the
year before; and the nomination of James Woods'
portrait of a sleazebag in *Salvador* took notice of the
critics' enthusiasm but was unlikely to win Academy
hearts. After forty years in movies, Newman continues to act at the same high level.

Mastrantonio is one of the most striking of Hollywood's younger actresses, with a strength and intensity that has carried her through some big-budget but
essentially flimsy movies, such as *The Abyss* and *Robin
Hood: Prince of Thieves.* She made her screen debut in
the 1983 *Scarface* but has never really found a star-
making role—a reflection of the scarcity of good
parts for actresses. Dianne Wiest won the Oscar for
Hannah and Her Sisters.

The art direction award went to *A Room With a
View.*

Newman: 3, 372, 443, 956, 964, 1444.5, 1645,
2198. Leven: 34, 77, 768, 1753, 1801, 1881, 1907,
2244.

423 • COLOR PURPLE, THE

WARNER BROS. PRODUCTION; WARNER BROS. 1985.

NOMINATIONS *Picture:* Steven Spielberg, Kathleen Ken-
nedy, Frank Marshall, and Quincy Jones, producers.
Actress: Whoopi Goldberg. *Supporting Actress:* Margaret
Avery. *Supporting Actress:* Oprah Winfrey. *Screenplay
Based on Material From Another Medium:* Menno Meyjes.
Cinematography: Allen Daviau. *Art Direction—Set Decora-
tion:* J. Michael Riva and Robert W. Welch; Linda
DeScenna. *Song:* "Miss Celie's Blues (Sister)," music
by Quincy Jones and Rod Temperton, lyrics by
Quincy Jones, Rod Temperton, and Lionel Richie.
Original Score: Quincy Jones, Jeremy Lubbock, Rod
Temperton, Caiphus Semenya, Andrae Crouch, Chris
Boardman, Jorge Calandrelli, Joel Rosenbaum, Fred
Steiner, Jack Hayes, Jerry Hey, and Randy Kerber.
Costume Design: Aggie Guerard Rogers. *Makeup:* Ken
Chase.

Goldberg plays Celie, who is separated from her beloved sister and married to a brutal, unloving man, played by Danny Glover. She recovers her self-esteem with the aid of jazz singer Avery and eventually triumphs over poverty and degradation. This adaptation of Alice Walker's epistolary novel sharply divided critics. Some loved its sweeping, romantic treatment of the story; others found it cloying and overproduced. Controversy raged over its portrayal of black men, and many blacks were offended that the project was handled by a white director. Spielberg was denounced for prettifying the material, but also praised for undertaking a project that employed so many black performers—the cast also includes Adolph Caesar [1857], Rae Dawn Chong, and Laurence Fishburne [2250.7]. Under the circumstances, it's not surprising that the Academy gave the film eleven nominations and then proceeded to vote it no Oscars, landing the film in a tie with *The Turning Point* for most nominations without winning. It's as if the Academy couldn't decide which side of the many controversies it was on. In hindsight *The Color Purple* may be seen as a very entertaining, often moving work—a tribute to its director and his crew and performers. And it can also be said that Spielberg was the wrong man for the job. One wishes it could be remade by a black woman director, such as Julie Dash or Euzhan Palcy.

As regards the Oscars, the greatest controversy about the film concerned the failure of the directors branch to include Spielberg among the nominees for best director. Spielberg was the only director of the year's best picture nominees not to be cited; his slot went to Akira Kurosawa for *Ran*. (Spielberg observed that being supplanted by Kurosawa took some of the sting out of the Academy's snub.) Then, in a stunning reversal, the Directors Guild named Spielberg the year's best director in their awards—an honor that in most cases has gone to the same person who wins the best director Oscar. Spielberg's omission pretty much doomed the movie's chances for the best picture Oscar, which went to *Out of Africa*. But the Academy sometimes seems to try to make amends, so the following year Spielberg was given the Irving G. Thalberg Memorial Award.

Goldberg was nominated for her film debut, as was Winfrey, who plays Goldberg's stepdaughter in the film. Goldberg has gone on to a highly successful movie career, but Winfrey has mostly withdrawn from acting and concentrated on her enormously popular TV talk show; she has occasionally produced programs for TV as well. Avery, an established actress, was cast in the part of the singer (though her singing was dubbed in the film) after Tina Turner decided not to take the role. The best actress Oscar went to Geraldine Page for *The Trip to Bountiful*. The supporting actress award was won by Anjelica Huston for *Prizzi's Honor*.

Out of Africa was the spoiler of the year, taking the awards for Kurt Luedtke's screenplay, David Watkin's cinematography, for art direction, and for John Barry's score. In the remaining categories in which *Color Purple* was nominated, Lionel Richie, who was one of the lyricists for the film's nominated song, won instead for "Say You, Say Me," from *White Nights*. The costuming Oscar went to Emi Wada for *Ran* and the makeup award to Michael Westmore and Zoltan Elek for *Mask*.

The Color Purple did make it into the Oscar record books in one way. The twelve people nominated for the film's score are the most ever nominated for a single film in a single category.

Spielberg: 416, 588, 1652, 1764.65. Kennedy: 588. Marshall: 1652. Jones: 144, 698, 987, 2299. Goldberg: 764. Daviau: 112, 308, 588, 613. DeScenna: 228, 1653, 1913, 2127.5. Richie: 616, 2271. Hayes: 2184.

424 • COME AND GET IT

SAMUEL GOLDWYN PRODUCTIONS; UNITED ARTISTS. 1936.
AWARD *Supporting Actor:* Walter Brennan.
NOMINATION *Film Editing:* Edward Curtiss.

Edward Arnold plays a lumberjack who falls in love with a dance hall girl, played by Frances Farmer, but his ambitions won't let him rest and he passes up a chance for happiness with her. Years later, after he's become a wealthy lumber magnate, he meets and makes a vain play for her granddaughter, also played by Farmer. This adaptation of one of Edna Ferber's blockbuster novels was produced by Samuel Goldwyn [102 . . .], who fought so with its first director, Howard Hawks [1779], that he finally had him replaced with William Wyler [175 . . .] and attempted to have Hawks' name removed from the credits. Wyler later commented that the best parts of the film belonged to Hawks, who was responsible for the casting of Farmer and the building up of Brennan's role into a substantial one. Farmer gives a strong performance, but her career was short-lived; her descent into mental illness is graphically portrayed in the movie *Frances*. The bagginess of the melodrama results from the disputed direction of the film and from the miscasting of Arnold in a role for which Goldwyn wanted Spencer Tracy [131 . . .]. The cast also includes Andrea Leeds [1899] in her debut role.

Brennan had been in Hollywood since 1923, working as an extra and a stuntman and gradually moving into character roles. He began a career as a scene-stealer when Hawks cast him in *Barbary Coast,* and over the years he became ubiquitous, appearing in more than one hundred films, winning three Oscars, and starring in several TV series, including *The Real McCoys.* He died in 1974.

The editing Oscar went to Ralph Dawson for *Anthony Adverse.*

Brennan: 1080, 1779, 2245.

425 • *COME BACK, LITTLE SHEBA*

Hal Wallis Productions; Paramount. 1952.
Award *Actress:* Shirley Booth.
Nominations *Supporting Actress:* Terry Moore. *Film Editing:* Warren Low.

Booth is the frumpy wife of an alcoholic former chiropractor, played by Burt Lancaster [107 . . .]. But sexy young boarder Moore introduces a disturbing element into the household. Rather drab little domestic melodrama, adapted by Ketti Frings from a play by William Inge [1894] in which Booth starred with great success on Broadway. Lancaster is badly miscast, though he tries valiantly to hide his robust, dynamic persona. Daniel Mann directs, and the cast includes Richard Jaeckel [1864].

Booth had been a Broadway actress since 1925 but didn't become a star until the forties, with an appearance in *My Sister Eileen.* The stage version of *Come Back* won her a Tony, and the film, her movie debut, brought her the New York Film Critics Award and the Cannes Festival best actress honor as well as the Oscar. But she made only a handful of movies afterward, the most memorable of them 1958's *The Matchmaker* —the original version of the play that became *Hello, Dolly!* She became best known for the title role in the TV sitcom *Hazel.* Most standard film and theater reference books list Booth's year of birth as 1907. But at her death in 1992, she was said to be ninety-four years old, which puts her year of birth nine years earlier. If true, this would make Booth fifty-four at the time of her Oscar win, and thus the only woman to win a best actress Oscar while in her fifties—so far as we know.

After working as a child model, Moore entered films in 1940 at the age of eleven, first under her real name, Helen Koford, then as Judy Ford—she plays Ingrid Bergman's character as a child in *Gaslight* under that name—or Jan Ford. She became Terry Moore in 1948 and began a publicity buildup as a sex goddess. After her nomination she appeared in a few major roles, but her career gradually faded. The award went to Gloria Grahame for *The Bad and the Beautiful.*

High Noon won the Oscar for Elmo Williams and Harry Gerstad's editing.

Low: 847, 1162, 1727.

426 • *COME BLOW YOUR HORN*

Essex-Tandem Enterprises Production; Paramount. 1963.
Nomination *Color Art Direction–Set Decoration:* Hal Pereira and Roland Anderson; Sam Comer and James Payne.

Bachelor Frank Sinatra [732 . . .] is idolized by his kid brother, played by Tony Bill [1927], but he's the despair of his father, played by Lee J. Cobb [301 . . .], in this gag-ridden adaptation by Norman Lear [553] of an early play by Neil Simon [332 . . .].

It hasn't worn well, but if you can forgive the sexism and the swinging bachelor shtick and the jokey cameo appearance of Dean Martin as a wino, it's occasionally amusing. This was Bill's debut as an actor, but he became more successful as a producer in the seventies. Directed by Bud Yorkin, with Molly Picon, Barbara Rush, and Jill St. John. The art direction Oscar went to *Cleopatra.*

Pereira: 278, 357, 363, 450, 736, 956, 1029, 1219, 1504, 1570, 1631, 1674, 1716, 1727, 1738, 1840, 1897, 1959, 2012, 2098, 2200, 2208. Anderson: 278, 363, 450, 649, 1029, 1194, 1214, 1219, 1452, 1570, 1668, 1674, 1880, 1994. Comer: 278, 357, 450, 726, 736, 925, 956, 1029, 1101, 1214, 1219, 1443, 1570, 1631, 1674, 1727, 1738, 1748, 1959, 1975, 1994, 2012, 2098, 2200, 2208. Payne: 1504, 1927.

427 • *COME FILL THE CUP*

WARNER BROS. 1951.

NOMINATION *Supporting Actor:* Gig Young.

Alcoholic newspaperman James Cagney [79 . . .] hits the skids, but with the help of recovered alcoholic James Gleason [904], he fights back and becomes editor of the paper from which he was fired. The publisher of the paper, Raymond Massey [1], enlists Cagney's aid in rescuing his nephew, Young, who has gotten involved with the mob. The movie betrays its origins, a novel by Harlan Ware, in its overplotting, but good performances keep it afloat. Directed by Gordon Douglas.

Young had begun in films not long after high school, having been discovered by Warners at the Pasadena Playhouse. After several bit parts, he landed a featured role in *The Gay Sisters* (1942), playing a character called Gig Young. He adopted the name because another actor shared his real name, Byron Barr. His career was interrupted by service in the Coast Guard in World War II. He became typed as a light comedian and second lead. The Oscar went to Karl Malden for *A Streetcar Named Desire.*

Young: 2007, 2047.

428 • *COME TO THE STABLE*

20TH CENTURY-FOX. 1949.

NOMINATIONS *Actress:* Loretta Young. *Supporting Actress:* Celeste Holm. *Supporting Actress:* Elsa Lanchester. *Motion Picture Story:* Clare Boothe Luce. *Black-and-White Cinematography:* Joseph LaShelle. *Black-and-White Art Direction—Set Decoration:* Lyle Wheeler and Joseph C. Wright; Thomas Little and Paul S. Fox. *Song:* "Through a Long and Sleepless Night," music by Alfred Newman, lyrics by Mack Gordon.

French nuns Young and Holm come to New England, where they charm and cajole the locals into building a children's hospital. Pretty much as icky as it sounds, this was one of those determinedly heartwarming efforts to recapture the magic (and the money and the Oscars) of *Going My Way.* It has only a few pleasures, among them a chance to see Dooley Wilson in a film other than *Casablanca,* but probably isn't worth the effort. Directed by Henry Koster [214].

Young retired from movies in 1953 and became one of the first major Hollywood stars to move into TV, where her half-hour anthology series, *The Loretta Young Show,* ran for eight seasons. She lost the Oscar to Olivia de Havilland for *The Heiress.*

Holm was far more impressive as the off-screen voice of the seductress in *A Letter to Three Wives* than as the sugary nun in this movie. This was Lanchester's first nomination, though she had performed memorably opposite her husband, Charles Laughton, as Anne of Cleves in *The Private Lives of Henry VIII* and even more memorably in the title role of *The Bride of Frankenstein.* The supporting actress award went to Mercedes McCambridge for *All the King's Men.*

Luce, the wife of *Time* magazine founder-publisher Henry Luce, was a formidable woman, the author of the classically bitchy play *The Women* (filmed in 1939), a Republican congresswoman, and ambassador to Italy during the Eisenhower administration. The Oscar went to Douglas Morrow for *The Stratton Story.*

The cinematography award went to Paul C. Vogel for *Battleground* and the art direction Oscar to *The Heiress.* Frank Loesser won the award for his song "Baby, It's Cold Outside," from *Neptune's Daughter.*

Young: 651. Holm: 46, 759. Lanchester: 2297.

LaShelle: 91, 357, 709, 953, 1017, 1149, 1283, 1391. Wheeler: 19, 46, 83, 356, 376, 476, 495, 530, 542, 719, 721, 798, 950, 1062, 1088, 1149, 1153, 1213, 1391, 1475, 1601, 1616, 1670, 1706, 1852, 2008, 2093, 2212. Wright: 235, 508, 569, 690, 746, 852, 1175, 1264, 1397, 1475, 2056. Little: 46, 83, 235, 495, 719, 721, 746, 950, 952, 1082, 1149, 1153, 1397, 1475, 1666, 1852, 1868, 2056, 2212, 2286. Fox: 376, 413, 476, 495, 530, 721, 950, 1088, 1601, 1666, 1706, 1852. Newman: 31, 34, 46, 72, 138, 182, 226, 333, 334, 347, 375, 437, 457, 476, 495, 542, 690, 797, 833, 952, 953, 959, 962, 1016, 1082, 1088, 1213, 1278, 1362, 1397, 1475, 1616, 1655, 1849, 1868, 1883, 1921, 2043, 2046, 2091, 2258, 2286, 2294, 2316. Gordon: 563, 569, 897, 1362, 1501, 1964, 1984, 2219.

429 • COMES A HORSEMAN

ROBERT CHARTOFF-IRWIN WINKLER PRODUCTION; UNITED ARTISTS. 1978.

NOMINATION *Supporting Actor:* Richard Farnsworth.

Rancher Jane Fonda [394 . . .] and drifter James Caan [784] battle ruthless cattle baron Jason Robards [54 . . .] in this western with a mid-twentieth-century setting. Rather murky and pretentious, with gloomy photography by Gordon Willis [786 . . .] and slow pacing by director Alan J. Pakula [54 . . .].

Farnsworth was a veteran stuntman who, in his fifties, was beginning to get sizable character roles in movies as men of crusty integrity—roles that also go to actors like Wilford Brimley and Ben Johnson [1139]. Though he lost the Oscar to Christopher Walken in *The Deer Hunter,* Farnsworth made a name for himself, and a few years later, in 1982, received excellent notices for his work in the lead role in *The Grey Fox.*

430 • COMING HOME

JEROME HELLMAN ENTERPRISES PRODUCTION; UNITED ARTISTS. 1978.

AWARDS *Actor:* Jon Voight. *Actress:* Jane Fonda. *Screenplay Written Directly for the Screen:* Nancy Dowd, story; Waldo Salt and Robert C. Jones, screenplay.

NOMINATIONS *Picture:* Jerome Hellman, producer. *Supporting Actor:* Bruce Dern. *Supporting Actress:* Penelope Milford. *Director:* Hal Ashby. *Film Editing:* Don Zimmerman.

Fonda plays a dutiful military wife who, when her husband, Dern, is shipped to Vietnam, volunteers for work at the veterans hospital. There she meets Voight, an old high school classmate whose war wounds confine him to a wheelchair. They have an affair and she turns into an opponent of the war, so that when Dern returns, there is an inevitable, and catastrophic, confrontation. A little too earnest, a little too obvious, the movie hasn't held up well. Playing out the vast international tragedy of the Vietnam War as a domestic drama is its first mistake. It lost the best picture Oscar to another movie about Vietnam, *The Deer Hunter,* a morally and politically confused film that nevertheless has a poetic, romantic sweep to it that made the moral and political correctness of *Coming Home* seem tepid and trivial. Fonda bitterly denounced the award to *The Deer Hunter*—and then admitted she hadn't seen the movie.

Voight began as a stage actor in 1960 and had appeared on Broadway in *The Sound of Music,* playing Rolf, the young man who joins the Nazis. He followed up his star-making performance in *Midnight Cowboy* with a mixture of little-seen films and one hit, *Deliverance.* He had originally been cast in the role of Fonda's husband in *Coming Home,* but when several actors, including Jack Nicholson [395 . . .] turned down the role of the paraplegic vet, he took it instead. Since the Oscar, his career has not been a distinguished one. He produced several films in which he starred but lately has been working primarily in TV movies.

Fonda's radical opposition to the Vietnam War made this a natural project for her, though it offended many of the paraplegic vets who were asked to participate in the movie. But Fonda's convictions have always seemed more strong than deep, and she had already begun to moderate her views. In the eighties, becoming better known for her aerobics videos than for her politics, she broke up with her husband, California Assemblyman Tom Hayden, and by the beginning of the nineties she started a new life with cable-TV magnate Ted Turner. She has announced her virtual retirement from acting—a reflection of the absence of good roles for women in their fifties. It will be interesting to see whether she comes out of retirement after she turns sixty (in 1997) and takes on the kind of roles that gave Shirley MacLaine [91 . . .], for example, a second career.

Dowd's first version of the *Coming Home* screenplay focused on a relationship between Fonda's character and another woman, not on an affair with the Voight character. Hellman hired Salt to rewrite the script, radically altering its nature. Salt had been working with paraplegic vet Ron Kovic on the manuscript that eventually became the book (and later the film) *Born on the Fourth of July,* and Kovic participated as an adviser on *Coming Home.* When Ashby took over the direction of the movie, replacing John Schlesinger [493 . . .], he brought in Jones, with whom he had worked as a film editor, to do a final version of the screenplay. Even then, the ending was uncertain, and the one that appears in the movie was worked out in a session of improvising by Voight, Fonda, and Dern.

Dern's family ties are interesting ones. He's a nephew of the poet Archibald MacLeish, and both his ex-wife, Diane Ladd [41 . . .], and their daughter, Laura Dern [1659], have been nominated for Oscars. He made his film debut in 1960 in *Wild River.* He's often cast as a lean, mean, sometimes psychotic type, and lost the Oscar to someone who also gets typecast in those parts, Christopher Walken, for *The Deer Hunter.*

Milford, who plays Fonda's more freewheeling friend Vi in the movie, lost to Maggie Smith in *California Suite.* Her post-Oscar career has been unimpressive. Her nomination helped earn *Coming Home* one distinction: It is among only thirteen films with nominations in all four acting categories. The others are *Bonnie and Clyde, For Whom the Bell Tolls, From Here to Eternity, Guess Who's Coming to Dinner, Johnny Belinda, Mrs. Miniver, My Man Godfrey, Network, Reds, A Streetcar Named Desire, Sunset Boulevard,* and *Who's Afraid of Virginia Woolf?*

Ashby lost the directing Oscar to Michael Cimino

for *The Deer Hunter,* for which Peter Zinner also won the film editing award.

Voight: 1312, 1734. Fonda: 394, 1066, 1104, 1356, 1473, 2047. Salt: 1312, 1780. Jones: 264, 843, 1032. Hellman: 1312. Ashby: 992, 1736.

431 • *COMING TO AMERICA*

EDDIE MURPHY PRODUCTION; PARAMOUNT. 1988.
NOMINATIONS *Costume Design:* Deborah Nadoolman. *Makeup:* Rick Baker.

African prince Eddie Murphy, accompanied by courtier Arsenio Hall, comes to America in search of a wife, rejecting the arranged marriage that his father, James Earl Jones [830], has planned for him. But though he may be a prince in Zamunda, he's a nobody in the ghettos of America, where he winds up working in a fast-food outlet. This amusing variation on themes drawn from tales such as *The Prince and the Pauper* and *Cinderella* is primarily a vehicle for Murphy, Paramount's biggest star of the eighties. He plays a variety of roles, including an elderly Jewish man. Some of it works, some of it doesn't, as is often the case with movies by director John Landis, but it's not as mean-spirited as some of Murphy's later films, such as *Harlem Nights* and his 1992 flop, *Boomerang.* Its chief claim to fame is as the focus of a famous lawsuit. Columnist Art Buchwald, who had sold Paramount a similar story idea, sued when he was not given credit on the film—the story is credited solely to Murphy. The trial revealed much about how Hollywood's accounting practices conceal profits, even on a huge hit such as this one, allowing almost no one to know how much money a given film actually earns. A detailed (if one-sided) account of the case is given by Buchwald's lawyer, Pierce O'Donnell, and journalist Dennis McDougal in *Fatal Subtraction: How Hollywood Really Does Business.*

Nadoolman's costumes for the royal family of Zamunda are a delightful blend of Ruritania and Vegas. She lost to James Acheson for *Dangerous Liaisons.* Baker, better known as a monster-maker, helps disguise Murphy and Hall for their multiple roles. The Oscar went to the team from *Beetlejuice.*

Baker: 68, 595.8, 839, 874.

432 • COMMANDOS STRIKE AT DAWN, THE

COLUMBIA. 1943.

NOMINATION *Scoring of a Dramatic or Comedy Picture:* Louis Gruenberg and Morris Stoloff.

Paul Muni [218.5 . . .] plays a Norwegian fisherman who helps lead the British in a commando raid on the occupying Nazi army. The posing and speechifying that afflict most war-effort movies are pretty heavy in this one, but it has its stirring moments still. Directed by John Farrow [101 . . .] from a screenplay by Irwin Shaw [1998] based on a story by C. S. Forester, the prestigious cast includes Cedric Hardwicke, Lillian Gish [584], and Alexander Knox [2286]. The Oscar went to Alfred Newman for *The Song of Bernadette.*

Gruenberg: 664, 1854. Stoloff: 13, 455, 596, 643, 677, 732, 773, 1057, 1058, 1115, 1206, 1862, 1872, 1873, 1998, 2110, 2329.

433 • COMMITMENTS, THE

BEACON COMMUNICATIONS PRODUCTION; 20TH CENTURY FOX (UNITED KINGDOM). 1991.

NOMINATION *Film Editing:* Gerry Hambling.

A group of young Dubliners get together to form a band dedicated to performing sixties soul music, but clashing temperaments prove stronger than individual commitments. (The title comes from the name of their group, of course.) Fresh, delightful comedy featuring a strong cast of almost complete unknowns; the most familiar face is that of Colm Meaney, best known as Chief O'Brien on *Star Trek: The Next Generation* and *Star Trek: Deep Space Nine,* in a small role. The Irish accents are occasionally impenetrable, but the music is a treat—even if Irish soul music is not exactly the real thing, it comes off as a splendid tribute to Motown. Directed by Alan Parker [1313 . . .]. The Oscar went to Joe Hutshing and Pietro Scalia for *JFK.*

Hambling: 641, 992.5, 1313, 1333.

434 • COMPETITION, THE

RASTAR FILMS PRODUCTION; COLUMBIA. 1980.

NOMINATIONS *Original Song:* "People Alone," music by Lalo Schifrin, lyrics by Wilbur Jennings. *Film Editing:* David Blewitt.

Richard Dreyfuss [803] and Amy Irving [2321] play concert pianists who are in the finals of a prestigious and, for the winner, lucrative international competition. Naturally they fall in love, and naturally, if one or the other wins, it may damage their relationship. Moreover, Dreyfuss is poor and Irving is rich, and if he loses the competition, he may have to give up his career. Formulaic as hell, with cardboard characters in mechanical dilemmas, but perversely watchable for the overacting of the leads, plus Lee Remick [508] as Irving's teacher and Sam Wanamaker as an egotistic lech of a conductor. The music is good, if you don't mind snippets of the classics. Written and directed by Joel Oliansky.

The forgettable song lost to Michael Gore and Dean Pitchford's title song from *Fame.* Thelma Schoonmaker won the editing Oscar for *Raging Bull.*

Schifrin: 70, 443, 720, 1928, 2218. Jennings: 1465.

435 • COMRADE X

MGM. 1940.

NOMINATION *Original Story:* Walter Reisch.

Newspaperman Clark Gable [798 . . .] falls in love with streetcar conductor Hedy Lamarr while on assignment in the Soviet Union. Rather obvious attempt to recapture the magic of *Ninotchka,* for which Reisch was one of the screenwriters, but Lamarr is no Garbo and Gable's heart doesn't seem in the project. Surprisingly flat, given the talents involved: writers Ben Hecht [78 . . .] and Charles Lederer, director King Vidor [378 . . .], and character actors Oscar Homolka [972], Eve Arden [1319], and Sig Ruman. The story Oscar went to Benjamin Glazer and John S. Toldy for *Arise, My Love.*

Reisch: 749, 1440, 2093.

436 • CONDEMNED

SAMUEL GOLDWYN PRODUCTIONS; UNITED ARTISTS. 1929–30.
NOMINATION *Actor:* Ronald Colman.

Colman is sent to Devil's Island for robbing a bank, but he falls in love with the warden's wife, escapes, and is reunited with her after the warden's death. Sheer nonsense, not helped by the slow pacing and overstated acting that often afflict early talkies, though it benefits from the production design of William Cameron Menzies [38 . . .] and the camera work of George Barnes [537 . . .] and Gregg Toland [407 . . .]. Directed by Wesley Ruggles [400]. Colman, who was also nominated for *Bulldog Drummond,* lost to George Arliss in *Disraeli.*

Colman: 311, 567, 1662.

437 • CONEY ISLAND

20TH CENTURY-FOX. 1943.
NOMINATION *Scoring of a Musical Picture:* Alfred Newman.

Betty Grable becomes a star thanks to the backing of George Montgomery, who then has to fight off romantic rival Cesar Romero. Routine musical with a turn-of-the-century setting and forgettable songs by Ralph Rainger [197 . . .] and Leo Robin [104 . . .]. Directed by Walter Lang. Newman lost to Ray Heindorf for *This Is the Army.*

Newman: 31, 34, 46, 72, 138, 182, 226, 333, 334, 347, 375, 428, 457, 476, 495, 542, 690, 797, 833, 952, 953, 959, 962, 1016, 1082, 1088, 1213, 1278, 1362, 1397, 1475, 1616, 1655, 1849, 1868, 1883, 1921, 2043, 2046, 2091, 2258, 2286, 2294, 2316.

438 • CONFIDENCE

MAFILM STUDIOS PRODUCTION (HUNGARY). 1980.
NOMINATION *Foreign Language Film.*

In 1944 a man and woman, each married to someone else, pose as husband and wife to evade the Nazis in Budapest. Understated but absorbing film by István Szabó. The Oscar went to the Soviet Union's *Moscow Does Not Believe in Tears.*

439 • CONFORMIST, THE

MARS FILM PRODUZIONE S.P.A.-MARIANNE PRODUCTIONS; PARAMOUNT (ITALY/FRANCE). 1971.
NOMINATION *Screenplay—Based on Material From Another Medium:* Bernardo Bertolucci.

Jean-Louis Trintignant plays an upper-class fascist, a repressed homosexual who marries a woman he doesn't love. Ordered by the party to assassinate his old professor, an antifascist, he becomes attracted to the professor's wife, but she in turn is attracted to Trintignant's wife. Bertolucci, who also directed, creates a superb evocation of Italy under Mussolini, handsomely photographed by Vittorio Storaro [92 . . .]. Bertolucci competed against a distinguished field: the screenplays for *A Clockwork Orange, The Garden of the Finzi-Continis, The Last Picture Show,* and the winner, Ernest Tidyman's script for *The French Connection.*

Bertolucci: 1136, 1141.

440 • CONQUEST

MGM. 1937.
NOMINATIONS *Actor:* Charles Boyer. *Interior Decoration:* Cedric Gibbons and William Horning.

Boyer plays Napoleon in this story of his affair with the Polish countess Marie Walewska, played by Greta Garbo [84 . . .]. The film was designed as a vehicle for Garbo, but the studio had been unable to cast a Napoleon until Boyer emerged as a star. Claude Rains [365 . . .] was under consideration at one point, but he was thought to be too old and not sexy enough to play opposite Garbo. The movie gets the full MGM treatment, with lavish sets and a screenplay worked on by Samuel Hoffenstein [572 . . .], Salka Viertel, and S. N. Behrman, direction by Clarence Brown [84 . . .] (the last of seven films he made with Garbo), and a supporting cast that includes Maria Ouspenskaya [560 . . .] and May Whitty [1371 . . .]. Unfortunately it's chock full of hokum and just a bit dull.

Boyer had become a star in France in the twenties, on both stage and screen. He had first come to Hollywood in 1929, when the studios, wrestling with the fact that the new technology of sound presented problems in the international market, experimented with remaking their features in various foreign languages. He stayed to make several features in English but returned to Europe from 1931 to 1934. His second trip to America made him a star. He lost this, the first of his four Oscar nominations, to Spencer Tracy for *Captains Courageous.*

The art direction Oscar was won by Stephen Goosson for *Lost Horizon.*

Boyer: 36, 643, 749. Gibbons: 66, 87, 130, 217, 227, 239, 285, 290, 629, 749, 831, 980, 1069, 1096, 1173, 1190, 1226, 1230, 1232, 1274, 1308, 1309, 1417, 1567, 1604, 1644, 1662, 1673, 1721, 1861, 1937, 2068, 2112, 2256, 2257, 2300, 2320, 2330. Horning: 175, 769, 1157, 1450, 1644, 1657, 2300.

441 • *CONSTANT NYMPH, THE*

WARNER BROS. 1943.

NOMINATION *Actress:* Joan Fontaine.

Fontaine is a Belgian waif who nurtures a love for a composer, played by Charles Boyer [36 . . .]. He marries Alexis Smith, however, as Fontaine wastes away with a heart condition. This well-done romance, from a novel by Margaret Kennedy, had been filmed twice before in England. It received the full Warners treatment, with a cast that includes Charles Coburn [535 . . .], May Whitty [1371 . . .], and Peter Lorre, and lush music by Erich Wolfgang Korngold [17 . . .]. Director Edmund Goulding wanted Robert Donat [406 . . .] or Leslie Howard [178 . . .] for the Boyer role, but both were doing their part for the British during the war—Howard was killed while this film was being made.

The movie was primarily a vehicle for Fontaine, who had won the Oscar two years before. It marked the peak of her career; the films that followed were mostly mediocre or showcases for her beauty, not her acting ability. The Oscar went to Jennifer Jones for *The Song of Bernadette.*

Fontaine: 1670, 1979.

442 • *CONVERSATION, THE*

A DIRECTORS COMPANY PRODUCTION; PARAMOUNT. 1974.

NOMINATIONS *Picture:* Francis Ford Coppola, producer; Fred Roos, coproducer. *Original Screenplay:* Francis Ford Coppola. *Sound:* Walter Murch and Arthur Rochester.

Professional snoop Gene Hackman [255 . . .] loves his work—eavesdropping on other people's conversations—until he's hired on a case involving murder and finds he can't detach himself from his work anymore. Technically brilliant, superbly acted film, directed by Coppola with a cast that includes John Cazale, Frederic Forrest [1726], Cindy Williams, Teri Garr [2113], and in one of his first substantial film roles, Harrison Ford [2296]. Often cited as one of the best films of the seventies, and certainly one of Coppola's best—in a low-key, low-budget style that seems unlike most of his other work.

While it was a critical success, *The Conversation* made little impression at the box office, which makes its inclusion among the best picture nominees something of a surprise. It was a strong slate: *Chinatown, The Godfather, Part II,* and *Lenny* were all worthy contenders, and only *The Towering Inferno* seemed tossed in to reward the people who had spent so much money on it. Coppola lost to himself, taking the award for *Godfather II* instead. The omission of Hackman from the actor nominees is a little hard to explain, however: Dustin Hoffman for *Lenny,* Jack Nicholson for *Chinatown,* and Al Pacino for *Godfather II* were shoo-ins, of course, and the sentimental winner, Art Carney in *Harry and Tonto,* is an understandable choice. But Hackman's gray, withdrawn Harry Caul is one of his finest creations, far superior to Albert Finney's show-offy and unconvincing turn as Hercule Poirot in *Murder on the Orient Express.* In the writing category, Coppola lost honorably: to Robert Towne's *Chinatown* script.

The loss by Murch and Rochester is unfortunate. *The Conversation* is *about* sound, and their work contributes both technically and thematically to the film's achievement. The sound team faced challenges ranging from finding the proper distortions for the recorded conversations to the right sound for the rustling of Hackman's plastic raincoat. But the Oscar went to a mere gimmick: the "Sensurround" effects created for *Earthquake.*

Coppola: 65, 92, 784, 785, 786, 1541. Roos: 92, 785. Murch: 92, 764, 786, 1066. Rochester: 411.5, 2293.

443 • COOL HAND LUKE

JALEM PRODUCTION; WARNER BROS.-SEVEN ARTS. 1967.
AWARD *Supporting Actor:* George Kennedy.
NOMINATIONS *Actor:* Paul Newman. *Screenplay—Based on Material From Another Medium:* Donn Pearce and Frank R. Pierson. *Original Music Score:* Lalo Schifrin.

Newman, a war hero down on his luck, is sentenced to a chain gang presided over by Strother Martin, who utters the film's famous catchphrase: "What we've got here is failure to communicate." Made in the year of *Bonnie and Clyde* and *The Graduate,* this otherwise rather routine prison flick has an aura of countercultural rebellion, especially in its ending, in which the rebel becomes a Christ figure. Very entertaining for its performances and for famous episodes such as the egg-eating contest, but its pretentious edge is annoying. The cast, directed by Stuart Rosenberg, includes Jo Van Fleet [593], Dennis Hopper [595 . . .], and such soon-to-be-familiar faces as Wayne Rogers, Joe Don Baker, Ralph Waite, and Harry Dean Stanton. Richard Davalos, who plays Blind Dick, played James Dean's brother in *East of Eden,* a part for which Newman tested unsuccessfully.

Kennedy, the son of show business people, worked in radio as a child, and after service in World War II began a career behind the scenes in TV. Eventually he worked on camera and entered films in the early sixties. Because of his size, he was often cast as a heavy, as in *Charade.* His role in *Cool Hand Luke* turns him in midpicture from a heavy, who enters a slugfest for superiority against Newman, into a more sympathetic character. Since the Oscar, he has been one of the movies' most durable character players.

Newman lost his fourth nomination to Rod Steiger in *In the Heat of the Night.*

The screenplay is based on Pearce's novel, which is drawn from personal experience. Pearce also appears in the film, as the convict known as Sailor. The Oscar went to Stirling Silliphant for *In the Heat of the Night.* The scoring award went to Elmer Bernstein for *Thoroughly Modern Millie.*

Newman: 3, 372, 422, 956, 964, 1444.5, 1645, 2198. Pierson: 371, 561. Schifrin: 70, 434, 720, 1928, 2218.

443.5 • COP, THE

DEMILLE PICTURES; PATHÉ. 1928–29.
NOMINATION *Writing Achievement:* Elliott Clawson.

This silent film, directed by Donald Crisp [952] and starring William Boyd, Alan Hale, and Robert Armstrong, has disappeared, leaving little information about its content. Clawson was not an official nominee this year, simply because the Academy announced only winners—in this case, Hans Kräly for *The Patriot* —and issued no certificates or other recognition to runners-up. He was, however, listed in the records of the writers branch as one of the people under consideration for the award.

Clawson: 1152, 1740.5, 1838.5.

444 • COQUETTE

PICKFORD; UNITED ARTISTS. 1928–29.
AWARD *Actress:* Mary Pickford.

Pickford is a contemporary southern belle whose flirtation with a social inferior enrages her father and leads to disaster. The long-forgotten film version of a Broadway play that starred Helen Hayes [31 . . .], it was an attempt by Pickford to change her "little Mary" image: She bobbed her long golden curls (some of which are still in museums) and made her first talkie. Audiences weren't happy with the change, and after three more films, including a disastrous version of *The Taming of the Shrew* in 1929 with her husband, Douglas Fairbanks, Pickford retired from the screen in 1933. She had entered show business at the age of five, to help support her widowed mother. Broadway producer David Belasco changed her name from Gladys Smith when she appeared in his play *The Warrens of Virginia* at the age of fourteen. Two years later, in 1909, she began her screen career, playing a little girl until well into her late twenties. In 1919 she joined with Fairbanks, D. W. Griffith, and Charles Chaplin [405 . . .] to found United Artists, designed to release their independent productions. She and Chaplin, the surviving founders, sold their interest in the company in 1953. In 1975, four years before her death, she received an honorary award from the Academy "in recognition of her unique contributions to the film industry and the development of film as an artistic medium."

445 • CORN IS GREEN, THE

WARNER BROS. 1945.

NOMINATIONS *Supporting Actor:* John Dall. *Supporting Actress:* Joan Lorring.

Aging spinster schoolteacher Bette Davis [46 . . .] goes to a Welsh mining town and fights poverty and prejudice in her efforts to send young miner Dall to the university. Emlyn Williams' play had been performed on stage by Ethel Barrymore [1445 . . .] and Sibyl Thorndike. Davis was too young for the part, and the film never quite makes the leap from the Warners soundstage into reality. Directed by Irving Rapper.

Neither Dall nor Lorring, as the girl who threatens to derail Davis' plans for Dall's future, had significant Hollywood careers. This was Dall's film debut, but apart from a leading part in *Rope,* directed by Alfred Hitchcock [1171 . . .] in 1948, and a small role in *Spartacus,* he made few significant films. Lorring, who was among the children evacuated from England to America in 1939, had a handful of film and TV roles, often as a troubled teenager. The supporting actor Oscar went to James Dunn for *A Tree Grows in Brooklyn.* Anne Revere won for *National Velvet.*

446 • CORSICAN BROTHERS, THE

EDWARD SMALL; UNITED ARTISTS. 1942.

NOMINATION *Scoring of a Dramatic or Comedy Picture:* Dimitri Tiomkin.

Douglas Fairbanks, Jr., plays the dual role of the twins who remain spiritually tied throughout their separation in this version of the story by Alexandre Dumas. Good swashbuckler with a fine cast, including Ruth Warrick, Akim Tamiroff [701 . . .], and J.

Carrol Naish [1294 . . .], under the direction of Gregory Ratoff. Tiomkin's score lost to Max Steiner's for *Now, Voyager.*

Tiomkin: 33, 286, 380, 638, 663, 730, 768, 850, 911, 912, 1206, 1347, 1370, 1470, 2006, 2127, 2282, 2335.

447 • CORVETTE K-225

UNIVERSAL. 1943.

NOMINATION *Black-and-White Cinematography:* Tony Gaudio.

Randolph Scott, commander of a small Canadian warship (that's what a corvette was before it became a car), fights off subs and bombers during World War II. Good wartime action picture, produced by Howard Hawks [1779], whose hand has been glimpsed by Hawksians in the direction, credited to Richard Rosson, the brother of cinematographer Hal Rosson [105 . . .]. The cast includes Barry Fitzgerald [787], Andy Devine, Noah Beery, Jr., Thomas Gomez [1695], and, in a blink-and-you'll-miss-him bit, Robert Mitchum [1935]. The cinematography Oscar went to Arthur Miller for *The Song of Bernadette.*

Gaudio: 90, 898, 1064, 1162, 1872.

448 • COTTON CLUB, THE

A TOTALLY INDEPENDENT PRODUCTION; ORION. 1984.

NOMINATIONS *Art Direction—Set Decoration:* Richard Sylbert; George Gaines and Les Bloom. *Film Editing:* Barry Malkin and Robert Q. Lovett.

Musician Richard Gere falls in love with gangster's moll Diane Lane, and tap dancer Gregory Hines falls in love with singer Lonette McKee. Their unhappy romances are the frail plot on which is hung this big, baggy gangster musical, which takes place largely in the legendary Harlem nightclub. Unfortunately writer-director Francis Coppola [65 . . .] never managed to get a focus to his story, written with William Kennedy, and this expensive production was one of the major box-office disasters of the eighties. Though he has prime dancing talent like Hines and his brother Maurice and legendary tap dancer Charles "Honi" Coles at his disposal, Coppola makes a mishmash of the dance sequences—he likes to show the dancers' faces rather than their feet! The film is bursting with interesting personalities—Bob Hoskins [1343], Nicolas Cage, Fred Gwynne, Gwen Verdon, Joe Dallesandro, Jennifer Grey, Tom Waits [1483], Woody Strode, Laurence Fishburne [2250.7]—who never get a chance to make an impression. The film developed a certain notoriety later because a girlfriend of producer Robert Evans [395] was convicted of the second-degree murder/kidnaping of one of the film's financial backers. Evans was not implicated in the case, but he was called as a witness in the trial and pleaded the Fifth Amendment. The affair came to be known as "the *Cotton Club* murder case."

The art direction award went to *Amadeus* and the editing Oscar to Jim Clark for *The Killing Fields*.

Sylbert: 395, 543, 1678, 1798, 2277. Gaines: 54, 890, 1798. Bloom: 1647. Malkin: 786.

449 • COUNTRY

TOUCHSTONE FILMS PRODUCTION; BUENA VISTA. 1984.
NOMINATION *Actress:* Jessica Lange.

Iowa farming couple Lange and Sam Shepard [1698] struggle to hold on to their land in the face of government foreclosure. Earnest and well crafted, with a powerful performance by Lange, but a little too issue-oriented to capture the imagination of urban America, which is where the ticket buyers are. Directed by Richard Pearce. The year saw three movies about the struggle of farm women, all of them in some ways responses to the policies of the Carter-Reagan years that accelerated the growth of agribusiness at the expense of individual farmers. The lead actresses in all three were nominated for Oscars; Sissy Spacek in *The River* and winner Sally Field in *Places in the Heart* were the other two. (The remaining nominations went to Judy Davis for *A Passage to India* and Vanessa Redgrave for *The Bostonians*.)

Lange: 244.5, 722, 1381, 1987, 2113.

450 • COUNTRY GIRL, THE

PERLBERG-SEATON PRODUCTION; PARAMOUNT. 1954.
AWARDS *Actress:* Grace Kelly. *Screenplay:* George Seaton.
NOMINATIONS *Picture:* William Perlberg, producer. *Actor:* Bing Crosby. *Director:* George Seaton. *Black-and-White Cinematography:* John F. Warren. *Black-and-White Art Direction—Set Decoration:* Hal Pereira and Roland Anderson; Sam Comer and Grace Gregory.

Broadway director William Holden [1424 . . .] is trying to help alcoholic has-been singer Crosby make a comeback. He thinks Crosby's biggest problem is his dependence on his wife, Kelly, when in fact the only backbone Crosby has comes from her. Drab and depressing adaptation of a drab and depressing play by Clifford Odets, this was an unexpected box-office success, perhaps because of the cast-against-type (but really miscast) stars. Everyone acts up a storm and you don't really believe a minute of it.

Oscars often go to performances in which you can see the effort, rather than to the performances that involve real acting, which may explain why Cary Grant [1445 . . .] never won an Oscar and Helen Hayes [31 . . .] won two. Kelly was superb in her sleek, romantic roles—*Rear Window, To Catch a Thief, High Society*—but here she is ruthlessly deglamorized, as far as a woman with her beauty can be, and naturally won the award that should have gone to Judy Garland for *A Star Is Born*. These were troubled times in the industry, however, and the success of a downer picture like *The Country Girl* was more than enough to carry Kelly to the Oscar after the box-office failure of *Star Is Born*.

Kelly, the rich Philadelphian who brought genuine class to the screen, was one of the phenomena of the fifties. She made her first screen appearance in 1951 in *Fourteen Hours,* but it was the supporting role in *High Noon* the next year that attracted attention. She made four films in 1954—*Dial M for Murder, Green Fire,* and *Rear Window* were the other three—so the Oscar can be seen as a tribute to her versatility. Though the camera loved her beauty, her appeal was heightened by her sensuous, slightly husky but patrician voice. She was noted for her amours as well—including both of her *Country Girl* costars—but she ended her career in 1956 with her marriage to Prince Rainier of Monaco. Perennial attempts were made to lure her back to the screen, but Rainier refused to allow it. She died in an automobile accident in Monaco in 1982.

Seaton and Perlberg entered into a production partnership in the early 1950s, of which *The Country Girl* is perhaps the most prestigious result. Seaton was a successful screenwriter, slightly less successful director, Perlberg a former assistant to Columbia boss Harry Cohn [1025 . . .]. The Oscar for best picture went to *On the Waterfront,* whose director, Elia Kazan, also won.

Crosby's performance had been highly praised by the critics. He was insecure about his acting ability, having built his film reputation as a crooner and as straight man to Bob Hope, but he was carefully coached by Seaton. Marlon Brando won the Oscar for *On the Waterfront.* Warren's cinematography, with its harsh, unflattering lighting, aided in giving Crosby's performance an air of realism. *On the Waterfront* also won for Boris Kaufman's cinematography and for art direction.

Kelly: 1339. Seaton: 31, 1325, 1868. Perlberg: 1325, 1868. Crosby: 173, 787. Pereira: 278, 357, 363, 426, 736, 956, 1029, 1219, 1504, 1570, 1631, 1674, 1716, 1727, 1738, 1840, 1897, 1959, 2012, 2098, 2200, 2208. Anderson: 278, 363, 426, 649, 1029, 1194, 1214, 1219, 1452, 1570, 1668, 1674, 1880, 1994. Comer: 278, 357, 426, 726, 736, 925, 956, 1029, 1101, 1214, 1219, 1443, 1570, 1631, 1674, 1727, 1738, 1748, 1959, 1975, 1994, 2012, 2098, 2200, 2208. Gregory: 1219.

451 • COUP DE TORCHON (CLEAN SLATE)

FILMS DE LA TOUR PRODUCTION (FRANCE). 1982.
NOMINATION *Foreign Language Film.*

The chief law officer of a small colonial township in West Africa begins to realize the potential power he wields, and starts to eliminate his enemies, including his wife. Director Bertrand Tavernier based the film on a novel by Jim Thompson, shifting its setting from the American South. Black humor with an edge, but its nastiness eventually becomes a bit too much. The Oscar went to the Spanish *Volver a Empezar.*

452 • COURSE COMPLETED

NICKEL ODEON DOS PRODUCTION (SPAIN). 1987.
NOMINATION *Foreign Language Film.*

A famous playwright experiences a midlife crisis. This film by director José Luis Garci (winner of the foreign language film Oscar for *Volver a Empezar)* has not been widely released in the United States. The Oscar went to Denmark's *Babette's Feast.*

453 • COURT-MARTIAL OF BILLY MITCHELL, THE

UNITED STATES PICTURES PRODUCTION; WARNER BROS. 1955.
NOMINATION *Story and Screenplay:* Milton Sperling and Emmett Lavery.

Gary Cooper [701 . . .] plays Mitchell, an aviation pioneer who had commanded American air forces in World War I, but in the 1920s got under the hide of the brass by his insistence that they were criminally neglecting the importance of airpower in future conflicts. The brass feared that any demonstration of the superiority of airpower would reduce funding for ground troops. When Mitchell disregarded orders in staging a demonstration of airpower, he was relieved of duty and subjected to the trial dramatized in this rather static film. Otto Preminger [73 . . .] directs a strong cast: Charles Bickford [651 . . .], Ralph Bellamy [114], Rod Steiger [992 . . .], and such future stalwarts of the tube as Elizabeth Montgomery, Jack Lord, Peter Graves, and Darren McGavin. The writing Oscar went to William Ludwig and Sonya Levien for *Interrupted Melody.*

454 • COUSIN, COUSINE

LES FILMS POMEREU-GAUMONT PRODUCTION; NORTHAL FILM DISTRIBUTORS LTD. (FRANCE). 1976.
NOMINATIONS *Actress:* Marie-Christine Barrault. *Screenplay—Written Directly for the Screen:* Jean-Charles Tacchella and Danièle Thompson. *Foreign Language Film.*

Barrault's mother weds Victor Lanoux's uncle, which makes Barrault and Lanoux cousins by marriage. But then Barrault's husband and Lanoux's wife have an affair, which brings Barrault and Lanoux reluctantly, and at first chastely, together. Easygoing

Gallic comedy, which writer-director Tacchella conceived in homage to the American screwball comedies of the thirties. It's very likable and was a huge international hit—one of the most successful imports ever released in America. It was remade in the States as *Cousins,* starring Isabella Rossellini and Ted Danson in the Barrault and Lanoux roles, in 1989.

Barrault, niece of the celebrated French actor Jean-Louis Barrault, made her screen debut in Eric Rohmer's *My Night at Maud's.* She achieved her Oscar nomination in one of the worst years for female leading roles in Hollywood history—so bad that two of the best actress nominees were from foreign films. The other was Liv Ullmann for *Face to Face.* The other contenders were Talia Shire for *Rocky* and Sissy Spacek for *Carrie,* but the Oscar went to Faye Dunaway for *Network.*

Network also won for Paddy Chayefsky's screenplay. The foreign language film award was a surprise. Both *Cousin, Cousine* and *Seven Beauties* had achieved nominations in other categories—*Seven Beauties* for its star, Giancarlo Giannini, and its director, Lina Wertmüller—but the award went to the Ivory Coast's entry, *Black and White in Color.* The upset is the result either of two strong entries splitting the vote, or perhaps of the introduction this year of a new rule in the rather anomalous foreign language award: Only voters who could certify that they had seen all nominated films were allowed to cast ballots. Designed to ensure fairness, this rule nevertheless encourages a certain amount of logrolling.

455 • COVER GIRL

COLUMBIA. 1944.
Award *Scoring of a Musical Picture:* Carmen Dragon and Morris Stoloff.
Nominations *Color Cinematography:* Rudolph Maté and Allen M. Davey. *Color Interior Decoration:* Lionel Banks and Cary Odell, art direction; Fay Babcock, set decoration. *Sound Recording:* John Livadary. *Song:* "Long Ago and Far Away," music by Jerome Kern, lyrics by Ira Gershwin.

Rita Hayworth is the model of the title, and Gene Kelly [74] the old pal she leaves behind when her career takes off. Will she wind up with one of the rich and powerful men (Lee Bowman and Otto Kruger) she meets at the top? Or will she go back to Brooklyn and Kelly, whom she really loves? If you don't know the answer to that, have you ever seen a movie? If this colorful musical had a better story, and more chemistry between Hayworth and Kelly, it might have been a classic, considering that it has superb production values and songs by Kern and Gershwin (though only the nominated song is among their best). The cast, directed by Charles Vidor, also has some appealing performers: Phil Silvers, Eve Arden [1319], and, in a tiny bit part that was her debut role, Shelley Winters [542 . . .]. The film helped make Hayworth—who seemed born for Technicolor—a superstar, and it served as a career boost for Kelly, too: He was loaned out by MGM for this movie, and it's the first musical since his debut in *For Me and My Gal* in 1942 in which he was given free rein—including the choreography, which he did with Stanley Donen. Both Kelly and Donen returned to MGM and glory.

Wilson won the awards for Leon Shamroy's cinematography and for art direction and sound. The song Oscar went to James Van Heusen and Johnny Burke for "Swinging on a Star," from *Going My Way.*

Stoloff: 13, 432, 596, 643, 677, 732, 773, 1057, 1058, 1115, 1206, 1862, 1872, 1873, 1998, 2110, 2329. Maté: 706, 1607, 1740, 2031. Davey: 217, 897, 1872, 1988. Banks: 13, 98, 928, 1115, 1370, 1998. Odell: 170, 1783. Babcock: 1998. Livadary: 330, 596, 732, 1058, 1206, 1215, 1303, 1366, 1370, 1488, 1521, 1740, 1872, 2111, 2325, 2327. Kern: 340, 375, 1117, 1707, 1990, 2327. Gershwin: 1797, 1910.

456 • COWBOY

PHOENIX PICTURES; COLUMBIA. 1958.
Nomination *Film Editing:* William A. Lyon and Al Clark.

Tenderfoot Jack Lemmon [91 . . .] goes West and more or less bribes trail boss Glenn Ford into letting him go along on a cattle drive. Good, not widely known film, directed by Delmer Daves, that nicely debunks some of the myths of the West. The cast includes Brian Donlevy [161] and Anna Kashfi, ex-wife of Marlon Brando [583 . . .]. The editing Oscar went to Adrienne Fazan for *Gigi*.

Lyon: 330, 732, 1058, 1566, 1776. Clark: 53, 114, 1370, 1550.

457 • *COWBOY AND THE LADY, THE*

SAMUEL GOLDWYN PRODUCTIONS; UNITED ARTISTS. 1938.
AWARD *Sound Recording:* Thomas Moulton
NOMINATIONS *Song:* "The Cowboy and the Lady," music by Lionel Newman, lyrics by Arthur Quenzer. *Original Score:* Alfred Newman.

Merle Oberon [487], whose father is running for president, falls in love with Gary Cooper [701 . . .], a rodeo cowboy, creating a variety of dilemmas. Wafer-thin comedy-romance that virtually defines the term "high concept," about fifty years before the phrase came into play. Producer Samuel Goldwyn [102 . . .], in need of a vehicle for contract players Cooper and Oberon, asked writer-director Leo McCarey [21 . . .] for an idea. McCarey snatched the phrase "the cowboy and the lady"—easy epithets for the two stars—from thin air and improvised a story on the spot. Later, he realized that he couldn't quite remember the plot he had told Goldwyn but managed to come up with an outline. Goldwyn then hired several teams of writers—including Anita Loos, Dorothy Parker [1845 . . .], Robert Riskin [905 . . .], and S. N. Behrman—to produce a workable screenplay. The result never satisfied anyone, including the stars, and William Wyler [175 . . .], assigned to direct it, managed to get himself fired from the project. H. C. Potter replaced him. The film was a box-office bomb.

The song Oscar went to Ralph Rainger and Leo Robin for "Thanks for the Memory," from *The Big Broadcast of 1938*. The scoring award was won by Erich Wolfgang Korngold for *The Adventures of Robin Hood*.

Moulton: 22, 46, 138, 366, 487, 560, 706, 798, 962, 1153, 1200, 1451, 1510, 1607, 1849, 2154, 2294. L. Newman: 183, 557, 795, 896, 981, 1160, 1273, 1585, 1762, 2043. Quenzer: 1306. A. Newman: 31, 34, 46, 72, 138, 182, 226, 333, 334, 347, 375, 428, 437, 476, 495, 542, 690, 797, 833, 952, 953, 959, 962, 1016, 1082, 1088, 1213, 1278, 1362, 1397, 1475, 1616, 1655, 1849, 1868, 1883, 1921, 2043, 2046, 2091, 2258, 2286, 2294, 2316.

458 • *CRASH DIVE*

20TH CENTURY-FOX. 1943.
AWARD *Special Effects:* Fred Sersen, photographic; Roger Heman, sound.

Submariners Tyrone Power and Dana Andrews are both in love with Anne Baxter [46 . . .]. At the end the war intrudes, but up to that point the movie is ordinary romantic fluff. The cast, directed by Archie Mayo, includes James Gleason [904], May Whitty [1371 . . .], and Harry Morgan, billed here as Henry Morgan. The action sequences, in color, are the film's saving grace. Sersen became so well known for the ocean scenes he staged in the Fox studio tank that it was named after him.

Sersen: 226, 241, 346, 520, 1655, 2286, 2317. Heman: 226, 346, 418, 520, 1041, 2286.

459 • *CRAZYLEGS*

HAL BARTLETT PRODUCTIONS; REPUBLIC. 1953.
NOMINATION *Film Editing:* Irvine "Cotton" Warburton.

Football star Elroy "Crazylegs" Hirsch plays himself in this silly exploitation pic very loosely based on his gridiron career. Directed by Francis D. Lyon. Hirsch had a small, unimpressive second career in movies; his only other memorable film is *Unchained*, best known for its theme song. Warburton's nomination takes note of the blend of actual game footage with studio film, but the Oscar went to William Lyon for *From Here to Eternity*.

Warburton: 1284.

460 • *CRIES AND WHISPERS*

SVENSKA FILMINSTITUTET-CINEMATOGRAPH AB PRODUCTION; NEW WORLD PICTURES (SWEDEN). 1973.
AWARD *Cinematography:* Sven Nykvist.
NOMINATIONS *Picture:* Ingmar Bergman, producer. *Director:* Ingmar Bergman. *Story and Screenplay—Based on*

Factual Material or Material Not Previously Published or Produced: Ingmar Bergman. *Costume Design:* Marik Vos.

Ingrid Thulin and Liv Ullmann [610 . . .] gather at the deathbed of their sister, Harriet Andersson, who has cancer. The three sisters represent types of women: Thulin is repressed, Ullmann passionate, Andersson innocent. The film works out the various relationships among them. Bergman's admirers count it among his masterworks; others regard it as morbid, talky, and pretentiously overwrought. It's certainly nobody's idea of a good time. But everyone recognizes the beauty and skill with which it is staged and filmed. The collaboration of Nykvist and Bergman that began in 1960 with *The Virgin Spring* has never been more stunning, with images that evoke the paintings of Edvard Munch, and colors—black for Thulin, red for Ullmann, white for Andersson—that are as carefully worked out as a piece of chamber music.

For all its artistry, it is still something of a surprise to find *Cries and Whispers* among the nominees for best picture, a place where foreign language films seldom wind up. The film was almost not released in the States until it was picked up by distributor Roger Corman, who had made his fortune producing quick, cheap thrillers that made no pretense at being art. It's even more of a jolt to see the curious mixture that constitutes the year's nominees: the sleeper teen comedy *American Graffiti,* the horror-shocker *The Exorcist,* the slapsticky romantic comedy *A Touch of Class,* and the winner, the overproduced buddy picture *The Sting.* An off year for Hollywood if ever there was one.

Bergman lost the directing Oscar to George Roy Hill and the writing Oscar to David S. Ward, both for *The Sting.* Edith Head's costumes for *The Sting* also won.

Nykvist: 644, 2173. Bergman: 111, 634, 644, 2082, 2283. Vos: 644, 2206.

461 • CRIMES AND MISDEMEANORS

JACK ROLLINS AND CHARLES H. JOFFE PRODUCTION; ORION. 1989.

NOMINATIONS *Supporting Actor:* Martin Landau. *Director:* Woody Allen. *Screenplay Written Directly for the Screen:* Woody Allen.

Landau wants to end his relationship with his mistress, Anjelica Huston [617 . . .], and winds up causing her to be murdered. Meanwhile, filmmaker Allen is courting Mia Farrow while trying to make a documentary about her boss, Alan Alda, an egotistic jerk. The stories run parallel, the comedy intersecting the melodrama at odd moments. The complex story is undeniably well handled, but the end result is curiously superficial and unsatisfying. There's a little too much self-conscious examining of themes like guilt and justice. The cast includes Claire Bloom, Jerry Orbach, Sam Waterston [1086], and an unbilled Daryl Hannah.

Landau lost to Denzel Washington in *Glory.* The directing Oscar went to Oliver Stone for *Born on the Fourth of July.* Tom Schulman won for his screenplay for *Dead Poets Society.*

Landau: 595.8, 2148. Allen: 39, 88, 294, 311.5, 863, 962.5, 1005, 1267, 1636, 1647.

462 • CRIMES OF THE HEART

CRIMES OF THE HEART PRODUCTION; DE LAURENTIIS ENTERTAINMENT GROUP. 1986.

NOMINATIONS *Actress:* Sissy Spacek. *Supporting Actress:* Tess Harper. *Screenplay Based on Material From Another Medium:* Beth Henley.

Spacek, Diane Keaton [88 . . .], and Jessica Lange [244.5 . . .] play three weird Mississippi sisters who reunite when Spacek is arrested for shooting her husband. Much talk, not much action, as is usual in plays that have been adapted for the screen. Henley's black comedy doubtless worked well on stage, but here it's just an excuse to put three—or four, counting Harper, who plays their nosy neighbor—of the best actresses of the eighties through their paces. Bruce Beresford [277 . . .] directs, and the cast includes Sam Shepard [1698]. It's not bad, it just doesn't add up to much.

Spacek lost to Marlee Matlin in *Children of a Lesser God,* Harper to Dianne Wiest in *Hannah and Her Sisters.* The screenplay Oscar went to Ruth Prawer Jhabvala for *A Room With a View.*

Spacek: 364, 418, 1330, 1701.

463 • CRIMINAL CODE, THE

COLUMBIA. 1930–31.
NOMINATION *Adaptation:* Seton I. Miller and Fred Niblo, Jr.

Phillips Holmes is sent to prison for a killing he committed in self-defense. District Attorney Walter Huston [50 . . .] is aware that Holmes might have been acquitted if he'd had a better defense, so when Huston is made warden of Holmes' prison, he tries to go easy on him. Unfortunately Holmes not only falls in love with Huston's daughter, played by Constance Cummings, he also witnesses a brutal prison murder, committed by Boris Karloff. When he abides by the "code" of the title and refuses to rat on Karloff, he is sent to solitary. Pretty good prison melodrama, with the stiffness that often afflicts early talkies, but well directed by Howard Hawks [1779] and photographed by James Wong Howe [1 . . .].

Miller and Niblo adapted a play by Martin Flavin, giving it a somewhat softer ending. Niblo is the son of the pioneering film director Fred Niblo. The Oscar went to Howard Estabrook for *Cimarron.*

Miller: 904.

464 • "CROCODILE" DUNDEE

RIMFIRE FILMS LTD. PRODUCTION; PARAMOUNT (AUSTRALIA). 1986.
NOMINATION *Screenplay Written Directly for the Screen:* Paul Hogan, story; Paul Hogan, Ken Shadie, and John Cornell, screenplay.

New York reporter Linda Kozlowski journeys to the Australian Outback in search of a legendary adventurer, played by Hogan. He returns with her to New York, where his wilderness skills prove surprisingly useful. Very good-natured little comedy, directed by Peter Faiman, that became a huge hit, making a star—at least for a while (his later films, including a sequel in 1988, have been much less suc-

cessful)—of Hogan, a former construction worker who had become a hit in his native country by spinning tales on TV talk shows. Before the movie, he was familiar to American audiences from his TV commercials for Australian tourism with the tag line "We'll put another shrimp on the barbie for you." Several studios passed up the distribution rights before Paramount picked up the movie, adding quotation marks in the title to make sure audiences didn't expect a nature film. The Oscar went to Woody Allen for *Hannah and Her Sisters.*

465 • CROMWELL

IRVING ALLEN LTD. PRODUCTION; COLUMBIA (UNITED KINGDOM). 1970.
AWARD *Costume Design:* Nino Novarese.
NOMINATION *Original Score:* Frank Cordell.

Richard Harris [660 . . .] plays the Puritan usurper Oliver Cromwell and Alec Guinness [287 . . .] the ill-fated King Charles I in this long, dull history lesson, an ill-advised attempt to make a spectacle out of an ideological struggle—though there are, of course, some big bloody battles. It needs a good shot of vulgar swashbuckling, but Harris isn't the man for that, and he's upstaged by the dry wit of Guinness' performance. Directed by Ken Hughes, with Robert Morley [1274], Dorothy Tutin, Frank Finlay [1506], and Timothy Dalton. It was a box-office debacle on both sides of the Atlantic. Novarese's costumes have historical accuracy to their credit, but as Pauline Kael observes, "Was there ever a period of history in which the clothes were less photogenic?" The Oscar for score went to Francis Lai for *Love Story.*

Novarese: 29, 413, 833, 1610.

466 • CROSS CREEK

ROBERT B. RADNITZ/MARTIN RITT/THORN EMI FILMS PRODUCTION; UNIVERSAL. 1983.
NOMINATIONS *Supporting Actor:* Rip Torn. *Supporting Actress:* Alfre Woodard. *Original Score:* Leonard Rosenman. *Costume Design:* Joe I. Tompkins.

Mary Steenburgen [1300] plays novelist Marjorie Kennan Rawlings, who moves to the Florida Everglades in search of material—which she finds in abundance. Pleasantly watchable film, long on atmospherics, short on plot, nicely directed by Martin Ritt [956]. Suggestion: Watch this one back-to-back with *The Yearling,* one of the works that came out of Rawlings' sojourn.

Torn began acting in films in the fifties, starting with *Baby Doll,* and while his name sounds like a parody of the press agentry that gave us Tab Hunter and Rock Hudson, it's for real: His real name is Elmore Torn, and Rip was a long-standing nickname. He studied at the Actors Studio and with dancer Martha Graham. He lost the Oscar to the performance in *Terms of Endearment* of Jack Nicholson—an actor he resembles in his ability to perform both subtly and over-the-top.

Woodard, one of the most gifted of the younger African-American actresses, has been hindered in her career by a lack of good roles, but she continues to make a strong impression in every performance. There were many who were shocked by the Academy's failure to nominate her for *Passion Fish,* for which her costar, Mary McDonnell, received a nomination. She lost the Oscar to Linda Hunt's tour de force trouser role in *The Year of Living Dangerously.*

The scoring award went to Bill Conti for *The Right Stuff.* Marik Vos won for her costumes for *Fanny & Alexander.*

Rosenman: 151, 264, 1914. Tompkins: 871.

467 • CROSSFIRE

RKO RADIO. 1947.

NOMINATIONS *Picture:* Adrian Scott, producer. *Supporting Actor:* Robert Ryan. *Supporting Actress:* Gloria Grahame. *Director:* Edward Dmytryk. *Screenplay:* John Paxton.

Police detective Robert Young investigates the murder of a Jewish salesman (Sam Levene), and the trail leads to Ryan, a psychotic anti-Semite. The fine cast includes Robert Mitchum [1935], and Paul Kelly. This excellent thriller was adapted from the novel *The Brick Foxhole,* by Richard Brooks [227 . . .], in which the victim was gay and the killer homophobic. The movie only occasionally becomes obtrusively preachy

in its handling of the theme of prejudice. A different kind of prejudice afflicted several participants in the film. Producer Scott and director Dmytryk were two of the Hollywood Ten, sentenced to prison for their refusal to testify before the House Un-American Activities Committee about alleged Communist Party affiliation. Scott, who had been a screenwriter as well as producer, left films after serving his sentence. Dmytryk served his one-year term, went to England for a few years, then returned to the States and testified before the committee, naming Scott and others as former communists. He was allowed to return to work and directed such films as *Broken Lance, The Caine Mutiny, Raintree County,* and *The Young Lions.* The best picture Oscar went to another film about anti-Semitism, *Gentleman's Agreement.*

Ryan started acting on stage in 1939 and made a few films before joining the marines during World War II. He appeared on Broadway in *Clash by Night* in 1940 and re-created his role in the 1952 film version. He was never a major star, but he was one of the most respected American actors in both film and theater, appearing opposite Katharine Hepburn [24 . . .] in the 1960 American Shakespeare Festival production of *Antony and Cleopatra.* He died of cancer in 1974. The Oscar went to Edmund Gwenn in *Miracle on 34th Street.*

Grahame lost to Celeste Holm for *Gentleman's Agreement,* whose director, Elia Kazan, also won.

Paxton also wrote the screenplay for the 1954 movie *The Wild One,* which helped make Marlon Brando [583 . . .] an icon of rebellion. He lost to George Seaton's screenplay for *Miracle on 34th Street.*

Grahame: 130.

468 • CROWD, THE

MGM. 1927–28.

NOMINATIONS *Unique and Artistic Picture. Director:* King Vidor.

A working-class family struggles to make ends meet in the impersonal, uncaring city. A film with nonstars—Eleanor Boardman, James Murray—and little in the way of conventional plot, it's one of the most critically acclaimed of the great silent films, and it still has much of its power. It was filmed on location in New York City, much of it with hidden cameras. The award for artistic quality, given only this first year of the awards, went to *Sunrise.* Frank Borzage took the directing award for *Seventh Heaven.*

Vidor: 378, 406, 857, 2228.

469 • CRUEL SEA, THE

J. Arthur Rank-Ealing; Universal-International (United Kingdom). 1953.

Nomination *Screenplay:* Eric Ambler.

Jack Hawkins commands a World War II warship and makes capable sailors out of men who held desk jobs in civilian life, such as lawyer Denholm Elliott [1725]. Well-filmed version of a novel by Nicholas Monsarrat, directed by Charles Frend, with Stanley Baker, Donald Sinden, Virginia McKenna, and Alec McCowen. The treatment of the ship's destruction and the plight of its survivors is particularly effective.

Ambler, best known as a spy-thriller novelist, began his film career in 1938 with Alexander Korda [1620] and was in charge of educational and morale films for the British War Office during World War II. The Oscar went to Daniel Taradash for *From Here to Eternity.*

470 • CRUSADES, THE

Paramount. 1935.

Nomination *Cinematography:* Victor Milner.

Loretta Young [428 . . .] plays Berengaria, princess of Navarre and wife of Richard the Lion-Hearted, played by Henry Wilcoxon. Everyone goes off to retake the Holy Land, gets captured, etc. Epic silliness from—who else?—Cecil B. DeMille [412 . . .]. The humongous cast includes Joseph Schildkraut [1169], Mischa Auer [1401], J. Carrol Naish [1294 . . .], and in a bit part, Ann Sheridan. For camp followers only. The cinematography award was won—in the Oscars' only successful write-in campaign—by Hal Mohr for *A Midsummer Night's Dream;* Milner came in third, after Gregg Toland for *Les Misérables.*

Milner: 304, 412, 740, 757, 827, 1217, 1452, 1668.

471 • CRY FREEDOM

Marble Arch Production; Universal. 1987.

Nominations *Supporting Actor:* Denzel Washington. *Song:* "Cry Freedom," music and lyrics by George Fenton and Jonas Gwangwa. *Original Score:* George Fenton and Jonas Gwangwa.

The attempts of Steve Biko (Washington) to marshal black opposition to apartheid attract the sympathetic attention of South African editor Donald Woods, played by Kevin Kline [670]. Biko is imprisoned and murdered, and Woods is forced to flee with his family. Filmed in Zimbabwe by director Richard Attenborough [745], who brings to it the same earnestness and attention to detail he brought to *Gandhi,* and with the same deadening results. What's wrong with this film is clear from the fact that Washington is a supporting actor—Attenborough tells the story from a white man's point of view. While the account of the Woods family's escape is full of suspense, it puts the focus of the film in the wrong place: on the suffering of the sympathetic white man, not the martyred black man and his many followers. Imagine if *Gandhi* had focused mainly on a British sympathizer. Both Washington and Kline, however, are excellent.

Though Washington lost to Sean Connery for *The Untouchables,* the film established him as one of the most powerful screen presences of our day. The music awards went to Franke Previte, John DeNicola, and Donald Markowitz's "(I've Had) The Time of My Life," from *Dirty Dancing,* and to the score by Ryuichi Sakamoto, David Byrne, and Cong Su for *The Last Emperor.*

Washington: 779, 1247.5. Fenton: 485, 671, 745.

472 • CRY IN THE DARK, A

Cannon Entertainment/Golan-Globus Production; Warner Bros. 1988.

Nomination *Actress:* Meryl Streep.

Streep and Sam Neill play an Australian Seventh-Day Adventist couple whose baby is carried off by a wild dog while the family is on a camping trip. The couple is tried for murdering the child, and the case becomes a media circus. Many Australians grow hostile to the couple because they belong to an out-of-the-mainstream religious group and because the woman played by Streep is seen as cold and unemotional in her testimony. Absorbing drama, well directed by Fred Schepisi in an effective semidocumentary style (it's based on a true story). Neill, one of the movies' most underrated actors, deserves as much credit as Streep, though his role is not as showy.

Streep was, as often, unfairly mocked for "doing another accent," adding Australian to her Polish *(Sophie's Choice)* and Danish *(Out of Africa)*. But she is entirely convincing—unflatteringly un-made-up, with a drab bowl-cut hairdo. The Oscar went to Jodie Foster for *The Accused.*

Streep: 521, 725, 1019, 1111, 1512, 1598, 1821, 1876.

472.5 • CRYING GAME, THE

PALACE PICTURES PRODUCTION; MIRAMAX FILMS (UNITED KINGDOM). 1992.
AWARD *Original Screenplay:* Neil Jordan.
NOMINATIONS *Picture:* Stephen Woolley, producer. *Actor:* Stephen Rea. *Supporting Actor:* Jaye Davidson. *Director:* Neil Jordan. *Film Editing:* Kant Pan.

Rea, a member of an IRA terrorist group, is assigned to guard a hostage, a British soldier played by Forest Whitaker. As they wait for the ransom, Rea and Whitaker unexpectedly become friends. After Whitaker is killed and the British attack the group's hideout, Rea flees. Disturbed by the sympathy he felt for Whitaker, Rea changes his identity, seeks out Whitaker's lover, and makes a shocking discovery. The survivors of the IRA group, including Miranda Richardson [478.5 . . .], find Rea and enlist him in another mission, but their plot goes awry. Witty, exciting thriller with several wonderful twists and surprises. Even if you know the film's secrets, it still works, largely because of Jordan's intelligent, provocative script and a gallery of entirely convincing performances. It was, interestingly, a bigger hit in America than it was in Great Britain, where IRA terrorism is not taken lightly: Imagine if the film had been set in the States with the leading character an antigovernment militiaman. The nominations for *The Crying Game* caused a mild stir when they were announced because they gave away one of the film's surprises. But they also boosted the movie's box office, and for a while there was some thought that this dark-horse candidate might even take the best picture award. That went, however, to *Unforgiven.* The other nominees were *A Few Good Men, Howards End,* and *Scent of a Woman.*

The success of *The Crying Game* made Jordan one of the hottest "new" directors in Hollywood, though the Irish-born filmmaker was hardly new. His *Mona Lisa* had been well received in 1986, earning Bob Hoskins an Oscar nomination. Jordan's subsequent attempts to work in Hollywood had not succeeded. His film *High Spirits* in 1988 was taken out of his hands and badly edited, and his remake of *We're No Angels,* with Robert De Niro [113 . . .] and Sean Penn, was a major box-office flop in 1989. On the strength of *The Crying Game,* he was given a plum assignment, the long-postponed film of the Anne Rice novel *Interview With the Vampire.*

Rea, an Irish-born actor, made his first film appearance in Jordan's debut film, *Angel* (1982), and appeared in Jordan's 1984 film *The Company of Wolves.* He also received a Tony nomination in 1993 for his appearance on Broadway in *Someone Who'll Watch Over Me.* He lost the Oscar to Al Pacino's performance in *Scent of a Woman.* Davidson, who was born in California but grew up in England, was working as a fashion assistant when he was cast in *The Crying Game.* He had never acted in a film before. The Oscar went to Gene Hackman in *Unforgiven.* The editing award was won by Joel Cox for *Unforgiven.*

473 • CYRANO DE BERGERAC

STANLEY KRAMER PRODUCTIONS; UNITED ARTISTS. 1950.
AWARD *Actor:* Jose Ferrer.

Ferrer plays the long-nosed poet-swordsman, who woos the woman he secretly loves, Roxane (Mala Powers), for a handsome but tongue-tied suitor, played by William Prince. Directed by Michael Gordon, this is a flat, stagy, low-budget version of the play by Edmond Rostand, much outclassed by the 1990 French version.

Ferrer started acting while he was at Princeton and made his Broadway debut in 1935. He was acclaimed for his performance as Iago in the 1942 production of *Othello* starring Paul Robeson, and made his screen debut in 1948 in *Joan of Arc,* which earned him his first Oscar nomination. His tendency to overact didn't hurt him in *Cyrano* or in his tour de force performance in *Moulin Rouge,* but it limited his effectiveness on screen. He did, however, have a long career as a character actor, lasting up till his death in 1992. He also directed a number of films. His son, Miguel Ferrer, is a well-known character player.

Ferrer: 1048, 1363.

474 • CYRANO DE BERGERAC

HACHETTE PREMIERE/CAMERA ONE PRODUCTION; ORION CLASSICS (FRANCE). 1990.

AWARD *Costume Design:* Franca Squarciapino.

NOMINATIONS *Actor:* Gérard Depardieu. *Art Direction—Set Decoration:* Ezio Frigerio; Jacques Rouxel. *Makeup:* Michele Burke and Jean-Pierre Eychenne. *Foreign Language Film.*

Depardieu plays the title role, with Anne Brochet as Roxane and Vincent Perez as Christian in this sumptuous film directed by Jean-Paul Rappeneau. The handsomeness of the production and the wholly affecting performances overcome the story's familiarity and its essentially theatrical, rather than cinematic, character. Things have to stand still for the speeches, and the death scene, while beautifully acted, stretches one's patience. It's definitely preferable to the 1950 version, but many of us think the 1987 Americanization with Steve Martin, *Roxanne,* gets closer to the heart of Cyrano.

Depardieu, one of the world's great actors, has been shockingly overlooked by the Academy through the years. He lost to Jeremy Irons in *Reversal of Fortune.* The art direction and makeup awards went to *Dick Tracy.*

The foreign language film award was one of the most controversial of recent years. It went to the Swiss *Journey of Hope* over *Cyrano,* the banned-in-China *Ju Dou,* and Germany's satiric *The Nasty Girl.* Many critics felt *Journey of Hope* ranked no better than

fourth in the nominees, just ahead of Italy's *Open Doors.*

Burke: 272.5, 409, 1641.

475 • DAD

UNIVERSAL/AMBLIN ENTERTAINMENT PRODUCTION; UNIVERSAL. 1989.

NOMINATION *Makeup:* Dick Smith, Ken Diaz, and Greg Nelson.

Busy yuppie Ted Danson goes home when his father, Jack Lemmon [91 . . .], suffers a heart attack, and stays to make up for the lost years of their relationship. Occasionally cutesy, occasionally poignant, always manipulative, but not enough to overcome one's resistance to it. The cast includes Olympia Dukakis [1351] as Danson's mother and Ethan Hawke as Danson's son, who is, you might have guessed, as estranged from Danson as Danson used to be from Lemmon. Adapted from a novel by William Wharton and directed by Gary David Goldberg, creator of the TV sitcom *Family Ties.* The makeup crew, who aged Lemmon well beyond his sixty-four years, lost to the team that made Jessica Tandy look both younger and older than her eighty years in *Driving Miss Daisy.*

Smith: 60.

476 • DADDY LONG LEGS

20TH CENTURY-FOX. 1955.

NOMINATIONS *Color Art Direction—Set Decoration:* Lyle Wheeler and John DeCuir; Walter M. Scott and Paul S. Fox. *Song:* "Something's Gotta Give," music and lyrics by Johnny Mercer. *Scoring of a Musical Picture:* Alfred Newman.

Fred Astaire [2126] is a millionaire playboy who is charmed by Leslie Caron [1113 . . .] when he sees her teaching the children at a French orphanage, so he decides to be the anonymous sponsor of her education at a college in the United States. Caron has only glimpsed his long-legged shadow on the orphanage wall, so from college she writes letters to her mysterious Daddy Long Legs. Complications ensue from his attempting to conceal his identity, and they are finally unraveled only with the aid of Astaire's secretary, the invaluable Thelma Ritter [46 . . .]. Directed by Jean

Negulesco [1052], with Fred Clark and Terry Moore [425]. Jean Webster's 1912 novel about an orphan who falls in love with her benefactor had been turned into a play in 1914, with the young Ruth Chatterton [1234 . . .], then into a silent movie with Mary Pickford [444] in 1919 and a talkie with Janet Gaynor [1792 . . .] in 1931. It also inspired a Shirley Temple movie, *Curly Top,* in 1936. So it was pretty shopworn by the time it was handed over to Phoebe [350] and Henry Ephron [350] to be turned into a musical for Astaire and Caron. Unfortunately Astaire and the ballet-trained Caron are not well matched as dancers, and the age difference (he was fifty-five, she twenty-four) accentuates their unsuitability as partners.

Mercer's score is delightful, and ''Something's Gotta Give'' is the last of the many great songs especially written for Astaire. The Academy voters, however, preferred the melodramatic theme song to *Love Is a Many-Splendored Thing.* Newman's orchestration lost to the scoring for *Oklahoma!* The art direction Oscar went to *Picnic.*

Wheeler: 19, 46, 83, 356, 376, 428, 495, 530, 542, 719, 721, 798, 950, 1062, 1088, 1149, 1153, 1213, 1391, 1475, 1601, 1616, 1670, 1706, 1852, 2008, 2093, 2212. DeCuir: 29, 201, 376, 413, 896, 950, 1088, 1391, 1852, 2000. Scott: 46, 376, 413, 530, 542, 557, 646, 896, 1088, 1213, 1391, 1475, 1706, 1753, 1881, 1907, 2008, 2120, 2247. Fox: 376, 413, 428, 495, 530, 721, 950, 1088, 1601, 1666, 1706, 1852. Mercer: 248, 278, 384, 494, 508, 636, 788, 825, 877, 903, 905, 1109, 1772, 1838, 1912, 2327, 2328. Newman: 31, 34, 46, 72, 138, 182, 226, 333, 334, 347, 375, 428, 437, 457, 495, 542, 690, 797, 833, 952, 953, 959, 962, 1016, 1082, 1088, 1213, 1278, 1362, 1397, 1475, 1616, 1655, 1849, 1868, 1883, 1921, 2043, 2046, 2091, 2258, 2286, 2294, 2316.

476.5 • DAENS

Favourite Films/Films Dérives/Titane & Shooting Star Filmcompany Production (Belgium). 1992.
Nomination *Foreign Language Film.*

A priest becomes active in the late-nineteenth-century Flemish labor movement. This film, by Stijn Coninx, has not yet been widely released in the United States. The Oscar went to the French *Indochine.*

477 • DAISY MILLER

A Directors Company Production; Paramount. 1974.
Nomination *Costume Design:* John Furness.

Cybill Shepherd plays Daisy, a naively independent American girl who is undone by her encounter with nineteenth-century Europe. Altogether disastrous adaptation of the Henry James novella, directed by Peter Bogdanovich [1139], whose first mistake was casting his protégée, Shepherd, in the lead. Though she later grew into a charming light comedian, she was too inexperienced and callow to carry so central a role. Strong supporting players such as Cloris Leachman [1139], Eileen Brennan [1617], and Mildred Natwick [147] only make Shepherd's inadequacy more obvious. The production is handsomely mounted by art director Ferdinando Scarfiotti [1136 . . .], and Furness' clothes—which lost to Theoni V. Aldredge's designs for *The Great Gatsby*—are lovely.

478 • DAM BUSTERS, THE

Associated British Picture Corporation Ltd.; Warner Bros. (United Kingdom). 1955.
Nomination *Special Effects.* (no individual citation.)

During World War II Michael Redgrave [1364] masterminds a British plan to blow up the Ruhr dam. Straightforward, exciting movie directed by Michael Anderson [101], with Richard Todd [878], Ursula Jeans, and Basil Sydney. The special effects Oscar went to *The Bridges of Toko-Ri.*

478.5 • DAMAGE

Skreba/Damage/NEF/Le Studio Canal+ Production; New Line (United Kingdom/France). 1992.
Nomination *Supporting Actress:* Miranda Richardson.

Rising British political figure Jeremy Irons [1689] falls into a passionate affair with Juliette Binoche, who just happens to be engaged to his son, Rupert Graves. The consequences for all, including Irons' wife, Richardson, are disastrous. Intelligent and well acted, though a little mechanical at heart—the denouement is so predictable one begins to get tired of waiting for it. This almost overwhelmingly moral tale, directed by Louis Malle [107 . . .], was nearly given the kiss of box-office death, an NC-17 rating, until Malle agreed to trim a few minutes from its somewhat acrobatic sex scenes. It's hard to guess what was cut. The controversy only served to highlight the continuing problems of the film industry's self-censorship system; though it's more flexible than the Production Code of old, it has its own peculiar unwritten standards of language, violence, and sexuality. Leslie Caron [1113 . . .] plays Binoche's mother.

Richardson had an amazing year, with equally fine —and completely different—performances in three films. She was a feline IRA assassin in *The Crying Game,* a mousy, dutiful wife in *Enchanted April,* and a practical, efficient political spouse in *Damage.* The scene in *Damage* in which her facade of cool efficiency is wiped away by the consequences of her husband's transgression is shattering. She lost, in one of the more controversial upsets of recent years, to Marisa Tomei in *My Cousin Vinny.*

Richardson: 2104.5.

479 • DAMN YANKEES

WARNER BROS. 1958.

NOMINATION *Scoring of a Musical Picture:* Ray Heindorf.

A baseball fan sells his soul to the devil (Ray Walston) and is transformed into a star player (Tab Hunter) for the Washington Senators. George Abbott [48] codirected with Stanley Donen this version of Abbott's Broadway hit musical based on Douglas Wallop's novel, *The Year the Yankees Lost the Pennant.* Gwen Verdon is the devil's vampish assistant, Lola, and the choreography is by Bob Fosse [49 . . .], who also dances with Verdon in "Who's Got the Pain (When They Do the Mambo)?" The fine song score by Richard Adler and Jerry Ross includes "Whatever Lola Wants," "Two Lost Souls," and "(You Gotta Have) Heart." Excellent as a record of a Broadway hit of the fifties—Walston, Verdon, Jean Stapleton, and others repeat their stage roles—but a lot of it seems trapped behind the footlights, and it's very much a period piece now, as its recent theatrical revival on Broadway

demonstrated. The Oscar went to André Previn for *Gigi.*

Heindorf: 331, 666, 930, 1043, 1204, 1385, 1408, 1430, 1690, 1719, 1750, 1910, 2058, 2186, 2243, 2310, 2318.

480 • DAMNED, THE

PEGASO-PRAESIDENS FILM PRODUCTION; WARNER BROS. (ITALY/ WEST GERMANY). 1969.

NOMINATION *Story and Screenplay—Based on Material Not Previously Published or Produced:* Nicola Badalucco, Enrico Medioli, and Luchino Visconti.

The von Essenbecks, a wealthy family of German industrialists, descend to various perversions—including an incestuous relationship between Helmut Berger and his mother, Ingrid Thulin—as Hitler comes to power. Visconti's X-rated film was a box-office success, but today it seems overheated, overstated, over-everything. And finally what's the point? To prove that the Nazis were nasty? We needed to see Berger in drag as Marlene Dietrich [1358] to learn that? The cast includes Dirk Bogarde and Charlotte Rampling, both of them sure to be called on when there's decadence to be shown. The Oscar went to William Goldman for *Butch Cassidy and the Sundance Kid.*

481 • DAMSEL IN DISTRESS, A

RKO RADIO. 1937.

AWARD *Dance Direction:* Hermes Pan.

NOMINATION *Interior Decoration:* Carroll Clark.

While doing a show in London, musical comedy star Fred Astaire [2126] falls for a British aristocrat, played by Joan Fontaine [441 . . .], but her family stands in the way. After his long Broadway collaboration with his sister, Adele, Astaire had wanted to avoid being trapped into a "dance team." But the success of the very first teaming with Ginger Rogers [1102] in *Flying Down to Rio* had led to picture after picture. In the five-picture contract he signed in 1936, Astaire insisted that one of the five be with someone other than Rogers. Rogers was similarly eager to play in something other than a musical, so while she made *Stage Door,* Astaire filmed this adaptation of a P. G. Wodehouse novel. Because Fontaine could neither sing nor dance, Astaire goes solo through much of the film, except when he's joined, as in Pan's award-winning number in a fun house, by George Burns [1976] and Gracie Allen, who play Astaire's publicists. The film was a flop, despite tidy direction by George Stevens [542 . . .], excellent comedy support from Burns and Allen and from Reginald Gardiner as a busybody butler, and, most of all, wonderful songs by George [1797] and Ira Gershwin [455 . . .]. That neither "A Foggy Day" nor "Nice Work If You Can Get It" was nominated for best song remains one of the Academy's mysteries, as does the lack of a scoring nomination for Victor Baravelle [358] and Robert Russell Bennett [1469].

Pan's Oscar was the last awarded in the dance direction category, which the Academy discontinued after this year. Born Hermes Panagiotopulos, he first became associated with Astaire on *Flying Down to Rio,* on which he was working as assistant to dance director Dave Gould [261 . . .]. When he aided Astaire in working out the steps for a number, the two struck up a friendship that lasted throughout their careers. Pan, who resembled Astaire, has often been called the star's alter ego. He was also the chief choreographer on numerous musicals without Astaire.

The art direction Oscar went to Steven Goosson for *Lost Horizon.*

Pan: 1990, 2115. Clark: 4, 686, 754, 1284, 1924, 2115.

482 • DANCES WITH WOLVES

Tig Production; Orion. 1990.

Awards *Picture:* Jim Wilson and Kevin Costner, producers. *Director:* Kevin Costner. *Screenplay Based on Material From Another Medium:* Michael Blake. *Cinematography:* Dean Semler. *Sound:* Jeffrey Perkins, Bill W. Benton, Greg Watkins, and Russell Williams II. *Original Score:* John Barry. *Film Editing:* Neil Travis.

Nominations *Actor:* Kevin Costner. *Supporting Actor:* Graham Greene. *Supporting Actress:* Mary McDonnell. *Art Direction–Set Decoration:* Jeffrey Beecroft; Lisa Dean. *Costume Design:* Elsa Zamparelli.

Costner, a soldier, is sent to a deserted fort in

Sioux territory where he waits alone for reinforcements to arrive. When he encounters the Indians, he finds them to be not the bloodthirsty savages he's been warned against, but a resourceful, humorous, loving people. He is aided in his attempts to communicate with the tribe by McDonnell, a white woman who survived a massacre as a child and has been raised by the Sioux. For his aid in a buffalo hunt and in fighting off an enemy tribe, he is adopted by the Sioux and given McDonnell as a bride. When the white soldiers arrive, however, he is arrested as a traitor. Rescued by the Sioux, he must choose a new way of life. Splendid, rousing film, a huge and unexpected box-office hit, and a critical success. Its epic moments, such as the buffalo hunt, are old-fashioned moviemaking at its best. A few prominent critics, however, were unenthusiastic, finding the treatment of the Indians sentimental and New Agey: Costner has "feathers in his hair, and feathers in his head," scoffed Pauline Kael.

Dances With Wolves became only the second western (the first was *Cimarron,* almost sixty years earlier) to win the best picture Oscar. Its only clear competitor for the award was Martin Scorsese's *GoodFellas,* which won the critics' near-universal praise, but was too chilly for most audiences and too quirkily self-referential to get the Academy's votes. The other contenders were the medical melodrama *Awakenings,* the sentimental comedy-fantasy *Ghost,* and the disappointing sequel *The Godfather, Part III.*

The success of *Dances With Wolves* is largely due to Costner's persistence—and money. He had begun his Hollywood career in bit parts in 1981 and was cut out of the hit *The Big Chill,* in which he was cast as Alex, the dead friend whose funeral precipitates the reunion. (He was to appear in flashbacks, but only his body, being dressed by the undertaker, appears in the released film.) However, Lawrence Kasdan, director of *The Big Chill,* provided Costner with a breakthrough role as the flamboyant younger brother in *Silverado,* and he became a major box-office draw in *No Way Out* (1987), *The Untouchables,* and *Field of Dreams.* He used his new celebrity to launch *Dances With Wolves,* based on his friend Blake's novel/screenplay. Costner insisted on going against the conventional Hollywood wisdom: casting unknowns (except for himself), making the film more than three hours long, using subtitles to translate Lakota Sioux dialogue, and most of all, filming a western, a genre that was thought to be dead. Rumors that the film was over budget had skeptics referring to "Kevin's Gate." Instead, it won seven Oscars and made Costner one of the most powerful people in Hollywood. He has said, however, that he has no plans to direct another movie.

Costner's acting nomination was one of the few the film received that generated controversy. Many felt the nomination should have gone instead to Robin Williams (whose costar, Robert De Niro, was nominated) for *Awakenings,* Al Pacino for *The Godfather, Part III,* or Ray Liotta for *GoodFellas.* There was no controversy about the winner: Jeremy Irons in *Reversal of Fortune.*

Greene was one of several Native American actors hired for the film, which departed from the old Hollywood practice of using Polish-Americans like Jeff Chandler [298] or Italian-Americans like Sal Mineo [630 . . .] to play Indians. Experienced but unknown, Greene was soon in demand for TV and movie roles, but he expressed a strong wish not to be typecast. He was impressive in the 1992 film *Thunderheart* as a contemporary Sioux lawman. The Oscar was won by Joe Pesci for *GoodFellas.*

McDonnell, a relatively unknown performer with stage and TV experience, had been seen in only a few films, such as *Matewan.* She rises beautifully to the challenge of playing a woman who has all but forgotten her native English during the years she has spent with the Sioux. Also trying not to be typed, she has chosen to play contemporary urban women in films such as *Grand Canyon* and *Passion Fish.* Whoopi Goldberg won the award for her performance in *Ghost.*

The art direction award went to *Dick Tracy,* the costuming Oscar to Franca Squarciapino for *Cyrano de Bergerac.*

Benton: 761.5. Watkins: 260. Williams: 779.

Barry: 259, 382.5, 1177, 1285, 1512. McDonnell: 1533.5.

483 • DANCING PIRATE

PIONEER PICTURES; RKO RADIO. 1936.
NOMINATION *Dance Direction:* Russell Lewis.

Dancing teacher Charles Collins is shanghaied by pirates but manages to escape when the ship docks in Mexico. He woos and wins the daughter of Frank Morgan [22 . . .], mayor of the village where he hides out. Minor musical with several claims to distinction: It has songs (though unmemorable ones) by Richard Rodgers [1921] and Lorenz Hart, it was an early Technicolor feature, and the cast includes the Royal Cansinos—the dancing team of Eduardo Cansino and Volga Haworth, who are better known as Rita Hayworth's parents. The Oscar went to Seymour Felix for the extravagant "A Pretty Girl Is Like a Melody" number from *The Great Ziegfeld.*

484 • DANGEROUS

WARNER BROS. 1935.
AWARD *Actress:* Bette Davis.

Davis is an alcoholic actress whose husband is crippled in an auto accident she causes. She redeems herself, of course, by giving up her lover, Franchot Tone [1387], to nurse her husband. Junky but enjoyable melodrama, the sort of film that usually had Davis chafing against the restrictions of her Warners contract. Directed by Alfred E. Green.

It's often thought that the Oscar for *Dangerous* was a consolation prize to Davis for not being nominated a year earlier for her much better performance in a much better film, *Of Human Bondage,* for which a strong write-in campaign had been mounted at the 1934 awards. (Davis came in third in that race, after winner Claudette Colbert in *It Happened One Night* and second-place finalist Norma Shearer for *The Barretts of Wimpole Street.*) But among the competing nominees—Elisabeth Bergner in *Escape Me Never,* Claudette Colbert in *Private Worlds,* Katharine Hepburn in *Alice Adams,* Miriam Hopkins in *Becky Sharp,* and Merle Oberon in *The Dark Angel*—only one other performance, Hepburn's, is in Davis' league. Hepburn and Colbert had already won Oscars, and at this point there were no two-time acting winners. Hepburn came in second, just ahead of Bergner.

Before coming to Hollywood in 1930, Davis had an undistinguished stage career—at one point she was apparently fired from a repertory company by its director, George Cukor [262 . . .], although in later years, when both became famous, Cukor denied that she had been dismissed. She signed with Universal but attracted little attention until George Arliss [550 . . .] requested her for a role in a Warners film, *The Man Who Played God,* in 1932. As a result, she moved to Warners and became one of the studio's biggest stars.

Davis: 46, 492, 1046, 1162, 1182, 1369, 1456, 1462.5, 1908, 2248.

485 • *DANGEROUS LIAISONS*

WARNER BROS. PRODUCTION; WARNER BROS. 1988.

AWARDS *Screenplay Based on Material From Another Medium:* Christopher Hampton. *Art Direction—Set Decoration:* Stuart Craig; Gerard James. *Costume Design:* James Acheson.

NOMINATIONS *Picture:* Norma Heyman and Hank Moonjean, producers. *Actress:* Glenn Close. *Supporting Actress:* Michelle Pfeiffer. *Original Score:* George Fenton.

Close and John Malkovich [992.3 . . .] play eighteenth-century French aristocrats who relieve their boredom by playing games of seduction. She wagers that he will be unable to make a conquest of Pfeiffer, a woman with a reputation for virtue. Naturally things don't turn out well for anyone. Stephen Frears [840] directs this witty, handsome adaptation by Hampton of his play, *Les Liaisons Dangereuses,* which itself is an adaptation of the novel by Choderlos de Laclos. The British-born Frears surprised many critics with his all-American cast, including Swoosie Kurtz, Keanu Reeves, Mildred Natwick [147], and Uma Thurman [1633.5]. In this, he was following the lead of Milos Forman in *Amadeus,* whose American performers likewise offended critics who expect English accents from people in periwigs. Forman, ironically, was the loser in a competition to get a version of

Liaisons to the screen: His own film, *Valmont,* came out a year later and flopped at the box office. *Liaisons* had also been filmed in France in 1959 in a modern-dress version directed by Roger Vadim, released in the States as *Dangerous Liaisons 1960.* Of all these versions, Frears' is far and away the best, and the Oscars went to its strongest elements: the wicked dialogue and the faithful re-creation of the period in the sets and costumes. The film's opening, showing the elaborate process by which Malkovich is dressed, is reason enough to give Acheson an Oscar.

Frears' omission from the directing nominees was something of a surprise, for the film is a tribute to his ability to elicit striking performances from unconventional performers such as Malkovich, Kurtz, and Reeves. In his place, and that of Lawrence Kasdan, director of best picture nominee *The Accidental Tourist,* the Academy nominated Charles Crichton for *A Fish Called Wanda* and Martin Scorsese for *The Last Temptation of Christ.* The omission of Frears from the directing nominees signaled that the Academy wasn't taking the picture seriously as a contender for the best picture Oscar, which went to *Rain Man,* whose director, Barry Levinson, also won.

Close lost the fifth of her unsuccessful nominations to Jodie Foster for *The Accused.*

This was the first nomination for Pfeiffer, and the role—along with two other performances in the same year, in *Married to the Mob* and *Tequila Sunrise*—clearly established that she was more than just an uncommonly beautiful woman. A former supermarket clerk and self-described Southern California surfer girl, she had begun to act in movies in 1980, cast in such unpromising stuff as *Charlie Chan and the Curse of the Dragon Queen* (1981). Although her first major film, *Grease 2* (1982), was a disaster, it helped her get stronger parts, in such films as *Scarface* (1983), *Ladyhawke,* and *The Witches of Eastwick.* Experience and self-confidence, combined with extraordinary talent, have made her one of the foremost film actresses of our day. She lost to Geena Davis in *The Accidental Tourist.*

The scoring award went to Dave Grusin for *The Milagro Beanfield War.*

Craig: 382.5, 608, 745, 1331. Acheson: 1136. Close: 199, 653, 1418, 2314. Pfeiffer: 633, 1212.5. Fenton: 471, 671, 745.

486 • DANGEROUS MOVES

ARTHUR COHN PRODUCTION (SWITZERLAND). 1984.
AWARD *Foreign Language Film.*

A Soviet chess champion faces the former champion, who had defected from the Soviet Union, in a tournament held in Geneva. Behind-the-scenes political intrigue echoes the action on the chessboard in this film directed by Richard Dembo. It may be a treat for chess lovers and geopolitics junkies, but it's slow going for most of the rest of us. The cast includes Leslie Caron [1113 . . .] and Liv Ullmann [610 . . .].

487 • DARK ANGEL, THE

SAMUEL GOLDWYN PRODUCTIONS; UNITED ARTISTS. 1935.
AWARD *Interior Decoration:* Richard Day.
NOMINATIONS *Actress:* Merle Oberon. *Sound Recording:* Goldwyn Sound Department, Thomas T. Moulton.

Oberon and Fredric March [184 . . .] are engaged, but he goes off to fight in World War I, accompanied by friend Herbert Marshall. March is blinded and taken prisoner by the Germans, and when he returns to England, he discovers that he is presumed dead. Rather than have Oberon marry him out of pity, he changes his identity and starts a new life. (Has this ever happened in real life?) But eventually Oberon and Marshall, who have announced their engagement, discover he is still alive. March arranges a meeting with them in which he tries to pretend he's not blind, but—well, you can guess the rest. Endearingly goopy stuff, directed by Sidney Franklin [799 . . .] from a screenplay in which Lillian Hellman [1182 . . .] had a hand. It started out as a play by Guy Bolton and was a huge hit as a silent film in 1925 with Ronald Colman [311 . . .] and Vilma Banky.

This was the first Oscar for Day, one of the industry's pioneer art directors, who began his work in Hollywood in 1918 for Erich von Stroheim [1975], a perfectionist whose quest for realism formed Day's style. Day's most enduring collaboration was perhaps with producer Samuel Goldwyn [102 . . .], another exacting perfectionist.

Oberon tried to conceal her origins with stories that she was born in Tasmania and educated in India, but it's now generally known that she was born in Bombay, daughter of an Indian mother and an Irish father, who was killed in World War I. She rose from poverty by using her exotic beauty to attract well-to-do patrons. Eventually she attracted producer Alexander Korda, who set out to make her a star. She had appeared in minor British films, but her first role of any consequence was as Anne Boleyn in Korda's *The Private Life of Henry VIII.* After appearing in *The Scarlet Pimpernel* (1935), she went to Hollywood, where she heard Goldwyn was planning to remake *The Dark Angel,* a film she had loved as a child. Goldwyn signed Oberon to a contract with his company and launched her Hollywood career, which lasted into the fifties, with a few appearances in the sixties. She died in 1979. The Oscar went to Bette Davis for *Dangerous.*

The sound award went to Douglas Shearer for *Naughty Marietta.*

Day: 22, 102, 235, 510, 560, 569, 797, 833, 864, 952, 1048, 1175, 1397, 1477, 1666, 1949, 2056, 2120, 2276. Moulton: 22, 46, 138, 366, 457, 560, 706, 798, 962, 1153, 1200, 1451, 1510, 1607, 1849, 2154, 2294.

488 • DARK AT THE TOP OF THE STAIRS, THE

WARNER BROS. 1960.
NOMINATION *Supporting Actress:* Shirley Knight.

Family drama set in Oklahoma in the twenties, with Robert Preston [2201] as an out-of-work traveling salesman and Dorothy McGuire [759] as the wife who doesn't understand him. Yet another tale of small-town repression based on a play by William Inge, who gave us *Picnic* and *Splendor in the Grass.* Thin and predictably plotted, with slack direction by Delbert Mann [1283] that saps all the drama from its climaxes and revelations. What energy the film has comes from the fine performances by Knight as the shy daughter, Eve Arden [1319] as McGuire's bossy sister, Angela Lansbury [749 . . .] as the gentle and understanding beautician who carries a torch for Preston, and particularly Preston, who grabs hold of his flimsy role and pumps life into it.

Knight received her first nomination in her second year in movies, while still in her early twenties. Her beauty and skill as an actress were oddly unappreciated in Hollywood, and after good roles failed to materialize, she turned primarily to stage and TV work. The Oscar went to Shirley Jones for *Elmer Gantry*.

Knight: 1985.

489 • DARK COMMAND

REPUBLIC. 1940.

NOMINATIONS *Black-and-White Interior Decoration:* John Victor Mackay. *Original Score:* Victor Young.

Walter Pidgeon [1232 . . .] as Quantrill squares off against lawman John Wayne [33 . . .] in this saga of 1860s Kansas. "Poverty row" studio Republic put a lot of money (for it) into this lively western with a strong director, Raoul Walsh, and better-than-average stars such as Pidgeon, Wayne, and Claire Trevor [510 . . .], though it also enlisted its contract regulars Roy Rogers and Gabby Hayes. The movie owes its nominations, however, to liberalized Academy rules that allowed individual studios to submit nominees in certain categories. The Oscars went to *Pride and Prejudice* for art direction and *Pinocchio* for score.

Mackay: 1257, 1269. Young: 97, 98, 100, 101, 280, 612, 693, 701, 794, 846, 925, 1214, 1257, 1396, 1452, 1748, 1823, 1994, 2235, 2315.

490 • DARK EYES

EXCELSIOR TV & RAI UNO PRODUCTION; ISLAND PICTURES (ITALY). 1987.

NOMINATION *Actor:* Marcello Mastroianni.

Mastroianni plays an aging womanizer who recalls an affair of his youth with a Russian woman at a health spa. Largely a showcase for its star's talent, based on several stories by Chekhov and directed by Nikita Mikhalkov, with Silvana Mangano and Marthe Keller. Mastroianni won the best actor prize at Cannes and his third Oscar nomination: He was nominated once

in the sixties, once in the seventies, and once in the eighties. This time he lost to Michael Douglas in *Wall Street*.

Mastroianni: 554, 1888.

491 • DARK MIRROR, THE

UNIVERSAL-INTERNATIONAL. 1946.

NOMINATION *Original Story:* Vladimir Pozner.

Olivia de Havilland [798 . . .] plays twins—one good, one evil—who pretend to be one person, putting the good twin in jeopardy when the evil one commits murder. Corny but effective pseudo-psychological melodrama, directed by Robert Siodmak [1085], from a screenplay by Nunnally Johnson [815 . . .] based on Pozner's story. With Lew Ayres [1052] as the psychologist who helps police lieutenant Thomas Mitchell [962 . . .] figure out what's going on. The Oscar went to Clemence Dane for *Vacation From Marriage*.

492 • DARK VICTORY

WARNER BROS.-FIRST NATIONAL. 1939.

NOMINATIONS *Picture:* David Lewis, producer. *Actress:* Bette Davis. *Original Score:* Max Steiner.

Snotty little rich girl Davis discovers she has a brain tumor and tries to party herself to death before she falls in love with her doctor, George Brent, and learns to accept death nobly. Wonderfully silly, sentimental melodrama with, thanks to Davis, a genuinely affecting ending and a handful of classic moments scattered throughout. Like *Now, Voyager,* it's one of the movies Davis turned from dross into gold almost single-handedly. Writer Casey Robinson persuaded Warners production head Hal Wallis [17 . . .] to buy the play on which it's based, which had been a flop with Tallulah Bankhead. Robinson was convinced he knew how to make it work on screen, which he did largely by adding Davis' self-destructive fling. Edmund Goulding directs a cast that includes Humphrey Bogart [24 . . .] as an Irish stable groom, complete with a fairly laughable brogue, Ronald Reagan as an effete, alcoholic playboy, and Geraldine Fitzgerald [2316] as Davis' understanding confidante. Remade in 1963 as *Stolen Hours* with Susan Hayward and for TV in 1976 with Elizabeth Montgomery—see them if you don't believe this movie needs Davis' nervous intensity to make it work.

Davis lost the Oscar to Vivien Leigh for *Gone With the Wind,* which of course took best picture as well. The scoring Oscar went to Herbert Stothart for *The Wizard of Oz.*

Lewis: 55. Davis: 46, 484, 1046, 1162, 1182, 1369, 1456, 1462.5, 1908, 2248. Steiner: 16, 154, 190, 330, 365, 385, 679, 747, 754, 798, 999, 1043, 1046, 1052, 1162, 1169, 1170, 1207, 1325, 1408, 1430, 1456, 1690, 1779, 1828.

493 • DARLING

ANGLO-AMALGAMATED LTD. PRODUCTION; EMBASSY PICTURES CORPORATION (UNITED KINGDOM). 1965.
AWARDS *Actress:* Julie Christie. *Story and Screenplay— Written Directly for the Screen:* Frederic Raphael. *Black-and-White Costume Design:* Julie Harris.
NOMINATIONS *Picture:* Joseph Janni, producer. *Director:* John Schlesinger.

Christie plays a swinging London model, who has an affair with a married man (Dirk Bogarde), ditches him for Laurence Harvey [1724], who gets her a movie role, and finally winds up the bored wife of an Italian nobleman. Now that casual sex, abortion, and homosexuality have lost their power to shock, *Darling* looks less like the sharp satire many critics thought it was, and more like a hollow little morality play spiced up with naughtiness. It has some points to make about the cult of celebrity and the emptiness of what constitutes success in the later twentieth century, but otherwise looks as dated as flapper movies of the twenties like *It* or *Our Dancing Daughters.*

Christie, however, gives the film what life it retains. She was a member of the Royal Shakespeare Company before her break into films, Schlesinger's *Billy Liar,* in 1963. In addition to *Darling,* she played Lara in *Doctor Zhivago,* another 1965 best picture nominee. In the seventies she began a relationship with Warren Beatty, with whom she costarred in *Mc-Cabe and Mrs. Miller, Shampoo,* and *Heaven Can Wait.* Her career faded, however, in the eighties, and the dearth of roles for mature women has limited her choices.

Raphael is a successful novelist as well as screenwriter. He dramatized his career, and his experiences with *Darling,* in a British TV miniseries, *The Glittering Prizes.*

By dressing Christie in miniskirts, costumer Harris —a British production designer, not the American actress—helped the fashion, originally introduced by designer Mary Quant, cross the ocean.

In addition to *Doctor Zhivago, Darling* competed in the best picture race against *Ship of Fools, A Thousand Clowns,* and the winner, *The Sound of Music,* whose director, Robert Wise, also won.

Christie: 1293. Raphael: 2160. Schlesinger: 1312, 1966.

494 • DARLING LILI

GEOFFREY PRODUCTIONS; PARAMOUNT. 1970.
NOMINATIONS *Song:* "Whistling Away the Dark," music by Henry Mancini, lyrics by Johnny Mercer. *Original Song Score:* Henry Mancini and Johnny Mercer. *Costume Design:* Donald Brooks and Jack Bear.

Julie Andrews [1284 . . .] is a spy for the Germans during World War I, and Rock Hudson [768] is the flying ace whose secrets she is out to get. Love, of course, transforms this improbable Mata Hari who, we discover, is being blackmailed into performing her nefarious duties. Flimsy stuff that was one of Andrews' many unsuccessful attempts to break out of the nursemaid mode of *Mary Poppins* and *The Sound of Music,* the films that had made her a star. It has pretty sets, nice music, and some good flying sequences, but the script and pacing—by writer-director Blake Edwards [2201]—are fairly leaden, and there's no chemistry between Andrews and Hudson. They just sort of twinkle at each other.

The song award went to "For All We Know," from *Lovers and Other Strangers.* The Beatles won for their song score for *Let It Be.* The costume Oscar went to Vittorio Nino Novarese for *Cromwell.*

Mancini: 122, 278, 384, 508, 512, 776, 825, 1573, 1574, 1864, 1970, 2011, 2037, 2201. Mercer: 248, 278, 384, 476, 508, 636, 788, 825, 877, 903,

905, 1109, 1772, 1838, 1912, 2327, 2328. Brooks: 356, 1907.

DAS BOOT
See 258.

494.5 • DAVE
WARNER BROS. PRODUCTION; WARNER BROS. 1993.
NOMINATION *Screenplay Written Directly for the Screen:* Gary Ross.

Kevin Kline [670] plays Dave Kovic, a guy who's so kindhearted he can barely make a go of his employment agency business, so he supports himself by doing look-alike appearances as the president of the United States, one Bill Mitchell (also played, of course, by Kline), who is as nasty as Dave is nice. The president's Haldemanian chief of staff, played by Frank Langella, gets the idea of using Dave as a stand-in for public appearances, which works fine until the president has a stroke while atop a woman not his wife. Eager to hold on to power, which he knows he'll lose if the kinder, gentler vice president, played by Ben Kingsley [308 . . .], succeeds to the office, Langella concocts a plan in which Dave will continue his masquerade full-time while Langella runs the country. Of course, this also involves trying to deceive the first lady, played by Sigourney Weaver [45 . . .], who hates her husband and has stayed with him only for appearance's sake. Played for charm rather than satire, this very agreeable comedy, essentially *The Prisoner of Zenda Goes to Washington,* runs down toward the end, when there's a little too much self-conscious evocation of Frank Capra, but it's kept aloft most of the time by the fine performances of Kline, Langella, Kingsley, and Weaver, plus Charles Grodin as Dave's accountant friend who figures out how to balance the budget while not cutting social programs, and Ving Rhames as a wary Secret Service man. Directed by Ivan Reitman. The Oscar went to Jane Campion for *The Piano.*

Ross: 195.

495 • DAVID AND BATHSHEBA
20TH CENTURY-FOX. 1951.
NOMINATIONS *Story and Screenplay:* Philip Dunne. *Color Cinematography:* Leon Shamroy. *Color Art Direction—Set Decoration:* Lyle Wheeler and George Davis; Thomas Little and Paul S. Fox. *Scoring of a Dramatic or Comedy Picture:* Alfred Newman. *Color Costume Design:* Charles LeMaire and Edward Stevenson.

Gregory Peck [759 . . .] is King David and Susan Hayward [973 . . .] Bathsheba in this biblical blockbuster directed by Henry King [1868 . . .]. It's nice to look at, and fun to spot Jayne Meadows being witchy as Michal, Francis X. Bushman being patriarchal as King Saul, and Gwen (billed as Gwyneth) Verdon being sinuous as a dancing girl. But it's just a little too dignified. Dunne was proud of his high-toned script, avoiding all those hoary old DeMille clichés, but he overlooks one thing: Without those hoary old DeMille clichés you've got little more than a soap opera in sandals.

After two decades as a screenwriter, Dunne moved into producing and directing in the mid-fifties, though without great distinction. A lifelong liberal Democrat, he also worked as a speechwriter for John F. Kennedy during the 1960 presidential campaign. The writing Oscar went to Alan Jay Lerner for *An American in Paris,* which also won for Alfred Gilks and John Alton's cinematography and for art direction and costume design. The scoring award went to Franz Waxman for *A Place in the Sun.*

Dunne: 952. Shamroy: 29, 226, 356, 413, 569, 602, 1088, 1153, 1213, 1592, 1610, 1706, 1852, 1883, 2013, 2286, 2334. Wheeler: 19, 46, 83, 356, 376, 428, 476, 530, 542, 719, 721, 798, 950, 1062, 1088, 1149, 1153, 1213, 1391, 1475, 1601, 1616, 1670, 1706, 1852, 2008, 2093, 2212. Davis: 46, 69, 401, 542, 736, 953, 1213, 1335, 1388, 1537, 1552, 1706, 1814, 2157, 2184, 2312. Little: 46, 83, 235, 428, 719, 721, 746, 950, 952, 1082, 1149, 1153, 1397, 1475, 1666, 1852, 1868, 2056, 2212, 2286. Fox: 376, 413, 428, 476, 530, 721, 950, 1088, 1601, 1666, 1706, 1852. Newman: 31, 34, 46, 72, 138, 182, 226, 333, 334, 347, 375, 428, 437, 457, 476, 542, 690, 797, 833, 952, 953, 959, 962, 1016,

1082, 1088, 1213, 1278, 1362, 1397, 1475, 1616, 1655, 1849, 1868, 1883, 1921, 2043, 2046, 2091, 2258, 2286, 2294, 2316. LeMaire: 21, 46, 376, 530, 542, 954, 1213, 1338, 1391, 1601, 1706, 2008, 2043, 2205, 2294. Stevenson: 636, 1374.

496 • DAVID AND LISA

HELLER-PERRY PRODUCTIONS; CONTINENTAL DISTRIBUTING INC. 1962.

NOMINATIONS *Director:* Frank Perry. *Screenplay—Based on Material From Another Medium:* Eleanor Perry.

Keir Dullea and Janet Margolin play the title roles, a boy who hates to be touched and a girl who speaks —and insists on being spoken to—only in rhymes. Howard Da Silva is the psychiatrist who helps the two when they are institutionalized. Based on a case history fictionalized in a book by Theodore Isaac Rubin, the film isn't as heavy-handed as some in placing blame for the young patients' condition, though as usual the implication is that the parents are at fault— at least in the case of David, who has the stereotypical dominating mother (Neva Patterson doing one of her witches) and ineffectual father (Richard McMurray). Margolin is particularly good at Lisa's swings from extremely annoying to charming, and the stunned gaze of Dullea's blank blue eyes provides a creepy intensity that would serve him well later as the haunted astronaut of *2001: A Space Odyssey.* The movie is a bit too melancholic, a tone made oppressive at times by Mark Lawrence's overstated score. A low-budget, independently made feature, it was a surprise box-office success.

The Perrys, husband and wife, had worked together in TV before making their debut with *David and Lisa.* They collaborated on such films as *The Swimmer* (1968), *Last Summer,* and *Diary of a Mad Housewife,* then went their separate ways in 1970. Eleanor Perry died in 1981. Frank Perry has continued to direct, though with little commercial success; his most notorious later film is the 1981 biopic about Joan Crawford, *Mommie Dearest.* The directing Oscar went to David Lean for *Lawrence of Arabia,* the writing award to Horton Foote for *To Kill a Mockingbird.*

497 • DAVID COPPERFIELD

MGM. 1935.

NOMINATIONS *Picture:* David O. Selznick, producer. *Assistant Director:* Joseph Newman. *Film Editing:* Robert J. Kern.

Freddie Bartholomew is young David and Frank Lawton grown-up David in this adaptation of the Charles Dickens classic. Magnificently, flawlessly cast: W. C. Fields as Mr. Micawber, Lionel Barrymore [723 . . .] as Mr. Peggotty, Maureen O'Sullivan as Dora, Edna May Oliver [581] as Aunt Betsy Trotwood, Roland Young [2117] as Uriah Heep, Basil Rathbone [979 . . .] as Mr. Murdstone, and scores of others, who make the original "Phiz" illustrations for the book come to life. George Cukor [262 . . .] directs from a screenplay by Hugh Walpole and Howard Estabrook [400 . . .]. One of the most successful of all Hollywood attempts to translate a great novel to the screen, and a delight from beginning to end.

The novel was a favorite of producer Selznick, who had to overcome studio resistance to so literary a project, though he had an advantage in that his father-in-law, Louis B. Mayer, ran the studio. Even then, Mayer wanted Selznick to cast Jackie Cooper [1836] in the title role to guarantee box-office success. Selznick insisted on the need for an English boy and discovered Bartholomew, who became a leading player for MGM in the later thirties. Fields was Selznick's second choice for Micawber: Charles Laughton [1387 . . .] was cast in the role, and Laughton's wife, Elsa Lanchester [428 . . .], was given the small part of the Micawber family maid. But Laughton brought no warmth to the role—he seemed more molester than mentor in his scenes with Bartholomew —and was quickly replaced, although Lanchester remained. Fields' performance is definitive—it is virtually impossible to read the novel without hearing his drawling delivery—and might have earned him an Oscar nomination if the supporting actor category (introduced in 1936) had existed. Selznick lost the Oscar to another MGM production, *Mutiny on the Bounty,* but his success in bringing Dickens to the screen made Margaret Mitchell feel that he might do her novel *Gone With the Wind* justice in the filming.

Assistant director Newman lost to Clem Beauchamp and Paul Wing's work on *Lives of a Bengal Lancer;* he came in third after write-in candidate Sherry Sourds for *A Midsummer Night's Dream.* The editing award went to Ralph Dawson for *A Midsummer Night's Dream.*

Selznick: 798, 1670, 1828, 1890, 1909, 1996, 2211. Newman: 1751. Kern: 1417.

498 • DAWN PATROL, THE

First National. 1930–31.
Award *Original Story:* John Monk Saunders.

Richard Barthelmess [1447 . . .] and Douglas Fairbanks, Jr., play World War I flying aces in the original "you can't send a kid up in a crate like that" movie. Primitive in technique, but it will be interesting to admirers of director Howard Hawks [1779], who was a World War I pilot himself. He's just beginning to get the hang of talkies here. The 1938 remake with Errol Flynn, Basil Rathbone [979 . . .], and David Niven [1778] is more polished technically, but it uses some of the same aerial footage.

Saunders also served in the Army Air Corps in the war and wrote the story for the first Oscar winner for best picture, *Wings.* He died in 1940.

499 • DAWNS HERE ARE QUIET, THE

Gorky Film Studios Production (USSR). 1972.
Nomination *Foreign Language Film.*

The story of a Soviet women's unit at the front during World War II, directed by Stanislav Rostotsky. Not widely released in the United States. The Oscar went to *The Discreet Charm of the Bourgeoisie.*

500 • DAY AT THE RACES, A

MGM. 1937.
Nomination *Dance Direction:* Dave Gould.

Groucho Marx is Dr. Hugo Z. Hackenbush, and the imperturbable Margaret Dumont is his wealthy sanitarium patient—she doesn't know he's really a veterinarian. Harpo and Chico, plus boring tenor Allan Jones and pretty Maureen O'Sullivan are there,

too. It's the only one of the classic Marx Brothers movies to get any sort of attention from the Academy, which *Duck Soup* (1933) and *A Night at the Opera* (1935) also deserved, and it was the wrong sort of attention: It's the sublime madness one remembers, not the interminable musical numbers. Eventually the Academy did the right thing and gave Groucho an honorary award ("in recognition of his brilliant creativity and for the unequalled achievements of the Marx Brothers in the art of motion picture comedy") at the 1972 ceremonies. The screenplay is by Robert Pirosh [157 . . .], George Seaton [31 . . .], and George Oppenheimer [2227]. Directed by Sam Wood [701 . . .].

Gould's nomination was for the "All God's Chillun Got Rhythm" number, in which a very young Dorothy Dandridge [361] may be glimpsed among the dancers. The award went to Hermes Pan for *A Damsel in Distress.*

Gould: 261, 297, 695.

501 • DAY FOR NIGHT

Les Films du Carrosse-P.E.C.F. (Paris)-P.I.C. (Rome) Production; Warner Bros. (France). 1974.
Award *Foreign Language Film (1973).*
Nominations *Supporting Actress:* Valentina Cortese. *Director:* François Truffaut. *Original Screenplay:* François Truffaut, Jean-Louis Richard, and Suzanne Schiffman.

Truffaut himself plays the director of a trivial movie, *Meet Pamela,* whose cast goes through as much off-camera intrigue as on-screen melodrama. It's all about the difficulties and the joys of making movies. For those of us who find that topic endlessly fascinating, it's a treat. Others may wish they were watching *Meet Pamela* instead. The cast includes Jacqueline Bisset, Jean-Pierre Léaud, and Jean-Pierre Aumont. The novelist and former film critic Graham Greene [639] has a bit part as an insurance salesman. Although *Day for Night* won the foreign language film Oscar for 1973, it did not meet the eligibility requirements for the other categories until the following year. The title, incidentally, alludes to the technique of shooting night scenes during daylight by underexposing the film.

Cortese, who plays an alcoholic actress whose career is on the skids, had begun acting in films in her native Italy but in the late forties and early fifties spent some time in Hollywood, where her name was spelled Cortesa. She appeared in *The Barefoot Contessa,* among other films. The Oscar went to Ingrid Bergman for *Murder on the Orient Express,* but during her acceptance speech, Bergman, who had worked with Cortese on the 1964 film *The Visit,* apologized to Cortese for winning.

The directing Oscar went to Francis Ford Coppola for *The Godfather, Part II.* Robert Towne won for his screenplay for *Chinatown.*

Truffaut: 716.

502 • DAY OF THE DOLPHIN, THE

ICARUS PRODUCTIONS; AVCO EMBASSY. 1973.

NOMINATIONS *Sound:* Richard Portman and Lawrence O. Jost. *Original Dramatic Score:* Georges Delerue.

George C. Scott [73 . . .] plays a dolphin trainer who teaches two of the animals to talk. But the dolphins are kidnaped and used in a plot to assassinate the president. This dumb, misguided movie is based on a best-seller by Robert Merle that fell into the wrong hands: director Mike Nichols [810 . . .] and screenwriter Buck Henry [810 . . .]. The sensibilities that created *The Graduate* are all wrong for this material—they can't have any fun with the thriller plot or the science fiction, but insist on turning out a "message picture" about how awful human beings are. The film ranges from cutesy (the baby-talking dolphin voices are supplied by Henry himself) to sour. The sound award was won by *The Exorcist.* The scoring Oscar went to Marvin Hamlisch for *The Way We Were.*

Portman: 339, 418, 521, 738, 784, 1109, 1473, 1526, 1701, 2331. Jost: 395, 1525. Delerue: 28, 85, 1066, 1187.

503 • DAY OF THE JACKAL, THE

WARWICK FILM PRODUCTIONS LTD.-UNIVERSAL PRODUCTIONS FRANCE S.A.; UNIVERSAL (UNITED KINGDOM/FRANCE). 1973.

NOMINATION *Film Editing:* Ralph Kemplen.

Edward Fox is the Jackal, a hired killer out to assassinate Charles de Gaulle. The British and French police know of the plot, but their internal conflicts, and the Jackal's intelligence, thwart them at nearly every turn. Smart, well-crafted thriller, based on a Frederick Forsyth novel, crisply directed by Fred Zinnemann [732 . . .]. The absence of big stars limited its box-office appeal—it plays somewhat like a well-made TV movie—but added to verisimilitude. There are, however, many familiar faces in the cast, including Cyril Cusack, Eric Porter, Delphine Seyrig, and Derek Jacobi. The editing Oscar went to William Reynolds for *The Sting.*

Kemplen: 1363, 1471.

504 • DAY OF THE LOCUST, THE

JEROME HELLMAN PRODUCTION; PARAMOUNT. 1975.

NOMINATIONS *Supporting Actor:* Burgess Meredith. *Cinematography:* Conrad Hall.

A nightmare vision of Hollywood in the thirties, as seen through the eyes of an art director, played by William Atherton, who encounters a variety of drifters and dreamers: would-be star Karen Black [672], her ex-vaudevillian father (Meredith), an inarticulate nobody (Donald Sutherland) obsessed with Black, and a sinister dwarf (Billy Barty). The climax is a riot at a movie premiere. A surrealist satire—the kind of thing Hollywood almost never does well—based on the novel by Nathanael West that is often cited as one of the key works of fiction about the movie industry. Unfortunately the film is a rather overheated and hysterical mess, though it has some fervent admirers. If you like *Barton Fink,* you'll find much to like here, too —and vice versa. The screenplay is by Waldo Salt [430 . . .], and the director is John · Schlesinger [493 . . .].

Meredith had a distinguished stage career, starting in 1929, and after an acclaimed performance in the play *Winterset,* he went to Hollywood for the film version in 1936. His career in movies of the thirties and forties, apart from a notable performance as George in *Of Mice and Men,* was unimpressive. In the sixties he returned to movies as a character actor, but he was probably best known for playing the Penguin on the sixties TV show *Batman*. He lost his first Oscar bid to George Burns in *The Sunshine Boys*.

Hall contributed greatly to what even those who dislike *Day of the Locust* will agree is strongest about it: the look of the film. Hall and Schlesinger agreed that it needed a rich, romantic aura to contrast with the sordid and depressing aspects of the story. "I thought that this was a story that involved everything that was golden, not only the times but the money, the sunsets, the era and the idea of the moth drawn to the flame," Hall commented. So golden tones predominate throughout the film. The Oscar went to John Alcott for *Barry Lyndon*.

Meredith: 1712. Hall: 317, 987, 1355, 1627, 1771.5, 2017.

505 • DAYS OF GLORY

RKO RADIO. 1944.
NOMINATION *Special Effects:* Vernon L. Walker, photographic; James G. Stewart and Roy Granville, sound.

Russians Tamara Toumanova and Gregory Peck [759 . . .] fight the Nazis in this mediocre wartime propaganda attempt to stir American sympathies for their Soviet allies. Directed by Jacques Tourneur from a screenplay by Casey Robinson, who was married to Toumanova, a Russian ballerina who had a brief, unspectacular film career. *Days of Glory* is chiefly remembered as the film in which Peck made his debut. The special effects award went to *Thirty Seconds Over Tokyo*.

Walker: 253, 1421, 1991. Stewart: 253, 1421, 1595. Granville: 253.

506 • DAYS OF HEAVEN

OP PRODUCTION; PARAMOUNT. 1978.
AWARD *Cinematography:* Nestor Almendros.
NOMINATIONS *Sound:* John K. Wilkinson, Robert W. Glass, Jr., John T. Reitz, and Barry Thomas. *Original Score:* Ennio Morricone. *Costume Design:* Patricia Norris.

Three early-twentieth-century drifters—Richard Gere, his sister, Linda Manz, and his lover (posing as his sister), Brooke Adams—go West in search of work, which they find in the fields owned by Sam Shepard [1698]. When Shepard falls in love with Ad-

ams, Gere encourages her to marry him because Shepard is said to be dying, and she will inherit his money. Writer-director Terrence Malick's film captivated the critics with the extraordinary beauty of its images and the elegiac tone of its narrative, though it now seems a little precious and arty. With two critical successes to his credit—the other one the 1974 film *Badlands*—Malick decided to quit filmmaking while he was ahead, saying he found that the burdens of dealing with Hollywood outweighed the pleasure of making movies.

Cuban-born Almendros worked on several propaganda films during the early Castro era, but left for France, where he won acclaim for his work on the films of Eric Rohmer [1402] and François Truffaut [501 . . .]. To achieve the look of *Days of Heaven*, many scenes were shot at "the magic hour"—about twenty minutes after sunset. Almendros died in 1992.

The sound award went to *The Deer Hunter*. Giorgio Moroder's score for *Midnight Express* took the music award, and Anthony Powell won for his costumes for *Death on the Nile*.

Almendros: 243, 1111, 1876. Wilkinson: 1513, 1584. Glass: 1513. Morricone: 308, 1331, 2185. Norris: 608, 1974, 2165, 2201.

507 • DAYS OF THUNDER

DON SIMPSON/JERRY BRUCKHEIMER PRODUCTION; PARAMOUNT. 1990.
NOMINATION *Sound:* Donald O. Mitchell, Rick Kline, Kevin O'Connell, and Charles Wilborn.

Cocky young race driver Tom Cruise [260] tries to prove he's the baddest dude on the track. After a life-threatening crash, he fights back with the aid of neurosurgeon Nicole Kidman and old pro Robert Duvall [92 . . .]. Formulaic moviemaking at its emptiest, reteaming the star and director (Tony Scott) of the 1986 hit *Top Gun*. The script, by Cruise and Robert Towne [395 . . .], is full of clichés minted in the thirties, and the noise level is set for metal-heads. Considering that they married after costarring here, Cruise and Kidman have remarkably little chemistry together, though that may be the fault of the script, which is just repeating the Cruise–Kelly McGillis re-

lationship from *Top Gun*. Some good performers—
Duvall, Randy Quaid [1135], Michael Rooker, Fred
Dalton Thompson—are wasted. It has to be noted
that audiences were indifferent to the movie, too,
another sign that the eighties recycling process that
gave us three *Rambo*s, five *Rocky*s, and countless sci-fi
movies about cute, friendly aliens had run its course.
The sound award went to *Dances With Wolves*.

Mitchell: 223, 398, 413.5, 734.5, 779, 1525,
1650, 1824, 1825, 2020, 2114, 2176.5. Kline:
658.5, 1333, 1825, 2020, 2114. O'Connell: 223,
586, 658.5, 1825, 2020, 2114.

508 • *DAYS OF WINE AND ROSES*

MARTIN MANULIS-JALEM PRODUCTION; WARNER BROS. 1962.
AWARD *Song:* "Days of Wine and Roses," music by
Henry Mancini, lyrics by Johnny Mercer.
NOMINATIONS *Actor:* Jack Lemmon. *Actress:* Lee Rem-
ick. *Black-and-White Art Direction–Set Decoration:* Jo-
seph Wright; George James Hopkins. *Black-and-White
Costume Design:* Don Feld.

Alcoholic Lemmon marries Remick, who follows
him into alcoholism. A steadily darkening story of
what we now call codependency, with strong performances from the leads and cast members Charles
Bickford [651 . . .], Jack Klugman, and Jack Albertson [1954], among others, well directed by Blake
Edwards [2201] from a screenplay adapted by J. P.
Miller from his *Playhouse 90* TV script. The TV version starred Cliff Robertson [387] and Piper Laurie
[364 . . .]. Losing the film role to Lemmon made
Robertson secure the rights to another TV drama in
which he appeared, the original version of *Charly,* for
which Robertson won the Oscar. Warners had little
confidence in *Days* and gave it only a perfunctory
opening release, but it developed a word-of-mouth
following. Not a lot of fun, but it's certainly interesting as an example of Edwards' work before he turned
his attention to the *Pink Panther* series and other high-
gloss entertainments.

The Mancini-Mercer song is not one of their more
distinguished creations, but it was a weak year for
song nominations. Every nominated song was the title
theme of a serious, nonmusical film: *Mutiny on the
Bounty, Two for the Seesaw, Tender Is the Night,* and *Walk
on the Wild Side.*

This was the fourth nomination for Lemmon—
who had won a supporting actor Oscar for *Mister
Roberts*—and his first for a serious dramatic role.
While he was typed as a light leading man and comic,
and such roles would continue to dominate his career
for the next decade, he would begin to move into
serious parts in the seventies. He lost to Gregory
Peck in *To Kill a Mockingbird.*

Remick's skills as an actress were sadly underused
by Hollywood, and she never became the major dramatic star that she might have been. She had made her
movie debut in a sexpot role, the teenage temptress
in the 1957 *A Face in the Crowd,* and the part would
type her for several more films, including *The Long
Hot Summer* (1958) and *Anatomy of a Murder.* Failing to
get substantial film roles after her nomination—she
lost to Anne Bancroft in *The Miracle Worker*—Remick
devoted as much time to TV and stage work as to
films. After marrying an English assistant director in
1970, she spent much of her later career in England.
She died of cancer in 1991, aged fifty-six.

The art direction award went to *To Kill a Mockingbird* and the costuming Oscar to Norma Koch for
What Ever Happened to Baby Jane?

Mancini: 122, 278, 384, 494, 512, 776, 825,
1573, 1574, 1864, 1970, 2011, 2037, 2201. Mercer:
248, 278, 384, 476, 494, 636, 788, 825, 877, 903,
905, 1109, 1772, 1838, 1912, 2327, 2328. Lemmon: 91, 394, 1330, 1337, 1761, 1860, 2140.
Wright: 235, 428, 569, 690, 746, 852, 1175, 1264,
1397, 1475, 2056. Hopkins: 110, 896, 1003, 1170,
1332, 1385, 1393, 1910, 1949, 1973, 2058, 2277.
Feld: 1625, 2047, 2107.

509 • *DEAD, THE*

LIFFEY FILMS PRODUCTION; VESTRON. 1987.
NOMINATIONS *Screenplay Based on Material From Another
Medium:* Tony Huston. *Costume Design:* Dorothy
Jeakins.

Donal McCann and his wife, Anjelica Huston
[617 . . .], go to a Christmas dinner party in turn-
of-the-century Dublin. As the party is breaking up, he

catches her lost in melancholy as she listens to an old song that reminds her of an old love, and he realizes how little they share of their inner lives. Superlative realization of a virtually unfilmable text, a short story by James Joyce that depends on the texture of its language and literary imagery for its evocation of the inner life of its characters. This is the last triumph of a great filmmaker, director John Huston [24 . . .], who died in the year of its release. Without tricks or technical fireworks, Huston lets the events of the story unfold, relying on a superb company of mostly Irish actors, some unfamiliar, some—such as Donal Donnelly and Dan O'Herlihy [18]—better known. The result is simple, poignant, perhaps uncinematic, but for those who yield themselves to it, deeply moving. Of course, some of the poignancy of the film comes from one's knowledge that it was Huston's last, and that his children, Anjelica, Tony, and, as the director's assistant, Danny Huston, were intimately involved in the making of the movie.

Tony Huston's screenplay lost to Bernardo Bertolucci's for *The Last Emperor,* which also won for James Acheson's costumes.

Jeakins: 393, 832, 882, 1048, 1385, 1391, 1432, 1748, 1881, 2012, 2238.

510 • DEAD END
SAMUEL GOLDWYN PRODUCTIONS; UNITED ARTISTS. 1937.
NOMINATIONS *Picture:* Samuel Goldwyn, with Merritt Hulburd, producers. *Supporting Actress:* Claire Trevor. *Cinematography:* Gregg Toland. *Interior Decoration:* Richard Day.

A slum on a dead-end street by the East River, next to an opulent apartment complex, is home to a variety of people: an aspiring but unemployed architect, Joel McCrea; a working woman who hopes to earn enough to move to a better neighborhood, Sylvia Sidney [1962]; a gangster named Baby Face Martin, Humphrey Bogart [24 . . .]; the gangster's moll, Trevor; and a bunch of street kids, Billy Halop, Leo Gorcey, Bernard Punsley, Huntz Hall, Bobby Jordan, and Gabriel Dell. The Dead End Kids, most of whom went on to become the Bowery Boys in endless B pictures of the forties, were the only members of the original cast of the play by Sidney Kingsley to repeat their Broadway roles on film. William Wyler [175 . . .] directs, and the screenplay is by Lillian Hellman [1182 . . .]. Though bowdlerized (in the play the character played by Trevor has a venereal disease; here she just looks a little under the weather) and sanitized (Day's realistic set was strewn with garbage, like a real New York street, before Goldwyn insisted that it be cleaned up), the movie still has intensity and power. Bogart was third choice for his role. James Cagney [79 . . .] lost the part because he was involved in a legal dispute with Warners and Goldwyn was nervous about intervening, and George Raft found the role too unpleasant. Bogart built his career on roles that Raft rejected. Later he would be cast in *The Maltese Falcon* after Raft decided not to work with a novice director, John Huston. One of the film's best scenes involves Bogart and his mother, Marjorie Main [601], in one of the few roles that gave her a chance to show that she was a fine, serious actress. The best picture Oscar went to *The Life of Emile Zola.*

Dead End gave Trevor a chance to break out of the B pictures in which she had been cast since coming to Hollywood in 1933. She lost to Alice Brady in *In Old Chicago.*

Toland lost to Karl Freund's work on *The Good Earth.* The art direction Oscar went to Stephen Goosson for *Lost Horizon.*

Goldwyn: 102, 184, 214, 560, 1182, 1607, 2316. Hulburd: 560. Trevor: 911, 1081. Toland: 407, 1006, 1200, 1327, 2316. Day: 22, 102, 235, 487, 560, 569, 797, 833, 864, 952, 1048, 1175, 1397, 1477, 1666, 1949, 2056, 2120, 2276.

511 • DEAD POETS SOCIETY
TOUCHSTONE PICTURES PRODUCTION IN ASSOCIATION WITH SILVER SCREEN PARTNERS IV; BUENA VISTA. 1989.
AWARD *Screenplay Written Directly for the Screen:* Tom Schulman.
NOMINATIONS *Picture:* Steven Haft, Paul Junger Witt, and Tony Thomas, producers. *Actor:* Robin Williams. *Director:* Peter Weir.

Williams, a new teacher at a stodgy New England prep school in the fifties, inspires his young students with his enthusiasm for poetry and life. Unfortunately one of the students, played by Robert Sean Leonard, wants to be an actor, defying his hard-nosed father, and when the father discovers he's appearing in a school play, there are disastrous consequences. The film gave Williams a chance to play something other than a manic wisecracker, but apart from his performance and a nice evocation of period and place, it's somewhat too contrived and melodramatic in its outcome. It was an unexpected box-office hit, however. The cast includes Ethan Hawke, Josh Charles, and Norman Lloyd.

Schulman was an unknown writer who beat the odds by selling his screenplay to Disney, seeing it produced and winning an Oscar over formidable competition: Woody Allen for *Crimes and Misdemeanors,* Spike Lee for *Do the Right Thing,* Steven Soderbergh for *sex, lies, and videotape,* and Nora Ephron for *When Harry Met Sally.* . . . He modeled Williams' character on both his own father, who had a great love of poetry, and a high school English teacher.

The best picture Oscar went to *Driving Miss Daisy.* The other contenders were *Born on the Fourth of July, Field of Dreams,* and *My Left Foot.*

Alec Baldwin and Liam Neeson [1764.65] were first considered for the lead, and Dustin Hoffman [810 . . .] would have played it if the right deal could have been struck. Williams, who had experienced a string of flops, was eager for the part, which he believed could change his screen image. He was the least likely contender for best actor in a field that included Kenneth Branagh for *Henry V,* Tom Cruise for *Born on the Fourth of July,* Morgan Freeman for *Driving Miss Daisy,* and the winner, Daniel Day-Lewis for *My Left Foot.*

Weir lost to Oliver Stone for *Born on the Fourth of July.*

Williams: 671, 800. Weir: 834, 2296.

512 • DEAR HEART

W.B.-THE OUT-OF-TOWNERS COMPANY PRODUCTION; WARNER BROS. 1964.
NOMINATION *Song:* "Dear Heart," music by Henry Mancini, lyrics by Jay Livingston and Ray Evans.

Middle-aged conventioneers Glenn Ford and Geraldine Page [935 . . .] meet and fall in love. Pleasant heart-tugger about ordinary people, somewhat in the *Marty* vein—which shouldn't be surprising, since it has the same director, Delbert Mann. Fifteen or twenty minutes longer than it needs to be, but it benefits from the presence of some good character actors, Angela Lansbury [749 . . .], Alice Pearce, Mary Wickes, and Richard Deacon among them. The song award went to "Chim Chim Cher-ee," from *Mary Poppins.*

Mancini: 122, 278, 384, 494, 508, 776, 825, 1573, 1574, 1864, 1970, 2011, 2037, 2201. Livingston: 344, 951, 1260, 1522, 2001, 2278. Evans: 344, 951, 1260, 1522, 2001, 2278.

513 • DEAR JOHN

A.B. SANDREW-ATELJEERNA (SWEDEN). 1965.
NOMINATION *Foreign Language Film.*

A waitress in a seaside town, an unwed mother, has a weekend affair with a sailor and fears that she'll never see him again. Simple, evocative film, told in flashbacks, written and directed by Lars Magnus Lindgren. The Oscar went to Czechoslovakia's *The Shop on Main Street.*

513.5 • DEATH BECOMES HER

UNIVERSAL PICTURES PRODUCTION; UNIVERSAL. 1992.
AWARD *Visual Effects:* Ken Ralston, Doug Chiang, Doug Smythe, and Tom Woodruff, Jr.

Vain, aging actress Meryl Streep [472 . . .] marries plastic surgeon Bruce Willis, stealing him from Goldie Hawn [323 . . .], who eats herself into obesity in despair. Years later, the two meet again, only Hawn has grown svelte and youthful while Streep is a wrinkling has-been. Streep discovers Hawn's secret: a potion that allows eternal youth—at a price. Shrill knockabout comedy, directed by Robert Zemeckis [127 . . .], that depends more on its amazing special effects and makeup wizardry than on its powerhouse cast and unfocused screenplay. Streep is contorted into pretzel shapes, and Hawn walks around with a hole in her middle, through which the sets can be quite clearly seen, thanks to state-of-the-art computer manipulation and matte effects. While it's possible to admire the technology, it's hard to overlook the misogynistic tone and the misuse of two gifted actresses. Besides, it's not very funny.

Ralston: 128, 419, 577, 708.5, 1684, 2274. Woodruff: 45.5.

514 • DEATH IN VENICE

ALFA CINEMATOGRAFICA-P.E.C.F. PRODUCTION; WARNER BROS. (ITALY/FRANCE). 1971.

NOMINATION *Costume Design:* Piero Tosi.

Dirk Bogarde plays an elderly German composer who, on a holiday in Venice, becomes obsessed with a beautiful young boy and ignores warnings that a cholera epidemic is spreading through the city. Luchino Visconti [480] adapts the novella by Thomas Mann with limited success. The evocation of the period (the turn of the century) and place is superb, but the film is far too long for the slightness of its narrative content. Mann's protagonist was a writer, but Visconti has made him a composer, and in place of Mann's philosophical meditations, there is the music of Gustav Mahler, which only adds to the film's languor. The cinematography is by Pasquale De Santis [1722]. The costume award went to Yvonne Blake and Antonio Castillo for *Nicholas and Alexandra.*

Tosi: 326, 1156, 1225, 2135.

515 • DEATH OF A SALESMAN

STANLEY KRAMER PRODUCTIONS; COLUMBIA. 1951.

NOMINATIONS *Actor:* Fredric March. *Supporting Actor:* Kevin McCarthy. *Supporting Actress:* Mildred Dunnock. *Black-and-White Cinematography:* Frank Planer. *Scoring of a Dramatic or Comedy Picture:* Alex North.

March is Willy Loman, the aging salesman driven to suicide by the meaninglessness of his life, in this faithful adaptation of Arthur Miller's play. Dunnock is his wife, and McCarthy and Cameron Mitchell his sons. As often, what makes a play work makes a movie seem stiff and talky. Even the "cinematic" elements of the play—the flashbacks—seem theatrical here: March walks out of the present into the past, and vice versa. The film has its admirers, but it was a box-office disappointment. Directed by Laslo Benedek. A made-for-TV version, based on a Broadway revival, starred Dustin Hoffman [810 . . .] in 1985.

This was the last Oscar nomination for March, a two-time winner, though he continued to be a reliable screen presence for two more decades, with memorable performances in *The Desperate Hours* (1955), *Inherit the Wind,* and *The Iceman Cometh* (1973). He died in 1975. The Oscar went to Humphrey Bogart for *The African Queen.*

Dunnock, like Mitchell, had appeared in the Broadway version of the play. She made her screen debut in 1945 in *The Corn is Green,* repeating another role she had played on stage. The Oscar went to Kim Hunter for *A Streetcar Named Desire.*

McCarthy had succeeded Arthur Kennedy [291 . . .] in the role of Biff on Broadway, and made his screen debut in the part. (Kennedy had already established himself in films and was nominated this year as best actor in *Bright Victory.)* The younger brother of writer Mary McCarthy, he has been a steady if not stellar performer on screen, TV, and stage ever since. He lost to Karl Malden for *Streetcar.*

William C. Mellor won for the cinematography of *A Place in the Sun,* which also won for Franz Waxman's score.

March: 184, 572, 1730, 1909. Dunnock: 119. Planer: 380, 393, 1457, 1716. North: 29, 215, 413, 577, 1654, 1727, 1802, 1814, 1886, 1949, 2174, 2177, 2212, 2277.

516 • DEATH ON THE NILE

JOHN BRABOURNE-RICHARD GOODWIN PRODUCTION; PARAMOUNT (UNITED KINGDOM). 1978.

AWARD *Costume Design:* Anthony Powell.

Who killed unpleasant heiress Lois Chiles? Was it Mia Farrow, whose lover, Simon MacCorkindale, was stolen from her by Chiles? Or Bette Davis [46 . . .], a dowager with a taste for pearls? Or Davis' sour spinster companion, Maggie Smith [332 . . .]? Or Angela Lansbury [749 . . .], author of naughty novels? Or crooked lawyer George Kennedy [443]? And how will Hercule Poirot, played by Peter Ustinov [943 . . .], and his colleague David Niven [1778] figure it out? Having made a big hit with their first all-star Agatha Christie adaptation, *Murder on the Orient Express,* producers John Brabourne [1533 . . .] and Richard Goodwin [1533] try the formula again, with indifferent results. Ustinov is a more convincing Poirot than Albert Finney was, but the film, directed by John Guillermin, is slackly paced. Still, any movie with both Bette Davis and Maggie Smith has to have its moments, and the location filming by Jack Cardiff [221 . . .] is splendid. Powell's costumes go beyond handsomeness into luxury: Chiles wears shoes, borrowed for the film, that are said to have diamond-studded heels.

Powell: 937, 1578, 2021, 2134.

517 • DECISION BEFORE DAWN

20TH CENTURY-FOX. 1951.

NOMINATIONS *Picture:* Anatole Litvak and Frank McCarthy, producers. *Film Editing:* Dorothy Spencer.

Oskar Werner [1812], a German soldier captured by the Americans in World War II, agrees to be parachuted back into his country as a spy for the Allies. Good thriller, directed by Litvak, with Richard Basehart, Gary Merrill, Hildegarde Neff, and the young Klaus Kinski in a small role.

Since it received only one other nomination, in what's generally regarded as a "minor" category, *Decision Before Dawn* stood little chance of winning the best picture Oscar, particularly against such impressive entries as *A Place in the Sun* and *A Streetcar Named Desire,* as well as the big-budget spectacle *Quo Vadis?,* and the winner, *An American in Paris.* And it seems obvious that a far more popular film, *The African Queen,* which was nominated in the actor, actress, director, and screenplay categories, and won Humphrey Bogart his sole Oscar, would have been a more viable candidate for best picture. But *Queen,* which was an independent production released through United Artists, was not nominated for best picture. The reason *Decision* displaced it is that it came from a major studio, headed by one of Hollywood's most powerful and charismatic figures, Darryl Zanuck [34 . . .]. The obvious conclusion is that Fox mustered its personnel in the nominating process, ensur-

ing that *Decision* made an appearance on the nominating ballots of every Academy member who worked for the studio. United Artists, a mere releasing organization, couldn't muster such influence. In a few years, as the studios withered away, things would change; in fact, the very next year, United Artists had two best picture candidates, *High Noon* and *Moulin Rouge,* and Fox had none—it was heavily involved in the development of CinemaScope, which it would introduce in 1953. But Fox, and Zanuck, would continue their logrolling efforts well into the sixties, engineering best picture nominations for such dubious candidates as the critical and box-office failures *Cleopatra* and *Doctor Dolittle.* The editing Oscar went to William Hornbeck for *A Place in the Sun.*

Litvak: 1849. McCarthy: 1541. Spencer: 413, 591, 1901.

518 • DECLINE OF THE AMERICAN EMPIRE, THE

MALOFILM GROUP/NATIONAL FILM BOARD OF CANADA PRODUCTION (CANADA). 1986.

NOMINATION *Foreign Language Film.*

Four male academics discuss their sex lives while preparing a dinner for four women, who are having a similar discussion at a health club. At dinner the conversation's intellectual tone shifts to the same topic. Provocative, perhaps a little arch, and certainly talky film directed by Denys Arcand. The Oscar went to *The Assault,* a film from the Netherlands.

519 • DEEP, THE

CASABLANCA FILMWORKS PRODUCTION; COLUMBIA. 1977.

NOMINATION *Sound:* Walter Goss, Dick Alexander, Tom Beckert, and Robin Gregory.

Scuba diving off Bermuda, Nick Nolte [1612] and Jacqueline Bisset happen upon an underwater stash of morphine and find themselves the target of villain Louis Gossett [1465]. Empty, dull adventure movie based on a novel by Peter Benchley, who also wrote *Jaws,* which this film desperately wants to be, even to the extent of casting Robert Shaw [1252] as yet another crusty seafaring man. It was a box-office hit, though it's hard to find anyone who admits seeing and liking it. Directed by Peter Yates [279 . . .]. The sound award went to *Star Wars.*

Alexander: 54, 209, 888, 1127, 1158.5, 2113, 2179.5. Beckert: 2293. Gregory: 1513.

520 • *DEEP WATERS*

20TH CENTURY-FOX. 1948.

NOMINATION *Special Effects:* Ralph Hammeras, Fred Sersen, and Edward Snyder, visual; Roger Heman, audible.

Orphan Dean Stockwell [1281], adopted by fisherman Dana Andrews, engineers a romance between Andrews and Jean Peters. Pedestrian tale, directed by Henry King [1868 . . .], with Anne Revere [759 . . .] and Ed Begley [1985] wasted in its cast. The effects Oscar went to *Portrait of Jennie.*

Hammeras: 1073, 1619. Sersen: 226, 241, 346, 458, 1655, 2286, 2317. Heman: 226, 346, 418, 458, 1041, 2286.

521 • *DEER HUNTER, THE*

EMI FILMS/MICHAEL CIMINO FILM PRODUCTION; UNIVERSAL. 1978.

AWARDS *Picture:* Barry Spikings, Michael Deeley, Michael Cimino, and John Peverall, producers. *Supporting Actor:* Christopher Walken. *Director:* Michael Cimino. *Sound:* Richard Portman, William McCaughey, Aaron Rochin, and Darin Knight. *Film Editing:* Peter Zinner.

NOMINATIONS *Actor:* Robert De Niro. *Supporting Actress:* Meryl Streep. *Screenplay Written Directly for the Screen:* Michael Cimino, Deric Washburn, Louis Garfinkle, and Quinn K. Redeker. *Cinematography:* Vilmos Zsigmond.

De Niro, Walken, and John Savage, steelworkers from a small Pennsylvania town, celebrate Savage's wedding, go on a deer hunt, and then go off to the Vietnam War. In Vietnam they are captured, tortured, and forced into playing Russian roulette. De Niro and Savage escape, but Walken is left behind. Back in the States, De Niro hears that Walken may be alive and returns to Vietnam to find him—but arrives too late to save him. Powerful, haunting, but deeply flawed, and one of the most controversial best picture choices ever. The passing years, and the subsequent career of writer-producer-director Cimino, have only deepened the controversy. One can glimpse something of the excess that would eventually undermine Cimino's *Heaven's Gate* in his lavish, prolonged treatment of the wedding party, which is brilliantly staged and photographed but advances the story not at all.

At the time, there was much debate about the picture's political correctness: whether it was pro- or antiwar, and whether the Oscar should have gone instead to the explicitly antiwar *Coming Home,* whose star, Jane Fonda, bitterly denounced the winning film without, she admitted, having seen it. The other contenders were the lightweight comedy *Heaven Can Wait,* the brutally exploitive *Midnight Express,* and the feminist comedy-drama *An Unmarried Woman*—none of them substantial enough to stand up against the two Vietnam War films. The central objection of many critics was to the portrayal of the brutal Vietnamese captors, and much was made of the fact that there were no actual reports of Russian roulette being used as either a torture device or a Vietnamese gambling pastime. But Cimino seems less interested in treating the Vietnam War literally than in showing how alien the experience of it was for Americans, and he chooses an isolated and in many ways unassimilated American subculture, the Polish-American steelworkers of Pennsylvania, to demonstrate the deeply radical effect of the Vietnam experience. In the end the award to Cimino's film can be seen as a recognition by Hollywood that newer, younger forces were at work—that this was the era of men like Francis Ford Coppola [65 . . .], George Lucas [65 . . .], and Steven Spielberg [416 . . .]. Cimino must have looked to many Academy members like a good candidate to join that pantheon of younger producer-directors.

The Deer Hunter was only the second film directed by Cimino. The first was *Thunderbolt and Lightfoot,* starring Clint Eastwood [2179.5], who had encouraged the young filmmaker, a writer on Eastwood's *Magnum Force* (1973). Cimino had served as a medic in Vietnam and got his start in films directing TV commercials. The Oscar catapulted Cimino to the top, and he immediately got the backing to do an epic western, *Heaven's Gate,* whose colossal cost overruns and disastrous premiere two years later led to the collapse of its releasing studio, United Artists. The title (ironically echoing "Watergate") became a by-word for Hollywood excess. Since then, Cimino has directed three more flops: *Year of the Dragon* (1985), which like *The Deer Hunter* outraged many Asian-Americans, *The Sicilian* (1987), and *Desperate Hours* (1990). Few Hollywood figures have risen so high so fast and fallen so swiftly.

Walken had been seen in a few minor films, and in a minor role in a major film—*Annie Hall,* as Diane Keaton's spooky brother. In *The Deer Hunter* he has an opportunity early in the film to display a certain attractiveness, but the madness into which he descends is the note that most directors have subsequently sought from him.

De Niro plays the film's moral center, a Hemingwayish figure who is (literally) a straight shooter. He lost to Jon Voight for *Coming Home.*

Streep's first nomination came for only her second film role. She made her debut a year earlier in a small part in *Julia.* It's a tribute to her skill that the *Deer Hunter* role attracted any notice at all, let alone an Oscar nomination, for as Walken's girlfriend she's scarcely more than a face in the crowd, with only a few lines of dialogue. She took the part to be near her lover, John Cazale, who has a small role in the film and was dying of cancer. The Oscar went to Maggie Smith for *California Suite.*

The screenplay award went to Nancy Dowd, Waldo Salt, and Robert C. Jones for *Coming Home.* Nestor Almendros won for his cinematography for *Days of Heaven.*

Portman: 339, 418, 502, 738, 784, 1109, 1473, 1526, 1701, 2331. McCaughey: 1089, 1310, 1712, 2287. Rochin: 641, 1089, 1310, 1711, 2124, 2165, 2231, 2287. Zinner: 784, 1465. De Niro: 113, 342, 785, 1650, 2005. Streep: 472, 725, 1019, 1111, 1512, 1598, 1821, 1876. Zsigmond: 416, 1701.

522 • DEFIANT ONES, THE

STANLEY KRAMER PRODUCTIONS; UNITED ARTISTS. 1958.
AWARDS *Story and Screenplay—Written Directly for the Screen:* Nedrick Young and Harold Jacob Smith. (The award was originally presented to Young under his pseudonym, Nathan E. Douglas, which he used during the period when he was blacklisted. The Academy restored official credit under his real name in 1992.) *Black-and-White Cinematography:* Sam Leavitt.
NOMINATIONS *Picture:* Stanley Kramer, producer. *Actor:* Tony Curtis. *Actor:* Sidney Poitier. *Supporting Actor:* Theodore Bikel. *Supporting Actress:* Cara Williams. *Director:* Stanley Kramer. *Film Editing:* Frederick Knudtson.

White convict Curtis and black convict Poitier, shackled together, escape from a southern chain gang. They overcome their racial animosity to cooperate in evading the police. Swift, exciting action and fine performances keep the message from overwhelming the story. Look for Carl "Alfalfa" Switzer, former child star of the Our Gang comedies, in a small role—the last before his death in a barroom brawl in 1959.

The blacklist that followed the House Un-American Activities Committee hearings on communists in the film industry blighted many careers in the early fifties. But many writers continued to work under pseudonyms or with other writers taking the credit for them, and several blacklistees received Oscars: See the entries for *The Brave One, The Bridge on the River Kwai,* and *Roman Holiday* for examples. In 1956 the Academy instituted a rule denying eligibility for nomination to anyone who had admitted membership in the Communist Party and had not renounced that membership, or who had refused to testify before a congressional committee investigating subversive activities. Two years later, when it was discovered that Oscar winner "Nathan E. Douglas" was actually blacklisted writer Nedrick Young, the Academy rescinded the rule, announcing that it was "unworkable." What was really unworkable, of course, was the blacklist itself, which virtually ended in 1960 when blacklistee Dalton Trumbo [273 . . .] was given a screen credit for his work on the script for *Spartacus.*

Kramer's film went up against a rather thin slate of best picture contenders: *Auntie Mame,* a rather too-literal translation of a Broadway hit; *Cat on a Hot Tin Roof,* a bowdlerized version of the Tennessee Williams play; *Separate Tables,* another play "opened up" for the screen; and the winner, *Gigi,* the opulent movie that marked the end of the golden era for MGM's film musicals. Out of the running were two movies that have earned more lasting critical acclaim than any of the nominees: Alfred Hitchcock's *Vertigo* and Orson Welles' *Touch of Evil.*

Curtis had begun his movie career as a teen idol in westerns and costume melodramas such as *The Prince Who Was a Thief* (1951) and *Son of Ali Baba* (1952) during his years as a Universal contract player. Critics joked about his Bronx accent and such deathless lines as "Yondah lies da castle of my foddah," but the studio contract, and his popularity, gave him the opportunity to work hard, and he matured as an actor, making strong impressions in a serious part in the 1957 drama *Sweet Smell of Success* and in a comic role in *Some Like It Hot.* His costar in the latter film, Jack Lemmon, has observed of Curtis: "He wanted to be a good actor, and he's the only guy I know who learned his craft successfully—literally, learned how to act—on film. Nobody else comes to my mind who did this." Curtis' career continued to be strong through the sixties, with one of his best dramatic performances coming in the title role of *The Boston Strangler* in 1968. He entered a career decline, accompanied by personal problems, including drug use, in the seventies, but still appears occasionally in films and on TV. The Oscar went to David Niven for *Separate Tables.*

Although Dorothy Dandridge had received an Oscar nomination for best actress in 1954, and Hattie McDaniel had won an Oscar for her supporting role in *Gone With the Wind,* black men were slower to achieve recognition from the Academy. Poitier's is the first nomination for an African-American man in either of the actor categories.

Bikel was born in Vienna but went to Palestine in the 1930s, where he began his acting career. After studying at the Royal Academy of Dramatic Art in London, he entered films, making his debut in *The African Queen.* He has also been active on the stage and is well known as a folksinger. He lost, interestingly, to another folksinger, Burl Ives in *The Big Country.*

Before her nomination Williams was better known as the wife of John Drew Barrymore, with whom she had several well-publicized spats before their divorce in 1959, than as an actress. The nomination, which she lost to Wendy Hiller for *Separate Tables,* was the highlight of her film career. She is now perhaps best remembered as a star of TV sitcoms, *Pete and Gladys* and *The Cara Williams Show.*

The Oscar for directing went to Vincente Minnelli for *Gigi,* which also won an award for its editor, Adrienne Fazan.

Young: 1000. Smith: 1000. Leavitt: 73, 630. Kramer: 330, 843, 912, 1065, 1812. Poitier: 1174. Knudtson: 1000, 1032, 1065, 1474, 2288.

523 • *DELIVERANCE*
WARNER BROS. 1972.

NOMINATIONS *Picture:* John Boorman, producer. *Director:* John Boorman. *Film Editing:* Tom Priestley.

Four Atlanta businessmen—Jon Voight [430 . . .], Burt Reynolds, Ned Beatty [1424], and Ronny Cox—go on a weekend canoe trip that ends in disaster when they encounter a pair of vicious mountain men. Based on a novel by James Dickey, who also did the screenplay and plays a sheriff in the movie, this gripping action film wants to have more meaning and resonance than most representatives of its genre, but doesn't. What one remembers after it's over are "Dueling Banjos" and the violence. The film helped make Reynolds a star after years of TV westerns and third-rate movies, and by the end of the decade he was the No. 1 box-office draw. But bad script choices—*Deliverance* is by far the best film he ever appeared in—and his own limitations as an actor sent his career into a steep decline in the eighties. Beatty and Cox make their film debuts in *Deliverance.*

Boorman got his start in British TV and directed his first movie, *Having a Wild Weekend,* in 1965. This copycat version of *Hard Day's Night,* starring the Dave Clark Five, led to Hollywood assignments on two films starring Lee Marvin [371], *Point Blank* (1967) and *Hell in the Pacific* (1968). Neither attracted much attention at the time, but *Point Blank* has become something of a cult film with the passage of time. *Deliverance,* which was a big box-office success, established Boorman among younger directors, but he followed it with the flops *Zardoz* (1974) and *Exorcist II: The Heretic* (1977), and didn't return to top form until the eighties and such films as *Excalibur* and *Hope and Glory*. His son, Charley, plays Voight's son in *Deliverance* and later played a major role in Boorman's *The Emerald Forest* (1985).

Deliverance received fewer nominations than any of the other films in competition for best picture and was never a serious contender in what amounted to a slugfest between *Cabaret* and *The Godfather*. (The other nominees were *The Emigrants* and *Sounder.*) *The Godfather* won the best picture Oscar, and *Cabaret* won for its director, Bob Fosse, and its film editor, David Bretherton.

Boorman: 940.

524 • DELUGE, THE

FILM POLSKI PRODUCTION (POLAND). 1974.
NOMINATION *Foreign Language Film.*

The Poles defend their homeland against an attempt by Sweden to take over the country in the seventeenth century in this adaptation of a novel by Henrik Sienkewicz, directed by Jerzy Hoffman. Not widely shown in the United States. The Oscar went to Federico Fellini's *Amarcord.*

525 • DERSU UZALA

MOSFILM STUDIOS PRODUCTION (USSR). 1975.
AWARD *Foreign Language Film.*

A turn-of-the-century Russian explorer relies on the wilderness savvy of his guide, Uzala, while charting territory near the border between Russia and Manchuria. When Uzala's eyesight begins to fail, the explorer brings him back to Moscow, which the man of nature finds oppressively alien. Akira Kurosawa [1661] directs this visually exciting film that's marred only by its rather obvious message: that the man close to nature is superior to the civilized man.

526 • DESERT RATS, THE

20TH CENTURY-FOX. 1953.
NOMINATION *Story and Screenplay:* Richard Murphy.

Richard Burton [85 . . .] is a British officer trying to halt Rommel's advances in North Africa during World War II. James Mason [761 . . .] plays Rommel, a role in which he had attracted attention in *The Desert Fox* two years earlier; this film was designed to cash in on the earlier one's success. It's a fairly routine war movie with good performances by Burton, Mason, and Robert Newton. Robert Wise [407 . . .] directed.

Murphy lost to Charles Brackett, Walter Reisch, and Richard Breen's script for *Titanic*.

Murphy: 257.

527 • DESERT SONG, THE

WARNER BROS. 1944.
NOMINATION *Color Interior Decoration:* Charles Novi, art direction; Jack McConaghy, set decoration.

Dennis Morgan leads North Africans in their fight against the Nazis in this updated version of the Sigmund Romberg operetta, a property Warners got a lot of mileage from: It filmed it first in 1929 and again in 1953. It got a lot of mileage from some of the sets, too: They were first used in *Casablanca*. Directed by Robert Florey, with Bruce Cabot, Gene Lockhart [36], Faye Emerson, Curt Bois, and Marcel Dalio, among others. The art directing Oscar went to *Wilson*.

McConaghy: 1750.

528 • DESIGNING WOMAN

MGM. 1957.
AWARD *Story and Screenplay—Written Directly for the Screen:* George Wells.

Fashion designer Lauren Bacall weds sportswriter Gregory Peck [759 . . .], but they have difficulty merging their sets of friends—hers are arty, his are thuggish—and when his old flame, Dolores Gray, shows up, Bacall's jealousy creates complications. At its best, this overextended trifle, directed by Vincente Minnelli [66 . . .], makes one long for the real thing: the Spencer Tracy–Katharine Hepburn comedies such as *Woman of the Year* on which it is obviously based. Today it seems more than a little sexist, and when the swishy choreographer played by Jack Cole pulls out the pictures of his wife and kids to prove he's straight, you know you're in the depths of the fifties. The film was originally set to star Grace Kelly [450 . . .] and James Stewart [73 . . .]—in roles much like the ones they had already played in *Rear Window*—but Kelly's marriage to Prince Rainier changed all that. The film's award, in the category designed for "original" scripts rather than "adapted" ones, seems a cheat in more ways than one. Not only is MGM contract writer Wells reworking old stuff, he's actually just fleshing out a story idea submitted by costume designer Helen Rose [130 . . .]. She didn't share in the Oscar for her story, and the clothes she designed for the movie didn't even get nominated.

529 • DESIRE UNDER THE ELMS

DON HARTMAN; PARAMOUNT. 1958.

NOMINATION *Black-and-White Cinematography:* Daniel L. Fapp.

New England farmer Burl Ives [200] marries Sophia Loren [1280 . . .], who falls in love with her stepson, Anthony Perkins [730]. Miscast, misdirected —by Delbert Mann [1283]—version of the Eugene O'Neill drama; it gets laughs in all the wrong places. The Oscar went to Sam Leavitt for *The Defiant Ones*.

Fapp: 675, 978, 1279, 1492, 2184, 2244.

530 • DESIRÉE

20TH CENTURY-FOX. 1954.

NOMINATIONS *Color Art Direction—Set Decoration:* Lyle Wheeler and Leland Fuller; Walter M. Scott and Paul S. Fox. *Color Costume Design:* Charles LeMaire and Rene Hubert.

Marlon Brando [583 . . .] plays Napoleon, who is in love with the young seamstress Desirée, Jean Simmons [858 . . .], but is forced to think of the Empire and his empress—Josephine, that is, played by Merle Oberon [487]. Romantic idiocy, adapted by Daniel Taradash [732] from a novel by Annemarie Selinko, made tolerable only by the fact that it's

Brando up there looking foolish. He was trapped into this nonsense when he refused to make *The Egyptian,* which is only a little worse than *Desirée.* Director Henry Koster [214] was unable to handle Brando, who clowned his way through the shooting.

The art direction award was won by *20,000 Leagues Under the Sea* and the costuming Oscar by Sanzo Wada for *Gate of Hell.*

Wheeler: 19, 46, 83, 356, 376, 428, 476, 495, 542, 719, 721, 798, 950, 1062, 1088, 1149, 1153, 1213, 1391, 1475, 1601, 1616, 1670, 1706, 1852, 2008, 2093, 2212. Fuller: 719, 1149, 1475, 1601, 2212. Scott: 46, 376, 413, 476, 542, 557, 646, 896, 1088, 1213, 1391, 1475, 1706, 1753, 1881, 1907, 2008, 2120, 2247. Fox: 376, 413, 428, 476, 495, 721, 950, 1088, 1601, 1666, 1706, 1852. LeMaire: 21, 46, 376, 495, 542, 954, 1213, 1338, 1391, 1601, 1706, 2008, 2043, 2205, 2294. Hubert: 2207.

531 • DESPERATE JOURNEY

WARNER BROS. 1942.

NOMINATION *Special Effects:* Byron Haskin, photographic; Nathan Levinson, sound.

Shot down in Nazi Germany, Americans Errol Flynn, Ronald Reagan, Alan Hale, and Arthur Kennedy [291 . . .] fight, connive, and double-talk their way across the border to freedom, thwarting monocled meanie Raymond Massey [1] at every turn. Silly? Yes. Improbable? Sure. Enjoyable? Absolutely. Suspend your disbelief and go along for the ride. Directed by Raoul Walsh. The special effects Oscar went to *Reap the Wild Wind.*

Haskin: 1621, 1768, 1769. Levinson: 16, 30, 343, 385, 689, 710, 712, 790, 930, 965, 1052, 1169, 1621, 1690, 1768, 1769, 1779, 1930, 1949, 2058, 2318.

532 • DESTINATION MOON

GEORGE PAL PRODUCTIONS; EAGLE LION CLASSICS. 1950.

AWARD *Special Effects.* (No individual citation.)

NOMINATION *Color Art Direction—Set Decoration:* Ernst Fegte; George Sawley.

An American inventor-entrepreneur puts together a private venture to send men to the moon. Now that we've actually been there, this journey conducted by producer George Pal may seem a little wide of the mark, and it certainly needs better dialogue, or at least better actors to speak it. But when you realize that it was done more than a decade before human beings ventured into space and almost two decades before they reached the moon, it's pretty impressive. Sci-fi writer Robert Heinlein contributed to the script, and the sets are based on the work of illustrator Chesley Bonestell. Directed by Irving Pichel. The art direction Oscar was won by *Samson and Delilah.*

Fegte: 674, 726, 1613. Sawley: 1668.

533 • DESTINATION TOKYO

WARNER BROS. 1943.

NOMINATION *Original Story:* Steve Fisher.

A submarine captained by Cary Grant [1445 . . .] makes its way past depth charges and underwater mines into Tokyo Harbor. The crew includes John Garfield [251 . . .], Alan Hale, Dane Clark, Tom Tully [330], and in his debut role, John Forsythe. Plenty of propaganda, but also plenty of suspense—one of the most watchable of the wartime impossible-mission movies, thanks to Grant, Garfield, and the no-nonsense direction of Delmer Daves. The screenplay from Fisher's story is by Daves and Albert Maltz [298 . . .]. The Oscar went to William Saroyan for *The Human Comedy.*

534 • DETECTIVE STORY

PARAMOUNT. 1951.

NOMINATIONS *Actress:* Eleanor Parker. *Supporting Actress:* Lee Grant. *Director:* William Wyler. *Screenplay:* Philip Yordan and Robert Wyler.

New York police detective Kirk Douglas [130 . . .] has built his career on an uncompromising hatred of crime, partly explained by his detestation of his own father, whose cruelty drove Douglas' mother insane. The one bright spot in his life is his love for Parker—until he learns a secret from her past that doesn't fit with his us-vs.-them attitude toward life. Meanwhile, the precinct house is the scene for a variety of small dramas involving eccentric shoplifter Grant and other cops and crooks played by William

Bendix [2222], Gladys George [2192], Joseph Wiseman, and others. Slightly too-theatrical version of a play by Sidney Kingsley, but Wyler, who had also directed an earlier adaptation of a Kingsley play, *Dead End,* keeps things moving along. The granddaddy of TV cop shows like *NYPD Blue,* the movie shows its age but wears it well, thanks to a good ensemble and a showy performance from Douglas.

Parker's second consecutive nomination put her in competition with Katharine Hepburn for *The African Queen,* Shelley Winters for *A Place in the Sun,* and Jane Wyman for *The Blue Veil.* The Oscar went to Vivien Leigh for *A Streetcar Named Desire.*

The twenty-two-year-old Grant was spotted by playwright Kingsley in an acting workshop and cast in the Broadway production of *Detective Story.* This led directly to the film version, an award at Cannes, and the Oscar nomination. (She lost to Kim Hunter for *Streetcar.*) But just as her film career was beginning, she was blacklisted for refusing to testify before the House Un-American Activities Committee about the alleged communist activities of her husband, playwright Arnold Manoff. She spent most of the fifties unemployed but resumed her career in the sixties.

William Wyler lost the directing Oscar to George Stevens for *A Place in the Sun.* His brother, Robert, and coauthor Yordan also lost to *A Place in the Sun*'s screenwriters, Michael Wilson and Harry Brown.

Parker: 328, 1007. Grant: 1130, 1798, 2218. W. Wyler: 175, 184, 420, 560, 730, 894, 1162, 1182, 1371, 1716, 2316. Yordan: 299, 545.

DEVIL AND DANIEL WEBSTER, THE
See 50.

535 • DEVIL AND MISS JONES, THE

ROSS-KRASNA; RKO RADIO. 1941.

NOMINATIONS *Supporting Actor:* Charles Coburn. *Original Screenplay:* Norman Krasna.

Millionaire department store owner Coburn, concerned about union unrest and grouchy employees, goes incognito as a salesclerk in the store. From Miss Jones, Jean Arthur [1353], he discovers that he's regarded as the very devil. But he smooths the course of love between her and Robert Cummings and soon has a thing going himself with Spring Byington [2325]. Semiclassic comedy with fine performances by all, including Edmund Gwenn [1325 . . .], S. Z. Sakall, and William Demarest [1058]. But it needs a lighter touch than director Sam Wood [701 . . .] brings to it. Wood, a staunch conservative, was reportedly disturbed that businessmen were being portrayed in the film as less than benevolent.

Coburn lost to Donald Crisp for *How Green Was My Valley.* Krasna said he based his story on his own experiences as an employee at Macy's while he was working his way through college in New York. The screenplay Oscar went to Herman J. Mankiewicz and Orson Welles for *Citizen Kane.*

Coburn: 838, 1353. Krasna: 741, 1615, 1694.

536 • *DEVIL CAME AT NIGHT, THE*
GLORIA FILM (FEDERAL REPUBLIC OF GERMANY). 1957.
NOMINATION *Foreign Language Film.*

An investigator of a series of murders in World War II Germany discovers that the killer is a member of the Gestapo, but the Gestapo covers up the evidence and pins the murders on an innocent man. Directed by Robert Siodmak [1085], who returned to Germany after spending the war years in Hollywood. Effective suspense thriller based on a true case discovered in the files of the Gestapo. Called in German *Nachts Wenn der Teufel Kamm,* it was released under several titles, including *The Devil Strikes at Night, Nazi Terror at Night,* and the literal translation, *Nights When the Devil Came.* The Oscar went to *The Nights of Cabiria.*

537 • *DEVIL DANCER, THE*
SAMUEL GOLDWYN PRODUCTIONS; UNITED ARTISTS. 1927–28.
NOMINATION *Cinematography:* George Barnes.

Adventure tale set in Tibet, with Clive Brook, Anna May Wong, and Gilda Gray. The film, produced by Samuel Goldwyn [102 . . .] and directed by Fred Niblo, is not in circulation today. Its chief claim to fame is that it was one of Goldwyn's first releases with a soundtrack, although it had only a musical score and no dialogue. One of three films for which

Barnes received nominations in this first year of the awards. The Oscar went to Charles Rosher and Karl Struss for *Sunrise.*

Barnes: 1236, 1509, 1670, 1739, 1748, 1885, 1890.

538 • *DEVIL PAYS OFF, THE*
REPUBLIC. 1941.
NOMINATION *Sound Recording:* Charles Lootens.

Former sailor tracks down spies infiltrating the navy. This feeble programmer, less than an hour long, with stars like J. Edward Bromberg and Osa Massen, owes its nomination to liberalized Academy rules that allowed each studio to submit a nominee in certain categories. The sound award went to *That Hamilton Woman.*

Lootens: 100, 168, 1257.

539 • *DEVIL'S HOLIDAY, THE*
PARAMOUNT PUBLIX. 1929–30.
NOMINATION *Actress:* Nancy Carroll.

Manicurist Carroll marries Phillips Holmes for money and is bought off by her husband's family. In the end she returns to him after he has gone insane. Written and directed by Edmund Goulding, with Paul Lukas [2233], ZaSu Pitts, and Ned Sparks. Carroll, a popular musical star, was persuaded by the studio to undertake more serious roles such as this one. Her career faded fast in the thirties, and she retired at the end of the decade. She died in 1965. The Oscar went to Norma Shearer for *The Divorcée.*

540 • *DIAMONDS ARE FOREVER*
ALBERT R. BROCCOLI-HARRY SALTZMAN PRODUCTION; UNITED ARTISTS. 1971.
NOMINATION *Sound:* Gordon K. McCallum, John Mitchell, and Alfred J. Overton.

Sean Connery [2185] as James Bond thwarts a plot involving the theft of diamonds that are being used in a satellite to focus a death ray. Though Connery was trying to shake the James Bond role, and had managed to escape from it for one film (*On Her Majesty's Secret Service* in 1969, with George Lazenby as Bond), he seems to be having a good time here, perhaps because the film has genuinely funny dialogue and situations, and a gallery of oddball characters including Jimmy Dean as a Howard Hughesish billionaire and Jill St. John as the fickle Tiffany Case, plus Lana Wood, Bruce Cabot, and Bond-film regulars Bernard Lee, Lois Maxwell, and Desmond Llewelyn. Directed by Guy Hamilton.

The sound award went to *Fiddler on the Roof.*

McCallum: 659, 1737, 1977. Mitchell: 1533. Overton: 215, 544, 606, 1548.

541 • DIARY OF A MAD HOUSEWIFE

FRANK PERRY FILMS PRODUCTION; UNIVERSAL. 1970.

NOMINATION *Actress:* Carrie Snodgress.

Her jerk of a husband, played by Richard Benjamin, drives Snodgress into an affair with a writer, Frank Langella, who turns out to be an even bigger jerk. Flat-footed satire, a good deal overpraised at the time. Directed by Frank Perry [496] from a script by Eleanor Perry [496] based on a novel by Sue Kaufman.

Snodgress was acclaimed for her performances in this film and *Rabbit, Run* the same year, but she gave up a chance at stardom and chose life with rocker Neil Young [1562.5] instead. When she returned to the screen, her roles in such movies as *The Fury* (1978), *Pale Rider* (1985), and *Murphy's Law* (1986) did nothing to restore her career to its early peak. The Oscar went to Glenda Jackson for *Women in Love.*

542 • DIARY OF ANNE FRANK, THE

20TH CENTURY-FOX. 1959.

AWARDS *Supporting Actress:* Shelley Winters. *Black-and-White Cinematography:* William C. Mellor. *Black-and-White Art Direction–Set Decoration:* Lyle R. Wheeler and George W. Davis; Walter M. Scott and Stuart A. Reiss.

NOMINATIONS *Picture:* George Stevens, producer. *Supporting Actor:* Ed Wynn. *Director:* George Stevens. *Scoring of Dramatic or Comedy Picture:* Alfred Newman. *Black-and-White Costume Design:* Charles LeMaire and Mary Wills.

Sympathizers in Amsterdam hide a group of Jews in an attic during World War II. They include Anne (Millie Perkins), her sister, Margot (Diane Baker), and her parents, played by Joseph Schildkraut [1169] and Gusti Huber. There are also the Van Daans (Winters and Lou Jacobi), and their son, Peter (Richard Beymer), plus the elderly Mr. Dussell (Wynn). Anne records their experiences in her diary: the terror, the frayed tempers, her budding romance with Peter, and the moments when the group draws together against the threat outside. The heartbreaking diary was well dramatized by Frances Goodrich [25 . . .] and Albert Hackett [25 . . .] on Broadway, and they adapted the play for the screen. But the pacing of the play is lost and much of its drama dissipated in the film version, and the decision to film in CinemaScope was unwise—the cramped attic seems to stretch endlessly. Audrey Hepburn [278 . . .] had been considered for the role of Anne, but at thirty she was clearly too old for the part, and she had serious reservations about it because it evoked painful memories of her own experiences in Holland under Nazi occupation. Perkins, a former model, just turned twenty, was chosen after a much-hyped Scarlett O'Hara–style "star search," but the role failed to make her a star.

Winters had been in films since 1943, but apart from her roles in *A Double Life* and *A Place in the Sun* (she was nominated for the latter), she had failed to make much impression. She left Hollywood for Broadway in the mid-fifties. Stevens, who had directed her in *A Place in the Sun,* brought her back for *Anne Frank,* and she stayed to play character parts, often shrill and blowsy roles like Mrs. Van Daan.

Both of Mellor's Oscars, and one of his two unsuccessful nominations, were for films directed by Stevens. He and the art directors work well together to create a sense of place—the attic shadowed by war, illuminated by hope—so it's doubly unfortunate that the CinemaScope lens undermines their efforts.

Stevens had a strong personal reason for wanting to film *Anne Frank.* During the war, he had served as a major in the Army Signal Corps film unit and was present at the liberation of Dachau. His film stood little chance against the year's blockbuster, *Ben-Hur,* which won for best picture and for its director, William Wyler.

Ben-Hur's Hugh Griffith took the supporting actor Oscar instead of Wynn, who had been in show business since his teens, becoming a vaudeville headliner and a *Ziegfeld Follies* star. Although he made a few films in the thirties, he was best known at that time as a radio star. After a business failure and a nervous breakdown in the forties, he became one of the first stars of a new medium, television, where he revived old vaudeville routines but also appeared in several dramatic roles. His son, Keenan Wynn, helped pave the way for his return to movies, a role in *The Great Man* in 1957. He continued to perform frequently, often in Disney films such as *The Absent-Minded Professor, Babes in Toyland,* and *Mary Poppins,* until his death in 1966 at the age of eighty.

The scoring Oscar went to Miklos Rozsa for *Ben-Hur.* The costume award was won by Orry-Kelly for *Some Like It Hot.*

Winters: 1537, 1579, 1596. Mellor: 833, 1558, 1579. Wheeler: 19, 46, 83, 356, 376, 428, 476, 495, 530, 719, 721, 798, 950, 1062, 1088, 1149, 1153, 1213, 1391, 1475, 1601, 1616, 1670, 1706, 1852, 2008, 2093, 2212. Davis: 46, 69, 401, 495, 736, 953, 1213, 1335, 1388, 1537, 1552, 1706, 1814, 2157, 2184, 2312. Scott: 46, 376, 413, 476, 530, 557, 646, 896, 1062, 1088, 1213, 1391, 1475, 1706, 1753, 1881, 1907, 2008, 2120, 2247. Reiss: 557, 646, 2008, 2093, 2247. Stevens: 768, 1353, 1579, 1799, 1998. Newman: 31, 34, 46, 72, 138, 182, 226, 333, 334, 347, 375, 428, 437, 457, 476, 495, 690, 797, 833, 952, 953, 959, 962, 1016, 1082, 1088, 1213, 1278, 1362, 1397, 1475, 1616, 1655, 1849, 1868, 1883, 1921, 2043, 2046, 2091, 2258, 2286, 2294, 2316. LeMaire: 21, 46, 376, 495, 530, 954, 1213, 1338, 1391, 1601, 1706, 2008, 2043, 2205, 2294. Wills: 376, 864, 1534, 2008, 2205, 2312.

543 • DICK TRACY

Touchstone Pictures Production; Buena Vista. 1990.

Awards *Art Direction–Set Decoration:* Richard Sylbert; Rick Simpson. *Song:* "Sooner or Later (I Always Get My Man)," music and lyrics by Stephen Sondheim. *Makeup:* John Caglione, Jr., and Doug Drexler.

Nominations *Supporting Actor:* Al Pacino. *Cinematography:* Vittorio Storaro. *Sound:* Chris Jenkins, David E. Campbell, D. M. Hemphill, and Thomas Causey. *Costume Design:* Milena Canonero.

Police detective Tracy, played by Warren Beatty [255 . . .], battles a gallery of oddball criminals, adopts a street kid (Charlie Korsmo), fends off a temptress (Madonna), and winds up with Tess Trueheart (Glenne Headly). Big, colorful, but empty version of the Chester Gould comic strip, produced and directed by Beatty. It has witty visuals, Sondheim songs, and a riotous performance by Pacino, so why isn't it more fun? Maybe because everyone is too busy spending money to take it seriously. The cast, many of them unrecognizable underneath the makeup that turns them into comic-strip grotesques, includes Charles Durning [180 . . .], Seymour Cassel [635], Dustin Hoffman [810 . . .] (both visually and verbally hilarious as Mumbles), James Caan [784], Michael J. Pollard [255], Estelle Parsons [255 . . .], and Kathy Bates [1328].

The Oscars went to all the right people: Sylbert and Simpson craft a three-dimensional Sunday comic-strip world, all primary colors and bold outlines. Sondheim, Broadway's wittiest composer, provides songs that have the right thirties supper-club sophistication—and aren't too difficult for Madonna, with her limited vocal abilities, to sing. And Caglione and Drexler work wonders with prosthetics, transforming the actors into Gouldian grotesques.

Pacino gives by far the best performance in the movie, as the head hood, a hilarious send-up of all the gangsters who surrounded him in the *Godfather* movies. The Oscar went to another actor playing an over-the-top hood, Joe Pesci in *GoodFellas.*

The cinematography Oscar went to Dean Semler for *Dances With Wolves,* which also won for sound. The costume award went to Franca Squarciapino for *Cyrano de Bergerac.*

Sylbert: 395, 448, 1678, 1798, 2277. Simpson: 2165. Pacino: 75, 561, 775.5, 784, 785, 1764.5, 1780. Storaro: 92, 1136, 1678. Jenkins: 1138.5, 1512. Campbell: 1154.5. Hemphill: 761.5, 1138.5. Canonero: 151, 386, 1512, 2148.

544 • DIE HARD

20TH CENTURY FOX PRODUCTION; 20TH CENTURY FOX. 1988.
NOMINATIONS *Sound:* Don Bassman, Kevin F. Cleary, Richard Overton, and Al Overton. *Film Editing:* Frank J. Urioste and John F. Link. *Visual Effects:* Richard Edlund, Al DiSarro, Brent Boates, and Thaine Morris. *Sound Effects Editing:* Stephen H. Flick and Richard Shorr.

New York cop Bruce Willis goes to L.A. to see his estranged wife, Bonnie Bedelia, at Christmas, and winds up battling terrorists who have taken over the high-rise corporate headquarters where she works. Exciting, noisy, violent, silly—in short, a typical eighties movie. Well directed by John McTiernan, with good performances by Willis and Bedelia, Alan Rickman and Alexander Godunov as terrorists, Hart Bochner as a hostage who's just too eager to collaborate, William Atherton as an anything-for-a-story journalist, and Reginald VelJohnson as the beat cop who is practically the only person outside the building who manages to keep his wits about him. Willis, Bedelia, Atherton, and VelJohnson went through it all over again in the sequel made in 1990.

The sound Oscar went to *Bird.* Arthur Schmidt won for editing *Who Framed Roger Rabbit,* which also won for visual effects and sound effects editing.

Bassman: 5, 961, 1541. Cleary: 5, 961. R. Overton: 5, 961. A. Overton: 215, 540, 606, 1548. Urioste: 152.5, 1711. Link: 701. Edlund: 45.5, 614, 766, 1589, 1590, 1652, 1684, 1916, 2165. Flick: 1589, 1711, 1888.5, 2124.

545 • DILLINGER

KING BROTHERS; MONOGRAM. 1945.
NOMINATION *Original Screenplay:* Philip Yordan.

Lawrence Tierney plays the man whose name became synonymous with gangster in this well-paced B movie directed by Max Nosseck, with Edmund Lowe, Anne Jeffreys, Eduardo Ciannelli, and Elisha Cook, Jr. The Oscar went to Richard Schweizer for *Marie-Louise.*

Yordan: 299, 534.

546 • DINER

JERRY WEINTRAUB PRODUCTION; MGM/UNITED ARTISTS. 1982.
NOMINATION *Screenplay Written Directly for the Screen:* Barry Levinson.

A group of college students in 1959 gather at their hangout, a Baltimore diner, and sort through their various problems, most of which involve women, whom they don't understand (and are perhaps incapable of understanding). More than a nostalgia piece, the movie scores some direct hits on the wall of misunderstanding that separated men and women in the fifties. This low-key ensemble comedy, less pretentious than the somewhat similar *The Big Chill,* resulted in various degrees of stardom for most of its cast, who were then comparative unknowns: Mickey Rourke, Ellen Barkin, Kevin Bacon, Steve Guttenberg, Daniel Stern, Paul Reiser, and Timothy Daly. It was also the directing debut for Levinson, then known primarily as a screenwriter. With *Tin Men* (1987) and *Avalon,* it forms a trilogy of films about his native Baltimore. The Oscar went to John Briley for *Gandhi.*

Levinson: 75, 112, 308, 1653.

547 • DIRTY DANCING

VESTRON PICTURES PRODUCTION IN ASSOCIATION WITH GREAT AMERICAN FILMS LTD. PARTNERSHIP; VESTRON. 1987.
AWARD *Song:* "(I've Had) The Time of My Life," music by Franke Previte, John DeNicola, and Donald Markowitz, lyrics by Franke Previte.

Idealistic teenager Jennifer Grey reluctantly accompanies her family to a Catskills resort in the early sixties and falls in love with dance teacher Patrick Swayze, a guy from the wrong side of the tracks. Dad (Jerry Orbach) objects, but it all comes out right in the end. Sweet, silly summertime fluff that became a huge popular hit thanks to nice performances by Grey, the daughter of Oscar winner Joel Grey [321], and Orbach, plus some cool moves by Swayze, and a soundtrack that blends oldies with some newer songs—not always smoothly. Directed by Emile Ardolino, with Cynthia Rhodes, Jack Weston, and Charles "Honi" Coles. One of the film's new songs, "She's

Like the Wind,'' was written by Swayze, who became a star thanks to the film. The Oscar-winning song is the most memorable of the new tunes, but like a lot of recent Oscar songs, it hasn't had much life outside the movie except on the film's soundtrack album, which was also a big success.

548 • DIRTY DOZEN, THE

MHK Productions Ltd.; MGM (U.S./United Kingdom). 1967.
Award *Sound Effects:* John Poyner.
Nominations *Supporting Actor:* John Cassavetes. *Sound:* MGM Studio Sound Department. *Film Editing:* Michael Luciano.

There's a job to be done during World War II, but it's a suicide mission. So the army comes up with a great idea: Get some men who are not only tough but have nothing to lose—namely, hardened convicts. Lee Marvin [371] is the major who gets the job of whipping into shape a bunch of riffraff that includes Cassavetes, Charles Bronson, Jim Brown, Telly Savalas [210], and Donald Sutherland. The military types who aid or interfere include Ernest Borgnine [1283], George Kennedy [443], Richard Jaeckel [1864], and Robert Ryan [467]. An action classic, thanks to better-than-average casting, a good script by Nunnally Johnson [815 . . .] and Lukas Heller, and unpretentious direction by Robert Aldrich. Often imitated, never bettered. John Wayne [33 . . .] was offered the Marvin role, but he was tied up making *The Green Berets.* Several very bad sequels were made for TV in the eighties.

Cassavetes shares with Charles Chaplin [405 . . .], John Huston [24 . . .], Orson Welles [407 . . .], Woody Allen [39 . . .], and Warren Beatty [255 . . .] the distinction of having been nominated for acting, writing, and directing. Like Welles and Huston, he often used the salary from his acting jobs, in films like *The Dirty Dozen* and *Rosemary's Baby,* to finance his own productions. He began his career on stage and in TV and made his first film as director, a low-budget feature called *Shadows,* in 1961. It was a critical success and won an award at the Venice Film Festival, but Cassavetes the writer-

director was never very successful in attracting audiences. He lost the Oscar this time to a costar from *The Dirty Dozen,* George Kennedy in *Cool Hand Luke.*

In the Heat of the Night won the Oscar for sound, and Hal Ashby won for editing it.

Cassavetes: 635, 2306. Luciano: 688, 963, 1202.

549 • DISCREET CHARM OF THE BOURGEOISIE, THE

Serge Silberman Production; 20th Century-Fox (France). 1972.
Award *Foreign Language Film.*
Nomination *Story and Screenplay—Based on Factual Material or Material Not Previously Published or Produced:* Luis Buñuel, story and screenplay, in collaboration with Jean-Claude Carrière.

Six wealthy friends attempt to sit down to dinner, but the meal keeps getting postponed by surreal events—the dream life of the would-be diners intruding into the real world. Superb satire that skewers most of writer-director Buñuel's favorite targets, especially the church. The writing award went to Jeremy Larner for *The Candidate.*

Buñuel: 2034. Carrière: 2034, 2173.

550 • DISRAELI

Warner Bros. 1929–30.
Award *Actor:* George Arliss.
Nominations *Production:* Jack L. Warner, with Darryl F. Zanuck, producers. *Writing Achievement:* Julian Josephson.

Arliss plays the Victorian statesman in this adaptation of a play he'd performed on stage and in a 1921 silent version. Among other things, Disraeli acts as matchmaker to Lady Clarissa (Joan Bennett) and Lord Deeford (Anthony Bushell). Florence Arliss, the actor's wife, plays Mrs. Disraeli. The film shows its age, but at the time it was a big hit. Directed by Alfred E. Green.

There's a curious anomaly about Arliss' award. The ballot this year listed him as a nominee for both *Disraeli* and *The Green Goddess,* but he was cited as winner only for the first. Academy records don't explain why, so it's possibly a clerical error or the result of voters indicating a preference for the *Disraeli* performance on their ballots. With his long horse face, Arliss was certainly an unlikely movie star, but he had cachet from his long stage career, so audiences turned out in the hinterlands to see what all the fuss was about. He had come to the States in 1902 with an English touring company and had been so well received he stayed, making a specialty of playing historical figures such as Voltaire, Richelieu, and Disraeli. In the early twenties he made a few films, including the first version of *Disraeli,* but returned to the stage until sound came in and the studios clamored for actors who could speak. He helped establish the film career of Bette Davis [46 . . .], who had attracted little attention until Arliss requested her for a role in *The Man Who Played God* (1932). Arliss retired in 1937 when his wife began going blind; he died in 1946. His son, Leslie Arliss, was a screenwriter and director of modest success.

All Quiet on the Western Front was the best picture winner. The screenwriting award went to Frances Marion for *The Big House.*

Arliss: 836. Warner: 55, 110, 689, 1393, 2318. Zanuck: 34, 46, 710, 759, 815, 946, 952, 990, 1201, 1327, 1666, 2154, 2286.

551 • DIVE BOMBER

WARNER BROS. 1941.

NOMINATION *Color Cinematography:* Bert Glennon.

A physician, Ralph Bellamy [114], tries to find out why pilots black out and what can be done about it. Errol Flynn and Fred MacMurray are fliers cooperating in the research. Good action film with fine aerial photography and less heavy propaganda than movies that came later in the war. Directed by Michael Curtiz [79 . . .], with Alexis Smith and, in a small role, Gig Young [427 . . .], billed as Byron Barr (his real name). Otherwise, the film provides an interesting footnote in Oscar history: It was originally announced as a nominee for special effects, crediting the work of Byron Haskin [531 . . .] and Nathan Levinson [16 . . .], but somehow, during the week after the nominations, it was replaced by *The Sea Wolf,* another Warner Bros. film with the same technicians credited

for special effects. The Academy has no record of how or why the switch took place.

Glennon received a solo nomination, although his screen credit is shared with Winton Hoch [1048 . . .], and the aerial photography is by Elmer Dyer [30]. The Oscar went to Ernest Palmer and Ray Rennahan for *Blood and Sand.*

Glennon: 581, 1901.

552 • DIVINE LADY, THE

FIRST NATIONAL. 1928–29.

AWARD *Director:* Frank Lloyd.

NOMINATIONS *Actress:* Corinne Griffith. *Cinematography:* John Seitz.

Griffith plays Lady Hamilton in this silent film, which was thought to be lost until a print turned up in a Czech archive a few years ago. It was reconstructed at UCLA. The cast includes Marie Dressler [611 . . .].

Lloyd, born in Scotland, began as an actor in Great Britain and came to the States in 1913. He started in films the following year as an actor but switched to directing—a profession he pursued for the next forty years. He directed his last film, appropriately titled *The Last Command,* in 1955, five years before his death. He is the only person to win the best director Oscar for a film not nominated for best picture.

Griffith was acclaimed as one of the most beautiful women in silent films, but her career faded quickly with the arrival of sound. She retired in 1932 and began to write, including the book *Papa's Delicate Condition,* which was filmed in 1963. She was among the six actresses considered for the Oscar this year—the only time the Academy chose to announce only the winner, Mary Pickford for *Coquette.* Although she and the other four runners-up were not official nominees, their names have been retained as such by the Academy records because they're listed by the actors branch as under consideration for the award.

Seitz was also an unofficial nominee. One of the most accomplished technicians among Hollywood's cinematographers, his contributions to films over more than forty years are singular, yet he never received an Oscar. In addition to his fine work on classic films by Preston Sturges *(Sullivan's Travels, The Miracle of Morgan's Creek,* and *Hail the Conquering Hero)* and Billy Wilder *(Double Indemnity, The Lost Weekend,* and *Sunset Boulevard),* Seitz also invented the matte shot—the technique of masking part of an image so that another image can be filled in later, without which much of the special effects of movies would be impossible. He retired from films in 1960 and concentrated on photographic research projects until his death in 1979. This time the Oscar went to Clyde DeVinna for *White Shadows in the South Seas.*

Lloyd: 374, 575, 1387, 2239. Seitz: 566, 674, 1208, 1714, 1975, 2262.

553 • *DIVORCE AMERICAN STYLE*

TANDEM PRODUCTIONS FOR NATIONAL GENERAL PRODUCTIONS; COLUMBIA. 1967.

NOMINATION *Story and Screenplay—Written Directly for the Screen:* Robert Kaufman; Norman Lear.

Breaking up really is hard to do, as Dick Van Dyke and Debbie Reynolds [2184] discover when they try it. Well-plotted comedy, but the mores—and the film's hard and garish visual style—plant it firmly in the late sixties. The strong supporting cast includes Jean Simmons [858 . . .], Jason Robards [54 . . .], Lee Grant [534 . . .], and Eileen Brennan [1617]. Director Bud Yorkin and writer-producer Lear first teamed in fifties television. They created Tandem Productions in 1959 and moved into films in the early sixties with the feature *Come Blow Your Horn.* Lear and Yorkin returned to TV in the seventies to create the seminal sitcom *All in the Family.* The writing award went to William Rose for *Guess Who's Coming to Dinner.*

554 • *DIVORCE—ITALIAN STYLE*

LUX-VIDES-GALATEA FILM PRODUCTION; EMBASSY PICTURES CORPORATION (ITALY). 1962.

AWARD *Story and Screenplay—Written Directly for the Screen:* Ennio De Concini, Alfredo Giannetti, and Pietro Germi.

NOMINATIONS *Actor:* Marcello Mastroianni. *Director:* Pietro Germi.

In a country that forbids divorce, what's Mastroi-

anni to do when he falls in love with a beautiful young woman but can't shed himself of his unlovely wife? He rekindles the ardor of one of his wife's old boyfriends so he can murder his wife *in flagrante*—a crime of passion treated lightly by the Sicilian courts. But the course of false love never did run smooth. Superb blend of farce and satire, handled with just the right touch—as a live-action animated cartoon—to mask the essential sourness of the concept.

Three of the five nominees in the "directly for the screen"—as opposed to based on a novel or play—writing category were foreign films. The others were Alain Robbe-Grillet for *Last Year at Marienbad* and Ingmar Bergman for *Through a Glass Darkly;* the more or less domestic nominees were the screenplays for *Freud* and *That Touch of Mink.* It's not so much that the Academy was suddenly becoming more generous toward foreign product as that the industry itself, as what remained of the old studio system turned to dust, was becoming internationalized. The year's best picture winner, *Lawrence of Arabia,* was an Anglo-American product, and one of its chief rivals for the Oscar, *The Longest Day,* had three directors—American, British, and German—and German and French dialogue with subtitles in English. As the American film industry reorganized itself, however, with the major studios absorbed into conglomerates, this international flavor faded.

Mastroianni was a beneficiary of the new internationalism, one of the few non-English-speaking actors to become a major star without going to Hollywood. He has more Oscar nominations for foreign language roles than any other performer, earning them for three very different films: the wildly farcical *Divorce,* the muted psychological drama *A Special Day,* and the Chekhovian *Dark Eyes.* His international fame began with *La Dolce Vita* and continued through scores of films, virtually all made in Europe, not Hollywood. He lost his first nomination to Gregory Peck for *To Kill a Mockingbird.*

Germi began his directing career in 1945, when the neorealist films of Vittorio De Sica [650] and Roberto Rossellini [1519] were gathering international acclaim. Although he worked in this vein for more than a decade, he is best known for the dark comedies he began producing with *Divorce.* Germi died in 1974, of hepatitis, at age sixty. Along with Frank Perry for *David and Lisa* and Arthur Penn for *The Miracle Worker,* he is one of three directorial nominees for this year whose films were not in contention for best picture. Since the 1928–29 awards, when Frank Lloyd won for *The Divine Lady,* no director whose film was not up for best picture has won the directing Oscar. This time the award went to David Lean for *Lawrence of Arabia.*

Mastroianni: 490, 1888.

555 • DIVORCÉE, THE

MGM. 1929–30.
AWARD *Actress:* Norma Shearer.
NOMINATIONS *Production:* Robert Z. Leonard, producer. *Director:* Robert Z. Leonard. *Writing Achievement:* John Meehan.

Fed up with philandering husband Chester Morris [38], Shearer gets her freedom and tries to play the field the way her ex did, having flings with Conrad Nagel and Robert Montgomery [904 . . .]. Alas, she realizes this life is not for her and reconciles with Morris. Clunky little drama, though historically somewhat interesting: It was made before the Production Code, so its attitudes toward sex and marriage seem in some ways more liberal than those of films of the later thirties and forties.

Shearer was nominated for her performance in this film and *Their Own Desire,* but the Academy cited only *The Divorcée* when it presented the Oscar. There's no explanation on record why the other film was omitted, but voters may have indicated a preference for this performance on their ballots. Of all the major female stars of the thirties—Dietrich, Garbo, Harlow, Crawford, Hepburn, Davis, Colbert, Stanwyck—Shearer is the one whose appeal has most faded with time. This may be because of her retirement from movies in 1942, although a similar move only heightened Garbo's mystery. To us, Shearer seems arch, mannered, ordinary in appearance—even slightly cross-eyed—and unconvincing as an actress. None of her thirties films is much revived today, with the exception of *The Women* (1939), in which

Joan Crawford [1319 . . .], Rosalind Russell [110 . . .], and the rest of the cast all but wipe her off the screen, even though Shearer has the leading role. The conventional wisdom holds that Shearer was a star, the "First Lady of the Screen," as MGM billed her, because Irving Thalberg [150 . . .] wanted her to be. Thalberg, the legendary production head at MGM, had spotted the young Shearer playing bit parts in movies in the early twenties and sought her out when he was putting together a company of players for Mayer studios in 1923. She married him in 1927, and he managed her career until his death in 1936. After *The Divorcée,* in which Shearer is lively and sexy, Thalberg started casting her in "prestige" productions, often adaptations of plays such as *Strange Interlude* and *The Barretts of Wimpole Street,* that had been vehicles for great stage actresses such as Lynn Fontanne [841] and Katharine Cornell. This later, more staid Shearer is the one most people are familiar with today. After Thalberg's death, she fell out of favor. Producers have always tried to make stars of their wives and mistresses, and unless the audience is willing, they rarely succeed. Shearer had intelligence and ambition, and it's unfair—and sexist—to suggest that she was nothing more than a powerful producer's puppet.

The best picture Oscar went to *All Quiet on the Western Front,* whose director, Lewis Milestone, also won. The writing award was won by Frances Marion for *The Big House.*

Shearer: 150, 723, 1274, 1721, 2038. Leonard: 831. Meehan: 271.

556 • DO THE RIGHT THING

FORTY ACRES AND A MULE FILMWORKS PRODUCTION; UNIVERSAL. 1989.
NOMINATIONS *Supporting Actor:* Danny Aiello. *Screenplay Written Directly for the Screen:* Spike Lee.

Aiello owns a pizzeria in Brooklyn's Bedford-Stuyvesant ghetto, where tensions between black and white simmer until they reach a violent boiling point one summer day. Lee's comedy-drama is both provocative and entertaining. It stirred controversy when several critics voiced concern that the film might provoke racial violence. Lee, quick to join in when there's a fight, denounced the critics, and with reason: His film is less violent than such contemporary action thrillers as *Lethal Weapon 2,* and it's a good deal more meaningful. The fine ensemble cast includes Ruby Dee, Ossie Davis, John Turturro, John Savage, Samuel L. Jackson [1633.5], Rosie Perez [656.5], and, in the key role of the delivery boy Mookie, Lee himself.

Aiello had worked on the New York stage before making his first film, *Bang the Drum Slowly,* in 1973, and continued to be seen in a variety of small roles over the next decade before emerging as a major character actor in films such as *The Purple Rose of Cairo, Moonstruck,* and *Do the Right Thing.* Though often typed as tough and streetwise, his performance as Cher's mousy mama's-boy fiancé in *Moonstruck* demonstrated his range. He lost to Denzel Washington for *Glory.*

Angry, abrasive, but hugely gifted, Lee is the dean of younger black filmmakers, mentor to rising talents such as John Singleton [272]. His first feature, *She's Gotta Have It,* in 1986, got strong critical support and helped him get lucrative work as a director of music videos and TV commercials, the proceeds from which he used to form his own production company. The box-office success of his next feature, *School Daze,* made in 1988 with partial funding from Columbia Pictures, demonstrated that Lee was in touch with an audience that Hollywood had underestimated. *Do the Right Thing,* the biggest critical and commercial success of the three, confirmed that, but Lee was bitter that the film received only two Oscar nominations. He lost the writing award to Tom Schulman for *Dead Poets Society,* which Lee noted was evidence that the Academy was more moved by the plight of white preppies than that of ghetto residents. His next two films, *Mo' Better Blues* (1990) and *Jungle Fever* (1991), were critically and commercially less successful. In 1992 Lee directed the epic *Malcolm X,* generating controversy throughout its filming by his battles with Warner Bros., and later when the film was largely slighted by the Academy.

557 • *DOCTOR DOLITTLE*

Apjac Productions; 20th Century-Fox. 1967.

Awards *Song:* "Talk to the Animals," music and lyrics by Leslie Bricusse. *Special Visual Effects:* L. B. Abbott.

Nominations *Picture:* Arthur P. Jacobs, producer. *Cinematography:* Robert Surtees. *Art Direction—Set Decoration:* Mario Chiari, Jack Martin Smith, and Ed Graves; Walter M. Scott and Stuart A. Reiss. *Sound:* 20th Century-Fox Studio Sound Department. *Original Music Score:* Leslie Bricusse. *Scoring of Music—Adaptation or Treatment:* Lionel Newman and Alexander Courage. *Film Editing:* Samuel E. Beetley and Marjorie Fowler.

Rex Harrison [413 . . .] plays the kindly English veterinarian who really can talk to animals—and understand them when they talk back—which leads his neighbors to think he's crazy. Awful, leaden musical based on the much-loved children's books by Hugh Lofting, substituting special effects and noisy songs— "Talk to the Animals" should be called "Shout at the Animals" the way Harrison is asked to deliver it—for the gentle whimsy of the books. Directed by Richard Fleischer, with Samantha Eggar [420], Anthony Newley [2285], Richard Attenborough [745], Peter Bull, and Geoffrey Holder.

This unfortunate affair was cooked up to imitate the success of *Mary Poppins,* but it lost buckets of money and almost bankrupted Fox, already swamped by the debts from *Cleopatra.* Harrison, though far from the plump little doctor of Lofting's books, was originally signed, along with lyricist Alan Jay Lerner [66 . . .], on the thought that if cloning *Mary Poppins* wasn't enough, marrying her to *My Fair Lady*'s Henry Higgins might do the trick. When Lerner got out, so did Harrison, but after an attempt to replace him with Christopher Plummer, he was persuaded back in. Location shooting at Castle Combe in England proved enormously expensive. After discovering the perfect little English village, the studio became aware of its imperfections and spent millions making it more perfect, in the end producing something that might as well have been shot on a soundstage and California locations. The animals proved fractious, and Harrison was bitten by a chimp, a dog, and a parrot. And after all the agony, audiences hated the film as much as the critics did.

So why is *Doctor Dolittle* among the nominees for best picture? As always with the big mysteries of the Academy, hard evidence is unavailable, so one has to fall back on informed speculation. The obvious candidate to replace it on the slate is *In Cold Blood,* whose director, Richard Brooks, was nominated for best director, as well as for his work on that movie's screenplay. Richard Fleischer, *Dolittle's* director, was not nominated. Strange things like that had happened before in the annals of Oscar. In 1951 *Decision Before Dawn* was nominated, and the far more popular and successful *The African Queen* wasn't. *The Longest Day,* but not its three directors, got a best picture nomination in 1962, while *The Miracle Worker,* not on the best picture slate, earned nominations for director Arthur Penn and Oscars for Patty Duke and Anne Bancroft. *Cleopatra* made the cut in 1963, but not *Hud,* whose director, Martin Ritt, was on the best director slate while *Cleopatra's* Joseph Mankiewicz wasn't. In all of these cases, the nominated film was an expensive project from 20th Century-Fox, one of the few studios able to hold out against the takeover of the industry by conglomerates in the sixties and seventies. Under Darryl F. Zanuck [34 . . .], Fox was able to muster studio loyalty, making sure that employees who were members of the Academy mentioned the studio's big pictures on their nominating ballots, as well as to mount the kind of publicity campaigns that persuade people—especially if they haven't seen the picture in question—that a film is deserving of consideration. *In Cold Blood, The African Queen, Hud,* and *The Miracle Worker* were all films made by independents, rebels, outsiders, and/or newcomers—people without a major studio backing them. The evidence of logrolling in these cases is circumstantial, of course. Believe it or don't.

As for the winners, Bricusse, the English-born songwriter, wasn't up against much competition. The nominees included songs from *The Jungle Book, Banning, Casino Royale,* and *Thoroughly Modern Millie,* of which only the Disney cartoon was a significant box-office success, and only "The Look of Love," by Burt

Bacharach and Hal David, from *Casino Royale,* was a song that would live on outside of its screen context. The year's best soundtrack, for *The Graduate,* was ineligible because the Simon and Garfunkel songs for which it is remembered had not been composed for the film. But when one thinks of the musical ferment of the late sixties, the great explosion of British rock, folk rock, acid rock, and soul, it's easy to see how retrograde Hollywood was—and how ready for the changes that would come to it in the seventies.

Abbott, in charge of the special effects that include, among other things, the creation of the Pushmi-Pullyu, which is sort of two llamas stuck together end-to-end, received the first of his four Oscars. He spent most of his fifty-five-year career in Hollywood at Fox. He died in 1985.

The best picture Oscar went to *In the Heat of the Night,* which also won for sound and for Hal Ashby's editing. Burnett Guffey won for the cinematography of *Bonnie and Clyde.* The Oscars for art direction and scoring of music (given to adapters and orchestrators) went to Alfred Newman and Ken Darby for *Camelot,* and the award for original score (given to composers) went to Elmer Bernstein for *Thoroughly Modern Millie.*

Bricusse: 805, 933, 937, 1766, 2037, 2201, 2285. Abbott: 1062, 1196, 1596, 2120. Surtees: 130, 175, 810, 917, 1094, 1139, 1388, 1469, 1644, 1747, 1911, 1927, 1960, 2055, 2152. Smith: 29, 413, 646, 896, 1230, 2008, 2120, 2247. Scott: 46, 376, 413, 476, 530, 542, 646, 896, 1062, 1088, 1213, 1391, 1475, 1706, 1753, 1881, 1907, 2008, 2120, 2247. Reiss: 542, 646, 2008, 2093, 2247. Newman: 183, 457, 795, 896, 981, 1160, 1273, 1585, 1762, 2043. Courage: 1585. Beetley: 1201.

558 • DOCTOR ZHIVAGO

Sostar S.A.-Metro-Goldwyn-Mayer British Studios Ltd. Production; MGM. 1965.

Awards *Screenplay—Based on Material From Another Medium:* Robert Bolt. *Color Cinematography:* Freddie Young. *Color Art Direction–Set Decoration:* John Box and Terry Marsh; Dario Simoni. *Music Score—Substantially Original:* Maurice Jarre. *Color Costume Design:* Phyllis Dalton.

NOMINATIONS *Picture:* Carlo Ponti, producer. *Supporting Actor:* Tom Courtenay. *Director:* David Lean. *Sound:* A. W. Watkins, sound director, MGM British Studio Sound Department, and Franklin E. Milton, sound director, MGM Studio Sound Department. *Film Editing:* Norman Savage.

Omar Sharif [1151] plays Zhivago, who marries Tonya (Geraldine Chaplin), but falls in love with Lara, played by Julie Christie [493 . . .], the mistress of Komarovsky, played by Rod Steiger [992 . . .], and the wife of the young revolutionary Pasha (Courtenay). World War I and the Bolshevik Revolution separate Zhivago and Lara except for brief, idyllic reunions. After Zhivago's death, his brother, played by Alec Guinness [287 . . .], seeks out a young girl, played by Rita Tushingham, who may be the daughter of Zhivago and Lara. This long, long epic based on the Boris Pasternak novel profits from the meticulousness of Lean and his team—Bolt, Young, Box, Simoni, and Jarre all worked on other films with the director. But it's a bit shapeless. The love affair of Zhivago and Lara is too thin a plotline to serve as a link between the spectacular reenactments of the revolution. And while Christie is wholly believable as an enigmatic beauty, Sharif makes an insipid Zhivago: There doesn't seem to be much going on behind those big brown eyes. The rest of the cast is fun to watch, even if their styles don't mesh well. Though Courtenay lost to Martin Balsam [2067] for *A Thousand Clowns,* his performance is one of the film's best because he holds back, suggesting banked fires within. Guinness, though miscast, is effective, as is Ralph Richardson [839 . . .] as Chaplin's sweetly dotty father.

Bolt's screenplay makes the most of a novel that was more poetic than cinematic—history provided the most filmable moments. The British playwright later turned to film directing—*Lady Caroline Lamb* (1972)—with little success.

This was the second of Young's three Oscars—all for films directed by Lean. He demonstrates an ability to shoot not only spectacle—the great scenes of war and revolution—but also moments of poetic intimacy, such as the lovely scenes shot through frosted panes illuminated by candlelight.

Although it's clear that no expense was spared on the art direction and costuming, they now seem somewhat dated, exhibiting the mid-sixties high-gloss style—too much obviously fake snow, too much red velvet before the revolution, and too much artful impoverishment afterward—that seems as passé as Christie's false eyelashes and high-maintenance coiffure. (Even at the height of the civil war, Lara seems to be able to get her hands on shampoo and conditioner.) Similarly, Jarre's score was enormously popular—"Lara's Theme" became an elevator-music classic—but it has grown monotonous with overfamiliarity.

Zhivago provided the sole best picture nomination for Carlo Ponti, who produced such foreign language Oscar winners as *La Strada* and *Yesterday, Today and Tomorrow,* as well as *Two Women,* for which his wife, Sophia Loren, won the best actress Oscar. *The Sound of Music* won for best picture and director Robert Wise, as well as for sound and for William Reynolds' editing.

Bolt: 1151, 1252. Young: 1035, 1151, 1429, 1737. Box: 1151, 1429, 1471, 1533, 2134. Marsh: 1285, 1471, 1766. Simoni: 29, 1151, 2000. Jarre: 764, 808, 1151, 1168, 1340, 1533, 1967, 2296. Dalton: 902, 1471. Courtenay: 579. Lean: 287, 289, 820, 1151, 1533, 1963. Watkins: 804, 1107, 1165. Milton: 175, 401, 814, 953, 2184.

559 • *DODES'KA-DEN*

TOHO COMPANY LTD.–YONKI NO KAI PRODUCTION (JAPAN). 1971.

NOMINATION *Foreign Language Film.*

In a Tokyo slum people live out their fantasies, some of them quite surreal. One of the less well received films by director Akira Kurosawa [1661], it was widely criticized as episodic, slack, overlong, and confused in tone, though it is, as always, visually stunning. The Oscar went to *The Garden of the Finzi-Continis.*

560 • DODSWORTH

SAMUEL GOLDWYN PRODUCTIONS; UNITED ARTISTS. 1936.

AWARD *Interior Decoration:* Richard Day.

NOMINATIONS *Picture:* Samuel Goldwyn, with Merritt Hulburd, producers. *Actor:* Walter Huston. *Supporting Actress:* Maria Ouspenskaya. *Director:* William Wyler. *Screenplay:* Sidney Howard. *Sound Recording:* Thomas T. Moulton.

Huston plays the title role, a retired industrialist who takes his wife, Fran, played by Ruth Chatterton [1234 . . .], on a trip to Europe. Unwilling to face middle age, she has romantic flings with David Niven [1778] and Paul Lukas [2233] before falling for an impoverished Austrian nobleman. She asks her husband for a divorce, but the nobleman's mother (Ouspenskaya) blocks the marriage. Meanwhile, Huston has fallen in love with Mary Astor [822]. A handsome production, a strong script by Howard (derived from the play he based on the Sinclair Lewis novel), fine direction, and, above all, splendid performances lift the film far above the soapsuds into which it seems destined to fall. It is, in fact, one of the best films of the thirties, a mature and intelligent drama for mature and intelligent audiences.

Wyler lost to Frank Capra and *Mr. Deeds Goes to Town*, but this was the first of the string of nominations that would make him the most nominated director in Oscar history, and only John Ford [815 . . .] would take home more Oscars. Wyler and Day were among the chief creators of the high-gloss style for which Goldwyn's films became famous. Unlike associate producer Hulburd, they managed to survive Goldwyn's penchant for meddling. Recruited from the *Saturday Evening Post* during one of Goldwyn's forays in search of East Coast talent, Hulburd lasted only a few years with the producer before returning to the magazine. His early death was attributed by many of his colleagues to the stress of his Hollywood experience. *Dodsworth* lost the Oscar to the more conventional *The Great Ziegfeld*.

The strong central core of the film is Huston. This quietly authoritative performance lost to Paul Muni's showier one in *The Story of Louis Pasteur*. Billed as "Mme Maria Ouspenskaya," the hammy little Rus-

sian actress made her film debut in *Dodsworth* but lost to another scenery-chewer, Gale Sondergaard in *Anthony Adverse*.

Howard's fine screenplay lost to Pierre Collings and Sheridian Gibney's for *The Story of Louis Pasteur*. The sound award went to Douglas Shearer and *San Francisco*.

Day: 22, 102, 235, 487, 510, 569, 797, 833, 864, 952, 1048, 1175, 1397, 1477, 1666, 1949, 2056, 2120, 2276. Goldwyn: 102, 184, 214, 510, 1182, 1607, 2316. Hulburd: 510. Huston: 50, 2136, 2318. Ouspenskaya: 1212. Wyler: 175, 184, 420, 534, 730, 894, 1162, 1182, 1371, 1716, 2316. Howard: 102, 798. Moulton: 22, 46, 138, 366, 457, 487, 706, 798, 962, 1153, 1200, 1451, 1510, 1607, 1849, 2154, 2294.

561 • DOG DAY AFTERNOON

WARNER BROS. 1975.

AWARD *Original Screenplay:* Frank Pierson.

NOMINATIONS *Picture:* Martin Bregman and Martin Elfand, producers. *Actor:* Al Pacino. *Supporting Actor:* Chris Sarandon. *Director:* Sidney Lumet. *Film Editing:* Dede Allen.

Pacino, with the aid of John Cazale, robs a bank to pay for a sex change operation for Sarandon, his lover. A tragicomedy of errors, kept percolating by Pacino's hyperactive characterization and a gallery of New York City characters, including Charles Durning [180 . . .] and Carol Kane [908]. Enjoyably offbeat drama based on a real incident—today it would probably be a lugubrious made-for-TV movie.

After two tries, Pierson finally won his Oscar. He turned from writing to directing, though his next film, the Barbra Streisand version of *A Star Is Born*, didn't advance his career very far.

Bregman, a former manager for several Hollywood stars, began an association with Pacino as producer on *Serpico* and subsequently also produced his films *Scarface* (1983) and *Sea of Love* (1989). Elfand, a former agent, became head of production for Warners in 1977. The best picture Oscar went to *One Flew Over the Cuckoo's Nest*.

For three consecutive years, Pacino and Jack Nicholson were considered the front-runners in the Oscar race, but they lost first to Jack Lemmon for *Save the Tiger* and then to Art Carney in *Harry and Tonto*. Nicholson finally broke the string by defeating Pacino this year with his performance in *Cuckoo's Nest*.

Sarandon credited Lumet with giving him the key to his character: Blanche DuBois as a hard hat. Unfortunately his subsequent career has yielded no more roles that brought him this sort of attention, and today he is largely known as the ex-husband of Susan Sarandon [107 . . .]. George Burns won the Oscar, for *The Sunshine Boys*.

Lumet lost to Milos Forman for *One Flew Over the Cuckoo's Nest*. The editing award went to Verna Fields' work on *Jaws*.

Pierson: 371, 443. Pacino: 75, 543, 775.5, 784, 785, 1764.5, 1780. Lumet: 1424, 1611, 2153, 2198. Allen: 1678.

562 • DOLCE VITA, LA

RIAMA FILM PRODUCTION; ASTOR PICTURES INC. (ITALY). 1961.

AWARD *Black-and-White Costume Design:* Piero Gherardi.

NOMINATIONS *Director:* Federico Fellini. *Story and Screenplay—Written Directly for the Screen:* Federico Fellini, Tullio Pinelli, Ennio Flaiano, and Brunello Rondi. *Black-and-White Art Direction–Set Decoration:* Piero Gherardi.

Marcello Mastroianni [490 . . .] plays a self-loathing tabloid journalist who spends his days and nights exploring the seamy side of Roman high society. There's no plot to speak of, but rather a series of episodes, all of which point to a deep spiritual malaise. What one remembers from the film, however, is the extraordinary vividness of its images—their vitality negates the film's message about spiritual emptiness. It was an enormous, eye-opening experience for many in the early sixties, and while it hasn't retained its power to shock and its message seems trite, it taught a generation about the potential of film, making some of Hollywood's best picture nominees— *Fanny, The Guns of Navarone, The Hustler, Judgment at*

Nuremberg, West Side Story—seem timid and formulaic. It also provided a star-making part for Mastroianni.

Gherardi was a former architect who began work in films after World War II and was a major influence on the look of Italian films up till his death in 1971. He lost the art direction Oscar to the designers of *The Hustler*.

Fellini was the only directing nominee whose film was not up for best picture. He took the slot that otherwise might have gone to Joshua Logan, who directed best picture nominee *Fanny*. The Oscar was won by Robert Wise and Jerome Robbins for *West Side Story*.

Three of the five nominees for original screenplay were foreign language films; the other two were the Soviet *Ballad of a Soldier* and the Italian *General Della Rovere*. The Oscar went to William Inge for *Splendor in the Grass*.

Gherardi: 603, 1068. Fellini: 61, 603, 657, 658, 1496, 1519, 1938, 2209. Pinelli: 603, 1938, 2209. Flaiano: 603, 2209. Rondi: 603.

563 • DOLLY SISTERS, THE

20TH CENTURY-FOX. 1946.

NOMINATION *Song:* "I Can't Begin to Tell You," music by James Monaco, lyrics by Mack Gordon.

Betty Grable and June Haver are the sisters, a vaudeville act who encounter the usual backstage tribulations that are primarily an excuse to string together a bunch of pleasant musical numbers. John Payne is the cause of much of the dissension, and the cast includes S. Z. Sakall and Reginald Gardiner, directed by Irving Cummings. Typical Fox musical, colorful and forgettable, produced by an old vaudevillian, George Jessel. The songs are a mixture of period oldies and new ones by Monaco and Gordon. "I Can't Begin to Tell You" competed with a slate of what have now become standards: Jerome Kern and Oscar Hammerstein's "All Through the Day," from *Centennial Summer;* Hoagy Carmichael and Jack Brooks' "Ole Buttermilk Sky," from *Canyon Passage;* Irving Berlin's "You Keep Coming Back Like a Song," from *Blue Skies;* and the winner, Harry Warren and Johnny Mercer's "On the Atchison, Topeka and Santa Fe," from *The Harvey Girls*.

Monaco: 1691, 1900, 1984. Gordon: 428, 569, 897, 1362, 1501, 1964, 1984, 2219.

564 • DOORWAY TO HELL

WARNER BROS. 1930–31.

NOMINATION *Original Story:* Rowland Brown.

Lew Ayres [1052] is a mob boss, with James Cagney [79 . . .] as the henchman who tries to take his place. Cagney's second film, for which he received sixth billing. Very dated and, in the case of Ayres, very miscast. Directed by Archie Mayo.

Three of the five original story nominees were films that featured Cagney; the other two are *The Public Enemy* and *Smart Money*. The Oscar went to the non-Cagney *The Dawn Patrol*.

Brown: 79.

565 • DOUBLE FEATURE

NICKEL ODEON S.A. PRODUCTION (SPAIN). 1984.

NOMINATION *Foreign Language Film.*

Director Jose Luis Garci's film, about the troubles of a pair of screenwriters, is a tribute to the Hollywood movies of the thirties and forties. The Oscar was won by the Swiss *Dangerous Moves*.

566 • DOUBLE INDEMNITY

PARAMOUNT. 1944.

NOMINATIONS *Picture:* Joseph Sistrom, producer. *Actress:* Barbara Stanwyck. *Director:* Billy Wilder. *Screenplay:* Raymond Chandler and Billy Wilder. *Black-and-White Cinematography:* John Seitz. *Sound Recording:* Loren Ryder. *Scoring of a Dramatic or Comedy Picture:* Miklos Rozsa.

Stanwyck persuades insurance salesman Fred Mac-Murray to join her in a plot to kill her husband and collect his insurance, but they reckon without insurance investigator Edward G. Robinson—and their own double-crossing natures. Wonderful, classic sleazy thriller, the essence of film noir, handled with wit and style. It was also the film that set the tone for Billy Wilder's later work: deeply but entertainingly cynical. The three stars never did better work. The

absence from the supporting actor nominees of Robinson—who never received an Oscar nomination —is one of the Academy's worst sins of omission. He's infinitely preferable to cuddly old Monty Woolley, nominated for *Since You Went Away*, or for that matter, the winner, Barry Fitzgerald's lovable priest in *Going My Way*.

The Academy was not very receptive to film noir, that product of war-weariness and uncertainty about the postwar future, but it found *Double Indemnity*'s critical and box-office success hard to ignore, and nominated it along with more conventional choices: the period melodrama *Gaslight*, the home-front sudser *Since You Went Away*, the flag-waving *Wilson*, and the winner, a feel-good favorite, *Going My Way*.

Stanwyck's third nomination found her at the peak of her career. In 1944 the Internal Revenue Service, which seems to have been inclined to publicity stunts in those days, announced that she was the highest-paid woman in America. She was at first reluctant to play the villainous Phyllis Dietrichson in *Double Indemnity*, but Wilder won her over by making her see what a great acting part it was. The Oscar went to Ingrid Bergman for *Gaslight*—an award that many saw as a belated recognition of her work in the previous year's *Casablanca* and *For Whom the Bell Tolls*.

This was Wilder's first nomination as a director, a role he had assumed in the States only two years earlier, on *The Major and the Minor*, although he had directed a film in France in 1933. He lost to Leo McCarey for *Going My Way*.

The intricate plots and hard-boiled dialogue of Chandler's novels were natural for film noir, as was his most famous character, Philip Marlowe, who has been played by actors as various as Humphrey Bogart (*The Big Sleep*, 1946), Dick Powell (*Murder, My Sweet*, 1944), Robert Montgomery (*Lady in the Lake*, 1946), James Garner (*Marlowe*, 1969), Elliot Gould (*The Long Goodbye*, 1973), and Robert Mitchum (*Farewell, My Lovely*, 1975). The flavor of Chandler's work is present in *Double Indemnity*, but it's so intermingled with Wilder's own sardonic tones that one wonders how much actual collaborating was done, especially given Chandler's notorious way of disappearing with a bottle. The screenplay Oscar went to Frank Butler and Frank Cavett for *Going My Way.*

Seitz was the cameraman on Wilder's second film as director, *Five Graves to Cairo,* and would work with him on two more films that rank among their finest: *The Lost Weekend* and *Sunset Boulevard.* He lost to Joseph LaShelle for *Laura.*

The Oscar for sound went to *Wilson.* Max Steiner won the scoring award for *Since You Went Away.*

Sistrom: 2222. Stanwyck: 138, 1879, 1923. Wilder: 91, 138, 198, 705, 709, 925, 1208, 1440, 1738, 1860, 1903, 1975, 2297. Chandler: 242. Seitz: 552, 674, 1208, 1714, 1975, 2262. Ryder: 827, 979, 1452, 1669, 1697, 1703, 1837, 1887, 2012, 2168, 2181, 2183, 2230, 2242. Rozsa: 175, 567, 604, 1035, 1069, 1070, 1085, 1208, 1227, 1644, 1872, 1890, 1968, 2050, 2304.

567 • DOUBLE LIFE, A

KANIN PRODUCTIONS; UNIVERSAL-INTERNATIONAL. 1947.

AWARDS *Actor:* Ronald Colman. *Scoring of a Dramatic or Comedy Picture:* Miklos Rozsa.

NOMINATIONS *Director:* George Cukor. *Original Screenplay:* Ruth Gordon and Garson Kanin.

Shakespearean actor Colman begins to go mad, as the characters he plays take over his life. Preparing for *Othello,* he murders an innocent waitress, Shelley Winters [542 . . .] and suspects publicist Edmond O'Brien [146 . . .] of having an affair with his wife and costar, Signe Hasso. Though Colman stretches credulity as a renowned tragedian, this is an enjoyable, literate melodrama.

The award to Colman is one of those Oscars the Academy sometimes presents to the right people for the wrong roles. This time the most deserving nominee was John Garfield for his bruisingly dedicated performance in *Body and Soul*—a role that may, in fact, have hastened his death. But the Academy loves to see acting that shows, and since playing Shakespeare and going mad weren't in Colman's usual repertoire, and since he had thirty years' experience in movies with no previous Oscars, this made him a shoo-in. Colman began his film career in Britain in 1918 and came to the States in 1920, where he soon

became a star. His beautiful voice made a transition to talkies easy, and he was a major performer up to the late forties. He took the Oscar as a signal to quit while he was ahead, however, and made only a few more appearances before his death in 1958.

This was the second of Rozsa's three Oscars. Like the first, for *Spellbound,* it was for a moody psychological drama. In the fifties he would find himself called on more often for big, brassy historical epics, such as *Quo Vadis?, Ivanhoe,* and his third Oscar-winning film, *Ben-Hur.*

Cukor lost to Elia Kazan for *Gentleman's Agreement.* Gordon and Kanin were in distinguished company: Abraham Polonsky's fine *Body and Soul* screenplay, Charles Chaplin's uncharacteristic black comedy *Monsieur Verdoux,* and the Italian neorealist classic *Shoeshine.* But the Oscar went, appallingly, to Sidney Sheldon's flimsy *The Bachelor and the Bobby-Soxer.*

Colman: 311, 436, 1662. Rozsa: 175, 566, 604, 1035, 1069, 1070, 1085, 1208, 1227, 1644, 1872, 1890, 1968, 2050, 2304. Cukor: 262, 1189, 1393, 1563. Gordon: 11, 1003, 1536, 1728. Kanin: 11, 1536.

568 • DOVE, THE

JOSEPH M. SCHENCK PRODUCTIONS; UNITED ARTISTS. 1927–28.

AWARD *Interior Decoration:* William Cameron Menzies.

Gilbert Roland plays a Mexican bandit who wagers that he can win Norma Talmadge. Silent romance, no longer in circulation, remade in 1939 by RKO as *The Girl and the Gambler,* a Tim Holt western. Menzies, who was cited by the Academy for both this film and *Tempest,* was an enormously influential production designer who, starting in 1921, helped move films out of the era of flimsy painted backdrops and into realistic three-dimensional sets. In the thirties he moved into directing and producing as well as art direction. His work on *Around the World in 80 Days,* though not officially recognized by the Academy, helped novice film producer Mike Todd win a best picture Oscar. He died in 1957.

Menzies: 38, 112.5, 311, 798, 1018, 2010.

569 • DOWN ARGENTINE WAY

20TH CENTURY-FOX. 1940.

NOMINATIONS *Color Cinematography:* Leon Shamroy and Ray Rennahan. *Color Interior Decoration:* Richard Day and Joseph C. Wright. *Song:* "Down Argentine Way," music by Harry Warren, lyrics by Mack Gordon.

Betty Grable and Argentine horse-breeder Don Ameche [419] have a romance, but the only thing most people remember about this empty-headed but colorful Fox musical is Carmen Miranda in her American film debut. This was a star-making vehicle for Grable, a replacement for the usual Fox star, Alice Faye, who had to bow out because of illness. Directed by Irving Cummings, with Charlotte Greenwood, J. Carrol Naish [1294 . . .], and Leonid Kinskey.

The Thief of Bagdad won for Georges Périnal's cinematography and Vincent Korda's art direction. Leigh Harline and Ned Washington's "When You Wish Upon a Star," from *Pinocchio,* was the best song winner.

Shamroy: 29, 226, 356, 413, 495, 602, 1088, 1153, 1213, 1592, 1610, 1706, 1852, 1883, 2013, 2286, 2334. Rennahan: 235, 241, 581, 701, 798, 1120, 1210. Day: 22, 102, 235, 487, 510, 560, 797, 833, 864, 952, 1048, 1175, 1397, 1477, 1666, 1949, 2056, 2120, 2276. Wright: 235, 428, 508, 690, 746, 852, 1175, 1264, 1397, 1475, 2056. Warren: 21, 324, 788, 791, 877, 897, 1072, 1367, 1501, 1964. Gordon: 428, 563, 897, 1362, 1501, 1964, 1984, 2219.

570 • DR. CYCLOPS

PARAMOUNT. 1940.

NOMINATION *Special Effects:* Farciot Edouart and Gordon Jennings, photographic.

Mad scientist Albert Dekker perfects a method of miniaturizing human beings. Groundbreaking special effects help salvage a slim and plodding narrative. Directed by Ernest Schoedsack. The Oscar went to *The Thief of Bagdad.*

Edouart: 56, 975, 1668, 1855, 1887, 1934, 2168, 2175, 2181. Jennings: 56, 975, 1668, 1855, 1887, 1934, 2168, 2175, 2181.

571 • DR. EHRLICH'S MAGIC BULLET

WARNER BROS. 1940.

NOMINATION *Original Screenplay:* Norman Burnside, Heinz Herald, and John Huston.

Edward G. Robinson is the nineteenth-century German scientist who first discovered a cure for venereal disease. Very interesting film that triumphs over squeamishness and censorship—you have to admire Warners for even trying to film the story and then handling it with taste and clarity. William Dieterle [1169] directs a strong cast: Ruth Gordon [11 . . .], Donald Crisp [952], Maria Ouspenskaya [560 . . .], Albert Basserman [706], Louis Calhern [1243], and others. Photographed by James Wong Howe [1 . . .]. The award for original screenplay went to Preston Sturges for *The Great McGinty.*

Herald: 1169. Huston: 24, 105, 356, 891, 1248, 1263, 1363, 1625, 1779, 2136.

572 • DR. JEKYLL AND MR. HYDE

PARAMOUNT PUBLIX. 1931–32.

AWARD *Actor:* Fredric March.

NOMINATIONS *Adaptation:* Percy Heath and Samuel Hoffenstein. *Cinematography:* Karl Struss.

The first sound version of Robert Louis Stevenson's 1885 tale of a scientist, played by March, who discovers a potion that releases the pure evil within his nature. A dramatization of the story was a sensation on the London stage only two years after the book was published, and it was a natural for the movies. There were at least two silent versions, including a still-watchable one with John Barrymore made in 1921. Of the two nominated sound versions, March's is superior, though it goes a bit over the top occasionally. Miriam Hopkins [165] plays the trollop Ivy, and the cast includes, in a bit part, the author's namesake nephew, Robert Louis Stevenson. Directed by Rouben Mamoulian.

March first came to Paramount's attention while parodying John Barrymore in a touring production of *The Royal Family*—a role that he repeated in the film version of the play, earning his first nomination. He shared his best actor Oscar with Wallace Beery, who tied with March for his performance in *The Champ.*

(Odd man out in the three-way race was Alfred Lunt, nominated for *The Guardsman.*) In fact, March out-polled Beery by one vote—the tally was not kept secret in those days—which by Academy rules constituted a tie. (The rule was later changed, and the only other tie in an acting category, between Barbra Streisand for *Funny Girl* and Katharine Hepburn for *The Lion in Winter,* was an actual dead heat.)

Heath and Hoffenstein lost to Edwin Burke's screenplay for *Bad Girl.* Struss is credited with a key effect in the scenes in which Jekyll becomes Hyde: On *Ben-Hur* (1926), Struss had filmed the healing of the lepers by having the deformities of leprosy painted on the actors in red. When a red filter was placed in front of the camera lens, the sores "miraculously" disappeared. He reversed the effect for Jekyll's transformation, painting lines on March's face in red that appeared when the filter was removed. The rest of the transformation was accomplished with the gradual addition of prostheses and wigs. The cinematography Oscar, however, went to Lee Garmes for *Shanghai Express.*

March: 184, 515, 1730, 1909. Hoffenstein: 754, 1149. Struss: 56, 582, 1819, 1972.

573 • DR. JEKYLL AND MR. HYDE

MGM. 1941.

NOMINATIONS *Black-and-White Cinematography:* Joseph Ruttenberg. *Scoring of a Dramatic Picture:* Franz Waxman. *Film Editing:* Harold F. Kress.

MGM's version of Robert Louis Stevenson's novella about the Victorian researcher who discovers a potion that transforms him into a sadistic monster features Spencer Tracy [131 . . .] in the title roles. While working for David O. Selznick [497 . . .] on *Gone With the Wind,* director Victor Fleming [798] had seen Selznick's new discovery, Ingrid Bergman [72 . . .], in screen tests and the rushes for her first American film, *Intermezzo.* So when he was set to direct *Dr. Jekyll,* Fleming wanted to use her in the part of Jekyll's virtuous fiancée. He cast newcomer Lana Turner [1558] as the prostitute Ivy. Bergman, however, recognized that Ivy was the showier part and succeeded in switching roles with Turner. Her performance is the best thing about the movie, though it's too obviously a case of an actress playing hard against type, and her Swedish accent overlaid with Culver City Cockney is a big problem. Tracy, that most American of actors, is miscast as both Victorian gentleman and monster, and Turner is merely pretty.

The transformation scenes were directed by Kress, who had been dissatisfied with the transformations in the 1921 John Barrymore and 1932 Fredric March versions. Working with studio makeup artist Jack Dawn, Kress devised a method of stopping the camera thirty-six times as each new layer of makeup was applied. Producer Victor Saville [406 . . .] was skeptical of Kress' idea and had him fired from the film. Kress was reinstated when Fleming and Tracy protested to the MGM front office; Saville was removed from the picture instead. Kress lost the Oscar to William Holmes' work on *Sergeant York.* The cinematography award went to Arthur Miller for *How Green Was My Valley.* The scoring Oscar was won by Bernard Herrmann for *All That Money Can Buy.*

Ruttenberg: 318, 749, 769, 828, 1069, 1232, 1371, 1861, 2234. Waxman: 958, 1457, 1459, 1579, 1670, 1822, 1975, 1979, 2004, 2334. Kress: 953, 1371, 1596, 2126, 2320.

574 • DR. STRANGELOVE OR: HOW I LEARNED TO STOP WORRYING AND LOVE THE BOMB

HAWK FILMS LTD. PRODUCTION; COLUMBIA (UNITED KINGDOM). 1964.

NOMINATIONS *Picture:* Stanley Kubrick, producer. *Actor:* Peter Sellers. *Director:* Stanley Kubrick. *Screenplay —Based on Material From Another Medium:* Stanley Kubrick, Peter George, and Terry Southern.

Right-wing Gen. Jack D. Ripper, played by Sterling Hayden, launches an atomic attack on the Soviets to forestall, among other things, the plot to fluoridate water. President Muffley (Sellers) is powerless to recall the attack, which sets off the Soviet doomsday machine, to the delight of nuclear scientist Dr. Strangelove (Sellers). Meanwhile, assorted military types run amok, including Gen. Buck Turgidson, played by George C. Scott [73 . . .], Col. Bat Guano, played by Keenan Wynn, Maj. King Kong, played by Slim Pickens, and British Group Capt. Lionel Mandrake, played by Sellers. Kubrick's dark slapstick satire is legendary in many ways. It has contributed a store of images to our cultural heritage: Kong astride the fatal bomb, Dr. Strangelove fighting off his gloved hand, General Ripper babbling about "precious bodily fluids." By becoming a popular success, it also demonstrated that the complacently paranoid view of the West as the bulwark against atheistic communism had ceased to be universally received as gospel. After the Cuban missile crisis and the Kennedy assassination, the deep vein of cynicism about American institutions would not be closed for a long time. But as a movie it has faded a bit with time. Its satire no longer shocks us, and its comic effects seem overstated. Its lasting delights are in some of the performances: Hayden's deranged babbling, Scott's blithe obtuseness in the face of universal destruction, and Sellers' three superbly delineated personae. No one who lived through the past forty years can fail to glimpse Gen. Curtis "Bomb 'em back to the Stone Age" LeMay in Hayden, or Gen. William Westmoreland and other straight shooters of Vietnam in Scott, or Henry Kissinger in Sellers' Strangelove (though in fact Kubrick and Sellers were unfamiliar with Kissinger at the time; Strangelove is actually a parody of Edward Teller, the proud father of the H-bomb). *Dr. Strangelove* is of an era, not for the ages. And perhaps we should be thankful for that.

The other best picture nominees for 1964, a year of painful healing, show how fragmented our culture was becoming. There was a stately historical epic, *Becket,* centering on a political assassination. There was a lively fantasy musical, *Mary Poppins,* that dealt with the loss of innocence. There was a dramatization of a novel, *Zorba the Greek,* about cultural miscommunication. And the winner was *My Fair Lady,* a musical about irreconcilable class differences.

Sellers was at his peak during the year. In addition to his three performances in *Dr. Strangelove*—he was

originally set to play Pickens' role, too, but was prevented by an injury—he also made the first two Inspector Clouseau comedies, *The Pink Panther* and *A Shot in the Dark,* and the charming *The World of Henry Orient.* Small wonder, then, that he also suffered a serious heart attack that year. He had made his film debut in 1951, but his first major role was in 1955's *The Ladykillers,* and the 1959 films *I'm All Right Jack* and *The Mouse That Roared* established him as a comic presence in movies. He never quite achieved the prestige of his performance in *Dr. Strangelove,* and his subsequent films, while usually filled with fine slapstick and eccentric characters, are a mixed bag. The Oscar went to Rex Harrison for *My Fair Lady.* George Cukor also won the directing award for that film.

George's novel *Red Alert,* on which *Strangelove* is based, is a thriller, not a satire. Kubrick began the project with the intention of playing it straight, but ran up against a similar doomsday thriller project, *Fail-Safe,* and decided to go for satire instead. His collaborator, Southern, is best known for the satiric-erotic novel *Candy,* which was badly filmed in 1968. The Oscar winner was Edward Anhalt for *Becket.*

Kubrick: 151, 415, 735, 2164. Sellers: 169. Southern: 595.

575 • *DRAG*

First National. 1928–29.

Nomination *Director:* Frank Lloyd.

Richard Barthelmess [1447 . . .] plays a Vermont newspaper editor who finds it a real drag when his wife's parents come to live with them. This comedy is no longer in circulation. Lloyd won the Oscar as best director for *The Divine Lady* at this ceremony, at which only the winners were announced. Academy records show that he was also considered for the award for his work on *Drag* and *Weary River,* and many lists of Oscar winners cite him as having won for all three. The most recent revision of the Academy's nominations and winners list, however, mentions only *The Divine Lady* as the film for which he won the award.

Lloyd: 374, 552, 1387, 2239.

576 • DRAGON SEED

MGM. 1944.

NOMINATIONS *Supporting Actress:* Aline MacMahon. *Black-and-White Cinematography:* Sidney Wagner.

Katharine Hepburn [24 . . .] plays Jade, a young woman of intelligence and spirit growing up in a Chinese village that values women not at all—until Jade becomes a hero in the village's struggle against the Japanese invaders. Tedious propagandistic version of a novel by Pearl S. Buck. Like most studios, MGM had capitulated to requests from the government for films glorifying our allies. It didn't work in this case: Nobody came to see the movie. MGM's *The Good Earth* was a prestigious film that never quite made it at the box office in 1937, so the studio should have known better than to try to film another of Buck's overrated novels about the Chinese peasantry. Though Hepburn tries mightily at a role that has the virtue of making a strong feminist statement, she is, like everyone else in the movie, ludicrously miscast; even with her eyelids taped back, her manner is much closer to Bryn Mawr than to Beijing. Other Asians are played by Walter Huston [50 . . .], Akim Tamiroff [701 . . .], Turhan Bey, Agnes Moorehead [963 . . .], Henry Travers [1371], and J. Carrol Naish [1294 . . .]. The few Chinese actors who appear in the movie play Japanese, since Japanese-American actors had all been shipped to internment camps. The film was directed by Jack Conway.

MacMahon plays Jade's tradition-minded, disapproving mother-in-law who turns out to be tough and resilient in the face of adversity. A likable, reliable character actress from the start of her Hollywood career in 1931, MacMahon was memorable as one of the sharper-tongued *Gold Diggers of 1933*. She lost her one bid at the Oscar to Ethel Barrymore for *None but the Lonely Heart*.

The cinematography award went to Joseph LaShelle for *Laura*.

Wagner: 1453.

577 • DRAGONSLAYER

BARWOOD/ROBBINS PRODUCTION; PARAMOUNT. 1981.

NOMINATIONS *Original Score:* Alex North. *Visual Effects:* Dennis Muren, Phil Tippett, Ken Ralston, and Brian Johnson.

Peter McNichol, young apprentice to sorcerer Ralph Richardson [839 . . .], answers the summons to slay a dragon that has been terrorizing a village. He is aided by Caitlin Clarke, a girl whose father has kept her disguised as a boy because of the annual sacrifice of a maiden to the beast. This wonderfully realized fairy tale, made in collaboration with the Disney studios, proved too scary for the younger trade and never quite found its theatrical audience. It remains one of the best fantasy films of recent years, with a strong script by Hal Barwood and director Matthew Robbins, superbly convincing dragons, and nice performances by the leads—especially Richardson, who brings his usual off-kilter manner to the wily sorcerer. The film's relatively poor box office, attributed to poor marketing, persuaded Disney to cease its joint-venture efforts and develop its own production and marketing unit for films aimed at more mature audiences. Three years later Touchstone Pictures began operations with the smash hit *Splash*.

North's fine score lost to Vangelis' *Chariots of Fire* score. The more successfully marketed adventure-fantasy *Raiders of the Lost Ark* won the special effects award.

North: 29, 215, 413, 515, 1654, 1727, 1802, 1814, 1886, 1949, 2174, 2177, 2212, 2277. Muren: 5, 588, 614, 997, 1002, 1071.5, 1684, 2019, 2284, 2339. Tippett: 1071.5, 1684, 2284. Ralston: 128, 419, 513.5, 708.5, 1684, 2274. Johnson: 44, 614.

578 • DREAM WIFE

MGM. 1953.

NOMINATION *Black-and-White Costume Design:* Helen Rose and Herschel McCoy.

Cary Grant [1445 . . .] wants to marry Deborah Kerr [599 . . .], but she refuses to give up her job with the State Department. So he proposes to Arab princess Betta St. John, who has been raised with the sole aim of pleasing men. Kerr, sent by her boss,

Walter Pidgeon [1232 . . .], to make sure Grant's marriage doesn't endanger diplomatic relations, teaches St. John that there's more to life than submitting to the whims of a man, and winds up with Grant in the end. Despite a feminist angle that's unusual for the era, this is a flimsy, tedious comedy that misuses two of the movies' most gifted stars. Written, produced, and directed by Sidney Sheldon [121]. The Oscar went to Edith Head for *Roman Holiday*.

Rose: 130, 629, 755, 817, 980, 1007, 1309, 1336, 1599. McCoy: 1644.

579 • DRESSER, THE

GOLDCREST FILMS/TELEVISION LTD./WORLD FILMS SERVICES PRODUCTION; COLUMBIA (U.S./UNITED KINGDOM). 1983.
NOMINATIONS *Picture:* Peter Yates, producer. *Actor:* Tom Courtenay. *Actor:* Albert Finney. *Director:* Peter Yates. *Screenplay Based on Material From Another Medium:* Ronald Harwood.

Finney is a self-obsessed, aging Shakespearean actor—a role based on Donald Wolfit, who can be seen in *Room at the Top, Lawrence of Arabia,* and *Becket.* Courtenay is his dresser, a dutiful but cynical backstage presence, much abused, but the force that gets the actor to the stage for every performance of *King Lear.* Brilliantly performed by the leads, though a little too theatrical in every way: too much a filmed play, and too much a film about players.

Yates, who trained at the Royal Academy of Dramatic Arts, knew the milieu of *The Dresser* well, though he had earned his fame for a very different kind of movie: *Bullitt,* the fast-paced action movie starring Steve McQueen. The inclusion of *The Dresser* among the best picture nominees suggests the thinness of the year's releases. The other nominees were *The Big Chill, The Right Stuff, Tender Mercies,* and the winner, *Terms of Endearment.* James L. Brooks won for his direction of *Terms.*

Finney's performance was widely noted as a tour de force. The actor was only forty-five, but he convincingly plays a much older man. Courtenay, nominated previously for his work in *Doctor Zhivago,* has devoted most of his career since the late sixties to the stage. The two actors lost to Robert Duvall's performance in *Tender Mercies.*

Harwood adapted his own play, which was based on his experiences working with Wolfit. The writing award went to James L. Brooks for *Terms of Endearment.*

Yates: 279. Courtenay: 558. Finney: 1378, 2106, 2177.

580 • DRIVING MISS DAISY

ZANUCK COMPANY PRODUCTION; WARNER BROS. 1989.
AWARDS *Picture:* Richard D. Zanuck and Lili Fini Zanuck, producers. *Actress:* Jessica Tandy. *Screenplay Based on Material From Another Medium:* Alfred Uhry. *Makeup:* Manlio Rocchetti, Lynn Barber, and Kevin Haney.
NOMINATIONS *Actor:* Morgan Freeman. *Supporting Actor:* Dan Aykroyd. *Art Direction–Set Decoration:* Bruno Rubeo; Crispian Sallis. *Film Editing:* Mark Warner. *Costume Design:* Elizabeth McBride.

When a suburban Atlanta matron, Daisy Werthan (Tandy), wrecks her car, her son, Boolie (Aykroyd), hires Hoke Colburn (Freeman) as her chauffeur—over her profound objections. But during the next twenty-five years Daisy and Hoke develop a friendship that transcends social and racial barriers. Uhry based his Pulitzer Prize–winning play on memories of his grandmother, and finely transforms the two-character play for film, adding such secondary characters as Boolie, the maid Idella (Esther Rolle), and Boolie's wife (Patti LuPone). The film was a sleeper hit. The Zanucks beat the odds against a movie with no youthful characters and a muted, somewhat downbeat ending. Many studios passed on releasing it before Warners took a chance. Its success seemed to take even the Academy by surprise: The director, Bruce Beresford [277 . . .], was omitted from the directorial nominees, so when the film won the best picture Oscar, it was the first best picture winner since *Grand Hotel* whose director was not in the running as well.

Richard Zanuck, the son of 20th Century-Fox head Darryl Zanuck [34 . . .], had served as production head at that studio, and briefly—before being fired by his own father—as studio head in 1970. *Driving Miss*

Daisy was Richard's first major film after dissolving a longtime partnership with David Brown [658.5 . . .] and forming a production company with his wife, Lili. She became only the second woman in Oscar history to receive an award for producing the best picture of the year. (The first was Julia Phillips for *The Sting*.)

Though born in London and trained on the British stage, Tandy became one of the most acclaimed actresses of the American theater, which she made her professional home after her marriage to Hume Cronyn [1791] in 1942. She made her film debut in 1944 in *The Seventh Cross*, for which Cronyn received a supporting actor nomination, but had to wait forty-five years for her first nomination. She was a sensation in the original Broadway production of *A Streetcar Named Desire* but lost the role of Blanche DuBois in the film version to Vivien Leigh, who won an Oscar for it. Her own film experiences were occasional and usually unmemorable until her Oscar triumph at age eighty-one, which made her the oldest performer to win an acting Oscar. She died in 1994.

Freeman, who grew up in Mississippi, created the role of Hoke in the original off-Broadway production of the play. In addition to this film, he also gave a strong performance in *Glory* in the same year, establishing himself as one of the screen's most important African-American actors. The race for best actor was seen by many as a three-way contest, with Freeman, Tom Cruise in *Born on the Fourth of July*, and the eventual winner, Daniel Day-Lewis in *My Left Foot*, running well ahead of Kenneth Branagh in *Henry V* and Robin Williams in *Dead Poets Society*.

Aykroyd surprised many by his low-key performance as Boolie. He had swiftly risen to fame on *Saturday Night Live*, and like many of that TV show's stars had moved over to the movies with only modest success. *Driving Miss Daisy* followed a series of rather bad flops, but the nomination helped revive his career. He competed in a strong field: Danny Aiello in *Do the Right Thing*, Marlon Brando in *A Dry White Season*, Martin Landau in *Crimes and Misdemeanors*, and the winner, Denzel Washington in *Glory*.

The art direction award went to *Batman*. *Born on the Fourth of July* won for film editing and *Henry V* for costumes.

R. Zanuck: 1041, 2198. Tandy: 728. Freeman: 1802.5, 1948. Sallis: 45.

581 • DRUMS ALONG THE MOHAWK
20TH CENTURY-FOX. 1939.

NOMINATIONS *Supporting Actress:* Edna May Oliver. *Color Cinematography:* Ray Rennahan and Bert Glennon.

Newlyweds Claudette Colbert [1025 . . .] and Henry Fonda [815 . . .] set up housekeeping in upstate New York, but their honeymoon is interrupted by the Revolutionary War. Well-made but episodic movie about a period that has been skimpily treated by Hollywood. Director John Ford [815 . . .], working from a novel by Walter D. Edmonds, adapted by Lamar Trotti [1516 . . .] and Sonya Levien [1007 . . .], has more success with it than most, though the life of the hardscrabble pioneers who have to fight off Indians and redcoats seems a little too cozy: The interiors look like they came from Ethan Allen—the furniture store, not the Revolutionary War hero. The fine cast includes the usual contingent of Ford stock company members: John Carradine, Arthur Shields, Francis Ford, and Ward Bond.

Oliver as usual plays a stiff but kindly figure, a variation on the perpetual maiden aunt that was her stock-in-trade from her film debut in 1924 to her death in 1942. She was memorable as Aunt March in *Little Women*, Betsey Trotwood in *David Copperfield*, the Nurse in *Romeo and Juliet* (1936), and Lady Catherine in *Pride and Prejudice*. She lost the Oscar to Hattie McDaniel in *Gone With the Wind*.

Rennahan and Glennon's work on *Drums Along the Mohawk* was eliminated from the final ballot for color cinematography after the Academy decided to winnow down its preliminary list of nominees to two finalists in each of the cinematography categories. But though Glennon lost his chance at the Oscar, Rennahan remained on the ballot for his work on *Gone With the Wind* and won, along with his co-cinematographer Ernest Haller.

Rennahan: 235, 241, 569, 701, 798, 1120, 1210. Glennon: 551, 1901.

582 • DRUMS OF LOVE

UNITED ARTISTS. 1927–28.

NOMINATION *Cinematography:* Karl Struss. (Disputed nomination.)

Betrothed to the hunchbacked Duke de Avilia, played by Lionel Barrymore [723 . . .], Emanuella (Mary Philbin) falls in love with his handsome brother, Count Leonardo (Don Alvarado), instead. Their romance is discovered by the duke's evil jester. This dated melodrama, one of the last films of the great D. W. Griffith, originally ended with the death of the lovers, but after initial release, Griffith reshot the ending with the death of Barrymore—and his blessing to the lovers—instead.

Three men were nominated for cinematography in the first year of the awards: George Barnes, Charles Rosher, and Struss. The awards could be for a single film, for several films, or for the total achievement during the nominating period. The winners, Rosher and Struss, were cited for *Sunrise,* but some lists show Struss as a nominee for *Drums of Love* as well—record keeping was sometimes lax about who was nominated for what in the early years of the Academy Awards— so we've included it, although the Academy's most recent revision of its nominees and winners list omits this film.

Struss: 56, 572, 1819, 1972.

583 • DRY WHITE SEASON, A

METRO-GOLDWYN-MAYER PRESENTATION OF A PAULA WEIN-STEIN PRODUCTION; MGM. 1989.

NOMINATION *Supporting Actor:* Marlon Brando.

When his gardener's son disappears, South African schoolteacher Donald Sutherland begins a painful process of awakening from his complacency to full knowledge of the enormity of apartheid. A passionately felt film, directed by Euzhan Palcy, that slips occasionally into melodrama but is full of telling details about the mechanism of racial injustice in South Africa in the seventies. Strong performances from Ja-net Suzman [1429], Zakes Mokae, Jurgen Prochnow, and Susan Sarandon [107 . . .].

Politically active like Sutherland and Sarandon, Brando accepted the minor but showy role of a South African barrister because of his commitment to the subject matter of the film. The Oscar went to Denzel Washington for *Glory.*

Brando: 784, 1069, 1141, 1477, 1763, 1949, 2212.

584 • DUEL IN THE SUN

VANGUARD FILMS; SELZNICK RELEASING ORGANIZATION. 1946.

NOMINATIONS *Actress:* Jennifer Jones. *Supporting Actress:* Lillian Gish.

Jones plays the sultry Pearl Chavez, who stirs enmity between the McCanles brothers—Lewt, played by Gregory Peck [759 . . .], and Jesse, played by Joseph Cotten. Overheated and often silly western whose finale, in which Jones and Peck shoot each other and crawl through the dirt to die together, justly earned the movie the nickname "Lust in the Dust." It's almost as famous for the off-screen passion that created it. David O. Selznick [497 . . .] produced the film to fulfill two major obsessions: surpassing his own *Gone With the Wind* and providing a vehicle for his mistress (and later wife), Jones. In the process, Selznick almost wrecked the film. Originally, novelist-screenwriter Niven Busch [990] had planned to produce a film version of his novel with John Wayne [33 . . .] as Lewt. But RKO, which had the rights to the book, sold it to Selznick, who rewrote the screenplay by Busch and Oliver Garrett, and cast Peck instead of Wayne. He hired King Vidor [378 . . .] to direct, but although Vidor is credited as director, he walked off the picture, unable to handle Selznick's constant interference. The film was completed by William Dieterle [1169], with the assistance of Josef von Sternberg [1358 . . .], as well as second unit directors Otto Brower and B. Reeves Eason; Selznick himself directed some scenes. Because of Selznick's constant fiddling, the film took more than two years to reach the screen—from the purchase of the script in 1944 to release in December 1946. It met with derisory reviews, but the outrage from the censors may have helped counter the bad reviews at the box office. Its disjointed storytelling undermines the effect of some good scenes, one of Peck's best performances, and the work of a strong cast that includes Lionel Barrymore [723 . . .], Walter Huston [50 . . .], Herbert Marshall, Charles Bickford [651 . . .], and Butterfly McQueen.

The film failed to give Jones' career the boost into the stratosphere that Selznick wanted, and he spent the next few years continually searching for the right vehicle for her, with little success. Not until 1955, with *Love Is a Many-Splendored Thing,* would she have another major box-office hit—or Oscar nomination. This time she lost to Olivia de Havilland in *To Each His Own.*

Duel did, however, provide the sole Oscar nomination for one of the legendary figures of movie history —Gish, who virtually invented screen acting and practiced it for seventy-five years, from her debut for D. W. Griffith in 1912 to *The Whales of August* in 1987. Her impressive career as one of the finest actresses of silent films might have continued into the sound era, but several box-office failures and a conflict with MGM head L. B. Mayer caused her to retire from the screen in 1933 and pursue a stage career. She returned for occasional character roles over the next five decades. She lost her sole nomination to Anne Baxter in *The Razor's Edge* but received an honorary award, "for superlative artistry and for distinguished contribution to the progress of motion pictures," at the 1970 awards ceremony. She died in 1993.

Jones: 1213, 1214, 1828, 1868.

585 • *DUMBO*

WALT DISNEY PRODUCTIONS; RKO RADIO. 1941.
AWARD *Scoring of a Musical Picture:* Frank Churchill and Oliver Wallace.
NOMINATION *Song:* "Baby Mine," music by Frank Churchill, lyrics by Ned Washington.

Mrs. Jumbo's baby boy is born with enormous ears, and when she takes revenge on those who laugh at him, she is shackled and caged. Dumbo, befriended by a mouse, Timothy, is put to work in a clown act. When the clowns celebrate their successful new act by boozing it up, Dumbo and Timothy accidentally get drunk as well and wake up in the treetops. Their discovery that Dumbo's ears enable him to fly leads to fame, fortune, and Mrs. Jumbo's freedom. Superlative animated classic, which many rank among Disney's greatest. It descends to sentimentality and sugary cuteness less often than many Disney films, and the "Pink Elephants" fantasy is a psychedelic riot long before psychedelia was ever heard of.

The Disney music department can't be called "unsung" heroes—for obvious reasons. But their contribution is sometimes ignored in the acclaim for the visual wit and charm of the films. *Dumbo*'s songs have a lively, contemporary swing character—particularly "Casey Jr." and "When I See an Elephant Fly"— that isn't present in those of the fairy-tale features *Snow White* and *Pinocchio.* And the verbal and melodic wit of "Pink Elephants on Parade" perfectly complements the images on screen. "Baby Mine," a lullaby that would not have been out of place in *Bambi,* is a more conventional song, but a charming one. It lost to Jerome Kern and Oscar Hammerstein's "The Last Time I Saw Paris," from *Lady Be Good.*

Churchill: 140, 1851. Wallace: 42, 402, 2202, 2273.5. Washington: 274, 911, 912, 1329, 1396, 1576, 1745, 2127, 2282, 2335.

586 • *DUNE*

DINO DE LAURENTIIS CORPORATION PRODUCTION; UNIVERSAL. 1984.
NOMINATION *Sound:* Bill Varney, Steve Maslow, Kevin O'Connell, and Nelson Stoll.

Interplanetary intrigue centers on control of the spice found on the planet known as Dune. At least, that's what we *think* the movie's about. One of its major problems is that the plot is virtually incomprehensible, except perhaps to the devotees of its source, the sci-fi novel by Frank Herbert. The movie was a notorious disaster, both critically and commercially. Written and directed by David Lynch [247 . . .], with a cast that includes Lynch regular Kyle MacLachlan, plus Francesca Annis, Brad Dourif [1481], Jose Ferrer [473 . . .], Linda Hunt [2319], Silvana Mangano, Sting, Dean Stockwell [1281], Max von Sydow [1546], Patrick Stewart, and Sean Young. An edition of the film with almost an hour more footage than the theatrical release is often shown on TV. Lynch had his name removed from that version and Allen Smithee —a pseudonym used on many movies whose directors decline to be credited—listed as director instead. The Oscar for sound went to *Amadeus*.

Varney: 127, 614, 1652. Maslow: 614, 1652, 1888.5. O'Connell: 223, 507, 658.5, 1825, 2020, 2114. Stoll: 2124.

587 • DYNAMITE

PATHÉ. 1928–29.

NOMINATION *Interior Decoration:* Mitchell Leisen.

Because of the terms of an inheritance, Kay Johnson marries a convict on death row, Charles Bickford [651 . . .], with the expectation that he'll be executed and she can then marry Conrad Nagel. But he's reprieved, and when he discovers her reasons for marrying him, he leaves her and goes to work as a miner. Because she'll lose the legacy if they don't live together, she follows him. An explosion traps all three of them in the mine, but Nagel sacrifices himself for the sake of the other two. Corny, extravagant melodrama from producer-director Cecil B. DeMille [412 . . .].

A one-year-only rules change in the awards deprived Leisen of his one chance at recognition by the Academy. This year only the winners were announced, and the others under consideration by the various branches of the Academy were not even recognized with certificates of nomination, as in later years. Because the names of the others who were considered for the Oscars were kept on file, however, Leisen and his fellow runners-up have traditionally been treated as if they were official nominees. Leisen began as a costume designer for DeMille and others, moved into art direction, and then in 1933 began an impressive directorial career. Among other films, he directed *Easy Living* (1937), *Midnight* (1939), *Remember the Night* (1940), *Arise My Love, Hold Back the Dawn, To Each His Own,* and *The Mating Season.* He lost the art direction Oscar to Cedric Gibbons for *The Bridge of San Luis Rey.*

588 • E.T. THE EXTRA-TERRESTRIAL

UNIVERSAL PICTURES PRODUCTION; UNIVERSAL. 1982.

AWARDS *Sound:* Buzz Knudson, Robert Glass, Don Digirolamo, and Gene Cantamessa. *Original Score:* John Williams. *Visual Effects:* Carlo Rambaldi, Dennis Muren, and Kenneth F. Smith. *Sound Effects Editing:* Charles L. Campbell and Ben Burtt.

NOMINATIONS *Picture:* Steven Spielberg and Kathleen Kennedy, producers. *Director:* Steven Spielberg. *Screenplay Written Directly for the Screen:* Melissa Mathison. *Cinematography:* Allen Daviau. *Film Editing:* Carol Littleton.

A botanizing crew of extraterrestrials is surprised during one of its missions in a forest near a suburban community. When the ship makes its escape, one crew member is left behind. He is discovered and befriended by a small boy, Elliott (Henry Thomas), and his siblings, played by Robert MacNaughton and Drew Barrymore. With their aid, the alien summons his ship and returns home, but not before drawing near-fatal attention from scientists who want to study him. Superlative sci-fi fantasy, and until Spielberg's *Jurassic Park,* the biggest moneymaker of all time. After more than a decade of knockoffs and imitations, the movie no longer has its original freshness, and the calculation and contrivance of some of its effects seem more obvious. But in its celebration of innocence and wonder, its evocation of both the pleasures and the miseries of childhood, it still ranks as one of the most memorable movies of the past twenty-five years.

The passing of a decade has also established more clearly what many said at the time of the Oscars: that the wrong film won the best picture award. The winner, *Gandhi,* is largely forgotten, while its chief rivals, *E.T.* and *Tootsie,* retain much of their popularity. (Neither of the other nominees, *Missing* and *The Verdict,* was taken seriously as a contender even at the time.) There are many ways of explaining *E.T.*'s loss at the awards ceremony. By the time of the awards, it had been in release for nearly a year, breaking box-office records and becoming a merchandising phenomenon

—books, records, toys—of enormous proportions. *Gandhi,* on the other hand, was a Christmas release, which has traditionally been better positioning for Oscar consideration. For film industry types grown bored with *E.T.* mania—and perhaps resentful that they hadn't cashed in on it—*Gandhi* looked like the real thing: serious, well made, and carrying with it a success story about the persistent struggle of producer-director Richard Attenborough to bring it to the screen. In comparison with Attenborough's struggle, Spielberg's success must have looked easy—he had the millions earned by *Jaws* and *Close Encounters* to help him in the making of *E.T.* Spielberg would further learn how deeply his enormous success was resented in the industry three years later, when his film *The Color Purple* raked in multiple nominations but none for its director.

Williams' fourth Oscar made him one of the most successful composers in the history of the awards, outranked at the time only by the nine Oscars won by Alfred Newman [31 . . .], whose position as head of the 20th Century-Fox music department virtually guaranteed him an annual nomination. In 1980 Williams succeeded the legendary Arthur Fiedler as conductor of the Boston Pops Orchestra and held the position until 1994.

Rambaldi had designed the hideous extraterrestrials of *Alien,* so creating the benign E.T. was in many ways a challenge to fabricate their antithesis. The creature is a combination of puppetry, electronics, and that old standby, a little person in a rubber suit. Muren and Smith supervised the flying bicycles and other effects.

E.T. also comes to life through sound effects. His voice is a filtered and rerecorded combination of several sources, including the voice of actress Debra Winger [1465 . . .]. But the film has a rich sonic texture throughout, including the characteristic jingle of the keys worn by actor Peter Coyote.

The rest of the awards belonged to *Gandhi,* including producer and director Attenborough, screenwriter John Briley, and editor John Bloom.

Knudson: 321, 516, 613, 631, 938, 1439, 1877, 1911, 2274. Glass: 416, 938, 1439, 1877, 1911.

Digirolamo: 613, 2274. Cantamessa: 339, 416, 1439, 1914, 2165, 2331. Williams: 6, 260, 403, 416, 613, 614, 659, 805, 933, 937, 982, 996, 997, 1041, 1047, 1596, 1652, 1679, 1684, 1701, 1765.65, 1916, 1977, 2107, 2126, 2194, 2293, 2322. Rambaldi: 44, 1089. Muren: 5, 577, 614, 997, 1002, 1071.5, 1684, 2019, 2284, 2339. Smith: 1002. Campbell: 127, 684, 2274. Burtt: 996, 1652, 1684, 1916, 2284. Spielberg: 416, 423, 1652, 1764.65. Kennedy: 423. Daviau: 112, 308, 423, 613.

589 • *EARL CARROLL VANITIES*
Republic. 1945.
Nomination *Song:* "Endlessly," music by Walter Kent, lyrics by Kim Gannon.

Constance Moore, European royalty down on her luck, lands a job singing in a nightclub. Vapid musical whose title tries to cash in on the reputation for naughtiness and nudity of the revues produced by Carroll in the thirties. It has little to recommend it except the wisecracks of Eve Arden [1319] and, for those consumed by nostalgia for the early days of TV, an appearance by Pinky Lee. Directed by Joseph Santley. The Oscar went to Richard Rodgers and Oscar Hammerstein for "It Might As Well Be Spring," from *State Fair.*

Kent: 1870. Gannon: 59, 1870.

590 • *EARRINGS OF MADAME DE . . . , THE*
Franco-London Productions; Arlan Pictures (France). 1954.
Nomination *Black-and-White Costume Design:* Georges Annenkov and Rosine Delamare.

Madame, played by Danielle Darrieux, pawns her earrings. Her husband, played by Charles Boyer [36 . . .], redeems them as a present for his mistress, who loses them while gambling. Vittorio De Sica [650] buys them and gives them to his mistress, Darrieux. And so on. A lavish, baroque film, directed by Max Ophüls [1582 . . .]. Some find it ravishing, others merely overproduced.

The costuming award went to Edith Head for *Sabrina.*

591 • *EARTHQUAKE*

Universal-Mark Robson-Filmakers Group Production; Universal. 1974.

Awards *Sound:* Ronald Pierce and Melvin Metcalfe, Sr. *Special Achievement Award for Visual Effects:* Frank Brendel, Glen Robinson, and Albert Whitlock.

Nominations *Cinematography:* Philip Lathrop. *Art Direction–Set Decoration:* Alexander Golitzen and E. Preston Ames; Frank McKelvy. *Film Editing:* Dorothy Spencer.

The Big One hits L.A., jeopardizing engineer Charlton Heston [175], his bitchy wife, Ava Gardner [1339], and his mistress, Genevieve Bujold [85], as well as George Kennedy [443], Richard Roundtree, and—in a brief cameo under the billing Walter Matuschanskayasky—Walter Matthau [709 . . .]. Awful, awful disaster flick, whose only thrill is watching people die horribly. An unpleasant subplot involves rapist Marjoe Gortner stalking Victoria Principal. The stars seem tired and dispirited, as well they might in a movie that casts Lorne Greene as Gardner's father—he was seven years old when she was born.

The Oscar for sound was awarded because of the film's use of Sensurround, a technique involving oversize speakers that produce a heavy bass rumble during the quake—unsubtle but more effective than what's going on in the movie. The Academy was so impressed with Sensurround that it gave its developers and engineers a Class II Scientific and Technical Award. The device hasn't been heard of since. Many think the Oscar should have gone instead to the fine, subtle work of Walter Murch and Arthur Rochester on *The Conversation,* a film that's *about* sound.

The disaster epic was at its peak this year, following the surprise success two years earlier of *The Poseidon Adventure. Earthquake* was up against another in the genre, *The Towering Inferno,* in several categories, losing to it for Fred Koenekamp and Joseph Biroc's cinematography and Harold F. Kress and Carl Kress' film editing. The art direction award went to *The Godfather, Part II.*

Pierce: 31, 1927. Robinson: 917, 1089, 1196. Whitlock: 917, 2104. Lathrop: 69. Golitzen: 31, 96, 414, 690, 706, 744, 1560, 1886, 1968, 1986, 2035, 2064, 2101. Ames: 31, 66, 290, 769, 1226, 1937, 2184. McKelvy: 917, 1450, 1570, 1631, 2047, 2200. Spencer: 413, 517, 1901.

592 • *EAST LYNNE*

Fox. 1930–31.

Nomination *Picture:* Winfield Sheehan, studio head.

Ann Harding [927] stars in the quintessential Victorian melodrama, about a woman who suffers and suffers and suffers—her husband divorces her, her lover deserts her, and she goes blind. Directed by Frank Lloyd [374 . . .] and produced with a sophistication the material doesn't deserve. The presence of this now little-seen film among the nominees reflects the confusion of an industry still struggling with the transition to sound. The Oscar went to *Cimarron,* generally regarded as one of the weakest films ever to win best picture, and the other nominees were *The Front Page, Skippy,* and *Trader Horn,* of which only *The Front Page* still gets respectful attention today. But the year's most interesting films were overlooked: *Morocco, Little Caesar, Public Enemy, The Blue Angel,* and *City Lights.*

Sheehan: 132, 374, 989, 1920.

593 • *EAST OF EDEN*

Warner Bros. 1955.

Award *Supporting Actress:* Jo Van Fleet.

Nominations *Actor:* James Dean. *Director:* Elia Kazan. *Screenplay:* Paul Osborn.

Dean is Cal Trask, growing up at odds with his stern, Bible-reading father, Adam, played by Raymond Massey [1], and his dutiful brother, Aron, played by Richard Davalos. This adaptation of the novel by John Steinbeck [1171 . . .] is a sometimes overobvious retelling of the Cain and Abel story, but it has staying power, despite its occasional pretentiousness. The extraordinary magnetism of Dean's performance is what holds it together and keeps the melodrama from turning laughable. Julie Harris [1301] and Albert Dekker provide strong support. Paul Newman [3 . . .] tested for the role that went to Davalos, who, twelve years later, had a small part in *Cool Hand Luke,* starring Newman.

Van Fleet made her screen debut as Dean's mother, though she was only eleven years his senior. An acclaimed Broadway actress and member of the Actors Studio, she has made only a handful of screen appearances.

This was the first of Dean's two posthumous nominations. *East of Eden* was, in fact, the only one of his three major films released before his death on September 30, 1955, in an auto accident. He can be glimpsed in the 1951 Korean War drama *Fixed Bayonets* and the Dean Martin–Jerry Lewis comedy *Sailor Beware* and in the 1952 musical *Has Anybody Seen My Gal?* But it was the posthumously released *Rebel Without a Cause* that established him as a screen legend. The Oscar went to Ernest Borgnine for *Marty,* which also won Oscars for its director, Delbert Mann, and its screenwriter, Paddy Chayefsky.

Dean: 768. Kazan: 63, 759, 1477, 1949. Osborn: 1763.

594 • *EASTER PARADE*
MGM. 1948.
Award *Scoring of a Musical Picture:* Johnny Green and Roger Edens.

When Ann Miller, the dance partner of turn-of-the-century musical star Fred Astaire [2126], walks out on him, he bets his friend Peter Lawford that he can make a star out of any chorus girl. The one he chooses happens to be Judy Garland [1065 . . .]. They go on to professional and romantic success, threatened only by Miller's attempts to break up their act. The plot is only a slight impediment to this lovely trifle. Not only is it the only film to team Garland and Astaire, it also has sixteen songs by Irving Berlin [34 . . .]. The star teaming happened by accident: Gene Kelly [74], originally set for the film, broke an ankle. Astaire, who had been in retirement for two years, was persuaded out of it by producer Arthur Freed [66 . . .]. Garland's husband, Vincente Minnelli [66 . . .], was scheduled to direct, but Garland's psychiatrist advised against their working together. Charles Walters [1173], a former dancer and choreographer, took over as director. The film's highlight is Astaire and Garland's duet to ''A Couple of Swells,'' which they perform in top-hatted (naturally) hobo garb.

Among the sixteen Berlin songs Green and Edens had to work with were seven new ones, none of which, however, made the slate of nominees for best song—a list that included, of all things, ''The Woody Woodpecker Song.''

Green: 66, 320, 662, 817, 914, 1298, 1471, 1550, 1657, 2047, 2244. Edens: 87, 115, 699, 801, 1476, 1950.

595 • *EASY RIDER*
Pando-Raybert Productions; Columbia. 1969.
Nominations *Supporting Actor:* Jack Nicholson. *Story and Screenplay—Based on Material Not Previously Published or Produced:* Peter Fonda, Dennis Hopper, and Terry Southern.

Wyatt (Fonda) and Billy (Hopper) take the money they've made from running drugs, buy motorcycles, and set out on a cross-country odyssey. Along the way, they're thrown in jail, where they meet alcoholic lawyer George Hanson (Nicholson), who tags along when they continue their ride. Hanson is killed before he reaches his destination, a New Orleans brothel, and at film's end, rednecks in a pickup truck shoot Wyatt and Billy. Hugely successful low-budget film, a paean to sex, drugs, and rock and roll, whose success—along with that of *Bonnie and Clyde, The Graduate,* and *2001: A Space Odyssey*—signaled the arrival of the baby boomers as the target movie audience. It's not in a league with those other films, however. Wyatt and Billy today look more like self-destructive dolts than role models for the revolution, and the film is gratingly sexist. About the best that can be said of it today is that it has a great soundtrack full of acid-rock classics, that it's better than the endless imitations that were spewed out of Hollywood in the next few years, and that it set Nicholson and cinematographer Laszlo Kovacs on the road to better things. For Fonda and Hopper, however, the career path was not so smooth. Fonda has continued in the shadow of his more famous father, Henry [815 . . .], and sister, Jane [394 . . .]—and more recently that of his daughter, Bridget. Hopper's debut as a director, after an acting career that began in 1955 with such films as *Rebel Without a Cause* and *Giant,* was promising, but personal crises and drug addiction sent his career into a tailspin. He began to reemerge in 1979 with his performance as a drugged-out photographer in *Apocalypse Now,* which many felt was a self-portrait. By the mid-eighties, with impressive performances in *Blue Velvet* and *Hoosiers,* he became a successful actor again, and his return to directing with the film *Colors* (1988) was critically well received. He has talked of making an *Easy Rider* sequel, though with the three central characters killed off in the first one, it's hard to imagine.

After spending a decade in Hollywood making low-budget features, mostly for Roger Corman, Nicholson received the first of his ten Oscar nominations. He was not the first choice for the role, however. Rip Torn [466] walked off the film after clashing with director Hopper. Bruce Dern [430], who had costarred with Fonda in the biker flick *The Wild Angels* (1966), was considered as a replacement, but Nicholson was more readily available. The Oscar went to Gig Young for *They Shoot Horses, Don't They?*

As with any successful film, legends have grown up about who contributed what to the success of *Easy Rider.* The screenplay, because it's loose, episodic, and partly improvised, is a particularly disputed area. Fonda has been credited with its genesis; he was supposedly inspired by a still from *The Wild Angels* showing him and Dern on their bikes, and spurred by a speech given by the sanctimonious Jack Valenti, head of the Motion Picture Association of America, about the need for more family films like *Doctor Dolittle.* Fonda and Hopper developed the story and presented it to producer Bert Schneider, whose family ties (his father was chairman and his brother president of Columbia) helped get the financing. At some point, Southern, who had collaborated on the screenplay for *Dr. Strangelove* and had written the script for *Barbarella* (1968), was called in for consultation—the extent of which became a matter of dispute after the film became a hit. Fonda and Hopper credited Southern with the film's title, but not much else. Southern claimed credit for much of the character played by Nicholson,

which he said was based on William Faulkner's lawyer Gavin Stevens, and for his famous speech about the Venusians. The Oscar went to William Goldman for a more conventional portrait of a pair of rebels on the run, *Butch Cassidy and the Sundance Kid.*

Nicholson: 395, 658.5, 672, 1019, 1135, 1481, 1625, 1678, 2020. Hopper: 939. Southern: 574.

595.5 • *EAT DRINK MAN WOMAN*
CENTRAL MOTION PICTURE CORPORATION PRODUCTION IN ASSOCIATION WITH ANG LEE PRODUCTIONS AND GOOD MACHINE; SAMUEL GOLDWYN COMPANY (REPUBLIC OF CHINA ON TAIWAN). 1994.

NOMINATION *Foreign Language Film.*

A celebrated Taiwanese chef is a widower with three unmarried daughters. He's a traditionalist who insists on preparing an elaborate Sunday dinner for them and trying to manage their lives, while they have Westernized ways—in fact, the youngest works at Wendy's. The film follows the intersecting lives and romances of the three daughters. This entertaining comedy was the second foreign film nominee—the first was *The Wedding Banquet*—directed by Ang Lee. The Oscar went to Russia's *Burnt by the Sun.*

595.8 • *ED WOOD*
TOUCHSTONE PICTURES PRODUCTION; BUENA VISTA. 1994.

AWARDS *Supporting Actor:* Martin Landau. *Makeup:* Rick Baker, Ve Neill, and Yolanda Toussieng.

Johnny Depp plays the title role, an actual fifties Hollywood director responsible for what have been celebrated as some of the most hilariously inept movies ever made, including *Plan 9 From Outer Space* (1959) and the "problem drama" about transvestism, *Glen or Glenda* (1953). Wood himself was a transvestite, who didn't think twice about donning women's clothes while directing a film. His star was the aging, drug-addicted Bela Lugosi (Landau). Slight but amusing and often quite affecting portrait of the Hollywood lunatic fringe, directed by Tim Burton from a script by Scott Alexander and Larry Karaszewski that's short on plot but full of atmosphere. But though many critics loved the movie, audiences weren't even remotely tempted to check it out, and it died a swift death at the box office. Accepting his Oscar, Landau quipped that everyone who saw the film was in the audience at the Shrine Auditorium. Too bad, because Depp is wonderful in the title role, and the supporting cast includes Sarah Jessica Parker as Wood's girlfriend, Bill Murray as the effeminate Bunny Breckenridge, Jeffrey Jones as the "amazing Criswell," and Vincent D'Onofrio in a letter-perfect cameo as Orson Welles [407 . . .]. The fine black-and-white cinematography by Stefan Czapsky should, many felt, have been nominated instead of the more conventionally picturesque work of Owen Roizman on *Wyatt Earp.*

Landau had become one of the most respected actors in Hollywood in part because of his reputation as an acting coach, but also because of his professionalism. He won the Screen Actors Guild award a month before the Oscars, and carried off most of the awards from the major critics' groups as well. But Landau had been considered the Oscar front-runner before, when he was nominated for *Tucker: The Man and His Dream,* but he was surprisingly upset by Kevin Kline for *A Fish Called Wanda.* He had also been nominated for *Crimes and Misdemeanors* and lost to Denzel Washington for *Glory.* The third time was apparently the charm.

Landau: 461, 2148. Baker: 68, 431, 839, 874. Neill: 153.5, 167, 600, 924.5, 1370.5. Toussieng: 1370.5.

596 • EDDY DUCHIN STORY, THE

COLUMBIA. 1956.

NOMINATIONS *Motion Picture Story:* Leo Katcher. *Color Cinematography:* Harry Stradling. *Sound Recording:* John Livadary, sound director, Columbia Studio Sound Department. *Scoring of a Musical Picture:* Morris Stoloff and George Duning.

Tyrone Power plays the pianist and bandleader who dies of leukemia after losing his wife, Kim Novak. Lots of music, which is the saving grace of this teary biopic, directed by George Sidney.

The writing award went to Dalton Trumbo (under the *nom de* blacklist of Robert Rich) for *The Brave One.* Lionel Lindon won for the cinematography of *Around*

the World in 80 Days. The King and I won for both sound recording and Alfred Newman and Ken Darby's scoring.

Stradling: 110, 149, 737, 852, 853, 864, 896, 957, 1246, 1393, 1567, 1949, 2338. Livadary: 330, 455, 732, 1058, 1206, 1215, 1303, 1366, 1370, 1488, 1521, 1740, 1872, 2111, 2325, 2327. Stoloff: 13, 432, 455, 643, 677, 732, 773, 1057, 1058, 1115, 1206, 1862, 1872, 1873, 1998, 2110, 2329. Duning: 732, 1057, 1442, 1566.

597 • EDISON, THE MAN

MGM. 1940.

NOMINATION *Original Story:* Hugo Butler and Dore Schary.

Spencer Tracy [131 . . .] plays the inventor as he struggles in poverty toward the breakthrough development of the lightbulb. Essentially the second half of a biopic saga that began the same year with *Young Tom Edison,* starring Mickey Rooney [115 . . .] in the title role. Sentimental, clichéd, and cavalier about matters of fact, but still watchable. Clarence Brown [84 . . .] directs a good cast: Rita Johnson, Charles Coburn [535 . . .], Gene Lockhart [36], and Henry Travers [1371]. The Oscar went to Benjamin Glazer and John S. Toldy for *Arise, My Love.*

Schary: 157, 271.

598 • EDUCATING RITA

ACORN PICTURES LTD. PRODUCTION; COLUMBIA (UNITED KINGDOM). 1983.

NOMINATIONS *Actor:* Michael Caine. *Actress:* Julie Walters. *Screenplay Based on Material From Another Medium:* Willy Russell.

Hairdresser Walters figures there must be more to life than doing hair, so she enrolls in alcoholic professor Caine's English literature class. As in *Pygmalion,* the tables are soon turned. Enjoyable adaptation by Russell of his two-character stage play. Not much of a movie, but Caine and Walters are terrific. Producer-director Lewis Gilbert [35], who launched Caine to stardom in *Alfie,* resisted the studio's desire to cast Dolly Parton [1438] in Walters' role.

Caine had become one of the busiest actors on

screen, appearing in two or three films a year when most stars barely make one. He lost to Robert Duvall in *Tender Mercies.*

Walters re-created the role she had played on stage, which earned her a Tony. It was her film debut, but her subsequent screen career has not been impressive. The Oscar went to Shirley MacLaine for *Terms of Endearment,* which also won for James L. Brooks' screenplay.

Caine: 35, 863, 1841.

599 • EDWARD, MY SON

MGM (UNITED KINGDOM). 1949.
NOMINATION *Actress:* Deborah Kerr.

The unhappy marriage of Kerr and Spencer Tracy [131 . . .] has led to the suicide of their son. Plodding and depressing adaptation by Donald Ogden Stewart [1148 . . .] of a play by Noel Langley and Robert Morley [1274]. Director George Cukor [262 . . .] never overcomes the theatrical origin of the work; in fact, by allowing Tracy to address the audience, he heightens it.

This was the first of Kerr's six unsuccessful nominations—a record for actresses that she shares with Thelma Ritter [46 . . .]. (Richard Burton [85 . . .] and Peter O'Toole [164 . . .] hold the record for actors at seven each.) Trained as a dancer at Sadlers Wells, she decided that she preferred acting and began a stage career that led to small film roles. Her first major part was in *Major Barbara* in 1941. The acclaim she received for her performance in *Black Narcissus* in 1947 led to a contract with MGM. Olivia de Havilland won the Oscar for *The Heiress.*

Kerr: 732, 891, 1088, 1778, 1969.

600 • EDWARD SCISSORHANDS

20TH CENTURY FOX PRODUCTION; 20TH CENTURY FOX. 1990.
NOMINATION *Makeup:* Ve Neill and Stan Winston.

Avon Lady Dianne Wiest [311.5 . . .] goes calling on the spooky mansion on the hill and discovers that its resident is a boy, played by Johnny Depp, with shears and knives in place of hands. His creator, mad scientist Vincent Price, died before he could attach the proper appendages. Wiest takes Depp home to husband Alan Arkin [884 . . .] and daughter Winona Ryder [27.5 . . .], where after a few mishaps such as a punctured water bed, Depp gains acceptance, and even acclaim, for his skill at topiary and hairdressing. But when Ryder starts to fall in love with Depp, jealous boyfriend Anthony Michael Hall stirs up hostility, causing Depp to flee. Quirky *Frankenstein*-in-suburbia fable from writer-director Tim Burton that has moments of wit and charm—Wiest and Depp are particularly fine—but never quite gets its tone and pacing smoothed out. Neill and Winston, who were later nominated for their work on Burton's *Batman Returns,* lost to John Caglione, Jr., and Doug Drexler for *Dick Tracy.*

Neill: 153.5, 167, 595.8, 924.5, 1370.5. Winston: 45, 153.5, 886, 1071.5, 1600, 2019.

601 • EGG AND I, THE

UNIVERSAL-INTERNATIONAL. 1947.
NOMINATION *Supporting Actress:* Marjorie Main.

Urbanite Claudette Colbert [1025 . . .] and her husband, Fred MacMurray, struggle with life on a chicken farm. Agreeable little situation comedy (the obvious inspiration for *Green Acres)* based on a best-selling book by Betty MacDonald. Directed by Chester Erskine, who cowrote the screenplay with Fred Finkelhoffe. Secondary characters Ma and Pa Kettle, played by Main and Percy Kilbride, were spun off into a series of low-budget features from Universal over the next decade.

Main had been a Broadway actress since 1916 and made her first film in 1931. Although she began her film career in relatively serious parts, most memorably as Humphrey Bogart's mother in *Dead End,* she is best remembered for bringing her raspy voice and folksy manner to comedy roles. During her period as an MGM contract player, she was the cook in *Meet Me in St. Louis* and a formidable frontier woman in *The Harvey Girls,* in which she even gets to sing and dance. The Oscar went to Celeste Holm for *Gentleman's Agreement.*

602 • EGYPTIAN, THE

20TH CENTURY-FOX. 1954.

NOMINATION *Color Cinematography:* Leon Shamroy.

Abandoned as an infant, Sinuhe (Edmund Purdom) grows up to be physician to the pharaoh Akhnaton (Michael Wilding). Tedious epic based on a now unreadable best-seller by Mika Waltari. Producer Darryl F. Zanuck [34 . . .] expected this to be a blockbuster, and he threw a lot of impressive talent at it: director Michael Curtiz [79 . . .], screenwriters Philip Dunne [495 . . .] and Casey Robinson, and a cast including Jean Simmons [858 . . .], Victor Mature, Gene Tierney [1153], Peter Ustinov [943 . . .], Judith Evelyn, Henry Daniell, John Carradine, and Zanuck's *protégée du jour,* Bella Darvi. Marlon Brando [583 . . .] was expected to play Sinuhe, but they made the mistake of letting him read the script, so he was replaced by Purdom, whose Hollywood career consisted largely of filling roles meant for others. (He also replaced Mario Lanza in *The Student Prince,* lip-synching the tenor's songs.) Shamroy's cinematography, by far the best thing about the movie, lost to Milton Krasner's for *Three Coins in the Fountain.*

Shamroy: 29, 226, 356, 413, 495, 569, 1088, 1153, 1213, 1592, 1610, 1706, 1852, 1883, 2013, 2286, 2334.

603 • 8¹/₂

CINERIZ PRODUCTION; EMBASSY PICTURES CORPORATION (ITALY). 1963.

AWARDS *Black-and-White Costume Design:* Piero Gherardi. *Foreign Language Film.*

NOMINATIONS *Director:* Federico Fellini. *Story and Screenplay—Written Directly for the Screen:* Federico Fellini, Ennio Flaiano, Tullio Pinelli, and Brunello Rondi. *Black-and-White Art Direction—Set Decoration:* Piero Gherardi.

Guido, a film director played by Marcello Mastroianni [490 . . .], is suffering from the cinematic equivalent of writer's block—he just can't seem to get his new film started. And he has all these complicated relationships with women: his wife, Anouk Aimée [1250]; his mistress, Sandra Milo; his ideal, the

potential star of his film, Claudia Cardinale; and even the memory of his first sexual encounter, the prostitute Saraghina, played by Edra Gale. So he drifts into fantasies of flight, of having them all in a harem, and finally, a liberating vision of the people in his life dancing in a ring. Hugely entertaining, baroque, provocative exploration of the director's own psyche. The title refers to the number of films Fellini had made through this one, with the fraction accounting for his contribution to several anthology films and his codirection of *Variety Lights* (1950). Art about art can sometimes turn self-indulgent, as in Paul Mazursky's explicit *hommage* to *8¹/₂, Alex in Wonderland* (1970), or Bob Fosse's *All That Jazz,* or Woody Allen's *Stardust Memories* (1980). But Fellini's wit and inventiveness, Mastroianni's superb performance, Gianni Di Venanzo's gorgeous cinematography, and Nino Rota's evocative score make this a classic. Its omission from the best picture nominees, even though the Academy recognized it in the foreign language category, is shocking. Most of the nominated films—*America, America, Cleopatra, How the West Was Won,* and *Lilies of the Field*—are forgotten or treated with derision today. Only the winner, *Tom Jones,* belongs in the company of *8¹/₂,* but its director, Tony Richardson, hardly deserved the Oscar in competition with Fellini.

The screenplay award went to James R. Webb for *How the West Was Won.* Gene Callahan's work on *America, America* won for art direction.

Gherardi: 562, 1068. Fellini: 61, 562, 657, 658, 1496, 1519, 1938, 2209. Flaiano: 562, 2209. Pinelli: 562, 1938, 2209. Rondi: 562.

EL AMOR BRUJO
See 71.

604 • EL CID

ALLIED ARTISTS. 1961.

NOMINATIONS *Color Art Direction—Set Decoration:* Veniero Colasanti and John Moore. *Song:* "Love Theme From *El Cid,*" music by Miklos Rozsa, lyrics by Paul Francis Webster. *Scoring of a Dramatic or Comedy Picture:* Miklos Rozsa.

Charlton Heston [175] plays the heroic leader of

the Spanish against the Moorish occupation in the eleventh century. Sophia Loren [1280 . . .] is his beloved Chimene. Big-budget epic with the usual virtues—lots of colorful action—and flaws—characters who don't make much sense. Though Heston ages throughout the film, Loren doesn't even get a gray hair or a wrinkle. Anthony Mann, a veteran director of westerns, treats this as if it were one, which works. Director Martin Scorsese [27.5 . . .], an admirer of the film, and of Mann's work, bankrolled a restoration and revival of the movie in 1993.

West Side Story won for art direction. The best song was Henry Mancini and Johnny Mercer's "Moon River," from *Breakfast at Tiffany's,* which also won the scoring award for Mancini.

Rozsa: 175, 566, 567, 1035, 1069, 1070, 1085, 1208, 1227, 1644, 1872, 1890, 1968, 2050, 2304. Webster: 33, 64, 95, 331, 376, 663, 730, 856, 1213, 1276, 1322, 1388, 1755, 1925, 2014.

EL NORTE
See 1449.

605 • ELECTRA
MICHAEL CACOYANNIS PRODUCTION (GREECE). 1962.
NOMINATION *Foreign Language Film.*

Irene Papas plays the title role, the Greek princess who plots with her brother, Orestes, to murder their mother, Clytemnestra, in revenge for the death of their father, Agamemnon. Michael Cacoyannis [2346] directs his own adaptation of the play by Euripides. He continued the trilogy with films of *The Trojan Women* (1971) and *Iphigenia* (1977), all starring Papas. Rather heavy-handed and as bleak as the landscapes—it was shot near Mycenae. The Oscar went to *Sundays and Cybèle.*

606 • ELECTRIC HORSEMAN, THE
RASTAR FILMS/WILDWOOD ENTERPRISES/S. POLLACK PRODUCTIONS; COLUMBIA. 1979.
NOMINATION *Sound:* Arthur Piantadosi, Les Fresholtz, Michael Minkler, and Al Overton.

Burned-out ex–rodeo star Robert Redford [1502 . . .] abducts a famous racehorse from a Las Vegas casino where a big conglomerate is using both of them to promote its products. Appalled at the company's exploitation of the horse, he plans to take it to open country and set it free to run with the wild horses. TV reporter Jane Fonda [394 . . .] tracks him down and gets converted to his cause. Critics dismissed this star vehicle as slick and contrived, another odd-couple-on-the-road movie. Perhaps it is, but there's a lot to be entertained by here. Both stars play it with conviction, and they get superb support from a gallery of pros: Valerie Perrine [1155] as Redford's ex-wife, Willie Nelson [936] as his partner, and John Saxon as an oily corporate honcho are the standouts. Director Sydney Pollack [1512 . . .] lets them all get the most out of their big scenes. The Oscar for sound went to *Apocalypse Now.*

Piantadosi: 54, 58, 215, 319, 1279, 2113. Fresholtz: 54, 58, 209, 215, 888, 1127, 1158.5, 1279, 1526, 2113. Minkler: 58, 260, 398, 413.5, 1047, 2144. Overton: 215, 540, 544, 1548.

607 • ELEMENTARY SCHOOL, THE
BARRANDOV FILM STUDIOS PRODUCTION (CZECHOSLOVAKIA). 1991.
NOMINATION *Foreign Language Film.*

Light, nostalgic film about a particularly disruptive elementary school class that drives one teacher mad. Directed by first-timer Jan Sverak, whose father, Zdenek Sverak, is a coauthor of the screenplay and a star of the film. Not yet widely released in the United States. The Oscar went to *Mediterraneo.*

608 • ELEPHANT MAN, THE
BROOKSFILMS LTD. PRODUCTION; PARAMOUNT. 1980.
NOMINATIONS *Picture:* Jonathan Sanger, producer. *Actor:* John Hurt. *Director:* David Lynch. *Screenplay Based on Material From Another Medium:* Christopher DeVore, Eric Bergren, and David Lynch. *Art Direction—Set Decoration:* Stuart Craig and Bob Cartwright; Hugh Scaife. *Original Score:* John Morris. *Film Editing:* Anne V. Coates. *Costume Design:* Patricia Norris.

Hurt plays John Merrick, victim of a neuromuscular disease that has left him so hideously deformed that he is exhibited at freak shows in turn-of-the-century England. Dr. Frederick Treves, played by Anthony Hopkins [1679.5 . . .], rescues him from this life and takes him to a hospital, where Merrick demonstrates that beneath his horrifying exterior he is a sensitive and cultivated man. His case makes him into a celebrity, and the actress Mrs. Kendal, played by Anne Bancroft [28 . . .], becomes his patron. The film, based on an actual case, takes horror movie and fairy-tale elements and makes them haunting. It's particularly distinguished by Lynch's fine direction and the superb black-and-white cinematography of Freddie Francis [779 . . .], who was curiously overlooked in the nominations. The cast also includes John Gielgud [103 . . .] and Wendy Hiller [1252 . . .].

The movie was produced by Brooksfilms, a company started by Mel Brooks [230 . . .] with the proceeds from such smash hits as *Blazing Saddles* and *Young Frankenstein*. Brooks was responsible not only for casting his wife, Bancroft, in the film but also for discovering Lynch, whose only previous feature film was the low-budget *Eraserhead* (1977), an eccentric horror movie about grotesques. *The Elephant Man* is not related to the Broadway play of the same name, by Bernard Pomerance, although its story is taken from the same historical sources. Brooks paid a settlement to the play's producers, who claimed that his film deprived them of income by making it impossible to sell the movie rights for the play. The film's competitors for best picture were *Coal Miner's Daughter, Raging Bull, Tess,* and the winner, *Ordinary People.*

Hurt's second nomination inspired jokes about the appropriateness of his surname: He had been tortured in *Midnight Express,* disemboweled in *Alien,* and deformed in *Elephant Man.* He continues to be a reliable and respected character actor, though none of his later films has given him the prominence for another Oscar try. He lost to Robert De Niro in *Raging Bull.*

Lynch's mainstream directorial debut was as impressive as any in recent memory. After studying painting in Washington, Boston, and Philadelphia, Lynch turned to film because of an interest in combining media. He received a grant from the American Film Institute for a short film in 1970 and studied and worked at the Institute's Center for Advanced Film Studies, writing, producing, directing, designing, editing, and even writing song lyrics for *Eraserhead.* After his Oscar nomination, which he lost to Robert Redford for *Ordinary People,* he was offered a chance to direct *Return of the Jedi* but decided instead to work on a project of his own that never materialized. He accepted the challenge of directing the film *Dune* in 1985 but was unable to impose order on the material, and the film was a catastrophic flop. He regained his status with the critics, however, with *Blue Velvet.*

Although not based on the Pomerance play, the screenplay was nominated in the "adaptation" category. The Academy has never quite been able to iron out the distinction between "written directly for the screen" and "based on material from another medium." Two of the nominees for "screenplay written directly for the screen" this year—*Brubaker* and the winning *Melvin and Howard*—were based in part on the experiences of actual people. The distinction seems to lie in the quotations from actual material that were incorporated into the *Elephant Man* screenplay. The Oscar went to Alvin Sargent for *Ordinary People.*

The award for art direction went to *Tess,* which also won for costume design. Thelma Schoonmaker won the Oscar for editing *Raging Bull.*

Hurt: 1313. Lynch: 247. Craig: 382.5, 485, 745, 1331. Cartwright: 164, 1285, 1766. Scaife: 1533, 1898. Morris: 230. Coates: 164, 992.3, 1151. Norris: 506, 1974, 2165, 2201.

609 • ELMER GANTRY

BURT LANCASTER-RICHARD BROOKS PRODUCTION; UNITED ARTISTS. 1960.

AWARDS *Actor:* Burt Lancaster. *Supporting Actress:* Shirley Jones. *Screenplay—Based on Material From Another Medium:* Richard Brooks.

NOMINATIONS *Picture:* Bernard Smith, producer. *Scoring of a Dramatic or Comedy Picture:* André Previn.

Lancaster plays Gantry, a charismatic, hypocritical Bible Belt evangelist of the twenties, in this adaptation of the Sinclair Lewis novel. Jean Simmons [858 . . .] is Sister Sharon, a character based on Aimee Semple

McPherson—as Lancaster's is based on Billy Sunday. Jones plays Lulu Bains, a prostitute, and the cast includes Dean Jagger [2154], Arthur Kennedy [291 . . .], and Patti Page as a gospel singer. Entertaining melodrama that pulls its punches a bit—the Catholic Legion of Decency made the filmmakers cut Lancaster's line "See you in hell, brother." Once dismissed as dated, the movie has since benefited from the fact that what goes around comes around: The spectacle of Jim Bakker and Jimmy Swaggart in the eighties made it seem timely again. Directed by Brooks, with cinematography by John Alton [66].

Gantry is a signature role for Lancaster, one that plays to his strengths—energy, charisma, sex appeal. When his fires were banked, in *Come Back, Little Sheba,* for example, or even his nominated role in *Birdman of Alcatraz,* he seemed itchy and uncomfortable. A former circus acrobat, he made his film debut in 1946 in *The Killers* and by 1948 had become established enough in Hollywood to form his own production company—one of the first actors to do so in the era of declining studio power. In later years he moved gracefully into character roles, memorably in *Local Hero* (1983) and *Field of Dreams,* and even a few leads, as in *Atlantic City,* until poor health forced his retirement. He died in 1995.

Jones benefited from an old truism: The Academy loves to see actors play against type. Her performance in *Elmer Gantry* is a reprise of the phenomenon that earned Donna Reed an Oscar for *From Here to Eternity:* an actress known for good-girl roles playing a whore. In fact, 1960 was the year of the prostitute at the Oscars: Elizabeth Taylor won the best actress Oscar as the high-class call girl in *Butterfield 8,* and her competition included Shirley MacLaine as the kept woman in *The Apartment* and Melina Mercouri as the happy hooker in *Never on Sunday.* Jones had made her film debut in *Oklahoma!* and followed it with *Carousel* (1956) and *April Love,* so she seemed destined to play sweet virgins for the rest of her career. The Oscar did little to change that, although she played a prostitute again in *The Cheyenne Social Club* (1970). Today she's probably most often remembered as the mother of the singing brood on *The Partridge Family.*

Brooks began his career writing for radio and had a few minor screenplays to his credit before he joined the marines in World War II. The result of his military experience was a novel, *The Brick Foxhole,* about the murder of a gay man, which was made into the film *Crossfire,* in which the homosexual became a Jew. He turned to directing in the fifties, making his strongest impression with *Blackboard Jungle.* He was one of the most respected writer-directors of the fifties and sixties, but he never quite achieved the stature of Billy Wilder [91 . . .] or John Huston [24 . . .].

Brooks was overlooked in the race for best director, pretty much dooming the chances of the film to take the best picture Oscar. Its competition was *The Alamo, Sons and Lovers, The Sundowners,* and the winner, *The Apartment.*

Ernest Gold won the scoring award for *Exodus.*

Lancaster: 107, 210, 732. Brooks: 227, 372, 987, 1627. Smith: 953. Previn: 172, 769, 1017, 1034, 1044, 1097, 1393, 1550, 1592, 2064, 2077, 2161.

610 • EMIGRANTS, THE

A.B. SVENSK FILMINDUSTRI PRODUCTION; WARNER BROS. (SWEDEN). 1972.

NOMINATIONS *Picture:* Bengt Forslund, producer. *Actress:* Liv Ullmann. *Director:* Jan Troell. *Screenplay— Based on Material From Another Medium:* Jan Troell and Bengt Forslund. *Foreign Language Film. (1971)*

Ullmann and Max von Sydow [1546] are among a group who emigrate from nineteenth-century Sweden to Minnesota. Troell shows the conditions that spurred them to leave their old homeland and the hardships they endured in reaching their new one. It's an impressive attempt at an epic, the first of two films; the sequel, *The New Land,* arrived in 1972. But it proceeds at its own pace, which is not always swift, nor is the narrative as involving as we could wish. Interestingly it was better received in the United States than in Sweden. Because of the peculiarities of Academy rules, it was eligible for consideration as a foreign language film a year before it qualified in the other categories. It lost the foreign language Oscar to *The Garden of the Finzi-Continis.* And it stood little chance in the best picture contest, which was a pitched battle between *Cabaret* and *The Godfather,* which the latter film won. (The other two nominees were *Deliverance* and *Sounder.)*

This was the first of two nominations, both unsuccessful, for Ullmann, one of the outstanding film actresses of the sixties and seventies, especially noted for her work with Ingmar Bergman [111 . . .] in films from *Persona* in 1966 to *Autumn Sonata* in 1978. The year after this nomination, she was misused in Hollywood in the flat-footed farce *40 Carats* and the tone-deaf musical *Lost Horizon.* But she has continued a somewhat diminishing screen career and a stronger stage career. She lost to Liza Minnelli in *Cabaret.*

The Emigrants is something of a tour de force for Troell, who not only wrote and directed it but also photographed and edited it. He began his screen career working with director Bo Widerberg and started directing in 1965. Like Ullmann, he accepted an offer to work in Hollywood, but of the two American films Troell has made, *Zandy's Bride* (1974) was a disappointment and *Hurricane* (1979) a disaster. The directing award went to Bob Fosse for *Cabaret.* Mario Puzo and Francis Ford Coppola won for the screenplay of *The Godfather.*

Ullmann: 634.

611 • EMMA

MGM. 1931–32.

NOMINATION *Actress:* Marie Dressler.

Dressler plays a maidservant who's so successful at keeping Jean Hersholt's household on an even keel after his wife dies, he eventually proposes and she marries him. Clarence Brown [84 . . .] directs, and the cast includes Myrna Loy, but Dressler is what keeps the movie from getting mired in its sentimental story. She lost to Helen Hayes in *The Sin of Madelon Claudet.*

Dressler: 1321.

612 • EMPEROR WALTZ, THE

PARAMOUNT. 1948.

NOMINATIONS *Scoring of a Musical Picture:* Victor Young. *Color Costume Design:* Edith Head and Gile Steele.

Phonograph salesman Bing Crosby [173 . . .] woos countess Joan Fontaine [441 . . .] in turn-of-the-century Vienna. Peculiar change of pace for director Billy Wilder [91 . . .], a period musical sandwiched between his Oscar-winning drama about alcoholism, *The Lost Weekend,* and his mordant satire set in postwar Berlin, *A Foreign Affair.* Despite some good lines, supplied by Wilder and cowriter Charles Brackett [705 . . .], and the contributions of character actors Lucile Watson [2233], Sig Rumann, and Richard Haydn (as Emperor Franz Joseph), it's a pretty flimsy affair. Crosby seems more somnolent than ever.

The scoring award went to Johnny Green and Roger Edens for *Easter Parade.* The costuming Oscar, the first ever awarded, went to Dorothy Jeakins and Karinska for *Joan of Arc.* Head was appalled, she later wrote, that "Ingrid Bergman's sackcloth and suits of armor could win over my Viennese finery."

Young: 97, 98, 100, 101, 280, 489, 693, 701, 794, 846, 925, 1214, 1257, 1396, 1452, 1748, 1823, 1994, 2235, 2315. Head: 31, 32, 46, 305, 357, 363, 636, 675, 736, 832, 894, 945, 1003, 1219, 1261, 1263, 1398, 1427, 1504, 1550, 1579, 1587, 1631, 1716, 1727, 1738, 1748, 1840, 1927, 1986, 2012, 2098, 2247, 2298. Steele: 817, 894, 1087, 1309, 1748.

613 • EMPIRE OF THE SUN

WARNER BROS. PRODUCTION; WARNER BROS. 1987.

NOMINATIONS *Cinematography:* Allen Daviau. *Art Direction—Set Decoration:* Norman Reynolds; Harry Cordwell. *Sound:* Robert Knudson, Don Digirolamo, John Boyd, and Tony Dawe. *Original Score:* John Williams. *Film Editing:* Michael Kahn. *Costume Design:* Bob Ringwood.

When the Japanese invade Shanghai at the start of World War II, young Christian Bale is separated from his parents, who live in the British enclave. He learns to live by his wits first on the streets of the city, then in a prison camp, before being reunited with them at war's end. Steven Spielberg [416 . . .] directs an adaptation by Tom Stoppard [275] of a J. G. Ballard novel. The film has epic ambitions, and sometimes achieves them, with great set pieces and moments of terror and beauty. But neither Stoppard nor Spielberg has found a shape for the material, so it never makes the impact on us it should. Unfortunately, in the year of its release it was also overshadowed by two better films about the period: *Hope and Glory,* which also deals with the wartime experiences of a young boy, and *The Last Emperor,* much of which takes place in Japanese-occupied China. Too bad, for Spielberg's film is well cast, with strong contributions coming from John Malkovich [992.3 . . .], Miranda Richardson [478.5 . . .], Nigel Havers, and Joe Pantoliano.

The Last Emperor swept all the categories in which *Empire of the Sun* was nominated, with awards for Vittorio Storaro's cinematography, Ferdinando Scarfiotti and Bruno Cesari's art direction, Bill Rowe and Ivan Sharrock's sound, Ryuichi Sakamoto, David Byrne, and Cong Su's score, Gabriella Cristiani's editing, and James Acheson's costumes.

Daviau: 112, 308, 423, 588. Reynolds: 614, 995, 1652, 1684, 1916. Cordwell: 2201. Knudson: 321, 516, 588, 631, 938, 1439, 1877, 1911, 2274. Digirolamo: 588, 2274. Boyd: 2274. Dawe: 996, 1684, 2274. Williams: 6, 260, 403, 416, 588, 614, 659, 805, 933, 937, 982, 996, 997, 1041, 1047, 1596, 1652, 1679, 1684, 1701, 1764.65, 1916, 1977, 2107, 2126, 2194, 2293, 2322. Kahn: 416, 653, 1652, 1764.65.

614 • EMPIRE STRIKES BACK, THE

LUCASFILM LTD. PRODUCTION; 20TH CENTURY-FOX. 1980.
AWARDS *Sound:* Bill Varney, Steven Maslow, Gregg Landaker, and Peter Sutton. *Special Achievement Award for Visual Effects:* Brian Johnson, Richard Edlund, Dennis Muren, and Bruce Nicholson.
NOMINATIONS *Art Direction–Set Decoration:* Norman Reynolds, Leslie Dilley, Harry Lange, and Alan Tomkins; Michael Ford. *Original Score:* John Williams.

Though the Rebel Alliance thwarted the forces of the evil Empire in *Star Wars,* the first sequel to that movie finds our heroes Luke Skywalker (Mark Hamill), Han Solo (Harrison Ford [2296]), and Princess Leia (Carrie Fisher) under attack by imperial forces on a frozen planet. Guided by the spirit of his mentor, Obi-Wan Kenobi, played by Alec Guinness [287 . . .], Luke escapes the attackers to seek the wisdom of the Jedi master Yoda, who turns out to be a gnomelike creature living in a swamp (and with a voice by Frank Oz that sounds like Miss Piggy after a stroke). Han, Leia, the Wookie Chewbacca, and the droids R2D2 and C3PO head for a planet ruled by an old crony of Han's, Lando Calrissian (Billy Dee Williams), where Han is captured by the Empire and put in suspended animation. Luke returns to do battle with Darth Vader (body by David Prowse, voice by James Earl Jones [830]); he loses a hand but gains a father. Wonderful, rousing comic-book adventure, with superlative special effects but perhaps not quite the mythmaking simplicity of the first film—it may be trying to do a bit too much to set up its sequel, *Return of the Jedi.* The Force was with all concerned, including director Irvin Kershner, who took over the chair from producer George Lucas [65 . . .], and the movie made gazillions. The screenplay is by Leigh Brackett and Lawrence Kasdan [6 . . .] from Lucas' story.

The art direction Oscar went to *Tess.* Michael Gore won the scoring award for *Fame.*

Varney: 127, 586, 1652. Maslow: 586, 1652, 1888.5. Landaker: 1047, 1652, 1888.5. Johnson: 44, 577. Edlund: 45.5, 544, 766, 1589, 1590, 1652, 1684, 1916, 2165. Muren: 5, 577, 588, 997, 1002, 1071.5, 1684, 2019, 2284, 2339. Nicholson: 1589, 1652. Reynolds: 613, 995, 1652, 1684, 1916. Dilley: 5, 44, 1652, 1916. Lange: 2164. Ford: 1652, 1684. Williams: 6, 260, 403, 416, 588, 613, 659, 805, 933, 937, 982, 996, 997, 1041, 1047, 1596, 1652, 1679, 1684, 1701, 1764.65, 1916, 1977, 2107, 2126, 2194, 2293, 2322.

614.5 • ENCHANTED APRIL

BBC FILMS PRODUCTION IN ASSOCIATION WITH GREENPOINT FILMS; MIRAMAX FILMS (UNITED KINGDOM). 1992.
NOMINATIONS *Supporting Actress:* Joan Plowright. *Screenplay Based on Material Previously Produced or Published:* Peter Barnes. *Costume Design:* Sheena Napier.

Four women, each discontented in some way with

her life, spend their holiday at a villa in Italy. Each has an epiphany that changes her. Charming but slight film, directed by Mike Newell, from a screenplay Barnes based on a novel by turn-of-the-century author Elizabeth von Arnim. Made memorable by a beautiful setting and by fine performances, especially Plowright as an elderly, crotchety woman who lives in the past, dropping names of the famous authors she once met, and Miranda Richardson [478.5 . . .] as a mousy housewife who stifles her sexuality with an insincere piety. The story was previously filmed in Hollywood in 1935 with Ann Harding [927] and Frank Morgan [22 . . .], but that version was a notorious box-office flop.

Plowright, who married Laurence Olivier [268 . . .] in 1961 after appearing with him in the film version of *The Entertainer,* had a distinguished career on the British stage but made few movies until the late eighties. She has recently begun to appear frequently in character roles, as a variety of matrons, dotty and otherwise. The Oscar went to Marisa Tomei for *My Cousin Vinny.*

The screenplay award went to Ruth Prawer Jhabvala for *Howards End.* Eiko Ishioka won for the costumes for *Bram Stoker's Dracula.*

615 • ENCHANTED COTTAGE, THE

RKO RADIO. 1945.
NOMINATION *Scoring of a Dramatic or Comedy Picture:* Roy Webb.

When disfigured veteran Robert Young and plain spinster Dorothy McGuire [759] fall in love, they're transformed into the beautiful people each sees in the other. Gooey updated version of a play by Arthur Wing Pinero, though it has to be noted that the movie still has admirers: Cher [1351 . . .], for one, has talked of remaking it. Directed by John Cromwell, with Herbert Marshall, Mildred Natwick [147], and Spring Byington [2325]. The Oscar went to Miklos Rozsa for *Spellbound.*

Webb: 640, 665, 969, 1049, 1394, 1639.

616 • ENDLESS LOVE

POLYGRAM/UNIVERSAL PICTURES/KEITH BARISH/DYSON LOVELL PRODUCTION; UNIVERSAL. 1981.
NOMINATION *Original Song:* "Endless Love," music and lyrics by Lionel Richie.

The obsessive passion of two teenagers, Martin Hewitt and Brooke Shields, leads to disaster. Howlingly awful movie, remembered today only because Tom Cruise [260] made his debut in a small role. Directed by Franco Zeffirelli [1722 . . .] from a screenplay by Judith Rascoe, based on a novel by Scott Spencer that, believe it or not, was rather good. Many first-rate performers are wasted in it: Shirley Knight [488 . . .] and Don Murray [314] as Shields' parents, Beatrice Straight [1424] and Richard Kiley as Hewitt's, plus James Spader (also a debut) and Penelope Milford [430]. At the Oscars Bette Midler [700 . . .], wisecracking her way through the list of song nominees, cheekily referred to it as "the endless movie *Endless Love.*" The award went to "Arthur's Theme (Best That You Can Do)," from *Arthur.*

Richie: 423, 2271.

617 • ENEMIES, A LOVE STORY

MORGAN CREEK PRODUCTION; 20TH CENTURY FOX. 1989.
NOMINATIONS *Supporting Actress:* Anjelica Huston. *Supporting Actress:* Lena Olin. *Screenplay Based on Material From Another Medium:* Roger L. Simon and Paul Mazursky.

Ron Silver hides out from the Nazis in wartime Poland. Believing his wife, Huston, to be dead, he marries the woman who has sheltered him, Margaret Sophie Stein, and immigrates with her to America. He takes a mistress, Olin, but finds himself in a predicament when Huston shows up alive. Extraordinary blend of tragedy and farce, from a novel by Isaac Bashevis Singer. With the help of a wonderful cast, director Mazursky manages to maintain the right blend of laughter and pathos. The New York Film Critics Circle gave Mazursky and Olin their awards for director and supporting actress.

Olin began her career as a member of the company of the Royal Dramatic Theater in Stockholm, under the direction of Ingmar Bergman [111 . . .], and appeared in his films *Fanny & Alexander* and *After the Rehearsal* (1984). Her appearance in *The Unbearable Lightness of Being* brought her international acclaim, but her career in Hollywood was not advanced by the failure of *Havana*. The supporting actress Oscar went to Brenda Fricker for *My Left Foot*.

Screenwriter Simon is best known for a series of detective novels featuring the character Moses Wine, one of which he adapted for the screen in 1978 as *The Big Fix,* starring Richard Dreyfuss [803]. The writing award went to Alfred Uhry for *Driving Miss Daisy*.

Huston: 840, 1625. Mazursky: 250, 875, 2182.

618 • ENEMY BELOW, THE

20TH CENTURY-FOX. 1957.
AWARD *Special Effects:* Walter Rossi.

Robert Mitchum [1935] and Curt Jurgens play underwater cat and mouse as captains of American and German submarines during World War II. Solid action movie, well directed by Dick Powell (yes, the actor). The Oscar went to Rossi for the sound effects. The unnominated photographic effects are by L. B. Abbott [557 . . .].

Rossi: 646, 2217.

619 • ENTERTAINER, THE

WOODFALL PRODUCTION; CONTINENTAL DISTRIBUTING INC. (UNITED KINGDOM). 1960.
NOMINATION *Actor:* Laurence Olivier.

Archie Rice (Olivier) is an aging vaudevillian who hates his apathetic audiences, his family, and most of all, perhaps, himself. The play, by John Osborne [2106], gave Olivier one of his greatest successes in a contemporary role, so the movie is important as a record of that performance. But it's an erratic piece of moviemaking that never finds a cinematic equivalent for what took place on stage. The distancing between audience and performer is gone, and Archie Rice close up is too repellent to be appreciated. This was only the second film directed by Tony Richardson [2106], and like the first, *Look Back in Anger,* it was a record of a stage production done in collaboration with Osborne. The cast is extraordinary: Brenda de Banzie plays Archie's wife, Roger Livesey his father,

and Joan Plowright [614.5], whom Olivier would soon marry, his daughter. Plus Daniel Massey [1907] and, in their screen debuts, Alan Bates [678] and Albert Finney [579 . . .]. Olivier lost to Burt Lancaster in *Elmer Gantry*.

Olivier: 268, 858, 901, 1272, 1506, 1670, 1693, 1841, 2316.

620 • ENTRE NOUS

PARTNERS PRODUCTION (FRANCE). 1983.
NOMINATION *Foreign Language Film.*

To escape the Nazis, Isabelle Huppert, a Russian Jew living in France, marries a man she doesn't love. After the war, she develops a close friendship with Miou-Miou, and the two women leave their husbands and go into business together. Director and coscreenwriter Diane Kurys based the film on the experiences of her mother. Sensitively done. The original French title was *Coup de Foudre*. The Oscar went to Ingmar Bergman's *Fanny & Alexander*.

621 • EQUUS

WINKAST COMPANY LTD.; P.B. LTD. PRODUCTION; UNITED ARTISTS. 1977.
NOMINATIONS *Actor:* Richard Burton. *Supporting Actor:* Peter Firth. *Screenplay—Based on Material From Another Medium:* Peter Shaffer.

Psychiatrist Burton investigates the case of a stableboy, Firth, accused of blinding the horses under his care. The cause is rooted in the boy's relationship with his parents, Colin Blakely and Joan Plowright [614.5], but Shaffer uses the psychology as a framework for philosophical exploration—not very successfully. Director Sidney Lumet [561 . . .] "opens up" the play by dramatizing key events that were shown in stylized form on stage, but the shocking images overwhelm the story.

Alcoholism, illness, and a turbulent personal life had severely damaged Burton's career, which could have been one of the most brilliant of any twentieth-century actor. *Equus,* in which he had performed on stage, was something of a comeback after almost a decade of mediocre (and worse) roles. The role is, however, almost too talky—a series of monologues that, however brilliantly delivered, can only wear down a film audience in the long run. The film was a failure at the box office. But Burton went into the awards a clear favorite. Three of his competitors, Woody Allen for *Annie Hall,* Richard Dreyfuss for *The Goodbye Girl,* and John Travolta for *Saturday Night Fever,* had never received acting nominations before, and the fourth, Marcello Mastroianni, was nominated for a foreign language role, in *A Special Day.* This was Burton's seventh nomination—no actor had ever received this many without winning. Dreyfuss, however, took the Oscar. Burton's career resumed its slump, and he died in 1984.

Like Burton, Firth had performed his role on stage. Since then, the English actor has been seen in occasional films, most notably in *Tess,* two years later. The Oscar went to Jason Robards for *Julia.*

Shaffer is the twin brother of playwright-screenwriter Anthony Shaffer, and the author of several plays with lofty philosophical aims and showy settings, such as *The Royal Hunt of the Sun* (filmed in 1969). He achieved his greatest stage and screen success with *Amadeus.* The Oscar went to Alvin Sargent for *Julia.*

Burton: 85, 164, 1391, 1706, 1897, 2277. Shaffer: 60.

622 • ESCAPE ME NEVER

BRITISH & DOMINIONS; UNITED ARTISTS (UNITED KINGDOM). 1935.
NOMINATION *Actress:* Elisabeth Bergner.

Unwed mother Bergner marries a man who doesn't love her. Long-forgotten melodrama remade in 1947 with Ida Lupino and Errol Flynn. Directed by Paul Czinner, Bergner's husband, with whom she fled the Nazis in 1933. She had been a major stage and screen star in Austria and Germany, and continued to perform with distinction on stage in London and New York, but her film career was unmemorable. Her most frequently seen performance today is in the 1936 version of Shakespeare's *As You Like It,* in which she plays Rosalind to the Orlando of Laurence Olivier [268 . . .]. Her German accent is a distraction in that role, however. In the Oscar race Bergner came in

third after Katharine Hepburn in *Alice Adams* and the winner, Bette Davis in *Dangerous.*

623 • ESKIMO

MGM. 1934.
AWARD *Film Editing:* Conrad Nervig.

Part documentary, part melodrama: an account of the struggles for survival of an Eskimo family, directed by W. S. Van Dyke [1751 . . .]. Remembered today only because of Nervig's Oscar, the first ever awarded for film editing.

Nervig: 1094, 1996.

E.T. THE EXTRA-TERRESTRIAL
See 588.

624 • ETERNALLY YOURS

WALTER WANGER; UNITED ARTISTS. 1939.
NOMINATION *Original Score:* Werner Janssen.

Loretta Young [428 . . .] grows resentful of the obsession of her husband, David Niven [1778], with his career: He's a magician. Slight romantic drama, directed by Tay Garnett, enlivened mostly by its supporting cast: Hugh Herbert, C. Aubrey Smith, Billie Burke [1306], Broderick Crawford [53], Eve Arden [1319], and ZaSu Pitts. Herbert Stothart won for the score of *The Wizard of Oz.*

Janssen: 233, 349, 757, 844, 1884.

625 • EUROPA, EUROPA

CCC-FILMKUNST AND LES FILMS DU LOSANGE PRODUCTION; ORION CLASSICS (WEST GERMANY/FRANCE/POLAND). 1991.
NOMINATION *Screenplay Based on Material From Another Medium:* Agnieszka Holland.

A Jewish teenager in Germany not only escapes detection by the Nazis but through an amazing chain of circumstances winds up in the Hitler Youth. Holland's superb film, which she also directed, became the focus of controversy—an almost annual occurrence where the Academy's foreign film award category is concerned. Nominees for this Oscar are submitted by representatives of the countries in which they are produced, but despite universal praise for Holland's film, which was made in the German language, Germany declined to submit it for consideration on the stated grounds that much of the backing for it was French and the writer-director Polish. Members of the committee responsible for choosing the German nominee also commented that they felt it wasn't up to their standards. There were accusations that the Germans were trying to forget the darkest era of their history, although the German entry in 1990 was *The Nasty Girl,* a film that dealt satirically with that very premise. Holland's nomination in the writing category was seen by many as a nose-thumbing by the Academy—or at least its writers branch—at the German committee.

Holland, born in Poland and educated in Czechoslovakia, is one of the most important filmmakers to come out of Eastern Europe since the Soviet repression of the late sixties that sent filmmakers such as Milos Forman [60 . . .], with whom Holland had studied, into exile. After being imprisoned in Czechoslovakia, Holland returned to Poland in 1972 and began her writing and directing career working with director Andrzej Wada. She fled to France in 1981 after martial law was imposed in Poland. Her film *Angry Harvest* was nominated by the West German government for an Oscar in 1985, and she wrote the story and screenplay for *Anna,* a film that earned a best actress nomination for Sally Kirkland in 1987. She directed her first American film, *The Secret Garden,* in 1993. Holland's screenplay for *Europa, Europa,* adapted from the autobiography of Solomon Perel, lost to Ted Tally's for *The Silence of the Lambs.*

626 • EUROPEANS, THE

MERCHANT IVORY PRODUCTIONS; LEVITT-PICKMAN (UNITED KINGDOM). 1979.

NOMINATION *Costume Design:* Judy Moorcroft.

Lee Remick [508] plays a woman whose marriage to a German baron is on the rocks, so she comes to visit her cousins in America, with her ne'er-do-well brother in tow, in search of a new fortune. Their arrival disturbs the equilibrium of a placid New England household. Rather stately and picturesque adaptation of the Henry James novel, with the usual poise and gloss one expects from the team of producer

Ismail Merchant [954.5 . . .], director James Ivory [954.5 . . .], and screenwriter Ruth Prawer Jhabvala [954.5 . . .]. Bloodless, but not boring. The costuming Oscar went to Albert Wolsky for *All That Jazz.*

Moorcroft: 1533.

627 • EVERY DAY'S A HOLIDAY

MAJOR PRODUCTIONS; PARAMOUNT. 1937.

NOMINATION *Interior Decoration:* Wiard Ihnen.

Mae West is a con woman so skilled she can sell the Brooklyn Bridge to suckers—and does. That gets her kicked out of town, but she gets her revenge by exposing a corrupt police chief (Lloyd Nolan). The Production Code was invented for the likes of West, whose earlier, bawdier films *She Done Him Wrong* and *I'm No Angel* are classics of the double-entendre genre. Depriving West of her lines left only her leer. That isn't enough to keep this middling comedy alive, despite an appearance by Louis Armstrong. Directed by Edward Sutherland. The art direction Oscar went to Stephen Goosson for *Lost Horizon.*

Ihnen: 237, 2286.

628 • EXCALIBUR

ORION PICTURES PRODUCTION; ORION. 1981.

NOMINATION *Cinematography:* Alex Thomson.

The story of King Arthur (Nigel Terry) from his conception through the establishment of the Round Table to its dissolution. Director John Boorman [523 . . .] breathes a lot more life into this version of the familiar story than was found in the dud musical *Camelot* or the wooden MGM epic *Knights of the Round Table.* It's full of blood and thunder and music by Carl Orff and Richard Wagner and Jungian archetypes and adultery in the woods and magic spells and enchanted swords and all sorts of good stuff. It's also a mess, but an enjoyable one. Like most versions of the story, its chief defect is that it never makes sense of Arthur himself—how did this callow youth and archetypal cuckold become the Great English Hero? Boorman's answer is that he had Merlin to help him and that when Morgana entrapped Merlin, everything went to pot. With Nicol Williamson muttering away madly as Merlin and Helen Mirren [1234.5] at her most literally and figuratively bewitching as Morgana, it makes sense—they're the best performances in the movie. Cherie Lunghi plays Guinevere as a teenybopper, and Nicholas Clay is a pretty little Lancelot. The cast also includes Corin Redgrave, Patrick Stewart, Gabriel Byrne, and Liam Neeson [1764.65]. The art direction is by Anthony Pratt [940].

Thomson had camera operator and second unit photographer credits on such films as *The Man Who Would Be King, The Seven-Per-Cent Solution,* and *Superman,* as well as cinematographer credits on numerous features, before receiving his sole nomination for *Excalibur.* The film seems to have typed him. He has subsequently shot the fantasy films *Legend* (1985) and *Labyrinth* (1986) as well as more realistic scripts. The Oscar went to Vittorio Storaro for *Reds.*

629 • EXECUTIVE SUITE

MGM. 1954.

NOMINATIONS *Supporting Actress:* Nina Foch. *Black-and-White Cinematography:* George Folsey. *Black-and-White Art Direction–Set Decoration:* Cedric Gibbons and Edward Carfagno; Edwin B. Willis and Emile Kuri. *Black-and-White Costume Design:* Helen Rose.

Power plays in the boardroom after the death of a corporation chief put stress on the marriage of rising exec William Holden [1424 . . .] and June Allyson in this dog-eat-dog *Grand Hotel* based on a novel by Cameron Hawley. The top dogs are Barbara Stanwyck [138 . . .], Fredric March [184 . . .], Walter Pidgeon [1232 . . .], Shelley Winters [542 . . .], Paul Douglas, Louis Calhern [1243], Dean Jagger [2154], and Foch, as the dead exec's secretary. With all that talent, it can't help but be watchable, though it isn't very good. Robert Wise [407 . . .] directed.

Foch, born in Holland to a Dutch composer and an American actress, grew up in New York and was a concert pianist before turning to acting. She began in B pictures in 1943 but graduated to larger roles, often variations of the chic conniver she plays in *An American in Paris.* She lost to Eva Marie Saint in *On the Waterfront.*

Boris Kaufman's cinematography and Richard Day's art direction also won Oscars for *On the Waterfront.* The costuming award went to Edith Head for *Sabrina.*

Folsey: 51, 137, 807, 835, 838, 1124, 1299, 1320, 1500, 1688, 1782, 2068, 2269. Gibbons: 66, 87, 130, 217, 227, 239, 285, 290, 440, 749, 831, 980, 1069, 1096, 1173, 1190, 1226, 1230, 1232, 1274, 1308, 1309, 1417, 1567, 1604, 1644, 1662, 1673, 1721, 1861, 1937, 2068, 2112, 2256, 2257, 2300, 2320, 2330. Carfagno: 130, 175, 917, 1069, 1552, 1644, 1814, 1937, 2312. Willis: 66, 87, 130, 227, 239, 290, 749, 831, 980, 1069, 1096, 1157, 1173, 1190, 1226, 1230, 1232, 1309, 1417, 1567, 1657, 1662, 1673, 1721, 1861, 1937, 2068, 2112, 2257, 2320, 2330. Kuri: 4, 166, 363, 894, 1284, 1823, 2155. Rose: 130, 578, 755, 817, 980, 1007, 1309, 1335, 1599.

630 • EXODUS

CARLYLE-ALPINA S.A. PRODUCTION; UNITED ARTISTS. 1960.

AWARD *Scoring of a Dramatic or Comedy Picture:* Ernest Gold.

NOMINATION *Supporting Actor:* Sal Mineo. *Color Cinematography:* Sam Leavitt.

Army nurse Kitty Fremont, played by Eva Marie Saint [1477], is on her way back to the States when she encounters a group of Jews facing resistance from the British in their attempts to get to Palestine. Their leader is the charismatic Ari Ben Canaan, played by Paul Newman [3 . . .], and among their numbers is the radical Dov Landau, played by Mineo. Kitty is particularly struck by a young blond girl, Karen, played by Jill Haworth, and plans to take her to the States. First, however, Karen wants to try to find her father, whom she believes to be still alive in Palestine. When Ari stages a hunger strike that wins passage for the Jews to Palestine, Kitty accompanies Karen. Though a Gentile, Kitty finds herself caught up in the formation of the new nation of Israel—and of course, falls in love with Ari, just as Karen falls for Dov. And so it goes for three and a half hours. This blockbuster epic is never dull, except when it decides to linger at the kibbutz and watch another folk dance, but it has too many cardboard characters and overstated performances. Saint seems edgy and uncertain, and though Newman does his usual strong, professional work throughout the film, he and Saint have no chemistry together. Otto Preminger [73 . . .] directed the adaptation of Leon Uris' novel by Dalton Trumbo [273 . . .], who received screen credits for *Exodus* and *Spartacus* this year, his first since being blacklisted as a member of the Hollywood Ten. The humongous cast includes Ralph Richardson [839 . . .], Peter Lawford, Lee J. Cobb [301 . . .], John Derek, and Hugh Griffith [175 . . .].

Gold's score contains one of the most familiar of epic themes, right up there with Max Steiner's for *Gone With the Wind* and Maurice Jarre's for *Doctor Zhivago* and *Lawrence of Arabia*. Gold emigrated from his native Austria in 1938 and became a film composer in the mid-forties. Much of his work was done for Stanley Kramer [330 . . .].

Mineo's second nomination found his career at a turning point, as he began to outgrow teen-idol status and look for a niche as an adult actor. He never quite found that niche, and his film career was largely at a standstill when he was murdered in 1976, apparently by a burglar. The Oscar went to Peter Ustinov for *Spartacus*, which also won for Russell Metty's cinematography.

Gold: 1032, 1474, 1776. Mineo: 1671. Leavitt: 73, 522.

631 • EXORCIST, THE

HOYA PRODUCTIONS; WARNER BROS. 1973.

AWARDS *Screenplay—Based on Material From Another Medium:* William Peter Blatty. *Sound:* Robert Knudson and Chris Newman.

NOMINATIONS *Picture:* William Peter Blatty, producer. *Actress:* Ellen Burstyn. *Supporting Actor:* Jason Miller. *Supporting Actress:* Linda Blair. *Director:* William Friedkin. *Cinematography:* Owen Roizman. *Art Direction–Set Decoration:* Bill Malley; Jerry Wunderlich. *Film Editing:* Jordan Leondopoulos, Bud Smith, Evan Lottman, and Norman Gay.

Divorced mother Burstyn, a movie star, discovers that her twelve-year-old daughter, Blair, is possessed by a demon. Burstyn calls on Miller, a Jesuit priest who is losing his faith, and he enlists the services of an elderly priest, Max von Sydow [1546], whose archaeological work has somehow unleashed this demon. Their attempt at exorcism is ultimately successful—but at a price. This enormously popular shocker became one of the movies' biggest box-office successes, despite almost universal critical loathing. And yes, it is junk, though well-made junk, with a prestige cast doing their best to make it convincing; it also has remarkable special effects. It has been endlessly and badly imitated, although in fact it was an imitation to start with: Blatty was partly inspired by the success of the film *Rosemary's Baby*.

Blatty adapted the screenplay from his own novel, which he sold to Warners even before it was published, basing it on newspaper reports of an alleged exorcism of a fourteen-year-old Maryland boy. Before the success of *The Exorcist,* he was best known as a screenwriter of mildly amusing comedies such as *A Shot in the Dark* (1964) and *Darling Lili.* Afterward, he devoted himself to horror shockers, including two *Exorcist* sequels. He also directed *The Exorcist III* (1990).

In addition to such visual effects as having Blair's head spin 360 degrees and spew green pea soup, much of the creepiness of the film comes from its audio track. Actress Mercedes McCambridge [53 . . .] spoke for the demon, but her voice was remixed and enhanced with various animal noises.

The presence of this tawdry shocker among the best picture nominees still gives one pause. There were certainly better, more interesting films available: the first major movie from Martin Scorsese [27.5 . . .], *Mean Streets;* the Robert Altman [1286 . . .] private-eye spoof *The Long Goodbye;* the controversial *Last Tango in Paris; The Last Detail; Paper Moon; Serpico; The Way We Were.* The competitors for the Oscar were George Lucas' *American Graffiti,* Ingmar Bergman's *Cries and Whispers,* the noisy farce *A Touch of Class,* and the winner, *The Sting.*

Burstyn's first nomination, for *The Last Picture Show,* had helped make her a bankable star, and the success of *The Exorcist* reinforced that status, enabling her to launch her own production of *Alice Doesn't Live*

Here Anymore, with newcomer Scorsese directing. It would win her the Oscar, but this time the award went to Glenda Jackson for *A Touch of Class.*

Miller has the distinction of being the partial answer to an Oscar trivia question: Which two Pulitzer Prize—winning playwrights were nominated for acting Oscars? Miller won his Pulitzer in 1973 for *That Championship Season;* the other is Sam Shepard, the Pulitzer winner for *Buried Child* in 1979, who was nominated for *The Right Stuff.* Miller has continued to act, and in 1982 he directed and acted in a film of his prize-winning play. The Oscar went to John Houseman for *The Paper Chase.*

Blair, a former child model who was said to have won the role over five hundred other candidates, was unable to create a post-*Exorcist* career of distinction. Her career has been much like that of an earlier supporting actress nominee, Patty McCormack, who was unable to move into more conventional roles after playing the killer child in *The Bad Seed.* By the eighties Blair was appearing in movies with titles like *Hell Night, Chained Heat,* and *Bad Blood.* In 1990 she appeared in a spoof of *The Exorcist* called *Repossessed.* The Oscar went to another child actress, Tatum O'Neal, in *Paper Moon.*

Friedkin was Hollywood's hottest young director after his Oscar for *The French Connection* and his box-office smash with *The Exorcist.* But subsequent missteps damaged his career: *Sorcerer* in 1977 was a hugely expensive box-office flop, and *Cruising* in 1980 was widely denounced as homophobic. The Oscar went to George Roy Hill for *The Sting.*

The Oscars for art direction and editing (William Reynolds) also went to *The Sting.* Sven Nykvist won the cinematography award for *Cries and Whispers.*

Knudson: 321, 516, 588, 613, 938, 1439, 1877, 1911, 2274. Newman: 60, 398, 641, 724, 784, 1820. Burstyn: 41, 1139, 1682, 1747. Friedkin: 724. Roizman: 724, 1424, 2113, 2316.5. Wunderlich: 1143. Smith: 682.

632 • EXPERIMENT PERILOUS

RKO RADIO. 1945.

NOMINATION *Black-and-White Interior Decoration:* Albert S. D'Agostino and Jack Okey, art direction; Darrell Silvera and Claude Carpenter, set decoration.

Hedy Lamarr lives in fear of her cruel husband, Paul Lukas [2233], but when psychologist George Brent falls in love with her and tries to help her, Lukas threatens all their lives. Tidy thriller, a little too derivative of *Gaslight,* but well directed by Jacques Tourneur, with a cast that includes Albert Dekker and Margaret Wycherly [1779]. The art direction award went to *Blood on the Sun.*

D'Agostino: 686, 1239, 1240, 1924. Okey: 1743. Silvera: 407, 686, 1239, 1264, 1341, 1924. Carpenter: 1924, 2212.

633 • FABULOUS BAKER BOYS, THE

GLADDEN ENTERTAINMENT PRESENTATION OF A MIRAGE PRODUCTION; 20TH CENTURY FOX. 1989.

NOMINATIONS *Actress:* Michelle Pfeiffer. *Cinematography:* Michael Ballhaus. *Original Score:* David Grusin. *Film Editing:* William Steinkamp.

The Bakers, played by Jeff Bridges [1139 . . .] and Beau Bridges, have a two-piano act that plays downscale cocktail lounges. Jeff is a bitter loner who longs to be a jazz musician, not a middle-of-the-road hack. Beau is a family man content to spend his days giving piano lessons and his nights doing cheery canned repartee and playing inane pop tunes with his brother. But both agree, after some canceled engagements, that the act needs sprucing up, so they hire a singer, Susie Diamond (Pfeiffer), a tough, cynical former call girl. Her presence revives the act but also drives another wedge between the brothers. A trio of first-rate performances and some bright dialogue keep this low-key character drama alive, though it bogs down toward the end, when it's clear that there's no particular place for the various relationships to go. Written and directed by Steve Kloves. Jennifer Tilly [311.5] has a nice bit as a ditzy would-be singer whose big number is "Candy Man."

Pfeiffer scored universal raves for her performance as Susie, with much astonishment that so beautiful a woman could both act and sing. Actually her voice is only passable—it's her delivery that makes her convincing as a singer, particularly in her celebrated piano-top performance of "Makin' Whoopee." Until the release of *Driving Miss Daisy,* Pfeiffer was considered the front-runner for the Oscar, but Jessica Tandy won, as much for her career as for the individual performance. (The other nominees were Isabelle Adjani for *Camille Claudel,* Pauline Collins for *Shirley Valentine,* and Jessica Lange for *Music Box.)*

After his first nomination, for *Broadcast News,* Ballhaus worked for Martin Scorsese on *The Last Temptation of Christ* and *GoodFellas* and has also filmed Mike Nichols' *Working Girl* and *Postcards From the Edge.* He lost to Freddie Francis for *Glory.*

Grusin not only scored *Baker Boys,* he also played the piano for Jeff Bridges. The Oscar went to Alan Menken for *The Little Mermaid.* The editing award was won by David Brenner and Joe Hutshing for *Born on the Fourth of July.*

Pfeiffer: 485, 1212.5. Ballhaus: 293. Grusin: 379, 667.5, 881, 890, 1318, 1473, 2113. Steinkamp: 1512, 2113.

634 • *FACE TO FACE*

Cinematograph A.B. Production; Paramount (Sweden). 1976.

Nominations *Actress:* Liv Ullmann. *Director:* Ingmar Bergman.

Psychiatrist Ullmann has a breakdown in this film edited from a four-part Swedish TV miniseries. For admirers of Ullmann and/or Bergman only—everyone else will find it unpleasantly trying. Ullmann lost to Faye Dunaway for *Network,* Bergman to John G. Avildsen for *Rocky.*

Ullmann: 610. Bergman: 111, 460, 644, 2082, 2283.

635 • *FACES*

John Cassavetes Production; Walter Reade-Continental Distributing. 1968.

Nominations *Supporting Actor:* Seymour Cassel. *Supporting Actress:* Lynn Carlin. *Story and Screenplay—Written Directly for the Screen:* John Cassavetes.

John Marley [1218], Gena Rowlands [777 . . .], Cassel, and Carlin, affluent middle-aged people, go through a variety of individual and marital crises. Writer-director Cassavetes' slice of private life was an unexpected success with audiences, though its pseudo-*cinéma-vérité* style no longer seems fresh and revealing today. Very much influenced by Ingmar Bergman [111 . . .], but without Bergman's poetry —or his performers.

Cassel was an acting student under Cassavetes and served as associate producer as well as actor in Cassavetes' first film as director, *Shadows* (1960). He continued to work with Cassavetes on almost all the director's films. The Oscar went to Jack Albertson for *The Subject Was Roses.*

Carlin's career in character roles has been relatively minor. She lost to Ruth Gordon in *Rosemary's Baby.*

Cassavetes was subsequently nominated as director for *A Woman Under the Influence,* earning him the distinction he shares with Charles Chaplin [405 . . .], John Huston [24 . . .], Orson Welles [407 . . .], Woody Allen [39 . . .], and Warren Beatty [255 . . .] of having been nominated as actor, writer, and director. The writing Oscar went to Mel Brooks for *The Producers.*

Cassavetes: 548, 2306.

636 • *FACTS OF LIFE, THE*

Panama and Frank Production; United Artists. 1960.

Award *Black-and-White Costume Design:* Edith Head and Edward Stevenson.

Nominations *Story and Screenplay—Written Directly for the Screen:* Norman Panama and Melvin Frank. *Black-and-White Cinematography:* Charles B. Lang, Jr. *Black-and-White Art Direction—Set Decoration:* Joseph McMillan Johnson and Kenneth A. Reid; Ross Dowd. *Song:* "The Facts of Life," music and lyrics by Johnny Mercer.

Bob Hope and Lucille Ball are married, but not to each other. They decide to have an affair, but things don't quite work out as planned. An interesting star team, but neither star can shake our ingrained expectations and play this material convincingly. A good example of what passed for sophisticated comedy in the early sixties, as well as an example of Hollywood's attempt to compete with TV by giving the audience something they couldn't see on the small screen: Hope and Ball as adulterers. Directed by Frank, with Ruth Hussey [1563], Don DeFore, and Louis Nye.

The Panama-Frank team, which had been together since the early forties, began to go their separate ways in the sixties, after this nomination. They lost to another celebrated writing-directing-producing team, Billy Wilder and I. A. L. Diamond, for *The Apartment*.

Lang lost to Freddie Francis' cinematography for *Sons and Lovers*. *The Apartment* also won for art direction. The song award went to Manos Hadjidakis for the title song from *Never on Sunday*.

Head: 31, 32, 46, 305, 357, 363, 612, 675, 736, 832, 894, 945, 1003, 1219, 1261, 1263, 1398, 1427, 1504, 1550, 1579, 1587, 1631, 1716, 1727, 1738, 1748, 1840, 1927, 1986, 2012, 2098, 2247, 2298. Stevenson: 495, 1374. Panama: 1108, 1705. Frank: 1108, 1705, 2125. Lang: 97, 250, 319, 649, 705, 765, 953, 1480, 1640, 1699, 1738, 1778, 1855, 1860, 1955, 1968, 2180. Johnson: 833, 978, 1388, 1595, 2098. Dowd: 101. Mercer: 248, 278, 384, 476, 494, 508, 788, 825, 877, 903, 905, 1109, 1772, 1838, 1912, 2327, 2328.

637 • FAIR CO-ED, THE

MGM. 1927–28.

AWARD *Title Writing:* Joseph Farnham.

Marion Davies, smitten with women's basketball coach Johnny Mack Brown, enrolls in college and goes out for his team in this featherweight comedy directed by Sam Wood [701 . . .]. Farnham was the sole winner of the title writing Oscar, made obsolete by sound and discontinued after this year. In some lists of Oscar nominations and awards, he's cited as a winner for the film *Telling the World* and as nominee for *The Fair Co-ed* and *Laugh, Clown, Laugh*. But the Academy's most recent revision of its nominations and winners list cites no titles after his name, because the Oscar was presented to him for the body of his work during the qualifying year. For the purposes of

this book, however, we've included the three films he worked on during the 1927–28 qualifying period.

Farnham: 1147, 2009.

638 • FALL OF THE ROMAN EMPIRE, THE

BRONSTON-ROMA PRODUCTION; PARAMOUNT. 1964.

NOMINATION *Music Score—Substantially Original:* Dimitri Tiomkin.

After the death of Marcus Aurelius, played by Alec Guinness [287 . . .], his mad son, Commodus (Christopher Plummer), takes over, and with the barbarians at the gates, it's only a matter of time before . . . well, the title kind of gives it away, doesn't it? Stately—perhaps too stately—epic directed by Anthony Mann that has its admirers because it doesn't go overboard in sex and violence. It flopped because sex and violence is what people go to costume epics to see. It has the usual blockbuster cast: Stephen Boyd is back in the old breastplate and greaves, and there's Sophia Loren [1280 . . .], James Mason [761 . . .], Anthony Quayle [85], John Ireland [53], Omar Sharif [1151], Mel Ferrer, and Eric Porter. The scoring award went to the Sherman brothers for *Mary Poppins*.

Tiomkin: 33, 286, 380, 446, 663, 730, 768, 850, 911, 912, 1206, 1347, 1370, 1470, 2006, 2127, 2282, 2335.

639 • FALLEN IDOL, THE

LONDON FILMS; SELZNICK RELEASING ORGANIZATION (UNITED KINGDOM). 1949.

NOMINATIONS *Director:* Carol Reed. *Screenplay:* Graham Greene.

Young Bobby Henrey plays an ambassador's son whose only friend in the huge embassy is the butler, played by Ralph Richardson [839 . . .]. When Richardson's shrill harpy of a wife dies accidentally, the boy believes the butler did it. His attempts to cover up for his friend draw suspicion to the man instead. Fine, gripping suspense film, one of a trio directed by Reed in the late forties. The others are *Odd Man Out* and *The Third Man*.

Reed's reputation as a director had begun to grow

before World War II with such films as *The Stars Look Down* (1939) and *Night Train to Munich* (1940). During the war, serving in the British propaganda filmmaking office, he codirected an Oscar-winning documentary, *The True Glory* (1945), with Garson Kanin [11 . . .]. He lost the directing Oscar to Joseph L. Mankiewicz for *A Letter to Three Wives*.

Greene, one of the major British novelists of the twentieth century, had also worked as a film critic for several English publications in the thirties. That career resulted in a notorious lawsuit brought against Greene and the magazine *Night and Day* in 1938 by 20th Century-Fox, after a review of Shirley Temple's *Wee Willie Winkie* in which Greene noted Temple's erotic effect on some of her audience: "Her admirers—middle-aged men and clergymen—respond to her dubious coquetry, to the sight of her well-shaped and desirable little body, packed with enormous vitality, only because the safety curtain of story and dialogue drops between their intelligence and their desire." Fox won the libel suit and Greene was fined £500. Greene wrote numerous screenplays in the years after the war, most of them adaptations of his own work. *The Fallen Idol* is based on his short story "The Basement Room." The Oscar went to Mankiewicz's screenplay for *A Letter to Three Wives*.

Reed: 1471, 2053.

640 • FALLEN SPARROW, THE

RKO RADIO. 1943.
NOMINATION *Scoring of a Dramatic or Comedy Picture:* C. Bakaleinikoff and Roy Webb.

John Garfield [251 . . .] is hunted by Nazis after returning to New York from fighting in the Spanish Civil War. Muddled thriller, directed by Richard Wallace, with Maureen O'Hara and Walter Slezak. The score lost to Alfred Newman's for *The Song of Bernadette*.

Bakaleinikoff: 916, 1445, 1863. Webb: 615, 665, 969, 1049, 1394, 1639.

641 • FAME

METRO-GOLDWYN-MAYER PRODUCTION; MGM. 1980.
AWARDS *Original Song:* "Fame," music by Michael Gore, lyrics by Dean Pitchford. *Original Score:* Michael Gore.
NOMINATIONS *Screenplay Written Directly for the Screen:* Christopher Gore. *Sound:* Michael Kohut, Aaron Rochin, Jay M. Harding, and Chris Newman. *Original Song:* "Out Here on My Own," music by Michael Gore, lyrics by Lesley Gore. *Film Editing:* Gerry Hambling.

Episodic intercutting of the stories of a group of students at New York's High School for Performing Arts. This was a big hit, thanks to a high energy level in its production numbers and some appealing performances, and it was made into a TV series, but it's pretty flimsy as drama. With the exception of Irene Cara [682], its young stars have mostly dropped from sight. Directed by Alan Parker [1313 . . .].

Gore and Pitchford's title tune won out against two songs by celebrated country singer-songwriters that have since become standards: Dolly Parton's title song for *9 to 5* and Willie Nelson's "On the Road Again," from *Honeysuckle Rose*. The remaining nominee was "People Alone," from *The Competition*.

The screenplay Oscar went to Bo Goldman for *Melvin and Howard*. *The Empire Strikes Back* won for sound and *Raging Bull* for Thelma Schoonmaker's editing.

M. Gore: 2020. Pitchford: 381, 697. Kohut: 1310, 1548, 1711, 2124, 2165, 2231. Rochin: 521, 1089, 1310, 1711, 2124, 2165, 2231, 2287. Harding: 1548. Newman: 60, 398, 631, 724, 784, 1820. Hambling: 433, 992.5, 1314, 1333.

642 • FAMILY, THE

MASSFILM-CINECITTA-LES FILMS ARIANE-CINEMAX PRODUCTION (ITALY). 1987.
NOMINATION *Foreign Language Film.*

Eighty years in the life of a well-to-do Italian family, from the birth of Carlo (Vittorio Gassman) to his eightieth birthday. Director and cowriter Ettore Scola's film, like his earlier *Le Bal,* is confined to a single set—in this case, the family's apartment. Slow and loosely structured, but interesting. The Oscar went to the Danish *Babette's Feast*.

643 • FANNY

MANSFIELD PRODUCTION; WARNER BROS. 1961.
NOMINATIONS *Picture:* Joshua Logan, producer. *Actor:* Charles Boyer. *Color Cinematography:* Jack Cardiff. *Scoring of a Dramatic or Comedy Picture:* Morris Stoloff and Harry Sukman. *Film Editing:* William H. Reynolds.

Fanny, played by Leslie Caron [1113 . . .], is left pregnant when Marius, Horst Buchholz, goes off to sea. She marries the elderly Panisse, played by Maurice Chevalier [203 . . .]. When Marius returns to claim Fanny and his son, he is dissuaded by his own father, César, played by Boyer. It's lovely, but a little slow, and stylistically all wrong. The screenplay is based on the middle play in a trilogy by Marcel Pagnol, regarded as a classic in France.

Pagnol himself adapted the three plays for the French screen in the thirties. MGM made its own adaptation in 1938, as *Port of the Seven Seas,* with Wallace Beery [202 . . .] as César, Maureen O'Sullivan as Fanny, and Frank Morgan [22 . . .] as Panisse. In 1954 Logan directed a Broadway musical version with a score by Harold Rome, and Ezio Pinza and Walter Slezak as César and Panisse. Studio head Jack Warner [55 . . .], however, insisted that the film be nonmusical and that the parts of Fanny and Marius be expanded to attract a younger audience. The songs were jettisoned, though the tunes were retained for the score. Their huge success in *Gigi* made the casting of Chevalier and Caron a natural choice, although Logan had originally planned to cast Audrey Hepburn [278 . . .] in the title role. Caron was reluctant at first to take the part because she feared the reaction of the French to an Americanization of the works. She agreed after she heard that Chevalier and Boyer were in the cast. The best picture Oscar went to *West Side Story.*

This was Boyer's fourth and final Oscar nomination. He was, as usual, a leading contender, but Maximilian Schell won for *Judgment at Nuremberg.* Although admired for his professionalism and respected for his success at the box office, Boyer remained undervalued by the Academy, perhaps because, like Spencer Tracy [131 . . .], he made acting look too easy. After *Fanny,* he was increasingly relegated to wise old Frenchman roles. He committed suicide in 1978, at the age of eighty, two days after his wife's death. Their only child had died, an apparent suicide, in 1965.

Cardiff increasingly turned his hand to directing in the late fifties, sometimes serving as both cinematographer and director. The Oscar went to Daniel Fapp for *West Side Story,* which also took the editing award. The scoring Oscar went to Henry Mancini for *Breakfast at Tiffany's.*

Logan: 1566, 1763. Boyer: 36, 440, 749. Cardiff: 221, 1875, 2228. Stoloff: 13, 432, 455, 596, 677, 732, 773, 1057, 1058, 1115, 1206, 1862, 1872, 1873, 1998, 2110, 2329. Sukman: 1833, 1873. Reynolds: 784, 896, 1753, 1881, 1927, 2152.

644 • FANNY & ALEXANDER

CINEMATOGRAPH A.B. FOR THE SWEDISH FILM INSTITUTE/SWEDISH TELEVISION SVT 1 (SWEDEN)/GAUMONT (FRANCE)/PERSONAFILM AND TOBIS FILMKUNST (BRD) PRODUCTION; EMBASSY PICTURES CORPORATION (SWEDEN). 1983.
AWARDS *Cinematography:* Sven Nykvist. *Art Direction–Set Decoration:* Anna Asp. *Costume Design:* Marik Vos. *Foreign Language Film.*
NOMINATIONS *Director:* Ingmar Bergman. *Screenplay Written Directly for the Screen:* Ingmar Bergman.

A year in the life of an extended Swedish family, seen largely through the eyes of ten-year-old Alexander. After his father, an actor, dies, his mother marries a harsh, sadistic clergyman. Alexander and his eight-year-old sister, Fanny, are rescued from this household by their grandmother. But plot, such as it is, is secondary to the extraordinary range of effects —some visual, as supplied by the deservedly honored team of cinematographer and designers, and some emotional, as communicated by Bergman's story, direction, and huge company of players. (Veterans Erland Josephson and Harriet Andersson are the most familiar performers, and Lena Olin [617] can be glimpsed in a small role as a maid.) The theme is simple and overobvious: the liberation of art vs. the oppression of religion. But the fantastic elaboration of it is what makes this one of Bergman's most enjoyable films. With four Oscars, it is the most honored foreign language film in Oscar history; only *Das Boot* has tied it among foreign language films for number of nominations.

Bergman lost the directing Oscar to James L. Brooks for *Terms of Endearment* and the writing Oscar to Horton Foote for *Tender Mercies*.

Nykvist: 460, 2173. Vos: 460, 2206. Bergman: 111, 460, 634, 2082, 2283.

645 • *FANTASIA*

WALT DISNEY PRODUCTIONS; RKO RADIO. 1941.

AWARDS *Special Award:* Leopold Stokowski and his associates for the creation of a new form of visualized music. *Special Award:* Walt Disney, William Garity, John N. A. Hawkins, and the RCA Manufacturing Company for advancement of the use of sound in motion pictures.

Eight pieces of classical music serve as the inspiration for animated cartoons. As a rule of thumb here, the less serious and "respectable" the work, the more successful the sequence. Hence, Dukas' light-classical *The Sorcerer's Apprentice* and Ponchielli's opera ballet *Dance of the Hours* are the most enjoyable segments, while the high-classical Beethoven *Pastoral* Symphony results in the kitschiest and Bach's Toccata and Fugue in D Minor the least inspired. Somewhere in between are the renditions of Tchaikovsky's *Nutcracker Suite,* images for which range from clever (the dancing mushrooms) to saccharine (the greeting-card fairies in the "Waltz of the Flowers"); Stravinsky's *Rite of Spring,* a visually exciting visit to the age of the dinosaurs but set to music in a truncated version that Stravinsky loathed; and Mussorgsky's "Night on Bare Mountain" and Schubert's "Ave Maria," moving from a phantasmagoria of ghosts and goblins (including witches with bare breasts and perceptible nipples that somehow passed the censors) to a smarmily pious religious processional.

The germ of *Fantasia* was *The Sorcerer's Apprentice,*

conceived by Disney from the start as a Mickey Mouse cartoon, one of the studio's Silly Symphonies animated shorts. (Dopey, rather than Mickey Mouse, was considered for the role of the apprentice, but Disney felt that it was a mistake to break up the Seven Dwarfs.) Stokowski, the Philadelphia Orchestra conductor who was a successful popularizer of classical music as well as something of a publicity hound, had come to Hollywood to appear in *One Hundred Men and a Girl.* He was excited by Disney's idea for animating the Dukas piece, but wanted an on-camera role. The initial collaboration grew into a feature film, involving narration by Deems Taylor, another popularizer of the classics. Along the way, several pieces of music were considered and discarded, including Debussy's "Clair de Lune" and "Perfumes of the Night." The latter even inspired a suggestion that theaters be equipped with devices to spray appropriate scents into the audience during the sequence. Likewise, the idea of expanding to a wide-screen technique during the "Ave Maria" sequence was discussed and discarded.

Technological innovation became the byword for the film, however, and also something of its undoing. Stokowski collaborated with Garity, the head of the Disney Studio sound department, on a four-track recording system that would allow stereo playback. Separate sections of the orchestra were recorded and then mixed so that individual sections could be emphasized at appropriate points in the film. But persuading theaters to install the sixty-eight speakers required for the technique, called Fantasound, was another thing, and the outbreak of war made RCA, which was set to produce the sound system, turn its resources to defense production.

Critical reaction to the movie was mixed, and after a road-show exhibition in major cities, Disney let RKO edit the film from two hours to eighty-two minutes for general release. The film was a huge money-loser, and not until the seventies, when it developed a cult reputation as a "head film," did it begin to recoup its losses. After its video release in 1991, the studio announced that the original version would no longer be shown, but that new sequences would be produced and interpolated among the old ones in future theatrical releases.

Disney: 1284, 1851.

646 · FANTASTIC VOYAGE

20TH CENTURY-FOX. 1966.

AWARDS *Color Art Direction—Set Decoration:* Jack Martin Smith and Dale Hennesy; Walter M. Scott and Stuart A. Reiss. *Special Visual Effects:* Art Cruickshank.

NOMINATIONS *Color Cinematography:* Ernest Laszlo. *Film Editing:* William B. Murphy. *Sound Effects:* Walter Rossi.

A famous scientist has a bloodclot on his brain, and only a radically experimental technique can save him. A miniaturized team of specialists, in a microscopic submarine, is injected into his bloodstream and sent to repair the damage. Colorfully idiotic sci-fi semi-classic, with the usual thundering clichés: the squabbles over whether to send a woman on the mission (even if she's Raquel Welch), the debates about playing God, the team member who's along to sabotage the mission, and so on. Naturally they have to take a detour along the way to the brain, and Welch (who else?) is attacked by antibodies. To their credit, the actors play all this with straight faces. They include Stephen Boyd, Edmond O'Brien [146 . . .], Donald Pleasence, Arthur O'Connell [73 . . .], and Arthur Kennedy [291 . . .]. Richard Fleischer directed. A quarter century later, the production design and special effects look charmingly dated. There's a toylike plastic brightness about the insides of the body, and some of the matte effects don't quite register correctly. But the script is plastic and kind of out-of-register, too, so it doesn't matter that much.

The cinematography Oscar went to Ted Moore for *A Man for All Seasons. Grand Prix* won for film editing and sound effects.

Smith: 29, 413, 557, 896, 1230, 2008, 2120, 2247. Hennesy: 86, 1196. Scott: 46, 376, 413, 476, 530, 542, 557, 896, 1088, 1213, 1391, 1475, 1706, 1753, 1881, 1907, 2008, 2120, 2247. Reiss: 542, 557, 2008, 2093, 2247. Cruickshank: 219. Laszlo: 31, 1000, 1032, 1065, 1196, 1812, 1907. Rossi: 618, 2217.

647 · FAR FROM THE MADDING CROWD

APPIA FILMS LTD. PRODUCTION; MGM (UNITED KINGDOM). 1967.

NOMINATION *Original Music Score:* Richard Rodney Bennett.

Julie Christie [493 . . .] plays Bathsheba Everdene, whose beauty enthralls three men: Gabriel, played by Alan Bates [678], who serves her faithfully; Sergeant Troy, played by Terence Stamp [206], who deserts another young woman to marry Bathsheba, whom he then abuses; and Boldwood, played by Peter Finch [1424 . . .], who kills Troy and goes mad. A quartet of fine performances keeps this version of the novel by Thomas Hardy, adapted by Frederic Raphael [493 . . .], from being merely depressing, but it has some of the stiff English-lit quality of *Masterpiece Theatre.* Directed by John Schlesinger [493 . . .], with fine photography by Nicolas Roeg. The Oscar went to Elmer Bernstein for *Thoroughly Modern Millie.*

Bennett: 1378, 1429.

647.5 · FAREWELL MY CONCUBINE

TOMSON (HK) FILMS COMPANY LTD. PRODUCTION; MIRAMAX (HONG KONG). 1993.

NOMINATIONS *Foreign Language Film. Cinematography:* Gu Changwei.

Two young boys are taken on as members of the Beijing Opera company and spend their lives as performers, while World War II, the communist revolution, and the Cultural Revolution transform the outside world. One of the men, who is gay, plays a woman on stage, a king's concubine. He is also attracted to the other actor, who plays the king, but that actor marries a beautiful prostitute. When the Cultural Revolution threatens to destroy the traditional arts, including the opera company, the two actors turn on each other, the one denouncing the other's homosexuality, the other retaliating by disclosing the scandalous past of the first actor's wife. Beautiful epic filmmaking, skillfully using the artificial world of theater as a window on history. Directed by Chen Kaige, whose father, a filmmaker, was imprisoned during the Cultural Revolution, after Chen turned informer against him. *Farewell My Concubine* is in some ways an attempt to make amends, and Chen's father served as an adviser on the film. Ironically, after sharing the top honors at Cannes with *The Piano*, *Farewell My Concubine* ran into trouble with the Chinese censors, who first approved its release and then banned it. Like *Raise the Red Lantern* two years earlier, *Farewell My Concubine* was not submitted for the Oscar by the Chinese government, but technicalities allowed the government of Hong Kong to submit it. The film was considered the front-runner for the foreign film award, but lost to *Belle Epoque*. The cinematography Oscar went to Janusz Kaminski for *Schindler's List*.

648 • FAREWELL, MY LOVELY

Elliott Kastner-ITC Production; Avco Embassy. 1975.
Nomination *Supporting Actress:* Sylvia Miles.

Robert Mitchum [1935] plays Philip Marlowe in this adaptation of the Raymond Chandler [242 . . .] novel that had been filmed in 1944 as *Murder, My Sweet.* A good re-creation of forties L.A. by director Dick Richards, screenwriter David Zelag Goodman [1221], and art director Dean Tavoularis [92 . . .]. The plot is the usual double-, triple-, and quadruple-crossing involving Charlotte Rampling, John Ireland [53], Anthony Zerbe, and, in minor roles, Harry Dean Stanton and (a year before fame struck) Sylvester Stallone [1712]. Miles' role is barely more than a cameo. She lost to Lee Grant for *Shampoo.*

Miles: 1312.

649 • FAREWELL TO ARMS, A

Paramount. 1932–33.
Awards *Cinematography:* Charles Bryant Lang, Jr. *Sound Recording:* Franklin B. Hansen.
Nominations *Picture:* Adolph Zukor, studio head. *Interior Decoration:* Hans Dreier and Roland Anderson.

Gary Cooper [701 . . .] plays the wounded World War I ambulance driver who falls in love with his nurse, played by Helen Hayes [31 . . .], in this adaptation of the Ernest Hemingway novel. It was filmed with two endings, in one of which she doesn't die. Rather stiff and sentimental in either case, with too many poignant gazes by Hayes. Hemingway hated the movie but liked Cooper, who became a close friend. Frank Borzage [132 . . .] directed.

This was the sole Oscar for Lang, though he tied with Leon Shamroy [29 . . .], a four-time winner, for the most nominations in the cinematography category—eighteen. Lang began his career in the Paramount photo lab in the early twenties and moved into work as a cinematographer in the latter part of the decade. He retired in 1973.

A Farewell to Arms and its art directors placed second in the balloting; the awards for best picture and art direction went to *Cavalcade.*

Lang: 97, 250, 319, 636, 705, 765, 953, 1480, 1640, 1699, 1738, 1778, 1855, 1860, 1955, 1968, 2180. Hansen: 412, 1194, 1217, 2024. Zukor: 1800, 1836. Dreier: 97, 161, 674, 701, 726, 925, 979, 1101, 1120, 1194, 1214, 1217, 1358, 1443, 1452, 1540, 1668, 1748, 1880, 1975, 1994, 2190. Anderson: 278, 363, 426, 450, 1029, 1194, 1214, 1219, 1452, 1570, 1668, 1674, 1880, 1994.

650 • FAREWELL TO ARMS, A

The Selznick Company Inc.; 20th Century-Fox. 1957.
Nomination *Supporting Actor:* Vittorio De Sica.

Second filming of the Ernest Hemingway novel, with Rock Hudson [768] as the wounded ambulance driver and Jennifer Jones [584 . . .] as the nurse with whom he falls in love. The thirty-two-year-old Hudson is too boyish for thirty-eight-year-old Jones, and the film moves sluggishly—it's almost exactly twice as long (152 minutes to 78 minutes) as its 1932 predecessor. The fault lies largely with its obsessive producer, David O. Selznick [497 . . .], who viewed the film primarily as a vehicle for his wife, Jones. Selznick hired Ben Hecht [78 . . .] to write the screenplay and persuaded John Huston [24 . . .] to direct. But there were problems from the start. Huston found the screenplay unfilmable and was unimpressed with Hudson's acting—he had suggested Gregory Peck [759 . . .] instead. So Huston quit and was replaced by Charles Vidor. Cinematographer Oswald Morris [659 . . .] also clashed with Selznick and was replaced by Piero Portalupi. Production designer Arthur Fellows and Selznick actually came to blows, so the screen credit for art direction went to Alfred Junge [221 . . .]. The result of all this was a box-office disaster and the end of Selznick's career as a producer.

Though he's best known today as a director of four films—*Shoeshine, The Bicycle Thief, Yesterday, Today and Tomorrow,* and *The Garden of the Finzi-Continis*—that received foreign language film Oscars, De Sica began as an actor and was a matinee idol in Italy in the late twenties and early thirties. He appeared in more than 150 films before his death in 1974. He lost his sole nomination to Red Buttons in *Sayonara.*

650.5 • FARINELLI: IL CASTRATO

K2 PRODUCTION/RTL/TVI/STEPHAN FILMS/ALINEA FILMS/LE STUDIO CANAL + /UGC IMAGES/FRANCE 2 CINEMA/MG S.R.L./ITALIAN INTERNATIONAL FILM S.R.L. PRODUCTION; MIRAMAX (BELGIUM). 1994.

NOMINATION *Foreign Language Film.*

Farinelli was an eighteenth-century opera singer whose phenomenal voice was the result of accidental castration when he was a small boy. The film, directed by Gerard Corbiau from a script he cowrote with his wife, Andree, deals with Farinelli's rivalry with the composer George Frederick Handel, as well as his relationship with his brother, Riccardo, a composer. The film is both visually and sonically opulent: To create the voice of the castrato, noted for having the voice of a choirboy with the lung power of an adult male, technicians electronically blended the voices of a contemporary soprano and countertenor. The practice of intentional castration to produce Farinelli-like voices was continued until the twentieth century, when the Pope banned it. Recordings of the last known castrato, Alessandro Moreschi, were made in the early years of the century, but the sound is poor. The Oscar went to Russia's *Burnt by the Sun.*

651 • FARMER'S DAUGHTER, THE

RKO RADIO. 1947.

AWARD *Actress:* Loretta Young.

NOMINATION *Supporting Actor:* Charles Bickford.

Swedish-American farm girl Young goes to work as a maid in a politically active household and winds up not only running for Congress but also marrying Congressman Joseph Cotten. Agreeable comedy, a bit heavy on the ain't-democracy-wonderful message, but made palatable by a good cast, including Ethel Barrymore [1445 . . .]. Directed by H. C. Potter.

Young made her first screen appearance in 1916, at the age of three, but didn't begin acting in films regularly until she was in her teens, in 1927. She appeared in scores of movies in the thirties, often in leads, but without becoming a major film star. She got the part that won her an Oscar only after Ingrid Bergman [72 . . .] turned it down. At the awards, Rosalind Russell was generally thought to be a shoo-in for her performance in *Mourning Becomes Electra.* But that film's miserable failure at the box office apparently damaged Russell's chances. The other nominees were Joan Crawford for *Possessed,* Susan Hayward for *Smash Up—the Story of a Woman,* and Dorothy McGuire for *Gentleman's Agreement.* Crawford had won two years earlier, and Hayward and McGuire were first-time nominees with what were presumed to be long careers ahead of them. So Young doubtless received the award as much for recognition of her twenty-year career as for her performance.

Bickford lost to Edmund Gwenn in *Miracle on 34th Street.*

Young: 428. Bickford: 1052, 1868.

652 • FAT CITY

RASTAR PRODUCTIONS; COLUMBIA. 1972.

NOMINATION *Supporting Actress:* Susan Tyrrell.

Life among the losers of Stockton, California, including has-been boxer Stacy Keach, would-be boxer Jeff Bridges [1139 . . .], and alcoholic Tyrrell. This film by John Huston [24 . . .] has admirers, but though it's well done, and very well played, it's one of those Statements About the Human Condition that aren't very convincing if you think hard about them. With Candy Clark [65] and Nicholas Colasanto. Tyrrell, an eccentric, flamboyant performer who got her start with the Andy Warhol circle, has been seen largely in offbeat movies, the most mainstream of which are *Big Top Pee-Wee* (1988) and John Waters'

Cry-Baby (1990). She lost to Eileen Heckart in *Butterflies Are Free.*

653 • *FATAL ATTRACTION*

Jaffe/Lansing Production; Paramount. 1987.
Nominations *Picture:* Stanley R. Jaffe and Sherry Lansing, producers. *Actress:* Glenn Close. *Supporting Actress:* Anne Archer. *Director:* Adrian Lyne. *Screenplay Based on Material From Another Medium:* James Dearden. *Film Editing:* Michael Kahn and Peter E. Berger.

Though happily married to Archer, Michael Douglas [1481 . . .] yields to temptation and has a fling with Close, who then pursues him, trying to break up his marriage or, failing that, kill him. Crass but creepy thriller that was a big box-office hit but certainly seems like a peculiar best picture nominee, odd company for the brightly satiric *Broadcast News,* the memory trip *Hope and Glory,* the charming *Moonstruck,* and the epic winner *The Last Emperor.* And there was other substantial fare available: *Wall Street, Good Morning, Vietnam, The Untouchables, Cry Freedom, My Life as a Dog, The Dead, Empire of the Sun, Radio Days, Au Revoir, Les Enfants, Babette's Feast, Full Metal Jacket, River's Edge* —any one of which seems like a more distinguished choice as a best picture contender.

Lansing, as the former president of 20th Century-Fox and hence the first woman to head a major studio, professed annoyance at the criticism of the film advanced by such feminists as Susan Faludi, who in her best-seller *Backlash* pointed out the film's subtext, that single women are a menace to society. To Lansing's credit, the following year she produced *The Accused,* a strong antirape drama. But then in 1993 Lansing, who had become head of Paramount, drew the ire of feminists again by producing *Indecent Proposal,* a melodrama, also directed by Lyne, in which a rich man pays a young married couple a million dollars for a night with the wife.

Close was not the first choice for the vindictive woman scorned. Isabelle Adjani [337 . . .] and Debra Winger [1465 . . .] turned the part down. Having spent her film career playing nurturing, self-sacrificing, and rather bland women, Close jumped at the chance to change her image. She succeeded, but the Oscar went to Cher for *Moonstruck.*

Archer was stuck with the more conventional role, one that might well have gone to Close under other circumstances: the warm, understanding mother who defends her household when it's under attack. Although she had been in films since 1972, few of her roles before *Fatal Attraction* had attracted much notice. Olympia Dukakis won the Oscar for *Moonstruck.*

Lyne is often grouped with other British directors such as Ridley Scott [2039] and Alan Parker [1313 . . .] who first attracted notice for their work in advertising. *Flashdance* was his first major hit, and its showy, music-video look is characteristic of all his work. He lost to Bernardo Bertolucci for *The Last Emperor.*

Fatal Attraction is actually a remake. Dearden himself had directed a short version of it under the title *Diversion* in 1980—hence his nomination in the adaptation rather than original screenplay category. As first shot, the film ended with the Close character committing suicide but in a manner that frames Douglas as her murderer. Preview audiences were unhappy with this ending, and it was rewritten and reshot with a more conventional vengeance scene for theatrical release. The original ending has been restored for one of the videotape releases. Dearden has since turned to feature direction, with *Pascali's Island* (1988) and *A Kiss Before Dying* (1991). The Oscar went to Mark Peploe and Bertolucci for *The Last Emperor,* which also won an Oscar for Gabriella Cristiani's editing.

Jaffe: 1111. Close: 199, 485, 1418, 2314. Kahn: 416, 613, 1652, 1764.65.

654 • *FATE IS THE HUNTER*

Arcola Pictures Production; 20th Century-Fox. 1964.
Nomination *Black-and-White Cinematography:* Milton Krasner.

Airline executive Glenn Ford tracks the cause of a fatal crash. Pedestrian who- or whatdunit with a capable second-string cast—Rod Taylor, Nancy Kwan, Suzanne Pleshette, Jane Russell, Wally Cox, Nehemiah Persoff—directed by Ralph Nelson [1174]. The cinematography Oscar went to Walter Lassally for *Zorba the Greek.*

Krasner: 21, 46, 96, 953, 1219, 2072.

655 • *FATHER GOOSE*

UNIVERSAL-GRANOX PRODUCTION; UNIVERSAL. 1964.
AWARD *Story and Screenplay—Written Directly for the Screen:* S. H. Barnett; Peter Stone and Frank Tarloff. **NOMINATIONS** *Sound:* Waldon O. Watson, sound director, Universal City Studio Sound Department. *Film Editing:* Ted J. Kent.

Crotchety recluse Cary Grant [1445 . . .] finds his South Sea island paradise in danger of being lost during World War II when Australian officer Trevor Howard [1875] presses him into service as a planespotter, and then a group of French schoolgirls, chaperoned by teacher Leslie Caron [1113 . . .] is deposited in his care while being evacuated from New Guinea. There's nothing new here. If you've seen *The African Queen* or *Heaven Knows, Mr. Allison,* you have a good idea of what to expect, and you've seen it much better done. Grant and Caron make it tolerable, however. Directed by Ralph Nelson [1174].

Stone had made his screenwriting debut in 1963 with the thriller *Charade,* which also starred Grant, and was called in for a rewrite for Tarloff's screenplay, which was based on Barnett's novel. The two screenwriters first met at the Oscars.

The award for sound went to *My Fair Lady.* The editing award was won by William Ziegler for *Mary Poppins.*

Watson: 350, 690, 744, 1810, 2035.

656 • *FATHER OF THE BRIDE*

MGM. 1950.
NOMINATIONS *Picture:* Pandro S. Berman, producer. *Actor:* Spencer Tracy. *Screenplay:* Frances Goodrich and Albert Hackett.

When daughter Elizabeth Taylor [318 . . .] announces that she's engaged, father Tracy begins to go to pieces. Somehow, with the help of wife Joan Bennett, he survives the wedding, which turns into an extravaganza against his will. This much-loved comedy of suburban manners, directed by Vincente Min-

nelli [66 . . .], has been derided as a typical MGM celebration of middle-class American family life. It spawned endless imitative TV sitcoms—*Father Knows Best, Make Room for Daddy,* and the like—as well as its own sequel, *Father's Little Dividend* (1951). But it gets its strong underpinning of integrity from Tracy, from Minnelli's respectful but unsentimental direction, and from the performances of a well-picked cast: Don Taylor as the groom, Moroni Olsen and Billie Burke [1306] as his parents, Leo G. Carroll as a supercilious caterer, Melville Cooper, Willard Waterman, and Russ (billed as Rusty) Tamblyn [1558]. Although he was the first choice for the role, Tracy almost refused to play it when he heard that production head Dore Schary [157 . . .] was also considering Jack Benny for the film. The 1991 remake with Steve Martin is inferior, but worth comparing to see what differences forty years have made: *Plus ça change, plus c'est la même chose?*

The best picture Oscar went to *All About Eve,* which also won for Joseph L. Mankiewicz's screenplay. Tracy lost to Jose Ferrer in *Cyrano de Bergerac.*

Berman: 40, 754, 1035, 1899, 2115. Tracy: 131, 271, 352, 843, 1000, 1065, 1470, 1751. Goodrich: 25, 1782, 2052. Hackett: 25, 1782, 2052.

656.5 • *FEARLESS*

WARNER BROS. PRODUCTION; WARNER BROS. 1993.
NOMINATION *Supporting Actress:* Rosie Perez.

When an airliner crashes, Jeff Bridges [1139 . . .], one of the survivors, heroically helps others from the flaming wreckage. But then Bridges disappears, to the consternation of his wife (Isabella Rossellini) and those like lawyer Tom Hulce [60] who want him to testify in a suit against the airline. When Bridges is located, he is strange, distant—and full of a curiously peaceful awe at having cheated death. The only person who understands that Bridges is overwhelmed by the tenuousness of existence is Perez, who also survived the crash and whose life was also changed, in a different way, by the experience. An intriguing, not wholly successful exploration of . . . well, the meaning of life, directed by Peter Weir [511 . . .] from a script that Rafael Yglesias based on his own novel. The film is fine at capturing the terror of the crash and the eerieness of Bridges' state of mind, but it has nowhere to go narratively. The cinematography is by Allen Daviau [112 . . .] and the score by Maurice Jarre [558 . . .]. Perez, whose previous credits include *Do the Right Thing* and *White Men Can't Jump* (1992), lost to Anna Paquin in *The Piano.*

657 • *FELLINI SATYRICON*

Alberto Grimaldi Production; United Artists (France/Italy). 1970.

Nomination *Director:* Federico Fellini.

Decadence in ancient Rome as reinterpreted by the man who chronicled decadence in modern Rome in *La Dolce Vita.* The story, if you can call it that, centers on the wanderings of two young men who have quarreled over a boy they both love. Not so much based on as an *hommage* to the work of the first century A.D. author Petronius, a favorite in the court of Nero who committed suicide when ordered by the emperor to do so. Chock full of grotesques and bizarre spectacle, with some amazing sets by Danilo Donati [658 . . .] and fine camera work by Giuseppe Rotunno [49], but the whole thing gets boring after half an hour or so.

Fellini and Ken Russell, for *Women in Love,* were the two directors this year whose films were not nominated for best picture. They took the slots that might have gone to George Seaton and Bob Rafelson, whose *Airport* and *Five Easy Pieces* were nominated. The Oscar went to Franklin J. Schaffner for *Patton.*

Fellini: 61, 562, 603, 658, 1496, 1519, 1938, 2209.

658 • *FELLINI'S CASANOVA*

P.E.A. Produzioni Europee Associate S.p.A. Production; Universal (Italy). 1976.

Award *Costume Design:* Danilo Donati.

Nomination *Screenplay—Based on Material From Another Medium:* Federico Fellini and Bernadino Zapponi.

Donald Sutherland plays the eighteenth-century sexual adventurer in this baroque adaptation of Casanova's *Memoirs.* The theme is alienation, which only results in an uninvolving film—two and a half hours of empty spectacle and meaningless copulation, with director Fellini's usual gallery of grotesques. A triumph only for Donati, who also designed the sets. The writing Oscar went to William Goldman for *All the President's Men.*

Donati: 809, 1266, 1722, 2000. Fellini: 61, 562, 603, 657, 1496, 1519, 1938, 2209.

658.5 • *FEW GOOD MEN, A*

Castle Rock Entertainment Production; Columbia. 1992.

Nominations *Picture:* David Brown, Rob Reiner, and Andrew Scheinman, producers. *Supporting Actor:* Jack Nicholson. *Film Editing:* Robert Leighton. *Sound:* Kevin O'Connell, Rick Kline, and Bob Eber.

Demi Moore, a young naval attorney with the Judge Advocate General's Office, is assigned to the defense of two marines accused of accidentally killing another marine in a supposedly unauthorized disciplinary action. She is assigned bright but rebellious hotshot Tom Cruise [260] as head of the defense team. Cruise, who has a reputation for brilliant plea bargaining but has never tried a case, senses a cover-up, and his suspicions lead him to Nicholson, the officer in charge of the base at Guantánamo, where the marine died. A courtroom confrontation is the result. An almost too well made drama, adapted by Aaron Sorkin from his hit Broadway play, it seems mechanically contrived to show off its big bright stars, and some of the characterization (Cruise's relationship with his father, Nicholson's devotion to the Marine Corps, the personal and professional tension between Cruise and Moore) is much too pat. There's nothing here you haven't seen before, especially if you've seen *The Caine Mutiny.* On the other hand, admirers of the stars will find it entertaining. Cruise has played this part—the showboater who gets serious—once too often, but he's very good at the parts that call for fine comic timing and quick repartee. He still lacks vocal range and heft for big dramatic scenes, however. There are good supporting performances by J. T. Walsh as Nicholson's second-in-command, Wolfgang Bodison as one of the marines on trial, Kevin Bacon as the prosecuting attorney, and Kiefer

Sutherland as a scarily gung-ho marine lieutenant (although when you spot the earring holes in Sutherland's earlobes during his close-ups, you may wonder if there's another plot twist in store).

The film had been produced, packaged, marketed, and promoted as an Oscar contender, so that its comparatively few nominations came as a shock to the team that brought it to the screen. Producer-director Reiner, who had been responsible for a string of well-received movies—*This Is Spinal Tap* (1984), *Stand By Me, When Harry Met Sally . . . , Misery*—had hoped for recognition as a director that might eclipse his earlier fame as ''Meathead'' on *All in the Family.* But he was the only director of a best picture nominee this year not to receive a nomination for directing; his slot went to Robert Altman for *The Player.* The other contenders for best picture were *The Crying Game, Howards End, Scent of a Woman,* and the winner, *Unforgiven. A Few Good Men* was the only best picture nominee this year to receive no Oscars in any category.

With this, his tenth nomination, Nicholson tied Laurence Olivier [268 . . .] for the most nominations received by an actor. Bette Davis [46 . . .] also received ten nominations, and among performers, only actress Katharine Hepburn [24 . . .], with twelve nominations, has more. The award went to Gene Hackman for *Unforgiven,* which also received an Oscar for Joel Cox's editing. The sound award went to *The Last of the Mohicans.*

Brown: 1041, 2198. Nicholson: 395, 595, 672, 1019, 1135, 1481, 1625, 1678, 2020. O'Connell: 223, 507, 586, 1825, 2020, 2114. Kline: 507, 1333, 1825, 2020, 2114.

659 • *FIDDLER ON THE ROOF*

Mirisch-Cartier Productions; United Artists. 1971.

Awards *Cinematography:* Oswald Morris. *Sound:* Gordon K. McCallum and David Hildyard. *Scoring— Adaptation and Original Song Score:* John Williams.

Nominations *Picture:* Norman Jewison, producer. *Actor:* Topol. *Supporting Actor:* Leonard Frey. *Director:* Norman Jewison. *Art Direction–Set Decoration:* Robert Boyle and Michael Stringer; Peter Lamont.

Topol plays Tevye, the milkman in a turn-of-the-century Ukrainian Jewish village, whose life centers on getting his daughters married off and then on surviving and immigrating to America when the pogroms start. Handsome translation to the screen of the Broadway musical based on the stories of Sholem Aleichem, with a book by Joseph Stein and songs by Sheldon Harnick and Jerry Bock. Only *Cabaret* the following year has surpassed it in making cinematic sense out of stage material. *Fiddler* was a hit in big cities but a box-office dud elsewhere, leading to trims of up to half an hour from its original three-hour running time.

Morris first received acclaim—though astonishingly no Oscar nomination—for his work on *Moulin Rouge* in 1952 and was a frequent collaborator with director John Huston [24 . . .] after that. He began his apprenticeship as a cameraman in England in the thirties and resumed his career after serving in the RAF during World War II. He is particularly noted for his use of filters and evocative lighting; *Fiddler* is said to have been shot through a woman's nylon stocking.

This was the first of five Oscars for Williams, the most acclaimed film composer of our time. He began his career as a composer working in TV in the fifties, providing theme music (often billed as Johnny Williams) for such series as *Lost in Space.* He began working in films in the sixties. The music of the eponymous fiddler is played in the film by Isaac Stern.

Jewison has been a successful director and producer in all respects except winning the Oscar. This time his film was up against *A Clockwork Orange, The Last Picture Show, Nicholas and Alexandra,* and the winner, *The French Connection.* William Friedkin took the directing Oscar for *The French Connection,* which also won a best actor award for Gene Hackman. Topol, an Israeli actor whose given name, Chaim, was believed by the studio to be unpronounceable by Americans, had played the role of Tevye in London. He was chosen over the American Tevye, Zero Mostel, because it was thought a younger, more virile Tevye would have a wider audience appeal. Topol has made only a few film appearances subsequently.

Frey, who plays Motel the tailor, made only occasional films after his nomination. He died of AIDS in 1988. The Oscar went to Ben Johnson in *The Last Picture Show*. The art direction award went to *Nicholas and Alexandra*.

Morris: 1471, 2299. McCallum: 540, 1737, 1977. Hildyard: 321. Williams: 6, 260, 403, 416, 588, 613, 614, 805, 933, 937, 982, 996, 997, 1041, 1047, 1596, 1652, 1679, 1684, 1701, 1764.65, 1916, 1977, 2107, 2126, 2194, 2293, 2322. Jewison: 992, 1351, 1736, 1857. Boyle: 743, 1450, 1816. Lamont: 45, 1898.

660 • FIELD, THE

GRANADA PRODUCTION; AVENUE PICTURES (IRELAND). 1990.
NOMINATION *Actor:* Richard Harris.

Irish farmer Harris, enraged when the owner of the land he has leased and cultivated for years decides to sell it, precipitates a bloody feud. Oppressive and uninvolving drama, directed by Jim Sheridan [992.5 . . .] with a good cast: John Hurt [608 . . .], Tom Berenger [1584], and Brenda Fricker [1399]. Harris lost to Jeremy Irons in *Reversal of Fortune*.

Harris: 2061.

661 • FIELD OF DREAMS

GORDON COMPANY PRODUCTION, UNIVERSAL. 1989.
NOMINATIONS *Picture:* Lawrence Gordon and Charles Gordon, producers. *Screenplay Based on Material From Another Medium:* Phil Alden Robinson. *Original Score:* James Horner.

Iowa farmer Kevin Costner [482] hears a voice one day: "If you build it, he will come." Gradually the message sinks in: Build a baseball diamond. When he does, the ghost of Shoeless Joe Jackson, played by Ray Liotta, shows up, followed by other players disgraced in the 1919 Black Sox scandal. Loopy, oddball premise for a fantasy that apparently struck the right chord in a lot of people, for it was a surprise box-office hit, going against the conventional wisdom that baseball movies always lose money. It seems to touch people in the same way as some of the films of Frank Capra [1025 . . .], evoking a nostalgia for a supposedly

simpler, more innocent era. Robinson directs his own adaptation of W. P. Kinsella's novel *Shoeless Joe,* keeping the material a few inches away from the saccharine—except for Costner's reconciliation scene with his dead father, when the syrup inevitably floods in. Strongly cast, with Amy Madigan [2156], Burt Lancaster [107 . . .], and James Earl Jones [830], who almost brings off his big speech about how baseball once reflected the best about America. But as many critics pointed out, this game being lauded by a great African-American actor was as rigidly segregated as the rest of American society until after World War II and the putative end to American innocence.

Field of Dreams competed against *Born on the Fourth of July, Dead Poets Society,* and *My Left Foot* for the best picture Oscar, losing to *Driving Miss Daisy,* which also won for Alfred Uhry's screenplay. The scoring award went to Alan Menken for *The Little Mermaid*.

Horner: 45, 67.

662 • FIESTA

MGM. 1947.
NOMINATION *Scoring of a Musical Picture:* Johnny Green.

Ricardo Montalban would rather be a musician and woo Esther Williams than fight bulls. Flimsy premise for a feeble musical, though it features a score by no less than Aaron Copland [894 . . .]. With Akim Tamiroff [701 . . .], Mary Astor [822], and Cyd Charisse. The Oscar went to Alfred Newman for *Mother Wore Tights*.

Green: 66, 320, 594, 817, 914, 1298, 1471, 1550, 1657, 2047, 2244.

663 • 55 DAYS AT PEKING

SAMUEL BRONSTON PRODUCTION; ALLIED ARTISTS. 1963.
NOMINATIONS *Song:* "So Little Time," music by Dimitri Tiomkin, lyrics by Paul Francis Webster. *Music Score—Substantially Original:* Dimitri Tiomkin.

Charlton Heston [175] takes charge of defending the international community of Peking when the dowager empress, played by Flora Robson [1759], incites the Boxer Rebellion of 1900. Big, flabby epic with lots of ridiculous casting: Ava Gardner [1339] as a Russian baroness, and Robson, Leo Genn [1644], and Robert Helpmann as Chinese. Plus David Niven [1778], John Ireland [53], Harry Andrews, and Paul Lukas [2233]. Directed by Nicholas Ray [1671]. The best song Oscar went to James Van Heusen and Sammy Cahn's "Call Me Irresponsible," from *Papa's Delicate Condition*. John Addison won for the score of *Tom Jones*.

Tiomkin: 33, 286, 380, 446, 638, 730, 768, 850, 911, 912, 1206, 1347, 1370, 1470, 2006, 2127, 2282, 2335. Webster: 33, 64, 95, 331, 376, 604, 730, 856, 1213, 1276, 1322, 1388, 1755, 1925, 2014.

664 • *FIGHT FOR LIFE, THE*
UNITED STATES FILM SERVICE; COLUMBIA. 1940.
NOMINATION *Original Score:* Louis Gruenberg.

A documentary about the work of the Chicago Maternity Center among the poor, made by Pare Lorentz for the U.S. Film Service. The scoring Oscar went to *Pinocchio*.

Gruenberg: 432, 1854.

665 • *FIGHTING SEABEES, THE*
REPUBLIC. 1944.
NOMINATION *Scoring of a Dramatic or Comedy Picture:* Walter Scharf and Roy Webb.

John Wayne [33 . . .] is a construction foreman with the navy's Construction Battalion (hence, Seabees) Unit in the South Pacific. Pretty good action film, packed with the usual propaganda, but also a romantic subplot involving war correspondent Susan Hayward [973 . . .]. Directed by Edward Ludwig. The Oscar went to Max Steiner for *Since You Went Away*.

Scharf: 174, 274, 737, 864, 921, 991, 1054, 1305, 2285. Webb: 615, 640, 969, 1049, 1394, 1639.

666 • *FINIAN'S RAINBOW*
WARNER BROS.-SEVEN ARTS. 1968.
NOMINATIONS *Sound:* Warner Bros.-Seven Arts Studio Sound Department. *Score of a Musical Picture—Original or Adaptation:* Ray Heindorf.

Irishman Fred Astaire [2126] and his daughter, Petula Clark, come to the American South so they can bury a pot of gold near Fort Knox. They're pursued by the leprechaun from whom Astaire has stolen the gold, Tommy Steele. Meanwhile, a group of sharecroppers are being kicked off their land by a bigoted southern senator, Keenan Wynn, so the leprechaun turns the senator black to teach him a lesson. The film's satire comes straight from the 1947 Broadway musical on which it was based, but by the late sixties it had become badly dated. What remains are some lovely songs by Burton Lane [117 . . .] and E. Y. Harburg [322 . . .] and Astaire's last film musical performance. Unfortunately Francis Ford Coppola [65 . . .] had never directed a musical and has admitted that his first attempt was a "disaster." He fired Astaire's longtime collaborator, Hermes Pan [481 . . .], as choreographer and staged the musical numbers rather hectically. The film has its admirers, but even they will admit that Steele is overbearing and the plot an encumbrance.

Oliver! took the Oscars for sound and John Green's scoring.

Heindorf: 331, 479, 930, 1043, 1204, 1385, 1408, 1430, 1690, 1719, 1750, 1910, 2058, 2186, 2243, 2310, 2318.

667 • *FIREMEN'S BALL, THE*
BARRANDOV FILM STUDIOS PRODUCTION (CZECHOSLOVAKIA). 1968.
NOMINATION *Foreign Language Film*.

Episodic comedy about the mishaps that take place during a ball in honor of the retiring chief of a small-town fire department. Slapstick satire on bureaucracy, directed by Milos Forman [60 . . .], his last film before the Soviet invasion forced him into exile in Hollywood. Ironically the Oscar went to the Soviet Union's *War and Peace*.

667.5 • *FIRM, THE*
JOHN DAVIS/SCOTT RUDIN/MIRAGE PRODUCTION; PARAMOUNT. 1993.
NOMINATIONS *Supporting Actress:* Holly Hunter. *Score:* Dave Grusin.

Just out of Harvard Law School, Mitch McDeere,

played by Tom Cruise [260], gets hired by a Memphis firm that provides the young lawyer and his wife (Jeanne Tripplehorn) with a new house, a big expensive car, and all sorts of terrific perks. Too good to be true, right? Soon McDeere notices stuff that makes him suspicious, and sure enough an FBI man (Ed Harris) confirms his suspicions: The firm is a front for the mob, and anyone who rats on the outfit or tries to leave it is going to meet with a mysterious accident. The thickening of the plot is provided by assorted supporting characters, all played by top-notch performers: Gene Hackman [255 . . .] as the partner who serves as McDeere's mentor in the firm, Hal Holbrook as the polished but menacing senior partner, Wilford Brimley as the folksy but menacing chief of security, Gary Busey [307] as the low-rent private eye McDeere enlists in his aid, Hunter as Busey's bleach-blond secretary, and David Strathairn as McDeere's jailbird brother. John Grisham's page-turner novel, on which the film is based, had all the ingredients for a first-rate movie thriller. But producer-director Sydney Pollack [1512 . . .] finds the wrong tone for the material. He turns what should have been a fast-moving paranoid nail-biter into something moody and languorous—it's two and a half hours long—with occasional bits of action, such as a chase sequence on an aerial tramway, that seem obligatory rather than essential to the plot. The script by screenwriters David Rabe, Robert Towne [395 . . .], and David Rayfiel scraps the hide-and-seek final section of Grisham's novel for a flat and confusing ending. And Grusin's jazz piano score makes the whole film seem like it's taking place in an upscale cocktail lounge. (Many felt that Grusin's nomination should have gone instead to Michael Nyman for *The Piano.*) Only the actors provide *The Firm* with energy and excitement, and Hunter is a particular standout as the tough, resourceful Tammy Hemphill. She received a simultaneous nomination as best actress for *The Piano,* winning that award, but losing this one to Anna Paquin, who plays her daughter in *The Piano.* The scoring award went to John Williams for *Schindler's List.*

Hunter: 293, 1563.5. Grusin: 379, 633, 881, 890, 1318, 1473, 2113.

668 • *FIRST LOVE*

UNIVERSAL. 1939.

NOMINATIONS *Black-and-White Cinematography:* Joseph Valentine. *Interior Decoration:* Jack Otterson and Martin Obzina. *Score:* Charles Previn.

Orphan Deanna Durbin is taken in by unpleasant relatives but is rescued from them when she falls in love with Robert Stack [2315]. Slight but amusing transmogrification of the Cinderella story, in which Durbin, Universal's biggest star, made headlines by receiving her first screen kiss. Directed by Henry Koster [214].

Valentine was in fact only a preliminary nominee for the Oscar. For the 1939 awards, the first year in which the cinematography awards were divided into black-and-white and color categories, the Academy announced a first round of nominations for cinematography and then placed only two finalists in each of the two divisions on the ballot: Bert Glennon for *Stagecoach* and the winner, Gregg Toland for *Wuthering Heights.* Lyle Wheeler's art direction won for *Gone With the Wind. Stagecoach* won for scoring.

Valentine: 776, 1048, 1229, 1896, 2291. Otterson: 96, 269, 681, 1229, 1240, 1895, 2342. Obzina: 681. Previn: 306, 1030, 1229, 1485, 1870, 1896.

669 • *FIRST LOVE*

ALFA PRODUCTIONS S.A.-SEITZ FILM PRODUCTION (SWITZERLAND). 1970.

NOMINATION *Foreign Language Film.*

Teenager John Moulder-Brown falls in love with Dominique Sanda, who is the mistress of his father, Maximilian Schell [1065 . . .]. Rather clumsy version of a Turgenev story, directed by Schell with an international cast that also includes Valentina Cortese [501]. Cinematography by Sven Nykvist [460 . . .]. The Oscar went to Italy's *Investigation of a Citizen Above Suspicion.*

670 • *FISH CALLED WANDA, A*

MICHAEL SHAMBERG-PROMINENT FEATURES PRODUCTION; MGM (UNITED KINGDOM). 1988.

AWARD *Supporting Actor:* Kevin Kline.

NOMINATIONS *Director:* Charles Crichton. *Screenplay Written Directly for the Screen:* John Cleese, screenplay; John Cleese and Charles Crichton, story.

Kline, Jamie Lee Curtis, and Michael Palin pull off a robbery, but they need the help of stuffy barrister Cleese to make their getaway. Hilarious farce with just enough bad taste to make it either memorable or offensive, depending on where you stand in these matters. Fans of the *Monty Python* TV series in which Cleese and Palin got their start won't object to it in the least. There were protests about the Palin character's speech impediment from people with similar disabilities.

Kline, who was already a respected stage actor, made his screen debut in *Sophie's Choice,* but Meryl Streep—who had suggested that Kline be cast in the film—walked off with the awards. His subsequent performance in the ensemble cast of *The Big Chill* established Kline in the movies, but he continued his work on stage as well, perhaps realizing that superstardom on screen was not coming his way. His work on *Silverado* brought him to the attention of Cleese, who was also in the cast, and won him the role of Otto, the somewhat dim would-be Nietzschean *Übermensch* in *Wanda.* The role exploited Kline's gift for physical comedy as no movie, with the exception of the little-seen *The Pirates of Penzance* (1983), had done before. The Oscar came as a surprise. The smart money had been on Martin Landau for *Tucker: The Man and His Dream.* Though Kline is a respected serious actor on stage—his Hamlet has been highly praised—his subsequent film roles have ranged from broad comedy, such as the vain soap-opera actor in *Soapdish* (1991), to mildly serious, such as the alienated L.A. doctor in *Grand Canyon.*

Crichton was in his late seventies when Cleese chose him to direct *Wanda.* He began as an editor in the British film industry in the thirties, and by the late forties had worked his way into directing. His most famous film, before *Wanda,* was *The Lavender Hill Mob,* one of the Ealing studios comedies of the early fifties that launched Alec Guinness to stardom. Unfortunately Crichton's star was not similarly launched, and from the sixties on, his directing was mostly confined to television. Putting together the package that became *Wanda,* Cleese sought out Crichton for his experience, saying, ''Charlie hasn't made a feature for over twenty years because they're all looking for exciting young directors, whereas I'm looking for unexciting old directors—who know what they're doing.'' During production Cleese was officially listed as codirector, but when the film was released, Crichton was given sole credit, Cleese claiming that the codirector status was only to placate MGM during the filming because the studio was concerned about Crichton's age and health. Crichton's Oscar nomination for directing was a surprise. Many thought the honor should have gone to Penny Marshall for *Big* or Jonathan Demme for *Married to the Mob* instead, especially as Cleese's contribution to the direction of *Wanda* was an open secret. The Oscar went to Barry Levinson for *Rain Man.*

Cleese had studied law at Cambridge, a fact that certainly informs his character in *Wanda,* barrister Archie Leach (a tongue-in-cheek tribute to Cary Grant [1445 . . .], whose real name that was). But at university Cleese became involved with the Footlights Dramatic Club, which has been the germ of the careers of such people as Jonathan Miller, Peter Cook, David Frost, Graham Chapman, Eric Idle, and Emma Thompson [954.5 . . .]. Cleese worked with Frost on the BBC's *That Was the Week That Was* in 1963, and his association with Chapman as writer and performer was the nucleus of *Monty Python's Flying Circus* in the late sixties and early seventies. After leaving the *Python* troupe, Cleese had a second triumph with the BBC TV sitcom *Fawlty Towers* in 1975 and 1979. Before *Wanda,* Cleese's film career had largely been confined to the various *Monty Python* spin-offs: *And Now for Something Completely Different* (1971), *Monty Python and the Holy Grail* (1974), and *Life of Brian* (1979), plus small roles in *Time Bandits* (1981) and *The Great Muppet Caper.* Cleese and Crichton went through thirteen drafts of the script before finally achieving what they wanted. The Oscar went to the writers of *Rain Man.*

671 • FISHER KING, THE

TriStar Pictures Production; TriStar. 1991.
Award *Supporting Actress:* Mercedes Ruehl.
Nominations *Actor:* Robin Williams. *Screenplay Written Directly for the Screen:* Richard LaGravenese. *Art Direction–Set Decoration:* Mel Bourne; Cindy Carr. *Original Score:* George Fenton.

Radio shock jock Jeff Bridges [1139 . . .] unwittingly inspires a psycho to shoot up a Manhattan restaurant and thereby brings about the death of college professor Williams' wife. Williams becomes a mad street person, and Bridges' life goes in the toilet—until their paths cross. Romantic morality tale, directed by Terry Gilliam [275], with moments of extravagant fantasy—contemporary New York becomes the setting for the quest for the Holy Grail. Somewhat overextended and sentimental, though an exceptional cast (including Amanda Plummer playing one of her gallery of eccentrics) pretty much brings it off.

Ruehl, who made her screen debut in 1979 in *The Warriors,* attracted little notice in a variety of supporting performances until 1988, when she played Dean Stockwell's wife in *Married to the Mob* and Tom Hanks' mother in *Big.* Though Stockwell and Hanks both received Oscar nominations, Ruehl had to wait until her widely acclaimed performance as Bridges' quirky girlfriend. She won over strong competition: Diane Ladd in *Rambling Rose,* Juliette Lewis in *Cape Fear,* Kate Nelligan in *The Prince of Tides,* and Jessica Tandy in *Fried Green Tomatoes.* She subsequently received a Tony Award for her performance in the Neil Simon [332 . . .] play *Lost in Yonkers,* a role she repeated in the 1993 screen version.

Williams lost his third nomination to Anthony Hopkins in *The Silence of the Lambs.* Callie Khouri's screenplay for *Thelma & Louise* won the writing award. The art direction Oscar went to *Bugsy,* and Alan Menken won for the score of *Beauty and the Beast.*

Williams: 511, 800. Bourne: 1005, 1418. Fenton: 471, 485, 745.

672 • FIVE EASY PIECES

BBS Productions; Columbia. 1970.
Nominations *Picture:* Bob Rafelson and Richard Wechsler, producers. *Actor:* Jack Nicholson. *Supporting Actress:* Karen Black. *Story and Screenplay—Based on Factual Material or Material Not Previously Published or Produced:* Bob Rafelson and Adrien Joyce.

Nicholson has given up a promising career as a concert pianist to become, to his artistic family's dismay, an oil-field roughneck living with a vulgar, clinging woman (Black). But he decides to return home for a last visit with his dying father. Celebrated character study and "road" movie, often compared with *Easy Rider,* though it's a much better film. Its most famous scene involves Nicholson's fight with a waitress in a roadside café over a chicken salad sandwich—often interpreted as the epitome of the rage many counterculture types felt at the plasticized conformity of American life. The film transcends such facile interpretations—Nicholson's character is too complex to serve as anyone's message-bearer.

The nominations for best picture of 1970 reflect the deep schisms of the era. At one extreme, there was the old-fashioned cornball all-star vehicle *Airport;* at the other, the wickedly nihilistic black comedy *MASH.* Somewhere in between came the mawkish *Love Story,* which centered on the generation gap, and the winner, the double-edged *Patton,* which was admired by hawks as a portrait of an American hero and seen by many doves as a portrait of a psychotic militarist. *Five Easy Pieces* looks like the most subtle and interesting work of all these nominees, but it was pretty much thrown out of contention when the Academy failed to nominate its director, Rafelson. On the other hand, Rafelson has yet to deliver on the promise shown with *Five Easy Pieces.* His subsequent films, which include *The King of Marvin Gardens* (1972) and *Mountains of the Moon* (1990), are for the most part interesting, but none is in the league of the film that brought him his first acclaim.

Nicholson, of course, has gone on to superstardom and wealth, having made his breakthrough into mainstream films with *Easy Rider* (of which Rafelson was an executive producer). He lost this, his second try at the Oscar, to George C. Scott for *Patton.*

Black had also appeared in *Easy Rider,* her second film after her debut in *You're a Big Boy Now.* For much of the seventies she was considered an important star, working in comparatively prestigious films such as *The Great Gatsby, Nashville,* and the last movie directed by Alfred Hitchcock [1171 . . .], *The Family Plot* (1976). But her looks were too unconventional and her dramatic range too narrow for a sustained career in leading roles, and she began to fade from sight in the eighties. She lost to Helen Hayes for *Airport.*

"Adrien Joyce" is a pseudonym for the screenwriter Carole Eastman. The writing Oscar went to Francis Ford Coppola and Edmund H. North for *Patton.*

Nicholson: 395, 595, 658.5, 1019, 1135, 1481, 1625, 1678, 2020.

673 • FIVE FINGERS

20TH CENTURY-FOX. 1952.

NOMINATIONS *Director:* Joseph L. Mankiewicz. *Screenplay:* Michael Wilson.

James Mason [761 . . .] plays the spy known as Cicero, who operates from within the British embassy in Ankara, Turkey, peddling secrets—including the plans for D-Day—to the Germans. Ironically the Germans don't believe him. Sophisticated, enjoyable melodrama based on the book *Operation Cicero,* by L. C. Moyzich, who appears as a character in the film, played by Oscar Karlweis. The cast also includes Danielle Darrieux, Michael Rennie, and Walter Hampden. According to Mankiewicz, the film's title, which means nothing, was thought up by Fox head Darryl F. Zanuck [34 . . .] because there had been a run of successful spy movies, all with numbers in their titles: *House on 92nd Street, 18 Rue Madeleine,* and *Call Northside 777.* (Zanuck may also have been inspired by the success of *The Third Man.)* The directing Oscar went to John Ford for *The Quiet Man.* Charles Schnee's screenplay for *The Bad and the Beautiful* won the writing award.

Mankiewicz: 46, 146, 1163, 1444, 1563, 1836, 1841. Wilson: 287, 730, 1579.

674 • FIVE GRAVES TO CAIRO

PARAMOUNT. 1943.

NOMINATIONS *Black-and-White Cinematography:* John Seitz. *Black-and-White Interior Decoration:* Hans Dreier and Ernst Fegte, art direction; Bertram Granger, set decoration. *Film Editing:* Doane Harrison.

Franchot Tone [1387] attempts to foil Field Marshal Rommel, played by Erich von Stroheim [1975] in this good espionage thriller directed by Billy Wilder [91 . . .]. A lively script, by Wilder and Charles Brackett [705 . . .], helps, as does the presence of Akim Tamiroff [701 . . .] and Anne Baxter [46 . . .] in the cast. Somewhat overshadowed by *Casablanca* when it comes to romantic intrigue in the desert, but still enjoyable.

The Song of Bernadette won for Arthur Miller's cinematography and for art direction. The editing Oscar went to George Amy for *Air Force.*

Seitz: 552, 566, 1208, 1714, 1975, 2262. Dreier: 97, 161, 649, 701, 726, 925, 979, 1101, 1120, 1194, 1214, 1217, 1358, 1443, 1452, 1540, 1668, 1748, 1880, 1975, 1994, 2190. Fegte: 532, 726, 1613. Granger: 701. Harrison: 1208, 1975.

675 • FIVE PENNIES, THE

DENA PRODUCTIONS; PARAMOUNT. 1959.

NOMINATIONS *Color Cinematography:* Daniel L. Fapp. *Song:* "The Five Pennies," music and lyrics by Sylvia Fine. *Scoring of a Musical Picture:* Leith Stevens. *Color Costume Design:* Edith Head.

Danny Kaye plays jazz musician Red Nichols in an okay biopic, enlivened mainly by the presence of the great Louis Armstrong. Nichols dubbed the trumpet playing, and the vocals, lip-synched by Barbara Bel Geddes [972], are by Eileen Wilson. Other musicians in the cast include Bob Crosby, Shelly Manne, and Ray Anthony. There's a guest appearance by Bob Hope, and Tuesday Weld [1205] plays Nichols' daughter. In addition to many jazz standards, the film includes several new songs written by Fine, who was Kaye's wife. Her nominated song lost to James Van Heusen and Sammy Cahn's "High Hopes," from *A Hole in the Head.*

Ben-Hur won the Oscars for Robert Surtees' cinematography and Elizabeth Haffenden's costumes. The Oscar for scoring a musical went to André Previn and Ken Darby for *Porgy and Bess.*

Fapp: 529, 978, 1279, 1492, 2184, 2244. Fine: 1348. Stevens: 1067, 1427. Head: 31, 32, 46, 305, 357, 363, 612, 636, 736, 832, 894, 945, 1003, 1219, 1261, 1263, 1398, 1427, 1504, 1550, 1579, 1587, 1631, 1716, 1727, 1738, 1748, 1840, 1927, 1986, 2012, 2098, 2247, 2298.

676 • FIVE STAR FINAL

FIRST NATIONAL. 1931–32.
NOMINATION *Picture:* Hal B. Wallis, producer.

Anything-for-a-story newspaper editor Edward G. Robinson does more harm than good in his pursuit of the news. Fast-moving melodrama with fine performances by Robinson and by Boris Karloff as an unethical reporter. Directed by Mervyn LeRoy [1662 . . .]. The Oscar went to *Grand Hotel.*

Wallis: 17, 55, 85, 164, 343, 365, 689, 712, 965, 1046, 1095, 1162, 1248, 1482, 1727, 1779, 2233, 2318.

677 • 5,000 FINGERS OF DR. T, THE

STANLEY KRAMER PRODUCTIONS; COLUMBIA. 1953.
NOMINATION *Scoring of a Musical Picture:* Frederick Hollander and Morris Stoloff.

Young Tommy Rettig, who hates to practice the piano, dreams of his piano teacher, Dr. Terwilliker (Hans Conreid), as a madman who keeps five hundred boys locked in his castle endlessly practicing at a mile-long keyboard. Oddball musical fantasy that was a huge box-office flop but has a cult following. The story is by Dr. Seuss, and the movie was produced by Stanley Kramer [330 . . .] and directed by Roy Rowland. The scoring Oscar went to Alfred Newman for *Call Me Madam.*

Hollander: 104, 1998, 2032. Stoloff: 13, 432, 455, 596, 643, 732, 773, 1057, 1058, 1115, 1206, 1862, 1872, 1873, 1998, 2110, 2329.

678 • FIXER, THE

JOHN FRANKENHEIMER-EDWARD LEWIS PRODUCTIONS; MGM. 1968.
NOMINATION *Actor:* Alan Bates.

In turn-of-the-century Russia, Bates, a Jewish handyman, is thrown in prison for a crime he didn't commit, and resists torture and inducements to confess. Endless, tedious drama that substitutes a message about the indomitability of man for the ironies of the Bernard Malamud novel on which it's based. Screenwriter Dalton Trumbo [273 . . .] is largely to blame. A lot of talent is wasted here: Dirk Bogarde, Georgia Brown, Hugh Griffith [175 . . .], Ian Holm [386], Jack Gilford [1761], Elizabeth Hartman [1537], and David Warner. Directed by John Frankenheimer.

This is, surprisingly, the sole nomination for Bates, one of the most prominent British actors of the generation that includes Peter O'Toole [164 . . .] and Albert Finney [579 . . .]. He's perhaps best known for his films of the sixties, including *Zorba the Greek, Georgy Girl, King of Hearts* (1966), and *Women in Love,* but he has continued to make memorable appearances. The Oscar went to Cliff Robertson for *Charly.*

679 • FLAME AND THE ARROW, THE

NORMA-F.R. PRODUCTION; WARNER BROS. 1950.
NOMINATIONS *Color Cinematography:* Ernest Haller. *Scoring of a Dramatic or Comedy Picture:* Max Steiner.

Burt Lancaster [107 . . .] plays a medieval Italian Robin Hood, leader of a band of rebels seeking to overthrow an evil tyrant. One of a couple of swashbucklers Lancaster made during the fifties that show off his training as a circus acrobat. Like *The Crimson Pirate* (1952), this one features his old circus partner Nick Cravat in several stunts. It's pure entertainment, directed by Jacques Tourneur from a screenplay by Waldo Salt [430 . . .], with Virginia Mayo, Robert Douglas, Aline MacMahon [576], and Norman Lloyd. The Oscars went to Robert Surtees for the cinematography of *King Solomon's Mines* and Franz Waxman for the score of *Sunset Boulevard.*

Haller: 55, 798, 1046, 1174, 1319, 2248. Steiner: 16, 154, 190, 330, 365, 385, 492, 747, 754, 798,

999, 1043, 1046, 1052, 1162, 1169, 1170, 1207, 1324, 1408, 1430, 1456, 1690, 1779, 1828.

680 • FLAME OF BARBARY COAST

REPUBLIC. 1945.

NOMINATIONS *Sound Recording:* Daniel J. Bloomberg. *Scoring of a Dramatic or Comedy Picture:* Dale Butts and Morton Scott.

Cowboy John Wayne [33 . . .] and gambler Joseph Schildkraut [1169] battle over Ann Dvorak in (menacing chords) 1906 San Francisco. Anyone who'd bet against Wayne would try to fill an inside straight. Yes, there's an earthquake, but the difference between this one and the one in *San Francisco* is the difference between Republic and MGM. Directed by Joseph Kane, with William Frawley and Virginia Grey. The Oscar for sound went to Stephen Dunn for *The Bells of St. Mary's.* Miklos Rozsa won for the score of *Spellbound.*

Bloomberg: 274, 693, 991, 1350, 1642, 1756. Scott: 922.

681 • FLAME OF NEW ORLEANS, THE

UNIVERSAL. 1941.

NOMINATION *Black-and-White Interior Decoration:* Martin Obzina and Jack Otterson, art direction; Russell A. Gausman, set decoration.

Gold digger Marlene Dietrich [1358] sets out to win rich, elderly Roland Young [2117] but falls for sailor Bruce Cabot instead. Dietrich is the main reason to watch this occasionally droll but mostly rather clumsy romance. She works hard, doing a turn at farce, in which she has to alternate between pretending to be a countess and pretending to be the countess' slovenly cousin. But there's no clue to what attracts her to Cabot, an actor she described later as "awfully stupid." Otherwise, the movie is full of good people: Young, Mischa Auer [1401], Andy Devine, Franklin Pangborn, and Laura Hope Crews. This was the first of four films director René Clair made in America during World War II. None of them is up to his classic *À Nous la Liberté.* The art direction Oscar went to *How Green Was My Valley.*

Obzina: 668. Otterson: 96, 269, 668, 1229, 1240, 1895, 2342. Gausman: 96, 414, 1560, 1572, 1886, 1895.

682 • FLASHDANCE

POLYGRAM PICTURES PRODUCTION; PARAMOUNT. 1983.

AWARD *Song:* "Flashdance . . . What a Feeling," music by Giorgio Moroder, lyrics by Keith Forsey and Irene Cara.

NOMINATIONS *Cinematography:* Don Peterman. *Song:* "Maniac," music and lyrics by Michael Sembello and Dennis Matkosky. *Film Editing:* Bud Smith and Walt Mulconery.

Jennifer Beals works as a welder in a Pittsburgh steel mill during the day and as a dancer (actually, her dancing is done by Marine Jahan) in a hard-hat bar by night. But she's got dreams: of being a ballet dancer and marrying the boss, Michael Nouri. And guess what—her dreams come true! Idiotic concoction of bits of *Rocky* and *Saturday Night Fever* brewed up with beer commercials and romance-novel clichés and teen sex fantasies. Today this hugely popular flick is largely forgotten, along with its stars, though its style lives on in Paula Abdul videos. Directed by Adrian Lyne [653] from a screenplay by Tom Hedley and the egregious Joe Eszterhas (author of *Basic Instinct).* The cast also includes Lilia Skala [1174].

With his second nomination and second Oscar, electronic composer Moroder was on his way to a three-for-three sweep as composer-songwriter. The pumping-pulsing style of composition that made him famous is today as dead as disco—though perhaps it's only as dead as Dracula.

If *Flashdance* is in any way distinguished, it's in its visuals and the rhythm of its editing, including the successful concealment of the fact that Jahan replaces Beals in the musical numbers. The Academy, however, preferred the work of Sven Nykvist as cinematographer for *Fanny & Alexander* and the team of five editors who cut *The Right Stuff.*

Moroder: 1313, 2114. Forsey: 189. Peterman: 1914. Smith: 631.

683 • FLAT TOP

MONOGRAM. 1952.

NOMINATION *Film Editing:* William Austin.

Sterling Hayden stars as the commander in charge of training naval aviators aboard aircraft carriers during World War II. Naturally he's a tough guy the men come to appreciate only after it's all over. Well-done programmer, with that perennial B-movie lead Richard Carlson, directed by Lesley Selander. The nomination for editing recognized Austin's skillful blending of documentary combat footage with the staged stuff, but the Oscar went to Elmo Williams and Harry Gerstad for *High Noon.*

684 • FLATLINERS

STONEBRIDGE ENTERTAINMENT PRODUCTION; COLUMBIA. 1990.

NOMINATION *Sound Effects Editing:* Charles L. Campbell and Richard Franklin.

Medical students Kiefer Sutherland, Julia Roberts [1603 . . .], Kevin Bacon, William Baldwin, and Oliver Platt experiment with inducing death and then reviving themselves to examine the near-death experience and theories of the afterlife. An impressive young cast and a good idea for a medical thriller, but it's all tarted up with Gothic effects and undermined by hack psychology. Directed by Joel Schumacher. The sound effects editing award went to *The Hunt for Red October.*

Campbell: 127, 588, 2274.

685 • FLIGHT COMMAND

MGM. 1941.

NOMINATION *Special Effects:* A. Arnold Gillespie, photographic; Douglas Shearer, sound.

Brash young pilot Robert Taylor learns self-discipline as he trains to be a naval aviator. Perennial plot —we'll see it again forty-five years later in *Top Gun*— that wastes the time of Ruth Hussey [1563], Walter Pidgeon [1232 . . .], Paul Kelly, and Red Skelton, not to mention the audience. Directed by Frank Borzage [132 . . .]. The special effects Oscar went to *I Wanted Wings.*

Gillespie: 175, 256, 704, 835, 1371, 1388, 1905, 2048, 2055, 2122, 2300. Shearer: 136, 202, 256, 817, 835, 1096, 1232, 1292, 1371, 1419, 1751, 1950, 1988, 2048, 2055, 2211, 2300.

686 • FLIGHT FOR FREEDOM

RKO RADIO. 1943.

NOMINATION *Black-and-White Interior Decoration:* Albert S. D'Agostino and Carroll Clark, art direction; Darrell Silvera and Harley Miller, set decoration.

Rosalind Russell [110 . . .] plays aviator Amelia Earhart. They shouldn't send a star up in a flimsy biopic like this. Fred MacMurray provides the overdone romantic interest. Directed by Lothar Mendes, with Herbert Marshall and Eduardo Ciannelli. The art direction Oscar went to *The Song of Bernadette.*

D'Agostino: 632, 1239, 1240, 1924. Clark: 4, 481, 754, 1284, 1924, 2115. Silvera: 407, 632, 1239, 1264, 1341, 1924.

687 • FLIGHT OF THE EAGLE, THE

BOLD PRODUCTIONS FOR THE SWEDISH FILM INSTITUTE, THE SWEDISH TELEVISION SVT 2, SVENSK FILMINDUSTRI, AND NORSK FILM A/S PRODUCTION (SWEDEN). 1982.

NOMINATION *Foreign Language Film.*

The story of an ill-fated attempt to reach the North Pole by balloon in 1897, with Max von Sydow [1546], directed by Jan Troell [610]. Not quite the epic it's intended to be. The Oscar went to Spain's *Volver a Empezar.*

688 • FLIGHT OF THE PHOENIX, THE

ASSOCIATES & ALDRICH COMPANY PRODUCTION; 20TH CENTURY-FOX. 1965.

NOMINATIONS *Supporting Actor:* Ian Bannen. *Film Editing:* Michael Luciano.

The survivors of a plane crash in the Arabian desert squabble among themselves. Pilot James Stewart [73 . . .] is filled with remorse because his error caused the crash, and an arrogant young German engineer (Hardy Kruger) thinks he can construct something flightworthy from the wreckage. Good adventure movie with no more clichés than are usual in the genre. Robert Aldrich directs, with Richard Attenborough [745], Peter Finch [1424 . . .], Ernest Borgnine [1283], George Kennedy [443], Dan Duryea, and others. Stunt pilot Paul Mantz was killed in a crash during the filming.

Scottish actor Bannen, who plays a cynical oil-field worker, has been a reliable presence in character roles (e.g., *Bite the Bullet, Hope and Glory*) since his screen debut in 1956. He lost to Martin Balsam in *A Thousand Clowns*. The editing Oscar went to William Reynolds for *The Sound of Music.*

Luciano: 548, 963, 1202.

689 • FLIRTATION WALK

FIRST NATIONAL. 1934.
NOMINATIONS *Picture:* Jack L. Warner and Hal Willis, with Robert Lord, producers. *Sound Recording:* Nathan Levinson.

West Point cadet Dick Powell falls for the general's daughter, Ruby Keeler, in this flimsy little musical. It needs Busby Berkeley [791 . . .] to put the cadets through their paces, but no such luck—Bobby Connolly [295 . . .] did the dance direction instead. Tyrone Power, who would get his own West Point movie, *The Long Gray Line,* twenty-one years later, is an extra. Directed by Frank Borzage [132 . . .]. The best picture Oscar went to *It Happened One Night* and the sound award to *One Night of Love.*

Warner: 55, 110, 550, 1393, 2318. Wallis: 17, 55, 85, 164, 343, 365, 676, 712, 965, 1046, 1095, 1162, 1248, 1482, 1727, 1779, 2233, 2318. Lord: 220, 1493. Levinson: 16, 30, 343, 385, 531, 710, 712, 790, 930, 965, 1052, 1169, 1621, 1690, 1768, 1769, 1779, 1930, 1949, 2058, 2318.

690 • FLOWER DRUM SONG

UNIVERSAL-INTERNATIONAL-ROSS HUNTER PRODUCTION IN ASSOCIATION WITH JOSEPH FIELDS; UNIVERSAL-INTERNATIONAL. 1961.
NOMINATIONS *Color Cinematography:* Russell Metty. *Color Art Direction—Set Decoration:* Alexander Golitzen and Joseph Wright; Howard Bristol. *Sound:* Waldon O. Watson, sound director, Revue Studio Sound Department. *Scoring of a Musical Picture:* Alfred Newman and Ken Darby. *Color Costume Design:* Irene Sharaff.

Miyoshi Umeki [1763] arrives in San Francisco's Chinatown to be the "picture bride" of nightclub owner Jack Soo, who's really in love with singer Nancy Kwan. But this leaves the way clear for student James Shigeta to marry Umeki. The stage musical by Richard Rodgers [1921] and Oscar Hammerstein [375 . . .] was one of their least successful, and it didn't fare any better on the screen. At least it's pretty and has some nice tunes ("Love, Look Away," "You Are Beautiful," "I Enjoy Being a Girl"). Hollywood had got out of the habit (as in *Dragon Seed* or *The Good Earth*) of casting Westerners as Asians, but it still treats Chinese-Americans as cute, childlike beings in a touristy ghetto, and some Chinese-Americans were offended by the casting of Japanese performers such as Umeki and Shigeta. The voice of dancer Reiko Sato in the "Love, Look Away" ballet is supplied by Marilyn Horne. Directed by Henry Koster [214].

As far as the Oscars were concerned, *Flower Drum Song* didn't have a chance. This was the year of *West Side Story,* which took the awards for Daniel L. Fapp's cinematography, for art direction, sound, scoring, and costumes—though at least in the last category Sharaff got to take home an Oscar anyway.

Metty: 1886. Golitzen: 31, 96, 414, 591, 706, 744, 1560, 1886, 1968, 1986, 2035, 2064, 2101. Wright: 235, 428, 508, 569, 746, 852, 1175, 1264, 1397, 1475, 2056. Bristol: 852, 864, 1182, 1451, 1607, 1613, 1907, 2064. Watson: 350, 655, 744, 1810, 2035. Newman: 31, 34, 46, 72, 138, 182, 226, 333, 334, 347, 375, 428, 437, 457, 476, 495, 542, 797, 833, 952, 953, 959, 962, 1016, 1082, 1088, 1213, 1278, 1362, 1397, 1475, 1616, 1655, 1849, 1868, 1883, 1921, 2043, 2046, 2091, 2258, 2286, 2294, 2316. Darby: 334, 953, 1088, 1592, 1883. Sharaff: 66, 290, 333, 338, 413, 852, 896, 1088, 1507, 1592, 1910, 2000, 2244, 2277.

691 • FLY, THE

BROOKSFILMS LTD. PRODUCTION; 20TH CENTURY FOX. 1986.
AWARD *Makeup:* Chris Walas and Stephan Dupuis.

Jeff Goldblum, a scientist experimenting with teleportation (like the *Star Trek* "beam me up" technology), manages to get his DNA scrambled with that of a fly, and the results, thanks to the makeup artistry of Walas and Dupuis, are grisly indeed. This begins as a witty, intelligent shocker but finally goes too far over the top. Directed and cowritten (with Charles Edward Pogue) by David Cronenberg. Geena Davis [6 . . .] costars. The premise is the same as that of the 1958 horror film of the same name.

After apprenticing as a special effects artist, Walas first achieved acclaim for the makeup effects he designed for *Raiders of the Lost Ark* and Cronenberg's 1981 film *Scanners*. He formed his own design company in the eighties, creating among other things the title creatures for *Gremlins* (1984). He also directed the 1989 sequel, *The Fly II*, a notorious flop.

692 • FLYING DOWN TO RIO

RKO RADIO. 1934.

NOMINATION *Song:* "Carioca," music by Vincent Youmans, lyrics by Edward Eliscu and Gus Kahn.

Gene Raymond pursues Dolores Del Rio to Rio de Janeiro, where he discovers that she's engaged to his best friend, Raul Roulien. In the midst of this mix-up, a couple of secondary characters get up and dance together, and film history is made: This wisp of a musical, directed by Thornton Freeland, is remembered mainly because it was the first to team Ginger Rogers [1102] and Fred Astaire [2126], who receive fourth and fifth billing in the credits. Their first dance together is in the nominated song, whose success inspired similar numbers in other Astaire-Rogers films: "The Continental" in *The Gay Divorcée* and "The Piccolino" in *Top Hat.* Their first top-billed teaming, in *The Gay Divorcée,* came so soon after *Flying Down to Rio* that Con Conrad and Herb Magidson's "The Continental" competed against "Carioca" for best song, and won. "Carioca" came in third.

Composer Youmans came to California to write the score for this film after a highly successful Broadway career that included *No, No, Nanette* and *Hit the Deck* and such standards as "Tea for Two" and "More Than You Know." Unfortunately this was his last score. He developed tuberculosis and was forced to retire.

Kahn: 1488, 1896.

693 • FLYING TIGERS

REPUBLIC. 1942.

NOMINATIONS *Sound Recording:* Daniel Bloomberg. *Scoring of a Dramatic or Comedy Picture:* Victor Young. *Special Effects:* Howard Lydecker, photographic; Daniel J. Bloomberg, sound.

John Wayne [33 . . .] takes on the Japanese as a fighter pilot with the Flying Tigers, stationed in China during World War II. Pretty much indistinguishable from every other movie in which Wayne fought the Japanese, but it's a good representative of the species. Directed by David Miller, with John Carroll, Anna Lee, Paul Kelly, Mae Clarke, and future head Mouseketeer James "Jimmie" Dodd. The sound award went to *Yankee Doodle Dandy,* the one for scoring to Max Steiner for *Now, Voyager,* and the one for special effects to *Reap the Wild Wind.*

Bloomberg: 274, 680, 991, 1350, 1642, 1756. Young: 97, 98, 100, 101, 280, 489, 612, 701, 794, 846, 925, 1214, 1257, 1396, 1452, 1748, 1823, 1994, 2235, 2315. Lydecker: 2308.

694 • FLYING WITH MUSIC

HAL ROACH; UNITED ARTISTS. 1942.

NOMINATIONS *Song:* "Pennies for Peppino," music by Edward Ward, lyrics by Chet Forrest and Bob Wright. *Scoring of a Musical Picture:* Edward Ward.

A man on the lam pretends to be a tour guide in Florida. This obscure B musical with obscure stars, George Givot and Marjorie Woodworth, owes its nominations to Hal Roach, the producer, who took advantage of the temporary liberalization of Academy rules in the years from 1937 through 1945, which allowed studios and independent production companies to supply nominees in certain categories. None of the dark horses from Roach or Monogram or Republic ever won anything, however. Irving Berlin's "White Christmas," from *Holiday Inn,* won the song Oscar. The scoring award went to Ray Heindorf and Heinz Roemheld for *Yankee Doodle Dandy.*

Ward: 47, 388, 1270, 1560, 2002. Forrest: 1270, 1384. Wright: 1270, 1384.

695 • FOLIES BERGÈRE

20TH CENTURY; UNITED ARTISTS. 1935.

AWARD *Dance Direction:* David Gould.

Maurice Chevalier [203 . . .], as a womanizing baron, hires Maurice Chevalier, as an entertainer at the Folies-Bergère, to imitate him and escort the baroness, Merle Oberon [487]. Easy enough, until Oberon gets wise and starts flirting with the fake baron to make the real one uneasy. Nifty musical farce, directed by Roy Del Ruth, with Ann Sothern [2246] and Eric Blore.

Gould is the first winner of the short-lived dance direction Oscar, receiving his award for his work on two films, *Broadway Melody of 1936* and this one. The citation was specifically for the "Straw Hat" number, the film's finale, involving humongous hats.

Gould: 261, 297, 500.

696 • FOLLOW THE BOYS

CHARLES K. FELDMAN PRODUCTIONS; UNIVERSAL. 1944.

NOMINATION *Song:* "I'll Walk Alone," music by Jule Styne, lyrics by Sammy Cahn.

There's a bit of a plot here, involving a marital spat between George Raft and Vera Zorina, but it's only an excuse for an all-star revue, featuring turns by Jeanette MacDonald, Dinah Shore, the Andrews Sisters, Arthur Rubinstein, and Sophie Tucker, among others. The best bits are W. C. Fields' pool-playing routine and the magic act of Orson Welles [407 . . .] that ends with him sawing Marlene Dietrich [1358] in half. (Welles was an accomplished magician, but the studio decided to resort to special effects for this finale, so that Dietrich's famous legs could walk off stage without the rest of her.) Such revues were a staple of wartime Hollywood; almost every studio mounted one with its contract talent, to try to show how they were doing their part to entertain the boys. Thus Warners did *Hollywood Canteen,* Paramount *Star Spangled Rhythm,* and MGM *Thousands Cheer.*

"I'll Walk Alone," sung by Dinah Shore, was a hit because it evoked the sentiments of couples separated by the war, but the winner was James Van Heusen and Johnny Burke's bouncy, optimistic "Swinging on a Star," from *Going My Way.*

Styne: 74, 737, 920, 921, 1031, 1719, 2072, 2110, 2343. Cahn: 74, 163, 182, 915, 926, 1031, 1056, 1216, 1524, 1587, 1692, 1708, 1719, 1859, 1907, 2016, 2064, 2072, 2103, 2110, 2125, 2263, 2264, 2315, 2343.

697 • FOOTLOOSE

DANIEL MELNICK PRODUCTION; PARAMOUNT. 1984.

NOMINATIONS *Song:* "Footloose," music and lyrics by Kenny Loggins and Dean Pitchford. *Song:* "Let's Hear It for the Boy," music and lyrics by Dean Pitchford and Tom Snow.

Kevin Bacon moves from the city to a small town where a local preacher, played by John Lithgow [2020 . . .], has succeeded in getting dancing and rock and roll banned. Utterly foolish movie that misuses the considerable talents not only of Lithgow and Bacon but also of Dianne Wiest [311.5 . . .] and Sarah Jessica Parker. This premise was trite when they made *Don't Knock the Rock* back in 1956. Songwriter Pitchford is responsible for the screenplay, and Herbert Ross [2152] directed. Stevie Wonder's "I Just Called to Say I Love You," from *The Woman in Red,* won the Oscar.

Pitchford: 381, 641. Snow: 381.

698 • FOR LOVE OF IVY

AMERICAN BROADCASTING COMPANIES-PALOMAR PICTURES INTERNATIONAL PRODUCTION; CINERAMA. 1968.

NOMINATION *Song:* "For Love of Ivy," music by Quincy Jones, lyrics by Bob Russell.

Sidney Poitier [522 . . .] is hired by a wealthy white family to pay court to their maid, Abby Lincoln, when she threatens to quit. Mediocre stuff, though it was Hollywood's first mainstream romantic comedy with black stars. Poitier supplied the story, which was turned into a screenplay by Robert Alan Aurthur [49]. The cast, directed by Daniel Mann, includes Beau Bridges and Carroll O'Connor. The song Oscar went to "The Windmills of Your Mind," written by Michel Legrand and Alan and Marilyn Bergman for *The Thomas Crown Affair.*

Jones: 144, 423, 2299. Russell: 144.

699 • *FOR ME AND MY GAL*

MGM. 1942.
NOMINATION *Scoring of a Musical Picture:* Roger Edens and Georgie Stoll.

Ambitious vaudevillian Gene Kelly [74] teams up with innocent young singer Judy Garland [1065 . . .]. When America enters World War I, Kelly deliberately breaks his fingers to dodge the draft. He and Garland go their separate ways, but Kelly proves his worth at the end. This was Kelly's film debut, in a role that echoes the one that made him a Broadway star, the amoral protagonist of *Pal Joey.* He's third-billed after George Murphy, but Kelly's chemistry with Garland makes this one a classic despite a hokey plot and rather drab production. Directed by Busby Berkeley [791 . . .], though with none of the mad inventiveness that was his signature.

After Kelly and Garland, the film's chief attraction is its score of period songs, including the title tune, plus "Oh You Beautiful Doll," "When You Wore a Tulip," "After You've Gone," "Ballin' the Jack," and many more. Edens and Stoll lost, however, to the arrangers of another period musical, Ray Heindorf and Heinz Roemheld, for *Yankee Doodle Dandy.*

Edens: 87, 115, 594, 801, 1476, 1950. Stoll: 74, 115, 207, 1216, 1298, 1299, 1950.

700 • *FOR THE BOYS*

20TH CENTURY FOX PRODUCTION; 20TH CENTURY FOX. 1991.
NOMINATION *Actress:* Bette Midler.

During World War II ambitious USO singer Midler teams up with headliner comedian James Caan [784]. Their partnership endures for several decades, as they entertain the troops through several wars and become big TV stars, but eventually they split, only to be reunited at a gala tribute half a century later. "For the birds," sneered the critics, and audiences agreed, sending this big, expensive project into red ink. On top of that, the producers were sued by Martha Raye, who claimed it was a rip-off of her own

story. (Bob Hope at least had the grace not to sue.) It has a sappy script, draggy direction by Mark Rydell [1473], zero chemistry between Midler and Caan, and god-awful old-age makeup for their reunion scenes. On the plus side are some lively musical numbers, and Midler's energy, which keeps things going even when you begin to wish they'd stop (the film runs almost two and a half hours). Midler had little chance at the Oscar, which was largely a three-way contest among winner Jodie Foster, for *The Silence of the Lambs,* and the two stars of *Thelma & Louise,* Susan Sarandon and Geena Davis. Laura Dern was the other nominee, for *Rambling Rose.*

Midler: 1726.

701 • *FOR WHOM THE BELL TOLLS*

PARAMOUNT. 1943.
AWARD *Supporting Actress:* Katina Paxinou.
NOMINATIONS *Picture:* Sam Wood, producer. *Actor:* Gary Cooper. *Actress:* Ingrid Bergman. *Supporting Actor:* Akim Tamiroff. *Color Cinematography:* Ray Rennahan. *Color Interior Decoration:* Hans Dreier and Haldane Douglas, art direction; Bertram Granger, set decoration. *Scoring of a Dramatic or Comedy Picture:* Victor Young. *Film Editing:* Sherman Todd and John Link.

American Robert Jordan (Cooper) joins guerrillas fighting in the Spanish Civil War and falls in love with Maria (Bergman), an emotionally traumatized woman who has been raped by the fascists. A handsome film, but Ernest Hemingway's book was too much for the censors, who weakened the story and sapped the flavor of the novel. Producer Wood also directed. The best picture Oscar went to *Casablanca.*

Paxinou was performing on stage in London when World War II began, and came to the United States because she was unable to return to her native Greece. Her performance as Pilar in *For Whom the Bell Tolls* was her screen debut, but she made only a few films afterward. She died in 1973.

Cooper was a natural choice for the role of Robert Jordan, since Hemingway's heroes are usually strong, silent types. He brings his usual taciturn authority to the part, but lost the Oscar to Paul Lukas in *Watch on the Rhine*.

The role of Maria was much sought after. Bergman had the support of Hemingway's wife, Martha Gellhorn, who suggested Bergman to the author as the ideal Maria after they met. But when Paramount started casting the film, Bergman had not yet established herself as a major star, and the studio considered Paulette Goddard [1855] and Betty Field for the part before signing Vera Zorina to play Maria. A disappointed Bergman agreed to do *Casablanca* instead, but during the last days of shooting on that film, Zorina was fired and Bergman took over the role. Ironically her performance in *Casablanca,* which at one point she feared would deprive her of the role of Maria, is the one that most people remember. She lost the Oscar to Jennifer Jones in *The Song of Bernadette*.

Tamiroff lost the supporting Oscar to Charles Coburn for *The More the Merrier*. The awards for cinematography (Hal Mohr and W. Howard Greene) and art direction went to *The Phantom of the Opera*. Alfred Newman won the scoring award for *The Song of Bernadette*. The editing Oscar went to George Amy for *Air Force*.

Wood: 804, 1095, 1102. Cooper: 912, 1366, 1607, 1779. Bergman: 72, 111, 173, 749, 1048, 1378. Tamiroff: 757. Rennahan: 235, 241, 569, 581, 798, 1120, 1210. Dreier: 97, 151, 649, 674, 726, 925, 979, 1101, 1120, 1194, 1214, 1217, 1358, 1443, 1452, 1540, 1668, 1748, 1880, 1975, 1994, 2190. Granger: 674. Young: 97, 98, 100, 101, 280, 489, 612, 693, 794, 846, 925, 1214, 1257, 1396, 1452, 1748, 1823, 1994, 2235, 2315. Todd: 1200. Link: 544.

702 • *FOR YOUR EYES ONLY*

EON PRODUCTIONS LTD.; UNITED ARTISTS (UNITED KINGDOM). 1981.

NOMINATION *Original Song:* "For Your Eyes Only," music by Bill Conti, lyrics by Mick Leeson.

Roger Moore is Bond, James Bond, for the fifth time, and it's one of the better efforts in the Moore series, substituting lots of chases and stunt work for the glitzy special effects and gadgets that had taken over in the preceding Bond movies. This is the one that takes place at a ski resort in the Alps and underwater off the coast of Greece, and has Carol Bouquet, Topol [659], Lynn-Holly Johnson, Julian Glover, Jill Bennett, and Cassandra Harris in the cast, directed by John Glen. The best song was "Arthur's Theme (Best That You Can Do)," from *Arthur*.

Conti: 1698, 1712.

703 • *FORBIDDEN GAMES*

SILVER FILMS; TIMES FILM CORPORATION (FRANCE). 1954.

AWARD *Honorary Award:* Best Foreign Language Film (1952).

NOMINATION *Motion Picture Story:* François Boyer.

Little Brigitte Fossey, orphaned when Nazi planes strafe the refugee group with which she is traveling, is taken in by a peasant family. When she and a young boy bury her dead puppy, it's the start of a game— they steal crosses to serve as the headstones for other buried animals. Exceptionally moving antiwar film by René Clément, one of the most celebrated works of the postwar European film renaissance. Though it received the Academy's honorary foreign film Oscar, the Venice Film Festival award, and the New York Film Critics Award for 1952, two more years passed before it received extensive distribution and became eligible for other Academy Awards. Jean Aurenche and Pierre Bost worked with Boyer to adapt his novel *Jeux Interdits* to the screen. The Oscar went to Philip Yordan for *Broken Lance*.

704 • *FORBIDDEN PLANET*

MGM. 1956.

NOMINATION *Special Effects:* A. Arnold Gillespie, Irving Ries, and Wesley C. Miller.

Space explorer Leslie Nielsen and his crew land on Altair-4, a planet inhabited only by reclusive scientist Walter Pidgeon [1232 . . .], his daughter, Anne Francis, and Robby the Robot. Well, there is someone, or something, else . . . a monster that's the Freudian id brought to dangerous life. Handsomely produced sci-fi near classic, based on Shakespeare's *The Tempest*. It needs better dialogue and better acting

—Nielsen never made it as a movie star until he learned to parody the kind of performance he gives here. Directed by Fred McLeod Wilcox. Every subsequent sci-fi movie and TV show is indebted to *Forbidden Planet,* especially the *Star Trek* series. The special effects, though extraordinary, lost to John Fulton's legendary work on *The Ten Commandments.*

Gillespie: 175, 256, 685, 835, 1371, 1388, 1905, 2048, 2055, 2122, 2300. Miller: 290, 1157, 1216.

705 • FOREIGN AFFAIR, A

PARAMOUNT. 1948.

NOMINATIONS *Screenplay:* Charles Brackett, Billy Wilder, and Richard L. Breen. *Black-and-White Cinematography:* Charles B. Lang, Jr.

Congresswoman Jean Arthur [1353], in Berlin on a postwar fact-finding tour, falls for officer John Lund, whose mistress, cabaret singer Marlene Dietrich [1358], is a former Nazi. Only writer-director Wilder might have tried to elicit comedy from black-marketing amid the rubble, but within certain limits it works. The limits are imposed in large part by Lund, an unimpressive actor under the best circumstances but particularly out of his depth in comedy. Arthur always needed a charmer like Cary Grant [1445 . . .] or James Stewart [73 . . .] to soften her edges. The honors here go to Dietrich, who was reluctant to take the role. She had spent the war in grueling tours entertaining the U.S. troops, which earned her the Medal of Freedom, the highest civilian honor. She incurred the wrath of her fellow Germans in the process, and playing a former Nazi didn't help toward reconciliation. When she finally returned to Germany as an entertainer in 1960, she was met with protests in the press and the streets—but also with considerable acclaim.

The writing Oscar went to John Huston for *The Treasure of the Sierra Madre.* Lang, who blended footage shot in Berlin with that taken on studio sets, lost to another blend of documentary and soundstage photography, William Daniels' work on *The Naked City.*

Brackett: 925, 1088, 1208, 1440, 1975, 2093, 2099. Wilder: 91, 138, 198, 566, 709, 925, 1208, 1440, 1738, 1860, 1903, 1975, 2297. Breen: 350, 2093. Lang: 97, 250, 319, 636, 649, 765, 953, 1480, 1640, 1699, 1738, 1778, 1855, 1860, 1955, 1968, 2180.

706 • FOREIGN CORRESPONDENT

WALTER WANGER; UNITED ARTISTS. 1940.

NOMINATIONS *Picture:* Walter Wanger, producer. *Supporting Actor:* Albert Basserman. *Original Screenplay:* Charles Bennett and Joan Harrison. *Black-and-White Cinematography:* Rudolph Maté. *Black-and-White Interior Decoration:* Alexander Golitzen. *Special Effects:* Paul Eagler, photographic; Thomas T. Moulton, sound.

Reporter Joel McCrea is sent to Europe just before the war; he falls in love with Laraine Day and exposes a bunch of spies. If that description is perfunctory, it's because this wonderful, first-rate Alfred Hitchcock [1171 . . .] film is so full of twists and turns that summarizing it is pointless—and if you've never seen it, you'll want to discover them for yourself. Hitchcock was disappointed when Gary Cooper [701 . . .] turned down the lead, but McCrea is fine, as is Day—anyway, their roles largely call for them to be islands of normality in the midst of more eccentric figures played by Herbert Marshall, George Sanders [46], Robert Benchley, Edmund Gwenn [1325 . . .], and Harry Davenport. (It's a measure of the wit of this film that Sanders is cast as a good guy and Gwenn as a bad guy.) The movie has what seems today a peculiarly detached tone about the impending war, largely because America's official neutrality had Hollywood walking on eggs; it's never really made explicit, for example, that the bad guys are working for the Nazis. But the end of the movie couldn't be clearer as an appeal to America to end its neutrality. Hitchcock's other film made during his first year in Hollywood, *Rebecca,* won the Oscar.

Basserman, who plays an elderly diplomat whose kidnaping sets much of the plot in motion, had fled the Nazis in 1933 after a distinguished stage and screen career in Germany. He came to Hollywood in 1939, and despite limited English found a variety of character roles, which he learned phonetically until he mastered the language. He lost to Walter Brennan in *The Westerner.*

The screenplay is nominally based on Vincent Sheean's *Personal History,* to which Wanger had bought the rights, but it bears no resemblance to the supposed source. Bennett, who had worked with Hitchcock in England on the screenplays for several films, had come to the States before the director. He claimed later that Harrison, Hitchcock's personal assistant, contributed nothing to the script but was given a credit as a personal favor. Robert Benchley provided much of his own dialogue. The Oscar went to Preston Sturges for *The Great McGinty.*

The cinematography Oscar went to George Barnes for *Rebecca. Pride and Prejudice* won for art direction and *The Thief of Bagdad* for special effects.

Wanger: 413, 1048, 1901. Harrison: 1670. Maté: 455, 1607, 1740, 2031. Golitzen: 31, 96, 414, 591, 690, 744, 1560, 1886, 1968, 1986, 2035, 2064, 2101. Eagler: 1595. Moulton: 22, 46, 138, 366, 457, 487, 560, 798, 962, 1153, 1200, 1451, 1510, 1607, 1849, 2154, 2294.

707 • FOREVER AMBER

20TH CENTURY-FOX. 1947.

NOMINATION *Scoring of a Dramatic or Comedy Picture:* David Raksin.

Linda Darnell is Amber, a young woman who sleeps her way to the top in the court of England's King Charles II, played by George Sanders [46]. This adaptation by Philip Dunne [495 . . .] and Ring Lardner, Jr. [1286 . . .], of a once-shocking bodice ripper by Kathleen Winsor is pretty silly, partly because of censorship, but mostly because it was silly to start with. Directed by Otto Preminger [73 . . .], who made his career—from here to *Anatomy of a Murder* by way of *The Moon Is Blue* and *The Man With the Golden Arm*—by filming the supposedly unfilmable and dueling the censors along the way. In most cases, it was worth the fight, but here it's doubtful. Still, it's fun to watch a cast that includes Cornel Wilde [1872], Richard Haydn, Jessica Tandy [580 . . .], Anne Revere [759 . . .], Leo G. Carroll, and Margaret Wycherly [1779] cavorting in periwigs and Res-

toration finery. Raksin's score lost to Miklos Rozsa's for *A Double Life.*

Raksin: 1778.

708 • FORMULA, THE

METRO-GOLDWYN-MAYER PRODUCTION; MGM. 1980.

NOMINATION *Cinematography:* James Crabe.

Detective George C. Scott [73 . . .], investigating the murder of a friend, discovers an international plot by the oil companies, led by Marlon Brando [583 . . .], to suppress a synthetic fuel formula. The chief interest of this not-very-thrilling thriller by writer Steve Shagan [1761 . . .] is watching the only screen teaming of two Oscar apostates, Brando and Scott, but their very dissimilar styles never quite mesh. The cast, under the less-than-sure direction of John G. Avildsen [1712], also includes John Gielgud [103 . . .] and Beatrice Straight [1424].

Crabe, who collaborated with Avildsen on *Save the Tiger, Rocky,* and other films, lost to Geoffrey Unsworth and Ghislain Cloquet for *Tess.*

708.5 • FORREST GUMP

STEVE TISCH/WENDY FINERMAN PRODUCTION; PARAMOUNT. 1994.

AWARDS *Picture:* Wendy Finerman, Steve Tisch, and Steve Starkey, producers. *Actor:* Tom Hanks. *Director:* Robert Zemeckis. *Screenplay Based on Material Previously Produced or Published:* Eric Roth. *Film Editing:* Arthur Schmidt. *Visual Effects:* Ken Ralston, George Murphy, Stephen Rosenbaum, and Allen Hall.

NOMINATIONS *Supporting Actor:* Gary Sinise. *Cinematography:* Don Burgess. *Art Direction–Set Decoration:* Rick Carter; Nancy Haigh. *Sound:* Randy Thom, Tom Johnson, Dennis Sands, and William B. Kaplan. *Original Score:* Alan Silvestri. *Makeup:* Daniel C. Striepeke, Hallie D'Amore, and Judith A. Cory. *Sound Effects Editing:* Gloria S. Borders and Randy Thom.

Forrest Gump (Hanks), a mildly retarded man, gladly shares the story of his life with strangers he encounters while sitting on a park bench. Those who listen to his story learn that he has achieved wealth and fame by following the precepts of his mother, played by Sally Field [1448 . . .]. He has, for example, met with Presidents Kennedy, Johnson, and Nixon, become a war hero and a ping-pong champion, made a fortune in the shrimp business, and even taught Elvis Presley how to swivel his hips. This adaptation of Winston Groom's modern picaresque novel became one of the most commercially successful films of all time, grossing more than $300 million in its first year of domestic release. It was also a critical success, although by no means a unanimous one: A critic for the *New York Times* put it on her "ten worst" list. Many others were disturbed by what they saw as an endorsement of sociopolitical do-nothing-ism—Forrest drifts through life, succeeding through a Horatio Algerish pluck-and-luck—much in tune with the country's rejection of government activism in the '94 elections. The film even opened some old Vietnam war wounds by what some saw as its endorsement of Forrest's naive patriotism, contrasted with a rather nastily portrayed group of antiwar activists. But most audiences were less inclined to examine the film's subtext than to enjoy its cinematic storytelling, its astonishing special effects—computerized imaging techniques that put Hanks in the company of dead presidents and convincingly turn Sinise, who plays Forrest's lieutenant in Vietnam, into a double amputee—and the wizardry of Hanks' performance. The cast also includes Robin Wright as Forrest's lifelong love, and Mykelti Williamson as Forrest's Vietnam buddy Bubba.

The producers were somewhat bemused by the harshness of the criticism leveled at the film: "I went to school at Berkeley and was involved in antiwar demonstrations in the sixties," Starkey has said. "I think many of the events depicted in this movie are strong memories for people of my generation." Finerman is largely responsible for discovering Groom's novel and persisting over several years in attempts to bring it to the screen, finally persuading Paramount to back it on the strength of the participation of Hanks and Zemeckis. No one, however, was prepared for the size of the Gump phenomenon, which extended itself into merchandising realms where so-called serious films never succeed, including a line of "Bubba Gump" seafood. There was some

fear that the success of the film might undermine it with Oscar voters, who reacted negatively to the *E.T.* phenomenon twelve years earlier. But among the nominees for best picture, only the critics' favorite, *Pulp Fiction,* was considered a serious challenger for the top award, and it was too dark and quirky for an honor that usually goes to films of serious moral purpose. *The Shawshank Redemption* and *Quiz Show* were handicapped by their poor box-office reception, and *Four Weddings and a Funeral* received only one nomination other than its best picture nod, a clear sign that it was not a strong contender.

The only handicap Hanks had in his run for the best actor Oscar was his previous year's win for *Philadelphia.* There was some sympathy for John Travolta, making a comeback after a long career downslide, in *Pulp Fiction,* and Morgan Freeman, who had made a strong run for the award in *Driving Miss Daisy* five years earlier, was thought to be due recognition not only for his quietly charismatic performance in *The Shawshank Redemption* but also for the body of his work. Paul Newman's performance in *Nobody's Fool* had also been praised as one of the best in his distinguished career. Only Nigel Hawthorne, a surprise nominee for *The Madness of King George,* was thought to be completely out of the running. But Hanks' portrayal of the gauche but genial Gump was so astonishingly different from his previous year's work as the lawyer dying of AIDS, and so carefully but convincingly nuanced, that it proved unbeatable. It made him only the second person to win consecutive best actor Oscars—the first was Spencer Tracy for 1937 and 1938—and the fifth performer to win back-to-back acting awards. The others are Luise Rainer (1936, 1937), Katharine Hepburn (1967, 1968), and Jason Robards (1976, 1977).

Zemeckis began his movie career as a screenwriter in collaboration with Bob Gale [127] on a likable low-budget feature about Beatlemania, *I Wanna Hold Your Hand* (1978), which he also directed. Although he continued his writing collaboration with Gale on such films as *1941, Used Cars* (1980), and *Back to the Future,* Zemeckis became better known as a director when *Romancing the Stone* was a smash success. With *Back to* the Future and its two sequels, as well as Who Framed Roger Rabbit and Death Becomes Her, he developed a specialty as director of special-effects-heavy comedies. Forrest Gump, with its elaborate but subtle use of computer-generated effects, is of a piece with Zemeckis' earlier work, but there is a depth of feeling not found in his previous films.

Sinise, one of the co-founders of the Chicago-based Steppenwolf Theatre Company, had begun his mainstream film career as a director with the 1988 film Miles From Home, a drama about the collapse of a family farm starring Richard Gere. It was poorly received, but Sinise's 1992 remake of Of Mice and Men, in which he also played the role of George, was critically praised. Forrest Gump was his first mainstream hit. The Oscar went to Martin Landau for Ed Wood, which also took the makeup award.

Among the other nominees, several are longtime collaborators with Zemeckis. Burgess was a second-unit photographer on the second and third Back to the Future films and Silvestri scored Romancing the Stone, the Back to the Future series, Who Framed Roger Rabbit, and Death Becomes Her. He also composed music for such movies as Predator and The Abyss. The cinematography Oscar went to John Toll for Legends of the Fall and the scoring award to Hans Zimmer for The Lion King. Speed won the sound and sound effects editing Oscars, and The Madness of King George won for art direction.

Hanks: 195, 1562.5. Zemeckis: 127. Schmidt: 418, 1763, 1975, 2274. Ralston: 128, 419, 513.5, 577, 1684, 2274. Hall: 129. Haigh: 152, 308. Thom: 129, 1425, 1684, 1698. Johnson: 2019. Kaplan: 127, 2114. Cory: 1764.65. Borders: 2019.

709 • FORTUNE COOKIE, THE

PHALANX-JALEM-MIRISCH CORPORATION OF DELAWARE PRODUCTION; UNITED ARTISTS. 1966.
Award Supporting Actor: Walter Matthau.
Nominations Story and Screenplay—Written Directly for the Screen: Billy Wilder and I. A. L. Diamond. Black-and-White Cinematography: Joseph LaShelle. Black-and-White Art Direction—Set Decoration: Robert Luthardt; Edward G. Boyle.

Matthau plays Whiplash Willie, an unscrupulous lawyer who persuades TV cameraman Jack Lemmon [91 . . .] to exaggerate the injuries Lemmon received when he was accidentally downed by a player while shooting a football game. The litigious society certainly seems fair game for Wilder's brand of cynical satire, but this thin comedy gets tiresome after the first hour. This was the first teaming of Matthau and Lemmon, who reestablished themselves as a duo in The Odd Couple two years later.

Since Matthau carries the picture, his placement in the supporting actor category is peculiar. But it reflects his status at the time of his first nomination. For the most part, Matthau had been seen in secondary character roles, usually in comedies but sometimes in serious parts. Oddly this most urban of actors, who seems perfectly cast as a weary New Yorker, made his film debut in two westerns, The Indian Fighter and The Kentuckian, in 1955. He benefited from a sympathy vote: He suffered a serious heart attack during the filming of The Fortune Cookie, and it's sometimes possible to spot the differences in the film between the leaner post-recovery Matthau and the out-of-shape pre-attack actor. The Oscar made him a star, though an unusual one, who played numerous leads in the next decade but found fewer good roles in the eighties.

The screenplay Oscar went to Claude Lelouch and Pierre Uytterhoeven for A Man and a Woman. Who's Afraid of Virginia Woolf? took the awards for Haskell Wexler's cinematography and for art direction.

Matthau: 1109, 1976. Wilder: 91, 138, 198, 566, 705, 925, 1208, 1440, 1738, 1860, 1903, 1975, 2297. Diamond: 91, 1860. LaShelle: 91, 357, 428, 953, 1017, 1149, 1283, 1391. Boyle: 91, 393, 743, 1783, 1860, 1866.

49TH PARALLEL
See 1008.

710 • 42ND STREET

WARNER BROS. 1932–33.
Nominations Picture: Darryl F. Zanuck, producer. Sound Recording: Nathan Levinson.

Director Warner Baxter [989] puts everything he's got into his big Broadway show, knowing that his heart condition may mean that it's his last. But then on opening night star Bebe Daniels breaks her ankle, and there's no one available but a green young understudy, Ruby Keeler, to play the part. She goes out a youngster and comes back a star. The fount of all movie musical clichés and still one of the best musicals ever, even though Keeler's clodhopper dancing and Dick Powell's sappy tenorizing are more forgivable than enjoyable. The delights are the songs by Al Dubin [791 . . .] and Harry Warren [21 . . .] ("Shuffle Off to Buffalo," "You're Getting to Be a Habit With Me," and others, including the title song), the performances of Baxter, Daniels, George Brent, Una Merkel [1959], Guy Kibbee, Ned Sparks, and Ginger Rogers [1102], and most of all, the first major work of Busby Berkeley [791 . . .], the inimitable director of surreal production numbers. Lloyd Bacon is the nominal director, but it's Berkeley's work one remembers. The film's huge success launched the careers of Berkeley, Keeler, Rogers, and Powell, and shaped the course of movie history. Today it's regarded as a classic, while the movie that won the best picture Oscar, *Cavalcade,* is largely forgotten.

Though Levinson had three out of the four nominations (the other two for *Gold Diggers of 1933* and *I Am a Fugitive From a Chain Gang),* he lost to Harold C. Lewis for *A Farewell to Arms.*

Zanuck: 34, 46, 550, 759, 815, 946, 952, 990, 1201, 1327, 1666, 2154, 2286. Levinson: 16, 30, 343, 385, 531, 689, 712, 790, 930, 965, 1052, 1169, 1621, 1690, 1768, 1769, 1779, 1930, 1949, 2058, 2318.

711 • *FOUL PLAY*

Miller-Miklis-Colin Higgins Picture Production; Paramount. 1978.

Nomination *Original Song:* "Ready to Take a Chance Again," music by Charles Fox, lyrics by Norman Gimbel.

Goldie Hawn [323 . . .] gets tangled up with some odd characters who are plotting to kill the pope during his visit to San Francisco, but everyone except detective Chevy Chase thinks she's nuts. Pleasant though unmemorable comedy thriller, directed by Colin Higgins. Hawn and Chase get good support from Dudley Moore [103], Burgess Meredith [504 . . .], Rachel Roberts [2061], and Brian Dennehy.

Fox and Gimbel, who also wrote the *Happy Days* TV show theme and Roberta Flack's hit "Killing Me Softly With His Song," had a modest success with Barry Manilow's recording of the nominated song. They lost to Paul Jabara's "Last Dance," from *Thank God It's Friday.*

Fox: 1508. Gimbel: 1448, 1508, 2172.

712 • *FOUR DAUGHTERS*

Warner Bros.-First National. 1938.

Nominations *Picture:* Hal B. Wallis, with Henry Blanke, producers. *Supporting Actor:* John Garfield. *Director:* Michael Curtiz. *Screenplay:* Lenore Coffee and Julius J. Epstein. *Sound Recording:* Nathan Levinson.

Claude Rains [365 . . .] is a musician, a widower who is raising four motherless daughters with the help of their elderly aunt, May Robson [1119]. The daughters are played by the Lane sisters, Priscilla, Rosemary, and Lola, plus Gale Page. All four fall in love with their father's pupil, Jeffrey Lynn, but Priscilla is the one he chooses. On the eve of the wedding, however, she realizes that Page is really in love with Lynn, so she gives him up and runs off with a boy from the wrong side of the tracks, Garfield. But Garfield is unable to support the two of them and commits suicide, so she goes back home, where things have sorted themselves out, romantically, and Lynn is still waiting for her. Well-made romantic drama, from a *Cosmopolitan* magazine story by Fannie Hurst. If soap gets in your eyes or you need to cut down on sweets, you may want to avoid this one, though you'll miss Garfield's powerfully watchable screen debut. Too bad he's matched with the annoyingly mannered Priscilla Lane. The best picture Oscar went to *You Can't Take It With You.*

Garfield grew up on the streets of New York, a background that he used to advantage in his debut role as the tough guy who doesn't quite fit in the sweetness-and-light world of the daughters. An acting student of Maria Ouspenskaya [560 . . .], he developed a naturalistic style and intense screen presence that anticipated that of Montgomery Clift [732 . . .] and Marlon Brando [583 . . .] by a decade or more. His performance in *Four Daughters* was so popular that Warners crafted a rehash called *Daughters Courageous* in 1939 to reunite him with the same cast (playing a different family) and provided him with a flashback scene in the sequel *Four Wives* (1939). The Oscar went to Walter Brennan for *Kentucky*.

Curtiz, who was also nominated for *Angels With Dirty Faces,* lost to Frank Capra for *You Can't Take It With You.* The screenplay award went to George Bernard Shaw and adapters Ian Dalrymple, Cecil Lewis, and W. P. Lipscomb for *Pygmalion. The Cowboy and the Lady* won for sound.

Wallis: 17, 55, 85, 164, 343, 365, 676, 689, 965, 1046, 1095, 1162, 1248, 1482, 1727, 1779, 2233, 2318. Blanke: 17, 90, 1046, 1169, 1315, 1457, 1936, 2136. Garfield: 251. Curtiz: 79, 365, 2318. Epstein: 365, 1555, 1687. Levinson: 16, 30, 343, 385, 531, 689, 710, 790, 930, 965, 1052, 1169, 1621, 1690, 1768, 1769, 1779, 1930, 1949, 2058, 2318.

713 • *FOUR DAYS OF NAPLES, THE*

Titanus-Metro; MGM (Italy). 1963.
NOMINATIONS *Story and Screenplay—Written Directly for the Screen:* Pasquale Festa Campanile, Massimo Franciosa, Nanni Loy, Vasco Pratolini, and Carlo Bernari. *Foreign Language Film* (1962).

A powerfully done re-creation of the Neapolitan resistance to the Nazis' attempt to round up all the male citizens in 1943. Directed by Loy. The screenplay award went to James R. Webb for *How the West Was Won.* The foreign language film Oscar was won by *Sundays and Cybèle.*

714 • *FOUR DEVILS*

Fox. 1928–29.
NOMINATION *Cinematography:* Ernest Palmer.

Four children grow up to be circus performers. As grown-ups, two of them, Janet Gaynor [1792 . . .] and Charles Morton, fall in love. The young Gaynor is played by Dawn O'Day, who later changed her cutesy screen name to Anne Shirley [1923]. This film by F. W. Murnau is only part talkie, and that part is primitively recorded. Murnau, the great German expressionist director, sought fluently moving camera effects and was unwilling to limit himself to the bolted-down cameras then necessary for sound. Palmer received no certification of his nomination from the Academy, which this year announced only the winners of the Oscars. But records of the various branches that made the selections in individual categories show that Palmer was under consideration for his work on this film and *Street Angel.* He lost to Clyde DeVinna for *White Shadows in the South Seas.*

Palmer: 235, 298, 1946.

715 • *FOUR FEATHERS, THE*

Alexander Korda; United Artists (United Kingdom). 1939.
NOMINATION *Color Cinematography:* Georges Périnal and Osmond Borradaile.

When he decides not to join his comrades and go to fight in the Sudan uprising, John Clements is presented with the feathers as a symbol of cowardice, so he disguises himself as a native and proves his valor by rescuing the blinded Ralph Richardson [839 . . .]. Handsome stiff-upper-lip stuff produced by Alexander Korda [1620], directed by his brother Zoltan, and designed by his brother Vincent [1070 . . .]. With C. Aubrey Smith and June Duprez. Filmed as a silent in Hollywood in 1921 and 1929, remade by Zoltan Korda as *Storm Over the Nile* in 1955 (using footage from the 1939 version), and remade again for TV in 1977. Obviously there's something about this material that's perennial—you can't keep good hokum down. Périnal and Borradaile were on the preliminary list of nominees for the cinematography Oscar but were removed from the final ballot when the Academy decided to reduce the list to two nominated films in each category—black and white and color. The official nominees became Sol Polito and W. Howard Greene for *The Private Lives of Elizabeth and Essex* and the winners, Ernest Haller and Ray Rennahan for *Gone With the Wind* (whose producer, ironists will note, was David O. Selznick, who produced the 1929 *Four Feathers*).

Périnal: 2050.

716 • 400 BLOWS, THE
Les Films du Carosse & SEDIF; Zenith International Film Corporation (France). 1959.
Nomination *Story and Screenplay—Written Directly for the Screen:* François Truffaut and Marcel Moussy.

A twelve-year-old boy, Antoine Doinel, played by Jean-Pierre Léaud, finds himself on his own, neglected by his sluttish mother and ineffectual father. So he plays hooky and turns petty thief, which lands him in reform school, from which he escapes. Writer-director Truffaut's first feature is one of the most celebrated in the history of French film, largely because of its freshness of outlook and technique, and because of the splendid performance by Léaud, who became the director's alter ego in a series of more or less autobiographical films about Antoine Doinel: the "Antoine et Colette" episode of *Love at Twenty* (1962), *Stolen Kisses* (1968), *Bed and Board* (1970), and *Love on the Run* (1979). The title, incidentally, is a slang phrase for getting into trouble, which Antoine certainly does.

The screenplay award went to the writing team that gave us *Pillow Talk*.

Truffaut: 501.

717 • FOUR MUSKETEERS, THE
Film Trust S.A. Production; 20th Century-Fox. 1975.
Nomination *Costume Design:* Yvonne Blake and Ron Talsky.

D'Artagnan (Michael York) becomes a full-fledged musketeer, joining forces with Porthos (Frank Finlay [1506]), Athos (Oliver Reed), and Aramis (Richard Chamberlain) to thwart the machinations of Rochefort (Christopher Lee), Lady De Winter (Faye Dunaway [255 . . .]), and Richelieu (Charlton Heston [175]). Sequel to *The Three Musketeers* (1974), which was filmed simultaneously but released separately, occasioning complaints and legal threats from cast and crew who claimed they weren't aware they were do-

ing two movies for the price of one. The first film was a brilliantly entertaining blend of traditional costume epic with contemporary slapstick, directed by Richard Lester. *Four* is a bit less entertaining than *Three*, partly because Alexandre Dumas' story turns darker—Constance, played as an endearing klutz by Raquel Welch, is killed off—and the plots and intrigues are a little stale. Still, it's a noisy, knockabout version of a classic, one of the best of its kind. The costuming honors went to Ulla-Britt Soderlund and Milena Canonero for *Barry Lyndon*.

Blake: 1429.

718 • FOUR POSTER, THE
Stanley Kramer Productions; Columbia. 1953.
Nomination *Black-and-White Cinematography:* Hal Mohr.

The bed of the title is the central setting for this drama about the forty-five-year married life of Rex Harrison [413 . . .] and Lilli Palmer, whose real-life marriage lasted considerably less long. Very much a performance piece, providing two fine actors with ample opportunity to wring tears and laughter from an audience, but it's really too theatrical for the movies. Jessica Tandy [580 . . .] and Hume Cronyn [1791] starred in the Jan de Hartog play on Broadway. The film was actually made in 1951 but held for release until the Broadway run was over. Instead of "opening up" the play, the film, directed by Irving Reis, uses animated cartoons from the UPA studio that created Mr. Magoo and Gerald McBoing-Boing as a bridge between episodes. The play was turned into the musical *I Do! I Do!* by Tom Jones and Harvey Schmidt. Burnett Guffey won the cinematography Oscar for *From Here to Eternity*.

Mohr: 1315, 1560.

718.5 • FOUR WEDDINGS AND A FUNERAL
Working Title Production; Gramercy Pictures (United Kingdom). 1994.
Nominations *Picture:* Duncan Kenworthy, producer. *Screenplay Written Directly for the Screen:* Richard Curtis.

At the first wedding, boy (Hugh Grant) meets girl (Andie MacDowell), and the same evening, boy gets girl. But at the second wedding, boy learns that he's losing girl, who's going to marry a rich, older Scotsman (Corin Redgrave). At the third wedding, of girl to Scotsman, boy also loses one of his closest friends. And the thoughts of mortality brought on by the friend's funeral lead to the fourth wedding, where all hell breaks loose. This rollicking romantic comedy, a big surprise hit on this side of the Atlantic, provided a starmaking role for Grant, who had acted in such films as *Maurice* (his debut) and *The Remains of the Day* without attracting much attention. The movie gets its energy from Curtis' script, Mike Newell's direction, and a wonderful gallery of supporting players, including Simon Callow and John Hannah as a gay couple. With only one other nomination, *Four Weddings* stood little chance at capturing the best picture Oscar, which went to *Forrest Gump*. The screenplay award went to Quentin Tarantino and Roger Avary for *Pulp Fiction*.

719 • FOURTEEN HOURS

20TH CENTURY-FOX. 1951.

NOMINATION *Black-and-White Art Direction—Set Decoration:* Lyle Wheeler and Leland Fuller; Thomas Little and Fred J. Rode.

Richard Basehart threatens to jump off a tall building, and various people try to talk him out of it. Good drama whose realistic style is undercut by too many clichés. Henry Hathaway [1194] directs a fascinating cast: Paul Douglas, Barbara Bel Geddes [972], Debra Paget, Agnes Moorehead [963 . . .], Howard da Silva, Jeffrey Hunter, Martin Gabel, and, in her screen debut, Grace Kelly [450 . . .]. Even the bit players are impressive: Ossie Davis, Harvey Lembeck, and Joyce Van Patten are among them. The art direction Oscar went to *A Streetcar Named Desire*.

Wheeler: 19, 46, 83, 356, 376, 428, 476, 495, 530, 542, 721, 798, 950, 1062, 1088, 1149, 1153, 1213, 1391, 1475, 1601, 1616, 1670, 1706, 1852, 2008, 2093, 2212. Fuller: 530, 1149, 1475, 1601, 2212. Little: 46, 83, 235, 428, 495, 721, 746, 950, 952, 1082, 1149, 1153, 1397, 1475, 1666, 1852, 1868, 2056, 2212, 2286.

720 • FOX, THE

RAYMOND STROSS-MOTION PICTURES INTERNATIONAL PRODUCTION; CLARIDGE PICTURES. 1968.

NOMINATION *Original Score—for a Motion Picture (Not a Musical):* Lalo Schifrin.

Sandy Dennis [2277] and Anne Heywood are struggling to keep their farm going when a stranger, Keir Dullea, happens on them. He helps kill the fox that has been preying on their chickens and gets the farm running. But his attraction to Heywood arouses Dennis' jealousy and resentment. Unsuccessful adaptation by Lewis John Carlino [970] and Howard Koch [365 . . .] of the short novel by D. H. Lawrence. The tensions and nuances of the story are lost, and though the women aren't quite vulgarized into stereotypical butch and femme lesbians, the film has a small-minded view of them that's false to Lawrence. Directed by Mark Rydell. The Oscar went to John Barry for *The Lion in Winter*.

Schifrin: 70, 434, 443, 1928, 2218.

721 • FOXES OF HARROW, THE

20TH CENTURY-FOX. 1947.

NOMINATION *Black-and-White Art Direction—Set Decoration:* Lyle Wheeler and Maurice Ransford; Thomas Little and Paul S. Fox.

Rex Harrison [413 . . .] plays a fortune-hunting rake in 1820s New Orleans. Silly costumer, based on a best-selling plotboiler by Frank Yerby. With Maureen O'Hara, Richard Haydn, Victor McLaglen [999 . . .], Vanessa Brown, Patricia Medina, and Gene Lockhart [36], directed by John M. Stahl [983]. The art direction Oscar went to *Great Expectations*.

Wheeler: 19, 46, 83, 356, 376, 428, 476, 495, 530, 542, 719, 798, 950, 1062, 1088, 1149, 1153, 1213, 1391, 1475, 1601, 1616, 1670, 1706, 1852, 2008, 2093, 2212. Ransford: 1153, 2093. Little: 46, 83, 235, 428, 495, 719, 746, 950, 952, 1082, 1149, 1153, 1397, 1475, 1666, 1852, 1868, 2056, 2212, 2286. Fox: 376, 476, 413, 428, 495, 530, 950, 1088, 1601, 1666, 1706, 1852.

722 • FRANCES

BROOKSFILM/EMI PRODUCTION; UNIVERSAL/AFD. 1982.

NOMINATIONS *Actress:* Jessica Lange. *Supporting Actress:* Kim Stanley.

Lange plays Frances Farmer, whose career as a screen and stage actress began promisingly in 1936 but was cut short by mental illness. Stanley plays her mother. Well acted and often harrowing biopic, but the screenplay doesn't shape the material into anything that makes dramatic or psychological sense. We're left to admire the acting, which is impressive in the showy way that screen madness usually is—and real madness never is. Then-unknown Kevin Costner [482] has a tiny bit part. Directed by Graeme Clifford.

Lange, whose career had been damaged by a typical starlet debut in the 1976 *King Kong* remake, established herself firmly as a major star with this and her simultaneous nomination as supporting actress in *Tootsie.* She won for the latter film. The best actress Oscar went to Meryl Streep for *Sophie's Choice.*

Lange: 244.5, 449, 1381, 1987, 2113. Stanley: 1770.

723 • FREE SOUL, A

MGM. 1930–31.

AWARD *Actor:* Lionel Barrymore.

NOMINATIONS *Actress:* Norma Shearer. *Director:* Clarence Brown.

Barrymore, who plays Shearer's father, saves hoodlum Clark Gable [798 . . .] from a murder rap, only to find that Shearer has fallen in love with Gable. When Shearer's ex-fiancé, Leslie Howard [178 . . .], shoots Gable, Barrymore defends Howard with a courtroom harangue, at the end of which he drops dead. The screenplay by John Meehan [271 . . .] is from a novel by Adela Rogers St. Johns [2250.3] that she based on her own father, lawyer Earl Rogers. Though Barrymore got the Oscar, the film is most notable as the one that made Gable a star. Barrymore had arranged for a screen test for Gable at MGM after an L.A. performance of the play *The Copperhead,* in which Barrymore starred and Gable had a supporting role. The studio signed Gable only after

audiences responded to him with enthusiasm. *A Free Soul* was remade in 1953 as *The Girl Who Had Everything,* with Elizabeth Taylor [318 . . .], William Powell [1170 . . .], and Fernando Lamas.

In his autobiography, *We Barrymores,* Barrymore claims that he did his big courtroom scene in one take, Brown having covered every angle with eight cameras. The logistics of placing eight cameras and lighting a set to accommodate them makes the story unlikely, however. It is the kind of scene designed to wring Oscars from the Academy, though to contemporary eyes it's impossibly hammy. Barrymore for the most part had given up the stage for movies, but he never quite broke the habit of playing to the balcony. Interestingly one of his chief competitors for the Oscar was Fredric March in *The Royal Family of Broadway,* playing a character modeled in large part on Lionel's brother, John.

The best actress Oscar went to Marie Dressler for *Min and Bill.* Norman Taurog was named best director for *Skippy.*

Barrymore: 1234. Shearer: 150, 555, 1274, 1721, 2038. Brown: 84, 957, 1417, 1718, 2320.

724 • FRENCH CONNECTION, THE

PHILIP D'ANTONI PRODUCTION IN ASSOCIATION WITH SCHINE-MOORE PRODUCTIONS; 20TH CENTURY-FOX. 1971.

AWARDS *Picture:* Philip D'Antoni, producer. *Actor:* Gene Hackman. *Director:* William Friedkin. *Screenplay —Based on Material From Another Medium:* Ernest Tidyman. *Film Editing:* Jerry Greenberg.

NOMINATIONS *Supporting Actor:* Roy Scheider. *Cinematography:* Owen Roizman. *Sound:* Theodore Soderberg and Christopher Newman.

Hackman is New York police detective Popeye Doyle, who with the aid of his partner, played by Scheider, exposes an international drug-smuggling operation. Hugely influential thriller, with tough, unlikable protagonists and an exciting and much-copied car chase. It made stars of Hackman and Scheider, and for a brief while made Friedkin Hollywood's hottest director. Today, after countless tough-cop movies and endless demolition derbies, it may be hard to see what all the enthusiasm was for, and particularly why the Academy, with its conservative humanist bent, named it the best picture of the year. The other nominees were Stanley Kubrick's perverse fantasia on violence, *A Clockwork Orange;* the excellent translation to film of the Broadway musical *Fiddler on the Roof;* Peter Bogdanovich's impressive mainstream debut, *The Last Picture Show;* and the more conventional costume epic *Nicholas and Alexandra.* But there are many who think the best picture might have been chosen from nonnominees such as *Sunday, Bloody Sunday, Klute,* and *McCabe and Mrs. Miller.*

Steve McQueen [1753] was Friedkin's first choice for the role of Popeye Doyle, but as a major box-office star he was uninterested in working for a relatively untested director. New York columnist Jimmy Breslin was also tested for the part. Hackman had a career breakthrough four years earlier with *Bonnie and Clyde* and had been recognized again in 1970 with a nomination for *I Never Sang for My Father* but had not yet made it as a leading player. The Oscar helped him become one of the most respected actors in the business.

Friedkin, on the other hand, rode the roller coaster down after his second monster hit, *The Exorcist,* two years later. He had begun his directing career in Chicago TV and broke into films with a movie that none of its principals cares to list on a résumé: *Good Times* (1967), a bit of fluff that starred Sonny and Cher (she prefers to call *Silkwood* her first movie, though it was her fifth). His best-received film before *The French Connection* was an adaptation of the Broadway play about gay men, *The Boys in the Band* (1970). Friedkin would later incur the wrath of gays with the unpleasantly homophobic *Cruising* (1980), which marked the beginning of a period of eclipse for the director.

Tidyman is a novelist perhaps best known for the creation of the title character in *Shaft.* His screenplay is based on a book by Robin Moore about real-life detectives Eddie Egan and Sonny Grosso, both of whom play small roles in the film.

Friedkin himself has spoken of *The French Connection* as a film that was made in the editing room, particularly the celebrated car chase. Greenberg, who

had edited *The Boys in the Band,* is also known for his work with director Brian De Palma on such films as *Dressed to Kill* (1980), *Body Double* (1984), and *The Untouchables.*

Scheider's appearances in *The French Connection* and *Klute* made 1971 a breakthrough year for the actor, who had appeared in low-budget or unsuccessful movies up to that point. His biggest hit was *Jaws*—a film for which he got little credit, being overshadowed by the shark, but which would have been less memorable without his nuanced portrayal of the island police chief who hates the water. His career in the eighties and nineties, however, has brought him few such roles. The supporting actor award went to Ben Johnson for *The Last Picture Show.*

The cinematography Oscar was won by Oswald Morris for *Fiddler on the Roof,* which also won for sound.

Hackman: 255, 971, 1333, 2179.5. Friedkin: 631. Greenberg: 92, 1111. Scheider: 49. Roizman: 631, 1424, 2113, 2316.5. Soderberg: 983, 1596, 1726, 2126, 2152. Newman: 60, 398, 631, 641, 784, 1820.

725 • FRENCH LIEUTENANT'S WOMAN, THE

PARLON PRODUCTION; UNITED ARTISTS (UNITED KINGDOM). 1981.

NOMINATIONS *Actress:* Meryl Streep. *Screenplay Based on Material From Another Medium:* Harold Pinter. *Art Direction—Set Decoration:* Assheton Gorton; Ann Mollo. *Film Editing:* John Bloom. *Costume Design:* Tom Rand.

Streep and Jeremy Irons [1689] play contemporary actors making a film in England about a mysterious Victorian woman and the passion she arouses in a rather conventional man. The actors are pulled into an off-screen affair. The novel by John Fowles on which Pinter based his screenplay is an intricate examination of both Victorian ideas and contemporary theories of fiction; it constantly addresses the reader and even provides alternative endings: a "Victorian" ending that neatly ties up all the plot threads and a "modern" one that leaves many of them unresolved. Faced with the dilemma of capturing the novel's themes of fictional illusion vs. reality, the filmmakers hit upon the idea of a film within a film. Unfortunately it doesn't work. We resent the modern intrusions into the period sections, and they don't shed any particular light on the changing relationships between men and women, or between art and life, as they're presumably intended to do. The leads are splendid, however, and the cinematography of Freddie Francis [779 . . .] helps keep past and present neatly separated. Karel Reisz directed. This was Irons' second film, and his first leading role, though he also appeared in the lead of the British TV miniseries *Brideshead Revisited* in 1981.

It's said that Vanessa Redgrave [263 . . .] was Fowles' choice for the lead, but Streep brings to it her accustomed skill and polish—for some, however, there's too much polish and not enough spontaneity. The best actress Oscar went to Katharine Hepburn for *On Golden Pond,* which also won for Ernest Thompson's screenplay.

Oscars went to *Raiders of the Lost Ark* for art direction and Michael Kahn's editing. Milena Canonero won for her *Chariots of Fire* costumes.

Streep: 472, 521, 1019, 1111, 1512, 1598, 1821, 1876. Pinter: 185. Bloom: 398, 745.

726 • FRENCHMAN'S CREEK

PARAMOUNT. 1945.

AWARD *Color Interior Decoration:* Hans Dreier and Ernst Fegte, art direction; Sam Comer, set decoration.

To escape a loveless marriage to Ralph Forbes and avoid the designs of his rakish friend Basil Rathbone [979 . . .] upon her person, Joan Fontaine [441 . . .] escapes to her family home in Cornwall, where she meets up with a handsome pirate, Arturo de Cordova. But then her husband and Rathbone show up, putting her and her pirate lover in jeopardy. Beautiful but empty-headed Restoration romance based on a novel by Daphne du Maurier. Handsomely photographed by George Barnes [537 . . .], who also shot *Rebecca,* which was written by du Maurier and starred Fontaine—but there the resemblance ends. Mitchell Leisen [587] directs, among others,

Nigel Bruce and Cecil Kellaway [843 . . .], who look a hoot in the Restoration finery designed by Raoul Pène du Bois [1120 . . .].

Dreier: 97, 151, 649, 674, 701, 925, 979, 1101, 1120, 1194, 1214, 1217, 1358, 1443, 1452, 1540, 1668, 1748, 1880, 1975, 1994, 2190. Fegte: 532, 674, 1613. Comer: 278, 357, 426, 450, 736, 925, 956, 1029, 1101, 1214, 1219, 1443, 1570, 1631, 1674, 1727, 1738, 1748, 1959, 1975, 1994, 2012, 2098, 2200, 2208.

727 • FREUD

UNIVERSAL-INTERNATIONAL-JOHN HUSTON PRODUCTION; UNIVERSAL-INTERNATIONAL. 1962.

NOMINATIONS *Story and Screenplay—Written Directly for the Screen:* Charles Kaufman and Wolfgang Reinhardt. *Music Score—Substantially Original:* Jerry Goldsmith.

Montgomery Clift [732 . . .] plays Freud in this account of the analysis of a patient, played by Susannah York [2047], that led to the formulation of the theory of the Oedipus complex. The movie has good performances and strong storytelling, but also silly and pretentious moments, and it was a box-office disappointment. The cast includes David McCallum, Susan Kohner [984], and in his return to the screen, Larry Parks [1058], who was blacklisted during the fifties. It was not a pleasant film in the making. Many of the cast resented the way director John Huston [24 . . .] bullied Clift, whose mental instability, exacerbated by alcohol and drug use, was increasing. But Huston elicited Clift's last first-rate performance in his next to last film.

The screenplay award went to *Divorce—Italian Style.* Maurice Jarre won for the score of *Lawrence of Arabia.*

Goldsmith: 152.5, 268, 395, 939, 1472, 1527, 1537, 1541, 1583, 1589, 1753, 1913, 2176, 2287.

728 • FRIED GREEN TOMATOES

ACT III COMMUNICATIONS IN ASSOCIATION WITH ELECTRIC SHADOW PRODUCTION; UNIVERSAL. 1991.

NOMINATIONS *Supporting Actress:* Jessica Tandy. *Screenplay Based on Material From Another Medium:* Fannie Flagg and Carol Sobieski.

The story of the friendship of two young women, played by Mary Stuart Masterson and Mary-Louise Parker, is told by Tandy, a nursing home resident, to Kathy Bates [1328]. It inspires Bates to lose weight and take charge of her life. Charming but somewhat derivative tale based on Flagg's novel *Fried Green Tomatoes at the Whistle Stop Cafe,* which owes much to the writings of Eudora Welty, Carson McCullers, and other chroniclers of southern eccentrics. (Flagg also has a cameo role in the movie.) The film, directed by Jon Avnet, sanitizes and sentimentalizes a period of brutal racism in its implausible account of the trial of a black man for murder, and glosses over the novel's more explicitly lesbian relationship between Masterson and Parker. But their performances, a splendid comic turn by Bates, and the glowing professionalism of Tandy and Cicely Tyson [1882] make it entertaining in spite of its compromises. It was a surprise box-office success. Tandy lost to Mercedes Ruehl in *The Fisher King,* and the writing award went to Ted Tally for *The Silence of the Lambs.*

Tandy: 580.

729 • FRIENDLY ENEMIES

EDWARD SMALL; UNITED ARTISTS. 1942.

NOMINATION *Sound Recording:* Jack Whitney, Sound Service Inc.

Charles Winninger and Charlie Ruggles, two elderly Americans of German extraction, find their friendship tested at the start of World War I. Unusual little comedy-drama that was filmed in 1925 with the vaudevillians Joe Weber and Lew Fields in the leads. It had a different resonance in the early years of World War II. The Oscar went to Nathan Levinson for Yankee Doodle Dandy.

Whitney: 862, 955, 1026, 1884, 2031, 2050, 2095.

730 • FRIENDLY PERSUASION

ALLIED ARTISTS. 1956.

NOMINATIONS *Picture:* William Wyler, producer. *Supporting Actor:* Anthony Perkins. *Director:* William Wyler. *Screenplay—Adapted:* Michael Wilson [Nomination withdrawn from final ballot]. *Sound Recording:*

Gordon R. Glennan, sound director, Westrex Sound Services Inc., and Gordon Sawyer, sound director, Samuel Goldwyn Studio Sound Department. *Song:* "Friendly Persuasion (Thee I Love)," music by Dimitri Tiomkin, lyrics by Paul Francis Webster.

When the Civil War starts, a group of Quakers in Indiana find their pacifism sorely tested, especially Gary Cooper [701 . . .] and Dorothy McGuire [759], whose son, Perkins, is itching to join the fight. A film of tasteful pathos and humor that's usually described as "homespun"—meaning it won't offend your grandmother. Those nostalgic for a kinder, gentler film era revere it; others know where the Schwarzenegger tapes are shelved. At 140 minutes *Friendly Persuasion* seems a bit padded, but it was a year of big pictures—the other nominees were *Giant, The King and I, The Ten Commandments,* and the winner, *Around the World in 80 Days.* In that company it looks modest indeed. Wyler lost the directing Oscar to George Stevens for *Giant.*

This was Perkins' third film. He made his debut in *The Actress* in 1953 and played Jimmy Piersall, a baseball player who suffered a bout of mental illness, in 1956's *Fear Strikes Out.* The edgy, disturbed note of the latter role would become his signature as an actor, and after his most famous role, Norman Bates in *Psycho,* he would never again be cast as a conventional leading man. His itchy mannerisms haven't developed by the time of *Friendly Persuasion,* however, and it's one of his best nonquirky roles. He lost the Oscar to Anthony Quinn in *Lust for Life.* Perkins died of AIDS in 1992.

The larger drama of conscience that surrounds Wilson's nonnomination is in some ways more compelling than the film itself. In Wilson's original screenplay, an adaptation of several stories about Quakers by Jessamyn West that was prepared for Frank Capra [1025 . . .], the boy so eager to fight in the war is disturbed by the realities of combat and becomes a medical aide instead. After Wilson had made an appearance before the House Un-American Activities Committee in 1951 and invoked the Fifth Amendment when asked about his knowledge of communist activities, he was blacklisted. Finding his own early, mildly populist films under suspicion, Capra distanced himself from Wilson and other writers under investigation. Wyler took over the production, and the script was changed so that the Quaker family is forced to give up their pacifism in defense of their homes.

The film was released with no writer credit, the result of a 1953 decision by the Screen Writers Guild to allow producers to remove the names of blacklisted writers from films. Wilson sued Wyler and Allied Artists, and the case was settled out of court. Though in later years Wyler insisted that he had no choice in the matter of giving Wilson screen credit, Wilson remained bitter about Wyler's role in the decision to the end of his life.

The writers branch of the Academy—many of whose members were tacitly in support of the writers who had been blacklisted—may have intended their nomination of the film's screenplay as an act of defiance. But a new Academy bylaw prohibited anyone who had refused to testify before a congressional committee from receiving a nomination. On February 6, 1957, the Academy ruled that a screenplay could be entered in nomination, even though its author was ineligible for the award, but in the end the *Friendly Persuasion* screenplay was not listed on the ballot. The draconian judgment that the work could be eligible even though its author wasn't was repealed as "unworkable" in 1959. The adapted screenplay Oscar went to the writers of *Around the World in 80 Days*. But at the same awards ceremony, an Oscar for the motion picture story of *The Brave One* was given to "Robert Rich," who turned out to be blacklistee Dalton Trumbo. Wilson likewise continued to work behind the scenes, and his coauthorship with fellow blacklistee Carl Foreman of the screenplay for *The Bridge on the River Kwai* in 1957 won an Oscar for Pierre Boulle, who could barely speak English and certainly didn't write it. Wilson resumed his credited career in the mid-sixties.

The sound award went to *The King and I*. The song Oscar was won by Jay Livingston and Ray Evans for "Whatever Will Be, Will Be (Que Será, Será)," from *The Man Who Knew Too Much*. Tiomkin and Webster's song was a big hit, however, in its recording by Pat Boone.

Wyler: 175, 184, 420, 534, 560, 894, 1162, 1182, 1371, 1716, 2316. Wilson: 287, 673, 1579. Sawyer: 33, 91, 184, 214, 393, 864, 882, 973, 974, 1032, 1511, 1592, 2244, 2297, 2310. Tiomkin: 33, 286, 380, 446, 638, 663, 768, 850, 911, 912, 1206, 1347, 1370, 1470, 2006, 2127, 2282, 2335. Webster: 33, 64, 95, 331, 376, 604, 663, 856, 1213, 1276, 1322, 1388, 1755, 1925, 2014.

731 • FROGMEN, THE

WARNER BROS. 1951.

NOMINATIONS *Motion Picture Story:* Oscar Millard. *Black-and-White Cinematography:* Norbert Brodine.

Richard Widmark [1098], Dana Andrews, Gary Merrill, Jeffrey Hunter, Robert Wagner, and Jack Warden [890 . . .] play underwater demolition experts during World War II. Solid if unexceptional action film, mercifully free of the propagandizing that would have slowed it down if it had been made six or seven years earlier. Directed by Lloyd Bacon. The writing Oscar went to Paul Dehn and James Bernard for *Seven Days to Noon*. William C. Mellor won the cinematography award for *A Place in the Sun*.

Brodine: 1306, 1464.

732 • FROM HERE TO ETERNITY

COLUMBIA. 1953.

AWARDS *Picture:* Buddy Adler, producer. *Supporting Actor:* Frank Sinatra. *Supporting Actress:* Donna Reed. *Director:* Fred Zinnemann. *Screenplay:* Daniel Taradash. *Black-and-White Cinematography:* Burnett Guffey. *Sound Recording:* John P. Livadary, sound director, Columbia Sound Department. *Film Editing:* William Lyon.

NOMINATIONS *Actor:* Montgomery Clift. *Actor:* Burt Lancaster. *Actress:* Deborah Kerr. *Scoring of a Dramatic or Comedy Picture:* Morris Stoloff and George Duning. *Black-and-White Costume Design:* Jean Louis.

On the eve of World War II a group of soldiers stationed at Pearl Harbor experience personal crises. Sergeant Warden (Lancaster) is having an affair with his captain's wife (Kerr). Private Prewitt (Clift) is getting the treatment because, having once blinded an opponent in the ring, he refuses to join the company boxing team. His friend Private Maggio (Sinatra) is being hassled by Sgt. Fatso Judson, played by Ernest Borgnine [1283]. Prewitt seeks the understanding company of a nightclub "hostess" (Reed). This hugely entertaining adaptation of the James Jones novel is one of the most mature films to come out of the Hollywood of the fifties. It still looks good today because of its marvelous casting and efficient story-telling, and because it makes as few compromises as possible with the censorship and jingoism of the age. It tied with *Gone With the Wind* by taking eight Oscars, a record the films held (being joined the following year by *On the Waterfront)* until *Gigi* won nine at the 1958 awards.

Producer Adler began his career as a screenwriter at MGM, working on short subjects, including the Oscar-winning short *Quicker 'n a Wink* in 1940. After army service in World War II, he became a producer at Columbia. *From Here to Eternity* was a pet project of studio boss Harry Cohn [1025 . . .], and it was a plum one for Adler, whose handful of previous productions were of no particular distinction. But he worked well with Zinnemann and Taradash and managed to hold firm against Cohn's initial insistence that Columbia contract players John Derek or Aldo Ray be cast as Prewitt instead of Clift. Three years later Adler was made head of production at 20th Century-Fox, where he remained until his death in 1960. He also received the Irving G. Thalberg Award in 1956.

Sinatra's obtaining the role of Maggio is the stuff of legend, including the myth that he obtained it with the help of the mob, which is the basis of the horse's head episode in *The Godfather*. It is said that he made an offer to do it for free and that Sinatra's then wife, Ava Gardner [1339], made a personal plea on his behalf with Cohn. And it is considered to be the role that revived his sinking career. The truth is probably less sensational. The hiatus in his career was partly real. Both he and the bobby-soxers who had made him famous had long since grown out of adolescence, and he suffered throat problems in 1952 that made him fear that his singing career was over. But it's unlikely that a man of his talents would have stayed in

eclipse for long, or that he needed special pleading for a role that suited him well. This was not, in fact, Sinatra's first serious role. In 1952 he had played in a melodrama, *Meet Danny Wilson,* which provided clear evidence that he could do more than croon. On the other hand, he got the role of Maggio only because Eli Wallach, who had been cast in the part, decided to do a Broadway play instead—*Camino Real,* by Tennessee Williams [119 . . .], which turned out to be as big a flop as *From Here to Eternity* was a hit. Unfortunately Sinatra didn't use the Oscar for *Eternity* as impetus to grow as an actor. He gave a few additional impressive dramatic performances in films such as *The Man With the Golden Arm* and *The Manchurian Candidate,* but much of his film career was spent in ephemeral movies such as the Rat Pack comedies he made with the likes of Dean Martin and Sammy Davis, Jr., in the sixties.

Like Shirley Jones for *Elmer Gantry,* Reed won her Oscar by playing against type. Both actresses were established as "nice girls" and surprised audiences and the Academy by playing prostitutes. Julie Harris [1301] is said to have been Zinnemann's first choice for the part, but Cohn felt she wasn't attractive enough. Reed had been a contract player at MGM, appearing primarily in B pictures, and almost her only memorable role before *Eternity* was in *It's a Wonderful Life,* in which she played the dutiful wife and mother that was her lot in most of her movies. The Oscar was no particular entree into better roles, hence her move into TV in the late fifties, where she played the good wife endlessly. She died in 1986 of pancreatic cancer.

Zinnemann was born in Vienna and started as a camera assistant in Europe in the twenties. He came to the States in 1929, finding work wherever he could in Hollywood, including a part as an extra in *All Quiet on the Western Front*. He worked his way into directing, and like Adler was hired by the short-subjects division of MGM in the thirties. He, too, made an Oscar-winning short, *That Mothers Might Live* in 1938. His early feature work in the forties was unimpressive until he went to Europe in 1948 for the American-Swiss coproduction *The Search,* which also launched the screen career of Montgomery Clift. With *The Men* in 1950 and *High Noon* in 1952, it became clear that Zinnemann was a major director.

The Harvard-educated Taradash had one of the most difficult screenwriting jobs imaginable—converting a novel that was notorious for its profanity, sex, and violence into something that would work on screen in the age of the Production Code. The book was thought to be unfilmable, and as written, it would have been. But the compromises made by Taradash, who worked patiently with the censors of the Code office, are surprisingly unobtrusive. It's quite clear that Reed's "hostess" does more than just chat with the soldiers, and as staged by Zinnemann, Lancaster and Kerr's famous love scene in the surf remains one of film's most erotic images. We don't want more than we get in the film, because what we get is strongly characterized and superbly directed. Taradash, who began his screenwriting career in 1939 on *Golden Boy,* reinforced his reputation as a capable adapter with an excellent screenplay for *Picnic,* but never received another Oscar nomination.

Guffey began as a Hollywood cameraman in 1923 and had a working career of nearly fifty years, becoming director of photography for Columbia in the forties. Both Guffey and editor Lyon were called on to conceal Clift's inability to box. Well-chosen camera angles and cuts do the trick.

Clift and Lancaster lost to William Holden for *Stalag 17,* an upset victory that may be attributable to the film's two nominees splitting the vote. (The other nominees were Marlon Brando for *Julius Caesar* and Richard Burton for *The Robe.)* Like virtually all the film's leads, Lancaster almost missed out on making the movie. He was the first choice for the role, but because he was tied up on another film, Edmond O'Brien [146 . . .] had been cast in the part. (The surf scene suddenly becomes unthinkable.)

Kerr, likewise, was a replacement, for Joan Crawford [1319 . . .]. The oft-told story that Crawford dropped out of the part because she didn't like the wardrobe sounds like a cruel, bitchy "bad Joan" legend and is very likely untrue. Crawford was in a position to request her own designer. As with Reed, Kerr was a stunning bit of reverse-type casting, for her roles were usually rather pallid and proper women. It's the hint that a devil lurks inside such women that makes her characterization of Karen Holmes so powerful and sexy. She lost the Oscar to Audrey Hepburn in *Roman Holiday.*

The scoring Oscar went to Bronislau Kaper for *Lili.* Edith Head's designs for *Roman Holiday* won the costuming award.

Adler: 1213. Sinatra: 1264. Zinnemann: 912, 1066, 1252, 1457, 1771, 1969. Guffey: 210, 255, 870, 1093. Livadary: 330, 455, 596, 1058, 1206, 1215, 1303, 1366, 1370, 1488, 1521, 1740, 1872, 2111, 2325, 2327. Lyon: 330, 456, 1058, 1566, 1776. Clift: 1065, 1579, 1771. Lancaster: 107, 210, 609. Kerr: 599, 891, 1088, 1778, 1969. Stoloff: 13, 432, 455, 596, 643, 677, 773, 1057, 1058, 1115, 1206, 1862, 1872, 1873, 1998, 2110, 2329. Duning: 596, 1057, 1442, 1566. Louis: 20, 126, 170, 262, 744, 1028, 1065, 1521, 1640, 1812, 1858, 1910, 2064.

733 • FRONT, THE

COLUMBIA. 1976.

NOMINATION *Screenplay—Written Directly for the Screen:* Walter Bernstein.

In the 1950s a Manhattan nobody, played by Woody Allen [39 . . .], is persuaded to become a "front"—to put his name on the TV scripts written by an old high school acquaintance, Michael Murphy, who is being blacklisted because of his earlier leftist activities. As other writers ask him to front for them, the work that appears under Allen's name develops such a reputation that he develops delusions of grandeur and begins to believe in his own writing ability, which doesn't exist. Promising comedy-drama that never quite delivers on its promise. Like other films that deal with the blacklisting era, such as *The Way We Were* or *Guilty by Suspicion* (1991), it oversimplifies a disgraceful epoch in American politics. On the other hand, it showcases a fine performance by Allen, one of his few appearances in a film he neither wrote nor directed. Many of the people responsible for the film, including Bernstein, director Martin Ritt [956], and actors Zero Mostel and Herschel Bernardi, were themselves blacklisted.

Bernstein was a magazine and TV writer who had written one screenplay, *Kiss the Blood off My Hands* (1948), before being blacklisted. When his name was removed from the blacklist in 1959, he resumed a screenwriting career, working on such films as *Fail-Safe* (1964) and *The Molly Maguires*. He returned to the McCarthy era for the screenplay of the 1988 thriller *The House on Carroll Street*. He lost the Oscar to Paddy Chayefsky for *Network*.

734 • FRONT PAGE, THE

THE CADDO COMPANY; UNITED ARTISTS. 1930–31.
NOMINATIONS *Picture:* Howard Hughes, producer. *Actor:* Adolphe Menjou. *Director:* Lewis Milestone.

Menjou plays irascible newspaper editor Walter Burns, who will stop at nothing to keep his star reporter, Hildy Johnson (Pat O'Brien), from getting married and leaving the paper. Eventually the plot involves an escaped murder suspect, political corruption, and an attempted suicide. The first filming of the play by Ben Hecht [78 . . .] and Charles MacArthur [1664 . . .] is fast-paced and funny, and still preferable to the 1974 remake. The best of all versions, however, is 1940's *His Girl Friday,* with Cary Grant [1445 . . .] as Burns and Rosalind Russell [110 . . .] as Hildy, directed by Howard Hawks [1779]—one of the funniest movies ever made, and a film unaccountably and inexcusably overlooked by the Academy. (Hildy's sex change was retained in yet another remake, *Switching Channels,* in 1988, in which Burt Reynolds plays Burns and Kathleen Turner [1545] Hildy, and the setting has been changed to a TV newsroom. It's the least successful of all four versions.)

The best picture Oscar went to *Cimarron,* generally dismissed as one of the weakest films ever to win the award. Today *The Front Page* seems like the best of the nominees, which also included *East Lynne* and *Skippy*. But the year's best pictures were the ones that weren't nominated: *City Lights, Little Caesar, Public Enemy, Morocco,* and *The Blue Angel*.

Menjou had a distinguished career that lasted from *The Blue Envelope Mystery* in 1916 to *Pollyanna* in 1960, three years before his death. He was a one-note character actor, but that note was elegant—in fact, he was publicized as one of the world's best-dressed men. He lost to Lionel Barrymore in *A Free Soul*.

Milestone had originally cast the star of his Oscar-winning *All Quiet on the Western Front,* Louis Wolheim, in Menjou's role, but Wolheim died before filming started. Milestone himself makes an appearance in the film, as does screenwriter Herman J. Mankiewicz [407 . . .]. The directing Oscar went to Norman Taurog for *Skippy*.

Hughes: 1646. Milestone: 48, 1464, 2159.

734.5 • FUGITIVE, THE

WARNER BROS. PRODUCTION; WARNER BROS. 1993.
AWARD *Supporting Actor:* Tommy Lee Jones.
NOMINATIONS *Picture:* Arnold Kopelson, producer. *Cinematography:* Michael Chapman. *Sound:* Donald O. Mitchell, Michael Herbick, Frank A. Montaño, and Scott D. Smith. *Original Score:* James Newton Howard. *Film Editing:* Dennis Virkler, David Finfer, Dean Goodhill, Don Brochu, Richard Nord, and Dov Hoenig. *Sound Effects Editing:* John Leveque and Bruce Stambler.

A Chicago surgeon, Dr. Richard Kimble, played by Harrison Ford [2296], is convicted of the brutal murder of his wife. But on the way to prison, the bus in which he is being transported is involved in a spectacular collision with a train, and Kimble escapes, determined to use his unexpected freedom to track down the one-armed man who really killed his wife. But an intelligent, single-minded U.S. marshal, Sam Gerard (Jones), is equally determined to track down Kimble and send him back to prison. The result is a terrific, nonstop action adventure, a battle of wits rather than bullets, beautifully paced by director Andrew Davis and screenwriters Jeb Stuart and David Twohy. Their immediate source is a sixties TV series, but what they've produced is more like an updated *Les Misérables* as Alfred Hitchcock [1171 . . .] might have done it. In a more conventionally made film, everything after the train wreck, which takes place near the beginning of the film (and is, incidentally, a textbook example of great editing), would have been anticli-mactic. Like most thrillers, *The Fugitive* stretches cre-dulity to the breaking point and won't hold up if you apply real-world logic to some of its plot contriv-ances. So don't.

The film also benefits greatly from the two lead performances. After the *Star Wars* and *Indiana Jones* films, Ford has become so identified with the action genre that critics often fail to give him credit for being so good at it. Imagine Kimble played by such supermen as Sylvester Stallone [1712] and Arnold Schwarzenegger, or a smart aleck like Bruce Willis, to see how right Ford is in this beleaguered everyman part. Or simply watch his expression when he gets on an elevator, only to be joined in it by the cops he's trying to elude. But even Ford is upstaged by Jones, who, though nominated as a supporting actor, shares top billing with him, and even has more lines in the script. Born in Texas, Jones attended Harvard, where he was a classmate of Stockard Channing [1835.5] and John Lithgow [2020 . . .], all of them active in stu-dent theater. Jones made his film debut (as Tom Lee Jones) by playing a Harvard student: Ryan O'Neal's roommate in *Love Story*. His movie career advanced slowly, however. He appeared opposite Faye Dunaway [255 . . .] in *Eyes of Laura Mars* (1978), played Sissy Spacek's husband in *Coal Miner's Daughter,* and had some substantial TV roles, playing Howard Hughes in a miniseries and winning an Emmy in 1982 as Gary Gilmore in *The Executioner's Song.* But lacking conven-tional good looks, he seemed doomed to playing heavies or cowboys—in an era when westerns were out of favor. In the late eighties, however, several good roles revived his career, one of them in a west-ern: the hit TV miniseries *Lonesome Dove* in 1989. The same year, he was cast by Andrew Davis in *The Pack-age,* a film that failed to attract much attention, but led to his casting in Davis' *Under Siege* and *The Fugitive.* And his 1991 nomination for his performance as the shadowy, decadent Clay Shaw in *JFK* made it clear that Jones was an actor of range and versatility. In *The Fugitive* Jones wittily underplays Gerard, proving as effective as in his earlier performance for Davis in

Under Siege, in which he went flamboyantly over the top.

The Fugitive was a mildly surprising nominee in the company of "serious" films such as *In the Name of the Father, The Piano, The Remains of the Day,* and the win-ner, *Schindler's List.* Many expected an equally serious entry such as *The Age of Innocence* or *Philadelphia* in its place, and *The Fugitive*'s chances of taking the top award were clearly doomed when Davis failed to re-ceive a nomination as director. (His slot went to Rob-ert Altman for *Short Cuts.*) But in recent years the Academy has grown more respectful of so-called genre films, giving the top award to westerns *(Dances With Wolves* and *Unforgiven)* and even to a horror thriller, *The Silence of the Lambs.* Action-adventure movies, which have been the bread and butter of Hollywood for a decade or more, may eventually re-ceive similar respect—if they're as well made as *The Fugitive.* This year, however, a major achievement in "serious" filmmaking, *Schindler's List,* had to be con-tended with. It took the award not only for best picture but also for Janusz Kaminiski's cinematogra-phy, John Williams' score, and Michael Kahn's edit-ing. The awards for sound and sound effects editing went to *Jurassic Park.*

Jones: 1047. Kopelson: 1584. Chapman: 1650. Mitchell: 223, 398, 411.5, 507, 779, 1525, 1650, 1824, 1825, 2020, 2114, 2176.5. Herbick: 411.5, 1802.5. Montaño: 411.5, 2176.5. Smith: 2176.5. Howard: 1071.3, 1612. Virkler: 961. Leveque: 411.5, 2176.5. Stambler: 411.5, 2176.5.

735 • FULL METAL JACKET

NATANT PRODUCTION; WARNER BROS. 1987.
NOMINATION *Screenplay Based on Material From Another Medium:* Stanley Kubrick, Michael Herr, and Gustav Hasford.

Matthew Modine, Adam Baldwin, and Vincent D'Onofrio are among the young marines being rigor-ously and brutally trained under the supervision of drill instructor Lee Ermey on Parris Island before shipping out to Vietnam, where very little that they have learned seems to apply. In fact, so sharp is the distinction between their training and their combat experience that the film breaks abruptly in two halves. The first, dealing primarily with Ermey's fateful harassment of the sluggish D'Onofrio, is so powerful that the second seems anticlimactic. Riddled with some of the roughest language ever spoken on screen, it certainly holds its own with *Platoon, Apocalypse Now,* and *The Deer Hunter* among Vietnam War films. Directed by Kubrick, it was filmed in England, which makes a surprisingly passable substitute for South Carolina and Vietnam.

The screenplay is based on Hasford's *The Short Timers.* Herr also wrote a celebrated account of combat in Vietnam, *Dispatches,* which has been the source, credited and otherwise, of many films about the war. The Oscar went to Mark Peploe and Bernardo Bertolucci for *The Last Emperor.*

Kubrick: 151, 415, 574, 2164.

736 • FUNNY FACE

PARAMOUNT. 1957.

NOMINATIONS *Story and Screenplay—Written Directly for the Screen:* Leonard Gershe. *Cinematography:* Ray June. *Art Direction–Set Decoration:* Hal Pereira and George W. Davis; Sam Comer and Ray Moyer. *Costume Design:* Edith Head and Hubert de Givenchy.

Fashion photographer Fred Astaire [2126] helps editor Kay Thompson discover a new face for her magazine: Audrey Hepburn [278 . . .]. The trouble is, Hepburn, a bookstore clerk with intellectual pretensions, doesn't want to be discovered—until she learns that it means a trip to Paris, where she can meet French existentialist philosopher Michel Auclair. But Auclair turns out to be a lecherous phony, and Hepburn and Astaire fall in love. As even its director, Stanley Donen, has noted, the picture really depends mostly on the charm of Astaire and Hepburn, but it has other pleasures: Thompson's kicky support; the work of real fashion photographer Richard Avedon, credited as a "special visual consultant," who supervised the sequences involving fashion photography; and the music, most of which is by George [1797] and Ira Gershwin [455 . . .], with agreeable additional songs by Roger Edens [87 . . .] and screenwriter Gershe. Hepburn, who had some

dance training, is not one of Astaire's better partners, but she sings quite winningly. Her solo number, "How Long Has This Been Going On," is one of the film's highlights, beautifully staged by Donen. She insisted on not being dubbed, and won—a battle she lost on *My Fair Lady.* Her deficiencies as a singer show up primarily in her duets with Astaire, who is more effectively partnered by Thompson in the "Clap Yo' Hands" number.

Gershe's screenplay was originally planned as a stage musical, but it attracted the attention of producer Edens, who thought it would make an ideal film for Astaire and Hepburn. Astaire had appeared in the Gershwin musical *Funny Face* on stage in 1927, but Gershe's screenplay has no resemblance to that show. The film's title apparently grew out of a line in the screenplay, when Hepburn says, "I think my face is perfectly funny." That in turn sparked the idea of using the Gershwin song in the musical. The writing Oscar went to George Wells for *Designing Woman*— this seems to have been the year for scripts about the fashion business.

Both the cinematography and art direction were greatly enhanced by the participation of Avedon, who was denied the kind of credit that might have earned him a nomination. Because of union regulations, his suggestions could not even be made directly to the technical crew, but had to be communicated through Donen. The cinematography Oscar went to Jack Hildyard for *The Bridge on the River Kwai,* the art direction award to *Sayonara.*

Givenchy was Hepburn's favorite designer, and she wears his clothes in virtually all the films she made after she became a star. This was the only one for which he received a nomination. The costuming Oscar went to Orry-Kelly for *Les Girls.*

June: 102, 145. Pereira: 278, 357, 363, 426, 450, 956, 1029, 1219, 1504, 1570, 1631, 1674, 1716, 1727, 1738, 1840, 1897, 1959, 2012, 2098, 2200, 2208. Davis: 46, 69, 401, 495, 542, 953, 1213, 1335, 1388, 1537, 1552, 1706, 1814, 2157, 2184, 2312. Comer: 278, 357, 426, 450, 726, 925, 956, 1029, 1101, 1214, 1219, 1443, 1570, 1631, 1674, 1727, 1738, 1748, 1959, 1975, 1994, 2012, 2098,

2200, 2208. Moyer: 278, 413, 833, 1101, 1120, 1214, 1674, 1738, 1748, 1975, 2012. Head: 31, 32, 46, 305, 357, 363, 612, 636, 675, 832, 894, 945, 1003, 1219, 1261, 1263, 1398, 1427, 1504, 1550, 1579, 1587, 1631, 1716, 1727, 1738, 1748, 1840, 1927, 1986, 2012, 2098, 2247, 2298.

737 • *FUNNY GIRL*

RASTAR PRODUCTIONS; COLUMBIA. 1968.

AWARD *Actress:* Barbra Streisand.

NOMINATIONS *Picture:* Ray Stark, producer. *Supporting Actress:* Kay Medford. *Cinematography:* Harry Stradling. *Sound:* Columbia Studio Sound Department. *Song:* "Funny Girl," music by Jule Styne, lyrics by Bob Merrill. *Score of a Musical Picture—Original or Adaptation:* Walter Scharf. *Film Editing:* Robert Swink, Maury Winetrobe, and William Sands.

Singer-comedian Fanny Brice (Streisand) comes out of Brooklyn to be a *Ziegfeld Follies* headliner, marry gambler Nicky Arnstein—played by Omar Sharif [1151]—and experience fame, fortune, and heartbreak. Directed by William Wyler [175 . . .], with the assistance of Herbert Ross [2152] on the musical numbers, it features Medford as Fanny's mother and Walter Pidgeon [1232 . . .] as Florenz Ziegfeld. Without Streisand, this big backstage musical would be nothing, and it certainly drags in the last third, as the Brice-Arnstein marriage begins to break up and the musical numbers grow fewer. Otherwise, it's chiefly memorable for its Styne-Merrill songs, including "Don't Rain on My Parade" and "People."

Streisand may be the most intensely controversial major star of our time—no one seems to be indifferent to her, and her fans and detractors are equally passionate. She shot to stardom in 1962, when she was twenty, with a showstopping number in the Broadway musical *I Can Get It for You Wholesale.* The Broadway version of *Funny Girl,* tailor-made for her, followed in 1964, and she made several celebrated TV specials before her movie debut in *Funny Girl.* It won her the Oscar in a startling tie with Katharine Hepburn for *The Lion in Winter*—the only one in the history of the best actress race, though Fredric March for *Dr. Jekyll and Mr. Hyde* and Wallace Beery for *The Champ* won in a nominal tie (March polled one vote more than Beery) at the 1931–32 awards. Efforts to capitalize on Streisand's musical talents followed immediately, but they were disasters: *Hello, Dolly!* and *On a Clear Day You Can See Forever* (1970), in both of which she was badly miscast. She had more success in nonmusical comedies such as *What's Up, Doc?* (1972) and comparatively serious roles such as *The Way We Were,* which earned her a second acting nomination. Like many contemporary stars, she moved into producing and eventually into directing. Even there, she has generated controversy, with much comment over the failure of the Academy to recognize her with nominations as the director of *Yentl* or *The Prince of Tides.*

Stark, a former agent, started a highly successful TV production company, Seven Arts, in 1957, and moved into film production with 1960's *The World of Suzie Wong.* He formed Rastar Productions in 1966, and the smash success of *Funny Girl* helped make him one of the most important producers in the business. *Funny Girl* was a project for which he was uniquely suited: Fanny Brice was his wife's mother. The Oscar went to another musical, *Oliver!* The other nominees were *The Lion in Winter, Rachel, Rachel,* and *Romeo and Juliet.*

With her wry underplaying, Medford is the only member of the cast who comes close to stealing scenes from Streisand. A durable but somewhat underutilized character actress, she inherited the mantle of Thelma Ritter [46 . . .] as the acerbic, lower-class sidekick and/or mom, though there weren't enough roles for her to play in the sixties and seventies. She died in 1980. The Oscar went to Ruth Gordon for *Rosemary's Baby.*

Most of the songs in *Funny Girl* were imported from the stage version and hence were ineligible for the Oscar. Styne and Merrill's new song for the film lost to "The Windmills of Your Mind," from *The Thomas Crown Affair.*

The cinematography Oscar went to Pasqualino De Santis for *Romeo and Juliet. Oliver!* won for sound and for John Green's scoring. The editing award went to Frank P. Keller for *Bullitt.*

Streisand: 1612, 1911, 2238. Stark: 803. Stradling: 110, 149, 596, 852, 853, 864, 896, 957, 1246, 1393, 1567, 1949, 2338. Styne: 74, 696, 920, 921, 1031, 1719, 2072, 2110, 2343. Scharf: 174, 274, 665, 864, 921, 991, 1054, 1305, 2285. Swink: 268, 1716.

738 • FUNNY LADY

RASTAR PICTURES PRODUCTION; COLUMBIA. 1975.

NOMINATIONS *Cinematography:* James Wong Howe. *Sound:* Richard Portman, Don MacDougall, Curly Thirlwell, and Jack Solomon. *Song:* "How Lucky Can You Get," music and lyrics by Fred Ebb and John Kander. *Scoring—Original Song Score and/or Adaptation:* Peter Matz. *Costume Design:* Ray Aghayan and Bob Mackie.

Fanny Brice, played by Barbra Streisand [737 . . .], after divorcing her gambler husband, Nicky Arnstein, played by Omar Sharif [1151], marries the producer of her show, Billy Rose, played by James Caan [784]. But her second marriage doesn't work out any better than her first did. Still, now Fanny's a rich and famous movie and radio star. Unnecessary and unmemorable sequel to *Funny Girl,* directed by Herbert Ross [2152], who had staged the musical numbers in the first film. There's no dramatic shape to the screenplay, by Jay Presson Allen [321 . . .] and Arnold Schulman [802 . . .], because there's not much of anywhere for it to go—Fanny's a success at the start and a success at the end, and the middle is made up of problems caused by her lousy taste in men. Caan does well with a role that he should be all wrong for: Rose was famously short and ugly. There are a few good musical numbers, but most of them are overproduced. The cast also includes Roddy McDowall and the cruelly underused Ben Vereen.

This was the last film shot by Howe, who died in 1976. The Oscar went to John Alcott for *Barry Lyndon.*

The sound award went to *Jaws.* Kander and Ebb's song lost to Keith Carradine's "I'm Easy," from *Nashville.* The scoring award was won by Leonard Rosenman for *Barry Lyndon,* which also won for Ulla-Britt Soderlund and Milena Canonero's costumes.

Howe: 1, 30, 36, 956, 1095, 1451, 1470, 1727, 1774. Portman: 339, 418, 502, 521, 784, 1109, 1473, 1526, 1701, 2331. MacDougall: 416, 938, 1439, 1916. Thirlwell: 307. Solomon: 896, 938, 1089, 1109, 1310. Aghayan: 743, 1126. Mackie: 1126, 1548.

739 • FUNNY THING HAPPENED ON THE WAY TO THE FORUM, A

MELVIN FRANK PRODUCTION; UNITED ARTISTS. 1966.

AWARD *Scoring of Music—Adaptation or Treatment:* Ken Thorne.

Pseudolus the slave (Zero Mostel) plots to win his freedom by aiding the lovers Hero (Michael Crawford) and Philia (Annette Andre) and thwarting the designs of Senex (Michael Hordern). Frantic, misdirected (by Richard Lester) filming of a hit Broadway musical adapted from Plautus by Burt Shevelove, Larry Gelbart [1467 . . .], and Stephen Sondheim [543]. The screenplay adaptation is by Melvin Frank [636 . . .] and Michael Pertwee. Farce doesn't need fancy camera work, jumpy editing, and superfluous sight gags, it needs timing, and when you've got a cast with such masters of timing as Phil Silvers, Buster Keaton, and Jack Gilford [1761], it's a crime not to let them show what they can do. The lively musical numbers are all hashed up, too. Sadly this was Keaton's last film, and he doesn't look at all well throughout, so that some of the physical comedy, even though it was done by a double, seems particularly cruel.

Thorne's Oscar came out of one of the strangest groups of competitors ever to be lumped into a single category: *The Gospel According to St. Matthew, Return of the Seven, The Singing Nun,* and *Stop the World—I Want to Get Off.* If you ever want a conversation-stopper, ask someone what *those* films have in common.

740 • FURIES, THE

HAL WALLIS PRODUCTIONS; PARAMOUNT. 1950.

NOMINATION *Black-and-White Cinematography:* Victor Milner.

Barbara Stanwyck [138 . . .] and her father, rancher Walter Huston [50 . . .], have a troubled relationship in this rather overwrought western directed by Anthony Mann. The cast also includes Judith Anderson [1670], Beulah Bondi [807 . . .], and Blanche Yurka, which may give you some clue to why it's called *The Furies*. This was Huston's last film. The Oscar went to Robert Krasker for *The Third Man*.

Milner: 304, 412, 470, 757, 827, 1217, 1452, 1668.

741 • FURY

MGM. 1936.
NOMINATION *Original Story:* Norman Krasna.

Spencer Tracy [131 . . .] plays an innocent man who is mistaken for a murderer and almost lynched. He escapes and returns to see that justice is done. Superb, gripping film, the first American movie of director Fritz Lang, with Sylvia Sidney [1962], Walter Abel, and Walter Brennan [424 . . .]. The cinematography is by Joseph Ruttenberg [318 . . .]. Lang, one of the most celebrated of German directors, fled the Nazis in 1933, and in 1934 was hired by David O. Selznick [497 . . .], then in charge of production at MGM. Lang was generally disliked at the studio, however, which may explain the lack of nominations for this first-rate work. He also wrote the screenplay, with Bartlett Cormack. Krasna based his story on an actual lynching that took place in San Jose in 1933. The Oscar went to Pierre Collings and Sheridan Gibney for *The Story of Louis Pasteur*.

Krasna: 535, 1615, 1694.

G.I. HONEYMOON

See 767.

741.5 • "G" MEN

WARNER BROS.-FIRST NATIONAL. 1935.
NOMINATION *Original Story:* Gregory Rogers. (Write-in candidate.)

James Cagney [79 . . .] was raised by a gangster, but he sees the error of their ways when a friend is gunned down, so he joins the FBI. Sure enough, he has to hunt down another old pal from the mob.

Smart, lively cops-and-robbers classic from a studio that knew how to make them. Warners was under some pressure because of a reaction against the violence of its gangster flicks, so it found a way to draw the crowds and appease the critics: send its star gangster, Cagney, to the other side, but still keep a gun in his hand. Directed by William Keighley, with Ann Dvorak, Margaret Lindsay, Robert Armstrong, Barton MacLane, and Lloyd Nolan. Seton I. Miller [463 . . .] adapted Rogers' story to the screen.

Though overlooked by the Academy's writers branch in the nominations, Rogers benefited from Warners' fury over the omission of many of its films from the nominees, especially *Captain Blood* and *A Midsummer Night's Dream*. Pressured by the studio, the Academy allowed write-in votes on the final ballot, and Warners made sure its employees had the studio's interests at heart when they voted. Rogers came in second, losing to Ben Hecht and Charles MacArthur for *The Scoundrel*.

742 • GABY—A TRUE STORY

G. BRIMMER PRODUCTION; TRI-STAR. 1987.
NOMINATION *Supporting Actress:* Norma Aleandro.

Rachel Levin plays Gaby Brimmer, a young woman born with cerebral palsy who surmounts grave disability to get an education and become an author. Well-done film, subsequently somewhat outshone by *My Left Foot*. Luis Mandoki directs, and the cast includes Liv Ullmann [610 . . .] and Robert Loggia [1039].

Aleandro, who plays the maid who devotes herself to Gaby and discovers that she can communicate with her, despite the girl's inability to speak, won the best actress award at Cannes for her performance in *The Official Story*. She is also well known in Argentina as a playwright and director. The Oscar went to Olympia Dukakis for *Moonstruck*.

743 • GAILY, GAILY

MIRISCH-CARTIER PRODUCTIONS; UNITED ARTISTS. 1969.
NOMINATIONS *Art Direction—Set Decoration:* Robert Boyle and George B. Chan; Edward Boyle and Carl

Biddiscombe. *Sound:* Robert Martin and Clem Portman. *Costume Design:* Ray Aghayan.

Beau Bridges plays Ben Harvey in this adaptation of the memoirs of Ben Hecht [78 . . .] dealing with his years as a young reporter in Chicago. Promising material, and it has a good director, Norman Jewison [659 . . .], and a strong cast: Melina Mercouri [1426] as a madam, Brian Keith as a veteran reporter, Hume Cronyn [1791] as a political hack, plus George Kennedy [443], Wilfred Hyde-White, and Margot Kidder in her film debut. But something went awry, and it's phony, busy, and unfunny. The art direction and sound awards went to *Hello, Dolly!* Margaret Furse won the costume Oscar for *Anne of the Thousand Days.*

R. Boyle: 659, 1450, 1816. E. Boyle: 91, 393, 709, 1783, 1860, 1866. Biddiscombe: 2120. Aghayan: 738, 1126.

744 • *GAMBIT*

UNIVERSAL. 1966.

NOMINATIONS *Color Art Direction—Set Decoration:* Alexander Golitzen and George C. Webb; John McCarthy and John Austin. *Sound:* Waldon O. Watson, sound director, Universal City Studio Sound Department. *Color Costume Design:* Jean Louis.

Michael Caine [35 . . .] plays a thief with his sights set on a priceless statuette owned by Herbert Lom. He enlists the aid of a Eurasian woman, played by Shirley MacLaine [91 . . .] to help him steal it. Entertaining caper movie and star vehicle, very much inspired by the success of *Topkapi.* There's nothing new here, but in a way that's what's so pleasant about it. Directed by Ronald Neame [289 . . .]. The Oscars went to *Fantastic Voyage* for art direction, *Grand Prix* for sound, and Elizabeth Haffenden and Joan Bridge for the costumes of *A Man for All Seasons.*

Golitzen: 31, 96, 414, 591, 690, 706, 1560, 1886, 1968, 1986, 2035, 2064, 2101. Webb: 32, 1986, 2064. McCarthy: 1642. Watson: 350, 655, 690, 1810, 2035. Louis: 20, 126, 170, 262, 732, 1028, 1065, 1521, 1640, 1812, 1858, 1910, 2064.

745 • *GANDHI*

INDO-BRITISH FILM PRODUCTION; COLUMBIA (UNITED KINGDOM). 1982.

AWARDS *Picture:* Richard Attenborough, producer. *Actor:* Ben Kingsley. *Director:* Richard Attenborough. *Screenplay Written Directly for the Screen:* John Briley. *Cinematography:* Billy Williams and Ronnie Taylor. *Art Direction—Set Decoration:* Stuart Craig and Bob Laing; Michael Seirton. *Film Editing:* John Bloom. *Costume Design:* John Mollo and Bhanu Athaiya.

NOMINATIONS *Sound:* Gerry Humphreys, Robin O'Donoghue, Jonathan Bates, and Simon Kaye. *Original Score:* Ravi Shankar and George Fenton. *Makeup:* Tom Smith.

Kingsley plays the Indian political and spiritual leader from his days as a young lawyer battling racial injustice in South Africa to his martyrdom after winning independence for India. Long (three hours plus) biopic of undeniable sweep and authenticity, but its reverential tone gets tedious after an hour or so. The enormous cast rounds up most of the Brits who usually do turns in costume epics: John Gielgud [103 . . .], Trevor Howard [1875], John Mills [1737], Michael Hordern, Edward Fox. Plus a few Americans: Candice Bergen [1919], Martin Sheen, John Ratzenberger. And some eminent international actors: Athol Fugard, Roshan Seth, Saeed Jaffrey. A then-unknown Daniel Day-Lewis [992.5 . . .] plays a young street punk who hassles Gandhi during his stay in England.

Gandhi was not the year's most popular film; that honor clearly belongs to *E.T. The Extra-Terrestrial.* Nor did it exhibit the most provocative blend of message and entertainment; that honor goes to *Tootsie,* the gender-switching comedy that acutely examined sexism. And in the long run, *Gandhi* certainly hasn't proved the most durable success. Even at the time, its triumph at the Oscars was seen as a manifestation of the Academy's tendency to reward earnest competence over inventive brilliance. Some thought the Academy was punishing Steven Spielberg for becoming too successful too fast, or Dustin Hoffman for being a difficult perfectionist. But *Gandhi* also benefited from being a late-year release, making it the movie freshest in the voters' minds as they filled out their Oscar ballots. *E.T.* had been in the theaters a long time, and its merchandising spin-offs—dolls, books, records—had been so ubiquitous in the Christmas season that they doubtless inspired a backlash, conscious or not. And *Tootsie* was ''just'' a comedy—no comedy has won best picture since *Annie Hall* in 1977. All things considered, *Gandhi* looked like the right blend of political correctness and dedicated filmmaking to most Academy voters.

Also influential in many voters' minds was Attenborough's well-publicized struggle to get the film made. He had begun planning a movie about Gandhi as early as 1963 and had talked at that time with Alec Guinness [287 . . .] about playing the role. Guinness grew too old, and Attenborough subsequently considered Albert Finney [579 . . .], Dirk Bogarde, Peter Finch [1424 . . .], Tom Courtenay [558 . . .], John Hurt [608 . . .], and Anthony Hopkins [1679.5 . . .] as he sought funding. He also worked with a series of screenwriters, including Donald Ogden Stewart [1148 . . .] and Robert Bolt [558 . . .]. Bolt wanted Fred Zinnemann [732 . . .] or David Lean [287 . . .] to direct if he did the screenplay. Eventually Attenborough assembled the funding, including $7 million from the government of India, and decided to direct the film himself. He had begun acting in his teens in the film *In Which We Serve* and had become an impressive character actor over the years. He turned to directing in 1969 with the film of the antiwar revue *Oh, What a Lovely War!* and followed with two epics, *Young Winston* and *A Bridge Too Far,* neither very successful at the box office, but clear evidence of his ability to handle the David Lean–style costume picture that *Gandhi* was destined to become. In recent years Attenborough has generously commented that Spielberg, in whose *Jurassic Park* he subsequently appeared, probably should have received the Oscar as director. Few of Attenborough's films show signs that he enjoyed making them very much. And while earnestness and efficiency may be appropriate in making a film like *Gandhi,* the absence of joy turned his film of *A Chorus Line* into a disaster, and the absence of wit made *Chaplin* into a

drag. In 1993 he directed perhaps his best film, *Shadowlands,* a small, quiet showcase for acting that suggests Attenborough's talents may have been sorely misapplied in overseeing blockbuster epics.

The best thing about *Gandhi* is the man who plays him. Kingsley, a Royal Shakespeare Company actor, is part Indian—he was born Krishna Banji. His versatility has been shown in parts as various as an American gangster in *Bugsy,* a domineering chess master in *Searching for Bobby Fischer,* and the Jewish bookkeeper in *Schindler's List.* Kingsley's Gandhi is saintly but also cunning, with a centered self-possession that grows perceptibly throughout the film. It's not easy to say that Kingsley deserved the Oscar more than Hoffman in *Tootsie* or Paul Newman in *The Verdict,* the two most impressive competitors for the award, but the Academy didn't disgrace itself by voting for him.

Briley started his work on the screenplay by trying to rewrite Bolt's script but eventually decided to do it himself. To assure the cooperation of the Indian government, the script sidesteps the darker aspects of Gandhi's life, including his troubled relationship with his children and the allegations that Gandhi broke his vow of chastity.

In the three categories in which *Gandhi* didn't win, the Oscars went to *E.T.* for sound and John Williams' score, and to the makeup team of *Quest for Fire.*

Kingsley: 308. Williams: 1473, 2307. Craig: 382.5, 485, 608, 1331. Laing: 2134. Seirton: 1678. Bloom: 398, 725. Mollo: 1916. Humphreys: 398. Kaye: 1138.5, 1584, 1678. Fenton: 471, 485, 671.

746 • *GANG'S ALL HERE, THE*

20TH CENTURY-FOX. 1943.

NOMINATION *Color Interior Decoration:* James Basevi and Joseph C. Wright, art direction; Thomas Little, set decoration.

Well-nigh indescribable musical, whose nugatory plot—something about the romantic rivalry of Alice Faye and Carmen Miranda over serviceman James Ellison—isn't worth going into. All you really need to know is that this was directed by Busby Berkeley [791 . . .] and that the musical numbers he staged have all the mad inventiveness of the ones he did for

Warners *Gold Diggers* series and other musicals in the thirties, with the addition of some of the most lurid Technicolor ever committed to celluloid. The highlight is Miranda's "The Lady in the Tutti-Frutti Hat," with chorus girls handling fruits and vegetables in ways that make you sure the censors had never read Freud. The cast also includes Benny Goodman and his orchestra, Eugene Pallette, Charlotte Greenwood, and Edward Everett Horton. How can you resist? Well, there *is* that plot. The art direction Oscar went to *The Phantom of the Opera*.

Basevi: 1082, 1868, 2245, 2316. Wright: 235, 428, 508, 569, 690, 852, 1175, 1264, 1397, 1475, 2056. Little: 46, 83, 235, 428, 495, 719, 721, 950, 952, 1082, 1149, 1153, 1397, 1475, 1666, 1852, 1868, 2056, 2212, 2286.

747 • GARDEN OF ALLAH, THE

Selznick International Pictures; United Artists. 1936.
Award *Special Award:* W. Howard Greene and Harold Rosson for color cinematography.
Nominations *Assistant Director:* Eric G. Stacey. *Score:* Selznick International Pictures Music Department, Max Steiner, head; score by Max Steiner.

Marlene Dietrich [1358], a rich woman sojourning in the desert, meets and marries Charles Boyer [36 . . .], who turns out to be a Trappist monk who has escaped the monastery and is inevitably drawn back by pangs of conscience. High-camp stuff from a novel by Robert Hichens that had been filmed twice as a silent. It was latched onto by David O. Selznick [497 . . .] for an early experiment with three-color Technicolor; Selznick's backer, multimillionaire Jock Whitney, owned stock in Technicolor and was eager to see it thrive on the screen. It was the last film completed by director Richard Boleslawski, who died, aged forty-eight, soon after its completion. (There are those who blame Selznick, that ineluctable meddler, for Boleslawski's premature demise.) The movie is more than a bit too much, as its supporting cast suggests: Basil Rathbone [979 . . .], Joseph Schildkraut [1169], John Carradine, C. Aubrey Smith, and dancer Tilly Losch—all of them prime hams. Dietrich and Boyer both regretted making the film.

"It's twash, isn't it?" Dietrich asked dialogue director Joshua Logan [643 . . .], who had been brought in to tame the accents of its stars.

The color is the film's chief claim to fame, but it is a bit on the garish side and tends to fade in and out. Greene had been experimenting with color since the twenties, including two-color sequences photographed for *Ben-Hur* in 1925. Rosson had worked as a cameraman since 1915 and continued in films until the late sixties.

The assistant director Oscar went to Jack Sullivan for *The Charge of the Light Brigade*. The scoring award was won by Erich Wolfgang Korngold's work on *Anthony Adverse*.

Greene: 96, 239, 1070, 1452, 1560, 1621, 1909, 2262. Rosson: 256, 2055, 2300. Stacey: 1327, 1909. Steiner: 16, 154, 190, 330, 365, 385, 492, 679, 754, 798, 999, 1043, 1046, 1052, 1162, 1169, 1170, 1207, 1324, 1408, 1430, 1456, 1690, 1779, 1828.

748 • GARDEN OF THE FINZI-CONTINIS, THE

Gianni Hecht Lucari-Arthur Cohn Production; Cinema 5 Ltd. (Italy). 1971.
Award *Foreign Language Film.*
Nomination *Screenplay—Based on Material From Another Medium:* Ugo Pirro and Vittorio Bonicelli.

The Finzi-Continis, a wealthy Jewish family in Ferrara, try to maintain their elegant, aristocratic lives behind their garden walls when the fascists begin to bar Jews from outside institutions. Their denial of the inevitable, of course, has a tragic end. Richly observed and poignant re-creation of an era by Vittorio De Sica [650]. Even the beautiful people, he seems to be saying, have souls, and he manages to make us care about them. The screenwriting award went to Ernest Tidyman for *The French Connection*.

Pirro: 1009.

749 • GASLIGHT

MGM. 1944.
Awards *Actress:* Ingrid Bergman. *Black-and-White Interior Decoration:* Cedric Gibbons and William Ferrari,

art direction; Edwin B. Willis and Paul Huldschinsky, set decoration.

NOMINATIONS *Picture:* Arthur Hornblow, Jr., producer. *Actor:* Charles Boyer. *Supporting Actress:* Angela Lansbury. *Screenplay:* John L. Balderston, Walter Reisch, and John Van Druten. *Black-and-White Cinematography:* Joseph Ruttenberg.

The psychotic Boyer tries to drive his young wife, Bergman, mad to prevent her uncovering his secrets. This thriller with a Victorian setting was actually a remake of a superior British film, released in the States in 1940 as *Angel Street.* MGM attempted to suppress the original version when it issued the remake. It's effective and well acted, but a little too lavish for its own good. George Cukor [262 . . .] directed, and the cast includes Joseph Cotten and May Whitty [1371 . . .].

Some have thought Bergman's Oscar a consolation prize for losing the year before, when she was nominated for *For Whom the Bell Tolls* and starred in that year's best picture, *Casablanca.* Bergman had been discovered by Kay Brown, who worked for David O. Selznick [497 . . .] in his New York office, in the 1936 Swedish film *Intermezzo,* to which Selznick bought the rights for an American remake. The 1939 film, costarring Leslie Howard, was a hit, and Selznick began to promote Bergman heavily. When *Gaslight* was being cast, he insisted on her receiving top billing. Boyer, who had been a star much longer, protested, and for a time there was thought of casting Greer Garson [239 . . .], Irene Dunne [114 . . .], or Hedy Lamarr instead. Selznick finally yielded on the billing when Hornblow agreed to cast Cotten, another Selznick player, in a supporting role.

Hornblow had received his law degree before World War I, but after the war he gave up the law to write and produce for Broadway. He came to Hollywood in 1927 and worked for Goldwyn and Paramount before moving to MGM in 1942. He became an independent producer in the fifties. The best picture Oscar went to *Going My Way.*

Bergman later referred to Boyer as ''the most intelligent actor I ever worked with.'' He had received an honorary award from the Academy in 1942 for his work in establishing the French Research Foundation in Los Angeles, a very personal charity, dedicated largely to teaching Hollywood about France, but also to aiding French exiles during the war. He was considered the leading contender for the Oscar after *Gaslight* became a hit, but Bing Crosby won for *Going My Way,* which was a bigger hit.

Lansbury was only seventeen when she made her film debut in *Gaslight,* but she appeared much older, and in later films often played the mothers of men her age. Born in London, she came to the United States during the war and studied drama in New York before winning an MGM contract. She lost the first of her three unsuccessful nominations to Ethel Barrymore in *None but the Lonely Heart.*

Balderston was a specialist in the suspense genre. He wrote the plays on which the 1931 horror films *Dracula* and *Frankenstein* were based, and worked on many fantasy, horror, and period adventure screenplays. Van Druten was a successful playwright, best known for the Broadway hits *The Voice of the Turtle* and *I Remember Mama.* Reisch was the most experienced screenwriter of the three. They lost to the writers of the *Going My Way* screenplay.

The cinematography award went to Joseph LaShelle for *Lifeboat.*

Bergman: 72, 111, 173, 701, 1048, 1378. Gibbons: 66, 87, 130, 217, 227, 239, 285, 290, 440, 629, 831, 980, 1069, 1096, 1173, 1190, 1226, 1230, 1232, 1274, 1308, 1309, 1417, 1567, 1604, 1644, 1662, 1673, 1721, 1861, 1937, 2068, 2112, 2256, 2257, 2300, 2320, 2330. Ferrari: 953. Willis: 66, 87, 130, 227, 239, 290, 629, 831, 980, 1069, 1096, 1157, 1173, 1190, 1226, 1230, 1232, 1309, 1417, 1567, 1657, 1662, 1673, 1721, 1861, 1937, 2068, 2112, 2257, 2320, 2330. Hornblow: 925, 1732, 2297. Boyer: 36, 440, 643. Lansbury: 1265, 1567. Balderston: 1194. Reisch: 435, 1440, 2093. Ruttenberg: 318, 573, 769, 828, 1069, 1232, 1371, 1861, 2234.

750 • GATE OF HELL

DAIEI PRODUCTION; EDWARD HARRISON (JAPAN). 1954.
AWARDS *Color Costume Design:* Sanzo Wada. *Honorary Award:* Best Foreign Language Film.

In twelfth-century Japan a samurai demands the wife of a nobleman as a reward, but she kills herself. Ravishingly beautiful film that makes up for its narrative simplicity with extraordinary visuals. Machiko Kyo is outstanding as the wife. Written and directed by Teinosuke Kinugasa and photographed by Kohei Sugiyama.

751 • GATES OF PARIS

FILMSONOR S.A. PRODUCTION (FRANCE). 1957.
NOMINATION *Foreign Language Film.*

Pierre Brasseur is an aimless, alcoholic layabout who conspires to hide a fugitive from the police but winds up killing him. Low-key, slowly paced character study by René Clair, not particularly well received at the time by the critics, though it has gained in stature over the years. The Oscar went to *The Nights of Cabiria.*

752 • GATHERING OF EAGLES, A

UNIVERSAL. 1963.
NOMINATION *Sound Effects:* Robert L. Bratton.

Rock Hudson [768] plays an officer assigned to make a Strategic Air Command base shape up, but his devotion to the task makes plenty of enemies and puts a strain on his marriage. Not badly done, but somewhat uninvolving. Directed by Delbert Mann [1283] from a screenplay by Robert Pirosh [157 . . .], with Rod Taylor, Barry Sullivan, and Kevin McCarthy [515]. The sound effects Oscar went to *It's a Mad, Mad, Mad, Mad World.*

Bratton: 1193.

753 • GAY DECEPTION, THE

JESSE L. LASKY; FOX. 1935.
NOMINATION *Original Story:* Don Hartman and Stephen Avery.

Francis Lederer plays a prince from a middle-European country who poses as a doorman and woos secretary Frances Dee. Pleasant, forgettable little Cin-

derella romance, nicely directed by William Wyler [175 . . .], with Benita Hume, Alan Mowbray, and Akim Tamiroff [701 . . .]. Ben Hecht and Charles MacArthur won the writing Oscar for *The Scoundrel.*

Hartman: 1703.

754 • GAY DIVORCÉE, THE

RKO RADIO. 1934.
AWARD *Song:* "The Continental," music by Con Conrad, lyrics by Herb Magidson.
NOMINATIONS *Picture:* Pandro S. Berman, producer. *Interior Decoration:* Van Nest Polglase and Carroll Clark. *Sound Recording:* Carl Dreher. *Score:* RKO Radio Studio Music Department, Max Steiner, head; score by Kenneth Webb and Samuel Hoffenstein.

Seeking a divorce, Ginger Rogers [1102] goes to an English seaside resort to meet a professional corespondent—a man who makes his living by spending the night (or appearing to spend the night) with women who want to obtain divorces. There she encounters Fred Astaire [2126] and develops the mistaken notion that he's the corespondent. The rest is the usual agreeable nonsense, made more agreeable by its stars and a supporting cast that includes Alice Brady [990 . . .], Edward Everett Horton, Erik Rhodes, Eric Blore, and seventeen-year-old Betty Grable, directed by Mark Sandrich. Astaire had starred in the stage version opposite Claire Luce, and RKO had first thought of reteaming them on screen. But the first Astaire-Rogers pairing, in *Flying Down to Rio,* made such an impression that Rogers was cast instead. The play had been called *The Gay Divorce,* and it's generally thought the Production Code's strictures about upholding the sanctity of marriage led to the title change, although some have suggested that the title of *The Gay Divorcée* is a witty paraphrase of *The Merry Widow,* which MGM filmed the same year.

The other major change from stage to screen involves the score. The New York and London productions had included thirteen songs by Cole Porter [261 . . .], but only one, "Night and Day," made it into the film version. Conrad and Magidson contributed two songs, Harry Revel [1291 . . .] and Mack Gordon [428 . . .] two more. "The Continental" is the first winner of a best song Oscar, beating the song that inspired it, "Carioca," from *Flying Down to Rio*.

The race for best picture contained twelve entries; the winner was *It Happened One Night*. *The Merry Widow* took the art direction Oscar, but not by much: Polglase and Clark came in second, only two votes behind the winners, Cedric Gibbons and Frederic Hope. The film placed third in the sound race and second in the competition for scoring; both of those awards went to *One Night of Love*.

Magidson: 907, 1830. Berman: 40, 656, 1035, 1899, 2115. Polglase: 358, 407, 1212, 1394, 2115. Clark: 4, 481, 686, 1284, 1924, 2115. Dreher: 966. Steiner: 16, 154, 190, 330, 365, 385, 492, 679, 747, 798, 999, 1043, 1046, 1052, 1162, 1169, 1170, 1207, 1324, 1408, 1430, 1456, 1690, 1779, 1828. Hoffenstein: 572, 1149.

755 • GAZEBO, THE

AVON PRODUCTIONS INC.; MGM. 1959.

NOMINATION *Black-and-White Costume Design:* Helen Rose.

Writer Glenn Ford thinks he's murdered a man who's blackmailing him, and tries to conceal his body in the gazebo in his backyard. Forgettable black-comedy farce from a play by Alec Coppel [354], directed by George Marshall and made tolerable by a bright cast: Debbie Reynolds [2184], Carl Reiner, Doro Merande, and John McGiver. The costumes by Orry-Kelly for *Some Like It Hot* won the Oscar.

Rose: 130, 578, 629, 817, 980, 1007, 1309, 1335, 1599.

756 • GENERAL DELLA ROVERE

ZEBRA & S. N. E. GAUMONT PRODUCTION; CONTINENTAL DISTRIBUTING INC. (ITALY). 1961.

NOMINATION *Story and Screenplay—Written Directly for the Screen:* Sergio Amidei, Diego Fabbri, and Indro Montanelli.

Con artist Vittorio de Sica [650] is persuaded by the Nazis to pose as the general, a leader of the Resistance, and spy on other members of the Resistance in prison. But he is so taken with the role, and with the character of the man he is impersonating,

that he becomes a hero instead. A tour de force performance by de Sica keeps this overlong film by Roberto Rossellini [1519] from falling into predictability and sentimentality. The Oscar went to William Inge for *Splendor in the Grass*.

Amidei: 1496, 1519, 1815.

757 • GENERAL DIED AT DAWN, THE

PARAMOUNT. 1936.

NOMINATIONS *Supporting Actor:* Akim Tamiroff. *Cinematography:* Victor Milner. *Score:* Paramount Studio Music Department, Boris Morros, head; score by Werner Janssen.

Gary Cooper [701 . . .] romances spy Madeleine Carroll and foils evil Chinese warlord Tamiroff. Fine romantic hokum from a screenplay by Clifford Odets, directed by Lewis Milestone [48 . . .]. In addition to Dudley Digges, Porter Hall, and William Frawley, the cast includes Milestone, Odets, novelist John O'Hara, and gossip columnist Sidney Skolsky in bit parts.

Tamiroff, a Russian-born actor trained at the Moscow Art Theater, was Hollywood's all-purpose foreigner—sometimes menacing, sometimes comic, sometimes Chinese, or Russian, or Mexican, or whatever—in films from *Queen Christina* in 1933 to *The Great Bank Robbery* in 1969. He lost the award—the first ever presented to a supporting actor—to Walter Brennan in *Come and Get It*.

Anthony Adverse (in which Tamiroff was Italian) won for Gaetano Gaudio's cinematography and for Erich Wolfgang Korngold's score.

Tamiroff: 701. Milner: 304, 412, 470, 740, 827, 1217, 1452, 1668. Morros: 1880, 2145. Janssen: 233, 349, 624, 844, 1884.

757.5 • GENERAL SPANKY

HAL ROACH; MGM. 1936.

NOMINATION *Sound Recording:* Elmer A. Raguse, sound director.

George "Spanky" McFarland, Billie "Buckwheat" Thomas, and Carl "Alfalfa" Switzer appear as their familiar characters from the Our Gang shorts, but in a feature-length film with a Civil War setting. Boring second-feature stuff, and the racial attitudes make it only barely tolerable today. The cast, which includes Phillips Holmes, Ralph Morgan, and Louise Beavers, is directed by Fred Newmeyer and Gordon Douglas. The sound Oscar went to Douglas Shearer for *San Francisco.*

Raguse: 345, 1306, 1464, 1487, 2117, 2118.

758 • GENEVIEVE

J. Arthur Rank-Sirius Productions Ltd.; Universal-International (United Kingdom). 1954.

Nominations *Story and Screenplay:* William Rose. *Scoring of a Dramatic or Comedy Picture:* Larry Adler. (The nominee originally announced was Muir Mathieson. In June 1986 the Board of Governors removed Mathieson's name from the Academy records and replaced it with that of the actual composer of the film's score, Larry Adler.)

The title refers to an antique car that John Gregson and Dinah Sheridan enter in a race from Brighton to London. Their archrivals are Kenneth More and Kay Kendall. Charming comedy, directed by Henry Cornelius and greatly enlivened by Kendall's peerless performance as a dizzy model who happens to play a wicked trumpet. It belongs to a period when the British seemed to have nothing going for them but charm, turning out one classic comedy after another. Meanwhile the Americans, anguished by the Cold War and McCarthyism, were concentrating on dramas like *On the Waterfront,* which won the Oscar for Budd Schulberg's screenplay. McCarthyism took its toll even on *Genevieve,* however: The original nominee for scoring, Mathieson, was the film's arranger and orchestra conductor, who had never claimed credit for the score. The actual composer was Larry Adler, a famous American harmonica virtuoso who was blacklisted in his native land. Mathieson's name was substituted for Adler's in the credits on prints distributed in the United States. The Academy Board of Governors made restitution to Adler thirty-two years later by inserting his name as the official nominee in the permanent record. The scoring award went to Dimitri Tiomkin for *The High and the Mighty.*

Rose: 843, 1128, 1736.

759 • GENTLEMAN'S AGREEMENT

20th Century-Fox. 1947.

Awards *Picture:* Darryl F. Zanuck, producer. *Supporting Actress:* Celeste Holm. *Director:* Elia Kazan.

Nominations *Actor:* Gregory Peck. *Actress:* Dorothy McGuire. *Supporting Actress:* Anne Revere. *Screenplay:* Moss Hart. *Film Editing:* Harmon Jones.

Peck plays a journalist who has an eye-opening experience when he poses as a Jew for a story about anti-Semitism. Today this earnest melodrama, based on a novel by Laura Z. Hobson, seems tame and somewhat too proud of being "controversial." There are too many stars making too many big speeches; in addition to the four nominees, the cast includes John Garfield [251 . . .], June Havoc, Albert Dekker, Jane Wyatt, Sam Jaffe [105], Gene Nelson, and eleven-year-old Dean Stockwell [1281]. But in the postwar years, when liberals hoped that the spirit of unity that defeated the Nazis would carry into the solution of social problems in America, the film was considered to be sincere and hard-hitting. It was the third best picture winner in a row with a social conscience, following *The Lost Weekend*'s look at alcoholism and *The Best Years of Our Lives'* concern about the reintegration of veterans into the social fabric. Zanuck, who was unique among the studio heads in not being Jewish, persisted in making the film over the objections of men like Louis B. Mayer, Sam Goldwyn [102 . . .], and Jack Warner [55 . . .], who were deeply concerned that a film about anti-Semitism would draw the fire of anti-Semites against the movie industry. In fact, Zanuck's was not the only film about anti-Semitism to be nominated for the best picture Oscar: *Crossfire* dealt with the same theme. (The other nominations were less controversial: *The Bishop's Wife, Great Expectations,* and *Miracle on 34th Street.*) Zanuck was vindicated when the movie was a critical and commercial success.

Holm had signed a contract with Fox only a year before her Oscar-winning role. She had become a Broadway star in 1943 with the comedy role of Ado Annie in the original production of *Oklahoma!* Usually cast in second leads, she was a reliable film presence into the mid-fifties, after which she divided her time more often among movies, TV, and theater. She is still seen in occasional character roles, most recently in *Three Men and a Baby* (1987).

Kazan was born in Turkey of Greek parents and came to the States as a small boy. Though he spent some time in Hollywood in the thirties, his early career was in the New York theater, where his renown as a director caused Zanuck to lure him to Hollywood. In the fifties his career was threatened when he refused to testify against former leftist colleagues before the House Un-American Activities Committee. But he changed his mind and in 1952 gave the committee the names they wanted. As a result, he was spared the blacklist but also earned the enmity of many who lost their jobs, as well as many who sympathized with them.

Peck lost his third nomination to Ronald Colman for *A Double Life.* McGuire, in her sole Oscar bid, lost to Loretta Young in *The Farmer's Daughter.*

Revere, who had won the award two years earlier for *National Velvet,* lost to Holm. In 1951 she would take the Fifth Amendment before HUAC and as a consequence be blacklisted. By the end of the fifties she would resume her acting career on Broadway but would not make another movie until 1970, when she appeared in *Tell Me That You Love Me, Junie Moon.*

Hart, a major Broadway director and playwright—often in collaboration with George S. Kaufman—wrote only a handful of screenplays, the most significant of which are this one and the script for the 1954 film of *A Star Is Born.* He lost to George Seaton for *Miracle on 34th Street.*

The editing Oscar went to Francis Lyon and Robert Parrish for *Body and Soul.*

Zanuck: 34, 46, 550, 710, 815, 946, 952, 990, 1201, 1327, 1666, 2154, 2286. Holm: 46, 428. Kazan: 63, 593, 1477, 1949. Peck: 1082, 2101, 2154, 2320. Revere: 1417, 1868. Hart: 297.

760 • *GEORGE WASHINGTON SLEPT HERE*

WARNER BROS. 1942.

NOMINATION *Black-and-White Interior Decoration:* Max Parker and Mark-Lee Kirk, art direction; Casey Roberts, set decoration.

City folk Jack Benny and Ann Sheridan decide to get away from it all and move to the country, but their ramshackle farmhouse and oddball neighbors prove more trying than the city. Somewhat flat-footed and predictable comedy, based on one of the lesser plays of George S. Kaufman and Moss Hart [297 . . .]. Fortunately it has a good supporting cast: Charles Coburn [535 . . .], Hattie McDaniel [798], Franklin Pangborn, and Percy Kilbride, whose similar character in a movie with a similar premise, *The Egg and I,* led to the *Ma and Pa Kettle* series. Directed by William Keighley. The art direction award went to *This Above All.*

Kirk: 1394, 1828. Roberts: 353, 1048.

761 • *GEORGY GIRL*

EVERGLADES PRODUCTIONS LTD.; COLUMBIA (UNITED KINGDOM). 1966.

NOMINATIONS *Actress:* Lynn Redgrave. *Supporting Actor:* James Mason. *Black-and-White Cinematography:* Ken Higgins. *Song:* ''Georgy Girl,'' music by Tom Springfield, lyrics by Jim Dale.

Plain and plump Redgrave takes on the job of mothering roommate Charlotte Rampling's illegitimate child and suddenly becomes the object of the attentions not only of Mason, her employer, but also of Alan Bates [678], Rampling's boyfriend. Once upon a time, this movie, directed by Silvio Narizzano, was thought to be rather naughty. Today, like such sagas of swinging London in the sixties as *Morgan!, Darling,* and *The Knack, and How to Get It* (1965), it seems to be trying a bit too hard. But all four stars are first-rate.

Redgrave found herself in the near-unique position of competing against her own sister, Vanessa, who was nominated for *Morgan!* The only other case of such sibling rivalry was between Joan Fontaine, who won for *Suspicion* when Olivia de Havilland was nominated for *Hold Back the Dawn* in 1941. The Redgraves lost to Elizabeth Taylor in *Who's Afraid of Virginia Woolf?* Lynn, the daughter of Michael Redgrave [1364] and Rachel Kempson, as well as sister of Vanessa and Corin Redgrave, and aunt to Joely and Natasha Richardson, has had a less spectacular career than Vanessa. She made her movie debut in a bit part in *Tom Jones* but is best known for TV work and for Weight Watchers commercials—the latter a direct consequence of the fame that came to her for *Georgy Girl,* after which she was determined not to be typed forever as fat and dowdy. In 1992 she won acclaim for a one-woman show, *Shakespeare for My Father,* that was part dramatic reading, part confessional about the difficulty of growing up as a perceived lesser talent in a theatrical household.

Mason's second nomination came four years after another celebrated role in which he played an older man in pursuit of a younger woman, *Lolita.* This time he lost to Walter Matthau in *The Fortune Cookie.*

Higgins lost to Haskell Wexler for *Who's Afraid of Virginia Woolf?* The best song was John Barry and Don Black's title song for *Born Free.*

Mason: 1910, 2198.

761.5 • GERONIMO: AN AMERICAN LEGEND

COLUMBIA PICTURES PRODUCTION; COLUMBIA. 1993.
NOMINATION *Sound:* Chris Carpenter, D. M. Hemphill, Bill W. Benton, and Lee Orloff.

Jason Patric plays Lt. Charles Gatewood, a young army officer who, aided by a scout, Al Sieber, played by Robert Duvall [92 . . .], attempts to track down and capture the Apache warrior Geronimo (Wes Studi). Gatewood comes to understand what drives his enemy and to sympathize with him but is unable to alter the course of events leading to the dispossession of the Apaches. A serious, intelligent attempt to look at American history from another point of view and to alter the image of the Indian that Hollywood helped create, though the film is somewhat undermined by its earnestness. It was released amid a barrage of other serious films—*Schindler's List, Philadelphia, In the Name of the Father*—and failed to find its own audience. For that matter, it was less audience-friendly—more brutal, less romantic—than *Dances With Wolves,* which had delivered a similar message several years earlier. Directed by Walter Hill from a screenplay by John Milius [92] and Larry Gross, *Geronimo* has a strong cast, including Gene Hackman [255 . . .] and Rodney A. Grant, fine cinematography by Lloyd Ahern, and an elegiac score by Ry Cooder. The sound Oscar went to *Jurassic Park.*

Hemphill: 543, 1138.5. Benton: 482. Orloff: 5, 2019.

762 • GERVAISE

AGNES DELAHAIE PRODUCTIONS CINÉMATOGRAPHIQUES & SILVER FILM; ANNIE DORFMANN, PRODUCER (FRANCE). 1956.
NOMINATION *Foreign Language Film.*

Maria Schell plays the title role, a woman who marries an alcoholic coworker in a laundry after she has been left with two children by her lover. She descends into alcoholism with him. The grimness of this adaptation of Zola's novel *L'Assommoir* is leavened somewhat by the picturesque re-creation of mid-nineteenth-century Paris. Directed by René Clement, with production design by Paul Bertrand and music by Georges Auric. The Oscar (the first competitive foreign film award) went to *La Strada.*

763 • GET OUT YOUR HANDKERCHIEFS

LES FILMS ARIANE-C.A.P.A.C. PRODUCTION (FRANCE). 1978.
AWARD *Foreign Language Film.*

Gérard Depardieu [474] is unable to make his wife happy, so he provides her with a lover who fails, too. Eventually a thirteen-year-old boy makes her both pregnant and contented. Eccentric comedy, directed by Bertrand Blier, that many find charming, but others regard as smutty and misogynistic.

764 • GHOST

HOWARD W. KOCH PRODUCTION; PARAMOUNT. 1990.
AWARDS *Supporting Actress:* Whoopi Goldberg. *Screenplay Written Directly for the Screen:* Bruce Joel Rubin.
NOMINATIONS *Picture:* Lisa Weinstein, producer. *Original Score:* Maurice Jarre. *Film Editing:* Walter Murch.

Yuppie Patrick Swayze is killed in an apparent

mugging but learns in the afterlife that the murderer was hired by someone he trusted. In his ectoplasmic state, he's unable to communicate with his girlfriend, Demi Moore, to warn her that she's in danger from the same person. Then he discovers someone who can hear but not see him—Goldberg, a con artist pretending to be a medium and surprised to learn that she's a real one. Can she persuade Moore that she's on the level and really does have a message from Swayze? What do you think? This very popular romantic comedy-drama bogs down in mush whenever Swayze and Moore are all there is to watch, but pops back to life whenever Goldberg appears. There's also good support from Tony Goldwyn and Vincent Schiavelli, the latter as a ghost who's really ticked off when Swayze turns up on his turf. Directed by Jerry Zucker.

Goldberg was born Caryn Johnson and began her career as a stand-up comedian, which led to a one-woman Broadway show in 1984. She made an impressive film debut in *The Color Purple* but spent the next five years in one bad movie after another. Just when it looked as if her career would consist of sitcom pilots and *Star Trek: The Next Generation* guest appearances, *Ghost* made her a star again—in some polls, the most popular female star in America, and one of the highest paid. *The Player* and *Sister Act* in 1992 reinforced her stature with critics and audiences. She is, it must be noted, only the second black woman to win an acting Oscar—fifty-one years after Hattie McDaniel's win for *Gone With the Wind.*

Rubin, who graduated from NYU film school in the same class as Martin Scorsese [806 . . .] and Brian De Palma, had two tales of the supernatural on screen in 1990. The other, *Jacob's Ladder,* was critically and commercially much less successful.

Ghost was a surprise nominee in the best picture category, competing against *Awakenings, The Godfather, Part III, GoodFellas,* and the winner, *Dances With Wolves.* Zucker was omitted from the directors' slate, however, and many felt the best picture nomination should have gone to either *The Grifters* or *Reversal of Fortune,* whose directors, Stephen Frears and Barbet Schroeder respectively, were nominated.

Jarre's score lost to John Barry's for *Dances With Wolves.* The most memorable music from *Ghost,* however, was not by Jarre at all, but a 1955 Oscar best song nominee, "Unchained Melody," from *Unchained.*

The editing award went to Neil Travis for *Dances With Wolves.*

Goldberg: 423. Jarre: 558, 808, 1151, 1168, 1340, 1533, 1967, 2296. Murch: 92, 442, 786, 1066.

765 • GHOST AND MRS. MUIR, THE
20TH CENTURY-FOX. 1947.
NOMINATION *Black-and-White Cinematography:* Charles Lang, Jr.

Widow Gene Tierney [1153] moves into a seaside cottage that's said to be haunted—and is, by Rex Harrison [413 . . .], a sea captain. Charming sentimental romance, with a screenplay by Philip Dunne [495 . . .]. This one could have gone overboard with too much whimsy or too many tears, but it manages a good balance, thanks to the intelligent direction of Joseph L. Mankiewicz [46 . . .] and an atmospheric score by Bernard Herrmann [50 . . .]. Good supporting cast, too: George Sanders [46], Edna Best, Vanessa Brown, Robert Coote, and nine-year-old Natalie Wood [1219 . . .]. The cinematography Oscar was won by Guy Green for *Great Expectations.*

Lang: 97, 250, 319, 636, 649, 705, 953, 1480, 1640, 1699, 1738, 1778, 1855, 1860, 1955, 1968, 2180.

766 • GHOSTBUSTERS
COLUMBIA PICTURES PRODUCTION; COLUMBIA. 1984.
NOMINATIONS *Song:* "Ghostbusters," music and lyrics by Ray Parker, Jr. *Visual Effects:* Richard Edlund, John Bruno, Mark Vargo, and Chuck Gasper.

Bill Murray, Dan Aykroyd [580], and Harold Ramis set up shop as Ghostbusters—exterminators of goblins and poltergeists and the like. Turns out there's a big call for that in New York City, especially after some heavy-duty demons invade the apartment of Sigourney Weaver [45 . . .] and take possession of her and Rick Moranis. The result is a paranormal showdown with all-out special effects. The movie cost a mint but made it all back with several hundred million to spare, though it's really rather clunky and heavy-handed. As long as Murray is on screen being unflappable, it's splendid, and Weaver makes a superb foil for him. But Aykroyd and Ramis, who wrote the script, forgot to write parts for themselves, and director Ivan Reitman hasn't found the right pacing for the action or the comedy. Basically it's a kids' movie with Murray and Weaver thrown in to keep the adults happy.

Stevie Wonder's "I Just Called to Say I Love You," from *The Woman in Red,* won the song Oscar. The visual effects award went to *Indiana Jones and the Temple of Doom.*

Edlund: 45.5, 544, 614, 1589, 1590, 1652, 1684, 1916, 2165. Bruno: 5, 153.5, 413.5, 1590, 2147.5.

767 • *G.I. HONEYMOON*

MONOGRAM. 1945.

NOMINATION *Scoring of a Dramatic or Comedy Picture:* Edward J. Kay.

Gale Storm marries a soldier, but his duties constantly keep them from consummating the marriage. Sniggery little comedy that was among the twenty-one nominees in this category thanks to Academy rules that allowed each studio or production company to submit an entry. The Oscar went to Miklos Rozsa for *Spellbound.*

Kay: 1092, 1103, 1121, 1965.

768 • *GIANT*

GIANT PRODUCTION; WARNER BROS. 1956.

AWARD *Director:* George Stevens.

NOMINATIONS *Picture:* George Stevens and Henry Ginsberg, producers. *Actor:* James Dean. *Actor:* Rock Hudson. *Supporting Actress:* Mercedes McCambridge. *Screenplay—Adapted:* Fred Guiol and Ivan Moffat. *Color Art Direction—Set Decoration:* Boris Leven; Ralph S. Hurst. *Scoring of a Dramatic or Comedy Picture:* Dimitri Tiomkin. *Film Editing:* William Hornbeck, Philip W. Anderson, and Fred Bohanan. *Color Costume Design:* Moss Mabry and Marjorie Best.

Easterner Elizabeth Taylor [318 . . .] marries rancher Hudson and goes with him to his enormous Texas spread, where she undergoes culture shock but finally proves her mettle. Among other things, she has to contend with Hudson's stubborn, resentful sister, McCambridge, and learn to deal with ne'er-do-well neighbor Dean. Then Dean strikes oil and his wealth and power exceed that of cattleman Hudson. Taylor and Hudson's children grow up to face new problems: Son Dennis Hopper [595 . . .] marries a Mexican-American, and daughter Carroll Baker [119] develops a thing for the aging Dean. The cliché description of this epic is "sprawling," and for once the cliché can't be bettered. The movie flops out over more than three hours' running time and throws dozens of characters at us—Chill Wills [33] as Hudson's uncle, Jane Withers as a blowsy, good-hearted neighbor, Sal Mineo [630 . . .] as a Mexican-American war hero, Earl Holliman, Judith Evelyn, Rod Taylor, Alexander Scourby—and somehow never loses our interest. It's a tribute to Stevens' ability to tell a story, even if the story, from a big flabby novel by Edna Ferber, is predictable. Unfortunately *Giant* also demonstrates Stevens' tendency to overstatement that would become a fatal flaw in his subsequent films, especially *The Diary of Anne Frank,* an overinflated version of what should have been an intimate, small-scale drama, and *The Greatest Story Ever Told,* a life of Christ so excessively star-stuffed as to be almost blasphemous. Critic Andrew Sarris once summed up Stevens as "a minor director with major virtues before *A Place in the Sun,* and a major director with minor virtues after." Stevens died in 1975.

Giant was the right movie for a year of excess. It was defeated for the best picture Oscar by the gargantuan *Around the World in 80 Days,* and one of its chief competitors was the whopping spectacular *The Ten Commandments.* The other two nominees, though not as overloaded as the big three, were still hefty: *The King and I* and *Friendly Persuasion.*

Among the performances, Dean's is the one that made the film legendary, which might not have been the case if Alan Ladd had agreed to play the part. Dean died on September 30, 1955, three days after he finished filming, and some of his dialogue was dubbed by Nick Adams [2157]. This was Dean's second posthumous nomination, and though his death created his mystique, this performance might have done it even if he had lived. It's itchy, offbeat, and marvelously watchable, and it sparks something in Hudson and Taylor that isn't there in the scenes they play without him. It also allows him to demonstrate more range—humor, pathos, rage—than his teen-rebel roles did.

Hudson, despite his physical stature, is too light-weight and boyish for his role, and though it's his only nomination, it's by no means his best performance. He had entered films in 1948 with no acting experience, and his astonishing good looks made him a teen heartthrob, which led to more film roles, eventually allowing him to grow and develop as an actor. He was best in comedies such as *Pillow Talk,* in which he parodies his *Giant* performance when he pretends to be a Texan. But he also gave a strong dramatic performance later in his career, in *Seconds.* As with Dean, his death in 1985 made him a symbol—in Hudson's case, of the tragedy of AIDS and homophobia. Dean and Hudson lost the Oscar to Yul Brynner in *The King and I.*

The supporting actress Oscar went to Hudson's *Written on the Wind* costar, Dorothy Malone. *Around the World in 80 Days* won for James Poe, John Farrow, and S. J. Perelman's screenplay, Victor Young's scoring, and Gene Ruggiero and Paul Weatherwax's editing. *The King and I* took the Oscars for art direction and Irene Sharaff's costumes.

Stevens: 542, 1353, 1579, 1799, 1998. Dean: 593. McCambridge: 53. Leven: 34, 77, 422, 1753, 1801, 1881, 1907, 2244. Tiomkin: 33, 286, 380, 446, 638, 663, 730, 850, 911, 912, 1206, 1347, 1370, 1470, 2006, 2127, 2282, 2335. Hornbeck: 973, 1033, 1579. Anderson: 1529, 1763. Mabry: 1355, 2238, 2247. Best: 15, 833, 1973.

769 • GIGI

ARTHUR FREED PRODUCTIONS INC.; MGM. 1958.

AWARDS *Picture:* Arthur Freed, producer. *Director:* Vincente Minnelli. *Screenplay—Based on Material From Another Medium:* Alan Jay Lerner. *Color Cinematography:* Joseph Ruttenberg. *Art Direction—Set Decoration:* William A. Horning and Preston Ames; Henry Grace and Keogh Gleason. *Song:* ''Gigi,'' music by Frederick Loewe, lyrics by Alan Jay Lerner. *Scoring of a Musical Picture:* André Previn. *Film Editing:* Adrienne Fazan. *Costume Design:* Cecil Beaton.

Leslie Caron [1113 . . .] plays the title role, a Parisian girl being raised in shabby-genteel surroundings by her mother (unseen) and her grandmother, played by Hermione Gingold. Like them, Gigi is expected to become a courtesan—with the hope that she'll have more luck than they at attracting a wealthy patron. To this end, they send her to be tutored in feminine wiles by her Aunt Alicia (Isabel Jeans). Gigi succeeds in attracting the bored but rich Gaston (Louis Jourdan), but more with her fresh and natural ways than with the artifice and sophistication her aunt supplies her. Maurice Chevalier [203 . . .] plays Gaston's uncle, Honoré, and serves as the ironic commentator on the story. This lavish musical sentimentalizes Colette's classic novella and buries it in too much finery and frippery, but it has a great deal of charm, supplied by a first-rate cast—who surprisingly didn't rate a single nomination. (Chevalier received an honorary Oscar ''for his contributions to the world of entertainment for more than half a century.'') Gingold in particular would seem to have merited a supporting actress nomination instead of Peggy Cass in *Auntie Mame,* Martha Hyer in *Some Came Running,* or Cara Williams in *The Defiant Ones.* But even without acting awards, *Gigi* set a new record by taking nine Oscars. The previous record was eight, held by *Gone With the Wind, From Here to Eternity,* and *On the Waterfront. Gigi*'s hold on the record would be short-lived: *Ben-Hur* won eleven the next year.

Gigi's triumph was a valedictory to the golden age of the MGM musical, which Freed had done more than anyone else to create. The studio's ''Freed unit'' had been responsible for such classics as *Meet Me in St. Louis, Easter Parade, Annie Get Your Gun, An American in Paris, Singin' in the Rain,* and *The Band Wagon,* as well as dozens more that are filled with memorable performances and musical numbers. After *Gigi,* Freed would produce only one more musical, *Bells Are Ringing*. He died in 1973.

Minnelli directed the only other Freed musical to win the best picture Oscar, *An American in Paris*. The child of theater people, he had begun his show business career as a set designer and moved into directing Broadway musicals. Freed hired him in 1940, and Minnelli began his screen directing career with *Cabin in the Sky* in 1943. Though best known for his musicals, he also directed such memorable nonmusicals as *Father of the Bride, Madame Bovary, The Bad and the Beautiful, Lust for Life,* and *Some Came Running*. Minnelli died in 1986.

Colette's story had been filmed in France in 1948 with a screenplay on which the author herself collaborated, and Anita Loos had dramatized it for the Broadway stage—a production for which Colette had discovered Audrey Hepburn [278 . . .]. (Hepburn was approached for the musical but declined; Caron, who had played Gigi in the London production of the Loos adaptation, was a natural second choice.) *Gigi* could not have been made in Hollywood five years earlier, when the censors were denying a code seal to *The Moon Is Blue* for uttering the forbidden words "virgin" and "seduce," and Lerner still had to be cautious to get by the censors. At one point Freed even suggested casting Irene Dunne [114 . . .] as Aunt Alicia, with the idea that such an eminently respectable Republican lady would blind the censors to the character's true nature. Dunne, however, was in retirement and not interested in the part. In the end the story's scandalous implications were mostly let slip by. As with *My Fair Lady,* there's a seamless interaction between Lerner's spoken dialogue and Lerner's lyrics. Lerner died in 1986.

This was the fourth and last of Ruttenberg's Oscars, and the only one for a color film. His major challenge on *Gigi* was a variety of Parisian locations, many of which, such as the famous sequence set in Maxim's, had to be lighted and shot quickly because of the limited time they were available. Ruttenberg and Minnelli moved on to filming *The Reluctant Debutante* once principal photography for *Gigi* was concluded, so several retake sequences were directed by

Charles Walters [1173] and shot by Ray June [102 . . .]. Ruttenberg died in 1983.

The music for *Gigi* echoes that of *My Fair Lady* in many ways, including the Oscar-winning title song, plus "It's a Bore" and "She's Not Thinking of Me," which were written for the nonsinger Louis Jourdan, just as *My Fair Lady*'s were designed for nonsinger Rex Harrison. Caron's singing voice was dubbed by Betty Wand.

Beaton, a celebrated designer and photographer, was more than costume designer for *Gigi;* he was the production designer, and the Oscar for art direction should properly have included him as well.

Freed: 66, 1950. Minnelli: 66. Lerner: 66, 1186, 1393, 1731. Ruttenberg: 318, 573, 749, 828, 1069, 1232, 1371, 1861, 2234. Horning: 175, 440, 1157, 1450, 1644, 1657, 2300. Ames: 31, 66, 290, 591, 1226, 1937, 2184. Grace: 69, 227, 401, 953, 1336, 1388, 1450, 1537, 1552, 2157, 2184, 2312. Gleason: 66, 130, 290, 1226, 1861, 1937. Loewe: 1186. Previn: 172, 609, 1017, 1034, 1044, 1097, 1393, 1550, 1592, 2064, 2077, 2161. Fazan: 66. Beaton: 1393.

770 • GIGOT

SEVEN ARTS PRODUCTIONS; 20TH CENTURY-FOX. 1962.
NOMINATION *Scoring of Music—Adaptation or Treatment:* Michel Magne.

Jackie Gleason plays a seriocomic role as a mute who acts as a father substitute to a Parisian waif. Pretty icky. If you suffered through Gleason's mime routines on TV while waiting for the *Honeymooners* sketches, you know what to expect here—except there's a lot more of it. Directed by Gene Kelly [74]. The Oscar went to Ray Heindorf for *The Music Man*.

771 • GIRL SAID NO, THE

GRAND NATIONAL. 1937.
NOMINATION *Sound Recording:* A. E. Kaye.

Dance hall hostess Irene Hervey takes sleazy customer Robert Armstrong for all he's worth. He plots to get even by posing as a theatrical agent, with the idea that when she gets her big break he can recoup his losses. Flimsy B picture whose only virtues are that it's short—about an hour—and that the latter half is filled with bits from, believe it or not, Gilbert and Sullivan operettas. Nominated only because of a rule change guaranteeing every studio an entry in the sound category. The award was won by Thomas Moulton for *The Hurricane*.

772 • GIRL WITH THE PISTOL, THE

DOCUMENTO FILM PRODUCTION (ITALY). 1968.

NOMINATION *Foreign Language Film.*

Monica Vitti plays a Sicilian woman who goes to London in pursuit of a man who abducted her but fled when he found she was more sexually insatiable than he. She falls in love with Stanley Baker. One of the less successful comedies by Mario Monicelli [367 . . .]. The Oscar went to the Soviet *War and Peace*.

773 • GIRLS' SCHOOL

COLUMBIA. 1938.

NOMINATION *Score:* Morris Stoloff and Gregory Stone.

Episodic comedy set in a boarding school for rich girls. The main plotline involves a love triangle centering on a student's pursuit of a man who elopes with one of the teachers. With Anne Shirley [1923], Ralph Bellamy [114], and Marjorie Main [601], among others, directed by John Brahm. Pleasant but terminally dated. Alfred Newman took the Oscar for *Alexander's Ragtime Band*.

Stoloff: 13, 432, 455, 596, 643, 677, 732, 1057, 1058, 1115, 1206, 1862, 1872, 1873, 1998, 2110, 2329.

774 • GIVE 'EM HELL, HARRY!

THEATROVISION PRODUCTION; AVCO EMBASSY. 1975.

NOMINATION *Actor:* James Whitmore.

Not so much a movie as a filmed record of Whitmore's one-man show, reading from the speeches and letters of President Harry S Truman. Fans of either Truman or Whitmore will enjoy it, but this nomination, like the one for Maximilian Schell's performance in another filmed play, *The Man in the Glass Booth*, certainly seems peculiar in a year that included the unnominated performances of Warren Beatty in

Shampoo, Gene Hackman in *Bite the Bullet*, Roy Scheider, Richard Dreyfuss and Robert Shaw in *Jaws*, or—most glaring oversight of all—Sean Connery and Michael Caine in *The Man Who Would Be King*. According to one theory, Schell and Whitmore owe their nominations to the Los Angeles pay-TV Z Channel (a now defunct forerunner of HBO), on which their productions were shown shortly before the nominating ballots were turned in. Jack Nicholson won the Oscar for *One Flew Over the Cuckoo's Nest*.

Whitmore: 157.

775 • GLASS CELL, THE

ROXY FILM PRODUCTION (FEDERAL REPUBLIC OF GERMANY). 1978.

NOMINATION *Foreign Language Film.*

When a school he has designed collapses, an architect serves time in prison. On his release, the person actually responsible for the accident tries to persuade him to commit murder. Thriller based on a novel by Patricia Highsmith, directed by Hans C. Geissendörfer. The cast includes Helmut Griem and Brigitte Fossey. The Oscar went to France's *Get Out Your Handkerchiefs*.

775.5 • GLENGARRY GLEN ROSS

STEPHANIE LYNN PRODUCTION; NEW LINE. 1992.

NOMINATION *Supporting Actor:* Al Pacino.

A group of real estate salesmen—Pacino, Jack Lemmon [91 . . .], Alan Arkin [884 . . .], and Ed Harris—are presented with the ultimate challenge: The one who sells the most real estate gets to keep his job; the runners-up don't. Alternately abrasive and depressing portrait of a group of losers, directed by Sidney Lumet [561 . . .] from a play by David Mamet [2198]. (The title is the name of a real estate development.) Mamet has a superb ear for the way people talk—the repetitions, non sequiturs, and idiosyncrasies of common speech. But whereas on stage the verbal rhythms, pauses, tics, spasms, and obscenities become hypnotic, they lose their coherence on film, from which we demand visual as well as verbal gratification. The cutting from set to set and character to character chops up the flow of the language and makes the fact that these guys really have nothing to say blatant and wearying. The performances are quite fine, but that's not enough.

Pacino had a dual nomination, bringing his total to eight, and won the best actor Oscar for *Scent of a Woman*. The supporting actor award went to Gene Hackman for *Unforgiven*.

Pacino: 75, 543, 561, 784, 785, 1764.5, 1780.

776 • GLENN MILLER STORY, THE
UNIVERSAL-INTERNATIONAL. 1954.
AWARD *Sound Recording:* Leslie I. Carey.
NOMINATIONS *Story and Screenplay:* Valentine Davies and Oscar Brodney. *Scoring of a Musical Picture:* Joseph Gershenson and Henry Mancini.

James Stewart [73 . . .] plays the bandleader, and June Allyson is his wife. The plot isn't much, just standard   rise-to-fame-with-the-help-of-a-good-woman stuff, then a tearjerker ending when Miller's plane is lost at sea during World War II. But if the music is what you came for, there's plenty of it, performed by Frances Langford, the Modernaires, Louis Armstrong, and Gene Krupa, and re-creations of all the Miller hits. Directed by Anthony Mann.

The writing Oscar went to Budd Schulberg for *On the Waterfront*. Adolph Deutsch and Saul Chaplin won for scoring *Seven Brides for Seven Brothers*.

Carey: 291, 1209, 1334, 1478, 2089. Davies: 1027, 1325. Gershenson: 2064. Mancini: 122, 278, 384, 494, 508, 512, 825, 1573, 1574, 1864, 1970, 2011, 2037, 2201.

777 • GLORIA
COLUMBIA PICTURES PRODUCTION; COLUMBIA. 1980.
NOMINATION *Actress:* Gena Rowlands.

When a mob hit wipes out a young boy's family, Rowlands, a mobster's ex-moll, takes charge of the boy and goes on the run, trying to outwit the mob, which wants some evidence the boy has. Obvious thriller premise, but handled by a writer-director who never deals in the obvious, John Cassavetes [548]. So this loopy film never quite delivers because we don't know whether to take it straight or as parody. As always, however, Rowlands, one of our best

and most misused actresses, is wonderful to watch. She was married to Cassavetes, for whom she did her best work, and since his death in 1989 has been shamefully underemployed. The Oscar went to Sissy Spacek for *Coal Miner's Daughter*.

Rowlands: 2306.

778 • GLORIOUS BETSY
WARNER BROS. 1927–28.
NOMINATION *Adaptation:* Anthony Coldeway.

Conrad Nagel and Dolores Costello star in a pioneering part-talkie about the romance of a brother of Napoleon and an American woman. Planned as a silent, episodes with dialogue were rushed into production when *The Jazz Singer* became a hit. *Glorious Betsy*'s sensational West Coast premiere (*The Jazz Singer* had made its debut in New York) spurred other studios to begin the rush to sound. The Oscar went to Benjamin Glazer for *Seventh Heaven*.

779 • GLORY
TRI-STAR PICTURES PRODUCTION; TRI-STAR. 1989.
AWARDS *Supporting Actor:* Denzel Washington. *Cinematography:* Freddie Francis. *Sound:* Donald O. Mitchell, Gregg C. Rudloff, Elliot Tyson, and Russell Williams II.
NOMINATIONS *Art Direction–Set Decoration:* Norman Garwood; Garrett Lewis. *Film Editing:* Steven Rosenblum.

Young Union officer Robert Gould Shaw, played by Matthew Broderick, takes charge of the 54th Massachusetts Regiment in the Civil War—a volunteer infantry unit made up of black soldiers, among them Washington and Morgan Freeman [580 . . .]. Stirring minor epic, fueled most of all by Washington's performance as a fiery, defiant man and Freeman's counterpoint portrayal of a gentle, centered one. Broderick and his second-in-command, Cary Elwes, seem callow and ineffectual in contrast, though that is, in fact, the point. Directed by Edward Zwick, better known for creating the TV series *thirtysomething*. The battle scenes, including the final hopeless, suicidal charge, are superb. The film's omission from the best picture nominees occasioned a great deal of comment; in the year of *Do the Right Thing,* Spike Lee's comedy-drama about urban violence, this portrait of the heroism of African-Americans certainly seems a better choice than the prep-school melodrama *Dead Poets Society* as an Oscar contender.

Washington's triumph somewhat mitigated the best picture oversight. Trained at the American Conservatory Theatre in San Francisco, Washington made his film debut in the lame, somewhat racist farce *Carbon Copy* (1981). But he went into the TV series *St. Elsewhere* in 1982 and delivered a fine performance in *A Soldier's Story* in 1984. Since then he has gone from strength to strength, including his stunning work in the title role of *Malcolm X,* his portrayal of a homophobic lawyer in *Philadelphia,* and his impressive performance in the ensemble cast of Kenneth Branagh's film of Shakespeare's *Much Ado About Nothing* in 1993.

Francis began his career in England as a camera operator for Alexander Korda [1620]. In addition to his work as a cinematographer, which is widely acclaimed, Francis has also been a director, chiefly of low-budget horror films.

The art direction Oscar went to *Batman.* David Brenner and Joe Hutshing won for the editing of *Born on the Fourth of July.*

Washington: 471, 1247.5. Francis: 1875. Mitchell: 223, 398, 411.5, 507, 734.5, 1525, 1650, 1824, 1825, 2020, 2114, 2176.5. Tyson: 1333, 1802.5. Williams: 482. Garwood: 275, 937. Lewis: 159, 272.5, 937.

780 • GO FOR BROKE!

MGM. 1951.

NOMINATION *Story and Screenplay:* Robert Pirosh.

Bigot Van Johnson gets assigned by the army to head the 442nd combat team made up of Japanese-Americans during World War II. Interesting postwar tolerance fable, with its share of war- and message-movie clichés, but some good action sequences, too. Many of the Japanese-American actors had been interned during the war. Directed by Pirosh, produced by Dore Schary [157 . . .]. The Oscar went to Alan Jay Lerner for *An American in Paris.*

Pirosh: 157.

781 • GO INTO YOUR DANCE

FIRST NATIONAL. 1935.

NOMINATION *Dance Direction:* Bobby Connolly.

Al Jolson is a big Broadway star who acts like it until newcomer Ruby Keeler helps take him down a peg or two. Routine backstage musical plot, but one of the films that give a clue why Jolson was a legendary entertainer. Directed by Archie L. Mayo, with Helen Morgan, Patsy Kelly, Glenda Farrell, and Akim Tamiroff [701 . . .], and songs by Harry Warren [21 . . .] and Al Dubin [791 . . .]. Keeler and Jolson married after the film was finished. The Oscar went to David Gould for *Broadway Melody of 1936* and *Folies Bergère.*

Connolly: 295, 329, 1667.

782 • GO-BETWEEN, THE

WORLD FILM SERVICES LTD. PRODUCTION; COLUMBIA (UNITED KINGDOM). 1971.

NOMINATION *Supporting Actress:* Margaret Leighton.

Young Leo (Dominic Guard) spends his school holiday at the country home of a friend, where he becomes the emissary between his friend's sister, played by Julie Christie [493 . . .], and her lover, played by Alan Bates [678]. Smitten with both Christie and Bates, Leo is shocked when he discovers that they are having an affair, and finally is forced to reveal their meeting place to her mother, Leighton. The experience leaves him emotionally traumatized. The tale is told by the aging bachelor Leo, played now by Michael Redgrave [1364], half a century later. Redgrave gets the film's most famous line, from the L. P. Hartley novel on which the movie is based: "The past is a foreign country. They do things differently there." Handsomely designed by Carmen Dillon [858 . . .] and photographed by Geoffrey Fisher, but a little too stately, and the psychological premise of both film and novel is dubious. *Masterpiece Theatre* fans will love it, as will admirers of Christie and Bates. Directed by

Joseph Losey from a screenplay by Harold Pinter [185 . . .].

Leighton was a member of the celebrated company of the postwar Old Vic, and won Tony Awards for her performances in the Broadway productions of *Separate Tables* and *The Night of the Iguana*. She died of multiple sclerosis in 1976. Cloris Leachman took the supporting actress Oscar for *The Last Picture Show*.

783 • GODDESS, THE

CARNEGIE PRODUCTIONS, INC.; COLUMBIA. 1958.
NOMINATION *Story and Screenplay—Written Directly for the Screen:* Paddy Chayefsky.

Neglected child Patty Duke [1326] grows up to be love-hungry, self-destructive movie star Kim Stanley [722] in this fable about the delusions of the American dream. Pretentious and overwrought, and Stanley is miscast as a sex symbol. (The role is usually said to be based on Marilyn Monroe, though there are elements of Jean Harlow, Frances Farmer, Rita Hayworth, Ava Gardner [1339], and lots of other stars in the character.) The film provided the debut roles of both Stanley and Duke. Directed by John Cromwell. The writing award went to Harold Jacob Smith and Nedrick Young (the latter under the pseudonym Nathan E. Douglas) for *The Defiant Ones*.

Chayefsky: 942, 1283, 1424.

784 • GODFATHER, THE

ALBERT S. RUDDY PRODUCTION; PARAMOUNT. 1972.
AWARDS *Picture:* Albert S. Ruddy, producer. *Actor:* Marlon Brando. *Screenplay—Based on Material From Another Medium:* Mario Puzo and Francis Ford Coppola. NOMINATIONS *Supporting Actor:* James Caan. *Supporting Actor:* Robert Duvall. *Supporting Actor:* Al Pacino. *Director:* Francis Ford Coppola. *Sound:* Bud Grenzbach, Richard Portman, and Christopher Newman. *Original Dramatic Score:* Nino Rota [nomination withdrawn because portions of the score had been used in a previous film also scored by Rota]. *Film Editing:* William Reynolds and Peter Zinner. *Costume Design:* Anna Hill Johnstone.

Michael Corleone (Pacino) returns from World War II just in time for the wedding of his sister, Connie, played by Talia Shire [785 . . .]. Michael has ambitions to escape his family's Mafia ties and to marry the WASP Kay, played by Diane Keaton [88 . . .]. But his father, Don Vito Corleone (Brando), is seriously wounded by a hit man from a rival family, and his hotheaded brother Sonny (Caan) is murdered. His remaining brother, Fredo (John Cazale), is a weakling, and the only other member of the immediate family, Tom Hagen (Duvall), adopted as a child by Don Vito, is the clan's *consigliere,* a lawyer who has to avoid anything that might get him disbarred. So Michael commits a revenge murder that sends him into exile in Sicily. Even there, the violent cycle continues, and Michael's young Sicilian wife dies in a hit. When it is safe to return to America, Michael marries Kay, promising to go straight. However, upon the death of Don Vito, Michael becomes the Godfather, arranging the murders of the family's enemies even as he is serving as godfather at the christening of his sister Connie's child.

The film was a huge commercial hit as well as a critical one. Today its status as a film classic, particularly when viewed in context with its two sequels, is unchallenged. Coppola's achievement seems the more remarkable in that his source material, Puzo's pop novel, could easily have produced what Paramount expected it to be: a routine action thriller. Ruddy, the nominal producer, was a stand-in for studio head Robert Evans [395], who chose Coppola because he was young, inexpensive, Italian, and had just won a writing Oscar for *Patton*. The Oscar race came down to two films—*Cabaret* and *The Godfather*—though the other nominees, *Deliverance, The Emigrants,* and *Sounder,* might have been respectable contenders in another year. Though *Cabaret* took the lion's share of Oscars—eight, to *The Godfather*'s three—the Academy voters seemed to recognize that *The Godfather* made a statement about American values and consequently worked on a higher level than *Cabaret*'s rather chilly portrait of pre–World War II decadence in Germany. But *The Godfather* was also curiously slighted in categories where one might have expected it to appear, most notably the magnificent cinematography of Gordon Willis [786 . . .] and the production design of Dean Tavoularis [92 . . .]. The score, by Nino Rota, was announced as a nominee and then withdrawn from competition when the Academy discovered that parts of it had been used in a 1958 Italian film, *Fortunella*.

Brando was Puzo's first choice for Don Corleone, but not the studio's. At one point, Danny Thomas was mentioned for the role; later, Ernest Borgnine [1283] was said to be the leading contender. When Coppola was put in charge, he was determined to cast either Brando or Laurence Olivier [268 . . .]. The latter was interested, but too ill to take on the part. To overcome Paramount's reluctance to cast Brando, who had not been in a hit film for more than a decade, and at forty-seven seemed too young to play the aging patriarch, Coppola engineered a crude screen test, filmed at Brando's home. The actor darkened his hair with shoe polish and stuffed his cheeks with Kleenex. The resulting footage won him the part. It reestablished Brando as a major film personality, although none of his subsequent appearances has been as successful as the role that won him his second Oscar. At the Oscar ceremony the statuette was picked up by a woman in Native American dress who identified herself as Sacheen Littlefeather. Brando's attempt at protesting the treatment of the American Indian was seen as eccentric rather than meaningful, particularly when Littlefeather was later identified as an actress named Maria Cruz.

It was a night of mixed triumph for Coppola, who joined a handful of directors who failed to receive Oscars for films that won the best picture award. Bob Fosse won for *Cabaret*.

The Godfather was the first movie since *On the Waterfront* to receive three nominations in the supporting actor category. The three nominees went from comparative obscurity to major stardom and, in the case of Duvall and Pacino, Oscar-winning performances as well. Caan, who had the flashiest role of the three as the volatile, sexy Sonny, seemed to suffer from overexposure in too many inferior movies in the midseventies, and his career went into eclipse in the eighties. In recent years he has returned as a versatile character player in such films as *Misery, Dick Tracy, For*

the Boys, and *Honeymoon in Vegas* (1992). Joel Grey's performance in *Cabaret* won for supporting actor.

Cabaret also won for sound and David Bretherton's editing. Anthony Powell took the costuming award for *Travels With My Aunt.*

Brando: 583, 1069, 1141, 1477, 1763, 1949, 2212. Puzo: 785. Coppola: 65, 92, 442, 785, 786, 1541. Duvall: 92, 826, 2015. Pacino: 75, 543, 561, 775.5, 785, 1764.5, 1780. Grenzbach: 395, 1584. Portman: 339, 418, 502, 521, 738, 1109, 1473, 1526, 1701, 2331. Newman: 60, 398, 631, 641, 724, 1820. Rota: 785. Reynolds: 643, 896, 1753, 1881, 1927, 2152. Zinner: 521, 1465. Johnstone: 1651.

785 • GODFATHER, PART II, THE

COPPOLA COMPANY PRODUCTION; PARAMOUNT. 1974.

AWARDS *Picture:* Francis Ford Coppola, producer; Gray Frederickson and Fred Roos, coproducers. *Supporting Actor:* Robert De Niro. *Director:* Francis Ford Coppola. *Screenplay Adapted From Other Material:* Francis Ford Coppola and Mario Puzo. *Art Direction—Set Decoration:* Dean Tavoularis and Angelo Graham; George R. Nelson. *Original Dramatic Score:* Nino Rota and Carmine Coppola.

NOMINATIONS *Actor:* Al Pacino. *Supporting Actor:* Michael V. Gazzo. *Supporting Actor:* Lee Strasberg. *Supporting Actress:* Talia Shire. *Costume Design:* Theadora Van Runkle.

Michael Corleone (Pacino) has wealth and power, but his way of life has become too much for his wife, Kay, played by Diane Keaton [88 . . .]. He is also at odds with his brother, Fredo (John Cazale), and his sister, Connie (Shire). He even alienates his most trusted adviser, his adopted brother and the family's *consigliere,* Tom Hagen, played by Robert Duvall [92 . . .]. As Michael grows increasingly isolated, he must also deal with the machinations of rival mobster Hyman Roth (Strasberg), who has drawn him into an alliance with the Batista regime in Cuba that falls apart with Castro's triumph. And a family associate, Frankie Pentangeli (Gazzo), threatens to expose Michael before a Senate committee. Interwoven with Michael's story are flashbacks to the childhood and youth of his father, Vito, who escapes a vendetta in his native Sicily, comes to America, and survives by his wits in Manhattan's turn-of-the-century Little Italy. As a young man, Vito (De Niro), is drawn into petty thievery to help his family survive, but also becomes a neighborhood hero by killing the predatory Don Fanucci, who runs a protection racket. Vito assumes Don Fanucci's power but with a kinder, gentler mien, and the Corleone dynasty is born. But where Vito is surrounded by admirers, his son, at film's end, is a lonely man, having separated from Kay and ordered the murder of Fredo.

The only sequel to win a best picture Oscar, *Part II* is a triumph of performance, direction, and design. Its narrative line is more complicated than that of the first film, and its tone darker and colder—which some contemporary critics found to be flaws. But for its admirers, who far outnumber its critics, it is, as Pauline Kael called it, "an epic vision of the corruption of America." It's a tribute to Coppola that he used the enormous commercial success of the first *Godfather* to launch something even stronger, putting the lie to the F. Scott Fitzgerald adage that "there are no second acts in American lives." It's also notable that *Part II* competed for the best picture Oscar against one of the outstanding films of the seventies, *Chinatown,* as well as Coppola's own superb *The Conversation.* (The other contenders were the dark biopic *Lenny* and the bloated disaster epic *The Towering Inferno.)* As with the first *Godfather* film, however, some key people were overlooked by the Academy: Once again, the magisterial cinematography of Gordon Willis [786 . . .] was not nominated. It has been suggested that the cinematographers branch of the Academy was still dominated by many old-timers from the studio era, when the practice was to flood the sets with light rather than indulge in the moody chiaroscuro at which Willis excels. Willis, who prefers to distance himself from Hollywood by living in New York, is philosophical about awards: "I don't make movies for cameramen," he has said. "I make movies for directors and producers." Also omitted from the nominees were editors Peter Zinner [521 . . .], Barry Malkin [448 . . .], and Richard Marks

[92 . . .], who helped create the intercutting of the stories of Vito and Michael. The original script, like the version later edited for television, told the stories sequentially. Intercutting them meant finding transitional images that would link the sequences, "repositioning shots," Malkin has explained, that were filmed for another context.

The first *Godfather* was a star-making film. It was the first major movie for Pacino, Keaton, and Shire, and provided career breakthroughs for James Caan and Duvall and a comeback role for Marlon Brando. Similarly, though De Niro had received good notices for *Bang the Drum Slowly* and *Mean Streets* (1973), playing the young Vito Corleone made him a star, and possibly the most sought-after serious actor of our time. Like Pacino, De Niro had studied acting with their *Part II* costar Strasberg. He got his start as an actor in movies by working for Brian De Palma in the 1968 countercultural comedy *Greetings.*

This is, surprisingly, the only Oscar nomination for Rota. He was originally nominated for *The Godfather,* but the nomination was withdrawn when it was discovered that portions of the score for that film had been used in a 1958 Italian film, *Fortunella.* Rota is celebrated for his long collaboration with Federico Fellini, including such films as *La Dolce Vita* and *8¹/₂.* He also composed scores for the 1956 *War and Peace* and the 1968 *Romeo and Juliet,* the latter providing a best-selling soundtrack album. He died in 1979. Carmine Coppola, the director's father, was a flutist in the NBC Symphony under Toscanini. His film scoring work has been primarily for his son.

Although Pacino had more screen time than best actor winner Marlon Brando in the first *Godfather,* he was nominated in the supporting actor category in that film. This time he clearly belonged in the leading actor category. Many felt the Oscar race was between Pacino and Jack Nicholson for *Chinatown,* but the Oscar went to Art Carney for *Harry and Tonto*—an upset that has been explained as either a result of Pacino and Nicholson splitting the vote or a reaction of older Academy members against younger actors (the other nominees were Albert Finney for *Murder on the Orient*

Express and Dustin Hoffman for *Lenny*) in favor of old pro Carney.

This is the only substantial film role for Gazzo, a playwright who adapted his Broadway success *A Hatful of Rain* for the screen. Strasberg was a celebrated acting teacher and artistic director of the Actors Studio, as well as father of actress Susan Strasberg. He had never appeared in a film before but subsequently made several more film appearances, including one as Pacino's father in . . . *And Justice for All,* before his death in 1982.

Shire, Coppola's sister, lost to Ingrid Bergman in *Murder on the Orient Express.* The costume award went to Theoni V. Aldredge for *The Great Gatsby.*

F. Coppola: 65, 92, 442, 784, 786, 1541. Frederickson: 92. Roos: 92. De Niro: 113, 342, 521, 1650, 2005. Puzo: 784. Tavoularis: 92, 292, 786, 2148. Graham: 92, 292, 1418. Nelson: 92, 292, 1698. Rota: 784. C. Coppola: 786. Pacino: 75, 543, 561, 775.5, 784, 1764.5, 1780. Shire: 1712. Van Runkle: 255, 1545.

786 • *GODFATHER, PART III, THE*

Zoetrope Studios Production; Paramount. 1990.

Nominations *Picture:* Francis Ford Coppola, producer. *Supporting Actor:* Andy Garcia. *Director:* Francis Ford Coppola. *Cinematography:* Gordon Willis. *Art Direction–Set Decoration:* Dean Tavoularis; Gary Fettis. *Song:* "Promise Me You'll Remember," music by Carmine Coppola, lyrics by John Bettis. *Film Editing:* Barry Malkin, Lisa Fruchtman, and Walter Murch.

Godfather Michael Corleone, played by Al Pacino [75 . . .], sees his son (Franc D'Ambrosio) beginning a promising career as an opera singer, and his daughter (Sofia Coppola) starting her own life. He longs to spare them from the vendettas that have decimated the family through the years, but extracting the family from crime isn't easy. He hopes to do it by working through the church, but on a visit to Italy he becomes caught up again in the ancient blood feuds, as well as ensnared (albeit on the right side for a change) in a complicated Vatican banking scandal. He steps down as Godfather, passing the role on to the illegitimate son (Garcia) of his brother Sonny. Though

he confesses the sin of having caused the death of his brother Fredo, achieves a sort of reconciliation with his ex-wife, Kay, played by Diane Keaton [88 . . .], and witnesses the triumph of his son's operatic debut, violence takes its toll again: His daughter is gunned down on the opera house steps shortly after her brother's triumphant performance in *Cavalleria Rusticana*—an opera about Sicilian vendettas. At the end the elderly Michael dies, more alone than ever.

Coppola's film trilogy is a tragedy in three acts, with the last act the least satisfactory. It is still visually stunning, with moments of great power and some memorable performances from Pacino and Garcia, and from Talia Shire [785 . . .] as the vindictive Connie, Eli Wallach as an oleaginously treacherous old Mafioso, Raf Vallone as the cardinal who becomes the short-lived Pope John Paul I, Donal Donnelly as a Vatican intriguer, and Joe Mantegna as a vicious rival mobster. But the film is thrown out of shape by the crucial miscasting of Sofia Coppola, an inexperienced actress who was thrust into the film by her father when Winona Ryder [27.5 . . .] fell ill and had to withdraw. One senses that the script was rewritten and the film edited to minimize her role, but it damages Garcia's part as her lover as well. Bridget Fonda, as a journalist trying for an exposé of the family, is largely wasted, as is George Hamilton, cast as the new *consigliere* because Robert Duvall [92 . . .] asked too much money to appear in the film. In addition to these flaws, there's a sense that the film doesn't advance us much beyond the end of *Part II* in delineating Michael's tragedy. It was also the least commercially successful of the three films.

On the other hand, *Part III*'s remarkable filmmaking deserved the recognition the Academy gave it: that is, nominations but not Oscars. Among the best picture nominees it runs a strong third after winner *Dances With Wolves* and a more contemporary gangster film, *GoodFellas* (which gets much of its resonance from the *Godfather* saga, including the presence of Robert De Niro [113 . . .] in its cast). And it's much more impressive than the other two nominees, *Awakenings* and *Ghost.*

Garcia, as the hotheaded offspring of Sonny Corleone, received less of a career boost than earlier *Godfather* film stars such as Pacino and De Niro. The Cuban-American actor had shown signs of becoming a star with a small role in *The Untouchables* and made a strong showing in *Black Rain.* But so far, he seems stuck in supporting roles in major films and leading roles in minor ones. He lost to Joe Pesci in *GoodFellas.*

Coppola lost the directing Oscar to Kevin Costner for *Dances With Wolves.* Willis, who was finally nominated for his glowing work on the *Godfather* films, lost to Dean Semler of *Dances With Wolves,* which also won for Neil Travis' editing. The art direction award went to *Dick Tracy,* which contained Stephen Sondheim's winning song, "Sooner or Later (I Always Get My Man)."

F. Coppola: 65, 92, 442, 784, 785, 1541. Willis: 2345. Tavoularis: 92, 292, 785, 2148. C. Coppola: 785. Malkin: 448. Fruchtman: 92, 1698. Murch: 92, 442, 764, 1066.

787 • *GOING MY WAY*

PARAMOUNT. 1944.

AWARDS *Picture:* Leo McCarey, producer. *Actor:* Bing Crosby. *Supporting Actor:* Barry Fitzgerald. *Director:* Leo McCarey. *Original Story:* Leo McCarey. *Screenplay:* Frank Butler and Frank Cavett. *Song:* "Swinging on a Star," music by James Van Heusen, lyrics by Johnny Burke.

NOMINATIONS *Actor:* Barry Fitzgerald. *Black-and-White Cinematography:* Lionel Lindon. *Film Editing:* Leroy Stone.

Crosby is a priest assigned to what we'd now call an inner-city parish which needs a lot of looking after, but his "modern" ways clash with those of conservative older priest Fitzgerald. This gooey heart-warmer was much beloved in its day, but now is pretty hard to take unless you have a high tolerance for cute kids, cute songs, and cute priests. It has its rewards, however: The great operatic mezzo Risë Stevens is one of them, and the cast includes Gene Lockhart [36], Porter Hall, Carl "Alfalfa" Switzer, and William Frawley. One of the few sentimental comedies to win the Oscar for best picture, it went up against the hard-nosed *Double Indemnity,* the melodramatic *Gaslight,* the home-fires-burning drama *Since You Went Away,* and the overproduced biopic *Wilson.* Some fine films didn't make the cut: *Hail the Conquering Hero, Laura, Lifeboat, Meet Me in St. Louis,* and *The Miracle of Morgan's Creek.* But *Going My Way*'s sentimental message that everything can be solved with a smile and a prayer was as good as gold with war-weary audiences and the Academy.

McCarey became the first person to receive three Oscars for a single picture. His wins as producer, director, and writer have been duplicated only by Billy Wilder for *The Apartment,* Francis Ford Coppola for *The Godfather, Part II,* and James L. Brooks for *Terms of Endearment.* It's hard to believe from McCarey's later sentimental films, such as *Going My Way,* its sequel *Bells of St. Mary's,* and his *Love Affair* remake *An Affair to Remember,* as well as his bizarre anticommunist diatribe *My Son John,* that he was a writer-director responsible for raucous comedies starring Laurel and Hardy, W. C. Fields, the Marx Brothers, and Mae West in the thirties. His last film, *Satan Never Sleeps* in 1962, combined both his devout Catholicism and his devout anticommunism in a tale about two priests battling the Chinese communists. He died in 1969.

Crosby's victory was a mild upset—the smart money was on Charles Boyer for *Gaslight.* (The other nominees, in addition to Fitzgerald, were Cary Grant, cast against type in *None but the Lonely Heart,* and Alexander Knox in the title role of *Wilson.*) There is little in Crosby's Oscar-winning performance that hadn't been seen in the dozens of movies he'd made since his debut in *King of Jazz* in 1930: an easygoing manner, an ability to make singing look as natural as talking, and good comic timing. Not until *The Country Girl* ten years later did Crosby attempt anything like a dramatic stretch.

Fitzgerald is such a natural as a priest that it's a little surprising to realize that he was actually a Lutheran. Trained at Dublin's Abbey Theatre, he was brought to Hollywood in 1936 by director John Ford [815 . . .]. He spent the next twenty-odd years reinforcing the stereotype of the silver-tongued, hard-drinking Irishman. His brother, Arthur Shields, played similar roles, though not so flamboyantly. They appeared together in several films, including *How Green Was My Valley* and *The Quiet Man.* Fitzgerald, who died in 1961, is the only person to have been nominated as both actor and supporting actor for the same role; the Academy immediately changed the rules to keep that from happening again. It only served to point up the difficulty of making the distinction between supporting and leading roles. Supporting performance Oscars have gone to players whose roles are so central to their films that they might easily have been nominated as leading performers, such as Haing S. Ngor in *The Killing Fields,* George Burns in *The Sunshine Boys,* Walter Matthau in *The Fortune Cookie,* Geena Davis in *The Accidental Tourist,* Meryl Streep in *Kramer vs. Kramer,* Tatum O'Neal in *Paper Moon,* and Tommy Lee Jones in *The Fugitive.* And there are some who argue that the Oscar-winning performances of Anthony Hopkins in *The Silence of the Lambs,* Michael Douglas in *Wall Street,* Lee Marvin in *Cat Ballou,* Louise Fletcher in *One Flew Over the Cuckoo's Nest,* Patricia Neal in *Hud,* and Luise Rainer in *The Great Ziegfeld*—all honored as leading roles— were really in supporting parts. The Academy takes the easy way out: It lets the voters decide which category a role belongs in.

Butler and Cavett receive screenplay credit, but as was common on McCarey's films, a fair amount of the dialogue and action were concocted in rehearsal rather than on the typewritten page. Butler had begun as an actor, but turned screenwriter with the advent of sound. During his period with Paramount, he worked on several of the Hope-Crosby *Road* pictures. Cavett had been an assistant director before turning mostly to writing in the forties.

Van Heusen changed his name from Edward Chester Babcock when he was in his teens and working as a radio announcer. He teamed with Burke in 1939, and their hit song for Tommy Dorsey, "Polka Dots and Moonbeams," launched Van Heusen's long association with Frank Sinatra [732 . . .]. Paramount hired the team to write the songs for Hope and Crosby's *Road* films. "Swingin' on a Star" was their first Oscar nomination, and it beat eleven competitors, including Jerome Kern and Ira Gershwin's "Long Ago and Far Away," from *Cover Girl,* Jule Styne and Sammy Cahn's "I'll Walk Alone," from *Follow the Boys,* and Ralph Blane and Hugh Martin's "The Trolley Song," from *Meet Me in St. Louis.*

Joseph LaShelle won the cinematography Oscar for *Laura,* and Barbara McLean won for editing *Wilson.*

McCarey: 21, 114, 173, 1212, 1394, 1404. Crosby: 173, 450. Butler: 1703, 2222. Cavett: 832, 1845. Van Heusen: 171, 173, 915, 926, 1056, 1524, 1587, 1708, 1859, 1907, 2016, 2064, 2263. Burke: 171, 173, 1547, 1691. Lindon: 101, 973.

788 • *GOING PLACES*

COSMOPOLITAN; WARNER BROS.-FIRST NATIONAL. 1938.
NOMINATION *Song:* "Jeepers Creepers," music by Harry Warren, lyrics by Johnny Mercer.

Dick Powell poses as a jockey, with the predictable consequences: He has to ride a horse and win a race. Flimsy musical, directed by Ray Enright, with Anita Louise and Ronald Reagan, forgettable except that all of a sudden Louis Armstrong and Maxine Sullivan are there to sing "Jeepers Creepers." The rest of the movie should be that good. The Oscar went to Ralph Rainger and Leo Robin for "Thanks for the Memory," from *The Big Broadcast of 1938.*

Warren: 21, 324, 569, 791, 877, 897, 1072, 1367, 1501, 1964. Mercer: 248, 278, 476, 384, 494, 508, 636, 825, 877, 903, 905, 1109, 1772, 1838, 1912, 2327, 2328.

789 • *GOLD*

AVTON FILM PRODUCTIONS LTD.; ALLIED ARTISTS. 1974.
NOMINATION *Song:* "Wherever Love Takes Me," music by Elmer Bernstein, lyrics by Don Black.

Roger Moore foils a plot by an international cartel, headed by John Gielgud [103 . . .], to flood a South African mine and thereby raise the price of gold. Ray Milland [1208] is the mine owner and Susannah York [2047] his daughter who falls in love with Moore although (because?) she's married to Bradford Dillman. Run-of-the-mine adventure, directed by Peter Hunt, with some good location filming and action sequences. The song, which doesn't have anything to do with the movie, lost to Al Kasha and Joel Hirschhorn's "We May Never Love Like This Again," from *The Towering Inferno,* which didn't either.

Bernstein: 27.5, 882, 1242, 1264, 1685, 1959, 2064, 2101, 2130, 2147, 2223. Black: 174, 259, 1574, 2147.

790 • *GOLD DIGGERS OF 1933*

WARNER BROS. 1932–33.

NOMINATION *Sound Recording:* Nathan Levinson.

Joan Blondell [246], Ruby Keeler, and Aline Mac-Mahon [576] are showgirls struggling to make ends meet, while Dick Powell is a well-to-do songwriter posing as a penniless one. This blissfully nonsensical backstage musical is one of the landmarks of movie musical history. Though Mervyn LeRoy [1662 . . .] directed the narrative section, which mainly deals with the women trying to help dig up enough gold from wealthy old foofs like Guy Kibbee to put on a show, the musical numbers were staged by Busby Berkeley [791 . . .] at his most surreal and antic. This is the one in which Ginger Rogers [1102] sings "We're in the Money" in pig Latin; neon-lighted dancers form a gigantic violin in "The Shadow Waltz"; dwarf Billy Barty, dressed as a baby, offers Powell a can opener to undo Keeler's suit of armor in "Pettin' in the Park"; and Blondell and Etta Moten sing a tribute to the unemployed in "Remember My Forgotten Man." The songs are by Harry Warren [21 . . .] and Al Dubin [791 . . .]. Berkeley himself has a bit part as the backstage call boy.

Levinson, who was also nominated for *42nd Street* and *I Was a Fugitive From a Chain Gang,* lost to Harold C. Lewis for *A Farewell to Arms.*

Levinson: 16, 30, 343, 385, 531, 689, 710, 712, 930, 965, 1052, 1169, 1621, 1690, 1768, 1769, 1779, 1930, 1949, 2058, 2318.

791 • *GOLD DIGGERS OF 1935*

FIRST NATIONAL. 1935.

AWARD *Song:* "Lullaby of Broadway," music by Harry Warren, lyrics by Al Dubin.

NOMINATION *Dance Direction:* Busby Berkeley.

Wealthy Alice Brady [990 . . .] has a show staged at her estate, giving performer Dick Powell a chance to fall in love with her daughter, Gloria Stuart. Meanwhile, Adolphe Menjou [734] has designs on Brady's fortune. The title, and the presence of Powell and director Berkeley, are all this movie has in common with the superior *Gold Diggers of 1933*. The cast also includes Glenda Farrell, Hugh Herbert, and Winifred Shaw as the "Broadway baby" in the "Lullaby of Broadway" number, the film's unquestioned highlight. The musical numbers reward one's endurance of the vapid plot.

Warren, born Salvatore Guaragna in Brooklyn, began his movie career as a pianist at the Vitagraph studios before World War I, providing mood music for the then-silent performers to emote to. But the war interrupted that career, and during the twenties he worked mostly as a song-plugger on Tin Pan Alley. He resumed his movie career when sound came in, and went to Hollywood in 1932, starting at Warners. Dubin, his partner until the late thirties, was already under contract to Warners when Warren arrived—in fact, Dubin is said to be the first lyricist ever signed by a studio. With composer Joe Burke, Dubin had written the songs for Warners' *Gold Diggers of Broadway* in 1929, the now forgotten original in the series (actually a remake of a 1923 silent). The most memorable of Burke and Dubin's songs for that film is "Tip-Toe Through the Tulips." Warren and Dubin's Oscar-winning "Lullaby" is an enduring but slightly dated standard that won over two superior nominees: Irving Berlin's "Cheek to Cheek," from *Top Hat,* and Jerome Kern, Dorothy Fields, and Jimmy McHugh's "Lovely to Look At," from *Roberta.*

Berkeley was never honored by the Academy for his unique achievements, partly because no awards category really quite fit him. "Dance direction" is a pale approximation of what he did; as Gerald Mast has commented, "Berkeley choreographed space, not people." It's possible that Berkeley's mad scenario for the "Lullaby of Broadway" number did as much as Warren's tune or Dubin's lyrics to win the Oscar for the songwriters, though Berkeley himself came in third in his category, after Hermes Pan's work on *Top*

Hat and the winner, David Gould for *Broadway Melody of 1936* and *Folies Bergère*. Berkeley's nomination also cited his work on the number "The Words Are in My Heart," but for many of his admirers, "Lullaby of Broadway" is the epitome of his art. In addition to the usual kaleidoscopic choreography, it climaxes with a chorus line spooking the Broadway baby of the song into a fall from a skyscraper. Some interpreters have seen the stone-faced, menacing, furiously tapping chorus as a Berkeleyan comment on the rise of fascism. Whatever was in his head, what's on screen is amazing.

Warren: 21, 324, 569, 788, 877, 897, 1072, 1368, 1501, 1964. Dubin: 1367, 1900. Berkeley: 792, 2196.

792 • *GOLD DIGGERS OF 1937*

WARNER BROS.-FIRST NATIONAL. 1936.

NOMINATION *Dance Direction:* Busby Berkeley.

Diggers Joan Blondell [246] and Glenda Farrell help persuade a group of insurance salesmen, including Victor Moore, to back their show. Dick Powell, as usual, is the tenor on hand. The cast also includes Osgood Perkins, best known today as the father of Anthony Perkins [730]. Lloyd Bacon directed the narrative parts of this film, but Berkeley's numbers, including "With Plenty of Money and You," are the main reason to sit through this one. The nomination cited his work on the "Love and War" number, but he lost to Seymour Felix's work on "A Pretty Girl Is Like a Melody," from *The Great Ziegfeld*—a number that emulates Berkeley's extravagant zaniness but lacks his wit.

Berkeley: 791, 2196.

793 • *GOLD RUSH, THE*

CHARLES CHAPLIN PRODUCTIONS; UNITED ARTISTS. 1942.

NOMINATIONS *Sound Recording:* James Fields, RCA Sound. *Scoring of a Dramatic or Comedy Picture:* Max Terr.

Charlie Chaplin [405 . . .] prospecting for gold in Alaska, joins up with Mack Swain, who has staked a gold claim but can't find it. In a mining town Chaplin falls for a pretty dance hall girl, Georgia Hale. When Chaplin helps Swain locate his lost claim, both men become rich, and Chaplin gets the girl. No plot synopsis can do justice to what many think is Chaplin's richest, funniest feature film, in which he eats a boiled shoe, turns a pair of dinner rolls into dancers, and fights for life in a cabin on the brink of a precipice. Written, produced, and directed by Chaplin. It often shows up near the top in critical surveys that name the greatest films of all time.

The Gold Rush was made in 1925, but when it was rereleased in 1942 with a music track, narration, and sound effects, the new additions were deemed eligible for awards. *Yankee Doodle Dandy* won for sound, and Max Steiner's score for *Now, Voyager* took the music Oscar.

Fields: 1856.

794 • *GOLDEN BOY*

COLUMBIA. 1939.

NOMINATION *Original Score:* Victor Young.

William Holden [1424 . . .], in his first major film role, plays Joe Bonaparte, a young violinist who becomes a prizefighter, lured by easy money. Barbara Stanwyck [138 . . .] plays the "dame" who encourages him to stay in the ring, and Adolphe Menjou [734] is his manager. Lee J. Cobb [301 . . .], actually only seven years older than Holden, plays his father. A little sappy, but redeemed by good performances and well-staged fight scenes. Rouben Mamoulian directed. Based on a play by Clifford Odets that was rewritten by Lewis Meltzer, Daniel Taradash [732], Sarah Y. Mason [1189], and Victor Heerman [1189] to provide a happy ending. Young lost to Victor Stothart for *The Wizard of Oz*.

Young: 97, 98, 100, 101, 280, 489, 612, 693, 701, 846, 925, 1214, 1257, 1396, 1452, 1748, 1823, 1994, 2235, 2315.

795 • *GOLDEN GIRL*

20TH CENTURY-FOX. 1951.

NOMINATION *Song:* "Never," music by Lionel Newman, lyrics by Eliot Daniel.

Mitzi Gaynor plays nineteenth-century entertainer Lotta Crabtree in a musical set in California during the Civil War, directed by Lloyd Bacon. A snoozer for anyone but fans of Gaynor or costars Dale Robertson and Dennis Day. (There must be some.) The song Oscar went to Hoagy Carmichael and Johnny Mercer for "In the Cool, Cool, Cool of the Evening," from *Here Comes the Groom*.

Newman: 183, 457, 557, 896, 981, 1160, 1273, 1585, 1762, 2043. Daniel: 1853.

796 • GOLDFINGER

EON PRODUCTIONS LTD.; UNITED ARTISTS (UNITED KINGDOM). 1964.

AWARD *Sound Effects:* Norman Wanstall.

Sean Connery [2185], as James Bond, takes on Gert Frobe as Auric Goldfinger, who has a plot to destroy Fort Knox, thereby increasing the value of his holdings in gold. Along the way, Connery has to battle Harold Sakata as Oddjob, a man with a lethal hat, and win over the very butch Honor Blackman as Pussy Galore. And the movie winds up with Bond handcuffed to a nuclear device. One of the best of the series, before the films began to be overloaded with technology. Directed by Guy Hamilton. Somehow the Academy overlooked the popular title tune, which was composed by Leslie Bricusse [557 . . .] and Anthony Newley [2285], and nominated instead the long-forgotten title tunes from *Dear Heart* and *Hush . . . Hush, Sweet Charlotte*. But then, this was the year that the Academy could have had its pick of eight songs by the Beatles, from *A Hard Day's Night,* and nominated none of them.

797 • GOLDWYN FOLLIES, THE

SAMUEL GOLDWYN PRODUCTIONS; UNITED ARTISTS. 1938.

NOMINATIONS *Interior Decoration:* Richard Day. *Score:* Alfred Newman.

Hollywood producer Adolphe Menjou [734], concerned that his latest films have flopped, hires as a consultant a young woman, played by Andrea Leeds [1899], whom he calls Miss Humanity because she represents the interests of the common folk. He falls in love with her, but she loves Kenny Baker instead. Inane premise, concocted by no less than Ben Hecht [78 . . .], to string together a group of musical

numbers and comedy routines by the Ritz Brothers, Edgar Bergen and Charlie McCarthy, and others. Directed by George Marshall. Producer Samuel Goldwyn [102 . . .] was imitating not only the big studio revues such as MGM's *Broadway Melody* series and Paramount's *Big Broadcast*s but also Florenz Ziegfeld's elaborate stage revues. To this end, he hired prestigious New York talent: choreographer George Balanchine and his ballet company, dancer Vera Zorina, and songwriters George [1797] and Ira Gershwin [455 . . .]. George Gershwin died during the preparations for the film, and the score was completed by Vernon Duke. *The Goldwyn Follies* turned out to be Goldwyn's folly: a horrid mishmash of high and low culture that flopped at the box office. And though the score includes four songs by the Gershwins, including "Love Walked In" and "Our Love Is Here to Stay" (the latter was George Gershwin's last composition), none of them was nominated for best song. The oversight was Goldwyn's, not the Academy's: A rules change allowed each studio to submit a single nominee for best song. For some reason, the Goldwyn entry was the forgettable title tune from *The Cowboy and the Lady*—could it have been because the song's composer was Lionel Newman, brother of Goldwyn's music director, Alfred?

The art direction Oscar went to Carl Weyl for *The Adventures of Robin Hood*. Though Newman lost for *Goldwyn Follies,* he won for *Alexander's Ragtime Band*.

Day: 22, 102, 235, 487, 510, 560, 569, 833, 864, 952, 1048, 1175, 1397, 1477, 1666, 1949, 2056, 2120, 2276. Newman: 31, 34, 46, 72, 138, 182, 226, 333, 334, 347, 375, 428, 437, 457, 476, 495, 542, 690, 833, 952, 953, 959, 962, 1016, 1082, 1088, 1213, 1278, 1362, 1397, 1475, 1616, 1655, 1849, 1868, 1883, 1921, 2043, 2046, 2091, 2258, 2286, 2294, 2316.

798 • GONE WITH THE WIND

SELZNICK INTERNATIONAL PICTURES; MGM. 1939.

AWARDS *Picture:* David O. Selznick, producer. *Actress:* Vivien Leigh. *Supporting Actress:* Hattie McDaniel. *Director:* Victor Fleming. *Screenplay:* Sidney Howard. *Color Cinematography:* Ernest Haller and Ray Rennahan. *Interior Decoration:* Lyle Wheeler. *Film Editing:* Hal C. Kern and James E. Newcom. *Special Award:* William Cameron Menzies for use of color for the enhancement of dramatic mood.

NOMINATIONS *Actor:* Clark Gable. *Supporting Actress:* Olivia de Havilland. *Sound Recording:* Thomas T. Moulton. *Original Score:* Max Steiner. *Special Effects:* John R. Cosgrove, photographic; Fred Albin and Arthur Johns, sound.

Scarlett O'Hara (Leigh) loves Ashley Wilkes, played by Leslie Howard [178 . . .], though he loves Melanie Hamilton (de Havilland). But the rakish Rhett Butler (Gable) knows that he and the fiery Scarlett are destined for each other. It takes the Civil War, Reconstruction, and being widowed twice to persuade Scarlett that he's right, but after the death of their daughter and what he considers to be evidence that Scarlett still loves Ashley, Rhett decides that he doesn't give a damn. Scarlett is devastated, but then tomorrow is another day and there's always Tara. Of these bits and pieces of romantic melodrama, stitched together with scraps of history and lots of myth by novelist Margaret Mitchell, was the most famous movie of all time made. It's huge and colorful and tremendously entertaining, though it bogs down in the last third, and perpetuates a lot of nonsense about the antebellum South—happy slaves and flirtatious belles and beaux—plus some pernicious stuff about sex: Rhett commits spousal rape and leaves Scarlett wreathed in smiles and chirping like a mockingbird. But for everyone who objects, there seem to be hundreds who think it's the greatest movie ever made.

For all its cast of thousands, *GWTW* is pretty nearly the product of a one-man band, that man being the then-inexhaustible Selznick. Fueled by ambition, cigarettes, and Benzedrine, Selznick oversaw every punctuation mark of the script and every frame of film, working himself into exhaustion, not to mention his cast and crew: Makeup artist Mont Westmore's death at the age of thirty-eight in 1940 was even ascribed by his physician to "his arduous work in charge of the makeup of the stars in *Gone With the Wind.*" Selznick is a key figure in Hollywood's second generation, the

son of a pioneer, Lewis J. Selznick, a distributor who made and lost a fortune in the early twenties. After working for his father, David joined the nascent MGM in 1926 as a story editor, but finding his ambitions as producer blocked by Metro's "boy wonder," Irving Thalberg [150 . . .], he moved over to Paramount and then to RKO, where he was, among other things, instrumental in launching the career of Katharine Hepburn [24 . . .]. When Thalberg became ill in 1933, Selznick returned to MGM, where his marriage to studio head Louis B. Mayer's daughter Irene inspired the wisecrack "The son-in-law also rises." But energy and talent rather than nepotism were responsible for Selznick's success, and after producing a series of hits, he left to become an independent producer, securing the considerable backing of millionaire John Hay Whitney to launch Selznick International Pictures. He had successes with the first *A Star Is Born, Nothing Sacred,* and *The Prisoner of Zenda,* but his greatest coup was securing the rights to Margaret Mitchell's best-seller. It is said that Mitchell's decision to let Selznick film the book was at least partly based on her admiration of his fine version of *David Copperfield.* To obtain the services of Gable, Selznick sold the distribution rights to MGM. The venture paid off famously. *GWTW* took the best picture Oscar against the stiffest competition in the history of the awards: *Dark Victory, Goodbye, Mr. Chips, Love Affair, Mr. Smith Goes to Washington, Ninotchka, Of Mice and Men, Stagecoach, The Wizard of Oz,* and *Wuthering Heights*—any one of which might have won the Oscar in a less-competitive year.

Key to the success of *GWTW* was the choice of a Scarlett, and that was Selznick's greatest coup of all. The nationwide hunt for an actress to play the part is legendary—and mostly, of course, a publicity stunt (although one candidate from that search, Alicia Rhett, made it into the film in the role of India Wilkes). Paulette Goddard [1855], Jean Arthur [1353], and Joan Bennett came closest to getting the role out of the roster of famous also-rans: Katharine Hepburn, Bette Davis [46 . . .], Joan Crawford [1319 . . .], Susan Hayward [973 . . .], Margaret Sullavan [2073], Tallulah Bankhead, Miriam Hopkins

[165], Ann Sheridan, Anita Louise, Lana Turner [1558], Frances Dee, and Catherine Campbell (the future mother of Patricia Hearst). Leigh wanted the part from the moment she read the novel and heard it was to be filmed. The English actress was not a complete unknown; her films *Fire Over England* (1937) and *A Yank at Oxford* (1938) had been widely seen. While filming the former, she fell in love with Laurence Olivier [268 . . .], whom she married in 1940 after both were divorced. She came to the States to be with Olivier during the filming of *Wuthering Heights*. The legend (too good to be entirely true, so it probably isn't) has it that she was first brought to Selznick's attention by his brother, agent Myron Selznick, during the filming of the burning of Atlanta, which took place on December 10, 1938. She was not finally set for the role until somewhere around Christmas Day. Her performance easily eclipsed even her formidable competition for the Oscar: Bette Davis in *Dark Victory,* Irene Dunne in *Love Affair,* Greta Garbo in *Ninotchka,* and Greer Garson in *Goodbye, Mr. Chips.* Yet between Scarlett O'Hara and her other great Oscar-winning film performance in *Streetcar Named Desire* more than a decade later, she made only a handful of films. The war, which she and Olivier spent in England, is partly to blame, as is her delicate physical and mental health, but Selznick, to whom she was under contract, also has to be blamed for not providing her with suitable roles.

Whatever one may say about the racial attitudes embodied in the character of Mammy, the role provided McDaniel with acting opportunities rarely granted to black performers of the era. Born in Kansas, she had to be trained in the dialect needed for the part. She began her career as a singer, a talent she rarely had a chance to use on screen, except in the 1936 film of *Show Boat.* Otherwise, both before and after *GWTW,* she was stuck playing maids—sometimes, as in *Alice Adams,* making even those stereotypical parts memorable. She was the first black performer to be nominated for an Oscar, and for more than half a century, until Whoopi Goldberg won for *Ghost,* she was the only black woman to win an acting award. On the other hand, McDaniel was not allowed

to attend the premiere of *GWTW* in Atlanta, and her photograph did not appear in the souvenir program. She died in 1952.

Though he not only won the Oscar for directing *GWTW* but also directed another famous and beloved nominee for best picture that year, *The Wizard of Oz,* Fleming is a comparatively uncelebrated director, partly because *GWTW* was Selznick's film, and Vivien Leigh's, and William Cameron Menzies', and Max Steiner's. And chunks of the movie were directed by other hands: George Cukor [262 . . .] began it, and his abrupt departure from the film, after directing such key scenes as the argument between Scarlett and Mammy before the Twelve Oaks barbecue and the birth of Melanie's baby in besieged Atlanta, has been the subject of rumor and speculation. One tale holds that Gable had him fired because he felt Cukor gave too much attention to the actresses. Another persistent but unsubstantiated story claims that Gable had supported himself in his prestardom days by prostitution among the Hollywood gay community, and that Cukor, who was gay, knew of Gable's past. The truth seems to be that both Selznick and Cukor realized Cukor was the wrong director for so huge a project. Fleming became his replacement partly because he was available but also because he was a close friend of Gable's. Fleming, who had begun his career in 1910 as a cameraman and had worked under D. W. Griffith, became a director in the twenties, working with Douglas Fairbanks, among others. His most famous pre-*GWTW* sound films were *Red Dust* in 1932, *Captains Courageous,* and *Test Pilot,* all of which suggested that he was better equipped to handle the film's action sequences than was the stage-trained and intellectual Cukor. But the task of directing *GWTW,* and of dealing with Selznick's incessant quibbles and changes, drove Fleming to collapse, and for about a month in midfilming the movie was directed by Sam Wood [701 . . .]. Menzies, too, directed a second unit. So all in all, *GWTW* had four directors, but only Fleming was credited. Although he also received credit as the director of the second most famous movie of 1939, *The Wizard of Oz,* Fleming's post-

Oscar career was relatively undistinguished. His last film before his death in 1949 was *Joan of Arc*.

Howard's Oscar was posthumous; he was killed in a tractor accident on his Massachusetts farm a few months before *GWTW* premiered. He had won the Pulitzer for his play *They Knew What They Wanted* (filmed in 1928, 1930, and 1940, but most memorably turned into the Broadway musical *The Most Happy Fella* in 1956), and had been lured to Hollywood by Samuel Goldwyn [102 . . .], for whom he wrote several screenplays, including *Dodsworth*. Howard did the first draft of the *GWTW* screenplay, which was four hundred pages long, enough for a six-and-a-half-hour film. So other hands were turned to it: Jo Swerling [1607], Oliver Garrett, F. Scott Fitzgerald, John Lee Mahin [352 . . .], John Van Druten [749], and Ben Hecht [78 . . .], who allegedly made his contributions without ever reading the novel. Selznick biographer David Thomson sums it up this way: Howard "was only designated writer, the figure around whom other efforts congregated. His was the draft to be rewritten, the wall against which every other ball could be thrown." But Howard got sole credit—in part as a gesture of respect to his memory—and his widow took home the Oscar.

Lee Garmes [201 . . .] was the first cinematographer hired for the film, but like most of the major cinematographers of the day, Garmes had little experience with Technicolor, and his conflicts with Technicolor's consultants, who were contractually obligated to be on every film shot in the process, led to his departure from the film. Haller, who replaced Garmes at much the same time that Fleming replaced Cukor, had never shot in color either, but Rennahan, a pioneer in color cinematography, joined him. For the first time, the Oscars for cinematography were divided into two categories—color and black and white. The following year the art direction award would be similarly divided, and when the costume design Oscar was introduced with the 1948 awards, it would also have color and black-and-white categories. These distinctions would persist until the 1967 awards, when the paucity of black-and-white films finally made the distinction unworkable. (The separate categories were briefly dropped in the late fifties but reinstated after protests from the artists who objected to the suddenly intensified competition.) *GWTW* became the first best picture winner shot in color.

Technicalities prevented Menzies, the production designer, from being nominated in the interior decoration category, but he is of course as much responsible for the look of *GWTW* as Wheeler. Consequently the Academy granted Menzies a special award. A similar courtesy might well have been extended to Walter Plunkett [9 . . .], the costume designer.

Gable was always a foregone conclusion as Rhett Butler—readers of the novel overwhelmingly demanded him—but other possibilities were considered. When it was thought that Warners might handle distribution of the film, and that Bette Davis might be its Scarlett, Errol Flynn was mentioned. Gary Cooper [701 . . .] was also under consideration. Gable himself, who hated the role because he was afraid he wouldn't be able to live up to the expectations people had for him, thought Ronald Colman [311 . . .] should play it. But Gable acquitted himself well, even though the Academy preferred the performance of Robert Donat in *Goodbye, Mr. Chips*. The other nominees were Laurence Olivier in *Wuthering Heights,* Mickey Rooney in *Babes in Arms,* and perhaps the best performance of all, James Stewart in *Mr. Smith Goes to Washington.* (It's generally thought that Stewart's Oscar the next year for *The Philadelphia Story* was a consolation prize for losing in 1939.)

De Havilland's performance as the saintly but surprisingly tough Melanie certainly ranks with Leigh's and McDaniel's. It was her first major serious role, after four years of being pretty and spunky in Errol Flynn swashbucklers. She and winner McDaniel stand head and shoulders above the competition: Geraldine Fitzgerald in *Wuthering Heights,* Edna May Oliver in *Drums Along the Mohawk,* and Maria Ouspenskaya in *Love Affair.*

Perhaps the most startling Oscar loss suffered by *GWTW* is that of Steiner. His score is perhaps the most famous of all film music, and the first four notes of the "Tara" theme affect some people the way the madeleine did Proust. The Oscar went, however, to Herbert Stothart for *The Wizard of Oz*—not for the songs, which were by Harold Arlen and E. Y. Harburg, but for the incidental music.

The loss in the special effects category, to *The Rains Came,* is equally puzzling—as if Academy voters felt they couldn't give *GWTW* everything. Cosgrove's singular contribution was in the area of glass painting, matte effects that, for example, transformed the back-lot facade of Tara into a plantation house in Georgia, and are used in subtle ways throughout the film.

The sound award went to *When Tomorrow Comes.*

Selznick: 497, 1670, 1828, 1890, 1909, 1996, 2211. Leigh: 1949. Howard: 102, 560. Haller: 55, 679, 1046, 1174, 1319, 2248. Rennahan: 235, 241, 569, 581, 701, 1120, 1210. Wheeler: 19, 46, 83, 356, 376, 428, 476, 495, 530, 542, 719, 721, 950, 1062, 1088, 1149, 1153, 1213, 1391, 1475, 1601, 1616, 1670, 1706, 1852, 2008, 2093, 2212. Kern: 1670, 1828. Newcom: 87, 1828, 2120. Menzies: 38, 112.5, 311, 568, 1018, 2010. Gable: 1025, 1387. De Havilland: 894, 925, 1849, 2099. Moulton: 22, 46, 138, 366, 457, 487, 560, 706, 962, 1153, 1200, 1451, 1510, 1607, 1849, 2154, 2294. Steiner: 16, 154, 190, 330, 365, 385, 492, 679, 747, 754, 999, 1043, 1046, 1052, 1162, 1169, 1170, 1207, 1324, 1408, 1430, 1456, 1690, 1779, 1828. Cosgrove: 1607, 1670, 1828, 1890. Johns: 1670, 1828, 2310.

799 • GOOD EARTH, THE

MGM. 1937.

Awards *Actress:* Luise Rainer. *Cinematography:* Karl Freund.

Nominations *Picture:* Irving Thalberg, with Albert Lewin, producers. *Director:* Sidney Franklin. *Film Editing:* Basil Wrangell.

Chinese peasant Wang, played by Paul Muni [218.5 . . .], marries the gentle O-lan (Rainer), whose discovery of some jewels makes them wealthy. Wang squanders their money on the spoiled and selfish Lotus, played by Tilly Losch, but a plague of locusts brings him back to reality. Long, expensive, but often tiresome adaptation of the novel by Pearl S.

Buck. Its chief virtues are the elaborate re-creations of China in California—costumes, livestock, and even whole buildings were transported from China for the sets that were built near Chatsworth—and special effects, particularly the locust plague. (Curiously the art direction went unnominated; the special effects Oscar was not introduced until the 1939 awards.) As usual, most of the roles of Asians were played by Westerners—in addition to Muni, Rainer, and Losch, all of whom were Austrian, the cast includes Walter Connolly, Jessie Ralph, and Charley Grapewin—although a few actors with Asian ancestry, notably Keye Luke, have secondary roles.

Rainer's second Oscar made her the first person to win two consecutive Oscars for acting—a feat that's been duplicated only by Spencer Tracy for *Captains Courageous* and *Boys Town,* Katharine Hepburn for *Guess Who's Coming to Dinner* and *The Lion in Winter,* Jason Robards for *All the President's Men* and *Julia,* and Tom Hanks for *Philadelphia* and *Forrest Gump.* She was also, until Jodie Foster's wins for *The Accused* and *The Silence of the Lambs,* the only person to win two acting Oscars while still under thirty. Today, her passive, long-suffering O-lan doesn't seem like much of a characterization when set against her competitors, particularly Greta Garbo's incandescent performance in *Camille* and Barbara Stanwyck's superb tear-jerking in *Stella Dallas,* which may well have split the vote. But even Janet Gaynor's steel-spined ingenue in *A Star Is Born* and Irene Dunne's dizzy comic turn in *The Awful Truth* have a lot more going for them. Rainer's triumph, however, was short-lived. MGM had trouble finding suitable roles for her, and when her marriage to playwright-screenwriter Clifford Odets hit the skids, she retired from films after only a few more unmemorable performances. She settled in London with her second husband.

Freund was one of cinematography's great pioneers, both a technical innovator and a fine artist. In his early career in Germany, he shot such expressionist classics as F. W. Murnau's *The Last Laugh* and Fritz Lang's *Metropolis.* He came to the States in 1929 as a consultant for Technicolor, and soon went to work for Universal, for which he shot the horror classic

Dracula (1931) and directed *The Mummy* (1932). He moved over to MGM, where he filmed *Camille* and *Pride and Prejudice,* among many others. In 1944 he founded Photo Research Corp., and in the fifties moved from films into TV, most notably as the head of cinematography for Desilu. He devised the three-camera setup for *I Love Lucy* that allowed the show to be filmed before a studio audience. He died in 1969.

The Good Earth was Thalberg's last production and bears the credit: "To the memory of Irving Grant Thalberg we dedicate this picture, his last great achievement." His death in 1936, at age thirty-seven, solidified his legend as MGM's "boy wonder," a producer of "prestige" films. Later generations have found many of his films glossy and devoid of life, and have blamed him for destroying the career of director Erich von Stroheim [1975], whose monumental *Greed* Thalberg ruthlessly edited. But it's clear that as creative director of MGM he helped establish that studio as the most celebrated of them all. The Irving G. Thalberg Award, honoring producers, was created in his memory and was first presented at the 1937 ceremony to Darryl F. Zanuck [34 . . .]. Lewin took over production of *The Good Earth* after Thalberg's death. The film lost the best picture Oscar to *The Life of Emile Zola.*

Leo McCarey won the directing Oscar for *The Awful Truth.* The editing award went to Gene Havlick and Gene Milford for *Lost Horizon.*

Rainer: 831. Freund: 239, 397. Thalberg: 150, 202, 812, 1387, 1721, 1846, 2129. Lewin: 1387. Franklin: 1232, 1371, 1440, 1662, 2320.

800 • *GOOD MORNING, VIETNAM*

TOUCHSTONE PICTURES PRODUCTION IN ASSOCIATION WITH SILVER SCREEN PARTNERS III; BUENA VISTA. 1987.
NOMINATION *Actor:* Robin Williams.

During the Vietnam War, deejay Adrian Cronauer (Williams) is sent by the Armed Forces Network to Saigon, where he battles army bureaucrats and incompetents, befriends the Vietnamese, and helps improve morale before the brass he has offended find evidence that he has fraternized with the enemy and succeed in shipping him out. Very, very loosely based on the experiences of the real-life Cronauer, the movie has nothing pointed or interesting to say about the American involvement in Vietnam. It might as well be set in the South Pacific during World War II or Seoul during the Korean War, except that its setting provides an excuse to play lots of golden oldies from the sixties. The movie is chiefly a vehicle for the high-flying improvisatory monologues and repartee of Williams. Fortunately the star gets good support from Forest Whitaker as a bemused aide, Bruno Kirby and J. T. Walsh as Cronauer's enemies, Robert Wuhl as a fellow deejay, and Noble Willingham as a sympathetic commanding officer. Directed by Barry Levinson [75 . . .].

Williams, who studied drama at Juilliard after graduating from college, developed a following as a stand-up comedian that led to a hit TV series, *Mork and Mindy,* in the late seventies. Starting with the title role in *Popeye* in 1980, he turned in a series of strong performances in films including *The World According to Garp* and *Moscow on the Hudson* (1984), without really striking fire at the box office until *Good Morning, Vietnam.* The Oscar went to Michael Douglas for *Wall Street.*

Williams: 511, 671.

801 • *GOOD NEWS*

MGM. 1947.
NOMINATION *Song:* "Pass That Peace Pipe," music and lyrics by Ralph Blane, Hugh Martin, and Roger Edens.

One of those they-don't-make-'em-like-that-anymore genres: the college musical, dealing with whether the star football player will pass French in time for the big game and with various romantic intrigues. Cheerful, colorfully inane remake of a 1930 movie based on a 1927 Broadway show, with a not-too-updated script by Betty Comden [141 . . .] and Adolph Green [141 . . .], and a few new songs added to the original score ("The Varsity Drag," "The Best Things in Life Are Free") by Buddy De Sylva [1212], Lew Brown [2214], and Ray Henderson. The very likable cast includes Peter Lawford,

June Allyson, Joan McCracken, and Mel Tormé. Directed by Charles Walters [1173].

The best song Oscar went to Allie Wrubel and Ray Gilbert for "Zip-A-Dee-Doo-Dah," from *Song of the South.*

Blane: 1299. Martin: 1299. Edens: 87, 115, 594, 699, 1476, 1950.

802 • GOODBYE, COLUMBUS

WILLOW TREE PRODUCTIONS; PARAMOUNT. 1969.
NOMINATION *Screenplay—Based on Material From Another Medium:* Arnold Schulman.

Librarian Richard Benjamin falls in love with rich young Ali MacGraw [1218] in this adaptation of Philip Roth's satiric novel about Jewish life in New York suburbia. Very much of its period—the *fin de* sixties—like *The Graduate, Bob & Carol & Ted & Alice,* and *The Landlord,* though not quite as assured as they are in exploring upper-middle-class angst and hang-ups. Directed by Larry Peerce. The writing Oscar went to Waldo Salt for *Midnight Cowboy.*

Schulman: 1219.

803 • GOODBYE GIRL, THE

RAY STARK PRODUCTION; MGM/WARNER BROS. 1977.
AWARD *Actor:* Richard Dreyfuss.
NOMINATIONS *Picture:* Ray Stark, producer. *Actress:* Marsha Mason. *Supporting Actress:* Quinn Cummings. *Screenplay—Written Directly for the Screen:* Neil Simon.

Dreyfuss plays an actor who, through a mix-up about the lease, winds up sharing an apartment with Mason, a former dancer who is now a single mother trying to raise her daughter, Cummings. You know the formula from here on out, and there are no surprises, just lots of wisecracks and a few sniffles. Directed by Herbert Ross [2152]. Adapted into a Broadway musical in 1992, by which time one of the film's best comic bits—Dreyfuss' performance of Richard III as a stereotypically swishy gay—had become politically incorrect.

Dreyfuss' win was an upset victory: The smart money was on Richard Burton to take the Oscar for *Equus,* his seventh nomination. Woody Allen in *Annie Hall,* Marcello Mastroianni in *A Special Day,* and John Travolta in *Saturday Night Fever* were not regarded as strong contenders. But Dreyfuss had also been seen that year in *Close Encounters of the Third Kind,* which may well have impressed voters that he was an actor with range. He had made his film debut in *The Graduate*—a bit part as an obnoxious neighbor in a Berkeley rooming house—and achieved stardom with *American Graffiti, The Apprenticeship of Duddy Kravitz,* and *Jaws.* But the Oscar did not propel his career upward. Instead, a string of flops in the early eighties, exacerbated by drug problems, sent his career into eclipse. He reemerged in the latter part of the decade, leaner, fitter, and grayer, to play mature men in *Down and Out in Beverly Hills* (1986) and *Tin Men* (1987) and even romantic leads in *Stakeout* (1987) and *Always* (1989). A second Oscar-caliber role, however, has eluded him.

Annie Hall took the Oscars for best picture, Diane Keaton's performance in the title role, and Woody Allen and Marshall Brickman's screenplay. Cummings, whose movie career ended with adolescence, lost to Vanessa Redgrave in *Julia.*

Stark: 737. Mason: 383, 403, 1495. Simon: 332, 1461, 1976.

804 • GOODBYE, MR. CHIPS

MGM (UNITED KINGDOM). 1939.
AWARD *Actor:* Robert Donat.
NOMINATIONS *Picture:* Victor Saville, producer. *Actress:* Greer Garson. *Director:* Sam Wood. *Screenplay:* Eric Maschwitz, R. C. Sheriff, and Claudine West. *Sound Recording:* A. W. Watkins. *Film Editing:* Charles Frend.

Schoolmaster Mr. Chipping (Donat), affectionately known as Chips, recalls his sixty years of service as classics master at an English public school, including his marriage to Garson, her death in childbirth, the devastation of World War I, and so on. Sentimental but not too gooey version of the James Hilton [1371] novel, done in the best MGM style, with a cast that includes John Mills [1737] and Paul Henreid (then billed as Von Hernreid) in his first English-language film. Cinematography by F. A. "Freddie" Young [558 . . .].

Donat triumphed over one of the most famous performances in the history of movies, Clark Gable's in *Gone With the Wind,* not to mention such formidable competitors as Laurence Olivier in *Wuthering Heights* and James Stewart in *Mr. Smith Goes to Washington.* (The remaining nominee, not quite so strong a competitor, was Mickey Rooney in *Babes in Arms.*) But it was a well-deserved win: Donat makes a meticulous passage from timorous young teacher to shy lover to devastated widower to beloved mentor. In his youth Donat looked like a strong rival for Olivier as both actor and matinee idol, but poor health—a lifelong battle with asthma—restricted his career. He made his greatest impression in the 1935 Alfred Hitchcock [1171 . . .] classic *The 39 Steps* and in his other nominated role in *The Citadel,* but his post-Oscar performances were scattered. His last screen appearance, just before his death at fifty-three, was in *The Inn of the Sixth Happiness* in 1958.

Otherwise, *Gone With the Wind* was the spoiler of the year, taking the best picture Oscar, as well as awards for actress Vivien Leigh, director Victor Fleming, screenwriter Sidney Howard, and editors Hal C. Kern and James E. Newcom. The sound award went to *When Tomorrow Comes.*

Though Garson stood little chance against Leigh, being nominated for her film debut role was a signal achievement amid such competition as veterans Bette Davis in *Dark Victory,* Irene Dunne in *Love Affair,* and Greta Garbo in *Ninotchka.* And the unnominated performances included Jean Arthur's in *Mr. Smith Goes to Washington,* Judy Garland's in *The Wizard of Oz,* Ginger Rogers' in *Bachelor Mother,* and Joan Crawford's in *The Women,* any one of which might have received a nomination in a less competitive year than 1939. It set Garson on a path to becoming MGM's leading actress in the early forties.

Donat: 406. Saville: 406. Garson: 239, 1232, 1371, 1372, 1973, 2193. Wood: 701, 1095, 1102. West: 1371, 1662. Watkins: 558, 1107, 1165.

805 • *GOODBYE, MR. CHIPS*

APJAC PRODUCTIONS; MGM (U.S./UNITED KINGDOM). 1969.
NOMINATIONS *Actor:* Peter O'Toole. *Score of a Musical Picture—Original or Adaptation:* Leslie Bricusse and John Williams.

In this musical version of the James Hilton [1371] novel previously filmed in 1939, O'Toole plays the schoolmaster of the title, with Petula Clark as his wife —she's a music hall performer in this version, to provide some cues for her musical numbers. The action is also updated, so that Clark dies in a World War II air raid, instead of in childbirth as in the earlier version. A lumbering dud, with bland and forgotten songs, made watchable only by O'Toole's performance and the support of Michael Redgrave [1364] and Sian Phillips. Directed by Herbert Ross [2152].

O'Toole's fourth nomination couldn't salvage a career that was entering a downward passage from which it would not recover until the eighties, when after having lost his youthful good looks, the actor turned to character roles. He lost the Oscar to John Wayne for *True Grit.* O'Toole was in good company: His fellow nominees were Richard Burton for *Anne of the Thousand Days* and Dustin Hoffman and Jon Voight for *Midnight Cowboy.*

The scoring award went to Lennie Hayton and Lionel Newman for *Hello, Dolly!*

O'Toole: 164, 1151, 1177, 1395, 1733, 1953. Bricusse: 557, 933, 937, 1766, 2037, 2201, 2285. Williams: 6, 260, 403, 416, 588, 613, 614, 659, 933, 937, 982, 996, 997, 1041, 1047, 1596, 1652, 1679, 1684, 1701, 1764.65, 1916, 1977, 2107, 2126, 2194, 2293, 2322.

806 • *GOODFELLAS*

WARNER BROS. PRODUCTION; WARNER BROS. 1990.
AWARD *Supporting Actor:* Joe Pesci.
NOMINATIONS *Picture:* Irwin Winkler, producer. *Supporting Actress:* Lorraine Bracco. *Director:* Martin Scorsese. *Screenplay Based on Material From Another Medium:* Nicholas Pileggi and Martin Scorsese. *Film Editing:* Thelma Schoonmaker.

Mobster Henry Hill (Ray Liotta) and his wife (Bracco) are put in the federal witness protection program after Hill decides it's the only way to save his hide. The film flashes back to his boyhood in Brooklyn and his fascination with the Mafiosi around him, such as Robert De Niro [113 . . .] and the snake-mean Pesci, who can snap from jocular to deadly in the blink of an eye. A superbly canny and assured piece of filmmaking, the work of a great American director, splendidly filmed by Michael Ballhaus [293 . . .]. Yet its excessive cleverness—asides to the camera, tricks of Brechtian alienation, astonishingly staged violence—keeps the viewer from warming to it. It aims at the head and the gut but it never captures the heart. Critics raved, but audiences and the Academy preferred *Dances With Wolves,* which got the best picture award. The omission of Liotta from the best actor roster surprised many. It's a splendid portrait of a rather stupid man who finds himself in well over his head. Liotta deserved to be nominated instead of Richard Harris, who campaigned harder and got a bid for *The Field.* De Niro was nominated for the more showy acting as the formerly comatose man in *Awakenings.*

Pesci was rightly cited for his hair-trigger performance. After breaking into films with his role in *Raging Bull,* he received little notice for his work over the next decade until he demonstrated a gift for manic comedy in *Lethal Weapon 2,* and in the same year as his Oscar-winning role, the knockabout part of the hapless burglar in *Home Alone.* The combination of the two megahits and the Oscar made Pesci a sought-after character performer for whom producers were willing to craft vehicles such as *My Cousin Vinny.*

Bracco was born in Brooklyn, but her first films were made in Europe, where she worked for Radio Luxembourg. She first attracted notice in American films in 1987's *Someone to Watch Over Me,* playing the tough-as-nails wife of a cop. She lost the Oscar to Whoopi Goldberg for *Ghost.*

Scorsese's versatility continues to astonish. Since 1986, he has made a glossy, star-studded sequel to a classic (*The Color of Money*), a moving but controversial religious epic (*The Last Temptation of Christ*), a gangster film (*GoodFellas*), a remake of a thriller (*Cape Fear*), and a costume drama from a novel by Edith Wharton (*The*

Age of Innocence). And somehow each one of those films has been a Scorsese film, not a prepackaged genre item. The Oscar has eluded him perhaps because the Academy prefers predictable competence to individual genius. This time he lost to a novice filmmaker, Kevin Costner for *Dances With Wolves.*

The screenplay for *GoodFellas,* based on Pileggi's book *Wiseguy,* lost to Michael Blake's for *Dances With Wolves,* which also won for Neil Travis' editing.

Pesci: 1650. Winkler: 1650, 1698, 1712. Scorsese: 27.5, 1142, 1650. Schoonmaker: 1650, 2312.5.

807 • GORGEOUS HUSSY, THE
MGM. 1936.

NOMINATIONS *Supporting Actress:* Beulah Bondi. *Cinematography:* George Folsey.

Lionel Barrymore [723 . . .] plays President Andrew Jackson, with Joan Crawford [1319 . . .] as Peggy Eaton, who precipitates a political crisis when the president comes to her defense. Historical drama with some distant relationship to the facts. Pretty silly, but watchable because of a gallery of performers including Robert Taylor, Melvyn Douglas [169 . . .], James Stewart [73 . . .], Franchot Tone [1387], Louis Calhern [1243], Melville Cooper, and Gene Lockhart [36]. Directed by Clarence Brown [84 . . .] and produced by Joseph L. Mankiewicz [46 . . .].

Bondi, who plays Mrs. Jackson, was one of the most durable of character actresses, playing battle-axes and frontier women in movies and on TV well into her eighties. She lost the supporting actress Oscar, the first ever awarded, to Gale Sondergaard in *Anthony Adverse,* for which Gaetano Gaudio also won the cinematography award.

Bondi: 1463. Folsey: 51, 137, 629, 835, 838, 1124, 1299, 1320, 1500, 1688, 1782, 2068, 2269.

808 • GORILLAS IN THE MIST
WARNER BROS. PRODUCTION; WARNER BROS./UNIVERSAL. 1988.

NOMINATIONS *Actress:* Sigourney Weaver. *Screenplay Based on Material From Another Medium:* Anna Hamilton Phelan, screenplay; Anna Hamilton Phelan and Tab

Murphy, story. *Sound:* Andy Nelson, Brian Saunders, and Peter Handford. *Original Score:* Maurice Jarre. *Film Editing:* Stuart Baird.

Weaver plays Dian Fossey, an American whose study of mountain gorillas in Africa brings her up against big-game hunters and native poachers, and whose growing obsession with preserving the animals eventually leads to her murder. Absorbing version of a true story, with excellent nature photography enhanced by special effects work. There is a needless romantic subplot involving Bryan Brown; Weaver and the gorillas more than carry the film. Directed by Michael Apted.

Weaver's performance, a study in an obsession that draws near to madness, earned her a best actress nomination simultaneously with a nomination for her supporting performance in *Working Girl.* Unfortunately she entered the Oscar record books as the first person to receive simultaneous nominations and lose both Oscars. (Later, Emma Thompson came along to keep her company by losing her simultaneous nominations as actress in *The Remains of the Day* and supporting actress in *In the Name of the Father.*) Weaver lost to Jodie Foster in *The Accused* for best actress and to Geena Davis in *The Accidental Tourist* for supporting actress.

The writing award went to Christopher Hampton for *Dangerous Liaisons.* The Oscar for sound went to *Bird.* Dave Grusin won for the score of *The Milagro Beanfield War.* The editing award went to Arthur Schmidt for *Who Framed Roger Rabbit.*

Weaver: 45, 2313. Nelson: 1764.65. Handford: 1512. Jarre: 558, 764, 1151, 1168, 1340, 1533, 1967, 2296. Baird: 1977.

809 • GOSPEL ACCORDING TO ST. MATTHEW, THE

Arco-Lux Cie Cinématografique de France Production; Walter Reade-Continental Distributing (France/Italy). 1966.
Nominations *Black-and-White Art Direction—Set Decoration:* Luigi Scaccianoce. *Scoring of Music—Adaptation or Treatment:* Luis Enrique Bacalov. *Black-and-White Costume Design:* Danilo Donati.

The life of Christ, played by a cast of unknown nonprofessional actors and filmed in a documentary style under the direction of a gay atheist Marxist, Pier Paolo Pasolini. Only Martin Scorsese's *The Last Temptation of Christ* comes close to this film in breaking free of the clichés and conventions of Hollywood biblical drama. That said, it's also something of a trial to sit through—it's more than two hours long—and there are many who think it overvalued because of its uniqueness.

Who's Afraid of Virginia Woolf? won the Oscars for art direction and Irene Sharaff's costume design. Ken Thorne won the scoring award for *A Funny Thing Happened on the Way to the Forum.*

Donati: 658, 1266, 1722, 2000.

810 • GRADUATE, THE

Mike Nichols-Lawrence Turman Production; Embassy Pictures Corporation. 1967.
Award *Director:* Mike Nichols.
Nominations *Picture:* Lawrence Turman, producer. *Actor:* Dustin Hoffman. *Actress:* Anne Bancroft. *Supporting Actress:* Katharine Ross. *Screenplay—Based on Material From Another Medium:* Calder Willingham and Buck Henry. *Cinematography:* Robert Surtees.

Benjamin Braddock (Hoffman) comes home after graduating from college and finds life with his wealthy parents in suburbia something of a bore until he's seduced by Mrs. Robinson (Bancroft), the wife of his father's best friend, and then falls in love with her daughter, Elaine (Ross). One of the films that defined a generation—the baby boomers who a few years later would follow the famous advice proffered to Benjamin and go into plastics (or computers or law or investment banking) and become yuppies. Though time has cast doubt on its countercultural values and imitation has deprived its cinematic and narrative innovations of their power to surprise, it's still enormously entertaining. For that we can thank all the nominees, plus a few distinguished contributors who didn't make the cut: production designer Richard Sylbert [395 . . .], editor Sam O'Steen [395 . . .], and songwriter Paul Simon (because they weren't written specifically for the film, the Simon and Garfunkel songs on the soundtrack were ineligible for the best song competition). Screenwriter Henry plays a desk clerk, and Richard Dreyfuss [803] makes one of his first screen appearances as an obnoxious (what else?) neighbor in a Berkeley rooming house.

Nichols' Oscar was interpreted by many as partly a consolation prize for his failure to win the previous year for his stunning directorial debut with *Who's Afraid of Virginia Woolf?* His win this year deprived Norman Jewison, director of best picture winner *In the Heat of the Night,* of the award. It was a signal that Nichols, previously known as a comedian teamed with Elaine May [890] and as a Broadway director, had arrived as a Hollywood force. Unfortunately Nichols followed *The Graduate* with an expensive flop, *Catch-22* (1970); a film admired by critics but not audiences, *Carnal Knowledge;* a major disaster, *The Day of the Dolphin;* and a dud comedy that even stars of the caliber of Jack Nicholson [395 . . .] and Warren Beatty [255 . . .] couldn't save, *The Fortune* (1975). At that point Nichols took a long leave from Hollywood and concentrated on theater work. His return in 1983 with *Silkwood* demonstrated that his skill as a film director had not left him, though he has never again had the critical and popular success that he experienced with his first two films. *The Graduate* is particularly notable for directorial choices that transform what could have been a conventional sex comedy into something more—for example, the famous final shot when, after Benjamin has rescued Elaine from her wedding, the two board a bus and the camera lingers on their faces far longer than is necessary, stirring the viewer's own uneasiness and doubt about their future.

Hoffman became a star because of *The Graduate,* in a role for which Robert Redford [1502 . . .] and Charles Grodin had been considered. He had worked in TV and in off-Broadway shows, where Nichols first spotted him. Though he was thirty, Hoffman's small stature made him convincing as the much younger Benjamin. He very shrewdly followed with a part that demonstrated his range: the tubercular street person in *Midnight Cowboy.* The Oscar went to Rod Steiger for *In the Heat of the Night.*

Doris Day [1572] was considered for the role of Mrs. Robinson, one of the more mind-boggling what-ifs in film history. It became a signature role for Bancroft, eclipsing even the performance in *The Miracle Worker* that won her the Oscar. Her icy assurance as Mrs. Robinson makes her moves on Benjamin is superbly done, as is the menace she projects when she learns of his love for Elaine, but Bancroft lost to Katharine Hepburn in *Guess Who's Coming to Dinner*—a performance that few people consider a landmark in that actress' career.

The promise Ross showed in *The Graduate* and two years later in *Butch Cassidy and the Sundance Kid* was never fulfilled, in part because of a paucity of good roles for actresses in the early seventies, when her career should have been established. In recent years she has concentrated primarily on TV work, often in collaboration with her husband, Sam Elliott. The supporting Oscar went to Estelle Parsons for *Bonnie and Clyde.*

The adaptation of the novel by Charles Webb bears the name of another novelist, Willingham, but the flavor of the screenplay is characteristic of Henry, who had been a TV writer for Steve Allen and Garry Moore and had collaborated with Mel Brooks [230 . . .] in the creation of the TV sitcom *Get Smart.* Henry was the son of silent film actress Ruth Taylor and appeared on stage at age sixteen in the original Broadway production of *Life With Father.* The Oscar went to Stirling Silliphant for *In the Heat of the Night.*

Burnett Guffey won for the cinematography for *Bonnie and Clyde.*

Nichols: 1679.5, 1821, 2277, 2313. Hoffman: 1111, 1155, 1312, 1653, 2113. Bancroft: 28, 1326, 1634, 2152. Henry: 890. Surtees: 130, 175, 557, 917, 1094, 1139, 1388, 1469, 1644, 1747, 1911, 1927, 1960, 2055, 2152.

811 • GRAND CANYON
20TH CENTURY FOX PRODUCTION; 20TH CENTURY FOX. 1991.
NOMINATION *Screenplay Written Directly for the Screen:* Lawrence Kasdan and Meg Kasdan.

Intersecting stories about several Los Angeles residents: Kevin Kline [670], a doctor who is feeling midlife malaise and a sense of being trapped in his marriage; his wife, Mary McDonnell [482 . . .], who has similar feelings that are altered when she discovers an abandoned baby and decides to keep it; Danny Glover, who comes to the rescue when Kline's car breaks down in a bad neighborhood; Steve Martin, a producer of ultraviolent movies who has a temporary conversion to nonviolence when he has a serious accident; and Alfre Woodard [466], whom Kline introduces to Glover in a successful matchmaking attempt. Well-acted comedy-drama in the vein of Kasdan's *The Big Chill,* but ultimately rather aimless: If these people weren't played by some of the most interesting actors around, it would be clearer that their epiphanies don't amount to much. Kasdan is too middle-of-the-road as writer and director to give this the eccentric spin that it needs, so it comes off as pretentious and glossy rather than—as presumably intended—bittersweet. The writing award went to Callie Khouri for *Thelma & Louise.*

L. Kasdan: 6, 199.

812 • GRAND HOTEL

MGM. 1931–32.

AWARD *Picture:* Irving Thalberg, producer.

People come, people go, Lewis Stone [1540] observes at the end of this melodrama set in an elegant Berlin hotel. But then he adds: "Nothing ever happens." Wrong. Ballerina Greta Garbo [84 . . .] falls in love with John Barrymore, a down-on-his-luck baron turned jewel thief. Stenographer Joan Crawford [1319 . . .] does some work for corrupt businessman Wallace Beery [202 . . .] and also brightens the final days of Lionel Barrymore [723 . . .], who has come to see how the rich people live before he dies. Undeniably a classic of sorts, though today the acting seems hammy and the dialogue hack. (The screenplay is by director Edmund Goulding from William A. Drake's stage play based on Vicki Baum's novel.) Garbo and Crawford come off best. The former, who really does say, "I want to be alone," is luminous, and the latter is lively and cute—adjectives that would cease to be applied to Crawford very shortly, when

she decided to become a Serious Actress. After sixty-plus years the movie also still looks pretty good, thanks to art director Cedric Gibbons [66 . . .], cinematographer William Daniels [84 . . .], and costumer Adrian. Director Goulding was bypassed in the nominations, so for fifty-seven years *Grand Hotel* had the distinction of being the only best picture winner whose director wasn't nominated, until *Driving Miss Daisy* won without a nomination for Bruce Beresford. But *Grand Hotel* is still the only winner to receive no nominations in any other category.

Thalberg's triumph with *Grand Hotel* came at the end of his reign as the studio's "boy wonder," which had begun when he went to work for Louis B. Mayer in 1923. In 1924 he became vice-president and supervisor of production at the newly formed MGM and presided over the passage of the studio from silents into sound. But a month after *Grand Hotel* received the Oscar, Thalberg had a serious heart attack, and after a European trip to recuperate, he discovered that his role at MGM had been greatly diminished. Even with reduced powers, he continued to be a formidable producer up to his death in 1937.

Thalberg: 150, 202, 799, 1387, 1721, 1846, 2129.

813 • GRAND ILLUSION

RÉALIZATION D'ART CINÉMATOGRAPHIQUE; WORLD PICTURES (FRANCE). 1938.

NOMINATION *Picture:* Frank Rollmer and Albert Pinkovitch, producers.

Erich von Stroheim [1975], the commandant of a prison camp during World War I, and Pierre Fresnay, a French officer, come to realize that as aristocrats they have much in common. More so, in fact, than Fresnay has in common with the other French officers, Jean Gabin, a former mechanic, and Marcel Dalio, a Jew. So when von Stroheim is forced to execute Fresnay for helping the others to escape, the film takes on a note of tragedy. One of the screen's enduring and unquestioned masterpieces, rich in character and narrative, and visually beautiful. Usually pigeonholed as an antiwar film, but it easily transcends any such label. Directed by Jean Renoir

[1884], who cowrote the screenplay with Charles Spaak, basing it, Renoir said, on stories told him by friends during the war. The cinematography is by Christian Matras and Claude Renoir (the director's nephew). The film was almost lost during World War II, but a negative was preserved, ironically, in Munich. *Grand Illusion* was the first foreign language film to receive a best picture nomination. It lost to *You Can't Take It With You.*

814 • GRAND PRIX

Douglas-Lewis-John Frankenheimer-Cherokee Production; MGM. 1966.

Awards *Sound:* Franklin E. Milton, sound director, MGM Studio Sound Department. *Film Editing:* Fredric Steinkamp, Henry Berman, Stewart Linder, and Frank Santillo. *Sound Effects:* Gordon Daniel.

Grand Hotel on wheels: the intersecting affairs and crises, personal and romantic, of drivers in a major European auto race. The big international cast, directed by John Frankenheimer, includes James Garner [1380], Eva Marie Saint [1477], Yves Montand, Toshiro Mifune, Brian Bedford, Jessica Walter, and Rachel Kempson. As you can tell from the awards, however, this is pretty much a show about cars going very fast and noisily around curves and sometimes not making it. Very handsome, with lots of split-screen work, but it goes on for almost three hours, so it's only for racing nuts—as the studio discovered when it stiffed at the box office.

Milton: 175, 401, 558, 953, 2184. Steinkamp: 1512, 2047, 2074, 2113. Linder: 1653.

815 • GRAPES OF WRATH, THE

20th Century-Fox. 1940.

Awards *Supporting Actress:* Jane Darwell. *Director:* John Ford.

Nominations *Picture:* Darryl F. Zanuck, with Nunnally Johnson, producers. *Actor:* Henry Fonda. *Screenplay:* Nunnally Johnson. *Sound Recording:* E. H. Hansen. *Film Editing:* Robert E. Simpson.

The drought and crop failures of the thirties, which turned Oklahoma into the dust bowl, send the Joad family on an odyssey to California in search of work and a better life, but they meet hostility, abuse, and exploitation. Fonda is Tom Joad, with Darwell as Ma and Russell Simpson as Pa, and the cast includes John Carradine, Charley Grapewin, John Qualen, Darryl Hickman, and Ward Bond, among many others. Superbly photographed by Gregg Toland [407 . . .]. This adaptation of the novel by John Steinbeck [1171 . . .] is celebrated by many as one of the greatest American films, but dissenters object to its sentimental melodramatizing and its tendency to pull back from strong political statement in favor of muzzily pious speeches about The People.

Beulah Bondi [807 . . .] and other character actresses campaigned for the role of Ma Joad, which was clearly a plum, but it went to Darwell, a veteran who made her film debut in 1913. Her career spanned half a century, and she was last seen on screen in *Mary Poppins,* three years before her death.

While today's critics find Ford's work on big studio projects like *Grapes of Wrath* and *How Green Was My Valley* less interesting than on the films, particularly the westerns, over which he exercised more individual control, *Grapes* is impressive because of the way the director's humanistic vision transforms Steinbeck's novel, in which the characters are symbolic vehicles for the author's ideas about social justice. Ford gives them greater depth, and while this may rob the film of its political edge, it also takes the story out of the context of the Depression and gives it universality.

Producer-writer Johnson worked as a journalist and magazine writer before coming to Hollywood in 1932 as screenwriter. He moved into producing after a few years, usually but not always on films from his own scripts. In 1943 he founded International Pictures, which merged with Universal three years later. Johnson returned to Fox for most of his remaining career, which lasted until 1967. The best picture Oscar went to *Rebecca.* Donald Ogden Stewart won for the screenplay of *The Philadelphia Story.*

Though Fonda is a screen legend, as well as the founder of a Hollywood acting dynasty now in its third generation, he was curiously slighted by the Academy. He made his film debut in 1935 and became a star in such movies as *Jezebel, Drums Along the Mohawk, Jesse James,* and *Young Mr. Lincoln.* His work with Ford on the last film earned him the role of Tom Joad over more-favored Fox contract players such as Don Ameche [419] and Tyrone Power. But it didn't lead to parts that he wanted, and after service in the navy during World War II, Fonda turned his attention to the theater, where his performance in the title role of *Mister Roberts* gained acclaim. The forty-one years that separate his two Oscar nominations—he won for *On Golden Pond* shortly before his death in 1982—is the longest stretch between acting nominations in Academy history. (He was, however, nominated as the producer of *Twelve Angry Men* in the interim.) He lost the Oscar to his close friend James Stewart in *The Philadelphia Story.*

The award for sound went to Douglas Shearer for *Strike Up the Band. Northwest Mounted Police* editor Anne Bauchens won the editing Oscar.

Ford: 952, 999, 1200, 1642, 1901. Zanuck: 34, 46, 550, 710, 759, 946, 952, 990, 1201, 1327, 1666, 2154, 2286. Johnson: 932, 1569. Fonda: 1473, 2153. Hansen: 143, 241, 952, 990, 1655, 1868, 1957, 2027, 2056, 2272, 2286, 2317.

816 • GREASE

Robert Stigwood/Allan Carr Production; Paramount. 1978.
Nomination *Song:* "Hopelessly Devoted to You," music and lyrics by John Farrar.

New girl in town Sandy (Olivia Newton-John) falls for Danny Zuko, a biker type, played by John Travolta [1633.5 . . .]. But she doesn't fit in with the good girls, and she's snubbed by the tough ones like Rizzo, played by Stockard Channing [1835.5]. The Broadway musical about the fifties was a huge hit, and the film was even huger—one of the biggest moneymakers in history. But why? It has occasional clumsy charm, but its parody of fifties teen mores is stale, and Randal Kleiser directs without wit or affection for the material. All the cleverness has gone into the casting: Though Newton-John is something of a pill, Travolta and Channing are excellent, and fifties teen idols Frankie Avalon and Edd Byrnes and such TV icons as

Eve Arden [1319], Sid Caesar, and Dody Goodman make amusing cameo appearances. Some of the musical numbers are brightly staged but badly integrated. The nominated song lost to Paul Jabara's "Last Dance," from *Thank God It's Friday.*

817 • GREAT CARUSO, THE

MGM. 1951.
Award *Sound Recording:* Douglas Shearer.
Nominations *Scoring of a Musical Picture:* Peter Herman Adler and Johnny Green. *Color Costume Design:* Helen Rose and Gile Steele.

Mario Lanza plays tenor Enrico Caruso in a biopic that follows him from boyhood in Naples through international operatic triumphs to his death. Ann Blyth [1319] plays his wife, and the cast, directed by Richard Thorpe, includes the distinguished sopranos Dorothy Kirsten and Jarmila Novotna. Unfortunately Lanza was not a distinguished tenor, and he gets most of the music, which is the only thing that makes this tedious, plotless business watchable. Essentially a vanity production designed to flatter the ego of its star, who had been signed by MGM in 1949 and had surprise hits with *That Midnight Kiss* (1949) and *The Toast of New Orleans.* Lanza's good looks and handsome but badly trained voice worked well on screen, but he turned to alcohol and pills and gained too much weight, so that by 1954 the studio was forced to remove him from *The Student Prince* and have Edmund Purdom lip-synch to Lanza's voice. Lanza died of a heart attack in 1959 at the age of thirty-eight.

This was the last Oscar of five won in competition by Shearer, one of MGM's major technical innovators. Over the years he also received six citations from the Academy for technical achievements, not only in sound but also for the development of a 65mm wide-screen process. He died in 1971.

An American in Paris took the Oscars for Johnny Green and Saul Chaplin's scoring and for Walter Plunkett and Irene Sharaff's costumes.

Shearer: 136, 202, 256, 685, 835, 1096, 1232, 1292, 1371, 1419, 1751, 1950, 1988, 2048, 2055, 2211, 2300. Green: 66, 320, 594, 662, 914, 1298, 1471, 1550, 1657, 2047, 2244. Rose: 130, 578, 629,

755, 980, 1007, 1309, 1335, 1599. Steele: 612, 894, 1087, 1309, 1748.

818 • GREAT DICTATOR, THE

CHARLES CHAPLIN PRODUCTIONS; UNITED ARTISTS. 1940. NOMINATIONS *Picture:* Charles Chaplin, producer. *Actor:* Charles Chaplin. *Supporting Actor:* Jack Oakie. *Original Screenplay:* Charles Chaplin. *Original Score:* Meredith Willson.

Chaplin plays both a Jewish barber and the dictator of Tomania, Adenoid Hynkel. While stirring up anti-Semitism, the latter is also plotting with his ally Benzino Napaloni (Oakie), the dictator of Bacteria, to invade the country of Austerlich. By accident, the barber is mistaken for Hynkel and gets the chance to make a speech in which he calls off the invasion and the anti-Semitic attacks. He delivers a message in favor of peace and brotherhood, some of it directed at the young woman, Hannah, played by Paulette Goddard [1855], who has befriended him. More than a decade after the introduction of sound, this is Chaplin's first talking picture, though its highlights remain its moments of pantomime, such as Hynkel's dance with a globe of the world he hopes to dominate. But the concluding speech goes on and on, undermining its high sentiments. Today, playing Hitler, Mussolini, Goebbels (Henry Daniell as Garbitsch), and Göring (Billy Gilbert as Herring) as mere comic-opera buffoons may seem tasteless. But as Chaplin notes in his autobiography, the reports coming out of Europe about the Nazis' terrorism and concentration camps "were so fantastic that few people believed them." Alexander Korda [1620] is credited with the suggestion that Chaplin play Hitler. Chaplin found Hitler's "face . . . obscenely comic—a bad imitation of me, with its absurd mustache, unruly, stringy hair and disgusting, thin little mouth. I could not take Hitler seriously. . . . The salute with the hand thrown back over the shoulder, the palm upward, made me want to put a tray of dirty dishes on it." Ironically *The Great Dictator* was controversial at the time because it dealt with Hitler unfavorably. The industry was reluctant to shut itself out of any foreign market, factions opposed to the American entry into the war protested, and even FDR, according to Chaplin, told the filmmaker, "Your picture is giving us a lot of trouble in the Argentine."

Chaplin was the first to receive simultaneous nominations as producer, actor, and writer, a feat that has been duplicated only by Orson Welles for *Citizen Kane* and Warren Beatty for *Heaven Can Wait* and *Reds.* The best picture Oscar went to *Rebecca,* James Stewart received the acting award for *The Philadelphia Story,* and the writing award went to Preston Sturges for *The Great McGinty.*

Oakie began his career on stage and moved to films with the advent of sound in 1928. Born Lewis Delaney Offield, he was raised in Oklahoma, whence his screen name. He made scores of films, most of them second features that are rarely seen today. Napolini is his most enduring performance, a spot-on parody of the dictator's mannerisms. The Oscar went to Walter Brennan for *The Westerner.*

Willson began his career as an orchestra flutist, then moved into radio as a music director for NBC on the West Coast. He did some film scoring work but turned his attention to songwriting and in 1957 wrote his first stage musical, the smash hit *The Music Man.* The Oscar for scoring went to *Pinocchio.*

Chaplin: 405, 1176, 1345. Willson: 1182.

819 • GREAT ESCAPE, THE

MIRISCH-ALPHA PICTURE PRODUCTION; UNITED ARTISTS. 1963. NOMINATION *Film Editing:* Ferris Webster.

Steve McQueen [1753], James Garner [1380], Richard Attenborough [745], Charles Bronson, Donald Pleasence, James Coburn, and David McCallum are among the POWs in a Nazi prison camp who engineer the breakout of the title. (The movie is actually a remake of a 1958 British film that was called *Breakout* in the States—Attenborough was in it, too.) Very entertaining action-adventure flick, though it's longer (168 minutes) than it needs to be. Produced and directed by John Sturges [131] from a screenplay by James Clavell and W. R. Burnett [2222], with music by Elmer Bernstein [27.5 . . .] and cinematography by Daniel Fapp [529 . . .]. McQueen did his own motorcycle stunts. The editing Oscar went to Harold F. Kress for *How the West Was Won.*

Webster: 227, 1265.

820 • GREAT EXPECTATIONS

J. ARTHUR RANK-CINEGUILD; UNIVERSAL-INTERNATIONAL (UNITED KINGDOM). 1947.

AWARDS *Black-and-White Cinematography:* Guy Green. *Black-and-White Art Direction—Set Decoration:* John Bryan, art direction; Wilfred Shingleton, set decoration.

NOMINATIONS *Picture:* Ronald Neame, producer. *Director:* David Lean. *Screenplay:* David Lean, Ronald Neame, and Anthony Havelock-Allan.

An orphaned boy named Pip encounters an escaped convict (Finlay Currie) in a churchyard and is kind to him. Later, Pip is summoned to the decaying mansion of Miss Havisham (Martita Hunt), where he meets the willful and beautiful girl Estella, played by Jean Simmons [858 . . .]. When he grows to be a young man, played by John Mills [1737], Pip learns that he will inherit a fortune (the expectations of the title). He believes Miss Havisham to be his benefactor and is shocked to learn that it is the convict instead. Chastened when his fortunes are lost, he is reunited at the end with Estella, now played by Valerie Hobson, who has also learned a lesson in humility from a disastrous marriage. This version of the novel by Charles Dickens is one of the finest adaptations of a literary classic to film, beautifully designed and photographed, and flawlessly acted. The cast also includes Alec Guinness [287 . . .] in his first important film role as Pip's friend Herbert Pocket.

Green began his career as a camera operator in the thirties and graduated to director of photography after the war. In the mid-fifties he moved into directing, with success on such films as *The Angry Silence, The Mark,* and *A Patch of Blue.*

Bryan began as a stage designer while still in his teens and moved into film in the early thirties, working on such films as *Pygmalion, Oliver Twist,* and *Becket.* He became a producer in the fifties, responsible for numerous British films, including *The Horse's Mouth.*

Gentleman's Agreement won the best picture Oscar, and Elia Kazan won for directing it. The screenplay award went to George Seaton for *Miracle on 34th Street.*

Bryan: 164, 325. Neame: 289, 1489. Lean: 287, 289, 558, 1151, 1533, 1963. Havelock-Allan: 289, 1722.

821 • GREAT GATSBY, THE

DAVID MERRICK PRODUCTION; PARAMOUNT. 1974.

AWARDS *Scoring—Original Song Score and/or Adaptation:* Nelson Riddle. *Costume Design:* Theoni V. Aldredge.

The arrival of the rich, young, handsome, and mysterious Jay Gatsby, played by Robert Redford [1502 . . .], causes quite a stir on Long Island one summer in the twenties. Caught up in his spell is a young neighbor, Nick Carraway, played by Sam Waterston [1086], who watches as others are drawn into Gatsby's aura: Gatsby's old flame, Daisy (Mia Farrow), and her husband, played by Bruce Dern [430], as well as Dern's mistress, played by Karen Black [672], and her jealous husband (Scott Wilson). The narrative line of the F. Scott Fitzgerald novel is followed fairly scrupulously in the screenplay by Francis Ford Coppola [65 . . .], but despite an opulent production and fine casting, the movie is all but comatose, languidly creeping from incident to incident, alluding to the book's themes and symbols rather than translating them into cinematic equivalents. Fitzgerald's Gatsby is an elusive, enigmatic American self-made man, but the film's Gatsby just seems like a good-looking guy who gets a bad deal. Jack Clayton [1724] directed, and the cinematography is by Douglas Slocombe [1066 . . .]. The film had been hyped as an event, with much promotion of Aldredge's designs as inspiration for the next big fashion trend: the Gatsby Look. But it was a big box-office flop, and the look was a flop in the stores.

Riddle: 338, 1172, 1518, 1708.

822 • GREAT LIE, THE

WARNER BROS. 1941.

AWARD *Supporting Actress:* Mary Astor.

Bette Davis [46 . . .] loves George Brent, but

selfish and conniving Astor steals him and marries him. When their marriage is annulled because Astor's divorce wasn't final, Davis marries Brent on the rebound. But then Brent is thought to have been killed in a plane crash, and Astor turns out to be carrying her ex-husband's child, so Davis agrees to pass off Astor's baby as her own so Astor, a concert pianist, can devote herself to her career. But is Brent really dead? What do you think? Astor herself called it a potboiler, and it's certainly ridiculous, but the two female leads give it everything they've got. Astor claimed that she and Davis rewrote much of the screenplay by Lenore Coffee [712], and even took some of the directing out of the hands of Edmund Goulding. If so, they made it a hell of a lot of fun. And Hattie McDaniel [798]—as a maid, of course—helps liven things up.

Astor said she would have preferred to win the Oscar for a film that was released the same year as *The Great Lie—The Maltese Falcon,* in which Astor also made one of her strongest screen impressions in a part that, interestingly, had previously been played by Davis in the inferior 1936 version *Satan Met a Lady.* The Oscar was no doubt in recognition of her work in both roles, as well as for a career that began in 1922. After the Oscar, MGM signed Astor to a contract that was her undoing as a film actress, since the studio cast her in maternal roles in such glossy films as *Meet Me in St. Louis* and the remake of *Little Women,* when Astor would have preferred grittier, bitchier parts. She made her last screen appearance in 1964's *Youngblood Hawke.* She died in 1987.

823 • GREAT MCGINTY, THE

PARAMOUNT. 1940.
Award *Original Screenplay:* Preston Sturges.

Brian Donlevy [161] is McGinty, who is rounded up off the street with other bums to stuff the ballot boxes on election day, and winds up in politics—becoming alderman, then mayor, then governor—by playing the game crookedly and doing what the boss, Akim Tamiroff [701 . . .], tells him to do. But along the way he also marries and has a family, and they awaken his conscience, leading to his political demise.

Brilliant, uproarious satire, slightly undermined by a few sentimental patches, but informed throughout by writer-director Sturges' loopy, affectionate take on humankind.

Though he had been a screenwriter since 1931, when he came to Hollywood to write the screenplay for his Broadway hit *Strictly Dishonorable,* this was Sturges' first directing job. It launched him into the major phase of his career, resulting in such classics as *Christmas in July* (1940), *The Lady Eve, Sullivan's Travels* (1941), *The Palm Beach Story* (1942), *Hail the Conquering Hero,* and *The Miracle of Morgan's Creek.* After leaving Paramount in 1944, however, Sturges entered a period of decline that lasted until his death in 1959. Of his later films, only *Unfaithfully Yours* (1948), which was a commercial failure at the time, now seems in a league with his great films of the early forties.

Sturges: 854, 1323.

824 • GREAT MUPPET CAPER, THE

JIM HENSON/ITC FILM ENTERTAINMENT LTD. PRODUCTION; UNIVERSAL (UNITED KINGDOM). 1981.
Nomination *Original Song:* "The First Time It Happens," music and lyrics by Joe Raposo.

The Muppets go to London to foil a jewel robbery in their second feature film, directed by Jim Henson and photographed by Oswald Morris [659 . . .]. The villains are Charles Grodin and Diana Rigg, and along the way John Cleese [670], Robert Morley [1274], Peter Ustinov [943 . . .], and Jack Warden [890 . . .] get caught up in the plot. Occasionally on the thin side, and a bit too long, but for the most part very engagingly performed, with some bright musical numbers for Miss Piggy and Kermit. The Oscar went to "Arthur's Theme (Best That You Can Do)," from *Arthur.*

825 • GREAT RACE, THE

PATRICIA-JALEM-REYNARD PRODUCTION; WARNER BROS. 1965.
Award *Sound Effects:* Tregoweth Brown.
Nominations *Color Cinematography:* Russell Harlan. *Sound:* George R. Groves, sound director, Warner Bros. Studio Sound Department. *Song:* "The Sweet-

heart Tree,'' music by Henry Mancini, lyrics by Johnny Mercer. *Film Editing:* Ralph E. Winters.

Tony Curtis [522] is the noble Leslie Gallant III and Jack Lemmon [91 . . .] the conniving Professor Fate, who square off in a New York-to-Paris auto race in 1908. Natalie Wood [1219 . . .] joins them as the feisty suffragist Maggie DuBois. Labored, overlong, pointless, but occasionally funny spoof of turn-of-the-century melodrama, with pie fights and duels and stunts and sight gags. Curtis and Lemmon give it everything they've got, as do Peter Falk [1377 . . .], Keenan Wynn, Arthur O'Connell [73 . . .], Vivian Vance, Dorothy Provine, and Larry Storch, among others, but it's still not enough to overcome the sense that this wasn't worth doing to start with. Blake Edwards [2201] directed and cowrote the story with Arthur Ross [303].

Freddie Young won the cinematography Oscar for *Doctor Zhivago. The Sound of Music* took the awards for sound and for William Reynolds' editing. The best song was ''The Shadow of Your Smile,'' by Johnny Mandel and Paul Francis Webster, from *The Sandpiper.*

Harlan: 204, 227, 879, 882, 2101. Groves: 1385, 1393, 1457, 1763, 1869, 1973, 2277. Mancini: 122, 278, 384, 494, 508, 512, 776, 1573, 1574, 1864, 1970, 2011, 2037, 2201. Mercer: 248, 278, 384, 476, 494, 508, 636, 788, 877, 903, 905, 1109, 1772, 1838, 1912, 2327, 2328. Winters: 175, 1094, 1109, 1644, 1782.

826 • GREAT SANTINI, THE

ORION PICTURES-BING CROSBY PRODUCTION; ORION PICTURES COMPANY. 1980.
NOMINATIONS *Actor:* Robert Duvall. *Supporting Actor:* Michael O'Keefe.

Duvall plays a marine pilot chafing against idleness during a time of peace (the film is set in 1962), so he takes his frustrations out on his family, bullying his teenage son, played by O'Keefe. Duvall's powerhouse performance saves the film from being just another monotonous drama about the generation gap, and he's well supported by O'Keefe and by Blythe Danner as his wife and Lisa Jane Persky as his daughter. If in the end you feel you're watching a performance

rather than getting to know a character, the fault lies less with Duvall than with the source, the autobiographical novel by Pat Conroy [1612], who fails to give dramatic shape to his experiences. The screenplay was written by Lewis John Carlino [970], who also directed. When the movie failed in several test markets, it received only a perfunctory release and was quickly sold to HBO. New York critics were enthusiastic about the movie, especially Duvall's performance, but the cable sale prevented the film from making much of an impact in theaters.

Duvall lost to Robert De Niro in *Raging Bull.* O'Keefe, who was twenty-five when he played the teenager in the film, has had little success finding substantial career-making roles. He lost to Timothy Hutton, as another troubled teenager in a dysfunctional family in *Ordinary People.*

Duvall: 92, 784, 2015.

827 • GREAT VICTOR HERBERT, THE

PARAMOUNT. 1939.
NOMINATIONS *Black-and-White Cinematography:* Victor Milner. *Sound Recording:* Loren Ryder. *Score:* Phil Boutelje and Arthur Lange.

Walter Connolly plays Herbert, the composer, who helps resolve the romantic difficulties of Allan Jones and Mary Martin. Not so much a biopic as an excuse to string together sixteen Herbert songs, including ''Ah, Sweet Mystery of Life,'' ''Tramp! Tramp! Tramp!,'' and ''Sweethearts.'' Nicely packaged fluff, and it's pleasant to see Martin in one of her handful of screen appearances. Directed by Andrew L. Stone.

Milner was only a preliminary nominee. For the 1939 awards, the first time that cinematography was divided into black-and-white and color categories, the Academy announced a first round of nominations for cinematography and then placed only two finalists, the official nominees, in each of the two divisions on the ballot: in this case, Bert Glennon for *Stagecoach* and the winner, Gregg Toland for *Wuthering Heights.* Bernard B. Brown won for the sound of *When Tomorrow Comes* and Richard Hageman, Frank Harling, John Leipold, and Leo Shuken for the score of *Stagecoach.*

Milner: 304, 412, 470, 740, 757, 1217, 1452, 1668. Ryder: 566, 979, 1452, 1669, 1697, 1703, 1837, 1887, 2012, 2168, 2181, 2183, 2230, 2242. Boutelje: 909. Lange: 171, 366, 1123, 2303.

828 • GREAT WALTZ, THE

MGM. 1938.

AWARD *Cinematography:* Joseph Ruttenberg.

NOMINATIONS *Supporting Actress:* Miliza Korjus. *Film Editing:* Tom Held.

Fernand Gravet plays Johann Strauss, with Luise Rainer [799 . . .] as his wife and Korjus as the soprano who tries to take him away from Rainer. Opulent but dopey, with one memorable sequence in which Strauss takes a carriage ride, and squeaky wheels, horse's hooves, birdcalls, and hunting horns inspire him to write "Tales From the Vienna Woods." Directed by Julien Duvivier.

Ruttenberg, born in Russia, came to the States as a boy and worked as a newspaperman before moving into the nascent field of newsreels. He went to work for Fox in 1915 and moved into feature film camera work in the twenties. This was the first of his four Oscars.

Korjus, a Polish-born coloratura soprano, was a star of the Berlin Opera. MGM came up with the memorable publicity line "Korjus—it rhymes with gorgeous," but this was her only Hollywood film. She lost the Oscar to Fay Bainter in *Jezebel.*

Though Held had two nominations—the other one for *Test Pilot*—the award for editing went to Ralph Dawson for *The Adventures of Robin Hood.*

Ruttenberg: 318, 573, 749, 769, 1069, 1232, 1371, 1861, 2234. Held: 2022.

829 • GREAT WAR, THE

DINO DE LAURENTIIS CINEMATOGRAFICA (ITALY). 1959.

NOMINATION *Foreign Language Film.*

Vittorio Gassman and Alberto Sordi, World War I soldiers, go AWOL during a big battle, but decide to return to the front when they learn that the rest of their company has been killed. Shambling, erratic comedy that turns serious toward the end. Directed

by Mario Monicelli [367 . . .]. The Oscar went to *Black Orpheus.*

830 • GREAT WHITE HOPE, THE

LAWRENCE TURMAN FILMS PRODUCTION; 20TH CENTURY-FOX. 1970.

NOMINATIONS *Actor:* James Earl Jones. *Actress:* Jane Alexander.

Jones plays heavyweight champ Jack Jefferson (a character modeled on Jack Johnson). Alexander is the white woman who becomes his lover, precipitating his fall. Howard Sackler adapted his Broadway play, but imperfectly—it's still much too theatrical. Directed by Martin Ritt [956], with Chester Morris [38] (his last film), Robert Webber, Hal Holbrook, Beah Richards [843], and Moses Gunn.

Jones is one of the strongest presences on stage and film, but this is his only nomination, a fact that underscores the lack of good roles for black actors. He made his Broadway debut in 1957 and became a star with the 1966 stage production of *Great White Hope.* His first film role was in 1964, in *Dr. Strangelove.* His familiar bass voice emanates from Darth Vader (whose body is that of David Prowse) in *Star Wars* and its two sequels. He lost the Oscar to George C. Scott in *Patton.*

Alexander won a Tony for her performance in the stage version of *Great White Hope.* The film version was her first screen appearance. She lost to Glenda Jackson in *Women in Love.*

Alexander: 54, 1111, 2023.

831 • GREAT ZIEGFELD, THE

MGM. 1936.

AWARDS *Picture:* Hunt Stromberg, producer. *Actress:* Luise Rainer. *Dance Direction:* Seymour Felix.

NOMINATIONS *Director:* Robert Z. Leonard. *Original Story:* William Anthony McGuire. *Interior Decoration:* Cedric Gibbons, Eddie Imazu, and Edwin B. Willis. *Film Editing:* William S. Gray.

William Powell [1170 . . .] plays the legendary Broadway producer Florenz Ziegfeld, with Rainer as his first wife, Anna Held, and Myrna Loy as his second, Billie Burke [1306]. Ziegfeld was noted for extravagant staging and so was MGM, so it's entertainingly huge but not hugely entertaining, if you get what we mean. The movie also features a lot of Ziegfeld's stars, such as Fanny Brice, Ray Bolger, and Gilda Gray, as well as actors playing other stars, such as Eddie Cantor and Will Rogers. But its selection as best picture of any year is a travesty. Among the nominated films, *Dodsworth, Libeled Lady,* and *Mr. Deeds Goes to Town* are superior, and the nonnominees include *My Man Godfrey, Fury, Show Boat, Swing Time,* and *Modern Times.*

Rainer was a twenty-six-year-old Viennese actress who had studied with Max Reinhardt. After introducing her in a minor film, *Escapade* (1935), in which she replaced Myrna Loy, who was involved in a contract dispute, MGM began a buildup for Rainer, whom it saw as a possible successor to Greta Garbo [84 . . .]. She won critical acclaim for her big scene in *The Great Ziegfeld,* in which she speaks to Ziegfeld on the telephone, congratulating him on his marriage to Burke. In later years Rainer's role in a three-hour film in which she has only a small amount of screen time would have been considered a supporting performance. Her competitors for the Oscar—Irene Dunne in *Theodora Goes Wild,* Gladys George in *Valiant Is the Word for Carrie,* Carole Lombard in *My Man Godfrey,* and Norma Shearer in *Romeo and Juliet*—all had bigger roles than Rainer. But MGM shrewdly pushed Rainer's performance, seeing an opportunity to create another major star. Unfortunately, after a second Oscar for *The Good Earth,* the studio found little for her to do, and her career was short-lived.

Felix had joined the exodus from Broadway to Hollywood that took place with the arrival of sound and the rise of the movie musical. He choreographed numerous musicals from 1929 through the early fifties. His nomination cited in particular his work on the number "A Pretty Girl Is Like a Melody." But what most people remember from that number is the extravagant tiered wedding cake set, not the dancing. The singer in the number, incidentally, is billed as Stanley Morner, who later changed his name to Dennis Morgan. But it's not Morner/Morgan's voice we hear, but Allan Jones'.

Leonard was one of MGM's reliable staff director-producers, usually assigned to musicals and light-weight romances. Of his films, only *Pride and Prejudice* stands out today as a first-rate achievement. The Oscar went to Frank Capra for *Mr. Deeds Goes to Town.*

Pierre Collings and Sheridan Gibney won the writing award for *The Story of Louis Pasteur.* The art direction award went to Richard Day for *Dodsworth.* Ralph Dawson won for the editing of *Anthony Adverse.*

Stromberg: 1419, 2052. Rainer: 799. Leonard: 555. Gibbons: 66, 87, 130, 217, 227, 239, 285, 290, 440, 629, 749, 980, 1069, 1096, 1173, 1190, 1226, 1230, 1232, 1274, 1308, 1309, 1417, 1567, 1604, 1644, 1662, 1673, 1721, 1861, 1937, 2068, 2112, 2256, 2257, 2300, 2320, 2330. Willis: 66, 87, 130, 227, 239, 290, 629, 749, 980, 1069, 1096, 1157, 1173, 1190, 1226, 1230, 1232, 1309, 1417, 1567, 1657, 1662, 1673, 1721, 1861, 1937, 2068, 2112, 2257, 2320, 2330.

832 • GREATEST SHOW ON EARTH, THE

CECIL B. DEMILLE PRODUCTIONS; PARAMOUNT. 1952.

AWARDS *Picture:* Cecil B. DeMille, producer. *Motion Picture Story:* Frederic M. Frank, Theodore St. John, and Frank Cavett.

NOMINATIONS *Director:* Cecil B. DeMille. *Film Editing:* Anne Bauchens. *Color Costume Design:* Edith Head, Dorothy Jeakins, and Miles White.

Love and intrigue at the circus, with Betty Hutton and Cornel Wilde [1872] as trapeze artists, Charlton Heston [175] as a cranky, put-upon ringmaster, Dorothy Lamour and Gloria Grahame [130 . . .] as specialty-act performers, and James Stewart [73 . . .] as a clown who never takes off his makeup because he has a deep, dark secret. There are also cameo appearances by Bing Crosby [173 . . .], Bob Hope, Edmond O'Brien [146 . . .], and Hopalong Cassidy (William Boyd), plus of course lots of real circus acts and the usual DeMille spectacle, in this case a big train wreck. Hutton and Wilde actually learned to do trapeze work for the film—in Wilde's case an instance of suffering for his art: The actor, an athlete with a long career of swashbucklers, was prone to acrophobia. A cornball classic, still quite watchable even though it's really a two-and-a-half-hour commercial for Ringling Brothers and Barnum & Bailey Circus. But best picture of the year? Better than nominees like *High Noon, Moulin Rouge,* and *The Quiet Man?* (We'll grant its superiority to *Ivanhoe,* the fifth nominee.) And what about the unnominated movies: the supernal *Singin' in the Rain,* the snarky *The Bad and the Beautiful* (which won five Oscars, more than any other film not nominated for best picture), or the great Alec Guinness comedies *The Man in the White Suit* and *The Lavender Hill Mob?*

The reasons for the best picture award probably lie in the complex love-hate relationship between Cecil B. DeMille and the film industry, and in the tormented politics of Cold War America. DeMille was often spoken of as the father of Hollywood, to which he had come in 1914 to film *The Squaw Man* in partnership with Jesse Lasky [1779 . . .] and Samuel Goldwyn [102 . . .]. The original plan had been to shoot the movie in Flagstaff, Arizona, but when DeMille got there, he was unimpressed with the landscape and decided to go on to California. As a result, *The Squaw Man* was the first feature-length movie shot in Hollywood. DeMille settled there and formed the nucleus of what would eventually become Paramount Studios, with which, except for a few years in the twenties, he was associated for the rest of his career. In his early years in Hollywood, he helped make a star of Gloria Swanson [1739 . . .] with a series of sexy comedies. Later he became celebrated for his epics, often on biblical themes, filled with spectacular orgies and decadence that were thoroughly and sometimes sadistically punished by a vengeful deity. Critics decried DeMille's vulgarity; audiences lapped it up. In the later thirties and in the forties DeMille went out of vogue, but he made a surprising comeback with *Samson and Delilah;* it became clear that he could give the public something they couldn't get on twelve-inch black-and-white TV screens: bigness. At the same time, DeMille's political conservatism, which had been out of vogue during the New Deal and war years, came back in fashion. In 1950 he fought a battle with Joseph L. Mankiewicz [46 . . .], a liberal, over control of the Directors Guild and the insti-

tution of a loyalty oath aimed at the communists and ex-communist liberals who were being investigated by the House Un-American Activities Committee. DeMille lost the battle, and also saw Mankiewicz's *All About Eve* win the Oscars for picture, director, and writer, when DeMille's *Samson and Delilah* was shut out of those categories. But by the 1952 awards, the witch-hunting of the McCarthy era had caused such nervousness and paranoia in Hollywood that it was politically unwise to take a stand against right-wingers like DeMille. So although the smart money at the Oscars was on the critically acclaimed and very popular *High Noon,* that film was tainted because its writer, Carl Foreman, had invoked the Fifth Amendment in testifying before HUAC. A vote for DeMille's movie may have looked like a perverse form of political correctness.

The film's other Oscar, for story, was an easier choice. The competition included three relatively low-wattage features—*The Narrow Margin, The Pride of St. Louis,* and *The Sniper*—and Leo McCarey's hysterically anticommunist melodrama *My Son John,* which had been a box-office flop. In this company the clichés and bland characterization of *The Greatest Show* look almost reassuring.

The Academy could still not bring itself to reward DeMille as a director (this was his only nomination in that category), though he remains one of the movies' best storytellers and most distinctive stylists (setting aside the question of the quality of both stories and style). Instead, they gave the Oscar to John Ford for *The Quiet Man.*

Perhaps deciding that film editing is a relatively noncontroversial task, the Academy voted the Oscar to Elmo Williams and Harry Gerstad for *High Noon.* Marcel Vertes won for the costumes for *Moulin Rouge.*

DeMille: 412, 2012. Cavett: 787, 1845. Bauchens: 412, 1452, 2012. Head: 31, 32, 46, 305, 357, 363, 612, 636, 675, 736, 894, 945, 1003, 1219, 1261, 1263, 1398, 1427, 1504, 1550, 1579, 1587, 1631, 1716, 1727, 1738, 1748, 1840, 1927, 1986, 2012, 2098, 2247, 2298. Jeakins: 393, 509, 882, 1048, 1385, 1391, 1432, 1748, 1881, 2012, 2238. White: 101, 2043.

833 • GREATEST STORY EVER TOLD, THE

GEORGE STEVENS PRODUCTION; UNITED ARTISTS. 1965.
NOMINATIONS *Color Cinematography:* William C. Mellor and Loyal Griggs. *Color Art Direction—Set Decoration:* Richard Day, William Creber, and David Hall; Ray Moyer, Fred MacLean, and Norman Rockett. *Music Score—Substantially Original:* Alfred Newman. *Color Costume Design:* Vittorio Nino Novarese and Marjorie Best. *Special Visual Effects:* J. McMillan Johnson.

The life of Christ, played by Max von Sydow [1546], with Dorothy McGuire [759] and Robert Loggia [1039] as Mary and Joseph, Charlton Heston [175] as John the Baptist, David McCallum as Judas, Telly Savalas [210] as Pontius Pilate, Claude Rains [365 . . .] as Herod, and (take a deep breath now) Robert Blake, Jamie Farr, Roddy McDowall, Janet Margolin, Sidney Poitier [522 . . .], Carroll Baker [119], Pat Boone, Van Heflin [1055], Sal Mineo [630 . . .], Shelley Winters [542 . . .], Ed Wynn [542], John Wayne [33 . . .], Angela Lansbury [749 . . .], Martin Landau [461 . . .], Joseph Schildkraut [1169], Jose Ferrer [473 . . .], Donald Pleasence, Richard Conte, "and members of the Inbal Dance Theatre of Israel." Whoppingly stultifying mega-epic, whose pretentiousness can be gauged by the screenplay credit "in Creative Association with Carl Sandburg." It is also the sad labor of love—or love's labor lost—of a major director, George Stevens [542 . . .], who devoted five years to making it only to find that the vogue for the religious epic had passed. After an initial release in a four-hour-and-twenty-minute version, it was cut to three hours and fifteen minutes and finally to less than two and a half hours, but never found an audience. Critics ridiculed it, most of them pointing out its most obvious flaw: the overlarding of the film with cameos that provoke whispers of "Isn't that . . . ?" instead of attention to the narrative, which in any case held no surprises.

Doctor Zhivago won the Oscars for cinematography (Freddie Young), art direction, score (Maurice Jarre), and costumes (Phyllis Dalton). The special effects award went to *Thunderball,* a film more in tune with the times.

Mellor: 542, 1558, 1579. Griggs: 988, 1799, 1887, 2012. Day: 22, 102, 235, 487, 510, 560, 569, 797, 864, 952, 1048, 1175, 1397, 1477, 1666, 1949, 2056, 2120, 2276. Creber: 1596, 2126. Hall: 2240. Moyer: 278, 413, 736, 1101, 1120, 1214, 1674, 1738, 1748, 1975, 2012. MacLean: 16, 1779. Rockett: 2120. Newman: 31, 34, 46, 72, 138, 182, 226, 333, 334, 347, 375, 428, 437, 457, 476, 495, 542, 690, 797, 952, 953, 959, 962, 1016, 1082, 1088, 1213, 1278, 1362, 1397, 1475, 1616, 1655, 1849, 1868, 1883, 1921, 2043, 2046, 2091, 2258, 2286, 2294, 2316. Novarese: 29, 413, 465, 1610. Best: 15, 768, 1973. Johnson: 636, 978, 1388, 1595, 2098.

834 • GREEN CARD

GREEN CARD COMPANY PRODUCTION; BUENA VISTA. 1990.
NOMINATION *Screenplay Written Directly for the Screen:* Peter Weir.

Prim Andie MacDowell agrees to marry shambling Gérard Depardieu [474] so he can stay in the States, with the understanding that they can go their separate ways once his residence is legally established. But the immigration authorities get suspicious, forcing her to let him move into her apartment. And—surprise!—they fall in love. Likable romantic comedy that could have been made in 1940 with Irene Dunne [114 . . .] and Charles Boyer [36 . . .], but seems a little old-fashioned half a century later. At least it avoids a cop-out happy ending. Depardieu, in his first English-language film, is delightful. Weir, who also directed the movie, lost to Bruce Joel Rubin for *Ghost.*

Weir: 511, 2296.

835 • GREEN DOLPHIN STREET

MGM. 1947.
AWARD *Special Effects:* A. Arnold Gillespie and Warren Newcombe, visual; Douglas Shearer and Michael Steinore, audible.
NOMINATIONS *Black-and-White Cinematography:* George Folsey. *Sound Recording:* MGM Studio Sound Department, Douglas Shearer, sound director. *Film Editing:* George White.

Lana Turner [1558] marries Richard Hart after he

proposes by mail seeking a helpmeet for his ranch in New Zealand. Actually it turns out that it was her sweet sister Donna Reed [732] that he really wanted to marry. With the aid of Van Heflin [1055], Lana endures mismating, an earthquake, and a Maori uprising. Galumphing, improbable saga based on a plot-heavy novel by Elizabeth Goudge. The earthquake, which won the Oscar, is the star, though the cast also includes Frank Morgan [22 . . .], Edmund Gwenn [1325 . . .], May Whitty [1371 . . .], and Gladys Cooper [1393 . . .]. Directed by Victor Saville [406 . . .].

The cinematography Oscar went to Guy Green for *Great Expectations. The Bishop's Wife* took the sound award, and Francis Lyon and Robert Parrish won for editing *Body and Soul.*

Gillespie: 175, 256, 685, 704, 1371, 1388, 1905, 2048, 2055, 2122, 2300. Newcombe: 1371, 2055. Shearer: 136, 202, 256, 685, 817, 1096, 1232, 1292, 1371, 1419, 1751, 1950, 1988, 2048, 2055, 2211, 2300. Steinore: 1905, 2048. Folsey: 51, 137, 629, 807, 838, 1124, 1299, 1320, 1500, 1688, 1782, 2068, 2269.

836 • GREEN GODDESS, THE

WARNER BROS. 1929–30.

NOMINATION *Actor:* George Arliss.

Arliss plays an oriental ruler who makes a group of British his prisoners. Stiff and stagy re-creation of a very dated melodrama by William Archer that was one of Arliss' stage hits. He also filmed it as a silent in 1923. This one is directed by Alfred E. Green, and the cast includes H. B. Warner [1206]. On the Oscar ballot, Arliss was listed as a candidate for his performances in both *The Green Goddess* and *Disraeli.* He was cited as a winner for the latter, and there's no explanation in Academy records why *The Green Goddess* was not also mentioned.

Arliss: 550.

837 • GREEN GRASS OF WYOMING

20TH CENTURY-FOX. 1948.

NOMINATION *Color Cinematography:* Charles G. Clarke.

Peggy Cummins, Robert Arthur, Charles Coburn [535 . . .], and Lloyd Nolan star in a story about horse ranchers, the third in a series of adaptations of novels by Mary O'Hara that began with *My Friend Flicka* (1943) and continued with *Thunderhead—Son of Flicka* in 1945. The first is the best, though they're all beautifully filmed. Directed by Louis King. Clarke lost to Joseph Valentine, William V. Skall, and Winton Hoch for *Joan of Arc.*

Clarke: 897, 1352, 1752.

838 • GREEN YEARS, THE

MGM. 1946.

NOMINATIONS *Supporting Actor:* Charles Coburn. *Black-and-White Cinematography:* George Folsey.

An Irish-born orphan, played first by Dean Stockwell [1281] and later by Tom Drake, grows up with his mother's large family in Scotland. A. J. Cronin's sentimental novel gets a lavishly sticky treatment from MGM, but it's chiefly notable only for Coburn's performance and for being the film in which Jessica Tandy [580 . . .] plays the daughter of Hume Cronyn [1791], her real-life husband. Tandy, who is two years older than Cronyn, was pregnant during the filming and gave birth the day after shooting finished. She's filmed behind tables and swathed in shawls throughout.

Coburn lost to Harold Russell in *The Best Years of Our Lives.* The cinematography award went to Arthur Miller for *Anna and the King of Siam.*

Coburn: 535, 1353. Folsey: 51, 137, 629, 807, 835, 1124, 1299, 1320, 1500, 1688, 1782, 2068, 2269.

839 • GREYSTOKE: THE LEGEND OF TARZAN, LORD OF THE APES

WARNER BROS. PRODUCTION; WARNER BROS. (UNITED KINGDOM). 1984.

NOMINATIONS *Supporting Actor:* Ralph Richardson. *Screenplay Based on Material From Another Medium:* P. H. Vazak [Robert Towne] and Michael Austin. *Makeup:* Rick Baker and Paul Engelen.

When his explorer parents are killed in the jungle, an infant is raised by apes. As a young man, played by Christopher Lambert, he is discovered by an explorer, played by Ian Holm [386], who brings him back to England and his inheritance, the estate of Greystoke. His eccentric grandfather, played by Richardson, accepts him as the next Lord Greystoke, and the young man (he is never called Tarzan in the film) is soon attracted to a woman named Jane, played by Andie MacDowell. But civilization, he will also learn, has its discontents. Promising material but very badly handled. Director Hugh Hudson [386] mangles the tone, sometimes playing the material for laughs, sometimes for pathos, but not delivering much of either. And he has no feel for the arc of a story—the material builds toward a climax that never comes. Lambert is a physically impressive Tarzan, but he's not given a character that makes much sense dramatically. MacDowell, in her film debut, is lovely, but the producers decided that her southern accent was a mistake and had her voice dubbed by Glenn Close [199 . . .].

Of the performers, Richardson, in his last film role, makes the strongest impression, perhaps because his eccentricity as an actor is in keeping with the scattered aimlessness of the narrative. He gives us nothing that we haven't seen before—he could be playing the same role he played in *The Wrong Box* almost twenty years earlier—but when his character dies, so does the film. The Oscar went to Haing S. Ngor for *The Killing Fields*.

Towne had originally written the screenplay as an updating of the Tarzan story that would reflect scientific discoveries about the kinship of apes and humans. When Hudson took over the film, he wanted to expand the material to make a statement about civilization and its impact on the environment and hired Austin to rewrite. Distressed by what had been done to his script, Towne had his name removed from the credits—P. H. Vazak is the name of Towne's dog. The Oscar went to Peter Shaffer for *Amadeus*.

What remains of Towne's concept, the scenes involving the infant Lord Greystoke and his ape family, demanded sophisticated makeup to turn actors into credible apes. The artists responsible for the apemen, Baker and Engelen, lost to Paul LeBlanc and Dick Smith for *Amadeus*.

Richardson: 894. Towne: 395, 1135, 1798. Baker: 68, 431, 595.8, 874. Engelen: 1285.5.

840 • GRIFTERS, THE

MARTIN SCORSESE PRODUCTION; MIRAMAX FILMS. 1990.
NOMINATION *Actress:* Anjelica Huston. *Supporting Actress:* Annette Bening. *Director:* Stephen Frears. *Screenplay Based on Material From Another Medium:* Donald E. Westlake.

John Cusack plays a small-time con artist who has teamed up with Bening, also a grifter. But then Cusack's mother, played by Huston, comes back in his life, and he's torn between her con games and Bening's. A film with a snaky fascination, brought about by three masterly performances, a coldhearted script, and first-rate direction. It's a triumph of the tawdry, one of the best efforts in the low-life genre since *Double Indemnity*. You don't have to like it, but it's certainly good at what it does.

Huston lost to Kathy Bates in *Misery*. Bening, who shot to stardom with this role and the following year's *Bugsy*, put her career on hold for marriage to Warren Beatty [255 . . .] and motherhood. She lost to Whoopi Goldberg in *Ghost*.

Frears began his film career as an assistant to director Karel Reisz on *Morgan!* and worked on several other features in the late sixties before turning his attention to television work. He emerged as a hot talent in 1985 with *My Beautiful Laundrette* and gained critical acclaim and wide popular attention with *Dangerous Liaisons* in 1988. Though that film was nominated for best picture, Frears was omitted from the directing nominees. The situation was reversed with a nomination for directing *The Grifters* but no nomination for the picture. After losing to Kevin Costner for *Dances With Wolves*, Frears had a career downturn with *Hero*, which received lukewarm critical and audience response in 1992, but his 1993 film, *The Snapper*, was warmly received by critics and art-house audiences.

Westlake's screenplay, an adaptation of a novel by Jim Thompson, lost to Michael Blake's for *Dances With Wolves*.

Huston: 617, 1625.

841 • GUARDSMAN, THE

MGM. 1931–32.

NOMINATIONS *Actor:* Alfred Lunt. *Actress:* Lynn Fontanne.

Lunt and Fontanne, a famous acting couple, play a famous acting couple. He's jealous, so he disguises himself and pays court to her to test her fidelity. But this is a no-win situation: If she doesn't respond, does that mean he's not a persuasive seducer? And if she does respond, does he really want her to? Not much of a movie, but welcome as a record of a celebrated stage performance. Directed by Sidney Franklin [799 . . .]; the cast includes Roland Young [2117] and ZaSu Pitts.

Lunt and Fontanne first played their roles in the Ferenc Molnar play on Broadway in 1924. Both had appeared in a few silent films, but this was their only talkie except for a cameo appearance in *Stage Door Canteen* in 1943. Lunt was the odd man out in a three-way race that saw Wallace Beery in *The Champ* and Fredric March in *Dr. Jekyll and Mr. Hyde* win the Oscar in a tie. (There is some speculation that Lunt's pique at coming in third made him decide to make no more movies.) Fontanne lost to another import from the Broadway stage, Helen Hayes, in *The Sin of Madelon Claudet.*

842 • GUERRE EST FINIE, LA

SOFRACIMA AND EUROPA-FILM PRODUCTION; BRANDON FILMS INC. (FRANCE/SWEDEN). 1967.

NOMINATION *Story and Screenplay—Written Directly for the Screen:* Jorge Semprun.

Yves Montand plays an aging anti-Franco revolutionary who wearily makes the rounds on behalf of a cause he knows was lost thirty years earlier. Ingrid Thulin is his mistress and Genevieve Bujold [85] his young student lover. Director Alan Resnais gives it his characteristic narrative complexity, including flash-forwards, but it doesn't really add up to much. At the time, it was much praised—like Resnais' *Last Year at Marienbad* and *Hiroshima, Mon Amour*—by critics and eagerly debated by film students. Today it just seems a rather aimless exploration of melancholia enlivened by some erotic sequences. Semprun's screenplay lost to William Rose's for *Guess Who's Coming to Dinner.*

Semprun: 2344.

843 • GUESS WHO'S COMING TO DINNER

COLUMBIA. 1967.

AWARDS *Actress:* Katharine Hepburn. *Story and Screenplay—Written Directly for the Screen:* William Rose. **NOMINATIONS** *Picture:* Stanley Kramer, producer. *Actor:* Spencer Tracy. *Supporting Actor:* Cecil Kellaway. *Supporting Actress:* Beah Richards. *Director:* Stanley Kramer. *Art Direction—Set Decoration:* Robert Clatworthy; Frank Tuttle. *Scoring of Music—Adaptation or Treatment:* DeVol. *Film Editing:* Robert C. Jones.

Well-to-do liberal San Franciscans Hepburn and Tracy have their values tested when their daughter, played by Katharine Houghton, brings home her fiancé, played by Sidney Poitier [522 . . .]. Well, it's not much of a test—Poitier is urbane, handsome, and up for a Nobel Prize. (The real question is what he sees in her.) Only the potent teaming of Hepburn and Tracy, in their ninth and last film together, redeems this problem comedy without a real problem: Tracy found more to worry about when his daughter was marrying a white guy in *Father of the Bride.* The film's lack of an edge, in a year when films with an edge such as *Bonnie and Clyde, The Graduate,* and *In Cold Blood* were attracting attention, didn't seem to matter, however. It was a box-office success, and the protests of white supremacists supplied the controversy that the film itself lacked. It was a natural for the Academy—a film that could validate the image of the Oscars as rewarding serious, socially relevant filmmaking without being too controversial. Unfortunately for Kramer, there was another nominee that had the same socially relevant theme, also starred Poitier, and had more bite: *In the Heat of the Night,* which won the best picture Oscar.

Hepburn was a driving force behind the film, putting her own money into it in order to allow the ailing and uninsurable Tracy to appear in it, as well as engineering the film debut of her niece, Houghton, whose career consists mainly of this movie. Hepburn was rewarded with the second of her four Oscars, thirty-four years after her first. While it's a performance with some of her usual steely assurance, it's essentially a backup role to Tracy—one catches her anxiety for him in every scene they share. And is it really superior to the performances of the other nominees: Anne Bancroft in *The Graduate,* Faye Dunaway in *Bonnie and Clyde,* Edith Evans in *The Whisperers,* and Audrey Hepburn in *Wait Until Dark?*

Rose's script, as several critics have noted, seems like an adaptation of a stage play, even though it was written for the screen. Though born in America, Rose began his career as a screenwriter in England, where he produced his earlier nominated scripts, for *Genevieve* and *The Ladykillers.* After Tracy's death, he and Hepburn had a brief relationship. He died in England in 1987.

The emphysema and heart trouble that killed Tracy only a few weeks after filming ended put constraints on the production, both financial and logistical—Tracy was on the set only a few hours each day. He lost the Oscar to Rod Steiger in *In the Heat of the Night.*

This was the next-to-last film for Kellaway, who plays Monsignor Ryan, a family friend. His final appearance, three years before his death, was in 1970's *Getting Straight.* The Oscar went to George Kennedy for *Cool Hand Luke.*

Richards plays Poitier's understanding mother and has a big scene in which she reassures Tracy about the marriage. Her films include *The Miracle Worker, In the Heat of the Night, The Great White Hope, Mahogany,* and *Drugstore Cowboy* (1989). She lost to Estelle Parsons in *Bonnie and Clyde.*

Kramer's middle-of-the-road liberalism, which seemed daring in the conservative fifties, went out of fashion in the socially and politically turbulent late sixties. In 1970 he tried making a movie about the campus protests of the era, *R.P.M.* It was laughed off the screen. *Guess Who's Coming* is his last major film. He lost the directing Oscar to Mike Nichols for *The Graduate.*

Camelot won the Oscars for art direction and for Alfred Newman and Ken Darby's scoring. The award for editing went to Hal Ashby for *In the Heat of the Night.*

Hepburn: 24, 40, 1177, 1199, 1357, 1473, 1563, 1654, 1956, 1963, 2305. Rose: 758, 1128, 1736. Kramer: 330, 522, 912, 1065, 1812. Tracy: 131, 271, 352, 656, 1000, 1065, 1470, 1751. Kellaway: 1224. Clatworthy: 1003, 1632, 1812, 2035. Tuttle: 1093, 2066. Devol: 371, 963, 1572. Jones: 264, 430, 1032.

844 • *GUEST IN THE HOUSE*

GUEST IN THE HOUSE INC.; UNITED ARTISTS. 1945.
NOMINATION *Scoring of a Dramatic or Comedy Picture:* Werner Janssen.

Anne Baxter [46 . . .] comes to visit Ralph Bellamy [114] and Ruth Warrick and turns out to be seriously disturbed—obsessed with their home and willing to do anything to possess it for herself. Nicely edgy thriller, directed by John Brahm, with good performances by the leads, plus Aline MacMahon [576] and Margaret Hamilton. Miklos Rozsa won the Oscar for the score of *Spellbound.*

Janssen: 233, 349, 624, 757, 1884.

845 • *GUEST WIFE*

GREENTREE PRODUCTIONS; UNITED ARTISTS. 1945.
NOMINATION *Scoring of a Dramatic or Comedy Picture:* Daniele Amfitheatrof.

Bachelor Don Ameche [419] wants to impress his family-oriented boss, so he persuades Claudette Colbert [1025 . . .], who is married to his best friend (Dick Foran), to pretend to be his wife. Silly farce with more star power than it deserves, directed by Sam Wood [701 . . .]. The Oscar went to Miklos Rozsa for *Spellbound.*

Amfitheatrof: 1871.

846 • *GULLIVER'S TRAVELS*

PARAMOUNT. 1939.
NOMINATIONS *Song:* "Faithful Forever," music by Ralph Rainger, lyrics by Leo Robin. *Original Score:* Victor Young.

The sailor Gulliver is cast ashore in the land of Lilliput, where the people are only a few inches tall.

He gets involved in the country's dispute with neighboring Blefuscu and helps further the romance between the daughter of the king of Lilliput and the son of the king of Blefuscu. Muddled animated cartoon based on the first book of Jonathan Swift's satire, eliminating the original's scatological humor and savage inquiry into the nature of man. Fleischer studios, the creators of the Betty Boop and Popeye shorts, were pressured by Paramount into this feature-length project after the huge success of *Snow White and the Seven Dwarfs.* "If Disney can make feature-length animated films, why can't we?" went the reasoning, and the question is still being asked, ruefully and after the fact, by the makers of such flops as *FernGully . . . The Last Rainforest* and *The Swan Princess.* In this case, it was because there wasn't a workable story, and the project was done in less than two years, compared with the Disney studios' four years of work on *Snow White.*

In the film the nominated song is the result of combining two rival national anthems, "Faithful" and "Forever," the film's equivalent of Swift's Lilliputian dispute over whether you open the little end or the big end of a boiled egg. The Oscar went to Harold Arlen and E. Y. Harburg's "Over the Rainbow," from *The Wizard of Oz,* another film said to have been inspired by the success of *Snow White. The Wizard* also won the Oscar for Herbert Stothart's scoring.

Rainger: 197, 1805. Robin: 104, 197, 368, 1072, 1805, 1843, 2032, 2088, 2310. Young: 97, 98, 100, 101, 280, 489, 612, 693, 701, 794, 925, 1214, 1257, 1396, 1452, 1748, 1823, 1994, 2235, 2315.

847 • GUNFIGHT AT THE O.K. CORRAL

HAL WALLIS PRODUCTIONS; PARAMOUNT. 1957.
NOMINATIONS *Sound Recording:* George Dutton. *Film Editing:* Warren Low.

Burt Lancaster [107 . . .] is Wyatt Earp and Kirk Douglas [130 . . .] Doc Holliday in this version of their classic showdown with the Clantons, directed by John Sturges [131] from a screenplay by Leon Uris. The big confrontation is well staged, but there's not a lot to hold our attention until we get to it except whether Doc will be sober enough to participate. The

movie suffers from the inevitable comparison to the superior John Ford [815 . . .] tale of the shoot-out, *My Darling Clementine* (1946). The good cast includes Jo Van Fleet [593], John Ireland [53], Dennis Hopper [595 . . .], and DeForest Kelley. The Oscar for sound went to *Sayonara.* Peter Taylor won for the editing of *The Bridge on the River Kwai.*

Dutton: 1855, 1934, 2175, 2200. Low: 425, 1162, 1727.

848 • GUNFIGHTER, THE

20TH CENTURY-FOX. 1950.
NOMINATION *Motion Picture Story:* William Bowers and Andre de Toth.

Gregory Peck [759 . . .] wants to lay down the guns that have given him his reputation, but every two-bit punk—e.g., Richard Jaeckel [1864]—wants to have a go at the champ. Solid, serious western—maybe a little too serious, though it has its share of well-staged action. Directed by Henry King, with exceptional crisp black-and-white cinematography by Arthur Miller [83 . . .]. The story award went to Edna and Edward Anhalt for *Panic in the Streets.*

Bowers: 1809.

849 • GUNGA DIN

RKO RADIO. 1939.
NOMINATION *Black-and-White Cinematography:* Joseph H. August.

Cary Grant [1445 . . .], Victor McLaglen [999 . . .], and Douglas Fairbanks, Jr., are an inseparable trio of roistering soldiers of the crown in India. But then Fairbanks threatens to break up the gang by marrying Joan Fontaine [441 . . .]. Loyal water-bearer Gunga Din, played by Sam Jaffe [105], longs to be a soldier, too. And meanwhile, the thuggee cult, devotees of Kali, are incited to mayhem by priest Eduardo Cianelli. Blissful nonsense, too light-hearted and light-headed to be taken seriously and criticized for being imperialist and racist, though some have done so. It may have been inspired by the poem by Rudyard Kipling, but screenwriters Ben Hecht [78 . . .] and Charles MacArthur [1664 . . .] were also inspired by their own play, *The Front Page,* from which they stole the bit about marriage breaking up the old gang. Joel Sayre and Fred Guiol [768] did the final screenplay, but director George Stevens [542 . . .] encouraged Grant to improvise much of his role—which he switched with Fairbanks at the last moment. The result is an enduring, endearing classic, which has in turn inspired a lot of inferior movies, including *Soldiers Three* (1951), *Sergeants 3* (a 1962 Rat Pack western version with Sammy Davis, Jr., in the Jaffe role), and *Indiana Jones and the Temple of Doom.* On the other hand, it also inspired a good movie, *The Man Who Would Be King,* and may have led to Grant's being cast in *His Girl Friday,* a more straightforward remake of *The Front Page* in 1940.

Underappreciated by the Academy, August was a pioneer, who began his career in 1911 with Thomas Ince and did memorable work on such films as *Twentieth Century* (1934), *The Informer,* and *The Hunchback of Notre Dame.* This time he was only a preliminary nominee for the Oscar. For the 1939 awards the Academy announced a first round of nominations for cinematography and then placed only two finalists in each of the two divisions—black and white and color—on the ballot. The official nominees were Bert Glennon for *Stagecoach* and the winner, Gregg Toland for *Wuthering Heights.*

August: 1595.

850 • GUNS OF NAVARONE, THE

CARL FOREMAN PRODUCTION; COLUMBIA (U.S./UNITED KINGDOM). 1961.

AWARD *Special Effects:* Bill Warrington, visual; Vivian C. Greenham, audible.

NOMINATIONS *Picture:* Carl Foreman, producer. *Director:* J. Lee Thompson. *Screenplay—Based on Material From Another Medium:* Carl Foreman. *Sound:* John Cox, sound director, Shepperton Studio Sound Department. *Scoring of a Dramatic or Comedy Picture:* Dimitri Tiomkin. *Film Editing:* Alan Osbiston.

Gregory Peck [759 . . .] heads an Allied suicide mission during World War II: an assault on a Greek island where the Nazis have two huge cannons that can easily destroy any invading force. Along for the attack are David Niven [1778], Anthony Quinn

[1226 . . .], Stanley Baker, Anthony Quayle [85], Irene Papas, and Richard Harris [660 . . .]. Fine action adventure based on a novel by Alistair MacLean. The special effects show their age a bit, but they were state-of-the-art at the time.

Today, when action flicks are the bread and butter of Hollywood, *Guns* seems like a peculiar choice as a best picture nominee. But its mission-impossible heroics seemed fresh until the James Bond series (which started up the next year) made them routine. One also suspects a certain eagerness of the Academy to make amends to Foreman, who had been blacklisted and moved to England during the fifties. He had not been credited for his work on the screenplay of *The Bridge on the River Kwai,* which received an Oscar in the name of Pierre Boulle, the French novelist who had written the book on which it was based. But the best picture Oscar went to *West Side Story,* and Foreman's screenplay lost to Abby Mann's for *Judgment at Nuremberg.*

Lee Thompson, a former actor and screenwriter, began his directing career in England in the fifties. His post-*Navarone* career hasn't produced any films of distinction; he is best known for the original version of *Cape Fear* (1962), several of the sequels to *Planet of the Apes,* and numerous Charles Bronson movies. The Oscar went to Robert Wise and Jerome Robbins for *West Side Story,* which also won for sound and Thomas Stanford's editing. Henry Mancini won the scoring Oscar for *Breakfast at Tiffany's.*

Foreman: 287, 380, 912, 1302, 2340. Cox: 164, 1151. Tiomkin: 33, 286, 380, 446, 638, 663, 730, 768, 911, 912, 1206, 1347, 1370, 1470, 2006, 2127, 2282, 2335.

851 • GUY NAMED JOE, A

MGM. 1944.

NOMINATION *Original Story:* David Boehm and Chandler Sprague.

Pilot Spencer Tracy [131 . . .] is killed in combat, but his ghost hangs around to kibitz as his girlfriend, played by Irene Dunne [114 . . .], is wooed by another soldier, Van Johnson. Unimpressive wartime fantasy-comedy weeper, not helped much by the disparity in age between Dunne, forty-three, and Johnson, twenty-eight. Victor Fleming [798] directs, and the cast includes Ward Bond, James Gleason [904], Lionel Barrymore [723 . . .], and Barry Nelson. Esther Williams appears in her second film role, just before she made a literal splash in *Bathing Beauty*. Future director-writer-producer Blake Edwards [2201] plays a flier. Steven Spielberg [416 . . .] remade the movie as *Always* in 1989 without improving on it. The writing Oscar went to Leo McCarey for *Going My Way*.

852 • GUYS AND DOLLS

SAMUEL GOLDWYN PRODUCTIONS; MGM. 1955.

NOMINATIONS *Color Cinematography:* Harry Stradling. *Color Art Direction—Set Decoration:* Oliver Smith and Joseph C. Wright; Howard Bristol. *Scoring of a Musical Picture:* Jay Blackton and Cyril Mockridge. *Color Costume Design:* Irene Sharaff.

Gambler Sky Masterson, played by Marlon Brando [583 . . .], makes a bet with Nathan Detroit, played by Frank Sinatra [732 . . .], that he can get Sarah Brown, played by Jean Simmons [858 . . .], who runs a street mission, to go to Havana with him. Meanwhile, Detroit is having trouble avoiding matrimony with the nightclub singer Adelaide (Vivian Blaine). The wonderful Frank Loesser [864 . . .] musical receives a stiff and stagy production here, despite (or perhaps because of?) the expensive talent. Brando and Simmons do their own singing, and though they're not bad, they're not right, either. Sinatra, who might have been expected to do better, seems ill at ease and not in the best voice. His style is more suited to the romantic tunes given to Brando than to the declamatory stuff that belongs to his own part.

Producer Samuel Goldwyn [102 . . .] decided to make the definitive Hollywood musical. He hired Joseph L. Mankiewicz [46 . . .] to direct and to rewrite the Jo Swerling [1607]–Abe Burrows book. For Sky Masterson, the producer and director considered Gene Kelly [74], Tony Martin, Kirk Douglas [130 . . .], Robert Mitchum [1935], Burt Lancaster [107 . . .], Bing Crosby [173 . . .], and Clark Ga-

ble [798 . . .]. At one point Goldwyn apparently seriously proposed Dean Martin and Jerry Lewis for the two male leads. Mankiewicz finally persuaded Brando, whom he had directed in *Julius Caesar,* to take the part. Grace Kelly [450 . . .] and Deborah Kerr [599 . . .] were the first choices for Sarah Brown, but when they were unavailable, the part fell to Brando's *Desirée* costar, Simmons. When Betty Grable was unable to play Adelaide, the part went to Blaine, who had been in the original Broadway cast. Loesser composed three new songs for the film, "Adelaide," "Pet Me Poppa," and "A Woman in Love," but except for the last, they're not equal to the songs from the Broadway version that were dropped: "I've Never Been in Love Before," "My Time of Day," and "More I Cannot Wish You."

In the end Goldwyn's obsessiveness about detail and his desire to have the money show up on the screen drained the show of its life. Stradling was wrestling with the comparatively new problems of wide-screen images and lost to Robert Burks' lush Riviera location photography for *To Catch a Thief.* Smith, a brilliant stage designer, was encouraged to make his sets artificial and stylized, which made the film seem more unreal than it needed to be. The small-town realism of *Picnic,* which had another famous stage designer, Jo Mielziner, on its art direction team, won the Oscar. *Oklahoma!* won the scoring award, and *Love Is a Many-Splendored Thing* won for costuming.

Stradling: 110, 149, 596, 737, 853, 864, 896, 957, 1246, 1393, 1567, 1949, 2338. Wright: 235, 428, 508, 569, 690, 746, 1175, 1264, 1397, 1475, 2056. Bristol: 690, 864, 1182, 1451, 1607, 1613, 1907, 2064. Blackton: 1469. Sharaff: 66, 290, 333, 338, 413, 690, 896, 1088, 1507, 1592, 1910, 2000, 2244, 2277.

853 • GYPSY

WARNER BROS. 1962.

NOMINATIONS *Color Cinematography:* Harry Stradling, Sr. *Scoring of Music—Adaptation or Treatment:* Frank Perkins. *Color Costume Design:* Orry-Kelly.

Rosalind Russell [110 . . .] plays stage mother

Rose, who pushes the career of her supposedly less attractive, less talented daughter, Louise, played by Natalie Wood [1219 . . .], when her favored daughter, June, played by Ann Jillian, elopes. Karl Malden [1477 . . .] is the faithful manager Herbie. Louise becomes the stripper Gypsy Rose Lee. Plodding adaptation of a superb Broadway show, with great songs by Jule Styne [74 . . .] and Stephen Sondheim [543], undermined by the leaden direction of Mervyn LeRoy [1662 . . .], who allows Russell to give an overstated, all-stops-out performance. The result was a box-office debacle, though it has to be noted that both the film and Russell's performance have passionate admirers. It should also be noted that some of Russell's vocals were dubbed by Lisa Kirk.

The Oscars went to Freddie Young for the cinematography of *Lawrence of Arabia,* Ray Heindorf for the scoring of *The Music Man,* and Mary Wills for the costumes of *The Wonderful World of the Brothers Grimm.*

Stradling: 110, 149, 596, 737, 852, 864, 896, 957, 1246, 1393, 1567, 1949, 2338. Orry-Kelly: 66, 1157, 1860.

854 • HAIL THE CONQUERING HERO

PARAMOUNT. 1944.
NOMINATION *Original Screenplay:* Preston Sturges.

Discharged from the marines because of hay fever, Eddie Bracken dreads going home. But a bunch of marines, headed by their sergeant, William Demarest [1058], hustle Bracken off back home with the claim that he's a war hero. (They don't want to disappoint his mom; the film also features the song "Home to the Arms of Mother," composed by Sturges.) Bracken's protestations of the truth are taken as false modesty, and one thing leads to another. Delirious comedy, kept furiously brewing by writer-director Sturges and his company of sublime character actors, including Franklin Pangborn, Elizabeth Patterson, Jimmy Conlin, and Chester Conklin. You might think wartime audiences would take offense at this lampoon of small-town patriotism, but it was a big hit. As he proved with his other great comedy of the year, *The Miracle of Morgan's Creek,* for which he also received a writing nomination, Sturges was one of the most sub-

versive wits ever to throw a curve ball past a censor. Academy sobersides, however, decided to give the Oscar to Lamar Trotti for the patriotic pageant *Wilson.*

Sturges: 823, 1323.

855 • HAIRY APE, THE

JULES LEVEY; UNITED ARTISTS. 1944.
NOMINATION *Scoring of a Dramatic or Comedy Picture:* Michel Michelet and Edward Paul.

William Bendix [2222] plays a crude, animalistic stoker on a luxury liner. When wealthy passenger Susan Hayward [973 . . .] recoils from him in disgust, he becomes obsessed with vengeance. Directed by Alfred Santell, with John Loder, Alan Napier, and Dorothy Comingore. Eugene O'Neill's play may have had some power on stage when it was performed by Louis Wolheim in 1922, but Bendix is not up to the demands of the role and the play's ape symbolism seems heavy-handed on screen. O'Neill disliked the movie because it resorted to a more conventional ending instead of the tragic-symbolic one of his play. Max Steiner won the Oscar for the score of *Since You Went Away.*

Michelet: 2215. Paul: 2187.

856 • HALF A HOUSE

LENRO PRODUCTIONS; FIRST AMERICAN FILMS. 1976.
NOMINATION *Original Song:* "A World That Never Was," music by Sammy Fain, lyrics by Paul Francis Webster.

A couple builds a house in the hope that it will bring them closer, but it doesn't. One of the most obscure films in the annals of Oscar, *Half a House* qualified for the awards with showings in New York and L.A. in 1976 but didn't receive general theatrical release until 1979. It came and went with no notice from the reviewers—even *Variety,* which can usually be counted on to make mention of the most ephemeral of the Bs. Its stars, Anthony Eisley and Pat Delaney, and director, Brice Mack, are obscure. Even the song by Fain and Webster, a first-rate composer and lyricist, is missing from standard reference books on popular music. Fain made an effort to attract the

Academy's notice to his song, taking out an ad in the trade papers to inform members that it was not on records and the film wasn't easy to find, and supplying a phone number for members to dial so they could listen to the tune. Its nomination was doubtless the result of the prestige of the songwriters, who were well known to the members of the music branch making the nominations. But it also reveals that the mid-seventies were one of the weakest periods for film songs in the history of Hollywood. The big flop musicals of the sixties—*Hello, Dolly!, Goodbye, Mr. Chips, Paint Your Wagon, Star!, Doctor Dolittle,* and so on—had succeeded in killing off a movie genre. Pop music was going through the doldrums, too, with rock in one of its fallow periods following the breakup of the Beatles and the deaths of Jimi Hendrix, Janis Joplin, and Jim Morrison. In 1976 the pickings were so slim that in addition to a minor song from an obscure movie, the Academy nominated Jerry Goldsmith's hymn to Satan, "Ave Satani," from *The Omen,* in a category that once honored the work of Kern, Berlin, Rodgers and Hammerstein, Carmichael, Mercer, Styne, Cahn, Van Heusen, and, yes, Fain and Webster. There were a couple of more mainstream nominees: Henry Mancini and Don Black's "Come to Me," from *The Pink Panther Strikes Again,* and the upbeat theme song from *Rocky,* "Gonna Fly Now," by Bill Conti, Carol Connors, and Ayn Robbins. The winner was Barbra Streisand and Paul Williams' "Evergreen (Love Theme from *A Star Is Born*)."

Fain: 95, 331, 376, 1213, 1276, 1681, 1925, 2014, 2214. Webster: 33, 64, 95, 331, 376, 604, 663, 730, 1213, 1276, 1322, 1388, 1755, 1925, 2014.

857 • HALLELUJAH

MGM. 1929–30.
Nomination *Director:* King Vidor.

Daniel Haynes plays a sharecropper who vows to change his ways after accidentally killing his brother. He becomes a preacher, but finds keeping his vow hard to do when confronted with the luminous Nina Mae McKinney. Fine if sometimes disjointed melodrama, stunningly filmed in Deep South locations, with some condescension toward rural black life, but also a great respect for those who endured it. Primitive in some regards, and there are plenty of signs that director Vidor hasn't completely made the transition from silents to sound: The actors are allowed to overstate emotions and to posture and roll their eyes too much, and transitions are often provided by titles, not narrative. In fact, much of *Hallelujah* was filmed without sound, and voices and sound effects were dubbed in later—a laborious process because nothing of the sort had ever been done before. So it's a true landmark—not only because of its technical innovations and the fact that it's the first all-black talking film but because its integration of music and story demonstrated what a sound film could do. In addition to spirituals, jazz, and folk songs, the music includes two songs by Irving Berlin [34 . . .]. The directing Oscar went to Lewis Milestone for *All Quiet on the Western Front.*

Vidor: 378, 406, 468, 2228.

858 • HAMLET

J. Arthur Rank-Two Cities Films; Universal-International (United Kingdom). 1948.
Awards *Picture:* Laurence Olivier, producer. *Actor:* Laurence Olivier. *Black-and-White Art Direction–Set Decoration:* Roger K. Furse; Carmen Dillon. *Black-and-White Costume Design:* Roger K. Furse.
Nominations *Supporting Actress:* Jean Simmons. *Director:* Laurence Olivier. *Scoring of a Dramatic or Comedy Picture:* William Walton.

Olivier is the prince of Denmark, with Simmons as Ophelia, Basil Sydney as Claudius, Eileen Herlie as Gertrude, and Felix Aylmer as Polonius, with some familiar faces in smaller roles: Stanley Holloway [1393] (the Grave Digger), Anthony Quayle [85] (Marcellus), and Peter Cushing (Osric). Olivier's Hamlet is a bit posy and broody for contemporary tastes—we go in for crisper, wittier Hamlets—and his decision to deliver the soliloquies in voice-overs, while it makes some cinematic sense, deprives us of an important emotional connection between audience and character. And the Freudian-influenced heavy breathing that goes on in the scenes between mother and son sometimes verges on silent-movie camp. That said, it's still a record of a great performance: mellifluously spoken—trippingly on the tongue, not mouthed—and athletically embodied. (Olivier hurt himself rather badly during some of his fight sequences.) Olivier may not be the greatest Hamlet of the century—as Peter Ustinov [943 . . .] has shrewdly observed, "Of all actors he is the most difficult to imagine as one who has not made up his mind"—but he's easily the best we have on film, since John Barrymore and John Gielgud [103 . . .] left no visual record of their performances.

The film also has the distinction of being the first British production to win the best picture Oscar. Its only real competition for the award, as far as posterity's judgment can see, was *The Treasure of the Sierra Madre.* The other nominees were the sentimental melodrama *Johnny Belinda,* the opulent dance film *The Red Shoes,* and the mental-illness shocker *The Snake Pit* —none of which, incidentally, stands up to some of the unnominated films of the year: *Red River, Fort Apache,* and *The Lady From Shanghai.*

Olivier became the first—and so far the only— person to win for both acting and producing, as well as the only person to direct himself to an acting award. His competition in the acting category was not stiff: Lew Ayres in a pallid, essentially supporting role in *Johnny Belinda,* Montgomery Clift in his debut role in *The Searchers,* Dan Dailey in the middling musical *When My Baby Smiles at Me,* and Clifton Webb as cute, cranky Mr. Belvedere in *Sitting Pretty.* (No one has satisfactorily explained the omission of Humphrey Bogart's remarkable work in *The Treasure of the Sierra Madre* from this list, or Henry Fonda's martinet cavalry commander in *Fort Apache,* or John Wayne's obsessive cattle-driver in *Red River.*)

Furse, who had also done the costumes for Olivier's *Henry V,* was the first person to win a black-and-white costume design Oscar, an award introduced this year. He also collaborated with Olivier as designer for many productions at the Old Vic. Dillon likewise worked with Olivier on other productions, including his film of *Richard III.*

Vivien Leigh [798 . . .] wanted to play Ophelia, but at thirty-five was too old for the role, although Olivier claimed that the Rank Organisation had made him bypass Leigh and cast Simmons, who was still in her teens and had already made a strong impression in such films as *Black Narcissus* and *Great Expectations,* but had never played a Shakespearean role. Though she lost to Claire Trevor in *Key Largo,* she was established as a star and came to Hollywood in the fifties.

Olivier lost the directing Oscar to John Huston for *The Treasure of the Sierra Madre.* Walton's score lost to Brian Easdale's for *The Red Shoes.*

Olivier: 268, 619, 901, 1272, 1506, 1670, 1693, 1841, 2316. Dillon: 901. Simmons: 867. Walton: 901.

859 • HAMLET

ICON PRODUCTION; WARNER BROS. 1990.

NOMINATIONS *Art Direction—Set Decoration:* Dante Ferretti, Francesca Lo Schiavo. *Costume Design:* Maurizio Millenotti.

Shakespeare's melancholy prince is played by Mel Gibson, with Glenn Close [199 . . .] as Gertrude, Alan Bates [678] as Claudius, Ian Holm [386] as Polonius, Helena Bonham Carter as Ophelia, and Paul Scofield [1252 . . .] as the Ghost. Directed by Franco Zeffirelli [1722 . . .] very much in the vein of his *Romeo and Juliet,* which means it's colorful and entertaining but doesn't break any new ground for the play. Like all screen versions, it has been severely pruned—uncut *Hamlet*s run more than four hours on stage—and in this case the sacrifices have been made in areas of poetry and motivation in favor of robust action. Gibson acquits himself well in the most famous of all Shakespearean roles, shaming the skeptics who joked that he would make his quietus with a Lethal Weapon, handcuff himself to the Ghost and jump from the battlements of Elsinore, or do Three Stooges routines with Rosencrantz and Guildenstern. Close is an attractive, poised Gertrude, though she stretches credibility as Gibson's mother—she's only nine years older than he. (On the other hand, Eileen Herlie was thirteen years *younger* than Olivier when she played his mother in the 1948 film.) Bates, Holm, and Scofield, all noted Hamlets in their day, are excellent, but Bonham Carter's role has suffered from cutting and she seems more messed up than mad.

Visually it's a feast, as most of Zeffirelli's films are; this Elsinore seems like a real place, not the usual papier-mâché Gothic castle. The art direction Oscar, however, went to *Dick Tracy* and the costuming award to Franca Squarciapino for *Cyrano de Bergerac.*

Ferretti: 14, 27.5, 1007.5. Lo Schiavo: 14, 1007.5. Millenotti: 1505.

860 • HANDFUL OF DUST, A

STAGE SCREEN PRODUCTION; NEW LINE. 1988.

NOMINATION *Costume Design:* Jane Robinson.

James Wilby and Kristen Scott Thomas are the naive, stodgy husband and bored, unfaithful wife in this adaptation by Tim Sullivan, Derek Granger, and director Charles Sturridge of Evelyn Waugh's novel about the not-too-bright young things of London between the wars. Sturridge, who was also responsible for TV's *Brideshead Revisited,* creates a dry, witty film that's a bit too preoccupied with period atmosphere and detail, but also thoughtful and well acted. Anjelica Huston [617 . . .], Alec Guinness [287 . . .], and Judi Dench have welcome cameo roles. James Acheson won the costume Oscar for *Dangerous Liaisons.*

861 • HANGING TREE, THE

BARODA PRODUCTIONS INC.; WARNER BROS. 1959.

NOMINATION *Song:* ''The Hanging Tree,'' music by Jerry Livingston, lyrics by Mack David.

Gary Cooper [701 . . .] plays a doctor trying to escape his past—he killed his wife—on the Montana frontier. Somber, well-done western, directed by Delmer Daves, with Maria Schell as a blind woman, Karl Malden [1477 . . .], and, in his film debut, George C. Scott [73 . . .]. The Oscar went to James Van Heusen and Sammy Cahn for ''High Hopes,'' from *A Hole in the Head.*

Livingston: 371, 402. David: 122, 371, 402, 882, 963, 1032, 2223.

862 • HANGMEN ALSO DIE

ARNOLD PRODUCTIONS; UNITED ARTISTS. 1943.

NOMINATIONS *Sound Recording:* Jack Whitney, Sound Service Inc. *Scoring of a Dramatic or Comedy Picture:* Hanns Eisler.

Brian Donlevy [161] kills Heydrich, the Nazi leader known as the Hangman, who was in charge of subduing Czechoslovakia, but the assassination precipitates the destruction of the village of Lidice. Fritz Lang produced and directed, and cowrote the screenplay with Bertolt Brecht, and the cinematography is by James Wong Howe [1 . . .]. The cast includes Walter Brennan [424 . . .], Gene Lockhart [36], and Margaret Wycherly [1779]. But despite some moments of excitement, it's somewhat overdone and, considering the talent involved, disappointing. The Oscar for sound went to *This Land Is Mine.* Alfred Newman won for the scoring of *The Song of Bernadette.*

Whitney: 729, 955, 1026, 1884, 2031, 2050, 2095. Eisler: 1445.

863 • HANNAH AND HER SISTERS

JACK ROLLINS AND CHARLES H. JOFFE PRODUCTION; ORION. 1986.

AWARDS *Supporting Actor:* Michael Caine. *Supporting Actress:* Dianne Wiest. *Screenplay Written Directly for the Screen:* Woody Allen.

NOMINATIONS *Picture:* Robert Greenhut, producer. *Director:* Woody Allen. *Art Direction—Set Decoration:* Stuart Wurtzel; Carol Joffe. *Film Editing:* Susan E. Morse.

Mia Farrow is Hannah, and Barbara Hershey and Wiest are her sisters. Formerly married to Allen, Hannah is now, she thinks, happily wed to Caine, but he lusts after Hershey, who is involved with a self-centered artist, Max von Sydow [1546]. Wiest is aimless, both personally and professionally, but once she finds herself as a writer, she and Allen, who also goes through various neurotic episodes, fall in love. The circling and intersecting stories also involve Lloyd Nolan and Maureen O'Sullivan as the sisters' parents (she is, of course, Farrow's real-life mother), Carrie Fisher, Daniel Stern, J. T. Walsh, Julie Kavner, Julia Louis-Dreyfus, and John Turturro. A lovely collection of incidents and characters, it doesn't really amount to much, but it's one of Allen's most likable movies since *Annie Hall*. The photography of Carlo Di Palma and Allen's usual well-chosen music score add greatly to the film's warmth and charm. One wishes, however, that the Caine and Allen characters didn't sound so much alike—the two actors could easily have switched roles.

Caine is now one of the movies' busiest actors—he was in four movies in 1986—but his film career was slow in taking off. Though he made his debut in 1956, it was a decade before *Alfie* brought him his first Oscar nomination and made him a star. Since then he has worked steadily, perfecting his craft largely on screen, unlike most British actors, who tend to oscillate between film and stage roles.

Allen provided Wiest's big career break. She made her film debut in 1980 in *It's My Turn* but attracted little attention until *Hannah,* her second film for Allen; the first was *The Purple Rose of Cairo*. Since the Oscar, she has often played rather eccentric women coping with motherhood, as in *The Lost Boys* (1987), *Parenthood,* and *Edward Scissorhands*.

This was Allen's second Oscar for a screenplay. Only Billy Wilder [91 . . .] has more writing nominations (twelve to Allen's eleven). Part of the secret of his success lies in working steadily: Since *Annie Hall* in 1977, Allen has turned out at least one film each year. When they bomb, as some have done badly of late, he simply moves on to the next project.

The best picture award went to *Platoon,* which also won for director Oliver Stone and film editor Claire Simpson. The art direction award went to *A Room With a View*.

Caine: 35, 598, 1841. Wiest: 311.5, 1530. Allen: 39, 88, 294, 311.5, 461, 962.5, 1005, 1267, 1636, 1647. Joffe: 1647.

864 • HANS CHRISTIAN ANDERSEN

SAMUEL GOLDWYN PRODUCTIONS; RKO RADIO. 1952.
NOMINATIONS *Color Cinematography:* Harry Stradling. *Color Art Direction–Set Decoration:* Richard Day and Clave; Howard Bristol. *Sound Recording:* Goldwyn Sound Department, Gordon Sawyer, sound director.

Song: "Thumbelina," music and lyrics by Frank Loesser. *Scoring of a Musical Picture:* Walter Scharf. *Color Costume Design:* Clave, Mary Wills, and Madame Karinska.

The shoemaker Andersen (Danny Kaye) journeys to Copenhagen, where he falls in love with a ballerina (Jeanmaire), not knowing that she's already married to a ballet master (Farley Granger). He writes the story "The Little Mermaid" to express his love for her, but she thinks it's just a plot for a ballet. He continues to turn out stories for children, which make him famous. But when the ballerina tells him she's married, he returns, heartbroken, to his home village, accompanied by his ward, Peter. As Granger summarized the plot: "Boy meets girl, boy loses girl, boy gets boy." Colorful but saccharine musical, produced by Samuel Goldwyn [102 . . .], directed by Charles Vidor from a screenplay by Moss Hart [297 . . .], that bears almost no relation to the real life of Andersen—a fact that infuriated the Danes, for whom Andersen is a national hero. Hart is not wholly to blame. He was hired to stitch together a script from thirty-two earlier versions commissioned by Goldwyn, who had been planning the film since 1938. The story is largely by Myles Connolly [1382]. The film is strictly for admirers of Kaye, although there are some nice dance sequences in which Jeanmaire is partnered by Erik Bruhn and choreographer Roland Petit. And Loesser's lovely songs include "No Two People" and "Anywhere I Wander."

The cinematography Oscar went to Winton Hoch and Archie Stout for *The Quiet Man. Moulin Rouge* won for art direction and Marcel Vertes' costumes. *Breaking the Sound Barrier* won for sound. Dimitri Tiomkin and Ned Washington won for the title song for *High Noon.* Alfred Newman took the scoring Oscar for *With a Song in My Heart*.

Stradling: 110, 149, 596, 737, 852, 853, 896, 957, 1246, 1393, 1567, 1949, 2338. Day: 22, 102, 235, 487, 510, 560, 569, 797, 833, 952, 1048, 1175, 1397, 1477, 1666, 1949, 2056, 2120, 2276. Bristol: 690, 852, 1182, 1451, 1607, 1613, 1907, 2064. Sawyer: 33, 91, 184, 214, 393, 730, 882, 973, 974, 1032, 1511, 1592, 2244, 2297, 2310. Loesser:

1131, 1422, 1551, 2026. Scharf: 174, 274, 665, 737, 921, 991, 1054, 1305, 2285. Wills: 376, 542, 1534, 2008, 2205, 2312. Karinska: 1048.

865 • HANUSSEN

OBJEKTIV STUDIO/CCC FILMKUNST/ZDF/HUNGAROFILM/ MOKEP PRODUCTION (HUNGARY). 1988.

NOMINATION Foreign Language Film.

Klaus Maria Brandauer [1512] plays a soldier who develops clairvoyant powers after he's wounded in World War I. Eventually his fame attracts the attention of the Nazis, but his foreknowledge of their fate is a problem. Third in the trilogy by István Szabó that includes *Mephisto* and *Colonel Redl*. Brandauer's compelling performance illuminates a powerful story. The Oscar went to *Pelle the Conqueror*.

866 • HAPPIEST MILLIONAIRE, THE

WALT DISNEY PRODUCTIONS; BUENA VISTA. 1967.

NOMINATION Costume Design: Bill Thomas.

Fred MacMurray plays Philadelphia millionaire Anthony J. Drexel Biddle, whose daughter, played by Lesley Ann Warren [2201], falls in love with Angie Duke, played by John Davidson. But the Biddles and the Dukes are not on speaking terms, so it falls to butler Tommy Steele to engineer a rapprochement. Seemingly endless musical, said to be the last film personally supervised by Disney before his death, but hardly a fitting monument. Over the years it has been reedited several times, trying to make it work, but to little avail. Prints range in length from 159 to 118 minutes. Even a cast that includes Greer Garson [239 . . .], Geraldine Page [935 . . .], Gladys Cooper [1393 . . .], and Hermione Baddeley [1724] can't save it. Directed by Norman Tokar. The costuming award went to John Truscott for *Camelot*.

Thomas: 116, 166, 254, 883, 1003, 1789, 1812, 1886, 2128.

867 • HAPPY ENDING, THE

PAX FILMS PRODUCTION; UNITED ARTISTS. 1969.

NOMINATIONS Actress: Jean Simmons. Song: "What Are You Doing the Rest of Your Life?," music by Michel Legrand, lyrics by Alan Bergman and Marilyn Bergman.

Simmons is a middle-aged woman so profoundly dissatisfied with her life as well-to-do lawyer John Forsythe's wife that she hits the bottle. Sometimes incisive but mostly superficial look at the institution of marriage, written and directed by Richard Brooks [227 . . .]. The cast includes Lloyd Bridges, Shirley Jones [609], Teresa Wright [1182 . . .], Nanette Fabray, and Bobby Darin [350].

After her first nomination, for *Hamlet*, Simmons came to Hollywood but never achieved major stardom against such formidable competition as Deborah Kerr [599 . . .], Audrey Hepburn [278 . . .], and Grace Kelly [450 . . .]. Her participation in big films such as *The Robe, Guys and Dolls, The Big Country, Elmer Gantry,* and *Spartacus* was significant, but it never quite struck sparks, either with audiences or with the Academy. In the seventies her film career dwindled, but in recent years she has been a frequent guest star on TV. The Oscar went to Maggie Smith for *The Prime of Miss Jean Brodie.*

Burt Bacharach and Hal David's "Raindrops Keep Fallin' on My Head," from *Butch Cassidy and the Sundance Kid,* won the song Oscar.

Simmons: 858. Legrand: 178, 1568, 1960, 2063, 2172, 2321, 2332. A. Bergman: 179, 1168, 1568, 1628, 1747, 1813, 1864, 2063, 2113, 2238, 2321, 2322. M. Bergman: 179, 1168, 1568, 1628, 1747, 1813, 1864, 2063, 2113, 2238, 2321, 2322.

868 • HAPPY NEW YEAR

COLUMBIA PICTURES PRODUCTION; COLUMBIA. 1987.

NOMINATION Makeup: Bob Laden.

Peter Falk [1377 . . .] and Charles Durning [180 . . .] plan a hit on a Palm Beach jewelry store run by Tom Courtenay [558 . . .]. But things keep getting screwed up. So does the movie, a remake of a 1973 French film by Claude Lelouch [76 . . .]. John Avildsen [1712] directs, in an interesting change of pace from his *Rocky*s and *Karate Kid*s, but this movie almost went straight to video. Laden's nomination was for the various disguises Falk assumes in the course of the film. The Oscar went to Rick Baker for *Harry and the Hendersons.*

869 • *HARD DAY'S NIGHT, A*

WALTER SHENSON PRODUCTION; UNITED ARTISTS (UNITED KINGDOM). 1964.

NOMINATIONS *Story and Screenplay—Written Directly for the Screen:* Alun Owen. *Scoring of Music—Adaptation or Treatment:* George Martin.

The Beatles [1158], as themselves, rebel against the constraints of celebrity—the packs of pursuing fans, the inanely questioning reporters, the busybody managers, the film and TV crews that treat them like furniture—but to little avail. They also have to look after Paul's foxy grandpa (Wilfrid Brambell), a bit of a problem even if he is a clean old man. Great good fun, a larky, extremely influential musical—the source of countless clichés in rock musicals and comedies about swinging London throughout the rest of the decade. The film established the individual Beatles personae that would annoy them through the rest of their existence as a group: brainy John, heartthrob Paul, droll George, and cuddly Ringo. Richard Lester's work made him an overnight star director, but though his pyrotechnical effects—odd camera angles, flashy cuts, overlapping dialogue, and eccentric asides—looked revolutionary at the time, they turned out to be little more than a footnote to the grammar of narrative filmmaking. The cinematography is by Gilbert Taylor, who also shot *Dr. Strangelove* and *Star Wars.*

The Academy's response to *Hard Day's Night* is incomprehensible. A nomination for Peter Glenville's stodgy direction of *Becket* but not for Lester? A story nomination for a film that had none? Nominations for the long-forgotten title songs for *Dear Heart* and *Hush . . . Hush, Sweet Charlotte,* but not for the title song of *A Hard Day's Night*—or for "And I Love Her," "Can't Buy Me Love," "If I Fell," "Tell Me Why," or the others? Of course, the Academy had never recognized the films of W. C. Fields or the Marx Brothers, either. The story and screenplay Oscar went to the writers of *Father Goose.* André Previn won the scoring award for *My Fair Lady.*

870 • *HARDER THEY FALL, THE*

COLUMBIA. 1956.

NOMINATION *Black-and-White Cinematography:* Burnett Guffey.

Sportswriter Humphrey Bogart [24 . . .] and fight promoter Rod Steiger [992 . . .] team up to push the career of a big but inept boxer, fixing his fights so he gets a chance at the title. When the guy gets slaughtered, Bogart is so disgusted he writes an exposé of the fight game. Well done, tough, and uncompromising, though Bogart's change of heart is a bit on the melodramatic side. Directed by Mark Robson [1001 . . .] from a screenplay by Philip Yordan [299 . . .] based on a novel by Budd Schulberg [1477]. Bogart is excellent in his last film, which also features Jan Sterling [911]. The cinematography award went to Joseph Ruttenberg for *Somebody Up There Likes Me*—it was a big year for boxing movies.

Guffey: 210, 255, 732, 1093.

871 • *HARLEM NIGHTS*

EDDIE MURPHY PRODUCTION; PARAMOUNT. 1989.

NOMINATION *Costume Design:* Joe I. Tompkins.

Nightclub owners Eddie Murphy and Richard Pryor battle mobster Danny Aiello [556] in thirties Harlem. Tiresome, unfunny vanity production. Murphy's plethora of credits, as producer, writer, and director, at the beginning of the film drew laughs from the audiences. Not that there was much in the way of audiences—the movie was Murphy's first big flop. Among the talents wasted are Redd Foxx, Michael Lerner [152], Della Reese, and Arsenio Hall. The period setting is nice to look at, however, and Tompkins' clothes are handsome. The Oscar went to Phyllis Dalton for *Henry V.*

Tompkins: 466.

872 • *HARP OF BURMA*

NIKKATSU CORPORATION; MASAYUKI TAKAGI, PRODUCER (JAPAN). 1956.

NOMINATION *Foreign Language Film.*

After the end of World War II, a Japanese soldier stays on in Burma, feeling a religious compulsion to bury the dead. Searing, poetic tale of the horrors of war, directed by Kon Ichikawa. Also known as *The Burmese Harp*. The first foreign language film Oscar went to *La Strada*.

873 • HARRY AND THE BUTLER

BENT CHRISTENSEN PRODUCTION (DENMARK). 1961.
NOMINATION *Foreign Language Film*.

When he inherits some money, an elderly man hires a valet, but his friends are offended by his pretentiousness and shun him. Directed by Bent Christensen. The Oscar went to the Ingmar Bergman [111 . . .] film *Through a Glass Darkly*.

874 • HARRY AND THE HENDERSONS

UNIVERSAL/AMBLIN ENTERTAINMENT PRODUCTION; UNIVERSAL. 1987.
AWARD *Makeup*: Rick Baker.

A vacationing family runs into Bigfoot—literally, with their car. They take him home and nurse him back to health, but the big guy, lovable though he is, proves more than they can handle. One of countless attempts to recapture the rapture of *E.T.,* but better than most, at least for kids. (It was produced by Steven Spielberg's company.) Likable cast, directed by William Dear: John Lithgow [2020 . . .], Melinda Dillon [3 . . .], David Suchet (TV's Hercule Poirot), Don Ameche [419], Lainie Kazan, and, as Harry, Kevin Peter Hall—though of course it could be anyone who's seven feet tall behind Baker's makeup.

Baker: 68, 431, 595.8, 839.

875 • HARRY AND TONTO

20TH CENTURY-FOX. 1974.
AWARD *Actor*: Art Carney.
NOMINATION *Original Screenplay*: Paul Mazursky and Josh Greenfeld.

Carney plays Harry, a seventy-year-old widower, who has had enough with being treated like a senior citizen, so he hits the road with his cat, Tonto, hitchhiking across country. Funny-sad episodic film, well directed by Mazursky, with a cast of pros: Ellen Burstyn [41 . . .], Chief Dan George [1179], Geral-

dine Fitzgerald [2316], Larry Hagman, and Arthur Hunnicutt [204], among others.

Carney, only fifty-five, took the role when Mazursky couldn't persuade James Cagney [79 . . .] out of retirement. He had made only a handful of film appearances before this one and was best known as Ed Norton of *The Honeymooners*. His Oscar was a controversial one. It beat two of the most celebrated performances in recent film history, Jack Nicholson's in *Chinatown* and Al Pacino's in *The Godfather, Part II*. And the other contenders were distinguished multiple nominees, Albert Finney for *Murder on the Orient Express* and Dustin Hoffman for *Lenny*. (Note for connoisseurs of oddball irony: Lenny Bruce's mother, Sally Marr, has a small role in *Harry and Tonto*.) Nicholson, Pacino, and Hoffman would go on to win Oscars, and Finney would get more chances to do so, but this was Carney's sole pass at the award. His post-Oscar film career was hampered by typecasting: Everyone wanted him to play cantankerous old men. His best subsequent performance was as a cantankerous old detective in *The Late Show* in 1977.

Robert Towne won the writing Oscar for *Chinatown*.

Mazursky: 250, 617, 2182.

876 • HARVEY

UNIVERSAL-INTERNATIONAL. 1950.
AWARD *Supporting Actress*: Josephine Hull.
NOMINATION *Actor*: James Stewart.

Genial bachelor alcoholic Elwood P. Dowd (Stewart) muddles through life, accompanied by a six-foot-three invisible white rabbit named Harvey. His exasperated sister, played by Hull, wants to have him committed. But of course Elwood is saner than the basket cases who surround him. Pleasant, not-too-whimsical version of a hit play by Mary Chase that actually won the Pulitzer Prize even though it's as evanescent as Harvey himself. Stewart and Hull are such enormously ingratiating performers that one readily forgives the film's staginess and the banality of the premise that cute drunks possess some higher wisdom. Directed by Henry Koster [214].

Hull had made a few films in the early thirties,

when everyone from Broadway made a try in Holly-wood, but her long acting career was mainly concentrated on stage. Her two most memorable film performances were both re-creations of roles she had played on Broadway—*Arsenic and Old Lace* (1944) and *Harvey*. She died in 1957.

Stewart lost to Jose Ferrer in *Cyrano de Bergerac*. Stewart: 73, 1033, 1370, 1563.

877 • HARVEY GIRLS, THE

MGM. 1946.

AWARD *Song:* "On the Atchison, Topeka and Santa Fe," music by Harry Warren, lyrics by Johnny Mercer.

NOMINATION *Scoring of a Musical Picture:* Lennie Hayton.

Judy Garland [1065 . . .] goes West and becomes a Harvey Girl—a waitress in a chain of restaurants being opened to serve passengers on the new railroads that are spanning the continent. The prim and starchy young women compete with the tawdry saloon girls for customers, and Judy competes with Angela Lansbury [749 . . .] for the affections of saloon-keeper John Hodiak. Guess who wins. Pleasing, brightly colored musical from MGM's vintage years. The plot's inane, and Hodiak is a dud as a leading man, but Garland is in fine form, and the supporting cast features Ray Bolger, Virginia O'Brien, Marjorie Main [601], Chill Wills [33], and Cyd Charisse. Directed by George Sidney.

This was Mercer's first Oscar (of four) and Warren's last (of three). Their winning song is the clear standout from a pleasant if otherwise unmemorable score. Mercer, who began as an actor on stage and a band singer, was a gifted lyricist for Hoagy Carmichael [341 . . .], Henry Mancini [122 . . .], Harold Arlen [248 . . .], and many others, but also a considerable composer—though he couldn't read music—on his own.

The scoring Oscar went to Morris Stoloff for *The Jolson Story*.

Warren: 21, 324, 569, 788, 791, 897, 1072, 1367, 1501, 1964. Mercer: 248, 278, 384, 476, 494, 508, 636, 788, 825, 903, 905, 1109, 1772, 1838, 1912, 2327, 2328. Hayton: 896, 1476, 1577, 1831, 1907.

878 • HASTY HEART, THE

WARNER BROS. 1949.

NOMINATION *Actor:* Richard Todd.

Todd is a rambunctious Scot in an army hospital in Burma who alienates his fellow patients until they learn that he's dying. Straightforward filming of a play by John Patrick adapted by Ranald MacDougall [1319] and directed by Vincent Sherman. It betrays its theatrical origin but still manages to wring a few tears. The cast includes Patricia Neal [956 . . .] and Ronald Reagan.

Todd, born in Dublin, began his acting career on stage in Britain before World War II. He had a modestly successful career in movies during the early fifties, playing the title roles in Disney's live-action *The Story of Robin Hood* (1952) and *Rob Roy—the Highland Rogue* (1953), Senate chaplain Peter Marshall in *A Man Called Peter,* and Sir Walter Raleigh in *The Virgin Queen,* among other roles. The Oscar went to Broderick Crawford for *All the King's Men*.

879 • HATARI!

MALABAR PRODUCTIONS; PARAMOUNT. 1962.

NOMINATION *Color Cinematography:* Russell Harlan.

John Wayne [33 . . .] heads a safari in Tanganyika, accompanied by Red Buttons [1763], Hardy Kruger, and Elsa Martinelli. Enjoyable, rambling, plotless adventure flick, with a screenplay credited to Leigh Brackett, though a lot of it was made up on the spot by producer-director Howard Hawks [1779] and the cast. One suspects that editor Stuart Gilmore [31 . . .] had a hand in making it make sense, too. Doesn't hold up to scrutiny from environmentalists, but it's a lot of fun if you can swallow the great-white-hunter stuff. Excellent score by Henry Mancini [122 . . .]. Harlan's cinematography lost to Fred A. "Freddie" Young's for *Lawrence of Arabia*.

Harlan: 204, 227, 825, 882, 2101.

880 • HATFUL OF RAIN, A

20TH CENTURY-FOX. 1957.

NOMINATION *Actor:* Anthony Franciosa.

Don Murray [314] plays a heroin addict who makes life difficult for his brother (Franciosa) and his wife, played by Eva Marie Saint [1477]. A solid melodrama that's lost the edge it had when drug abuse was a new and shocking topic for the movies. Directed by Fred Zinnemann [732 . . .] from a screenplay adapted by Michael V. Gazzo [785] from his own play. The cast includes Lloyd Nolan, Henry Silva, and William Hickey [1625].

Franciosa played his role in the stage production as well. His screen career got off to a strong start in 1957, with roles in *A Face in the Crowd* and *Wild Is the Wind,* and in *The Long Hot Summer* the following year. But it petered out in the sixties, and he turned to TV series work. The Oscar went to Alec Guinness for *The Bridge on the River Kwai.*

881 • HAVANA

UNIVERSAL PICTURES LTD. PRODUCTION; UNIVERSAL. 1990.

NOMINATION *Original Score:* David Grusin.

Gambler Robert Redford [1502 . . .] is hanging on in Cuba, though it's clear that the impending Castro revolution is about to deprive him of his livelihood. In the meantime, he has an affair with Lena Olin [617] that forces him—very much à la Bogart in *Casablanca*—to become politically engaged. The movie is too long, and there's no chemistry between Redford and Olin, but it's not as bad as the reviews made it out to be at the time. Still, it was a whopping box-office disaster and put a serious dent in the careers of Redford, Olin, and director Sydney Pollack [1512 . . .]. It has enjoyable performances by Alan Arkin [884 . . .], Richard Farnsworth [429], and an unbilled Raul Julia, among others. Grusin's score lost to John Barry's for *Dances With Wolves.*

Grusin: 379, 633, 667.5, 890, 1318, 1473, 2113.

882 • HAWAII

MIRISCH CORPORATION OF DELAWARE PRODUCTION; UNITED ARTISTS. 1966.

NOMINATIONS *Supporting Actress:* Jocelyne LaGarde. *Color Cinematography:* Russell Harlan. *Sound:* Gordon E. Sawyer, sound director, Samuel Goldwyn Studio Sound Department. *Song:* "My Wishing Doll," music by Elmer Bernstein, lyrics by Mack David. *Original Music Score:* Elmer Bernstein. *Color Costume Design:* Dorothy Jeakins. *Special Visual Effects:* Linwood G. Dunn.

Missionary Max von Sydow [1546] sets out to bring Christianity to the islands with the help of wife Julie Andrews [1284 . . .], who is still in love with her first boyfriend, two-fisted sailor Richard Harris [660 . . .]. Galumphing blockbuster from James Michener's doorstop of a novel, adapted by Daniel Taradash [732] and Dalton Trumbo [273 . . .], and directed by George Roy Hill [317 . . .]. Trumbo and Hill said that they had America's involvement in Vietnam in mind when they made the film, which deals with the havoc wrought by men of good intentions. The cast includes Gene Hackman [255 . . .], Carroll O'Connor, John Cullum, and George Rose. Von Sydow's sons, Henrik and Clas, play his son in the film at different ages. Bette Midler [700 . . .], who grew up in Hawaii, is said to be an extra in the shipboard scenes.

LaGarde—who had never acted, didn't speak English, and learned the role phonetically—was chosen for the role because of her size: She weighed more than four hundred pounds. She had no subsequent film career. She lost to Sandy Dennis for *Who's Afraid of Virginia Woolf? A Man for All Seasons* won for Ted Moore's cinematography and Elizabeth Haffenden and Joan Bridge's costumes. The award for sound went to *Grand Prix. Born Free* won for John Barry and Don Black's title song and for Barry's score. The special effects award went to *Fantastic Voyage.*

Harlan: 204, 227, 825, 879, 2101. Sawyer: 33, 91, 184, 393, 730, 864, 973, 974, 1032, 1592, 2244, 2297, 2310. Bernstein: 27.5, 789, 1242, 1264, 1685, 1959, 2064, 2101, 2130, 2147, 2223. David: 122, 371, 402, 861, 963, 1032, 2223.

Jeakins: 393, 509, 832, 1048, 1385, 1391, 1432, 1748, 1881, 2012, 2238.

883 • HAWAIIANS, THE

UNITED ARTISTS. 1970.

NOMINATION *Costume Design:* Bill Thomas.

Sequel to *Hawaii,* starring Charlton Heston [175] as an island empire-builder. No worse than its predecessor, and maybe a little tidier in its narrative, adapted by James R. Webb [953] from the Michener novel and directed by Tom Gries. The cast includes Geraldine Chaplin, Tina Chen, Alec McCowen, Mako [1753], and Keye Luke. The costuming Oscar went to Vittorio Nino Novarese for *Cromwell.*

Thomas: 116, 166, 254, 866, 1003, 1789, 1812, 1886, 2128.

884 • HEART IS A LONELY HUNTER, THE

WARNER BROS.-SEVEN ARTS. 1968.

NOMINATIONS *Actor:* Alan Arkin. *Supporting Actress:* Sondra Locke.

Arkin plays a deaf-mute in a small southern town who has an effect on the lives of Locke, Stacy Keach, and Cicely Tyson [1882], among others. Melancholy mood piece, based on a novel by Carson McCullers, distinguished primarily for its performances—Locke and Keach made their screen debuts in it—and the photography of James Wong Howe [1 . . .]. Directed by Robert Ellis Miller.

Arkin's second nomination, for a performance that received the New York Film Critics Award, seemed to certify that he was a major film actor. He had, after all, received his first for the bemused Russian sailor in *The Russians Are Coming, the Russians Are Coming,* and in the interim had played a terrifying villain in *Wait Until Dark.* With such astonishing versatility, how could he fail? But he followed with a series of box-office flops, including the much-anticipated *Catch-22,* in which he landed the plum role of Yossarian. There seemed to be few roles to fit his talents, and the emergence of Dustin Hoffman [810 . . .], another short, intense urban actor with greater presence on camera, eliminated Arkin's chances for some

key parts. Arkin blends into ensembles with ease, however, so he has established a solid career as a character actor. The Oscar went to Cliff Robertson for *Charly.*

Locke, who lost to Ruth Gordon in *Rosemary's Baby,* did not see a sharp rise in her career after her nomination. She made a few unmemorable films over the next few years but gained more exposure in the mid-seventies when she began a relationship with Clint Eastwood [2179.5] and costarred in several of his films. In the later eighties she began a second career as a director with the film *Ratboy* (1986) under the aegis of Eastwood. They have since gone their separate ways.

Arkin: 1736.

885 • HEART LIKE A WHEEL

AURORA FILM PARTNERS/20TH CENTURY-FOX PRODUCTION; 20TH CENTURY-FOX. 1983.

NOMINATION *Costume Design:* William Ware Theiss.

Bonnie Bedelia plays Shirley Muldowney, a race-car driver who, with the aid of manager Beau Bridges, overcomes the usual obstacles of prejudice and stupidity to become a champ. Entertaining biopic with a nice but not too heavily applied feminist edge and few *Rocky*esque heroics. Directed by Jonathan Kaplan, with cinematography by Tak Fujimoto. The Oscar went to Marik Vos for *Fanny & Alexander.*

Theiss: 264, 316.

886 • HEARTBEEPS

MICHAEL PHILLIPS/UNIVERSAL PICTURES PRODUCTION; UNIVERSAL. 1981.

NOMINATION *Makeup:* Stan Winston.

Robots Bernadette Peters and Andy Kaufman fall in love. Dumb, laughless, and expensive waste of talent that expired swiftly at the box office. Directed by Allan Arkush, with Randy Quaid [1135], Kenneth McMillan, and Melanie Mayron. You know a film's in trouble when critics pay more attention to the makeup than to the performances, but Winston's work lost to Rick Baker's for *An American Werewolf in London.*

Winston: 45, 153.5, 600, 1071.5, 1600, 2019.

887 • HEARTBREAK KID, THE

PALOMAR PICTURES INTERNATIONAL PRODUCTION; 20TH CENTURY-FOX. 1972.

NOMINATIONS *Supporting Actor:* Eddie Albert. *Supporting Actress:* Jeannie Berlin.

Nice Jewish boy Charles Grodin marries nice Jewish girl Berlin but falls in love with gorgeous shiksa Cybill Shepherd while he's on his honeymoon. Despite the premise, this is not nearly so offensive or thin as it sounds, or as gag-ridden as you might expect from the scenarist, Neil Simon [332 . . .]. It's quite skillfully directed by Elaine May [890] and makes its satiric points without shouting them at you. Based on a short story by Bruce Jay Friedman [1893], "A Change of Plan." Cinematography by Owen Roizman [631 . . .].

Albert, who plays Shepherd's disapproving father, had spent much of the sixties playing opposite Eva Gabor and Arnold the pig on *Green Acres.* His return to the movies put him in line for numerous character roles over the next two decades. He lost the Oscar to Joel Grey in *Cabaret.*

Berlin, who is May's daughter, had appeared in several films before the one that earned her an Oscar nomination. But her film career stalled at this point, and she has made only occasional appearances in later years. The Oscar went to Eileen Heckart for *Butterflies Are Free.*

Albert: 1716.

888 • HEARTBREAK RIDGE

WARNER BROS. PRODUCTION; WARNER BROS. 1986.

NOMINATION *Sound:* Les Fresholtz, Dick Alexander, Vern Poore, and William Nelson.

Marine sergeant Clint Eastwood [2179.5] whips a group of raw recruits into shape, and they go out and . . . invade Grenada. Apart from that anticlimax, this is fairly entertaining, a cut above most of the Reagan-era Ramboid stuff, thanks almost entirely to Eastwood. He's in fine form as an actor here, though as director he needs better material than the collection of misapplied clichés supplied him by screenwriter James Carabatsos. Good support from Marsha Mason [383 . . .] in one of her few roles not written by Neil Simon [332 . . .], Moses Gunn, Eileen Heckart [133 . . .], and Mario Van Peebles. The Oscar went to a somewhat better war movie, *Platoon.*

Fresholtz: 54, 58, 209, 215, 606, 1127, 1158.5, 1279, 1526, 2113, 2179.5. Alexander: 54, 209, 519, 1127, 1158.5, 2113, 2179.5. Poore: 209, 1127, 1158.5, 2179.5. Nelson: 1158.5.

889 • HEAVEN CAN WAIT

20TH CENTURY-FOX. 1943.

NOMINATIONS *Picture:* Ernst Lubitsch, producer. *Director:* Ernst Lubitsch. *Color Cinematography:* Edward Cronjager.

Don Ameche [419] has spent his life in a series of flirtations and amorous escapades, so when he dies he goes to the devil, played by Laird Cregar. Believing what he's been told about sex being sinful, Ameche tells his life story to His Excellency (as the film calls him), expecting to roast eternally. Recognizing that Ameche was really a kind, sweet fellow, the devil packs him off to the other place. Delicious charmer of a film, from a screenplay by Samson Raphaelson based on a play called *Birthday,* by Laszlo Bus-Fekete. With Gene Tierney [1153] as Ameche's wife and Charles Coburn [535 . . .] as his grandfather, plus Marjorie Main [601], Spring Byington [2325], Eugene Pallette, Signe Hasso, and Louis Calhern [1243]. Lubitsch and Raphaelson wanted Fredric March [184 . . .] or Rex Harrison [413 . . .], but studio head Darryl Zanuck [34 . . .] pressed contract player Ameche on them. Ameche turned in one of his best performances.

The film is generally ranked among Lubitsch's best, but there was little chance it would win the best picture Oscar—the studio was pushing its big picture of the year, *The Song of Bernadette,* and the voters preferred *Casablanca,* which also won for its director, Michael Curtiz. So although Lubitsch was one of the most acclaimed directors and producers in Hollywood, a former head of production at Paramount, he never received a competitive Oscar. At the 1946 awards, which took place shortly before his death in 1947, he was given an honorary award by the Academy, "for his distinguished contributions to the art of the motion picture."

The Oscar for cinematography went to Hal Mohr and W. Howard Greene for *The Phantom of the Opera*.

Lubitsch: 1217, 1484, 1540, 1847. Cronjager: 176, 400, 934, 1569, 1964, 2102.

890 • HEAVEN CAN WAIT

DOGWOOD PRODUCTIONS; PARAMOUNT. 1978.

AWARD *Art Direction—Set Decoration:* Paul Sylbert and Edwin O'Donovan; George Gaines.

NOMINATIONS *Picture:* Warren Beatty, producer. *Actor:* Warren Beatty. *Supporting Actor:* Jack Warden. *Supporting Actress:* Dyan Cannon. *Director:* Warren Beatty and Buck Henry. *Screenplay Based on Material From Another Medium:* Elaine May and Warren Beatty. *Cinematography:* William A. Fraker. *Original Score:* Dave Grusin.

L.A. Rams quarterback Joe Pendleton (Beatty) is in an accident and is whisked off to heaven by an eager angel, played by codirector Henry, only to discover that his time wasn't up yet. So the supervising angel, Mr. Jordan, played by James Mason [761 . . .], gives Pendleton a second chance. The problem is, the only available body is that of a rich, mean millionaire, who's being murdered by his unfaithful wife (Cannon), and his assistant, played by Charles Grodin. Pendleton is determined to use the millionaire's body to fulfill his dream of playing in the Super Bowl, but he has to convince his trainer, Max Corkle (Warden), that he's returned to life in another man's body. And meanwhile, he falls in love with a woman, played by Julie Christie [493 . . .], who has come to protest the environmental damage being done by the millionaire's company. Very likable remake of *Here Comes Mr. Jordan* that doesn't amount to much, but has a comforting warm fuzziness about it that is fortunately kept from becoming too cloying by the lively conniving of Cannon and Grodin, who are by far the best thing about the film. It made Beatty only the second person in Oscar history to receive simultaneous nominations as producer, actor, director, and writer. (The other was Orson Welles for *Citizen Kane*.) Its other distinction, as far as Oscar

nominations are concerned, is that Beatty and Warden received nominations for roles that earned Robert Montgomery and James Gleason nominations in the earlier film. In the original, Montgomery played a boxer, and Beatty is said to have written the lead role with Muhammad Ali in mind, deciding to play it himself and to change the character to a football player only when Ali turned him down. Both Beatty and Henry made their directing debuts with *Heaven Can Wait,* and they were the first dual nominees for directing since Robert Wise and Jerome Robbins won for *West Side Story*. The film's Oscar-winning art director, Sylbert, is the twin brother of the multiply nominated designer Richard Sylbert [395 . . .].

The Oscars were a duel between two Vietnam films, *The Deer Hunter* and *Coming Home*. The former won for best picture, supporting actor Christopher Walken, and director Michael Cimino. Jon Voight won the acting Oscar for *Coming Home*.

This is the sole nomination for May, who became famous for her comedy act with Mike Nichols [810 . . .] in the late fifties and went on to success as an actress *(California Suite),* director *(The Heartbreak Kid),* and writer. Unfortunately her career received a bad setback when the expensive comedy *Ishtar,* which she wrote and directed for Beatty and Dustin Hoffman [810 . . .], was a major flop in 1987. The writing award went to Oliver Stone for *Midnight Express*.

Nestor Almendros won for the cinematography of *Days of Heaven* and Giorgio Moroder for the score of *Midnight Express*.

Sylbert: 1612. Gaines: 54, 448, 1798. Beatty: 255, 308, 1678, 1798. Warden: 1798. Cannon: 250. Henry: 810. Fraker: 1205, 1380, 1439, 2231. Grusin: 379, 633, 667.5, 881, 1318, 1473, 2113.

891 • HEAVEN KNOWS, MR. ALLISON

20TH CENTURY-FOX. 1957.

NOMINATIONS *Actress:* Deborah Kerr. *Screenplay—Based on Material From Another Medium:* John Lee Mahin and John Huston.

Marine corporal Allison, played by Robert Mitchum [1935], is stranded on a Pacific island during World War II with a nun, Sister Angela, played by

Kerr. Enormously appealing performances by the stars make this rather obvious adventure movie work. It's a bit of a rehash of the odd-couple-in-adversity formula that fired *The African Queen,* which like this film was directed by Huston, though this one has to shy away from getting its characters sexually involved, depriving the movie of some of the tension it needs. Photographed by Oswald Morris [659 . . .]. Based on a novel by Charles Shaw.

This was the fourth of Kerr's six unsuccessful tries at the Oscar. She was considered a favorite after winning the New York Film Critics Award, but Joanne Woodward took the Oscar for *The Three Faces of Eve.* The writing award went to Pierre Boulle (fronting for blacklistees Carl Foreman and Michael Wilson) for *The Bridge on the River Kwai.*

Kerr: 599, 732, 1088, 1778, 1969. Mahin: 352. Huston: 24, 105, 356, 571, 1248, 1263, 1363, 1625, 1779, 2136.

891.5 • *HEAVENLY CREATURES*

WINGNUT FILMS PRODUCTION; MIRAMAX (NEW ZEALAND). 1994.

NOMINATION *Screenplay Written Directly for the Screen:* Frances Walsh and Peter Jackson.

In the fifties, two teenagers at a New Zealand girls' school, Pauline Parker (Melanie Lynskey) and Juliet Hulme (Kate Winslet), develop a close friendship—too shockingly close, in the eyes of some—based on a rich and shared fantasy life. But when events threaten to separate the girls, they turn to murder in order to preserve the world they've created for themselves. Fascinating, sometimes chilling, and very well-acted version of a true story, directed by Jackson. The accuracy of the film, however, was challenged by the former Juliet Hulme, now the mystery novelist Anne Perry, who had successfully concealed her identity until the film's release provoked a reporter to check out a rumor that Perry was in fact Juliet. Although she refused to see the film, Perry denounced what she considered distortions in it, including the suggestion of a lesbian relationship between the girls. More disinterested critics, however, found the film imaginative

and not at all sensational in its handling of the story, an absorbing study of folie à deux. The Oscar went to Quentin Tarantino and Roger Avary for *Pulp Fiction.*

892 • *HEAVEN'S GATE*

PARTISAN PRODUCTIONS LTD.; UNITED ARTISTS. 1981.

NOMINATION *Art Direction–Set Decoration:* Tambi Larsen; Jim Berkey.

Immigrants and cattlemen battle it out in late-nineteenth-century Wyoming. A famous disaster—not just the Johnson County range war, but the movie too. Michael Cimino had become the most sought-after director in Hollywood after the success of *The Deer Hunter,* and he was given carte blanche on his next movie. Cost overruns on the production destroyed the studio, United Artists. And the film—rambling, plotless, visually beautiful, and more than three hours long—destroyed Cimino's career. The very title, perhaps because it echoes "Watergate," another famous debacle, has become synonymous with Hollywood excess. To be fair, the movie has its defenders, including some prominent French critics, who claim that it has been unfairly maligned by American journalists eager to savage the successful. Superbly filmed by Vilmos Zsigmond [416 . . .]. The huge cast includes Kris Kristofferson [1874], Christopher Walken [521], Isabelle Huppert, Jeff Bridges [1139 . . .], John Hurt [608 . . .], Sam Waterston [1086], Brad Dourif [1481], Joseph Cotten, Mickey Rourke, and Willem Dafoe [1584]. The art direction Oscar went to *Raiders of the Lost Ark.*

Larsen: 956, 1341, 1727, 1897.

892.5 • *HEDD WYN*

PENDEFIG CYF PRODUCTION (UNITED KINGDOM). 1993.

NOMINATION *Foreign Language Film.*

A Welsh farmer's son seeks his country's prize for poetry but dies in World War I. Moving antiwar drama directed by Paul Turner and starring Huw Garmon, Sue Roderick, and Judith Humphreys. The film, which has not yet been widely distributed in the United States, is the first entry in the Welsh language to be nominated. The Oscar went to *Belle Epoque.*

893 • HEDDA

Royal Shakespeare-Brut Productions-George Barrie/Robert Enders Film Production; Brut Productions (United Kingdom). 1975.

Nomination *Actress:* Glenda Jackson.

Hedda Gabler (Jackson), bored with her marriage, tries to take revenge on an old lover, but her machinations finally entrap her. Straightforward, uncinematic rendering of the Ibsen play by the Royal Shakespeare Company, with Peter Eyre, Timothy West, Jennie Linden, and Patrick Stewart, directed by Trevor Nunn. Heavy going for all but devoted Ibsenites and fans of Jackson.

Fine actress that Jackson is, her performance in this little-seen drama would scarcely have drawn notice from the Academy in other years. But 1975 is perhaps the nadir for roles for women in Hollywood film, as the nominations demonstrate: Jackson competed against a foreign language performance, Isabelle Adjani in *The Story of Adele H.;* a bizarre turn in a relatively minor role, Ann-Margret in *Tommy;* a lead in a low-budget, minimally distributed movie, Carol Kane in *Hester Street;* and the winner, Louise Fletcher in *One Flew Over the Cuckoo's Nest*—a role that might have been classified as supporting in other years. The Academy overlooked the performances of Julie Christie and Goldie Hawn in *Shampoo,* Barbra Streisand in *Funny Lady,* Candice Bergen in *Bite the Bullet* and *The Wind and the Lion,* Diana Ross in *Mahogany,* and Diane Keaton in *Love and Death,* but even these also-rans show that there were few memorable roles for women in the mid-seventies. This was Jackson's last nomination before she retired from films to enter politics as a member of Parliament.

Jackson: 1966, 2125, 2307.

894 • HEIRESS, THE

Paramount. 1949.

Awards *Actress:* Olivia de Havilland. *Black-and-White Art Direction—Set Decoration:* John Meehan and Harry Horner; Emile Kuri. *Scoring of a Dramatic or Comedy Picture:* Aaron Copland. *Black-and-White Costume Design:* Edith Head and Gile Steele.

Nominations *Picture:* William Wyler, producer. *Supporting Actor:* Ralph Richardson. *Director:* William Wyler. *Black-and-White Cinematography:* Leo Tover.

Catherine Sloper (de Havilland) is the plain, dutiful daughter of the wealthy, arrogant, and emotionally abusive Dr. Sloper (Richardson). When handsome but penniless young Morris Townsend, played by Montgomery Clift [732 . . .], pays court to Catherine, Dr. Sloper recognizes him as a fortune hunter and vows to disinherit Catherine if she marries Townsend. They arrange to elope anyway, but Townsend fails to show up. When he returns some years later, after Dr. Sloper has died and she has come into her inheritance, Catherine, who has become as cold and self-possessed as her father, turns the tables on Townsend and jilts him. Elegant, absorbing adaptation by Ruth and Augustus Goetz of their play based on the novella *Washington Square,* by Henry James. Clift is a bit too edgily modern for the period role, but de Havilland, Richardson, and Miriam Hopkins [165], as Catherine's conniving, featherbrained Aunt Lavinia, are very fine indeed. The film is especially adroit in capturing the central ambiguity of the story: Is Townsend really just a fortune hunter, or is he genuinely attracted to Catherine, whose gentleness and patience show through her awkwardness?

De Havilland's second Oscar came at the end of the major phase of her Hollywood career. In the fifties she made fewer and fewer film appearances, concentrating instead on stage work. She didn't return to the screen until 1953's *My Cousin Rachel* and in 1955 took up residence in France with her husband, the editor of *Paris Match.* In recent years she has made occasional appearances in cameo roles in TV miniseries.

Production designer Horner came from Broadway to Hollywood in 1940 to work on *Our Town* and became a protégé of the celebrated production designer William Cameron Menzies [38 . . .]. Horner, who turned to directing for a while in the fifties, said the main set for the film, the house in Washington Square, was designed to reflect the three principal characters: It is Dr. Sloper's elegant but sterile shrine to his dead wife; its heavy walls and doors turn it into a cage for Catherine; and its opulence fuels Townsend's desire for possessions. The central element, the staircase, was made particularly steep to draw attention to Catherine's ascension at the film's end, when she rejects Townsend. Art director Meehan is occasionally confused with the screenwriter (see 271, 555) of the same name.

Copland, born in Brooklyn, began his studies with Rubin Goldmark, who also taught George Gershwin [1797]. But where Gershwin moved from popular musical into classical, Copland did the reverse, studying with Nadia Boulanger in Paris and beginning his career with compositions much influenced by Stravinsky. In the thirties he began to blend classical forms with jazz and folk influences, producing the ballets *Billy the Kid* and *Appalachian Spring.* Hollywood called in 1939, and he began writing occasional film scores. The score for *The Heiress* was his fourth nomination, but the only one to win him an Oscar.

This was the first of Head's eight Oscars, and the second in a string of annual nominations that would be unbroken until 1967. She was remarkable for her ability to produce not only chic clothes for stars who wanted to look good but also, as in the case of de Havilland's deliberately unbecoming wardrobe in *The Heiress,* designs that would help create the characters —although some have maintained that, as head of costuming for Paramount, Head claimed credit for work that was actually done by others.

Richardson was one of the Big Three of the twentieth-century English theater, along with his frequent costars Laurence Olivier [268 . . .] and John Gielgud [103 . . .], although like Gielgud's, his fame was primarily as a stage player and his film roles mostly character parts, while Olivier had the matinee-idol looks that made him a successful leading man in movies. He lost to Dean Jagger in *Twelve O'Clock High.*

The best picture Oscar went to *All the King's Men.* Joseph L. Mankiewicz won for directing *A Letter to Three Wives.* The cinematography award went to Paul C. Vogel for *Battleground.*

de Havilland: 798, 925, 1849, 2099. Meehan: 1975, 2155. Horner: 964, 2047. Kuri: 4, 166, 363, 629, 1284, 1823, 2155. Copland: 1451, 1464, 1510.

Head: 31, 32, 46, 305, 357, 363, 612, 636, 675, 736, 832, 945, 1003, 1219, 1261, 1263, 1398, 1427, 1504, 1550, 1579, 1587, 1631, 1716, 1727, 1738, 1748, 1840, 1927, 1986, 2012, 2098, 2247, 2298. Steele: 612, 817, 1087, 1309, 1748. Wyler: 175, 184, 420, 534, 560, 730, 1162, 1182, 1371, 1716, 2316. Richardson: 839. Tover: 925.

895 • HELL AND HIGH WATER

20TH CENTURY-FOX. 1954.

NOMINATION *Special Effects [no individual citation].*

Cold War thriller about a submarine mission in the Arctic to foil a plot hatched by the Chinese commies. It's really designed mainly to show off Fox's new toy, CinemaScope. Cult director Samuel Fuller also wrote the screenplay, and the cast includes Richard Widmark [1098], Cameron Mitchell, David Wayne, and Bella Darvi—one of the least impressive of the many protégées of studio head Darryl F. Zanuck [34 . . .]. The special effects award went to *20,000 Leagues Under the Sea.*

896 • HELLO, DOLLY!

CHENAULT PRODUCTIONS; 20TH CENTURY-FOX. 1969.

AWARDS *Art Direction—Set Decoration:* John DeCuir, Jack Martin Smith, and Herman Blumenthal; Walter M. Scott, George Hopkins, and Raphael Bretton. *Sound:* Jack Solomon and Murray Spivack. *Score of a Musical Picture—Original or Adaptation:* Lennie Hayton and Lionel Newman.

NOMINATIONS *Picture:* Ernest Lehman, producer. *Cinematography:* Harry Stradling. *Film Editing:* William Reynolds. *Costume Design:* Irene Sharaff.

Matchmaker Dolly Gallagher Levi, played by Barbra Streisand [737 . . .], sets her cap for a wealthy Yonkers merchant, played by Walter Matthau [709 . . .]. In the course of her manipulations, she also helps Matthau's young clerk, played by Michael Crawford, find love with a milliner, played by Marianne McAndrew. Big, dull musical whose problem is not so much that it's overproduced as that nobody seems to be having much fun spending all that money. The Jerry Herman score is full of catchy tunes, and Streisand certainly knows how to sing them, but they overwhelm the wisp of a plot, which was derived by producer-writer Lehman from Michael Stewart's Broadway book, which in turn came from Thornton Wilder's play *The Matchmaker*. Wilder's play was charmingly filmed in 1958 with Shirley Booth [425], Paul Ford, Anthony Perkins [730], Shirley MacLaine [91 . . .], and Robert Morse. Seeing the same story without the whopping production numbers makes one wonder why anyone thought so slight a vehicle would bear the weight of musicalization. The answer is the effervescent Carol Channing [2064], who starred in the original Broadway *Hello, Dolly!* Channing desperately wanted a chance at the film, as did most of her successors in the part, who included Ginger Rogers [1102], Dorothy Lamour, and Betty Grable. But Fox bet that its new superstar, Streisand, would pull in the most money. They were wrong: The film was a flop at the box office. At twenty-seven Streisand was a couple of decades too young for the part, a fact she obviously recognized. Her Dolly Levi is less a character than a collection of mannerisms, some of them borrowed from Mae West. Director Gene Kelly [74] was unable to help much. Still, it's watchable, and the big title number in which Streisand is teamed with Louis Armstrong is a showpiece on its own—the rest of the movie should be that good. Crawford and Tommy Tune, who plays his fellow clerk, are engaging, though McAndrew and E. J. Peaker, as their love interests, are forgettable.

The film probably owes its best picture nomination to the usual logrolling by Fox, which had been able to get a similar nomination for its disastrous *Doctor Dolittle* two years earlier. So it edged out much worthier potential nominees such as *They Shoot Horses, Don't They?*, *Easy Rider*, *The Wild Bunch*, and *Medium Cool*. The award went to a film about as antithetical in spirit to *Hello, Dolly!* as one can imagine: *Midnight Cowboy*.

Conrad Hall won for the cinematography of *Butch Cassidy and the Sundance Kid*. The editing Oscar went to Françoise Bonnot for *Z*. Margaret Furse won for the costumes for *Anne of the Thousand Days*.

DeCuir: 29, 201, 376, 413, 476, 950, 1088, 1391, 1852, 2000. Smith: 29, 413, 557, 646, 1230, 2008, 2120, 2247. Blumenthal: 413, 1062. Scott: 46,

376, 413, 476, 530, 542, 557, 646, 1062, 1088, 1213, 1391, 1475, 1706, 1753, 1881, 1907, 2008, 2120, 2247. Hopkins: 110, 508, 1003, 1170, 1332, 1385, 1393, 1910, 1949, 1973, 2058, 2277. Bretton: 963, 1596, 2126. Solomon: 738, 938, 1089, 1109, 1310. Spivack: 2120. Hayton: 877, 1476, 1577, 1831, 1907. Newman: 183, 457, 557, 795, 981, 1160, 1273, 1585, 1762, 2043. Lehman: 1450, 1738, 2244, 2277. Stradling: 110, 149, 596, 737, 852, 853, 864, 957, 1246, 1393, 1567, 1949, 2338. Reynolds: 643, 784, 1753, 1881, 1927, 2152. Sharaff: 66, 290, 333, 338, 413, 690, 852, 1088, 1507, 1592, 1910, 2000, 2244, 2277.

897 • HELLO FRISCO, HELLO

20TH CENTURY-FOX. 1943.
AWARD *Song:* "You'll Never Know," music by Harry Warren, lyrics by Mack Gordon.
NOMINATION *Color Cinematography:* Charles G. Clarke and Allen Davey.

Social-climbing Barbary Coast saloon-keeper John Payne and rising star singer Alice Faye fall in love. Oh, there's more going on in this stale Fox musical trifle, but do you really want to know about it? Directed by H. Bruce Humberstone, with Jack Oakie [818], Laird Cregar, June Havoc, and Ward Bond. Chiefly designed to keep people's minds off the war, although the Oscar-winning song, performed by Faye in her most misty-eyed fashion, was a big hit because it expressed the sentiments of couples separated by the conflict. It beat out some pretty impressive (and superior) competitors: Harold Arlen and E. Y. Harburg's "Happiness Is a Thing Called Joe," from *Cabin in the Sky;* Arlen and Johnny Mercer's "My Shining Hour," from *The Sky's the Limit;* Arlen and Mercer's "That Old Black Magic," from *Star Spangled Rhythm;* and Cole Porter's "You'd Be So Nice to Come Home To," from *Something to Shout About;* plus five other songs.

The cinematography Oscar went to Hal Mohr and W. Howard Greene for *The Phantom of the Opera*.

Warren: 21, 324, 569, 788, 791, 877, 1072, 1367, 1501, 1964. Gordon: 428, 563, 569, 1362,

1501, 1964, 1984, 2219. Clarke: 837, 1352, 1752. Davey: 217, 455, 1872, 1988.

898 • HELL'S ANGELS

THE CADDO COMPANY; UNITED ARTISTS. 1929–30.

NOMINATION *Cinematography:* Gaetano Gaudio and Harry Perry.

The eternal triangle ensnares World War I fliers Ben Lyon and James Hall and a hot little number called Jean Harlow. This is the film in which she offers to slip into something more comfortable. What makes this a classic is not the campy story, though it helped make Harlow a star, but the truly spectacular aerial sequences, involving not only the usual aerobatic dogfights but also zeppelin battles. Produced and directed by Howard Hughes [734 . . .] as if he had all the money in the world. Actually, much of it was written and directed by James Whale, who took over the film after Hughes decided to turn it into a talkie in midproduction. There were four deaths and numerous injuries during the shooting, and Hughes himself crashed a plane while demonstrating how he wanted one of the flying stunts to be performed. Some think the aerial photography, supervised by Perry and using twenty-six cameramen, has never been surpassed—it has certainly been endlessly imitated. However, the cinematography Oscar went to Joseph T. Rucker and Willard Van Der Veer for *With Byrd at the South Pole.*

Gaudio: 90, 447, 1064, 1162, 1872.

899 • HELLZAPOPPIN'

MAYFAIR; UNIVERSAL. 1942.

NOMINATION *Song:* "Pig Foot Pete," music by Gene de Paul, lyrics by Don Raye.

Film version of a famous Broadway revue that featured variety acts and audience participation routines and starred Ole Olsen and Chic Johnson. The film has a little plot to hold it together—something about the romantic difficulties of a rich man staging a show at his mansion. Silly, dated, often tedious, but occasionally very funny. In addition to Olsen and Johnson, the cast includes Martha Raye, Mischa Auer [1401], Hugh Herbert, Shemp Howard, and Elisha Cook, Jr. How-

ever, there's a little problem about the nominated song: It doesn't appear in the movie. It was one of ten nominees, all of them submitted by their respective studios under an Academy open-door policy that lasted from 1940 through 1945. "Pig Foot Pete" was sung by Raye in *Keep 'Em Flying,* a Bud Abbott and Lou Costello movie released a year earlier. So whoever submitted Universal's entry may have forgotten which movie the song was in—not surprising, given the quality of the films. The mystery nominee lost to Irving Berlin's "White Christmas," from *Holiday Inn.*

Raye: 306.

900 • HENRY & JUNE

WALRUS & ASSOCIATES PRODUCTION; UNIVERSAL. 1990.

NOMINATION *Cinematography:* Philippe Rousselot.

Henry is Henry Miller, the American expatriate writer, played by Fred Ward, and June is his wife, played by Uma Thurman [1633.5]. Their relationship is examined through the eyes of his lover, Anaïs Nin, played by Maria de Medeiros. Interesting portrait of an erotic triangle, splendidly re-creating Paris in the early thirties. The film became notorious as the first to receive the NC-17 rating that was created to replace the X, much exploited by pornographers, with a designation that would encourage adult but not pornographic films. The new rating failed miserably, as the films labeled NC-17 became sitting ducks for conservative pressure groups, who prevented them from being booked in mainstream theaters, advertised in newspapers, and stocked in video stores. Only the most conservative will find *Henry & June* offensive, however. Written and directed by Philip Kaufman [2173]. Rousselot lost to Dean Semler for *Dances With Wolves.*

Rousselot: 940, 1701.5.

901 • HENRY V

J. ARTHUR RANK-TWO CITIES FILMS, UNITED ARTISTS (UNITED KINGDOM). 1946.

AWARD *Special Award:* Laurence Olivier for outstanding achievement as actor, producer and director.

NOMINATIONS *Picture:* Laurence Olivier, producer. *Actor:* Laurence Olivier. *Color Interior Decoration:* Paul

Sheriff and Carmen Dillon. *Scoring of a Dramatic or Comedy Picture:* William Walton.

Young King Henry V of England, played by Olivier, leads his people into war against the French and wins not only the battle of Agincourt but also the hand of the French king's daughter, Katharine, played by Renee Asherson. This superlative version of Shakespeare's play, originally planned as a wartime morale booster, has become a cinematic landmark. It moves from a re-creation of the "wooden O"—the Elizabethan Globe theater—into a stylized representation of the action of the play and then into a stunningly realistic battle. Olivier is at his unbeatable best, and he's well supported by Asherson, Leo Genn [1644], Felix Aylmer, Robert Newton, Max Adrian, Robert Helpmann, Ernest Thesiger, and many others. The splendid color cinematography for *Henry V* by Robert Krasker [2053] was curiously omitted from the nominations, in part because the Academy decided to cut down on the number of nominations, and limited the cinematography candidates to two each in the color and black-and-white categories.

Olivier made his film debut in 1930, but it was not until *Wuthering Heights* in 1939 that his reputation as a movie actor began to equal his acclaim as a stage performer. But the war, during which he served in the aviation branch of the royal navy, took him away from Hollywood. Most of his wartime film work was done in England, with a strong propaganda bias. In 1944 he became codirector with Ralph Richardson [839 . . .] of the Old Vic and began preparations for filming *Henry V*. He first approached William Wyler [175 . . .], who had directed him in *Wuthering Heights,* about directing *Henry V* but decided to assume the task himself—his first work as film director. Olivier's intention to cast his wife, Vivien Leigh [798 . . .], as Katharine fell afoul of David O. Selznick [497 . . .], who owned her contract and was reluctant to let her play so small a role.

The special award to Olivier was well planned, because it was unlikely that any film, especially an English one, would triumph over *The Best Years of Our Lives,* which touched a special chord in postwar audiences and took best picture, the best actor award for Fredric March, and the scoring award for Hugo Friedhofer. The art direction award went to *The Yearling.*

Olivier: 268, 619, 858, 1272, 1506, 1670, 1693, 1841, 2316. Sheriff: 1363. Dillon: 858. Walton: 858.

902 • HENRY V

RENAISSANCE FILMS PRODUCTION IN ASSOCIATION WITH BBC; SAMUEL GOLDWYN COMPANY (UNITED KINGDOM). 1989.
AWARD *Costume Design:* Phyllis Dalton.
NOMINATIONS *Actor:* Kenneth Branagh. *Director:* Kenneth Branagh.

Branagh plays Shakespeare's monarch in an adaptation of the play that interpolates a bit of the *Henry IV* plays to establish the king's relationship with Falstaff (Robbie Coltrane). The cast also includes Emma Thompson [954.5 . . .] as the French princess Katharine, Paul Scofield [1252 . . .] as King Charles VI of France, Ian Holm [386] as Fluellen, Judi Dench as Mistress Quickly, Derek Jacobi as the Chorus, and Robert Stephens as Pistol. Inevitably compared with Olivier's magisterial 1946 film, it nevertheless succeeds on its own terms, thanks to Branagh's astonishingly assured direction and performance, a flawless cast, a stirring score by Pat Doyle, and fine photography by Kenneth MacMillan. Branagh's film takes a harsher view of war than Olivier's, which was designed to honor a country that had just survived a long and destructive conflict.

Born in Belfast in 1960, raised in England, and trained at the Royal Academy of Dramatic Art, Branagh has experienced both the adulation and the abuse that someone who achieves much at an early age is bound to know. He played Henry V at Stratford at twenty-three, the youngest person ever to do so. He started his own company, the Renaissance Theatre Company, in 1987. And he directed his first film—which earned him two Oscar nominations—before he was thirty. Moreover, it was based on the same play that Laurence Olivier [268 . . .], often proclaimed the greatest actor of our century, had filmed. Branagh's chutzpah even extended to writing his memoirs, titled *Beginning,* before he was thirty. "Branagh-bashing" was an inevitable consequence, but his talent is manifest and he downplays the comparison with Olivier by presenting a boyish charm in contrast to Oliver's regal hauteur. (In his second film, the 1991 thriller *Dead Again,* Branagh risks a cheeky parody of the master, playing the composer accused of murder with Olivier's hooded eyes and plummy projection.) The other frequent comparison is to the boy wonder Orson Welles [407 . . .], whose famous long tracking shot at the beginning of *Touch of Evil* Branagh admittedly imitated in the scene after the battle of Agincourt, when Branagh carries Christian Bale across the battlefield as voices swell in the hymn "Non Nobis." Branagh continues to work hard on a wide range of projects, from *Dead Again* to the 1992 domestic comedy *Peter's Friends* (which earned further invidious comparisons, this time to *The Big Chill*) to 1993's film of *Much Ado About Nothing* to *Mary Shelley's Frankenstein* (1994). He was nominated for another Oscar in 1992 for his short film *Swan Song.* His most frequent collaborator has been his wife, Emma Thompson, whose career threatens to eclipse his. The acting Oscar went to Daniel Day-Lewis for *My Left Foot.* Oliver Stone won for directing *Born on the Fourth of July.*

Dalton: 558, 1471.

903 • *HERE COME THE WAVES*

PARAMOUNT. 1945.
NOMINATION *Song:* "Ac-cent-tchu-ate the Positive," music by Harold Arlen, lyrics by Johnny Mercer.

Betty Hutton plays twins—one smart, one silly—who have a nightclub sister act but decide to do their part during World War II by joining the Waves. When the smart twin falls in love with Bing Crosby [173 . . .], the silly twin tries to break up their romance by masquerading as her sister. Goofy wartime nonsense, directed by Mark Sandrich, the movie is now remembered almost solely for Crosby's introduction of an Arlen-Mercer classic. "Ac-cent-tchu-ate the Positive" had to compete against an incredible thirteen other songs in this year of liberalized nominating rules. The winner was Richard Rodgers and Oscar Hammerstein's "It Might As Well Be Spring," from *State Fair.*

Arlen: 248, 322, 368, 1838, 1910, 1912, 2186, 2300. Mercer: 248, 278, 384, 476, 494, 508, 636, 788, 825, 877, 905, 1109, 1772, 1838, 1912, 2327, 2328.

904 • *HERE COMES MR. JORDAN*

COLUMBIA. 1941.
AWARDS *Original Story:* Harry Segall. *Screenplay:* Sidney Buchman and Seton I. Miller.
NOMINATIONS *Picture:* Everett Riskin, producer. *Actor:* Robert Montgomery. *Supporting Actor:* James Gleason. *Director:* Alexander Hall. *Black-and-White Cinematography:* Joseph Walker.

Heavyweight contender Joe Pendleton (Montgomery) is in a plane crash, and his soul is whisked off to heaven by a busybody angel, played by Edward Everett Horton, who discovers to his horror that Pendleton was supposed to survive the crash. Mr. Jordan, played by Claude Rains [365 . . .], is the angel in charge of sorting things out, which he does by returning Pendleton to earth in the body of a murdered millionaire. Pendleton is determined to get a chance at the title and manages to convince his old manager, Max Corkle (Gleason), that it's really him in the millionaire's body. There's also a romantic subplot involving Evelyn Keyes. If all this sounds familiar, it's because it was done twice—the second time by Warren Beatty as *Heaven Can Wait,* which kept the plotline and even the characters' names, but made Pendleton a quarterback instead of a boxer. The first version is brisker, if slightly more sentimental, than the second. On the other hand, imagining Montgomery as a champion boxer is more of a stretch than imagining Beatty as a star quarterback. On the whole it's a small-scale charmer, the product of good writing and casting, one of those fine movies that occasionally happen to be turned out by otherwise undistingished directors—Hall never made another film of its caliber.

The screenplay is based on Segall's play *Halfway to Heaven.* Buchman had been a screenwriter in Hollywood since 1930 and was one of the star writers at Columbia. He moved into producing and in the forties became a studio production executive. His career was cut short by the blacklist, however, after he admitted to the House Un-American Activities Committee in 1951 that he had been a member of the Communist Party, but refused to name other party members. He returned to producing for 20th Century-Fox in the sixties. Miller, who had been a writer in Hollywood since the mid-twenties, also turned to producing in the forties.

The best picture Oscar went to *How Green Was My Valley,* which also won for supporting actor Donald Crisp, director John Ford, and cinematographer Arthur Miller. Gary Cooper won as best actor for *Sergeant York.*

Buchman: 1057, 1370, 1998. Miller: 463. Riskin: 114, 1488. Montgomery: 1431. Walker: 1058, 1494, 2325.

905 • HERE COMES THE GROOM

PARAMOUNT. 1951.
AWARD *Song:* "In the Cool, Cool, Cool of the Evening," music by Hoagy Carmichael, lyrics by Johnny Mercer.
NOMINATION *Motion Picture Story:* Robert Riskin and Liam O'Brien.

With the aid of some war orphans he has brought into the country, a reporter, played by Bing Crosby [173 . . .], courts a reluctant Jane Wyman [246 . . .], who plans to marry her boss, played by Franchot Tone [1387]. Tired comedy directed by Frank Capra [1025 . . .]. One of his ickiest movies, dragged down by too many cute kids and inane musical numbers, including Anna Maria Alberghetti shrilling "Caro Nome." Louis Armstrong, Dorothy Lamour, Phil Harris, and some other Paramount contract players have cameos, but by the time they show up, nobody cares.

On the other hand, the movie does have a thoroughly engaging song, well performed by Crosby (not unexpected) and Wyman (a true surprise). Carmichael, one of the great songwriters of the golden age of American pop songwriting, had been composing for movies off and on since the thirties, as well as acting in such films as *The Best Years of Our Lives* and *To Have and Have Not* (1944). Somehow the Academy

managed to ignore much of Carmichael's work for films, including the sassy "Baltimore Oriole," written with Paul Francis Webster [33 . . .] for 1945's *Johnny Angel,* and Carmichael and Mercer's "How Little We Know," from *To Have and Have Not.*

This was the last time Capra and Riskin, one of the great directing-writing teams, would collaborate. In December 1950 Riskin had a severe stroke that left him paralyzed until his death in 1955. The Oscar went to Paul Dehn and James Bernard for *Seven Days to Noon.*

Carmichael: 341. Mercer: 248, 278, 384, 476, 494, 508, 636, 788, 825, 877, 903, 1109, 1772, 1838, 1912, 2327, 2328. Riskin: 1025, 1119, 1366, 2325.

906 • HERE COMES THE NAVY

WARNER BROS. 1934.
NOMINATION *Picture:* Lou Edelman, producer.

Shipyard worker James Cagney [79 . . .] joins the navy and discovers he's in a unit headed by Pat O'Brien, with whom he's had a pre-enlistment dustup. He complicates things by falling in love with O'Brien's sister but becomes a hero and thereby sets things right. Pleasant stuff, directed by Lloyd Bacon, that was the first of nine films—including the last either actor made, *Ragtime*—that Cagney and O'Brien appeared in together. Its appearance in the best picture slate, especially given that it received no other nominations, is inexplicable, except that Warners had no other viable candidates that year. Edelman, a Warners staff producer of no particular distinction, ended his career as a TV producer, responsible for such series as *Wyatt Earp* and *Big Valley.* The Oscar went to *It Happened One Night.*

907 • HERS TO HOLD

UNIVERSAL. 1943.
NOMINATION *Song:* "Say a Pray'r for the Boys Over There," music by Jimmy McHugh, lyrics by Herb Magidson.

Deanna Durbin goes to work in an airplane factory, doing her part for the war effort, but also managing to be near pilot Joseph Cotten. Sentimental flag-waving romance, directed by Frank Ryan, with Durbin singing everything from "Begin the Beguine" to the Seguidilla from *Carmen.* The nominated song lost to "You'll Never Know," by Harry Warren and Mack Gordon, from *Hello Frisco, Hello.*

McHugh: 916, 1707, 2028, 2328. Magidson: 754, 1830.

908 • HESTER STREET

MIDWEST FILM PRODUCTIONS. 1975.
NOMINATION *Actress:* Carol Kane.

Kane joins her immigrant husband (Steven Keats), who came to turn-of-the-century New York several years before her, and discovers that he is no longer the modest, religiously observant man she knew. He has picked up American slang, while she speaks only Yiddish; he is also smitten with a flashly Americanized woman. The small-scale, low-budget film, well directed by Joan Micklin Silver, deals with Kane's attempts to assimilate before she loses her husband for good.

Kane had appeared in secondary roles in *Carnal Knowledge, The Last Detail,* and *Dog Day Afternoon* before winning the lead in Silver's film. It didn't exactly make her a star, but she would become more widely known a few years later in the TV series *Taxi,* playing the immigrant wife of Andy Kaufman—almost a parody of her *Hester Street* role. She owes her Oscar nomination to the dearth of roles for established actresses in major productions in 1975. She lost to Louise Fletcher in *One Flew Over the Cuckoo's Nest.*

909 • HI DIDDLE DIDDLE

ANDREW STONE PRODUCTIONS; UNITED ARTISTS. 1943.
NOMINATION *Scoring of a Dramatic or Comedy Picture:* Phil Boutelje.

Young lovers Martha Scott [1510] and Dennis O'Keefe find life complicated by their parents, who are con artists. Ephemeral fluff, with Adolphe Menjou [734], Pola Negri, Billie Burke [1306], and June Havoc, produced and directed by Andrew L. Stone [1067]. The scoring Oscar went to Alfred Newman for *The Song of Bernadette.*

Boutelje: 827.

910 • HIDE-OUT

MGM. 1934.
NOMINATION *Original Story:* Mauri Grashin.

Racketeer Robert Montgomery [904 . . .], wounded and on the run, winds up on Maureen O'Sullivan's farm, where she nurses his wounds, reforms him, and of course falls in love with him. Crowd-pleasing melodrama without much to recommend it other than some good character performers —Edward Arnold, Elizabeth Patterson, and the young Mickey Rooney [115 . . .]—directed by W. S. Van Dyke [1751 . . .]. Grashin came in third: The story Oscar went to Arthur Caesar for *Manhattan Melodrama.*

911 • HIGH AND THE MIGHTY, THE

WAYNE-FELLOWS PRODUCTIONS; WARNER BROS. 1954.
AWARD *Scoring of a Dramatic or Comedy Picture:* Dimitri Tiomkin.
NOMINATIONS *Supporting Actress:* Jan Sterling. *Supporting Actress:* Claire Trevor. *Director:* William Wellman. *Song:* "The High and the Mighty," music by Dimitri Tiomkin, lyrics by Ned Washington. *Film Editing:* Ralph Dawson.

Airline pilot John Wayne [33 . . .] not only has a crippled plane, but he's over the Pacific with a bunch of panicky passengers including Trevor and Sterling. Yes, you've seen this one before, but it's still one of the best of a well-worn genre, played more for suspense than for soap opera.

This is the sole nomination for Sterling, who got terminally typecast as a tough blonde. She and Trevor, who also wound up in such roles a lot, lost to a more ladylike blonde, Eva Marie Saint in *On the Waterfront.* Director Elia Kazan and editor Gene Milford also won for *On the Waterfront.* The song, which needlessly stuck words onto Tiomkin's main theme, lost to the title tune by Jule Styne and Sammy Cahn for *Three Coins in the Fountain.*

Tiomkin: 33, 286, 380, 446, 638, 663, 730, 768, 850, 912, 1206, 1347, 1370, 1470, 2006, 2127, 2282, 2335. Trevor: 510, 1081. Wellman: 157, 1909. Washington: 274, 585, 912, 1329, 1396,

1576, 1745, 2127, 2282, 2335. Dawson: 17, 90, 1315.

912 • *HIGH NOON*

STANLEY KRAMER PRODUCTIONS; UNITED ARTISTS. 1952.

AWARDS *Actor:* Gary Cooper. *Song:* "High Noon (Do Not Forsake Me, Oh My Darlin')," music by Dimitri Tiomkin, lyrics by Ned Washington. *Scoring of a Dramatic or Comedy Picture:* Dimitri Tiomkin. *Film Editing:* Elmo Williams and Harry Gerstad.

NOMINATIONS *Picture:* Stanley Kramer, producer. *Director:* Fred Zinnemann. *Screenplay:* Carl Foreman.

Will Kane (Cooper), the marshal of a small western town, gets married to a Quaker, played by Grace Kelly [450 . . .], planning to adopt her peaceful ways, hang up his badge, and settle down. Then word comes that four bad men are arriving on the noon train, planning to even old scores with Kane. Should Kane choose fight or flight? If the former, will he lose his pacifist bride, if not his life? If he leaves, can he live with his conscience? And can he get any of the craven townspeople he's protected over the years to help him out in this showdown? Spare, simple, classically structured (the time span of the action is precisely that of the film's running time) and widely regarded as one of the best westerns of all time. There are dissenters who find it pretentious and too reliant on music and editing to cover up its weaknesses of plot and characterization; they cite the story that after a disastrous preview, editor Williams was called in to recut the movie—introducing the famous cuts to a clock face that give the film the suspense of a prelaunch countdown. In any case, it's a movie of fine craftsmanship, with a solid supporting cast: Thomas Mitchell [962 . . .], Lloyd Bridges, Katy Jurado [299], Otto Kruger, Lon Chaney, Jr., Harry (billed as Henry) Morgan, and Lee Van Cleef, among others. The cinematography is by Floyd Crosby [1993].

Cooper had been in a career slump since his last nomination, for *For Whom the Bell Tolls* in 1943. *High Noon* and the Oscar helped restart his career. At the 1960 awards, held just a month before Cooper's death in 1961, he received an honorary award "for his many memorable screen performances and the international recognition he, as an individual, has gained for the motion picture industry."

The Tiomkin-Washington song, which was a jukebox hit at the time, has otherwise had little life outside of the context of the film. To its credit, it's a simple narrative ballad that's wholly in keeping with the style and theme of the film—almost like a chorus commenting on the action, as those who liken the movie to Greek drama have noted. (In this case, the chorus is Tex Ritter, who sings the song off camera.) On the other hand, it started the vogue for movie theme songs, usually irrelevant to the action and often to the mood of the films in which they appeared. Tiomkin's percussive melody for the song is also the primary theme of his score, which has a tick-tock pulse reinforcing the clock motif.

As popular as *High Noon* was, it lost the best picture Oscar to *The Greatest Show on Earth.* One explanation for this is the Academy's perpetual snubbing of genre films—westerns, thrillers, science fiction, mysteries, action adventures—in favor of psychological dramas and literary adaptations. Until *Dances With Wolves,* only one other western, *Cimarron,* had received the best picture award, and very few had even been nominated. It's doubtful that the Academy really considered the hokey circus melodrama *Greatest Show* high art, so it's more likely that *High Noon* was handicapped at the Oscars by other forces. It was independently produced and released through United Artists, a studio that would become the dominant distributor of best picture winners in the sixties, but at this point had released only one such winner, *Rebecca,* in 1940. UA didn't have the promotional muscle of the majors —Paramount, MGM, 20th Century-Fox, Warners— who then dominated the Oscars. And *High Noon* was written by Foreman, who had just taken the Fifth Amendment in testifying before the House Un-American Activities Committee. Somewhat after the fact, some—including Foreman himself—saw *High Noon* as a parable about a loner (Foreman) abandoned by the people who ordinarily might have supported him (Hollywood liberals) but were terrified into silence by the forces of repression (HUAC and Senator Joseph McCarthy). The Academy gave the best picture award to a film produced by Cecil B. DeMille, one of Hollywood's archreactionaries. The directing Oscar went to a conservative, John Ford, for *The Quiet Man.* (To be fair, Ford was no admirer of DeMille, having spoken out against him in a recent battle over control of the Screen Directors Guild, so by choosing Ford over DeMille, the Academy had it both ways.) And in a nice bit of irony, the writing award went to Charles Schnee for *The Bad and the Beautiful,* a not-terribly-flattering portrait of the filmmaking community.

Cooper: 701, 1366, 1607, 1779. Tiomkin: 33, 286, 380, 446, 638, 663, 730, 768, 850, 911, 1206, 1347, 1370, 1470, 2006, 2127, 2282, 2335. Washington: 274, 585, 911, 1329, 1396, 1576, 1745, 2127, 2282, 2335. Williams: 2155. Gerstad: 380. Kramer: 330, 522, 843, 1065, 1812. Zinnemann: 732, 1066, 1252, 1457, 1771, 1969. Foreman: 287, 380, 850, 1302, 2340.

913 • HIGH SOCIETY

ALLIED ARTISTS. 1956.

NOMINATION *Motion Picture Story:* Edward Bernds and Elwood Ullman. (Nominated in error; withdrawn from final ballot.)

One of the Bowery Boys is mistaken for the heir to a fortune, so they move into a mansion and . . . A *Bowery Boys* movie, nominated for an *Oscar,* for *writing?* Well, not really, though this is one of the most ludicrous and mysterious mix-ups in the history of the awards. The writers branch clearly intended to nominate the MGM musical remake of *The Philadelphia Story,* which had the same title as the Bowery Boys movie, and Bernds and Ullman graciously withdrew their names from contention. But how the mistake happened is the mystery. Possibly it was a simple clerical error; the person typing up the list of nominees and checking the Writers Guild credits to see who wrote the story may have simply looked up the wrong *High Society.* But it's hard to believe that the writers branch nominating committee would have placed the MGM *High Society* in the story category, because it was clearly not an original story; it was common knowledge that the film was a musical remake of a 1941 movie that had won an Oscar for Donald Ogden Stewart's screenplay, which had been

adapted from a hit Broadway play by Philip Barry. However this peculiar snafu happened, it was only one of three embarrassments in the writing category this year. The Oscar for story was awarded to Robert Rich for *The Brave One.* When he failed to show up to collect his statuette, it became known that "Robert Rich" was a pseudonym for the blacklisted writer Dalton Trumbo. And the Academy was forced to rule that writer Michael Wilson could not be cited as the author of the screenplay for *Friendly Persuasion*—the anonymous screenplay was announced as a nominee but withdrawn from the final ballot—because of a new Academy bylaw prohibiting nominations to anyone who refused to testify before a congressional committee or to renounce earlier membership in the Communist Party. Hollywood writers have always complained of mistreatment, but 1956 was a nadir. As for the Bowery Boys' *High Society, Gunsmoke* fans might want to check it out to see what Amanda Blake's career amounted to just before she became famous as Miss Kitty.

914 • HIGH SOCIETY

SOL C. SIEGEL PRODUCTION; MGM. 1956.

NOMINATIONS *Song:* "True Love," music and lyrics by Cole Porter. *Scoring of a Musical Picture:* Johnny Green and Saul Chaplin.

Spoiled, rich Tracy Lord, played by Grace Kelly [450 . . .], is about to have a big society wedding in Newport to the rather stuffy George Kittredge, played by John Lund, when her ex-husband, C. K. Dexter-Haven, played by Bing Crosby [173 . . .], shows up to play host for the Newport Jazz Festival. At the same time, reporter Mike Connor, played by Frank Sinatra [732 . . .], and photographer Liz Imbrie, played by Celeste Holm [46 . . .], arrive to cover the wedding and perhaps uncover some dirt about the Lord family. Tracy falls out of love with George, in and out of love with Mike, and back in love with Dex. This remake of *The Philadelphia Story* sacrifices some of the wit and romance of the original for the sake of its musical numbers, the highlights of which are duets: Crosby and Sinatra on "Well, Did You Evah?" (a song not composed for the film but borrowed from Porter's 1939 Broadway show

DuBarry Was a Lady) and Crosby and Louis Armstrong on "Now You Has Jazz." Kelly would seem ideally cast, but the image of the original Tracy Lord, Katharine Hepburn, superimposes itself on every movement and every line. This was the last screen appearance for Louis Calhern [1243], as droll and lecherous Uncle Willie. Directed by Charles Walters [1173].

"True Love," sung in the film by Crosby with Kelly backing him on a chorus, was the biggest hit of the songs Porter wrote for High Society, one of his last scores before retiring in 1958 after an old riding injury forced him to have a leg amputated. The Oscar went to Jay Livingston and Ray Evans' "Whatever Will Be, Will Be (Que Será, Será)," from The Man Who Knew Too Much. Alfred Newman and Ken Darby took the scoring award for The King and I.

Porter: 261, 1862, 2329. Green: 66, 320, 594, 662, 817, 1298, 1471, 1550, 1657, 2047, 2244. Chaplin: 66, 1097, 1782, 2244.

915 • HIGH TIME

BING CROSBY PRODUCTIONS INC.; 20TH CENTURY-FOX. 1960.
NOMINATION Song: "The Second Time Around," music by James Van Heusen, lyrics by Sammy Cahn.

Widower Bing Crosby [173 . . .] decides to go back to college, and naturally he has trouble fitting in with the younger generation, who include Tuesday Weld [1205], Fabian, and Richard Beymer. Tedious and formulaic—and no, the title doesn't have anything to do with marijuana, which didn't become a college fixture until a few years later. Directed by Blake Edwards [2201]. The Oscar went to Manos Hadjidakis for the title song from Never on Sunday.

Van Heusen: 171, 173, 787, 926, 1056, 1524, 1587, 1708, 1859, 1907, 2016, 2064, 2263. Cahn: 74, 163, 182, 696, 926, 1031, 1056, 1216, 1524, 1587, 1692, 1708, 1719, 1859, 1907, 2016, 2064, 2072, 2103, 2110, 2125, 2263, 2264, 2315, 2343.

916 • HIGHER AND HIGHER

RKO RADIO. 1944.
NOMINATIONS Song: "I Couldn't Sleep a Wink Last Night," music by Jimmy McHugh, lyrics by Harold Adamson. Scoring of a Musical Picture: C. Bakaleinikoff.

When his fortune goes down the tubes, Leon Errol calls on the aid of his servants to get the money back. Moderately dumb comedy with music, notable for a cast that includes Frank Sinatra [732 . . .] (third-billed, in his first film acting role), Michele Morgan, Jack Haley, Victor Borge, Mary Wickes, and Mel Tormé. Directed by Tim Whelan. The music awards went to James Van Heusen and Johnny Burke's "Swinging on a Star," from Going My Way, and Carmen Dragon and Morris Stoloff's scoring of Cover Girl.

McHugh: 907, 1707, 2028, 2328. Adamson: 21, 921, 1980, 2028. Bakaleinikoff: 640, 1445, 1863.

917 • HINDENBURG, THE

ROBERT WISE-FILMAKERS GROUP-UNIVERSAL PRODUCTION; UNIVERSAL. 1975.
AWARDS Special Achievement Award for Sound Effects: Peter Berkos. Special Achievement Award for Visual Effects: Albert Whitlock and Glen Robinson.
NOMINATIONS Cinematography: Robert Surtees. Art Direction—Set Decoration: Edward Carfagno; Frank McKelvy. Sound: Leonard Peterson, John A. Bolger, Jr., John Mack, and Don K. Sharpless.

A saboteur causes the 1937 crash of the German dirigible Hindenburg in New Jersey. On board are Anne Bancroft [28 . . .], George C. Scott [73 . . .], Gig Young [427 . . .], Burgess Meredith [504 . . .], Charles Durning [180 . . .], and lots of others. A real disaster, and we don't just mean the crash. Director Robert Wise [407 . . .] finds no way to make the sluggish intertwining soap-opera plots entertain us, so he lets the handsome production effects do the job. The climactic scene, intercutting actual newsreel footage with dramatic re-creations of the fates of the various passengers, comes off in the worst possible taste, as a crassly sensational use of the lives and deaths of real people. Other disaster flicks of the era, such as The Poseidon Adventure and The Towering Inferno, at least had the virtue of being pure fiction, so that we could have our cheap thrills while knowing that nobody got hurt in real life. The film's premise that the Hindenburg was sabotaged is based on mere speculation.

The film's two Oscars were noncompetitive

awards. In the other categories, Surtees lost to John Alcott for *Barry Lyndon,* which also won for art direction. The award for sound went to *Jaws.*

Whitlock: 591, 2104. Robinson: 591, 1089, 1196. Surtees: 130, 175, 557, 810, 1094, 1139, 1388, 1469, 1644, 1747, 1911, 1927, 1960, 2055, 2152. Carfagno: 130, 175, 629, 1069, 1552, 1644, 1814, 1937, 2312. McKelvy: 591, 1450, 1570, 1631, 2047, 2200.

918 • HIROSHIMA, MON AMOUR

Argos Films-Como Films-Daiei Pictures Ltd.-Pathé Overseas Production; Zenith International Film Corporation (France-Japan). 1960.

Nomination *Story and Screenplay—Written Directly for the Screen:* Marguérite Duras.

A French actress and a Japanese architect have an affair while she is making a film in Hiroshima. Trying to understand his experience of the atomic bombing of the city, she recalls her wartime affair with a German, which led to her being shunned by her neighbors. Much-explicated first feature by Alain Resnais, more profoundly felt than his subsequent exercises in fragmented narrative such as *Last Year at Marienbad, Muriel* (1963), and *La Guerre Est Finie.* If today it seems excessively mannered and tricksy, it's because the shock of the new has worn off and its tricks and mannerisms have become the stuff of perfume commercials and music videos. Duras, an eminent French novelist, lost to Billy Wilder and I. A. L. Diamond's story and screenplay for *The Apartment.*

919 • HIS BUTLER'S SISTER

Universal. 1944.

Nomination *Sound Recording:* Bernard B. Brown.

Deanna Durbin, who wants to be a singer, goes to work as a maid for composer Franchot Tone [1387], whose butler is Durbin's half brother, Pat O'Brien. (Still with us?) Naturally Durbin gets to be a singer and gets Tone in the bargain, but not without the usual difficulties. Passable vehicle for Universal's chief moneymaker, Durbin, whose charm seems to elude today's audiences. A good supporting cast includes

Akim Tamiroff [701 . . .], Alan Mowbray, and Hans Conreid. Directed by Frank Borzage [132 . . .]. The sound award went to E. H. Hansen for *Wilson.*

Brown: 93, 96, 269, 1010, 1011, 1125, 1560, 1896, 2028, 2260.

920 • HIT PARADE OF 1941

Republic. 1940.

Nominations *Song:* "Who Am I?," music by Jule Styne, lyrics by Walter Bullock. *Score:* Cy Feuer.

Musical revue set in a radio station, held together by a plot about the owner's attempt to substitute his girlfriend as a vocalist in place of the sponsor's daughter. The cast includes Kenny Baker, Frances Langford, Hugh Herbert, Mary Boland, Ann Miller, Patsy Kelly, Phil Silvers, Sterling Holloway, Franklin Pangborn, and Borrah Minevitch and His Harmonica Rascals. A period piece, to say the least. Directed by John H. Auer. The song award went to Leigh Harline and Ned Washington for "When You Wish Upon a Star," from *Pinocchio.* Alfred Newman won for the score of *Tin Pan Alley.*

Styne: 74, 696, 737, 921, 1031, 1719, 2072, 2110, 2343. Bullock: 1829. Feuer: 321, 976, 1305, 1806, 1932.

921 • HIT PARADE OF 1943

Republic. 1943.

Nominations *Song:* "Change of Heart," music by Jule Styne, lyrics by Harold Adamson. *Scoring of a Musical Picture:* Walter Scharf.

The hits keep coming. This time the musical numbers are strung on a plot about a songwriter accused of plagiarism. With John Carroll, Susan Hayward [973 . . .], Gail Patrick, Eve Arden [1319], Melville Cooper, and the young Dorothy Dandridge [361], directed by Albert S. Rogell. Harry Warren and Mack Gordon's "You'll Never Know," from *Hello Frisco, Hello,* won for best song. The scoring Oscar went to Ray Heindorf for *This Is the Army.*

Styne: 74, 696, 737, 920, 1031, 1719, 2072, 2110, 2343. Adamson: 21, 916, 1980, 2028. Scharf: 174, 274, 665, 737, 864, 991, 1054, 1305, 2285.

922 • HITCHHIKE TO HAPPINESS

REPUBLIC. 1945.

NOMINATION *Scoring of a Musical Picture:* Morton Scott.

Queen of the Cowgirls Dale Evans goes East and helps a songwriter and a waiter write a hit Broadway show. Forgettable minor musical, with William Frawley. Georgie Stoll won for the scoring of *Anchors Aweigh.*

Scott: 680.

923 • HITTING A NEW HIGH

RKO RADIO. 1937.

NOMINATION *Sound Recording:* John Aalberg.

A nightclub singer, played by Lily Pons, wants to be an opera star, so her agent, played by Jack Oakie [818] sends her in pursuit of a wealthy opera lover, played by Edward Everett Horton, who's gone to Africa on safari. Pons dresses up as Ooga-Hunga the Bird Girl, wows him with her voice, and gets a contract with the Met. Truly idiotic movie, directed by the otherwise esteemed Raoul Walsh. Its box-office failure put an end to attempts to make Pons a movie star. Though charming on stage, she registered poorly on camera, and after three increasingly deadly films returned to her distinguished stage career. The sound award went to Thomas Moulton for *The Hurricane.*

Aalberg: 407, 959, 1033, 1102, 1978, 1991, 2030, 2166, 2213.

924 • HOA-BINH

MADELEINE-PARC-LA GUEVILLE-C.A.P.A.C. PRODUCTION (FRANCE). 1970.

NOMINATION *Foreign Language Film.*

Life in Vietnam, as seen through the eyes of a ten-year-old boy whose mother dies while his father is away fighting for the Viet Cong. Moving antiwar statement by director Raoul Coutard, who had lived in Vietnam as a combat photographer. The title means "peace." The Oscar went to *Investigation of a Citizen Above Suspicion.*

924.5 • HOFFA

20TH CENTURY-FOX PRODUCTION; 20TH CENTURY-FOX. 1992.

NOMINATIONS *Cinematography:* Stephen H. Burum. *Makeup:* Ve Neill, Greg Cannom, John Blake.

Jack Nicholson [395 . . .] plays Jimmy Hoffa, boss of the Teamsters Union, who survives investigations by Congress and Robert Kennedy but is eventually done in by the mob. Danny DeVito, who plays his sidekick-protector, also directed this choppy, muddled, and eventually unconvincing biopic that tries too hard to prove that Hoffa was a good guy, not a goon. The screenplay is by David Mamet [2198], and the cast includes such fine character actors as J. T. Walsh, Armand Assante, and Robert Prosky. Nicholson is almost unrecognizable, thanks to the makeup, which turns him round and puffy. He labors hard at the characterization, too, but finally just seems miscast. The cinematography award went to Philippe Rousselot for *A River Runs Through It.* Cannom, along with Michele Burke and Matthew Mungle, won for the makeup for *Bram Stoker's Dracula.*

Neill: 153.5, 167, 595.8, 600, 1370.5. Cannom: 272.5, 937, 1370.5.

925 • HOLD BACK THE DAWN

PARAMOUNT. 1941.

NOMINATIONS *Picture:* Arthur Hornblow, Jr., producer. *Actress:* Olivia de Havilland. *Screenplay:* Charles Brackett and Billy Wilder. *Black-and-White Cinematography:* Leo Tover. *Black-and-White Interior Decoration:* Hans Dreier and Robert Usher, art direction; Sam Comer, set decoration. *Scoring of a Dramatic Picture:* Victor Young.

Charles Boyer [36 . . .] is a Romanian stranded in a Mexican border town along with a number of other hopeful immigrants to the United States. He marries schoolteacher de Havilland to gain entry, planning to desert her and link up with his girlfriend, Paulette Goddard [1855]. The film has a few problems of tone that are overcome primarily by the skillful players—Boyer succeeds in making a heel likable, and de Havilland redeems what could have been a truly thankless role. Brian Donlevy [161] and Veronica Lake have cameo roles on a film set, as does the film's director, Mitchell Leisen [587]. The best picture Oscar went to *How Green Was My Valley.*

This was de Havilland's second nomination, and her first in a leading role. She made the film on a loan-out from Warner Bros., with which she had begun a battle that would lead to her suspension in 1943 but ultimately to a legal victory that would break the hold of the studios on their stars. This nomination was bittersweet, however: She lost to her sister, Joan Fontaine, who won for *Suspicion,* widening a rift between them. (Fontaine and de Havilland would remain the only sisters to receive simultaneous acting nominations until 1966, when Lynn Redgrave was nominated for *Georgy Girl* and her sister, Vanessa, for *Morgan!)*

The story of *Hold Back the Dawn* is based on the experiences of Kurt Frings, who fled Germany in 1937 and went to Paris, where he met an American journalist, Katharine "Ketti" Hartley, whom he would marry. Her novel, *Hold Back the Dawn,* based on the experience of helping him get to the United States, was bought by Paramount. But Wilder had his own experiences entering the United States via Mexico, which he blended with the Fringses' story—to Kurt Frings' dismay, when he discovered that the character in the film he thought was based on himself had been turned into a gigolo. Kurt Frings became a successful agent; Ketti became a screenwriter and playwright, and won the 1958 Pulitzer Prize for her stage adaptation of *Look Homeward, Angel.* This was the second nomination for the Brackett-Wilder screenwriting team, and while it was not up to their first nominated screenplay, for *Ninotchka,* it cemented a partnership that would grow as Brackett moved into producing and Wilder into directing. The Oscar went to Sidney Buchman and Seton I. Miller for *Here Comes Mr. Jordan.*

Tover had begun his career at the age of sixteen in silent films. Reliable but not brilliant, he was a mainstay at Paramount and later at Fox. The Oscar went to Arthur Miller for *How Green Was My Valley,* which also took the art direction award. The scoring Oscar went to Bernard Herrmann for *All That Money Can Buy.*

Hornblow: 749, 1732, 2297. de Havilland: 798, 894, 1849, 2099. Brackett: 705, 1088, 1208, 1440, 1975, 2093, 2099. Wilder: 91, 138, 198, 566, 705, 709, 1208, 1440, 1738, 1860, 1903, 1975, 2297. Tover: 894. Dreier: 97, 151, 649, 674, 701, 726, 979, 1101, 1120, 1194, 1214, 1217, 1358, 1443, 1452, 1540, 1668, 1748, 1880, 1975, 1994, 2190. Usher: 97, 1443. Comer: 278, 357, 426, 450, 726, 736, 956, 1029, 1101, 1214, 1219, 1443, 1570, 1631, 1674, 1727, 1738, 1748, 1959, 1975, 1994, 2012, 2098, 2200, 2208. Young: 97, 98, 100, 101, 280, 489, 612, 693, 701, 794, 846, 1214, 1257, 1396, 1452, 1748, 1823, 1994, 2235, 2315.

926 • *HOLE IN THE HEAD, A*
SINCAP PRODUCTIONS; UNITED ARTISTS. 1959.

AWARD *Song:* "High Hopes," music by James Van Heusen, lyrics by Sammy Cahn.

A small-time Miami Beach hotel owner, played by Frank Sinatra [732 . . .], is on the verge of losing his hotel, so he courts a rich widow, played by Eleanor Parker [328 . . .], but hasn't the heart to go through with the sleazy business of marrying her for her money. Meanwhile, his elder brother, played by Edward G. Robinson, agrees to put up the money if he can have custody of Sinatra's son, played by Eddie Hodges. Finally Sinatra and Parker admit they really love each other, Robinson gives in and lets Hodges stay, and everybody is happy. Tired, implausible, sweet-and-sour comedy directed by Frank Capra [1025 . . .] at the depressing end of a brilliant career. Though the cast also includes Carolyn Jones [124], Thelma Ritter [46 . . .], and Keenan Wynn, and the cinematography was by William Daniels [84 . . .], the best thing about the movie is its buoyant Oscar-winning song, which later became a theme song for the Kennedy campaign. Van Heusen and Cahn both became three-time Oscar winners, though it was only their second award as a team—they would win one more best song Oscar together, for "Call Me Irresponsible," from *Papa's Delicate Condition.*

Van Heusen: 171, 173, 787, 915, 1056, 1524, 1587, 1708, 1859, 1907, 2016, 2064, 2263. Cahn: 74, 163, 182, 696, 915, 1031, 1056, 1216, 1524, 1587, 1692, 1708, 1719, 1859, 1907, 2016, 2064, 2072, 2103, 2110, 2125, 2263, 2264, 2315, 2343.

927 • HOLIDAY

PATHÉ. 1930–31.

NOMINATIONS *Actress:* Ann Harding. *Adaptation:* Horace Jackson.

Harding plays Linda Seton, who falls in love with John Case, played by Robert Ames, who is engaged to her sister, Julia, played by Mary Astor [822]. It becomes clear that Linda and John are kindred free spirits, not ready to settle down to the life of wealth and respectability for which Linda, Julia, and their alcoholic brother, Ned, have been raised. Polished, well-done early talkie version of the play by Philip Barry that was remade with more stellar performers in 1938. Astor is quite good, however—superior to Doris Nolan in the same role eight years later. Edward Everett Horton plays Nick Potter in both films; in this one his wife is played by Hedda Hopper. Directed by Edward H. Griffith.

Harding, a Broadway star, joined the exodus to Hollywood that took place when sound came in, and soon became known for her performances in movies about long-suffering women. Such films had a brief vogue in the early thirties and helped make Irene Dunne [114 . . .] and Norma Shearer [150 . . .] into major stars. Others, like Harding and Ruth Chatterton [1234 . . .], were simply trapped in them, and when the vogue for weepies passed, so did their careers. Harding had the misfortune to be cast in a major flop, *Enchanted April,* in 1935. Harding married composer-conductor Werner Janssen [233 . . .] in 1937 and partially retired from the screen, making occasional appearances in matronly roles through the forties and fifties. She died in 1981. She lost her one Oscar bid to Marie Dressler in *Min and Bill.*

The writing award went to Howard Estabrook for *Cimarron.*

928 • HOLIDAY

COLUMBIA. 1938.

NOMINATION *Interior Decoration:* Stephen Goosson and Lionel Banks.

Cary Grant [1445 . . .] plays poor but proud Johnny Case, who has charmed Julia Seton (Doris Nolan) into an engagement and who further impresses her wealthy father (Henry Kolker) with his business acumen. The problem is, Case doesn't want to settle down, but Julia does. On the other hand, Julia's sister, Linda, played by Katharine Hepburn [24 . . .], is disillusioned with the life of wealth and privilege, whereupon it becomes painfully clear that she and Johnny are meant for each other. Superb romantic comedy, directed by George Cukor [262 . . .], with Grant and Hepburn at their shining best, and fine contributions by Lew Ayres [1052] as the trapped, alcoholic Seton son; Edward Everett Horton and Jean Dixon as Case's friends, the Potters; and Binnie Barnes and Henry Daniell as the ultrasnobbish Crams. The screenplay, based on the play by Philip Barry that was previously filmed in 1930, is by Donald Ogden Stewart [1148 . . .] and Sidney Buchman [904 . . .]. Horton re-creates the role he played in the earlier film; Hepburn understudied the role of Linda on Broadway in 1928 but never had a chance to appear in it before an audience. Oddly the film was a box-office disappointment, which may account for its paucity of nominations. Another Grant-Hepburn teaming of the same year, *Bringing Up Baby,* was also a flop, certifying Hepburn as box-office poison. Today both films are regarded as classics.

The art direction Oscar went to Carl J. Weyl for *The Adventures of Robin Hood.*

Goosson: 1073, 1182, 1206, 2066. Banks: 13, 98, 455, 1115, 1370, 1998.

929 • HOLIDAY INN

PARAMOUNT. 1942.

AWARD *Song:* "White Christmas," music and lyrics by Irving Berlin.

NOMINATIONS *Original Story:* Irving Berlin. *Scoring of a Musical Picture:* Robert Emmett Dolan.

Bing Crosby [173 . . .] and Fred Astaire [2126] are both in love with Virginia Dale, their partner in a nightclub act, causing the act to split up. Astaire and Dale continue to team, but Crosby retires to a farm in Connecticut. Country living soon proves such a burden that he decides to turn the farmhouse into a nightclub that will be open only for holidays; he hires Marjorie Reynolds to sing in the club and soon falls in love with her. But Astaire, who has gone on a bender because Dale has walked out on their act, shows up at Holiday Inn and falls for Reynolds, too. Eventually the triangle resolves itself, with Dale returning and Crosby and Reynolds getting together. Not as good as it should be—partly because Dale and Reynolds are low-wattage partners for the male stars. The main thing is the musical numbers, each of which celebrates a different holiday—an idea that comes from a Broadway revue Berlin once planned, which is why he received story credit for the movie. Producer-director Mark Sandrich hired Claude Binyon and Elmer Rice to write the screenplay. Of the twelve songs Berlin wrote for the film, only "White Christmas" and the Valentine's Day song, "Be Careful, It's My Heart," are still much performed. (The score also includes "Easter Parade," which was not composed for the film.)

Virtually overnight, "White Christmas" became one of the most popular songs of all time. Berlin had written the song in the thirties and set it aside for future use. Its instant popularity owed much to the film's appearance during the first year of United States involvement in World War II, when it captured the mood of homesick soldiers. It earned Berlin his sole Oscar, even though he composed dozens of great songs for the movies, notably for the great Fred Astaire–Ginger Rogers musicals of the thirties, *Top Hat, Follow the Fleet* (1936), and *Carefree*. A Berlin song, "Blue Skies," was one of the first ever sung on screen—in 1927's *The Jazz Singer*. His last work for the movies came thirty years later, the title song for *Sayonara* (which had once been planned as a Broadway musical for Berlin).

The Oscar for original story went to Emeric Pressburger for *The Invaders*. *Yankee Doodle Dandy* won the scoring award for Ray Heindorf and Heinz Roemheld.

Berlin: 34, 244, 358, 1773, 2115, 2268. Dolan: 173, 213, 244, 994, 1120, 1704, 1912.

930 • HOLLYWOOD CANTEEN

WARNER BROS. 1944.

NOMINATIONS *Sound Recording:* Nathan Levinson. *Song:* "Sweet Dreams Sweetheart," music by M. K. Je-

rome, lyrics by Ted Koehler. *Scoring of a Musical Picture:* Ray Heindorf.

Several stars, including Bette Davis [46 . . .] and John Garfield [251 . . .], both of whom appear as themselves in the film, set up the Hollywood Canteen to entertain servicemen during World War II. The movie consists largely of star cameos and variety acts, strung together by a wispy plotlet involving servicemen played by Robert Hutton and Dane Clark, directed by Delmer Daves. Mainly of historical interest, and for the now-you-see-them-now-you-don't appearances of Jack Benny, Joe E. Brown, Eddie Cantor, the Andrews Sisters, Joan Crawford [1319], Sydney Greenstreet [1248], Paul Henreid, Peter Lorre, Eleanor Parker [328 . . .], Roy Rogers, Trigger, Barbara Stanwyck [138 . . .], Jane Wyman [246 . . .], Dorothy Malone [2315], and lots of others. Among the songs written for the film is "Don't Fence Me In," by Cole Porter [261 . . .], which has proved to be a more durable standard than the nominee, which lost to James Van Heusen and Johnny Burke's "Swinging on a Star," from *Going My Way.*

The sound award went to E. H. Hansen for *Wilson.* Carmen Dragon and Morris Stoloff won for scoring *Cover Girl.*

Levinson: 16, 30, 343, 385, 531, 689, 710, 712, 790, 965, 1052, 1169, 1621, 1690, 1768, 1769, 1779, 1930, 1949, 2058, 2318. Jerome: 1750. Koehler: 1750, 2186. Heindorf: 331, 479, 666, 1043, 1204, 1385, 1408, 1430, 1690, 1719, 1750, 1910, 2058, 2186, 2243, 2310, 2318.

931 • HOLLYWOOD REVUE OF 1929, THE

MGM. 1928–29.

NOMINATION *Production:* Harry Rapf, producer.

Primitive demonstration of the wonders of talking pictures, with emcees Jack Benny and Conrad Nagel introducing a bunch of MGM contract players in specialty acts: e.g, Joan Crawford [1319 . . .] doing a hilariously awful dance, Norma Shearer [150 . . .] and John Gilbert doing an even more hilariously awful updated version of the balcony scene from *Romeo and Juliet.* Plus Buster Keaton, Laurel and Hardy, Marion Davies, Marie Dressler [611 . . .], Lionel Barrymore [723 . . .], Bessie Love [296], and such variety acts as the Brox Sisters and Ernest Belcher's Dancing Tots. (One of the tots, Belcher's daughter, grew up to be Marge Champion.) Directed by Charles Riesner. The best picture Oscar went to *Broadway Melody*.

Rapf: 296.

932 • *HOLY MATRIMONY*

20TH CENTURY-FOX. 1943.
NOMINATION *Screenplay:* Nunnally Johnson.

Publicity-shy artist Monty Woolley [1569 . . .] is knighted, but when his butler dies, he assumes the servant's identity, having the butler buried in Westminster Abbey instead. He then marries Gracie Fields and tries to live happily ever after, but suddenly finds himself accused of his own murder. Droll little comedy with a sterling company of great character actors: Una O'Connor, Alan Mowbray, Melville Cooper, and Franklin Pangborn. Directed by John Stahl [983]. Johnson's screenplay is based on Arnold Bennett's novel *Buried Alive,* which was also filmed in 1933 as *His Double Life.* The Oscar went to Julius and Philip Epstein and Howard Koch for *Casablanca.*

Johnson: 815, 1569.

933 • *HOME ALONE*

20TH CENTURY FOX PRODUCTION; 20TH CENTURY FOX. 1990.
NOMINATIONS *Song:* "Somewhere in My Memory," music by John Williams, lyrics by Leslie Bricusse. *Original Score:* John Williams.

When his large, scatterbrained family goes off for a Christmas vacation trip to Paris and accidentally leaves him behind, a small boy, played by Macaulay Culkin, delights in having the freedom of the house until two burglars, played by Joe Pesci [806 . . .] and Daniel Stern, decide to rob the place. Culkin's elaborate booby traps foil their plot. Silly live-action cartoon (with Culkin as the Road Runner and Pesci/Stern as the Coyote) that came out of nowhere to become a humongous hit—one of the biggest box-office successes of all time. Probably more violent than a kids' movie ought to be, but it caught the fantasies of the latchkey generation perfectly. Culkin became the biggest child star since Shirley Temple,

and writer-producer John Hughes became a gazillionaire. Directed by Chris Columbus.

The song award went to Stephen Sondheim for "Sooner or Later (I Always Get My Man)," from *Dick Tracy.* John Barry won for the score of *Dances With Wolves.*

Williams: 6, 260, 403, 416, 588, 613, 614, 659, 805, 937, 982, 996, 997, 1041, 1047, 1596, 1652, 1679, 1684, 1701, 1764.65, 1916, 1977, 2107, 2126, 2194, 2293, 2322. Bricusse: 557, 805, 937, 1766, 2037, 2201, 2285.

934 • *HOME IN INDIANA*

20TH CENTURY-FOX. 1944.
NOMINATION *Color Cinematography:* Edward Cronjager.

Spunky Jeanne Crain [1575] and flirty June Haver are sisters in a family that raises racehorses. Crain can ride as well as any man, but she'd really like to attract Lon McCallister's attentions, too. Unfortunately he's snared by Haver's girlish ways—until he wises up. Rural nostalgia as only Hollywood can serve it up, with Walter Brennan [424 . . .], Charlotte Greenwood, and Ward Bond, directed by Henry Hathaway [1194]. Leon Shamroy won for the cinematography for *Wilson.*

Cronjager: 176, 400, 889, 1569, 1964, 2102.

935 • *HONDO*

WAYNE-FELLOWS PRODUCTIONS; WARNER BROS. 1953.
NOMINATIONS *Supporting Actress:* Geraldine Page. *Motion Picture Story:* Louis L'Amour. (Nomination withdrawn.)

Hondo, a cavalry scout played by John Wayne [33 . . .], comes across a woman (Page) whose husband has left her and their small son on a homestead in a territory threatened by the Apaches. Solid, unpretentious western originally released in 3-D. John Farrow [101 . . .] directed, and the cast includes Ward Bond and James Arness.

This was the first film starring role and the first nomination for Page, who despite a relatively narrow range—she specialized in characters that ranged from tense to scatty—was one of the most celebrated actresses of the postwar era, racking up seven nominations before finally winning on her eighth try, for *The Trip to Bountiful*. This time she lost to Donna Reed in *From Here to Eternity*.

For a while in the fifties it seemed that the writers branch of the Academy was under a curse—see the entries for *The Brave One, The Bridge on the River Kwai,* and *Friendly Persuasion* and the first listing for *High Society* for further evidence. In this case they nominated western novelist Louis L'Amour, one of the most prolific writers of our time, for a story that, he informed them two days after the nominations were announced, had been published in *Collier's* magazine on July 5, 1952, under the title "The Gift of Cochise," and technically wasn't eligible for consideration. The nomination was withdrawn, but even the winning entry in the story category would eventually prove something of an embarrassment to the Academy: Ian McLellan Hunter, who took the Oscar for *Roman Holiday,* was actually fronting for blacklisted writer Dalton Trumbo.

Page: 1005, 1555, 1591, 1959, 1985, 2142, 2341.

936 • HONEYSUCKLE ROSE

WARNER BROS. PRODUCTION; WARNER BROS. 1980.
NOMINATION *Original Song:* "On the Road Again," music and lyrics by Willie Nelson.

Nelson plays a country-music singer married to Dyan Cannon [250 . . .]. When his longtime guitarist, Slim Pickens, retires, Pickens' daughter, Amy Irving [2321], joins the band and enters into an affair with Nelson. Straightening out these tangled relationships makes up the thin plot of the film, which is a C&W translation of *Intermezzo*. The main thing is the music. Cannon and Irving do their own singing, and Emmylou Harris makes a guest appearance. Directed by Jerry Schatzberg.

Nelson made his screen debut as an actor in a supporting role in 1979's *The Electric Horseman,* and his extremely likable screen presence made Hollywood think he might become a star. But *Honeysuckle Rose* and other films in which he starred, such as *Barbarosa* (1982) and *Songwriter* (1984), were box-office disappointments, so Nelson returned to doing what he does best: writing and performing songs.

"On the Road Again," which has become his theme song, competed with the work of another country singer-songwriter-actor, Dolly Parton's title tune from *9 to 5*. But the Academy wasn't ready for country music yet: The Oscar went to Michael Gore and Dean Pitchford's title song from *Fame*.

937 • HOOK

TRISTAR PICTURES PRODUCTION; TRISTAR. 1991.
NOMINATIONS *Art Direction–Set Decoration:* Norman Garwood; Garrett Lewis. *Song:* "When You're Alone," music by John Williams, lyrics by Leslie Bricusse. *Costume Design:* Anthony Powell. *Makeup:* Christina Smith, Monty Westmore, and Greg Cannom. *Visual Effects:* Eric Brevig, Harley Jessup, Mark Sullivan, and Michael Lantieri.

Peter Pan has grown up, married, had children, and become a weary yuppie, played by Robin Williams [511 . . .], who has forgotten his magical childhood. On a trip to England with his family, he visits Wendy, now an elderly woman, played by Maggie Smith [332 . . .]. When his children are kidnaped by Captain Hook, played by Dustin Hoffman [810 . . .], Peter must recapture his youthful vigor and innocence. Aided by Tinker Bell, played by Julia Roberts [1603 . . .], he vanquishes Hook. Even though the casting of Williams, Smith, and Hoffman seems inspired, and the film's central premise is a good one, this super-expensive movie, produced and directed by Steven Spielberg [416 . . .], doesn't fly. It's noisy, busy, and dull. Never-Neverland seems like a penal colony for hyperactive children, and Williams' natural buoyancy is stifled by the production. It was a big hit anyway. Glenn Close [199 . . .] appears in drag as one of the pirates.

Bugsy won the Oscars for art direction and Albert Wolsky's costumes. The title song by Alan Menken and Howard Ashman for *Beauty and the Beast* took the song award. *Terminator 2: Judgment Day* won for makeup and special effects.

Garwood: 275, 779. Lewis: 159, 272.5, 779. Williams: 6, 260, 403, 416, 588, 613, 614, 659, 805, 933, 982, 996, 997, 1041, 1047, 1596, 1652, 1679, 1684, 1701, 1764.65, 1916, 1977, 2107, 2126,

2194, 2293, 2322. Bricusse: 557, 805, 933, 1766, 2037, 2201, 2285. Powell: 516, 1578, 2021, 2134. Smith: 1764.65. Cannom: 272.5, 924.5, 1370.5. Brevig: 2124. Jessup: 1002. Lantieri: 128, 1071.5.

937.5 • HOOP DREAMS

KARTEMQUIN FILMS PRODUCTION; FINE LINE. 1994.

NOMINATION *Film Editing:* Frederick Marx, Steve James, and Bill Haugse.

While in the eighth grade, William Gates and Arthur Agee are recruited from the Chicago ghetto by the suburban St. Joseph's High School because they are promising basketball players—St. Joseph's previously produced the superstar Isiah Thomas. This terrific documentary was planned by its makers as a short film, but turned into a six-year project, following the boys through the first year of college. It's a portrait not only of the making of a star athlete, but also of life in an American inner city, rich with absorbing details of what it's like to be poor and black, and full of authentic human drama. Directed by James, written by James, Marx, and Peter Gilbert, and photographed by Gilbert, *Hoop Dreams* received rave reviews and became one of the most commercially successful documentaries in history. Praise for the film had been so high that there had even been talk that it might be nominated for best picture.

But you can't succeed these days without causing controversy, and *Hoop Dreams* has had its share. First, St. Joseph's and its head coach, Gene Pingatore, sued, saying they had been misled by the filmmakers and misrepresented in the final product. (The case was settled out of court.) And the film's admirers were thunderstruck when *Hoop Dreams* was not among the nominees for best documentary feature. The documentary award had drawn fire several times before: Such critical and commercial successes as *The Thin Blue Line* (1988), *Roger & Me* (1989), and *Paris Is Burning* (1990) had also been overlooked by the committee that nominates documentaries. Some critics also pointed out that one of the year's nominated documentaries, *Maya Lin: A Strong Clear Vision,* had been made by Frieda Lee Mock—the previous year's chairman of the documentary committee. Mock had, however, disqualified herself from judging the 1994 entries, and her film went on to win the documentary Oscar. The documentary committee is composed of volunteer members who undertake the arduous task of screening scores of films, both short and feature-length. It has been charged that the committee's bias is toward the most conventional and traditional documentary forms, and that they automatically exclude experimental works or films without strong social or political messages. Another entry for 1994, *Crumb,* a film about the underground comic artist R. Crumb, had received acclaim at the Sundance Festival and excellent reviews from critics, but the screening of *Crumb* was reportedly shut off after only a few minutes by the documentary committee. The firestorm of criticism after the snubbing of *Hoop Dreams* was so intense, including a full-page newspaper protest ad signed by many prominent Academy members, that Academy president Arthur Hiller [1218] was forced to announce, "We'll be taking a close, hard look at the procedures of the documentary committee to see if changes need to be made."

The damage to *Hoop Dreams* had been done, however—although it was mitigated somewhat by the increased box office generated by the controversy—and the film lost its one nomination when Arthur Schmidt won for the editing of *Forrest Gump.*

938 • HOOPER

WARNER BROS. PRODUCTION; WARNER BROS. 1978.

NOMINATION *Sound:* Robert Knudson, Robert J. Glass, Don MacDougall, and Jack Solomon.

Burt Reynolds plays an aging stuntman, Jan-Michael Vincent the young guy who taunts him into risking his neck, and Sally Field [1448 . . .] the girlfriend who suffers through all this macho nonsense. Formulaic filmmaking, directed by former stuntman Hal Needham, that assumes you're smitten with its star and will watch him do almost anything. Consider yourself warned. The sound Oscar went to *The Deer Hunter.*

Knudson: 321, 416, 588, 613, 631, 1439, 1877, 1911, 2274. Glass: 416, 588, 1439, 1877, 1911.

MacDougall: 416, 738, 1439, 1916. Solomon: 738, 896, 1089, 1109, 1310.

939 • HOOSIERS

CARTER DE HAVEN PRODUCTION; ORION. 1986.

NOMINATIONS *Supporting Actor:* Dennis Hopper. *Original Score:* Jerry Goldsmith.

Gene Hackman [255 . . .], a college basketball coach with his career on the skids, gets a chance to redeem himself by coaching an Indiana high school team to the state championship. Conventional against-the-odds drama, directed by David Anspaugh, that aims to please and hits its mark, though you may hate yourself for being so neatly manipulated. Hackman is terrific, and Hopper does the small-town basketball nut routine flawlessly. Along with *Blue Velvet* the same year, it signaled his comeback from a decade or so of drug abuse and self-destructiveness. The Oscar went to Michael Caine for *Hannah and Her Sisters.* Herbie Hancock won for scoring *'Round Midnight.*

Hopper: 595. Goldsmith: 152.5, 268, 395, 727, 1472, 1527, 1537, 1541, 1583, 1589, 1753, 1913, 2176, 2287.

940 • HOPE AND GLORY

DAVROS PRODUCTION SERVICES LTD. PRODUCTION; COLUMBIA (UNITED KINGDOM). 1987.

NOMINATIONS *Picture:* John Boorman, producer. *Director:* John Boorman. *Screenplay Written Directly for the Screen:* John Boorman. *Cinematography:* Philippe Rousselot. *Art Direction—Set Decoration:* Anthony Pratt; Joan Woolard.

A look through a small boy's eyes at how an English family survived the air raids and bombings of World War II. It's nothing like *Mrs. Miniver.* Instead of stiff-upper-lip sentiment, there's raucous humor, sex, knavery, terror, and occasional beauty and even a bit of heroism. Boorman based his film on his own experiences. The boy is Sebastian Rice-Edwards, with Sarah Miles [1737] as his mother and Ian Bannen [688] as his grandfather. The producer-writer-director's son, Charley, appears as a downed German pilot.

World War II loomed large in the films of the year. The wartime experiences of another young English boy were dealt with in *Empire of the Sun,* and the big winner at the awards was *The Last Emperor,* which focused in part on the role of Pu Yi during the war. *The Last Emperor* was the spoiler for *Hope and Glory;* it took the best picture Oscar, plus awards for Bernardo Bertolucci's direction, Vittorio Storaro's cinematography, and the art direction of Ferdinando Scarfiotti and Bruno Cesari. The screenplay award went to John Patrick Shanley for *Moonstruck.*

Boorman: 523. Rousselot: 900, 1701.5.

941 • HORSE'S MOUTH, THE

KNIGHTSBRIDGE FILMS; UNITED ARTISTS (UNITED KINGDOM). 1958.

NOMINATION *Screenplay—Based on Material From Another Medium:* Alec Guinness.

Guinness plays a shabby, unscrupulous artist named Gulley Jimson in his adaptation of Joyce Cary's novel. What there is in the way of plot deals with Jimson's belief that genius (i.e., his) must be served, especially when it comes to finding new places to cover with his paintings. The movie lacks dramatic shape, but it's a lot of fun to watch Guinness at work, and the cinematography by Arthur Ibbetson [85] is especially handsome. Ronald Neame [289 . . .] directed. The music is adapted from Prokofiev's *Lieutenant Kije* themes. Jimson's paintings were done by John Bratby.

As Guinness' fine autobiography, *Blessings in Disguise,* reveals, he is not only a great actor, he's also a skillful writer. He adapted Dickens' *Great Expectations* for the stage in 1939. His performance in that production led eventually to his screen debut in the film version after the war, when Neame and David Lean [287 . . .] recalled him and cast him in their movie. *The Horse's Mouth* is Guinness' only screenplay to be filmed. The Oscar went to Alan Jay Lerner for *Gigi.*

Guinness: 287, 1150, 1181, 1916.

942 • HOSPITAL, THE

HOWARD GOTTFRIED-PADDY CHAYEFSKY PRODUCTION IN ASSOCI-
ATION WITH ARTHUR HILLER; UNITED ARTISTS. 1971.

AWARD *Story and Screenplay—Based on Factual Material
or Material Not Previously Published or Produced:* Paddy
Chayefsky.

NOMINATION *Actor:* George C. Scott.

Scott plays a burned-out physician at a big-city
hospital who's being driven over the edge by lunatics,
incompetents, bureaucrats, and a serial killer. Usually
on-target satire that does for the medical establishment what Chayefsky tried to do for the TV business
in *Network* but is keener and wittier than that more
celebrated movie. Chayefsky had moved a long way
from the softer and more sentimental celebration of
the little people that won him his first Oscar for
Marty. Directed by Arthur Hiller [1218], with Diana
Rigg, Bernard Hughes, Nancy Marchand, Richard
Dysart, Frances Sternhagen, and, in her film debut,
Stockard Channing [1835.5]. The Academy averted a
second controversial award to Scott, who snubbed the
ceremony the previous year and failed to pick up his
Oscar for *Patton;* this time the award went to Gene
Hackman for *The French Connection.*

Chayefsky: 783, 1283, 1424. Scott: 73, 964,
1541.

943 • HOT MILLIONS

MILDRED FREED ALBERG PRODUCTION; MGM (UNITED KING-
DOM). 1968.

NOMINATION *Story and Screenplay—Written Directly for
the Screen:* Ira Wallach and Peter Ustinov.

Con man Ustinov, aided by Maggie Smith
[332 . . .], uses his computer expertise to siphon
off money into phony corporations. Delicious performances by the leads, plus Bob Newhart, Karl Malden
[1477 . . .], and Robert Morley [1274], make this
otherwise rather ephemeral caper comedy memorable. Directed by Eric Till. The Oscar went to Mel
Brooks for *The Producers.*

Ustinov: 1644, 1886, 2116.

944 • HOT ROCK, THE

LANDERS-ROBERTS PRODUCTION; 20TH CENTURY-FOX. 1972.

NOMINATION *Film Editing:* Frank P. Keller and Fred
W. Berger.

Robert Redford [1502 . . .] heads a group of
particularly inept burglars in their attempt to make
off with a spectacular diamond. Well-done caper
comedy, a little grittier than many in the genre, with
excellent performances by George Segal [2277], Ron
Leibman, Paul Sand, and Zero Mostel. Peter Yates
[279 . . .] directs an adaptation by William
Goldman [54 . . .] of a novel by Donald Westlake
[840]. David Bretherton took the editing Oscar for
Cabaret.

Keller: 158, 313, 1059.

945 • HOUSE IS NOT A HOME, A

CLARENCE GREENE-RUSSELL ROUSE PRODUCTION; EMBASSY PIC-
TURES CORPORATION. 1964.

NOMINATION *Black-and-White Costume Design:* Edith
Head.

Shelley Winters [542 . . .] plays Polly Adler,
once New York's most celebrated madam. Dull,
cheesy movie, made in that twilight zone when the
Production Code was dying and before the ratings
system cordoned off movies into G, PG, R, and X, so
that it smirks for a while, then turns ponderously
moral about sins hinted at but not shown. Robert
Taylor, Cesar Romero, and Broderick Crawford [53]
are among the people trapped in this debacle, written
by Clarence Greene [1572 . . .] and Russell Rouse
[1572 . . .] and directed by Rouse. Not Head's finest hour: One suspects that she was almost relieved to
see her frequent rival Dorothy Jeakins win the Oscar
this time, for *The Night of the Iguana.* Whom would
Head have found to thank?

Head: 31, 32, 46, 305, 357, 363, 612, 636, 675,
736, 832, 894, 1003, 1219, 1261, 1263, 1398,
1427, 1504, 1550, 1579, 1587, 1631, 1716, 1727,
1738, 1748, 1840, 1927, 1986, 2012, 2098, 2247,
2298.

946 • *HOUSE OF ROTHSCHILD, THE*

20TH CENTURY; UNITED ARTISTS. 1934.

NOMINATION *Picture:* Darryl F. Zanuck, with William Goetz and Raymond Griffith, producers.

George Arliss [550 . . .] plays Nathan Rothschild, the head of the banking family, in this opulent costumer set at the time of the Napoleonic wars. Loretta Young [428 . . .], his daughter, is courted by Captain Fitzroy, played by Robert Young in a wig that makes him look like he's having a bad hair century. The big cast includes Boris Karloff as the villainous Count Ledrantz, C. Aubrey Smith as the Duke of Wellington, Alan Mowbray as Metternich, and Florence Arliss as Hannah Rothschild. Stately but not stuffy. Directed by Alfred R. Werker. The best picture Oscar went to the much more down-to-earth *It Happened One Night,* but *The House of Rothschild* came in third, after *The Barretts of Wimpole Street.*

Zanuck: 34, 46, 550, 710, 759, 815, 952, 990, 1201, 1327, 1666, 2154, 2286. Goetz: 1763.

947 • *HOUSE OF THE SEVEN GABLES, THE*

UNIVERSAL. 1940.

NOMINATION *Original Score:* Frank Skinner.

George Sanders [46] railroads his brother, Vincent Price, for the murder of their father, but gets his just deserts in the end. Somewhat hokey and truncated version of a segment of Nathaniel Hawthorne's moody classic, directed by Joe May as if it were a horror movie, with lots of portentous gloom. The cinematography is by Milton Krasner [21 . . .]. The scoring award went to Leigh Harline, Paul J. Smith, and Ned Washington for *Pinocchio.*

Skinner: 62, 96, 125, 1229.

948 • *HOUSE ON CHELOUCHE STREET, THE*

NOAH FILMS LTD. PRODUCTION (ISRAEL). 1973.

NOMINATION *Foreign Language Film.*

The dawning of Israel's independence as seen through the eyes of a Sephardic family. Directed by Moshe Mizrahi and produced by Menahem Golan and Yoram Globus. Not widely released commercially, but you may be able to catch it at festivals of Jewish films. The Oscar went to *Day for Night.*

949 • *HOUSE ON 92ND STREET, THE*

20TH CENTURY-FOX. 1945.

AWARD *Original Story:* Charles G. Booth.

FBI operatives foil the attempts of Nazi agents to steal A-bomb secrets during World War II. Effective docudrama with good location filming in Washington and New York. A few spy-movie clichés along the way, but pretty credible for the most part. Henry Hathaway [1194] directs, with William Eythe, Lloyd Nolan, Signe Hasso, Gene Lockhart [36], Leo G. Carroll, and, in a bit part as a morgue attendant, E. G. Marshall (billed as Edward Marshall).

950 • *HOUSE ON TELEGRAPH HILL, THE*

20TH CENTURY-FOX. 1951.

NOMINATION *Black-and-White Art Direction—Set Decoration:* Lyle Wheeler and John DeCuir; Thomas Little and Paul S. Fox.

Concentration camp survivor Valentina Cortese [501] comes to San Francisco after World War II by assuming the identity of a woman who died in the camp, but discovers that her life is in danger from the woman's enemies. Good thriller, directed by Robert Wise [407 . . .], with Richard Basehart. The art direction award went to Richard Day and George James Hopkins for *A Streetcar Named Desire.*

Wheeler: 19, 46, 83, 356, 376, 428, 476, 495, 530, 542, 719, 721, 798, 1062, 1088, 1149, 1153, 1213, 1391, 1475, 1601, 1616, 1670, 1706, 1852, 2008, 2093, 2212. DeCuir: 29, 201, 376, 413, 476, 896, 1088, 1391, 1852, 2000. Little: 46, 83, 235, 428, 495, 719, 721, 746, 952, 1082, 1149, 1153, 1397, 1475, 1666, 1852, 1868, 2056, 2212, 2286. Fox: 376, 413, 428, 476, 495, 530, 721, 1088, 1601, 1666, 1706, 1852.

951 • *HOUSEBOAT*

PARAMOUNT AND SCRIBE; PARAMOUNT. 1958.

NOMINATIONS *Story and Screenplay—Written Directly for the Screen:* Melville Shavelson and Jack Rose. *Song:*

"Almost in Your Arms (Love Song From *Houseboat*)," music and lyrics by Jay Livingston and Ray Evans.

Diplomat's daughter Sophia Loren [1280 . . .] pretends to be a domestic servant and is hired by Cary Grant [1445 . . .], a widower with three children, to help him set up housekeeping on a boat. Naturally Grant and Loren fall in love. Agreeable high-gloss romantic comedy with powerful star chemistry, directed by Shavelson. With Martha Hyer [1859], Harry Guardino, and Eduardo Ciannelli. The writing award went to Nedrick Young (under his blacklist-era pseudonym Nathan E. Douglas) and Harold Jacob Smith for *The Defiant Ones*. Frederick Loewe and Alan Jay Lerner's title song for *Gigi* won the song Oscar.

Shavelson: 1786. Rose: 1786, 2125. Livingston: 344, 512, 1260, 1522, 2001, 2278. Evans: 344, 512, 1260, 1522, 2001, 2278.

952 • HOW GREEN WAS MY VALLEY

20TH CENTURY-FOX. 1941.

AWARDS *Picture:* Darryl F. Zanuck, producer. *Supporting Actor:* Donald Crisp. *Director:* John Ford. *Black-and-White Cinematography:* Arthur Miller. *Black-and-White Interior Decoration:* Richard Day and Nathan Juran, art direction; Thomas Little, set decoration.
NOMINATIONS *Supporting Actress:* Sara Allgood. *Screenplay:* Philip Dunne. *Sound Recording:* E. H. Hansen. *Scoring of a Dramatic Picture:* Alfred Newman. *Film Editing:* James B. Clark.

Huw Morgan, played on screen by Roddy McDowall and in voice-over by Irving Pichel, remembers the disintegration of his Welsh mining family and the devastation of their village in the 1890s. This splendid "prestige" mounting of the novel by Richard Llewellyn has grown controversial over the years because it was the film that beat *Citizen Kane* for the best picture Oscar. Today *Kane* is an acknowledged masterpiece and *How Green* is often dismissed as sentimental and melodramatic, even by admirers of its director. Most critics would rank *How Green* no better than third among the candidates for best picture, with *The Maltese Falcon* taking second place. That said, *How Green* is still a classic example of Hollywood filmmaking at its most effective, with remarkable sets, eloquent camera work, and a screenplay that leaves no handkerchief unwrung. The fine cast includes Walter Pidgeon [1232 . . .], Maureen O'Hara, Barry Fitzgerald [787], and Arthur Shields. The detractors who denounce its tear-jerking are countered by defenders who maintain that such criticism is superficial and that Ford clearly shows Huw's sentimentalizing of the past to be at odds with the reality.

Donald Crisp, who plays Huw's father, was born in Scotland and came to the United States in 1906. He began his acting career on stage but moved into film work in 1908, as both actor and director. One of his most memorable early performances was as the abusive father of Lillian Gish [584] in D. W. Griffith's *Broken Blossoms*. He continued as director until 1930, when he began to devote himself entirely to acting, becoming one of the most durable character players in the business. He made his last screen appearance in 1963's *Spencer's Mountain*, fifty-five years after his first. He died in 1974, aged ninety-four.

With this award, Ford became the first director to win two consecutive Oscars (a feat equaled only by Joseph L. Mankiewicz for *A Letter to Three Wives* and *All About Eve*) and the first since Frank Capra [1025 . . .] to have won three directing awards. At this point the war interrupted Ford's Hollywood career: He went to work, with the commission of lieutenant commander in the navy, producing documentaries in support of the war effort, two of which, *The Battle of Midway* and *December 7th*, won Oscars. After the war, his work was dismissed by contemporary critics as evidence of a decline in talent but is now seen by many critics and film historians as his finest period, including such great westerns as *My Darling Clementine* (1946), *Fort Apache* (1948), and *The Searchers* (1956), all of which were, it now seems shocking to observe, ignored by the Academy.

Miller was another industry pioneer, who began as a bit player and camera assistant while he was in his teens, and worked as photographer on the 1914 serial *The Perils of Pauline*. This was the first of his three Oscars, all of which he won for his work at 20th Century-Fox in the forties.

Allgood, born in Dublin, had been a member of the celebrated Abbey Theatre company and was acclaimed for her performance as Juno in Sean O'Casey's *Juno and the Paycock,* which was filmed by Alfred Hitchcock [1171 . . .] in 1930. After a handful of films in England, she went to America in 1940 and appeared in movies until her death in 1950. The Oscar went to Mary Astor for *The Great Lie.*

Sidney Buchman and Seton I. Miller won the screenplay award for *Here Comes Mr. Jordan. That Hamilton Woman* took the Oscar for sound. Bernard Herrmann won for the score of *All That Money Can Buy* and William Holmes for editing *Sergeant York.*

Zanuck: 34, 46, 550, 710, 759, 815, 946, 990, 1201, 1327, 1666, 2154, 2286. Ford: 815, 999, 1200, 1642, 1901. Miller: 83, 241, 1082, 1655, 1868, 2056. Day: 22, 102, 235, 487, 510, 560, 569, 797, 833, 864, 1048, 1175, 1397, 1477, 1666, 1949, 2056, 2120, 2276. Juran: 1666. Little: 46, 83, 235, 428, 495, 719, 721, 746, 950, 1082, 1149, 1153, 1397, 1475, 1666, 1852, 1868, 2056, 2212, 2286. Dunne: 495. Hansen: 241, 815, 990, 1655, 1868, 1957, 2027, 2056, 2272, 2286, 2317. Newman: 31, 34, 46, 72, 138, 182, 226, 333, 334, 347, 375, 428, 437, 457, 476, 495, 542, 690, 797, 833, 953, 959, 962, 1016, 1082, 1088, 1213, 1278, 1362, 1397, 1475, 1616, 1655, 1849, 1868, 1883, 1921, 2043, 2046, 2091, 2258, 2286, 2294, 2316.

953 • *HOW THE WEST WAS WON*

Metro-Goldwyn-Mayer and Cinerama; MGM. 1963.

Awards *Story and Screenplay—Written Directly for the Screen:* James R. Webb. *Sound:* Franklin E. Milton, sound director, MGM Studio Sound Department. *Film Editing:* Harold F. Kress.

Nominations *Picture:* Bernard Smith, producer. *Color Cinematography:* William H. Daniels, Milton Krasner, Charles Lang, Jr., and Joseph LaShelle. *Color Art Direction–Set Decoration:* George W. Davis, William Ferrari, and Addison Hehr; Henry Grace, Don Greenwood, Jr., and Jack Mills. *Music Score—Substantially Original:* Alfred Newman and Ken Darby. *Color Costume Design:* Walter Plunkett.

In the 1830s Karl Malden [1477 . . .] and Agnes Moorehead [963 . . .] go West, with daughters Carroll Baker [119] and Debbie Reynolds [2184]. They're rescued from difficulties by trapper James Stewart [73 . . .], but when Malden and Moorehead are killed, Baker and Stewart get married and settle down, and Reynolds continues West, where she meets up with gambler Gregory Peck [759 . . .], performs in saloons, and eventually strikes gold and marries Peck, settling in San Francisco. Stewart and Baker's son, George Peppard, goes off to fight in the Civil War, encountering General Sherman, played by John Wayne [33 . . .], and General Grant, played by Harry Morgan. After the war, he returns to find both his parents dead, so he sets out for the West, too, encountering his father's old trapping colleague, Henry Fonda [815 . . .], and working for a while as a buffalo hunter for railroad builder Richard Widmark [1098]. Eventually he settles in Arizona, becomes a lawman, and marries Carolyn Jones [124]. Now a widow, Reynolds sells her San Francisco mansion and goes to live with nephew Peppard and his family, getting there just in time for Peppard's showdown with the bad guys, headed by Eli Wallach, a climactic shoot-out on a runaway train. (Stuntman Bob Morgan, doubling for Peppard, lost a leg in the spectacular final sequence.) The movie is about as bloated as it sounds, but it's not boring, especially if you like to spot stars—Lee J. Cobb [301 . . .], Robert Preston [2201], Walter Brennan [424 . . .], Andy Devine, Raymond Massey [1], Thelma Ritter [46 . . .], and Russ Tamblyn [1558] show up along the way, and the narrator is Spencer Tracy [131 . . .]. Henry Hathaway [1194] directed the part leading up to the Civil War, John Ford [815 . . .] did the war section, and George Marshall handled the rest. Originally released in Cinerama, a technique that used three cameras and a curved screen for its illusion of depth. The result is that there are seams where the three separate images are joined, even in the subsequent release in a conventional wide-screen print. Since Cinerama is defunct, the movie has lost some of the panoramic effects that it was designed for and might never again be shown as it was originally intended to be seen.

Webb, a former magazine writer, had spent some

time writing westerns for Roy Rogers at Republic before World War II. Afterward, he became a prominent screenwriter, concentrating largely on westerns such as *Apache* (1954) and *The Big Country* and action films. He also did the screenplay for the first version of *Cape Fear* in 1963. He died in 1974.

Kress, an editor since 1939, has also worked as a director of both documentaries and feature films. His son, Carl Kress [2126], is also an editor.

Tom Jones won the best picture award and took the Oscar for John Addison's score as well. *Cleopatra* won for Leon Shamroy's cinematography, for art direction, and for the costumes by Irene Sharaff, Vittorio Nino Novarese, and Renie.

Milton: 175, 401, 558, 814, 2184. Kress: 573, 1371, 1596, 2126, 2320. Smith: 609. Daniels: 84, 372, 1410. Krasner: 21, 46, 96, 654, 1219, 2072. Lang: 97, 250, 319, 636, 649, 705, 765, 1480, 1640, 1699, 1738, 1778, 1855, 1860, 1955, 1968, 2180. LaShelle: 91, 357, 428, 709, 1017, 1149, 1283, 1391. Davis: 46, 69, 401, 495, 542, 736, 1213, 1335, 1388, 1537, 1552, 1706, 1814, 2157, 2184, 2312. Ferrari: 749. Hehr: 401. Grace: 69, 227, 401, 769, 1335, 1388, 1450, 1537, 1552, 2157, 2184, 2312. Newman: 31, 34, 46, 72, 138, 182, 226, 333, 334, 347, 375, 428, 437, 457, 476, 495, 542, 690, 797, 833, 952, 959, 962, 1016, 1082, 1088, 1213, 1278, 1362, 1397, 1475, 1616, 1655, 1849, 1868, 1883, 1921, 2043, 2046, 2091, 2258, 2286, 2294, 2316. Darby: 334, 690, 1088, 1592, 1883. Plunkett: 9, 66, 1087, 1243, 1587, 1657, 1859, 2029, 2330.

954 • HOW TO MARRY A MILLIONAIRE

20TH CENTURY-FOX. 1953.
NOMINATION *Color Costume Design:* Charles LeMaire and Travilla.

Fashion models Lauren Bacall, Betty Grable, and Marilyn Monroe lease an extravagant penthouse in Manhattan and set out to do exactly what the title says. Trouble is, they keep falling for guys who either seem to be rich but aren't, or are rich but don't seem to be. Sexist but amusing gold-digger comedy, a little too stiffly staged—it was the first film made in CinemaScope, although not the first released, an honor that fell to *The Robe*. It's one of Grable's last movies; she saw the handwriting on the wall after this film, in which she is upstaged by Bacall's dry, feline delivery and Monroe's peerless comic performance as the bumbling, nearsighted Pola, who has taken to heart the Dorothy Parker [1845 . . .] couplet "Men seldom make passes/At girls who wear glasses." Written and produced by Nunnally Johnson [815 . . .], directed by Jean Negulesco [1052], with David Wayne, Rory Calhoun, Cameron Mitchell, and William Powell [1170 . . .]. Preceded by an interminable overture in which Alfred Newman [31 . . .] conducts "Street Scene" to demonstrate the wonders of stereophonic sound. LeMaire, along with Emile Santiago, won the costuming Oscar for *The Robe*.

LeMaire: 21, 46, 376, 495, 530, 542, 1213, 1338, 1391, 1601, 1706, 2008, 2043, 2205, 2294. Travilla: 15, 1952, 2043.

954.5 • HOWARDS END

MERCHANT IVORY PRODUCTIONS; SONY PICTURES CLASSICS (UNITED KINGDOM/U.S.). 1992.
AWARDS *Actress:* Emma Thompson. *Adapted Screenplay:* Ruth Prawer Jhabvala. *Art Direction:* Luciana Arrighi and Ian Whittaker.
NOMINATIONS *Picture:* Ismail Merchant, producer. *Supporting Actress:* Vanessa Redgrave. *Director:* James Ivory. *Cinematography:* Tony Pierce-Roberts. *Costume Design:* Jenny Beavan, John Bright. *Original Score:* Richard Robbins.

The Schlegel sisters, Margaret (Thompson) and Helen (Helena Bonham Carter), are well-to-do members of the intellectual and artistic fringe of Edwardian London. Helen's brief engagement to Paul Wilcox, the younger son of a very wealthy mercantile family, precipitates a split between the Wilcoxes and Schlegels that begins to heal when Margaret becomes friends with Mrs. Wilcox (Redgrave). But after Mrs. Wilcox dies, the misunderstandings are renewed when the Wilcoxes learn that she has left instructions that her country house, Howards End, should go to Margaret; they destroy Mrs. Wilcox's handwritten note, so that Margaret is unaware of the legacy. However, Mr. Wilcox, played by Anthony Hopkins [1679.5 . . .], finds Margaret attractive and a year or so later proposes marriage. Before they can wed, however, Helen shows up with a bank clerk, Leonard Bast, and his wife, Jacky. The Schlegels, who have taken an interest in Leonard because he wants to improve himself, have acted on some remarks by Wilcox about the company at which Leonard worked, advising Leonard to seek another job, which he has lost, so that the Basts are living in poverty. Jacky, spotting Wilcox, reveals that they were once lovers. Wilcox's moral obtuseness suddenly becomes apparent to Margaret, but she decides to marry him anyway, causing a split with Helen. Some months later, Helen informs Margaret that she has returned to England from traveling on the Continent and wishes to collect her belongings, which are being stored at Howards End. There Margaret has a few more revelations about Helen, Leonard Bast, and the character of her husband. More than just another pretty coffee-table movie, this fine, subtle adaptation of the E. M. Forster novel goes well beyond the re-creation of place and period for which the Merchant-Ivory-Jhabvala team has become famous. It's a tragicomedy of manners, whose problems of caste and class are metaphors for the profound difficulty of human communication—especially between the sexes. For once, the manners and mores of the past seem relevant, and not just an excuse for opulent costumes and sets.

Thompson creates a woman who is witty, engaged, and warm but also uncertain of her own needs and desires, and perhaps too quick to give others—especially her husband—the benefit of the doubt. Although well known in England for her work on stage and TV, before the Oscar she had just begun to attract notice on this side of the Atlantic, primarily for her work with her husband, Kenneth Branagh [902], with whom she has appeared in *Henry V, Dead Again* (1991), *Peter's Friends* (1992), and *Much Ado About Nothing* (1993). Her fine performance opposite Hopkins in this film led to their reteaming in *The Remains of the Day.*

The second Oscar for Jhabvala followed a well-received but generally less successful adaptation of

two Evan Connell novels into the film *Mr. and Mrs. Bridge,* also done in partnership with Merchant and Ivory.

The best picture Oscar went to *Unforgiven,* which also won for Clint Eastwood's directing. Marisa Tomei won as best supporting actress for *My Cousin Vinny.* Philippe Rousselot won for the cinematography for *A River Runs Through It.* Eiko Ishioka took the award for the costumes for *Bram Stoker's Dracula.* The scoring Oscar went to Alan Menken for *Aladdin.*

Thompson: 992.5, 1679.5. Jhabvala: 1679.5, 1725. Arrighi: 1679.5. Whittaker: 44, 1679.5. Merchant: 1679.5, 1725. Redgrave: 263, 1021, 1066, 1285, 1354. Ivory: 1679.5, 1725. Pierce-Roberts: 1725. Beavan: 263, 1290, 1679.5, 1725. Bright: 263, 1290, 1679.5, 1725. Robbins: 1679.5.

955 • HOWARDS OF VIRGINIA, THE

FRANK LLOYD; COLUMBIA. 1940.

NOMINATIONS *Sound Recording:* Jack Whitney, General Service. *Original Score:* Richard Hageman.

Cary Grant [1445 . . .] plays a backwoodsman who woos aristocrat Martha Scott [1510] in Revolutionary War–era Virginia. Laborious historical pageant, in which Founding Fathers such as Jefferson and Washington make cameo appearances. Like virtually every Hollywood film about the era, it was a box-office flop, not helped by the miscasting of Grant in a role more suited to Henry Fonda [815 . . .], James Stewart [73 . . .], or Gary Cooper [701 . . .]. Directed by Frank Lloyd [374 . . .] from a Sidney Buchman [904 . . .] screenplay based on Elizabeth Page's novel *The Tree of Liberty.* The sound Oscar went to Douglas Shearer for *Strike Up the Band. Pinocchio* won for Leigh Harline, Paul J. Smith, and Ned Washington's score.

Whitney: 729, 862, 1026, 1884, 2031, 2050, 2095. Hageman: 979, 1200, 1801, 1901, 2062.

956 • HUD

SALEM-DOVER PRODUCTION; PARAMOUNT. 1963.

AWARDS *Actress:* Patricia Neal. *Supporting Actor:* Melvyn Douglas. *Black-and-White Cinematography:* James Wong Howe.

NOMINATIONS *Actor:* Paul Newman. *Director:* Martin Ritt. *Screenplay—Based on Material From Another Medium:* Irving Ravetch and Harriet Frank, Jr. *Black-and-White Art Direction–Set Decoration:* Hal Pereira and Tambi Larsen; Sam Comer and Robert Benton.

Newman plays the title role, a Texas rancher who's as unscrupulous and hedonistic as his father (Douglas) is upright and ascetic. Among other things, Hud is a bad example for his young nephew, played by Brandon de Wilde [1799], and bad news for the housekeeper, Alma (Neal). This adaptation of the novel *Horseman, Pass By,* by Larry McMurtry [1139], has a sweaty authenticity often lacking in character dramas. It's not formulaic or pretentious in the least, thanks to superb performances and a solid script. The Academy was generous in honoring the key people responsible for it, except for producers Ritt and Ravetch, whose film should have been in contention for the best picture Oscar instead of the oddly dim crew of features that was nominated: *America, America, Cleopatra, How the West Was Won,* and *Lilies of the Field. Hud* is easily in a class with the best picture winner, *Tom Jones.*

Neal's Oscar honored a true survivor. She had been in films since 1949, the year that she made *The Fountainhead,* initiating an affair with costar Gary Cooper [701 . . .] that concluded several years later, when Neal suffered a nervous collapse. Her earlier films, except for the sci-fi cult classic *The Day the Earth Stood Still* (1951), were nothing special, but in the later fifties she began to get good supporting roles in such movies as *A Face in the Crowd* (1957) and *Breakfast at Tiffany's.* She suffered a devastating loss in 1962 when her young daughter died of measles, two years after her son had been struck by a taxicab and had to undergo several major operations for head injuries. While her Oscar triumph may have been in part the result of a sympathy vote, her performance was clearly the standout among the nominees: Leslie Caron for *The L-Shaped Room,* Shirley MacLaine for *Irma la Douce,* Rachel Roberts for *This Sporting Life,* and Natalie Wood for *Love With the Proper Stranger.* The award did not immediately lead to better roles, however, and two years later she suffered a massive cerebral hemorrhage that impaired her speech and left her paralyzed. Her courageous fight to recover was the subject of a made-for-TV movie in 1981, *The Patricia Neal Story,* starring Glenda Jackson [893 . . .].

Douglas had been one of Hollywood's most reliable leading men in the thirties, most famous for his performance opposite Greta Garbo in *Ninotchka.* After service in World War II, he found his Hollywood career stalled—in part because his liberal politics were unpopular in the era of the blacklist. His wife, Helen Gahagan Douglas, had been a congresswoman, but she lost a bitter contest for the Senate in 1950 to Richard M. Nixon, who insinuated that Mrs. Douglas was soft on communism. The Douglases left Hollywood for Broadway, and Melvyn did not return until the sixties, when he established a solid career as a character actor that lasted until his death in 1981.

Howe's second Oscar rewards the superbly textured and innovative camera work that made him one of the most celebrated—if not most highly honored —cinematographers in the industry.

This was Newman's third nomination, and it is one of his signature roles. A man who could give convincing performances in such mediocre movies as *The Young Philadelphians, From the Terrace* (1960), and the overblown *Exodus* found complexities in Hud that more limited performers would have missed. It's easy for him to use his own charisma to make Hud attractive; making him repellent, which he does, is the trick. The Oscar went to Sidney Poitier for *Lilies of the Field.*

Ritt was one of the first major talents to emerge from the shadow of the blacklist, which had stymied his early career as a TV director—an experience that he later turned into the film *The Front.* He had a long-standing professional relationship with Newman, whom he had taught at the Actors Studio in the fifties, as well as with Newman's Oscar nemesis, Poitier, who starred in the first Hollywood film Ritt directed, 1958's *Edge of the City.* Although he would later direct Sally Field to an Oscar in *Norma Rae,* Ritt never received another nomination. He died in 1990. The Oscar went to Tony Richardson for *Tom Jones.*

Ravetch and Frank, husband and wife, collaborated with Ritt several times, starting with *The Long Hot Summer* (also starring Newman, in 1958) and continuing through *Norma Rae*. They lost to John Osborn for *Tom Jones*.

The art direction award went to Gene Callahan for *America, America*.

Neal: 1954. Douglas: 169, 971. Howe: 1, 30, 36, 738, 1095, 1451, 1470, 1727, 1774. Newman: 3, 372, 422, 443, 964, 1444.5, 1645, 2198. Ravetch: 1448. Frank: 1448. Pereira: 278, 357, 363, 426, 450, 736, 1029, 1219, 1504, 1570, 1631, 1674, 1716, 1727, 1738, 1840, 1897, 1959, 2012, 2098, 2200, 2208. Larsen: 892, 1341, 1727, 1897. Comer: 278, 357, 426, 450, 726, 736, 925, 1029, 1101, 1214, 1219, 1443, 1570, 1631, 1674, 1727, 1738, 1748, 1959, 1975, 1994, 2012, 2098, 2200, 2208. Benton: 69, 1504, 1840.

957 • HUMAN COMEDY, THE

MGM. 1943.
Award *Original Story:* William Saroyan.
Nominations *Picture:* Clarence Brown, producer. *Actor:* Mickey Rooney. *Director:* Clarence Brown. *Black-and-White Cinematography:* Harry Stradling.

Rooney plays Homer Macauley, who delivers telegrams in the small town of Ithaca, California, but one day has to deliver heartbreaking wartime news to his own family. One of MGM's more successful sentimental celebrations of the American family, made palatable by good performances and straightforward direction, but in need of a spoonful of medicine to make the sugar go down. With Frank Morgan [22 . . .], Fay Bainter [393 . . .], Van Johnson, Donna Reed [732], S. Z. Sakall, and, in one of his first screen appearances, Robert Mitchum [1935] as a soldier on leave.

''Will Saroyan ever write a great play?'' asks the song ''Zip'' in *Pal Joey*. The answer, sadly, was no. Though much acclaimed in his day for a prolific outpouring of stories, novels, and plays, celebrating a joie de vivre that seemed tonic during the Depression years, this Fresno-born writer is little read or studied today. His most enduring works are the play *The Time of Your Life,* which received a mediocre film treatment in 1948, and the novel *The Human Comedy,* here adapted by Howard Estabrook [400 . . .]. In 1992, a little over a decade after his death, Saroyan's Oscar turned up in a San Francisco pawnshop.

The best picture Oscar went to *Casablanca,* which also won for Michael Curtiz's direction. Rooney lost to Paul Lukas in *Watch on the Rhine*. The cinematography award went to Arthur Miller for *The Song of Bernadette*.

Brown: 84, 723, 1417, 1718, 2320. Rooney: 115, 225, 252. Stradling: 110, 149, 596, 737, 852, 853, 864, 896, 1246, 1393, 1567, 1949, 2338.

958 • HUMORESQUE

WARNER BROS. 1946.
Nomination *Scoring of a Dramatic or Comedy Picture:* Franz Waxman.

Wealthy Joan Crawford [1319 . . .] takes violinist John Garfield [251 . . .] for her lover but realizes that she is only retarding his career. Classic camp, with much froufrou dialogue contributed by Clifford Odets and Zachary Gold, adapting a novel by Fannie Hurst that was filmed as a silent in 1920. Fortunately there's a generous amount of music, played by Isaac Stern, and some dry kibitzing by Oscar Levant to blow away the suds occasionally. Directed by Jean Negulesco [1052] as if he believed every word. Crawford fans—or those who want to see why there *are* Crawford fans—shouldn't miss it; everyone else is duly warned. With J. Carrol Naish [1294 . . .]. The fourteen-year-old Robert Blake plays Garfield as a boy. The scoring award went to Hugo Friedhofer for *The Best Years of Our Lives*.

Waxman: 573, 1457, 1459, 1579, 1670, 1822, 1975, 1979, 2004, 2334.

959 • HUNCHBACK OF NOTRE DAME, THE

RKO RADIO. 1939.
Nominations *Sound Recording:* John Aalberg. *Score:* Alfred Newman.

Charles Laughton [1387 . . .] plays Quasimodo, the title character, who saves the Gypsy Esmeralda, played by Maureen O'Hara, when she's accused of being a witch. Fine, atmospheric version of the Victor Hugo romance *Nôtre-Dame de Paris,* celebrated for Laughton's elaborate makeup and the handsome re-creation of medieval Paris. The cast includes Cedric Hardwicke, Thomas Mitchell [962 . . .], Harry Davenport, and, in his screen debut, Edmond O'Brien [146 . . .]. Directed by William Dieterle [1169] from a screenplay by Sonya Levien [1007 . . .] and Bruno Frank. Perhaps the best of the many versions of the Hugo novel, which was filmed in 1923 with Lon Chaney, in 1957 with Anthony Quinn [1226 . . .], and for TV in 1982 with Anthony Hopkins [1679.5 . . .]. It is said that Laughton was filming the scene in which he rings the bells of Notre Dame on the day when news came that England had declared war against Germany. Laughton continued to ring the bells long after the cameras had ceased to turn.

The award for sound went to Bernard B. Brown for *When Tomorrow Comes.* The scoring award went to the four composers and arrangers who worked on *Stagecoach.*

Aalberg: 407, 923, 1033, 1102, 1978, 1991, 2030, 2166, 2213. Newman: 31, 34, 46, 72, 138, 182, 226, 333, 334, 347, 375, 428, 437, 457, 476, 495, 542, 690, 797, 833, 952, 953, 962, 1016, 1082, 1088, 1213, 1278, 1362, 1397, 1475, 1616, 1655, 1849, 1868, 1883, 1921, 2043, 2046, 2091, 2258, 2286, 2294, 2316.

960 • HUNGARIANS

DIALOG STUDIO PRODUCTION (HUNGARY). 1978.
NOMINATION *Foreign Language Film.*

Hungarian farmers seek better wages in Germany during World War II but encounter the difficulty of being foreigners among the Nazis. Written and directed by Zoltan Fabri, based on a novel by Jozsef Balazs. The Oscar went to *Get Out Your Handkerchiefs.*

961 • HUNT FOR RED OCTOBER, THE

MACE NEUFELD/JERRY SHERLOCK PRODUCTION; PARAMOUNT. 1990.
AWARD *Sound Effects Editing:* Cecelia Hall and George Watters II.
NOMINATIONS *Sound:* Don Bassman, Richard Overton, Kevin F. Cleary, and Richard Bryce Goodman. *Film Editing:* Dennis Virkler and John Wright.

Soviet sub captain Sean Connery [2185] masterminds a plot to defect to the West with a new atomic submarine that could greatly alter the balance between the United States and the USSR. American agent Alec Baldwin is sent to figure out what Connery is up to in this thriller, set in the pre-glasnost era, from the novel by Tom Clancy. Lots of twists and turns of plot, and some icy confrontations between good guys and bad—a mixture of each on both teams. Just enough techie talk—a Clancy specialty—to make it convincing but not retard the plot. Splendidly directed by John McTiernan, a master of action-adventure movies, though in this case the action is less impressive than the characters brought to life by Scott Glenn, Sam Neill, James Earl Jones [830], and lots of others at top form. Connery is as usual superb, though he was not the first choice for the part: Klaus Maria Brandauer [1512] was originally cast but had to bow out because of a schedule conflict. *Dances With Wolves* won the Oscars for sound and Neil Travis' editing.

Hall: 2114. Watters: 1915, 2114. Bassman: 5, 544, 1541. Overton: 5, 544. Cleary: 5, 544. Virkler: 734.5. Wright: 1888.5.

962 • HURRICANE, THE

SAMUEL GOLDWYN PRODUCTIONS; UNITED ARTISTS. 1937.
AWARD *Sound Recording:* Thomas Moulton.
NOMINATIONS *Supporting Actor:* Thomas Mitchell. *Score:* Samuel Goldwyn Studio Music Department, Alfred Newman, head; score by Alfred Newman.

Terangi (Jon Hall), a South Pacific islander and mate on a trading ship, is imprisoned for the accidental death of a white man. He escapes and makes it back home to his wife, Marama (Dorothy Lamour). But the governor of the island on which they live,

DeLaage, played by Raymond Massey [1], is a hide-bound believer that the white man has to teach the natives respect for law. He insists on returning Terangi to justice, over the objections of the other whites on the island, including his own wife, played by Mary Astor [822], as well as the priest, played by C. Aubrey Smith, and the doctor, played by Mitchell. Then a whopper of a hurricane strikes, in the midst of which Terangi saves the life of Mme DeLaage, softening even the governor's heart. Corny but very entertaining melodrama, with a truly spectacular hurricane, supervised by James Basevi [746 . . .], who also created the earthquake in *San Francisco*. Directed by John Ford [815 . . .], with second unit work by Stuart Heisler shot in Pago Pago. The screenplay, based on the novel by Charles Nordhoff and James Norman Hall, is credited to Dudley Nichols [30 . . .] and Oliver H. P. Garrett, but producer Samuel Goldwyn [102 . . .] hired Ben Hecht [78 . . .] for a rewrite over Ford's objections because Goldwyn felt that there wasn't enough dialogue. This was the first major film for both Lamour and Hall; the latter was hired when Goldwyn contract player Joel McCrea, originally set for the part, persuaded the producer that he couldn't play a South Sea islander convincingly.

Mitchell's two Oscar nominations (the other was for *Stagecoach)* seemed to certify him as a specialist in boozy medics. This time he lost to Joseph Schildkraut in *The Life of Emile Zola.* The scoring award went to Charles Previn for *One Hundred Men and a Girl.*

Moulton: 22, 46, 138, 366, 457, 487, 560, 706, 798, 1153, 1200, 1451, 1510, 1607, 1849, 2154, 2294. Mitchell: 1901. Newman: 31, 34, 46, 72, 138, 182, 226, 333, 334, 347, 375, 428, 437, 457, 476, 495, 542, 690, 797, 833, 952, 953, 959, 1016, 1082, 1088, 1213, 1278, 1362, 1397, 1475, 1616, 1655, 1849, 1868, 1883, 1921, 2043, 2046, 2091, 2258, 2286, 2294, 2316.

962.5 • *HUSBANDS AND WIVES*

TriStar Pictures Production; TriStar. 1992.
Nominations *Supporting Actress:* Judy Davis. *Original Screenplay:* Woody Allen.

When their close friends, played by Davis and Sydney Pollack [1512 . . .], reveal that their marriage is falling apart, a couple, played by Allen and Mia Farrow, begins to experience marital difficulties, too. Among other things, Allen, a college professor, suddenly finds himself attracted to one of his students, played by Juliette Lewis [342]. This might have been received as one of writer-director Allen's more straightforwardly amusing films of recent years, except that it was released after the notorious breakup of Allen and Farrow, in which it was revealed that Allen had been having an affair with Farrow's adopted daughter, Soon-Yi Previn, a college student about the age of the character played by Lewis. This uncomfortable intersection of art and life makes it difficult to take the film on its own terms.

Davis lost to Marisa Tomei in *My Cousin Vinny.* The writing award went to Neil Jordan for *The Crying Game.*

Davis: 1533. Allen: 39, 88, 294, 311.5, 461, 863, 1005, 1267, 1636, 1647.

963 • *HUSH . . . HUSH, SWEET CHARLOTTE*

20th Century-Fox. 1964.
Nominations *Supporting Actress:* Agnes Moorehead. *Black-and-White Cinematography:* Joseph Biroc. *Black-and-White Art Direction—Set Decoration:* William Glasgow; Raphael Bretton. *Song:* "Hush . . . Hush, Sweet Charlotte," music by Frank DeVol, lyrics by Mack David. *Score—Substantially Original:* Frank DeVol. *Film Editing:* Michael Luciano. *Black-and-White Costume Design:* Norma Koch.

Charlotte, played by Bette Davis [46 . . .], is an aging eccentric living in a moldering southern mansion. She believes she was responsible for the death of her fiancé many years ago—then gradually the truth emerges. Gothic goings-on, very much in the vein of *What Ever Happened to Baby Jane?,* which was also produced and directed by Robert Aldrich. He planned to reteam Davis with her *Baby Jane* costar, Joan Crawford [1319 . . .], as wicked cousin Miriam, but Crawford was ill, so Olivia de Havilland [798 . . .] took the role instead. The Aldrich films are sometimes accused of trashy exploitation of no-longer-young actresses—the cast also includes Davis' *Great Lie* costar Mary Astor—but the actresses themselves seem to be having fun playing out their campy roles, taking the old melodramatics of their Warner Bros. heyday and going over the top. Moorehead is the spooky housekeeper, and the cast also includes Joseph Cotten, Cecil Kellaway [843 . . .], Victor Buono [2248], Bruce Dern [430], and George Kennedy [443].

Moorehead, a distinguished actress who would spend her final years (she died in 1974) playing a witch on the TV sitcom *Bewitched,* lost to Lila Kedrova in *Zorba the Greek.* Walter Lassally's cinematography and Vassilis Fotopoulos' art direction also won awards for *Zorba.* Richard M. Sherman and Robert B. Sherman won for the song "Chim Chim Cher-ee" and the score for *Mary Poppins,* which also won for Cotton Warburton's editing. Dorothy Jeakins took the costume Oscar for *The Night of the Iguana.*

Moorehead: 1052, 1239, 1372. Biroc: 2126. Bretton: 896, 1596, 2126. DeVol: 371, 843, 1572. David: 122, 371, 402, 861, 882, 1032, 2223. Luciano: 548, 688, 1202. Koch: 1126, 2248.

964 • HUSTLER, THE

Robert Rossen Productions; 20th Century-Fox. 1961.

Awards *Black-and-White Cinematography:* Eugen Shuftan. *Black-and-White Art Direction—Set Decoration:* Harry Horner; Gene Callahan.

Nominations *Picture:* Robert Rossen, producer. *Actor:* Paul Newman. *Actress:* Piper Laurie. *Supporting Actor:* Jackie Gleason. *Supporting Actor:* George C. Scott. *Director:* Robert Rossen. *Screenplay—Based on Material From Another Medium:* Sidney Carroll and Robert Rossen.

Newman plays Fast Eddie Felson, a young poolroom hustler who takes on the best in the game, Minnesota Fats (Gleason). Laurie is an alcoholic young woman who becomes Felson's lover, and Scott is Felson's slimy, conniving, treacherous manager. Absorbing, entertaining, and often very moving character drama, with astonishingly assured performances by all four nominated players, plus fine support from

Myron McCormick, Murray Hamilton, Michael Constantine, and in small roles as bartenders, Vincent Gardenia [142 . . .] and the Raging Bull himself, Jake LaMotta. Surprisingly omitted from the nominees: editor Dede Allen [561 . . .], who worked with miles of pool-playing footage (assisted by the uncredited Evan Lottman [631] on some of the montage sequences), convincingly turning some of Willie Mosconi's plays into Newman's. (Gleason shot his own game.)

Shuftan, who changed the spelling of his name from Schüfftan for American screen credits, began his career in Germany in the twenties, working on, among other films, *Menschen am Sonntag,* famous for launching the careers of directors Robert Siodmak [1085] and Edgar Ulmer, writer Billy Wilder [91 . . .], and Schüfftan's camera assistant, Fred Zinnemann [732 . . .]. When the Nazis came to power, Schüfftan went to France and eventually to the United States. He is also known for the invention of the Schüfftan process, which used a mirror to combine live action with miniature sets, a trick first achieved in Fritz Lang's 1927 film *Metropolis.*

Horner's work on *The Hustler* is in sharp contrast to his other Oscar-winning designs, the elegant period sets for *The Heiress.* Though the run-down pool halls of the film have the look of actual locations, they are for the most part constructed sets, built not in Hollywood but in New York City. Horner found the theatrical craftspeople of New York more dedicated to realism than those of the Hollywood studio system. If you wanted cracks in the plaster, he said, a Hollywood set builder would paint them on; in New York you'd get real cracks.

One reason *The Hustler* was made in New York is that producer-director-writer Rossen had exiled himself from Hollywood after giving the names of fellow former communists to the House Un-American Activities Committee in 1953. The action cleared him from blacklisting, but Rossen shunned the mainstream film community for the rest of his career. After *The Hustler,* he made only one more film, *Lilith* (1964), a box-office failure, before his death in 1966. He lost the best picture award to *West Side Story,* which also won for directors Robert Wise and Jerome Robbins. The screenplay, adapted from the novel by Walter Tevis, lost to Abby Mann's work on *Judgment at Nuremberg*.

Many consider Newman's Fast Eddie Felson his finest performance, but it would take the Academy twenty-five years to come around to that point of view, finally giving him the Oscar for his work in *The Hustler*'s sequel, *The Color of Money*. This was only Newman's second nomination, but his loss to Maximilian Schell in *Judgment at Nuremberg* is still one of the Academy's great shockers.

Laurie's early film career had been disastrously mishandled by Universal, the studio to which she was under contract, which wanted her to be a pretty little ingenue and cast her in drivel like *The Prince Who Was a Thief* (1951), *Francis Goes to the Races* (1951), and *Son of Ali Baba* (1952). Breaking free of her contract, she did TV and stage work that demonstrated her dramatic abilities and led to her casting in *The Hustler*. But she decided to retire from films and did not return to the screen until 1976, when she began a successful second career as a character actress in *Carrie*. She lost to Sophia Loren in *Two Women*.

Gleason had likewise had only a mediocre early career in films but became a major TV star in the fifties. When he returned to the movies in the sixties, he preferred at first to play more serious roles, as in *The Hustler, Gigot,* and *Requiem for a Heavyweight* (1962). But though he was a skilled actor, his TV persona haunted him, and his film career never amounted to much. At the end of it, before his death in 1987, he spent much time in popular junk like the *Smokey and the Bandit* series that started in 1977. Gleason and Scott lost to George Chakiris, an upset winner (the smart money was on Montgomery Clift for *Judgment at Nuremberg)* for his performance in *West Side Story*.

Horner: 894, 2047. Callahan: 63, 356, 1143. Rossen: 53. Newman: 3, 372, 422, 443, 956, 1444.5, 1645, 2198. Laurie: 364, 390. Scott: 73, 942, 1541.

965 • I AM A FUGITIVE FROM A CHAIN GANG

WARNER BROS. 1932–33.

NOMINATIONS *Picture:* Hal B. Wallis, producer. *Actor:* Paul Muni. *Sound Recording:* Nathan Levinson.

Muni plays a World War I veteran who falls in with bad company after returning home and winds up sentenced to a chain gang. After brutal treatment, he escapes and creates a new life, but is persuaded to give himself up with the expectation that he will be exonerated. When his pardon fails to come through, he is forced to escape once more. The film ends with a haunting encounter with the woman he loves, who asks him how he lives. "I steal," whispers Muni, and slips back into the shadows. Still powerful after sixty years because of the simplicity, even naïveté, of its storytelling, and Muni's fine performance. Based on a true story by Robert E. Burns, published as *I Am a Fugitive From a Georgia Chain Gang*. Warners, under pressure from southern exhibitors and the state of Georgia, eliminated the particulars of the story's location. Burns himself, traveling under an assumed name, worked on the screenplay, but the credit went to Sheridan Gibney [1936]. Directed by Mervyn LeRoy [1662 . . .]. The movie was a big hit, and it established its studio as the principal source of social-conscious realism in the thirties. The Oscar for best picture, however, went to *Cavalcade*.

Muni lost his second nomination to Charles Laughton in *The Private Life of Henry VIII,* coming in second, according to Academy records, in a three-man race that also included Leslie Howard for *Berkeley Square*. Levinson, who had three of the four nominations for sound, placed second to Harold C. Lewis for *A Farewell to Arms*.

Wallis: 17, 55, 85, 164, 343, 365, 676, 689, 712, 1046, 1095, 1162, 1248, 1482, 1727, 1779, 2233, 2318. Muni: 218.5, 1133, 1169, 1936, 2191. Levinson: 16, 30, 343, 385, 531, 689, 710, 712, 790, 930, 1052, 1169, 1621, 1690, 1768, 1769, 1779, 1930, 1949, 2058, 2318.

966 • I DREAM TOO MUCH

RKO Radio. 1935.

Nomination *Sound Recording:* Carl Dreher.

Singer Lily Pons marries American composer Henry Fonda [815 . . .], but they find their careers in conflict. The first of three attempts by RKO to make opera star Pons as successful on screen as Columbia's Grace Moore [1488] or MGM's Jeanette MacDonald. Though Pons was the most talented singer of the three, and was celebrated for her charm on stage, she photographed unbecomingly, and her films were not well received. This one, directed by John Cromwell, also features Eric Blore, Osgood Perkins, and Lucille Ball. The Oscar went to Douglas Shearer for his work on a MacDonald vehicle, *Naughty Marietta.*

Dreher: 754.

967 • I EVEN MET HAPPY GYPSIES

Avala Film Production (Yugoslavia). 1967.

Nomination *Foreign Language Film.*

A Gypsy traveling salesman rescues a young girl from her sexually abusive stepfather. The title, obviously, is ironic. The chief strength of the film is its examination of the life and culture of the Gypsies of what was then Yugoslavia. Directed by Aleksander Petrovic. The Oscar went to *Closely Watched Trains.*

968 • I LOVE YOU ROSA

Noah Films Ltd. Production (Israel). 1972.

Nomination *Foreign Language Film.*

When her husband dies, twenty-one-year-old Rosa discovers that by Jewish law she now belongs to her late husband's brother. Trouble is, he's only eleven years old. Pleasant Jewish family comedy set in nineteenth-century Jerusalem, with interesting glimpses into traditions of the past. Directed by Moshe Mizrahi, whose *The House on Chelouche Street* would receive a nomination the following year, and whose *Madame Rosa* won the foreign film Oscar in 1977. This time the Oscar went to *The Discreet Charm of the Bourgeoisie.*

969 • I MARRIED A WITCH

Paramount-Cinema Guild; United Artists. 1942.

Nomination *Scoring of a Dramatic or Comedy Picture:* Roy Webb.

Witch Veronica Lake and her warlock father, Cecil Kellaway [843 . . .], are burned at the stake in seventeenth-century Salem, but they come back three hundred years later to take revenge on the descendant of their persecutors, Fredric March [184 . . .]. Instead, Lake falls in love with March. Wispy but pleasant fantasy-comedy, nicely directed by René Clair from a script by Robert Pirosh [157 . . .] and Marc Connelly [352], based on a novel by Thorne Smith. Good support from Robert Benchley, Susan Hayward [973 . . .], and Elizabeth Patterson. The Oscar went to Max Steiner for *Now, Voyager.*

Webb: 640, 665, 1049, 1394, 1639.

970 • I NEVER PROMISED YOU A ROSE GARDEN

Scherick/Blatt Production; New World Pictures. 1977.

Nomination *Screenplay—Based on Material From Another Medium:* Gavin Lambert and Lewis John Carlino.

A schizophrenic teenager, played by Kathleen Quinlan, battles her psychiatrist, played by Bibi Andersson, who is determined to find a treatment for her. Grim but simplistic adaptation of the autobiographical novel by Hannah Green, worth checking out for an interesting cast: Lorraine Gary, Susan Tyrrell [652], Signe Hasso, Jeff Conaway, Diane Varsi [1558], Sylvia Sidney [1962], and Dennis Quaid, directed by Anthony Page. The Oscar went to Alvin Sargent for *Julia.*

Lambert: 1875.

971 • I NEVER SANG FOR MY FATHER

Jamel Productions; Columbia. 1970.

Nominations *Actor:* Melvyn Douglas. *Supporting Actor:* Gene Hackman. *Screenplay—Based on Material From Another Medium:* Robert Anderson.

Hackman plays a middle-aged man forced to deal with his elderly, disagreeable, demanding father, played by Douglas. Estelle Parsons [255 . . .] plays Hackman's sister, whom Douglas has disowned because she married a Jew. The hopelessness of the situation makes this a real downer, but exceptional performances make it watchable. Directed by Gilbert Cates.

Douglas lost to George C. Scott in *Patton*. Hackman, rather oddly placed in the supporting category, although his role is at least as large as Douglas', lost to John Mills in *Ryan's Daughter*.

Anderson first received acclaim for his play *Tea and Sympathy,* once considered daring for its treatment of homosexuality, and filmed in a tepid, bowdlerized version—adapted by Anderson himself—in 1956. *I Never Sang* also began as a play, but Anderson was more fortunate in being able to adapt it without the censors' scissors. He lost to Ring Lardner, Jr., for *MASH*.

Douglas: 169, 956. Hackman: 255, 724, 1333, 2179.5. Anderson: 1457.

972 • I REMEMBER MAMA

RKO RADIO. 1948.

NOMINATIONS *Actress:* Irene Dunne. *Supporting Actor:* Oscar Homolka. *Supporting Actress:* Barbara Bel Geddes. *Supporting Actress:* Ellen Corby. *Black-and-White Cinematography:* Nicholas Musuraca.

Mama (Dunne) is a Norwegian immigrant, a fount of wisdom and strength for her family in turn-of-the-century San Francisco. Bel Geddes is Katrin, the daughter who grows up to write her memoirs and hence serves as the central consciousness of this warmly entertaining family drama. It's not for those who shun sentiment, of course, and it could be a little more cinematic—its origins in the Broadway hit by John Van Druten [749] are a little too obvious, despite some excellent work by designers Albert D'Agostino [632 . . .] and Carroll Clark [4 . . .] in re-creating early twentieth-century San Francisco. Philip Dorn plays Papa, Homolka is the black sheep Uncle Chris, and Corby Aunt Trina. The cast also includes Cedric Hardwicke, Edgar Bergen, Rudy Vallee, and Barbara O'Neil [55]. George Stevens [542 . . .] directed. The ultimate source is Kathryn Forbes' novel *Mama's Bank Account.*

This was the last of Dunne's five unsuccessful nominations—she lost this time to Jane Wyman in *Johnny Belinda*—and one of her last films before her retirement from movies in 1952, when she was in her mid-fifties, an age at which important roles for actresses become few. She made occasional TV appearances but never acted again. Instead, Dunne became active in Republican politics and held a minor diplomatic position at the United Nations during the Eisenhower administration. She was ninety-two when she died in 1990.

Homolka, born in Vienna, worked in German silent films and early talkies before choosing exile first in England and then in the United States during the Third Reich. He was usually cast in comic character roles, although he played his share of villains, as well as a memorable General Kutuzov in the 1956 *War and Peace.* He died in 1978. The Oscar went to Walter Huston for *The Treasure of the Sierra Madre.*

Bel Geddes, daughter of the stage designer Norman Bel Geddes, had a far more successful stage than screen career. On Broadway she created Maggie the Cat in *Cat on a Hot Tin Roof* and appeared in numerous other roles that went to movie stars when they were filmed. Corby, who began her career in Hollywood behind the camera as a production assistant and ''script girl,'' moved into character roles in the mid-forties, often playing mousy types and gradually moving into grandmotherly parts like the one for which she is most famous—the matriarch on the TV series *The Waltons.* The supporting actress award went to Claire Trevor for *Key Largo.*

Musuraca began his career in the silent era and by the late thirties had become a leading cameraman for RKO, helping create such dark, atmospheric films as *The Spiral Staircase* and *Out of the Past.* When RKO collapsed in the fifties, Musuraca turned primarily to TV work. The Oscar went to William Daniels for *The Naked City.*

Dunne: 114, 400, 1212, 2041.

I VITELLONI

See 2209.

973 • I WANT TO LIVE!

FIGARO INC.; UNITED ARTISTS. 1958.

AWARD *Actress:* Susan Hayward.

NOMINATIONS *Director:* Robert Wise. *Screenplay—Based on Material From Another Medium:* Nelson Gidding and Don Mankiewicz. *Black-and-White Cinematography:* Lionel Lindon. *Sound:* Gordon E. Sawyer, sound director, Samuel Goldwyn Studio Sound Department. *Film Editing:* William Hornbeck.

Barbara Graham (Hayward) was a prostitute and a thief, but was she a murderer? This film, which we'd now call a docudrama, puts the case that she was framed and that she didn't deserve to die in the gas chamber in San Quentin in 1955. Based on the reporting of Ed Montgomery (played by Simon Oakland in the movie) and Graham's own letters, it's a pretty effective indictment of the death penalty, if nothing else, though occasionally a bit overwrought and too proud of being "controversial." Hayward gives it everything she's got. The jazz score, composed by Johnny Mandel [64 . . .] and performed by Gerry Mulligan, Shelly Manne, Art Farmer, and others, dates it as late-fifties hip—which is better than late-fifties square, of course. The supporting performers include Theodore Bikel [522], John Marley [1218], and in very small roles, Gavin MacLeod and Jack Weston. Produced by Walter Wanger [413 . . .].

No one worked harder for the Oscar than Hayward, who had received four previous nominations. She was up against two other actresses who also had multiple unsuccessful nominations; Deborah Kerr, nominated for *Separate Tables,* also had four priors, and Rosalind Russell, up for *Auntie Mame,* three. The nominees also included second-timer Elizabeth Taylor in *Cat on a Hot Tin Roof* and first-timer Shirley MacLaine in *Some Came Running.* While the Oscar was the climax of a career that had spanned twenty years, Hayward fell afoul of the middle-age curse that Hollywood imposes on actresses, winding up in mediocre tearjerkers in the sixties. She died in 1975 of a brain tumor, but even though she knew she was terminally ill, she made an appearance at the awards ceremony a year earlier to present the best actress Oscar.

The Oscar for directing went to Vincente Minnelli for *Gigi.* Mankiewicz, the son of Oscar winner Herman Mankiewicz [407 . . .] and nephew of multiple winner Joseph Mankiewicz [46 . . .], failed to become the third in his family to take home the award: It went to Alan Jay Lerner, also for *Gigi,* which won for Adrienne Fazan's editing as well. The cinematography Oscar went to Sam Leavitt for *The Defiant Ones. South Pacific* won for sound.

Hayward: 980, 1396, 1845, 2294. Wise: 407, 1753, 1881, 2244. Lindon: 101, 787. Sawyer: 33, 91, 184, 214, 393, 730, 864, 882, 974, 1032, 1511, 1592, 2244, 2297, 2310. Hornbeck: 768, 1033, 1579.

974 • I WANT YOU

SAMUEL GOLDWYN PRODUCTIONS; RKO RADIO. 1951.

NOMINATION *Sound Recording:* Gordon Sawyer.

Farley Granger plays a young high school graduate who gets drafted into the Korean War, and after trying to get out of it, goes off and becomes a man—persuading his older brother, a World War II vet played by Dana Andrews, that enlisting is the right thing to do. Chillingly naive Cold War recruiting film—the title comes from the posters outside the recruitment offices. This was nobody's finest hour, least of all producer Samuel Goldwyn [102 . . .], who wanted it to be a kind of sequel to *The Best Years of Our Lives* and recruited major talent: cinematographer Harry Stradling [110 . . .], art director Richard Day [22 . . .], and novelist Irwin Shaw [1998], who did the screenplay. Shaw later admitted that he was "whoring" when he wrote it. Directed by Mark Robson [1001 . . .], with Dorothy McGuire [759], Peggy Dow, Ray Collins, Mildred Dunnock [119 . . .], Martin Milner, and Jim Backus. It was as big a flop as it deserved to be. The Oscar went to Douglas Shearer for *The Great Caruso.*

Sawyer: 33, 91, 184, 214, 393, 730, 864, 882, 973, 1032, 1511, 1592, 2244, 2297, 2310.

975 • I WANTED WINGS

PARAMOUNT. 1941.

AWARD *Special Effects:* Farciot Edouart and Gordon Jennings, photographic; Louis Mesenkop, sound.

Ray Milland [1208], William Holden [1424 . . .], and Wayne Morris join the air force, and Brian Donlevy [161] has to train them. Routine eve-of-war melodrama, directed by Mitchell Leisen [587], with Veronica Lake. The award recognizes the efforts to blend the aerial photography of Elmer Dyer [30] with in-studio action.

Edouart: 56, 570, 1668, 1855, 1887, 1934, 2168, 2175, 2181. Jennings: 56, 570, 1668, 1855, 1887, 1934, 2168, 2175, 2181. Mesenkop: 56, 1668, 1887.

976 • ICE CAPADES
REPUBLIC. 1941.
NOMINATION *Scoring of a Musical Picture:* Cy Feuer.

A minimal plot involving a newsreel journalist played by James Ellison is the basis for a series of specialty ice-skating acts and comedy routines involving Jerry Colonna, Alan Mowbray, Phil Silvers, and Barbara Jo Allen doing her "Vera Vague" character. Among the skaters is Vera Hruba, a Czech who came in second to Sonja Henie at the 1936 Olympics, and like Henie went to Hollywood. Unlike Henie, she moved out of ice-skating musicals and into straight acting roles in Republic's westerns and adventure melodramas, first as Vera Hruba Ralston, then as Vera Ralston. She was the protégée of Republic studio head Herbert Yates, whom she married in 1952. Like many of the more obscure films that received Oscar nominations, *Ice Capades* owes its nomination to liberalized rules that allowed each studio to submit nominees. The Oscar went to Frank Churchill and Oliver Wallace for *Dumbo.*

Feuer: 321, 920, 1305, 1806, 1932.

977 • ICE CASTLES
INTERNATIONAL CINEMEDIA CENTRE LTD. PRODUCTION; COLUMBIA. 1979.
NOMINATION *Song:* "Theme From *Ice Castles* (Through the Eyes of Love)," music by Marvin Hamlisch, lyrics by Carole Bayer Sager.

Hockey player Robby Benson and figure skater Lynn-Holly Johnson fall in love; but her hopes for a big-time career are dashed when she's accidentally blinded. Okay schmaltzfest with a good cast—Col-

leen Dewhurst, Jennifer Warren, and Tom Skerritt in particular—but a routine triumph-over-adversity script, directed by Donald Wrye. The Oscar went to David Shire and Norman Gimbel for "It Goes Like It Goes," from *Norma Rae.*

Hamlisch: 398, 1109, 1747, 1813, 1876, 1898, 1927, 2238. Sager: 103, 166.5, 1071.3, 1898.

978 • ICE STATION ZEBRA
FILMWAYS PRODUCTION; MGM. 1968.
NOMINATIONS *Cinematography:* Daniel L. Fapp. *Special Visual Effects:* Hal Millar and J. McMillan Johnson.

A satellite plunges to earth with a capsule containing information that could touch off World War III if it falls into the wrong hands, so both the Americans and the Soviets head for the North Pole to retrieve it. Routine adaptation of an Alistair MacLean thriller, directed by John Sturges [131], with Rock Hudson [768], Ernest Borgnine [1283], Patrick McGoohan, Jim Brown, and Tony Bill [1927]. The cinematography Oscar went to Pasqualino De Santis for *Romeo and Juliet.* The special effects award was won by Stanley Kubrick for *2001: A Space Odyssey.*

Fapp: 529, 675, 1279, 1492, 2184, 2244. Johnson: 636, 833, 1388, 1595, 2098.

979 • IF I WERE KING
PARAMOUNT. 1938.
NOMINATIONS *Supporting Actor:* Basil Rathbone. *Interior Decoration:* Hans Dreier and John Goodman. *Sound Recording:* Loren L. Ryder. *Original Score:* Richard Hageman.

Poet-swordsman François Villon, played by Ronald Colman [311 . . .], matches wits and rapiers with Louis XI (Rathbone), while wooing the fair lady played by Frances Dee. Amusing swashbuckler, based on a play by Justin McCarthy that also became the Rudolf Friml operetta *The Vagabond King,* which was filmed in 1930 and 1955. The screenplay is by Preston Sturges [823 . . .]. Frank Lloyd [374 . . .] directed.

Rathbone lost to Walter Brennan in *Kentucky.* The art direction Oscar went to Carl J. Weyl for *The Adventures of Robin Hood,* which also won for Erich

Wolfgang Korngold's score. Thomas Moulton won for the sound for *The Cowboy and the Lady.*

Rathbone: 1721. Dreier: 97, 151, 649, 674, 701, 726, 925, 1101, 1120, 1194, 1214, 1217, 1358, 1443, 1452, 1540, 1668, 1748, 1880, 1975, 1994, 2190. Goodman: 414, 1560, 1895. Ryder: 566, 827, 1452, 1669, 1697, 1703, 1837, 1887, 2012, 2168, 2181, 2183, 2230, 2242. Hageman: 955, 1200, 1801, 1901, 2062.

980 • I'LL CRY TOMORROW

MGM. 1955.
AWARD *Black-and-White Costume Design:* Helen Rose.
NOMINATIONS *Actress:* Susan Hayward. *Black-and-White Cinematography:* Arthur E. Arling. *Black-and-White Art Direction–Set Decoration:* Cedric Gibbons and Malcolm Brown; Edwin B. Willis and Hugh B. Hunt.

Stage and screen star Lillian Roth (Hayward) descends into alcoholism and a succession of bad marriages that destroy her career. The cast includes Richard Conte as one of Roth's abusive husbands, plus Eddie Albert [887 . . .] and Jo Van Fleet [593]. Exploitive weeper, directed by Daniel Mann. The screenplay by Helen Deutsch [1173] and Jay Richard Kennedy is based on Roth's autobiography, which she wrote after the appearance on TV's *This Is Your Life* that is the film's final scene. Roth had dropped out of sight in the thirties after appearances in such films as *The Love Parade* and the Marx Brothers' 1930 *Animal Crackers.* Though it spans some thirty years, this movie makes little effort to create a sense of period in either design or costume—it looks fifties throughout.

Hayward lost to Anna Magnani in *The Rose Tattoo,* which also won for James Wong Howe's cinematography and for art direction.

Rose: 130, 578, 629, 755, 817, 1007, 1309, 1335, 1599. Hayward: 973, 1396, 1845, 2294. Arling: 2320. Gibbons: 66, 87, 130, 217, 227, 239, 285, 290, 440, 629, 749, 831, 1069, 1096, 1173, 1190, 1226, 1230, 1232, 1274, 1308, 1309, 1417, 1567, 1604, 1644, 1662, 1673, 1721, 1861, 1937, 2068, 2112, 2256, 2257, 2300, 2320, 2330. Brown:

1861. Willis: 66, 87, 130, 227, 239, 290, 629, 749, 831, 1069, 1096, 1157, 1173, 1190, 1226, 1230, 1232, 1309, 1417, 1567, 1657, 1662, 1673, 1721, 1861, 1937, 2068, 2112, 2257, 2320, 2330. Hunt: 175, 401, 1069, 1232, 1335, 1388, 1567, 1644, 1657, 1673, 2157, 2184.

981 • I'LL GET BY

20TH CENTURY-FOX. 1950.
NOMINATION *Scoring of a Musical Picture:* Lionel Newman.

Featherweight musical about songwriters William Lundigan and Dennis Day and singers June Haver and Gloria DeHaven, with Thelma Ritter [46 . . .], directed by Richard Sale. A remake of the ten-year-old *Tin Pan Alley,* for which Lionel's brother, Alfred, won the scoring Oscar. Lionel wasn't so lucky: He lost to Adolph Deutsch and Roger Edens for *Annie Get Your Gun.*

Newman: 183, 457, 557, 795, 896, 1160, 1273, 1585, 1762, 2043.

982 • IMAGES

HEMDALE GROUP LTD.-LION'S GATE FILMS PRODUCTION; COLUMBIA (U.S./IRELAND). 1972.
NOMINATION *Original Dramatic Score:* John Williams.

Susannah York [2047] plays a schizophrenic children's book author trying to sort out what is real and what is hallucination. Exhausting and unsatisfactory drama, written and directed by Robert Altman [1286 . . .], with some stunning cinematography by Vilmos Zsigmond [416 . . .]. The movie has ardent admirers, as almost all of Altman's do, but while you can't fault it for ambition and daring, it doesn't really repay the effort of sitting through it. Williams lost to Charles Chaplin, Raymond Rasch, and Larry Russell for the score of *Limelight,* a film that became eligible for the Oscar twenty years after it was made.

Williams: 6, 260, 403, 416, 588, 613, 614, 659, 805, 933, 937, 996, 997, 1041, 1047, 1596, 1652, 1679, 1684, 1701, 1764.65, 1916, 1977, 2107, 2126, 2194, 2293, 2322.

983 • IMITATION OF LIFE

UNIVERSAL. 1934.

NOMINATIONS *Picture:* Produced by John M. Stahl. *Sound Recording:* Theodore Soderberg. *Assistant Director:* Scott Beal.

Widow Claudette Colbert [1025 . . .], left penniless with a young daughter, gets rich off a pancake recipe devised by her maid, Louise Beavers. But Colbert and Beavers are faced with trouble when their daughters grow up. Beavers' daughter, played by Fredi Washington, can pass for white, and she rejects her mother. And Colbert's daughter, Rochelle Hudson, falls in love with her mother's boyfriend (Warren William). Classic melodrama from a novel by Fannie Hurst, almost made credible by terrific performances from Colbert, Beavers, and Washington, but undermined by its racial attitudes—Beavers is perfectly happy to let Colbert be the one who gets rich off her recipe—and by the underlying premise that career women must suffer. The 1959 remake is more sophisticated and hip, but that's not necessarily a good thing when you're dealing with tear-jerking material like this. And at least in this version the daughter who passes for white is actually played by an African-American. Stahl also directed the film, and the screenplay is by William Hurlbut.

The best picture Oscar went to Colbert's other triumph of the year, *It Happened One Night.* The sound award went to Paul Neal for *One Night of Love.* Beals placed third in the competition in which John Waters was named best assistant director for *Viva Villa!*

Soderberg: 724, 1596, 1726, 2126, 2152.

984 • IMITATION OF LIFE

UNIVERSAL-INTERNATIONAL. 1959.

NOMINATIONS *Supporting Actress:* Susan Kohner. *Supporting Actress:* Juanita Moore.

A widow, played by Lana Turner [1558], comes to New York with her young daughter, hoping to become an actress. By chance, she encounters a homeless black woman, played by Moore, who has a daughter the same age as Turner's. Moore agrees to be a live-in housekeeper while Turner looks for work. A young photographer, played by John Gavin, helps the women and begins to fall in love with Turner. But her career comes first, and eventually she is a star and the mistress of a famous director, played by Dan O'Herlihy [18]. She and Moore now share an opulent home, but both have problems with their daughters. Moore's, played by Kohner, wants to pass for white; and Turner's, played by Sandra Dee, falls for Gavin just as Turner finds that he was the love of her life all along. Super-slick redo of the 1934 melodrama, with Turner's character an altogether harder type than the one played by Claudette Colbert in the original. It's trash, but it's played out with such flair, under the direction of Douglas Sirk, that you don't hate yourself for wallowing in it. Its racial attitudes, while slightly more sophisticated than those of the earlier film, still seem to prefer subservient blacks, like Moore's character, to those like Kohner's who want to escape from their second-class status.

The parallel character in the first *Imitation* was played by a black actress, Fredi Washington. But Kohner was white, the daughter of Hollywood agent Paul Kohner and Mexican actress Lupita Tovar. After a handful of films in the late fifties and early sixties, the last of which was *Freud* in 1962, she married designer John Weitz and retired from acting. Moore had been in films since the early fifties, but this was her first major role—and her last, thanks to the dearth of substantial parts for black performers. The supporting actress Oscar went to Shelley Winters for *The Diary of Anne Frank.*

985 • IMMORTAL LOVE

SHOCHIKU COMPANY LTD. (JAPAN). 1961.

NOMINATION *Foreign Language Film.*

While a young woman waits for her fiancé's return, her family decides to sell her to a wealthy landowner. Written and directed by Keisuke Kinoshita. The Oscar went to *Through a Glass Darkly.*

986 • IMPORTANT MAN, THE

PELICULAS RODRIGUEZ S.A. (MEXICO). 1961.

NOMINATION *Foreign Language Film.*

Toshiro Mifune plays a drunken thug rejected by even his own family. He buys an election and becomes mayor but still gets no respect. Eventually he is convicted of murdering a prostitute. Not much of a character arc in this film directed by Ismael Rodriguez, but as always Mifune is worth watching. The Oscar went to *Through a Glass Darkly*.

987 • *IN COLD BLOOD*

PAX ENTERPRISES PRODUCTION; COLUMBIA. 1967.

NOMINATIONS *Director:* Richard Brooks. *Screenplay— Based on Material From Another Medium:* Richard Brooks. *Cinematography:* Conrad Hall. *Original Music Score:* Quincy Jones.

Two drifters, played by Robert Blake and Scott Wilson, slaughter a Kansas family just for kicks, and are caught, tried, and executed. Chillingly effective adaptation of Truman Capote's celebrated ''nonfiction novel'' that set the standard by which subsequent ''docudramas'' should be tried and mostly found wanting. In the year of *Bonnie and Clyde* and *The Graduate,* it dealt in a more extreme fashion with the sense of rootlessness and alienation portrayed in those more celebrated and certainly more likable movies. *In Cold Blood* is too long, indulges in too much naive psychologizing, and by today's standards for screen violence seems to pull its punches, but it was far more deserving of a best picture nomination than the dud musical *Doctor Dolittle* or the syrupy problem comedy *Guess Who's Coming to Dinner.* Perhaps it failed to receive one because Columbia, which also released *Guess Who's Coming,* put its promotional efforts behind that film, under the assumption that it had a better chance at the award than *In Cold Blood.*

Brooks lost the directing award to Mike Nichols for *The Graduate* and the writing Oscar to Stirling Silliphant for *In the Heat of the Night.* Burnett Guffey won for the cinematography for *Bonnie and Clyde.* The scoring award went to Elmer Bernstein for *Thoroughly Modern Millie.*

Brooks: 227, 372, 609, 1627. Hall: 317, 504, 1355, 1627, 1771.5, 2017. Jones: 144, 423, 698, 2299.

988 • *IN HARM'S WAY*

SIGMA PRODUCTIONS; PARAMOUNT. 1965.

NOMINATION *Black-and-White Cinematography:* Loyal Griggs.

Naval officers John Wayne [33 . . .] and Kirk Douglas [130 . . .] spearhead retaliatory efforts after the attack on Pearl Harbor. Mixed in with the military escapades are some romantic ones and a plethora of star cameos involving Patricia Neal [956 . . .], Paula Prentiss, Brandon de Wilde [1799], Dana Andrews, Stanley Holloway [1393], Burgess Meredith [504 . . .], Franchot Tone [1387], Carroll O'Connor, Slim Pickens, Henry Fonda [815 . . .], George Kennedy [443], Larry Hagman, and others. But it's dull and draggy and goes on for almost three hours. Produced and directed by Otto Preminger [73 . . .]. Griggs lost to Ernest Laszlo for *Ship of Fools.*

Griggs: 833, 1799, 1887, 2012.

989 • *IN OLD ARIZONA*

FOX. 1928–29.

AWARD *Actor:* Warner Baxter.

NOMINATIONS *Production:* Winfield Sheehan, studio head. *Director:* Irving Cummings. *Writing Achievement:* Tom Barry. *Cinematography:* Arthur Edeson.

Baxter plays the Cisco Kid, the character created by O. Henry and later made famous in a series of B-movie westerns starring first Baxter, then Cesar Romero, Gilbert Roland, and Duncan Renaldo. A TV series in the fifties featured Renaldo, with Leo Carrillo as the sidekick Pancho, a character who doesn't appear in this film. A primitive talkie, it's remarkable for being shot on location in Zion National Park and the Mojave Desert at a time when studios were treating sound equipment gingerly. The novelty of such atmospheric effects as birds singing, roosters crowing, and horses' hooves galloping into the distance wowed audiences, and the film helped revive the western as a movie genre.

Baxter had an undistinguished film career to this point and was cast only at the last moment, when Raoul Walsh, who was both directing and starring in the film, lost an eye in an auto accident on location in

Utah. Baxter's deep voice and good looks caught on, but he never became a major star. His best-known subsequent performance was as the ailing director in *42nd Street* who sends Ruby Keeler out with instructions to come back a star. He died in 1951, aged sixty.

The nominees in all the other categories were unofficial ones. Only the winners were announced this year, but the various branches that selected them kept lists of the runners-up who had been considered for the awards. The best picture Oscar went to *Broadway Melody*. The directing award was won by Frank Lloyd for *The Divine Lady*. Clyde DeVinna won for the cinematography of *White Shadows in the South Seas*.

Sheehan: 132, 374, 592, 1920. Barry: 2191. Edeson: 48, 365.

990 • IN OLD CHICAGO
20TH CENTURY-FOX. 1937.

AWARDS *Supporting Actress:* Alice Brady. *Assistant Director:* Robert Webb.

NOMINATIONS *Picture:* Darryl F. Zanuck, with Kenneth MacGowan, producers. *Original Story:* Niven Busch. *Sound Recording:* E. H. Hansen. *Score:* 20th Century-Fox Studio Music Department, Louis Silvers, head.

Brady plays Mrs. O'Leary, the one whose cow kicked over a lantern and started the Chicago fire. But most of the film deals with the rivalry of her good son, played by Don Ameche [419], and her bad 'un, played by Tyrone Power. Alice Faye, as Power's nightclub-singer girlfriend, gets to sing some unmemorable songs. If you detect more than a shade of resemblance between this big, dumb, and very entertaining movie and *San Francisco,* the previous year's hit about a major disaster in a raucous turn-of-the-century American city, go to the head of the class. Directed by Henry King [1868 . . .], with Andy Devine, Brian Donlevy [161], and Sidney Blackmer. The screenplay, based on Busch's novel *We the O'Learys,* is by Lamar Trotti [1516 . . .] and Sonya Levien [1007 . . .].

Brady was born in a trunk, so to speak, the daughter of an eminent producer. She became a stage star, first as an operetta singer and then as a dramatic actress, in the early years of the century. Though she made a number of silent films, her major screen career came in the thirties, as a character player, usually in comic parts. Her last film, before her death from cancer in 1939, was *Young Mr. Lincoln*.

Webb was best known as a second unit director on action films, but he was also the director in charge of numerous B pictures starting in the mid-forties, including Elvis Presley's debut film, *Love Me Tender* (1956).

In Old Chicago lost the best picture Oscar to *The Life of Emile Zola*. The award for original story went to William A. Wellman and Robert Carson for *A Star Is Born*. Thomas Moulton won the sound award for *The Hurricane*. The scoring award went to Charles Previn for *One Hundred Men and a Girl*.

Brady: 1401. Zanuck: 34, 46, 550, 710, 759, 815, 946, 952, 1201, 1327, 1666, 2154, 2286. Mac-Gowan: 1189. Hansen: 241, 815, 952, 1655, 1868, 1957, 2027, 2056, 2272, 2286, 2317. Silvers: 1488, 1957, 1982.

991 • IN OLD OKLAHOMA
REPUBLIC. 1943.

NOMINATIONS *Sound Recording:* Daniel J. Bloomberg. *Scoring of a Dramatic or Comedy Picture:* Walter Scharf.

Oil driller John Wayne [33 . . .] battles it out with assorted rivals and bad guys in this okay action saga. The love interest is provided by Martha Scott [1510], and the cast, directed by Albert S. Rogell, includes Albert Dekker, Marjorie Rambeau [1609 . . .], and Sidney Blackmer, plus Republic contract players Gabby Hayes and Dale Evans. Also known as *War of the Wildcats*. The Oscars went to Stephen Dunn for the sound for *This Land Is Mine* and Alfred Newman for the score of *The Song of Bernadette*.

Bloomberg: 274, 680, 693, 1350, 1642, 1756. Scharf: 174, 274, 665, 737, 864, 921, 1054, 1305, 2285.

992 • IN THE HEAT OF THE NIGHT
MIRISCH CORPORATION PRODUCTION; UNITED ARTISTS. 1967.

AWARDS *Picture:* Walter Mirisch, producer. *Actor:* Rod Steiger. *Screenplay—Based on Material From Another Me-*

dium: Stirling Silliphant. *Sound:* Samuel Goldwyn Studio Sound Department. *Film Editing:* Hal Ashby.
NOMINATIONS *Director:* Norman Jewison. *Sound Effects:* James A. Richard.

Virgil Tibbs, a black police officer from the North, played by Sidney Poitier [522 . . .], finds himself stranded in a small Mississippi town where he is first accused of a murder and then allowed by the local sheriff, played by Steiger, to assist in solving it. Very entertaining movie that's far more subtle than it sounds. It could have been a tedious racial-tolerance problem drama on the order of *Guess Who's Coming to Dinner,* one of the films it beat for best picture. Instead, it's a witty, observant, frequently funny thriller, playing off the odd-couple relationship of Poitier and Steiger in endearing and sometimes surprising ways. The solid cast includes Warren Oates, Lee Grant [534 . . .], Beah Richards [843], and Scott Wilson. It's not a landmark film like *Bonnie and Clyde* or *The Graduate,* which it also beat for best picture, but it holds up well after all these years, while the countercultural hipness of those movies has begun to look a bit passé. There's something to be said for mainstream moviemaking at its best, after all.

Few people knew mainstream moviemaking better than Mirisch, who was vice-president in charge of production for the Mirisch Co., which he formed with his brothers Harold and Marvin in 1957. Walter Mirisch learned the ropes on poverty row, as a producer at Monogram and later at its higher-quality subsidiary, Allied Artists. The Mirisch Co. was responsible, at least in part, for the best picture winners *The Apartment* and *West Side Story,* as well as such movies as *Some Like It Hot, The Great Escape, The Pink Panther, The Russians Are Coming, the Russians Are Coming,* and *Fiddler on the Roof.* In addition to serving as president of the Academy from 1973 to 1977, Mirisch also received both the Irving G. Thalberg Memorial Award for 1977 and the Jean Hersholt Humanitarian Award for 1982.

Steiger was a product of the Actors Studio, and his first major screen appearance was with a fellow alumnus, Marlon Brando, in *On the Waterfront,* for which Steiger received his first nomination. He was, how-

ever, an actor it was easy to miscast, as in his next role, as Jud Fry in *Oklahoma!,* so his career has had frequent ups and downs. A man to whom overacting comes as naturally as breathing, he gives a notably controlled performance in *Heat.*

Silliphant began his Hollywood career in the advertising and promotion departments of Disney and 20th Century-Fox and has subsequently been both a writer and a producer. *Heat* is his best work. In the seventies he became known for screenplays for disaster flicks such as *The Poseidon Adventure* and *The Towering Inferno.*

Ashby turned from editing to directing in 1970, when he succeeded Jewison as the director of *The Landlord.* Before his death in 1988, he was responsible for such films as the cult favorite *Harold and Maude* (1971), *The Last Detail, Shampoo, Bound for Glory,* and *Being There.*

Jewison is a notorious Oscar also-ran, although it's hard to put credence in the suggestion of one Oscar historian that the Academy has turned its back on Jewison because of prejudice against Canadians. Still, whenever the director of a best picture winner fails to get the Oscar for directing, too, there's a tendency to wonder why. This time Jewison lost to Mike Nichols for *The Graduate,* an award that many interpreted as recognition for Nichols' failure to win the previous year for *Who's Afraid of Virginia Woolf?*

The award for sound effects went to John Poyner for *The Dirty Dozen.*

Steiger: 1477, 1543. Ashby: 430, 1736. Jewison: 659, 1351, 1736, 1857.

992.3 • *IN THE LINE OF FIRE*

CASTLE ROCK ENTERTAINMENT AND COLUMBIA PICTURES PRODUCTION; COLUMBIA. 1993.
NOMINATIONS *Supporting Actor:* John Malkovich. *Screenplay Written Directly for the Screen:* Jeff Maguire. *Film Editing:* Anne V. Coates.

Someone is threatening to assassinate the president, and aging Secret Service man Clint Eastwood [2179.5] is determined that it isn't going to happen. For one thing, he's haunted by the fact that he was in the motorcade in Dallas on November 22, 1963, and was unable to prevent Kennedy's assassination. The trouble is, the would-be assassin (Malkovich) knows this about Eastwood and uses it to taunt him. A fine-tuned, very effective thriller, directed by Wolfgang Petersen [258]. Like *The Fugitive,* 1993's other great action thriller, *In the Line of Fire* relies on characters who use their brains, not just their guns, and the script provides them with room to grow in. In one of his best performances, Eastwood displays his usual weary grit, this time undercut with the vulnerability that has made his characters more appealing in recent years. Rene Russo is the perfect foil as his fellow agent: He's old, she's young; he's macho, she's a feminist. Sure, they fall in love, but they make a very witty team. Dylan McDermott, Fred Dalton Thompson, and John Mahoney provide solid support. The music is by Ennio Morricone [308 . . .], who came to prominence along with Eastwood with *A Fistful of Dollars* thirty years earlier.

Malkovich plays a cold-blooded killer who's a renegade intelligence agent, a character that's on its way to becoming a movie cliché: A year earlier, Tommy Lee Jones, who took this year's supporting actor Oscar for his performance in *The Fugitive,* played a CIA renegade in *Under Siege.*

The screenplay award went to Jane Campion for *The Piano.* The Oscar for editing was won by Michael Kahn for *Schindler's List.*

Malkovich: 1580. Coates: 164, 608, 1151.

992.5 • *IN THE NAME OF THE FATHER*

HELL'S KITCHEN/GABRIEL BYRNE PRODUCTION; UNIVERSAL (IRELAND). 1993.

NOMINATIONS *Picture:* Jim Sheridan, producer. *Actor:* Daniel Day-Lewis. *Supporting Actor:* Pete Postlethwaite. *Supporting Actress:* Emma Thompson. *Director:* Jim Sheridan. *Screenplay Based on Material Previously Published or Produced:* Terry George and Jim Sheridan. *Film Editing:* Gerry Hambling.

Gerry Conlon (Day-Lewis) is a bit of a lout. He travels from his native Belfast to England in 1974, supposedly looking for work, but mostly loafing and doping with members of a hippie commune. He also robs a prostitute and returns home to Belfast, where he flashes the money he's stolen. Soon he finds himself in jail, accused of bombing a pub in the English town of Guilford, where he had been staying. His father, Guiseppe (Postlethwaite), a hardworking man who has been at odds with his layabout son, is also arrested, along with other members of Conlon's family and several residents of the commune. The British are so eager to bring the Irish Republican Army under control that they accuse the Conlons of being terrorists, and under torture, Gerry confesses. The experience of prison transforms Gerry Conlon, who begins the long process of trying to prove his innocence. Finally a lawyer (Thompson) decides to take his case. Fifteen years after his arrest, Conlon is freed. The wrenching, nightmarish tale, based on Conlon's book *Proved Innocent,* is well told by Sheridan, though like all movies with a political edge, it occasionally tips over into melodrama to make its points. Sheridan has also admitted that he fictionalized some details and characters for dramatic effect. But Day-Lewis and Postlethwaite are extraordinary, and Corin Redgrave makes a fine villain as the police official who extorts Gerry's confession and conceals exculpating evidence. Daniel Massey [1907] also appears, as the prosecuting attorney. The cinematography is by Peter Biziou [1333] and the music by Trevor Jones.

The best picture Oscar went to *Schindler's List,* which also received awards for Steven Spielberg's direction, Steven Zaillian's screenplay, and Michael Kahn's direction.

Day-Lewis once again demonstrates his apparent unwillingness to do the same thing twice: His Gerry Conlon is as different from his previous performance as the repressed Newland Archer in *The Age of Innocence* as that role was from the dashing Hawkeye in *The Last of the Mohicans.* Recognized as one of the screen's major performers since his Oscar for Sheridan's *My Left Foot,* he lost to Tom Hanks in *Philadelphia.*

Postlethwaite is relatively unknown as a film actor (his previous screen credits include a bit part in Day-Lewis' *Last of the Mohicans*), but he's a respected veteran of the British stage. The Oscar went to Tommy Lee Jones in *The Fugitive.*

Thompson's nomination generated mild controversy. Because of her previous year's Oscar, she shared top billing with Day-Lewis, but her role in *In the Name of the Father* is small and the courtroom theatrics it involves are fairly routine. Many felt she should have been recognized for her luminous performance as Beatrice in *Much Ado About Nothing* instead. She was simultaneously nominated for best actress for *The Remains of the Day.* She lost both Oscars—best actress went to Holly Hunter and supporting actress to Anna Paquin, both for *The Piano*—and became only the second person in the history of the awards to receive simultaneous nominations without winning in either category. (The other double loser is Sigourney Weaver for *Gorillas in the Mist* and *Working Girl.*)

Sheridan: 1399. Day-Lewis: 1399. Thompson: 954.5, 1679.5. Hambling: 433, 641, 1313, 1333.

993 • IN WHICH WE SERVE

Two Cities; United Artists (United Kingdom). 1943.

Award *Special Award:* Noël Coward, for his outstanding production achievement. (1942)

Nominations *Picture:* Noël Coward, producer. *Original Screenplay:* Noël Coward.

The lives of the crew of a torpedoed destroyer flash before their eyes—and ours, of course. Super World War II British patriotic opus, pulling out every stop in its paean to England, home, and duty. Anglophiles will love it—others are duly warned. Coward based the film on the experiences of Lord Mountbatten, whose ship was sunk early in the war. In addition to writing and producing, Coward codirected with David Lean [287 . . .]. The cast includes Richard Attenborough [745] and Celia Johnson [289] in their film debuts, plus John Mills [1737], Bernard Miles, and Michael Wilding, among others. Nine-year-old Daniel Massey, who would one day be nominated for playing Noël Coward in *Star!,* also appears, as does the infant Juliet Mills—as her father's son.

Coward received an honorary award for the film a year before it met the eligibility requirements for competitive Oscars, which it lost to *Casablanca* for best picture, and to Norman Krasna for the screenplay of *Princess O'Rourke.* One of the twentieth century's most versatile figures, Coward was actor, com-

poser, playwright, novelist, producer, and director. He made his first screen appearance while still in his teens in a bit part in D. W. Griffith's *Hearts of the World* (1918) and wrote his first screenplay, *The Queen Was in the Parlor,* in 1927. Many of his plays were adapted for the screen, including *Cavalcade,* the best picture winner for 1932–33. His last film appearance, in *The Italian Job,* came in 1969; he died in 1973.

994 • INCENDIARY BLONDE

Paramount. 1945.

Nomination *Scoring of a Musical Picture:* Robert Emmett Dolan.

Betty Hutton plays the queen of the speakeasies, Texas Guinan, in a tolerable musical biopic. Directed by George Marshall, with Arturo de Cordova, Charlie Ruggles, Albert Dekker, and Barry Fitzgerald [787]. Handsomely photographed by Ray Rennahan [235 . . .]. The scoring Oscar went to Georgie Stoll for *Anchors Aweigh.*

Dolan: 173, 213, 244, 929, 1120, 1704, 1912.

995 • INCREDIBLE SARAH, THE

Helen M. Strauss-Reader's Digest Films Ltd. Production; Seymour Borde & Associates (United Kingdom). 1976.

Nominations *Art Direction—Set Decoration:* Elliot Scott and Norman Reynolds; Peter Howitt. *Costume Design:* Anthony Mendleson.

Glenda Jackson [893 . . .] plays Sarah Bernhardt in a survey of the great actress' early career. As fine an actress as Jackson is, she's profoundly miscast, and the flimsy script by Ruth Wolff doesn't help. Directed by Richard Fleischer, with Daniel Massey [1907]. The art direction award went to *All the President's Men.* Danilo Donati won for the costumes for *Fellini's Casanova.*

Scott: 69, 2274. Reynolds: 613, 614, 1652, 1684, 1916. Howitt: 1285, 1651, 2274. Mendleson: 2340.

996 • INDIANA JONES AND THE LAST CRUSADE

Lucasfilm Ltd. Production; Paramount. 1989.

Award *Sound Effects Editing:* Ben Burtt and Richard Hymns.

NOMINATIONS *Sound:* Ben Burtt, Gary Summers, Shawn Murphy, and Tony Dawe. *Original Score:* John Williams.

Harrison Ford [2296] as Indy joins forces with Sean Connery [2185], who plays Indy's father, in a search for the Holy Grail. The third film in the trilogy that began with *Raiders of the Lost Ark* is a rousing affair, with nice support from Denholm Elliott [1725] and, in the opening sequence, River Phoenix [1735] as the young Indy. The imagination of director Steven Spielberg [416 . . .] is as fertile as ever, but you may find yourself overstimulated by the time it's all over. Connery's droll performance is the film's highlight, but interestingly, producer George Lucas [65 . . .] was skeptical of casting him, having imagined someone less vigorous in the part. Along the way, Connery contributed script ideas such as the fact that Jones *père* and *fils* have both enjoyed the favors of the female lead, played by Alison Doody—a joke that Lucas and Spielberg reportedly at first found in bad taste.

The sound Oscar went to *Glory.* Alan Menken's music for *The Little Mermaid* won the scoring Oscar.

Burtt: 588, 1652, 1684, 1916, 2284. Hymns: 129, 1071.5, 2284. Summers: 129, 1071.5, 1684, 2019. Murphy: 1071.5. Dawe: 613, 1684, 2274. Williams: 6, 260, 403, 416, 588, 613, 614, 659, 805, 933, 937, 982, 997, 1041, 1047, 1596, 1652, 1679, 1684, 1701, 1764.65, 1916, 1977, 2107, 2126, 2194, 2293, 2322.

997 • *INDIANA JONES AND THE TEMPLE OF DOOM*

LUCASFILM LTD. PRODUCTION; PARAMOUNT. 1984.
AWARD *Visual Effects:* Dennis Muren, Michael McAlister, Lorne Peterson, and George Gibbs.
NOMINATION *Original Score:* John Williams.

Archaeologist Jones, played by Harrison Ford [2296], finds himself trekking across India accompanied by a gold-digging woman, played by Kate Capshaw, and a Chinese orphan, played by Ke Huy Quan, to rescue a village's missing children and a magic stone. Along the way they tangle with the cult of Kali, the movie's homage to *Gunga Din.* Silly, souped-up

sequel (actually a prequel) to *Raiders of the Lost Ark,* directed by Steven Spielberg [416 . . .] with endless inventiveness but not much warmth. Full of kids' gross-out jokes, kinetic effects stolen from amusement park rides, and perilous situations taken from old comic books; in short, there's not much here for anyone over the age of fifteen. (Ironically the movie stirred so much controversy because of a gruesome bit in which a man's heart is torn from his chest that it resulted in the creation of the PG-13 rating.) Spielberg and producer George Lucas [65 . . .] later admitted that they felt the movie had gone a bit too far over the top, and their next Indiana Jones outing, *Indiana Jones and the Last Crusade,* is a somewhat more restrained affair. Maurice Jarre won the scoring Oscar for *A Passage to India*—a very different India.

Muren: 5, 577, 588, 614, 1002, 1071.5, 1684, 2019, 2284, 2339. McAlister: 2284. Gibbs: 45.5, 2274. Williams: 6, 260, 403, 416, 588, 613, 614, 659, 805, 933, 937, 982, 996, 1041, 1047, 1596, 1652, 1679, 1684, 1701, 1764.65, 1916, 1977, 2107, 2126, 2194, 2293, 2322.

998 • *INDISCRETION OF AN AMERICAN WIFE*

VITTORIO DE SICA PRODUCTIONS; COLUMBIA (U.S./ITALY). 1954.
NOMINATION *Black-and-White Costume Design:* Christian Dior.

Two lovers, an American woman played by Jennifer Jones [584 . . .] and an Italian man played by Montgomery Clift [732 . . .], have their final meeting in the Roman railway station. Misbegotten collaboration of director Vittorio De Sica [650] and producer David O. Selznick [497 . . .], seriously damaged by Selznick's overprotectiveness toward his wife, Jones. Among other things, Selznick called in his own cameraman, Oswald Morris [659 . . .], to shoot close-ups that De Sica didn't want and his own cameraman, G. R. Aldo, was not trained to do. And Selznick hired Carson McCullers, Paul Gallico [1607], and finally Truman Capote to rewrite the script provided by De Sica's frequent collaborator Cesare Zavattini [194 . . .] and Mario Soldati. Clift, never the sturdiest of actors, finally gave up and turned in one of his limpest performances. The version originally released was only a little over an hour, although a reedited version, closer to De Sica's vision for the film, was released as *Terminal Station* in 1983. Dior lost to Edith Head for *Sabrina*.

998.5 • *INDOCHINE*

Paradis Films/La Générale d'Images/BAC Films/Orly Films/Ciné Cinq Production; Sony Pictures Classics (France). 1992.

Award *Foreign Language Film.*
Nomination *Actress:* Catherine Deneuve.

Deneuve plays the French owner of an Indochinese rubber plantation. She and her adopted Vietnamese daughter both fall in love with the same man during the course of the film, directed by Regis Wargnier, which covers thirty years of recent Southeast Asian history. Lushly romantic, but pretentious and muddled in its attempt to say something about the political conflicts of the region.

Because of her astonishing beauty, many were blinded to the fact that Deneuve is also a compelling and gifted actress, who gave particularly fine performances under the direction of Luis Buñuel [549 . . .] in *Belle du Jour* (1967) and *Tristana,* François Truffaut [501 . . .] in *Mississippi Mermaid* (1968) and *The Last Metro,* and Roman Polanski [395 . . .] in *Repulsion* (1965). She owes her nomination for *Indochine,* however, largely to the lack of strong leading roles for women in Hollywood's 1992 output. She lost to Emma Thompson in *Howards End.*

999 • *INFORMER, THE*

RKO Radio. 1935.

Awards *Actor:* Victor McLaglen. *Director:* John Ford. *Screenplay:* Dudley Nichols. *Score:* RKO Radio Studio Music Department, Max Steiner, head; score by Max Steiner.
Nominations *Picture:* Cliff Reid, producer. *Film Editing:* George Hively.

McLaglen plays Gypo Nolan, a rather slow-witted barfly who rats on an Irish revolutionary leader, played by Wallace Ford, to collect the reward money.

Vivid, well-staged adaptation of the novel by Liam O'Flaherty, but a little dated in style and performance. With Heather Angel, Preston Foster, Una O'Connor, and Donald Meek, among others.

McLaglen, a former soldier, prizefighter, and circus performer, began his screen career in England before coming to the United States in 1924. He spent his long career playing big lugs, most memorably in *Gunga Din* as well as numerous films directed by Ford. The story has it that Ford coaxed the Oscar-winning performance out of McLaglen by keeping the actor boozed up, disoriented, and thoroughly intimidated throughout the shooting. But it's also the kind of showy part in which even a moderately competent actor—and McLaglen was somewhat more than that—could make an impression. McLaglen's three competitors for the best actor award all came from the same film: Clark Gable, Charles Laughton, and Franchot Tone were nominated for *Mutiny on the Bounty.* Splitting the MGM bloc vote may have helped McLaglen over the top in the Oscar race.

This was the first of Ford's record four Oscars for directing. Ford had followed his brother, Francis (who appears in the role of Flynn in *The Informer*), into the movie business in 1913. Beginning as a bit player, he moved into directing, turning out endless westerns during the silent era. With the coming of sound, he became one of the most important directors in the history of Hollywood. Interestingly, although Ford won more Oscars than any other director, he never received one for a western, the genre with which he is most closely identified.

Nichols entered the annals of Oscar as the first person to refuse the award. The 1935 ceremony took place in the thick of union battles, and many members of the Screen Writers Guild, such as Nichols, chose to boycott the awards because the Academy had been founded as a sort of company union—an attempt to stave off the organization of Hollywood labor. Nichols returned his Oscar with a note saying, "To accept it would be to turn my back on nearly a thousand members who ventured everything in the long-drawn-out fight for a genuine writers' organization." (Ford, on the other hand, although he was treasurer of the Screen Directors Guild, kept his.) Two years later, when the Academy had been persuaded to accept the guilds and to divorce itself from any union-busting activities, Nichols accepted the award. A former newspaperman, Nichols came to Hollywood with the advent of sound and began his most fruitful collaboration, with Ford, in 1934, when he scripted *The Lost Patrol* and *Judge Priest*. He also directed several films, including *Sister Kenny* and *Mourning Becomes Electra*.

This was the first Oscar for Steiner, a Viennese-born composer who studied with Gustav Mahler and was an orchestra conductor before emigrating to the United States in 1914. He first worked as a Broadway orchestrator and conductor. In 1929 he went to Hollywood, where he worked primarily for RKO and Warners, although his most famous score was done for an independent production: *Gone With the Wind*.

The Informer came in second for the best picture Oscar, which went to *Mutiny on the Bounty*. Hively was third in the competition for the editing award, which Ralph Dawson won for *A Midsummer Night's Dream*.

McLaglen: 1642. Ford: 815, 952, 1200, 1642, 1901. Nichols: 30, 1200, 2092. Steiner: 16, 154, 190, 330, 365, 385, 492, 679, 747, 754, 798, 1043, 1046, 1052, 1162, 1169, 1170, 1207, 1324, 1408, 1430, 1456, 1690, 1779, 1828.

1000 • INHERIT THE WIND

STANLEY KRAMER PRODUCTIONS; UNITED ARTISTS. 1960.
NOMINATIONS *Actor:* Spencer Tracy. *Screenplay—Based on Material From Another Medium:* Nedrick Young and Harold Jacob Smith. (Young was nominated under a pseudonym, Nathan E. Douglas, which he used while he was blacklisted. The Academy restored the credit under his real name in 1992.) *Black-and-White Cinematography:* Ernest Laszlo. *Film Editing:* Frederic Knudtson.

A young southern schoolteacher, played by Dick York, breaks his state's law against teaching the theory of evolution and is brought to trial. The case attracts national attention, and two eminent attorneys volunteer their services. The prosecutor is a silver-tongued fundamentalist, played by Fredric March [184 . . .];

his adversary is a celebrated trial lawyer, played by Tracy. Commenting on the events is a cynical newspaperman played by Gene Kelly [74]. Somewhat ham-handed version of a play by Jerome Lawrence and Robert E. Lee, based quite obviously on the Scopes "monkey trial" of 1925, in which William Jennings Bryan and Clarence Darrow squared off under the jaundiced eye of reporter H. L. Mencken. Why the playwrights found it necessary to change the names of the protagonists is unclear, but it puts a glaze of artifice over both play and film. Produced and directed by Stanley Kramer [330 . . .], notorious for "message films" in which the message is often compromised, watered-down, and irrelevant. Everyone concerned with this film—especially blacklisted screenwriter Young—obviously knew that the subtext was McCarthyism and its suppression of heterodoxy. But that subtext barely peeps through the showy goings-on, the florid acting, and the historical distancing. The climactic upbraiding of the cynical journalist played by Kelly is particularly off-kilter: He's denounced for being a loner. The chief fun, however, is seeing two of the screen's most formidable actors, March and Tracy, trying to upstage each other.

Tracy lost to Burt Lancaster in *Elmer Gantry,* which also won for Richard Brooks' screenplay. The cinematography Oscar went to Freddie Francis for *Sons and Lovers.* Daniel Mandell won for editing *The Apartment.*

Tracy: 131, 271, 352, 656, 843, 1065, 1470, 1751. Young: 522. Smith: 522. Laszlo: 31, 646, 1032, 1065, 1196, 1812, 1907. Knudtson: 522, 1032, 1065, 1474, 2288.

1001 • INN OF THE SIXTH HAPPINESS, THE

20TH CENTURY-FOX. 1958.
NOMINATION *Director:* Mark Robson.

Ingrid Bergman [72 . . .] plays Gladys Aylward, an English servant who longs to go to China to work as a missionary. After scrimping and saving for years, she gets her chance. She wins over the local mandarin, played by Robert Donat [406 . . .] in his last film appearance, and captures the heart of a Nationalist general, played by Curt Jurgens. As World War II begins, she single-handedly saves a flock of orphans from the invading Japanese. Isobel Lennart's somewhat saccharine script, based on the book *The Small Woman,* by Alan Burgess, is redeemed by fine performances, handsome cinematography by Freddie Young [558 . . .], and a stirring score by Malcolm Arnold [287]. Not only are occidental actors such as Donat and Jurgens cast as Asians, but even the scenery is Western: Wales stands in for China, which was off-limits to American film crews.

Given that the film received no other nominations, Robson's directorial nomination seems rather odd. He was, however, at the peak of his career, after the multiple nominations received by his *Peyton Place* a year earlier. In subsequent years he also produced his own films. The directing Oscar went to Vincente Minnelli for *Gigi.*

Robson: 1558.

1002 • INNERSPACE

WARNER BROS. PRODUCTION; WARNER BROS. 1987.
AWARD *Visual Effects:* Dennis Muren, William George, Harley Jessup, and Kenneth Smith.

Dennis Quaid plays a navy test pilot whose assignment is to be miniaturized (à la *Fantastic Voyage*) for an experimental trip through the bloodstream of a laboratory animal. Instead, through the machinations of the bad guys, he accidentally winds up inside a mousy hypochondriac, played by Martin Short. Silly odd-coupling sci-fi farce, directed by Joe Dante, who takes the right comic-book approach to the subject, and has some good people to work with——Meg Ryan, Kevin McCarthy [515], Henry Gibson, and Orson Bean among them. But it's a little draggy, which is unfortunate, since you don't want to give anyone time to think about the implausibility of the whole thing. The special effects are just right, though, with just enough evocation of the somewhat cheesy effects of *Fantastic Voyage* to come off as both *hommage* and parody.

Muren: 5, 577, 588, 614, 997, 1071.5, 1684, 2019, 2284, 2339. Jessup: 937. Smith: 588.

1003 • INSIDE DAISY CLOVER

PARK PLACE PRODUCTION; WARNER BROS. 1965.
NOMINATIONS *Supporting Actress:* Ruth Gordon. *Color Art Direction—Set Decoration:* Robert Clatworthy; George James Hopkins. *Color Costume Design:* Edith Head and Bill Thomas.

In thirties Hollywood, Natalie Wood [1219 . . .] is a teen star facing the transition into adult roles and getting no help from her mother (Gordon), her narcissistic and possibly gay husband, played by Robert Redford [1502 . . .] in one of his first major screen roles, or the head of the studio, played by Christopher Plummer. Though the movie is meant to be satiric, screenwriter Gavin Lambert [970 . . .], adapting his own novel, and director Robert Mulligan [2101] never quite get the tone right. Over the years, the movie, which was a flop at the time, has developed a cult following, based partly on its occasional over-the-top moments, including Gordon's typically oddball performance, and partly on the perceived correspondence between Daisy's career and Wood's.

Gordon lost to Shelley Winters in *A Patch of Blue.* *Doctor Zhivago* won the awards for art direction and for Phyllis Dalton's costumes.

Gordon: 11, 567, 1536, 1728. Clatworthy: 843, 1632, 1812, 2035. Hopkins: 110, 508, 896, 1170, 1332, 1385, 1393, 1910, 1949, 1973, 2058, 2277. Head: 31, 32, 46, 305, 357, 363, 612, 636, 675, 736, 832, 894, 945, 1219, 1261, 1263, 1398, 1427, 1504, 1550, 1579, 1587, 1631, 1716, 1727, 1738, 1748, 1840, 1927, 1986, 2012, 2098, 2247, 2298. Thomas: 116, 166, 254, 866, 883, 1789, 1812, 1886, 2128.

1004 • INSIDE MOVES

GOODMARK PRODUCTION; ASSOCIATED FILM DISTRIBUTION. 1980.
NOMINATION *Supporting Actress:* Diana Scarwid.

After a suicide attempt, John Savage meets a group of variously disabled people in a bar and begins to come to terms with life. Sometimes wry, sometimes talky, sometimes mushy little film, written by Valerie Curtin [75] and Barry Levinson [75 . . .] and directed by Richard Donner. Notable for the first screen appearance of Harold Russell since his Oscar-winning performance in *The Best Years of Our Lives* thirty-four years earlier.

Scarwid made her first screen appearance in *Pretty Baby* in 1978. After losing the Oscar to Mary Steenburgen in *Melvin and Howard,* Scarwid appeared as Christina Crawford in the career-damaging *Mommie Dearest* in 1981. Her subsequent work has done little to establish her as a screen presence.

1005 • INTERIORS

JACK ROLLINS AND CHARLES H. JOFFE PRODUCTION; UNITED ARTISTS. 1978.

NOMINATIONS *Actress:* Geraldine Page. *Supporting Actress:* Maureen Stapleton. *Director:* Woody Allen. *Screenplay Written Directly for the Screen:* Woody Allen. *Art Direction—Set Decoration:* Mel Bourne; Daniel Robert.

Page plays a perfectionist but suicidal interior designer whose ex-husband, played by E. G. Marshall, marries a woman (Stapleton) who is florid, somewhat messy, but vital—in short, Page's antithesis. Page and Marshall have three daughters, played by Diane Keaton [88 . . .], Kristin Griffith, and Mary Beth Hurt. Allen's first ''serious'' movie, an examination of the relationships among these people, has strong admirers and defenders, but the majority opinion seems to be that it's pretentious and dull, a too-obvious emulation of Ingmar Bergman [111 . . .] with borrowings from Chekhov. Allen reworked the theme of the relationship of three sisters more successfully in *Hannah and Her Sisters.*

Page lost her sixth nomination to Jane Fonda in *Coming Home.* The supporting actress award went to Maggie Smith in *California Suite.* Michael Cimino won for directing *The Deer Hunter.* The screenplay Oscar went to Nancy Dowd, Waldo Salt, and Robert C. Jones for *Coming Home.* The award for art direction went to *Heaven Can Wait.*

Page: 935, 1555, 1591, 1959, 1985, 2142, 2341. Stapleton: 31, 1198, 1678. Allen: 39, 88, 294, 311.5, 461, 863, 962.5, 1267, 1636, 1647. Bourne: 671, 1418.

1006 • INTERMEZZO: A LOVE STORY

SELZNICK INTERNATIONAL PICTURES; UNITED ARTISTS. 1939.

NOMINATIONS *Black-and-White Cinematography:* Gregg Toland. *Score:* Lou Forbes.

Violinist Leslie Howard [178 . . .] falls in love with his daughter's piano teacher, Ingrid Bergman [72 . . .]. She becomes his accompanist and his mistress but inevitably has to suffer the consequences. An entertainingly sentimental romance, set to dollops of classical music, it was Bergman's first American movie. She had filmed the story first in Sweden and was spotted in that movie by Kay Brown, the New York story editor for producer David O. Selznick [497 . . .]. William Wyler [175 . . .] was set to direct and Harry Stradling [110 . . .] to film, but both were fired by Selznick shortly into production. Gregory Ratoff nominally succeeded Wyler, with Toland as cinematographer, but it is said that Toland actually directed much of the film, with Howard's help.

On Oscar night, Toland won for *Wuthering Heights.* His work on *Intermezzo,* in fact, had not even made the final ballot: For the 1939 awards, the first year in which the cinematography Oscars were divided into black-and-white and color categories, the Academy announced a first round of nominations for cinematography and then placed only two finalists in each of the two divisions on the ballot. Toland's official competitor for the award was Bert Glennon for *Stagecoach.* In addition to the classical selections, the film features theme music written by Robert Henning and Heinz Provost for the 1936 Swedish film. Forbes' arrangements lost the scoring Oscar to Richard Hageman, Frank Harling, John Leipold, and Leo Shuken for *Stagecoach.*

Toland: 407, 510, 1200, 1327, 2316. Forbes: 282, 2057, 2186, 2310.

1007 • INTERRUPTED MELODY

MGM. 1955.

AWARD *Story and Screenplay:* William Ludwig and Sonya Levien.

NOMINATIONS *Actress:* Eleanor Parker. *Color Costume Design:* Helen Rose.

Opera singer Marjorie Lawrence (Parker) is stricken with polio, but with the help of her doctor, played by Glenn Ford, she makes a comeback and sings at the Met. Standard triumph-over-adversity bi-opic, most memorable for the off-screen use of so-prano Eileen Farrell as Parker/Lawrence's singing voice. (Farrell also makes an on-screen appearance as a voice student.) The cast includes Roger Moore and Cecil Kellaway [843 . . .], and Stuart Whitman [1277] can be spotted in a bit part.

Ludwig, a contract writer for MGM, paid his dues churning out scripts for the Andy Hardy series and second-string musicals such as *The Great Caruso*. On the latter, he first collaborated with Levien, a Holly-wood veteran who began her screenwriting career providing scenarios for silent movies.

Parker lost her third and final nomination to Anna Magnani in *The Rose Tattoo*. The costuming Oscar went to Charles LeMaire for *Love Is a Many-Splendored Thing*.

Levien: 1920. Parker: 328, 534. Rose: 130, 578, 629, 755, 817, 980, 1309, 1335, 1599.

1007.5 • *INTERVIEW WITH THE VAMPIRE*

Geffen Pictures Production; Geffen Pictures through Warner Bros. 1994.
Nominations *Art Direction—Set Decoration:* Dante Ferretti; Francesca Lo Schiavo. *Original Score:* Elliot Goldenthal.

A young writer (Christian Slater) interviews a man he has met on the nighttime streets of San Francisco and hears a fantastic tale: The man, Louis (Brad Pitt), is two hundred years old, having been turned into a vampire at the end of the eighteenth century when, after losing his wife and child, he was so sunk in grief that he succumbed to the advances of a suave vampire, Lestat, played by Tom Cruise [260]. The film follows Louis' un-life, as he and Lestat take on a third com-panion, a twelve-year-old girl, Claudia (Kirsten Dunst). Louis and Claudia free themselves from the oppressive Lestat and journey to Europe, where they encounter still more vampires, played by Antonio Banderas and Stephen Rea [472.5]. Superbly stylish horror movie—moody, bloody, perverse, and often very funny—that transcends its genre with an acute psychological portrait of what it might actually be like to be a vampire. Anne Rice wrote the screenplay—very likely with some uncredited help from the direc-tor, Neil Jordan [472.5]—based on her own novel. But Rice, like many of the devotees of the novel, was appalled at the casting of Cruise as Lestat, a role in which many envisioned Daniel Day-Lewis [992.5 . . .] or Jeremy Irons [1689]. Then, just be-fore the film's release, Rice took back her earlier denunciation of the movie in a full-page newspaper ad, praising Cruise's performance. Though Rice's re-cantation smells suspiciously like a publicity stunt, Cruise is in fact quite good, playing with a sinister and sophisticated wit that most were surprised to find within his range. The movie is almost stolen, how-ever, by young Dunst, who convincingly plays a ma-ture woman trapped in a child's body. Her omission from the supporting actress nominees was surprising, especially after an equally impressive performance in a very different role, the young Amy in *Little Women*. (Some suspected that Anna Paquin's win the previous year for *The Piano* made Academy members reluctant to nominate another child actress.) The film's atmo-sphere comes not only from the art direction and score but also from the cinematography of Philippe Rousselot [900 . . .]. The makeup is by Stan Win-ston [45 . . .]. The Oscar for art direction went to *The Madness of King George*. Hans Zimmer won for the scoring of *The Lion King*.

Ferretti: 14, 27.5, 859. Lo Schiavo: 14, 859.

1008 • *INVADERS, THE*

Ortus; Columbia (United Kingdom). 1942.
Award *Original Story:* Emeric Pressburger.
Nominations *Picture:* Michael Powell, producer. *Screenplay:* Rodney Ackland and Emeric Pressburger.

Five Nazis, survivors of a sunken U-boat, try to make their way across Canada. Fine, suspenseful war-time melodrama, with the usual propagandistic edge: The enemy is sneaky and cowardly. The cast includes Anton Walbrook, Eric Portman, Leslie Howard [178 . . .], Raymond Massey [1], Glynis Johns

[1969], Finlay Currie, and Laurence Olivier [268 . . .] in a cameo as a French-Canadian fur trapper. Directed by Powell, with music by Ralph Vaughan Williams. Now generally known by its original British title, *49th Parallel*.

Pressburger, born in Hungary, began his career as a screenwriter in Germany and Austria and went to England in 1936. *The Invaders* is the beginning of his long collaboration with Powell, with whom he formed a production company known as the Archers. From 1942 to 1956 they co-wrote, -produced, and -directed a series of opulent and impressive films that included *Black Narcissus, The Tales of Hoffman,* and *The Red Shoes.*

The best picture award went to *Mrs. Miniver,* which also won for the screenplay by George Froeschel, James Hilton, Claudine West, and Arthur Wimperis. Pressburger: 1489, 1677. Powell: 1489, 1677.

1009 • INVESTIGATION OF A CITIZEN ABOVE SUSPICION

VERA FILMS S.P.A. PRODUCTION; COLUMBIA (ITALY). 1971.
AWARD *Foreign Language Film, 1970.*
NOMINATION *Story and Screenplay—Based on Factual Material or Material Not Previously Published or Produced:* Elio Petri and Ugo Pirro.

A policeman, the head of the Rome homicide division, murders his mistress and then decides to plant clues that should lead his investigators to him. His theory is that he is above suspicion by virtue of his office. Sure enough, the investigators turn in the direction of a leftist that they would like to see convicted. Effective, if unpleasant, thriller with a political edge, directed by Petri. Music by Ennio Morricone [308 . . .]. The writing award went to Paddy Chayefsky for *The Hospital.*
Pirro: 748.

1010 • INVISIBLE AGENT

UNIVERSAL. 1942.
NOMINATION *Special Effects:* John Fulton, photographic; Bernard B. Brown, sound.

The formula for invisibility that passed from hand to hand in Universal films starting with *The Invisible Man* in 1933 now goes to war, as Jon Hall uses it to thwart Nazis and the Japanese, including Peter Lorre (in the same makeup he used before the war to play the nice Mr. Moto, perhaps). Cornball fun, directed by Edwin L. Marin. The special effects award went to *Reap the Wild Wind.*
Fulton: 269, 1011, 1012, 2012, 2310. Brown: 93, 96, 269, 919, 1011, 1125, 1560, 1896, 2028, 2260.

1011 • INVISIBLE MAN RETURNS, THE

UNIVERSAL. 1940.
NOMINATION *Special Effects:* John P. Fulton, photographic; Bernard B. Brown and William Hedgecock, sound.

Cedric Hardwicke frames Vincent Price for a murder Hardwicke committed. Luckily for Price, he has access to Universal's invisibility potion. Okay sequel to the 1933 classic. Directed by Joe May, with John Sutton, Nan Grey, and Cecil Kellaway [843 . . .]. The special effects award was won by *The Thief of Bagdad.*
Fulton: 269, 1010, 1012, 2012, 2310. Brown: 93, 96, 269, 919, 1010, 1125, 1560, 1896, 2028, 2260.

1012 • INVISIBLE WOMAN, THE

UNIVERSAL. 1941.
NOMINATION *Special Effects:* John Fulton, photographic; John Hall, sound.

Mad scientist John Barrymore turns Virginia Bruce invisible, and she uses it to get even with him. Thin but pleasant comedy, with Barrymore doing a parody of his brother Lionel's Kringelein character in *Grand Hotel.* The cast, directed by A. Edward Sutherland, includes Charlie Ruggles, Oscar Homolka [972], Margaret Hamilton, and Shemp Howard. The special effects award went to *I Wanted Wings.*
Fulton: 269, 1010, 1011, 2012, 2310.

1013 • INVITATION, L'

GROUPE 5 GENÈVE-TÉLÉVISION SUISSE ROMANDE-CITEL FILMS-PLANFILM (PARIS) PRODUCTION (SWITZERLAND). 1973.
NOMINATION *Foreign Language Film.*

A man throws a party at his country house for the people who work in his office, and the group discovers things they never knew about one another. Lightly diverting film directed by Claude Goretta. The Oscar went to *Day for Night*.

1014 • IPHIGENIA

GREEK FILM CENTRE PRODUCTION (GREECE). 1977.
NOMINATION *Foreign Language Film*.

The Greek fleet is becalmed on its way to Troy to recover Helen of Troy, and the priest Calchas persuades Agamemnon that he must sacrifice his daughter, Iphigenia. Her mother, Clytemnestra, played by Irene Papas, opposes the sacrifice. Last in the trilogy of plays by Euripides directed by Michael Cacoyannis [2346] that began with *Electra* in 1962 and continued with *The Trojan Women* (1972). Too overstated to be cinematically successful. The Oscar went to *Madame Rosa*.

1015 • IRENE

IMPERADIO PICTURES; RKO RADIO. 1940.
NOMINATION *Score*: Anthony Collins.

Anna Neagle, in the title role, is sent by her employer to do some work for a wealthy customer, played by Ray Milland [1208]. He is so taken with her he gets her a job as a model for a designer played by Roland Young [2117]. Since this also involves pretending to be a socialite, complications ensue. The outcome is easy to guess, however. Somewhat labored version of a musical first seen on Broadway in 1919, so it was something of an antique. (It had also been filmed as a silent in 1926.) This version was designed as a vehicle for Neagle, who was a huge star in England but never made an equivalent impression in the States. It was directed by her husband, Herbert Wilcox. The cast also includes May Robson [1119], Billie Burke [1307], and Arthur Treacher. The Oscar went to Alfred Newman for *Tin Pan Alley*.

Collins: 1458, 1971.

1016 • IRISH EYES ARE SMILING

20TH CENTURY-FOX. 1944.
NOMINATION *Scoring of a Musical Picture*: Alfred Newman.

Dick Haymes plays Ernest R. Ball, turn-of-the-century composer of songs like the title tune, "Mother Machree," "Will You Love Me in December as You Do in May?" and others. One of the countless cornball period musicals churned out by Fox in the forties, this one is distinguished by the presence of Metropolitan Opera greats Leonard Warren and Blanche Thebom, the acerbic Monty Woolley [1569 . . .], some Technicolored production numbers choreographed by Hermes Pan [481 . . .], but not much else. Gregory Ratoff directed, with June Haver, Anthony Quinn [1226 . . .], Maxie Rosenbloom, and Veda Ann Borg. The scoring award went to Carmen Dragon and Morris Stoloff for *Cover Girl*.

Newman: 31, 34, 46, 72, 138, 182, 226, 333, 334, 347, 375, 428, 437, 457, 476, 495, 542, 690, 797, 833, 952, 953, 959, 962, 1082, 1088, 1213, 1278, 1362, 1397, 1475, 1616, 1655, 1849, 1868, 1883, 1921, 2043, 2046, 2091, 2258, 2286, 2294, 2316.

1017 • IRMA LA DOUCE

MIRISCH-PHALANX PRODUCTION; UNITED ARTISTS. 1963.
AWARD *Scoring of Music—Adaptation or Treatment*: André Previn.
NOMINATIONS *Actress*: Shirley MacLaine. *Color Cinematography*: Joseph LaShelle.

A Parisian cop, played by Jack Lemmon [91 . . .], falls for Irma (MacLaine), a Parisian streetwalker, and resorts to a variety of ruses to make her exclusively his. Frantic, itchy farce, a little too sniggery for contemporary tastes, but very popular at the time. Directed by Billy Wilder [91 . . .] from a screenplay he cowrote with I. A. L. Diamond [91 . . .]. Originally a stage musical that began life in Paris, moved to London and finally to New York in 1960. The screen version eliminated the song lyrics, but their tunes, by Marguerite Monnot, are the basis of the score, which earned Previn the third of his four Oscars.

This was MacLaine's third nomination, and like the first two, for *Some Came Running* and *The Apartment*, she received it for playing a woman of questionable virtue. She lost to Patricia Neal in *Hud*.

LaShelle, who was also nominated this year along

with three other eminent cinematographers for *How the West Was Won,* lost to Leon Shamroy for *Cleopatra.*

Previn: 172, 609, 769, 1034, 1044, 1097, 1393, 1550, 1592, 2064, 2077, 2161. MacLaine: 91, 1859, 2020, 2152. LaShelle: 91, 357, 428, 709, 953, 1149, 1283, 1391.

1018 • IRON MASK, THE

UNITED ARTISTS. 1928–29.

NOMINATION *Interior Decoration:* William Cameron Menzies. (Disputed nomination.)

D'Artagnan, played by Douglas Fairbanks, comes to the aid when the scheming Rochefort tries to pass off an imposter as the heir to the throne of France. Based on Alexandre Dumas' *Ten Years After,* this part-talkie was Fairbanks' last swashbuckler. It was rereleased in 1940 with a narration by Douglas Fairbanks, Jr. Directed by Allan Dwan.

For many years Menzies has been cited in lists of Oscar nominees for his work on this film. But in fact, there were no official announcements of nominations for the 1928–29 awards; the Academy revealed only the names of the winners at the banquet in 1930, presenting the art direction award to Cedric Gibbons for *The Bridge of San Luis Rey* "and other pictures." The names of others under consideration by the individual branches of the Academy that actually voted the awards this year were kept in in-house records. In later years nominees were given certificates and official recognition, so that in published records of Academy nominees, the also-rans of 1928–29 have been listed as if they were official nominees. But some confusion has crept in about which of the several films Menzies worked on during this eligibility period put him under consideration for the award. Some lists published by the Academy have cited this film; others, including the most recent revision by the Academy of its nominations and winners list, say he was being considered for his work on *Alibi* and *The Awakening.* With that in mind, we've included all three films in this book.

Menzies: 38, 112.5, 311, 568, 798, 2010.

1019 • IRONWEED

TAFT ENTERTAINMENT PICTURES/KEITH BARISH PRODUCTION; TRI-STAR. 1987.

NOMINATIONS *Actor:* Jack Nicholson. *Actress:* Meryl Streep.

In Depression-era Albany, New York, Francis Phelan (Nicholson), an alcoholic bum who was once a baseball player, tries to make connection again with the family he abandoned after accidentally causing the death of his infant son. Streep is his equally down-and-out lover who is on the verge of death. Evocative, melancholy film that unfortunately lacks dramatic shape, so that its bleakness finally becomes tiring. William Kennedy adapted his Pulitzer-winning novel, and it's directed by Hector Babenco [1099] with a stunning cast: Carroll Baker [119], Michael O'Keefe [826], Diane Venora, Fred Gwynne, Margaret Whitton, Tom Waits [1483], Nathan Lane, Ted Levine, and Frank Whaley, among others. The two leads are at the peak of their powers, but the film failed with both critics and audiences. Nicholson lost to Michael Douglas in *Wall Street* and Streep to Cher in *Moonstruck.*

Nicholson: 395, 595, 658.5, 672, 1135, 1481, 1625, 1678, 2020. Streep: 472, 521, 725, 1111, 1512, 1598, 1821, 1876.

1020 • IS PARIS BURNING?

TRANSCONTINENTAL FILMS-MARIANNE PRODUCTIONS; PARAMOUNT (U.S./FRANCE). 1966.

NOMINATIONS *Black-and-White Cinematography:* Marcel Grignon. *Black-and-White Art Direction—Set Decoration:* Willy Holt; Marc Frederix and Pierre Guffroy.

The question in the title was asked by Adolf Hitler (played here by Billy Frick), who ordered the torching of the city in 1944, and the film is a three-hour attempt to explain why not. The book, by Larry Collins and Dominique Lapierre, was a best-seller; the film, written by Gore Vidal and Francis Ford Coppola [65 . . .] and directed by René Clement, was a flop, even with a cast that included Jean-Paul Belmondo, Charles Boyer [36 . . .], Leslie Caron [1113 . . .], George Chakiris [2244], Kirk Douglas [130 . . .] as General Patton, Glenn Ford as General Bradley, Yves

Montand, Anthony Perkins [730], Simone Signoret [1724 . . .], and Orson Welles [407 . . .]. Absence of dramatic structure and the usual distractions of celebrity-spotting fatally weaken the movie.

Who's Afraid of Virginia Woolf? won for Haskell Wexler's cinematography and for the art direction of Richard Sylbert and George James Hopkins.

Guffroy: 2021.

1021 • *ISADORA*

ROBERT AND RAYMOND HAKIM-UNIVERSAL LTD. PRODUCTION; UNIVERSAL (UNITED KINGDOM). 1968.

NOMINATION *Actress:* Vanessa Redgrave.

Redgrave plays Isadora Duncan, one of the major creative forces in modern dance, and a woman who shocked people on two continents. This fine but somewhat loose-jointed biopic was bungled in its initial release by a studio that couldn't quite figure how to market it. After it flopped, it was reedited in a shorter version and titled *The Loves of Isadora*. Director Karel Reisz succeeded in getting a third version in distribution in 1987. Whichever version one sees, it's Redgrave's extraordinary performance that makes it work, although it has a fine score by Maurice Jarre [558 . . .] and strong support from James Fox, Jason Robards [54 . . .], and Bessie Love [296], among others. The best actress race resulted in a tie: Katharine Hepburn for *The Lion in Winter* and Barbra Streisand for *Funny Girl.*

Redgrave: 263, 954.5, 1066, 1285, 1354.

1022 • *ISLAND AT THE TOP OF THE WORLD, THE*

WALT DISNEY PRODUCTIONS; BUENA VISTA. 1974.

NOMINATION *Art Direction—Set Decoration:* Peter Ellenshaw, John B. Mansbridge, Walter Tyler, and Al Roelofs; Hal Gausman.

At the turn of the century a wealthy English explorer (Donald Sinden) sets out to find his missing son, accompanied by an American archaeologist (David Hartman), a French balloonist (Jacques Marin), and an Eskimo guide, played by Mako [1753]. They discover a strange island inhabited by Viking warriors. Dud attempt by Disney to repeat the success of *20,000 Leagues Under the Sea* with an adventure that looks like it was written by Jules Verne but wasn't. (It's based on a book by Ian Cameron, *The Lost Ones.*) The absence of star power—*20,000 Leagues,* after all, had James Mason, Kirk Douglas, and Peter Lorre—is only one of the film's problems. Robert Stevenson [1284] directed, and the score is by Maurice Jarre [558 . . .]. The art direction award went to *The Godfather, Part II.*

Ellenshaw: 166, 219, 1284. Mansbridge: 166. Tyler: 357, 1101, 1716, 1738, 1748, 1959, 2012, 2208. Gausman: 4, 166, 1284, 2185.

1023 • *ISLANDS IN THE STREAM*

PETER BART/MAX PALEVSKY PRODUCTION; PARAMOUNT. 1977.

NOMINATION *Cinematography:* Fred J. Koenekamp.

George C. Scott [73 . . .] plays an artist living on an island in the Bahamas at the beginning of World War II. After a visit by his three sons, he decides to return to the mainland, but the war changes his plans. Based on a novel by Ernest Hemingway, the film naturally involves a variety of tests of manhood. It's expensively produced, glossy, and dull, though Scott acts his heart out, and he's well supported by Claire Bloom, David Hemmings, Gilbert Roland, Susan Tyrrell [652], and Hart Bochner. Franklin Schaffner [1541] directed, and the score is by Jerry Goldsmith [152.5 . . .]. Koenekamp lost to Vilmos Zsigmond for *Close Encounters of the Third Kind.*

Koenekamp: 1541, 2126.

1024 • *IT HAPPENED ON 5TH AVENUE*

ROY DEL RUTH; ALLIED ARTISTS. 1947.

NOMINATION *Original Story:* Herbert Clyde Lewis and Frederick Stephani.

A group of homeless men take over a Manhattan mansion while the owner is away, and change his life and that of his daughter when they return. Minor comedy made up of intelligent borrowings from the plays of George S. Kaufman and Moss Hart [297 . . .] and the films of Frank Capra [1025 . . .]. Directed by Roy Del Ruth, with Gale Storm, Don DeFore, Ann Harding [927], Charlie Ruggles, and Victor Moore. The writing award went to Valentine Davies for *Miracle on 34th Street*—it was a busy year in New York City.

1025 • *IT HAPPENED ONE NIGHT*

COLUMBIA. 1934.

AWARDS *Picture:* Harry Cohn, producer. *Actor:* Clark Gable. *Actress:* Claudette Colbert. *Director:* Frank Capra. *Adaptation:* Robert Riskin.

Heiress Ellie Andrews (Colbert) jumps ship—literally—after her father (Walter Connolly) disapproves of her choice of a husband. On a bus bound for New York, a reporter (Gable) recognizes her and decides to claim the reward that's been posted for the runaway heiress after first spending enough time with her to get a story. They fall in love, hard-boiled reporter softens, and spoiled rich girl learns humility. A legendary film whose success (along with the contemporaneous success of *The Thin Man*) made the romantic comedy one of the major genres of the thirties. Without it, would we have had such classics as *My Man Godfrey, The Awful Truth, Nothing Sacred, Easy Living, Bringing Up Baby,* or *Libeled Lady?* Certainly, without it we wouldn't have such indelible images as "the walls of Jericho," Colbert hitchhiking, the busload of passengers singing "The Man on the Flying Trapeze," and Colbert fleeing her wedding, her long veil trailing in the breeze. Or such essential elements of Hollywood mythology as the stories that Gable's taking off his shirt to reveal a bare chest almost ruined the underwear industry or that the creators of Bugs Bunny were inspired by Gable's chomping down on a carrot. No sixty-year-old film is going to retain its freshness, of course; there have been too many imitations of *It Happened* over the years, and there have been romantic comedies, such as the ones mentioned above, that have equaled or bettered it. But the charm of its performers, the skill and inventiveness of its direction, the lovely filigree of character bits, the wit of the dialogue, have endured. It became the first film to sweep all five of the "top" Oscar categories. (Only two others, *One Flew Over the Cuckoo's Nest* and *The Silence of the Lambs,* have achieved that feat.) It's also the first best picture winner that still shows up on people's lists of their favorite films. In that respect, it

signals the maturing of the sound film, and serves as well as any movie as a milestone for defining the golden age of Hollywood—the period that lasted until the outbreak of World War II—when movie attendance reached unprecedented highs and the major studios raked in unprecedented profits.

The irony here is that Columbia was not one of the major studios. Along with Universal, it is usually classified as a "major minor"—a notch above "poverty row" studios such as Republic and Monogram, but not in the league of MGM, Fox, Paramount, Warners, or RKO, all of which owned theaters that could serve as outlets for their product. (Columbia and Universal would find that not owning theaters worked to their advantage after 1948, when an antitrust ruling forced the majors to divest themselves of their theaters.) So the Oscar sweep of *It Happened* was particularly sweet to the studio head, Harry Cohn. Like other moguls of the golden age, Cohn was a self-made man, an immigrant's son who worked through various jobs before beginning his career in the fledgling film industry at Universal, working for its founder, Carl Laemmle. With his brother, Jack Cohn, and Joe Brandt, Harry founded what became Columbia in 1920. In 1932 he prevailed over a power play by Jack and became unquestioned head of the studio, which he ran like a petty tyrant, gouging, spying, and bullying. So disliked was Cohn that a famous quip about the crowd that showed up for his funeral in 1958— "It just proves that if you give the people what they want, they'll turn out for it"—has been attributed to everyone from Ben Hecht [78 . . .] to Red Skelton.

Gable was not the first choice for the lead of *It Happened.* The script had been prepared with Robert Montgomery [904 . . .] in mind, but MGM refused to loan him out, providing Gable instead—it is said as a punishment for Gable's refusal to take a role he had been offered. Though audiences later made him "King of Hollywood," Gable was just one leading man among many in 1934. He had begun his Hollywood career in the twenties with little success, but his stage work had brought him to the attention of Lionel Barrymore [723 . . .], who arranged for a screen test and helped get him cast in *A Free Soul,* the film that launched Gable's career. The Oscar and its attendant publicity helped make him a major star. Though he is one of the movies' enduring icons, thanks to his great sex appeal and especially to his performance as Rhett Butler in *Gone With the Wind,* his reign as King was in fact quite brief. His film career was interrupted by World War II, which he entered shortly after his wife, Carole Lombard [1401], was killed in a plane crash. He was decorated for his service in the army air force. His postwar films, however, were mostly undistinguished, and audiences soon discovered other icons such as Marlon Brando [583 . . .] and James Dean [593 . . .]. He died in 1961, shortly after filming *The Misfits.*

Colbert likewise was not the first choice for the film. Myrna Loy, Miriam Hopkins [165], and Margaret Sullavan [2073] turned it down. Bette Davis [46 . . .] was eager to play the role, but Warners wouldn't loan her out for it, producing a bit of Oscar irony: Davis was loaned out instead for *Of Human Bondage,* which earned her universal acclaim and produced a storm of controversy when she was not nominated for best actress. By Oscar night it looked as if Davis might actually be the first person to win the award on a write-in vote. Colbert was so certain of it, in fact, that she made no plans to attend the ceremony. She was summoned to the awards at the last minute, as she was preparing to board a train for New York. (Davis came in third in the race, after Norma Shearer in *The Barretts of Wimpole Street.*) Years later, Colbert would inadvertently repay Davis by withdrawing from *All About Eve* because of a back injury, handing Davis one of her signature roles. Born in France, Colbert had come to the States as a child and began her acting career on Broadway. She made her screen debut in a film directed by Capra, *For the Love of Mike,* in 1927. After playing rather ludicrous vamps in the Cecil B. DeMille epics *The Sign of the Cross* and *Cleopatra,* she made a solid impression in the melodramatic *Imitation of Life.* But by revealing her gift for comedy, *It Happened One Night* established her screen persona more effectively than any previous film. She continued her film career into the early fifties, then retired except for occasional appearances, including

several TV and Broadway roles when she was well into her eighties—and looked thirty years younger.

Of all Capra's major films, *It Happened* is the least afflicted with the tendency to sentimentality and soft-minded populism that have stuck the epithet "Capracorn" on his work. Born in Sicily, raised in California, and educated at what is now Caltech, Capra began his film work as a writer and director of shorts for Hal Roach and Mack Sennett. After breaking into features with several films starring Harry Langdon, Capra was hired by Columbia in 1928 and soon became the studio's most valuable property. Today, after Alfred Hitchcock [1171 . . .] and perhaps Cecil B. DeMille [412 . . .], Capra may be the best-known name among general audiences of all the golden age directors.

How much of Capra's success he actually owes to Riskin will continue to be debated. Riskin had gotten into the movie business before World War I when two shirt makers for whom he worked invested in the movies and made him a producer of comedy shorts. The war interrupted that career, but after it he joined up with his brother, Everett Riskin [114 . . .], to produce short films and plays. He also dabbled in magazine writing. After losing money in the stock market crash, the Riskins went to Hollywood; both wound up at Columbia, Robert as a writer and Everett as a producer. In 1931 Capra filmed *The Miracle Woman,* based on a play written by Robert, who warned Capra that the play had been a flop and that the film would be, too. It was. The same year, Riskin contributed dialogue to a Capra film, *Platinum Blonde,* that became one of Jean Harlow's earliest hits. With *American Madness* in 1932 and *Lady for a Day* in 1933, Capra and Riskin became a team. "Frank provided the schmaltz and Bob provided the acid," observed screenwriter Philip Dunne [495 . . .], who, like many, felt that the social conscience of the Capra films stemmed much more from Riskin's New Deal liberalism than from any political views of Capra's. Though Capra in later years was reluctant to acknowledge the writer's influence, most of his major work —with the exception of *Mr. Smith Goes to Washington* and *It's a Wonderful Life*—was done with Riskin. On the other hand, *all* of Riskin's major work was done with Capra.

Cohn: 1488. Gable: 798, 1387. Colbert: 1623, 1828. Capra: 1033, 1119, 1206, 1366, 1370, 2325. Riskin: 905, 1119, 1366, 2325.

1026 • IT HAPPENED TOMORROW
ARNOLD PRODUCTIONS; UNITED ARTISTS. 1944.

NOMINATIONS *Sound Recording:* Jack Whitney. *Scoring of a Dramatic or Comedy Picture:* Robert Stolz.

Reporter Dick Powell is given the power to see tomorrow's headlines today, which is a great advantage until he turns up in those future headlines. Nicely handled fantasy, directed by René Clair and written by Clair and Dudley Nichols [30 . . .], with Linda Darnell, Jack Oakie [818], and Edgar Kennedy. The sound award went to E. H. Hansen for *Wilson*. Max Steiner won for the score of *Since You Went Away*.

Whitney: 729, 862, 955, 1884, 2031, 2050, 2095. Stolz: 1896.

1027 • IT HAPPENS EVERY SPRING
20TH CENTURY-FOX. 1949.

NOMINATION *Motion Picture Story:* Shirley W. Smith and Valentine Davies.

Scientist Ray Milland [1208] discovers a chemical that repels wood, so he becomes a superstar baseball pitcher. Formulaic fantasy with a good deal of charm, directed by Lloyd Bacon, with Jean Peters, Paul Douglas, Ed Begley [1985], and Jessie Royce Landis. The Oscar went to Douglas Morrow for *The Stratton Story*.

Davies: 776, 1325.

1028 • IT SHOULD HAPPEN TO YOU
COLUMBIA. 1954.

NOMINATION *Black-and-White Costume Design:* Jean Louis.

Gladys Glover, played by Judy Holliday [262], is getting nowhere in the big city when she suddenly hits on a way to make her name known all over New York: She rents a billboard in Columbus Circle and puts her name on it. This makes her an instant celebrity, to the dismay of her infatuated neighbor, played by Jack Lemmon [91 . . .] in his film debut. Bright, eminently likable little satire whose target, the obsession with fame, is still current today, when people jostle for their fifteen Warholian minutes of fame. Written by Ruth Gordon [11 . . .] and Garson Kanin [11 . . .] and directed by George Cukor [262 . . .]. Holliday is super, as is Lemmon, and they're well supported by Peter Lawford, as a wolfish executive who wants Holliday for her prime location, and Michael O'Shea as a sleaze who wants to cash in on Gladysmania. Oddly underrated by the Academy, as were other Gordon-Kanin-Cukor films such as *Adam's Rib* and *Pat and Mike*. Louis lost to Edith Head for *Sabrina*.

Louis: 20, 126, 170, 262, 732, 744, 1065, 1521, 1640, 1812, 1858, 1910, 2064.

1029 • IT STARTED IN NAPLES
PARAMOUNT AND CAPRI PRODUCTION; PARAMOUNT. 1960.

NOMINATION *Color Art Direction—Set Decoration:* Hal Pereira and Roland Anderson; Sam Comer and Arrigo Breschi.

When his brother dies, lawyer Clark Gable [798 . . .] goes to Naples to settle the estate and bring his brother's young son back to America. But the boy's aunt, Sophia Loren [1280 . . .], protests. You know the rest: Uncle meets aunt, uncle loses aunt, uncle gets aunt. Not as much fun as it might have been: Fifty-nine-year-old Gable and twenty-six-year-old Loren were not exactly made for each other. This was Gable's next-to-last film. He died shortly after making *The Misfits* the next year. Directed by Melville Shavelson [951 . . .], who also wrote the screenplay with Jack Rose [951 . . .] and Suso Cecchi D'Amico [367]. Naples is handsomely filmed by Robert Surtees [130 . . .]. The art direction Oscar went to *Spartacus*.

Pereira: 278, 357, 363, 426, 450, 736, 956, 1219, 1504, 1570, 1631, 1674, 1716, 1727, 1738, 1840, 1897, 1959, 2012, 2098, 2200, 2208. Anderson: 278, 363, 426, 450, 649, 1194, 1214, 1219, 1452, 1570, 1668, 1674, 1880, 1994. Comer: 278, 357, 426, 450, 726, 736, 925, 956, 1101, 1214, 1219,

1443, 1570, 1631, 1674, 1727, 1738, 1748, 1959, 1975, 1994, 2012, 2098, 2200, 2208.

1030 • IT STARTED WITH EVE

UNIVERSAL. 1942.

NOMINATION *Scoring of a Musical Picture:* Charles Previn and Hans Salter.

Robert Cummings persuades perfect stranger Deanna Durbin to pose as his fiancée to please his cranky old millionaire father, Charles Laughton [1387 . . .], who is supposedly on his deathbed. But then Laughton is taken with Durbin and decides not to die, which complicates things when Cummings' real fiancée shows up. One of the better vehicles concocted by Universal for Durbin, with a good script by Norman Krasna [535 . . .] and Leo Townsend based on a story by Hans Kräly [1137.5 . . .]. Directed by Henry Koster [214]. The scoring award went to Ray Heindorf and Heinz Roemheld for *Yankee Doodle Dandy.*

Previn: 306, 668, 1229, 1485, 1870, 1896. Salter: 62, 340, 399, 1307, 2060.

1031 • IT'S A GREAT FEELING

WARNER BROS. 1949.

NOMINATION *Song:* "It's a Great Feeling," music by Jule Styne, lyrics by Sammy Cahn.

Jack Carson and Dennis Morgan are trying to get a movie made, but Carson's ego keeps getting in the way. Meanwhile, Morgan is romancing Doris Day [1572]. No *Singin' in the Rain* by a long shot, but still an amusing lampoon of Hollywood types, as well as a showcase for Warners talent. Directed by David Butler. There are cameo appearances by Gary Cooper [701 . . .], Joan Crawford [1319 . . .], Errol Flynn, Sydney Greenstreet [1248], Danny Kaye, Patricia Neal [956 . . .], Edward G. Robinson, Jane Wyman [246 . . .], Eleanor Parker [328 . . .], Ronald Reagan, and directors Michael Curtiz [79 . . .], King Vidor [378 . . .], and Raoul Walsh. The song Oscar went to Frank Loesser for "Baby, It's Cold Outside," from *Neptune's Daughter.*

Styne: 74, 696, 737, 920, 921, 1719, 2072, 2110, 2343. Cahn: 74, 163, 182, 696, 915, 926, 1056,

1216, 1524, 1587, 1692, 1708, 1719, 1859, 1907, 2016, 2064, 2072, 2103, 2110, 2125, 2263, 2264, 2315, 2343.

1032 • IT'S A MAD, MAD, MAD, MAD WORLD

CASEY PRODUCTION; UNITED ARTISTS. 1963.

AWARD *Sound Effects:* Walter G. Elliott.

NOMINATIONS *Color Cinematography:* Ernest Laszlo. *Sound:* Gordon E. Sawyer, sound director, Samuel Goldwyn Studio Sound Department. *Song:* "It's a Mad, Mad, Mad, Mad World," music by Ernest Gold, lyrics by Mack David. *Music Score—Substantially Original:* Ernest Gold. *Film Editing:* Frederic Knudtson, Robert C. Jones, and Gene Fowler, Jr.

When word of a buried treasure gets out in L.A., all sorts of people go nuts trying to find it. Policeman Spencer Tracy [131 . . .] is the one in charge of trying to keep order. Enormous, overblown comedy that goes on and on and on for more than three hours without much in the way of pacing or narrative or character development or anything that holds one's interest. Produced and directed by Stanley Kramer [330 . . .], who was not particularly known, before or after, as a maker of funny films. A lot of the people involved are TV or stage comics whose shtick is too large-scale for the movies—especially a movie filmed in Cinerama. The cast includes Milton Berle, Sid Caesar, Buddy Hackett, Ethel Merman, Mickey Rooney [115 . . .], Dick Shawn, Phil Silvers, Terry-Thomas, Jonathan Winters, Edie Adams, Dorothy Provine, Eddie "Rochester" Anderson, Jim Backus, Ben Blue, William Demarest, Peter Falk [1377 . . .], Paul Ford, Leo Gorcey, Edward Everett Horton, Buster Keaton, Don Knotts, Carl Reiner, the Three Stooges, Joe E. Brown, Andy Devine, Sterling Holloway, ZaSu Pitts, Arnold Stang, Stan Freberg, Norman Fell, Jimmy Durante, Jack Benny, and Jerry Lewis.

The Oscar for cinematography went to Leon Shamroy for *Cleopatra. How the West Was Won* took the awards for sound and for Harold Kress' editing. The best song was "Call Me Irresponsible," by James Van Heusen and Sammy Cahn, from *Papa's Delicate Condition.* John Addison won for the score of *Tom Jones.*

Laszlo: 31, 646, 1000, 1065, 1196, 1812, 1907. Sawyer: 33, 91, 184, 214, 393, 730, 864, 882, 973, 974, 1511, 1592, 2244, 2297, 2310. Gold: 630, 1474, 1776. David: 122, 371, 402, 861, 882, 963, 2223. Knudtson: 522, 1000, 1065, 1474, 2288. Jones: 264, 430, 843.

1033 • *IT'S A WONDERFUL LIFE*

LIBERTY FILMS; RKO RADIO. 1946.

NOMINATIONS *Picture:* Frank Capra, producer. *Actor:* James Stewart. *Director:* Frank Capra. *Sound Recording:* John Aalberg. *Film Editing:* William Hornbeck.

Distressed that his building and loan institution in the small town of Bedford Falls is losing out to the bank run by the grasping Mr. Potter, played by Lionel Barrymore [723 . . .], George Bailey (Stewart) contemplates suicide, only to be rescued at the last minute by Clarence, played by Henry Travers [1371]. Clarence turns out to be an angel, and he gives George a chance to see what Bedford Falls would have been like if George Bailey had never been born. It's not a pretty sight, and George happily returns to his wife, played by Donna Reed [732], and family, and learns that the citizens of Bedford Falls have come to the rescue of his lending institution and that they'll all have a merry Christmas together. Enormously popular fantasy that now ranks alongside *Gone With the Wind, Casablanca,* and *The Wizard of Oz* as one of the favorite American films. But like *Wizard,* it was something of a flop at the time of its release. Repeated showings on TV, usually at Christmastime, however, and its widespread availability on videocassette (because the copyright on the film had been allowed to lapse, numerous companies released it on tape) solidified it in the hearts of its admirers. That said, there is also a sturdy contingent that finds the movie saccharine and simple-minded, pandering to a nostalgia for a small-town America that never existed. The vogue for the film seemed to reach a peak during the Reagan era, when celebrations of "basic American values" were in vogue—at the same time that people who ran lending institutions were behaving more like Mr. Potter than like George Bailey. Ironically, many of the people who brought this paean to the American

way into existence were victims of the witch-hunts of the fifties; the script was worked on by Dalton Trumbo [273 . . .], Michael Wilson [287 . . .], and Dorothy Parker [1845 . . .], all of whom were blacklisted, as well as by Clifford Odets, who escaped blacklisting by admitting that he had been a communist and by naming others. The screenplay is credited to Capra and to Frances Goodrich [25 . . .] and Albert Hackett [25 . . .]. The cast also includes Thomas Mitchell [962 . . .], Beulah Bondi [807 . . .], Ward Bond, and Gloria Grahame [130 . . .], with Ellen Corby [972] in a bit part.

It's a Wonderful Life marks the end of the major phase of Capra's career, which, starting with *Lady for a Day* in 1933, had been one of the most celebrated in Hollywood history. Driven by a desire for recognition, the Sicilian-born Capra had become an ultra-American director, crafting an image of the country as home to upright individualists like George Bailey, Mr. Deeds, Mr. Smith, and the eccentrics of *You Can't Take It With You.* He had spent the war years creating the propagandistic documentary series *Why We Fight.* But he found himself at the Academy Awards facing a more successful film, *The Best Years of Our Lives,* that suggested that simple American virtues had eroded, and that we may have known why we fought but weren't so sure what we would do now that the fighting was over. *Best Years* took the awards for picture and for director William Wyler, as well as for actor Fredric March and editor Daniel Mandell. (The sound award went to John Livadary for *The Jolson Story.*) Capra made only five more comparatively unsuccessful films, from *State of the Union* in 1948 to *A Pocketful of Miracles* in 1961, though he lived on till 1991, when he died at the age of ninety-four.

The film did help relaunch Stewart's career, which had been interrupted by World War II, during which he served with great distinction, rising to the rank of colonel in the army air force. George Bailey has become one of his most famous roles, and Stewart has called it a personal favorite.

Capra: 1025, 1119, 1206, 1366, 1370, 2325. Stewart: 73, 876, 1370, 1563. Aalberg: 407, 923,

959, 1102, 1978, 1991, 2030, 2166, 2213. Hornbeck: 768, 973, 1579.

1034 • IT'S ALWAYS FAIR WEATHER

MGM. 1955.

NOMINATIONS *Story and Screenplay:* Betty Comden and Adolph Green. *Scoring of a Musical Picture:* André Previn.

World War II buddies Gene Kelly [74], Dan Dailey [2258], and Michael Kidd have a reunion ten years later and find that their lives have gone rather sour. A spree on the town, however, sends them off with a new appreciation for one another and new direction to their lives. Time has removed the barbs from this musical satire, but the three principals are first-rate dancers, which makes their big numbers a treat, especially the one in which they dance with garbage-can lids on their feet. Kelly, who codirected the film with Stanley Donen, also does a great routine on roller skates. The cast includes Cyd Charisse and Dolores Gray. The movie, however, was a box-office flop.

Comden and Green had taken on the movies in *Singin' in the Rain* and the theater in *The Band Wagon,* so it was to be expected that they'd get around to television—and specifically to TV commercials—in this one. They lost to William Ludwig and Sonya Levien for *Interrupted Melody.* The scoring award went to Robert Russell Bennett, Jay Blackton, and Adolph Deutsch for *Oklahoma!*

Comden: 141. Green: 141. Previn: 172, 609, 769, 1017, 1044, 1097, 1393, 1550, 1592, 2064, 2077, 2161.

1035 • IVANHOE

MGM. 1952.

NOMINATIONS *Picture:* Pandro S. Berman, producer. *Color Cinematography:* F. A. Young. *Scoring of a Dramatic or Comedy Picture:* Miklos Rozsa.

Ivanhoe (Robert Taylor) loves the fair Rowena, played by Joan Fontaine [441 . . .], who is the ward of his father, Cedric (Finlay Currie). But Cedric opposes their marriage, so Ivanhoe has gone off to the crusades with Richard the Lion-Hearted. He returns to find things in a pretty mess, what with the intrigues of Sir Brian de Bois-Guilbert, played by George Sanders [46], and Prince John (Guy Rolfe). Eventually he has to fight to save the life of Rebecca, played by Elizabeth Taylor [318 . . .], the daughter of the Jew Isaac (Felix Aylmer), as well as vanquish Bois-Guilbert and choose between Rebecca and Rowena. Big, handsome MGMization of the Walter Scott novel that's also just a wee bit dull, owing to the merely competent direction of Richard Thorpe, the plodding screenplay of Noel Langley and Aeneas Mac-Kenzie, and Robert Taylor's typically stiff performance. On the plus side, twenty-year-old Elizabeth Taylor is astonishingly beautiful. The abiding mystery here is that *Ivanhoe* was MGM's entry in the best picture contest, and not *The Bad and the Beautiful,* which won five Oscars, more than any other film not nominated for best picture. Or for that matter, that MGM's real best picture of the year, *Singin' in the Rain,* was not among the contenders. The best picture award went to *The Greatest Show on Earth,* an upset winner over the front-runner, *High Noon.*

The cinematography award went to Winton C. Hoch and Archie Stout for *The Quiet Man.* Dimitri Tiomkin won for the score of *High Noon.*

Berman: 40, 656, 754, 1899, 2115. Young: 558, 1151, 1429, 1737. Rozsa: 175, 566, 567, 604, 1069, 1070, 1085, 1208, 1227, 1644, 1872, 1890, 1968, 2050, 2304.

1036 • JACK LONDON

BRONSTON; UNITED ARTISTS. 1944.

NOMINATION *Scoring of a Dramatic or Comedy Picture:* Frederic E. Rich.

Michael O'Shea plays the turn-of-the-century writer in a second-rate biopic that mixes his adventures with some anachronistic wartime anti-Japanese propaganda. Susan Hayward [973 . . .] is the love interest. Directed by Alfred Santell. The scoring award went to Max Steiner for *Since You Went Away.*

Rich: 1900.

1037 • JACOB THE LIAR

VEB/DEFA PRODUCTION (GERMAN DEMOCRATIC REPUBLIC). 1976.

NOMINATION *Foreign Language Film.*

In a Polish ghetto during World War II, Jacob becomes a hero to his community by telling lies that keep the hopes of his fellow Jews alive. Bittersweet comedy, directed by Frank Beyer. The Oscar went to *Black and White in Color.*

1038 • JACQUELINE SUSANN'S ONCE IS NOT ENOUGH

HOWARD W. KOCH PRODUCTION; PARAMOUNT. 1975.

NOMINATION *Supporting Actress:* Brenda Vaccaro.

Deborah Raffin plays a young woman named January (which should give you a clue about this movie, even if the presence of the novelist's name in the title hasn't already). She falls in with a bad lot: the jet-set coterie of her movie producer father, played by Kirk Douglas [130 . . .]. Among others, these include some cliché predatory lesbians, played by Alexis Smith and Melina Mercouri [1426], a boozy, brawling writer (David Janssen), a playboy (George Hamilton), and a sex-crazed magazine editor, played by Vaccaro. Wretched junk from a lot of very talented people: writer Julius Epstein [365 . . .], cinematographer John Alonzo [395], art director John DeCuir [29 . . .], and composer Henry Mancini [122 . . .]. Directed by an Oscar-winning cinematographer, Guy Green [820]. Perhaps the worst movie for which anyone ever received an acting nomination, it did little for Vaccaro's career. She made her screen debut in *Midnight Cowboy,* but her career slumped in the later seventies. She can occasionally be seen in TV movies. The Oscar went to Lee Grant for *Shampoo.*

1039 • JAGGED EDGE

COLUMBIA PICTURES PRODUCTION; COLUMBIA. 1985.

NOMINATION *Supporting Actor:* Robert Loggia.

Lawyer Glenn Close [199 . . .] agrees to defend a San Francisco newspaper editor, Jeff Bridges [1139 . . .], accused of murdering his wife. She also falls in love with him, which becomes a big problem when Loggia, her investigator, turns up evidence that Bridges is guilty. Good nail-biting thriller that asks a little too much suspension of disbelief at times, particularly since Close, Bridges, Loggia, and Peter Coyote, who plays the prosecutor, are performers who radiate so much intelligence you can't believe they haven't spotted the holes in the plot. Still, the screenplay helped Joe Eszterhas *(Basic Instinct)* become one of Hollywood's highest-paid writers. Directed by Richard Marquand, with a score by John Barry [259 . . .]. The cast includes Leigh Taylor-Young and Lance Henriksen, and if Trekkers look quick, they can spot Michael Dorn without his Klingon makeup.

Loggia, who trained at the Actors Studio, has been in movies since 1956, when he appeared in *Somebody Up There Likes Me,* but *Jagged Edge* was the first film in which he attracted widespread critical attention. He has subsequently been seen in more prominent character roles, most notably as the toy manufacturer in *Big* who taps out "Heart and Soul" with Tom Hanks on a giant keyboard. The Oscar went to Don Ameche for *Cocoon.*

1040 • JANIE

WARNER BROS. 1944.

NOMINATION *Film Editing:* Owen Marks.

Joyce Reynolds plays a teenager who's crazy for guys in uniform and finally settles on Robert Hutton. Extremely dated home-front romantic comedy directed by Michael Curtiz [79 . . .], with Edward Arnold, Ann Harding [927], Robert Benchley, and Hattie McDaniel [798]. The Oscar went to Barbara McLean for *Wilson.*

Marks: 365.

1041 • JAWS

UNIVERSAL-ZANUCK/BROWN PRODUCTION; UNIVERSAL. 1975.

AWARDS *Sound:* Robert L. Hoyt, Roger Heman, Earl Madery, and John Carter. *Original Score:* John Williams. *Film Editing:* Verna Fields.

NOMINATION *Picture:* Richard D. Zanuck and David Brown, producers.

A great white shark turns up off a New England

resort island at the peak of tourist season, and it takes three men to get rid of it: the landlubber police chief, played by Roy Scheider [49 . . .]; a puckish ichthyologist, played by Richard Dreyfuss [803]; and a macho old salt, played by Robert Shaw [1252]. Funny, scary blockbuster that gets into people's heads the way *Psycho* did—making possible the famous ad line for *Jaws 2:* "Just when you thought it was safe to go back in the water." The movie's huge success launched the phenomenal career of director Steven Spielberg [416 . . .], who was the only director of a best picture nominee that year not to receive a nomination. (His slot went to Federico Fellini for *Amarcord.*) This was the beginning of Spielberg's mysteriously troubled relationship with the Oscars that would culminate a decade later when his film *The Color Purple* received eleven nominations but none for its director. In the case of *Jaws,* as with *E.T. The Extra-Terrestrial,* many felt that Spielberg was being punished for too much success. There were also rumors that the film had been "saved" by its editor, Fields, particularly since there were plenty of stories about difficulties and disasters during the shoot: The mechanical sharks repeatedly malfunctioned, and one of the boats used in the film sank, taking cameras and film with it. Since Spielberg was a Hollywood newcomer, with only a few TV movies and the feature *The Sugarland Express* (1974) to his credit, it was therefore easy to dismiss his achievement as beginner's luck aided by a skilled crew. Now that Spielberg's films from *Jaws* to *Jurassic Park* dominate the list of the biggest money-makers of all time, and he's attained artistic stature as well as Oscars with *Schindler's List,* nobody's dismissing that achievement. On the other hand, though Spielberg's subsequent career has scotched the rumor that Fields saved the film, she undoubtedly helped more than anyone to create the pacing and tension that make *Jaws* such a mind and gut grabber.

The ominous chugging theme of *Jaws* made Williams the most famous composer in Hollywood. Though he had previously won the Oscar for *Fiddler on the Roof,* this was his first original score—as opposed to adaptation—to take the award. Since then, he has been associated with many of the biggest films

ever made—the *Star Wars* series, the *Superman* films, the Indiana Jones cycle—and has accumulated more nominations than any musician except Alfred Newman [31 . . .].

The best picture Oscar went to *One Flew Over the Cuckoo's Nest.*

Heman: 226, 346, 418, 458, 520, 2286. Williams: 6, 260, 403, 416, 588, 613, 614, 659, 805, 933, 937, 982, 996, 997, 1047, 1596, 1652, 1679, 1684, 1701, 1764.65, 1916, 1977, 2107, 2126, 2194, 2293, 2322. Fields: 65. Zanuck: 580, 2198. Brown: 658.5, 2198.

1042 • *JAZZ SINGER, THE*

WARNER BROS. 1927–28.

AWARD *Special Award:* Warner Bros., for producing *The Jazz Singer,* the pioneer outstanding talking picture, which has revolutionized the industry.

NOMINATIONS *Adaptation:* Alfred Cohn. *Engineering Effects:* Nugent Slaughter.

Jakie Rabinowitz (Al Jolson) makes it big in show-biz under the name Jack Robin, but this leads to a split with his father, a cantor, played by Warner Oland. Jack redeems himself by filling in when his father is too ill to perform the Kol Nidre on Yom Kippur. Directed by Alan Crosland, with Eugenie Besserer as Jakie's mother, William Demarest [1058], and Roscoe Karns. Legendary as the film that, as the Academy put it, revolutionized the industry, and still watchable today, even though everything about it—from the acting to the story to Jolson's performing style—is archaic. Though its fame is as the first talkie, there are really only a few moments of speech in it. After a huge success with their 1926 *Don Juan,* which featured a synchronized score and sound effects, Warners had planned to move gradually into sound. Only Jolson's songs were to be recorded for *The Jazz Singer,* but when the performer ad-libbed the famous "You ain't heard nothin' yet" as an intro to a number, a decision was made to leave it in and to have Jolson and Besserer ad-lib a bit of dialogue later in the film. The sensational audience reaction to these bits of speech, which contrast sharply with the miming and title cards in the rest of the movie, emboldened

Warners to move swiftly into production on their first "all-talking" feature, the 1928 *Lights of New York*—now long-forgotten. There are a few ironies attendant on the birth of the talkies. Jolson was not the first choice for the role. George Jessel, who had starred in the play on Broadway, was asked to do it but wanted too much money. Eddie Cantor was a second choice, but declined. And the man who was perhaps most responsible for hastening the arrival of sound, Sam Warner, never got a chance to witness the revolution he created: He died a few days before the opening of *The Jazz Singer*. Although Hollywood was in the throes of converting to sound by the time the first Academy Awards were presented in May 1929, the Academy ruled *The Jazz Singer* ineligible for competition for best picture, believing it unfair to let sound films compete with silents. In the two categories in which it was allowed to compete, the awards went to Benjamin Glazer for the adaptation of *Seventh Heaven* and to Roy Pomeroy for the engineering effects of *Wings*.

1043 • JAZZ SINGER, THE

WARNER BROS. 1952.

NOMINATION *Scoring of a Musical Picture:* Ray Heindorf and Max Steiner.

Danny Thomas plays the cantor's son whose showbiz career causes a split with his father (Eduard Franz). Needless, goopy remake, wasting the talents of director Michael Curtiz [79 . . .] and stars Peggy Lee [1554], Mildred Dunnock [119 . . .], and Tom Tully [330]. About the best things one can say about it is that some of the music is nice and that it's a lot better than the next remake, the 1980 debacle that starred Neil Diamond and Laurence Olivier [268 . . .]. The scoring award went to Alfred Newman for *With a Song in My Heart*.

Heindorf: 331, 479, 666, 930, 1204, 1385, 1408, 1430, 1690, 1719, 1750, 1910, 2058, 2186, 2243, 2310, 2318. Steiner: 16, 154, 190, 330, 365, 385, 492, 679, 747, 754, 798, 999, 1046, 1052, 1162, 1169, 1170, 1207, 1324, 1408, 1430, 1456, 1690, 1779, 1828.

1044 • JESUS CHRIST SUPERSTAR

UNIVERSAL-NORMAN JEWISON-ROBERT STIGWOOD PRODUCTION; UNIVERSAL. 1973.

NOMINATION *Scoring—Original Song Score and/or Adaptation:* André Previn, Herbert Spencer, and Andrew Lloyd Webber.

Young tourists in Israel do their own musical version of the last week in the life of Christ. Curious film version of a curious phenomenon: a stage musical that grew out of a concept album by composer Lloyd Webber and lyricist Tim Rice [32.5 . . .]. The movie has its admirers, and it has to be said that the performers—Ted Neeley (Jesus), Carl Anderson (Judas), Yvonne Elliman (Mary Magdalene), and Josh Mostel (Herod)—give it everything they've got. But the feel-good effect of the stage version is lost on screen, and the play-within-a-play framing, provided by writer-director Norman Jewison [659 . . .], is pointless. The handsome cinematography is by Douglas Slocombe [1066 . . .]. The scoring award went to Marvin Hamlisch for *The Sting*.

Previn: 172, 609, 769, 1017, 1034, 1097, 1393, 1550, 1592, 2064, 2077, 2161. Spencer: 1766.

1045 • JESUS OF MONTREAL

MAX FILMS/GERARD MITAL PRODUCTION (CANADA). 1989.

NOMINATION *Foreign Language Film.*

A theater group in Montreal decides to stage a Passion play, but their modernized version causes the church to try to close them down. Lively satire that takes on a few too many targets but manages to hit most of them. Directed by Denys Arcand. The Oscar went to *Cinema Paradiso*.

1046 • JEZEBEL

WARNER BROS. 1938.

AWARDS *Actress:* Bette Davis. *Supporting Actress:* Fay Bainter.

NOMINATIONS *Picture:* Hal B. Wallis, with Henry Blanke, producers. *Cinematography:* Ernest Haller. *Score:* Max Steiner.

Davis plays an airheaded antebellum New Orleans belle whose stubborn individuality and her efforts to arouse the jealousy of her beau, played by Henry

Fonda [815 . . .], lead to grief. She atones for her big sin, which amounts to wearing the wrong-color dress to a ball, by heroic service during an outbreak of yellow fever. Superb version of a cornball melodrama, one of the many times that a Davis performance, and Warners' production values, triumphed over questionable material. Davis is ably abetted by her leading man, as well as director William Wyler [175 . . .] and a screenplay by Clements Ripley, Abem Finkel [1779], and an up-and-coming screenwriter by the name of John Huston [24 . . .]. The solid cast includes George Brent, Donald Crisp [952], Spring Byington [2325], and Eddie ''Rochester'' Anderson. It is often said that *Jezebel* was Warners' attempt to get the jump on *Gone With the Wind* or that it was a consolation prize to Davis for not getting the part of Scarlett O'Hara. Interestingly both cinematographer Haller and composer Steiner would go on to work on *GWTW,* and Anderson appears in both films.

Though Davis had previously won an Oscar for *Dangerous, Jezebel* was the film that marked her ascendance as a superstar. It was her first major role after an epic battle with the studio. Infuriated by the poor quality of the post-Oscar roles she was offered, she tried to break her contract and sailed for England, intending to make films there. A court ruling in the studio's favor returned her to the fold, but she had apparently gotten the message across, for the studio paid her court costs and offered her a series of superior scripts. The lead in *Jezebel* was much desired by both Tallulah Bankhead and Miriam Hopkins [165]. The latter had played the role on stage, and losing out to Davis would spark a famous feud that raged off stage during the filming of *The Old Maid* (1939), in which both Davis and Hopkins starred. Though her second Oscar was her last, Davis would accumulate ten nominations before her death in 1989.

Also nominated as best actress in *White Banners,* Bainter was the first person to receive simultaneous nominations in both leading and supporting performance categories. She made her Broadway debut in 1912 but didn't make her first film until 1934. A reliable character actress, she was also nominated for her last film, *The Children's Hour,* in 1961. She died in 1968.

The best picture Oscar went to *You Can't Take It With You.* Joseph Ruttenberg won for the cinematography of *The Great Waltz.* The scoring award went to Alfred Newman for *Alexander's Ragtime Band.*

Davis: 46, 484, 492, 1162, 1182, 1369, 1456, 1462.5, 1908, 2248. Bainter: 393, 2266. Wallis: 17, 55, 85, 164, 343, 365, 676, 689, 712, 965, 1095, 1162, 1248, 1482, 1727, 1779, 2233, 2318. Blanke: 17, 90, 712, 1169, 1315, 1457, 1936, 2136. Haller: 55, 679, 798, 1174, 1319, 2248. Steiner: 16, 154, 190, 330, 365, 385, 492, 679, 747, 754, 798, 999, 1043, 1052, 1162, 1169, 1170, 1207, 1324, 1408, 1430, 1456, 1690, 1779, 1828.

1047 • JFK

WARNER BROS. 1991.

AWARDS *Cinematography:* Robert Richardson. *Film Editing:* Joe Hutshing and Pietro Scalia.

NOMINATIONS *Picture:* A. Kitman Ho and Oliver Stone, producers. *Supporting Actor:* Tommy Lee Jones. *Director:* Oliver Stone. *Screenplay Based on Material From Another Medium:* Oliver Stone and Zachary Sklar. *Sound:* Michael Minkler, Gregg Landaker, and Tod A. Maitland. *Original Score:* John Williams.

New Orleans D.A. Jim Garrison, played by Kevin Costner [482], becomes obsessed with the assassination of John F. Kennedy and starts his own investigation, which leads him to accuse New Orleans businessman Clay Shaw (Jones) of involvement in a conspiracy to kill the president. But Shaw, it seems, is only the tip of the iceberg . . . Provocative, infuriating movie that takes endless liberties with the facts —for starters, it turns the showboating Garrison (who had the gall to appear in the film as Earl Warren) into a naive shining knight. With all its giddy paranoia, the movie is a stunning demonstration of what a talented filmmaker can do when he gets the wrong idea in his head: He makes something both worthless and watchable. Taken as fact, the film is absurd. Taken as a fantasia on the American obsession with the Kennedy assassination, it can get into your head and under your skin. On the plus side are some terrific performances from Gary Oldman (a creepily banal Lee Harvey Oswald), Joe Pesci [806 . . .], Donald Sutherland, Jack Lemmon [91 . . .], Walter Matthau [709 . . .], Kevin Bacon, and Ed Asner. And the Oscars honored the real heroes of the movie: Richardson shot film that Hutshing and Scalia could seamlessly blend with documentary footage, so that one is never quite sure, for example, where the Zapruder film ends and Stone's begins. On the other hand, Costner is no more successful at sustaining a New Orleans accent than he was at the British one he essayed in *Robin Hood: Prince of Thieves.* The scenes with Garrison and his wife, played by Sissy Spacek [364 . . .], resort to the moldiest clichés, of the "Honey, please stop reading the Warren Commission Report and come to bed" variety. Costner is also given a big courtroom speech heavily indebted to *Mr. Smith Goes to Washington,* at the end of which he walks away in a golden glow, surrounded by his adoring and now reconciled family. For all his contention that the establishment done it, Stone displays a reverence for conventional family values that would warm Dan Quayle's heart. Stone's treatment of Clay Shaw and his coterie displays some of the rankest homophobia to be seen since *Cruising* in 1980.

The Academy clearly admires Stone's audacity, but it preferred the less politically eccentric *The Silence of the Lambs,* its director, Jonathan Demme, and its screenwriter, Ted Tally. Jones lost to Jack Palance in *City Slickers.* The sound Oscar was won by *Terminator 2: Judgment Day.* The scoring award went to Alan Menken for *Beauty and the Beast.*

Richardson: 260, 1584. Hutshing: 260. Ho: 260. Stone: 260, 1313, 1584, 1746. Jones: 734.5. Minkler: 58, 260, 398, 413.5, 606, 2144. Landaker: 614, 1652, 1888.5. Maitland: 260. Williams: 6, 260, 403, 416, 588, 613, 614, 659, 805, 933, 937, 982, 996, 997, 1041, 1596, 1652, 1679, 1684, 1701, 1764.65, 1916, 1977, 2107, 2126, 2194, 2293, 2322.

1048 • JOAN OF ARC

SIERRA PICTURES; RKO RADIO. 1948.

AWARDS *Color Cinematography:* Joseph Valentine, William V. Skall, and Winton Hoch. *Color Costume Design:* Dorothy Jeakins and Karinska. *Special Award:* Walter Wanger, for distinguished service to the industry in adding to its moral stature by his production.

NOMINATIONS *Actress:* Ingrid Bergman. *Supporting Actor:* Jose Ferrer. *Color Art Direction—Set Decoration:* Richard Day; Edwin Casey Roberts and Joseph Kish. *Scoring of a Dramatic or Comedy Picture:* Hugo Friedhofer. *Film Editing:* Frank Sullivan.

Bergman plays the Maid of Orleans in an adaptation by Maxwell Anderson [48] and Andrew Solt of Anderson's play *Joan of Lorraine,* in which Bergman had appeared on Broadway. Ferrer is the Dauphin, and scattered through the huge cast are such familiar faces as Gene Lockhart [36], Ward Bond, John Ireland [53], and Cecil Kellaway [843 . . .]. Much too long and talky, it was a major box-office disappointment. It was the last film of director Victor Fleming [798], who had seen Bergman's Broadway Joan and persuaded producer Wanger to back the film project. Fleming, cinematographer Valentine, and set decorator Roberts all died shortly after completing the film —a presage of the ill fortune that would follow others associated with the project.

Though the film was designed as a religious experience, the sins of two of its principals, Bergman and Wanger, would make headlines soon after its release. Bergman's leaving her husband and child for director Roberto Rossellini [1519] shocked many people precisely because of the saintly image she had presented in films such as *Joan of Arc* and *The Bells of St. Mary's.* And Wanger would be tried and jailed two years later for shooting Jennings Lang, agent and lover of Wanger's wife, Joan Bennett. One of Hollywood's most important independent producers, Wanger never won an Oscar but received two special awards, including one for his service as president of the Academy. The award for *Joan of Arc* was seen by some as the Academy's attempt to make amends for not nominating the film for best picture. Wanger was forced into bankruptcy by the film's failure. He later recouped his fortunes but lost them again on *Cleopatra.*

Jeakins and Karinska were, along with the designer of the black-and-white costumes for *Hamlet,* the first winners of the newly introduced costume award. Their win was greeted with bitterness by Edith Head [31 . . .], who was nominated for *The Emperor Waltz.* "To my mind," Head wrote in her memoirs, "there was no way Ingrid Bergman's sackcloths and suits of armor could win over my Viennese finery."

Bergman was greatly disappointed by the failure of the film, which followed one flop, *Arch of Triumph* (1948), and would be succeeded by another, *Under Capricorn* (1949). This stall in her Hollywood career may have contributed to her decision to pursue her fortunes in Europe with Rossellini. The Oscar went to Jane Wyman for *Johnny Belinda.*

Ferrer was two years away from his Oscar triumph in *Cyrano de Bergerac* when he was nominated for his performance as the Dauphin. A successful Broadway actor-director, he made his film debut in *Joan of Arc* and was responsible for the few good notices the picture received. He lost to Walter Huston in *The Treasure of the Sierra Madre.*

The Red Shoes won for art direction and Brian Easdale's score. The Oscar for editing was won by Paul Weatherwax for *The Naked City.*

Valentine: 668, 776, 1229, 1896, 2291. Skall: 96, 208, 1170, 1317, 1453, 1644, 1668, 1822, 2102. Hoch: 1642, 1807. Jeakins: 393, 509, 832, 882, 1385, 1391, 1432, 1748, 1881, 2012, 2238. Karinska: 864. Wanger: 413, 706, 1901. Bergman: 72, 111, 173, 701, 749, 1378. Ferrer: 473, 1363. Day: 22, 102, 235, 487, 510, 560, 569, 797, 833, 864, 952, 1175, 1397, 1477, 1666, 1949, 2056, 2120, 2276. Roberts: 353, 760. Kish: 13, 1062, 1812, 1840. Friedhofer: 2, 21, 184, 187, 214, 267, 2303, 2336.

1049 • JOAN OF PARIS

RKO RADIO. 1942.

NOMINATION *Scoring of a Dramatic or Comedy Picture:* Roy Webb.

A Resistance fighter, played by Michele Morgan, sacrifices herself to save some Allied pilots. Enjoyable, even stirring, adventure-romance in which the wartime propaganda never gets in the way. Directed by Robert Stevenson [1284], with Paul Henreid, Thomas Mitchell [962 . . .], May Robson [1119], and Alan Ladd. The scoring Oscar went to Max Steiner for *Now, Voyager.*

Webb: 640, 665, 969, 1394, 1639.

1050 • JOB'S REVOLT

MAFILM TARSULAS STUDIO/HUNGARIAN TELEVISION (BUDAPEST)/ZDF (MAINZ) PRODUCTION (HUNGARY). 1983.

NOMINATION *Foreign Language Film.*

An elderly Jewish couple must find a way to protect their adopted son when the Nazis begin to round up the Jews. Directed by Imre Gyöngyössi and Barna Kabay. The Oscar went to *Fanny & Alexander.*

1051 • JOE

CANNON GROUP PRODUCTION; CANNON RELEASING. 1970.

NOMINATION *Story and Screenplay—Based on Factual Material or Material Not Previously Published or Produced:* Norman Wexler.

Peter Boyle plays a hard hat who discovers that the businessman (Dennis Patrick) he's met in a bar not only hates hippies, too, but has murdered his daughter's druggie boyfriend. They join forces to hunt for the runaway daughter. A sleeper hit of the day, now long-forgotten and terminally dated. Its celebrity at the time seemed to have something to do with the fact that the movie both satirizes and sympathizes with its titular hero, thereby attracting the widest possible audience. Now best remembered as the first major film of director John G. Avildsen [1712] and as the debut film for Susan Sarandon [107 . . .], who plays the daughter. Wexler lost to Francis Ford Coppola and Edmund H. North for *Patton.*

Wexler: 1780.

1052 • JOHNNY BELINDA

WARNER BROS. 1948.

AWARD *Actress:* Jane Wyman.

NOMINATIONS *Picture:* Jerry Wald, producer. *Actor:* Lew Ayres. *Supporting Actor:* Charles Bickford. *Sup-*

porting Actress: Agnes Moorehead. *Director:* Jean Negulesco. *Screenplay:* Irmgard Von Cube and Allen Vincent. *Black-and-White Cinematography:* Ted Mc-Cord. *Black-and-White Art Direction–Set Decoration:* Robert Haas; William Wallace. *Sound Recording:* Warner Bros. Studio Sound Department, Nathan Levinson, sound director. *Scoring of a Dramatic or Comedy Picture:* Max Steiner. *Film Editing:* David Weisbart.

Wyman plays Belinda McDonald, a deaf-mute living with her father (Bickford) and aunt (Moorehead) on a remote Canadian island. Belinda is thought by the villagers to be retarded, but a visiting doctor (Ayres) helps her learn sign language and demonstrate her intelligence. Then she is raped by the local bully and bears a child, and because she is unable to communicate what happened, the village suspects the doctor of being the father. Well-done melodrama that was considered daring in its day because of its presentation of rape and illegitimacy. A strong cast and effective location filming—Mendocino, California, fills in for Nova Scotia—give the script's earnestness heart and its tear-jerking credibility.

The film was a particular triumph for Wyman, who had started as a bit player and chorus girl in 1936 and gradually worked her way into larger parts, finally getting a big break, after a decade in Hollywood, with *The Lost Weekend* in 1945. Her work on *Johnny Belinda* coincided with the breakup of her marriage to Ronald Reagan. Her film career began to fade in the mid-fifties, and she turned to TV work. In the eighties she had a long run on the prime-time soap opera *Falcon Crest.*

Ayres was starting a second career in Hollywood. He had begun by playing opposite Greta Garbo [84 . . .] in the 1929 silent *The Kiss,* which he followed up with the lead in the best picture winner *All Quiet on the Western Front.* But beginning at the top often means you have no way to go but down, and his career through most of the thirties was unspectacular until, after making a solid impression as Katharine Hepburn's alcoholic brother in *Holiday,* he landed the lead in *Young Dr. Kildare* in 1938, beginning a successful string of Kildare features into the early forties. But

when the United States entered the war, Ayres declared himself a conscientious objector, and his career stopped. He served with distinction, however, as a noncombatant medical corpsman and returned to films after the war. *Johnny Belinda* is the most memorable of his postwar films, but Ayres continued to appear in films and on TV into this decade, well into his eighties. He lost the Oscar to Laurence Olivier in *Hamlet,* which also took the best picture award.

Johnny Belinda has the distinction of being one of the thirteen films that received nominations in all four acting categories. (For a complete list, see the entry for *Coming Home.*) Bickford lost to Walter Huston in *The Treasure of the Sierra Madre,* Moorehead to Claire Trevor in *Key Largo.*

A Romanian-born former painter and stage designer, Negulesco started his career as an assistant producer and second unit director. In the forties he became a director for Warners, turning out a series of well-crafted and relatively low-key films, such as *The Mask of Dimitrios* (1944). In the fifties, after his success with *Johnny Belinda,* he moved to 20th Century-Fox, where he became a specialist in CinemaScope romances such as *How to Marry a Millionaire* and *Three Coins in the Fountain.* While critics prefer his earlier work at Warners, it's the audience-pleasers that he's currently most remembered for. He lost to John Huston for *The Treasure of the Sierra Madre.*

Huston also won the writing award for *Treasure.* The Oscar for cinematography went to William Daniels for *The Naked City,* which also won for Paul Weatherwax's editing. *Hamlet* won for art direction. The award for sound went to *The Snake Pit.* Brian Easdale won the scoring Oscar for *The Red Shoes.*

Wyman: 246, 1241, 2320. Wald: 1319, 1558, 1875. Bickford: 651, 1868. Moorehead: 963, 1239, 1372. McCord: 1881, 2161. Haas: 1170. Levinson: 16, 30, 343, 385, 531, 689, 710, 712, 790, 930, 965, 1169, 1621, 1690, 1768, 1769, 1779, 1930, 1949, 2058, 2318. Steiner: 16, 154, 190, 330, 365, 385, 492, 679, 747, 754, 798, 999, 1043, 1046, 1162, 1169, 1170, 1207, 1324, 1408, 1430, 1456, 1690, 1779, 1828.

1053 • JOHNNY COME LATELY

CAGNEY PRODUCTIONS; UNITED ARTISTS. 1943.
NOMINATION *Scoring of a Dramatic or Comedy Picture:* Leigh Harline.

Newspaperman James Cagney [79 . . .] is hired as editor of a paper owned by elderly widow Grace George and leads a crusade against corrupt local officials. Pleasant but not special, the movie takes a wrong turn into melodrama in the last third, but it features a gallery of fine character actors, including Marjorie Main [601], Hattie McDaniel [798], and Margaret Hamilton. Directed by William K. Howard from a screenplay by John Van Druten [749]. The first film from the independent production company founded by Cagney and his brother William [2318], it was a box-office failure.

The scoring Oscar was won by Alfred Newman for *The Song of Bernadette.*

Harline: 1576, 1607, 1838, 1851, 2312, 2327.

1054 • JOHNNY DOUGHBOY

REPUBLIC. 1942.
NOMINATION *Scoring of a Musical Picture:* Walter Scharf.

Jane Withers stars as a stagestruck teenager who runs away from home and gets into show business, entertaining the troops as part of the Hollywood Victory Caravan. Flimsy little musical with a gimmick: The cast is filled with kiddie stars such as Bobby Breen, Baby Sandy, and Spanky McFarland, most of whom, like Withers, who later gained fame as Josephine the Plumber in TV commercials, were at the end of their popularity. The Oscar went to Ray Heindorf and Heinz Roemheld for *Yankee Doodle Dandy.*

Scharf: 174, 274, 665, 737, 864, 921, 991, 1305, 2285.

1055 • JOHNNY EAGER

MGM. 1942.
AWARD *Supporting Actor:* Van Heflin.

Lana Turner [1558], as the daughter of District Attorney Edward Arnold, has the misfortune to fall in love with gangster Johnny Eager, played by Robert Taylor. MGM was never very good at gangster fare—that was Warners' forte—because of its high-gloss style and its tendency to cast such waxworks as Turner and Taylor in roles for which Warners might have used Davis and Bogart. Heflin, as Taylor's alcoholic buddy, steals the show, not to mention the Oscar. Directed by Mervyn LeRoy [1662 . . .] from a screenplay by John Lee Mahin [352 . . .] and James Edward Grant [1809].

Heflin was discovered on Broadway by Katharine Hepburn [24 . . .], who had him cast in *A Woman Rebels* (1936) and later in the stage version of *The Philadelphia Story.* But *A Woman Rebels* was one of Hepburn's most notorious flops, and when the film of *The Philadelphia Story* was being cast, Heflin's role went to James Stewart, who won the Oscar for it. Heflin's own Oscar helped restart his career, and he went on to a variety of second leads and character roles, the most memorable being the besieged homesteader in *Shane* and the mad bomber in *Airport.* The latter was his last film role; he died of a heart attack in 1971.

1056 • JOKER IS WILD, THE

A.M.B.L. PRODUCTION; PARAMOUNT. 1957.
AWARD *Song:* "All the Way," music by James Van Heusen, lyrics by Sammy Cahn.

Frank Sinatra [732 . . .] plays nightclub singer Joe E. Lewis, who falls afoul of the mob, loses his voice, and makes a comeback as a comedian. Jeanne Crain [1575] and Mitzi Gaynor are the women in his life, and the cast includes Eddie Albert [887 . . .], Beverly Garland, Jackie Coogan, and Sophie Tucker. Good biopic, with a role tailor-made for Sinatra. Directed by Charles Vidor.

The Oscar-winning song was such a big hit that the film was retitled *All the Way* when it was rereleased in 1966. According to popular-music historian David Ewen, Van Heusen composed the song to fit the plot: "The big jump musically at the end of the second bar to the middle of the third bar was specifically designed to be difficult for him to sing, and he was supposed to break down dramatically," Van Heusen said.

Van Heusen: 171, 173, 787, 915, 926, 1524, 1587, 1708, 1859, 1907, 2016, 2064, 2263. Cahn:

74, 163, 182, 696, 915, 926, 1031, 1216, 1524, 1587, 1692, 1708, 1719, 1859, 1907, 2016, 2064, 2072, 2103, 2110, 2125, 2263, 2264, 2315, 2343.

1057 • JOLSON SINGS AGAIN

SIDNEY BUCHMAN PRODUCTIONS; COLUMBIA. 1949.
NOMINATIONS *Story and Screenplay:* Sidney Buchman. *Color Cinematography:* William Snyder. *Scoring of a Musical Picture:* Morris Stoloff and George Duning.

Sequel to *The Jolson Story* that follows Al Jolson, played by Larry Parks [1058], through the war years, when he entertains the troops and meets the woman who will be his second wife, played by Barbara Hale. Too obviously cobbled together to capitalize on the success of the first film, it was nevertheless a big hit. Famous mainly for a trick shot in which Jolson is introduced to the actor who will play him in *The Jolson Story,* and Parks shakes hands with Parks. As in the original, it's Jolson's voice on the soundtrack. Directed by Henry Levin.

The writing award went to Robert Pirosh for *Battleground.* Winton Hoch won for the cinematography for *She Wore a Yellow Ribbon.* Stoloff (who appears on screen as an orchestra leader) and Duning lost to Roger Edens and Lennie Hayton for *On the Town.*

Buchman: 904, 1370, 1998. Snyder: 56, 1223. Stoloff: 13, 432, 455, 596, 643, 677, 732, 773, 1058, 1115, 1206, 1862, 1872, 1873, 1998, 2110, 2329. Duning: 596, 732, 1442, 1566.

1058 • JOLSON STORY, THE

COLUMBIA. 1946.
AWARDS *Sound Recording:* John Livadary. *Scoring of a Musical Picture:* Morris Stoloff.
NOMINATIONS *Actor:* Larry Parks. *Supporting Actor:* William Demarest. *Color Cinematography:* Joseph Walker. *Film Editing:* William Lyon.

Parks plays Al Jolson, the cantor's son who became one of the century's legendary entertainers. A phenomenally popular biopic, it's not much seen today because Jolson's performing style, and the music he sang, now seem corny and archaic. In fact, at the time the film was made, several producers passed on the project for those very reasons. But Columbia boss

Harry Cohn [1025 . . .], a former song-plugger, had been a Jolson fan and took on the project. The film was a hit because there were still many who had grown up with Jolson's recordings and had seen him giving his all on stage—in his heyday, the teens and twenties, Jolson was a superstar. The movie is cliché-ridden and gives no hint that its subject was a temperamental egomaniac, but Parks' performance (with songs dubbed by Jolson) captures the singer's charisma. Evelyn Keyes plays "Julie Benson," Jolson's first wife, who was actually Ruby Keeler; Demarest is Jolson's mentor-manager.

Parks was a Columbia contract player with a five-year career in B movies when he landed the biggest role of his life. The part had been turned down by James Cagney [79 . . .] and Danny Thomas (the latter declined because Columbia wanted him to have his nose bobbed for the part). Jose Ferrer [473 . . .] and Richard Conte were also tested. With *The Jolson Story* and its sequel, *Jolson Sings Again,* Parks seemed to have arrived. Then he was called before the House Un-American Activities Committee, admitted that he had been a member of the Communist Party, and his Hollywood career was over. His last screen appearance was in *Freud* in 1962. He died in 1975. The Oscar went to Fredric March for *The Best Years of Our Lives.*

Demarest was a durable character actor who made his film debut in 1927—one of his first movies, in fact, was *The Jazz Singer,* starring Jolson. Specializing in irascible types, he was an indispensable member of the de facto stock company that made up the casts of the films of Preston Sturges [823 . . .], including *The Great McGinty, The Lady Eve, Sullivan's Travels* (1941), *Hail the Conquering Hero,* and *The Miracle of Morgan's Creek.* In later years, before his death in 1983, he was best known as Uncle Charley on the TV sitcom *My Three Sons.* The Oscar went to Harold Russell for *The Best Years of Our Lives.*

The cinematography award went to Charles Rosher, Leonard Smith, and Arthur Arling for *The Yearling.* Daniel Mandell won for the editing of *The Best Years of Our Lives.*

Livadary: 330, 455, 596, 732, 1206, 1215, 1303,

1366, 1370, 1488, 1521, 1740, 1872, 2111, 2325, 2327. Stoloff: 13, 432, 455, 596, 643, 677, 732, 773, 1057, 1115, 1206, 1862, 1872, 1873, 1998, 2110, 2329. Walker: 904, 1494, 2325. Lyon: 330, 456, 732, 1566, 1776.

1059 • JONATHAN LIVINGSTON SEAGULL

JLS LTD. PARTNERSHIP PRODUCTION; PARAMOUNT. 1973.
NOMINATIONS *Cinematography:* Jack Couffer. *Film Editing:* Frank P. Keller and James Galloway.

Jonathan wants to test the limits of flight instead of sticking with his flock, and achieves a mystical transcendence. Few contemporary critics could resist using the phrase "for the birds" or noting later that the film had laid an egg. The dopey mysticism of Richard Bach's bizarre adaptation of his hippie-era best-seller doesn't work, especially when stretched out over two hours with a goopy score by Neil Diamond. The voices on the soundtrack belong to James Franciscus, Juliet Mills, Hal Holbrook, Dorothy McGuire [759], and Richard Crenna. Visually impressive, but the Academy was more impressed by the cinematography of Sven Nykvist for *Cries and Whispers* and the editing of William Reynolds for *The Sting*.

Keller: 158, 313, 944.

1060 • JOURNEY OF HOPE

CATPICS/CONDOR FEATURES PRODUCTION (SWITZERLAND). 1990.
AWARD *Foreign Language Film.*

Impoverished Turkish couple and their son set out to find work in Switzerland, disastrously entrusting their lives to those who smuggle illegal immigrants. Though the film deals with the plight of European "guest workers," and obviously makes a statement relevant to the American problem of exploited illegal immigrants, it avoids preachiness. Directed by Xavier Koller, who cowrote the screenplay with Feride Çiçekoglu.

1061 • JOURNEY OF NATTY GANN, THE

WALT DISNEY PICTURES AND SILVER SCREEN PARTNERS II PRODUCTION; BUENA VISTA. 1985.
NOMINATION *Costume Design:* Albert Wolsky.

In the depths of the Depression, Natty (Meredith Salenger), a teenage girl, sets out from Chicago to find her father, who has gone West in search of work. Along the way she is befriended and protected by a wolf and a young man (John Cusack). Good Disney film with a grittiness and realism that wouldn't have been present if the studio had made it a decade or so earlier. Directed by Jeremy Kagan. The costume Oscar went to Emi Wada for *Ran*.

Wolsky: 49, 308, 1876, 2127.5.

1062 • JOURNEY TO THE CENTER OF THE EARTH

JOSEPH M. SCHENCK ENTERPRISES & COOGA MOOGA FILM PRODUCTIONS INC.; 20TH CENTURY-FOX. 1959.
NOMINATIONS *Color Art Direction—Set Decoration:* Lyle R. Wheeler, Franz Bachelin, and Herman A. Blumenthal; Walter M. Scott and Joseph Kish. *Sound:* Carl Faulkner, sound director, 20th Century-Fox Studio Sound Department. *Special Effects:* L. B. Abbott and James B. Gordon, visual; Carl Faulkner, audible.

James Mason [761 . . .] plays a professor from the University of Edinburgh who leads a team of explorers, including Pat Boone and Arlene Dahl, into an extinct volcano in an attempt to reach the earth's core. They have to contend with cave-ins, a rival explorer, and giant lizards before they're through. Larky, cornball version of the Jules Verne story, adapted by Walter Reisch [435 . . .] and Charles Brackett [705 . . .]—though it's a far cry from *Ninotchka*, on which they also collaborated. Directed by Henry Levin. The score is by Bernard Herrmann [50 . . .]. The brightly unconvincing sets and special effects perfectly complement the comic-book tone of the script. The Academy preferred *Ben-Hur* in all the categories for which *Journey* was nominated.

Wheeler: 19, 46, 83, 356, 376, 428, 476, 495, 530, 542, 719, 721, 798, 950, 1088, 1149, 1153, 1213, 1391, 1475, 1601, 1616, 1670, 1706, 1852, 2008, 2093, 2212. Blumenthal: 413, 896. Scott: 46,

376, 413, 476, 530, 542, 557, 646, 896, 1088, 1213, 1391, 1475, 1706, 1753, 1881, 1907, 2008, 2120, 2247. Kish: 13, 1048, 1812, 1840. Faulkner: 1088, 1213, 2336. Abbott: 557, 1196, 1596, 2120.

1063 • JU DOU

CHINA FILM CO-PRODUCTION CORPORATION/TOKUMA SHOTEN PUBLISHING PRODUCTION (PEOPLE'S REPUBLIC OF CHINA). 1990.

NOMINATION *Foreign Language Film.*

Abused by her elderly husband, Ju Dou has an affair with his nephew and becomes pregnant. The old man believes the child to be his, but the boy grows up hating him. Powerful, visually stunning film, directed by Zhang Yimou, with Gong Li, who also appeared in Zhang's *Red Sorghum* (1987) and *Raise the Red Lantern,* in the title role. Because the film was thought to be an allegory of China's rebellion against its aging rulers, it was banned and the people responsible for submitting it to the Academy were disciplined. The Oscar went to *Journey of Hope.*

1064 • JUAREZ

WARNER BROS. 1939.

NOMINATIONS *Supporting Actor:* Brian Aherne. *Black-and-White Cinematography:* Tony Gaudio.

Paul Muni [218.5 . . .] plays the title role, the president of Mexico who leads his people in their fight for independence after Louis Napoleon, played by Claude Rains [365 . . .], makes Maximilian (Aherne) emperor of Mexico. Big all-star affair that's something of a snooze, despite a cast that includes Bette Davis [46 . . .] as the Empress Carlota, John Garfield [251 . . .] as Porfirio Díaz, Gale Sondergaard [83 . . .] as the Empress Eugénie, and Donald Crisp [952], Gilbert Roland, Harry Davenport, and Louis Calhern [1243]. Directed by William Dieterle [1169] from a screenplay by John Huston [24 . . .], Wolfgang Reinhardt [727], and Aeneas MacKenzie.

Aherne was a child actor in England who interrupted his career for schooling, then returned to the stage and made his first films in England in the twenties. In 1931 he came to America to appear on Broadway in *The Barretts of Wimpole Street,* which brought

him a film contract. Though suave and handsome, he never became a major star. He lost the Oscar to Thomas Mitchell in *Stagecoach.* Aherne died in 1986.

Gaudio did not in fact make the final ballot for the Oscar. For the 1939 awards, the first year in which the cinematography awards were divided into black-and-white and color categories, the Academy announced a first round of nominations for cinematography and then placed only two finalists in each of the two divisions on the ballot. Bert Glennon for *Stagecoach* and the winner, Gregg Toland for *Wuthering Heights,* were the official black-and-white cinematography contenders.

Gaudio: 90, 447, 898, 1162, 1872.

1065 • JUDGMENT AT NUREMBERG

STANLEY KRAMER PRODUCTIONS; UNITED ARTISTS. 1961.

AWARDS *Actor:* Maximilian Schell. *Screenplay—Based on Material From Another Medium:* Abby Mann.

NOMINATIONS *Picture:* Stanley Kramer, producer. *Actor:* Spencer Tracy. *Supporting Actor:* Montgomery Clift. *Supporting Actress:* Judy Garland. *Director:* Stanley Kramer. *Black-and-White Cinematography:* Ernest Laszlo. *Black-and-White Art Direction—Set Decoration:* Rudolph Sternad; George Milo. *Film Editing:* Frederic Knudtson. *Black-and-White Costume Design:* Jean Louis.

Tracy is the American judge who presides over the 1948 war-crimes trial. Schell plays a German defense attorney, Clift a man who was sterilized by the Nazis, and Garland a woman sent to the camps for befriending Jews. The cast also includes Burt Lancaster [107 . . .], Richard Widmark [1098], and Marlene Dietrich [1358] as the widow of a Nazi general. The individual performances are gripping, but as in most of Kramer's movies, the message is delivered with earnestness but also with a polish that makes it seem glib.

Schell had first played his role in a *Playhouse 90* TV version of the story. His family had fled their native Austria to Switzerland after the *Anschluss.* He began his acting career on stage and made his first films in Germany. In 1958 he made his first American film, *The Young Lions.* The Oscar that followed three years later established his international reputation, but despite two subsequent nominations, he has never been among the first rank of film actors. He has directed two films, *First Love* and *The Pedestrian,* that were nominated for foreign language film Oscars. His older sister is the actress Maria Schell.

Mann got his start as a writer for TV in the so-called golden age of television drama. The script for *Judgment* was first performed on *Playhouse 90,* then greatly expanded for the movies.

Kramer was once again unsuccessful, both as producer and as director, in winning the competition, but the Academy board gave him the Irving G. Thalberg Memorial Award at the 1961 ceremonies. Robert Wise won as producer and shared the director Oscar with Jerome Robbins for *West Side Story.*

For the second year in a row, Tracy was up for best actor in a film produced by Kramer, for whom he would make two more movies, *It's a Mad, Mad, Mad, Mad World* and *Guess Who's Coming to Dinner*—the latter would earn him his final nomination.

Clift was a physical and mental wreck going into the film. The serious automobile accident he suffered in 1957 had robbed him of his looks, he thought, and he had begun to drink heavily. The harrowing confession his character is forced to make, in a seven-minute scene, required four takes. Witnesses to the filming said they found it hard to separate performer from character. He lost his final chance at an Oscar to George Chakiris in *West Side Story* and died five years later.

After her near win for *A Star Is Born,* Garland's life continued to be tumultuous. But she conquered her problems temporarily for a celebrated Carnegie Hall recital in the same year that she delivered her strong dramatic performance in *Judgment.* She would make only three more films, however, one of them a voice-over for the 1962 animated feature *Gay Purr-ee.* The ups and downs of her personal life continued, and she died in circumstances that will always provoke speculation, of an overdose of sleeping pills, in 1969. This time the Oscar was won by Rita Moreno for *West Side Story,* which also won for Thomas Stanford's editing.

The Hustler won the Oscars for Eugen Shuftan's cinematography and for art direction. The costuming Oscar went to Piero Gherardi for *La Dolce Vita.*

Schell: 1066, 1253. Mann: 1812. Kramer: 330, 522, 843, 912, 1812. Tracy: 131, 271, 352, 656, 843, 1000, 1470, 1751. Clift: 732, 1579, 1771. Garland: 1910. Laszlo: 31, 646, 1000, 1032, 1196, 1812, 1907. Sternad: 1998, 2066. Milo: 1632, 2035. Knudtson: 522, 1000, 1032, 1474, 2288. Louis: 20, 126, 170, 262, 732, 744, 1028, 1521, 1640, 1812, 1858, 1910, 2064.

1066 • JULIA

20TH CENTURY-FOX PRODUCTION; 20TH CENTURY-FOX. 1977.
AWARDS *Supporting Actor:* Jason Robards. *Supporting Actress:* Vanessa Redgrave. *Screenplay—Based on Material From Another Medium:* Alvin Sargent.
NOMINATIONS *Picture:* Richard Roth, producer. *Actress:* Jane Fonda. *Supporting Actor:* Maximilian Schell. *Director:* Fred Zinnemann. *Cinematography:* Douglas Slocombe. *Original Score:* Georges Delerue. *Film Editing:* Walter Murch. *Costume Design:* Anthea Sylbert.

Fonda plays playwright Lillian Hellman [1182 . . .], whose friend from childhood, Julia (Redgrave), asks her to undertake a perilous mission —smuggle money to her in Nazi Germany for use by the Resistance. A fine re-creation of life among the left-wing intelligentsia of the thirties, the film nevertheless seems unfocused. It's a memory piece, drawn from Hellman's *Pentimento,* but it's never quite clear why we're expected to share these memories. Though meticulously done, it's somehow lifeless, despite stunning performances from all the nominees, as well as Meryl Streep [472 . . .] in her screen debut.

Robards, who plays Dashiell Hammett [2233], won his second consecutive Oscar—one of only five performers to win two in a row. (The others are Luise Rainer [799 . . .] for 1936 and 1937, Spencer Tracy [131 . . .] for 1937 and 1938, Katharine Hepburn [24 . . .] for 1967 and 1968, and Tom Hanks [195 . . .] for 1993 and 1994.) Except for his superlative turn as Howard Hughes in *Melvin and Howard,* Robards' subsequent film roles have been routine; he makes numerous appearances in character parts on film and TV.

Redgrave's Oscar gave her a chance to make a famous speech denouncing ''Zionist hoodlums''—a reference to protesters outside the Dorothy Chandler Pavilion who were demonstrating against Redgrave's pro-Palestinian stance. When it came his turn to present the writing awards, Paddy Chayefsky [783 . . .] in turn denounced Redgrave as one of the people who use the ceremony ''for the propagation of their own personal propaganda.'' In context, however, Redgrave's speech was a rather evenhanded statement against anti-Semitism and fascism—a position that most of the Academy probably shared. Which is not to say that Redgrave has never been guilty of extreme and sometimes eccentric statements—one reason, perhaps, that despite continued memorable performances, and two subsequent nominations, she has yet to find a role that would bring her another Oscar.

Sargent, a former TV writer who began his screenwriting career in 1966 with *Gambit,* subsequently won another Oscar for *Ordinary People,* marking him as a specialist in serious topics. His most recent work, however, has included the story for the Bill Murray comedy *What About Bob?* (1991).

Annie Hall took the Oscars for best picture, actress Diane Keaton, and director Woody Allen. Vilmos Zsigmond won for the cinematography for *Close Encounters of the Third Kind. Star Wars* won for John Williams' score, Paul Hirsch, Marcia Lucas, and Richard Chew's editing, and John Mollo's costumes.

Robards: 54, 1300. Redgrave: 263, 954.5, 1021, 1285, 1354. Sargent: 1502, 1526. Fonda: 394, 430, 1104, 1356, 1473, 2047. Schell: 1065, 1253. Zinnemann: 732, 912, 1252, 1457, 1771, 1969. Slocombe: 1652, 2134. Delerue: 28, 85, 502, 1187. Murch: 92, 442, 764, 786. Sylbert: 395.

1067 • JULIE
ARWIN PRODUCTIONS; MGM. 1956.
NOMINATIONS *Screenplay—Original:* Andrew L. Stone. *Song:* ''Julie,'' music by Leith Stevens, lyrics by Tom Adair.

Doris Day [1572] plays a woman whose second husband, a concert pianist played by Louis Jourdan, murdered her first husband. Now she's next. Silly woman-in-jeopardy thriller that has a few good moments of suspense. Stone also directed, but he lost the writing Oscar to Albert Lamorisse for *The Red Balloon,* a short film that had no dialogue. (There are those who think *Julie* would have been better off with no dialogue, too.) As for the song, the Oscar went to ''Whatever Will Be, Will Be (Que Será, Será),'' written by Jay Livingston and Ray Evans, and sung by Day in *The Man Who Knew Too Much.*

Stevens: 675, 1427.

1068 • JULIET OF THE SPIRITS
RIZZOLI FILMS S.P.A. PRODUCTION; RIZZOLI FILMS (FRANCE/ITALY/WEST GERMANY). 1966.
NOMINATIONS *Color Art Direction—Set Decoration:* Piero Gherardi. *Color Costume Design:* Piero Gherardi.

Giulietta Masina plays a Roman housewife who consults a medium when she suspects that her husband is cheating on her. As a result, she enters a fantastic spirit world that has a symbolic resonance with her real life. The first feature-length color film directed by Federico Fellini [61 . . .] has been called a feminist $8^1/2$, but aside from its entertaining phantasmagoria, it doesn't have much to offer, and it remains a male director-screenwriter's vision of a woman's fantasy life, which seems, as Pauline Kael observes, to be made up of ''leftover decor from MGM musicals.'' The award for art direction went to *Fantastic Voyage.* Elizabeth Haffenden and Joan Bridge won for the costumes for *A Man for All Seasons.*

Gherardi: 562, 603.

1069 • JULIUS CAESAR
MGM. 1953.
AWARD *Black-and-White Art Direction—Set Decoration:* Cedric Gibbons and Edward Carfagno; Edwin B. Willis and Hugh Hunt.
NOMINATIONS *Picture:* John Houseman, producer. *Actor:* Marlon Brando. *Black-and-White Cinematography:* Joseph Ruttenberg. *Scoring of a Dramatic or Comedy Picture:* Miklos Rozsa.

Shakespeare's tragedy centering on the plot to assassinate Caesar, played by Louis Calhern [1243], received an effective if somewhat stodgy treatment from

MGM. The fifties were the heyday of Roman sex-and-sandals epics such as *Quo Vadis?*, *The Robe,* and *Ben-Hur,* so Shakespeare's play fit right in. Portions of the sets done by Gibbons, Carfagno, and Hunt for *Quo Vadis?* two years earlier were shipped to Hollywood from Rome for this film. Unlike the epics, however, *Julius Caesar* had a script that made sense, and MGM decided to make the most of it, casting James Mason [761 . . .] as Brutus, John Gielgud [103 . . .] as Cassius, and Edmond O'Brien [146 . . .] as Casca. Greer Garson [239 . . .] and Deborah Kerr [599 . . .] more than fill the play's two small women's roles, Calpurnia and Portia.

Joseph L. Mankiewicz [46 . . .], who directed, considered Paul Scofield [1252 . . .] for Antony, but Scofield was a comparative unknown in America. Brando was cast at the suggestion of Houseman, who had seen the actor on stage in New York, in the play *A Flag Is Born,* in which he gave an oration similar to the one Antony delivers over Caesar's body. Brando worked hard to deepen his voice, and Gielgud coached him on speaking blank verse. While the acting honors in the film more properly belong to Mason and Gielgud, Brando's performance is a strong one: He speaks it well and looks it even better. The Oscar, however, went to William Holden for *Stalag 17.*

Houseman had come to Hollywood with Orson Welles [407 . . .], with whom he had cofounded the Mercury Theater in New York. He was an uncredited writer on the screenplay of *Citizen Kane* but quarreled with Welles and went to work for David O. Selznick [497 . . .] briefly before World War II. He was primarily a producer for much of his Hollywood career but later became a ubiquitous character actor. The Oscar for best picture went to *From Here to Eternity,* for which Burnett Guffey received the cinematography award. The scoring Oscar went to Bronislau Kaper for *Lili.*

Gibbons: 66, 87, 130, 217, 227, 239, 285, 290, 440, 629, 749, 831, 980, 1096, 1173, 1190, 1226, 1230, 1232, 1274, 1308, 1309, 1417, 1567, 1604, 1644, 1662, 1673, 1721, 1861, 1937, 2068, 2112, 2256, 2257, 2300, 2320, 2330. Carfagno: 130, 175,

629, 917, 1552, 1644, 1814, 1937, 2312. Willis: 66, 87, 130, 227, 239, 290, 629, 749, 831, 980, 1096, 1157, 1173, 1190, 1226, 1230, 1232, 1309, 1417, 1567, 1657, 1662, 1673, 1721, 1861, 1937, 2068, 2112, 2257, 2320, 2330. Hunt: 175, 401, 980, 1232, 1335, 1388, 1567, 1644, 1657, 1673, 2157, 2184. Houseman: 1525. Brando: 583, 784, 1141, 1477, 1763, 1949, 2212. Ruttenberg: 318, 573, 749, 769, 828, 1232, 1371, 1861, 2234. Rozsa: 566, 567, 604, 1035, 1070, 1085, 1208, 1227, 1644, 1872, 1890, 1968, 2050, 2304.

JUMBO
See 207.

1070 • *JUNGLE BOOK*
Alexander Korda; United Artists. 1942.

Nominations *Color Cinematography:* W. Howard Greene. *Color Interior Decoration:* Vincent Korda, art direction; Julia Heron, set decoration. *Scoring of a Dramatic or Comedy Picture:* Miklos Rozsa. *Special Effects:* Lawrence Butler, photographic; William H. Wilmarth, sound.

Sabu plays Rudyard Kipling's Mowgli, raised by wolves and befriended by other animals—a friendship that he puts to good advantage when he grows up and faces danger. Good adventure story, very loosely based by screenwriter Laurence Stallings on Kipling's stories. This version by the Korda brothers—Alexander [1620] produced, Zoltan directed—is today less popular with kids than the Disney animated version, but adults may find it more romantic and exciting. It's clearly one of the films that inspired *Raiders of the Lost Ark.*

The cinematography Oscar went to Leon Shamroy for *The Black Swan. My Gal Sal* took the art direction award. Max Steiner won for the score of *Now, Voyager.* The special effects award went to *Reap the Wild Wind.*

Greene: 96, 239, 747, 1452, 1560, 1621, 1909, 2262. Korda: 1201, 2031, 2050. Heron: 201, 366, 1886, 2031. Rozsa: 175, 566, 567, 604, 1035, 1069, 1085, 1208, 1227, 1644, 1872, 1890, 1968, 2050, 2304. Butler: 2031, 2050, 2066. Wilmarth: 2031.

1071 • JUNGLE BOOK, THE

WALT DISNEY PRODUCTIONS; BUENA VISTA. 1967.

NOMINATION *Song:* "The Bare Necessities," music and lyrics by Terry Gilkyson.

The panther Bagheera (voice of Sebastian Cabot) tells the "man-cub" Mowgli, who has been raised in the jungle by the animals, that it's time for him to join the human race. Mowgli doesn't want to, however, so he runs away. He's befriended by the bear Baloo (voice of Phil Harris), but threatened by the ape king (voice of Louie Prima), the tiger Shere Khan (voice of George Sanders [46]), and the python Kaa (voice of Sterling Holloway). Lively and irreverent version of the Rudyard Kipling stories, with good music and some funny if unpolished animation. It was a big box-office hit. The Oscar, however, went to a song from a big box-office flop, also about a human being who can communicate with animals: Leslie Bricusse's "Talk to the Animals," from *Doctor Dolittle.*

1071.3 • JUNIOR

NORTHERN LIGHTS ENTERTAINMENT PRODUCTION; UNIVERSAL. 1994.

NOMINATION *Song:* "Look What Love Has Done," Music and lyrics by Carole Bayer Sager, James Newton Howard, James Ingram, and Patty Smyth.

Arnold Schwarzenegger plays a scientist working on a fertility drug who is goaded by his research partner (Danny DeVito) into an extraordinary experiment, in the course of which he becomes pregnant. What sounds like a tired and obvious high-concept premise produces a very likable, even touching comedy—a reminder that some very good movies, e.g., *Tootsie* and *Big,* have been made from rather banal ideas. It may not be in their league, but *Junior* has some of the sweetness of the latter and some of the shrewd analysis of male-female roles of the former. It benefits from a very talented cast, including Emma Thompson [954.5 . . .], Pamela Reed, Frank Langella, and Judy Collins, and a well-crafted script by Kevin Wade and Chris Conrad. And Schwarzenegger, nicely directed by Ivan Reitman, who also directed his *Kindergarten Cop* and *Twins,* has grown into a

surprisingly skillful comic actor. Unfortunately for the film's box office, Schwarzenegger's hard-core fans weren't interested in seeing him get in touch with his feminine side, and the movie never found its audience. The Oscar for best song went to "Can You Feel the Love Tonight," by Elton John and Tim Rice, from *The Lion King.*

Sager: 103, 166.5, 977, 1898. Howard: 734.5, 1612. Ingram: 166.5.

1071.5 • JURASSIC PARK

AMBLIN ENTERTAINMENT PRODUCTION; UNIVERSAL. 1993.

AWARDS *Sound:* Gary Summers, Gary Rydstrom, Shawn Murphy, and Ron Judkins. *Sound Effects Editing:* Gary Rydstrom and Richard Hymns. *Visual Effects:* Dennis Muren, Stan Winston, Phil Tippett, and Michael Lantieri.

A billionaire, played by Richard Attenborough [745], has bankrolled the ultimate theme park: an island on which dinosaurs of all sorts have been brought to life, genetically engineered from traces of dinosaur DNA found in prehistoric mosquitoes preserved in amber. He invites paleontologists Sam Neill and Laura Dern [1659] and mathematician Jeff Goldblum to join him, along with his own grandchildren, on a preopening tour of the park. But all too soon, everything goes haywire, thanks to an unscrupulous employee who plans to smuggle embryonic saurians to the outside world. Steven Spielberg [416 . . .] directs the ultimate monster movie, the lineal descendant of *King Kong* and Spielberg's own *Jaws,* and it grossed more money than any film in history, including the previous box-office champ, Spielberg's *E.T. The Extra-Terrestrial.* It is undeniably a triumph of special effects, a revolutionary use of computer animation to bring to vivid life creatures not seen on earth for millions of years. And if what you're looking for is nonstop excitement, it delivers that, too. Yet this product of Spielberg's *annus mirabilis,* in which he brought forth not only his most profitable film but also his finest, *Schindler's List,* was a disappointment to those among his admirers who cherished his ability to instill childlike wonder in the viewer and to mix thrills with humor. Spielberg himself seemed a little embarrassed by the product, and he left the editing, in which he has traditionally been deeply involved, in the hands of others so he could devote himself full-time to *Schindler's List*. (Both films are edited by Michael Kahn, who won an Oscar for *Schindler's List*.) The movie is aimed at thirteen-year-old kids of all ages, all over the world. To judge from its box-office receipts, there must be a lot of them.

Summers: 129, 996, 1684, 2019. Rydstrom: 129, 2019. Murphy: 996. Judkins: 1764.65. Hymns: 129, 996, 2284. Muren: 5, 577, 588, 614, 997, 1002, 1684, 2019, 2284, 2339. Winston: 45, 153.5, 600, 886, 1600, 2019. Tippett: 577, 1684, 2284. Lantieri: 128, 937.

1072 • JUST FOR YOU

PARAMOUNT. 1952.
NOMINATION *Song:* "Zing a Little Zong," music by Harry Warren, lyrics by Leo Robin.

Bing Crosby [173 . . .] plays a workaholic producer who neglects his teenage son until the boy falls for Crosby's fiancée, Jane Wyman [246 . . .]. Passable little musical, featuring Ethel Barrymore [1445 . . .] and Natalie Wood [1219 . . .], directed by Elliott Nugent. The song Oscar went to "High Noon (Do Not Forsake Me, Oh My Darlin')," the title tune by Dimitri Tiomkin and Ned Washington.

Warren: 21, 324, 569, 788, 791, 877, 897, 1367, 1501, 1964. Robin: 104, 197, 368, 846, 1805, 1843, 2032, 2088, 2310.

1073 • JUST IMAGINE

FOX. 1930–31.
NOMINATION *Interior Decoration:* Stephen Goosson and Ralph Hammeras.

Comedian El Brendel dies in 1930 but is revived fifty years later. Primitive sci-fi musical that's chiefly of interest today for what people in 1930 thought 1980 might look like. Naturally there are lots of art deco skyscrapers, people go by numbers rather than names, and Brendel (a long-forgotten Swedish-dialect comic) winds up on a rocket to Mars. Directed by

David Butler, with Maureen O'Sullivan. The art direction Oscar went to Max Ree for *Cimarron*.

Goosson: 928, 1182, 1206, 2066. Hammeras: 520, 1619.

1074 • KAGEMUSHA (THE SHADOW WARRIOR)

TOHO COMPANY LTD.-KUROSAWA PRODUCTIONS LTD. COPRODUCTION; 20TH CENTURY-FOX (JAPAN). 1980.
NOMINATIONS *Art Direction—Set Decoration:* Yoshiro Muraki. *Foreign Language Film.*

The life of a thief is spared because he resembles a sixteenth-century warlord and can be used as a double after the warlord dies. Elaborately pictorial film directed by Akira Kurosawa [1661] that was the most expensive production in the history of Japanese film. It was partly bankrolled by Francis Ford Coppola [65 . . .], George Lucas [65 . . .], and 20th Century-Fox. Though clearly the work of a master filmmaker, it's a bit stiff and remote.

The art direction award went to Pierre Guffroy and Jack Stevens for *Tess. Moscow Does Not Believe in Tears* won the foreign film Oscar.

Muraki: 1661, 2120, 2324.

1075 • KANSAN, THE

SHERMAN; UNITED ARTISTS. 1943.
NOMINATION *Scoring of a Dramatic or Comedy Picture:* Gerard Carbonara.

Sharpshooter Richard Dix [400] is the new marshal who sets out to clean up the town. Uncomplicated, unsophisticated western with Jane Wyatt, Eugene Pallette, Albert Dekker, Victor Jory, and Robert Armstrong, directed by George Archainbaud. Carbonara lost to Alfred Newman for *The Song of Bernadette*.

1076 • KAPO

VIDES-ZEBRAFILM-CINERIZ (ITALY). 1960.
NOMINATION *Foreign Language Film.*

Susan Strasberg plays a French Jew who is saved from the gas chambers by a doctor, who gives her the identity of a non-Jewish prisoner. She becomes a Kapo, a prisoner who is allowed to serve as a guard in the camps, and is brutalized by the experience. Too melodramatic for its tragic subject. Directed by Gillo Pontecorvo [155]. The Oscar went to Ingmar Bergman's *The Virgin Spring*.

1077 • KARATE KID, THE

COLUMBIA PICTURES PRODUCTION; COLUMBIA. 1984.
NOMINATION *Supporting Actor:* Noriyuki "Pat" Morita.

Daniel (Ralph Macchio), the new kid in a Southern California suburb, has trouble adjusting until the handyman in his apartment complex, Mr. Miyagi (Morita), teaches him karate; Daniel beats the bullies and wins the girl (Elizabeth Shue). Simple, straightforward, and quite enjoyable crowd-pleaser that, like an earlier film also directed by John G. Avildsen [1712], *Rocky,* came out of nowhere and became a box-office champion. Also like *Rocky,* it spawned a succession of increasingly feeble sequels, but the original has undeniable charm, thanks to likable performances and a good script by Robert Mark Kamen.

Berkeley-born Morita was a character actor with a couple of decades of film and TV credits when he landed the role of the sagacious Mr. Miyagi. He lost the Oscar to Haing S. Ngor for *The Killing Fields*.

1078 • KARATE KID, PART II, THE

COLUMBIA PICTURES PRODUCTION; COLUMBIA. 1986.
NOMINATION *Song:* "Glory of Love," music by Peter Cetera and David Foster, lyrics by Peter Cetera and Diane Nini.

After winning a karate championship, Daniel (Ralph Macchio) accompanies his teacher, Mr. Miyagi, played by Noriyuki "Pat" Morita [1077], to Okinawa, where the two must face Miyagi's old enemies as well as a typhoon. Overcalculating sequel that lacks the low-budget freshness of the original but did huge box-office business. Tamlyn Tomita is the love interest for Daniel, Nobu McCarthy for Miyagi. Like the first movie, it was directed by John G. Avildsen [1712] and written by Robert Mark Kamen. The nominated song is as mindlessly upbeat as the movie. It lost to Giorgio Moroder and Tom Whitlock's "Take My Breath Away" from *Top Gun*.

Foster: 251.5

1079 • KEEPER OF PROMISES (THE GIVEN WORD), THE

CINEDISTRI (BRAZIL). 1962.
NOMINATION *Foreign Language Film.*

A priest refuses a peasant's offering to the church when he learns that the peasant has been practicing voodoo. A simple drama of cultural conflict that ends tragically, the film, written and directed by Anselmo Duarte, won the top award at the Cannes Festival but lost the Oscar to *Sundays and Cybèle*.

1080 • KENTUCKY

20TH CENTURY-FOX. 1938.
AWARD *Supporting Actor:* Walter Brennan.

Romeo and Juliet in the bluegrass: Loretta Young [428 . . .] and Richard Greene belong to rival horse-raising clans but somehow manage to get together. An early Technicolor feature, handsomely filmed by Ernest Palmer [235 . . .] but otherwise pretty routine. Directed by David Butler. This was the second Oscar for Brennan, on his way to his record-setting three wins.

Brennan: 424, 1779, 2245.

1081 • KEY LARGO

WARNER BROS. 1948.
AWARD *Supporting Actress:* Claire Trevor.

Gangster Edward G. Robinson and his henchmen take over a hotel in the Florida Keys run by Lionel Barrymore [723 . . .] and daughter Lauren Bacall. Fortunately Humphrey Bogart [24 . . .] is a guest in the hotel, too, so Robinson eventually meets his match. Fine, atmospheric drama directed by John Huston [24 . . .], who adapted a Maxwell Anderson [48] play with the help of Richard Brooks [227 . . .], improving it in the process. Superb acting and the photography of Karl Freund [239 . . .] make this a standout. Ordinarily Huston might have received a nomination for his direction, but he was already in the running for *The Treasure of the Sierra Madre* (for which he won). So the only puzzle is why Robinson, who gives one of his finest performances as the gangster, failed to receive a nomination. In fact, Robinson was never nominated for an Oscar, an oversight the Academy finally remedied a few months before his death with an honorary award at the 1972 ceremonies; the citation read: "Edward G. Robinson who achieved greatness as a player, a patron of the arts and a dedicated citizen . . . in sum, a Renaissance man. From his friends in the industry he loves."

Trevor spent her Hollywood career being typecast as shady ladies—most memorably, the syphilitic prostitute in *Dead End,* the whore cast out by the respectable townswomen in *Stagecoach,* and Robinson's alcoholic mistress in *Key Largo.* After a start on Broadway in the late twenties, she came to Hollywood in 1932, toiling steadily in B pictures, but occasionally making it into good films. Her career tapered off in the later fifties, but she made a few films in the sixties and had a small role in the 1982 movie *Kiss Me Goodbye.*

Trevor: 510, 911.

1082 • KEYS OF THE KINGDOM, THE

20TH CENTURY-FOX. 1945.

NOMINATIONS *Actor:* Gregory Peck. *Black-and-White Cinematography:* Arthur Miller. *Black-and-White Interior Decoration:* James Basevi and William Darling, art direction; Thomas Little and Frank E. Hughes, set decoration. *Scoring of a Dramatic or Comedy Picture:* Alfred Newman.

Peck plays Father Francis Chisholm, a saintly Scot who finds adventure and his true calling as a missionary in China. Too long and too uplifting, but watchable because of a strong cast: Thomas Mitchell [962 . . .], Vincent Price, Roddy McDowall (as the young Francis Chisholm), Edmund Gwenn [1325 . . .], Cedric Hardwicke, Peggy Ann Garner, James Gleason [904], Anne Revere [759 . . .], Arthur Shields, and Sara Allgood [952]. Joseph L. Mankiewicz [46 . . .] and Nunnally Johnson [815 . . .] adapted the novel by A. J. Cronin. John M. Stahl [983] directed. Today the movie is remembered mainly as one of the three 1945 movies (the others were *Spellbound* and *The Valley of Decision*) that made Peck a star. He lost to Ray Milland in *The Lost Weekend.*

The cinematography Oscar went to Harry Stradling for *The Picture of Dorian Gray. Blood on the Sun* took the art direction award. Miklos Rozsa won for the score of *Spellbound.*

Peck: 759, 2101, 2154, 2320. Miller: 83, 241, 952, 1655, 1868, 2056. Basevi: 746, 1868, 2245, 2316. Darling: 83, 374, 1195, 1655, 1868, 2240. Little: 46, 83, 235, 428, 495, 719, 721, 746, 950, 952, 1149, 1153, 1397, 1475, 1666, 1852, 1868, 2056, 2212, 2286. Hughes: 83. Newman: 31, 34, 46, 72, 138, 182, 226, 333, 334, 347, 375, 428, 437, 457, 476, 495, 542, 690, 797, 833, 952, 953, 959, 962, 1016, 1088, 1213, 1278, 1362, 1397, 1475, 1616, 1655, 1849, 1868, 1883, 1921, 2043, 2046, 2091, 2258, 2286, 2294, 2316.

1083 • KHARTOUM

JULIAN BLAUSTEIN PRODUCTION; UNITED ARTISTS (UNITED KINGDOM). 1966.

NOMINATION *Story and Screenplay—Written Directly for the Screen:* Robert Ardrey.

Charlton Heston [175] plays General Gordon, sent by the British to quell an uprising led by the Mahdi, played by Laurence Olivier [268 . . .], in 1885. Plodding would-be epic that strives to stick close to history while providing the usual action heroics. But if you're going to try to be accurate, why have an American actor play an Englishman and an English actor play an Arab? Directed by Basil Dearden, with Ralph Richardson [839 . . .], Richard Johnson, Alexander Knox [2286], and Michael Hordern.

Ardrey, born and educated in Chicago, taught anthropology at the University of Chicago for several years before Thornton Wilder helped him get started as a playwright. After some Broadway success in the thirties, he went to Hollywood in the forties, where he worked on numerous films. In the sixties he returned to his original interest in anthropology and wrote some best-selling popular works on behavioral evolution, including *African Genesis* and *The Territorial Imperative.* The Oscar went to Claude Lelouch and Pierre Uytterhoeven for *A Man and a Woman.*

1084 • KHOVANSHCHINA

MOSFILM STUDIOS PRODUCTION; ARTKINO PICTURES (USSR). 1961.

NOMINATION *Scoring of a Musical Picture:* Dimitri Shostakovich.

A film of the opera by Modest Mussorgsky about political intrigue at the court of Peter the Great. The work, left unfinished at the composer's death in 1881, was completed and rescored by the Soviet composer Shostakovich for a production at the Kirov in 1958; more music was added for the film. The Oscar went to the scoring for *West Side Story*.

1085 • KILLERS, THE

MARK HELLINGER PRODUCTIONS; UNIVERSAL. 1946.

NOMINATIONS *Director:* Robert Siodmak. *Screenplay:* Anthony Veiller. *Scoring of a Dramatic or Comedy Picture:* Miklos Rozsa. *Film Editing:* Arthur Hilton.

Burt Lancaster [107 . . .] is the Swede, an ex-boxer turned gas station attendant. He's murdered by a couple of goons (Charles McGraw and a remarkably slim William Conrad), but he doesn't seem to resist being bumped off. In the Ernest Hemingway story on which the film is based, there's not much more plot than that. But Veiller, aided by an uncredited John Huston [24 . . .], crafted a whydunit, as insurance investigator Edmond O'Brien [146 . . .] puts the pieces of the puzzle together. The result is one of the finest film noirs, providing a smashing debut for Lancaster, plus one of the roles that made Ava Gardner [1339] a star.

Siodmak was born in Memphis, Tennessee, while his family was in the States on a business trip. But he was raised in Germany and began his film directing career there. He fled the Nazis, going first to Paris in 1933 and then to America in 1940. During his Hollywood years he directed quite a few atmospheric melodramas—*Christmas Holiday, The Spiral Staircase*—as well as horror movies such as *Son of Dracula* (1943) and the fun swashbuckler *The Crimson Pirate* (1952). He returned to Germany in the 1950s, where his credits included the 1957 foreign language film nominee *The Devil Came at Night*. The Oscar went to William Wyler for *The Best Years of Our Lives,* which also won for Robert E. Sherwood's screenplay, Hugo Friedhofer's score, and Daniel Mandell's editing.

Veiller: 1899. Rozsa: 175, 566, 567, 604, 1035, 1069, 1070, 1208, 1227, 1644, 1872, 1890, 1968, 2050, 2304.

1086 • KILLING FIELDS, THE

ENIGMA PRODUCTIONS LTD.; WARNER BROS. (UNITED KINGDOM). 1984.

AWARDS *Supporting Actor:* Haing S. Ngor. *Cinematography:* Chris Menges. *Film Editing:* Jim Clark.

NOMINATIONS *Picture:* David Puttnam, producer. *Actor:* Sam Waterston. *Director:* Roland Joffé. *Screenplay Based on Material From Another Medium:* Bruce Robinson.

Waterston plays Sydney Schanberg, a *New York Times* reporter, who stays on in Cambodia to cover the takeover by the Khmer Rouge after other Americans have been evacuated. With him are an English reporter (Julian Sands) and an American photographer, played by John Malkovich [992.3 . . .]. They are aided by Dith Pran (Ngor), their Cambodian interpreter, but when the Westerners are forced to leave the country, Pran is separated from them. The film details his attempts to survive the massacres and atrocities of the Pol Pot regime, as Schanberg, back in the States, does what he can to locate him. Harrowing but rewarding look at one of the century's worst episodes, though the emphasis on Schanberg's feelings of guilt sometimes seems overstated—as if American pangs of conscience were on a par with the deep and bitter suffering of the Cambodians. Similarly the placement of Waterston in the leading role category and Ngor in the supporting one seems somehow topsy-turvy. It seems to be hard for Westerners to make movies about oppression in other parts of the world without filtering it through their own experience—a similar flaw afflicted Richard Attenborough's film about South Africa, *Cry Freedom*. The supporting cast includes Craig T. Nelson, Athol Fugard, and Spalding Gray, who turned his experiences during the filming in Thailand into a stage monologue that was filmed as *Swimming to Cambodia* (1987).

Ngor, a physician, had seen his family wiped out by the Khmer Rouge before he escaped to America.

He was chosen from hundreds of Cambodians who were tested for the role, and it launched him on a new career. Unlike another nonactor, Harold Russell, who won an Oscar for *The Best Years of Our Lives* but had virtually no subsequent acting career, Ngor has continued to perform in films and on TV. The film was also instrumental in reuniting him with surviving members of his family.

British photographer Menges began as a documentary-film maker and moved into feature films in the seventies. He worked as a camera operator on *The Empire Strikes Back* and was cinematographer on such movies as *Local Hero* (1983) and *Comfort and Joy* (1984) before his big break with *The Killing Fields*.

Clark, a British editor, previously worked on such films as *Charade, Darling, The Day of the Locust,* and *Marathon Man.*

Puttnam, who had won the Oscar for *Chariots of Fire* three years earlier, would parlay his success at the Oscars into a brief and troubled tenure as head of production for Columbia in 1986. This time the Oscar went to *Amadeus.*

Waterston has been primarily a stage actor, with mostly unmemorable screen credits except for several Woody Allen features, such as *Interiors, Hannah and Her Sisters,* and *Crimes and Misdemeanors.* More recently he has been seen in the TV series *I'll Fly Away* and *Law and Order.* The Oscar went to F. Murray Abraham for *Amadeus,* which also won for Milos Forman's direction and Peter Shaffer's screenplay. Robinson's script for *The Killing Fields* was based on a *New York Times Magazine* article, "The Death and Life of Dith Pran," by Schanberg.

Menges: 1331. Clark: 1331. Puttnam: 386, 1313, 1331. Joffé: 1331.

1087 • KIND LADY

MGM. 1951.

NOMINATION *Black-and-White Costume Design:* Walter Plunkett and Gile Steele.

Maurice Evans is a con man who takes over the household of elderly invalid Ethel Barrymore [1445 . . .]. Well-handled thriller, directed by John Sturges [131]. Based on a play by Edward Chodorov,

who cowrote the screenplay with Jerry Davis and Charles Bennett [706]. The cast includes Angela Lansbury [749 . . .], Betsy Blair, and Keenan Wynn. The costuming Oscar went to Edith Head for *A Place in the Sun.*

Plunkett: 9, 66, 953, 1243, 1587, 1657, 1859, 2029, 2330. Steele: 612, 817, 897, 1309, 1748.

1088 • KING AND I, THE

20TH CENTURY-FOX. 1956.

AWARDS *Actor:* Yul Brynner. *Color Art Direction—Set Decoration:* Lyle R. Wheeler and John DeCuir; Walter M. Scott and Paul S. Fox. *Sound Recording:* Carl Faulkner, sound director, 20th Century-Fox Studio Sound Department. *Scoring of a Musical Picture:* Alfred Newman and Ken Darby. *Color Costume Design:* Irene Sharaff.

NOMINATIONS *Picture:* Charles Brackett, producer. *Actress:* Deborah Kerr. *Director:* Walter Lang. *Color Cinematography:* Leon Shamroy.

Kerr plays an Englishwoman who, after the death of her husband, goes to Thailand with her young son to be governess to the household of the king of Siam (Brynner). Lush filming of the musical by Richard Rodgers [1921] and Oscar Hammerstein II [375 . . .], which was based as much on the movie *Anna and the King of Siam* as on the Margaret Landon book that was the source of the first film. It's an elaborately artificial concoction, not a moment of which seems to be taking place in the real world—it's not stagy, it's soundstagy. The screenplay is flimsy, largely a matter of will-she-stay-or-will-she-go, with a subplot involving the illicit love of Tuptim, played by Rita Moreno [2244], and Lun Tha (Carlos Rivas). But thanks to Brynner and Kerr, who are in top form (even though Kerr's singing voice is the colorless Marni Nixon), it's possibly the best translation of a Rodgers and Hammerstein musical to film. *South Pacific* was woefully miscast, *Oklahoma!* too awkwardly blended location filming with staged sequences, *Carousel* (1956) was slackly directed and missing some of its best music, and the well-scrubbed wholesomeness of *The Sound of Music* sets some people's teeth on edge. *The King and I* also has splendid choreography by Jerome Robbins [2244], who staged the "Small House of Uncle Thomas" ballet. And of course there are some great songs: "Getting to Know You," "Hello, Young Lovers," "Something Wonderful," and so on.

Hollywood is notorious for overlooking the original Broadway stars when casting film musicals, but Brynner was an all-but-inevitable choice for the king. It's said, however, that Brynner wanted to direct the film but not appear in it, suggesting Marlon Brando [583 . . .] for the king instead. Interestingly Brynner was not the first choice when the Broadway production was being cast; he was a comparative unknown, and Rex Harrison [413 . . .], who had played the king in the 1946 film, and Alfred Drake were considered first. Born on Sakhalin Island, off the coast of Siberia north of Japan, Brynner had been a circus performer in Paris before becoming an actor. He was discovered by Michael Chekhov [1890], who brought Brynner to the States with his touring company in 1940. The war intervened, during which Brynner served as a French-language radio commentator for the Office of War Information. He made his Broadway debut in 1946 opposite Mary Martin in *Lute Song* and his film debut in *Port of New York* in 1949. Brynner was all over the place in 1956, appearing in two other major films: *Anastasia* and *The Ten Commandments*. After the Oscar, he continued to be a film presence over the next twenty years, but his exotic shaven-headed image is more memorable than most of the films he played in. In the decade before his death from lung cancer in 1985, he toured in revivals of *The King and I*, racking up more than four thousand performances.

Gertrude Lawrence, the original Anna of *The King and I*, persuaded Rodgers and Hammerstein to turn the material into a musical for her—after Cole Porter [261 . . .] turned her down. She created the part in 1951 but died in 1952. The part was subsequently played by Celeste Holm [46 . . .] and in the London production by Valerie Hobson. Dinah Shore sought the role when the film was being cast, but Brynner insisted on Kerr. The Oscar went to Brynner's *Anastasia* costar, Ingrid Bergman.

The best picture Oscar went to *Around the World in 80 Days,* which also won for Lionel Lindon's cinematography.

Lang, a Fox contract director of no particular distinction, received his sole nomination for *The King,* but rumor has it that Brynner and choreographer Robbins did most of the directing. The Oscar went to George Stevens for *Giant.*

Wheeler: 19, 46, 83, 356, 376, 428, 476, 495, 542, 719, 721, 798, 950, 1062, 1149, 1153, 1213, 1391, 1475, 1601, 1616, 1670, 1706, 1852, 2008, 2093, 2212. DeCuir: 29, 201, 376, 413, 476, 896, 950, 1391, 1852, 2000. Scott: 46, 376, 413, 476, 530, 542, 557, 646, 896, 1062, 1213, 1391, 1475, 1706, 1753, 1881, 1907, 2008, 2120, 2247. Fox: 376, 413, 428, 476, 495, 530, 721, 950, 1601, 1666, 1706, 1852. Faulkner: 1062, 1213, 2336. Newman: 31, 34, 46, 72, 138, 182, 226, 333, 334, 347, 375, 428, 437, 457, 476, 495, 542, 690, 797, 833, 952, 953, 959, 962, 1016, 1082, 1213, 1278, 1362, 1397, 1475, 1616, 1655, 1849, 1868, 1883, 1921, 2043, 2046, 2091, 2258, 2286, 2294, 2316. Darby: 334, 690, 953, 1592, 1883. Sharaff: 66, 290, 333, 338, 413, 690, 852, 896, 1507, 1592, 1910, 2000, 2244, 2277. Brackett: 705, 925, 1208, 1440, 1975, 2093, 2099. Kerr: 599, 732, 891, 1778, 1969. Shamroy: 29, 226, 356, 413, 495, 569, 602, 1153, 1213, 1592, 1610, 1706, 1852, 1883, 2013, 2286, 2334.

1089 • KING KONG

Dino de Laurentiis Production; Paramount. 1976.

Award *Special Achievement Award for Visual Effects:* Carlo Rambaldi, Glen Robinson, and Frank Van Der Veer.

Nominations *Cinematography:* Richard H. Kline. *Sound:* Harry Warren Tetrick, William McCaughey, Aaron Rochin, and Jack Solomon.

Paleontologist Jeff Bridges [1139 . . .] stows away aboard a tanker headed for Skull Island, where oil company exec Charles Grodin hopes to make a big strike. Along the way, they pick up Jessica Lange [244.5 . . .], who's found floating in a life raft—she was on a movie producer's yacht when it sank. On

Skull Island they find Kong, a forty-foot-tall ape, whom Grodin captures and brings back to New York. Kong and Lange wind up on top of the World Trade Center. John Guillermin directed this pumped-up remake of the 1933 classic that's not as bad as its reputation, thanks mainly to its three stars and some good special effects. But trying to judge this movie without comparing it to the original is like playing the Tolstoy family's game in which the winner was the person who went the longest without thinking about a white bear. (Nights were long at Yasnaya Polyana.) The 1933 film is one of the most influential of all time, retaining its freshness sixty years later, when most of its contemporaries, including best picture winner *Cavalcade,* have been forgotten. Yet it received no notice from the Academy—in part because the award for special effects had not yet been created. If it had been, chief technician Willis O'Brien would surely have been cited. The remake was the debut film for Lange, who went on to greater things and would prefer to forget where she started, although the wit underlying her performance as the addlebrained starlet who captivates the beast has become more obvious since she demonstrated depth and intelligence in her later serious roles.

The special effects award was a noncompetitive one voted by the Academy board. Not cited in the award was makeup artist Rick Baker [68 . . .], who wears an ape suit for some of the effects. The cinematography Oscar went to Haskell Wexler for *Bound for Glory. All the President's Men* won for sound.

Rambaldi: 44, 588. Robinson: 591, 917, 1196. Kline: 334. Tetrick: 1712, 2287. McCaughey: 521, 1310, 1712, 2287. Rochin: 521, 641, 1310, 1711, 2124, 2165, 2231, 2287. Solomon: 738, 896, 938, 1109, 1310.

1090 • KING OF BURLESQUE

20TH CENTURY-FOX. 1935.

NOMINATION *Dance Direction:* Sammy Lee.

An impresario from the world of burlesque, Warner Baxter [989], decides to go upscale with a big Broadway production. Not much plot, and what there is is dumb, but there are plenty of musical numbers, and nice work from Alice Faye, Jack Oakie [818], and Fats Waller, among others, directed by Sidney Lanfield. Lee, nominated for the "Lovely Lady" and "Too Good to Be True" numbers, lost to David Gould's work on *Broadway Melody of 1936* and *Folies Bergère.*

Lee: 37.

1091 • KING OF JAZZ

UNIVERSAL. 1929–30.

AWARD *Interior Decoration:* Herman Rosse.

Musical revue spotlighting Paul Whiteman and his orchestra, with lavish production numbers in two-color Technicolor. Invaluable historical record of a musical epoch, with a performance of Gershwin's "Rhapsody in Blue" and musical numbers by various artists, among them the Rhythm Boys, a trio that included Bing Crosby [173 . . .], making his film debut. Directed by John Murray Anderson.

1092 • KING OF THE ZOMBIES

MONOGRAM. 1941.

NOMINATION *Scoring of a Dramatic Picture:* Edward Kay.

Mad scientist plots to send zombies into combat in the war. Low-budget no-brainer from "poverty row" studio Monogram that owes its nomination to a rules change allowing studios and production companies to submit candidates. There were twenty nominees in this scoring category. The winner was Bernard Herrmann for *All That Money Can Buy.*

Kay: 767, 1103, 1121, 1965.

1093 • KING RAT

COLEYTOWN PRODUCTION; COLUMBIA. 1965.

NOMINATIONS *Black-and-White Cinematography:* Burnett Guffey. *Black-and-White Art Direction—Set Decoration:* Robert Emmet Smith; Frank Tuttle.

George Segal [2277] plays Corporal King, a POW in a Japanese camp in Malaya during World War II whose cunning, guile, and unscrupulousness enable him to survive, and even live comfortably. Intelligent, probing, sometimes grim but also entertaining study of the ethics of survival. King's character and morality are scrutinized from two viewpoints: that of the upper-class Brit played by James Fox, who is fascinated by the amoral American loner-hustler, and that of the moralist played by Tom Courtenay [558 . . .], who is determined to expose King as evil. Directed by Bryan Forbes [81], who also adapted the novel by James Clavell. The cast includes John Mills [1737] and Denholm Elliott [1725]. The Oscars went to *Ship of Fools* for Ernest Laszlo's cinematography and Robert Clatworthy and Joseph Kish's art direction–set decoration.

Guffey: 210, 255, 732, 870. Tuttle: 843, 2066.

1094 • *KING SOLOMON'S MINES*

MGM. 1950.

AWARDS *Color Cinematography:* Robert Surtees. *Film Editing:* Ralph E. Winters and Conrad A. Nervig. NOMINATION *Picture:* Sam Zimbalist, producer.

Deborah Kerr [599 . . .] persuades great white hunter Stewart Granger to help her look for her husband, lost in darkest Africa during a search for the fabled treasure of King Solomon's mines. Silly, splendid epic whose assumptions about the white man's burden are archaic, so it's best to overlook them and enjoy the spectacular scenery, the wildlife footage, and the succession of perils into which the characters keep stepping. Kerr and Granger are a fine, sexy team—they were one off screen, too, for a while. Compton Bennett directed the narrative stuff, while Andrew Marton directed the action, which includes a breathtaking animal stampede. There was so much footage left over that MGM kept using it for the next twenty years in various African adventures.

Surtees, who came to Hollywood in 1927 and served an apprenticeship under such masters as Gregg Toland [407 . . .] and Joseph Ruttenberg [318 . . .], was himself one of the masters of color cinematography and a specialist in location filming. He returned to Africa in 1953 for *Mogambo.* This was the first of his three Oscars.

The best picture Oscar went to *All About Eve.*

Surtees: 130, 175, 557, 810, 917, 1139, 1388, 1469, 1644, 1747, 1911, 1927, 1960, 2055, 2152. Winters: 175, 825, 1109, 1644, 1782. Nervig: 623, 1996. Zimbalist: 175, 1644.

1095 • *KINGS ROW*

WARNER BROS. 1942.

NOMINATIONS *Picture:* Hal B. Wallis, producer. *Director:* Sam Wood. *Black-and-White Cinematography:* James Wong Howe.

Randy (Ann Sheridan), Parris (Robert Cummings), and Drake (Ronald Reagan) grow up in a small midwestern town that's chock full of passion, madness, intrigue, and plain old meanness. Grand melodrama that almost seems designed by Warners as an antidote to the syrupy images of small-town life then being poured out by MGM. The Henry Bellamann novel on which it's based was thought to be unfilmable, but screenwriter Casey Robinson was willing to work with the Breen office to get it made. The result may be supertrash, but it gave Reagan the best role of his career—his screen career, that is— and the title of his autobiography: *Where's the Rest of Me?*, which refers to his character's response to waking up and discovering he's had a leg amputated. The cast includes Betty Field, Charles Coburn [535 . . .], Claude Rains [365 . . .], Judith Anderson [1670], Maria Ouspenskaya [560 . . .], and Harry Davenport. The score is by Erich Wolfgang Korngold [17 . . .].

The Oscars all went to *Mrs. Miniver,* for best picture, director William Wyler, and cinematographer Joseph Ruttenberg.

Wallis: 17, 55, 85, 164, 343, 365, 676, 689, 712, 965, 1046, 1162, 1248, 1482, 1727, 1779, 2233, 2318. Wood: 701, 804, 1102. Howe: 1, 30, 36, 738, 956, 1451, 1470, 1727, 1774.

1096 • *KISMET*

MGM. 1944.

NOMINATIONS *Color Cinematography:* Charles Rosher. *Color Interior Decoration:* Cedric Gibbons and Daniel B. Cathcart, art direction; Edwin B. Willis and Richard Pefferle, set decoration. *Sound Recording:* Douglas Shearer. *Scoring of a Dramatic or Comedy Picture:* Herbert Stothart.

Ronald Colman [311 . . .] plays the roguish hero, whose daughter (Joy Ann Page, who played Annina in *Casablanca)* is wooed by a young prince, as an evil vizier (is there any other kind?), played by Edward Arnold, plots malfeasance. Marlene Dietrich [1358] has a smallish part as one of the vizier's harem dancers; she's coated with gold paint and judiciously aided by body doubles in long shots for the actual dancing. This kitschy stuff, directed by William Dieterle [1169], seems more suited to Universal's Jon Hall–Maria Montez series than to the glossy MGM treatment it receives here. The old warhorse of a play on which it's based opened originally on Broadway in 1911. It was filmed in 1920 and 1930, and after this was turned into a hit Broadway musical that was filmed by MGM in 1955 with Howard Keel and Ann Blyth [1319].

Wilson took the Oscars for Leon Shamroy's cinematography and for art direction and sound. The scoring award went to Max Steiner for *Since You Went Away.*

Rosher: 22, 87, 1818, 1972, 2320. Gibbons: 66, 87, 130, 217, 227, 239, 285, 290, 440, 629, 749, 831, 980, 1069, 1173, 1190, 1226, 1230, 1232, 1274, 1308, 1309, 1417, 1567, 1604, 1644, 1662, 1673, 1721, 1861, 1937, 2068, 2112, 2256, 2257, 2300, 2320, 2330. Cathcart: 2068. Willis: 66, 87, 130, 227, 239, 290, 629, 749, 831, 980, 1069, 1157, 1173, 1190, 1226, 1230, 1232, 1309, 1417, 1567, 1657, 1662, 1673, 1721, 1861, 1937, 2068, 2112, 2257, 2320, 2330. Pefferle: 87, 1157, 1230, 1552, 2312. Shearer: 136, 202, 256, 397, 685, 817, 835, 1232, 1292, 1371, 1419, 1751, 1950, 1988, 2048, 2055, 2211, 2300. Stothart: 397, 1232, 1274, 1292, 1387, 1662, 1988, 2068, 2193, 2234, 2300.

1097 • KISS ME KATE

MGM. 1953.
Nomination *Scoring of a Musical Picture:* André Previn and Saul Chaplin.

Backstage at a Broadway production of a musical version of Shakespeare's *Taming of the Shrew,* the leads, Howard Keel and Kathryn Grayson, are squabbling. Formerly married, they are now trying to go their separate ways but keep discovering that, as the song has it, they are "So in Love." The Cole Porter [261 . . .] lyrics for this adaptation of the great stage hit have been bowdlerized, and much of the movie seems to be trying too hard. Grayson's acidulous soprano and limited acting ability have never been more unwelcome: As Kate she runs the gamut from pouty to petulant. Keel, however, looks and sounds great, and even in sanitized versions the show is full of wonderful songs. Interestingly one of the movie's highlights is a number set to "From This Moment On," which was not in the original score of *Kiss Me Kate*—it was borrowed from another Porter show, *Out of This World.* It's terrifically danced by Ann Miller, Bob Fosse [49 . . .], Tommy Rall, and Bobby Van, with choreography by Hermes Pan [481]. The movie was filmed in 3-D, which accounts for some of the in-your-lap staging. Directed by George Sidney, with Keenan Wynn and James Whitmore [157 . . .] as the gangsters who advise "Brush Up Your Shakespeare." The scoring award went to Alfred Newman for *Call Me Madam.*

Previn: 172, 609, 769, 1017, 1034, 1044, 1393, 1550, 1592, 2064, 2077, 2161. Chaplin: 66, 914, 1782, 2244.

1098 • KISS OF DEATH

20TH CENTURY-FOX. 1947.
Nominations *Supporting Actor:* Richard Widmark. *Original Story:* Eleazar Lipsky.

When ex-mobster Victor Mature decides to inform on his former partners in crime, hired killer Widmark is dispatched to get rid of him. Gripping thriller that gave Widmark an attention-getting film debut role, though Widmark felt that the part handicapped him and spent the rest of his career avoiding roles that might type him as a giggling psychotic who pushes old ladies downstairs. Ben Hecht [78 . . .] and Charles Lederer turned Lipsky's story into a screenplay, and it was directed by Henry Hathaway [1194] with splendidly atmospheric New York location photography by Norbert Brodine [731 . . .]. The cast includes Brian Donlevy [161], Karl Malden [1477 . . .], and Mildred Dunnock [119 . . .]. Widmark lost to Santa Claus—Edmund Gwenn in *Miracle on 34th Street,* which also won for Valentine Davies' story.

1099 • KISS OF THE SPIDER WOMAN

H.B. FILMES PRODUCTION IN ASSOCIATION WITH SUGARLOAF FILMS; ISLAND ALIVE (BRAZIL). 1985.

AWARD *Actor:* William Hurt.

NOMINATIONS *Picture:* David Weisman, producer. *Director:* Hector Babenco. *Screenplay Based on Material From Another Medium:* Leonard Schrader.

A gay man (Hurt) and a revolutionary leader (Raul Julia) are confined together in a South American prison where the authorities hope to coerce the former into spying on the latter. Hurt begins to understand the political passion of his cellmate, while Julia is entertained by Hurt's flamboyant retellings of the plots of exotic movie melodramas. Sonia Braga is the star of the movies within the movie. Absorbing character drama that did surprisingly well at the box office —at least it was surprising to those who thought that homosexuality, dialogue about political responsibility, and a downer ending would drive away the audiences. It always helps to have top-notch performers and a strong script, of course. Manuel Puig's novel has subsequently been the basis of a hit Broadway musical, too.

Hurt was one of the hottest actors in Hollywood during the eighties, from his debut in *Altered States* through such films as *Body Heat* (1981), *The Big Chill,* the post-Oscar *Children of a Lesser God* and *Broadcast News,* for which he was nominated, and *The Accidental Tourist.* But in the nineties, except for a well-received performance in *The Doctor* (1991), he seemed to drop from sight. He was not the first choice for his Oscar-winning role: Burt Lancaster [107 . . .] had to pull out of the film because of heart surgery.

Out of Africa was the spoiler for the remaining *Kiss* nominees, winning for best picture, director Sydney Pollack, and screenwriter Kurt Luedtke. Babenco, a leading Brazilian director, used his success with his first Hollywood venture to obtain backing for his next film, *Ironweed,* which was as significant a flop as *Kiss* was a success. Screenwriter Schrader is the brother and sometime collaborator of writer-director Paul Schrader.

Hurt: 293, 390.

1100 • KISSES FOR MY PRESIDENT

PEARLAYNE PRODUCTION; WARNER BROS. 1964.

NOMINATION *Black-and-White Costume Design:* Howard Shoup.

Polly Bergen becomes president of the United States, creating problems for first husband Fred Mac-Murray. Dumb, dated comedy milking its premise for predictable role-reversal humor. Directed by Curtis Bernhardt. The Oscar went to Dorothy Jeakins for *The Night of the Iguana.*

Shoup: 410, 1649, 1700, 2338.

1101 • KITTY

PARAMOUNT. 1946.

NOMINATION *Black-and-White Interior Decoration:* Hans Dreier and Walter Tyler, art direction; Sam Comer and Ray Moyer, set decoration.

Paulette Goddard [1855] plays the title role, an eighteenth-century wench passed off as a duchess with the aid of a down-at-the-heels nobleman played by Ray Milland [1208]. This bodice-ripper version of *Pygmalion* is handsomely produced, but it doesn't amount to much. Mitchell Leisen [587] directed, and the cast includes Cecil Kellaway [843 . . .], Constance Collier, Sara Allgood [952], and Eric Blore. The Oscar went to *Anna and the King of Siam.*

Dreier: 97, 151, 649, 674, 701, 726, 925, 979, 1120, 1194, 1214, 1217, 1358, 1443, 1452, 1540, 1668, 1748, 1880, 1975, 1994, 2190. Tyler: 357, 1022, 1716, 1738, 1748, 1959, 2012, 2208. Comer: 278, 357, 426, 450, 726, 736, 925, 956, 1029, 1214, 1219, 1443, 1570, 1631, 1674, 1727, 1738, 1748, 1959, 1975, 1994, 2012, 2098, 2200, 2208. Moyer: 278, 413, 736, 833, 1120, 1214, 1674, 1738, 1748, 1975, 2012.

1102 • KITTY FOYLE

RKO RADIO. 1940.

AWARD *Actress:* Ginger Rogers.

NOMINATIONS *Picture:* David Hempstead, producer. *Director:* Sam Wood. *Screenplay:* Dalton Trumbo. *Sound Recording:* John Aalberg.

Kitty (Rogers) is an ambitious young woman from the poorer side of Philadelphia who lands a job as secretary to the upper-class Dennis Morgan. They fall in love and elope, but his family objects to their marriage—they think she's okay but want to send her to finishing school and give her some polish—whereupon Kitty, in her pride, walks out. The marriage is annulled, but then Kitty discovers she's pregnant. Just as she's about to break the news to Morgan, she also discovers that he's engaged to a woman of his own class. She decides to have the child on her own, without telling Morgan. The baby dies, but Kitty meets a handsome young doctor (James Craig), who eventually proposes to her. Then Morgan returns to say he's decided to leave his wife and that he wants Kitty to live with him and be his love in South America. Decisions, decisions. The movie, based on a novel by Christopher Morley, is weepy, talky, and whimsical, a very mixed bag that was quite popular in its day, but hasn't held up well at all—especially the jaw-droppingly antifeminist prologue. The cast includes Eduardo Ciannelli and Gladys Cooper [1393 . . .].

Rogers' Oscar looks like one of those semihonorary awards that often get presented to performers who have done better work in better films but somehow never got rewarded for it. She had been in the movies since the early thirties, and in addition to the magical teaming with Fred Astaire [2126], had given delightful performances in *Stage Door* and *Bachelor Mother,* among other films. Her career would last into the fifties, and in 1965 she came out of semiretirement to appear on Broadway in *Hello, Dolly!* She had a special quality of being bold but not brassy—the girl next door, if that girl happens to be a sensational dancer and gifted comedian.

The best picture Oscar went to *Rebecca.* John Ford won for directing *The Grapes of Wrath.* The award for sound went to Douglas Shearer for *Strike Up the Band.*

This was Trumbo's sole nomination under his own name, although he won two Oscars. One he received under the pseudonym Robert Rich for *The Brave One;* the other was presented to Ian McLellan Hunter for *Roman Holiday,* although Hunter later let it be known that he was fronting for Trumbo, who had been cited for contempt of Congress for his failure to testify to the satisfaction of the House Un-American Activities Committee. After serving a prison term, Trumbo was blacklisted but continued to write sub rosa, and returned to the screen under his own name in the sixties with the films *Spartacus* and *Exodus.* Donald Ogden Stewart [1148 . . .], who was credited with "additional dialogue" on *Kitty Foyle,* defeated Trumbo in the Oscar race with his screenplay for *The Philadelphia Story.*

Wood: 701, 804, 1095. Trumbo: 273, 1716. Aalberg: 407, 923, 959, 1033, 1978, 1991, 2030, 2166, 2213.

1103 • *KLONDIKE FURY*

MONOGRAM. 1942.

NOMINATION *Scoring of a Dramatic or Comedy Picture:* Edward Kay.

When a patient dies during an operation, a doctor gives up his practice and flies to the Yukon to start a new life. Paper-thin adventure-romance with Edmund Lowe and Lucille Fairbanks. Another Monogram entry that received a nomination because studios were allowed to submit candidates for certain awards. The Oscar went to Max Steiner for *Now, Voyager.*

Kay: 767, 1092, 1121, 1965.

1104 • *KLUTE*

GUS PRODUCTION; WARNER BROS. 1971.

AWARD *Actress:* Jane Fonda.

NOMINATION *Story and Screenplay—Based on Factual Material or Material Not Previously Published or Produced:* Andy Lewis and Dave Lewis.

Klute (Donald Sutherland) is a cop from a small town who comes to New York in search of a missing friend. The trail leads to Bree Daniels (Fonda), a hooker whom Klute winds up protecting from a killer. Exceptionally well done thriller, with superb performances by the leads and crisply effective direction by Alan J. Pakula [54 . . .]. The neo-expressionist cinematography of Gordon Willis [786 . . .] is a big plus. The cast includes Roy Scheider [49 . . .], Rita Gam, and Jean Stapleton.

After starting her film career in 1960 with *Tall Story,* Fonda went through a typical ingenue period of good but unexceptional performances in films ranging from vapid—*The Chapman Report* (1962)—to fluffy—*Cat Ballou, Barefoot in the Park*—to exploitive—*Barbarella* (1968). The last was made during her marriage to French director Roger Vadim. But the following year she had her first strong and impressive dramatic role in *They Shoot Horses, Don't They?*, which earned her critical acclaim and her first nomination. In the meantime, she had also become involved with activist Tom Hayden and turned into an outspoken critic of the Vietnam War. Even *Klute*, she claimed, was a political statement about the exploitation of women. She received both boos and applause when she accepted her Oscar, pointedly thanked everyone "who applauded," and declined to turn her acceptance speech into a more explicit political statement. She subsequently used her success at the box office and the Oscars to produce such agitprop films as *FTA* (1972)—the initials standing for either "Free . . ." or "Fuck the Army"—and the documentary on her trip to North Vietnam, *Introduction to the Enemy* (1974). But by the mid-seventies, she began to back off from her more aggressive activism.

The screenplay award went to Paddy Chayefsky for *The Hospital*.

Fonda: 394, 430, 1066, 1356, 1473, 2047.

1105 • KNICKERBOCKER HOLIDAY

PCA; United Artists. 1944.
Nomination *Scoring of a Musical Picture:* Werner R. Heymann and Kurt Weill.

Charles Coburn [535 . . .] plays Peter Stuyvesant, the tyrannical governor of seventeenth-century New Amsterdam. Nelson Eddy is his rival, a believer in democracy. Dull translation to the screen of a celebrated but seldom revived stage musical with songs by Weill and Maxwell Anderson [48], the most famous of which is "September Song." Coburn plays the role that won acclaim for Walter Huston [50 . . .] on Broadway. The cast, directed by Harry Brown, includes Shelley Winters [542 . . .].

This is the only nomination for Weill, a composer celebrated for his collaboration with Bertolt Brecht in the late twenties and early thirties in Berlin. Together they produced *Die Dreigroschenoper (The Threepenny Op-*era*)* and *Mahagonny* before both were forced into exile by the Nazis. Weill came to New York, where he became a major figure in the musical theater, creating such works as *Lady in the Dark, One Touch of Venus,* and *Street Scene*. The Oscar went to Carmen Dragon and Morris Stoloff for *Cover Girl*.

Heymann: 1487, 2036, 2096.

1106 • KNIFE IN THE WATER

Film Polski Kamera Unit (Poland). 1963.
Nomination *Foreign Language Film.*

A married couple picks up a young hitchhiker and invites him to join them for the weekend on their boat. The resulting sexual conflicts become increasingly violent. Compelling feature film debut by director Roman Polanski [395 . . .], who collaborated on the screenplay with Jakub Goldberg and Jerzy Skolimowski. The Polish government denounced the film, hastening Polanski's exile in the West. The Oscar went to *8¹/₂*.

1107 • KNIGHTS OF THE ROUND TABLE

MGM. 1953.
Nominations *Color Art Direction–Set Decoration:* Alfred Junge and Hans Peters; John Jarvis. *Sound Recording:* A. W. Watkins, sound director, MGM Sound Department.

Robert Taylor is Lancelot, Ava Gardner [1339] Guinevere, and Mel Ferrer Arthur in this galumphingly dull version of the old familiar triangle, designed mainly as MGM's first CinemaScope film. At least *Camelot* had songs. Directed by Richard Thorpe, with Stanley Baker and Felix Aylmer.

The art direction award went to the very first CinemaScope epic, *The Robe*. The sound Oscar was won by *From Here to Eternity*.

Junge: 221. Peters: 69, 1226, 1567, 1673. Watkins: 558, 804, 1165.

1108 • KNOCK ON WOOD

Dena Productions; Paramount. 1954.
Nomination *Story and Screenplay:* Norman Panama and Melvin Frank.

Ventriloquist Danny Kaye somehow gets involved

in international espionage in this busy farce. Kaye fans get their money's worth; others may just get a headache. Produced and directed by Panama and Frank, with Mai Zetterling, Torin Thatcher, and David Burns. The Oscar went to Budd Schulberg for *On the Waterfront.*

Panama: 636, 1705. Frank: 636, 1705, 2125.

1109 • KOTCH

KOTCH COMPANY PRODUCTION; ABC PICTURES PRESENTATION; CINERAMA. 1971.

NOMINATIONS *Actor:* Walter Matthau. *Sound:* Richard Portman and Jack Solomon. *Song:* "Life Is What You Make It," music by Marvin Hamlisch, lyrics by Johnny Mercer. *Film Editing:* Ralph E. Winters.

Matthau plays one of his grumpy old men, an elderly widower whose family underestimates his abilities. Very much a vehicle for its star, who at fifty-one had already begun to play characters several decades older. He's directed by his frequent costar, Jack Lemmon [91 . . .], whose sole effort at feature directing turned out quite nicely—it's a very pleasant little film.

Matthau lost to Gene Hackman in *The French Connection,* which also won for Jerry Greenberg's editing. The award for sound went to *Fiddler on the Roof.* Isaac Hayes won the song Oscar for "Theme From *Shaft.*"

Matthau: 709, 1976. Portman: 339, 418, 502, 521, 738, 784, 1473, 1526, 1701, 2331. Solomon: 738, 896, 938, 1089, 1310. Hamlisch: 398, 977, 1747, 1813, 1876, 1898, 1927, 2238. Mercer: 248, 278, 384, 476, 494, 508, 636, 788, 825, 877, 903, 905, 1772, 1838, 1912, 2327, 2328. Winters: 175, 825, 1094, 1644, 1782.

1110 • KRAKATOA, EAST OF JAVA

AMERICAN BROADCASTING COMPANIES-CINERAMA PRODUCTION; CINERAMA. 1969.

NOMINATION *Special Visual Effects:* Eugene Lourie and Alex Weldon.

A boatload of Victorian adventurers led by Maximilian Schell [1065 . . .] sets out in search of sunken treasure and winds up at ground zero when the volcanic island of Krakatoa explodes. Big, silly, incoherent spectacular originally shown in Cinerama. As the reference books will tell you, Krakatoa was *west* of Java, but the filmmakers didn't have accuracy, logic, plot, characterization, or much of anything else in mind. The cast, directed by Bernard Kowalski, also includes Diane Baker, Brian Keith, Rossano Brazzi, and Sal Mineo [630 . . .]. The special effects Oscar went to Robbie Robertson for *Marooned.*

Weldon: 1541.

1111 • KRAMER VS. KRAMER

STANLEY JAFFE PRODUCTIONS; COLUMBIA. 1979.

AWARDS *Picture:* Stanley R. Jaffe, producer. *Actor:* Dustin Hoffman. *Supporting Actress:* Meryl Streep. *Director:* Robert Benton. *Screenplay Based on Material From Another Medium:* Robert Benton.

NOMINATIONS *Supporting Actor:* Justin Henry. *Supporting Actress:* Jane Alexander. *Cinematography:* Nestor Almendros. *Film Editing:* Jerry Greenberg.

Workaholic ad exec Hoffman neglects his family, until one day his wife, Streep, walks out, leaving him with their small son, Henry. Hoffman learns to cope with single-parenting and turns into a kinder, gentler fellow. Then Streep returns and seeks custody of Henry, leading to a brutal courtroom confrontation. For all the high-powered performers, first-rate production, and thoughtful and heartfelt direction, it doesn't add up to quite enough. For one thing, the script doesn't fill in enough of the blanks in Streep's character to explain why this intelligent and obviously loving woman would abandon her child. It's suggested that her departure was part temporary breakdown, part quest for selfhood. But it looks like just a plot contrivance, no matter how hard Streep works to put the character together. The movie was a huge hit—it spoke particularly to maturing baby boomers who were finding the balance of career and family hard to manage. But its triumph at the Oscars was at the expense of some films that look a lot more interesting today. The competitors for best picture included the cheerful sleeper *Breaking Away,* the upbeat melodrama *Norma Rae,* and two flawed, overwrought, but fascinating films, *All That Jazz* and *Apocalypse Now,* that were perhaps the last gasp of the daring moviemaking of the seventies, when directors like Bob Fosse and Francis Coppola stretched the limits of the mainstream film. *Kramer vs. Kramer* signals Hollywood's retreat into the crowd-pleasing sentimental earnestness of the eighties that would produce, in succession, such slick but unadventurous best picture winners as *Ordinary People, Chariots of Fire, Gandhi, Terms of Endearment, Amadeus,* and *Out of Africa.*

Jaffe, a former head of Paramount, had moved over to Columbia as an executive but went independent with *Kramer,* and subsequently teamed up with former Fox executive Sherry Lansing [653] for Jaffe-Lansing Productions, a modestly successful company whose major hit was *Fatal Attraction.*

Hoffman rose swiftly to stardom with *The Graduate* and demonstrated his versatility two years later in *Midnight Cowboy,* making him one of the most talked-about actors in Hollywood. But he had bad-mouthed the Oscars on a talk show in 1975, when he was up for an award for *Lenny,* allegedly calling the awards "obscene," so it's not surprising that he was persona non grata with the Academy for a while. *Kramer* marked Hoffman's movement into the mainstream—for a change he wasn't playing a weirdo or a loner, but a middle-class workaholic father.

Streep had made her debut in a small role in *Julia* in 1977 and had been nominated for her work in *The Deer Hunter* the following year. By 1979 she was emerging as a major figure, even though her roles were still smallish, as in *Manhattan,* or in second-string features, as in *The Seduction of Joe Tynan.* When *Kramer* was being cast, Streep tested for the role played in the film by JoBeth Williams. Kate Jackson was the leading candidate for the role of Joanna Kramer, but when Jackson had to fulfill a commitment to the *Charlie's Angels* TV series, Jaffe's future associate, Lansing, proposed Streep for the more important role. In the eighties Streep became a major figure, astonishing audiences and critics with her ability to subsume herself in roles and to master a variety of accents.

Benton burst on the scene about the same time as Hoffman, with his screenplay in collaboration with David Newman for *Bonnie and Clyde.* Born in Texas,

he teamed up with Newman in the sixties, when they were both editors at *Esquire* magazine. He made his directing debut with the little-seen but critically well received *Bad Company* in 1972 and continued with *The Late Show* in 1977. Along the way, he also contributed to the screenplays for *What's Up, Doc?* (1977) and *Superman. Kramer vs. Kramer* was adapted from a novel by Avery Corman. Some parts of the film were improvised or reworked by the actors—Henry, for example, was told what his scenes were about and allowed to use his own words in some of them.

At nine Henry was the youngest person ever nominated for an Oscar. He has made a few subsequent appearances in films, including *Sixteen Candles* (1984) and *Sweet Hearts Dance* (1988). He lost to Melvyn Douglas, who at seventy-nine was then the oldest person to win an acting Oscar.

The award for cinematography went to Vittorio Storaro for *Apocalypse Now.* Alan Heim won for the editing of *All That Jazz.*

Jaffe: 653. Hoffman: 810, 1155, 1312, 1653, 2113. Streep: 472, 521, 725, 1019, 1512, 1598, 1821, 1876. Benton: 255, 1146, 1444.5, 1580. Alexander: 54, 830, 2023. Almendros: 243, 506, 1876. Greenberg: 92, 724.

1112 • KWAIDAN

Toho Company Ltd. Production (Japan). 1965.
Nomination *Foreign Language Film.*

Four Japanese ghost stories collected by Lafcadio Hearn, directed by Masaki Kobayashi. Eerie, atmospheric, beautifully composed and filmed, with avant-garde music by Toru Takemitsu. The Oscar went to *The Shop on Main Street.*

1113 • L-SHAPED ROOM, THE

Romulus Productions Ltd.; Columbia (United Kingdom). 1963.
Nomination *Actress:* Leslie Caron.

Finding herself pregnant, a young Frenchwoman (Caron) goes to England to have an abortion but changes her mind and stays on in a run-down rooming house populated by other lonely people. A writer, played by Tom Bell, falls in love with her but breaks off their relationship when he discovers she's pregnant. Drab, moody, longish film made watchable by some fine performers, including Brock Peters, Emlyn Williams, Cicely Courtneidge, and Bernard Lee. Directed by Bryan Forbes [81], who wrote the screenplay based on a novel by Lynne Reid Banks.

Caron, who was moving out of the soubrette roles that had made her a star, lost to Patricia Neal in *Hud*.

Caron: 1173.

LA CAGE AUX FOLLES
See 326.

LA DOLCE VITA
See 562.

LA GUERRE EST FINIE
See 842.

LA RONDE
See 1723.

LA STRADA
See 1938.

LA TRAVIATA
See 2135.

LA VENGANZA
See 2197.

LA VÉRITÉ
See 2199.

1114 • *LACOMBE, LUCIEN*
NEF-UPF (Paris)-Vides Film (Rome)-Hallelujah Film (Munich) Production (France). 1974.
Nomination *Foreign Language Film.*

Lucien is a teenage thug enlisted by the Gestapo in 1944 as an agent after being turned down by the Resistance. He moves in on a Jewish family in hiding but falls in love with their daughter and saves her from execution. After the liberation, he is executed as a collaborator. Director Louis Malle [107 . . .]

treats the material with cool detachment, which makes it all the more chilling. The Oscar went to *Amarcord*.

1115 • *LADIES IN RETIREMENT*
Cowan-Miller; Columbia. 1941.
Nominations *Black-and-White Interior Decoration:* Lionel Banks and George Montgomery. *Scoring of a Dramatic Picture:* Morris Stoloff and Ernst Toch.

Housekeeper Ida Lupino murders her employer and sets up the household for her two mad sisters, Elsa Lanchester [428 . . .] and Edith Barrett. Then the employer's wicked nephew, Louis Hayward, arrives and figures out what she's done. Creepy old-dark-house melodrama adapted by Reginald Denham, Edward Percy, and Garrett Fort from Denham and Percy's play. Directed by Charles Vidor, with cinematography by George Barnes [537 . . .]. The art direction award went to *How Green Was My Valley*. Bernard Herrmann won for the score of *All That Money Can Buy*.

Banks: 13, 98, 455, 928, 1370, 1998. Stoloff: 13, 432, 455, 596, 643, 677, 732, 773, 1057, 1058, 1206, 1862, 1872, 1873, 1998, 2110, 2329. Toch: 13, 1556.

1116 • *LADY AND GENT*
Paramount Publix. 1931–32.
Nomination *Original Story:* Grover Jones and William Slavens McNutt.

Boxer George Bancroft [2085] and nightclub owner Wynne Gibson adopt the orphaned child of his manager. Forgotten—and possibly lost—little heart-tugger with a fifth-billed John Wayne [33 . . .], plus Charles Starrett, James Gleason [904], and Charles Winninger. The Oscar went to Frances Marion for a more durable movie about a boxer and a kid, *The Champ*.

Jones: 1194. McNutt: 1194.

1117 • *LADY BE GOOD*
MGM. 1941.
Award *Song:* "The Last Time I Saw Paris," music by Jerome Kern, lyrics by Oscar Hammerstein II.

Songwriters Ann Sothern [2246] and Robert Young, married to each other, overcome career and marital difficulties. Flimsy plot, but attractive performances and splendid songs keep this backstage musical going. The cast, directed by Norman Z. McLeod, includes Red Skelton, Eleanor Powell, Lionel Barrymore [723 . . .], and Dan Dailey [2258]. No connection—other than the title song and the song "Fascinating Rhythm"—with the Broadway musical by George [1797] and Ira Gershwin [455 . . .].

"The Last Time I Saw Paris" has often been treated as a song about lost love, but it was in fact a response to the fall of the city to the Nazis—an event that so moved Hammerstein that he wrote the lyrics before asking Kern to provide a tune, the reverse of his usual procedure with his songwriting partners. Producer Arthur Freed [66 . . .] asked Hammerstein also to write the bit of dialogue preceding the song in the film, which makes explicit that it's designed as a "salute to a lost city." Hammerstein, whose career was centered in the theater, not Hollywood, used this opportunity to obtain a favor from MGM: the screen rights to the play *Green Grow the Lilacs,* which the studio held. Three years later his musical adaptation of the play would be staged as *Oklahoma!* Kern had settled in Hollywood in 1930, and much of his later career, until his death in 1945, was spent working on film song scores.

Kern: 340, 375, 455, 1707, 1990, 2327. Hammerstein: 375, 1122, 1921, 1951.

1118 • LADY EVE, THE

PARAMOUNT. 1941.

NOMINATION *Original Story:* Monckton Hoffe.

Henry Fonda [815 . . .], heir to a brewery fortune, falls—figuratively, literally, and frequently—for Barbara Stanwyck [138 . . .]. Their shipboard romance ends when she's unmasked as a con artist. But since she's begun to fall in love with him, and wants to get even for the cold way in which he drops her, she disguises herself as an English aristocrat and wangles an introduction to his family. He falls in love again, but she gets her revenge on the honeymoon. Howlingly funny lunatic farce, though the Academy

missed the point: The film's genius is not in the story by Hoffe, which the screenplay by Preston Sturges [823 . . .] resembles hardly at all. Sturges kept only a few incidental details and its basic premise, that of a woman who deceives a man by pretending to be her own twin—or in Sturges' version, a black-sheep half sister. The real strengths of the movie are in Sturges' cheeky dialogue and lightning-paced direction, Fonda's endearingly dazed dopiness, Stanwyck's superb blend of toughness and chic, and the peerless supporting work of Charles Coburn [535 . . .], Eugene Pallette, William Demarest [1058], Eric Blore, and Melville Cooper. The story award went to Harry Segall for *Here Comes Mr. Jordan.* One wonders: If Hoffe had won, would he have thanked Sturges for completely ignoring his story?

1119 • LADY FOR A DAY

COLUMBIA. 1932–33.

NOMINATIONS *Picture:* Frank Capra, producer. *Actress:* May Robson. *Director:* Frank Capra. *Adaptation:* Robert Riskin.

Robson plays Apple Annie, a boozy old street vendor who has a daughter she hasn't seen since infancy. When the daughter, who has been raised in a convent in Europe, announces that she is engaged to a Spanish nobleman and is coming to New York to introduce Annie to the future in-laws, Annie is in despair. In her letters she has pretended to be a wealthy socialite. But her street companions rally around, and Dave the Dude, a gambler played by Warren William, stages a grand reception by blackmailing some of the town's most prominent citizens. Fine adaptation of a Damon Runyon story, "Madame la Gimp," with just enough grit to keep the sentimental story from being cloying. The movie's critical and commercial success helped establish Capra as a major director. It also showed that Columbia was a studio on the rise: The first production from the studio to receive a best picture nomination, it lost to *Cavalcade.*

The Academy's records show that Capra came in second in the race for the directing Oscar. Capra himself recalled that at the Oscar ceremony Will Rogers called out, "Come up and get it, Frank!" when announcing the winner for best director. Whereupon Capra headed for the stage only to slink back in embarrassment when he realized that Rogers meant Frank Lloyd, who won for *Cavalcade*. But Capra's biographer, Joseph McBride, notes that no contemporary reports mention Capra's gaffe, and that Capra and George Cukor, who came in third for *Little Women*, were invited to join Lloyd on the stage after the Oscar had been presented. Capra's hunger for the Oscar, McBride believes, made him oversensitive to being singled out as an also-ran.

In the Oscar balloting, Robson came in second to Katharine Hepburn in *Morning Glory* and ahead of Diana Wynyard, nominated for *Cavalcade*. Robson was second choice for Apple Annie, after Marie Dressler [611 . . .], whom MGM refused to lend for the role. Robson had made a few appearances in silent films, but her major career was on Broadway until the thirties, when she became a regular performer in dowager roles on screen. She was seventy-five when she made *Lady for a Day* and continued performing well into her eighties, making her last appearance in *Joan of Paris* in 1942, the year of her death.

Riskin, who would continue as Capra's most frequent collaborator, came in second to Victor Heerman and Sarah Y. Mason for *Little Women*.

Capra: 1025, 1033, 1206, 1366, 1370, 2325. Riskin: 905, 1025, 1366, 2325.

1120 • LADY IN THE DARK

PARAMOUNT. 1944.

NOMINATIONS *Color Cinematography:* Ray Rennahan. *Color Interior Decoration:* Hans Dreier and Raoul Pène du Bois, art direction; Ray Moyer, set decoration. *Scoring of a Musical Picture:* Robert Emmett Dolan.

Liza Elliott, played by Ginger Rogers [1102], is a successful magazine editor, but she is tormented by feelings of insecurity, so she undergoes psychoanalysis. Turns out all she needs is a good man—or rather Ray Milland [1208], a male chauvinist who craves not only her but also her job. Sexist hooey, and a thunderingly dull version of a celebrated Broadway musical. Moss Hart [297 . . .] wrote the original play

after his own psychoanalysis, and Kurt Weill [1105] and Ira Gershwin [455 . . .] supplied the songs for the show, which starred Gertrude Lawrence as Liza and brought cast members Macdonald Carey (in the Milland role), Victor Mature (as a movie star played in the film by Jon Hall), and Danny Kaye (whose part is played in the film by Mischa Auer [1401]) to the attention of Hollywood. In fact, the show seems to have succeeded mainly because of its original cast, for it's seldom revived, partly because the plot's sexism wouldn't be tolerated today. The film, with a screenplay by Frances Goodrich [25 . . .] and Albert Hackett [25 . . .] and directed by Mitchell Leisen [587], is expensively produced, but it hashes up the songs and production numbers. The cast also includes Warner Baxter [989].

Leon Shamroy won for the cinematography for *Wilson*, which also took the art direction Oscar. Carmen Dragon and Morris Stoloff won for the scoring of *Cover Girl*.

Rennahan: 235, 241, 569, 581, 701, 798, 1210. Dreier: 97, 151, 649, 674, 701, 726, 925, 979, 1101, 1194, 1214, 1217, 1358, 1443, 1452, 1540, 1668, 1748, 1880, 1975, 1994, 2190. Pène du Bois: 1210. Moyer: 278, 413, 736, 833, 1101, 1214, 1674, 1738, 1748, 1975, 2012. Dolan: 173, 213, 244, 929, 994, 1704, 1912.

1121 • LADY LET'S DANCE

SCOTT R. DUNLAP; MONOGRAM. 1944.

NOMINATIONS *Song:* "Silver Shadows and Golden Dreams," music by Lew Pollack, lyrics by Charles Newman. *Scoring of a Musical Picture:* Edward Kay.

Slender little programmer set in a California resort. The big star is the ice skater Belita, and the comic relief is by Frick and Frack. You got it. Yet another film that nominated itself, thanks to liberalized Academy rules in the early forties. The song Oscar went to James Van Heusen and Johnny Burke's "Swinging on a Star," from *Going My Way*. The scoring award was won by Carmen Dragon and Morris Stoloff for *Cover Girl*.

Kay: 767, 1092, 1103, 1965.

1122 • LADY OBJECTS, THE

COLUMBIA. 1938.

NOMINATION *Song:* "A Mist Over the Moon," music by Ben Oakland, lyrics by Oscar Hammerstein II.

Young marrieds Lanny Ross and Gloria Stuart find their union tested when she becomes more successful as a lawyer than he is as an architect. There's also a subplot in which Ross gets accused of the murder of a nightclub singer. Hammerstein is surprisingly prestigious talent to be associated with this ephemeral programmer, directed by Erle C. Kenton. The Oscar went to Ralph Rainger and Leo Robin for "Thanks for the Memory," from *Big Broadcast of 1938.*

Hammerstein: 375, 1117, 1921, 1951.

1123 • LADY OF BURLESQUE

HUNT STROMBERG; UNITED ARTISTS. 1943.

NOMINATION *Scoring of a Dramatic or Comedy Picture:* Arthur Lange.

Someone is bumping off people backstage at the burlesque house, and stripper Barbara Stanwyck [138 . . .] is determined to find out who. Enjoyable mystery-comedy based on Gypsy Rose Lee's *The G-String Murders,* though this is burlesque filtered through the Breen office, and hence about as decorous as *Swan Lake.* Fortunately Stanwyck's gritty tough-girl manner makes the milieu seem real, and she's well supported by Michael O'Shea and Pinky Lee, among others. Directed by William Wellman [157 . . .]. The scoring Oscar went to Alfred Newman for *The Song of Bernadette.*

Lange: 171, 366, 827, 2303.

1124 • LADY OF THE TROPICS

MGM. 1939.

NOMINATION *Black-and-White Cinematography:* George Folsey.

Adventurer Robert Taylor falls in love with Eurasian Hedy Lamarr in Saigon, but villainous Joseph Schildkraut [1169] prevents their happiness. This probably began as someone's idea of a great romantic teaming: the star of *Camille* paired with the star of *Algiers.* Unfortunately it was the wrong star from each: Instead of Greta Garbo [84 . . .] and Charles Boyer [36 . . .], they got the beautiful but wooden Taylor and Lamarr, who strike no sparks. Folsey was among the preliminary nominees for the Oscar but did not in fact make the final ballot, which listed only two contenders for black-and-white cinematography: Bert Glennon for *Stagecoach* and the winner, Gregg Toland for *Wuthering Heights.* Perhaps because of confusion over its new division of cinematography into black-and-white and color categories, for the 1939 awards the Academy chose to winnow down its original slate to two finalists in each division.

Folsey: 51, 137, 629, 807, 835, 838, 1299, 1320, 1500, 1688, 1782, 2068, 2269.

1125 • LADY ON A TRAIN

UNIVERSAL. 1945.

NOMINATION *Sound Recording:* Bernard B. Brown.

From her window on a train, Deanna Durbin witnesses an apparent murder, but she can't get the police to believe her. Eventually, with the help of a mystery writer, she finds the murderer, but first she has to get involved with the victim's eccentric relatives. Pleasant mystery-comedy if you don't expect too much. Durbin sings, as usual. The cast includes Ralph Bellamy [114], Edward Everett Horton, Patricia Morison, Dan Duryea, and William Frawley, directed by Charles David. The sound award went to Stephen Dunn for *The Bells of St. Mary's.*

Brown: 93, 96, 269, 919, 1010, 1011, 1560, 1896, 2028, 2260.

1126 • LADY SINGS THE BLUES

MOTOWN-WESTON-FURIE PRODUCTION; PARAMOUNT. 1972.

NOMINATIONS *Actress:* Diana Ross. *Story and Screenplay —Based on Factual Material or Material Not Previously Published or Produced:* Terence McCloy, Chris Clark, and Suzanne de Passe. *Art Direction—Set Decoration:* Carl Anderson; Reg Allen. *Scoring—Adaptation and Original Song Score:* Gil Askey. *Costume Design:* Bob Mackie, Ray Aghayan, and Norma Koch.

Ross plays Billie Holiday, who battled racism, drug addiction, and her own self-destructiveness in her rise to fame. Unfortunately the movie, directed by Sidney Furie, never shakes free of biopic conventions and clichés, hemming in a superb performance by Ross and excellent support from Billy Dee Williams and Richard Pryor. On the other hand, the songs keep breaking through the soapsuds of the plot, and while Ross doesn't have Holiday's gift of living the lyrics, she compensates by giving all the vocal sweetness she's got. The cinematography of John Alonzo [395] is another plus.

Lady was tailor-made by Ross' Motown mentor Berry Gordy for her film debut. He had discovered her while she was still in high school in Detroit, and by 1964 had sent her trio, the Supremes, to the top of the pop charts. Eventually Ross' ambitions broke up the group, and in 1970 she became an even bigger star as a solo artist. Despite an auspicious debut in films that earned her an Oscar nomination, her follow-up film, the 1975 *Mahogany,* in which she reteamed with Billy Dee Williams, was not a hit, and she made only one more feature, *The Wiz,* which was an outright disaster. The Oscar went to Liza Minnelli for *Cabaret,* which also won for art direction and Ralph Burns' scoring.

Jeremy Larner won the writing award for *The Candidate.* The costume Oscar went to Anthony Powell for *Travels With My Aunt.*

Anderson: 1133. Mackie: 738, 1548. Aghayan: 738, 743. Koch: 963, 2248.

1127 • LADYHAWKE

WARNER BROS. AND 20TH CENTURY FOX PRODUCTION; WARNER BROS. 1985.

NOMINATIONS *Sound:* Les Fresholtz, Dick Alexander, Vern Poore, and Bud Alper. *Sound Effects Editing:* Bob Henderson and Alan Murray.

In medieval Europe an evil bishop (John Wood) has cast a spell on two lovers, played by Rutger Hauer and Michelle Pfeiffer [485 . . .]. She is transformed during the day into a hawk, while he turns into a wolf at night. Undoing this spell involves enlisting a young thief, played by Matthew Broderick, and an elderly priest, played by Leo McKern. This very promising adventure fantasy-romance has been botched somewhat by director Richard Donner, who doesn't give us quite enough magic and wonder, and considering

that he's made his reputation of late as an action director with the *Lethal Weapon* movies, he stages the big fight scenes confusingly. And Broderick is forced, by both direction and script, to play his role as Ferris Bueller in *Camelot.* Still, there are some lovely scenes, photographed by Vittorio Storaro [92 . . .], and Hauer and Pfeiffer make a smashing pair of lovers, even though they're rarely on screen together. The film was one of Pfeiffer's breakthrough roles.

The award for sound went to *Out of Africa. Back to the Future* won for sound effects editing.

Fresholtz: 54, 58, 209, 215, 606, 888, 1279, 1526, 2113, 2179.5. Alexander: 54, 209, 519, 888, 2113, 2179.5. Poore: 209, 888, 2179.5. Alper: 1712. Henderson: 1159. Murray: 1159.

1128 • LADYKILLERS, THE

EALING STUDIOS LTD.; CONTINENTAL DISTRIBUTING INC. (UNITED KINGDOM). 1956.

NOMINATION *Screenplay—Original:* William Rose.

A band of thieves takes up lodgings in the home of a sweetly dotty little old lady. When she discovers that they have pulled off a robbery, they plot to kill her, but their efforts to do so keep backfiring, and one by one they die instead. Droll little entry from the golden age of British film comedy, starring Alec Guinness [287 . . .], Peter Sellers [169 . . .], and Herbert Lom, and Katie Johnson as their elderly nemesis. Directed by Alexander Mackendrick [1255]. Not quite as polished as Guinness' other great fifties comedies *The Lavender Hill Mob, The Man in the White Suit,* or *Kind Hearts and Coronets* (1949), perhaps, but still a treat. It was Sellers' first major film. Rose would go on to win an Oscar for the saccharine *Guess Who's Coming to Dinner.* But this sharp black-comedy script lost to the wordless screenplay by Albert Lamorisse for *The Red Balloon.*

Rose: 758, 843, 1736.

1129 • LAND OF PROMISE

FILM POLSKI PRODUCTION (POLAND). 1975.

NOMINATION *Foreign Language Film.*

Turn-of-the-century industrialists encounter difficulties with their workforce. The three men who run the plant are a Pole, a German, and a Jew; the character of the Jewish industrialist was criticized by some in the States as anti-Semitic. Written and directed by Andrzej Wada from a novel by the 1924 Nobel Prize laureate Wladyslaw S. Reymont. The Oscar went to *Dersu Uzala.*

1130 • LANDLORD, THE

MIRISCH-CARTIER II PRODUCTION; UNITED ARTISTS. 1970.
NOMINATION *Supporting Actress:* Lee Grant.

A naive rich young white guy, played by Beau Bridges, buys a run-down rooming house in the ghetto, planning to fix it up and live there after relocating the tenants. They, however, have a few things to teach him. Sharp, funny satire that may have lost some of its teeth with the passage of time, and the accommodations that the characters reach seem unreal after the increasing polarization of black and white, rich and poor, that took place in the eighties. But it was the first film to deal with gentrification, and it was written by a black screenwriter, William Gunn, from a novel by a black author, Kristin Hunter. Hal Ashby [430 . . .] directs a fine cast: Pearl Bailey, Diana Sands, Louis Gossett [1465], and Susan Anspach. Grant, who plays Bridges' mother, has a hilarious scene with Bailey. The Oscar went to Helen Hayes for *Airport.*

Grant: 534, 1798, 2218.

1131 • LAS VEGAS NIGHTS

PARAMOUNT. 1941.
NOMINATION *Song:* ''Dolores,'' music by Lou Alter, lyrics by Frank Loesser.

Very minor musical about the misadventures of a group of vaudevillians stranded in Vegas. The stars are Bert Wheeler, Virginia Dale, Phil Regan, and Tommy Dorsey and his orchestra, but it's most notable for the first screen appearance of Dorsey's soloist—Frank Sinatra [732 . . .]. The song Oscar went to Jerome Kern and Oscar Hammerstein II's ''The Last Time I Saw Paris,'' from *Lady Be Good.*

Alter: 2131. Loesser: 864, 1422, 1551, 2026.

1132 • LASSIE COME HOME

MGM. 1943.
NOMINATION *Color Cinematography:* Leonard Smith.

The indomitable collie makes an arduous cross-country journey to rejoin the family that was forced to sell her. The first film in the series not only made a star of the dog but also helped launch the career of Elizabeth Taylor [318 . . .], who appears in a minor role. It was her second film (the first was a dim little comedy at Universal in 1942, *There's One Born Every Minute*). The rest of the film's cast is pretty good, too: Roddy McDowall, Donald Crisp [952], May Whitty [1371 . . .], Edmund Gwenn [1325 . . .], Nigel Bruce, and Elsa Lanchester [428 . . .]. There were six more Lassie films, a radio series, and an endlessly mutating TV series before *Lassie Come Home* was remade in 1978 as *The Magic of Lassie;* the dog turned up in yet another movie in 1994. But the first was, as usual, the best. The cinematography Oscar went to Hal Mohr and W. Howard Greene for *The Phantom of the Opera.*

Smith: 208, 1417, 2320.

1133 • LAST ANGRY MAN, THE

FRED KOHLMAR PRODUCTIONS; COLUMBIA. 1959.
NOMINATIONS *Actor:* Paul Muni. *Black-and-White Art Direction—Set Decoration:* Carl Anderson; William Kiernan.

TV producer David Wayne wants to do a documentary on the life and work of a Brooklyn physician (Muni) who has spent his life tending to his poor neighbors. The doctor decides to participate so he can expose the venality of his profession, especially doctors who think more of money than of people, but at the last minute he goes to the aid of a young patient, played by Billy Dee Williams, and collapses of a heart attack. Too-sentimental, too-preachy adaptation by Gerald Green and Richard Murphy [257 . . .] of Green's novel, but Muni, in his last film, is worth watching, as are supporting players Betsy Palmer, Luther Adler, Godfrey Cambridge, and Claudia McNeil. Another plus is the fine location photography by James Wong Howe [1 . . .]. Directed by Daniel Mann.

The acting Oscar went to Charlton Heston for *Ben-Hur*. *The Diary of Anne Frank* won for art direction.

Muni: 218.5, 965, 1169, 1936, 2191. Anderson: 1126. Kiernan: 1521, 1550, 1753, 1858, 2238.

1134 • *LAST COMMAND, THE*

PARAMOUNT FAMOUS LASKY. 1927–28.
AWARD *Actor:* Emil Jannings.
NOMINATION *Original Story:* Lajos Biro.

Exiled by the Bolshevik Revolution, an old Russian general ekes out a living as a Hollywood extra. But when he is called on to appear in a film that re-creates the events of the revolution, he goes insane. Celebrated silent film, directed by Josef von Sternberg [1358 . . .], with Evelyn Brent and William Powell [1170 . . .].

Born in Switzerland and raised in Germany, Jannings became an important stage actor with Max Reinhardt's company in Berlin in the early years of the century. He made his film debut in 1914 and by the mid-twenties was acclaimed as one of the movies' greatest actors. His most celebrated role before coming to Hollywood was in F. W. Murnau's 1924 film *The Last Laugh*. Paramount signed him to a contract in 1927, and his roles in *The Last Command* and *The Way of All Flesh* won him the first acting Oscar ever presented. But the coming of sound made his Hollywood career a short one, and he returned to Germany before the awards ceremony in May 1929. The following year he gave perhaps his most famous performance, as the professor who degrades himself for love of Marlene Dietrich [1358] in *The Blue Angel*. His international career was ended when he became an enthusiastic supporter of the Nazis. He died in 1950.

Biro, a Hungarian-born writer, had been working in Hollywood since 1924. He went to England in 1932 to work for Alexander Korda [1620] and wrote some of the most successful British films of the thirties, including *The Private Life of Henry VIII, The Scarlet Pimpernel* (1935), *The Four Feathers,* and *The Thief of Bagdad*. The Oscar went to Ben Hecht for *Underworld*.

Some lists cite *The Last Command* as one of the nominees for best picture of 1927–28. The Academy's latest revision of its nominees and winners list, however, does not include it in this category.

Jannings: 2236.

1135 • *LAST DETAIL, THE*

ACROBAT FILMS PRODUCTION; COLUMBIA. 1973.
NOMINATIONS *Actor:* Jack Nicholson. *Supporting Actor:* Randy Quaid. *Screenplay—Based on Material From Another Medium:* Robert Towne.

Naval petty officers Nicholson and Otis Young transfer Quaid, a sailor convicted of a minor theft, to a military prison where he's to serve an eight-year sentence. The disparity between punishment and crime irks Nicholson, who decides to give Quaid a good time as a send-off. Gritty, profane comedy-drama adapted by Towne from a novel by Darryl Ponicsan and finely directed by Hal Ashby [430 . . .]. The principals are superb, and the solid supporting cast includes Clifton James, Carol Kane [908], Michael Moriarty, Nancy Allen, and, in a tiny role, Gilda Radner.

This was Nicholson's third nomination, and the beginning of a string of performances in the mid-seventies that, for three consecutive years, would make him a leading contender for the Oscar that he finally won for *One Flew Over the Cuckoo's Nest*. This time he lost to Jack Lemmon for *Save the Tiger*.

Quaid made his debut in *The Last Picture Show*, whose director, Peter Bogdanovich, cast him the following year in *What's Up, Doc?* But *The Last Detail* was the first film to allow him to show the range of which he was capable. Although he's subsequently been overshadowed by his more charismatic younger brother, Dennis, he continues to be one of the most reliable character actors of his generation. The Oscar went to John Houseman for *The Paper Chase*.

Like Nicholson, Towne began his screen career working for quickie director Roger Corman. He did uncredited work on *Bonnie and Clyde*, but *The Last Detail* was the first major screenplay in his name. It would start a string of three consecutive nominations —*Chinatown* and *Shampoo* were the follow-ups—and make him one of the most sought-after writers and script doctors in Hollywood. The Oscar went to William Peter Blatty for *The Exorcist*.

Nicholson: 395, 595, 658.5, 672, 1019, 1481, 1625, 1678, 2020. Towne: 395, 839, 1798.

1136 • LAST EMPEROR, THE

HEMDALE FILM PRODUCTION; COLUMBIA (UNITED KINGDOM). 1987.

AWARDS *Picture:* Jeremy Thomas, producer. *Director:* Bernardo Bertolucci. *Screenplay Based on Material From Another Medium:* Mark Peploe and Bernardo Bertolucci. *Cinematography:* Vittorio Storaro. *Art Direction–Set Decoration:* Ferdinando Scarfiotti; Bruno Cesari and Osvaldo Desideri. *Sound:* Bill Rowe and Ivan Sharrock. *Original Score:* Ryuichi Sakamoto, David Byrne, and Cong Su. *Film Editing:* Gabriella Cristiani. *Costume Design:* James Acheson.

Crowned emperor of China at the age of three, Pu Yi grows up in the seclusion of the Forbidden City, but gradually the outside world intrudes. First a Scottish tutor, played by Peter O'Toole [164 . . .], comes to introduce him to the ways of the West. Then a revolution drives Pu Yi from the Forbidden City, and he spends the twenties as a jazz-age playboy. When the Japanese invade Manchuria in 1932, he agrees to serve as the puppet emperor of Manchukuo. After the war and the communist revolution he is imprisoned, and he ends his days as a gardener in Beijing's botanical gardens. Sweeping, sumptuous film about an empty life—an extraordinary technical achievement that certainly deserved the Oscars it received for photography, design, sound, and music. And Bertolucci's audacity and persistence in wearing down the Chinese bureaucracy so he can take us places that movies have never gone before, such as the Forbidden City itself, also deserved recognition. But *The Last Emperor* is one of only eight best picture winners—the first since *Gigi* in 1958—to receive no nominations for acting, which suggests the hollowness at the film's core. Even though John Lone as the grown-up Pu Yi and Joan Chen as his empress are excellent, the characters they play are passive little figures swept along by history. Pu Yi doesn't seem to deserve so lavish a biopic.

The film's Oscar sweep echoed an earlier one: Like *Gandhi, The Last Emperor* was a big-budget, meticulously produced epic that overcame the odds against filming in an exotic location. It lacked *Gandhi*'s earnest high-mindedness, however, so some suspected that its success at the awards was a reflection of the film community's shock at the ousting of David Puttnam [386 . . .] as head of Columbia. Puttnam had been involved in the studio's picking up the Bertolucci film before his departure. Some Academy voters may have wanted to thumb their noses at Columbia's management for its treatment of Puttnam. If so, they overlooked a less ambitious but more human-scaled competitor for the best picture Oscar, *Hope and Glory*, which had also been one of Puttnam's acquisitions for Columbia. Hollywood also loves movies in which the money shows on the screen, so that may have tipped the balance in favor of *The Last Emperor* over *Hope and Glory*, *Moonstruck*, and *Broadcast News*, all critically praised but less showy productions. (The fifth film, *Fatal Attraction*, was probably nominated because it made tons of money and caused endless controversy, but it was never a serious contender.)

Bertolucci's Oscars recognized a filmmaker whose explorations of sex and politics—and sexual politics —in *The Conformist* and *Last Tango in Paris* brought both acclaim and controversy. In 1976 he wrote and directed *1900*, an epic more than five hours long (released, unsuccessfully, in the States in a four-hour version) starring Gérard Depardieu [474] and Robert De Niro [113 . . .] that viewed the class struggle with a Marxist bias. *The Last Emperor* continued his examination of his favorite themes, but in a more decorous fashion than some of his earlier works. (*Last Tango* remains one of the most sexually audacious mainstream films, and when *1900* was rereleased in 1991 in its uncut version it received an NC-17 rating.) So the Academy's honoring an Italian Marxist director whose work is decidedly unconventional seems like a rather daring move for so conservative an institution. Interestingly Bertolucci and his competitors form the first entirely foreign-born slate of director nominees, including two Britons, John Boorman *(Hope and Glory)* and Adrian Lyne *(Fatal Attraction)*, a

Swede, Lasse Hallstrom *(My Life as a Dog),* and a Canadian, Norman Jewison *(Moonstruck).* Accepting the Oscar, Bertolucci referred to Hollywood as "the Big Nipple." His post-Oscar films, *The Sheltering Sky* (1990) and *Little Buddha* (1994), however, have been critical and commercial failures.

Peploe, a British screenwriter, has worked largely with European directors, including Jacques Demy *(The Pied Piper,* 1972) and Michelangelo Antonioni *(The Passenger,* 1975). He also cowrote the screenplay for Bertolucci's *The Sheltering Sky.*

Storaro has been a continual collaborator with Bertolucci, working on all of his major films, and is also one of the most sought-after cinematographers in Hollywood, having done notable work with directors such as Francis Ford Coppola *(Apocalypse Now, One From the Heart, Tucker: The Man and His Dream)* and Warren Beatty *(Reds, Dick Tracy).* Scarfiotti is also a Bertolucci regular, having worked as production designer on *Last Tango.*

The music is the cross-cultural product of a Japanese composer, Sakamoto, an American, Byrne, and a Chinese, Su. Sakamoto, who also has a small acting role in the film, now lives in the United States, where he is less well known than in his native Japan. Celebrated for his fusion of the rhythms and instruments of many countries and the mixture of classical and pop elements, he composed music for the opening ceremonies of the 1992 Olympics in Barcelona and has done scores for such films as *The Sheltering Sky* and *The Handmaid's Tale* (1990). Byrne, who rose to fame as the songwriter and lead singer for the Talking Heads, is one of the major American pop musicians exploring international influences. Trained in photography and video at the Rhode Island School of Design, he wrote, directed, and acted in the feature *True Stories* in 1986, and composed the score for the film *Married to the Mob.* Su's career has not extended much beyond his native China.

By winning two consecutive Oscars, the second for *Dangerous Liaisons,* Acheson has developed a reputation as one of the leading designers of period costumes. *The Last Emperor* is said to have required some nine thousand costumes.

Bertolucci: 439, 1141. Storaro: 92, 543, 1678. Scarfiotti: 2127.5. Acheson: 485.

1137 • LAST METRO, THE

Les Films du Carrosse Production (France). 1980.
Nomination *Foreign Language Film.*

During the Nazi occupation of Paris, Catherine Deneuve [998.5] runs a small theater that also shelters several people in danger of being arrested: The theater's prewar manager, her husband, who is Jewish, hides in the cellar; one of the actors, played by Gérard Depardieu [474], is a member of the Resistance; and a director is gay. Directed by François Truffaut [501 . . .] and photographed by Nestor Almendros [243 . . .] with music by Georges Delerue [28 . . .]. The Oscar went to *Moscow Does Not Believe in Tears.*

1137.5 • LAST OF MRS. CHENEY, THE

MGM. 1928–29.
Nomination *Writing Achievement:* Hans Kräly.

Norma Shearer [150 . . .] plays the title role, a glamorous American jewel thief making her way through London high society. Very dated early talkie —shooting was held up one day because the fabric of one of Shearer's gowns was making so much noise the dialogue was inaudible. Directed by Sidney Franklin [799 . . .] from an adaptation by Kräly and Claudine West [804 . . .] of a play by Frederick Lonsdale. The cast includes Basil Rathbone [979 . . .] and Hedda Hopper. None of the film versions of Lonsdale's play was a success on screen, but MGM kept trying, casting it with Joan Crawford [1319 . . .] in 1937 and, under the title *The Law and the Lady,* with Greer Garson [239 . . .] in 1951. Kräly won the Oscar for *The Patriot,* but Academy records show that the writers branch was also considering his work on this film for the award. Only the winners were announced this year, and the unofficial nominees received no recognition from the Academy.

Kräly: 1485, 1540.

1138 • LAST OF THE MOHICANS, THE

RELIANCE PICTURES; UNITED ARTISTS. 1936.

NOMINATION *Assistant Director:* Clem Beauchamp.

Hawkeye (Randolph Scott), a scout raised by the Indians, rescues a British officer's daughter (Binnie Barnes) from the clutches of the evil Magua (Bruce Cabot) during the French and Indian War. Entertaining version of the James Fenimore Cooper novel. The screenplay by Philip Dunne [495 . . .] was the acknowledged basis of the very successful 1992 remake. Directed by George Seitz, with cinematography by Robert Planck [74 . . .] and music by Roy Webb [615 . . .]. The assistant director Oscar went to Jack Sullivan for *The Charge of the Light Brigade.*

Beauchamp: 1194.

1138.5 • LAST OF THE MOHICANS, THE

20TH CENTURY FOX PRODUCTION; 20TH CENTURY FOX. 1992.

AWARD *Sound:* Chris Jenkins, Doug Hemphill, Mark Smith, and Simon Kaye.

Daniel Day-Lewis [992.5 . . .] plays Hawkeye, the intrepid trapper raised by the Mohican Chingachgook, played by American Indian activist Russell Means. During the French and Indian War, the two men, joined by Chingachgook's son, Uncas (Eric Schweig), come to the aid of two Englishwomen, Cora (Madeleine Stowe) and her sister, Alice (Jodhi May), and escort them to their father, a British officer (Maurice Roëves). Along the way, Hawkeye and Cora fall in love. The fortunes of war go against the British, and when the women fall into the hands of the vengeful Magua (Wes Studi), Hawkeye, Chingachgook, and Uncas must come to the rescue again. Exciting, highly romantic action epic directed by Michael Mann from a screenplay that Mann and Christopher Crowe based in part on the Philip Dunne [495 . . .] script for the 1936 version of the James Fenimore Cooper novel. Day-Lewis is a sensational romantic hero, and the film is greatly helped by a stirring score by Trevor Jones and Randy Edelman and the cinematography of Dante Spinotti.

Jenkins: 543, 1512. Hemphill: 543, 761.5. Kaye: 745, 1584, 1678.

1139 • LAST PICTURE SHOW, THE

BBS PRODUCTIONS; COLUMBIA. 1971.

AWARDS *Supporting Actor:* Ben Johnson. *Supporting Actress:* Cloris Leachman.

NOMINATIONS *Picture:* Stephen J. Friedman, producer. *Supporting Actor:* Jeff Bridges. *Supporting Actress:* Ellen Burstyn. *Director:* Peter Bogdanovich. *Screenplay— Based on Material From Another Medium:* Larry McMurtry and Peter Bogdanovich. *Cinematography:* Robert Surtees.

Anarene is a bleak little West Texas town where the grown-ups lead lives of quiet desperation but the kids are a little more noisy about it. High school senior Sonny Crawford (Timothy Bottoms) has an affair with the lonely wife (Leachman) of his football coach. His friend Duane (Bridges) is trying to persuade his spoiled rich girlfriend, Jacy (Cybill Shepherd), to sleep with him. Meanwhile, her mother (Burstyn) is having an affair with an oilfield roughneck (Clu Gulager). The conscience of the town is Sam the Lion (Johnson), who runs the pool hall and the movie theater. This provocative, poignant, sometimes satiric coming-of-age-in-the-fifties saga, adapted from McMurtry's novel, made Bogdanovich a big name overnight. It launched the careers of Bottoms, Bridges, and Shepherd, as well as Randy Quaid [1135], making his screen debut in a smaller role, and it gave Eileen Brennan [1617], who plays an understanding waitress, one of her first important movie roles.

Johnson's part as the voice of experience in the film was reinforced by the fact that he was the most experienced member of the cast. He came to Hollywood in the forties to work as a horse wrangler and stuntman and began acting in small roles in films directed by John Ford [815 . . .]. Though he played the lead in Ford's *The Wagonmaster* (1950), most of his career has been spent in supporting roles. Ford, the subject of a biography by Bogdanovich, reportedly pressured Johnson into taking the role of Sam the Lion, after the actor objected to the film's language and nudity. The Oscar heightened Johnson's name recognition but did little to alter the size of the roles he received.

Leachman, who had been a finalist in the 1946

Miss America contest, made her screen debut in 1955 in *Kiss Me Deadly* but did mostly stage and TV work until her Oscar-winning role. Although her part in *The Last Picture Show* was a serious one, she has since been best known for her work in comedy, including *Young Frankenstein* and the TV series *The Mary Tyler Moore Show* and its spin-off, *Phyllis.*

One critic likened Bogdanovich's film to *Citizen Kane* in its revelation of what appeared to be a major young talent (Bogdanovich was thirty-two). He had begun as a film critic and wrote books on Ford, Howard Hawks [1779], and Orson Welles [407 . . .] before doing apprentice work for low-budget producer Roger Corman. His first film, *Targets* (1968), attracted some favorable critical attention if not much in the way of audiences. He followed *The Last Picture Show* with a homage to Howard Hawks' screwball classic *Bringing Up Baby,* the 1972 *What's Up, Doc?,* with Barbra Streisand [737 . . .] and Ryan O'Neal [1218]. It was a box-office success but received mixed reviews. His next film, *Paper Moon,* was considerably more successful with the critics, but in 1974 his career began to decline, starting with a clunky adaptation of Henry James' *Daisy Miller,* featuring an inadequately prepared Cybill Shepherd, and followed by the disastrous musical *At Long Last Love* (1975), in which Shepherd and Burt Reynolds attempted to sing Cole Porter [261 . . .]. Of his subsequent films, only *Mask,* which featured a strong performance by Cher [1351 . . .], has attracted wide critical praise and acceptance at the box office. In 1990 he directed an unsuccessful sequel to *The Last Picture Show, Texasville,* reuniting Bridges, Shepherd, Bottoms, Leachman, Quaid, and Brennan.

The best picture Oscar went to *The French Connection,* for which William Friedkin won as director and Ernest Tidyman for screenplay. The cinematography award went to Oswald Morris for *Fiddler on the Roof.*

Bridges: 1918, 2086. Burstyn: 41, 631, 1682, 1747. Surtees: 130, 175, 557, 810, 917, 1094, 1388, 1469, 1644, 1747, 1911, 1927, 1960, 2055, 2152.

1140 • *LAST SUMMER*

FRANK PERRY-ALSID PRODUCTION; ALLIED ARTISTS. 1969.
NOMINATION *Supporting Actress:* Catherine Burns.

Teenagers Richard Thomas, Barbara Hershey, and Bruce Davison [1203] are spending the summer on the beach, coming to terms with their awakening sexuality. When shy, homely newcomer Burns arrives, their games of exploration suddenly become destructive. Provocative melodrama about the loss of innocence, directed by Frank Perry [496] from a script by Eleanor Perry [496] based on a novel by Evan Hunter. The movie was originally rated X because of its use of the word "fuck." It has since been downrated to R. Of the gifted quartet of young performers, Thomas, Hershey, and Davison went on to successful careers. But nominee Burns made only one more film, *Red Sky at Morning* (1971), also with Thomas, before dropping from sight. The Oscar went to Goldie Hawn for *Cactus Flower.*

1141 • *LAST TANGO IN PARIS*

P.E.A. PRODUZIONI EUROPÉE ASSOCIATE S.A.A.-LES PRODUCTIONS ARTISTES ASSOCIÉS S.A. PRODUCTION; UNITED ARTISTS (ITALY/FRANCE). 1973.
NOMINATIONS *Actor:* Marlon Brando. *Director:* Bernardo Bertolucci.

After his wife's suicide, expatriate American Brando tries to purge himself by entering into a purely sexual liaison with a young Parisian woman, Maria Schneider. The movie's explicit sexuality still has the power to shock, though it has not lived up to its reputation as a breakthrough film, and its treatment of women is questionable. It is, however, one of Brando's most compelling performances, largely because the torment and menace are so nakedly presented. No films he has made since this one and the previous year's *The Godfather* have presented him so impressively. Originally X-rated, it exists in an R-rated version as well.

The Academy apparently found the film too strong for their consideration, presenting the actor award to Jack Lemmon for *Save the Tiger* and the directing award to George Roy Hill for *The Sting.*

Brando: 583, 784, 1069, 1477, 1763, 1949, 2212. Bertolucci: 439, 1136.

1142 • *LAST TEMPTATION OF CHRIST, THE*

TESTAMENT PRODUCTION; UNIVERSAL/CINEPLEX ODEON. 1988. **NOMINATION** *Director:* Martin Scorsese.

Jesus, played by Willem Dafoe [1584], goes about his mission on earth much as the Gospels report it. But his last temptation, as he hangs on the cross, is to give up his role as savior of mankind and live an ordinary mortal life. Scorsese's extraordinarily powerful, if deeply flawed, version of the novel by Nikos Kazantzakis became a cause célèbre, thanks to protests from evangelical Christians, disturbed that a major Hollywood studio should produce what they believed to be a blasphemous version of the life of Christ. It is nothing of the sort, of course. It is fairly explicit in showing the work of the prostitute Mary Magdalene (Barbara Hershey), it portrays the disciples as gritty, rather common men, and its staging of the crucifixion is gruesomely realistic. The flaws of the film are some rather banal dialogue by screenwriter Paul Schrader and an overlong and confusing "last temptation" sequence. Dafoe and Harvey Keitel [308], who plays Judas, give fine performances, and Peter Gabriel's score, using Middle Eastern and African instruments and rhythms, is brilliant. Also in the cast are Harry Dean Stanton, David Bowie, Verna Bloom, André Gregory, Roberts Blossom, Irvin Kershner, and Nehemiah Persoff.

Scorsese had been intrigued with the idea of filming Kazantzakis' book since he was given a copy of it by Hershey, the star of his early film *Boxcar Bertha* (1972). Paramount gave him a go-ahead in 1982, and Aidan Quinn was cast as Jesus, but the studio was pressured into backing out of the deal. By nominating Scorsese but ignoring his film in other categories, the Academy seemed to be patting him on the back for finally getting the film made while signaling that they didn't really care much for it. Not since Frank Lloyd's win for *The Divine Lady* at the 1928–29 awards has an Oscar gone to a director whose film was not also nominated for best picture. This time it went to Barry Levinson for *Rain Man*.

Scorsese: 27.5, 806, 1650.

1143 • *LAST TYCOON, THE*

SAM SPIEGEL-ELIA KAZAN FILM PRODUCTION; PARAMOUNT. 1976. **NOMINATION** *Art Direction–Set Decoration:* Gene Callahan and Jack Collis; Jerry Wunderlich.

Robert De Niro [113 . . .] plays Monroe Stahr, in charge of production at a major Hollywood studio in the thirties and involved in a power struggle with the studio head, Brady, played by Robert Mitchum [1935]. He also has an affair with a woman (Ingrid Boulting) who reminds him of his dead wife. Muddled and slow-moving adaptation, by Harold Pinter [185 . . .], of the unfinished novel by F. Scott Fitzgerald. The movie seems unfinished, too, despite a magnetic performance by De Niro and a powerhouse cast: Tony Curtis [522] as an aging, impotent star, Jeanne Moreau as a fading leading lady, Jack Nicholson [395 . . .] as a union organizer, plus Ray Milland, Dana Andrews, Theresa Russell, and, in a very small part, Anjelica Huston [617 . . .]. Fitzgerald modeled Monroe Stahr on Irving G. Thalberg [150 . . .] and Brady on Louis B. Mayer. This was the last film directed by Elia Kazan [63 . . .] and produced by three-time Oscar winner Sam Spiegel [287 . . .]. The art direction Oscar went to *All the President's Men*.

Callahan: 63, 356, 964. Wunderlich: 631.

1144 • *LAST VOYAGE, THE*

ANDREW AND VIRGINIA STONE PRODUCTION; MGM. 1960. **NOMINATION** *Special Effects:* A. J. Lohman.

An explosion sinks a luxury liner, and passengers and crew struggle for their lives. Well-done adventure flick made more than a decade before the vogue for disaster epics like *The Poseidon Adventure* and *The Towering Inferno*. Along for the ride are Robert Stack [2315], Dorothy Malone [2315], George Sanders [46], and Edmond O'Brien [146 . . .]. Written and directed by Andrew L. Stone [1067]. A decommissioned liner was actually sunk for the film, but the

Academy preferred the special effects of *The Time Machine*.

1145 • *LAST YEAR AT MARIENBAD*

PRECEITEL-TERRA FILM PRODUCTION; ASTOR PICTURES INC. (FRANCE/ITALY). 1962.

NOMINATION *Story and Screenplay—Written Directly for the Screen:* Alain Robbe-Grillet.

A small group of elegantly dressed men and women wander through a grand palace and its elaborately geometrical gardens as one of the men tries to persuade a woman that they had met the previous year at the Marienbad spa, where they had an affair. Celebrated film directed by Alain Resnais that forsakes narrative logic and aims instead at the meaningless complexity of music. Highly regarded in its day, it's now often dismissed as precious and arid. Still, there's something hypnotic about it, and it's full of striking images. The cinematography is by Sacha Vierny.

Robbe-Grillet, a French novelist and theorist of fiction, went on to direct his own films, starting with *L'Immortelle* in 1963, but none has achieved the celebrity of *Marienbad*. His screenwriting nomination was one in a very curious mixed bag of international entries, ranging from Ingmar Bergman's script for *Through a Glass Darkly* to Stanley Shapiro and Nate Monaster's Doris Day comedy *That Touch of Mink*. The other contenders were Charles Kaufman and Wolfgang Reinhardt for *Freud* and the winners, Ennio de Concini, Alfredo Giannetti, and Pietro Germi for *Divorce—Italian Style*.

1146 • *LATE SHOW, THE*

LION'S GATE FILM PRODUCTION; WARNER BROS. 1977.

NOMINATION *Screenplay—Written Directly for the Screen:* Robert Benton.

Lily Tomlin [1415] plays an eccentric woman who hires an elderly private eye, played by Art Carney [875], to find her cat, which has been kidnaped by some hoods she has ripped off. The case results in the death of his partner (Howard Duff) and involves both detective and client in more weirdness than they expected. Offbeat and, thanks to Tomlin and Carney,

very entertaining return to the world created by Dashiell Hammett [2233], Raymond Chandler [242 . . .], and film noir, but with contemporary twists that are all Benton's own. He directed, too. The film was produced by Robert Altman [1286 . . .], whose influence shows in its loose and laid-back style. The Oscar went to Woody Allen and Marshall Brickman for *Annie Hall*.

Benton: 255, 1111, 1444.5, 1580.

1147 • *LAUGH, CLOWN, LAUGH*

MGM. 1927–28.

AWARD *Title Writing:* Joseph Farnham.

Lon Chaney plays a circus clown who smiles though his heart is breaking because of love for his ward, played by Loretta Young [428 . . .]. In the end he kills himself doing a dangerous stunt, clearing the way for her to marry another. Directed by Herbert Brenon [1878], with cinematography by James Wong Howe [1 . . .]. Farnham was the sole winner of the title writing Oscar, made obsolete by sound and discontinued after this year. In some lists of Oscar nominees, he's cited as a winner for the film *Telling the World* and as nominee for *The Fair Co-ed* and *Laugh, Clown, Laugh*. But the Academy's most recent revision of its nominations and winners list cites no titles after his name, because the Oscar was presented to him for the body of his work during the qualifying year. For the purposes of this book, however, we've included his name as winner under the three films he worked on during the 1927–28 qualifying period.

Farnham: 637, 2009.

1148 • *LAUGHTER*

PARAMOUNT PUBLIX. 1930–31.

NOMINATION *Original Story:* Harry d'Abbadie d'Arrast, Douglas Doty, and Donald Ogden Stewart.

Showgirl Nancy Carroll [539] marries Frank Morgan [22 . . .] for his money, but it doesn't make her happy. Then an old flame, Fredric March [184 . . .], comes back into her life. Romantic comedy with a bright and witty script, hindered a bit by the stiffness of most early talkies and d'Arrast's direction. Herman Mankiewicz [407 . . .], who produced, also contributed to the script. The Oscar went to John Monk Saunders for *The Dawn Patrol.*

Stewart: 1563.

1149 • *LAURA*

20TH CENTURY-FOX. 1944.

AWARD *Black-and-White Cinematography:* Joseph La-Shelle.

NOMINATIONS *Supporting Actor:* Clifton Webb. *Director:* Otto Preminger. *Screenplay:* Jay Dratler, Samuel Hoffenstein, and Betty Reinhardt. *Black-and-White Interior Decoration:* Lyle Wheeler and Leland Fuller, art direction; Thomas Little, set decoration.

Detective Dana Andrews goes to investigate the murder of Laura Hunt, played by Gene Tierney [1153], a beautiful advertising executive with a lousy taste in men. The chief ones in her life are her patron, the bitchy columnist and radio personality Waldo Lydecker (Webb), and the ne'er-do-well southerner Shelby Carpenter, played by Vincent Price. As he sorts through the clues in her apartment and gazes at her portrait, the detective begins to fall in love with the dead woman. Fortunately she isn't dead after all —the corpse, disfigured by a close-range shotgun blast, belonged to someone who was staying in the apartment while Laura was out of town. So whodunit? Waldo? Shelby? Laura's rival for Shelby's affections, Ann Treadwell, played by Judith Anderson [1670]? Or maybe Laura herself? Wonderful, classic thriller, full of lovable nasties and memorable lines, most of them given to Webb. Everyone concerned is at peak form, including composer David Raksin [707 . . .], whose theme music is one of the movies' most familiar tunes. Raksin's omission from the scoring nominees is probably the result of studio politics: Fox head Darryl F. Zanuck [34 . . .] was eager to promote his big biopic *Wilson,* and at the time each studio was allowed a single entry of its own choosing in the music categories. So Alfred Newman's score for *Wilson* was nominated instead of Raksin's. (Lyrics by Johnny Mercer [248 . . .] were added to Raksin's tune after the film became a hit, so the song, because it didn't actually appear in the film, was ineligible for an Oscar.) It's likely that *Laura* would have been a best picture nominee under less politically dicey circumstances, but though *Laura* was a smash hit and *Wilson* a flop, the latter film got the best picture nod.

LaShelle was trained as an electrical engineer and went to work in Hollywood in 1924 as a lab assistant. But an interest in photography caused him to pursue a career as a cameraman, and after working as a camera operator on such films as *How Green Was My Valley* and *The Song of Bernadette,* he became a director of photography. *Laura* earned him his first nomination and only Oscar. He died in 1989.

Webb started as a dancer and by the twenties was a leading Broadway musical performer, thought by many to be a rival to Fred Astaire [2126]. He also made a few silent films in the twenties, but *Laura* was his first screen appearance in almost twenty years. It launched a successful movie career. He lost the Oscar to Barry Fitzgerald in *Going My Way.*

Preminger began as a stage producer and director in his native Austria and came to the States in the thirties, first to Broadway and then to Hollywood. But after directing a few films at Fox in the mid-thirties, he clashed with Zanuck and returned to Broadway as director and actor. His performance as a Nazi officer in the Broadway play *Margin for Error* caused Fox to sign him for a similar role in *The Pied Piper.* When the studio decided to film *Margin for Error* in 1943, he agreed to repeat his Broadway role if he could also direct the movie. Zanuck had taken a leave from the studio during the early years of the war, but on his return, he vetoed plans to have Preminger direct *Laura.* The film was then begun under the direction of Rouben Mamoulian, but Zanuck was disappointed with the way the film was going, and agreed to let Preminger take it over. In later years Mamoulian and Preminger feuded over the extent of the respective contributions to the movie, which had given a boost to Preminger's career as director. The directing Oscar went to Leo McCarey for *Going My Way,* which also won the screenplay award for Frank Butler and Frank Cavett. The Oscar for art direction went to *Gaslight.*

LaShelle: 91, 357, 428, 709, 953, 1017, 1283, 1391. Webb: 1666, 1835. Preminger: 73, 356. Hoffenstein: 572, 754. Wheeler: 19, 46, 83, 356, 376, 428, 476, 495, 530, 542, 719, 721, 798, 950, 1062, 1088, 1153, 1213, 1391, 1475, 1601, 1616, 1670, 1706, 1852, 2008, 2093, 2212. Fuller: 530, 719, 1475, 1601, 2212. Little: 46, 83, 235, 428, 495, 719, 721, 746, 950, 952, 1082, 1153, 1397, 1475, 1666, 1852, 1868, 2056, 2212, 2286.

1150 • LAVENDER HILL MOB, THE

J. ARTHUR RANK-EALING; UNIVERSAL-INTERNATIONAL (UNITED KINGDOM). 1952.
AWARD *Story and Screenplay:* T. E. B. Clarke.
NOMINATION *Actor:* Alec Guinness.

Mousy bank clerk Guinness masterminds a perfect crime, the theft of gold from the Bank of England. Of course, nothing goes quite as planned, but if it did, we wouldn't have one of the small masterpieces of British comedy. Directed by Charles Crichton [670], with Stanley Holloway [1393] as Guinness' partner in crime, and in a one-line walk-on, the then-unknown Audrey Hepburn [278 . . .]. The cinematography is by Douglas Slocombe [1066 . . .].

Clarke, educated at Cambridge, worked as a journalist before joining the Ealing studios as a screenwriter. He died in 1989.

This was Guinness' first nomination, although he had received great critical acclaim for playing eight members of the D'Ascoyne family in the 1949 comedy *Kind Hearts and Coronets,* as well as for his chilling Fagin in the 1948 film of *Oliver Twist.* The Oscar went to Gary Cooper for *High Noon.*

Clarke: 1535, 1875. Guinness: 287, 941, 1181, 1916.

1151 • LAWRENCE OF ARABIA

HORIZON PICTURES (G.B.) LTD.-SAM SPIEGEL-DAVID LEAN PRODUCTION; COLUMBIA (UNITED KINGDOM). 1962.
AWARDS *Picture:* Sam Spiegel, producer. *Director:* David Lean. *Color Cinematography:* Fred A. Young. *Color Art Direction—Set Decoration:* John Box and John Stoll; Dario Simoni. *Sound:* John Cox, sound director, Shepperton Studio Sound Department. *Music Score— Substantially Original:* Maurice Jarre. *Film Editing:* Anne Coates.

NOMINATIONS *Actor:* Peter O'Toole. *Supporting Actor:* Omar Sharif. *Screenplay—Based on Material From Another Medium:* Robert Bolt.

T. E. Lawrence (O'Toole), an eccentric, rebellious British officer, is sent to act as a liaison between the British and the Arabs and winds up uniting various Arab tribes and leading them in a splendid victory against the Turks. Eventually, however, Lawrence's charisma proves insufficient to hold the Arabs together, and he is pulled back from megalomania when he is captured by the Turks and tortured and raped by the bey, played by Jose Ferrer [473 . . .]. Lawrence is also finessed in the high-level power plays of Prince Faisal, played by Alec Guinness [287 . . .], General Allenby (Jack Hawkins), and the British foreign office, represented by Dryden, played by Claude Rains [78 . . .]. Disillusioned, Lawrence retires to England, where he dies in a motorcycle accident but is celebrated with a funeral at St. Paul's. Breathtaking "literate epic" that wisely subordinates the complicated politics of the Middle East to a highly romanticized portrait of Lawrence, who was more introverted, and much plainer and shorter, than the flamboyant, handsome figure created by O'Toole. Sharif plays Lawrence's quietly centered Arab alter ego, Ali, and the cast includes Anthony Quinn [1226 . . .] as the bloodthirsty Auda, Anthony Quayle [85] as a British colonel, and Arthur Kennedy [291 . . .] as an American journalist based on the man who made Lawrence an international celebrity, Lowell Thomas.

This was Spiegel's third Oscar for best picture, a record equaled only by Darryl F. Zanuck [34 . . .]. Though Spiegel would also collect the Irving G. Thalberg Award at the 1963 awards, his subsequent career as a producer was less impressive. After two flops in 1966, *The Chase* and *The Night of the Generals,* he made another attempt at an epic, *Nicholas and Alexandra,* that despite a lackluster run at the box office earned him another nomination. His final film, *The Last Tycoon,* was smaller in scale and commercially unsuccessful. He died in 1985. Even in its first years of release, despite critical acclaim and seven Oscars, *Lawrence of Arabia* would prove something of a disappointment at the box office, and yielding to pressure from exhibitors, Columbia would trim more than half an hour from the film. Originally 222 minutes long, it was reedited in 1989, restoring the excised footage but also tightening some of the existing scenes. Its current length is 216 minutes.

After *Lawrence,* Lean's reputation began a decline. Although *Doctor Zhivago,* which reunited many of the talents who worked on *Lawrence* (Sharif, Guinness, Bolt, Young, Box, Simoni, Jarre), was a box-office hit and won five Oscars, many critics found it beautiful but empty. The subsequent *Ryan's Daughter* was both a critical disappointment and a commercial disaster, an expensive spectacle that put a halt to Lean's career for fourteen years. In the seventies there seemed to be little demand for the sweeping historical drama with which Lean was identified, but in 1984 he returned to the screen with a well-received version of *A Passage to India.* At the time of his death in 1991, Lean was planning to film Joseph Conrad's *Nostromo.*

For many, the real star of *Lawrence of Arabia* is the desert, its ravishing vistas captured in Super Panavision 70 by Young's camera. Young's work in film spanned more than half a century, starting in the late twenties in England, and including such movies as the 1939 *Goodbye, Mr. Chips, Ivanhoe, Mogambo, Lust for Life,* and *The Inn of the Sixth Happiness,* before his memorable collaboration with Lean, which won him three Oscars (the other two for *Zhivago* and *Ryan's Daughter*).

Jarre likewise benefited from the collaboration with Lean, winning Oscars for *Zhivago* and *Passage to India* as well as for *Lawrence.* Educated at the Sorbonne, he studied music at the Paris Conservatoire and began work as a film composer in France in the fifties. He was nominated for an Oscar for *Sundays and Cybèle,* but his work on *Lawrence* was his first score for a non-French film. He has since become one of the movies' most prolific composers.

Coates was a relatively unknown editor when she was hired for *Lawrence* after cutting some tests that had been run with Albert Finney [579 . . .] in the title role. Lean, who had been an editor himself, was a close collaborator in the editing of the picture.

Coates subsequently participated in the restoration of the film.

Finney's decision to bow out of *Lawrence* made O'Toole a star. Others considered for the role include Marlon Brando [583 . . .], Anthony Perkins [730], and Guinness—who was the only one of the contenders who remotely resembled the real T. E. Lawrence, but was nearing fifty and was thus too old to play the young adventurer. O'Toole had made a few film appearances, but it was his stage work at Bristol Old Vic and the Royal Shakespeare Theatre at Stratford that brought him to Lean's attention. Although O'Toole's performance was the sensation of the year, he lost the Oscar to the sentimental favorite, Gregory Peck, in *To Kill a Mockingbird.* This was the beginning of a long string of bad Oscar luck for O'Toole—seven nominations without winning, a record tied only by Richard Burton [85 . . .].

Sharif had made some films in his native Egypt before being cast in *Lawrence.* As with O'Toole, the film launched him as a star, but his subsequent casting in the title role of *Doctor Zhivago* exposed his inadequacy as an actor. He has since proved to be a latter-day Robert Taylor, a limited actor but a decorative addition to a film, easy to watch even when profoundly miscast, as in *Funny Girl,* in which he plays an American Jewish gambler. His recent career has been largely made up of TV movies and cameo roles in theatrical films, and he has concentrated more on his expertise at the game of bridge than on acting. The Oscar went to Ed Begley for *Sweet Bird of Youth.*

The screenwriting award went to Horton Foote for *To Kill a Mockingbird.*

Spiegel: 287, 1429, 1477. Lean: 287, 289, 558, 820, 1533, 1963. Young: 558, 1035, 1429, 1737. Box: 558, 1429, 1471, 1533, 2134. Simoni: 29, 558, 2000. Cox: 164, 850. Jarre: 558, 764, 808, 1168, 1340, 1533, 1967, 2296. Coates: 164, 608, 992.3. O'Toole: 164, 805, 1177, 1395, 1733, 1953. Bolt: 558, 1252.

LE BAL
See 135.

LE PLAISIR
See 1582.

1152 • LEATHERNECK, THE

RALPH BLOCK; PATHÉ. 1928–29.

NOMINATION *Writing Achievement:* Elliott Clawson.

Court-martialed for desertion and murdering a fellow marine, William Boyd is acquitted at the last moment by the testimony of his Russian wife. Part-talkie with Alan Hale and Robert Armstrong. A pioneer screenwriter, Clawson's most famous screenplay was the adaptation, in collaboration with Raymond Schrock, of Gaston Leroux's novel *The Phantom of the Opera,* for the 1925 Lon Chaney film. Clawson was not an official nominee this year, simply because the Academy announced only winners—in this case, Hans Kräly for *The Patriot*—and issued no certificates or other recognition to runners-up. He was, however, listed in the records of the writers branch as one of the people under consideration for the award.

Clawson: 443.5, 1740.5, 1838.5.

1153 • LEAVE HER TO HEAVEN

20TH CENTURY-FOX. 1945.

AWARD *Color Cinematography:* Leon Shamroy. **NOMINATIONS** *Actress:* Gene Tierney. *Color Interior Decoration:* Lyle Wheeler and Maurice Ransford, art direction; Thomas Little, set decoration. *Sound Recording:* Thomas T. Moulton.

Cornel Wilde [1872] makes the very serious mistake of falling in love with Tierney, whom we glimpse early in the film dashing around a New Mexico resort on a horse, scattering her beloved father's ashes as the Alfred Newman [31 . . .] score thunders behind her. Turns out she's a spoiled psychopath, who will stop at nothing to hold on to the man she loves—including letting Wilde's crippled brother (Darryl Hickman) drown and falling downstairs to abort the baby she fears will distract Wilde from devoting his life to adoring her. When it becomes clear that Wilde is attracted to her cousin, Jeanne Crain [1575], Tierney commits suicide, making it look like Wilde murdered her. Truly weird and overheated supersoap, from a Ben Ames Williams novel adapted by Jo

Swerling [1607] and directed by John M. Stahl [983], who had a gift for turning melodramas into movies that seem more substantial than they really are—he also did the 1932 *Back Street,* the 1934 *Imitation of Life,* and the 1935 *Magnificent Obsession.* The cast, going at it with everything they've got, includes Vincent Price, Ray Collins, Gene Lockhart [36], and Chill Wills [33].

This was the year for films about obsessions of various kinds: *The Lost Weekend, Mildred Pierce, Spellbound, The Picture of Dorian Gray, The Woman in the Window.* But what sets *Leave Her to Heaven* apart from these other psychological dramas is that it was filmed in color, a medium to this point usually reserved for musicals, historical romances, and costume dramas. Some critics felt the story needed the moody high contrast of black and white, but *Leave Her* was a harbinger of things to come, and the opulent hues of Shamroy's camera work won him the third of his record-setting four Oscars, all of them for color films. The only other cinematographer with four Oscars is Joseph Ruttenberg [318 . . .], but Shamroy has more nominations than any other director of photography except Charles B. Lang [97 . . .], who also racked up eighteen.

Tierney was discovered by Fox head Darryl Zanuck [34 . . .] while she was performing on Broadway, and she made her debut in *The Return of Jesse James* in 1940. Her film appearances were rather routine until *Laura* was a hit in 1944, and she became Fox's major leading lady in dramatic roles. Her career began to fade in the fifties, and a nervous breakdown in 1955 led to her retirement from the screen. Her daughter from her first marriage, to designer Oleg Cassini, was born retarded in 1943 after Tierney contracted German measles during her pregnancy. After that marriage ended in 1952, she had a tempestuous affair with Aly Khan that ended badly. She returned to the screen briefly in the 1960s. *Leave Her to Heaven* was something of a departure from type for Tierney, who usually played more sweetly passive roles, but she handles quite well a part that might have been done by Bette Davis [46 . . .], Olivia de Havilland [798 . . .], or, for that matter, Joan Crawford, who won the Oscar for *Mildred Pierce*. Tierney died in 1991.

The art direction award went to *Frenchman's Creek*. *The Bells of St. Mary's* won for sound.

Shamroy: 29, 226, 356, 413, 495, 569, 602, 1088, 1213, 1592, 1610, 1706, 1852, 1883, 2013, 2286, 2334. Wheeler: 19, 46, 83, 356, 376, 428, 476, 495, 530, 542, 719, 721, 798, 950, 1062, 1088, 1149, 1213, 1391, 1475, 1601, 1616, 1670, 1706, 1852, 2008, 2093, 2212. Ransford: 721, 2093. Little: 46, 83, 235, 428, 495, 719, 721, 746, 950, 952, 1082, 1149, 1397, 1475, 1666, 1852, 1868, 2056, 2212, 2286. Moulton: 22, 46, 138, 366, 457, 487, 560, 706, 798, 962, 1200, 1451, 1510, 1607, 1849, 2154, 2294.

1154 • LEGEND

LEGEND COMPANY PRODUCTION; UNIVERSAL. 1986.

NOMINATION *Makeup:* Rob Bottin and Peter Robb-King.

Young lovers Tom Cruise [260] and Mia Sara fall afoul of demon Tim Curry in this fantasy directed by Ridley Scott [2039]. An opulent flop that none of its participants places prominently on his or her résumé, except perhaps production designer Assheton Gorton [725] and the nominated makeup artists. They lost, however, to Chris Walas and Stephan Dupuis for *The Fly*.

Bottin: 2124.

1154.5 • LEGENDS OF THE FALL

TRISTAR PICTURES PRODUCTION; TRISTAR. 1994.

AWARD *Cinematography:* John Toll.

NOMINATIONS *Art Direction—Set Decoration:* Lilly Kilvert; Dorree Cooper. *Sound:* Paul Massey, David Campbell, Christopher David, and Douglas Ganton.

Anthony Hopkins [1679.5 . . .] plays the patriarch of the Ludlow clan: three sons, Alfred (Aidan Quinn), Tristan (Brad Pitt), and Samuel (Henry Thomas), raised on a Montana ranch. Samuel gets engaged to Susannah (Julia Ormond), but when he brings her home to meet the family a lot of messy passions get aroused. And then World War I breaks out to complicate things even more. As more than

one critic observed, it's something like *The Brothers Karamazov* being performed as an episode of *Bonanza*. Still, if you have a taste for old-fashioned popcorn epics of the fifties like *Broken Lance* and *The Big Country,* this is a reasonably acceptable nineties equivalent. The screenplay by Susan Shilliday and Bill Wittliff, based on a story by Jim Harrison, encourages everyone to overact, and director Edward Zwick lets them. The score is by James Horner [45 . . .].

Toll specializes in outdoors work, as in the commercially unsuccessful but spectacularly visual film about yacht racing, *Wind* (1992), but some critics of the award argued that Toll was honored more for the handsomeness of the scenery he was photographing than for his skill as a camera director.

The art direction award went to *The Madness of King George*. *Speed* won for sound.

Campbell: 543.

1155 • LENNY

MARVIN WORTH PRODUCTION; UNITED ARTISTS. 1974.

NOMINATIONS *Picture:* Marvin Worth, producer. *Actor:* Dustin Hoffman. *Actress:* Valerie Perrine. *Director:* Bob Fosse. *Screenplay Adapted From Other Material:* Julian Barry. *Cinematography:* Bruce Surtees.

Hoffman plays the hipster comedian Lenny Bruce, who was constantly in trouble with the law for the obscenities in his routines, and who died young of a drug overdose. Perrine is Bruce's stripper wife, Honey, and Jan Miner (best known as Madge the manicurist in those ''you're soaking in it'' detergent commercials) plays Bruce's mother, Sally Marr. Bleak, effective pseudo-documentary whose aim is to show Bruce as a victim of fifties prudery. The film errs in trying to show too much of the nice guy hiding under Bruce's abrasive exterior, but it's admirably free of biopic clichés (though it may have minted some new ones, to be found in subsequent self-destructive-entertainer movies such as *Bird* and the 1989 flop about John Belushi, *Wired*—or for that matter in Fosse's own autobiographical *All That Jazz*).

The Oscar contest was an interesting rematch between Fosse and Francis Ford Coppola, who had faced off two years earlier when Coppola's *The Godfather* took best picture and Fosse won as director. Coppola had two films in the running—*The Godfather, Part II,* which won, and *The Conversation.* But Fosse and his film were running behind not only Coppola, who won as director, but also director Roman Polanski and his film *Chinatown.* (The fifth nominee, *The Towering Inferno,* was there as a tribute to money, not art.)

The best actor race was likewise a race dominated by young men who represented a new generation of American film actors, none of them conventionally handsome, all demonstrating an intensity of performance that had been missing from the screen since the early-fifties heyday of Marlon Brando [583 . . .], Montgomery Clift [732 . . .], and James Dean [593 . . .]. But unlike Dean and Clift, and to a lesser degree Brando, there was nothing self-destructive about Hoffman and competitors Jack Nicholson, who was up for *Chinatown,* and Al Pacino, nominated for *Godfather II.* They were quirky and unpredictable but basically professional. The Oscar, perhaps the result of a split vote, or more likely a sentimental favoring of an old pro, went to Art Carney for *Harry and Tonto,* in which, interestingly, Bruce's real-life mother, Sally Marr, had a small role. (The fifth nominee was Albert Finney in an over-made-up caricature role as Hercule Poirot in *Murder on the Orient Express.*)

Perrine, a former Vegas showgirl, had appeared in a few small roles before landing the plum part of Honey Bruce. An untrained actress, she held the screen convincingly and was immediately acclaimed as a new star. But apart from a comic turn as a stereotypical blowsy broad in *Superman* and a small role as Robert Redford's ex-wife in *The Electric Horseman,* her subsequent screen career has been a minor one. She lost to Ellen Burstyn in *Alice Doesn't Live Here Anymore.*

Barry adapted his own stage play, which had starred Cliff Gorman on Broadway. He lost to Coppola and Mario Puzo's script for *Godfather II.*

Surtees is the son of Robert Surtees, one of the most celebrated of Hollywood cinematographers. Bruce Surtees began his career as a cinematographer in 1971 on three Clint Eastwood [2179.5] movies—*The Beguiled, Dirty Harry,* and *Play Misty for Me.* He continued to work for Eastwood on numerous films.

His sole nomination is for work in now-uncommon black and white. The Oscar went to Fred Koenekamp and Joseph Biroc for *The Towering Inferno.*

Hoffman: 810, 1111, 1312, 1653, 2113. Fosse: 49, 321.

1156 • *LEOPARD, THE*

TITANUS PRODUCTION; 20TH CENTURY-FOX (ITALY/U.S.). 1963.

NOMINATION *Color Costume Design:* Piero Tosi.

Burt Lancaster [107 . . .] plays an Italian prince in the 1860s who regrets the passing of the old aristocratic order, symbolized by the marriage of his nephew, played by Alain Delon, to a merchant's daughter, played by Claudia Cardinale. Beautifully done film, written and directed by Luchino Visconti [480], with cinematography by Giuseppe Rotunno [49] and music by Nino Rota [784]. The last third of the almost three-hour film, a banquet and ball, is one of the most celebrated set pieces in recent cinema history. The movie was not a success when first released in the States—it had been trimmed by more than forty minutes and badly dubbed. It was restored to its original length in 1983. The costume Oscar went to *Cleopatra.*

Tosi: 326, 514, 1225, 2135.

1157 • *LES GIRLS*

SOL C. SIEGEL PRODUCTION; MGM. 1957.

AWARD *Costume Design:* Orry-Kelly.

NOMINATIONS *Art Direction–Set Decoration:* William A. Horning and Gene Allen; Edwin B. Willis and Richard Pefferle. *Sound:* Wesley C. Miller, sound director, MGM Studio Sound Department.

Kay Kendall writes a tell-all book about the nightclub act in which she, Mitzi Gaynor, and Taina Elg performed with Gene Kelly [74]. In the resulting libel suit the three women testify about their relationship to Kelly, each of them giving a different account of the way the act split up. Considering the talent involved—director George Cukor [262 . . .], songwriter Cole Porter [261 . . .], and cinematographer Robert Surtees [130 . . .]—this ought to be a lot better than it is. When the gorgeous, funny Kendall is on screen, it lives up to expectations, but Porter's songs are not his best, and Kelly was at the end of his career as a dancer—this was the last musical in which he starred. His subsequent on-screen roles were largely dramatic ones, with occasional musical cameos. The art direction and sound awards went to *Sayonara*.

Orry-Kelly: 66, 853, 1860. Horning: 175, 440, 769, 1450, 1644, 1657, 2300. Allen: 1393, 1910. Willis: 66, 87, 130, 227, 239, 290, 629, 749, 831, 980, 1069, 1096, 1173, 1190, 1226, 1230, 1232, 1309, 1417, 1567, 1657, 1662, 1673, 1721, 1861, 1937, 2068, 2112, 2257, 2320, 2330. Pefferle: 87, 1096, 1230, 1552, 2312. Miller: 290, 704, 1216.

LES MISÉRABLES
See 1327.

1158 • LET IT BE
BEATLES-APPLE PRODUCTIONS; UNITED ARTISTS (UNITED KINGDOM). 1970.
AWARD *Original Song Score:* The Beatles.

The Beatles gather for a recording session in this documentary made by director Michael Lindsay-Hogg just before the group's breakup. Having passed over their songs for *A Hard Day's Night* and *Help!* (1965), the Academy finally decided to make amends and give the Beatles an Oscar. Even so, the music branch ignored two eligible songs by John Lennon and Paul McCartney [1191] from *Let It Be,* the title song and "The Long and Winding Road." (The best song Oscar went to "For All We Know," from *Lovers and Other Strangers*.) And it can't be said that the Beatles faced brutal competition in the song score category: The other entries were from *The Baby Maker, A Boy Named Charlie Brown, Darling Lili,* and *Scrooge*.

1158.5 • LETHAL WEAPON
WARNER BROS. PRODUCTION; WARNER BROS. 1987.
NOMINATION *Sound:* Les Fresholtz, Dick Alexander, Vern Poore, Bill Nelson.

Mel Gibson plays Martin Riggs, an L.A. police detective who's so distraught over the recent death of his wife that his behavior becomes self-destructive.

This naturally dismays his new partner, Roger Murtaugh (Danny Glover), but the two gradually establish a rapport, helped by Murtaugh's lively, understanding family. When the two cops' investigation of the suicide of a runaway teenager leads them to uncover a drug ring, Riggs narrowly escapes death and Murtaugh's own daughter (Traci Wolfe) is kidnaped. Slam-bang action-adventure flick with hugely attractive performances by Gibson and Glover that help one tolerate some of the film's excessive violence—including a particularly nasty torture scene. It was, of course, a monster hit and spawned sequels in 1989 and 1992. Directed by Richard Donner, with Gary Busey [307] as a bad guy and Darlene Love as Murtaugh's wife. The Oscar for sound went to *The Last Emperor*.

Fresholtz: 54, 58, 209, 215, 606, 888, 1127, 1279, 1526, 2113. Alexander: 54, 209, 519, 888, 1127, 2113, 2179.5. Poore: 209, 888, 1127, 2179.5. Nelson: 888.

1159 • LETHAL WEAPON 2
WARNER BROS. PRODUCTION; WARNER BROS. 1989.
NOMINATION *Sound Effects Editing:* Robert Henderson and Alan Robert Murray.

High-strung police detective Riggs (Mel Gibson) and his family-man partner Murtaugh (Danny Glover) uncover a smuggling operation run by a South African consular official (Joss Ackland). Violent, noisy, formulaic action-adventure thriller made palatable by first-rate performers, including Joe Pesci [806 . . .] as the hyperactive Leo Getz, whom Riggs and Murtagh are forced to keep in protective custody. This sequel to the 1987 hit does nothing new, unless you call demolishing an entire house new, but Gibson and Glover are such an engaging team you don't mind being in their company even when the movie is junk. Directed, like the first film and the 1992 sequel, by Richard Donner. The sound effects editing Oscar seems to have been devised to honor Hollywood's most profitable products, the expensive action epics that came in vogue in the mid-eighties. The award went to *Indiana Jones and the Last Crusade*.

Henderson: 1127. Murray: 1127.

1160 • LET'S MAKE LOVE

COMPANY OF ARTISTS INC.; 20TH CENTURY-FOX. 1960.

NOMINATION *Scoring of a Musical Picture:* Lionel Newman and Earle H. Hagen.

When super-wealthy Yves Montand learns that he's to be lampooned in a Broadway show, he visits rehearsals to put a stop to it, but is mistaken for a look-alike and drafted into the cast. He decides to go along with it when he gets a look at cast member Marilyn Monroe, so he hires Bing Crosby [173 . . .] as singing teacher, Gene Kelly [74] as dance instructor, and Milton Berle as comedy coach. Big, empty musical brought to life occasionally by its performers, but Monroe's unhappiness with being put in this fluffy nonsense after demonstrating her talent in movies like *Bus Stop* and *Some Like It Hot* infected the whole project, and it isn't much fun. With Tony Randall, Wilfred Hyde-White, and Frankie Vaughan, whom Fox hoped to make into a star. They didn't. The script is by Norman Krasna [535 . . .]. George Cukor [262 . . .] directed. Morris Stoloff and Harry Sukman won the scoring Oscar for *Song Without End.*

Newman: 183, 457, 557, 795, 896, 981, 1273, 1585, 1762, 2043.

1161 • LETTER, THE

PARAMOUNT FAMOUS LASKY. 1928–29.

NOMINATION *Actress:* Jeanne Eagels.

Eagels, the wife of a rubber plantation owner in Malaya, kills a man in what appears to be self-defense, but the letter of the title reveals that he was her lover and that she murdered him in cold blood. Somerset Maugham turned his story into a play, which was a Broadway hit for Katharine Cornell before this early talkie was made. Directed by Jean de Limur, with O. P. Heggie, Reginald Owen, and Herbert Marshall.

Eagels had made a few silent films but was best known for her stage work, particularly as Sadie Thompson in another Somerset Maugham play, *Rain.* Paramount had hopes for her as a star of the talkies, but she died of a heroin overdose in 1929. Although she's often cited as the first person to be nominated for an Oscar posthumously, she wasn't officially nominated at all. This year the Academy chose to announce only the winners, in this case, Mary Pickford for *Coquette.* Eagels and the four others being considered by the actors branch for the award didn't even receive a certificate of nomination. But because their names are maintained in Academy records as among the people being considered, they have traditionally been considered nominees.

1162 • LETTER, THE

WARNER BROS. 1940.

NOMINATIONS *Picture:* Hal B. Wallis, producer. *Actress:* Bette Davis. *Supporting Actor:* James Stephenson. *Director:* William Wyler. *Black-and-White Cinematography:* Gaetano Gaudio. *Original Score:* Max Steiner. *Film Editing:* Warren Low.

Somerset Maugham's melodrama about a woman (Davis) who hides infidelity and murder behind a mask of respectability receives a second filming. Stephenson is the lawyer who defends her when she's tried for shooting a man, and Herbert Marshall (who also appeared in the 1929 film) plays her plantation-owner husband. Very classy stuff for the most part, though softened around the edges by the Production Code. Davis is simply terrific in one of her finest, if less celebrated, roles. Gale Sondergaard [83 . . .] does one of her patented sinister women, this time a Eurasian, and the cast also includes Frieda Inescort and Cecil Kellaway [843 . . .]. The screenplay is by Howard Koch [365 . . .].

The best picture Oscar went to *Rebecca,* which also won for George Barnes' cinematography. Ginger Rogers won best actress for *Kitty Foyle.* Walter Brennan took his third Oscar for *The Westerner.* The scoring award went to Leigh Harline, Paul J. Smith, and Ned Washington for *Pinocchio.* Anne Bauchens won for editing *Northwest Mounted Police.*

Wallis: 17, 55, 85, 164, 343, 365, 676, 689, 712, 965, 1046, 1095, 1248, 1482, 1727, 1779, 2233, 2318. Davis: 46, 484, 492, 1046, 1182, 1369, 1456, 1462.5, 1908, 2248. Wyler: 175, 184, 420, 534, 560, 730, 894, 1182, 1371, 1716, 2316. Gaudio: 90, 447, 898, 1064, 1872. Steiner: 16, 154, 190, 330, 365, 385, 492, 679, 747, 754, 798, 999, 1043,

1046, 1052, 1169, 1170, 1207, 1324, 1408, 1430, 1456, 1690, 1779, 1828. Low: 425, 847, 1727.

1163 • LETTER TO THREE WIVES, A

20TH CENTURY-FOX. 1949.

AWARDS *Director:* Joseph L. Mankiewicz. *Screenplay:* Joseph L. Mankiewicz.

NOMINATION *Picture:* Sol C. Siegel, producer.

Three suburban women receive a letter from an acquaintance informing them that she's run off with one of their husbands. Is it rich guy Jeffrey Lynn, married to poor girl Jeanne Crain [1575]? Or girl from the wrong side of the tracks Linda Darnell's hard-to-land Paul Douglas? Or has busy career woman Ann Sothern [2246] lost her schoolteacher husband, Kirk Douglas [130 . . .]? We get anxious flashbacks as the women wait for the truth. We also get bits of satire, social commentary, and witty dialogue. And if the end's a comedown, the rest of the movie makes it easy to forgive. Sothern is wonderful as usual, Darnell gives her best screen performance, and Crain, who has the least interesting role, is lovely to look at. The men match them, although Kirk Douglas seems odd casting as an English teacher—it was one of the roles he played before *Champion* made him a star and typed him as the ruthless but charming loner. Thelma Ritter [46 . . .], in one of her first important roles, launches her career as scene stealer, and the off-screen voice of the letter writer is that of Celeste Holm [46 . . .]. Originally the screenplay, based on a *Cosmopolitan* story, called for four wives, and Anne Baxter [46 . . .] had been cast as No. 4 before studio head Darryl Zanuck [34 . . .] decided that four stories would make the film too long.

Mankiewicz, a former journalist, followed his older (by twelve years) brother, Herman [407 . . .], to Hollywood and began his film career as a writer. In the mid-thirties he became a producer and in 1946 replaced Ernst Lubitsch [889 . . .], who was ill, as director of *Dragonwyck,* beginning a successful writer-director career. Although Mankiewicz defeated Robert Rossen in the directing and writing categories, Rossen triumphed by taking the best picture Oscar for *All the King's Men.*

Mankiewicz: 46, 146, 673, 1444, 1563, 1836, 1841. Siegel: 2072.

1164 • LETTERS FROM MARUSIA

CONACINE PRODUCTION (MEXICO). 1975.

NOMINATION *Foreign Language Film.*

The Chilean militia massacres striking miners at Marusia in 1907. Directed by Miguel Littin, a Chilean exile, the film is a grim allegory of life in that country under Pinochet. *Letters from Marusia* received a limited commercial release in the United States in 1985. The Oscar went to *Dersu Uzala.*

1165 • LIBEL

ANATOLE DE GRUNWALD; MGM (UNITED KINGDOM). 1959.

NOMINATION *Sound:* A. W. Watkins, sound director, MGM London Sound Department.

Dirk Bogarde is a baronet and a former prisoner of war—or is he? When he's accused of being an imposter, he finds it very difficult to prove his identity in court. Interesting but rather stiff-jointed courtroom melodrama whose cast—Olivia de Havilland [798 . . .], Robert Morley [1274], Wilfred Hyde-White—keeps its theatrical origins (a play by Edward Wooll) from getting too obvious. Screenplay by Anatole de Grunwald and Karl Tunberg [175 . . .], directed by Anthony Asquith. The sound award went to Franklin E. Milton for *Ben-Hur.*

Watkins: 558, 804, 1107.

1166 • LIBELED LADY

MGM. 1936.

NOMINATION *Picture:* Lawrence Weingarten, producer.

Heiress Myrna Loy sues newspaper editor Spencer Tracy [131 . . .] for printing an erroneous rumor about her, so Tracy hires William Powell [1170 . . .] to woo Loy so he can then expose her for carrying on with a married man. Trouble is, Powell isn't married, but Tracy knows how to fix that: He persuades his own girlfriend, Jean Harlow, to marry Powell—temporarily, of course. But then Powell falls for Loy, and Harlow falls for Powell, and so on. Lively screwball farce with a powerful star quartet. It's a little on the heavy side—director Jack Conway doesn't have the lightness of touch that Howard Hawks brought to *Bringing Up Baby* or Leo McCarey to *The Awful Truth* or Frank Capra to *It Happened One Night,* the classics of the genre. The screenplay is by Maurine Watkins, Howard Emmett Rogers, and George Oppenheimer [2227] from a story by Wallace Sullivan. The absence of nominations other than for best picture can be partly explained away: Powell was nominated for *My Man Godfrey* and Tracy for *San Francisco.* MGM was pushing its First Lady, Norma Shearer, for her role in *Romeo and Juliet,* and its new discovery Luise Rainer, who won, for *The Great Ziegfeld,* which left Loy and Harlow out in the cold— even though Shearer is a mannered, overage Juliet, Rainer's part in *The Great Ziegfeld* is an extended cameo, and both Loy and Harlow give better performances than either. The best picture Oscar went to *The Great Ziegfeld.*

Weingarten: 372.

1167 • LIES MY FATHER TOLD ME

Pentimento Productions Ltd.-Pentacle VIII Productions Ltd.; Columbia (Canada). 1975.

Nomination *Original Screenplay:* Ted Allan.

Coming-of-age story set in the Montreal Jewish ghetto in the 1920s, about a boy's relationship with his grandfather. Sentimental little story, directed by the Czech émigré Jan Kadar. Writer Allan, whose screenplay is based on his book, also appears in the film as Mr. Baumgarten. The Oscar went to Frank Pierson for *Dog Day Afternoon.*

1168 • LIFE AND TIMES OF JUDGE ROY BEAN, THE

First Artists Production Company Ltd. Production; National General Pictures. 1972.

Nomination *Song:* "Marmalade, Molasses & Honey," music by Maurice Jarre, lyrics by Marilyn Bergman and Alan Bergman.

Outlaw Roy Bean, played by Paul Newman [3 . . .], rides into a small Texas town whose inhabitants promptly lynch him. Surviving the assault, he returns to blow away his assailants and set himself up as law west of the Pecos. Pop antiwestern that sounds like it ought to be a lot of fun: After all, it's directed by John Huston [24 . . .], who also makes a cameo appearance, and in addition to Newman features Ava Gardner [1339] as Lily Langtry, plus Victoria Principal, Jacqueline Bisset, Anthony Perkins [730], Tab Hunter, Stacy Keach, Roddy McDowall, and Ned Beatty [1424]. But it's something of a mess, larded with countercultural self-consciousness and a few surreal touches. The screenplay is by John Milius [92]. The song award went to Al Kasha and Joel Hirschhorn's "The Morning After," from *The Poseidon Adventure.*

Jarre: 558, 764, 808, 1151, 1340, 1533, 1967, 2296. M. Bergman: 179, 867, 1568, 1628, 1747, 1813, 1864, 2063, 2113, 2238, 2321, 2322. A. Bergman: 179, 867, 1568, 1628, 1747, 1813, 1864, 2063, 2113, 2238, 2321, 2322.

1169 • LIFE OF EMILE ZOLA, THE

Warner Bros. 1937.

Awards *Picture:* Henry Blanke, producer. *Supporting Actor:* Joseph Schildkraut. *Screenplay:* Heinz Herald, Geza Herczeg, and Norman Reilly Raine.
Nominations *Actor:* Paul Muni. *Director:* William Dieterle. *Original Story:* Heinz Herald and Geza Herczeg. *Interior Decoration:* Anton Grot. *Sound Recording:* Nathan Levinson. *Assistant Director:* Russ Saunders. *Score:* Warner Bros. Studio Music Department, Leo Forbstein, head; score by Max Steiner.

Muni plays the nineteenth-century French writer, who comes to the defense of Alfred Dreyfus (Schildkraut), a French officer unjustly convicted of espionage and sentenced to Devil's Island. Rich, vivid, and surprisingly exciting film, though the title is misleading, since it deals with only one episode in Zola's life. Curiously the film glosses over a central element of the Dreyfus Affair—the anti-Semitism that led to his conviction. Despite (or perhaps, as some have suggested, because of) the fact that most studio heads, including the Warner brothers, were Jewish, Hollywood didn't attempt to deal with anti-Semitism as a theme until after World War II, in films such as *Crossfire* and *Gentleman's Agreement.* The huge cast includes Gale Sondergaard [83 . . .], Donald Crisp [952],

Morris Carnovsky, Louis Calhern [1243], and Harry Davenport.

This was the first best picture Oscar for Warners, and in part it honored a genre, the socially conscious biopic, at which the studio excelled: *I Was a Fugitive From a Chain Gang, The Story of Louis Pasteur,* and *Juarez,* all starring Muni, and *Dr. Ehrlich's Magic Bullet,* with Edward G. Robinson, came from Warners. Producer Blanke, often listed as an associate producer with Hal Wallis [17 . . .], was one of the major overseers of Warners' ''prestige'' output. He had begun his career in Germany as an assistant to Ernst Lubitsch [889 . . .] and accompanied Lubitsch to America in the twenties. Blanke died in 1981.

Born in Vienna, Schildkraut studied acting under Albert Basserman [706] in Germany and became a star in the company headed by Max Reinhardt before coming to America in 1920. He was a major Broadway star in the twenties and made several important silent films, including D. W. Griffith's *Orphans of the Storm* (1922) and the 1927 *King of Kings,* directed by Cecil B. DeMille [412 . . .], in which Schildkraut played Judas. In the sound era he largely played character roles, on both stage and screen. His last major film role was as the father in *The Diary of Anne Frank,* a part he had created on stage. He died in 1964.

Muni lost to Spencer Tracy in *Captains Courageous.* The Oscar for directing went to Leo McCarey for *The Awful Truth.* William A. Wellman and Robert Carson won for the story of *A Star Is Born.* Stephen Goosson took the art direction Oscar for *Lost Horizon.* Thomas Moulton won for sound for *The Hurricane.* Robert Webb was named best assistant director for *In Old Chicago.* And the scoring award went to Charles Previn for *One Hundred Men and a Girl.*

Blanke: 17, 90, 712, 1046, 1315, 1457, 1936, 2136. Herald: 571. Muni: 218.5, 965, 1133, 1936, 2191. Grot: 90, 1621, 1768, 1981. Levinson: 16, 30, 343, 385, 531, 689, 710, 712, 790, 930, 965, 1052, 1621, 1690, 1768, 1769, 1779, 1930, 1949, 2058, 2318. Forbstein: 90, 385. Steiner: 16, 154, 190, 330, 365, 385, 492, 679, 747, 754, 798, 999, 1043, 1046, 1052, 1162, 1170, 1207, 1324, 1408, 1430, 1456, 1690, 1779, 1828.

1170 • *LIFE WITH FATHER*
WARNER BROS. 1947.

NOMINATIONS *Actor:* William Powell. *Color Cinematography:* Peverell Marley and William V. Skall. *Color Art Direction—Set Decoration:* Robert M. Haas; George James Hopkins. *Scoring of a Dramatic or Comedy Picture:* Max Steiner.

Powell plays Clarence Day, head of a large family of redheaded boys in turn-of-the-century New York. Irene Dunne [114 . . .] is his slightly scatterbrained passive-aggressive wife, Vinnie, in this adaptation of a long-running hit Broadway show by Howard Lindsay and Russel Crouse, which was in turn adapted from the stories of the younger Clarence Day (played in the film by Jimmy Lydon). Agreeable family comedy, though it's hard to separate it in the memory from other tales of turn-of-the-century family life such as *Meet Me in St. Louis, Cheaper by the Dozen* (1950), and numerous Disney flicks that focus on a fuming late-Victorian paterfamilias and his mildly rebellious offspring. Donald Ogden Stewart [1148 . . .] did the screenplay and lost a battle with the censors over Father Day's characteristic explosions of ''damn!'' This made hash of the play's famous curtain line: ''I'm going to be baptized, dammit!'' Directed by Michael Curtiz [79 . . .] and featuring the world's least awkward adolescent, fifteen-year-old Elizabeth Taylor [318 . . .], plus Edmund Gwenn [1325 . . .], ZaSu Pitts, and, as one of the Day boys, Martin *(Route 66)* Milner.

Powell's long career had taken a downturn in the forties, when he found himself stuck in the increasingly tedious series of sequels to *The Thin Man.* But *Life With Father* launched him into an autumnal phase, playing suave elderly men in such films as *Mr. Peabody and the Mermaid* (1948) and *How to Marry a Millionaire.* His last screen appearance was in *Mister Roberts* in 1955. He died in 1984, in his nineties. This was his third unsuccessful nomination. He lost the Oscar to a fellow film veteran, Ronald Colman, for *A Double Life.*

Jack Cardiff won for the cinematography of *Black Narcissus,* which also won for Alfred Junge's art direction. The scoring award went to Miklos Rozsa for *A Double Life.*

Powell: 1401, 2052. Marley: 1957. Skall: 96, 208, 1048, 1317, 1453, 1644, 1668, 1822, 2102. Haas: 1052. Hopkins: 110, 508, 896, 1003, 1332, 1385, 1393, 1910, 1949, 1973, 2058, 2277. Steiner: 16, 154, 190, 330, 365, 385, 492, 679, 747, 754, 798, 999, 1043, 1046, 1052, 1162, 1169, 1207, 1324, 1408, 1430, 1456, 1690, 1779, 1828.

1171 • LIFEBOAT

20TH CENTURY-FOX. 1944.

NOMINATIONS *Director:* Alfred Hitchcock. *Original Story:* John Steinbeck. *Black-and-White Cinematography:* Glen MacWilliams.

The survivors of a torpedoed ship battle the elements and each other. They include Tallulah Bankhead as a journalist, William Bendix [2222] as a wounded sailor, Walter Slezak as the Nazi U-boat commander responsible for sinking their ship, and Hume Cronyn [1791] as the ship's radio operator. Ultimately Hitchcock's technique becomes more interesting than the plot or the characters, although the film gives one a rare chance to see Bankhead in fine form. It also produced a famous anecdote: A complaint was reportedly lodged with the studio because a visitor to the set had seen Bankhead hike up her skirts to climb into the lifeboat, thereby revealing that she wore no underwear. Hitchcock, asked to discuss the incident with Bankhead, declined, saying it was unclear who should take responsibility for the matter: wardrobe, makeup, or hairdressing.

When it was released, the film was assailed by some critics as unpatriotic, because the Slezak character was a proudly defiant Nazi rather than a sniveling coward, while some of the representatives of the Allies on board the lifeboat were obvious weaklings. On the other hand, admirers of Hitchcock regard *Lifeboat* as an inferior member of the director's canon because the obligatory patriotism of the script undermines his usual wit and suspense. Though it's less impressive than his other films of the period, particularly *Shadow of a Doubt* and *Notorious, Lifeboat* earned him his second nomination largely because of his skill at using a confined single set. He even found an ingenious way to make his usual cameo appearance—in a before-

and-after reducing ad in a newspaper on the lifeboat. The Oscar went to Leo McCarey for *Going My Way*.

Steinbeck's story, adapted for the screen by Jo Swerling [1607], exhibits many of the weaknesses of the novelist's work, particularly a heavy-handed reliance on rather obvious symbolism. McCarey received this Oscar, too.

MacWilliams was a second-string Fox cameraman, perhaps entrusted with this A picture because it involved only one set, and Hitchcock was well known for dominating the placement of the camera. The Oscar went to Joseph LaShelle for *Laura*.

Hitchcock: 1632, 1669, 1670, 1890. Steinbeck: 1294, 2212.

1172 • LI'L ABNER

PANAMA AND FRANK PRODUCTION; PARAMOUNT. 1959.

NOMINATION *Scoring of a Musical Picture:* Nelson Riddle and Joseph J. Lilley.

Dogpatch is chosen, because of its essential worthlessness, as an atomic test site. Silly, stagy filming of the Broadway musical based on the Al Capp comic strip, with many of the original cast members repeating their stage roles: Peter Palmer as Li'l Abner, Stubby Kaye as Marryin' Sam, Howard St. John as General Bullmoose, and Julie Newmar as Stupefyin' Jones. Leslie Parrish replaces Edie Adams as Daisy Mae. Norman Panama [636 . . .] and Melvin Frank [636 . . .] adapt their own stage book and also direct the movie. The best thing about it is the songs by Johnny Mercer [248 . . .] and Gene DePaul, which include "Jubilation T. Cornpone" and "Namely You." The scoring Oscar went to André Previn and Ken Darby for *Porgy and Bess*.

Riddle: 338, 821, 1518, 1708.

1173 • LILI

MGM. 1953.

AWARD *Scoring of a Dramatic or Comedy Picture:* Bronislau Kaper.

NOMINATIONS *Actress:* Leslie Caron. *Director:* Charles Walters. *Screenplay:* Helen Deutsch. *Color Cinematography:* Robert Planck. *Color Art Direction–Set Decoration:*

Cedric Gibbons and Paul Groesse; Edwin B. Willis and Arthur Krams.

Caron plays the title role, an orphan who joins a traveling carnival troupe and falls in love with the magician, played by Jean-Pierre Aumont. Meanwhile, puppeteer Mel Ferrer falls in love with her but can express his love only through his puppets. Few films divide audiences and critics more radically: Some find it adorable, others claim it makes them want to hit something. Sometimes thought of as a musical, because of its stylized settings and ballet sequences, and the song ''Hi-Lili, Hi-Lo,'' with lyrics by Deutsch and tune by Kaper, but it's not technically one—as the Academy's nomination of Kaper's score in the nonmusical category indicates. It was, however, turned into a Broadway musical, *Carnival,* in 1961, with songs by Bob Merrill [737]. The cast includes Zsa Zsa Gabor, Amanda Blake, and Kurt Kasznar. The screenplay is based on a story by Paul Gallico [1607].

Kaper, born in Poland, began his career as a composer for the screen in Germany and joined the migration to Hollywood that took place with the rise of Hitler. He spent most of his career at MGM. He died in 1983.

Caron, trained as a ballet dancer, was a member of Roland Petit's company in Paris when Gene Kelly [74] spotted her and cast her in *An American in Paris.* Through the fifties she played ingenues, but after her most famous performance, in *Gigi,* she turned to more serious parts. She lost her first nomination to an actress who had been celebrated as Gigi on stage, Audrey Hepburn in *Roman Holiday.*

Walters had been hired by MGM as a choreographer and worked in that capacity on such films as *Meet Me in St. Louis* and *Ziegfeld Follies* before turning director on *Good News* in 1947. Never quite in the league of such musical directors as Vincente Minnelli [66 . . .] or Stanley Donen, he still turned out some likable films, *Easter Parade, High Society, Billy Rose's Jumbo,* and *The Unsinkable Molly Brown* among them. His nonmusical work includes the last film made by Cary Grant [1445 . . .], *Walk, Don't Run* (1966). He died in 1982. The Oscar went to Fred Zinnemann for *From Here to Eternity,* which also won for Daniel Taradash's screenplay.

The Oscar for cinematography went to Loyal Griggs for *Shane. The Robe* won the art direction award.

Kaper: 397, 1388. Caron: 1113. Planck: 74, 1190, 2079. Gibbons: 66, 87, 130, 217, 227, 239, 285, 290, 440, 629, 749, 831, 980, 1069, 1096, 1190, 1226, 1230, 1232, 1274, 1308, 1309, 1417, 1567, 1604, 1644, 1662, 1673, 1721, 1861, 1937, 2068, 2112, 2256, 2257, 2300, 2320, 2330. Groesse: 87, 1190, 1232, 1309, 1335, 1385, 1604, 2112, 2157, 2320. Willis: 66, 87, 130, 227, 239, 290, 629, 749, 831, 980, 1069, 1096, 1157, 1190, 1226, 1230, 1232, 1309, 1417, 1567, 1657, 1662, 1673, 1721, 1861, 1937, 2068, 2112, 2257, 2320, 2330. Krams: 357, 1309, 1727, 1937, 1959, 2098, 2208.

1174 • *LILIES OF THE FIELD*

RAINBOW PRODUCTIONS; UNITED ARTISTS. 1963.

AWARD *Actor:* Sidney Poitier.

NOMINATIONS *Picture:* Ralph Nelson, producer. *Supporting Actress:* Lilia Skala. *Screenplay—Based on Material From Another Medium:* James Poe. *Black-and-White Cinematography:* Ernest Haller.

Five East German nuns, exiled in the American Southwest, prevail on handyman Poitier to build a chapel for them. Unassuming little heartwarmer that became a sleeper hit, though it hardly deserved a best picture nomination over *8¹/₂* or *Hud.* Nelson, who also directed and acted in the film, put together the project on a shoestring, finally getting the backing he needed when Poitier agreed to play the lead.

Poitier was not only the first black male to win an Oscar, he is also, to this date, the only African-American of either sex to win for a leading role. Born in Florida to Bahamian parents and raised in the Bahamas, he began his acting career with the American Negro Theater and made his film debut in *No Way Out* in 1950. His breakthrough role came five years later as a high school student in *Blackboard Jungle,* but it was not until the sixties that he reached major stardom. During the black power movement later in that decade, Poitier was sometimes attacked by militants for playing middle-class blacks, as in his most famous roles in *Guess Who's Coming to Dinner* and *In the Heat of the Night*. In the seventies Poitier turned to directing, mostly on films with black performers, and began to make fewer on-screen appearances.

Nelson, a stage actor, began directing in fifties TV. He won an Emmy for *Requiem for a Heavyweight* and made his screen directing debut with the film of that TV drama in 1962. He died in 1987. The best picture Oscar went to *Tom Jones*.

Skala, a Viennese stage performer, made her film debut in *Lilies* as the nuns' mother superior. She has subsequently been seen in such films as *Charly* (also produced and directed by Nelson) and *Flashdance*. The Oscar went to Margaret Rutherford for *The V.I.P.'s*.

Poe lost to John Osborne for *Tom Jones*. James Wong Howe won for the cinematography of *Hud*.

Poitier: 522. Poe: 101, 372, 2047. Haller: 55, 679, 798, 1046, 1319, 2248.

1175 • LILLIAN RUSSELL

20TH CENTURY-FOX. 1940.

NOMINATION *Black-and-White Interior Decoration:* Richard Day and Joseph C. Wright.

Alice Faye plays the title role, the Gay Nineties entertainer who was the toast of New York. Cornball biopic, directed by Irving Cummings, one of dozens of period musicals turned out by Fox apparently to keep its huge supply of feather boas and swallowtail coats out of mothballs. This one has only a remote connection with the facts, and mainly exists to allow Faye to sing a lot of period and pseudo-period songs and flirt with Don Ameche [419], Henry Fonda [815 . . .], and Edward Arnold, who plays Diamond Jim Brady, a role he'd had in his own biopic at Universal in 1935. The cast includes Leo Carrillo as Tony Pastor, Weber and Fields as themselves, Eddie Foy, Jr., as his own father, and Nigel Bruce and Una O'Connor. The art direction award went to Cedric Gibbons and Paul Groesse for *Pride and Prejudice*.

Day: 22, 102, 235, 487, 510, 560, 569, 797, 833, 864, 952, 1048, 1397, 1477, 1666, 1949, 2056, 2120, 2276. Wright: 235, 428, 508, 569, 690, 746, 852, 1264, 1397, 1475, 2056.

1176 • LIMELIGHT

CHARLES CHAPLIN PRODUCTIONS; COLUMBIA. 1972.

AWARD *Original Dramatic Score:* Charles Chaplin, Raymond Rasch, and Larry Russell.

Chaplin, an alcoholic has-been music hall comedian, rescues a young woman, Claire Bloom, from suicide. He nurses her back to health, and when she finds work as a dancer, she gets him a job with the company. When Chaplin realizes that Bloom's devotion to him is endangering her chance at a suitable marriage, he disappears. Later he is discovered and enlisted for a benefit show in which she is appearing. He does an act with Buster Keaton—the only screen teaming of the great comedians—but suffers a heart attack and dies in the wings as he watches Bloom dance. Too mawkish, too long, too talky, but it has some wonderful Chaplinesque moments.

Limelight was made in 1952, but because it was not shown in Los Angeles that year, it was deemed eligible for the Academy Awards when it was rereleased and played there in 1972. It is the last important Chaplin film. *A King in New York,* which was made in England in 1957, is a misfired satire on McCarthyism and popular culture that was withheld from release in America until 1973. *A Countess From Hong Kong,* made in 1967, stars Marlon Brando [583 . . .] and Sophia Loren [1280 . . .], but looks like the work of an inept amateur. Chaplin seems to have spent the last of his energy as a filmmaker on *Limelight,* which is one of his most personal films. The setting—the Edwardian London theater—evokes his childhood. Chaplin's children, Sydney, Charles, Jr., Geraldine, Josephine, and Michael, all appear in the film. Claire Bloom, who shot to stardom with the role, was cast, as she has observed, because of her strong resemblance to Chaplin's wife Oona. The character she plays is in some ways based on Chaplin's mother, a musical performer who went insane. By restoring her to health and success, Chaplin is rewriting his mother's life with a happy ending.

In 1952, however, the happy ending for Chaplin

was a few years off. As *Limelight* was opening, U.S. immigration authorities, responding to anticommunist political pressure, investigated Chaplin, who had never become an American citizen. He sailed to England for the premiere of *Limelight* and didn't return to the States until 1972, when he received an honorary Oscar from the Academy at a ceremony that remains one of the award's sentimental highlights. The following year he won the only competitive award he ever received from the Academy. Ironically the man whose brilliance as a performer had made him one of the century's legendary figures, and whose skills as producer, director, and writer had created a handful of screen classics, won for music, a field in which he was decidedly an amateur.

Chaplin: 405, 818, 1345.

L'INVITATION
See 1013.

1177 • *LION IN WINTER, THE*
HAWORTH PRODUCTIONS LTD.; AVCO EMBASSY. 1968.
AWARDS *Actress:* Katharine Hepburn. *Screenplay—Based on Material From Another Medium:* James Goldman. *Original Score—for a Motion Picture (Not a Musical):* John Barry.
NOMINATIONS *Picture:* Martin Poll, producer. *Actor:* Peter O'Toole. *Director:* Anthony Harvey. *Costume Design:* Margaret Furse.

O'Toole, as Henry II of England, and Hepburn, as his estranged wife, Eleanor of Aquitaine, get together at Christmas and battle over who is going to be his successor. Very, very talky costume drama, played to —and maybe through—the hilt by the leads, with able support from two young actors making their film debuts: Timothy Dalton and Anthony Hopkins [1679.5 . . .]. Some find it compelling, while others think it's just a high-toned, overblown gabfest.

Hepburn won her second consecutive Oscar, bringing her total to three, though she had to share the honor with Barbra Streisand, who tied for her performance in *Funny Girl.* There was, as often, an element of sentimentality in the Academy's voting: This was Hepburn's first film since the death of Spen-cer Tracy [131 . . .]. The period following her third award was something of a muddled one for Hepburn. Her next film was the disastrous *The Madwoman of Chaillot,* which, despite a cast that included Charles Boyer [36 . . .], Edith Evans [377 . . .], Paul Henreid, Giulietta Masina, Richard Chamberlain, Yul Brynner [1088], and Danny Kaye, was all but unreleasable. She fared only slightly better on Broadway with the musical *Coco.* Not until the amusing pairing with John Wayne [33 . . .] in *Rooster Cogburn* in 1975 and the sentimental *On Golden Pond,* which won her a fourth Oscar, did she find roles that attracted film audiences again.

Goldman, the older brother of William Goldman [54 . . .], adapted his own Broadway play for the film and has subsequently done screenplays for *Nicholas and Alexandra, Robin and Marian* (1976) and *White Nights.* He also cowrote the book for the Broadway musical *Follies* with Stephen Sondheim [543].

Barry had first attracted attention with his scores for James Bond movies, starting with *From Russia With Love* in 1963, and won two awards for the score and title song of *Born Free* in 1966. He has since become one of the movies' most prolific composers, second only, perhaps, to John Williams [6 . . .] in public awareness. In the music categories, only Alfred Newman [31 . . .] and songwriter Alan Menken [1184 . . .] have taken home more Oscars than Barry, who has won five.

The Lion in Winter, as an "intellectual" costume drama with big stars spouting what sounded like big thoughts, looked like a strong contender for best picture. The other contenders included a small psychological drama, *Rachel, Rachel,* Franco Zeffirelli's lively version of *Romeo and Juliet,* and two musicals—*Funny Girl* and *Oliver!* The latter was a somewhat surprising winner, also taking an Oscar for director Carol Reed. (Harvey, a former film editor, has not fulfilled the promise some saw in his direction of *Lion.*) There were, as usual, many who thought the year's most interesting films had been slighted by the Academy, *2001: A Space Odyssey, Rosemary's Baby, Belle du Jour,* and the Soviet Union's spectacular *War and Peace* among them.

In another Oscar upset, the award went to Cliff Robertson for *Charly,* adding to O'Toole's record-setting string of unsuccessful nominations. But for what it's worth, O'Toole became the second performer to receive nominations for playing the same character in two different films, having also played Henry II in *Becket.* Bing Crosby had been nominated for two outings as Father O'Malley in *Going My Way* and *The Bells of St. Mary's.* Subsequently Al Pacino was nominated twice as Michael Corleone in *The Godfather* and *The Godfather, Part II.* And Paul Newman was Fast Eddie Felson in both *The Hustler* and *The Color of Money.*

The costume award went to Danilo Donati for *Romeo and Juliet.*

Hepburn: 24, 40, 843, 1199, 1357, 1473, 1563, 1654, 1956, 1963, 2305. Barry: 259, 382.5, 482, 1285, 1512. O'Toole: 164, 805, 1151, 1395, 1733, 1953. Furse: 85, 164, 1285, 1374, 1766.

1177.5 • LION KING, THE

WALT DISNEY PICTURES PRODUCTION; BUENA VISTA. 1994.

AWARDS *Original Score:* Hans Zimmer. *Song:* "Can You Feel the Love Tonight," music by Elton John, lyrics by Tim Rice.

NOMINATIONS *Song:* "Circle of Life," music by Elton John, lyrics by Tim Rice. *Song:* "Hakuna Matata," music by Elton John, lyrics by Tim Rice.

When the lion king Mufasa is accidentally killed, the king's evil brother, Scar, tricks the heir apparent, the cub Simba, into believing that he has caused his father's death. Simba flees into the wilderness where he grows up befriended by a meerkat and a warthog. But then the day comes when he must summon the courage to return and face down Scar, whose rule has turned the lion kingdom into a wasteland. Phenomenally successful cartoon feature that continued the renaissance of Disney animation, topping even *The Little Mermaid, Beauty and the Beast,* and *Aladdin* at the box office, though some critics felt it was a shade inferior to those films—especially the songs. One of the few Disney animated features based on an original

story rather than a fairy tale or children's book—the credited writers are Irene Mecchi, Jonathan Roberts, and Linda Woolverton. One wonders what Walt Disney would think of a cartoon bearing his name that includes fart jokes, but the film is a tribute to traditional Disney character animation, enhanced by some groundbreaking work in computer animation. It also has some very well-chosen actors on the soundtrack. Jeremy Irons [1689] is the standout as the villainous Scar—the script even works in a sly allusion to his Oscar-winning role as Claus Von Bulow in *Reversal of Fortune*—but the cast also includes Jonathan Taylor Thomas as young Simba and Matthew Broderick as grown-up Simba, James Earl Jones [830] as Mufasa, Nathan Lane as Timon the meerkat, Ernie Sabella as Pumbaa the warthog, and Whoopi Goldberg [423 . . .] and Cheech Marin as hyenas.

One of Hollywood's busiest composers, Zimmer had scored two best picture winners, *Rain Man* and *Driving Miss Daisy,* but this was his first Oscar. John has been one of pop music's biggest stars since the seventies, and has made a few on-camera appearances as a performer, as in *Tommy.* This was Rice's second Oscar-winning collaboration; his first award was with Alan Menken for "A Whole New World" from *Aladdin.*

Zimmer: 1653. Rice: 32.5.

1178 • LITTLE ARK, THE

ROBERT RADNITZ PRODUCTIONS LTD.; CINEMA CENTER FILMS PRESENTATION; NATIONAL GENERAL PICTURES. 1972.

NOMINATION *Song:* "Come Follow, Follow Me," music by Fred Karlin, lyrics by Marsha Karlin.

Two Dutch children are swept away in a houseboat by a flood and try to find safety. Children's film from producer Robert Radnitz, whose *Sounder* was both critically and commercially more successful. Directed by James B. Clark; the cast includes Theodore Bikel [522]. The song Oscar went to Al Kasha and Joel Hirschhorn for "The Morning After," from *The Poseidon Adventure.*

F. Karlin: 120, 1221, 1926.

1179 • LITTLE BIG MAN

HILLER PRODUCTIONS LTD.-STOCKBRIDGE PRODUCTIONS; CINEMA CENTER FILMS PRESENTATIONS; NATIONAL GENERAL PICTURES. 1970.

NOMINATION *Supporting Actor:* Chief Dan George.

Dustin Hoffman [810 . . .] plays Jack Crabb, who ventures West and undergoes a series of picaresque adventures, among other things, surviving the battle of Little Big Horn and living to be 121 (which necessitated a five-hour makeup job for Hoffman). It's a wildly uneven two-and-a-half-hour satiric epic that now looks a little dated, as many of the once-hip late-sixties moves do. The targets—white stupidity and venality—seem too easy, and the analogies with the American involvement in Vietnam too obvious. The shifts in tone, from slapstick to tragedy, throw the movie out of shape. Wags referred to it as *The Graduate Goes West.* Still, it's very watchable and has plenty of admirers. Hoffman is joined by Faye Dunaway [255 . . .] as a horny preacher's wife, Jeff Corey as Wild Bill Hickok, Richard Mulligan as Custer, and Martin Balsam [2067]. Arthur Penn [43 . . .] directed from a screenplay by Calder Willingham [810] based on Thomas Berger's novel. The cinematographer is Harry Stradling, Jr. [1790 . . .].

George, seventy-one-year-old honorary chief of a Canadian tribe, plays an Indian patriarch, mentor of Hoffman, who is adopted by the Indians. After his Oscar nomination, George appeared in several more films, including *Harry and Tonto* and *The Outlaw Josey Wales,* before his death in 1981. The award went to John Mills for *Ryan's Daughter.*

1180 • LITTLE CAESAR

FIRST NATIONAL. 1930–31.

NOMINATION *Adaptation:* Francis Faragoh and Robert N. Lee.

Edward G. Robinson plays the gangster Caesar Enrico Bandello—clearly modeled on Al Capone. Little Rico meets his famous end on the steps of a church. Still something of a classic, though of the great early-thirties triad of gangster flicks that includes *Public Enemy* and *Scarface* (1932), it's the most primitively

made. Directed by Mervyn LeRoy [1662 . . .], with Douglas Fairbanks, Jr., and Glenda Farrell. The movie made Robinson a star, and he went on to be one of the movies' most distinguished actors, though he never received an Oscar nomination. The writing Oscar went to Howard Estabrook for *Cimarron.*

1181 • LITTLE DORRIT

SANDS FILMS PRODUCTION; CANNON RELEASING (UNITED KINGDOM). 1988.

NOMINATIONS *Supporting Actor:* Alec Guinness. *Screenplay Based on Material From Another Medium:* Christine Edzard.

Guinness plays William Dorrit, who has lived so long in the debtors' prison in London that he has come to be known as the Father of the Marshalsea. The title character is his daughter Amy, played by Sarah Pickering. The Dorrits are befriended by Arthur Clennam, played by Derek Jacobi, a man who is instrumental in restoring the fortunes of the family, while in the meantime his own are destroyed. Edzard's adaptation of the novel by Charles Dickens, which she also directed, is certainly ambitious. The film was shown in two parts, subtitled *Nobody's Fault* and *Little Dorrit's Story,* totaling six hours. But ultimately the film is undone by its literalness; those who have read the book will miss the texture of Dickens' language, while those who haven't may be baffled by the intricacies of the plot (even though the second part begins by virtually recapitulating the action of the first). Guinness and Jacobi are superb, and the well-chosen cast includes Roshan Seth, Miriam Margolyes, Cyril Cusack, Eleanor Bron, Joan Greenwood, and Robert Morley [1274]. The Los Angeles film critics gave it their award for best picture. But *Masterpiece Theatre* has become the accepted venue for this kind of literary adaptation, and it really seems like a better-than-average TV serialization.

Guinness lost to Kevin Kline in *A Fish Called Wanda.* The writing Oscar went to Christopher Hampton for *Dangerous Liaisons.*

Guinness: 287, 941, 1150, 1916.

1182 • LITTLE FOXES, THE

Samuel Goldwyn Productions; RKO Radio. 1941.

Nominations *Picture:* Samuel Goldwyn, producer. *Actress:* Bette Davis. *Supporting Actress:* Patricia Collinge. *Supporting Actress:* Teresa Wright. *Director:* William Wyler. *Screenplay:* Lillian Hellman. *Black-and-White Interior Decoration:* Stephen Goosson, art direction; Howard Bristol, set decoration. *Scoring of a Dramatic Picture:* Meredith Willson. *Film Editing:* Daniel Mandell.

Davis plays Regina Giddens, whose brothers (Charles Dingle and Carl Benton Reid) are involved in a scheme to bring industry to their small southern town but need the capital of her banker husband, Horace (Herbert Marshall), to float the deal. Horace, who is an invalid, wants no part of the scheme despite Regina's entreaties. Regina's nephew, Leo (Dan Duryea), who works in the bank, steals some bonds from Horace's safe-deposit box so the deal will go through. When Regina learns of this theft, she blackmails her brothers into giving her a majority interest in the project. Horace, however, wants to forgive and forget, and informs Regina that he's changing his will in favor of their daughter, Alexandra (Wright). But before he can do this, he suffers a seizure, and Regina refuses to give him the medicine that would forestall his fatal heart attack. Almost everyone in this very dysfunctional southern family is up to no good, except perhaps Alexandra and her mousy, alcoholic Aunt Birdie (Collinge). Entertaining melodrama, made into something more distinguished than its plot would suggest by the subtle characterization and intelligent dialogue of Hellman's screenplay, based on her own Broadway hit. Many of the cast, including Collinge and Duryea, repeat roles they had played on stage. Davis assumes the role created on Broadway by Tallulah Bankhead.

Goldwyn had an edge in buying the rights to the play because Hellman had been a contract writer for him. To obtain Davis' services was a more complex business—it finally involved loaning out Goldwyn player Gary Cooper [701 . . .] to Warners for *Sergeant York,* which won the actor his first Oscar. Even then, Jack Warner was reluctant to allow his biggest star, Davis, to work for another studio, until Goldwyn reminded Warner that he owed him a sizable gambling debt. The best picture Oscar went to *How Green Was My Valley.*

Davis modeled her performance on Bankhead's—to Wyler's dismay: He wanted a more subtly insidious and charming character. The fights between actress and director—who were former lovers—were legendary, including a three-week sick-out by Davis. The resulting performance is highly watchable but not first-rate Davis, and she lost the Oscar to Joan Fontaine in *Suspicion.*

Both Collinge and Wright made their film debuts in *The Little Foxes.* Born in Ireland, Collinge had begun acting in London when she was ten and came to America four years later, in 1908. She became a major Broadway player but made only a few films after *The Little Foxes,* the most important being *Shadow of a Doubt* and *The Nun's Story.* She died in 1974. Wright was discovered by Goldwyn in the cast of the long-running Broadway hit *Life With Father* and signed to a contract. Her big year at the Oscars would be 1942, when she received two nominations and won for *Mrs. Miniver.* This year the supporting actress award went to Mary Astor for *The Great Lie.*

Wyler's direction, greatly aided by the cinematography of Gregg Toland [407 . . .], led Hellman to say that much of the film worked better than the play. The deep-focus scene in which an impassive Davis sits on a sofa as Marshall collapses on the stairs behind her is justly admired. The directing award went to John Ford for *How Green Was My Valley.*

Hellman had rewritten her play so often that when Goldwyn demanded yet another rewrite—largely to work on the love story subplot involving Wright and Richard Carlson, whose character was not in the play—she suggested that the work be done by her friends Arthur Kober, Dorothy Parker [1845 . . .], and Alan Campbell [1909]. Hellman received sole screen credit, however. The Oscar went to Seton I. Miller and Sidney Buchman for *Here Comes Mr. Jordan.*

The art direction Oscar went to *How Green Was My Valley.* William Holmes won for editing *Sergeant York.*

Goldwyn: 102, 184, 214, 510, 560, 1607, 2316.

Davis: 46, 484, 492, 1046, 1162, 1369, 1456, 1462.5, 1908, 2248. Wright: 1371, 1607. Wyler: 175, 184, 420, 534, 560, 730, 894, 1162, 1371, 1716, 2316. Hellman: 1451. Goosson: 928, 1073, 1206, 2066. Bristol: 690, 852, 864, 1451, 1607, 1613, 1907, 2064. Willson: 818. Mandell: 91, 184, 1607, 2297.

1183 • LITTLE FUGITIVE

LITTLE FUGITIVE PRODUCTION COMPANY; JOSEPH BURSTYN INC. 1953.

NOMINATION *Motion Picture Story:* Ray Ashley, Morris Engel, and Ruth Orkin.

Young Richie Andrusco plays a boy who thinks he has caused his brother's death, so he runs away and spends the day wandering around Coney Island. This small, low-budget independent film was an art-house phenomenon of the early fifties, hailed by some as an American equivalent of the Italian neorealist films of Vittorio De Sica [650] and Roberto Rossellini [1519]. It's no *Bicycle Thief,* but it has its charms. Engel and Orkin, husband and wife, made two more low-budget films in the fifties, one of which, *Weddings and Babies,* won the Critics Prize at the Venice Festival in 1948. The Oscar went to Ian McLellan Hunter, fronting for Dalton Trumbo, for *Roman Holiday.*

1183.5 • LITTLE KIDNAPPERS, THE

RANK/NOLBANDOV-PARKYN. 1954.

AWARDS *Honorary Award:* Jon Whitely for his outstanding juvenile performance. *Honorary Award:* Vincent Winter for his outstanding juvenile performance.

Forbidden by their grandfather (Duncan Macrae) to have a dog, orphans Whitely and Winter discover an abandoned baby whom they secretly try to raise in the woods. Charming little film, set in Nova Scotia, directed by Philip Leacock from a screenplay by Neil Paterson [1724]. Whitely and Winter made other film appearances over the next decade. The latter emigrated to Australia, where he is a stage actor.

1184 • LITTLE MERMAID, THE

WALT DISNEY PICTURES PRODUCTION IN ASSOCIATION WITH SILVER SCREEN PARTNERS IV; BUENA VISTA. 1989.

AWARDS *Song:* "Under the Sea," music by Alan Menken, lyrics by Howard Ashman. *Original Score:* Alan Menken.

NOMINATION *Song:* "Kiss the Girl," music by Alan Menken, lyrics by Howard Ashman.

Ariel, a young mermaid filled with curiosity about life on the land, rescues a handsome prince from drowning. Making a bargain with Ursula, the sea witch, Ariel receives legs that will let her walk on the land, but a terrible fate awaits her if she's unable to win the prince's love. Splendid Disney animated film, the first in the trilogy of Menken-Ashman cartoon features that continued with *Beauty and the Beast* and concluded, after Ashman's death, with *Aladdin.* A tremendous hit, *The Little Mermaid* revived Disney's near moribund animation department and made Menken and Ashman the hottest songwriting team in Hollywood. Both nominated songs were sung by Samuel E. Wright, the voice for the crab Sebastian. Jodi Benson is the voice of Ariel, and Pat Carroll that of Ursula; other characters are voiced by Kenneth Mars, Buddy Hackett, and René Auberjonois.

Ashman and Menken were introduced in 1978 by Broadway conductor Lehman Engel, teacher of a class on writing for the musical theater. They began their collaboration with an off-off-Broadway show, *God Bless You, Mr. Rosewater,* based on a novel by Kurt Vonnegut. Their second show, *Little Shop of Horrors,* was a big off-Broadway hit and led to their work on the film version, for which they wrote additional songs, including an Oscar nominee. The film also caught the attention of Disney's Jeffrey Katzenberg, who signed them to a contract with the studio.

Menken: 32.5, 162, 1188. Ashman: 32.5, 162, 1188.

1185 • LITTLE NIGHT MUSIC, A

SASCHA-WIEN FILM PRODUCTION IN ASSOCIATION WITH ELLIOTT KASTNER; NEW WORLD PICTURES (AUSTRIA/WEST GERMANY). 1977.

AWARD *Original Song Score and Its Adaptation or Adaptation Score:* Jonathan Tunick.

NOMINATION *Costume Design:* Florence Klotz.

On a weekend outing at the country home of Mme Armfeldt (Hermione Gingold), a lawyer (Len Cariou), married to a much younger woman (Lesley-Anne Down), encounters his former mistress, Desirée, played by Elizabeth Taylor [318 . . .]. Various romantic realignments ensue. The adaptation of the Broadway musical based on the Ingmar Bergman [111 . . .] film *Smiles of a Summer Night,* with songs by Stephen Sondheim [543], was a colossal flop. Hugh Wheeler, who wrote the book for the stage musical, also did the screenplay, and Harold Prince directed both, but they don't do enough to disguise the piece's stage origins. Filmed on location in Austria, it's at once too stylized and too awkwardly opened up. Taylor was added to give the film star quality, but Down, Gingold, and Diana Rigg are far more fun to watch—and to listen to: Taylor's inability to sing is especially glaring because she is given the musical's most famous number, "Send in the Clowns." The film's Oscar reflects the poverty of the year's musical offerings; the Academy could muster only two competitors, *Pete's Dragon* and *The Slipper and the Rose—the Story of Cinderella,* in a category that would normally have five contenders. The costume award went to John Mollo for *Star Wars.*

1186 • LITTLE PRINCE, THE

STANLEY DONEN ENTERPRISES LTD. PRODUCTION; PARAMOUNT (UNITED KINGDOM). 1974.

NOMINATIONS *Song:* "Little Prince," music by Frederick Loewe, lyrics by Alan Jay Lerner. *Scoring—Original Song Score and/or Adaptation:* Alan Jay Lerner, Frederick Loewe, Angela Morley, and Douglas Gamley.

A pilot (Richard Kiley) who crashes in the desert encounters a small boy who has come here from a tiny planet to learn about life on earth. The pilot, too, has things to learn—something about getting in touch with the inner child, it would seem. This musical adaptation of the delicate little allegory by Antoine de Saint Exupéry founders under the weight of its own overproduced whimsy. Its failure pounded another nail in the coffin of the film musical, done in by such late-sixties/early-seventies duds as *Darling Lili, Goodbye, Mr. Chips, Star!,* and *Doctor Dolittle.* Stanley Donen directed, and the cast includes Bob Fosse [49 . . .] as a snake and Gene Wilder [1626 . . .] as a fox. This was the last collaboration of Lerner and Loewe. History will honor them for *My Fair Lady* and *Gigi,* but the quality of this score is indicated by the fact that their nominated song lost to Al Kasha and Joel Hirschhorn's "We May Never Love Like This Again," from *The Towering Inferno.* The scoring award went to Nelson Riddle for *The Great Gatsby.*

Loewe: 769. Lerner: 66, 769, 1393, 1731. Morley: 1842.

1187 • LITTLE ROMANCE, A

PAN ARTS ASSOCIATES PRODUCTION; ORION PICTURES CORPORATION. 1979.

AWARD *Original Score:* Georges Delerue.

NOMINATION *Screenplay Based on Material From Another Medium:* Allan Burns.

Diane Lane, an American girl living in France, and Thelonious Bernard, a young Frenchman, run away together, accompanied by Laurence Olivier [268 . . .], a charming old con artist. Pleasantly lightweight little comedy romance, with Olivier having the time of his life. Directed by George Roy Hill [317 . . .], with Arthur Hill, Sally Kellerman [1286], and Broderick Crawford [53].

Delerue first came to prominence in the late fifties as the composer for such attention-getting French New Wave films as *Hiroshima, Mon Amour* and *Jules and Jim* (1961). His international career blossomed in the later sixties and seventies with work on *A Man for All Seasons* and *Women in Love,* as well as countless French films. He is now in equal demand on both sides of the Atlantic.

The screenplay award went to Robert Benton for *Kramer vs. Kramer*.

Delerue: 28, 85, 502, 1066.

1188 • *LITTLE SHOP OF HORRORS*

Geffen Company Production; Geffen Company through Warner Bros. 1986.

Nominations *Song:* "Mean Green Mother From Outer Space," music by Alan Menken, lyrics by Howard Ashman. *Visual Effects:* Lyle Conway, Bran Ferren, and Martin Gutteridge.

Shy, mousy Seymour (Rick Moranis) works in a flower shop in a slum, where he's bullied by his boss, played by Vincent Gardenia [142 . . .], until he discovers a strange new plant. Suddenly Seymour's the toast of the town, and the object of the affections of the woman he's adored from afar, Audrey (Ellen Greene). The trouble is, the little plant thrives on blood, and Seymour is forced to provide more and more nourishment; soon the little plant isn't so little anymore. Lively, hilarious horror musical that began life off-Broadway, when Menken and Ashman adapted for the stage the low-budget cult film produced by Roger Corman in 1960, adding their songs. This film version is niftily directed by Frank Oz and wonderfully cast, with Steve Martin as Audrey's sadistic dentist boyfriend and Bill Murray as his perfect patient, a masochist. (Murray's role was played in the 1960 film by then-unknown Jack Nicholson [395 . . .].) There's also a girl-group trio who serve as chorus commenting on the action. The real standout in the cast, though, may be Levi Stubbs as the voice of Audrey II, the plant. Stubbs gets to use his intimidating bass voice full out in performing the nominated song, which was not in the original stage version. For some reason, the Academy preferred the tedious techno-pop "Take My Breath Away," from *Top Gun*. And the visual effects lost to those for *Aliens*.

Menken: 32.5, 162, 1184. Ashman: 32.5, 162, 1184.

1189 • *LITTLE WOMEN*

RKO Radio. 1932–33.

Award *Adaptation:* Victor Heerman and Sarah Y. Mason.

Nominations *Picture:* Merian C. Cooper, with Kenneth MacGowan, producers. *Director:* George Cukor.

The wife and four daughters of a Civil War officer keep the home fires burning while he's away and have various romantic problems while growing up. Katharine Hepburn [24 . . .] is Jo, the spirited "tomboy" writer-to-be; Frances Dee plays Meg, Joan Bennett is the flibbertigibbet Amy, and Jean Parker is poor, doomed Beth. Spring Byington [2325] is Marmee, Douglass Montgomery Jo's adoring neighbor Laurie, Paul Lukas [2233] the burly Professor Bhaer, and Edna May Oliver [581] Aunt March. Perfect casting and a luminous performance by Hepburn make this adaptation of the Louisa May Alcott novel one of the classics of the thirties. Its flaws are those of the novel —a tendency to the saccharine being the major one —but its power to charm has lasted more than sixty years.

Heerman and Mason, husband and wife, were frequent collaborators. Born in England, Heerman was raised in America and began acting as a child. He turned to directing in the silent era but gave it up in the early thirties. His most accessible work as director is the Marx Brothers' *Animal Crackers* (1930). Among the films credited to Heerman and Mason are *Magnificent Obsession, Stella Dallas,* and *Golden Boy*.

Little Women was a project planned by David O. Selznick [497 . . .] while he was head of production at RKO, but not begun until after he had left for MGM. It came in third in the race for best picture, after *A Farewell to Arms* and the winner, *Cavalcade*.

Both Cukor and Hepburn can credit much of their early career advances to the enthusiasm of Selznick. This was her fourth film, and while she was not nominated for it, she received the Oscar for *Morning Glory* at the same ceremony. Cukor came in third in the three-man Oscar race, behind Frank Capra for *Lady for a Day* and the winner, Frank Lloyd for *Cavalcade*.

Cooper: 1642. MacGowan: 990. Cukor: 262, 567, 1393, 1563.

1190 • LITTLE WOMEN

MGM. 1949.

AWARD *Color Art Direction—Set Decoration:* Cedric Gibbons and Paul Groesse; Edwin B. Willis and Jack D. Moore.

NOMINATION *Color Cinematography:* Robert Planck and Charles Schoenbaum.

Louisa May Alcott's novel receives a second filming, but where the 1933 version is warm and fuzzy, the 1949 one is bright and hard. Mervyn LeRoy [1662 . . .] directed, and the cast features June Allyson as Jo, Janet Leigh [1632] as Meg, Elizabeth Taylor [318 . . .] as Amy, and Margaret O'Brien as Beth, with Mary Astor [822] playing Marmee and Peter Lawford as Laurie. Victor Heerman and Sarah Y. Mason, who won Oscars for the 1933 film, also worked on the screenplay with Andrew Solt, and even the Adolph Deutsch [87 . . .] score is an adaptation of the one Max Steiner [16 . . .] did for the original film. But Allyson, who is merely spunky, is no substitute for Katharine Hepburn, who brought a rare delicacy to her portrayal of the bumptious Jo.

The cinematography Oscar went to Winton Hoch for *She Wore a Yellow Ribbon.*

Gibbons: 66, 87, 130, 217, 227, 239, 285, 290, 440, 629, 749, 831, 980, 1069, 1096, 1173, 1226, 1230, 1232, 1274, 1308, 1309, 1417, 1567, 1604, 1644, 1662, 1673, 1721, 1861, 1937, 2068, 2112, 2256, 2257, 2300, 2320, 2330. Groesse: 87, 1173, 1232, 1309, 1335, 1385, 1604, 2112, 2157, 2320. Willis: 66, 87, 130, 227, 239, 290, 629, 749, 831, 980, 1069, 1096, 1157, 1173, 1226, 1230, 1232, 1309, 1417, 1567, 1657, 1662, 1673, 1721, 1861, 1937, 2068, 2112, 2257, 2320, 2330. Moore: 31, 1662, 1937, 1986, 2112, 2330. Planck: 74, 1173, 2079.

1190.5 • LITTLE WOMEN

DI NOVI PICTURES; COLUMBIA. 1994.

NOMINATIONS *Actress:* Winona Ryder. *Original Score:* Thomas Newman. *Costume Design:* Colleen Atwood.

Ryder plays Jo March, one of the four daughters of a Civil War–era family living in Concord, Massachu-

setts. The others are Meg (Trini Alvarado), Beth (Claire Danes), and Amy, the youngest, played first by Kirsten Dunst and then by Samantha Mathis. While their father is away, the household is held together by Marmee, played by Susan Sarandon [107 . . .]. Eventually, the little women encounter men—next-door neighbor Laurie (Christian Bale), his tutor John Brooke (Eric Stoltz), and Professor Friedrich Bhaer (Gabriel Byrne). Robin Swicord's screenplay and Gillian Armstrong's direction give this filming of Louisa May Alcott's novel a more pronounced feminist spin than the 1933 and 1949 versions, but it works in ways that one feels Alcott, that product of the Transcendentalist movement, would have approved. It is also exceptionally well acted by an ensemble that seems to have grown up together. The film was a critical favorite and a modest box-office success. Many critics felt that it deserved a best picture nomination, or at least nominations for Swicord's screenplay, Armstrong's direction, or Danes' touching performance as Beth, and there was some speculation that its lack of appeal to male audiences extended to the largely male membership of the Academy.

Ryder took a risk by accepting the role of Jo, who was almost definitively embodied by Katharine Hepburn [24 . . .] in the 1933 film, but she brings her own luminosity to the role, as well as an astonishing gift for letting the camera see her thoughts. Watch, for example, the mixture of astonishment, envy, and relief that fly across Ryder's face in the scene in which Amy arrives with her fiancé. The role had a special meaning for Ryder, who had been deeply affected by the kidnaping and murder of Polly Klaas, a girl from Ryder's hometown of Petaluma, California—*Little Women* was Klaas' favorite book. The best actress Oscar went to Jessica Lange for *Blue Sky.* The award for scoring was won by Hans Zimmer for *The Lion King.* The costuming award went to Lizzy Gardiner and Tim Chappel for *The Adventures of Priscilla, Queen of the Desert.*

Ryder: 27.5. Newman: 1802.5.

1191 • LIVE AND LET DIE

EON PRODUCTIONS LTD.; UNITED ARTISTS (UNITED KINGDOM). 1973.

NOMINATION *Song:* "Live and Let Die," music and lyrics by Paul McCartney and Linda McCartney.

Roger Moore makes his first appearance as James Bond in this adventure involving drug smugglers and voodoo. Jane Seymour is the fortune-teller Domino, who loses her gift when she also loses her virginity— to Bond, of course. Despite good performances by Yaphet Kotto and the sinuous Geoffrey Holder as villains, this is one of the least memorable Bonds, better known for the McCartneys' song than anything else. Directed by Guy Hamilton. The Oscar went to Marvin Hamlisch and Alan and Marilyn Bergman for the title song from *The Way We Were.*

1192 • LIVE FOR LIFE

LES FILMS ARIANE-LES PRODUCTIONS ARTISTES ASSOCIÉS-VIDES FILMS PRODUCTION (FRANCE). 1967.

NOMINATION *Foreign Language Film.*

Yves Montand is a French TV journalist who falls for fashion model Candice Bergen [1919]. She accompanies him on trips to Africa and New York, while wife Annie Girardot languishes at home. A high-gloss but dull film, almost as dopey as its title. Written and directed by Claude Lelouch [76 . . .] as a kind of follow-up to his megahit *A Man and a Woman.* The Oscar went to *Closely Watched Trains.* ·

1193 • LIVELY SET, THE

UNIVERSAL. 1964.

NOMINATION *Sound Effects:* Robert L. Bratton.

College student James Darren drops out of school to become a race car driver. Remake of the 1954 *Johnny Dark,* which starred Tony Curtis [522]. Unlike Curtis, Darren was just another pretty face, but racing fans may enjoy the action scenes. Directed by Jack Arnold, with Pamela Tiffin, Doug McClure, Marilyn Maxwell, and Greg Morris. The sound effects Oscar went to Norman Wanstall for *Goldfinger.*

Bratton: 752.

1194 • LIVES OF A BENGAL LANCER

PARAMOUNT. 1935.

AWARDS *Assistant Director:* Clem Beauchamp. *Assistant Director:* Paul Wing.

NOMINATIONS *Picture:* Louis D. Lighton, producer. *Director:* Henry Hathaway. *Screenplay:* Achmed Abdullah, John L. Balderston, Grover Jones, William Slavens McNutt, and Waldemar Young. *Interior Decoration:* Hans Dreier and Roland Anderson. *Sound Recording:* Franklin Hansen. *Film Editing:* Ellsworth Hoagland.

Gary Cooper [701 . . .] is Captain McGregor and Franchot Tone [1387] Lieutenant Fortescue, Lancers stationed on the edge of the British Empire in northwest India. Splendid stiff-upper-lip stuff, not quite as good as *Gunga Din,* but in a league with such imperialist classics as *Beau Geste* and *The Four Feathers.* With C. Aubrey Smith, of course, plus Richard Cromwell, Guy Standing, Douglass Dumbrille, Mischa Auer [1401], Leonid Kinskey, and those masters of all ethnicities, Akim Tamiroff [701 . . .] and J. Carrol Naish [1294 . . .]. The all-American Cooper takes a bit of getting used to as a Brit, but the whole thing is essentially a western with puttees and turbans instead of chaps and warbonnets, as Paramount displayed when they recycled the plot in the 1939 *Geronimo.* The best picture Oscar went to *Mutiny on the Bounty.*

Hathaway had been an actor and an assistant director in the silent era and started his directing career with low-budget westerns. *Bengal Lancer* was his first big project. His career lasted into the seventies and was capped by directing John Wayne's Oscar-winning performance in *True Grit.* He lost his sole Oscar nomination to John Ford for *The Informer,* coming in third after a write-in candidate, Michael Curtiz, for *Captain Blood. The Informer* also won for Dudley Nichols' screenplay.

Lives also placed third in the art direction competition, which was won by Richard Day for *The Dark Angel,* and in the sound race, won by Douglas Shearer for *Naughty Marietta.* Ralph Dawson took the Oscar for editing *A Midsummer Night's Dream.*

Beauchamp: 1138. Lighton: 352, 2022. Balderston: 749. Jones: 1116. McNutt: 1116. Dreier: 97,

161, 674, 649, 701, 726, 925, 979, 1101, 1120, 1214, 1217, 1358, 1443, 1452, 1540, 1668, 1748, 1880, 1975, 1994, 2190. Anderson: 278, 363, 426, 450, 649, 1029, 1214, 1219, 1452, 1570, 1668, 1674, 1880, 1994. Hansen: 412, 649, 1217, 2024.

1195 • LLOYD'S OF LONDON

20TH CENTURY-FOX. 1936.

NOMINATIONS *Interior Decoration:* William S. Darling. *Film Editing:* Barbara McLean.

Pseudo-history (far more pseudo than history) of the eighteenth-century founding of the legendary insurance company, with Freddie Bartholomew growing up to be Tyrone Power, who battles George Sanders [46] for the love of Madeleine Carroll. Entertaining costume epic, directed by Henry King [1868 . . .], with C. Aubrey Smith, Montagu Love, Una O'Connor, and other members of the Hollywood outpost of the British Empire, plus bit players imitating the prince of Wales, Benjamin Franklin, Lord Nelson and Captain Hardy, and Samuel Johnson and James Boswell. The art direction award went to Richard Day for *Dodsworth.* Ralph Dawson won for editing *Anthony Adverse.*

Darling: 83, 374, 1082, 1655, 1868, 2240. McLean: 34, 46, 1327, 1655, 1868, 2286.

1196 • LOGAN'S RUN

SAUL DAVID PRODUCTION; MGM. 1976.

AWARD *Special Achievement Award for Visual Effects:* L. B. Abbott, Glen Robinson, and Matthew Yuricich.

NOMINATIONS *Cinematography:* Ernest Laszlo. *Art Direction–Set Decoration:* Dale Hennesy; Robert de Vestel.

Three hundred years in the future, human life is limited to a thirty-year span, kept rigidly fixed by euthanasia. Naturally there are rebels against this forced termination. Michael York plays the "Sandman" Logan, a cop whose job is to track down these recalcitrant seniors and terminate them. Instead, he falls in love with Jenny Agutter and joins in their rebellion. Passable sci-fi fantasy, muddled by its obvious allegorical intent, the thinness and predictability of its plotting, and a flat ending. Good casting helps, especially Peter Ustinov [943 . . .] as the pa-

triarch of the rebels, muttering T. S. Eliot poems from *Old Possum's Book of Practical Cats.* With Richard Jordan, Roscoe Lee Browne, and, in one of her first important roles, Farrah Fawcett (then Fawcett-Majors). Michael Anderson [101] directed.

The special effects include a pioneering use of laser holography, which fails, however, to make much impact on a two-dimensional movie screen. Much of the film was shot in Dallas, with matte effects isolating that city's futuristic City Hall and other locations from the surrounding older city. The Oscar was a noncompetitive award. In the competitive categories, Haskell Wexler won for the cinematography for *Bound for Glory,* and the art direction Oscar went to George Jenkins and George Gaines for *All the President's Men.*

Abbott: 557, 1062, 1596, 2120. Robinson: 591, 917, 1089. Yuricich: 416. Laszlo: 31, 646, 1000, 1032, 1065, 1812, 1907. Hennesy: 86, 646. De Vestel: 2107.

1197 • LOLITA

SEVEN ARTS PRODUCTIONS; MGM (U.S./UNITED KINGDOM). 1962.

NOMINATION *Screenplay—Based on Material From Another Medium:* Vladimir Nabokov.

James Mason [761 . . .] plays Humbert Humbert, a middle-aged European intellectual obsessed with pubescent girls—"nymphets." When he discovers the girl of his dreams, Lolita (Sue Lyon), he rents a room from her mother, Charlotte, played by Shelley Winters [542 . . .]. Discovering Humbert's passion, Charlotte ships Lolita off to camp and demands Humbert's sexual favors for herself. Humbert decides he has no choice but to do away with Charlotte. Dogging Humbert's every move, however, is the strange Clare Quilty, played by Peter Sellers [169 . . .]. Either the nadir of bad taste or a brilliantly satiric black comedy—there doesn't seem to be much of a middle ground on this film. The only consensus is that filming it at all was audacious—which inspired the movie's advertising campaign line: "How did they ever make a movie of *Lolita*?" It took director Stanley Kubrick [151 . . .], who subsequently broke screen taboos on violence in *A Clockwork*

Orange, to do it. Kubrick's treatment necessarily eliminates the novel's celebrated intricacy of language in favor of visual intricacies. The eloquent cinematography of Oswald Morris [659 . . .] and flawless casting helped, although Mason seems not to have been the first choice for Humbert; Cary Grant [1445 . . .], Noël Coward [993], and Laurence Olivier [268 . . .] were all considered for the role. Grant was reportedly shocked that he was even considered.

Though both the novel and film versions of *Lolita* are keen satires on American sexual attitudes, for many people the story obscures the satire. One wonders how, or if, *Lolita* would be filmed today, when increasing public candor about sexuality has led to a heightened awareness of child sexual abuse. Nabokov's adaptation of his notorious novel is faithful to its narrative line, although Lolita's age has been advanced from twelve to the early teens (Lyon was sixteen). The script that Nabokov later published is not the one used in the film, leading one to suspect much reworking by Kubrick, but the author expressed approval of the movie. The Academy seems to have felt *Lolita* was too hot to handle, bypassing its fine performers and director, and giving the writing Oscar to Horton Foote for *To Kill a Mockingbird.*

1198 • LONELYHEARTS

SCHARY PRODUCTIONS INC.; UNITED ARTISTS. 1958.
NOMINATION *Supporting Actress:* Maureen Stapleton.

Reporter Montgomery Clift [732 . . .], assigned to write the newspaper's advice-to-the-lovelorn column under the byline "Miss Lonelyhearts," is inevitably drawn into the lives of the people with whom he corresponds. Earnest and melodramatic transformation by Dore Schary [157 . . .] of Nathanael West's darkly satiric novel. Directed by Vincent J. Donehue, with Robert Ryan [467], Myrna Loy, Dolores Hart, and Jackie Coogan. Stapleton, making her film debut, lost to Wendy Hiller in *Separate Tables.*

Stapleton: 31, 1005, 1678.

1199 • LONG DAY'S JOURNEY INTO NIGHT

ELY LANDAU PRODUCTIONS; EMBASSY PICTURES CORPORATION. 1962.
NOMINATION *Actress:* Katharine Hepburn.

Hepburn is Mary Tyrone, addicted to morphine, married to a pompous, fading actor, James, played by Ralph Richardson [839 . . .], and mother of two sons: the alcoholic Jamie, played by Jason Robards [54 . . .], and the tubercular Edmund, played by Dean Stockwell [1281]. Their long day wanes through various recriminations and reconciliations. Harrowing, absorbing, sometimes annoyingly verbose, but ultimately rewarding film of a classic American play by Eugene O'Neill. Director Sidney Lumet [561 . . .] makes no effort to "open up" the play, but he doesn't simply film it. With the aid of cinematographer Boris Kaufman [119 . . .] he draws us nearer to the characters. Though stagy, it's a meticulous presentation of four astonishing performances— all of which could, and perhaps should, have been nominated. (The jury at the Cannes Festival cited the entire cast; the National Board of Review gave its award to Robards.) The original version of the film ran nearly three hours. It was subsequently cut to 134 minutes, sacrificing large chunks of Robards' role.

For many, this is Hepburn's greatest performance, reinforcing what many have noted: that her four Oscars—for *Morning Glory, Guess Who's Coming to Dinner, The Lion in Winter,* and *On Golden Pond*—were not necessarily granted for her best work. Critics, and perhaps audiences, would cite her work in other movies such as *Little Women, Alice Adams, The Philadelphia Story, Adam's Rib,* and *The African Queen* instead. This time she lost to Anne Bancroft in *The Miracle Worker.*

Hepburn: 24, 40, 843, 1177, 1357, 1473, 1563, 1654, 1956, 1963, 2305.

1200 • LONG VOYAGE HOME, THE

ARGOSY-WANGER; UNITED ARTISTS. 1940.
NOMINATIONS *Picture:* John Ford, producer. *Screenplay:* Dudley Nichols. *Black-and-White Cinematography:* Gregg Toland. *Original Score:* Richard Hageman. *Film Editing:* Sherman Todd. *Special Effects:* R. T. Layton

and R. O. Binger, photographic; Thomas T. Moulton, sound.

Intersecting stories of the crew of a cargo-hauling ship on shore leave. The central tale is that of Ole Olson, played by John Wayne [33 . . .], who wants to give up his life at sea and return home to Sweden. Entertaining, ambitious reworking of four one-act plays by Eugene O'Neill: *The Moon of the Caribbees, Bound East for Cardiff, In the Zone,* and *The Long Voyage Home.* Its flaws are the wordiness of the original plays and the tendency of Ford to indulge in macho horse-play—and Wayne's Swedish accent takes some getting used to. But it's full of wonderful moments and fine performances, including the film debut of Mildred Natwick [147], for once playing a real person, not a mousy eccentric. The other performers include a large contingent from Ford's repertory company: Thomas Mitchell [962 . . .], Barry Fitzgerald [787], John Qualen, Ward Bond, and Arthur Shields. The best picture Oscar went to *Rebecca.*

Nichols lost to Donald Ogden Stewart for *The Philadelphia Story.* The cinematography Oscar went to George Barnes for *Rebecca. Pinocchio* won for score. Anne Bauchens took the Oscar for editing *Northwest Mounted Police. The Thief of Bagdad* received the special effects award.

Ford: 815, 952, 999, 1642, 1901. Nichols: 30, 999, 2092. Toland: 407, 510, 1006, 1327, 2316. Hageman: 955, 979, 1801, 1901, 2062. Todd: 701. Binger: 1451, 1607. Moulton: 22, 46, 138, 366, 457, 487, 560, 706, 798, 962, 1153, 1451, 1510, 1607, 1849, 2154, 2294.

1201 • LONGEST DAY, THE

Darryl F. Zanuck Productions; 20th Century-Fox. 1962.
Awards *Black-and-White Cinematography:* Jean Bourgoin and Walter Wottitz. *Special Effects:* Robert MacDonald, visual; Jacques Maumont, audible.
Nominations *Picture:* Darryl F. Zanuck, producer. *Black-and-White Art Direction—Set Decoration:* Ted Haworth, Leon Barsacq, and Vincent Korda; Gabriel Bechir. *Film Editing:* Samuel E. Beetley.

D-Day restaged by Zanuck, at a cost of $10 million, with 167 featured actors, including John Wayne [33 . . .], Robert Mitchum [1935], Henry Fonda [815 . . .], Robert Ryan [467], Rod Steiger [992 . . .], Sal Mineo [630 . . .], Stuart Whitman [1277], Eddie Albert [887 . . .], Edmond O'Brien [146 . . .], Red Buttons [1763], Alexander Knox [2286], Richard Burton [85 . . .], Richard Todd [878], Leo Genn [1644], and Sean Connery [2185], not to mention Paul Anka, Fabian, and Tommy Sands. It's a bit too big to be enjoyable, especially when you realize that on or near the spots where stars and stuntmen are going through their paces, actual people fought and died.

The cinematography and special effects awards were well deserved—much of the film matches documentary and newsreel images closely. There is, however, a mystery about the Oscars awarded to Bourgoin and Wottitz. The nominations, when announced, also included Henri Persin, and the credits for the film include a fourth director of photography, Pierre Levent. Why Levent was excluded from the nominations and Persin from the final awards is unknown. Both the program for the ceremony and the letter from Price Waterhouse that makes the award official include Persin's name, but at some point his name was "whited-out" from the official records.

The best picture Oscar went to a better, if not bigger, epic, *Lawrence of Arabia,* which also won for Anne Coates' editing. The art direction Oscar went to *To Kill a Mockingbird.*

The Longest Day proved to be Zanuck's last hurrah. As many of his bigger films did, it muscled out potential best picture candidates that have received more long-lasting critical and audience acclaim: *Jules and Jim, The Man Who Shot Liberty Valance, The Manchurian Candidate.* But it made a lot of money, which Fox, embroiled in the production of *Cleopatra,* sorely needed. As a result of its success, Zanuck was called back by the Fox board to head the studio. But the great days of the studios, the era that shaped Zanuck, were over, and though *The Sound of Music* would recoup some of the losses of *Cleopatra,* subsequent mistakes like *Doctor Dolittle* and *Hello, Dolly!* would put Zanuck on the spot, too. By 1970 he was out again.

MacDonald: 175, 2048. Zanuck: 34, 46, 550, 710, 759, 815, 947, 952, 990, 1327, 1666, 2154, 2286. Haworth: 1283, 1550, 1763, 1860, 2247. Korda: 1070, 2031, 2050. Beetley: 557.

1202 • LONGEST YARD, THE

ALBERT S. RUDDY PRODUCTION; PARAMOUNT. 1974.
NOMINATION *Film Editing:* Michael Luciano.

Football player Burt Reynolds lands in prison, where he is forced by the sadistic warden, played by Eddie Albert [887 . . .], to captain a convict football team in a game against the prison guards. Violent action comedy that was a big hit with audiences and solidified Reynolds' standing as a big box-office draw —a position he was to undermine with too many similar but less well made vehicles. Director Robert Aldrich, working from a script by Tracy Keenan Wynn, is in some ways remaking his own *The Dirty Dozen* but with less heart. The cast includes Ed Lauter, Michael Conrad, Bernadette Peters, Mike Henry, and Richard Kiel. The editing Oscar went to Harold F. and Carl Kress for *The Towering Inferno.*

Luciano: 548, 688, 963.

1203 • LONGTIME COMPANION

AMERICAN PLAYHOUSE PRODUCTION; SAMUEL GOLDWYN COMPANY. 1990.
NOMINATION *Supporting Actor:* Bruce Davison.

AIDS decimates a group of gay men in eighties New York. Well-acted, well-written (by Craig Lucas), and well-meaning drama that some critics felt was a little too self-conscious and earnest about treating a topic that mainstream Hollywood had avoided. But though it's sentimental and occasionally a little too artily elegiac—as in the imagined reunion of the living and the dead at film's end—it's also very moving and sometimes very funny as well. Produced in cooperation with the Public Broadcasting System's *American Playhouse.* The cast, directed by Norman René, includes Patrick Cassidy, Dermot Mulroney, Mary-Louise Parker, Michael Schoeffling, and Campbell Scott. The Oscar went to Joe Pesci for *GoodFellas.*

1204 • LOOK FOR THE SILVER LINING

WARNER BROS. 1949.
NOMINATION *Scoring of a Musical Picture:* Ray Heindorf.

June Haver plays twenties musical star Marilyn Miller in a series of production numbers strung together by a tired old biopic plot. Directed by David Butler, with Gordon MacRae, Ray Bolger, Charles Ruggles, Rosemary DeCamp, and S. Z. Sakall. Roger Edens and Lennie Hayton won the Oscar for scoring *On the Town.*

Heindorf: 331, 479, 666, 930, 1043, 1385, 1408, 1430, 1690, 1719, 1750, 1910, 2058, 2186, 2243, 2310, 2318.

1205 • LOOKING FOR MR. GOODBAR

FREDDIE FIELDS PRODUCTION; PARAMOUNT. 1977.
NOMINATIONS *Supporting Actress:* Tuesday Weld. *Cinematography:* William A. Fraker.

Diane Keaton [88 . . .] plays Terry Dunn, a teacher in a school for the deaf, who picks up men for casual sex and is murdered by one of them. Writer-director Richard Brooks [227 . . .] turns Judith Rossner's novel into a shrill, boring indictment of the sexual revolution, undermining some good performances with hack psychology, portentous symbolism, and too-flashy camera work. The *Harvard Lampoon* named it Worst Film of the Year—over such truly awesome competition as *Airport '77, The Other Side of Midnight,* and *You Light Up My Life.* The cast includes Richard Gere, William Atherton, Richard Kiley, LeVar Burton, Tom Berenger [1584], and Brian Dennehy.

Weld, who plays Keaton's older sister, began her career as a teenager, usually playing bad girls and adolescent vamps. A talented actress, often wasted in inferior movies, she never had the career-making part she deserved. She lost the Oscar to Vanessa Redgrave in *Julia.*

The cinematography award went to Vilmos Zsigmond for *Close Encounters of the Third Kind.*

Fraker: 890, 1380, 1439, 2231.

1205.5 • *LORENZO'S OIL*

KENNEDY MILLER FILM PRODUCTION; UNIVERSAL (AUSTRALIA). 1992.

NOMINATIONS *Actress:* Susan Sarandon. *Original Screenplay:* George Miller and Nick Enright.

Sarandon plays Michaela Odone, who with her husband, Augusto, played by Nick Nolte [1612], sets out to find a treatment for their young son, Lorenzo, when they discover that he has the terrible degenerative disease adrenoleukodystrophy. Battling what they see as indifference in the medical profession and shortsightedness in the foundation ostensibly searching for a cure, the Odones comb through the medical literature for clues that ultimately lead them to what seems to be a breakthrough treatment. Uncompromising in its presentation of the way the disease ravages Lorenzo (played by Zack O'Malley Greenburg), the film is sometimes hard to watch, but the intensity of Sarandon's and Nolte's performances makes the film compelling. The story is based on fact, although Lorenzo's oil—the dietary supplement discovered by the real Odones—has not proved to be quite so miraculous as the film suggests. Peter Ustinov [943 . . .] plays a physician who aids the Odones in their research. Tautly directed by screenwriter Miller, heretofore better known for creating Mad Max and the *Road Warrior* movies. *Lorenzo's Oil* is a far cry from those demolition derbies, but Miller had studied medicine in his native Australia before becoming a filmmaker.

Sarandon lost to Emma Thompson for *Howards End*. The writing Oscar went to Neil Jordan for *The Crying Game*.

Sarandon: 107, 413.3, 2039.

LOS TARANTOS
See 2003.

1206 • *LOST HORIZON*

COLUMBIA. 1937.

AWARDS *Interior Decoration:* Stephen Goosson. *Film Editing:* Gene Havlick and Gene Milford.

NOMINATIONS *Picture:* Frank Capra, producer. *Supporting Actor:* H. B. Warner. *Sound Recording:* John Livadary. *Assistant Director:* C. C. Coleman, Jr. *Score:* Columbia Studio Music Department, Morris Stoloff, head; score by Dimitri Tiomkin.

A planeload of Westerners escape from a revolution in China, but the plane is forced down in the Himalayas, where they discover a paradisal valley called Shangri-La. Ronald Colman [311 . . .], a famous diplomat, is enchanted by the place, where everyone seems peaceful, contented, and contemplative. They also, he learns, never grow old. But his restless brother (John Howard) finds Shangri-La oppressive and sinister and forces Colman to accompany him on his attempt to return to the outside world. Colman alone survives this flight from Shangri-La and at film's end is making his way back to it. Robert Riskin [905 . . .] adapted the novel by James Hilton [1371], a much-admired fable in the politically and economically jittery thirties. Though admirers of Capra's work have turned *Lost Horizon* into a legendary film, in its time it was something of a disappointment not only critically but also financially: It was Columbia's most expensive film to that point, and battles between cost-containing studio head Harry Cohn [1025 . . .] and director Capra were intense. Before it entered general release, the film was cut by about ninety minutes from its first preview length, and it lost another large chunk when it was rereleased in 1943. The American Film Institute restored much of the film in the eighties, using 16mm prints and supplementing missing footage with stills shown over the extant soundtrack. Admirers of the film respond to its Capraesque optimism about the essential goodness of humanity, which has been corrupted by a ruthlessly competitive civilization. (This implicit critique of capitalism would later land Capra, whose political views were not so firmly fixed, in trouble with fifties Red-hunters.) Detractors find much of the movie dull and talky and point out that the leisurely, contemplative life of Shangri-La is built on the labor of a peasant class. The rest of the cast includes Jane Wyatt and Margo as the love interests for Colman and Howard respectively. Margo comes to a bad end when she strays from the confines of Shangri-La and her true age is revealed. Edward Everett Horton and

Thomas Mitchell [962 . . .] provide what's supposed to be comic relief (perhaps a little too much of which was provided in the AFI restoration). Sam Jaffe [105] is the High Lama and Warner his majordomo, Chang.

It's possible to applaud the Academy's award to Goosson while at the same time admitting the truth of the comment by Graham Greene [639] that Shangri-La "resembles a film star's luxurious estate in Beverly Hills." It was, in fact, built on Columbia's Burbank Ranch. The snow scenes were filmed in an L.A. icehouse that was later used in *The Magnificent Ambersons*. And the editors were rewarded for going beyond the call of duty, though the film's subsequent parings-down now make it hard to assess their work. According to Capra's biographer, Joseph McBride, Capra shot more than a million feet of film, a ratio of ninety-three feet shot for every one used.

The Life of Emile Zola won for best picture, and Joseph Schildkraut's performance in it took the best supporting actor Oscar. Warner, a veteran of silent films, is otherwise best known for his performance as Jesus in the 1927 *King of Kings*. The award for sound went to Thomas Moulton for *The Hurricane*. Robert Webb won as assistant director of *In Old Chicago*. The scoring award went to Universal music department head Charles Previn for *One Hundred Men and a Girl*.

Goosson: 928, 1073, 1182, 2066. Havlick: 1370, 2325. Milford: 1477, 1488. Capra: 1025, 1033, 1119, 1366, 1370, 2325. Livadary: 330, 455, 596, 732, 1058, 1215, 1303, 1366, 1370, 1488, 1521, 1740, 1872, 2111, 2325, 2327. Stoloff: 13, 432, 455, 596, 643, 677, 732, 773, 1057, 1058, 1115, 1862, 1872, 1873, 1998, 2110, 2329. Tiomkin: 33, 286, 380, 446, 638, 663, 730, 768, 850, 911, 912, 1347, 1370, 1470, 2006, 2127, 2282, 2335.

1207 • LOST PATROL, THE
RKO RADIO. 1934.

NOMINATION *Score:* RKO Radio Studio Music Department, Max Steiner, head; score by Max Steiner.

Victor McLaglen [999 . . .] is the sergeant in charge of an ill-fated group of British soldiers, lost in the desert and under siege from Arabs. Entertaining adventure directed by John Ford [815 . . .] from a screenplay by Dudley Nichols [30 . . .], with Boris Karloff, Wallace Ford, Reginald Denny, and Alan Hale. Steiner's score came in third in the Oscar race. The winner was *One Night of Love*.

Steiner: 16, 154, 190, 330, 365, 385, 492, 679, 747, 754, 798, 999, 1043, 1046, 1052, 1162, 1169, 1170, 1324, 1408, 1430, 1456, 1690, 1779, 1828.

1208 • LOST WEEKEND, THE
PARAMOUNT. 1945.

AWARDS *Picture:* Charles Brackett, producer. *Actor:* Ray Milland. *Director:* Billy Wilder. *Screenplay:* Charles Brackett and Billy Wilder.
NOMINATIONS *Black-and-White Cinematography:* John F. Seitz. *Scoring of a Dramatic or Comedy Picture:* Miklos Rozsa. *Film Editing:* Doane Harrison.

Don Birnam (Milland) and his brother, Wick (Philip Terry), are preparing to go to the country for the weekend in an attempt by Wick to help Don stay off booze. But Don persuades Wick to go to a concert with Don's girlfriend, Helen St. James, played by Jane Wyman [246 . . .], and take a later train. Wick has taken the precaution of clearing all the liquor bottles from their apartment and leaving Don with no money, but Don is a good deal more wily than Wick realizes. Returning to find his brother gone, Wick, fed up with the situation, leaves for the country alone, whereupon Don sets out on an odyssey of boozing, cadging the money he needs and finally resorting to outright theft when that runs out. By Saturday night he has wound up in the alcoholic ward of Bellevue, from which he escapes only by chance. After a grisly hallucination, he resolves to commit suicide, and only the timely arrival of the persistent Helen saves his life. A tough, confrontive melodrama, based on the novel by Charles Jackson, that softens up only with a hopeful ending that's not in the same key as what has gone before. The movie was a big hit, not to mention an award winner, despite the studio's reluctance to back the project—it was thought to be uncommercial and likely to draw protests from the liquor industry. Its success at the Oscars launched a postwar series of hard-hitting adult problem dramas.

Over the next four years, best picture Oscars went to films about the difficulties faced by returning servicemen *(The Best Years of Our Lives)*, anti-Semitism *(Gentleman's Agreement)*, and political demagoguery *(All the King's Men)*. (The fourth winner, *Hamlet,* was a problem drama of a different order.) The excellent cast includes Howard da Silva and, as Wyman's mother, Lillian Fontaine—mother of Olivia de Havilland [798 . . .] and Joan Fontaine [441 . . .].

Brackett received his law degree from Harvard and began practicing law in the twenties but soon dropped that profession to concentrate on writing. In addition to working as drama critic for the *New Yorker* magazine, he published several novels and sold numerous stories to the movies in the twenties. Paramount hired him as a staff writer in 1932, but his career as screenwriter didn't take off until he joined up with Wilder on *Bluebeard's Eighth Wife* in 1938. Their writing collaboration lasted until 1950. Brackett's producing career started with *Eight Graves to Cairo* in 1943 and lasted till the early sixties.

Brackett and Wilder wanted to cast Jose Ferrer [473 . . .] in *The Lost Weekend,* but the studio forced them to settle on Milland, whose career to this point had been largely in light comedy and romantic roles. Born in Wales, Milland made a few English films before coming to Hollywood in 1930. The Oscar did little to establish him as a leading dramatic player, however. His later film career, in the seventies, was largely as a crusty, villainous sort, in films ranging from *Love Story* to *The Thing With Two Heads* (1972). He died in 1986.

Wilder's double Oscar triumph marked the beginning of the writer-director's peak period, which lasted until his triple win for *The Apartment* in 1960. Born in Austria, Wilder worked as a reporter in Berlin before breaking into the German film industry. When Hitler came to power, Wilder left for Hollywood, where, after mastering the English language, he worked his way into screenwriting. The collaboration with Brackett beginning in 1938 soon made him one of Hollywood's most sought-after writers. He began directing in 1942 on *The Major and the Minor.*

Harry Stradling won for the cinematography for

The Picture of Dorian Gray. Rozsa, who had three scoring nominations, including one for his collaboration with Morris Stoloff on *A Song to Remember,* won the Oscar for *Spellbound.* The editing award went to Robert J. Kern for *National Velvet.*

Brackett: 705, 925, 1088, 1440, 1975, 2093, 2099. Wilder: 91, 138, 198, 566, 705, 709, 925, 1440, 1738, 1860, 1903, 1975, 2297. Seitz: 552, 566, 674, 1714, 1975, 2262. Rozsa: 175, 566, 567, 604, 1035, 1069, 1070, 1085, 1227, 1644, 1872, 1890, 1968, 2050, 2304. Harrison: 674, 1975.

1209 • LOUISA

UNIVERSAL-INTERNATIONAL. 1950.

NOMINATION *Sound Recording:* Leslie I. Carey, Universal-International Sound Department.

Spring Byington [2325] goes to live with her son, Ronald Reagan, and his wife, Ruth Hussey [1563], and becomes the object of the romantic attentions of two men, Edmund Gwenn [1325 . . .] and Charles Coburn [535 . . .]. At the same time, her granddaughter, played by Piper Laurie [364 . . .] in her film debut, is also having love problems. Pleasantly tolerable fluff, directed by Alexander Hall [904], with more good performers than it deserves. Byington's success in this film led to the TV sitcom *December Bride.* The sound award went to *All About Eve.*

Carey: 291, 776, 1334, 1478, 2089.

1210 • LOUISIANA PURCHASE

PARAMOUNT. 1941.

NOMINATIONS *Color Cinematography:* Harry Hallenberger and Ray Rennahan. *Color Interior Decoration:* Raoul Pène du Bois, art direction; Stephen A. Seymour, set decoration.

U.S. Senator Oliver P. Loganberry (Victor Moore) heads an investigation into political corruption in Louisiana that New Orleans lawyer Jim Taylor (Bob Hope) attempts to thwart by putting temptation in the senator's way. Rather silly film of a somewhat dated Broadway musical, with songs by Irving Berlin [34 . . .]—not his best work. Except most notably for Hope, much of the cast was drawn from the Broadway show, including Moore, Vera Zorina, and

Irene Bordoni. Rennahan won an Oscar for his work, with Ernest Palmer, on *Blood and Sand* instead. The art direction award went to *Blossoms in the Dust*.

Rennahan: 235, 241, 569, 581, 701, 798, 1120.
Pène du Bois: 1120.

1211 • LOUISIANA STORY, THE

ROBERT FLAHERTY; LOPERT FILMS. 1948.

NOMINATION *Motion Picture Story:* Frances Flaherty and Robert Flaherty.

The work of an oil exploration and drilling crew in the Louisiana bayous is seen through the eyes of a young boy. Splendidly done fictionalized documentary that was the last major work of Robert Flaherty, the pioneering documentary-film maker, and his wife, Frances. Produced by Standard Oil, the film doesn't dodge the implications that industrial "progress" may be a mixed blessing, though considering the widespread pollution of the Louisiana bayous, it now seems naive in not examining that question more directly. But it's a fine example of the Flahertys' work. Robert, the son of a gold prospector, grew up exploring the wilderness, and on his journeys among the Eskimos in 1913 he took along a movie camera. The footage from that first journey was lost, but in 1920 he returned to make the enormously influential documentary *Nanook of the North*. Distributed in 1922, it was a huge commercial success, leading to subsequent films set in far-off places, *White Shadows in the South Seas, Tabu, Man of Aran* (1934), and *Elephant Boy* (1937) among them. Of these, only *Man of Aran* is technically a documentary, the genre with which Flaherty is identified, and even it has a strong, obviously scripted narrative line, as does *Nanook,* which some have criticized for its oversentimentalized man-against-the-elements theme. But Flaherty's ability to capture the actuality of daily life in remote regions set the standard that all documentarians aspire to. Andrew Sarris has perhaps summed up Flaherty's achievement best: "Today Flaherty seems touchingly romantic in his desire to find people who have escaped the corruption of civilization. Flaherty's cinema is one of the last testaments of the 'cult of nature,' and, as such, is infinitely precious." The

Flahertys' sole nomination came at a time when Hollywood was beginning to break free of the confines of the soundstages and studio back lots and take cameras on location. Of the five nominees for motion picture story, three had a documentary feel to them: *The Naked City* was a crime drama shot in New York, and the winner, *The Search,* written by Richard Schweizer and David Wechsler, took place in the rubble of postwar Berlin.

1212 • LOVE AFFAIR

RKO RADIO. 1939.

NOMINATIONS *Picture:* Leo McCarey, producer. *Actress:* Irene Dunne. *Supporting Actress:* Maria Ouspenskaya. *Original Story:* Mildred Cram and Leo McCarey. *Interior Decoration:* Van Nest Polglase and Al Herman. *Song:* "Wishing," music and lyrics by Buddy De Sylva.

Playboy artist Charles Boyer [36 . . .] and nightclub singer Dunne have a shipboard romance, though each is engaged to someone else. They vow to meet on their return to the States, but Dunne is injured in an accident on her way to the tryst. She chooses not to reveal to Boyer the fact that she has been paralyzed, but they are united at the end. The first half of the film, with its witty sparring between the lovers, is a delight; your enjoyment of the second half depends on your tolerance for soap-operatic motivation. Superior to its remake, *An Affair to Remember,* largely because it's shorter and sweeter, though the second team, Cary Grant [1445 . . .] and Deborah Kerr [599 . . .], are at least as good as Boyer and Dunne. Interestingly the two films star four of the most talented people never to receive Oscars for acting—a fact perhaps Warren Beatty [255 . . .] and Annette Bening [840] should have kept in mind when they did yet another remake, this one once again called *Love Affair,* in 1994.

McCarey had conceived the film for the talents of Boyer and Dunne, and Boyer considered it one of his best films. Dunne has the showier part, and those who find her mannered and arch should avoid the movie at all costs. The same goes for the diminutive Maria Ouspenskaya, whose tendency to overact finally landed her in B movies and horror flicks such as *The Wolf Man* (1941). Here she plays—or overplays—Boyer's lovable old grandmother. *Gone With the Wind* captured four of the categories in which *Love Affair* was nominated: picture, actress (Vivien Leigh), supporting actress (Hattie McDaniel), and art direction. The story award went to Lewis R. Foster for *Mr. Smith Goes to Washington*. The best song was Harold Arlen and E. Y. Harburg's "Over the Rainbow," from *The Wizard of Oz*.

McCarey: 21, 114, 173, 787, 1394, 1404. Dunne: 114, 400, 972, 2041. Ouspenskaya: 560. Polglase: 358, 407, 754, 1394, 2115.

1212.5 • LOVE FIELD

SANFORD/PILLSBURY PRODUCTION; ORION. 1992.

NOMINATION *Actress:* Michelle Pfeiffer.

Pfeiffer plays a bored Dallas housewife who idolizes JFK and Jackie, so when Kennedy is assassinated, she leaves her husband and takes a bus for Washington to attend the funeral. But along the way she strikes up an acquaintance with a black man (Dennis Haysbert) traveling with his small daughter. Pfeiffer's clumsy involvement with them nearly precipitates disaster. Interesting but awkwardly structured film, held together largely by Pfeiffer's witty performance as an airhead with a heart of gold. The interracial romance is ultimately unconvincing—why would a man as proud and wary as Haysbert's character jeopardize himself and especially his daughter by an involvement with a loose cannon like the woman played by Pfeiffer? Directed by Jonathan Kaplan. The title, incidentally, refers to the old Dallas airport. Pfeiffer lost to Emma Thompson in *Howards End.*

Pfeiffer: 485, 633.

1213 • LOVE IS A MANY-SPLENDORED THING

20TH CENTURY-FOX. 1955.

AWARDS *Song:* "Love Is a Many-Splendored Thing," music by Sammy Fain, lyrics by Paul Francis Webster. *Scoring of a Dramatic or Comedy Picture:* Alfred Newman. *Color Costume Design:* Charles LeMaire.

NOMINATIONS *Picture:* Buddy Adler, producer. *Actress:* Jennifer Jones. *Color Cinematography:* Leon Shamroy. *Color Art Direction—Set Decoration:* Lyle Wheeler and George W. Davis; Walter M. Scott and Jack Stubbs. *Sound Recording:* Carl W. Faulkner.

War correspondent Mark Elliott, played by William Holden [1424 . . .], and Eurasian doctor Han Suyin (Jones) fall in love during the Korean War, but . . . This big, slushy romance, based on Suyin's book, was the top box-office film of the year, but the overstated score and once-ubiquitous theme song are probably the most memorable things about it. The Fain-Webster song won them their second Oscar as a team, but it beat some much better competitors: Johnny Mercer's "Something's Gotta Give," from *Daddy Long Legs,* and Alex North and Hy Zaret's durable title tune, "Unchained Melody." (Try to imagine Demi Moore and Patrick Swayze in *Ghost* making out to "Love Is a Many-Splendored Thing" instead of "Unchained Melody.")

Many-Splendored lost to one of the most unpretentious movies ever to win the best picture Oscar, *Marty,* and Jones lost to the earthy Anna Magnani in *The Rose Tattoo.* The cinematography Oscar went to Robert Burks for *To Catch a Thief. Picnic* won for art direction and *Oklahoma!* for sound.

Fain: 95, 331, 376, 856, 1276, 1681, 1925, 2014, 2214. Webster: 33, 64, 95, 331, 376, 604, 663, 730, 856, 1276, 1322, 1388, 1755, 1925, 2014. Newman: 31, 34, 46, 72, 138, 182, 226, 333, 334, 347, 375, 428, 437, 457, 476, 495, 542, 690, 797, 833, 952, 953, 959, 962, 1016, 1082, 1088, 1278, 1362, 1397, 1475, 1616, 1655, 1849, 1868, 1883, 1921, 2043, 2046, 2091, 2258, 2286, 2294, 2316. LeMaire: 21, 46, 376, 495, 530, 542, 954, 1338, 1391, 1601, 1706, 2008, 2043, 2205, 2294. Adler: 732. Jones: 584, 1214, 1828, 1868. Shamroy: 29, 226, 356, 413, 495, 569, 602, 1088, 1153, 1592, 1610, 1706, 1852, 1883, 2013, 2286, 2334. Wheeler: 19, 46, 83, 356, 376, 428, 476, 495, 530, 542, 719, 721, 798, 950, 1062, 1088, 1149, 1153, 1391, 1475, 1601, 1616, 1670, 1706, 1852, 2008, 2093, 2212. Davis: 46, 69, 401, 495, 542, 736, 953, 1335, 1388, 1537, 1552, 1706, 1814, 2157, 2184, 2312. Scott: 46, 376, 413, 476, 530, 542, 557, 646, 896,

1062, 1088, 1391, 1475, 1706, 1753, 1881, 1907, 2008, 2120, 2247. Faulkner: 1062, 1088, 2336.

1214 • LOVE LETTERS

HAL WALLIS PRODUCTIONS; PARAMOUNT. 1945.

NOMINATIONS *Actress:* Jennifer Jones. *Black-and-White Interior Decoration:* Hans Dreier and Roland Anderson, art direction; Sam Comer and Ray Moyer, set decoration. *Song:* "Love Letters," music by Victor Young, lyrics by Edward Heyman. *Scoring of a Dramatic or Comedy Picture:* Victor Young.

Joseph Cotten writes love letters to Jones on behalf of a fellow soldier. Taken with the eloquence of the letters, Jones marries the man she believes to be the author. But he turns out to be an abusive jerk, and when he's killed, she develops amnesia and goes to prison for his murder. After she's released, she meets and falls in love with Cotten, who helps her recover her memory. Dull, overplotted melodrama, with a screenplay by Ayn Rand from a novel by Chris Massie. William Dieterle [1169] directed, and the cinematography is by Lee Garmes [201 . . .]. The cast includes Anita Louise, Cecil Kellaway [843 . . .], Gladys Cooper [1393 . . .], and Reginald Denny.

Jones lost to Joan Crawford in *Mildred Pierce.* The art direction award went to *Blood on the Sun.* Richard Rodgers and Oscar Hammerstein won for "It Might As Well Be Spring," from *State Fair.* Miklos Rozsa took the Oscar for his score for *Spellbound.*

Jones: 584, 1213, 1828, 1868. Dreier: 97, 151, 649, 674, 701, 726, 925, 979, 1101, 1120, 1194, 1217, 1358, 1443, 1452, 1540, 1668, 1748, 1880, 1975, 1994, 2190. Anderson: 278, 363, 426, 450, 649, 1029, 1194, 1219, 1452, 1570, 1668, 1674, 1880, 1994. Comer: 278, 357, 426, 450, 726, 736, 925, 956, 1029, 1101, 1219, 1443, 1570, 1631, 1674, 1727, 1738, 1748, 1959, 1975, 1994, 2012, 2098, 2200, 2208. Moyer: 278, 413, 736, 833, 1101, 1120, 1674, 1738, 1748, 1975, 2012. Young: 97, 98, 100, 101, 280, 489, 612, 693, 701, 794, 846, 925, 1257, 1396, 1452, 1748, 1823, 1994, 2235, 2315.

1215 • LOVE ME FOREVER

COLUMBIA. 1935.

NOMINATION *Sound Recording:* John Livadary.

Opera singer Grace Moore [1488] becomes the protégée of gangster and nightclub owner Leo Carrillo, who backs her appearance at the Metropolitan Opera in *La Bohème.* Goofy blend of gangster movie and backstage melodrama that takes some jaw-dropping liberties with opera: In the *Bohème* production, Moore apparently sings both Mimi and Musetta. Directed by Victor Schertzinger [1488 . . .] from a script by Jo Swerling [1607] and Sidney Buchman [904 . . .]. The sound award went to Douglas Shearer for *Naughty Marietta.*

Livadary: 330, 455, 596, 732, 1058, 1206, 1303, 1366, 1370, 1488, 1521, 1740, 1872, 2111, 2325, 2327.

1216 • LOVE ME OR LEAVE ME

MGM. 1955.

AWARD *Motion Picture Story:* Daniel Fuchs.

NOMINATIONS *Actor:* James Cagney. *Screenplay:* Daniel Fuchs and Isobel Lennart. *Sound Recording:* Wesley C. Miller. *Song:* "I'll Never Stop Loving You," music by Nicholas Brodszky, lyrics by Sammy Cahn. *Scoring of a Musical Picture:* Percy Faith and George Stoll.

Doris Day [1572] plays singer Ruth Etting, whose career was launched by her brutal hood of a manager, Martin Synder (Cagney). Vastly superior to most musical biopics, largely because of Fuchs' strong script, Cagney's compellingly vicious performance, and Day's superb singing. For those who think of her as the fluffy virgin of the Universal comedies, the tough broad she plays here should come as a revelation, even if she's not much like Etting, whose style was less brassy. Well directed by Charles Vidor, with Cameron Mitchell, Robert Keith, and Tom Tully [330].

The peculiar division between story and screenplay that allowed Fuchs to win but his collaboration with Lennart to lose was eventually abandoned by the Academy. The Oscar for screenplay went to Paddy Chayefsky for *Marty.*

Cagney lost the last of his three nominations to Ernest Borgnine in *Marty.* The sound award was won by *Oklahoma!,* which also took the scoring Oscar. The lovely song, which held its own in the film among the standards "Shaking the Blues Away," "Mean to Me," and "Ten Cents a Dance," lost to Sammy Fain and Paul Francis Webster's title song from *Love Is a Many-Splendored Thing.*

Cagney: 79, 2318. Lennart: 1969. Miller: 290, 704, 1157. Brodszky: 163, 1692, 1843, 2103. Cahn: 74, 163, 182, 696, 915, 926, 1031, 1056, 1524, 1587, 1692, 1708, 1719, 1859, 1907, 2016, 2064, 2072, 2103, 2110, 2125, 2263, 2264, 2315, 2343. Stoll: 74, 115, 207, 699, 1298, 1299, 1950.

1217 • *LOVE PARADE, THE*

PARAMOUNT FAMOUS LASKY. 1929–30.

NOMINATIONS *Production:* Ernst Lubitsch, producer. *Actor:* Maurice Chevalier. *Director:* Ernst Lubitsch. *Cinematography:* Victor Milner. *Interior Decoration:* Hans Dreier. *Sound Recording:* Franklin Hansen.

Chevalier plays a military attaché from a Ruritanian country. His amorous escapades get him recalled home, where he falls in love with the queen, played by Jeanette MacDonald. But once they're married, he finds being her consort—and subordinate—confining. Eventually she comes round to accepting him as her equal. Charmingly spicy musical comedy, with songs by Victor Schertzinger [1488 . . .] and Clifford Grey that are mostly forgettable, except for "Dream Lover." The movie was a big hit, hailed as a breakthrough in the early days of sound, though it's technically still a little too stiff and clunky. Lubitsch and Hansen managed one pioneering effect in the film: a quartet involving Chevalier and MacDonald in one set, and their servants, Lupino Lane and Lillian Roth, in another. Because dubbing of voices had not yet become common, Lubitsch had adjacent sets built, and the action on each was filmed by a separate camera, with Lubitsch perched between the two sets to direct the two pairs of actors.

All of the nominees from *The Love Parade* were unofficial. The Academy announced only the winners, but the names of the contenders, though not recognized in any way, were kept on record by the various branches of the Academy that chose the year's win-

ners. The best picture Oscar went to *All Quiet on the Western Front,* which also won for its director, Lewis Milestone. George Arliss won the best actor award for *Disraeli.* Joseph T. Rucker and Willard Van Der Veer won for the cinematography of *With Byrd at the South Pole. King of Jazz* won for Herman Rosse's art direction, and Douglas Shearer took the first Oscar ever given for sound for *The Big House.*

Lubitsch: 889, 1484, 1540, 1847. Chevalier: 203. Milner: 304, 412, 470, 740, 757, 827, 1452, 1668. Dreier: 97, 151, 649, 674, 701, 726, 925, 979, 1101, 1120, 1194, 1214, 1358, 1443, 1452, 1540, 1668, 1748, 1880, 1975, 1994, 2190. Hansen: 412, 649, 1194, 2024.

1218 • *LOVE STORY*

THE LOVE STORY COMPANY PRODUCTION; PARAMOUNT. 1970.

AWARD *Original Score:* Francis Lai.

NOMINATIONS *Picture:* Howard G. Minsky, producer. *Actor:* Ryan O'Neal. *Actress:* Ali MacGraw. *Supporting Actor:* John Marley. *Director:* Arthur Hiller. *Story and Screenplay—Based on Factual Material or Material Not Previously Published or Produced:* Erich Segal.

Boy meets girl, boy gets girl, girl dies. Preppie Harvard student O'Neal falls in love with musical Cliffie MacGraw, but his mean, snobby father, played by Ray Milland [1208], opposes the marriage because she's not their sort. Then she comes down with leukemia. Icky, but oddly remote and dull movie that was hugely popular with people who had apparently never seen this sort of thing done right—like by Bette Davis in *Dark Victory.* It made stars of O'Neal and MacGraw, who spent the rest of their careers trying to live it down, and it provided a debut role for Tommy (billed as Tom) Lee Jones [734.5 . . .], as O'Neal's Harvard roommate. But it's suggestive that none of the people who received Oscar nominations for this film ever received another: The Academy clearly let the film's popularity blind them to its quality—or lack of it.

Lai's first big hit as a film composer came with *A Man and a Woman,* a score surprisingly overlooked by the Academy, considering that it sold records by the crateful. The record of the *Love Story* score was an even bigger hit. He has continued as a highly prolific film composer, mostly for French films.

The best picture Oscar went to *Patton,* for which George C. Scott won as actor and Franklin Schaffner as director. Hiller is currently president of the Academy.

MacGraw, who had made her film debut a year earlier in *Goodbye, Columbus,* lost to Glenda Jackson in *Women in Love.* Her private life subsequently became more interesting than her acting career: She married Paramount head Robert Evans [395] but left him for Steve McQueen [1753]. Though touted as a big new star for her *Love Story* role, she made only a few more films. Her performance in the 1983 TV miniseries *The Winds of War* was so severely panned that she retired from the screen.

Marley, a respected character actor, plays Mac-Graw's father. He lost to John Mills in *Ryan's Daughter.*

Francis Ford Coppola and Edmund H. North also edged out Segal in the story and screenplay category with their *Patton* script. But Segal, a Yale classics professor, proceeded to turn his screenplay into a best-selling novel, and then to produce a sequel, *Oliver's Story,* a few years later. It too was filmed, in 1978, but by that time, whatever magic *Love Story* held had faded.

1219 • LOVE WITH THE PROPER STRANGER

BOARDWALK-RONA PRODUCTION; PARAMOUNT. 1963.

NOMINATIONS *Actress:* Natalie Wood. *Story and Screenplay—Written Directly for the Screen:* Arnold Schulman. *Black-and-White Cinematography:* Milton Krasner. *Black-and-White Art Direction—Set Decoration:* Hal Pereira and Roland Anderson; Sam Comer and Grace Gregory. *Black-and-White Costume Design:* Edith Head.

Wood and footloose musician Steve McQueen [1753], neither of them ready to commit to settling down, have a fling—but she gets pregnant. Good dramatic comedy, with a nice sense of place—New York City's Italian neighborhoods. The solid supporting cast includes Edie Adams, Herschel Bernardi, Tom Bosley, and Harvey Lembeck. Produced by Alan J.

Pakula [54 . . .] and directed by Robert Mulligan [2102].

Wood lost to Patricia Neal in *Hud,* which also won for James Wong Howe's cinematography. The writing Oscar went to James R. Webb for *How the West Was Won.* Gene Callahan won for the art direction for *America, America.* Piero Gherardi took the costume Oscar for *8½.*

Wood: 1671, 1894. Schulman: 802. Krasner: 21, 46, 96, 654, 953, 2072. Pereira: 278, 357, 363, 426, 450, 736, 956, 1029, 1504, 1570, 1631, 1674, 1716, 1727, 1738, 1840, 1897, 1959, 2012, 2098, 2200, 2208. Anderson: 278, 363, 426, 450, 649, 1029, 1194, 1214, 1452, 1570, 1668, 1674, 1880, 1994. Comer: 278, 357, 426, 450, 726, 736, 925, 956, 1029, 1101, 1214, 1443, 1570, 1631, 1674, 1727, 1738, 1748, 1959, 1975, 1994, 2012, 2098, 2200, 2208. Gregory: 450. Head: 31, 32, 46, 305, 357, 363, 612, 636, 675, 736, 832, 894, 945, 1003, 1261, 1263, 1398, 1427, 1504, 1550, 1579, 1587, 1631, 1716, 1727, 1738, 1748, 1840, 1927, 1986, 2012, 2098, 2247, 2298.

1219.5 • LOVER, THE

RENN PRODUCTION/BURRILL PRODUCTIONS/FILMS A2, MGM/ UNITED ARTISTS (FRANCE/UNITED KINGDOM). 1992.

NOMINATION *Cinematography:* Robert Fraisse.

An adolescent girl (Jane March) has an affair with a Westernized Chinese man (Tony Leung) in Southeast Asia in the twenties. Beautiful but empty erotic melodrama, based on a novel by Marguérite Duras [918], directed by Jean-Jacques Annaud. The cinematography Oscar went to Philippe Rousselot for *A River Runs Through It.*

1220 • LOVER COME BACK

UNIVERSAL-INTERNATIONAL-THE 7 PICTURES CORPORATION, NOB HILL PRODUCTIONS INC., ARWIN PRODUCTIONS INC.; UNIVERSAL-INTERNATIONAL. 1961.

NOMINATION *Story and Screenplay—Written Directly for the Screen:* Stanley Shapiro and Paul Henning.

Advertising account execs Doris Day [1572] and Rock Hudson [768] work for rival agencies. In the course of trying to wrest clients away from one another's firms, Day pays court to Hudson, who poses as a scientist working on a product that doesn't exist. He of course is perfectly willing to be wooed. Essentially an unofficial remake of *Pillow Talk* (which Shapiro also wrote): Day once again plays a brittle career woman who doesn't know she needs love; Hudson is again the womanizer who pretends to be sexually repressed; and Tony Randall is once again Hudson's neurotic pal. It's harder and more calculating than *Pillow Talk,* very much aware of the formula it's based on, but it has bright and amusing moments (along with sniggery, sexist ones), as well as a bit of a satiric edge, although advertising is a barn-size target where satire is concerned. Of the three Day-Hudson comedies (the other one is the 1964 *Send Me No Flowers*) this is the one that most conforms to the stereotype of Day as the virgin defending her honor—she's rarely allowed to soften into humanity in this movie. The supporting cast includes Edie Adams, Jack Oakie [818], Jack Kruschen [91], Ann B. Davis, and Jack Albertson [1954]. Directed by Delbert Mann [1283]. The screenplay Oscar went to William Inge for *Splendor in the Grass.*

Shapiro: 1498, 1572, 2035.

1221 • LOVERS AND OTHER STRANGERS

ABC Pictures Production; Cinerama. 1970.
Award *Song:* "For All We Know," music by Fred Karlin, lyrics by Robb Royer and James Griffin (a.k.a. Robb Wilson and Arthur James).
Nominations *Supporting Actor:* Richard Castellano. *Screenplay—Based on Material From Another Medium:* Renee Taylor, Joseph Bologna, and David Zelag Goodman.

Bonnie Bedelia and Michael Brandon, who have been living together, decide to get married, but their encounters with friends, family, and prospective in-laws give them some second thoughts. Witty, episodic comedy, adapted by the screenwriters from their Broadway play, with a big, skillful cast: Gig Young [427 . . .], Bea Arthur, Anne Jackson, Harry Guardino, Cloris Leachman [1139], and Anne Meara, among others. Diane Keaton [88 . . .] makes her screen debut in a small role. Directed by Cy Howard.

When he was a teenager, Karlin was inspired to become a musician by a movie, *Young Man With a Horn* (1950). After graduating from Amherst College, he played in a jazz band and later became an orchestrator for the Radio City Music Hall orchestra.

Castellano, who had appeared in the Broadway production of *Lovers and Other Strangers,* made his screen debut in a bit part in *A Fine Madness* (1966). His subsequent screen career, except for the role of Clemenza in *The Godfather,* was not a major one. He died in 1988. The Oscar went to John Mills for *Ryan's Daughter.*

The screenplay award went to Ring Lardner, Jr., for *MASH.*

Karlin: 120, 1178, 1926.

1222 • LOVES OF A BLONDE

Barrandov Film Studios Production (Czechoslovakia). 1966.
Nomination *Foreign Language Film.*

A young woman in a small factory town falls in love with a traveling musician and pursues him to his family's home in Prague. Charming minor comedy directed by Milos Forman [60 . . .]. The Oscar went to *A Man and a Woman.*

1223 • LOVES OF CARMEN, THE

The Beckworth Corporation; Columbia. 1948.
Nomination *Color Cinematography:* William Snyder.

Rita Hayworth is the Gypsy Carmen, who leads the young soldier Don Jose (Glenn Ford) into temptation—and both of them to their doom. Colorful but dull, especially without Bizet's music to underscore it all—the score is by Mario Castelnuovo-Tedesco. Hayworth is certainly watchable, but Ford looks painfully awkward in his period uniform and curly wig. Charles Vidor directed, and the cast includes Victor Jory, Luther Adler, and Margaret Wycherly [1779]. The Oscar went to Joseph Valentine, William V. Skall, and Winton Hoch for *Joan of Arc.*

Snyder: 56, 1057.

1224 • LUCK OF THE IRISH, THE

20TH CENTURY-FOX. 1948.

NOMINATION *Supporting Actor:* Cecil Kellaway.

Newspaperman Tyrone Power's encounter with a leprechaun (Kellaway) in New York City complicates his relationship with Anne Baxter [46 . . .]. Flimsy whimsy, directed by Henry Koster [214], with Lee J. Cobb [301 . . .] and Jayne Meadows. Kellaway lost to Walter Huston in *The Treasure of the Sierra Madre.*

Kellaway: 843.

1225 • LUDWIG

MEGA FILM S.P.A. PRODUCTION; MGM (ITALY/FRANCE/WEST GERMANY). 1973.

NOMINATION *Costume Design:* Piero Tosi.

Helmut Berger plays Ludwig II of Bavaria, who descends into madness during his long reign. Ponderous and silly epic, directed by Luchino Visconti [480]. Like most of Visconti's later films, such as *The Damned* and *Death in Venice,* it uses homosexuality as metaphor for decadence—a tired and offensive trope. The big international cast includes Trevor Howard [1875] as Richard Wagner, whose music was a ruling passion of Ludwig's, plus Romy Schneider, Silvana Mangano, Helmut Griem, and Gert Frobe. Handsomely filmed in Ludwig's own extravagant Bavarian castles. The costuming Oscar went to Edith Head for *The Sting.*

Tosi: 326, 514, 1156, 2135.

1226 • LUST FOR LIFE

MGM. 1956.

AWARD *Supporting Actor:* Anthony Quinn.

NOMINATIONS *Actor:* Kirk Douglas. *Screenplay—Adapted:* Norman Corwin. *Color Art Direction—Set Decoration:* Cedric Gibbons, Hans Peters, and Preston Ames; Edwin B. Willis and F. Keogh Gleason.

Douglas plays Vincent van Gogh in this well-received and splendidly filmed account of the last third of the painter's life, from his early work in the grim, gray mining communities of Holland to the blazing mad last years in Provence. Inevitably but not overwhelmingly Hollywoodized—one is always conscious that the neurasthenic van Gogh is really the physically robust Douglas. The Irving Stone novel gives the film

its title, but not much else; MGM bought the rights to the book in 1946 to forestall others from capitalizing on its status as a best-seller. The project stayed on the shelf for several years, until *Moulin Rouge,* another biography of an artist, became a hit. John Houseman [1069 . . .] was assigned to produce and Vincente Minnelli [66 . . .] to direct. The splendid cinematography, overlooked in the nominations, is by Freddie Young [558 . . .] and Russell Harlan [204 . . .]. The score is by Miklos Rozsa [175 . . .]. Though liked by the critics, *Lust for Life* was a disappointment at the box office.

Quinn, who plays Paul Gauguin, won his second Oscar for one of the shortest on-screen appearances—his screen time amounts to about nine minutes—ever to receive an award.

Douglas, who won the New York Film Critics Award as best actor, was passed over by the Academy once again, this time in favor of Yul Brynner in *The King and I.*

Corwin was best known for his work as a writer and narrator on radio and was chosen as screenwriter because he specialized in re-creations of historical events and personalities. The Oscar went to James Poe, John Farrow, and S. J. Perelman for *Around the World in 80 Days.*

Although Peters received screen credit, he was replaced during filming by Preston Ames, after conflicts with Minnelli, a former set designer who insisted on having his way on his films. The art direction Oscar went to *The King and I.*

Quinn: 2212, 2282, 2346. Douglas: 130, 380. Gibbons: 66, 87, 130, 217, 227, 239, 285, 290, 440, 629, 749, 831, 980, 1069, 1096, 1173, 1190, 1230, 1232, 1274, 1308, 1309, 1417, 1567, 1604, 1644, 1662, 1673, 1721, 1861, 1937, 2068, 2112, 2256, 2257, 2300, 2320, 2330. Peters: 69, 1107, 1567, 1673. Ames: 31, 66, 290, 591, 769, 1937, 2184. Willis: 66, 87, 130, 227, 239, 290, 629, 749, 831, 980, 1069, 1096, 1157, 1173, 1190, 1230, 1232, 1309, 1417, 1567, 1657, 1662, 1673, 1721, 1861, 1937, 2068, 2112, 2257, 2320, 2330. Gleason: 66, 130, 290, 769, 1861, 1937.

1227 • LYDIA

ALEXANDER KORDA; UNITED ARTISTS. 1941.

NOMINATION *Scoring of a Dramatic Picture:* Miklos Rozsa.

Merle Oberon [487] plays an elderly woman who gathers her former suitors to recall their flirtations, discovering that memory is colored by nostalgia. Charmingly sentimental version of a French film, *Un Carnet de Bal* (1937), remade by its director, Julien Duvivier. Ben Hecht [78 . . .] and Samuel Hoffenstein [572 . . .] adapted the French film's screenplay, by Duvivier and others. Handsomely filmed by Lee Garmes [201 . . .]. The art direction is by Vincent Korda [1070 . . .], whose brother, Alexander [1620], produced the film. With Joseph Cotten, Edna May Oliver [581], George Reeves, and Sara Allgood [952]. The scoring Oscar went to Bernard Herrmann for *All That Money Can Buy.*

Rozsa: 175, 566, 567, 604, 1035, 1069, 1070, 1085, 1208, 1644, 1872, 1890, 1968, 2050, 2304.

1228 • MACARIO

CLASA FILMS MUNDIALES S.A. (MEXICO). 1960.

NOMINATION *Foreign Language Film.*

A starving peasant bargains with Death and is rewarded with the power to heal. Adaptation of a retelling by B. Traven of a fable by the Brothers Grimm, directed by Roberto Gavaldon, with cinematography by Gabriel Figueroa [1432]. The Oscar went to *The Virgin Spring.*

1229 • MAD ABOUT MUSIC

UNIVERSAL. 1938.

NOMINATIONS *Original Story:* Marcella Burke and Frederick Kohner. *Cinematography:* Joseph Valentine. *Interior Decoration:* Jack Otterson. *Score:* Charles Previn and Frank Skinner.

Hollywood star Gail Patrick doesn't want fans to know she has a teenage daughter (Deanna Durbin), so she ships the kid off to a Swiss boarding school. Forced to conceal her parent's identity, Durbin invents a dashing explorer father and, when another student threatens to expose her as a liar, traps Herbert Marshall into playing the part of Dad. Third in

Universal's endless series of Durbin vehicles, and not too bad at that. Directed by Norman Taurog [271 . . .], with Arthur Treacher and William Frawley. The story award went to Eleanore Griffin and Dore Schary for *Boys Town.* Joseph Ruttenberg won for the cinematography for *The Great Waltz,* Carl J. Weyl for the art direction of *The Adventures of Robin Hood,* and Alfred Newman for the score for *Alexander's Ragtime Band.*

Valentine: 668, 776, 1048, 1896, 2291. Otterson: 96, 269, 668, 681, 1240, 1895, 2342. Previn: 306, 668, 1030, 1485, 1870, 1896. Skinner: 62, 96, 125, 947.

1230 • MADAME BOVARY

MGM. 1949.

NOMINATION *Black-and-White Art Direction—Set Decoration:* Cedric Gibbons and Jack Martin Smith; Edwin B. Willis and Richard A. Pefferle.

Young Emma, played by Jennifer Jones [584 . . .], her head full of romantic nonsense, marries a dull provincial doctor, Charles Bovary, played by Van Heflin [1055]. Her hunger for a more passionate existence drives her to take lovers, played by Louis Jourdan and Christopher Kent. (The latter is the Swedish actor Alf Kjellin, making his American debut under a name he used only for this film.) Eventually she commits suicide. Controversial version of the Flaubert novel, initially well received, later dismissed as a glossy mishandling of a great novel, and more recently lauded as a fine example of the work of its director, Vincente Minnelli [66 . . .]. He has been particularly celebrated for the staging of the ball scene, filmed by Robert Planck [74 . . .] with swirling, 360-degree pans, set to an eerie waltz theme by Miklos Rozsa [175 . . .] and culminating with windows being smashed when Emma faints. The screenplay is by Robert Ardrey [1083], who added a framing device: the trial of Flaubert, played by James Mason [761 . . .], on charges of obscenity. It has been suggested that the frame story was devised to put the Production Code enforcers off the scent— suicide and adultery were taboo, but the Hollywood censors could hardly find themselves cracking down on something that had survived a nineteenth-century court challenge and been proclaimed a literary classic. The cast also includes Gene Lockhart [36] and Gladys Cooper [1393 . . .]. The art direction, primarily the work of Smith, lost to *The Heiress*.

Gibbons: 66, 87, 130, 217, 227, 239, 285, 290, 440, 629, 749, 831, 980, 1069, 1096, 1173, 1190, 1226, 1232, 1274, 1308, 1309, 1417, 1567, 1604, 1644, 1662, 1673, 1721, 1861, 1937, 2068, 2112, 2256, 2257, 2300, 2320, 2330. Smith: 29, 413, 557, 646, 896, 2008, 2120, 2247. Willis: 66, 87, 130, 227, 239, 290, 629, 749, 831, 980, 1069, 1096, 1157, 1173, 1190, 1226, 1232, 1309, 1417, 1567, 1657, 1662, 1673, 1721, 1861, 1937, 2068, 2112, 2257, 2320, 2330. Pefferle: 87, 1096, 1157, 1552, 2312.

1231 • MADAME BOVARY

MK2/C.E.D./FR3 Films Production; Samuel Goldwyn Company (France). 1991.

Nomination *Costume Design:* Corinne Jorry.

Isabelle Huppert plays Flaubert's doomed heroine in this version directed by Claude Chabrol. Although it's more faithful to the novel than the 1949 MGM version, it's not nearly so much fun to watch. The costume Oscar went to Albert Wolsky for *Bugsy*.

1232 • MADAME CURIE

MGM. 1943.

Nominations *Picture:* Sidney Franklin, producer. *Actor:* Walter Pidgeon. *Actress:* Greer Garson. *Black-and-White Cinematography:* Joseph Ruttenberg. *Black-and-White Interior Decoration:* Cedric Gibbons and Paul Groesse, art direction; Edwin B. Willis and Hugh Hunt, set decoration. *Sound Recording:* Douglas Shearer. *Scoring of a Dramatic or Comedy Picture:* Herbert Stothart.

Facing down opposition and ridicule from the scientific establishment, the Curies, Marie (Garson) and Pierre (Pidgeon), discover radium. Hokey "prestige" production, based on the memoirs of the Curies' daughter, Eve. Directed by Mervyn LeRoy [1662 . . .], with Henry Travers [1371], Albert Basserman [706], Robert Walker, C. Aubrey Smith, May

Whitty [1371 . . .], Van Johnson, Margaret O'Brien, and a narration by James Hilton [1371]. So many people connected with this film—Franklin, Garson, Pidgeon, Ruttenberg, Travers, Whitty, and so on—also worked on *Mrs. Miniver* that this movie seems like a sequel: It has the same noble-pair-triumphs-over-adversity quality.

The best picture Oscar went to *Casablanca*. Paul Lukas won as best actor for *Watch on the Rhine*. Jennifer Jones was named best actress for *The Song of Bernadette,* which also won for Arthur Miller's cinematography, for art direction, and for Alfred Newman's score. The sound award went to Stephen Dunn for *This Land Is Mine*.

Franklin: 799, 1371, 1440, 1662, 2320. Pidgeon: 1371. Garson: 239, 804, 1371, 1372, 1973, 2193. Ruttenberg: 318, 573, 749, 769, 828, 1069, 1371, 1861, 2234. Gibbons: 66, 87, 130, 217, 227, 239, 285, 290, 440, 629, 749, 831, 980, 1069, 1096, 1173, 1190, 1226, 1230, 1274, 1308, 1309, 1417, 1567, 1604, 1644, 1662, 1673, 1721, 1861, 1937, 2068, 2112, 2256, 2257, 2300, 2320, 2330. Groesse: 87, 1173, 1190, 1309, 1335, 1385, 1604, 2112, 2157, 2320. Willis: 66, 87, 130, 227, 239, 290, 629, 749, 831, 980, 1069, 1096, 1157, 1173, 1190, 1226, 1230, 1309, 1417, 1567, 1657, 1662, 1673, 1721, 1861, 1937, 2068, 2112, 2257, 2320, 2330. Hunt: 175, 401, 980, 1069, 1335, 1388, 1567, 1644, 1657, 1673, 2157, 2184. Shearer: 136, 202, 256, 397, 685, 817, 835, 1096, 1292, 1371, 1419, 1751, 1950, 1988, 2048, 2055, 2211, 2300. Stothart: 397, 1096, 1274, 1292, 1387, 1662, 1988, 2068, 2193, 2234, 2300.

1233 • MADAME ROSA

Lira Films Production (France). 1977.

Award *Foreign Language Film.*

Simone Signoret [1724 . . .] plays an aging woman, a survivor of Auschwitz, who has earned her living caring for the children of her fellow prostitutes in Paris. In her last days she is looked after by an Arab boy she has raised. Directed by Moshe Mizrahi, with Claude Dauphin and the director, Constantin Costa-Gavras [1330 . . .], in a dramatic role. Well received by critics and audiences, but it's somewhat sentimental and sanitized. Signoret is excellent. The cinematography is by Nestor Almendros [243 . . .].

1234 • MADAME X

MGM. 1928–29.

NOMINATIONS *Actress:* Ruth Chatterton. *Director:* Lionel Barrymore.

A woman on trial for murder is defended by a man who is really her long-lost son, although he doesn't know it. The tale, from a play by Alexandre Bisson, is a Hollywood perennial: There were three silent versions preceding it and two more sound remakes (1937 and 1966), not to mention a TV movie version in 1981. This movie sometimes appears under the title *Absinthe.* Chatterton is the long-suffering heroine, with Lewis Stone [1540] her stern, unforgiving husband.

Chatterton's and Barrymore's nominations are unofficial. This year the Academy announced only the winners of the Oscars, which in these cases were Mary Pickford for *Coquette* and Frank Lloyd for *The Divine Lady.* The names of the others who were being considered by the actors and directors branches for the awards are on record with the Academy, but the unofficial nominees never received an official recognition.

After a successful stage career, Chatterton came to Hollywood in 1928. She was considered a major star in the early thirties, although few would list her among Hollywood's legendary leading ladies today. Her most memorable film is *Dodsworth;* it was also her last in Hollywood. After it, she made two British films and went into semiretirement, emerging only for several Broadway productions.

In his autobiography, *We Barrymores,* Lionel Barrymore claims that, with the advent of sound, he was drafted into directing by the studio, which needed directors with stage experience to handle speaking actors. He directed five features in all. To overcome the unwieldy sound equipment, which limited the movement of actors, he says he persuaded the sound engineers to rig a microphone to the end of a fishing pole which could then track a moving actor around

the set—in short, that he invented the microphone boom. There are plenty of others who have laid claim to this innovation, however, as Barrymore notes: ''All I can say is that in 1929 I recorded Miss Ruth Chatterton's voice with a fishing pole.''

Chatterton: 1758. Barrymore: 723.

1234.5 • *MADNESS OF KING GEORGE, THE*

CLOSE CALL FILMS; SAMUEL GOLDWYN COMPANY IN ASSOCIATION WITH CHANNEL FOUR (UNITED KINGDOM). 1994.

AWARD *Art Direction–Set Decoration:* Ken Adam; Carolyn Scott.

NOMINATIONS *Actor:* Nigel Hawthorne. *Supporting Actress:* Helen Mirren. *Screenplay Based on Material Previously Produced or Published:* Alan Bennett.

Hawthorne plays King George III of England, whose mental state in the years after the Revolutionary War almost precipitates a constitutional crisis, in part because of the machinations of the Prince of Wales (Rupert Everett). Mirren is Queen Charlotte, and Ian Holm [386] plays a physician who uses unconventional methods (for the time) in an attempt to bring about a cure. Witty, literate, handsomely mounted but occasionally talky adaptation by Bennett of his play *The Madness of George III.* It was also Nicholas Hytner's impressive debut as a film director. Hawthorne himself claims to have suggested that the American distributors change the title to keep audiences from thinking that the movie was a sequel. Bennett has rejected suggestions that he had the disarray of the contemporary British royal household in mind when he wrote the play.

Hawthorne created the role of George III in the original British and American productions of the play. His film appearances have been rare, but he is a highly regarded stage performer, including a Tony win for his performance in the Broadway production of *Shadowlands.* The Oscar went to Tom Hanks for *Forrest Gump.*

Mirren, one of the most gifted British actresses, has had a rather peculiar film career, including the arty porn of *Caligula* (1979) as well as supporting roles in more mainstream films such as *Excalibur,*

White Nights, 2010, and The Mosquito Coast (1986) and art-house fare such as The Cook, the Thief, His Wife, and Her Lover (1989). She is best known to American audiences for her appearances on PBS in the superb British TV miniseries Prime Suspect and its two sequels. Dianne Wiest won the Oscar for Bullets Over Broadway.

Bennett first came to prominence in the late sixties in the British revue Beyond the Fringe, which launched a quartet of talented writer-performers—Dudley Moore [103], Peter Cook, and Jonathan Miller were the others. He is best known today as a writer, author of numerous successful stage and television plays, as well as screenplays for such films as A Private Function (1984) and Prick Up Your Ears (1987). He has also acted in such films as Dreamchild (1985) and Little Dorrit, and plays a small role in The Madness of King George. The screenplay Oscar went to Eric Roth for Forrest Gump.

Adam: 12.5, 101, 151, 1898.

1235 • MADRON

EDRIC-ISRACINE-ZEV BRAUN PRODUCTIONS; FOUR STAR-EXCELSIOR RELEASING COMPANY. 1970.
NOMINATION Song: "Till Love Touches Your Life," music by Riz Ortolani, lyrics by Arthur Hamilton.

Nun Leslie Caron [1113 . . .] survives an Apache attack on a wagon train and is rescued by gunfighter Richard Boone, whom she must accompany through Indian territory to safety. Mediocre western, filmed in Israel—"a matzoh western," in the words of one wit—and directed by Jerry Hopper. The Oscar went to Fred Karlin, Robb Royer, and James Griffin for "For All We Know," from Lovers and Other Strangers.

Ortolani: 1344.

1236 • MAGIC FLAME, THE

SAMUEL GOLDWYN PRODUCTIONS; UNITED ARTISTS. 1927–28.
NOMINATION Cinematography: George Barnes.

Ronald Colman [311 . . .] plays two roles, a clown and a villainous count, in this silent Ruritanian romance also starring Vilma Banky and directed by Henry King [1868 . . .]. Barnes lost to Charles Rosher and Karl Struss for Sunrise.

Barnes: 537, 1509, 1670, 1739, 1748, 1885, 1890.

1237 • MAGIC FLUTE, THE

SVERIGES RADIO A.B. PRODUCTION; SURROGATE RELEASING (SWEDEN). 1975.
NOMINATION Costume Design: Henny Noremark and Karin Erskine.

Prince Tamino and the birdcatcher Papageno are sent by the Queen of the Night to rescue her daughter, Pamina, from the sorcerer Sarastro—who turns out to be the good guy. Brilliant version of the Mozart opera, directed by Ingmar Bergman [111 . . .], who adapted the libretto by Schikaneder, trying to make it make sense. (He almost succeeds.) Instead of trying to make the opera itself cinematic, Bergman films it as a stage production, with backstage glimpses of the performers, and though there are perhaps too many reaction shots of the audience, the whole thing is irresistible—one of the finest opera films ever made. Filmed by Sven Nykvist [460 . . .] for Swedish TV, and sung in Swedish. For American audiences, the best-known performer is the Papageno, Hakan Hagegard. The costume award went to Ulla-Britt Soderlund and Milena Canonero for Barry Lyndon.

1238 • MAGIC OF LASSIE, THE

LASSIE PRODUCTIONS; THE INTERNATIONAL PICTURE SHOW COMPANY. 1978.
NOMINATION Original Song: "When You're Loved," music and lyrics by Richard M. Sherman and Robert B. Sherman.

James Stewart [73 . . .] stars in this remake of Lassie Come Home, as the owner of the indomitable collie, whom he is forced to hand over to meanie Pernell Roberts. About the only thing this version has going for it is Stewart, plus Alice Faye and Mickey Rooney [115 . . .]. Directed by Don Chaffey. A movie that didn't need remaking isn't helped by the addition of songs, especially when they're sung by Pat and Debby Boone. The Oscar went to Paul Jabara's "Last Dance," from Thank God It's Friday.

R. M. Sherman: 166, 396, 1284, 1842, 2107.
R. B. Sherman: 166, 396, 1284, 1842, 2107.

1239 • MAGNIFICENT AMBERSONS, THE

MERCURY; RKO RADIO. 1942.

NOMINATIONS *Picture:* Orson Welles, producer. *Supporting Actress:* Agnes Moorehead. *Black-and-White Cinematography:* Stanley Cortez. *Black-and-White Interior Decoration:* Albert S. D'Agostino, art direction; Al Fields and Darrell Silvera, set decoration.

Young Eugene Morgan (Joseph Cotten) loves Isabel Amberson (Dolores Costello), a member of the turn-of-the-century midwestern town's wealthiest family, but she marries someone else. Twenty years later Eugene returns to the town and once again begins to court the widowed Isabel, but her headstrong, spoiled son, George (Tim Holt), breaks up their relationship. Eugene prospers, making his fortune in the nascent automotive industry, while the Ambersons' wealth evaporates. Director-screenwriter Welles improves on Booth Tarkington's novel, adding psychological depth and making its commentary on the effect of the Industrial Revolution on American society more subtle. Splendidly designed and photographed, superbly acted, *Ambersons* is a fascinating movie, flawed by a shapeless narrative.

That shapelessness, however, is not entirely Welles' fault. *Ambersons* is the most notorious instance in the sound era of the disastrous effect of miscommunication and/or antagonism between director and studio. After filming on *Ambersons* was completed, Welles was enlisted in a documentary project in Brazil, part of the wartime propaganda effort to keep Latin American countries on our side. While he was out of the country, the first cut of *Ambersons,* slightly over two hours long, was previewed. The audience reaction was devastatingly negative. After a somewhat more favorable but not promising preview, RKO head George Schaefer put editor Robert Wise [407 . . .] in charge of cutting and reshooting scenes, since Welles was unavailable to do the job himself. Wise recut the film to its current eighty-eight-minute running time. Meanwhile, Schaefer was replaced as studio head, and the new management decided to cut its losses by giving *Ambersons* only a limited, unpromoted release. With this record of mutilation and indifference, it seems odd to find *Ambersons* among the Oscar contenders, especially as the Academy's treatment of *Citizen Kane* the year before was less than an enthusiastic endorsement of Welles as filmmaker. One can only speculate that many in the Academy membership found something to sympathize with in Welles' treatment by the Hollywood studio system. In the long run, even the flawed *Ambersons* has to be judged a finer artistic achievement than *Mrs. Miniver,* which won the Oscars for best picture, supporting actress Teresa Wright, and cinematographer Joseph Ruttenberg.

The *Ambersons* debacle has become central to the Welles legend. For those to whom Welles is a hero, it's an instance of the abuse of genius by commercial-minded dolts. Others see it as evidence of Welles' self-destructiveness and ambivalence: He himself ordered significant cuts in the film before the first preview—cuts that Wise mostly restored before the more successful second screening. Even as scripted, *Ambersons* has a difficult and unsatisfactory ending. After the commercial failure of *Kane* and *Ambersons,* the remainder of Welles' film career—more than forty years—was spent scrounging for money, acting in movies of wildly varying (but mostly low) quality, doing TV commercials, and producing movies of fitful brilliance. As late as 1970 he was still talking about assembling surviving members of the cast—Cotten, Moorehead, Holt, and Anne Baxter [46 . . .], who played Cotten's daughter—to film a new ending for *Ambersons.* Welles never received another Oscar nomination but was given an honorary award at the 1970 ceremonies: "for superlative artistry and versatility in the creation of motion pictures."

If anyone came out well from *Ambersons,* it was Moorehead, who plays George's spinster Aunt Fanny. She began her association with Welles in 1940 as a member of his Mercury Theater Company and came to Hollywood for the small part of Kane's mother in *Citizen Kane.* After her first nomination, she became a steadily employed character actress, always in somewhat vinegary roles.

Cortez was born Stanley Krantz, but his older

brother, Jacob Krantz, became a silent-film star as a Latin lover under the name Ricardo Cortez. So when Stanley came to Hollywood, he became Cortez, too. He had worked as an assistant to still photographer Edward Steichen. After apprenticing as an assistant cameraman, he became a director of photography in 1937, working largely on B pictures until Welles tapped him at the last minute for *Ambersons* because his *Citizen Kane* cinematographer, Gregg Toland, was unavailable.

The *fin de siècle* sets for the Amberson mansion are among the most convincing period re-creations in an era when Hollywood rarely bothered with verisimilitude. Welles said that Anne Baxter's grandfather, Frank Lloyd Wright, visited the set and was appalled at their gloomy clutter—precisely what his own domestic architecture had aimed at ending. Welles had been disappointed by the snow scenes in *Citizen Kane* because you couldn't see the actors' breath. He had the snow scenes for *Ambersons* staged in a Los Angeles icehouse, which had also been used for *Lost Horizon* and would be used in 1951 for *The Thing*. The art direction Oscar went to *This Above All*.

Welles: 407. Moorehead: 963, 1052, 1372. Cortez: 1828. D'Agostino: 632, 686, 1240, 1924. Fields: 407. Silvera: 407, 632, 686, 1264, 1341, 1924.

1240 • MAGNIFICENT BRUTE, THE
UNIVERSAL. 1936.
NOMINATION *Interior Decoration:* Albert S. D'Agostino and Jack Otterson.

Victor McLaglen [999 . . .] and William Hall are steelworker rivals for the affections of Binnie Barnes in this forgettable melodrama directed by John G. Blystone. The art direction Oscar went to Richard Day for *Dodsworth*.

D'Agostino: 632, 686, 1239, 1924. Otterson: 96, 269, 668, 681, 1229, 1895, 2342.

1241 • MAGNIFICENT OBSESSION
UNIVERSAL-INTERNATIONAL. 1954.
NOMINATION *Actress:* Jane Wyman.

Playboy Rock Hudson [768] accidentally blinds Wyman, so in his remorse he goes to medical school, becomes a surgeon, and restores her sight. Blame novelist Lloyd C. Douglas for the ridiculous plot, with its overlay of sentimental religiosity, but blame producer Ross Hunter [31] for remaking it—the whole slurpy business had already been done in 1935 with Robert Taylor and Irene Dunne [114 . . .]. At least director Douglas Sirk knew how to turn such drivel into entertainment—you can't stop watching even though you know you should. With Agnes Moorehead [963 . . .] and Barbara Rush. Wyman lost to Grace Kelly in *The Country Girl*.

Wyman: 246, 1052, 2320.

MAGNIFICENT SEVEN, THE (JAPAN, 1956)
See 1788.

1242 • MAGNIFICENT SEVEN, THE
MIRISCH-ALPHA PRODUCTION; UNITED ARTISTS. 1960.
NOMINATION *Scoring of a Dramatic or Comedy Picture:* Elmer Bernstein.

A small Mexican town, harassed by bandits, hires a pack of gunslingers for protection. Highly entertaining remake of the Akira Kurosawa [1661] classic, *Seven Samurai,* directed by John Sturges [131]. The seven are Yul Brynner [1088], Steve McQueen [1753], Horst Buchholz, James Coburn, Charles Bronson, Robert Vaughn [2338], and Brad Dexter. Eli Wallach plays the bandit chief. Bernstein's main theme was later used in Marlboro cigarette commercials. The Oscar went to Ernest Gold for the score for *Exodus*.

Bernstein: 27.5, 789, 882, 1264, 1685, 1959, 2064, 2101, 2130, 2147, 2223.

1243 • MAGNIFICENT YANKEE, THE
MGM. 1950.
NOMINATIONS *Actor:* Louis Calhern. *Black-and-White Costume Design:* Walter Plunkett.

Calhern plays Justice Oliver Wendell Holmes, with Ann Harding [927] as his wife in an adaptation of a play by Emmett Lavery [453]. Solid though unexciting biopic directed by John Sturges [131].

Calhern made his screen debut while still in his twenties, in 1921, but turned his attention to the stage until talkies came in. He is best remembered for numerous character roles in the forties and fifties, in films such as *Notorious, Annie Get Your Gun,* and *The Asphalt Jungle* and in the title role of *Julius Caesar.* He died in 1956, shortly after completing his last film role in *High Society.* He lost the Oscar to Jose Ferrer in *Cyrano de Bergerac.*

The costuming Oscar went to Edith Head and Charles LeMaire for *All About Eve.*

Plunkett: 9, 66, 953, 1087, 1587, 1657, 1859, 2029, 2330.

1244 • MAHOGANY

JOBETE FILM PRODUCTION; PARAMOUNT. 1975.
NOMINATION *Song:* "Theme From *Mahogany* (Do You Know Where You're Going To)," music by Michael Masser, lyrics by Gerry Goffin.

Diana Ross [1126] plays a Chicago secretary who breaks the color bar as a fashion model and then goes on to success as a designer. But she decides to give it all up and settle down with politician Billy Dee Williams. Draggy, incoherent soap opera, misdirected by Ross' Motown mentor, Berry Gordy, who fired the original director, Tony Richardson [2106]. With Beah Richards [843], Nina Foch [629], Jean-Pierre Aumont, and Anthony Perkins [730]. (Foch and Perkins play the types in which they were most often cast, a bitch and a creep respectively.) This flop helped wreck Ross' film career, which had begun promisingly with *Lady Sings the Blues.* After one more film, *The Wiz,* Ross abandoned the movies. Though it yielded a song nominee that was a big hit for Ross, *Mahogany* is not a musical. The Oscar went to Keith Carradine for "I'm Easy," from *Nashville.*

1245 • MAIDS OF WILKO, THE

POLISH CORPORATION FOR FILM PRODUCTION (POLAND). 1979.
NOMINATION *Foreign Language Film.*

A World War I veteran visits his aunt and uncle at Wilko, where the five unmarried sisters at the neighboring estate all once had crushes on him. As they renew old acquaintance, they come to realize how much they have changed with the passing years. Delicately handled film with a good deal of wistful charm.

Directed by Andrzej Wada. The Oscar went to *The Tin Drum.*

1246 • MAJORITY OF ONE, A

WARNER BROS. 1961.
NOMINATION *Color Cinematography:* Harry Stradling, Sr.

Rosalind Russell [110 . . .] plays a middle-aged Jewish widow who takes an ocean cruise and falls in love with a middle-aged widower. The punch line is that he's Japanese. The capper is that he's played by Alec Guinness [287 . . .]. On Broadway this little character comedy by Leonard Spiegelgass [1409] apparently had some charm. But the screen version, also by Spiegelgass, is just tiresome, not helped much by Russell's overplaying and Guinness' obvious embarrassment. Directed by Mervyn LeRoy [1662 . . .]. Daniel L. Fapp won the cinematography Oscar for *West Side Story.*

Stradling: 110, 149, 596, 737, 852, 853, 864, 896, 957, 1393, 1567, 1949, 2338.

1247 • MAKE A WISH

PRINCIPAL PRODUCTIONS; RKO RADIO. 1937.
NOMINATION *Score:* Hugo Riesenfeld, musical director; score by Hugo Riesenfeld.

Composer Basil Rathbone [979 . . .] visits a summer camp where he discovers singer Bobby Breen. Vapid little musical that failed to make Breen RKO's answer to Fox's Shirley Temple or Universal's Deanna Durbin. And to add to the insult, Durbin's musical *One Hundred Men and a Girl* won the scoring Oscar.

1247.5 • MALCOLM X

BY ANY MEANS NECESSARY CINEMA PRODUCTION; WARNER BROS. 1992.
NOMINATIONS *Actor:* Denzel Washington. *Costume Design:* Ruth Carter.

Washington plays the title role, the man who started life as Malcolm Little, turned to crime as a young man, was converted to Islam in prison, and became one of the most important figures in the struggle for black civil rights in the sixties. Searing, stirring, first-class biopic—heads above most representatives of the genre, including such Oscar winners as *Gandhi* and *The Last Emperor*. The movie covers an amazing range, from the exhilarating jitterbug sequences in the early part of the film to the unbearable tension of the events leading up to Malcolm's assassination. Directed by Spike Lee [556], who also coproduced with Marvin Worth [1155] and cowrote with Arnold Perl. The superb cast includes Angela Bassett [2250.7] as Malcolm's wife, Al Freeman, Jr., as Elijah Muhammad, and Lee himself as Malcolm's friend Shorty. Lee tirelessly promoted the film, often abrasively—by taking public his behind-the-scenes fights with Warner Bros. over funding the movie, and by urging students to cut school to see his film. But it was a serious box-office disappointment, despite strong reviews. Still, it deserved far more attention than the Academy gave it and certainly belonged in the best picture and best director competition instead of *Scent of a Woman* and its director, Martin Brest. It can also be argued that Washington's performance was finer, fuller, and deeper than Al Pacino's winning show-offy turn in *Scent,* although Pacino's prior neglect by the Academy tipped things in his favor. Also overlooked was Ernest Dickerson's fine cinematography, which was preferable to the candy-box eroticism of Robert Fraisse for *The Lover* or the easy picturesqueness of the Oscar-winning work of Philippe Rousselot for *A River Runs Through It*. Though this time, more than ever, Lee had clear evidence of Hollywood racism, he was uncommonly muted in his disappointment at being shunned by the Academy. Ruth Carter's witty zoot suits and period designs lost to Eiko Ishioka's extravaganzas in *Bram Stoker's Dracula.*

Washington: 471, 779.

1248 • MALTESE FALCON, THE

WARNER BROS. 1941.

NOMINATIONS *Picture:* Hal B. Wallis, producer. *Supporting Actor:* Sydney Greenstreet. *Screenplay:* John Huston.

Humphrey Bogart [24 . . .] plays Sam Spade, a San Francisco detective who is drawn by a client, Brigid O'Shaugnessy, played by Mary Astor [822],

into the quest for a mysterious statuette of a black bird. In the process, he crosses paths with the florid Casper Gutman (Greenstreet) and his henchmen, Joel Cairo (Peter Lorre) and Wilmer (Elisha Cook, Jr.). One of the most popular films of all time and probably the best of its genre, the hard-boiled private eye. It also provided a stunning directorial debut for Huston. Its success came as a surprise, since the novel by Dashiell Hammett [2233] had been filmed twice before—under the same title with Ricardo Cortez and Bebe Daniels in 1931 and as *Satan Met a Lady* with Warren William and Bette Davis [46 . . .] in 1936. George Raft backed out of the Sam Spade role reportedly because he didn't want to do a remake or to work with a novice director, thereby giving Bogart the role that boosted him out of the pack of Warners contract players and made him one of the true Hollywood superstars—and one of the most unlikely. Mary Astor's description of Bogart captures him superbly: "He wasn't very tall; vocally he had a range from A to B; his eyes were like shiny coal nuggets pressed deep into his skull; and his smile was a mistake that he tried to keep from happening. He was no movie hero. He was no hero at all." And that very unheroic quality is what makes his Spade—a mean little man—so memorable. Astor claimed that she hyperventilated before each scene to give her Brigid that eerie instability. The film provided definitive roles for her, for Lorre, and especially for Greenstreet, who as Astor notes never "did a picture later in which that evil, hiccupy laugh wasn't exploited." The cast also includes Gladys George [2192], Lee Patrick, Ward Bond, Jerome Cowan, and, in a bit part as Captain Jacobi, the director's father, Walter Huston [50 . . .].

It comes as a shock, then, to realize that *The Maltese Falcon* was a washout at the Oscars. The best picture Oscar (which should have gone to *Citizen Kane* in any case) went to *How Green Was My Valley,* for which Donald Crisp took the supporting actor award. The writing Oscar went to Sidney Buchman and Seton I. Miller for *Here Comes Mr. Jordan*. The closest *The Maltese Falcon* came to an Oscar was Astor's supporting actress win for *The Great Lie,* released the same year, which many interpret as honoring her performance in both films—and Astor herself said she wished it had been for *Falcon* instead.

Wallis: 17, 55, 85, 164, 343, 365, 676, 689, 712, 965, 1046, 1095, 1162, 1482, 1727, 1779, 2233, 2318. Huston: 24, 105, 356, 571, 891, 1263, 1363, 1625, 1779, 2136.

1249 • MAMA TURNS A HUNDRED

ELIAS QUEREJETA P.C. PRODUCTION (SPAIN). 1979.
NOMINATION *Foreign Language Film.*

A family gathers for the matriarch's birthday, eager for her to kick off, but Mama has life in her yet. Satiric look at the Spanish version of momism, in which the mother is also a symbol of Franco's rule over the Spanish people. Directed by Carlos Saura. The cast includes Geraldine Chaplin. The Oscar went to *The Tin Drum*.

1249.5 • MAMBO KINGS, THE

NORTHWEST PRODUCTION; WARNER BROS. 1992.
NOMINATION *Song:* "Beautiful Maria of My Soul," music by Robert Kraft, lyrics by Arne Glimcher.

Brothers Armand Assante and Antonio Banderas emigrate from Cuba in the fifties, start a band, and have romantic and professional conflicts. Eventually they appear on an episode of *I Love Lucy*—a sequence in which Desi Arnaz, Jr., plays his own father. Inconsequential version of the Pulitzer Prize–winning novel *The Mambo Kings Play Songs of Love,* by Oscar Hijuelos. The music, including appearances by Tito Puente and Celia Cruz, is the best thing about the movie, but there's not enough of it to make up for the lack of story. The cast includes Cathy Moriarty [1650] and Roscoe Lee Browne. Directed by Glimcher, whose song lost to Alan Menken and Tim Rice's "A Whole New World," from *Aladdin*.

1250 • MAN AND A WOMAN, A

LES FILMS 13 PRODUCTION; ALLIED ARTISTS (FRANCE). 1966.
AWARDS *Story and Screenplay—Written Directly for the Screen:* Claude Lelouch and Pierre Uytterhoeven. *Foreign Language Film.*

NOMINATIONS *Actress:* Anouk Aimée. *Director:* Claude Lelouch.

A race car driver (Jean-Louis Trintignant) and a movie "script girl" (Aimée), both of them widowed, meet while visiting their respective children. They fall in love, but her memories of her dead husband cast a pall over the relationship. Eventually love, accompanied by the familiar theme music of Francis Lai [1218], conquers all. Lush but paper-thin romance that was a huge international success—one of the most popular French films of all time. In addition to the foreign film Oscar, it also won the prize at Cannes. The movie's soft-focus emptiness has lost a lot of its charm, perhaps because its images of romance have been endlessly copied by TV commercials and parodied by everyone from Woody Allen to the Zucker brothers. Lelouch found out how times had changed when he remade it in 1977 as *Another Man, Another Chance,* with Genevieve Bujold [85] and James Caan [784], and turned out a sequel, *A Man and a Woman: 20 Years Later,* in 1986. Both of them bombed.

Aimée lost to Elizabeth Taylor in *Who's Afraid of Virginia Woolf?* The directing Oscar went to Fred Zinnemann for *A Man for All Seasons.*

Lelouch: 76. Uytterhoeven: 76.

1251 • MAN CALLED PETER, A

20TH CENTURY-FOX. 1955.
NOMINATION *Color Cinematography:* Harold Lipstein.

Richard Todd [878] plays Peter Marshall, a Scottish clergyman who became chaplain to the U.S. Senate, but died young. Susan Peters [1662] plays his wife, Catherine, on whose book this middling, pious, weepy biopic is based. Directed by Henry Koster [214], with Marjorie Rambeau [1609 . . .] and Jill Esmond. Lipstein lost to Robert Burks for *To Catch a Thief*.

1252 • MAN FOR ALL SEASONS, A

HIGHLAND FILMS LTD. PRODUCTION; COLUMBIA (UNITED KINGDOM). 1966.
AWARDS *Picture:* Fred Zinnemann, producer. *Actor:* Paul Scofield. *Director:* Fred Zinnemann. *Screenplay—Based on Material From Another Medium:* Robert Bolt.

Color Cinematography: Ted Moore. *Color Costume Design:* Elizabeth Haffenden and Joan Bridge.

NOMINATIONS *Supporting Actor:* Robert Shaw. *Supporting Actress:* Wendy Hiller.

Scofield plays Thomas More, whose refusal to countenance the divorce of Henry VIII (Shaw) from Catherine of Aragon leads to More's execution. Fine, serious filming of Bolt's play, handsomely opened up by eliminating some stylized theatrical characters, such as one representing the Common Man, and filming in settings where the events took place, or at least in their near equivalents—the modern Thames was too commercial and too polluted. It's still a little more talky than a film should be, and the motives, relationships, and dialogue have a "modern" flavor that's occasionally jarring. But of Hollywood's flurry of anglophile historical pageants, which include *Becket, The Lion in Winter,* and *Anne of the Thousand Days,* it's by far the best directed, best written, and best cast, with Leo McKern as Thomas Cromwell, Orson Welles [407 . . .] as Cardinal Wolsey, John Hurt [608 . . .] as the perfidious Rich, Susannah York [2047] as More's daughter, and, in a wordless walk-on, Vanessa Redgrave [263 . . .] as Anne Boleyn. Redgrave had originally been cast in the role played by York, but stage commitments kept her from making the film. She agreed to do the walk-on but insisted on not being billed in the credits. She later played Hiller's role, More's wife, in a TV version starring Charlton Heston [175] in 1988.

Although *A Man for All Seasons* is an exceptional film, its best picture Oscar is often held up as an example of the Academy's conservatism. The nominees it defeated are all in some ways more daring: The satiric portrait of a sexual predator, *Alfie,* and the saga of a brawling academic couple, *Who's Afraid of Virginia Woolf?,* both broke screen taboos about language and sex. And both the farcical *The Russians Are Coming, the Russians Are Coming* and the epic *The Sand Pebbles* attempted to make antiwar statements that were slightly before their time. Still, the sober humanism of *A Man for All Seasons,* with its portrait of a man who followed the dictates of conscience and faith though it meant his own death, had its own contemporary relevance.

Scofield is one of the finest of the generation of British actors that came to prominence in the immediate postwar years, including Richard Burton [85 . . .], Richard Attenborough [745], Denholm Elliott [1725], and Ian Bannen [688]—a generation that, with the exception of Burton, was overshadowed in the movies by both older performers like Laurence Olivier [268 . . .] and Alec Guinness [287 . . .] and younger ones like Albert Finney [579 . . .], Alan Bates, [678] and Peter O'Toole [164 . . .]. Apart from *A Man for All Seasons,* Scofield has made few films of note, although he has left a record of his exceptional performance as King Lear in the Peter Brook stage production that was filmed in 1971, as well as small roles in Kenneth Branagh's *Henry V* and (as the Ghost) in the Franco Zeffirelli *Hamlet.* In 1994 he received acclaim, and a second nomination, for his portrayal of Mark Van Doren in *Quiz Show.*

Zinnemann's second directing Oscar did not initiate a new period in his exceptional career. It was six years before he made another film, *The Day of the Jackal,* and he would make only one more significant one, *Julia,* before retiring.

Bolt, previously honored for his screenplay for *Doctor Zhivago,* followed his second Oscar by work with his frequent collaborator David Lean on *Ryan's Daughter,* a notorious flop. He turned to directing in 1972 with *Lady Caroline Lamb,* but critical and commercial reaction was discouraging. He subsequently wrote the screenplays for *The Bounty* (1984) and *The Mission.* Bolt died in 1995.

Moore began his work as cameraman in England after World War II, serving as camera operator on *The African Queen,* among other films. His career as cinematographer began in the mid-fifties and entered its major phase in 1962, when he was assigned to an adventure thriller called *Dr. No,* the first James Bond movie. He has subsequently shot many of the films in that series.

Shaw, who made his film debut in 1954's *The Dam Busters,* had his own career breakthrough in the Bond series, as the rock-solid blond villain in *From Russia With Love* (1963). A novelist and playwright, he adapted his novel *The Man in the Glass Booth* for the stage, and the film version earned an Oscar nomination for actor Maximilian Schell in 1975. By that time Shaw had become a major character actor, with memorable roles in *The Sting* and *Jaws*. He died suddenly of a heart attack in 1978, aged fifty-one. His Oscar nomination makes him one of three actors to receive notice from the Academy for playing Henry VIII. The others were Charles Laughton, who won for *The Private Life of Henry VIII,* and Richard Burton, who was nominated for *Anne of the Thousand Days*. Shaw lost to Walter Matthau in *The Fortune Cookie*.

Hiller lost to Sandy Dennis in *Who's Afraid of Virginia Woolf?*

Zinnemann: 732, 912, 1066, 1457, 1771, 1969. Scofield: 1643.5. Bolt: 558, 1151. Haffenden: 175. Hiller: 1637, 1778.

1253 • MAN IN THE GLASS BOOTH, THE

ELY LANDAU ORGANIZATION PRODUCTION; AFT DISTRIBUTING. 1975.

NOMINATION *Actor:* Maximilian Schell.

A Jewish industrialist (Schell) is suspected of being a Nazi war criminal and put on trial. A direct translation to film of the play by Robert Shaw [1252] based on the trial of Adolph Eichmann, directed by Arthur Hiller [1218]. Not at all cinematic and hence not very satisfactory, a clear demonstration of the difference between stage and film. Several experiments were made in the mid-seventies with direct filming of plays, but they were critically and commercially unsuccessful. This one was produced by Ely Landau in his American Film Theatre series. Another such venture, called Theatrovision, produced *Give 'Em Hell, Harry!*, for which James Whitmore was also nominated for an Oscar. Both filmed plays were shown during the nominating period on the Los Angeles Z Channel, a predecessor of current cable movie channels, and both Schell and Whitmore doubtless owe their nominations to this exposure. (More recently, nominations have been generated by the widespread mailing of videocassettes to Academy members.) Unfortunately some very fine performances were overlooked: Roy Scheider, Richard Dreyfuss, and Shaw himself in *Jaws,* Sean Connery and Michael Caine in *The Man Who Would Be King,* and Warren Beatty in *Shampoo*. The Oscar went to Jack Nicholson for *One Flew Over the Cuckoo's Nest.*

Schell: 1065, 1066.

1254 • MAN IN THE IRON MASK, THE

EDWARD SMALL; UNITED ARTISTS. 1939.

NOMINATION *Original Score:* Lud Gluskin and Lucien Moraweck.

Louis Hayward plays twins, one of whom becomes Louis XIV of France, the other a swashbuckling adventurer keeping company with D'Artagnan (Warren William) and the Three Musketeers. Enjoyable version of the Dumas novel, directed by James Whale, with Joan Bennett, Joseph Schildkraut [1169], and Alan Hale. The Oscar went to Herbert Stothart for *The Wizard of Oz.*

1255 • MAN IN THE WHITE SUIT, THE

J. ARTHUR RANK-EALING; UNIVERSAL-INTERNATIONAL (UNITED KINGDOM). 1952.

NOMINATION *Screenplay:* Roger MacDougall, John Dighton, and Alexander Mackendrick.

Research chemist Alec Guinness [287 . . .] discovers a miracle synthetic fabric that repels dirt and lasts forever. But when he announces his discovery, both labor and management are appalled. It would put the textile companies, not to mention the dry cleaners and dye works (it repels dye as well as dirt), out of business. So the scientist becomes a pariah and is forced to flee, wearing his suit, which glows in the dark. Wonderful premise, wonderfully executed. Mackendrick also directed, and the peerless cast includes Joan Greenwood, Cecil Parker, Michael Gough, and Ernest Thesiger. One of the unchallenged classics of British fifties comedy. The Oscar went to Charles Schnee for *The Bad and the Beautiful.*

Dighton: 1716.

1256 • MAN OF A THOUSAND FACES

UNIVERSAL-INTERNATIONAL. 1957.

NOMINATION *Story and Screenplay—Written Directly for the Screen:* story by Ralph Wheelwright; screenplay by R. Wright Campbell, Ivan Goff, and Ben Roberts.

James Cagney [79 . . .] plays Lon Chaney, the great horror film actor and makeup expert, with Dorothy Malone [2315] as Chaney's first wife and Jane Greer as his second. It's a little too long, and the psychologizing is hack—Chaney's physical expressiveness is "explained" as an outgrowth of his childhood attempts to communicate with his deaf-mute parents. Nor are Cagney's re-creations of Chaney's film performances particularly impressive if you've seen the originals. Producer-to-be Robert Evans [395] plays producer Irving Thalberg [150 . . .]; he was personally selected for the role by Thalberg's widow, Norma Shearer [150 . . .]. With Marjorie Rambeau [1609 . . .], Jim Backus, Jeanne Cagney, and Jack Albertson [1954], directed by Joseph Pevney. The writing Oscar went to George Wells for *Designing Woman.*

1257 • MAN OF CONQUEST

REPUBLIC. 1939.

NOMINATIONS *Interior Decoration:* John Victor Mackay. *Sound Recording:* C. T. Lootens. *Original Score:* Victor Young.

Richard Dix [400] plays Texas hero Sam Houston in this somewhat draggy biopic, with Gail Patrick and Joan Fontaine [441 . . .], directed by George Nicholls, Jr. One of Republic's "prestige" efforts that surely would have been lost sight of in the Hollywood *annus mirabilis* 1939, if the Academy hadn't liberalized its nominating rules, allowing studios to submit their own candidates in certain award categories. The Oscars went to Lyle Wheeler for the art direction for *Gone With the Wind,* Bernard B. Brown for the sound for *When Tomorrow Comes,* and Herbert Stothart for the score for *The Wizard of Oz.*

Mackay: 489, 1269. Lootens: 100, 168, 538. Young: 97, 98, 100, 101, 280, 489, 612, 693, 701, 794, 846, 925, 1214, 1396, 1452, 1748, 1823, 1994, 2235, 2315.

1258 • MAN OF IRON

POLISH CORPORATION FOR FILM, UNIT "X" PRODUCTION (POLAND). 1981.

NOMINATION *Foreign Language Film.*

An account of the 1980 Gdansk shipyard strike and the rise of the Solidarity movement, blending documentary footage with a narrative about a shipyard worker and his documentary-film maker wife. Solidarity leader Lech Walesa makes an appearance as himself in the film, directed by Andrzej Wada, which is a sequel to the 1972 film *Man of Marble.* The Oscar went to *Mephisto.*

1259 • MAN OF LA MANCHA

P.E.A. PRODUZIONI EUROPEE ASSOCIATE S.P.A. PRODUCTION; UNITED ARTISTS (ITALY). 1972.

NOMINATION *Scoring—Adaptation and Original Song Score:* Laurence Rosenthal.

Imprisoned by the Inquisition, Cervantes, played by Peter O'Toole [164 . . .], tells the inmates the story of Don Quixote (also played by O'Toole), Sancho Panza, played by James Coco [1495], and the don's love for Dulcinea, who is actually the sluttish servant Aldonza, played by Sophia Loren [1280 . . .]. Muddled, unsuccessful translation of a hit Broadway show to the screen. Although well cast, O'Toole, Coco, and Loren are undermined by the theatricality of the concept—Dale Wasserman adapted his own play—and the slack direction of Arthur Hiller [1218]. Rosenthal's scoring of the songs by Mitch Leigh and Joe Darion lost to Ralph Burns' work on *Cabaret.*

Rosenthal: 164.

1260 • MAN WHO KNEW TOO MUCH, THE

FILWITE PRODUCTIONS INC.; PARAMOUNT. 1956.

AWARD *Song:* "Whatever Will Be, Will Be (Que Será, Será)," music and lyrics by Jay Livingston and Ray Evans.

Doris Day [1572] and James Stewart [73 . . .], a couple vacationing in Marrakesh, witness a murder that, it turns out, is connected to a political assassination plot. To ensure their silence, their young son is kidnaped. The climax occurs in London, at a concert in Albert Hall, where an assassin's bullet is to be fired simultaneously with the crash of cymbals. Remake by Alfred Hitchcock [1171 . . .] of his 1934 film, one of the biggest successes of his pre-Hollywood career. Since it's the only film Hitchcock remade, gallons of critical ink have been used in debating the relative merits of the two films. The majority opinion seems to favor the first version, but there is a vociferous, articulate minority on the side of the remake. Hitchcock himself, in a typically double-edged statement, said, "The first version is the work of a talented amateur and the second was made by a professional." It's the high-gloss professionalism—handsome location filming by Robert Burks [1537 . . .], thundering Bernard Herrmann [50 . . .] score, and Hollywood star performances—that many critics feel saps the suspense from the story. The remake is more than half an hour longer than the original, which also featured the first English-language performance of Peter Lorre.

The Livingston-Evans song, their third Oscar winner, is the subject of a frequently asked trivia question: What's the only song from a Hitchcock movie to win an Oscar? It was a huge hit on records and became Day's theme song.

Livingston: 344, 512, 951, 1522, 2001, 2278. Evans: 344, 512, 951, 1522, 2001, 2278.

1261 • MAN WHO SHOT LIBERTY VALANCE, THE

JOHN FORD PRODUCTION; PARAMOUNT. 1962.

NOMINATION *Black-and-White Costume Design:* Edith Head.

Timid easterner James Stewart [73 . . .] plans to set up a law practice in the West, but he's robbed and bullied by the outlaw Valance, played by Lee Marvin [371]. Stewart is befriended by John Wayne [33 . . .], however, who finally guns down Valance in a fight for which Stewart receives the credit. Stewart's celebrity as the man who . . . gains him respect and power, and he eventually become a U.S. senator. The film is framed by Senator Stewart's return to Shinbone for Wayne's funeral, occasioning a

confession to the local newspaper editor that Wayne was the one who deserved the credit. The editor's response is one of the movies' most famous catchphrases: "When the legend becomes fact, print the legend." One of the last westerns directed by John Ford [815 . . .], it has become one of the most critically celebrated—a sharp reversal from the reception at the time of its release, when many reviewers found it tedious and cliché-ridden. This was, it should be remembered, the heyday of the TV western, a period so saturated with gunfights and showdowns that it was easy to overlook Ford's ironic valedictory to the Old West, especially since *Liberty Valance* is visually one of the most uninteresting of the director's films; it's shot, by William Clothier [33 . . .], in black and white and largely on a soundstage—your typical episode of *Bonanza* has more visual rewards. Its virtues lie in its script, by James Warner Bellah and Willis Goldbeck, and its performances: Stewart and Wayne are unsurpassable, of course. (This is the film in which Wayne calls Stewart "Pilgrim.") Marvin's sneering villainy provides something for him to parody in his Oscar-winning performance in *Cat Ballou*. Edmond O'Brien [146 . . .] is an alcoholic newspaper editor, and a good contingent of Ford regulars—Andy Devine, Woody Strode, John Qualen, and John Carradine—shows up, along with Vera Miles, Strother Martin, and Lee Van Cleef. The film's sole nomination was the virtually obligatory annual one to Head, who lost to Norma Koch for *What Ever Happened to Baby Jane?*

Head: 31, 32, 46, 305, 357, 363, 612, 636, 675, 736, 832, 894, 945, 1003, 1219, 1263, 1398, 1427, 1504, 1550, 1579, 1587, 1631, 1716, 1727, 1738, 1748, 1840, 1927, 1986, 2012, 2098, 2247, 2298.

1262 • MAN WHO WALKED ALONE, THE

PRC. 1945.

NOMINATION *Scoring of a Dramatic or Comedy Picture:* Karl Hajos.

A returning serviceman's involvement with a rich woman lands him in trouble. Ephemeral little melodrama starring Dave "Tex" O'Brien, which gives you a clue to its star power. This was the last year for an open nominations policy instituted in 1937 to beef up Academy membership in a period when the Academy's conflict with the unions had caused membership to dwindle to virtually nothing. Individual studios were allowed to submit nominees in certain categories. In this scoring category alone, there were twenty-one entries. Like its fellow "poverty row" studios Monogram and Republic, PRC (short for Producers Releasing Corporation) took advantage of the Oscar nomination as a publicity gimmick, but never succeeded at the awards. This time the Oscar went to Miklos Rozsa for *Spellbound*.

Hajos: 1961.

1263 • MAN WHO WOULD BE KING, THE

ALLIED ARTISTS-COLUMBIA PICTURES PRODUCTION; ALLIED ARTISTS. 1975.

NOMINATIONS *Screenplay Adapted From Other Material:* John Huston and Gladys Hill. *Art Direction—Set Decoration:* Alexander Trauner and Tony Inglis; Peter James. *Film Editing:* Russell Lloyd. *Costume Design:* Edith Head.

British soldiers Sean Connery [2185] and Michael Caine [35 . . .] set out to make their fortunes in nineteenth-century India, Afghanistan, and Kafiristan. They succeed by passing off Connery as the reincarnated Alexander the Great, but that's when their problems start. Based on a Rudyard Kipling story, with Christopher Plummer as Kipling. Splendid, exciting, funny, with two great screen actors at their peak. Huston, who also directed, had wanted to make Kipling's story with Humphrey Bogart [24 . . .] and Clark Gable [798 . . .] but was never able to get the project off the ground while those actors were alive. The success of *Butch Cassidy and the Sundance Kid* and *The Sting* inspired Huston to dust off the project for Robert Redford and Paul Newman, but Newman balked at the notion of playing an Englishman. Fortunately Huston found the perfect team. The mystery is that neither Connery nor Caine was nominated. Instead the slate contained two lesser performances in forgotten movies: Maximilian Schell in *The Man in the Glass Booth* and James Whitmore in *Give 'Em Hell,*

Harry! The cinematography is by Oswald Morris [659 . . .] and the score by Maurice Jarre [558 . . .].

The writing award went to Lawrence Hauben and Bo Goldman for *One Flew Over the Cuckoo's Nest. Barry Lyndon* won for art direction and Ulla-Britt Soderlund and Milena Canonero's costumes. *Jaws* took the Oscar for Verna Fields' editing.

Huston: 24, 105, 356, 571, 891, 1248, 1363, 1625, 1779, 2136. Trauner: 91. James: 2340. Head: 31, 32, 46, 305, 357, 363, 612, 636, 675, 736, 832, 894, 945, 1003, 1219, 1261, 1398, 1427, 1504, 1550, 1579, 1587, 1631, 1716, 1727, 1738, 1748, 1840, 1927, 1986, 2012, 2098, 2247, 2298.

1264 • MAN WITH THE GOLDEN ARM, THE

OTTO PREMINGER PRODUCTIONS; UNITED ARTISTS. 1955.

NOMINATIONS *Actor:* Frank Sinatra. *Black-and-White Art Direction—Set Decoration:* Joseph C. Wright; Darrell Silvera. *Scoring of a Dramatic or Comedy Picture:* Elmer Bernstein.

Sinatra plays an ex-junkie who gets hooked again, with Eleanor Parker [328 . . .] as his wife, plus Kim Novak, Arnold Stang, Darren McGavin, and Robert Strauss. Time has filed the edge off this once-controversial melodrama, but Sinatra's performance still makes it watchable. Producer-director Otto Preminger [73 . . .], who had dared the censors with his film of *The Moon Is Blue* two years earlier, chopped another prop out from under film censorship when he decided to make the movie despite the Production Code's strictures against any depiction of drug use. It was released without the Code seal, but the Catholic Legion of Decency passed it—an inconsistency that showed how shaky the twenty-year-old system of insitutional self-censorship had become. The movie was a success at the box office. Walter Newman [198 . . .] and Lewis Meltzer adapted the novel by Nelson Algren. The jazz sequences by Shorty Rogers and Shelly Manne, and Saul Bass's hip, stylish title credits, also attracted attention.

In his second nomination, Sinatra lost to Ernest Borgnine as the mild-mannered butcher in *Marty*. The art direction Oscar went to *The Rose Tattoo*. Alfred Newman won for the score for *Love Is a Many-Splendored Thing*.

Sinatra: 732. Wright: 235, 428, 508, 569, 690, 746, 852, 1175, 1397, 1475, 2056. Silvera: 407, 632, 686, 1239, 1341, 1924. Bernstein: 27.5, 789, 882, 1242, 1685, 1959, 2064, 2101, 2130, 2147, 2223.

1265 • *MANCHURIAN CANDIDATE, THE*

M.C. PRODUCTION; UNITED ARTISTS. 1962.

NOMINATIONS *Supporting Actress:* Angela Lansbury. *Film Editing:* Ferris Webster.

Frank Sinatra [732 . . .] gradually uncovers a fiendish political assassination plot: Lansbury, mother of Korean War hero Laurence Harvey [1724], is maneuvering her right-wing husband, James Gregory, into the presidency, and as part of the plot, Harvey, Sinatra, and others had been brainwashed during captivity by the Chinese. Creepy, loopy, and sometimes very funny thriller, a real gem, based on a novel by Richard Condon [1625], adapted by George Axelrod [278], and directed by John Frankenheimer. The cast includes Janet Leigh [1632], Henry Silva, and John McGiver. The film was not a box-office success at the time of its release, and after the assassination of John F. Kennedy it was pulled from circulation, not to resurface until 1987. So far as we know, however, no conspiracy buffs have linked the film, or its suppression, to the JFK assassination, despite the coincidence of names: Laurence Harvey? Lee Harvey Oswald? (Hey, we're just kidding.)

Throughout much of her early career, Lansbury found herself cast as older women. Here, for example, at thirty-seven, she plays mother to Harvey, who was thirty-four. She lost this, her third nomination, to Patty Duke in *The Miracle Worker*. She wisely turned her attention to the stage, where she's a multiple Tony winner, acclaimed for her performances in *Mame, Gypsy,* and *Sweeney Todd*.

The editing Oscar went to Anne Coates for *Lawrence of Arabia*.

Lansbury: 749, 1567. Webster: 227, 819.

1266 • *MANDRAGOLA*

EUROPIX-CONSOLIDATED (FRANCE/ITALY). 1966.

NOMINATION *Black-and-White Costume Design:* Danilo Donati.

A wealthy man poses as a doctor and seduces the wife of a man seeking a cure for her infertility. Alberto Lattuada directs this handsomely designed version of the sixteenth-century comedy by Machiavelli. The cast includes Rosanna Schiaffino, Philippe Leroy, Totò, and Jean-Claude Brialy. The Oscar went to Irene Sharaff for *Who's Afraid of Virginia Woolf?*

Donati: 658, 809, 1722, 2000.

1267 • *MANHATTAN*

JACK ROLLINS AND CHARLES H. JOFFE PRODUCTION; UNITED ARTISTS. 1979.

NOMINATIONS *Supporting Actress:* Mariel Hemingway. *Screenplay Written Directly for the Screen:* Woody Allen and Marshall Brickman.

Allen plays a TV comedy writer involved with a teenager, played by Hemingway. This relationship is complicated when he meets Diane Keaton [88 . . .], who first annoys him with her intellectual pretentiousness but finally attracts him. Allen's first film after *Annie Hall* delighted the critics with its risk-taking May–December (or perhaps April–September) romance, its elegant black-and-white cinematography by the perennially unnominated Gordon Willis [786 . . .], and its all–George Gershwin [1797] score. It was not quite the crowd-pleaser that *Annie Hall* had been, however, and while it retains some passionate admirers who believe it's Allen's masterwork, others feel that its not much of an advance beyond the earlier film. The same themes—the love of New York, the protagonist's neuroses and sexual hang-ups, the lampooning of intellectual fads—dominate both movies. *Manhattan*'s excellent cast includes Michael Murphy, Wallace Shawn, and, as Allen's lesbian ex-wife, Meryl Streep [472 . . .].

Streep defeated Hemingway in the supporting actress competition with her role in *Kramer vs. Kramer*. Hemingway made her film debut in 1976 in *Lipstick*, which starred her sister, Margaux. Mariel was seventeen when she made *Manhattan* and landed leading roles in *Personal Best* (1982) and *Star 80* (1983). The box-office failure of both movies did nothing to advance her career, however, and she has been seen only occasionally in films since then.

The screenplay Oscar went to Steve Tesich for *Breaking Away.*

Allen: 39, 88, 294, 311.5, 461, 863, 962.5, 1005, 1636, 1647. Brickman: 88.

1268 • MANHATTAN MELODRAMA
COSMOPOLITAN; MGM. 1934.
AWARD *Original Story:* Arthur Caesar.

Two kids from the wrong side of the tracks grow up to become gangster Clark Gable [798 . . .] and District Attorney William Powell [1170 . . .]. Eventually Powell is forced to prosecute his old chum. The title says it all: This is a solid melodrama with fine star performances, including Myrna Loy as the woman both men love, the usual crisp, get-on-with-it direction of W. S. Van Dyke [1751 . . .], and the fine cinematography of James Wong Howe [1 . . .]. It also provided a couple of items for trivia buffs: It was the movie John Dillinger saw just before he was gunned down outside the theater, and the young Gable is played by Mickey Rooney [115 . . .].

Oliver H. P. Garrett and Joseph L. Mankiewicz [46 . . .] were credited with the screenplay from Caesar's story, which spawned other movies about kids who grow up to be on opposite sides of the law, including *Angels With Dirty Faces* and *Cry of the City* (1948).

1269 • MANHATTAN MERRY-GO-ROUND
REPUBLIC. 1937.
NOMINATION *Interior Decoration:* John Victor Mackay.

Gangster Leo Carrillo acquires a record company, providing a skeletal plot on which to hang a series of musical numbers by artists ranging from Cab Calloway to Gene Autry [1696], and taking in an appearance by Joe DiMaggio along the way. The cast includes Phil Regan, Ann Dvorak, and James Gleason [904]. Mackay probably owes his nomination to the Academy's desire to beef up its membership after a disastrous period when union members resigned from

it en masse. A rules change effective this year, and lasting through the 1947 awards, allowed each studio to submit a nominee in certain categories. Smaller studios such as Republic took advantage of the free publicity but seldom received Oscars. This time the award went to Stephen Goosson for *Lost Horizon.*

Mackay: 489, 1257.

1270 • MANNEQUIN
MGM. 1938.
NOMINATION *Song:* "Always and Always," music by Edward Ward, lyrics by Chet Forrest and Bob Wright.

Joan Crawford [1319 . . .] leaves her poor but sleazy husband, Alan Curtis, and makes a better life for herself by landing a job as a model and meeting rich guy Spencer Tracy [131 . . .]. Despite some grit and realism in its earlier scenes, this romantic drama winds up in the soap. A prime example of MGM in its gilded age, but mainly for Crawford fans. Directed by Frank Borzage [132 . . .]. The song Oscar went to "Thanks for the Memory," by Ralph Rainger and Leo Robin, from *Big Broadcast of 1938.*

Ward: 47, 388, 694, 1560, 2002. Forrest: 694, 1384. Wright: 694, 1384.

1271 • MANNEQUIN
GLADDEN ENTERTAINMENT PRODUCTION; 20TH CENTURY FOX. 1987.
NOMINATION *Song:* "Nothing's Gonna Stop Us Now," music and lyrics by Albert Hammond and Diane Warren.

Kim Cattrall is the spirit of an ancient Egyptian trapped in a department store dummy until window dresser Andrew McCarthy accidentally brings her to life. Witless romantic comedy, a rip-off of *One Touch of Venus* (1948), which at least had Ava Gardner [1339], Robert Walker, and songs by Kurt Weill [1105] and Ogden Nash. This one has some likable performers—James Spader, Estelle Getty, Meshach Taylor—but they can't save it. Directed by Michael Gottlieb. The song Oscar went to Franke Previte, John DeNicola, and Donald Markowitz for "(I've Had) The Time of My Life" from *Dirty Dancing.*

1272 • MARATHON MAN

ROBERT EVANS-SIDNEY BECKERMAN PRODUCTION; PARAMOUNT. 1976.

NOMINATION *Supporting Actor:* Laurence Olivier.

Graduate student Dustin Hoffman [810 . . .] accidentally becomes drawn into a conflict with Nazi war criminal Olivier, who has been hiding out in South America but comes to New York to retrieve a fortune in diamonds. The two leads, strongly supported by Roy Scheider [49 . . .], William Devane, and Fritz Weaver, keep this busy but badly constructed thriller interesting. The scene in which Olivier tortures Hoffman with a dentist's drill made "Is it safe?" a catchphrase of the day. Directed by John Schlesinger [493 . . .] from a screenplay William Goldman [54 . . .] adapted from his own novel.

The teaming of Olivier and Hoffman provides a demonstration of two schools of acting—British classicism and American naturalism—and shows that the end results can coexist. But it also provided a famous anecdote: Hoffman deprived himself of sleep for several nights before the torture scene, so that he would arrive on the set exhausted and edgy. Olivier, appalled at the condition of his costar, is said to have exclaimed, "Dear boy, wouldn't it be easier to *act?*" The Oscar went to Jason Robards for *All the President's Men.*

Olivier: 268, 619, 858, 901, 1506, 1670, 1693, 1841, 2316.

1273 • MARDI GRAS

JERRY WALD PRODUCTIONS INC.; 20TH CENTURY-FOX. 1958.

NOMINATION *Scoring of a Musical Picture:* Lionel Newman.

Military school student Pat Boone wins a date with movie star Christine Carere at Mardi Gras time in New Orleans. Forgettable attempt by Fox to turn the well-scrubbed Boone into a movie musical moneymaker as big as Elvis. It was the last film directed by Edmund Goulding, who never received an Oscar nomination, though he worked on such classics as *Grand Hotel* and *Dark Victory.* The Oscar went to André Previn for *Gigi.*

Newman: 183, 457, 557, 795, 896, 981, 1160, 1585, 1762, 2043.

1274 • MARIE ANTOINETTE

MGM. 1938.

NOMINATIONS *Actress:* Norma Shearer. *Supporting Actor:* Robert Morley. *Interior Decoration:* Cedric Gibbons. *Original Score:* Herbert Stothart.

Shearer plays the ill-fated queen of France in this long, long, expensive dud of a movie, now celebrated more as an example of MGM's extravagant golden age production values than for acting or storytelling. It was virtually a studio gift to Shearer, who as widow of production head Irving G. Thalberg [150 . . .] still had substantial clout—not to mention large stock holdings. In addition to Morley as Louis XVI, the cast includes Tyrone Power (on loan from 20th Century-Fox) as the romantic interest, the Swedish Count Axel de Fersen, John Barrymore as Louis XV, Gladys George [2192] as Madame DuBarry, and Anita Louise, Joseph Schildkraut [1169], Reginald Gardiner, Peter Bull, Cora Witherspoon, Joseph Calleia, Scotty Beckett, Henry Daniell, Mae Busch, and Barry Fitzgerald [787]. Directed by W. S. Van Dyke [1751 . . .] from a screenplay by Claudine West [804 . . .], Donald Ogden Stewart [1148 . . .], and Ernest Vajda based on a book by Stefan Zweig. The cinematography is by William Daniels [84 . . .] and the costumes by Adrian. All this opulence, however, has one rooting for the Revolution.

Shearer may have read the film's box-office failure as a signal that her career was heading toward an end. She made only five more films before retiring in 1942, marrying her ski instructor and spending the remaining forty-one years of her life as a whatever-happened-to item. The Oscar went to Bette Davis for *Jezebel.*

Morley made his film debut in a role that had been offered to Charles Laughton [1387 . . .]. He had made his stage debut in England in 1929 and scored his first big success in a play based on the life of Oscar Wilde. His performance in that part on Broadway in 1938 brought him to the attention of MGM. He continued to be a major character performer on both sides of the Atlantic, as well as writing plays, including *Edward My Son,* which was filmed in 1949. He died in 1992. The supporting actor Oscar went to Walter Brennan for *Kentucky.*

The Adventures of Robin Hood won for Carl J. Weyl's art direction and Erich Wolfgang Korngold's score.

Shearer: 150, 555, 723, 1721, 2038. Gibbons: 66, 87, 130, 217, 227, 239, 285, 290, 440, 629, 749, 831, 980, 1069, 1096, 1173, 1190, 1226, 1230, 1232, 1308, 1309, 1417, 1567, 1604, 1644, 1662, 1673, 1721, 1861, 1937, 2068, 2112, 2256, 2257, 2300, 2320, 2330. Stothart: 397, 1096, 1232, 1292, 1387, 1662, 1988, 2068, 2193, 2234, 2300.

1275 • MARIE-LOUISE

PRAESENS FILMS (SWITZERLAND). 1945.
AWARD *Original Screenplay:* Richard Schweizer.

The story of a young French girl, a wartime refugee in Switzerland, and her struggle to overcome her fears. Directed by Leopold Lindtberg. Schweizer, a Swiss screenwriter, was the first person to win an Oscar for the screenplay of a foreign language film. It has to be noted that the competition in the original screenplay category was composed of mostly forgotten movies: *Dillinger, Music for Millions, Salty O'Rourke,* and *What Next, Corporal Hargrove?* Schweizer's simple, sentimental story was aimed right at the hearts of postwar audiences, but the movie is almost unlocatable today.

Schweizer: 1771.

1276 • MARJORIE MORNINGSTAR

BEACHWOLD PICTURES; WARNER BROS. 1958.
NOMINATION *Song:* ''A Very Precious Love,'' music by Sammy Fain, lyrics by Paul Francis Webster.

Marjorie Morgenstern, played by Natalie Wood [1219 . . .], has the usual adolescent fantasies of stardom, which include changing her name. But after a fling with an older man, played by Gene Kelly [74], she settles for Martin Milner and suburbia. Muddled adaptation of a best-seller by Herman Wouk. Its dullness is surprising, considering its cast: Ed Wynn [542], Claire Trevor [510 . . .], Everett Sloane, Carolyn Jones [124], and Martin Balsam [2067]. Di-

rected by Irving Rapper. The Oscar went to Alan Jay Lerner and Frederick Loewe for the title song from *Gigi.*

Fain: 95, 331, 376, 856, 1213, 1681, 1925, 2014, 2214. Webster: 33, 64, 95, 331, 376, 604, 663, 730, 856, 1213, 1322, 1388, 1755, 1925, 2014.

1277 • MARK, THE

RAYMOND STROSS-SIDNEY BUCHMAN PRODUCTION; CONTINENTAL DISTRIBUTING INC. (UNITED KINGDOM). 1961.
NOMINATION *Actor:* Stuart Whitman.

Paroled after serving three years in prison for molesting a young girl, Whitman tries to start a new life in a town in the British Midlands with the aid of his psychiatrist, played by Rod Steiger [992 . . .]. He falls in love with Maria Schell, whose ten-year-old daughter reminds Whitman of the girl he molested, though he finds that he has overcome his old urges. But a reporter uncovers Whitman's identity and prints an exposé in the local newspaper. Somewhat formulaic, but well-handled and exceptionally well-acted problem drama, directed by Guy Green [820].

Whitman made his screen debut in bit parts in two sci-fi classics, *When Worlds Collide* and *The Day the Earth Stood Still,* in 1951, but though he has worked regularly in films and TV for more than forty years, he has never achieved major stardom. The Oscar went to Maximilian Schell for *Judgment at Nuremberg.*

1278 • MARK OF ZORRO, THE

20TH CENTURY-FOX. 1940.
NOMINATION *Original Score:* Alfred Newman.

Diego de Vega (Tyrone Power) comes home to California after studying in Spain and discovers that the people are under the thumb of tyranny. So he disguises himself as the masked bandit Zorro and sets out to restore freedom. Very enjoyable hokum, somewhat weakened by Power's lack of flash and dazzle, especially obvious when he faces Errol Flynn's old adversary Basil Rathbone [979 . . .] in the big duel. Director Rouben Mamoulian, designers Richard Day [22 . . .] and Joseph C. Wright [235 . . .], and cinematographer Arthur Miller [83 . . .] give the whole thing a great look. The cast includes Linda

Darnell, Gale Sondergaard [83 . . .], and Eugene Pallette. All the many versions of Zorro—it was filmed in 1920 by Douglas Fairbanks and later turned into a TV series by Disney—stem from a story, "The Curse of Capistrano," by Johnston McCulley. The script for this one is by John Tainton Foote, Garrett Fort, and Bess Meredyth [2303.5 . . .]. Newman's score lost to Leigh Harline, Paul J. Smith, and Ned Washington's for *Pinocchio.*

Newman: 31, 34, 46, 72, 138, 182, 226, 333, 334, 347, 375, 428, 437, 457, 476, 495, 542, 690, 797, 833, 952, 953, 959, 962, 1016, 1082, 1088, 1213, 1362, 1397, 1475, 1616, 1655, 1849, 1868, 1883, 1921, 2043, 2046, 2091, 2258, 2286, 2294, 2316.

1279 • MAROONED

Frankovich-Sturges Production; Columbia. 1969.

Award *Special Visual Effects:* Robbie Robertson.

Nominations *Cinematography:* Daniel Fapp. *Sound:* Les Fresholtz and Arthur Piantadosi.

Astronauts Gene Hackman [255 . . .], James Franciscus, and Richard Crenna are stranded when a rocket malfunctions. Gregory Peck [759 . . .] is the mission control guy in charge of getting them home. Meanwhile, wives Lee Grant [534 . . .], Nancy Kovack, and Mariette Hartley agonize on earth as astronaut David Janssen tries to rig up a rescue operation. What could have been a plausible thriller falls short because of a cliché-clotted script by Mayo Simon from Martin Caidin's novel. Director John Sturges [131], who handled earthbound action well in *The Great Escape* and *The Magnificent Seven,* doesn't seem to know how to give this one the pace it needs. The winning special effects are the main show. The cinematography Oscar went to Conrad Hall for *Butch Cassidy and the Sundance Kid. Hello, Dolly!* took the award for sound.

Fapp: 529, 675, 978, 1492, 2184, 2244. Fresholtz: 54, 58, 209, 215, 606, 888, 1127, 1526, 2113. Piantadosi: 54, 58, 215, 319, 606, 2113.

1280 • MARRIAGE ITALIAN STYLE

C.C. Champion-Les Films Concordia Production; Embassy Pictures Corporation (France/Italy). 1964.

Nominations *Actress:* Sophia Loren. *Foreign Language Film.* (1965)

Hearing that his mistress, Loren, is dying, Marcello Mastroianni [490 . . .] hurries to her bedside, where they recall their life together. He agrees to honor her dying wish, that they be married, only to discover afterward that she's tricked him: She's not dying at all, but wanted to prevent him from marrying a younger woman. He has the marriage annulled, but Loren has a card or two left up her sleeve . . . Deliciously vulgar little comedy, directed by Vittorio De Sica [650], that's a perfect vehicle for its stars. The cast includes Pia Lindstrom, daughter of Ingrid Bergman [72 . . .]. Loren lost to Julie Andrews in *Mary Poppins.* A year later the movie was Italy's entry in the foreign language film category. The foreign film award has a different set of rules from the other categories, requiring a nomination by the country in which it was produced. It lost to *The Shop on Main Street.*

Loren: 2167.

1281 • MARRIED TO THE MOB

Mysterious Arts-Demme Production; Orion. 1988.

Nomination *Supporting Actor:* Dean Stockwell.

When her Mafioso husband (Alec Baldwin) is rubbed out for fooling around with the mistress of mob boss Stockwell, Michelle Pfeiffer [485 . . .] decides it's time to make a new life for herself and her young son, especially since Stockwell starts coming on to her at the funeral, attracting the notice of his wife, Mercedes Ruehl [671]. But divorce from the mob isn't easy, what with Stockwell's persistent attentions, Ruehl's jealous interference, and the attempts of FBI agent Matthew Modine to use Pfeiffer to get the goods on Stockwell. Wonderfully loopy comedy, written by Barry Strugatz and Mark R. Burns and directed by Jonathan Demme [1820], who gets top-notch performances from everyone. The score is by David Byrne [1136], the production design by Kristi Zea, and the cinematography by Tak Fujimoto. The cast also includes Joan Cusack [2313], Nancy Travis, and, in a bit as a hit man, rocker Chris Isaak.

Stockwell is in his sixth decade as a movie actor. Born in Hollywood (his father, an actor, was the voice for Prince Charming in *Snow White and the Seven Dwarfs*), he made his debut at nine in *Anchors Aweigh* and was a leading child star, with appearances in such films as *The Green Years, Gentleman's Agreement, The Boy With Green Hair* (1948), and *Kim* (1950). With adolescence, he disappeared from the screen but returned in his twenties as a handsome young leading man, best known for his work as "sensitive" types in *Compulsion* (1959), *Sons and Lovers,* and *Long Day's Journey Into Night*. In the later sixties and the seventies, he again dropped out of mainstream movies and supported himself primarily by selling real estate. But he surfaced as a major character actor in the eighties, most memorably in *Blue Velvet* and his nominated role. The Oscar went to Kevin Kline for *A Fish Called Wanda*.

1282 • MARTIN LUTHER

LUTHERAN CHURCH PRODUCTIONS AND LUTHER-FILM GMBH; LOUIS DE ROCHEMONT ASSOCIATES. 1953.

NOMINATIONS *Black-and-White Cinematography:* Joseph C. Brun. *Black-and-White Art Direction—Set Decoration:* Fritz Maurischat and Paul Markwitz.

Niall MacGinnis plays the cleric who sparked the Reformation in this biography partly produced by the Lutheran church. Directed by Irving Pichel. The cinematography Oscar went to Burnett Guffey for *From Here to Eternity*. *Julius Caesar* took the award for art direction.

1283 • MARTY

HECHT AND LANCASTER'S STEVEN PRODUCTIONS; UNITED ARTISTS. 1955.

AWARDS *Picture:* Harold Hecht, producer. *Actor:* Ernest Borgnine. *Director:* Delbert Mann. *Screenplay:* Paddy Chayefsky.

NOMINATIONS *Supporting Actor:* Joe Mantell. *Supporting Actress:* Betsy Blair. *Black-and-White Cinematography:* Joseph LaShelle. *Black-and-White Art Direction—Set Deco-*

ration: Edward S. Haworth and Walter Simonds; Robert Priestley.

Homely, middle-aged Marty (Borgnine) usually pals around with Angie (Mantell) and the other guys because he's too shy to chase girls. Then he happens to meet Clara (Blair), who's just as timid as he is. Sweet-natured little sleeper hit that's probably the most unassuming movie ever to win the best picture award—as well as the shortest (ninety-one minutes). Today *Marty*'s sentimentalizing of the common man has lost its appeal, and among the movies of 1955, the other nominees for best picture—*Love Is a Many-Splendored Thing, Mister Roberts, Picnic,* and *The Rose Tattoo*—and such nonnominees as *Rebel Without a Cause, Bad Day at Black Rock, East of Eden,* and *Blackboard Jungle* have a stronger hold on our affections. But its triumph at the Oscars is something of a Hollywood milestone. For one thing, it was a movie that began life as a TV drama—the small-screen version starred Rod Steiger [992 . . .]—signaling a new accommodation of Hollywood with the medium that it saw as its biggest threat. For another, the studio that released it, United Artists, had won only one best picture Oscar before, and that was for *Rebecca,* produced by David O. Selznick [497 . . .] when he was on top of the world. As the power of the major studios—MGM, Fox, Paramount, Warners—waned over the next decade, UA would emerge as a major force, winning more best picture Oscars in the sixties than any other releasing organization. But *Marty* certainly didn't signal a turn to intimate dramas about the little people: The following year the awards would be dominated by such opulent superproductions as *Giant, The Ten Commandments,* and *Around the World in 80 Days*.

Hecht was a former dancer who had been a member of the Martha Graham company and had come to Hollywood in the thirties as a choreographer at Paramount. He became an agent and discovered Burt Lancaster [107 . . .], with whom he formed an independent production company in the late forties. Hecht died in 1985.

Squat, gap-toothed Borgnine studied acting after being discharged from the navy after World War II and made his film debut in 1951. His breakthrough role was the sadistic Sgt. Fatso Judson in *From Here to Eternity*, and he came close to being typed as a villain until he was cast in *Marty*. This succession of lucky breaks established Borgnine in Hollywood, but he's never had another Oscar-caliber role.

Mann likewise benefited from the lucky accident that was *Marty*, triumphing in his first major film directing assignment over such veterans as Elia Kazan *(East of Eden)*, David Lean *(Summertime)*, Joshua Logan *(Picnic)*, and John Sturges *(Bad Day at Black Rock)*. He began his directing career in television, including the original TV version of *Marty*. His subsequent film work is competent but undistinguished.

Before World War II, Chayefsky did a turn as a stand-up comedian but began writing plays after the war, finding a hungry market in the new medium of TV. From his early slice-of-life works such as *Marty, The Catered Affair* (1956), and *The Bachelor Party*, he moved to more satiric works, such as *The Goddess, The Americanization of Emily, Network,* and *The Hospital*.

Like many supporting performers, Mantell slipped back into obscurity after the one perfect role. He lost to Jack Lemmon in *Mister Roberts*. Blair, who was married to Gene Kelly [74] at the time of *Marty*, likewise found no suitable parts after her nomination. She moved to Europe in the later fifties and made a few appearances in foreign films. The Oscar went to Jo Van Fleet for *East of Eden*.

The Rose Tattoo won the awards for James Wong Howe's cinematography and for art direction.

Hecht: 1778. Chayefsky: 783, 942, 1424. LaShelle: 91, 357, 428, 709, 953, 1017, 1149, 1391. Haworth: 1201, 1550, 1763, 1860, 2247. Priestley: 1566, 1763.

1284 • MARY POPPINS

WALT DISNEY PRODUCTIONS; BUENA VISTA. 1964.

AWARDS *Actress:* Julie Andrews. *Song:* "Chim Chim Cher-ee," music and lyrics by Richard M. Sherman and Robert B. Sherman. *Music Score—Substantially Original:* Richard M. Sherman and Robert B. Sherman. *Film Editing:* Cotton Warburton. *Special Visual Effects:* Peter Ellenshaw, Hamilton Luske, and Eustace Lycett.

NOMINATIONS *Picture:* Walt Disney and Bill Walsh, producers. *Director:* Robert Stevenson. *Screenplay—Based on Material From Another Medium:* Bill Walsh and Don DaGradi. *Color Cinematography:* Edward Colman. *Color Art Direction–Set Decoration:* Carroll Clark and William H. Tuntke; Emile Kuri and Hal Gausman. *Sound:* Robert O. Cook, sound director, Walt Disney Studio Sound Department. *Scoring of Music—Adaptation or Treatment:* Irwin Kostal. *Color Costume Design:* Tony Walton.

Mary Poppins (Andrews) arrives with a change of the wind to serve as nanny for the mischievous Banks children. In addition to setting young Jane and Michael in order, she manages to take some of the starch out of their stuffed-shirt father (David Tomlinson) and focus the attention of their scatterbrained mother, played by Glynis Johns [1969]. The cast also includes Dick Van Dyke, Hermione Baddeley [1724], Elsa Lanchester [428 . . .], Ed Wynn [542], Jane Darwell [815], Arthur Treacher, Reginald Owen, Reta Shaw, and Arthur Malet. Charming if slightly overextended musical, based on the children's books of P. L. Travers. It has become one of the movies' best-loved classics, but recapturing its charm has eluded subsequent imitators. Producers have given us numerous thundering dud fantasy musicals, ranging from *Doctor Dolittle* to the Disney studios' own *Bedknobs and Broomsticks,* which reunited many members of the creative team that produced *Mary Poppins*.

Andrews' Oscar was seen by many as a consolation prize for the slight she received from Warner Bros., which bypassed her in casting the film version of *My Fair Lady* and gave the role of Liza Doolittle, which Andrews had created on Broadway, to Audrey Hepburn. The Disney studios had considered Bette Davis [46 . . .] and Mary Martin for the role of Mary Poppins before settling on Andrews, whom Disney himself had seen in *Camelot* on Broadway. Born to British stage performers, Andrews began appearing on stage as a child. Her role in a New York company of the musical *The Boy Friend* led to *My Fair Lady* and stardom. But the hits of *Mary Poppins* and *The Sound of*

Music, in which she played another cheerful governess, limited her career, typing her as a purveyor of spoonfuls of sugar, and the decline of the film musical provided her with few opportunities to do what she does best.

The Sherman brothers, sons of songwriter Al Sherman, came to the attention of Disney when they wrote songs recorded by Mouseketeer Annette Funicello in the late fifties. They were hired by the studios and contributed to a string of its films through the sixties before going freelance in the seventies. They also worked as screenwriters on such films as *The Slipper and the Rose.*

Receiving a Golden Globe Award for *Mary Poppins,* Andrews had joked by thanking "the man who made all this possible, Jack Warner." But Warner got his own last laugh: *My Fair Lady* was a spoiler in most of the other categories for which *Mary Poppins* was nominated, taking Oscars for best picture, director George Cukor, cinematographer Harry Stradling, art directors Gene Allen, Cecil Beaton, and George James Hopkins, sound director George Groves, music adapter André Previn, and costume designer Beaton. The award for screenplay went to Edward Anhalt for *Becket.*

Andrews: 1881, 2201. R. M. Sherman: 166, 396, 1238, 1842, 2107. R. B. Sherman: 166, 396, 1238, 1842, 2107. Warburton: 459. Ellenshaw: 166, 219, 1022. Lycett: 4, 166, 219. Disney: 645, 1851. Colman: 4. Clark: 4, 481, 686, 754, 1924, 2115. Tuntke: 77. Kuri: 4, 166, 363, 629, 894, 1823, 2155. Gausman: 4, 166, 1022, 2185. Cook: 254, 1529. Kostal: 166, 1557, 1881, 2244. Walton: 49, 1379, 2299.

1285 • *MARY, QUEEN OF SCOTS*

HAL B. WALLIS-UNIVERSAL PICTURES LTD. PRODUCTION; UNIVERSAL (UNITED KINGDOM). 1971.
NOMINATIONS *Actress:* Vanessa Redgrave. *Art Direction—Set Decoration:* Terence Marsh and Robert Cartwright; Peter Howitt. *Sound:* Bob Jones and John Aldred. *Original Dramatic Score:* John Barry. *Costume Design:* Margaret Furse.

The ill-fated Queen Mary (Redgrave) is out-

matched in the Tudor power game by Elizabeth I, played by Glenda Jackson [893 . . .]. Plodding pageant, produced by Hal Wallis [17 . . .], who seems to have had a thing for English history: He gave us *Becket* and *Anne of the Thousand Days,* too. What fun there is to be had comes from seeing the two best English actresses of their day going at it. Historians say that Mary and Elizabeth never met, but that doesn't stop screenwriter John Hale [85] from imagining what might have happened if they did. Directed by Charles Jarrott, with Patrick McGoohan, Timothy Dalton, Trevor Howard [1875], Daniel Massey [1907], and Ian Holm [386].

Redgrave lost to Jane Fonda in *Klute.* The art direction Oscar went to *Nicholas and Alexandra,* which also won for Yvonne Black and Antonio Castillo's costumes. *Fiddler on the Roof* won for sound. The scoring award went to Michel Legrand for *Summer of '42.*

Redgrave: 263, 954.5, 1021, 1066, 1354. Marsh: 558, 1471, 1766. Cartwright: 164, 608, 1766. Howitt: 995, 1651, 2274. Aldred: 85. Barry: 259, 382.5, 482, 1177, 1512. Furse: 85, 164, 1177, 1374, 1766.

1285.5 • *MARY SHELLEY'S FRANKENSTEIN*

TRISTAR PICTURES PRODUCTION; TRISTAR. 1994.
NOMINATION *Makeup:* Daniel Parker, Paul Engelen and Carol Hemming.

Kenneth Branagh [902] plays Victor Frankenstein, the scientist who makes a monster, played by Robert De Niro [113 . . .], in this version of Mary Shelley's novel. Designed by its producer, Francis Ford Coppola [65 . . .], as a companion piece to his *Bram Stoker's Dracula,* it has the flaws of that film, including awkward efforts to give the material a contemporary psychological and thematic spin as well as a willingness to indulge in excessive blood and guts. Both films also attempt to humanize their monsters more than the Universal horror movies of the early thirties did, but the melodrama of the story and treatment overwhelm these efforts. De Niro is interesting to watch, but as both actor and director, Branagh trips and falls as he goes over the top. The supporting cast includes Tom Hulce [60], Helena Bonham Carter, Aidan

Quinn, Ian Holm [386], and an almost unrecognizable John Cleese [670] as a German professor. The screenplay is by Steph Lady and Frank Darabont [1802.5], and the cinematography by Roger Pratt. The makeup Oscar went to Rick Baker, Ve Neill, and Yolanda Toussieng for *Ed Wood.*

Engelen: 839.

1286 • *MASH*

ASPEN PRODUCTIONS; 20TH CENTURY-FOX. 1970.
AWARD *Screenplay—Based on Material From Another Medium:* Ring Lardner, Jr.
NOMINATIONS *Picture:* Ingo Preminger, producer. *Supporting Actress:* Sally Kellerman. *Director:* Robert Altman. *Film Editing:* Danford B. Greene.

Rebellious doctors at a Mobile Army Surgical Hospital during the Korean War do battle with the military bureaucracy while trying to save lives. Uproarious and truly subversive film—despite its setting, the film was clearly more about Vietnam than Korea—that revolutionized movie comedy with its hip attitudes, its blending of farce with violence, and its wildly overlapping dialogue. Seen today, some of the sexist, frat-boy humor is a little too grating, and some bad movies resulted from imitating *MASH*'s attitudes, such as the *Porky's* and *Police Academy* series. The fine cast includes Donald Sutherland as Hawkeye, Elliott Gould [250] as Trapper John, and Tom Skerritt as Duke, the three principal pranksters. Robert Duvall [92 . . .] as the pious Major Burns and Kellerman as Maj. "Hotlips" Houlihan are their prime targets. The great popular success of *MASH* made it impossible for the Academy to ignore, even though the old guard, especially Fox head Darryl F. Zanuck [34 . . .], considered director Altman a difficult maverick. Hollywood could hardly ignore the signals that had been sent by the success of films like *Bonnie and Clyde, The Graduate,* and *Easy Rider* that the new moviegoing generation was on the lookout for movies that seemed relevant to their lives. But the membership of the Academy was made up of the survivors of the studio era, practitioners of polished craftsmanship that the new filmmakers—admirers of the spontaneous, the natural, the rough-hewn—seemed to scorn. So *MASH*

was not nominated in some categories where it was most revolutionary—sound, for example, or the cinematography of Harold E. Stine [1596].

And the one Oscar *MASH* received was something of a backhanded compliment: Lardner's screenplay, based on a novel by Richard Hooker, was only a framework for Altman's free, improvisatory style. Lardner himself resented Altman's hogging the credit for the movie and ignored him in his acceptance speech. Then fifty-five, Lardner had grown up in the Hollywood of the studio era and won his previous Oscar in 1942 for *Woman of the Year.* But he also had credentials as a maverick: One of the Hollywood Ten, convicted of contempt of Congress for his refusal to testify about membership in the Communist Party before the House Un-American Activities Committee in 1949, he served a year in prison and was blacklisted through the fifties. He had reemerged in 1965 with a well-received script for *The Cincinnati Kid.* The Oscar for *MASH,* however, did not signal the start of a new phase in Lardner's career.

The best picture Oscar went to *Patton,* another portrait of the arrogance of military power, but one so subtle that it had plenty of admirers among the Vietnam hawks, including Richard Nixon. *MASH* producer Preminger is the brother of producer-director Otto Preminger [73 . . .].

Kellerman made her film debut in a grade-Z movie, *Reform School Girl,* in 1957, and found few good roles until *MASH.* She played leads for a few years afterward but gradually moved into the ranks of character players. The Oscar went to Helen Hayes for *Airport.*

MASH was a breakthrough film for Altman, at the age of forty-five. He started his career making industrial films in Kansas City and moved into television. His first Hollywood films, *Countdown* (1968) and *That Cold Day in the Park* (1969), were little seen, so *MASH* took everyone by surprise with its lively, improvisatory style—including, it is said, the film's stars, Sutherland and Gould, who wanted Altman replaced because they thought he didn't know what he was doing. Altman's post-*MASH* career has been full of ups and very long downs, and the Oscar has continued to elude him. This time it went to Franklin J. Schaffner for *Patton,* which also won for Hugh S. Fowler's editing.

Lardner: 2305. Altman: 1415, 1584.5, 1817.5. Greene: 230.

1287 • MASK

UNIVERSAL PICTURES PRODUCTION; UNIVERSAL. 1985.
AWARD *Makeup:* Michael Westmore and Zoltan Elek.

Eric Stoltz plays Rocky Dennis, a teenager disfigured by a rare bone disease, who survives because his mother, played by Cher [1351 . . .], has taught him self-esteem. Entertaining and often very moving film that rises above its disease-of-the-week genre (it's based on a true story) because of a strong script by Anna Hamilton Phelan [808] and fine performances by Stoltz, Sam Elliott as Cher's biker boyfriend, Laura Dern [1659] as a blind girl who befriends Rocky, and especially Cher, who won the best actress award at Cannes and was considered a sure thing for an Oscar nomination. Failing that, she nevertheless agreed to be a presenter at the Oscars and showed up in a hilariously outlandish getup designed by Bob Mackie [738 . . .] to hand a bemused Don Ameche his award for *Cocoon. Mask* was directed by Peter Bogdanovich [1139], and though it is his most successful film of recent years, the success was marred by his battles with Universal over the music track. Bogdanovich wanted songs by Bruce Springsteen [1562.5], but the studio was unwilling to pay the royalties and forced him to settle for Bob Seger [189] instead.

Westmore: 409, 2165.

1287.5 • MASK, THE

KATJA MOTION PICTURE PRODUCTION; NEW LINE. 1994.
NOMINATION *Visual Effects:* Scott Squires, Steve Williams, Tom Bertino and John Farhat.

Jim Carrey is Stanley Ipkiss, a meek bank clerk terrorized by his boss and his landlady until he discovers an ancient mask with magical powers: It transforms him into a superbeing able to mold his body into all sorts of fantastical shapes, and gives him a prankish personality to match. As a result, he's able to foil the plots of a gangster (Peter Greene), and win the affections of the gangster's moll-with-a-heart-of-gold (Cameron Diaz). Lively, very entertaining comic book adventure with great visual inventiveness. It's the best of the three 1994 films—the others were *Ace Ventura, Pet Detective* and *Dumb and Dumber*—that made Carrey a superstar. His comic plasticity is perfectly keyed to the special effects that allow him to do the impossible, and the makeup by Greg Cannom [272.5 . . .] smartly exaggerates Carrey's features without hindering the actor's own ability to distort them. The cast, directed by Charles Russell, includes Richard Jeni, Peter Riegert, and a very gifted dog named Max. The special effects award went to *Forrest Gump.*

1288 • MATEWAN

RED DOG FILMS PRODUCTION; CINECOM PICTURES. 1987.
NOMINATION *Cinematography:* Haskell Wexler.

A strike by miners in Matewan, West Virginia, in the twenties against appalling conditions in the coal mines ends in disaster. Powerful drama written and directed by John Sayles [1533.5], with Chris Cooper, Mary McDonnell [482 . . .], and James Earl Jones [830]. The Oscar went to Vittorio Storaro for *The Last Emperor.*

Wexler: 229, 264, 1481, 2277.

1289 • MATING SEASON, THE

PARAMOUNT. 1951.
NOMINATION *Supporting Actress:* Thelma Ritter.

Hardworking and ambitious John Lund marries Gene Tierney [1153], the daughter of an ambassador. Ritter, Lund's working-class mother, who has been forced to sell her hamburger joint, shows up to meet her daughter-in-law just as the newlyweds are throwing a Very Important Party. Tierney mistakes Ritter for the cook and presses her into service. For reasons that make sense only in the movies, Lund and Ritter decide to continue the deception until Miriam Hopkins [165], Tierney's snobbish harpy of a mother, precipitates a disclosure. A story with overtones of soap opera (compare *Stella Dallas)* is played for laughs in this script by Walter Reisch [435 . . .], Richard Breen [350 . . .], and Charles Brackett [705 . . .], directed by Mitchell Leisen [587]. The result is surprisingly entertaining, though Lund and Tierney are uncharismatic as the supposed leads. He is dull and puffy-looking, and she is unflatteringly photographed by Charles Lang [97 . . .], who manages to emphasize her overbite. The secret of the film's success is Ritter, in one of her best performances. This was the second of her six unsuccessful nominations. This time she lost to Kim Hunter in *A Streetcar Named Desire*.

Ritter: 46, 210, 1564, 1572, 2294.

1290 • MAURICE
MERCHANT IVORY PRODUCTIONS; CINECOM PICTURES (UNITED KINGDOM). 1987.
NOMINATION *Costume Design:* Jenny Beavan and John Bright.

James Wilby plays the title role, a middle-class Cambridge undergraduate who's had a long, physically unconsummated relationship with an upper-class friend, Clive (Hugh Grant). But then he has a physical relationship with Clive's gamekeeper, Scudder (Rupert Graves), and has to come to terms with the problem of being gay in Edwardian England. Handsome version of the novel by E. M. Forster, produced by Ismail Merchant [954.5 . . .] and directed by James Ivory [954.5 . . .]; the latter collaborated on the screenplay with Kit Hesketh-Harvey. It's one of Forster's weakest novels—it was not published during his lifetime, though more because of the strictures against homosexuality than because of its quality— and the film is a little too glossy and earnest. The cast includes Billie Whitelaw, Denholm Elliott [1725], Simon Callow, and Ben Kingsley [308 . . .]. The Oscar went to James Acheson for *The Last Emperor*.

Beavan: 263, 954.5, 1679.5, 1725. Bright: 263, 954.5, 1679.5, 1725.

1290.5 • MAVERICK
ICON PRODUCTION; WARNER BROS. 1994.
NOMINATION *Costume Design:* April Ferry.

Mel Gibson plays Bret Maverick, an easygoing gambler-con artist whose chief goal is to win enough money to enter a poker game being staged by the Commodore (James Coburn) on a riverboat at St.

Louis. But first he has to outwit his opponents, who include the flirtatious Annabelle, played by Jodie Foster [7 . . .], and a lawman, Zane Cooper, played by James Garner [1380]. Of course, the plot takes a few twists as each of the principals tries to out-con the others. Larky, likable Western spoof that's sometimes over-frantic, as are many of the films of its director, Richard Donner. (There are several in-jokey references to his earlier movies, including cameos by Danny Glover from the *Lethal Weapon* movies and Margot Kidder from *Superman*.) Fortunately, Gibson and Garner are great fun to watch, and it's a delight to see Foster take a break from serious roles. Graham Greene [482] does an amusing bit that parodies his role in *Dances With Wolves*. The screenplay by William Goldman [54 . . .] is based on the late-fifties TV series that made Garner a star. The cinematography is by Vilmos Zsigmond [416 . . .] and the music by Randy Newman [112 . . .]. The costuming Oscar went to Lizzy Gardiner and Tim Chappel for *The Adventures of Priscilla, Queen of the Desert*.

1291 • MAYOR OF 44TH STREET, THE
RKO RADIO. 1942.
NOMINATION *Song:* "There's a Breeze on Lake Louise," music by Harry Revel, lyrics by Mort Greene.

Hoods bilk dance bands in a protection racket in this thin gangster drama/musical. It has a pretty good cast—George Murphy, Anne Shirley [1923], Richard Barthelmess [1447 . . .], William Gargan [2045], Mary Wickes, and Freddie Martin and his orchestra —but not much else. Directed by Alfred E. Green. Revel and Greene's song lost to Irving Berlin's "White Christmas," from *Holiday Inn*.

Revel: 1322.

1292 • MAYTIME
MGM. 1937.
NOMINATIONS *Sound Recording:* Douglas Shearer. *Score:* MGM Studio Music Department, Nat W. Finston, head; score by Herbert Stothart.

Opera singer Jeanette MacDonald loves Nelson Eddy, but she marries impresario John Barrymore. Bad mistake. Still, it resulted in one of MacDonald and Eddy's best musicals. The screenplay by Noel Langley is loosely based on an operetta by Sigmund Romberg, but most of Romberg's music was discarded and a variety of songs from other sources interpolated. There's a big, bad opera sequence based on themes from Tchaikovsky's Fifth Symphony with lyrics by Bob Wright [694 . . .] and Chet Forrest [694 . . .]. Directed by Robert Z. Leonard [555 . . .]. The Oscar for sound went to Thomas Moulton for *The Hurricane*. Charles Previn won for the score of *One Hundred Men and a Girl*.

Shearer: 136, 202, 256, 397, 685, 817, 835, 1096, 1232, 1371, 1419, 1751, 1950, 1988, 2048, 2055, 2211, 2300. Finston: 1387. Stothart: 397, 1096, 1232, 1274, 1387, 1662, 1988, 2068, 2193, 2234, 2300.

1293 • MCCABE AND MRS. MILLER

ROBERT ALTMAN-DAVID FOSTER PRODUCTION; WARNER BROS. 1971.

NOMINATION *Actress:* Julie Christie.

Roguish drifter McCabe, played by Warren Beatty [255 . . .] becomes a brothel keeper in a mining town; Mrs. Miller (Christie) is the madam. Episodic fantasia on western themes, written by Robert Altman [1286 . . .] and Brian McKay (with substantial help from Beatty) and directed by Altman (with substantial help from Beatty, though there were some substantial ego clashes along the way). Altman's Old West is a muddy, messy place full of eccentrics drawn from the director's large supply of regulars—Rene Auberjonois, John Schuck, Bert Remsen, Keith Carradine [1415], Shelley Duvall, Michael Murphy. The ocher-toned images are supplied by Vilmos Zsigmond [416 . . .]. The Academy, as usual, didn't know what to make of Altman's work. Christie lost to Jane Fonda in *Klute*.

Christie: 493.

1294 • MEDAL FOR BENNY, A

PARAMOUNT. 1945.

NOMINATIONS *Supporting Actor:* J. Carrol Naish. *Original Story:* John Steinbeck and Jack Wagner.

Naish plays the father of a young man who has always been scorned by the citizens of a small town, but when they learn that he is to be posthumously awarded the Congressional Medal of Honor, they rush to cash in on the media attention. Nicely done little satire, with Dorothy Lamour and Arturo de Cordova, directed by Irving Pichel.

Naish, who was of Irish descent, became a ubiquitous character actor in ethnic roles because he was small, dark, and had a gift for accents. But because he didn't fit the Hollywood stereotype for his own ethnicity, he never played Irishmen. He lost to James Dunn in *A Tree Grows in Brooklyn*.

The story by Steinbeck and Wagner was adapted for the screen by Frank Butler [787 . . .]. The Oscar went to Charles G. Booth for *The House on 92nd Street*.

Naish: 1740. Steinbeck: 1171, 2212.

1295 • MEDITERRANEO

PENTAFILM S.p.A./A.M.A. FILM S.r.l. PRODUCTION (ITALY). 1991.

AWARD *Foreign Language Film, 1991.*

Italian soldiers, stranded on a Greek island, make the best advantage of the fact that the local men are off fighting World War II. Directed by Gabriele Salvatores. A thin but handsomely filmed comedy whose triumph over the very highly regarded *Raise the Red Lantern* by the Chinese director Zhang Yimou raised a small storm of controversy. The foreign language film Oscar is voted on by only those members of the Academy who can certify that they have seen all five nominees. This results in a significant amount of logrolling by those producers and distributors that can bankroll publicity campaigns among the handful of qualifying members.

1296 • MEDIUM, THE

TRANSFILM; LOPERT FILMS (ITALY). 1952.

NOMINATION *Scoring of a Musical Picture:* Gian-Carlo Menotti.

Marie Powers plays a fake clairvoyant who, in the throes of an unexpectedly real encounter with spirits, accidentally kills her assistant, a mute (Leo Coleman). Fourteen-year-old Anna Maria Alberghetti makes her film debut as the girl who boards in the medium's apartment. Eerie filming of the opera by Menotti, who also directed. Though the film was made in Rome, the libretto was written and is sung in English. Menotti was one of the few opera composers of the latter half of the twentieth century to achieve widespread popular success, in part because of his willingness to explore new media such as the movies and, in the case of his most famous work, *Amahl and the Night Visitors,* television. The Oscar went to Alfred Newman for the score of *With a Song in My Heart.*

1297 • *MEET JOHN DOE*

FRANK CAPRA; WARNER BROS. 1941.

NOMINATION *Original Story:* Richard Connell and Robert Presnell.

Journalist Barbara Stanwyck [138 . . .] concocts a publicity stunt for her paper: She plants a letter to the editor from "John Doe," who says he's so disgusted with political corruption that he's going to commit suicide by jumping from the roof of City Hall. When the public's interest is excited, the paper needs to find a real John Doe, so they hire a homeless man, played by Gary Cooper [701 . . .]. The paper's right-wing publisher, played by Edward Arnold, gets into the act, turning John Doe into a figurehead for his fascist movement. But Cooper realizes how far things have gone and decides that the only way to stop it is really to commit suicide. This promising satire goes awry because its director, Frank Capra [1025 . . .], and screenwriter, Robert Riskin [905 . . .], couldn't figure out how to end it. Several versions were previewed, including one in which Cooper actually kills himself, before Capra settled on one in which "the people" persuade Cooper not to go through with it. The political satire also goes awry —sometimes the film seems to be on the side of the common man, at other times it seems to be treating the common man as a mindless dope. Often grouped with *Mr. Deeds Goes to Town* and *Mr. Smith Goes to Washington* as Capra's trilogy about American rugged individuals, it's the least successful of the three, despite a strong cast that also includes Walter Brennan [424 . . .], Spring Byington [2325], James Gleason

[904], and Gene Lockhart [36]. Capra's sentimentality and political muddleheadedness have rarely been more painfully exposed. The movie's failure at the box office put an end to the major period of Capra's career, and except for the un-Capraesque *Arsenic and Old Lace* (made in 1941 but not released until 1944), he didn't make another commercial release until *It's a Wonderful Life* in 1946, concentrating instead on wartime documentaries.

The story on which *Meet John Doe* is based was written for a magazine by Connell in 1922, and Connell collaborated with Presnell on a film treatment in 1939, which was the basis of the Riskin screenplay. The Oscar for original story went to Harry Segall for *Here Comes Mr. Jordan.*

Connell: 2162.

1298 • *MEET ME IN LAS VEGAS*

MGM. 1956.

NOMINATION *Scoring of a Musical Picture:* George Stoll and Johnny Green.

Dan Dailey [2258] is a rancher whose luck at the Vegas gaming tables changes when he encounters ballet dancer Cyd Charisse. Tiresome, routine musical, directed by Roy Rowland, with Agnes Moorehead [963 . . .] and guest stars Jerry Colonna, Lena Horne, and Frankie Laine, among others. The Oscar went to Alfred Newman and Ken Darby for *The King and I.*

Stoll: 74, 115, 207, 699, 1216, 1299, 1950. Green: 66, 320, 594, 662, 817, 914, 1471, 1550, 1657, 2047, 2244.

1299 • *MEET ME IN ST. LOUIS*

MGM. 1944.

NOMINATIONS *Screenplay:* Irving Brecher and Fred F. Finklehoffe. *Color Cinematography:* George Folsey. *Song:* "The Trolley Song," music and lyrics by Ralph Blane and Hugh Martin. *Scoring of a Musical Picture:* Georgie Stoll.

The year before the St. Louis World's Fair of 1904, the Smith family is stunned when the head of the household (Leon Ames) suddenly announces that he's accepted a job that will require them to move to

New York City. This puts a crimp in the budding romance of daughter Judy Garland [1065 . . .] with the boy next door, Tom Drake. Mother Mary Astor [822] rallies the family's support, but by Christmas, the misery of their youngest daughter, Margaret O'Brien, shocks them into a realization that they belong where they are. This paper-thin plot, from the *New Yorker* stories of Sally Benson [83], is made into one of the most memorable of Hollywood musicals by the performers, who include Harry Davenport as Grandpa and Marjorie Main [601] as the maid, Katie; the wonderful Blane-Martin score that includes "The Boy Next Door" and "Have Yourself a Merry Little Christmas"; the studio's picture-postcard re-creation of an America that never was; and the meticulous direction of Vincente Minnelli [66 . . .], which keeps the nostalgia strong but not soggy. The absence of nominations in the picture, acting, directing, and art direction categories is surprising, although it may stem from the studio's desire to promote *Gaslight* at the awards, and perhaps also from a desire to punish Garland and Minnelli. The former was emphatic in her desire not to play any more juvenile roles and fought against being cast in the part; once she accepted, she missed many scheduled shoots because of illness—one of the first signs of her coming physical and mental disintegration. Minnelli annoyed both the art department and the head office with his constant preoccupation with the design and decor of the film; having begun as a scenic designer, he had more specific notions about what he wanted than most directors. He also quarreled constantly with Technicolor consultant Natalie Kalmus, who was required by contractual arrangement with Technicolor Corp. to be on the set of any film shot in the process. The omission of O'Brien from the supporting actress nominees was compensated for by a special award, a miniature Oscar, as outstanding child actress of 1944. The oft-told tale that Minnelli induced the seven-year-old O'Brien's hysterics in the Christmas scene by a graphic description of the death of her dog may or may not be true: O'Brien rarely needed coaching to bring on tears—it was her forte.

Finklehoffe, a contract writer with the MGM pro-duction unit headed by Arthur Freed [66 . . .], had brought the Benson stories to Freed's attention and was a logical choice to write the screenplay. He enlisted the aid of fellow contract writer Brecher, who put together the final version of the script in collaboration with Minnelli. The Oscar went to Frank Butler and Frank Cavett for *Going My Way*.

Folsey's recollections of the shoot include two of the film's most memorable moments. One is the Christmas Eve sequence, which features a complexly lighted view of the yard full of snowmen, seen from O'Brien's bedroom window. Once the various elements of the scene had been put in place and filmed, an electrician told Folsey that his readings showed the sequence to be underexposed. Instead, the results were haunting. The sequence in which Drake helps Garland extinguish the gaslights throughout the house was still more complicated, involving as it did not only lighting changes as each fixture is extinguished but also a camera and sound boom in constant motion as the actors move through the house. Venetian blinds, rather than dimmer switches, controlled many of the lighting changes. Folsey lost to Leon Shamroy's work on *Wilson*.

Blane and Martin, also under contract to the Freed unit, originally were stymied by Freed's insistence that they write a song about the trolley. As Blane recalled, in one of those Hollywood memories that sound like the work of a screenwriter, he did some library research and discovered a photograph of a St. Louis trolley with the caption "Clang, Clang, Clang, Went the Trolley." "I dashed back," Blane remembered, "told Hugh the title, and we wrote it in about ten minutes." Over the years, "Have Yourself a Merry Little Christmas," thanks in large part to Garland's perennial performances of it, has proved more enduring than the nominated song, but it may have been thought too derivative of Irving Berlin's "White Christmas," from *Holiday Inn,* which had won the Oscar two years earlier. "The Trolley Song" lost to a similarly upbeat tune, James Van Heusen and Johnny Burke's "Swinging on a Star," from *Going My Way*.

Although Stoll, the film's music director, received sole nomination for the score, much of the work was done by vocal arrangers Blane and Martin under the supervision of Roger Edens [87 . . .], by arranger and orchestrator Conrad Salinger [1818], and by assistant music director Lennie Hayton [877 . . .]. The Oscar went to Carmen Dragon and Morris Stoloff for *Cover Girl.*

Folsey: 51, 137, 629, 807, 835, 838, 1124, 1320, 1500, 1688, 1782, 2068, 2269. Blane: 801. Martin: 801. Stoll: 74, 115, 207, 699, 1216, 1298, 1950.

1300 • MELVIN AND HOWARD

LINSON/PHILLIPS/DEMME-UNIVERSAL PICTURES PRODUCTION; UNIVERSAL. 1980.
AWARDS *Supporting Actress:* Mary Steenburgen. *Screenplay Written Directly for the Screen:* Bo Goldman.
NOMINATION *Supporting Actor:* Jason Robards.

Melvin Dummar (Paul LeMat) picks up a raggedy stray in the Nevada desert and gives him a lift. The bum turns out to be Howard Hughes (Robards), who leaves Dummar a fortune in his will. But that's the beginning of Dummar's problems, as he's besieged by fortune hunters, reporters, and lawyers. Wonderful eccentric comedy, brilliantly realized by director Jonathan Demme [1820], cinematographer Tak Fujimoto, and a cast that includes Pamela Reed, Dabney Coleman, Michael J. Pollard [255], and Gloria Grahame [130 . . .]. The real Melvin Dummar plays a bus station counterman. The movie is one of the small classics of recent years, but it was a flop at the box office. Universal, unable to figure out how to market the film, kept it on the shelf for more than a year. It was a sensation at the New York Film Festival but failed to find audiences elsewhere.

Steenburgen plays Dummar's first wife, who supports the household by working as a go-go dancer. She was discovered by Jack Nicholson [395 . . .] and made her debut in one of his directorial outings, the 1978 *Goin' South.* The Oscar boosted her name recognition, and she has continued to work steadily and impressively. She reunited with Demme in 1993 on his *Philadelphia.*

Goldman spent a good deal of time with the real Melvin Dummar and his family and friends before finishing his script, his first solo effort after collabo-

rating on screenplays for *One Flew Over the Cuckoo's Nest* and *The Rose.* He has since written the critically praised *Shoot the Moon* (1982) and received a third nomination for *Scent of a Woman.* Though not a prolific screenwriter, he's one of the most respected, often called on for uncredited script-fixing.

Robards lost to Timothy Hutton in *Ordinary People.* Goldman: 1481, 1764.5. Robards: 54, 1066.

1301 • MEMBER OF THE WEDDING, THE

STANLEY KRAMER PRODUCTIONS; COLUMBIA. 1952.
NOMINATION *Actress:* Julie Harris.

Harris plays twelve-year-old Frankie, whose only companions are a small cousin, John Henry, played by Brandon de Wilde [1799], and the family cook, Berenice Sadie Brown, played by Ethel Waters [1575]. Clinging to childhood as she's forced into adolescence, Frankie is forced to confront the future when her older brother gets married and John Henry dies. Delicate filming of the novella-play by Carson McCullers, adapted by Edward Anhalt [164 . . .] and Edna Anhalt [1523 . . .], with the original Broadway stars repeating their roles. The movie, produced by Stanley Kramer [330 . . .] and directed by Fred Zinnemann [732 . . .], was a box-office bomb, but it launched the film careers of Harris and de Wilde.

Harris, who was twenty-seven when she made her film debut, has become one of the most acclaimed American stage performers, but she was less successful on screen. She is best remembered for her performances in *East of Eden, I Am a Camera* (1955), and *The Haunting* (1963). In recent years she has made occasional appearances in small character roles. She lost to another stage actress also making her screen debut, Shirley Booth, in *Come Back, Little Sheba.*

1302 • MEN, THE

STANLEY KRAMER PRODUCTIONS; UNITED ARTISTS. 1950.
NOMINATION *Story and Screenplay:* Carl Foreman.

Paraplegic veteran Marlon Brando [583 . . .] overcomes the psychological trauma of his disability with the aid of his fellow patients in a hospital ward. Brando's impressive debut is helped by the straightforward direction of Fred Zinnemann [732 . . .].

Foreman's screenplay lapses into some predictable clichés, particularly where Brando's fiancée, Teresa Wright [1182 . . .], is concerned, but it also provides Brando with solid material. Brando did not get along with other actors in the cast, such as Everett Sloane and Jack Webb, but hit it off well with the nonprofessional actors, real paraplegics, on location at a California veterans hospital. The screenplay Oscar went to Charles Brackett, Billy Wilder, and D. M. Marshman, Jr., for *Sunset Boulevard*.

Foreman: 287, 380, 850, 912, 2340.

1303 • MEN IN HER LIFE, THE

GREGORY RATOFF; COLUMBIA. 1941.

NOMINATION *Sound Recording:* John Livadary.

Under the tutelage of Conrad Veidt, circus performer Loretta Young [428 . . .] becomes a famous ballerina, rejecting love for the sake of her career. At the peak of her success, she marries wealthy Dean Jagger [2154], who forces her to give up her career. When an opportunity to dance again presents itself, however, she leaves Jagger. Finding that she's pregnant, she decides to conceal the fact from Jagger and raise the child, a girl, on her own. When she finds true love with Shepperd Strudwick (billed as John Shepperd), she goes to Jagger for a divorce, but he learns of the child and demands his daughter as the price of setting her free. She consents, but Shepperd is killed and she is left on her own again. Finally, years later, mother and daughter are reunited. Tedious, overplotted weeper, seemingly designed to show that women should think twice about having careers. Directed by Gregory Ratoff from a screenplay by Frederick Kohner [1229], Michael Wilson [287 . . .], and Paul Trivers. The sound Oscar went to *That Hamilton Woman*.

Livadary: 330, 455, 596, 732, 1058, 1206, 1215, 1366, 1370, 1740, 1872, 2111, 2325, 2327.

1304 • MEPHISTO

MAFILM-OBJEKTIV STUDIO AND MANFRED DURNIOK PRODUCTION (HUNGARY). 1981.

AWARD *Foreign Language Film.*

A leftist actor, played by Klaus Maria Brandauer [1512], betrays his political principles—and ultimately his friends and family—for the sake of his career when the Nazis come to power. A stunning performance by Brandauer fires this excellent film by István Szabó, the first of a trilogy continued by *Colonel Redl* and *Hanussen*. The source, a novel by Klaus Mann, is based on the career of the actor Gustav Gründgens, who was married to Mann's sister, and is also said to have been his lover.

1305 • MERCY ISLAND

REPUBLIC. 1941.

NOMINATION *Scoring of a Dramatic Picture:* Cy Feuer and Walter Scharf.

A fishing party off the Florida Keys turns into a harrowing adventure when the group is wrecked on an apparently deserted island. Passable action programmer with Ray Middleton, Gloria Dickson, and Otto Kruger. The Oscar went to Bernard Herrmann for *All That Money Can Buy*.

Feuer: 321, 920, 976, 1806, 1932. Scharf: 174, 274, 665, 737, 864, 921, 991, 1054, 2285.

1306 • MERRILY WE LIVE

HAL ROACH; MGM. 1938.

NOMINATIONS *Supporting Actress:* Billie Burke. *Cinematography:* Norbert Brodine. *Interior Decoration:* Charles D. Hall. *Sound Recording:* Elmer Raguse. *Song:* "Merrily We Live," music by Phil Craig, lyrics by Arthur Quenzer.

Writer Brian Aherne [1064], in search of material, is hired as a butler by wealthy matron Burke and ends up straightening out her spoiled daughter, Constance Bennett. Forgettable but fun, though it's much too close to *My Man Godfrey* in its plot, and the madcap family is an awful lot like the one in the year's best picture winner, *You Can't Take It With You*. Directed by Norman Z. McLeod, with Alan Mowbray, Bonita Granville [2045], Ann Dvorak, and Patsy Kelly.

Burke, the daughter of a circus clown, was born in Washington, D.C., but grew up in England, where she made her stage debut. Celebrated for her beauty, she came to America in 1907 and married impresario Florenz Ziegfeld in 1914. She had a brief film career in the early silent era but chose to concentrate her career on the Broadway stage until Ziegfeld lost his fortune in the 1929 stock market crash. She returned to Hollywood, where she soon made a name for herself as a character actress, playing scatterbrained roles with great charm, most memorably in *Topper.* She also served as an adviser on *The Great Ziegfeld,* in which she's played by Myrna Loy. She's perhaps best known as Glinda, the Good Witch, in *The Wizard of Oz.* She made her last screen appearances in 1960, in *Sergeant Rutledge* and *Pepe.* She died in 1970. The Oscar went to Fay Bainter for *Jezebel.*

The cinematography Oscar went to Joseph Ruttenberg for *The Great Waltz.* Carl J. Weyl won for the art direction of *The Adventures of Robin Hood.* The award for sound went to Thomas Moulton for *The Cowboy and the Lady.* Ralph Rainger and Leo Robin won for ''Thanks for the Memory,'' from *Big Broadcast of 1938.*

Brodine: 731, 1464. Hall: 348. Raguse: 345, 757.5, 1464, 1487, 2117, 2118. Quenzer: 457.

1307 • MERRY MONAHANS, THE
UNIVERSAL. 1944.
NOMINATION *Scoring of a Musical Picture:* H. J. Salter.

Backstage musical about a vaudeville family that's largely an excuse for nostalgic period songs. The cast —Donald O'Connor, Jack Oakie [818], Ann Blyth [1319], Rosemary De Camp—is a lot better than the movie deserves. Directed by Charles Lamont. The Oscar went to Carmen Dragon and Morris Stoloff for *Cover Girl.*

Salter: 62, 340, 399, 1030, 2060.

1308 • MERRY WIDOW, THE
MGM. 1934.
AWARD *Interior Decoration:* Cedric Gibbons and Frederic Hope.

The widow, Sonia (Jeanette MacDonald), is far from merry in her Ruritanian homeland, so she announces that she's moving to Paris. But she's so rich that this move would wreck the economy of the country, so its king commissions the womanizing Prince Danilo, played by Maurice Chevalier [203 . . .], to woo and marry Sonia and bring her back home. A few mistaken identities and plot twists later, all goes well. Delightful version of the Franz Lehar musical, with additional music by Richard Rodgers [1921] and new lyrics by Gus Kahn [692 . . .] and Lorenz Hart, and a book by Samson Raphaelson and Ernest Vajda. A soufflé whipped up by director Ernst Lubitsch [889 . . .], but with some of the lightness taken out by studio meddling and personality conflicts between Chevalier and Lubitsch. The then-new Production Code office was shocked by all the Parisian immorality, so some three minutes were cut from the distributed prints of the film to please the censors. The negative was untouched, however, so that contemporary versions available on videotape and laser disc are unscathed. Unfortunately the box-office reception of the movie was poor, and this was the last teaming of Chevalier and MacDonald. The latter went on to a collaboration with Nelson Eddy that was more popular in its day but now looks like a long stride in the wrong direction.

Gibbons: 66, 87, 130, 217, 227, 239, 285, 290, 440, 629, 749, 831, 980, 1069, 1096, 1173, 1190, 1226, 1230, 1232, 1274, 1309, 1417, 1567, 1604, 1644, 1662, 1673, 1721, 1861, 1937, 2068, 2112, 2256, 2257, 2300, 2320, 2330. Hope: 1721.

1309 • MERRY WIDOW, THE
MGM. 1952.
NOMINATIONS *Color Art Direction—Set Decoration:* Cedric Gibbons and Paul Groesse; Edwin B. Willis and Arthur Krams. *Color Costume Design:* Helen Rose and Gile Steele.

Lana Turner [1558] plays Sonia and Fernando Lamas is Prince Danilo in this tired Technicolor remake of the Franz Lehar musical, directed by Curtis Bernhardt, with Una Merkel [1959] and Richard Haydn. The leads are dubbed, of course, but Lana and Fernando look marvelous, thanks to the work of the nominees and the cinematography of Robert Surtees [130 . . .]. The Oscars, however, went to Paul Sheriff and Marcel Vertes for art direction and to Vertes alone for costumes for *Moulin Rouge.*

Gibbons: 66, 87, 130, 217, 227, 239, 285, 290,

440, 629, 749, 831, 980, 1069, 1096, 1173, 1190, 1226, 1230, 1232, 1274, 1308, 1417, 1567, 1604, 1644, 1662, 1673, 1721, 1861, 1937, 2068, 2112, 2256, 2257, 2300, 2320, 2330. Groesse: 87, 1173, 1190, 1232, 1335, 1385, 1604, 2112, 2157, 2320. Willis: 66, 87, 130, 227, 239, 290, 629, 749, 831, 980, 1069, 1096, 1157, 1173, 1190, 1226, 1230, 1232, 1417, 1567, 1657, 1662, 1673, 1721, 1861, 1937, 2068, 2112, 2257, 2320, 2330. Krams: 357, 1173, 1727, 1937, 1959, 2098, 2208. Rose: 130, 578, 629, 755, 817, 980, 1007, 1335, 1599. Steele: 612, 817, 897, 1087, 1748.

1310 • METEOR

METEOR PRODUCTIONS; AMERICAN INTERNATIONAL. 1979.
NOMINATION *Sound:* William McCaughey, Aaron Rochin, Michael J. Kohut, and Jack Solomon.

Killer meteor dooms earth, and along with it a cast that includes Sean Connery [2185], Natalie Wood [1219 . . .], Karl Malden [1477 . . .], Henry Fonda [815 . . .], Martin Landau [461 . . .], and Trevor Howard [1875]. What, you may ask, are all these fine actors doing in this piece of junk? They probably asked themselves that, after the trouble-plagued shoot ran well over budget, and then the film stiffed at the box office. Directed by Ronald Neame [289 . . .]. The sound Oscar went to *Apocalypse Now,* another troubled budget-buster that at least had the merit of being good.

McCaughey: 521, 1089, 1712, 2287. Rochin: 521, 641, 1089, 1711, 2124, 2165, 2231, 2287. Kohut: 641, 1548, 1711, 2124, 2165, 2231. Solomon: 738, 896, 938, 1089, 1109.

1311 • METROPOLITAN

WESTERLY FILM-VIDEO PRODUCTION; NEW LINE. 1990.
NOMINATION *Screenplay Written Directly for the Screen:* Whit Stillman.

A group of twentysomethings from the Manhattan privileged classes get together during the Christmas holidays. Entertaining slice-of-upper-class-life comedy with a satiric edge, featuring a cast of unknowns directed by newcomer Stillman. Perhaps too brittle for most tastes, but an impressive debut for Stillman,

who had another critical success in 1994 with *Barcelona.* The Oscar went to Bruce Joel Rubin for *Ghost.*

1312 • MIDNIGHT COWBOY

JEROME HELLMAN-JOHN SCHLESINGER PRODUCTION; UNITED ARTISTS. 1969.
AWARDS *Picture:* Jerome Hellman, producer. *Director:* John Schlesinger. *Screenplay—Based on Material From Another Medium:* Waldo Salt.
NOMINATIONS *Actor:* Dustin Hoffman. *Actor:* Jon Voight. *Supporting Actress:* Sylvia Miles. *Film Editing:* Hugh A. Robertson.

Voight plays Joe Buck, a Texan who comes to New York thinking he can make a big score by hustling rich women for his sexual services. Disillusioned and down on his luck, he's educated in the ways of the street by a scruffy, impoverished con artist, Ratso Rizzo (Hoffman). Astonishing performances by the leads make the film work even today, despite its obtrusively flashy editing and camera tricks and tiresomely shrill satire of urban attitudes. Some of what seemed hip and knowing at the time seems smart-alecky today, particularly the treatment of the women, Miles and Brenda Vaccaro [1038], whom Voight hustles. The film appeared in the first year of the new Motion Picture Association rating system and earned an X for its language and depictions of sex. Its triumph at the Oscars made it the only X-rated best picture winner, but it has since been rereleased with an R rating. Considering that the previous year's winner was the family musical *Oliver!,* something certainly seemed to be happening to the American movie. The best picture slate was one of the most schizophrenic in the history of the awards: *Midnight Cowboy* defeated *Anne of the Thousand Days,* a historical pageant produced by Hollywood veteran Hal B. Wallis; *Butch Cassidy and the Sundance Kid,* a smash-hit revisionist western; *Hello, Dolly!,* a disastrous big-budget musical; and the Algerian-made leftist political melodrama *Z.*

After completing his education at Oxford, where he began his involvement with theater, Schlesinger first worked as an actor and gradually moved into filmmaking with a series of BBC documentaries. His first feature film, *A Kind of Loving,* appeared in 1962, and he followed it with satiric looks at British life in *Billy Liar* (1962) and *Darling. Midnight Cowboy* established him on this side of the Atlantic, but except for *Sunday, Bloody Sunday,* his later films have not had much impact.

Salt's Hollywood career, which began in 1938, was interrupted by the blacklisting that resulted from his refusal to testify before the House Un-American Activities Committee in 1951. He resumed work in the mid-sixties. His career was the subject of a documentary, *Waldo Salt: A Screenwriter's Journey,* that received an Oscar nomination in 1990.

Hoffman's performance as Ratso Rizzo was a shrewd move: It demonstrated his range, saving him from further casting in roles cloned from Benjamin Braddock in *The Graduate.* Voight, who had made a couple of forgotten movies before *Midnight Cowboy,* was also hailed as a new star, but except for his Oscar-winning role in *Coming Home,* he has not demonstrated staying power as a screen actor. The Oscar went to John Wayne in *True Grit.*

Miles lost to Maggie Smith in *The Prime of Miss Jean Brodie.* The editing Oscar went to Françoise Bonnot for *Z.*

Hellman: 430. Schlesinger: 493, 1966. Salt: 430, 1780. Hoffman: 810, 1111, 1155, 1653, 2113. Voight: 430, 1734. Miles: 648.

1313 • *MIDNIGHT EXPRESS*

Casablanca Filmworks Production; Columbia (United Kingdom). 1978.

Awards *Screenplay Based on Material From Another Medium:* Oliver Stone. *Original Score:* Giorgio Moroder. **Nominations** *Picture:* Alan Marshall and David Puttnam, producers. *Supporting Actor:* John Hurt. *Director:* Alan Parker. *Film Editing:* Gerry Hambling.

Billy Hayes (Brad Davis), imprisoned in Turkey for trying to smuggle hashish out of the country, is brutalized and tortured. Hurt and Randy Quaid [1135] are among Hayes' fellow prisoners. Over-the-top prison drama that abuses the audience almost as much as it does its characters, and yet was a big box-office success—which doubtless explains its Oscar nomina-

tions. In addition to being excessively violent, the film is also racist—all Turks in it are portrayed as either sadists or fools—and homophobic, but *Midnight Express* helped jump-start the Hollywood careers of several of its nominees, particularly Stone, Moroder, Puttnam, and Parker.

Though it's based on a true story, the real Billy Hayes was tougher and more resourceful than the one in the film, who is largely a beautiful victim of the lustful Turks. But Stone's career has been built on extravagant fictions based on the lives of real people, from Richard Boyle in *Salvador* to Ron Kovic in *Born on the Fourth of July* to Jim Garrison in *JFK* and Le Ly Hayslip in *Heaven and Earth* (1993). Stone, who had only a couple of minor credits before this one, got a major career boost from the Oscar, but it would take him eight more years to establish a career as director that has eclipsed his work as writer.

Midnight Express also established Moroder, who was better known as a composer of pop dance music. His electronic score set a trend in film music that now seems to have run its course.

Puttnam, who subsequently turned to producing more earnest work such as *Chariots of Fire, The Killing Fields,* and *The Mission,* professed to be embarrassed by the excesses of *Midnight Express.* But it made him a hot property in Hollywood, leading to a brief and controversial tenure as head of production at Columbia eight years later. The best picture Oscar went to *The Deer Hunter,* which also won for Christopher Walken's supporting performance, Michael Cimino's direction, and Peter Zinner's editing.

Stone: 260, 1047, 1584, 1746. Moroder: 682, 2114. Puttnam: 386, 1086, 1331. Hurt: 608. Parker: 1333. Hambling: 433, 641, 992.5, 1333.

1314 • *MIDNIGHT LACE*

Ross Hunter-Arwin Production; Universal-International. 1960.

Nomination *Color Costume Design:* Irene.

Doris Day [1572], married to wealthy businessman Rex Harrison [413 . . .], begins receiving ominous phone calls that make her fear for her life. The suspects include John Gavin, Roddy McDowall, and Herbert Marshall. Slick but flimsy thriller—the surprise ending isn't much of a surprise if you've sat through more than one of these wife-in-jeopardy affairs. Directed by David Miller and produced by Ross Hunter [31] with his usual style-over-substance production values. The costuming award went to Valles and Bill Thomas for *Spartacus*.

Irene: 192.

1315 • *MIDSUMMER NIGHT'S DREAM, A*

WARNER BROS. 1935.

AWARDS *Cinematography:* Hal Mohr. (Write-in vote.) *Film Editing:* Ralph Dawson.

NOMINATION *Picture:* Henry Blanke, producer.

In a wood near Athens, the fairies play tricks on two pairs of young lovers and a group of workingmen preparing a play to celebrate the wedding of Theseus and Hippolyta. Lavish and entertaining filming of Shakespeare's play, with James Cagney [79 . . .] as Bottom, Olivia de Havilland [798 . . .] as Hermia, Mickey Rooney [115 . . .] as Puck, and Dick Powell, Joe E. Brown, Hugh Herbert, Victor Jory, Anita Louise, Arthur Treacher, and Billy Barty, among many others. It has to be seen to be believed—and believe it or not, it's worth seeing. It was based on the stage production of Max Reinhardt, a major European theatrical director and impresario. Reinhardt receives codirector credit with William Dieterle [1169]. Shakespeare purists were appalled, but we rather think Shakespeare would have loved it. The fairy scenes, with luminous, shimmering effects and gauzy costumes, are more magical than they usually are on stage, greatly enhanced by Erich Wolfgang Korngold's [17 . . .] adaptation of Felix Mendelssohn's incidental music for the play. Jory and Louise make a splendid-looking Oberon and Titania, though neither is up to the demands of the verse. Cagney is quite wonderful, and his teaming with Brown in the Pyramus and Thisbe scene is hilarious. Rooney gets on some people's nerves, but it's an amazing performance for someone in his early teens. This was de Havilland's film debut; she had played the role in Reinhardt's 1934 production in the Hollywood Bowl.

Warner Bros. had lost money on *A Midsummer Night's Dream* and was hoping for as much publicity as possible from the awards. Upset at the film's failure to receive more nominations, the studio mounted an aggressive write-in campaign, similar to the one a year earlier that had been launched in support of Bette Davis, whose failure to be nominated for *Of Human Bondage* had shocked Hollywood. In the case of *A Midsummer Night's Dream,* Mohr's omission from the slate of cinematography nominees in particular had caused much comment, especially since Mohr had been a Hollywood cameraman—and a particularly innovative one, noted for his use of a moving camera and crane shots—since 1921. He filmed Warners' legendary first talkie, *The Jazz Singer.* The studio's write-in campaign for Mohr succeeded: He became the first write-in winner and—since the rules were subsequently rewritten to exclude write-ins—the only one. Attempts to produce write-in winners for the film in other categories were not successful, although assistant director Sherry Sourds came in second to Clem Beauchamp and Paul Wing, who won for *Lives of a Bengal Lancer. A Midsummer Night's Dream*'s other winner, Dawson, was, like Mohr, an industry veteran—a film editor since 1919.

The best picture Oscar went to *Mutiny on the Bounty.*

Mohr: 718, 1560. Dawson: 17, 90, 911. Blanke: 17, 90, 712, 1046, 1169, 1457, 1936, 2136.

1316 • *MIGHTY JOE YOUNG*

ARKO PRODUCTION; RKO RADIO. 1949.

AWARD *Special Effects.* (No individual citation.)

Terry Moore [425] has a pet gorilla named Joe, who adores her but also has this growth hormone problem. Robert Armstrong discovers them in Africa and brings them back to the States as a nightclub attraction. Unfortunately Joe doesn't take to nightlife. Silly attempt to recapture the magic of *King Kong* (1933), which was also made by some of the same people, including producer Merian C. Cooper [1189 . . .], director Ernest B. Schoedsack, and special effects man Willis O'Brien, who shared the Oscar with Ray Harryhausen, though the Academy chose not to cite individuals by name in this category in the years from 1949 through 1955. Armstrong was also in the original film. Ben Johnson [1139] costars.

1317 • MIKADO, THE

UNIVERSAL (UNITED KINGDOM). 1939.
NOMINATION *Color Cinematography:* William V. Skall and Bernard Knowles.

Kenny Baker is Nanki-Poo and Martyn Green the lord high executioner in this agreeably colorful version of the Gilbert and Sullivan operetta, featuring members of the D'Oyle Carte Company. Directed by Victor Schertzinger [1488 . . .]. When the Academy decided to reduce the number of official nominees on the final ballot to two nominated films in each cinematography category, black and white and color, Skall and Knowles were eliminated from the competition. The Oscar went to Ernest Haller and Ray Rennahan for *Gone With the Wind.*

Skall: 96, 208, 1048, 1170, 1453, 1644, 1668, 1822, 2102.

1318 • MILAGRO BEANFIELD WAR, THE

ROBERT REDFORD/MOCTESUMA ESPARZA PRODUCTION; UNIVERSAL. 1988.
AWARD *Original Score:* Dave Grusin.

Scruffy, small-time New Mexico farmer Chick Vennera decides to divert some water from a big development to keep his bean plants alive, and touches off all sorts of conflicts. Lively, rambling, eccentric film (there's an angel involved in the goings-on), directed by Robert Redford [1502 . . .], that went nowhere at the box office, but has a cult following—just as the novel by John Nichols on which it's based does. Very much a matter of taste, but there are some very engaging performers involved in it, including Ruben Blades, Sonia Braga, Melanie Griffith [2313], John Heard, Daniel Stern, Christopher Walken [521], Freddy Fender, and M. Emmet Walsh. The screenplay is by Nichols and David Ward [1839.5 . . .], the cinematography by Robbie Greenberg.

Grusin began his career composing for the movies in 1967 on *Divorce American Style* and has since become one of the most prolific film scorers, and has done television work as well, notably on *St. Elsewhere.* Though he's a favorite of several filmmakers, including Sydney Pollack [1512 . . .], his light jazz strikes some detractors as only a step up from elevator music. He is also a successful recording artist.

Grusin: 379, 633, 667.5, 881, 890, 1473, 2113.

1319 • MILDRED PIERCE

WARNER BROS. 1945.
AWARD *Actress:* Joan Crawford.
NOMINATIONS *Picture:* Jerry Wald, producer. *Supporting Actress:* Eve Arden. *Supporting Actress:* Ann Blyth. *Screenplay:* Ranald MacDougall. *Black-and-White Cinematography:* Ernest Haller.

In the title role, Crawford plays a determined woman who makes a fortune in business but is almost undone by her poor taste in husbands and her spoiled daughter Veda (Blyth). Classic melodrama that neatly merges two genres: film noir and the woman's picture. Everybody in it is at peak form, including Jack Carson as Mildred's weak, adoring buddy, Zachary Scott as her rotter of a second husband, and Butterfly McQueen as Prissy—uh, Lottie. Directed by Michael Curtiz [79 . . .]—reluctantly at first, because he thought Crawford a mannered has-been, but with growing respect when it became clear she was giving the performance of her lifetime.

Few stars have fought harder to become and remain a star than Crawford, who spent almost half a century in movies. Born in San Antonio, she supported herself as a waitress and saleswoman before breaking into movies by winning a Charleston contest. She made her first movies in 1925, playing assorted flappers. By the time she made *Grand Hotel* in 1932, she was a major MGM star, but she had to compete for roles with the studio's other leading ladies, Norma Shearer [150 . . .], Greta Garbo [84 . . .], Luise Rainer [799 . . .], Jean Harlow, and Myrna Loy, and her career slumped in the early forties. She was signed by Warner Bros. in 1943, in part to provide competition for Bette Davis [46 . . .] on the studio roster, but not until *Mildred Pierce* did she find the role that would establish her most familiar persona: the hard-boiled, long-suffering, absolutely ruthless woman. Like most screen actresses, she found her career declining as she moved into her late forties and fifties. Her marriage to the chairman of Pepsi-Cola could have provided her with a comfortable retirement, but she persisted in her film career, and after the success of the grotesque *What Ever Happened to Baby Jane?* accepted roles in low-budget sixties horror movies like *Berserk!, The Karate Killers,* and *Trog.* She died in 1977, but her image was tarnished posthumously by the tell-all memoir *Mommie Dearest,* by her adopted daughter Christina, which was made into a 1981 movie starring Faye Dunaway [255 . . .].

The best picture Oscar went to *The Lost Weekend,* which also won for Charles Brackett and Billy Wilder's screenplay.

Anne Revere won the supporting actress Oscar for *National Velvet.* Arden, whose radio and TV character in the series *Our Miss Brooks* made her one of the most beloved performers of the forties and fifties, made a couple of early talkies under her real name, Eunice Quedens. She didn't become a regular performer in movies until 1937 when, under her new name, she was seen in *Stage Door.* She became a type: the heroine's wisecracking, good-hearted sidekick—a part she plays even in her Oscar-nominated role. Although her career was largely concentrated in TV after the mid-fifties, she made a few scattered but welcome film appearances, in *Anatomy of a Murder, The Dark at the Top of the Stairs,* and *Grease,* among others, before her death in 1990. Blyth, an operatic-trained soprano, first appeared in films in 1944 but was usually cast in nonsinging roles in the early years of her career. She made a few musicals, including *The Great Caruso, Rose Marie* (1954), *The Student Prince* (1954), *Kismet,* and her last film, *The Helen Morgan Story,* before retiring from movies in 1957.

Harry Stradling won for the cinematography for *The Picture of Dorian Gray.*

Crawford: 1597, 1955. Wald: 1052, 1558, 1875. Haller: 55, 679, 798, 1046, 1174, 2248.

1320 • MILLION DOLLAR MERMAID

MGM. 1952.

NOMINATION *Color Cinematography:* George J. Folsey.

Esther Williams plays Annette Kellerman, an Australian swimmer who came to America and became a star in the Hippodrome extravaganzas in the early years of this century. She also scandalized civic authorities by inventing the one-piece bathing suit. Fairly flimsy stuff as far as plot and character go, chiefly notable for some outrageous aquatic numbers staged by Busby Berkeley [791 . . .]. Directed by Mervyn LeRoy [1662 . . .], with Victor Mature, Walter Pidgeon [1232 . . .], and, as Anna Pavlova, Maria Tallchief. The Oscar went to Winton Hoch and Archie Stout for *The Quiet Man.*

Folsey: 51, 137, 629, 807, 835, 838, 1124, 1299, 1500, 1688, 1782, 2068, 2269.

1321 • MIN AND BILL

MGM. 1930–31.

AWARD *Actress:* Marie Dressler.

Dressler is Min and Wallace Beery [202 . . .] Bill in this creaky antique about a waterfront couple who fight the authorities over the custody of her adopted daughter. Directed by George Hill, the cast also includes Marjorie Rambeau [1609 . . .]. Beery and Dressler were so popular a pair that MGM reunited them in 1933 in *Tugboat Annie.*

Dressler's warmth and superb comic timing made her a top box-office star in the early thirties, but she died at the peak of her success in 1934. She had been a Broadway star before the turn of the century and moved from vaudeville into movies, making her debut opposite Charles Chaplin [405 . . .] in *Tillie's Punctured Romance* in 1914. By the late twenties her career had faded. It was revived by screenwriter Frances Marion [202 . . .], who tailor-made some scripts for her. Her most memorable performances are opposite Greta Garbo in *Anna Christie* and in the ensemble cast of *Dinner at Eight* (1933). Nowhere is Dressler's peerless comic timing better seen than in the latter film's concluding moments, a classic exchange with Jean Harlow.

Dressler: 611.

1322 • MINSTREL MAN

PRC. 1944.

NOMINATIONS *Song:* "Remember Me to Carolina," music by Harry Revel, lyrics by Paul Webster. *Scoring of a Musical Picture:* Leo Erody and Ferde Grofé.

Musical drama about the search of a minstrel performer for his daughter, interesting primarily for its re-creation of the nineteenth-century minstrel theater, with Benny Fields and Gladys George [2192], directed by Joseph H. Lewis. The Oscars went to James Van Heusen and Johnny Burke for the song "Swinging on a Star," from *Going My Way,* and to Carmen Dragon and Morris Stoloff for the score for *Cover Girl.*

Revel: 1291. Webster: 33, 64, 95, 331, 376, 604, 663, 730, 856, 1213, 1276, 1388, 1755, 1925, 2014.

1323 • MIRACLE OF MORGAN'S CREEK, THE

PARAMOUNT. 1944.

NOMINATION *Original Screenplay:* Preston Sturges.

Trudy Kockenlocker (Betty Hutton) does her part for the war effort by going to a party with some servicemen on the night before they ship out. But in the middle of the fun, she bumps her head, and the rest of the evening turns into a blur. So when she discovers she's pregnant, she hasn't the foggiest idea who the father is, except that his name was something like "Ratzkiwatzki." And it seems that she married the man, which means that she can't marry anyone else, like Norval Jones (Eddie Bracken), who would like to. And then the *babies* arrive . . . One of the three or four funniest movies ever made, a subversive masterpiece that finds nothing sacred, least of all Motherhood and Our Boys Overseas. That the movie was made and released at all in a year when audiences were weeping through *Since You Went Away, A Guy Named Joe, The Sullivans,* and other war-effort films is astonishing. Mostly it's a tribute to Sturges' sly wit and supersonic direction, and to his performers, who also include William Demarest [1058] as Trudy's volatile father, Diana Lynn as her cynical kid sister, and, reprising their roles from *The Great McGinty,* Brian

Donlevy [161] and Akim Tamiroff [701 . . .]. Sturges was a double nominee, for the equally subversive *Hail the Conquering Hero,* but he lost to Lamar Trotti's screenplay for *Wilson.*

Sturges: 823, 854.

1324 • MIRACLE OF OUR LADY OF FATIMA, THE

WARNER BROS. 1952.

NOMINATION *Scoring of a Dramatic or Comedy Picture:* Max Steiner.

The Virgin Mary appears to Portuguese children in a vision during World War I. Sticky, pious, and dull movie, directed by John Brahm, with Gilbert Roland and, as one of the children, Sherry Jackson, later best known as Danny Thomas' TV sitcom daughter. The Oscar went to Dimitri Tiomkin for *High Noon.*

Steiner: 16, 154, 190, 330, 365, 385, 492, 679, 747, 754, 798, 999, 1043, 1046, 1052, 1162, 1169, 1170, 1207, 1408, 1430, 1456, 1690, 1779, 1828.

1325 • MIRACLE ON 34TH STREET

20TH CENTURY-FOX. 1947.

AWARDS *Supporting Actor:* Edmund Gwenn. *Original Story:* Valentine Davies. *Screenplay:* George Seaton. **NOMINATION** *Picture:* William Perlberg, producer.

Macy's public relations executive Maureen O'Hara hires Gwenn as department store Santa—though he raises eyebrows when he gives his name as Kris Kringle. Moreover, on his first day on the job, he causes a sensation by referring customers to other stores— even Gimbels—when Macy's doesn't have what they want. Kris moves in with lawyer John Payne, who's trying to attract the attention of O'Hara, a divorcée raising her young daughter, played by Natalie Wood [1219 . . .], to be skeptical of legends like Santa Claus. When he makes an enemy of the store psychologist (Porter Hall), Kris winds up in a hearing to determine his sanity. Payne agrees to be his lawyer but finds himself challenged to prove that his client is who he persists in saying he is: Santa Claus. Charming Christmas story that has maintained its status as a perennial partly because it has more of an edge in its humor than most, taking sharp hits at politics and pseudo-psychology in particular. It also benefits from its appealing performers: O'Hara, Payne, Gwenn, and Wood are perfectly cast, and they're well supported by Gene Lockhart [36] as the judge who finds his reelection bid jeopardized by having to put Santa on trial, William Frawley as his cigar-puffing campaign manager, and Jerome Cowan as the district attorney prosecuting Santa. Thelma Ritter [46 . . .] makes her film debut in the small role of a Macy's customer, and Jack Albertson [1954] has a bit as a postal worker.

Gwenn was born in Wales and established himself on the London stage in the early years of the century. He made his first film in 1916. Before World War II, he divided his film appearances between Britain and the United States, but he became a major Hollywood character actor in the forties, working steadily until a few years before his death in 1959.

Miracle is one of a handful of films to win two writing Oscars. Screenwriter Davies turned director for one film, *The Benny Goodman Story,* in 1955. Seaton, who also directed *Miracle,* started as a screenwriter and in partnership with Perlberg became one of the most commercially successful producers of the fifties.

The best picture Oscar went to *Gentleman's Agreement.*

Gwenn: 1336. Davies: 776, 1027. Seaton: 31, 450, 1868. Perlberg: 450, 1868.

1326 • MIRACLE WORKER, THE

PLAYFILMS PRODUCTION; UNITED ARTISTS. 1962.

AWARDS *Actress:* Anne Bancroft. *Supporting Actress:* Patty Duke.

NOMINATIONS *Director:* Arthur Penn. *Screenplay—Based on Material From Another Medium:* William Gibson. *Black-and-White Costume Design:* Ruth Morley.

Teacher Anne Sullivan (Bancroft) goes to live with a family whose daughter, Helen Keller (Duke), is deaf and blind. The parents, played by Victor Jory and Inga Swenson, have found it impossible to manage the child, and at first they resist Sullivan's attempts to discipline Helen. Sullivan persists and eventually breaks through the barrier to communicate with the child. Absorbing, exciting drama that occasionally betrays its stage origins—director Penn and stars Bancroft and Duke had been involved in the original Broadway production—but has considerable power as cinema.

Bancroft made her screen debut in *Don't Bother to Knock* in 1952 but found herself stuck in mediocre movies—*Demetrius and the Gladiators* (1954) or, worse, *Gorilla at Large* (1954)—through the fifties. She turned her attention to the theater and won a Tony in 1958 for her performance in Gibson's *Two for the Seesaw.* She received another Tony for *The Miracle Worker,* which became her ticket back to Hollywood and serious stardom.

Duke had been a stage and TV performer from the age of seven and made her film debut at the age of twelve in 1958 in *The Goddess.* The following year she was cast in the Broadway production of *The Miracle Worker.* She was sixteen when she won the Oscar— the youngest person ever to win the award in competition, a distinction she held until ten-year-old Tatum O'Neal won for *Paper Moon.* Her subsequent film career has not been distinguished, and she became better known for her work on the sixties sitcom *The Patty Duke Show.* In 1979 she played Anne Sullivan in a made-for-TV version of *The Miracle Worker* and is frequently seen in TV dramas. She has also served as president of the Screen Actors Guild and has written a memoir dealing with her struggle with serious emotional problems.

Penn, whose directing career began in television, had made only one film, *The Left-Handed Gun* (1958), before *The Miracle Worker.* He lost to David Lean for *Lawrence of Arabia.*

Gibson was a novelist before he turned playwright, making his first success with the play *Two for the Seesaw.* Before it was staged, *The Miracle Worker* was seen as a TV drama on the *Playhouse 90* series in 1957. The Oscar went to Horton Foote for *To Kill a Mockingbird.*

The costume award went to Norma Koch for *What Ever Happened to Baby Jane?*

Bancroft: 28, 810, 1634, 2152. Penn: 43, 255.

1327 • MISÉRABLES, LES

20TH CENTURY; UNITED ARTISTS. 1935.

NOMINATIONS *Picture:* Darryl F. Zanuck, producer. *Cinematography:* Gregg Toland. *Assistant Director:* Eric Stacey. *Film Editing:* Barbara McLean.

Jean Valjean, played by Fredric March [184 . . .], serves time in prison for petty theft, but his attempts to start a new life are hindered by the implacable police inspector Javert, played by Charles Laughton [1387 . . .]. Big, handsome production of the Victor Hugo novel—first-class entertainment that does honor to its source. Directed by Richard Boleslawski, with art direction by Richard Day [22 . . .] and a cast that includes Cedric Hardwicke, Jessie Ralph, John Carradine, and Leonid Kinskey. Made on the eve of the merger of 20th Century and Fox studios, *Les Misérables* was a clear sign that 20th Century-Fox, under the leadership of Zanuck, would emerge as one of the major players of the golden age of the studio system. Adaptations of literary classics were as hot a trend in the mid-thirties as, say, muscular action adventures were in the mid-eighties: *Les Misérables* competed for best picture against MGM's version of *David Copperfield* and Warners' adaptation of *A Midsummer Night's Dream,* and other contenders included such filmed novels as Booth Tarkington's *Alice Adams,* Rafael Sabatini's *Captain Blood,* Liam O'Flaherty's *The Informer,* and the winner, Nordhoff and Hall's *Mutiny on the Bounty.*

Toland came in second for the Oscar, losing out to the write-in campaign for Hal Mohr's work on *A Midsummer Night's Dream.* The assistant director award went to Clem Beauchamp and Paul Wing for *Lives of a Bengal Lancer.* Ralph Dawson won for the editing for *A Midsummer Night's Dream.*

Zanuck: 34, 46, 550, 710, 759, 815, 946, 952, 990, 1201, 1666, 2154, 2286. Toland: 407, 510, 1006, 1200, 2316. Stacey: 747, 1909. McLean: 34, 46, 1195, 1655, 1868, 2286.

1328 • MISERY

CASTLE ROCK ENTERTAINMENT PRODUCTION; COLUMBIA. 1990.

AWARD *Actress:* Kathy Bates.

When he wrecks his car on an icy road, novelist James Caan [784] is rescued by Bates, who turns out to be a major fan of his work—but also a psychopath. Gripping adaptation of a Stephen King novel by William Goldman [54 . . .], tautly directed by Rob Reiner. You come away from it feeling thoroughly exploited, but the terrific performances by the leads, plus Richard Farnsworth [429], Frances Sternhagen, and Lauren Bacall, give it some redeeming qualities.

Bates, born in Memphis, developed a reputation as a major stage actress, a favorite of both critics and playwrights; Terrence McNally, for example, wrote the play *Frankie and Johnny in the Clair de Lune* specifically for her. But her plainness caused Hollywood to shy away from casting Bates in major roles, even when she had created them on stage, so her part in Marsha Norman's *'Night, Mother* went to Sissy Spacek [364 . . .] when it was filmed in 1986, and Michelle Pfeiffer [485 . . .], of all people, was called on to play the drab, repressed waitress in *Frankie and Johnny* (1991). The Oscar gave Bates the name recognition she needed for more important screen roles, as in *Fried Green Tomatoes* and *Used People* (1992), although even those films treat her as an ensemble performer rather than a leading player.

1329 • MISS SADIE THOMPSON

THE BECKWORTH CORPORATION; COLUMBIA. 1953.

NOMINATION *Song:* ''Sadie Thompson's Song (Blue Pacific Blues),'' music by Lester Lee, lyrics by Ned Washington.

Rita Hayworth plays Sadie, a nightclub entertainer on a South Pacific island during World War II, who draws the ire of the puritanical Mr. Davidson, played by Jose Ferrer [473 . . .]. Davidson claims he's protecting the morals of the troops by shutting down Sadie's performances, but he's really trying to suppress his lust for her. Meanwhile, Sadie falls for a marine (Aldo Ray). Directed by Curtis Bernhardt. Colorful but tepid version of the Somerset Maugham story that had become the play *Rain,* which starred Jeanne Eagels [1161] on stage, Gloria Swanson in the 1928 film called *Sadie Thompson,* and Joan Crawford in a 1932 version again called *Rain.* The earlier films, pre–Production Code, were more explicit about the professions of its leads: Sadie was a prostitute and Davidson a minister. But although the industry's censors were being put to the test in 1953 by *The Moon Is Blue,* Columbia capitulated to their demands and cleaned up Sadie's act and made Davidson a layman. Even so, several local censor boards saw fit to ban the film, thereby boosting its box office. Charles Bronson, billed as Buchinsky, has a small role. The movie was originally made in 3-D. Hayworth's singing is dubbed by Jo Ann Greer. The Oscar went to Sammy Fain and Paul Francis Webster for "Secret Love," from *Calamity Jane.*

Washington: 274, 585, 911, 912, 1396, 1576, 1745, 2127, 2282, 2335.

1330 • MISSING

UNIVERSAL PICTURES/POLYGRAM PICTURES PRESENTATION OF AN EDWARD LEWIS PRODUCTION; UNIVERSAL. 1982.

AWARD *Screenplay Based on Material From Another Medium:* Costa-Gavras and Donald Stewart.

NOMINATIONS *Picture:* Edward Lewis and Mildred Lewis, producers. *Actor:* Jack Lemmon. *Actress:* Sissy Spacek.

American businessman Ed Horman (Lemmon) goes to a South American country to investigate the disappearance of his son (played in flashbacks by John Shea) after a military takeover. Staunchly conservative, he is at odds with his son's left-leaning wife, Beth (Spacek), and at first rejects the claim that Charles Horman was executed by the government with the acquiescence of American officials. But the weight of the evidence eventually shatters his illusions. Tough but ultimately too-shrill political drama, the first American film directed by Costa-Gavras. Based on actual events in Chile in 1973 (the country is not named in the movie, which was filmed in Mexico), *Missing* drew angry denials from the American State Department, and a lawsuit against the studio was filed by several officials depicted in the film. Though a harsh indictment of American complicity in maintaining right-wing domination in Latin America, *Missing* is undermined by sentimentality, melodrama, and a touch of smugness.

The Academy membership, which had grown younger and more politically liberal in the late seventies and was conscious of Hollywood's dark political era in the fifties, was sympathetic with the political stance taken by Costa-Gavras, a Greek who had been blacklisted in his own country and forced into exile by a right-wing government. Costa-Gavras' subsequent American films have, however, lacked the edge of earlier work such as *Z, State of Siege* (1973), and *Missing: Betrayed* (1988) is a mixed-up melodrama about the unlikely romance of an FBI agent and a white supremacist, and *Music Box* undercuts its exploration of guilt and innocence with too much courtroom melodrama.

The best picture Oscar went to *Gandhi,* which also won the best actor award for Ben Kingsley. The best actress award went to Meryl Streep for *Sophie's Choice.*

Costa-Gavras: 2344. Lemmon: 91, 394, 508, 1337, 1761, 1860, 2140. Spacek: 364, 418, 462, 1701.

1331 • MISSION, THE

WARNER BROS./GOLDCREST AND KINGSMERE PRODUCTION; WARNER BROS. 1986.

AWARD *Cinematography:* Chris Menges.

NOMINATIONS *Picture:* Fernando Ghia and David Puttnam, producers. *Director:* Roland Joffé. *Art Direction–Set Decoration:* Stuart Craig; Jack Stephens. *Original Score:* Ennio Morricone. *Film Editing:* Jim Clark. *Costume Design:* Enrico Sabbatini.

The work of eighteenth-century Jesuit missionaries in the Brazilian jungles is undermined by colonial business interests and infighting within the church itself. Stunningly filmed and interestingly cast—Robert De Niro [113 . . .], Jeremy Irons [1689], Ray McAnally, Aidan Quinn, Liam Neeson [1764.65], and radical activist Daniel Berrigan—*The Mission* falls apart because it never quite decides whether to be a historical epic, political drama, or moral fable, and screenwriter Robert Bolt [558 . . .] fails to come up with a plot that would hold all these elements together. Although both box-office and critical reception was tepid, the Academy chose to recognize it at least in part because it's the kind of high-minded prestige production that usually qualifies for Oscars.

Many, however, felt that the best picture nomination should have gone to more daring work such as *Blue Velvet* or *My Beautiful Laundrette.*

This was the second Oscar for Menges, who had won his first for *The Killing Fields,* a film also put together by Puttnam, Joffé, and Clark. Menges subsequently turned to directing, making his debut in 1988 with *A World Apart,* a drama about apartheid.

Platoon won the best picture Oscar, as well as awards for director Oliver Stone and editor Claire Simpson. *A Room With a View* took the awards for art direction and costuming. The scoring award went, in a controversial decision, to Herbie Hancock for *'Round Midnight.*

Menges: 1086. Puttnam: 386, 1086, 1313. Joffé: 1086. Craig: 382.5, 485, 608, 745. Stephens: 2021. Morricone: 308, 506, 2185. Clark: 1086.

1332 • *MISSION TO MOSCOW*

WARNER BROS. 1943.

NOMINATION *Black-and-White Interior Decoration:* Carl Weyl, art direction; George J. Hopkins, set decoration.

U.S. Ambassador Joseph Davies, played by Walter Huston [50 . . .], goes to the Soviet Union and discovers a bunch of happy, peace-loving folks who really aren't so bad even if they *are* commies. An exercise in forced naïveté, put together by Warners at the behest of the Office of War Information, which wanted Hollywood to contribute to the war effort by propagandizing on behalf of the Allies. Unfortunately a few years later this particular ally was our worst enemy, and studios like Warners that had lionized the Soviets were being combed by the House Un-American Activities Committee in search of Reds. Screenwriter Howard Koch [365 . . .] would be one of the victims of the blacklists of the fifties, though as much for his political affiliations in the thirties as for his contribution to this film. Mediocre as entertainment and ludicrous as history, *Mission to Moscow* is still a fascinating document of the attitudes of an era, particularly since Warners threw some of its best talent— director Michael Curtiz [79 . . .], composer Max Steiner [16 . . .], and actors Ann Harding [927],

Oscar Homolka [972], Gene Lockhart [36], Eleanor Parker [328 . . .], Frieda Inescort, Helmut Dantine, Henry Daniell, and lots of others—into so commercially dubious a project. The art direction Oscar went to *The Song of Bernadette.*

Weyl: 17. Hopkins: 110, 508, 896, 1003, 1170, 1385, 1393, 1909, 1949, 1973, 2058, 2277.

1333 • *MISSISSIPPI BURNING*

FREDERICK ZOLLO PRODUCTION; ORION. 1988.

AWARD *Cinematography:* Peter Biziou.

NOMINATIONS *Picture:* Frederick Zollo and Robert F. Colesberry, producers. *Actor:* Gene Hackman. *Supporting Actress:* Frances McDormand. *Director:* Alan Parker. *Sound:* Robert Litt, Elliot Tyson, Rick Kline, and Danny Michael. *Film Editing:* Gerry Hambling.

When three civil rights workers are murdered in Mississippi in 1964, FBI agents Hackman and Willem Dafoe [1584] are sent to investigate. Hackman is an ex-sheriff whose casual, ingratiating manner irritates no-nonsense professional Dafoe, but Hackman uses his tactics to get close to the wife (McDormand) of one of the suspects. Well-made melodrama with a serious flaw: its wrongheadedness about history. Many who were involved in the civil rights movement were outraged at the portrayal of blacks in the film as passive victims, and at the notion that the FBI acted with dispatch to solve the murders of James Chaney, Andrew Goodman, and Michael Schwerner on which this film is based. Under J. Edgar Hoover, the FBI was a good deal more interested in trying to find communists in the civil rights movement than in bringing its brutal opponents to justice. A somewhat more accurate account of the case was presented in the 1990 TV movie *Murder in Mississippi.*

Biziou previously worked with director Parker on *Bugsy Malone* and *Pink Floyd—the Wall* (1982) and has also worked with former members of the *Monty Python* group, Terry Jones on *Life of Brian* (1979) and Terry Gilliam [275] on *Time Bandits* (1981), and with Adrian Lyne [653] on *9¹/₂ Weeks* (1986). Since the Oscar, he has filmed the directorial debut of fellow cinematographer Chris Menges [1086 . . .], *A World Apart* (1988).

The controversy over the accuracy of *Mississippi Burning* broke well before the awards and did it no good in the voting. The best picture award went to *Rain Man,* which also won for actor Dustin Hoffman and director Barry Levinson. McDormand lost to Geena Davis in *The Accidental Tourist. Bird* took the Oscar for sound. The award for editing went to Arthur Schmidt for *Who Framed Roger Rabbit.*

Hackman: 255, 724, 971, 2179.5. Parker: 1313. Litt: 1802.5. Tyson: 779, 1802.5. Kline: 507, 658.5, 1825, 2020, 2114. Hambling: 433, 641, 992.5, 1313.

1334 • *MISSISSIPPI GAMBLER*
UNIVERSAL-INTERNATIONAL. 1953.
NOMINATION *Sound Recording:* Leslie I. Carey, sound director, Universal-International Sound Department.

Riverboat gambler Tyrone Power gets involved with flirtatious Scarlett O'Hara clone Piper Laurie [364 . . .] and more demure Julia Adams in this piece of stale cornpone. Director Rudolph Maté [455 . . .] is better known for his work as a cinematographer, so this one looks good, though Irving Glassberg is nominally in charge of the camera. The cast includes Dennis Weaver. The Oscar for sound went to John Livadary for *From Here to Eternity.*

Carey: 291, 776, 1209, 1478, 2089.

1335 • *MISTER BUDDWING*
DDD-CHEROKEE PRODUCTION; MGM. 1966.
NOMINATIONS *Black-and-White Art Direction—Set Decoration:* George W. Davis and Paul Groesse; Henry Grace and Hugh Hunt. *Black-and-White Costume Design:* Helen Rose.

James Garner [1380] comes down with that old standby ailment of melodrama and farce, amnesia, and spends the rest of the movie trying to figure out who he is and what his relationship is to Jean Simmons [858 . . .], Suzanne Pleshette, Angela Lansbury [749 . . .], and Katharine Ross [810], among others. Unfortunately this one is played for melodrama, not farce, and director Delbert Mann [1283] makes it a pretty draggy affair. *Who's Afraid of Virginia Woolf?* won the Oscars for art direction and Irene Sharaff's costumes.

Davis: 46, 69, 401, 495, 542, 736, 953, 1213, 1388, 1537, 1552, 1706, 1814, 2157, 2184, 2312. Groesse: 87, 1173, 1190, 1232, 1309, 1385, 1604, 2112, 2157, 2320. Grace: 69, 227, 401, 769, 953, 1388, 1450, 1537, 1552, 2157, 2184, 2312. Hunt: 175, 401, 980, 1069, 1232, 1388, 1567, 1644, 1657, 1673, 2157, 2184. Rose: 130, 578, 629, 755, 817, 980, 1007, 1309, 1599.

1336 • *MISTER 880*
20TH CENTURY-FOX. 1950.
NOMINATION *Supporting Actor:* Edmund Gwenn.

Gwenn is a kindly little old counterfeiter, who continually foils the efforts of treasury agent Burt Lancaster [107 . . .] to track him down. Pleasant little comedy directed by Edmund Goulding that gets its Capraesque flavor from the screenplay by Capra collaborator Robert Riskin [905 . . .]. The cast includes Dorothy McGuire [759] and Millard Mitchell. Gwenn lost to George Sanders in *All About Eve.*

Gwenn: 1325.

1337 • *MISTER ROBERTS*
ORANGE PRODUCTION; WARNER BROS. 1955.
AWARD *Supporting Actor:* Jack Lemmon.
NOMINATIONS *Picture:* Leland Hayward, producer. *Sound Recording:* William A. Mueller.

Roberts, played by Henry Fonda [815 . . .], is a lieutenant on a cargo ship during World War II. He longs to see combat, but his tyrannical, paranoid captain, James Cagney [79 . . .], blocks his efforts to obtain a transfer. Lemmon plays Ensign Pulver, the amiable goof-off whose every move is designed to avoid the captain's notice. William Powell [1170 . . .], in his last film, is the ship's doctor. The play by Thomas Heggen and Joshua Logan [643 . . .], based on Heggen's novel, was a huge hit on Broadway, where Fonda created the title role. It lost something in the translation to screen, partly because censorship took some of the salt out of the dialogue, and partly because "opening up" the play and filming on location means that things stop from time to time to look at the scenery. Worse yet, director John Ford [815 . . .] and Fonda quarreled, Ford sulked and began to drink, letting actor Ward Bond, who had a small role in the film, take over as director. Eventually Ford withdrew from the film and was replaced by Mervyn LeRoy [1662 . . .], who claimed to have directed as much as 90 percent of the movie. In his memoirs Logan claims to have done the final cutting, polishing, and some reshooting. He had directed the play and had planned to direct the film as well, but after a dispute with Fonda, he considered filming it with Marlon Brando [583 . . .] instead. Producer Hayward finally persuaded Logan, who had not directed a movie since 1938, that the teaming of Ford and Fonda would enable the film to get the financial backing it needed. Logan received cowriter credit on the screenplay with Frank Nugent [1642], whose work on the film Logan despised.

After graduating from Harvard and serving as an ensign in the navy, Lemmon had done stage and TV work in New York. He made his film debut in 1954 and won his first Oscar in only his fourth movie.

Hayward was an agent and a Broadway producer who had spent some time early in his career as a publicist for United Artists and a writer for First National pictures. *Mister Roberts* was the first of three pictures he produced during the late fifties. The best picture Oscar went to *Marty*.

The sound award went to *Oklahoma!*

Lemmon: 91, 394, 508, 1330, 1761, 1860, 2140. Mueller: 331.

1338 • MODEL AND THE MARRIAGE BROKER, THE

20TH CENTURY-FOX. 1951.

NOMINATION *Black-and-White Costume Design:* Charles LeMaire and Renie.

Jeanne Crain [1575] is the first half of the title and Thelma Ritter [46 . . .] the second in this pleasant comedy about the efforts of the latter to bring together the former and Scott Brady. Ritter is, as usual, a delight, and she's well supported by Zero Mostel and Nancy Kulp among others, not to mention well directed by George Cukor [262 . . .]. The screenplay is by Charles Brackett [705 . . .], Richard Breen [350 . . .], and Walter Reisch [435 . . .]. The costuming award went to Edith Head for *A Place in the Sun.*

LeMaire: 21, 46, 376, 495, 530, 542, 954, 1213, 1391, 1601, 1706, 2008, 2043, 2205, 2294. Renie: 201, 355, 413, 1601.

1339 • MOGAMBO

MGM. 1953.

NOMINATIONS *Actress:* Ava Gardner. *Supporting Actress:* Grace Kelly.

African big-game hunter Clark Gable [798 . . .] has a fling with showgirl Gardner when she's accidentally stranded in Kenya. But then his client, Donald Sinden, shows up for a gorilla hunt, bringing along his beautiful young wife, Kelly, creating a couple of interlocking triangles. Colorful, lively, and very likable remake of *Red Dust* (1932), with Gardner in the role originally played by Jean Harlow, Kelly in the one played by Mary Astor [822], and Gable in the one played by—Gable. Director John Ford [815 . . .] works from a screenplay by John Lee Mahin [352 . . .], who also wrote the first version. Ford is not at home in this kind of romance, built on sexual tension, so it's not quite the equal of *Red Dust,* which was directed by Victor Fleming [798] and features one of Harlow's finest performances. Perhaps because he's done it all before, Gable seems to be walking through his part, but name another fifty-two-year-old man who could do as little acting as he does here and still make you believe that he had Ava Gardner and Grace Kelly fighting over him. The cinematography by Robert Surtees [130 . . .] and Freddie Young [558 . . .] was worthy of a nomination, though there are some poorly matched scenes during the gorilla hunt, which mixes footage shot in the wild with more obviously staged sequences.

Gardner never gave a freer, funnier performance than this one. Though her career was built on her astonishing beauty and not on acting ability, the camera found something genuine in her, a saucy openness. Born in near poverty in North Carolina, she was discovered when MGM's casting department spotted her photograph and arranged a screen test. She made her screen debut in 1942 and performed in B pictures and bit parts until she made a strong impression in *The Killers* four years later. *Mogambo* was made at the peak of her career. In the mid-fifties, after three disastrous celebrity marriages, to Mickey Rooney [115 . . .], Artie Shaw [1772], and Frank Sinatra [732 . . .], she moved to Spain, where she became the delight of the paparazzi. She continued to make screen appearances until 1980. She died in 1990. The best actress Oscar went to Audrey Hepburn for *Roman Holiday.*

Mogambo was Kelly's third film and the one that established her as a major star. The Oscar went to Donna Reed for *From Here to Eternity.*

Kelly: 450.

1340 • MOHAMMAD, MESSENGER OF GOD

FILMCO INTERNATIONAL PRODUCTION; IRWIN YABLANS COMPANY (UNITED KINGDOM). 1977.

NOMINATION *Original Score:* Maurice Jarre.

Anthony Quinn [1226 . . .] plays Hamza, the uncle of the prophet Mohammad, in this attempt at an epic about the founding of Islam. Because of the religion's tradition against depiction of Mohammad, he is never shown in the film. Nevertheless, the production stirred intense controversy within the Muslim community and never found an audience. Directed by Moustapha Akkad, with Irene Pappas and cinematography by Jack Hildyard [287]. The scoring Oscar went to John Williams for *Star Wars.*

Jarre: 558, 764, 808, 1151, 1168, 1533, 1967, 2296.

1341 • MOLLY MAGUIRES, THE

TAMM PRODUCTIONS; PARAMOUNT. 1970.

NOMINATION *Art Direction—Set Decoration:* Tambi Larsen; Darrell Silvera.

Irish immigrant coal miners form a secret society in 1870s Pennsylvania to fight for better working conditions. Detective Richard Harris [660 . . .] infiltrates the group, which is headed by Sean Connery [2185], and has an affair with local woman Samantha

Eggar [420]. Director Martin Ritt [956] gets strong performances from a cast that also includes Frank Finlay [1506], but the film is relentlessly heavy and plodding. The screenplay is by Walter Bernstein [733] who, like Ritt, had been blacklisted in the fifties. Both writer and director are clearly interested in using the movie to make a political statement. They succeeded much better a few years later in *The Front,* which is explicitly about the blacklist era, and Ritt would make a more successful film about the labor movement in *Norma Rae.* The expensive art direction, re-creating a nineteenth-century mining village on location in a small Pennsylvania town, caused problems for the studio when the film crashed and burned at the box office. The Oscar went to *Patton.*

Larsen: 892, 956, 1727, 1897. Silvera: 407, 632, 686, 1239, 1264, 1924.

1342 • MON ONCLE D'AMÉRIQUE

PHILIPPE DUSSART-ANDREA FILMS T.F. 1 PRODUCTION; NEW WORLD PICTURES (FRANCE). 1980.

NOMINATION *Screenplay Written Directly for the Screen:* Jean Gruault.

The theories of behaviorist psychologist Henri Laborit are demonstrated in the lives of three people: factory manager Gérard Depardieu [474], actress Nicole Garcia, and TV executive Roger Pierre. The title —"my American uncle"—is a slang phrase for the good luck one hopes will turn up. Provocative but eventually somewhat wearying satire, directed by Alain Resnais. The Oscar went to Bo Goldman for *Melvin and Howard.*

1343 • MONA LISA

PALACE/HANDMADE PRODUCTION; ISLAND PICTURES (UNITED KINGDOM). 1986.

NOMINATION *Actor:* Bob Hoskins.

Hoskins plays George, a London mobster who's so loyal to his boss, the sinister Mortwell, played by Michael Caine [35 . . .], that he is willing to go to prison in his place. When George gets out, Mortwell gives him a job as chauffeur to Simone (Cathy Tyson), a high-priced prostitute in his employ. Gradually her loathing of Mortwell and her introduction of George to the sleaziest parts of London open his eyes, leading to a climactic confrontation. The three principals are superb, as is the direction by Neil Jordan [472.5], who cowrote the screenplay with David Leland. It's not a pleasant film, but it certainly holds your interest.

Hoskins won best actor awards at Cannes and from the New York and L.A. film critics, but the Oscar—for services long rendered but never before honored—went to Paul Newman for *The Color of Money*. The film also made a very unlikely star of Hoskins, who began his career on stage in England, achieved a triumph on British TV in the miniseries *Pennies From Heaven,* and had been working steadily in movies since the early eighties. A facility with accents allowed him to play something other than cockney thugs and made him credible as the toon-beset L.A. detective in *Who Framed Roger Rabbit,* among many other character leads.

1344 • *MONDO CANE*

CINERIZ PRODUCTION; TIMES FILM CORPORATION (ITALY). 1963.

NOMINATION *Song:* "More," music by Riz Ortolani and Nino Oliviero, lyrics by Norman Newell.

Gross-out pseudo-documentary about eccentric and often revolting human behavior around the world. (The title means "dog world.") Produced by Gualtiero Jacopetti, it was a surprise box-office hit, and the nominated song was a success on the charts, though it lost to James Van Heusen and Sammy Cahn's "Call Me Irresponsible," from *Papa's Delicate Condition.*

Ortolani: 1235.

1345 • *MONSIEUR VERDOUX*

THE CHAPLIN STUDIOS; UNITED ARTISTS. 1947.

NOMINATION *Original Screenplay:* Charles Chaplin.

Verdoux (Chaplin), happily married and the father of a son, supports himself and his family (who are unaware of his activities) by bigamy and murder: He marries unpleasant wealthy women and bumps them off. He is eventually caught and executed, but not before he has delivered a speech in which he notes how much lesser are his crimes than those of men who cause and profit from wars. Chaplin's most sophisticated film is undermined by such muddleheaded philosophizing, by slack pacing, and by inconsistency of tone. However, it's also often very funny, particularly the scenes involving Martha Raye, who proves resistant to all attempts to do her in. Critics disliked it, and it was withdrawn from release for seventeen years. On its reissue, it was greeted by many as a masterpiece. The critical consensus has swung to the middle by now, but it has passionate adherents.

Chaplin considered it his best film, but it was a box-office disaster, its release hindered by the poor reviews and by protests from various patriotic groups and religious organizations. Chaplin had recently concluded a paternity-suit trial, and though a blood test had demonstrated his innocence, the hint of scandal lingered. As the postwar Red scare began to gather momentum, there were questions about his politics, focused primarily on a speech he had given advocating a "second front" for the war to defend the Soviet Union. Although he had lived and worked in the United States for more than forty years, the English-born Chaplin had never become an American citizen, which fueled the ire of right-wing newspapers and the American Legion. In the midst of all this turmoil, *Verdoux* is an audacious nose-thumbing.

The screen credit for writing goes to Chaplin, but it also carries a note: "Based on an idea by Orson Welles." "Had I foreseen the kudos he eventually tried to make out of it," Chaplin sourly notes in his autobiography, "I would have insisted on no screen credit at all." In Chaplin's version of the story, Welles [407 . . .] had come to Chaplin with the idea of a series of documentaries, one of which would be of the French "Bluebeard" murderer, Landru. When Chaplin found material for comedy in the story of Landru, he offered Welles $5,000 for the idea. Welles agreed if he could have screen credit, too. Welles, however, had a different story: He wrote a screenplay with the intention of producing it for Chaplin at RKO, but Chaplin wanted to direct it himself and bought the script. At first, Welles claimed, Chaplin had withheld even the token screen credit but added it after the film's first critical drubbing. In any case, here's plenty of fuel for Oscar bashers: Even though the screenplay is attributable to the men who gave us *The Gold Rush* and *Citizen Kane,* the Oscar went to the man who gave us *The Other Side of Midnight* and *Bloodline*—Sidney Sheldon won for *The Bachelor and the Bobby-Soxer.*

Chaplin: 405, 818, 1176.

1346 • *MONSIEUR VINCENT*

EDIC/UGC (FRANCE). 1948.

AWARD *Special Award:* Voted by the Academy Board of Governors as the most outstanding foreign language film released in the United States during 1948.

Pierre Fresnay stars as Vincent de Paul, who devoted himself to helping the poor in seventeenth-century France and was later canonized. Intelligent religious biopic, directed by Maurice Cloche, greatly helped by Fresnay's performance, a screenplay by Jean Anouilh, and the cinematography of Claude Renoir. From 1948 through 1955, before the establishment of the competitive foreign film category, the Academy annually honored a foreign language film, including such distinguished work as *The Bicycle Thief, Rashomon, Forbidden Games,* and *Gate of Hell.* The competitive award established in 1956 has proved to be an awkwardly administered category, whose behind-the-scenes politics and sometimes disappointing choices have caused many critics to suggest that the less democratic method of selection used in earlier years might be preferable.

1347 • *MOON AND SIXPENCE, THE*

LOEW-LEWIN; UNITED ARTISTS. 1943.

NOMINATION *Scoring of a Dramatic or Comedy Picture:* Dimitri Tiomkin.

George Sanders [46] plays a London stockbroker who finally makes his dream come true: He leaves his wife and family and chilly old England and moves first to Paris to become an artist and then to Tahiti, where he eventually dies. Directed by Albert Lewin, who also adapted the story by Somerset Maugham—played in the film by Herbert Marshall—which is based on the life of Gauguin. Good attempt at transferring the novel to screen, and Sanders is excellent in the lead, nicely blending the romantic and unscrupulous elements of the character. Parts of the film are in color. With Doris Dudley, Eric Blore, Elena Verdugo, and Albert Basserman [706]. Tiomkin lost to Alfred Newman for *The Song of Bernadette.*

Tiomkin: 33, 286, 380, 446, 638, 663, 730, 768, 850, 911, 912, 1206, 1370, 1470, 2006, 2127, 2282, 2335.

1348 • *MOON IS BLUE, THE*

PREMINGER-HERBERT PRODUCTION; UNITED ARTISTS. 1953.

NOMINATIONS *Actress:* Maggie McNamara. *Song:* "The Moon Is Blue," music by Herschel Burke Gilbert, lyrics by Sylvia Fine. *Film Editing:* Otto Ludwig.

McNamara is a young woman whose major charm is her candor, which she uses to attract both David Niven [1778] and William Holden [1424 . . .]. Tepid little comedy, adapted by F. Hugh Herbert from his own play, that was notorious at the time because of the way in which the heroine teasingly maintained her virginity, and because the words "virgin," "seduce," "mistress," and "pregnant" were actually spoken on screen. The film was denied the Production Code seal and the approval of the Catholic Legion of Decency, which was precisely what producer-director Otto Preminger [73 . . .] was aiming for. As a result of the publicity gained by his persistence in releasing it, *The Moon Is Blue* not only cleaned up at the box office but entered the history books as the film that undermined the industry's system of self-censorship, which had been in effect for nearly twenty years. It goes without saying that no one would be shocked by the movie today, but in fact hardly anyone was really shocked by it at the time. Audiences, drawn in by the promise that they'd see something risqué, were disappointed and incredulous at the controversy, turning the censorship board into a nationwide laughingstock and causing its rigid chairman, Joseph Breen, to resign. The Academy played both sides of the street, giving Breen an honorary Oscar "for his conscientious, open-minded and dignified management of the Motion Picture Production Code" at the 1953 ceremonies.

McNamara, a former model, had been in the second cast of the Broadway version of *Moon,* replacing Barbara Bel Geddes [972]. She made only three more films—*Three Coins in the Fountain, Prince of Players* (1955), and *The Cardinal*—and dropped from sight. After several serious emotional breakdowns, she committed suicide in 1978. Her film career was partly hindered because she bore a strong resemblance to a more gifted actress, Jean Simmons [858 . . .]. The Oscar went to Audrey Hepburn for *Roman Holiday.*

The song award went to Sammy Fain and Paul Francis Webster for ''Secret Love,'' from *Calamity Jane.* William Lyon won for editing *From Here to Eternity.*

Gilbert: 361, 2049. Fine: 675.

1349 • MOONRAKER

EON PRODUCTIONS LTD.; UNITED ARTISTS. 1979.
NOMINATION *Visual Effects:* Derek Meddings, Paul Wilson, and John Evans.

James Bond (Roger Moore) thwarts the plot of an industrialist (Michael Lonsdale) to conquer the world with weapons launched from a space station. Overblown and clunky, perhaps the worst of the Bond movies, with expensive special effects and stunt work trying to make up for a far-fetched script and the pedestrian acting of Moore and Lois Chiles. Directed by Lewis Gilbert [35]. The special effects award went to *Alien.*

Meddings: 1977.

1350 • MOONRISE

MARSHALL GRANT PICTURES; REPUBLIC. 1948.
NOMINATION *Sound Recording:* Daniel J. Bloomberg.

Dane Clark is ostracized in his hometown because his father was executed for murder, but things go from bad to worse when he accidentally kills one of his chief tormentors. Okay melodrama, given some distinction by a strong cast—Gail Russell, Ethel Barrymore [1445 . . .], Harry Morgan, Lloyd Bridges, Rex Ingram, and Harry Carey, Jr.—and a good director, Frank Borzage [132 . . .]. The sound award went to *The Snake Pit.*

Bloomberg: 274, 680, 693, 991, 1642, 1756.

1351 • MOONSTRUCK

PATRICK PALMER & NORMAN JEWISON PRODUCTION; MGM. 1987.
AWARDS *Actress:* Cher. *Supporting Actress:* Olympia Dukakis. *Screenplay Written Directly for the Screen:* John Patrick Shanley.
NOMINATIONS *Picture:* Patrick Palmer and Norman Jewison, producers. *Supporting Actor:* Vincent Gardenia. *Director:* Norman Jewison.

Cher plays a middle-aged widowed bookkeeper who lives with her parents, Dukakis and Gardenia, and her grandfather (Feodor Chaliapin), in New York City. She agrees to marry her long-standing boyfriend, Danny Aiello [556], even though she doesn't really love him, but then she falls in love with his younger brother, played by Nicolas Cage. Endlessly amusing romantic comedy, filled with peerless performances and lovingly observed eccentrics. Wittily counterpointed on the soundtrack by everything from Dean Martin's ''That's Amore'' to Vikki Carr's ''It Must Be Him'' to Puccini's *La Bohème.*

Cher's triumph capped the third phase of a remarkable career that began in the sixties when she teamed up with Sonny Bono as a singing duo. Together, they made two very forgettable films—*Wild on the Beach* (1965) and *Good Times* (1967)—and Cher also went solo in 1969 for the movie *Chastity.* (Later, Cher would conveniently forget her early efforts. Accepting the Oscar, she thanked Meryl Streep, with whom, she said, she had made her ''first movie,'' *Silkwood.* But it was in fact her fifth film.) The second stage of her career came in the seventies, when Sonny and Cher starred in a top-rated TV variety show before splitting up in middecade. And finally in the eighties she emerged as an actress, with a well-received performance in *Come Back to the 5 & Dime, Jimmy Dean, Jimmy Dean* (1982), followed by her first nominated performance in *Silkwood.* Her failure to receive a nomination for *Mask,* which had won her an award at Cannes, made her a sentimental favorite for the Oscar for *Moonstruck.* She faced less-than-formidable competition: Glenn Close for the controversial shocker *Fatal Attraction,* newcomer Holly Hunter for *Broadcast News,* Sally Kirkland, whose nomination for the little-seen *Anna* was the result of a strenuous publicity campaign, and Meryl Streep, in the critical and box-office failure *Ironweed.* Cher had reinforced her chances by appearing in two other films in 1987, *Suspect* and *The Witches of Eastwick,* demonstrating her versatility. Her post-Oscar film career has been skimpy: the 1990 dramatic comedy *Mermaids* and a cameo in *The Player.* She has devoted herself primarily to recording and music videos.

Dukakis was best known for stage work, although she had made film appearances, mostly in small roles, since 1964, when she made her debut in *Lilith.* She is the cousin of 1988 presidential candidate Michael Dukakis. Her post-Oscar career has been busy, with substantial roles in such films as *Dad* and *Steel Magnolias.*

Shanley was better known as a playwright before making his mark in films with *Moonstruck.* He has failed to repeat his success, following the Oscar with a disastrous effort, the confused *The January Man* in 1989 and an interesting but ultimately unsuccessful directorial debut with *Joe Versus the Volcano,* which he also wrote, in 1990.

Moonstruck was a critical and audience favorite, but the Academy was persuaded that the epic aims of *The Last Emperor* and its director, Bernardo Bertolucci, were superior. Gardenia, who died in 1992, lost to a universal favorite: Sean Connery in *The Untouchables.*

Cher: 1821. Palmer: 390, 1857. Jewison: 659, 992, 1736, 1857. Gardenia: 142.

1352 • MOONTIDE

20TH CENTURY-FOX. 1942.

NOMINATION *Black-and-White Cinematography:* Charles Clarke.

Sailor Jean Gabin rescues Ida Lupino from suicide in an interesting if minor romantic drama with Thomas Mitchell [962 . . .] and Claude Rains [365 . . .], directed by Archie Mayo. The screenplay is by John O'Hara, from a novel by Willard Robertson. The Oscar went to Joseph Ruttenberg for *Mrs. Miniver.*

Clarke: 837, 897, 1752.

1353 • MORE THE MERRIER, THE

COLUMBIA. 1943.

AWARD *Supporting Actor:* Charles Coburn.

NOMINATIONS *Picture:* George Stevens, producer. *Actress:* Jean Arthur. *Director:* George Stevens. *Original Story:* Frank Ross and Robert Russell. *Screenplay:* Richard Flournoy, Lewis R. Foster, Frank Ross, and Robert Russell.

In wartime Washington, Arthur, who works for the government, rents out part of her flat to Coburn, who in turn sublets his part to Joel McCrea—to Arthur's shock. Coburn plays Cupid to bring his fellow housemates together, even though Arthur is engaged to someone else—a real drip. Delicious romantic comedy, not seen as often as it should be, perhaps because its problems-of-wartime situation dates it a bit. It was remade as *Walk, Don't Run* (1966), in which the housing shortage is that of Tokyo during the Olympics, but the remake is notable only as the last film of Cary Grant [1445 . . .]. The three principals are excellent, and while Coburn and Arthur got the Academy's attention, McCrea also deserved it: Few leading men of his day played both comic and action roles with his finesse, yet he never received an Oscar nomination.

Often cast as an Englishman, Coburn was actually born in Georgia. He spent most of his early career on stage and finally made his film debut, in his late fifties, in the title role of *Boss Tweed* in 1933. His career as a lovable, sophisticated grandfatherly type flourished in the forties but extended through the fifties, including two memorable outings with Marilyn Monroe, *Monkey Business* (1952) and *Gentlemen Prefer Blondes* (1953). He made his last screen appearance in 1960, at the age of eighty-three, in *Pepe.* He died in 1961.

This was, remarkably, the only nomination for Arthur, even though she starred in a number of classics: *Mr. Deeds Goes to Town, Easy Living* (1937), *You Can't Take It With You, Only Angels Have Wings, Mr. Smith Goes to Washington,* and others. Her career in movies began in 1923, while she was still in her teens. Though she made numerous silent movies, she survived the transition to sound because of her distinctive voice. She made her last screen appearance in 1953 in *Shane,* and after a TV sitcom in 1956 retired from acting. She died in 1991, in her mid-eighties. The Oscar went to Jennifer Jones for *The Song of Bernadette.*

Stevens lost to *Casablanca,* which took the awards for best picture and for director Michael Curtiz. Although Garson Kanin [11 . . .] has claimed authorship of the first version of the screenplay for *The More the Merrier* in collaboration with Russell, he was denied credit on the finished film. Ross (who was married to Arthur at the time) and Russell lost to William Saroyan for *The Human Comedy.* The screenplay Oscar went to *Casablanca*'s Julius and Philip Epstein and Howard Koch.

Coburn: 535, 838. Stevens: 542, 768, 1579, 1799, 1998. Ross: 1706. Foster: 1370.

1354 • MORGAN!

QUINTRA FILMS LTD. PRODUCTION; CINEMA V DISTRIBUTING (UNITED KINGDOM). 1966.
NOMINATIONS *Actress:* Vanessa Redgrave. *Black-and-White Costume Design:* Jocelyn Rickards.

Artist Morgan Delt (David Warner) goes nuts when his wife (Redgrave) announces that she's leaving him for an art dealer (Robert Stephens). Morgan's eccentric behavior reflects his obsession with the gorillas that form the subject of his paintings. Funny-sad but somewhat pointless satire, directed by Karel Reisz from a script adapted by David Mercer from his own play. Like a lot of the comedies that came out of Britain in the sixties, including *Georgy Girl* and *The Knack, and How to Get It* (1965), it hasn't held up too well; its cheekiness now seems rather juvenile, and its depiction of Morgan's breakdown strikes a lot of people today as more painful than funny. Redgrave was nominated along with her sister, Lynn, who was up for her performance in *Georgy Girl.* They were the first sisters to receive simultaneous nominations since Joan Fontaine was nominated for *Rebecca* in the same year Olivia de Havilland was up for *Hold Back the Dawn.* The Oscar went to Elizabeth Taylor for *Who's Afraid of Virginia Woolf?* The costuming award went to Irene Sharaff, also for *Virginia Woolf.*

Redgrave: 263, 954.5, 1021, 1066, 1285.

1355 • MORITURI

ARCOLA-COLONY PRODUCTION; 20TH CENTURY-FOX. 1965.
NOMINATIONS *Black-and-White Cinematography:* Conrad Hall. *Black-and-White Costume Design:* Moss Mabry.

Secret agent Marlon Brando [583 . . .] poses as an SS officer to help the British capture a German freighter during World War II. Routine action thriller, made by Brando to fulfill a contractual obligation to Fox. Directed by Bernhard Wicki, with Yul Brynner [1088], Trevor Howard [1875], Janet Margolin, and Wally Cox. The title is an allusion to the words supposedly spoken to the Roman emperors by gladiators before a combat: *Morituri te salutamus*—we who are about to die salute you. When the film failed at the box office, it was retitled *Saboteur: Code Name Morituri,* because some felt the title was to blame for the poor audiences. A stronger, tighter script might have helped.

The cinematography award went to Ernest Laszlo for another seafaring film set in wartime, *Ship of Fools.* The costuming Oscar was won by Julie Harris for *Darling.*

Hall: 317, 504, 987, 1627, 1771.5, 2017. Mabry: 768, 2238, 2247.

1356 • MORNING AFTER, THE

LORIMAR MOTION PICTURES PRODUCTION; 20TH CENTURY FOX. 1986.
NOMINATION *Actress:* Jane Fonda.

Fonda plays an alcoholic who wakes up in bed with a corpse with a knife in his back, but she doesn't remember how she got there. Jeff Bridges [1139 . . .] comes to her aid in unraveling the mystery. The first-rate performances by the leads keep this routine thriller afloat, even though nothing about it makes a lot of sense. Sidney Lumet [561 . . .] directed, and the cast includes Raul Julia. The Oscar went to Marlee Matlin for *Children of a Lesser God.*

Fonda: 394, 430, 1066, 1104, 1473, 2047.

1357 • MORNING GLORY

RKO RADIO. 1932–33.
AWARD *Actress:* Katharine Hepburn.

Hepburn plays Eva Lovelace, a small-town girl

who comes to the big city determined to become a star on Broadway. Among the city folk who take note of her beauty, if not her talent, which is questionable anyway, are Douglas Fairbanks, Jr., and Adolphe Menjou [743]. Interesting if sometimes stiffly directed by Lowell Sherman, this backstage drama would probably be long forgotten if it hadn't helped launch one of Hollywood's greatest careers. It's based on a play by Zoë Akins and was remade in 1958 as *Stage Struck,* in which the inadequacy of Susan Strasberg in the Hepburn role exposed the flimsiness of the vehicle.

To some extent, *Morning Glory* recapitulates Hepburn's own experiences. Born to a well-to-do New England family, she was also stagestruck and managed to launch an acting career in 1928 without much training or experience. Her first success, in a play called *The Warrior's Husband* in 1932, attracted the attention of RKO, which like most Hollywood studios was raiding Broadway for talent to replace stars whose careers had faded with the coming of sound. Her screen debut in *A Bill of Divorcement* (1932) was a sensation, and the Oscar the next year certified her arrival in Hollywood. On the other hand, Hollywood wasn't entirely sure about this new arrival. Hepburn was unconventional in appearance and somewhat mannered in acting style. For her part, Hepburn was unhappy in Hollywood and returned to New York in 1933 to appear in *The Lake* on Broadway. But disastrous reviews caused the play to close quickly and she came back to RKO. For the rest of the decade, Hepburn's career reflected Hollywood's ambivalence about her, as well as the immaturity and poor training that undermined her enormous talent. At her best, in *Alice Adams, Stage Door, Bringing Up Baby* (1938), and *Holiday,* she demonstrated an appealing mixture of the earnest and the playful, an attractive vulnerability showing through the armor. But she was more often at her worst in the thirties: miscast in *Christopher Strong* (1933) and *Spitfire* (1934) and misdirected in *Mary of Scotland* (1936), or given material that drew out her worst mannerisms in *The Little Minister* (1934) and *Quality Street* (1937). As a result, she was on the infamous ''box-office poison'' list drawn up by a prominent exhibitor, which damaged the careers of Marlene Dietrich [1358], Mae West, and others. Her career was salvaged in the forties by the success of *The Philadelphia Story* and a potent teaming with Spencer Tracy [131 . . .] that began with *Woman of the Year.*

Hepburn: 24, 40, 843, 1177, 1199, 1473, 1563, 1654, 1956, 1963, 2305.

1358 • *MOROCCO*

PARAMOUNT PUBLIX. 1930–31.

NOMINATIONS *Actress:* Marlene Dietrich. *Director:* Josef von Sternberg. *Cinematography:* Lee Garmes. *Interior Decoration:* Hans Dreier.

Cabaret singer Dietrich comes to Morocco to cut a swath through the Foreign Legion. Though Adolphe Menjou [734] offers her a life of luxury and wealth, she gives it up for legionnaire Gary Cooper [701 . . .]. Sublime nonsense that transcends all notions of taste and art and dramatic credibility—enjoy it for what it is.

This was Dietrich's first American film, and the second (after 1930's *The Blue Angel,* the film that made her a star) in the series of seven films she made with Sternberg. Paramount snapped her up as a potential competitor to Greta Garbo [84 . . .], and a legendary career was born. Sternberg and cameraman Garmes carefully crafted her image as an exotic, sexually ambiguous temptress. By the end of the thirties she and Sternberg had gone their separate ways, in part because of the poor box office of their later films. *Destry Rides Again* (1940) initiated a second stage in her career, in which she became looser and funnier and more self-mocking. When war broke out, she spent much of her time entertaining the American troops, often putting herself at risk. She earned the American Medal of Freedom, but also the enmity of her fellow Germans, many of whom regarded her anti-Nazi activities as treason. She gave some of her best performances in postwar films such as *A Foreign Affair* and *Witness for the Prosecution* but became most celebrated for her nightclub performances, carefully crafted to display her as alluring well into her seventies. Eventually she made a celebrated return to Germany, where she triumphed over protesters. After a bad fall during an Australian tour in 1975, she retired, spending most of the years before her death in 1992 in seclusion, except for a cameo appearance in 1979 in the film *Just a Gigolo* and off-camera interviews by Maximilian Schell [1065 . . .] for his fine 1984 documentary *Marlene.* She lost her sole Oscar nomination to Marie Dressler for *Min and Bill.*

Von Sternberg was born without the ''von,'' which was added either by a producer who thought it looked classy in the credits or by Sternberg himself—the stories vary. Born in Vienna, he spent much of his childhood in the United States. He began his film career before World War I as a cutter and writer and assistant director, and made training films for the army during the war. He gradually became an important Hollywood director in the twenties and in 1930 went to Germany to direct Emil Jannings [1134 . . .] in *The Blue Angel.* In Berlin he discovered Dietrich, whom he molded into a star. It's been said that she was Trilby to his Svengali, but that underestimates her talent and her will to learn her trade. The seven films they made together became increasingly more bizarre in subject matter and style, climaxing perhaps in the extravagant 1934 *The Scarlet Empress,* in which Dietrich plays Catherine the Great in a Russia that exists only in fevered dreams. The directing Oscar this time went to Norman Taurog for *Skippy.*

Garmes lost to Floyd Croby for *Tabu.* The art direction Oscar went to *Cimarron.*

Von Sternberg: 1800. Garmes: 201, 1800, 1828. Dreier: 97, 151, 649, 674, 701, 726, 925, 979, 1101, 1120, 1194, 1214, 1217, 1443, 1452, 1540, 1668, 1748, 1880, 1975, 1994, 2190.

1359 • MOSCOW DOES NOT BELIEVE IN TEARS

MosFILM STUDIOS PRODUCTION (USSR). 1980.
AWARD *Foreign Language Film.*

Three young women come to Moscow in 1958 and wind up as roommates. The film follows their lives as they pursue careers and mates—only one of them with much success—and ends with their reunion twenty years later. The kind of movie that Hollywood might have made in 1958 with Diane Varsi, Sandra Dee, and Jill St. John, it's interesting as a self-portrait of Soviet life. Directed by Vladimir Menshov.

1360 • MOTHER INDIA

MEHBOOB PRODUCTIONS (INDIA). 1957.
NOMINATION *Foreign Language Film.*

A family struggles to survive after the father is disabled, but when the son murders the man to whom they are in debt, the mother kills him for dishonoring the family. Directed by Mehboob, a leading filmmaker in Bombay, *Mother India* has been described as ''Bombay's answer to *Pather Panchali,''* the internationally acclaimed film by Satyajit Ray made in 1955 in the rival film center of Calcutta. But *Mother India* has been little seen in the United States, and the Oscar went to *The Nights of Cabiria.*

1361 • MOTHER IS A FRESHMAN

20TH CENTURY-FOX. 1949.
NOMINATION *Color Costume Design:* Kay Nelson.

Widow Loretta Young [428 . . .] shocks daughter Betty Lynn with her decision to go back to college, especially since it's the college Lynn is attending. And she only makes matters worse by becoming the most popular coed on campus and by winning the affections of professor Van Johnson, on whom Lynn has a crush. Corny romantic situation comedy that in play form became a staple of high school drama clubs in the fifties. Directed by Lloyd Bacon. The costuming award went to Leah Rhodes, Travilla, and Marjorie Best for *The Adventures of Don Juan.*

1362 • MOTHER WORE TIGHTS

20TH CENTURY-FOX. 1947.
AWARD *Scoring of a Musical Picture:* Alfred Newman.
NOMINATIONS *Color Cinematography:* Harry Jackson. *Song:* ''You Do,'' music by Josef Myrow, lyrics by Mack Gordon.

Mother is Betty Grable and Father is Dan Dailey [2258], trying to raise a family and keep their vaudeville act together at the same time. One of the best of the endless stream of period musicals churned out by Fox in the forties, this one, directed by Walter Lang [1088], has handsome production values and a strong supporting cast: Mona Freeman, Vanessa Brown, Sara Allgood [952], William Frawley, Veda Ann Borg, Sig Rumann, Lee Patrick, and—this is a really big show —Señor Wences. The off-screen narrator is Anne Baxter [46 . . .]. The cinematography Oscar went to Jack Cardiff for *Black Narcissus*. Allie Wrubel and Ray Gilbert's "Zip-A-Dee-Doo-Dah," from *Song of the South,* won the song Oscar.

Newman: 31, 34, 46, 72, 138, 182, 226, 333, 334, 347, 375, 428, 437, 457, 476, 495, 542, 690, 797, 833, 952, 953, 959, 962, 1016, 1082, 1088, 1213, 1278, 1397, 1475, 1616, 1655, 1849, 1868, 1883, 1921, 2043, 2046, 2091, 2258, 2286, 2294, 2316. Myrow: 2219. Gordon: 428, 563, 569, 897, 1501, 1964, 1984, 2219.

1363 • *MOULIN ROUGE*

ROMULUS FILMS LTD. PRODUCTION; UNITED ARTISTS. 1952.
AWARDS *Color Art Direction–Set Decoration:* Paul Sheriff; Marcel Vertes. *Color Costume Design:* Marcel Vertes.
NOMINATIONS *Picture:* John Huston, producer. *Actor:* Jose Ferrer. *Supporting Actress:* Colette Marchand. *Director:* John Huston. *Film Editing:* Ralph Kemplen.

Ferrer plays Henri de Toulouse-Lautrec, the *fin de siècle* Parisian artist, whose dwarfism was the result of a childhood accident. As drama, *Moulin Rouge* lacks a compelling plotline, but its stunning design, re-creating the milieu that inspired a great artist, and its exploration of the world from Lautrec's point of view make it very watchable. The screenplay is by Huston and Anthony Veiller [1085 . . .], and the unforgivably unnominated cinematography is by Oswald Morris [659 . . .]. Morris had fierce battles with the Technicolor consultants who were contractually obligated to be present on every film made in their process. His desire for a soft, diffused look, echoing the palette and texture of the artist's works, was at odds with Technicolor's insistence on crisp, bold colors. The cinematography branch of the Academy, which has often been wary of experimentation, bypassed Morris in favor of more conventional work on mediocre films such as *Million Dollar Mermaid* and *The Snows of Kilimanjaro*. Although the art direction and costuming certainly deserved recognition, it's doubtful that

they would have appeared to such good effect without Morris' lighting and filters.

The omission of Morris was not, however, the most controversial move by the Academy this year: Awarding the best picture Oscar to *The Greatest Show on Earth* was, especially since the other nominees included *High Noon* and *The Quiet Man*. (*Ivanhoe* was the fifth nominee, supplanting worthier contenders such as *The Bad and the Beautiful,* which went on to win more Oscars than any other film in the history of the awards that was not nominated for best picture, and *Singin' in the Rain,* which has become one of the most celebrated of all Hollywood musicals.) The failure of the superior contenders can be explained by the fact that both *High Noon* and *Moulin Rouge* were independent productions released through United Artists, and *The Quiet Man* was released through a minor studio, Republic. At this point, the studio system, though crumbling, still held sway at the Oscars. That would begin to change in 1955, when *Marty,* a United Artists release, took the big one, initiating a period in which UA would dominate the top award.

Ferrer, who had won the Oscar two years earlier for *Cyrano de Bergerac,* gained more acclaim for the stunt used to diminish his stature—an apparatus that allowed him to walk on his knees—than for his acting, although he plays two roles, the artist and his father, in the film. The Oscar went to Gary Cooper for *High Noon,* which also won for editors Elmo Williams and Harry Gerstad.

Marchand, who plays Marie Charlet, had no significant international career after her nomination, which she lost to Gloria Grahame in *The Bad and the Beautiful.*

The Oscar for directing went to John Ford for *The Quiet Man.*

Sheriff: 901. Huston: 24, 105, 356, 571, 891, 1248, 1263, 1625, 1779, 2136. Ferrer: 473, 1048. Kemplen: 503, 1471.

1364 • *MOURNING BECOMES ELECTRA*

RKO RADIO. 1947.
NOMINATIONS *Actor:* Michael Redgrave. *Actress:* Rosalind Russell.

At the end of the Civil War, Gen. Ezra Mannon, played by Raymond Massey [1], returns to his home in New England, to find that his wife, Christine, played by Katina Paxinou [701], has been unfaithful to him with a seafaring man, Adam Brant, played by Leo Genn [1644]. Christine poisons Mannon, whereupon her children, Lavinia (Russell) and Orin (Redgrave), murder Brant. Christine commits suicide, and the children are so guilt-ridden that Orin also kills himself and Lavinia shuts herself up in the Mannon mansion to live out her life alone. Dreary, endless (nearly three hours long) adaptation of the Eugene O'Neill play based on Aeschylus' *Oresteia,* helped not at all by the eccentric casting: Massey is Canadian, Paxinou Greek, Russell American, and Redgrave English. As Pauline Kael observed, "It is apparent from their accents that they have only recently become a family." Dudley Nichols [30 . . .], who also directed, wrote the screenplay, but although he had successfully adapted O'Neill to the screen in *The Long Voyage Home,* this time it doesn't work. The cast also includes Kirk Douglas [130 . . .] as the suitor Lavinia rejects at the end of the film.

This was the only nomination for Redgrave, one of the great actors of the English stage, although he gave strong performances in such films as *The Lady Vanishes* (1938), *Dead of Night* (1945), *The Browning Version* (1951), *The Importance of Being Earnest* (1952), and *The Innocents* (1961). Connoisseurs of Oscar trivia will note that he's the only acting nominee to have fathered two acting nominees: Lynn [761] and Vanessa [263 . . .]. The Oscar went to Ronald Colman for *A Double Life.*

Russell's nomination was the result of both canny publicity and strong goodwill from the Hollywood community, where she was well liked. And despite the film's failure at the box office, she was considered the front-runner in a race against Joan Crawford for *Possessed,* Susan Hayward for *Smash Up—the Story of a Woman,* and Dorothy McGuire for *Gentleman's Agreement.* Crawford had won two years earlier, and both Hayward and McGuire were first-time nominees. But the surprise winner was Loretta Young, for *The Farmer's Daughter.* Young had the advantage of being even more of a Hollywood veteran than Russell, with a career stretching back to the silent era, and of having appeared in a film that Academy voters had actually seen.

Russell: 110, 1403, 1834.

1365 • MR. & MRS. BRIDGE

Merchant Ivory Productions; Miramax Films. 1990.
Nomination *Actress:* Joanne Woodward.

The Bridges, played by Woodward and Paul Newman [3 . . .], are a middle-aged midwestern couple who have grown so familiar with one another over the years that they scarcely notice the routines that they have fallen into in their relationship, until events in the lives of their children (Kyra Sedgwick and Robert Sean Leonard) and the outside world intrude, and they must make individual and sometimes conflicting choices. Delicate, evocative, and occasionally very funny character drama that works principally because of the consummate artistry of Woodward and Newman, who have no trouble at all playing a long-married couple. The film's chief flaw lies in its screenplay, by Ruth Prawer Jhabvala [954.5 . . .], which is an adaptation of two novels by Evan Connell. In the two books, *Mr. Bridge* and *Mrs. Bridge,* Connell tells the same story from separate points of view, a narrative tour de force that also makes plain the author's point: that even in the closest relationships, communication never fully succeeds. Jhabvala's uniting the two stories into one narrative shifts the angle of vision in one direction, so that Mrs. Bridge, because she's a warmer and more sympathetic character, becomes the central consciousness of the film. As with most of the films by the team of producer Ismail Merchant [954.5 . . .], director James Ivory [954.5 . . .], and writer Jhabvala, you feel the rightness of the design and performances and texture of the film, even if you come away somewhat unsatisfied. Woodward lost the Oscar to Kathy Bates in *Misery.*

Woodward: 1645, 1962, 2075.

1366 • MR. DEEDS GOES TO TOWN

COLUMBIA. 1936.

AWARD *Director:* Frank Capra.

NOMINATIONS *Picture:* Frank Capra, producer. *Actor:* Gary Cooper. *Screenplay:* Robert Riskin. *Sound Recording:* John Livadary.

Longfellow Deeds (Cooper), who lives in a small town in Vermont and loves to write greeting-card doggerel and play the tuba, inherits a fortune. Ace reporter Babe Bennett, played by Jean Arthur [1353], is assigned the task of finding out what makes this hick tick. She feigns affection for Deeds to get close to him but finds herself falling in love. When he discovers her identity, he decides he's had enough of the big time and announces he's going to give his millions away. But his lawyer, afraid of losing his meal ticket, decides to have him declared insane. Only Babe's confession that she really loves him persuades Deeds to fight the charges. Artful blend of screwball comedy, social comment, whimsy, and pathos, adapted from a magazine story by Clarence Budington Kelland, *Deeds* is one of the essential films of the thirties and like all Capra films, it has adoring admirers. But others find that its message—the little people are better than the fat cats, and country folk are superior to city slickers—is presented too ham-handedly. The movie made Jean Arthur a star after more than a decade in the business. The cast includes Lionel Stander, Douglass Dumbrille, Raymond Walburn, Charles Lane, Irving Bacon, Walter Catlett, H. B. Warner [1206], Franklin Pangborn, and even Gabby Hayes.

Capra had parlayed his first Oscar triumph for *It Happened One Night* into special status at Columbia, and *Deeds* is the first film that bears his name as producer as well as director. The best picture Oscar went to *The Great Ziegfeld.*

This was the first nomination for Cooper, in a role that was tailor-made for his ability to play both rugged and gentle. It's hard to imagine another actor bringing off Deeds' eccentricities—his tuba playing, fire-engine chasing, and banister sliding—without making a fool of himself. But as often, the Academy preferred high earnestness and gave the award to Paul Muni for *The Story of Louis Pasteur,* which also won for the screenplay by Pierre Collings and Sheridan Gibney.

The sound award went to Douglas Shearer for *San Francisco.*

Capra: 1025, 1033, 1119, 1206, 1370, 2325. Cooper: 701, 912, 1607, 1779. Riskin: 905, 1025, 1119, 2325. Livadary: 330, 455, 596, 732, 1058, 1206, 1215, 1303, 1370, 1488, 1521, 1740, 1872, 2111, 2325, 2327.

1367 • MR. DODD TAKES THE AIR

WARNER BROS. 1937.

NOMINATION *Song:* "Remember Me," music by Harry Warren, lyrics by Al Dubin.

Minor musical comedy about a small-town guy who becomes a hit on the radio as a singer, with Kenny Baker, Jane Wyman [246 . . .], and Alice Brady [990 . . .], directed by Alfred E. Green. The Oscar went to Harry Owens' "Sweet Leilani," from *Waikiki Wedding.*

Warren: 21, 324, 569, 788, 791, 877, 897, 1072, 1501, 1964. Dubin: 791, 1900.

1368 • MR. HULOT'S HOLIDAY

FRED ORAIN PRODUCTION; GBD INTERNATIONAL RELEASING CORPORATION (FRANCE). 1955.

NOMINATION *Story and Screenplay:* Jacques Tati and Henri Marquet.

Hulot (Tati), a storklike figure with an engagingly out-of-it manner, takes his vacation by the sea and initiates a series of enchanting and hilarious calamities. Writer, director, and star Tati, a former rugby player and music hall star, launched his feature film career in 1949 with *Jour de Fête,* a comedy about a provincial postman that was a hit, provoking comparisons with great silent comedians such as Buster Keaton and Harold Lloyd. *Mr. Hulot* brought him international fame, although many think *My Uncle* (1958) and *Playtime* (1968), with their satiric glances at modern life and technology, are even better. The Oscar went to William Ludwig and Sonya Levien for *Interrupted Melody.*

1368.5 • MR. SATURDAY NIGHT

CASTLE ROCK ENTERTAINMENT PRODUCTION; COLUMBIA. 1992.
NOMINATION *Supporting Actor:* David Paymer.

Billy Crystal plays a stand-up comedian who moves from the Borscht Belt to nightclubs to TV to an old age of working retirement communities and cruise ships, but usually winds up alienating his audiences as well as everyone behind the scenes. His brother (Paymer) patiently endures the years of abuse. Crystal also wrote—in collaboration with Lowell Ganz [1893] and Babaloo Mandel [1893]—and directed this occasionally amusing but often tedious showbiz saga. Its chief flaw is that Crystal, an engaging comedian with superb timing and a lightning wit, is unable to convert himself into his antithesis, a hostile comic undone by bad taste and poor judgment—an amalgam of the worst elements of Don Rickles, Milton Berle, and numerous lesser comedians. The excellent supporting cast includes Julie Warner as Crystal's wife, Helen Hunt, Jerry Orbach, and Ron Silver, with cameos from Slappy White and Jerry Lewis. Paymer, a fine character actor with a decade or so of work in TV (*Cagney and Lacey*) and movies, lost to Gene Hackman in *Unforgiven.*

1369 • MR. SKEFFINGTON

WARNER BROS. 1944.
NOMINATIONS *Actress:* Bette Davis. *Supporting Actor:* Claude Rains.

Beautiful but flighty Davis marries Skeffington (Rains) for his money, so she can help her brother out of a jam. When her frivolity and her indifference toward their daughter finally become too much for him, he has an affair, whereupon Davis divorces him. But the years pass and her beauty fades, while he goes blind, so at the end they are reunited in a perfect union; she redeems herself by tending him, and he can't see that she is no longer beautiful. One of the classic Davis melodramas, not quite on a par with *Dark Victory* or *Now, Voyager,* and a bit longer (146 minutes) than it needs to be, but always fun to watch. The screenplay is by Julius [365 . . .] and Philip Epstein [365] and the director is Vincent Sherman. The cast includes Walter Abel, George Coulouris,

Jerome Cowan, Gigi Perreau, and Dolores Gray. Davis lost to Ingrid Bergman in *Gaslight.* Barry Fitzgerald took the supporting actor award for *Going My Way.*

Davis: 46, 484, 492, 1046, 1162, 1182, 1456, 1462.5, 1908, 2248. Rains: 365, 1370, 1455.

1370 • MR. SMITH GOES TO WASHINGTON

COLUMBIA. 1939.
AWARD *Original Story:* Lewis R. Foster.
NOMINATIONS *Picture:* Frank Capra, producer. *Actor:* James Stewart. *Supporting Actor:* Harry Carey. *Supporting Actor:* Claude Rains. *Director:* Frank Capra. *Screenplay:* Sidney Buchman. *Interior Decoration:* Lionel Banks. *Sound Recording:* John Livadary. *Score:* Dimitri Tiomkin. *Film Editing:* Gene Havlick and Al Clark.

When an incumbent U.S. senator dies, the state's other senator, Joseph Paine (Rains), decides the best way to keep his delegation in line is to have a naive young patriot, Jefferson Smith (Stewart), appointed to the position. But Smith's innocence makes him a laughingstock until he discovers that his idol, Paine, is corrupt. With only his secretary, played by Jean Arthur [1353] behind him, Smith launches into a desperate filibuster to show the country the truth about what's going on in Washington. A classic, thanks largely to one of Stewart's finest performances and a magnificent cast that also includes Edward Arnold, Guy Kibbee, Thomas Mitchell [962 . . .], Eugene Pallette, Beulah Bondi [807 . . .], H. B. Warner [1206], Porter Hall, Charles Lane, William Demarest [1058], H. V. Kaltenborn, and Jack Carson. It's certainly not subtle, but it has an energy and enthusiasm that make its harangue about truth, justice, and the American Way tolerable. Ironically this great flag-waver got under the thin skin of some members of the U.S. Senate—though there were others who praised it—and Capra claimed that Joseph P. Kennedy, then the ambassador to Great Britain, tried to prevent the film's being exported.

Foster's original story was called ''The Gentleman From Montana,'' although in the film the state Mr. Smith represents is never named. Foster had begun his career writing gags for the silent comedies produced by Hal Roach. He also began directing in 1936 but was more successful as a screenwriter.

In a year of formidable competition, *Mr. Smith* lost the best picture Oscar to *Gone With the Wind*, which also won for Victor Fleming's direction, Sidney Howard's screenplay, Lyle Wheeler's art direction, and Hal C. Kern and James E. Newcom's editing.

To give Smith the proper hoarseness as his filibuster wore on, Stewart asked a doctor to prescribe something that would give him a sore throat. His performance boosted his career, and it's generally thought that Stewart's Oscar the following year, for *The Philadelphia Story*, was a consolation prize for losing to Robert Donat in *Goodbye, Mr. Chips*.

Carey, best known for his long career in westerns, plays the vice president. He and Rains lost to a fellow cast member, Thomas Mitchell, for his performance in *Stagecoach*.

The sound award went to Bernard B. Brown for *When Tomorrow Comes*. Richard Hageman, Frank Harling, John Leipold, and Leo Shuken shared the scoring award for *Stagecoach*.

Foster: 1353. Capra: 1025, 1033, 1119, 1206, 1366, 2325. Stewart: 73, 876, 1033, 1563. Rains: 365, 1369, 1455. Buchman: 904, 1057, 1998. Banks: 13, 98, 455, 928, 1115, 1998. Livadary: 330, 455, 596, 732, 1058, 1206, 1215, 1303, 1366, 1488, 1521, 1740, 1872, 2111, 2325, 2327. Tiomkin: 33, 286, 380, 446, 638, 663, 730, 768, 850, 911, 912, 1206, 1347, 1470, 2006, 2127, 2282, 2335. Havlick: 1206, 2325. Clark: 53, 114, 456, 1550.

1370.5 • MRS. DOUBTFIRE

20TH CENTURY FOX PRODUCTION; 20TH CENTURY FOX. 1993.
AWARD *Makeup:* Greg Cannom, Ve Neill, and Yolanda Toussieng.

Life with her eccentric husband, Daniel, played by Robin Williams [511 . . .], grows so difficult that Miranda, played by Sally Field [1448 . . .], sues for divorce and wins custody of their three children. Daniel, desperate to see more of the kids he's allowed to visit only on weekends, persuades his brother, a makeup artist played by Harvey Fierstein, to disguise him as a woman, and gets hired on as his own children's nanny, Mrs. Doubtfire. Things get even more complicated when Miranda starts a romance with Stu (Pierce Brosnan) that Daniel is determined to break up, and when Daniel gets a chance at a job that would satisfy the court's requirement that he be gainfully employed—but the crucial interview is scheduled for a time and place when he has to show up as Mrs. Doubtfire. The nifty farce premise is tailor-made for the volatile talents of Williams, but unfortunately the script, by Randi Mayem Singer and Leslie Dixon, takes an excessively sentimental turn. As long as it showcases Williams, who is usually a hoot, the movie is fine. Audiences, however, didn't seem to mind the movie's draggy stretches, or its bashing of the career woman played by Field, as much as the critics did. *Mrs. Doubtfire* became a megahit, adding to the fortunes of its director, Chris Columbus, who was already raking it in from having directed the *Home Alone* movies.

Cannom: 272.5, 924.5, 937. Neill: 153.5, 167, 595.8, 600, 924.5. Toussieng: 595.8.

1371 • MRS. MINIVER

MGM. 1942.
AWARDS *Picture:* Sidney Franklin, producer. *Actress:* Greer Garson. *Supporting Actress:* Teresa Wright. *Director:* William Wyler. *Screenplay:* George Froeschel, James Hilton, Claudine West, and Arthur Wimperis. *Black-and-White Cinematography:* Joseph Ruttenberg.
NOMINATIONS *Actor:* Walter Pidgeon. *Supporting Actor:* Henry Travers. *Supporting Actress:* May Whitty. *Sound Recording:* Douglas Shearer. *Film Editing:* Harold F. Kress. *Special Effects:* A. Arnold Gillespie and Warren Newcombe, photographic; Douglas Shearer, sound.

The Minivers, Garson and Pidgeon, residents of an idyllic English village, face the onset of World War II with chins high and upper lips stiff. Mrs. M. is doughty through Dunkirk, valiantly shelters her brood through the bombings, and fends off a downed German flier (Helmut Dantine) in her own kitchen. She also marries off her son (Richard Ney) to Wright, who herself becomes a casualty of war. In short, a tidy little microcosm of England suffering but enduring. Phony, hokey, sappy—and somehow still enjoyable, if only for its historical value as the slickest and most sentimental of all Hollywood contributions to the war effort. Its purpose was to instill support for our British allies, but only the patriotic fervor of America's first year of the war could possibly justify giving it the best picture Oscar over *The Magnificent Ambersons* or *Yankee Doodle Dandy* among the nominees, or *To Be or Not to Be, Sullivan's Travels,* or *Now, Voyager* among the nonnominees.

Garson was discovered by no less than Louis B. Mayer, when the MGM head, traveling in London, spotted her in a stage production. He signed her to an MGM contract and cast her in *Goodbye, Mr. Chips,* creating a new Metro star virtually overnight. The retirement of Greta Garbo [84 . . .] and Norma Shearer [150 . . .] in 1941 gave Garson her choice of roles at the studio, including Mrs. Miniver, which had first been offered to Shearer. Garson was a major star through the war years, but her career began to decline in the fifties. She caused a scandal by marrying Richard Ney, her son in *Mrs. Miniver,* who was a decade younger than she. And her Oscar acceptance speech has become legendary for its length—it lasted a little more than five minutes, although mythmakers have claimed that it was much longer.

Wright was discovered by another mogul, Samuel Goldwyn [102 . . .], in the cast of *Life With Father* on Broadway, and made her screen debut in *The Little Foxes,* for which she received her first nomination. A year later she entered the record books as only the second person to receive simultaneous nominations in both leading and supporting role categories—she was also nominated for her role in *The Pride of the Yankees.* (The first dual nominee was Fay Bainter for *White Banners* and *Jezebel* in 1938.) But aside from *Shadow of a Doubt* and *The Best Years of Our Lives,* her subsequent films were mostly undistinguished. In recent years she has sometimes been seen in character roles in both films and TV.

Wyler, born in Germany, came to America in 1922 at the behest of Carl Laemmle, the head of Universal Pictures, who was a distant relative of Wyler's mother. (Laemmle was notorious for putting family members on the Universal payroll.) Wyler be-

gan directing in 1925, when he was only twenty-three, and turned out dozens of westerns in the silent era. In the thirties he was signed by Samuel Goldwyn, who appreciated Wyler's perfectionism, and began to rack up a string of Oscar nominations that make him the most nominated director in Academy annals. After winning his first Oscar, for *Mrs. Miniver,* Wyler joined the army air force and made several wartime documentaries.

The screenplay was based on a novel by Jan Struther. Hilton was perhaps the best known of the screenwriting team because of his novels, including *Lost Horizon* and *Goodbye, Mr. Chips,* both of which were filmed. Wimperis can be seen in the cast of *Mrs. Miniver,* in the role of Sir Henry.

This was the second Oscar for Ruttenberg, who was born in Russia and began as a newsreel photographer before going to work for Fox in the silent era. He joined MGM in 1926 and remained with the studio till the early sixties.

Garson first teamed with Pidgeon for *Blossoms in the Dust.* They made a pleasant, handsome, but rather bland pairing that led to a series of costarring assignments. Pidgeon lost to James Cagney in *Yankee Doodle Dandy.*

Travers, born in Ireland, was a veteran stage performer on both sides of the Atlantic when he made his screen debut in 1933. Usually cast as a cherubic elderly gentleman, he is best remembered as the angel Clarence in *It's a Wonderful Life.* The Oscar went to Van Heflin for *Johnny Eager.*

Whitty, born in 1865, was a major stage actress at the turn of the century and became Dame May Whitty in 1918, in recognition of her work entertaining the troops during World War I. She made occasional appearances in silent films and became a regular character player in the late thirties, with a particularly memorable performance in the title role of *The Lady Vanishes,* directed by Alfred Hitchcock [1171 . . .], in 1938.

The award for sound went to Nathan Levinson for *Yankee Doodle Dandy.* Daniel Mandell won for editing *The Pride of the Yankees.* The special effects Oscar was won by *Reap the Wild Wind.*

Franklin: 799, 1232, 1440, 1662, 2320. Garson: 239, 804, 1232, 1372, 1973, 2193. Wright: 1182, 1607. Wyler: 175, 184, 420, 534, 560, 730, 894, 1162, 1182, 1716, 2316. Froeschel: 1662. West: 804, 1662. Wimperis: 1662. Ruttenberg: 318, 573, 749, 769, 828, 1069, 1232, 1861, 2234. Pidgeon: 1232. Whitty: 1431. Shearer: 136, 202, 256, 397, 685, 817, 835, 1096, 1232, 1292, 1419, 1751, 1950, 1988, 2048, 2055, 2211, 2300. Kress: 573, 953, 1596, 2126, 2320. Gillespie: 175, 256, 685, 704, 835, 1388, 1905, 2048, 2055, 2122, 2300. Newcombe: 835, 2055.

1372 • MRS. PARKINGTON

MGM. 1944.

NOMINATIONS *Actress:* Greer Garson. *Supporting Actress:* Agnes Moorehead.

Garson plays a poor American woman who marries wealthy Walter Pidgeon [1232 . . .] and sets out to conquer Victorian society. Moorehead is a Frenchwoman who was Pidgeon's mistress and becomes Garson's confidante. Sometimes plodding saga, based on a novel by Louis Bromfield, with no surprises but some entertaining performances. The cast includes Edward Arnold, Cecil Kellaway [843 . . .] (as the prince of Wales), Gladys Cooper [1393 . . .], Frances Rafferty, Tom Drake, Peter Lawford, Dan Duryea, Lee Patrick, Rod Cameron, Kay Medford [737], and Hans Conreid. Directed by Tay Garnett and handsomely photographed by Joseph Ruttenberg [318 . . .]. Garson lost to Ingrid Bergman in *Gaslight,* Moorehead to Ethel Barrymore in *None but the Lonely Heart.*

Garson: 239, 804, 1232, 1371, 1973, 2193. Moorehead: 963, 1052, 1239.

1373 • MUDDY RIVER

KIMURA PRODUCTION (JAPAN). 1981.

NOMINATION *Foreign Language Film.*

A nine-year-old boy's parents object to his new friendship with a boy whose mother is a prostitute. Absorbing, beautifully photographed (by Shohei Ando) coming-of-age story set in Osaka in the fifties. Directed by Kohei Oguri. The Oscar went to *Mephisto.*

1374 • MUDLARK, THE

20TH CENTURY-FOX (UNITED KINGDOM). 1951.

NOMINATION *Black-and-White Costume Design:* Edward Stevenson and Margaret Furse.

The widowed Queen Victoria, played by Irene Dunne [114 . . .], is a recluse. But a young boy sneaks into the palace to catch a glimpse of the queen and awakens her interest in the outside world. Amusing little historical drama, with a padded-out Dunne in one of her last screen roles, and Alec Guinness [287 . . .] in one of his first, as Disraeli, plus Finlay Currie as Victoria's gruff Scottish manservant, John Brown. Directed by Jean Negulesco [1052] from a screenplay by Nunnally Johnson [815 . . .] based on a novel by Theodore Bonnet. The costuming award went to Edith Head for *A Place in the Sun.*

Stevenson: 495, 636. Furse: 85, 164, 1177, 1285, 1766.

1375 • MUPPET MOVIE, THE

JIM HENSON PRODUCTIONS; LORD GRADE/MARTIN STAARGER PRESENTATION; AFD. 1979.

NOMINATIONS *Song:* "The Rainbow Connection," music and lyrics by Paul Williams and Kenny Ascher. *Original Song Score and Its Adaptation or Adaptation Score:* Paul Williams and Kenny Ascher.

The first big-screen outing for the Muppets is a how-it-all-got-started saga, showing how Kermit left his swamp and linked up with Miss Piggy, Fozzie Bear, and the rest of the crew on their way to stardom. Amusing but slightly overextended, and stuffed with star cameos by Bob Hope, Milton Berle, Steve Martin, Orson Welles [407 . . .], and others. Directed by James Frawley. The best song Oscar went to David Shire and Norman Gimbel for "It Goes Like It Goes," from *Norma Rae.* Ralph Burns won for the score for *All That Jazz.*

Williams: 309, 403, 1561, 1911.

1376 • MUPPETS TAKE MANHATTAN, THE

TRI-STAR PICTURES PRODUCTION; TRI-STAR. 1984.

NOMINATION *Original Song Score:* Jeff Moss.

Kermit, Miss Piggy, and the gang try to get backing to stage their show on Broadway. Charming, well-paced spoof of the Mickey Rooney–Judy Garland musicals, written by Tom Patchett, Jay Tarses, and director Frank Oz (who also speaks for the pig). Probably the best of the Muppet movies. The cast includes Dabney Coleman, Art Carney [875], James Coco [1495], Joan Rivers, and Gregory Hines. The Oscar went to Prince for *Purple Rain.*

1377 • MURDER, INC.

20TH CENTURY-FOX. 1960.

NOMINATION *Supporting Actor:* Peter Falk.

A look inside the thirties crime syndicate, with Falk as Abe Reles, the No. 1 hired killer of the mob. It's not up to the standards set in the Warners gangster movies of the real thirties, but it has a lot of interesting people to watch: Stuart Whitman [1277], Simon Oakland, Morey Amsterdam, Vincent Gardenia [142 . . .], Sylvia Miles [648 . . .], and Seymour Cassel [635] among them, plus singer Sarah Vaughan in one of her rare dramatic appearances. Directed by Burt Balaban. The nomination helped boost Falk's name recognition, but he lost to Peter Ustinov in *Spartacus.*

Falk: 1587.

1378 • MURDER ON THE ORIENT EXPRESS

G.W. FILMS LTD. PRODUCTION; PARAMOUNT (UNITED KINGDOM). 1974.

AWARD *Supporting Actress:* Ingrid Bergman.

NOMINATIONS *Actor:* Albert Finney. *Screenplay Adapted From Other Material:* Paul Dehn. *Cinematography:* Geoffrey Unsworth. *Original Dramatic Score:* Richard Rodney Bennett. *Costume Design:* Tony Walton.

When nasty businessman Richard Widmark [1098] is murdered aboard the famous train, Hercule Poirot (Finney) is called in to investigate. The suspects and standbys include mousy missionary Bergman, Lauren Bacall, Martin Balsam [2067], Jacqueline Bisset, Sean Connery [2185], John Gielgud [103 . . .], Wendy Hiller [1252 . . .], Anthony Perkins [730], Vanessa Redgrave [263 . . .], Rachel Roberts [2061], and Michael York. Sidney Lumet [561 . . .] directs what was planned as a triumph of style, but is mostly an evening of celebrity-spotting.

Bergman provides the highlight of the movie. She had been offered the role played by Hiller, an imperious Russian princess, but shrewdly recognized that the missionary was the better, although smaller part. She delivers what amounts to a delicious parody of her role in *The Inn of the Sixth Happiness.* She was stunned when she won the Oscar, and at the ceremony blurted out her embarrassment that she had won rather than Valentina Cortese, whose performance in *Day for Night* Bergman thought ''beautiful.'' Later she realized that she had slighted the other nominees—Madeline Kahn for *Blazing Saddles,* Diane Ladd for *Alice Doesn't Live Here Anymore,* and Talia Shire for *The Godfather, Part II*—and said she wished she'd kept her mouth shut. With her third award, she tied Walter Brennan [424 . . .] and Katharine Hepburn for the most Oscars won for acting. (Hepburn would pick up a fourth for *On Golden Pond* seven years later.)

Finney's nomination recognizes his versatility, but his performance is mostly a collection of eccentric mannerisms and a triumph of makeup. Art Carney won the Oscar for *Harry and Tonto.*

Dehn's adaptation of the Agatha Christie novel lost to Francis Ford Coppola and Mario Puzo's *The Godfather, Part II,* for which Carmine Coppola and Nino Rota also won the scoring Oscar. The cinematography award went to Fred Koenekamp and Joseph Biroc for *The Towering Inferno* and the costuming award to Theoni V. Aldredge for *The Great Gatsby.*

Bergman: 72. Finney: 579, 2106, 2177. Dehn: 1784. Unsworth: 164, 321, 2021. Bennett: 647, 1429. Walton: 49, 1285, 2299.

1379 • MURMUR OF THE HEART
Nouvelles Éditions de Films-Marianne Productions-Vides Cinematografica-Franz Seitz Filmproduktion; Continental Distributing Inc. (France). 1972.
Nomination *Story and Screenplay—Based on Factual Material or Material Not Previously Published or Produced:* Louis Malle.

A brilliant pubescent boy in fifties France is obsessed with losing his virginity. Meanwhile, his mother is carrying on an affair that ends unhappily. When the boy is left with a heart murmur after an illness, his mother takes him to a spa, where they console one another in bed. Delicious comedy about growing up that's not as shocking or as titillating as its plot outline makes it sound. Directed by Malle. The Oscar went to Jeremy Larner for *The Candidate.*

Malle: 107, 109.

1380 • MURPHY'S ROMANCE
Fogwood Films Production; Columbia. 1985.
Nominations *Actor:* James Garner. *Cinematography:* William A. Fraker.

Divorcée Sally Field [1448 . . .], trying to start a new life with her son (Corey Haim) in Arizona, falls in love with the local pharmacist (Garner). Easygoing little romance that depends on the considerable charisma of its two stars to flesh out the pleasant predictability of its story, by Irving Ravetch [956 . . .] and Harriet Frank, Jr. [956 . . .]. Directed by Martin Ritt [956]. The movie's chief claim to fame is that it provided Garner with the sole Oscar nomination in a career that began in 1956 and has been marked by solid, reliable performances in comic, dramatic, and action roles. The Oscar went to William Hurt for *Kiss of the Spider Woman.* David Watkin won for the cinematography for *Out of Africa.*

Fraker: 890, 1205, 1439, 2231.

1381 • MUSIC BOX
Carolco Pictures Production; Tri-Star. 1989.
Nomination *Actress:* Jessica Lange.

When her father, played by Armin Mueller-Stahl, is fingered as an ex-Nazi war criminal, Lange, an attorney, comes to his defense. But she finds disturbing evidence of his guilt. The great potential of the story is sapped when it's played for melodrama instead of exploring the characters and their moral dilemmas. Directed by Costa-Gavras [1330 . . .] from a screenplay by Joe Eszterhas, with Frederic Forrest [1726], Donald Moffat, Lukas Haas, and Michael Rooker. Lange lost to Jessica Tandy in *Driving Miss Daisy.*

Lange: 244.5, 449, 722, 1987, 2113.

1382 • MUSIC FOR MILLIONS
MGM. 1945.
Nomination *Original Screenplay:* Myles Connolly.

Musician June Allyson, who is pregnant, waits for her husband to return from the war. Meanwhile, Jose Iturbi's orchestra plays lots of light classics, and Allyson's kid sister Margaret O'Brien kibitzes. Forgettable sentimental musical, directed by Henry Koster [214]. The best thing about it is Jimmy Durante's clowning. The Academy apparently had to scrape to come up with five nominees in this category; they also included the screenplays for the low-budget gangster movie *Dillinger,* the unmemorable *Salty O'Rourke,* and the lightweight service comedy *What's Next, Corporal Hárgrove?.* The Oscar went to the Swiss film *Marie-Louise.*

1383 • MUSIC IN MANHATTAN
RKO Radio. 1944.
Nomination *Sound Recording:* Stephen Dunn.

Anne Shirley [1923] and Dennis Day star as a song-and-dance team trying to make it big on Broadway. Minor programmer with some nice musical support from the Charlie Barnet Orchestra. The cast includes Jane Darwell [815]. The award for sound went to E. H. Hansen for *Wilson.*

Dunn: 173, 1479, 2059.

1384 • MUSIC IN MY HEART
Columbia. 1940.
Nomination *Song:* "It's a Blue World," music and lyrics by Chet Forrest and Bob Wright.

Tony Martin plays a singer from an unspecified European country who faces deportation unless he can get work. He lands a job in a show with Rita Hayworth—and of course he gets Rita, too. Second-feature stuff of no particular distinction except that it was the first musical for Hayworth, who was on the cusp of fame. The cast, directed by Joseph Santley, includes the fussbudget support of Eric Blore and Alan Mowbray and features Andre Kostelanetz and his orchestra. The song Oscar went to Leigh Harline and Ned Washington for "When You Wish Upon a Star," from *Pinocchio*.

Forrest: 694, 1270. Wright: 694, 1270.

1385 • MUSIC MAN, THE

WARNER BROS. 1962.
AWARD *Scoring of Music—Adaptation or Treatment:* Ray Heindorf.
NOMINATIONS *Picture:* Morton Da Costa, producer. *Color Art Direction—Set Decoration:* Paul Groesse; George James Hopkins. *Sound:* George R. Groves, sound director, Warner Bros. Studio Sound Department. *Film Editing:* William Ziegler. *Color Costume Design:* Dorothy Jeakins.

Con man Harold Hill, played by Robert Preston [2201], persuades a small turn-of-the-century Iowa town that what it really needs to avoid "trouble, right here in River City," is a marching band to keep the kids occupied. His plot—to take the money for the instruments and run—is undone when he falls in love with the town librarian, Marian, played by Shirley Jones [609]. As a transcription of a Broadway musical smash hit, the movie, directed by Da Costa, who also directed the stage version, is invaluable, though it's too obviously pitched to an audience that's expected to hold up the show for applause. Still, if movie audiences applauded, they'd find plenty of reasons to do so—chief among them Preston's superb, charismatic performance. The Academy's failure to recognize it is a mystery. It has been suggested that voters regarded it as simply a Broadway performance re-created for the screen, but that didn't stop them from giving Oscars to Yul Brynner for *The King and I* or Rex Harrison for *My Fair Lady*. Preston's performance is certainly in the same league as Brynner's or Harrison's, not to mention the actors who were nominated

instead: Burt Lancaster for *Birdman of Alcatraz,* Jack Lemmon for *Days of Wine and Roses,* Marcello Mastroianni for *Divorce—Italian Style,* Peter O'Toole for *Lawrence of Arabia,* and the winner, Gregory Peck for *To Kill a Mockingbird*. Preston is well supported by Jones, Buddy Hackett, Paul Ford, Hermione Gingold, Pert Kelton, and eight-year-old Ron (billed as Ronny) Howard. (The future director's father, Rance Howard, has a small role, too.)

Heindorf's third Oscar is probably as much a tribute to the material he had to work with as to his own skill in arranging it. The songs by Meredith Willson [818 . . .] cover a range from ingenious novelty (the re-creation of a train journey in "Rock Island") to nostalgic evocation of an era ("Shipoopi," "Gary, Indiana") to soaring lyricism ("Till There Was You") to rousing showstopper ("76 Trombones"). Willson was urged to write the show by Frank Loesser [864 . . .], who thought Willson's Iowa boyhood would provide material for a musical. The Broadway version opened in December 1957 and ran for 1,375 performances.

The best picture award went to *Lawrence of Arabia,* which also won for art direction, sound, and Anne Coates' editing. The costume Oscar went to Mary Wills for *The Wonderful World of the Brothers Grimm.*

Heindorf: 331, 479, 666, 930, 1043, 1204, 1408, 1430, 1690, 1719, 1750, 1910, 2058, 2186, 2243, 2310, 2318. Groesse: 87, 1173, 1190, 1232, 1309, 1335, 1604, 2112, 2157, 2320. Hopkins: 110, 508, 896, 1003, 1170, 1332, 1393, 1910, 1949, 1973, 2058, 2277. Groves: 825, 1393, 1457, 1763, 1869, 1973, 2277. Ziegler: 110, 1393. Jeakins: 393, 509, 832, 882, 1048, 1391, 1432, 1748, 1881, 2012, 2238.

1386 • MUSIC TEACHER, THE

RTBF/K2 ONE PRODUCTION (BELGIUM). 1988.
NOMINATION *Foreign Language Film.*

The eminent operatic bass-baritone Jose Van Dam stars as a singer who retires from the stage and takes on a pair of students—a beautiful young woman and a man who's also a pickpocket. The film deals with their romance and their performance in a singing contest run by a bisexual count who's attracted to both of them. Silly and florid, but saved by the music and by Van Dam's performance. Directed by Gerard Corbiau. The Oscar went to *Pelle the Conqueror*.

1387 • MUTINY ON THE BOUNTY

MGM. 1935.

AWARD *Picture:* Irving Thalberg with Albert Lewin, producers.

NOMINATIONS *Actor:* Clark Gable. *Actor:* Charles Laughton. *Actor:* Franchot Tone. *Director:* Frank Lloyd. *Screenplay:* Jules Furthman, Talbot Jennings, and Carey Wilson. *Score:* MGM Studio Music Department, Nat W. Finston, head; score by Herbert Stothart. *Film Editing:* Margaret Booth.

Fletcher Christian (Gable) leads a rebellion against Captain Bligh (Laughton), whom Christian believes to be leading the ship into disaster. Tone plays Byam, the officer who separates from the mutineers before their journey to Pitcairn Island, and returns to England to stand trial. Handsome, rousing adventure classic, somewhat at odds with the facts—which were more evenhandedly presented in the 1985 *The Bounty*—but a prime example of MGM filmmaking at its best, full of juicy performances and technical finesse. Laughton's performance is regarded as one of his best, managing to present Bligh as neither evil nor incompetent, but nevertheless the kind of captain who might inspire a mutiny. The cinematography is by Arthur Edeson [48 . . .]. The cast also includes Dudley Digges, Henry Stephenson, Donald Crisp [952], Spring Byington [2325], and Movita, who plays Fletcher Christian's Polynesian lover and later married Marlon Brando, who played Christian in the 1962 remake. Connoisseurs of Oscar minutiae will note that *Mutiny* is the last best picture winner to have received no other Oscars; the others are *Broadway Melody* and *Grand Hotel,* and all three were MGM productions. And that *Mutiny* is the only film to have received three nominations in the best actor category, possibly because the supporting actor Oscar, for which Tone might have been more properly nominated, was not created until the 1936 awards. In the final balloting, Laughton came in third, after a write-in candidate, Paul Muni [218.5 . . .], in *Black Fury.* The winner was Victor McLaglen in *The Informer,* which also won for John Ford's direction, Dudley Nichols' screenplay, and Max Steiner's score. *Mutiny on the Bounty*'s screenplay and score both placed second.

This was the sole nomination for writer Furthman, one of the most prolific and distinctive screenwriters in Hollywood history. Furthman began writing for the movies in 1918 and was responsible for screenplays for such movies as *Morocco, Shanghai Express, Blonde Venus* (1932), *Only Angels Have Wings, The Outlaw* (1943), *To Have and Have Not* (1944), *The Big Sleep* (1946), and *Rio Bravo* (1959).

Another distinguished Hollywood veteran, Booth, also received her sole nomination for *Mutiny,* coming in second to Ralph Dawson for *A Midsummer Night's Dream.* She began her career as an assistant editor in 1921 with the Mayer studios. Her appointment as head of MGM's editing department in 1939 took her out of direct competition for the Oscars, though she became legendary as a supervisor at the studio, a position she held until 1968. Her work was recognized with an honorary Oscar "for her exceptional contribution to the art of film editing in the motion picture industry" at the 1977 awards.

Thalberg: 150, 202, 799, 812, 1721, 1846, 2129. Lewin: 799. Gable: 798, 1025. Laughton: 1620, 2297. Lloyd: 374, 552, 575, 2239. Jennings: 83. Finston: 1292. Stothart: 397, 1096, 1232, 1274, 1292, 1662, 1988, 2068, 2193, 2234, 2300.

1388 • MUTINY ON THE BOUNTY

ARCOLA PRODUCTION; MGM. 1962.

NOMINATIONS *Picture:* Aaron Rosenberg, producer. *Color Cinematography:* Robert L. Surtees. *Color Art Direction—Set Decoration:* George W. Davis and J. McMillan Johnson; Henry Grace and Hugh Hunt. *Song:* "Love Song From *Mutiny on the Bounty,*" music by Bronislau Kaper, lyrics by Paul Francis Webster. *Music Score—Substantially Original:* Bronislau Kaper. *Film Editing:* John McSweeney, Jr. *Special Effects:* A. Arnold Gillespie, visual; Milo Lory, audible.

The remake of the 1935 best picture winner features Marlon Brando [583 . . .] as Fletcher Christian and Trevor Howard [1875] as Captain Bligh, with Richard Harris [660 . . .] and Hugh Griffith [175 . . .] in supporting roles. Unfortunately it was an expensive disaster. The script went through multiple rewrites. The first version, by Eric Ambler [469], was thrown out and a new version by John Gay [1778] commissioned. Drafts followed from William Driscoll, Borden Chase [1676], Howard Clewes, and finally Charles Lederer. Location shooting at Tahiti proved expensive because of the unpredictable weather. The first director, Carol Reed [639 . . .], was replaced by Lewis Milestone [48 . . .]. Illness felled the crew, and an action sequence went awry, resulting in one fatality and multiple injuries. Finally Milestone left the picture, irked at Brando's resentment of his having replaced Reed, who had worked closely with Brando on his characterization of Christian as a fop made into a man by his confrontation with Bligh. George Seaton [31 . . .] completed the film, which was a box-office disaster.

As the film's nominations show, its chief strengths were in the technical categories. The best picture Oscar went to *Lawrence of Arabia,* which dominated the technical categories in which *Mutiny on the Bounty* might otherwise have captured a few awards. *Lawrence* also won for Fred A. Young's cinematography, for art direction, and for Maurice Jarre's score and Anne Coates' editing. The special effects award went to *The Longest Day.* The song category was made up entirely of title tunes from the year's movies—Webster had another nomination for the theme from *Tender Is the Night*—and the Oscar went to Henry Mancini and Johnny Mercer's "Days of Wine and Roses."

Surtees: 130, 175, 557, 810, 917, 1094, 1139, 1469, 1644, 1747, 1911, 1927, 1960, 2055, 2152. Davis: 46, 69, 401, 495, 542, 736, 953, 1213, 1336, 1537, 1552, 1706, 1814, 2157, 2184, 2312. Johnson: 636, 833, 978, 1595, 2098. Grace: 69, 227, 401, 769, 953, 1336, 1450, 1537, 1552, 2157, 2184, 2312. Hunt: 175, 401, 980, 1069, 1232, 1336, 1567, 1644, 1657, 1673, 2157, 2184. Kaper: 397, 1173. Webster: 33, 64, 95, 331, 376, 604, 663, 730, 856, 1213, 1276, 1322, 1755, 1925, 2014. Gillespie: 175, 256, 685, 704, 835, 1372, 1905, 2048, 2055, 2122, 2300. Lory: 175.

1389 • *MY BEAUTIFUL LAUNDRETTE*

WORKING TITLE LTD./SAF PRODUCTION FOR FILM FOUR INTERNATIONAL ORION CLASSICS (UNITED KINGDOM). 1986.
NOMINATION *Screenplay Written Directly for the Screen:* Hanif Kureishi.

Gordon Warnecke plays Omar, a young Pakistani living in London, who persuades his uncle (Roshan Seth) to help him set up business with a run-down Laundromat. With the aid of his working-class punk lover, Johnny, played by Daniel Day-Lewis [992.5 . . .], he turns the operation into a combination laundry and disco called Powders. Funny, offbeat movie, originally made for British TV, directed by Stephen Frears [840]. Kureishi and Frears subsequently teamed up for *Sammy and Rosie Get Laid* (1987), which like *Laundrette* explores sex and racism in contemporary London, but with a darker vision. The Oscar went to Woody Allen for *Hannah and Her Sisters.*

1390 • *MY BRILLIANT CAREER*

MARGARET FINK FILMS PTY. LTD. PRODUCTION; ANALYSIS FILM RELEASING (AUSTRALIA). 1980.
NOMINATION *Costume Design:* Anna Senior.

Sybylla, played by Judy Davis [962.5 . . .], is a young woman growing up in the Australian Outback at the turn of the century. Her family is poor, and they don't know quite what to do with the dreamy, intelligent Sybylla, who wants to be a writer. So her mother, who has married beneath her socially, sends Sybylla off to live with her wealthy grandmother, where Sybylla gets a little polish and attracts the attention of a handsome young man (Sam Neill). This idyll among the upper classes is interrupted when she is sent to tutor a slovenly outback family. In the end Sybylla rejects her handsome suitor's proposal and sets out to find her own way in the world. Very enjoyable coming-of-age story, based on a novel by sixteen-year-old Miles Franklin—some of the film's enigmas of characterization stem from the source, which was adapted by Eleanor Whitcombe. The Australian-made movie, directed by Gillian Armstrong, made stars of Davis and Neill. The costuming Oscar went to Anthony Powell for *Tess*.

1391 • *MY COUSIN RACHEL*
20TH CENTURY-FOX. 1952.
NOMINATIONS *Supporting Actor:* Richard Burton. *Black-and-White Cinematography:* Joseph LaShelle. *Black-and-White Art Direction—Set Decoration:* Lyle Wheeler and John DeCuir; Walter M. Scott. *Black-and-White Costume Design:* Charles LeMaire and Dorothy Jeakins.

Burton's elderly foster father marries a young woman, played by Olivia de Havilland [798 . . .], and then dies. Burton then falls in love with her, but she spurns his offer of marriage. Then he begins to suspect not only that she murdered her husband but that she's also trying to murder him. Rather muddled melodrama, based on the novel by Daphne du Maurier and directed by Henry Koster [214]. Burton and de Havilland were somewhat at odds during the filming, but he earned good reviews for his performance, which marked his American film debut. Though his part was clearly a leading role, the studio scoped out the competition and decided to put his name forward in the supporting actor category. He lost this, the first of his seven unsuccessful nominations, to Anthony Quinn for *Viva Zapata! The Bad and the Beautiful* won the remaining Oscars, for Robert Surtees' cinematography, for art direction, and for Helen Rose's costumes.

Burton: 85, 164, 621, 1706, 1897, 2277. LaShelle: 91, 357, 428, 709, 953, 1017, 1149, 1284. Wheeler: 19, 46, 83, 356, 376, 428, 476, 495, 530, 542, 719, 721, 798, 950, 1062, 1088, 1149, 1153, 1213, 1475, 1601, 1616, 1670, 1706, 1852, 2008, 2093, 2212. DeCuir: 29, 201, 376, 413, 476, 896, 950, 1088, 1852, 2000. Scott: 46, 376, 413, 476, 530, 542, 557, 646, 1062, 1088, 1213, 1475, 1706, 1753, 1881, 1907, 2008, 2120, 2247. LeMaire: 21, 46, 376, 495, 530, 542, 954, 1213, 1339, 1601, 1706, 2008, 2043, 2205, 2294. Jeakins: 393, 509, 832, 882, 1048, 1385, 1432, 1748, 1881, 2012, 2238.

1391.5 • *MY COUSIN VINNY*
20TH CENTURY FOX PRODUCTION; 20TH CENTURY FOX. 1992.
AWARD *Supporting Actress:* Marisa Tomei.

When New Yorkers Ralph Macchio and Mitchell Whitfield are arrested on suspicion of murder in a small southern town, Macchio calls on his cousin Vinny, played by Joe Pesci [806 . . .], to serve as his defense attorney. But Vinny's legal training and certification are, to put it mildly, suspect, and the judge (Fred Gwynne) in charge of the case is a Yale graduate and a stickler for proper court procedure. Fortunately Vinny's street smarts and the unusual expertise of his girlfriend Mona Lisa Vito (Tomei) who accompanies him help him win the case. Featherweight but enjoyable comedy, directed by Jonathan Lynn, that seems to have about half an hour of padding in it.

Tomei, still in her twenties, gives a superb comic performance, but she was still a surprise winner against a heavyweight lineup: Judy Davis in *Husbands and Wives,* Joan Plowright in *Enchanted April,* Vanessa Redgrave in *Howards End,* and Miranda Richardson in *Damage.* The difficulty of choosing among candidates with the credentials of those actresses may have tipped the voters in the direction of newcomer Tomei. But a legend has also grown up that presenter Jack Palance [408 . . .] was either unable to read the name he found in the envelope or unwilling to give the Oscar to the real winner—said to be Redgrave in some versions of the story—so he simply read off the last name on the cue card: Tomei. The Academy has firmly denied the rumor, as has the accounting firm of Price Waterhouse, the legendary keepers of the ballots.

1392 • *MY DEAREST SEÑORITA*
EL IMÁN PRODUCTION (SPAIN). 1972.
NOMINATION *Foreign Language Film.*

The lady of the title is Adela, who is actually Juan, masquerading to see what life is like as a woman. Directed by Jaime de Armiñán. The Oscar went to *The Discreet Charm of the Bourgeoisie.*

1393 • *MY FAIR LADY*

WARNER BROS. 1964.

AWARDS *Picture:* Jack L. Warner, producer. *Actor:* Rex Harrison. *Director:* George Cukor. *Color Cinematography:* Harry Stradling. *Color Art Direction—Set Decoration:* Gene Allen and Cecil Beaton; George James Hopkins. *Sound:* George R. Groves, sound director, Warner Bros. Studio Sound Department. *Scoring of Music—Adaptation or Treatment:* André Previn. *Color Costume Design:* Cecil Beaton.

NOMINATIONS *Supporting Actor:* Stanley Holloway. *Supporting Actress:* Gladys Cooper. *Screenplay—Based on Material From Another Medium:* Alan Jay Lerner. *Film Editing:* William Ziegler.

Linguistics professor Henry Higgins (Harrison) wagers that he can train a Cockney flower girl, Eliza Doolittle, played by Audrey Hepburn [278 . . .], to speak so well that people will think she's a duchess. He succeeds, of course, but at what cost? The most successful Broadway musical of all time if judged not only by its initial run of 2,717 performances in New York but also by its 2,281 performances in London, its two best-selling (mono and stereo) original cast albums, and its numerous revivals, including one on Broadway in 1993. And then it became a very, very big film musical. Size, unfortunately, isn't everything, and the delights of the movie—which include the witty dialogue adapted from Shaw's *Pygmalion* and the superb songs by Lerner and Frederick Loewe [769 . . .]—are weighted down quite a bit by the opulent sets and costumes. Warner, having spent a bundle to get the film rights, was determined to make the film distinct from the stage version and planned to give the show an entirely new cast. As a result, Julie Andrews [1284 . . .], who had created the part of Eliza, was denied a chance to leave her legendary performance on film. The widespread resentment at this helped make Andrews the winner for her performance in *Mary Poppins;* it may have also deprived Hepburn of a nomination. Though Hepburn is delightful in the role, accepting it may have been a bad career move, especially after she was forced to have her singing voice dubbed by Marni Nixon. Warner was, however, stymied in his attempts to recast other

roles: His first choice for Higgins, Cary Grant [1445 . . .], flatly refused, saying he wouldn't even see the movie if someone other than Harrison played the part. Peter O'Toole [164 . . .], who has subsequently played the *Pygmalion* Higgins, was also considered. James Cagney [79 . . .] declined to come out of retirement to play the part of Eliza's father, so it went to its creator, Holloway. The remaining cast includes Wilfred Hyde-White as Colonel Pickering, Cooper as Higgins' mother, Jeremy Brett as Freddy Eynsford-Hill, Theodore Bikel [522] as Higgins' Hungarian rival Zoltan Karpathy, and Mona Washbourne as Mrs. Pearce.

The best picture Oscar was the last triumph for the ruthless Warner, the youngest of the four brothers who founded the studio in 1917. They struggled through the twenties, a second-rank studio, until their pioneering work with sound in *The Jazz Singer* launched them into the major leagues. In 1956 Jack Warner engineered a coup that forced out his surviving brothers, Harry and Albert (Sam died in 1927), and became the chief stockholder and studio boss. After his triumph with *My Fair Lady,* however, Warner's next attempt at a prestige production, Lerner and Loewe's *Camelot,* was a box-office disaster. With *Camelot* he had his way, completely replacing the original cast, with unfortunate consequences. In 1967 he sold his interest in the studio to Seven Arts and became an independent producer, but with little success. He died in 1978.

Harrison had made his career on stage largely in light comedy roles—unlike other eminent British actors, he never played Shakespeare—and made a screen debut in Great Britain in 1930. His film career didn't take shape until the mid-forties, with movies such as *Anna and the King of Siam, Blithe Spirit,* and *The Ghost and Mrs. Muir.* But it was the original production of *My Fair Lady* in 1956 that made him a major star. Lerner and Loewe tailor-made the songs for Harrison's limited singing range, and his performance of Higgins, because it has been so well documented on both records and film, is the standard by which all others, even the nonsinging Higgins of *Pygmalion,* are now judged. But the film version seems a bit overrehearsed, as one might expect from someone who had played the role hundreds of times. The original cast recording documents a subtler, warmer characterization than the one on film.

Cukor's Oscar was long overdue—so long, in fact, that he is the oldest person, at sixty-five, ever to receive the best director award. A stage director, he was hired by Hollywood with the advent of sound and first worked as dialogue coach on *All Quiet on the Western Front* and served an apprenticeship as codirector on several films in 1930. In 1932 he went to work for David O. Selznick [497 . . .] at RKO, where one of his first assignments was *A Bill of Divorcement,* the debut film of Katharine Hepburn [24 . . .], with whom he would work off and on over the next forty years—their last collaboration was a TV movie, *Love Among the Ruins,* in 1975. In addition to the films for which he was nominated, Cukor was responsible for such movies as *David Copperfield, Camille, Gaslight, Adam's Rib,* and the 1954 *A Star Is Born.* Often labeled a "woman's director," frequently a euphemism to indicate that a director is gay, he was above all a superb director of actors of both sexes. He died in 1983 and is buried alongside his old friend Frances Goldwyn and her husband Samuel [102 . . .].

Though it was much admired at the time, and probably deserved the Academy's honors, the look of *My Fair Lady* has dated. Beaton, who received the art direction credit that was denied him for *Gigi,* provides designs for both sets and costumes that are mannered, an uneasy blend of Edwardian elegance and sixties Hollywood excess. Higgins' home is particularly fussy, with touches of art nouveau set off against Pre-Raphaelite paintings and Julia Margaret Cameron photographs—not at all the kind of austere bachelor digs one expects of the character. Hairstyles and makeup also have a sixties overdoneness. Allen, the studio art director, who was treated with condescension by Beaton, later served as president of the Academy from 1983 to 1985.

The supporting player awards went to Peter Ustinov for *Topkapi* and Lila Kedrova for *Zorba the Greek.* Lerner's screenplay, which departs only a little from the stage version, lost to Edward Anhalt's for *Becket.*

The editing award went to Cotton Warburton for *Mary Poppins.*

Warner: 55, 110, 550, 689, 2318. Harrison: 413. Cukor: 262, 567, 1189, 1563. Stradling: 110, 149, 596, 737, 852, 853, 864, 896, 957, 1246, 1567, 1949, 2338. Allen: 1157, 1910. Beaton: 769. Hopkins: 110, 508, 896, 1003, 1170, 1332, 1385, 1910, 1949, 1973, 2058, 2277. Groves: 825, 1385, 1457, 1763, 1869, 1973, 2277. Previn: 172, 609, 769, 1017, 1034, 1044, 1097, 1550, 1592, 2064, 2077, 2161. Cooper: 1456, 1868. Lerner: 66, 769, 1186, 1731. Ziegler: 110, 1393.

1394 • *MY FAVORITE WIFE*

RKO Radio. 1940.

NOMINATIONS *Original Story:* Leo McCarey, Bella Spewack, and Samuel Spewack. *Black-and-White Interior Decoration:* Van Nest Polglase and Mark-Lee Kirk. *Original Score:* Roy Webb.

Cary Grant [1445 . . .] has just married Gail Patrick, when who should show up but Irene Dunne [114 . . .], his wife who was lost at sea seven years ago and has just been declared legally dead. It turns out she was shipwrecked on a desert island with Randolph Scott, who'd be happy to let Grant and Patrick stay married so he can make things legal with Dunne. Nifty romantic farce, directed by Garson Kanin [11 . . .]. The story isn't all that original; it's based on Tennyson's "Enoch Arden," as the script makes plain: Dunne's name is Ellen Arden. But it's the best of all the versions of the story, which include not only some silent melodramas but also the contemporaneous *Too Many Husbands* (1940) and its musical remake, *Three for the Show* (1955), not to mention the official 1963 remake of *My Favorite Wife, Move Over, Darling.* (The last was begun as *Something's Gotta Give,* the film Marilyn Monroe had started shortly before her death.)

This was the sole nomination for the Spewacks, a husband-and-wife writing team that had a string of Broadway successes, culminating in their Tony Award–winning book for *Kiss Me, Kate.* The Oscar went to Benjamin Glazer and John S. Toldy for *Arise,*

My Love. The scoring award went to Leigh Harline, Paul J. Smith, and Ned Washington for *Pinocchio.*

McCarey: 21, 114, 173, 787, 1212, 1404. Polglase: 358, 407, 754, 1212, 2115. Kirk: 760, 1828. Webb: 640, 665, 969, 1049, 1639.

1395 • *MY FAVORITE YEAR*

METRO-GOLDWYN-MAYER/BROOKSFILM/MICHAEL GRUSKOFF PRODUCTION; MGM/UNITED ARTISTS. 1982.

NOMINATION *Actor:* Peter O'Toole.

Mark Linn-Baker, a young comedy writer on a fifties TV variety show, is assigned the task of chaperoning the guest star, an Errol Flynn–like film idol, Alan Swann (O'Toole), noted for his wicked, wicked —but mostly inebriated—ways. Bright, funny little film, directed by Richard Benjamin, with a first-rate cast, including Joseph Bologna [1221] as the temperamental star of the TV show, modeled on Sid Caesar, and Lainie Kazan as Linn-Baker's mom back in Brooklyn. O'Toole is hilarious in the most recent of his seven unsuccessful nominations. He lost to Ben Kingsley in *Gandhi.* In 1992 the movie was made into an unsuccessful Broadway musical, in which Kazan repeated her film role.

O'Toole: 164, 805, 1151, 1177, 1733, 1953.

1396 • *MY FOOLISH HEART*

SAMUEL GOLDWYN PRODUCTIONS; RKO RADIO. 1949.

NOMINATIONS *Actress:* Susan Hayward. *Song:* "My Foolish Heart," music by Victor Young, lyrics by Ned Washington.

Hayward's wartime romance with Dana Andrews ends with her pregnant, so she marries Kent Smith and spends the rest of her life suffering, which Hayward does, as usual, superbly. Well-done sentimental drama, with the title song squeezing every extra tear. Mark Robson [1001 . . .] directed from a screenplay by Julius Epstein [365 . . .] and Philip Epstein [365] based, believe it or not, on a short story by J. D. Salinger, "Uncle Wiggily in Connecticut." Salinger's dismay at having his spare, ironic story turned into a Susan Hayward weeper may explain why he's never allowed *The Catcher in the Rye* or any other work of his to be filmed. Hayward lost to Olivia de Havil-

land in *The Heiress.* The song Oscar went to Frank Loesser for "Baby, It's Cold Outside," from *Neptune's Daughter.*

Hayward: 973, 980, 1845, 2294. Young: 97, 98, 100, 101, 280, 489, 612, 693, 701, 794, 846, 925, 1214, 1257, 1452, 1748, 1823, 1994, 2235, 2315. Washington: 274, 585, 911, 912, 1329, 1576, 1745, 2127, 2282, 2335.

1397 • *MY GAL SAL*

20TH CENTURY-FOX. 1942.

AWARD *Color Interior Decoration:* Richard Day and Joseph Wright, art direction; Thomas Little, set decoration.

NOMINATION *Scoring of a Musical Picture:* Alfred Newman.

Victor Mature plays turn-of-the-century songwriter Paul Dresser, who falls in love with singer Sally Elliott (Rita Hayworth). Naturally he writes a song about her. In real life Sal was a prostitute Dresser had known in his youth, but no one expects fidelity to the truth in a Fox musical biopic, even when it purports to be based on the memoirs of Dresser's brother, novelist Theodore Dreiser. Hayworth, whose singing voice is dubbed by Nan Wynn, replaced a pregnant Alice Faye in the cast, which also includes James Gleason [904], Phil Silvers, and, in a bit part billed as Judy Ford, Terry Moore [425]. Directed by Irving Cummings. Choreographer Hermes Pan [481 . . .] dances with Hayworth in the "Gay White Way" number. Enjoyable enough, thanks to its stars, the color cinematography of Ernest Palmer [235], and the award-winning art direction. The scoring Oscar went to Ray Heindorf and Heinz Roemheld for *Yankee Doodle Dandy.*

Day: 22, 102, 235, 487, 510, 560, 569, 797, 833, 864, 952, 1048, 1175, 1477, 1666, 1949, 2056, 2120, 2276. Wright: 235, 428, 508, 569, 690, 746, 852, 1175, 1264, 1475, 2056. Little: 46, 83, 235, 428, 495, 719, 721, 746, 950, 952, 1082, 1149, 1153, 1475, 1666, 1852, 1868, 2056, 2212, 2286. Newman: 31, 34, 46, 72, 138, 182, 226, 333, 334, 347, 375, 428, 437, 457, 476, 495, 542, 690, 797, 833, 952, 953, 959, 962, 1016, 1082, 1088, 1213,

1278, 1362, 1475, 1616, 1655, 1849, 1868, 1883, 1921, 2043, 2046, 2091, 2258, 2286, 2294, 2316.

1398 • MY GEISHA

SACHIKO PRODUCTION; PARAMOUNT. 1962.

NOMINATION *Color Costume Design:* Edith Head.

Director Yves Montand is making a movie in Japan and wife Shirley MacLaine [91 . . .] wants a part in it, so guess what she disguises herself as? This sounds like an old *I Love Lucy* episode, except Lucy did it better. Handsomely filmed by cinematographer Shunichuro Nakao, working with director Jack Cardiff [221 . . .], himself a major cinematographer. The fitfully amusing script is by Norman Krasna [535 . . .], and the cast includes Robert Cummings and Edward G. Robinson. The costuming Oscar went to Mary Wills for *The Wonderful World of the Brothers Grimm.*

Head: 31, 32, 46, 305, 357, 363, 612, 636, 675, 736, 832, 894, 945, 1003, 1219, 1261, 1263, 1427, 1504, 1550, 1579, 1587, 1631, 1716, 1727, 1738, 1748, 1840, 1927, 1986, 2012, 2098, 2247, 2298.

1399 • MY LEFT FOOT

FERNDALE/GRANADA PRODUCTION; MIRAMAX FILMS (IRELAND). 1989.

AWARDS *Actor:* Daniel Day-Lewis. *Supporting Actress:* Brenda Fricker.

NOMINATIONS *Picture:* Noel Pearson, producer. *Director:* Jim Sheridan. *Screenplay Based on Material From Another Medium:* Jim Sheridan and Shane Connaughton.

Born with cerebral palsy to an impoverished Dublin family, Christy Brown (Day-Lewis and, as a boy, Hugh O'Conor) is thought to be little more than a vegetable until his mother (Fricker) discovers that she can communicate with him. Gradually he learns to draw and write with his left foot and becomes celebrated as an artist and writer. Wonderful, funny, touching movie that makes no false moves, avoiding cheesy sentiment and pious pleas for understanding the handicapped. The entire cast, including Ray McAnally as Christy's father, Fiona Shaw, and Cyril Cusack, is superb, though some advocates for the disabled protested that Christy should have been played by actual people with cerebral palsy.

A succession of radically differing film roles—the gay punk in *My Beautiful Laundrette,* the prissy fiancé Cyril in *A Room With a View,* and the womanizing Czech doctor in *The Unbearable Lightness of Being*—had already given Day-Lewis a reputation as a chameleon before he astonished everyone with his fierce and vulnerable Christy Brown. Born in London in 1958, he is the son of the late English poet laureate C. Day Lewis and actress Jill Balcon. He made his film debut in a bit part in *Sunday, Bloody Sunday.* The Oscar made him a much sought-after star, and he has continued to demonstrate astonishing versatility by playing, in swift succession, the virile Hawkeye in *The Last of the Mohicans,* the repressed Newland Archer in *The Age of Innocence,* and the wrongfully imprisoned Gerry Conlon in *In the Name of the Father.* The last film reunited him with Sheridan.

Fricker, a respected Irish actress who was little known on this side of the Atlantic, has continued to be seen in more mainstream films, such as *Home Alone 2: Lost in New York* (1992).

Day-Lewis triumphed over the early favorites for the Oscar, Tom Cruise in *Born on the Fourth of July* and Morgan Freeman in *Driving Miss Daisy,* but the Academy gave the best picture Oscar to *Miss Daisy* and the directing Oscar to Oliver Stone for *Born.* But Sheridan, who made his film directing debut with *My Left Foot,* was clearly on the brink of a new career; he was already established as a playwright and stage director in Dublin and New York. The writing Oscar went to Alfred Uhry for *Driving Miss Daisy.*

Day-Lewis: 992.5. Sheridan: 992.5.

1400 • MY LIFE AS A DOG

SVENSK FILMINDUSTRI/FILMTEKNICK PRODUCTION; SKOURAS PICTURES (SWEDEN). 1987.

NOMINATIONS *Director:* Lasse Hallström. *Screenplay Based on Material From Another Medium:* Lasse Hallström, Reidar Jönsson, Brasse Brännström, and Per Berglund.

Twelve-year-old Ingemar, feeling as unwanted and in the way as the dog he has to leave behind, is sent to stay with relatives in the country because his mother is dying. In a village of odd characters, he comes to terms with the loss of his mother and his own awakening sexuality. Engaging bittersweet comedy, with a terrific central performance by young Anton Glanzelius. The movie's success introduced Hallström to American audiences and gave him an entree to Hollywood, where he has directed the offbeat films *Once Around* (1991) and *What's Eating Gilbert Grape.* He was the sole directing nominee whose film was not also a candidate for best picture; he took the slot that might otherwise have gone to James L. Brooks for *Broadcast News,* a substitution that took a good many people by surprise. The directing Oscar went to Bernardo Bertolucci for *The Last Emperor,* which also won for the screenplay by Bertolucci and Mark Peploe.

1401 • *MY MAN GODFREY*

UNIVERSAL. 1936.

NOMINATIONS *Actor:* William Powell. *Actress:* Carole Lombard. *Supporting Actor:* Mischa Auer. *Supporting Actress:* Alice Brady. *Director:* Gregory La Cava. *Screenplay:* Eric Hatch and Morris Ryskind.

Nitwit socialite Lombard, in search of a "forgotten man" as part of a scavenger hunt, finds Powell at the city dump. Not knowing that he's a down-and-out former socialite, her equally scatty family—Brady and her husband, Eugene Pallette, and their other daughter, Gail Patrick—hires Powell as their butler. He sorts out their very confused lives and winds up with Lombard for his pains. Definitive screwball comedy, a bit dated, sometimes overfrantic, but certainly a classic. It's also the first film to receive nominations in all four acting categories. The supporting categories were new this year, but not until *Mrs. Miniver,* six years later, did another film achieve this distinction. (See the entry for *Coming Home* for a complete list of these movies.) And *My Man Godfrey* is the only one of the thirteen films with nominations in all four categories not also nominated for best picture—which is a pity, because it's a lot better than most of the year's nominees, including the best picture winner, *The Great Ziegfeld.* Look for Jane Wyman [246 . . .] among the party guests.

Powell's career was at its peak in 1936, when he also appeared in the title role of *The Great Ziegfeld* as well as *Libeled Lady* and *After the Thin Man.* He lost the Oscar to Paul Muni in *The Story of Louis Pasteur.*

This was the sole nomination for Lombard, who had once been married to her costar, Powell, but was more famous for her passionate affair with and marriage to Clark Gable [798 . . .]. She had made her screen debut at the age of twelve, in 1921, and was signed to a Fox contract in 1925. She didn't become a major star until her appearance opposite John Barrymore in *Twentieth Century* in 1934. Her major films were all comedies, including *Nothing Sacred* and *To Be or Not to Be.* The last was released after her death in January 1942 in a plane crash on her way back from a tour selling war bonds. She lost the Oscar to Luise Rainer in *The Great Ziegfeld.*

Auer, who plays an artist under the patronage of Brady, was born in Russia. After appearing on Broadway, he made his film debut in 1928. The Oscar nomination launched his career as a comic supporting player, and he popped up in dozens of films over the next decade. After the war, he moved to Europe and made numerous appearances in French and Italian films before his death in 1967. He lost the Oscar to Walter Brennan in *Come and Get It.*

The supporting actress Oscar was won by Gale Sondergaard for *Anthony Adverse.* La Cava lost to Frank Capra for *Mr. Deeds Goes to Town.* The screenwriting award went to Pierre Collings and Sheridan Gibney for *The Story of Louis Pasteur.*

Powell: 1170, 2052. Brady: 990. La Cava: 1899. Ryskind: 1899.

1402 • *MY NIGHT AT MAUD'S*

FILMS DU LOSANGE-F.F.P.-FILMS DU CAROSSE-FILMS DES DEUX MONDES-LES FILMS DE LA PLÉIADE-PRODUCTIONS LA GUEVILLE-RENN FILMS-SIMAR FILMS PRODUCTION; PATHÉ CONTEMPORARY FILMS (FRANCE). 1970.

NOMINATIONS *Story and Screenplay—Based on Factual Material or Material Not Previously Published or Produced:* Eric Rohmer. *Foreign Language Film* (1969).

Jean-Louis Trintignant is a devout Catholic who plans to marry Marie-Christine Barrault [454], whom he has met in church. But he's also attracted to Maud (Françoise Fabian), who's a freethinker. Their night is spent in intellectual discourse about religion and morality, but it's still pretty sexy. The third of Rohmer's series of films called "Six Moral Tales," and many think it's the best, although *Claire's Knee* (1970) and *Chloe in the Afternoon* (1972) have more popular appeal. The writing award went to Francis Ford Coppola and Edmund H. North for *Patton*. The foreign film award, for which the movie was eligible a year earlier, was won by *Z*.

1403 • *MY SISTER EILEEN*

COLUMBIA. 1942.

NOMINATION *Actress:* Rosalind Russell.

Would-be writer Ruth (Russell) and her pretty would-be actress sister, Eileen (Janet Blair), come to New York, where they rent an odd little basement flat in Greenwich Village and try to make their way in Manhattan. Pleasant adaptation by Joseph Fields and Jerome Chodorov of their play based on the *New Yorker* stories of Ruth McKenney. The stage origins show, despite some attempts at "opening up," including the addition of the girls' parents, played by Elizabeth Patterson and Grant Mitchell. The cast, directed by Alexander Hall [904], includes Brian Aherne [1064] as the editor who takes an interest in Ruth's stories—and in her. Something about this material keeps people coming back to it: Richard Quine, who plays a drugstore clerk in this film, directed a movie musical remake in 1955 that starred Betty Garrett, Janet Leigh [1632], and Jack Lemmon [91 . . .], and Russell reprised her role as Ruth in the 1953 stage musical *Wonderful Town*.

This was Russell's first Oscar nomination, though she had been in films since 1934 and had played substantial roles in such movies as *Craig's Wife* (1936), *Night Must Fall, The Women* (1939), and the marvelous *His Girl Friday* (1940). This time the Oscar went to Greer Garson for *Mrs. Miniver*.

Russell: 110, 1364, 1834.

1404 • *MY SON JOHN*

RAINBOW PRODUCTIONS; PARAMOUNT. 1952.

NOMINATION *Motion Picture Story:* Leo McCarey.

Parents Helen Hayes [31 . . .] and Dean Jagger [2154] discover to their horror that their son (Robert Walker) is . . . a commie! Shrill, wacky, paranoid—and a huge box-office flop. McCarey, who had given the world such comedy classics as *Duck Soup* (1933) and *The Awful Truth,* as well as such heartwarmers as *Going My Way* and *Love Affair/An Affair to Remember,* let his right-wing Catholic streak take over for this one, which he also directed and produced. It's full of nonsense: Walker is clearly a communist because he's bookish and nonathletic, unlike his muscular straight-arrow younger brother, played by Richard Jaeckel [1864]. Worth seeing as a benchmark for Cold War hysteria, Hollywood style, and for the performance by Walker. Sadly it was his last; he died, apparently from a combination of alcohol and tranquilizers, during the filming. Some footage of him in the movie was borrowed from *Strangers on a Train*. The Oscar went to Frederic Frank, Theodore St. John, and Frank Cavett for *The Greatest Show on Earth*.

McCarey: 21, 114, 173, 787, 1212, 1394.

1405 • *MY SON, MY SON*

EDWARD SMALL; UNITED ARTISTS. 1940.

NOMINATION *Black-and-White Interior Decoration:* John DuCasse Schulze.

Brian Aherne [1064] pulled himself up by his bootstraps, and he's determined that his son is not going to have to struggle the way he did. Big mistake. Plodding adaptation by Lenore Coffee [712] of a bestseller by Howard Spring, with Madeleine Carroll, Louis Hayward, and Laraine Day, directed by Charles Vidor and photographed by Harry Stradling [110 . . .]. The art direction Oscar went to Cedric Gibbons and Paul Groesse for *Pride and Prejudice*.

Schulze: 1866.

1406 • MY SWEET LITTLE VILLAGE

BARRANDOV FILM STUDIOS PRODUCTION (CZECHOSLOVAKIA). 1986.

NOMINATION *Foreign Language Film.*

Comic episodes in the daily life of a small village, nicely textured but somewhat too whimsical. Directed by Jiri Menzel. The Oscar went to *The Assault.*

1407 • MY UNCLE

SPECTRA-GRAY-ALTER FILMS IN ASSOCIATION WITH FILMS DEL CENTAURE (FRANCE). 1958.

AWARD *Foreign Language Film.*

Jacques Tati [1368] makes his second screen appearance as Mr. Hulot, who lives in a ramshackle old-fashioned neighborhood while his sister has a suburban house with every modern inconvenience. Hulot goes to work for his brother-in-law and comes close to demolishing his plastics factory, not to mention the ultramodern house. Superb slapstick comedy, with a shade more satiric edge—and a few more slack moments—than *Mr. Hulot's Holiday.* Tati directed and cowrote (with Jacques Lagrange) the film.

1408 • MY WILD IRISH ROSE

WARNER BROS. 1947.

NOMINATION *Scoring of a Musical Picture:* Ray Heindorf and Max Steiner.

Dennis Morgan plays turn-of-the-century songwriter Chauncey Olcott, who wrote the title tune. Naturally there's a Rose he wrote it for, and she's played by Arlene Dahl. Middling nostalgia piece, directed by David Butler, with Alan Hale, Sara Allgood [952], Ben Blue, and William Frawley. The Oscar went to Alfred Newman for a much better nostalgic musical—an all-too-common forties genre—*Mother Wore Tights.*

Heindorf: 331, 479, 666, 930, 1043, 1204, 1385, 1430, 1690, 1719, 1750, 1910, 2058, 2186, 2243, 2310, 2318. Steiner: 16, 154, 190, 330, 365, 385, 492, 679, 747, 754, 798, 999, 1043, 1046, 1052, 1162, 1169, 1170, 1207, 1324, 1430, 1456, 1690, 1779, 1828.

1409 • MYSTERY STREET

MGM. 1950.

NOMINATION *Motion Picture Story:* Leonard Spiegelgass.

Forensic medicine at Harvard helps the Boston cops solve a murder. Good documentary-style thriller, written by Sidney Boehm and Richard Brooks [227 . . .] and directed by John Sturges [131], with Ricardo Montalban, Sally Forrest, Elsa Lanchester [428 . . .], and Jan Sterling [911]. The Oscar went to Edward and Edna Anhalt for another documentary-style thriller, *Panic in the Streets.*

1410 • NAKED CITY, THE

MARK HELLINGER PRODUCTIONS; UNIVERSAL-INTERNATIONAL. 1948.

AWARDS *Black-and-White Cinematography:* William Daniels. *Film Editing:* Paul Weatherwax.

NOMINATION *Motion Picture Story:* Malvin Wald.

Police lieutenant Dan Muldoon, played by Barry Fitzgerald [787], heads the investigation of the murder of a young woman. Fast-moving and enormously influential manhunt melodrama that was an eye-opener in its day because of its location shooting in New York City. If it seems routine and clichéd today, it's partly because of the endless imitations in both movies and TV, including the TV series based on it. That's not to say, however, that the script by Wald and Albert Maltz [298 . . .] isn't lacking in stuff that was already clichéd, but crisp direction by Jules Dassin [1426] and especially Daniels' cinematography made it look fresh at the time. The cast includes Howard Duff, Don Taylor, Jean Adair, and Arthur O'Connell [73 . . .]. It's also rumored that the blond corpse was played by Shelley Winters [542 . . .].

Daniels began his long and extraordinarily distinguished career behind the camera in 1917 and became famous for his work with Erich von Stroheim [1975] —*Blind Husbands* (1919), *Foolish Wives* (1922), *Greed* (1925), and *The Merry Widow* (1925)—and as the favored cinematographer of Greta Garbo [84 . . .]. He went into semiretirement because of illness in the early forties but returned to work in 1947 and was active throughout the fifties and for much of the sixties. His last film, *Move,* was shot in the year of his death, 1970, at the age of seventy-five.

The Oscar for story went to Richard Schweizer and David Wechsler for *The Search.*

Daniels: 84, 372, 953. Weatherwax: 101.

1411 • NAKED PREY, THE

THEODORA PRODUCTIONS; PARAMOUNT (U.S./SOUTH AFRICA). 1966.

NOMINATION *Story and Screenplay—Written Directly for the Screen:* Clint Johnston and Don Peters.

Victorian big-game hunter Cornel Wilde [1872] and his party are attacked by a warlike African tribe. Impressed by his courage in defending himself, the tribesmen give Wilde a chance to live—if he can survive being hunted down like the animals he once pursued. Exciting, violent action film, produced and directed by Wilde. The Oscar went to Claude Lelouch and Pierre Uytterhoeven for *A Man and a Woman.*

1412 • NAKED SPUR, THE

MGM. 1953.

NOMINATION *Story and Screenplay:* Sam Rolfe and Harold Jack Bloom.

Bounty hunter James Stewart [73 . . .] pursues and snares Robert Ryan [467], but the trick is getting him back to the authorities. Superb western, directed by Anthony Mann—one of eight films Mann and Stewart made in the fifties, and one of their very best. The cast also includes Janet Leigh [1632], Ralph Meeker, and Millard Mitchell. The Colorado scenery, photographed by William Mellor [542 . . .], is impressive. The writing Oscar went to Charles Brackett, Walter Reisch, and Richard Breen for *Titanic.*

1413 • NAPOLEON AND SAMANTHA

WALT DISNEY PRODUCTIONS; BUENA VISTA. 1972.

NOMINATION *Original Dramatic Score:* Buddy Baker.

When his grandfather dies, Napoleon (Johnny Whitaker) and his friend Samantha, played by ten-year-old Jodie Foster [7 . . .], take their pet lion and go in search of their grown-up friend Danny, played by Michael Douglas [1481 . . .]. Routine Disney wilderness adventure, memorable only as one of Foster's first films. The scoring award went to Charles Chaplin, Raymond Rasch, and Larry Russell for *Limelight.*

1414 • NARROW MARGIN, THE

RKO RADIO. 1952.

NOMINATION *Motion Picture Story:* Martin Goldsmith and Jack Leonard.

Cop Charles McGraw is assigned to escort gangster's moll Marie Windsor on a train journey to the trial at which she'll testify against the mob. But also on board the train are some hit men who will stop at nothing to make sure she doesn't get there. Exciting low-budget action thriller that delivers more than you might expect from its B-movie cast. The 1990 remake, with A-list stars Gene Hackman [255 . . .] and Anne Archer [653], isn't half as good. Tautly directed by Richard Fleischer and shot by George Diskant to emphasize the cramped quarters in which the action takes place. The Oscar went to Frederic M. Frank, Theodore St. John, and Frank Cavett for *The Greatest Show on Earth.*

1415 • NASHVILLE

ABC ENTERTAINMENT-JERRY WEINTRAUB-ROBERT ALTMAN PRODUCTION; PARAMOUNT. 1975.

AWARD *Original Song:* "I'm Easy," music and lyrics by Keith Carradine.

NOMINATIONS *Picture:* Robert Altman, producer. *Supporting Actress:* Ronee Blakley. *Supporting Actress:* Lily Tomlin. *Director:* Robert Altman.

An assorted group of characters gather in the country music capital, where their paths crisscross. They include Blakley as the current queen of the country music world; Tomlin as a gospel singer whose children are deaf; Ned Beatty [1424] as her neglectful husband; Carradine as the womanizing rock star who sleeps with Tomlin; Michael Murphy as the advance man for a presidential candidate preparing for a big rally; Henry Gibson as an unctuously hypocritical *Grand Ole Opry* star; Barbara Harris [2275] as an aspirant to country stardom; Gwen Welles as a truly lousy singer who is forced to become a stripper instead; plus Karen Black [672], Shelley Duvall, Geraldine Chaplin, Allen Garfield, Keenan Wynn, Scott Glenn, and Jeff Goldblum, as well as cameos by Elliott Gould [250] and Julie Christie [493 . . .]. Rambling, messy, funny, occasionally touching—and now and then a little dull, thanks to Altman's willingness to let his performers improvise their roles, which not all of them are up to. At the time, it was a critical sensation because of its endearingly shambling quality, and because it was the perfect antidote to bicentennial hoopla and presidential politics, which it deftly satirizes. Today it seems like a not entirely successful experiment. The Academy neglected a key player: editor Sidney Levin, who was faced with assembling something that made sense out of some seventy hours' worth of footage.

Most of the musical performers in *Nashville* composed their own songs, with predictably varying results. Carradine belongs to one of Hollywood's most successful extended families: He's the son of John Carradine, brother of Robert and David, and his daughter is Martha Plimpton. After appearing in *Hair* on Broadway, he returned to Hollywood, making one of his first appearances in Altman's *McCabe and Mrs. Miller.* He also starred in Altman's *Thieves Like Us* (1974). His career has largely been in out-of-the-mainstream movies.

Altman, as usual, was not to the Academy's taste. The best picture Oscar went to *One Flew Over the Cuckoo's Nest,* which also won for director Milos Forman.

Blakley was an established singer-songwriter who made her acting debut in *Nashville,* in a role that was originally to have starred Susan Anspach. She has made only occasional and mostly unmemorable screen appearances.

Tomlin shot to stardom on TV's *Rowan and Martin's Laugh-In. Nashville* was her first film. She has subsequently divided her time between the stage, where she has performed in two critically acclaimed one-woman shows written by her longtime collaborator Jane Wagner, and such movies as *The Late Show, 9 to 5, All of Me* (1984), and Altman's *Short Cuts.* The

supporting actress Oscar went to Lee Grant for *Shampoo.*

Altman: 1286, 1584.5, 1817.5.

1416 • NASTY GIRL, THE

Sentana Filmproduktion (Germany). 1990.
Nomination *Foreign Language Film.*

A student in a small German town enters a national competition with an essay about her town during the Third Reich. In the course of her research, she uncovers the truth about some respected citizens and becomes the target of furious protest. The film follows her from teenage years into married life, with star Lena Stolze giving an accomplished performance at all stages. A funny and sometimes rather frightening movie, based on the actual story of Anja Rosmus but presented in a fictionalized form by writer-director Michael Verhoeven. The Oscar went to *Journey of Hope.*

1417 • NATIONAL VELVET

MGM. 1945.
Awards *Supporting Actress:* Anne Revere. *Film Editing:* Robert J. Kern.
Nominations *Director:* Clarence Brown. *Color Cinematography:* Leonard Smith. *Color Interior Decoration:* Cedric Gibbons and Urie McCleary, art direction; Edwin B. Willis and Mildred Griffiths, set decoration.

Velvet Brown, played by twelve-year-old Elizabeth Taylor [318 . . .], wins a horse in a raffle and, with the aid of scruffy Mi Taylor, played by Mickey Rooney [115 . . .], trains it to run in the Grand National Steeplechase. What's more, when a rider can't be found, she disguises herself as a boy and rides the horse herself. Wonderful classic that created a generation of horse-mad little girls. Taylor is almost unnervingly beautiful, and she has splendid support from everyone involved, including Rooney, Revere as her mother, Donald Crisp [952] as her father, and Angela Lansbury [749 . . .] as her older sister.

Revere's performance as the mother who was once a champion swimmer and who wants her daughter to have the same chance to prove herself is one of the film's highlights. Revere made her Broadway debut in

1931, but except for a single film in 1934, didn't come to Hollywood until 1940. She was a prominent character player, sometimes as a villain, but also in motherly roles. The blacklist interrupted her career in 1951, when she invoked the Fifth Amendment in testifying about communist activities in Hollywood before the House Un-American Activities Committe. She was unable to find work until 1958, when she resumed her stage career, winning a Tony in 1960 for her role in *Toys in the Attic.* In 1970 she returned to the screen in *Tell Me That You Love Me, Junie Moon* but made only a few more movies after that. She died in 1990.

The Oscar for directing went to Billy Wilder for *The Lost Weekend.* Leon Shamroy took the award for the color cinematography of *Leave Her to Heaven.* The art direction award went to *Frenchman's Creek.*

Revere: 759, 1868. Kern: 497. Brown: 84, 723, 957, 1718, 2320. Smith: 208, 1132, 2320. Gibbons: 66, 87, 130, 217, 227, 239, 285, 290, 440, 629, 749, 831, 980, 1069, 1096, 1173, 1190, 1226, 1230, 1232, 1274, 1308, 1309, 1567, 1604, 1644, 1662, 1673, 1721, 1861, 1937, 2068, 2112, 2256, 2257, 2300, 2320, 2330. McCleary: 239, 1537, 1541, 1657, 2330. Willis: 66, 87, 130, 227, 239, 290, 629, 749, 831, 980, 1069, 1096, 1157, 1173, 1190, 1226, 1230, 1232, 1309, 1567, 1657, 1662, 1673, 1721, 1861, 1937, 2068, 2112, 2257, 2320, 2330.

1418 • NATURAL, THE

TRI-STAR PICTURES PRODUCTION; TRI-STAR. 1984.

NOMINATIONS *Supporting Actress:* Glenn Close. *Cinematography:* Caleb Deschanel. *Art Direction–Set Decoration:* Angelo Graham, Mel Bourne, James J. Murakami, and Speed Hopkins; Bruce Weintraub. *Original Score:* Randy Newman.

Robert Redford [1502 . . .] plays Roy Hobbs, a young baseball player on his way to greatness when he is waylaid by a mysterious woman (Barbara Hershey), who guns him down. Fifteen years later, no longer young, he tries to make a comeback—but will he fall to the temptress Kim Basinger, or be kept on the straight and narrow by the pure love of his childhood sweetheart, played by Close? Overly self-conscious mythologizing view of baseball that lacks the energetic raunch of *Bull Durham* or the likable sentiment of *Field of Dreams.* Directed by Barry Levinson [75 . . .] from a screenplay by Roger Towne and Phil Dusenberry, based on a novel by Bernard Malamud. The movie has a powerhouse cast—Robert Duvall [92 . . .], Wilford Brimley, Richard Farnsworth, Robert Prosky, Darren McGavin, and Joe Don Baker are also featured—and superb production values, but it doesn't hold together.

Close lost to Peggy Ashcroft in *A Passage to India,* which also won for Maurice Jarre's score. The cinematography award went to Chris Menges for *The Killing Fields,* and *Amadeus* won for art direction.

Close: 199, 485, 653, 2314. Deschanel: 1698. Graham: 92, 292, 785. Bourne: 671, 1005. Newman: 112, 1524.5, 1530, 1651.

1419 • NAUGHTY MARIETTA

MGM. 1935.

AWARD *Sound Recording:* Douglas Shearer.

NOMINATION *Picture:* Hunt Stromberg, producer.

Princess Marie of France (Jeanette MacDonald) disguises herself to escape marrying a man she doesn't love and winds up in North America, where she's rescued from peril by Captain Warrington (Nelson Eddy), an Indian scout. The first MacDonald-Eddy teaming and one of the best—they haven't been embalmed yet, and they've got a great Victor Herbert score to sing, including, yes, "Ah, Sweet Mystery of Life" and "Tramp, Tramp, Tramp." Directed by W. S. Van Dyke [1751 . . .], with Frank Morgan [22 . . .], Elsa Lanchester [428 . . .], Akim Tamiroff [701 . . .], and, in a bit part, Marjorie Main [601]. The best picture award went to *Mutiny on the Bounty.*

Shearer: 136, 202, 256, 397, 685, 817, 835, 1096, 1232, 1292, 1371, 1751, 1950, 1988, 2048, 2055, 2211, 2300. Stromberg: 831, 2052.

1420 • NAVAJO

BARTLETT-FOSTER PRODUCTIONS; LIPPERT PICTURES INC. 1952.
NOMINATION *Black-and-White Cinematography:* Virgil E. Miller.

A young Navajo boy resists a teacher's attempt to make him learn English. Semidocumentary, directed by Norman Foster. The Oscar went to Robert Surtees for *The Bad and the Beautiful.*

1421 • NAVY COMES THROUGH, THE

RKO RADIO. 1942.
NOMINATION *Special Effects:* Vernon L. Walker, photographic; James G. Stewart, sound.

Win-the-war action/propaganda flick featuring the men of the merchant marine, including Pat O'Brien, George Murphy, Jackie Cooper [1836], and Desi Arnaz, directed by A. Edward Sutherland. The special effects award went to *Reap the Wild Wind.*

Walker: 253, 505, 1991. Stewart: 253, 505, 1595.

1421.5 • NELL

20TH CENTURY FOX PRODUCTION; 20TH CENTURY FOX. 1994.
NOMINATION *Actress:* Jodie Foster.

A delivery boy has been taking provisions to a woman hermit living in an isolated Appalachian cabin, but one day she's found dead. When a county health officer, played by Liam Neeson [1764.65], goes to investigate, he discovers the woman's daughter, Nell (Foster), whose existence was unknown. Because her mother had suffered a speech-impairing stroke and Nell has had no other contact with the outside world, she has developed a private language that she once shared with a twin sister who died as a child. The discovery of Nell attracts the attention of university scientists, one of whom, played by Natasha Richardson, is dispatched to investigate. The doctor and the scientist spy on Nell, but when they win her confidence and learn to communicate with her, they become convinced that she must remain in isolation—that the needs of the individual outweigh the needs of science. But the professor (Richard Libertini) in charge of Nell's case insists that she must be brought to a university hospital and isolated for further study.

The results, calamitous for Nell, lead to a courtroom confrontation. Michael Apted's direction and fine performances by Foster, Neeson, and Richardson animate an often unconvincing and predictable story, drawn from the play *Idioglossia,* by Mark Handley, who co-wrote the screenplay with William Nicholson [1795.5]. The cold-hearted scientist played by Libertini is a caricature, the climactic courtroom scene is mechanical, and the subplot romance that develops between the characters played by Neeson and Richardson is trite.

The screenplay ultimately undermines the effect of Foster's often daring performance, which initially earned raves from critics but then suffered a backlash from those who found it mannered and showy. Because the script brings nothing new to bear on the central theme of the film, nature vs. civilization, coming down with heavy obviousness in favor of the former, *Nell* is given no room to grow and change. But Foster has some moments of real power, as in a scene in which Nell strays into a poolroom and is menaced by some hoods—although even there the situation is haunted by déjà vu, as it inevitably recalls Foster's first Oscar-winning role in *The Accused.* The Oscar went to Jessica Lange for *Blue Sky.*

Foster: 7, 1820, 2005.

1422 • NEPTUNE'S DAUGHTER

MGM. 1949.
AWARD *Song:* "Baby, It's Cold Outside," music and lyrics by Frank Loesser.

Esther Williams stars as a swimsuit designer who falls for Ricardo Montalban. There's a subplot in which Red Skelton is mistaken for a polo player, and the cast includes Betty Garrett, Keenan Wynn, Mel Blanc, and Xavier Cugat and his orchestra, directed by Edward Buzzell. Pretty inane, but you guessed that already.

One of the century's finest songwriters, Loesser was both a great melodist and a witty lyricist. Born in 1910, Loesser spent the first phase of his career as a lyricist, providing words for such songs as "The Moon of Manakoora," based on a theme from Alfred Newman's score for *The Hurricane,* and "The Boys in the Back Room,'' sung by Marlene Dietrich [1358] in *Destry Rides Again* (1939), with music by Frederick Hollander [104 . . .]. His first big hit as his own composer was "Praise the Lord and Pass the Ammunition," written just after Pearl Harbor. During the war, as a PFC in Special Services, he wrote the song scores for musicals that toured military bases. His first Broadway show was *Where's Charley?* in 1948, and two years later he wrote one of the finest of all musicals, *Guys and Dolls.* He returned to Hollywood to compose the score for *Hans Christian Andersen* for Samuel Goldwyn, who also bought the rights to *Guys and Dolls* and commissioned several new songs for the film version. Loesser's 1956 show *The Most Happy Fella* further demonstrated his astonishing versatility, with music that ranges from operatic ensemble ("How Beautiful the Days") to Broadway showstopper ("Big D") to jukebox hit ("Standing on the Corner"). His last show, *How to Succeed in Business Without Really Trying,* was in 1962, seven years before his death.

Loesser: 864, 1131, 1551, 2026.

1423 • NEST, THE

A. Punto E. L. S. A. Production (Spain). 1980.
Nomination *Foreign Language Film.*

A wealthy man, past middle age, is drawn to a thirteen-year-old girl, with predictably unhappy consequences. Written and directed by Jaime De Armiñán. The Oscar went to *Moscow Does Not Believe in Tears.*

1424 • NETWORK

Howard Gottfried-Paddy Chayefsky Production; MGM/United Artists. 1976.
Awards *Actor:* Peter Finch. *Actress:* Faye Dunaway. *Supporting Actress:* Beatrice Straight. *Screenplay—Written Directly for the Screen:* Paddy Chayefsky.
Nominations *Picture:* Howard Gottfried, producer. *Actor:* William Holden. *Supporting Actor:* Ned Beatty. *Director:* Sidney Lumet. *Cinematography:* Owen Roizman. *Film Editing:* Alan Heim.

When the UBS TV network is taken over by a conglomerate headed by Beatty, the network's head, played by Robert Duvall [92 . . .], fires Holden, the head of the news division, because his solid, responsible programs are down in the ratings. Dunaway, a ratings-mad V.P. of programming, is put in charge of the news. The chief anchorman, Finch, goes nuts on camera and urges viewers to open their windows and scream, "I'm mad as hell and I'm not going to take this anymore," and the ratings soar. As Finch becomes a messianic cult hero, Dunaway and Holden, who is married to Straight, have an affair. Then Finch announces that he's going to commit suicide on the air. Shrill, scattershot satire that spares no one, including the audience. Chayefsky's script is long on big speeches and short on wit, though it's undeniably prescient: Real TV today sometimes looks loonier than *Network*'s version of it, with the rise of tabloid TV, "infotainment" shows, and cult commentators like Rush Limbaugh.

Finch died of a heart attack on January 14, 1977, and became the only posthumous winner of an acting Oscar in Academy history. (Posthumous nominations were given to Jeanne Eagels for *The Letter* and twice to James Dean, for *East of Eden* and *Giant.)* Born in London, Finch was raised in Australia, where he began his career on stage in 1935 and in Australian films the following year. He was "discovered" by Laurence Olivier [268 . . .], who was touring Australia in 1949, and came to England, where he emerged as a leading man in plays and films of the fifties.

Dunaway was born in Florida and studied acting at Boston University, beginning her career on stage with the Lincoln Center Repertory Company in 1962. She shot to film stardom with her performance in *Bonnie and Clyde* and was a major Hollywood leading lady throughout the seventies. But she began to be cast in too many tense, neurotic, predatory-woman roles, capped by her performance as Joan Crawford [1319 . . .] in the 1981 *Mommie Dearest,* which set her career on a downward path from which it has yet to recover, despite a critically well received performance as an aging alcoholic in the 1987 *Barfly.*

The part of Holden's wife was a small one with a big attention-getting speech. Straight had made a few film appearances before *Network,* including a performance as a nun in *The Nun's Story,* which also starred

Finch, but her acting career had been primarily on stage. Lumet was familiar with her work because she was the cousin of his ex-wife, Gloria Vanderbilt. Straight made several screen appearances after *Network,* but except for the horror thriller *Poltergeist* they were in little-seen films.

Network earned Chayefsky his third Oscar. His last screenplay, before his death in 1981, was for the film *Altered States,* but Chayefsky was so annoyed with what director Ken Russell had done with the script that he asked for credit under a pseudonym, Sidney Aaron.

Network was considered a leading contender for the best picture Oscar in a field that also included *All the President's Men, Bound for Glory,* and *Taxi Driver,* but the award went to the crowd-pleaser of the year, *Rocky,* which also won Oscars for director John G. Avildsen and editors Richard Halsey and Scott Conrad.

Though *Network* was something of a comeback for Holden, a major star of the fifties whose career had declined as age and alcoholism eroded his looks, it was his last important film. He died in 1981.

Beatty, born in Kentucky, made his screen debut in *Deliverance* and has become one of the movies' most versatile and appealing character players, in films that include *Nashville, All the President's Men,* and *Superman.* The Oscar went to Jason Robards for *All the President's Men.*

Haskell Wexler won the cinematography Oscar for *Bound for Glory.*

Finch: 1966. Dunaway: 255, 395. Chayefsky: 783, 942, 1283. Holden: 1903, 1975. Lumet: 561, 1611, 2153, 2198. Roizman: 631, 724, 2113, 2316.5. Heim: 49.

1425 • *NEVER CRY WOLF*

Walt Disney Productions; Buena Vista. 1983.
Nomination *Sound:* Alan R. Splet, Todd Boekelheide, Randy Thom, and David Parker.

Charles Martin Smith plays a naturalist who goes to live among the wolves of the Arctic and learns about the ecological role of these supposedly fierce predators. Entertaining nature film based on a book by Farley Mowat, and somewhat more daring than the traditional Disney fare—including a scene in which

Smith runs naked amid a caribou herd to study what it's like to be a wolf. Stunningly photographed by Hiro Narita under the direction of Carroll Ballard, who also directed *The Black Stallion.* The sound award went to *The Right Stuff.*

Splet: 225. Boekelheide: 60. Thom: 129, 708.5, 1684, 1698.

1426 • *NEVER ON SUNDAY*

Melinafilm Production; Lopert Pictures Corporation (Greece). 1960.
Award *Song:* "Never on Sunday," music and lyrics by Manos Hadjidakis.
Nominations *Actress:* Melina Mercouri. *Director:* Jules Dassin. *Story and Screenplay—Written Directly for the Screen:* Jules Dassin. *Black-and-White Costume Design:* Deni Vachlioti.

Writer-director Dassin plays an American professor who tries to educate a Greek prostitute (Mercouri), who likes to go to performances of the Greek tragedies which she gives her own peculiar spin: Oedipus, she says, was so nice to his mother. Culture-clash comedy that manages to be amusing despite its trite mind-body dualities and happy hooker clichés. It was a huge hit in a year of weakening censorship, when prostitution suddenly ceased to be taboo on screen: Elizabeth Taylor and Shirley Jones won the actress and supporting actress Oscars this year for playing prostitutes in *Butterfield 8* and *Elmer Gantry.*

Hadjidakis was a Greek bouzouki player hired to improvise a score for the film, which Dassin made on a shoestring. The song became a chart-topping hit in America, although the record's English lyrics were not the ones heard in the film—a fact that touched off a small controversy at the Oscars, when Connie Francis performed the recorded version of the song, not Hadjidakis' nominated lyrics.

Mercouri, a prominent actress on the Greek stage, made her film debut in Greece in 1955. *Never on Sunday,* her first major international success, won her the best actress award at Cannes. She married Dassin and subsequently acted in his *Phaedra* and *Topkapi.* After the military takeover in Greece in 1967, she was politically exiled until 1974. In 1977 she was elected to the Greek Parliament. She died in 1994.

Dassin had his own experience as a political exile. Born in Connecticut, he began his career as an actor and moved into writing for radio and directing short films. He became a feature film director in 1942 and was critically praised for the realistic style of *Brute Force* in 1947 and *The Naked City* the following year. But in 1950 he was cited as a communist in the testimony of fellow director Edward Dmytryk [467] before the House Un-American Activities Committee and had to leave the country to continue his career. He made films in England and France, including the well-received suspense film *Rififi* (1955). After *Never on Sunday,* he again received American backing for his films but chose to live and work primarily in Europe. His most successful later film is *Topkapi,* which also starred Mercouri and had a score by Hadjidakis. *The Apartment* won the Oscars for director Billy Wilder and writers Wilder and I. A. L. Diamond. The costuming award went to Edith Head and Edward Stevenson for *The Facts of Life.*

Vachlioti: 1559.

1427 • NEW KIND OF LOVE, A

LLENROC PRODUCTIONS; PARAMOUNT. 1963.
NOMINATIONS *Scoring of Music—Adaptation or Treatment:* Leith Stevens. *Color Costume Design:* Edith Head.

Department store fashion buyer Joanne Woodward [1365 . . .] and scruffy journalist Paul Newman [3 . . .] loathe each other at first sight. But if you don't think they'll get together eventually, you haven't seen *Designing Woman* or *Woman of the Year* or any of the dozens of romantic comedies from which this movie is derived. Even the Parisian setting and the support of Maurice Chevalier [203 . . .] and Thelma Ritter [46 . . .] don't lift this one above routine. Written and directed by Melville Shavelson [951 . . .]. André Previn won the scoring award for *Irma la Douce.* The costuming Oscar went to Irene Sharaff, Vittorio Nino Novarese, and Renie for *Cleopatra.*

Stevens: 675, 1067. Head: 31, 32, 46, 305, 357, 363, 612, 636, 675, 736, 832, 894, 945, 1003, 1219, 1261, 1263, 1398, 1504, 1550, 1579, 1587, 1631, 1716, 1727, 1738, 1748, 1840, 1927, 1986, 2012, 2098, 2247, 2298.

1428 • NEW LAND, THE

A. B. SVENSK FILMINDUSTRI PRODUCTION (SWEDEN). 1972.
NOMINATION *Foreign Language Film.*

In this sequel to *The Emigrants,* the characters played by Max von Sydow [1546] and Liv Ullmann [610 . . .] arrive in America and carve out their new life in nineteenth-century Minnesota. Rich, absorbing continuation of the saga directed, photographed, edited, and cowritten (with Bengt Forslund) by Jan Troell [610]. The Oscar went to *The Discreet Charm of the Bourgeoisie.*

1429 • NICHOLAS AND ALEXANDRA

A HORIZON PICTURES PRODUCTION; COLUMBIA (UNITED KINGDOM). 1971.
AWARDS *Art Direction—Set Decoration:* John Box, Ernest Archer, Jack Maxsted, and Gil Parrondo; Vernon Dixon. *Costume Design:* Yvonne Blake and Antonia Castillo.
NOMINATIONS *Picture:* Sam Spiegel, producer. *Actress:* Janet Suzman. *Cinematography:* Freddie Young. *Original Dramatic Score:* Richard Rodney Bennett.

Michael Jayston is Czar Nicholas II and Suzman his wife, Alexandra, in this elaborate account of their lives in the years leading up to the Bolshevik Revolution, based on a best-seller by Robert K. Massie. Unfortunately it's both stately and sketchy, with screenwriter James Goldman [1177] and director Franklin Schaffner [1541] trying to cram too much history and too many characters into three very long hours. The huge cast includes the usual string of cameos by actors like Harry Andrews, Jack Hawkins, Laurence Olivier [268 . . .], Michael Redgrave [1364], Alexander Knox [2286], Irene Worth, and Eric Porter, among others. The visual splendor honored by the Academy only served to make the movie the equivalent of a coffee-table book—beautiful but unwieldy and unread, or in this case unseen. Only Spiegel's aggressive advertising campaign can explain its presence among the best picture nominees, supplanting movies that were better received by critics and audiences, such as *Klute, McCabe and Mrs. Miller,* and *Sunday, Bloody Sunday.* The Oscar went to *The French Connection.*

Suzman, born in South Africa, was a member of the Royal Shakespeare Company who had made her film debut in 1970 in *A Day in the Death of Joe Egg.* Her career has largely been on the stage, but she has made occasional films, such as the antiapartheid drama *A Dry White Season.* The Oscar went to Jane Fonda for *Klute.*

Oswald Morris won for the cinematography for *Fiddler on the Roof.* The scoring award went to Michel Legrand for *Summer of '42.*

Box: 558, 1151, 1471, 1533, 2134. Archer: 2164. Parrondo: 1541, 2134. Dixon: 151, 1471. Blake: 717. Spiegel: 287, 1151, 1477. Young: 558, 1035, 1151, 1737. Bennett: 647, 1378.

1430 • NIGHT AND DAY

WARNER BROS. 1946.
NOMINATION *Scoring of a Musical Picture:* Ray Heindorf and Max Steiner.

Cary Grant [1445 . . .] plays Cole Porter [261 . . .] in this lame, hokey biopic of the great songwriter. A monumental disappointment considering the talents involved: The producer was composer Arthur Schwartz [2026 . . .], the director Michael Curtiz [79 . . .], and the cast includes Alexis Smith, Monty Woolley [1569 . . .], Ginny Simms, Jane Wyman [246 . . .], Eve Arden [1319], Dorothy Malone [2315], and Mary Martin, who plays herself and re-creates her star-making performance of ''My Heart Belongs to Daddy'' in Porter's show *Leave It to Me!* The movie's only virtue is that it's packed wall-to-wall with Porter songs, making it one of those films that seem tailor-made for videotape—you can fast-forward from song to song and skip the stale story provided by Charles Hoffman, Leo Townsend, and William Bowers [848 . . .]. The Oscar went to Morris Stoloff for *The Jolson Story.*

Heindorf: 331, 479, 666, 930, 1043, 1204, 1385, 1408, 1690, 1719, 1750, 1910, 2058, 2186, 2243, 2310, 2318. Steiner: 16, 154, 190, 330, 365, 385,

492, 679, 747, 754, 798, 999, 1043, 1046, 1052, 1162, 1169, 1170, 1207, 1324, 1408, 1456, 1690, 1779, 1828.

1431 • NIGHT MUST FALL

MGM. 1937.
NOMINATIONS *Actor:* Robert Montgomery. *Supporting Actress:* May Whitty.

Rosalind Russell [110 . . .] gradually comes to realize that Montgomery is a serial killer and that Whitty, into whose household he has wheedled and flattered his way, is his next victim. Tense adaptation by John Van Druten [749] of a stage melodrama by Emlyn Williams. Directed by Richard Thorpe.

Montgomery, who had made his film debut in 1929 and was an MGM contract player, was best known as a light comedian and romantic leading man. He lost to Spencer Tracy in *Captains Courageous.*

The supporting actress Oscar went to Alice Brady for *In Old Chicago.*

Montgomery: 904. Whitty: 1371.

1432 • NIGHT OF THE IGUANA, THE

SEVEN ARTS PRODUCTIONS; MGM. 1964.
AWARD *Black-and-White Costume Design:* Dorothy Jeakins.
NOMINATIONS *Supporting Actress:* Grayson Hall. *Black-and-White Cinematography:* Gabriel Figueroa. *Black-and-White Art Direction—Set Decoration:* Stephen Grimes.

Defrocked alcoholic clergyman Richard Burton [85 . . .] arrives at a Mexican hotel run by Ava Gardner [1339] with a busload of tourists for whom he is serving as guide. They include Deborah Kerr [599 . . .] as a spinster in charge of her nonagenarian grandfather; Sue Lyon, who had played Lolita, as yet another Lolita, bent this time on seducing Burton; and Hall as the leader of the group of sight-seeing schoolteachers. As usual, when the author is Tennessee Williams [119 . . .], passions spin the plot. It's more than a bit overdone, but fun in a shabby sort of way. John Huston [24 . . .] directed, or perhaps refereed, for the location shoot at Puerto Vallarta became an object of international gossip, especially when Elizabeth Taylor [318 . . .] came to stay there with Burton, whom she had not yet married. The supporting actress award went to Lila Kedrova for *Zorba the Greek,* which also won for Walter Lassally's cinematography and for Vassilis Fotopoulos' art direction. This is the sole nomination for Figueroa, an internationally acclaimed Mexican cinematographer, who studied with Gregg Toland [407 . . .] and is perhaps best known for his work with director Luis Buñuel [549 . . .].

Jeakins: 393, 509, 832, 882, 1048, 1385, 1391, 1748, 1881, 2012, 2238. Grimes: 1512, 2238.

1433 • NIGHT PEOPLE

20TH CENTURY-FOX. 1954.
NOMINATION *Motion Picture Story:* Jed Harris and Tom Reed.

Cold War spy thriller about an American serviceman abducted by the Soviets in Berlin. Though obviously dated in its political posturings, and somewhat undermined by Fox's decision to shoot what should have been a shadowy and claustrophobic story in Technicolor and the fledgling CinemaScope process, it's well scripted and directed by Nunnally Johnson [815 . . .]. The cast includes Gregory Peck [759 . . .], Broderick Crawford [53], Anita Bjork, Walter Abel, Rita Gam, Buddy Ebsen, and Jill Esmond. The Oscar went to Philip Yordan for *Broken Lance.*

1434 • NIGHT TRAIN

20TH CENTURY-FOX (UNITED KINGDOM). 1941.
NOMINATION *Original Story:* Gordon Wellesley.

A Czech inventor and his daughter escape from the Nazis to Britain, but he's kidnaped and returned to Germany. British agent Rex Harrison [413 . . .] poses as a German general and rescues him. Nifty thriller, now generally known by its original British title, *Night Train to Munich,* directed by Carol Reed [639 . . .], with Margaret Lockwood as the daughter and Paul Henreid—still billed as Von Hernreid—as the man who helps her escape from a concentration camp but turns out to be a Nazi agent. Screenwriters Frank Launder and Sidney Gilliat adapted Wellesley's novel *Report on a Fugitive,* interpolating two characters

they had introduced in the Alfred Hitchcock [1171 . . .] film *The Lady Vanishes* (1938), Charters and Caldicott (Basil Radford and Naunton Wayne). Charters and Caldicott were spun off into a series of six more British comedies in which the duo bumbles its way through chance encounters with spies. Wellesley lost to Harry Segall for *Here Comes Mr. Jordan.*

1434.5 • NIGHTMARE BEFORE CHRISTMAS, THE

TOUCHSTONE PICTURES PRODUCTION; BUENA VISTA. 1993.
NOMINATION *Visual Effects:* Pete Kozachik, Eric Leighton, Ariel Velasco Shaw, and Gordon Baker.

Out of boredom, Jack the Pumpkin King, ruler of Halloweentown, kidnaps Santa Claus and proposes that they switch roles. The consequences, as you might imagine, are disastrous. Imaginative animated musical fantasy, using stop-motion puppets instead of drawings—a painstaking process that took nearly two years to accomplish. The mixture of whimsy and the gently macabre is not to all tastes, but the movie is often dazzlingly beautiful. The story idea came from Tim Burton, the creator of *Beetlejuice, Edward Scissorhands,* and the *Batman* movies. The script is by Caroline Thompson. Henry Selick directed, and the score and songs are by Danny Elfman. The visual effects Oscar went to *Jurassic Park.*

1435 • NIGHTS AND DAYS

POLISH CORPORATION FOR FILM-"KADR" FILM UNIT PRODUCTION (POLAND). 1976.
NOMINATION *Foreign Language Film.*

The life of a Polish married couple is used as a perspective on the first half of the twentieth century. This ambitious blend of *Scenes From a Marriage* and *Cavalcade,* based on a novel by Maria Dabrowska and directed by Jerzy Antczak, lasts more than four and a half hours and was little seen in the United States. The Oscar went to *Black and White in Color.*

1436 • NIGHTS OF CABIRIA

DINO DE LAURENTIIS PRODUCTION (ITALY). 1957.
AWARD *Foreign Language Film.*

Giulietta Masina plays Cabiria, a Roman prostitute

who remains naively optimistic through endless misfortunes: She's picked up and then dumped by a movie star, a man proposes to her but just wants to steal her purse, and so on. Masina's endearing performance and the observant direction of Federico Fellini [61 . . .] make what could have been a sentimental downer into a classic. (There are those, of course, who maintain it *is* a sentimental downer, but they seem to be in a minority.) The screenplay is by Fellini, Ennio Flaiano [562 . . .], Tullio Pinelli [562 . . .], and Pier Paolo Pasolini. It was adapted into the Broadway and film musical *Sweet Charity*.

1437 • NINE LIVES

A/S Nordsjøfilm (Norway). 1957.
NOMINATION *Foreign Language Film.*

A Norwegian sailor struggles to survive in the wilderness after his ship is destroyed by the Germans in World War II. Based on the true story of Jan Baalsrud. Written and directed by Arne Skouen. The Oscar went to *Nights of Cabiria*.

1438 • 9 TO 5

20TH CENTURY-FOX PRODUCTION; 20TH CENTURY-FOX. 1980.
NOMINATION *Original Song:* "9 to 5," music and lyrics by Dolly Parton.

Three office workers—Lily Tomlin [1415], Jane Fonda [394 . . .], and Parton—take revenge on their crooked, sexist boss (Dabney Coleman). Uneven comedy, written by Colin Higgins and Patricia Resnick and directed by Higgins. Tomlin has the film's best scene, in which she fantasizes herself as Snow White and, accompanied by cartoon animals, poisons Coleman. Parton, in her film debut, is charming, but Fonda plays her meek and mousy character too well —she almost disappears from the film.

Parton had established herself as one of the top country music singers, with frequent successful crossovers to the mainstream pop charts, long before she made her first film. Her spectacularly endowed figure helped her gain fame, which she held on to by virtue of personal charm, a lovely singing voice, and true songwriting gifts. She followed *9 to 5* with two somewhat unsuccessful films, *The Best Little Whorehouse in*

Texas and *Rhinestone* (1984), but was well received as the owner of the beauty parlor in which much of the action of *Steel Magnolias* takes place. She has continued her career as a songwriter, including the smash hit "I Will Always Love You," which she originally recorded but which Whitney Houston turned into a phenomenon when she sang it in *The Bodyguard*. She lost the Oscar to Michael Gore and Dean Pitchford for the title song from *Fame*.

1439 • 1941

A-TEAM/STEVEN SPIELBERG FILM PRODUCTION; UNIVERSAL-COLUMBIA PRESENTATION; UNIVERSAL. 1979.
NOMINATIONS *Cinematography:* William A. Fraker. *Sound:* Robert Knudson, Robert J. Glass, Don MacDougall, and Gene S. Cantamessa. *Visual Effects:* William A. Fraker, A. D. Flowers, and Gregory Jein.

Just after Pearl Harbor, a Japanese submarine surfaces off of Los Angeles, and everyone goes nuts. Frantic, noisy, special-effects-dominated farce, directed by Steven Spielberg [416 .. . .] from a script by Robert Zemeckis [127] and Bob Gale [127]. Critics hated it and audiences were indifferent; it was Spielberg's first flop. It does, however, have some defenders who like its high energy level and its technical finesse. The cast of thousands includes Dan Aykroyd [580], Ned Beatty [1424], John Belushi, Treat Williams, Nancy Allen, Robert Stack [2315], Toshiro Mifune, Christopher Lee, Warren Oates, Slim Pickens, and John Candy. The cinematography award went to Vittorio Storaro for *Apocalypse Now,* which also won for sound. The visual effects Oscar went to *Alien.*

Fraker: 890, 1205, 1380, 2231. Knudson: 321, 416, 588, 613, 631, 938, 1877, 1911, 2274. Glass: 416, 588, 938, 1877, 1911. MacDougall: 416, 738, 938, 1916. Cantamessa: 339, 416, 588, 1914, 2165, 2331. Flowers: 1596, 2120. Jein: 416.

1440 • NINOTCHKA

MGM. 1939.
NOMINATIONS *Picture:* Sidney Franklin, producer. *Actress:* Greta Garbo. *Original Story:* Melchior Lengyel.

Screenplay: Charles Brackett, Walter Reisch, and Billy Wilder.

Garbo is a Soviet official sent to Paris to find three commissars who have gone there to sell jewels and have been seduced by the decadent bourgeois lifestyle. She meets—and falls in love with—an exiled Russian count, played by Melvyn Douglas [169 . . .]. Wonderful romantic comedy, directed by Ernst Lubitsch [889 . . .] with his usual inventive charm. The cast includes Ina Claire as the Grand Duchess Swana; Sig Rumann, Felix Bressart, and Alexander Granach as the wayward commissars Iranoff, Buljanoff, and Kopalski; and Bela Lugosi as Commissar Razinin. The movie was at the time only a modest box-office success, and there were partisans on the left who objected to its implication that communists would turn capitalist to have the worldly goods of Paris, and partisans on the right who felt it trivialized what they saw as the Soviet menace. But if imitation is the surest test of a classic, *Ninotchka* ranks high: MGM used the central plot theme of thawing an icy Soviet woman the next year in *Comrade X,* and an updated version called *The Iron Petticoat,* with the very unlikely pairing of Bob Hope and Katharine Hepburn [24 . . .], appeared in 1956. And it was musicalized, first for stage and then for screen, as *Silk Stockings* (1957). *Ninotchka* lost the best picture award to *Gone With the Wind.*

Garbo's last nomination—she made only one more film, the disappointing *Two-Faced Woman,* before leaving movies for good in 1941—came for a role that was virtually tailor-made for her. She was skilled at suggesting banked fires behind a mask of impassiveness, but usually used that technique in tragic, or at least melodramatic, roles. There are moments in *Ninotchka* when she's clearly parodying her screen image —an image that had grown overfamiliar to audiences, leading to declining returns for her films at the box office. She was, however, extremely insecure about her ability to play comedy, especially the scene in which she becomes drunk on champagne, and insisted on having the set closed to nonessential personnel. She had requested Lubitsch as her director, and con-

temporary acquaintances recall that she was happy with the film, but years later she told others that he was "a vulgar little man" and she hadn't enjoyed working with him. She lost her fourth unsuccessful nomination to Vivien Leigh in *Gone With the Wind.* The Academy gave her an honorary Oscar at the 1954 awards show, although Garbo didn't attend the ceremony.

Lengyel conceived the original story in three sentences: "Russian girl saturated with Bolshevist ideals goes to fearful, capitalistic, monopolistic Paris. She meets romance and has an uproarious good time. Capitalism not so bad after all." After he completed a first script in January 1938, Gottfried Reinhardt, Jacques Deval, and S. N. Behrman worked on it. Reinhardt and Behrman contributed the scene in the restaurant in which, as the ads proclaimed, "Garbo Laughs!" When Lubitsch was signed, he brought in Walter Reisch, who added the jewelry subplot, and finally Brackett and Wilder joined the team. Brackett, Reisch, and Wilder all urged that Lubitsch be given screen credit with them because of his work on the final script, but to no avail. The Oscar for original story went to Lewis R. Foster for *Mr. Smith Goes to Washington,* and Sidney Howard took the award for the screenplay of *Gone With the Wind.*

Franklin: 799, 1232, 1371, 1662, 2320. Garbo: 84, 336, 1718. Brackett: 705, 925, 1088, 1208, 1975, 2093, 2099. Reisch: 435, 749, 2093. Wilder: 91, 138, 198, 566, 705, 709, 925, 1208, 1738, 1860, 1903, 1975, 2297.

1441 • NINTH CIRCLE, THE

JADRAN FILM PRODUCTION (YUGOSLAVIA). 1960.
NOMINATION *Foreign Language Film.*

A Jewish girl in Croatia marries a Catholic boy to escape being sent to a concentration camp during World War II. The first film to deal with the collaboration of Croatian Nationalists with the Nazis is moving in its portrait of the heroine's plight and harrowing in its depiction of wartime atrocities. Directed by France Stiglic. The Oscar went to *The Virgin Spring.*

1442 • NO SAD SONGS FOR ME

COLUMBIA. 1950.

NOMINATION *Scoring of a Dramatic or Comedy Picture:* George Duning.

Margaret Sullavan [2073] learns that she has only six months to live but chooses not to tell husband Wendell Corey or daughter Natalie Wood [1219 . . .]. Instead, she tries to prepare them to live on without her, even doing a little matchmaking between Corey and Viveca Lindfors. As teary as it sounds, but saved from mawkishness by Sullavan's intelligent performance (her last on screen), a solid script by Howard Koch [365 . . .], and the direction of Rudolph Maté [455 . . .]. The scoring award went to Franz Waxman for *All About Eve.*

Duning: 596, 732, 1057, 1566.

1443 • NO TIME FOR LOVE

PARAMOUNT. 1944.

NOMINATION *Black-and-White Interior Decoration:* Hans Dreier and Robert Usher, art direction; Sam Comer, set decoration.

Magazine photographer Claudette Colbert [1025 . . .], sent to cover the construction of the Lincoln Tunnel, falls for sandhog foreman Fred Mac-Murray. Predictable odd-couple romantic comedy, with very likable stars directed by Mitchell Leisen [587]. The support includes Ilka Chase, Richard Haydn, and June Havoc. The art direction Oscar went to *Gaslight.*

Dreier: 97, 151, 649, 674, 701, 726, 925, 979, 1101, 1120, 1194, 1214, 1217, 1358, 1452, 1540, 1668, 1748, 1880, 1975, 1994, 2190. Usher: 97, 925. Comer: 278, 357, 426, 450, 726, 736, 925, 956, 1029, 1101, 1214, 1219, 1570, 1631, 1674, 1727, 1738, 1748, 1959, 1975, 1994, 2012, 2098, 2200, 2208.

1444 • NO WAY OUT

20TH CENTURY-FOX. 1950.

NOMINATION *Story and Screenplay:* Joseph L. Mankiewicz and Lesser Samuels.

When his brother dies in a hospital under the care of a black doctor, played by Sidney Poitier [522 . . .], gangster Richard Widmark [1098] takes revenge by inciting race riots. Solid but dated problem drama that's chiefly notable for the screen debuts of Poitier, Ossie Davis, and Ruby Dee. Mankiewicz also directed, but his achievement here was overshadowed by his work the same year on *All About Eve,* for which he won directing and screenplay Oscars. The story and screenplay award went to Charles Brackett, Billy Wilder, and D. M. Marshman, Jr., for *Sunset Boulevard.*

Mankiewicz: 46, 146, 673, 1163, 1563, 1836, 1841. Samuels: 198.

1444.5 • NOBODY'S FOOL

SCOTT RUDIN/CINEHAUS PRODUCTION; PARAMOUNT IN ASSOCIATION WITH CAPELLA INTERNATIONAL. 1994.

NOMINATIONS *Actor:* Paul Newman. *Screenplay Based on Material Previously Produced or Published:* Robert Benton.

Newman is Sully, a small-town odd-jobs man who has mostly thrown away his life, as well as his marriage. His existence as an aimless ne'er-do-well is threatened by the arrival of his son (Dylan Walsh), whose own marriage has broken up and who has given up a job as a college teacher. Seeing his son entering a life much like his own arouses Sully's concern—not only for the son but for his grandson—and provokes him to thoughts of mending his ways. Absorbing, low-key character drama, centered on a beautifully understated performance by Newman—one of the best in a career built of beautifully understated performances. But director Benton also has a fine ensemble to work with, including Jessica Tandy [580 . . .] as Sully's landlady, Bruce Willis as his sometime employer, and Melanie Griffith [2313] as Willis' disaffected wife, with whom Sully flirts. Benton's screenplay is based on a novel by Richard Russo. The Oscars went to Tom Hanks as actor and Eric Roth as writer for *Forrest Gump.*

Newman: 3, 372, 422, 443, 956, 964, 1645, 2198. Benton: 255, 1111, 1146, 1580.

1445 • *NONE BUT THE LONELY HEART*

RKO RADIO. 1944.

AWARD *Supporting Actress:* Ethel Barrymore.

NOMINATIONS *Actor:* Cary Grant. *Scoring of a Dramatic or Comedy Picture:* C. Bakaleinikoff and Hanns Eisler. *Film Editing:* Roland Gross.

Grant plays a Cockney ne'er-do-well who tries to get his life in order when he finds that his mother (Barrymore) is dying. Intriguing but not wholly successful character drama, marred by the Hollywood phoniness of its sets and costumes. It was the directing debut of Clifford Odets, who also wrote the screenplay based on Richard Llewellyn's novel. The cast includes Barry Fitzgerald [787], June Duprez, Jane Wyatt, and Dan Duryea.

Barrymore was not the first choice for her role: Grant wanted Laurette Taylor, but her alcoholism took her out of the running. Of the three Barrymores, Ethel was the most reluctant film star. Lionel [723 . . .] much preferred movies to the stage and made more than two hundred films. John oscillated between films and the stage until his drinking made remembering lines too difficult, whereupon he devoted himself to movies, increasingly relying on off-camera cue cards to prompt him. But though Ethel made a handful of silent films, she found the gratification of live audiences preferable, and had consented to make only one talkie, *Rasputin and the Empress,* before returning to the screen in *None but the Lonely Heart.* The good reviews, the generous pay, the Oscar, and her advancing age—she was sixty-five—persuaded her that the time was right for a film career, and she made a score of movies before her death in 1959.

This was the second of Grant's two unsuccessful nominations, and he seems to have consciously chosen the material as a departure from his suave romantic comedian image. It also resonated deeply with his own life: Grant was born to a poverty-stricken family in Bristol, England. His mother had been institutionalized after a breakdown when he was nine years old, and in his early teens he had run away from home to join a theatrical troupe. He was not reunited with his mother until 1933, when she was released from the institution after twenty years. His father died the same year, and Grant became the dutiful support of his mother, who lived into her nineties. After the box-office disappointment of *None but the Lonely Heart* and the loss of the Oscar to Bing Crosby in *Going My Way,* Grant resumed his more familiar screen persona and was a durable and ageless superstar up to his retirement from the screen in 1966. He received an honorary award from the Academy at the 1969 ceremonies, "for his unique mastery of the art of screen acting with the respect and affection of his colleagues." He died at the age of eighty-two in 1986, while on a lecture tour.

The scoring Oscar went to Max Steiner for *Since You Went Away.* Barbara McLean won for the editing of *Wilson.*

Barrymore: 1528, 1575, 1891. Grant: 1549. Bakaleinikoff: 640, 916, 1863. Eisler: 862.

1446 • *NONE SHALL ESCAPE*

COLUMBIA. 1944.

NOMINATION *Original Story:* Alfred Neumann and Joseph Thau.

Flashbacks from the war-crimes trial of a German officer, played by Alexander Knox [2286], trace his increasing involvement with the Nazi Party. Wounded in World War I, he tries to resume a career as a teacher in a Polish village, but his brutal nature leads to his dismissal and he joins the Nazis, determined to revenge himself on the villagers after the invasion of Poland. Solid, tense melodrama that's a little dated because it was made several years before the actual war-crimes trials and the full disclosure of the horrors of the Holocaust. Directed by Andre de Toth [848] from a screenplay by Lester Cole. The cast includes Marsha Hunt and Henry Travers [1371]. The story Oscar went to Leo McCarey for *Going My Way.*

1447 • *NOOSE, THE*

FIRST NATIONAL. 1927–28.

NOMINATION *Actor:* Richard Barthelmess.

Barthelmess plays a gangster whose mother has remarried—to the governor of the state. When his father, her ex-husband, proves a threat to her,

Barthelmess kills him, and the only person who can save him from execution is the governor. Solid melodrama that sank into the obscurity of most silent films released at the dawn of sound.

One of the most popular actors of the silent era, Barthelmess gained fame as a leading man for D. W. Griffith in such films as *Broken Blossoms* (1919) and *Way Down East* (1920), and as the star of films made by his own production company such as *Tol'able David* (1921). He survived the transition to sound, but as a character actor—most notably in *Only Angels Have Wings*—not as a major star. He retired from films in 1942 and died in 1963. The Oscar went to Emil Jannings for *The Last Command* and *The Way of All Flesh*.

Barthelmess: 1538.

1448 • NORMA RAE

20TH CENTURY-FOX PRODUCTION; 20TH CENTURY-FOX. 1979. AWARDS *Actress:* Sally Field. *Original Song:* "It Goes Like It Goes," music by David Shire, lyrics by Norman Gimbel. NOMINATIONS *Picture:* Tamara Asseyev and Alex Rose, producers. *Screenplay Based on Material From Another Medium:* Irving Ravetch and Harriet Frank, Jr.

In the title role, Field plays a southern textile worker who becomes the fiery head of a movement to organize the workers in a mill. Ron Leibman is the labor organizer who inspires her to join the cause. The cast, directed by Martin Ritt [956], includes Beau Bridges, Pat Hingle, Barbara Baxley, Gail Strickland, Noble Willingham, and Grace Zabriskie. A rousing star-making performance by Field helps the film overcome the occasional obviousness of its script.

Field was born and raised in the movie industry. Her mother was a fifties B-movie actress who appeared under the name Margaret Field and later, after her marriage to Jock Mahoney, as Maggie Mahoney. While still in her teens, Sally landed the lead in the 1965–66 TV series *Gidget* and followed that one with *The Flying Nun*—roles that she has spent her later career trying to live down. Although she studied at the Actors Studio, she was not taken seriously until she won an Emmy in 1976 for the TV movie *Sybil,* about a young woman with multiple personality dis-

order. Still, her big-screen career was mostly limited to roles supporting her then lover, Burt Reynolds, in such movies as *Smokey and the Bandit* (1977), *The End* (1978), and *Hooper* (1978). *Norma Rae* was a true breakthrough for Field, who has continued to demonstrate equal ability at both drama and comedy.

Shire, a Yale-educated composer, began his career writing for films in 1971 and provided the musical scores for such major pictures as *The Conversation, All the President's Men,* and *Saturday Night Fever* before winning an Oscar as a songwriter. He was formerly married to Talia Shire [785 . . .]. Among Gimbel's credits are the theme song for the TV series *Happy Days,* the Teresa Brewer hit "Ricochet," and Roberta Flack's "Killing Me Softly With His Song."

The best picture award went to *Kramer vs. Kramer,* which also won for Robert Benton's screenplay. Interestingly Field would win her second Oscar for a film written and directed by Benton, *Places in the Heart.*

Field: 1580. Shire: 1628. Gimbel: 711, 1508, 2172. Ravetch: 956. Frank: 956.

1449 • NORTE, EL

INDEPENDENT PRODUCTION; CINECOM INTERNATIONAL/ISLAND ALIVE. 1984. NOMINATION *Screenplay Written Directly for the Screen:* Gregory Nava and Anna Thomas.

Two Guatemalans, brother and sister, decide to flee their country when their parents are killed during a struggle to organize plantation workers. They first go to Mexico, where they learn to deal with the authorities and the unscrupulous men who prey on would-be immigrants to the United States. When they finally reach Los Angeles, they find the struggle to survive will continue. Earnest and heartfelt film, directed by Nava, that's occasionally crudely made and conventionally scripted, but is still extraordinarily moving at times. Made independently, on a low budget, with support in its distribution from the PBS *American Playhouse* series. Nava was born in San Diego and educated at UCLA. On the strength of *El Norte,* he and his wife, Thomas, were given studio support to make the 1988 film *A Time of Destiny,* with William

Hurt [293 . . .] and Timothy Hutton [1502]. The movie was, however, a critical and commercial disappointment. The Oscar went to Robert Benton for *Places in the Heart*.

1450 • NORTH BY NORTHWEST

MGM. 1959.
NOMINATIONS *Story and Screenplay—Written Directly for the Screen:* Ernest Lehman. *Color Art Direction–Set Decoration:* William A. Horning, Robert Boyle, and Merrill Pye; Henry Grace and Frank McKelvy. *Film Editing:* George Tomasini.

Roger Thornhill, played by Cary Grant [1445 . . .], is having one of those weeks when everything goes wrong: He's mistaken for a federal agent, abducted, filled full of alcohol and set behind the wheel of a car, picked up for drunk driving, mistaken for an assassin at the U.N., forced to flee on a train, seduced by a mysterious woman, pursued from New York to South Dakota by the police, attacked by a crop-dusting plane, and finally forced to battle for his life while dangling from the presidents' faces on Mount Rushmore. Superb, high-flying nonsense, and one of the most entertaining movies ever made by Alfred Hitchcock [1171 . . .] or anyone else. Eva Marie Saint [1477] is the seductress, James Mason [761 . . .] the chief spy, Martin Landau [461 . . .] his henchman, Jessie Royce Landis (who was born ten months after Grant) Grant's mother, Leo G. Carroll the professorial government agent, and Hitchcock the man who just misses a bus. The superb location photography is by Robert Burks [1537 . . .] and the score by Bernard Herrmann [50 . . .].

The Academy's perpetual undervaluing of Hitchcock—and of the action-thriller genre in general—continued, though *North by Northwest* is a far more enduringly popular movie than any of the best picture nominees, which included *Anatomy of a Murder, The Diary of Anne Frank, The Nun's Story,* and *Room at the Top.* Its failure to win more nominations, particularly for Grant, Mason, Landis, Hitchcock, Burks, and Herrmann, is probably due to MGM's decision to push its gargantuan *Ben-Hur* at the Oscars—a tactic

that obviously worked. In addition to best picture, *Ben-Hur* won more Oscars than any film in history, including the awards for art direction and the editing of Ralph E. Winters and John D. Dunning. In the only category in which *North by Northwest* didn't face competition from *Ben-Hur,* Lehman's screenplay lost to Russell Rouse, Clarence Greene, Stanley Shapiro, and Maurice Richlin's for *Pillow Talk.*

Lehman: 896, 1738, 2244, 2277. Horning: 175, 440, 769, 1157, 1644, 1657, 2300. Boyle: 659, 743, 1816. Grace: 69, 227, 401, 769, 953, 1335, 1388, 1537, 1552, 2157, 2184, 2312. McKelvy: 591, 917, 1570, 1631, 2047, 2200.

1451 • NORTH STAR, THE

SAMUEL GOLDWYN PRODUCTIONS; RKO RADIO. 1943.
NOMINATIONS *Original Screenplay:* Lillian Hellman. *Black-and-White Cinematography:* James Wong Howe. *Black-and-White Interior Decoration:* Perry Ferguson, art direction; Howard Bristol, set decoration. *Sound Recording:* Thomas Moulton. *Scoring of a Dramatic or Comedy Picture:* Aaron Copland. *Special Effects:* Clarence Slifer and R. O. Binger, photographic; Thomas T. Moulton, sound.

A village on a collective farm is one of the first targets of the Nazi invasion of the Soviet Union. Anne Baxter [46 . . .] and Farley Granger are the young lovers whose lives are changed by the coming of the war; the heroic villagers include Dana Andrews, Walter Huston [50 . . .], Ann Harding [927], Jane Withers, and Walter Brennan; and the vilest of the Nazis is—of course—Erich von Stroheim [1975]. Glossy, sentimental, propagandistic claptrap, produced by Samuel Goldwyn [102 . . .] as a contribution to the war effort—in the same get-to-love-your-Russkie-allies vein as Warners' *Mission to Moscow.* Lewis Milestone [48 . . .] directed. The movie received tepidly respectable reviews but died at the box office. In the Cold War–era fifties it was reedited, with footage of the Soviet repression of the 1956 Hungarian revolution added, and metamorphosed into an anticommunist movie called *Armored Attack.*

The film was the end of the long working relationship of Goldwyn and Hellman. She had gone to work for Goldwyn in 1935, as a cowriter on *The Dark Angel,* and continued through such films as *These Three, Dead End,* and *The Little Foxes.* But she felt betrayed by the alterations Goldwyn and Milestone made in her script for *The North Star* and, after a violent confrontation, bought her way out of her contract. Her work on the film would come back to haunt her again when the House Un-American Activities Committee investigated her in the fifties. The screenplay award went to Norman Krasna for *Princess O'Rourke.*

Arthur Miller won the cinematography Oscar for *The Song of Bernadette,* which also won for art direction and Alfred Newman's score. The award for sound went to Stephen Dunn for *This Land Is Mine. Crash Dive* took the special effects award.

Hellman: 1182. Howe: 1, 30, 36, 738, 956, 1095, 1470, 1727, 1774. Ferguson: 366, 407, 1607, 2292. Bristol: 690, 852, 864, 1182, 1607, 1613, 1907, 2064. Moulton: 22, 46, 138, 366, 457, 487, 560, 706, 798, 962, 1153, 1200, 1510, 1607, 1849, 2154, 2294. Copland: 894, 1464, 1510. Slifer: 1595. Binger: 1200, 1607.

1452 • *NORTH WEST MOUNTED POLICE*
PARAMOUNT. 1940.
AWARD *Film Editing:* Anne Bauchens.
NOMINATIONS *Color Cinematography:* Victor Milner and W. Howard Greene. *Color Interior Decoration:* Hans Dreier and Roland Anderson. *Sound Recording:* Loren Ryder. *Original Score:* Victor Young.

The Mounties always get their man, and so do the Texas Rangers, so you know how things will turn out when Ranger Dusty Rivers, played by Gary Cooper [701 . . .], pursues his man north of the border. Silly Cecil B. DeMille [412 . . .] adventure without the jaw-dropping extravagance of DeMille's biblical epics, so there's not much left to recommend it. Nice cast, though: Madeleine Carroll, Paulette Goddard [1855], Preston Foster, Robert Preston [2201], Akim Tamiroff [701 . . .], Walter Hampden, Lon Chaney, Jr., and Robert Ryan [467].

Georges Périnal won the cinematography Oscar for *The Thief of Bagdad,* which also won for Vincent Korda's art direction. Douglas Shearer took the sound

award for *Strike Up the Band.* The scoring award went to Leigh Harline, Paul J. Smith, and Ned Washington for *Pinocchio.*

Bauchens: 412, 832, 2012. Milner: 304, 412, 470, 740, 757, 827, 1217, 1668. Greene: 96, 239, 747, 1070, 1560, 1621, 1909, 2262. Dreier: 97, 151, 649, 674, 701, 726, 925, 979, 1101, 1120, 1194, 1214, 1217, 1358, 1443, 1540, 1668, 1748, 1880, 1975, 1994, 2190. Anderson: 278, 363, 426, 450, 649, 1029, 1194, 1214, 1219, 1570, 1668, 1674, 1880, 1994. Ryder: 566, 827, 979, 1669, 1697, 1703, 1837, 1887, 2012, 2168, 2181, 2183, 2230, 2242. Young: 97, 98, 100, 101, 280, 489, 612, 693, 701, 794, 846, 925, 1214, 1257, 1396, 1748, 1823, 1994, 2235, 2315.

1453 • *NORTHWEST PASSAGE*
MGM. 1940.
NOMINATION *Color Cinematography:* Sidney Wagner and William V. Skall.

Under the hard-nosed leadership of Maj. Robert Rogers, played by Spencer Tracy [131 . . .], a group of rangers blaze a trail through the prerevolutionary American wilderness. Colorful action epic with spectacular scenery but also an attitude toward the American Indian that now seems distasteful. Directed by King Vidor [378 . . .] from a script by Laurence Stallings and Talbot Jennings [83 . . .] based on the novel by Kenneth Roberts. The cast includes Robert Young, Walter Brennan [424 . . .], and Ruth Hussey [1563]. Though the movie is subtitled *Book One— Rogers' Rangers,* MGM never got around to filming the rest of the story. The cinematography award went to Georges Périnal for *The Thief of Bagdad.*

Wagner: 576. Skall: 96, 208, 1048, 1170, 1317, 1644, 1668, 1822, 2102.

1454 • *NOT AS A STRANGER*
STANLEY KRAMER PRODUCTIONS; UNITED ARTISTS. 1955.
NOMINATION *Sound Recording:* Watson Jones, sound director, RCA Sound Department.

Medical student Robert Mitchum [1935] marries nurse Olivia de Havilland [798 . . .], who helps put him through school despite his roving ways. Somewhat soapy version of a soapy best-seller by Morton Thompson, produced and directed by Stanley Kramer [330 . . .] from a script by Edward Anhalt [164 . . .] and Edna Anhalt [1523 . . .]. Helped greatly by a stellar cast: Frank Sinatra [732 . . .], Gloria Grahame [130 . . .], Broderick Crawford [53], Charles Bickford [651 . . .], and Lee Marvin [371]. The Oscar for sound went to Fred Hynes for *Oklahoma!*

1455 • *NOTORIOUS*

RKO RADIO. 1946.

NOMINATIONS *Supporting Actor:* Claude Rains. *Original Screenplay:* Ben Hecht.

Ingrid Bergman [72 . . .], the playgirl daughter of a convicted Nazi spy, is enlisted by government agent Cary Grant [1445 . . .] to infiltrate a group of her father's old associates in Rio de Janeiro. When she encounters Rains, an old admirer, intelligence chief Louis Calhern [1243] decides the quickest way to find out what the Nazis are up to is for Bergman to woo Rains. Grant, who has fallen for Bergman despite her shady past, reluctantly agrees, even when Bergman is forced into marrying Rains. But when Rains and his sinister mother, Leopoldine Konstantin, discover the truth about Bergman, they attempt to do away with her by slowly poisoning her. One of director Alfred Hitchcock's [1171 . . .] finest films, with top-notch performances by all, powerful star chemistry between Grant and Bergman, and wonderful nail-biting moments. So why didn't it receive more nominations? *Notorious* began as a David O. Selznick [497 . . .] production, but Selznick had become deeply embroiled in his would-be blockbuster *Duel in the Sun,* so he farmed the film out to RKO, which was also releasing two films with powerful egos at the helm: Samuel Goldwyn's *The Best Years of Our Lives* and Frank Capra's *It's a Wonderful Life.* What resources the financially troubled studio had to promote films for Oscars went into those pictures, which gained best picture nominations. Heavyweight Fox studio head Darryl Zanuck [34 . . .] invariably managed to wangle a nomination for one of his films, so *The Razor's Edge* also gained a slot. MGM likewise had immense power at nomination time, which it used on behalf of *The Yearling.* And Laurence Olivier's *Henry V* was a prestigious hands-across-the-sea nominee. That left no room for *Notorious,* or *The Big Sleep, My Darling Clementine,* or *Brief Encounter,* all films that have stood the test of time far better than either *The Razor's Edge* or *The Yearling.* In the directing race, Hitchcock was passed over for Clarence Brown for *The Yearling,* Capra, David Lean for *Brief Encounter,* Robert Siodmak for *The Killers,* and William Wyler (who won) for *The Best Years.*

Rains' tortured mama's boy is one of his finest portrayals—menace tinged with charm tinged with guilt and a bit of psychopathology. He lost to Harold Russell in *The Best Years of Our Lives.*

Hecht's screenplay kept company with some of the most varied nominees in Oscar history, including Raymond Chandler's *The Blue Dahlia,* Jacques Prévert's masterly *Children of Paradise,* and Norman Panama and Melvin Frank's Hope and Crosby outing *The Road to Utopia.* The Oscar was won by Muriel and Sydney Box's melodrama *The Seventh Veil.*

Rains: 365, 1369, 1371. Hecht: 78, 1765, 2179, 2211, 2316.

1456 • *NOW, VOYAGER*

WARNER BROS. 1942.

AWARD *Scoring of a Dramatic or Comedy Picture:* Max Steiner.

NOMINATIONS *Actress:* Bette Davis. *Supporting Actress:* Gladys Cooper.

Charlotte Vale (Davis) is a middle-aged spinster in a wealthy Boston family, totally dominated by her elderly mother (Cooper). But Dr. Jaquith, a kindly psychiatrist played by Claude Rains [365 . . .], encourages the swan inside the ugly duckling to emerge. On a cruise, Charlotte encounters the handsome Jerry Durrence (Paul Henreid) and has an affair, even though he's married (unhappily) and has a daughter. A transfigured Charlotte returns to Boston, where she proclaims her liberation from the maternal bonds and becomes engaged to an eminent Bostonian (John Loder). But when she meets Jerry again, she breaks off her engagement, precipitating her mother's fatal stroke. At Jaquith's sanitarium, where she has gone to try to resolve her feelings of guilt, Charlotte meets Jerry's daughter, Tina (Janis Wilson), in whom she recognizes a shy, withdrawn girl very much like the earlier Charlotte. And in growing close to Tina, she brings Jerry back into her life. Quintessential ''woman's picture''—a genre scorned by critics until feminist writers began to question why portrayals of women's emotions and problems had been dismissed by them as inferior material for the movies, and began to seriously examine the themes and subtexts of such films. And the message of *Now, Voyager* is that a woman really can lead an independent life. It's also the quintessential Bette Davis movie—a film that triumphs as entertainment (if not art) largely because of her performance. The director was the otherwise undistinguished Irving Rapper; the real auteur of the movie was Davis, skillfully showing the steel inside the mousy, withdrawn Charlotte, and later showing the insecurity lingering in the poised and self-confident Charlotte. She is well supported by Cooper, Rains, and Henreid, as well as Bonita Granville [2044], Ilka Chase, Lee Patrick, and Mary Wickes. Casey Robinson did the screenplay from a novel by Olive Higgins Prouty, who also wrote *Stella Dallas,* this movie's chief rival as the archetypal Hollywood weeper.

Between his first Oscar, for *The Informer,* and this one, Steiner had also composed the most famous of all film scores for *Gone With the Wind.* The next year he would write the music for *GWTW*'s chief rival as the Great American Movie, *Casablanca.* The unstintingly romantic *Now, Voyager* score is one of his best.

The acting Oscars went to *Mrs. Miniver*'s Greer Garson and Teresa Wright, depriving Davis of her chance to win a third award on her record-setting sixth nomination. This was the first of three nominations for Cooper, who had been a celebrated early-twentieth-century beauty in London and made a few silent films in Britain. In 1940 she settled in Hollywood, where she played grandes dames for the next three decades. She died in 1971 at the age of eighty-three.

Steiner: 16, 154, 190, 330, 365, 385, 492, 679, 747, 754, 798, 999, 1043, 1046, 1052, 1162, 1169, 1170, 1207, 1324, 1408, 1430, 1690, 1779, 1828. Davis: 46, 484, 492, 1046, 1162, 1182, 1369, 1462.5, 1908, 2248. Cooper: 1393, 1868.

1457 • NUN'S STORY, THE

WARNER BROS. 1959.

NOMINATIONS *Picture:* Henry Blanke, producer. *Actress:* Audrey Hepburn. *Director:* Fred Zinnemann. *Screenplay—Based on Material From Another Medium:* Robert Anderson. *Color Cinematography:* Franz Planer. *Sound:* George R. Groves, sound director, Warner Bros. Studio Sound Department. *Scoring of a Dramatic or Comedy Picture:* Franz Waxman. *Film Editing:* Walter Thompson.

Hepburn plays Sister Luke, a young nun who goes to work in the Belgian Congo with a doctor, played by Peter Finch [1424 . . .], and begins to question her vocation. Fine, serious filmmaking and a stunning cast—Edith Evans [377 . . .], Peggy Ashcroft [1533], Dean Jagger [2154], Mildred Dunnock [119 . . .], Beatrice Straight [1424], Paricia Collinge [1182], Barbara O'Neil [55], and Colleen Dewhurst —make this adaptation of the book by Kathryn C. Hulme well worth seeing, even if one questions whether it deserves a best picture slot over such non-nominees as *Some Like It Hot, The 400 Blows, Wild Strawberries, Rio Bravo,* and *North by Northwest.*

This was the year of the *Ben-Hur* blitz, which swept away the Oscars for picture, director William Wyler, cinematographer Robert Surtees, Franklin E. Milton's sound direction, and Miklos Rozsa's score. *Room at the Top* deprived *The Nun's Story* of the other two Oscars: Simone Signoret won as best actress and Neil Paterson for his screenplay.

Blanke: 17, 90, 712, 1046, 1169, 1315, 1936, 2136. Hepburn: 278, 1716, 1738, 2221. Zinnemann: 732, 912, 1066, 1252, 1771, 1969. Anderson: 971. Planer: 380, 393, 515, 1716. Groves: 825, 1385, 1393, 1763, 1869, 1973, 2277. Waxman: 573, 958, 1459, 1579, 1670, 1822, 1975, 1979, 2004, 2334. Thompson: 2056.

1458 • NURSE EDITH CAVELL

RKO RADIO. 1939.

NOMINATION *Original Score:* Anthony Collins.

Cavell (Anna Neagle) tends to the wounded in Belgium during World War I but is caught and executed by the Germans as a spy. Earnest and somewhat stodgy, with obvious propagandizing aims. The cast, directed by Herbert Wilcox, includes Edna May Oliver [581], George Sanders [46], ZaSu Pitts, and May Robson [1119]. The scoring award went to Herbert Stothart for *The Wizard of Oz.*

Collins: 1015, 1971.

1459 • OBJECTIVE, BURMA!

WARNER BROS. 1945.

NOMINATIONS *Original Story:* Alvah Bessie. *Scoring of a Dramatic or Comedy Picture:* Franz Waxman. *Film Editing:* George Amy.

Errol Flynn leads his paratroopers against a Japanese outpost in World War II Burma. Well-done war movie with plenty of action and mercifully few flag-waving speeches, although the script's characterization of the Japanese as subhuman beings is pretty hard to take. At the time, however, its racism attracted less attention than the fact that the movie ignored the British role in Burma, which was more significant than that of the Americans. Directed by Raoul Walsh.

This was the sole nomination for Bessie, who five years later would become one of the Hollywood Ten, imprisoned for contempt of Congress for his failure to testify before the House Un-American Activities Committee. He later wrote a book about the experience, *Inquisition in Eden.* He lost the Oscar to Charles G. Booth's story for *The House on 92nd Street.*

The scoring award went to Miklos Rozsa for *Spellbound.* Robert J. Kern won the editing Oscar for *National Velvet.*

Waxman: 573, 958, 1457, 1579, 1670, 1822, 1975, 1979, 2004, 2334. Amy: 30, 2318.

1460 • OBSESSION

GEORGE LITTO PRODUCTIONS; COLUMBIA. 1976.

NOMINATION *Original Score:* Bernard Herrmann.

Twenty years after his wife and daughter were sup-posedly murdered by their kidnapers, businessman Cliff Robertson [387] meets a young woman, played by Genevieve Bujold [85], who looks exactly like the wife he lost. He proceeds to try to remake her in the dead wife's image. This *hommage* to Hitchcock's *Vertigo* is entertaining enough, but there's too much show-offy camera work by Vilmos Zsigmond [416 . . .], under the direction of Brian DePalma, and the plot twists of Paul Schrader's script don't take us anywhere we haven't been before. The cast also includes John Lithgow [2020 . . .] in one of his earliest important film roles.

Herrmann, who died before the film was released, received two posthumous nominations, the other one for *Taxi Driver.* The Oscar went to Jerry Goldsmith for *The Omen.*

Herrmann: 50, 83, 407, 2005.

1461 • ODD COUPLE, THE

HOWARD W. KOCH PRODUCTION; PARAMOUNT. 1968.

NOMINATIONS *Screenplay—Based on Material From Another Medium:* Neil Simon. *Film Editing:* Frank Bracht.

Jack Lemmon [91 . . .] is Felix and Walter Matthau [709 . . .] is Oscar in this straightforward adaptation of Simon's stage hit about two men—a neatnik and a slob—who room together after their divorces. Perfect star performances make it work, despite its obvious stage origins. The subsequent TV sitcom with Tony Randall and Jack Klugman has made the characters overfamiliar, so it's hard to appreciate how good Lemmon and Matthau are. Directed by Gene Saks, who did the Broadway version, too.

Simon lost to James Goldman for *The Lion in Winter.* The editing Oscar went to Frank P. Keller for *Bullitt.*

Simon: 332, 803, 1976.

1462 • ODD MAN OUT

J. ARTHUR RANK-TWO CITIES FILMS; UNIVERSAL-INTERNATIONAL (UNITED KINGDOM). 1947.

NOMINATION *Film Editing:* Fergus McDonnell.

James Mason [761 . . .] plays an Irish revolutionary who is wounded in an encounter with the police and spends his last hours fleeing them through the streets of Belfast, encountering a variety of sympathizers and betrayers. A superb performance by Mason, who thought it was his best film, and taut direction by Carol Reed [639 . . .] make it first-rate. The cast includes Robert Newton, Kathleen Ryan, Cyril Cusack, and Dan O'Herlihy [18]. Splendidly filmed by Robert Krasker [2054]. The editing Oscar went to Francis Lyon and Robert Parrish for *Body and Soul.*

1462.5 • *OF HUMAN BONDAGE*

RKO RADIO. 1934.

NOMINATION *Actress:* Bette Davis. (Write-in candidate.)

Davis plays Mildred, a trashy waitress who manages to get her hooks into a young doctor played by Leslie Howard [178 . . .]; she nearly ruins his life. Good version of the book by W. Somerset Maugham, adapted by Lester Cohen and directed by John Cromwell, with Frances Dee, Kay Johnson, Reginald Denny, Alan Hale, and Reginald Owen.

Davis' flamboyant performance made her a star after three years in Hollywood and a dozen mediocre-to-lousy films. It also resulted in one of Oscar history's most notorious oversights, when the nominations were announced and Davis was not among them. The official candidates were Grace Moore for *One Night of Love,* Norma Shearer for *The Barretts of Wimpole Street,* and the eventual winner, Claudette Colbert for *It Happened One Night.* An outcry resulted, much of it led by Davis' studio, Warner Bros., which hoped to reap a publicity bonanza from the arrival of a new star—whom it had, ironically, loaned out for the film that made her one. The Academy capitulated, allowing write-ins on the final ballot, a practice that continued for one more year before it was outlawed. Davis came in third, ahead of Moore but behind Shearer. But the publicity helped her earn the award for her performance in *Dangerous* the following year.

Davis: 46, 484, 492, 1046, 1162, 1182, 1369, 1456, 1908, 2248.

1463 • *OF HUMAN HEARTS*

MGM. 1938.

NOMINATION *Supporting Actress:* Beulah Bondi.

Backwoods preacher Walter Huston [50 . . .] is at odds with his son, James Stewart [73 . . .], in this wholesome bit of sentimental Americana that features John Carradine as Abraham Lincoln, plus Gene Reynolds, Charles Coburn [535 . . .], Guy Kibbee, Gene Lockhart [36], and Ann Rutherford. Directed by Clarence Brown [84 . . .]. Bondi, who plays Stewart's mother, lost to Fay Bainter in *Jezebel.*

Bondi: 807.

1464 • *OF MICE AND MEN*

HAL ROACH; UNITED ARTISTS. 1939.

NOMINATIONS *Picture:* Lewis Milestone, producer. *Black-and-White Cinematography:* Norbert Brodine. *Sound Recording:* Elmer Raguse. *Score:* Aaron Copland. *Original Score:* Aaron Copland.

Two itinerant farm workers, George, played by Burgess Meredith [504 . . .], and Lennie (Lon Chaney, Jr.), are hired on at a farm in California. Lennie is big and strong but retarded, and his inability to control both his strength and his urge to pet soft things has tragic consequences when he encounters Mae (Betty Field), the flirtatious wife of the sadistic Curley (Bob Steele). Well-made adaptation of the novel by John Steinbeck [1171 . . .], adapted by Eugene Solow and directed by Milestone. A strong cast includes Charles Bickford [651 . . .] and Noah Beery, Jr. As in many of Steinbeck's works, the characters have been freighted with more symbolism than they can bear, but the story still makes a strong emotional impact.

Gone With the Wind took the best picture Oscar. Brodine was only a preliminary nominee for the cinematography award, losing to Gregg Toland for *Wuthering Heights* after the Academy decided to whittle down its first slate of cinematography nominees and place only two names in each of the categories, black and white and color, on the final ballot. The other official nominee was Bert Glennon for *Stagecoach.* The award for sound went to Bernard B. Brown for *When Tomorrow Comes. Of Mice and Men* was one of Copland's first film scores, and it was the only one to receive nominations in both scoring categories. The first category was primarily for adaptation and arranging, and the winners were Richard Hageman, Frank Harling, John Leipold, and Leo Shuken for *Stagecoach,* the score for which was largely made up of folk melodies. The second category was for composition, and the winner was Herbert Stothart for the incidental music —not the songs—for *The Wizard of Oz,* although even that score has elements of pastiche, with classical music interpolations. Because the two scoring categories, introduced at the 1938 awards, were so awkwardly defined, the Academy maintained them only three years. At the 1941 Oscars they were replaced with awards for scoring dramatic films and musical films, a distinction that lasted until the paucity of musicals in the mid-eighties made the pickings too slim for an award in that category.

Milestone: 48, 734, 2159. Brodine: 731, 1306. Raguse: 345, 757.5, 1306, 1487, 2117, 2118. Copland: 894, 1451, 1510.

1465 • OFFICER AND A GENTLEMAN, AN

LORIMAR PRODUCTION IN ASSOCIATION WITH MARTIN ELFAND; PARAMOUNT. 1982.

AWARDS *Supporting Actor:* Louis Gossett, Jr. *Song:* ''Up Where We Belong,'' music by Jack Nitzsche and Buffy Sainte-Marie, lyrics by Will Jennings.
NOMINATIONS *Actress:* Debra Winger. *Screenplay Written Directly for the Screen:* Douglas Day Stewart. *Original Score:* Jack Nitzsche. *Film Editing:* Peter Zinner.

Richard Gere enrolls in Naval Officer Candidate School and meets factory worker Winger. Gossett is the tough drill instructor who helps Gere turn from a misfit punk into—well, you've read the title. Formula moviemaking that manages to be entertaining even though you can see the clichéd plot turns coming long before they arrive on the screen. Taylor Hackford directs as if the clichés were fresh, and he sometimes makes you think they are. The huge success of the film launched a series of eighties recruiting-poster movies, including *Top Gun* and *Iron Eagle* (1986). Gere is too soft-focus an actor for his role, but Winger and Gossett are terrific, and they're well supported by

David Keith as Gere's buddy, Robert Loggia [1039] as Gere's roving sailor father, and Lisa Blount, Lisa Eilbacher, David Caruso, and Grace Zabriskie.

Gossett became the third African-American actor to win an Oscar—after Hattie McDaniel for *Gone With the Wind* and Sidney Poitier for *Lilies of the Field.* He made his film debut in 1961 supporting Poitier in *A Raisin in the Sun* but didn't return to the screen until 1970, when he made a strong impression as an angry tenant in *The Landlord.* The following year he demonstrated his skill in a comic role opposite James Garner [1380] in *Skin Game.* Since the Oscar, Gossett has had both leading roles and supporting ones, although the quality of the films he has appeared in, such as the three *Iron Eagle* movies (1986, 1988, 1992), hasn't been the highest.

Previously nominated for *One Flew Over the Cuckoo's Nest,* Nitzsche, a composer who also scored *The Exorcist,* lost the scoring award to John Williams for *E.T. The Extra-Terrestrial.* His collaborator on the music for the winning song, Sainte-Marie, is best known as a folksinger. A Cree Indian born in Saskatchewan, she has been active in Native American affairs and is familiar to the younger set from her appearances on *Sesame Street.*

After several minor films, Winger shot to stardom with an appearance opposite John Travolta [1760] in *Urban Cowboy* (1980). She lost her first nomination to Meryl Streep in *Sophie's Choice.* The screenplay Oscar went to John Briley for *Gandhi,* which also won for John Bloom's editing.

Nitzsche: 1481. Jennings: 434. Winger: 1795.5, 2020. Zinner: 521, 784.

1466 • OFFICIAL STORY, THE

HISTORIAS CINEMATOGRÁFICAS/CINEMANIA AND PROGRESS COMMUNICATIONS PRODUCTION; ALMI PICTURES (ARGENTINA). 1985.

AWARD *Foreign Language Film.*
NOMINATION *Screenplay Written Directly for the Screen:* Luis Puenzo and Aida Bortnik.

Norma Aleandro, married to a wealthy Argentine businessman, gradually realizes that her adopted daughter may be one of the children who were taken away from members of the political opposition to the Argentine junta. Powerful, chilling film, with a beautiful performance by Aleandro. Puenzo, who also directed, and Bortnik make a devastating political statement without propagandizing. On the strength of this film, which was only Puenzo's second feature as a director, he was invited to Hollywood. Unfortunately his first attempt at directing a big-budget American movie, *The Old Gringo* (1989), was a flop. The screenplay Oscar went to Earl W. Wallace, William Kelley, and Pamela Wallace for *Witness*.

1467 • OH, GOD!

WARNER BROS. PRODUCTION; WARNER BROS. 1977.

NOMINATION *Screenplay—Based on Material From Another Medium:* Larry Gelbart.

God, played by George Burns [1976], appears to supermarket manager John Denver and tells him to spread the word. Sweetly inoffensive little high-concept comedy-fantasy that goes a long way on the strength of Burns' impeccable comic timing and a likable cast that includes Teri Garr [2113], Paul Sorvino, Ralph Bellamy [114], William Daniels, Donald Pleasence, and Barnard Hughes. Directed by Carl Reiner, who also has a cameo as himself. There were two rather lame sequels: *Oh God! Book II* (1980) and *Oh, God! You Devil* (1984). Gelbart lost to Alvin Sargent for *Julia*.

Gelbart: 2113.

1468 • OH KAY!

FIRST NATIONAL. 1927–28.

NOMINATION *Title Writing:* George Marion, Jr.

Colleen Moore plays Lady Kay Rutledge, who flees a marriage she doesn't want and winds up with a handsome bootlegger (Lawrence Gray). Silent film based on a Broadway musical whose chief glory was its song score, by George [1797] and Ira Gershwin [455 . . .], which included "Clap Yo' Hands" and "Someone to Watch Over Me." Without the music, the film depends heavily on a plot based on Guy Bolton and P. G. Wodehouse's book for the show, and that was largely designed as something to hang the songs on. So when sound came in, the film sank

into obscurity—as did Moore, who was one of the silents' big stars. The title writing award, given only once before sound made it obsolete, went to Joseph Farnham for cumulative achievements during the nominating period, including *Telling the World*. The Academy's most recent revision of its nominations and winners list cites no titles after either Farnham's or Marion's name, because nominees could be recognized for the body of their work during the qualifying year. But because this book is an examination of films as well as the people who've worked on them, we've listed Marion as a nominee for *Oh, Kay!*, as other compilations of Oscar lore have previously done.

1469 • OKLAHOMA!

RODGERS & HAMMERSTEIN PICTURES INC.; MAGNA THEATRE CORPORATION. 1955.

AWARDS *Sound Recording:* Fred Hynes, sound director, Todd-AO Sound Department. *Scoring of a Musical Picture:* Robert Russell Bennett, Jay Blackton, and Adolph Deutsch.

NOMINATIONS *Color Cinematography:* Robert Surtees. *Film Editing:* Gene Ruggiero and George Boemler.

The cowboy Curly (Gordon MacRae) is smitten with Laurey, played by Shirley Jones [609], but she decides to play hard to get and go to the box social with the sinister hired hand Jud Fry, played by Rod Steiger [992 . . .]. Meanwhile, the promiscuous Ado Annie, played by Gloria Grahame [130 . . .], is squabbling with her own boyfriend, Will Parker (Gene Nelson), by throwing herself at the itinerant peddler Ali Hakim, played by Eddie Albert [887 . . .]. Jud is accidentally killed in a scuffle with Curly, but everything winds up literally OK. The landmark 1943 Broadway musical, often credited as the work that changed the course of the American musical theater from revues strung on a thread of story to "book musicals" focusing on character and plot development, receives a less-than-epochal filming here. It's still entertaining, and no one can fault the songs of Richard Rodgers [1921] and Oscar Hammerstein II [375 . . .]. But it suffers from the usual problems of adapting a stage musical to the screen—the two media have different and often incompatible conventions. Director Fred Zinnemann [732 . . .] and screenwriters Sonya Levien [1007 . . .] and William Ludwig [1007] fail to find a comfortable cinematic way of translating Hammerstein's stage book. Rodgers and Hammerstein insisted that the book be adhered to on all of the earlier films of their musicals, including *Carousel* (1956), *South Pacific,* and *The King and I.* The result was that most—with the exception of *The King and I,* whose exotic setting lent itself to a stylized treatment—were poorly translated to the screen. The chief concession to the medium is location shooting—in Maine for *Carousel,* in the real South Pacific, and for this one in Arizona, which was judged more photogenic than Oklahoma. But the locations don't match well with the scenes that were obviously shot on a soundstage, especially during Laurey's dream, a celebrated ballet by Agnes De Mille, that moves from a realistic location setting to a very undreamlike soundstage set. Instead of echoing the film's story, the ballet merely brings it to a halt.

Zinnemann and producer Arthur Hornblow, Jr. [749 . . .], wisely resisted the temptation to cast Curly and Laurey with box-office stars, although Paul Newman [3 . . .] and Joanne Woodward [1365 . . .] were considered for the roles. MacRae and Jones (in her screen debut) look and sound fine. Grahame is inspired casting as Ado Annie, though Nelson is a bit too mature for Will Parker. Steiger's method acting is out of key with the other performers, who include Charlotte Greenwood as Aunt Eller and James Whitmore [157 . . .] as Annie's shotgun-toting father. The dancers include James Mitchell, Bambi Linn, Kelly Brown, and Marc Platt. The film of *Oklahoma!* also suffered by comparison with the previous year's *Seven Brides for Seven Brothers,* a work that clearly derived from *Oklahoma!* but was written and designed from the start for the movies.

Oklahoma! might have fared better at the Oscars if it had had the support of a major studio behind it. Magna Theatre Corp. had been founded by Michael Todd [101] to promote his 65mm wide-screen process, Todd-AO, which had met resistance from the studios, already beginning to convert to other processes such as CinemaScope and VistaVision. Todd

had the last laugh the following year, when he won the best picture Oscar with *Around the World in 80 Days.*

The cinematography Oscar went to Robert Burks for *To Catch a Thief.* Charles Nelson and William A. Lyon won for the editing of *Picnic.*

Hynes: 33, 413, 1592, 1881, 1883, 2244. Bennett: 1517. Blackton: 852. Deutsch: 87, 141, 1782, 1818. Surtees: 130, 175, 557, 810, 917, 1094, 1139, 1388, 1644, 1747, 1911, 1927, 1960, 2055, 2152. Ruggiero: 101.

1470 • OLD MAN AND THE SEA, THE

LELAND HAYWARD; WARNER BROS. 1958.
AWARD *Scoring of a Dramatic or Comedy Picture:* Dimitri Tiomkin.
NOMINATIONS *Actor:* Spencer Tracy. *Color Cinematography:* James Wong Howe.

An old fisherman (Tracy) lands the giant marlin he's dreamed of catching all his life, but nearly dies when sharks attack the fish as he attempts to bring it back to shore. Ernest Hemingway's fable about human endurance might have made an interesting short film, but even at eighty-six minutes this version seems overextended. Tracy gives it his considerable all, but his star quality prevents him from becoming anything other than Spencer Tracy pretending to be an old fisherman. Directed by John Sturges [131]. Hemingway's wife, Mary, appears as a tourist in one scene.

This was the last of four Oscars received by Tiomkin during a career that began with the arrival of sound and lasted until his own production of *Tchaikovsky* in 1970. He died in 1979.

Tracy lost to David Niven in *Separate Tables.* Howe's work, supplemented in this film with location footage shot by Floyd Crosby [1993] and Tom Tutwiler and underwater camera work by Lamar Boren, lost to Joseph Ruttenberg's for *Gigi.*

Tiomkin: 33, 286, 380, 446, 638, 663, 730, 768, 850, 911, 912, 1206, 1347, 1370, 2006, 2127, 2282, 2335. Tracy: 131, 271, 352, 656, 843, 1000, 1065, 1751. Howe: 1, 30, 36, 738, 956, 1095, 1451, 1727, 1774.

1471 • *OLIVER!*

ROMULUS FILMS LTD. PRODUCTION; COLUMBIA (UNITED KINGDOM). 1968.

AWARDS *Picture:* John Woolf, producer. *Director:* Carol Reed. *Art Direction–Set Decoration:* John Box and Terence Marsh; Vernon Dixon and Ken Muggleston. *Sound:* Shepperton Studio Sound Department. *Score of a Musical Picture—Original or Adaptation:* John Green. *Honorary Award:* Onna White, for her outstanding choreography achievement.

NOMINATIONS *Actor:* Ron Moody. *Supporting Actor:* Jack Wild. *Screenplay—Based on Material From Another Medium:* Vernon Harris. *Cinematography:* Oswald Morris. *Film Editing:* Ralph Kemplen. *Costume Design:* Phyllis Dalton.

The young orphan Oliver Twist (Mark Lester) falls in with Fagin (Moody) and his band of juvenile pickpockets, led by the Artful Dodger (Wild). Surprisingly successful musical version of the Charles Dickens novel, with Shani Wallis as the understanding prostitute Nancy and Oliver Reed (the director's nephew) as the brutal Bill Sikes. Though the songs by Lionel Bart are only so-so, they're performed with extraordinary energy and skill, and Carol Reed's direction and the superb production values resulted in one of the last great film musicals. It has to be noted, however, that *Oliver!* is one of the most controversial of the Academy's choices for best picture. Some of the contempt that has been expressed for the film stems from the era in which it appeared: 1968, a year of assassinations and violent protest, was not a year in which a costume musical based on a Victorian novel was likely to be thought relevant, however dark it might be—and *Oliver!* is a very dark musical indeed. On the other hand, none of the other nominees was particularly in keeping with the spirit of the age either: They include the period musical *Funny Girl,* the historical costume drama *The Lion in Winter,* the psychological melodrama *Rachel, Rachel,* and the jazzed-up Shakespeare film *Romeo and Juliet.* Four of the five nominees, in fact, were set in the past. Missing from the nominees was Stanley Kubrick's enigmatic *2001: A Space Odyssey,* perhaps the only film of the year that has achieved legendary status, and much of the animus

directed against the Academy's choice of *Oliver!* is based on its failure to recognize Kubrick's achievement. The following year the Academy would reward a gritty, contemporary work, *Midnight Cowboy.*

Reed, a former actor, began his screen directing career in England in the 1930s, and by the outbreak of World War II was considered one of Britain's leading directors, with such films as *Night Train* to his credit. During the war he was assigned to producing documentaries and propaganda films. With Garson Kanin [11 . . .], he codirected *The True Glory,* a film about the last years of the war, which won the documentary feature Oscar for 1945. After the war, his reputation as a director reached its peak with such films as *Odd Man Out, The Fallen Idol,* and *The Third Man.* His work in Hollywood, however, was inferior, reaching its lowest point when he was fired from the remake of *Mutiny on the Bounty* in 1962 and when he directed the leaden *The Agony and the Ecstasy* in 1965. *Oliver!* was a stunning comeback, a tribute to Reed's ability, demonstrated in his best films, to create an atmosphere that permeates an entire production. Unfortunately neither of Reed's two subsequent films, *Flap* (1970) and *The Public Eye* (a.k.a. *Follow Me;* 1972), was a success. He died in 1976.

Of the technical awards received by *Oliver!,* White's honorary Oscar for choreography deserves special mention. Since it abandoned the "dance direction" category in which it gave awards from 1935 to 1937, the Academy had only once before singled out a film's choreographer for a special award: Jerome Robbins, for *West Side Story.* (Gene Kelly received a special award for 1951 "specifically for his brilliant achievements in the art of choreography," but also noting his "versatility as an actor, singer, director and dancer." That award was not, however, for a specific film, although it was given the same year that *An American in Paris* won for best picture.) White, born in Nova Scotia, has devoted most of her career to the Broadway stage, where she first gained acclaim for her work on *The Music Man*—the film version of which she also choreographed.

Moody created the role of Fagin in the original 1960 London production of *Oliver!* As a character player he has been seen in numerous films and TV series, primarily in England, but has not had a success comparable to his role in this film. The Oscar went to Cliff Robertson for *Charly.*

Wild was sixteen when he made his film debut in *Oliver!* He was the star of a children's TV series, *H. R. Pufnstuf,* in 1969 and made several films in the early seventies before disappearing from the screen. He has a small role in the 1991 *Robin Hood: Prince of Thieves.* Jack Albertson won the supporting actor award for *The Subject Was Roses.*

The screenplay Oscar went to James Goldman for *The Lion in Winter.* Pasqualino De Santis won for the cinematography for *Romeo and Juliet,* which also won for Danilo Donati's costumes. Frank P. Keller took the award for editing for *Bullitt.*

Woolf: 1724. Reed: 639, 2053. Box: 558, 1151, 1429, 1533, 2134. Marsh: 558, 1285, 1766. Dixon: 151, 1429. Green: 66, 320, 594, 662, 817, 914, 1298, 1550, 2047, 2244. Morris: 659, 2299. Kemplen: 503, 1363. Dalton: 558, 902.

1472 • OMEN, THE

20TH CENTURY-FOX PRODUCTIONS LTD.; 20TH CENTURY-FOX. 1976.

AWARD *Original Score:* Jerry Goldsmith.

NOMINATION *Original Song:* "Ave Satani," music and lyrics by Jerry Goldsmith.

Gregory Peck [759 . . .] and Lee Remick [508] discover, a little too late, that their son, Damien, is the Antichrist. One of the best of the *Exorcist*-inspired nail-biters, which just makes it the best of a bad lot. Directed by Richard Donner from a screenplay by David Seltzer, with David Warner, Billie Whitelaw, and Leo McKern. There were two big-screen sequels —*Damien—Omen II* (1978) and *The Final Conflict* (1981)—plus a TV movie, *Omen IV: The Awakening* (1991).

This is the sole Oscar so far for Goldsmith, who began his work as a composer for radio and TV, writing, among other familiar themes, the music for *Gunsmoke.* He began his work for the movies in the late fifties and has written dozens of film scores. Because he has been considered a specialist in action

pictures, his work has been somewhat overshadowed by that of John Williams [6 . . .]. The song Oscar went to Barbra Streisand and Paul Williams for "Evergreen (Love Theme From *A Star Is Born*)."

Goldsmith: 152.5, 268, 395, 727, 939, 1527, 1537, 1541, 1583, 1589, 1753, 1913, 2176, 2287.

1473 • ON GOLDEN POND

ITC FILMS/IPC PRODUCTION; UNIVERSAL. 1981.

AWARDS *Actor:* Henry Fonda. *Actress:* Katharine Hepburn. *Screenplay Based on Material From Another Medium:* Ernest Thompson.

NOMINATIONS *Picture:* Bruce Gilbert, producer. *Supporting Actress:* Jane Fonda. *Director:* Mark Rydell. *Cinematography:* Billy Williams. *Sound:* Richard Portman and David Ronne. *Original Score:* Dave Grusin. *Film Editing:* Robert L. Wolfe.

The Thayers, Norman (Henry Fonda) and Ethel (Hepburn), arrive at their summer cabin where they're soon joined by their daughter, Chelsea (Jane Fonda), who brings along her lover (Dabney Coleman) and his thirteen-year-old son, Billy (Doug McKeon). Crabby old Norman is fretting about getting old—he's nearing eighty—and has never gotten along with Chelsea, but when Billy is left with him for a few days, he somehow gets through the kid's veneer of toughness. Eventually, with the aid of his wife, he effects a reconciliation with his daughter, too. Just as slushy as it sounds—perhaps even more. Only the inspired casting makes the film work, and even then it's closer to a *Hallmark Hall of Fame* TV drama than to anything that resembles a theatrical movie. But it's worth watching as the only screen teaming of the two Fondas, whose real-life relationship was reportedly as tense and wary as that of Norman and Chelsea. It was also the only screen teaming of Henry Fonda and Hepburn. Unfortunately the film seems to preen itself on that fact; director Rydell allows the two great actors to become adorable icons instead of persuading them to give performances of control and depth.

Henry Fonda's only previous nomination for acting was for 1940's *The Grapes of Wrath*—a forty-one-year gap between acting nominations that's the longest on record. (He did, however, receive a nomination at the

1957 awards as producer of *12 Angry Men,* so some would count the thirty-eight-year gaps between Helen Hayes' nominations for *The Sin of Madelon Claudet* and *Airport* and Jack Palance's for *Shane* and *City Slickers* as an Academy record.) The Academy overlooked numerous fine performances by Fonda, including the title role in *Young Mr. Lincoln;* a dizzy turn at slapstick romance in *The Lady Eve;* his fine Wyatt Earp in *My Darling Clementine* (1946); the martinet cavalry commander in *Fort Apache* (1948); the title role in *Mister Roberts,* which he first created on stage; the earnest juror in *12 Angry Men;* and the icy villain in *Once Upon a Time in the West* (1969). Fonda's stubborn independence and standoffish temperament may have worked against him—he was inaccessible to the press when other actors of his era, such as his friend James Stewart [73 . . .], were more forthcoming. Fonda was also attracted to the stage at the expense of his film career. He had begun acting in his native Omaha, where one of his first mentors was the mother of Marlon Brando [583 . . .]. In 1928 he joined a New England summer company, the University Players, which had been founded at Princeton by Joshua Logan [643 . . .] and came to include Stewart, Mildred Natwick [147], and Fonda's first wife, Margaret Sullavan [2073]. After several Broadway roles, Fonda joined Stewart and Sullavan in Hollywood, making his debut in *The Farmer Takes a Wife* (1935). He signed a contract with 20th Century-Fox, where he began a long association with director John Ford with the film *Drums Along the Mohawk.* The war and service in the navy interrupted Fonda's movie career, and he increasingly sought stage work after the war. He was absent from the screen from 1948 to 1955. During that time he created the role of Mister Roberts on Broadway and returned to movies for the film version. His later career was spread among movies, TV, and the stage. While Fonda's performance in *On Golden Pond* was neither one of his best nor even the year's best—Burt Lancaster's nominated performance in *Atlantic City* was clearly superior—the Oscar was a sentimental gesture on the part of the Academy, which was well aware that Fonda had been overlooked—he had been given an honorary Oscar at

the previous year's ceremony as "the consummate actor, in recognition of his brilliant accomplishments and enduring contribution to the art of motion pictures." It was also widely known that he was terminally ill with a heart condition. Jane, his daughter by Frances Brokaw, the second of his five wives, accepted the award for her father that made them the only father and daughter to win Oscars for acting. Henry Fonda died a few months later.

Hepburn's record-setting fourth Oscar came more than a decade after her back-to-back wins for *Guess Who's Coming to Dinner* and *The Lion in Winter.* During that time she made only half a dozen films, the most successful of which was *Rooster Cogburn* (1975), another teaming with a legendary star, John Wayne [33 . . .]. Still physically active well into her eighties, Hepburn made one theatrical film, *The Ultimate Solution of Grace Quigley* (1985), which received only scant release, and several TV movies. In 1994 she was persuaded to return to the screen in the Warren Beatty [255 . . .] remake of *Love Affair/An Affair to Remember,* in the role of the grandmother previously played by Maria Ouspenskaya and Cathleen Nesbitt. Hepburn failed to show up at the 1981 ceremonies to claim her Oscar; she has made only one appearance at an Academy Awards show: to present her friend Lawrence Weingarten [372 . . .] the 1973 Irving G. Thalberg Award.

Thompson, a former actor, based his screenplay on his own successful Broadway play. In 1988 Thompson made his debut as a film director with an unsuccessful movie, *1969.*

The best picture Oscar went to *Chariots of Fire,* which also won for Vangelis' score. Jane Fonda lost to Maureen Stapleton in *Reds,* which took Oscars for Warren Beatty's direction and Vittorio Storaro's cinematography. *Raiders of the Lost Ark* won the awards for sound and for Michael Kahn's editing.

H. Fonda: 815, 2153. Hepburn: 24, 40, 843, 1177, 1199, 1357, 1563, 1654, 1956, 1963, 2305. J. Fonda: 394, 430, 1066, 1104, 1356, 2047. Williams: 745, 2307. Portman: 339, 418, 502, 521, 738, 784, 1109, 1526, 1701, 2331. Ronne: 1701, 1825.

Grusin: 379, 633, 667.5, 881, 890, 1318, 2113. Wolfe: 54, 1726.

1474 • ON THE BEACH

LOMITAS PRODUCTIONS INC.; UNITED ARTISTS. 1959.
NOMINATIONS *Scoring of a Dramatic or Comedy Picture:* Ernest Gold. *Film Editing:* Frederic Knudtson.

In Australia a group of survivors await the arrival of a cloud of lethal atomic fallout that is wiping out life on earth. They include Gregory Peck [759 . . .], Ava Gardner [1339], Anthony Perkins [730], and, in his first nonmusical role, Fred Astaire [2126]. The end of the world played as domestic drama interrupted by high-minded speeches, *On the Beach* is a pretty good sampling of Hollywood-style Cold War pessimism, but most people prefer the nihilistic satiric spin put on the topic by *Dr. Strangelove* five years later. Produced and directed by Stanley Kramer [330 . . .]. The screenplay, by John Paxton [467] and James Lee Barrett, is based on a novel by Nevil Shute, who hated the movie. The Oscars went to *Ben-Hur*'s Miklos Rozsa for score and Ralph E. Winters and John D. Dunning for editing.

Gold: 630, 1032, 1776. Knudtson: 522, 1000, 1032, 1065, 2288.

1475 • ON THE RIVIERA

20TH CENTURY-FOX. 1951.
NOMINATIONS *Color Art Direction—Set Decoration:* Lyle Wheeler and Leland Fuller; Joseph C. Wright, Thomas Little, and Walter M. Scott. *Scoring of a Musical Picture:* Alfred Newman.

Danny Kaye plays both an entertainer and the war hero he resembles; the former is persuaded to pose as the latter in this remake of *Folies Bergère.* Colorful and amusing musical farce, though your enjoyment of it may depend on how much of Kaye you can take. The cast also includes Gene Tierney [1153], Corinne Calvet, and Marcel Dalio. Directed by Walter Lang [1088] and handsomely photographed by Leon Shamroy [29 . . .]. The screenplay is by Valentine Davies [776 . . .], Phoebe Ephron [350], and Henry Ephron [350]. The art direction and scoring awards went to *An American in Paris.*

Wheeler: 19, 46, 83, 356, 376, 428, 476, 495, 530, 542, 719, 721, 798, 950, 1062, 1088, 1149, 1153, 1213, 1391, 1601, 1616, 1670, 1706, 1852, 2008, 2093, 2212. Fuller: 530, 719, 1149, 1601, 2212. Wright: 235, 428, 508, 569, 690, 746, 852, 1175, 1264, 1397, 2056. Little: 46, 83, 235, 428, 495, 719, 721, 746, 950, 952, 1082, 1149, 1153, 1397, 1666, 1852, 1868, 2056, 2212, 2286. Scott: 46, 376, 413, 476, 530, 542, 557, 646, 896, 1062, 1088, 1213, 1391, 1706, 1753, 1881, 1907, 2008, 2120, 2247. Newman: 31, 34, 46, 72, 138, 182, 226, 333, 334, 347, 375, 428, 437, 457, 476, 495, 542, 690, 797, 833, 952, 953, 959, 962, 1016, 1082, 1088, 1213, 1278, 1362, 1397, 1616, 1655, 1849, 1868, 1883, 1921, 2043, 2046, 2091, 2258, 2286, 2294, 2316.

1476 • ON THE TOWN

MGM. 1949.
AWARD *Scoring of a Musical Picture:* Roger Edens and Lennie Hayton.

Sailors Gene Kelly [74], Frank Sinatra [732 . . .], and Jules Munshin, on shore leave in New York, meet Vera-Ellen, Betty Garrett, and Ann Miller. Thinly plotted but likable musical, adapted by Betty Comden [141 . . .] and Adolph Green [141 . . .] from their Broadway show, for which they also provided lyrics for music written by Leonard Bernstein [1477]. The show stemmed from a Bernstein ballet, *Fancy Free,* which had been choreographed by Jerome Robbins [2244]. Kelly, however, did the film's choreography and codirected with Stanley Donen. The movie was one of the first musicals to be shot—at least in part—on location. The cinematography is by Harold Rosson [105 . . .]. Considering all the talent and innovation involved, it's a pity the movie's not better than it is. One mistake was jettisoning most of the Comden-Green-Bernstein songs, including the lovely "Some Other Time," which gave the show a coherence that its cobbled-together plot couldn't supply. Kelly's desire to be taken seriously as a dancer also inspires a rather draggy ballet sequence.

Edens, associate producer for Arthur Freed [66 . . .], who headed the legendary MGM musical production unit, had come to Hollywood in 1933 and joined MGM's music department in 1935 as composer and arranger. Hayton, who joined MGM in the forties, was married for a time to Lena Horne.

Edens: 87, 115, 594, 699, 801, 1950. Hayton: 877, 896, 1577, 1831, 1907.

1477 • ON THE WATERFRONT

HORIZON-AMERICAN CORPORATION; COLUMBIA. 1954.

AWARDS *Picture:* Sam Spiegel, producer. *Actor:* Marlon Brando. *Supporting Actress:* Eva Marie Saint. *Director:* Elia Kazan. *Story and Screenplay:* Budd Schulberg. *Black-and-White Cinematography:* Boris Kaufman. *Black-and-White Art Direction—Set Decoration:* Richard Day. *Film Editing:* Gene Milford.

NOMINATIONS *Supporting Actor:* Lee J. Cobb. *Supporting Actor:* Karl Malden. *Supporting Actor:* Rod Steiger. *Scoring of a Dramatic or Comedy Picture:* Leonard Bernstein.

Longshoreman Terry Malloy (Brando) risks his life by blowing the whistle on corrupt boss Johnny Friendly (Cobb) after Malloy's brother (Steiger) is killed. Saint is the shy young girl who falls in love with Brando. Malden is a waterfront priest. The film was a huge critical success and still has much of its power, though it pulls its punches with an upbeat ending. It has also been continually imitated over the years, particularly Brando's "coulda been a contender" speech, to which Martin Scorsese paid affectionate homage in the final scene of *Raging Bull.* Look for Martin Balsam [2067], Fred Gwynne, and Pat Hingle in small roles.

Spiegel had just had his first big success with *The African Queen,* which had been unaccountably bypassed by the Academy for a best picture nomination. He picked up the Kazan-Schulberg screenplay after it had been turned down by most of the major studios, and arranged a deal with United Artists. Brando turned it down when Spiegel first sent it his way, so the producer passed it on to Frank Sinatra [732 . . .], who was eager to play the role. But Spiegel also continued wooing Brando, who finally agreed to play it—provoking a lawsuit from Sinatra. (Kazan also tested a young newcomer whom he knew from the Actors

Studio, Paul Newman [3 . . .], who had not yet made a movie.) Spiegel also moved the project from United Artists to Columbia, whose boss, Harry Cohn [1025 . . .], had turned down the project twice, but was won over by the idea of having Brando star in a Columbia picture. Spiegel cut himself a lucrative deal with the studio, which along with the Oscar made him a major film industry player. He had spent years hustling his way in Hollywood, where the Austrian-born producer began in 1927 as a story translator, and in Europe, where he produced a number of films before returning to the States in 1935. For a time, he used the name S. P. Eagle, thinking it more distinguished than his real one.

Brando shot to film stardom with his first movie, *The Men,* and had three consecutive unsuccessful nominations before winning on his fourth try. Along with his contemporary, Montgomery Clift [732 . . .], he revolutionized the nature of screen acting, bringing an emotional nakedness to movies. It's hard to think of a major film actor, from Paul Newman to Daniel Day-Lewis [992.5 . . .], who doesn't derive something from him. Though his special quality as an actor is often traced to the Stanislavskian "method" he learned at the Actors Studio, there's also a freedom and intensity of performance that is Brando's own and that no acting school could teach—and that few of his contemporaries from the Actors Studio seemed to have learned. Born in Omaha, where his mother was prominent in community theater, Brando went to New York in the forties and landed roles in such conventional Broadway plays as *I Remember Mama* and *Candida.* But it took an unconventional drama, Tennessee Williams' *A Streetcar Named Desire,* also directed by Kazan, to make him a star. The sensation he made as Stanley Kowalski quickly brought him to Hollywood—and, sadly, ended one of the theater's most promising careers. Brando has been accused of squandering his considerable resources, but he may have just been in the right place (Hollywood) at the wrong time (the fifties). His eccentricity and outspokenness didn't endear him to an industry fearful of boat-rockers and nervous about the effects of TV, the breakup of the studio system, and the congressional inquiries into Hollywood's politics. He might have found more room to grow as an artist and made fewer powerful enemies in a less conservative era. For a time after his Oscar, Brando made an effort at performing in mainstream Hollywood product—*Guys and Dolls, The Teahouse of the August Moon* (1956), *Sayonara, The Young Lions*—but it soon became clear that material worthy of his talent wasn't being offered to him. After a disastrous directorial debut with *One-Eyed Jacks* and a legendarily troubled production of *Mutiny on the Bounty,* his career began to decline, and until Francis Ford Coppola chose him for *The Godfather* Brando was considered unemployable.

Saint made her film debut in *On the Waterfront.* She had starred in TV and Broadway plays before coming to Hollywood. The Oscar made her a star, but not a major one, and of her subsequent pictures, only *North by Northwest* shows her to best advantage.

Kazan's first Oscar, for *Gentleman's Agreement,* had established his Hollywood career, but he continued to spend as much time in the theater as in Hollywood. In 1947 he helped found the Actors Studio, which gave him his first contact with Brando, whom he directed in both stage and screen versions of *Streetcar* as well as in *Viva Zapata!* Kazan's career was jeopardized in the early fifties, when he was called before the House Un-American Activities Committee, but he chose to testify and to name former communists in his testimony. Some have felt Kazan's decision to name names not only cowardly but unnecessary: that a man with Kazan's stage and screen credentials could have been a leader in the fight against the Red-baiters. Kazan remained conscience-stricken throughout his life, and his memoirs are an extended apologia. *On the Waterfront* is also seen as an apologia, turning an informer, Terry Malloy, into a hero. This was, in fact, why Brando was reluctant to take the role; he had been critical of Kazan's decision, but in the end his loyalty to the man who had been his mentor proved stronger than his political convictions.

The identification of Terry Malloy with the HUAC informers also stems from the experience of the film's screenwriter. Like many writers of the thirties, Schulberg had his flirtation with communism and was subpoenaed by HUAC in 1951. Like Kazan, he named names. Schulberg was the son of an industry pioneer, B. P. Schulberg. The younger Schulberg worked his experiences growing up in Hollywood into a novel, *What Makes Sammy Run?,* that shocked the film town with its portrait of the community's greed and vulgarity when it was published in 1941. After the Oscar, Schulberg concentrated on writing novels, books, and articles about boxing (including a biography of Muhammad Ali), and his autobiography, *Moving Pictures: Memories of a Hollywood Prince.* In 1995, Schulberg's stage version of *Waterfront* was a Broadway flop.

Kaufman was born in Poland and educated in France, where he began his career as a cameraman. He came to the States in 1942 and worked on wartime documentaries before moving into feature films. His documentary training served him well during the location shooting of *On the Waterfront,* which was filmed during a raw New Jersey winter. His most effective work was done in black and white, including such films as *Long Day's Journey Into Night* and *The Pawnbroker.* He died in 1980.

This was the last of Day's seven Oscars, the climax of a career in Hollywood that lasted more than half a century, from his work with Erich von Stroheim [1975] starting in 1918 through his last film, *Tora! Tora! Tora!,* in 1970, two years before his death.

On the Waterfront is one of a handful of films to receive multiple acting nominations in a single category. As often happens, these tend to cancel one another out. The supporting actor Oscar went to Edmond O'Brien for *The Barefoot Contessa.*

The music Bernstein wrote for *On the Town* and *West Side Story* won Oscars for other people: the studio arrangers. Ironically the one original score he composed for the movies was passed over by the Academy in favor of Dimitri Tiomkin's for *The High and the Mighty.*

Spiegel: 287, 1151, 1429. Brando: 583, 784, 1069, 1141, 1763, 1949, 2212. Kazan: 63, 593, 759, 1949. Kaufman: 119. Day: 22, 102, 235, 487, 510, 560, 569, 797, 833, 864, 952, 1048, 1175, 1397,

1666, 1949, 2056, 2120, 2276. Milford: 1206, 1488. Cobb: 301. Malden: 1949. Steiger: 992, 1543.

1478 • ONCE MORE, MY DARLING

NEPTUNE FILMS; UNIVERSAL-INTERNATIONAL. 1949.

NOMINATION *Sound Recording:* Universal-International Studio Sound Department, Leslie I. Carey, sound director.

Robert Montgomery [904 . . .] is sent by the army to investigate the source of some jewelry Ann Blyth [1319] has been given by a man with apparent Nazi connections. She falls in love with Montgomery, they elope, and are involved in a chase. Flimsy romantic comedy, produced and directed by Montgomery from a script by Robert Carson [1908]. The sound award went to *Twelve O'Clock High.*

Carey: 291, 776, 1209, 1334, 2089.

1479 • ONCE UPON A HONEYMOON

RKO RADIO. 1942.

NOMINATION *Sound Recording:* Steve Dunn.

Burlesque star Ginger Rogers [1102] marries Austrian baron Walter Slezak and accompanies him to Europe. When he turns out to be a Nazi, foreign correspondent Cary Grant [1445 . . .] tries to open her eyes to what's happening in Europe. Weird attempt to blend screwball comedy with wartime drama. When Grant and Rogers are thought to be Jewish and almost become victims of the Holocaust, you may think someone's put on a reel from an entirely different movie. To be fair, contemporary audiences were unaware of the real horrors of the Nazi concentration camps, but it's hard to believe director Leo McCarey [21 . . .] and his cowriter, Sheridan Gibney [1936], didn't have some inkling how appallingly unfunny this film would someday seem. The sound Oscar went to Nathan Levinson for *Yankee Doodle Dandy.*

Dunn: 173, 1383, 2059.

1480 • ONE-EYED JACKS

PENNEBAKER PRODUCTION; PARAMOUNT. 1961.

NOMINATION *Color Cinematography:* Charles Lang, Jr.

Outlaw Marlon Brando [583 . . .] seeks revenge on Karl Malden [1477 . . .], an old friend who has become a sheriff. The film is also Brando's only attempt at directing; he took over after forcing Stanley Kubrick [151 . . .] off the picture, ostensibly because of difficulties with the screenplay. The script had been begun by Niven Busch [990], adapting a novel by Louis L'Amour [935]. Busch's version was rewritten by Sam Peckinpah [2280]. When Kubrick was hired to direct, he called in Calder Willingham [810]. Guy Trosper [1605] was also hired to rewrite the script, which was incomplete when shooting began, and some scenes were improvised. Another point of contention was the casting of Malden—Kubrick wanted Spencer Tracy [131 . . .]. The film went hugely over budget, with six times as much footage shot for it as for the typical Hollywood feature. Working with editor Archie Marchek, Brando made a first cut that was eight hours long. It was reduced to three hours, but Paramount took it out of Brando's hands and issued a 141-minute version. The result is a cult favorite that despite good reviews failed at the box office and damaged Brando's flagging career. The cast also includes Katy Jurado [299] and Ben Johnson [1139]. The cinematography Oscar went to Daniel L. Fapp for *West Side Story.*

Lang: 97, 250, 319, 636, 649, 705, 765, 953, 1640, 1699, 1738, 1778, 1855, 1860, 1955, 1968, 2180.

1481 • ONE FLEW OVER THE CUCKOO'S NEST

UNITED ARTISTS. 1975.

AWARDS *Picture:* Saul Zaentz and Michael Douglas, producers. *Actor:* Jack Nicholson. *Actress:* Louise Fletcher. *Director:* Milos Forman. *Screenplay Adapted From Other Material:* Lawrence Hauben and Bo Goldman.

NOMINATIONS *Supporting Actor:* Brad Dourif. *Cinematography:* Haskell Wexler and Bill Butler. *Original Score:* Jack Nitzsche. *Film Editing:* Richard Chew, Lynzee Klingman, and Sheldon Kahn.

Nicholson plays McMurphy, a rebellious patient in a mental institution where the inmates are kept under the stern supervision of Nurse Ratched (Fletcher).

But McMurphy's natural ebullience infects others in the ward, and one of them, Billy (Dourif), commits suicide after McMurphy arranges for him to lose his virginity and Nurse Ratched threatens to tell Billy's mother. Enraged by this, McMurphy attacks Ratched, an act that results in his being lobotomized. Terrific performances by a cast that also includes the then-unknown Danny DeVito and Christopher Lloyd, a solid script, and the intelligently straightforward direction of Forman result in a fine film that steers clear of an awful lot of traps. A few years earlier, it would, for example, have been played for obvious counter-cultural messages about the rebel against the establishment. It also might have fallen into sentimental nonsense about how the insane are somehow nearer to the truth than the ostensibly sane. Or it could have had the explicit antifeminism of Ken Kesey's novel, in which women represent the repressive civilizing forces that threaten to emasculate men. Fortunately the movie transcends all these subtexts. It became the first movie since 1934's *It Happened One Night* to win all five top Oscars—for picture, actor, actress, director, and writer. Only one other, *The Silence of the Lambs,* has done so.

Kirk Douglas [130 . . .] had played McMurphy on Broadway in 1963 and had bought the property for the movies, intending to star in it. Unable to get studio backing, he realized that he had grown too old for the role and gave it to his son Michael. The younger Douglas had made a handful of second-rank movies but was better known for his work on TV in the series *The Streets of San Francisco*. Not yet a bankable film star, he realized the best chance to get it filmed was to attract a major star. When he engaged Nicholson, he attracted the support of Zaentz, a Berkeley-based record producer who had made his fortune with the Fantasy Records label, particularly a string of hits by Creedence Clearwater Revival. The smash success of *Cuckoo's Nest* established both Douglas and Zaentz as important Hollywood figures. As producers, they went their separate ways—Douglas with the prescient *The China Syndrome,* Zaentz with several less successful films before striking Oscar gold again with *Amadeus.*

Nicholson had been in Hollywood for a decade, acting in Roger Corman's low-budget movies and writing and producing his own little-seen films, when he suddenly became a star with his performance as the alcoholic southern lawyer in *Easy Rider*. His hip, cynical persona was right for the times, but Nicholson's skill as an actor and on-screen vitality have enabled him to endure as a film star when contemporaries such as James Caan [784], Elliott Gould [250], and Burt Reynolds have gone into decline. *Cuckoo's Nest* was his fifth nomination, and he has gone on to five more, tying Laurence Olivier [268 . . .] and Bette Davis [46]. Only Katharine Hepburn [24 . . .], with twelve nominations, has more.

Fletcher won the role of Nurse Ratched only after a series of better-known actresses, including Anne Bancroft [28 . . .], Ellen Burstyn [41 . . .], Angela Lansbury [749 . . .], and Geraldine Page [935 . . .], had turned it down. She had begun her acting career in television in the fifties, but she retired in 1962 to raise a family. Robert Altman [1286 . . .] brought her back to the screen when he cast her in *Thieves Like Us* (1974), in which she attracted the attention of Milos Forman. She has continued her career as a character actress, though largely in films of no particular distinction. Her acceptance speech at the Academy Awards included an emotional moment in which she spoke in sign language to her parents, both of whom were deaf.

Forman fled his native Czechoslovakia after the Soviet invasion of 1968. He had been one of his country's most important filmmakers, with such credits as *Loves of a Blonde* and *The Firemen's Ball,* both of which received foreign language film Oscar nominations. His first American film, *Taking Off* (1971), was a box-office disappointment. After winning the Oscar, he directed the less well received *Hair* (1979) and *Ragtime* before reuniting with producer Zaentz for *Amadeus.*

Hauben has had no subsequent credits of importance, but Goldman has continued to be one of the movies' most intelligent—if not especially prolific—screenwriters. In addition to his other nominations, he wrote the script for *Shoot the Moon* (1982). Kesey, incidentally, hated their version of his novel.

The supporting actor Oscar went to George Burns for *The Sunshine Boys.* John Alcott took the cinematography award for *Barry Lyndon.* John Williams won for the score for *Jaws,* which also received an Oscar for Verna Fields' editing.

Zaentz: 60. Douglas: 2224. Nicholson: 395, 595, 658.5, 672, 1019, 1135, 1625, 1678, 2020. Forman: 60. Goldman: 1300, 1764.5. Wexler: 229, 264, 1288, 2277. Nitzsche: 1465. Chew: 1916. Kahn: 1512.

1482 • ONE FOOT IN HEAVEN

Warner Bros. 1941.

Nomination *Picture:* Hal B. Wallis, producer.

Fredric March [184 . . .] is the Reverend William Spence, with Martha Scott [1510] as his wife in this story of the life of a turn-of-the-century minister. Pleasant, well-meaning little nostalgia piece, somewhat overshadowed by others in the genre, such as *Life With Father, Meet Me in St. Louis,* and *Cheaper by the Dozen.* A little too wholesome for contemporary tastes. Adapted by Casey Robinson from the book by Hartzell Spence, with Beulah Bondi [807 . . .], Gene Lockhart [36], Harry Davenport, Laura Hope Crews, and, in a bit as the groom in a wedding scene, Gig Young [427 . . .], still billed under his real name, Byron Barr. Directed by Irving Rapper. The Oscar went to *How Green Was My Valley.*

Wallis: 17, 55, 85, 164, 343, 365, 676, 689, 712, 965, 1046, 1095, 1162, 1248, 1727, 1779, 2233, 2318.

1483 • ONE FROM THE HEART

Zoetrope Studios Production; Columbia. 1982.

Nomination *Original Song Score and Its Adaptation or Adaptation Score:* Tom Waits.

In Las Vegas, lovers Teri Garr [2113] and Frederic Forrest [1726] quarrel. He takes up with showgirl Nastassia Kinski, she with waiter Raul Julia. Meanwhile Garr confides in her friend Lainie Kazan, and Forrest in his friend Harry Dean Stanton. And singers Waits and Crystal Gayle comment on the action with their songs. Flashy, empty exercise in film technique —an experiment by director Francis Ford Coppola [65 . . .] gone expensively awry, destroying, when it flopped at the box office, Coppola's attempt to create his own film studio, American Zoetrope. There's always something to watch, thanks to production designer Dean Tavoularis [92 . . .] and cinematographer Vittorio Storaro [92 . . .], and the performers are engaging ones, but the script, by Coppola and Armyan Bernstein, gives them nothing interesting to do.

Waits, a singer-songwriter with something of a cult following, has acted in numerous movies, including several directed by Coppola—*Rumble Fish* (1983), *The Cotton Club,* and *Bram Stoker's Dracula.* He lost the Oscar to Leslie Bricusse and Henry Mancini for *Victor/Victoria.*

1484 • ONE HOUR WITH YOU

Paramount Publix. 1931–32.

Nomination *Picture:* Ernst Lubitsch, producer.

Maurice Chevalier [203 . . .] and Jeanette MacDonald are happily married, but Genevieve Tobin, who has quarreled with her husband, Roland Young [2117], sets her sights on Chevalier. Delicious sophisticated musical comedy directed by Lubitsch, although George Cukor [262 . . .] receives codirector credit. The film was begun by Cukor, but Lubitsch took it over soon after shooting started. Some legal posturing that took place after the film premiered resulted in screen credit for both men, although it's generally agreed that it's a Lubitsch film—for one thing, it's a remake of one of his silent pictures, *The Marriage Circle* (1924). Lubitsch also contributed heavily to the screenplay credited to Samson Raphaelson. The movie has rhymed dialogue blending with the songs, which have music by Oscar Straus and Richard Whiting [1829] and lyrics by Leo Robin [104 . . .]. The best picture Oscar went to *Grand Hotel.*

Lubitsch: 889, 1217, 1540, 1847.

1485 • ONE HUNDRED MEN AND A GIRL

UNIVERSAL. 1937.

AWARD *Score:* Universal Studio Music Department, Charles Previn, head.

NOMINATIONS *Picture:* Charles R. Rogers, with Joe Pasternak, producers. *Original Story:* Hans Kräly. *Sound Recording:* Homer G. Tasker. *Film Editing:* Bernard W. Burton.

Deanna Durbin's father, Adolphe Menjou [734], is an out-of-work musician. Determined to find work for him and ninety-nine of his closest friends, she inveigles conductor Leopold Stokowski (playing himself) into hiring them. Enjoyable nonsense that made Durbin a superstar—she almost single-handedly rescued the studio, Universal, from financial disaster. Though she never received so much as a nomination, the Academy gave her an honorary award, in tandem with Mickey Rooney [115 . . .], at the 1938 ceremonies, citing them "for their significant contribution in bringing to the screen the spirit and personification of youth, and as juvenile players setting a high standard of ability and achievement." Henry Koster [214] directed, and the cast includes a gallery of classic thirties character players, Alice Brady [990 . . .], Eugene Pallette, Mischa Auer [1401], Billy Gilbert, and Leonid Kinskey among them.

Previn was born in Brooklyn and began his career as a conductor of theater orchestras in New York before moving to Hollywood and establishing a career as orchestrator and composer. He would later be instrumental in launching the career of his nephew, André Previn [172 . . .], in Hollywood, when André's family, forced to leave their native Berlin after the rise of the Nazis, settled in Los Angeles.

The best picture Oscar went to *The Life of Emile Zola.* William A. Wellman and Robert Carson won for the story for *A Star Is Born.* Thomas Moulton took the sound award for *The Hurricane,* and Gene Havlic and Gene Milford won for editing *Lost Horizon.*

Previn: 306, 668, 1030, 1229, 1870, 1896. Rogers: 2081. Pasternak: 74, 2081. Kräly: 1137.5, 1540. Tasker: 2081.

1486 • ONE IN A MILLION

20TH CENTURY-FOX. 1936.

NOMINATION *Dance Direction:* Jack Haskell.

Sonja Henie makes her papa, Jean Hersholt, proud by winning a gold medal at the Winter Olympics. Sweetly corny debut vehicle for Henie, a three-time Olympic gold medalist, who went on to a series of carbon-copy ice-skating movies. Compared with such sexy contemporary skaters as Katarina Witt, Henie looks endearingly klunky. The cast, directed by Sidney Lanfield, includes Adolphe Menjou [734], the Ritz Brothers, Don Ameche [419], and—how can you resist?—Borrah Minevich and His Harmonica Rascals. Haskell, nominated for his skating ensembles, lost to Seymour Felix's direction of the "A Pretty Girl Is Like a Melody" number from *The Great Ziegfeld.*

1487 • ONE MILLION B.C.

HAL ROACH; UNITED ARTISTS. 1940.

NOMINATIONS *Original Score:* Werner Heymann. *Special Effects:* Roy Seawright, photographic; Elmer Raguse, sound.

Cave people Victor Mature, Carole Landis, and Lon Chaney, Jr., battle the elements, dinosaurs, and each other in this camp classic, directed by Hal Roach, Hal Roach, Jr., and allegedly D. W. Griffith. The 1966 remake, *One Million Years B.C.,* with Raquel Welch falling out of her animal-skin bikini, is a little better, thanks to Ray Harryhausen's animated dinosaurs. In this one the dinosaurs are lizards roaming around miniaturized sets. No one cares that the dinosaurs really vanished from the earth long before the advent of humans, of course. The scoring award went to Leigh Harline, Paul J. Smith, and Ned Washington for *Pinocchio.* The special effects Oscar was won by Lawrence Butler for the photographic effects and Jack Whitney for the sound for *The Thief of Bagdad.*

Heymann: 1105, 2036, 2096. Seawright: 2118, 2119. Raguse: 345, 757.5, 1306, 1464, 2117, 2118.

1488 • ONE NIGHT OF LOVE

COLUMBIA. 1934.

AWARDS *Sound Recording:* John Livadary. *Score:* Columbia Studio Music Department, Louis Silvers, head; thematic music by Victor Schertzinger and Gus Kahn. **NOMINATIONS** *Picture:* Harry Cohn, with Everett Riskin, producers. *Actress:* Grace Moore. *Director:* Victor Schertzinger. *Film Editing:* Gene Milford.

Aspiring soprano Moore has a tiff with her teacher, Tullio Carminati, and almost gives up her career for Lyle Talbot. She comes to her senses in time, though. Entertaining vehicle for the Metropolitan Opera star, with Nydia Westman, Jessie Ralph, and Jane Darwell [815]. Moore sings excerpts from *Madame Butterfly, Lucia di Lammermoor,* and *Carmen,* as well as program stuff like "Ciri-Biri-Bin" and Kahn and Schertzinger's title song.

Schertzinger was born in Pennsylvania and began his musical career as a concert violinist. After working as a theater conductor, he agreed to compose music to accompany Thomas Ince's silent films and soon found himself directing movies as well as writing scores for them. His career as director began in 1917 and lasted until his death in 1941.

Kahn was one of the most prolific lyricists in the golden age of the American popular song, working with composers such as Sigmund Romberg and George Gershwin [1797] as well as Schertzinger. His songs include "Pretty Baby," "Ain't We Got Fun," "My Buddy," "Toot Toot Tootsie, Goodbye," "Yes Sir, That's My Baby," "Love Me or Leave Me," "Makin' Whoopee," and "San Francisco." He died in 1941. In 1952 he was played by Danny Thomas in the biopic *I'll See You in My Dreams,* the title of which is one of his songs.

The box-office success of *One Night of Love* was a tonic for Columbia, a studio that in the fifties became a major Hollywood player but in the thirties was still on the fringe. Cohn had followed Schertzinger's suggestion that he sign Moore for films when she was dropped by MGM, where she had made two films in the early thirties but had been fired for gaining too much weight—an occupational hazard for opera singers. A beautiful woman, Moore also appealed to American movie audiences because she was scarcely an exotic: She was born in Slabtown, Tennessee. She made a series of successful movies over the next three years, inspiring other studios to seek out operatic talent: RKO signed Lily Pons and MGM tried out Miliza Korjus [828], but with much less success.

Along with the success of *One Night,* Columbia also earned its first best picture Oscar, for *It Happened One Night,* which also took awards for actress Claudette Colbert and director Frank Capra. Milford came in third in the race for the editing award, which went to Conrad Nevig for *Eskimo.*

Livadary: 330, 455, 596, 732, 1058, 1206, 1215, 1303, 1366, 1370, 1521, 1740, 1872, 2111, 2325, 2327. Silvers: 990, 1957, 1982. Schertzinger: 1863. Kahn: 692, 1896. Cohn: 1025. Riskin: 114, 904. Milford: 1206, 1477.

1489 • ONE OF OUR AIRCRAFT IS MISSING

MICHAEL POWELL; UNITED ARTISTS (UNITED KINGDOM). 1942. **NOMINATIONS** *Original Screenplay:* Michael Powell and Emeric Pressburger. *Special Effects:* Ronald Neame, photographic; C. C. Stevens, sound.

An RAF crew parachute out of their bomber, crippled in a run over Germany, and land in Holland, where the Dutch help them make their way across country. Entertaining variation on a familiar wartime theme (see also *Desperate Journey),* with a good cast that includes Peter Ustinov [943 . . .] and Joyce Redman [1506 . . .] in secondary roles. Powell and Pressburger also directed, Neame was cinematographer, and the film was edited by David Lean [287 . . .]. The screenplay award went to Michael Kanin and Ring Lardner, Jr., for *Woman of the Year. Reap the Wild Wind* won for special effects.

Powell: 1008, 1677. Pressburger: 1008, 1677. Neame: 289, 820.

1490 • ONE POTATO, TWO POTATO

BAWALCO PICTURE PRODUCTION; CINEMA V DISTRIBUTING. 1964. **NOMINATION** *Story and Screenplay—Written Directly for the Screen:* Orville H. Hampton and Raphael Hayes.

An interracial couple, played by Barbara Barrie [279] and Bernie Hamilton, encounters prejudice and discrimination. Once daring, now dated problem drama directed by Larry Peerce, with Richard Mulligan and Robert Earl Jones. The Oscar went to S. H. Barnett, Peter Stone, and Frank Tarloff for *Father Goose.*

1491 • $1,000 A MINUTE

REPUBLIC. 1935.
NOMINATION *Sound Recording:* Republic Sound Department.

Roger Pryor and Edgar Kennedy make a bet on how fast they can spend money. Minor comic programmer based on a screenplay by Joseph Fields, who later wrote *My Sister Eileen.* The Oscar went to Douglas Shearer for *Naughty Marietta.*

1492 • ONE, TWO, THREE

MIRISCH COMPANY INC. IN ASSOCIATION WITH PYRAMID PRODUCTIONS A.G.; UNITED ARTISTS. 1961.
NOMINATION *Black-and-White Cinematography:* Daniel L. Fapp.

James Cagney [79 . . .] is a Coca-Cola executive in West Berlin trying to open up the Soviet market. To his horror, his daughter (Pamela Tiffin) falls in love with a communist (Horst Buchholz). Arlene Francis plays Cagney's wife. This satirical farce written by Billy Wilder [91 . . .] and I. A. L. Diamond [91 . . .] was a box-office hit, but critics either loved it or found it loud and vulgar. There seems to be no middle ground. Cagney is a dynamo in the last film he made until he returned for *Ragtime* twenty years later, and director Wilder never lets the pace flag.

Fapp was nominated in both black-and-white and color categories. He lost this one to Eugen Shuftan for *The Hustler* but took home the color cinematography Oscar for *West Side Story.*

Fapp: 529, 675, 978, 1280, 2184, 2244.

1493 • ONE WAY PASSAGE

WARNER BROS. 1932–33.
AWARD *Original Story:* Robert Lord.

William Powell [1170 . . .] and Kay Francis fall in love aboard an ocean liner, but note the title: He's a con artist headed for prison; she's dying. Tidy little tearjerker, with welcome comic relief from Frank McHugh and Aline MacMahon [576]. Directed by Tay Garnett.

Lord went to Hollywood as a screenwriter in the mid-twenties after working on the staff of the *New Yorker.* He turned producer for Warners in the thirties, heading up such films as *The Private Lives of Elizabeth and Essex* and *The Letter.* In the late forties he formed Santana Productions with Humphrey Bogart [24 . . .] but retired in the early fifties. He died in 1976.

Lord: 220, 689.

1494 • ONLY ANGELS HAVE WINGS

COLUMBIA. 1939.
NOMINATIONS *Black-and-White Cinematography:* Joseph Walker. *Special Effects:* Roy Davidson, photographic; Edwin C. Hahn, sound.

Cary Grant [1445 . . .] is in charge of a group of pilots whose job is to transport mail and freight over the Andes from Ecuador to Peru. The company they work for, however, doesn't spend much money on upkeep, so the job is hazardous. Adding to the hazards are Jean Arthur [1353] and Rita Hayworth, the former a showgirl stranded in the town where the pilots are based, the latter an old flame of Grant's who is now married to Richard Barthelmess [1447 . . .], a flier who's trying to redeem himself after causing the death of another pilot. Hugely entertaining hooey, directed by Howard Hawks [1779], who also wrote the story on which the screenplay, by Jules Furthman [1387], is based. It may be derivative of such movies as *Red Dust* (1932) and *The Dawn Patrol,* but *Only Angels* has its own charm, thanks to an enormously likable cast, playing Hawks' usual game of cracking wise in the face of adversity. The cast also includes Thomas Mitchell [962 . . .], Allyn Joslyn, and Noah Beery, Jr. The success of the movie helped make Hayworth a star.

Walker was on the preliminary slate of black-and-white cinematography nominees, which was reduced to two candidates, Bert Glennon for *Stagecoach* and winner Gregg Toland for *Wuthering Heights,* for the final ballot. E. H. Hansen and Fred Sersen won the special effects award for *The Rains Came.*

Walker: 904, 1058, 2325.

1495 • *ONLY WHEN I LAUGH*

COLUMBIA PICTURES PRODUCTION; COLUMBIA. 1981.
NOMINATIONS *Actress:* Marsha Mason. *Supporting Actor:* James Coco. *Supporting Actress:* Joan Hackett.

Mason is an alcoholic actress, just out of rehab and trying to work out her problems with her daughter, Kristy McNichol. Coco and Hackett play Mason's close friends, an out-of-work gay actor and a socialite. Though Neil Simon [332 . . .] completely reworked his play *The Gingerbread Lady* for this film, it still seems stagy, perhaps because Simon's plays get their energy from a live audience's response to his wisecracks. The actors in his films don't get that zap of laughter and applause, and they seem a little frantic as a consequence, especially in this movie, which tries to mix poignancy and gags.

This is the last of Mason's four unsuccessful nominations, three of which were for films written by her then husband, Simon. After their marriage ended, Mason's career declined, and she has been seen only occasionally in recent films. She lost to Katharine Hepburn in *On Golden Pond.*

Coco made his screen debut in 1969 in *Ensign Pulver* and did comic supporting roles in movies through the seventies and eighties, though he was more successful as a Broadway actor. He died at the age of fifty-seven in 1987. The Oscar went to John Gielgud for *Arthur.*

Hackett began as a model and became a prominent Broadway actress. She made her film debut in 1966 in *The Group,* making occasional film appearances before her death from cancer in 1983 at the age of forty-one.

Maureen Stapleton won the supporting actress award for *Reds.*

Mason: 383, 403, 803.

1496 • *OPEN CITY*

MINERVA FILMS; MAYER-BURSTYN (ITALY). 1946.
NOMINATION *Screenplay:* Sergio Amidei and Federico Fellini.

Fleeing the Gestapo, Roman Resistance leader Marcello Pagliero hides out with a friend's pregnant girlfriend, Anna Magnani [1727 . . .]. When she is killed, he moves in with Maria Michi, who eventually betrays him along with an activist priest, played by Aldo Fabrizi. A landmark film in many ways, not least of them that it introduced the world to the talents of Fellini and director Roberto Rossellini [1519]. It also set the style for postwar Italian cinema, creating the movement known as neorealism, which not only included such filmmakers as Vittorio De Sica [650] but also inspired Americans in such documentary-style melodramas as *The Naked City.* On top of it, *Open City* is an exciting drama, still more impressive because the war ended only a few months before the film was made, giving the events it dramatizes a poignant immediacy.

The screenplay Oscar went to Robert E. Sherwood for *The Best Years of Our Lives.*

Amidei: 756, 1519, 1815. Fellini: 61, 562, 603, 657, 658, 1519, 1938, 2209.

1497 • *OPEN DOORS*

ERRE PRODUZIONI/ISTITUTO LUCE PRODUCTION (ITALY). 1990.
NOMINATION *Foreign Language Film.*

Gian Maria Volonte plays a judge, a member of a panel trying a murder case in fascist Italy. His objection to the death penalty causes him to explore all the evidence in detail, even though the accused man is brutal and unrepentant, and the other judges are impatient with Volonte's meticulousness. Intelligent but not wholly successful exploration of the issue of crime and punishment, directed by Gianni Amelio. The Oscar went to *Journey of Hope.*

1498 • OPERATION PETTICOAT

GRANART COMPANY; UNIVERSAL-INTERNATIONAL. 1959.

NOMINATION *Story and Screenplay—Written Directly for the Screen:* Paul King and Joseph Stone; Stanley Shapiro and Maurice Richlin.

Cary Grant [1445 . . .] is a World War II submarine commander whose ship is in such bad condition that the navy wants to scuttle it. But with the aid of his roguish, unscrupulous supply officer, Tony Curtis [522], he gets the sub back into action, even though it involves painting the ship pink and taking on as passengers a contingent of nurses, who have to share close quarters with the horny crew. Very funny service comedy whose strength is not in its script but in the peerless comedy teamwork of Grant and Curtis, nicely directed by Blake Edwards [2201] and supported by Dina Merrill, Arthur O'Connell [73 . . .], and a couple of performers who would later become more famous for their TV work, Gavin McLeod and Marion Ross. Curtis, who had just done a hilarious imitation of Grant in *Some Like It Hot,* insisted that the studio cast Grant in the film.

King and Stone, who wrote the story for the film, went home empty-handed, but not screenplay authors Shapiro and Richlin. They took home Oscars for their work on *Pillow Talk* instead, as did the authors of that story, Russell Rouse and Clarence Greene.

Shapiro: 1220, 1572, 2035. Richlin: 1572.

1499 • OPERATION THUNDERBOLT

GOLAN-GLOBUS PRODUCTION (ISRAEL). 1977.

NOMINATION *Foreign Language Film.*

When terrorists hijack a planeload of Israelis to the Entebbe airport in Uganda, Israeli commandos stage a daring and successful raid to rescue the hostages. Exciting docudrama, directed by Menahem Golan, with a cast that includes Klaus Kinski and Assaf Dayan (son of Israeli General Moshe Dayan). Made with the enthusiastic support of the Israeli government, it has the virtue of seeming more real than the star-studded made-for-TV movies *Raid on Entebbe* (1977) and *Victory at Entebbe* (1976). The Oscar went to *Madame Rosa.*

1500 • OPERATOR 13

COSMOPOLITAN; MGM. 1934.

NOMINATION *Cinematography:* George Folsey.

Marion Davies plays a spy for the Yankees during the Civil War who falls in love with Rebel officer Gary Cooper [701 . . .]. Extremely silly but entertaining romantic adventure, directed by Richard Boleslavsky, with a cast that includes the Mills Brothers. Folsey came in second to Victor Milner for *Cleopatra* in the cinematography race.

Folsey: 51, 137, 629, 807, 835, 838, 1124, 1299, 1320, 1688, 1782, 2068, 2269.

1501 • ORCHESTRA WIVES

20TH CENTURY-FOX. 1942.

NOMINATION *Song:* "I've Got a Gal in Kalamazoo," music by Harry Warren, lyrics by Mack Gordon.

A trumpet player (George Montgomery) and a girl (Ann Rutherford) he encounters on the tour elope, but when she joins him on the road, she discovers he's had a thing going with the band's singer (Lynn Bari). Likable excuse for great numbers by Glenn Miller and his orchestra. The cast, directed by Archie Mayo, includes Cesar Romero, Jackie Gleason [964], and, making her screen debut in a bit part, Dale Evans. The nominated song would have been a hit on its own, but what makes it special in the movie is the dancing of the Nicholas Brothers. The Oscar went to Irving Berlin for "White Christmas," from *Holiday Inn.*

Warren: 21, 324, 569, 788, 791, 877, 897, 1072, 1367, 1964. Gordon: 428, 563, 569, 897, 1362, 1964, 1984, 2219.

1502 • ORDINARY PEOPLE

WILDWOOD ENTERPRISES INC. PRODUCTION; PARAMOUNT. 1980.

AWARDS *Picture:* Ronald L. Schwary, producer. *Supporting Actor:* Timothy Hutton. *Director:* Robert Redford. *Screenplay Based on Material From Another Medium:* Alvin Sargent.

NOMINATIONS *Actress:* Mary Tyler Moore. *Supporting Actor:* Judd Hirsch.

An affluent suburban couple suffers a crippling loss

when their older son is accidentally drowned. The younger son (Hutton) blames himself and attempts suicide. The father (Donald Sutherland) is unable to help his son deal with his guilt feelings, and the mother (Moore) doesn't even try. Only with the aid of a psychiatrist (Hirsch) do father and son come to terms with their loss—but the mother is a hopeless case. Intelligent but ultimately too formulaic domestic drama that relies more on the performers than on any real insights into character to make its effect. The film's central antithesis—the psychiatrist (warm, sloppy, Jewish, male) vs. the mother (cold, meticulous, Protestant, female)—is particularly obvious.

Ordinary People is now remembered as one of the weakest choices for best picture in recent years. The nominees it defeated included *Raging Bull,* which was chosen as the best film of the eighties in a survey of critics at the end of the decade, and *The Elephant Man,* a critically praised movie that launched the Hollywood career of David Lynch. The other nominees, *Coal Miner's Daughter* and *Tess,* had less claim on the top Oscar, but there were some impressive films that didn't even make the list: *Melvin and Howard, The Stunt Man, The Empire Strikes Back,* and *My Brilliant Career.* In this company, *Ordinary People* just looks like an ordinary movie.

At nineteen Hutton entered the record books as the youngest male to win an acting Oscar. Supporting actress Oscars had previously gone to sixteen-year-old Patty Duke for *The Miracle Worker* and ten-year-old Tatum O'Neal for *Paper Moon,* but actors' careers typically begin later and last longer than actresses'. No man in his twenties, for example, has ever won the best actor Oscar. Hutton made his screen debut at the age of five in a film starring his father, Jim Hutton, *Never Too Late* (1965), but worked primarily in TV before returning to the big screen for *Ordinary People.* Although he has played leads in his post-Oscar career, he has not been able to establish himself as a major star.

Redford was born in the shadow of the movie industry in Santa Monica, California, but he studied acting in New York and made his breakthrough as an actor on Broadway in 1963 in *Barefoot in the Park,*

playing a role he repeated in the 1967 film version. His extraordinary good looks made him a natural for the movies, but he didn't become a major star until his seventh film, *Butch Cassidy and the Sundance Kid.* And his looks may have actually been a liability when it comes to recognition from the Academy for his acting, in an era when less conventionally handsome men such as Dustin Hoffman [810 . . .], Jack Nicholson [395 . . .], and Robert De Niro [113 . . .] were receiving Oscars. Redford, whose only acting nomination was for *The Sting,* was overlooked for strong performances in *The Candidate, Jeremiah Johnson* (1972), *The Way We Were,* and *All the President's Men.* But he was the first to benefit from a phenomenon of the poststudio era in Hollywood, the ability of a star to use his or her box-office clout and turn director. Although performers as far back as Lillian Gish [584] had taken turns at directing, and a few of them, such as Charles Chaplin [405 . . .], Orson Welles [407 . . .], and Woody Allen [39 . . .], are as acclaimed for their directing as for their on-camera work, Redford is the first superstar to turn director at the height of his acting career and win an Oscar for it—but not, of course, the last, as Warren Beatty's win for *Reds,* Kevin Costner's for *Dances With Wolves,* and Clint Eastwood's for *Unforgiven* demonstrate. Redford has said that he was drawn to the Judith Guest novel on which Sargent's screenplay is based because it reminded him of his own emotionally repressive childhood, and he bought the rights to the book in 1976, four years before he made his directing debut. Redford's next two films as director, *The Milagro Beanfield War* and *A River Runs Through It,* received mixed notices, but his 1994 film *Quiz Show* was acclaimed as his finest work yet.

This is the second Oscar for Sargent, and the psychotherapeutic theme of *Ordinary People* seems to have shaped his later career: He also wrote the screenplay for *Nuts* (1987), about a woman whose parents want to have her committed, and the story for *What About Bob?* (1991), a comedy about a psychiatrist hounded by an overdependent patient.

Moore is one of the most popular actresses ever to appear on television, first gaining fame with her role on *The Dick Van Dyke Show* in the sixties. On the strength of her popularity in that show, she attempted a film career, but after a series of unsuccessful movies that ranged from *Thoroughly Modern Millie* to the last Elvis Presley vehicle, *Change of Habit* (1969), she gave it up and returned to TV, achieving even greater success in *The Mary Tyler Moore Show.* She was praised by the critics for her first dramatic role in *Ordinary People,* but once again film roles failed to materialize. She has, however, played serious parts in TV dramas and on Broadway in *Whose Life Is It Anyway?* The Oscar went to Sissy Spacek for *Coal Miner's Daughter.*

Hirsch has likewise found greater success as a TV performer, on *Taxi* and *Dear John,* than in the movies. He was cast in *Ordinary People* after Redford decided not to appear in the film, and moved Donald Sutherland, who had previously been cast as the psychiatrist, into the role of the father.

Schwary: 1857. Redford: 1643.5, 1927. Sargent: 1066, 1526.

1503 • ORGANIZER, THE

Lux-Vides-Méditerranée Cinema Production; Walter Reade-Sterling-Continental Distributing (France/Italy/Yugoslavia). 1964.
Nomination *Story and Screenplay—Written Directly for the Screen:* Age, Scarpelli, and Mario Monicelli.

Marcello Mastroianni [490 . . .] plays a schoolteacher who helps organize a strike by textile workers in late-nineteenth-century Italy. Solid, entertaining drama directed by Monicelli, whose reputation was built on his comic films. Though serious in theme and purpose, *The Organizer* is helped by Monicelli's sense of humor, and Mastroianni gives an impressively restrained performance. The Oscar went to S. H. Barnett, Peter Stone, and Frank Tarloff for *Father Goose.*

Age: 367. Scarpelli: 367. Monicelli: 367.

1503.5 • ORLANDO

Adventures Pictures Production; Sony Pictures Classics (United Kingdom). 1993.
Nominations *Art Direction:* Ben Van Os, Jan Roelfs. *Costume Design:* Sandy Powell.

Orlando (Tilda Swinton) is an Elizabethan courtier who magically lives for more than four hundred years without growing older, but in the middle of things changes sexes and becomes a woman. An intriguing but rather languid fable of sexual identity, based by writer-director Sally Potter on the novel by Virginia Woolf. Queen Elizabeth I is amusingly played by writer Quentin Crisp. Beautifully filmed by Alexei Rodionov on locations in St. Petersburg and Uzbekistan, the movie was a modest art-house success of the sort that sparks heated discussions afterward. The award for art direction went to *Schindler's List.* Gabriella Pescucci won for the costumes for *The Age of Innocence.*

1504 • OSCAR, THE

Clarence Greene-Russell Rouse Production; Embassy Pictures Corporation. 1966.
Nominations *Color Art Direction—Set Decoration:* Hal Pereira and Arthur Lonergan; Robert Benton and James Payne. *Color Costume Design:* Edith Head.

Flashbacks show Oscar contender Stephen Boyd's ruthless climb to success. Amazingly the Academy sanctioned the use of its trademark by the producers of this wonderfully lurid heap of trash, directed and cowritten—with Harlan Ellison and Clarence Greene [1572 . . .]—by Russell Rouse [1572 . . .]. The cast includes singer Tony Bennett in a dramatic role, Elke Sommer, Eleanor Parker [328 . . .], Milton Berle, Joseph Cotten, Jill St. John, Ernest Borgnine [1283], Ed Begley [1985], Walter Brennan [424 . . .], James Dunn [2137], Peter Lawford, Edie Adams, and cameos by Bob Hope, Hedda Hopper, Merle Oberon [487], and Frank Sinatra [732 . . .].

The art direction Oscar went to *Fantastic Voyage.* Designer Head got her own cameo in *The Oscar,* as befits the most honored woman in Academy history, but she lost the award this time to Elizabeth Haffenden and Joan Bridge for *A Man for All Seasons.*

Pereira: 278, 357, 363, 426, 450, 736, 956, 1029, 1219, 1570, 1631, 1674, 1716, 1727, 1738, 1840, 1897, 1959, 2012, 2098, 2200, 2208. Benton: 69, 956, 1840. Payne: 426, 1927. Head: 31, 32, 46, 305, 357, 363, 612, 636, 675, 736, 832, 894, 945, 1003, 1219, 1261, 1263, 1398, 1427, 1550, 1579, 1587,

1631, 1716, 1727, 1738, 1748, 1840, 1927, 1986, 2012, 2098, 2247, 2298.

1505 • OTELLO

CANNON PRODUCTION; CANNON RELEASING (ITALY). 1986.

NOMINATION *Costume Design:* Anna Anni and Maurizio Millenotti.

The Moorish military hero Othello (Placido Domingo) is tricked by his aide-de-camp, Iago (Justino Diaz), into believing his wife, Desdemona (Katia Ricciarelli), has been unfaithful. Visually stunning version of the Verdi opera based on Shakespeare's play, directed by Franco Zeffirelli [1722 . . .]. The film is faulted by many because of Zeffirelli's reworking of the opera, which he trimmed in an attempt to make the work more cinematic. Some cuts, such as Desdemona's "Willow Song," are unforgivable—for people familiar with the opera, it's like leaving Ophelia's mad scene out of *Hamlet* (which Zeffirelli didn't do when he filmed that play). On the other hand, the three principals are in excellent voice and, unlike many opera singers, look good even in close-ups. The costuming Oscar went to Jenny Beavan and John Bright for *A Room With a View.*

Millenotti: 859.

1506 • OTHELLO

B.H.E. PRODUCTION; WARNER BROS. (UNITED KINGDOM). 1965.

NOMINATIONS *Actor:* Laurence Olivier. *Supporting Actor:* Frank Finlay. *Supporting Actress:* Joyce Redman. *Supporting Actress:* Maggie Smith.

Olivier is Shakespeare's noble Moor, whose jealousy, roused by Iago (Finlay), causes him to murder his innocent wife, Desdemona (Smith). The most controversial of all of Olivier's Shakespeare films, directed by Stuart Burge from Olivier's National Theatre Company production. It's uncut and unadorned by any "opening up" of the play, so it's not quite a movie. But as a record of a great actor's most daring performance, it's invaluable.

Most of the controversy centers on Olivier's characterization and makeup: His Othello is a vivid, flawed, sensitive, and passionate man, clearly an eth-

nic outsider. Olivier gives him an indeterminate accent with West Indian undertones that, while they're false to the Moorish origins of the play's character, were evocative for contemporary British audiences. Othello is now a part that few white actors play, and those who do downplay his race. This heightened racial sensitivity is for the good, but considered merely from the standpoint of seeing what a great actor can do—even if what he's doing seems to us misguided—Olivier's Othello is a performance not to be missed. The Oscar went to Lee Marvin for *Cat Ballou.*

Finlay underplays Iago, which makes his villainy all the more chilling—the menace lies in this Iago's wit, his insidiously taking the audience into his confidences. It's easy for an Iago to steal the show from an Othello, but while Finlay scarcely does that, he has some of the film's most memorable moments. On the whole, Finlay, who made his screen debut in *The Loneliness of the Long Distance Runner* (1962), has been underused in the movies. His most memorable subsequent appearances have been as Porthos in Richard Lester's *The Three Musketeers* (1974) and *The Four Musketeers.* The Oscar went to Martin Balsam for *A Thousand Clowns.*

Redman—who plays Iago's wife, Emilia—and Smith lost to Shelley Winters in *A Patch of Blue.*

Olivier: 268, 619, 858, 901, 1272, 1670, 1693, 1841, 2316. Redman: 2106. Smith: 332, 1608, 1725, 2134.

1507 • OTHER SIDE OF MIDNIGHT, THE

FRANK YABLANS PRESENTATIONS PRODUCTION; 20TH CENTURY-FOX. 1977.

NOMINATION *Costume Design:* Irene Sharaff.

Marie-France Pisier plays a woman whose amatory adventures in pre– and post–World War II Paris involve American flier John Beck and shipping tycoon Raf Vallone, setting the two men up for a confrontation. Boring trash that makes about as much sense as its title, adapted by Herman Raucher [1960] and Daniel Taradash [732] from the novel by Sidney Sheldon [121]. The cast, directed by Charles Jarrott, includes Susan Sarandon [107 . . .], Clu Gulager, and Howard Hesseman. John Mollo won the Oscar for the costumes for *Star Wars*.

Sharaff: 66, 290, 333, 338, 413, 690, 852, 896, 1088, 1592, 1910, 2000, 2244, 2277.

1508 • OTHER SIDE OF THE MOUNTAIN, THE

FILMWAYS-LARRY PEERCE-UNIVERSAL PRODUCTION; UNIVERSAL. 1975.

NOMINATION *Song:* "Richard's Window," music by Charles Fox, lyrics by Norman Gimbel.

Marilyn Hassett plays Jill Kinmont, a competition skier crippled in an accident that dooms her hopes for the Olympics. Sentimental comeback-trail drama that works too hard at milking tears from the audience. Kinmont's true story should have been told without phony melodrama. The cast, directed by Larry Peerce, includes Beau Bridges, Dabney Coleman, and Griffin Dunne. The song Oscar went to Keith Carradine's "I'm Easy," from *Nashville*.

Fox: 711. Gimbel: 711, 1448, 2172.

1509 • OUR DANCING DAUGHTERS

COSMOPOLITAN; MGM. 1928–29.

NOMINATION *Writing Achievement:* Josephine Lovett. *Cinematography:* George Barnes.

Flapper Joan Crawford [1319 . . .] loves hunky Johnny Mack Brown, but her naughty friend Anita Page marries him instead. But Anita falls downstairs while drunk, leaving the way open for good-girl Joan after all. Hugely popular semisilent (it has music and sound effects but not synchronized dialogue) that made Crawford a star. Directed by Harry Beaumont [296]. Both Lovett and Barnes were unofficial nominees, recorded by the branches that presented the Oscars this year as under consideration for the awards. Only the winners were officially announced. The Oscar for writing went to Hans Kräly for *The Patriot*. Clyde DeVinna won the cinematography award for *White Shadows in the South Seas*.

Barnes: 537, 1236, 1670, 1739, 1748, 1885, 1890.

1510 • OUR TOWN

SOL LESSER; UNITED ARTISTS. 1940.

NOMINATIONS *Picture:* Sol Lesser, producer. *Actress:* Martha Scott. *Black-and-White Interior Decoration:* Lewis J. Rachmil. *Sound Recording:* Thomas Moulton. *Score:* Aaron Copland. *Original Score:* Aaron Copland.

In the small community of Grovers Corners, New Hampshire, young Emily Webb (Scott) falls in love with George Gibbs, played by William Holden [1424 . . .]. Frank Craven plays the Narrator who tells us about their lives and those of others in the town. Craven, who created his role in the original Broadway production, also worked with Thornton Wilder and Harry Chandlee [1779] to adapt Wilder's Pulitzer Prize–winning play for the screen. It's a good movie, even though it doesn't measure up to the play, one of the most loved American works, which has become a staple of amateur companies and high schools but also receives frequent professional revivals. The film lacks the play's freshness and immediacy: Performed without scenery and only a few props, the play draws a theater audience into creating Grovers Corners for themselves. The movie, however, has conventionally realistic scenery, and an awful cop-out Hollywood ending undermines the poetry of the play's last act. Sam Wood [701 . . .] directed, and the cast includes Thomas Mitchell [962 . . .] and Fay Bainter [393 . . .] as Dr. and Mrs. Gibbs, Guy Kibbee and Beulah Bondi [807 . . .] as the Webbs, and Stuart Erwin [1571] as Howie Newsome. The best picture Oscar went to *Rebecca*.

Scott created the role of Emily Webb in the original Broadway production and made her screen debut in the film version. After a few movies in the early forties, she began to divide her time among films, Broadway, and TV. In her later career she played supporting roles and cameos in films such as *The Ten Commandments, Sayonara, Ben-Hur* (as Judah Ben-Hur's mother), and *The Turning Point*. The best actress Oscar went to Ginger Rogers for *Kitty Foyle*.

Although Rachmil received the official recognition from the Academy for the art direction of *Our Town*, his work was done under the supervision of production designer William Cameron Menzies [38 . . .].

The award went to Cedric Gibbons and Paul Groesse for *Pride and Prejudice*. The sound award went to Douglas Shearer for *Strike Up the Band*.

For the second year in a row, Copland was placed in both scoring categories. The first was designed for orchestrators, arrangers, and adapters, the second for composers, but the haziness of the distinction between the two categories led the Academy to switch to a different division the following year and give separate awards for scoring "dramatic pictures" and "musical pictures." Copland lost to Alfred Newman for *Tin Pan Alley* in the "score" category and to Leigh Harline, Paul J. Smith, and Ned Washington for *Pinocchio* in the "original score" category.

Moulton: 22, 46, 138, 366, 457, 487, 560, 706, 798, 962, 1153, 1200, 1451, 1607, 1849, 2154, 2294. Copland: 894, 1451, 1464.

1511 • OUR VERY OWN

SAMUEL GOLDWYN PRODUCTIONS; RKO RADIO. 1950.
NOMINATION *Sound Recording:* Samuel Goldwyn Studio Sound Department, Gordon Sawyer, sound director.

A middle-class family is thrown into turmoil by the reaction of their eldest daughter, high school senior Ann Blyth [1319], when she learns that she's adopted. Thin and unconvincing drama, directed by David Miller, with Jane Wyatt and Donald Cook as Blyth's parents, Farley Granger as her boyfriend, and Natalie Wood [1219 . . .] as her younger sister. Produced by Samuel Goldwyn [102 . . .] with his usual high production values—sets by Richard Day [22 . . .], cinematography by Lee Garmes [201 . . .], music by Victor Young [97 . . .]—but there's not enough to the script by F. Hugh Herbert to sustain this one. The award for sound went to *All About Eve*.

Sawyer: 33, 91, 184, 214, 393, 730, 864, 882, 973, 974, 1032, 1592, 2244, 2297, 2310.

1512 • OUT OF AFRICA

UNIVERSAL PICTURES LTD. PRODUCTION; UNIVERSAL. 1985.
AWARDS *Picture:* Sydney Pollack, producer. *Director:* Sydney Pollack. *Screenplay Based on Material From Another Medium:* Kurt Luedtke. *Cinematography:* David Watkin. *Art Direction–Set Decoration:* Stephen Grimes;

Josie MacAvin. *Sound:* Chris Jenkins, Gary Alexander, Larry Stensvold, and Peter Handford. *Original Score:* John Barry.
NOMINATIONS *Actress:* Meryl Streep. *Supporting Actor:* Klaus Maria Brandauer. *Film Editing:* Fredric Steinkamp, William Steinkamp, Pembroke Herring, and Sheldon Kahn. *Costume Design:* Milena Canonero.

Streep plays Karin Blixen, wife of a philandering Danish baron (Brandauer), whom she doesn't love. When he gives her syphilis, she kicks him out of the house they have shared on a Kenya coffee plantation. Loving the land, she stays on, trying to make a go of the plantation and falling in love with a dashing adventurer-pilot, Denys Finch-Hatton, played by Robert Redford [1502 . . .]. In the end, however, she is forced to return to Denmark, where in the years that follow the conclusion of the film, Karin Blixen became famous as the writer Isak Dinesen. Intelligently written and beautifully filmed romantic character study that, while it's a pleasure to watch, doesn't have enough dramatic tension—Streep's performance is all that holds the film together. The starry miscasting of Redford further damages the film; while he cuts a dashing figure and gives his usual engaging performance, he makes no effort at an English accent, knowing perhaps that he would receive the same ridicule that later greeted Kevin Costner's accent in *Robin Hood: Prince of Thieves*. Meanwhile, Streep, who never met an accent she couldn't mimic, is doing apparently letter-perfect Danish intonations. Their performances simply don't mesh.

Out of Africa is typical of the films that dominated the best picture Oscar in the eighties: meticulously produced "prestige" costume dramas without a lot of freshness or relevance, such as *Chariots of Fire, Gandhi, Amadeus,* and *The Last Emperor*. The Academy seemed to be honoring these films as a way of pretending that the industry was fundamentally serious—that its heart wasn't in the *Star Wars, Indiana Jones, Star Trek, Ghostbusters, Rocky,* and *Rambo* sequels, but rather in works that aspired to art and high seriousness. *Out of Africa* defeated *The Color Purple* (which likewise had pretentions to seriousness), *Kiss of the Spider Woman* (a surprising sleeper hit), *Prizzi's Honor* (a superb black comedy, a genre that has never won a best picture award), and *Witness* (a well-made thriller—another genre usually scorned by the Academy).

As producer and director, Pollack has built a reputation for good-looking, well-made films that showcase top stars: Redford (who has made seven films for Pollack), Jane Fonda *(They Shoot Horses, Don't They?* and *The Electric Horseman)*, Barbra Streisand *(The Way We Were)*, Paul Newman *(Absence of Malice)*, Dustin Hoffman *(Tootsie)*, and Tom Cruise *(The Firm)*, among others. Pollack began as an actor in New York and in recent years has given some well-received performances on screen, in *Tootsie* and *Husbands and Wives.* But after working as an acting coach, he moved into TV as a director, including work on the *Ben Casey* series. He moved from TV to movies in 1965, when he directed Anne Bancroft and Sidney Poitier in *The Slender Thread,* and over the years has become one of the industry's leading directors. His first major success as a movie director, *They Shoot Horses, Don't They?,* was also Pollack's first film as producer, a role he has assumed more frequently in recent years.

Luedtke, a former reporter, broke into films with the newspaper drama *Absence of Malice.* His screenplay is based on Isak Dinesen's stories as well as on biographical material.

Watkin, born in England, began his career filming documentaries and moved into features when he was hired by director Richard Lester in 1965 for two movies, *The Knack . . . and How to Get It* and *Help!* He has since become one of England's premier cinematographers, although he has surprisingly been overlooked by the Academy—this is his sole nomination. His work includes *Chariots of Fire, Moonstruck,* and the 1990 Franco Zeffirelli *Hamlet.*

With previous Oscars for *Born Free* and its title song and for *The Lion in Winter,* Barry continued to be one of the movies' most prolific and versatile composers, ranging from the brassy, flashy scores for the James Bond movies to the moody, noirish jazz score for *Body Heat* (1981). The sweeping, romantic themes of the *Out of Africa* score evoked comparisons with such old-style Hollywood masters as Max Steiner

[16 . . .], and he returned to the same mode for his next Oscar-winning score, for *Dances With Wolves.*

Despite some jokes about the accent—she had previously done a British accent for *The French Lieutenant's Woman,* a Polish accent for *Sophie's Choice,* and an Okie accent for *Silkwood*—this was one of Streep's best-received performances, an impressive demonstration of acting technique. She lost the Oscar to a strong sentimental favorite, Geraldine Page, who had been nominated seven times without winning and finally took the award for *The Trip to Bountiful.*

Austrian-born Brandauer is one of Europe's most acclaimed younger actors. His performance in *Mephisto* helped that film win the best foreign language film award, but he had never previously been nominated for an acting Oscar. He lost to another sentimental favorite, Don Ameche in *Cocoon.*

The award for editing went to Thom Noble for *Witness.* Emi Wada won for the costumes for *Ran.*

Pollack: 2047, 2113. Luedtke: 3. Grimes: 1432, 2238. MacAvin: 1897, 2106. Jenkins: 543, 1138.5. Handford: 808. Barry: 259, 382.5, 482, 1177, 1285. Streep: 472, 521, 725, 1019, 1111, 1598, 1821, 1876. F. Steinkamp: 814, 2047, 2074, 2113. W. Steinkamp: 633, 2113. Herring: 264, 2120. Kahn: 1481. Canonero: 151, 386, 543, 2148.

1513 • OUTLAND

Ladd Company Production; The Ladd Company. 1981.
Nomination *Sound:* John K. Wilkinson, Robert W. Glass, Jr., Robert M. Thirlwell, and Robin Gregory.

Sean Connery [2185] is a marshal investigating some mysterious deaths on the third moon of Jupiter, which is being mined for titanium. The boss of the mining operation, Peter Boyle, tries to thwart Connery with some hired guns. The basic outline is lifted from *High Noon,* but it's a mediocre movie with lame dialogue and a flimsy plot; only that consummate professional Connery gives it substance. Written and directed by Peter Hyams, with Frances Sternhagen, James B. Sikking, and John Ratzenberger. The sound award went to *Raiders of the Lost Ark.*

Wilkinson: 506, 1584. Glass: 506. Thirlwell: 127, 1701. Gregory: 519.

1514 • OUTLAW—JOSEY WALES, THE

MALPASO COMPANY FILM PRODUCTION; WARNER BROS. 1976.
NOMINATION *Original Score:* Jerry Fielding.

Clint Eastwood [2179.5] tracks down the men who murdered his family; meanwhile, bounty hunters are tracking Eastwood down. Bloody revenge saga, directed by Eastwood after Philip Kaufman [2173], who also cowrote the screenplay (with Sonia Chernus), left the film. Eastwood's hard-core admirers rate it highly; those who have come around to Eastwood only in recent years may find it harder to take. The cast includes Chief Dan George [1179] and Sondra Locke [884]. The fine cinematography is by Bruce Surtees [1155]. The scoring Oscar went to Jerry Goldsmith for *The Omen.*

Fielding: 1944, 2280.

1515 • OX, THE

SWEETLAND FILMS AB/JEAN DOUMANIAN PRODUCTION (SWEDEN). 1991.
NOMINATION *Foreign Language Film.*

A family struggles to survive the famine that caused thousands of Swedes to leave their native land in the mid-nineteenth century. The topic was also treated in *The Emigrants,* whose stars, Max von Sydow [1546] and Liv Ullmann [610 . . .], have supporting roles in this film. Written and directed by Sven Nykvist [460 . . .]. The Oscar went to *Mediterraneo.*

1516 • OX-BOW INCIDENT, THE

20TH CENTURY-FOX. 1943.
NOMINATION *Picture:* Lamar Trotti, producer.

Outsider Henry Fonda [815 . . .] rides into a small western town where a lynching is about to take place and finds that he and the few people of goodwill are unable to dissuade the mob. Small, serious ''adult'' western that's a few years ahead of its time —*Shane* and *High Noon* would make the genre respectable. Considering that it's exceptionally well written, acted, and directed, it's surprising that the film received only one Oscar bid—it's the last movie ever to be nominated for best picture with no other nominations. Studio head Darryl F. Zanuck [34 . . .] was not among its backers; Fonda, Trotti

(who also wrote the screenplay, based on the novel by Walter Van Tilburg Clark), and director William Wellman [157 . . .] had to persist in their attempts to get it made. Fonda in particular deserved an acting nomination over either Walter Pidgeon in *Madame Curie* or Mickey Rooney in *The Human Comedy,* but those actors had the support of their studio, MGM. The fine cast includes Dana Andrews, Anthony Quinn [1226 . . .], and Francis Ford as the victims, Harry (billed as Henry) Morgan as Fonda's sidekick, and Jane Darwell [815], Harry Davenport, and Margaret Hamilton among the townspeople. The best picture Oscar went to *Casablanca.*

Trotti: 2043, 2286, 2337.

1517 • PACIFIC LINER

RKO RADIO. 1938.
NOMINATION *Original Score:* Robert Russell Bennett.

A cholera epidemic breaks out on a ship bound for San Francisco from China. A slow boat from China at that—rather tedious melodrama with a good cast: Victor McLaglen [999 . . .], Chester Morris [38], Wendy Barrie, and Barry Fitzgerald [787]. Bennett, best known as an orchestrator for Broadway musicals, lost to Erich Wolfgang Korngold's score for *The Adventures of Robin Hood.*

Bennett: 1469.

1518 • PAINT YOUR WAGON

ALAN JAY LERNER PRODUCTION; PARAMOUNT. 1969.
NOMINATION *Score of a Musical Picture—Original or Adaptation:* Nelson Riddle.

Miners Lee Marvin [371] and Clint Eastwood [2179.5] set up a household in which they share a wife, Jean Seberg. The Broadway musical by Alan Jay Lerner [66 . . .] and Frederick Loewe [769 . . .] becomes a big wide-screen production that bombed with audiences and critics but has since gained something of a following. Spectacular location shooting clashes with the conventional musical elements, and the casting of nonsingers like Marvin and Eastwood is more than a little ludicrous, although in Eastwood's case the problem is more one of image than of technique. As a jazz aficionado, Eastwood has some musical sense and possesses a surprisingly pleasant voice. But it's hard to forget Dirty Harry and the Man With No Name when Eastwood is singing "I Talk to the Trees." Fortunately the most familiar song in the score, "They Call the Wind Maria," goes to a real singer, Harve Presnell. The filming was hindered by clashes between Lerner, who produced, and director Joshua Logan [643 . . .]. The screenplay is by Paddy Chayefsky [783 . . .].

The scoring award went to Lennie Hayton and Lionel Newman for *Hello, Dolly!*

Riddle: 338, 821, 1172, 1708.

1519 • *PAISAN*

ROBERTO ROSSELLINI PRODUCTIONS; MAYER-BURSTYN (ITALY). 1949.

NOMINATION *Story and Screenplay:* Alfred Hayes, Federico Fellini, Sergio Amidei, Marcello Pagliero, and Roberto Rossellini.

Six episodes that take place between the Allied landing in Sicily in 1943 and the end of the war in Europe two years later, involving the interaction between the American troops and the people they meet —a black soldier whose shoes are stolen by a poor family, a nurse who tries to find an old lover who's a member of the underground, and so on. The cast is made up mostly of nonprofessional actors, and some of the dialogue is improvised, but the total effect is impressive—a vivid dramatization of life in wartime Italy. Directed by Rossellini. The Oscar went to Robert Pirosh for *Battleground.*

Hayes: 2018. Fellini: 61, 562, 603, 657, 658, 1496, 1938, 2209. Amidei: 756, 1496, 1815.

1520 • *PAIX SUR LES CHAMPS*

PHILIPPE COLLETTE-E.G.C. PRODUCTION (BELGIUM). 1970.
NOMINATION *Foreign Language Film.*

A farmer whose mother was accused of being a witch commits murder. Directed by Jacques Boigelet, who collaborated with Rene Wheeler [327] on the screenplay, based on a true story. Little seen in the United States. The Oscar went to *Investigation of a Citizen Above Suspicion.*

1521 • *PAL JOEY*

ESSEX-GEORGE SIDNEY PRODUCTION; COLUMBIA. 1957.
NOMINATIONS *Art Direction—Set Decoration:* Walter Holscher; William Kiernan and Louis Diage. *Sound Recording:* Columbia Studio Sound Department, John P. Livadary, sound director. *Film Editing:* Viola Lawrence and Jerome Thoms. *Costume Design:* Jean Louis.

Frank Sinatra [732 . . .] plays Joey, a nightclub singer who wants to start his own club and courts wealthy Rita Hayworth to obtain the money, though his heart really belongs to chorus girl Kim Novak. Lame "cleaned-up" version of the great musical by Richard Rodgers [1921] and Lorenz Hart that in its original 1940 Broadway version had a book by John O'Hara based on his *New Yorker* stories, about a scheming rotter who dumps the nice girl for the rich one and is then dumped himself. It gave Gene Kelly [74] his big break, and Columbia bought the rights to the show with the idea that Kelly would repeat his success on screen. But in the meantime, Kelly became a big star at MGM, which refused to lend him out. The project stayed on the shelf until Sinatra agreed to do it. The O'Hara book didn't pass muster with the Production Code, so Dorothy Kingsley [1782] did a screenplay in which Joey became a nice guy, even though Sinatra's tough-guy persona would have been ideal for the original role. Censorship also robbed Hart's racy lyrics of their bite and sass, and some of the show's songs—"You Mustn't Kick It Around," "Den of Iniquity," and others—were dropped. In their place, such Rodgers and Hart classics as "The Lady Is a Tramp," "I Didn't Know What Time It Was," "There's a Small Hotel," and "My Funny Valentine" were borrowed from other shows. These songs, and others from the Broadway *Pal Joey,* such as "Bewitched, Bothered and Bewildered" and "I Could Write a Book," keep the movie from being a total dud. George Sidney directed. Novak's singing voice was dubbed by Trudy Erwin, Hayworth's by Jo Ann Greer. *Sayonara* won for art direction and sound. The editing Oscar went to Peter Taylor for *The Bridge on the River Kwai.* Orry-Kelly won for the costumes for *Les Girls.*

Holscher: 13. Kiernan: 1133, 1550, 1753, 1858,

2238. Diage: 170, 1858. Livadary: 330, 455, 596, 732, 1058, 1206, 1215, 1303, 1366, 1370, 1488, 1740, 1872, 2111, 2325, 2327. Lawrence: 1550. Louis: 20, 126, 170, 262, 732, 744, 1028, 1065, 1640, 1812, 1858, 1910, 2064.

1522 • PALEFACE, THE

PARAMOUNT. 1948.

AWARD Song: "Buttons and Bows," music and lyrics by Jay Livingston and Ray Evans.

Jane Russell plays Calamity Jane, who marries a tenderfoot dentist played by Bob Hope to conceal her identity. She spends much of the movie helping Hope look like a sharpshooting hero and avoiding consummating the marriage. Silly but endearing. One of Hope's best movies, although the sequel, *Son of Paleface,* is even better. Directed by Norman Z. McLeod.

Though they won three best song Oscars, Livingston and Evans don't get much respect from the standard historians of popular music—Alec Wilder mentions them not at all in his *American Popular Song,* for example. They teamed up while in college at the University of Pennsylvania and began their songwriting career in radio. Aside from their nominated songs, their hits include "To Each His Own" and the theme song for TV's *Bonanza.*

Livingston: 344, 512, 951, 1260, 2001, 2278. Evans: 344, 512, 951, 1260, 2001, 2278.

1523 • PANIC IN THE STREETS

20TH CENTURY-FOX. 1950.

AWARD Motion Picture Story: Edna Anhalt and Edward Anhalt.

Public health officer Richard Widmark [1098] tries to track down Zero Mostel and Jack Palance [408 . . .], two fugitives who are carrying a deadly plague in the New Orleans waterfront area. Tense, exciting manhunt thriller that's given real zip by the direction of Elia Kazan [63 . . .], the excellent location photography of Joe MacDonald [1550 . . .], and fine performances, including Paul Douglas as the police captain and Barbara Bel Geddes [972] as Widmark's wife. This was one of Palance's first films; he's billed as Walter Jack Palance.

Each of the three writing categories this year contained a husband-and-wife team among its nominees: Frances Goodrich and Albert Hackett were nominated in the screenplay category for *Father of the Bride,* and Ruth Gordon and Garson Kanin in the story and screenplay category for *Adam's Rib.* The Anhalts, however, were the only pair to take home Oscars that night. Not mentioned in the nominations were Richard Murphy [257 . . .] and Daniel Fuchs [1216], who worked with the Anhalts on the screenplay from their story.

Edna Anhalt: 1850. Edward Anhalt: 164, 1850.

1524 • PAPA'S DELICATE CONDITION

AMRO PRODUCTIONS; PARAMOUNT. 1963.

AWARD Song: "Call Me Irresponsible," music by James Van Heusen, lyrics by Sammy Cahn.

Jackie Gleason [964] stars as the lovable but alcoholic head of a turn-of-the-century family. Pleasant family comedy based on the memoirs of silent film star Corinne Griffith [552], with a good cast: Glynis Johns [1969], Charles Ruggles, Juanita Moore [984], and Elisha Cook, Jr., among others, directed by George Marshall.

Papa's Delicate Condition was originally planned to star Fred Astaire [2126]—to the great delight of Cahn, who had never written a song for the actor many consider one of the greatest interpreters of popular songs. But Astaire had other commitments and the project was shelved, along with what would be Van Heusen and Cahn's fourth Oscar-winning song, until the script was reworked for Gleason. With the award, the team of Van Heusen and Cahn tied the record for most songwriting Oscars set the previous year by Johnny Mercer [248 . . .]. With a total of twenty-six nominations, Cahn is tied with Max Steiner [16 . . .] and behind only John Williams [6 . . .], who has thirty-one, and Alfred Newman [31 . . .], who accumulated forty-five, for the most nominations in the music categories.

Van Heusen: 171, 173, 787, 915, 926, 1056, 1587, 1708, 1859, 1907, 2016, 2064, 2263. Cahn: 74, 163, 182, 696, 915, 926, 1031, 1056, 1216,

1587, 1692, 1708, 1719, 1859, 1907, 2016, 2064, 2072, 2103, 2110, 2125, 2263, 2264, 2315, 2343.

1524.5 • PAPER, THE

IMAGINE ENTERTAINMENT PRODUCTION; UNIVERSAL. 1994.
NOMINATION *Song:* ''Make Up Your Mind,'' music and lyrics by Randy Newman.

Michael Keaton plays a city editor on a New York newspaper whose love for what he does and determination to get things right is sometimes compromised by his relationships with the people he lives and works with: his wife, played by Marisa Tomei [1391.5], who has put her career as a reporter on hold to have a baby; his managing editor, played by Glenn Close [199 . . .], who is torn between reporting the news and appeasing the bean-counting owners of the paper; his executive editor, played by Robert Duvall [92 . . .], a man of integrity but uncertain health; and his star columnist, played by Randy Quaid [1135], whose personal and journalistic standards are sometimes questionable. Fast-moving and entertainingly old-fashioned newspaper melodrama that plays less like a movie than like a prestige-cast episode of a good TV drama series such as *NYPD Blue* or *ER.* Directed by Ron Howard from a screenplay by David Koepp and Stephen Koepp, with a cast that also includes Jason Robards [54 . . .], Jason Alexander, and Spalding Gray. Newman, who also did the film's score, lost to Elton John and Tim Rice's ''Can You Feel the Love Tonight'' from *The Lion King.*

Newman: 112, 1418, 1530, 1651.

1525 • PAPER CHASE, THE

THOMPSON-PAUL PRODUCTIONS; 20TH CENTURY-FOX. 1973.
AWARD *Supporting Actor:* John Houseman.
NOMINATIONS *Screenplay—Based on Material From Another Medium:* James Bridges. *Sound:* Donald O. Mitchell and Lawrence O. Jost.

Timothy Bottoms plays a Harvard law student whose professors include the aloof and demanding Kingsfield (Houseman). Bottoms falls for a girl (Lindsay Wagner) who's derisive about the law and everything it represents—and then he discovers that she's Kingsfield's daughter. An interesting re-creation of a milieu that anyone who's ever done time in law/business/medical/graduate school will instantly recognize, but the movie doesn't have enough dramatic substance to sustain it. Bridges directed his adaptation of a novel by John Jay Osborn, Jr. The cinematography is by Gordon Willis [786 . . .] and the score by John Williams [6 . . .].

Born in Romania and raised in England, Houseman came to the United States in the twenties and worked as a writer and translator before establishing himself as a director, producer, and writer on Broadway. He founded the Mercury Theater with Orson Welles [407 . . .] in 1937 and came to Hollywood with Welles to work on *Citizen Kane.* His contributions to *Kane* as adviser, writer, and story editor were, he thought, insufficiently acknowledged by Welles, and the two men went their separate ways. While keeping one foot in the theater, Houseman also became a successful film producer, with credits such as *The Bad and the Beautiful, Julius Caesar, Executive Suite,* and *Lust for Life.* Although he had made a few on-screen appearances before *The Paper Chase,* Kingsfield was his first substantial film role. He continued to act for the rest of his life, although the characters he played were mostly variations on the Kingsfield persona, including the TV series based on the movie. He died in 1988.

The screenplay award went to William Peter Blatty for *The Exorcist,* which also won for sound.

Houseman: 1069. Bridges: 394. Mitchell: 223, 398, 411.5, 507, 734.5, 779, 1650, 1824, 1825, 2020, 2114, 2176.5. Jost: 395, 502.

1526 • PAPER MOON

A DIRECTORS COMPANY PRODUCTION; PARAMOUNT. 1973.
AWARD *Supporting Actress:* Tatum O'Neal.
NOMINATIONS *Supporting Actress:* Madeline Kahn. *Screenplay—Based on Material From Another Medium:* Alvin Sargent. *Sound:* Richard Portman and Les Fresholtz.

Con artist Ryan O'Neal [1218], who runs a Bible-selling scam in rural Kansas during the Depression, teams up with an orphan (Tatum O'Neal) who's as good at fleecing people as he is. Amusingly cynical comedy, directed by Peter Bogdanovich [1139], with

John Hillerman and Randy Quaid [1135]. The evocative black-and-white cinematography is by Laszlo Kovacs. At one time the film was set to be directed by John Huston [24 . . .] and to star Paul Newman [3 . . .] and Newman's daughter, Nell Potts.

At ten O'Neal became the youngest person ever to win a competitive Oscar. The daughter of Ryan O'Neal and actress Joanna Moore, Tatum had modest success in the movies. Her next film, *The Bad News Bears* (1976), was a hit. But both *Nickelodeon* (1976) and *International Velvet* (1978) were box-office disappointments, and as she moved into her twenties, she seemed destined to go the way of such child actresses as Patty McCormack [133] and Linda Blair [631]— into cheesy exploitation movies. In 1986 she married tennis star John McEnroe and became largely known for her appearances in supermarket tabloids. After separating from McEnroe, she has recently made some attempts to resume her acting career.

Sargent's screenplay, adapted from the novel *Addie Pray,* by Joe David Brown, lost to William Peter Blatty's for *The Exorcist,* which also won for sound.

Kahn: 230. Sargent: 1066, 1502. Portman: 339, 418, 502, 521, 738, 784, 1109, 1473, 1701, 2331. Fresholtz: 54, 58, 209, 215, 606, 888, 1127, 1158.5, 1279, 2113.

1527 • PAPILLON

CORONA-GENERAL PRODUCTION COMPANY PRODUCTION; ALLIED ARTISTS. 1973.
NOMINATION *Original Dramatic Score:* Jerry Goldsmith.

Steve McQueen [1753] plays Henri Charrière, nicknamed Papillon—he has a butterfly tattoo. Sentenced to imprisonment on Devil's Island, he is determined to escape. His friend and fellow prisoner, Louis, played by Dustin Hoffman [810 . . .], aids in his efforts. Potentially exciting adventure yarn undermined by being stretched out over two and a half hours, and by the occasional pretentiousness of the screenplay, based on Charrière's memoirs, by Dalton Trumbo [273 . . .] and Lorenzo Semple, Jr. The writers and director Franklin J. Schaffner [1541] seem more interested in the grimness of imprison-

ment than in the exhilaration of escape. This was Trumbo's last screenplay, and he makes an on-camera appearance as the prison commandant. The cast also includes Victor Jory in his last film appearance. The scoring award went to Marvin Hamlisch for *The Way We Were*.

Goldsmith: 152.5, 268, 395, 727, 939, 1472, 1537, 1541, 1583, 1589, 1753, 1913, 2176, 2287.

1528 • PARADINE CASE, THE

VANGUARD FILMS; SELZNICK RELEASING ORGANIZATION. 1947.
NOMINATION *Supporting Actress:* Ethel Barrymore.

Barrister Anthony Keane, played by Gregory Peck [759 . . .], falls in love with his client, Mrs. Paradine (Alida Valli), who is accused of killing her husband. Dull, miscast, and talky drama, directed by Alfred Hitchcock [1171 . . .], but with none of his usual wit and imagination; it's one of Hitchcock's worst films, and even his most ardent admirers find little to say in its defense. They do, on the other hand, have an easy excuse: The movie was produced by David O. Selznick [497 . . .], who is responsible for the muddled casting—Peck as an Englishman, the ineffective Valli in the title role, the inexperienced Louis Jourdan in his first English-language film, all of them under some form of contractual obligation to the producer. Selznick also wrote the screenplay. He had acquired the property, a novel by Robert Hichens, for MGM in 1933, seeing it as a vehicle for Greta Garbo [84 . . .], who showed no interest in it. After he left MGM, Selznick bought the rights for his own production company and tried to persuade Garbo to return to the screen in it. When she declined, he considered it for Ingrid Bergman [72 . . .] or Vivien Leigh [798 . . .], who weren't interested either. So Selznick decided to make a new star, choosing Valli, who was then one of Italy's rising stars. Although Valli would make a stronger impression in *The Third Man* the following year, her appeal to American audiences was slight. The cast also includes Charles Laughton [1387 . . .], Charles Coburn [535 . . .], Ann Todd, and Leo G. Carroll. (Hitchcock carries a cello in his signature appearance.) Barrymore, who plays Laughton's wife, lost to Celeste Holm in *Gentleman's Agreement*.

Barrymore: 1445, 1575, 1891.

1529 • PARENT TRAP, THE

WALT DISNEY PRODUCTIONS; BUENA VISTA. 1961.

NOMINATIONS *Sound:* Robert O. Cook, sound director, Walt Disney Studio Sound Department. *Film Editing:* Philip W. Anderson.

Twins, both played by Hayley Mills [1588.5], meet at summer camp—to their great surprise, because neither twin knew of the existence of the other. It seems their parents, Maureen O'Hara and Brian Keith, divorced while the girls were infants and agreed to raise each twin separately. So the girls swap parents—the twin raised by O'Hara goes home with Keith, and vice versa—in an effort to reunite the family. Good Disney family comedy that's more memorable for Mills' performance, and the trick photography that makes it possible, than for its predictable gags and plot. Joanna Barnes gets to play one of her familiar snotty dames, trying to get her hooks into Keith's money. The cast also includes Una Merkel [1959], Charlie Ruggles, Leo G. Carroll, Cathleen Nesbitt, and Nancy Kulp. David Swift directed and wrote the screenplay, based on a novel by Erich Kästner, *Das Doppelte Lottchen*. The Oscar for sound went to *West Side Story,* which also won for Thomas Stanford's editing.

Cook: 254, 1284. Anderson: 768, 1763.

1530 • PARENTHOOD

IMAGINE ENTERTAINMENT PRODUCTION; UNIVERSAL. 1989.

NOMINATIONS *Supporting Actress:* Dianne Wiest. *Song:* "I Love to See You Smile," music and lyrics by Randy Newman.

Though he's no role model as a parent, Jason Robards [54 . . .] has four children: Steve Martin, Wiest, Harley Kozak, and Tom Hulce [60]. Martin, married to Mary Steenburgen [1300], is worried that his devotion to his career is harming his children. Wiest is a divorcée whose teenage daughter, Martha Plimpton, has taken up with spacy Keanu Reeves, while her younger son, Leaf Phoenix, seems to be in

his own world. Kozak is married to Rick Moranis, a fanatic about "parenting" theories who is determined to raise their daughter, barely out of diapers, to be a genius. Hulce, who is Robards' favorite child, is a screwup, a gambler on the run from people he owes money. The intersection of these lives produces an entertaining though slightly too glossy comedy-drama, directed by Ron Howard from a screenplay by Lowell Ganz [1893] and Babaloo Mandel [1893] to which Howard contributed story ideas. Martin as usual is terrific, especially when he has to rescue a kid's birthday party from disaster.

Wiest lost to Brenda Fricker in *My Left Foot*. The song Oscar went to Alan Menken and Howard Ashman for "Under the Sea," from *The Little Mermaid*.

Wiest: 331.5, 863. Newman: 112, 1418, 1524.5, 1651.

1531 • PARIS BLUES

PENNEBAKER PRODUCTION; UNITED ARTISTS. 1961.

NOMINATION *Scoring of a Musical Picture:* Duke Ellington.

Jazz musicians Paul Newman [3 . . .] and Sidney Poitier [522 . . .] meet tourists Joanne Woodward [1365 . . .] and Diahann Carroll [411] in Paris. Despite the starry foursome, the real star of the film is Ellington's music—there's just enough story not to get in the way of it, too. Martin Ritt [956] directed, and the cast includes Louis Armstrong.

Though he was one of the greatest American composers, racism prevented Ellington from making a contribution to films comparable to that of white musicians of his stature, such as George Gershwin [1797], Irving Berlin [34 . . .], and Aaron Copland [894 . . .]. With his orchestra, Ellington made occasional appearances in films such as the all-black musical *Cabin in the Sky*. But his first complete film score was not commissioned until late in his career, when Otto Preminger asked him to provide the music for *Anatomy of a Murder*. (He was passed over in the nominations that year in favor of such forgettable scores as those for *On the Beach* and *Pillow Talk*.) After *Paris Blues,* Ellington wrote only one more film score, for *Assault on a Queen* (1966). He lost the Oscar to Saul

Chaplin, Johnny Green, Sid Ramin, and Irwin Kostal for *West Side Story*—an instance of the anomalous nature of the music scoring category, for while Ellington was the author of the *Paris Blues* score, the *West Side Story* team only arranged the music that had been written by Leonard Bernstein [1477].

1532 • PARIS UNDERGROUND

Constance Bennett; United Artists. 1945.

Nomination *Scoring of a Dramatic or Comedy Picture:* Alexander Tansman.

American Constance Bennett and Englishwoman Gracie Fields join the French Resistance after the Nazis invade. Forgettable wartime potboiler, directed by Gregory Ratoff. The Oscar went to Miklos Rozsa for *Spellbound.*

1533 • PASSAGE TO INDIA, A

G.W. Films Ltd. Production; Columbia (United Kingdom). 1984.

Awards *Supporting Actress:* Peggy Ashcroft. *Original Score:* Maurice Jarre.

Nominations *Picture:* John Brabourne and Richard Goodwin, producers. *Actress:* Judy Davis. *Director:* David Lean. *Screenplay Based on Material From Another Medium:* David Lean. *Cinematography:* Ernest Day. *Art Direction—Set Decoration:* John Box and Leslie Tomkins; Hugh Scaife. *Sound:* Graham Hartstone, Nicolas Le Messurier, Michael A. Carter, and John Mitchell. *Film Editing:* David Lean. *Costume Design:* Judy Moorcroft.

Adela Quested (Davis) journeys from England to India to meet her fiancé (Nigel Havers), accompanied by her prospective mother-in-law, Mrs. Moore (Ashcroft). In India Mrs. Moore meets the young Dr. Aziz (Victor Banerjee), who invites the two women to join him on an excursion to the Marabar Caves. Disaster ensues: Mrs. Moore, finding the caves mysterious and sinister, is overcome by the experience and is forced to rest. Miss Quested, who continues the exploration of the caves with Aziz, succumbs to hysteria and accuses the Indian of attempting to rape her. The resulting arrest and trial escalate into a major incident. Lean's last film is a remarkably effective adaptation

of E. M. Forster's novel about the ways in which East is East and West is West. It has both the virtues and the faults of most Lean films. The virtues include great picturesqueness, as well as a gallery of fine performers, including James Fox as the English intellectual who tries to bring about understanding between his people and the Indians—and only makes matters worse. The film's faults include excessive length and a sometimes slack narrative flow. The appearance by Alec Guinness [287 . . .] as the Indian Godbole comes off as an embarrassing cameo; the other Indian roles are played by native performers.

Perhaps the greatest achievement of the film is that it provided a vehicle for the talents of Ashcroft, an actress often cited as the equal of John Gielgud [103 . . .] and Laurence Olivier [268 . . .]. Renowned for her Shakespeare (she has been called the century's greatest Juliet), Chekhov, and Ibsen as well as Brecht and Beckett, Ashcroft was not seen often on screen. Although she made her film debut in a classic, *The 39 Steps* (1935), directed by Alfred Hitchcock [1171 . . .], most of her film roles were small and conventional supporting parts. She also appeared in *The Nun's Story* and *Sunday, Bloody Sunday.* In the same year that *A Passage to India* was released, she received acclaim as another Englishwoman in India in the British TV miniseries *The Jewel in the Crown.* In *A Passage to India* Ashcroft makes a vivid presence out of a character who lacks clear definition in Forster's novel. Lean's direction was of little help to her, Ashcroft told her biographer, Michael Billington: "It seemed as if he wanted her to be a mystical and mysterious person, whereas I saw her as someone with her feet planted firmly on the ground." The New York film critics gave Ashcroft their award for best actress, but Academy voters followed the lead of the Los Angeles film critics, who gave her their supporting actress award. Ashcroft died in 1991.

Jarre's win was his third—all three of them for films by David Lean. (*Lawrence of Arabia* and *Doctor Zhivago* are the others.)

Amadeus won the best picture Oscar, as well as the ones for director (Milos Forman), screenplay (Peter Shaffer), art direction (Patrizia Von Brandenstein and

Karel Cerny), sound and costuming (Theodor Pistek). Davis was defeated by Sally Field in *Places in the Heart*. *The Killing Fields* took awards for Chris Menges' cinematography and Jim Clark's editing.

Jarre: 558, 764, 808, 1151, 1168, 1340, 1967, 2296. Brabourne: 1722. Davis: 962.5. Lean: 287, 289, 558, 820, 1151, 1963. Box: 558, 1151, 1429, 1471, 2134. Tomkins: 2321. Scaife: 608, 1898. Hartstone: 45, 1977. Le Messurier: 45, 1977. Carter: 45. Mitchell: 540. Moorcroft: 626.

1533.5 • PASSION FISH

ATCHAFALAYA FILMS PRODUCTION; MIRAMAX FILMS. 1992.
NOMINATIONS *Actress:* Mary McDonnell. *Original Screenplay:* John Sayles.

McDonnell plays a soap-opera actress who's paralyzed in an accident. Confined to a wheelchair, she goes home to the Louisiana bayou country, fully intending to drink herself to death. She hires as an attendant a woman, played by Alfre Woodard [466], whose rebellion against her family landed her in jail. Naturally there's a clash of wills when Woodard, who wants to restore her own self-respect, is disgusted by McDonnell's self-indulgence. What could have been merely a predictable melodrama about overcoming adversity turns into a fine character study, thanks to writer-director-editor Sayles, who is fortunately more interested in the characters than in preaching sermons about self-esteem. The principals are nicely supported by David Strathairn as an old beau of McDonnell's who has made a bad marriage and now bums around the bayous, and a visiting trio of McDonnell's fellow soap stars, played hilariously by Angela Bassett [2250.7], Nora Dunn, and Sheila Kelley. Sayles nicely uses the soap-opera background of his character for irony, lifting her real-life struggle out of the suds.

Many critics of the Oscars were justifiably perturbed at the failure of the Academy to nominate Woodard as well as McDonnell—individually the two actresses are terrific; together they're dynamite. Woodard seems a far better choice as an Oscar nominee than, for example, Catherine Deneuve, who was nominated for the glossy *Indochine*. The award went to Emma Thompson for *Howards End*.

Sayles won a MacArthur Foundation "genius grant" in 1983, partly in recognition of his work as a filmmaker able to work independently of the Hollywood studios and to produce intelligent, offbeat films. Sayles is also a well-received novelist and short story writer, and he has occasionally acted in his own and other people's movies. Like numerous major Hollywood talents, including Francis Ford Coppola [65 . . .], Martin Scorsese [806 . . .], Jack Nicholson [395 . . .], and Robert Towne [395 . . .], he began his film career working for low-budget exploitation-flick producer Roger Corman. Sayles gave his own witty spin to otherwise silly movies like *Piranha* (1978) and made an impressive directing debut in 1980 with the extremely low-budget *The Return of the Secaucus Seven,* about the reunion of a group of sixties activists, which anticipated the slicker and more expensively produced *The Big Chill* by three years. Other Sayles films that have received critical praise include *The Brother From Another Planet* (1984), *Matewan, Eight Men Out* (1988), and *City of Hope* (1991). But the Academy, which has a blind spot for independent filmmakers, ignored Sayles until this nomination. He lost to Neil Jordan for *The Crying Game*.

McDonnell: 482.

1534 • PASSOVER PLOT, THE

COAST INDUSTRIES-GOLAN-GLOBUS PRODUCTIONS LTD.; ATLAS FILMS (U.S./ISRAEL). 1976.
NOMINATION *Costume Design:* Mary Wills.

Offbeat religious drama based on a theory that Jesus (played by Zalman King) was a revolutionary actively battling the Roman rule and that he didn't actually die on the cross but that he and his disciples staged his death and resurrection. Needless to say, this one is intensely controversial—and little seen. There are some interesting names in the cast, however: Harry Andrews as John the Baptist, Hugh Griffith [175 . . .] as Caiaphas, and Donald Pleasence as Pontius Pilate. The costuming Oscar went to Danilo Donati for *Fellini's Casanova*.

Wills: 376, 542, 864, 2008, 2205, 2312.

1535 • PASSPORT TO PIMLICO

J. ARTHUR RANK-EALING; EAGLE LION (UNITED KINGDOM). 1949.

NOMINATION *Story and Screenplay:* T. E. B. Clarke.

In the midst of postwar austerity, the London borough of Pimlico suddenly discovers that an ancient document makes it part of France, not England, with the result that it's exempt from rationing laws and other restrictions. This makes it the hottest spot in town. Classic British comedy of the golden age just following the war that produced such gems as *The Lavender Hill Mob, Kind Hearts and Coronets, The Man in the White Suit,* and others. Because its satire is directed at the drabness of the postwar era in Britain, that part of the film has lost its edge. But that hardly matters when we can watch such splendid character performers as Stanley Holloway [1393], Hermione Baddeley [1724], Margaret Rutherford [2204], and, as the quintessential British bureaucrats, Basil Radford and Naunton Wayne. Directed by Henry Cornelius, who collaborated on the screenplay with Clarke, who got his story idea from a wartime news item about Canada's deeding to the Netherlands the room in which the exiled Princess Juliana was about to give birth. The Oscar went to Robert Pirosh for *Battleground.*

Clarke: 1150, 1875.

1536 • PAT AND MIKE

MGM. 1952.

NOMINATION *Story and Screenplay:* Ruth Gordon and Garson Kanin.

Pat is amateur athlete Katharine Hepburn [24 . . .]. Mike is down-at-the-heels sports promoter Spencer Tracy [131 . . .], who sees her as a potential meal ticket and signs up to manage her professional career. Of course, they're going to fall in love, even though they're from opposite sides of the tracks, but first Pat's upper-crust boyfriend (William Ching) has to be dealt with, as well as the mobsters— including Charles Bronson, billed as Buchinski—that Mike is involved with. First-rate in all respects, including the direction by George Cukor [262 . . .] and cinematography by William Daniels [84 . . .]. Hepburn and Tracy play together so well it's almost

like watching one performer rather than two, and she's wholly convincing as a sports star, even in the company of real athletes such as Gussie Moran, Babe Didrikson Zaharias, and Don Budge. The supporting players include Aldo Ray, Sammy White, Jim Backus, Chuck Connors, Carl "Alfalfa" Switzer, and sportscaster Tom Harmon. The only mystery is why this one—like its Tracy/Hepburn/Cukor/Gordon/Kanin predecessor *Adam's Rib*—received only one nomination. As a movie, it's far more memorable than best picture winner *The Greatest Show on Earth* or nominee *Ivanhoe,* although the presence of the latter among the contenders probably explains *Pat and Mike*'s absence: Both were released by MGM, but *Ivanhoe* was the studio's big-ticket item. Among the other MGM films bumped out of contention because of the studio's desire to promote *Ivanhoe* were *The Bad and the Beautiful* (which nevertheless won more Oscars than any other movie not nominated for best picture) and *Singin' in the Rain.* Garson and Kanin lost the Oscar to T. E. B. Clarke for *The Lavender Hill Mob.*

Gordon: 11, 567, 1003, 1728. Kanin: 11, 567.

1537 • PATCH OF BLUE, A

PANDRO S. BERMAN-GUY GREEN PRODUCTION; MGM. 1965.

AWARD *Supporting Actress:* Shelley Winters.

NOMINATIONS *Actress:* Elizabeth Hartman. *Black-and-White Cinematography:* Robert Burks. *Black-and-White Art Direction–Set Decoration:* George W. Davis and Urie McCleary; Henry Grace and Charles S. Thompson. *Music Score—Substantially Original:* Jerry Goldsmith.

Hartman, who is blind, falls in love with Sidney Poitier [522 . . .], not realizing he's black. Her harpy of a mother (Winters) knows, however. Problem drama whose heart is in the right place, especially for the times in which it was made, but whose preachiness and lack of subtlety make it tiresome today. Directed by Guy Green [820].

Winters' flamboyance as an actress—and as a talk-show personality—only increased in the later years of her career, and she has continued to work in both TV and movies, usually playing a blowsy vulgarian, particularly in campy or cult movies like *Bloody Mama*

(1970) or *What's the Matter With Helen?,* but also in more mainstream fare such as *The Poseidon Adventure* and *Pete's Dragon.* She cultivated her image as a no-holds-barred type by publishing two notorious volumes of memoirs in the eighties, naming the names of her various famous lovers, some of whom denied her allegations.

Hartman made her film debut in *A Patch of Blue* and followed with *The Group,* in which she established as her specialty the role of nervous, fragile young women. After similar roles in such films as *You're a Big Boy Now, The Beguiled* (1971), and *Walking Tall* (1973), she faded from the screen. After a history of psychiatric problems, she died in 1987 when she fell from her fifth-floor Manhattan apartment. The Oscar went to Julie Christie for *Darling.*

Ernest Laszlo won for the cinematography for *Ship of Fools,* which also took the award for art direction. The scoring Oscar went to Maurice Jarre for *Doctor Zhivago.*

Winters: 542, 1579, 1596. Burks: 1669, 1941, 2098. Davis: 46, 69, 401, 495, 542, 736, 953, 1213, 1335, 1388, 1552, 1706, 1814, 2157, 2184, 2312. McCleary: 239, 1417, 1541, 1657, 2330. Grace: 69, 227, 401, 769, 953, 1335, 1388, 1450, 1552, 2157, 2184, 2312. Thompson: 1642. Goldsmith: 152.5, 268, 395, 727, 939, 1472, 1527, 1541, 1583, 1589, 1753, 1913, 2176, 2287.

1538 • PATENT LEATHER KID, THE

FIRST NATIONAL. 1927–28.
NOMINATION *Actor:* Richard Barthelmess.

Barthelmess stars in a World War I drama based on a novel by Rupert Hughes. This silent film, directed by Alfred Santell, is not in circulation today. Emil Jannings won the Oscar for his performances in *The Last Command* and *The Way of All Flesh.*

Barthelmess: 1447.

1539 • PATHFINDER

FILMKAMERATENE PRODUCTION (NORWAY). 1987.
NOMINATION *Foreign Language Film.*

In frozen Lapland, an adolescent boy returns from hunting to find that a group of fierce bandits has slaughtered his family. He seeks shelter among other Lapps, but they shun him, thinking the bandits may be on his trail, and head for a larger encampment, leaving the boy behind. He meets up with the bandits and offers to lead them to the Lapps, but instead tricks them. Exciting adventure saga, based on an old Lapp folktale. Written and directed by Nils Gaup, whose son, Mikkel, plays the boy. The Oscar went to *Babette's Feast.*

1540 • PATRIOT, THE

PARAMOUNT FAMOUS LASKY. 1928–29.
AWARD *Writing Achievement:* Hans Kräly.
NOMINATIONS *Production:* Ernst Lubitsch, producer. *Actor:* Lewis Stone. *Director:* Ernst Lubitsch. *Interior Decoration:* Hans Dreier.

Emil Jannings [1134 . . .] plays the vicious Czar Paul I in a historical drama about the events leading up to Paul's assassination, masterminded by Stone, the patriot of the title. Some crowd footage from this extravagant production was used later in *The Scarlet Empress* (1934), but the remainder of the film, a silent with some synchronized sound effects, is apparently lost.

Kräly began his career writing for the movies in Germany, where he met Lubitsch, whom he accompanied to Hollywood in 1923. He retired from screenwriting in the early forties and died in 1950.

The best picture Oscar went to *Broadway Melody.* Stone, who began in films in 1915 as a leading man and matured into character roles in the sound era, becoming best known as Andy Hardy's father in the long-running MGM series, lost to Warner Baxter in *In Old Arizona.* Stone, Lubitsch, and Dreier were "unofficial" nominees for the 1928–29 awards—the Academy announced only the winners this year. The lists of the others under consideration by the branches that voted the awards were, however, kept on record, and although the unofficial nominees received no certificates or other recognition from the Academy, they have traditionally been listed alongside the official nominees from other years. Frank Lloyd won the directing Oscar for *The Divine Lady.* The award for art direction was won by Cedric Gibbons for *The Bridge of San Luis Rey.*

Kräly: 1137.5, 1485. Lubitsch: 889, 1217, 1484, 1847. Dreier: 97, 151, 649, 674, 701, 726, 925, 979, 1101, 1120, 1194, 1214, 1217, 1358, 1443, 1452, 1668, 1748, 1880, 1975, 1994, 2190.

1541 • PATTON

20TH CENTURY-FOX. 1970.

AWARDS *Picture:* Frank McCarthy, producer. *Actor:* George C. Scott. *Director:* Franklin J. Schaffner. *Story and Screenplay—Based on Factual Material or Material Not Previously Published or Produced:* Francis Ford Coppola and Edmund H. North. *Art Direction—Set Decoration:* Urie McCleary and Gil Parrondo; Antonio Mateos and Pierre-Louis Thevenet. *Sound:* Douglas Williams and Don Bassman. *Film Editing:* Hugh S. Fowler.

NOMINATIONS *Cinematography:* Fred Koenekamp. *Original Score:* Jerry Goldsmith. *Special Visual Effects:* Alex Weldon.

Scott plays Gen. George Patton, whose arrogance and eccentricity sometimes undermine his effectiveness as a commander during World War II. Huge, sweeping, and enormously effective war movie. Somehow, in the midst of the intense protests against the Vietnam War, Hollywood managed to make a movie that both hawks and doves liked—the former because they saw the film as a glorification of Patton as a heroic figure, the latter because they saw it as portraying him as the kind of nut who was causing people to die in Southeast Asia. (A similar ambiguity later attracted both sides to *The Deer Hunter,* which was read by some as a testament to American heroism, by others as a demonstration of American folly.) The film effectively plays off the abrasive Patton against the more diplomatic Gen. Omar Bradley, played by Karl Malden [1477 . . .].

McCarthy, himself a retired brigadier general, had wanted to make a film about Patton since the end of World War II. He finally found the backing of Fox head Darryl Zanuck [34 . . .], who had also acquired one of *Patton*'s chief competitors for the best picture Oscar, the more explicitly antiwar *MASH.*

Scott was not the first choice for the role; he landed it after Burt Lancaster [107 . . .], Rod Steiger [992 . . .], Lee Marvin [371], and Robert Mitchum [1935] had either rejected the role or proved unavailable, and after John Wayne [33 . . .], who wanted it, was turned down. In films since 1959, when he received his first nomination for *Anatomy of a Murder,* Scott started off well, with memorable performances in *The Hustler* and *Dr. Strangelove,* but by the time of *Patton* his career was in something of a slump. The Oscar revived it somewhat, even though —or some say because—he rejected the honor in advance, announcing that he would decline the award because he felt the suspense of the competition was phony. In recent years Scott has been little seen in films, concentrating his career on stage and TV.

Schaffner began his directing career in the early years of TV, working for CBS News and such programs as Edward R. Murrow's *Person to Person* interview series, then moving into TV drama, winning several Emmys, one of them for the famous tour of the White House conducted by Jacqueline Kennedy. His first film was *The Stripper* (1963), but his biggest hit before *Patton* was *Planet of the Apes.* His post-Oscar career was less impressive, dwindling from the big-budget spectacle *Nicholas and Alexandra* to flops such as the Luciano Pavarotti feature *Yes, Giorgio* (1982). He died in 1989.

Coppola was a few years out of UCLA film school, having worked for exploitation film producer Roger Corman, and directed several features—*You're a Big Boy Now, Finian's Rainbow,* and *The Rain People* (1969) —when he received the commission from McCarthy to do the *Patton* screenplay. North, a veteran screenwriter who had been a major in the Army Signal Corps during World War II, was called in as a collaborator. The Oscar for *Patton* was a major break for Coppola, helping him land the job of writing and directing *The Godfather.*

The cinematography Oscar went to Freddie Young for *Ryan's Daughter.* Francis Lai took the award for the score for *Love Story. Tora! Tora! Tora!* won for special effects.

McCarthy: 517. Scott: 73, 942, 964. Coppola: 65,

92, 442, 784, 785, 786. McCleary: 239, 1417, 1537, 1657, 2330. Parrondo: 1429, 2134. Williams: 1726, 1824, 2152. Bassman: 5, 544, 961. Koenekamp: 1023, 2126. Goldsmith: 152.5, 268, 395, 727, 939, 1472, 1527, 1537, 1583, 1589, 1753, 1913, 2176, 2287. Weldon: 1110.

1542 • PAW

LATERNA FILM (DENMARK). 1959.
NOMINATION *Foreign Language Film.*

A boy whose father is Danish and mother American Indian goes to live with his aunt in a small Danish village. Stung by the community's bigotry, he runs away. Directed by Astrid Henning-Jensen. The Oscar went to *Black Orpheus.*

1543 • PAWNBROKER, THE

ELY LANDAU PRODUCTIONS; AMERICAN INTERNATIONAL PICTURES. 1965.
NOMINATION *Actor:* Rod Steiger.

Steiger plays Sol Nazerman, an aging survivor of the Nazi concentration camps who now runs a pawnshop in Harlem, where the misery of his customers only exacerbates the misery he feels in recalling the past. Uncompromisingly grim but also deeply moving character drama that provoked controversy in its day because of a scene in which a prostitute bares her breasts for the pawnbroker. It's far from a perfect film—it has the self-consciousness of an American film striving for the harshness of European neorealism, and it's determinedly downbeat—but it still has an impact, thanks largely to fine performances by Steiger, Geraldine Fitzgerald [2316], Brock Peters, Jaime Sanchez, Thelma Oliver, Juano Hernandez, and Raymond St. Jacques. It's at least as good as most of the year's best picture nominees—*Darling, Doctor Zhivago, Ship of Fools,* and *A Thousand Clowns*—and it seems to be taking place in an entirely different part of the galaxy from the winner, *The Sound of Music.* Sidney Lumet [561 . . .] directed, the cinematography is by Boris Kaufman [119 . . .], and the score is by Quincy Jones [144 . . .]. Steiger, who gives one of his best performances, lost to Lee Marvin in *Cat Ballou.*

Steiger: 992, 1477.

1544 • PEDESTRIAN, THE

ALFA GLARUS-MFG-SEITZ-ZEV BRAUN PRODUCTION (FEDERAL REPUBLIC OF GERMANY). 1973.
NOMINATION *Foreign Language Film.*

A German industrialist is accused by a newspaper of war crimes committed in Greece in 1943. As his case is debated on TV, his guilt is linked to more contemporary events such as the war in Vietnam. Rather pretentious and muddled film, written and directed by Maximilian Schell [1065 . . .]. Many critics found it highly provocative, but one suspects that the film's country of origin made them receptive to its too-sweeping theme of collective guilt. Schell also appears in the film, and Peggy Ashcroft [1533], Elisabeth Bergner [622], and Françoise Rosay make cameo appearances. The Oscar went to *Day for Night.*

1545 • PEGGY SUE GOT MARRIED

RASTAR PRODUCTIONS; TRI-STAR. 1986.
NOMINATIONS *Actress:* Kathleen Turner. *Cinematography:* Jordan Cronenweth. *Costume Design:* Theadora Van Runkle.

At her twenty-fifth high school class reunion, Turner, who's about to break up with her husband (Nicolas Cage) and is depressed by what she and her classmates have become, gets knocked unconscious and transported back to her senior year—with a chance to set things on a different course. Amusing and occasionally poignant fantasy-comedy-drama that needs a better script to succeed, especially since *Back to the Future* had covered the same ground with more wit and ingenuity a year earlier. The characters need to be a lot sharper, and there's too much fooling around when it comes to getting Turner back to the future. Francis Coppola [65 . . .] directs a cast that includes Barry Miller, Catherine Hicks, Jim Carrey, Lisa Jane Persky, Barbara Harris [2275], Don Murray [314], Maureen O'Sullivan, Leon Ames, Helen Hunt, and John Carradine.

This is the sole nomination for Turner, who leaped

to stardom with a sizzling performance in her debut film, *Body Heat* (1981), and solidified her presence in films with *Romancing the Stone* and *Prizzi's Honor*. She lost to Marlee Matlin in *Children of a Lesser God*.

Cronenweth, whose credits include such visually impressive films as *Altered States* and *Blade Runner*, lost to Chris Menges for *The Mission*. The costuming Oscar went to Jenny Beaven and John Bright for *A Room With a View*.

Van Runkle: 255, 785.

1546 • PELLE THE CONQUEROR

PER HOLST / KAERNE FILMS PRODUCTION; MIRAMAX FILMS (DENMARK). 1988.
AWARD *Foreign Language Film.*
NOMINATION *Actor:* Max von Sydow.

Von Sydow plays a widowed Swedish farmer who takes his young son, Pelle, to Denmark in search of a better life. But he is cruelly treated by his employers, and Pelle, who is bullied by the locals, decides to seek a better life elsewhere on his own. Moving adaptation by director-screenwriter Bille August of a portion of an epic-length novel by Martin Andersen Nexo.

Von Sydow is one of Sweden's most acclaimed actors, known throughout the world for his work for Ingmar Bergman [111 . . .] in such films as *The Seventh Seal* (1957), *Wild Strawberries, The Magician* (1958), *The Virgin Spring,* and many others. He has also had an astonishingly successful international career, appearing in such American movies as *The Greatest Story Ever Told, Hawaii, The Exorcist, Three Days of the Condor,* and *Hannah and Her Sisters,* among many others, so it's a bit of a surprise to find that this is his only Oscar nomination. He lost to Dustin Hoffman in *Rain Man.*

1547 • PENNIES FROM HEAVEN

COLUMBIA. 1936.
NOMINATION *Song:* "Pennies From Heaven," music by Arthur Johnston, lyrics by Johnny Burke.

Sent to jail by mistake, Bing Crosby [173 . . .] promises a fellow inmate he'll look up his family when he gets out, which leads him to little Edith Fellows and her grandfather, Donald Meek, whom he

aids. Very pedestrian musical, directed by Norman Z. McLeod, depending heavily on the charm of its star and performances by Louis Armstrong and Lionel Hampton. The song is a classic, but the movie isn't. The Oscar went to Jerome Kern and Dorothy Fields for "The Way You Look Tonight," from *Swing Time.*

Burke: 171, 173, 787, 1691.

1548 • PENNIES FROM HEAVEN

METRO-GOLDWYN-MAYER / HERBERT ROSS / HERA PRODUCTION; MGM. 1981.
NOMINATIONS *Screenplay Based on Material From Another Medium:* Dennis Potter. *Sound:* Michael J. Kohut, Jay M. Harding, Richard Tyler, and Al Overton. *Costume Design:* Bob Mackie.

Steve Martin plays a Depression-era traveling salesman who has a frigid wife (Jessica Harper); he seduces a small-town schoolteacher (Bernadette Peters). Astonishing blend of Dreiseresque tragic realism with musical comedy—the hopes and desires of the characters are all expressed in fantasy re-creations of movie musical numbers. For example, Martin and Peters go to the movies to see *Follow the Fleet* and wind up joining in the great Astaire-Rogers number "Let's Face the Music and Dance." Still more astonishing, Martin is a terrific dancer. The movie almost works, thanks to its principals, which also include Christopher Walken [521] as a sleazy pimp; he brings down the house with a high-energy song-and-dance number. The cinematography of Gordon Willis [786 . . .] and the brilliant period re-creations—including some impressive stagings based on Edward Hopper paintings—of production designer Ken Adam [12.5 . . .] are also first-rate. Unfortunately director Herbert Ross [2152] can't find the right tone for the nonmusical sections, so the film loses the ironic lift the musical numbers give it. Audiences, expecting another Steve Martin put-on like his previous movie, *The Jerk* (1979), didn't know when, whether, or how to laugh, and the movie was a huge box-office flop.

The film is based on a critically acclaimed six-part British TV series written by Potter, which starred Bob Hoskins [1343] in the Martin role. Potter subsequently wrote another well-received series, *The Sing-*

ing Detective, which, like *Pennies From Heaven,* has been shown on American public TV. Potter's other screenplays include *Gorky Park* (1983) and *Dreamchild* (1985). The Oscar went to Ernest Thompson for *On Golden Pond.* The award for sound went to *Raiders of the Lost Ark.* Milena Canonero won the costuming Oscar for *Chariots of Fire.*

Kohut: 641, 1310, 1711, 2124, 2165, 2231. Harding: 641. Tyler: 215, 1824, 1877. Overton: 215, 540, 544, 606. Mackie: 738, 1126.

1549 • PENNY SERENADE

COLUMBIA. 1941.

NOMINATION *Actor:* Cary Grant.

Grant and Irene Dunne [114 . . .] play a childless couple who adopt a baby after Dunne miscarries. But the child dies when it's six years old. Classic heartbreaker, directed by George Stevens [542 . . .] from a screenplay by Morrie Ryskind [1401 . . .]. A film that some find intensely moving and others find merely exploitive. It earned Grant the first of his two Oscar nominations, both of them for "serious" roles. He deserved to be recognized instead for such movies as *The Awful Truth, Bringing Up Baby* (1938), *Holiday, Gunga Din, Only Angels Have Wings, His Girl Friday* (1940), *The Philadelphia Story, Notorious, An Affair to Remember, North by Northwest, Operation Petticoat, That Touch of Mink,* and *Charade.* Does any actor in the history of movies have a better filmography? This time the Oscar went to Gary Cooper for *Sergeant York.*

Grant: 1445.

1550 • PEPE

G.S.-POSA FILMS INTERNATIONAL PRODUCTION; COLUMBIA. 1960.

NOMINATIONS *Color Cinematography:* Joe MacDonald. *Color Art Direction–Set Decoration:* Ted Haworth; William Kiernan. *Sound:* Charles Rice, sound director, Columbia Studio Sound Department. *Song:* "Faraway Part of Town," music by André Previn, lyrics by Dory Langdon. *Scoring of a Musical Picture:* Johnny Green. *Film Editing:* Viola Lawrence and Al Clark. *Color Costume Design:* Edith Head.

When the magnificent horse he has raised gets bought by director Dan Dailey [2258], Pepe, a Mexican peasant played by Cantinflas, journeys to Hollywood to persuade Dailey that he should be hired to take care of it. Boring three-hour musical fiasco of the bigger-is-better school, directed by George Sidney. The main plot, such as it is, is carried on by characters played by Shirley Jones [609], Ernie Kovacs, William Demarest [1058], and others. But the film's gimmick is that Pepe has supposedly hilarious encounters with movie stars, including Maurice Chevalier [203 . . .], Bing Crosby [173 . . .], Charles Coburn [535 . . .], Tony Curtis [522], Bobby Darin [350], Sammy Davis, Jr., Jimmy Durante, Zsa Zsa Gabor, Greer Garson [239 . . .], Janet Leigh [1632], Jack Lemmon [91 . . .], Kim Novak, Donna Reed [732], Debbie Reynolds [2184], Edward G. Robinson, and Frank Sinatra [732 . . .]. Without them, *Pepe* would be unwatchable; with them, it's merely tedious.

When a major studio sinks as much talent as Columbia did into something that turns out to be a turkey, the Academy has often felt compelled to hand out consolatory nominations. *Spartacus* won the Oscars for Russell Metty's cinematography, for art direction, and for Valles and Bill Thomas' costumes. *The Alamo* took the award for sound. The best song was Manos Hadjidakis' title tune for *Never on Sunday.* Morris Stoloff and Harry Sukman won the scoring award for *Song Without End.* And Daniel Mandell took the editing Oscar for *The Apartment.*

MacDonald: 1753, 2336. Haworth: 1201, 1283, 1763, 1860, 2247. Kiernan: 1133, 1521, 1753, 1858, 2238. Rice: 320. Previn: 172, 609, 769, 1017, 1034, 1044, 1097, 1393, 1592, 2064, 2077, 2161. Langdon: 1926, 2161. Green: 66, 320, 594, 662, 817, 914, 1298, 1471, 1657, 2047, 2244. Lawrence: 1521. Clark: 53, 114, 456, 1370. Head: 31, 32, 46, 305, 357, 363, 612, 636, 675, 736, 832, 894, 945, 1003, 1219, 1261, 1263, 1398, 1427, 1504, 1579, 1587, 1631, 1716, 1727, 1738, 1748, 1840, 1927, 1986, 2012, 2098, 2247, 2298.

1551 • PERILS OF PAULINE, THE

PARAMOUNT. 1947.
NOMINATION Song: "I Wish I Didn't Love You So," music and lyrics by Frank Loesser.

Betty Hutton plays Pearl White, the star of the silent-movie cliff-hanger serials, and in addition to John Lund, Billy De Wolfe, Constance Collier, and William Demarest [1058], the cast includes many veterans of the golden age of slapstick, such as William Farnum, Snub Pollard, Chester Coklin, and Hank Mann. Unfortunately the re-creations of the old routines, directed by George Marshall, are pale and awkward copies of the real thing. Still, it's an interesting nostalgia piece, and the songs *are* by Loesser. The Oscar, however, went to Allie Wrubel and Ray Gilbert for "Zip-A-Dee-Doo-Dah," from *Song of the South.*

Loesser: 864, 1131, 1422, 2026.

1552 • PERIOD OF ADJUSTMENT

MARTEN PRODUCTION; MGM. 1962.
NOMINATION *Black-and-White Art Direction—Set Decoration:* George W. Davis and Edward Carfagno; Henry Grace and Dick Pefferle.

Newlyweds Jane Fonda [394 . . .] and Jim Hutton try to help an older married couple, Tony Franciosa [880] and Lois Nettleton, who are having problems because of Franciosa's sexual dysfunction. Interesting comedy adapted by Isobel Lennart [1216 . . .] from an uncharacteristic work by Tennessee Williams [119 . . .]. Notable chiefly for the film directing debut of George Roy Hill [317 . . .] and as one of Fonda's earliest films. The cast includes John McGiver and Jack Albertson [1954]. The art direction Oscar went to *To Kill a Mockingbird.*

Davis: 46, 69, 401, 495, 542, 736, 953, 1213, 1335, 1388, 1537, 1706, 1814, 2157, 2184, 2312. Carfagno: 130, 175, 629, 917, 1069, 1644, 1814, 1937, 2312. Grace: 69, 227, 401, 769, 953, 1335, 1388, 1450, 1537, 2157, 2184, 2312. Pefferle: 87, 1096, 1157, 1230, 2312.

1553 • PERRI

WALT DISNEY PRODUCTIONS; BUENA VISTA. 1957.
NOMINATION *Score:* Paul Smith.

A young squirrel learns to survive in the wilderness in this interesting blend of live-action animal footage with studio backgrounds; it features an impressive dream sequence with animation by Ub Iwerks [211], Peter Ellenshaw [166 . . .], and Joshua Meador. *Perri* was based on a book by Felix Salten, making it a sort of live-action companion to *Bambi.* The scoring Oscar went to Malcolm Arnold for *The Bridge on the River Kwai.*

Smith: 402, 1576, 1745, 1851, 1871, 2071, 2202.

1554 • PETE KELLY'S BLUES

MARK VII LTD. PRODUCTION; WARNER BROS. 1955.
NOMINATION *Supporting Actress:* Peggy Lee.

Bandleader Kelly (Jack Webb) gets involved with gangsters in the twenties, giving in to pressure from mob boss Edmond O'Brien [146 . . .] and hiring the boss' girlfriend (Lee) as a singer. Eventually Lee provides the evidence Kelly needs to bring the boss down. The music, featuring singers Lee and Ella Fitzgerald, is the best thing about this otherwise rather routine drama. Webb, who had made a fortune from his *Dragnet* TV series, also produced and directed the film, which has an interesting cast: Janet Leigh [1632], Andy Devine, Lee Marvin [371], Martin Milner, and, in her first appearance, Jayne Mansfield. Too bad the screenplay, by Richard L. Breen [350 . . .], doesn't give them anything interesting to do.

Lee began her singing career as a teenager in her native North Dakota and was barely into her twenties when she became the lead singer for the Benny Goodman Orchestra. She made appearances as a singer in two films before taking on a dramatic role in the 1950 remake of *The Jazz Singer. Pete Kelly's Blues* is her only other acting role. She also wrote the lyrics to melodies by Sonny Burke for the films *Tom Thumb* and *Lady and the Tramp* (1955). She provided several character voices in the latter film, which is, remarkably, one of the few major Disney animated features to receive no notice from the Academy. After the great success of the videotape release of *Lady and the Tramp,* Lee sued

Disney because she had not shared in the enormous profits of the video. She lost her one Oscar nomination to Jo Van Fleet in *East of Eden*.

1555 • *PETE 'N' TILLIE*

UNIVERSAL-MARTIN RITT-JULIUS J. EPSTEIN PRODUCTION; UNIVERSAL. 1972.

NOMINATIONS *Supporting Actress:* Geraldine Page. *Screenplay—Based on Material From Another Medium:* Julius J. Epstein.

Pete, played by Walter Matthau [709 . . .], is a shambling bachelor who uses his humor as a defense mechanism. Somehow he and Tillie (Carol Burnett) get together and marry, but the death of their young son drives them apart again. Bittersweet but rather confused drama that's a lot better when Matthau and Burnett are allowed to be funny. Director Martin Ritt [956] has apparently encouraged Burnett to underplay, which is a waste of resources. The cast also includes René Auberjonois, Barry Nelson, Henry Jones, and Kent Smith. Page, who has some good moments in an underdeveloped role as Burnett's bitchy friend, lost to Eileen Heckart in *Butterflies Are Free*. Epstein's screenplay, based on the novel *Witch's Milk,* by Peter de Vries, lost to Francis Ford Coppola and Mario Puzo's for *The Godfather*.

Page: 935, 1005, 1591, 1959, 1985, 2142, 2341. Epstein: 365, 712, 1687.

1556 • *PETER IBBETSON*

PARAMOUNT. 1935.

NOMINATION *Score:* Paramount Studio Music Department, Irvin Talbot, head; score by Ernst Toch.

Gary Cooper [701 . . .] and Ann Harding [927], who were childhood sweethearts, meet as adults, but she's married. Then Cooper's imprisoned for murdering her husband and she dies—but comes back to visit him from heaven, where they are finally united. Exceedingly strange fantasy that counted among its admirers the surrealist-minded Luis Buñuel [549 . . .]. Directed by Henry Hathaway [1194] from a screenplay by Vincent Lawrence, Waldemar Young [1194], and Constance Collier, based on a novel by George du Maurier. The cinematography by

Charles Lang [97 . . .] is exceptional. The scoring Oscar went to Max Steiner for *The Informer*.

Toch: 13, 1115.

1557 • *PETE'S DRAGON*

WALT DISNEY PRODUCTIONS; BUENA VISTA. 1977.

NOMINATIONS *Original Song:* "Candle on the Water," music and lyrics by Al Kasha and Joel Hirschhorn. *Original Song Score and Its Adaptation or Adaptation Score:* Al Kasha, Joel Hirschhorn, and Irwin Kostal.

Elliott, a thirty-foot-tall invisible dragon, is the only friend that the orphaned Pete (Sean Marshall) has, until the dragon helps Pete run away from his cold and greedy foster parents, played by Shelley Winters [542 . . .] and Charles Tyner. Pete is befriended by a lighthouse keeper, played by Mickey Rooney [115 . . .], and his daughter, Helen Reddy. And the well-meaning but rather klutzy Elliott helps foil the villains. Dull, silly musical, a misbegotten attempt to make another *Mary Poppins*–style smash, but without the wit or style of that film. The cast also includes Jim Dale, Red Buttons [1763], and Jim Backus, but everyone either overacts or (in the case of Reddy) can't act. The animated-cartoon dragon is the only redeeming element. The song award went to Joseph Brooks for the title tune from *You Light Up My Life*. Jonathan Tunick won the scoring award for *A Little Night Music*. (If you want a date for the death of the movie musical, 1977 might be it.)

Kasha: 1596, 2126. Hirschhorn: 1596, 2126. Kostal: 166, 1284, 1881, 2244.

1558 • *PEYTON PLACE*

JERRY WALD PRODUCTIONS INC.; 20TH CENTURY-FOX. 1957.

NOMINATIONS *Picture:* Jerry Wald, producer. *Actress:* Lana Turner. *Supporting Actor:* Arthur Kennedy. *Supporting Actor:* Russ Tamblyn. *Supporting Actress:* Hope Lange. *Supporting Actress:* Diane Varsi. *Director:* Mark Robson. *Screenplay—Based on Material From Another Medium:* John Michael Hayes. *Cinematography:* William Mellor.

Turner plays Constance MacKenzie, whose daughter, Allison (Varsi), is scandalized when Mom takes up with the sexy outsider Michael Rossi (Lee Philips).

Lange plays Allison's friend Selena Cross, the nice girl from the wrong side of the tracks, and Kennedy is Selena's abusive stepfather. The tangled passions of adolescence and middle age seem to ensnare everyone in this scenic little New England hamlet—Peyton Place is probably just over the hill from Grovers Corners, the scene of *Our Town,* but the two villages seem to be in different universes. Hayes' adaptation of Grace Metalious' tawdry best-seller becomes a surprisingly good—or at least extremely entertaining— movie. While toeing the line drawn by the censors, the film gets away with murder, as well as incest and miscellaneous promiscuity. It may just be the quintessential fifties film: It shows the randy dopiness of the sixties bottled up within the smug small-town family values. (Not surprisingly, the movie inspired a hugely popular prime-time TV soap opera in the sixties.) Though the film is set in the pre–World War II thirties, nothing about fashions or hairstyles, especially Turner's, clues you in to that. The very attractive cast also includes Lloyd Nolan, Terry Moore [425], David Nelson, Betty Field, Mildred Dunnock [119 . . .], Leon Ames, and Lorne Greene.

The best picture Oscar went to *The Bridge on the River Kwai,* which also won for David Lean's direction, Pierre Boulle's (actually Carl Foreman and Michael Wilson's) screenplay, and Jack Hildyard's cinematography.

Turner, legendarily "discovered" when she was a sixteen-year-old Hollywood High School student, began as a bit player and was gradually molded into a star by MGM. Never taken seriously as an actress, she was nevertheless convincing in an endless series of tough-lady roles, the most memorable of which was the classic 1946 film noir, *The Postman Always Rings Twice.* Her Oscar nomination, in her twentieth year in the movies, is as much a recognition of her position as a survivor as anything else. Countless other attractive women had undergone the star-making treatment— Lizabeth Scott, Veronica Lake, Arlene Dahl, Rhonda Fleming, Yvonne DeCarlo—but none of these would-be glamour queens had careers that equaled Turner's. Even scandal—the headline-making murder of her lover, Johnny Stompanato, by her daughter, Cheryl

Crane, in 1958—couldn't derail her career, although eventually age would do so. She was last seen on the movie screen in 1978's *Witches' Brew.* She lost the Oscar to Joanne Woodward in *The Three Faces of Eve.*

Kennedy and Tamblyn, who plays Norman Page, lost to Red Buttons in *Sayonara.* Lange and Varsi lost to Buttons' costar, Miyoshi Umeki.

Wald: 1052, 1319, 1875. Kennedy: 291, 380, 1859, 2139. Robson: 1001. Hayes: 1669. Mellor: 542, 833, 1579.

1559 • PHAEDRA

Jules Dassin-Melinafilm Production; Lopert Pictures Corporation (U.S./Greece). 1962.
Nomination *Black-and-White Costume Design:* Denny Vachlioti.

Melina Mercouri [1462], the second wife of shipping tycoon Raf Vallone, runs away with his son, Anthony Perkins [730], in this updated version of the tragedy by Euripides. Enjoyable for the soap operatics, but undermined by pretentiousness and bad casting. Written and directed by Jules Dassin [1426]. The Oscar went to Norma Koch for *What Ever Happened to Baby Jane?*

Vachlioti: 1426.

1560 • PHANTOM OF THE OPERA, THE

Universal. 1943.
Awards *Color Cinematography:* Hal Mohr and W. Howard Greene. *Color Interior Decoration:* Alexander Golitzen and John B. Goodman, art direction; Russell A. Gausman and Ira S. Webb, set decoration.
Nominations *Sound Recording:* Bernard B. Brown. *Scoring of a Musical Picture:* Edward Ward.

Disfigured by acid, composer Claude Rains [365 . . .] takes refuge in the vaults beneath the Paris Opera and manipulates the career of singer Susanna Foster while menacing Miles Mander, Nelson Eddy, Hume Cronyn [1791], and others. Gaston Leroux's old chestnut achieved film fame with the 1925 Lon Chaney version, and the remakes keep coming: in 1962 with Herbert Lom, for TV in 1983 with Maximilian Schell [1065 . . .], for the big screen again in 1989 with Robert Englund of the *Nightmare* on *Elm Street* series, for TV again in 1990 with Charles Dance. The Andrew Lloyd Webber [1044] stage musical version will no doubt be filmed eventually. They're all, except the Chaney original, pretty awful, with long dull stretches between the moments of horror: the scarring, the chandelier's fall, the unmasking. This one has moments of comic byplay between Foster's rival suitors, and high-camp operatic pastiches, based on themes from Tchaikovsky and Chopin, that rival Susan Alexander Kane's operatic debut in *Citizen Kane* for dreadfulness. In other words, it's watchable for all the wrong reasons. To their credit, Mohr, Greene, and the design team make all this nonsense look extremely good. Midwar economies had made many studios cut back on color productions, but Universal went all out for this one. Still, though the studio has a reputation for its horror films, it's the low-budget black-and-white ones that we remember most fondly.

The sound award went to *This Land Is Mine*. The scoring Oscar was won by Ray Heindorf for *This Is the Army*.

Mohr: 718, 1315. Greene: 96, 239, 747, 1070, 1452, 1621, 1909, 2262. Golitzen: 31, 96, 414, 591, 690, 706, 744, 1886, 1968, 1986, 2035, 2064, 2101. Goodman: 414, 979, 1895. Gausman: 96, 414, 681, 1572, 1886, 1895. Webb: 96, 414. Brown: 93, 96, 269, 919, 1010, 1011, 1125, 1896, 2028, 2260. Ward: 47, 388, 694, 1270, 2002.

1561 • *PHANTOM OF THE PARADISE*

HARBOR PRODUCTIONS; 20TH CENTURY-FOX. 1974.

NOMINATION *Scoring—Original Song Score and/or Adaptation:* Paul Williams and George Aliceson Tipton.

Songwriter William Finley is framed by a demonic record producer (Williams), who steals Finley's songs. Finley escapes from prison to take his revenge on Williams but is accidentally disfigured when he gets his head caught in a record-pressing machine. So he becomes the Phantom who haunts the Paradise, the Fillmore-style rock arena that's Williams' latest project. Finley also falls in love with Williams' new star, Jessica Harper. Lively, witty, anything-goes parody of *The Phantom of the Opera,* written and directed

by Brian De Palma. Gerrit Graham is particularly good as the vain, zonked glitter-rock star ''Beef.'' The production designer is Jack Fisk, who was assisted by his wife, Sissy Spacek [364 . . .]. The scoring Oscar went to Nelson Riddle for *The Great Gatsby*.

Williams: 309, 403, 1375, 1911.

1562 • *PHARAOH*

KADR FILM UNIT PRODUCTION (POLAND). 1966.

NOMINATION *Foreign Language Film.*

Prince Rameses, who later becomes Rameses III, battles the high priest Herihor in this intriguing historical epic, a genre one thinks of as purely Hollywood. It's interesting to see it done without superstar actors and expensive special effects. Directed by Jerzy Kawalerowicz. The Oscar went to *A Man and a Woman*.

1562.5 • *PHILADELPHIA*

TRISTAR PICTURES PRODUCTION; TRISTAR. 1993.

AWARDS *Actor:* Tom Hanks. *Song:* ''Streets of Philadelphia,'' music and lyrics by Bruce Springsteen.

NOMINATIONS *Screenplay Written Directly for the Screen:* Ron Nyswaner. *Makeup:* Carl Fullerton and Alan D'Angerio. *Song:* ''Philadelphia,'' music and lyrics by Neil Young.

Lawyer Andrew Beckett (Hanks) is fired by his firm when they discover he has AIDS. When Beckett tries to sue for wrongful termination, no other reputable Philadelphia firm will take the case, so Beckett turns to Joe Miller, an ambulance-chaser played by Denzel Washington [471 . . .]. The homophobic Miller at first doesn't want to take the case, but he's intrigued by the thought of facing down the Establishment fat cats, and witnessing the prejudice against Beckett stirs something in Miller, who is black. Hollywood's first big-star, big-budget film about AIDS is solidly and occasionally imaginatively directed by Jonathan Demme [1820] and brilliantly performed by Hanks and Washington, and it was a box-office success. But many critics likened it to *Guess Who's Coming to Dinner,* another big-name project on a ''controversial'' topic that set out to educate its audiences and pulled some of its punches to do so. Some gays found

Philadelphia's portrait of the relationship between Beckett and his lover (Antonio Banderas) overcautious. And some accused Demme of making the film to ease his conscience for having made a presumably gay man the villain in *The Silence of the Lambs*. *Philadelphia* is certainly guilty of oversimplification and sentimentality: It sets up Beckett as a paragon and his chief adversary, the senior partner of the firm, as a hissable villain—played in his most narrow-eyed style by Jason Robards [54 . . .]—and Beckett's gushingly supportive family sometimes stretches credulity. But there's nothing in *Guess Who's Coming to Dinner* as daring as the scene in which Beckett demonstrates his love of life by explicating the aria "La Mamma Morta," sung by Maria Callas. The cast also includes Mary Steenburgen [1300] as the attorney who opposes Miller in court and Joanne Woodward [1365 . . .] as Beckett's mother. The cinematography is by Demme's frequent collaborator Tak Fujimoto.

After his nomination for *Big*, Hanks' career stalled a bit. *Turner and Hooch* (1989), *The Burbs* (1989), and *Joe Versus the Volcano* (1990) were unworthy of his talents, and *The Bonfire of the Vanities* (1990) was a notorious disaster. Hanks was absent from the screen for two years after *Bonfire*, returning in a supporting role as the overweight, tobacco-chewing coach of a women's baseball team in *A League of Their Own*, a hit that revived his screen career. In the summer before *Philadelphia* he was also praised for his performance in the romantic comedy *Sleepless in Seattle*. Hanks is often compared to Jack Lemmon [91 . . .] for his ability to play light comedy and serious dramatic roles with equal finesse. At the Oscars, Hanks delivered a deeply felt acceptance speech, paying tribute not only to his coworkers but also to the people who have died from AIDS.

Springsteen, one of rock music's superstars, had never composed a song for the movies before, but both the film's subject matter and Demme's considerable reputation for intelligent and imaginative use of music in his movies persuaded him—as well as fellow rock artists Young and Peter Gabriel—to contribute to a distinguished song score. Springsteen's gentle,

elegiac song about loss sets the tone of the film effectively. Both Springsteen and Young gave eloquent performances of their songs at the Oscar ceremonies.

Nyswaner, who is gay, was the focus of much of the criticism from the gay community, articulated in a widely published article by writer Larry Kramer [2307]. He lost to Jane Campion for *The Piano*. The makeup Oscar went to *Mrs. Doubtfire*.

Hanks: 195, 708.5. Fullerton: 1680.

1563 • *PHILADELPHIA STORY, THE*

MGM. 1940.

AWARDS *Actor:* James Stewart. *Screenplay:* Donald Ogden Stewart.

NOMINATIONS *Picture:* Joseph L. Mankiewicz, producer. *Actress:* Katharine Hepburn. *Supporting Actress:* Ruth Hussey. *Director:* George Cukor.

Tracy Lord (Hepburn) is about to marry stuffy George Kittredge (John Howard). But then Tracy's ex-husband, C. K. Dexter Haven, played by Cary Grant [1445 . . .], shows up. And *Spy* magazine editor Sidney Kidd (Henry Daniell) has sent a reporter, Mike Connor (Stewart), and photographer, Liz Imbrie (Hussey), to cover the wedding, in the hope they'll also uncover some dirt about Tracy's father (John Halliday), who's been having an affair with a showgirl. The brittle, unforgiving Tracy is irked by Dexter's presence, but she finds Mike intriguing, especially when she discovers that he's a fiction writer who works for *Spy* only to pay the bills. After a little too much champagne at the party the night before the wedding, she and Mike slip off for a moonlight swim. Suddenly the goddesslike Tracy is a mortal woman confronted with three men: the one she used to love, Dexter; the one she says she loves, George; and the one she thinks she now loves, Mike. One of the most professionally made romantic comedies ever to come out of Hollywood, a tribute to taste and talent—particularly that of Mankiewicz, Cukor, and Donald Ogden Stewart—and the star system at its most efficient. There are also fine performances by Roland Young [2117] as lecherous Uncle Willie, Virginia Weidler as kid sister Dinah, and Mary Nash as the somewhat distracted Mrs. Lord. It's one of the few adaptations of a Broadway hit that don't seem awkwardly "opened up" or too cramped and talky for the screen. Philip Barry had written the play for—and with—Hepburn, turning what had often seemed like her weaknesses—artificiality and condescension—into integral parts of the character, and then allowing her to transcend them at the end. She had bought the rights to the play and used it to revive her screen career, which had stalled.

James Stewart's Oscar is thought to have been at least partly for his performance in *Mr. Smith Goes to Washington* the previous year, when he lost to Robert Donat in *Goodbye, Mr. Chips.* One of the legendary figures of the screen, Stewart started acting at Princeton and joined a company formed by his classmate Joshua Logan [643 . . .] that did summer stock and included Henry Fonda [815 . . .] and Margaret Sullavan [2073]. After some work on Broadway, he came to Hollywood, where Sullavan, who had already established her career, was instrumental in getting him started. He made his first appearance in 1935's *The Murder Man* and soon became an MGM contract player. But it was his work for Frank Capra at Columbia, *You Can't Take It With You* and *Mr. Smith Goes to Washington,* that made Stewart a major star. His career was interrupted soon after the Oscar by distinguished wartime service. When he returned to the screen in 1947, it was in Capra's *It's a Wonderful Life,* one of his most famous roles.

Donald Ogden Stewart was a logical choice to adapt Philip Barry's play for the screen: He and Barry had been classmates at Yale. Barry wrote the role of Nick Potter in *Holiday* with Stewart in mind, and Stewart played the part on Broadway and later adapted the play for the screen. Finding success as a humorist, Stewart migrated to Hollywood in 1930 at the advent of sound and worked on the screenplays of such films as *Smilin' Through, Dinner at Eight* (1934), *The Barretts of Wimpole Street, The Prisoner of Zenda, Marie Antoinette,* and *Love Affair.* Though known largely for his witty, sophisticated dialogue, in the thirties Stewart, born to privilege, developed a social conscience and joined several leftist organizations. During the era of the House Un-American Activities

Committee investigations into communism in Hollywood, Stewart was blacklisted. He chose exile in London, where he lived until his death in 1980.

The best picture Oscar went to *Rebecca.* Hepburn lost to Ginger Rogers in *Kitty Foyle.* The supporting actress award went to Jane Darwell for *The Grapes of Wrath,* for which John Ford received the directing Oscar.

J. Stewart: 73, 876, 1033, 1370. D. O. Stewart: 1148. Mankiewicz: 46, 146, 673, 1163, 1444, 1836, 1841. Hepburn: 24, 40, 843, 1177, 1199, 1357, 1473, 1654, 1956, 1963, 2305. Cukor: 262, 567, 1189, 1393.

1563.5 • PIANO, THE

JAN CHAPMAN & CIBY 2000 PRODUCTION; MIRAMAX FILMS (AUSTRALIA/FRANCE). 1993.

AWARDS *Actress:* Holly Hunter. *Supporting Actress:* Anna Paquin. *Screenplay Written Directly for the Screen:* Jane Campion.

NOMINATIONS *Picture:* Jan Chapman, producer. *Director:* Jane Campion. *Cinematography:* Stuart Dryburgh. *Costume Design:* Janet Patterson. *Film Editing:* Veronika Jenet.

Ada (Hunter) and her daughter, Flora (Paquin), arrive from Scotland at a remote spot on the New Zealand coast, where Ada has agreed to an arranged marriage with the settler Stewart (Sam Neill). Ada, who is mute, has brought her most prized possession: a piano. But Stewart balks at the prospect of carting the instrument home and leaves it to ruin on the beach. However, a neighbor, Baines, played by Harvey Keitel [308], hauls it to his own home and invites Ada over to play it. Gradually they strike a bargain: He'll allow her to buy back the piano—a bit at a time—by granting him small, but increasingly larger, intimacies. A provocative, enigmatic fable that became one of the most talked-about movies of the year, winning widespread critical acclaim and numerous awards, including the top prize at the Cannes Festival. There were some who felt *The Piano* was a little too enigmatic for its own good—that the sum of its very intriguing parts was not great. But it was the major competitor against *Schindler's List* for the top Oscars, and some thought that Campion might deprive Steven Spielberg of the best director Oscar, especially after the New York and Los Angeles critics passed him over and gave her their award, even though they named *Schindler's List* best picture. There was also much comment when the Oscar nominations bypassed Michael Nyman's score, integral to the texture of the film.

Above all, the film was a triumph for Hunter, who speaks only in voice-overs. Born in Georgia, Hunter made a few appearances in films in the early eighties but shot to stardom in 1987 when she was cast in *Broadcast News* and the eccentric comedy *Raising Arizona*. But Hunter didn't fit any established Hollywood types: She was no sexy romantic heroine, tough action-adventure foil, or high-toned leading lady, so her career seemed to go nowhere for a while. Spielberg cast her in *Always,* his 1989 remake of *A Guy Named Joe,* but it bombed. Like many actresses unable to find movie roles, Hunter accepted TV movies and managed to find some good ones, winning Emmys for *Roe vs. Wade* (1989) and *The Positively True Adventures of the Alleged Texas Cheerleader-Murdering Mom* (1993). Finally she landed two radically differing roles in major films, *The Firm* and *The Piano,* and was nominated for both. She lost her supporting actress nomination for *The Firm* to her *Piano* costar, Paquin.

At eleven Paquin is the second-youngest winner of a competitive Oscar—Tatum O'Neal was the youngest, at ten, when she won for *Paper Moon.* Campion chose Paquin for the role of the sly, inquisitive Flora over hundreds of young New Zealanders. Paquin reportedly went along with an older sister who wanted to audition and then decided to try for the part herself. At the Oscars she was something of a surprise winner over Hunter, Emma Thompson in *In the Name of the Father,* Rosie Perez in *Fearless,* and the actress who was thought to be the front-runner, Winona Ryder in *The Age of Innocence.*

Campion, born in New Zealand, made several acclaimed short films and the features *Sweetie* (1989) and *An Angel at My Table* (1990) before receiving international acclaim for *The Piano.* She became only the second woman in the history of the Oscars to be nominated as a director. (The first was Lina Wertmüller for *Seven Beauties.*) She lost that award to Steven Spielberg for *Schindler's List,* which also won for Janusz Kaminski's cinematography and Michael Kahn's editing. The award for costumes went to Gabriella Pescucci for *The Age of Innocence.*

Hunter: 293, 667.5.

1564 • PICKUP ON SOUTH STREET

20TH CENTURY-FOX. 1953.

NOMINATION *Supporting Actress:* Thelma Ritter.

Pickpocket Richard Widmark [1098] picks the wrong pocket—it contains top-secret microfilm, and the commies will stop at nothing to get it from him. Exciting, violent, paranoid thriller written and directed by cult favorite Samuel Fuller; unlike some of the Cold War Red-baiting movies, this one is more interested in shocks than politics. The cast includes Jean Peters, Richard Kiley, and Milburn Stone. Ritter, in the fourth of her six unsuccessful nominations, lost to Donna Reed in *From Here to Eternity.*

Ritter: 46, 210, 1289, 1572, 2294.

1565 • PICKWICK PAPERS, THE

RENOWN PRODUCTION; KINGSLEY INTERNATIONAL PICTURES (UNITED KINGDOM). 1955.

NOMINATION *Black-and-White Costume Design:* Beatrice Dawson.

The portly Mr. Pickwick (James Hayter), his manservant Sam Weller (Harry Fowler), and the bachelor members of the Pickwick Club set out for a series of Pickwickian adventures. Nigel Patrick plays the rascally Jingle, and James Donald is Winkle. Cheerful and amusing skim through the Dickens novel, adapted and directed by Noel Langley. Very, *very* British, and consequently not terribly successful this side of the Atlantic, though lovers of the book will be gratified by its comparative faithfulness to the text. The cast includes Donald Wolfit, Hermione Baddeley [1724], Hermione Gingold, and Joyce Grenfell. The costuming award went to Helen Rose for *I'll Cry Tomorrow.*

1566 • PICNIC

COLUMBIA. 1955.

AWARDS *Color Art Direction–Set Decoration:* William Flannery and Joe Mielziner; Robert Priestley. *Film Editing:* Charles Nelson and William A. Lyon.

NOMINATIONS *Picture:* Fred Kohlmar, producer. *Supporting Actor:* Arthur O'Connell. *Director:* Joshua Logan. *Scoring of a Dramatic or Comedy Picture:* George Duning.

Hunky drifter William Holden [1424 . . .] shows up in a small Kansas town in search of old frat brother Cliff Robertson [387] and stirs lust in local ladies of all ages, from Susan Strasberg to Verna Felton. Kim Novak's mom, Betty Field, wants her to do the proper fifties thing and marry rich boy Robertson, but at the town's Labor Day picnic, Holden's sex appeal causes the women to do strange things: Beauty queen Novak decides to run away with him, her brainy little sister Strasberg gets drunk, and old-maid schoolteacher Rosalind Russell [110 . . .] loses her cool and tricks O'Connell into marrying her. This adaptation by Daniel Taradash [732] of the play by William Inge [1894] is one of the key films for students of fifties sexual mores, but its staginess keeps it from being a really good movie. The fine cinematography is by James Wong Howe [1 . . .], and some of the second unit camera work, such as the final helicopter shot of Novak's bus following Holden's freight train, was done by the young Haskell Wexler [229 . . .]. The winning art direction (Mielziner designed the original stage production) blends location work in Salina, Kansas, with studio sets.

Picnic is the first and best (along with the contemporaneous *Bus Stop)* in a string of films directed by Logan, who had made his mark as a preeminent Broadway director with the original stage versions of *Annie Get Your Gun, Mister Roberts,* and *South Pacific.* He had worked in Hollywood in the late thirties, most notably as dialogue director on *The Garden of Allah,* but had returned to New York. His stage directing career had been interrupted twice by serious nervous breakdowns—he was diagnosed as manic-depressive. Recovering from the second of these breakdowns, he was called on by Columbia head Harry Cohn [1025 . . .] to direct the film of *Picnic,* which Logan had also directed on stage. Cohn was hoping to use the movie to boost the career of Novak, whom he was grooming as a replacement for Rita Hayworth. Logan agreed to direct if he could be given a free hand with the casting, and also tested Janice Rule, who had played the role on Broadway, and Carroll Baker [119], the suggestion of screenwriter Daniel Taradash [732]. Rule, however, did not film well, and Baker was deemed too young-looking to play opposite Holden. In the end Novak, the least gifted member of the cast, in many ways gives the most affecting performance: Her character is meant to be lovely and shallow but longing to be taken more seriously; the part fits the insecure actress perfectly. Holden was already cast when Logan signed on. He is, as Logan noted in his memoirs, too old for the part, but his sexual magnetism carries him through the role convincingly. Because Cohn wanted another marquee name in the film, Russell was signed for the part originally played on stage by Eileen Heckart [133 . . .]. Strasberg, the eighteen-year-old daughter of famous acting teachers Paula and Lee Strasberg [785], was signed to replace Kim Stanley [722 . . .], who at thirty-one was too old to play Novak's kid sister on screen. Robertson, whom Logan remembered from a Chicago production of *Mister Roberts,* makes his film debut in a role played on stage by Paul Newman [3 . . .], who had been signed by Warner Bros. (Newman met his future wife, Joanne Woodward [1365 . . .], while performing in *Picnic* on Broadway; she was an understudy to Stanley and Rule and had a smaller role.) In *Picnic* Logan has not yet learned—if indeed he ever did—that on film less is more, and as a consequence betrays many of his performers, particularly Russell and Strasberg (both of whom rarely needed encouragement in this regard), into going over the top. Scene climaxes that were powerful on stage are merely overpowering on screen when hyped with Duning's music. Logan lost to Delbert Mann for *Marty,* which also took the best picture award.

O'Connell, a reliable character actor, gives one of the best performances in the film as Russell's reluctant fiancé, re-creating his Broadway role; he lost to Jack Lemmon in *Mister Roberts.*

Duning's score produced a hit record, the melding of the film's main theme with the jazz standard "Moonglow," but lost to Alfred Newman's *Love Is a Many-Splendored Thing* score.

Priestley: 1283, 1763. Nelson: 371, 1872. Lyon: 330, 456, 732, 1058, 1776. O'Connell: 73. Logan: 643, 1763. Duning: 596, 732, 1057, 1442.

1567 • PICTURE OF DORIAN GRAY, THE

MGM. 1945.

AWARD *Black-and-White Cinematography:* Harry Stradling.

NOMINATIONS *Supporting Actress:* Angela Lansbury. *Black-and-White Interior Decoration:* Cedric Gibbons and Hans Peters, art direction; Edwin B. Willis, John Bonar, and Hugh Hunt, set decoration.

Hurd Hatfield plays Gray, a young man who descends into debauchery and vice but remains youthful. Meanwhile, however, his portrait, which he keeps locked away, grows increasingly hideous. Intelligent but occasionally heavy-handed filming of Oscar Wilde's story, with George Sanders [46] standing in for Wilde as the epigrammatic Sir Henry Wotton, Lansbury as the innocent Sibyl Vane, and Donna Reed [732] and Peter Lawford. Written and directed by Albert Lewin [799 . . .].

Stradling, born in England, came to the United States as a boy and worked as a cameraman in silent films. He began his career as a cinematographer in France, filming Jacques Feyder's celebrated *Carnival in Flanders* (1935), and worked in England before returning to Hollywood in the late thirties. In the later forties he became known as a specialist in color photography, and *The Picture of Dorian Gray* includes some Technicolor inserts. His son, Harry Stradling, Jr. [1790 . . .], has followed the same profession. The elder Stradling died in 1970.

Lansbury lost to Anne Revere in *National Velvet.* The art direction award went to *Blood on the Sun.*

Stradling: 110, 149, 596, 737, 852, 853, 864, 896, 957, 1246, 1393, 1949, 2338. Lansbury: 749, 1265. Gibbons: 66, 87, 130, 217, 227, 239, 285, 290, 440, 629, 749, 831, 980, 1069, 1096, 1173, 1190, 1226, 1230, 1232, 1274, 1308, 1309, 1417, 1604, 1644, 1662, 1673, 1721, 1861, 1937, 2068, 2112, 2256, 2257, 2300, 2320, 2330. Peters: 69, 1107, 1226, 1673. Willis: 66, 87, 130, 227, 239, 290, 629, 749, 831, 980, 1069, 1096, 1157, 1173, 1190, 1226, 1230, 1232, 1309, 1417, 1657, 1662, 1673, 1721, 1861, 1937, 2068, 2112, 2257, 2320, 2330. Hunt: 175, 401, 980, 1069, 1232, 1335, 1388, 1644, 1657, 1673, 2157, 2184.

1568 • PIECES OF DREAMS

RFB ENTERPRISES PRODUCTION; UNITED ARTISTS. 1970.

NOMINATION *Song:* "Pieces of Dreams," music by Michel Legrand, lyrics by Alan Bergman and Marilyn Bergman.

Robert Forster plays a young priest whose faith is tested when he falls in love with Lauren Hutton. Soaper that seems to have vanished from circulation, directed by Daniel Haller from a script by Roger O. Hirson, based on the novel *The Wine and the Music,* by William E. Barrett. The Oscar went to Fred Karlin, Robb Royer, and James Griffin for the song "For All We Know," from *Lovers and Other Strangers.*

Legrand: 179, 867, 1960, 2063, 2172, 2321, 2332. A. Bergman: 179, 867, 1168, 1628, 1747, 1813, 1864, 2063, 2113, 2238, 2321, 2322. M. Bergman: 179, 867, 1168, 1628, 1747, 1813, 1864, 2063, 2113, 2238, 2321, 2322.

1569 • PIED PIPER, THE

20TH CENTURY-FOX. 1942.

NOMINATIONS *Picture:* Nunnally Johnson, producer. *Actor:* Monty Woolley. *Black-and-White Cinematography:* Edward Cronjager.

Crusty, child-hating old bachelor Woolley finds himself entrusted with the safety of young Roddy McDowall and Peggy Ann Garner when war breaks out in Europe. Making their way back to England, they pick up even more children fleeing from the approaching Nazis. Anne Baxter [46 . . .] shows up to help, but then they have to contend with a Nazi officer, played by Otto Preminger [73 . . .]. Corny but entertaining. Directed by Irving Pichel from

Johnson's screenplay, based on a story by Nevil Shute. The cast also includes J. Carrol Naish [1294 . . .], Jill Esmond, and Marcel Dalio. The best picture Oscar went to *Mrs. Miniver,* which also won for Joseph Ruttenberg's cinematography.

Woolley, a Yale classmate (and some say lover) of Cole Porter [261 . . .], returned to his alma mater as an English and drama teacher, but followed his theatrical friends and students to Broadway in 1936. He won his greatest acclaim for creating the role of the lovably irascible Sheridan Whiteside in the original Broadway production of *The Man Who Came to Dinner* in 1939, and repeated the role in the 1942 film version—and indeed, in most of the characters he played on screen. He lost the first of his two Oscar nominations to James Cagney in *Yankee Doodle Dandy.*

Johnson: 815, 932. Woolley: 1828. Cronjager: 176, 400, 889, 934, 1964, 2102.

1570 • PIGEON THAT TOOK ROME, THE

LLENROC PRODUCTIONS; PARAMOUNT. 1962.

NOMINATION *Black-and-White Art Direction—Set Decoration:* Hal Pereira and Roland Anderson; Sam Comer and Frank R. McKelvy.

Undercover agent Charlton Heston [175] uses carrier pigeons to send espionage information out of Nazi-occupied Rome while wooing Elsa Martinelli. Routine comedy, written and directed by Melville Shavelson [951 . . .], with Harry Guardino, Salvatore Baccaloni, and Brian Donlevy [161]. The art direction Oscar went to *To Kill a Mockingbird.*

Pereira: 278, 357, 363, 426, 450, 736, 956, 1029, 1219, 1504, 1631, 1674, 1716, 1727, 1738, 1840, 1897, 1959, 2012, 2098, 2200, 2208. Anderson: 278, 363, 426, 450, 649, 1029, 1194, 1214, 1219, 1452, 1668, 1674, 1880, 1994. Comer: 278, 357, 426, 450, 726, 736, 925, 956, 1029, 1101, 1214, 1219, 1443, 1631, 1674, 1727, 1738, 1748, 1959, 1975, 1994, 2012, 2098, 2200, 2208. McKelvy: 591, 917, 1450, 1631, 2047, 2200.

1571 • PIGSKIN PARADE

20TH CENTURY-FOX. 1936.

NOMINATION *Supporting Actor:* Stuart Erwin.

Erwin plays Amos Dodd, a farmer who's recruited for a college football team because he can hurl melons. Silly college musical that's remembered today chiefly because of the young actress making her feature film debut as Erwin's sister: Judy Garland [1065 . . .]. The movie also features her *Wizard of Oz* costar, Jack Haley, plus Patsy Kelly, Betty Grable, Tony Martin, Elisha Cook, Jr., and, in a bit part, Alan Ladd. Though he's top-billed, Erwin became one of the first nominees in the new supporting performance category, losing to Walter Brennan in *Come and Get It.* After countless comic relief roles in major features and leads in B-movie comedy quickies, Erwin earned his chief fame as one of TV's earliest stars, in the sitcom *The Trouble With Father,* which was renamed *The Stuart Erwin Show.* He died in 1967.

1572 • PILLOW TALK

ARWIN PRODUCTIONS; UNIVERSAL-INTERNATIONAL. 1959.

AWARD *Story and Screenplay—Written Directly for the Screen:* Russell Rouse and Clarence Greene; Stanley Shapiro and Maurice Richlin.

NOMINATIONS *Actress:* Doris Day. *Supporting Actress:* Thelma Ritter. *Color Art Direction—Set Decoration:* Richard H. Riedel; Russell A. Gausman and Ruby R. Levitt. *Scoring of a Dramatic or Comedy Picture:* Frank DeVol.

Interior designer Day and womanizing songwriter Rock Hudson [768] share a telephone party line. Her attempts to dislodge him from the telephone, on which he's usually serenading a girlfriend, make them enemies—until he finds out what she looks like. Determined to add her to his conquests, he assumes the identity of a shy Texan. You know the rest. Tremendously popular comedy that's really very good in its occasionally sniggery sort of way. The director is Michael Gordon; the film marks his return to Hollywood after being blacklisted in the early fifties. The principals get fine support from Ritter as Day's perpetually hung-over housekeeper and Tony Randall as Hudson's bemused pal, and the cast also includes

Nick Adams [2157], Julia Meade, Marcel Dalio, and Lee Patrick. Day's wardrobe is by Jean Louis [20 . . .] and the cinematography is by Arthur Arling [980 . . .].

Rouse and Greene were a moderately successful directing-producing team who also collaborated on screenplays for several of their films, which include *A House Is Not a Home* and *The Oscar.* Shapiro and Richlin, who did the screenplay from Rouse and Greene's story, found themselves in the unusual position of competing against themselves—their screenplay for *Operation Petticoat* was nominated in the same category. Although *Pillow Talk* is an agreeable romantic farce, one has to question its Oscar win over some of its other competitors: Ernest Lehman's ingenious screenplay for *North by Northwest,* François Truffaut and Marcel Moussy's *The 400 Blows,* and Ingmar Bergman's *Wild Strawberries.*

Day began her career as a singer in the era of the big bands. From 1948, when she made her screen debut in *Romance on the High Seas,* she had been the star of a successful series of lightweight musicals made at Warner Bros. She also tried more serious roles, such as the singer Ruth Etting in *Love Me or Leave Me* and the mother of a kidnaped child in *The Man Who Knew Too Much. Pillow Talk* launched a new phase of her career: a string of romantic comedies that sophisticates derided as the Doris-defends-her-virginity series. In fact, Day's virginity is the central issue in only a couple of the dozen or so films that she made after *Pillow Talk.* Perhaps the concept of virginity seemed so anachronistic in the swinging sixties that Day became stereotyped in the popular imagination. The Oscar went to Simone Signoret in *Room at the Top.*

Ritter lost the fifth of her six unsuccessful nominations to Shelley Winters in *The Diary of Anne Frank.* The art direction award went to *Ben-Hur,* which also won for Miklos Rozsa's score.

Rouse: 2241. Greene: 2241. Shapiro: 1220, 1498, 2035. Richlin: 1498. Ritter: 46, 210, 1289, 1564, 2294. Gausman: 96, 414, 681, 1560, 1886, 1895. Levitt: 77, 395, 1881. DeVol: 371, 843, 963.

1573 • PINK PANTHER, THE

Mirisch-G-E-Production; United Artists. 1964.
Nomination *Music Score—Substantially Original:* Henry Mancini.

Peter Sellers [169 . . .] plays Inspector Clouseau, pursuing a mysterious jewel thief known as the Phantom whose target is the Pink Panther—a fabulous gem possessed by Princess Dala (Claudia Cardinale). The trail leads to Cortina d'Ampezzo, where David Niven [1778], Robert Wagner, and Capucine also become involved in the plot. The first of a hugely successful series that gave Sellers an indelible identity as the accident-prone detective with the impenetrable accent. In fact, Niven was the nominal lead of the film; Clouseau was meant to be a secondary character, but he proved so popular that Sellers' next vehicle, *A Shot in the Dark,* was quickly reworked to develop the Clouseau character even further. Blake Edwards [2201] directed, and also wrote the screenplay in collaboration with Maurice Richlin [1498 . . .]. The Pink Panther itself ceased to be a jewel and became a cartoon character with a life of its own, accompanied by Mancini's jaunty, pouncing theme. The scoring Oscar, however, went to Richard and Robert Sherman for *Mary Poppins.*

Mancini: 122, 278, 384, 494, 508, 512, 776, 825, 1574, 1864, 1970, 2011, 2037, 2201.

1574 • PINK PANTHER STRIKES AGAIN, THE

Amjo Productions Ltd.; United Artists. 1976.
Nomination *Original Song:* "Come to Me," music by Henry Mancini, lyrics by Don Black.

Herbert Lom plays former Chief Inspector Dreyfus of the Sûreté, who has been driven insane by previous dealings with the bumbling Inspector Clouseau, played by Peter Sellers [169 . . .]. So he hatches a fiendish plot, hiring assassins from around the world to bump off Clouseau, and abducting a famous scientist to construct a ray gun that could destroy the world. The fourth Sellers-Clouseau film—there was one, *Inspector Clouseau,* in 1968, that starred Alan Arkin [884 . . .] in the part, but it bombed—and the most extravagant. It may also be the funniest—or else the stupidest, depending on the extent of your affection for the series. Lesley-Anne Down is the Russian agent hired to dispatch Clouseau; she falls in love with him after an encounter in the dark with the Egyptian agent (Omar Sharif [1151] in a cameo) whom she mistakes—don't ask why—for Clouseau. Burt Kwouk is back as Clouseau's manservant/martial arts partner Kato. As usual, Blake Edwards [2201] directs. The nominated song is actually a throwaway parody— an overblown love song that accompanies Sellers' ludicrous wooing of Down. It lost to Barbra Streisand and Paul Williams' ''Evergreen (Love Theme from *A Star Is Born*).''

Mancini: 122, 278, 384, 494, 508, 512, 776, 825, 1573, 1864, 1970, 2011, 2037, 2201. Black: 174, 259, 789, 2147.

1575 • PINKY

20TH CENTURY-FOX. 1949.

NOMINATIONS *Actress:* Jeanne Crain. *Supporting Actress:* Ethel Barrymore. *Supporting Actress:* Ethel Waters.

Crain plays a black woman whose skin is so fair she can easily pass for white, so she goes to the North and trains as a nurse. She and a white doctor, played by William Lundigan, fall in love. But Crain, reluctant to tell him the truth about her race, returns to the South and tends an elderly white woman, Barrymore, who leaves her big old house to Crain in her will. She now faces a decision: Marry Lundigan, who has learned her secret and is willing to start a new life with her somewhere else, or remain in the South and turn the house into a clinic for blacks? Somewhat daring problem drama for its age, though *Pinky* has worn less well than other contemporary racial-conflict dramas such as *Home of the Brave, Intruder in the Dust,* and *No Way Out,* partly because of the miscasting of Crain, who is scarcely credible as Waters' granddaughter. Philip Dunne [495 . . .] and Dudley Nichols [30 . . .] based their screenplay on a novel by Cid Ricketts Sumner. Elia Kazan [63 . . .] took over as director of the film from John Ford [815 . . .], who had clashed with Waters. Kazan later found the film ''predictable and tedious.'' The cast includes Nina Mae McKinney (the dazzling Chick of *Hallelujah),* Evelyn Varden, Arthur Hunnicutt [204], and, in a small role as a nurse, Juanita Moore, who later earned her own Oscar nomination as the mother of a young woman trying to pass for white in *Imitation of Life.* The three nominations for *Pinky's* actresses reflect the power of the film's producer, Darryl F. Zanuck [34 . . .]— the far superior *Home of the Brave* and *Intruder in the Dust,* made the same year, received no attention from the Academy.

In his memoirs Kazan discreetly refrains from mentioning Crain by name while still indicating how inept he found her as an actress. Her lack of expressiveness, he said, he finally used to an advantage, contrasting her with the more volatile and skilled performers such as Waters and Barrymore, suggesting the character's position as a social outsider. Known far more as a wholesome beauty than as a dramatic actress, Crain made her film debut in *The Gang's All Here* in 1943 and became a mainstay of Fox Technicolor musicals and romantic comedies such as *Home in Indiana, State Fair,* and *Centennial Summer.* Her career faded in the mid-fifties and by the sixties was limited to Italian costume epics such as *Pontius Pilate* and *Queen of the Nile* (in which she played Nefertiti). The Oscar went to Olivia de Havilland for *The Heiress.*

Waters was the first black performer to be nominated for an acting Oscar since Hattie McDaniel won for *Gone With the Wind.* Born in poverty, she began her singing career while still in her teens and worked her way up through small-time clubs to stardom in Harlem and eventually in 1927 on Broadway. She made a few film appearances in the late twenties and early thirties, but her major Hollywood career began in 1942, with an appearance in *Tales of Manhattan,* followed by a memorable performance the following year in *Cabin in the Sky.* Her finest dramatic role was in the stage and screen versions of *Member of the Wedding.* Her last screen appearance was as Dilsey in the otherwise unfortunate film version of Faulkner's *The Sound and the Fury* (1959). She died in 1977. Waters and Barrymore lost the Oscar to Mercedes McCambridge in *All the King's Men.*

Barrymore: 1445, 1528, 1891.

1576 • PINOCCHIO

WALT DISNEY PRODUCTIONS; RKO RADIO. 1940.

AWARDS *Song:* ''When You Wish Upon a Star,'' music by Leigh Harline, lyrics by Ned Washington. *Original Score:* Leigh Harline, Paul J. Smith, and Ned Washington.

An elderly wood-carver, Geppetto, who lives alone with only a kitten named Figaro and a goldfish named Cleo as his companions, carves a puppet he names Pinocchio. A fairy hears Geppetto's wish for a son and grants Pinocchio life, with the promise that if he earns it he will one day be a real boy. And to help him along the way, she also dubs an attendant cricket, named Jiminy, Pinocchio's official conscience. First, however, Pinocchio must resist the temptations put in his way by a conniving fox and a stupid cat, survive being exploited by the evil puppet master Stromboli, endure growing donkey ears and tail when he's sent to the sinister Pleasure Island, and rescue Geppetto from the belly of the great whale Monstro. Maybe the greatest of all Disney animated cartoons, certainly one of the most beautifully drawn and richly characterized. The story is based on a book by Carlo Collodi, but as generations of lovers of the movie who have gone to the source have discovered, the original is a much darker, more satiric business: Pinocchio is a young lout, and Jiminy is an unnamed cricket whose good advice only gets him squashed with a mallet. The voices for the characters are supplied by Dickie Jones (Pinocchio), Cliff Edwards (Jiminy Cricket), Christian Rub (Geppetto), and Evelyn Venable (the Blue Fairy). Marge Champion was the figure model for the fairy.

Over the years, other filmmakers have tried to equal the success of the Disney animated features but have failed, and not for want of animating skill. The great Disney films have a way of connecting with the audience that is unsurpassed, and one of the key elements lies in their scores: Only the Astaire-Rogers musicals of the thirties produced more memorable songs, and they did it by hiring the finest songwriters of the day: Irving Berlin [34 . . .], Jerome Kern [340 . . .], and George [1797] and Ira Gershwin [455 . . .]. Disney did it with less celebrated songwriters: Harline and Washington, Frank Churchill [140 . . .] and Larry Morey [140 . . .], the Sherman brothers [166 . . .], Mack David [122 . . .], Al Hoffman [402] and Jerry Livingston [371 . . .], Terry Gilkyson [1071], and Alan Menken [32.5 . . .], Howard Ashman [32.5 . . .], and Tim Rice [32.5 . . .]. These and many other composers and lyricists produced some of the most familiar songs ever written, with the images that accompanied them on screen providing the ultimate *aide-mémoire. Pinocchio*'s song score was the first from Disney to receive recognition by the Academy. Harline was a studio veteran, having joined Disney in 1932 as an arranger and moved up to head the music department. As lyricist, Washington also has to his credits a string of Oscar-nominated songs, as well as ''I'm Gettin' Sentimental Over You'' and the theme song from the TV western *Rawhide*. But Harline and Washington are remembered best for what has become, via Cliff Edwards' ethereal falsetto, the Disney studios' theme song.

Harline: 1053, 1607, 1838, 1851, 2312, 2327. Washington: 274, 585, 911, 912, 1329, 1396, 1745, 2127, 2282, 2335. Smith: 402, 1553, 1745, 1851, 1871, 2071, 2202.

1577 • PIRATE, THE

MGM. 1948.

NOMINATION *Scoring of a Musical Picture:* Lennie Hayton.

Manuela, played by Judy Garland [1065 . . .], a young woman engaged to the portly Don Pedro (Walter Slezak), imagines the street performer Serafin, played by Gene Kelly [74], to be a notorious pirate. It turns out that the pirate is actually her unlovely fiancé. Rather thin stuff, despite all the talent lavished on it: Garland, Kelly, director Vincente Minnelli [66 . . .], and composer Cole Porter [261 . . .]. Kelly is at his most dashing and virile, but the others are off their peak form; Garland was going through a bad period psychologically, putting strain on her marriage to Minnelli, and Porter had experienced a series of flops on Broadway. The screenplay, by Frances Goodrich [25 . . .] and Albert Hackett [25 . . .], is based on an S. N. Behrman play that was a hit on Broadway for Alfred Lunt [841] and Lynn Fontanne [841]. MGM bought the rights to the play in 1942, while it was still running, intending to film it as a nonmusical with William Powell [1170 . . .], Hedy Lamarr, and Charles Laughton [1387 . . .]. Producer Arthur Freed [66 . . .] suggested that it be musicalized. Kelly is well supported in some of his numbers by the Nicholas Brothers, and the cast also includes Gladys Cooper [1393 . . .] and Reginald Owen. The most memorable number from Porter's score is ''Be a Clown.'' The scoring award went to Johnny Green and Roger Edens for another Garland musical, *Easter Parade*.

Hayton: 877, 896, 1476, 1831, 1907.

1578 • PIRATES

Carthago Films Production in association with Accent Cominco; Cannon Releasing. 1986.

Nomination *Costume Design:* Anthony Powell.

English pirate Walter Matthau [709 . . .], set adrift on a raft, is picked up by a Spanish ship that he proceeds to demolish. Very odd slapstick comedy from a very unlikely director, Roman Polanski [395 . . .]. A critical and box-office bomb. The Oscar went to Jenny Beavan and John Bright for *A Room With a View*.

Powell: 516, 937, 2021, 2134.

1579 • PLACE IN THE SUN, A

Paramount. 1951.

Awards *Director:* George Stevens. *Screenplay:* Michael Wilson and Harry Brown. *Black-and-White Cinematography:* William C. Mellor. *Scoring of a Dramatic or Comedy Picture:* Franz Waxman. *Film Editing:* William Hornbeck. *Black-and-White Costume Design:* Edith Head.

Nominations *Picture:* George Stevens, producer. *Actor:* Montgomery Clift. *Actress:* Shelley Winters.

Poor boy Clift and poor girl Winters form an attachment. But then rich girl Elizabeth Taylor [318 . . .] enters his life, and the choice between Taylor and Winters hardly seems a fair contest. He contemplates murder to rid himself of Winters, but at

the crucial moment, alone with her on a lake, he realizes he can't go through with it—just before she accidentally falls in and drowns anyway, with the result that he is tried and sentenced to death for a crime he wanted to commit but didn't. Impressive but overstated reworking of Theodore Dreiser's novel *An American Tragedy,* which had been filmed in 1931 by director Josef von Sternberg [1358 . . .]. Something in the material seems to prevent successful adaptation to the screen; perhaps it's Dreiser's heavy-handed insistence on society as fate, which translates here to rather ludicrous portraits of the frivolous rich vs. the downtrodden poor. The Production Code also deprived the plot of a key element: the pregnancy of the character played by Winters. To compensate, she's made shrill and clinging, characteristics that Winters believed prevented her from ever again being cast in a conventional romantic leading role. On the other hand, the scenes between Clift and the nineteen-year-old Taylor are some of the most powerfully romantic in the annals of Hollywood. The cast also includes Anne Revere [759 . . .] as Clift's mother, Shepperd Strudwick and Frieda Inescort as Taylor's parents, and Raymond Burr as the prosecutor who gets the book thrown at Clift.

Stevens, the son of actors, began his film career as a cameraman and moved into directing via short subjects. His first important feature film was also one of his best, *Alice Adams,* and he built his reputation with such varied work as *Swing Time, Gunga Din,* and *Woman of the Year*. He moved into producing as well as directing, receiving his first nomination as producer of *Talk of the Town* and his second as director of *The More the Merrier*. He interrupted his Hollywood career for wartime service and was present at the liberation of Dachau, an experience that may have helped turn him away from the lighter work of his prewar career and toward more serious subjects. *A Place in the Sun* is seen by some as the first film in a trilogy, completed by *Shane* and *Giant,* about American life. It lost the best picture Oscar, in one of the most surprising upsets in the history of the awards, to *An American in Paris*. Some believe that *A Place in the Sun* and *A Streetcar Named Desire,* the two most serious contenders, split the vote, tipping the award to the MGM musical. (The other two nominees, *Decision Before Dawn* and *Quo Vadis?,* were not strong candidates.)

Wilson's Oscar did nothing to save him from the blacklisting that occurred when he refused to testify before the House Un-American Activities Committee about Communist Party membership. He would, however, remain a thorn in the side of the Academy, which deprived him of a credit for his work on the screenplay of *Friendly Persuasion* and gave an Oscar to Pierre Boulle for the screenplay for *The Bridge on the River Kwai,* which Wilson coauthored. His collaborator on *A Place in the Sun,* Brown, had used his experiences in World War II to launch his screenwriting career, earning his first nomination for *Sands of Iwo Jima.* He continued to specialize largely in war films and westerns.

Mellor provided one of the movies' most powerful erotic moments with his extreme close-ups of Clift and Taylor in *A Place in the Sun.* He started as a lab assistant at Paramount and moved into cinematography in 1934. His work on *A Place in the Sun* began a collaboration with Stevens that continued on *Giant, The Diary of Anne Frank,* and *The Greatest Story Ever Told.* He died during work on the last film, in 1963.

This was the second consecutive scoring award for Waxman, who won the year before for *Sunset Boulevard.* He continued to work as a film composer until his death in 1967.

Hornbeck was a Hollywood veteran whose career extended back to early days at Keystone and as editor for Mack Sennett. He moved to England in the thirties, where he worked on the films of Alexander Korda [1620], but returned to America during the war to work as supervisory editor on the famous series of *Why We Fight* documentaries made by Frank Capra [1025 . . .]. After his Oscar, he moved into studio administration, rising to vice-president of Universal in 1966. He died in 1983.

This was the fourth of Head's eight Oscars. Taylor's white dress became one of the most copied designs in the history of film fashions.

Clift lost to Humphrey Bogart in *The African Queen.*

Vivien Leigh took the best actress award for *A Streetcar Named Desire.*

Stevens: 542, 768, 1353, 1799, 1998. Wilson: 287, 673, 730. Brown: 1756. Mellor: 542, 833, 1558. Waxman: 573, 958, 1457, 1459, 1670, 1822, 1975, 1979, 2004, 2334. Hornbeck: 768, 973, 1033. Head: 31, 32, 46, 305, 357, 363, 612, 636, 675, 736, 832, 894, 945, 1003, 1219, 1261, 1263, 1398, 1427, 1504, 1550, 1587, 1631, 1716, 1727, 1738, 1748, 1840, 1927, 1986, 2012, 2098, 2247, 2298. Clift: 732, 1065, 1771. Winters: 542, 1537, 1596.

1579.5 • PLACE IN THE WORLD, A

ADOLFO ARISTARAIN / OSVALDO PAPALEO / MIRNA ROSALES PRODUCTION (URUGUAY). 1992.

NOMINATION *Foreign Language Film.* (Withdrawn from final ballot.)

Growing up on an Argentine sheep ranch is the subject of this film directed by Adolfo Aristarain. Shortly after it was announced as one of the nominees, the film was withdrawn by the Academy from competition on the grounds that it had not been made in Uruguay. It was, in fact, Argentine-made, with an Argentine director and a largely Argentine cast. But Argentina declined to sponsor the film for the Oscars, a prerequisite for being considered in the category, so the producers, who included a Uruguayan investor, arranged to have it submitted as a Uruguayan entry. The Academy stipulated that "individuals with producer credit whose contributions were essentially financial will not be regarded as satisfying the requirement" that a film be made by citizens of the country sponsoring it for the award. Aristarain protested the Academy's decision, even taking the matter to court, but to no avail. The case only increased the already widespread dissatisfaction with the foreign film category, and attempts by the Academy to clarify the eligibility rules were not completely successful. During the nominating process the following year, for example, the Academy disqualified an entry from Poland, *Blue,* on the grounds that the film was set in France and the dialogue was entirely in French, although the director, Krzysztof Kieslowski [1671.5], as well as the writers, cinematographer, and composer were all Polish. ''I don't think the rules take into account the realities of filmmaking in Europe,'' protested the producer of *Blue*, Marin Karmitz. Kieslowski again fell foul of this rule when Switzerland sponsored his 1994 film, *Red*, for the Oscar; it was ruled ineligible for the foreign film Oscar on the same grounds. But this time the sympathy generated by the controversy earned *Red* nominations in other categories, including one for best director. To add to an already confusing situation, the Academy seemed to ignore its own rules when the 1993 nominees were announced: They included *The Wedding Banquet,* an entry from Taiwan that was set in the United States, used an American production team, and had almost as much dialogue in English as in Chinese.

1580 • PLACES IN THE HEART

TRI-STAR PICTURES PRODUCTION; TRI-STAR. 1984.
AWARDS *Actress:* Sally Field. *Screenplay Written Directly for the Screen:* Robert Benton.
NOMINATIONS *Picture:* Arlene Donovan, producer. *Supporting Actor:* John Malkovich. *Supporting Actress:* Lindsay Crouse. *Director:* Robert Benton. *Costume Design:* Ann Roth.

When her husband, the sheriff in Waxahachie, Texas, is shot and killed, Field tries to hold her family together through the Depression by raising cotton and taking in boarders, including a blind man (Malkovich). But when things go from bad to worse, it looks like only winning a cotton-picking contest can save her from foreclosure. Earnest and occasionally entertaining heart-tugger, although for many people the supporting characters—including Danny Glover as a sharecropper, Crouse as Field's sister, Ed Harris as Crouse's husband, and Amy Madigan [2156] as the woman Harris is having an affair with—are far more interesting than Field's struggling farm woman. (This was the year of the struggling farm woman at the Oscars: Jessica Lange and Sissy Spacek were nominated for similar roles in *Country* and *The River* respectively.) The fine cinematography is by Nestor Almendros [243 . . .], a master of atmospherics.

With her second nomination and second win, Field demonstrated that she was an actress of considerable ability, if not a great deal of range—her character here, Edna Spalding, could be Norma Rae's cousin. Her win seems to have taken Field by surprise. She responded with a now notorious acceptance speech in which she gushed, ''The first time I didn't feel it, but this time I feel it and I can't deny the fact you like me —right now, you *like* me!'' However heartfelt her surprise at being accepted as an actress, the emotion was seen by some as a little too unfettered and subsequently became the stuff of parody. Field has continued her career apparently with determination to prove that she does have a range: from the housewife who dreams of stardom as a stand-up comic in *Punchline* (1988), to the mother struggling with anger at her daughter's death in *Steel Magnolias,* to the mother desperate to escape with her child from Iran in *Not Without My Daughter* (1990), to the aging soap-opera star in the slapstick farce *Soapdish* (1991). She has also had some success as a producer of both her own films, such as *Punchline,* and others', such as the Julia Roberts [1603 . . .] vehicle *Dying Young* (1991).

Benton, who made an impressive debut with the screenplay for *Bonnie and Clyde* and reached the top with his double win for *Kramer vs. Kramer,* wrote *Places in the Heart* as a conscious return to his roots: He grew up in Waxahachie and modeled the Field character on stories he'd heard about his great-grandmother. A subsequent writing-directing effort, *Nadine* (1987), also returned to his Texas background, but with less success.

The best picture Oscar went to *Amadeus,* which also won for Milos Forman's direction and Theodor Pistek's costume design. The supporting actor award went to Haing S. Ngor for *The Killing Fields,* in which Malkovich, in his first year as a screen actor, had also appeared. Crouse, the daughter of playwright Russel Crouse (and named after Crouse's writing partner, Howard Lindsay), lost to Peggy Ashcroft in *A Passage to India.*

Field: 1448. Benton: 255, 1111, 1146, 1444.5. Malkovich: 992.3.

1581 • PLÁCIDO

Jet Films (Spain). 1961.

Nomination *Foreign Language Film.*

A satire on Spanish charitable institutions, directed and cowritten by Luis Garcia Berlanga. Not widely released in the United States. The Oscar went to *Through a Glass Darkly.*

1582 • PLAISIR, LE

Stera Film-CCFC Production; Arthur Mayer-Edward Kingsley Inc. (France). 1954.

Nomination *Black-and-White Art Direction–Set Decoration:* Max Ophuls.

Three tales by Guy de Maupassant: "Le Masque," in which an old man tries to recapture his youth by wearing an enchanted mask; "La Maison Tellier," about the excursion of the residents of a brothel to attend the first communion of the madam's niece; and "Le Modèle," in which the mistress-model of an artist forces him to marry her by attempting suicide. Directed by Ophuls, who also wrote the screenplay with Jacques Natanson [1723]. Elegantly styled, with a gallery of fine actors: Claude Dauphin, Madeleine Renaud, Danielle Darrieux, Jean Gabin, Pierre Brasseur, and Simone Simon, among others. The art direction award went to Richard Day for *On the Waterfront.*

Ophuls: 1723.

1583 • PLANET OF THE APES

Apjac Productions; 20th Century-Fox. 1968.

Award *Honorary Award:* John Chambers, for his outstanding makeup achievement.

Nominations *Original Score—for a Motion Picture (Not a Musical):* Jerry Goldsmith. *Costume Design:* Morton Haack.

Astronauts led by Charlton Heston [175] crashland on a planet on which the apes have evolved into rational creatures while retaining their simian features, while humans have regressed into nasty, brutish creatures thought by the apes to be of a lower order. Very entertaining sci-fi classic, with a famous surprise ending that's beautifully staged. Directed by Franklin Schaffner [1541] from a screenplay by Michael Wilson

[287 . . .] and Rod Serling based on a novel by Pierre Boulle [287]. Kim Hunter [1949], Roddy McDowall, and Maurice Evans play the cultivated apes, with James Whitmore [157 . . .], James Daly, and Linda Harrison among the human contingent. The cinematography is by Leon Shamroy [29 . . .]. The film was followed by four sequels as well as both live-action and animated TV series.

Chambers' makeup involved elaborate rubber prosthetics, carefully attached to the face to allow the actors a range of expressions. Its extreme discomfort caused Edward G. Robinson to bow out of the role played in the film by Evans. Chambers was only the second person to be honored by the Academy for makeup achievement—the first was William Tuttle for *7 Faces of Dr. Lao*—before the competitive award for makeup was finally established in 1981.

The scoring award went to John Barry for *The Lion in Winter.* Danilo Donati won for the costumes for *Romeo and Juliet.*

Goldsmith: 152.5, 268, 395, 727, 939, 1472, 1527, 1537, 1541, 1589, 1753, 1913, 2176, 2287. Haack: 2184, 2252.

1584 • PLATOON

Hemdale Film Production; Orion. 1986.

Awards *Picture:* Arnold Kopelson, producer. *Director:* Oliver Stone. *Sound:* John "Doc" Wilkinson, Richard Rogers, Charles "Bud" Grenzbach, and Simon Kaye. *Film Editing:* Claire Simpson.

Nominations *Supporting Actor:* Tom Berenger. *Supporting Actor:* Willem Dafoe. *Screenplay Written Directly for the Screen:* Oliver Stone. *Cinematography:* Robert Richardson.

Charlie Sheen plays a young soldier who volunteers for the war in Vietnam and finds the experiences there are nothing like the war movies he watched as a kid. Berenger and Dafoe play two experienced sergeants, Barnes and Elias, who are radically differing products of the war: Barnes, badly scarred, is fierce and brutal; Elias has taken to drugs as an escape but is gentle and almost saintly. The success of *Platoon* stems largely from the high-energy direction of Stone (aided greatly by Simpson's editing and Richardson's camera work); he stages some of the most convincing battle scenes ever put on film, and never lets the movie's pace slacken. One suspects that the film's popularity was centered in the visceral excitement of the combat sequences, which gave the crowd that cheered the *Rambo* movies a lot of action, while those who found the *Rambo* films politically repugnant examples of Reagan-era jingoism could appreciate *Platoon* because it was on the opposite side of the political fence. But as storytelling, *Platoon* is something of a disappointment: The characters are crudely drawn, used primarily as cannon fodder, and there's no plot to speak of. Perhaps recognizing the thinness of *Platoon*'s story, Stone has treated many of his subsequent films as sequels to or glosses on *Platoon,* especially the two films that he has said form a trilogy with *Platoon: Born on the Fourth of July,* which deals with the stateside experience of a paraplegic Vietnam vet, and *Heaven and Earth* (1993), which looks at the war and its aftermath from the point of view of a Vietnamese woman.

Stone had been turned down by all the major studios in his efforts to get funding for *Platoon,* which he had conceived ten years earlier, and the enthusiastic reviews and huge box-office success of the film took the industry by surprise. Released late in the year, it was an unexpected dark horse in the Oscar race. Before *Platoon* took off at the theaters, the smart money for the best picture Oscar was on Woody Allen's intricately amusing *Hannah and Her Sisters* or the sumptuous Merchant Ivory adaptation of E. M. Forster's *A Room With a View.* The other nominees were *Children of a Lesser God,* essentially a well-made filming of a well-made play, and *The Mission,* a disappointingly muddled historical epic. But *Platoon*'s popularity, as well as its political correctness, helped it win out with the increasingly liberal Academy members.

Though he has become one of Hollywood's most celebrated filmmakers, *Platoon* remains Stone's most impressive achievement, perhaps because it's the one closest to his own experiences. After a career boost from his first Oscar, for the screenplay for *Midnight Express,* Stone floundered a bit. His first major directing job was a botched horror film, *The Hand*

(1981), based on his own screenplay. He returned exclusively to screenwriting for the next five years, although none of the films he wrote is distinguished: *Conan the Barbarian* (1982), *Scarface* (1983), *Year of the Dragon* (1985), and *8 Million Ways to Die* (1986). But in 1986 he seemed to find himself suddenly, getting critical acclaim for two films, *Platoon* and *Salvador,* which he both wrote and directed. Since then, he has been one of Hollywood's most visible, and most controversial, writer-directors. His films have been denounced as shrill and manipulative and sometimes as wrongheadedly propagandistic. But they do maintain a coherent point of view: that corporate America is morally corrupt. His next movie after *Platoon, Wall Street,* also starred Charlie Sheen, this time as a naive young man who gets hardened by his encounters with the world of high finance, which Stone sees as the moral equivalent of the war in Vietnam. Stone is also fascinated by the culture of the sixties, which he explored not only in his Vietnam films but also in the 1991 Jim Morrison biopic *The Doors* and in *JFK.*

The supporting actor Oscar went to Michael Caine for *Hannah and Her Sisters,* which also won for Woody Allen's screenplay. Richardson lost to Chris Menges' work on *The Mission.*

Kopelson: 734.5. Stone: 260, 1047, 1313, 1746. Wilkinson: 506, 1513. Grenzbach: 395, 784. Kaye: 745, 1138.5, 1678. Richardson: 260, 1047.

1584.5 • *PLAYER, THE*

AVENUE PICTURES PRODUCTION; FINE LINE FEATURES. 1992. **NOMINATIONS** *Director:* Robert Altman. *Screenplay Based on Material Previously Produced or Published:* Michael Tolkin. *Film Editing:* Geraldine Peroni.

Hollywood studio executive Griffin Mill (Tim Robbins) suddenly starts getting mysterious threatening messages, apparently from a writer whose script he has rejected. Thinking he's identified the poison penman, Mill tracks him to his house, where he discovers that the writer has a beautiful girlfriend (Greta Scacchi). His encounter with the writer (Vincent D'Onofrio), however, ends disastrously: In a shoving match, Mill accidentally causes his death. Mill slips away, covers his tracks, and even starts an affair with the girlfriend. But some police detectives, played by Lyle Lovett and Whoopi Goldberg [423 . . .], begin to investigate Mill in connection with the writer's death. The texture of Altman's delicious satire on wheeling-dealing Hollywood depends more on the milieu in which it's set than on the film-noirish/thrillerish plot. There are lots of wonderful secondary characters: Peter Gallagher as the rival who threatens to supplant Mill, Fred Ward as a rather thick studio security chief, Dean Stockwell [1281] as an agent, and an endless stream of cameo appearances by the likes of Cher [1351 . . .], Bruce Willis, Julia Roberts [1603 . . .], Jack Lemmon [91 . . .], Burt Reynolds, and many others.

The film was a triumphant return to top form for Altman, who had been the most sensational director in Hollywood after *MASH* in the early seventies but was almost invisible in the eighties after a series of disastrous releases. *The Player* was acclaimed by critics, and while it was no blockbuster, it did quite well at the box office. The directing Oscar, however, went to Clint Eastwood for *Unforgiven,* which also won for Joel Cox's editing. Ruth Prawer Jhabvala won the writing award for *Howards End.*

Altman: 1286, 1415, 1817.5.

1585 • PLEASURE SEEKERS, THE

20TH CENTURY-FOX. 1965.
NOMINATION *Scoring of Music—Adaptation or Treatment:* Lionel Newman and Alexander Courage.

Tourists Ann-Margret [362 . . .], Pamela Tiffin, and Carol Lynley have romantic adventures in Madrid. Unnecessary remake of *Three Coins in the Fountain,* which was, like this one, directed by Jean Negulesco [1052]. The cast includes Tony Franciosa [880], Gene Tierney [1153], Brian Keith, and Gardner McKay. The Oscar went to Irwin Kostal for *The Sound of Music.*

Newman: 183, 457, 557, 795, 896, 981, 1160, 1273, 1762, 2043. Courage: 557.

1586 • PLYMOUTH ADVENTURE

MGM. 1952.
AWARD *Special Effects.* (No individual citation.)

Spencer Tracy [131 . . .], Gene Tierney [1153], Van Johnson, Leo Genn [1644], and Lloyd Bridges come over on the *Mayflower* to settle New England. History as only Hollywood in a high-minded mood can tell it. Dull and dated, including the not-very-special effects, which mostly have to do with the stormy voyage. Some big names are involved—director Clarence Brown [84 . . .], screenwriter Helen Deutsch [1173], cinematographer William Daniels [84 . . .], and composer Miklos Rozsa [175 . . .] —but a Thanksgiving pageant put on by Miss Dooley's third grade would be more entertaining.

1587 • POCKETFUL OF MIRACLES

FRANTON PRODUCTION; UNITED ARTISTS. 1961.
NOMINATIONS *Supporting Actor:* Peter Falk. *Song:* "Pocketful of Miracles," music by James Van Heusen, lyrics by Sammy Cahn. *Color Costume Design:* Edith Head and Walter Plunkett.

Bette Davis [46 . . .] plays Apple Annie, an aging street vendor, whose daughter, played by Ann-Margret [362 . . .], has been raised in Europe. When the daughter announces that she's coming to America to introduce her aristocratic fiancé to her mother, Annie calls on her gangster chum Dave the Dude (Glenn Ford) to help her pose as the society woman she's pretended to be in her letters. Remake by director Frank Capra [1025 . . .] of his 1933 film *Lady for a Day,* but wholly lacking the original's charm. After producer Hal Wallis [17 . . .] expressed interest in buying the rights to the original film as a vehicle for Shirley Booth [425] in the fifties, Capra himself decided to remake it, but he was unable to get the script to work in an updated version. His return to it in the sixties was a serious mistake—the original film had relevance to a Depression-era audience, but not to a Kennedy-era one. Davis, at a low point in her career, took the lead after Booth, Helen Hayes [31 . . .], Jean Arthur [1353], and Katharine Hepburn [24 . . .] turned it down. Frank Sinatra [732 . . .] accepted the role of Dave the Dude, but then backed out when the script couldn't be fixed to his satisfaction; Kirk Douglas [130 . . .], Jackie Gleason [964], and Dean Martin also refused it. Though the supporting cast is a mix of veterans—Arthur O'Connell [73 . . .], Thomas Mitchell [962 . . .] (in his last film), and Edward Everett Horton—and newcomers such as Falk, as a hood known as Joy Boy, and Ann-Margret (in her first film), the result is tedious. Its failure at the box office put an end to Capra's distinguished career.

Falk lost to George Chakiris in *West Side Story,* which also won for Irene Sharaff's costumes. The best song was Henry Mancini and Johnny Mercer's "Moon River," from *Breakfast at Tiffany's.*

Falk: 1377. Van Heusen: 171, 173, 787, 915, 926, 1056, 1524, 1708, 1859, 1907, 2016, 2064, 2263. Cahn: 74, 163, 182, 696, 915, 926, 1031, 1056, 1216, 1524, 1692, 1708, 1719, 1859, 1907, 2016, 2064, 2072, 2103, 2110, 2125, 2263, 2264, 2315, 2343. Head: 31, 32, 46, 305, 357, 363, 612, 636, 675, 736, 832, 894, 945, 1003, 1219, 1261, 1263, 1398, 1427, 1504, 1550, 1579, 1631, 1716, 1727, 1738, 1748, 1840, 1927, 1986, 2012, 2098, 2247, 2298. Plunkett: 9, 66, 953, 1087, 1243, 1657, 1859, 2029, 2330.

1587.5 • POETIC JUSTICE

COLUMBIA PICTURES PRODUCTION; COLUMBIA. 1993.
NOMINATION *Song:* "Again," music and lyrics by Janet Jackson, James Harris III, and Terry Lewis.

Jackson plays Justice, a beautician in South-Central L.A., who, after her boyfriend is killed in a senseless quarrel, agrees to join a friend (Khandi Alexander) on a trip to Oakland with a mail carrier (Tupac Shakur). The loose string of episodes that results makes up this intriguing but ultimately disappointing road movie, written and directed by John Singleton [272]. The title alludes to Justice's own verse, which we hear on the soundtrack, and which was in fact written by Maya Angelou, who also appears in the film. Jackson, a member of a celebrated, indeed notorious, musical family, makes her acting debut in the movie. The song Oscar went to Bruce Springsteen for "Streets of Philadelphia," from *Philadelphia.*

1588 • POLICEMAN, THE

EPHI-ISRAELI MOTION PICTURE STUDIO PRODUCTION (ISRAEL). 1971.
NOMINATION *Foreign Language Film.*

Shay K. Ophir plays a kind-hearted but ineffective Israeli policeman who is in danger of losing his job. The local crooks, knowing that he may be replaced with a more effective cop, stage a crime that even he can solve—making him a hero, though he loses his job anyway. Slight and amusing comedy written and directed by Ephraim Kishon. The Oscar went to *The Garden of the Finzi-Continis.*

1588.5 • POLLYANNA

WALT DISNEY PRODUCTIONS; BUENA VISTA. 1960.
AWARD *Honorary Award:* Hayley Mills for *Pollyanna,* the most outstanding juvenile performance during 1960.

Mills, in the title role, plays an orphan who goes to live with her prim Aunt Polly, played by Jane Wyman [246 . . .] in a turn-of-the-century New England town. Spunky, energetic, perpetually optimistic Pollyanna wins the hearts of everyone in the town, converting even sourpusses like Adolphe Menjou [734] (in his last film) and Agnes Moorehead [963 . . .], and engineers a romance between Wyman and the town doctor, Richard Egan. Agreeable Disney version of the Eleanor H. Porter story that had been a famous vehicle for Mary Pickford [444] in 1920. It could have been cloying, but it's not, though this sort of period Americana is not to everyone's taste. Mills gives a natural, unaffected performance, and is supported by a solid cast that includes Karl Malden [1477 . . .], Nancy Olson [1975], and Donald Crisp [952]. The screenplay is by David Swift, who also directed.

Mills is the last winner of a miniature Oscar statuette, an honor first devised for Shirley Temple in 1934 which became a traditional way for the Academy to recognize child performers. It was given to Deanna Durbin and Mickey Rooney [115 . . .] at the 1938 ceremonies, to Judy Garland [1065 . . .] for 1939, to Margaret O'Brien for 1944, Peggy Ann Garner for 1945, Claude Jarman, Jr., for 1946, Ivan Jandl for *The Search* at the 1948 awards, Bobby Driscoll for 1949, and to Jon Whiteley and Vincent Winter for

The Little Kidnappers at the 1954 awards. After Mills received the honor, the Academy decided to include child performers among the regular competitive awards. Child stars had earlier received nominations, including Jackie Cooper for *Skippy* and Patty McCormack for *The Bad Seed,* but the first to win a competitive Oscar was sixteen-year-old Patty Duke for *The Miracle Worker*. Mills had been signed to a five-year contract with the Disney studios when Walt Disney himself screened her first British film, *Tiger Bay* (1960), while her father, John Mills [1737], was making *Swiss Family Robinson* for the studio. After the success of *Pollyanna,* she made an equally big hit, *The Parent Trap,* for Disney, plus several films, including *The Moon-Spinners* and *That Darn Cat,* that did less spectacularly at the box office. Her career stalled when she entered her twenties. She married producer-director Roy Boulting, who was well into his fifties, in 1971. In recent years she has returned to acting, primarily on television, with appearances in the British miniseries *The Flame Trees of Thika* as well as several Disney TV sequels to *The Parent Trap*.

1589 • POLTERGEIST

METRO-GOLDWYN-MAYER/STEVEN SPIELBERG PRODUCTION; MGM/UNITED ARTISTS. 1982.
NOMINATIONS *Original Score:* Jerry Goldsmith. *Visual Effects:* Richard Edlund, Michael Wood, and Bruce Nicholson. *Sound Effects Editing:* Stephen Hunter Flick and Richard L. Anderson.

A couple, played by Craig T. Nelson and JoBeth Williams, move with their three children to a new subdivision. But increasingly weird things begin to happen in the house, until finally the youngest child (Heather O'Rourke) is kidnaped by spirits who enter via the TV set. Parapsychologist Beatrice Straight [1424] and medium Zelda Rubinstein eventually set things right, discovering that the house was built over an Indian burial ground. Flashy, creepy, often funny shocker, produced, cowritten, and reportedly at least partially directed by Steven Spielberg [416 . . .]. The credited director is Tobe Hooper, who had been hired on the strength of his cult horror film *The Texas Chainsaw Massacre* (1974). *Poltergeist* was a hit with fans

of horror comic books, but too far over the top for more conventional members of the audience. Because of the early death of two of its young stars, a legend has grown up that the production was somehow cursed: Dominique Dunne, who played the teenage daughter, died soon after it opened. O'Rourke, who appeared in the film's two sequels in 1986 and 1988, died shortly before the third film in the series opened.

The scoring Oscar went to John Williams for Spielberg's other big hit of the year, *E.T. The Extra-Terrestrial,* which also won for visual effects and sound effects editing.

Goldsmith: 152.5, 268, 395, 727, 939, 1472, 1527, 1537, 1541, 1583, 1753, 1913, 2176, 2287. Edlund: 45.5, 544, 614, 766, 1590, 1652, 1684, 1916, 2165. Nicholson: 614, 1652. Flick: 544, 1711, 1888.5, 2124. Anderson: 1652.

1590 • POLTERGEIST II: THE OTHER SIDE

VICTOR-GRAIS PRODUCTION; MGM. 1986.
NOMINATION *Visual Effects:* Richard Edlund, John Bruno, Garry Waller, and William Neil.

Just when you thought it was safe to go back in the house, the family of Craig T. Nelson and JoBeth Williams is once again pestered by poltergeists. Mediocre sequel that doesn't have the guiding hand of the first film's producer, Steven Spielberg [416 . . .], to make it anything other than a routine special effects festival. Directed by Brian Gibson, with Heather O'Rourke and Zelda Rubinstein returning from the first movie, plus Will Sampson, Julian Beck, and Geraldine Fitzgerald [2316]. *Aliens* won the special effects award.

Edlund: 45.5, 544, 614, 766, 1589, 1652, 1684, 1916, 2165. Bruno: 5, 153.5, 413.5, 766, 2147.5.

1591 • POPE OF GREENWICH VILLAGE, THE

UNITED ARTISTS-KOCH/KIRKWOOD PRODUCTION; MGM/UNITED ARTISTS. 1984.
NOMINATION *Supporting Actress:* Geraldine Page.

Cousins Charlie (Mickey Rourke) and Paulie,

played by Eric Roberts [1734], are two-bit crooks who manage to pull off a big job that lands them in trouble with the Mafia. Loose-jointed, not particularly successful film that was undermined in part by the confused management of MGM. At one point, Michael Cimino [521] was called in as consultant, even though he had recently been responsible for the major debacle of *Heaven's Gate.* Rourke and Roberts were cast after Al Pacino [75 . . .] and Robert De Niro [113 . . .], who had initially expressed interest in the script, turned down the film. Stuart Rosenberg directed, but the major interest of the film is supplied by its supporting cast: Daryl Hannah, Kenneth Mc-Millan, Tony Musante, M. Emmet Walsh, Burt Young [1712], and Philip Bosco. Page, who plays the mother of a corrupt policeman (Jack Kehoe), received her seventh nomination, and lost to Peggy Ashcroft in *A Passage to India.*

Page: 935, 1005, 1555, 1959, 1985, 2142, 2341.

1592 • PORGY AND BESS

SAMUEL GOLDWYN PRODUCTIONS; COLUMBIA. 1959.

AWARD *Scoring of a Musical Picture:* André Previn and Ken Darby.
NOMINATIONS *Color Cinematography:* Leon Shamroy. *Sound:* Gordon E. Sawyer, sound director, Samuel Goldwyn Studio Sound Department, and Fred Hynes, sound director, Todd-AO Sound Department. *Color Costume Design:* Irene Sharaff.

Porgy, played by Sidney Poitier [522 . . .], is a crippled beggar in the Catfish Row section of Charleston, South Carolina. He and Bess, played by Dorothy Dandridge [361], fall in love, but she meets up with her old lover, Crown (Brock Peters), who is in hiding because he killed a man. Crown wants her back, but Porgy kills him and is jailed. Meanwhile, Bess is persuaded by the dope-peddler Sportin' Life (Sammy Davis, Jr.) to accompany him to New York. When Porgy is freed from jail, he sets out for New York in his goat-drawn cart. The great music drama by George [1797] and Ira Gershwin [455 . . .] receives a respectful, unimaginative treatment in this Samuel Goldwyn [102 . . .] production, directed by Otto Preminger [73 . . .]. The music is wonderful, of course, and it's well performed by Robert McFerrin (dubbing Poitier), Adele Addison (dubbing Dandridge), Davis, Pearl Bailey as Maria, and Diahann Carroll [411] as Clara. But the production, Goldwyn's last, was famously troubled. A fire destroyed the sets and costumes just as shooting was about to start. The first director, Rouben Mamoulian (who had directed the original 1935 Broadway production), wanted to open up the film, using locations rather than soundstage sets and a more contemporary jazz orchestration; he was fired when he wouldn't adhere to Goldwyn's wishes. Poitier was reluctant to take the role of Porgy, feeling the drama presented a retrograde image of blacks, and there were many protests about the script and the costumes from the cast: Bailey refused to appear in anything in which women wore bandannas—the old emblem of Aunt Jemima—and the lyrics were purged of as much dialect as possible. Preminger, infamous as a directorial tyrant, caused Dandridge to break down in tears and Poitier to walk off the set. And once it was released, the picture, crippled by protests from black organizations, was a box-office disaster. It is seldom seen today, and legal difficulties concerning rights to the music have prevented its release on videotape.

The Oscars to Previn and Darby were deserved, although they faced feeble competition: 1959 was a weak year for the Hollywood musical, and except for the Disney *Sleeping Beauty,* the other competitors have mostly been forgotten—*The Five Pennies, Li'l Abner,* and *Say One for Me.* In the other categories, *Porgy and Bess* was blitzed by the *Ben-Hur* sweep: Robert L. Surtees won for cinematography, Franklin E. Milton for sound, and Elizabeth Haffenden for costumes.

Previn: 172, 609, 769, 1017, 1034, 1044, 1097, 1393, 1550, 2064, 2077, 2161. Darby: 334, 690, 953, 1088, 1883. Shamroy: 29, 226, 356, 413, 495, 569, 602, 1088, 1153, 1213, 1610, 1706, 1852, 1883, 2013, 2286, 2334. Sawyer: 33, 91, 184, 214, 393, 730, 864, 882, 973, 974, 1032, 1511, 2244, 2297, 2310. Hynes: 33, 413, 1469, 1881, 1883, 2244. Sharaff: 66, 290, 333, 338, 413, 690, 852, 896, 1088, 1507, 1910, 2000, 2244, 2277.

1593 • PORTIA ON TRIAL

REPUBLIC. 1937.

NOMINATION *Score:* Republic Studio Music Department, Alberto Colombo, head; score by Alberto Colombo.

Frieda Inescort stars in a melodrama about a woman who once lost custody of a child in a court battle, and years later uses her skills as a lawyer to settle old scores. Respectable production from a low-budget studio, directed by George Nicholls, Jr. The cast includes Walter Abel and Heather Angel. The scoring award went to Charles Previn for *One Hundred Men and a Girl.*

1594 • PORTRAIT OF CHIEKO

SHOCHIKU COMPANY LTD. (JAPAN). 1967.

NOMINATION *Foreign Language Film.*

Chieko, the wife of a poet and sculptor, tries to become a painter but is frustrated by her inability to capture the beauty she imagines. In despair, she attempts suicide and eventually goes insane. Beautifully photographed by Hiroshi Takamura and directed by Noboru Nakamura. The Oscar went to *Closely Watched Trains.*

1595 • PORTRAIT OF JENNIE

VANGUARD FILMS; SELZNICK RELEASING ORGANIZATION. 1948.

AWARD *Special Effects:* Paul Eagler, J. McMillan Johnson, Russell Shearman, and Clarence Slifer, visual; Charles Freeman and James G. Stewart, audible.

NOMINATION *Black-and-White Cinematography:* Joseph August.

In Central Park, artist Joseph Cotten encounters a young girl, played by Jennifer Jones [584 . . .], dressed in turn-of-the-century clothing. He asks if he can paint her portrait, but each time she comes for a sitting, she seems to have aged several years more. They fall in love, but when she becomes a mature young woman, she dies. She is, of course, a ghost, who could not rest until fulfilled by her love for Cotten. A very odd business based on a novel by Robert Nathan, the film is a testament to the obsession of its producer, David O. Selznick [497 . . .], with its star, Jones—the whole thing is very much a portrait

of Jennifer. Selznick, as usual, constantly tinkered and revised and introduced new elements during the filming, at one point hiring Jerome Robbins [2244] to choreograph a sequence that was cut from the film. The special effects Oscar was won for a spectacular hurricane and tidal wave at the film's climax, which Selznick added when it was clear that the story alone was not enough to make the film succeed. William Dieterle [1169] directed, and the cast includes Ethel Barrymore [1445 . . .], Lillian Gish [584], Cecil Kellaway [843 . . .], and David Wayne. The score, by Dimitri Tiomkin [33 . . .], is based on Debussy. August, who died before the film was completed, lost the cinematography Oscar to William Daniels for *The Naked City.*

Eagler: 706. Johnson: 636, 833, 978, 1388, 2098. Slifer: 1451. Stewart: 253, 505, 1421. August: 849.

1596 • POSEIDON ADVENTURE, THE

IRWIN ALLEN PRODUCTION; 20TH CENTURY-FOX. 1972.

AWARDS *Song:* "The Morning After," music and lyrics by Al Kasha and Joel Hirschhorn. *Special Achievement Award for Visual Effects:* L. B. Abbott and A. D. Flowers.

NOMINATIONS *Supporting Actress:* Shelley Winters. *Cinematography:* Harold E. Stine. *Art Direction—Set Decoration:* William Creber; Raphael Bretton. *Sound:* Theodore Soderberg and Herman Lewis. *Original Dramatic Score:* John Williams. *Film Editing:* Harold F. Kress. *Costume Design:* Paul Zastupnevich.

A cruise ship is capsized by an enormous tidal wave, and the survivors, trapped in the upside-down vessel, try to find their way to the bottom of the ship, which is now its top. Very entertaining junk, directed by Ronald Neame [289 . . .], that launched (if that's the word) the most inexplicably popular film genre of the seventies, the disaster flick. This one, produced by Irwin Allen [2126], who became the master of the genre, has the virtue of an entertaining premise, taken from a novel by Paul Gallico [1607], which allows for a lot of nightmarishly askew locations and intensely claustrophobic sensations. And though the script by Stirling Silliphant [992] and Wendell Mayes [73] doesn't give them anything worth saying, the movie has a top-notch cast: Gene Hackman [255 . . .], Ernest Borgnine [1283], Red Buttons [1763], Roddy McDowall, Stella Stevens, Jack Albertson [1954], Arthur O'Connell [73 . . .], Leslie Nielsen, Carol Lynley, and Pamela Sue Martin. Winters steals scenes as a kind-hearted (but also weak-hearted) Jewish grandmother who saves the day with her swimming skills. The sets were modeled on the *Queen Mary,* and the actual ship, docked at Long Beach, was used for some exteriors. The Oscar-winning song is sung by Maureen McGovern.

Winters lost to Eileen Heckart in *Butterflies Are Free.* The award for cinematography went to Geoffrey Unsworth for *Cabaret,* which also won for art direction, sound, and David Bretherton's editing. The scoring award went to Charle Chaplin, Raymond Rasch, and Larry Russell for *Limelight.* Anthony Powell won for the costumes for *Travels With My Aunt.*

Kasha: 1557, 2126. Hirschhorn: 1557, 2126. Abbott: 557, 1062, 1196, 2120. Flowers: 1439, 2120. Winters: 542, 1537, 1579. Creber: 833, 2126. Bretton: 896, 963, 2126. Soderberg: 724, 983, 1726, 2126, 2152. Lewis: 2120, 2126. Williams: 6, 260, 403, 416, 588, 613, 614, 659, 805, 933, 937, 982, 996, 997, 1041, 1047, 1652, 1679, 1684, 1701, 1764.65, 1916, 1977, 2107, 2126, 2194, 2293, 2322. Kress: 573, 953, 1371, 2126, 2320. Zastupnevich: 1983, 2259.

1597 • POSSESSED

WARNER BROS. 1947.

NOMINATION *Actress:* Joan Crawford.

Crawford loves Van Heflin [1055], but he's wrapped up in his career as an engineer and doesn't reciprocate, so she marries Raymond Massey [1] and then goes insane when Heflin falls in love with her stepdaughter, Geraldine Brooks. Enjoyable all-stops-out melodrama, directed by Curtis Bernhardt. The 1931 film of this name, also with Crawford, is based on a completely different story. The best actress Oscar went to Loretta Young for *The Farmer's Daughter.*

Crawford: 1319, 1955.

1598 • POSTCARDS FROM THE EDGE

COLUMBIA PICTURES PRODUCTION; COLUMBIA. 1990.

NOMINATIONS *Actress:* Meryl Streep. *Song:* "I'm Checkin' Out," music and lyrics by Shel Silverstein.

Streep plays a movie actress who takes a few too many pills and, after getting her stomach pumped and going through rehab, tries to sort out her life and career. But she has to contend with the well-meant interference of her mother, a fading, alcoholic star, played by Shirley MacLaine [91 . . .]. Enjoyable comedy-drama adapted by Carrie Fisher from her clearly autobiographical novel, though in the movie version Fisher has put more distance between herself and the character played by Streep, not to mention between her real mother, Debbie Reynolds [2184], and the character played by MacLaine. Mike Nichols [810 . . .] directs with his usual cold amusement. The movie overflows with Hollywood in-jokes and a gallery of fine performers: Dennis Quaid as an actor who is Streep's boyfriend/fellow rehab grad, Gene Hackman [255 . . .] as her director, Richard Dreyfuss [803] as her doctor, plus Rob Reiner, Mary Wickes, Annette Bening [840], and Simon Callow, among others. MacLaine gets to do a big musical number, too, a powerhouse rendition of "I'm Still Here."

After a series of highly praised dramatic performances, culminating in the deadly serious *Ironweed* and *A Cry in the Dark,* Streep seemed to make a conscious decision—although she has denied that it was anything of the sort—to send her career in a different direction by taking on comedy roles. The first of these, *She-Devil* (1989), was a critical and box-office disappointment, though she received great praise for her performance as a vain romance novelist. *Postcards* was a success, however, and she followed with two more comedies, *Defending Your Life* (1991) and *Death Becomes Her.* In 1994, she tried yet another career turn, starring in the action-adventure movie *The River Wild.* At the end of *Postcards* Streep also demonstrates that she has a way with a song, belting out Silverstein's country tune with great energy. The Oscars went to Kathy Bates for *Misery* and Stephen Sondheim for the song "Sooner or Later (I Always Get My Man)," from *Dick Tracy*.

Streep: 472, 521, 725, 1019, 1111, 1512, 1821, 1876.

1599 • POWER AND THE PRIZE, THE

MGM. 1956.

NOMINATION *Black-and-White Costume Design:* Helen Rose.

Corporate capo Burl Ives [200] picks Robert Taylor as both his successor and his son-in-law. But Taylor not only proves unwilling to get involved in an unscrupulous deal engineered by Ives, he also falls in love with a German woman who is suspected of being a commie. Forgettable drama, directed by Henry Koster [214], with Mary Astor [822], Charles Coburn [535 . . .], and Cedric Hardwicke—all of whom are more fun to watch than Taylor. The Oscar went to Jean Louis for *The Solid Gold Cadillac*.

Rose: 130, 578, 629, 755, 817, 980, 1007, 1309, 1335.

1600 • PREDATOR

20TH CENTURY FOX PRODUCTION; 20TH CENTURY FOX. 1987.

NOMINATION *Visual Effects:* Joel Hynek, Robert M. Greenberg, Richard Greenberg, and Stan Winston.

Arnold Schwarzenegger heads a rescue team on a mission in the South American jungles, but the team discovers that they're the prey for an alien that's most often glimpsed as a sort of shimmer among the trees. Enjoyably tense, if overbloody, action adventure, tailor-made for Schwarzenegger's limited acting talents, and directed with great efficiency by John McTiernan. The visual effects Oscar went to *Innerspace*.

Winston: 45, 153.5, 600, 886, 1071.5, 2019.

1601 • PRESIDENT'S LADY, THE

20TH CENTURY-FOX. 1953.

NOMINATIONS *Black-and-White Art Direction—Set Decoration:* Lyle Wheeler and Leland Fuller; Paul S. Fox. *Black-and-White Costume Design:* Charles LeMaire and Renie.

Charlton Heston [175] plays Andrew Jackson, with Susan Hayward [973 . . .] as his wife, Rachel, a di-

vorcée whom Jackson married before her divorce had become final. The scandal that arose during the political campaign hastened her death shortly before his inauguration as president. Oversentimental historical romance from a screenplay by John Patrick [1939] based on a novel by Irving Stone. Henry Levin directed, and the cast includes John McIntire, Fay Bainter [393 . . .], and Carl Betz. The art direction Oscar went to *Julius Caesar,* the costuming award to Edith Head for *Roman Holiday*.

Wheeler: 19, 46, 83, 356, 376, 428, 476, 495, 530, 542, 719, 721, 798, 950, 1062, 1088, 1149, 1153, 1213, 1391, 1475, 1616, 1670, 1706, 1852, 2008, 2093, 2212. Fuller: 530, 719, 1149, 1475, 2212. Fox: 376, 413, 428, 476, 495, 530, 721, 950, 1088, 1666, 1706, 1852. LeMaire: 21, 46, 376, 495, 530, 542, 954, 1213, 1338, 1391, 1706, 2008, 2043, 2205, 2294. Renie: 201, 355, 413, 1338.

1602 • PRETTY BABY

LOUIS MALLE FILM PRODUCTION; PARAMOUNT (U.S./FRANCE). 1978.

NOMINATION *Original Song Score and Its Adaptation or Adaptation Score:* Jerry Wexler.

A photographer, played by Keith Carradine [1415], becomes infatuated with a twelve-year-old prostitute (Brooke Shields) in a New Orleans brothel. An intriguing theme so "tastefully" handled that it becomes boring—one of the few times that's happened in a film directed by Louis Malle [107 . . .]. This was his first American film. The cast includes Susan Sarandon [107 . . .], who would subsequently star in Malle's *Atlantic City,* and Diana Scarwid [1004]. The film looks great: Polly Platt [2020], who cowrote the script with Malle, designed the World War I–period settings, and the cinematography is by Sven Nykvist [460 . . .]. The Oscar went to Joe Renzetti for *The Buddy Holly Story*.

1603 • PRETTY WOMAN

TOUCHSTONE PICTURES PRODUCTION; BUENA VISTA. 1990.

NOMINATION *Actress:* Julia Roberts.

Restless, ruthless financial wheeler-dealer Richard Gere meets an L.A. hooker (Roberts) when he gets lost on the way to his hotel. Finding her outlook on the world intriguing, he offers her $3,000 to spend the weekend with him—not for sex but for companionship. He proceeds to make her over, providing a new wardrobe as well as a new outlook on the world; she reciprocates by softening his view of humanity. An enormously popular sleeper hit that made Roberts a superstar and revived Gere's career. It's enjoyable light entertainment if you don't think about it too much—ironically, the original screenplay by J. F. Lawton was a gritty downer, intended to make you think. The transmogrification of the *Pretty Woman* screenplay is lampooned in Robert Altman's *The Player,* in which a writer's determinedly downbeat screenplay gets transformed into an upbeat movie starring Julia Roberts. Garry Marshall directed, and the cast includes Ralph Bellamy [114], Jason Alexander, Laura San Giacomo, and Hector Elizondo. Roberts, a surprise nominee (many felt the slot should have gone to Glenn Close for *Reversal of Fortune),* lost to Kathy Bates in *Misery.*

Roberts: 1922.

1604 • PRIDE AND PREJUDICE

MGM. 1940.

AWARD *Black-and-White Interior Decoration:* Cedric Gibbons and Paul Groesse.

Mr. Bennet, played by Edmund Gwenn [1325 . . .], is the father of five marriageable daughters. Elizabeth, played by Greer Garson [239 . . .], is a woman of intelligence and spirit, and her elder sister, Jane (Maureen O'Sullivan), is lovely and gentle. But the younger sisters Lydia (Ann Rutherford) and Kitty (Heather Angel) are silly flirts, and Mary (Marsha Hunt) is plain and bookish. The marital fortunes of the girls brighten, at least in the eyes of their mother (Mary Boland), when some eligible young men come to stay at a nearby country house. One, Mr. Bingley (Bruce Lester), is attracted to Jane. The other, the handsome and snobbish Mr. Darcy, played by Laurence Olivier [268 . . .], is offended by the vulgarity of Mrs. Bennet and the flirtatiousness of Kitty and Lydia, but can't help noticing the handsome, witty Elizabeth. Just when it looks as if Jane

and Bingley are going to hit it off, however, Darcy and Bingley leave. Then Elizabeth receives a proposal of marriage from Mr. Collins (Melville Cooper), a foolish man who continually fawns on his patroness, the formidable Lady Catherine de Bourgh, played by Edna May Oliver [581]. When Elizabeth turns him down, Collins, who has been ordered by Lady Catherine to marry, immediately marries a friend of Elizabeth's. Encountering Darcy again, Elizabeth is astonished when he too proposes marriage, but he can't conceal his distaste for the rest of her family, and reveals that he engineered the earlier departure of Bingley because he thought his friend's interest in Jane was unsuitable. Elizabeth indignantly refuses him. Then word comes that Lydia has eloped with Mr. Wickham (Edward Ashley), an old enemy of Darcy's, threatening social ruin for the Bennets. Elizabeth realizes that perhaps she really does love Darcy, but now it's too late—or is it? Wonderfully entertaining MGMization of the Jane Austen novel. Janeites may cavil at some of the things that have been done to the book: It has been moved up in time so that the women can be dressed in Victorian hoops and crinoline rather than Regency styles. Lady Catherine has been given a wholly unconvincing change of heart at film's end. And thanks to the Production Code's strictures against making light of clergymen, Mr. Collins is no longer a man of the cloth. The result, as Pauline Kael observes, is "more Dickens than Austen," but at least that's translating one kind of greatness into another. Olivier, in top form, is the definitive Darcy, and Garson, though a bit too mature for her role, plays well opposite him. The film is directed by Robert Z. Leonard [555 . . .] from a screenplay by Aldous Huxley and Jane Murfin. The immediate source for the screenplay is a stage adaptation made by Helen Jerome, to which MGM production head Irving Thalberg [150 . . .] had bought the rights in 1933, with the intention of starring his wife, Norma Shearer [150 . . .], as Elizabeth. Thalberg had died in 1936, and studio head Louis B. Mayer insisted that Garson, rather than the forty-year-old Shearer, star in the film, which may have hastened Shearer's decision to retire from the screen.

Gibbons: 66, 87, 130, 217, 227, 239, 285, 290, 440, 629, 749, 831, 980, 1069, 1096, 1173, 1190, 1226, 1230, 1232, 1274, 1308, 1309, 1417, 1567, 1644, 1662, 1673, 1721, 1861, 1937, 2068, 2112, 2256, 2257, 2300, 2320, 2330. Groesse: 87, 1173, 1190, 1232, 1309, 1335, 1385, 2112, 2157, 2320.

1605 • PRIDE OF ST. LOUIS, THE

20TH CENTURY-FOX. 1952.

NOMINATION *Motion Picture Story:* Guy Trosper.

Dan Dailey [2258] plays baseball pitcher Dizzy Dean, who turns commentator after an accident ends his career on the field. Directed by Harmon Jones [759], with Joanne Dru and Richard Crenna. The screenplay from Trosper's story is by Herman J. Mankiewicz [407 . . .]. The Oscar went to Frederic M. Frank, Theodore St. John, and Frank Cavett for *The Greatest Show on Earth.*

1606 • PRIDE OF THE MARINES

WARNER BROS. 1945.

NOMINATION *Screenplay:* Albert Maltz.

John Garfield [251 . . .] plays Al Schmid, a marine blinded during an attack by the Japanese. Solid, often moving true story, directed by Delmer Daves. The cast includes Eleanor Parker [328 . . .], Dane Clark, and Rosemary DeCamp. The Oscar went to Charles Brackett and Billy Wilder for *The Lost Weekend.*

Maltz: 298.

1607 • PRIDE OF THE YANKEES, THE

SAMUEL GOLDWYN PRODUCTIONS; RKO RADIO. 1942.

AWARD *Film Editing:* Daniel Mandell.

NOMINATIONS *Picture:* Samuel Goldwyn, producer. *Actor:* Gary Cooper. *Actress:* Teresa Wright. *Original Story:* Paul Gallico. *Screenplay:* Herman J. Mankiewicz and Jo Swerling. *Black-and-White Cinematography:* Rudolph Maté. *Black-and-White Interior Decoration:* Perry Ferguson, art direction; Howard Bristol, set decoration. *Sound Recording:* Thomas Moulton. *Scoring of a Dramatic or Comedy Picture:* Leigh Harline. *Special Effects:* Jack Cosgrove and Ray Binger, photographic; Thomas T. Moulton, sound.

Cooper plays Yankee first baseman Lou Gehrig, who became a baseball legend before he was forced to retire on July 4, 1939, because he was suffering from amyotrophic lateral sclerosis, which became known as Lou Gehrig's disease. With the possible exception of *Field of Dreams,* this is the most popular baseball movie of all, drenched in sentiment, pumped full of uplift. Goldwyn bought the rights to the story on the urging of Niven Busch [990], who was working for the producer as a story editor. Unfamiliar with baseball, and aware that sports movies rarely succeeded at the box office, Goldwyn was convinced the story would work after watching the newsreel of Gehrig's famous farewell speech in Yankee Stadium. (The real thing is a simpler, less tear-drenched affair than Cooper's rendition of it in the film.) Shrewdly, Goldwyn insisted that the script concentrate heavily on the struggles of Gehrig's immigrant parents and Gehrig's shy romancing of the woman he married, played by Wright. The love element, heavily underscored with the Irving Berlin [34 . . .] song "Always," helped draw the audience that would have stayed away from a baseball movie. But baseball fans were rewarded with the presence of real players, most notably Babe Ruth, in the cast. The formula worked: It was Goldwyn's most profitable movie to that date. The movie is directed by Sam Wood [701 . . .], and the cast includes Walter Brennan [424 . . .] and Dan Duryea.

Editor Mandell is credited with the solution to one of the film's major technical problems: Gehrig was left-handed, Cooper right-handed. So Mandell suggested that Cooper bat normally, but run to third base instead of first. The images in those sequences would then be printed in reverse. This also necessitated reversing the insignia on the players' uniforms so they'd come out the right way on screen. This ingenious solution also helps explain the film's nomination for special effects, though the Oscar in that category went to *Reap the Wild Wind.*

The best picture Oscar went to *Mrs. Miniver,* which also earned Wright an Oscar in a supporting role. She was the second double nominee in Oscar history; the first was Fay Bainter, who had been nominated as actress in *White Banners* and won as supporting actress in *Jezebel.* Wright lost in the actress category to her *Mrs. Miniver* costar, Greer Garson. *Mrs. Miniver* also took the awards for the screenplay by George Froeschel, James Hilton, Claudine West, and Arthur Wimperis, and for Joseph Ruttenberg's cinematography.

Cooper lost to James Cagney in *Yankee Doodle Dandy,* which also won for Nathan Levinson's sound engineering. The Oscar for original story went to Emeric Pressburger for *The Invaders.* The scoring award was won by Max Steiner for *Now, Voyager.*

Mandell: 91, 184, 1182, 2297. Goldwyn: 102, 184, 214, 510, 560, 1182, 2316. Cooper: 701, 912, 1366, 1779. Wright: 1182, 1371. Mankiewicz: 407. Maté: 455, 706, 1740, 2031. Ferguson: 366, 407, 1451, 2292. Bristol: 690, 852, 864, 1182, 1451, 1613, 1907, 2064. Moulton: 22, 46, 138, 366, 457, 487, 560, 706, 798, 962, 1153, 1200, 1451, 1510, 1849, 2154, 2294. Harline: 1053, 1576, 1838, 1851, 2312, 2327. Cosgrove: 798, 1670, 1828, 1890. Binger: 1200, 1451.

1608 • PRIME OF MISS JEAN BRODIE, THE

20TH CENTURY-FOX PRODUCTIONS LTD.; 20TH CENTURY-FOX. 1969.

AWARD *Actress:* Maggie Smith.
NOMINATION *Song:* ''Jean,'' music and lyrics by Rod McKuen.

In the title role, Smith plays a teacher at a girls' school in Edinburgh. Jean Brodie is undeniably charismatic, but she's also something of a fascist, and the time is the 1930s, which bodes ill for the pupils influenced by her. Celia Johnson [289] is the teacher who spots the danger of Brodieism, Robert Stephens is Brodie's artist lover, and Pamela Franklin the sexy student who becomes her rival for Stephens' affections. Enjoyable adaptation of the novel by Muriel Spark, with a screenplay by Jay Presson Allen [321 . . .] that's based as much on Allen's stage version as on the novel itself, though the chief delights are in the acting rather than the script or the direction by Ronald Neame [289 . . .].

Smith made her stage debut in London in 1952 and her first Broadway appearance in 1956 but did not begin appearing regularly in films until the sixties. Her nuanced, technically dazzling performance in *Jean Brodie* signaled her emergence as a major screen presence, but also established her as a character performer, not a leading lady. On stage she had been able to play more conventional roles, including many Shakespeare heroines. But the camera typed her as an eccentric, angular figure, even when she was playing a straight dramatic role such as Desdemona in *Othello,* for which she received her first nomination. She is most often seen now as a prim spinster like the ones she played in *A Room With a View* and *The Lonely Passion of Judith Hearne* (1987). But her skill is so remarkable that she can individualize even the types in which she is cast.

McKuen's inappropriately slurpy song lost to Burt Bacharach and Hal David's ''Raindrops Keep Fallin' on My Head,'' from *Butch Cassidy and the Sundance Kid.*

Smith: 332, 1506, 1725, 2134. McKuen: 266.

1609 • PRIMROSE PATH, THE

RKO RADIO. 1940.

NOMINATION *Supporting Actress:* Marjorie Rambeau.

Ginger Rogers [1102] falls in love with Joel McCrea, but their romance is complicated by the fact that her mother (Rambeau) has been a prostitute, though of course the Production Code keeps that fact rather murky. Misfired melodrama that's still worth seeing for Rambeau's fine performance. Directed by Gregory La Cava [1401 . . .], with Henry Travers [1371] and Miles Mander. Rambeau lost to Jane Darwell in *The Grapes of Wrath.*

Rambeau: 2121.

1610 • PRINCE OF FOXES

20TH CENTURY-FOX. 1949.

NOMINATIONS *Black-and-White Cinematography:* Leon Shamroy. *Black-and-White Costume Design:* Vittorio Nino Novarese.

Renaissance rogue Tyrone Power tangles with Cesare Borgia, played by Orson Welles [407 . . .]. Opulent but dull costume drama that, unlike most of

Fox's costumers, was filmed on location in Italy. Unfortunately the studio didn't spring for the color photography that might have made the settings more opulent. An adaptation of a novel by Samuel Shellabarger, directed by Henry King [1868 . . .] (with some, but perhaps not enough, assistance from Welles). The cast includes Wanda Hendrix, Felix Aylmer, Everett Sloane, and Katina Paxinou [701]. The cinematography award went to Paul C. Vogel for *Battleground*. Edith Head and Gile Steele won for the costumes for *The Heiress*.

Shamroy: 29, 226, 356, 413, 495, 569, 602, 1088, 1153, 1213, 1592, 1706, 1852, 1883, 2013, 2286, 2334. Novarese: 29, 413, 465, 833.

1611 • PRINCE OF THE CITY

ORION PICTURES/WARNER BROS. PRODUCTION; ORION/WARNER BROS. 1981.

NOMINATION *Screenplay Based on Material From Another Medium:* Jay Presson Allen and Sidney Lumet.

New York cop Treat Williams turns informer to expose corruption in the narc squad and suffers the consequences. Long, slow docudrama, based on facts reported in Robert Daley's book. Williams overacts, but the good supporting cast includes Jerry Orbach, Bob Balaban, James Tolkan, Lindsay Crouse [1580], Lane Smith, and Lance Henriksen. Lumet also directed. The screenplay Oscar went to Ernest Thompson for *On Golden Pond*.

Allen: 321. Lumet: 561, 1424, 2153, 2198.

1612 • PRINCE OF TIDES, THE

BARWOOD/LONGFELLOW PRODUCTION; COLUMBIA. 1991.

NOMINATIONS *Picture:* Barbra Streisand and Andrew Karsch, producers. *Actor:* Nick Nolte. *Supporting Actress:* Kate Nelligan. *Screenplay Based on Material From Another Medium:* Pat Conroy and Becky Johnston. *Cinematography:* Stephen Goldblatt. *Art Direction–Set Decoration:* Paul Sylbert; Caryl Heller. *Original Score:* James Newton Howard.

Nolte, a South Carolina teacher and football coach whose marriage to Blythe Danner is in trouble, goes to New York to see his sister, played by Melinda Dillon [3 . . .], who has just attempted suicide—

not for the first time. He meets her psychiatrist, played by Streisand, and in the course of attempting to help Dillon, Nolte and Streisand become involved. She's married to a cold, arrogant musician (Jeroen Krabbe), and her son (played by Streisand's real-life son, Jason Gould) is at odds with his father because the boy wants to play football more than he wants to practice the violin. Nolte coaches the boy and helps Streisand split up with Krabbe. In turn, Streisand helps Nolte come to terms with events in the past that traumatized his whole family, including Nolte's mother, played by Nelligan. Florid, silly, but very watchable melodrama—it's like what *Now, Voyager* might have been if Bette Davis had slept with Claude Rains and not with Paul Henreid. Conroy helped adapt his own novel, which perhaps accounts for the movie's excess of plot: It's often hard to follow unless you've read the book.

The Prince of Tides was successful enough at the box office to make it a contender for the best picture slate, particularly since it was a late-year "prestige" production, and 1991 was a year of badly flawed films. The other nominees included the first animated feature ever nominated for best picture, *Beauty and the Beast;* the brilliantly made but coldly unlikable *Bugsy;* Oliver Stone's weirdly paranoid rewriting of history, *JFK;* and perhaps the most uncharacteristic winner of the best picture Oscar in the history of the award, *The Silence of the Lambs.* But observers and critics of the Oscars were startled when the Academy failed to nominate the director of *The Prince of Tides:* Barbra Streisand. The directors of *Bugsy, JFK,* and *The Silence of the Lambs* received nominations, but the other two slots were filled by John Singleton for *Boyz N the Hood* and Ridley Scott for *Thelma & Louise.* Many critics would have nominated one or the other of those films for best picture instead of *The Prince of Tides,* but omitting Streisand from the slate after singling out her film seemed like a deliberate snub—and politically very incorrect, given that the Hollywood establishment had been much criticized for allowing few women to rise to top management positions and for the declining number of good movie roles for actresses. Streisand became the third woman director to fail to receive a nomination for a film that was nominated for best picture; the others are Randa Haines, unnominated for her work on *Children of a Lesser God,* and Penny Marshall, whose work on *Awakenings* was ignored by the Academy. Only two women, Lina Wertmüller for *Seven Beauties* and Jane Campion for *The Piano,* have ever been nominated for directing Oscars. Was it Streisand's reputation as a perfectionist who had often clashed with her own directors that kept her from receiving the nomination? Was it that the directors branch thought recognizing a black director, Singleton, or a director whose film had been hailed as a feminist fable, Scott, was more politically correct? Were there suspicions that Streisand had taken advantage of her position as producer to upgrade her role from a secondary one in the novel to a leading one in the film? Or was it simply that the directors branch is dominated by aging white males? Whatever the reason, Streisand took the apparent snub with extreme grace, declining to make a show of her bitterness and making a very well received appearance at the awards ceremony.

The major reason for the mostly positive critical reception of *The Prince of Tides* is Nolte's extremely fine performance as Tom Wingo, which gives the film a plausible center in reality that the script doesn't provide. Nolte runs the gamut from tenderness to brute physicality, from witty self-assurance to profound despair. But Anthony Hopkins, playing the indelible character of Hannibal Lecter in *The Silence of the Lambs,* deprived Nolte of the Oscar.

Nelligan, a Canadian-born, British-trained actress whose work has been seen more often on stage than on screen, lost to Mercedes Ruehl in *The Fisher King.* Ted Tally took the screenplay award for *The Silence of the Lambs.* The cinematography Oscar went to Robert Richardson for *JFK. Bugsy* won for art direction. Alan Menken won for the score of *Beauty and the Beast.*

Streisand: 737, 1911, 2238. Sylbert: 890. Howard: 734.5, 1071.3.

1613 • PRINCESS AND THE PIRATE, THE

REGENT PICTURES; RKO RADIO. 1944.

NOMINATIONS *Color Interior Decoration:* Ernst Fegte, art direction; Howard Bristol, set decoration. *Scoring of a Dramatic or Comedy Picture:* David Rose.

Bob Hope is an eighteenth-century entertainer who somehow winds up on a ship with a princess (Virginia Mayo) trying to escape from a forced marriage. They get hijacked by pirate Victor McLaglen [999 . . .] and have to match wits with villain Walter Slezak. Amusing vehicle for Hope, though it's overproduced by Samuel Goldwyn [102 . . .], so it seems weighted down. Directed by David Butler, with Walter Brennan [424 . . .] and a cameo by Bing Crosby [173 . . .]. The art direction Oscar went to *Wilson.* Max Steiner won for the score for *Since You Went Away.*

Fegte: 532, 674, 726. Bristol: 690, 852, 864, 1182, 1451, 1607, 1907, 2064. Rose: 2310.

1614 • PRINCESS BRIDE, THE

ACT III COMMUNICATIONS PRODUCTION; 20TH CENTURY FOX. 1987.

NOMINATION *Song:* "Storybook Love," music and lyrics by Willy DeVille.

An elderly man, played by Peter Falk [1377 . . .], tells a fairy tale to his grandson (Fred Savage) about a commoner (Cary Elwes) and a princess (Robin Wright), who fall in love but have to endure a series of adventures before all can end happily ever after. The adventures involve a dashing swordsman (Mandy Patinkin), a giant (Andre the Giant) under the thrall of a diminutive bully (Wallace Shawn), a bickering old couple played by Billy Crystal and Carol Kane [908], and villains Chris Sarandon [561] and Christopher Guest. It's supposed to be a romp, and sometimes it is, but sometimes it gets too self-conscious and tongue-in-cheeky for its own good. Written by William Goldman [54 . . .] and directed by Rob Reiner, with a music score by Mark Knopfler. The song Oscar went to Franke Previte, John De-Nicola, and Donald Markowitz for "(I've Had) The Time of My Life," from *Dirty Dancing.*

1615 • *PRINCESS O'ROURKE*

WARNER BROS. 1943.

AWARD *Original Screenplay:* Norman Krasna.

Olivia de Havilland [798 . . .] is the princess and Robert Cummings is the pilot she falls in love with, causing a diplomatic incident. Flimsy wartime propaganda-comedy, directed by Krasna, with Charles Coburn [535 . . .], Jack Carson, Jane Wyman [246 . . .], Harry Davenport, and Gladys Cooper [1393 . . .].

Krasna worked as a film critic and newspaper editor in his native New York before becoming a publicist for Warner Bros. He began writing stage plays, stories, and screenplays in the thirties and moved into directing and producing in the forties. He died in 1984.

Krasna: 535, 741, 1694.

1616 • *PRISONER OF ZENDA, THE*

SELZNICK INTERNATIONAL PICTURES; UNITED ARTISTS. 1937.

NOMINATIONS *Interior Decoration:* Lyle Wheeler. *Score:* Selznick International Pictures Music Department, Alfred Newman, musical director; score by Alfred Newman.

Ronald Colman [311 . . .] plays the double role of the commoner Rudolph Rassendyl and King Rudolf V in this Ruritanian romance classic about the look-alike who is drafted into impersonating the king to foil a dastardly plot to prevent Rudolf's coronation. Douglas Fairbanks, Jr., is the dashing villain, Rupert of Hentzau; Madeleine Carroll the beautiful Princess Flavia, the king's intended, with whom the commoner falls in love; Mary Astor [822] the woman caught in the middle of the intrigue; Raymond Massey [1] the sinister Black Michael; David Niven [1778] the stalwart Capt. Fritz von Tarlenheim; and C. Aubrey Smith Colonel Zapt, who masterminds the impersonation. Sheer delight, with a perfect cast and a witty script, adapted from the novel by Anthony Hope and the play by Edward Rose. The screenplay is credited to John Balderston [749 . . .], Wills Root, and Donald Ogden Stewart [1148 . . .], but it was worked on by others, including Sidney Howard [102 . . .], George Cukor [262 . . .], and the film's ineluctable producer, David O. Selznick [497 . . .]. The credited directors are John Cromwell and W. S. Van Dyke [1751 . . .], but Cukor also worked on it. The wonder is that all these cooks made such a palatable broth: The remake in 1952 follows it almost frame by frame, but despite attractive stars such as Stewart Granger, Deborah Kerr [599 . . .], and James Mason [761 . . .], and lush Technicolor, it's only passable. The art direction award went to Stephen Goosson for *Lost Horizon.* Charles Previn won for the score for *One Hundred Men and a Girl.*

Wheeler: 19, 46, 83, 356, 376, 428, 476, 495, 530, 542, 719, 721, 798, 950, 1062, 1088, 1149, 1153, 1213, 1391, 1475, 1601, 1670, 1706, 1852, 2008, 2093, 2212. Newman: 31, 46, 78, 138, 182, 226, 333, 334, 347, 375, 428, 437, 457, 476, 495, 542, 690, 797, 833, 952, 953, 959, 962, 1016, 1082, 1088, 1213, 1278, 1362, 1397, 1475, 1655, 1849, 1868, 1883, 1921, 2043, 2046, 2091, 2258, 2286, 2294, 2316.

1617 • *PRIVATE BENJAMIN*

WARNER BROS. PRODUCTION; WARNER BROS. 1980.

NOMINATIONS *Actress:* Goldie Hawn. *Supporting Actress:* Eileen Brennan. *Screenplay Written Directly for the Screen:* Nancy Meyers, Charles Shyer, and Harvey Miller.

When her bridegroom, played by Albert Brooks [293], expires on their wedding night, Hawn is so distraught that she joins the army, which turns out to be somewhat different from what the recruiting sergeant (Harry Dean Stanton) made her think it would be. So much for the silly setup of this very popular service comedy, which clearly grew out of its "high concept" premise—Goldie in the army—and doesn't have to bother making sense. Fortunately Hawn provides plenty of charm and is well supported by Brennan as her sergeant, Armand Assante as the smooth Frenchman who almost woos her away from the army, Sam Wanamaker and Barbara Barrie [279] as her parents, plus Robert Webber, Mary Kay Place, P. J. Soles, Sally Kirkland [82], Gretchen Wyler, and Craig T. Nelson. But the movie bogs down when it tries to convince us that the army really is the right place for Pvt. Judy Benjamin—there must be other places where a spoiled rich girl can learn to be a mensch. Howard Zieff directed.

In the decade after her Oscar for *Cactus Flower,* Hawn established herself as a star without actually having a major hit. The most successful film in which she appeared was *Shampoo,* in which she had a secondary role, and the most interesting film was *The Sugarland Express* (1974), the first feature directed by Steven Spielberg [416 . . .], which was not a box-office success. But *Private Benjamin,* which she also produced in collaboration with writers Meyers, Shyer, and Miller, was a smash, giving Hawn the kind of clout in Hollywood that few women possess. Although her subsequent films haven't had the box-office appeal of *Private Benjamin,* she has maintained her stardom by virtue of an appealing persona. She lost the Oscar to Sissy Spacek in *Coal Miner's Daughter.*

Brennan had a well-established stage career before entering the movies. Among other things, she played the ingenue, Irene Molloy, in the original production of *Hello, Dolly!* on Broadway in 1964. She made her film debut in a small role in *Divorce American Style* but first attracted notice as the hard-bitten waitress in *The Last Picture Show.* Since then, she has typically appeared as tough, world-weary women. In 1983 she was seriously injured when she was hit by a car, but after a two-year absence from the screen she resumed her career. The Oscar went to Mary Steenburgen for *Melvin and Howard,* which also won an award for Bo Goldman's screenplay.

Hawn: 323.

1618 • PRIVATE LIFE

Mosfilm Studios Production (USSR). 1982.
Nomination *Foreign Language Film.*

A middle-aged Russian businessman quits his job when he's passed over for a promotion but finds himself unable to communicate with the family he's neglected over the years. He has an affair with his former secretary but is forced to come to terms with himself and his family. Surprising subject matter for a Soviet film, but the midlife crisis is apparently univer-

sal. Directed by Yuli Raizman. The Oscar went to *Volver a Empezar (To Begin Again).*

1619 • PRIVATE LIFE OF HELEN OF TROY, THE

First National. 1927–28.
Nominations *Title Writing:* Gerald Duffy. *Engineering Effects:* Ralph Hammeras.

Maria Corda plays Helen, with Ricardo Cortez as Paris and Lewis Stone [1540] as Menelaus in a film that has the same title as a novel by John Erskine about the postwar life of Helen and Menelaus. The movie, however, is really a tongue-in-cheek treatment of the story told by Homer. Alexander Korda [1620], husband of the film's Helen, directed from a screenplay by Carey Wilson [1387]. The cinematography is by Lee Garmes [201 . . .] and Sid Hickox. Although Duffy received the nomination, titles are also credited to Ralph Spence and Casey Robinson. The Oscar went to Joseph Farnham for *Telling the World* and other films. Hammeras was not nominated for a particular film, but for cumulative achievement during the year. Although the Academy's most recent revision of its nominees and winners list cites no titles by his name, many older lists of nominees give this film as one of the ones for which he was considered. The engineering effects award was won by Roy Pomeroy for *Wings.*

Hammeras: 520, 1073.

1620 • PRIVATE LIFE OF HENRY VIII, THE

London Films; United Artists (United Kingdom). 1932–33.
Award *Actor:* Charles Laughton.
Nomination *Picture:* Alexander Korda, producer.

Laughton plays the corpulent king, with Merle Oberon [487] as Anne Boleyn, Binnie Barnes as Catherine Howard, Wendy Barrie as Jane Seymour, and, best of all, Elsa Lanchester [428 . . .] as Anne of Cleves. Played more for comedy than for history, the movie permanently established the popular image of the monarch as a gluttonous lecher. It's still very entertaining if you're not looking for insight into Tudor statecraft. Directed by Korda from a screenplay by Lajos Biro [1134] and Arthur Wimperis [1371 . . .]. The cast includes Robert Donat [406 . . .], Miles Mander, and John Loder.

More actors have received Oscar nominations for playing Henry VIII than any other figure of literature or history; the others are Robert Shaw for *A Man for All Seasons* and Richard Burton for *Anne of the Thousand Days*. But Laughton's is the one that sticks in the memory best. After serving in World War I, Laughton studied at the Royal Academy of Dramatic Art and became a prominent stage actor in London. He met Lanchester while performing in a play, and she persuaded him to appear with her in some short comic films. They married in 1929, partly because Laughton wanted to conceal his homosexuality from the world. In 1931 they came to America to appear on Broadway in the play *Payment Deferred* and the following year came to Hollywood for the film version of the play. Laughton soon became a leading character player, appearing as Nero in *The Sign of the Cross* (1932), as Mr. Barrett in *The Barretts of Wimpole Street*, as Javert in *Les Misérables*, as Captain Bligh in *Mutiny on the Bounty*, and as Quasimodo in *The Hunchback of Notre Dame* (1939). In 1955 he made his only film as director, the critically acclaimed *The Night of the Hunter*. He made his last screen appearance in the year of his death, 1962, in *Advise and Consent*.

Korda began his film career in his native Hungary in 1916. After working in Austria and Germany, he came to Hollywood in 1926, where he stayed for four years. But his major career was in England, where he founded London Films, the most important British production unit of the 1930s. As producer, he is best remembered for his elaborate costume dramas, *The Four Feathers, The Thief of Bagdad, Jungle Book,* and *That Hamilton Woman*. He worked closely with his brothers, art director Vincent Korda [1070 . . .] and director Zoltan Korda. *The Private Life of Henry VIII* was the first foreign-made film to receive a nomination for best picture. It lost to *Cavalcade*.

Laughton: 1387, 2297.

1621 • *PRIVATE LIVES OF ELIZABETH AND ESSEX, THE*

WARNER BROS. 1939.

NOMINATIONS *Color Cinematography:* Sol Polito and W. Howard Greene. *Interior Decoration:* Anton Grot. *Sound Recording:* Nathan Levinson. *Score:* Erich Wolfgang Korngold. *Special Effects:* Byron Haskin, photographic; Nathan Levinson, sound.

Elizabeth I of England, played by Bette Davis [46 . . .], falls in love with the Earl of Essex (Errol Flynn), but after a quarrel, he rebels against her and she is forced to execute him. Lively, entertaining historical pageant, less pretentious than such later efforts at filming English history as *Becket, The Lion in Winter,* and *A Man for All Seasons,* perhaps because Warners knew how to blend some swashbuckling into the mix. But though Davis is every inch the queen, Flynn is stiff and uncomfortable playing opposite her—their teaming a year earlier in *The Sisters* had not gone well, either, perhaps because he didn't take acting seriously enough to suit her. Michael Curtiz [79 . . .] directed from a script by Norman Reilly Raine [1169] and Aeneas MacKenzie based on the play *Elizabeth the Queen*—a title under which the film is sometimes shown—by Maxwell Anderson [48]. The cast includes Olivia de Havilland [798 . . .], Donald Crisp [952], Vincent Price, Alan Hale, Henry Daniell, James Stephenson [1162], Leo G. Carroll, and Nanette Fabray (billed as Fabares). Davis played Elizabeth I again sixteen years later in *The Virgin Queen*.

The cinematography Oscar went to Ernest Haller and Ray Rennahan for *Gone With the Wind,* which also won for Lyle Wheeler's art direction. The Oscar for sound was won by Bernard B. Brown for *When Tomorrow Comes. Stagecoach* won for score and *The Rains Came* for special effects.

Polito: 353, 1779. Greene: 96, 239, 747, 1070, 1452, 1560, 1909, 2262. Grot: 90, 1169, 1768, 1981. Levinson: 16, 30, 343, 385, 531, 689, 710, 712, 790, 930, 965, 1052, 1169, 1690, 1768, 1769, 1779, 1930, 1949, 2058, 2318. Korngold: 17, 90, 1768. Haskin: 531, 1768, 1769.

1622 • PRIVATE WAR OF MAJOR BENSON, THE

UNIVERSAL-INTERNATIONAL. 1955.

NOMINATION *Motion Picture Story:* Joe Connelly and Bob Mosher.

Benson, played by Charlton Heston [175], is an irascible officer sent by his superiors to head a military school run by nuns. Predictably icky little heart-warmer with cute kids, including Sal Mineo [630 . . .], and a love interest supplied by the school doctor, Julie Adams. Jerry Hopper directed, and the cast also includes William Demarest [1058], Tim Considine, David Janssen, and Milburn Stone. It's hard to believe there wasn't a better motion picture story to fill out the nomination slate. The Oscar went to Daniel Fuchs for *Love Me or Leave Me.*

1623 • PRIVATE WORLDS

WALTER WANGER; PARAMOUNT. 1935.

NOMINATION *Actress:* Claudette Colbert.

Colbert and Charles Boyer [36 . . .] are doctors in a mental hospital whose colleagues include Joel McCrea, whose wife, Joan Bennett, has a breakdown. Directed by Gregory La Cava [1401 . . .], whom Boyer credited with a crucial bit of advice: His acting would improve if instead of just speaking English, Boyer would think in it, too. A watchable melodrama with a naive treatment of mental illness, it's mainly interesting because the film's success made Boyer a star. Colbert lost to Bette Davis in *Dangerous,* an award that was seen by most as a consolation prize to Davis for failing to be nominated the previous year for her work in *Of Human Bondage.* Had Davis been nominated, Colbert might not have won that year for *It Happened One Night.*

Colbert: 1025, 1828.

1624 • PRIZEFIGHTER AND THE LADY, THE

MGM. 1932–33.

NOMINATION *Original Story:* Frances Marion.

The prizefighter is played by a real one, Max Baer. His troubles start when he falls for the lady (Myrna Loy), who is a gangster's mistress. Mostly for fight

fans: The supporting cast includes Jack Dempsey, Primo Carnera, Jess Willard, and James J. Jeffries, plus some actors—Otto Kruger and Walter Huston [50 . . .]. Directed by W. S. Van Dyke [1751 . . .]. Marion came in second to Robert Lord for *One Way Passage.*

Marion: 202, 378.

1625 • PRIZZI'S HONOR

ABC MOTION PICTURES PRODUCTION; 20TH CENTURY FOX. 1985.

AWARD *Supporting Actress:* Anjelica Huston.

NOMINATIONS *Picture:* John Foreman, producer. *Actor:* Jack Nicholson. *Supporting Actor:* William Hickey. *Director:* John Huston. *Screenplay Based on Material From Another Medium:* Richard Condon and Janet Roach. *Film Editing:* Rudi Fehr and Kaja Fehr. *Costume Design:* Donfeld.

Nicholson plays Charley Partanna, a Mafia hit man who falls in love with and marries Irene, a beautiful blonde, played by Kathleen Turner [1545], who is also a killer for hire. Eventually, however, the couple is faced with a terrible dilemma because Irene has made a serious mistake involving the mob's money—well, as Charley puts it, "I love ya, but I gotta kill ya." Wonderful, one-of-a-kind comedy of Mafia manners, full of great scenes and characters, including Anjelica Huston as Charley's old girlfriend, in disgrace with the family because she had an affair to spite him; Hickey as the octogenarian don who holds his aging sons, Robert Loggia [1039] and Lee Richardson, firmly in check; and John Randolph as the don's *consigliere* and Charley's father.

Anjelica's award made the Hustons the first family with three generations of Oscar winners and made John Huston the only person to direct both his father and his daughter in Oscar-winning roles; Walter Huston had won his award for John's *The Treasure of the Sierra Madre.* Ironically it once looked as if John Huston had ruined his daughter's career instead of launching it; her first major role, in his *A Walk With Love and Death* (1969), was a critical and commercial flop. She turned instead to modeling in the seventies, playing only a couple of small film roles. But in the early eighties she came back to movies, at first in small parts in such films as *The Postman Always Rings Twice* (1981) and *Frances*. Her performance as the cunning Maerose Prizzi was a revelation, and by the end of the decade she had established herself as one of the most versatile and talented Hollywood actresses.

Prizzi's Honor was the fortieth film to be directed by John Huston, who was seventy-eight when he made it. But its droll, dark tone, straight from Condon's novel, was not to the taste of the Academy, which prefers straightforward "prestige" products like *Out of Africa,* for which Sydney Pollack won the directing Oscar and Kurt Luedtke the writing award.

To create Charley, Nicholson downplayed his demonic eyebrows and smile, and created a slightly dim but sweet little killer with a prominent upper lip that makes him look like he's just been to the dentist and the Novocain hasn't worn off. He lost to William Hurt's more flamboyant performance in *Kiss of the Spider Woman*.

Hickey, a character player who first appeared on screen in 1957 in *A Hatful of Rain,* had made only casual appearances in films over the years, working primarily on stage and as an acting teacher. The Oscar went to Don Ameche for *Cocoon*.

The award for editing was won by Thom Noble for *Witness*. Emi Wada took the costuming Oscar for *Ran*.

A. Huston: 617, 840. Foreman: 317. Nicholson: 395, 595, 658.5, 672, 1019, 1135, 1481, 1678, 2020. J. Huston: 24, 105, 356, 571, 891, 1248, 1263, 1363, 1779, 2136. Donfeld: 508, 2047, 2107.

1626 • PRODUCERS, THE

SIDNEY GLAZIER PRODUCTION; AVCO EMBASSY. 1968.
AWARD *Story and Screenplay—Written Directly for the Screen:* Mel Brooks.
NOMINATION *Supporting Actor:* Gene Wilder.

Zero Mostel plays a hard-luck Broadway type who hits on a brilliant scheme: He'll find the worst possible play and, with the help of his accountant (Wilder), sell 25,000 percent in shares of it to gullible backers, so when it flops he can pocket the dough. And he finds the perfect vehicle, he thinks: neo-Nazi nut Kenneth Mars' paean to *der Führer,* which Mostel

turns into a musical, *Springtime for Hitler*. Trouble is, the audience thinks the awful play is a put-on and it's a big hit. Brooks' first outing as a director suffered from poor distribution and critical scorn at first, but over the years it has grown into a cult favorite. It's very silly, in the worst of taste, with Brooks' usual tiresome fag jokes and sexist gags, and Mostel is an overbearing performer. But somehow, just like *Springtime for Hitler,* it transcends everything that's wrong with it. You may start giggling nervously and then say what the hell and start laughing out loud. The cast includes Dick Shawn, Estelle Winwood, Renee Taylor, and William Hickey [1625].

Brooks' Oscar is one of the rare signs that the Academy has a sense of humor. He defeated the authors of the very serious *The Battle of Algiers* and *Faces,* the enigmatic *2001: A Space Odyssey,* and the more conventional caper comedy *Hot Millions*. Brooks began his writing career in TV, on the classic Sid Caesar–Imogene Coca vehicle *Your Show of Shows,* and created the popular sitcom *Get Smart,* before launching his screen career with *The Producers*. He planned at first to act in the film, in the part played by Mars, but instead appears only in the chorus of *Springtime for Hitler*. With his next film, *The Twelve Chairs* (1970), he began regularly appearing on screen. Not until 1974, however, with the two hits *Blazing Saddles* and *Young Frankenstein,* did Brooks become a success as a director. In recent years he has been more successful as a producer—*The Elephant Man, The Fly*—than as a writer, director, or performer.

Bonnie and Clyde provided Wilder's film debut after several years on Broadway. His screen career has been most successful when he teamed with others, first Brooks and later, in *Silver Streak* (1976) and *Stir Crazy* (1980), with Richard Pryor. He lost the Oscar to Jack Albertson in *The Subject Was Roses*.

Brooks: 230, 2331. Wilder: 2331.

1627 • PROFESSIONALS, THE

PAX ENTERPRISES PRODUCTION; COLUMBIA. 1966.
NOMINATIONS *Director:* Richard Brooks. *Screenplay—Based on Material From Another Medium:* Richard Brooks. *Color Cinematography:* Conrad Hall.

Wealthy Ralph Bellamy [114] hires gunmen Burt Lancaster [107 . . .], Lee Marvin [371], Robert Ryan [467], and Woody Strode to rescue his wife, Claudia Cardinale, who has been kidnaped by Jack Palance [408 . . .]. Solid, exciting western that may have almost too many stars for its own good, and a screenplay that's a little overwrought. The score is by Maurice Jarre [558 . . .]. Brooks lost the directing Oscar to Fred Zinnemann and the writing award to Robert Bolt, both for *A Man for All Seasons,* which also won for Ted Moore's cinematography.

Brooks: 227, 372, 609, 987. Hall: 317, 504, 987, 1355, 1771.5, 2017.

1628 • PROMISE, THE

FRED WEINTRAUB-PAUL HELLER PRESENT/UNIVERSAL PRODUCTION; UNIVERSAL. 1979.

NOMINATION *Song:* "Theme From *The Promise* (I'll Never Say 'Goodbye')," music by David Shire, lyrics by Alan Bergman and Marilyn Bergman.

Kathleen Quinlan is hideously disfigured in a car crash, and rather than confront her boyfriend, Stephen Collins, with her deformity, she lets his mother, played by Beatrice Straight [1424], tell him she died. She starts a new life in California, where plastic surgery gives her a wholly different face. Then, one day, she meets Collins, who doesn't recognize her, but is strangely attracted to her, and . . . do you really want to know more? Hoary drivel that Bette Davis [46 . . .] and George Brent, with Gladys Cooper [1393 . . .] as the mother, might have made entertaining forty years earlier. Perhaps the producers—Fred Weintraub and Paul Heller, who also came up with the story—thought they had another *Love Story* on their hands. Nope. Directed by Gilbert Cates. Shire won an Oscar anyway, but it was for his song with Norman Gimbel, "It Goes Like It Goes," from *Norma Rae.*

Shire: 1448. A. Bergman: 179, 867, 1168, 1568, 1747, 1813, 1864, 2063, 2113, 2238, 2321, 2322. M. Bergman: 179, 867, 1168, 1568, 1747, 1813, 1864, 2063, 2113, 2238, 2321, 2322.

1629 • PROMOTER, THE

J. ARTHUR RANK-RONALD NEAME; UNIVERSAL-INTERNATIONAL (UNITED KINGDOM). 1952.

NOMINATION *Sound Recording:* Pinewood Studios Sound Department.

Alec Guinness [287 . . .] plays a young man who rises from poverty to become mayor of his town, but not through pluck and luck or other Horatio Alger schemes. He uses forgery, cunning, deceit, and other wiles—and not only gets away with it, he makes everyone else better off in the process. Delightful entry from the golden age of British comedy, directed by Ronald Neame [289 . . .] with a sterling cast that includes Glynis Johns [1969], Valerie Hobson, and Petula Clark. Based on a story by Arnold Bennett, adapted by Eric Ambler [469]. The cinematography is by Oswald Morris [659 . . .]. In Britain the movie is known as *The Card.* The sound Oscar went to another British entry, *Breaking the Sound Barrier.*

1630 • PROUD AND THE BEAUTIFUL, THE

LA COMPAGNIE INDUSTRIELLE COMMERCIALE CINÉMATOGRAPHIQUE; KINGSLEY INTERNATIONAL PICTURES (FRANCE). 1956.

NOMINATION *Motion Picture Story:* Jean-Paul Sartre.

Michèle Morgan is stranded in a squalid Mexican seaside town when her husband dies of a plague. But she joins up with alcoholic doctor Gérard Philipe to fight the disease. Rather conventional tale of redemption treated with intense realism by director Yves Allégret—an interesting but oppressive film. It's also known as *Les Orgueilleux* and *The Proud Ones.* Although Sartre, the existentialist philosopher and novelist, was nominated for his story, he made no direct contribution to the film. It's based on his novel *L'Amour Rédempteur,* adapted for the screen by Allégret, Jean Aurenche, Pierre Bost, and Jean Clouzot. The Oscar went to Dalton Trumbo, under his *nom de* blacklist of Robert Rich, for *The Brave One.*

1631 • *PROUD AND THE PROFANE, THE*

PERLBERG-SEATON PRODUCTION; PARAMOUNT. 1956.

NOMINATIONS *Black-and-White Art Direction—Set Decoration:* Hal Pereira and A. Earl Hedrick; Samuel M. Comer and Frank R. McKelvy. *Black-and-White Costume Design:* Edith Head.

Widow Deborah Kerr [599 . . .] and army officer William Holden [1424 . . .] have one of those ill-fated wartime romances. Routine to say the least. Directed by George Seaton [31 . . .], who also wrote the screenplay based on the novel *The Magnificent Bastards,* by Lucy Herndon Crockett. (Maybe that's where the "Profane" comes from.) The cast includes Thelma Ritter [46 . . .], Dewey Martin, Ross Bagdasarian, and Marion Ross. The art direction Oscar went to *Somebody Up There Likes Me.* Jean Louis won for the costumes for *The Solid Gold Cadillac.*

Pereira: 278, 357, 363, 426, 450, 736, 956, 1029, 1219, 1504, 1570, 1674, 1716, 1727, 1738, 1840, 1897, 1959, 2012, 2098, 2200, 2208. Comer: 278, 357, 426, 450, 726, 736, 925, 956, 1029, 1101, 1214, 1219, 1443, 1570, 1674, 1727, 1738, 1748, 1959, 1975, 1994, 2012, 2098, 2200, 2208. McKelvy: 591, 917, 1450, 1570, 2047, 2200. Head: 31, 32, 46, 305, 357, 363, 612, 636, 675, 736, 832, 894, 945, 1003, 1219, 1261, 1263, 1398, 1427, 1504, 1550, 1579, 1587, 1716, 1727, 1738, 1748, 1840, 1927, 1986, 2012, 2098, 2247, 2298.

1632 • *PSYCHO*

ALFRED J. HITCHCOCK PRODUCTIONS INC.; PARAMOUNT. 1960.

NOMINATIONS *Supporting Actress:* Janet Leigh. *Director:* Alfred Hitchcock. *Black-and-White Cinematography:* John L. Russell. *Black-and-White Art Direction—Set Decoration:* Joseph Hurley and Robert Clatworthy; George Milo.

Marion Crane (Leigh) is having an affair with Sam Loomis (John Gavin), who can't afford to marry her. When she's entrusted with a large amount of money from the office where she works, she takes it and runs, planning to join up with Sam. But she's forced to stop for the night at the lonely Bates Motel, run by a jittery young man named Norman, played by Anthony Perkins [730]. And so begins one of the most famous and influential of all Hollywood movies, which was dismissed by some critics at the time as a sordid, tawdry little shocker. It is, for many, the most frightening movie ever made, but repeat watching reveals it to be also deliciously witty, a masterly demonstration of filmmaking designed purely to manipulate an audience in every way possible. It's famous for having been cheaply made by a crew that also worked on Hitchcock's TV series—in marked contrast to the showy, expensive *North by Northwest* that preceded it in 1959. And it's famous, too, for dispatching its "star," Leigh, in the first third of the film—not to mention for the way in which she's dispatched: a montage remarkable for suggesting things (full frontal nudity, knife ripping into flesh) that aren't really on screen. Some controversy has been generated over the years by the claim that designer Saul Bass, who storyboarded the shower scene and reportedly also arranged camera setups during the filming of it, should receive credit for directing it. That's a debate better left to partisans who think that the "authorship" of a film is of paramount importance. In any case, editor George Tomasini [1450] deserves at least as much credit as Bass and should have been included among the editing nominees. Also omitted from the nominations was the famous score by Bernard Herrmann [50 . . .], whose yelping violins have been endlessly imitated. Joseph Stefano's screenplay, from a novel by Robert Bloch, could also have been among the nominees, although Stefano may be responsible for the moments when *Psycho* runs out of juice, such as the boring "explanation" at the film's end by the psychiatrist played by Simon Oakland. The cast also includes Vera Miles, Martin Balsam [2067], John McIntire, Frank Albertson, and Patricia Hitchcock, whose father makes his appearance as a man in a cowboy hat outside the real estate office.

Hitchcock's devotees and critics of the Academy make common cause on *Psycho*'s failure to receive a nomination for best picture. With good reason: John Wayne's bloated epic *The Alamo* had no place being nominated in its stead; *Elmer Gantry* is a film distinguished largely by Burt Lancaster's charismatic performance; *Sons and Lovers* and *The Sundowners* are solid, serious films that fade from the memory not long after one sees them. Only the winner, Billy Wilder's *The Apartment,* has anything near *Psycho*'s stature thirty-odd years later, but even it seems dated where *Psycho* remains timeless. It would take the Academy thirty-one years to come around to the realization that so-called genre films, and specifically horror films, could be works of distinction: When it honored *The Silence of the Lambs,* perhaps the Academy was also in its way honoring that movie's most distinctive ancestor.

This is the sole nomination for Leigh, who began her film career in 1947 after being spotted by Norma Shearer [150 . . .], the retired diva of MGM, who recommended the young actress to her old studio. In 1951 Leigh married Tony Curtis [522], with whom she was teamed in several films. Their daughter, Jamie Lee Curtis, made her own film debut in a movie deeply indebted to *Psycho, Halloween* (1978). For the most part, Leigh was a decorative presence in pleasant, routine films, but she appeared in a few more substantial works, including Orson Welles' *Touch of Evil* (1958) and John Frankenheimer's paranoid thriller *The Manchurian Candidate.* Now retired from the screen, Leigh was last seen in a horror movie, *The Fog* (1980), that starred her daughter. She lost the Oscar to Shirley Jones in *Elmer Gantry.*

This was the last of Hitchcock's five unsuccessful nominations. Though he never won as director, in 1967 he was given the Irving G. Thalberg Award, which honors film producers. This time he lost to Billy Wilder for *The Apartment.*

The cinematography Oscar went to Freddie Francis for *Sons and Lovers.* Alexander Trauner and Edward G. Boyle won for the art direction of *The Apartment.*

Hitchcock: 1171, 1669, 1670, 1890. Clatworthy: 843, 1003, 1812, 2035. Milo: 1065, 2035.

1633 • PUBLIC ENEMY, THE

WARNER BROS. 1930–31.

NOMINATION *Original Story:* John Bright and Kubec Glasmon.

James Cagney [79 . . .] plays Tom Powers, a young punk who becomes a big shot during Prohibi-

tion before he's finally gunned down. Powerful gangster flick with a live-wire role for Cagney, in his fourth film, the one that made him a star. He was originally cast in the secondary role played by Edward Woods. Legends have grown up about how the switch took place: Warners contract writers Bright and Glasmon said they wrote the script originally with Cagney in mind; studio head Jack Warner [55 . . .] also claimed credit for the casting. Cagney said that director William Wellman [157 . . .] made the switch, over the objections of Darryl F. Zanuck [34 . . .], then head of production at Warners, until Zanuck saw the rushes and realized that the wrong actor was playing the lead. The film also helped advance the career of Jean Harlow, playing the rival for Cagney's affections to Mae Clarke, who gets a grapefruit smashed in her face by Cagney in the film's signature scene. Though it was a popular success, the Academy passed over the film for best picture nominations in favor of such forgotten movies as *East Lynne* and *Skippy.* It has certainly lasted longer than even the best picture winner, *Cimarron,* thanks to Cagney's dynamite performance, which also escaped the Academy's notice.

Of the five films nominated for original story, three starred Cagney. (The other two were *Doorway to Hell* and *Smart Money.*) The winner, however, was John Monk Saunders' story for *The Dawn Patrol.*

1633.5 • PULP FICTION

BAND APART/JERSEY FILMS PRODUCTION; MIRAMAX. 1994.

AWARD *Screenplay Written Directly for the Screen:* Quentin Tarantino, screenplay; Quentin Tarantino and Roger Avary, stories.

NOMINATIONS *Picture:* Lawrence Bender, producer. *Actor:* John Travolta. *Supporting Actor:* Samuel L. Jackson. *Supporting Actress:* Uma Thurman. *Director:* Quentin Tarantino. *Film Editing:* Sally Menke.

Vincent (Travolta) and Jules (Jackson) are hit men in the hire of underworld boss Marsellus Wallace (Ving Rhames). Thurman plays Mia, Wallace's wife, whom Vincent must entertain one evening; he's nervously aware of the rumors of what has happened to people who got a bit too intimate with her. Their stories are mingled with those of a couple who call

each other "Pumpkin" (Tim Roth) and "Honey
Bunny" (Amanda Plummer) and are bent on robbing
the diner where they've just had breakfast, and Butch
(Bruce Willis), a boxer who double-crosses Wallace.
Audacious, bloody, and hilarious reworking of film
noir material into something fresh and unique. It was
a huge critical success, though from the first there
were dissenters: When it was given the top prize at
Cannes there were boos mingled with the cheers.
Audiences flocked to it as well, and were similarly
divided, though in the end the cheers far outnumbered the boos. Also in the cast are Harvey Keitel
[308] as a gangland cleanup specialist, Maria De
Medeiros as Butch's girlfriend, Eric Stoltz as a drug
pusher, and Christopher Walken [521] in a very funny
flashback cameo. Although it's far from the kind of
morally centered drama that usually wins the best
picture Oscar, *Pulp Fiction* was considered the only
strong contender against *Forrest Gump,* which won.

Tarantino claims to have learned the craft of filmmaking when he worked as a video store clerk and
steeped himself in all kinds of movies, particularly
relishing the imaginatively violent films of Hong Kong
director John Woo. Tarantino obtained the backing
for his first feature, the hyperviolent *Reservoir Dogs*
(1992), by persuading Keitel to star in and coproduce
it. He also funded his career as a director by selling
two screenplays, *True Romance* (1993) and *Natural Born
Killers* (1994). In *Pulp Fiction,* Tarantino, collaborating
with his friend Avary, backs off from the excessive
violence of *Reservoir Dogs* and concentrates instead on
developing quirky characters and narrative surprises
that have been called "Dickensian"—an adjective
that works well if one recalls the Dickens who was
fascinated with the criminal underworld of his day and
whose moments of horror often spill over into grotesque comedy. Though he lost the directing Oscar to
Robert Zemeckis for *Forrest Gump, Pulp Fiction* established Tarantino as one of the most promising new
talents in movies.

At the same time that *Pulp Fiction* was establishing a
new career, it was reviving a moribund one. At the
start of the eighties, Travolta was one of the movies'
biggest stars, after the smash hits of *Saturday Night*

Fever and *Grease.* But he seemed unable to choose material that would maintain that stardom, and he had a
string of disastrous flops through the rest of the decade. Only *Look Who's Talking* in 1989 was a box-office
hit, and that film's success was predicated more on
the appeal of a wisecracking baby than on Travolta's
performance. But *Pulp Fiction* put him on the A-list
once again, and he was considered the chief contender against Tom Hanks, who won as best actor for
Forrest Gump.

Many critics of the awards felt relegating Jackson
to supporting actor status was unfair and perhaps even
racist: Jackson's role is almost as large as Travolta's.
Jackson made his film debut in *Ragtime* in 1981, but
spent most of the decade in stage work. He gained
prominence in movies when he was cast by Spike Lee
[556] in *Do the Right Thing,* and followed with strong
roles in Lee's *Mo' Better Blues* (1990) and *Jungle Fever*
(1991). He has also been seen in a variety of parts in
such films as *GoodFellas, Patriot Games* (1992), and *Jurassic Park.* The Oscar went to Martin Landau for *Ed
Wood.*

Thurman made her film debut at seventeen in *Kiss
Daddy Goodnight* (1987), and established her career
with performances in *Dangerous Liaisons* and *Henry &
June,* and as the blind heroine of *Jennifer 8* (1992). The
Oscar went to Dianne Wiest for *Bullets Over Broadway.*

The editing award went to Arthur Schmidt for
Forrest Gump.

Travolta: 1760.

1634 • PUMPKIN EATER, THE

ROMULUS FIMS LTD. PRODUCTION; ROYAL FILMS INTERNATIONAL
(UNITED KINGDOM). 1964.

NOMINATION *Actress:* Anne Bancroft.

Bancroft, the mother of eight children, leaves her
second husband, Richard Johnson, for screenwriter
Peter Finch [1424 . . .], but finds that he's incurably
unfaithful. Intelligent, serious, downer film directed
by Jack Clayton [1724] from a screenplay by Harold
Pinter [185 . . .] based on a novel by Penelope
Mortimer. Full of exceptional performers doing their
best, including James Mason [761 . . .], Cedric
Hardwicke, Maggie Smith [332 . . .], and Eric Por-

ter. Bancroft, who does a flawless British accent throughout, lost to Julie Andrews in *Mary Poppins*.

Bancroft: 28, 810, 1326, 2152.

1635 • *PURPLE RAIN*

PURPLE FILMS COMPANY PRODUCTION; WARNER BROS. 1984.

AWARD *Original Song Score:* Prince.

Prince stars in a story about a Minneapolis musician's struggle to escape from an oppressive homelife and establish himself as a musician. As a concert flick it's terrific—providing you like Prince. As a narrative film it stinks, full of narcissism and sexism wrapped in moldy struggling-artist clichés. Written and directed by Albert Magnoli, although the real auteur is Prince. The cast includes Apollonia Kotero, Morris Day, and Clarence Williams III.

The award to Prince seemed to signal a change in the Academy, which had shunned rock in the late sixties and early seventies, passing over the work of the Beatles in *Hard Day's Night* and *Help!* Born Prince Rogers Nelson, the musician, noted for sexually suggestive performances, became one of the most important figures in popular music in the mid-eighties, rivaled as composer and performer only by Michael Jackson and Bruce Springsteen [1562.5]. After the Oscar, Prince directed as well as acted in three more films—*Under the Cherry Moon* (1986), *Sign o' the Times* (1987), and *Graffiti Bridge* (1990)—but they were critical and commercial failures.

1636 • *PURPLE ROSE OF CAIRO, THE*

JACK ROLLINS AND CHARLES H. JOFFE PRODUCTION; ORION. 1985.

NOMINATION *Screenplay Written Directly for the Screen:* Woody Allen.

Mia Farrow is a lonely woman whose husband, played by Danny Aiello [556], is abusive and unfaithful. She spends her days at the movies—the film is set in the thirties—where one day Jeff Daniels, a character in the film she's watching, notices her in the audience and, smitten, comes to life and steps off the screen. The other actors on screen are shocked at the alteration in their fictional life, and soon a group from the movie studio arrives to try to persuade the errant character back into the film. An ingenious little charmer, Allen's film, which he also directed but doesn't act in, turns needlessly melancholy at the end, when Farrow returns to her grim everyday life. The delightful cast also includes Dianne Wiest [311.5 . . .], Van Johnson, Zoe Caldwell, Milo O'Shea, Edward Herrmann, Michael Tucker, and Glenne Headly. The cinematography is by Gordon Willis [786 . . .]. Allen lost to William Kelley, Pamela Wallace, and Earl W. Wallace for *Witness*.

Allen: 39, 88, 294, 311.5, 461, 863, 962.5, 1005, 1267, 1647.

1637 • *PYGMALION*

MGM (UNITED KINGDOM). 1938.

AWARD *Screenplay:* George Bernard Shaw, adaptation by Ian Dalrymple, Cecil Lewis, and W. P. Lipscomb. **NOMINATIONS** *Picture:* Gabriel Pascal, producer. *Actor:* Leslie Howard. *Actress:* Wendy Hiller.

Linguistics professor Henry Higgins (Howard) wagers with Colonel Pickering (Scott Sunderland) that he can pass off the flower girl Eliza Doolittle (Hiller) as a duchess. He succeeds, but he radically changes her life and that of her dustman father (Wilfred Lawson). Shaw's play, now better known to most people in the musical version, *My Fair Lady,* is superbly translated to the screen, thanks to producer Pascal, who somehow charmed the irascible playwright into allowing the work to be filmed. It was codirected by Leslie Howard and Anthony Asquith. The cast includes Marie Lohr as Mrs. Higgins, Jean Cadell as Mrs. Pearce, and David Tree as Freddy Eynsford-Hill. Cathleen Nesbitt, who played Mrs. Higgins in the original production of *My Fair Lady,* has a smaller role in the film, and Anthony Quayle [85] can be glimpsed in a bit part. The cinematography is by Harry Stradling [110 . . .] and the musical score by Arthur Honegger.

Because it's one of the least preachy of Shaw's plays and has a measure of romance, *Pygmalion* is well suited for the screen. Pascal's later version of *Major Barbara* (1941) doesn't work quite as well because its plot, characterization, and ideas are more complex. Shaw himself wrote dialogue for several scenes, such as the Embassy Ball, which "open up" the play. He was famously miffed, however, at being nominated for the Oscar, blustering that it was "as if they had never heard of me—and it's very likely they never have." But it's also said that visitors to his home at Ayot St. Lawrence found the statuette on display. Shaw would doubtless be irate at the fact that he has become an Oscar trivia item: He is the only person to win both a Nobel Prize and an Academy Award.

The best picture Oscar went to *You Can't Take It With You.* This was the second of two nominations for Howard, who was on the brink of filming his most famous role: Ashley Wilkes in *Gone With the Wind.* He lost to Spencer Tracy in *Boys Town.* Hiller, who had appeared in only one film before this one, was chosen by Shaw for the role of Eliza. She lost to Bette Davis in *Jezebel.*

Dalrymple: 406. Howard: 178. Hiller: 1252, 1778.

1638 • QIVITOQ

A/S Nordisk Films Kampagni (Denmark). 1956.
Nomination *Foreign Language Film.*

A film about the cultural confrontation of Danes and Eskimos in Greenland, directed by Erik Balling and handsomely shot in color by Poul Pedersen, *Qivitoq* was made to celebrate the fiftieth anniversary of Nordisk, the oldest continuously operating film company in the world. In its eighty-first year, Nordisk would win Denmark's first foreign-film Oscar, for *Babette's Feast,* but this year it lost to the Italian producers of *La Strada.*

1639 • QUALITY STREET

RKO Radio. 1937.
Nomination *Score:* RKO Radio Studio Music Department, Roy Webb, musical director; score by Roy Webb.

Katharine Hepburn [24 . . .] wins the heart of Franchot Tone [1387], but he's an officer in the British army and has to go off and fight Napoleon. During his decade-long absence, she loses the first bloom of youth; when he returns, rather than confront him with her changed self, she poses as her own flighty

niece. One of the films that made Hepburn "box-office poison" and stymied her career until she could revive it with *The Philadelphia Story.* This whimsy based on a play by James Barrie, who was trying to emulate Jane Austen, brought out the worst of Hepburn's mannerisms and fluttery archness, but she looks lovely, and there are some good performances by Fay Bainter [393 . . .], Eric Blore, Cora Witherspoon, Estelle Winwood, and Joan Fontaine [441 . . .]. George Stevens [542 . . .] directs. The scoring award went to Charles Previn for *One Hundred Men and a Girl.*

Webb: 615, 640, 665, 969, 1049, 1394.

1640 • QUEEN BEE

Columbia. 1955.
Nominations *Black-and-White Cinematography:* Charles Lang. *Black-and-White Costume Design:* Jean Louis.

Joan Crawford [1319 . . .] plays a contemporary southern matron who interferes destructively in the lives of others: She drives her husband, Barry Sullivan, to drink, and his sister, Betsy Palmer, to suicide —in the latter case by thwarting Palmer's romance with Crawford's own former lover, John Ireland [53]. If you enjoy Crawford's eye-popping, you'll love it. Otherwise, it's a rather cheesy attempt to update *The Little Foxes.* The screenplay, based on a novel by Edna Lee, and the direction are by Ranald MacDougall [1319], who did the script for *Mildred Pierce.* The cinematography Oscar went to James Wong Howe for *The Rose Tattoo.* Helen Rose won for the costumes for *I'll Cry Tomorrow.*

Lang: 97, 250, 319, 636, 649, 705, 765, 953, 1480, 1699, 1738, 1778, 1855, 1860, 1955, 1968, 2180. Louis: 20, 126, 170, 262, 732, 744, 1028, 1065, 1521, 1812, 1858, 1910, 2064.

1640.5 • QUEEN MARGOT

Renn Productions; Miramax (France). 1994.
Nomination *Costume Design:* Moidele Bickel.

Isabelle Adjani [337 . . .] plays the title role, Marguerite de Valois, the Catholic wife of the Protestant Henri de Navarre (Daniel Auteuil), who becomes King Henri IV of France. Virna Lisi is Catherine de

Medici, Margot's mother. Margot's promiscuity, particularly her affair with La Mole (Vincent Perez), and the virulent religious conflicts of the sixteenth century form the central story of this lavish but often impenetrable (at least to those not versed in French history) epic, culminating in the St. Bartholomew's Day massacre of the Huguenots. Directed by Patrice Chereau and filmed by Philippe Rousselot [900 . . .]. Lisi won the best actress award at Cannes and the film was given a special jury prize, but it was poorly received by both critics and art-house audiences in the States. The costuming award went to Lizzy Gardiner and Tim Chappel for *The Adventures of Priscilla, Queen of the Desert.*

1641 • *QUEST FOR FIRE*

International Cinema Corporation Production; 20th Century-Fox (France/Canada). 1982.

Award *Makeup:* Sarah Monzani and Michele Burke.

Three Stone Age warriors set out to find fire, which they have not yet discovered how to produce. They battle predators and Neanderthals, and rescue from cannibals a woman who belongs to a more advanced tribe that has mastered the art of fire. Interesting try at a prehistoric epic, directed by Jean-Jacques Annaud from a screenplay by Gérard Brach. Attempts have been made to advance it far beyond such campy howlers as *One Million B.C.;* novelist Anthony Burgess created a language for the characters, and pop anthropologist Desmond Morris served as a consultant on body movements and other physical traits. The makeup is the real star; underneath it are Everett McGill, Rae Dawn Chong, Ron Perlman, and Nameer El-Kadi. Philippe Sarde [2021] did the score, and the production was designed by Guy Comtois and Brian Morris. It was filmed, by Claude Agostini, on locations in Africa, Canada, Scotland, and Iceland.

Burke: 272.5, 409, 474.

1642 • *QUIET MAN, THE*

Argosy Pictures; Republic. 1952.

Awards *Director:* John Ford. *Color Cinematography:* Winston C. Hoch and Archie Stout.

Nominations *Picture:* John Ford and Merian C.

Cooper, producers. *Supporting Actor:* Victor McLaglen. *Screenplay:* Frank S. Nugent. *Color Art Direction—Set Decoration:* Frank Hotaling; John McCarthy, Jr., and Charles Thompson. *Sound Recording:* Republic Sound Department, Daniel J. Bloomberg, sound director.

American Sean Thornton, played by John Wayne [33 . . .], moves to the Irish village of Inisfree and buys the cottage he was born in, infuriating Will Danaher (McLaglen), who had been planning to expand his own land holdings by buying the cottage, which was owned by the Widow Tillane, played by Mildred Natwick [147]. He's further enraged when Thornton falls in love with Danaher's sister, Mary Kate (Maureen O'Hara). Wanting to encourage the likable American, some of the locals tell Danaher that he could expand his holdings by marrying the widow, and that she'd be willing as long as there's no other woman—i.e., Mary Kate—in the house, so Danaher agrees to allow Thornton and Mary Kate to marry. But when the widow refuses his proposal, Danaher learns he's been deceived. Furious, he denies Mary Kate her dowry. When Thornton refuses to fight Danaher for the money, Mary Kate runs away. Only the Reverend Playfair (Arthur Shields), a boxing aficionado, knows why Thornton won't fight: He once killed a man in the ring. Playfair persuades Thornton that some things are worth fighting for, so Thornton pursues Mary Kate, drags her over hill and dale, and returns her to her brother's house. Danaher relents and gives her the money, which she and Thornton throw into the fire. Spoiling for a fight, Danaher throws a punch at Thornton, who returns it. After an epic brawl, Thornton goes home to Mary Kate and Danaher goes off to court the widow. Rich, rousing romantic comedy-drama that transcends its stereotypes of the Irish as drinkers and brawlers. It's an Ireland where people talk like poets and where Protestants and Catholics get along amicably; the town is squeaky-clean and prosperous, and the countryside is impossibly green. But there are also hints of darkness, of the subjugation of women, which Mary Kate battles, and of the impoverished, politically turbulent past that caused Thornton's family to leave the village. Like most of Ford's best films, it has a sentimental, even cornball, surface but a suggestive subtext. It also has a remarkable cast, including Barry Fitzgerald [787] as the matchmaker Michaeleen Flynn and Ward Bond as Father Lonergan. Perhaps because it came from "poverty row" Republic—the only studio Ford could find that would back him in making the picture the way he wanted it: in color and on location—the film was overlooked in some Oscar categories where it should have been included. Maureen O'Hara, for example, who never received a nomination, deserved one far more than Joan Crawford in *Sudden Fear,* Bette Davis in *The Star,* or Susan Hayward in *With a Song in My Heart.* And the score by Victor Young [97 . . .] is more memorable than that by Max Steiner for *The Miracle of Our Lady of Fatima* or Herschel Burke Gilbert's for *The Thief.*

Ford's fourth Oscar set a record for directors that has yet to be broken. But contemporary critics dismissed much of Ford's later career as routine, and the director was at odds with the Hollywood establishment, especially after the troubled filming of *Mister Roberts,* from which personal demons caused Ford to withdraw in midfilming. So this was his last nomination, despite subsequent films such as *The Searchers* (1956) and *The Man Who Shot Liberty Valance* that later critics rank among the director's best. Ford's last films, *Seven Women* and *Young Cassidy,* were made in 1965, half a century after John joined his elder brother, Francis (who plays Dan Tobin in *The Quiet Man),* in Hollywood. John Ford died in 1973 of cancer.

The cinematography Oscar was richly deserved. The only conceivable challenger to Hoch and Stout, Oswald Morris [659 . . .], wasn't nominated for his work on *Moulin Rouge.* Hoch had gone three for three at the Oscars. Subsequently he would shoot one of the most remarkable films ever to be completely ignored by the Academy, Ford's *The Searchers,* and become a pioneer in developing color photography for TV. He died in 1979. This was Stout's sole nomination in a career that began in 1914, when he went to work for Mack Sennett's Keystone. His specialty was outdoor work, and much of his later career was in association with John Wayne on such films as *Angel and the Badman* (1947), *Fort Apache* (1948), *Hondo,* and *The High and the Mighty,* which was his last film. He retired in 1954 after a heart attack but lived until 1965.

Ford had bought the rights to the story by Maurice Walsh on which *The Quiet Man* is based in the thirties. He persuaded Republic to give him the backing he needed by first making *Rio Grande* (with many from the *Quiet Man* cast, including Wayne, O'Hara, and McLaglen) for the studio in 1950. In the best picture race, *The Quiet Man* faced such competitors as *High Noon, Ivanhoe,* and *Moulin Rouge* and lost to *The Greatest Show on Earth.*

McLaglen lost to Anthony Quinn in *Viva Zapata!* Charles Schnee won the screenplay award for *The Bad and the Beautiful. Moulin Rouge* took the Oscar for art direction and *Breaking the Sound Barrier* for sound.

Ford: 815, 952, 999, 1200, 1901. Hoch: 1048, 1807. Cooper: 1189. McLaglen: 999. McCarthy: 744. Thompson: 1537. Bloomberg: 274, 680, 693, 991, 1350, 1756.

1643 • QUIET ONE, THE

FILM DOCUMENTS; MAYER-BURSTYN. 1949.

NOMINATION *Story and Screenplay:* Helen Levitt, Janice Loeb, and Sidney Meyers.

A ten-year-old boy in Harlem turns delinquent but is helped by a special school. Though it won an award at the 1949 Venice Film Festival, this low-budget docudrama is no longer in general circulation. Directed by Meyers, who also plays a psychiatrist in the film. James Agee [24] wrote commentary and dialogue, and Gary Merrill provides the off-screen narration. Writer Loeb was also the film's producer, and Levitt receives a cinematography credit. The Oscar went to Robert Pirosh for *Battleground.*

1643.5 • QUIZ SHOW

HOLLYWOOD PICTURES PRESENTATION OF A WILDWOOD ENTERPRISES/BALTIMORE PICTURES PRODUCTION; BUENA VISTA. 1994.

NOMINATIONS *Picture:* Robert Redford, Michael Jacobs, Julian Krainin, and Michael Nozik, producers. *Supporting Actor:* Paul Scofield. *Director:* Robert Redford. *Screenplay Based on Material Previously Produced or Published:* Paul Attanasio.

John Turturro plays Herb Stempel, an abrasive nerd who becomes a celebrity in the fifties with his string of wins on the TV quiz show "Twenty-One" —wins that are carefully orchestrated by the show's producers. But then the producers decide to end Stempel's winning streak and replace him with a more appealing egghead, young college professor Charles Van Doren, played by Ralph Fiennes [1764.65], who is also coached in the answers. Stempel, believing that there is a streak of anti-Semitism in the network's decision to bump him from the show in favor of the patrician WASP Van Doren, finally gets the ear of a congressional investigator, Richard Goodwin (Rob Morrow). An entertaining skeptical look at an American epoch—wittily written, skillfully directed, and finely cast, with Scofield as Charles Van Doren's upright father, Mark; David Paymer [1368.5] as producer Dan Enright; and Christopher McDonald as quiz show host Jack Barry. There are also amusing cameos by two major film directors: Martin Scorsese [27.5 . . .] as the representative of the quiz show's sponsor, Geritol, and Barry Levinson [75 . . .] as *Today* show host Dave Garroway. The cinematography is by Michael Ballhaus [293 . . .].

The screenplay by Attanasio, a former *Washington Post* film critic, is based on Goodwin's memoir, *Remembering America: A Voice From the Sixties*. But though the movie uses the real names of the participants in the quiz show scandals, its dramatic effects are achieved by scrambling chronology and beefing up the role of Goodwin in exposing the fraud. Though some critics carped about these deviations from fact, on the whole *Quiz Show* received some of the best reviews of any film of 1994, and it was hailed as Redford's best directing job to date. But audiences couldn't be persuaded to see it: *Quiz Show* was one of the year's biggest box-office disappointments. Some blamed the studio's marketing campaign: The film opened as a "prestige" production in New York and L.A., and only gradually widened into other urban and suburban theaters after the first publicity barrage had spent itself. Others wondered if the topic of the film was too intellectual in a year that celebrated the "dumbness" of *Forrest Gump*. Still others wondered if audiences weren't waiting to see a film *about* television *on* television—*Quiz Show* lacked action and romance, making it the sort of thing one could wait to see on video. In any case, the film's box-office demise seemed to doom its chances for Oscars, which went to *Forrest Gump* for best picture, director Robert Zemeckis, and screenwriter Eric Roth. On the other hand, poor box-office didn't seem to hurt *Ed Wood* in the awards, and Scofield lost to Martin Landau's performance in that film.

Redford: 1502, 1927. Scofield: 1252.

1644 • *QUO VADIS?*

MGM. 1951.
NOMINATIONS *Picture:* Sam Zimbalist, producer. *Supporting Actor:* Leo Genn. *Supporting Actor:* Peter Ustinov. *Color Cinematography:* Robert Surtees and William V. Skall. *Color Art Direction—Set Decoration:* William A. Horning, Cedric Gibbons, and Edward Carfagno; Hugh Hunt. *Scoring of a Dramatic or Comedy Picture:* Miklos Rozsa. *Film Editing:* Ralph E. Winters. *Color Costume Design:* Herschel McCoy.

Marcus Vinicius (Robert Taylor) is a noble Roman in the army of the Emperor Nero (Ustinov), and therefore a sworn enemy of the new sect of Christians said to be stirring up trouble in Rome. He's also a favorite of the Empress Poppaea (Patricia Laffan). But then he falls in love with the beautiful Christian Lygia, played by Deborah Kerr [599 . . .], and to get even, Poppaea has the lot of them thrown to the lions. Meanwhile, Nero has Rome burned so he can build a more impressive imperial capital. The episodes of sadistic violence are sugarcoated—or perhaps Nutra-Sweet-coated, since there's nothing "natural" about this film—with a phony religiosity. Apart from the spectacle, the movie's best moments belong to Ustinov, who's an even hammier Nero than Charles Laughton [1387 . . .], who played the part in *The Sign of the Cross,* which *Quo Vadis?* greatly resembles. Mervyn LeRoy [1662 . . .] directed, and the cast includes Genn as Petronius, Finlay Currie as Peter, Abraham Sofaer as Paul, Buddy Baer as Ursus, Felix

Aylmer as Plautius, Rosalie Crutchley as Acte, and it's said that both Elizabeth Taylor [318 . . .] and Sophia Loren [1280 . . .] are extras—Taylor because she was honeymooning in Rome with Nicky Hilton and thought it would be fun, Loren because she was an unknown who needed the money.

Quo Vadis? has much in common with the later and more successful *Ben-Hur*. Both were based on pious old warhorse novels: *Quo Vadis?* on a work by Henryk Sienkewicz, *Ben-Hur* on Gen. Lew Wallace's tome. Both enlisted prestigious "name" writers for their screenplays: *Ben-Hur* had Gore Vidal and Christopher Fry, *Quo Vadis?* playwright S. N. Behrman, along with Hollywood veterans John Lee Mahin [352 . . .] and Sonya Levien [1007 . . .]. And Zimbalist, Surtees, Horning, Carfagno, Hunt, Rozsa, and Winters all worked on both pictures. But where *Ben-Hur* took more Oscars than any other picture in history, *Quo Vadis?* struck out in all the categories for which it was nominated. MGM's other contender, *An American in Paris,* took the award for best picture, for the color cinematography of Alfred Gilks and John Alton, for art direction, and for Walter Plunkett and Irene Sharaff's costumes. The supporting actor Oscar went to Karl Malden for *A Streetcar Named Desire,* and *A Place in the Sun* was the winner for Franz Waxman's score and William Hornbeck's editing.

Zimbalist: 175, 1094. Ustinov: 943, 1886, 2116. Surtees: 130, 175, 557, 810, 917, 1094, 1139, 1388, 1469, 1747, 1911, 1927, 1960, 2055, 2152. Skall: 96, 208, 1048, 1170, 1317, 1453, 1668, 1822, 2102. Horning: 175, 440, 769, 1157, 1450, 1657, 2300. Gibbons: 66, 87, 130, 217, 227, 239, 285, 290, 440, 629, 749, 831, 980, 1069, 1096, 1173, 1190, 1226, 1230, 1232, 1274, 1308, 1309, 1417, 1567, 1604, 1662, 1673, 1721, 1861, 1937, 2068, 2112, 2256, 2257, 2300, 2320, 2330. Carfagno: 130, 175, 629, 917, 1069, 1552, 1814, 1937, 2312. Hunt: 175, 401, 980, 1069, 1232, 1335, 1388, 1567, 1657, 1673, 2157, 2184. Rozsa: 175, 566, 567, 604, 1035, 1069, 1070, 1085, 1208, 1227, 1872, 1890, 1968, 2050, 2304. Winters: 175, 825, 1094, 1109, 1782. McCoy: 578.

1645 • RACHEL, RACHEL

WARNER BROS.-SEVEN ARTS. 1968.
NOMINATIONS *Picture:* Paul Newman, producer. *Actress:* Joanne Woodward. *Supporting Actress:* Estelle Parsons. *Screenplay—Based on Material From Another Medium:* Stewart Stern.

Woodward plays a lonely, unmarried middle-aged schoolteacher in a small Connecticut town, who gets a chance at love in the form of lonely, unmarried middle-aged James Olson. The kind of film often described as "sensitive"—code for "don't go expecting sex, violence, or laughs." Of its kind, it's particularly well done, with Woodward giving a subtly appealing performance and getting good support from Parsons, Kate Harrington, Donald Moffat, and Geraldine Fitzgerald [2316].

The failure of the Academy to nominate Newman as director—he made his directorial debut with the film and won the New York Film Critics Award for it —infuriated his wife, Woodward, who was determined to boycott the Oscars until he talked her out of it. Newman was one of the two best picture directors passed over for a directing nomination this year; the other was William Wyler for *Funny Girl*. In their place, the Academy nominated Stanley Kubrick for *2001: A Space Odyssey* and Gillo Pontecorvo for *The Battle of Algiers*. The award went to Carol Reed for *Oliver!,* which also won the best picture Oscar. Woodward lost to the only women to tie for a best actress Oscar: Katharine Hepburn in *The Lion in Winter* and Barbra Streisand in *Funny Girl*. Parsons lost to Ruth Gordon for *Rosemary's Baby*. The writing award went to James Goldman for *The Lion in Winter*.

Newman: 3, 372, 422, 443, 956, 964, 1444.5, 2198. Woodward: 1365, 1962, 2075. Parsons: 255. Stern: 2018.

1646 • RACKET, THE

THE CADDO COMPANY; PARAMOUNT FAMOUS LASKY. 1927–28.
NOMINATION *Production:* Howard Hughes, producer.

Silent gangster film about a big-city police officer (Thomas Meighan) trying to control the mob, led by Lewis Wolheim, but hamstrung by municipal corruption. Directed by Lewis Milestone [48 . . .] from a screenplay by Harry Behn, Del Andrews [48], and Bartlett Cormack based on Cormack's play. The cinematography is by Tony Gaudio [90 . . .]. Hughes remade it in 1951; the first version is apparently lost. The Oscar went to *Wings.*

Hughes: 734.

1647 • *RADIO DAYS*
ORION. 1987.
NOMINATIONS *Screenplay Written Directly for the Screen:* Woody Allen. *Art Direction–Set Decoration:* Santo Loquasto; Carol Joffe, Les Bloom, and George De Titta, Jr.

Scenes from the lives of a family living in Queens during World War II are mixed with those of a group of radio actors the family listens to on the radio. Pleasant nostalgia drawn from writer-director Allen's own childhood—it's his *Amarcord.* The big cast, made up of many regulars from Allen's previous films, includes Seth Green as the small boy modeled on Allen (the real Allen does voice-over narration), Julie Kavner and Michael Tucker as his parents, Mia Farrow as a hopeful who wants to break into radio, plus Josh Mostel, Dianne Wiest [311.5 . . .], Wallace Shawn, Tito Puente, Danny Aiello [556], Jeff Daniels, Tony Roberts, Diane Keaton [88 . . .], Kitty Carlisle Hart, Kenneth Mars, and Mercedes Ruehl [671]. The Oscar for screenplay went to John Patrick Shanley for *Moonstruck. The Last Emperor* won for art direction.

Allen: 39, 88, 294, 311.5, 461, 863, 962.5, 1005, 1267, 1636. Loquasto: 311.5, 2345. Joffe: 863. Bloom: 448. De Titta: 1651.

1648 • *RAFFLES*
SAMUEL GOLDWYN PRODUCTIONS; UNITED ARTISTS. 1929–30.
NOMINATION *Sound Recording:* Oscar Lagerstrom.

Ronald Colman plays a cricket-playing gentleman who has had a successful career as a thief but is determined to go straight. Then a friend in need contacts him, and he agrees to one last heist. Thanks to Colman's suave performance, this is probably the most successful of the four film versions of the story, from a turn-of-the-century novel, *Raffles the Amateur Cracksman,* by E. W. Hornung. John Barrymore had starred in a silent version in 1917, another one came along in 1925, and Goldwyn remade the 1930 version almost scene for scene—though with an ending more in line with the Production Code—in 1939 with David Niven [1778]. Directed by Harry D'Arrast [1148] and —after producer Samuel Goldwyn [102 . . .] fired D'Arrast—George Fitzmaurice; the screenplay is by Sidney Howard [102 . . .]. The cast includes Kay Francis as the romantic lead. The Oscar for sound, the first ever given, went to Douglas Shearer for *The Big House.*

Lagerstrom: 560.

1649 • *RAGE TO LIVE, A*
MIRISCH CORPORATION OF DELAWARE-ARAHO PRODUCTION; UNITED ARTISTS. 1965.
NOMINATION *Black-and-White Costume Design:* Howard Shoup.

A promiscuous woman (Suzanne Pleshette) finds that marriage doesn't satisfy her needs. Dull version of a once-shocking novel by John O'Hara. The film is franker than it would have been five years earlier, when the Production Code was still being enforced, but not as explicit as it would have been five years later, after the MPAA ratings system had taken effect. A decidedly second-string cast—Bradford Dillman, Ben Gazzara, Peter Graves, Bethel Leslie, and James Gregory—doesn't help, nor does the direction of Walter Grauman. The Oscar went to designer Julie Harris for *Darling.*

Shoup: 410, 1100, 1700, 2338.

1650 • *RAGING BULL*
ROBERT CHARTOFF-IRWIN WINKLER PRODUCTION; UNITED ARTISTS. 1980.
AWARDS *Actor:* Robert De Niro. *Film Editing:* Thelma Schoonmaker.
NOMINATIONS *Picture:* Irwin Winkler and Robert Chartoff, producers. *Supporting Actor:* Joe Pesci. *Supporting Actress:* Cathy Moriarty. *Director:* Martin Scorsese. *Cinematography:* Michael Chapman. *Sound:* Donald O. Mitchell, Bill Nicholson, David J. Kimball, and Les Lazarowitz.

De Niro is fighter Jake La Motta, with Pesci as his brother, Joey, and Moriarty as La Motta's second wife, Vikki. The film is an ironic biopic, avoiding the clichés of the genre while at the same time alluding to those clichés, and those of boxing films such as *Golden Boy* and *Champion*—it's clearly a movie made by a man in love with movies. That may explain why film critics praise it so highly. It took first place in a critics' poll to name the best films of the eighties—admittedly a decade without a lot of high points. It's an easy film to admire; it's made with consummate skill and has three terrific performances. But it's a hard film to love, largely because it's about a most unlovable man—a crude, brutal fighter who becomes tolerable only after he self-destructs. So although the Academy's failure to honor it more highly is often cited as an example of the institution's blindness, it's also understandable: Unlike *Ordinary People,* the film that won best picture, *Raging Bull* doesn't have the high moral tone that the Academy has traditionally sought from movies. Still, it's difficult to explain the Academy's failure to nominate the screenplay by Paul Schrader and Mardik Martin.

De Niro was celebrated as much for the physical exertion of the role as for the intensity of his characterization. He trained with La Motta before filming started, and the boxer said that he believed the actor could have turned professional fighter with ease. And then, to film the sequences of the older, out-of-shape La Motta, Scorsese shut down production while De Niro ate himself out of shape, gaining more than fifty pounds. The Oscar attested to the fact that in the six years since his first Academy Award, De Niro had become the foremost American film actor of his generation. (He was born in 1943.) On the other hand, although he has worked steadily in a wide range of films and roles ranging from the vicious Al Capone in *The Untouchables* to the tormented comatose patient in *Awakenings* to the monster in *Mary Shelley's Frankenstein,* he has not recently had a role that captures the imagination the way his great performances of the late seventies did.

Schoonmaker's career has been identified with that of Scorsese, whose very first feature, *Who's That Knocking at My Door?,* she edited in 1968. Together, they worked as editors on *Woodstock,* for which she received her first nomination, and their collaboration as director and editor has continued to this day.

Pesci had begun as a nightclub singer, guitar player, and comedian, and had made only one film, a low-budget affair called *Death Collector* (1975), before he was cast in *Raging Bull.* He was managing a restaurant when De Niro suggested him for the role. The Oscar nomination—he lost to Timothy Hutton in *Ordinary People*—put Pesci back into the acting business, but stardom would wait another decade, until his Oscar-winning role in another Scorsese film, *GoodFellas.*

Stardom would also elude Moriarty, a model still in her teens who had no significant acting experience when Pesci noted her resemblance to the real Vikki La Motta and suggested her to Scorsese. After the Oscar nomination, she slipped back into obscurity for a decade, reemerging in the early nineties as a character actress, playing bombshell types with wit and style in such films as *The Mambo Kings, Soapdish* (1991), and *Matinee* (1993). The Oscar went to Mary Steenburgen for *Melvin and Howard.*

Scorsese, who continues to be ranked by critics as America's most interesting director, lost to Robert Redford for *Ordinary People.*

Interestingly there were two black-and-white films nominated for best picture this year; the other was *The Elephant Man,* whose cinematographer, Freddie Francis, was not among the nominees. Chapman lost to Geoffrey Unsworth and Ghislain Cloquet for *Tess.*

The Oscar for sound went to *The Empire Strikes Back.*

De Niro: 113, 342, 521, 785, 2005. Schoonmaker: 806, 2312.5. Winkler: 806, 1698, 1712. Chartoff: 1698, 1712. Pesci: 806. Scorsese: 27.5, 806, 1142. Chapman: 734.5. Mitchell: 223, 398, 411.5, 507, 734.5, 779, 1525, 1824, 1825, 2020, 2114, 2176.5. Lazarowitz: 2113.

1651 • RAGTIME

RAGTIME PRODUCTION; PARAMOUNT. 1981.

NOMINATIONS *Supporting Actor:* Howard E. Rollins, Jr. *Supporting Actress:* Elizabeth McGovern. *Screenplay*

Based on Material From Another Medium: Michael Weller. *Cinematography:* Miroslav Ondricek. *Art Direction—Set Decoration:* John Graysmark, Patrizia Von Brandenstein, and Anthony Reading; George De Titta, Sr., George De Titta, Jr., and Peter Howitt. *Original Song:* "One More Hour," music and lyrics by Randy Newman. *Original Score:* Randy Newman. *Costume Design:* Anna Hill Johnstone.

Rollins plays a young black musician in turn-of-the-century New York who becomes a terrorist because of his apparent mistreatment by whites he had trusted. This episode was a subplot in E. L. Doctorow's best-selling novel, but it becomes the central one in the film, directed by Milos Forman [60 . . .]. It is interwoven with others, such as the murder of architect Stanford White, who is played by novelist Norman Mailer. McGovern is White's mistress, Evelyn Nesbit. The large cast also includes Mary Steenburgen [1300], James Olson, Brad Dourif [1481], Kenneth McMillan, Mandy Patinkin, Donald O'Connor, Pat O'Brien, Debbie Allen, Moses Gunn, Jeff Daniels, and John Ratzenberger. The film's major casting coup was James Cagney [79 . . .] as the commissioner of police. Cagney was persuaded by Forman, who lived nearby on Martha's Vineyard, to make a comeback after twenty years' absence from the screen. A big-budget project, *Ragtime* was a critical and commercial disappointment. Screenwriter Weller fails to capture the intricacy of Doctorow's novel, a witty fantasia on historical themes. The novel had originally been bought by Dino de Laurentiis for director Robert Altman [1286 . . .], who might have captured its texture, but producer and director had a parting of the ways, so de Laurentiis took it to Forman.

Rollins landed the role after a Scarlett O'Hara–style talent search. Unfortunately the failure of the film didn't help Rollins' career much. He has been seen in occasional films, most notably *A Soldier's Story,* but is best known for his work on the TV series based on the film *In the Heat of the Night.* His recent career, however, has been hindered by serious personal problems, including several headline-making run-ins with the law. The Oscar went to John Gielgud for *Arthur.*

McGovern was similarly hailed as a new star for her work in the film, but good roles for women are hard to come by, and she has been seen in a mixture of film, TV, and stage work. Maureen Stapleton won for *Reds.*

Weller's screenplay lost to Ernest Thompson's adaptation of his own play, *On Golden Pond.* Vittorio Storaro took the cinematography Oscar for *Reds.* The art direction award went to *Raiders of the Lost Ark.*

Newman was already established as a major songwriter and performer, but his nominations marked the emergence of the second generation of Newmans in the film scoring business. His uncles, Alfred [31 . . .] and Lionel [183 . . .], had multiple nominations to their credit. He lost the song Oscar to the team that wrote "Arthur's Theme (Best That You Can Do)." The scoring award went to Vangelis for *Chariots of Fire.*

Ondricek: 60. Graysmark: 2340. Von Brandenstein: 60, 2185. De Titta, Jr.: 1647. Howitt: 995, 1285, 2274. Newman: 112, 1418, 1524.5, 1530. Johnstone: 784.

1652 • *RAIDERS OF THE LOST ARK*

Lucasfilm Ltd. Production; Paramount. 1981.

Awards *Art Direction—Set Decoration:* Norman Reynolds and Leslie Dilley; Michael Ford. *Sound:* Bill Varney, Steve Maslow, Gregg Landaker, and Roy Charman. *Film Editing:* Michael Kahn. *Visual Effects:* Richard Edlund, Kit West, Bruce Nicholson, and Joe Johnston. *Special Achievement Award for Sound Effects Editing:* Benjamin P. Burtt, Jr., and Richard L. Anderson.

Nominations *Picture:* Frank Marshall, producer. *Director:* Steven Spielberg. *Cinematography:* Douglas Slocombe. *Original Score:* John Williams.

Adventurous archaeologist Indiana Jones, played by Harrison Ford [2296], is enlisted in the search for the Ark of the Covenant—which the Nazis are also seeking, with the belief that whoever possesses it will have ultimate power. Indy endures all sorts of perils, escaping by a hair's breadth every time, until the wrath of God dispatches the villains at film's end. Larky action adventure that became an enormous phenomenon, setting off Hollywood's quest for bigger and bigger blockbusters. It was conceived as an affectionate tribute to the kind of movies that Spielberg and executive producer George Lucas [65 . . .] loved when they were kids: Saturday matinee thrillers and cliff-hanger serials. The previous successes of both filmmakers gave them the clout to make any kind of movie they wanted. It turned out that audiences wanted to see the same kind of movie, and this led to two more *Indiana Jones* movies, plus countless less entertaining knockoffs. Lucas and Spielberg thus became the agents of what has been called the "dumbing down" of American movies. Lucas wrote the screenplay in collaboration with Lawrence Kasdan [6 . . .], who received the screen credit. The cast includes Karen Allen as Indiana's spunky girlfriend, Paul Freeman as a Nazi archaeologist, and Denholm Elliott [1725] as one of Indy's colleagues. Ford, who was already well established as Han Solo in Lucas' *Star Wars* trilogy, was not initially considered for the role of Indiana. The part was offered to Tom Selleck, who declined because he had been signed for the TV series that made him famous, *Magnum, P.I.*

Like the *Star Wars* films, *Raiders* raked in the technical awards but was not considered a serious contender for the more prestigious Oscars such as picture and director. Those honors went to *Chariots of Fire* and to Warren Beatty for *Reds*. The latter film also won for Vittorio Storaro's cinematography, while *Chariots* took the Oscar for Vangelis' score.

Reynolds: 613, 614, 995, 1684, 1916. Dilley: 5, 44, 614, 1916. Ford: 614, 1684. Varney: 127, 586, 614. Maslow: 586, 614, 1888.5. Landaker: 614, 1047, 1888.5. Charman: 45, 1977, 2287. Kahn: 416, 613, 653, 1764.65. Edlund: 45.5, 544, 614, 766, 1589, 1590, 1684, 1916, 2165. West: 2339. Nicholson: 614, 1589. Burtt: 588, 996, 1684, 1916, 2284. Anderson: 1589. Marshall: 423. Spielberg: 416, 423, 588, 1764.65. Slocombe: 1066, 2134. Williams: 6, 260, 403, 416, 588, 613, 614, 659, 805, 933, 937, 982, 996, 997, 1041, 1047, 1596, 1679, 1684, 1701, 1764.65, 1916, 1977, 2107, 2126, 2194, 2293, 2322.

1653 • RAIN MAN

GUBER-PETERS COMPANY PRODUCTION; UNITED ARTISTS. 1988.
AWARDS *Picture:* Mark Johnson, producer. *Actor:* Dustin Hoffman. *Director:* Barry Levinson. *Screenplay Written Directly for the Screen:* Ronald Bass and Barry Morrow, screenplay; Barry Morrow, story.
NOMINATIONS *Cinematography:* John Seale. *Art Direction—Set Decoration:* Ida Random; Linda DeScenna. *Original Score:* Hans Zimmer. *Film Editing:* Stu Linder.

Tom Cruise [260] plays Charlie Babbitt, a flashy car salesman who discovers at his father's death that he has an older brother, Raymond (Hoffman), who has been institutionalized because, although he's a mathematical genius, he's autistic. Furious that he's been cut out of the father's will in favor of Raymond, Charlie "liberates" Raymond from the institution and the two set out on a cross-country odyssey during which they develop a closeness that will be unexpected only to people who have never seen a movie before. Entertaining vehicle for two surprisingly complementary stars, though Cruise's contribution to the film was underestimated by the Academy: Hoffman has the showier part, but it's essentially a collection of mannerisms, while Cruise is called on to develop a character that actually changes in the course of the film. The film was originally offered to Hoffman and Bill Murray, with Hoffman as Charlie and Murray as Raymond. But Murray turned it down, while Hoffman, who had been intrigued by an installment of *60 Minutes* on autistic savants, wanted to play Raymond. Cruise's eagerness to play the part of Charlie was welcomed: He would attract a younger audience. Finding a director was more complicated. Martin Brest [1764.5] was originally attached to the project but withdrew after disagreements with Hoffman. Steven Spielberg [416 . . .] agreed to do it but was committed to finishing *Indiana Jones and the Last Crusade*. Sydney Pollack [1512 . . .] was also briefly attached to the project before Levinson finally signed on. After all the trouble—plus numerous script revisions—*Rain Man* turned out to be a solid critical success and a huge box-office success.

The combination of critical and financial success, as well as the fact that *Rain Man* opened at year's end, which always gives a film an edge at Oscar time, made it nearly unbeatable. Its competition was flawed. *The Accidental Tourist* was a rather too low-key movie that disappointed admirers of the novel on which it was based and failed to attract an audience; *Dangerous Liaisons,* perhaps the best of the contenders, was too cynical and downbeat for the Academy; *Mississippi Burning* had drawn sharp criticism for its historical and political inaccuracies; and *Working Girl* was a crowd-pleasing romantic comedy—a genre that has only rarely taken the top award.

Hoffman's award was also considered a sure thing, although his competition was quite strong. Gene Hackman had been praised for his work in *Mississippi Burning,* and many felt he was overdue for recognition again by the Academy; since his award seventeen years earlier for *The French Connection,* Hackman, one of Hollywood's best actors, had not even been nominated. Tom Hanks was highly praised for his tour de force as a thirteen-year-old in a thirty-year-old's body in *Big.* Edward James Olmos had given a charismatic performance as math teacher Jaime Escalante in *Stand and Deliver.* And Max von Sydow, who had been recognized as one of the world's most distinguished actors for thirty years, had never been nominated before his performance in *Pelle the Conqueror.* But Hoffman, once a bitter critic of the Academy, as well as a notoriously difficult perfectionist, had become a Hollywood legend. There were perhaps also many who felt that he had been shortchanged by the Academy six years earlier when his brilliant performance in *Tootsie* had been passed over in favor of Ben Kingsley in *Gandhi.* This was Hoffman's second Oscar. Since winning it, he has given several interesting performances—including the incomprehensible Mumbles in *Dick Tracy* and the sinister pirate captain in *Hook*—but has not found a more substantial vehicle for his talent.

Levinson also has an on-screen role in *Rain Man* as the psychiatrist who evaluates Charlie's petition to be named guardian of Raymond at the film's end. He had begun his career as a TV comedy writer and moved over into films in the later seventies. He turned director in 1982 with *Diner,* the first of several movies he

has made about his native Baltimore. After the *Rain Man* Oscar, Levinson's career has had one high point, the stylish but cold *Bugsy,* and two lows, the flops *Toys* and *Jimmy Hollywood* (1994).

Writer Morrow came up with the story idea for *Rain Man* while doing research for a book about a mentally retarded man, *Bill,* which was turned into a TV movie starring Mickey Rooney [115 . . .]. His original screenplay was first handed over to Bass for rewrites, but as directors came and went on the project, writers Richard Price, Michael Bortman, David Rayfiel, and Kurt Luedtke [3 . . .] were also involved, and there was heavy input from Hoffman in the shaping of Raymond's character, as well as from the final director, Levinson. In the end, however, only Bass and Morrow received credit.

The Oscar for cinematography went to Peter Biziou for *Mississippi Burning. Dangerous Liaisons* won for Stuart Craig and Gerard James' art direction. Dave Grusin took the scoring award for *The Milagro Beanfield War,* and Arthur Schmidt won for editing *Who Framed Roger Rabbit.*

Johnson: 308. Hoffman: 810, 1111, 1155, 1312, 2113. Levinson: 75, 112, 308, 546. Seale: 2296. Descenna: 228, 423, 1913, 2127.5. Zimmer: 1177.5. Linder: 814.

1654 • RAINMAKER, THE

HAL WALLIS PRODUCTIONS; PARAMOUNT. 1956.
NOMINATIONS *Actress:* Katharine Hepburn. *Scoring of a Dramatic or Comedy Picture:* Alex North.

Con man Burt Lancaster [107 . . .] arrives in a drought-stricken prairie town, claiming to be able to bring rain. What he brings instead, through his poetic gift of causing others to dream, is a new hope for Hepburn, a lonely spinster. The leads, who are at peak form even though both are somewhat too old for their roles, bring to life this adaptation by N. Richard Nash of his successful Broadway play, directed by Joseph Anthony, who also did the stage version. The cast includes Wendell Corey, Earl Holliman, and Lloyd Bridges. The cinematography is by Charles Lang [97 . . .]. Hepburn lost to Ingrid Bergman in

Anastasia. The scoring Oscar went to Victor Young for *Around the World in 80 Days.*

Hepburn: 24, 40, 843, 1177, 1199, 1357, 1473, 1563, 1956, 1963, 2305. North: 29, 215, 413, 515, 577, 1727, 1802, 1814, 1886, 1949, 2174, 2177, 2212, 2277.

1655 • RAINS CAME, THE

20TH CENTURY-FOX. 1939.

AWARD *Special Effects:* E. H. Hansen, photographic; Fred Sersen, sound.

NOMINATIONS *Black-and-White Cinematography:* Arthur Miller. *Interior Decoration:* William Darling and George Dudley. *Sound Recording:* E. H. Hansen. *Original Score:* Alfred Newman. *Film Editing:* Barbara McLean.

Lady Edwina Esketh (Myrna Loy) falls in love with Major Rama Safti (Tyrone Power), and one just didn't do that sort of thing in India during the Raj. Entertaining if hokey ''prestige'' production that culminates in a spectacular flood; the film is now remembered chiefly as the one whose special effects were judged better than those of *Gone With the Wind* and *The Wizard of Oz.* Louis Bromfield's novel was adapted by Philip Dunne [495 . . .] and Julian Josephson [550]. The director is Clarence Brown [84 . . .], and the cast includes George Brent, Brenda Joyce, Nigel Bruce, Maria Ouspenskaya [560 . . .], Joseph Schildkraut [1169], Jane Darwell [815], Henry Travers [1371], Marjorie Rambeau [1609 . . .], H. B. Warner [1206], and Laura Hope Crews. Remade sixteen years later as *The Rains of Ranchipur.*

Miller was excluded from the final ballot for black-and-white cinematography after the Academy decided to winnow down its preliminary list of nominees to two candidates: Bert Glennon for *Stagecoach* and the winner, Gregg Toland for *Wuthering Heights. Gone With the Wind* won for art direction and Hal Kern and James Newcom's editing. The Oscar for sound was won by Bernard B. Brown for *When Tomorrow Comes.* Herbert Stothart took the award for original score for *The Wizard of Oz.*

Hansen: 143, 241, 815, 952, 990, 1868, 1957, 2027, 2056, 2272, 2286, 2317. Sersen: 226, 241, 346, 458, 520, 2286, 2317. Miller: 83, 241, 952, 1082, 1868, 2056. Darling: 83, 374, 1082, 1195, 1868, 2240. Newman: 31, 34, 46, 72, 138, 182, 226, 333, 334, 347, 375, 428, 437, 457, 476, 495, 542, 690, 797, 833, 952, 953, 959, 962, 1016, 1082, 1088, 1213, 1278, 1362, 1397, 1475, 1616, 1849, 1868, 1883, 1921, 2043, 2046, 2091, 2258, 2286, 2294, 2316. McLean: 34, 46, 1195, 1327, 1868, 2286.

1656 • RAINS OF RANCHIPUR, THE

20TH CENTURY-FOX. 1955.

NOMINATION *Special Effects.* (No individual citation.)

Socialite Lana Turner [1558] falls in love with Hindu doctor Richard Burton [85 . . .], but the heavens show what they think of their affair by providing a big flood. Burton's boredom—''It never rains but it Ranchipurs,'' he cracked—is evident in his performance. The rains are the star, though the special effects here are inferior to those in the 1939 original, *The Rains Came.* Jean Negulesco [1052] directs a cast that includes Fred MacMurray, Joan Caulfield, Michael Rennie, and Eugenie Leontovich. The Oscar went to *The Bridges at Toko-Ri.*

1657 • RAINTREE COUNTY

MGM. 1957.

NOMINATIONS *Actress:* Elizabeth Taylor. *Art Direction—Set Decoration:* William A. Horning and Urie McCleary; Edwin B. Willis and Hugh Hunt. *Score:* Johnny Green. *Costume Design:* Walter Plunkett.

Southern belle Taylor falls in love with Yankee schoolteacher Montgomery Clift [732 . . .], but the Civil War and her fragile mental state threaten their happiness. Rambling adaptation by Millard Kaufman [131 . . .] of Ross Lockridge's rambling best-seller is undone by the inability of director Edward Dmytryk [467] to put a dramatic shape on the material. Clift was seriously injured in an automobile accident in midfilming, delaying production. The alteration of his appearance is painfully apparent in some segments of the film. The huge cast includes Eva Marie Saint [1477], Nigel Patrick, Lee Marvin [371], Rod Taylor,

Agnes Moorehead [963 . . .], Walter Abel, Tom Drake, and DeForest Kelley. The cinematography is by Robert Surtees [130 . . .].

This was Taylor's first Oscar nomination, which some thought was recompense for having been overlooked a year earlier for her work in *Giant.* She lost to Joanne Woodward in *The Three Faces of Eve.* The art direction Oscar went to *Sayonara.* Malcolm Arnold won for the score of *The Bridge on the River Kwai.* Orry-Kelly took the costuming award for *Les Girls.*

Taylor: 318, 372, 1956, 2277. Horning: 175, 440, 769, 1157, 1450, 1644, 2300. McCleary: 239, 1417, 1537, 1541, 2330. Willis: 66, 87, 130, 227, 239, 290, 629, 749, 831, 980, 1069, 1096, 1157, 1173, 1190, 1226, 1230, 1232, 1309, 1417, 1567, 1662, 1673, 1721, 1861, 1937, 2068, 2112, 2257, 2320, 2330. Hunt: 175, 401, 980, 1069, 1232, 1335, 1388, 1567, 1644, 1673, 2157, 2184. Green: 66, 320, 594, 662, 817, 914, 1298, 1471, 1550, 2047, 2244. Plunkett: 9, 66, 953, 1087, 1243, 1587, 1859, 2029, 2330.

1658 • *RAISE THE RED LANTERN*

ERA INTERNATIONAL (HK) LTD. PRESENTATION IN ASSOCIATION WITH CHINA FILM CO-PRODUCTION CORPORATION PRODUCTION (HONG KONG). 1991.

NOMINATION *Foreign Language Film.*

Gong Li plays a young woman who is sold to be the concubine, the "Fourth Wife," of a rich merchant. Gradually she is drawn into the intrigue of the household, a world in itself, sealed off from outside realities. (The red lantern is hung outside the room of the wife being favored that night.) An absorbing story, stunningly acted by Gong Li and filmed with great beauty. Directed by Zhang Yimou. The Oscar went to *Mediterraneo.*

1659 • *RAMBLING ROSE*

CAROLCO PICTURES PRODUCTION; SEVEN ARTS. 1991.

NOMINATIONS *Actress:* Laura Dern. *Supporting Actress:* Diane Ladd.

Rose (Dern), a country girl whose attitude toward sex is that it's wholly natural and nothing to make a fuss about, goes to work for a family in thirties Geor-gia. The lady of the house, Ladd, is only slightly perturbed by Rose's unfettered libido, but her husband, played by Robert Duvall [92 . . .], and son, Lukas Haas, find Rose more than a little unsettling. And the town where they live is considerably less tolerant. Droll, delightful film, directed by Martha Coolidge, who sets a nice pace and tone for material that might have become sleazy in the hands of a less intelligent director. The screenplay is by Calder Willingham [810], from his own novel. Duvall's performance, one of his best, was surprisingly overlooked by the Academy.

Dern and Ladd became the first mother and daughter to receive simultaneous Oscar nominations. Dern's father, Bruce Dern, received his own nomination thirteen years earlier for *Coming Home,* so he and Ladd became the only people with acting nominations whose child has also been nominated for acting. Laura Dern lost to Jodie Foster in *The Silence of the Lambs,* Ladd to Mercedes Ruehl in *The Fisher King.*

Ladd: 41, 2279.

1660 • *RAMBO: FIRST BLOOD PART II*

ANABASIS INVESTMENTS PRODUCTION; TRI-STAR. 1985.

NOMINATION *Sound Effects Editing:* Frederick J. Brown.

Sylvester Stallone [1712] plays John Rambo, a former Green Beret, who single-handedly rescues American MIAs who are being secretly imprisoned in Cambodia. Stupid, noisy, extremely violent, and a huge box-office hit. *First Blood* (1982), the original Rambo film, also with Stallone, was a pointlessly violent game of hide-and-seek between Rambo and a small-town police force that unjustly arrested him, but it made a certain amount of sense and was not quite so badly written, acted, or directed. It was only a modest success, but the sequel reached near-mythic status. Many saw it as the epitome of the violent jingoism of the Reagan years, the purging of the American malaise over our failure in Vietnam, and the cinematic correlative for the huge Pentagon expenditures of the eighties. Seen today, it's merely a tawdry affair glorifying Stallone's muscles and indulging in some unsavory sadomasochistic display of its hero. Even the worst of the World War II zap-the-Japs movies, however, couldn't equal the racist relish with which the mostly Asian bad guys are dispatched. The screenplay is credited to Stallone and James Cameron; one suspects from Cameron's other films—*The Terminator* (1984), *Aliens, The Abyss, Terminator 2: Judgment Day,* which are much cleverer examples of the action-adventure genre—that a lot of the worst excesses of *Rambo* were contributed by its star. George Pan Cosmatos directed, and the cast includes Richard Crenna, Julia Nickson, and Steven Berkoff. The cinematography is by Jack Cardiff [221 . . .]. The sequel, *Rambo III* (1988), is not quite so dumb, sadistic, and racist. The Oscar for sound effects editing went to Charles L. Campbell and Robert Rutledge for *Back to the Future.*

1661 • *RAN*

GREENWICH FILM/NIPPON HERALD FILMS/HERALD ACE PRODUCTION; ORION CLASSICS (JAPAN). 1985.
AWARD *Costume Design:* Emi Wada.
NOMINATIONS *Director:* Akira Kurosawa. *Cinematography:* Takao Saito, Masaharu Ueda, and Asakazu Nakai. *Art Direction–Set Decoration:* Yoshiro Muraki and Shinobu Muraki.

When a feudal lord decides to stand down in favor of the eldest of his three sons, the resulting power struggle destroys him and his kingdom. Spectacular adaptation by Kurosawa and fellow screenwriters Hideo Oguni and Masato Ide of Shakespeare's *King Lear,* changing the daughters to sons and making other alterations in the plot, but keeping the essential tragic force.

Kurosawa, the most internationally celebrated of the postwar Japanese directors, had never before received a nomination, although his *Rashomon* had received an honorary Oscar at the 1951 ceremonies as the outstanding foreign film of the year—an award regularly given before the establishment of the competitive foreign language film Oscar five years later. But Kurosawa's nomination rather shockingly bumped Steven Spielberg from the slate, even though Spielberg's *The Color Purple* had racked up eleven other nominations, including one for best picture. If he had won, the seventy-five-year-old Kurosawa

would have been the oldest winner for best director in the history of the awards, but he lost to Sydney Pollack for *Out of Africa.* Four years later, at the 1989 awards, Kurosawa received an honorary Oscar "for accomplishments that have inspired, delighted, enriched and entertained audiences and influenced filmmakers throughout the world."

Out of Africa also took the awards for David Watkin's cinematography and Stephen Grimes and Josie MacAvin's art direction.

Y. Muraki: 1074, 2120, 2324.

1662 • *RANDOM HARVEST*

MGM. 1942.
NOMINATIONS *Picture:* Sidney Franklin, producer. *Actor:* Ronald Colman. *Supporting Actress:* Susan Peters. *Director:* Mervyn LeRoy. *Screenplay:* George Froeschel, Claudine West, and Arthur Wimperis. *Black-and-White Interior Decoration:* Cedric Gibbons and Randall Duell, art direction; Edwin B. Willis and Jack Moore, set decoration. *Scoring of a Dramatic or Comedy Picture:* Herbert Stothart.

Colman has been left with amnesia after his experience in the trenches of World War I, and even the authorities don't know who he is. The day of the armistice, he wanders away from the institution and gets lost in the jubilant crowds. He is rescued by a music hall entertainer played by Greer Garson [239 . . .], whom he marries and settles down with in a quaint little cottage. Then one day, on a journey into town by himself, he recovers his memory— which wipes out all memory of his more recent life with Garson. Turns out he's the wealthy head of an important family, so he takes over the family business and makes a huge success of it, helped by a very efficient secretary, Garson, who has tracked him down and gotten herself hired on, but won't tell him the truth about their life together until he remembers for himself, even when he is on the verge of marrying a young woman, played by Peters. On the eve of the wedding, however, Peters recognizes that their relationship is not what it should be and calls it off. But since he's become a very important person, Colman feels he needs a consort and asks Garson to marry him—with the understanding that there need not be, you know, any of that sort of thing. Lower lip quivering and eyes misty, she accepts. But will he ever come to his senses and remember her? Loony, marshmallowy stuff, based on a best-seller by James Hilton [1371], done with such straight-faced conviction and with such high-forties MGM polish that you can't help loving it. It's much more entertaining than the more earnest *Mrs. Miniver,* the best picture winner, with which it shares Garson, the screenwriters, and the same there'll-always-be-an-England tone. To be fair, though we can now scoff at the silliness and sentimentality of *Random Harvest,* many who saw it in 1942—women whose husbands were away fighting the war—must have identified with Garson, a woman threatened with permanently losing her husband. The cast includes Philip Dorn, Reginald Owen, Edmund Gwenn [1325 . . .], Henry Travers [1371], Margaret Wycherly [1779], Jill Esmond, Melville Cooper, Arthur Shields, Norma Varden, Henry Daniell, Una O'Connor, and Peter Lawford.

Colman lost to James Cagney in *Yankee Doodle Dandy.* This was the most important film role for Peters, who was paralyzed in a hunting accident in 1944, made a few films afterward in which she was confined to a wheelchair, and died at the age of thirty-one in 1952. The supporting actress Oscar went to Teresa Wright for *Mrs. Miniver,* which also won for William Wyler's direction and for its screenplay, which was written by Froeschel, West, Wimperis, and Hilton. The art direction Oscar went to *This Above All.* Max Steiner won for the score of *Now, Voyager.*

Franklin: 799, 1232, 1371, 1440, 2320. Colman: 311, 436, 567. LeRoy: 2300. Froeschel: 1371. West: 804, 1371. Wimperis: 1371. Gibbons: 66, 87, 130, 217, 227, 239, 285, 290, 440, 629, 749, 831, 980, 1069, 1096, 1173, 1190, 1226, 1230, 1232, 1274, 1308, 1309, 1417, 1567, 1604, 1644, 1673, 1721, 1861, 1937, 2068, 2112, 2256, 2257, 2300, 2320, 2330. Duell: 227, 2257. Willis: 66, 87, 130, 227, 239, 290, 629, 749, 831, 980, 1069, 1096, 1157, 1173, 1190, 1226, 1230, 1232, 1309, 1417, 1567, 1657, 1673, 1721, 1861, 1937, 2068, 2112, 2257,

2320, 2330. Moore: 31, 1190, 1937, 1986, 2112, 2330. Stothart: 397, 1096, 1232, 1274, 1292, 1387, 1988, 2068, 2193, 2234, 2300.

1663 • *RASHOMON*

DAIEI PRODUCTION; RKO RADIO (JAPAN). 1952.
AWARD *Honorary Award:* Outstanding foreign language film released during 1951.
NOMINATION *Black-and-White Art Direction—Set Decoration:* Takashi Matsuyama; H. Motsumoto. (1952)

In a violent encounter with a bandit in the forest, a woman is raped and her husband killed. But at the trial that follows, four different versions of the story are told, and dramatized in flashback, and the guilt and innocence of the principals are brought into question. Landmark work, directed by Akira Kurosawa [1661], that was the first postwar Japanese film widely exhibited in the United States. It helped make Toshiro Mifune, who plays the bandit, an international star. And the title, which refers to the gateway to the city of Kyoto that forms the backdrop for the trial, has become a byword for the subjective nature of the truth.

Because of the vagaries of distribution, *Rashomon* became eligible for its honorary award a year before it became eligible for competitive ones. In the art direction competition, it lost to *The Bad and the Beautiful.*

Matsuyama: 1788.

1664 • *RASPUTIN AND THE EMPRESS*

MGM. 1932–33.
NOMINATION *Original Story:* Charles MacArthur.

The monk Rasputin, played by Lionel Barrymore [723 . . .], has the Empress Alexandra of Russia, played by Ethel Barrymore [1445 . . .], under his spell because he claims to be able to heal the ailing tsarevitch. Nicholas II (Ralph Morgan) is no help, so it falls to Prince Paul Chegodieff (John Barrymore) to assassinate the mad monk. The prime hamming of the three Barrymores in their only screen appearance together is the main reason to see this otherwise rather plodding historical pageant. Each tries to upstage the other, as their biographer, Margot Peters, has noted: "No one analyzed how the trio acted together, yet their technique was simple. Resolved: If I—or John or Ethel—do not look at my sibling, then the audience won't either. Ethel keeps her eyes so resolutely downcast throughout the film that she might be a blushing maiden rather than Empress of All the Russias. . . . John is even more adept at the game. In the long 'I know my destiny' scene, Lionel . . . is forced to orate the whole time to John's back as John poses on a table, cocks his leg, plays with his sword, and keeps his face . . . militantly toward the camera. . . . But then Lionel gets his revenge by playing with his long wavy beard so determinedly . . . that it becomes a fourth Barrymore.'' The cast also includes Diana Wynyard [374], Edward Arnold, and, as Anastasia, Anne Shirley [1923], under her first screen name, Dawn O'Day. William Daniels [84 . . .] did the cinematography and Richard Boleslavsky refereed—uh, directed. MacArthur, who was dragooned by Ethel into doing the screenplay, came in third in the Oscar race, losing to Robert Lord for *One Way Passage.*

MacArthur: 1765, 2316.

1665 • *RAVEN'S END*

AB EUROPA FILM (SWEDEN). 1964.
NOMINATION *Foreign Language Film.*

Thommy Berggren plays a young writer living with his mother and father in an impoverished Depression-era household. The film, directed by Bo Widerberg, depicts their struggles to better themselves. The Oscar went to *Yesterday, Today and Tomorrow.*

1666 • *RAZOR'S EDGE, THE*

20TH CENTURY-FOX. 1946.
AWARD *Supporting Actress:* Anne Baxter.
NOMINATIONS *Picture:* Darryl F. Zanuck, producer. *Supporting Actor:* Clifton Webb. *Black-and-White Interior Decoration:* Richard Day and Nathan Juran, art direction; Thomas Little and Paul S. Fox, set decoration.

After World War I, Larry Darrell (Tyrone Power) gives up his socialite girlfriend, played by Gene Tierney [1153], to search the world for the meaning of life. Meanwhile his old girlfriend Sophie (Baxter) loses her husband and child and becomes a Parisian *poule.* Big, corny saga that doesn't make a lot of sense but is fun anyway. Edmund Goulding directed, from a screenplay by Lamar Trotti [1516 . . .] based on the novel by Somerset Maugham, who is himself a character in the film, portrayed by Herbert Marshall. Webb plays one of his snide wasps, and the cast includes John Payne, Lucile Watson [2233], and Elsa Lanchester [428 . . .].

Baxter, the granddaughter of Frank Lloyd Wright, began acting as a child, studying with Maria Ouspenskaya [560 . . .], appearing on Broadway while she was still in her teens, and making her film debut in 1940. Her first important role was as the ingenue in *The Magnificent Ambersons.* In her memoirs, *Intermission,* she recalls how illness forced her absence from the production of *The Razor's Edge* and that when she returned, she found the cast had grown so close she felt herself an outsider—a feeling that she used to heighten her character as the self-destructive Sophie. After her nomination for *All About Eve,* she found few good roles. Often she was stuck playing bitchy temptresses of the sort epitomized by the seductive Egyptian princess in *The Ten Commandments,* which under the direction of Cecil B. DeMille turned into high camp. She went into semiretirement in the 1960s, when she married and moved to a cattle ranch in Australia. Much of her later career was spent on stage, and in 1971 she appeared in the musical *Applause,* based on *All About Eve,* playing Margo Channing, the Bette Davis role. Her final screen appearance was in *Jane Austen in Manhattan* (1980). She died in 1985.

The best picture Oscar went to *The Best Years of Our Lives,* for which Harold Russell took the supporting actor award. The art direction Oscar was won by *Anna and the King of Siam.*

Baxter: 46. Zanuck: 34, 46, 550, 710, 759, 815, 946, 952, 990, 1201, 1327, 2154, 2286. Webb: 1149, 1835. Day: 22, 102, 235, 487, 510, 560, 569, 797, 833, 864, 952, 1048, 1175, 1397, 1477, 1949, 2056, 2120, 2276. Juran: 952. Little: 46, 83, 235, 428, 495, 719, 721, 746, 950, 952, 1082, 1149, 1153, 1397, 1475, 1852, 1868, 2056, 2212, 2286.

Fox: 376, 413, 428, 476, 495, 530, 721, 950, 952, 1088, 1601, 1852.

1667 • *READY, WILLING AND ABLE*

WARNER BROS. 1937.

NOMINATION *Dance Direction:* Bobby Connolly.

To land the big part in a Broadway musical, Ruby Keeler pretends to be an English actress. Silly Warners fluff, directed by Ray Enright, with Lee Dixon, Allen Jenkins, Louise Fazenda, Ross Alexander, Winifred Shaw, and, in a small part, Jane Wyman [246 . . .]. Connolly was nominated for choreographing a number sometimes mistakenly attributed to Busby Berkeley [791 . . .], in which Keeler and Dixon dance on the keys of a giant typewriter. But the movie is best remembered for the song introduced in the number: "Too Marvelous for Words," by Richard Whiting [1829] and Johnny Mercer [248 . . .]. Somehow Connolly got the nomination and the song didn't, but he lost to Hermes Pan for the "Fun House" number from *A Damsel in Distress*.

Connolly: 295, 329, 781.

1668 • *REAP THE WILD WIND*

PARAMOUNT. 1942.

AWARD *Special Effects:* Farciot Edouart, Gordon Jennings, and William L. Pereira, photographic; Louis Mesenkop, sound.

NOMINATIONS *Color Cinematography:* Victor Milner and William V. Skall. *Color Interior Decoration:* Hans Dreier and Roland Anderson, art direction; George Sawley, set decoration.

Paulette Goddard [1855], who runs a marine salvage business off the coast of Georgia, enlists shipowner John Wayne [33 . . .] and lawyer Ray Milland [1208] in her battle with villainous Raymond Massey [1], but naturally her allies are also rivals for her affections. Goddard finally gets to play Scarlett O'Hara, for which she was a leading contender, though she's called Loxi Claiborne here. And one of her chief rivals for the role of Scarlett, Susan Hayward [973 . . .], shows up, too. Typically bombastic Cecil B. DeMille [412 . . .] spectacle, whose climactic battle with a giant squid in a hurricane won the film

its special effects award. The cast includes Robert Preston [2201], Charles Bickford [651 . . .], Walter Hampden, Louise Beavers, Hedda Hopper, Oscar Polk, and Milburn Stone. The underwater photography, pretty impressive for its day, is by Dewey Wrigley.

The cinematography Oscar went to Leon Shamroy for *The Black Swan*. *My Gal Sal* won the art direction award.

Edouart: 56, 570, 975, 1855, 1887, 1934, 2168, 2175, 2181. Jennings: 56, 570, 975, 1855, 1887, 1934, 2168, 2175, 2181. Mesenkop: 56, 975, 1887. Milner: 304, 412, 470, 740, 757, 827, 1217, 1452. Skall: 96, 208, 1048, 1170, 1317, 1453, 1644, 1822, 2102. Dreier: 97, 151, 649, 674, 701, 726, 925, 979, 1101, 1120, 1194, 1214, 1217, 1358, 1443, 1452, 1540, 1748, 1880, 1975, 1994, 2190. Anderson: 278, 363, 426, 450, 649, 1029, 1194, 1214, 1219, 1452, 1570, 1674, 1880, 1994. Sawley: 532.

1669 • *REAR WINDOW*

PATRON INC.; PARAMOUNT. 1954.

NOMINATIONS *Director:* Alfred Hitchcock. *Screenplay:* John Michael Hayes. *Color Cinematography:* Robert Burks. *Sound Recording:* Loren L. Ryder.

Photographer James Stewart [73 . . .], confined to his apartment with a broken leg, begins observing the lives of his neighbors and soon comes to suspect one of them (Raymond Burr) of murder. Despite the efforts of a police detective friend (Wendell Corey) to dissuade him, Stewart, aided by his girlfriend, Grace Kelly [450 . . .], and his nurse, Thelma Ritter [46 . . .], persists in trying to find out the truth. But then Burr discovers that he's being watched . . . Superb Hitchcock thriller, full of suspense and wit, heightened by a surprising erotic charge between Stewart and Kelly. Perhaps because of the character's broken leg, the Production Code officials overlooked the implications of Kelly's spending the night in Stewart's apartment, but it's plain to see from their foreplay that the two are not about to let a little thing like a plaster cast get in the way. The film is also a tour de force of staging: Hitchcock views all the action from the point of view of Stewart's apartment, resisting the temptation to take the camera along with Kelly on her excursion into Burr's apartment and otherwise to "open up" the action. The bits of other lives glimpsed through apartment windows become movies within the movie: There's a composer (Ross Bagdasarian) struggling with his music, a sexy young dancer (Georgine Darcy) fending off various admirers, and a lonely middle-aged woman (Judith Evelyn) who drinks too much and almost takes too many pills. And there's the director's signature cameo, as a butler winding a clock in the composer's apartment. Given the importance of *Rear Window*'s set, the omission of art directors Hal Pereira [278 . . .] and Joseph McMillan Johnson [636 . . .], and set decorators Sam Comer [278 . . .] and Ray Moyer [278 . . .], from the nominations is puzzling. But so are the omissions of editor George Tomasini [1450] and composer Franz Waxman [573 . . .]. And for that matter, *Rear Window* looks like a much more plausible candidate for best picture than *Three Coins in the Fountain,* which was nominated thanks to the usual logrolling by its studio, 20th Century-Fox. But *Rear Window*'s failure to be nominated probably resulted from Paramount's own logrolling: The studio pushed *The Country Girl* for the awards, resulting in a nomination for that film as best picture and a best actress win by Kelly for her deglamorized role in it.

Rear Window's relatively few nominations gives credence to those who assert that there was an Academy bias against Hitchcock, perhaps the most famous of all Hollywood directors. This time he lost the directing Oscar, which he never won, to Elia Kazan for *On the Waterfront.*

This was the first collaboration of Hayes and Hitchcock, who would also work together on *To Catch a Thief, The Trouble With Harry* (1955), and the remake of *The Man Who Knew Too Much.* Hayes' screenplay, an adaptation of a Cornell Woolrich short story, lost to George Seaton's for *The Country Girl.*

Burks lost to Milton Krasner's work on *Three Coins in the Fountain,* an elaborate CinemaScope travelogue that's the virtual antithesis of the claustrophobic *Rear Window.* Ryder's sound work, perfectly capturing the echoes and reverberations of noises in an urban inner courtyard, lost to Leslie I. Carey's for *The Glenn Miller Story.*

Hitchcock: 1171, 1632, 1670, 1890. Hayes: 1558. Burks: 1537, 1941, 2098. Ryder: 566, 827, 979, 1452, 1697, 1703, 1837, 1887, 2012, 2168, 2181, 2183, 2230, 2242.

1670 • *REBECCA*

SELZNICK INTERNATIONAL PICTURES; UNITED ARTISTS. 1940.

AWARDS *Picture:* David O. Selznick, producer. *Black-and-White Cinematography:* George Barnes.

NOMINATIONS *Actor:* Laurence Olivier. *Actress:* Joan Fontaine. *Supporting Actress:* Judith Anderson. *Director:* Alfred Hitchcock. *Screenplay:* Robert E. Sherwood and Joan Harrison. *Black-and-White Interior Decoration:* Lyle Wheeler. *Original Score:* Franz Waxman. *Film Editing:* Hal C. Kern. *Special Effects:* Jack Cosgrove, photographic; Arthur Johns, sound.

Fontaine plays a shy, rather plain impoverished gentlewoman, the paid companion to a wealthy, unpleasant dowager (Florence Bates). On a trip with her employer to the South of France, she meets and falls in love with a handsome, brooding widower, Maxim de Winter (Olivier). They marry and return to his estate, Manderley, which is managed by the severe housekeeper Mrs. Danvers (Anderson), from whom the young woman learns that the previous Mrs. de Winter, Rebecca, was her antithesis: stunningly beautiful and vivacious. The fear that she can never equal Rebecca in her husband's affections torments the young woman, and Mrs. Danvers does nothing to allay those fears. And then the second Mrs. de Winter stumbles on the truth about Rebecca . . . This version of the paradigmatic gothic romance by Daphne du Maurier—itself based on the paradigm supplied by Charlotte Bronte in *Jane Eyre*—is Hitchcock's first American film. It has a superb cast, also including George Sanders [46] as a cad (what else?), Nigel Bruce, Gladys George [2192], Reginald Denny, Melville Cooper, Leo G. Carroll, and, as a man outside a phone booth, the director. The material is not wholly suited to Hitchcock's temperament: He gets the ominousness right, of course, and has fun with the malicious dowager played by Bates, who extinguishes a cigarette in a jar of cold cream. He's also quite adept at suggesting the lesbianism of the relationship between Rebecca and Mrs. Danvers without betraying it to the censors. But he doesn't take seriously the Byronic moody broodiness of Olivier's character and doesn't make the love story as credible as a "woman's director" such as George Cukor [262 . . .] might have done. Still, it's a highly entertaining product, if a rather surprising best picture winner over such nominees as *The Grapes of Wrath, The Great Dictator,* and *The Philadelphia Story.*

Selznick bought the rights to the novel before its publication in 1938, thinking of it as a possible vehicle for Hitchcock, whom he had just put under contract. From the beginning, producer and director were at odds over the screenplay, Hitchcock's technique being to tell the story as much as possible through images, Selznick feeling a commitment to the words and insisting on fidelity to the novel. (Changes from book to film were, however, necessary. In the novel, de Winter is goaded into killing Rebecca. In the film, though the circumstances of her death throw suspicion on de Winter, she's really a suicide; the censors would not allow a murderer to escape punishment.) Selznick, who loved to tinker with his films in the editing room, was also perturbed at Hitchcock's tendency to "edit in the camera"—carefully rehearsing the action and setting up the camera angles so that very little excess film was shot. Fortunately for Hitchcock, much of Selznick's time that might otherwise have been spent on tinkering and second-guessing was being spent on *Gone With the Wind* instead. The film's triumph at the awards ceremony, the year after *GWTW,* made Selznick the first producer to win back-to-back best picture Oscars. But the strain of this achievement, physically, emotionally, and financially, undermined the producer. It would be four years before he produced another film, *Since You Went Away,* and he never again achieved the success that he had known in the thirties. His later career was spent largely in trying to find the right vehicle for his mistress and later wife, Jennifer Jones [584 . . .]. He died in 1965.

Barnes began his career in 1919 with film pioneer Thomas Ince and was a major force in cinematography until his death in 1953, among other things serving as mentor to Gregg Toland [407 . . .]. In addition to his nominated work, he shot such films as *Footlight Parade* (1933), *Dames* (1934) and *Gold Diggers of 1935, Meet John Doe, Frenchman's Creek, Jane Eyre* (1944), *None but the Lonely Heart, The Greatest Show on Earth,* and *War of the Worlds.*

Hitchcock wanted Ronald Colman [311 . . .] to play Maxim de Winter, but Colman declined the role. When he was cast, Olivier hoped that *Rebecca* would team him with Vivien Leigh [798 . . .], but her casting in *Gone With the Wind* precluded that. Fontaine, who had met Selznick during the casting of *GWTW,* in which her sister, Olivia de Havilland [798 . . .], appeared, was eager for the part, and Selznick was instantly smitten with her, although Fontaine insists that she dodged his advances. Fontaine and Leigh were tested along with Loretta Young [428 . . .], Margaret Sullavan [2073], and Anne Baxter [46 . . .], but Leigh, Young, and Sullavan were thought too knowing and experienced for the shy heroine, and Baxter was only sixteen years old. Fontaine had been in films since 1935, mostly in supporting roles and bit parts, and her most notable leading role, with Fred Astaire in *A Damsel in Distress,* showed her at a disadvantage opposite the suave, experienced Astaire. But her inexperience and nervousness worked to an advantage in *Rebecca,* particularly opposite the imperious Olivier and Anderson, and Hitchcock did everything he could to heighten it. She lost the Oscar to Ginger Rogers in *Kitty Foyle* but became a star. Olivier lost to James Stewart in *The Philadelphia Story.*

This is the sole nomination for Anderson, an Australian-born actress who made her Broadway debut in 1918, at the age of twenty, and became known for her performances in classical drama, playing Gertrude to the Hamlet of John Gielgud [103 . . .] in 1936 and achieving her greatest acclaim as Medea in 1947. Usually typed as a villain in movies, she had made only one film appearance before *Rebecca.* Subsequently she was seen in such films as *Kings Row, Laura, The Ten Commandments, Cat on a Hot Tin Roof,* and *Star Trek III: The Search for Spock* (1984). She became Dame Judith in 1960 and died in 1992. She lost to Jane Darwell in *The Grapes of Wrath*.

Hitchcock was England's most celebrated director when Selznick lured him to Hollywood. Beginning as an art director in British films in 1921, he worked as an assistant director, editor, and screenwriter before directing his first film, *The Pleasure Garden* in 1925. He began to reach international acclaim in the mid-thirties and to achieve his identity as a specialist in thrillers with such films as *The Man Who Knew Too Much* (1934), *The 39 Steps* (1935), and *The Lady Vanishes* (1938). Although under contract to Selznick through most of his first decade in Hollywood, he managed to elude the director's interference and to establish his personal style in works on loan-out to other studios. The Oscar would always elude him, however. This time it went to John Ford for *The Grapes of Wrath*.

The screenplay Oscar went to Donald Ogden Stewart for *The Philadelphia Story*. Cedric Gibbons and Paul Groesse won for the art direction for *Pride and Prejudice*. *Pinocchio* took the scoring award for Leigh Harline, Paul J. Smith, and Ned Washington. Anne Bauchens won the editing Oscar for *Northwest Mounted Police*. *The Thief of Bagdad* took the Oscar for special effects.

Selznick: 497, 798, 1828, 1890, 1909, 1996, 2211. Barnes: 537, 1236, 1509, 1739, 1748, 1885, 1890. Olivier: 268, 619, 858, 901, 1272, 1506, 1693, 1841, 2316. Fontaine: 441, 1979. Hitchcock: 1171, 1632, 1669, 1890. Sherwood: 184. Harrison: 706. Wheeler: 19, 46, 83, 356, 376, 428, 476, 495, 530, 542, 719, 721, 798, 950, 1062, 1088, 1149, 1153, 1213, 1391, 1475, 1601, 1616, 1706, 1852, 2008, 2093, 2212. Waxman: 573, 958, 1457, 1459, 1579, 1822, 1975, 1979, 2004, 2334. Kern: 798, 1828. Cosgrove: 798, 1607, 1828, 1890. Johns: 798, 1828, 2310.

1671 • *REBEL WITHOUT A CAUSE*

Warner Bros. 1955.

Nominations *Supporting Actor:* Sal Mineo. *Supporting Actress:* Natalie Wood. *Motion Picture Story:* Nicholas Ray.

James Dean [593 . . .] plays Jim, a new kid in town who gets in trouble and at the police station meets up with Judy (Wood) and Plato (Mineo), two other troubled teens. They bond against the adult world, symbolized by Jim's parents (Jim Backus and Ann Doran) and Judy's parents (William Hopper and Rochelle Hudson). Plato's parents are in absentia; he's being taken care of by the maid (Marietta Canty). But they're also at odds with other teenagers played by Corey Allen, Nick Adams [2157], and Dennis Hopper [595 . . .]. Only the death of one of the trio, it seems, can effect a reconciliation with the rest of the world. One of the quintessential films of the fifties and a triumph of iconography. In every outward respect—fashions, music, psychology, sociology—*Rebel* is badly dated. But the image of Dean slouching in his red windbreaker seems to transcend all eras, reincarnating as Steve McQueen [1753] in the sixties, as John Travolta [1633.5 . . .] in the seventies, as Richard Gere in the eighties, and as Johnny Depp in the nineties—to name only some of the more talented avatars. Dean's self-destructiveness has also, sadly, replicated itself, most recently in the career of River Phoenix [1735]. *Rebel Without a Cause* still has the power to hold an audience, and not just because of Dean's charisma. Ray, who also directed the film, gives his simple story—the screenplay is by Stewart Stern [1645 . . .]—the right touches of myth. The scenes in the empty swimming pool, which was originally created for *Sunset Boulevard* on the grounds of the deserted Getty mansion, and at the Planetarium have a poetry to them, greatly helped by the cinematography of Ernest Haller [55 . . .]. Nobody who saw the movie as a teenager—or at least, no white suburbanite—has ever quite forgotten the impact it had.

Mineo, born in the Bronx, began his acting career as a child on Broadway, appearing in *The Rose Tattoo* and *The King and I*. He was still in his teens when he came West to appear in the movies in 1954, making his debut in *Six Bridges to Cross*. After *Rebel*, he was usually typed as a juvenile delinquent, and because of his "ethnic" looks and small stature, never moved out of character roles. He lost to Jack Lemmon in *Mister Roberts*.

Wood is one of the few child stars who made a

reasonably smooth transition through adolescence and became a star as an adult. She began her film career in 1946 at the age of eight and worked steadily up to her death by drowning in 1981. Much has been made of the early deaths of many of *Rebel*'s cast: Dean's automobile accident, Mineo's murder, and Nick Adams' drug-related death. Wood lost her first nomination to Jo Van Fleet in *East of Eden*.

Ray himself exhibited some of the self-destructiveness demonstrated by his characters in *Rebel* as well as in many of the films he directed: *They Live by Night* (1948), *In a Lonely Place* (1950), and *Johnny Guitar* (1954) are among the most celebrated. His reputation in America was not high until the French auteur critics discovered him in the sixties. It is hard, however, to discern much in the way of a personal style in some of his later big-budget flops—*King of Kings* (1961) and *55 Days at Peking*—which, although made for the money they brought him, were his last major directing efforts. In 1979, when he was dying of cancer, he collaborated with German director Wim Wenders on a documentary about his last months, *Lightning Over Water*. The Oscar for story went to Daniel Fuchs for *Love Me or Leave Me*.

Mineo: 630. Wood: 1219, 1894.

1671.5 • RED

CAB/MK2/TOR Production; Miramax (Switzerland/ France/Poland). 1994.

Nominations *Director:* Krzysztof Kieslowski. *Screenplay Written Directly for the Screen:* Krzysztof Piesiewicz and Krzysztof Kieslowski. *Cinematography:* Piotr Sobocinski.

Irene Jacob plays Valentine, a model living in Geneva, who accidentally runs over a dog with her car one day, which causes her to meet its owner, a retired judge played by Jean-Louis Trintignant, who spends his days idly spying on a neighbor. Their stories intermingle with those of Valentine's neighbor Auguste (Jean-Pierre Lorit) and his girlfriend Karin (Frédérique Feder), and the film concludes with the accidental meeting of characters from *Blue* (1993) and *White* (1994), the other two films in Kieslowski's trilogy called *Three Colors*. The colors are those of the French flag, and they dominate the three films not only visually but also thematically—blue symbolizes liberty, white equality, and red fraternity—although there's nothing mechanical or contrived in Kieslowski's development of these themes, and each film in the trilogy stands on its own.

Red was an immense critical success, heading many critics' lists of the best films of the year, but it was declared ineligible for the foreign-language film Oscar on a technicality: Contenders for that award must be nominated by a committee from the country producing them, but when Switzerland entered *Red* as its candidate, the film was ruled insufficiently Swiss because the director, his cowriter, and the cinematographer were Polish, and the producer was French. This was the second year in a row that one of Kieslowski's films had been excluded from the competition: *Blue* was disqualified as the Polish entry for the 1993 awards on the grounds that the film was set in France, with French actors, and its dialogue was entirely in French. The controversy over the exclusion of *Red,* which included a full-page newspaper protest ad signed by many prominent Academy members, may have helped the film earn its three nominations in more mainstream categories, but so far it has not stirred the Academy to revise the rules that prevent internationally made films—or films that offend the political sensitivities of the countries that might submit them—from being considered for the foreign film Oscar.

Kieslowski came to prominence in the seventies, drawing attention in 1979 with *Camera Buff,* a satire on film censorship in Poland, and with several films that were banned in his native country but exhibited at film festivals. He is best known for his ten-part *Decalogue,* a series of films made for TV in 1988, each based on one of the Ten Commandments, and the 1991 film *The Double Life of Veronique.* His sometimes enigmatic exploration of private lives is reminiscent of the European filmmaking of the sixties, when directors such as Michelangelo Antonioni [240], Ingmar Bergman [111 . . .], and Luis Buñuel [549 . . .] attempted to revolutionize cinematic storytelling. Kieslowski has said that *Red* will be his last film.

The Oscars went to director Robert Zemeckis for *Forrest Gump,* writers Quentin Tarantino and Roger Avary for *Pulp Fiction,* and cinematographer John Toll for *Legends of the Fall.*

1672 • RED BALLOON, THE

FILMS MONTSOURIS; LOPERT FILMS (FRANCE). 1956.
AWARD *Screenplay—Original:* Albert Lamorisse.

On his way to school, a small boy finds a red balloon that trails him on his wanderings through Paris. Charming fantasy, directed by Lamorisse, whose son, Pascal, plays the boy. Beautifully photographed by Edmond Séchan. It was a prize winner at Cannes, and it became the only short film—its running time is a little over half an hour—to win a screenplay Oscar, even though it has no spoken dialogue.

Lamorisse's career consisted primarily of short films, usually about children. He was killed in a helicopter accident in Iran in 1970 while filming *The Lover's Wind,* which was posthumously completed by his widow and released in 1978. It was nominated for best feature-length documentary but lost to *Scared Straight!*

1673 • RED DANUBE, THE

MGM. 1950.
NOMINATION *Black-and-White Art Direction—Set Decoration:* Cedric Gibbons and Hans Peters; Edwin B. Willis and Hugh Hunt.

Agents begin rounding up Soviet citizens in postwar Vienna to return them to the USSR, but ballerina Janet Leigh [1632], among others, doesn't want to go, and boyfriend Peter Lawford is willing to help her. Propagandizing turns a poignant human situation into a tiresome Cold War melodrama. Directed by George Sidney, with Walter Pidgeon [1232 . . .], Ethel Barrymore [1445 . . .], Angela Lansbury [749 . . .], Louis Calhern [1243], and Melville Cooper. The art direction award went to *Sunset Boulevard.*

Gibbons: 66, 87, 130, 217, 227, 239, 285, 290, 440, 629, 749, 831, 980, 1069, 1096, 1173, 1190, 1226, 1230, 1232, 1274, 1308, 1309, 1417, 1567, 1604, 1644, 1662, 1721, 1861, 1937, 2068, 2112, 2256, 2257, 2300, 2320, 2330. Peters: 69, 1107, 1226, 1567. Willis: 66, 87, 130, 227, 239, 290, 629, 749, 831, 980, 1069, 1096, 1157, 1173, 1190, 1226, 1230, 1232, 1309, 1417, 1567, 1657, 1662, 1721, 1861, 1937, 2068, 2112, 2257, 2320, 2330. Hunt: 175, 401, 980, 1069, 1232, 1335, 1388, 1567, 1644, 1657, 2157, 2184.

1674 • RED GARTERS

PARAMOUNT. 1954.
NOMINATION *Color Art Direction—Set Decoration:* Hal Pereira and Roland Anderson; Sam Comer and Ray Moyer.

Cowboy Guy Mitchell rides into the town of Paradise Lost to avenge the death of his brother, but gets caught up in various romantic intrigues. Good-natured tongue-in-cheek musical spoof that tried something truly experimental (for a major Hollywood studio, that is): boldly colored stylized sets. Unfortunately it flopped, though not so much because of the experiment as because the songs, by Jay Livingston [344 . . .] and Ray Evans [344 . . .], were unmemorable, and the cast, though attractive and talented, was made up of low-wattage stars: Rosemary Clooney, Jack Carson, Pat Crowley, Gene Barry, Cass Daley, and Buddy Ebsen. The art direction Oscar went to *20,000 Leagues Under the Sea.*

Pereira: 278, 357, 363, 426, 450, 736, 956, 1029, 1219, 1504, 1570, 1631, 1716, 1727, 1738, 1840, 1897, 1959, 2012, 2098, 2200, 2208. Anderson: 278, 363, 426, 450, 649, 1029, 1194, 1214, 1219, 1452, 1570, 1668, 1880, 1994. Comer: 278, 357, 426, 450, 726, 736, 925, 956, 1029, 1101, 1214, 1219, 1443, 1570, 1631, 1727, 1738, 1748, 1959, 1975, 1994, 2012, 2098, 2200, 2208. Moyer: 278, 413, 736, 833, 1101, 1120, 1214, 1738, 1748, 1975, 2012.

1675 • RED LANTERNS, THE

TH. DAMASKINOS & V. MICHAELIDES A.E. (GREECE). 1963.
NOMINATION *Foreign Language Film.*

A film about the lives of five prostitutes in a

Piraeus brothel, directed by Vassilis Georgiades. The Oscar went to *8¹/₂*.

1676 • *RED RIVER*

Monterey Productions; United Artists. 1948.
Nominations *Motion Picture Story:* Borden Chase. *Film Editing:* Christian Nyby.

Tom Dunson, played by John Wayne [33 . . .], founds a huge ranch in Texas, aided by old saddle pal Groot Nadine, played by Walter Brennan [424 . . .], and a boy, Matthew Garth, whom they rescued after Garth's wagon train was massacred by Indians. Garth grows up, goes off to fight in the Civil War, and returns, now played by Montgomery Clift [732 . . .], to find that the herd has grown so large that the cattle need to be driven to market. But on the way, Dunson's obsessiveness becomes unbearable, and the men turn against him. Garth is forced to take charge of the cattle drive, causing Dunson to swear to pursue Garth and kill him. One of the greatest of all westerns, superbly orchestrated by director Howard Hawks [1779], beautifully filmed by Russell Harlan [204 . . .], with a magnificent score by Dimitri Tiomkin [33 . . .]. Wayne was never better, and Clift, in his first film, is every inch a star, surprisingly believable as a tough, wiry cowpoke. As in most of Hawks' films, the supporting cast is a top-notch ensemble: Joanne Dru as the woman Garth rescues from Indians and falls in love with, John Ireland [53] as Cherry Valance (a role, however, that seems to have mostly landed on the cutting-room floor reportedly because of a conflict between actor and director over the affections of Dru, whom Ireland subsequently married), and such western standbys as Noah Beery, Jr., Hank Worden, Chief Yowlatchie, and both Harry Carey Sr. and Jr. You can also spot Shelley Winters [542 . . .] as an extra among the women in the wagon train. *Red River*'s status as a classic grows with the years, but at the time, the Academy—and most film critics—undervalued westerns, dismissing them as mere crowd-pleasers. Wayne, however, certainly deserved a nomination far more than Lew Ayres in *Johnny Belinda*, Dan Dailey in *When My Baby Smiles at Me*, and Clifton Webb in *Sitting Pretty*. Clift was nomi-

nated for his other film appearance of the year, in *The Search*. (The Oscar went to Laurence Olivier for *Hamlet*.)

Chase collaborated with Charles Schnee [130] on the screenplay from his story, which lost to Richard Schweizer and David Wechsler's for *The Search*.

Nyby, who lost to Paul Weatherwax for *The Naked City*, would go on to direct, most notably on *The Thing* (1952), although some attribute that film's success to its producer, Hawks.

1677 • *RED SHOES, THE*

J. Arthur Rank-Archers; Eagle Lion (United Kingdom). 1948.
Awards *Color Art Direction–Set Decoration:* Hein Heckroth; Arthur Lawson. *Scoring of a Dramatic or Comedy Picture:* Brian Easdale.
Nominations *Picture:* Michael Powell and Emeric Pressburger, producers. *Motion Picture Story:* Emeric Pressburger. *Film Editing:* Reginald Mills.

Ballet impresario Anton Walbrook discovers a young dancer, Moira Shearer, and composer Marius Goring writes a ballet for her, based on Hans Christian Andersen's fairy tale about a young woman who puts on some magical red dancing slippers and dances herself to death. Shearer falls in love with Goring, incurring Walbrook's fury, and abandons her career for love. When she finds herself drawn back to the world of ballet, the tragic results echo the fairy tale. The great beauty of the production makes up for the melodramatic clichés of the story and the tritely sexist moral that a woman can't have both a marriage and a career. The leads are admirably supported by Robert Helpmann, Leonide Massine, Albert Basserman [706], and Ludmilla Tcherina. The long central ballet, choreographed by Helpmann, is dazzling in both performance and staging, and clearly influenced the climactic ballet of *An American in Paris* three years later. As far as the Oscars are concerned, the chief mystery is why the magnificent color cinematography of Jack Cardiff [221 . . .] failed to receive a nomination. The only explanation is that Hollywood was increasingly nervous about the revival of European competition after World War II—demonstrated by the presence of two best picture nominees from Britain, *The Red Shoes* and *Hamlet;* the latter won. Cardiff had won the cinematography award the previous year for *Black Narcissus,* but the cinematographers branch ducked the possibility of back-to-back British wins by omitting him from the nominees. Oddly, although the 1948 black-and-white cinematography slate contains five entries, the one for color cinematography has only four.

Of the winners, Heckroth had the most interesting career. Born in Germany, he had been a set designer for the ballet and began his film career after World War II working on such British color productions as *Caesar and Cleopatra* and several Powell-Pressburger productions, including *Black Narcissus.* He died in 1970.

Powell and Pressburger were perhaps the most successful producing-writing-directing team in the history of British film. Powell had worked in British films since the late twenties, most notably as director of *The Thief of Bagdad,* and the Hungarian-born Pressburger had begun his career in Germany, before coming to England to work for Alexander Korda [1620]. In 1942 Powell and Pressburger formed their own production company, the Archers, which averaged a film a year over the next fourteen years, including such titles as *The Life and Death of Colonel Blimp* (1944), *I Know Where I'm Going* (1945), and their most acclaimed films, *Black Narcissus, The Red Shoes,* and *The Tales of Hoffman.* Their separate careers after the partnership broke up in 1956 were not particularly distinguished. Pressburger died in 1988, Powell in 1990.

The Oscar for story went to Richard Schweizer and Davis Wechsler for *The Search.* Paul Weatherwax won the editing Oscar for *The Naked City.*

Heckroth: 1997. Powell: 1008, 1489. Pressburger: 1008, 1489.

1678 • *REDS*

J.R.S. Production; Paramount. 1981.
Awards *Supporting Actress:* Maureen Stapleton. *Director:* Warren Beatty. *Cinematography:* Vittorio Storaro. **Nominations** *Picture:* Warren Beatty, producer. *Actor:* Warren Beatty. *Actress:* Diane Keaton. *Supporting Actor:*

Jack Nicholson. *Screenplay Written Directly for the Screen:* Warren Beatty and Trevor Griffiths. *Art Direction—Set Decoration:* Richard Sylbert; Michael Seirton. *Sound:* Dick Vorisek, Tom Fleischman, and Simon Kaye. *Film Editing:* Dede Allen and Craig McKay. *Costume Design:* Shirley Russell.

Beatty plays journalist John Reed, who went to Russia to cover the Bolshevik Revolution and was filled with youthful enthusiasm for the communist cause. Keaton is Louise Bryant, Reed's lover, who tracks him down when he's imprisoned in Finland for smuggling diamonds and currency to aid the Bolsheviks. Ambitious attempt at an epic that founders because it lacks a strong central story line, and the characters of Reed and Bryant are not well defined. But it's certainly watchable, thanks to a cast that includes Stapleton as Emma Goldman, Nicholson as Eugene O'Neill, plus Jerzy Kosinski, Paul Sorvino, Edward Herrmann, Gene Hackman [255 . . .], William Daniels, M. Emmet Walsh, Bessie Love [296], George Plimpton, and Josef Sommer. And there are intriguing snippets of interviews with real-life "witnesses" to the events Reed reported on, including Rebecca West, Henry Miller, Will Durant, Adela Rogers St. Johns [2250.3], and others, giving the film a pseudo-documentary quality. Unfortunately these people are not identified while they're on screen, so we lose some of the context of what they have to say.

Stapleton's earth-motherly Emma Goldman is one of the film's high points. A product of the Actors Studio, she first gained acclaim in the original Broadway production of *The Rose Tattoo* but lost her part to Anna Magnani when the film was made. She was, however, nominated for an Oscar for her first film, *Lonelyhearts,* and has continued to be a major actress in character roles on stage, screen, and TV.

Beatty is the only person other than Orson Welles [407 . . .] to receive simultaneous nominations as producer, actor, director, and writer—and the only person to do it twice. (The other time is for *Heaven Can Wait.)* He also joins Robert Redford [1502 . . .], Kevin Costner [482], and Clint Eastwood [2179.5] in the gallery of superstars who have never received acting Oscars but have been honored for directing. The younger brother of Shirley MacLaine [91 . . .], he made his film debut in 1961 in *Splendor in the Grass* and *The Roman Spring of Mrs. Stone.* But he was not taken seriously by critics until the triumph of *Bonnie and Clyde* six years later. After the Oscar for *Reds,* Beatty was absent from the screen for a long time, and his return, in the big-budget flop comedy *Ishtar* (1987), was not propitious. Of his most recent films, *Dick Tracy* and *Bugsy* were only modestly successful at the box office, and *Love Affair* (1994) was a major flop. Still, Beatty remains one of Hollywood's most charismatic stars.

This was the second of three Oscars for Storaro, who has subsequently worked for Beatty on *Ishtar* and *Dick Tracy* and has continued his long association with Bernardo Bertolucci [439 . . .].

Reds was thought to be the front-runner for the best picture Oscar. It had nominations in all the right areas, including all four acting categories—one of only thirteen films to have that distinction. (See the entry for *Coming Home* for the complete list.) Its competitors were not particularly strong: *Atlantic City,* although possibly the best of all the nominees, was a critical favorite that had been poorly distributed; *On Golden Pond* was thin and sentimental; and *Raiders of the Lost Ark* was rousing entertainment with no pretentions to the high seriousness that has traditionally won best picture Oscars. But the upset winner was *Chariots of Fire,* a British import that also happened to be a box-office success, which *Reds* wasn't. *Chariots* also took the Oscars for Colin Welland's screenplay and Milena Canonero's costumes.

The actor and actress awards went to Henry Fonda and Katharine Hepburn for *On Golden Pond.* John Gielgud won as supporting actor for *Arthur. Raiders of the Lost Ark* took the remaining awards, for art direction, sound, and Michael Kahn's editing.

Stapleton: 31, 1005, 1198. Beatty: 255, 308, 890, 1798. Storaro: 92, 543, 1136. Keaton: 88. Nicholson: 395, 595, 658.5, 672, 1019, 1135, 1481, 1625, 2020. Sylbert: 395, 448, 543, 1798, 2277. Seirton: 745. Fleischman: 1820. Kaye: 745, 1138.5, 1584. Allen: 561. McKay: 1820. Russell: 27.

1679 • REIVERS, THE

IRVING RAVETCH-ARTHUR KRAMER-SOLAR PRODUCTIONS; CINEMA CENTER FILMS PRESENTATION; NATIONAL GENERAL PICTURES. 1969.

NOMINATIONS *Supporting Actor:* Rupert Crosse. *Original Score—for a Motion Picture (Not a Musical):* John Williams.

The McCaslin family is the proud owner of a fine automobile, one of the few in Jefferson, Mississippi, in 1905. But one day their hired man, Boon, played by Steve McQueen [1753], decides to borrow it for a trip to Memphis to visit a brothel. He winds up accompanied by twelve-year-old Lucius McCaslin (Mitch Vogel) and the McCaslins' black servant, Ned (Crosse). Their episodic adventures form the substance of this charmingly aimless period piece, based on William Faulkner's last novel. Neither the novel nor the movie is a classic, but both have plenty of good moments. Mark Rydell [1473] directed from a script by Irving Ravetch [956 . . .] and Harriet Frank, Jr. [956 . . .]. The fine cast includes Sharon Farrell, Ruth White, Juano Hernandez, Will Geer, and Michael Constantine. The off-camera narrator is Burgess Meredith [504 . . .]. Crosse, who died of cancer in 1973, was the first black performer to be nominated for a supporting actor award and only the second black man, the first being Sidney Poitier [522 . . .], to receive an acting nomination. He lost to Gig Young in *They Shoot Horses, Don't They?* Burt Bacharach took the scoring award for *Butch Cassidy and the Sundance Kid.*

Williams: 6, 260, 403, 416, 588, 613, 614, 659, 805, 933, 937, 982, 996, 997, 1041, 1047, 1596, 1652, 1684, 1701, 1764.65, 1916, 1977, 2107, 2126, 2194, 2293, 2322.

1679.5 • REMAINS OF THE DAY, THE

MIKE NICHOLS/JOHN CALLEY/MERCHANT IVORY PRODUCTION; COLUMBIA (UNITED KINGDOM). 1993.

NOMINATIONS *Picture:* Mike Nichols, John Calley, and Ismail Merchant, producers. *Actor:* Anthony Hopkins. *Actress:* Emma Thompson. *Director:* James Ivory. *Screenplay Based on Material Previously Produced or Published:* Ruth Prawer Jhabvala. *Art Direction:* Luciana

Arrighi and Ian Whittaker. *Costume Design:* Jenny Beavan and John Bright. *Original Score:* Richard Robbins.

Hopkins plays Stevens, the head butler of a great English country house, and Thompson is Miss Kenton, the housekeeper. A model servant, Stevens concerns himself solely with the running of the household, blinding himself to things that might disturb his concentration on the task at hand; he ignores the illness and death of his elderly father (Peter Vaughan), the Nazi sympathies of his employer, Lord Darlington (James Fox), and most especially the attraction that has developed between himself and Miss Kenton. Finally, unable to take Stevens' remoteness any longer, Miss Kenton accepts the proposal of another man (Tim Piggott-Smith) and leaves Lord Darlington's service. Years later, after the war, and Darlington's death, the house is sold to an American businessman (Christopher Reeve), and Stevens journeys to see Miss Kenton, with whom he has corresponded, hoping to persuade her to come back to work at Darlington Hall——and to reenter his very changed life. A delicately touching story of regret for missed opportunities, handled with the usual Merchant-Ivory gift for period detail, which never, however, overwhelms the human drama. The superb cast also includes Hugh Grant as Darlington's godson. The cinematography is by Tony Pierce-Roberts [954.5 . . .].

Nichols had bought the rights to Kazuo Ishiguro's novel intending to film it with Jeremy Irons [1689] and Meryl Streep [472 . . .]. When that project fell through, and Merchant and Ivory expressed interest in filming the book, Nichols agreed to enter into partnership with them on the production. Bringing in the Merchant-Ivory team was a shrewd move, because the film needed a writer of the caliber of Jhabvala, who is skilled at adapting subtle, interior works. Interestingly 1993 was a year for films about frustrated passion in opulent period settings: *The Age of Innocence* beat *The Remains of the Day* to the theaters, which may explain why the Academy, which tends to favor films that open at year's end, chose to honor *Remains,* and not *Age,* with a best picture nomination. By doing so,

the Academy also fueled the suspicion of many of its critics that it has something against Martin Scorsese, who directed *Age.* But there is also a strong anglophile streak in the Academy's choices that may have given *Remains* the edge. In any case, the best picture Oscar went to *Schindler's List,* which also won for Steven Spielberg's direction, Steven Zaillian's screenplay, Allan Starski and Ewa Braun's art direction, and John Williams' score.

Catapulted to stardom by their earlier Oscars, both Hopkins and Thompson found themselves among the industry's busiest performers. Hopkins had been equally acclaimed for his work in *Shadowlands,* and there was much prenomination speculation about which film would earn him an Oscar bid. Thompson was simultaneously nominated for her work as supporting actress in *In the Name of the Father* and had received critical acclaim earlier in the year for *Much Ado About Nothing.* The Oscars went to Tom Hanks for *Philadelphia* and Holly Hunter for *The Piano.*

The Age of Innocence did have one last laugh: It beat out *Remains* in the costume awards, for which Gabriella Pescucci took the Oscar.

Nichols: 810, 1821, 2277, 2313. Merchant: 954.5, 1725. Hopkins: 1820. Thompson: 954.5, 992.5. Ivory: 954.5, 1725. Jhabvala: 954.5, 1725. Arrighi: 954.5. Whittaker: 44, 954.5. Beavan: 263, 954.5, 1290, 1725. Bright: 263, 954.5, 1290, 1725. Robbins: 954.5.

1680 • REMO WILLIAMS: THE ADVENTURE BEGINS

Dick Clark/Larry Spiegel/Mel Bergman Production; Orion. 1985.

Nomination *Makeup:* Carl Fullerton.

Begins——and ends. This tongue-in-cheek action adventure is about a cop (Fred Ward) recruited for a top-secret mission by a top-secret organization and trained by an inscrutable master of ancient oriental martial arts, played by Joel Grey [321] underneath the nominated makeup. It's very silly and only fitfully entertaining. It's clear from the title that the producers expected it to turn into a moneymaking series like the Indiana Jones or James Bond movies—they even hired as its director Guy Hamilton, who had done four Bond films. But *Remo* went nowhere at the box office. And the makeup Oscar went to Michael Westmore and Zoltan Elek for *Mask.*

Fullerton: 1562.5.

1681 • RESCUERS, THE

WALT DISNEY PRODUCTIONS; BUENA VISTA. 1977.
NOMINATION *Original Song:* "Someone's Waiting for You," music by Sammy Fain, lyrics by Carol Connors and Ayn Robbins.

Penny, a small orphan, is kidnaped by the wicked Madame Medusa and carried off to a swamp to aid in the search for the fabulous Devil's Eye diamond. But the Rescue Aid Society sends out two mice, the reluctant Bernard and the intrepid Bianca, to save Penny. One of the best Disney animated features between the golden age that ended sometime in the fifties and the renaissance that took place in the eighties, when *The Little Mermaid, Beauty and the Beast,* and *Aladdin* restored the studio's supremacy in the field of animation. *The Rescuers* isn't in the league of what went before or came after, but it's nicely done, with an exciting story, good comic detail, and a particularly well chosen cast doing the voices: Bob Newhart as Bernard, Eva Gabor as Bianca, and especially Geraldine Page [935 . . .] as Madame Medusa. One of the supervising animators was Don Bluth, who later left the studio to start his own series of animated features, such as *The Secret of NIMH* (1982) and *An American Tail. The Rescuers* lacks the lively song score that the great earlier Disney films and the recent blockbuster hits both possess—the melancholy nominated ballad is sweet but unmemorable. It lost to Joseph Brooks' title tune from *You Light Up My Life.*

Fain: 95, 331, 376, 856, 1213, 1276, 1925, 2014, 2214. Connors: 1712. Robbins: 1712.

1682 • RESURRECTION

UNIVERSAL PICTURES PRODUCTION; UNIVERSAL. 1980.
NOMINATIONS *Actress:* Ellen Burstyn. *Supporting Actress:* Eva Le Gallienne.

A car crash that kills her husband allows Burstyn a near-death experience, after which she develops the power to heal. Intriguing New Agey drama about spiritual awakening that flopped at the box office despite mostly strong reviews. Burstyn herself commissioned the script by Lewis John Carlino [970]. Daniel Petrie directs a cast that includes Sam Shepard [1698] as the boyfriend who turns against Burstyn, believing her powers to be satanic; Richard Farnsworth [429] as the mysterious proprietor of a service station in the desert; Roberts Blossom as Burstyn's father; and Le Gallienne as her grandmother. The music by Maurice Jarre [558 . . .] anticipates his similarly celestial score for *Ghost* a decade later.

Burstyn lost to Sissy Spacek in *Coal Miner's Daughter.* Le Gallienne, a celebrated stage actress, director, and impresario, makes one of her few screen appearances in the film. At eighty-two she was the oldest person to have been nominated for an acting Oscar. (Jessica Tandy would later beat the record by a few months with her nomination for *Fried Green Tomatoes.*) The Oscar went to Mary Steenburgen for *Melvin and Howard.*

Burstyn: 41, 631, 1139, 1747.

1683 • RETURN OF MARTIN GUERRE, THE

SOCIÉTÉ FRANÇAISE DE PRODUCTION CINÉMATOGRAPHIQUE/SOCIÉTÉ DE PRODUCTIONS DES FILMS MARCEL DASSAULT-FR 3 PRODUCTION; EUROPEAN INTERNATIONAL DISTRIBUTION (FRANCE). 1983.
NOMINATION *Costume Design:* Anne-Marie Marchand.

A man claiming to be Martin Guerre, played by Gérard Depardieu [474], arrives in a sixteenth-century French village, where he is reunited after a seven-year absence with his young wife (Nathalie Baye) and the son he has never seen. But is this man really Guerre, whom everyone remembers as a cruder, less robust sort? Eventually the suspicions, exacerbated by the claims of some transients that this Guerre is an imposter and that the real one was crippled in the war, lead to a trial and the truth. Entertaining romantic mystery, directed by Daniel Vigne, that was a big art-house hit and was remade in 1993 as *Sommersby.* The costume award went to Marik Vos for *Fanny & Alexander.*

1684 • RETURN OF THE JEDI

LUCASFILM LTD. PRODUCTION; 20TH CENTURY-FOX. 1983.
AWARD *Special Achievement Award for Visual Effects:* Richard Edlund, Dennis Muren, Ken Ralston, and Phil Tippett.
NOMINATIONS *Art Direction—Set Decoration:* Norman Reynolds, Fred Hole, and James Schoppe; Michael Ford. *Sound:* Ben Burtt, Gary Summers, Randy Thom, and Tony Dawe. *Original Score:* John Williams. *Sound Effects Editing:* Ben Burtt.

Han Solo, played by Harrison Ford [2296], has been betrayed to the forces of Jabba the Hutt, a desert potentate who looks like a cross between a garden slug and Sydney Greenstreet [1284]. But his friends Luke Skywalker (Mark Hamill), Princess Leia (Carrie Fisher), Chewbacca (Peter Mayhew), Lando Calrissian (Billy Dee Williams), and the droids C3PO (Anthony Daniels) and R2D2 (Kenny Baker and assorted models and sound effects) rescue him and set off to do battle with the Empire, finally vanquishing the evil emperor after the last-minute rebellion of his chief henchman, Darth Vader, whose voice is that of James Earl Jones [830]. Of course, they get a fair amount of help from a forest-dwelling tribe of teddy-bear-like creatures called Ewoks, as well as the disembodied spirits of Luke's Jedi mentors, Yoda (voice by Frank Oz) and Obi-Wan Kenobi, played by Alec Guinness [287 . . .]. Entertaining finale—at least so far—to the saga begun by producer George Lucas [65 . . .] six years earlier in *Star Wars.* Richard Marquand directed, and the screenplay was by Lucas and Lawrence Kasdan [6 . . .]. A few critics grumbled that they were getting tired of the series, and some of the actors betray a bit of ennui, too, but audiences clearly weren't a bit bored: The returns for *Return* topped those of its predecessor in the series, *The Empire Strikes Back.* Until *Jurassic Park* became the all-time box-office champ, *Return of the Jedi* was the third highest grosser in the history of movies, after *E.T. The Extra-Terrestrial* and *Star Wars.*

Starting with the 1972 awards, the Academy decided to eliminate special effects as a regular competitive category and to present Oscars for special effects only as "special achievement awards." Over the next two decades, however, the Academy has vacillated: Sometimes the special effects Oscars—for visual effects and sound effects editing—are competitive, the next year they become honorary again. During this time, the field, and the special effects awards, have been dominated by Lucas' Industrial Light and Magic, one of the products of the fortune he amassed from the *Star Wars* trilogy.

In the competitive categories, *Return of the Jedi* lost to *Fanny & Alexander* for art direction and to *The Right Stuff* for sound, Bill Conti's score, and Jay Boekelheide's sound effects editing.

Edlund: 45.5, 544, 614, 766, 1589, 1590, 1652, 1916, 2165. Muren: 5, 577, 588, 614, 997, 1002, 1071.5, 2019, 2284, 2339. Ralston: 128, 419, 513.5, 577, 708.5, 2274. Tippett: 577, 1071.5, 2284. Reynolds: 613, 614, 995, 1652, 1916. Ford: 614, 1652. Burtt: 588, 996, 1652, 1916, 2284. Summers: 129, 996, 1071.5, 2019. Thom: 129, 708.5, 1425, 1698. Dawe: 613, 996, 2274. Williams: 6, 260, 403, 416, 588, 613, 614, 659, 805, 933, 937, 982, 996, 997, 1041, 1047, 1596, 1652, 1679, 1701, 1764.65, 1916, 1977, 2107, 2126, 2194, 2293, 2322.

1685 • RETURN OF THE SEVEN

MIRISCH PRODUCTIONS; UNITED ARTISTS (U.S./SPAIN). 1966.
NOMINATION *Scoring of Music—Adaptation or Treatment:* Elmer Bernstein.

Slack sequel to *The Magnificent Seven,* with Yul Brynner [1088] returning as the head of the gang of samurailike gunfighters, but the rest of the seven, which included Steve McQueen [1753], James Coburn, and Charles Bronson, have been replaced with less charismatic actors. Burt Kennedy directs from a screenplay by Larry Cohen. Bernstein, nominated for adapting his own themes from the superior original, lost to Ken Thorne for *A Funny Thing Happened on the Way to the Forum.*

Bernstein: 27.5, 789, 882, 1242, 1264, 1959, 2064, 2101, 2130, 2147, 2223.

1686 • RETURN TO OZ

WALT DISNEY PICTURES AND SILVER SCREEN PARTNERS II PRO-
DUCTION; BUENA VISTA. 1985.

NOMINATION *Visual Effects:* Will Vinton, Ian Wingrove,
Zoran Perisic, and Michael Lloyd.

Fairuza Balk plays Dorothy, whose well-meaning
Aunt Em, played by Piper Laurie [364 . . .], disturbed by the girl's fantastic tales of a land called Oz,
has sent her for treatment in a sinister sanitarium.
Dorothy escapes and is swept back to the magic land
—this time by a flood rather than a tornado. She
discovers, however, that Oz has been conquered by
the evil Nome King (Nicol Williamson). Escaping
from the clutches of the witch Mombi (Jean Marsh,
who also plays the matron of the sanitarium), Dorothy is aided by Jack Pumpkinhead and the mechanical
man Tik Tok in freeing Oz from the Nome King's
sway. This dark fantasy, directed and cowritten (with
Gill Dennis) by Walter Murch [92 . . .], was
shunned by critics and audiences brought up on the
1939 *The Wizard of Oz.* But many readers of the original Oz books by L. Frank Baum recognized that this
nonmusical film was in many ways much closer to the
source than the Judy Garland classic. *Return to Oz* has,
for example, Baum's turn-of-the-century ambivalence
about technology, which can be both malevolent (the
bizarre shock-treatment mechanisms of the sanitarium) and kind (the genial Tik Tok). Too gloomy for
kids, but also too much a kiddie movie for adults, it
never found an audience. Too bad, because it's one of
the most imaginatively designed and creatively executed films of recent years, as worthy of cult status as
Blade Runner, which initially suffered a similar fate at
the box office. Of the special effects nominees, the
most familiar name is that of Will Vinton, whose
Claymation techniques previously earned him an Oscar for the animated short film *Closed Mondays* in
1974, as well as three more nominations for animated
shorts. In *Return to Oz* he brings the very rocks to life.
The special effects Oscar went to the far more conventional work for *Cocoon.*

Perisic: 1977.

1687 • REUBEN, REUBEN

SALTAIR/WALTER SHENSON PRODUCTION PRESENTED BY THE
TAFT ENTERTAINMENT COMPANY; 20TH CENTURY-FOX INTERNA-
TIONAL CLASSICS. 1983.

NOMINATIONS *Actor:* Tom Conti. *Screenplay Based on
Material From Another Medium:* Julius J. Epstein.

Conti plays a drunken, womanizing Scottish poet
who makes the most of his literary celebrity by playing the academic "writer in residence" game until he
falls in love with a beautiful student, played by Kelly
McGillis in her first film. Amusingly literate little
movie, directed by Robert Ellis Miller.

Conti won a Tony for his performance on Broadway in *Whose Life Is It Anyway?* but lost the part in the
1981 film version to Richard Dreyfuss [803]. Born in
Scotland, trained in Glasgow, Conti has had little luck
getting good film roles; his most recent performance
of note was in the role of Pauline Collins' Greek lover
in *Shirley Valentine.* The Oscar went to Robert Duvall
for *Tender Mercies.*

Epstein's screenplay was based on a novel by Peter
DeVries that had been turned into a play, *Spofford,* by
Herman Shumlin. The writing award went to James
L. Brooks for *Terms of Endearment.*

Epstein: 365, 712, 1555.

1688 • REUNION IN VIENNA

MGM. 1932–33.

NOMINATION *Cinematography:* George J. Folsey.

An exiled duke, Rudolph von Hapsburg (John Barrymore), returns to Austria and tries to pick up
where he left off with his old love, played by Diana
Wynyard [374], whose husband, played by Frank
Morgan [22 . . .], is unconcerned by the duke's dalliance. Barrymore gives this stage-bound version of a
Broadway hit by Robert E. Sherwood [184 . . .] a
fair amount of life, but it needs more. Directed by
Sidney Franklin [799 . . .] from a screenplay by Ernest Vajda and Claudine West [804 . . .], with May
Robson [1119], Eduardo Ciannelli, Una Merkel
[1959], and Henry Travers [1371]. Folsey came in
second to Charles B. Lang, Jr., for *A Farewell to Arms.*

Folsey: 51, 137, 629, 807, 835, 838, 1124, 1299,
1320, 1500, 1782, 2068, 2269.

1689 • *REVERSAL OF FORTUNE*

REVERSAL FILMS PRODUCTION; WARNER BROS. 1990.

AWARD *Actor:* Jeremy Irons.

NOMINATIONS *Director:* Barbet Schroeder. *Screenplay Based on Material From Another Medium:* Nicholas Kazan.

Did Claus von Bulow (Irons) attempt to murder his wife, Sunny, played by Glenn Close [199 . . .]? She can't say, because she now lies in a coma. A jury thinks so, but Harvard law professor Alan Dershowitz (Ron Silver) agrees to handle von Bulow's appeal because the evidence used against him in the first trial is shaky. A very odd relationship develops between the elegant, Eurotrashy von Bulow and the shambling, hustling Dershowitz. Meanwhile, from her comatose state, Sunny narrates the film for us, taking us back into her early life with Claus and speculating on what brought them to this state of affairs. Deliciously witty version of a case about which everyone had an opinion but nobody—except possibly Claus—had any facts. A tour de force of writing, directing, and acting, the film's chief flaws may be that the only point it seems designed to make is that even the rich deserve a fair trial, and that it enhanced the mystique of Mr. Chutzpah, Dershowitz—the only one of the principals in a position to exert any influence over the film, which is nominally based on his own book. The strong supporting cast includes Annabella Sciorra, Uta Hagen, and Fisher Stevens, but it's really the three leads that make the film work. Close in particular is a surprising omission from the candidates for best actress—certainly more deserving than Julia Roberts, who was nominated for *Pretty Woman*. And the film, which was produced by Edward R. Pressman and Oliver Stone [260 . . .], would have made a more distinguished candidate for best picture than *Awakenings* (1990 was a good year for comas) or *Ghost*.

There was no controversy about the Oscar for Irons, whose Claus von Bulow is one of the most subtly etched characterizations in years: arrogant, abrasive, yet oddly charming and strangely vulnerable. His chief competitor in one of the weakest best actor races of recent years was Gérard Depardieu in *Cyrano de Bergerac*. Otherwise, Kevin Costner's nomi-

nation as actor was more a tribute to the film he directed, *Dances With Wolves,* than a recognition of his performance in it; Robert De Niro spent much of *Awakenings* asleep, and many believed the nomination should have gone to his costar, Robin Williams, instead; and Richard Harris had earned a nomination with an aggressive publicity campaign, but his film, *The Field,* had not been widely seen. Irons, trained at the Bristol Old Vic, had at first been something of a reluctant movie star, finding the piecemeal process of moviemaking at odds with his stage training. But after his appearance in the British TV miniseries *Brideshead Revisited* in 1981 made him an overnight sensation, billed as "the thinking woman's sex symbol" in some publicity, he was sought for the lead in *The French Lieutenant's Woman*. Over the next few years he appeared in a handful of mostly arty movies, receiving good reviews but not becoming the star that many had expected. Critical acclaim for his performance in David Cronenberg's shocker *Dead Ringers* (1988), in which he played murderous twin gynecologists, led to his casting in *Reversal of Fortune*—a debt he acknowledged in his Oscar acceptance speech, specifically thanking Cronenberg. Since the Oscar, Irons has continued his film career primarily in out-of-the-mainstream work such as *Damage, M. Butterfly* (1993), and *The House of the Spirits* (1994). He also did the voice for the villain of *The Lion King,* working in a witty allusion to his Oscar-winning role.

Schroeder's film career began in France, primarily as a producer in association with director Eric Rohmer. He moved into directing in the seventies and made his first American film, *Barfly,* in 1987. He lost the Oscar to Kevin Costner for *Dances With Wolves,* which also won for Michael Blake's screenplay. Writer Kazan is the son of director Elia Kazan [63 . . .].

1690 • *RHAPSODY IN BLUE*

WARNER BROS. 1945.

NOMINATIONS *Sound Recording:* Nathan Levinson. *Scoring of a Musical Picture:* Ray Heindorf and Max Steiner.

Robert Alda plays George Gershwin [1797] in a mostly pedestrian biopic that at least has the virtue of generous servings of some of the greatest music ever composed by an American. Alda's solid performance, and the screenplay, by Howard Koch [365 . . .] and Elliot Paul from a story by Sonya Levien [1007 . . .], make it a notch or two better than the subsequent year's travesty on Cole Porter's life, *Night and Day*. Irving Rapper is the director, and the cast includes Joan Leslie, Alexis Smith, Charles Coburn [535 . . .], Albert Basserman [706], Morris Carnovsky, Rosemary De Camp, and, as "themselves," Al Jolson, Paul Whiteman and his orchestra, Oscar Levant, and Hazel Scott. The award for sound went to *The Bells of St. Mary's*. Georgie Stoll won for the scoring of *Anchors Aweigh*.

Levinson: 16, 30, 343, 385, 531, 689, 710, 712, 790, 930, 965, 1052, 1169, 1621, 1768, 1769, 1779, 1930, 1949, 2058, 2318. Heindorf: 331, 479, 666, 930, 1043, 1204, 1385, 1408, 1430, 1719, 1750, 1909, 2058, 2186, 2243, 2310, 2318. Steiner: 16, 154, 190, 330, 365, 385, 492, 679, 747, 754, 798, 999, 1043, 1046, 1052, 1162, 1169, 1170, 1207, 1324, 1408, 1430, 1456, 1779, 1828.

1691 • RHYTHM ON THE RIVER

PARAMOUNT. 1940.
NOMINATION *Song:* "Only Forever," music by James Monaco, lyrics by Johnny Burke.

Songwriters Bing Crosby [173 . . .] and Mary Martin are dragooned into ghosting for supposed songwriter Basil Rathbone [979 . . .], but they find a way to expose him as a phony and get the recognition they deserve. Pleasant musical nonsense, directed by Victor Schertzinger [1488 . . .] from a screenplay by Dwight Taylor, Billy Wilder [91 . . .], and Jacques Théry. Oscar Levant, Charley Grapewin, and William Frawley provide welcome support to the stars. Leigh Harline and Ned Washington won the song Oscar for "When You Wish Upon a Star," from *Pinocchio*.

Monaco: 563, 1900, 1984. Burke: 171, 173, 787, 1547.

1692 • RICH, YOUNG AND PRETTY

MGM. 1951.
NOMINATION *Song:* "Wonder Why," music by Nicholas Brodszky, lyrics by Sammy Cahn.

An American in Paris, but this one is Jane Powell, a naive young Texan who accompanies her father (Wendell Corey) to Europe, where she meets her sophisticated mother (Danielle Darrieux) for the first time and gets involved in romantic intrigue in the form of Fernando Lamas and Vic Damone. Pretty, inane MGM musical, a reminder that not everything that glittered in the golden age was truly golden. Directed by Norman Taurog [271 . . .] from a screenplay by Dorothy Cooper and Sidney Sheldon [121]. The supporting cast includes Marcel Dalio and Una Merkel [1959]. The song Oscar went to Hoagy Carmichael and Johnny Mercer for "In the Cool, Cool, Cool of the Evening," from *Here Comes the Groom*.

Brodszky: 163, 1216, 1843, 2103. Cahn: 74, 163, 182, 696, 915, 926, 1031, 1056, 1216, 1524, 1587, 1708, 1719, 1859, 1907, 2016, 2064, 2072, 2103, 2110, 2125, 2263, 2264, 2315, 2343.

1693 • RICHARD III

LONDON FILMS; LOPERT FILMS (UNITED KINGDOM). 1956.
NOMINATION *Actor:* Laurence Olivier.

Olivier plays Shakespeare's malevolent hunchbacked monarch, busily wooing the lady Anne (Claire Bloom), matching wits against Buckingham, played by Ralph Richardson [839 . . .], drowning the duke of Clarence, played by John Gielgud [103 . . .], and plotting against Edward IV (Cedric Hardwicke). Despite the presence of these theatrical luminaries, plus Stanley Baker, Pamela Brown, Michael Gough, and others, it's mainly Olivier's show. In addition to giving one of his finest, wittiest performances, he also produced (in association with Alexander Korda [1620]), directed, and adapted the play, tightening and trimming one of Shakespeare's less well made historical dramas. The film earned a footnote in the history of Hollywood because it was shown on television simultaneously with its American theatrical premiere—an experimental one-time-only testing of the relationship between the two media. Olivier lost the Oscar to Yul Brynner in *The King and I.*

Olivier: 268, 619, 858, 901, 1272, 1506, 1670, 1841, 2316.

1694 • RICHEST GIRL IN THE WORLD, THE

RKO RADIO. 1934.

NOMINATION *Original Story:* Norman Krasna.

Miriam Hopkins [165] poses as her own secretary to find out if she can land a man who loves her for herself and not for her gold. Amusing romantic trifle, somewhat eclipsed at the dawn of the golden age of the romantic comedy by *It Happened One Night.* The cast also includes Joel McCrea, Fay Wray, and Reginald Denny. The director is William A. Seiter. Krasna came in second in the Oscar race, losing to Arthur Caesar's *Manhattan Melodrama.*

Krasna: 535, 741, 1615.

1695 • RIDE THE PINK HORSE

UNIVERSAL-INTERNATIONAL. 1947.

NOMINATION *Supporting Actor:* Thomas Gomez.

Robert Montgomery [904 . . .] plays an ex-serviceman who travels to New Mexico with evidence that he plans to use to blackmail Fred Clark, a gangster responsible for the death of Montgomery's army buddy. But as in most film noir, nothing—and nobody—is that simple. Much celebrated by fans of the genre, and the screenplay by Ben Hecht [78 . . .] and Charles Lederer is full of entertainingly baroque characters and dialogue. Montgomery also directed. Gomez, who plays the man who runs the carousel that gives the film its title, lost to Edmund Gwenn in *Miracle on 34th Street.*

1696 • RIDIN' ON A RAINBOW

REPUBLIC. 1941.

NOMINATION *Song:* "Be Honest With Me," music and lyrics by Gene Autry and Fred Rose.

Cattleman Autry helps nab a bank robber who only stole the money because he wanted to help his daughter. Agreeable musical oater, made at the peak of Autry's prewar career; from 1938 to 1942 he was one of the top ten box-office draws. He was also a songwriter of some prominence, responsible for the standard "Here Comes Santa Claus" as well as his theme song, "Back in the Saddle Again," but he owes his only Oscar nomination to Academy rules that in the late thirties and early forties permitted each studio, even lowly Republic, to submit a candidate in certain categories. He lost to Jerome Kern and Oscar Hammerstein II's "The Last Time I Saw Paris," from *Lady Be Good.* But if you ever want to bet someone that Gene Autry was once nominated for an Oscar, you'll win.

1697 • RIDING HIGH

PARAMOUNT. 1943.

NOMINATION *Sound Recording:* Loren L. Ryder.

Dick Powell dreams of finding the mother lode in a silver mine while romancing Dorothy Lamour, a burlesque star who's gone home to Arizona to help friends run a dude ranch. Dud musical, directed by George Marshall, with Victor Moore and Cass Daley. The sound award went to Stephen Dunn for *This Land Is Mine.*

Ryder: 566, 827, 979, 1452, 1669, 1703, 1837, 1887, 2012, 2168, 2181, 2183, 2230, 2242.

1698 • RIGHT STUFF, THE

ROBERT CHARTOFF-IRWIN WINKLER PRODUCTION; THE LADD COMPANY THROUGH WARNER BROS. 1983.

AWARDS *Sound:* Mark Berger, Tom Scott, Randy Thom, and David MacMillan. *Original Score:* Bill Conti. *Film Editing:* Glenn Farr, Lisa Fruchtman, Stephen A. Rotter, Douglas Stewart, and Tom Rolf. *Sound Effects Editing:* Jay Boekelheide.

NOMINATIONS *Picture:* Irwin Winkler and Robert Chartoff, producers. *Supporting Actor:* Sam Shepard. *Cinematography:* Caleb Deschanel. *Art Direction—Set Decoration:* Geoffrey Kirkland, Richard J. Lawrence, W. Stewart Campbell, and Peter Romero; Pat Pending and George R. Nelson.

The saga of the Mercury astronauts—test pilots recruited for America's entry into the space race, without much forethought that the job was more suited to human cannonballs than to skilled fliers.

Among other things, the movie deals with the attempts of the publicity machine to turn the earthy, human astronauts into the squeaky-clean paragons featured in *Life* magazine. Lively, entertaining saga, based on the remarkable book by Tom Wolfe. Writer-director Philip Kaufman [2173] doesn't quite find a satisfactory tone for the film: His test pilots and their families are heroic; everyone else—German rocket scientists, doctors and nurses, journalists, and especially politicians, and most especially Lyndon B. Johnson (Donald Moffat)—is a caricature. The result is an uneasy blend of *Twelve O'Clock High* and *Dr. Strangelove.* For some reason, perhaps because many moviegoers thought they'd already seen the real thing on TV, the film stiffed at the box office. There was also some negative publicity because John Glenn (played by Ed Harris in the movie) was running for the presidential nomination, and many of his opponents bad-mouthed the movie as unfair competition. Technically, however, the movie is a triumph, and it has some very fine performances, including Shepard as Chuck Yeager, Scott Glenn as Alan Shepard, Dennis Quaid as Gordon Cooper, Fred Ward as Gus Grissom, Veronica Cartwright as Betty Grissom, Pamela Reed as Trudy Cooper, Mary Jo Deschanel (the cinematographer's wife) as Annie Glenn, and Barbara Hershey, Kim Stanley [722 . . .], Kathy Baker, Levon Helm, Scott Wilson, David Clennon, Jeff Goldblum, and Harry Shearer.

Conti came to prominence as a film composer in the early seventies, working on several films directed by Paul Mazursky [250 . . .]: *Blume in Love* (1973), *Harry and Tonto,* and *Next Stop, Greenwich Village* (1976). He made his mark with the upbeat scoring and song from *Rocky,* which earned him his first nomination. He has continued his association with Mazursky, as well as with Stallone through the long series of *Rocky* sequels.

The Right Stuff was treated well by the Academy, although its omission of Kaufman from the writing and directing categories may have been a consequence of the film's failure at the box office. The best picture award went to *Terms of Endearment.* Shepard, an important playwright who turned increasingly to acting in the eighties, lost to Jack Nicholson—playing, ironically, a former astronaut—in *Terms of Endearment.* *Fanny & Alexander* took the awards for Sven Nykvist's cinematography and for art direction.

Berger: 60, 92. Scott: 60. Thom: 129, 708.5, 1425, 1684. MacMillan: 1888.5. Conti: 702, 1712. Fruchtman: 92, 786. Winkler: 806, 1650, 1712. Chartoff: 1650, 1712. Deschanel: 1418. Campbell: 395, 1798. Nelson: 92, 292, 785.

1699 • RIGHT TO LOVE, THE

PARAMOUNT PUBLIX. 1930–31.
NOMINATION *Cinematography:* Charles Lang.

Ruth Chatterton [1234 . . .] stars as a woman whose lover dies before they can wed. She marries to give her daughter a name, and the girl—also played by Chatterton—grows up to be a missionary, maintaining a sort of psychic connection with her mother. Offbeat romantic melodrama, directed by Richard Wallace, with Paul Lukas [2233] and David Manners. Lang lost to Floyd Crosby for *Tabu.*

Lang: 97, 250, 319, 636, 649, 705, 765, 953, 1480, 1640, 1738, 1778, 1855, 1860, 1955, 1968, 2180.

1700 • RISE AND FALL OF LEGS DIAMOND, THE

UNITED STATES PICTURES PRODUCTION; WARNER BROS. 1960.
NOMINATION *Black-and-White Costume Design:* Howard Shoup.

Ray Danton plays the Depression-era gangster in this B movie directed with considerable flair by Budd Boetticher [312]. It has a small cult following among auteurist admirers of Boetticher, and the cinematography by Lucien Ballard [359] makes it look a lot better than it is. The unstarry cast features Karen Steele, Elaine Stewart, Jesse White, Simon Oakland, and Warren Oates, with Dyan Cannon [250 . . .] in a bit part, nine years before *Bob & Carol & Ted & Alice* made her famous. The costuming Oscar went to Edith Head and Edward Stevenson for *The Facts of Life.*

Shoup: 410, 1100, 1649, 2338.

1701 • RIVER, THE

Universal Pictures Production; Universal. 1984.
Award *Special Achievement Award for Sound Effects Editing:* Kay Rose.
Nominations *Actress:* Sissy Spacek. *Cinematography:* Vilmos Zsigmond. *Sound:* Nick Alphin, Robert Thirlwell, Richard Portman, and David Ronne. *Original Score:* John Williams.

A farm family headed by Spacek and Mel Gibson struggles to make a go of it, fighting against the floods that devastate their crops. Designed, like the same year's *Country,* to raise the consciousness of audiences about the plight of American farmers threatened by financial policies that favor big agribusiness, but the film is marred by mediocre plotting and weak characterization. Directed by Mark Rydell [1473], with Scott Glenn, Billy Green Bush, and James Tolkan. The flood sequences, which are responsible for Rose's Oscar, are impressive.

Spacek lost to the third of the trio of indomitable farm wives featured in the year's films, Sally Field in *Places in the Heart.* Jessica Lange, of *Country,* was also a nominee. In fact, the three actresses were invited to testify before a congressional committee hearing on the plight of farmers.

The cinematography Oscar went to Chris Menges for *The Killing Fields.* The award for sound was won by *Amadeus,* and Maurice Jarre took the Oscar for his score for *A Passage to India.*

Spacek: 364, 418, 462, 1330. Zsigmond: 416, 521. Thirlwell: 127, 1513. Portman: 339, 418, 502, 521, 738, 784, 1109, 1473, 1526, 2331. Ronne: 1473, 1825. Williams: 6, 260, 403, 416, 588, 613, 614, 659, 805, 933, 937, 982, 996, 997, 1041, 1047, 1596, 1652, 1679, 1684, 1764.65, 1916, 1977, 2107, 2126, 2194, 2293, 2322.

1701.5 • RIVER RUNS THROUGH IT, A

Columbia. 1992.
Award *Cinematography:* Philippe Rousselot.
Nominations *Screenplay Based on Material Previously Produced or Published:* Richard Friedenberg. *Original Score:* Mark Isham.

Craig Sheffer is the good boy and Brad Pitt the black sheep of a Montana family, but they're united in their love of fly-fishing, which they were taught by their preacher father, played by Tom Skerritt. Handsomely mounted version of a short novel by Norman Maclean celebrated for its lyricism. Under the direction of Robert Redford [1502 . . .], who also does the voice-over narration, the cast and cinematographer Rousselot find a pleasantly elegiac tone, but lovers of the Maclean story were disappointed, and you have to be passionate about fly-fishing or Montana scenery to get really enthusiastic about the movie. Nevertheless, it did respectably at the box office.

Rousselot apprenticed with Nestor Almendros [243 . . .] and became a leading cinematographer in France before making his first English-language film for director John Boorman [523 . . .], *The Emerald Forest,* in 1985. In addition to his nominated work, he was also cinematographer on such visually stunning films as *Dangerous Liaisons* and *The Bear.*

The writing Oscar went to Ruth Prawer Jhabvala for *Howards End.* The Oscar for score was won by Alan Menken for *Aladdin.*

Rousselot: 900, 940.

1702 • ROAD A YEAR LONG, THE

Jadran Film Production (Yugoslavia). 1958.
Nomination *Foreign Language Film.*

As a Yugoslav village struggles to build an access to the sea that will bring it out of poverty, the film tells the stories of the lives and loves of several citizens. Ambitious semidocumentary, directed by Giuseppe de Santis [216], who also wrote the screenplay with Maurizio Ferrara, Tonino Guerra [61 . . .], Elio Petri [1009], Gianni Puccini, and Mario Socrate. The cinematography is by Pasqualino De Santis [1722]. The Oscar went to *My Uncle.*

1703 • ROAD TO MOROCCO, THE

Paramount. 1942.
Nominations *Original Screenplay:* Frank Butler and Don Hartman. *Sound Recording:* Loren Ryder.

Bing Crosby [173 . . .] and Bob Hope are, as the title song by Johnny Burke [171 . . .] and Jimmy Van Heusen [171 . . .] puts it, just like Webster's dictionary—Morocco-bound. And both are determined, when they get there, to win Princess Shalmar (Dorothy Lamour). But they have Mullay Kasim, played by Anthony Quinn [1226 . . .], to contend with. The third Hope-Crosby-Lamour *Road* picture is entirely agreeable nonsense, though a lot of the topical gags have dated. The huge goodwill generated by the casualness of the performers is what keeps these otherwise forgettable comedies alive, though the Burke–Van Heusen songs, which also include "Moonlight Becomes You," help a good deal. David Butler directs, and Yvonne De Carlo can be spotted among the harem girls.

Michael Kanin and Ring Lardner, Jr., took the screenplay Oscar for *Woman of the Year*. The award for sound went to Nathan Levinson for *Yankee Doodle Dandy*.

Butler: 787, 2222. Hartman: 753. Ryder: 566, 827, 979, 1452, 1669, 1697, 1837, 1887, 2012, 2168, 2181, 2183, 2230, 2242.

1704 • ROAD TO RIO
BING CROSBY ENTERPRISES AND HOPE ENTERPRISES; PARAMOUNT. 1947.
NOMINATION *Scoring of a Musical Picture:* Robert Emmett Dolan.

Musicians Bob Hope and Bing Crosby [173 . . .] hit the road for the fifth time, with predictable results. This time, Dorothy Lamour is a Brazilian heiress in the sinister clutches of Gale Sondergaard [83 . . .]. The songs, once again by Johnny Burke [171 . . .] and Jimmy Van Heusen [171 . . .], include "But Beautiful," and to sing them Bing gets help from the Andrews Sisters. The cast, directed by Norman Z. McLeod, includes Frank Faylen, Jerry Colonna, Raul Roulien, and Charles Middleton. The scoring Oscar went to Alfred Newman for *Mother Wore Tights*.

Dolan: 173, 213, 244, 929, 994, 1120, 1912.

1705 • ROAD TO UTOPIA
PARAMOUNT. 1946.
NOMINATION *Original Screenplay:* Norman Panama and Melvin Frank.

The fourth of the Bob Hope–Bing Crosby [173 . . .] *Road* comedies is the most insouciant about matters of plot, logic, or anything else, and it may be the funniest. This time they're prospecting for gold in the Klondike, Dorothy Lamour is a dance hall girl with a heart of anything but gold, and Robert Benchley is the narrator. Even Santa Claus shows up. Once again, the songs are by Johnny Burke [171 . . .] and James Van Heusen [171 . . .]. They include "Personality." Hal Walker [1880] directed. Panama and Frank lost the screenplay award to Muriel and Sydney Box for *The Seventh Veil*.

Panama: 636, 1108. Frank: 636, 1108, 2125.

1706 • ROBE, THE
20TH CENTURY-FOX. 1953.
AWARDS *Color Art Direction–Set Decoration:* Lyle Wheeler and George W. Davis; Walter M. Scott and Paul S. Fox. *Color Costume Design:* Charles LeMaire and Emile Santiago.
NOMINATIONS *Picture:* Frank Ross, producer. *Actor:* Richard Burton. *Color Cinematography:* Leon Shamroy.

Burton plays a Roman centurion who participates in the crucifixion but is converted to Christianity with the aid of Jean Simmons [858 . . .] and slave Victor Mature, and is sent to martyrdom. The robe of the title is the one worn by Christ when he went to Calvary, which the dissolute Burton wins in a dice game. A typical sin-and-sanctity epic, based on a novel by Lloyd C. Douglas, with a screenplay attributed to Philip Dunne [495 . . .]. However, in his autobiography, *Take Two,* Dunne disclaimed responsibility for the screenplay, saying he was assigned to the project by studio head Darryl Zanuck [34 . . .], with the task of rewriting a script that producer Ross claimed was his own work. Eventually Dunne learned that the script was actually "the work of one or more blacklisted writers, who had agreed to forgo credit as a condition of their employment." The following year Dunne wrote the screenplay for the sequel, *Demetrius and the Gladiators,* which because it concentrates on action at the expense of religiosity, may be a better movie. *The Robe* has only its technical distinction to keep it memorable: It was the first movie released in

CinemaScope. Otherwise, Jay Robinson's juicy performance as Caligula is what people most remember about it. Henry Koster [214] directed, and the cast includes Michael Rennie, Dean Jagger [2154], Torin Thatcher, Richard Boone, and Ernest Thesiger. The voice of Jesus was supplied by Cameron Mitchell. The Oscar for best picture went to *From Here to Eternity*.

Burton was cast only after Tyrone Power and Laurence Olivier [268 . . .] had turned down the part. He was not fond of his role in the film, describing it as "prissy," but it established him as a major box-office star and won him his second nomination—his first for a leading role. The Oscar went to William Holden for *Stalag 17*.

The cinematography award was won by Loyal Griggs for *Shane*.

Wheeler: 19, 46, 83, 356, 376, 428, 476, 495, 530, 542, 719, 721, 798, 950, 1062, 1088, 1149, 1153, 1213, 1391, 1475, 1601, 1616, 1670, 1852, 2008, 2093, 2212. Davis: 46, 69, 401, 495, 542, 736, 953, 1213, 1335, 1388, 1537, 1552, 1814, 2157, 2184, 2312. Scott: 46, 376, 413, 476, 530, 542, 557, 646, 896, 1062, 1088, 1213, 1391, 1475, 1753, 1881, 1907, 2008, 2120, 2247. Fox: 376, 413, 428, 476, 495, 530, 721, 950, 1088, 1601, 1666, 1852. LeMaire: 21, 46, 376, 495, 530, 542, 954, 1213, 1338, 1391, 1601, 2008, 2043, 2205, 2294. Ross: 1353. Burton: 85, 164, 621, 1391, 1897, 2277. Shamroy: 29, 226, 356, 413, 495, 569, 602, 1088, 1153, 1213, 1592, 1610, 1852, 1883, 2013, 2286, 2334.

1707 • ROBERTA

RKO Radio. 1935.
Nomination *Song:* "Lovely to Look At," music by Jerome Kern, lyrics by Dorothy Fields and Jimmy McHugh.

An American football player, Randolph Scott, inherits a Parisian dress shop when his aunt dies. He falls in love with the shop's manager, a Russian princess played by Irene Dunne [114 . . .]. Though Scott and Dunne are the nominal romantic leads, the film really belongs to Ginger Rogers [1102] and Fred Astaire [2126], who after starring together in *The Gay*

Divorcée are relegated to the sidekick roles they played in their first film together, *Flying Down to Rio*. Producer Pandro S. Berman [40 . . .] bought the rights to the play as a vehicle for Dunne, and after the teaming of Astaire and Ginger Rogers became a hit, he decided to adapt it for their talents as well. Dunne's rather chilly role and Scott's awkward miscasting—his inability to sing necessitated throwing out some of the original Broadway show's songs—put most of the burden of carrying the movie on Rogers and Astaire. Astaire's role is a fusion of two characters in the stage show: a bandleader played by Bob Hope in his first important stage role and a hoofer played by George Murphy. Rogers plays the ersatz Countess Scharwenka, a.k.a. Lizzie Gatz. Despite a weak book, *Roberta* had been a big hit on stage, largely because its most famous song, "Smoke Gets in Your Eyes," was an instant smash. Astaire suggested adding "I Won't Dance," a Kern song from another show, to the film's score, which also includes "Yesterdays," "I'll Be Hard to Handle," and "The Touch of Your Hand."

"Lovely to Look At" was composed for the film to be sung during a fashion show; it has served that purpose, in countless fashion parades and beauty pageants, ever since. One of the models in the film's fashion show is Lucille Ball, then a blonde. The song Oscar went to Harry Warren and Al Dubin's "Lullaby of Broadway," from *Gold Diggers of 1935*. "Lovely to Look At" came in third, after Irving Berlin's "Cheek to Cheek," from *Top Hat*.

Kern: 340, 375, 455, 1117, 1990, 2327. Fields: 1990. McHugh: 907, 916, 2028, 2328.

1708 • ROBIN AND THE SEVEN HOODS

P-C Production; Warner Bros. 1964.
Nominations *Song:* "My Kind of Town," music by James Van Heusen, lyrics by Sammy Cahn. *Scoring of Music—Adaptation or Treatment:* Nelson Riddle.

Musical gangster spoof set in the Chicago of the Roaring Twenties, with members of the Frank Sinatra [732 . . .] set of the sixties, the notorious Rat Pack, playing roles based on the Robin Hood legend. Sinatra is Robbo, Dean Martin plays John, Sammy Davis, Jr., is Will, Bing Crosby [173 . . .] is Allen A. Dale, Barbara Rush is Marian. Peter Falk [1377 . . .] plays a bad guy—Guy Gisborne—and Edward G. Robinson is Big Jim. You can tell from this the level of the film's wit, but for admirers of the principals it's easy to take. Directed by Gordon Douglas from a screenplay by David Schwartz. The song Oscar went to Richard and Robert Sherman's "Chim Chim Cheree," from *Mary Poppins.* André Previn won the scoring award for *My Fair Lady.*

Van Heusen: 171, 173, 787, 915, 926, 1056, 1524, 1587, 1859, 1907, 2016, 2064, 2263. Cahn: 74, 163, 182, 696, 915, 926, 1031, 1056, 1216, 1524, 1587, 1692, 1719, 1859, 1907, 2016, 2064, 2072, 2103, 2110, 2125, 2263, 2264, 2315, 2343. Riddle: 338, 821, 1172, 1518.

1709 • *ROBIN HOOD*

WALT DISNEY PRODUCTIONS; BUENA VISTA. 1973.
NOMINATION *Song:* "Love," music by George Bruns, lyrics by Floyd Huddleston.

Animated version of the Robin Hood legend, in which the characters are animals: Robin (voice of Brian Bedford) is a fox, Little John (voice of Phil Harris) a bear. Peter Ustinov [943 . . .] supplies the voice for the villain, Prince John, who is a lion, and Terry-Thomas is Sir Hiss, a snake. Other voices are supplied by Roger Miller, Andy Devine, and Pat Buttram. Mildly amusing feature from the weakest period of Disney animation. The nominated song lost to the title song from *The Way We Were,* by Marvin Hamlisch and Alan and Marilyn Bergman.

Bruns: 116, 1839, 1992.

1710 • *ROBIN HOOD: PRINCE OF THIEVES*

MORGAN CREEK PRODUCTION; WARNER BROS. 1991.
NOMINATION *Song:* "(Everything I Do) I Do It for You," music by Michael Kamen, lyrics by Bryan Adams and Robert John Lange.

Kevin Costner [482] is the famous outlaw, with Mary Elizabeth Mastrantonio [422] as his Maid Marian and Morgan Freeman [580 . . .] as a Moorish sidekick. There are lots of things wrong with this movie,

from Costner's on-again-but-mostly-off-again British(?) accent to the overdone violence, but it's passably entertaining. The highlight is a splendidly over-the-top performance by Alan Rickman as the sheriff of Nottingham. Sean Connery [2185] makes a cameo appearance as King Richard at the film's end. The cast also includes Christian Slater, Brian Blessed, and Jack Wild [1471]. Kevin Reynolds directed.

The song, a fairly pedestrian rocker, is tacked on to the movie's final credits and has little to do with the film that preceded it. It lost to the title song from *Beauty and the Beast,* by Howard Ashman and Alan Menken.

1711 • *ROBOCOP*

TOBOR PICTURES PRODUCTION; ORION. 1987.
AWARD *Special Achievement Award for Sound Effects Editing:* Stephen Flick and John Pospisil.
NOMINATIONS *Sound:* Michael J. Kohut, Carlos De Larios, Aaron Rochin, and Robert Wald. *Film Editing:* Frank J. Urioste.

Peter Weller plays a Detroit cop of the not-too-far-away future who is left more dead than alive by a gang of very bad guys. The technology exists to refit what's left of him with various bionic parts that leave him more machine than man—but what a machine! He returns to service ostensibly on the side of law and order, but as his memories of his pre-Robocop life come back to him, he realizes that many of the people who have refitted him are as bad as the people he's out to arrest. Bone-crunchingly and blood-spurtingly violent, but occasionally funny and even touching in its way, this film directed by Paul Verhoeven was a big hit with the action crowd, but also provoked comment from intellectual analysts of pop culture. It probably doesn't merit too much of the latter, but if you can tolerate the mayhem and the noise, it's fairly entertaining. The cast includes Nancy Allen, Daniel O'Herlihy [18], Ronny Cox, Kurtwood Smith, and Miguel Ferrer. A couple of mediocre sequels and two TV series, one of them animated, followed. The special visual effects, supervised by animator Phil Tippett [577 . . .], were surprisingly overlooked in the nominations. *The Last Emperor* won the Oscars for sound and for Gabriella Cristiani's editing.

Flick: 544, 1589, 1888.5, 2124. Kohut: 641, 1310, 1548, 2124, 2165, 2231. De Larios: 2124, 2165, 2231. Rochin: 521, 641, 1089, 1310, 2124, 2165, 2231, 2287. Urioste: 152.5, 544.

1712 • *ROCKY*

ROBERT CHARTOFF-IRWIN WINKLER PRODUCTION; UNITED ARTISTS. 1976.

AWARDS *Picture:* Irwin Winkler and Robert Chartoff, producers. *Director:* John G. Avildsen. *Film Editing:* Richard Halsey and Scott Conrad.

NOMINATIONS *Actor:* Sylvester Stallone. *Actress:* Talia Shire. *Supporting Actor:* Burgess Meredith. *Supporting Actor:* Burt Young. *Screenplay Written Directly for the Screen:* Sylvester Stallone. *Sound:* Harry Warren Tetrick, William McCaughey, Lyle Burbridge, and Bud Alper. *Original Song:* "Gonna Fly Now," music by Bill Conti, lyrics by Carol Connors and Ayn Robbins.

Rocky Balboa (Stallone) is a down-on-his-luck Philadelphia boxer who gets a chance to take on the champ, Apollo Creed (Carl Weathers), and succeeds, thanks in part to the support of his shy girlfriend, Adrian (Shire), his loudmouth brother, Paulie (Young), and a savvy old trainer, Mickey (Meredith). No one, not even Stallone, knew at the time what a phenomenon this movie would become: a low-budget, sometimes grimy, but ultimately crowd-pleasing film, written by and starring an unknown, that was a huge box-office success and carried off the top Oscar against such formidable competition as *All the President's Men, Bound for Glory, Network,* and *Taxi Driver. Rocky* the movie, in short, recapitulated the story of Rocky the fighter. It was followed by four increasingly monotonous sequels, which are really more like remakes—in each, Rocky starts at the bottom and fights his way to the top. And it spawned countless imitations, including Stallone's own *Rambo* series and Avildsen's *Karate Kid* films. In its way, *Rocky* is the first film of the eighties, an era in which movies were increasingly packaged, promoted, and otherwise tailor-made to draw the widest possible audience. And Stallone's overnight stardom also marks the birth of

the new star system in Hollywood, in which popular performers increasingly held enormous power, drawing huge salaries and, with the aid of superagents such as Michael Ovitz of CAA, dominating the shape of filmmaking the way they were never allowed to do in the era of the studio system. On the one hand, this new star power enabled some creative actor-directors—Woody Allen [39 . . .], Clint Eastwood [2179.5], Warren Beatty [255 . . .], Kevin Costner [482], Barbra Streisand [737 . . .], and Robert Redford [1502 . . .], for example—to take on interesting projects and make some good movies. But it also resulted in overblown vanity projects such as Eddie Murphy's *Harlem Nights* and Bruce Willis' *Hudson Hawk* (1991), or routine and tawdry work such as many of Stallone's later films.

Winkler and Chartoff, however, shouldn't be blamed for the *Rocky* phenomenon; instead, they should be credited for having seen the potential in Stallone's script and allowed him to make the film. Partners since the mid-sixties, Winkler and Chartoff had been responsible for several interesting projects, including the 1967 thriller *Point Blank,* a John Boorman [523 . . .] film that attracted little attention at the time but has since developed a cult following, and *They Shoot Horses, Don't They?,* a film that helped establish Jane Fonda's reputation as an actress. And the proceeds from the *Rocky* series helped them produce two subsequent best picture nominees, *Raging Bull* and *The Right Stuff.* Chartoff and Winkler parted company in the mid-eighties. Winkler has gone on to produce *GoodFellas* and made his directing debut in 1991 with a drama about Hollywood blacklisting, *Guilty by Suspicion.*

Avildsen served his apprenticeship as an assistant director and production manager in the sixties and first made his name as a director in 1970 with *Joe.* He also directed Jack Lemmon's Oscar-winning performance in *Save the Tiger.* A director of no particular style, he seems most at home with feel-good material such as the *Rocky* and *Karate Kid* films and the 1989 drama about a get-tough inner-city school principal, *Lean on Me.*

Seeing *Rocky* today, after the years that Stallone has

devoted to bodybuilding, is something of a revelation. Although well muscled, the original Rocky Balboa looks like a human being—and like a fighter. But Stallone's excessively pumped-up body is almost a metaphor for his career, which began in the early seventies, usually in work designed to pay the rent. After Stallone's first success, an enterprising distributor unearthed a soft-porn movie in which Stallone had appeared in 1971, and retitled the flick *The Italian Stallion*. But Stallone's mainstream career began in bit parts in such movies as Woody Allen's *Bananas* (1971). He had larger roles in *The Lord's of Flatbush* (1974), *Death Race 2000* (1975), and *Farewell My Lovely*. *Rocky* made him a star, and Stallone tried to use his newfound clout to make serious films at first. But his next two films failed to find an audience: *F.I.S.T.* (1978) was a drama about labor union corruption that he wrote and starred in, and *Paradise Alley* (1978), a "mean streets" saga, was his directing debut. The success of *Rocky II* (1979) showed Stallone the way: Find a sure thing and stick with it. Subsequently Stallone's career at the box office has been full of peaks and valleys, the peaks being the *Rocky* and *Rambo* series, the valleys being almost everything else he has tried to do. He lost the acting Oscar to Peter Finch in *Network* and the writing award to Paddy Chayefsky for the same film.

Shire lost to Beatrice Straight in *Network*. Jason Robards took the supporting actor award for *All the President's Men,* which also won for sound. The best song was Barbra Streisand and Paul Williams' "Evergreen (Love Theme From *A Star Is Born)."*

Winkler: 806, 1698, 1650. Chartoff: 1650, 1698. Shire: 785. Meredith: 504. Tetrick: 1089, 2287. McCaughey: 521, 1089, 1310, 2287. Alper: 1127. Conti: 702, 1698. Connors: 1681. Robbins: 1681.

1713 • ROCKY III

ROBERT CHARTOFF-IRWIN WINKLER/UNITED ARTISTS PRODUCTION; MGM/UNITED ARTISTS. 1982.
NOMINATION *Song:* "Eye of the Tiger," music and lyrics by Jim Peterik and Frankie Sullivan III.

Rocky Balboa, played by Sylvester Stallone [1712], who also wrote and directed the movie, loses his title to the flamboyant but dirty fighter Clubber Lang (Mr. T). But Rocky's old antagonist, Apollo Creed, helps him train for the rematch. All the characters from the first movie are back: Talia Shire [785 . . .] weeps and worries as Adrian, Burt Young [1712] connives as Paulie, and Burgess Meredith [504 . . .] dispenses ringside wisdom as Mickey. Tired, predictable, and profitable. The best song Oscar went to Jack Nitzsche, Buffy Sainte-Marie, and Will Jennings for "Up Where We Belong," from *An Officer and a Gentleman.*

1714 • ROGUE COP

MGM. 1954.
NOMINATION *Black-and-White Cinematography:* John Seitz.

When his brother is killed, policeman Robert Taylor, who's on the mob's payroll, finds reasons to suspect his criminal associates. Passable attempt at something like film noir from a studio where it usually didn't find a home. Directed by Roy Rowland, with Janet Leigh [1632], George Raft, Anne Francis, and Vince Edwards. The screenplay, by Sidney Boehm, is based on a novel by William P. McGivern. The cinematography award went to Boris Kaufman for *On the Waterfront.*

Seitz: 552, 566, 674, 1208, 1975, 2262.

1715 • ROGUE SONG, THE

MGM. 1929–30.
NOMINATION *Actor:* Lawrence Tibbett.

Tibbett plays a bandit who woos a princess (Catherine Dale Owen) in this version of the Franz Lehar operetta *Gypsy Love*. The film seems to be lost, although its soundtrack exists and has been released on record. It was directed by Lionel Barrymore [723 . . .], who recalled it as "one of the first talking pictures in color," that is, two-color Technicolor, an expensive process whose unsatisfactory colors didn't justify its use for long. The film also featured comic relief from Laurel and Hardy, whose routines were directed by Hal Roach.

Metropolitan Opera baritone Tibbett, who made a handful of musicals in the early years of sound, was a California-born singer around whom legends have grown up: among other things, that his father was a sheriff who was killed by cattle rustlers and that the baritone himself fell afoul of the mob, in the form of Bugsy Siegel. The latter story makes its way into the film *Bugsy,* although the character portrayed in that movie bears little resemblance to the singer, whose baby-faced virility and magnificent voice made him a potential box-office draw. His career on the opera stage came first, and he made only cameo appearances in films after 1931. The acting Oscar went to George Arliss for *Disraeli.*

1716 • *ROMAN HOLIDAY*

PARAMOUNT. 1953.

AWARDS *Actress:* Audrey Hepburn. *Motion Picture Story:* Dalton Trumbo. (The Oscar was originally awarded to Ian McLellan Hunter, who fronted for Trumbo during the blacklist period; Trumbo's name was inserted into the official Academy records as the author of the story and winner of the Oscar on December 15, 1992.) *Black-and-White Costume Design:* Edith Head.

NOMINATIONS *Picture:* William Wyler, producer. *Supporting Actor:* Eddie Albert. *Director:* William Wyler. *Screenplay:* Ian McLellan Hunter and John Dighton. *Black-and-White Cinematography:* Frank Planer and Henry Alekan. *Black-and-White Art Direction—Set Decoration:* Hal Pereira and Walter Tyler. *Film Editing:* Robert Swink.

Hepburn plays Princess Anne, a member of the royal family of an unspecified European country. On a goodwill tour of Rome, she grows bored with being cooped up in the palace and trotted out for ceremonial occasions, so she slips out to see the world for herself. She winds up under the supervision of an American journalist, played by Gregory Peck [759 . . .], and his photographer pal, played by Albert. But will the Princess give up her kingdom to be the wife of a reporter? Delightful fairy-tale romance, brimful of charm—a slip of a story given classic status by enormously winning performances and solid direction. It has to be noted that some critics feel Wyler's direction is one of the film's flaws—that it needed the wit that an Ernst Lubitsch [889 . . .] might have

provided or the sentiment of a Frank Capra [1025 . . .]. In fact, Capra was originally scheduled to direct the film but decided to pass it on to Wyler, who has the sense to let winning performers like Hepburn and Peck carry the film without dressing them up in tricks of directorial style.

The phrase "a star is born" has become such a cliché that it astonishes us when it actually happens. Certainly critics and audiences were astonished when *Roman Holiday* revealed Audrey Hepburn to them for the first time and were even more surprised to learn that *Roman Holiday* was her seventh film. For the most part, she'd been seen in bits—most notably in a walk-on, with one line, in *The Lavender Hill Mob.* She had more substantial roles in the 1951 British films *Secret People* and *Young Wives' Tale.* But it was a chance encounter with the novelist Colette, while Hepburn was filming a French movie, *Nous Irons à Monte Carlo* (released as *Monte Carlo Baby* in America), that made her a star. Colette was helping Anita Loos prepare a Broadway version of *Gigi* and felt that Hepburn was the embodiment of her heroine. The stage role led to her casting in *Roman Holiday.* Born in Belgium, of Dutch and English parentage, Hepburn attended school in England but was in Holland with her mother when World War II began and spent the war years under German occupation. She studied ballet but was not physically suited for a career as a dancer, so she turned to acting. She was a major star until 1967, when she decided to retire from the screen. She made a comeback in 1976's *Robin and Marian* but appeared in only a handful of not-very-successful films after that. Her last screen appearance was in *Always* in 1989. In her later years she devoted herself to work for UNICEF, which led the Academy to present her the Jean Hersholt Award at the 1992 ceremonies. The award was given posthumously: Hepburn died of cancer in early 1993.

The inspiration for *Roman Holiday* was reportedly the Italian adventures of Britain's Princess Margaret, a fact that made Paramount initially rather nervous, fearing reprisals from the British censors. The writing of the screenplay was a collaborative effort that reportedly involved Ben Hecht [78 . . .] and the Italian writers Ennio Flaiano [562 . . .] and Suso Cecchi d'Amico [367], as well as the nominees. Credit for the story was denied Trumbo because he was one of the Hollywood Ten, imprisoned for contempt of Congress for failing to answer questions to the satisfaction of the House Un-American Activities Committee. But Hunter, who fronted for Trumbo, was subsequently also blacklisted. Despite the later ruling of the Writers Guild that Trumbo should be credited with the story, and the Academy's 1992 rectification of the award citation, partisans of Hunter and Hecht continue to claim a portion of the credit for their men.

The Oscar for best picture went to *From Here to Eternity,* for which Frank Sinatra also won as supporting actor, Fred Zinnemann as director, Daniel Taradash as author of the screenplay, Burnett Guffey as cinematographer, and William Lyon as editor. The award for art direction went to *Julius Caesar.*

Hepburn: 278, 1457, 1738, 2221. Trumbo: 273, 1102. Head: 31, 32, 46, 305, 357, 363, 612, 636, 675, 736, 832, 894, 945, 1003, 1219, 1261, 1263, 1398, 1427, 1504, 1550, 1579, 1587, 1631, 1727, 1738, 1748, 1840, 1927, 1986, 2012, 2098, 2247, 2298. Wyler: 175, 184, 420, 534, 560, 730, 894, 1162, 1182, 1371, 2316. Albert: 887. Dighton: 1255. Planer: 380, 393, 515, 1457. Pereira: 278, 357, 363, 426, 450, 736, 956, 1029, 1219, 1504, 1570, 1631, 1674, 1727, 1738, 1840, 1897, 1959, 2012, 2098, 2200, 2208. Tyler: 357, 1022, 1101, 1738, 1748, 1959, 2012, 2208. Swink: 268, 737.

1717 • ROMAN SPRING OF MRS. STONE, THE

SEVEN ARTS PRODUCTIONS; WARNER BROS. (U.S./UNITED KINGDOM). 1961.

NOMINATION *Supporting Actress:* Lotte Lenya.

Vivien Leigh [798 . . .] is Mrs. Stone, a wealthy, widowed actress idling in Rome, where she finds that the most efficient release from loneliness and ennui is picking up handsome young men, chief among them a gigolo played by Warren Beatty [255 . . .]. The cast —which also includes Lenya as a procuress, Coral Browne as one of Mrs. Stone's catty friends, and Ernst Thesiger, Jill St. John, Cleo Laine, Bessie Love [296], and Jean Marsh—enlivens this adaptation by Gavin Lambert [970 . . .] of a Tennessee Williams [119 . . .] story, though it's awkwardly paced by director José Quintero, a celebrated theatrical director with little film experience. The "daring" subject matter of the film now seems dated, and only the most naive viewers miss the fact that the story is really about the loneliness of an aging gay man—very much like the story's author.

Lenya had made only one screen appearance before *Roman Spring,* in the 1931 film version of *Die Dreigroschenoper (The Threepenny Opera),* the celebrated musical created by Bertolt Brecht and Lenya's husband, Kurt Weill [1105]. Lenya had gained fame in Berlin for her performances in the Brecht-Weill musicals. She accompanied Weill to the United States after the Nazis rose to power, and retired from the stage after his death in 1950. Her appearance in the 1954 New York production of *Threepenny Opera* revived her career. She made only a few films and is perhaps best known to moviegoers as the villainous Rosa Klebb in the 1963 James Bond film, *From Russia With Love.* The Oscar went to Rita Moreno for *West Side Story.*

1718 • ROMANCE

MGM. 1929–30.

NOMINATIONS *Actress:* Greta Garbo. *Director:* Clarence Brown.

Garbo is an opera star forced to choose between her wealthy "patron," Lewis Stone [1540], and a young clergyman (Gavin Gordon), who falls in love with her. Stiff, dull early talkie with an inadequate leading man. Garbo and Brown were also nominated for their work on her first talkie, *Anna Christie.* She lost to Norma Shearer in *The Divorcée,* he to Lewis Milestone for *All Quiet on the Western Front.*

Garbo: 84, 336, 1440. Brown: 84, 723, 957, 1417, 2320.

1719 • ROMANCE ON THE HIGH SEAS

MICHAEL CURTIZ PRODUCTIONS; WARNER BROS. 1948.

NOMINATIONS *Song:* "It's Magic," music by Jule Styne, lyrics by Sammy Cahn. *Scoring of a Musical Picture:* Ray Heindorf.

The title says it all: engaging musical precursor to *The Love Boat,* with various shipboard romances involving Jack Carson, Janis Paige, Don DeFore, and, in her screen debut, Doris Day [1572]. Pleasant but somewhat disappointing considering the talents involved: director Michael Curtiz [79 . . .], screenwriters Julius J. Epstein [365 . . .], Philip G. Epstein [365], and I. A. L. Diamond [91 . . .], and character players Oscar Levant, S. Z. Sakall, Fortunio Bonanova, Eric Blore, and Franklin Pangborn. (A little more star power at the top might have helped.) And there's a fine song score by Styne and Cahn. Their nominated song, which was a big hit for Day, lost to Jay Livingston and Ray Evans' "Buttons and Bows," from *The Paleface.* The scoring Oscar went to Johnny Green and Roger Edens for *Easter Parade.*

Styne: 74, 696, 737, 920, 921, 1031, 2072, 2110, 2343. Cahn: 74, 163, 182, 696, 915, 926, 1031, 1056, 1216, 1524, 1587, 1692, 1708, 1859, 1907, 2016, 2064, 2072, 2103, 2110, 2125, 2263, 2264, 2315, 2343. Heindorf: 331, 479, 666, 930, 1043, 1204, 1385, 1408, 1430, 1690, 1750, 1910, 2058, 2186, 2243, 2310, 2318.

1720 • ROMANCING THE STONE

EL CORAZON PRODUCCIONES S.A. PRODUCTION; 20TH CENTURY-FOX. 1984.

NOMINATION *Film Editing:* Donn Cambern and Frank Morriss.

Romance novelist Kathleen Turner [1545] creates intrepid fictional heroines who fall in love with dashing men, but her own life centers on her cat until her sister is abducted in Colombia because she has the secret to a fabulous treasure. Setting out to rescue her, Turner gets increasingly embroiled in a dizzying adventure with dastardly villains (Manuel Ojeda, Danny DeVito) and the hero she has dreamed of only in her novels, Michael Douglas [1481 . . .] (who also produced the movie). Delightful adventure spoof

with a terrific performance by Turner, whose transformation from shy, prissy, and mousy to intrepid, sexy, and funny is a marvel. Turner should have been nominated instead of the routinely lugubrious work of Jessica Lange in *Country* or Sissy Spacek in *The River.* Director Robert Zemeckis [127 . . .], working from a script by novice screenwriter Diane Thomas, keeps things moving. The handsome cinematography is by Dean Cundey [2274]. Check out the vastly inferior sequel, *The Jewel of the Nile* (1985), with the same stars but a different director and screenwriters, to discover what a good director and script are worth. The editing Oscar went to Jim Clark for *The Killing Fields.*

Morriss: 245.

1721 • ROMEO AND JULIET

MGM. 1936.

NOMINATIONS *Picture:* Irving Thalberg, producer. *Actress:* Norma Shearer. *Supporting Actor:* Basil Rathbone. *Interior Decoration:* Cedric Gibbons, Frederic Hope, and Edwin B. Willis.

Shakespeare's star-crossed lovers are played by Leslie Howard [178 . . .] and Shearer, with Rathbone as Tybalt, Edna May Oliver [581] as the Nurse, John Barrymore as Mercutio, and C. Aubrey Smith, Andy Devine, Henry Kolker, Violet Kemble-Cooper, and Reginald Denny. Huge, reverent, tedious film with superannuated stars playing Shakespeare's teenagers: Howard was forty-three, Shearer thirty-six, Rathbone forty-four, and Barrymore fifty-four. On the other hand, Barrymore's amusingly over-the-top performance may be the film's highlight—at least it has the energy the rest of the movie sorely needs. George Cukor [262 . . .] directed from a screenplay prepared by Talbot Jennings [83 . . .] in consultation with Elizabethan scholars John Tucker Murray and William Strunk. The cinematography is by William Daniels [84 . . .].

Thalberg was led astray by his quest for vehicles for his wife, Shearer, that would establish her as the leading dramatic actress of the screen. Her previous excursions into "prestige" drama, *Strange Interlude* (1932) and *The Barretts of Wimpole Street,* had not drawn the audiences, or the critical respect, Thalberg and Shearer desired. The notion of filming *Romeo and Juliet* grew out of Katharine Cornell's success in the role on Broadway—Cornell was the role model Thalberg had in mind for Shearer. But studio head Louis B. Mayer opposed the idea, believing Shakespeare not a good commercial venture—a 1929 filming of *The Taming of the Shrew* with Mary Pickford and Douglas Fairbanks had been a notorious bomb, and Warners' 1935 *A Midsummer Night's Dream* had been only a critical success. Thalberg went over Mayer's head to Nicholas Schenck, the president of Loew's Inc., MGM's parent company, to secure funding, and thereby secured Mayer's enmity all the more firmly. Thalberg was, however, thwarted by Mayer in a plan to film *Romeo and Juliet* on location in Verona, and Thalberg's hiring of stage designer Oliver Messel to oversee production design was sabotaged by Gibbons and the MGM art department. In the end, Mayer was proved right: *Romeo and Juliet* was a financial disaster, and the critical reception was merely respectful. The best picture Oscar went to another MGM production, *The Great Ziegfeld,* which also won a best actress Oscar for Luise Rainer, whom the studio was grooming as a rival to Shearer.

Rathbone, one of the first people to be nominated in the newly created supporting performance categories, lost to Walter Brennan in *Come and Get It.* The art direction award went to Richard Day for *Dodsworth.*

Thalberg: 150, 202, 799, 812, 1387, 1846, 2129. Shearer: 150, 555, 723, 1274, 2038. Rathbone: 979. Gibbons: 66, 87, 130, 217, 227, 239, 285, 290, 440, 629, 749, 831, 980, 1069, 1096, 1173, 1190, 1226, 1230, 1232, 1274, 1308, 1309, 1417, 1567, 1604, 1644, 1662, 1673, 1861, 1937, 2068, 2112, 2256, 2257, 2300, 2320, 2330. Hope: 1308. Willis: 66, 87, 130, 227, 239, 290, 629, 749, 831, 980, 1069, 1096, 1157, 1173, 1190, 1226, 1230, 1232, 1309, 1417, 1567, 1657, 1662, 1673, 1861, 1937, 2068, 2112, 2257, 2320, 2330.

1722 • *ROMEO AND JULIET*

B.H.E. Film-Verona Production-Dino de Laurentiis Cinematografica S.p.A. Production; Paramount (United Kingdom/Italy). 1968.

Awards *Cinematography:* Pasqualino De Santis. *Costume Design:* Danilo Donati.

Nominations *Picture:* Anthony Havelock-Allan and John Brabourne, producers. *Director:* Franco Zeffirelli.

Zeffirelli's version of Shakespeare's play casts real teenagers, seventeen-year-old Leonard Whiting and sixteen-year-old Olivia Hussey, as the young lovers, plus Milo O'Shea as Friar Laurence, Michael York as Tybalt, John McEnery as Mercutio, and Laurence Olivier [268 . . .] as the unbilled off-screen narrator. Though Zeffirelli and scenarists Franco Brusati and Masolino D'Amico sacrifice verse for vivacity, cutting much of Shakespeare's dialogue, *Romeo and Juliet* is not only the most commercially successful Shakespeare film but also one of the most entertaining. The discreet nudity and realistic fights elicited comment at the time, and the ostentation, including exaggerated codpieces, of Donati's costumes caused the youthful Veronans to be compared to hippies. It's certainly a long way from the 1936 MGM version, though many traditionalists think the best *Romeo and Juliet* movie is the 1954 British-Italian version with Laurence Harvey [1724] and Susan Shentall in the leads, beautifully filmed on location in Verona by Robert Krasker [2053]. Zeffirelli's version uses locations in smaller towns in Tuscany. Surprisingly omitted from the Oscar nominations is the score by Nino Rota [785], which was a big hit on records.

De Santis had worked as a camera operator on several of the most important Italian films of the early sixties, including Michelangelo Antonioni's *La Notte* and *The Eclipse* and Federico Fellini's *8¹/₂. Romeo and Juliet* was his first big assignment as a director of photography. His subsequent career has been largely in Europe, where he has worked with such directors as Luchino Visconti [480] and Robert Bresson.

Zeffirelli began his career as an art director and in the sixties became one of the most acclaimed directors of theater and opera, noted for his elaborate sets and costumes and extravagant stage business. His first international success as a film director was the 1967 version of *The Taming of the Shrew,* starring Richard Burton and Elizabeth Taylor. His attempts to make films with contemporary settings—*The Champ, Endless Love*—have mostly been disastrous. His film versions of the classics, such as his 1990 film of *Hamlet,* and of operas, such as *La Traviata* and *Otello,* have been better received. *Romeo and Juliet* lost the best picture Oscar to *Oliver!,* which also won for director Carol Reed.

Donati: 658, 809, 1266, 2000. Havelock-Allan: 289, 820. Brabourne: 1533. Zeffirelli: 2135.

1723 • RONDE, LA

SACHA GORDINE PRODUCTION; COMMERCIAL PICTURES (FRANCE). 1951.

NOMINATIONS *Screenplay:* Jacques Natanson and Max Ophuls. *Black-and-White Art Direction—Set Decoration:* Jean D'Eaubonne.

The merry-go-round of sex is the theme of this sophisticated drama set in nineteenth-century Austria. It features an all-star mostly French cast: Anton Walbrook, Simone Signoret [1724 . . .], Danielle Darrieux, Simone Simon, Jean-Louis Barrault, and Gérard Philipe, among others. The circle begins with the liaison of a prostitute and a soldier; the soldier has an affair with a chambermaid, the maid with her master, and so on, until we return to the prostitute. The story is based on a play by Arthur Schnitzler. Ophuls also directed this elegant entertainment, a far more daring story than the Production Code permitted of Hollywood at the time, as the writers branch of the Academy surely recognized by giving it a nomination. Such European "art films" of the fifties were a significant contributor to the eventual demise of the Code. The screenplay Oscar went to Michael Wilson and Harry Brown for *A Place in the Sun.* Richard Day and George James Hopkins took the art direction award for *A Streetcar Named Desire.*

Ophuls: 1582.

1724 • ROOM AT THE TOP

ROMULUS FILMS LTD. PRODUCTION; CONTINENTAL DISTRIBUTING INC. (UNITED KINGDOM). 1959.

AWARDS *Actress:* Simone Signoret. *Screenplay—Based on Material From Another Medium:* Neil Paterson.

NOMINATIONS *Picture:* John Woolf and James Woolf, producers. *Actor:* Laurence Harvey. *Supporting Actress:* Hermione Baddeley. *Director:* Jack Clayton.

Harvey plays a lad from the industrial north of England, who after serving time in a German prison camp during World War II figures that England owes him a good deal more than just a pigeonhole in the class system. On his way to the top, he has an affair with Signoret but throws her over for a less interesting but wealthy young woman, played by Heather Sears. Baddeley plays a friend of Signoret's who sees through Harvey from the start. Superbly intelligent drama, adapted from a novel by John Braine. It impressed contemporary critics and audiences with its daringly profane language—mild by current standards—and frankness about sex, which got it banned in several cities. The cinematography is by Freddie Francis [779 . . .].

Signoret became a major star in France in the years after World War II, giving memorable performances in such films as *La Ronde* and *Diabolique* (1955). The Oscar for *Room at the Top* caused a brief flurry of interest in Hollywood, but apart from a few English-language films, such as *Ship of Fools,* for which she received her second nomination, she spent her later career primarily in France. She died in 1985.

Paterson was a novelist, a pioneer in British TV, and a governor of the British Film Institute in addition to his work as a screenwriter, which included scripts for *The Little Kidnappers* (1953) and *The Spiral Road* (1962).

Although Harvey had been in movies for a decade, starring in the 1954 *Romeo and Juliet* and the 1955 *I Am a Camera,* he had attracted little attention until *Room at the Top.* For a while in the early sixties he was a major leading man, giving perhaps his most memorable performance as the brainwashed would-be assassin in *The Manchurian Candidate.* His career tapered off in the later decade. He died of cancer in 1973, aged forty-five. He lost the Oscar to Charlton Heston for *Ben-Hur,* which also won for best picture and for director William Wyler.

Baddeley was a familiar character actress of British stage and screen, whose most famous role in later years, before her death in 1986, was as Mrs. Naugatuck on *Maude.* She lost the Oscar to Shelley Winters in *The Diary of Anne Frank.*

Clayton had worked as an assistant director and editor for Alexander Korda [1620] in the thirties and forties and was an associate producer for John Huston on *Moulin Rouge* and *Beat the Devil* (1953). He first attracted attention as a director in 1956 when his short film *The Bespoke Overcoat* won the Oscar for best two-reel short subject. *Room at the Top* was his first feature as director, and he followed with a few impressive works, including *The Innocents* (1961), a taut adaptation of Henry James' story "The Turn of the Screw," and *The Pumpkin Eater.* His subsequent work as a director has been only occasional, ranging from the major flop *The Great Gatsby* in 1974 to the critically praised *The Lonely Passion of Judith Hearne* in 1987.

Signoret: 1812. John Woolf: 1471.

1725 • ROOM WITH A VIEW, A

MERCHANT IVORY PRODUCTION FOR GOLDCREST AND CINECOM; CINECOM PICTURES (UNITED KINGDOM). 1986.
AWARDS *Screenplay Based on Material From Another Medium:* Ruth Prawer Jhabvala. *Art Direction—Set Decoration:* Gianni Quaranta and Brian Ackland-Snow; Brian Savegar and Elio Altamura. *Costume Design:* Jenny Beavan and John Bright.
NOMINATIONS *Picture:* Ismail Merchant, producer. *Supporting Actor:* Denholm Elliott. *Supporting Actress:* Maggie Smith. *Director:* James Ivory. *Cinematography:* Tony Pierce-Roberts.

Lucy Honeychurch (Helena Bonham Carter), while traveling in Italy with her chaperon, Charlotte (Smith), encounters the eccentric Mr. Emerson (Elliott) and his son, George (Julian Sands). For the Edwardian upper-middle-class British, Italy is a sensuous, exotic land, and it proves to be a bit too much

for Lucy when George falls head over heels in love with her. She flees back to England, where she becomes engaged to the prissy, scholarly Cecil Vyse, played by Daniel Day-Lewis [992.5 . . .]. But then Emerson and George show up in her own neighborhood, and Lucy is forced to question whether she's really so conventional as she would like to be thought. Entertaining version of a rather trifling novel by E. M. Forster—it lacks the depth of *Howards End* or *A Passage to India,* in both novel and film versions. But it's hardly worth quibbling when a movie is so wittily performed, so beautifully filmed, and so gorgeously scored—it has music by Richard Robbins [954.5 . . .], but it also made a hit of Kiri Te Kanawa's version of "O mio babbino caro," from Puccini's *Gianni Schicchi.* Simon Callow, Judi Dench, and Rupert Graves are also in the cast.

Jhabvala has become the most celebrated literary adapter in contemporary movies through her work with Merchant and Ivory. She is also a novelist in her own right, and two of her books, *The Householder* and *Heat and Dust,* have been adapted by her for the movies. Born in Germany, she came to England as a child and moved to India in 1959 with her husband.

The best picture Oscar went to *Platoon,* which also won for Oliver Stone's direction.

Elliott appeared in films starting in the fifties, with substantial roles in such films as *Breaking the Sound Barrier* and *The Cruel Sea.* In the sixties he became a character player, often as lowlifes, but more frequently in his later years as absentminded intellectuals, as in *Indiana Jones and the Last Crusade.* He died in 1992. The Oscar went to Michael Caine for *Hannah and Her Sisters,* for which Dianne Wiest also won the supporting actress award.

The cinematography Oscar went to Chris Menges for *The Mission.*

Jhabvala: 954.5, 1679.5. Quaranta: 300, 2135. Beavan: 263, 954.5, 1290, 1679.5. Bright: 263, 954.5, 1290, 1679.5. Merchant: 954.5, 1679.5. Smith: 332, 1506, 1608, 2134. Ivory: 954.5, 1679.5. Pierce-Roberts: 954.5.

1726 • ROSE, THE

20TH CENTURY-FOX PRODUCTION; 20TH CENTURY-FOX. 1979.
NOMINATIONS *Actress:* Bette Midler. *Supporting Actor:* Frederic Forrest. *Sound:* Theodore Soderberg, Douglas Williams, Paul Wells, and Jim Webb. *Film Editing:* Robert L. Wolfe and C. Timothy O'Meara.

Midler plays a self-destructive rock star modeled on Janis Joplin. Her all-out performance in her first starring role is the best reason to see this otherwise rather depressing movie, directed by Mark Rydell [1473]. It's a far cry from the comic performances she later became better known for, although there are elements of bawdy humor in her portrayal and some of her musical numbers. Forrest plays her dropout boyfriend, and Alan Bates [678] is her manager. The screenplay is by Bill Kerby and Bo Goldman [1300 . . .], the cinematography by Vilmos Zsigmond [416 . . .].

Born in Honolulu, Midler can be glimpsed as an extra in the film *Hawaii,* made when she was twenty. In the seventies she gained her first fame as a flamboyant cabaret performer, most notoriously at the Continental Baths, a pre-AIDS gay bathhouse and club in Manhattan. She followed *The Rose* with the concert film *Divine Madness,* but her career came a-cropper with a big flop, appropriately titled *Jinxed!* (1982). Absent from movies for four years, she returned with a series of knockabout comedies—*Down and Out in Beverly Hills* (1986), *Ruthless People* (1986), and *Outrageous Fortune* (1987)—that restarted her career. She lost the Oscar to Sally Field in *Norma Rae.*

Well-received supporting performances in *Apocalypse Now* and *The Rose* gave Forrest a crack at a few leads, most notably in Wim Wenders' *Hammett* (1982), but he subsequently returned to character roles in such films as *Tucker: The Man and His Dream* and *Music Box.* The Oscar went to Melvyn Douglas for *Being There.*

Apocalypse Now took the award for sound. Alan Heim won for editing *All That Jazz.*

Midler: 700. Soderberg: 724, 983, 1596, 2126, 2152. Williams: 1541, 1824, 2152. Wells: 2152. Webb: 54. Wolfe: 54, 1473.

1727 • ROSE TATTOO, THE

HAL WALLIS PRODUCTIONS; PARAMOUNT. 1955.
AWARDS *Actress:* Anna Magnani. *Black-and-White Cinematography:* James Wong Howe. *Black-and-White Art Direction—Set Decoration:* Hal Pereira and Tambi Larsen; Sam Comer and Arthur Krams.
NOMINATIONS *Picture:* Hal Wallis, producer. *Supporting Actress:* Marisa Pavan. *Scoring of a Dramatic or Comedy Picture:* Alex North. *Film Editing:* Warren Low. *Black-and-White Costume Design:* Edith Head.

Magnani plays Serafina Delle Rose, a Sicilian widow in a Gulf Coast town. She is devoted to the memory of her virile husband, despite evidence of his philandering, until one day a hunky but somewhat dim-witted truck driver, played by Burt Lancaster [107 . . .], enters her life and pays court to her—even going so far as to have a rose tattooed on his chest, in imitation of Serafina's dead husband. Meanwhile, Serafina is also obsessed with protecting the virginity of her daughter, Rosa (Pavan), from the advances of a naive young sailor (Ben Cooper). Enjoyable filming of a lesser work of Tennessee Williams [119 . . .], with a dazzling performance by Magnani in her first English-language role. She is said to have learned the part phonetically, although the claim is scarcely credible, given the nuances of her line readings. Lancaster, on the other hand, gives one of his few really awful performances: He was never good at playing dumb, and he is hamstrung by the role of an amorous goof, playing the part with lots of teeth and energy—he's like a very handsome, very large puppy badly in need of obedience school, or at least a stronger directorial hand than Daniel Mann can supply. Williams, who adapted his play for the screen, wrote it with Magnani in mind, but she declined the offer to appear in it on Broadway, where the part was played by Maureen Stapleton [31 . . .]. The cast also includes Virginia Grey and Jo Van Fleet [593].

Magnani, born in Egypt and raised in poverty in Rome, made her first film, a silent, while still a teenager in 1927. She established herself as a film and stage actress in the thirties and forties but first gained international acclaim in *Open City* in 1945. She made only four American films; the others were *Wild Is the*

Wind, for which she received a second Oscar nomination, *The Fugitive Kind* (1960), and *The Secret of Santa Vittoria.* She died in 1973 of pancreatic cancer.

This was the first of two Oscars for Howe. Born in China, he came to America as a small child and began work in films in 1917, starting in menial tasks and becoming a director of photography in 1923. His eloquent, moody, deep-focus photography helped make him one of the most famous of all Hollywood cinematographers, with a career that spanned more than half a century.

The best picture Oscar went to *Marty.* Pavan, the twin sister of actress Pier Angeli, had a modest career in films of the fifties. She lost to Jo Van Fleet in *East of Eden.* The award for scoring went to Alfred Newman for *Love Is a Many-Splendored Thing.* Charles Nelson and William A. Lyon won for editing *Picnic.* Helen Rose took the costuming Oscar for *I'll Cry Tomorrow.*

Magnani: 2282. Howe: 1, 30, 36, 738, 956, 1095, 1451, 1470, 1774. Pereira: 278, 357, 363, 426, 450, 736, 956, 1029, 1219, 1504, 1570, 1631, 1674, 1716, 1738, 1840, 1897, 1959, 2012, 2098, 2200, 2208. Larsen: 892, 956, 1341, 1897. Comer: 278, 357, 426, 450, 726, 736, 925, 956, 1029, 1101, 1214, 1219, 1443, 1570, 1631, 1674, 1738, 1748, 1959, 1975, 1994, 2012, 2098, 2200, 2208. Krams: 357, 1173, 1309, 1937, 1959, 2098, 2208. Wallis: 17, 55, 85, 164, 343, 365, 676, 689, 712, 965, 1046, 1095, 1162, 1248, 1482, 1779, 2233, 2318. North: 29, 215, 413, 515, 577, 1654, 1802, 1814, 1886, 1949, 2174, 2177, 2212, 2277. Low: 425, 847, 1162. Head: 31, 32, 46, 305, 357, 363, 612, 636, 675, 736, 832, 894, 945, 1003, 1219, 1261, 1263, 1398, 1427, 1504, 1550, 1579, 1587, 1631, 1716, 1738, 1748, 1840, 1927, 1986, 2012, 2098, 2247, 2298.

1728 • ROSEMARY'S BABY

William Castle Enterprises Production; Paramount. 1968.

Award *Supporting Actress:* Ruth Gordon.
Nomination *Screenplay—Based on Material From Another Medium:* Roman Polanski.

Mia Farrow plays Rosemary, and John Cassavetes [548 . . .] is her husband—a striving young actor who, we discover, will do anything to advance his career. The young couple moves into a sinister-looking old Manhattan apartment house, where their next-door neighbors are a nosy but apparently well-meaning elderly couple, played by Sidney Blackmer and Gordon. Then Rosemary gets pregnant and begins to suspect that something diabolical is going on. Superb horror thriller that unfortunately inspired a couple of decades of bad imitations, the best of which is *The Exorcist.* Polanski directed his adaptation of a novel by Ira Levin, and the terrific cast includes Maurice Evans, Ralph Bellamy [114], Patsy Kelly, Elisha Cook, Jr., and Charles Grodin. The atmospheric cinematography and production design are by William Fraker [890 . . .] and Richard Sylbert [395 . . .] respectively.

Gordon made her first films as a bit player while trying to make it on the New York stage in 1915 and 1916. She became one of the most celebrated stage actresses of the first half of the twentieth century, and one of the few Americans to have a great success in England as well as New York. In the early forties she came to Hollywood to appear in a few films, including *Abe Lincoln in Illinois, Dr. Ehrlich's Magic Bullet,* and *Action in the North Atlantic.* But where the movies are concerned, her off-screen career was more successful. With her husband, Garson Kanin [11 . . .], she wrote several of the wittiest screenplays of the late forties and early fifties, including *A Double Life, Adam's Rib,* and *Pat and Mike.* She returned to the screen as an actress in the mid-sixties, usually playing eccentrics and harridans in movies that have developed a cult following, such as *Where's Poppa?* (1970) and *Harold and Maude* (1971). She died in 1985.

James Goldman won the screenplay Oscar for *The Lion in Winter.*

Gordon: 11, 567, 1003, 1536. Polanski: 395, 2021.

1729 • ROUND MIDNIGHT

Irwin Winkler Production; Warner Bros. 1986.
Award *Original Score:* Herbie Hancock.
Nomination *Actor:* Dexter Gordon.

Gordon plays an expatriate, alcoholic jazz musician in fifties Paris, whose friendship with a fan (François Cluzet) helps him experience a creative breakthrough. One of the finest films about jazz, directed by Bertrand Tavernier and written by Tavernier and David Rayfiel, who based their story on that of musicians Bud Powell and Lester Young. Hancock appears in the film, along with Lonette McKee, Wayne Shorter, Martin Scorsese [27.5 . . .], and Philippe Noiret.

Hancock, one of the most talented jazz pianists to emerge in the sixties, worked with Miles Davis before developing his own sound. He was a pioneer in bringing electronic instruments into jazz and in integrating jazz with rock and dance pop. His Oscar, however, caused a small controversy, with many members of the Academy's music branch protesting an award to a film that was only partly scored by Hancock—much of the music in *Round Midnight* is made up of jazz standards such as the song that gives the film its title. The eligibility requirements for the awards were subsequently amended to exclude films that contained substantial amounts of "preexisting music."

Gordon, a celebrated tenor saxophonist, had made only one previous film appearance, thirty-one years earlier, in *Unchained*. He died in 1990. The Oscar went to Paul Newman for *The Color of Money*.

1730 • ROYAL FAMILY OF BROADWAY, THE

PARAMOUNT PUBLIX. 1930–31.
NOMINATION *Actor:* Fredric March.

March plays John Barrymore—though not by that name; the character is called Tony Cavendish—in this amusing if stagy version of a play by George S. Kaufman and Edna Ferber that lampooned the Barrymore family. Ina Claire is the Ethel Barrymore [1445 . . .] character. The plot is something about how theater people can't stop acting even when they're off stage, but it's mainly an excuse for flamboyant poses and entertaining rant. The adaptation is by Herman J. Mankiewicz [407 . . .] and Gertrude Purcell, and it provided George Cukor [262 . . .] with one of his earliest film directing jobs, though he

had to share credit with Cyril Gardner, a former film editor turned director who was brought in because of his greater experience in working with the camera. Cukor, however, did the lion's share of the work of preparing the actors and staging the scenes. In a nifty bit of irony, March lost the Oscar to the one member of the Barrymore clan not parodied in the film: Lionel, who won for *A Free Soul*.

March: 184, 515, 572, 1909.

1731 • ROYAL WEDDING

MGM. 1951.
NOMINATION *Song:* "Too Late Now," music by Burton Lane, lyrics by Alan Jay Lerner.

Fred Astaire [2126] and Jane Powell play a brother-sister dance team who journey to London at the time of the wedding of Princess Elizabeth and Prince Philip. Powell falls in love with an English nobleman, Peter Lawford, and Astaire falls for Sarah Churchill. The screenplay, by Lerner, is based in part on the experiences of Astaire and his sister, Adele, in the twenties. Like Powell's character, Adele wound up marrying into the nobility. There is also a shipboard dance number during heavy seas that is based on the Astaires' experiences. It's an agreeable film, directed by Stanley Donen, with nice songs, the best of which are the nominated tune and the raucous "How Could You Believe Me When I Said I Loved You When You Know I've Been a Liar All My Life?," which is said to be the longest song title on record. The highlights are the famous gimmick number in which Astaire dances on the walls and ceilings, and a sharply contrasting (and superior) one in which he dances solo on a bare stage with a hat rack for a partner. The film was the highlight of Sarah Churchill's brief film career. Although she trained as a dancer, she dances only briefly with Astaire in this film. MGM was forbidden to use the fact that she was Sir Winston's daughter in publicity for the movie.

The best song Oscar went to Hoagy Carmichael and Johnny Mercer for "In the Cool, Cool, Cool of the Evening," from *Here Comes the Groom*.

Lane: 117. Lerner: 66, 769, 1186, 1393.

1732 • RUGGLES OF RED GAP

PARAMOUNT. 1935.

NOMINATION *Picture:* Arthur Hornblow, Jr., producer.

Englishman Roland Young [2117] makes the mistake of playing poker with American Egbert Froud (Charlie Ruggles), and in the process bets—and loses—his butler, Ruggles, played by Charles Laughton [1387 . . .], who is forced to accompany Froud and his social-climbing wife, Effie (Mary Boland), to the Wild West town of Red Gap. The remainder of the film might be called "How the West Was Tamed"—by Ruggles, who in turn falls for the widow Judson (ZaSu Pitts). Classic comedy, based on a story and play by Harry Leon Wilson that had been filmed twice before as a silent, and would be remade again as *Fancy Pants* in 1950, with Bob Hope and Lucille Ball. This one owes much to its director, Leo McCarey [21 . . .], and to its peerless cast of character actors. The film was edited by future director Edward Dmytryk [467]. The best picture Oscar went to another film starring Laughton: *Mutiny on the Bounty*.

Hornblow: 925, 2297.

1733 • RULING CLASS, THE

KEEP FILMS LTD. PRODUCTION; AVCO EMBASSY (UNITED KINGDOM). 1972.

NOMINATION *Actor:* Peter O'Toole.

When his eccentric father (Harry Andrews) dies, the even madder Jack (O'Toole) becomes the earl of Gurney, who sometimes thinks he's Jesus Christ and is rich enough to persuade people to go along with the delusion. But then he switches identities and decides he's Jack the Ripper, commits murder, pins the rap on the butler (Arthur Lowe), and enters the House of Lords. Way over-the-top satire, written and directed by Peter Medak, that has become a cult favorite. It's certainly one of a kind (for which many are thankful) and features the invaluable support of Alastair Sim. Very much worth sitting through the parts that don't work (of which there are too many) to get to the parts that do. O'Toole gives one of his most amazing performances, but he lost again, this time to Marlon Brando in *The Godfather*.

O'Toole: 164, 805, 1151, 1177, 1395, 1953.

1734 • RUNAWAY TRAIN

CANNON FILMS PRODUCTION; CANNON RELEASING. 1985.

NOMINATIONS *Actor:* Jon Voight. *Supporting Actor:* Eric Roberts. *Film Editing:* Henry Richardson.

Convicts Voight and Roberts break out of prison and wind up on a train whose brakes have failed, leaving them careening across Canada. Dark, brutal, nonstop action film with an impressive pedigree: It was based on a screenplay by Akira Kurosawa [1661], who never got the backing to film it himself. Directed by Andrei Konchalovsky, with Rebecca DeMornay and Kenneth McMillan.

Voight lost to William Hurt in *Kiss of the Spider Woman*. Roberts, whose screen career has subsequently been overshadowed by that of his younger sister, Julia [1603 . . .], lost to Don Ameche in *Cocoon*. The editing award went to Thom Noble for *Witness*.

Voight: 430, 1312.

1735 • RUNNING ON EMPTY

LORIMAR PRODUCTION; WARNER BROS. 1988.

NOMINATIONS *Supporting Actor:* River Phoenix. *Screenplay Written Directly for the Screen:* Naomi Foner.

Annie and Arthur Pope, played by Christine Lahti [1989] and Judd Hirsch [1502], have been on the run for years—ever since their student radical days when they blew up a building and accidentally killed a man. Now their son, Danny (Phoenix), is graduating from high school; he's a talented musician who's been offered a scholarship to Juilliard, and he has a girlfriend (Martha Plimpton). It's time for the Popes to make a very painful decision about their future: Should they let Danny stay underground with them, as he's willing to do? Or should they let him go, knowing that they may never see him again? Effective problem drama, a bit too mechanically plotted, but the fine performances and the sensitive direction by Sidney Lumet [561 . . .] keep it from falling into TV-movie predictability.

At the time of his drug-related death in 1994, Phoenix, still in his early twenties, was considered one of the finest film actors of his generation. He had first gained acclaim in 1986, at the age of sixteen, with two films, *The Mosquito Coast* and *Stand by Me,* playing troubled but strong teenagers. He subsequently gave memorable performances as a naive young soldier having a last romantic fling before he's shipped off to Vietnam in *Dogfight* (1991) and as a narcoleptic male prostitute in *My Own Private Idaho* (1991). He lost the Oscar to Kevin Kline in *A Fish Called Wanda.*

The screenplay Oscar went to Ronald Bass and Barry Morrow for *Rain Man.*

1736 • RUSSIANS ARE COMING, THE RUSSIANS ARE COMING, THE

Mirisch Corporation of Delaware Production; United Artists. 1966.
Nominations *Picture:* Norman Jewison, producer. *Actor:* Alan Arkin. *Screenplay—Based on Material From Another Medium:* William Rose. *Film Editing:* Hal Ashby and J. Terry Williams.

A Soviet submarine runs aground off the coast of New England, sending the villagers into a tizzy. Arkin is a sailor who goes ashore and tries to talk sense into the natives, who include Carl Reiner, Eva Marie Saint [1477], Brian Keith, Jonathan Winters, Paul Ford, Tessie O'Shea, Ben Blue, Parker Fennelly, Doro Merande, and Michael J. Pollard [255]. The sub crew includes Theodore Bikel [522] and John Philip Law. Pleasant situation comedy that today seems awfully tame, but was treated as if it were trenchant satire when it was released. It certainly seems like a peculiar candidate for best picture, especially since Jewison was denied a directorial nomination—as were, remarkably, two more of the directors of the year's best picture nominees: *Alfie*'s Lewis Gilbert and *The Sand Pebbles*' Robert Wise. In their places, the Academy nominated Michelangelo Antonio for *Blowup,* Richard Brooks for *The Professionals,* and Claude Lelouch for *A Man and a Woman.* The two best picture directors who did get nominated were Mike Nichols for *Who's Afraid of Virginia Woolf?* and Fred Zinnemann for *A Man for All Seasons,* which won the best picture and directing Oscars. The thinness of the films of 1966 seems pretty obvious from this sampling, but Hollywood was on the brink of a new era that resulted from the demise of the Production Code and the emergence of a younger, hipper audience, raised on rock and roll and rebellion, reflected in the following year's youth-cult successes, *Bonnie and Clyde* and *The Graduate. The Russians Are Coming* looks pale indeed when set against those movies.

Arkin lost to Paul Scofield in *A Man for All Seasons,* which also won for Robert Bolt's screenplay. The editing award went to the team that put together the car-racing action of *Grand Prix.*

Jewison: 659, 992, 1351, 1857. Arkin: 884. Rose: 758, 843, 1128. Ashby: 430, 992.

1737 • RYAN'S DAUGHTER

Faraway Productions A.G.; MGM (United Kingdom). 1970.
Awards *Supporting Actor:* John Mills. *Cinematography:* Freddie Young.
Nominations *Actress:* Sarah Miles. *Sound:* Gordon K. McCallum and John Bramall.

In a village on the coast of Ireland, Miles marries the schoolteacher, played by Robert Mitchum [1935], but she has an affair with a British soldier (Christopher Jones). Since the time is 1916, she is suspected of betraying Irish revolutionaries to the British. Director David Lean [287 . . .], known for epics such as *Lawrence of Arabia* and *Doctor Zhivago,* unfortunately tries to turn this small story by Robert Bolt [558 . . .] into something with epic sweep and heft. It isn't capable of it, so a tale that could have been told neatly and effectively in ninety minutes is pounded out thin to cover twice that length. Young's magnificent photography covers some of the thin spots, and there are some fine actors around trying to beef out their parts: Trevor Howard [1875] as a priest, Mills as the village idiot, and Leo McKern as Miles' father. The film was a box-office bomb anyway, and Lean's career was seriously damaged by it: It was fourteen years before he made another movie, and that one would be his last, *A Passage to India.*

Mills' Oscar may have been as much a recognition of his contribution to the movies—he had never been nominated before—as for his performance in this one. He had begun his screen career in the thirties but came to prominence in the forties with such films as *In Which We Serve* and *Great Expectations* and continued to be a character actor of considerable range over the next four decades. He also became known as the father of two actresses, Hayley [1588.5] and Juliet Mills. He died in 1982.

This was the third of Young's Oscars, all of them for films directed by Lean. In 1985, at the age of eighty-three, Young turned director, on a movie called *Arthur's Hallowed Ground,* which, however, received little commercial distribution.

Miles, who was married to screenwriter Bolt, lost to Glenda Jackson in *Women in Love.* The Oscar for sound went to *Patton.*

Young: 558, 1035, 1151, 1429. McCallum: 540, 659, 1977.

1738 • *SABRINA*

PARAMOUNT. 1954.

AWARD *Black-and-White Costume Design:* Edith Head. **NOMINATIONS** *Actress:* Audrey Hepburn. *Director:* Billy Wilder. *Screenplay:* Billy Wilder, Samuel Taylor, and Ernest Lehman. *Black-and-White Cinematography:* Charles Lang, Jr. *Black-and-White Art Direction—Set Decoration:* Hal Pereira and Walter Tyler; Sam Comer and Ray Moyer.

Sabrina Fairchild (Hepburn) is the daughter of the chauffeur (John Williams) to the Larrabees, a wealthy Long Island family. Hopelessly smitten with the younger Larrabee son, David, played by William Holden [1424 . . .], a playboy who scarcely knows she exists, Sabrina attempts suicide in a fit of adolescent lovesickness. She is rescued by the older Larrabee son, Linus, played by Humphrey Bogart [24 . . .], who is as businesslike as David is philandering. Linus persuades Sabrina to go to Paris, where plans have already been made for her to attend cooking school, and forget about David. In Paris Sabrina comes under the tutelage of an elderly baron (Marcel Dalio), who recognizes that she lacks culinary talent, so he teaches her about style instead. She returns to Long Island the picture of elegance and sophistication, whereupon David falls in love with her. Unfortunately he's supposed to marry Elizabeth Tyson, played

by Martha Hyer [1859], and his infatuation with Sabrina threatens a business deal between the Larrabees and the Tysons. So Linus sets out to break up the romance of Sabrina and David by wooing her himself —and you can guess the rest. Several things are wrong with this romantic comedy: Sabrina's suicide attempt, which seems wholly out of character, strikes a sour note that the film has to work hard to recover from; there's some unfunny business involving Holden and a pair of champagne glasses; and Bogart, though he has endearing and amusing moments, is badly miscast in a role for which Cary Grant [1445 . . .] was the first choice. (In the early fifties there was a dearth of young romantic leads who could assume the roles once played by Grant, Ray Milland [1208], and Robert Montgomery [904 . . .]. Later in the decade, Jack Lemmon [91 . . .], Tony Curtis [522], and Rock Hudson [768] would emerge to take their place, but for the meantime actresses like Hepburn and Grace Kelly [450 . . .] were often partnered with men old enough to be their fathers.) Nevertheless, *Sabrina* is highly entertaining, thanks largely to Hepburn's extraordinary rapport with her fellow actors and with the camera, though it's only her second film as a star. To gauge Hepburn's contribution to *Sabrina,* try to imagine any other contemporary ingenue—Mitzi Gaynor, for example—in the title role. She is ably supported by Bogart, Holden, Williams, Walter Hampden as the Larrabee patriarch, and Francis X. Bushman, Ellen Corby [972], and Nancy Kulp, among others. And for all the flaws of his screenplay (based on Taylor's Broadway play *Sabrina Fair),* Wilder is a director whose pacing can't be faulted, even if his taste can. The production is handsomely designed and filmed, much of it on location on Long Island: The Larrabee estate is actually that of Paramount exec Barney Balaban.

This was the fifth of Head's record-setting (for costumers and for women) eight Oscars. However, although Head claimed credit by virtue of her status as head of the Paramount costuming department, much of Hepburn's wardrobe is by the actress' favorite couturier, Hubert de Givenchy [736]. The Oscars went to *The Country Girl*—actress Grace Kelly and screenwriter George Seaton—and to *On the Waterfront* —director Elia Kazan, cinematographer Boris Kaufman, and art director Richard Day.

Head: 31, 32, 46, 305, 357, 363, 612, 636, 675, 736, 832, 894, 945, 1003, 1219, 1261, 1263, 1398, 1427, 1504, 1550, 1579, 1587, 1631, 1716, 1727, 1748, 1840, 1927, 1986, 2012, 2098, 2247, 2298. Hepburn: 278, 1457, 1716, 2221. Wilder: 91, 138, 198, 566, 705, 709, 925, 1208, 1440, 1860, 1903, 1975, 2297. Lehman: 896, 1450, 2244, 2277. Lang: 97, 250, 319, 636, 649, 705, 765, 953, 1480, 1640, 1699, 1778, 1855, 1860, 1955, 1968, 2180. Pereira: 278, 357, 363, 426, 450, 736, 956, 1029, 1219, 1504, 1570, 1631, 1674, 1716, 1727, 1897, 1959, 2012, 2098, 2200, 2208. Tyler: 357, 1022, 1101, 1716, 1748, 1959, 2012, 2208. Comer: 278, 357, 426, 450, 726, 736, 925, 956, 1029, 1101, 1214, 1219, 1443, 1570, 1631, 1674, 1727, 1748, 1959, 1975, 1994, 2012, 2098, 2200, 2208. Moyer: 278, 413, 736, 833, 1101, 1120, 1214, 1674, 1748, 1975, 2012.

1739 • SADIE THOMPSON

GLORIA SWANSON PRODUCTIONS; UNITED ARTISTS. 1927–28.
NOMINATIONS *Actress:* Gloria Swanson. *Cinematography:* George Barnes.

Sadie (Swanson) is a prostitute who follows the fleet to Pago Pago, from which an antivice crusader played by Lionel Barrymore [732 . . .] tries to banish her. But he's ultimately undone by his repressed passion for her. Meanwhile, Sadie dallies with a marine, played by Raoul Walsh, who also directed the film. This silent version is perhaps the best of the many filmings of the story by W. Somerset Maugham: Joan Crawford [1319 . . .] played Sadie in a 1932 version, titled *Rain,* and Rita Hayworth was in the 1953 film known as *Miss Sadie Thompson.* Unfortunately the last reel of the film is now missing, though a version patched out with still photographs and the original title cards is available on video. The production design is by William Cameron Menzies [38 . . .].

Thanks to *Sunset Boulevard,* Swanson is perhaps the best known of all the great silent film actresses. She began her screen acting career while still a teenager in 1913, appearing in Mack Sennett comedies and becoming famous in Cecil B. DeMille [412 . . .] films of the early twenties. Both *Sadie Thompson* and *The Trespasser,* for which she would receive a nomination two years later, were financed by her lover, Joseph P. Kennedy. She lost the Oscar this time to Janet Gaynor, who was nominated for *Seventh Heaven, Street Angel,* and *Sunrise.*

The cinematography Oscar went to Charles Rosher and Karl Struss for *Sunrise.*

Swanson: 1975, 2138. Barnes: 537, 1236, 1509, 1670, 1748, 1885, 1890.

1740 • SAHARA

COLUMBIA. 1943.
NOMINATIONS *Supporting Actor:* J. Carrol Naish. *Black-and-White Cinematography:* Rudolph Maté. *Sound Recording:* John Livadary.

A tank crew headed by Humphrey Bogart [24 . . .] rescues a group of Allied soldiers, plus an Italian POW (Naish), a Nazi pilot (Kurt Krueger) whose plane has crashed, and a Sudanese soldier (Rex Ingram), after the fall of Tobruk in 1942. Lost in the desert, they reach a well, but have to make a stand there against a Nazi batallion that also wants the water. Outstanding wartime action film, written by John Howard Lawson [233] and by Zoltan Korda, who also directed. Lawson, one of the Hollywood Ten imprisoned in the fifties because of his refusal to testify about his earlier Communist Party activities, was inspired partly by a 1937 Soviet film, *The Thirteen.* The propagandizing that occasionally gets in the way of the action was endemic to most movies of the war years. The cast includes Bruce Bennett, Lloyd Bridges, and Dan Duryea.

The supporting actor Oscar went to Charles Coburn for *The More the Merrier.* Arthur Miller won for the cinematography for *The Song of Bernadette.* The award for sound went to Stephen Dunn for *This Land Is Mine.*

Naish: 1294. Maté: 455, 706, 1607, 2031. Livadary: 330, 455, 596, 732, 1058, 1206, 1215, 1303, 1366, 1370, 1488, 1521, 1872, 2111, 2325, 2327.

1740.5 • SAL OF SINGAPORE

PATHÉ. 1928–29.

NOMINATION *Writing Achievement:* Elliott Clawson.

Sal (Phyllis Haver), a tough waterfront type, is enlisted by Captain Erickson (Alan Hale) to look after a baby he has found in a lifeboat. Mostly silent film, with eighteen minutes of dialogue on the final reel. Clawson was only an unofficial nominee; the Academy announced only the winners this year—in this case, Hans Kräly for *The Patriot*. The runners-up received no certificates or other recognition, but their names have been preserved in Academy records as under consideration for the award.

Clawson: 443.5, 1152, 1838.5.

1741 • SALAAM BOMBAY!

MIRABAI PRODUCTION (INDIA). 1988.

NOMINATION *Foreign Language Film.*

A twelve-year-old boy, bullied by his older brother, runs away from home and tries to make a living on the streets of Bombay. After encounters with prostitutes, thieves, and drug peddlers, he is arrested and thrown into a grim juvenile detention center. Exceptional documentary-style drama, the first feature film made by Mira Nair, who began her career as a documentary filmmaker. Most of the cast members are actual residents of the streets of Bombay, and the locations are all too real. The Oscar went to *Pelle the Conqueror*.

1742 • SALLAH

SALLAH FILM LTD. PRODUCTION (ISRAEL). 1964.

NOMINATION *Foreign Language Film.*

Haym Topol [659] plays the title role, a man who emigrates to Israel in 1948 with his wife and seven children. Fundamentally lazy, Sallah finds ways to take care of his family that don't involve real work. Pleasant satiric comedy-drama, directed by Ephraim Kishon. The Oscar went to *Yesterday, Today and Tomorrow*.

1743 • SALLY

FIRST NATIONAL. 1929–30.

NOMINATION *Interior Decoration:* Jack Okey.

Marilyn Miller plays Sally, a restaurant dishwasher who dreams of becoming a dancer, masquerades as one at a fancy party, and winds up a star of the *Ziegfeld Follies*. Attempt to capture on film a celebrated Broadway musical that launched Miller's stardom in 1920. Despite music by Jerome Kern [340 . . .] that includes Miller's signature "Look for the Silver Lining," an elaborate production and filming in early two-color Technicolor, the movie was not a success. While she was apparently charming on stage, Miller was not photogenic, and she made only two more films. The cast, directed by John Francis Dillon, includes Joe E. Brown, Pert Kelton, and Ford Sterling. The art direction Oscar went to Herman Rosse for *King of Jazz*.

Okey: 632.

1744 • SALTY O'ROURKE

PARAMOUNT. 1945.

NOMINATION *Original Screenplay:* Milton Holmes.

Alan Ladd is a con artist who thinks he has the perfect scam involving a jockey (Stanley Clements). Then schoolteacher Gail Russell enters his life and complicates it. Passable but predictable dramatic comedy, directed by Raoul Walsh, with William Demarest [1058], Bruce Cabot, and Spring Byington [2325]. The original screenplay Oscar went to Richard Schweizer for *Marie-Louise*.

1745 • SALUDOS AMIGOS

WALT DISNEY PRODUCTIONS; RKO RADIO. 1943.

NOMINATIONS *Sound Recording:* C. O. Slyfield. *Song:* "Saludos Amigos," music by Charles Wolcott, lyrics by Ned Washington. *Scoring of a Musical Picture:* Edward H. Plumb, Paul J. Smith, and Charles Wolcott.

Short feature made up of four animated sequences, introduced by live-action footage from a goodwill tour of South America made by Walt Disney [645 . . .] and some of his staff as part of the wartime Good Neighbor Policy designed to keep Latin America neutral. The cartoons feature Donald Duck as a tourist, first at Lake Titicaca and later, in the colorful finale, joined by José Carioca at the carnival in Rio; Goofy appears in a segment called "El Gaucho Goofy," which demonstrates the differences between the American cowboy and the Argentine gaucho; and there's a story about Pedro, a little plane that flies the mail over the Andes. Minor Disney, with nice music, but the more ambitious *The Three Caballeros,* released the following year, is much better at both entertaining and propagandizing. The award for sound went to Stephen Dunn for *This Land Is Mine.* The best song was Harry Warren and Mack Gordon's "You'll Never Know," from *Hello, Frisco, Hello.* The scoring award went to Ray Heindorf for *This Is the Army.*

Slyfield: 140, 402, 2071. Wolcott: 1871, 2071. Washington: 274, 585, 911, 912, 1329, 1396, 1576, 2127, 2282, 2335. Plumb: 140, 2071, 2202. Smith: 402, 1553, 1576, 1851, 1871, 2071, 2202.

1746 • SALVADOR

HEMDALE FILM PRODUCTION; HEMDALE RELEASING. 1986.
NOMINATIONS *Actor:* James Woods. *Screenplay Written Directly for the Screen:* Oliver Stone and Richard Boyle.

Woods plays a boozy, druggy journalist modeled on screenwriter Boyle and bearing his name. He and a similarly dissipated deejay called Dr. Rock (James Belushi) set out for El Salvador in search of some action —a story for Boyle, more booze and women for Dr. Rock. They soon find, however, that the action in El Salvador is very real indeed and that their lives are in danger. Brutal, profane drama that has all the earmarks of Stone's work (he also directed): It's designed to demonstrate the folly of American involvement in Central America, but Stone doesn't just preach, he harangues. It does, however, have a powerful performance by Woods as an almost complete sleaze, and fine support from Michael Murphy as a well-meaning American ambassador undermined by his own government, John Savage as a photojournalist, and Elpedia Carrillo, Tony Plana, and Cynthia Gibb. *Salvador* made little impression at the box office, but it was released in the same year as *Platoon,* which made Stone an important player in Hollywood.

Woods made his screen debut in 1972 and, though he played a few more or less likable parts such as Barbra Streisand's communist friend in *The Way We Were,* soon found himself cast as a psychotic or a weirdo. The Oscar nomination for *Salvador* helped him win respect as a serious actor, although his subsequent attempts to play comic and even romantic roles haven't quite erased his image as a creep. He lost the Oscar to Paul Newman in *The Color of Money.*

The screenplay award went to Woody Allen for *Hannah and Her Sisters.*

Stone: 260, 1047, 1313, 1584.

1747 • SAME TIME, NEXT YEAR

WALTER MIRISCH-ROBERT MULLIGAN PRODUCTION; MIRISCH CORPORATION/UNIVERSAL PICTURES PRESENTATION; UNIVERSAL. 1978.
NOMINATIONS *Actress:* Ellen Burstyn. *Screenplay Based on Material From Another Medium:* Bernard Slade. *Cinematography:* Robert Surtees. *Original Song:* "The Last Time I Felt Like This," music by Marvin Hamlisch, lyrics by Alan Bergman and Marilyn Bergman.

Burstyn and Alan Alda play two people who first meet at a country inn in the fifties and have a one-night stand—one night a year, that is, for the next twenty-five years—even though each is married to someone else. Tiresome adaptation by Slade of his Broadway comedy-drama, which was thin and cutesy on stage and doesn't improve at all on screen, where the actors have to labor harder to suggest the passage of time. The satiric glances at changing American manners and mores are predictable. In the end it depends on two enormously likable actors to bring it off, so your tolerance of it probably is proportional to your fondness for Burstyn and Alda. Directed by Robert Mulligan [2101]. Burstyn lost to Jane Fonda in *Coming Home.* The cinematography Oscar went to Nestor Almendros for *Days of Heaven.* The best song was Paul Jabara's "Last Dance," from *Thank God It's Friday.*

Burstyn: 41, 631, 1139, 1682. Surtees: 130, 175, 557, 810, 917, 1094, 1139, 1388, 1469, 1644, 1911, 1927, 1960, 2055, 2152. Hamlisch: 398, 977, 1109, 1813, 1876, 1898, 1927, 2238. A. Bergman:

179, 867, 1168, 1568, 1628, 1813, 1864, 2063, 2113, 2238, 2321, 2322. M. Bergman: 179, 867, 1168, 1568, 1628, 1813, 1864, 2063, 2113, 2238, 2321, 2322.

1748 • SAMSON AND DELILAH

CECIL B. DeMILLE PRODUCTIONS; PARAMOUNT. 1950.
AWARDS *Color Art Direction—Set Decoration:* Hans Dreier and Walter Tyler; Sam Comer and Ray Moyer. *Color Costume Design:* Edith Head, Dorothy Jeakins, Elois Jenssen, Gile Steele, and Gwen Wakeling.
NOMINATIONS *Color Cinematography:* George Barnes. *Scoring of a Dramatic or Comedy Picture:* Victor Young. *Special Effects.* (No individual citation.)

The Hebrew strongman Samson (Victor Mature) is seduced by the Philistine Delilah (Hedy Lamarr), but, enslaved and blinded, he brings the temple down on his pagan enemies—and himself. It's impossible to take seriously, but it's lots of fun if you don't try. Director Cecil B. DeMille [412 . . .], of course, took it seriously, saying in his autobiography that he was aiming for a "poignant drama of faith." But it's his usual serving of sex and violence tricked out with a moral lesson. Unfortunately the sex isn't that enjoyable—Mature is flabby and Lamarr has lost the bloom that made her sensationally appealing in *Algiers* more than a decade earlier—so all we have left is the violence: Mature and his doubles struggling with a lethargic lion and jawboning a few score of his foes, plus the destruction of the temple, which is spectacular, if scarcely worth waiting two hours for. George Sanders [46] is the ruler of the Philistines, and twenty-five-year-old Angela Lansbury [749 . . .] plays thirty-seven-year-old Lamarr's older sister. Also in the cast are Henry Wilcoxon, Russ (billed as Rusty) Tamblyn [1558], Moroni Olsen, Fay Holden, Mike Mazurki, and George Reeves.

The Oscar for cinematography went to Robert Surtees for *King Solomon's Mines.* Franz Waxman won for the score for *Sunset Boulevard.* The award for special effects went to *Destination Moon.*

Dreier: 97, 151, 649, 674, 701, 726, 925, 979, 1101, 1120, 1194, 1214, 1217, 1358, 1443, 1452, 1540, 1668, 1880, 1975, 1994, 2190. Tyler: 357, 1022, 1101, 1716, 1738, 1959, 2012, 2208. Comer: 278, 357, 426, 450, 726, 736, 925, 956, 1029, 1101, 1214, 1219, 1443, 1570, 1631, 1674, 1727, 1738, 1959, 1975, 1994, 2012, 2098, 2200, 2208. Moyer: 278, 413, 736, 833, 1101, 1120, 1214, 1674, 1738, 1975, 2012. Head: 31, 32, 46, 305, 357, 363, 612, 636, 675, 736, 832, 894, 945, 1003, 1219, 1261, 1263, 1398, 1427, 1504, 1550, 1579, 1587, 1631, 1716, 1727, 1738, 1840, 1927, 1986, 2012, 2098, 2247, 2298. Jeakins: 393, 509, 832, 882, 1048, 1385, 1391, 1432, 1881, 2012, 2238. Jenssen: 2144. Steele: 612, 817, 894, 1087, 1309. Barnes: 537, 1236, 1509, 1670, 1739, 1885, 1890. Young: 97, 98, 100, 101, 280, 489, 612, 693, 701, 794, 846, 925, 1214, 1257, 1396, 1452, 1823, 1994, 2235, 2315.

1749 • SAMURAI, THE LEGEND OF MUSASHI

TOHO (JAPAN). 1955.
AWARD *Honorary Award:* Best Foreign Language Film first released in the United States during 1955.

Toshiro Mifune stars as a man who begins as an outlaw but is changed by his experiences and becomes a famous samurai, Miyamoto Musashi. Slow, thoughtful epic, in three parts, each about one hundred minutes, directed by Hiroshi Inagaki and beautifully filmed in color.

1750 • SAN ANTONIO

WARNER BROS. 1945.
NOMINATIONS *Color Interior Decoration:* Ted Smith, art direction; Jack McConaghy, set decoration. *Song:* "Some Sunday Morning," music by Ray Heindorf and M. K. Jerome, lyrics by Ted Koehler.

Cowboy Errol Flynn romances dance hall girl Alexis Smith but has to battle saloon owner Victor Francen to get her. Okay western, with a colorful cast: S. Z. Sakall, Florence Bates, Paul Kelly, Monte Blue, Chris-Pin Martin, and Doodles Weaver, among others. Directed by David Butler from a screenplay by Alan LeMay and W. R. Burnett [2222]. The cinematography is by Bert Glennon [551 . . .]. The art direction Oscar went to *Frenchman's Creek.* Richard

Rodgers and Oscar Hammerstein won for "It Might As Well Be Spring," from *State Fair*.

Smith: 353. McConaghy: 527. Heindorf: 331, 479, 666, 930, 1043, 1204, 1385, 1408, 1430, 1690, 1719, 1910, 2058, 2186, 2243, 2310, 2318. Jerome: 930. Koehler: 930, 2186.

1751 • SAN FRANCISCO

MGM. 1936.

AWARD *Sound Recording:* Douglas Shearer.
NOMINATIONS *Picture:* John Emerson and Bernard H. Hyman, producers. *Actor:* Spencer Tracy. *Director:* W. S. Van Dyke. *Original Story:* Robert Hopkins. *Assistant Director:* Joseph Newman.

Clark Gable [798 . . .] plays a Barbary Coast saloon owner who hires aspiring opera singer Jeanette MacDonald as a performer and then falls in love with her. Tracy, meanwhile, plays a priest who, though he's an old buddy of Gable's, is determined to clean up the Coast. He doesn't have to: The earthquake of '06 does it for him. Hugely enjoyable melodrama-with-music, including the title song by Gus Kahn [692 . . .] and Bronislau Kaper [397 . . .], which somehow failed to make the cut for a best song nomination, but has become the city's official song. The earthquake sequence is a classic, but unlike some movies with big special effects climaxes, the rest of *San Francisco* is worth sitting through for it, thanks especially to the solid screenplay by Anita Loos and the performances of Gable and Tracy. (MacDonald is a bit too arch and coy for contemporary tastes.) The supporting cast includes Jack Holt, Ted Healy, Jessie Ralph, and Al Shean. Reportedly, director Van Dyke assigned the legendary D. W. Griffith to direct one of the crowd sequences.

Although the special effects Oscar was not introduced until three years later, the award to Shearer (the third of the five he won) and the nomination of assistant director Newman are clearly for their work on the movie's most famous sequence.

The best picture Oscar went to *The Great Ziegfeld*. This was the first nomination for Tracy; he lost to Paul Muni in *The Story of Louis Pasteur,* which also won for the story by Pierre Collings and Sheridan Gibney.

Frank Capra received the directing Oscar for *Mr. Deeds Goes to Town*. Jack Sullivan won as assistant director for *The Charge of the Light Brigade*.

Shearer: 136, 202, 256, 397, 685, 817, 835, 1096, 1232, 1292, 1371, 1419, 1950, 1988, 2048, 2055, 2211, 2300. Tracy: 131, 271, 352, 656, 843, 1000, 1065, 1470. Van Dyke: 2052. Newman: 497.

1752 • SAND

20TH CENTURY-FOX. 1949.

NOMINATION *Color Cinematography:* Charles G. Clarke.

The title character is a horse that has been raised to be shown but in the end is allowed to go wild. Brief (seventy-eight minutes) second programmer distinguished only for Clarke's handsome photography. Louis King directs Mark Stevens, Rory Calhoun, Colleen Gray, and Charley Grapewin. The Oscar went to Winston Hoch for *She Wore a Yellow Ribbon*.

Clarke: 837, 897, 1352.

1753 • SAND PEBBLES, THE

ARGYLE-SOLAR PRODUCTION; 20TH CENTURY-FOX. 1966.

NOMINATIONS *Picture:* Robert Wise, producer. *Actor:* Steve McQueen. *Supporting Actor:* Mako. *Color Cinematography:* Joseph MacDonald. *Color Art Direction–Set Decoration:* Boris Leven; Walter M. Scott, John Sturtevant, and William Kiernan. *Sound:* James P. Corcoran, sound director, 20th Century-Fox Studio Sound Department. *Original Music Score:* Jerry Goldsmith. *Film Editing:* William Reynolds.

McQueen is a sailor on a gunboat, the *San Pablo* (the title is a pun on the ship's name), patrolling the Yangtze River in China in 1926. He is a loner, shunned by other members of the crew because of his kind treatment of the coolie Po-Han (Mako) who assists him. When McQueen interrupts an assault on a young Chinese woman, he becomes the center of an international incident. The cast also includes Richard Attenborough [745], Richard Crenna as the ship's captain, and Candice Bergen [1919] as an American missionary with whom McQueen becomes romantically involved, plus Larry Gates, Simon Oakland, and Gavin MacLeod. A handsome production, filmed in Taiwan and Hong Kong, but the screenplay by Robert

Anderson [971 . . .] gets rather muddled when it tries to suggest a relevance to the American involvement in Vietnam, and the whole thing goes on much too long—about three hours. Something of a stiff at the box office, *The Sand Pebbles* was a default nominee in a year of generally unsatisfactory films: the other nominees were *Alfie, The Russians Are Coming, the Russians Are Coming, Who's Afraid of Virginia Woolf,* and the winner, *A Man for All Seasons.* Wise also directed, but failed to receive a nomination in that category. In fact, only two of the directors of the year's best picture nominees, Mike Nichols for *Virginia Woolf* and Fred Zinnemann for *A Man for All Seasons,* were so cited.

McQueen was at his peak both as an actor and as a box-office draw. A genuine tough guy, he had done time in reform school and the marines and had worked as a lumberjack, a carnival barker, a bartender, and at numerous other odd jobs before taking up acting. Trained at the Actors Studio, he did stage and TV work and made his debut in 1955 in a bit part in *Somebody Up There Likes Me.* He first made his mark as a screen actor in *The Magnificent Seven* and established his image in *The Great Escape* in 1963. Not content to be typed as an action hero, he formed his own production company. His most ambitious project, however, a film of Ibsen's *An Enemy of the People* (1979), was a flop that received limited distribution. He died of cancer in 1980. The Oscar went to Paul Scofield for *A Man for All Seasons.*

Mako, a Japanese-born actor, makes his screen debut in *The Sand Pebbles.* He has been seen in many character roles on stage, TV, and in films. Walter Matthau won the supporting actor award for *The Fortune Cookie.*

The cinematography award went to Ted Moore for *A Man for All Seasons. Fantastic Voyage* won the art direction award. The Oscar for sound went to the auto racing film *Grand Prix,* which also won for film editing. John Barry's score for *Born Free* won the music Oscar.

Wise: 407, 973, 1881, 2244. MacDonald: 1550, 2336. Leven: 34, 77, 422, 768, 1801, 1881, 1907, 2244. Scott: 46, 376, 413, 476, 530, 542, 557, 646, 896, 1062, 1088, 1213, 1391, 1475, 1706, 1881, 1907, 2008, 2120, 2247. Kiernan: 1133, 1521, 1550, 1858, 2238. Corcoran: 29, 413, 1881. Goldsmith: 152.5, 268, 395, 727, 939, 1472, 1527, 1537, 1541, 1583, 1589, 1913, 2176, 2287. Reynolds: 643, 784, 896, 1881, 1927, 2152.

1754 • SANDAKAN NO. 8

TOHO COMPANY LTD.-HAIYUZA PRODUCTION (JAPAN). 1975.
NOMINATION *Foreign Language Film.*

The title refers to a brothel in Borneo where a young woman works so that she can support her family in Japan. The film, directed by Kei Kumai, tells her story in flashback, as the elderly woman, now living in Japan, is interviewed by a journalist. The result is a strong political statement on the role of women in Japan. The Oscar went to *Dersu Uzala.*

1755 • SANDPIPER, THE

FILMWAYS-VENICE PRODUCTION; MGM. 1965.
AWARD *Song:* "The Shadow of Your Smile," music by Johnny Mandel, lyrics by Paul Francis Webster.

Unwed mother Elizabeth Taylor [318 . . .] gets involved with Episcopalian minister Richard Burton [85 . . .], the headmaster of her young son's school. Burton is, however, married to Eva Marie Saint [1477], while Taylor, a Big Sur hippie artist, has been carrying on with sculptor Charles Bronson—a part that Taylor wanted Sammy Davis, Jr., to play. Incredible drivel, concocted by a prestigious pair of screenwriters, the formerly blacklisted Dalton Trumbo [273 . . .] and Michael Wilson [287 . . .], from bits and pieces of old stories such as *The Garden of Allah* and Somerset Maugham's *Rain.* Aware of the flimsiness of the script, Burton and Taylor, who were in it for the money, insisted that producer Martin Ransohoff hire a first-rate director. When William Wyler [175 . . .] backed out, Vincente Minnelli [66 . . .] took on the project. It did nothing for anybody's career, though it was a box-office hit, thanks to the notoriety of Burton and Taylor.

Mandel has been a screen composer since 1958, with scoring credits on such films as *I Want To Live!, The Americanization of Emily, The Russians Are Coming,* the Russians Are Coming, MASH, Being There, and The Verdict. "The Shadow of Your Smile" also won a Grammy as song of the year.

Mandel: 64. Webster: 33, 64, 95, 331, 376, 604, 663, 730, 856, 1213, 1276, 1322, 1388, 1925, 2014.

1756 • SANDS OF IWO JIMA
REPUBLIC. 1949.

NOMINATIONS *Actor:* John Wayne. *Motion Picture Story:* Harry Brown. *Sound Recording:* Republic Studio Sound Department, Daniel J. Bloomberg, Sound Director. *Film Editing:* Richard L. Van Enger.

Wayne is Marine Sgt. John M. Stryker, in charge of whipping his young recruits into shape for the recapture of Iwo Jima. Quintessential war movie, a classic of the genre in spite of (because of?) its clichés, with well-staged action footage blended with actual combat film. Directed by Allan Dwan, with John Agar, Forrest Tucker, Arthur Franz, Richard Jaeckel [1864], Martin Milner, and three survivors of the iconic flag-raising on Mount Suribachi: Rene A. Gagnon, Ira H. Hayes, and John H. Bradley. It's certainly not subtle, especially not the score by Victor Young [97 . . .], or the Duke's final scene, but would you want it to be?

Wayne had been in the movies for twenty years when he received his first nomination, and his career would last more than a quarter century longer. Like many of the screen's more natural and unaffected performers, particularly those who made their careers in war movies or westerns, Wayne was underestimated by the Academy. He had been a major star since *Stagecoach* in 1939, and the year before *Sands of Iwo Jima* gave one of his finest performances as the martinet Dunson in *Red River,* but the most memorable phase of his career was about to begin: the series of performances he gave for John Ford in the fifties and early sixties, in *The Quiet Man, The Searchers* (1956), and *The Man Who Shot Liberty Valance.* He lost his first nomination to Broderick Crawford in *All the King's Men.*

Douglas Morrow won the writing Oscar for *The Stratton Story.* The award for sound went to *12 O'Clock High.* Harry Gerstad won for editing *Champion.*

Wayne: 33, 2147. Brown: 1579. Bloomberg: 274, 680, 693, 991, 1350, 1642.

1757 • SARABAND
J. ARTHUR RANK-EALING; EAGLE LION (UNITED KINGDOM). 1949.

NOMINATION *Color Art Direction—Set Decoration:* Jim Morahan, William Kellner, and Michael Relph.

Joan Greenwood plays Sophie Dorothea of Hanover, the wife of the future George I of England. Stewart Granger is her roguish true love, whom she must forsake for royal duties. Slow-motion historical drama, handsomely photographed by Douglas Slocombe [1066 . . .], but essentially one of those movies in which the scenery upstages the actors. Greenwood seems miscast as a romantic heroine—her purry voice was better suited to comic or villainous roles. Directed by Basil Dearden, from a screenplay by John Dighton [1255 . . .] and Alexander Mackendrick [1255], with Flora Robson [1759], Françoise Rosay, Peter Bull, Anthony Quayle [85], Michael Gough, and Christopher Lee. The British title is *Saraband for Dead Lovers.* The award for art direction went to *Little Women.*

Kellner: 1956.

1758 • SARAH AND SON
PARAMOUNT FAMOUS LASKY. 1929–30.

NOMINATION *Actress:* Ruth Chatterton.

Chatterton plays a vaudeville singer who marries the partner in her act, a lazy lout whom she winds up supporting. When he leaves her, he gives away their child to a rich couple. Years later, after she has become a famous opera singer, Chatterton hires lawyer Fredric March [184 . . .] to help her find her son. Mother and child are finally united when the boy, awaking from a coma, finds both Chatterton and his adoptive mother at his bedside—and reaches out for Chatterton. Silly, gooey stuff, directed by Dorothy Arzner from a screenplay by Zoë Akins. Chatterton lost to Norma Shearer in *The Divorcée.*

Chatterton: 1234.

1759 • SARATOGA TRUNK

WARNER BROS. 1946.

NOMINATION *Supporting Actress:* Flora Robson.

Ingrid Bergman [72 . . .] plays a shady New Orleans lady named Clio Dulaine who vamps Gary Cooper [701 . . .], playing a Texan named Clint Maroon, at Saratoga Springs. Silly, rambling drivel based on an Edna Ferber best-seller, made tolerable by Bergman's lively performance, handsome photography by Ernest Haller [55 . . .], and music by Max Steiner [16 . . .]. Directed by Sam Wood [701 . . .] from a screenplay by Casey Robinson.

Robson is most improbably miscast as a mulatto servant. One of England's finest actresses, she was made a Dame of the British Empire in 1960. Her film career was largely in character roles, including two performances as Queen Elizabeth I: *Fire Over England* (1937) and *The Sea Hawk*. She can also be seen in *Wuthering Heights* and *Black Narcissus*. She died in 1984. The Oscar went to Anne Baxter for *The Razor's Edge*.

1760 • SATURDAY NIGHT FEVER

ROBERT STIGWOOD ORGANISATION LTD. PRODUCTION; PARAMOUNT. 1977.

NOMINATION *Actor:* John Travolta.

Travolta is Tony, a Brooklyn kid who works in a hardware store but lives for weekends at the disco, where he meets Stephanie (Karen Lynn Gorney), his female equivalent. Crowded with incidents but unencumbered by plot, *Saturday Night Fever* is the movie that for many sums up the seventies by providing its most potent icon: Travolta in a tight white suit dancing to the music of the Bee Gees. The screenplay by Norman Wexler [1051 . . .] is based on a story in *New York* magazine, "Tribal Rites of the New Saturday Night," by Nik Cohn. John Badham directed, and the cinematography is by Ralf D. Bode [418]. In addition to the songs by the Bee Gees (Barry, Robin, and Maurice Gibb), the film is scored by David Shire [1448 . . .]. The movie was a huge hit at the box office, and the soundtrack album was a phenomenal success, particularly the song "Staying Alive." But the Academy cold-shouldered the film and its music.

While the monotony of the flood of inane disco music that followed from the success of *Saturday Night Fever* has tarnished the aura of the Bee Gees, the failure of the music branch to nominate even one of their songs remains one of the Academy's most astonishing oversights. Instead, the nominees included such bland and forgettable tunes as "Candle on the Water," from *Pete's Dragon,* "The Slipper and the Rose Waltz (He Danced With Me/She Danced With Me)," from *The Slipper and the Rose,* and "Someone's Waiting for You," from *The Rescuers*. And the annoying title song from *You Light Up My Life* beat the sole contender of any distinction, "Nobody Does It Better," from *The Spy Who Loved Me*. The following year the Academy would fall over itself to make amends, giving the best song Oscar to a disco hit, "Last Dance," from *Thank God It's Friday*—a lousy film that was one of the many rushed into production to capitalize on the *Saturday Night Fever* phenomenon.

Travolta was one aspect of the *Fever* phenomenon, however, that the Academy could not ignore. Already a teen idol from his work on the TV sitcom *Welcome Back, Kotter,* the actor, in his early twenties, had made two films—he had a bit part in the mediocre *Exorcist* clone *The Devil's Rain* (1975) and a more substantial supporting role in *Carrie*—before *Saturday Night Fever* made him a superstar. His stature was apparently confirmed the following year when *Grease* became one of the biggest moneymakers of all time. But Travolta was unable to find roles that would keep him on top: *Moment by Moment* (1978) was a ridiculous drama about the affair of an older woman (Lily Tomlin) and a younger man (Travolta) that seemed to jinx both stars. *Urban Cowboy* (1980) was essentially a remake of *Saturday Night Fever* set in the kicker bars of Houston, and costars Debra Winger [1465 . . .] and Scott Glenn got the most notice from the reviewers. *Staying Alive* (1983) was an ill-conceived sequel to *Saturday Night Fever*. By the end of the eighties poor career management had turned Travolta, an actor of real talent, into a Hollywood has-been, lucky to get a role in the talking-baby movie *Look Who's Talking* (1989) and its two sequels. In 1994, however, he seemed poised for a comeback after a sensational performance in *Pulp Fiction*. He lost the Oscar to Richard Dreyfuss in *The Goodbye Girl*.

Travolta: 1633.5.

1761 • SAVE THE TIGER

FILMWAYS-JALEM-CIRANDINHA PRODUCTIONS; PARAMOUNT. 1973.

AWARD *Actor:* Jack Lemmon.

NOMINATIONS *Supporting Actor:* Jack Gilford. *Story and Screenplay—Based on Factual Material or Material Not Previously Published or Produced:* Steve Shagan.

Lemmon plays an L.A. garment manufacturer who regrets the course his life has taken, away from youthful innocence and heroic idealism—he's a World War II veteran—and deep into the sordidness and corruption of the business world. But he has to struggle hard —using the same old corrupt methods—to save his firm and protect the jobs of the people who work for him. Writer-producer Shagan joins in the condemnation of American values that was characteristic of Watergate-era filmmaking, but the movie is monotonous and talky, and it died at the box office. John G. Avildsen [1712] directed, none too subtly. The score is by Marvin Hamlisch [398 . . .].

Lemmon's Oscar made him the first person to win an award for a leading role after receiving one for a supporting performance. After the first Oscar, for *Mister Roberts,* Lemmon had distinguished himself as a comic actor, particularly in films directed by Billy Wilder, such as *Some Like It Hot* and *The Apartment,* and other movies such as *The Odd Couple.* But like many actors adept at comedy, he knew that recognition as an actor wouldn't come until he could demonstrate skill in dramatic roles. Only *Days of Wine and Roses,* however, gave him much chance to do so before *Save the Tiger.* After the second Oscar, he began to devote himself to serious roles, with occasional sidesteps into comedy, and all of his subsequent nominations—for *The China Syndrome, Tribute,* and *Missing*— have been for dramatic parts. He overcame some formidable competition to win this Oscar: The other nominees were Marlon Brando for *Last Tango in Paris,* Jack Nicholson for *The Last Detail,* Al Pacino for *Serpico,* and Robert Redford for *The Sting.*

Gilford, who plays Lemmon's business partner, began his career on stage and did substantial work in TV in the fifties. He had only a few film credits before the mid-sixties, when he began appearing more frequently in character roles, as a shy, mousy "little guy." The Oscar went to John Houseman for *The Paper Chase.*

Shagan lost to David S. Ward for *The Sting.*

Lemmon: 91, 394, 508, 1330, 1337, 1860, 2140. Shagan: 2218.

1762 • SAY ONE FOR ME

BING CROSBY PRODUCTIONS INC.; 20TH CENTURY-FOX. 1959.

NOMINATION *Scoring of a Musical Picture:* Lionel Newman.

Bing Crosby [173 . . .] plays a priest whose parish includes Broadway, which gets him involved in sorting out the lives of various theatrical types, including chorus girl Debbie Reynolds [2184]. Misbegotten musical, clearly inspired by *Going My Way.* The blend of showbiz and sanctity doesn't work, and nobody—including Crosby, Reynolds, Robert Wagner, Ray Walston, Stella Stevens, Sebastian Cabot, and songwriters Sammy Cahn [74 . . .] and James Van Heusen [171 . . .]—is at his or her best. Directed by Frank Tashlin. The scoring Oscar went to André Previn and Ken Darby for *Porgy and Bess.*

Newman: 183, 457, 557, 795, 896, 981, 1160, 1273, 1585, 2043.

1763 • SAYONARA

WILLIAM GOETZ PRODUCTION; WARNER BROS. 1957.

AWARDS *Supporting Actor:* Red Buttons. *Supporting Actress:* Miyoshi Umeki. *Art Direction—Set Decoration:* Ted Haworth; Robert Priestley. *Sound:* George Groves, sound director, Warner Bros. Studio Sound Department.

NOMINATIONS *Picture:* William Goetz, producer. *Actor:* Marlon Brando. *Director:* Joshua Logan. *Screenplay— Based on Material From Another Medium:* Paul Osborn. *Cinematography:* Ellsworth Fredericks. *Film Editing:* Arthur P. Schmidt and Philip W. Anderson.

Brando, an air force major stationed in Japan, falls in love with a beautiful dancer, Miiko Taka, a member of a celebrated but cloistered all-female troupe. His enlisted-man acquaintance, Buttons, likewise falls for a Japanese girl, Umeki. Their romances encounter hostility from both Americans and Japanese. The cast includes James Garner [1380], Martha Scott [1510], and Kent Smith, with Ricardo Montalban as a Kabuki actor—reverting to the old Hollywood tradition of casting Westerners as Asians, in which Brando himself had participated for the previous year's *Teahouse of the August Moon.* This handsomely filmed sentimental romance takes its edge from America's growing awareness of its complex relationship with Japan. Logan, the director and coauthor of the Broadway production of *South Pacific,* based on a book by James Michener, wanted to turn Michener's novel *Sayonara* into a stage musical, hoping to persuade Irving Berlin [34 . . .] to write the score. However, Michener offered the rights to several others simultaneously, including Goetz, and after legal hassles, the film version was a compromise worked out by the parties involved. Berlin did, however, contribute the title song. Brando was the first choice of Logan and Goetz, but he was initially reluctant, so Rock Hudson [768] was considered for the role. His unavailability led the producer and director to consider making the female lead the more important part and casting Audrey Hepburn [278 . . .] as the dancer. She declined, saying that no one would believe her as an Asian. Brando finally stated his chief objection, that the American leaves the Japanese woman, as in *Madame Butterfly,* and agreed to play the part if the ending was changed so that they remained together. Ironically one of the film's chief flaws is Brando's undisciplined performance; unhappy with Logan's direction, he alternately walked through his part and overstated it, adopting an often ludicrous southern accent. It is the weakest of his nominated performances. Taka, a Japanese-American with no previous acting experience, was cast in the role of the dancer. Her only other significant screen role was in *Walk, Don't Run,* the 1966 movie that was the last film made by Cary Grant [1445 . . .].

Buttons started in show business in his teens as a singing bellboy, picking up his stage name from the

uniform he wore and from the color of his hair. After working the Borscht Belt as a comedian and appearing in burlesque, he landed Broadway stage work and made his film debut in 1944's *Winged Victory,* based on the stage play in which he had also appeared. In the early fifties he became a star on TV. *Sayonara* was his first major film role, and he appeared frequently in character parts after winning the Oscar.

Umeki had been a nightclub singer in Japan, and her appearance on Japanese TV helped her win the role in *Sayonara.* She appeared in *Flower Drum Song* on Broadway after winning the Oscar and re-created her stage role for the film of that musical. She was also in the cast of the TV sitcom *The Courtship of Eddie's Father* in the late sixties, but her appearances on both big and little screens have been rare in recent years.

Goetz was the "other" producer son-in-law of MGM head Louis B. Mayer, the more famous one being David O. Selznick [497 . . .]. He became a vice-president of 20th Century-Fox when the studio was created by merger in 1933, and later served as production head. He left to found International Pictures and became head of production for Universal-International in 1946. In 1954 he formed an independent production company. *Sayonara* is typical of his films: pleasant but not first-rate. The best picture Oscar went to *The Bridge on the River Kwai,* which took all the other awards for which *Sayonara* was nominated: Alec Guinness won as best actor, David Lean as director, Pierre Boulle (fronting for the blacklisted Michael Wilson and Carl Foreman) for screenplay, Jack Hildyard for cinematography, and Peter Taylor for editing.

Haworth: 1201, 1283, 1550, 1860, 2247. Priestley: 1283, 1566. Groves: 825, 1385, 1393, 1457, 1869, 1973, 2277. Goetz: 946. Brando: 583, 784, 1069, 1141, 1477, 1949, 2212. Logan: 643, 1566. Osborn: 593. Schmidt: 418, 708.5, 1975, 2274. Anderson: 768, 1529.

1764 • SCENT OF A WOMAN

DEAN FILM PRODUCTION; 20TH CENTURY-FOX (ITALY). 1975. **NOMINATIONS** *Screenplay Adapted From Other Material:* Ruggero Maccari and Dino Risi. *Foreign Language Film.*

Vittorio Gassman plays a retired army officer whose blindness deprives him of his chief pleasure in life: beautiful women. So he ropes a young cadet into accompanying him on a trip to Naples and describing the women they encounter. The developing relationship between the blind man and his guide is the core of this darkly sentimental comedy-drama, based on a novel by Giovanni Arpino. Directed by Risi, it's more tightly focused, but also considerably more sexist, than the 1992 American film that was based on it. The screenplay Oscar went to Laurence Hauben and Bo Goldman for *One Flew Over the Cuckoo's Nest.* Coincidentally Goldman did the screenplay for the 1992 remake. *Dersu Uzala* took the foreign language film award.

1764.5 • SCENT OF A WOMAN

UNIVERSAL RELEASE/CITY LIGHT FILMS PRODUCTION; UNIVERSAL. 1992.

AWARD *Actor:* Al Pacino.

NOMINATIONS *Picture:* Martin Brest, producer. *Director:* Martin Brest. *Adapted Screenplay:* Bo Goldman.

Pacino plays Col. Frank Slade, an embittered retired army officer whose blindness makes him dependent on a family he despises. When they go away for a long weekend, they hire Charlie Simms (Chris O'Donnell), a student at a local prep school, to look after Slade. Charlie is himself something of a misfit: He's there on a scholarship, surrounded by rich kids who don't have to earn money by baby-sitting an irascible blind man. He's also facing a dilemma: a hearing to determine who was responsible for a practical joke played on the school's headmaster. If Charlie, who knows the truth, doesn't fess up, his hopes of graduating and getting into a prestigious college could be dead. But if he rats on his fellow students, he breaks the code of silence that binds them against the odious headmaster. To Charlie's astonishment, he's roped into accompanying Slade to New York, where the colonel plans to have one last fling before killing himself. But the colonel's zest for the life he can no longer see around him—particularly the women whom he can identify by the perfume they wear—is strong, and Charlie's predicament touches him.

Pacino's vivid, enjoyable performance, helped by solid support from O'Donnell, makes this otherwise predictable movie work. He was a shoo-in for the Oscar, which often goes to actors playing at handicaps they don't possess—e.g., Dustin Hoffman as the autistic savant in *Rain Man,* Daniel Day-Lewis as a cerebral palsy victim in *My Left Foot,* Jane Wyman and Holly Hunter as the mutes in *Johnny Belinda* and *The Piano.* Like these, Pacino's performance is a tour de force, particularly the tenuous grace of the tango he dances with Gabrielle Anwar in a celebrated scene. Unfortunately the prep school plot drags the film down in its last section, winding up with a conventional scene in which a spellbinding speech from Pacino makes everything come out right. *Scent of a Woman* was a box-office hit, but the thinness of its plot and the derivativeness (from the 1975 Italian film) of its central premise make it a dubious choice as a best picture nominee; the honor should have gone to *Malcolm X, Passion Fish,* or *The Player* instead.

But only those who feel that the Oscar should have gone to Denzel Washington's performance in *Malcolm X* would deny Pacino his award after two decades as an Oscar also-ran. If Pacino had lost this one—and his simultaneous nomination for supporting actor in *Glengarry Glen Ross*—he would have broken the record for most nominations without winning now held by Peter O'Toole [164 . . .] and Richard Burton [85 . . .]. Pacino, who trained at the High School for the Performing Arts and the Actors Studio in New York, had made two forgettable films before vaulting to stardom in *The Godfather.* Through the seventies he was one of the hottest actors in Hollywood. But his career nosedived in the eighties with such artistic and commercial disasters as *Cruising* (1980) and *Revolution* (1985), and he turned his attention to stage work. He returned to films with a typically dynamic performance in *Sea of Love* (1989), and the following year demonstrated his versatility in both a hilarious turn as a mobster in *Dick Tracy* and a finely crafted portrayal of the aging Michael Corleone in *The Godfather, Part III.* And Pacino's new willingness to help publicize his film, even granting occasional uneasy interviews, didn't hurt him with Academy voters, many of whom had resented his earlier standoffishness and dismissed him as a New York snob.

Brest, who had his biggest previous hit as a director with *Beverly Hills Cop,* lost the directing Oscar to Clint Eastwood for *Unforgiven,* which also took the award for best picture. The writing Oscar went to Ruth Prawer Jhabvala for *Howards End.*

Pacino: 75, 543, 561, 775.5, 784, 785, 1780. Goldman: 1300, 1481.

1764.6 • *SCENT OF GREEN PAPAYA, THE*

LES PRODUCTIONS LAZENNEC (PARIS)/GIAI PHONG FILM STUDIO (HO CHI MINH CITY) PRODUCTION (VIETNAM). 1993.

NOMINATION *Foreign Language Film.*

In the prewar Vietnam of the fifties, a young woman comes of age as a servant in a well-to-do household. Eventually the family loses its fortune, and she is sent to work for a sophisticated young man. She falls in love with him, but at first he scarcely notices the beautiful young woman. Simple, exquisitely designed and photographed film, written and directed by Tran Anh Hung, with cinematography by Benoit Delhomme. Although the cast and director are Vietnamese, the film was produced and filmed in France. The Oscar went to *Belle Epoque.*

1764.65 • *SCHINDLER'S LIST*

UNIVERSAL PICTURES/AMBLIN ENTERTAINMENT PRODUCTION; UNIVERSAL. 1993.

AWARDS *Picture:* Steven Spielberg, Gerald R. Molen, and Branko Lustig, producers. *Director:* Steven Spielberg. *Screenplay Based on Material Previously Produced or Published:* Steven Zaillian. *Art Direction:* Allan Starski and Ewa Braun. *Cinematography:* Janusz Kaminski. *Film Editing:* Michael Kahn. *Original Score:* John Williams.

NOMINATIONS *Actor:* Liam Neeson. *Supporting Actor:* Ralph Fiennes. *Costume Design:* Anna Biedrzycka-Sheppard. *Makeup:* Christina Smith, Matthew Mungle, and Judy Alexander Cory. *Sound:* Andy Nelson, Steve Pederson, Scott Millan, and Ron Judkins.

Oskar Schindler (Neeson), a German industrialist, comes to Cracow seeking his fortune: He knows that if he can get on the right side of the Nazi occupying forces, they will supply him with cheap labor—Jews —for his factory. He succeeds, and with the aid of a Jewish accountant, Itzhak Stern, played by Ben Kingsley [308 . . .], he soon has his factory humming. But there's a spark of humanity within the money-driven, hard-drinking, womanizing Schindler, and as the brutality of the Nazis becomes more apparent, he slowly begins to use his skill at manipulating the Germans to save the lives of the Jews who work for him. He wins concessions from the psychotic Amon Goeth (Fiennes), the concentration camp commandant who thinks nothing of using the inmates who pass by his windows for target practice. Uncompromising in its presentation of the horrors of the Holocaust, *Schindler's List* avoids the melodrama that many felt cheapened earlier attempts at dealing with the twentieth century's most appalling episode, such as *Sophie's Choice* and *Judgment at Nuremberg.* Its central theme is the unknowable source of goodness: how a flawed human being like Oskar Schindler, a man who had lived for what he could get out of others, could turn into a hero, performing good deeds with no apparent hope of reward. Spielberg, Zaillian, and Thomas Keneally, the author of the book on which the film is based, are content to leave such things a mystery, inexplicable by conventional attempts at analyzing motives. The result is a film of astonishing power that despite scenes of harrowing brutality doesn't leave its audience brutalized.

That *Schindler's List* is also a work of astonishing technical skill is not surprising: No filmmaker of the latter half of the century had a surer command of the medium than Spielberg, and the movie is remarkable for the documentarylike quality of Kaminski's black-and-white cinematography, for the unobtrusive skill of Kahn's editing, particularly in its central episode, the destruction of the ghetto, and for the movingly understated score by Williams. But many critics were surprised at the maturity of Spielberg's treatment of the subject—phrases like "coming of age" were commonplace from reviewers amazed that the man who had made blockbuster entertainments like *Jaws, E.T.,* and *Jurassic Park* could also make an adult drama of tragic force. Others, however, saw that *Schindler's*

List is consistent with Spielberg's previous work, which has often dealt with the capacity for extraordinary endeavor that dwells in apparently ordinary people, such as the characters played by Roy Scheider in *Jaws,* Richard Dreyfuss in *Close Encounters of the Third Kind,* or Whoopi Goldberg in *The Color Purple.* The master of presenting childhood experience on screen in *E.T.* uses this skill with almost unbearable poignancy in depicting the plight of the children of the ghetto. And the craftsman of *Jaws,* the Indiana Jones trilogy, and *Jurassic Park* clearly knows how different make-believe terror is from the real thing.

Spielberg had been notoriously snubbed by the Academy. When *Jaws* and *The Color Purple* were nominated for best picture, Spielberg had been passed over for a directing nomination. *E.T.* was the most successful film of all time (until Spielberg's own *Jurassic Park* eclipsed it), but the best picture Oscar went to the conventional and dull *Gandhi.* (Spielberg may have privately enjoyed the irony of casting *Gandhi*'s Oscar-winning director, Richard Attenborough, in *Jurassic Park* and its Oscar-winning actor, Kingsley, in *Schindler's List.*) By the time of the Oscars there was little doubt that *Schindler's List* would take the top award. But there was a suspicion that Spielberg might lose as director to Jane Campion for *The Piano;* Campion had earlier won the directing honors from the New York and Los Angeles film critics. On Oscar night a clearly relieved Spielberg could only comment that the awards were like "a cool drink after the longest drought of my life." His work on *Schindler's List,* he said, was the most satisfying of his career, among other things because it enabled him to affirm his identity as a Jew. His coproducer Lustig was an Auschwitz survivor.

Like many films, *Schindler's List* had been through several false starts before finally reaching the screen. Keneally, an Australian writer, had stumbled on the story through an accidental encounter with one of the people who had been on Schindler's list of Jews to be spared from shipment to Auschwitz, ostensibly so they could work in Schindler's munitions factory (which never produced a usable weapon). His semifictional account won the Booker Prize in Great Britain

(under its original title, *Schindler's Ark).* Spielberg bought the rights to the book when it was published, then gave the project to Martin Scorsese [27.5 . . .] and finally got it back in a trade when Scorsese expressed interest in doing *Cape Fear,* to which Spielberg had the rights. Zaillian, who had made a name for himself with the screenplay for *Awakenings,* and would begin his directing career in 1993 with the critically well received *Searching for Bobby Fischer,* was assigned to the project after several other writers, including Keneally and Kurt Luedtke [3 . . .], had made an attempt at it. Zaillian's solution to the problem of telling the story, which in the book involves a multiplicity of characters, was to focus on Schindler's choice between good as represented by Stern and evil as embodied by Goeth.

Kaminski was born in Poland but came to America in 1980. His American career had been largely spent on second- and third-rate projects, such as the vehicle for rapper Vanilla Ice, *Cool as Ice* (1991). The choice of filming in black and white—in an era when films were routinely being colorized for TV showing—was daring, and perhaps only a filmmaker with Spielberg's clout could have prevailed over the pleas of the studio for color. Black and white, Spielberg explained, is "completely unforgiving. . . . If you wake up with a pimple in the morning, black and white will accentuate the blemish more than color will. . . . I knew the minute I read the book that I would be making this film someday in black and white." *Schindler's List* was the first film made in black and white to receive the Oscar since 1960's *The Apartment,* and the first to be nominated since *Raging Bull* and *The Elephant Man* in 1980.

Casting was also crucial to the realism of the film. Spielberg resisted pressure to place a major star in the part of Schindler, although Harrison Ford [2296], Mel Gibson, and Kevin Costner [482] were apparently seriously considered. Neeson, an Irish actor, made his first film appearance in *Excalibur* in 1981. While an accomplished and recognized actor, he had not achieved major stardom. Fiennes was considerably less well known, with most of his previous exposure to American audiences in the form of British television imports; he has, for example, a small role in the first of the *Prime Suspect* dramas that were broadcast in the PBS *Mystery!* series. He gained weight and stopped exercising to become the unpleasantly bloated Goeth. The acting Oscars went to Tom Hanks for *Philadelphia* and Tommy Lee Jones for *The Fugitive.*

The award for costume design went to Gabriella Pescucci for *The Age of Innocence.* Greg Cannom, Ve Neill, and Yolanda Tousseing won for the makeup for *Mrs. Doubtfire.* The Oscar for sound went to *Jurassic Park.*

Spielberg: 416, 423, 588, 1652. Zaillian: 113. Kahn: 416, 613, 653, 1652. Williams: 6, 260, 403, 416, 588, 613, 614, 659, 805, 933, 937, 982, 996, 997, 1041, 1047, 1596, 1652, 1679, 1684, 1701, 1916, 1977, 2107, 2126, 2194, 2293, 2322. Smith: 937. Mungle: 272.5. Nelson: 808. Judkins: 1071.5. Cory: 708.5.

1764.7 • SCHTONK

BAVARIA FILM GMBH PRODUCTION (GERMANY). 1992.

NOMINATION *Foreign Language Film.*

A satire on the vogue for Hitler memorabilia and other Nazi-era nostalgia, inspired by the notorious faked Hitler diaries. Written and directed by Helmut Dietl. Not yet widely released in the United States. The Oscar went to *Indochine.*

1765 • SCOUNDREL, THE

PARAMOUNT. 1935.

AWARD *Original Story:* Ben Hecht and Charles MacArthur.

Noël Coward [993] plays a bad-tempered, meddling, universally loathed New York publisher who dies but gets a chance at redemption if he can find someone who'll weep for him. Amusingly sophisticated fantasy-comedy-drama, directed by the authors, who also make cameo appearances in the film, as do their famous Algonquin roundtable companions, Alexander Woollcott and Edna Ferber, plus MacArthur's wife, Helen Hayes [31 . . .]. With Julie Haydon, Eduardo Ciannelli, and Lionel Stander.

Hecht and MacArthur both began their writing careers on newspapers and later transformed their experiences into their most famous play, *The Front Page.* They also collaborated on the play *Twentieth Century,* which was memorably filmed in 1934. They worked together as film directors on three movies in addition to *The Scoundrel: Crime Without Passion* (1934), *Once in a Blue Moon* (1935), and *Soak the Rich* (1936). Hecht was the first to come to Hollywood, arriving in the late twenties and receiving an Oscar for *Underworld* in the first year of the awards. One of the most prolific of all screenwriters, he received credits on some seventy films, but also worked without credit on many others, including *Gone With the Wind* and *Roman Holiday.* He died in 1964. MacArthur came to Hollywood in the thirties, but Hayes found the stage more congenial to her talents than films, so she concentrated most of her career in New York. Their son, James MacArthur, became a well-known film and TV actor. Charles MacArthur died in 1956.

Hecht: 78, 1455, 2179, 2211, 2316. MacArthur: 1664, 2316.

1766 • SCROOGE

WATERBURY FILMS LTD. PRODUCTION; CINEMA CENTER FILMS PRESENTATION; NATIONAL GENERAL PICTURES (UNITED KINGDOM). 1970.

NOMINATIONS *Art Direction–Set Decoration:* Terry Marsh and Bob Cartwright; Pamela Cornell. *Song:* "Thank You Very Much," music and lyrics by Leslie Bricusse. *Original Song Score:* Leslie Bricusse, Ian Fraser, and Herbert W. Spencer. *Costume Design:* Margaret Furse.

Musical version of Charles Dickens' tale about the miserly Scrooge, played by Albert Finney [579 . . .], who is reformed by ghostly visitors on Christmas Eve. Passable attempt to imitate the much better *Oliver!* Its chief distinction is the supporting cast: Alec Guinness [287 . . .], Edith Evans [377 . . .], Kenneth More, Lawrence Naismith, Gordon Jackson, and Roy Kinnear. Directed by Ronald Neame [289 . . .] from a screenplay by Bricusse and filmed by Oswald Morris [659 . . .]. The art direction Oscar went to *Patton.* The best song was "For All We Know," from *Lovers and Other Strangers,* by Fred Karlin, Robb Royer, and James Griffin. The Beatles won for the song score for *Let It Be.* Vittorio

Nino Novarese took the costuming award for *Crom-well.*

Marsh: 558, 1285, 1471. Cartwright: 164, 608, 1285. Bricusse: 557, 805, 933, 937, 2037, 2201, 2285. Spencer: 1044. Furse: 85, 164, 1177, 1285, 1374.

1767 • SCROOGED

ART LINSON PRODUCTION; PARAMOUNT. 1988.

NOMINATION *Makeup:* Tom Burman and Bari Dreiband-Burman.

Bill Murray is a mean TV network exec who overworks and underrewards his secretary, played by Alfre Woodard [466], but gets his comeuppance from ghosts played by David Johansen and Carol Kane [908]. Updating Dickens' "A Christmas Carol," especially with Murray as the Scrooge figure, doesn't sound like a bad idea, but the movie is leaden and overproduced. The screenplay by Mitch Glazer and Michael O'Donoghue is partly to blame, but so is director Richard Donner's pacing. The attractive but mostly wasted cast includes Karen Allen, John Forsythe, John Glover, Bobcat Goldthwait, Robert Mitchum [1935], and Michael J. Pollard [255], with cameos by people ranging from Robert Goulet to John Houseman [1069 . . .] to Mary Lou Retton. The makeup award went to Ve Neill, Steve LaPorte, and Robert Short for *Beetlejuice.*

1768 • SEA HAWK, THE

WARNER BROS. 1940.

NOMINATIONS *Black-and-White Interior Decoration:* Anton Grot. *Sound Recording:* Nathan Levinson. *Score:* Erich Wolfgang Korngold. *Special Effects:* Byron Haskin, photographic; Nathan Levinson, sound.

Errol Flynn sets out at the behest of Queen Elizabeth, played by Flora Robson [1759], to make a nuisance of himself with the Spanish; he also woos Brenda Marshall in the process. One of Flynn's most entertaining swashbucklers, with phenomenally staged action sequences given an operatic oomph by Korngold's tremendous score. Directed by Michael Curtiz [79 . . .] from a screenplay by Seton I. Miller [463 . . .] and Howard Koch [365 . . .]. The cast

has about every character player Warners could find, including Henry Daniell, Claude Rains [365 . . .], Donald Crisp [952], Alan Hale, Una O'Connor, James Stephenson [1162], and Gilbert Roland. The bit of wartime propagandizing for England, home, and duty at the end is forgivable, even stirring.

The art direction award went to Cedric Gibbons and Paul Groesse for *Pride and Prejudice.* Douglas Shearer won for the sound for *Strike Up the Band.* Alfred Newman's score for *Tin Pan Alley* was judged superior to Korngold's. *The Thief of Bagdad* took the special effects Oscar.

Grot: 90, 1169, 1621, 1981. Levinson: 16, 30, 343, 385, 531, 689, 710, 712, 790, 930, 965, 1052, 1169, 1621, 1690, 1769, 1779, 1930, 1949, 2058, 2318. Korngold: 17, 90, 1621. Haskin: 531, 1621, 1769.

1769 • SEA WOLF, THE

WARNER BROS. 1941.

NOMINATION *Special Effects:* Byron Haskin, photographic; Nathan Levinson, sound.

Edward G. Robinson is Wolf Larsen, a Nietzschean freighter captain who terrorizes his reluctant passengers, including John Garfield [251 . . .], Ida Lupino, Alexander Knox [2286], Gene Lockhart [36], and Barry Fitzgerald [787]. Handsome version of a much-filmed story by Jack London; in addition to several silent films, the tale has been told as a western called *Barricade* (1950) and under the titles *Wolf Larsen* (1958) and *Wolf of the Seven Seas* (1975). This one is probably the best, thanks to a script by Robert Rossen [53 . . .] and some top-notch Warners production personnel: director Michael Curtiz [79 . . .], cinematographer Sol Polito [353 . . .], composer Erich Wolfgang Korngold [17 . . .], and editor George Amy [30 . . .]. Some of the film's footage was reused, in a colorized version, in the 1993 made-for-cable movie starring Charles Bronson and Christopher Reeve.

Interestingly *The Sea Wolf* was not among the nominees for the special effects Oscar when they were announced on February 9, 1942. But sometime between then and February 19, the original nominee,

Dive Bomber, another Warner Bros. film also credited to Haskin and Levinson, was replaced by *The Sea Wolf.* The Academy has no record of how or why the switch took place. The special effects Oscar went to *I Wanted Wings.*

Haskin: 531, 1621, 1768. Levinson: 16, 30, 343, 385, 531, 689, 710, 712, 790, 930, 965, 1052, 1169, 1621, 1690, 1768, 1779, 1930, 1949, 2058, 2318.

1770 • *SEANCE ON A WET AFTERNOON*

RICHARD ATTENBOROUGH-BRYAN FORBES PRODUCTIONS; ARTIXO PRODUCTIONS LTD. (UNITED KINGDOM). 1964.

NOMINATION *Actress:* Kim Stanley.

Stanley plays Myra Savage, a medium who browbeats her husband, Billy, played by Richard Attenborough [745], into kidnaping a little girl as a publicity stunt. Myra will then reveal the child's whereabouts through her "supernatural" powers. But once the plot is under way, Billy realizes that the child will give away their secret and therefore must be killed. Tense, gloomy drama in which writer-director Bryan Forbes [81] tries to downplay the thriller plot and concentrate on the characters, with mixed results. The film is dominated by Stanley's florid performance, although Attenborough's more subtle and complex characterization is perhaps the better of the two. The cast includes Patrick Magee and Nanette Newman, and the score is by John Barry [259 . . .].

Stanley gained acclaim on the New York stage as one of the most impressive products of the Actors Studio and made her film debut in 1958 in *The Goddess* but otherwise has made only a few movies. She lost to Julie Andrews in *Mary Poppins.*

Stanley: 722.

1771 • *SEARCH, THE*

PRAESENS FILMS; MGM (SWITZERLAND/U.S.). 1948.

AWARDS *Motion Picture Story:* Richard Schweizer and David Wechsler. *Special Award:* Ivan Jandl, outstanding juvenile performance of 1948.

NOMINATIONS *Actor:* Montgomery Clift. *Director:* Fred Zinnemann. *Screenplay:* Richard Schweizer and David Wechsler.

In postwar Germany little Karel Malik (Jandl) runs away and hides when the group of children he is with is being loaded onto a Red Cross ambulance—he thinks the ambulance is going to carry him to the gas chambers. Meanwhile, his mother, played by Jarmila Novotna, having also survived the concentration camps, is looking for him. Karel is accidentally discovered by an American soldier (Clift), who wins his confidence and eventually reunites him with his mother. Touching drama whose impact is heightened by filming among the rubble of occupied Germany and by the impressive film debut of Clift. (He had actually made his first film, *Red River,* a year earlier, but it was released after *The Search.)* The cast includes Aline MacMahon [576] and Wendell Corey.

Although the Oscars went to the Swiss screenwriters—whose script was supplemented with "additional dialogue" by Paul Jarrico [2105]—and to the nine-year-old Jandl, who spoke only Czech and learned his English dialogue phonetically, their subsequent American film careers were nonexistent. The same can't be said for the star and his director, however. With the release of *Red River,* Clift became a star whose naturalistic, unactorish delivery—abetted by undeniable good looks—helped revolutionize screen acting. And *The Search* was the film that made Zinnemann a major director, even though he had been in Hollywood since the early thirties, had won an Oscar for his short subject, *That Mothers Might Live,* at the 1938 awards, and had been a feature director since 1942. Clift lost the Oscar to Laurence Olivier in *Hamlet.* John Huston won for both the direction and the screenplay of *The Treasure of the Sierra Madre.*

Schweizer: 1275. Clift: 732, 1065, 1579. Zinnemann: 732, 912, 1066, 1252, 1457, 1969.

1771.5 • *SEARCHING FOR BOBBY FISCHER*

SCOTT RUDIN/MIRAGE PRODUCTION; PARAMOUNT. 1993.

NOMINATION *Cinematography:* Conrad L. Hall.

Josh Waitzkin (Max Pomeranc) is a small New York boy who has learned the game of chess, first by watching players in the park and then by coming under the tutelage of Vinnie, played by Laurence

Fishburne [2250.7], who makes his living hustling chess games. When his parents, Fred (Joe Mantegna) and Bonnie (Joan Allen), realize that their son could be the next Bobby Fischer, they hire a brilliant but volatile tutor, Bruce Pandolfini, played by Ben Kingsley [308 . . .]. But the parents soon come to wonder if they should sacrifice their son's childhood for the high-powered, neurotic world of tournament chess. Intriguing, absorbing film that neatly dodges the clichés and easy emotional resolutions that most films about child prodigies readily fall into. Steven Zaillian [113 . . .] makes an impressive directing debut, working from his own screenplay based on a book by the real Fred Waitzkin. With a first-rate cast that also includes David Paymer [1368.5] and a fine score by James Horner [45 . . .], the movie was a critical favorite that never found an audience. The studio was reportedly stymied by the esoteric subject matter and considered various ways of hyping the film, including a title change. Failing that, in a year of exceptional films, *Searching for Bobby Fischer* got lost in the crowd. Hall lost to Janusz Kaminski's work on *Schindler's List*.

Hall: 317, 504, 987, 1355, 1627, 2017.

1772 • SECOND CHORUS

NATIONAL PICTURES; PARAMOUNT. 1940.
NOMINATIONS *Song:* "Love of My Life," music by Artie Shaw, lyrics by Johnny Mercer. *Score:* Artie Shaw.

Trumpeters Fred Astaire [2126] and Burgess Meredith [504 . . .] try to land jobs with Artie Shaw's orchestra and compete for the affections of Paulette Goddard [1855]. Astaire once called this "the worst film I ever made." He's probably right, but how bad can a film in which Astaire performs to music by Shaw be? The movie, directed by H. C. Potter, was really designed as a vehicle for clarinetist-bandleader Shaw, who had leaped to fame in 1938 with a recording of "Begin the Beguine" and continued to make headlines by recovering from a life-threatening illness and by a string of eight marriages. At the time of this film he was married to Lana Turner [1558], his third wife. Astaire signed on because he wanted to work with a real swing orchestra like Shaw's. *Second Chorus*

is also Astaire's first film collaboration with Mercer, with whom he had written a 1936 song hit, "I'm Building Up to an Awful Letdown." Astaire and Mercer would work on four more films together.

Shaw and Mercer's song lost to Leigh Harline and Ned Washington's "When You Wish Upon a Star," from *Pinocchio*. The Oscar for scoring went to Alfred Newman for *Tin Pan Alley*.

Mercer: 248, 278, 384, 476, 494, 508, 636, 788, 825, 877, 903, 905, 1109, 1838, 1912, 2327, 2328.

1773 • SECOND FIDDLE

20TH CENTURY-FOX. 1939.
NOMINATION *Song:* "I Poured My Heart Into a Song," music and lyrics by Irving Berlin.

Sonja Henie plays a midwestern schoolteacher whose skating talents send her to Hollywood and a romance with Tyrone Power. Fluff notable only for its Berlin song score, which isn't among his better efforts. Directed by Sidney Lanfield, with Rudy Vallee, Edna May Oliver [581], and Lyle Talbot. The Oscar went to Harold Arlen and E. Y. Harburg for "Over the Rainbow," from *The Wizard of Oz*.

Berlin: 34, 244, 358, 929, 2215, 2268.

1774 • SECONDS

THE SECONDS COMPANY; PARAMOUNT. 1966.
NOMINATION *Black-and-White Cinematography:* James Wong Howe.

Tired middle-aged businessman John Randolph discovers a secret outfit that promises rejuvenation through plastic surgery and a new identity. The operation turns him into Rock Hudson [768] on the outside, but on the inside he's still John Randolph. And not only does he not enjoy his new life any more than his old, he has a further shock coming. Dazzling but depressing thriller, directed by John Frankenheimer from a screenplay by Lewis John Carlino [970] based on a novel by David Ely. Though the movie has one of Hudson's best performances, and solid support from Salome Jens, Will Geer, Jeff Corey, and Murray Hamilton, it was a box-office flop, possibly because it's a real downer. Howe's cinematography is full of impressive technical accomplishments, though like many film experiments of the sixties, the film seems too often to be indulging in technique for technique's sake. The Oscar went to Haskell Wexler for *Who's Afraid of Virginia Woolf?*

Howe: 1, 30, 36, 738, 956, 1095, 1451, 1470, 1727.

1775 • SECRET COMMAND

COLUMBIA. 1944.

NOMINATION *Special Effects:* David Allen, Ray Cory, and Robert Wright, photographic; Russell Malmgren and Harry Kusnick, sound.

Pat O'Brien plays an FBI agent whose top-secret task involves posing as a shipyard worker to uncover a Nazi sabotage plot. Carole Landis poses as his wife— and becomes the real thing at film's end. Chester Morris [38] is O'Brien's brother, who, because he's not let in on the secret, almost gives the plot away to the bad guys. War-effort stuff, but passably entertaining anyway. Directed by Edward Sutherland, with Ruth Warrick, Barton MacLane, and Tom Tully [330]. The special effects Oscar went to *Thirty Seconds Over Tokyo.*

Allen: 2339.

1776 • SECRET OF SANTA VITTORIA, THE

STANLEY KRAMER COMPANY PRODUCTION; UNITED ARTISTS. 1969.

NOMINATIONS *Original Score—for a Motion Picture (Not a Musical):* Ernest Gold. *Film Editing:* William Lyon and Earle Herdan.

During World War II the village of Santa Vittoria devises elaborate schemes to hide its wine from the Nazi occupation. Long, loud comedy full of Italian peasant stereotypes played by Anthony Quinn [1226 . . .], Anna Magnani [1727 . . .], Virna Lisi, Sergio Franchi, Eduardo Ciannelli, Giancarlo Giannini [1781], and Valentina Cortese [501], all of whom need a director with a lighter touch than Stanley Kramer [330 . . .] possesses. The screenplay is by William Rose [758 . . .] and Ben Maddow [105], from a best-selling novel by Robert Crichton. The scoring Oscar went to Burt Bacharach for *Butch Cas-*

sidy and the Sundance Kid. Françoise Bonnot won for editing *Z.*

Gold: 630, 1032, 1474. Lyon: 330, 456, 732, 1058, 1566.

1777 • SENSATIONS OF 1945

ANDREW STONE PRODUCTIONS; UNITED ARTISTS. 1944.

NOMINATION *Scoring of a Musical Picture:* Mahlon Merrick.

Dennis O'Keefe runs a publicity agency that's in trouble until Eleanor Powell comes along to teach him a thing or two. But the plot is just an excuse for the movie to revive vaudeville and present specialty acts by Powell, W. C. Fields (in his last film), Sophie Tucker, and the Cab Calloway and Woody Herman orchestras, among others. Directed by Andrew L. Stone [1067], with Eugene Pallette, C. Aubrey Smith, and Lyle Talbot. The scoring Oscar went to Carmen Dragon and Morris Stoloff for *Cover Girl.*

1778 • SEPARATE TABLES

CLIFTON PRODUCTIONS INC.; UNITED ARTISTS. 1958.

AWARDS *Actor:* David Niven. *Supporting Actress:* Wendy Hiller.

NOMINATIONS *Picture:* Harold Hecht, producer. *Actress:* Deborah Kerr. *Screenplay—Based on Material From Another Medium:* Terence Rattigan and John Gay. *Black-and-White Cinematography:* Charles Lang, Jr. *Scoring of a Dramatic or Comedy Picture:* David Raksin.

Though they sit at separate tables at an English seaside hotel, the guests soon find their private lives growing public. Burt Lancaster [107 . . .] is thinking of ending his involvement with Hiller and returning to his ex-wife, Rita Hayworth. Kerr is a spinster under the watchful eye of her mother—Gladys Cooper [1393 . . .] repeating her *Now, Voyager* role. Niven is a courtly imposter whose guilty secret is shockingly exposed. And Cathleen Nesbitt, Felix Aylmore, Rod Taylor, and Audrey Dalton are on hand, too. Rattigan and Gay's adaptation and interweaving of Rattigan's pair of one-act plays, a substantial hit on the London stage, is somewhat too drab and stagy to make a good movie, but the performers are certainly worth watching, even the miscast Lancaster and Hayworth. Delbert Mann [1283] directed.

Niven had been a familiar, suave presence in films for more than twenty years when he received his sole Oscar nomination. Forsaking a conventional career, he set out to see the world as a young man and wound up in Hollywood, where he charmed his way into the movies. Appearance as an extra in *Mutiny on the Bounty,* combined with a letter of introduction from a mutual friend in England, won him a contract with Samuel Goldwyn [102 . . .] and a one-line bit in Goldwyn's *Barbary Coast.* Larger parts, in films such as *Dodsworth, Wuthering Heights,* and *Bachelor Mother,* were to follow, and by the start of World War II, Niven had become a reliable second-string leading man, heir to roles that Robert Montgomery [904 . . .], Ray Milland [1208], and Cary Grant [1445 . . .] either refused or were unavailable for. But the outbreak of war stirred Niven's latent patriotism—his father and grandfather had been professional soldiers, and Niven had attended Sandhurst—and he joined the British army. He resumed his career after the war in the same light comedy and costume-drama roles, most notably in *The Bishop's Wife, The Moon Is Blue,* and *Around the World in 80 Days.* As often, the performance in a heavyweight role of an actor thought to be a lightweight drew the Academy's attention, and Niven triumphed over strong competitors: Tony Curtis and Sidney Poitier in *The Defiant Ones,* Paul Newman in *Cat on a Hot Tin Roof,* and Spencer Tracy in *The Old Man and the Sea.* Niven was wise enough not to test his limits as an actor further, and he returned for the most part to roles that exploited his considerable charm and gift for comedy. He died in 1983.

Hiller scored a triumph in only her second film, as Eliza Doolittle in *Pygmalion,* and followed with another Shaw heroine, the title character of *Major Barbara* (1941). But the major part of her early career was spent on the stage in England. After her Oscar, she began to appear more frequently, performing with distinction in such films as *Sons and Lovers, A Man for All Seasons,* and *Murder on the Orient Express.* She became Dame Wendy Hiller in 1975.

The best picture Oscar went to *Gigi,* which also won for Alan Jay Lerner's screenplay. Kerr lost the fifth of her six unsuccessful tries for an Oscar to Susan Hayward in *I Want to Live!* The cinematography award went to Sam Leavitt for *The Defiant Ones,* and Dimitri Tiomkin won for the score of *The Old Man and the Sea.*

Hiller: 1252, 1637. Hecht: 1283. Kerr: 599, 732, 891, 1088, 1969. Rattigan: 281. Lang: 97, 250, 319, 636, 649, 705, 765, 953, 1480, 1640, 1699, 1738, 1855, 1860, 1955, 1968, 2180. Raksin: 707.

1779 • SERGEANT YORK

WARNER BROS. 1941.

AWARDS *Actor:* Gary Cooper. *Film Editing:* William Holmes.

NOMINATIONS *Picture:* Jesse L. Lasky and Hal B. Wallis, producers. *Supporting Actor:* Walter Brennan. *Supporting Actress:* Margaret Wycherly. *Director:* Howard Hawks. *Original Screenplay:* Harry Chandlee, Abem Finkel, John Huston, and Howard Koch. *Black-and-White Cinematography:* Sol Polito. *Black-and-White Interior Decoration:* John Hughes, art direction; Fred MacLean, set decoration. *Sound Recording:* Nathan Levinson. *Scoring of a Dramatic Picture:* Max Steiner.

Cooper plays Alvin York, a Tennessee mountaineer who gives up his hell-raising ways when he falls in love with Gracie Williams (Joan Leslie) and finds religion when a bolt of lightning disrupts his plans to take revenge on a man he believes cheated him in a business deal. But his newfound belief in the biblical precepts against killing is tested when he is drafted in World War I. Overcoming his pacifism, he uses the marksmanship skills he learned back home to kill Germans instead, single-handedly capturing an enemy regiment and becoming a national hero. For all the wartime propagandizing, the sentimentalizing of "simple folk," and the big-picture packaging, this tale of a real-life American hero is still quite affecting, thanks to the hugely likable performance of Cooper and fine support from Brennan as Pastor Pile, Wycherly as York's mother, plus George Tobias, Ward Bond, Noah Beery, Jr., Howard Da Silva, and June Lockhart, among others. Hawks' cunning and energetic direction helps, too, though many find it ironic that he earned his sole nomination for this film, whose moments of Hollywood-style piety and patriotism make it one of his least characteristic works.

Of all the major Hollywood filmmakers, Hawks received the most cavalier treatment from the Academy, possibly because he freelanced his way around the system instead of being tied down to one of the big studios which might have given his films more promotion at Oscar time. He began his film career after World War I as a screenwriter and moved into directing in the mid-twenties. In his later career, he continued to work as a writer—usually uncredited—on his own films and gradually became his own producer as well. When he was subjected to other equally strong-willed producers, like *Sergeant York*'s Wallis or *Ball of Fire*'s Samuel Goldwyn, Hawks' work lost some of its edge and energy. Perhaps no director made so many sheerly enjoyable films, but many of Hawks' finest movies were completely ignored by the Academy, including the best of all the thirties gangster films, *Scarface* (1932); the dizziest of the screwball comedies, *Twentieth Century* (1934), *Bringing Up Baby* (1938), and *His Girl Friday* (1938); the quintessential Bogart and Bacall movies, *To Have and Have Not* (1944) and *The Big Sleep* (1946); and the star-making Marilyn Monroe musical *Gentlemen Prefer Blondes* (1953). But Hawks was also mostly ignored by American film scholars and historians until the sixties, when the French auteur theory took hold on this side of the Atlantic, and critics such as Andrew Sarris and young filmmakers such as Peter Bogdanovich [1139] began championing him. At the urging of the younger generation, the Academy finally voted Hawks an honorary Oscar at the 1974 ceremony, recognizing him as "a master American filmmaker whose creative efforts hold a distinguished place in world cinema."

Cooper was the real Sergeant York's choice for the role. For more than a decade, the Montana-born actor had been the symbol of American integrity, the quintessential strong silent type. His break as a feature player had come in 1926, when he was cast at the last minute in *The Winning of Barbara Worth*, replacing an actor who failed to show up for a location shoot. The following year he appeared in a supporting role in the first best picture winner, *Wings*. Surviving the transition to sound, he soon became a major leading man in such films as *Morocco, A Farewell to Arms,* and *Lives of a Bengal Lancer*. It was Frank Capra's *Mr. Deeds Goes to Town* that, more than any other film, established the Cooper persona: shy but two-fisted.

The best picture Oscar went to *How Green Was My Valley,* which also won for supporting actor Donald Crisp, director John Ford, cinematographer Arthur Miller, and for the art direction of Richard Day, Nathan Juran, and Thomas Little. Wycherly lost to Mary Astor in *The Great Lie*. The screenplay award went to Orson Welles and Herman J. Mankiewicz for *Citizen Kane*. The award for sound was won by Jack Whitney for *That Hamilton Woman,* and Bernard Herrmann took the Oscar for scoring for *All That Money Can Buy*.

Cooper: 701, 912, 1366, 1607. Lasky: 2272. Wallis: 17, 55, 85, 164, 343, 365, 676, 689, 712, 965, 1046, 1095, 1162, 1248, 1482, 1727, 2233, 2318. Brennan: 424, 1080, 2245. Huston: 24, 105, 356, 571, 891, 1248, 1263, 1363, 1625, 2136. Koch: 365. Polito: 353, 1621. Hughes: 16, 2058. MacLean: 16, 833. Levinson: 16, 30, 343, 385, 531, 689, 710, 712, 790, 930, 965, 1052, 1169, 1621, 1690, 1768, 1769, 1930, 1949, 2058, 2318. Steiner: 16, 154, 190, 330, 365, 385, 492, 679, 747, 754, 798, 999, 1043, 1046, 1052, 1162, 1169, 1170, 1207, 1324, 1408, 1430, 1456, 1690, 1828.

1780 • SERPICO

Produzioni de Laurentiis International Manufacturing Company S.p.A. Production; Paramount. 1973.
Nominations *Actor:* Al Pacino. *Screenplay—Based on Material From Another Medium:* Waldo Salt and Norman Wexler.

Pacino plays Frank Serpico, a New York cop who grows disillusioned with the corruption within the force but is unable to find anyone who'll listen to his tales about the crookedness of his fellow cops, who shun him as a snitch. Gradually he turns into a hippie dropout and finally exiles himself from this country. Pacino's lively, intense performance drives this solid adaptation of the Peter Maas book. The real Serpico, who had supporters among younger cops, was less isolated than the one depicted in the film. Sidney Lumet [561 . . .] directs a cast that includes John Randolph, Tony Roberts, James Tolkan, Lewis J. Stadlen, M. Emmet Walsh, F. Murray Abraham [60], and Kenneth McMillan. Pacino lost to Jack Lemmon in *Save the Tiger.* The screenplay Oscar went to William Peter Blatty for *The Exorcist.*

Pacino: 75, 543, 561, 775.5, 784, 785, 1764.5. Salt: 430, 1312. Wexler: 1051.

1781 • *SEVEN BEAUTIES*

Medusa Distribuzione Production; Cinema 5 Ltd. (Italy). 1976.

NOMINATIONS *Actor:* Giancarlo Giannini. *Director:* Lina Wertmüller. *Screenplay—Written Directly for the Screen:* Lina Wertmüller. *Foreign Language Film.*

In fascist Italy, Pasqualino (Giannini) is a Neapolitan layabout who has seven sisters—the "beauties" of the title, though in fact they're all overweight and unattractive. After he kills the pimp for one of the sisters, Pasqualino joins the army to avoid prosecution, but deserts and is sent to a Nazi concentration camp run by a monstrous woman (Shirley Stoler), whom he services sexually in order to survive. Grotesque satiric drama that was critically praised at the time. It makes a show of playing with ideas, largely in the persona of the anarchist played by Fernando Rey, who drowns himself in a vat of excrement, but whatever it offers in the way of intellectual stimulation is small compensation for the film's unpleasantness. Wertmüller's apparent misogyny—the film's women are grotesque—is truly ironic, considering that she was the first woman ever nominated for a directing Oscar. Born in Rome to an aristocratic Swiss family, Wertmüller worked in theater and TV, served as a production assistant on Fellini's *8½,* and began her collaboration with Giannini when she directed him on TV in 1966. A succession of films—*The Seduction of Mimi* (1972), *Love and Anarchy* (1973), *All Screwed Up* (1974), and *Swept Away* . . . (1974)—made Wertmüller an art-house favorite, and *Seven Beauties,* the most ambitious collaboration of the director and the star, earned her a contract with Warner Bros. But at the peak of her success, the Wertmüller phenome-

non suddenly evaporated. Her next film, *The End of the World in Our Usual Bed in a Night Full of Rain* (1978), was a critical and commercial bomb, and the Warners deal was terminated. Wertmüller has continued to make films in Italy, but they have received little attention on this side of the Atlantic.

The best actor Oscar went to Peter Finch for *Network,* which also won for Paddy Chayefsky's screenplay. John G. Avildsen won for directing a film that, in its enthusiastically upbeat nature, may be the very antithesis of *Seven Beauties: Rocky.* The foreign film award went to *Black and White in Color.*

1782 • *SEVEN BRIDES FOR SEVEN BROTHERS*

MGM. 1954.

AWARD *Scoring of a Musical Picture:* Adolph Deutsch and Saul Chaplin.

NOMINATIONS *Picture:* Jack Cummings, producer. *Screenplay:* Albert Hackett, Frances Goodrich, and Dorothy Kingsley. *Color Cinematography:* George Folsey. *Film Editing:* Ralph E. Winters.

Howard Keel and his six younger brothers are mountain men in nineteenth-century Oregon. When Keel comes home with a wife, Jane Powell, the brothers decide to follow suit and carry off young women from the nearby villages. A rescue party sets out to retrieve the unwilling brides, but an avalanche closes the road between the villages and the brothers' mountain cabin. Powell and Keel are there to chaperon and make sure that nothing happens that shouldn't between the brothers and the young women until the spring thaw. Naturally love blossoms. Much-praised musical that has dated somewhat, especially the sexual politics of the situation—derived from Stephen Vincent Benét's version of the rape of the Sabine women, a story he called "The Sobbin' Women." The film is seldom seen to its best advantage today; it was one of the first movies made in CinemaScope and uses the full width of the screen in its big dance numbers. And it *is* one of the great dance musicals. Though the songs by Johnny Mercer [248 . . .] and Gene de Paul [899] are pleasant but unmemorable, the dancing, choreographed by Michael Kidd and directed by Stanley Donen, is terrific. The brothers are played by Jeff Richards, Russ Tamblyn [1558], Tommy Rall, Marc Platt, Matt Mattox, and Jacques d'Amboise, and each dancer seems determined to outdo the other.

The best picture Oscar went to *On the Waterfront,* which also won for Gene Milford's editing. The screenplay award went to George Seaton for *The Country Girl.* Milton Krasner won for the cinematography for *Three Coins in the Fountain.*

Deutsch: 87, 141, 1469, 1818. Chaplin: 66, 914, 1097, 2244. Hackett: 25, 656, 2052. Goodrich: 25, 656, 2052. Folsey: 51, 137, 629, 807, 835, 838, 1124, 1299, 1320, 1500, 1688, 2068, 2269. Winters: 175, 825, 1094, 1109, 1644.

1783 • SEVEN DAYS IN MAY

JOEL PRODUCTIONS; PARAMOUNT. 1964.
NOMINATIONS *Supporting Actor:* Edmond O'Brien. *Black-and-White Art Direction—Set Decoration:* Cary Odell; Edward G. Boyle.

An army colonel, played by Kirk Douglas [130 . . .], discovers that his general, played by Burt Lancaster [107 . . .], is the mastermind of a plot to overthrow pacifist President Jordan Lyman, played by Fredric March [184 . . .]. Good political paranoia thriller, somewhat overshadowed by the more inventive *Dr. Strangelove,* released the same year, but full of enjoyable performances. O'Brien plays a senator, and the cast includes Ava Gardner [1339], Martin Balsam [2067], Hugh Marlowe, and, in a small role, John Houseman [1069 . . .]. Directed by John Frankenheimer, though it's not as juicy as his earlier *The Manchurian Candidate.* The screenplay is by Rod Serling from a novel by Fletcher Knebel and Charles W. Bailey II. O'Brien lost to Peter Ustinov in *Topkapi.* The art direction Oscar went to Vassilis Fotopoulos for *Zorba the Greek.*

O'Brien: 146. Odell: 170, 455. Boyle: 91, 393, 709, 743, 1860, 1866.

1784 • SEVEN DAYS TO NOON

BOULTING BROTHERS; MAYER-KINGSLEY-DISTINGUISHED FILMS (UNITED KINGDOM). 1951.
AWARD *Motion Picture Story:* Paul Dehn and James Bernard.

An atomic scientist played by Barry Jones threatens to destroy London with a hidden A-bomb unless the government agrees to stop producing the weapons. Fine suspense thriller that manages not to let the message overwhelm the story. Directed by John Boulting. The screenplay from Dehn and Bernard's story is by Roy Boulting and Frank Harvey. The cast, largely made up of unknowns, includes Joan Hickson, who is best known for her portrayal, many years later, of Agatha Christie's Miss Marple on British television.

Both Dehn and Bernard were newcomers to screenwriting but continued to have substantial careers in film. Dehn was a poet, opera librettist, playwright, and song lyricist as well as a screenwriter. His film credits include *Goldfinger, The Spy Who Came in From the Cold,* several of the *Planet of the Apes* sequels, and *Murder on the Orient Express.* Bernard was more famous as a composer, specializing in scores for horror films, particularly those turned out by Britain's Hammer Films, such as *The Curse of Frankenstein* (1957).

Dehn: 1378.

1785 • 7 FACES OF DR. LAO

GALAXY-SCARUS PRODUCTION; MGM. 1964.
AWARD *Honorary Award:* William Tuttle, for his outstanding makeup achievement.
NOMINATION *Special Visual Effects:* Jim Danforth.

A traveling circus, run by an elderly Chinese man, comes to a small western town and changes the lives of the citizens. Tony Randall plays the title role—or rather roles, thanks to Tuttle's makeup. Randall's performance is the highlight of this interesting but somewhat sticky fantasy, adapted by Charles G. Finney from his own novel and directed by George Pal. The cast includes Barbara Eden, Arthur O'Connell [73 . . .], John Ericson, Noah Beery, Jr., Minerva Urecal, John Qualen, and Lee Patrick. The special effects Oscar went to Peter Ellenshaw, Hamilton Luske, and Eustace Lycett for *Mary Poppins*.

Danforth: 2253.

1786 • SEVEN LITTLE FOYS, THE

HOPE ENTERPRISES INC. AND SCRIBE PRODUCTIONS; PARAMOUNT. 1955.

NOMINATION *Story and Screenplay:* Melville Shavelson and Jack Rose.

Bob Hope plays entertainer Eddie Foy, who enlisted his seven children in his vaudeville act. A moderately entertaining if oversentimental biopic, greatly enlivened by the cameo appearance of James Cagney [79 . . .] as George M. Cohan. TV trivia collectors will note the appearance of Jerry Mathers, from *Leave It to Beaver,* as the five-year-old version of Foy's oldest son, who is played later in the film by Billy Gray, of *Father Knows Best.* Shavelson also directed and, with Rose, coproduced the movie; the two were frequent writers for Hope. They lost the Oscar to William Ludwig and Sonya Levien for *Interrupted Melody.*

Shavelson: 951. Rose: 951, 2125.

1787 • SEVEN-PER-CENT SOLUTION, THE

HERBERT ROSS FILM/WINITSKY-SELLERS PRODUCTION; UNIVERSAL (UNITED KINGDOM). 1976.

NOMINATIONS *Screenplay—Based on Material From Another Medium:* Nicholas Meyer. *Costume Design:* Alan Barrett.

Disturbed by his friend's addiction to cocaine (the title refers, as Holmesians know, to the amount of the drug used in an injection), Dr. Watson, played by Robert Duvall [92 . . .], brings his friend Sherlock Holmes (Nicol Williamson) to Vienna for treatment by a young physician just beginning to make a name for himself—Sigmund Freud, played by Alan Arkin [884 . . .]. Once Holmes is on the road to recovery, the detective and the doctor team up to solve a mystery: the disappearance of one of Freud's patients, played by Vanessa Redgrave [263 . . .]. Holmes is still obsessed by the fiendish Dr. Moriarty, but when we meet the archvillain, he turns out to be apparently a meek old man, played by Laurence Olivier [268 . . .]. Generosity of casting is the chief of this

amusing film's virtues, which also has handsome production design by Ken Adam [12.5 . . .] and cinematography by Oswald Morris [659 . . .]. In the hands of a more clever director than Herbert Ross [2152], it might have been a top-notch entertainment. It just misses, but it's still one of the best of the Holmesian pastiches. Also in the cast are Joel Grey [321], Samantha Eggar [420], and Jeremy Kemp. Meyer's screenplay is based on his own novel—with a twist at the end of the film that's not found in the first editions of the book. A clever writer, Meyer turned to directing and is responsible for the best of the *Star Trek* films, the even-numbered ones: He directed *II* and *VI* and wrote the screenplay for *IV.* The writing Oscar went to William Goldman for *All the President's Men,* the costume award to Danilo Donati for *Fellini's Casanova.*

1788 • SEVEN SAMURAI, THE

TOHO PRODUCTION; KINGSLEY INTERNATIONAL PICTURES (JAPAN). 1956.

NOMINATIONS *Black-and-White Art Direction—Set Decoration:* Takashi Matsuyama. *Black-and-White Costume Design:* Kohei Ezaki.

A farming village, plagued by marauding bandits who annually carry off much of their harvest, decides to hire some masterless samurai to defend them. Samurai are as scornful of peasants as the farmers are mistrustful of warriors, but necessity makes strange bedfellows, and finally an elderly samurai (Takashi Shimura) gathers a band of seven, including a brash youngster (Toshiro Mifune) who wants to be a samurai. The group, outnumbered more than five to one, manages to emerge victorious—but at what cost? One of the most satisfying movies ever made, outstanding not only as an action film but also as a study of human values. Directed by Akira Kurosawa [1661], who also cowrote the screenplay. It has been endlessly imitated, including the American western version, *The Magnificent Seven,* and Roger Corman's sci-fi version, *Battle Beyond the Stars* (1980), but this is the real thing. The original American-release version was titled *The Magnificent Seven,* but it was subsequently released under the title given here. Although the

Academy records cite it as *The Magnificent Seven,* to avoid confusion we've adopted the alternate title. The film's three-and-a-half-hour length intimidated American exhibitors, so it was shown in a chopped-up version for many years. The art direction Oscar went to *Somebody There Likes Me.* Jean Louis won the costuming award for *The Solid Gold Cadillac.*

Matsuyama: 1663.

1789 • *SEVEN THIEVES*

20TH CENTURY-FOX. 1960.

NOMINATION *Black-and-White Costume Design:* Bill Thomas.

Edward G. Robinson plays an aging thief who wants one last stab at glory, so he plots to knock over the casino at Monte Carlo. Amusing caper, directed by Henry Hathaway [1194], with Rod Steiger [992 . . .], Joan Collins, Eli Wallach, and Sebastian Cabot. The costuming Oscar went to Edith Head and Edward Stevenson for *The Facts of Life.*

Thomas: 116, 166, 254, 866, 883, 1003, 1812, 1886, 2128.

1790 • *"1776"*

JACK L. WARNER PRODUCTION; COLUMBIA. 1972.

NOMINATION *Cinematography:* Harry Stradling, Jr.

The events leading up to the Declaration of Independence are turned into a musical comedy. It worked on Broadway, where the show ran more than twelve hundred performances, but the film version went the way of almost all of Hollywood's attempts to dramatize the American Revolution. It also suffered the fate of most of the musicals Hollywood has attempted in the past twenty-five years: agonizing death at the box office. Most of the actors, including William Daniels as John Adams, Howard da Silva as Benjamin Franklin, and Ken Howard as Thomas Jefferson, were in the original Broadway cast. Blythe Danner, who wasn't, plays Martha Jefferson. Director Peter H. Hunt hasn't taught them how to scale down their performances for the screen, and the whole thing comes off as very silly. The screenplay is by Peter Stone [655], who also did the book for the Broadway version. The songs—none of which has

survived the show—are by Sherman Edwards. Stradling lost to Geoffrey Unsworth's work on a successful translation of a Broadway musical, *Cabaret.*

Stradling: 2238.

1791 • *SEVENTH CROSS, THE*

MGM. 1944.

NOMINATION *Supporting Actor:* Hume Cronyn.

Seven men escape from a concentration camp in Nazi Germany and are pursued by the Gestapo. Good wartime melodrama, not too heavily overlaid with propaganda. The director, in one of his first important feature assignments, is Fred Zinnemann [732 . . .]. The cast includes Spencer Tracy [131 . . .], Signe Hasso, Felix Bressart, Ray Collins, and Agnes Moorehead [963 . . .]. Jessica Tandy [580 . . .] makes her American film debut playing Cronyn's wife—the first performance together of this famous husband-and-wife acting team. In his memoir, *A Terrible Liar,* Cronyn also notes the presence in the cast of the great German actresses Helene Thimig and Helene Weigel, both exiles reduced to playing bit parts. The cinematography is by Karl Freund [239 . . .].

Cronyn, a Canadian-born actor better known for his stage work than his movies, made his film debut in Hitchcock's *Shadow of a Doubt* and has been seen over the years in a variety of character roles. He was often teamed with Tandy on stage, though less frequently on screen. His most memorable screen performances have been in *Lifeboat,* the original 1946 version of *The Postman Always Rings Twice, Sunrise at Campobello, Cleopatra,* and *Cocoon.* The Oscar went to Barry Fitzgerald for *Going My Way.*

1792 • *SEVENTH HEAVEN*

Fox. 1927–28.

AWARDS *Actress:* Janet Gaynor. *Director:* Frank Borzage. *Adaptation:* Benjamin Glazer.

NOMINATIONS *Production:* William Fox, producer. *Interior Decoration:* Harry Oliver.

Parisian sewer worker Charles Farrell rescues waif Gaynor, they get married, he goes to war and comes back blind. Lachrymose and very popular silent film that made Farrell and Gaynor a star team in the early thirties. Tastes change, and this sugary romance gets snickers today. Glazer's scenario is based on a play by Austin Strong.

Gaynor, who was twenty-two when she received the Oscar—which also cited her performances in *Street Angel* and *Sunrise*—held the record as the youngest recipient of the best actress award until 1987, when twenty-one-year-old Marlee Matlin took the honor for *Children of a Lesser God.* After appearing in comedy shorts, she made her first features in 1926. She retired from films in 1938 and made only one return to the screen, in *Bernadine* (1957), although she did occasional radio and television work. She died in 1984.

This was the first of two Oscars for Borzage, a director mostly forgotten today because his work tends to a sentimentality now passé. He began his film career as an actor in 1912 and became a director in 1916. He also directed *Street Angel,* one of the three films that won Gaynor her Oscar. He died in 1962.

Glazer, a former attorney and journalist, became a playwright and turned to screenwriting in the early twenties. In the thirties he became a producer, working mostly at Paramount. He received a second Oscar for *Arise My Love.* He died in 1958.

Wings won the Oscar as best production. The art direction award went to William Cameron Menzies for *The Dove* and *The Tempest.*

Gaynor: 1909, 1946, 1972. Borzage: 132. Glazer: 97. Oliver: 1946.

1793 • SEVENTH VEIL, THE

J. Arthur Rank-Sydney Box-Ortus; Universal (United Kingdom). 1946.
Award *Original Screenplay:* Muriel Box and Sydney Box.

Concert pianist Ann Todd has a breakdown, and psychiatrist Herbert Lom is called in for the cure. Evidence points to the Svengali-like influence of James Mason [761 . . .], her cousin and guardian. Enjoyable melodrama that critics and audiences of the day took a good deal more seriously when dramas based on psychiatry, such as the previous year's *Spell-*

bound, were in vogue. Directed by Compton Bennett, the movie was one of the signs of revival in the post-war British film industry, though it's now overshadowed by other British films of the year, such as *Henry V* and *Brief Encounter.*

The Boxes were important figures in the renaissance of British film. She began her work in the industry in 1927 as an assistant to director Anthony Asquith and began writing for the screen in 1935, the year she married Sydney. He was a producer of training and propaganda films during the war, after which husband and wife teamed to write, produce, and direct numerous films. In 1958 Sydney became a British television executive, but Muriel continued her career as a director. They divorced in 1969 and Sydney died in 1983.

1794 • SEX, LIES, AND VIDEOTAPE

Outlaw Production; Miramax Films. 1989.
Nomination *Screenplay Written Directly for the Screen:* Steven Soderbergh.

Graham (James Spader) comes to Baton Rouge, Louisiana, to visit an old college buddy, John (Peter Gallagher), who is married to Ann (Andie MacDowell) but having an affair with her sister, Cynthia (Laura San Giacomo). Over the next few days, the four will explore sex (Graham's impotence, Ann's frigidity) and lies (John's infidelity, Cynthia's betrayal of her sister) through videotape—Graham has a collection of interviews he has done with women about their sex lives. Witty, absorbing film that was a career-maker not only for its four actors but also for writer-director Soderbergh, who was twenty-six when his film won the top award at the Cannes Festival. The Academy, less receptive to low-budget independent filmmaking, overlooked the movie in favor of more mainstream product and gave the Oscar to the decidedly less original screenplay by Tom Schulman for *Dead Poets Society.*

Soderbergh was singled out as a hot property, but he has dodged the chance to become a major mainstream director, choosing instead projects that intrigue him. His next movie, *Kafka* (1991), based on a screenplay by Lem Dobbs, received mixed reviews and sparse distribution. *King of the Hill* (1993), which he both wrote and directed, was much better received by the critics but failed to find an audience. It is, however, one of the better films of a year that saw an exceptional number of good movies in release.

1795 • *SHADOW OF A DOUBT*

UNIVERSAL. 1943.

NOMINATION *Original Story:* Gordon McDonell.

Uncle Charley (Joseph Cotten) returns to his hometown, Santa Rosa, California, where his namesake niece, played by Teresa Wright [1182 . . .], gradually discovers that he is a serial killer. Alfred Hitchcock [1171 . . .] claimed that this was his favorite among the films he directed in America, and while it's risky to take anything Hitchcock said at face value, it's possible to see why he liked it so much: It's one of the few unsentimental portraits of small-town America made during the war, when American values were more sacred than ever. Perhaps Hitchcock's acerbic treatment of this American scene spooked the Academy, for the film deserved more recognition than it received. The fine cast includes Henry Travers [1372], Patricia Collinge [1182], and, making his screen debut, Hume Cronyn [1791]. In particular, Cotten's chilling performance seems far more deserving of a nomination than Walter Pidgeon's warm and fuzzy support of Greer Garson in *Madame Curie,* yet Cotten never received an Oscar nomination—or even one of the Academy's honorary consolation prizes. The location photography (the real Santa Rosa puts Hollywood's back-lot re-creations of small-town America to shame) by Joseph Valentine [668 . . .] is superb, and the score by Dimitri Tiomkin [33 . . .] is effective in its spooky manipulation of the "Merry Widow" motif. The screenplay was written by Hitchcock's wife, Alma Reville, and two famous chroniclers of American family life: Sally Benson [83], whose *New Yorker* stories became *Meet Me in St. Louis,* and Thornton Wilder, the author of *Our Town.* Reville, Benson, and Wilder deserved as much credit as McDonell, who lost the Oscar to William Saroyan for a more sentimental portrait of small-town America, *The Human Comedy.*

1795.5 • *SHADOWLANDS*

SHADOWLANDS PRODUCTION; SAVOY PICTURES (UNITED KINGDOM). 1993.

NOMINATIONS *Actress:* Debra Winger. *Screenplay Based on Material Previously Produced or Published:* William Nicholson.

Anthony Hopkins [1679.5 . . .] plays C. S. Lewis, the Oxford don and writer of literary history and criticism, science fiction, children's books, and theological essays. A lifelong bachelor, set in his ways and sharing quarters with his brother, Warnie (Edward Hardwicke), he finds his life transformed when he falls in love with Joy Gresham (Winger), an American divorcée who has a bracing openness to experience that's quite different from Lewis' complacent academic existence. His fondness for Gresham leads him to make an in-name-only marriage that will enable her to stay in England with her young son, Douglas. But when she becomes ill with cancer, he realizes he truly loves her, and his well-reasoned belief in God is sorely tested by her death. Low-key but moving drama, with luminous performances. Directed by Richard Attenborough [745]; it's probably his finest work as a director, playing to his strengths—an attention to character and an awareness of detail—that were sacrificed to the epic ambitions of *Gandhi.*

After her nomination for *Terms of Endearment,* Winger was absent from the screen for several years. A tough-minded perfectionist, she earned a reputation for being "difficult," and her subsequent career has been marked by poor choices of material—the lame comedy *Legal Eagles* (1986), the ill-conceived thriller *Betrayed* (1988)—and overpublicized squabbles with directors, such as the one with Penny Marshall that led to her departure from the cast of *A League of Their Own* (1992). After the critical and commercial failure of *The Sheltering Sky* (1990), Winger was again absent from the screen, but she received excellent notices for two late-1993 films, *Shadowlands* and *A Dangerous Woman.* The Oscar went to Holly Hunter for *The Piano.*

Nicholson had adapted his stage play for the screen once before, with Joss Ackland and Claire Bloom in the leads, in 1985. Both actors are quite good, but

Hopkins and Winger are exceptional—Bloom, for example, brings a quietly appealing intelligence to the role, but Winger adds an energy and abrasiveness that don't seem to be in Bloom's range. The writing award went to Steven Zaillian for *Schindler's List*.

Winger: 1465, 2020.

1796 • SHAFT

SHAFT PRODUCTIONS LTD.; MGM. 1971.

AWARD *Song:* "Theme from *Shaft*," music and lyrics by Isaac Hayes.

NOMINATION *Original Dramatic Score:* Isaac Hayes.

Private eye John Shaft (Richard Roundtree) is hired to locate the daughter of a Harlem gang lord played by Moses Gunn. The charismatic black action hero was something new to Hollywood filmmaking, and films such as *Shaft* and *Superfly* (1972) quickly got a label: "blaxploitation." At the time, the sex and violence of these movies provided a visceral shock, heightened by the racial politics of the era. But now that black action heroes such as Eddie Murphy, Danny Glover, and Wesley Snipes have been mainstreamed by Hollywood, *Shaft* can be seen for what it is, a fairly effective contribution to the traditional private-eye genre. Gordon Parks directs, from a screenplay by Ernest Tidyman [724] and John D. F. Black.

Hayes' Oscar was a sign of change in one of the awards' most controversial categories and one of the Academy's most conservative and politicized divisions, the music branch. The other nominees were the Sherman brothers' "The Age of Not Believing," from *Bedknobs and Broomsticks,* Henry Mancini and Alan and Marilyn Bergman's "All His Children," from *Sometimes a Great Notion,* the title tune by Barry DeVorzon and Perry Botkin, Jr., from *Bless the Beasts and Children,* and Marvin Hamlisch and Johnny Mercer's "Life Is What You Make It," from *Kotch*—all tunes of sentimental uplift, most of them by some of the Academy's most honored traditional songwriters. But the award went to one of the kings of soul, the child of sharecroppers, whose funky "Memphis Sound" was a long way from the Tin Pan Alley- and Broadway-influenced tunes that had always dominated the awards. It's possible that the Academy was react-ing to the perennial criticism that it had been deaf to the changes that rock had brought to popular music—most notoriously in its failure to recognize the contribution of the Beatles in their movies *A Hard Day's Night* and *Help!* (1965). But the award to Hayes proved only a temporary turn away from tradition: Six years later, the Academy would be zinged again for failing to nominate the music of the Bee Gees for *Saturday Night Fever.* Hayes has gone on to play occasional character roles in such films as *It Could Happen to You* (1994).

The scoring Oscar went to Michel Legrand for *Summer of '42.*

1797 • SHALL WE DANCE

RKO RADIO. 1937.

NOMINATION *Song:* "They Can't Take That Away From Me," music by George Gershwin, lyrics by Ira Gershwin.

Fred Astaire [2126] plays a supposedly Russian ballet dancer named Petrov who is actually an American, Pete Peters. On board a ship to America, he gets involved with nightclub dancer Linda Keene, played by Ginger Rogers [1102]. The plot eventually obliges them to pose as husband and wife and to suffer the consequences. As usual, the plot's not the thing in an Astaire-Rogers musical, especially when the score is by the Gershwins and includes, in addition to the title song and the Oscar nominee, "Let's Call the Whole Thing Off," "I've Got Beginner's Luck," "Slap That Bass," and "They All Laughed." The plot's ballet setting has its origins in the 1936 Broadway musical *On Your Toes,* whose songwriters, Richard Rodgers [1921] and Lorenz Hart, wanted Astaire as the star. Astaire declined, fearful that he wouldn't fit into a show that was being choreographed by George Balanchine. When *On Your Toes* became a big hit, however, that reinforced an idea that had been kicked around at RKO of giving one of the Astaire-Rogers musicals a ballet setting. Mark Sandrich directs, and the cast includes Edward Everett Horton, Eric Blore, Jerome Cowan, and the exceedingly odd specialty dancer Harriet Hoctor, whose specialty has to be seen to be believed.

The Gershwins composed song scores for three Hollywood films; *A Damsel in Distress* and *The Goldwyn Follies* are the other two, and the songs in them include "A Foggy Day," "Nice Work If You Can Get It," "Love Walked In," and "Our Love Is Here to Stay," among many others. Incredibly this was the only nomination for George Gershwin, who died of a brain tumor in 1937; Ira was nominated for his work with other composers. The loss by "They Can't Take That Away From Me" to "Sweet Leilani," from *Waikiki Wedding*, was blamed by some on an Academy rules change that had recently allowed members of the Screen Extras Guild to vote in the Oscar balloting —an attempt to overcome resentment for the Academy's perceived antiunion stance. That had meant an increase in the number of voters from eight hundred the previous year to fifteen thousand. Admirers of the Gershwins' music claimed that it was too sophisticated for the extras and argued that they should be disqualified from future voting. The following year the extras were not allowed to vote in the song category, but they were not excluded from participation in the awards until 1944.

I. Gershwin: 455, 1910.

1798 • SHAMPOO

RUBEEKER PRODUCTIONS; COLUMBIA. 1975.
AWARD *Supporting Actress:* Lee Grant.
NOMINATIONS *Supporting Actor:* Jack Warden. *Original Screenplay:* Robert Towne and Warren Beatty. *Art Direction—Set Decoration:* Richard Sylbert and W. Stewart Campbell; George Gaines.

On the eve of Nixon's election to the presidency in 1968, a Beverly Hills hairdresser named George (Beatty) finds himself in a complicated situation: He has promised his current girlfriend, Jill, played by Goldie Hawn [323 . . .], that they'll make their relationship permanent once he gets his own salon. He's sleeping with Felicia (Grant), who's married to Hollywood big shot Lester (Warden), who might be persuaded by Felicia to bankroll George's salon. But Lester's mistress, Jackie, played by Julie Christie [493 . . .], is also one of George's old girlfriends. George also beds Felicia's daughter, played by Carrie

Fisher in her film debut. Because George is a hairdresser, Lester thinks he's gay, but when he finds out the truth of George's involvements, there's hell to pay. What sounds like a conventional sex farce turns into a meditation on men, women, politics, ambition, business, and other enigmas of life. Some critics hated it, finding it nasty and self-involved because of Beatty's reputation as a womanizer; others found it richly satiric, with an underlying melancholy—a Hollywood version of Ingmar Bergman's *Smiles of a Summer Night* (1955) or Jean Renoir's *Rules of the Game* (1939). While it doesn't deserve the latter comparisons, *Shampoo* is no more cheap and tawdry than its ultimate source: the Restoration comedy by William Wycherley, *The Country Wife*. The performances, directed by Hal Ashby [430 . . .], are first-rate, as is the cinematography by Laszlo Kovacs.

After her first Oscar nomination, for *Detective Story*, Grant was blacklisted because she refused to testify against her husband, Arnold Manoff, before the House Un-American Activities Committee. She resumed her film career in the early sixties and has become one of Hollywood's most respected character actresses. She turned to directing in the eighties, working in both TV and movies, and her film *Down and Out in America* won the 1986 documentary feature Oscar.

Warden lost to George Burns in *The Sunshine Boys*. The screenplay Oscar went to Frank Pierson for *Dog Day Afternoon*. *Barry Lyndon* won the award for art direction.

Grant: 534, 1130, 2218. Warden: 890. Towne: 395, 839, 1135. Beatty: 255, 308, 890, 1678. Sylbert: 395, 448, 543, 1678, 2277. Campbell: 395, 1698. Gaines: 54, 448, 890.

1799 • SHANE

PARAMOUNT. 1953.
AWARD *Color Cinematography:* Loyal Griggs.
NOMINATIONS *Picture:* George Stevens, producer. *Supporting Actor:* Brandon de Wilde. *Supporting Actor:* Jack Palance. *Director:* George Stevens. *Screenplay:* A. B. Guthrie, Jr.

The Starretts, played by Jean Arthur [1353] and

Van Heflin [1055], are in danger of being driven off their homestead until Shane (Alan Ladd), a former gunfighter, rides into their lives and helps vanquish their foes, particularly the snake-mean Wilson (Palance). Undeniably one of the classic westerns, with its iconographic pairing of good (Ladd) vs. evil (Palance) and its hero-worshiping small boy (de Wilde). But there are many who find it "over-elaborated . . . in comparison with the greater spontaneity of Ford and Hawks," as Andrew Sarris puts it, or "overplanned and uninspired: Westerns are better when they're not so self-importantly self-conscious," in Pauline Kael's words—a rare concurrence of two critics who are often at odds. The cast includes Ben Johnson [1139], Edgar Buchanan, Elisha Cook, Jr., Ellen Corby [972], and Nancy Kulp. It's Ladd's best performance—or most fortuitous casting—and the actor was said to be devastated at the Academy's failure to nominate him. One theory holds that he was blackballed by Paramount, which he had recently left after being a contract player there for a decade. He was certainly denied the full benefit of the studio's publicity, which was used to help William Holden win the best actor Oscar for *Stalag 17.*

There can hardly be any controversy about the Oscar to Griggs—unquestionably the best thing about *Shane* is the spectacular clarity of its images, filmed in Jackson Hole, Wyoming. Griggs had begun his career in Paramount's special effects department and had only recently graduated to cinematographer when he received the Oscar. He died in 1978.

The best picture Oscar went to *From Here to Eternity,* which also won for Frank Sinatra's supporting performance, Fred Zinnemann's direction, and Daniel Taradash's screenplay. Palance would go on to a long career as a character player, mostly playing villains, and win his Oscar thirty-eight years later for *City Slickers.* De Wilde, who had made his screen debut the year before in *Member of the Wedding,* continued his career into his twenties, with a solid performance a decade after *Shane* in *Hud,* but was killed in a traffic accident at the age of thirty, in 1972.

Griggs: 833, 988, 1887, 2012. Stevens: 542, 768, 1353, 1579, 1998. Palance: 408, 1955.

1800 • SHANGHAI EXPRESS

PARAMOUNT PUBLIX. 1931–32.
AWARD *Cinematography:* Lee Garmes.
NOMINATIONS *Picture:* Adolph Zukor, studio head. *Director:* Josef von Sternberg.

Marlene Dietrich [1358], as Shanghai Lily, meets up with former lover Clive Brook on the train passing through strife-torn China. Revolutionaries, led by warlord Warner Oland, attack the train, and all manner of intrigue takes place. Wonderfully hokey melodrama of the kind that's usually called dated, but probably never got taken very seriously at any time. Full of cheeky dialogue by Jules Furthman [1387], including Dietrich's classic "It took more than one man to change my name to Shanghai Lily." The cast includes Eugene Pallette and Anna May Wong doing her usual sinister bit. A more appealing leading man than the rather pasty-looking Brook might have given this a real jolt.

Garmes, who along with Sternberg is one of the chief architects of the Dietrich mystique, began in films in 1916. He became known for his artful lighting, departing from naturalism for dramatic and poetic effects. He is said to have shot as much as a third of *Gone With the Wind,* though he received no screen credit. His career lasted until 1968, and he died a decade later.

The directing Oscar went to Frank Borzage for *Bad Girl. Shanghai Express* was the third of the seven films Sternberg made with Dietrich, but as the series progressed, the box office declined. Eventually Sternberg split with Paramount and Dietrich. He went to England in 1937 to direct a film of Robert Graves' *I, Claudius,* but producer Alexander Korda [1620] called a halt to the filming after several weeks, sensing that the production was going to become a serious financial drain. Sternberg's later career in Hollywood was spotty, including uncredited work on *Duel in the Sun* and a disastrous attempt to work with the unstable Howard Hughes [734 . . .]. He died in 1969.

The best picture Oscar was won by *Grand Hotel.*

Garmes: 201, 1358, 1828. Zukor: 649, 1836. Sternberg: 1358.

1801 • SHANGHAI GESTURE, THE

ARNOLD PRODUCTIONS; UNITED ARTISTS. 1942.

NOMINATIONS *Black-and-White Interior Decoration:* Boris Leven. *Scoring of a Dramatic or Comedy Picture:* Richard Hageman.

Ona Munson plays Mother Gin Sling, proprietor of a Shanghai gambling den, who employs a rich young woman, played by Gene Tierney [1153], to get even with an old flame, played by Walter Huston [50 . . .]. Laughably bowdlerized version of an old stage melodrama in which the character was called Mother Goddam and the gambling joint was clearly a brothel. But why anyone would have wanted to film this claptrap, even if they could have gotten it past the censors, is hard to figure. The director, in his period of decline, is Josef von Sternberg [1358 . . .]. The cast includes Victor Mature, Albert Basserman [706], Maria Ouspenskaya [560 . . .], Eric Blore, Marcel Dalio, and Mike Mazurki. The art direction Oscar went to *This Above All.* Max Steiner won for the score of *Now, Voyager.*

Leven: 34, 77, 422, 768, 1753, 1881, 1907, 2244. Hageman: 955, 979, 1200, 1901, 2062.

1802 • SHANKS

WILLIAM CASTLE ENTERPRISES PRODUCTION; PARAMOUNT. 1974.

NOMINATION *Original Dramatic Score:* Alex North.

Marcel Marceau plays a dual role: a puppeteer and a dying inventor who gives the puppeteer a device that can animate the dead. Exceedingly weird horror-fantasy, and definitely not for people who have a thing about mimes. Directed by William Castle. The scoring Oscar went to Nino Rota and Carmine Coppola for *The Godfather, Part II.*

North: 29, 215, 413, 515, 577, 1654, 1727, 1814, 1886, 1949, 2174, 2177, 2212, 2277.

1802.5 • SHAWSHANK REDEMPTION, THE

CASTLE ROCK ENTERTAINMENT PRODUCTION; COLUMBIA. 1994.

NOMINATIONS *Picture:* Niki Marvin, producer. *Actor:* Morgan Freeman. *Screenplay Based on Material Previ-* *ously Produced or Published:* Frank Darabont. *Cinematography:* Roger Deakins. *Sound:* Robert J. Litt, Elliot Tyson, Michael Herbick, and Willie Burton. *Original Score:* Thomas Newman. *Film Editing:* Richard Francis-Bruce.

Andy Dufresne (Tim Robbins) is sentenced to life in Shawshank Prison for murdering his wife—a crime he didn't commit. After being brutalized by other inmates, he is befriended by a savvy fellow prisoner, Red (Freeman), who helps him learn the ropes—and also tells us Andy's story in voice-over narration. In his earlier life, Andy was a banker, and he uses his skill with money to win over first the guards and then the warden (Bob Gunton). Soon, he is an accomplice to the warden's crooked kickback schemes. But there's more going on behind Andy's somewhat innocent facade than even Red knows. Very entertaining prison melodrama based on a short novel by Stephen King, *Rita Hayworth and the Shawshank Redemption.* The film benefits greatly from first-time director Darabont's amazingly assured narrative skills. Though the story is full of contrivances that don't bear close scrutiny, Darabont makes them work by allowing the characters time to develop. It helps that he has first-rate actors to work with: Robbins uses the glints of devilish intelligence in his baby face skillfully, and Freeman radiates integrity, inner strength, and a sly wit. James Whitmore [157 . . .] has an affecting role as an elderly prisoner who doesn't know what to do when he's finally paroled. The movie's failure at the box office was attributed by many to its title, which gave no hint of its contents. *Forrest Gump* took the Oscars for best picture, for actor Tom Hanks, for Eric Roth's screenplay, and for Arthur Schmidt's editing. The award for cinematography went to John Toll for *Legends of the Fall. Speed* won for sound, and the scoring Oscar went to Hans Zimmer for *The Lion King.*

Freeman: 580, 1948. Litt: 1333. Tyson: 779, 1333. Herbick: 411.5, 734.5. Burton: 58, 209, 307, 2231. Newman: 1190.5.

1803 • SHE

RKO RADIO. 1935.

NOMINATION *Dance Direction:* Benjamin Zemach.

Helen Gahagan plays the title role, the ruler of a mysterious kingdom. She (who must be obeyed) has been kept alive and young for centuries by a magic flame. But then an archaeological expedition—Randolph Scott, Nigel Bruce, Helen Mack—arrives, and She falls in love with Scott and tries to bump off Mack. Entertainingly campy version of H. Rider Haggard's old warhorse of an adventure-fantasy, adapted by Ruth Rose and Dudley Nichols [30 . . .], directed by Irving Pichel and Lansing C. Holden, and produced by Merian C. Cooper [1189 . . .]. The story had produced numerous silent film versions and has subsequently been adapted for the talents of Ursula Andress in 1965 and Sandahl Bergman in 1985. This was the only important film role for Gahagan, a former opera singer and Broadway actress, who was married to Melvyn Douglas [169 . . .]. She later went into politics, which, considering her performance here, was not a bad career move—at least until she fell afoul of a Richard Nixon dirty tricks campaign in the 1950 Senate race. Zemach, nominated for the "Hall of Kings" number, lost to David Gould's work on *Broadway Melody of 1936* and *Folies Bergère.*

1804 • SHE DONE HIM WRONG

PARAMOUNT. 1932–33.

NOMINATION *Picture:* William LeBaron, producer.

Mae West runs a saloon and seduces Cary Grant [1445 . . .], an undercover cop posing as a mission worker in the Bowery of the Gay Nineties. There's also some chicanery involving Gilbert Roland and Rafaela Ottiano, the latter as a character called Russian Rita. But mainly it's an excuse for West to sing "Frankie and Johnny," "I Wonder Where My Easy Rider's Gone," and "I Like a Man Who Takes His Time," and to mutter endless double entendres. Terrific movie based on West's 1928 Broadway play *Diamond Lil,* and while Harvey Thew and John Bright [1633] get credited with the adaptation and Lowell Sherman with the direction, West is the film's real auteur. Historians have long cited West's two films of 1933—the other is *I'm No Angel*—as the chief cause of the strict enforcement of the Production Code, the industry's self-censoring mechanism, which was put in the hands of Joseph I. Breen in 1934 and bowdlerized American movies for the next thirty-four years. Feminists have noted that it was a woman's cheerful carnality that spooked the censors into overdrive. West's 1933 movies were huge hits at the box office and saved Paramount from bankruptcy, which explains this movie's candidacy for best picture, even though it received no other nominations. The best picture Oscar went to *Cavalcade.*

LeBaron: 400.

1805 • SHE LOVES ME NOT

PARAMOUNT. 1934.

NOMINATION *Song:* "Love in Bloom," music by Ralph Rainger, lyrics by Leo Robin.

On the run from the mob, showgirl Curly Flagg, played by Miriam Hopkins [165], dresses as a man and hides out in the Princeton dorm room of a student played by Bing Crosby [173 . . .]. Agreeable musical comedy, with one of Hopkins' best performances. The screenplay by Benjamin Glazer [97 . . .] is an adaptation of a play by Howard Lindsay based on a novel by Edward Hope. With such a high-concept premise, it's not surprising that there have been imitations and remakes—*True to the Army* (1946) and *How to Be Very, Very Popular* (1955). Elliott Nugent directed, and the cast includes Kitty Carlisle. Except for the nominated song, most of the music is forgettable. "Love in Bloom" later became associated with Jack Benny, making Rainger-Robin the only songwriting team with two Oscar-nominated songs that became theme songs for comedians: Their Oscar-winning "Thanks for the Memory," from *Big Broadcast of 1938,* was Bob Hope's signature song. They lost the Oscar this time, coming in second to Con Conrad and Herb Magidson's "The Continental," from *The Gay Divorcée.*

Rainger: 197, 846. Robin: 104, 197, 368, 846, 1072, 1843, 2032, 2088, 2310.

1806 • SHE MARRIED A COP

REPUBLIC. 1939.

NOMINATION *Score:* Cy Feuer.

She (Jean Parker) is an actress; he, the cop played by Phil Regan, is tricked by her into doing the voice of an animated pig. Long-forgotten little musical, directed by Sidney Salkow, with songs by Ralph Freed and Burton Lane [117 . . .]. The animation was supervised by Leon Schlesinger, best known as the producer of the *Looney Tunes* and *Merrie Melodies* series at Warner Bros. The Oscar went to Richard Hageman, Frank Harling, John Leipold, and Leo Shuken for *Stagecoach.*

Feuer: 321, 920, 976, 1305, 1932.

1807 • SHE WORE A YELLOW RIBBON

ARGOSY PICTURES; RKO RADIO. 1949.

AWARD *Color Cinematography:* Winton Hoch.

Retirement is being forced upon cavalry captain Nathan Brittles, played by John Wayne [33 . . .], and he doesn't like it one bit, especially since the cavalry has recently experienced the defeat of Custer at the Little Big Horn. He manages to hold on for one last campaign. Spectacularly handsome John Ford [815 . . .] western, with one of Wayne's best performances and the usual fine support from Ford's stock company, including Ben Johnson [1139], Harry Carey, Jr., Victor McLaglen [999 . . .], Mildred Natwick [147], and Arthur Shields. The romantic subplot involving Joanne Dru and John Agar is a bit tedious. The screenplay, by Frank Nugent [1642] and Laurence Stallings, is based on a *Saturday Evening Post* story by James Warner Bellah. The film is usually grouped with *Fort Apache* (1948) and *Rio Grande* (1950) as Ford's "cavalry trilogy."

Hoch was instructed to give the film the look of the paintings of Frederic Remington. A pioneer in color cinematography, he began his career as a technician with the Technicolor Corp. In 1940 he began working as cinematographer, but that career was interrupted by service in World War II. Though he squabbled a bit with Ford over the filming of *She Wore a Yellow Ribbon,* once lodging a protest with the union when Ford ordered him to stop packing up his gear and shoot a sunset, he continued to work with the director on such films as *The Quiet Man,* which won him his third Oscar, and *The Searchers* (1956). He was also a pioneer in color photography for television.

Hoch: 1048, 1642.

1808 • SHEEP HAS FIVE LEGS, THE

RAOUL PLOQUIN; UNITED MOTION PICTURE ORGANIZATION (FRANCE). 1955.

NOMINATION *Motion Picture Story:* Jean Marsan, Henry Troyat, Jacques Perret, Henri Verneuil, and Raoul Ploquin.

. . . and Fernandel has six roles: He plays the father of quintuplet sons as well as all five sons. The plot involves the estrangement of the father from his offspring, and the desire of the village where he lives to reap the publicity benefits of a family reunion. The brothers include an effeminate beautician, an impoverished father of a huge family, an alcoholic sea captain, an advice-to-the-lovelorn columnist, and a priest whose resemblance to Don Camillo (the cleric played by Fernandel in other films) is a trial he must bear. Amusing tour de force, except to those for whom a little Fernandel goes a long way. Directed by Verneuil. The Oscar went to Daniel Fuchs for *Love Me or Leave Me.*

1809 • SHEEPMAN, THE

MGM. 1958.

NOMINATION *Story and Screenplay—Written Directly for the Screen:* James Edward Grant and William Bowers.

"The land was made for the cattle," went the old cry of the western rancher. Not so, responds sheepman Glenn Ford, as he tries to stake out his own turf, romance Shirley MacLaine [91 . . .], and fight Leslie Nielsen. Pleasant if unmemorable western comedy directed by George Marshall. The Oscar went to Nedrick Young (under his blacklist pseudonym Nathan E. Douglas) and Harold Jacob Smith for *The Defiant Ones.*

Bowers: 848.

1810 • SHENANDOAH

UNIVERSAL. 1965.

NOMINATION *Sound:* Waldon O. Watson, sound director, Universal City Studio Sound Department.

Widower James Stewart [73 . . .] tries to raise his family—six sons and a daughter—and hold on to his land in Civil War–era Virginia, without becoming involved in the conflict. Well-done family drama, written by James Lee Barrett and directed by Andrew V. McLaglen. The cast includes Patrick Wayne as one of the sons, Katharine Ross [810] in her film debut as Wayne's wife, and Doug McClure, Glenn Corbett, Rosemary Forsyth, Phillip Alford, Denver Pyle, George Kennedy [443], Tim McIntire, Warren Oates, Strother Martin, and Harry Carey, Jr. The Oscar for sound went to *The Sound of Music*.

Watson: 350, 655, 690, 744, 2035.

1811 • SHIP COMES IN, A

DeMILLE PICTURES; PATHÉ. 1927–28.

NOMINATION *Actress:* Louise Dresser.

Dresser plays Mrs. Plecznik, a Polish immigrant, in this silent film, directed by William K. Howard, which received scant distribution at the time and has apparently vanished. Dresser was a veteran character actress who played Catherine the Great opposite Rudolph Valentino in *The Eagle* (1925), was Al Jolson's mother in *Mammy* (1930), costarred with Will Rogers in *State Fair* and *David Harum* (1934), and returned to Catherine the Great's Russia in 1934 to play the Empress Elizabeth in *The Scarlet Empress*. She retired from the screen in 1937 and died in 1965 at the age of eighty-six. The Oscar went to Janet Gaynor for *Seventh Heaven, Street Angel,* and *Sunrise*.

1812 • SHIP OF FOOLS

COLUMBIA. 1965.

AWARDS *Black-and-White Cinematography:* Ernest Laszlo. *Black-and-White Art Direction–Set Decoration:* Robert Clatworthy; Joseph Kish.

NOMINATIONS *Picture:* Stanley Kramer, producer. *Actor:* Oskar Werner. *Actress:* Simone Signoret. *Supporting Actor:* Michael Dunn. *Screenplay–Based on Material From Another Medium:* Abby Mann. *Black-and-White Costume Design:* Bill Thomas and Jean Louis.

A German ship sails from Vera Cruz to Bremerhaven in 1933, carrying a variety of passengers: Vivien Leigh [798 . . .] is a divorcée appalled by the notion of growing old; Signoret is a Spanish countess; Werner is her lover, the ship's doctor; Lee Marvin [371] a loutish former baseball player; Jose Ferrer [473 . . .] a vicious anti-Semite; Elizabeth Ashley a rich young woman; George Segal [2277] her artist lover; and Dunn a dwarf who is the film's central consciousness and perhaps most "normal" character. Also on board are Jose Greco, Lilia Skala [1174], and Werner Klemperer. This somewhat overheated melodrama was widely praised at the time but hasn't held up well, partly because, like the novel by Katherine Anne Porter on which it was based, it tries too hard to make metaphorical connections between its shipboard soap-operatics and the rise of the Third Reich. Kramer also directed but was not included among the nominees in that category.

Laszlo, born in Hungary, came to the United States in 1926 and worked as a camera operator at Paramount until the late forties when he was promoted to cinematographer. His son, Andrew, is also a cinematographer. Ernest died in 1984.

The Sound of Music—a very different kind of treatment of the rise of the Third Reich—was named best picture. Lee Marvin defeated his *Ship of Fools* costar, Werner, in the best actor race with his performance in *Cat Ballou*—many felt Marvin's Oscar was in recognition of his work in both films. Werner had appeared in films in Austria as a bit player before World War II. Injuries from a bombing kept him out of combat in the war, and he resumed his screen career in 1948, making his strongest impression in *Jules and Jim* (1961) before essaying his first English-language role in *Ship of Fools*. He subsequently appeared in such movies as *The Spy Who Came in From the Cold, Fahrenheit 451* (1966), and *Voyage of the Damned* (1976), before his death in 1984.

Dunn, born in Oklahoma, first came to attention on Broadway in *The Ballad of the Sad Café*. After his nomination, he appeared in several films and on TV, but in 1973 was found dead in a London hotel, apparently a suicide. The supporting actor award went to Martin Balsam for *A Thousand Clowns*.

Julie Christie won as best actress for *Darling*. Robert Bolt won the screenplay award for *Doctor Zhivago*.

Laszlo: 31, 646, 1000, 1032, 1065, 1196, 1907. Clatworthy: 843, 1003, 1632, 2035. Kish: 13, 1048. Kramer: 330, 522, 843, 912, 1065. Signoret: 1724. Mann: 1065. Thomas: 116, 166, 254, 866, 883, 1003, 1789, 1886, 2128. Louis: 20, 126, 170, 262, 732, 744, 1028, 1065, 1521, 1640, 1858, 1910, 2064.

1813 • *SHIRLEY VALENTINE*

LEWIS GILBERT/WILLY RUSSELL PRODUCTION; PARAMOUNT (UNITED KINGDOM). 1989.

NOMINATIONS *Actress:* Pauline Collins. *Song:* "The Girl Who Used to Be Me," music by Marvin Hamlisch, lyrics by Alan Bergman and Marilyn Bergman.

Collins plays the title role, a middle-aged British housewife bored with her life and her complacent husband (Bernard Hill) until she gets the chance to vacation alone in Greece. There she meets a charismatic Greek, played by Tom Conti [1687], and has a romantic fling that changes her life. As banal as the plot sounds—bored Brits are always flying off to Greece to get jolts of life, as in *Zorba the Greek*—Collins' terrific performance makes this predictable little movie watchable. It was probably better in its first incarnation: a one-woman show, also with Collins, written by Willy Russell [598]. His screenplay opens things up and lets us see the people Collins had to create on her own in the stage version, but that's not necessarily a good thing: The movie is still a one-woman show. Lewis Gilbert [35] directs, as he also did with Russell's *Educating Rita*. Collins, whose film career has been minimal, although she is a familiar face to watchers of TV's *Upstairs, Downstairs* and other imported British fare, lost to Jessica Tandy in *Driving Miss Daisy*. The song Oscar went to Alan Menken and Howard Ashman for "Under the Sea," from *The Little Mermaid*.

Hamlisch: 398, 977, 1109, 1747, 1876, 1898, 1927, 2238. A. Bergman: 179, 867, 1168, 1568, 1628, 1747, 1864, 2063, 2113, 2238, 2321, 2322. M. Bergman: 179, 867, 1168, 1568, 1628, 1747, 1864, 2063, 2113, 2238, 2321, 2322.

1814 • *SHOES OF THE FISHERMAN, THE*

GEORGE ENGLUND PRODUCTIONS; MGM. 1968.

NOMINATIONS *Art Direction—Set Decoration:* George W. Davis and Edward Carfagno. *Original Score—for a Motion Picture (Not a Musical):* Alex North.

Anthony Quinn [1226 . . .] plays a Russian archbishop, a survivor of the gulag, who becomes pope and has to deal with all sorts of personal and world crises. Tiresome, half-baked all-star epic, with Laurence Olivier [268 . . .], Oskar Werner [1812], David Janssen, Vittorio de Sica [650], Leo McKern, and John Gielgud [103 . . .] trudging dutifully through under the direction of Michael Anderson [101]. The screenplay by John Patrick and James Kennaway [2150] is based on a best-selling plotboiler by Morris West. The award for art direction went to *Oliver!* John Barry won for the score of *The Lion in Winter*.

Davis: 46, 69, 401, 495, 542, 736, 953, 1213, 1335, 1388, 1537, 1552, 1706, 2157, 2184, 2312. Carfagno: 130, 175, 629, 917, 1069, 1552, 1644, 1937, 2312. North: 29, 215, 413, 515, 577, 1654, 1727, 1802, 1886, 1949, 2174, 2177, 2212, 2277.

1815 • *SHOESHINE*

A.L.F.A. CINEMATOGRAFICA; LOPERT FILMS (ITALY). 1947.

AWARD *Special Award:* The high quality of this motion picture, brought to eloquent life in a country scarred by war, is proof to the world that the creative spirit can triumph over adversity.

NOMINATION *Original Screenplay:* Sergio Amidei, Adolfo Franci, C. G. Viola, and Cesare Zavattini.

Two shoeshine boys in the rubble of postwar Rome are apprehended for trafficking in the black market and are sent to reform school, which poisons their friendship and their lives. Superb film, directed by Vittorio De Sica [650]. *Shoeshine* and *The Bicycle Thief* announced that a new era of filmmaking was at hand —the label given it was "neorealist"—and it influenced American directors as profoundly as it did European ones. The Academy's special award to *Shoeshine* also initiated the practice of annually honoring a foreign language film, which was turned, with decidedly mixed results, into a competitive award at the 1956 ceremonies. The Academy clearly wasn't ready for too much neorealism, however, for the screenplay award went, rather scandalously, to Sidney Sheldon for *The Bachelor and the Bobby-Soxer.*

Amidei: 756, 1496, 1519. Zavattini: 194, 2171.

1816 • SHOOTIST, THE

FRANKOVICH/SELF PRODUCTION; DINO DE LAURENTIIS PRESENTATION; PARAMOUNT. 1976.

NOMINATION *Art Direction—Set Decoration:* Robert F. Boyle; Arthur Jeph Parker.

John Wayne [33 . . .] plays a famous gunfighter who, dying of cancer, tries to return to his hometown and die in peace. The townspeople, of course, aren't ready to let him go gentle. The cast, directed by Don Siegel, includes James Stewart [73 . . .], Lauren Bacall, Ron Howard, Richard Boone, Hugh O'Brian, Harry Morgan, John Carradine, Sheree North, and Scatman Crothers. Because the film was Wayne's last and, like the character he plays, he knew he was dying of cancer, it has taken on some added layers of emotional significance. It's a little too elegiac to be completely satisfactory as entertainment, but it's certainly well acted, thoughtfully scripted by Miles Hood Swarthout and Scott Hale from a novel by Glendon Swarthout, and handsomely filmed by Bruce Surtees [1155]. The art direction Oscar went to *All the President's Men.*

Boyle: 659, 743, 1450. Parker: 394.

1817 • SHOP ON MAIN STREET, THE

CESKOSLOVENSKY FILM COMPANY PRODUCTION; PROMINENT FILMS (CZECHOSLOVAKIA). 1966.

AWARD *Foreign Language Film (1965).*

NOMINATION *Actress:* Ida Kaminska.

Kaminska plays an elderly Jewish shopkeeper in Nazi-occupied Czechoslovakia. Deaf and a bit dotty, she doesn't realize the peril she's in. Then a mousy carpenter (Josef Kroner) is appointed by his collaborationist brother-in-law to be "Aryan controller" of

her shop, and he finds himself trying to protect her from the Nazis, with disastrous results. Undeniably affecting tragicomic fable, with a wonderful performance by Kaminska, but it's a little too sentimental and about half an hour longer than it needs to be. Directed by Jan Kadar and Elmar Klos, who cowrote the screenplay with Ladislav Grosman. Differing eligibility requirements in the foreign language category and the other competitive categories made Kaminska eligible for an award a year after the film won its first Oscar. She lost to Elizabeth Taylor in *Who's Afraid of Virginia Woolf?*

1817.5 • SHORT CUTS

AVENUE PICTURES PRODUCTION; FINE LINE FEATURES. 1993.

NOMINATION *Director:* Robert Altman.

Like Altman's *Nashville, Short Cuts* is a collage of individual stories, this time set in Los Angeles. The screenplay, by Altman and Frank Barhydt, is based on the stories of Raymond Carver. The characters include a couple, played by Andie MacDowell and Bruce Davison [1203], whose son has been struck down on his birthday by a driver, played by Lily Tomlin [1415], who leaves the scene, though she's not technically a hit-and-run (she thinks the boy is okay). Tomlin is a waitress married to a drunk, played by Tom Waits [1483]. Lyle Lovett is the baker who has made a cake for the boy's birthday, and then torments them with anonymous phone calls because he's pissed off that they didn't pick it up. Jack Lemmon [91 . . .] is the boy's self-obsessed grandfather. And these lives intersect with others, played by Tim Robbins, Madeleine Stowe, Jennifer Jason Leigh, Chris Penn, Julianne Moore, Matthew Modine, Peter Gallagher, Anne Archer [653], Lori Singer, Annie Ross, Buck Henry [810 . . .], and Huey Lewis [127]. Most critics were enthusiastic about Altman's film, although there were some articulate dissenters who found the director's attitude toward his characters cold and condescending—unlike the author of the stories, Raymond Carver, who communicated the poignancy in these lonely lives. It's certainly not as entertaining as Altman's most commercially successful works—*MASH, Nashville, The Player*—and at more than three hours long it can try one's patience. The cinematography is by Walt Lloyd and the score by Mark Isham [1701.5]. As usual, Altman's editor, Geraldine Peroni [1584.5], deserves notice.

Altman was the sole candidate for a directing Oscar whose film was not in the running for best picture. (In that race, *The Fugitive,* directed by Andrew Davis, supplanted *Short Cuts.)* Altman joins the company of other directors who were nominated for films that received no other nominations; recently these have included Martin Scorsese and David Lynch, nominated for *The Last Temptation of Christ* and *Blue Velvet* respectively. The only thing these three movies have in common seems to be that they are unsettling personal statements, difficult for the Academy to ignore, but apparently more difficult for them to reward. Altman lost to Steven Spielberg for *Schindler's List.*

Altman: 1286, 1415, 1584.5.

1818 • SHOW BOAT

MGM. 1951.

NOMINATIONS *Color Cinematography:* Charles Rosher. *Scoring of a Musical Picture:* Adolph Deutsch and Conrad Salinger.

When it's disclosed that Julie Laverne, played by Ava Gardner [1339], is part black, she has to leave the acting company on the *Cotton Blossom* showboat. The only person who can replace her as leading lady is Magnolia (Kathryn Grayson), the young daughter of the riverboat's captain, Andy Hawks (Joe E. Brown) and his wife, Parthy, played by Agnes Moorehead [963 . . .]. Because the leading man, Julie's husband, has also left, a handsome drifter, Gaylord Ravenal (Howard Keel), is enlisted to play opposite Magnolia. Magnolia and Gaylord fall in love and marry, but his gambling breaks up their marriage. Handsomely filmed but flimsy version of the great musical by Jerome Kern [340 . . .] and Oscar Hammerstein II [375 . . .]. It has some strong points: Gardner is ravishingly beautiful, Keel is in fine voice, Marge and Gower Champion do some good dance numbers, and William Warfield, as Joe, sings "Ol' Man River" stirringly. But the pert and acidulous

Grayson is a real trial, and the screenplay, by John Lee Mahin [352 . . .], is bland. George Sidney directed, and the cast includes Robert Sterling, Adele Jergens, Leif Erickson, and Regis Toomey. Although Gardner wanted to do her own singing and took voice lessons, she is dubbed by Annette Warren; interestingly Gardner's own voice is heard on the soundtrack album from the film. Lena Horne was crushed at not being cast in the part of Julie, but MGM feared the film wouldn't be shown in the South. Horne did get to sing "Can't Help Lovin' That Man" in the 1946 Jerome Kern biopic *Till the Clouds Roll By. Show Boat* had been filmed twice before. The first version was a part-talkie in 1929, but the best of all, inexplicably overlooked by the Academy, is the 1936 film, directed by James Whale, with the definitive performances of Paul Robeson as Joe and Helen Morgan as Julie, plus Irene Dunne [114 . . .] as Magnolia, Allan Jones as Gaylord, Charles Winninger as Captain Andy, and Hattie McDaniel [798] as Queenie.

Show Boat was overshadowed by a better MGM musical, *An American in Paris,* which won for the cinematography of Alfred Gilks and John Alton and the scoring of Johnny Green and Saul Chaplin.

Rosher: 22, 87, 1096, 1972, 2320. Deutsch: 87, 141, 1469, 1782.

1819 • SIGN OF THE CROSS, THE

PARAMOUNT PUBLIX. 1932–33.

NOMINATION *Cinematography:* Karl Struss.

Fredric March [184 . . .] is Marcus Superbus, a Roman officer who falls in love with a Christian woman, Mercia (Elissa Landi), to the fury of the Empress Poppaea, played by Claudette Colbert [1025 . . .], who wants him for herself. To get even with the Christians, she provokes her husband, Nero, played by Charles Laughton [1387 . . .], into all sorts of persecutions. As usual in the religious epics of Cecil B. DeMille [412 . . .], the villains make it all worthwhile: Colbert is terrifically sexy, lounging around in a vat of asses' milk, and Laughton is deliciously decadent. There's plenty of sadistic violence, too—the film was made before the Production Code was enforced. And of course the divine comeuppance meted out to the bad guys sends us away purged of all those naughty thoughts we had earlier in the movie—doesn't it? In 1944 the film was reedited and rereleased, with a prologue set during World War II added on and some of the sex and violence that wouldn't pass the Code trimmed out. Recently the film has been restored to its original shape. The screenplay by Waldemar Young [1194] and Sidney Buchman [904 . . .] is based on a play by Wilson Barrett, though the plot sure does resemble *Quo Vadis?* an awful lot, and that was based on a novel by Henryk Sienkewicz. The cast includes Nat Pendleton, Charles Middleton, Kent Taylor, and John Carradine. Struss placed third in a three-man race for the cinematography Oscar, which went to Charles B. Lang for *A Farewell to Arms.*

Struss: 56, 572, 582, 1972.

1820 • SILENCE OF THE LAMBS, THE

STRONG HEART/DEMME PRODUCTION; ORION. 1991.

AWARDS *Picture:* Edward Saxon, Kenneth Utt, and Ron Bozman, producers. *Actor:* Anthony Hopkins. *Actress:* Jodie Foster. *Director:* Jonathan Demme. *Screenplay Based on Material From Another Medium:* Ted Tally. **NOMINATIONS** *Sound:* Tom Fleischman and Christopher Newman. *Film Editing:* Craig McKay.

Clarice Starling (Foster), a young FBI trainee, is called on by a senior agent, Jack Crawford (Scott Glenn), to interview a notorious serial killer, Hannibal Lecter (Hopkins), who is held in a high-security mental institution. The inexperienced but clever young woman and the suavely menacing psychopath develop a working relationship that helps her find another killer, known as Buffalo Bill because he skins his victims. She unmasks Buffalo Bill as one Jame Gumb (Ted Levine), who is holding his current victim (Brooke Smith) still alive in his cellar. Extraordinarily gripping thriller that, like the best films in its genre, such as Hitchcock's *Psycho,* actually gets better on repeat viewings, when you can relax a bit and enjoy the wit of the direction and the script, based on Thomas Harris' book, and the terrific performances. It's certainly one of the most unusual best picture winners in the history of the award, which has tradi-

tionally gone to earnest dramas with strong social, political, or moral messages. *The Silence of the Lambs* is anything but earnest, although it can be said to send a strong feminist message through its portrayal of Clarice, one of the most intelligent and appealing women in recent movies. Watch Clarice as she manipulates a roomful of good-ol'-boy deputies who clearly don't take her seriously, for example, or subtly fends off the unwanted sexual interest of various men in the film. In a year of stiffer competition, the movie might not have had as much success at the Oscars, but it was up against a weak slate. Its strongest competitor, *Bugsy,* had received admiring reviews but had been rejected by audiences that found it chilly and uninvolving. *Beauty and the Beast* was tremendously popular, but it was an anomalous nominee, the only animated feature ever to be a candidate for best picture. *JFK* had been undermined by the controversy over its version of the Kennedy assassination. And *The Prince of Tides,* a rather florid melodrama, had drawn attention mainly because of the failure to nominate its director, Barbra Streisand. So *The Silence of the Lambs* beat the odds: For years, few films released before Labor Day had even been nominated for best picture. Demme's movie appeared on Valentine's Day 1991 and by Oscar night had already been released on videotape—accessibility that may have boosted its chances. It went on to do what only two other films, *It Happened One Night* and *One Flew Over the Cuckoo's Nest,* have done: sweep the five top Oscars—picture, actor, actress, director, and writer. And it became the only "horror movie" ever to win the top award.

Hopkins' portrayal of Hannibal Lecter was thought at the time of the film's release to be a sure thing for a supporting actor nomination. But the character so caught the public imagination that it was boosted to leading role status. Born in Wales and trained at the Royal Academy of Dramatic Art in London, Hopkins had made his film debut early in his acting career, in *The Lion in Winter,* but had received more attention as a stage actor than for his work in films. The Oscar made him one of the most sought-after actors in the business, and his eagerness to work has made him one of the busiest.

Foster became the second actress in history—the first was Luise Rainer [799 . . .]—to win two best actress Oscars before the age of thirty. She has, like many successful Hollywood actors, moved into producing and directing. Her first film as director, *Little Man Tate* (1991), received respectable reviews.

Demme's win was a triumph for a director who had been thought of as the maker of quirky comedies—*Melvin and Howard, Something Wild* (1986), *Married to the Mob*—that did well with critics but not so well at the box office. He revealed himself as the most successful of all the so-called heirs to Alfred Hitchcock [1171 . . .], achieving not only the master's ability to shock but also his macabre wit. He is also one of the most skillful directors of actors in Hollywood. As Tom Hanks noted when accepting the best actor Oscar for Demme's *Philadelphia,* a lot of people who worked for Demme have received Oscars, including Mary Steenburgen for *Melvin and Howard* as well as Foster and Hopkins. Like many filmmakers of his generation—Francis Ford Coppola [65 . . .], Peter Bogdanovich [1139], Martin Scorsese [27.5 . . .], John Sayles [1533.5], among others—Demme began his career working for quickie producer Roger Corman (who has a small role in *The Silence of the Lambs*). The first film of Demme's that attracted widespread critical notice was the comedy *Citizens Band* (a.k.a. *Handle With Care,* 1977), which was, however, poorly distributed and publicized and failed to find an audience. *Melvin and Howard* brought him more acclaim and a chance to direct a major studio project, *Swing Shift,* but conflicts on the latter with producer-star Goldie Hawn [323 . . .] seriously damaged the film. He has been more successful working on films on which he has a free hand, including the superb Talking Heads concert movie *Stop Making Sense* (1984) and the fine filming of monologist Spalding Gray's *Swimming to Cambodia* (1987). His most recent film, *Philadelphia,* was a solid box-office success, but many critics felt it was compromised by sentimentality, and some traced that flaw to the controversy that arose over the portrait of the putatively gay villain of *The Silence of the Lambs,* Jame Gumb, who many gay activists felt was an offensive stereo-type. Some theorized that Demme's fear of offending both the gay community and straight audiences fatally weakened *Philadelphia.*

Tally's most important previous screenwriting credit was the film *White Palace* (1990). His screenplay for *The Silence of the Lambs* follows the Harris novel closely, but wisely keeps the focus on the two principals, reducing the role of the FBI agent played by Scott Glenn. The ending is a witty stroke found only in the movie.

The award for sound was won by *Terminator 2: Judgment Day.* The editing Oscar went to Joe Hutshing and Pietro Scalia for *JFK.*

Hopkins: 1679.5. Foster: 7, 1421.5, 2005. Fleischman: 1678. Newman: 60, 398, 631, 641, 724, 784. McKay: 1678.

1821 • *SILKWOOD*

ABC Motion Pictures Production; 20th Century-Fox. 1983.

Nominations *Actress:* Meryl Streep. *Supporting Actress:* Cher. *Director:* Mike Nichols. *Screenplay Written Directly for the Screen:* Nora Ephron and Alice Arlen. *Film Editing:* Sam O'Steen.

Streep plays Karen Silkwood, a worker at the Kerr-McGee nuclear fuel plant in Oklahoma, whose unionizing activities and her determination to expose unsafe practices that are exposing workers to radiation may have caused her death: She was killed in an automobile accident on her way to a meeting with a *New York Times* reporter. Even before her death, she was an outsider, regarded as a troublemaker not only by the plant's management but also by fellow workers who feared losing their jobs. Her closest relationships in the film are with her boyfriend Drew (Kurt Russell) and her roommate Dolly (Cher), a lesbian whose attraction to Karen is unrequited. Streep gives a technically accomplished performance in the lead, but the less actorish playing of Russell and Cher is more satisfying—Streep's intensity tends to subvert the ensemble work needed for a really effective film. The movie marks Nichols' return to feature film directing after an eight-year absence, but his rather chilly treatment of his characters isn't what's needed in a film that's supposed to have a political edge; we don't care enough about the people in the movie. The cinematography is by Miroslav Ondricek [60 . . .], and the cast includes Craig T. Nelson, Diana Scarwid [1004], Fred Ward, Ron Silver, Josef Sommer, David Strathairn, M. Emmet Walsh, and Tess Harper [462].

Streep lost to Shirley MacLaine in *Terms of Endearment,* which also won for director James L. Brooks. The supporting actress Oscar went to Linda Hunt for *The Year of Living Dangerously.* Horton Foote took the writing award for *Tender Mercies,* and the editing Oscar went to the team of five editors who worked on *The Right Stuff.*

Streep: 472, 521, 725, 1019, 1111, 1512, 1598, 1876. Cher: 1351. Nichols: 810, 1679.5, 2277, 2313. Ephron: 1839.5, 2255. O'Steen: 395, 2277.

1822 • SILVER CHALICE, THE

Victor Saville Production; Warner Bros. 1954.
Nominations *Color Cinematography:* William V. Skall. *Scoring of a Dramatic or Comedy Picture:* Franz Waxman.

Paul Newman [3 . . .] makes his film debut in this story about a Greek slave who crafts the silver cup holder used at the Last Supper. Boring biblical blockbuster, with Virginia Mayo as the vamp, Pier Angeli as the virgin, and Jack Palance [408 . . .] as the villain—the requisite three V's of the genre. The cast, directed by Victor Saville [406 . . .], includes Walter Hampden, Joseph Wiseman, Alexander Scourby, Lorne Green (also making his debut), E. G. Marshall, and Natalie Wood [1219 . . .]. Lesser Samuels [198 . . .] adapted a pious page-turner by Thomas B. Costain. The cinematography Oscar went to Milton Krasner for *Three Coins in the Fountain.* Dimitri Tiomkin won for the score of *The High and the Mighty.*

Skall: 96, 208, 1048, 1170, 1317, 1453, 1644, 1668, 2102. Waxman: 573, 958, 1457, 1459, 1579, 1670, 1975, 1979, 2004, 2334.

1823 • SILVER QUEEN

Sherman; United Artists. 1942.
Nominations *Black-and-White Interior Decoration:* Ralph Berger, art direction; Emile Kuri, set decoration. *Scoring of a Dramatic or Comedy Picture:* Victor Young.

Priscilla Lane, George Brent, and Bruce Cabot form a romantic triangle in this tale about Lane's attempt to recoup the fortune, including the deed to a silver mine, her father (Eugene Pallette) lost at gambling. Routine melodrama, directed by Lloyd Bacon. The art direction award went to *This Above All,* the scoring Oscar to Max Steiner for *Now, Voyager.*

Kuri: 4, 166, 363, 629, 894, 1284, 2155. Young: 97, 98, 100, 101, 280, 489, 612, 693, 701, 794, 846, 925, 1214, 1257, 1396, 1452, 1748, 1994, 2235, 2315.

1824 • SILVER STREAK

Frank Yablans Presentations Production; 20th Century-Fox. 1976.
Nomination *Sound:* Donald Mitchell, Douglas Williams, Richard Tyler, and Hal Etherington.

Book publisher Gene Wilder [1626 . . .] meets Jill Clayburgh [1919 . . .] on a train, where he witnesses the murder of a man who turns out to be her boss. With the help of a thief on the run, played by Richard Pryor, they solve the case, but not before getting stuck on the runaway train. This action comedy, written by Colin Higgins and directed by Arthur Hiller [1218], can't make up its mind whether it wants to go for thrills or romance or jokes, readily apparent in the unlikely casting of Wilder in a Cary Grant [1445 . . .] role. It was a big hit, however, and if you can put up with its illogical switchbacks, a lot of it is fun, especially the interplay of Wilder and Pryor in their first screen teaming. The cast includes Patrick McGoohan, Ned Beatty [1424], Ray Walston, Richard Kiel, and Fred Willard. The Oscar for sound went to *All the President's Men.*

Mitchell: 223, 398, 411.5, 507, 734.5, 779, 1525, 1650, 1825, 2020, 2114, 2176.5. Williams: 1541, 1726, 2152. Tyler: 215, 1548, 1877.

1825 • SILVERADO

COLUMBIA PICTURES PRODUCTION; COLUMBIA. 1985.
NOMINATIONS *Sound:* Donald O. Mitchell, Rick Kline, Kevin O'Connell, and David Ronne. *Original Score:* Bruce Broughton.

Kevin Kline [670] and Scott Glenn team up with Glenn's younger brother, Kevin Costner [482], and a black settler, Danny Glover, against a longtime foe of Kline's, Brian Dennehy, who has become sheriff of Silverado. Overlong, self-conscious, and choppy movie—some chunks of characterization and bits of plot, particularly where Rosanna Arquette is concerned, are probably on an editing-room floor somewhere. Nevertheless, what's left is often very entertaining, particularly Costner, who comes alive on screen for the first time—literally. In *The Big Chill* he was seen as the corpse, and to make up for it, director Lawrence Kasdan [6 . . .] gave him a big role in the next movie he directed. *Silverado* helped launch Costner to superstardom, but it didn't jumpstart the western back to life, as Kasdan had hoped. Some critics dubbed *Silverado* a "yuppie western" because of Kasdan's *Big Chill,* which also featured Kline and Jeff Goldblum, who plays a bad guy here. The cast includes Linda Hunt [2319], Joe Seneca, Lynn Whitfield, and Jeff Fahey. The screenplay is by Kasdan and his brother Mark, the cinematography by John Bailey. *Out of Africa* took the Oscars for sound and John Barry's score.

Mitchell: 223, 398, 411.5, 507, 734.5, 779, 1525, 1650, 1824, 2020, 2114, 2176.5. Kline: 507, 658.5, 1333, 2020, 2114. O'Connell: 223, 507, 586, 658.5, 2020, 2114. Ronne: 1473, 1701.

1826 • SIMPLE STORY, A

RENN PRODUCTIONS/SARA FILMS/F.R.3/RIALTO FILMS PRODUCTION (FRANCE). 1979.
NOMINATION *Foreign Language Film.*

Divorcée Romy Schneider, about to turn forty, discovers she is pregnant. She has an abortion and breaks up with her lover, Claude Brasseur. She tries to reconcile with her ex-husband and becomes pregnant again, but although he's not willing to come back to her permanently, she decides to bear the child. Interesting character study that might be called "Midlife Crisis, French Style." Directed by Claude Sautet. The Oscar went to *The Tin Drum.*

1827 • SIN OF MADELON CLAUDET, THE

MGM. 1931–32.
AWARD *Actress:* Helen Hayes.

Deserted by her lover, Madelon (Hayes) gives birth to his son and then must find ways to support the boy. She falls into bad company and is sent to prison; when she gets out, she finds the boy, whom she hasn't seen for ten years, tells him his mother is dead, and proceeds to raise him, even putting him through medical school, by turning to prostitution. Irresistible drivel, reluctantly adapted for Hayes' debut in talking pictures by her husband, Charles MacArthur [1664 . . .], from a 1924 Broadway play by Edward Knoblock. When the first version of the film, directed by Edgar Selwyn, was a disaster at the previews, producer Irving Thalberg [150 . . .] had about a third of it thrown out, rewritten, and replaced with new footage. The cast includes Lewis Stone [1540], Robert Young, Jean Hersholt, Karen Morley, Charles Winninger, and Alan Hale.

Hayes had been a stage actress since she was a child and had made a few silent films while she was in her teens. She had been a major Broadway star for more than a decade when she and MacArthur were lured to Hollywood because the advent of sound required both writers who could create dialogue and actors who could speak it. But Hayes was uncomfortable with filmmaking and dissatisfied with the roles presented to her, so after a few pictures, the best of which were *Arrowsmith* and *A Farewell to Arms,* she returned to the stage in 1935 and became one of the most famous and beloved actresses of the century. She made only occasional film appearances over the rest of her career, most notably in *Anastasia* and *Airport,* the film that won her a second Oscar thirty-eight years after the first.

Hayes: 31.

1828 • SINCE YOU WENT AWAY

SELZNICK INTERNATIONAL PICTURES; UNITED ARTISTS. 1944.
AWARD *Scoring of a Dramatic or Comedy Picture:* Max Steiner.
NOMINATIONS *Picture:* David O. Selznick, producer. *Actress:* Claudette Colbert. *Supporting Actor:* Monty Woolley. *Supporting Actress:* Jennifer Jones. *Black-and-White Cinematography:* Stanley Cortez and Lee Garmes. *Black-and-White Interior Decoration:* Mark-Lee Kirk, art direction; Victor A. Gangelin, set decoration. *Film Editing:* Hal C. Kern and James E. Newcom. *Special Effects:* John R. Cosgrove, photographic; Arthur Johns, sound.

Colbert plays Anne Hilton, left to manage a household that consists of two daughters, Jane (Jones) and Bridget (Shirley Temple), when her husband goes off to war. Joseph Cotten plays a bachelor who has always been in love with Anne, and Robert Walker is the young soldier with whom Jane falls in love. Highly accomplished sentimental portrait of the home front's fears, trials, and heartbreak, directed by John Cromwell with constant close supervision by Selznick, who also wrote the screenplay, based on a novel by Margaret Buell Wilder. The huge cast includes Lionel Barrymore [723 . . .], Hattie McDaniel [798], Agnes Moorehead [963 . . .], Guy Madison, Craig Stevens, Keenan Wynn, Albert Basserman [706], Nazimova, and Dorothy Dandridge [361]. It's hardly a great film, but it's an enduring sentimental portrait of an era. Ironically this tribute to family values was made by a man involved in breaking up two households: Selznick's affair with Jones put an end to both her marriage to Walker and the producer's own marriage to Irene Mayer Selznick.

This was the third Oscar for Steiner, who is said to have written the scores for more than 250 films in his career, which spanned more than thirty years, from the advent of sound to 1965. He died in 1971.

The best picture Oscar went to *Going My Way,* which also won for supporting actor Barry Fitzgerald. Colbert lost to Ingrid Bergman in *Gaslight,* which took the art direction Oscar as well. Ethel Barrymore won the supporting actress award for *None but the Lonely Heart.* Cortez—who had to leave the film for his own military service—and Garmes lost to Joseph LaShelle's cinematography for *Laura.* The Oscar for editing went to Barbara McLean for *Wilson,* and the special effects Oscar was won by *Thirty Seconds Over Tokyo.*

Steiner: 16, 154, 190, 330, 365, 385, 492, 679, 747, 754, 798, 999, 1043, 1046, 1052, 1162, 1169, 1170, 1207, 1324, 1408, 1430, 1456, 1690, 1779. Selznick: 497, 798, 1670, 1890, 1909, 1996, 2211. Colbert: 1025, 1623. Woolley: 1569. Jones: 584, 1213, 1214, 1868. Cortez: 1239. Garmes: 201, 1358, 1800. Kirk: 760, 1394. Gangelin: 2244. Kern: 798, 1670. Newcom: 87, 798, 2120. Cosgrove: 798, 1607, 1670, 1890. Johns: 798, 1670, 2310.

1829 • SING, BABY, SING

20TH CENTURY-FOX. 1936.
NOMINATION *Song:* "When Did You Leave Heaven," music by Richard A. Whiting, lyrics by Walter Bullock.

Shakespearean actor Adolphe Menjou [734] falls for nightclub singer Alice Faye in this musical takeoff on the relationship of John Barrymore and his fourth wife, Elaine Barrie. Directed by Sidney Lanfield from a script by Milton Sperling [453], Jack Yellen, and Harry Tugend. The cast includes Gregory Ratoff, Patsy Kelly, Tony Martin, and the Ritz Brothers. The song Oscar went to Jerome Kern and Dorothy Fields for "The Way You Look Tonight," from *Swing Time.*

Bullock: 920.

1830 • SING YOUR WAY HOME

RKO RADIO. 1945.
NOMINATION *Song:* "I'll Buy That Dream," music by Allie Wrubel, lyrics by Herb Magidson.

Shipboard musical with a low-wattage cast headed by Jack Haley and Anne Jeffreys. The director is Anthony Mann, who would go on to bigger and better things, including some of the finest westerns of the fifties: *Winchester '73, Bend of the River,* and *The Naked Spur.* The Oscar went to Richard Rodgers and Oscar Hammerstein II for "It Might As Well Be Spring," from *State Fair.*

Wrubel: 1871. Magidson: 754, 907.

1831 • SINGIN' IN THE RAIN

MGM. 1952.

NOMINATIONS *Supporting Actress:* Jean Hagen. *Scoring of a Musical Picture:* Lennie Hayton.

Don Lockwood, played by Gene Kelly [74], and Lina Lamont (Hagen) are the premier couple of silent movies, but the advent of sound threatens their careers—especially Lina's, since she has a voice that would curdle milk. After a disastrous preview of their first talkie, Don and his former vaudeville partner, Cosmo (Donald O'Connor), a studio musician, have an idea: turn the film into a musical and dub Lina's voice with that of Don's girlfriend, an aspiring actress named Kathy Selden, played by Debbie Reynolds [2184]. The picture is a big hit, but the shrewish Lina demands that Kathy be prevented from starting her own screen career and do nothing but provide her voice. Can Don and Cosmo find a way to thwart Lina? Fabulous musical with all its players in peak form, a rich and witty screenplay by Adolph Green [141 . . .] and Betty Comden [141 . . .], and a cornucopia of songs by Arthur Freed [66 . . .] and Nacio Herb Brown. Freed also produced, and the codirectors are Stanley Donen and Kelly. The cinematography is by Harold Rosson [105 . . .], and the cast includes Millard Mitchell, Rita Moreno [2244], Cyd Charisse, Madge Blake, King Donovan, and Kathleen Freeman. Since the plot hinges on the dubbing of voices, it's amusing to note that Reynolds' singing voice is dubbed by Betty Royce; it's also said that Hagen uses her own voice in the film-within-a-film sequence in which her dialogue is supposedly dubbed by Reynolds.

Today, *Singin' in the Rain* is the most celebrated of all Hollywood musicals, and it frequently turns up on critics' lists of the best films—musical and nonmusical—of all time. Kelly's glorious performance of the title tune is his finest moment on film, and O'Connor's "Make 'Em Laugh" number is a slapstick classic. (Freed and Brown wrote the song especially for the movie: its resemblance to the Cole Porter [261 . . .] song "Be a Clown," from *The Pirate,* which Freed also produced, is much too close for comfort, but Porter chose to ignore it.) The movie isn't even seriously harmed by its weakest section, the overextended "Broadway Rhythm" ballet, with a *pas de deux* by Kelly and Charisse that's at odds with the period style of the rest of the film. At the time, however, critics and audiences treated *Singin' in the Rain* as just another MGM musical—evidence that too rich a diet can dull the palate. *An American in Paris* had won the best picture Oscar the year before, and the studio chose to push its big historical costume drama, *Ivanhoe,* for best picture, bypassing both *Singin' in the Rain* and another satire on Hollywood, *The Bad and the Beautiful.* The latter film went on to win more Oscars than any other movie not nominated for best picture, but *Singin' in the Rain* was shut out of the awards.

Hagen had made her screen debut as the woman who breaks up Judy Holliday's home in *Adam's Rib,* and she pays homage to Holliday by modeling Lina Lamont's shrill nasality on the voice that won Holliday an Oscar in *Born Yesterday.* But aside from a solid performance in *The Asphalt Jungle* and the role that won her a nomination, Hagen found few parts in movies that suited her talents either as actress or as comedian. She is otherwise remembered as Danny Thomas' wife in the fifties sitcom *Make Room for Daddy.* She died in 1977 of throat cancer. The Oscar went to Gloria Grahame for *The Bad and the Beautiful.*

Alfred Newman won the scoring award for *With a Song in My Heart.*

Hayton: 877, 896, 1476, 1577, 1907.

1832 • SINGING GUNS

PALOMAR PICTURES CORPORATION; REPUBLIC. 1950.

NOMINATION *Song:* "Mule Train," music and lyrics by Fred Glickman, Hy Heath, and Johnny Lange.

Cowboy Vaughn Monroe has to battle for a gold mine that's rightfully his. Saturday matinee programmer, directed by R. G. Springsteen, with crooner Monroe trying to make it as a movie star. He didn't, even with the support of Ella Raines, Walter Brennan [424 . . .], Ward Bond, Jeff Corey, and Billy Gray. The film's only claim to fame is the hit song "Mule Train," which wasn't even Monroe's hit: Frankie Laine's version was the one that topped the charts.

The Oscar went to Ray Evans and Jay Livingston's "Mona Lisa," from *Captain Carey, USA.*

1833 • SINGING NUN, THE

MGM. 1966.
NOMINATION *Scoring of Music—Adaptation or Treatment:* Harry Sukman.

Sister Ann, played by Debbie Reynolds [2184], writes a hit song, "Dominique," and is confused by the worldly attention it attracts. Saccharine but calculated attempt to cash in on two huge phenomena: the blockbuster success of *The Sound of Music* and the unexpected (and inexplicable) success of "Dominique," a chart-topper composed by a Belgian nun called Soeur Sourire. For a while, cute nuns were everywhere, including TV, on which the series that Sally Field [1448 . . .] would like to forget, *The Flying Nun,* ran for three seasons. A lot of talent was wasted on this one: director Henry Koster [214], screenwriters Sally Benson [83] and John Furia, cinematographer Milton Krasner [21 . . .], and cast members Greer Garson [239 . . .], Ricardo Montalban, Agnes Moorehead [963 . . .], Chad Everett, Katharine Ross [810], Juanita Moore [984]—and Ed Sullivan as himself. The songs were by Soeur Sourire and Randy Sparks. The Oscar went to Ken Thorne for *A Funny Thing Happened on the Way to the Forum.*

Sukman: 643, 1873.

1834 • SISTER KENNY

RKO RADIO. 1946.
NOMINATION *Actress:* Rosalind Russell.

Russell plays the title role, the Australian nurse Elizabeth Kenny, who developed a controversial therapeutic treatment for polio. Conventional medicine of the day immobilized victims of the disease, but Kenny, working in remote areas of Australia where medical guidance was hard to come by, fought the paralysis with exercises designed to stimulate and retrain the muscles. Despite evidence of success, the medical establishment resisted Kenny's methods. In addition to playing Kenny, Russell became an ardent supporter of the Kenny treatment and a backer of the foundation that promoted her methods. The film has some of the clichés of the loner-against-the-establishment medical biopic genre, but Russell's conviction makes them believable, and she's well supported by Alexander Knox [2286], Dean Jagger [2154], and Beulah Bondi [807 . . .]. Dudley Nichols [30 . . .] directed, and cowrote the screenplay, based on Kenny's autobiography, with Knox and Mary McCarthy. Russell lost the second of her four unsuccessful tries at an Oscar to Olivia de Havilland in *To Each His Own.*

Russell: 110, 1364, 1403.

1835 • SITTING PRETTY

20TH CENTURY-FOX. 1948.
NOMINATION *Actor:* Clifton Webb.

A busy young couple, Robert Young and Maureen O'Hara, advertise for a nanny and are most impressed by the credentials they receive in the mail from Lynn Belvedere, whom they assume to be a sweet old lady. Mr. Belvedere (Webb) turns out to be neither a lady nor sweet—he's a genius, a snob, and a veritable whiz at bringing order out of the chaos of their household. But the town gossips, led by next-door neighbor Richard Haydn, are scandalized by his presence. Very amusing situation comedy that produced two sequels —*Mr. Belvedere Goes to College* (1949) and *Mr. Belvedere Rings the Bell* (1951), also starring Webb—and, a generation later, the inevitable TV sitcom. Directed by Walter Lang [1088] from a screenplay by F. Hugh Herbert based on a novel by Gwen Davenport. The cast includes Louise Allbritton and Ed Begley [1985]. Webb's acerbic manner and fine comic timing are wonderful, but was his Lynn Belvedere really more deserving of a nomination than Humphrey Bogart's unforgettable Fred C. Dobbs in *The Treasure of the Sierra Madre?* Or John Wayne's driven Tom Dunson in *Red River?* Or Henry Fonda's martinet Colonel Thursday in *Fort Apache?* Anyway, the Oscar went to Laurence Olivier for *Hamlet.*

Webb: 1149, 1666.

1835.5 • SIX DEGREES OF SEPARATION

METRO-GOLDWYN-MAYER PRODUCTION; MGM/UNITED ARTISTS. 1993.

NOMINATION *Actress:* Stockard Channing.

Channing and Donald Sutherland play a pretentious New York couple whose lives are changed when a young black con artist (Will Smith) shows up at their apartment one evening, claiming to be a mugging victim, a classmate of their children's at Harvard, and the son of Sidney Poitier [522 . . .]. Amusing if sometimes rather arch satire on Manhattan manners and racial attitudes, adapted by John Guare [107] from his Broadway play and shrewdly directed by Fred Schepisi, who manages to give the film some visual oomph but can't do much about its talkiness. The cast includes Mary Beth Hurt, Bruce Davison [1203], Anthony Michael Hall, Richard Masur, and Ian McKellen.

Channing began acting as a student at Radcliffe in the sixties, performing on Harvard's stages with fellow students John Lithgow [2020 . . .] and Tommy Lee Jones [734.5 . . .]. She made her film debut in a small role in *The Hospital* and won her first leading role opposite Warren Beatty [255 . . .] and Jack Nicholson [395 . . .] under the direction of Mike Nichols [810 . . .] in *The Fortune* (1975). Unfortunately that film, despite the constellation of talent, was a flop, and though she gave a standout performance as Rizzo in the blockbuster *Grease,* Channing was unable to establish herself as a star in films. Broadway was another matter, however, and she has become one of the New York stage's most sought-after performers. She created the part of Ouisa Kittredge in the original Broadway production of *Six Degrees of Separation.* The Oscar went to Holly Hunter for *The Piano.*

1836 • SKIPPY

PARAMOUNT PUBLIX. 1930–31.

AWARD *Director:* Norman Taurog.

NOMINATIONS *Picture:* Adolph Zukor, studio head. *Actor:* Jackie Cooper. *Adaptation:* Joseph L. Mankiewicz and Sam Mintz.

In the title role ten-year-old Cooper, a middle-class kid, teams up with a boy from the slums to try to make money to buy a license for the slum kid's dog. A pleasant antique, based on a popular comic strip of the day now remembered mainly for the eponymous peanut butter.

Taurog's rapport with child actors may come from having been one himself; he entered movies as a teenager and became a director at the age of twenty, in 1919. He worked primarily on short subjects until the advent of sound, when he moved into features, working steadily until 1968, directing countless light entertainments at Paramount and MGM, including vehicles for Dean Martin and Jerry Lewis—*The Stooge* (1953), *The Caddy, Living It Up* (1954)—and Elvis Presley—*G.I. Blues* (1960), *Blue Hawaii* (1961), *Girls! Girls! Girls!* (1962). He died in 1981.

Cooper, who was Taurog's nephew, is one of the most successful former child stars in the history of the movies, with a career that spans more than half a century. He appeared in the Our Gang series of the late twenties and worked steadily in features until World War II. After his career as an actor began to fade in the late forties, he worked on stage and then moved into TV as actor, director, and producer. In recent years he returned to movies to play Perry White in the *Superman* films. The Oscar went to Lionel Barrymore for *A Free Soul.*

The best picture Oscar was won by *Cimarron,* which also took the award for Howard Estabrook's screenplay.

Taurog: 271. Zukor: 649, 1800. Mankiewicz: 46, 146, 673, 1163, 1444, 1563, 1841.

1837 • SKYLARK

PARAMOUNT. 1941.

NOMINATION *Sound Recording:* Loren Ryder.

Feeling neglected by workaholic husband Ray Milland [1208], Claudette Colbert [1025 . . .] heads for Reno, where she flirts with Brian Aherne [1064] and gets somewhat more attention than she wanted. Agreeable romantic comedy, even if you know what's going to happen. Mark Sandrich directs this adaptation of a play by Samson Raphaelson, with Binnie

Barnes and Walter Abel. The sound award went to Jack Whitney for *That Hamilton Woman*.

Ryder: 566, 827, 979, 1452, 1669, 1697, 1703, 1887, 2012, 2168, 2181, 2183, 2230, 2242.

1838 • SKY'S THE LIMIT, THE

RKO Radio. 1943.

NOMINATIONS *Song:* "My Shining Hour," music by Harold Arlen, lyrics by Johnny Mercer. *Scoring of a Musical Picture:* Leigh Harline.

Flying ace Fred Astaire [2126] falls in love with Joan Leslie while on leave, but realizing that the war makes permanent relationships impossible, he breaks up with her. Robert Benchley brings about a bittersweet reconciliation as Astaire flies off to war at the film's end. More somber than most of Astaire's musicals, it climaxes with an unusual dramatic dance number by Astaire to Arlen-Mercer's "One for My Baby," in which a remorseful, drunken Astaire smashes the glassware in a bar. Directed by Edward H. Griffith from a screenplay by Frank Fenton and Lynn Root. The cast also features Robert Ryan [467] and Elizabeth Patterson.

In addition to "My Shining Hour," Arlen had two more songs in the running in 1943: "Happiness Is Just a Thing Called Joe," from *Cabin in the Sky*, with lyrics by E. Y. Harburg, and "That Old Black Magic," which had lyrics by Mercer, from *Star Spangled Rhythm*. The Oscar went to Harry Warren and Mack Gordon's "You'll Never Know," from *Hello, Frisco, Hello*. The scoring award went to Ray Heindorf for *This Is the Army*.

Arlen: 248, 322, 368, 903, 1910, 1912, 2186, 2300. Mercer: 248, 278, 384, 476, 494, 636, 788, 825, 877, 903, 905, 1109, 1772, 1912, 2328. Harline: 1053, 1576, 1607, 1851, 2312, 2327.

1838.5 • SKYSCRAPER

DeMille Pictures; Pathé. 1928–29.

NOMINATION *Writing Achievement:* Elliott Clawson.

William Boyd, Alan Hale, and the future wife of Alan Ladd, Sue Carol, star in a silent melodrama directed by Howard Higgin; the film has apparently disappeared. The screenplay was apparently cowritten with Tay Garnett, but only Clawson received recognition from the Academy, and even that was unofficial: The Academy announced only the winners this year —in this case, Hans Kräly for *The Patriot*. Names of the runners-up were preserved by the writers branch.

Clawson: 443.5, 1152, 1740.5.

1839 • SLEEPING BEAUTY

Walt Disney Productions; Buena Vista. 1959.

NOMINATION *Scoring of a Musical Picture:* George Bruns.

The wicked fairy Maleficent (voice of Eleanor Audley) puts a curse on the Princess Aurora (voice of Mary Costa): On her sixteenth birthday, the princess will prick her finger on a spinning wheel and die. Despite the efforts of the good fairies Flora, Fauna, and Merryweather (voiced by Verna Felton, Barbara Jo Allen, and Barbara Luddy), the curse—somewhat mitigated by their magic, which puts Aurora and her kingdom into a deep slumber—is fulfilled. But Prince Philip (voiced by Bill Shirley) comes to the rescue. Handsome Disney animated feature whose box-office failure marks the end of the golden age of Disney animation that began a little over two decades earlier with *Snow White and the Seven Dwarfs*. Actually the animated features had been secondary products at Disney for much of the fifties, as the studio moved into live-action films and theme park development, but *Sleeping Beauty* was an ambitious attempt to reenter the field, with the biggest budget and longest production schedule of any of the cartoon films. It was done in a wide-screen process with stereophonic sound, using elaborate production design and a complicated blend of "rotoscoping" (superimposing cartoon images on live-action footage) and conventional animation. The musical score, for once, was not original; it was based on Tchaikovsky's ballet music with words supplied by various lyricists. There's a terrific final battle in which Philip contends with Maleficent, who has turned herself into a dragon, but the rest of the film lacks the comedy of the early features—the plump little good fairies are only mildly amusing. Disney animation would not fully recover from the failure of *Sleeping Beauty* until *The Little Mermaid* launched a new era of Disney supremacy thirty years later. The scoring Oscar went to André Previn and Ken Darby for *Porgy and Bess*.

Bruns: 116, 1709, 1992.

1839.5 • *SLEEPLESS IN SEATTLE*

TRISTAR PICTURES PRODUCTION; TRISTAR. 1993.
NOMINATIONS *Screenplay Written Directly for the Screen:* Nora Ephron, David S. Ward, and Jeff Arch, screenplay; Jeff Arch, story. *Song:* "A Wink and a Smile," music by Marc Shaiman, lyrics by Ramsey McLean.

After the death of his wife, Sam Baldwin, played by Tom Hanks [195 . . .], has moved to Seattle with his young son, Jonah (Ross Malinger), in an attempt to start a new life in a place without so many painful memories. But Sam's restlessness and insomnia disturb Jonah, who one evening places a phone call to a radio-talk-show therapist to try to help his dad. Sam winds up on the phone, and millions of people across the country hear his touching story of how deeply he loved his wife. One of them is Annie Reed (Meg Ryan), who lives in Baltimore and is engaged to a man (Bill Pullman) she wants to be in love with but really isn't. She's haunted by Sam's story and eventually, after a whole film full of false starts, they wind up meeting on top of the Empire State Building—the way Cary Grant and Deborah Kerr were supposed to in *An Affair to Remember*. A charmingly old-fashioned romantic comedy filtered through modern attitudes toward sex and psychology and media phenomena like talk shows and videotape. The two stars—who are together for only a few minutes of screen time—are brimful of charm, and are nicely supported by Rosie O'Donnell as her confidant and Rob Reiner [658.5] as his. Ephron also directed, and the plushy cinematography of Sven Nykvist [460 . . .] gives the whole thing a touch of moonglow. The screenplay Oscar went to Jane Campion for *The Piano*. The best song was Bruce Springsteen's "Streets of Philadelphia," from *Philadelphia*.

Ephron: 1821, 2255. Ward: 1927.

1840 • *SLENDER THREAD, THE*

PARAMOUNT. 1965.
NOMINATIONS *Black-and-White Art Direction—Set Decoration:* Hal Pereira and Jack Poplin; Robert Benton and Joseph Kish. *Black-and-White Costume Design:* Edith Head.

Sidney Poitier [522 . . .] is a suicide-hot-line worker who takes a call from Anne Bancroft [28 . . .] and tries to keep her on the line while rescue workers locate her. The film's premise is slender, too—more suited for a one-hour TV drama than a full-length movie with prestigious stars attached. Sydney Pollack [1512 . . .], a veteran of one-hour TV dramas, makes his feature film directing debut, working from a screenplay by Stirling Silliphant [992]. The supporting cast includes Telly Savalas [210], Steven Hill, Edward Asner, and Dabney Coleman. The score is by Quincy Jones [144 . . .]. *Ship of Fools* won for art direction. The costuming Oscar went to Julie Harris for *Darling*.

Pereira: 278, 357, 363, 426, 450, 736, 956, 1029, 1219, 1504, 1570, 1631, 1674, 1716, 1727, 1738, 1897, 1959, 2012, 2098, 2200, 2208. Benton: 69, 956, 1504. Kish: 13, 1048, 1062, 1812. Head: 31, 32, 46, 305, 357, 363, 612, 636, 675, 736, 832, 894, 945, 1003, 1219, 1261, 1263, 1398, 1427, 1504, 1550, 1579, 1587, 1631, 1716, 1727, 1738, 1748, 1927, 1986, 2012, 2098, 2247, 2298.

1841 • *SLEUTH*

PALOMAR PICTURES INTERNATIONAL PRODUCTION; 20TH CENTURY-FOX (UNITED KINGDOM). 1972.
NOMINATIONS *Actor:* Michael Caine. *Actor:* Laurence Olivier. *Director:* Joseph L. Mankiewicz. *Original Dramatic Score:* John Addison.

A wealthy, snobbish mystery writer (Olivier) devises a plot to get even with his wife's lover (Caine), but his adversary is more than a match for him. An amusingly intricate stage play becomes an overextended showcase for two superb actors—the film's entire cast. It should be better, and the fault lies in part with Anthony Shaffer's adaptation of his play, which runs to the pretentious. The cinematography is by Oswald Morris [659 . . .]. Marlon Brando won the acting Oscar for *The Godfather*. This was Mankiewicz's last work as a director, and he lost to Bob Fosse for *Cabaret*. Addison's score had not been included among the original five nominees, but when the Academy discovered that one of those nominees, the score by Nino Rota [2] for *The Godfather,* included music that had been used in an earlier film, Rota was declared ineligible. The music branch took a vote to come up with a replacement nominee, which turned out to be Addison's score. The scoring award went to Charles Chaplin, Raymond Rasch, and Larry Russell for the twenty-year-old *Limelight,* just now meeting eligibility requirements for the Oscar.

Caine: 35, 598, 863. Olivier: 268, 619, 858, 901, 1272, 1506, 1670, 1693, 2316. Mankiewicz: 46, 146, 673, 1163, 1444, 1563, 1836. Addison: 2106.

1842 • SLIPPER AND THE ROSE—THE STORY OF CINDERELLA, THE

PARADINE CO-PRODUCTIONS LTD.; UNIVERSAL (UNITED KINGDOM). 1977.

NOMINATIONS *Original Song:* "The Slipper and the Rose Waltz (He Danced With Me/She Danced With Me)," music and lyrics by Richard M. Sherman and Robert B. Sherman. *Original Song Score and Its Adaptation or Adaptation Score:* Richard M. Sherman, Robert B. Sherman, and Angela Morley.

Gemma Craven is Cinderella and Richard Chamberlain her prince in this okay family musical, which didn't make the impact at the box office its producers (David Frost and Stuart Lyons) hoped it would. Directed by Bryan Forbes, who wrote the screenplay with the Sherman brothers. The cast includes Annette Crosbie, Michael Hordern, Christopher Gable, Kenneth More, and Edith Evans [377 . . .]. The best song Oscar went to Joseph Brooks' title tune from *You Light Up My Life.* Jonathan Tunick won the scoring award for *A Little Night Music.*

R. M. Sherman: 166, 396, 1238, 1284, 2107. R. B. Sherman: 166, 396, 1238, 1284, 2107. Morley: 1186.

1843 • SMALL TOWN GIRL

MGM. 1953.

NOMINATION *Song:* "My Flaming Heart," music by Nicholas Brodszky, lyrics by Leo Robin.

Jane Powell makes a play for city slicker Farley Granger, who has been arrested by her father, the sheriff, for speeding through their town. Minor MGM musical with some big production numbers, directed by Busby Berkeley [791 . . .], thrown in. Leslie Kardos directed the more forgettable part of the film, and the cast includes Ann Miller, S. Z. Sakall, Billie Burke, Nat King Cole, and Bobby Van, who does an amazingly goofy specialty number in which he literally bounces around the town. The best song was "Secret Love," by Sammy Fain and Paul Francis Webster, from *Calamity Jane.*

Brodszky: 163, 1216, 1692, 2103. Robin: 104, 197, 368, 846, 1072, 1805, 2032, 2088, 2310.

1844 • SMART MONEY

WARNER BROS. 1930–31.

NOMINATION *Original Story:* Lucien Hubbard and Joseph Jackson.

Small-town barber Edward G. Robinson goes to the city looking for gambling action, accompanied by his friend James Cagney [79 . . .]. They hit the big time but have a fatal disagreement after Cagney unmasks a girlfriend of Robinson's as a police informer. Modest film that is the only teaming of the movies' most famous gangsters. Directed by Alfred E. Green. The writing Oscar went to John Monk Saunders for *The Dawn Patrol.*

Hubbard: 1917, 2290.

1845 • SMASH UP—THE STORY OF A WOMAN

WALTER WANGER; UNIVERSAL-INTERNATIONAL. 1947.

NOMINATIONS *Actress:* Susan Hayward. *Original Story:* Dorothy Parker and Frank Cavett.

Hayward plays an aspiring young singer who marries another singer, Lee Bowman, and helps him build his career, giving up her chance at stardom when their child is born. As he becomes famous and wealthy, she grows bored with staying home and begins to drink. Her alcoholism breaks up their marriage, and she's unable to restart her singing career. She hits bottom but is redeemed when she rescues her child—whom Bowman has kept because she's an unfit mother—from a fire. Rather plodding melodrama, with the usual career vs. marriage dilemma (always the woman's problem, of course, never the man's) worked out according to formula. Directed by Stuart Heisler and filmed by Stanley Cortez [1239 . . .], with Marsha Hunt and Eddie Albert [887 . . .]. Hayward lost her first try at the Oscar to Loretta Young in *The Farmer's Daughter*. John Howard Lawson [233] did the screenplay from Parker and Cavett's not-very-original story (it's derived from, among other things, *A Star Is Born*, on which Parker had worked, and is indebted to *The Lost Weekend*, which had made alcoholism a hot topic for the movies). The Oscar went to Valentine Davies for *Miracle on 34th Street*.

Hayward: 973, 980, 1396, 2294. Parker: 1909. Cavett: 787, 832.

1846 • SMILIN' THROUGH

MGM. 1932–33.

NOMINATION *Picture:* Irving Thalberg, producer.

On his wedding day Leslie Howard [178 . . .] loses his bride, played by Norma Shearer [150 . . .], when she is accidentally killed by an embittered suitor, played by Fredric March [184 . . .], who then flees from prosecution. Howard remains single for the next fifty years, devoted to the memory of the wife he lost. But then he agrees to be the ward of an orphaned niece—who looks just like the dead woman and is, of course, played by Shearer. Devoted to this young woman, who seems to restore to him what he lost so long ago, he is horrified when she falls in love with the son of the man who caused his wife's death, also played by March. He forbids them to see one another, and March goes off to serve in World War I. But the ghost of the dead wife appears to Howard and persuades him to let bygones be bygones. All-stops-out sentimental chestnut, from a play by Jane Cowl and Jane Murfin that had been filmed with Norma Talmadge in 1922 and got another going-over in

1941, with Jeanette MacDonald. This one has all the virtues of a Thalberg showpiece for Shearer: Cedric Gibbons [66 . . .] sets, Adrian gowns, Lee Garmes [201 . . .] cinematography—it looks yummy, but it's just empty calories. Sidney Franklin [799 . . .] directed, and the screenplay is by Ernest Vajda, Claudine West [804 . . .], Donald Ogden Steward [1148 . . .], and Bernard Fagan. The best picture Oscar went to *Cavalcade*.

Thalberg: 150, 202, 799, 812, 1387, 1721, 2129.

1847 • SMILING LIEUTENANT, THE

PARAMOUNT PUBLIX. 1931–32.

NOMINATION *Picture:* Ernst Lubitsch, producer.

Ruritanian princess Miriam Hopkins [165], who is a bit of a frump, is irked because the title character, played by Maurice Chevalier [203 . . .], is more interested in Claudette Colbert [1025 . . .] than in her, so she determines to marry him and no one else. Finally Colbert takes pity on her and does a makeover that gets Chevalier's attention. Amusingly frivolous musical directed by Lubitsch, who also wrote the screenplay in collaboration with Ernest Vajda and Samson Raphaelson; it's based on a novel by Hans Muller and the operetta *The Waltz Dream*. The songs, by Oscar Straus and Clifford Grey, serve the plot but don't linger in the memory. There are plenty of pre–Production Code innuendoes, in the Lubitsch manner, and Colbert, who plays the leader of an all-girl orchestra, is so sexy it's scarcely credible when she doesn't wind up with Chevalier at the end. The cast also includes Charles Ruggles, George Barbier, and Elizabeth Patterson. The best picture Oscar went to *Grand Hotel*.

Lubitsch: 889, 1217, 1484, 1540.

1848 • SMOKEY AND THE BANDIT

UNIVERSAL-RASTAR PRODUCTION; UNIVERSAL. 1977.

NOMINATION *Film Editing:* Walter Hannemann and Angelo Ross.

Burt Reynolds is the Bandit, a good-ol'-boy who, while trying to win a racing bet and deliver some bootleg beer, picks up a runaway bride, played by Sally Field [1448 . . .], only to discover that the father of the man she's supposed to marry is a sheriff, played by Jackie Gleason [964]. A bonehead classic, directed by former stuntman Hal Needham, that's the car-chase movie to end all car-chase movies, but unfortunately it didn't. It made zillions of dollars and turned Reynolds into the No. 1 box-office star—a position he was unable to maintain, partly because he got stuck in too many bad imitations of this movie. The screenplay is by James Lee Barrett, Charles Shyer [1617], and Alan Mandel. The editing award went to Paul Hirsch, Marcia Lucas, and Richard Chew for *Star Wars*.

Hannemann: 2163.

1849 • SNAKE PIT, THE

20TH CENTURY-FOX. 1948.

AWARD *Sound Recording:* Thomas T. Moulton, 20th Century-Fox Sound Department.

NOMINATIONS *Picture:* Anatole Litvak and Robert Bassler, producers. *Actress:* Olivia de Havilland. *Director:* Anatole Litvak. *Screenplay:* Frank Partos and Millen Brand. *Scoring of a Dramatic or Comedy Picture:* Alfred Newman.

De Havilland suffers a severe mental breakdown and is sent to a grim, primitive mental institution from which she is finally rescued by psychoanalyst Leo Genn [1644], who helps her come to terms with some unresolved feelings about her father. Well-produced message picture, based on a novel by Mary Jane Ward, from the late-forties era when Hollywood's idea of a prestige production was one that tackled—or at least feinted at—a social problem: alcoholism (*The Lost Weekend*), anti-Semitism (*Gentleman's Agreement*), racism (*Pinky*), or in this case, the treatment of the mentally ill. The quick-fix therapy and the squeamishness of the Production Code date the film badly, but de Havilland's performance is impressive. The cast also includes Mark Stevens, Celeste Holm [46 . . .], Leif Erickson, Beulah Bondi [807 . . .], Lee Patrick, Natalie Schafer, Frank Conroy, and Betsy Blair [1283].

The best picture Oscar went to *Hamlet*. Jane Wyman won the best actress award for *Johnny Belinda*. John Huston took both the directing Oscar and the screenplay award for *The Treasure of the Sierra Madre*. Brian Easdale won for the score of *The Red Shoes*.

Moulton: 22, 46, 138, 366, 457, 487, 560, 706, 798, 962, 1153, 1200, 1451, 1510, 1607, 2154, 2294. Litvak: 517. De Havilland: 798, 894, 925, 2099. Newman: 31, 34, 46, 72, 138, 182, 226, 333, 334, 347, 375, 428, 437, 457, 476, 495, 542, 690, 797, 833, 952, 953, 959, 962, 1016, 1082, 1088, 1213, 1278, 1362, 1397, 1475, 1616, 1655, 1868, 1883, 1921, 2043, 2046, 2091, 2258, 2286, 2294, 2316.

1850 • SNIPER, THE

STANLEY KRAMER PRODUCTIONS; COLUMBIA. 1952.

NOMINATION *Motion Picture Story:* Edna Anhalt and Edward Anhalt.

San Francisco police detective Adolphe Menjou [734] tries to track down a man who's gunning down women. Arthur Franz is the killer and Marie Windsor is among his victims. Good stop-him-before-he-kills-again manhunt flick, crisply directed by Edward Dmytryk [467] from a screenplay by Harry Brown [1579 . . .]. Filmed in a documentary style by Burnett Guffey [210 . . .]. The Oscar went to Frederic M. Frank, Theodore St. John, and Frank Cavett for *The Greatest Show on Earth*.

Edna Anhalt: 1523. Edward Anhalt: 164, 1523.

1851 • SNOW WHITE AND THE SEVEN DWARFS

WALT DISNEY PRODUCTIONS; RKO RADIO. 1937.

AWARD *Special Award:* Walt Disney, for *Snow White and the Seven Dwarfs*, recognized as a significant screen innovation which has charmed millions and pioneered a great new entertainment field for the motion picture cartoon. (1938)

NOMINATION *Score:* Walt Disney Studio Music Department, Leigh Harline, head; score by Frank Churchill, Leigh Harline, and Paul J. Smith.

A wicked queen (voice of Lucille La Verne) consults her magic mirror (voice of Moroni Olsen) and discovers that she's no longer the fairest in the land. So she arranges to have the beautiful young Snow White (voice of Adriana Caselotti) murdered. The girl, however, charms the Huntsman (voice of Stuart Buchanan) commissioned to kill her and is abandoned in a forest, where she takes refuge in the home of seven dwarfs. (Roy Atwell is the voice of Doc, Otis Harlan is Happy, Scotty Mattraw is Bashful, Billy Gilbert is Sneezy, and Pinto Colvig does both Sleepy and Grumpy; the seventh, Dopey, is mute.) With the aid of the dwarfs, a heroic young prince (voice of Harry Stockwell) rescues Snow White after the queen discovers the girl is still alive, disguises herself as an old crone, and presents the girl with a poisoned apple. One of Hollywood's landmarks, right up there with *The Birth of a Nation* and *The Jazz Singer* as a definitive event in the history of an industry. It was the first commercially successful feature-length animated cartoon, and although it was neither the first Technicolor feature nor even the first color cartoon, its use of color to affect mood and create the tone of scenes was enormously influential. It also established the Disney studios as an enduring force in the industry. (*Snow White* was the first Disney film distributed by RKO. Up to this point, Disney had worked through United Artists, but that studio wanted him to sign over the television rights to the films. Even though TV would not be commercially viable for more than a decade, Disney was prescient in realizing that he could become a player in the new medium. RKO distributed Disney's films until 1953, when the Disney studios formed their own distribution company, Buena Vista.) *Snow White* also created the enduring formula for Disney features: a classic tale, populated with memorable comic characters, featuring at least one moment of hair-raising terror and lots of hummable songs. (The omission from the best song competition of *Snow White*'s songs by Churchill and Larry Morey [140 . . .], including "Heigh Ho," "Whistle While You Work," and "Someday My Prince Will Come," is hard to explain.) The Disney animated-feature formula would work like a charm for another decade or so, resulting in what some call a golden age of Disney animation, including *Pinocchio, Fantasia, Bambi, Dumbo,* and *Cinderella.* In the early fifties, however, as the studio ventured into live-action films, nature films, television, and amusement parks, the

animated feature declined. *Sleeping Beauty,* an expensive attempt to revive it in 1959, was also a failure, and despite occasional features throughout the sixties, seventies, and eighties, animation did not become a major Disney project again until the success of *The Little Mermaid* in 1989 and the subsequent blockbusters *Beauty and the Beast, Aladdin,* and *The Lion King.* The advent of videotape, meanwhile, helped keep the classics of the golden age alive, especially with Disney's shrewd policy of releasing the films on tape for a limited period only. *Snow White* was the one treasure kept back from video until late in 1994.

Snow White had its premiere in December 1937 but did not go into general release until February 1938. It was, therefore, eligible for the 1937 Oscars, losing its sole nomination to *One Hundred Men and a Girl,* whose star, Deanna Durbin, had been one of the singers considered and rejected for the voice of Snow White. The extent of the *Snow White* phenomenon wasn't apparent at the time of the 1937 awards, but by the time the 1938 awards were given out, the movie had grossed more than $8 million. (It cost $1.5 million to make.) At the 1938 awards ceremony, Disney received an honorary Oscar flanked by seven miniature Oscars, and before his death in 1966 would receive more awards from the Academy than any other person. His first had been for the cartoon short *Flowers and Trees* at the 1931–32 awards, at which he also received his first honorary Oscar, for the creation of Mickey Mouse. In addition to Oscars as producer of cartoons, live-action shorts, and documentaries, he also received the Irving G. Thalberg Award at the 1941 ceremonies, plus another special award for *Fantasia.* The four awards he received at the 1953 ceremonies—for the cartoon *Toot, Whistle, Plunk and Boom,* the short film *Bear Country,* the documentary short *The Alaskan Eskimo,* and the documentary feature *The Living Desert*—set a record for Oscars won by a person at a single ceremony. Disney detractors point out that these Oscars, like the others presented to him, went to a studio executive, not to the creative personnel who actually worked on the films. Disney supporters retort that it took Walt Disney's vision to get the films made.

Disney: 645, 1284. Harline: 1053, 1576, 1607, 1838, 2312, 2327. Churchill: 140, 585. Smith: 402, 1553, 1576, 1745, 1871, 2071, 2202.

1852 • SNOWS OF KILIMANJARO, THE

20TH CENTURY-FOX. 1952.

NOMINATIONS *Color Cinematography:* Leon Shamroy. *Color Art Direction—Set Decoration:* Lyle Wheeler and John DeCuir; Thomas Little and Paul S. Fox.

Gregory Peck [759 . . .] plays a writer who is wounded while on safari in Africa. As he and his wife, played by Susan Hayward [973 . . .], wait for help, he recalls the past and the events that have caused tension in their marriage. Tedious, overproduced film centered in the Ernest Hemingway story that gives it a title, but with bits and pieces collected from other Hemingway works by screenwriter Casey Robinson. Peck's nice-guy image works against him in the role of a Hemingway stalwart. The cast includes Ava Gardner [1339], Hildegarde Neff, Leo G. Carroll, Torin Thatcher, and Marcel Dalio. Directed by Henry King [1868 . . .], with a score by Bernard Herrmann [50 . . .]. The cinematography Oscar went to Winton C. Hoch and Archie Stout for *The Quiet Man.* Paul Sheriff and Marcel Vertes won for the art direction of *Moulin Rouge.*

Shamroy: 29, 226, 356, 413, 495, 569, 602, 1088, 1153, 1213, 1592, 1610, 1706, 1883, 2013, 2286, 2334. Wheeler: 19, 46, 83, 356, 376, 428, 476, 495, 530, 542, 719, 721, 798, 950, 1062, 1088, 1149, 1153, 1213, 1391, 1475, 1601, 1616, 1670, 1706, 2008, 2093, 2212. DeCuir: 29, 201, 376, 413, 476, 896, 950, 1088, 1391, 2000. Little: 46, 83, 235, 428, 495, 719, 721, 746, 950, 952, 1082, 1149, 1153, 1397, 1475, 1666, 1868, 2056, 2212, 2286. Fox: 376, 413, 428, 476, 495, 530, 721, 950, 1088, 1601, 1666, 1706.

1853 • SO DEAR TO MY HEART

WALT DISNEY PRODUCTIONS; RKO RADIO. 1949.

NOMINATION *Song:* "Lavender Blue," music by Eliot Daniel, lyrics by Larry Morey.

Bobby Driscoll plays a farm boy who raises a black sheep that constantly gets into mischief. The film is more memorable for the animated inserts that preach the morals of the story than for the live-action sections, directed by Harold Schuster. It's an obvious attempt to repeat the success of the more entertaining *The Song of the South,* which also blended animation with live action and likewise starred Driscoll and Luanna Patten, but was less preachy and cloyingly nostalgic. The cast includes Burl Ives [200], Beulah Bondi [807 . . .], and Harry Carey. Adapted by John Tucker Battle from a novel by Sterling North. Driscoll received an honorary Oscar as "outstanding juvenile actor" for his work in this film and the same year's *The Window.* The song Oscar went to Frank Loesser for "Baby, It's Cold Outside," from *Neptune's Daughter.*

Daniel: 795. Morey: 140.

1854 • SO ENDS OUR NIGHT

LOEW-LEWIN; UNITED ARTISTS. 1941.

NOMINATION *Scoring of a Dramatic Picture:* Louis Gruenberg.

German officer Fredric March [184 . . .], unwilling to serve the Nazis, is pursued by their agents across Europe. Fine, serious drama adapted by Talbot Jennings [83 . . .] from a novel by Erich Maria Remarque. Directed by John Cromwell, with Margaret Sullavan [2073], Frances Dee, Glenn Ford, Anna Sten, and Erich von Stroheim [1975]. The production design is by William Cameron Menzies [38 . . .] and the cinematography by William Daniels [84 . . .]. The scoring award went to Bernard Herrmann for *All That Money Can Buy.*

Gruenberg: 432, 664.

1855 • SO PROUDLY WE HAIL!

PARAMOUNT. 1943.

NOMINATIONS *Supporting Actress:* Paulette Goddard. *Original Screenplay:* Allan Scott. *Black-and-White Cinematography:* Charles Lang. *Special Effects:* Farciot Edouart and Gordon Jennings, photographic; George Dutton, sound.

Army nurses Claudette Colbert [1025 . . .], Goddard, Veronica Lake, and Barbara Britton save lives and lose a few of their own, too, in the Pacific during World War II. This sincere tribute to war nurses occasionally gets smarmy and condescending but is entertaining if you can make allowances for the time and place in which it was made. Mark Sandrich directed, and the cast includes George Reeves, Walter Abel, and Sonny Tufts.

Goddard was a former Ziegfeld Girl who became a star under the patronage of Charles Chaplin [405 . . .], whom she married; he starred her in *Modern Times* and *The Great Dictator.* She gave her best performances in *The Women* (1939), *North West Mounted Police, Hold Back the Dawn,* and *Reap the Wild Wind,* but narrowly lost the role that might have made her a legend: Scarlett O'Hara in *Gone With the Wind.* Her career ended in the mid-fifties, except for an appearance in an Italian movie in 1964 and a made-for-TV movie, *The Snoop Sisters,* in 1972. She died in 1990. The Oscar went to Katina Paxinou for *For Whom the Bell Tolls.*

The writing award went to Norman Krasna for *Princess O'Rourke.* Arthur Miller won for the cinematography for *The Song of Bernadette,* and the special effects award went to Fred Sersen and Roger Heman for *Crash Dive.*

Lang: 97, 250, 319, 636, 649, 705, 765, 953, 1480, 1640, 1699, 1738, 1778, 1860, 1955, 1968, 2180. Edouart: 56, 570, 975, 1668, 1887, 1934, 2168, 2175, 2181. Jennings: 56, 570, 975, 1668, 1887, 1934, 2168, 2175, 2181. Dutton: 847, 1934, 2175, 2200.

1856 • SO THIS IS WASHINGTON

VOTION; RKO RADIO. 1943.
NOMINATION *Sound Recording:* J. L. Fields, RCA Sound.

Long-forgotten programmer featuring a popular radio comedy team of the day, Lum and Abner (Chester Lauk and Norris Goff), who go to Washington to try to establish a patent for a rubber substitute. With Alan Mowbray and Minerva Urecal. The Oscar went to Stephen Dunn for *This Land Is Mine.*

Fields: 793.

1857 • SOLDIER'S STORY, A

CALDIX FILMS PRODUCTION; COLUMBIA. 1984.
NOMINATIONS *Picture:* Norman Jewison, Ronald L. Schwary, and Patrick Palmer, producers. *Supporting Actor:* Adolph Caesar. *Screenplay Based on Material From Another Medium:* Charles Fuller.

An army attorney, Captain Davenport, played by Howard E. Rollins, Jr. [1651], is sent to an all-black army camp in Louisiana to investigate the murder of a martinet drill sergeant (Caesar). In flashbacks we learn how the sergeant's expressions of contempt for the country-boy draftees—the film is set in 1944—provide an apparent motive; Davenport has to struggle against the racism of the white officers in charge of the camp to get to the truth. Tense, well-done adaptation by Fuller of his Pulitzer Prize–winning stage success, *A Soldier's Play,* with fine performances, including the then-little-known Denzel Washington [471 . . .], and Larry Riley, David Allan Grier, Robert Townsend, and Patti LaBelle. Many members of the cast were in the original staging of the play by the Negro Ensemble Company. What could be a routine problem drama becomes a solid, effective movie in the hands of Jewison, who was the only director of a best picture nominee this year to be overlooked in the directing category; his slot went to Woody Allen for *Broadway Danny Rose.*

The best picture Oscar went to *Amadeus,* which also won for Peter Shaffer's screenplay. Haing S. Ngor won the supporting actor award for *The Killing Fields.*

Jewison: 659, 992, 1351, 1736. Schwary: 1502. Palmer: 390, 1351.

1858 • SOLID GOLD CADILLAC, THE

COLUMBIA. 1956.
AWARD *Black-and-White Costume Design:* Jean Louis.
NOMINATION *Black-and-White Art Direction—Set Decoration:* Ross Bellah; William R. Kiernan and Louis Diage.

Laura Partridge, played by Judy Holliday [262], decides to go to the annual shareholders' meeting of a large corporation in which she holds a few shares of stock. The questions she raises about the company hit a nerve, one thing leads to another, and she winds up running the company, marrying its founder (Paul Douglas), who had been ousted by the unscrupulous board members Laura exposes, and being rewarded with the titular car—which appears in a Technicolor scene at the end. Entertaining if formulaic comedy that betrays its stage origins: It was a Broadway hit for George S. Kaufman and Howard Teichmann; Abe Burrows adapted it for the screen. On Broadway Laura Partridge was played by Josephine Hull [876]; Holliday's casting allows the film a romantic subplot. Directed by Richard Quine, with Fred Clark, John Williams, Hiram Sherman, Neva Patterson, Ray Collins, Arthur O'Connell [73 . . .], and Richard Deacon. George Burns [1976] provides an off-screen narration.

Louis was born in Paris and worked for Hattie Carnegie in New York before moving to Hollywood, where he was a designer for Columbia from 1944 to 1958. He then moved over to Universal for a few years but went freelance in the late sixties. The art direction Oscar went to *Somebody Up There Likes Me.*

Louis: 20, 126, 170, 262, 732, 744, 1028, 1065, 1521, 1640, 1812, 1910, 2064. Kiernan: 1133, 1521, 1550, 1753, 2238. Diage: 170, 1521.

1859 • SOME CAME RUNNING

SOL C. SIEGEL PRODUCTION; MGM. 1958.

NOMINATIONS *Actress:* Shirley MacLaine. *Supporting Actor:* Arthur Kennedy. *Supporting Actress:* Martha Hyer. *Song:* "To Love and Be Loved," music by James Van Heusen, lyrics by Sammy Cahn. *Costume Design:* Walter Plunkett.

Discharged from the army, writer Dave Hirsh, played by Frank Sinatra [732 . . .], goes home to the Midwest where, bored with the monotony of the life led by his older brother, Frank (Kennedy), and frustrated by his encounters with the chilly schoolteacher Gwen French (Hyer), he takes up with the town lowlife: gambler 'Bama Dillert (Dean Martin) and a waifish factory girl, Ginny (MacLaine). Overheated but also reticent, in the manner of a lot of late-fifties movies trying to slip past the enfeebled Production Code, this version of the novel by James Jones gets what class and energy it can from its performers and director, Vincente Minnelli [66 . . .]. (It's a little hard to believe the same director did *Gigi* the same year.) The screenplay is by John Patrick [1939] and Arthur Sheekman.

MacLaine had made her film debut three years earlier in Alfred Hitchcock's *The Trouble With Harry* and had an important role in *Around the World in 80 Days* but had not yet become a star. *Some Came Running* gave her a showy part that helped her get there, although it also typed her as a hooker with a heart of gold, a role she would play off and on for the next decade, in *The Apartment, Irma la Douce,* and *Sweet Charity,* among others. She lost to Susan Hayward in *I Want to Live!*

This was the last in Kennedy's string of five unsuccessful tries at the Oscar. He lost to Burl Ives in *The Big Country.* Kennedy continued to appear in movies up till his death in 1990, although much of his later career was spent in minor European films.

Hyer made her film debut in 1946 and spent much of her career playing the "other woman" to leads like Audrey Hepburn in *Sabrina* and Sophia Loren in *Houseboat.* In 1966 she married producer Hal Wallis [17 . . .] and made only a few subsequent screen appearances. She lost to Wendy Hiller in *Separate Tables.*

The best song was the title tune by Alan Jay Lerner and Frederick Loewe from Minnelli's other 1958 movie, *Gigi,* which also won for Cecil Beaton's costumes.

MacLaine: 91, 1017, 2020, 2152. Kennedy: 291, 380, 1558, 2139. Van Heusen: 171, 173, 787, 915, 926, 1056, 1524, 1587, 1708, 1907, 2016, 2064, 2263. Cahn: 74, 163, 182, 696, 915, 926, 1031, 1056, 1216, 1524, 1587, 1692, 1708, 1719, 1907, 2016, 2064, 2072, 2103, 2110, 2125, 2263, 2264, 2315, 2343. Plunkett: 9, 66, 953, 1087, 1243, 1587, 1657, 2029, 2330.

1860 • *SOME LIKE IT HOT*

ASHTON PRODUCTIONS & THE MIRISCH COMPANY; UNITED ART-
ISTS. 1959.

AWARD *Black-and-White Costume Design:* Orry-Kelly.
NOMINATIONS *Actor:* Jack Lemmon. *Director:* Billy Wilder. *Screenplay—Based on Material From Another Medium:* Billy Wilder and I. A. L. Diamond. *Black-and-
White Cinematography:* Charles Lang, Jr. *Black-and-
White Art Direction—Set Decoration:* Ted Haworth; Edward G. Boyle.

Tony Curtis [522] plays Joe and Lemmon is Jerry,
Chicago musicians who accidentally witness the St.
Valentine's Day massacre and are forced to flee to
Miami disguised as Josephine and Daphne, members
of an all-girl orchestra whose featured vocalist is the
luscious Sugar Kane (Marilyn Monroe). To pursue
her, Joe sneaks out of drag and adopts the persona of
an impotent millionaire who sounds like Cary Grant
[1445 . . .] ("Nobody talks like that!" objects
Jerry). This also involves secretly borrowing the yacht
owned by Osgood Fielding III (Joe E. Brown), and to
that end, Jerry/Daphne is enlisted to court Fielding
to keep him ashore during Joe's assignation with
Sugar. Meanwhile, the gangsters, led by Spats
Columbo (George Raft), have also shown up . . .
Hilarious farce and one of the sweetest natured of
Wilder's usually acerbic comedies, thanks to endearing performances by Lemmon and Brown, Curtis'
high-spirited mimicry of Grant, and Monroe's breathtaking luminosity. Her failure to receive a nomination
for one of her most celebrated performances may owe
something to the stories of her misbehavior during
the production. In a fragile emotional state, heightened by a pregnancy that ended in a miscarriage,
Monroe was deeply dependent on her acting coach,
Paula Strasberg, and required multiple takes in even
the simplest scenes, to the annoyance of Wilder and
Curtis. The latter's bitterness over her behavior man-
ifested itself in a famous statement that kissing her
was "like kissing Hitler." Even the more judicious
Lemmon has described Monroe as "selfish," and
Wilder has commented, "I never met anyone as utterly mean as Marilyn Monroe. Nor as utterly fabulous on the screen, and that includes Garbo." Fortu-

nately only the fabulousness shows. Curtis, who eerily
resembles Eve Arden [1319] when he's in drag, was
likewise overlooked by the Academy, provoking a
comment in his autobiography: "As for the Oscars, I
always believed the old saying that the only thing you
can rely on the Academy for is free movies at the end
of the year."

This was the second Oscar for Orry-Kelly, who
was born John Kelley in Australia, worked on Broadway, and started his film costuming career in 1923.
He died in 1964.

Some Like It Hot began the long association of Lemmon with Wilder, although Wilder's first choice for
the role was Frank Sinatra [732 . . .]. (Wilder had
rejected the studio's suggestions of Bob Hope and
Danny Kaye for the Joe and Jerry roles and Mitzi
Gaynor for Sugar Kane.) Lemmon would make six
more films with Wilder: *The Apartment, Irma la Douce,
The Fortune Cookie* (1966), *Avanti!* (1972), *The Front
Page* (1974), and *Buddy Buddy* (1981). Lemmon lost
the best actor Oscar to Charlton Heston in *Ben-Hur,*
for which William Wyler received the directing
award.

Wilder and Diamond's screenplay is classified as an
adaptation, although it only remotely resembles its
supposed source, a 1932 German musical called
Fanfaren der Liebe, which concerns two musicians who
put on various disguises, including women's clothing,
to find work in different orchestras. Wilder and Diamond added the gangster plot and almost everything
else. The Oscar went to Neil Paterson for a more
direct "adaptation," *Room at the Top.*

Wilder was no fan of color photography and was
backed up in his decision to shoot the film in black
and white by color tests, which showed the makeup of
Curtis and Lemmon in their drag roles to be harsh
and unconvincing. Lang lost to William C. Mellor for
The Diary of Anne Frank, which also won for art direction.

Orry-Kelly: 66, 853, 1157. Lemmon: 91, 394,
508, 1330, 1337, 1761, 2140. Wilder: 91, 138, 198,
566, 705, 709, 925, 1208, 1440, 1738, 1903, 1975,
2297. Diamond: 91, 709. Lang: 93, 250, 319, 636,
649, 705, 765, 953, 1480, 1640, 1699, 1738, 1778,

1855, 1955, 1968, 2180. Haworth: 1201, 1283, 1550, 1763, 2247. Boyle: 91, 393, 709, 743, 1783, 1866.

1861 • *SOMEBODY UP THERE LIKES ME*

MGM. 1956.

AWARDS *Black-and-White Cinematography:* Joseph Ruttenberg. *Black-and-White Art Direction—Set Decoration:* Cedric Gibbons and Malcolm F. Brown; Edwin B. Willis and F. Keogh Gleason.

NOMINATION *Film Editing:* Albert Akst.

Paul Newman [3 . . .] stars in this fictionalized version of the autobiography of middleweight champ Rocky Graziano. A solid if somewhat conventional fable of the kid who works his way from the streets to fame, not unlike the later *Rocky.* The movie is notable for the careers it helped launch: It was Newman's first distinctive screen performance after his lackluster debut in the turgid *The Silver Chalice,* and the supporting players include Steve McQueen [1753] and Robert Loggia [1039] in their screen debuts. Robert Wise [407 . . .] directs from a screenplay by Ernest Lehman [896 . . .], and the cast also includes Pier Angeli, Everett Sloane, Eileen Heckart [133 . . .], and Sal Mineo [630 . . .].

This was the third of Ruttenberg's four Oscars. The award for film editing went to Gene Ruggiero and Paul Weatherwax for *Around the World in 80 Days.*

Ruttenberg: 318, 573, 749, 769, 828, 1069, 1232, 1371, 2234. Gibbons: 66, 87, 130, 217, 227, 239, 285, 290, 440, 629, 749, 831, 980, 1069, 1096, 1173, 1190, 1226, 1230, 1232, 1274, 1308, 1309, 1417, 1567, 1604, 1644, 1662, 1673, 1721, 1937, 2068, 2112, 2256, 2257, 2300, 2320, 2330. Brown: 980. Willis: 66, 87, 130, 227, 239, 290, 629, 749, 831, 980, 1069, 1096, 1157, 1173, 1190, 1226, 1230, 1232, 1309, 1417, 1567, 1657, 1662, 1673, 1721, 1937, 2068, 2112, 2257, 2320, 2330. Gleason: 66, 130, 290, 769, 1226, 1937.

1862 • *SOMETHING TO SHOUT ABOUT*

COLUMBIA. 1943.

NOMINATIONS *Song:* "You'd Be So Nice to Come Home To," music and lyrics by Cole Porter. *Scoring of a Musical Picture:* Morris Stoloff.

Well, not really. Just a routine musical with Don Ameche [419] helping Janet Blair get her big break on Broadway by supplanting an untalented star on opening night. Directed by Gregory Ratoff, with Jack Oakie [818], William Gaxton, Veda Ann Borg, Hazel Scott, Teddy Wilson, and one Lily Norwood—who'd soon change her name to Cyd Charisse. How a composer of the stature of Porter wound up working on this forgotten and forgettable nothing is a mystery, but only the nominated song is among his better work. It lost to Harry Warren and Mack Gordon's "You'll Never Know," from *Hello, Frisco, Hello.* The scoring award went to Ray Heindorf for *This Is the Army.*

Porter: 261, 914, 2329. Stoloff: 13, 432, 455, 596, 643, 677, 732, 773, 1057, 1058, 1115, 1206, 1872, 1873, 1998, 2110, 2329.

1863 • *SOMETHING TO SING ABOUT*

GRAND NATIONAL. 1937.

NOMINATION *Score:* Grand National Studio Music Department, Constantin Bakaleinikoff, musical director; score by Victor Schertzinger.

Bandleader James Cagney [79 . . .] is wooed by Hollywood but hates the grooming the studio subjects him to. He loses his temper during the filming of his first movie and starts a brawl with everyone on the set. He leaves to marry the singer in his band, but when they return from their honeymoon, they discover the studio has incorporated his real fight in their movie, which has become a hit. The studio still wants to make him a star, but they insist he keep his marriage a secret. One of Cagney's most forgettable movies, this low-budget programmer was made for the very minor Grand National studio while the star was feuding with Warner Bros. The cast includes William Frawley and Gene Lockhart [36].

Bakaleinikoff had been a member of the Los Angeles Philharmonic before becoming a music director at

Paramount and MGM. In 1941 he became head of the RKO music department. Schertzinger began his film composing career in 1916, when he composed a score to accompany Thomas Ince's *Civilization.* He also directed many films, including this one, before his death in 1941. The Oscar went to *One Hundred Men and a Girl.*

Bakaleinikoff: 640, 916, 1445. Schertzinger: 1488.

1864 • *SOMETIMES A GREAT NOTION*

UNIVERSAL-NEWMAN-FOREMAN COMPANY PRODUCTION; UNIVERSAL. 1971.

NOMINATIONS *Supporting Actor:* Richard Jaeckel. *Song:* "All His Children," music by Henry Mancini, lyrics by Alan Bergman and Marilyn Bergman.

Paul Newman [3 . . .] both directs and stars in this adaptation by John Gay [1778] of a Ken Kesey novel about a logging family in Oregon. Tensions arise both within the family and with other loggers when Newman tries to stay uninvolved in a labor dispute. Henry Fonda [815 . . .] is Newman's father, Lee Remick [508] his wife, and Michael Sarrazin and Jaeckel his brothers. Unfortunately Newman and Gay are unable to put an effective dramatic shape on the material, and the family relationships are predictable. The film's rather elliptical title was changed to *Never Give an Inch* when it was shown on TV.

Jaeckel followed the classic career path that starts in the mail room: He was a delivery boy at 20th Century-Fox and made his debut in *Guadalcanal Diary* in 1943, when he was still in his teens. Never a star, he has always been a reliable second lead, especially in war films and westerns: *Battleground, Sands of Iwo Jima, The Gunfighter, The Naked and the Dead* (1958), *The Dirty Dozen, Pat Garrett and Billy the Kid* (1973), and so on. The Oscar went to Ben Johnson for *The Last Picture Show.*

The song award went to Isaac Hayes for "Theme from *Shaft.*"

Mancini: 122, 278, 384, 494, 508, 512, 776, 825, 1573, 1574, 1970, 2011, 2037, 2201. A. Bergman: 179, 867, 1168, 1568, 1628, 1747, 1813, 2063, 2113, 2238, 2321, 2322. M. Bergman: 179, 867, 1168, 1568, 1628, 1747, 1813, 2063, 2113, 2238, 2321, 2322.

1865 • *SOMEWHERE IN TIME*

RASTAR-STEPHEN DEUTSCH-UNIVERSAL PICTURES PRODUCTION; UNIVERSAL. 1980.

NOMINATION *Costume Design:* Jean-Pierre Dorleac.

Christopher Reeve plays a playwright who becomes fascinated with a seventy-year-old picture of a woman (Jane Seymour) and finds himself traveling back in time, where he discovers that he was her lover in a previous life. Richard Matheson adapts his own novel, *Bid Time Return,* but the movie, directed by Jeannot Szwarc, is sentimental and derivative: a bit of *Portrait of Jennie,* a touch of *Berkeley Square,* a whiff of *On a Clear Day You Can See Forever.* Though the film failed at the box office, it has its admirers. Reeve and Seymour are attractive, and they're supported by Christopher Plummer, Teresa Wright [1182 . . .], Bill Erwin, and George Wendt. There's also a fine, evocative score by John Barry [259 . . .]. The costuming award went to Anthony Powell for *Tess.*

1866 • *SON OF MONTE CRISTO, THE*

EDWARD SMALL: UNITED ARTISTS. 1941.

NOMINATION *Black-and-White Interior Decoration:* John DuCasse Schulze, art direction; Edward G. Boyle, set decoration.

Louis Hayward plays the son of Edmond Dantes, the famous count; he foils the machinations of George Sanders [46] and gets Joan Bennett as a reward. Pleasant swashbuckler, though Hayward is no Errol Flynn. Who is that unmasked man in a supporting role? Why, that's the Lone Ranger, Clayton Moore. Directed by Rowland V. Lee. The art direction Oscar went to *How Green Was My Valley.*

Schulze: 1405. Boyle: 91, 393, 709, 743, 1783, 1860.

1867 • *SON OF PALEFACE*

HOPE ENTERPRISES INC.; PARAMOUNT. 1952.

NOMINATION *Song:* "Am I in Love," music and lyrics by Jack Brooks.

Bob Hope and Roy Rogers team up in this endearing western spoof, part sequel to *The Paleface,* part knockoff of the Hope-Crosby *Road* series, but mostly just silly fun. Jane Russell is the good-hearted bad girl, and the cast includes Bill Williams, Lloyd Corrigan, Douglass Dumbrille, Harry Von Zell, Iron Eyes Cody, and, of course, Trigger. There are gag cameos by Bing Crosby [173 . . .] and Cecil B. DeMille [412 . . .]. Directed by Frank Tashlin, who cowrote the screenplay with Robert L. Welch and Joseph Quillan. The Oscar went to Dimitri Tiomkin and Ned Washington's title song from *High Noon.*

Brooks: 324, 341.

1868 • *SONG OF BERNADETTE, THE*

20TH CENTURY-FOX. 1943.

AWARDS *Actress:* Jennifer Jones. *Black-and-White Cinematography:* Arthur Miller. *Black-and-White Interior Decoration:* James Basevi and William Darling, art direction; Thomas Little, set decoration. *Scoring of a Dramatic or Comedy Picture:* Alfred Newman.
NOMINATIONS *Picture:* William Perlberg, producer. *Supporting Actor:* Charles Bickford. *Supporting Actress:* Gladys Cooper. *Supporting Actress:* Anne Revere. *Director:* Henry King. *Screenplay:* George Seaton. *Sound Recording:* E. H. Hansen. *Film Editing:* Barbara McLean.

Jones plays Bernadette of Lourdes, whose vision of the Virgin Mary (Linda Darnell!) attracts the faithful but irks the people of her own town. This long, sentimental, ponderously reverent religious fable, adapted from a novel by Franz Werfel, was a big hit but hasn't stood up well with the passage of time. Still, it's a must-see for those interested in Hollywood's treatment of religion and as a demonstration of the technical resources available to a big studio going all out on a prestige project. And if one yields to the production's blandishments, it can be a moving experience. The huge cast includes Vincent Price, Lee J. Cobb [301 . . .], Patricia Morison, Sig Rumann, Blanche Yurka, Marcel Dalio, Jerome Cowan, Moroni Olsen, and Mae Marsh.

The film was a star-maker for Jones, who was born Phylis Isley in Oklahoma. She had married actor Robert Walker while studying acting in New York, and the two came to Hollywood, where she began her film career in 1939, playing small roles in B movies and the serial *Dick Tracy's G-Men.* She interrupted her career briefly to have children before she was discovered by David O. Selznick [497 . . .]—or rather, Selznick's invaluable East Coast story editor/talent scout, Kay Brown, who had been instrumental in persuading Selznick to buy the rights to *Gone With the Wind* and had discovered Ingrid Bergman [72 . . .] for him. Selznick signed the actress to a contract, changed her name to Jennifer Jones, and began a publicity buildup for her, but was unable to find his own property for her debut under her new name. So Jones had her breakthrough role and earned her Oscar on a loan-out to Fox. She also became Selznick's mistress and married him in 1949, after divorcing Walker. Her later career was obsessively managed by her patron. After Selznick's death in 1965, she made only a handful of screen appearances, the last one of note in *The Towering Inferno.*

This was the second of Miller's three Oscars and the third of Newman's record-setting nine music awards.

Because of its twelve nominations, *The Song of Bernadette* was considered the front-runner for the best picture Oscar, but that award went to one of the most enduring Hollywood films of all time, *Casablanca,* which also won for its director, Michael Curtiz, and for the screenplay by Julius and Philip Epstein and Howard Koch. Bickford lost the first of his three unsuccessful nominations to Charles Coburn in *The More the Merrier.* Cooper and Revere lost to Katina Paxinou in *For Whom the Bell Tolls.* The award for sound went to Stephen Dunn for *This Land Is Mine.* The film editing Oscar was won by George Amy for *Air Force.*

Jones: 584, 1213, 1214, 1828. Miller: 83, 241, 952, 1082, 1655, 2056. Basevi: 746, 1082, 2245, 2316. Darling: 83, 374, 1082, 1195, 1655, 2240. Little: 46, 83, 235, 428, 495, 719, 721, 746, 950, 952, 1082, 1149, 1153, 1397, 1475, 1666, 1852, 2056, 2212, 2286. Newman: 31, 34, 46, 72, 138, 182, 226, 333, 334, 347, 375, 428, 437, 457, 476, 495, 542, 690, 797, 833, 952, 953, 959, 962, 1016, 1082, 1088, 1213, 1278, 1362, 1397, 1475, 1616,

1655, 1849, 1883, 1921, 2043, 2046, 2091, 2258, 2286, 2294, 2316. Perlberg: 450, 1325. Bickford: 651, 1052. Cooper: 1393, 1456. Revere: 759, 1417. King: 2286. Seaton: 31, 450, 1325. Hansen: 143, 241, 815, 952, 990, 1655, 1957, 2027, 2056, 2272, 2286, 2317. McLean: 34, 46, 1327, 1195, 1655, 2286.

1869 • SONG OF THE FLAME

FIRST NATIONAL. 1929–30.
NOMINATION *Sound Recording:* George Groves.

Early musical, set during the Russian Revolution but with little real connection to historical fact. The source is a 1925 operetta with music by George Gershwin [1797], though the Gershwin songs have been discarded. The cast, directed by Alan Crosland, includes Alexander Gray, Bernice Claire, and Noah Beery. Douglas Shearer received the Oscar, the first ever presented for sound, for *The Big House.*

Groves: 825, 1385, 1393, 1457, 1763, 1973, 2277.

1870 • SONG OF THE OPEN ROAD

CHARLES ROGERS PRODUCTIONS; UNITED ARTISTS. 1944.
NOMINATIONS *Song:* "Too Much in Love," music by Walter Kent, lyrics by Kim Gannon. *Scoring of a Musical Picture:* Charles Previn.

Lightweight musical about a bored child star who tries to check out "real life" and winds up staging a benefit variety show that features Edgar Bergen and Charlie McCarthy trading insults with W. C. Fields. Directed by S. Sylvan Simon [262], with Bonita Granville [2044], Reginald Denny, Sammy Kaye and his orchestra, and Jane Powell in her film debut. The best song was "Swinging on a Star," by James Van Heusen and Johnny Burke, from *Going My Way.* Morris Stoloff and Carmen Dragon won for the score of *Cover Girl.*

Kent: 589. Gannon: 59, 589. Previn: 306, 668, 1030, 1229, 1485, 1896.

1871 • SONG OF THE SOUTH

WALT DISNEY PRODUCTIONS; RKO RADIO. 1947.
AWARDS *Song:* "Zip-A-Dee-Doo-Dah," music by Allie Wrubel, lyrics by Ray Gilbert. *Special Award:* James Baskett, for his able and heart-warming characterization of Uncle Remus, friend and story teller to the children of the world.
NOMINATION *Scoring of a Musical Picture:* Daniele Amfitheatrof, Paul J. Smith, and Charles Wolcott.

Young Johnny (Bobby Driscoll) goes to live on an Old South plantation with his mother (Ruth Warrick) and grandmother, played by Lucile Watson [2233], but is unhappy and determined to run away until Uncle Remus (Baskett) tells him the stories of Brer Rabbit, Brer Fox, and Brer Bear. A controversial Disney classic that's undeniably executed with finesse: The animated versions of the Joel Chandler Harris tales are wonderful, and the live-action episodes are beautifully filmed by Gregg Toland [407 . . .]—one of his few works in color. The cast, directed by Harve Foster, includes Luana Patten and Hattie McDaniel [798]. But the film drew fire for racial stereotyping and is one of the few Disney features that fail to get periodic revivals and videotape release. The animated sequences turn up on TV from time to time, out of context of the main story. The real loss in this case is the fine performance of Baskett, a veteran character actor who also does the voice of Brer Fox in the cartoons. The honorary award was presented to him in lieu of a supporting actor nomination; it would be a decade before a black man, Sidney Poitier in *The Defiant Ones,* was nominated for an acting award. Baskett died in 1948.

The scoring Oscar went to Alfred Newman for *Mother Wore Tights.*

Wrubel: 1830. Amfitheatrof: 845. Smith: 402, 1553, 1576, 1745, 1851, 2071, 2202. Wolcott: 1745, 2071.

1872 • SONG TO REMEMBER, A

COLUMBIA. 1945.
NOMINATIONS *Actor:* Cornel Wilde. *Original Story:* Ernst Marischka. *Color Cinematography:* Tony Gaudio and Allen M. Davey. *Sound Recording:* John Livadary. *Scoring of a Dramatic or Comedy Picture:* Miklos Rozsa and Morris Stoloff. *Film Editing:* Charles Nelson.

Wilde plays Frederick Chopin, with Merle Oberon [487] as George Sand and Paul Muni [218.5 . . .] as

Chopin's teacher in this colorful cornball biopic that was a surprising box-office hit. It's awful, thanks to the cliché-cluttered screenplay by Sidney Buchman [904 . . .] that had been written back in 1937 at the suggestion of Frank Capra [1025 . . .], who had planned to make the movie with Spencer Tracy [131 . . .] as Chopin and Marlene Dietrich [1358] as George Sand. But Capra broke with Columbia, leaving the script behind. When *A Song to Remember* was a hit, Capra sued for a percentage of the profits, but withdrew the suit after an examination of his settlement with Columbia showed his legal status to be weak. Capra might have given the film more life and interest than its director, Charles Vidor, did. The cast includes Stephen Bekassy as Franz Liszt, and Nina Foch [629], George Coulouris, and Sig Arno.

An excellent athlete, Wilde gave up a slot on the 1936 Olympic fencing team because of his decision to pursue a stage career. He got the break that would take him to Hollywood when he was hired as fencing coach to Laurence Olivier [268 . . .] for a 1940 Broadway production of *Romeo and Juliet* and was cast in the part of Tybalt. He made his film debut in 1940 but didn't become a star until five years later, when he appeared in *A Song to Remember, Leave Her to Heaven,* and the swashbuckler *The Bandit of Sherwood Forest.* His career was not of the first rank, however, and after *The Greatest Show on Earth* in 1952, he found few good roles. He moved into producing and directing and is best known in that field for the gripping adventure thriller *The Naked Prey.* He died in 1989. The Oscar went to Ray Milland for *The Lost Weekend.*

Charles G. Booth won the award for story for *The House on 92nd Street.* The cinematography award went to Leon Shamroy for *Leave Her to Heaven.* Stephen Dunn won for the sound for *The Bells of St. Mary's.* Rozsa took home an Oscar for the score for *Spellbound.* Robert J. Kern won for editing *National Velvet.*

Gaudio: 90, 447, 898, 1064, 1162. Davey: 217, 455, 897, 1988. Livadary: 330, 455, 596, 732, 1058, 1206, 1215, 1303, 1366, 1370, 1488, 1521, 1740, 2111, 2325, 2327. Rozsa: 175, 566, 567, 604, 1035, 1069, 1070, 1085, 1208, 1227, 1644, 1890, 1968, 2050, 2304. Stoloff: 13, 432, 455, 596, 643, 677, 732, 773, 1057, 1058, 1115, 1206, 1862, 1873, 1998, 2110, 2329. Nelson: 371, 1566.

1873 • SONG WITHOUT END

GOETZ-VIDOR PICTURES PRODUCTION; COLUMBIA. 1960.
AWARD *Scoring of a Musical Picture:* Morris Stoloff and Harry Sukman.

Dirk Bogarde plays Franz Liszt in this attempt to recapture the box-office magic of *A Song to Remember,* made fifteen years earlier by director Charles Vidor, who began this film but died and was replaced by George Cukor [262 . . .]. Capucine is Princess Carolyne and Genevieve Page Countess Marie, with Patricia Morison as George Sand and a cast that includes Martita Hunt, Lou Jacobi, and Marcel Dalio. It looks and sounds great: The cinematography is by James Wong Howe [1 . . .], the production was designed by Walter Holscher [13 . . .], and the piano is played by Jorge Bolet. But it's the usual dull biopic stuff, from a screenplay by Oscar Millard [731].

Stoloff: 13, 432, 455, 596, 643, 677, 732, 773, 1057, 1058, 1115, 1206, 1862, 1872, 1998, 2110, 2329. Sukman: 643, 1833.

1874 • SONGWRITER

TRI-STAR PICTURES PRODUCTION; TRI-STAR. 1984.
NOMINATION *Original Song Score:* Kris Kristofferson.

Willie Nelson [936] plays a country-music star who's getting taken by a shady legal deal that eats up his profits, so he turns promoter himself, managing the career of his buddy, Kristofferson. Lightweight satire-with-music, written by Bud Shrake and directed by Alan Rudolph, with Melinda Dillon [3 . . .], Rip Torn [466], Lesley Ann Warren [2201], and Nelson's harmonica player, Mickey Raphael, and other members of his backup band. The film was a box-office dud, more or less stalling attempts to make Nelson a movie star.

After establishing himself as a major writer-performer of country music in the sixties, with such hits as "Help Me Make It Through the Night" and "Me and Bobby McGee," Kristofferson, a former Rhodes Scholar, became a busy leading man in movies of the seventies, performing in such films as *Alice Doesn't Live*

Here Anymore, The Sailor Who Fell From Grace With the Sea (1975), the 1976 remake of A Star Is Born, and Semi-Tough (1977). His acting career seemed to stall at about the time of his appearance in the famous flop Heaven's Gate in 1980, though he has continued to make occasional film appearances and frequently performs in concert with Nelson and others. The Oscar went to Prince for Purple Rain.

1875 • SONS AND LOVERS

COMPANY OF ARTISTS INC.; 20TH CENTURY-FOX. 1960.
AWARD Black-and-White Cinematography: Freddie Francis.
NOMINATIONS Picture: Jerry Wald, producer. Actor: Trevor Howard. Supporting Actress: Mary Ure. Director: Jack Cardiff. Screenplay—Based on Material From Another Medium: Gavin Lambert and T. E. B. Clarke. Black-and-White Art Direction—Set Decoration: Tom Morahan; Lionel Couch.

Dean Stockwell [1281] plays Paul Morel, who is coddled and manipulated by his mother, played by Wendy Hiller [1252 . . .], who wants him to become something better than his rough, boorish coal-miner father (Howard). Paul's first love is the sensitive Miriam (Heather Sears), but her distaste for sex is a disastrous barrier, and he turns to a married woman, Clara (Ure). Meanwhile, the influence of his mother, strong and encouraging at first, grows oppressive: She scorns the timid Miriam and fears the experienced Clara. Well-done adaptation of D. H. Lawrence's novel, with some of the book's weaknesses—too-obvious relationships, a choppy narrative flow. The cast also includes Donald Pleasence and Ernest Thesiger.

Francis had apprenticed in the British film industry before World War II, but his career really began after the war, during which he served as a director of photography in the British army. He worked as a camera operator on such films as Moulin Rouge and Beat the Devil (1954) and was a second unit director of photography on Moby Dick (1956). His first notice as cinematographer came on such films as Room at the Top and Saturday Night and Sunday Morning (1960). After winning the Oscar, Francis turned director,

specializing in horror films, the most notable of which are The Day of the Triffids (1962) and Dr. Terror's House of Horrors (1964). In 1980 he returned to cinematography with great distinction, particularly on such films as The Elephant Man, The French Lieutenant's Woman, and the movie that won him a second Oscar, Glory.

Howard rose to fame with only his second film, Brief Encounter. Before his death in 1988, he gave memorable performances in The Third Man, Mutiny on the Bounty, Von Ryan's Express (1965), The Charge of the Light Brigade (1968), Ryan's Daughter, Gandhi, and many others. The Oscar went to Burt Lancaster for Elmer Gantry, for which Shirley Jones took the supporting actress award. Ure, who had gained acclaim on stage for her performance in Look Back in Anger, and subsequently appeared in the 1959 film version, made only a few films before her death in 1975 from a combination of alcohol and barbiturates that was ruled accidental.

The best picture Oscar went to The Apartment, which also won for its director, Billy Wilder, and for art direction. The screenplay award went to Richard Brooks for Elmer Gantry.

Francis: 779. Wald: 1052, 1319, 1558. Cardiff: 221, 643, 2228. Lambert: 970. Clarke: 1150, 1535. Couch: 85.

1876 • SOPHIE'S CHOICE

ITC ENTERTAINMENT PRESENTATION OF A PAKULA-BARISH PRODUCTION; UNIVERSAL/A.F.D. 1982.
AWARD Actress: Meryl Streep.
NOMINATIONS Screenplay Based on Material From Another Medium: Alan J. Pakula. Cinematography: Nestor Almendros. Original Score: Marvin Hamlisch. Costume Design: Albert Wolsky.

Sophie (Streep) is a Polish immigrant living in Brooklyn after World War II. Stingo (Peter MacNicol), a southern writer, lives in the same apartment house, and he is drawn to Sophie and her lover, Nathan, played by Kevin Kline [670]. Gradually he learns the horrifying story of what Sophie did to survive a Nazi concentration camp, and the revelation leads to further disaster. Ploddingly faithful adaptation by

Pakula, who also directed, of the novel by William Styron. Both book and film are unequal to the task set for them: illuminating the century's most profound moral enigma, the complexity of evil and guilt embodied by the Holocaust. The performances of the three leads are powerfully watchable, although they never quite merge into the ensemble the script demands, in part because of Streep's intensity. Kline, who was suggested by Streep for his role, makes his film debut.

Sophie was, not surprisingly, a much sought-after role, for which the director initially wanted Liv Ullman [610 . . .]. Streep became the first actress to take an Oscar for a leading role after a previous win —for *Kramer vs. Kramer*—in a supporting part. (Jessica Lange subsequently also won a best actress Oscar, for *Blue Sky,* after an earlier win for *Tootsie.*) Learning German and Polish for the film, she also established herself as a master of accents, subsequently adopting an Oklahoma accent for *Silkwood,* a Danish one for *Out of Africa,* and an Australian one for *A Cry in the Dark.* (This linguistic facility became the subject of so many jokes that she seems to have avoided it in her more recent films.)

Pakula lost to Costa-Gavras and Donald Stewart for the screenplay for *Missing. Gandhi* took the awards for Billy Williams and Ronnie Taylor's cinematography and for John Mollo and Bhanu Athaiya's costumes. The scoring award went to John Williams for *E.T. The Extra-Terrestrial.*

Streep: 472, 521, 725, 1019, 1111, 1512, 1598, 1821. Pakula: 54, 2101. Almendros: 243, 506, 1111. Hamlisch: 398, 977, 1109, 1747, 1813, 1898, 1927, 2238. Wolsky: 308, 1061, 2127.5.

1877 • *SORCERER*
WILLIAM FRIEDKIN FILM PRODUCTION; PARAMOUNT-UNIVERSAL. 1977.
NOMINATION *Sound:* Robert Knudson, Robert J. Glass, Richard Tyler, and Jean-Louis Ducarme.

Roy Scheider [49 . . .] stars in this remake of *The Wages of Fear* (1952), about the efforts of a team of truckers to deliver nitroglycerine across rugged South American terrain. This version, directed by William Friedkin [631 . . .], was a costly flop that did serious damage to the career of a director who had back-to-back megahits—*The French Connection* and *The Exorcist*—earlier in the decade. The original film, directed by Henri-Georges Clouzot, is regarded as a suspense classic. The remake has some remarkable stunts and special effects but lacks the tension which is its main *raison d'être.* The screenplay is by Walon Green [2280]. The Oscar for sound went to *Star Wars.*

Knudson: 321, 416, 588, 613, 631, 938, 1439, 1911, 2274. Glass: 417, 588, 938, 1439, 1911. Tyler: 215, 1548, 1824.

1878 • *SORRELL AND SON*
ART CINEMA; UNITED ARTISTS. 1927–28.
NOMINATION *Director:* Herbert Brenon.

H. B. Warner [1206] plays a man who, after his wife leaves him, devotes his life to his son, who proves ungrateful. This silent film was remade with sound in 1933, also with Warner but with a different director, Jack Raymond. Brenon, who also did the screenplay for the silent version, began his film directing career in 1912. His films include a silent version of *The Great Gatsby* (1926) and *Neptune's Daughter,* starring swimmer Annette Kellerman. Brenon was hurt during the making of the latter film when a glass-sided tank was overfilled and exploded; the incident is depicted, in a heavily fictionalized manner, in the 1952 Esther Williams biopic of Kellerman, *Million Dollar Mermaid.* Brenon resisted the arrival of sound, and his Hollywood career declined in the early thirties. In 1934 he moved to England, which he had left as a boy, and directed a handful of films there before retiring in 1940. He died in 1958. The Oscar went to Frank Borzage for *Seventh Heaven.*

1879 • *SORRY, WRONG NUMBER*
HAL WALLIS PRODUCTIONS: PARAMOUNT. 1948.
NOMINATION *Actress:* Barbara Stanwyck.

When she makes a telephone call to her husband's office, Stanwyck, a wealthy hypochondriac, accidentally overhears a plot for her own murder. Her performance is the best thing about this thriller, adapted by Lucille Fletcher from her radio play that starred

Agnes Moorehead [963 . . .]. What was compact and claustrophobic on radio is thin and jumbled on screen, however, and a bad performance by Burt Lancaster [107 . . .] as the husband doesn't help—Lancaster was always unconvincing in roles that called for him to restrain his physicality. Directed by Anatole Litvak [517 . . .], with Wendell Corey, Ed Begley [1985], Leif Erickson, and William Conrad. The cinematography is by Sol Polito [353 . . .].

This was the last of Stanwyck's four unsuccessful nominations; the award went to Jane Wyman for *Johnny Belinda*. As Stanwyck's big-screen career began to fade in the fifties, she moved into television, where she had great success on several series, including *Big Valley* in the late sixties. Regarded by her coworkers as a consummate professional, she received an honorary Oscar "for superlative creativity and unique contribution to the art of screen acting" at the 1981 awards ceremony. She died in 1990.

Stanwyck: 138, 566, 1923.

1880 • SOULS AT SEA

PARAMOUNT. 1937.
NOMINATIONS *Interior Decoration:* Hans Dreier and Roland Anderson. *Assistant Director:* Hal Walker. *Score:* Paramount Studio Music Department, Boris Morros, head; score by W. Franke Harling and Milan Roder.

After a shipwreck, nineteenth-century naval officer Gary Cooper [701 . . .] undergoes a court-martial for failing to do his duty, but he's really an undercover agent investigating the illegal slave trade. Solid action-adventure with a melodramatic script that bites off a bit too much to handle in an hour and a half, partly because it was trimmed after filming when the studio decided it didn't have a blockbuster on its hands. Directed by Henry Hathaway [1194], with George Raft, Frances Dee, Henry Wilcoxon, Harry Carey, Robert Cummings, Porter Hall, and Joseph Schildkraut [1169]. The screenplay is by Grover Jones [1116 . . .] and Dale Van Every [352].

The art direction Oscar went to Stephen Goosson for *Lost Horizon*. Robert Webb won as assistant director for *In Old Chicago*. The scoring award went to Charles Previn for *One Hundred Men and a Girl*.

Dreier: 97, 161, 649, 674, 701, 726, 925, 979, 1101, 1120, 1194, 1214, 1217, 1358, 1443, 1452, 1540, 1668, 1748, 1975, 1994, 2190. Anderson: 278, 363, 426, 450, 649, 1029, 1194, 1214, 1219, 1452, 1570, 1668, 1674, 1994. Morros: 757, 2145. Harling: 1901, 2080.

1881 • SOUND OF MUSIC, THE

ARGYLE ENTERPRISES PRODUCTION; 20TH CENTURY-FOX. 1965.
AWARDS *Picture:* Robert Wise, producer. *Director:* Robert Wise. *Sound:* James P. Corcoran, sound director, 20th Century-Fox Studio Sound Department, and Fred Hynes, sound director, Todd-AO Sound Department. *Scoring of Music—Adaptation or Treatment:* Irwin Kostal. *Film Editing:* William Reynolds.
NOMINATIONS *Actress:* Julie Andrews. *Supporting Actress:* Peggy Wood. *Color Cinematography:* Ted McCord. *Color Art Direction—Set Decoration:* Boris Leven; Walter M. Scott and Ruby Levitt. *Color Costume Design:* Dorothy Jeakins.

Maria (Andrews), a novice in an Austrian nunnery, is so obviously unsuited for a life of quiet obedience that she's persuaded by the mother abbess (Wood) to take a job as governess to the family of the widowed Captain Von Trapp (Christopher Plummer) of the Austrian navy. The seven children have succeeded in running off several previous governesses, but Maria wins them over with her humor and good sense. She also wins over their father, who suddenly realizes that he's in love with her and not with his fiancée, a baroness played by Eleanor Parker [328 . . .]. The baroness tries a preemptive strike that sends Maria running back to the nunnery in alarm, but Maria soon comes to her senses and returns to face the fact that she's in love with the captain, too. They get married, but then comes the *Anschluss,* and the captain is called to serve the Third Reich. With the aid of the captain's friend, Max Detweiler (Richard Haydn), an impresario in charge of acts at the Salzburg Folk Festival, plus the help of Maria's friends at the nunnery, the Von Trapps elude the Nazis and escape over the mountains to Switzerland. Phenomenally successful film musical, and one of the last of its kind, though the attempts to mimic its success—e.g., *Doctor Dolit-*

tle, Goodbye, Mr. Chips—may have been what killed off the family-oriented musical. The criticisms usually leveled at The Sound of Music are that it's "manipulative," although manipulation is precisely what one expects of this kind of movie: "You'll laugh! You'll cry! You'll come out humming the tunes!" And you do, unless you're made of sterner critical stuff. The tunes are, of course, by Richard Rodgers [1921] and Oscar Hammerstein II [375 . . .]. The screenplay by Ernest Lehman [896 . . .] is based on the book for the 1959 stage musical by Howard Lindsay and Russel Crouse, which in turn came from Maria Von Trapp's autobiographical book and a German film based on it. The cast includes Charmian Carr, Heather Menzies, Nicolas Hammond, Duane Chase, Angela Cartwright, Debbie Turner, and Kym Karath as the Von Trapp brood. Among the nuns are Anna Lee as Sister Margaretta, Portia Nelson as Sister Berthe, and Marni Nixon—the off-screen voice of Deborah Kerr in The King and I, Audrey Hepburn in My Fair Lady, and Natalie Wood in West Side Story—as Sister Sophia.

The Sound of Music is perhaps the most successful of all the film versions of the musicals of Rodgers and Hammerstein, not only for what it made at the box office but also in converting a theatrical experience into a cinematic one. Despite location filming, Oklahoma!, Carousel (1956), and South Pacific remained stubbornly stage-bound. But Wise found fresh and imaginative ways to use the scenic qualities musically, as for example in the famous opening sequence, in which the camera searches through the Alps until it finds Andrews, who bursts into the title song, or the rousing "Do-Re-Mi" number, brilliantly edited to integrate various Salzburg locations into the song. The screenplay, too, is somewhat different from the stage version, in part because Hammerstein, who exercised rigid control over the scripts for the earlier films, had died in 1960.

The two Oscars were especially gratifying for Wise, who had won the same two awards four years earlier for West Side Story but had reluctantly shared the directing trophy for that film with Jerome Robbins. Wise's post–Sound of Music career was not so distinguished, however. The Sand Pebbles received good

reviews but was less than stellar at the box office, and Star! was a reunion with Julie Andrews that proved disastrous for both their careers. The failure of The Hindenburg helped put an end to the disaster-movie cycle. And Star Trek: The Motion Picture was not the success that was anticipated; only the later films in the series, in which Wise had no part, eventually helped the first into profitability. Wise's most recent film, Rooftops (1989), was an odd excursion into West Side Story territory: a little-seen dance musical with a contemporary urban setting. In the eighties Wise served several terms as president of the Academy.

Reynolds, whose editing helps the film's musical numbers immeasurably, began working in Hollywood in the late thirties and was editor on such films as Algiers and the sci-fi classic The Day the Earth Stood Still (1951), which was directed by Wise. He also edited two of the earlier Rodgers and Hammerstein films, South Pacific and Carousel.

The back-to-back success of Mary Poppins and The Sound of Music typed Andrews as the eternal governess, and no amount of type-breaking roles—including the film S.O.B. (1981), in which she bared her breasts —has succeeded in changing that. She lost to Julie Christie in Darling.

Wood, a veteran actress, made her first film in 1919 but otherwise was seen in only a handful of movies. She played the title role in a fifties TV series Mama, based on the stories that had been filmed as I Remember Mama; her acting career was primarily spent on stage. Although trained as a singer, Wood is dubbed in "Climb Every Mountain" by Marni Nixon. Wood died in 1978. The supporting actress Oscar went to Shelley Winters for A Patch of Blue.

The cinematography award was won by Freddie Young for Doctor Zhivago, which also took the Oscars for art direction and for Phyllis Dalton's costumes.

Wise: 407, 973, 1753, 2244. Corcoran: 29, 413, 1753. Hynes: 33, 413, 1469, 1592, 1883, 2244. Kostal: 166, 1284, 1557, 2244. Reynolds: 643, 784, 896, 1753, 1927, 2152. Andrews: 1284, 2201. McCord: 1052, 2161. Leven: 34, 77, 422, 768, 1753, 1801, 1907, 2244. Scott: 46, 376, 413, 476, 530, 542, 557, 646, 896, 1062, 1088, 1213, 1391, 1475,

1706, 1753, 1907, 2008, 2120, 2247. Levitt: 77, 395, 1572. Jeakins: 393, 509, 832, 882, 1048, 1385, 1391, 1432, 1748, 2012, 2238.

1882 • SOUNDER

20TH CENTURY-FOX. 1972.

NOMINATIONS *Picture:* Robert B. Radnitz, producer. *Actor:* Paul Winfield. *Actress:* Cicely Tyson. *Screenplay—Based on Material From Another Medium:* Lonne Elder III.

Winfield and Tyson play the father and mother of three children—a sharecropper family trying to scrape by in Depression-era Louisiana—in this fine, simple film, one of the few "family films" worthy of the name: It's for families and about families, and explains what's good about families. Fortunately the earnestness of its aims never saps its value as entertainment. Directed by Martin Ritt [956] and expressively filmed by John Alonzo [395]. The cast includes Kevin Hooks as the oldest son and Taj Mahal, who also did the music, as Ike. Based on a novel by William H. Armstrong. Ritt was unfairly omitted from the directing slate; his slot went to the veteran Joseph L. Mankiewicz for the inferior *Sleuth.*

The best picture Oscar went to *The Godfather,* for which Marlon Brando also won as best actor. *Sounder* provided Winfield with his first major film role. He had previously appeared in the TV sitcom *Julia* and would continue his film career, primarily in character roles, in such movies as *Star Trek II: The Wrath of Khan, The Terminator* (1984), and *Presumed Innocent* (1990).

Tyson had also made her first major appearance in a TV series, *East Side, West Side.* Her film appearances in later years have been less celebrated than her work on television, particularly the acclaimed TV movie *The Autobiography of Miss Jane Pittman* (1974). The Oscar went to Liza Minnelli for *Cabaret.*

1883 • SOUTH PACIFIC

SOUTH PACIFIC ENTERPRISES INC.; MAGNA THEATRE CORPORATION. 1958.

AWARD *Sound:* Fred Hynes, sound director, Todd-AO Sound Department.

NOMINATIONS *Color Cinematography:* Leon Shamroy. *Scoring of a Musical Picture:* Alfred Newman and Ken Darby.

Stationed on a South Pacific island during World War II, navy nurse Nellie Forbush, played by Mitzi Gaynor, finds herself falling in love with French planter Emile de Becque (Rossano Brazzi). She is disturbed, however, because he has had children with a native woman who is now dead. Meanwhile, Lieutenant Cable, a young officer played by John Kerr, falls in love with Liat (France Nuyen), daughter of the raffish Bloody Mary (Juanita Hall). Despite a magnificent score by Richard Rodgers [1921] and Oscar Hammerstein II [375 . . .], poor casting and slack direction turn one of the greatest American musicals into one of the screen's biggest disappointments. The irony is that the director, Joshua Logan [643 . . .], was largely responsible for the success of the stage version, cowriting the book and directing the original production. The Broadway musical had memorably starred Mary Martin and Ezio Pinza, but Pinza had died and Martin was too old for her role by the time it was filmed. Logan, Rodgers and Hammerstein, and producer Buddy Adler [732 . . .] briefly considered Audrey Hepburn [278 . . .] for the role of Nellie, but perhaps the thought of Hepburn claiming to be "as corny as Kansas in August" struck them as implausible. The same thought might have warned them away from Elizabeth Taylor [318 . . .], who was encouraged to pursue the role by then-husband Michael Todd [101], who owned Magna Corp., the releasing organization for the film. But Taylor froze in a singing audition before Rodgers, who refused to consider dubbing Nellie. Doris Day [1572], whom one might have thought an ideal choice, lost the part because Logan felt she was typed in the public's mind: "she would make Nellie into Doris Day." Ironically the final choice makes Nellie into Mitzi Gaynor—hard and perky and unlovable, though she works like a demon to put the role across. As producer Arthur Hornblow [749 . . .] said to Logan: "Mitzi gives you too much for your money." Rodgers and Hammerstein changed their mind about dubbing and decided that Brazzi, whose singing voice they had earlier approved, should be dubbed by Giorgio Tozzi, the

Metropolitan Opera bass. Tozzi, who later performed the role on stage, might have seemed a good choice for Emile de Becque, but Brazzi had become a hot romantic lead after appearances in *Three Coins in the Fountain, The Barefoot Contessa,* and *Summertime.* Brazzi's ego was wounded by the decision to dub, and his performance lacks fire. Oddly Rodgers and Hammerstein also insisted that Hall, the only member of the cast who had been in the original company, also be dubbed, by Muriel Smith. Bill Lee sings for Kerr.

It's difficult to ascribe blame for one of the film's most notorious mistakes: the wash of color that sweeps in during musical numbers. In his memoirs Logan says he wanted to avoid a picture-postcard look and was advised by photographer Eliot Elisofon, who had consulted with John Huston on the color for *Moulin Rouge,* to shoot the South Pacific locations in unconventional ways. Logan also wanted to re-create the effect of the stage musical, in which the lighting changed to focus the audience's attention on the performer of the songs. Shamroy agreed to test color filters during the songs, filming the numbers both with and without the color changes. Producer Adler agreed, but according to Logan, after filming started Adler decided to cut costs by filming the sequences only with the color changes—the color could be corrected in the lab, he said, if they decided it didn't work. When the film was previewed, Logan hated the garish color transformations but was told it was too late to change them back. The final effect is obtrusive, although *South Pacific* shares with many filmed stage musicals the problem of reconciling realistic location photography with stylized musical numbers. The cinematography award went to Joseph Ruttenberg for *Gigi,* for which André Previn won the scoring Oscar.

Hynes: 33, 413, 1469, 1592, 1881, 2244. Shamroy: 29, 226, 356, 413, 495, 569, 602, 1088, 1153, 1213, 1592, 1610, 1706, 1852, 2013, 2286, 2334. Newman: 31, 34, 46, 72, 138, 182, 226, 333, 334, 347, 375, 428, 437, 457, 476, 495, 542, 690, 797, 833, 952, 953, 959, 962, 1016, 1082, 1088, 1213, 1278, 1362, 1397, 1475, 1616, 1655, 1849, 1868, 1921, 2043, 2046, 2091, 2258, 2286, 2294, 2316. Darby: 334, 690, 953, 1088, 1592.

1884 • SOUTHERNER, THE

Loew-Hakim; United Artists. 1945.

Nominations *Director:* Jean Renoir. *Sound Recording:* Jack Whitney, General Service. *Scoring of a Dramatic or Comedy Picture:* Werner Janssen.

Sam Tucker (Zachary Scott), a Texas farmer, moves his family to a small farm where they are to be sharecroppers in the cotton fields. Despite storms and a flood that ruin his crop, Sam resists the enticement of a job in a factory to remain on the land. A fine, small, relatively uncelebrated classic, with a screenplay based on the novel *Hold Autumn in Your Hand,* by George Sessions Perry. The first draft of the script was by Hugo Butler [597], but it was rewritten by Renoir with the uncredited help of William Faulkner. The cinematography is by Lucien Andriot, and the production was designed by Renoir's longtime collaborator, Eugene Lourié [1110]. The excellent cast includes Betty Field as Sam's wife, and Beulah Bondi [807 . . .], Percy Kilbride, Blanche Yurka, J. Carrol Naish [1294 . . .], and Norman Lloyd.

Renoir, one of the most esteemed directors in the history of film, was the son of the painter Auguste Renoir. He made his first film, *La Fille de l'Eau,* in 1924, but didn't really come into his own as a director until after the advent of sound, with such films as *Boudu Sauvé des Eaux* (1932), *Madame Bovary* (1934), *Le Crime de Monsieur Lange* (1935), and the two often regarded as his masterpieces, *Grand Illusion* and *The Rules of the Game* (1939). With the outbreak of war, Renoir came to America, where he directed several films, including *This Land Is Mine* and *The Diary of a Chambermaid* (1946). *The Southerner* is the best of his work in America, and Renoir later looked back on the American experience ruefully, not only because the films he produced here were inferior but also because his exile was resented in France. In 1950 he made one of his most beautiful films, *The River,* shot in color by his nephew Claude Renoir, entirely in India. He resumed work in Europe in 1953 with *The Golden Coach,* starring Anna Magnani [1727 . . .], and followed it with such films as *Eléna et les Hommes* (American title: *Paris Does Strange Things*) in 1956, and *Le Déjeuner sur l'Herbe* (1959). He lost his one nomination to Billy Wilder for *The Lost Weekend*. Renoir received an honorary Oscar at the 1974 awards ceremony: ''To Jean Renoir—a genius who, with grace, responsibility and enviable devotion through silent film, sound film, feature, documentary and television, has won the world's admiration.'' He died in 1979.

The award for sound went to Stephen Dunn for *The Bells of St. Mary's*. Miklos Rozsa took the scoring Oscar for *Spellbound*.

Whitney: 729, 862, 955, 1026, 2031, 2050, 2095. Janssen: 233, 349, 624, 757, 844.

1885 • SPANISH MAIN, THE

RKO RADIO. 1945.

NOMINATION *Color Cinematography:* George Barnes.

Pirate Paul Henreid abducts Maureen O'Hara, who proves quite a handful. Amusing swashbuckler, though you've seen it all before, and Henreid is a little too gentlemanly for his role. Directed by Frank Borzage [132 . . .] from a script by George Worthing Yates and Herman J. Mankiewicz [407 . . .], with Binnie Barnes and Walter Slezak. The Oscar went to Leon Shamroy for *Leave Her to Heaven*.

Barnes: 537, 1236, 1509, 1670, 1739, 1748, 1890.

1886 • SPARTACUS

BRYNA PRODUCTIONS INC.; UNIVERSAL-INTERNATIONAL. 1960.

AWARDS *Supporting Actor:* Peter Ustinov. *Color Cinematography:* Russell Metty. *Color Art Direction—Set Decoration:* Alexander Golitzen and Eric Orbom; Russell A. Gausman and Julia Heron. *Color Costume Design:* Valles and Bill Thomas.

NOMINATIONS *Scoring of a Dramatic or Comedy Picture:* Alex North. *Film Editing:* Robert Lawrence.

Kirk Douglas [130 . . .] plays the title role, a slave who leads a revolt against the forces of Rome, epitomized by the haughty sadist Crassus, played by Laurence Olivier [268 . . .]. The cast also includes Tony Curtis [522] as Antoninus, Crassus' favorite; Jean Simmons [858 . . .] as Varinia, the slave girl loved by Spartacus and sought by Crassus; Charles Laughton [1387 . . .] as the senator Gracchus; Ustinov as Batiatus, a slave trader; and John Gavin as the young Julius Caesar; plus Nina Foch [629], Herbert Lom, John Ireland [53], Joanna Barnes, and Woody Strode. One of the most admired of Hollywood's historical blockbusters, without the stale religiosity of *Ben-Hur* or the cliché-ridden dialogue of *Quo Vadis?* It's long and occasionally rather brutal, but very wittily performed. The screenplay, based on a novel by Howard Fast, is by Dalton Trumbo [273 . . .], who receives one of the first screen credits granted to anyone who was blacklisted during the fifties, even though during that period Trumbo won two Oscars —under the pseudonym Robert Rich for *The Brave One,* and behind the front supplied by Ian McLellan Hunter for *Roman Holiday*. Douglas, who produced the film, was instrumental in hiring Trumbo. Stanley Kubrick [151 . . .] replaced the first director chosen by Douglas, Anthony Mann. Kubrick, who was two years away from the notoriety brought him by *Lolita* and four from the celebrity brought him by *Dr. Strangelove,* was mistrusted by the studio and by many of the veteran technicians, including cinematographer Metty, as well as many members of the cast. His perfectionism and insistence on doing things his way may have cost him an Oscar nomination for *Spartacus*. The film was rereleased in 1991 with footage that had been excised in part by the censors for the original release and in part by the studio after the initial run. Some of the soundtrack was missing, particularly in a famous censored scene in which the homosexual attentions of Crassus to Antoninus are made moderately clear; Curtis dubbed his own voice in the restored version, but Olivier had died, so his role was dubbed by Anthony Hopkins [1679.5 . . .].

Ustinov is one of the most gifted performers of our time: a successful novelist, playwright, and director, as well as a superb character actor, usually in comic parts. He had made several films in the early forties as actor, director, and writer but first gained fame in this country with his performance as Nero in the 1951 *Quo Vadis?*

Metty began his career as cinematographer in the

mid-thirties and shot such films as *Bringing Up Baby* (1938), *The Story of G.I. Joe, Magnificent Obsession, Written on the Wind, Touch of Evil* (1958), and *Imitation of Life* (1959) before winning his Oscar for *Spartacus.* He died in 1978.

The scoring Oscar went to Ernest Gold for *Exodus.* Daniel Mandell won for editing *The Apartment.*

Ustinov: 943, 1644, 2116. Metty: 690. Golitzen: 31, 96, 414, 591, 690, 706, 744, 1560, 1968, 1986, 2035, 2064, 2101. Gausman: 96, 414, 681, 1285, 1572, 1895. Heron: 201, 366, 1070, 2031. Valles: 2029. Thomas: 116, 166, 254, 866, 883, 1003, 1789, 1812, 2128. North: 29, 215, 413, 515, 577, 1654, 1727, 1802, 1814, 1949, 2174, 2177, 2212, 2277.

1887 • SPAWN OF THE NORTH

PARAMOUNT. 1938.

AWARD *Special Award: For outstanding achievement in creating special photographic and sound effects:* Special effects by Gordon Jennings, assisted by Jan Domela, Dev Jennings, Irmin Roberts and Art Smith; transparencies by Farciot Edouart, assisted by Loyal Griggs; sound effects by Loren Ryder, assisted by Harry Mills, Louis H. Mesenkop and Walter Oberst.

Henry Fonda [815 . . .] and George Raft costar as Alaskan salmon fishermen taking on Russian poachers in turn-of-the-century Alaska. When they're not fighting the Russkies, they're jostling each other for the love of Dorothy Lamour. Enjoyably lively action adventure, directed by Henry Hathaway [1194] and photographed by Charles Lang [97 . . .]. The screenplay is by Jules Furthman [1387] and Talbot Jennings [83 . . .] and the score by Dimitri Tiomkin [33 . . .]. The supporting cast includes John Barrymore and Akim Tamiroff [701 . . .]. The honorary award was the first ever given by the Academy for special effects, which became a regular competitive award the following year.

G. Jennings: 56, 570, 975, 1668, 1855, 1934, 2168, 2175, 2181. D. Jennings: 2175. Edouart: 56, 570, 975, 1668, 1855, 1934, 2168, 2175, 2181. Griggs: 833, 988, 1799, 2012. Ryder: 566, 827,

979, 1452, 1669, 1697, 1703, 1837, 2012, 2168, 2181, 2183, 2230, 2242. Mesenkop: 56, 975, 1668.

1888 • SPECIAL DAY, A

CANAFOX FILMS PRODUCTION; CINEMA 5 LTD. (ITALY/CANADA). 1977.

NOMINATIONS *Actor:* Marcello Mastroianni. *Foreign Language Film.*

The day is May 6, 1938, when Hitler and Mussolini made the alliance of the fascists and the Nazis official, and all Rome turned out to celebrate—except for a tired housewife, played by Sophia Loren [1280 . . .], and a suicidal gay man (Mastroianni), who meet, talk, and make love. Interesting but contrived star teaming that seems to preen itself on casting its stars against type. Both of them are fun to watch as usual, but only marginally convincing, and the film doesn't have much of a point to make otherwise. Directed by Ettore Scola, who cowrote the screenplay with Ruggero Maccari [1764] and Maurizio Costanzo. The cinematography is by Pasqualino De Santis [1722]. Mastroianni lost to Richard Dreyfuss in *The Goodbye Girl.* The foreign language film Oscar went to *Madame Rosa.*

Mastroianni: 490, 554.

1888.5 • SPEED

20TH CENTURY FOX PRODUCTION; 20TH CENTURY FOX. 1994.

AWARDS *Sound:* Gregg Landaker, Steve Maslow, Bob Beemer, and David R. B. MacMillan. *Sound Effects Editing:* Stephen Hunter Flick.

NOMINATION *Film Editing:* John Wright.

After foiling an earlier plot by a mad bomber played by Dennis Hopper [595 . . .], L.A. bomb-squad officer Jack Traven (Keanu Reeves) finds himself playing a dangerous game with the bomber, who has rigged a city bus with a bomb that is armed once the driver goes over fifty miles per hour, and will explode once the bus drops below that speed. Slambang rollercoaster of a movie, wonderfully mindless entertainment that succeeds not only because of its endless stunts, but also because they take place in situations we recognize—an elevator, a bus, a subway train—and because it manages to include some characters whose fates we can care about. Reeves is a surprisingly engaging action hero, and Sandra Bullock became a star with her performance as a passenger who winds up in the driver's seat of the fatal bus. Also on hand are Joe Morton, Jeff Daniels, and Alan Ruck. Directed by Jan De Bont, who was the cinematographer on such films as *Die Hard, Black Rain, Total Recall,* and *The Hunt for Red October,* and obviously used those opportunities to learn how to make action movies. The editing Oscar went to Arthur Schmidt for *Forrest Gump.*

Landaker: 614, 1047, 1652. Maslow: 586, 614, 1652. Beemer: 413.5. MacMillan: 1698. Flick: 544, 1589, 1711, 2124. Wright: 961.

1889 • SPEEDY

HAROLD LLOYD CORP.; PARAMOUNT FAMOUS LASKY. 1927–28.

NOMINATION *Comedy Direction:* Ted Wilde.

Harold Lloyd plays a baseball nut who keeps getting fired because of his passion for the game. He redeems himself in the eyes of his girlfriend by his efforts to save her grandfather's horse-drawn streetcar, the last one in New York. Lloyd's last silent film is not as well known as such signature works as *Safety Last* (1923) or *The Freshman* (1925), but it's still fun, with a great chase sequence filmed on location in New York. Babe Ruth makes a cameo appearance. Wilde began his career as a gag writer for Lloyd and served as director on a few of the comedian's later features. His career, like Lloyd's, faded with the arrival of sound, though he made a couple of non-Lloyd talkies, *Clancy in Wall Street* and *Loose Ankles,* in 1930. Wilde lost to Lewis Milestone for *Two Arabian Knights.* The division of the directing award into comedy and drama was discontinued after this year.

1890 • SPELLBOUND

SELZNICK INTERNATIONAL PICTURES; UNITED ARTISTS. 1945.

AWARD *Scoring of a Dramatic or Comedy Picture:* Miklos Rozsa.

NOMINATIONS *Picture:* David O. Selznick, producer. *Supporting Actor:* Michael Chekhov. *Director:* Alfred Hitchcock. *Black-and-White Cinematography:* George Barnes. *Special Effects:* Jack Cosgrove, photographic.

A man played by Gregory Peck [759 . . .] arrives at a psychiatric clinic claiming to be its new director, Dr. Edwardes, but it soon becomes apparent that he's an imposter—an amnesiac who may have murdered the real Dr. Edwardes. A staff psychiatrist, played by Ingrid Bergman [72 . . .], helps him uncover his identity—and that of the real murderer. Inspired by Selznick's fascination with psychoanalysis (his own shrink, May Romm, receives screen credit as "psychiatric advisor"), but flawed by his pretensions and his meddling, which resulted in a fair amount of ludicrous nonsense, not helped at all by the very bad idea of having Salvador Dali stage dream sequences. Even Selznick's wife, Irene, called it "a terrible piece of junk." It's not quite as bad as that, since Hitchcock didn't take it nearly as seriously as the producer did, and it has eminently watchable stars, well supported by Chekhov as Bergman's mentor and Leo G. Carroll as Dr. Murchison. Hitchcock makes his signature appearance carrying a violin. The screenplay is by Ben Hecht [78 . . .] and Angus MacPhail from a novel by Hilary St. John Saunders and Leslie Palmer (under the pseudonym Francis Breeding).

Rozsa, born in Hungary, won the first of his three Oscars. He had begun his film scoring career in England with Alexander Korda [1620] and came to the States during World War II.

Chekhov was a nephew of the playwright Anton Chekhov and had worked as actor and director in collaboration with Stanislavski. He emigrated first to England and later to the United States, founding acting schools in both countries. His role as Bergman's mentor was his most important film part. The Oscar went to James Dunn for *A Tree Grows in Brooklyn.*

The Lost Weekend took the honors for best picture and for director Billy Wilder. The cinematography award went to Harry Stradling for *The Picture of Dorian Gray* and the special effects Oscar to *Wonder Man.*

Rozsa: 175, 566, 567, 604, 1035, 1069, 1070, 1085, 1208, 1227, 1644, 1872, 1968, 2050, 2304. Selznick: 497, 798, 1670, 1828, 1908, 1996, 2211. Hitchcock: 1171, 1632, 1669, 1670. Barnes: 537, 1236, 1509, 1670, 1739, 1748, 1885. Cosgrove: 798, 1607, 1670, 1828.

1891 • SPIRAL STAIRCASE, THE

RKO RADIO. 1946.

NOMINATION *Supporting Actress:* Ethel Barrymore.

A serial killer is on the loose in a turn-of-the-century New England village, and his targets are young women who have physical defects—like Dorothy McGuire [759], the mute paid companion for Barrymore, a dowager who lives in an old dark house. Nifty gothic thriller, well directed by Robert Siodmak [1085], with George Brent, Kent Smith, Rhonda Fleming, Elsa Lanchester [428 . . .], and Sara Allgood [952]. The screenplay, by Mel Dinelli, is based on a novel by Ethel Lina White. The cinematographer is Nicholas Musuraca [972] and the music is by Roy Webb [615 . . .]. Barrymore lost to Anne Baxter in *The Razor's Edge.*

Barrymore: 1445, 1528, 1575.

1892 • SPIRIT OF ST. LOUIS, THE

LELAND HAYWARD-BILLY WILDER; WARNER BROS. 1957.

NOMINATION *Special Effects:* Louis Lichtenfield.

James Stewart [73 . . .] plays Charles Lindbergh in this re-creation of the famous solo flight across the Atlantic in 1927. Virtually a one-man show, with Stewart giving his considerable all. Billy Wilder [91 . . .], who directed and cowrote the screenplay with Wendell Mayes [73], somehow dropped his customary cynicism for this portrait of an American hero. Too bad, because the film could use a little of it —much of the movie is taken up with a man talking to a fly. Filmed in CinemaScope, which reduces the claustrophobic sense that some of the in-flight sequences need, by cinematographers Robert Burks [1537 . . .] and Peverell Marley [1170 . . .], with aerial camera work by Thomas Tutwiler. Lichtenfield's visual effects lost to Walter Rossi's sound effects for *The Enemy Below*—a curious case of apples vs. oranges that the Academy remedied in 1963 by dividing visual effects and sound effects into separate categories.

1893 • SPLASH

TOUCHSTONE FILMS PRODUCTION; BUENA VISTA. 1984.

NOMINATION *Screenplay Written Directly for the Screen:* Lowell Ganz, Babaloo Mandel, and Bruce Jay Friedman; screen story by Bruce Jay Friedman, story by Brian Grazer.

Tom Hanks [195 . . .] plays a New Yorker whose love life is a disaster until he meets the right woman —except she's not a woman, she's a mermaid, played by Daryl Hannah. Dealing with this beautiful fish-out-of-water—who magically loses her piscine attributes as long as she stays dry—is hard enough, but then a scientist (Eugene Levy) gets wise and wants to experiment on her. Delightful if slightly overextended comedy that launched Disney's Touchstone Pictures division—a production branch created for movies that were a little too risqué for the regular Disney label that had traditionally meant "bring the whole family." A big hit, the movie was a career-maker for several participants: Hanks, who had made only two big-screen movies before this one; Hannah, whose only memorable role before this one was in *Blade Runner;* John Candy, who plays Hanks' brother, and whose likability had never come across on screen so well before; and director Ron Howard, following up his well-received *Night Shift* (1982) and establishing himself as a major young director. Ganz and Mandel had also written the screenplay for *Night Shift* and would team up again with Howard and Grazer (who is also *Splash*'s producer) on *Parenthood.* Friedman is a humorist whose writing was also adapted in 1984 for the Steve Martin movie *The Lonely Guy.* The screenplay Oscar went to Robert Benton for *Places in the Heart.*

1894 • SPLENDOR IN THE GRASS

NBI PRODUCTION; WARNER BROS. 1961.

AWARD *Story and Screenplay—Written Directly for the Screen:* William Inge.

NOMINATION *Actress:* Natalie Wood.

Deanie Loomis (Wood) and Bud Stamper, played by Warren Beatty [255 . . .] in his film debut, are teen sweethearts in a Kansas town in the twenties, but his bullying father (Pat Hingle) and her prudish mother (Audrey Christie) want to break up the kids before they get too serious. Sexual frustration sends Bud chasing after bad girls and Deanie to a mental institution. She gets cured, and he gets married, to the earthy Angelina (Zohra Lampert), whom he meets while away at college. Cooked-up but tasty coming-of-age melodrama. Even though the movie is set in the twenties and its release date puts it in the sixties, it's one of the key films for understanding what it was like to grow up in the fifties—along with Inge's *Picnic* and Wood's *Rebel Without a Cause,* plus *Peyton Place* and a few other troubled-youth tales. Somehow overlooked by the Academy are the director, Elia Kazan [63 . . .], who handles this florid and messy stuff as if he believed every word, and cinematographer Boris Kaufman [119 . . .], art director Richard Sylbert [395 . . .], and costumer Anna Hill Johnstone [784 . . .], who give the movie a rich, handsome gleam. The supporting cast includes Barbara Loden as Bud's rebellious sister, Sandy Dennis [2277] as one of Deanie's sidekicks, and Inge himself as a minister. The movie made Beatty a star.

As far-fetched as *Splendor in the Grass* seems, Inge was writing about the world he knew. He was born in Independence, Kansas, in 1913, and his plays *Picnic* and *The Dark at the Top of the Stairs* (which were later filmed) also grew out of the experiences of a solitary, bookish boyhood. He became a journalist and teacher in St. Louis, and a meeting with a playwright who had lived in St. Louis, Tennessee Williams [119 . . .], set Inge on the course to becoming a playwright. *Come Back, Little Sheba* launched a successful Broadway career in 1949. It was also adapted for the movies, as was his later play, *Bus Stop.* Inge's career as a playwright fizzled in the sixties. He wrote only one more screenplay, *All Fall Down* (1962), which also starred Beatty. Inge committed suicide in 1973.

The best actress Oscar went to Sophia Loren for *Two Women.*

Wood: 1219, 1671.

1895 • SPOILERS, THE

FRANK LLOYD; UNIVERSAL. 1942.

NOMINATION *Black-and-White Interior Decoration:* John B. Goodman and Jack Otterson, art direction; Russell A. Gausman and Edward R. Robinson, set decoration.

In the gold rush Yukon, John Wayne [33 . . .] has been railroaded by Randolph Scott, but Wayne breaks out of jail and settles his scores with Scott in an epic fistfight and wins saloon singer Marlene Dietrich [1358] in the process. Fine old hokum from a novel by Rex Beach that had been filmed three times before and would be remade in 1955—but this is the best version because of its stars and because it doesn't take itself seriously. The screenplay is by Lawrence Hazard and Tom Reed [1433] and the director is Ray Enright. The cast includes Margaret Lindsay, Harry Carey, and Richard Barthelmess [1447 . . .]. The art direction Oscar went to *This Above All.*

Goodman: 414, 979, 1560. Otterson: 96, 269, 668, 681, 1229, 1240, 2342. Gausman: 414, 681, 1285, 1572, 1886.

1896 • SPRING PARADE

UNIVERSAL. 1940.

NOMINATIONS *Black-and-White Cinematography:* Joseph Valentine. *Sound Recording:* Bernard B. Brown. *Song:* "Waltzing in the Clouds," music by Robert Stolz, lyrics by Gus Kahn. *Score:* Charles Previn.

A Deanna Durbin vehicle *mit Schlag.* The setting is nineteenth-century Vienna, and she's a baker's assistant (the baker is S. Z. Sakall) who falls for army officer Robert Cummings, who is not quite what he seems. A pleasant enough excuse for lots of songs, including Strauss' "Blue Danube," with lyrics supplied by Kahn. Directed by Henry Koster [214] from a screenplay by Bruce Manning and Felix Jackson [123] and a story by Ernst Marischka [1872]. The cast includes Mischa Auer [1401], Allyn Joslyn, Reginald Denny, and Franklin Pangborn.

The cinematography Oscar went to George Barnes for *Rebecca.* Douglas Shearer won for the sound for *Strike Up the Band. Pinocchio* took the awards for Leigh Harline and Ned Washington's "When You Wish

Upon a Star'' and for Harline, Washington, and Paul J. Smith's scoring.

Valentine: 668, 776, 1048, 1229, 2291. Brown: 93, 96, 269, 919, 1010, 1011, 1125, 1560, 2028, 2260. Stolz: 1026. Kahn: 692, 1488. Previn: 306, 668, 1030, 1229, 1485, 1870.

1897 • SPY WHO CAME IN FROM THE COLD, THE

SALEM FILMS LTD. PRODUCTION; PARAMOUNT (UNITED KINGDOM). 1965.

NOMINATIONS *Actor:* Richard Burton. *Black-and-White Art Direction—Set Decoration:* Hal Pereira, Tambi Larsen, and Edward Marshall; Josie MacAvin.

Burton is an aging British spy who, nearing the end of his career, gets a chance to go over the Berlin Wall as a mole. A grimly deglamorized film, designed in part as a counterpoint to the James Bond image of the spy as hip and swashbuckling, this adaptation of the John Le Carré novel by Paul Dehn [1378 . . .] and Guy Trosper [1605] is well directed by Martin Ritt [956], but it's not a lot of fun. The bleak photography —the Cold War never looked chillier—is by Oswald Morris [659 . . .]. The cast includes Oskar Werner [1812], Claire Bloom, Sam Wanamaker, Cyril Cusack, Michael Hordern, and the ''M'' of the James Bond series, Bernard Lee.

Burton's career was at its peak at the box office and at its nadir with the critics, thanks to the crowd-pleasing teamings with Elizabeth Taylor [318 . . .] in *Cleopatra, The V.I.P.'s,* and *The Sandpiper. Spy* gave him a chance to redeem himself with the critics, and he did, though he resisted and resented the direction he received from Ritt, who wanted him to look shabby and anonymous and even to damp down the resonance of his famous voice. In other years, such playing against type might have won Burton an Oscar, but he was up against the world's most famous actor, Laurence Olivier in *Othello,* and another actor playing a shabby, faceless type, Rod Steiger in *The Pawnbroker,* as well as his own *Spy* costar, Werner, in *Ship of Fools.* But despite all these high-powered, serious contenders, Lee Marvin slipped through and won for one of the few comedy performances ever recognized by the Academy, in *Cat Ballou.*

Ship of Fools won the art direction Oscar.

Burton: 85, 164, 621, 1391, 1706, 2277. Pereira: 278, 357, 363, 426, 450, 736, 956, 1029, 1219, 1504, 1570, 1631, 1674, 1716, 1727, 1738, 1840, 1959, 2012, 2098, 2200, 2208. Larsen: 892, 956, 1341, 1727. Marshall: 2106. MacAvin: 1512, 2106.

1898 • SPY WHO LOVED ME, THE

EON PRODUCTIONS LTD.; UNITED ARTISTS (UNITED KINGDOM). 1977.

NOMINATIONS *Art Direction—Set Decoration:* Ken Adam and Peter Lamont; Hugh Scaife. *Original Song:* ''Nobody Does It Better,'' music by Marvin Hamlisch, lyrics by Carole Bayer Sager. *Original Score:* Marvin Hamlisch.

James Bond (Roger Moore) teams with a Russian spy (Barbara Bach) to thwart a plot by a villain (Curt Jurgens) who has his own underwater kingdom and a seven-foot-tall henchman (Richard Kiel) nicknamed Jaws because of his stainless-steel dentures. One of the better Roger Moore Bonds, with a script by Christopher Wood and Richard Maibaum that as usual has only its title and its hero in common with its supposed source, a novel by Ian Fleming. Directed by Lewis Gilbert [35], with cinematography by Claude Renoir. The nominated song is sung by Carly Simon.

The art direction Oscar went to the year's biggest pop adventure, *Star Wars,* which also won for John Williams' score. The best song was judged to be the title tune by Joseph Brooks for *You Light Up My Life,* but posterity has been kinder to Hamlisch and Sager's entry.

Adam: 12.5, 101, 151, 1234.5. Lamont: 45, 659. Scaife: 608, 1533. Hamlisch: 398, 977, 1109, 1747, 1813, 1876, 1927, 2238. Sager: 103, 166.5, 977, 1071.3.

1899 • STAGE DOOR

RKO RADIO. 1937.

NOMINATIONS *Picture:* Pandro S. Berman, producer. *Supporting Actress:* Andrea Leeds. *Director:* Gregory La Cava. *Screenplay:* Morris Ryskind and Anthony Veiller.

Katharine Hepburn [24 . . .] plays Terry Randall, an aspiring actress who's also a rich girl slumming: She checks into a boardinghouse full of other Broadway hopefuls and winds up rooming with Jean Maitland, played by Ginger Rogers [1102], a poor girl who thinks Terry is a poseur and a pain. Things get even more tense between the two when both get involved with rich producer Anthony Powell, played by Adolphe Menjou [734], and when Terry lands a part that by rights should have gone to the more talented Kaye Hamilton (Leeds), a fellow resident of the boardinghouse. Terrific comedy-drama, loosely based on a play by Edna Ferber and George S. Kaufman—so loosely that Kaufman groused that it should have been called "Screen Door." (In fact, the movie is better than the play.) Hepburn and Rogers are in peak sparring form, and they have one of the all-time great supporting casts: Gail Patrick, Constance Collier, Lucille Ball, Jack Carson, Franklin Pangborn, Grady Sutton, Eve Arden [1319], and Ann Miller. The abiding mystery is why neither Hepburn nor Rogers landed a nomination. Either would have been preferable to the year's best actress winner, Luise Rainer in *The Good Earth*. Rogers never gave a better nonmusical performance, and Hepburn does a tremendous self-parody. In fact, her famous line from the play in *Stage Door,* "The calla lilies are in bloom again," was lifted from the play in which she made her own disastrous return to Broadway in 1933, *The Lake*. The movie is filled with such in-jokes: The title of the play in which Hepburn is appearing in *Stage Door* is *Enchanted April*—which was the title of a notorious RKO flop movie of 1935 (remade with more success in 1991).

The best picture Oscar went to *The Life of Emile Zola,* which also won for the screenplay by Norman Reilly Raine, Heinz Herald, and Geza Herczeg. Leeds, who made her screen debut in *Come and Get It* in 1936, retired from movies in 1940 after only a few film roles, most of them unmemorable. She lost to Alice Brady in *In Old Chicago*. Leo McCarey won for directing *The Awful Truth*.

Berman: 40, 656, 754, 1035, 2115. La Cava: 1401. Ryskind: 1401. Veiller: 1085.

1900 • *STAGE DOOR CANTEEN*

PRINCIPAL ARTISTS-LESSER; UNITED ARTISTS. 1943.
NOMINATIONS *Song:* "We Mustn't Say Good Bye," music by James Monaco, lyrics by Al Dubin. *Scoring of a Musical Picture:* Frederic E. Rich.

Young soldiers about to be shipped overseas spend their last days in New York courting the hostesses of the Stage Door Canteen, a Broadway wartime institution staffed by the great performers of the day. The sentimental screenplay, by Delmer Daves, is only a framework for vaudeville turns and cameo appearances by an endless stream of performers, including Judith Anderson [1670], Tallulah Bankhead, Ray Bolger, Katharine Cornell, Jane Darwell [815], Dorothy Fields [1707 . . .], Arlene Francis, Helen Hayes [31 . . .], Jean Hersholt, George Jessel, Alfred Lunt [841], Harpo Marx, Yehudi Menuhin, Cornelia Otis Skinner, Ethel Waters [1575], May Whitty [1371 . . .], Ralph Bellamy [114], Helen Broderick, William Demarest [1058], Gracie Fields, Katharine Hepburn [24 . . .], Sam Jaffe [105], Gertrude Lawrence, Elsa Maxwell, Ethel Merman, Merle Oberon [487], Johnny Weissmuller, Ed Wynn [542], Edgar Bergen, Ina Claire, Lynn Fontanne [841], Gypsy Rose Lee, Aline MacMahon [576], Paul Muni [218.5 . . .], Franklin Pangborn, George Raft, Martha Scott [1510], Peggy Lee [1554], and the bands of Count Basie, Xavier Cugat, Benny Goodman, Kay Kyser, Freddy Martin, and Guy Lombardo. Directed by Frank Borzage [132 . . .].

The song Oscar went to "You'll Never Know," by Harry Warren and Mack Gordon, from *Hello, Frisco, Hello*. The scoring award was won by Ray Heindorf for *This Is the Army*.

Monaco: 563, 1691, 1984. Dubin: 791, 1367. Rich: 1036.

1901 • *STAGECOACH*

WALTER WANGER; UNITED ARTISTS. 1939.
AWARDS *Supporting Actor:* Thomas Mitchell. *Score:* Richard Hageman, Frank Harling, John Leipold, and Leo Shuken.
NOMINATIONS *Picture:* Walter Wanger, producer. *Director:* John Ford. *Black-and-White Cinematography:* Bert

Glennon. *Interior Decoration:* Alexander Toluboff. *Film Editing:* Otho Lovering and Dorothy Spencer.

The stage sets out through hostile Indian country, bound for Lordsburg, Arizona, with a group of passengers that includes Dallas, a woman of ill repute, played by Claire Trevor [510 . . .]; the alcoholic Doc Boone (Mitchell); Hatfield (John Carradine), a saturnine southerner; Lucy Mallory (Louise Platt), a pregnant woman on the way to meet her husband; Peacock (Donald Meek), a whiskey salesman whose sample case Doc Boone decimates; and Gatewood (Berton Churchill), a pompous banker who's trying to get away with robbery. Along the way, the drivers, Curley, played by George Bancroft [2085], and Buck (Andy Devine), stop to pick up the Ringo Kid, played by John Wayne [33 . . .], who has a score to settle with some bad guys in Lordsburg. Landmark western, with a rich screenplay by Dudley Nichols [30 . . .] based on a story by Ernest Haycox and ultimately, it has been said, on the Guy de Maupassant story "Boule de Suif," although one wonders if that attribution hasn't been tacked on by the movie's intellectual admirers to make it seem more respectable. If so, it doesn't need it: Though it has its share of clichés and sentimental moments, this is one of the definitive American movies, full of plausible, detailed characterization and great action sequences, including the oft-imitated stuntwork of Yakima Canutt. Above all, the movie created an American icon. Wayne was no stranger to westerns: He'd been bumming around Hollywood for a decade appearing in endless poverty-row oaters before Ford gave him the part that would make him one of the most colossal of all Hollywood superstars, heralding his first appearance in the movie with a sweeping bit of camera work which leaves no doubt that this character is someone special.

Mitchell's Oscar may have been particularly for *Stagecoach,* but it would have been hard to overlook him in 1939, when he also appeared in *Only Angels Have Wings, Gone With the Wind, Mr. Smith Goes to Washington,* and *The Hunchback of Notre Dame.* Though he had made one appearance in silent films in 1924, Mitchell was a stage actor and a playwright until 1936, when he came to Hollywood and became one

of the most ubiquitous performers in movies. He continued to be busy through the forties, but his career tapered off in the fifties. He made his last screen appearance in 1961, a year before his death, in *Pocketful of Miracles.*

The best picture of the year was *Gone With the Wind,* which also won for Victor Fleming's direction, Lyle Wheeler's art direction, and Hal C. Kern and James E. Newcom's editing. Glennon was one of the two official nominees for black-and-white cinematography. The Academy announced a preliminary slate with eleven nominees before reducing it to two candidates on the final ballot. The Oscar went to Gregg Toland for *Wuthering Heights.*

Mitchell: 962. Hageman: 955, 979, 1200, 1801, 2062. Harling: 1880, 2080. Shuken: 2184. Wanger: 413, 706, 1048. Ford: 815, 952, 999, 1200, 1642. Glennon: 551, 581. Toluboff: 36, 2214. Spencer: 413, 517, 591.

1902 • *STAGECOACH TO FURY*

REGAL FILMS INC. PRODUCTION; 20TH CENTURY-FOX. 1956. NOMINATION *Black-and-White Cinematography:* Walter Strenge.

A stagecoach is held up by bandits, and its passengers fear for their lives until a former cavalry officer, played by Forrest Tucker, engineers a plan that saves the day. Mediocre western programmer, directed by William Claxton with Mari Blanchard and Wallace Ford. By 1956 color had taken hold solidly as one of Hollywood's weapons against television—this was the first year that all five nominees for best picture were color films. But it's hard to believe that there were no more impressive candidates to fill out the black-and-white cinematography slate—like Asaichi Nakai for *Seven Samurai,* for example. Strenge, who worked primarily on B pictures from 1929 to 1968, lost to Joseph Ruttenberg for *Somebody Up There Likes Me.*

1903 • *STALAG 17*

PARAMOUNT. 1953. AWARD *Actor:* William Holden. NOMINATIONS *Supporting Actor:* Robert Strauss. *Director:* Billy Wilder.

Holden plays the cynical loner Sergeant Sefton, a POW in a German camp during World War II. His abrasive contempt for his fellow prisoners makes him the object of suspicion when it becomes apparent that one of them is a spy working for the Nazis. Entertainingly tough-minded comedy, based on a play by Donald Bevan and Edmund Trzcinski, who had been inmates of the real Stalag 17. The movie shows signs of its stage origins—too many expository speeches—despite the attempts of scenarists Wilder and Edwin Blum to loosen it up for the movies. The camp commandant is played by Otto Preminger [73 . . .], and the other prisoners include Don Taylor, Peter Graves, Neville Brand, Ross Bagdasarian, and Trzcinski himself as "Triz." Sig Rumann plays Schulz, the comic Nazi. Strauss, as the gross Stosh (a.k.a. "Animal"), and Harvey Lembeck, as his buddy Harry, were in the original Broadway company. The cinematography is by Ernest Laszlo [31 . . .]. About the worst thing you can say about *Stalag 17* is that it inspired the inane copycat TV sitcom *Hogan's Heroes*.

Holden made his film debut in 1938, when he was twenty, and achieved stardom the following year in *Golden Boy*. War service interrupted his early screen career, and he was little more than a pleasant second-string leading man until he was cast in *Sunset Boulevard*, a role that gave him a chance to show an edge beneath his handsomeness. He became one of the major stars of the fifties, in films such as *The Moon Is Blue, The Country Girl, Executive Suite, Sabrina, Love Is a Many-Splendored Thing, Picnic,* and *The Bridge on the River Kwai,* among others. As his looks began to fade in the sixties, he turned toward character leads, giving memorable performances as hard-bitten types in *The Wild Bunch* and *Network*. He died in 1981. His Oscar was won over some formidable competitors: Marlon Brando in *Julius Caesar,* Richard Burton in *The Robe,* and Montgomery Clift and Burt Lancaster in *From Here to Eternity*.

Strauss played a variety of character parts, usually working-class urbanites, in films and on TV through the fifties and sixties. He died in 1975. The Oscar went to Frank Sinatra for *From Here to Eternity,* which also won for director Fred Zinnemann.

Holden: 1424, 1975. Wilder: 91, 138, 198, 566, 705, 709, 925, 1208, 1440, 1738, 1860, 1975, 2297.

1904 • *STAND AND DELIVER*

MENENDEZ/MUSCA & OLMOS PRODUCTION; WARNER BROS. 1988.

NOMINATION *Actor:* Edward James Olmos.

Olmos plays Jaime Escalante, a math teacher in a high school in the Los Angeles barrio, who inspires his students, mostly poor Chicano kids, to excel. His efforts to get them to pass advance placement tests in calculus pay off stunningly, but the testing board grows suspicious: Surely these inner-city kids can't be that good? So after having fired the kids up to beat the system once, Escalante has to fire them up again to battle prejudice. Terrifically inspiring beating-the-odds movie—a *Rocky* about math. Olmos is a powerhouse, and he gets great support from the young actors playing his students, especially Lou Diamond Phillips as a kid who doesn't want his buddies to know how smart he is. Also impressive are Rosana de Soto as Escalante's wife and Andy Garcia [786] as one of the testing board's skeptics—who's caught in a bind because he's Chicano himself. Directed by Ramon Menendez, who cowrote the screenplay with Tom Musca. The story is all the better for being true.

Olmos, who was born in the East L.A. that serves as the setting for *Stand and Deliver,* began his career as a rock musician and got his start as an actor in *Zoot Suit,* a musical play by Luis Valdez that was first staged in Los Angeles, went to Broadway, and was filmed in 1981. After small but impressive roles in movies that did mediocre business but have developed a cult following, *Wolfen* (1981) and *Blade Runner,* Olmos achieved stardom on TV as the taciturn police chief on *Miami Vice*. Despite the acclaim he received for *Stand and Deliver,* his subsequent screen performances have not attracted wide audiences, but he has been prominent as a spokesman for the Mexican-American community. He made an impressive directorial debut in 1992 with the grim prison film *American Me*. The Oscar went to Dustin Hoffman for *Rain Man*.

1905 • *STAND BY FOR ACTION*

MGM. 1943.

NOMINATION *Special Effects:* A. Arnold Gillespie and Donald Jahraus, photographic; Michael Steinore, sound.

War-effort drama about Robert Taylor's initiation into battle aboard a destroyer. Routine flag-waver, directed by Robert Z. Leonard [555 . . .], with a better cast than it deserves: Charles Laughton [1387 . . .], Brian Donlevy [161], and Walter Brennan [424 . . .]. Written by George Bruce, Herman J. Mankiewicz [407 . . .], and John L. Balderston [749 . . .] and photographed by Charles Rosher [22 . . .]. The special effects award went to Fred Sersen and Roger Heman for *Crash Dive.*

Gillespie: 175, 256, 685, 704, 835, 1371, 1388, 2048, 2055, 2122, 2300. Jahraus: 2048, 2055. Steinore: 835, 2048.

1906 • *STAND BY ME*

ACT III PRODUCTION; COLUMBIA. 1986.

NOMINATION *Screenplay Based on Material From Another Medium:* Raynold Gideon and Bruce A. Evans.

Four boys—Wil Wheaton, River Phoenix [1735], Corey Feldman, and Jerry O'Connell—hear a rumor that there's a corpse in the nearby woods and set out to investigate, encountering their own fears and insecurities, as well as a gang of older bullies led by Kiefer Sutherland. Richard Dreyfuss [803] is the narrator—the Wheaton character grown up—and the cast includes Casey Siemaszko and John Cusack. Fine, insightful coming-of-age comedy-drama, one of the best movies ever made from something written by Stephen King—in this case, a story called "The Body." Directed by Rob Reiner. A few critics have protested that the screenplay is full of dirty words that weren't common in the fifties, when the film takes place. If they're old enough to remember the fifties, those critics must have spent all their time at the movies. The Oscar went to Ruth Prawer Jhabvala for *A Room With a View.*

1907 • *STAR!*

ROBERT WISE PRODUCTION; 20TH CENTURY-FOX. 1968.

NOMINATIONS *Supporting Actor:* Daniel Massey. *Cinematography:* Ernest Laszlo. *Art Direction—Set Decoration:* Boris Leven; Walter M. Scott and Howard Bristol. *Sound:* 20th Century-Fox Sound Department. *Song:* "Star!," music by Jimmy Van Heusen, lyrics by Sammy Cahn. *Score of a Musical Picture—Original or Adaptation:* Lennie Hayton. *Costume Design:* Donald Brooks.

Julie Andrews [1284 . . .] plays Gertrude Lawrence, the celebrated musical comedy star, with Massey as Noël Coward [993], her friend and confidant. Disastrous dud musical, overextended (nearly three hours long) and centrally miscast. Andrews works hard to create a character who is demanding and egotistic off stage and adorable on stage, but her Mary Poppins–Maria Von Trapp image had become a screen through which all else must be strained, and you can see the effort. Despite the work of people who had made *The Sound of Music* a smash—Andrews, director Robert Wise, designers Leven and Scott—*Star!* was one of the flops that killed the movie musical. It was undermined by the lack of story—the screenplay is by William Fairchild—and by a central character who was not only unlovable but also a figure who had no resonance for movie audiences: Lawrence had made only a handful of films. Fox attempted to salvage the movie by cutting it to 120 minutes and releasing it under the inane title *Those Were the Happy Times,* but to no avail. The cast also includes Richard Crenna, Robert Reed, Beryl Reid, and Jenny Agutter, and the choreography is by Michael Kidd.

Massey was not only the godson of the man he plays in *Star!* but he had made his first screen appearance as a small boy in Coward's film *In Which We Serve.* The son of Raymond Massey [1] and brother of actress Anna Massey, he has spent his career primarily on stage, making only occasional movie appearances. The Oscar went to Jack Albertson for *The Subject Was Roses.*

Pasqualino De Santis won for the cinematography for *Romeo and Juliet,* which also won for Danilo Donati's costumes. The Oscar for art direction went

to another, far more successful musical with an ex-
clamatory title, *Oliver!,* which also took the awards
for sound and for John Green's adaptation score.
"The Windmills of Your Mind," by Michel Legrand
and Alan and Marilyn Bergman, from *The Thomas
Crown Affair,* won the song Oscar.

Laszlo: 31, 646, 1000, 1032, 1065, 1196, 1812.
Leven: 34, 77, 422, 768, 1753, 1801, 1881, 2244.
Scott: 46, 376, 413, 476, 530, 542, 557, 646, 896,
1062, 1088, 1213, 1391, 1475, 1706, 1753, 1881,
2008, 2120, 2247. Bristol: 690, 852, 864, 1182,
1451, 1607, 1613, 2064. Van Heusen: 171, 173,
787, 915, 926, 1056, 1524, 1587, 1708, 1859,
2016, 2064, 2263. Cahn: 74, 163, 182, 696, 915,
926, 1031, 1056, 1216, 1524, 1587, 1692, 1708,
1719, 1859, 2016, 2064, 2072, 2103, 2110, 2125,
2263, 2264, 2315, 2343. Hayton: 877, 896, 1476,
1577, 1831. Brooks: 356, 494.

1908 • STAR, THE

BERT E. FRIEDLOB PRODUCTIONS; 20TH CENTURY-FOX. 1952.
NOMINATION *Actress:* Bette Davis.

Davis plays an Oscar-winning actress who has hit
the midlife skids. Sterling Hayden is the former actor
who helps her sort things out after she's arrested for
drunken driving. Disappointingly meandering drama
that gets what energy it can from Davis' performance
and from the resonance of the story with her own
career: After leaving Warner Bros. and going out on
her own in the late forties, she had one triumph, *All
About Eve,* followed by a series of forgettable films.
Although she was called on for a few serious roles,
through much of the remainder of her career she
would receive most attention for films like *The Star*
and *What Ever Happened to Baby Jane?* that exploited
her former eminence as an actress. Stuart Heisler
directs from a screenplay by Katherine Albert and
Dale Eunson that was reportedly written with Joan
Crawford [1319 . . .] in mind for the lead. The cast
includes Natalie Wood [1219 . . .] and Warner Anderson. The Oscar went to Shirley Booth for *Come
Back, Little Sheba.*

Davis: 46, 484, 492, 1046, 1162, 1182, 1369,
1456, 1462.5, 2248.

1909 • STAR IS BORN, A

SELZNICK INTERNATIONAL PICTURES; UNITED ARTISTS. 1937.
AWARDS *Original Story:* William A. Wellman and Rob-
ert Carson. *Special Award:* W. Howard Greene for the
color photography.
NOMINATIONS *Picture:* David O. Selznick, producer.
Actor: Fredric March. *Actress:* Janet Gaynor. *Director:*
William Wellman. *Screenplay:* Alan Campbell, Robert
Carson, and Dorothy Parker. *Assistant Director:* Eric
Stacey.

Young hopeful Esther Blodgett (Gaynor) comes to
Hollywood, where she encounters a star, Norman
Maine (March), who helps her launch a career in
movies under the name Vicki Lester. Norman and
Vicki marry, but as her star ascends, his career stalls
and he sinks into alcoholism. Very entertaining
drama, well laced with comedy and some satiric
glances at the movie industry. The stars are well supported by Adolphe Menjou [734] as a producer, May
Robson [1119] as Granny, Lionel Stander as a publicist, and Andy Devine, Clara Blandick, Peggy Wood
[1881], Franklin Pangborn, and Edgar Kennedy. Future stars Carole Landis and Lana Turner [1558] can
be spotted as extras in the Santa Anita bar scene.

A Star Is Born obviously captured a central Hollywood myth, as the film's two remakes demonstrate,
but the Oscar for original story is a bit odd, considering that Adela Rogers St. Johns and Jane Murfin had
received nominations for a very similar story, for the
film *What Price Hollywood?,* five years earlier. Selznick
had also produced that film, which is about an alcoholic director who turns a waitress into a movie star
and spirals into decline as she becomes more successful; it's more satiric, less sentimental than *A Star Is
Born.* According to Selznick's biographer David
Thomson, Wellman said he and Carson wrote the
story for *A Star Is Born* and presented it to Selznick,
who wasn't very interested until Wellman talked to
Selznick's wife, Irene, who loved the idea and persuaded her husband to film it. But both David and
Irene Selznick said the idea originated with David,
who was interested in improving on *What Price Hollywood?,* which had grown dated. Wellman himself gave
credence to that version of the film's origin when,

accepting the Oscar for the film, he said the award really belonged to Selznick. Norman Maine is often said to be modeled on John Gilbert and John Barrymore. In Wellman and Carson's original draft, Vicki, distraught over Norman's suicide, gives up her career and goes home to Canada. Parker and Campbell, who were hired to aid Carson in writing the screenplay, retained that ending. The current ending, with its now-famous last line, "This is Mrs. Norman Maine," has been attributed to still other writers: David Thomson says Ring Lardner, Jr. [1286 . . .], and Budd Schulberg [1477] came up with it, but Ronald Haver, in his fine book on the filming of the 1954 musical remake, says the line was the contribution of writer John Lee Mahin [352 . . .].

Greene had shared a special award for color photography with Harold Rosson a year earlier, for their work on Selznick's *The Garden of Allah.* As color became more and more common in the late thirties, the Academy asked a committee of cinematographers to screen all the color pictures made during 1937 and choose one for a special award. It repeated this practice the following year, when Oliver Marsh and Allen Davey were given a special award for the color cinematography of *Sweethearts.* Color cinematography was finally made a competitive award starting with the 1939 Oscars. To contemporary eyes, the color of *A Star Is Born* is drab and muted—it looks like a "colorized" black-and-white film. Imperfect technology is partly to blame, but Hollywood art directors, set decorators, costumers, and makeup artists were just beginning to learn how to design for color and often erred on the side of restraint. Compare, for example, the vivid hues of Walt Disney's cartoons, such as the same year's *Snow White and the Seven Dwarfs,* whose artists were not laboring under the difficulty of working with real people and places.

The best picture Oscar went to *The Life of Emile Zola,* which also won for the screenplay by Norman Reilly Raine, Heinz Herald, and Geza Herczeg. Spencer Tracy won the best actor award for *Captains Courageous,* and Luise Rainer took her second Oscar in a row for *The Good Earth.* Leo McCarey was named best director for *The Awful Truth.* The assistant director

award, discontinued after this year, went to Robert Webb for *In Old Chicago.*

Wellman: 157, 911. Greene: 96, 239, 747, 1070, 1452, 1560, 1621, 2262. Selznick: 497, 798, 1670, 1828, 1890, 1996, 2211. March: 184, 515, 572, 1730. Gaynor: 1792, 1946, 1972. Parker: 1845. Stacey: 747, 1327.

1910 • *STAR IS BORN, A*

Transcona Enterprises Production; Warner Bros. 1954.

Nominations *Actor:* James Mason. *Actress:* Judy Garland. *Color Art Direction—Set Decoration:* Malcolm Bert, Gene Allen, and Irene Sharaff; George James Hopkins. *Song:* "The Man That Got Away," music by Harold Arlen, lyrics by Ira Gershwin. *Scoring of a Musical Picture:* Ray Heindorf. *Color Costume Design:* Jean Louis, Mary Ann Nyberg, and Irene Sharaff.

Garland is Esther Blodgett, who becomes the star Vicki Lester under the patronage of Norman Maine (Mason), who ruins his own career with drink and finally commits suicide. Superb musical remake of the 1937 film, equaling it in most ways and surpassing it in the nominated performances: Garland is a far more convincing star than Janet Gaynor was, and Mason is so appealing in his initial appearances that his disintegration is all the more shattering. The scene in which he drunkenly interrupts Garland's Oscar speech is a chilling classic. The supporting cast includes Charles Bickford [651 . . .] as a producer, Jack Carson as a publicist, and Tom Noonan, Amanda Blake, and Dub Taylor. The director is George Cukor [262 . . .], who had also directed the film regarded as the source for all three *Star Is Born* movies, *What Price Hollywood?* The screenplay is by Moss Hart [297 . . .]. Both Cukor and Hart were curiously overlooked in the nominations. For that matter, the film itself would have made a more distinguished best picture candidate than some of the ones that were nominated, such as *The Caine Mutiny, The Country Girl,* and *Three Coins in the Fountain.* But at its premiere, *A Star Is Born* was criticized for being overlong, so studio head Jack Warner [55 . . .] ordered it drastically cut, eliminating several musical numbers and large chunks of characterization. It originally ran three hours; it was cut to 152 minutes, and later to 110 minutes. The studio had sunk a great deal of money in the film, its first venture into CinemaScope, but when it was a disappointment at the box office, Warner chose not to promote it for the awards. In 1983 a 170-minute version was released that restored the missing musical numbers and the excised dialogue, using production stills when the visuals were missing. Ronald Haver's 1988 account of the making of the film and the restoration, in which he took part, is one of the best books ever written about filmmaking and the studio system.

Above all, the film is a tribute to the immense talent and troubled life of Garland, who had been absent from the screen for four years—and would be absent for six more years after the twin disappointments of the movie's poor box office and her own failure to win the Oscar. She lost, in one of the award's most stunning upsets, to Grace Kelly in *The Country Girl.* Garland had given birth to a son, Joey Luft, two days before the awards show; because she was considered the front-runner, TV cameras had been stationed outside her hospital room for a special remote presentation. Garland's loss has been attributed in part to the intense gossip that emanated from the filming of *A Star Is Born,* alleging constant displays of temperament and alcohol and drug abuse. Most of her coworkers on the film praised her hard work, while admitting that her frequent absences from the set caused the film to run over budget.

Mason, one of the most distinguished performers to be overlooked by the Academy, lost to Marlon Brando for *On the Waterfront.* The art direction award went to *20,000 Leagues Under the Sea.* Arlen and Gershwin's song, which gave Garland one of her most powerful moments on film, lost to the title tune by Jule Styne and Sammy Cahn from *Three Coins in the Fountain.* The scoring award went to Adolph Deutsch and Saul Chaplin for *Seven Brides for Seven Brothers.* Sanzo Wada won for the costumes for *Gate of Hell.*

Mason: 761, 2198. Garland: 1065. Bert: 110. Allen: 1157, 1393. Sharaff: 66, 290, 333, 338, 413, 690, 852, 896, 1088, 1507, 1592, 2000, 2244, 2277. Hopkins: 110, 508, 896, 1003, 1170, 1332, 1385, 1393, 1949, 1973, 2058, 2277. Arlen: 248, 322, 368, 903, 1838, 1912, 2186, 2300. Gershwin: 455, 1797. Heindorf: 331, 479, 666, 930, 1043, 1204, 1385, 1408, 1430, 1690, 1719, 1750, 2058, 2186, 2243, 2310, 2318. Louis: 20, 126, 170, 262, 732, 744, 1028, 1065, 1521, 1640, 1812, 1858, 2064. Nyberg: 141.

1911 • STAR IS BORN, A

BARWOOD/JON PETERS PRODUCTION; FIRST ARTISTS PRESENTATION; WARNER BROS. 1976.

AWARD *Original Song:* "Evergreen (Love Theme From *A Star Is Born),*" music by Barbra Streisand, lyrics by Paul Williams.

NOMINATIONS *Cinematography:* Robert Surtees. *Sound:* Robert Knudson, Dan Wallin, Robert Glass, and Tom Overton. *Original Song Score and Its Adaptation or Adaptation Score:* Roger Kellaway.

Third time, but no charm. Streisand is Esther Hoffman, a pop singer who attracts the attention of a rock star, John Norman Howard, played by Kris Kristofferson [1874]. Her career soars, his plummets, and he ends it all by crashing his Ferrari. Tedious, unconvincing version of the story originally hatched by William Wellman and Robert Carson in 1937, and stylishly updated by Moss Hart in 1954. Here, the writing credits go to Joan Didion and John Gregory Dunne—both of whom have disavowed the final version—and director Frank Pierson [371 . . .], who claimed that the project was taken over by Streisand and her then lover, Jon Peters, the film's coproducers. Streisand's musical numbers give the movie what energy it has, although she's an unconvincing rock star—the music in the film, including the Oscar-winning song, is all strings and no soul. And because there's no chemistry between Streisand and Kristofferson, at the end of the movie there's not a damp eye in the house. The supporting cast includes Gary Busey [307], Paul Mazursky [250 . . .], and Sally Kirkland [82].

A Star Is Born marked a turning point in Streisand's career. After her sensational debut in *Funny Girl,* she became one of the biggest box-office stars, but by the mid-seventies, as her salary escalated, she began to make fewer films and to exercise increasing control over them. *A Star Is Born* was the first film on which she also served as producer, and in 1983 she made her debut as a director with *Yentl*. She is also the only person to win Oscars for both acting and songwriting.

Williams began his film career as an actor in the mid-sixties and launched a successful songwriting career in the seventies with the Carpenters' recording of "We've Only Just Begun"—originally written as a commercial jingle for a California bank. He has continued to appear as a character actor in films, but songwriting has been his primary career.

The Oscar for cinematography went to Haskell Wexler for *Bound for Glory,* which also won for the adaptation scoring by Leonard Rosenman. *All the President's Men* took the award for sound.

Streisand: 737, 1612, 2238. Williams: 309, 403, 1375, 1561. Surtees: 130, 175, 557, 810, 917, 1094, 1139, 1388, 1469, 1644, 1747, 1927, 1960, 2055, 2152. Knudson: 321, 416, 588, 613, 631, 938, 1439, 1877, 2274. Wallin: 2312.5. Glass: 417, 588, 938, 1439, 1877.

1912 • STAR SPANGLED RHYTHM

PARAMOUNT. 1943.

NOMINATIONS *Song:* "(That Old) Black Magic," music by Harold Arlen, lyrics by Johnny Mercer. *Scoring of a Musical Picture:* Robert Emmett Dolan.

Part commercial for Paramount, part flag-waving "salute to the boys in blue," this all-star revue strings its musical numbers on a story about a studio gatekeeper (Victor Moore) pretending to be the head of the studio. Switchboard operator Betty Hutton tries to keep Moore's son, a sailor played by Eddie Bracken, from learning the truth. Meanwhile, the studio musters its resources to put on a show for the navy. Those resources include Bing Crosby [173 . . .], Bob Hope, Fred MacMurray, Franchot Tone [1387], Ray Milland [1208], Dorothy Lamour, Paulette Goddard [1855], Vera Zorina, Mary Martin, Dick Powell, Veronica Lake, Alan Ladd, Eddie "Rochester" Anderson, William Bendix [2222], Jerry Colonna, Macdonald Carey, Walter Abel, Susan Hayward [973 . . .], Arthur Treacher, Sterling Hol-

loway, Cecil Kellaway [843 . . .], Anne Revere [759 . . .], and directors Cecil B. DeMille [412 . . .] and Preston Sturges [823 . . .] playing themselves. Pretty good for what it is, thanks to an unobtrusive screenplay by Harry Tugend and no-nonsense direction by George Marshall, but especially to a handful of fine Arlen-Mercer songs, of which the nominee and "Time to Hit the Road to Dreamland" are the most familiar.

Arlen had three nominated songs this year, including "Happiness Is a Thing Called Joe," from *Cabin in the Sky,* and "My Shining Hour," from *The Sky's the Limit.* The latter also had lyrics by Mercer. But the Oscar went to Harry Warren and Mack Gordon's "You'll Never Know," from *Hello, Frisco, Hello.* The scoring award was won by Ray Heindorf for *This Is the Army.*

Arlen: 248, 322, 368, 903, 1838, 1910, 2186, 2300. Mercer: 248, 278, 384, 476, 494, 508, 636, 788, 825, 877, 903, 905, 1109, 1772, 1838, 2327, 2328. Dolan: 173, 213, 244, 929, 994, 1120, 1704.

1913 • STAR TREK—THE MOTION PICTURE

CENTURY ASSOCIATES PRODUCTION; PARAMOUNT. 1979.

NOMINATIONS *Art Direction–Set Decoration:* Harold Michelson, Joe Jennings, Leon Harris, and John Vallone; Linda DeScenna. *Original Score:* Jerry Goldsmith. *Visual Effects:* Douglas Trumbull, John Dykstra, Richard Yuricich, Robert Swarthe, Dave Stewart, and Grant McCune.

The starship *Enterprise* sets out, once again under the command of James T. Kirk (William Shatner), to deal with a mysterious alien force that threatens earth. Along for the ride as usual are Spock (Leonard Nimoy), McCoy (DeForest Kelley), Scotty (James Doohan), Uhura (Nichelle Nichols), Chekhov (Walter Koenig), and Sulu (George Takei), plus Stephen Collins, Persis Khambatta, Majel Barrett, Grace Lee Whitney, and Mark Lenard. The original series had a not-particularly-successful run on network TV in the sixties, but over the next decade its syndicated reruns attracted a huge cult following, and that and the success of *Star Wars* led Paramount to think that reuniting the original cast in a film version would be a huge moneymaker. So the studio hired a prestigious director, Robert Wise [407 . . .], and poured millions into the special effects. But history repeated itself: The first *Star Trek* movie was a box-office disappointment, and only gradually moved into profitability as the sequels in 1982, 1984, 1986, 1989, and 1991 and the spin-off TV series *Star Trek: The Next Generation* spread the cult. The problem with the first film is that it's slow and rather pretentious, with a script by Harold Livingstone and Alan Dean Foster that doesn't allow for enough of the witty interplay of the crew which made the series so much fun. On paper, Wise must have looked like a good choice for director; not only had he overseen such big Oscar-winning projects as *West Side Story* and *The Sound of Music,* but he had also directed one of the most highly regarded sci-fi films of all time, *The Day the Earth Stood Still* (1951). Unfortunately his *Star Trek* movie resembles those films less than it does one of his later attempts at science fiction, the slow and talky *The Andromeda Strain.* Producer Gene Roddenberry, who created the TV series, is perhaps also to blame: The movie tends to be preachy, a trait Roddenberry had developed as his creation produced a cult.

The art direction Oscar went to *All That Jazz.* Georges Delerue won the scoring award for *A Little Romance.* The visual effects Oscar went to the year's big sci-fi smash, *Alien.*

Michelson: 2020. DeScenna: 228, 423, 1653, 2127.5. Goldsmith: 152.5, 268, 395, 727, 939, 1472, 1527, 1537, 1541, 1583, 1589, 1753, 2176, 2287. Trumbull: 228, 416. Dykstra: 1916. Yuricich: 228, 416. McCune: 1916.

1914 • *STAR TREK IV: THE VOYAGE HOME*

Harve Bennett Production; Paramount. 1986.
Nominations *Cinematography:* Don Peterman. *Sound:* Terry Porter, Dave Hudson, Mel Metcalfe, and Gene S. Cantamessa. *Original Score:* Leonard Rosenman. *Sound Effects Editing:* Mark Mangini.

Once again, only the crew of the *Enterprise* can save earth from destruction. This time, an alien probe is destroying earth's weather patterns, and the only creatures that can communicate with it and get it to stop are humpback whales, which have become extinct. So Kirk (William Shatner) and crew must travel back to twentieth-century San Francisco (presumably one of the few cities on earth where they won't seem out of place) to pick up some whales. Lively, funny adventure—perhaps the best of the *Star Trek* movie series, thanks to a witty script by Harve Bennett (who also produced), Steve Meerson, Peter Krikes, and Nicholas Meyer [1787]. As observers have noticed, the even-numbered films in this series are the best. Perhaps not coincidentally, they're the ones in which Meyer participated as writer and/or director—he was director of *Star Trek II: The Wrath of Khan* (1982) and cowrote and directed *Star Trek VI: The Undiscovered Country.* This one, which was directed by Leonard Nimoy, gets most of its fun from seeing old familiar characters in a contemporary setting: the dour Spock (Nimoy) silencing a punk on a bus with a Vulcan nerve pinch; cranky Dr. McCoy (DeForest Kelley) fulminating about primitive twentieth-century medical technology; Chekhov (Walter Koenig) inquiring of passersby for the location of "nuclear wessels," and so on. Scotty (James Doohan), Uhura (Nichelle Nichols), and Sulu (George Takei) are along for the trip, too. The cast also includes Jane Wyatt, Catherine Hicks, Mark Lenard, John Schuck, and Brock Peters.

The cinematography Oscar went to Chris Menges for *The Mission. Platoon* won for sound. Herbie Hancock took the scoring Oscar for *'Round Midnight.* Don Sharpe won for the sound effects editing for *Aliens.*

Peterman: 682. Porter: 32.5, 162. Hudson: 32.5, 162. Metcalfe: 32.5, 162. Cantamessa: 339, 416, 588, 1439, 2165, 2331. Rosenman: 151, 264, 466. Mangini: 32.5.

1915 • *STAR TREK VI: THE UNDISCOVERED COUNTRY*

Paramount Pictures Production; Paramount. 1991.
Nominations *Makeup:* Michael Mills, Edward French, and Richard Snell. *Sound Effects Editing:* George Watters II and F. Hudson Miller.

The Klingon Empire is crumbling as a result of its

overexpenditure on military preparedness, and the United Federation of Planets is trying to avoid crisis by entering into an alliance with its old enemy. In the midst of all this, Admiral Kirk (William Shatner) is sent into a delicate negotiation with the Klingons, whom he has always hated, especially since they killed his son—in *Star Trek III: The Search for Spock* (1984). But a power-hungry, Shakespeare-spouting Klingon general (Christopher Plummer) uses this opportunity to frame Kirk and McCoy (DeForest Kelley) and get them sentenced to an icebound penal-colony planet. It takes all the efforts of Kirk's old *Enterprise* crew— Spock (Leonard Nimoy), Scotty (James Doohan), Uhura (Nichelle Nichols), Chekhov (Walter Koenig), and Sulu (George Takei)—to free them, find out who really committed the crime of which they are accused, and avert interplanetary chaos. Though the cast, in what was planned as a last screen appearance together, is getting a bit stiff in the joints and thick around the middle to be involved in such derring-do, this valedictory to the series is also one of the most entertaining. The script by Nicholas Meyer [1787] (who also directed) and Denny Martin Flinn is based on an idea suggested by Nimoy, that the Klingon Empire should undergo a crisis like that of the Soviet Union, including a Chernobyl-like disaster. But most of the fun comes from witty riffs on familiar characters. The cast includes Mark Lenard, Brock Peters, Kurtwood Smith, Rosana DeSoto, David Warner, Iman, John Schuck, and—playing the grandfather of Worf, his character on *Star Trek: The Next Generation*— Michael Dorn.

Terminator 2: Judgment Day took the Oscars for Stan Winston and Jeff Dawn's makeup and for Gary Rydstrom and Gloria S. Borders' sound effects editing.

Watters: 961, 2114.

1916 • *STAR WARS*

Lucasfilm Ltd. Production; 20th Century-Fox. 1977.
Awards *Art Direction–Set Decoration:* John Barry, Norman Reynolds, and Leslie Dilley; Roger Christian. *Sound:* Don MacDougall, Ray West, Bob Minkler, and Derek Ball. *Original Score:* John Williams. *Film Editing:* Paul Hirsch, Marcia Lucas, and Richard Chew. *Cos-*

tume Design: John Mollo. *Visual Effects:* John Stears, John Dykstra, Richard Edlund, Grant McCune, and Robert Blalack. *Special Achievement Award for creation of the alien, creature and robot voices:* Benjamin Burtt, Jr. **Nominations** *Picture:* Gary Kurtz, producer. *Supporting Actor:* Alec Guinness. *Director:* George Lucas. *Screenplay—Written Directly for the Screen:* George Lucas.

A long time ago in a galaxy far, far away, a young man, Luke Skywalker (Mark Hamill), finds himself in the company of an elderly sage, Obi-Wan Kenobi (Guinness); a roguish space jockey, Han Solo, played by Harrison Ford [2296]; a huge furry Wookie (Peter Mayhew); and the droids C3PO (Anthony Daniels) and R2D2 (Kenny Baker). They set out to rescue Princess Leia (Carrie Fisher), a leader of rebel forces against the evil Empire who is being held captive by the sinister Darth Vader (body of David Prowse, voice of James Earl Jones [830]). And so the legend begins: *Star Wars* quickly became one of the most successful films of all time, setting box-office records and establishing George Lucas as one of the most important men in his industry. It was greatly helped by advances in special effects technology that gave its spacecraft a fluid realism never before seen, but it's also an entertainingly old-fashioned blend of adventure-movie character types—the callow youth who has to prove himself, the cynical loner, the spunky heroine, the bumbling sidekicks, the black-clad villain—in situations borrowed from westerns, serials, and swashbucklers. Somehow, Lucas made it all seem new, generating two sequels, *The Empire Strikes Back* and *The Return of the Jedi,* and enough cash to create a special effects factory known as Industrial Light and Magic. Critics also blame *Star Wars* for infantilizing movies over the next decade, as imitators sought the formula that would pack in audiences hungry for new thrills.

The seven Oscar wins show that the Academy regarded *Star Wars* as a technological phenomenon but not an artistic achievement. The best picture award went to a movie very much of this galaxy: *Annie Hall,* which also won for director Woody Allen and for the screenplay by Allen and Marshall Brickman. The supporting actor Oscar went to Jason Robards for *Julia.*

Reynolds: 613, 614, 995, 1652, 1684. Dilley: 5, 44, 614, 1652. Christian: 44. MacDougall: 416, 738, 938, 1439. Minkler: 2144. Williams: 6, 260, 403, 416, 588, 613, 614, 659, 805, 933, 937, 982, 996, 997, 1041, 1047, 1596, 1652, 1679, 1684, 1701, 1764.65, 1977, 2107, 2126, 2194, 2293, 2322. M. Lucas: 65. Chew: 1481. Mollo: 745. Stears: 2084. Dykstra: 1913. Edlund: 45.5, 544, 614, 766, 1589, 1590, 1652, 1684, 2165. McCune: 1913. Burtt: 588, 996, 1652, 1684, 2284. Kurtz: 65. Guinness: 287, 941, 1150, 1181. G. Lucas: 65.

1917 • STAR WITNESS

WARNER BROS. 1931–32.

NOMINATION *Original Story:* Lucien Hubbard.

Thugs try to keep a family from testifying in court about a battle between gangsters they have accidentally witnessed. Good melodrama directed by William Wellman [157 . . .], with Walter Huston [50 . . .], Chic Sale, Sally Blane, and Grant Mitchell. The Oscar went to Frances Marion for *The Champ.*

Hubbard: 1844, 2290.

1918 • STARMAN

COLUMBIA PICTURES PRODUCTION; COLUMBIA. 1984.

NOMINATION *Actor:* Jeff Bridges.

Karen Allen, a widow, is astonished when a man (Bridges) who looks exactly like her dead husband appears in her home. Turns out he's an alien whose spaceship has crashed in the woods nearby. Though he has the ability to assume human form, he must learn human speech and manners in order to make his way to the place—a meteor crater in Arizona—where he can meet the mother ship. Overcoming her shock and skepticism, Allen aids him, and the two fall in love. Meanwhile, the feds, led by Richard Jaeckel [1864], are hot on his trail, eager to collect the starman, dead or alive, as a specimen for research. There's certainly nothing new in the story, but director John Carpenter resists the temptation to play with special effects and instead makes one of the few sci-fi adventures with a heart, as well as a believable love story. Bridges is particularly fine in his transformation of the alien from a geeky outsider to a figure of otherworldly self-

possession, and he and Allen have real chemistry together. Charles Martin Smith provides nice support as a scientist appalled at what his own government plans to do with the alien. The screenplay is by Bruce A. Evans [1906] and Raynold Gideon [1906]. The music is by Jack Nitzsche [1465 . . .]. The Oscar went to F. Murray Abraham for *Amadeus.*

Bridges: 1139, 2086.

1919 • STARTING OVER

ALAN J. PAKULA/JAMES L. BROOKS PRODUCTION; PARAMOUNT. 1979.

NOMINATIONS *Actress:* Jill Clayburgh. *Supporting Actress:* Candice Bergen.

Burt Reynolds and Bergen split up because of her desire to pursue a singing career. Clayburgh is his new love interest, but something keeps drawing him back to Bergen. This comedy of modern manners, written by James L. Brooks [293 . . .] and directed by Alan J. Pakula [54 . . .], has its moments, but it's ultimately a bit thin and self-conscious. Reynolds used it to try to change his image: He had been typed as a roistering good-ol'-boy, and that had made him a top box-office star. Playing a man who hyperventilates in Bloomingdale's was a radical departure, but fans preferred the good-ol'-boy, and Reynolds' career began a decline that was swift and startling. The supporting cast includes Charles Durning [180 . . .], Frances Sternhagen, Austin Pendleton, Mary Kay Place, Wallace Shawn, Daniel Stern, and, in a bit part, Kevin Bacon.

Like Reynolds, Clayburgh was at the peak of a career that declined sharply in the next decade, partly because she took on too many roles that seemed the same: liberated women having trouble with unliberated men—an extension of her first Oscar-nominated role in *An Unmarried Woman.* The dearth of strong parts for women, and the emergence of younger, more versatile actresses such as Meryl Streep [472 . . .], Glenn Close [199 . . .], and Jessica Lange [244.5 . . .], relegated Clayburgh to character roles in offbeat films. The Oscar was won by Sally Field for *Norma Rae.*

Bergen was born and raised in Hollywood, the

daughter of ventriloquist-comedian Edgar Bergen, who received an honorary Academy Award in 1937 for the creation of Charlie McCarthy. Beautiful, intelligent, but rather spoiled, Candice Bergen fell into movies while still a college student when she was recruited for the 1966 movie *The Group.* Something of a dilettante, she continued to act, model, and work as a photojournalist without much distinction in any field until the mid-seventies, when she began to take acting more seriously. She developed a sharp and feisty persona in films such as *Bite the Bullet* and *The Wind and the Lion.* In *Starting Over* she's called on to play an airhead, a woman who thinks she can sing when she can't, and she accomplishes a delicious self-parody. She had wanted the Clayburgh role, she says in her autobiography, *Knock Wood,* but accepted the other part in order to work with director Pakula. She is married to director Louis Malle [107 . . .] and has most recently achieved success in the TV sitcom *Murphy Brown.* The Oscar went to Meryl Streep for *Kramer vs. Kramer.*

Clayburgh: 2182.

1920 • STATE FAIR

Fox. 1932–33.

NOMINATIONS *Picture:* Winfield Sheehan, studio head. *Adaptation:* Paul Green and Sonya Levien.

The Frake family goes to the fair: Abel (Will Rogers) to show his prize pig; his wife, Melissa, played by Louise Dresser [1811], to enter the canned-goods contest; and their children, Margy, played by Janet Gaynor [1792 . . .], and Wayne (Norman Foster) to find romance—she with a nice young man played by Lew Ayres [1052], he with a trapeze artist (Sally Eilers). Pleasantly dated piece of Norman Rockwelliana, adapted by Green and Levien from a novel by Phil Stong and tidily directed by Henry King [1868 . . .]. Rogers is the main reason to watch, the romantic plots an excuse not to. The cast includes Frank Craven, Victor Jory, and Doro Merande. It was pleasantly remade in 1945 as a musical, and poorly remade as another musical in 1962.

The best picture Oscar went to *Cavalcade.* Victor Heerman and Sarah Y. Mason won for the screenplay for *Little Women;* Green and Levien came in third, after Robert Riskin's script for *Lady for a Day.*

Sheehan: 132, 374, 592, 989. Levien: 1007.

1921 • STATE FAIR

20TH CENTURY-FOX. 1945.

AWARD *Song:* "It Might As Well Be Spring," music by Richard Rodgers, lyrics by Oscar Hammerstein II. **NOMINATION** *Scoring of a Musical Picture:* Charles Henderson and Alfred Newman.

Musical version of the 1933 film, with Charles Winninger and Fay Bainter [393 . . .] in the parts originally played by Will Rogers and Louise Dresser. But their roles have been pared down to emphasize the stories of the young lovers—Jeanne Crain [1575], Dana Andrews, Dick Haymes, and Vivian Blaine. Hammerstein did the screenplay, based on the first film's adaptation by Paul Green and Sonya Levien of Phil Stong's novel. If it weren't for the songs by Rodgers and Hammerstein, it would be pretty sticky. In addition to the Oscar winner, the songs include "It's a Grand Night for Singing" and "That's for Me." Walter Lang [1088] directed and the cinematography is by Leon Shamroy [29 . . .]. Louanne Hogan dubs Jeanne Crain in the performance of the Oscar-winning song.

This was Rodgers' sole nomination, but although *State Fair* was the only film musical written by Rodgers and Hammerstein, both composer and lyricist had collaborated separately with others on numerous songs for the movies. Rodgers and his earlier lyricist, Lorenz Hart, had composed memorable song scores for *Love Me Tonight* (1932), *Hallelujah I'm a Bum* (1933), and *Mississippi* (1935). The first two antedated the song award, and the third, which included "Easy to Remember" and "Soon," was somehow overlooked in the nominations. The collaboration of Rodgers and Hart was celebrated in a typically inane biopic, *Words and Music* (1948), that did, however, feature some lively production numbers—it's one of those musicals that work better on videotape with a thumb on the fast-forward button. Hammerstein had more success with the Academy: He had already won for "The Last Time I Saw Paris," from *Lady Be Good,* and amassed three more nominations. The Rodgers and Hammerstein Broadway hits were made into a string of film musicals of varying quality from 1955 to 1965, starting with *Oklahoma!* and continuing with *Carousel* (1956), *The King and I, South Pacific, Flower Drum Song,* and *The Sound of Music.* (To date, no films have been made of Rodgers and Hammerstein's lesser collaborations: *Allegro, Me and Juliet,* and *Pipe Dream.*) Rodgers died in 1979, Hammerstein in 1960.

The scoring award went to Georgie Stoll for *Anchors Aweigh.*

Hammerstein: 375, 1117, 1122, 1951. Newman: 31, 34, 46, 72, 138, 182, 226, 333, 334, 347, 375, 428, 437, 457, 476, 495, 542, 690, 797, 833, 952, 953, 959, 962, 1016, 1082, 1088, 1213, 1278, 1362, 1397, 1475, 1616, 1655, 1849, 1868, 1883, 2043, 2046, 2091, 2258, 2286, 2294, 2316.

1922 • STEEL MAGNOLIAS

RASTAR PRODUCTIONS; TRI-STAR. 1989.

NOMINATION *Supporting Actress:* Julia Roberts.

The women of a small Louisiana town gather at the beauty parlor run by Truvy, played by Dolly Parton [1438], for a sort of support group. They include M'Lynn, played by Sally Field [1448 . . .], whose daughter, Shelby (Roberts), is about to get married. M'Lynn is concerned because Shelby, who is diabetic, has been told that having a baby would be unwise. There to provide advice are Ouiser, a pinched and sharp-tongued eccentric, played by Shirley MacLaine [91 . . .]; Claree, played by Olympia Dukakis [1351], whose chief joy in life is needling Ouiser; and the spacy Annelle (Daryl Hannah), Truvy's assistant. The men are decidedly secondary, but they include Tom Skerritt as M'Lynn's husband, Sam Shepard [1698] as Truvy's, and Dylan McDermott as Shelby's. Entertaining but superficial comedy that turns serious in the latter third. It's mostly a showcase for the actresses, though none of them does anything new: Fields is plucky, Roberts is winsome, MacLaine is sarcastic, Dukakis is feisty, Parton is warm, and Hannah is loopy. But at least they get some funny lines from the screenplay by Robert Harling, adapted from his stage play. Herbert Ross [2152] gives it his usual high gloss.

Roberts, who would become a superstar the following year with the release of *Pretty Woman,* lost to Brenda Fricker in *My Left Foot.*

Roberts: 1603.

1923 • STELLA DALLAS

SAMUEL GOLDWYN PRODUCTIONS; UNITED ARTISTS. 1937.

NOMINATIONS *Actress:* Barbara Stanwyck. *Supporting Actress:* Anne Shirley.

Stanwyck is Stella, a New England factory worker whose good looks and determination to get ahead attract the attention of her boss, Stephen Dallas (John Boles). They marry and have a daughter, Laurel (Shirley), but it soon grows obvious that the marriage won't work out: He's the son of a man who went bankrupt, and wants to recoup the family fortunes; Stella's common origins and cheerfully vulgar manner seem likely to retard his career. When he takes a plum job in New York, she remains behind with their daughter in New England. In his absence, Stella's vulgarity causes Laurel to be snubbed by people of Stephen's class. Realizing this, Stella sacrifices herself for Laurel; she gives Stephen a divorce so he can marry a woman, played by Barbara O'Neil [55], of his own social class, and lets Laurel go to live with them. At the end, Stella, who has cut herself off from Laurel, believing this to be the best thing she can do for her daughter, stands alone gazing through the windows into the mansion where Laurel is being married to a wealthy young man. Terrific "woman's picture," and a solid rebuke to critics and film historians (mostly male) who have traditionally treated that genre as a minor one. Though it has become a synonym for "tearjerker," *Stella Dallas* has genuine depth of character and power to move an audience—and people who ask more than that of a movie are doomed to near-perpetual disappointment. The screenplay is by Victor Heerman [1189] and Sarah Y. Mason [1189] from a novel by Olive Higgins Prouty. King Vidor [378 . . .] directed, and the cinematography is by Rudolph Maté [455 . . .]. The cast includes Alan Hale, Tim Holt, and Marjorie Main [601]. Produced by Samuel Goldwyn [102 . . .], who had made a silent version of the story in 1925 that was one of the biggest moneymakers of his career. The 1990 remake, *Stella,* with Bette Midler [700 . . .] in the title role, is a curious botch and a demonstration of how times have changed.

Above all, the film is a tribute to the talent of Stanwyck. Though her career lasted nearly half a century longer, many think Stella Dallas is her finest performance, and it made her one of the top stars in Hollywood. Ironically she had to overcome Goldwyn's resistance to land the role. After failing to sign Ruth Chatterton [1234 . . .] or Gladys George [2192] for the part, Goldwyn insisted that Stanwyck, already an established performer, do a screen test. Insulted, Stanwyck at first refused, but was persuaded by friends that the part was worth swallowing her pride. This was the first of her four unsuccessful nominations. Her failure to receive the Oscar this time may have been caused by the presence of a formidable competitor, Greta Garbo in *Camille,* who was thought to be the front-runner. One can only surmise that Stanwyck and Garbo split the vote, handing the award to Luise Rainer for *The Good Earth.*

Shirley had begun her film career in 1922 at the age of five, under the silly screen name Dawn O'Day, which she used until 1934 when she adopted the name of the character she played in *Anne of Green Gables.* Never a major performer, she made her last film, *Murder My Sweet,* in 1944, retiring while still in her thirties. She lost to Alice Brady in *In Old Chicago.*

Stanwyck: 138, 566, 1879.

1924 • STEP LIVELY

RKO RADIO. 1944.
NOMINATION *Black-and-White Interior Decoration:* Albert S. D'Agostino and Carroll Clark, art direction; Darrell Silvera and Claude Carpenter, set decoration.

When their money runs out, a theatrical troupe has to use their wits to keep from being kicked out of a hotel until the producer (George Murphy) can come up with the cash. Musical version of *Room Service* (1938) that's more frantic than fun, despite the presence of Frank Sinatra [732 . . .], Adolphe Menjou

[734], Eugene Pallette, and Walter Slezak, and songs by Jule Styne [74 . . .] and Sammy Cahn [74 . . .]. Directed by Tim Whelan. The Oscar went to *Gaslight.*

D'Agostino: 632, 686, 1239, 1240. Clark: 4, 481, 686, 754, 1284, 2115. Silvera: 407, 632, 686, 1239, 1264, 1341. Carpenter: 632, 2212.

1925 • STEPMOTHER, THE

MAGIC EYE OF HOLLYWOOD PRODUCTIONS; CROWN INTERNATIONAL. 1972.
NOMINATION *Song:* "Strange Are the Ways of Love," music by Sammy Fain, lyrics by Paul Francis Webster.

Routine low-budget thriller about a killer stepmother, with a routine low-budget cast: Alejandro Rey, John Anderson, Katherine Justice, and John D. Garfield, the son of John Garfield [251 . . .]. Directed by Hikmet Avedis. The presence of distinguished songwriters like Fain and Webster in the credits of such an undistinguished film suggests how little opportunity there was for placing songs in the films of the early seventies. So do the other nominees: the title song from *Ben;* "Come Follow, Follow Me," from *The Little Ark;* "Marmalade, Molasses and Honey," from *The Life and Times of Judge Roy Bean*—mostly forgotten songs from mostly forgotten movies. The Oscar went to Al Kasha and Joel Hirschhorn for "The Morning After," from *The Poseidon Adventure.*

Fain: 95, 331, 376, 856, 1213, 1276, 1681, 2014, 2214. Webster: 33, 64, 95, 331, 376, 604, 663, 730, 856, 1213, 1276, 1322, 1388, 1755, 2014.

1926 • STERILE CUCKOO, THE

BOARDWALK PRODUCTIONS; PARAMOUNT. 1969.
NOMINATIONS *Actress:* Liza Minnelli. *Song:* "Come Saturday Morning," music by Fred Karlin, lyrics by Dory Previn.

Minnelli plays Pookie Adams, an eccentric college student who makes a play for a freshman (Wendell Burton) in this low-key but sweetly funny adaptation of a novel by John Nichols. The screenplay is by Alvin Sargent [1066 . . .] and the director is Alan J. Pakula [54 . . .].

This was the first nomination for Minnelli, the daughter of Vincente Minnelli [66 . . .] and Judy

Garland [1065 . . .]. An established stage performer, Minnelli's only previous film—apart from an
appearance as an infant in her mother's movie *In the
Good Old Summertime* (1949)—was *Charlie Bubbles*
(1967). Pookie Adams established Minnelli's "type"
—nervous, intense, offbeat, like her Oscar-winning
Sally Bowles in *Cabaret*. Unfortunately the type would
also limit her opportunities in movies. She lost this
time to Maggie Smith in *The Prime of Miss Jean Brodie*.

The song Oscar went to Burt Bacharach and Hal
David for "Raindrops Keep Fallin' on My Head,"
from *Butch Cassidy and the Sundance Kid*.

Minnelli: 321. Karlin: 120, 1178, 1221. Previn:
1550, 2161.

1927 • STING, THE

UNIVERSAL-BILL/PHILLIPS-GEORGE ROY HILL PRODUCTION;
ZANUCK/BROWN PRESENTATION; UNIVERSAL. 1973.

AWARDS *Picture:* Tony Bill, Michael Phillips, and Julia
Phillips, producers. *Director:* George Roy Hill. *Story
and Screenplay—Based on Factual Material or Material
Not Previously Published or Produced:* David S. Ward.
Art Direction–Set Decoration: Henry Bumstead; James
Payne. *Scoring—Original Song Score and/or Adaptation:*
Marvin Hamlisch. *Film Editing:* William Reynolds.
Costume Design: Edith Head.

NOMINATIONS *Actor:* Robert Redford. *Cinematography:*
Robert Surtees. *Sound:* Ronald K. Pierce and Robert
Bertrand.

An old pro of a con artist, Paul Newman
[3 . . .], takes a brash young tyro (Redford) under
his wing, and the two team up to swindle a murderous gangster, Robert Shaw [1252]. The supporting
cast includes Charles Durning [180 . . .], Ray Walston, Eileen Brennan [1617], Harold Gould, and Sally
Kirkland [82]. Very lightweight material given a lot of
production muscle and the stellar teaming of Newman, Redford, and their *Butch Cassidy and the Sundance
Kid* director, Hill. It's glamorous and entertaining—
the kind of movie that Hollywood turned to increasingly in the eighties, but which looks somewhat out of
place in the early seventies, when projects of some
artistic heft were being produced, such as *Five Easy
Pieces, MASH, The French Connection, The Last Picture

Show, Cabaret,* the two *Godfather* films, *Chinatown,
Nashville, One Flew Over the Cuckoo's Nest,* and *All the
President's Men*. In that company, *The Sting* seems slick
and mechanical. It was, however, a major box-office
success.

The best picture Oscar for *The Sting* is something
of an unusual one. The Academy almost never rewards films that are "pure entertainment," preferring to honor movies of serious import and lofty
aims. But the best picture slate was a curious mixture
this year. Perhaps the most enduring of the nominees
is *American Graffiti,* the low-budget sleeper produced
and directed by George Lucas [65 . . .]. The others
include Ingmar Bergman's grim *Cries and Whispers,* the
phenomenal shocker *The Exorcist,* and a very dark
horse, the slapstick romantic comedy *A Touch of Class*.
To come up with this slate, the Academy ignored the
first major directing venture of Martin Scorsese
[27.5 . . .], *Mean Streets;* the jolting Marlon Brando–
Bernardo Bertolucci film about sexual obsession, *Last
Tango in Paris;* and a more mainstream romantic
drama, *The Way We Were*.

The young team of producers, all of them in their
early thirties, were hailed as the latest phenomena in
the generation of "movie brats," joining the company
of such others as Francis Ford Coppola [65 . . .],
Peter Bogdanovich [1139], and Lucas, who had come
from film schools and universities into an industry
whose old-line studio personnel were dying off or
retiring. Bill began as an actor, making his debut in
Come Blow Your Horn in 1963, but after little success in
that career, he teamed with a friend, Michael Phillips,
and Phillips' wife, Julia, in a production company
whose first film, *Steelyard Blues,* which had a script by
Ward, was released in 1972. Bill and the Phillipses
went their separate ways after the Oscar for *The Sting*.
Bill has continued to produce, act, and direct, but
with only modest success. After a critical triumph
with *Taxi Driver* and another big box-office hit with
Close Encounters of the Third Kind, the Phillipses split
up, in an acrimonious divorce compounded by drugs
and infidelity, that Julia Phillips detailed in a much-
talked-about best-seller, *You'll Never Eat Lunch in This
Town Again*. Julia Phillips was the first woman to re-

ceive an Oscar as the producer of a best picture winner. Michael Phillips has continued to produce such films as *Heartbeeps, Cannery Row* (1982), *The Flamingo Kid* (1984), and most recently, *Mom and Dad Save the World* (1992)—a far cry from the triumphs of the seventies.

Hill, a former stage and TV director, began his film directing career in 1962 with *Period of Adjustment,* and after a couple of small-scale films, including the amusing Peter Sellers [169 . . .] comedy *The World of Henry Orient* (1964), landed the blockbuster *Hawaii,* which made him a mainstream big-picture director. His first major success was the previous teaming of Newman and Redford, *Butch Cassidy and the Sundance Kid.* He subsequently directed Redford in *The Great Waldo Pepper* (1975) and Newman in *Slap Shot* (1977), but both films were box-office failures, and Hill has lost the stature he had at the time of his Oscar.

Ward, a graduate of UCLA's film school, was still in his twenties when his script for *The Sting* was picked up for production. Although he received a second nomination for his work on the screenplay for *Sleepless in Seattle,* his career in the twenty years between the two films, including the script for the sequel, *The Sting II,* a decade later, was not distinguished.

In addition to the award for *The Sting,* Hamlisch received two more Oscars that evening, for his work on the original score and title song of *The Way We Were,* making him the only person to sweep the three music categories. Hamlisch's adaptation score set off a rage for the ragtime music of Scott Joplin, a turn-of-the-century black composer whose reputation had been in eclipse. (Purists quibbled that the use of Joplin's music is anachronistic in *The Sting,* which is set in thirties Chicago.) Hamlisch, who studied at Juilliard, began his film music career in 1968. In 1976 he received a Pulitzer Prize for drama along with four other collaborators in the creation of the musical *A Chorus Line.*

Reynolds began his career as an editor in 1937 and worked on such films as *Algiers, The Day the Earth Stood Still* (1951), *Three Coins in the Fountain, Bus Stop,* and *South Pacific* before winning his first Oscar for *The*

Sound of Music. He also edited another best picture winner, *The Godfather.* In 1980 he was an executive in charge of postproduction on the disastrous *Heaven's Gate,* which was edited and reedited in an attempt to salvage the film.

This was Head's eighth and final Oscar win. Only studio head Walt Disney [645 . . .], art director Cedric Gibbons [66 . . .], and composer Alfred Newman [34 . . .] took home more awards. Head died in 1981.

Redford's role earned him his only nomination for acting, although he subsequently received the award as director of *Ordinary People.* He had agreed to do *The Sting* after Jack Nicholson [395 . . .] turned it down. Nicholson also earned a nomination, for *The Last Detail,* but the Oscar went to Jack Lemmon for *Save the Tiger.*

The award for cinematography went to Sven Nykvist for *Cries and Whispers. The Exorcist* won the Oscar for sound.

M. Phillips: 2005. J. Phillips: 2005. Hill: 317. Ward: 1839.5. Bumstead: 2101, 2179.5, 2200. Payne: 426, 1504. Hamlisch: 398, 977, 1109, 1747, 1813, 1876, 1898, 2238. Reynolds: 643, 784, 896, 1753, 1881, 2152. Head: 31, 32, 46, 305, 357, 363, 612, 636, 675, 736, 832, 894, 945, 1003, 1219, 1261, 1263, 1398, 1427, 1504, 1550, 1579, 1587, 1631, 1716, 1727, 1738, 1748, 1840, 1986, 2012, 2098, 2247, 2298. Redford: 1502, 1643.5. Surtees: 130, 175, 557, 810, 917, 1094, 1139, 1388, 1469, 1644, 1747, 1911, 1960, 2055, 2152. Pierce: 31, 591.

1928 • STING II, THE

JENNINGS LANG/UNIVERSAL PICTURES PRODUCTION; UNIVERSAL. 1983.

NOMINATION *Original Song Score or Adaptation Score:* Lalo Schifrin.

A decade after the Oscar-winning original, Jackie Gleason [964] and Mac Davis play the roles created by Paul Newman and Robert Redford respectively, in this mediocre sequel about their attempt to con Karl Malden [1477 . . .], using Oliver Reed, in the role played by Robert Shaw in the earlier movie, as a pawn. Unconvincing casting is only the start of the movie's problems. The screenplay is by David S. Ward, who wrote the original, and the cast includes Teri Garr [2113], who deserves better. Directed by Jeremy Paul Kagan. Michel Legrand, Alan Bergman, and Marilyn Bergman won for the song score for *Yentl*.

Schifrin: 70, 434, 443, 720, 2218.

1929 • STOLEN KISSES

LES FILMS DU CAROSSE-LES PRODUCTIONS ARTISTES ASSOCIÉS PRODUCTION (FRANCE). 1968.
NOMINATION *Foreign Language Film.*

The film follows twenty-year-old Antoine Doinel (Jean-Pierre Léaud), the hero of *The 400 Blows,* as Doinel wanders through a variety of odd jobs and affairs. Charming and funny, with Léaud getting good support from Delphine Seyrig, Michel Lonsdale, and Claude Jade. Directed by François Truffaut [501 . . .]. The Oscar went to *War and Peace*.

1930 • STOLEN LIFE, A

WARNER BROS. 1946.
NOMINATION *Special Effects:* William McGann, visual; Nathan Levinson, audible.

Bette Davis [46 . . .] plays twins—one good and one evil, of course. The evil one steals Glenn Ford away from the good one. But then evil twin is accidentally drowned, and good twin has an opportunity to have Ford after all—by masquerading as evil twin, whose death she alone has witnessed. But to her dismay she learns that Ford has fallen out of love with his wife because evil twin was fooling around. Good twin, unable to handle this new life, runs away, but Ford figures out the truth and—music up, fade out. Campy claptrap in which Davis gives her considerable all, but even that's not enough to make it remotely credible. Directed by Curtis Bernhardt, with Dane Clark, Walter Brennan [424 . . .], and Charlie Ruggles. The script by Catherine Turney is based on an earlier film, made in England in 1939, that starred Elisabeth Bergner [622] and Michael Redgrave [1364]. The special effects Oscar went to Thomas Howard for *Blithe Spirit*.

Levinson: 16, 30, 343, 385, 531, 689, 710, 712, 790, 930, 965, 1052, 1169, 1621, 1690, 1768, 1769, 1779, 1949, 2058, 2318.

1931 • STOP THE WORLD—I WANT TO GET OFF

WARNER BROS. PRODUCTIONS LTD.; WARNER BROS. (UNITED KINGDOM). 1966.
NOMINATION *Scoring of Music—Adaptation or Treatment:* Al Ham.

Tony Tanner plays a character known as Littlechap in this allegorical musical by Leslie Bricusse [557 . . .] and Anthony Newley [2285]. That should be enough to tell you whether you'd like it. Those who cheered when Dustin Hoffman pushed the mime in *Tootsie* had better stay away. The film, directed by Philip Savile, is a direct transcription of the stage version presented in England in 1961 and on Broadway the following year. Though this filming was not successful, it's better than the 1979 remake, *Sammy Stops the World,* starring Sammy Davis, Jr., whose recording of the show's song "What Kind of Fool Am I?" had been a hit. The Oscar went to Ken Thorne for *A Funny Thing Happened on the Way to the Forum*.

1932 • STORM OVER BENGAL

REPUBLIC. 1938.
NOMINATION *Score:* Cy Feuer.

Forgotten programmer about intrigue in India, starring Patric Knowles, Richard Cromwell, Rochelle Hudson, and Douglas Dumbrille and directed by Sidney Salkow. Essentially a Republic western with an exotic setting, it owes its nomination to liberalized rules, designed to increase Academy membership, that allowed each studio to submit its own nominees in certain categories. The Oscar went to Alfred Newman for *Alexander's Ragtime Band*.

Feuer: 321, 920, 976, 1305, 1806.

1933 • STORY OF ADELE H., THE

LES FILMS DU CAROSSE-LES PRODUCTIONS ARTISTES ASSOCIÉS PRODUCTION; NEW WORLD PICTURES (FRANCE). 1975.
NOMINATION *Actress:* Isabelle Adjani.

Adele (Adjani), the daughter of Victor Hugo, falls

in love with an English officer and becomes obsessed with him long after it's clear that he doesn't requite her passion and that he's not worthy of the attentions of the gifted daughter of a famous man. The film, directed by François Truffaut [501 . . .], who also cowrote the screenplay, is based on the diaries Adele wrote in code that were deciphered in 1955. Adjani's astonishing performance—she was only nineteen, playing a woman in her thirties—fuels the film, which some find otherwise remote and uninvolving. The Oscar went to Louise Fletcher for *One Flew Over the Cuckoo's Nest.*

Adjani: 337.

1934 • STORY OF DR. WASSELL, THE

PARAMOUNT. 1944.

NOMINATION *Special Effects:* Farciot Edouart and Gordon Jennings, photographic; George Dutton, sound.

Gary Cooper [701 . . .] plays the doctor, a heroic World War II navy surgeon who saved lives in the Pacific. Unfortunately his tale is told by director Cecil B. DeMille [412 . . .], who fills what could have been a simple, exciting story with gaseous clichés. The cast includes Laraine Day, Signe Hasso, and Dennis O'Keefe. The screenplay, by Alan LeMay and Charles Bennett [706], is based on a book by James Hilton [1371]. The special effects Oscar went to *Thirty Seconds Over Tokyo.*

Edouart: 56, 570, 975, 1668, 1855, 1887, 2168, 2175, 2181. Jennings: 56, 570, 975, 1668, 1855, 1887, 2168, 2175, 2181. Dutton: 847, 1855, 2175, 2200.

1935 • STORY OF G.I. JOE, THE

LESTER COWAN; UNITED ARTISTS. 1945.

NOMINATIONS *Supporting Actor:* Robert Mitchum. *Screenplay:* Leopold Atlas, Guy Endore, and Philip Stevenson. *Song:* "Linda," music and lyrics by Ann Ronell. *Scoring of a Dramatic or Comedy Picture:* Louis Applebaum and Ann Ronell.

Burgess Meredith [504 . . .] plays Ernie Pyle, the most famous of the World War II frontline correspondents, in a straightforward, intelligent account of the men (there are no women in the cast) who fought in North Africa, Sicily, and Italy, adapted from Pyle's book. The cast includes many actual veterans of the Italian campaign. Directed by William Wellman [157 . . .].

This is the sole Oscar nomination for Mitchum, who plays Lieutenant Walker. He began his screen career in 1943 playing villains in Hopalong Cassidy westerns and moved gradually into larger roles in more important films, such as *Thirty Seconds Over Tokyo.* His career was briefly interrupted after *The Story of G.I. Joe* when he was drafted—he had been exempted from service early in the war, before his movie career began, because he had a young son and was working on the assembly line at Lockheed Aircraft. (One of his fellow workers at Lockheed was Jim Dougherty, whose wife, Norma Jean, would be Mitchum's costar in *River of No Return* in 1954, after she changed her name to Marilyn Monroe.) Mitchum was a reliable leading man in such movies as *Out of the Past* (1947), *Crossfire, Heaven Knows, Mr. Allison, Home From the Hill* (1960), *The Sundowners* (1960), *El Dorado* (1967), and *Ryan's Daughter,* and gave his most impressive performances as two psychotic villains, in *Night of the Hunter* (1955) and *Cape Fear* (1962). His most recent big-screen appearances have been in the 1991 remake of *Cape Fear* (a cameo role) and in the 1993 western *Tombstone.* The Oscar went to James Dunn for *A Tree Grows in Brooklyn.*

Charles Brackett and Billy Wilder won for their screenplay for *The Lost Weekend.* The song Oscar went to Richard Rodgers and Oscar Hammerstein II for "It Might As Well Be Spring," from *State Fair.* Miklos Rozsa won for the score for *Spellbound.*

1936 • STORY OF LOUIS PASTEUR, THE

COSMOPOLITAN; WARNER BROS.-FIRST NATIONAL. 1936.

AWARDS *Actor:* Paul Muni. *Original Story:* Pierre Collings and Sheridan Gibney. *Screenplay:* Pierre Collings and Sheridan Gibney.

NOMINATION *Picture:* Henry Blanke, producer.

Pasteur (Muni) battles prejudice and bureaucracy to establish his theories about microorganisms and inoculation against disease. The granddaddy of all scientific-pioneer biopics, whose surprise box-office success started a vogue that continued at Warners with *Dr. Ehrlich's Magic Bullet* and spread to MGM with *Young Tom Edison* (1939), *Edison the Man,* and *Madame Curie,* to 20th Century-Fox with *The Story of Alexander Graham Bell* (1939), and to RKO with *Sister Kenny.* If the original seems cliché-ridden, that's because it's where the clichés started—although they really started in schoolbook celebrations of Great Men. William Dieterle [1169] directed, and the cast includes Josephine Hutchinson, Anita Louise, Donald Woods, Porter Hall, and Akim Tamiroff [701 . . .].

Muni, born in a town in Eastern Europe that was, during his lifetime, a part of Austria, Poland, and the Soviet Union in swift succession, came to the United States as a child. He began his acting career in Yiddish theater, moved to Broadway, and made his film debut in 1929 in *The Valiant,* for which he received his first Oscar nomination. He returned to Broadway for several years but came back in 1932 with two films that made him a star: *Scarface* and *I Am a Fugitive From a Chain Gang.* His Oscar-winning role seemed to type him in biopics: He played the title roles in *The Life of Emile Zola* and *Juarez* as well. But he was unhappy with his contract at Warners and left Hollywood for the stage again in the early forties, making only a few films after that. His last screen appearance was in *The Last Angry Man* in 1959, after which he retired from acting because of poor health. He died in 1967.

Collings and Gibney are the only screenwriters to win two Oscars apiece for their work on a single film, a feat made possible by the division of the writing award into story and screenplay categories. Starting with the 1940 awards, the writing category had three divisions: story, ''original'' screenplay, and ''adapted'' screenplay, and definitions of eligibility in those categories shifted a bit over the years. The current division of the award into ''original'' and ''adapted'' screenplays, merging the story credit into the scenario writing Oscar, did not take place until the 1957 awards. Several other films received more than one writing award, such as *Here Comes Mr. Jordan, Going My Way,* and *Miracle on 34th Street.* But in those cases, the story authors were different people from the writers credited with the screenplay. Despite the distinction, Collings had no substantial post-Oscar screenwriting career. Gibney, who had also written the screenplay for *I Am a Fugitive From a Chain Gang,* later worked on such films as *Anthony Adverse, Cheers for Miss Bishop,* and *Once Upon a Honeymoon.*

The best picture Oscar went to *The Great Ziegfeld.*

Muni: 218.5, 965, 1133, 1169, 2191. Blanke: 17, 90, 712, 1046, 1169, 1315, 1457, 2136.

1937 • STORY OF THREE LOVES, THE
MGM. 1953.

NOMINATION *Color Art Direction—Set Decoration:* Cedric Gibbons, Preston Ames, Edward Carfagno, and Gabriel Scognamillo; Edwin B. Willis, Keogh Gleason, Arthur Krams, and Jack D. Moore.

Three short films loosely linked by a frame story in which passengers on an ocean liner recall the past. Two of the stories are directed by Gottfried Reinhardt: ''The Jealous Lover'' stars Moira Shearer and James Mason [761 . . .] as a ballet dancer and her infatuated but stern impresario in a plot reminiscent of *The Red Shoes,* in which Shearer also starred. ''Equilibrium'' is about a young woman (Pier Angeli) who is rescued from suicide by a circus performer, played by Kirk Douglas [130 . . .]. The most interesting of the three, ''Mademoiselle,'' is directed by Vincente Minnelli [66 . . .]: The son (Ricky Nelson) of a rich family living in Rome wishes he were a grown-up so he could avoid the lessons given him by a young French governess played by Leslie Caron [1113 . . .]. A mysterious old woman, played by Ethel Barrymore [1445 . . .], makes the wish come true, and suddenly Ricky Nelson is transformed to Farley Granger. Naturally he and Caron fall in love, but the spell can't last . . . The cast also includes Agnes Moorehead [963 . . .] and Zsa Zsa Gabor. Slickly produced, but ultimately forgettable. The art direction award went to *The Robe.*

Gibbons: 66, 87, 130, 217, 227, 239, 285, 290, 440, 629, 749, 831, 980, 1069, 1096, 1173, 1190, 1226, 1230, 1232, 1274, 1308, 1309, 1417, 1567, 1604, 1644, 1662, 1673, 1721, 1861, 2068, 2112, 2256, 2257, 2300, 2320, 2330. Ames: 31, 66, 290,

591, 769, 1226, 2184. Carfagno: 130, 175, 629, 917, 1069, 1552, 1644, 1814, 2312. Willis: 66, 87, 130, 227, 239, 290, 629, 749, 831, 980, 1069, 1096, 1157, 1173, 1190, 1226, 1230, 1232, 1309, 1417, 1567, 1657, 1662, 1673, 1721, 1861, 2068, 2112, 2257, 2320, 2330. Gleason: 66, 130, 290, 769, 1226, 1861. Krams: 357, 1173, 1309, 1727, 1959, 2098, 2208. Moore: 31, 1190, 1662, 1986, 2112, 2330.

1938 • STRADA, LA

PONTI-DE LAURENTIIS PRODUCTION; TRANS-LUX DISTRIBUTING CORPORATION (ITALY). 1956.
AWARD *Foreign Language Film.*
NOMINATION *Screenplay—Original:* Federico Fellini and Tullio Pinelli.

Anthony Quinn [1226 . . .] plays Zampano, an itinerant strong man working the small villages of Italy, who buys a young woman, Gelsomina (Giulietta Masina), from her impoverished family and puts her to work as a clown, as well as his servant and bedmate. Although he treats her with scorn, she loves him. When an acrobat known as the Fool (Richard Basehart) takes pity on her and becomes her friend, Zampano kills him. Gelsomina's despair at his crime becomes so oppressive that Zampano abandons her. Later, when he learns of her death, he is overcome with grief. Fellini's direction and the trio of performers transform this simple, grim fable into one of the most celebrated of all films. It was the first recipient of the competitive foreign language film Oscar—from 1947 through 1955, the award had been honorary.

La Strada helped establish Fellini as one of the most important European directors. Born in Rimini, Fellini began his film career as a writer, making his first mark in that field with *Open City* in 1945. His first work as a director was *Variety Lights* (1950), followed by *The White Sheik* (1952) and *I Vitelloni*. Masina, his wife, also starred in *Nights of Cabiria* in 1956. In 1959 Fellini's international reputation was furthered by *La Dolce Vita,* his satirical portrait of life in Italy, and in 1963 he made what many regard as his finest film, *8¹/₂*. For some critics, Fellini's significance as a filmmaker ends here; the later movies, they say, are simply a reworking of the themes of the earlier ones, especially the desire to return to a childhood seen as more innocent and pure than the decadence and grotesquerie of the contemporary adult world. There are, nevertheless, moments of imaginative brilliance in the later works, such as *Juliet of the Spirits, Fellini's Satyricon,* and *Amarcord.* Fellini received an honorary award at the 1992 Oscars. He died in 1993.

The writing award went to Albert Lamorisse for *The Red Balloon.*

Fellini: 61, 562, 603, 657, 658, 1496, 1519, 2209. Pinelli: 562, 603, 2209.

1939 • STRANGE LOVE OF MARTHA IVERS, THE

HAL WALLIS PRODUCTIONS; PARAMOUNT. 1946.
NOMINATION *Original Story:* Jack Patrick.

As a teenager, Martha causes the death of her mean, wealthy aunt, played by Judith Anderson [1670]. Two boys, friends of Martha's, witness the deed but remain silent—the old lady had it coming, anyway. The death is ruled accidental and Martha inherits her aunt's fortune. Eventually she marries one of the witnesses, while the other runs away from home and becomes a ne'er-do-well gambler. When the latter, played by Van Heflin [1055], returns to town some years later, he discovers that Martha, played by Barbara Stanwyck [138 . . .], is held in a loveless marriage by her mousy husband, played by Kirk Douglas [130 . . .], whose power over the willful Martha is based on his knowledge of her guilty secret and the fact that he also happens to be district attorney. The triangle is the basis of the plot of this nifty, noirish melodrama that provided an impressive, if uncharacteristic, debut role for Douglas—wimps would not be his stock-in-trade for long. Lewis Milestone [48 . . .] directs from a screenplay by Robert Rossen [53 . . .].

Patrick, a screenwriter since the mid-thirties, is also known as John Patrick—the name under which he won the Pulitzer Prize for drama in 1954 for *The Teahouse of the August Moon,* which was filmed in 1956. His other film credits include *The President's Lady, Three Coins in the Fountain, Love Is a Many-Splendored*

Thing, Les Girls, and *Some Came Running.* The Oscar went to Clemence Dane for *Vacation From Marriage.*

1940 • STRANGER, THE

INTERNATIONAL PICTURES; RKO RADIO. 1946.

NOMINATION *Original Story:* Victor Trivas.

Nazi war criminal Orson Welles [407 . . .] escapes to America and settles down in a small New England town, where he marries Loretta Young [428 . . .] and lives peacefully until FBI investigator Edward G. Robinson shows up. This modest thriller was the first credited directing job by Welles after the disaster of *The Magnificent Ambersons.* He did it in part to prove he could work within the studio system, and later claimed it was his worst picture. Even if it is, it's still full of showy Wellesian touches—odd camera angles, dramatic lighting effects—which overcome its artificial plot and uninvolving characters. The original version included preliminary material showing the Nazi's pursuit and escape in South America that was cut when the film was released. Welles wanted Agnes Moorehead [963 . . .] to play the FBI agent but was overruled. The cinematography is by Russell Metty [690 . . .] and the screenplay is by Anthony Veiller [1085 . . .] and an uncredited John Huston [24 . . .], not to mention Welles.

Trivas, born in Russia, began his film career in Germany as an art director and worked there as screenwriter and director before being exiled by the Nazis. The Oscar for original story went to Clemence Dane's *Vacation From Marriage.*

1941 • STRANGERS ON A TRAIN

WARNER BROS. 1951.

NOMINATION *Black-and-White Cinematography:* Robert Burks.

The strangers are professional tennis player Guy Haines (Farley Granger) and rich psycho Bruno Antony (Robert Walker). Bruno wants to get rid of his father; Guy would like to be rid of his trampy wife, Miriam (Laura Elliott), and marry Anne Morton (Ruth Roman), the daughter of a U.S. senator (Leo G. Carroll). Discovering this, Bruno hatches a tit-for-tat plot: He'll murder the wife if Guy will murder the

father. Guy wants no part of this, but Bruno proceeds to murder the wife anyway—and then to blackmail Guy into holding up his end of the deal. Delicious, dazzling thriller directed by Alfred Hitchcock [1171 . . .], with a superlatively creepy performance by Walker. The witty screenplay was adapted from a Patricia Highsmith novel by Raymond Chandler [242 . . .], Czenzi Ormonde, and Whitfield Cook. The peerless supporting cast includes Patricia Hitchcock (the director's daughter) as Anne's younger sister, Barbara, whose resemblance to Miriam puts her in harm's way; Marion Lorne as Bruno's dithery mother; Norma Varden as a society matron nearly offed by Bruno during a parlor trick; and the director as a man trying to board a train with a bass violin. And there's a smashing, nail-biting climax involving an unmoored merry-go-round. The real mystery, of course, is that the Academy took no notice of these achievements. Walker would make only one more film, *My Son John,* before his death in August 1951 at the age of thirty-two; footage of him from *Strangers on a Train* was used in that film to patch out sequences not yet shot at the time of his death. He merited a nomination, as did the film—which was passed over in favor of the long-forgotten *Decision Before Dawn* and the hackneyed *Quo Vadis?*—and the director, whose work is at least as impressive as William Wyler's nominated work on *Detective Story.* The only explanation for these oversights is that Hitchcock, who also produced the film, was unable to mount an Oscar publicity campaign, or wasn't interested in doing so, and that Warner Bros. was eager to promote its big "prestige" movie, *A Streetcar Named Desire,* at the expense of the others it had released during the year.

Burks lost to William C. Mellor for *A Place in the Sun.*

Burks: 1537, 1669, 2098.

1942 • STRATEGIC AIR COMMAND

PARAMOUNT. 1955.

NOMINATION *Motion Picture Story:* Beirne Lay, Jr.

Dutch Holland, played by James Stewart [73 . . .], gets called up for active duty in the air force. He doesn't want to give up his career as a professional baseball player, and his sweet wifey, Sally (June Allyson), isn't wild about the idea either. But soon he's persuaded that even though there isn't a war going on out there, the sneaky commies can't be trusted and flying bombers for SAC is a nobler calling than even baseball. The gooey domestic drama saps the energy from this Cold War agitprop, but some of the aerial photography by Thomas Tutwiler is impressive, and Stewart gives it his full aw-shucks conviction. With Frank Lovejoy as the aptly named General Hawkes, Barry Sullivan, Jay C. Flippen, Bruce Bennett, Rosemary De Camp, and Strother Martin. Directed by Anthony Mann, with ground-level cinematography by William Daniels [84 . . .]. The story Oscar went to Daniel Fuchs for *Love Me or Leave Me*.

Lay: 2.

1943 • STRATTON STORY, THE

MGM. 1949.

Award *Motion Picture Story:* Douglas Morrow.

Monty Stratton, played by James Stewart [73 . . .], is on his way to stardom as a major league baseball player when he loses a leg in a hunting accident. He makes an astonishing, unique comeback. Standard inspirational biopic played with conviction by Stewart, with June Allyson as his wife—a role she would reprise, without much variation in manner (adoring and self-sacrificing) or dialogue (sweetly supportive), in *The Glenn Miller Story* and *Strategic Air Command*. Director Sam Wood [701 . . .] had a genuine feeling for this kind of corn, and he gets the most out of the screenplay by Morrow and Guy Trosper [1605] and a cast that includes Frank Morgan [22 . . .], Agnes Moorehead [963 . . .], and real ballplayers Bill Dickey and Jimmy Dykes.

1944 • STRAW DOGS

Talent Associates Ltd.-Amerbroco Films Ltd. Production; ABC Pictures Presentation; Cinerama (United Kingdom). 1971.

Nomination *Original Dramatic Score:* Jerry Fielding.

In an attempt to escape the social upheaval of his own country, an American mathematician played by Dustin Hoffman [810 . . .] settles in a small, isolated village in Cornwall with his wife (Susan George), a native of the town. But the apparently peaceful community is actually a nest of unspeakably vicious types who resent his presence and his possession of the sexy woman they have coveted for themselves. After being harassed and seeing his wife gang-raped, Hoffman sheds his civilized pacifism and takes bloody revenge. Intensely controversial film that is either an ultraviolent pornographic fantasy or a serious look at the dark forces underlying human nature, depending on your reading of it. Somehow one doubts that very many in the audiences that made it a box-office smash went home to discuss its supposed intellectual subtext: the pop anthropological theories about behavioral evolution advanced in the best-selling books by former screenwriter Robert Ardrey [1083], including *The Territorial Imperative*. The movie was directed by Sam Peckinpah [2280], but even many of the director's admirers found *Straw Dogs* repellent, especially its portrayal of the rape victim, stereotyped as a provocateur. And unlike Peckinpah's *The Wild Bunch,* or some recent movies about the consequences of violence, such as *Boyz N the Hood* and *Unforgiven,* the ending of *Straw Dogs* seems not only to justify Hoffman's revenge but even to endorse it as therapeutic. The screenplay is by Peckinpah and David Zelag Goodman [1221], from a novel, *The Siege of Trencher's Farm,* by Gordon M. Williams. The cast includes Peter Vaughan and David Warner. The Oscar for score went to Michel Legrand for *Summer of '42.*

Fielding: 1514, 2280.

1944.5 • STRAWBERRY AND CHOCOLATE

ICAIC/IMCINE/Telemadrid/S.G.A.E./Tabasco Films Production; Miramax (Cuba). 1994.

Nomination *Foreign Language Film.*

Diego (Jorge Perrugoria), a gay man living in Havana, meets David (Vladimir Cruz), a straight, Marxist university student, at a café and invites him back to his apartment. David resists Diego's seduction attempts, but is intrigued by how different this new acquaintance is from the people he knows. When he is persuaded to spy on Diego he agrees, if only to explore Diego's ideas for himself. Cuba's first-ever foreign language film nominee, directed by Tomás Gutiérez Alea, is an interesting, often witty exploration of life and politics in Castro's Cuba, although some Cuban exiles protested that the freedom of expression displayed in the film was purely fictional, and some American gays found the characterization of Diego naive and stereotypical. The Oscar went to Russia's *Burnt by the Sun.*

1945 • STRAWBERRY BLONDE, THE

WARNER BROS. 1941.

NOMINATION *Scoring of a Musical Picture:* Heinz Roemheld.

James Cagney [79 . . .] and Jack Carson go on a blind date with Olivia de Havilland [798 . . .] and Rita Hayworth. Cagney falls for Hayworth (the title character), but she elopes with Carson, so he marries de Havilland instead. Cagney goes to work for Carson and is forced to take the fall and go to jail because of Carson's shady dealings. While in jail, he learns dentistry and takes his revenge on Carson when the latter comes to him with a toothache. Pleasantly meandering comedy-drama, set in turn-of-the-century Brooklyn. Director Raoul Walsh never lets it sink into sentimental nostalgia, and he gets good help in this line from Cagney's ebullient performance. De Havilland, too, is adept at purging the sentimentality and finding the shrewdness in what could have been a pallid role: the woman whose husband keeps wondering if he missed out by not marrying the strawberry blonde. The film is a remake of a 1931 Gary Cooper [701 . . .] picture called *One Sunday Afternoon.* It was remade under that title as a musical in 1948. This version, which has a screenplay by Julius J. Epstein [365 . . .] and Philip G. Epstein [365], is the best of the three. The cinematography is by James Wong Howe [1 . . .].

The scoring Oscar went to Frank Churchill and Oliver Wallace for *Dumbo.*

Roemheld: 2318.

1946 • STREET ANGEL

FOX. 1927–28.

AWARD *Actress:* Janet Gaynor.

NOMINATIONS *Cinematography:* Ernest Palmer. (1928–29) *Interior Decoration:* Harry Oliver. (1928–29)

Poverty leaves Gaynor with no alternative but prostitution, but the police spot her and she's forced to flee. She takes refuge with a circus, which hires her, and meets a young painter (Charles Farrell), with whom she falls in love. Sentimental vehicle made to capitalize on the success of the Gaynor-Farrell team in *Seventh Heaven,* one of the other films for which Gaynor was cited as the first best actress winner—the third was *Sunrise.* Frank Borzage [132 . . .] directed. The scenario, by Marion Orth, is based on a play by Monckton Hoffe [1118].

Confusion about eligibility dates allowed *Street Angel*'s cinematography and art direction to be considered for Oscars a year after Gaynor had already been cited for her performance in the film. In fact, for the 1928–29 awards, only winners were announced, so Palmer and Oliver's nominations were unofficial: They were on the lists of people being considered for the awards but were given no official recognition of their candidacy. Interestingly Palmer's experimental work on the film, with much use of fog filters, was originally rejected by the processing lab as unprintable. He lost to Clyde De Vinna's cinematography for *White Shadows in the South Seas.* The art direction Oscar went to Cedric Gibbons for *The Bridge of San Luis Rey* "and other pictures."

Gaynor: 1792, 1909, 1972. Palmer: 235, 298, 714. Oliver: 1792.

1947 • STREET OF CHANCE

PARAMOUNT. 1929–30.

NOMINATION *Writing Achievement:* Howard Estabrook.

William Powell [1170 . . .] plays a suave hood whose attempt to cure his younger brother (Regis Toomey) of gambling backfires. Powell becomes the target of the mob and is forced to sacrifice himself to save his brother's life. Well-done early talkie, directed by John Cromwell, who also has a small role. The cast includes Kay Francis and Jean Arthur [1353]. Estabrook, assisted by Lenore Coffee [712], worked from a story by Oliver H. P. Garrett. The Oscar went to Frances Marion for *The Big House*.

Estabrook: 400.

1948 • STREET SMART

CANNON FILMS PRODUCTION; CANNON RELEASING. 1987.
NOMINATION *Supporting Actor:* Morgan Freeman.

Christopher Reeve plays a magazine writer whose proposed story about prostitutes and their pimps doesn't pan out, so he makes one up. The story is so good that his career takes off, but the pimp in the phony story coincidentally resembles a real one, Fast Black (Freeman), who's a suspect in a murder case. So Reeve finds himself in deep trouble: He can't admit to his editor that he lied. He can't reveal sources to the police that he doesn't have. And when his girlfriend (Mimi Rogers) is hurt and a prostitute (Kathy Baker) he has talked to is killed, Reeve has to find a way out of the mess. Intriguing premise for a thriller that's nicely executed but a little too tidy at the end, and Reeve's lack of charisma doesn't give the audience enough to identify with in the central role, so that Freeman and Baker, both of whom are terrific, steal the movie out from under his nose. Jerry Schatzberg directed from a script by David Freeman, who based it on his own *New York* magazine story about a pimp.

Street Smart and the nomination gave a big boost to Freeman's screen career, which had consisted up to this point of smallish secondary roles. He was better known for his stage and TV work, though he has said he wants to forget the time he put in as Easy Reader on the children's show *The Electric Company*. His nomination two years later for *Driving Miss Daisy,* combined with a fine performance the same year in *Glory,* made him one of the screen's preeminent black actors. Leading roles have been hard to come by, but he has given fine support in films such as *Robin Hood: Prince of Thieves* and *Unforgiven*. The Oscar went to Sean Connery for *The Untouchables*.

Freeman: 580, 1802.5.

1949 • STREETCAR NAMED DESIRE, A

CHARLES K. FELDMAN GROUP PRODUCTIONS; WARNER BROS. 1951.
AWARDS *Actress:* Vivien Leigh. *Supporting Actor:* Karl Malden. *Supporting Actress:* Kim Hunter. *Black-and-White Art Direction—Set Decoration:* Richard Day; George James Hopkins.
NOMINATIONS *Picture:* Charles K. Feldman, producer. *Actor:* Marlon Brando. *Director:* Elia Kazan. *Screenplay:* Tennessee Williams. *Black-and-White Cinematography:* Harry Stradling. *Sound Recording:* Nathan Levinson. *Scoring of a Dramatic or Comedy Picture:* Alex North. *Black-and-White Costume Design:* Lucinda Ballard.

Blanche DuBois (Leigh) comes to stay with her sister, Stella (Hunter), and Stella's husband, Stanley Kowalski (Brando), in a shabby two-room apartment in the New Orleans French Quarter. Blanche's southern-belle affectations irritate the rough, vulgar Stanley, but Stella, who's passionately in love with her earthy husband, manages to keep the peace for a while. Blanche even begins a flirtation with one of Stanley's card-playing buddies, Mitch (Malden), who has never married because he lives with his ailing mother. But Stanley discovers the embarrassing truth about why Blanche had to leave her job as a schoolteacher, and uses it to break up the relationship between Blanche and Mitch. When Stella goes to the hospital to have a baby, Stanley and Blanche are left alone in the apartment, and after an argument, he rapes her. At the end, Blanche is led away to a mental institution, and Stella vows to have no more to do with her husband. One of the greatest American plays becomes an extremely fine movie, marred only by the fact that it is very much a filmed play whose scenes are shaped for the stage. The niggling excisions of the censors also sometimes result in scenes that build to a climax that never comes. The censors wanted no mention of Blanche's homosexual husband or her nymphomania. They tamed the rape scene and wanted indications that Stanley would be punished by the loss of Stella's love. (In 1994 a version using alternative footage that had been censored from the original-release version was made available. Among other things, it makes it clear that Stella returned to

Stanley at the end.) Whatever its weaknesses, *Streetcar* has a quartet of performers who constitute one of the finest acting ensembles ever captured on film. Brando, Malden, and Hunter had worked together on the Broadway production, which was directed by Kazan. Warners felt that the film needed a bigger box-office name than Broadway's original Blanche, Jessica Tandy [580 . . .], and persuaded Kazan to cast Olivia de Havilland [798 . . .] instead. But de Havilland asked for more money than the producers were willing to pay, so they turned to Leigh, who had appeared in the London production. The Broadway production was produced by Irene Mayer Selznick, the daughter of MGM czar Louis B. Mayer and the ex-wife of David O. Selznick [497 . . .]; the latter tried to persuade Kazan and Williams to cast his second wife, Jennifer Jones [584 . . .], as Blanche in the film.

After her triumph in *Gone With the Wind,* Leigh had made only four films: *Waterloo Bridge, That Hamilton Woman, Caesar and Cleopatra,* and *Anna Karenina* (1948). In part, David Selznick was to blame, because her contractual obligation to him kept her from taking parts in films produced by others. But her marriage to Laurence Olivier [268 . . .], who had returned to England during World War II, also restricted her film career. Sometimes the two men who dominated her professional life collided: Selznick prevented Olivier from casting Leigh in *Henry V,* for example. Olivier had directed her in the London production of *Streetcar,* and he came to the States to appear in the film *Carrie* while Leigh was filming her stunning performance as Blanche. Kazan had some difficulties reconciling his own conception of Blanche with the one that Olivier had helped Leigh develop in London, but in the end, her performance ranks among the finest on film. After winning the Oscar for *Streetcar,* Leigh would make only three more movies—*The Deep Blue Sea* (1955), *The Roman Spring of Mrs. Stone,* and *Ship of Fools*—before her death in 1967.

Malden made his film debut in 1940 in *They Knew What They Wanted* and played secondary roles in such movies as *13 Rue Madeleine* and *Kiss of Death,* but he had made his name as an actor primarily on stage before *Streetcar.* He gave some of his most memorable screen performances in films directed by Kazan: *Streetcar, On the Waterfront,* and *Baby Doll.* Mostly he's known for somewhat stolid character roles in films such as *How the West Was Won, Gypsy,* and *Patton,* among many others, and for his work on the TV series *Streets of San Francisco.* He has recently served as president of the Academy.

Hunter had made a handful of films in the early forties and worked for a while in England before landing the part of Stella on Broadway and being cast in the film version. But because she was blacklisted for her political affiliations shortly after receiving the Oscar, she left Hollywood again and concentrated on stage work. She returned to Hollywood infrequently, though she is popular with sci-fi cultists because of her appearance—heavily made up—as one of the ape people in *Planet of the Apes* and several of its sequels.

Feldman started as an agent and became a producer in the early forties. *Streetcar* resulted in his sole nomination, though he was responsible for a number of interesting films, ranging from *Red River* to *What's New Pussycat?* The best picture Oscar went to *An American in Paris,* in what was seen as an upset victory: The other nominees included the now-forgotten *Decision Before Dawn* and the galumphing costume epic *Quo Vadis?,* both of which were nominated thanks to strenuous campaigning by the powerful studios that made them. The fifth nominee was *A Place in the Sun.* It's thought that the more serious films, *Streetcar* and *Place,* may have split the votes, giving the award to *An American in Paris.*

Brando had made his film debut a year earlier in *The Men* and was only twenty-seven when he appeared in *Streetcar*—try to think of a contemporary screen actor in his twenties who would be even remotely credible in the part of Stanley Kowalski. Although the stereotype of Brando's Stanley is the inarticulate brute or the man in the torn T-shirt wailing ''Stella!,'' he plays the part for boyishness as much as brutishness and makes clear the powerful erotic spell that Stanley has cast over Stella. No performer in his twenties has ever won the award for best actor, and Brando lost this, his first nomination, to Humphrey

Bogart for *The African Queen.* Brando's reluctance to do publicity was thought to have hurt him, and there was a strong sentiment that Bogart was due a "career" Oscar.

Williams received sole credit for the screenplay, with a subordinate credit for adaptation going to Oscar Saul, who, along with Kazan, did most of the real work of turning the play into a movie. The writing Oscar went to Michael Wilson and Harry Brown for *A Place in the Sun,* which also won for George Stevens' direction, William C. Mellor's cinematography, Franz Waxman's scoring, and Edith Head's costumes. The sound award went to *The Great Caruso.*

Leigh: 798. Malden: 1477. Day: 22, 102, 235, 487, 510, 560, 569, 797, 833, 864, 952, 1048, 1175, 1397, 1477, 1666, 2056, 2120, 2276. Hopkins: 110, 508, 896, 1003, 1170, 1332, 1385, 1393, 1910, 1973, 2058, 2277. Brando: 583, 784, 1069, 1141, 1477, 1763, 2212. Kazan: 63, 593, 759, 1477. Williams: 119. Stradling: 110, 149, 596, 737, 852, 853, 864, 896, 957, 1246, 1393, 1567, 2338. Levinson: 16, 30, 343, 385, 531, 689, 710, 712, 790, 930, 965, 1052, 1169, 1621, 1690, 1768, 1769, 1779, 1930, 2058, 2318. North: 29, 215, 413, 515, 577, 1654, 1727, 1802, 1814, 1886, 2174, 2177, 2212, 2277.

1950 • STRIKE UP THE BAND

MGM. 1940.

AWARD *Sound Recording:* Douglas Shearer.

NOMINATIONS *Song:* "Our Love Affair," music and lyrics by Roger Edens and Arthur Freed. *Score:* Georgie Stoll and Roger Edens.

High school students Mickey Rooney [115 . . .] and Judy Garland [1065 . . .] organize a swing band and put on a show to enter a national radio band contest. But when a band member becomes ill, they use the money to pay for an operation he needs. The band is rescued by a rich man, and they win the contest. The second in the series of hey-kids-let's-put-on-a-show musicals starring Rooney and Garland, which began with *Babes in Arms,* is something of a drag where plot is concerned. The charisma of the leads helps, however, as does the staging of the musical

numbers by director Busby Berkeley [792 . . .], even though his work at MGM was always more restrained than in his great Warners musicals. The film bears no relationship to the Broadway musical by George [1797] and Ira Gershwin [455 . . .], though it retains the title song. The remaining songs are by Edens and Freed.

This was the fourth of Shearer's five Oscars for sound. The award for best song went to Leigh Harline and Ned Washington's "When You Wish Upon a Star," from *Pinocchio.* The scoring award was won by Alfred Newman for *Tin Pan Alley.*

Shearer: 136, 202, 256, 397, 685, 817, 835, 1096, 1232, 1292, 1371, 1419, 1751, 1988, 2048, 2055, 2211, 2300. Edens: 87, 115, 594, 699, 801, 1476. Freed: 66, 769. Stoll: 74, 115, 207, 699, 1216, 1298, 1299.

1951 • STRIP, THE

MGM. 1951.

NOMINATION *Song:* "A Kiss to Build a Dream On," music and lyrics by Bert Kalmar, Harry Ruby, and Oscar Hammerstein II.

Mickey Rooney [115 . . .] plays a jazz drummer on the Sunset Strip who has a run-in with the mob. Average melodrama directed by Leslie Kardos, with Sally Forrest, William Demarest [1058], and James Craig, and musical performances by Louis Armstrong, Earl Hines, and Jack Teagarden, with cinematography by Robert Surtees [130 . . .]—in short, a B picture as only MGM could make one.

The nominated song had a long genesis. Kalmar and Ruby originally composed it as "Moonlight on the Meadow," but it went unperformed. Then Hammerstein was hired to provide new lyrics for Allan Jones and Kitty Carlisle to sing in the Marx Brothers' film *A Night at the Opera* (1935), but it was cut from that movie and shelved for sixteen years, until MGM pulled it from the vaults and gave it to Louis Armstrong in *The Strip.* Ruby, like many songwriters of the twenties and thirties, the golden age of Tin Pan Alley, began his career as a pianist and song plugger. While working in vaudeville, he teamed up with Kalmar, who was a music publisher as well as performer.

Together, Ruby and Kalmar wrote such songs as "Thinking of You," "I Wanna Be Loved by You," "Three Little Words," and "Who's Sorry Now." Though never among the top rank of songwriters, the team earned its own MGM musical biopic, *Three Little Words,* in 1950. The Oscar went to Hoagy Carmichael and Johnny Mercer for "In the Cool, Cool, Cool of the Evening," from *Here Comes the Groom.*

Hammerstein: 375, 1117, 1122, 1921.

1952 • STRIPPER, THE

JERRY WALD PRODUCTIONS INC.; 20TH CENTURY-FOX. 1963. **NOMINATION** *Black-and-White Costume Design:* Travilla.

Joanne Woodward [1365 . . .] plays a former small-town beauty queen who dreamed of Hollywood stardom but now works as a carnival stripper. Stranded in her old hometown, she moves in with Claire Trevor [510 . . .], for whom she used to baby-sit. The baby has grown up into Richard Beymer, with whom Woodward has an affair that leaves everyone sadder but wiser. Formulaic William Inge [1894] drama originally titled *A Loss of Roses,* immeasurably helped by Woodward's performance. Meade Roberts adapted the play for the screen. Franklin Schaffner [1541] makes his film directing debut, and the cast includes Carol Lynley, Robert Webber, Louis Nye, Gypsy Rose Lee, and Michael J. Pollard [255]. The cinematography is by Ellsworth Fredericks [1763]. The costuming Oscar went to Piero Gherardi for *8½.*

Travilla: 15, 954, 2043.

1953 • STUNT MAN, THE

MELVIN SIMON PRODUCTIONS; 20TH CENTURY-FOX. 1980. **NOMINATIONS** *Actor:* Peter O'Toole. *Director:* Richard Rush. *Screenplay Based on Material From Another Medium:* Lawrence B. Marcus and Richard Rush.

Running from the cops, a drifter named Cameron (Steve Railsback) blunders into a movie location shooting and accidentally causes the death of a stuntman. But the film's director, Eli Cross (O'Toole), seizes the opportunity, conceals the death, hides Cameron from the police, and drafts him as the new stuntman—setting up an intricately comic illu-

sion-and-reality tale. The cast also includes Barbara Hershey as the film's star, who becomes Cameron's lover, and Allen Goorwitz as the film-within-the-film's screenwriter. Rush's ingenious movie was made independently, after original deals to make it for Columbia and Warners had fallen through, and languished without a distributor for more than a year after it was completed, although it earned raves in test screenings and at film festivals in Seattle, Dallas, Montreal, and elsewhere. Fox finally agreed to distribute the film, but the box office was spotty. Critical reaction, too, was mixed, ranging from wild enthusiasm to cool skepticism—the latter group admits the movie's ingenuity but finds it flawed in tone and just this side of pretentious.

There's little debate over O'Toole's performance, however, which is a masterly comic creation, a parody of such legendary director deities as Von Stroheim, Welles, Ford, and Huston. (Perhaps Eli Cross is a relative of Noah Cross, the character Huston played in *Chinatown.*) This was the sixth of O'Toole's seven unsuccessful acting nominations, a record he shares with Richard Burton [85 . . .]. He lost to Robert De Niro in *Raging Bull.*

Rush began his directing career on low-budget exploitation flicks, such as *Hell's Angels on Wheels* (1967) and *Psych-Out* (1968), both of which featured the then-unknown Jack Nicholson [395 . . .]. He graduated to major-studio projects, such as *Getting Straight* (1970) and *Freebie and the Bean* (1974). But the relative lack of commercial success of *The Stunt Man* seemed to bring a halt to Rush's directing career, despite two Oscar nominations, and he didn't make another movie for fourteen years, returning in 1994 with the poorly received Bruce Willis thriller *Color of Night.* No one has won the directing Oscar for a film that wasn't in the running for best picture since Frank Lloyd won, in the second year of the Oscars, for directing *The Divine Lady,* so Rush had little chance at the award. The Oscar for directing went to Robert Redford for *Ordinary People,* which also won for Alvin Sargent's screenplay.

O'Toole: 164, 805, 1151, 1177, 1395, 1733.

1954 • SUBJECT WAS ROSES, THE

MGM. 1968.

AWARD *Supporting Actor:* Jack Albertson.
NOMINATION *Actress:* Patricia Neal.

Soldier Martin Sheen returns from World War II to his family in the Bronx but finds his experiences have made communication with his parents, Albertson and Neal, much harder. Well-meaning but stagy version of a Pulitzer Prize–winning play, adapted for the screen by its author, Frank Gilroy, and directed by Ulu Grosbard.

After starting in vaudeville and burlesque in his teens, Albertson established himself on Broadway and early TV and made his film debut in 1954 in *Top Banana,* based on a Broadway show in which he had also appeared. He continued to work steadily on stage and both large and small screens, in such films as *Man of a Thousand Faces, Days of Wine and Roses,* and *Period of Adjustment* and the TV sitcom *Chico and the Man,* for which he won an Emmy. He also won a Tony for the stage version of *The Subject Was Roses,* making him one of a handful of performers who have won all three awards. After the Oscar, he appeared in such films as *Justine* (1969), *Willy Wonka and the Chocolate Factory,* and *The Poseidon Adventure* and did his last film work as one of the voices for the Disney animated feature *The Fox and the Hound* in the year of his death, 1981.

Neal's performance marked her return to the screen after a devastating series of strokes in 1965 that severely affected her speech and mobility. The story of her recuperation was dramatized in a 1981 TV movie, *The Patricia Neal Story,* with Glenda Jackson [893 . . .] in the title role. The Oscar went, in the only tie vote in the history of the best actress award, to Katharine Hepburn for *The Lion in Winter* and Barbra Streisand for *Funny Girl.*

Neal: 956.

1955 • SUDDEN FEAR

JOSEPH KAUFMAN PRODUCTIONS INC.; RKO RADIO. 1952.

NOMINATIONS *Actress:* Joan Crawford. *Supporting Actor:* Jack Palance. *Black-and-White Cinematography:* Charles B. Lang, Jr. *Black-and-White Costume Design:* Sheila O'Brien.

Playwright Myrna Hudson (Crawford) marries ambitious actor Lester Blaine (Palance), who's really after her money. When she accidentally finds out that Lester and his mistress, Irene Neves, played by Gloria Grahame [130 . . .], are planning to kill her, Myrna decides to kill him first, plotting out the murder as if it were one of her plays. But when the time comes, Myrna can't go through with it. Lester plans to run her down in a car, making it look like a hit-and-run, but you know what they say about the best-laid plans. Nifty little suspense thriller, written by Lenore Coffee [712] and Robert Smith from a story by Edna Sherry, and tightly directed by David Miller.

Crawford lost to Shirley Booth in *Come Back, Little Sheba.* This was the first nomination for Palance, who had made only two previous films, one of them, *Panic in the Streets,* for director Elia Kazan [63 . . .], who had worked with Palance when the actor assumed the role of Stanley Kowalski in the Broadway production of *A Streetcar Named Desire.* Palance lost to Anthony Quinn (another former Stanley) in *Viva Zapata!* The cinematography Oscar went to Robert Surtees for *The Bad and the Beautiful,* which also won for Helen Rose's costumes.

Crawford: 1319, 1597. Palance: 408, 1799. Lang: 97, 250, 319, 636, 649, 705, 765, 953, 1480, 1640, 1699, 1738, 1778, 1855, 1860, 1968, 2180.

1956 • SUDDENLY, LAST SUMMER

HORIZON PRODUCTION; COLUMBIA. 1959.

NOMINATIONS *Actress:* Katharine Hepburn. *Actress:* Elizabeth Taylor. *Black-and-White Art Direction–Set Decoration:* Oliver Messel and William Kellner; Scot Slimon.

Hepburn plays the wealthy dowager Mrs. Venable, who is determined to have her niece, Catherine Holly (Taylor), lobotomized because of what Mrs. Venable regards as Catherine's insane stories regarding the death of Sebastian, Mrs. Venable's son. Montgomery Clift [732 . . .] plays the neurosurgeon Dr. Cukrowicz, who is not so sure Catherine is insane and manages to get at the truth: Sebastian, who was gay, was using his beautiful cousin, Catherine, to attract boys during their vacation in North Africa the previous summer. But the boys turned on Sebastian and not only killed him but also ate him. Of course, you might not quite get at the truth yourself through the veil that the censors pulled over this adaptation by Gore Vidal of a one-act play by Tennessee Williams [119 . . .]. The play has been somewhat overextended to fill out nearly two hours of movie. Still, it's a treat to watch Hepburn throw herself into the rococo oddities of Williams' plot and dialogue, and Taylor, then twenty-seven, was never more beautiful. Clift, on the other hand, was on the downward slope of his career, suffering from the effects of alcohol and drugs, and his performance shows it. Reportedly, director Joseph L. Mankiewicz [46 . . .] had to bully Clift in order to keep him on track through the film, which upset Taylor and Hepburn so much that, after shooting her last scene, Hepburn walked up to the director and spat in his face or at his feet—accounts vary. The cast also included Albert Dekker and Mercedes McCambridge [53 . . .]. The cinematography is by Jack Hildyard [287].

The best actress Oscar went to Simone Signoret for *Room at the Top*. The award for art direction was won by *The Diary of Anne Frank*.

Hepburn: 24, 40, 843, 1177, 1199, 1357, 1473, 1563, 1654, 1963, 2305. Taylor: 318, 372, 1657, 2277. Kellner: 1757.

1957 • *SUEZ*

20TH CENTURY-FOX. 1938.

NOMINATIONS *Cinematography:* Peverell Marley. *Sound Recording:* Edmund Hansen. *Original Score:* Louis Silvers.

How Tyrone Power built the Suez Canal. Well, Ferdinand de Lesseps, a French engineer, really built it, but in this bio-epic, de Lesseps/Power is preoccupied with Loretta Young [428 . . .] and Annabella as much as with digging his way from Mediterranean to Gulf. Enjoyable Hollywoodization of history, as rewritten by Philip Dunne [495 . . .] and Julian Josephson [550]. Allan Dwan directed a cast that includes Henry Stephenson, Joseph Schildkraut [1169], Sidney Blackmer, J. Edward Bromberg, Sig Rumann, Nichel Bruce, Miles Mander, and Leon Ames.

The Oscar for cinematography went to Joseph

Ruttenberg for *The Great Waltz*. *The Cowboy and the Lady* won for sound. Erich Wolfgang Korngold took the award for scoring for *The Adventures of Robin Hood*.

Marley: 1170. Hansen: 143, 241, 815, 952, 990, 1485, 1655, 1868, 2027, 2056, 2286, 2317. Silvers: 990, 1488, 1982.

1958 • *SULLIVANS, THE*

20TH CENTURY-FOX. 1944.

NOMINATION *Original Story:* Edward Doherty and Jules Schermer.

Five brothers, serving together in World War II, go down on the same ship. Wartime heartbreaker based on a true incident that provoked Congress to enact a law forbidding members of the same family from serving together. You really have to be in the mood for a good cry to sit through it, but it has a fine cast—Anne Baxter [46 . . .], Thomas Mitchell [962 . . .], Selena Royle, Ward Bond, Bobby Driscoll, and five otherwise unfamiliar actors as the brothers: Edward Ryan, John Campbell, James Cardwell, John Alvin, and George Offerman, Jr. Directed by Lloyd Bacon. The Oscar went to Leo McCarey for *Going My Way*.

1959 • *SUMMER AND SMOKE*

HAL WALLIS PRODUCTIONS; PARAMOUNT. 1961.

NOMINATIONS *Actress:* Geraldine Page. *Supporting Actress:* Una Merkel. *Color Art Direction—Set Decoration:* Hal Pereira and Walter Tyler; Sam Comer and Arthur Krams. *Scoring of a Dramatic or Comedy Picture:* Elmer Bernstein.

Page plays Alma Winemiller, repressed spinster daughter of a minister in a small Mississippi town. Laurence Harvey [1724] is John Buchanan, the dissipated son of the town doctor. Alma has nursed a love for John since childhood, but her primness and his wildness have kept them apart. Eventually, traumatic events bring each round to the other's point of view —he learning to value her spirituality, she recognizing the demands of the flesh. Somewhat too formulaic Tennessee Williams [119 . . .] play, adapted for the screen by James Poe [101 . . .] and Meade Roberts. Page is as usual fascinating to watch, but Harvey doesn't have the magnetism the part needs, the staging is slick and artificial, and the direction by Peter Glenville [164] allows things to drag. The supporting cast includes Rita Moreno [2244], John McIntire, Thomas Gomez [1695], Pamela Tiffin, Lee Patrick, and Earl Holliman.

Page lost to Sophia Loren in *Two Women*. Merkel, who plays Alma's increasingly dotty mother, was a veteran Hollywood character actress who began her career as a stand-in for Lillian Gish [584] on several films directed by D. W. Griffith. She established herself as an actress in her own right on Broadway before returning to Hollywood to play Ann Rutledge in Griffith's 1930 *Abraham Lincoln*. She stayed for a long career, often in comic roles, in such films as *42nd Street, Born to Dance, Destry Rides Again* (1939), *The Bank Dick* (1940), and many others. She died in 1986. Merkel lost her one Oscar bid to another member of the *Summer and Smoke* cast, Moreno, who won for *West Side Story*, which also took the Oscar for art direction. The scoring award went to Henry Mancini for *Breakfast at Tiffany's*.

Page: 935, 1005, 1555, 1591, 1985, 2142, 2341. Pereira: 278, 357, 363, 426, 450, 736, 956, 1029, 1219, 1504, 1570, 1631, 1674, 1716, 1727, 1738, 1840, 1897, 2012, 2098, 2200, 2208. Tyler: 357, 1022, 1101, 1716, 1738, 1748, 2012, 2208. Comer: 278, 357, 426, 450, 726, 736, 925, 956, 1029, 1101, 1214, 1219, 1443, 1570, 1631, 1674, 1727, 1738, 1748, 1975, 1994, 2012, 2098, 2200, 2208. Krams: 357, 1173, 1309, 1727, 1937, 2098, 2208. Bernstein: 27.5, 789, 882, 1242, 1264, 1685, 2064, 2101, 2130, 2147, 2223.

1960 • *SUMMER OF '42*

ROBERT MULLIGAN-RICHARD ALAN ROTH PRODUCTION; WARNER BROS. 1971.

AWARD *Original Dramatic Score:* Michel Legrand. **NOMINATIONS** *Story and Screenplay—Based on Factual Material or Material Not Previously Published or Produced:* Herman Raucher. *Cinematography:* Robert Surtees. *Film Editing:* Folmar Blangsted.

Coming-of-age story about the sexual initiation of a teenage boy (Gary Grimes) on a New England is-

land in the first summer of World War II. Pleasant, well-done box-office hit whose jokes about adolescent sexual awkwardness now seem a little dated. Directed by Robert Mulligan [2101], with Jennifer O'Neill as a lonely young woman whose husband is away at war.

This was the second of Legrand's three Oscar wins. The award for writing went to Paddy Chayefsky for *The Hospital*. Oswald Morris won for the cinematography for *Fiddler on the Roof*. The editing award went to Jerry Greenberg for *The French Connection*.

Legrand: 179, 867, 1568, 2063, 2172, 2321, 2332. Surtees: 130, 175, 557, 810, 917, 1094, 1139, 1388, 1469, 1644, 1747, 1911, 1927, 2055, 2152.

1961 • *SUMMER STORM*

ANGELUS; UNITED ARTISTS. 1944.

NOMINATION *Scoring of a Dramatic or Comedy Picture:* Karl Hajos.

A beautiful woman (Linda Darnell) does irreparable harm when she attracts the attentions of a judge, played by George Sanders [46]. Interesting attempt by Hollywood to film a story by Anton Chekhov, ''The Shooting Party.'' Directed by Douglas Sirk from a script by Rowland Leigh, and featuring Edward Everett Horton, Sig Rumann, and Anna Lee. The scoring Oscar went to Max Steiner for *Since You Went Away*.

Hajos: 1262.

1962 • *SUMMER WISHES, WINTER DREAMS*

RASTAR PICTURES PRODUCTION; COLUMBIA. 1973.

NOMINATIONS *Actress:* Joanne Woodward. *Supporting Actress:* Sylvia Sidney.

After the death of her mother (Sidney), a middle-aged woman (Woodward) finds herself depressed by the meaninglessness of her life, her lack of love for her gentle, affectionate husband, played by Martin Balsam [2067], and her estrangement from her gay son (Ron Rickards) and overweight daughter (Dori Brenner). Not enough happens in this drab, plodding domestic drama, written by Stewart Stern [1645 . . .], who also did Woodward's earlier drama about loneliness, *Rachel, Rachel*. Directed by

Gilbert Cates. Woodward lost to Glenda Jackson in *A Touch of Class.*

Sidney had become a Broadway leading actress while still in her teens and began her film career in 1929. Her delicate, melancholy beauty often caused her to be cast in victim roles, but she gave fine performances in such films as *An American Tragedy* (1931), *Street Scene* (1931), *Madame Butterfly* (1932), *Fury, You Only Live Once* (1937), and *Dead End.* In the forties and fifties she concentrated primarily on stage work and was absent from the screen from 1956 until she made her movie comeback in the film for which she received her sole nomination. She continued to do character roles well into her eighties, often as eccentric elderly women, as in *Beetlejuice* and *Used People* (1992). The Oscar went to Tatum O'Neal in *Paper Moon.*

Woodward: 1365, 1645, 2075.

1963 • *SUMMERTIME*

ILYA LOPERT-DAVID LEAN; UNITED ARTISTS (UNITED KINGDOM/ U.S.). 1955.
NOMINATIONS *Actress:* Katharine Hepburn. *Director:* David Lean.

Hepburn is Jane Hudson, an unmarried middle-aged woman who has a romantic fling with a suave Italian (Rossano Brazzi) while on vacation in Venice. Handsomely filmed—by Jack Hildyard [287]—romantic travelogue, a genre that was very popular in the fifties (you might call this one "Three Coins in the Canal"). The screenplay, based on the play *The Time of the Cuckoo,* by Arthur Laurents, is by Lean and H. E. Bates. Hepburn's performance and the Venetian scenery are the main reasons to see the movie, whose cast also includes Isa Miranda, Darren McGavin, and Mari Aldon. The film is more in the vein of Lean's earlier *Brief Encounter* than that of the blockbuster epics—*The Bridge on the River Kwai, Lawrence of Arabia, Doctor Zhivago*—he became known for in the later fifties and the sixties.

Hepburn lost to Anna Magnani in *The Rose Tattoo.* Interestingly only two of the men up for best director this year were nominated for films that were also in the running for best picture: Joshua Logan for *Picnic*

and the winner, Delbert Mann for *Marty.* The other directorial contenders were John Sturges for *Bad Day at Black Rock* and Elia Kazan for *East of Eden,* but their pictures and *Summertime* were supplanted on the best picture slate by *Love Is a Many-Splendored Thing, Mister Roberts,* and *The Rose Tattoo.*

Hepburn: 24, 40, 843, 1177, 1199, 1357, 1473, 1563, 1654, 1956, 2305. Lean: 287, 289, 558, 820, 1151, 1533.

1964 • *SUN VALLEY SERENADE*

20TH CENTURY-FOX. 1941.
NOMINATIONS *Black-and-White Cinematography:* Edward Cronjager. *Song:* "Chattanooga Choo Choo," music by Harry Warren, lyrics by Mack Gordon. *Scoring of a Musical Picture:* Emil Newman.

Figure skater Sonja Henie plays a refugee from wartime Norway who winds up at the Sun Valley resort in Idaho, where she falls for John Payne. The needless plot exists mainly to bridge a bunch of musical numbers, skating turns, and comedy routines, involving Glenn Miller and his orchestra, Milton Berle, Joan Davis, Dorothy Dandridge [361], and the spectacular Nicholas Brothers. Directed by H. Bruce Humberstone.

The cinematography award went to Arthur Miller for *How Green Was My Valley.* The best song was Jerome Kern and Oscar Hammerstein II's "The Last Time I Saw Paris," from *Lady Be Good.* Frank Churchill and Oliver Wallace won the scoring Oscar for *Dumbo.*

Cronjager: 176, 400, 889, 934, 1569, 2102. Warren: 21, 324, 569, 788, 791, 877, 897, 1072, 1367, 1501. Gordon: 428, 563, 569, 897, 1362, 1501, 1984, 2219.

1965 • *SUNBONNET SUE*

MONOGRAM. 1945.
NOMINATION *Scoring of a Musical Picture:* Edward J. Kay.

Gale Storm loves to sing in her father's saloon, but her social-climbing relatives object. This B musical with a Gay Nineties setting would scarcely have been noticed if studios hadn't been allowed to submit their own nominees in this category—a practice begun in the thirties to build Academy membership that ended with the 1946 awards. Kay lost to Georgie Stoll for *Anchors Aweigh.*

Kay: 767, 1092, 1103, 1121.

1966 • *SUNDAY, BLOODY SUNDAY*

JOSEPH JANNI PRODUCTION; UNITED ARTISTS (UNITED KINGDOM). 1971.

NOMINATIONS *Actor:* Peter Finch. *Actress:* Glenda Jackson. *Director:* John Schlesinger. *Story and Screenplay—Based on Factual Material or Material Not Previously Published or Produced:* Penelope Gilliatt.

Finch plays a middle-aged physician who is having an affair with a young man (Murray Head) who is simultaneously having an affair with a divorced woman (Jackson) in her thirties. Intelligent, unmelodramatic exploration of what it means to be an adult—which the characters played by Jackson and Finch are and their shared lover isn't. One of the most subtle and provocative films of its day, sometimes amusing, sometimes quite moving, and always watchable. The supporting cast includes Peggy Ashcroft [1533], Maurice Denham, Bessie Love [296], Vivian Pickles, and Jon Finch, with thirteen-year-old Daniel Day-Lewis [992.5 . . .] making his first screen appearance in a bit as a tough street kid. The cinematography is by Billy Williams [745 . . .], and Luciana Arrighi [954.5 . . .] was the production designer.

Finch lost to Gene Hackman in *The French Connection,* for which William Friedkin took the directing Oscar. Jackson lost to Jane Fonda for *Klute.* Gilliatt, a novelist, also served for a time as film critic for the *New Yorker.* The screenplay Oscar went to Paddy Chayefsky for *The Hospital.*

Finch: 1424. Jackson: 893, 2125, 2307. Schlesinger: 493, 1312.

1967 • *SUNDAYS AND CYBÈLE*

TERRA FILM-FIDES-ORSAY FILMS-LES FILMS DU TROCADERO; COLUMBIA (FRANCE). 1963.

AWARD *Foreign Language Film. (1962)*
NOMINATIONS *Screenplay—Based on Material From An-*

other Medium: Serge Bourguignon and Antoine Tudal. *Scoring of Music—Adaptation or Treatment:* Maurice Jarre.

A German (Hardy Kruger) who has suffered severe emotional damage from a wartime plane crash is accidentally mistaken for the father of a girl (Patricia Gozzi) in a French boarding school. The two form a friendship and begin to spend their Sundays together. But his nurse spots him with the girl in the woods and fears the worst, with disastrous consequences. Well-done drama, with fine camera work by Henri Decaë, but its charm and poignancy haven't held up with the years. Bourguignon also directed.

Because the foreign language film nominees have different eligibility rules from those in other Oscar categories, *Sundays and Cybèle* became eligible for the screenplay and scoring awards a year after it had taken the foreign film Oscar. The writing award went to John Osborne for *Tom Jones.* André Previn won the scoring Oscar for *Irma la Douce.*

Jarre: 558, 764, 808, 1151, 1168, 1340, 1533, 2296.

1968 • *SUNDOWN*

WALTER WANGER; UNITED ARTISTS. 1941.

NOMINATIONS *Black-and-White Cinematography:* Charles Lang. *Black-and-White Interior Decoration:* Alexander Golitzen, art direction; Richard Irvine, set decoration. *Scoring of a Dramatic Picture:* Miklos Rozsa.

Gene Tierney [1153] plays an Arab woman who aids the British in foiling a German plot to arm African rebels at the beginning of World War II. Passable action picture also featuring Bruce Cabot, George Sanders [46], Harry Carey, Joseph Calleia, Cedric Hardwicke, Reginald Gardiner, and Dorothy Dandridge [361]. Directed by Henry Hathaway [1194]. The cinematography award went to Arthur Miller for *How Green Was My Valley,* which also won for art direction. Bernard Herrmann won for the score for *All That Money Can Buy.*

Lang: 97, 250, 319, 636, 649, 705, 765, 953, 1480, 1640, 1699, 1738, 1778, 1855, 1860, 1955, 2180. Golitzen: 31, 96, 414, 591, 690, 706, 744, 1560, 1886, 1986, 2035, 2064, 2102. Rozsa: 175,

566, 567, 604, 1035, 1069, 1070, 1085, 1208, 1227, 1644, 1872, 1890, 2050, 2304.

1969 • SUNDOWNERS, THE

WARNER BROS. 1960.

NOMINATIONS *Picture:* Fred Zinnemann, producer. *Actress:* Deborah Kerr. *Supporting Actress:* Glynis Johns. *Director:* Fred Zinnemann. *Screenplay—Based on Material From Another Medium:* Isobel Lennart.

Kerr plays Ida Carmody and Robert Mitchum [1935] is her husband, Paddy, in this story about an Irish sheepherding family trying to strike roots in Australia. Johns is an innkeeper and Peter Ustinov [943 . . .] plays her suitor. The cast also includes Dina Merrill, Chips Rafferty, Michael Anderson, Jr., and Mervyn Johns. Good family film with solid performances and handsome scenery, filmed by Jack Hildyard [287], but it's a bit too slow and predictable. Australian films of recent years have given us an authentic view of the country that makes this movie's artifice, and its nonnative cast, more apparent. Lennart's screenplay is based on a novel by Jon Cleary. The music is by Dimitri Tiomkin [33 . . .]. *The Sundowners* was only a modest success at the box office, and it seems a rather weak choice for a best picture nomination in a year that included such impressive nonnominees as *Psycho* and *Spartacus.* The best picture Oscar went to *The Apartment,* which also won for director Billy Wilder.

This was the last of Kerr's six unsuccessful tries at an Oscar. She finally received an honorary one, "in appreciation for a full career's worth of elegant and beautifully crafted performances," at the 1993 awards. She lost this time to Elizabeth Taylor in *Butterfield 8.*

Johns, whose father, Mervyn, also appears in *The Sundowners,* began her stage career in 1935 at the age of twelve and began appearing in movies three years later. Best known for her light comedy and romantic roles, she also had her own American TV sitcom, *Glynis,* in the sixties. She lost to Shirley Jones in *Elmer Gantry,* which also received an award for Richard Brooks' screenplay.

Zinnemann: 732, 912, 1066, 1252, 1457, 1771. Kerr: 599, 732, 891, 1088, 1778. Lennart: 1216.

1970 • SUNFLOWER

SOSTAR S.A. PRODUCTION; AVCO EMBASSY (FRANCE/ITALY). 1970.

NOMINATION *Original Score:* Henry Mancini.

Sophia Loren [1280 . . .] plays a woman whose husband, Marcello Mastroianni [490 . . .], is reported missing at the Eastern front during World War II. She goes to hunt for him after the war and they're finally reunited. Oversentimental romance whose only distinction is that much of it was filmed in the Soviet Union. Directed by Vittorio De Sica [650]. The Oscar went to Francis Lai for *Love Story.*

Mancini: 122, 278, 384, 494, 508, 512, 776, 825, 1573, 1574, 1864, 2011, 2037, 2201.

1971 • SUNNY

WILCOX; RKO RADIO. 1941.

NOMINATION *Scoring of a Musical Picture:* Anthony Collins.

Anna Neagle plays the title role, a circus bareback rider who stows away on a ship to avoid marrying a man she doesn't love, and winds up in love with a rich one, played by John Carroll. Thin stuff that was a famous Broadway vehicle in 1925 for Marilyn Miller, who made a film of it in 1930. This version was designed as a showcase for Neagle by her husband, Herbert Wilcox, who also directed it. It also features Ray Bolger and Edward Everett Horton. Neagle never achieved the popularity on this side of the Atlantic that she had in England, and *Sunny* didn't help much. The song score is by Jerome Kern [340 . . .] and Oscar Hammerstein II [375 . . .]; the most famous number from it is "Who?" The scoring Oscar went to Frank Churchill and Oliver Wallace for *Dumbo.*

Collins: 1015, 1458.

1972 • SUNRISE

FOX. 1927–28.

AWARDS *Unique and Artistic Picture. Actress:* Janet Gaynor. *Cinematography:* Charles Rosher and Karl Struss. NOMINATION *Interior Decoration:* Rochus Gliese.

Farmer George O'Brien falls for a seductress from the city (Margaret Livingston) who persuades him to murder his wife (Gaynor). One of the most celebrated of all silent films, brilliantly directed by F. W. Murnau as a tale with mythic resonance, transcending the potboiling melodrama its plot suggests. Unfortunately it came along just as silent films were dying out, so it didn't have the impact it might have had a few years earlier. American directors such as John Ford [815 . . .] studied Murnau's techniques carefully, but the exigencies of early sound recording made impossible the sweeping camera movements that Murnau used so effectively. An international panel of critics in the seventies voted *Sunrise* second only to *Citizen Kane* as the "most important" American film.

The Academy originally planned to grant two "best picture" awards: one for "most outstanding motion picture production, considering all elements that contribute to a picture's greatness," and one for "the most unique *[sic],* artistic, worthy and original production without reference to cost or magnitude." The distinction is certainly muddy, and it was abandoned after the first year, but it's generally been interpreted as a bit like the distinction some critics make between "movies"—stuff to enjoy with popcorn—and "films"—the subject of learned essays and critical scrutiny. And the winners of the two awards for 1927–28, *Wings* and *Sunrise,* certainly belong to those two genres. *Wings* was a product of traditional Hollywood moviemaking—a lively, star-studded adventure romance—while *Sunrise* has pretenses to art, not mere commercial success. But as the Academy perhaps recognized, there's nothing that says a movie can't be artful—and besides, isn't the commerce/culture distinction something of an embarrassment for an organization claiming to be an Academy of Motion Picture Arts and Sciences? On the other hand, it's hard to explain why, in later years, the Academy has always cited *Wings,* and not *Sunrise,* as its first "best picture" winner—failing to admit that it gave two "best picture" Oscars on its first outing.

Gaynor, who was also cited for her work in *Seventh Heaven* and *Street Angel,* is the only best actress winner to receive an Oscar for more than one performance in a single year. Gaynor was twenty-two, and in only her second year as a film actress, when she won. Until Marlee Matlin received the Oscar for *Children of a Lesser God,* Gaynor was the youngest recipient of the best actress award.

Rosher was a Hollywood pioneer, beginning his career in 1911. He was cameraman on many of the most successful films of Mary Pickford [444]. Before *Sunrise,* Rosher spent a year working with Murnau in Germany. He spent much of his later career at MGM, where he shot many of the Technicolor musicals of the late forties and early fifties, such as *Annie Get Your Gun, Show Boat, Kiss Me Kate,* and his last film, *Jupiter's Daughter.* He died in 1974. His son, Charles Rosher, Jr., is also a cinematographer.

Struss began as a still photographer in New York and came to Hollywood in 1919, where he was hired by Cecil B. DeMille [412 . . .]. He spent much of his later career at Paramount, but he also worked for Charles Chaplin on *The Great Dictator* and *Limelight.* He retired in 1959 and died in 1981.

Gliese was brought over from Germany by Murnau to supervise the production design. He lost to William Cameron Menzies, who was cited for his work on *The Dove* and *The Tempest.*

Gaynor: 1792, 1909, 1946. Rosher: 22, 87, 1096, 1818, 2320. Struss: 56, 572, 582, 1819.

1973 • *SUNRISE AT CAMPOBELLO*

SCHARY PRODUCTIONS INC.; WARNER BROS. 1960.
NOMINATIONS *Actress:* Greer Garson. *Color Art Direction–Set Decoration:* Edward Carrere; George James Hopkins. *Sound:* George R. Groves, sound director, Warner Bros. Studio Sound Department. *Color Costume Design:* Marjorie Best.

Ralph Bellamy [114] plays Franklin D. Roosevelt and Garson is his wife, Eleanor, in this account of FDR's bout with polio, his recovery and return to politics. Hume Cronyn [1791] is political adviser Louis Howe, Jean Hagen [1831] secretary Missy Le Hand, Anne Shoemaker FDR's mother, Sara, and Alan Bunce presidential candidate Al Smith. Dore

Schary [157 . . .] produced his own adaptation of his hit Broadway play, which also starred Bellamy, who won a Tony for his performance. Though it's fairly standard inspirational biopic stuff, it's interesting to see the two stars go through their paces as Franklin and Eleanor. Garson was fitted with outsize teeth to give her Mrs. Roosevelt's overbite. Directed by Vincent J. Donehue.

The Oscar for best actress went to Elizabeth Taylor for *Butterfield 8*. *Spartacus* won for art direction and for the costumes by Valles and Bill Thomas. The award for sound went to *The Alamo*.

Garson: 239, 804, 1232, 1371, 1372, 2193. Carrere: 15, 334. Hopkins: 110, 508, 896, 1003, 1170, 1332, 1385, 1393, 1910, 1949, 2058, 2277. Groves: 825, 1385, 1393, 1457, 1763, 1869, 2277. Best: 15, 768, 833.

1974 • SUNSET

HUDSON HAWK PRODUCTION; TRI-STAR. 1988.

NOMINATION *Costume Design:* Patricia Norris.

Bruce Willis is Tom Mix and James Garner [1380] Wyatt Earp in this murder mystery set in silent-era Hollywood, which speculates on what might have happened if the cowboy star and legendary lawman had teamed up to solve a case. (They did, in fact, know each other.) Unfortunately the movie is a dreadful botch, with Willis miscast and/or misdirected by Blake Edwards [2201]. Garner's considerable charm, and an interesting supporting cast that includes Malcolm McDowell, Mariel Hemingway [1267], Kathleen Quinlan, and Joe Dallesandro, can't save it. The costuming Oscar went to James Acheson for *Dangerous Liaisons*.

Norris: 506, 608, 2165, 2201.

1975 • SUNSET BOULEVARD

PARAMOUNT. 1950.

AWARDS *Story and Screenplay:* Charles Brackett, Billy Wilder, and D. M. Marshman, Jr. *Black-and-White Art Direction–Set Decoration:* Hans Dreier and John Meehan; Sam Comer and Ray Moyer. *Scoring of a Dramatic or Comedy Picture:* Franz Waxman.

NOMINATIONS *Picture:* Charles Brackett, producer. *Ac-*

tor: William Holden. *Actress:* Gloria Swanson. *Supporting Actor:* Erich von Stroheim. *Supporting Actress:* Nancy Olson. *Director:* Billy Wilder. *Black-and-White Cinematography:* John F. Seitz. *Film Editing:* Arthur Schmidt and Doane Harrison.

Holden plays Joe Gillis, a down-on-his-luck screenwriter who eludes some repo men by hiding his car on the Sunset Boulevard estate of Norma Desmond (Swanson), a once-famous silent film star. Living alone, except for her faithful butler, Max (von Stroheim), who was once not only her director but also her husband, Norma plots a comeback and hires Gillis to write the screenplay—and to be her lover, too. Gillis would rather be with the young scriptreader and aspiring screenwriter Betty Schaefer (Olson), but Norma won't let go—ever. Perhaps the most acclaimed movie about Hollywood, and certainly one of the best, its chief rivals being *Singin' in the Rain* and *The Player*. The supporting cast includes Fred Clark, Jack Webb, and, playing themselves, Cecil B. DeMille [412 . . .], Hedda Hopper, Buster Keaton, silent stars Anna Q. Nilsson and H. B. Warner [1206], columnist Sidney Skolsky, and songwriters Ray Evans and Jay Livingston, who perform their Oscar-winning song from *The Paleface*, "Buttons and Bows," in a party scene. (Evans and Livingston also wrote a new song, "Paramount-Don't-Want-Me Blues," that was cut from the finished film.) The intersection of the real Hollywood and the movie's version of it is fascinating: The scene in which Norma meets DeMille takes place on the set of *Samson and Delilah*, which was then being shot at Paramount. DeMille greets Norma as "young fellow," which was his nickname for Swanson, whose screen career was launched by him. And the silent footage that Norma shows to Gillis comes from her own disastrous, uncompleted 1928 film *Queen Kelly*, which was directed by von Stroheim and bankrolled by Swanson's lover, Joseph P. Kennedy.

This was the last collaboration of Brackett and Wilder, whose first teaming as writers took place in 1938 on *Bluebeard's Eighth Wife*. Brackett often acted as producer and Wilder as director on their films. Brackett continued a successful career on his own, primarily as producer, and received an honorary Oscar at the 1957 ceremonies ''for outstanding service to the Academy''—he was its president from 1949 to 1955. Wilder became his own producer and received the 1987 Irving G. Thalberg Award. In 1957 Wilder began a second successful long-term writing collaboration with I. A. L. Diamond [91 . . .] on the film *Love in the Afternoon.* Marshman, the third member of the writing team for *Sunset Boulevard,* had been a film critic for *Life* magazine. The germ of the story for *Sunset Boulevard,* according to Wilder, was a jotting Wilder had made about doing a movie centering on a star whose career had ended with the arrival of sound. Marshman is said to have come up with the concept of the relationship between the aging star and a younger man. Wilder was also eager to disguise the fact that he was filming a satire on Hollywood, so the film was referred to during production as ''A Can of Beans.'' In the original draft, the film opened with Joe Gillis as a corpse in the morgue telling his story to the other dead bodies there; the sequence was actually filmed but discarded when preview audiences reacted negatively.

Sunset Boulevard gets much of its texture from the inversion of a cliché: Hollywood, the land of sunshine, becomes a city of dreadful night, much of it taking place in a gloomy overdressed mansion from which sunlight is excluded. The exterior of Norma's house was a Wilshire Boulevard mansion formerly owned by J. Paul Getty—a Getty Oil office building stands there today. The famous swimming pool, which was constructed for the film, was only a tank, without the circulatory equipment needed to make it usable. The empty pool was, however, reused five years later for a well-known scene in *Rebel Without a Cause.* In addition to the interior of Norma's house, the winning art direction team also meticulously recreated the interior of Schwab's Drug Store, the Hollywood landmark that was, according to myth, the place where Lana Turner [1558] was discovered.

This was the first of Waxman's two consecutive wins for scoring. Born in a section of Germany now a part of Poland, Waxman trained in Dresden and Berlin and began his film scoring career for the German UFA studios. The rise of the Nazis brought him to the United States, where he scored such films as *The Bride of Frankenstein, Suspicion,* and *Sorry, Wrong Number,* gaining recognition as a specialist in suspense. In 1947 he founded the Los Angeles Musical Festival.

Hollywood's reaction to *Sunset Boulevard* was generally admiring, although at the premiere Wilder was reportedly the subject of a vicious denunciation by MGM mogul Louis B. Mayer. ''I said to him, 'Fuck you,' '' Wilder recalls. *Sunset Boulevard*'s loss to *All About Eve* in the best picture race provokes the suspicion that the Academy was a good deal more comfortable with a movie satirizing theater folk than with a biting portrait of its own industry, a notion that was given some support two years later when another satire of Hollywood, *The Bad and the Beautiful,* failed to be nominated for best picture, though it went on to win more Oscars than any film in history that wasn't in the running for the top award.

Joe Gillis was a breakthrough role for Holden, at that point only a moderately successful leading man. Montgomery Clift [732 . . .] had originally been signed to play Gillis, but had withdrawn, some think because playing a young man in love with a much older woman might have drawn attention to Clift's own relationship with singer Libby Holman, who like Norma Desmond had been a star in the twenties but had faded into obscurity. Holden lost his first Oscar nomination to Jose Ferrer in *Cyrano de Bergerac.*

Swanson was likewise not the first choice for her role. Wilder had visualized Mae West in the part, when he was still thinking of the film as a broader and more outrageous satire than the noirish film it ultimately became. West's ego forbade her to play a fading star, especially one who, like West, was noted for her taste for younger men. Wilder also considered Pola Negri, whose thick accent had ended her career with the advent of sound—and made her unsuitable for Norma as well. Mary Pickford [444], approached for the role, felt that the predatory older woman ran counter to her image, with which Wilder and Brackett were forced to agree. Swanson was finally cast at the suggestion of George Cukor [262 . . .], who persuaded her to test for the part. After fitful attempts to continue her career into the sound era, the last in *Father Takes a Wife* in 1941, Swanson had retired. Because the role of Norma Desmond had such resonance with her own life, taking it was an act of artistic courage. And it's hard to say whether it paid off: On the one hand, it's one of the indelible screen performances, but it also fixed Swanson permanently in the memory as the campy fading star, not as the sexy comedian of her best silent movies. And it did little to restart her career, which consisted of a couple of forgotten films in the early fifties and a cameo in the disaster flick *Airport 1975*. The Oscar race was one of the most intense in the history of the best actress category, with Bette Davis up for one of her definitive performances in *All About Eve* and competing with her costar, Anne Baxter, just as their characters in the film had competed for stage stardom. Eleanor Parker, perhaps the only candidate not seen as a front-runner, was up for *Caged*. The Oscar went to Judy Holliday for *Born Yesterday*. Swanson died in 1983 at the age of eighty-six.

Von Stroheim was born without the "von," which he added to his surname to suggest noble origins. He came to America while in his twenties and began his film career around 1914, working as an actor. He gained fame as a villain in movies made during World War I, often playing sadistic German officers—an image he would use for its resonance in perhaps his best screen performance, in 1937's *Grand Illusion*. After the war, he became one of the most famous and controversial directors of the silent era, noted for his attention to detail and his fascination with sexual obsession. His first film as director, *Blind Husbands* (1919), was a commercial smash. Its companion piece, *Foolish Wives* (1922), was equally successful at the box office, and even more acclaimed by the critics, but his extravagance sapped the film's profits, and he was fired from his next directing project by Irving G. Thalberg [150 . . .], then head of production at Universal. He then began what is considered his masterwork, *Greed* (1925), a page-by-page filming of the Frank Norris novel *McTeague,* the first cut of which has been estimated to have run between seven and ten hours. Von Stroheim began *Greed* for what was then

the Goldwyn Studios, but it was absorbed by the merger that created MGM. The new studio brought in von Stroheim's nemesis, Thalberg, to head production. Under Thalberg's supervision, *Greed* was reduced to a little over two hours in length. The version that now exists is fascinating, but also jumpy and sketchy, an imperfect representation of what the director had in mind. After *Greed,* von Stroheim directed only four more films, including Swanson's *Queen Kelly,* from which he was fired before completion. His last film as director, and only work in sound, *Walking Down Broadway* (1932), was never released. Von Stroheim continued his career as an actor, working in France but returning to the States at the outbreak of the war. He first worked for Wilder in *Five Graves to Cairo,* in which he plays Field Marshal Rommel. After his supporting actor nomination, which he lost to George Sanders for *All About Eve,* von Stroheim appeared in only a few more films, all of them in Europe, before his death in 1957.

Olson's nomination makes *Sunset Boulevard* one of a handful of films with nominees in all four acting categories. (See the entry for *Coming Home* for the complete list.) She had been signed by Paramount shortly after her graduation from UCLA and made her first screen appearance in 1949. She made little impact in Hollywood, however, and retired from the screen in 1955. After a brief comeback in the early sixties in several Disney films such as *Pollyanna* and *The Absent-Minded Professor,* her subsequent roles were scattered, including a reunion with Swanson in the cast of *Airport 1975*. The Oscar went to Josephine Hull for *Harvey*.

The directing Oscar went to Joseph L. Mankiewicz for *All About Eve*. Robert Krasker won for the cinematography for *The Third Man*. The award for editing went to Ralph E. Winters and Conrad A. Nervig for *King Solomon's Mines*.

Brackett: 705, 925, 1088, 1208, 1440, 2093, 2099. Wilder: 91, 138, 198, 566, 705, 709, 925, 1208, 1440, 1738, 1860, 1903, 2297. Dreier: 97, 151, 649, 674, 701, 726, 925, 979, 1101, 1120, 1194, 1214, 1217, 1358, 1443, 1452, 1540, 1668, 1748, 1880, 1994, 2190. Meehan: 894, 2155. Comer: 278, 357, 426, 450, 726, 736, 925, 956,

1029, 1101, 1214, 1219, 1443, 1570, 1631, 1674, 1727, 1738, 1748, 1959, 1994, 2012, 2098, 2200, 2208. Moyer: 278, 413, 736, 833, 1101, 1120, 1214, 1674, 1738, 1748, 2012. Waxman: 573, 958, 1457, 1459, 1579, 1670, 1822, 1979, 2004, 2334. Holden: 1424, 1903. Swanson: 1739, 2138. Seitz: 552, 566, 674, 1208, 1714, 2262. Schmidt: 418, 708.5, 1763, 2274. Harrison: 674, 1208.

1976 • SUNSHINE BOYS, THE

RAY STARK PRODUCTION; MGM. 1975.

AWARD *Supporting Actor:* George Burns.

NOMINATIONS *Actor:* Walter Matthau. *Screenplay— Adapted From Other Material:* Neil Simon. *Art Direction —Set Decoration:* Albert Brenner; Marvin March.

Burns and Matthau are Lewis and Clark, an old vaudeville team who, eleven years after an acrimonious breakup, are persuaded by Clark's nephew (Richard Benjamin), an agent, to reunite for a TV special. A premise without a plot, this little variation on the love-hate relationship already well worked in *The Odd Couple* has nowhere to go, but Burns manages to infuse some humanity into what is otherwise one of the most mechanical of Simon's filmed plays. Directed by Herbert Ross [2152], with Lee Meredith, Howard Hesseman, Fritz Feld, and F. Murray Abraham [60].

Burns assumed the role of Lewis after the death of Jack Benny, originally cast in the part. He had first become a success as a comedian in vaudeville when he teamed up with Gracie Allen, whom he married a few years after they formed their act. The team made films in the thirties, including *International House* (1933), *We're Not Dressing* (1934), and *A Damsel in Distress,* but largely concentrated on radio and, after 1950, TV. Gracie retired in 1958 and died six years later, but Burns carried on as a stand-up comedian without her. His last big-screen appearance before *The Sunshine Boys* was in 1939, although he did a narrative voice-over for *The Solid Gold Cadillac* in 1956. The Oscar, which he received at the age of eighty, restarted a modest film career for Burns, particularly in the series of movies in which he played the deity, starting with *Oh, God!* in 1977. He was still making

public appearances and giving lively interviews well into his nineties.

Matthau, who plays Burns' contemporary, though he's some twenty-four years younger, lost to Jack Nicholson in *One Flew Over the Cuckoo's Nest,* which also won for Laurence Hauben and Bo Goldman's screenplay. The art direction Oscar went to *Barry Lyndon.*

Matthau: 709, 1109. Simon: 332, 803, 1461. Brenner: 159, 332, 2152, 2165. March: 12.5, 86, 332, 2152.

1977 • SUPERMAN

DOVEMEAD LTD. PRODUCTION; ALEXANDER SALKIND PRESENTATION; WARNER BROS. (UNITED KINGDOM). 1978.

AWARD *Special Achievement Award for Visual Effects:* Les Bowie, Colin Chilvers, Denys Coop, Roy Field, Derek Meddings, and Zoran Perisic.

NOMINATIONS *Sound:* Gordon K. McCallum, Graham Hartstone, Nicolas Le Messurier, and Roy Charman. *Original Score:* John Williams. *Film Editing:* Stuart Baird.

With their planet, Krypton, about to explode, Jor-El, played by Marlon Brando [583 . . .], and his wife, played by Susannah York [2047], place their infant son in a spaceship and send him hurtling off to earth, where he's discovered by the Kents (Glenn Ford and Phyllis Thaxter), who name him Clark and raise him as their own, though they soon become aware that this child has extraordinary powers. Years pass, and Clark Kent (Christopher Reeve) has become a newspaper reporter at the *Metropolis Daily Planet,* concealing his alter ego, Superman. His fellow reporter, Lois Lane (Margot Kidder), is smitten with the Man of Steel, but Superman's mission, to promote truth, justice, and the American way, means that he doesn't have much time for romance. Instead, he has to deal with the megalomaniac aims of Lex Luthor, played by Gene Hackman [255 . . .]. Blockbuster comic-strip fantasy that manages to be entertaining despite its lack of style—which may in fact be part of its charm: Such later comic-strip fantasies as *Batman* and *Dick Tracy* were loaded with style but weren't as much fun. It's designed to wow, which results in some pointless star casting: i.e., Brando as Jor-El. The filmmakers also wanted to cast the title role with a big name, and reportedly asked Robert Redford [1502 . . .], Warren Beatty [255 . . .], and other superstars to take the part. Fortunately they settled on Reeve, who is just about perfect—convincingly shy and awkward as Clark Kent, dazzlingly handsome as Superman. Kidder and Hackman also seem to have fun with their roles. They are supported by Ned Beatty [1424] and Valerie Perrine [1155] as Lex Luthor's henchpersons, Jackie Cooper [1836] as Perry White, Marc McClure as Jimmy Olsen, and Trevor Howard [1875], Maria Schell, Terence Stamp [206], Sarah Douglas, Harry Andrews, Larry Hagman, and John Ratzenberger. Noel Neill and Kirk Alyn, the original Lois Lane and Superman from the late-forties serials, were cast as Lois Lane's parents but cut from the release version. Their footage was restored when the film was shown on television. Richard Donner directs from a screenplay attributed to Mario Puzo [784 . . .], David Newman [255], Robert Benton [255 . . .], and Leslie Newman. The film is dedicated to cinematographer Geoffrey Unsworth [164 . . .], who died shortly after its completion.

The award for sound went to *The Deer Hunter,* which also won for Peter Zinner's editing. Giorgio Moroder won for the score for *Midnight Express.*

Meddings: 1349. Perisic: 1686. McCallum: 540, 659, 1737. Hartstone: 45, 1533. Le Messurier: 45, 1533. Charman: 45, 1652, 2287. Williams: 6, 260, 403, 416, 588, 613, 614, 659, 805, 933, 937, 982, 996, 997, 1041, 1047, 1596, 1652, 1679, 1684, 1701, 1764.65, 1916, 2107, 2126, 2194, 2293, 2322. Baird: 808.

1978 • SUSAN SLEPT HERE
RKO Radio. 1954.
Nominations *Sound Recording:* John O. Aalberg. *Song:* "Hold My Hand," music and lyrics by Jack Lawrence and Richard Myers.

Screenwriter Dick Powell, doing research for a film about juvenile delinquency, takes charge of a teenage troublemaker played by Debbie Reynolds

[2184]. Clumsy, dated comedy that's supposed to be racy but is merely sniggery. Directed by Frank Tashlin from a screenplay by Alex Gottlieb. For some reason, the Academy, normally wary of the use of its trademark, agreed to let the film be narrated by the Oscar supposedly belonging to Powell's character. The cast includes Anne Francis, Glenda Farrell, and Horace McMahon. The award for sound went to *The Glenn Miller Story.* Jule Styne and Sammy Cahn won for the title song from *Three Coins in the Fountain.*

Aalberg: 407, 923, 959, 1033, 1102, 1991, 2030, 2166, 2213.

1979 • SUSPICION
RKO Radio. 1941.
Award *Actress:* Joan Fontaine.
Nominations *Picture:* RKO Radio. *Scoring of a Dramatic Picture:* Franz Waxman.

Lina (Fontaine) marries the handsome, charming playboy Johnnie, played by Cary Grant [1445 . . .], then slowly begins to unearth clues that he's planning to kill her. One of the weakest of the films directed by Alfred Hitchcock [1171 . . .] in his first years in America, it has its moments, but studio meddling and censorship pressure gutted the ending. The screenplay is by Samson Raphaelson, Joan Harrison [706 . . .], and Alma Reville from a novel by Francis Iles. The cast also includes Cedric Hardwicke, Nigel Bruce, May Whitty [1371 . . .], Isabel Jeans, Heather Angel, and Leo G. Carroll. The cinematography is by Harry Stradling [110 . . .], who helped light the famous scene in which Grant carries a possibly poisoned glass of milk upstairs: To draw attention to the glass, it was lighted from within—a trickier feat in 1941 than it might be today.

Fontaine's early film career was overshadowed by that of her older sister, Olivia de Havilland [798 . . .], who became an established star in her first year in movies, 1935. The same year, Fontaine had made her first film, *No More Ladies,* under the name Joan Burfield, but it was a minor part in a forgettable movie. In 1937, as Joan Fontaine, she began to play secondary roles and occasional leads, but even in leading roles, such as the one she played opposite Fred Astaire in *A Damsel in Distress,* she seemed tentative and awkward, though she was undeniably beautiful. Hitchcock took advantage of this awkwardness by casting her as the shy second Mrs. DeWinter in *Rebecca,* which made her a star and earned Fontaine her first Oscar nomination. The role in *Suspicion* was hardly a stretch from the part she had played in *Rebecca*—in both, she's the passive spouse of strong-willed men. It's possible that her Oscar win was in fact a kind of consolation prize for losing the award for *Rebecca,* but it was a peculiar triumph in another respect: Fontaine's sister, de Havilland, was also a nominee, for *Hold Back the Dawn.* Only one other time have sisters been competitors for the same acting award, when Vanessa Redgrave was nominated for *Morgan!* and Lynn Redgrave for *Georgy Girl.* Fontaine and de Havilland had never been particularly affectionate siblings, but the competition drew a wedge between the two that may have been overdramatized in the press as a "feud." It certainly helped put a lifelong chill on their relationship. Though Fontaine continued to be a star through the forties and into the fifties, she was not successful in finding memorable film roles, so in the end de Havilland had the more substantial screen career, finally winning her own Oscars for *To Each His Own* and *The Heiress.*

The Oscar for best picture went to *How Green Was My Valley.* Bernard Herrmann won for the score for *All That Money Can Buy.*

Fontaine: 441, 1670. Waxman: 573, 958, 1457, 1459, 1579, 1670, 1822, 1975, 2004, 2334.

1980 • *SUZY*

MGM. 1936.

NOMINATION *Song:* "Did I Remember," music by Walter Donaldson, lyrics by Harold Adamson.

World War I flying ace Cary Grant [1445 . . .] falls in love with showgirl Jean Harlow. They marry, but then her first husband, Franchot Tone [1387], who was thought to be dead, shows up. Aimless but occasionally pleasant fluff, though something of a disappointment considering the talent involved: The cast also includes Benita Hume, Lewis Stone [1540], and Una O'Connor, and the screenplay was written by

Dorothy Parker [1845 . . .], Alan Campbell [1909], Horace Jackson [927], and Lenore Coffee [712]. Maybe the problem is that director George Fitzmaurice doesn't know how to give this one the lift it needs—the comedy keeps sinking into the suds, and Harlow wasn't confident enough as an actress to bring off so complex a part. Grant is fun, though, and he even gets to sing the nominated song, which lost to Jerome Kern and Dorothy Fields' "The Way You Look Tonight," from *Swing Time.*

Adamson: 21, 916, 921, 2028.

1981 • *SVENGALI*

WARNER BROS. 1930–31.

NOMINATIONS *Cinematography:* Barney "Chick" McGill. *Interior Decoration:* Anton Grot.

John Barrymore plays the title role, the musician whose hypnotic powers turn a young woman, Trilby (Marian Marsh), into an opera diva, but are insufficient to make her love him. Vivid, expressionist version of the old chestnut by George Du Maurier, directed by Archie Mayo. Barrymore, made up to look repellently fascinating, is superb; his omission from the Oscar nominees is not only mysterious—Jackie Cooper was nominated for *Skippy*—but also ironic: Fredric March was nominated for playing a character based on John Barrymore in *The Royal Family of Broadway,* and the award went to John's brother, Lionel, for *A Free Soul.* John Barrymore is possibly the most distinguished major film actor never to receive an Oscar nomination. The cast also includes Donald Crisp [952], Bramwell Fletcher, and Carmel Myers.

The cinematography Oscar went to Floyd Crosby for *Tabu.* Max Ree was cited for the art direction of *Cimarron.*

Grot: 90, 1169, 1621, 1768.

1982 • *SWANEE RIVER*

20TH CENTURY-FOX. 1939.

NOMINATION *Score:* Louis Silvers.

Don Ameche [419] plays the nineteenth-century songwriter Stephen Foster in this colorful, corny biopic that also features Al Jolson as Edwin P. Christy, whose minstrel shows gave Foster's music its popularity. If you can put up with the racial attitudes on display, the movie has an energy that's quite enjoyable, not to mention lots of old, old familiar songs. Directed by Sidney Lanfield from a screenplay by John Taintor Foote and Philip Dunne [495 . . .], with Andrea Leeds [1899], Felix Bressart, and Russell Hicks. The scoring award went to Richard Hageman, Frank Harling, John Leipold, and Leo Shuken for *Stagecoach*.

Silvers: 990, 1488, 1957.

1983 • SWARM, THE

WARNER BROS. PRODUCTION; WARNER BROS. 1978.

NOMINATION *Costume Design:* Paul Zastupnevich.

The killer bees are coming! And right in their way are Michael Caine [35 . . .], Katharine Ross [810], Richard Widmark [1098], Richard Chamberlain, Olivia de Havilland [798 . . .], Fred MacMurray, Ben Johnson [1139], Lee Grant [534 . . .], Jose Ferrer [473 . . .], Patty Duke Astin [1326], Slim Pickens, Cameron Mitchell, Bradford Dillman, and Henry Fonda [815 . . .]. You might think all those stars would make this dumb disaster epic watchable. You'd be wrong. Produced and directed by the man who made his career in the seventies with such crash-and-burners as *The Poseidon Adventure* and *The Towering Inferno,* Irwin Allen [2126]. The screenplay is by Stirling Silliphant [992] and the music by Jerry Goldsmith [152.5 . . .]. The failure of *The Swarm* and the following year's *Meteor* made it clear that the disaster-flick vogue had run its course. The costuming Oscar went to Anthony Powell for *Death on the Nile*.

Zastupnevich: 1596, 2259.

1984 • SWEET AND LOWDOWN

20TH CENTURY-FOX. 1944.

NOMINATION *Song:* "I'm Making Believe," music by James V. Monaco, lyrics by Mack Gordon.

Benny Goodman and his orchestra star in this swing musical that has some sensational numbers linked by a thin plotlet involving a romance between Linda Darnell and trombonist James Cardwell. The cast, directed by Archie Mayo, includes Jack Oakie [818], Lynn Bari, Allyn Joslyn, and Dickie Moore.

The Oscar went to James Van Heusen and Johnny Burke's "Swinging on a Star," from *Going My Way*.

Monaco: 563, 1691, 1900. Gordon: 428, 563, 569, 897, 1362, 1501, 1964, 2219.

1985 • SWEET BIRD OF YOUTH

ROXBURY PRODUCTION; MGM. 1962.

AWARD *Supporting Actor:* Ed Begley.

NOMINATIONS *Actress:* Geraldine Page. *Supporting Actress:* Shirley Knight.

Page is Alexandra Del Lago, a movie queen whose career is declining into a haze of sex and drugs. She and her current boy toy, Chance Wayne, played by Paul Newman [3 . . .], are visiting his Gulf Coast hometown, where the local politico, Boss Finley (Begley), has vowed to take his revenge on Chance for seducing the Boss' daughter, Heavenly (Knight). In the stage version of the Tennessee Williams [119 . . .] play, Boss had vowed to castrate Chance, but the censors forced adapter-director Richard Brooks [227 . . .] to emasculate the emasculation. The play is so overheated to start with that the movie version can't really be called tepid, what with Page and Knight flinging themselves at Newman whenever possible, but it elicits laughs when gasps are intended. Also in the cast are Rip Torn [466] as the Boss' son—Torn later played the Boss in the 1989 TV movie starring Elizabeth Taylor [318 . . .] as Alexandra—plus Mildred Dunnock [119 . . .], Madeleine Sherwood, Philip Abbott, and Dub Taylor. The cinematography is by Milton Krasner [21 . . .].

Begley worked as a radio announcer before beginning his stage career. His appearance on Broadway in the original production of *All My Sons* in 1947 led to work in Hollywood that same year when the play's director, Elia Kazan [63 . . .], was casting the film *Boomerang*. He continued to work steadily as a film, TV, and stage character actor, scoring his biggest triumphs as the character based on William Jennings Bryan in the original Broadway version of *Inherit the Wind,* and in the TV dramas *Patterns* and *12 Angry Men*. (He appeared in the films based on the teleplays, but lost the movie version of *Inherit the Wind* to Fredric

March.) Begley died in 1970. His tall blond son, Ed Begley, Jr., is a well-known character actor.

This was the third in Page's record-setting string of seven unsuccessful nominations that finally ended when she won for *The Trip to Bountiful* on her eighth try. This time she lost to Anne Bancroft in *The Miracle Worker,* for which Patty Duke also took the supporting actress Oscar.

Page: 935, 1005, 1555, 1591, 1959, 2142, 2341. Knight: 488.

1986 • *SWEET CHARITY*
UNIVERSAL. 1969.

NOMINATIONS *Art Direction–Set Decoration:* Alexander Golitzen and George C. Webb; Jack D. Moore. *Score of a Musical Picture—Original or Adaptation:* Cy Coleman. *Costume Design:* Edith Head.

Shirley MacLaine [91 . . .] is Charity Hope Valentine, a dance hall hooker who wants a better life but isn't quite bright enough to get it. Rather messy filming of the Broadway musical based on the Federico Fellini film *Nights of Cabiria.* It has some terrific songs by Coleman and Dorothy Fields [1707 . . .], including "Hey, Big Spender" and "If They Could See Me Now," and showcases some wonderful dancing by Chita Rivera, Paula Kelly, and others. But it was the first directing effort of Bob Fosse [49 . . .], who also did the choreography, and he hasn't yet found a way to integrate the artifice of the musical numbers with the realism of film—he would figure it out by the time he made *Cabaret.* MacLaine, who had already played the golden-hearted whore once too often in her career, seems to be searching for ways to make this one new. The cast also includes Ricardo Montalban as a movie star, John McMartin as the naive guy who falls in love with Charity, and Sammy Davis, Jr., as an evangelist, plus Stubby Kaye and Ben Vereen. The screenplay by Peter Stone [655] is based on the book written by Neil Simon [332 . . .] for the Broadway version. The cinematography is by Robert Surtees [130 . . .].

The Oscar for art direction went to *Hello, Dolly!,* which also won for the scoring by Lennie Hayton and Lionel Newman. Margaret Furse took the costuming award for *Anne of the Thousand Days.*

Golitzen: 31, 96, 414, 591, 690, 706, 744, 1560, 1886, 1968, 2035, 2064, 2101. Webb: 32, 744, 2064. Moore: 31, 1190, 1662, 1937, 2112, 2330. Head: 31, 32, 46, 305, 357, 363, 612, 636, 675, 736, 832, 894, 945, 1003, 1219, 1261, 1263, 1398, 1427, 1504, 1550, 1579, 1587, 1631, 1716, 1727, 1738, 1748, 1840, 1927, 2012, 2098, 2247, 2298.

1987 • *SWEET DREAMS*
HBO PICTURES PRODUCTION IN ASSOCIATION WITH SILVER SCREEN PARTNERS; TRI-STAR. 1985.

NOMINATION *Actress:* Jessica Lange.

Lange plays country singer Patsy Cline, with Ed Harris as her husband, Charlie, in this predictable biopic; most people know of Cline's plane-crash death, so the foreshadowings of doom become tiresome. But Lange is superbly, likably vivid as Cline—it's a good change of pace from the psychotic movie star she played in *Frances,* or from the anxious, put-upon women she's played in more recent films. Unlike Sissy Spacek, who did her own singing as Loretta Lynn in *Coal Miner's Daughter,* Lange lip-syncs to Cline's recordings—a wise choice, as Cline's voice was distinctive. The cast includes Anne Wedgeworth as Cline's mother, plus David Clennon, P. J. Soles, and John Goodman. Directed by Karel Reisz from a screenplay by Robert Getchell [41 . . .]. Lange lost to Geraldine Page in *The Trip to Bountiful.*

Lange: 244.5, 449, 722, 1381, 2113.

1988 • *SWEETHEARTS*
MGM. 1938.

AWARD *Special Award:* Oliver Marsh and Allen Davey for color cinematography.

NOMINATIONS *Sound Recording:* Douglas Shearer. *Score:* Herbert Stothart.

Jeanette MacDonald and Nelson Eddy play a married theatrical couple who make beautiful music together on stage but bicker constantly when they're off —the tiffs abetted by their producer, played by Frank Morgan [22 . . .]. Among the best of the MacDonald-Eddy musicals because the fights, scripted by Dorothy Parker [1845 . . .] and Alan Campbell [1909], prevent the sugariness that afflicts the singing team's other films. The songs are by Victor Herbert, with lyrics by Chet Forrest [694 . . .] and Bob Wright [694 . . .]. Directed by W. S. Van Dyke [1751 . . .], with Ray Bolger, Mischa Auer [1401], Florence Rice, Fay Holden, Reginald Gardiner, Allyn Joslyn, Lucile Watson [2233], and Gene Lockhart [36].

The production was designed to show off MGM's first use of three-color Technicolor. Marsh was a veteran Hollywood cinematographer whose career began in 1918 and included such films as *The Dove, The Sin of Madelon Claudet, David Copperfield, The Great Ziegfeld,* and several of the MacDonald-Eddy teamings. He died in 1941. Davey was a specialist in color who usually consulted and shared credit with an experienced studio cinematographer. From 1936 through 1938 the Academy gave a special award for color cinematography, but by 1939 the use of color had grown so widespread that the cinematography award was divided into color and black-and-white categories, a division that persisted through the 1966 awards, after which the decline in the number of black-and-white films made a separate award unnecessary.

The award for sound went to Thomas T. Moulton for *The Cowboy and the Lady.* Alfred Newman took the scoring Oscar for *Alexander's Ragtime Band.*

Marsh: 217. Davey: 217, 455, 897, 1872. Shearer: 136, 202, 256, 397, 685, 817, 835, 1096, 1232, 1293, 1371, 1419, 1751, 1950, 2048, 2055, 2211, 2300. Stothart: 397, 1096, 1232, 1274, 1292, 1387, 1662, 2068, 2193, 2234, 2300.

1989 • SWING SHIFT

WARNER BROS. PRODUCTION; WARNER BROS. 1984.
NOMINATION *Supporting Actress:* Christine Lahti.

Goldie Hawn [323 . . .] plays a woman whose husband (Ed Harris) joins the navy after the attack on Pearl Harbor, so she goes to work in an aircraft factory alongside Lahti. Hawn also has an affair with the foreman, played by Kurt Russell. Otherwise, not a lot happens in this botched movie that's supposed to be about life on the home front in World War II—which is, in any case, a curious subject for a movie forty-odd years later, unless one has a fresh point to make about the situation and the people in it. Part of the problem may lie in the troubled relationship between the star, Hawn, whose production company made it, and the director, Jonathan Demme [1820]. After Demme was finished with the film, Hawn reportedly had it reedited with additional material shot by another director. But the screenplay, credited to a pseudonym, Rob Morton, also seems never to have taken shape: It was worked on by Nancy Dowd [430], Bo Goldman [1300 . . .], Ron Nyswaner [1562.5], and Robert Towne [395 . . .]. The cast also includes Fred Ward, Holly Hunter [293 . . .], Roger Corman, and Belinda Carlisle. The cinematography is by Demme regular Tak Fujimoto.

Reviewers almost unanimously panned *Swing Shift* but also unanimously praised Lahti, who has been giving solid, lively performances in films since her debut in . . . *And Justice for All* in 1979. Unfortunately most of the movies she has appeared in have been critical and/or commercial disappointments, including *Housekeeping* (1987), *Running on Empty, The Doctor* (1991), and *Leaving Normal* (1993). She lost the Oscar to Peggy Ashcroft in *A Passage to India.*

1990 • SWING TIME

RKO RADIO. 1936.
AWARD *Song:* "The Way You Look Tonight," music by Jerome Kern, lyrics by Dorothy Fields.
NOMINATION *Dance Direction:* Hermes Pan.

Fred Astaire [2126] has gotten himself engaged to hometown girl Betty Furness, which makes things difficult when he goes to the city and encounters Ginger Rogers [1102]—but the rather ineptly contrived plot, credited to Howard Lindsay and Allan Scott [1855], is not what this great musical is all about. To some critics, particularly dance critics, *Swing Time* is the chief rival to *Top Hat* for best Astaire-Rogers film. After all, it contains the "Pick Yourself Up" duet; the "Waltz in Swing Time"; Astaire's tribute to Bill Robinson, "Bojangles of Harlem"; and "Never Gonna Dance," a number whose finale required forty-seven takes (Rogers' feet were bleeding before the ten-hour shooting day was over). Director George Stevens [542 . . .] is not as comfortable with musicals as was Mark Sandrich, who had done three of the five preceding Astaire-Rogers films, but the best parts of *Swing Time*—the musical numbers—were really directed by Astaire and Pan. The stars are supported by Victor Moore, Helen Broderick, Eric Blore, and Georges Metaxa.

It's a mark of the musical riches of the era that Astaire and Rogers made two musicals in 1936, and that the other one, *Follow the Fleet,* had an Irving Berlin [34 . . .] score that includes "Let Yourself Go" and "Let's Face the Music and Dance." Astonishingly *Follow the Fleet* received no Oscar nominations, even though forgettable songs like "Did I Remember," from *Suzy,* and "A Melody From the Sky," from *Trail of the Lonesome Pine,* were among the nominees. Kern and Fields' song won out over one of Cole Porter's classics, "I've Got You Under My Skin," from *Born to Dance.* Kern had come to Hollywood in 1930, during the great migration from Broadway that was initiated by sound. Fields, too, spent much of the thirties in Hollywood. The daughter of vaudevillian Lew Fields, of Weber and Fields, she had teamed with composer Jimmy McHugh [907 . . .] in 1926 on songs for the floor shows at the Cotton Club. In addition to the lyrics for more than three hundred songs, she wrote the books for many Broadway musicals, including *Annie Get Your Gun.*

Pan's nomination was specifically for the "Bojangles of Harlem" number, which is sometimes excised from TV showings of the film in a misguided attempt at political correctness. The dance direction Oscar went to Seymour Felix for the "A Pretty Girl Is Like a Melody" extravaganza in *The Great Ziegfeld.*

Kern: 340, 375, 455, 1117, 1707, 2327. Fields: 1707. Pan: 481, 2115.

1991 • SWISS FAMILY ROBINSON

RKO RADIO. 1940.

NOMINATION *Special Effects:* Vernon L. Walker, photographic; John O. Aalberg, sound.

Thomas Mitchell [962 . . .] and Edna Best, and their sons, Freddie Bartholomew, Tim Holt, and Terry Kilburn, emigrate to Australia but are shipwrecked on the way and have to develop survival skills. Good filming of the Johann Wyss novel, with more action and less comedy than the 1960 Disney remake. Directed by Edward Ludwig from a script by Gene Towne, Graham Baker, and Walter Ferris. The Oscar for special effects went to Lawrence Butler and Jack Whitney for *The Thief of Bagdad.*

Walker: 253, 505, 1421. Aalberg: 407, 923, 959, 1033, 1102, 1978, 2030, 2166, 2313.

1992 • SWORD IN THE STONE, THE

WALT DISNEY PRODUCTIONS; BUENA VISTA. 1963.

NOMINATION *Scoring of Music—Adaptation or Treatment:* George Bruns.

A boy nicknamed Wart is befriended by the magician Merlin who, aided by a talking owl named Archimedes, educates the boy for the day when he will reveal himself as King Arthur by drawing the sword Excalibur from the stone in which it has been planted. Minor animated feature from the period in which Disney animation had been relegated to third or fourth place after live-action films, amusement parks, and television projects. There are some lively moments when Merlin battles the sorceress Mim, but it's fairly flat stuff otherwise. The screenplay by Bill Peet is based on the first book of the trilogy *The Once and Future King,* whose other two volumes were the source for the musical *Camelot.* The long-forgotten songs are by Richard M. Sherman [166 . . .] and Robert B. Sherman [166 . . .]. The scoring award went to André Previn for *Irma la Douce.*

Bruns: 116, 1709, 1839.

1993 • TABU

PARAMOUNT PUBLIX. 1930–31.

AWARD *Cinematography:* Floyd Crosby.

A Tahitian pearl fisher falls in love with a young woman who's been proclaimed taboo. Part documentary, part melodrama, filmed on location, *Tabu* is the intriguing collaboration—or rather failed collaboration—of two great directors, the documentarian Robert Flaherty [1211] and the German F. W.

Murnau, who died in an automobile accident shortly before the film was released. Flaherty and Murnau had distinctly different views of the subject matter they were undertaking. The documentary maker wanted to demonstrate the relationship of the natives to nature, while Murnau, the creator of *Nosferatu* (1922), *The Last Laugh* (1924), and *Sunrise,* was interested in the interplay of character and fate. Flaherty left the project before its completion. While *Tabu* is dated by a cornball plot and a condescension toward non-Western people characteristic of the times, it has been called the last great silent film, if only because of the beauty and strangeness of its images.

No other winner of the cinematography Oscar had as little prior experience behind a motion picture camera as Crosby, who had worked as a still photographer before being hired by Flaherty for *Tabu.* The Oscar caused some controversy, with some contending that the voters were more impressed with the exotic subject matter than with the technical skill of the cinematographer—a position reinforced by the fact that the two previous winners of the cinematography Oscar had also been shot in exotic locales: *White Shadows in the South Seas* and *With Byrd at the South Pole.* So the following year, eligibility for the cinematography award was narrowed to films "photographed in America under normal production conditions." Crosby continued his career as a documentary cameraman, working for Pare Lorentz on *The River* (1937) and *The Fight for Life.* In the fifties he moved into feature films, shooting *High Noon* and sharing a cinematography credit with James Wong Howe [1 . . .] on *The Brave Bulls* (1951), as well as doing second unit work on films such as *Oklahoma!* and *The Old Man and the Sea.* Much of his later career, however, was spent on B movies and exploitation films, many of them for quickie master Roger Corman. Crosby, whose son is rocker David Crosby, died in 1985.

1994 • *TAKE A LETTER, DARLING*

PARAMOUNT. 1942.

NOMINATIONS *Black-and-White Cinematography:* John Mescall. *Black-and-White Interior Decoration:* Hans Dreier and Roland Anderson, art direction; Sam Comer, set decoration. *Scoring of a Dramatic or Comedy Picture:* Victor Young.

Rosalind Russell [110 . . .], the co-owner of an ad agency, hires a new secretary, Fred MacMurray. As usual in such role-reversal comedies, there's a certain amount of posturing to establish the heterosexuality of the leads, and of course an ending that confirms it. Overlook the messages about the boss' and secretary's "proper places," and you might enjoy the sparring of Russell and MacMurray, scripted by Claude Binyon and directed by Mitchell Leisen [587]. The supporting cast includes Robert Benchley, Macdonald Carey, Constance Moore, Cecil Kellaway [843 . . .], and Dooley Wilson.

This was the sole nomination for Mescall, whose career as cinematographer began in 1920 and included such films as *The Bride of Frankenstein* and the 1936 *Show Boat.* In the mid-forties he became a consultant on special effects photography. The cinematography Oscar went to Joseph Ruttenberg for *Mrs. Miniver.*

The art direction award was won by *This Above All.* Max Steiner won for the score for *Now, Voyager.*

Dreier: 97, 151, 649, 674, 701, 726, 925, 979, 1101, 1120, 1194, 1214, 1217, 1358, 1443, 1452, 1540, 1668, 1748, 1880, 1975, 2190. Anderson: 278, 363, 426, 450, 649, 1029, 1194, 1214, 1219, 1452, 1570, 1668, 1674, 1880. Comer: 278, 357, 426, 450, 726, 736, 925, 956, 1029, 1101, 1214, 1219, 1443, 1570, 1631, 1674, 1727, 1738, 1748, 1959, 1975, 2012, 2098, 2200, 2208. Young: 97, 98, 100, 101, 280, 489, 612, 693, 701, 794, 846, 925, 1214, 1257, 1396, 1452, 1748, 1823, 2235, 2315.

1995 • *TAKE THE HIGH GROUND*

MGM. 1953.

NOMINATION *Story and Screenplay:* Millard Kaufman.

Drill sergeant Richard Widmark [1098] whips recruits Carleton Carpenter, Russ Tamblyn [1558], and others into shape at Fort Bliss. Cold War preparedness propaganda handled with appropriate toughness by director Richard Brooks [227 . . .] and a cast that includes Karl Malden [1477 . . .], Elaine Stewart, and Steve Forrest. The writing Oscar went to Charles Brackett, Walter Reisch, and Richard Breen for *Titanic*.

Kaufman: 131.

1996 • *TALE OF TWO CITIES, A*

MGM. 1936.

NOMINATIONS *Picture:* David O. Selznick, producer. *Film Editing:* Conrad A. Nervig.

Ronald Colman [311 . . .] plays Sydney Carton, who loves Lucie Manette (Elizabeth Allan), but goes to the guillotine to save the life of Charles Darnay (Donald Woods), the man she loves. Entertaining version of the Dickens classic that occasionally gets a little stiff and poky but comes to rousing life with the crowd scenes, which were directed by Val Lewton and Jacques Tourneur—a team later responsible for some classics of atmospheric horror, *Cat People* (1942) and *I Walked With a Zombie* (1943). The rest of the movie is directed by Jack Conway from a screenplay by W. P. Lipscomb [1637] and S. N. Behrman. Blanche Yurka is the splendidly sinister Madame DeFarge, Edna May Oliver [581] is Miss Pross, Basil Rathbone [979 . . .] the Marquis St. Evremonde, and Henry B. Walthall Dr. Manette.

This was Selznick's last production at MGM before forming his own production company, which would eventually turn out *A Star Is Born, Gone With the Wind,* and *Rebecca*. The best picture Oscar went to *The Great Ziegfeld*. Ralph Dawson won for the editing of *Anthony Adverse*.

Selznick: 497, 798, 1670, 1828, 1890, 1909, 2211. Nervig: 623, 1094.

1997 • *TALES OF HOFFMAN*

MICHAEL POWELL & EMERIC PRESSBURGER PRODUCTION; LOPERT FILMS (UNITED KINGDOM). 1951.

NOMINATIONS *Color Art Direction—Set Decoration:* Hein Heckroth. *Color Costume Design:* Hein Heckroth.

This adaptation of the opera by Offenbach about a poet who has three bizarre romances, including one with a mechanical doll, reunited many of the people responsible for *The Red Shoes:* writer-producer-directors Michael Powell [1008 . . .] and Emeric Press-burger [1008 . . .], dancers Moira Shearer, Léonide Massine, Robert Helpmann, and Ludmilla Tcherina, and designer Heckroth. It's extravagant and messy, and it was a box-office flop. The musical side is handled by Sir Thomas Beecham and the Royal Philharmonic, and singers Robert Rounseville (in the title role) and Ann Ayars. *An American in Paris* took the Oscars for art direction and for the costumes by Orry-Kelly, Walter Plunkett, and Irene Sharaff.

Heckroth: 1677.

1998 • *TALK OF THE TOWN, THE*

COLUMBIA. 1942.

NOMINATIONS *Picture:* George Stevens, producer. *Original Story:* Sidney Harmon. *Screenplay:* Sidney Buchman and Irwin Shaw. *Black-and-White Cinematography:* Ted Tetzlaff. *Black-and-White Interior Decoration:* Lionel Banks and Rudolph Sternad, art direction; Fay Babcock, set decoration. *Scoring of a Dramatic or Comedy Picture:* Frederick Hollander and Morris Stoloff. *Film Editing:* Otto Meyer.

Factory worker Leopold Dilg, played by Cary Grant [1445 . . .], is on the run from the police, who want him for murder and arson. He's been framed, but finds refuge in the home of Nora Shelley, played by Jean Arthur [1353], where he hopes to hide until he can prove his innocence. But Shelley has sub-let the house to Michael Lightcap, a Supreme Court justice, played by Ronald Colman [311 . . .], a strict law-and-order man. The premise could easily have been used in film noir or manhunt melodrama, but it's played (not entirely successfully) for comedy —even farce, as when Shelley attempts to hide Dilg from her tenant and must pass him off as the gardener. Fortunately the stellar presence and skilled playing of Grant, Arthur, and Colman make up for much of the film's lapses in logic and tone, and for the occasional sermons about justice and tolerance we have to sit through. Stevens also directed, and the cast includes Edgar Buchanan, Glenda Farrell, Emma Dunn, Rex Ingram, Leonid Kinskey, and Lloyd Bridges.

The Academy somewhat overrated the film, nominating it for best picture instead of Preston Sturges' magisterial *Sullivan's Travels,* a movie that more successfully blends farce and seriousness, or the superb Bette Davis vehicle *Now, Voyager.* It lost to *Mrs. Miniver,* which also took Oscars for its screenplay by Arthur Wimperis, George Froeschel, James Hilton, and Claudine West, and for Joseph Ruttenberg's cinematography. The award for story went to Emeric Pressburger for *The Invaders. This Above All* won the art direction award. Max Steiner won for the score for *Now, Voyager.* Daniel Mandell took the Oscar for editing *The Pride of the Yankees.*

Stevens: 542, 768, 1353, 1579, 1799. Buchman: 904, 1057, 1370. Banks: 13, 98, 455, 928, 1115, 1370. Sternad: 1065, 2066. Babcock: 455. Hollander: 104, 677, 2032. Stoloff: 13, 432, 455, 596, 643, 677, 732, 773, 1057, 1058, 1115, 1206, 1862, 1872, 1873, 2110, 2329. Meyer: 2041.

1999 • TALL, DARK AND HANDSOME
20TH CENTURY-FOX. 1941.

NOMINATION *Original Screenplay:* Karl Tunberg and Darrell Ware.

Cesar Romero, a suave gangster with a heart of gold, falls for good girl Virginia Gilmore. Passable comedy, ersatz Damon Runyon with a supporting cast —Charlotte Greenwood, Milton Berle, Sheldon Leonard—that's a good deal more interesting than the leads. Directed by H. Bruce Humberstone. The Oscar wound up in another universe: It went to Herman J. Mankiewicz and Orson Welles for *Citizen Kane.*

Tunberg: 175.

2000 • TAMING OF THE SHREW, THE
ROYAL FILMS INTERNATIONAL-FILMS ARTISTICI INTERNAZIONALI S.R.L. PRODUCTION; COLUMBIA (U.S./ITALY). 1967.

NOMINATIONS *Art Direction—Set Decoration:* Renzo Mongiardino, John DeCuir, Elven Webb, and Giuseppe Mariani; Dario Simoni and Luigi Gervasi. *Costume Design:* Irene Sharaff and Danilo Donati.

The rakish bachelor Petruchio, played by Richard Burton [85 . . .], arrives in Padua, determined to take a wealthy wife. The most eligible one is Katharine, played by Elizabeth Taylor [318 . . .], but she's well known for her bad temper and is determined to remain single. Busy, noisy, colorful version of Shakespeare's comedy, directed by Franco Zeffirelli [1722 . . .], who adapted the play with the aid of Paul Dehn [1378 . . .] and Suso Cecchi D'Amico [367]—quite successfully, too, for this is one of the least stagy versions of Shakespeare on film. But the play's not the thing here, the star power and slapstick are. Zeffirelli had originally thought of casting Sophia Loren [1280 . . .] and Marcello Mastroianni [490 . . .] in the leads; when they failed to make a commitment to the project, the Burtons gladly joined for a percentage of profits in lieu of salary because of Taylor's eagerness to play a Shakespearean role. Reviews were mixed, but the Burtons made money off their deal. The cast includes Michael Hordern as Baptista, Cyril Cusack as Grumio, and Michael York, making his film debut, as Lucentio. The rich, handsome cinematography is by Oswald Morris [659 . . .] and Luciano Trasatti.

Burton may have found some irony in the fate of the film at the Oscars, where the art direction and costuming awards went to *Camelot*—the musical in which he had starred on Broadway, but for which he was passed over in favor of Richard Harris.

Mongiardino: 300. DeCuir: 29, 201, 376, 413, 476, 896, 950, 1088, 1391, 1852. Webb: 413. Simoni: 29, 558, 1151. Sharaff: 66, 290, 333, 338, 413, 690, 852, 896, 1088, 1507, 1592, 1910, 2244, 2277. Donati: 658, 809, 1266, 1722.

2001 • TAMMY AND THE BACHELOR
UNIVERSAL-INTERNATIONAL. 1957.

NOMINATION *Song:* "Tammy," music and lyrics by Ray Evans and Jay Livingston.

Tammy, played by Debbie Reynolds [2184], lives in the bayous with her grandpa, played by Walter Brennan [424 . . .], but when she rescues a young pilot (Leslie Nielsen) whose plane has crashed, and Gramps is busted for bootlegging, Tammy is invited to stay at Nielsen's plantation. Her simple country ways are in sharp contrast with the affectations of the plantation folk, who include Fay Wray as Nielsen's dotty mother, Sidney Blackmer as his stuffy father, and Mildred Natwick [147] as his spinster aunt. Oh, and there's Nielsen's predatory fiancée, Mala Powers, to be dealt with, too. It's sort of like Tennessee Williams for teenyboppers, and it produced two sequels and a TV series before Tammy finally expired, possibly of hyperglycemia. The song, a gushy ballad that was a huge hit, lost to James Van Heusen and Sammy Cahn's "All the Way," from *The Joker Is Wild.*

Evans: 344, 512, 951, 1260, 1522, 2278. Livingston: 344, 512, 951, 1260, 1522, 2278.

2002 • *TANKS A MILLION*

Hal Roach; United Artists. 1941.

Nomination *Scoring of a Dramatic Picture:* Edward Ward.

Tiny (fifty minutes) second-feature service comedy starring William Tracy, James Gleason [904], and Noah Beery, Jr. Directed by Fred Guiol. The movie owes its nomination to the rules that allowed each studio—in this case Hal Roach—to submit a candidate in this category. There were twenty contenders —ranging from *Citizen Kane* to *King of the Zombies*—in this category. The winner was Bernard Herrmann for *All That Money Can Buy.*

Ward: 47, 388, 694, 1270, 1560.

2003 • *TARANTOS, LOS*

Tecisa-Films R.B. (Spain). 1963.

Nomination *Foreign Language Film.*

A tragic Romeo and Juliet–style romance involving two lovers from warring Gypsy families, directed by Rovira-Beleta. The Oscar went to *8¹/₂.*

2004 • *TARAS BULBA*

Harold Hecht Productions; United Artists. 1962.

Nomination *Music Score—Substantially Original:* Franz Waxman.

Yul Brynner [1088] plays the title role, a sixteenth-century Cossack leader who has vowed revenge on the Poles for an act of treachery. But his son, Andrei, played by Tony Curtis [522], falls in love with a Polish girl (Christine Kaufmann). Action-filled but unconvincing would-be epic, based on a novel by Nikolai Gogol, with a screenplay by Karl Tunberg [175 . . .]

and Waldo Salt [430 . . .]—the latter's first credited work for the screen since being blacklisted a decade earlier. Directed by J. Lee Thompson [850], with a cast that includes Sam Wanamaker and George Macready. Filmed in Argentina, with gauchos doing much of the stunt riding. The cinematography is by Joe MacDonald [1550 . . .]. The scoring Oscar went to Maurice Jarre for *Lawrence of Arabia.*

Waxman: 573, 958, 1457, 1459, 1579, 1670, 1822, 1975, 1979, 2334.

2005 • *TAXI DRIVER*

Bill/Phillips Production of a Martin Scorsese Film; Columbia. 1976.

Nominations *Picture:* Michael Phillips and Julia Phillips, producers. *Actor:* Robert De Niro. *Supporting Actress:* Jodie Foster. *Original Score:* Bernard Herrmann.

De Niro plays Travis Bickle, a New York cabbie who is so inarticulate and alienated that his attempts to make human contact—for example, by dating a pretty political campaign worker (Cybill Shepherd)— are doomed to failure. Obsessed by the squalid life of the city, he singles out a child prostitute, Iris (Foster), for rescue, and guns down her pimp, played by Harvey Keitel [308]. A brilliant, bloody movie that appalled and disgusted some critics, *Taxi Driver* became one of the essential films of the late twentieth century when a deranged loner named John Hinckley, obsessed with Jodie Foster, tried to assassinate Ronald Reagan. But even if the movie hadn't made such a tragic irruption into the real world, its dense portrayal of urban evil would have haunted us anyway. It has to be noted that *Taxi Driver,* like other successful movies about lurking horror, is often very funny— although perhaps the only reaction one can have to its shocks is to laugh. The cast also includes Peter Boyle, Albert Brooks [293], Leonard Harris, and Joe Spinell. The film's director, Martin Scorsese [27.5 . . .], has a cameo as a gun-wielding passenger in Bickle's cab.

As with many films that stretch the envelope in which Hollywood movies are wrapped, the Academy was forced to take notice of *Taxi Driver* but not compelled to reward it. Hence the lack of nominations for the people most responsible for its creation: Scorsese, screenwriter Paul Schrader, cinematographer Michael Chapman [734.5 . . .], and editor Tom Rolf [1698]. This was the beginning of Scorsese's curious relationship with the Academy, which has honored his actors with numerous nominations and three awards—Ellen Burstyn for *Alice Doesn't Live Here Anymore,* De Niro for *Raging Bull,* Joe Pesci for *GoodFellas*—but has sent mixed messages about its assessment of the director's own work. This time it nominated the film but not the director; Ingmar Bergman for *Face to Face* and Lina Wertmüller for *Seven Beauties* took the slots that might have gone to the directors of best picture nominees *Taxi Driver* and *Bound for Glory* (Hal Ashby, in the latter case). In 1988 Scorsese would receive a nomination for directing *The Last Temptation of Christ,* but the film would receive no other nominations.

Schrader, a writer who later turned director, has worked on numerous films that explore, with varying degrees of success, the nature of sin—a product, some think, of his intensely Calvinist midwestern childhood. Among the films he both wrote and directed are *Blue Collar* (1978), *Hardcore* (1979), *American Gigolo* (1980), and *Light of Day* (1987). He also did the screenplays for *Raging Bull, The Mosquito Coast* (1986), and *The Last Temptation of Christ,* and directed *Patty Hearst* (1988). In short, he's one of the most interesting filmmakers to receive no notice from the Academy.

The best picture Oscar, one of the most astonishing choices of recent years, went to *Rocky,* which won out over *All the President's Men, Bound for Glory,* and *Network* as well as *Taxi Driver.* Peter Finch won the best actor award for *Network,* for which Beatrice Straight also received the supporting actress Oscar.

This was the last score composed by Herrmann, who died, at the age of sixty-four, a day after he finished recording it. The Oscar went to Jerry Goldsmith for *The Omen.*

M. Phillips: 1927. J. Phillips: 1927. De Niro: 113, 342, 521, 785, 1650. Foster: 7, 1421.5, 1820. Herrmann: 50, 83, 407, 1460.

2006 • *TCHAIKOVSKY*

DIMITRI TIOMKIN-MOSFILM STUDIOS PRODUCTION (USSR). 1971.

NOMINATIONS *Scoring—Adaptation and Original Song Score:* Dimitri Tiomkin. *Foreign Language Film.*

Innokenti Smoktunovsky plays the Russian composer in this biopic produced by Tiomkin, who had long wanted to make it in Hollywood but had been unable to persuade a studio to back him. Born near St. Petersburg, Tiomkin came to the States in 1925 and became a citizen in 1937. The thaw in U.S.-Soviet relations in the sixties made a collaboration with Mosfilm possible, and Warner Bros.-Seven Arts provided American backing. The film was released in the United States with a narration provided by Laurence Harvey [1724], but it was heavily cut—the Soviet version runs 191 minutes, the American one a little over an hour and a half. The music is great, the story routine—sanitizing and sentimentalizing the composer's life, ignoring his homosexuality. Directed by Igor Talankin. The Oscar went to John Williams for the adaptation score for *Fiddler on the Roof.*

Tiomkin: 33, 286, 380, 446, 638, 663, 730, 768, 850, 911, 912, 1206, 1347, 1370, 1470, 2127, 2282, 2335.

2007 • *TEACHER'S PET*

PERLBERG-SEATON PRODUCTION; PARAMOUNT. 1958.

NOMINATIONS *Supporting Actor:* Gig Young. *Story and Screenplay—Written Directly for the Screen:* Fay Kanin and Michael Kanin.

Clark Gable [798 . . .] plays a newspaper city editor who learned his trade the hard way, from the ground up. Scornful of people who think they can learn journalism in a classroom, he enrolls in a course taught by Doris Day [1572] with the intent of exposing her inadequacy. You can guess the rest, but smart performers and a pleasant script make it tolerable anyway. Directed by George Seaton [31 . . .]. Young plays a neurotic rival for Day's affections, and the cast includes Mamie Van Doren, Nick Adams [2157], and Charles Lane. The supporting actor Oscar went to Burl Ives for *The Big Country.* The writing award went to Nedrick Young (under the blacklist pseudonym Nathan E. Douglas) and Harold Jacob Smith for *The Defiant Ones.*

Young: 427, 2047. M. Kanin: 2305.

2008 • *TEENAGE REBEL*

20TH CENTURY-FOX. 1956.

NOMINATIONS *Black-and-White Art Direction—Set Decoration:* Lyle R. Wheeler and Jack Martin Smith; Walter M. Scott and Stuart A. Reiss. *Black-and-White Costume Design:* Charles LeMaire and Mary Wills.

Ginger Rogers [1102] plays a woman whose daughter (Betty Lou Keim) from a previous marriage comes to live with her and causes all sorts of trouble. Hollow, dated generation-gap drama that suffers by comparison with more energetic members of the genre like *Rebel Without a Cause.* Edmund Goulding directs from a screenplay by Walter Reisch [435 . . .] and Charles Brackett [705 . . .]—hard to believe they were two of the writers on *Ninotchka.* With Michael Rennie, Mildred Natwick [147], Warren Berlinger, and Louise Beavers. The art direction award went to *Somebody Up There Likes Me.* Jean Louis won for the costumes for *The Solid Gold Cadillac.*

Wheeler: 19, 46, 83, 356, 376, 428, 476, 495, 530, 542, 719, 721, 798, 950, 1062, 1088, 1149, 1153, 1213, 1391, 1475, 1601, 1616, 1670, 1706, 1852, 2093, 2212. Smith: 29, 413, 557, 646, 896, 1230, 2120, 2247. Scott: 46, 376, 413, 476, 530, 542, 557, 646, 896, 1062, 1088, 1213, 1391, 1475, 1706, 1753, 1881, 1907, 2120, 2247. Reiss: 542, 557, 646, 2093, 2247. LeMaire: 21, 46, 376, 495, 530, 542, 954, 1213, 1338, 1391, 1601, 1706, 2043, 2205, 2294. Wills: 376, 542, 864, 1534, 2205, 2312.

2009 • *TELLING THE WORLD*

MGM. 1927–28.

AWARD *Title Writing:* Joseph Farnham.

When his wealthy father disinherits him, William Haines goes to work as a reporter and turns out to be very good at it: He solves a murder and saves his sweetheart, Anita Page, from a revolution in China. Lively romantic adventure-comedy, directed by Sam Wood [701 . . .], from a screenplay by Raymond L. Schrock and a story by Dale Van Every [352].

Farnham's citation by the Academy, which made him the sole winner of an award discontinued after this year, was not for his work on any particular film —the awards for 1927–28 could be for general achievement during the qualifying period. But *Telling the World* is listed in many histories of the awards as among three works for which he won the Oscar.

Farnham: 637, 1147.

2010 • *TEMPEST*

ART CINEMA; UNITED ARTISTS. 1927–28.

AWARD *Interior Decoration:* William Cameron Menzies.

John Barrymore plays a peasant who joins the army and falls in love with the general's daughter (Camilla Horn), who scorns him. Then the Russian Revolution gives people of his class control over people of hers, whereupon he must choose between love and the revolution. This being Hollywood, the revolutionaries are a pretty scuzzy bunch, which makes Barrymore's choice a little easier. The screenplay for this silent film was begun by Erich von Stroheim [1975], who planned to direct as well, but it was taken out of his hands by the studio, much rewritten, and given to Sam Taylor to direct. The cast also includes Louis Wolheim, and the cinematography is by Charles Rosher [22 . . .].

Menzies was cited by the Academy for both this film and *The Dove.* His career in Hollywood began in 1921 and lasted until the year before his death, when he served as associate producer on *Around the World in 80 Days,* helping novice producer Mike Todd win a best picture Oscar. He also directed several films, including *Address Unknown* and the sci-fi cult classic *Invaders From Mars* (1953).

Menzies: 38, 112.5, 311, 568, 798, 1018.

2011 • *10*

GEOFFREY PRODUCTIONS; ORION PICTURES COMPANY. 1979.

NOMINATIONS *Song:* ''Song From *10* (It's Easy to Say),'' music by Henry Mancini, lyrics by Robert Wells. *Original Score:* Henry Mancini.

Composer Dudley Moore [103], in the throes of

midlife crisis, encounters the nubile girl of his dreams, Bo Derek, the perfect 10 on a scale of 1 to . . . But when it comes down to actual sex, Moore realizes that he really belongs with Julie Andrews [1284 . . .]. Hugely popular at the time, the movie made Derek a star for a while—at least until audiences came to the same conclusion as Moore, that real women are more interesting than fantasy ones. Now the movie just seems tiresome and only fitfully funny. Written and directed by Blake Edwards [2201], with Robert Webber, Dee Wallace, Sam Jones, and Brian Dennehy. The Oscar for best song went to David Shire and Norman Gimbel for "It Goes Like It Goes," from *Norma Rae.* Georges Delerue won for the score for *A Little Romance.*

Mancini: 122, 278, 384, 494, 508, 512, 776, 825, 1573, 1574, 1864, 1970, 2037, 2201.

2012 • TEN COMMANDMENTS, THE

MOTION PICTURE ASSOCIATES INC.; PARAMOUNT. 1956.
AWARD *Special Effects:* John Fulton.
NOMINATIONS *Picture:* Cecil B. DeMille, producer. *Color Cinematography:* Loyal Griggs. *Color Art Direction–Set Decoration:* Hal Pereira, Walter H. Tyler, and Albert Nozaki; Sam M. Comer and Ray Moyer. *Sound Recording:* Loren L. Ryder, sound director, Paramount Studio Sound Department. *Film Editing:* Anne Bauchens. *Color Costume Design:* Edith Head, Ralph Jester, John Jensen, Dorothy Jeakins, and Arnold Friberg.

Charlton Heston [175] as Moses and Yul Brynner [1088] as Rameses square off in what looks for a time like a battle of big bare chests. But then, everything about this blockbuster biblical epic is big—the screen, the sets, the special effects, and the cast. It may be the most entertaining biblical epic ever made, not because it's good, but because it's impossible to take seriously and there's always something to watch—for three and a half hours, as the children of Israel win their right to head for the promised land, wander in the desert, turn to idolatry, etc. In 1923 DeMille had made a silent version in which the biblical story is only a setup for a modern morality tale. In this version he ignores thirty years of screen acting technique and reverts to the stylized acting of the silent film, staging tableaux full of stained-glass attitudes—people in postures and gestures straight out of nineteenth-century melodrama—and directing his actors to the broadest possible performances. When you've got actors capable of going over the top in a single bound, like Anne Baxter [46 . . .], Edward G. Robinson, Cedric Hardwicke, Nina Foch [629], Judith Anderson [1670], Vincent Price, and John Carradine, the result is something to see. Also on hand are Yvonne DeCarlo, Debra Paget, John Derek, Martha Scott [1510], Eduard Franz, Olive Deering, H. B. Warner [1206], Henry Wilcoxon, and, in bit parts, Woody Strode, Michael Connors, Clint Walker, Michael Ansara, and Robert Vaughn [2338]. Heston's son Fraser plays the infant Moses. The screenplay is credited to Aeneas MacKenzie, Jesse L. Lasky, Jr., Jack Gariss, and Frederic M. Frank [832]. But there's no telling which one of them came up with Baxter's line: "Oh, Moses, you splendid stubborn fool!"

The best picture nominees demonstrate that 1956 was a watershed year for Hollywood. For the first time, all five nominated films were in color, and all of them ran well over two hours in length—the shortest, *The King and I,* was 133 minutes, the next shortest, *Friendly Persuasion,* 140 minutes. *Giant* ran for more than three hours, and the winner, *Around the World in 80 Days,* for 167 minutes. By contrast, the previous year's best picture winner, *Marty,* is the shortest film to win the award, only 91 minutes long. In its attempt to win audiences away from TV, Hollywood had adapted a bigger-is-better strategy that would shape movies from now on, as demonstrated by the next three best picture winners, *The Bridge on the River Kwai, Gigi,* and *Ben-Hur,* all color spectaculars, two of them of epic proportions. Fulton's special effects, also something that the small TV screen couldn't encompass, would likewise set a trend for the movies.

Around the World in 80 Days also took the awards for Lionel Lindon's cinematography and for Gene Ruggiero and Paul Weatherwax's editing. *The King and I* won for art direction, sound, and Irene Sharaff's costumes.

Fulton: 269, 1010, 1011, 1012, 2310. DeMille: 412, 832. Griggs: 833, 988, 1799, 1887. Pereira: 278, 357, 363, 426, 450, 736, 956, 1029, 1219, 1504, 1570, 1631, 1674, 1716, 1727, 1738, 1840, 1897, 1959, 2098, 2200, 2208. Tyler: 357, 1022, 1101, 1716, 1738, 1748, 1959, 2208. Comer: 278, 357, 426, 450, 726, 736, 925, 956, 1029, 1101, 1214, 1219, 1443, 1570, 1631, 1674, 1727, 1738, 1748, 1959, 1975, 1994, 2098, 2200, 2208. Moyer: 278, 413, 736, 833, 1101, 1120, 1214, 1674, 1738, 1748, 1975. Ryder: 566, 827, 979, 1452, 1669, 1697, 1703, 1837, 1887, 2168, 2181, 2183, 2230, 2242. Bauchens: 412, 832, 1452. Head: 31, 32, 46, 305, 357, 363, 612, 636, 675, 736, 832, 894, 945, 1003, 1219, 1261, 1263, 1398, 1427, 1504, 1550, 1579, 1587, 1631, 1716, 1727, 1738, 1748, 1840, 1927, 1986, 2098, 2247, 2298. Jester: 305. Jensen: 305. Jeakins: 393, 509, 832, 882, 1048, 1385, 1391, 1432, 1748, 1881, 2238.

2013 • TEN GENTLEMEN FROM WEST POINT

20TH CENTURY-FOX. 1942.

NOMINATION *Black-and-White Cinematography:* Leon Shamroy.

A sentimental, patriotic saga about the founding of the U.S. Military Academy, with Laird Cregar giving the standout performance as a martinet commander. Also in the cast are George Montgomery, Maureen O'Hara, Harry Davenport, Ward Bond, and Tom Neal. Written by Richard Maibaum and George Seaton [31 . . .] and directed by Henry Hathaway [1194]. The Oscar went to Joseph Ruttenberg for *Mrs. Miniver.*

Shamroy: 29, 226, 356, 413, 495, 569, 602, 1088, 1153, 1213, 1592, 1610, 1706, 1852, 1883, 2286, 2334.

2014 • TENDER IS THE NIGHT

20TH CENTURY-FOX. 1962.

NOMINATION *Song:* "Tender Is the Night," music by Sammy Fain, lyrics by Paul Francis Webster.

Jennifer Jones [584 . . .] plays the fragile, neurotic Nicole Diver and Jason Robards [54 . . .] is her husband, Dick, in this adaptation by Ivan Moffat [768] of the F. Scott Fitzgerald novel about European café society in the years between two world wars. Draggy and uninvolving product of the failed hopes of David O. Selznick [497 . . .] that the novel might provide a great role for his wife, Jones. After years of trying to assemble the package, in the process considering everyone from Cary Grant [1445 . . .] to Montgomery Clift [732 . . .] to Paul Newman [3 . . .] as a costar for Jones, he was finally forced to relinquish the project to the studio, which put it in the hands of an inexperienced producer, Henry T. Weinstein, and an aging, unsympathetic director, Henry King [1868 . . .]. Robards is miscast and Jones too old for her role. The cast also includes Joan Fontaine [441 . . .], Tom Ewell, Jill St. John, and Paul Lukas [2233]. The somewhat inappropriate theme song lost to Henry Mancini and Johnny Mercer's title song from *Days of Wine and Roses.*

Fain: 95, 331, 376, 856, 1213, 1276, 1681, 1925, 2214. Webster: 33, 64, 331, 376, 604, 663, 730, 856, 1213, 1276, 1322, 1388, 1755, 1925.

2015 • TENDER MERCIES

EMI PRESENTATION OF AN ANTRON MEDIA PRODUCTION; UNIVERSAL/A.F.D. 1983.

AWARDS *Actor:* Robert Duvall. *Screenplay Written Directly for the Screen:* Horton Foote.

NOMINATIONS *Picture:* Philip S. Hobel, producer. *Director:* Bruce Beresford. *Song:* "Over You," music and lyrics by Austin Roberts and Bobby Hart.

Former country-music star Mac Sledge (Duvall) has hit the skids, thanks to his drinking. Divorced from his wife, Dixie (Betty Buckley), who is still a big star, he is rescued by the patient attention of Rosa Lee, played by Tess Harper [462], a widow who runs a small motel and service station on a lonely stretch of Texas highway. Harper makes her film debut, and Ellen Barkin has one of her first film roles as Sue Anne, Mac's daughter. The cast also includes Wilford Brimley. Very muted character study that depends on skillful performances to make its quiet impact.

Duvall, who did his own singing for the film and even wrote some of his songs, made his film debut as Boo Radley in *To Kill a Mockingbird* and played a series of fairly colorless supporting roles in such movies as *Captain Newman, M.D., Bullitt,* and *True Grit* before attracting attention as the religious fanatic Major Burns in *MASH* and as the *consigliere* Tom Hagen in *The Godfather.* He has also directed two films, a documentary called *We're Not the Jet Set* (1975) and a feature, blending documentary and scripted footage, called *Angelo, My Love* (1983). He has continued to be one of the busiest, and best-reviewed, actors in Hollywood.

Foote, a Texas-born writer, won acclaim for his 1953 teleplay *The Trip to Bountiful,* which he adapted for the screen thirty-two years later. His first screenplay, *Storm Fear,* was produced in 1955. His association with Duvall began with *To Kill a Mockingbird,* for which Foote received his first Oscar. In 1971 Foote adapted a William Faulkner story for the film *Tomorrow,* giving Duvall one of his most impressive—if little-seen—screen roles.

Terms of Endearment won the Oscars for best picture and for director James L. Brooks. This is the sole directorial nomination for Beresford, who began his career in Australia and made his reputation with the film *Breaker Morant,* for which he received a writing nomination. *Tender Mercies* was Beresford's first film made in America. He was surprisingly overlooked by the Academy six years later, when his film *Driving Miss Daisy* took the best picture Oscar, making Beresford the first person to direct a best picture winner without receiving a nomination since the 1931–32 awards, when *Grand Hotel,* directed by nonnominee Edmund Goulding, took the top honor.

The Oscar for best song went to Giorgio Moroder, Keith Forsey, and Irene Cara for ''Flashdance . . . What a Feeling,'' from *Flashdance.*

Duvall: 92, 784, 826. Foote: 2101, 2142. Beresford: 277.

2016 • TENDER TRAP, THE

MGM. 1955.

NOMINATION *Song:* ''(Love Is) The Tender Trap,'' music by James Van Heusen, lyrics by Sammy Cahn.

Bachelor womanizer Frank Sinatra [732 . . .] finds that Debbie Reynolds [2184]—somewhat aided by David Wayne and Celeste Holm [46 . . .]—has him hooked. Amusing if stagy little comedy, adapted by Julius J. Epstein [365 . . .] from a play by Max Shulman and Robert Paul Smith and directed by Charles Walters [1173]. With Carolyn Jones [124], Lola Albright, and James Drury. The song Oscar went to the title tune by Sammy Fain and Paul Francis Webster from *Love Is a Many-Splendored Thing.*

Van Heusen: 171, 173, 787, 915, 926, 1056, 1524, 1587, 1708, 1859, 1907, 2064, 2263. Cahn: 74, 163, 182, 696, 915, 926, 1031, 1056, 1216, 1524, 1587, 1692, 1708, 1719, 1859, 1907, 2064, 2072, 2103, 2110, 2125, 2263, 2264, 2315, 2343.

2017 • TEQUILA SUNRISE

MOUNT COMPANY PRODUCTION; WARNER BROS. 1988.

NOMINATION *Cinematography:* Conrad L. Hall.

A former drug dealer (Mel Gibson) has been trying to go straight, but now the feds suspect he's back in the business. Fortunately he has a friend on the force (Kurt Russell), who believes in him and helps make an end run around the heavy-footed narcs, led by J. T. Walsh. Their friendship is complicated, however, when both men fall in love with the same woman, played by Michelle Pfeiffer [485 . . .], a restaurateur under surveillance by the narcs. Meanwhile, one of Gibson's old drug connections (Raul Julia) shows up, posing as a Mexican narcotics agent. High-gloss romantic adventure-drama that doesn't add up to much but is a lot of fun if you hang loose and go where its rather rambling plot leads you. Written and directed by Robert Towne [365 . . .]. Gibson, Russell, and Pfeiffer have all had better roles, but their star chemistry here could propel a dozen vehicles. The cinematography Oscar went to Peter Biziou for *Mississippi Burning.*

Hall: 317, 504, 987, 1355, 1627, 1771.5.

2018 • TERESA

MGM. 1951.

NOMINATION *Motion Picture Story:* Alfred Hayes and Stewart Stern.

Veteran John Ericson's marriage to an Italian girl, Pier Angeli, is the cause of friction with his mother, Patricia Collinge [1182]. Thin and dated problem drama, directed by Fred Zinnemann [732 . . .], with Peggy Ann Garner, Ralph Meeker, Bill Mauldin, and, in his film debut, Rod Steiger [992 . . .]. The Oscar went to Paul Dehn and James Bernard for *Seven Days to Noon*.

Hayes: 1519. Stern: 1645.

2019 • *TERMINATOR 2: JUDGMENT DAY*

CAROLCO PICTURES PRODUCTION; TRISTAR. 1991.

AWARDS *Sound:* Tom Johnson, Gary Rydstrom, Gary Summers, and Lee Orloff. *Makeup:* Stan Winston and Jeff Dawn. *Visual Effects:* Dennis Muren, Stan Winston, Gene Warren, Jr., and Robert Skotak. *Sound Effects Editing:* Gary Rydstrom and Gloria S. Borders. **NOMINATIONS** *Cinematography:* Adam Greenberg. *Film Editing:* Conrad Buff, Mark Goldblatt, and Richard A. Harris.

Killer cyborgs from the future, Arnold Schwarzenegger and Robert Patrick, battle it out over a boy, Edward Furlong, who is destined to be the leader of rebel human forces after a nuclear calamity leaves the world under the domination of artificially intelligent machines. Schwarzenegger is the good cyborg, but he unfortunately looks exactly like the bad one that had earlier been sent from the future to terminate Furlong's mother, Linda Hamilton. This causes a bit of trouble when the cyborg and the boy have to spring her from the mental institution in which she's been confined because of her ravings about the coming apocalypse. Once she's released, they not only have to dodge the bad cyborg, a technically advanced model that has the ability to shape its liquid metal body into almost any form it chooses, but also persuade a scientist (Joe Morton) to destroy his own research, which will prevent the future calamity from occurring. Ingenious, technically dazzling sci-fi movie by writer-director James Cameron. It is, of course, a sequel, and the first film in the series, *The Terminator* (1984), is probably a better movie—less pretentious about its apocalyptic visions, less dominated by demolition-derby car chases. But this one caught the public's—not to mention the Academy's—fancy with its expensive and innovative special effects. The effects team, from Industrial Light and Magic, built on the computer-generated effects pioneered in *The Abyss,* for which Orloff, Muren, and Skotak also received nominations. *Terminator 2* had no serious competition in the categories in which it won. The other Oscars went to *JFK* for Robert Richardson's cinematography and Joe Hutshing and Pietro Scalia's editing.

Johnson: 708.5. Rydstrom: 129, 1071.5. Summers: 129, 996, 1071.5, 1684. Orloff: 5, 761.5. Winston: 45, 153.5, 600, 886, 1071.5, 1600. Muren: 5, 577, 588, 614, 997, 1002, 1071.5, 1684, 2284, 2339. Skotak: 45. Borders: 708.5.

2020 • *TERMS OF ENDEARMENT*

PARAMOUNT. 1983.

AWARDS *Picture:* James L. Brooks, producer. *Actress:* Shirley MacLaine. *Supporting Actor:* Jack Nicholson. *Director:* James L. Brooks. *Screenplay Based on Material From Another Medium:* James L. Brooks. **NOMINATIONS** *Actress:* Debra Winger. *Supporting Actor:* John Lithgow. *Art Direction–Set Decoration:* Polly Platt and Harold Michelson; Tom Pedigo and Anthony Mondello. *Sound:* Donald O. Mitchell, Rick Kline, Kevin O'Connell, and James Alexander. *Original Score:* Michael Gore. *Film Editing:* Richard Marks.

Aurora Greenway (MacLaine) is a rather prickly widow who devotes herself to her daughter, Emma (Winger), and dodges her lecherous next-door neighbor, the former astronaut Garrett Breedlove (Nicholson). Eventually Emma rebels against Aurora's constant attentions, marries a feckless college professor (Jeff Daniels), and moves away. Aurora finally succumbs to the courtship of Garrett, while Emma, who has discovered that her husband is sleeping with one of his graduate students, has her own affair with a meek bank officer (Lithgow). Aurora and Emma are reconciled only when Emma develops cancer. Entertainingly messy hodgepodge of family comedy and tearjerker that comes to life largely because of the vivid, eccentric performances of MacLaine, Winger, and Nicholson—you're never quite sure what they're going to do next, but you know it's going to be fun to watch. Danny DeVito has a small role as one of Aurora's spurned suitors. The cinematography is by Andrzej Bartkowiak.

The rights to the novel by Larry McMurtry [1139] on which the film is based originally belonged to Jennifer Jones [584 . . .], who planned to make Aurora her comeback role. But Brooks persuaded Paramount to buy the rights from her and proceeded to cast it his own way, considering Anne Bancroft [28 . . .] and Louise Fletcher [1481] for the role of Aurora before casting MacLaine. Sissy Spacek [364 . . .] had the role of Emma before Winger replaced her. Burt Reynolds, who had starred in *Starting Over,* which Brooks had written and produced, wanted to play Garrett but had prior commitments—he made the bombs *The Man Who Loved Women* and *Stroker Ace* in 1983 instead, putting an end to his reign as a top box-office draw. *Terms* was Brooks' debut as a feature film director. He was already famous as the creator of the hit TV series *Room 222, The Mary Tyler Moore Show,* and *Taxi.* After his triple play at the Oscars, Brooks waited four years before trying again with *Broadcast News,* which was critically praised but only moderately successful at the box office. For the next few years, Brooks concentrated primarily on producing such films as *Big, Say Anything* (1989), and *The War of the Roses* (1989). His return to feature film directing in 1993 was an outright disaster: *I'll Do Anything,* which was conceived as a musical but recut to eliminate the songs when preview audiences hated it; without the songs, the movie was choppy and thin, and although a few reviewers admired its flashes of wit, audiences stayed away.

MacLaine had four previous tries at an acting Oscar, spread out over twenty-five years; her first nomination was for *Some Came Running* in 1958. She had also received a nomination as producer of a documentary, *The Other Half of the Sky: A China Memoir* (1974). The sister of Warren Beatty [255 . . .], she made her first films, *Artists and Models* and *The Trouble With Harry,* in 1955, after a classic leap to fame on Broadway: She was understudy for Carol Haney in the musical *Pajama Game* and went on to great acclaim when

the star was injured. A specialist in quirky characters and golden-hearted hookers, she worked steadily through the sixties and seventies. She claimed to have modeled the tense and determined Aurora Greenway on Martha Mitchell, the irrepressible wife of Watergate-era Attorney General John Mitchell. After her Oscar, about which MacLaine forthrightly said, "I deserve this," she was absent from the screen for five years, devoting herself to writing several eccentric memoirs about her beliefs in reincarnation and other spiritual phenomena. She returned to the screen in *Madame Sousatzka* (1988) and has become a specialist in character roles, particularly women not far removed from Aurora, in such films as *Steel Magnolias, Postcards From the Edge, Used People* (1992), and *Guarding Tess* (1994).

Nicholson began his career in Roger Corman B movies, but after *Easy Rider* made him a star, he became one of the movies' most celebrated and admired actors; only Laurence Olivier [268 . . .] and Bette Davis [46 . . .] have scored as many acting nominations as Nicholson, and only Katharine Hepburn [24 . . .] has more. In 1993 he received the American Film Institute's Lifetime Achievement Award. The Oscar for *Terms* made him the first person to receive the award as supporting actor after a prior win for best actor. (Actresses Helen Hayes for *Airport,* Ingrid Bergman for *Murder on the Orient Express,* and Maggie Smith for *California Suite* had previously won supporting actress Oscars after leading-role wins.) Nicholson has continued to give strong performances in films, although the enormous salary he now commands limits his availability for movies, and he is usually called on for intense or flamboyant roles, as in *Batman, A Few Good Men,* and *Wolf* (1994).

Winger's fierce dedication to preparing for her role caused some friction with MacLaine, who in her Oscar speech made a somewhat double-edged tribute to Winger's "turbulent brilliance." Following this film, Winger's career seemed to slump. Her next movie, made three years later, was the muddled *Legal Eagles,* and subsequent films, such as *Made in Heaven* (1987), in which she played a cameo role as a man, *Betrayed* (1988), *Everybody Wins* (1990), and *The Shel-*

tering *Sky* (1990) were critical and commercial failures. In 1993, however, she made two films, *A Dangerous Woman* and *Shadowlands,* that drew critical praise for her versatility, and she received a nomination for the latter.

Lithgow, one of the most admired character players in Hollywood, began to devote himself to acting while a student at Harvard, where his fellow performers included Stockard Channing [1835.5] and Tommy Lee Jones [734.5 . . .].

The award for art direction went to Anna Asp for *Fanny & Alexander. The Right Stuff* won the remaining awards, for sound, Bill Conti's score, and a team of five film editors.

Brooks: 293. MacLaine: 91, 1017, 1859, 2152. Nicholson: 395, 595, 658.5, 672, 1019, 1135, 1481, 1625, 1678. Winger: 1465, 1795.5. Lithgow: 2314. Michelson: 1913. Mitchell: 223, 398, 411.5, 507, 734.5, 779, 1525, 1650, 1824, 1825, 2114, 2176.5. Kline: 507, 658.5, 1333, 1825, 2114. O'Connell: 223, 507, 586, 658.5, 1825, 2114. Alexander: 418. Gore: 641. Marks: 92, 293.

2021 • TESS

RENN-BURRILL CO-PRODUCTION WITH THE PARTICIPATION OF THE SOCIÉTÉ FRANÇAISE DE PRODUCTION (S.F.P.); COLUMBIA (FRANCE/UNITED KINGDOM). 1980.

AWARDS *Cinematography:* Geoffrey Unsworth and Ghislain Cloquet. *Art Direction—Set Decoration:* Pierre Guffroy and Jack Stephens. *Costume Design:* Anthony Powell.

NOMINATIONS *Picture:* Claude Berri, producer; Timothy Burrill, coproducer. *Director:* Roman Polanski. *Original Score:* Philippe Sarde.

Nastassia Kinski plays the title role in this adaptation of the novel *Tess of the D'Urbervilles,* by Thomas Hardy. The peasant kinswoman of a wealthy family, she's seduced by her rich cousin, Alec (Leigh Lawson), and has a baby who dies. When a young minister, Angel Clare, played by Peter Firth [621], marries her, he is shocked by her wedding night revelation about the baby. Rejected by him, she returns to Alec, setting a chain of tragic events into play. The screenplay by Polanski, Gerard Brach, and John Brownjohn

is faithful to the novel, although admirers of Hardy will find plenty to fault in the tone of the film and in the choice of the delicate German actress Kinski for the role of the earthy Tess. The film's visual finesse—France substitutes nicely for Hardy's Wessex—makes its nearly three-hour length rewarding. This was the first film made by Polanski after his exile from the United States, where he is under indictment for unlawful sexual relations with a thirteen-year-old girl.

Unsworth came to prominence during the fifties in his native England and worked on many British and American films through the sixties and seventies, including *2001: A Space Odyssey.* His last completed film, *Superman,* is dedicated to him. Unsworth died of a heart attack during the filming of *Tess,* which was completed by Cloquet, a Belgian cinematographer who first gained fame in France in the fifties. Cloquet shot, among other films, Alain Resnais' Holocaust documentary *Night and Fog* (1955), Arthur Penn's *Mickey One* (1965), and Woody Allen's *Love and Death* (1975). He died in 1982.

Guffroy's work as a production designer has been for some of the most famous names in French film: Jean Cocteau's *The Testament of Orpheus* (1959), Robert Bresson's *The Trial of Joan of Arc* (1962), Jean-Luc Godard's *Pierrot le Fou* (1965), and François Truffaut's *The Bride Wore Black* (1968), among many others. He has also worked on Luis Buñuel's *The Discreet Charm of the Bourgeoisie, The Phantom of Liberty* (1974), and *That Obscure Object of Desire* (1977), Philip Kaufman's *The Unbearable Lightness of Being,* and Milos Forman's *Valmont.*

The best picture Oscar went to *Ordinary People,* which also won for director Robert Redford. The scoring award went to Michael Gore for *Fame.*

Unsworth: 164, 321, 1378. Guffroy: 1020. Stephens: 1331. Powell: 516, 937, 1578, 2134. Polanski: 395, 1728.

2022 • TEST PILOT

MGM. 1938.

NOMINATIONS *Picture:* Louis D. Lighton, producer. *Original Story:* Frank Wead. *Film Editing:* Tom Held.

Clark Gable [798 . . .] plays the pilot, with

Myrna Loy as the woman in his life and Spencer Tracy [131 . . .] as his loyal mechanic. Enjoyable if predictable. Fortunately it cuts the expected ''men must work and women must weep'' treacle with some light comedy well played by a trio that's as fine as they come. Victor Fleming [798] directed, and the cast includes Lionel Barrymore [723 . . .] and Marjorie Main [601]. Wead, who had been a flying ace in World War I, knew his subject well—his own life story is dramatized in the John Ford [815 . . .] film *The Wings of Eagles* (1957). The best picture Oscar went to *You Can't Take It With You*. Dore Schary and Eleanore Griffin won the story Oscar for *Boys Town*. The editing award went to Ralph Dawson for *The Adventures of Robin Hood*.

Lighton: 352, 1194. Wead: 406. Held: 828.

2023 • TESTAMENT

ENTERTAINMENT EVENTS PRODUCTION IN ASSOCIATION WITH AMERICAN PLAYHOUSE; PARAMOUNT. 1983.

NOMINATION *Actress:* Jane Alexander.

Nuclear war has broken out, and in a small California town a family headed by William Devane and Alexander prepares for the end. A well-meaning movie, written by John Sacret Young and directed by Lynne Littman, that's meant to be wrenching and provocative, but the realism the material needs doesn't quite come through because the actors are so familiar to us as actors. The cast includes Roxana Zal, Lukas Haas, Lilia Skala [1174], Leon Ames, Rebecca DeMornay, Mako [1753], Lurene Tuttle, and, in a small prestardom role, Kevin Costner [482]. The Oscar went to Shirley MacLaine for *Terms of Endearment*.

Alexander: 54, 830, 1111.

2024 • TEXAS RANGERS, THE

PARAMOUNT. 1936.

NOMINATION *Sound Recording:* Franklin Hansen.

Fred MacMurray, Jack Oakie [818], and Lloyd Nolan are saddle pals who wind up on opposing sides of the law when MacMurray and Oakie become Rangers and Nolan turns bad. Pleasant if rather obvious western, directed by King Vidor [378 . . .]. The Oscar went to Douglas Shearer for *San Francisco*.

Hansen: 412, 649, 1194, 1217.

2025 • THANK GOD IT'S FRIDAY

CASABLANCA-MOTOWN PRODUCTION; COLUMBIA. 1978.

AWARD *Original Song:* ''Last Dance,'' music and lyrics by Paul Jabara.

It's Friday night at the Zoo, an L.A. disco, and the customers come and go and pair and split as the beat goes on. Dreary reminder of why disco died. Somewhere in the mess are a couple of people who deserved better and got it: Jeff Goldblum and Debra Winger [1465 . . .]. Directed by Robert Klane and written by Barry Armyan Bernstein, and featuring Donna Summer, Chick Vennera, and Lionel Richie [423 . . .] with the Commodores. Having completely ignored the far superior songs by the Bee Gees in the previous year's *Saturday Night Fever*—which was, of course, the movie that spurred this quickie into production—the Academy seemed determined to prove its hipness by rewarding Jabara's song. Jabara, who had a modest career as songwriter and performer (he's seen in this film, too), died of AIDS in 1993.

2026 • THANK YOUR LUCKY STARS

WARNER BROS. 1943.

NOMINATION *Song:* ''They're Either Too Young or Too Old,'' music by Arthur Schwartz, lyrics by Frank Loesser.

A ''Hey, kids, let's put on a show!'' musical, except in this cast the kids are Warner Bros. contract players, involved in staging a for-the-boys wartime patriotic revue. The plot has something to do with Eddie Cantor being mistaken for a cabdriver who looks just like him, but it's really an excuse to allow stars like Bette Davis [46 . . .] to sing (sort of—she does the nominated song), dance (she does a jitterbug), and clown. Produced by Mark Hellinger and directed by David Butler, who appear as themselves within their film. The cast, either playing themselves or getting caught in the plot, includes Humphrey Bogart [24 . . .], Jack Carson, Olivia de Havilland

[798 . . .], Errol Flynn, John Garfield [251 . . .], Ida Lupino, Alan Hale, Ann Sheridan, Spike Jones and his City Slickers, Hattie McDaniel [798], Dinah Shore, S. Z. Sakall, Edward Everett Horton, Joan Leslie, and Dennis Morgan. Songwriter Schwartz also collaborated on the story with Everett Freeman; the screenplay is by Norman Panama [636 . . .], Melvin Frank [636 . . .], and James V. Kern. The Oscar went to Harry Warren and Mack Gordon for "You'll Never Know," from *Hello, Frisco, Hello.*

Schwartz: 2088. Loesser: 864, 1131, 1422, 1551.

2027 • THANKS A MILLION
20TH CENTURY-FOX. 1935.
NOMINATION *Sound Recording:* E. H. Hansen.

Pop singer Dick Powell runs for governor and Fred Allen manages his campaign in this pleasant little musical featuring Ann Dvorak, Patsy Kelly, and Paul Whiteman and his orchestra. Directed by Roy Del Ruth from a story by Nunnally Johnson [815 . . .]. The songs are by Arthur Johnston [1547] and Gus Kahn [692 . . .]. The Oscar for sound went to Douglas Shearer for *Naughty Marietta.*

Hansen: 143, 241, 815, 952, 990, 1655, 1868, 1957, 2056, 2272, 2286, 2317.

2028 • THAT CERTAIN AGE
UNIVERSAL. 1938.
NOMINATIONS *Sound Recording:* Bernard B. Brown. *Song:* "My Own," music by Jimmy McHugh, lyrics by Harold Adamson.

Deanna Durbin develops a crush on Melvyn Douglas [169 . . .] but winds up with a more suitable boyfriend, Jackie Cooper [1836]. Fluffy teen comedy, tailored for Durbin, Universal's profit machine. Directed by Edward Ludwig from a story by F. Hugh Herbert scripted by Bruce Manning, Charles Brackett [705 . . .], and Billy Wilder [91 . . .], believe it or not.

The award for sound went to Thomas T. Moulton for *The Cowboy and the Lady.* "Thanks for the Memory," by Ralph Rainger and Leo Robin, from *The Big Broadcast of 1938,* won the song Oscar.

Brown: 93, 96, 269, 919, 1010, 1011, 1125, 1560, 1896, 2260. McHugh: 907, 916, 1707, 2328. Adamson: 21, 916, 921, 1980.

2029 • THAT FORSYTE WOMAN
MGM. 1950.
NOMINATION *Color Costume Design:* Walter Plunkett and Valles.

That woman is Irene, played by Greer Garson [239 . . .], married to the arrogant Soames Forsyte (Errol Flynn), whose coldness drives her into the arms of a young man (Robert Young) engaged to her niece, June, played by Janet Leigh [1632]. Walter Pidgeon [1232 . . .] is Soames' artistic cousin Jo, the Forsyte family black sheep. Handsomely mounted but stiff and dull adaptation of part of John Galsworthy's *The Forsyte Saga.* Directed by Compton Bennett from a screenplay by Jan Lustig, Ivan Tors, and James B. Williams. Blunted by censorship and not nearly as interesting or as well acted as the famous BBC TV serial. The costume Oscar went to Edith Head, Dorothy Jeakins, Elois Jenssen, Gile Steele, and Gwen Wakeling for *Samson and Delilah.*

Plunkett: 9, 66, 953, 1087, 1243, 1587, 1657, 1859, 2330. Valles: 1886.

2030 • THAT GIRL FROM PARIS
RKO RADIO. 1936.
NOMINATION *Sound Recording:* J. O. Aalberg.

Lily Pons runs out on her French fiancé and stows away on an ocean liner, falling in love with bandleader Gene Raymond. Inane romantic comedy designed as a showcase for opera singer Pons, in the hope that she might be as successful on the screen as soprano Grace Moore [1488] had been. She wasn't. Directed by Leigh Jason from a screenplay by P. J. Wolfson, Dorothy Yost, and Jane Murfin [2250.3]. The cast includes Jack Oakie [818], Herman Bing, Mischa Auer [1401], and Lucille Ball. The award for sound went to Douglas Shearer for *San Francisco.*

Aalberg: 407, 923, 959, 1033, 1102, 1978, 1991, 2166, 2213.

2031 • THAT HAMILTON WOMAN

ALEXANDER KORDA; UNITED ARTISTS. 1941.

AWARD *Sound Recording:* Jack Whitney, General Service.

NOMINATIONS *Black-and-White Cinematography:* Rudolph Maté. *Black-and-White Interior Decoration:* Vincent Korda, art direction; Julia Heron, set decoration. *Special Effects:* Lawrence Butler, photographic; William H. Wilmarth, sound.

Vivien Leigh [798 . . .] is Emma, Lady Hamilton, a woman of common origins whose beauty earned her a position as trophy wife to the British ambassador to Naples. Lord Hamilton (Alan Mowbray) loves his art collection more than his wife, so when the dashing young Admiral Horatio Nelson, played by Laurence Olivier [268 . . .], comes to Naples to ask its king and queen for support in the fight against Napoleon, Emma and Horatio, who is also married, fall in love. After defeating Napoleon at sea and losing his right eye and arm, Nelson returns to Naples, just in time to rescue the Hamiltons and the Neapolitan royal family from a revolution. Nelson's attentions to Emma have not gone unnoticed, however, and he is careful to keep up appearances when they return to England by being seen in public with his stern and unforgiving wife, Lady Nelson, played by Gladys Cooper [1393 . . .]. Lord Hamilton dies penniless, but Lady Nelson refuses to divorce her husband so he can marry Emma. Nelson makes a home for Emma and their child in the country, but when he is killed at the Battle of Trafalgar, she is left destitute. Enjoyable romantic drama that mixes a propagandistic view of history—Nelson has a big speech about how the English have always fought tyrants—with its love story. The Oliviers were at their most luscious, which made audiences happy, and the flag-waving is appropriately stirring, which made it Winston Churchill's favorite film. (Rumor has it that Churchill not only had a financial interest in the film but also wrote Nelson's speech about destroying dictators.) There was also a bit of real-life background to add piquancy to the on-screen romance: Before they received the divorces that allowed them to marry in 1940, Leigh and Olivier had also been lovers unhap-pily married to other people. Alexander Korda [1620] produced and directed, making the film in Hollywood —again with Churchill's encouragement, partly because filmmaking was an effective cover for British spies in then-neutral America. The cast also includes Sara Allgood [952] as Emma's mother and Henry Wilcoxon as Captain Hardy. The stirring score is by Miklos Rozsa [175 . . .].

The Oscar for cinematography went to Arthur Miller for *How Green Was My Valley,* which also won for art direction. The award for special effects went to *I Wanted Wings.*

Whitney: 729, 862, 955, 1026, 1884, 2050, 2095. Maté: 455, 706, 1607, 1740. Korda: 1070, 1201, 2050. Heron: 201, 366, 1070, 1886. Butler: 1070, 2050, 2066. Wilmarth: 1070.

2032 • THAT LADY IN ERMINE

20TH CENTURY-FOX. 1948.

NOMINATION *Song:* "This Is the Moment," music by Frederick Hollander, lyrics by Leo Robin.

Ruritanian romance in which figures from the past take a hand in the lives and loves of people in the present. Pleasant but undistinguished musical begun under the direction of Ernst Lubitsch [889 . . .] and completed after his death by Otto Preminger [73 . . .]. Starring Betty Grable, who is badly miscast, plus Douglas Fairbanks, Jr., Cesar Romero, Walter Abel, Reginald Gardiner, and Harry Davenport. The screenplay is by Samson Raphaelson and Lubitsch. The song Oscar went to "Buttons and Bows," by Jay Livingston and Ray Evans, from *The Paleface.*

Hollander: 104, 677, 1998. Robin: 104, 197, 368, 846, 1072, 1805, 1843, 2088, 2310.

2033 • THAT MAN FROM RIO

ARIANE-LES ARTISTES PRODUCTION; LOPERT PICTURES CORPORATION (FRANCE/ITALY). 1964.

NOMINATION *Story and Screenplay—Written Directly for the Screen:* Jean-Paul Rappeneau, Ariane Mnouchkine, Daniel Boulange, and Philippe de Broca.

Jean-Paul Belmondo plays a pilot who sets out on a wild chase from Paris to the Amazon when his archaeologist girlfriend (Françoise Dorleac) is kidnaped by a thief (Jean Servais) trying to get his hands on some priceless statuettes. Energetically performed and directed (by de Broca) adventure-movie spoof that was a big hit at the time but now looks like it could have used a little more discipline and coordination on both sides of the camera. The story and screenplay Oscar went to S. H. Barnett, Peter Stone, and Frank Tarloff for *Father Goose*.

2034 • *THAT OBSCURE OBJECT OF DESIRE*

GREENWICH-LES FILMS GALAXIE-INCINE COMPAÑÍA INDUSTRIAL, S.A. PRODUCTION; FIRST ARTISTS (SPAIN). 1977.
NOMINATIONS *Screenplay—Based on Material From Another Medium:* Luis Buñuel and Jean-Claude Carrière. *Foreign Language Film.*

A suave middle-aged man (Fernando Rey) is obsessed with his maid (played by two actresses, Carole Bouquet and Angela Molina), who constantly teases and frustrates his passion. Buñuel's last film is an intriguing and amusing version of a story by Pierre Louÿs that had been filmed numerous times before, including a version with Marlene Dietrich [1358] directed by Josef von Sternberg [1358 . . .], *The Devil Is a Woman* (1935). Buñuel gives it his own surreal touch, including the double casting of the femme fatale. The screenplay award went to Alvin Sargent for *Julia*. The foreign film award was won by *Madame Rosa*.

Buñuel: 549. Carrière: 549, 2173.

2035 • *THAT TOUCH OF MINK*

UNIVERSAL-INTERNATIONAL-GRANLEY-ARWIN-NOB HILL PRODUCTION; UNIVERSAL-INTERNATIONAL. 1962.
NOMINATIONS *Story and Screenplay—Written Directly for the Screen:* Stanley Shapiro and Nate Monaster. *Color Art Direction—Set Decoration:* Alexander Golitzen and Robert Clatworthy; George Milo. *Sound:* Waldon O. Watson, sound director, Universal City Studio Sound Department.

Wealthy businessman Cary Grant [1445 . . .] and unemployed secretary Doris Day [1572] eventually wind up together, though at first the consummation of their romance is constantly frustrated—as when Day breaks out in a psychosomatic rash brought on by the very thought of losing her virginity. Amusing if sniggery farce, with formulaic plotting and characterization that would be nothing without its stars—imagine what it would have been like with John Gavin and Sandra Dee in the leads—which makes the nomination for its script a little puzzling. Shapiro, after all, had already won an Oscar for a variation on the formula, *Pillow Talk*. Gig Young [427 . . .] and Audrey Meadows have bright moments as Grant's and Day's respective sidekicks, and John Astin is a wonderfully sleazy lech. There are also cameos by Mickey Mantle, Roger Maris, and Yogi Berra. Directed by Delbert Mann [1283].

The writing Oscar went to Ennio de Concini, Alfred Giannetti, and Pietro Germi for *Divorce—Italian Style*. *Lawrence of Arabia* won for art direction and sound.

Shapiro: 1220, 1498, 1572. Golitzen: 31, 96, 414, 591, 690, 706, 744, 1560, 1886, 1968, 1986, 2064, 2101. Clatworthy: 843, 1003, 1632, 1812. Milo: 1065, 1632. Watson: 350, 655, 690, 744, 1810.

2036 • *THAT UNCERTAIN FEELING*

ERNST LUBITSCH; UNITED ARTISTS. 1941.
NOMINATION *Scoring of a Dramatic Picture:* Werner Heymann.

Merle Oberon [487], frustrated and bored in her marriage to Melvyn Douglas [169 . . .], develops psychosomatic hiccups, so she goes to a psychiatrist, where she meets a creatively blocked concert pianist, played by Burgess Meredith [504 . . .]. He causes such turmoil in their lives that Oberon happily settles down again with Douglas. Often funny, sometimes flat comedy directed by Ernst Lubitsch [889 . . .]— one of his lesser works, a remake of one of his silent films, *Kiss Me Again* (1925). Oberon doesn't have the comic gift to bring off a role that needs a Carole Lombard [1401]. The screenplay is by Donald Ogden Stewart [1148 . . .] and Walter Reisch [435 . . .], with the usual uncredited assist from Lubitsch. The cast also includes Alan Mowbray, Harry Davenport, Sig Rumann, and Eve Arden [1319]. The scoring Oscar went to Bernard Herrmann for *All That Money Can Buy*.

Heymann: 1105, 1487, 2096.

2037 • THAT'S LIFE!

PARADISE COVE/UBILAM PRODUCTION; COLUMBIA. 1986.

NOMINATION *Song:* "Life in a Looking Glass," music by Henry Mancini, lyrics by Leslie Bricusse.

Jack Lemmon [91 . . .] fears turning sixty, and his wife, Julie Andrews [1284 . . .], fears that she may have cancer. Serious-funny family problem drama, with the emphasis on family: The director is Blake Edwards [2201], who is married to Andrews. Her daughter, Emma Walton, plays her daughter in the film, as does his daughter, Jennifer Edwards. And Lemmon's son, Chris Lemmon, plays their son. Moreover, Lemmon's wife, Felicia Farr, has a role, and the film was shot at the home of Edwards and Andrews. Cast members not caught in this web of nepotism include Sally Kellerman [1286], Robert Loggia [1039], Matt Lattanzi, and Cynthia Sikes. It's as self-indulgent as it sounds. Edwards cowrote the screenplay with Milton Wexler. The Oscar for song went to "Take My Breath Away," by Giorgio Moroder and Tom Whitlock, from *Top Gun*.

Mancini: 122, 278, 384, 494, 508, 512, 776, 825, 1573, 1574, 1864, 1970, 2011, 2201. Bricusse: 557, 805, 933, 937, 1766, 2201, 2285.

2038 • THEIR OWN DESIRE

MGM. 1929–30.

NOMINATION *Actress:* Norma Shearer.

Shearer's father, Lewis Stone [1540], is having an affair, and Shearer is appalled to discover that her boyfriend, Robert Montgomery [904 . . .], is the son of her father's mistress. Things turn out all right when Shearer and Montgomery are lost at sea, and Stone repents when they are rescued. Thin melodrama directed by E. M. Hopper from a screenplay by Frances Marion [202 . . .]. Shearer won the Oscar this year for *The Divorcée,* according to the Academy's official citation, even though the Oscar ballot listed her as a nominee for both this film and *The Divorcée*. The Academy has no explanation on record of why

the performance for *The Divorcée* was singled out on the citation, but speculates that some voters may have marked their ballots with a preference for that film over *Their Own Desire,* which was both a critical and commercial dud.

Shearer: 150, 555, 723, 1274, 1721.

2039 • THELMA & LOUISE

PATHÉ ENTERTAINMENT PRODUCTION; MGM. 1991.

AWARD *Screenplay Written Directly for the Screen:* Callie Khouri.

NOMINATIONS *Actress:* Geena Davis. *Actress:* Susan Sarandon. *Director:* Ridley Scott. *Cinematography:* Adrian Biddle. *Film Editing:* Thom Noble.

Thelma (Davis) is married to a jerk, and Louise (Sarandon) is going with a guy who can't commit. One evening the two women go out together, and Thelma flirts with a man who then tries to rape her in the parking lot, whereupon Louise guns him down. Terrified to face the consequences, not only from the law but also from Thelma's husband, the two hit the road, where they have a variety of adventures, including a fling for Thelma with a sexy hitchhiker (Brad Pitt), who also robs them. What the hell, say Thelma and Louise, and they turn bandits on the run. Lively and entertaining, *Thelma & Louise* isn't quite the groundbreaking feminist road movie some reviewers made it out to be, but the script and direction have a freshness and style that make it closer to *Bonnie and Clyde* than to what it might have been—a gender-switched *Smokey and the Bandit*. It's fortunate in having terrific leads, as well as strong support from Harvey Keitel [308] as a lawman who understands the two fugitives better than they realize, and Christopher McDonald as Thelma's thickheaded husband. Unfortunately, in the end Thelma and Louise, like the movie they're in, have nowhere to go.

The Oscar capped a stunning debut for Khouri. Davis and Sarandon lost to Jodie Foster for *The Silence of the Lambs,* which also took the award for Jonathan Demme's direction.

This is the sole nomination for Scott, who began his career as a set designer for the BBC, moved into directing, and became hugely successful making TV commercials. He made an impressive feature film debut with *The Duellists* (1977), a costume drama that flopped at the box office but is still widely admired for the beauty of its photography. His second film, *Alien,* was a monster hit in every sense of the word, and he followed that with *Blade Runner,* whose initial box-office failure was eventually redeemed by its status as a cult favorite. *Legend* and *Someone to Watch Over Me* (1987) were also box-office disappointments, but *Black Rain* was a commercial success. After *Thelma & Louise,* Scott was involved in a critical and commercial disaster, *1492: Conquest of Paradise* (1992). All of Scott's films are marked by sumptuous and imaginative visuals, which carry the movies a long way even when their stories don't. When he's working with a good script and fine actors, as in *Thelma & Louise,* he's among the best directors around. His brother is director Tony Scott, best known for *Top Gun.*

JFK won the Oscars for Robert Richardson's cinematography and Joe Hutshing and Pietro Scalia's editing.

Davis: 6. Sarandon: 107, 413.3, 1205.5. Noble: 2296.

2040 • THEM!
WARNER BROS. 1954.

NOMINATION *Special Effects.* (No individual citation.)

Atomic fallout produces ants the size of semitrailers in this classic fifties sci-fi adventure, starring Edmund Gwenn [1325 . . .], James Whitmore [157 . . .], and James Arness. When we were kids, we thought the movie was about big bugs, but then we grew up to read that it was really an allegory about the Cold War. Don't mistake this one, anyway, for the run-of-the-mill giant insect schlockers—it's smart and funny and genuinely scary at times, even if you know the scientific explanations about how giant ants would collapse under the weight of their own exoskeletons. Directed by Gordon Douglas from a screenplay by Ted Sherdeman based on a story by George Worthing Yates. Fess Parker has a bit part and Leonard Nimoy an even smaller bit. The special ef-

fects involve hauling about giant models rather than stop-motion photography, but they're effective enough, even if the Academy preferred the ones for *20,000 Leagues Under the Sea.*

2041 • THEODORA GOES WILD
COLUMBIA. 1936.

NOMINATIONS *Actress:* Irene Dunne. *Film Editing:* Otto Meyer.

Theodora (Dunne) writes a steamy best-selling novel that scandalizes her hometown but lands her a suave New Yorker, played by Melvyn Douglas [169 . . .]. Bright and busy screwball comedy that demonstrated Dunne's versatility—up to this point, she was best known as the suffering heroine of movies like *Back Street* and *Magnificent Obsession.* Richard Boleslawski directed, from a screenplay by Sidney Buchman [904 . . .] based on a story by Mary McCarthy. The cast includes Thomas Mitchell [962 . . .] and Spring Byington [2325]. Dunne lost to Luise Rainer in *The Great Ziegfeld.* The editing award went to Ralph Dawson for *Anthony Adverse.*

Dunne: 114, 400, 972, 1212. Meyer: 1998.

2042 • THERE GOES MY HEART
HAL ROACH; UNITED ARTISTS. 1938.

NOMINATION *Score:* Marvin Hatley.

Virginia Bruce is a runaway heiress, and Fredric March [184 . . .] is the reporter on her trail. *It Happened One Night* was three years old by the time this one was made, so maybe writers Jack Jevne and Eddie Moran thought nobody would notice their script's resemblance to the classic. Not bad if you can shake off the déjà vu, thanks to a cast that includes Patsy Kelly, Alan Mowbray, Nancy Carroll [539], Eugene Pallette, Harry Langdon, and Arthur Lake. Directed by Norman Z. McLeod. The score isn't really anything special—every studio was allowed to come up with a nominee, and this is the one Hal Roach picked as an entry. The Oscar went to Alfred Newman for *Alexander's Ragtime Band.*

Hatley: 234, 2237.

2043 • *THERE'S NO BUSINESS LIKE SHOW BUSINESS*

20TH CENTURY-FOX. 1954.

NOMINATIONS *Motion Picture Story:* Lamar Trotti. *Scoring of a Musical Picture:* Alfred Newman and Lionel Newman. *Color Costume Design:* Charles LeMaire, Travilla, and Miles White.

Ethel Merman and Dan Dailey [2258] play the Donahues, who with their three kids form a vaudeville family act. But when the kids grow up to be Donald O'Connor, Mitzi Gaynor, and Johnnie Ray, the act begins to fall apart. Flimsy backstage musical with a boring plot but terrific musical numbers—all of them to songs by Irving Berlin [34 . . .]. Marilyn Monroe, who plays O'Connor's girlfriend, gets to do "Heat Wave," Dailey and O'Connor get to dance, and Merman gets to belt. Even Gaynor, whose role is smallish, comes across well. The only drawback in the cast is the inexplicable Ray, who had a big jukebox smash with the lugubrious "Cry," so he was hustled into the movies, where neither his acting nor his singing passed muster. Here, he's the son who decides to become a priest, and he bleats a nauseating song called "If You Believe." The movie would be ideal for the VCR, on which you can fast-forward through Ray and the plot, except that it was designed to show off CinemaScope, which means that about half of every frame won't fit on a TV screen. Directed by Walter Lang [1088], with Hugh O'Brian, Frank McHugh, and Lee Patrick.

Trotti, whose nomination is hard to countenance, lost to Philip Yordan for *Broken Lance.* The scoring award went to Adolph Deutsch and Saul Chapin for *Seven Brides for Seven Brothers.* The Oscar for costumes went to Sanzo Wada for *Gate of Hell.*

Trotti: 1516, 2286, 2337. A. Newman: 31, 34, 46, 72, 138, 182, 226, 333, 334, 347, 375, 428, 437, 457, 476, 495, 542, 690, 797, 833, 952, 953, 959, 962, 1016, 1082, 1088, 1213, 1278, 1362, 1397, 1475, 1616, 1655, 1849, 1868, 1883, 1921, 2046, 2091, 2258, 2286, 2294, 2316. L. Newman: 183, 457, 557, 795, 896, 981, 1160, 1273, 1585, 1762. LeMaire: 21, 46, 376, 495, 530, 542, 954, 1213, 1338, 1391, 1601, 1706, 2008, 2205, 2294. Travilla: 15, 954, 1952. White: 101, 832.

2044 • *THESE THREE*

SAMUEL GOLDWYN PRODUCTIONS; UNITED ARTISTS. 1936.

NOMINATION *Supporting Actress:* Bonita Granville.

Miriam Hopkins [165] and Merle Oberon [487] play schoolteachers whose lives are ruined when one of their pupils (Granville) starts a malicious rumor that both women are having affairs with a young doctor (Joel McCrea). Very fine adaptation by Lillian Hellman [1182 . . .] of her play *The Children's Hour,* in which the child's lie was that the women were lesbians. (This gave rise to a story about the film's producer, Samuel Goldwyn [102 . . .], who was legendary for his malapropisms. Goldwyn was supposedly informed that the play could not be filmed because the women were lesbians. "So what?" Goldwyn allegedly replied. "We'll make them Americans.") So sensational was the theme of lesbianism at the time, that the Production Code office forbade not only mentioning it in the film but even the use of the play's original title. Interestingly this version is superior to the 1961 remake, *The Children's Hour,* in which the women are explicitly accused of lesbianism. Hellman admitted that she had no problem in changing her play, because the less sensational charge of adultery put more focus on the theme of her story: the power of a lie. William Wyler [175 . . .] directed, and the success of this film and *Dodsworth* the same year made his career. The cinematography is by Gregg Toland [407 . . .]. The cast also includes Alma Kruger, Margaret Hamilton, and Walter Brennan [424 . . .].

Granville began her career on stage at the age of three and made her first films in 1932, when she was nine. She also starred as girl detective Nancy Drew in a series of movies in the later thirties. Her career continued into her early twenties, including a supporting role in *Now, Voyager.* She retired from the screen in the fifties. One of the first nominees for the new supporting actress category, she lost to Gale Sondergaard in *Anthony Adverse.*

2045 • THEY KNEW WHAT THEY WANTED

RKO Radio. 1940.

Nomination *Supporting Actor:* William Gargan.

Charles Laughton [1387 . . .] plays an Italian winemaker in the Napa Valley who woos a San Francisco waitress, played by Carole Lombard [1401], by mail, sending her the picture of his foreman (Gargan) instead of his own. Shocked at the deception when she arrives for their wedding, she has an affair with the foreman. Well-filmed version of a play by Sidney Howard [102 . . .], adapted by Robert Ardrey [1083] and directed by Garson Kanin [11 . . .]. Unfortunately Lombard is miscast in a role that asks her to suppress her giddiness, and Laughton carries on too much in a very peculiar accent. The Howard play was so well thought of that it had been filmed twice before, in 1928 as *The Secret Love* and in 1930 as *A Lady in Love*. Today it's probably best known as the source of the Broadway musical *The Most Happy Fella,* by Frank Loesser [864 . . .].

Gargan had come to Hollywood from Broadway in the early years of sound, but his career was largely in B movies. He also played the title role in the fifties TV detective series *Martin Kane* and made a series of hard-hitting antismoking public service TV commercials in the seventies after suffering throat cancer—he spoke with the aid of an artificial larynx. He died in 1979. The supporting actor Oscar went to Walter Brennan for *The Westerner*.

2046 • THEY SHALL HAVE MUSIC

Samuel Goldwyn Productions; United Artists. 1939.

Nomination *Score:* Alfred Newman.

A slum kid (Gene Reynolds) accidentally wanders into a recital by Jascha Heifetz and is so impressed that he takes up the violin. Moreover, Heifetz is so touched by the story that he gives a benefit for the struggling music school where the kid is studying. Cornball showcase for Heifetz provided by producer Samuel Goldwyn [102 . . .] in one of his bids for prestige. This is the one in which Walter Brennan [424 . . .] plays a music teacher! Joel McCrea, Andrea Leeds [1899], Marjorie Main [601], and Porter Hall also star. Archie Mayo directs from a script by John Howard Lawson [233] and Irmgard Von Cube [1052]. Gregg Toland [407 . . .] did the cinematography, but the main thing is Heifetz's playing, of which there's plenty. The scoring award went to Richard Hageman, Frank Harling, John Leipold, and Leo Shuken for *Stagecoach*.

Newman: 31, 34, 46, 72, 138, 182, 226, 333, 334, 347, 375, 428, 437, 457, 476, 495, 542, 690, 797, 833, 952, 953, 959, 962, 1016, 1082, 1088, 1213, 1278, 1362, 1397, 1475, 1616, 1655, 1849, 1868, 1883, 1921, 2043, 2091, 2258, 2286, 2294, 2316.

2047 • THEY SHOOT HORSES, DON'T THEY?

Chartoff-Winkler-Pollack Production; ABC Pictures Presentation; Cinerama. 1969.

Award *Supporting Actor:* Gig Young.

Nominations *Actress:* Jane Fonda. *Supporting Actress:* Susannah York. *Director:* Sydney Pollack. *Screenplay—Based on Material From Another Medium:* James Poe and Robert E. Thompson. *Art Direction—Set Decoration:* Harry Horner; Frank McKelvy. *Score of a Musical Picture—Original or Adaptation:* John Green and Albert Woodbury. *Film Editing:* Fredric Steinkamp. *Costume Design:* Donfeld.

Penniless people, many of them aspiring actors who came to Depression-era Hollywood hoping to break into the movies, perform in a dance marathon presided over by a cynical emcee (Young). Grim but absorbing adaptation of a novel by Horace McCoy. Fonda and York are among the contestants, as are Michael Sarrazin, Red Buttons [1763], Bonnie Bedelia, and Bruce Dern [430]. The film's narrative disjointedness—it uses flash-forwards as well as flashbacks—has been criticized, but it adds an energy to what might have been a weary, nihilistically plodding movie. The cinematography is by Philip Lathrop [69 . . .]. Though it racked up an impressive collection of nominations, *They Shoot Horses* was shut out of the top award, perhaps because of the clout wielded by 20th Century-Fox, which mustered enough votes to place its big flop *Hello, Dolly!* among the nominees for best picture. That award went, however, to another grimly uncompromising film, *Midnight Cowboy.*

Young had made his film debut in 1940 under his own name, Byron Barr, but because there was already another actor with that name, he took the name of the character he played in a 1942 movie, *The Gay Sisters,* and became known as Gig Young. Through much of his career, he was typed as a lightweight, often as the hero's wisecracking sidekick, as in *That Touch of Mink.* After the Oscar, he made a handful of films before his death in 1978; he apparently shot his wife, German actress Kim Schmidt, to whom he had been married only three weeks, and then killed himself.

Fonda had never before demonstrated the ability to carry so serious a role, and it provided her with something of a comeback after *Barbarella* (1968), made during her liaison with Roger Vadim, threatened to type her as a sex kitten. She lost to Maggie Smith for *The Prime of Miss Jean Brodie.*

York was still in her teens when she made her screen debut in *Tunes of Glory* in 1960, and she became a star three years later when she played Sophie Western in *Tom Jones.* She lost the Oscar to Goldie Hawn in *Cactus Flower.*

Pollack's previous work as director had attracted little attention from critics or audiences, but *They Shoot Horses,* which he also produced, provided a career breakthrough, making him one of the most important producer-directors of the seventies and eighties. He lost to John Schlesinger for *Midnight Cowboy,* for which Waldo Salt also took the screenplay award.

The placement of *They Shoot Horses* among the nominees for musicals is one of the Academy's odder moves. Although it's filled with period music, it's hardly what anyone would call a musical. The scoring Oscar went to Lennie Hayton and Lionel Newman for *Hello, Dolly!,* which also won for art direction.

The award for editing went to Françoise Bonnot for *Z.* Margaret Furse won for the costumes for *Anne of the Thousand Days.*

Young: 427, 2007. Fonda: 394, 430, 1066, 1104, 1356, 1473. Pollack: 1512, 2113. Poe: 101, 372, 1174. Horner: 894, 964. McKelvy: 591, 917, 1450, 1570, 1631, 2200. Green: 66, 320, 594, 662, 817, 914, 1298, 1471, 1550, 1657, 2244. Steinkamp: 814, 1512, 2074, 2113. Donfeld: 508, 1625, 2107.

2048 • THEY WERE EXPENDABLE

MGM. 1945.

NOMINATIONS *Sound Recording:* Douglas Shearer. *Special Effects:* A. Arnold Gillespie, Donald Jahraus, and R. A. MacDonald, photographic; Michael Steinore, sound.

"They" are members of the PT (patrol torpedo) boat squadron in the Philippines during World War II, and they include Robert Montgomery [904 . . .], John Wayne [33 . . .], Jack Holt, Ward Bond, Marshall Thompson, Cameron Mitchell, and future director Blake Edwards [2201] in a bit part as one of the crewmen. The modest and well-handled love interest is provided by Donna Reed [732] as a nurse. Produced and directed by John Ford [815 . . .], it's mercifully free of the phony heroics that mar so many war-effort movies, so it doesn't seem dated. The screenplay is by Frank "Spig" Wead [406 . . .], whose own life story would be told by Ford in *The Wings of Eagles* (1957). The cinematography is by Joseph August [849 . . .]. The Oscar for sound went to Stephen Dunn for *The Bells of St. Mary's.* The special effects award went to *Wonder Man.*

Shearer: 136, 202, 256, 397, 685, 817, 835, 1096, 1232, 1293, 1371, 1419, 1751, 1950, 1988, 2055, 2211, 2300. Gillespie: 175, 256, 685, 704, 835, 1371, 1388, 1905, 2055, 2122, 2300. Jahraus: 1905, 2055. MacDonald: 175, 1201. Steinore: 835, 1905.

2049 • THIEF, THE

FRAN PRODUCTIONS INC.; UNITED ARTISTS. 1952.

NOMINATION *Scoring of a Dramatic or Comedy Picture:* Herschel Burke Gilbert.

Accused of treason, nuclear physicist Ray Milland [1208] attempts to elude the FBI. Cold War thriller with a gimmick: There is no dialogue. Unfortunately the efforts of screenwriters Clarence Greene [1572 . . .] and Russell Rouse [1572 . . .] to maintain this tour de force for eighty-five minutes soon get boring. Greene also produced and Rouse directed. The cast includes Rita Gam and Martin Gabel. The scoring Oscar went to Dimitri Tiomkin for *High Noon*.

Gilbert: 361, 1348.

2050 • THIEF OF BAGDAD, THE

ALEXANDER KORDA; UNITED ARTISTS (UNITED KINGDOM/ U.S.). 1940.
AWARDS *Color Cinematography:* Georges Périnal. *Color Interior Decoration:* Vincent Korda. *Special Effects:* Lawrence Butler, photographic; Jack Whitney, sound.
NOMINATION *Original Score:* Miklos Rozsa.

Sabu plays the title role, a street urchin who enlists the aid of a genie (Rex Ingram) to outwit an evil vizier (Conrad Veidt). (If you still think the makers of Disney's *Aladdin* were unfamiliar with this film, we'd like to interest you in a nice bridge we're selling.) One of the great pictures for kids, which means it's great fun for grown-ups, too. The screenplay is by Miles Malleson (who also plays the sultan) and Lajos Biro [1134], and there are three credited directors: Michael Powell [1008 . . .], Ludwig Berger, and Tim Whelan. Producer Alexander Korda [1620] and his associate producers, William Cameron Menzies [38 . . .] and Zoltan Korda, are also said to have had a hand in directing. John Justin and June Duprez are the romantic leads.

Périnal worked on some of the most celebrated French films of the late twenties and early thirties, including Jean Cocteau's *Blood of a Poet* (1930) and René Clair's *Sous les Toits de Paris* (1930), *Le Million* (1931), and *A Nous la Liberté*. He was hired by Alexander Korda in 1933 and helped Korda advance the British film industry by shooting such films as *The Private Life of Henry VIII* and *Things to Come*. After the Oscar, he continued his career primarily in England, with such films as *Vacation from Marriage* and *The Fallen Idol*. He died in 1965.

Vincent Korda was primarily known for his work for his brother Alexander, although he continued his career after Alexander's death in 1956 on such films as *The Longest Day* and *The Yellow Rolls-Royce* (1964). Vincent died in 1979.

The scoring award went to Leigh Harline, Paul J. Smith, and Ned Washington for *Pinocchio*.

Périnal: 715. Korda: 1070, 1201, 2031. Butler: 1070, 2031, 2066. Whitney: 729, 862, 955, 1026, 1884, 2031, 2095. Rozsa: 175, 566, 567, 604, 1035, 1069, 1070, 1085, 1208, 1227, 1644, 1872, 1890, 1968, 2304.

2051 • THIN ICE

20TH CENTURY-FOX. 1937.
NOMINATION *Dance Direction:* Harry Losee.

As you might have guessed from the title, figure skater Sonja Henie is the star of this pleasantly trifling musical romance with an Alpine setting and Tyrone Power as a prince with whom she falls in love. Sidney Lanfield directs a cast that includes Arthur Treacher, Joan Davis, Alan Hale, Sig Rumann, and Melville Cooper. Losee, nominated for the "Prince Igor" production number, lost to Hermes Pan for *A Damsel in Distress*.

2052 • THIN MAN, THE

MGM. 1934.
NOMINATIONS *Picture:* Hunt Stromberg, producer. *Actor:* William Powell. *Director:* W. S. Van Dyke. *Adaptation:* Frances Goodrich and Albert Hackett.

Powell is Nick Charles and Myrna Loy is his wife, Nora. He's a private eye with a gallery of yeggs for friends, she's an heiress who enjoys slumming. Together, they're delightful, though they tend to drink a bit too much. The mystery plot has something to do with a murdered inventor, but the film gets its lift from the repartee of the Charleses, the invention of writer Dashiell Hammett [2233], supposedly modeled on himself and Lillian Hellman [1182 . . .]. This celebrated movie is a little stiff in the joints, partly because it was rushed through production in only sixteen days—reportedly because studio head Louis B. Mayer had no faith in the material and wanted it treated as a B movie. It launched a series of five more *Thin Man* movies, even though the title character, played by Edward Ellis, appears only in this one. The cinematography is by James Wong Howe [1 . . .], and the cast includes Maureen O'Sullivan, Nat Pendleton, Cesar Romero, Porter Hall, and Skippy, the terrier who plays Asta; he also appeared in *Bringing Up Baby* (1938) and *The Awful Truth.*

This was the year that *It Happened One Night* became the first film to sweep all the top awards, including best picture, best actor, best director, and best adapted screenplay. Powell came in third in the three-man race won by Clark Gable; Frank Morgan came in second for his role in *The Affairs of Cellini.* Van Dyke was a second-place finisher after Frank Capra, and Goodrich and Hackett also placed second after Robert Riskin.

Stromberg: 831, 1419. Powell: 1170, 1401. Van Dyke: 1751. Goodrich: 25, 656, 1782. Hackett: 25, 656, 1782.

2053 • THIRD MAN, THE

SELZNICK ENTERPRISES IN ASSOCIATION WITH LONDON FILMS PRO- DUCTIONS LTD.; SELZNICK RELEASING ORGANIZATION (UNITED KINGDOM). 1950.

AWARD *Black-and-White Cinematography:* Robert Krasker.

NOMINATIONS *Director:* Carol Reed. *Film Editing:* Oswald Hafenrichter.

An American writer (Joseph Cotten) comes to postwar Vienna in search of an old friend, Harry Lime, but is told that Lime is dead. But Lime, played by Orson Welles [407 . . .], turns out to be alive, and the object of a considerable manhunt that culminates in a chase through the Viennese sewers. Great thriller written by Graham Greene [639], with substantial additions by Welles, whose suave and evil Lime is one of his finest creations. The coproducers, Alexander Korda [1620] and David O. Selznick [497 . . .], originally wanted Cary Grant [1445 . . .] or James Stewart [73 . . .] to play the writer, but when they were unavailable, Cotten, who was under contract to Selznick, got the part. Noël Coward [993] was Selznick's choice to play Lime, but Reed felt he was wrong for the role. Selznick also considered Robert Mitchum [1935] for the role; when Mitchum was busted for marijuana, Selznick reluctantly consented to casting Welles. The film was a surprising hit, as was Anton Karas' theme music,

played on a zither. The failure to nominate *The Third Man* in the picture, writing, and music categories, or to single out Welles as a supporting actor, is simply baffling.

Krasker, born in Australia, started his career in France before going to England, where he became a major cinematographer. The moody off-angle visuals of *The Third Man* are his most famous work, but he contributed with distinction to many subsequent films, including *Billy Budd, Birdman of Alcatraz,* and *The Collector,* before his death in 1981.

Reed seems to have accommodated to working with Welles, who was never shy about taking over. Years later, in an interview with Peter Bogdanovich [1139], Welles took credit for "a very few *ideas,* like the fingers coming through the grille." Reed asserted, however, that the hand in the shot was his own and that the scene had been filmed before Welles arrived on the set. The Oscar for directing went to Joseph L. Mankiewicz for *All About Eve.*

The editing Oscar went to Ralph E. Winters and Conrad A. Nervig for *King Solomon's Mines.*

Reed: 639, 1471.

2054 • "38"

ARABELLA FILM/SATEL FILM PRODUCTION (AUSTRIA). 1986.

NOMINATION *Foreign Language Film.*

On the eve of the *Anschluss,* when Hitler annexed Austria, a naive young couple, an actress and a Jewish playwright, try to lead their lives as if nothing unusual were happening. The results are disastrous for both. Adaptation of a novel by Friedrich Torberg, *Auch Das War Wien,* directed by Wolfgang Gluck. The film received a limited commercial release in the United States in 1988 under the title *38: Vienna Before the Fall.* The Oscar went to *The Assault.*

2055 • THIRTY SECONDS OVER TOKYO

MGM. 1944.

AWARD *Special Effects:* A. Arnold Gillespie, Donald Jahraus, and Warren Newcombe, photographic; Douglas Shearer, sound.

NOMINATION *Black-and-White Cinematography:* Robert Surtees and Harold Rosson.

Spencer Tracy [131 . . .] plays Lt. Col. Jimmy Doolittle in this account of the first bombing raids on Japan, but his part is secondary to the depictions of the preparation and planning for the raid, with the usual family tensions, preflight jitters, and do-or-die speechifying. Dated but watchable. Directed by Mervyn LeRoy [1662 . . .] from a screenplay by Dalton Trumbo [273 . . .], who despite his flag-waving here would be imprisoned as one of the Hollywood Ten in the fifties. The cast includes Van Johnson, Robert Walker, Phyllis Thaxter, Scott McKay, Don DeFore, Robert Mitchum [1935], Leon Ames, Moroni Olsen, and, in a bit part, future director Blake Edwards [2201]. The cinematography Oscar went to Joseph LaShelle for *Laura*.

Gillespie: 175, 256, 685, 704, 835, 1371, 1388, 1905, 2048, 2122, 2300. Jahraus: 1905, 2048. Newcombe: 835, 1371. Shearer: 136, 202, 256, 397, 685, 817, 835, 1096, 1232, 1293, 1371, 1419, 1751, 1950, 1988, 2048, 2211, 2300. Surtees: 130, 175, 557, 810, 917, 1094, 1139, 1388, 1469, 1644, 1747, 1911, 1927, 1960, 2152. Rosson: 105, 133, 256, 747, 2300.

2056 • THIS ABOVE ALL

20TH CENTURY-FOX. 1942.

AWARD *Black-and-White Interior Decoration:* Richard Day and Joseph Wright, art direction; Thomas Little, set decoration.

NOMINATIONS *Black-and-White Cinematography:* Arthur Miller. *Sound Recording:* E. H. Hansen. *Film Editing:* Walter Thompson.

The speech by Polonius in *Hamlet* completes the phrase begun in the title: "to thine own self be true," which is what deserter Tyrone Power learns to do when he falls in love with Joan Fontaine [441 . . .] in wartime London and her patriotism stirs him to heroic action. Sentimental but enjoyable adaptation by R. C. Sheriff [804] of a novel by Eric Knight. Directed by Anatole Litvak [517 . . .], with Thomas Mitchell [962 . . .], Henry Stephenson, Nigel Bruce, Gladys Cooper [1393 . . .], Sara Allgood [952], Alexander Knox [2286], Melville Cooper, Jill Esmond, Arthur Shields, and Miles Mander. MGM's contribution to the war effort, *Mrs. Miniver,* took the Oscar in the cinematography category, which was won by Joseph Ruttenberg. The award for sound went to Nathan Levinson for Warners' musical flag-waver, *Yankee Doodle Dandy*. Daniel Mandell won the editing Oscar for *The Pride of the Yankees*.

Day: 22, 102, 235, 487, 510, 560, 569, 797, 833, 864, 952, 1048, 1175, 1397, 1477, 1666, 1949, 2120, 2276. Wright: 235, 428, 508, 569, 690, 746, 852, 1175, 1264, 1397, 1475. Little: 46, 83, 235, 428, 495, 719, 721, 746, 950, 952, 1082, 1149, 1153, 1397, 1475, 1666, 1852, 1868, 2212, 2286. Miller: 83, 241, 952, 1082, 1655, 1868. Hansen: 143, 241, 815, 952, 990, 1655, 1868, 1957, 2027, 2272, 2286, 2317. Thompson: 1457.

2057 • THIS IS CINERAMA

CINERAMA PRODUCTIONS CORPORATION. 1953.

NOMINATION *Scoring of a Dramatic or Comedy Picture:* Louis Forbes.

A travelogue designed to show off what was billed as "the eighth wonder of the world," the widescreen process called Cinerama, this movie offered audiences a series of hyperkinetic thrills, including a ride on a roller coaster. Using a huge curved screen and three projectors for exciting three-dimensional effects, Cinerama was one of the film industry's first attempts to give audiences something they couldn't get on their new TV sets. *This Is Cinerama* was a big hit at the box office, but the process had some serious defects. For one thing, the three images didn't blend seamlessly: There were visible bands between them. The effect was best viewed from the center of the theater—to the sides, the distortion of the curved screen became distracting. The expense of converting a theater to the process limited it to a few big-city venues—a drawback at a time when Americans were moving to the suburbs. And the process worked best when the camera was in motion, making the seams dividing the screen less noticeable. For that reason, most Cinerama films were nonnarrative. The first fiction films made in the medium, *How the West Was Won* and *The Wonderful World of the Brothers Grimm,* were not released until 1962. Eventually both of these films were released in conventional wide-screen formats, but the earlier travelogues like *This Is Cinerama* have disappeared, along with the big screens on which they were shown. Cinerama was developed by Fred Waller, a Paramount special effects man, for the 1939 World's Fair in New York, where it involved eleven projectors. Waller received one of the Academy's special scientific and technical awards, "for designing and developing the multiple photographic and projection systems which culminated in Cinerama," at the 1953 ceremonies. The Oscar for scoring went to Bronislau Kaper for *Lili*.

Forbes: 282, 1006, 2186, 2310.

2058 • THIS IS THE ARMY

WARNER BROS. 1943.
AWARD *Scoring of a Musical Picture:* Ray Heindorf.
NOMINATIONS *Color Interior Decoration:* John Hughes and Lt. John Koenig, art direction; George J. Hopkins, set decoration. *Sound Recording:* Nathan Levinson.

Originally a hit Broadway revue that also toured military bases, and was entirely performed by soldiers, this film version supplies a frame story about Jerry Jones (George Murphy), who writes a World War I revue called *Yip, Yip, Yaphank,* which was a real show written, like *This Is the Army,* by Irving Berlin [34 . . .]. Comes the next war, and it's the turn of his son, Johnny (Ronald Reagan), to write his own show. The spectacle of two famous future California politicos playing father and son is enough to get a lot of people's attention, but there's a good deal more to enjoy in the movie. Such as Berlin himself singing "Oh, How I Hate to Get Up in the Morning," or Kate Smith doing (natch) "God Bless America." Also on hand, either in the frame story or as performers, are Joan Leslie, George Tobias, Alan Hale, Charles Butterworth, Rosemary De Camp, Dolores Costello, Una Merkel [1959], Frances Langford, and Joe Louis. Michael Curtiz [79 . . .] directs from a screenplay by Casey Robinson and Claude Binyon.

This was the second of Heindorf's three scoring awards. The Oscar for art direction went to *The Phan-*

tom of the Opera. Stephen Dunn took the award for sound for *This Land Is Mine.*

Heindorf: 331, 479, 666, 930, 1043, 1204, 1385, 1408, 1430, 1690, 1719, 1750, 1910, 2186, 2243, 2310, 2318. Hughes: 16, 1779. Hopkins: 110, 508, 896, 1003, 1170, 1332, 1385, 1393, 1910, 1949, 1973, 2277. Levinson: 16, 30, 343, 385, 531, 689, 710, 712, 790, 930, 965, 1052, 1169, 1621, 1690, 1768, 1769, 1779, 1930, 1949, 2318.

2059 • THIS LAND IS MINE

RKO RADIO. 1943.
AWARD *Sound Recording:* Stephen Dunn.

Schoolteacher Charles Laughton [1387 . . .] tries to lead a quiet, normal life when his country is invaded by the Nazis, but eventually he is forced to take a stand. Too-glossy wartime propaganda that's perhaps the weakest film from one of the greatest of all directors, Jean Renoir [1884]. The screenplay is by Dudley Nichols [30 . . .], and the cast includes Maureen O'Hara, George Sanders [46], Walter Slezak, Kent Smith, and Una O'Connor.

Dunn: 173, 1383, 1479.

2060 • THIS LOVE OF OURS

UNIVERSAL. 1945.
NOMINATION *Scoring of a Dramatic or Comedy Picture:* H. J. Salter.

Merle Oberon [487] has been separated from her husband (Charles Korvin) for twelve years, after he accused her of infidelity. She has supported herself in a nightclub act with Claude Rains [365 . . .]. But then Korvin reenters her life, tells her that he knows she was faithful, and takes her back again. The trouble is, he has told their daughter (Sue England) that her mother is dead, so they decide to conceal Oberon's true identity from the girl. But the daughter takes an intense dislike to her "stepmother." Thin sentimental drama, with a typically enjoyable performance by Rains but not much else. It's loosely based on a play by Luigi Pirandello that had earlier been filmed with Greta Garbo [84 . . .] under the title *As You Desire*

Me (1932). William Dieterle [1169] directs. The Oscar went to Miklos Rozsa for *Spellbound.*

Salter: 62, 340, 399, 1030, 1307.

2061 • THIS SPORTING LIFE

Julian Wintle-Leslie Parkyn Production; Walter Reade-Sterling-Continental Distributing (United Kingdom). 1963.

Nominations *Actor:* Richard Harris. *Actress:* Rachel Roberts.

Coal miner Frank Machin (Harris) works his way out of the mines by becoming a professional rugby star. He also has an affair—a love-hate relationship—with his landlady, played by Roberts. Grim, unlovable movie about a grim, unlovable pair, but the performers and the direction of Lindsay Anderson give it a hard-edged realism that's undeniably powerful. Adapted by David Storey from his novel. The cast includes Alan Badel, Colin Blakely, and, making her film debut in a minor role, Glenda Jackson [893 . . .].

Harris, born in Ireland, made his stage debut in London in 1956 and entered films in 1959. Though he had substantial parts in *The Guns of Navarone* and *Mutiny on the Bounty, This Sporting Life* was his breakthrough role, leading to starring parts in such big Hollywood productions as *Hawaii* and *Camelot.* He lost to Sidney Poitier in *Lilies of the Field.*

Roberts had made a few films in Britain in the fifties but had concentrated largely on her stage career. Her performances in two early-sixties British realist movies, *Saturday Night and Sunday Morning* (1960) and *This Sporting Life,* drew wide attention, but her subsequent films were a mixed bag, ranging from the western *Wild Rovers* (1971) to the glossy *Murder on the Orient Express.* Roberts was married at the time of her nomination for *This Sporting Life* to Rex Harrison, who was also a nominee for *Cleopatra.* They are one of five married couples to have received simultaneous Oscar nominations; the others are Alfred Lunt and Lynn Fontanne, nominated for *The Guardsman;* Richard Burton and Elizabeth Taylor, nominees for *Who's Afraid of Virginia Woolf?;* Frank Sinatra and Ava Gardner, nominated for *From Here to Eternity* and *Mogambo*

respectively; and Charles Laughton and Elsa Lanchester, nominees for *Witness for the Prosecution.* Roberts committed suicide in 1980 at the age of fifty-three. The Oscar went to Patricia Neal for *Hud.*

Harris: 660.

2062 • THIS WOMAN IS MINE

Frank Lloyd; Universal. 1941.

Nomination *Scoring of a Dramatic Picture:* Richard Hageman.

Carol Bruce is the woman in question. She stows away on a fur traders' ship bound for Oregon and becomes the object of interest for both Franchot Tone [1387] and John Carroll. Also on board are Walter Brennan [424 . . .], Nigel Bruce, and Leo G. Carroll. Tedious stuff, directed by Frank Lloyd [374 . . .] from a screenplay by Seton I. Miller [463 . . .]. The scoring award went to Bernard Herrmann for *All That Money Can Buy.*

Hageman: 955, 979, 1200, 1801, 1901.

2063 • THOMAS CROWN AFFAIR, THE

Mirisch-Simkoe-Solar Production; United Artists. 1968.

Award *Song:* "The Windmills of Your Mind," music by Michel Legrand, lyrics by Alan Bergman and Marilyn Bergman.

Nomination *Original Score—for a Motion Picture (Not a Musical):* Michel Legrand.

Steve McQueen [1753] is a bored millionaire plotting to rob a bank, and Faye Dunaway [255 . . .] is the insurance investigator out to see that he doesn't get away with it. Sleek, sexy caper movie that doesn't take itself seriously; it's a glittering toy and it knows it, using all sorts of camera hijinks, provided by cinematographer Haskell Wexler [229 . . .], to keep you amused. The Legrand-Bergman song is the perfect whirligig equivalent of what's going on on screen. Norman Jewison [659 . . .] directs from a screenplay by Alan R. Trustman. Also on screen are Jack Weston, Paul Burke, and Yaphet Kotto.

This was the first Oscar for both Legrand and the Bergmans. The composer, born in Paris, started his film composing career in France in the fifties and began working on this side of the Atlantic in the late sixties. The Bergmans, husband and wife, have written songs for dozens of films over the past twenty-five years.

The scoring Oscar went to John Barry for *The Lion in Winter.*

Legrand: 179, 867, 1568, 1960, 2172, 2321, 2332. A. Bergman: 179, 867, 1168, 1568, 1628, 1747, 1813, 1864, 2113, 2238, 2321, 2322. M. Bergman: 179, 867, 1168, 1568, 1628, 1747, 1813, 1864, 2113, 2238, 2321, 2322.

2064 • *THOROUGHLY MODERN MILLIE*

Ross Hunter-Universal Production; Universal. 1967.
Award *Original Music Score:* Elmer Bernstein.
Nominations *Supporting Actress:* Carol Channing. *Art Direction—Set Decoration:* Alexander Golitzen and George C. Webb; Howard Bristol. *Sound:* Universal City Studio Sound Department. *Song:* "Thoroughly Modern Millie," music and lyrics by James Van Heusen and Sammy Cahn. *Scoring of Music—Adaptation or Treatment:* André Previn and Joseph Gershenson. *Costume Design:* Jean Louis.

The plot of this outsize musical has something to do with the determinedly modern (for the twenties, that is) Millie, played by Julie Andrews [1284 . . .], and naive heiress Dorothy Brown, played by Mary Tyler Moore [1502], being stalked by white slavers, played by Beatrice Lillie, Jack Soo, and Pat Morita [1077]. James Fox and John Gavin are the young men who woo Millie and Dorothy, and Channing is the social lioness Muzzy Van Hossmere. Everyone works very hard to entertain, but the strain begins to show as the movie enters its second hour. The attempt to convert the wisp of a story into a blockbuster musical is a bit like trying to pump a cupcake full of air to turn it into a wedding cake. The inspiration for the film was *The Boy Friend,* the 1954 Broadway musical spoof of the twenties that launched Andrews' career —and was itself turned into an overblown movie musical in 1971. George Roy Hill [317 . . .], who directs from a screenplay by Richard Morris, blamed producer Ross Hunter [31] for the movie's excesses. *Thoroughly Modern Millie* does have its admirers— many of them fans of Andrews or Moore or Channing

or Lillie—and there are amusing moments, especially when Lillie, a performer who wasn't done justice by the movies, is on screen. The film even has some fun with Gavin's handsome woodenness—when he's paralyzed by a poison dart, it takes a while for people to notice.

This is the sole Oscar for Bernstein, one of the most prolific and versatile of film composers. He began his career writing for movies in 1952 and first gained notice for the jazz-tinged score for *The Man With the Golden Arm.* He later composed one of the most familiar of all movie themes for *The Magnificent Seven.* Still composing regularly in his seventies, in recent years he has scored films as various as *An American Werewolf in London, Ghostbusters, My Left Foot, The Grifters,* and *The Age of Innocence.*

This is the sole nomination for Channing, a beloved Broadway performer whose manner is a bit too large-scale for the movies, of which she has made only a few. She first became famous for her portrayal of Lorelei Lee in the 1949 Broadway musical *Gentlemen Prefer Blondes,* but she lost that role to Marilyn Monroe in the 1953 film version, just as she would lose her most famous role, as Dolly Gallagher Levi in *Hello, Dolly!,* to Barbra Streisand when that musical was filmed. Channing lost the Oscar to Estelle Parsons in *Bonnie and Clyde.*

The award for art direction went to *Camelot,* which also won for Alfred Newman and Ken Darby's adaptation score and John Truscott's costumes. *In the Heat of the Night* took the Oscar for sound. "Talk to the Animals," written by Leslie Bricusse for *Doctor Dolittle,* was named best song.

Bernstein: 27.5, 789, 882, 1242, 1264, 1685, 1959, 2101, 2130, 2147, 2223. Golitzen: 31, 96, 414, 591, 690, 706, 744, 1560, 1886, 1968, 1986, 2035, 2101. Webb: 32, 744, 1986. Bristol: 690, 852, 864, 1182, 1451, 1607, 1613, 1907. Van Heusen: 171, 173, 787, 915, 926, 1056, 1524, 1587, 1708, 1859, 1907, 2016, 2263. Cahn: 74, 163, 182, 696, 915, 926, 1031, 1056, 1216, 1524, 1587, 1692, 1708, 1719, 1859, 1907, 2016, 2072, 2103, 2110, 2125, 2263, 2264, 2315, 2343. Previn: 172, 609, 769, 1017, 1034, 1044, 1097, 1393, 1550, 1592,

2077, 2161. Gershenson: 776. Louis: 20, 126, 170, 262, 732, 744, 1028, 1065, 1521, 1640, 1812, 1858, 1910.

2065 • *THOSE MAGNIFICENT MEN IN THEIR FLYING MACHINES*

20TH CENTURY-FOX LTD. PRODUCTION; 20TH CENTURY-FOX (UNITED KINGDOM). 1965.

NOMINATION *Story and Screenplay—Written Directly for the Screen:* Jack Davies and Ken Annakin.

The subtitle of the film goes on a bit more: *Or, How I Flew From London to Paris in 25 Hours and 11 Minutes,* which pretty much sums up this adventure comedy about a cross-Channel air race in 1910. Stuart Whitman [1277] and James Fox are the American and British rivals, not just for the trophy but also for Sarah Miles [1737]. Robert Morley [1274] is Miles' father, and the other contestants in the race include Alberto Sordi, Gert Frobe, Jean-Pierre Cassel, and Terry-Thomas. There are also appearances by Benny Hill, Flora Robson [1759], Gordon Jackson, Sam Wanamaker, and, in the prefatory history of flight, Red Skelton. It's too long and works too hard at being a blockbuster, but it has its share of laughs. Annakin also directed. The writing Oscar went to Frederic Raphael for *Darling.*

2066 • *THOUSAND AND ONE NIGHTS, A*

COLUMBIA. 1945.

NOMINATIONS *Color Interior Decoration:* Stephen Goosson and Rudolph Sternad, art direction; Frank Tuttle, set decoration. *Special Effects:* L. W. Butler, photographic; Ray Bomba, sound.

Cornel Wilde [1872] is Aladdin and Phil Silvers (!) is his sidekick in this spoofy version of the story. Rex Ingram, who was the genie in *The Thief of Bagdad,* is another one here, as is Evelyn Keyes. Shelley Winters [542 . . .] has a bit part as one of the attendant ladies. Directed by Alfred E. Green. The art direction award went to *Frenchman's Creek. Wonder Man* won for special effects.

Goosson: 928, 1073, 1182, 1206. Sternad: 1065, 1998. Tuttle: 843, 1093. Butler: 1070, 2031, 2050.

2067 • *THOUSAND CLOWNS, A*

HARRELL PRODUCTION; UNITED ARTISTS. 1965.

AWARD *Supporting Actor:* Martin Balsam.

NOMINATIONS *Picture:* Fred Coe, producer. *Screenplay —Based on Material From Another Medium:* Herb Gardner. *Scoring of Music—Adaptation or Treatment:* Don Walker.

Jason Robards [54 . . .] plays a Manhattan dropout from the rat race, who's raising his young nephew (Barry Gordon) to share his nonconformist attitude toward bourgeois strivings. But the guardians of bourgeois values, social workers played by William Daniels and Barbara Harris [2275], show up and threaten to put Robards back on track. Their plan is somewhat undermined when Harris is attracted to Robards. Balsam is Robards' brother, who is very much caught in the rat race. Engaging but formulaic comedy that's more than a little derivative from *You Can't Take It With You, Auntie Mame,* and other such mild digs at conventional values. Historically it provides an interesting transition between the Organization Man ethos of the fifties and the hippie era of the later sixties. Many people recall the movie fondly as a kind of touchstone of their youth, when the notion that one didn't have to work nine to five like one's parents seemed incredibly liberating. (A lot of those people went on to be yuppies, working nine to nine.) Gardner adapts his own Broadway play, and it remains stagebound except for a memorable opening sequence in which Robards and Gordon watch hordes of working stiffs flood into the city. Gardner and editor Ralph Rosenblum conceived the sequence together after principal filming under the direction of Coe had ended.

After beginning his acting career on stage and TV, Balsam entered movies in a small role in *On the Waterfront* and established himself as a regular character player, usually an aggressive urbanite, in such films as *12 Angry Men, Marjorie Morningstar, Psycho,* and *Breakfast at Tiffany's.* His most memorable post-Oscar roles have been in *Little Big Man, Murder on the Orient Express,* and *All the President's Men,* and he has been seen frequently in TV dramas.

Coe is one of the key figures of early television as

producer and director of *Marty* and other dramas on the series *Philco Television Playhouse* and *Playhouse 90*. He moved into Broadway producing in the later fifties, with hits such as *Two for the Seesaw, The Miracle Worker,* and *A Thousand Clowns*. He produced the latter two when they were adapted for the screen, and made his debut as a screen director with *A Thousand Clowns*. He died in 1979. The best picture Oscar went to *The Sound of Music,* which also won for Irwin Kostal's scoring. Robert Bolt took the writing award for *Doctor Zhivago*.

2068 • THOUSANDS CHEER

MGM. 1943.

NOMINATIONS *Color Cinematography:* George Folsey. *Color Interior Decoration:* Cedric Gibbons and Daniel Cathcart, art direction; Edwin B. Willis and Jacques Mersereau, set decoration. *Scoring of a Musical Picture:* Herbert Stothart.

A romance between an officer's daughter (Kathryn Grayson) and a private played by Gene Kelly [74] is the premise for MGM to put on one of those all-star patriotic reviews beloved of wartime Hollywood— e.g., Paramount's *Star Spangled Rhythm,* Universal's *Follow the Boys,* and Warner's *Thank Your Lucky Stars*. This one mixes pop music with pseudo-classical uplift provided by José Iturbi and a piece specially commissioned from Dimitri Shostakovich [1084]. The pop music comes off best, especially when Lena Horne sings "Honeysuckle Rose." But then Iturbi falls into the cracks between the keys trying to let his hair down and play boogie-woogie. Also on hand are Mary Astor [822], Ben Blue, Lionel Barrymore [723 . . .], Donna Reed [732], Margaret O'Brien, June Allyson, Mickey Rooney [115 . . .], Judy Garland [1065 . . .], Red Skelton, Eleanor Powell, Frank Morgan [22 . . .], Ann Sothern [2246], and Lucille Ball. Directed by George Sidney from a screenplay by Paul Jarrico [2105] and Richard Collins.

The cinematography Oscar went to Hal Mohr and W. Howard Greene for *Phantom of the Opera,* which also won for art direction. Ray Heindorf won for scoring *This Is the Army*.

Folsey: 51, 137, 629, 807, 835, 838, 1124, 1299, 1320, 1500, 1688, 1782, 2269. Gibbons: 66, 87, 130, 217, 227, 239, 285, 290, 440, 629, 749, 831, 980, 1069, 1096, 1173, 1190, 1226, 1230, 1232, 1274, 1308, 1309, 1417, 1567, 1604, 1644, 1662, 1673, 1721, 1861, 1937, 2112, 2256, 2257, 2300, 2320, 2330. Cathcart: 1096. Willis: 66, 87, 130, 227, 239, 290, 629, 749, 831, 980, 1069, 1096, 1157, 1173, 1190, 1226, 1230, 1232, 1309, 1417, 1567, 1657, 1662, 1673, 1721, 1861, 1937, 2112, 2257, 2320, 2330. Stothart: 397, 1096, 1232, 1274, 1292, 1387, 1662, 1988, 2193, 2234, 2300.

2069 • THREE

AVALA FILM PRODUCTION (YUGOSLAVIA). 1966.

NOMINATION *Foreign Language Film*.

A drama about the wartime experiences of a young man and the three people whose deaths he witnesses or causes, directed by Aleksander Petrovic. The Oscar went to *A Man and a Woman*.

2070 • THREE BROTHERS

ITER FILM (ROME)/GAUMONT (PARIS) PRODUCTION (ITALY). 1981.

NOMINATION *Foreign Language Film*.

The brothers have taken very different paths in their lives: One is a judge in Rome, another is a teacher in Naples, and the third is a factory worker in Turin. When their mother dies, they reunite at the farm where they were born. The film is somewhat formulaic in working out the relationship among the brothers, who represent three aspects and regions of Italian life, politics, and society, but is more successful in depicting their relationship with their father. Directed by Francesco Rosi, who cowrote the screenplay with Tonino Guerra [61 . . .]. The cinematography is by Pasqualino De Santis [1722]. The Oscar went to *Mephisto*.

2071 • THREE CABALLEROS, THE

WALT DISNEY PRODUCTIONS; RKO RADIO. 1945.

NOMINATIONS *Sound Recording:* C. O. Slyfield. *Scoring of a Musical Picture:* Edward Plumb, Paul J. Smith, and Charles Wolcott.

A collection of Disney animated shorts blended

with some live-action footage that like the earlier *Saludos Amigos* grew out of a State Department–sponsored trip by Walt Disney [645 . . .] and some studio personnel to Latin America. By the time the film was released, the Good Neighbor Policy designed to prevent Central and South American countries from allying with the Axis powers was outmoded, so *The Three Caballeros* is less propagandistic than the earlier film—and a good deal better. The title characters are Donald Duck, the Brazilian parrot Joe Carioca, and the Mexican rooster Panchito. They feature in the film's most elaborate and extended sequences, in which Donald goes to Baía and then to Mexico. Donald's encounter with some dancing cacti on the latter trip results in some of the studio's most astonishingly psychedelic animation—if you thought *Fantasia* was a "head film," check this one out. Other episodes involve Pablo, a penguin who hates the cold, and a little gaucho who encounters a donkey with wings. The blend of live action and animation is sophisticated, and the songs include "You Belong to My Heart," "Baía," and the title tune.

The Oscar for sound went to Stephen Dunn for *The Bells of St. Mary's.* Georgie Stoll won for the scoring of *Anchors Aweigh.*

Slyfield: 140, 402, 1745. Plumb: 140, 1745, 2202. Smith: 402, 1553, 1576, 1745, 1851, 1871, 2202. Wolcott: 1745, 1871.

2072 • *THREE COINS IN THE FOUNTAIN*

20TH CENTURY-FOX. 1954.

AWARDS *Color Cinematography:* Milton Krasner. *Song:* "Three Coins in the Fountain," music by Jule Styne, lyrics by Sammy Cahn.

NOMINATION *Picture:* Sol C. Siegel, producer.

Dorothy McGuire [759], Jean Peters, and Maggie McNamara [1348], vacationing in Rome, make wishes at the Trevi fountain and wind up being wooed by Clifton Webb [1149 . . .], Rossano Brazzi, and Louis Jourdan. Lush travelogue designed to show off Rome in CinemaScope, which is why you might wonder what all the fuss was about when you see this one on TV today. Director Jean Negulesco [1052] gives this insubstantial film a good deal of style, as do art directors Lyle Wheeler [19 . . .] and John DeCuir [29 . . .]. The screenplay is by John Patrick, and the cast includes Howard St. John and Cathleen Nesbitt, but the Academy spotted the people most responsible for the film's success: Krasner probably did more for Italian tourism than anyone since Marco Polo, and the Styne-Cahn ballad was a chart-topper. The film's best picture nomination, however, owes more to the aggressive publicity campaign put on by the studio than to its true worth; it displaced superior films such as *A Star Is Born* and *Rear Window.* The Oscar went to *On the Waterfront.*

This was the sole award for Krasner, an enormously prolific cinematographer who worked at Universal in the thirties and forties and moved over to Fox after the war. His last film was *Beneath the Planet of the Apes* (1970). He died in 1988.

This was the first of four Oscars for Cahn but the only one for Styne. They first teamed up in 1942, when Styne was working as a vocal coach, arranger, and composer at Fox and Cahn was a lyricist at "poverty row" Republic Pictures. Their collaboration on "It Seems I've Heard That Song Before" for Republic's *Youth on Parade,* which earned their first Oscar nomination, established them as a songwriting team. After numerous hits, they broke up because of Styne's distaste for Hollywood. He moved to New York, while Cahn remained behind, establishing a fruitful partnership with James Van Heusen [171 . . .]. Styne's post-Oscar career was primarily on Broadway, where his songwriting partners included Leo Robin [104 . . .] on *Gentlemen Prefer Blondes,* Betty Comden [141 . . .] and Adolph Green [141 . . .] on *Bells Are Ringing* and others, Stephen Sondheim [543] on *Gypsy,* and Bob Merrill [737] on *Funny Girl* and other shows. Styne died in 1994.

Krasner: 21, 46, 96, 654, 953, 1219. Styne: 74, 696, 737, 920, 921, 1031, 1719, 2110, 2343. Cahn: 74, 163, 182, 696, 915, 926, 1031, 1056, 1216, 1524, 1587, 1692, 1708, 1719, 1859, 1907, 2016, 2064, 2103, 2110, 2125, 2263, 2264, 2315, 2343. Siegel: 1163.

2073 • THREE COMRADES

MGM. 1938.

NOMINATION Actress: Margaret Sullavan.

The comrades—Robert Taylor, Franchot Tone [1387], and Robert Young—are all Germans facing the hardships of life in post–World War I Germany, and all are in love with Sullavan, who is dying. F. Scott Fitzgerald and Edward E. Paramore adapted the novel by Erich Maria Remarque, but though doomed youth was a specialty of both Fitzgerald and Remarque, the story has been sapped by too much MGM prettifying and nervousness about making the movie too explicitly anti-Nazi, and by the fact that Taylor, Tone, and Young are mediocre actors at best. Sullavan is enormously appealing, however. Frank Borzage [132 . . .] directed, and the cast includes Guy Kibbee, Lionel Atwill, Henry Hull, Charley Grapewin, Monty Woolley [1569 . . .], and Marjorie Main [601].

This is the sole nomination for Sullavan, who began her acting career with a theatrical group founded at Princeton by Joshua Logan [643 . . .] and others that grew to include Henry Fonda [815 . . .] and James Stewart [73 . . .]. Her success on Broadway led to a film contract with Universal in 1933, and she was instrumental in bringing Fonda, whom she married, and Stewart to Hollywood. During a decade in Hollywood, she made such films as *The Good Fairy* (1935), *The Shop Around the Corner* (1940), and *Back Street,* but was perhaps more successful on stage than on screen. She left Hollywood in 1943 and made only one more film, *No Sad Songs for Me,* in 1950. After divorcing Fonda, she married William Wyler [175 . . .] and Leland Hayward [1337]. She died of an overdose of barbiturates in 1960, at the age of forty-nine. The Oscar went to Bette Davis in *Jezebel.*

2074 • THREE DAYS OF THE CONDOR

DINO DE LAURENTIIS PRODUCTION; PARAMOUNT. 1975.

NOMINATION Film Editing: Frederic Steinkamp and Don Guidice.

Robert Redford [1502 . . .] is a researcher for a publishing company that's really a front for the CIA. One day he returns from lunch to discover that every-body in the small brownstone office building has been murdered. On the run from the assassins, who belong to a network within the CIA that's trying to take it over, he grabs a frightened young woman, played by Faye Dunaway [255 . . .], and hides out with her, gradually persuading her that his fantastic, paranoid tale is the truth. Max von Sydow [1546] is the chief assassin and Cliff Robertson [387] and John Houseman [1069 . . .] are the guys in the CIA he's supposed to trust, though in movies like this, you never really know. Good thriller with some nice star turns, but it takes itself a little too seriously, like a lot of Watergate-era movies. The following year, Redford would make the definitive Watergate-era movie, *All the President's Men,* and that true story would have a lot more chilling menace than this cooked-up one does. Directed by Sydney Pollack [1512 . . .] from a screenplay by Lorenzo Semple, Jr., and David Rayfiel, based on a novel, *Six Days of the Condor,* by James Grady. The cinematography is by Owen Roizman [631 . . .] and the music by Dave Grusin [379 . . .]. The editing Oscar went to Verna Fields for *Jaws.*

Steinkamp: 814, 1512, 2047, 2113.

2075 • THREE FACES OF EVE, THE

20TH CENTURY-FOX. 1957.

AWARD Actress: Joanne Woodward.

A mousy young southern housewife (Woodward) develops multiple-personality disorder—she sometimes turns into a sexy floozy. A psychiatrist, played by Lee J. Cobb [301 . . .], manages to uncover a third personality that's the "real" one, mature and self-confident, by getting her to confront the childhood trauma that set her off. Formulaic, simplistic hokum, but Woodward's marvelously accomplished performance almost persuades you to believe in it—more so than the pretentious introduction delivered by Alistair Cooke. Director Nunnally Johnson [815 . . .] also did the screenplay, based on a case study by two doctors. The cinematography is by Stanley Cortez [1239 . . .], and the cast includes David Wayne, Nancy Kulp, and Vince Edwards.

Born in Georgia and educated at Louisiana State

University, Woodward came to New York in the early fifties to break into the theater. She was an understudy for the original Broadway production of *Picnic,* where she met Paul Newman [3 . . .], a cast member whom she would marry in 1958. She made her film debut in 1955 in *Count Three and Pray.* Her career has been linked with that of Newman, with whom she has costarred in eleven films, starting with *The Long Hot Summer* in 1958. He has also directed her in several films, including *Rachel, Rachel* and *The Glass Menagerie* (1987). Their most recent on-screen pairing was in *Mr. and Mrs. Bridge.* In recent years Woodward has done frequent TV work, including the 1976 TV movie *Sybil,* in which she plays the psychiatrist who helps patient Sally Field [1448 . . .] overcome multiple-personality disorder. Woodward recently also provided a deliciously nuanced off-screen narrative for *The Age of Innocence.*

Woodward: 1365, 1645, 1962.

2076 • *THREE IS A FAMILY*

MASTER PRODUCTIONS; UNITED ARTISTS. 1945.

NOMINATION *Sound Recording:* W. V. Wolfe, RCA Sound.

Sitcom-style programmer about a family and its overcrowded apartment, with an impressive cast: Fay Bainter [393 . . .], Charlie Ruggles, Helen Broderick, Marjorie Reynolds, Arthur Lake, and Hattie McDaniel [798]. Directed by Edward Ludwig from a screenplay by Harry Chandlee [1779] and Marjorie L. Pfaelzer based on a play by Phoebe [350] and Henry Ephron [350]. The Oscar went to Stephen Dunn for *The Bells of St. Mary's.*

2077 • *THREE LITTLE WORDS*

MGM. 1950.

NOMINATION *Scoring of a Musical Picture:* André Previn.

Fred Astaire [2126] and Red Skelton play the songwriting team of Bert Kalmar [1951] and Harry Ruby [1951] in a routine and rather cheesy-looking musical biopic. The plot revolves around the attempts of Astaire and Vera-Ellen, who plays his wife, to find a spouse for Skelton, but it's mainly there to string songs on. Unfortunately, except for "Who's Sorry Now?," most of Kalmar and Ruby's songs were not very interesting. Debbie Reynolds [2184] makes one of her first screen appearances, playing Helen Kane, the "boop-boop-a-doop" girl. Kane herself dubbed Reynolds' singing of "I Wanna Be Loved by You." Directed by Richard Thorpe, with Arlene Dahl and Keenan Wynn. Previn lost to Adolph Deutsch and Roger Edens for *Annie Get Your Gun.*

Previn: 172, 609, 769, 1017, 1034, 1044, 1097, 1393, 1550, 1592, 2064, 2161.

2078 • *THREE MEN AND A CRADLE*

FLACH FILM PRODUCTION (FRANCE). 1985.

NOMINATION *Foreign Language Film.*

Three bachelors suddenly have the task of taking care of an infant that one of them has fathered. Amusing role-reversal comedy, written and directed by Coline Serreau, that was remade in Hollywood as the hugely popular *Three Men and a Baby* (1987). The Oscar went to *The Official Story.*

2079 • *THREE MUSKETEERS, THE*

MGM. 1948.

NOMINATION *Color Cinematography:* Robert Planck.

Gene Kelly [74] plays the swordsman D'Artagnan, a kid from the country who first tangles with and then joins the musketeers—Athos, played by Van Heflin [1055]; Porthos, played by Gig Young [427 . . .]; and Aramis (Robert Coote)—in their fight against the villainy embodied by Milady DeWinter, played by Lana Turner [1558], and Richelieu (Vincent Price). With June Allyson as Constance, Angela Lansbury [749 . . .] as Queen Anne, and Frank Morgan [22 . . .] as Louis XIII. Kelly's athleticism—he makes swordplay into dancing—is the best thing about this lavishly staged version of the Alexandre Dumas novel. But it's routinely directed by George Sidney from a screenplay by Robert Ardrey [1083]. This was the third version made in sound by Hollywood. The first, in 1935, stars Walter Abel as D'Artagnan; a musical version in 1939 featured Don Ameche [419] and the Ritz Brothers. The 1974 British version directed by Richard Lester and starring Michael York, along with its simultaneously filmed sequel, *The Four Musketeers,* is the best and liveliest telling of the tale. The Oscar for cinematography went to Joseph Valentine, William V. Skall, and Winton Hoch for *Joan of Arc.*

Planck: 74, 1173, 1190.

2080 • THREE RUSSIAN GIRLS

R&F Productions; United Artists. 1944.

Nomination *Scoring of a Dramatic or Comedy Picture:* Franke Harling.

Anna Sten stars as a nurse at the front in this wartime propaganda effort designed to stir audience sympathies for their Soviet allies. Based on a Soviet movie, *Girl From Stalingrad,* and directed by Fedor Ozep and Henry Kesler, with Kent Smith, Mimi Forsythe, Kathy Frye, and Feodor Chaliapin. The Oscar went to Max Steiner for *Since You Went Away.*

Harling: 1880, 1901.

2081 • THREE SMART GIRLS

Universal. 1936.

Nominations *Picture:* Joseph Pasternak, with Charles Rogers, producers. *Original Story:* Adele Comandini. *Sound Recording:* Homer G. Tasker.

When their father, Charles Winninger, falls prey to gold digger Binnie Barnes and her scheming mother, Alice Brady [990 . . .], the girls—Nan Grey, Barbara Read, and Deanna Durbin—plot to reunite him with their mother, Nella Walker. Amusingly predictable stuff, well laced with musical numbers. Grey and Read went nowhere, but Durbin, a fourteen-year-old lyric soprano making her feature film debut, became Universal's biggest star—her pictures are credited with saving the studio from bankruptcy. Durbin was way down the cast list here—below Ray Milland [1208] and even Mischa Auer [1401]—but she obviously had something special for audiences of the day. Most people under fifty, however, even lovers of old movies, have never seen a Durbin film. Henry Koster [214] is the director. He and producer Pasternak had just fled Berlin, where they were in charge of Universal's German operations.

The Great Ziegfeld won the best picture Oscar. The award for story went to Pierre Collings and Sheridan Gibney for *The Story of Louis Pasteur.* Douglas Shearer took the sound Oscar for *San Francisco.*

Pasternak: 74, 1485. Rogers: 1485. Tasker: 1485.

2082 • THROUGH A GLASS DARKLY

A.B. Svensk Filmindustri Production; Janus Films (Sweden). 1962.

Award *Foreign Language Film.* (1961)

Nomination *Story and Screenplay—Written Directly for the Screen:* Ingmar Bergman.

Harriet Andersson plays a schizophrenic married to a doctor, played by Max von Sydow [1546], who has been unable to help her. After a spell in a mental hospital, she joins her husband, her father (Gunnar Björnstrand), and her younger brother (Lars Passgärd) on a lonely island in the Baltic, where they proceed to torment one another. Gloomy first film in a trilogy writer-director Bergman designed to explore questions of religious faith—or rather the loss or lack of it. The other two films are *Winter Light* (1962) and *The Silence* (1963). Some find these powerfully acted and literate films utterly absorbing. Others find them pretentious and arid. There is no middle ground. The cinematography is by Sven Nykvist [460 . . .]. The writing Oscar went to Ennio de Concini, Alfredo Giannetti, and Pietro Germi for *Divorce—Italian Style.*

Bergman: 111, 460, 634, 644, 2283.

2083 • THROW MOMMA FROM THE TRAIN

Rollins, Morra and Brezner Production; Orion. 1987.

Nomination *Supporting Actress:* Anne Ramsey.

Inspired by watching Hitchcock's *Strangers on a Train,* Danny De Vito proposes a tit-for-tat murder arrangement to his writing teacher, Billy Crystal: If Crystal will off De Vito's horrible old harridan of a mother (Ramsey), De Vito will kill Crystal's ex-wife, who has infuriated Crystal by ripping off one of his ideas and coming up with a best-seller. Hit-or-miss comedy, with some fine talent on screen but not enough inventiveness in the script by Stu Silver. De Vito also directed, and the cinematography is by Barry Sonnenfeld. Ramsey, a short, gravel-voiced character player, died the year after her most prominent role. The Oscar went to Olympia Dukakis for *Moonstruck.*

2084 • *THUNDERBALL*

ALBERT R. BROCCOLI-HARRY SALTZMAN PRODUCTION; UNITED ARTISTS. 1965.

AWARD *Special Visual Effects:* John Stears.

The fourth James Bond film with Sean Connery [2185] involves the theft by the villain Largo (Adolfo Celi) of two H-bomb-laden bombers, with which he holds the world hostage. The climax comes in a huge underwater battle. Directed by Terence Young from a screenplay by Richard Maibaum and John Hopkins. Noisy and gimmicky, it's one of the weakest of Connery's Bond movies. It had been planned as the first in the series, but legal problems made rights to the Ian Fleming novel temporarily unavailable, so *Dr. No* was filmed instead. Producer Kevin McClory retained the rights, and in 1983 he persuaded Connery to reprise the role of Bond in *Never Say Never Again,* which is essentially a remake of *Thunderball.*

Stears: 1916.

2085 • *THUNDERBOLT*

PARAMOUNT FAMOUS LASKY. 1928–29.

NOMINATION *Actor:* George Bancroft.

The title is Bancroft's nickname: He's a mobster whose moll is Fay Wray. When her old boyfriend, a bank clerk played by Richard Arlen, wants to marry her, Thunderbolt frames him for murder and then winds up on death row alongside him. Director Josef von Sternberg [1358 . . .] gives real atmosphere to this gangster movie begun as a silent and completed with sound. The screenplay is by Jules Furthman [1387] and Herman J. Mankiewicz [407 . . .].

For a few years in the late twenties, Bancroft was a big star, especially in a series of gangster movies directed by Sternberg—*Underworld, The Dragnet* (1928), and *The Docks of New York* (1928). But his career soon faded, and he turned to character roles in such films as *Mr. Deeds Goes to Town, Angels With Dirty Faces, Stagecoach,* and *North West Mounted Police.* He retired

from films in 1942 and died in 1956. He was not an "official" nominee for the Oscar—this year the Academy announced only the winners—but his name is on record as one of the five people being considered for the award, which was voted by a committee from the actors branch. The award went to Warner Baxter for *In Old Arizona.*

2086 • *THUNDERBOLT AND LIGHTFOOT*

MALPASO COMPANY FILM PRODUCTION; UNITED ARTISTS. 1974.

NOMINATION *Supporting Actor:* Jeff Bridges.

Prison escapee Clint Eastwood [2179.5] joins up with a young drifter (Bridges) and Eastwood's old bank-robbing team, George Kennedy [443] and Geoffrey Lewis, to recover the loot he has hidden from an earlier theft. Unfortunately someone has built a building over the stash. Solid action drama, laced with comedy, written and directed by Michael Cimino [521], his first work as a director. Eastwood, whose production company, Malpaso, made this film, served as something of a mentor to Cimino, who had written the screenplay for Eastwood's 1973 *Magnum Force.* The cast includes Catherine Bach, Gary Busey [307], Vic Tayback, and Dub Taylor. Bridges lost to Robert De Niro in *The Godfather, Part II.*

Bridges: 1139, 1918.

2087 • *TIME MACHINE, THE*

GALAXY FILMS PRODUCTION; MGM. 1960.

AWARD *Special Effects:* Gene Warren and Tim Baar.

Victorian scientist Rod Taylor's invention rockets him into the distant future, where he discovers that humankind has evolved into two warring races: the lovely but ineffective Eloi and the vicious Morlocks. Entertaining version of the H. G. Wells novel, adapted with great liberties by David Duncan, but provided with imaginative designs and special effects by producer-director George Pal. Art directors George W. Davis [46 . . .] and William Ferrari [749 . . .] deserve a large share of the credit. The cast includes Yvette Mimieux, Alan Young, and Sebastian Cabot.

2088 • TIME, THE PLACE AND THE GIRL, THE

WARNER BROS. 1947.

NOMINATION *Song:* "A Gal in Calico," music by Arthur Schwartz, lyrics by Leo Robin.

Dennis Morgan and Jack Carson have trouble making a go of their nightclub. Thin and forgettable musical, with Martha Vickers, Janis Paige, S. Z. Sakall, and Alan Hale, directed by David Butler. The best song was "Zip-A-Dee-Doo-Dah," from *Song of the South,* by Allie Wrubel and Ray Gilbert.

Schwartz: 2026. Robin: 104, 197, 368, 846, 1072, 1805, 1843, 2032, 2310.

2089 • TIME TO LOVE AND A TIME TO DIE, A

UNIVERSAL-INTERNATIONAL. 1958.

NOMINATION *Sound:* Leslie I. Carey, sound director, Universal-International Sound Department.

John Gavin plays a German soldier in World War II who falls in love with Lilo Pulver when he is home on leave, but is killed when he returns to the front. Slow-paced attempt to repeat the theme—the futility of war—of *All Quiet on the Western Front,* which was, like this film, based on a novel by Erich Maria Remarque, who plays a small role as a schoolteacher. Unconvincing casting—Gavin, Jock Mahoney, Don DeFore, and Keenan Wynn as Germans—undermines the direction by Douglas Sirk and the location filming of Russell Metty [690 . . .]. Jim Hutton, billed as Dana Hutton, makes his film debut, and the cast also includes Klaus Kinski in a small role. The sound Oscar went to Fred Hynes for *South Pacific.*

Carey: 291, 776, 1209, 1334, 1478.

2090 • TIN DRUM, THE

FRANZ SEITZ FILM/BIOSKOP FILM/ARTEMIS FILM/HALLELUJAH FILM/GGB 14.KG/ARGOS FILMS PRODUCTION (FEDERAL REPUBLIC OF GERMANY). 1979.

AWARD *Foreign Language Film.*

Oskar (David Bennent) decides at the age of three that the world is too absurd to grow up in, so he stops growing. Meanwhile, the Nazis come to power, and the hideousness of Germany under the Third Reich is viewed from Oskar's warped perspective. Intriguing, sometimes shrill, sometimes hilarious satire, based on a novel by Günter Grass, adapted by Jean-Claude Carrière [549 . . .], Franz Seitz, and the film's director, Volker Schlöndorff. As Oskar, twelve-year-old Bennent gives an astonishing performance.

2091 • TIN PAN ALLEY

20TH CENTURY-FOX. 1940.

AWARD *Score:* Alfred Newman.

Alice Faye and Betty Grable both fall for songwriter John Payne. Enjoyable musical set in New York City during World War I and the twenties that's typical of its studio: handsome production values, good songs, but second-rank stars. Comic turns by Jack Oakie [818] and Billy Gilbert and the sensational dancing of the Nicholas Brothers help make up for the dullness of the story and the top-billed performers. Directed by Walter Lang [1088], with cinematography by Leon Shamroy [29 . . .]. The choreography is by Seymour Felix [831]. This is the second of Newman's record-setting nine Oscars.

Newman: 31, 34, 46, 72, 138, 182, 226, 333, 334, 347, 375, 428, 437, 457, 476, 495, 542, 690, 797, 833, 952, 953, 959, 962, 1016, 1082, 1088, 1213, 1278, 1362, 1397, 1475, 1616, 1655, 1849, 1868, 1883, 1921, 2043, 2046, 2258, 2286, 2294, 2316.

2092 • TIN STAR, THE

PERLBERG-SEATON PRODUCTION; PARAMOUNT. 1957.

NOMINATION *Story and Screenplay—Written Directly for the Screen:* Barney Slater and Joe Kane; Dudley Nichols.

Anthony Perkins [730] gets made sheriff of a small western town. (How did *that* happen?) Fortunately former sheriff Henry Fonda [815 . . .] arrives on the scene to help the kid take care of things. Good western that owes much to Nichols' screenplay and Anthony Mann's direction. The cast includes Betsy Palmer, Neville Brand, Lee Van Cleef, and John McIntire. The Oscar went to George Wells for *Designing Woman.*

Nichols: 30, 999, 1200.

2093 • TITANIC

20TH CENTURY-FOX. 1953.

AWARD *Story and Screenplay:* Charles Brackett, Walter Reisch, and Richard Breen.

NOMINATION *Black-and-White Art Direction–Set Decoration:* Lyle Wheeler and Maurice Ransford; Stuart Reiss.

It was sad when that great ship went down, but by the time it does in this movie, you may have grown tired of the cardboard characters who go with it. Clifton Webb [1149 . . .] and Barbara Stanwyck [138 . . .] are the world's most unlikely married couple. Brian Aherne [1064] is the ship's captain, and Thelma Ritter [46 . . .] is an unsinkable-Molly-Brown type. Also on board are Robert Wagner, Richard Basehart, and Allyn Joslyn. Jean Negulesco [1052] directed. A superior British account of the doomed voyage, *A Night to Remember,* was made in 1958.

The writing Oscar for this predictable and clichéd screenplay seems even more incredible when one sees that it was up against the bright and witty work of Betty Comden and Adolph Green on *The Band Wagon.* The only possible explanation for *Titanic's* win in this category is that the contest was very much a battle of the studios: MGM had three entries (Sam Rolfe and Harold Jack Bloom's *The Naked Spur* and Millard Kaufman's *Take the High Ground* in addition to the Comden-Green script) and Fox had two (its other entry was Richard Murphy's *The Desert Rats*), so MGM's vote was split three ways and Fox's only two. Brackett may have also had a bit of an edge in the voting because he was president of the Academy at the time. This was his third writing Oscar—and his only one not in collaboration with Billy Wilder, the partner from whom he split after *Sunset Boulevard.* Both of his partners on *Titanic,* Reisch and Breen, had also earlier been collaborators on the Brackett-Wilder team: Reisch on *Ninotchka* and Breen on *A Foreign Affair.* Unfortunately *Titanic* is lacking Wilder's keen-edged wit. Brackett died in 1969, Reisch in 1983, and Breen in 1967.

The Oscar for art direction went to *Julius Caesar.*

Brackett: 705, 925, 1088, 1208, 1440, 1975, 2099. Reisch: 435, 749, 1440. Breen: 350, 705.

Wheeler: 19, 46, 83, 356, 376, 428, 476, 495, 530, 542, 719, 721, 798, 950, 1062, 1088, 1149, 1153, 1213, 1391, 1475, 1601, 1616, 1670, 1706, 1852, 2008, 2212. Ransford: 721, 1153. Reiss: 542, 557, 646, 2008, 2247.

2094 • TLAYUCAN

PRODUCCIONES MATOUK S.A. (MEXICO). 1962.

NOMINATION *Foreign Language Film.*

A poor man steals from the church to pay for medicine for his child. When he's caught, the towns-people support him instead of the priest. Simple anticlerical fable, directed by Carlos Sarage. The Oscar went to *Sundays and Cybèle.*

2095 • T-MEN

RELIANCE PICTURES; EAGLE LION. 1947.

NOMINATION *Sound Recording:* Sound Service Inc., Jack R. Whitney, sound director.

Dennis O'Keefe leads a team of government agents on the trail of counterfeiters. Good documentary-style melodrama, effectively directed by Anthony Mann and imaginatively filmed by John Alton [66]. With Alfred Ryder, June Lockhart, Wallace Ford, and Charles McGraw. The Oscar for sound went to Gordon Sawyer for *The Bishop's Wife.*

Whitney: 729, 862, 955, 1026, 1884, 2031, 2050.

2096 • TO BE OR NOT TO BE

ERNST LUBITSCH; UNITED ARTISTS. 1942.

NOMINATION *Scoring of a Dramatic or Comedy Picture:* Werner Heymann.

Jack Benny and Carole Lombard [1401] play Josef and Maria Tura, the stars of a shabby little Polish theatrical company who become involved in a plot to assassinate a Nazi spy. Astonishing blend of farce and melodrama that almost works, although there are critics who think that a comedy set in Nazi-occupied Warsaw is too tasteless and offensive to bear. Director Ernst Lubitsch [889 . . .] collaborated with Melchior Lengyel [1440] on the story and Edwin Justus Mayer on the screenplay. Andrew Sarris comments: ''For Lubitsch, it was sufficient to say that

Hitler had bad manners, and no evil was then inconceivable." The movie was also shadowed by the death of Lombard, only two weeks after its completion. The cast includes Robert Stack [2315] as Lombard's lover, plus Felix Bressart, Lionel Atwill, and Sig Rumann. Rudolph Maté [455 . . .] did the cinematography. Among those who were deeply offended by the film's premise was Miklos Rozsa [175 . . .], then music director for its producer, Alexander Korda [1620]. Rozsa refused to compose the score, and Heymann was assigned to it instead—although when Lubitsch objected to Heymann's heavy-handedness in some scenes, Rozsa reluctantly agreed to compose a part of the score. The scoring Oscar went to Max Steiner for *Now, Voyager.*

Heymann: 1105, 1487, 2036.

2097 • TO BE OR NOT TO BE

Brooksfilms Production; 20th Century-Fox. 1983.
Nomination *Supporting Actor:* Charles Durning.

Mel Brooks [230 . . .] and Anne Bancroft [28 . . .] play the Bronskis, the husband-and-wife stars of a Polish theatrical group, in this remake of the 1942 film that satirized the Nazis. By the time of the remake, however, the Nazis were hardly in line for satire, so the point of the film is blunted—instead of the daring wit of the original, we get lots of Brooksian horseplay, some of it funny, much of it lame. The film, directed by Alan Johnson from a screenplay by Thomas Meehan and Ronny Graham, follows the original almost scene for scene, adding a few new characters and interpolating a lot of old gags. Tim Matheson plays the young pilot with whom the Bancroft character is having an affair; Durning is "Concentration Camp" Erhardt, played in the original by Sig Rumann; Jose Ferrer [473 . . .] is the spy whom the theatrical troupe is enlisted to catch; and the cast is filled out by Christopher Lloyd, George Gaynes, Jack Riley, and Lewis J. Stadlen. Durning lost to Jack Nicholson in *Terms of Endearment.*

Durning: 180.

2098 • TO CATCH A THIEF

Paramount. 1955.
Award *Color Cinematography:* Robert Burks.
Nominations *Color Art Direction–Set Decoration:* Hal Pereira and Joseph McMillan Johnson; Sam Comer and Arthur Krams. *Color Costume Design:* Edith Head.

John Robie, played by Cary Grant [1445 . . .], is a former cat burglar who specialized in jewels. So when a new thief starts ripping off the wealthy sojourners on the French Riviera, he comes under suspicion and has to nab the copycat burglar to clear himself. He's aided by a glamorous, wealthy American, Frances Stevens, played by Grace Kelly [450 . . .], and her mother, played by Jessie Royce Landis. Stylish film directed by Alfred Hitchcock [1171 . . .] from a screenplay by John Michael Hayes [1558 . . .]. Hitchcock eschews thrills and suspense and goes for elegance and romance—and thanks to Grant and Kelly, who are a powerfully sexy team, it works. Landis is far more plausible playing Kelly's mother than playing Grant's, as she did in *North by Northwest*—she and Grant were born in the same year. She also gets to reprise one of Hitchcock's most famous gross-outs: In *Rebecca* the dowager played by Florence Bates extinguishes a cigarette in a jar of cold cream; Landis stubs hers out in the yolk of a fried egg. During the filming, Kelly met her husband-to-be, Prince Rainier of Monaco.

Burks began in the special effects department of Warner Bros. and moved into cinematography in 1949. His career was linked with Hitchcock's starting in 1951, when he shot *Strangers on a Train,* and continued through eleven more of the director's movies, including *The Man Who Knew Too Much, Vertigo, North by Northwest,* and *The Birds.* He died in 1968.

The art direction Oscar went to *Picnic.* Charles LeMaire won for the costumes for *Love Is a Many-Splendored Thing.*

Burks: 1537, 1669, 1941. Pereira: 278, 357, 363, 426, 450, 736, 956, 1029, 1219, 1504, 1570, 1631, 1674, 1716, 1727, 1738, 1897, 1959, 2012, 2200, 2208. Johnson: 636, 833, 978, 1388, 1595. Comer: 278, 357, 426, 450, 726, 736, 925, 956, 1029, 1101, 1214, 1219, 1443, 1570, 1631, 1674, 1727,

1738, 1748, 1959, 1975, 1994, 2012, 2200, 2208.
Krams: 357, 1173, 1309, 1727, 1937, 1959, 2208.
Head: 31, 32, 46, 305, 357, 363, 612, 636, 675,
736, 832, 894, 945, 1003, 1219, 1261, 1263, 1398,
1427, 1504, 1550, 1579, 1587, 1631, 1716, 1727,
1738, 1748, 1840, 1927, 1986, 2012, 2247, 2298.

2099 • TO EACH HIS OWN

PARAMOUNT. 1946.

AWARD *Actress:* Olivia de Havilland.

NOMINATION *Original Story:* Charles Brackett.

A spirited young woman (de Havilland) in a small
town has a romance with a young pilot (John Lund)
who is killed. Finding herself pregnant, she has the
baby, arranges for it to be adopted, but is shut out of
her son's life when the adoptive mother guesses the
truth. So she goes off to the city and becomes rich by
starting a cosmetics company. Finally she's reunited
with her son (also played by Lund), when he's grown
up and a World War II pilot. Entertaining sentimental
drama that might have been a lot better with a more
colorful supporting cast—it has Mary Anderson, Roland Culver, Virginia Welles, Phillip Terry, and the
reliably bland Lund in his film debut. Mitchell Leisen
[587] directs skillfully enough, but the show is mostly
de Havilland's.

After two previous losses—one of them to her
sister, Joan Fontaine, for *Suspicion*—de Havilland, one
of the most capable Hollywood stars, was overdue for
an Oscar. She made her debut in 1935, shot to stardom with her frequent costar, Errol Flynn, in *Captain
Blood,* and four years later landed the plum role of
Melanie in *Gone With the Wind.* In 1943 she began a
celebrated court battle with her studio, Warner
Bros., challenging the contract system that allowed
studios to punish rebellious stars by suspending them
and then tacking on the term of the suspension at the
end of their contract—a device that had been used to
punish Bette Davis [46 . . .] and James Cagney
[79 . . .], among others. The suit was decided in
her favor, setting a precedent that gave stars far more
power over the choice of scripts than they had during
the thirties and early forties. The legal maneuverings
had kept de Havilland off the screen from 1943 to
1946, so the Oscar for her return performance was
perhaps an even sweeter triumph than it might have
been earlier.

The writing award went to Clemence Dane for
Vacation From Marriage.

De Havilland: 798, 894, 925, 1849. Brackett:
705, 925, 1088, 1208, 1440, 1975, 2093.

2100 • TO FORGET VENICE

RIZZOLI FILM/ACTION FILM PRODUCTION (ITALY). 1979.

NOMINATION *Foreign Language Film.*

Nicky and his young lover, Picchio, go to a country house near Venice to visit Nicky's aunt, Marta,
who is looked after by her adopted niece, Anna, and
Anna's lover, Claudia. Nicky and Anna share childhood memories and discover that they have differing
views of the past. Slow-moving character drama, directed by Franco Brusati. The Oscar went to *The Tin
Drum.*

2101 • TO KILL A MOCKINGBIRD

UNIVERSAL-INTERNATIONAL-PAKULA-MULLIGAN-BRENTWOOD
PRODUCTION; UNIVERSAL-INTERNATIONAL. 1962.

AWARDS *Actor:* Gregory Peck. *Screenplay—Based on
Material From Another Medium:* Horton Foote. *Black-
and-White Art Direction—Set Decoration:* Alexander
Golitzen and Henry Bumstead; Oliver Emert.

NOMINATIONS *Picture:* Alan J. Pakula, producer. *Supporting Actress:* Mary Badham. *Director:* Robert Mulligan. *Black-and-White Cinematography:* Russell Harlan.
Music Score—Substantially Original: Elmer Bernstein.

Widower Atticus Finch (Peck) is trying to raise
two small children, Scout (Badham) and Jim (Philip
Alford), in an Alabama town. A lawyer, he finds his
position in the town jeopardized when he agrees to
defend a black man (Brock Peters) accused of raping a
white woman. A much-loved film that has critics who
deride its sentimentality, but it manages to make its
points about tolerance without being preachy, a real
achievement in the context of the racially troubled
early sixties. Its strength is the strength of the autobiographical novel by Harper Lee on which it's based.
Though it's nostalgic for the simplicity of childhood,
it also recognizes that some things change for the

better with time. The cast includes Rosemary Murphy, Ruth White, Alice Ghostley, and, in his film debut, Robert Duvall [92 . . .], playing the key role of Boo Radley. The film's off-screen narrator is Kim Stanley [722 . . .].

Peck's low-key earnestness never found a better vehicle. The part of Atticus Finch was his favorite—the closest, Peck said, to "the real me"—and Lee thought him perfect in a role based on her own father, who died during the filming. Rock Hudson [768] had wanted the part and urged Universal to buy the rights for him. Peck prevailed, however, and won his sole competitive Oscar, although his triumph over the critically favored Peter O'Toole in *Lawrence of Arabia* is often cited, along with John Wayne's for *True Grit* and Henry Fonda's for *On Golden Pond,* as evidence of the Academy's tendency to reward career longevity over performance. Peck had made his debut in 1944 in *Days of Glory* and received his first nomination the following year. Never an actor of wide range —as his miscasting as Captain Ahab in *Moby Dick* (1956) perhaps most painfully demonstrates—he was nevertheless a warm and attractive presence on screen, allowing him a long career. He served as president of the Academy from 1967 to 1970.

This was the first of two wins for Foote, a Texas-born novelist and screenwriter whose teleplay *The Trip to Bountiful* had earned him acclaim in the early days of television; he would later adapt it for both stage and screen. *To Kill a Mockingbird* would also begin a fruitful relationship with Robert Duvall. Foote adapted a William Faulkner story for Duvall, who gives one of his best screen performances in the little-seen film, *Tomorrow* (1971), that resulted. And both Foote and Duvall would win Oscars for their work on *Tender Mercies.*

The film looks like it was shot on location but was made on the Universal lot, a fact that surely contributed to the win for art direction. The artifice shows only occasionally, as in the set for the courtroom, which isn't beat-up enough for a small-town southern courthouse in the Depression.

Lawrence of Arabia took the best picture Oscar, winning for director David Lean and composer Maurice

Jarre as well. After seven films together, starting in 1956 with *Fear Strikes Out,* Pakula and Mulligan went their separate ways in 1967. In the seventies producer Pakula turned director, achieving greater success in that field than Mulligan, who has never surpassed or even equaled his work on this film.

Badham was defeated in the Oscar race by another child star, Patty Duke in *The Miracle Worker.* Duke's career, unlike Badham's, continued into adulthood. Badham, who was nine when the film was made, now lives on a farm near Richmond, Virginia, where she manages a clothing store. Her brother, John Badham, has had a more successful Hollywood career. He rose from the Universal mail room to become a director, best known for *Saturday Night Fever.*

The cinematography Oscar went to Jean Bourgoin and Walter Wottitz for *The Longest Day.*

Peck: 759, 1082, 2154, 2320. Foote: 2015, 2142. Golitzen: 31, 96, 414, 591, 690, 706, 744, 1560, 1886, 1968, 1986, 2035, 2064. Bumstead: 1927, 2179.5, 2200. Pakula: 54, 1876. Harlan: 204, 227, 825, 879, 882. Bernstein: 27.5, 789, 882, 1242, 1264, 1685, 1959, 2064, 2130, 2147, 2223.

2102 • *TO THE SHORES OF TRIPOLI*

20TH CENTURY-FOX. 1942.

NOMINATION *Color Cinematography:* Edward Cronjager and William V. Skall.

John Payne joins the marines—notice we said *Payne,* not Wayne—who proceed to make a real man of him. Typical wartime recruiting-poster stuff with Maureen O'Hara, Randolph Scott, and Nancy Kelly, directed by H. Bruce "Lucky" Humberstone. The screenplay is by Lamar Trotti [1516 . . .]. The Oscar went to Leon Shamroy for *The Black Swan.*

Cronjager: 176, 400, 889, 934, 1569, 1964. Skall: 96, 208, 1048, 1170, 1317, 1453, 1644, 1668, 1822.

2103 • *TOAST OF NEW ORLEANS, THE*

MGM. 1950.

NOMINATION *Song:* "Be My Love," music by Nicholas Brodszky, lyrics by Sammy Cahn.

Tenor Mario Lanza gets plucked off his fishing boat

and turned into an opera star in New Orleans. Corny and awful—but also kind of fun if you're in the mood. Costar Kathryn Grayson reportedly loathed Lanza, and it sometimes shows—Grayson wasn't actress enough to conceal it. Rita Moreno [2244] and J. Carrol Naish [1294 . . .] are there to do ethnic bits, and David Niven [1778] tries to stay out of the cross fire between the two singing stars. Norman Taurog [271 . . .] directed. The Oscar went to Ray Evans and Jay Livingston for "Mona Lisa," from *Captain Carey, U.S.A.*

Brodszky: 163, 1216, 1692, 1843. Cahn: 74, 163, 182, 696, 915, 926, 1031, 1056, 1216, 1524, 1587, 1692, 1708, 1719, 1859, 1907, 2016, 2064, 2072, 2110, 2125, 2263, 2264, 2315, 2343.

2104 • TOBRUK

Gibraltar Productions-Corman Company-Universal Production; Universal. 1967.

Nomination *Special Visual Effects:* Howard A. Anderson, Jr., and Albert Whitlock.

During the World War II North African campaign, American Rock Hudson [768], Brit Nigel Green, and German Jew George Peppard join forces to blow up Rommel's fuel supply. Potentially exciting action film that bogs down too often in talk. Directed by Arthur Hiller [1218]. The Oscar went to L. B. Abbott for *Doctor Dolittle.*

Whitlock: 591, 917.

2104.5 • TOM & VIV

New Era Entertainment Production; Miramax. 1994.

Nominations *Actress:* Miranda Richardson. *Supporting Actress:* Rosemary Harris.

Richardson plays Vivienne Haigh-Wood, the first wife of poet T. S. Eliot, played by Willem Dafoe [1584], in this account of the marriage of a passionate, unstable young woman to a repressed but ambitious writer. Eventually, Viv's eccentricity, explained as stemming from a hormonal problem now easily treated, leads Tom to commit her to a mental institution for the rest of her life. Well-played but often superficial and unsatisfying scenes from a marriage, directed by Brian Gilbert from a screenplay by Michael Hastings and Adrian Hodges based on Hastings' play.

The best actress Oscar went to Jessica Lange for playing another unstable wife in *Blue Sky.* Harris, who plays Vivienne's mother, is a distinguished stage actress who has made only occasional appearances in films; she lost to Dianne Wiest in *Bullets Over Broadway.*

Richardson: 478.5.

2105 • TOM, DICK AND HARRY

RKO Radio. 1941.

Nomination *Original Screenplay:* Paul Jarrico.

Ginger Rogers [1102] plays a woman who has trouble deciding which of her three boyfriends she wants to marry: Tom (George Murphy) is a car salesman, Dick (Alan Marshall) is a millionaire, and Harry, played by Burgess Meredith [504 . . .], is an eccentric. Much of the film is taken up with her daydreams about what life would be like with each. Charming comedy, directed by Garson Kanin [11 . . .], with Phil Silvers in a funny turn as an ice cream man. The Oscar went to Herman J. Mankiewicz and Orson Welles for *Citizen Kane.*

2106 • TOM JONES

Woodfall Production; United Artists-Lopert Pictures (United Kingdom). 1963.

Awards *Picture:* Tony Richardson, producer. *Director:* Tony Richardson. *Screenplay—Based on Material From Another Medium:* John Osborne. *Music Score—Substantially Original:* John Addison.

Nominations *Actor:* Albert Finney. *Supporting Actor:* Hugh Griffith. *Supporting Actress:* Diane Cilento. *Supporting Actress:* Edith Evans. *Supporting Actress:* Joyce Redman. *Color Art Direction—Set Decoration:* Ralph Brinton, Ted Marshall, and Jocelyn Herbert; Josie MacAvin.

Jones (Finney), a foundling, has been raised by the kindly Mr. Allworthy (George Devine), as if he were Allworthy's own son. But Jones' amorous dalliance with the sluttish Molly Seagrim (Cilento) and the machinations of his enemies, including the priggish young Blifil (David Warner), lead to his expulsion, to

the dismay of the young woman he really loves, Sophie Western, played by Susannah York [2047]. Her
father, Squire Western (Griffith), though he thinks
Jones a fine lad, is persuaded by his snobbish sister
(Evans) that the marriage of Sophie to a young man of
questionable birth would be unthinkable. On the
road, Jones encounters the lusty Mrs. Waters
(Redman), with whom, after a famous scene in which
dinner serves as foreplay, he goes to bed. They are
soon to discover, to their mutual shock, that she may
well be his mother. Reaching London, the handsome
young Jones catches the eye of Lady Bellaston (Joan
Greenwood). When Sophie arrives soon afterward,
Lady Bellaston engineers a plot to have the young
woman fall into the clutches of a foppish rake, Lord
Fellamar (David Tomlinson). Several hair's-breadth
escapes later, Jones' true parentage is revealed. Enjoyably loosey-goosey treatment of the eighteenth-
century novel by Henry Fielding. Richardson's inspiration was to break away from the stateliness of movie
costume dramas and infuse the film with the grubbi-
ness and energy of real life. Some contemporary critics found the result forced and frantic rather than
witty, and Richardson himself later wrote that he
"felt the movie to be incomplete and botched in
much of its execution." But it was a huge hit, thanks
in large part to some charismatic performers, and it
made stars of Finney and York. Lynn Redgrave [761]
makes her film debut in a bit part. The cinematography is by Walter Lassally [2346].

Tom Jones' best picture win was a fairly easy one.
The opponents were *America, America,* producer-director Elia Kazan's semiautobiographical movie about a
young immigrant, which did poorly at the box office;
the mammoth debacle *Cleopatra;* the Cinerama spectacle *How the West Was Won;* and the low-key sentimental
comedy *Lilies of the Field.* Two very fine films, *Hud* and
8½, were not in the running.

Richardson and Osborne came to prominence in
1956, when the former directed a play written by the
latter, *Look Back in Anger.* The title of this drama about
working-class rage in postwar Britain provided a label
for Osborne, Richardson, and several other young
artists of the fifties: "angry young men." In 1958

Richardson and Osborne also collaborated on the play
The Entertainer—another bitter attack on British com-
placency. They did the film versions of both plays in
1959 and 1960, attracting the attention of Holly-
wood. Richardson also served as producer on *Saturday
Night and Sunday Morning* in 1960, which provided
Finney's first starring role on screen. Summoned to
Hollywood, Richardson got off to a bad start with a
censor-gutted version of William Faulkner's novel
Sanctuary (1961), but his next two British films, *A
Taste of Honey* (1961) and *The Loneliness of the Long
Distance Runner* (1962), were solid art-house successes. After winning the Oscar, Richardson returned
to Hollywood in 1965 to make the extravagant satire
The Loved One, but critical and commercial success
eluded him for the rest of his film directing career.
He died of AIDS in 1991, after completing *Blue Sky,*
which was held from release until 1994 because its
studio, Orion, went bankrupt. Osborne has continued his career as playwright, but like many of the
angry young men, he mellowed on reaching middle
age.

Addison began his film scoring career in Britain in
the early fifties and provided the scores for the films
of *Look Back in Anger* and *The Entertainer.* His work on
Tom Jones, a lively pastiche of eighteenth-century clas-
sical-sounding themes, was a sharp change of pace.
He has continued his work primarily in England.

Finney lost to Sidney Poitier in *Lilies of the Field.*
The supporting actor Oscar went to Melvyn Douglas
for *Hud* and the supporting actress award to Margaret
Rutherford for *The V.I.P.s. Cleopatra* won for art direction.

Addison: 1841. Finney: 579, 1378, 2177. Griffith:
175. Evans: 377, 2265. Redman: 1506. Marshall:
1897. MacAvin: 1512, 1897.

2107 • *TOM SAWYER*

Arthur P. Jacobs Production; Reader's Digest Presentation; United Artists. 1973.

Nominations *Art Direction–Set Decoration:* Philip Jefferies; Robert de Vestel. *Scoring—Original Song Score
and/or Adaptation:* Richard M. Sherman, Robert B.

Sherman, and John Williams. *Costume Design:* Donfeld.

Johnnie Whitaker plays the title role, with Jeff East as Huck Finn and Jodie Foster [7 . . .] as Becky Thatcher, in this musical version of Mark Twain's novel about a wheeler-dealer kid in pre–Civil War Hannibal, Missouri. Like most movies based on Twain's books, it sacrifices satire and social comment in the name of wholesomeness—as you might expect in a film produced under the auspices of *Reader's Digest*. Directed by Don Taylor from a screenplay by the Sherman brothers and featuring Celeste Holm [46 . . .] and Warren Oates. *The Sting* took all three Oscars: for art direction, Marvin Hamlisch's scoring, and Edith Head's costumes.

De Vestel: 1196. R. M. Sherman: 166, 396, 1238, 1284, 1842. R. B. Sherman: 166, 396, 1238, 1284, 1842. Williams: 6, 260, 403, 416, 588, 613, 614, 659, 805, 933, 937, 982, 996, 997, 1041, 1047, 1596, 1652, 1679, 1684, 1701, 1764.65, 1916, 1977, 2126, 2194, 2293, 2322. Donfeld: 508, 1625, 2047.

2108 • TOM THUMB

George Pal Productions; MGM. 1958.
Award *Special Effects:* Tom Howard.

Russ Tamblyn [1558] is the two-inch-high hero who outwits villains Terry-Thomas and Peter Sellers [169 . . .] in this likable musical fantasy, directed by George Pal, that blends live-action performers with Pal's stop-motion Puppetoons. The songs are by Peggy Lee [1554] and Sonny Burke and the cinematography by Georges Périnal [715 . . .].

Howard: 232.

2109 • TOMMY

Robert Stigwood Organisation Ltd. Production; Columbia (United Kingdom). 1975.
Nominations *Actress:* Ann-Margret. *Scoring—Original Song Score and/or Adaptation:* Peter Townshend.

Tommy (Roger Daltrey) has been deaf, dumb, and blind since he witnessed the murder of his father. But despite his afflictions, he becomes a pinball whiz. When he suddenly is cured, he uses the celebrity he has already acquired to found a new religion. Over-the-top adaptation of the Who's rock opera, directed by Ken Russell [2307] with characteristic excess—in one appalling scene, Ann-Margret, who plays Tommy's mother, is inundated with baked beans. Still, it's perversely watchable and the music is great. The cast includes Oliver Reed as Ann-Margret's brutal lover, Robert Powell as the father, Keith Moon as Uncle Ernie, and Elton John [1177.5], Eric Clapton, and Jack Nicholson [395 . . .]. The standout appearance, though, is by Tina Turner, whose number as the Acid Queen is one of the most sensational rock performances on film.

Though she proved herself a fine actress again and again, major film roles eluded Ann-Margret, and her one nomination for a leading role was something of a fluke: Her role in *Tommy* might well have been classified as supporting. But it was a year in which many important films—*Jaws, Dog Day Afternoon, The Sunshine Boys, The Man Who Would Be King*—had only token roles for women. And though *Nashville* featured numerous women, the episodic nature of the film meant there were no leading roles. As a result, the 1975 nominees for best actress constituted probably the weakest slate in Oscar history. Three of the nominations were for performances in films that received only minimal distribution: Isabelle Adjani in *The Story of Adele H.,* Glenda Jackson in *Hedda,* and Carol Kane in *Hester Street.* And the winner, Louise Fletcher, had what might have been classified as a supporting role in other years, as Nurse Ratched in *One Flew Over the Cuckoo's Nest.* Though Ann-Margret has continued her film career, she has received her best notices for TV work, particularly for a 1984 performance as Blanche DuBois in *A Streetcar Named Desire.*

Townshend wrote the book, lyrics, and music for the 1968 British TV production of *Tommy* that featured the other members of the Who, Daltrey, Moon, and John Entwhistle. It became a phenomenally successful record album and was performed widely, usually in a concert version, throughout the early seventies. Townshend, who would receive a Tony Award in 1993 for the Broadway revival of

Tommy, lost the Oscar to Leonard Rosenman for *Barry Lyndon.*

Ann-Margret: 362.

2110 • *TONIGHT AND EVERY NIGHT*

COLUMBIA. 1945.

NOMINATIONS *Song:* "Anywhere," music by Jule Styne, lyrics by Sammy Cahn. *Scoring of a Musical Picture:* Marlin Skiles and Morris Stoloff.

Rita Hayworth and Janet Blair are performers in a London musical theater that firmly believes the show must go on—through the blitz and other hazards of World War II. Nicely colorful musical, with Hayworth stunningly photographed by Rudolph Maté [455 . . .] (and dubbed by Martha Mears). Victor Saville [406 . . .] directs, and the musical numbers are staged by Jack Cole. The screenplay by Lesser Samuels [198 . . .] and Abem Finkel [1779] is based on a play by Lesley Storm, *Heart of a City,* that paid tribute to London's Windmill Theatre—called the Music Box in the movie. The song Oscar went to "It Might As Well Be Spring," by Richard Rodgers and Oscar Hammerstein II, from *State Fair.* Georgie Stoll won the scoring award for *Anchors Aweigh.*

Styne: 74, 696, 737, 920, 921, 1031, 1719, 2072, 2343. Cahn: 74, 163, 182, 696, 915, 926, 1031, 1056, 1216, 1524, 1587, 1692, 1708, 1719, 1859, 1907, 2016, 2064, 2072, 2103, 2125, 2263, 2264, 2315, 2343. Stoloff: 13, 432, 455, 596, 643, 677, 732, 773, 1057, 1058, 1115, 1206, 1862, 1872, 1873, 1998, 2329.

2111 • *TOO MANY HUSBANDS*

COLUMBIA. 1940.

NOMINATION *Sound Recording:* John Livadary.

Believing her husband, Fred MacMurray, to be dead, Jean Arthur [1353] marries Melvyn Douglas [169 . . .]. Of course, MacMurray isn't dead, so when he shows up, Arthur decides to make the most of it and let the two husbands compete for her affections. Pleasant but slightly thin comedy, based on a play by Somerset Maugham, *Home and Beauty.* The adaptation is by Claude Binyon, and the director is Wesley Ruggles [400]. The cast includes Harry Dav-

enport, Edgar Buchanan, and Melville Cooper. For an intriguing glimpse at Hollywood's view of the relative roles of men and women in a marriage, check out *My Favorite Wife,* made the same year, in which Cary Grant finds himself with two wives and doesn't like it at all. The award for sound went to Douglas Shearer for *Strike Up the Band.*

Livadary: 330, 455, 596, 732, 1058, 1206, 1215, 1303, 1366, 1370, 1488, 1521, 1740, 1872, 2325, 2327.

2112 • *TOO YOUNG TO KISS*

MGM. 1951.

NOMINATION *Black-and-White Art Direction—Set Decoration:* Cedric Gibbons and Paul Groesse; Edwin B. Willis and Jack D. Moore.

Pianist June Allyson pretends to be a child prodigy to advance her career but falls in love with Van Johnson, who thinks she's underage. Pleasantly formulaic romantic comedy, directed by Robert Z. Leonard [555 . . .] from a screenplay by Frances Goodrich [25 . . .] and Albert Hackett [25 . . .]. The cast includes Gig Young [427 . . .] and Hans Conreid. The art direction Oscar went to *A Streetcar Named Desire.*

Gibbons: 66, 87, 130, 217, 227, 239, 285, 290, 440, 629, 749, 831, 980, 1069, 1096, 1173, 1190, 1226, 1230, 1232, 1274, 1308, 1309, 1417, 1567, 1604, 1644, 1662, 1673, 1721, 1861, 1937, 2068, 2256, 2257, 2300, 2320, 2330. Groesse: 87, 1173, 1190, 1232, 1309, 1335, 1385, 1604, 2157, 2320. Willis: 66, 87, 130, 227, 239, 290, 629, 749, 831, 980, 1069, 1096, 1157, 1173, 1190, 1226, 1230, 1232, 1309, 1417, 1567, 1657, 1662, 1673, 1721, 1861, 1937, 2068, 2257, 2320, 2330. Moore: 31, 1190, 1662, 1937, 1986, 2330.

2113 • *TOOTSIE*

MIRAGE/PUNCH PRODUCTION; COLUMBIA. 1982.

AWARD *Supporting Actress:* Jessica Lange.

NOMINATIONS *Picture:* Sydney Pollack and Dick Richards, producers. *Actor:* Dustin Hoffman. *Supporting Actress:* Teri Garr. *Director:* Sydney Pollack. *Screenplay Written Directly for the Screen:* Larry Gelbart and Mur-

ray Schisgal, screenplay; Don McGuire and Larry
Gelbart, story. *Cinematography:* Owen Roizman.
Sound: Arthur Piantadosi, Les Fresholtz, Dick Alexan-
der, and Les Lazarowitz. *Song:* "It Might Be You,"
music by Dave Grusin, lyrics by Alan Bergman and
Marilyn Bergman. *Film Editing:* Fredric Steinkamp and
William Steinkamp.

Out-of-work New York actor Hoffman has a bright
idea: When his girlfriend, Garr, is turned down for a
part in a soap opera, Hoffman disguises himself as a
woman and wins the role. Discovering what it's like
to be treated as a woman by sexist producer Dabney
Coleman and lecherous actor George Gaynes, Hoffman, while staying in character, strikes back, giving
his alter ego, Dorothy Michaels, a no-nonsense feminist persona. The character catches on big with audiences, turning what Hoffman thought would be a
short gig into a long-term project, which complicates
things because he's falling in love with the leading
lady, Lange, who doesn't know he's really a man.
Moreover, he has to deal with Garr, who doesn't
realize that Dorothy Michaels is really her boyfriend,
and with Lange's widowed father, Charles Durning
[180 . . .], who falls for Dorothy when s/he comes
home for a weekend with his daughter. A farce premise develops unexpected depth and poignancy in this
brilliantly managed comedy—the gags fall naturally
into place without sounding like punch lines, and the
characterizations, even mere caricatures like Coleman's and Gaynes' roles, are spot on. The richness of
the supporting performances reminds one of the heyday of Hollywood character acting: Director Pollack
plays Hoffman's exasperated agent, an unbilled Bill
Murray brings perfect timing to his part as Hoffman's
roommate, and Geena Davis [6 . . .] makes a droll,
sexy film debut as a member of the soap opera's cast.
Interestingly this finely tuned, classic Hollywood
comedy, with its solid feminist message, had to pass
through chaos to achieve greatness: In addition to the
credited writers, the screenplay was worked on at
various stages by Don McGuire (who receives story
credit), Robert Kaufman [553], Elaine May [890],
Barry Levinson [75 . . .], Valerie Curtin [75], and
Robert Garland. Producer Richards was originally set

to direct, and Hal Ashby [430 . . .] replaced him
before Pollack finally signed on. And the on-set quar-
rels of Hoffman and Pollack became part of Hollywood legend. But none of this matters when what
shows up on screen is as good as *Tootsie.*

Lange finally arrived as a star in 1982, receiving
simultaneous nominations for supporting work in
Tootsie and the leading role in *Frances*—films and characters so sharply contrasting that Hollywood could
hardly fail to take notice. Lange had worked hard to
overcome the image left by her debut role six years
earlier, the bimbo beloved of a giant ape in the remake of *King Kong.* In the interim she played a small
but key role in *All That Jazz,* although the part was
still more decorative than a challenge to her acting
ability. Her next film, *How to Beat the High Co$t of
Living* (1980), was a flop comedy, and the torrid remake of *The Postman Always Rings Twice* (1981) could
have stuck her in sexpot roles forever. By demonstrating her range in the two Oscar-nominated films,
Lange commanded respect and much better parts.
Unfortunately her determination to be taken seriously
has also landed her in many films that audiences regard as downers, and with the exception of her second Oscar-winning role in *Blue Sky,* in recent years
her career has been unspectacular.

Tootsie, with its box-office success and its critical
acclaim, might seem like a sure thing for the top
Oscar. But the Academy, which likes to take itself
seriously as the body that defines the industry's claims
to greatness, has never been inclined to honor comedies. After somehow letting *Annie Hall* slip through
and win the top award five years before, the Academy
had honored more earnest works, such as *The Deer
Hunter, Kramer vs. Kramer, Ordinary People,* and *Chariots
of Fire.* Consequently, although *Tootsie* and *E.T. The
Extra-Terrestrial* were both the year's most popular
films and the year's most critically praised ones, the
clear choice for Academy members devoted to demonstrating the high seriousness of their profession was
Gandhi. So the awards went to that film for best picture and for its leading actor, Ben Kingsley; its director, Richard Attenborough; its screenwriter, John
Briley; its cinematographers, Billy Williams and Ron-

nie Taylor; and its editor, John Bloom. The award for sound went to *E.T.* Jack Nitzsche, Buffy Sainte-Marie, and Will Jennings won the song award for "Up Where We Belong," from *An Officer and a Gentleman.*

Lange: 244.5, 449, 722, 1381, 1987. Pollack: 1512, 2047. Hoffman: 810, 1111, 1155, 1312, 1653. Gelbart: 1467. Roizman: 631, 724, 1424, 2316.5. Piantadosi: 54, 58, 215, 319, 606, 1279. Fresholtz: 54, 58, 209, 215, 606, 888, 1127, 1158.5, 1279, 1526. Alexander: 54, 209, 519, 888, 1127, 1158.5, 2179.5. Lazarowitz: 1650. Grusin: 379, 633, 667.5, 881, 890, 1318, 1473. A. Bergman: 179, 867, 1168, 1568, 1628, 1747, 1813, 1864, 2063, 2238, 2321, 2322. M. Bergman: 179, 867, 1168, 1568, 1628, 1747, 1813, 1864, 2063, 2238, 2321, 2322. F. Steinkamp: 814, 1512, 2047, 2074. W. Steinkamp: 633, 1512.

2114 • *TOP GUN*

Don Simpson/Jerry Bruckheimer Production; Paramount. 1986.
Award *Song:* "Take My Breath Away," music by Giorgio Moroder, lyrics by Tom Whitlock.
Nominations *Sound:* Donald O. Mitchell, Kevin O'Connell, Rick Kline, and William B. Kaplan. *Film Editing:* Billy Weber and Chris Lebenzon. *Sound Effects Editing:* Cecelia Hall and George Watters II.

Tom Cruise [260] is a cocky kid determined to be the top fighter pilot in the navy's training program. But he has to learn to follow orders and join the team before he can really be a good pilot. Banal plot, borrowed by screenwriters Jim Cash and Jack Epps, Jr., from old World War II flicks, then juiced up by the flashy direction of Tony Scott, provided with a souped-up music score by Harold Faltermeyer [189] larded with occasional songs, and edited at a cut-to-the-chase pace. In short, the quintessential eighties film: an audience-grabber made with all the conviction of a diet-soda commercial, selling a Reaganoid vision of quick techno-military fixes to the world's political crises. Although it cemented Cruise as the movies' top box-office draw, he is helped immeasurably by an attractive supporting cast: Val Kilmer as his chief rival, Anthony Edwards as Cruise's ill-fated co-

pilot, Meg Ryan as Edwards' wife, and Tom Skerritt as the old hand in charge of training the young hotshots. Only Kelly McGillis, as the love interest, is miscast: She seems more like Cruise's big sister than his lover. The huge box-office success of the movie made producers Don Simpson and Jerry Bruckheimer, previously responsible for *Flashdance* and *Beverly Hills Cop,* the hottest producers of the eighties. But their attempt to recycle the *Top Gun* formula in *Days of Thunder* four years later was a flop.

This was the third Oscar in three tries for Moroder, whose popularity as a film composer has waned with the vogue for synthesizer-based dance pop.

Platoon, which was designed as a counter to the militaristic jingoism of films like *Top Gun,* won the Oscars for sound and for Claire Simpson's film editing. Don Sharpe took the award for the sound effects editing for *Aliens.*

Moroder: 682, 1313. Mitchell: 223, 398, 411.5, 507, 734.5, 779, 1525, 1650, 1824, 1825, 2020, 2176.5. O'Connell: 223, 507, 586, 658.5, 1825, 2020. Kline: 507, 658.5, 1333, 1825, 2020. Kaplan: 127, 708.5. Hall: 961. Watters: 961, 1915.

2115 • *TOP HAT*

RKO Radio. 1935.
Nominations *Picture:* Pandro S. Berman, producer. *Interior Decoration:* Carroll Clark and Van Nest Polglase. *Song:* "Cheek to Cheek," music and lyrics by Irving Berlin. *Dance Direction:* Hermes Pan.

Ginger Rogers [1102] thinks Fred Astaire [2126] is something he isn't: the husband of her best friend, Helen Broderick, who is really married to Edward Everett Horton. The rest of the plot is much the same as *The Gay Divorcée,* leading some to refer to it as a remake. The presence of much of the *Divorcée* cast—Erik Rhodes, Eric Blore, Horton—adds to the similarity, as does the big dance-craze number, "The Piccolino," which evokes *Divorcée's* "The Continental" (which was in turn derived from *Flying Down to Rio's* "Carioca"). Since *Divorcée,* Astaire and Rogers had become a phenomenally popular and highly polished team, and *Top Hat* may be their finest film. It helps, too, that *Top Hat* has six great Berlin songs, including the title song, which became a signature number for Astaire. Directed by Mark Sandrich from a screenplay by Dwight Taylor and Allan Scott [1855]. Lucille Ball has a bit as a flower seller.

Mutiny on the Bounty took the best picture Oscar. The art direction award went to Richard Day for *The Dark Angel,* although Polglase and Clark came in second. Harry Warren and Al Dubin's "Lullaby of Broadway," from *Gold Diggers of 1935,* won the song Oscar. Berlin's "Cheek to Cheek" came in second, with Jerome Kern, Dorothy Fields, and Jimmy McHugh's "Lovely to Look At," from the other Astaire-Rogers film of the year, *Roberta,* in third place. Pan, nominated for the "Piccolino" and "Top Hat, White Tie and Tails" numbers, took second place to David Gould's work on *Broadway Melody of 1936* and *Folies Bergère.*

Berman: 40, 656, 754, 1035, 1899. Clark: 4, 481, 686, 754, 1284, 1924. Polglase: 358, 407, 754, 1212, 1394. Berlin: 34, 244, 358, 929, 1773, 2268. Pan: 481, 1990.

2116 • *TOPKAPI*

FILMWAYS PRODUCTION; UNITED ARTISTS. 1964.
AWARD *Supporting Actor:* Peter Ustinov.

The title refers to the Istanbul museum that a gang of highly specialized thieves plots to rob. They include Melina Mercouri [1426], Maximilian Schell [1065 . . .], Robert Morley [1274], Akim Tamiroff [701 . . .], and Ustinov. This brightly colored and entertaining caper movie, directed by Jules Dassin [1426] and filmed on location by Henry Alekan [1716], has been imitated so often that it has lost its freshness, but performers like Ustinov and Morley in particular are still a treat to watch. The score is by Manos Hadjidakis [1426].

This was the second Oscar for Ustinov, whose film career is now reaching the half-century mark. His most recent appearance was in *Lorenzo's Oil.*

Ustinov: 943, 1644, 1886.

2117 • *TOPPER*

HAL ROACH; MGM. 1937.
NOMINATIONS *Supporting Actor:* Roland Young. *Sound Recording:* Elmer Raguse.

When a giddy young rich couple, George and Marion Kirby, played by Cary Grant [1445 . . .] and Constance Bennett, are killed in a car wreck, their ghosts decide to have a little fun by haunting their banker, Cosmo Topper (Young), whose life with his feather-headed wife, played by Billie Burke [1306], is in dire need of spicing up. Endearing screwball fantasy given style and wit by the performers and their supporting cast, which includes Alan Mowbray, Eugene Pallette, Arthur Lake, and Hedda Hopper. The screenplay, based on a novel by Thorne Smith that was once thought quite racy, is by Jack Jevne, Eric Hatch [1401], and Eddie Moran. It's directed by Norman Z. McLeod.

In a golden age of character actors, Young stands out as one of the most accomplished. *Topper* gives him a chance to demonstrate his gift for physical comedy, using hilarious contortions to suggest his manipulation by the invisible ghosts. Born in England, he made his stage debut in London in 1908 but emigrated to America in 1912. He played Dr. Watson to John Barrymore's Sherlock Holmes in a couple of silent films but didn't become a regular in movies until the arrival of sound. He was typically cast as Milquetoast types and gave one of his most memorable performances as the sinisterly obsequious Uriah Heep in *David Copperfield.* He also played the lecherous Uncle Willy in *The Philadelphia Story.* He died in 1953. He lost the Oscar to Joseph Schildkraut in *The Life of Emile Zola.*

The Oscar for sound went to Thomas T. Moulton for *The Hurricane.*

Raguse: 345, 757.5, 1306, 1464, 1487, 2118.

2118 • *TOPPER RETURNS*

HAL ROACH; UNITED ARTISTS. 1941.
NOMINATIONS *Sound Recording:* Elmer Raguse. *Special Effects:* Roy Seawright, photographic; Elmer Raguse, sound.

Murdered by mistake, Joan Blondell [246] looks around for someone with experience dealing with ghosts and calls on Cosmo Topper, played by Roland Young [2117], to help her find the killer and warn his intended victim. Third in the series of *Topper* films, and though it misses Constance Bennett, who dropped out after the second, and Cary Grant [1445 . . .], who left after the first, it's fun anyway. Billie Burke [1306] is still around as Mrs. Topper, and the supporting cast includes Carole Landis, Dennis O'Keefe, Patsy Kelly, and—doing some unfortunately stereotypical shtick—Eddie "Rochester" Anderson. Roy Del Ruth directs this one. The award for sound went to Jack Whitney for *That Hamilton Woman. I Wanted Wings* won for special effects.

Raguse: 345, 979, 1306, 1464, 1487, 2117. Seawright: 1487, 2119.

2119 • TOPPER TAKES A TRIP

HAL ROACH; UNITED ARTISTS. 1939.

NOMINATION *Special Effects:* Roy Seawright.

The Toppers, played by Roland Young [2117] and Billie Burke [1306], are on the verge of a divorce, so Marion Kirby (Constance Bennett), Topper's ghostly friend, helps save their marriage. Second in the series of three *Topper* movies, and almost as amusing as the first, though Cary Grant [1445 . . .] isn't around anymore. The cast, directed by Norman Z. McLeod, includes Alan Mowbray, Franklin Pangborn, and Skippy, the terrier who was Asta in the *Thin Man* movies and played key roles in *Bringing Up Baby* (1938) and *The Awful Truth*. The special effects Oscar went to *The Rains Came.*

Seawright: 1487, 2118.

2120 • TORA! TORA! TORA!

20TH CENTURY-FOX (U.S./JAPAN). 1970.

AWARD *Special Visual Effects:* A. D. Flowers and L. B. Abbott.

NOMINATIONS *Cinematography:* Charles F. Wheeler, Osami Furuya, Sinsaku Himeda, and Masamichi Satoh. *Art Direction–Set Decoration:* Jack Martin Smith, Yoshiro Muraki, Richard Day, and Taizoh Kawashima; Walter M. Scott, Norman Rockett, and Carl Biddiscombe. *Sound:* Murray Spivack and Herman Lewis.

Film Editing: James E. Newcom, Pembroke J. Herring, and Inoue Chikaya.

Ambitious docudrama, an American and Japanese coproduction, that attempts to tell the story of the attack on Pearl Harbor from both sides. Fascinating for World War II history buffs but a bit draggy for less committed audiences. Richard Fleischer directed the U.S. sequences, Toshio Masuda and Kinji Fukasuku the Japanese ones. The American cast includes Martin Balsam [2067], Jason Robards [54 . . .], Joseph Cotten, E. G. Marshall, and James Whitmore [157 . . .]. The chief Japanese performers are Tatsuya Mihashi, Soh Yamamura, and Takahiro Tamura. The cinematography Oscar went to Freddie Young for *Ryan's Daughter. Patton* won for art direction, sound, and Hugh S. Fowler's editing.

Flowers: 1439, 1596. Abbott: 557, 1062, 1196, 1596. Smith: 29, 413, 557, 646, 896, 1230, 2008, 2247. Muraki: 1074, 1661, 2324. Day: 22, 102, 235, 487, 510, 560, 569, 797, 833, 864, 952, 1048, 1175, 1397, 1477, 1666, 1949, 2056, 2276. Scott: 46, 376, 413, 476, 530, 542, 557, 646, 896, 1088, 1213, 1391, 1475, 1706, 1753, 1881, 1907, 2008, 2247. Rockett: 833. Biddiscombe: 743. Spivack: 896. Lewis: 1596, 2126. Newcom: 87, 798, 1828. Herring: 264, 1512.

2121 • TORCH SONG

MGM. 1953.

NOMINATION *Supporting Actress:* Marjorie Rambeau.

Musical comedy star Joan Crawford [1319 . . .] puts her career above all else, until she falls in love with a blind pianist (Michael Wilding). This musical melodrama marked Crawford's return to her old studio, MGM, after her *Mildred Pierce* triumph at Warners. But the result is a ludicrous camp-fest whose absurdity was pointed up in *That's Entertainment, Part III* (1994), in which Crawford's performance of "Two-Faced Woman" was shown alongside Cyd Charisse's performance of the same song, cut from *The Band Wagon*. Both actresses lip-synched to the same recording of singer India Adams, but Charisse's is the convincing one. Charles Walters [1173], the unfortunate director, also appears as Crawford's dance partner in the opening number. The cast includes Gig Young [427 . . .] and Harry (billed as Henry) Morgan. Rambeau, who plays Crawford's mother, lost to Donna Reed in *From Here to Eternity*.

Rambeau: 1609.

2122 • TORPEDO RUN

MGM. 1958.

NOMINATION *Special Effects:* A. Arnold Gillespie, visual; Harold Humbrock, sound.

Glenn Ford, a World War II submarine commander, is forced to destroy a Japanese ship with his own family aboard. Routine war-is-hell flick that might have made more impact fifteen years earlier. Directed by Joseph Pevney, with Ernest Borgnine [1283] and Dean Jones. The special effects award went to *tom thumb*.

Gillespie: 175, 256, 685, 704, 835, 1371, 1388, 1905, 2048, 2055, 2300.

2123 • TORTILLA FLAT

MGM. 1942.

NOMINATION *Supporting Actor:* Frank Morgan.

Spencer Tracy [131 . . .], John Garfield [251 . . .], Hedy Lamarr, and others pose as the denizens of a picturesque waterfront slum in the fishing town of Monterey, California. Though they're scarcely credible in their roles, this adaptation of a novel by John Steinbeck [1171 . . .] is amusing. Victor Fleming [798] directs from a screenplay by John Lee Mahin [352 . . .] and Benjamin Glazer [97 . . .], and the cast includes Akim Tamiroff [701 . . .], Sheldon Leonard, Donald Meek, and John Qualen. Morgan, who plays a dog-loving old beggar, lost to Van Heflin in *Johnny Eager*.

Morgan: 22.

2124 • TOTAL RECALL

CAROLCO PICTURES PRODUCTION; TRI-STAR. 1990.

AWARD *Special Achievement Award:* Eric Brevig, Rob Bottin, Tim McGovern, and Alex Funke for visual effects.

NOMINATIONS *Sound:* Michael J. Kohut, Carlos de Larios, Aaron Rochin, and Nelson Stoll. *Sound Effects Editing:* Stephen H. Flick.

Arnold Schwarzenegger suspects that his mind has been programmed with someone else's memories—they can do that sort of thing in the twenty-first century. Eventually this leads him to go to Mars to try to uncover the plot and, of course, to decimate the bad guys. Hyperviolent cartoony sci-fi flick with astonishing special effects, though they were soon superseded in Schwarzenegger's next sci-fi adventure, *Terminator 2: Judgment Day*. The plot, based on a story by Philip K. Dick adapted by Ronald Shusett, Dan O'Bannon, and Gary Goldman, is full of switch-backs, several of them involving Schwarzenegger's wife, played by Sharon Stone. But mostly it's a slam-bang adventure that may leave you feeling a little queasy—a specialty of the film's director, Paul Verhoeven. Also in the cast are Rachel Ticotin, Ronny Cox, and Michael Ironside. The award for sound went to *Dances With Wolves*. *The Hunt for Red October* took the Oscar for sound effects editing.

Brevig: 937. Bottin: 1154. Kohut: 641, 1310, 1548, 1711, 2165, 2231. De Larios: 1711, 2165, 2231. Rochin: 521, 641, 1089, 1310, 1711, 2165, 2231, 2287. Stoll: 586. Flick: 544, 1589, 1711, 1888.5.

2125 • TOUCH OF CLASS, A

BRUT PRODUCTIONS; AVCO EMBASSY (UNITED KINGDOM). 1973.

AWARD *Actress:* Glenda Jackson.

NOMINATIONS *Picture:* Melvin Frank, producer. *Story and Screenplay—Based on Factual Material or Material Not Previously Published or Produced:* Melvin Frank and Jack Rose. *Song:* "All That Love Went to Waste," music by George Barrie, lyrics by Sammy Cahn. *Original Dramatic Score:* John Cameron.

George Segal [2277], an American in London, decides to have an extramarital fling but finds himself falling in love with the woman (Jackson) he's planned to have only casual sex with. Noisy, clumsy, and hugely popular comedy directed by Frank, with Paul Sorvino and Hildegarde Neil. Some contemporary reviewers called it the kind of screwball farce that might have been made in the thirties if Hollywood had been free of censors, but it's really just dumb and vulgar. People were astonished that Jackson, known for serious movies like *Marat/Sade* (1966), *Women in Love, Mary, Queen of Scots,* and *Sunday, Bloody Sunday,* could do knockabout comedy. Truth be told, she isn't really very good at it, and her Oscar for this film is one of the most inexplicable in the history of the award, although it's hard to pick an alternative from the other nominees: Ellen Burstyn for *The Exorcist,* Marsha Mason in *Cinderella Liberty,* Barbra Streisand in *The Way We Were,* and Joanne Woodward in *Summer Wishes, Winter Dreams*—all fine actresses in flawed movies. After this, her second Oscar, Jackson had a string of mostly flop movies through the seventies and eighties. Her most successful was *House Calls* (1978), in which she costarred with Walter Matthau [709 . . .]; it's a better demonstration of her comic talents. In 1990 she gave up her acting career to enter politics and won a seat in Parliament.

Jackson's win can be explained by weak competition, but the movie's nomination for best picture can't: To make it a contender, the Academy overlooked *Last Tango in Paris, The Last Detail, Serpico, The Way We Were, Paper Moon, Mean Streets, The Long Goodbye,* and *Blume in Love.* The best picture Oscar went to *The Sting,* which also won for David Ward's screenplay.

Barrie, an aspiring songwriter, was an executive for the Brut cosmetics company, which financed the film. The best song was Marvin Hamlisch and Marilyn and Alan Bergman's title tune for *The Way We Were,* which also won for Hamlisch's score.

Jackson: 893, 1966, 2307. Frank: 636, 1108, 1705. Rose: 951, 1786. Barrie: 2264. Cahn: 74, 163, 182, 696, 915, 926, 1031, 1056, 1216, 1524, 1587, 1692, 1708, 1719, 1859, 1907, 2016, 2064, 2072, 2103, 2110, 2263, 2264, 2315, 2343.

2126 • TOWERING INFERNO, THE

Irwin Allen Production; 20th Century-Fox/Warner Bros. 1974.
Awards *Cinematography:* Fred Koenekamp and Joseph Biroc. *Song:* "We May Never Love Like This Again,"

music and lyrics by Al Kasha and Joel Hirschhorn. *Film Editing:* Harold F. Kress and Carl Kress.
Nominations *Picture:* Irwin Allen, producer. *Supporting Actor:* Fred Astaire. *Art Direction–Set Decoration:* William Creber and Ward Preston; Raphael Bretton. *Sound:* Theodore Soderberg and Herman Lewis. *Original Dramatic Score:* John Williams.

The world's tallest skyscraper is being dedicated in San Francisco, and sure enough the damn thing catches fire, trapping all sorts of people inside. Can fire chief Steve McQueen [1753] and architect Paul Newman [3 . . .] figure out a way to save them? Will builder William Holden [1424 . . .] and electrical contractor Richard Chamberlain get fried by their own sloppy work? And what about Faye Dunaway [255 . . .], or Robert Wagner, or Susan Blakely, or Jennifer Jones [584 . . .], or O. J. Simpson, or Robert Vaughn [2338]? It would be nice to say this expensive disaster epic went down in flames, but it was a big hit—to the immense relief of the two studios that teamed up to make it. They had each bought books about skyscraper disasters—*The Tower,* by Richard Martin Stern, and *The Glass Inferno,* by Thomas M. Scortia and Frank M. Robinson—so they decided to pool their resources rather than go broke making competing movies. This made the expensive cast possible, as well as the extravagant sets that got burned down. But in attempting to recapture the pop thrills of *The Poseidon Adventure,* screenwriter Stirling Silliphant [992] and producer Allen, who did both movies, made the mistake of thinking like the builders of the movie's skyscraper, that bigger was better—or at least that longer was better: *The Towering Inferno* spreads its repetitive cremations and plummetings over nearly three hours, while *The Poseidon Adventure* packed them in neatly in less than two. Interestingly, in the category in which one might have thought *The Towering Inferno* would be a shoo-in for the Oscar, special effects, the award, which was honorary rather than competitive at this point, went to the year's other big shake-and-baker, *Earthquake.* These overextended blockbusters seemed to sate the audience's taste for disaster, for the genre itself crashed and burned with *The Hindenburg* the following year.

Koenekamp became a director of photography in 1966 after serving an apprenticeship as a camera operator, and distinguished himself with his work on such films as *Patton* and *Papillon* before receiving the Oscar. Biroc had served as an assistant to George Folsey [51 . . .] before making his debut as a cinematographer on *It's a Wonderful Life* in 1946. He also photographed the movie that started the 3-D craze in the early fifties, *Bwana Devil* (1952).

This was the second Oscar for the Kasha-Hirschhorn team, who won their first for *The Poseidon Adventure.*

Carl Kress took over as editor of *The Towering Inferno* when his father, Harold, was hospitalized as a result of an automobile accident. Later, Carl would complain that the Oscar had done little for his career because people assumed he had merely been assisting his father, when in fact he had done the lion's share of the cutting of the film. Harold Kress' career extends back to 1939 and includes such films as *Random Harvest, Cabin in the Sky, Madame Curie,* and other movies from the heyday of MGM. Carl Kress began his editing career in 1966; he has been active in TV work as well as movies and has won two Emmys.

The film's nomination for best picture can be explained by the considerable clout possessed by the two big studios that produced it. Clearly it didn't belong in the company of the other nominees: *Chinatown, The Conversation, Lenny,* and the winner, *The Godfather, Part II.* And hardly anyone believes it was better than some other films of a remarkable year: *Alice Doesn't Live Here Anymore, Day for Night, Young Frankenstein, Badlands, Harry and Tonto,* or *The Three Musketeers.* Producer Allen shared directing credit with John Guillermin, but they were not among the directorial nominees.

The Towering Inferno has one thing to its credit: It provided Astaire, one of the movies' legendary figures, with his sole nomination. He brings his usual charm to a stock character: a con artist who finds (and loses) love during the harrowing rescue. Astaire had begun to do nonmusical performances in 1959 with *On the Beach* and made only one musical film,

Finian's Rainbow, in the years that followed. His last work as a film actor was in *Ghost Story* in 1981. He had been given an honorary Oscar at the 1949 ceremonies "for his unique artistry and his contributions to the technique of musical pictures," but he lost the competition for supporting actor to Robert De Niro in *The Godfather, Part II.* Astaire died, at the age of eighty-eight, in 1987.

Godfather II also took the awards for art direction and for the scoring of Nino Rota and Carmine Coppola. *Earthquake* won for sound.

Koenekamp: 1023, 1541. Biroc: 963. Kasha: 1557, 1596. Hirschhorn: 1557, 1596. H. Kress: 573, 953, 1371, 1596, 2320. Creber: 833, 1596. Bretton: 896, 963, 1596. Soderberg: 724, 983, 1596, 1726, 2152. Lewis: 1596, 2120. Williams: 6, 260, 403, 416, 588, 613, 614, 659, 805, 933, 937, 982, 996, 997, 1041, 1047, 1596, 1652, 1679, 1684, 1701, 1764.65, 1916, 1977, 2107, 2194, 2293, 2322.

2127 • *TOWN WITHOUT PITY*

Mirisch Company Inc. in association with Gloria Films; United Artists (U.S./Switzerland/West Germany). 1961. **Nomination** *Song:* "Town Without Pity," music by Dimitri Tiomkin, lyrics by Ned Washington.

Kirk Douglas [130 . . .] plays the defense attorney in the trial of four American GIs accused of raping a German woman. By portraying the victim, played by Christine Kaufmann, as a provocative slut, he gets the rapists off with a light sentence, but he ruins the young woman's life. A promising story flatly handled, despite an accomplished cast including E. G. Marshall, Robert Blake, and Richard Jaeckel [1864]. Directed by Gottfried Reinhardt and filmed on location in Germany. The hit title song, sung by Gene Pitney, seems rather cheesy in context. It lost to Henry Mancini and Johnny Mercer's "Moon River," from *Breakfast at Tiffany's.*

Tiomkin: 33, 286, 380, 446, 638, 663, 730, 768, 850, 911, 912, 1206, 1347, 1370, 1470, 2006, 2282, 2335. Washington: 274, 585, 911, 912, 1329, 1396, 1576, 1745, 2282, 2335.

2127.5 • TOYS

20TH CENTURY FOX PRODUCTION; 20TH CENTURY FOX. 1992.
NOMINATIONS *Art Direction:* Ferdinando Scarfiotti, Linda DeScenna. *Costume Design:* Albert Wolsky.

Toy maker Donald O'Connor wills his factory to his brother, a general (Michael Gambon), who wants to replace its bright, whimsical creations with sinister war toys. O'Connor's children, Robin Williams [511 . . .] and Joan Cusack [2313], are forced to struggle to regain the factory. Thick, cloying, confused whimsy weighs down this scattershot allegory, the brainchild of its producer-director-writer, Barry Levinson [75 . . .], who had dreamed all his career of filming it and finally, having gained clout with *Rain Man,* was able to do so. Some dreams are better left up in the clouds—*Toys* was a catastrophic critical and commercial flop. It was, however, brilliantly designed and is worth zipping through on videotape to glimpse Scarfiotti's delightful sets. The Oscars went to *Howards End* for art direction and to Eiko Ishioka for the costumes for *Bram Stoker's Dracula.*

Scarfiotti: 1136. DeScenna: 228, 423, 1653, 1913. Wolsky: 49, 308, 1061, 1876.

2128 • TOYS IN THE ATTIC

MIRISCH-CLAUDE PRODUCTIONS; UNITED ARTISTS. 1963.
NOMINATION *Black-and-White Costume Design:* Bill Thomas.

Con man Dean Martin comes home to New Orleans with his young wife, Yvette Mimieux, to see his unmarried sisters, Geraldine Page [935 . . .] and Wendy Hiller [1252 . . .], but Page's jealousy of Mimieux almost leads to Martin's death. Thanks to Page and Hiller, this passable adaptation by James Poe [101 . . .] of a play by Lillian Hellman [1182 . . .] is quite watchable, though director George Roy Hill [317 . . .] is unable to find ways to overcome its staginess. It also features one of the last screen appearances of Gene Tierney [1153], who plays Mimieux's mother. The costuming Oscar went to Piero Gherardi for *8½.*

Thomas: 116, 166, 254, 866, 883, 1003, 1789, 1812, 1886.

2129 • TRADER HORN

MGM. 1930–31.
NOMINATION *Picture:* Irving G. Thalberg, producer.

Harry Carey is the intrepid Horn, who carries the white man's burden into darkest Africa. The explorers discover Edwina Booth, a "white goddess"—Booth spends much of the movie clad in her long blond hair and a few shreds of clothes. If you can ignore the racism and sexism, it's entertaining, and impressive when you realize the hardships the camera crew—headed by Clyde DeVinna [2273]—and the actors went through to make a sound film on location in Nairobi, Lake Victoria, Tanganyika, Uganda, the Belgian Congo, and Kenya in the early thirties. In the end most of the narrative footage shot on location was deemed unusable and had to be reshot on the MGM back lot, but the footage of African wildlife and natives was impressive—and profitable: MGM reused it again and again in the Johnny Weissmuller *Tarzan* series. Directed by W. S. Van Dyke [1751 . . .] from a screenplay by Richard Schayer, Dale Van Every [352], John Thomas Neville, and Cyril Hume. Avoid the exceedingly stupid 1973 remake that reuses footage from *King Solomon's Mines.* The best picture Oscar went to *Cimarron.*

Thalberg: 150, 202, 799, 812, 1387, 1721, 1846.

2130 • TRADING PLACES

AARON RUSSO PRODUCTION; PARAMOUNT. 1983.
NOMINATION *Original Song Score or Adaptation Score:* Elmer Bernstein.

Two wealthy old codgers, Ralph Bellamy [114] and Don Ameche [419], make a wager about heredity vs. environment, and use rich white stockbroker Dan Aykroyd [580] and poor black con artist Eddie Murphy as their guinea pigs: Aykroyd gets kicked out into the streets, while Murphy gets Aykroyd's job. But the guinea pigs get even, with the help of hooker Jamie Lee Curtis and Aykroyd/Murphy's butler, Denholm Elliott [1725]. All these bright performers are needed to bring life to a rather thin script by Timothy Harris and Herschel Weingrod, because director John Landis isn't much help. Though the parts are definitely better than the whole, it was a big hit, and it made

Murphy a superstar. Bernstein's score is based in part on Mozart—the credits run to the overture from *The Marriage of Figaro*. The Oscar went to Michel Legrand and Alan and Marilyn Bergman for *Yentl*.

Bernstein: 27.5, 789, 882, 1242, 1264, 1685, 1959, 2064, 2101, 2147, 2223.

2131 • *TRAIL OF THE LONESOME PINE*

WALTER WANGER; PARAMOUNT. 1936.

NOMINATION *Song:* "A Melody From the Sky," music by Louis Alter, lyrics by Sidney Mitchell.

Sylvia Sidney [1962] and Henry Fonda [815 . . .], sister and brother, are caught up in an Appalachian family feud which is complicated by the arrival of the railroad and young construction engineer Fred Mac-Murray. Handsome, well-acted version of an old novel by John Fox, Jr., that had been filmed by Cecil B. DeMille [412 . . .] in 1915. This one was directed by Henry Hathaway [1194]. It was also the first outdoors film made in three-color Technicolor—the cinematographer is W. Howard Greene [96 . . .]. The cast includes Fuzzy Knight, Beulah Bondi [807 . . .], Nigel Bruce, and Spanky McFarland. It's said that, after seeing this film, cartoonist Al Capp used Fonda as the model for Li'l Abner. His costar MacMurray served as the model for another cartoon character, Captain Marvel. The screenplay is by Grover Jones [1116 . . .], Horace McCoy, and Harvey Thew. The Oscar for song went to Jerome Kern and Dorothy Fields for "The Way You Look Tonight," from *Swing Time*.

Alter: 1131.

2132 • *TRAIN, THE*

LES PRODUCTIONS ARTISTES ASSOCIÉS; UNITED ARTISTS (U.S./FRANCE/ITALY). 1965.

NOMINATION *Story and Screenplay—Written Directly for the Screen:* Franklin Coen and Frank Davis.

With things looking bad for the Germans in 1944, a Nazi colonel, played by Paul Scofield [1252 . . .], tries to ship the Impressionist masterworks from the Jeu de Paume from Paris to Germany. Burt Lancaster [107 . . .], a French railway inspector, is persuaded by members of the Resistance, including Jeanne

Moreau, to try to stop the train. Fine, exciting action thriller, directed by John Frankenheimer. The writing award went to Frederic Raphael for *Darling*.

Davis: 2137.

2133 • *TRANSATLANTIC*

FOX. 1931–32.

AWARD *Interior Decoration:* Gordon Wiles.

Intersecting stories of the passengers on a luxury liner: a gambler pursued by the mob, a married man having a fling with a dancer, and so on. Even at the time, this one was compared to *Grand Hotel*. It has one of that movie's cast members, Jean Hersholt, though the rest of the cast isn't quite as stellar as the MGM blockbuster: Myrna Loy, Edmund Lowe, Lois Moran, John Halliday, and Greta Nissen. William K. Howard directs from a script by Guy Bolton and Lynn Starling.

2134 • *TRAVELS WITH MY AUNT*

ROBERT FRYER PRODUCTIONS; MGM (UNITED KINGDOM). 1972.

AWARD *Costume Design:* Anthony Powell.

NOMINATIONS *Actress:* Maggie Smith. *Cinematography:* Douglas Slocombe. *Art Direction—Set Decoration:* John Box, Gil Parrondo, and Robert W. Laing.

A mild-mannered, middle-aged accountant (Alec McCowen) is dragooned by his flamboyant elderly aunt (Smith) into a mysterious mission that takes them across Europe. Determinedly wacky stuff that soon wears out its welcome. Director George Cukor [262 . . .] was instrumental in getting it made: He was an admirer of the novel by Graham Greene [639] on which the film is based, and persuaded Katharine Hepburn [24 . . .] to star in it. But before filming started, Hepburn left or was fired from the project— the details have been somewhat veiled. Smith was not an ideal replacement; she is nine years younger than McCowen, who in the film is supposed to be a quarter century or so younger than his aunt—who may in fact be his mother. The first version of the screenplay was written by Hugh Wheeler. After several revisions, many of them to please Hepburn, Wheeler was replaced by Chester Erskine, though the final version of the script is credited to Wheeler and Jay Presson Allen [321 . . .]. Management turmoil at MGM under owner Kirk Kerkorian and president James T. Aubrey left the project without much solid support from the home office. The resulting film is a mess with a few bright moments. The cast includes Louis Gossett, Jr. [1465], as Smith's lover, Robert Stephens as the man Smith and McCowen set out to rescue from sinister forces, and Cindy Williams as a hippie who seduces McCowen.

This was the first of three Oscars for costumer Powell. Smith lost to Liza Minnelli in *Cabaret,* which also won for Geoffrey Unsworth's cinematography and for art direction.

Powell: 516, 937, 1578, 2021. Smith: 332, 1506, 1608, 1725. Slocombe: 1066, 1652. Box: 558, 1151, 1429, 1471, 1533. Parrondo: 1429, 1541. Laing: 745.

2135 • *TRAVIATA, LA*

ACCENT FILMS B.V. PRODUCTION IN ASSOCIATION WITH RAI-RADIOTELEVISIONE ITALIANA, THROUGH PSO; UNIVERSAL CLASSICS (ITALY/FRANCE). 1982.

NOMINATIONS *Art Direction–Set Decoration:* Franco Zeffirelli; Gianni Quaranta. *Costume Design:* Piero Tosi.

Teresa Stratas is Violetta, the doomed young courtesan who falls in love with Alfredo (Placido Domingo), a naive young man from the country, but is persuaded by his father, Giorgio Germont (Cornell MacNeill), to give him up. Alfredo curses her, but returns in time for a reconciliation at her deathbed. Exciting all-stops-out filming of Verdi's opera with singers who can really act. As with most of director Zeffirelli's films of opera or Shakespeare, there are some cuts that people familiar with the work will resent, and his determination to keep things from getting stagy sometimes simply results in overbusyness. The orchestra is conducted by James Levine and the cinematography is by Ennio Guarnieri. *Gandhi* took the Oscars for art direction and for John Mollo and Bhanu Athaiya's costumes.

Zeffirelli: 1722. Quaranta: 300, 1725. Tosi: 326, 514, 1156, 1225.

2136 • *TREASURE OF THE SIERRA MADRE, THE*

WARNER BROS. 1948.

AWARDS *Supporting Actor:* Walter Huston. *Director:* John Huston. *Screenplay:* John Huston.
NOMINATION *Picture:* Henry Blanke, producer.

Humphrey Bogart [24 . . .] is Fred C. Dobbs, an American on the make in Mexico, who teams up with a kid (Tim Holt) and an old-timer (Walter Huston) to hunt for gold—an adventure that eventually destroys them. A genuine classic—one of those movies in which script, direction, and cast are perfectly in sync, which shouldn't be surprising when you notice who won the Oscars. Based on the novel by the enigmatic B. Traven, whom John Huston claimed to have consulted during the filming in Mexico and the Mojave Desert. The cinematography is by Ted McCord [1052 . . .]. Smaller roles are played by Bruce Bennett, Barton MacLane, Alfonso Bedoya, young Robert Blake (billed as Bobby), and the director himself. The chief mystery, as far as the Oscars are concerned, is how Bogart, in one of his finest performances, was passed over for a nomination in favor of Lew Ayres for *Johnny Belinda,* Dan Dailey for *When My Baby Smiles at Me,* or Clifton Webb for *Sitting Pretty.* The only answer is that his Fred C. Dobbs, itchy, paranoid, and unlikable, was so shocking a departure from his established image as a toughie who's really good at heart (Fred C. Dobbs isn't good *anywhere*) that it turned off audiences who expected a last-reel redemption. The studio, disappointed by the film's poor box office, failed to promote Bogart for the Oscar, won by Laurence Olivier for *Hamlet,* which also took the best picture award. (Montgomery Clift, for his debut film *The Search,* was the fifth nominee for best actor.)

Walter Huston had been a vaudevillian who switched over to serious drama in the twenties and came to Hollywood with the arrival of sound. By the mid-thirties he was an established and respected performer in movies. He first acted for his son in a small part in *The Maltese Falcon.* After receiving the Oscar, he made two more films before his death in 1950.

John Huston became the first person to direct his own father to an acting Oscar, just as, thirty-seven years later, he would be the first person to direct his own daughter to an acting Oscar, when Anjelica Huston won for *Prizzi's Honor*. He had begun as an actor at about the time his father entered movies, but soon moved over to screenwriting, and in 1941 made one of the most assured directing debuts in the history of movies, with *The Maltese Falcon*. For the next forty-six years, he remained one of the most interesting—if not always the most successful—directors. His flops —*Phobia* (1980), *Victory* (1981), *Annie* (1982)—were as catastrophic as his successes were brilliant. Everyone has his or her own canon of Huston's greatest hits, but most would include *The Asphalt Jungle*, *The African Queen*, *The Man Who Would Be King*, and *Prizzi's Honor* as well as *Maltese Falcon* and *Sierra Madre*. In the sixties he returned to acting occasionally, often to finance his own films, receiving an Oscar nomination as supporting actor for *The Cardinal* and creating one of the most memorable of all screen villains, Noah Cross, in *Chinatown*. He died in 1987, after completing one of his finest films, *The Dead*.

W. Huston: 50, 560, 2318. J. Huston: 24, 105, 356, 571, 891, 1248, 1263, 1363, 1625, 1779. Blanke: 17, 90, 712, 1046, 1169, 1315, 1457, 1936.

2137 • TREE GROWS IN BROOKLYN, A

20TH CENTURY-FOX. 1945.
AWARD *Supporting Actor:* James Dunn.
NOMINATION *Screenplay:* Frank Davis and Tess Slesinger.

Peggy Ann Garner plays Francie Nolan, a girl growing up in the slums of Brooklyn in the twenties. Her mother, played by Dorothy McGuire [759], works hard to keep the family going, while her father (Dunn) is an easygoing lovable drunk. Francie idolizes him and is at odds with her mother, who favors Francie's brother, but the father's death brings mother and daughter closer together. Very well done sentimental drama, adapted from a best-selling novel by Betty Smith, with fine performances. Garner received the Academy's miniature Oscar as "outstanding child actress of 1945," primarily for this film, though she made two others, *Nob Hill* and *Junior Miss,* the same year. The large and colorful supporting cast

includes Joan Blondell [246], Lloyd Nolan, and James Gleason [904]. The film also marked the feature directing debut of Elia Kazan [63 . . .], who claimed in his autobiography that he suggested that cinematographer Leon Shamroy [29 . . .], who helped Kazan with the rudiments of camera setups, be given a credit as codirector.

Dunn made his Broadway debut in 1930 and his film debut the following year in *Bad Girl*. Most of his career was spent in B pictures, in which he often played leads, but his alcoholism limited his career in major features. From 1950 to his death in 1967, he was seen more often on TV than in films.

The screenplay Oscar went to Charles Brackett and Billy Wilder for *The Lost Weekend*.

Davis: 2132.

2138 • TRESPASSER, THE

JOSEPH P. KENNEDY PRODUCTIONS; UNITED ARTISTS. 1929–30.
NOMINATION *Actress:* Gloria Swanson.

Swanson plays a secretary who weds a rich man (Robert Ames), to the dismay of his father (William Holden, but not the William Holden whom Swanson would costar with twenty years later in *Sunset Boulevard;* many books and articles have made the mistake of confusing the two actors). After Holden persuades them to have their marriage annulled, Ames remarries, but his wife is seriously injured in an accident. Meanwhile, Swanson has Ames' son, whose existence —as is the custom in such melodramas—she conceals from him. She is rescued from poverty by her former employer and becomes his mistress until he dies. When Ames' wife discovers the existence of the child, she conveniently dies, clearing the way for a happy ending. The quintessential star vehicle, designed by Swanson's lover, Joseph P. Kennedy, for her entrance into talking pictures—she even got to sing in it. Written and directed by Edmund Goulding, with cinematography by George Barnes [537 . . .]. Remade by Goulding as *That Certain Woman* in 1937 with Bette Davis [46 . . .] and Henry Fonda [815 . . .]. Swanson lost to Norma Shearer in *The Divorcée*.

Swanson: 1739, 1975.

2139 • TRIAL

MGM. 1955.

NOMINATION *Supporting Actor:* Arthur Kennedy.

Lawyer Glenn Ford defends a Chicano youth (Rafael Campos) accused of murder and finds himself not only caught up in the racial tensions surrounding the case but also being duped by the commies, led by Kennedy. The Cold War politics date the movie, but they also make it more interesting than most courtroom melodramas. Don Mankiewicz [973]—the son of Herman J. Mankiewicz [407 . . .] and nephew of Joseph L. Mankiewicz [46 . . .]—based the screenplay on his own novel. Mark Robson [1001 . . .] directs a strong cast: Dorothy McGuire [759], John Hodiak, Katy Jurado [299], Juano Hernandez, and Elisha Cook, Jr. Kennedy lost the third of his five unsuccessful tries at an Oscar to Jack Lemmon in *Mister Roberts.*

Kennedy: 291, 380, 1558, 1859.

2140 • TRIBUTE

LAWRENCE TURMAN-DAVID FOSTER PRESENTATION OF A JOEL B. MICHAELS-GARTH H. DRABINSKY PRODUCTION; 20TH CENTURY-FOX (CANADA/U.S.). 1980.

NOMINATION *Actor:* Jack Lemmon.

Lemmon plays a wheeler-dealer type who finds he's dying of cancer, so he makes a last-ditch effort to get to know his son, Robby Benson, who has been raised by Lemmon's ex-wife, Lee Remick [508]. Tiresome sentimental exercise adapted by Bernard Slade from his play, which also starred Lemmon. Neither Slade nor director Bob Clark (best known for the *Porky's* movies) succeeds in making it cinematic, but it has some attractive performers, including Colleen Dewhurst and John Marley [1218] as well as the leads. Lemmon lost to Robert De Niro in *Raging Bull.*

Lemmon: 91, 394, 508, 1330, 1337, 1761, 1860.

2141 • TRIO

J. ARTHUR RANK-SYDNEY BOX; PARAMOUNT (UNITED KINGDOM). 1950.

NOMINATION *Sound Recording:* Pinewood Studio Sound Department, Cyril Crowhurst, sound director.

Anthology film of three short stories by W. Somerset Maugham. "The Verger" deals with a church custodian who becomes a successful small businessman after his illiteracy causes a vicar to fire him. "Mr. Knowall" takes place on a cruise, during which an obnoxious jerk redeems himself. "Sanatorium" is about a doomed love affair in a tuberculosis hospital. The stories were adapted for the screen by Maugham, R. C. Sheriff [804], and Noel Langley, and directed by Ken Annakin [2065] and Harold French. The casts include James Hayter, Michael Hordern, Felix Aylmer, Nigel Patrick, Naunton Wayne, Wilfred Hyde White, Michael Rennie, Jean Simmons [858 . . .], and Finlay Currie. The award for sound went to Thomas T. Moulton for *All About Eve.*

2142 • TRIP TO BOUNTIFUL, THE

BOUNTIFUL PRODUCTION; ISLAND PICTURES. 1985.

AWARD *Actress:* Geraldine Page.

NOMINATION *Screenplay Based on Material From Another Medium:* Horton Foote.

Depressed by her life with her son (John Heard) and daughter-in-law (Carlin Glynn), the widowed Mrs. Watts (Page) sneaks out one day and takes the bus to Bountiful, the small Texas town where she grew up. Along the way, she tells the story of her life to a sympathetic young woman (Rebecca DeMornay). Sentimental mood piece, full of fine period detail (the late forties) and excellent performances, but not quite enough to sustain a full-length film. Foote wrote it first as a television play in 1953, with Lillian Gish [584], and later turned it into a Broadway play. Directed by Peter Masterson.

Page had a record-setting seven unsuccessful nominations before winning the Oscar for her last film role. Presenter F. Murray Abraham [60] gushed, "I consider this woman the greatest actress in the English language," before reading out her name to the audience at the awards ceremony. There were many who agreed with him—but also quite a few others who found Page mannered and limited in range. Her characters on film were mostly eccentrics, often frustrated spinsters, but she brought great commitment to each part. She had attained stardom in 1952 in an off-Broadway production of *Summer and Smoke,* playing a role that she later re-created on film, and entered movies the following year with her Oscar-nominated part in *Hondo*. She died in 1987.

The screenplay award went to Kurt Luedtke for *Out of Africa*.

Page: 935, 1005, 1555, 1591, 1959, 1985, 2341. Foote: 2015, 2101.

2143 • TRISTANA

Forbes Films Ltd.-United Cineworld-Epoca Films S.A.-Talia Film S.A.-Les Films Corona-Selenia Cinematográfica S.r.l. Production (Spain). 1970.

Nomination *Foreign Language Film.*

Catherine Deneuve [998.5] plays the title role, a young woman who is seduced by her guardian (Fernando Rey), whom she leaves for a virile young painter (Franco Nero). A comparatively straightforward narrative for a film by Luis Buñuel [549 . . .] but nevertheless filled with his typically surreal and bizarre touches. The Oscar went to *Investigation of a Citizen Above Suspicion*.

2144 • TRON

Walt Disney Productions; Buena Vista. 1982.

Nominations *Sound:* Michael Minkler, Bob Minkler, Lee Minkler, and Jim La Rue. *Costume Design:* Elois Jenssen and Rosanna Norton.

Jeff Bridges [1139 . . .] plays a computer genius who enters the computer itself to do battle with the program created by mad scientist David Warner. Dazzling settings designed by Syd Mead, Jean Moebius Giraud, and Peter Lloyd and animation supervised by Harrison Ellenshaw [219]. Unfortunately the visual wizardry couldn't make up for the thinness of the story by director Steven Lisberger, and the movie, designed to attract video-gamers, was a big flop. The cast includes Bruce Boxleitner and Bernard Hughes. The award for sound went to *E.T. The Extra-Terrestrial*. John Mollo and Bhanu Athaiya took the costuming award for *Gandhi*.

M. Minkler: 58, 260, 398, 413.5, 606, 1047. B. Minkler: 1916. Jenssen: 1748.

2145 • TROPIC HOLIDAY

Paramount. 1938.

Nomination *Score:* Boris Morros.

Screenwriter Ray Milland [1208] goes to Mexico and falls in love with Dorothy Lamour. Mediocre musical, with Martha Raye, Bob Burns, Binnie Barnes, and Tito Guizar, directed by Theodore Reed. The Oscar went to Alfred Newman for *Alexander's Ragtime Band*.

Morros: 757, 1880.

2146 • TRUCE, THE

Tamames-Zemborain Production (Argentina). 1974.

Nomination *Foreign Language Film.*

A middle-aged widower, at odds with his sons, starts a new life with a twenty-four-year-old woman. Directed by Sergio Renan from a screenplay by Mario Benedetti. The Oscar went to *Amarcord*.

2147 • TRUE GRIT

Hal Wallis Productions; Paramount. 1969.

Award *Actor:* John Wayne.

Nomination *Song:* "True Grit," music by Elmer Bernstein, lyrics by Don Black.

Kim Darby plays a young woman whose father has been murdered, so she hires a fat, one-eyed old marshal, Rooster Cogburn (Wayne), to find the killer. Enjoyable comic western directed by Henry Hathaway [1194] from a screenplay by Marguerite Roberts based on a novel by Charles Portis. The cast includes Glen Campbell, Robert Duvall [92 . . .], Strother Martin, and Dennis Hopper [595 . . .]. Photographed by Lucien Ballard [359].

Some sort of award to Wayne was long overdue, and it seems appropriate that the Oscar was presented to him thirty years after *Stagecoach* made him an American icon. But it was also one of the Academy's most controversial awards: an honor to one of Hollywood's most hidebound conservatives at a time when the country was being torn apart by the politics of protest. And there are many who are still shocked that this mere movie star should be given an award over serious actors like his four competitors: Richard Burton for *Anne of the Thousand Days*, Dustin Hoffman and Jon Voight for *Midnight Cowboy,* and Peter O'Toole for *Goodbye, Mr. Chips.* But thirty years of giving performances that people want to pay money to see isn't something to be dismissed casually, and though all of John Wayne's characterizations partake of John Wayne the star, they're also remarkably distinct: The Ringo Kid of *Stagecoach* is a very different person from Tom Dunson in *Red River,* and Ethan Edwards in *The Searchers* (1956) is a long way from Rooster Cogburn. Because Wayne spent his career in genre films—westerns and war movies—he was never taken seriously by the critics. But it takes skill to bring life to the two-dimensional characters of most genre films, and Wayne did just that for more than forty years. He died in 1979.

The Oscar for best song went to "Raindrops Keep Fallin' on My Head," by Burt Bacharach and Hal David, from *Butch Cassidy and the Sundance Kid.*

Wayne: 33, 1756. Bernstein: 27.5, 789, 882, 1242, 1264, 1685, 1959, 2064, 2101, 2130, 2223. Black: 174, 259, 789, 1574.

2147.5 • *TRUE LIES*

Lightstorm Entertainment Production; 20th Century Fox. 1994.

Nomination *Visual Effects:* John Bruno, Thomas L. Fisher, Jacques Stroweis, and Patrick McClung.

Harry Tasker (Arnold Schwarzenegger) leads a double life: His wife, Helen (Jamie Lee Curtis), thinks he's a mild-mannered businessman when in fact he's a spy for a top-secret government agency. Eventually, the deception falls apart when he's persuaded by his colleague Gib (Tom Arnold) that Helen may be having an affair; his attempts to get the goods on her—and to punish both her and her supposed lover (Bill Paxton)—help put both Harry and Helen in peril from some Middle Eastern nuclear terrorists. Megabudget spoof that begins nicely as a James Bond *hommage,* but often threatens to collapse under the weight of the money that's being piled on it. It finally holds up because writer-director James Cameron has a sure hand with this sort of action nonsense, having directed such big-budget blow-'em-ups as the *Terminator* films and *Aliens.* The movie is packed with outra-

geous stunts, such as Schwarzenegger's pursuit on horseback of a bad guy on a motorcycle, which takes them through the lobby, up the elevator, and onto the roof of a luxury hotel. And it has some ingratiating performers to watch: Curtis and Arnold are skilled comic actors, but even Schwarzenegger has become humanized as a performer. He knows how to put the right spin on his punchlines, as when Curtis is shocked to learn that her husband has killed people. His retort, "Yes, but they were all bad," has just the right small-boyish sincerity. On the downside, many critics objected to a sour note of misogyny in the script, such as a scene in which Helen is degraded by having to pose as a hooker and perform a striptease, and to the conventional dehumanizing of the villains. The visual effects Oscar went to *Forrest Gump.*

Bruno: 5, 153.5, 413.5, 766, 1590.

2148 • *TUCKER: THE MAN AND HIS DREAM*

Lucasfilm Production; Paramount. 1988.

Nominations *Supporting Actor:* Martin Landau. *Art Direction—Set Decoration:* Dean Tavoularis, art direction; Armin Ganz, set decoration. *Costume Design:* Milena Canonero.

Jeff Bridges [1139 . . .] plays Preston Tucker, who dreams of taking on the Big Three automakers with a car that would give people high quality at a reasonable price. Naturally he's shot down. An interesting attempt by director Francis Ford Coppola [65 . . .] to portray an old-fashioned American hero, though it gets sentimental and contrived. It's also an allegory of Coppola's failed attempts to create his own movie studio. Landau plays the partner who loses his shirt in the venture, and the supporting cast includes Joan Allen, Frederic Forrest [1726], Mako [1753], Dean Stockwell [1281], and Christian Slater. The movie was a box-office disappointment. Landau lost to Kevin Kline for *A Fish Called Wanda.* The art direction and costuming nominations reflect the film's snazzy re-creation of the forties, but the Oscars went to an even more ambitious re-creation of a period: the eighteenth-century decor created by Stuart Craig and Gerard James and clothes designed by James Acheson for *Dangerous Liaisons*.

Landau: 461, 595.8. Tavoularis: 92, 292, 785, 786. Canonero: 151, 386, 543, 1512.

2149 • *TULSA*

WALTER WANGER; EAGLE LION. 1949.

NOMINATION *Special Effects.* (No individual citation.)

Susan Hayward [973 . . .] is determined to make it in the oil business. Naturally, like all ambitious career women in the movies, she has to suffer for her hubris. Still, this is pretty solid entertainment if you can forgive its clichés. Directed by Stuart Heisler with a good cast: Robert Preston [2201], Pedro Armendariz, Chill Wills [33], and Ed Begley [1985]. The Technicolor cinematography of Winton Hoch [1048 . . .] helps, too. The screenplay is by Frank Nugent [1642] and Curtis Kenyon. The Oscar for special effects went to *Mighty Joe Young*.

2150 • *TUNES OF GLORY*

H.M. FILMS LTD. PRODUCTION; LOPERT PICTURES CORPORATION (UNITED KINGDOM). 1960.

NOMINATION *Screenplay—Based on Material From Another Medium:* James Kennaway.

John Mills [1737], a by-the-book disciplinarian, comes to replace Alec Guinness [287 . . .], the popular, casual, boozy commander of a Scottish regiment. Sparks fly. Watching two great actors sparring is the chief pleasure of this otherwise drab-looking and thinly plotted movie, directed by Ronald Neame [289 . . .]. Susannah York [2047] makes her film debut as Guinness' daughter. Kennaway's adaptation of his own novel lost to Richard Brooks' screenplay for *Elmer Gantry*.

2151 • *TURKISH DELIGHT*

ROB HOUWER FILM PRODUCTION (THE NETHERLANDS). 1973.

NOMINATION *Foreign Language Film.*

Rutger Hauer plays an artist whose marriage to a middle-class woman grows stale, so he enters into a period of mad promiscuity. Abrasive, erotic film directed by Paul Verhoeven and photographed by Jan De Bont. The Oscar went to *Day for Night*.

2152 • *TURNING POINT, THE*

HERA PRODUCTIONS; 20TH CENTURY-FOX. 1977.

NOMINATIONS *Picture:* Herbert Ross and Arthur Laurents, producers. *Actress:* Anne Bancroft. *Actress:* Shirley MacLaine. *Supporting Actor:* Mikhail Baryshnikov. *Supporting Actress:* Leslie Browne. *Director:* Herbert Ross. *Screenplay—Written Directly for the Screen:* Arthur Laurents. *Cinematography:* Robert Surtees. *Art Direction—Set Decoration:* Albert Brenner; Marvin March. *Sound:* Theodore Soderberg, Paul Wells, Douglas O. Williams, and Jerry Jost. *Film Editing:* William Reynolds.

Old friends Bancroft and MacLaine reunite when Bancroft's ballet company stops in Oklahoma City on tour. MacLaine gave up her career as a dancer when she married Tom Skerritt, but Bancroft chose career over marriage and is now facing her postcareer years alone. MacLaine and Skerritt's daughter, Browne, who is also Bancroft's goddaughter, is an aspiring dancer who has an affair with the ballet company's star, Baryshnikov. When Bancroft starts trying to manage Browne's career, MacLaine objects to having her maternal privileges usurped and the two women have a slugfest, after which they kiss, make up, and settle down to the task together. Though the film makes a nod to feminism, it falls back on the tired old premise that a woman can't be a success in both career and marriage. If the plot didn't get in the way of the dancing, the movie would be terrific: Not only do we get generous amounts of Baryshnikov, who is at his sensational peak as a dancer (and who's not bad as an actor, too), but there are also glimpses of Suzanne Farrell, Peter Martins, Antoinette Sibley, Marcia Haydée, and Fernando Bujones. But the characters are thinly and predictably drawn, so they need all the oomph the actors can give them. The nominees are all equal to the task, fortunately, as is the invaluable Skerritt—who belongs with Sam Neill and Scott Glenn on any list of the most underrated actors in movies. Martha Scott [1510] plays the ballet company founder.

The Turning Point was conceived by Ross, Laurents, and Nora Kaye, a former dancer who, like the character played by MacLaine, gave up her career when she married Ross. The producers tried to persuade Grace Kelly [450 . . .] to play either of the leading roles, but Prince Rainier squelched Princess Grace's eagerness to return to the screen. When Audrey Hepburn [278 . . .] learned of the film, she sought the role played by Bancroft, but the contract had already been signed.

The film did surprisingly well at the box office, confounding studio types who were convinced that a ballet picture would bomb, and that doubtless accounts for its eleven nominations. But on Oscar night it would set a record—later tied by *The Color Purple*—for most nominations without a single win. The best picture award went to *Annie Hall,* for which Diane Keaton also won as best actress, Woody Allen as best director, and Allen and Marshall Brickman for best screenplay. Baryshnikov, who made his acting debut in the film, lost to Jason Robards in *Julia.* Browne, like Baryshnikov, was a dancer who had never acted on screen before, but unlike him she chose not to appear in movies again; she lost to Vanessa Redgrave in *Julia.* The cinematography Oscar went to Vilmos Zsigmond for *Close Encounters of the Third Kind.* The art direction award went to *Star Wars,* which also won for sound and for the editing of Paul Hirsch, Marcia Lucas, and Richard Chew.

Bancroft: 28, 810, 1326, 1634. MacLaine: 91, 1017, 1859, 2020. Surtees: 130, 175, 557, 810, 917, 1094, 1139, 1388, 1469, 1644, 1747, 1911, 1927, 1960, 2055. Brenner: 159, 332, 1976, 2165. March: 12.5, 86, 332, 1976. Soderberg: 724, 983, 1596, 1726, 2126. Wells: 1726. Williams: 1541, 1726, 1824. Reynolds: 643, 784, 896, 1753, 1881, 1927.

2153 • 12 ANGRY MEN

ORION-NOVA PRODUCTION; UNITED ARTISTS. 1957.
NOMINATIONS *Picture:* Henry Fonda and Reginald Rose, producers. *Director:* Sidney Lumet. *Screenplay— Based on Material From Another Medium:* Reginald Rose.

A young Latino (John Savoca) is on trial for murder, and Fonda is the only juror who believes he's innocent. So for the next ninety minutes or so, he battles it out with the others, who are a predictable gallery of character types: the Bigot, the Milquetoast,

the Impatient Businessman, etc. Within its limitations —it began as a TV play and has the talkiness and claustrophobic look of its source, and it's a little too earnest in its liberalism—this is a solid, entertaining drama. And of course it's a showcase for actors: The other jurors are played by Lee J. Cobb [301 . . .], Martin Balsam [2067], Ed Begley [1985], Jack Warden [890 . . .], E. G. Marshall, Jack Klugman, Robert Webber, George Voskovec, John Fielder, Joseph Sweeney, and Edward Binns. The cinematography is by Boris Kaufman [119 . . .].

This was Fonda's sole turn as producer, and it earned him his only nomination in the forty-one years that separated his two acting nominations. Coproducer Rose adapted his own teleplay. The film marked the movie directing debut of Lumet, who was a well-established director of TV dramas. *The Bridge on the River Kwai* won for best picture, director David Lean, and screenwriters Pierre Boulle, Michael Wilson, and Carl Foreman, although the blacklisted Wilson and Foreman were granted their awards posthumously twenty-seven years later.

Fonda: 815, 1473. Lumet: 561, 1424, 1611, 2198.

2154 • TWELVE O'CLOCK HIGH

20TH CENTURY-FOX. 1949.
AWARDS *Supporting Actor:* Dean Jagger. *Sound Recording:* 20th Century-Fox Sound Department, Thomas T. Moulton, sound director.
NOMINATIONS *Picture:* Darryl F. Zanuck, producer. *Actor:* Gregory Peck.

The commander of an American air base in England during World War II has a grim task: sending young fliers off on missions that are near suicidal. When the air corps decides that Gary Merrill is too soft for the job, he's replaced with grim, icy Peck. But eventually the job gets to Peck, too, and he has a nervous breakdown. Fine, tough-minded war drama, just distant enough from the actual events to have a realistic psychological edge that a win-the-war epic would have lacked. It also nicely avoids phony romance with an all-male cast that includes Hugh Marlowe, Millard Mitchell, and Paul Stewart. The screenplay, by Sy Bartlett and Beirne Lay, Jr. [2 . . .], is based on their novel. Directed by Henry King [1868 . . .]. The cinematography, by Leon Shamroy [29 . . .], is supplemented with actual combat footage.

Jagger, who plays a major under Peck's command, made his film debut in 1929 and spent more than half a century on screen, playing countless character roles. His career reached its peak in the fifties, including such films as *My Son John, The Robe, Executive Suite, White Christmas, Bad Day at Black Rock, The Nun's Story,* and *Elmer Gantry.* He died in 1991.

The award for best picture went to *All the King's Men,* for which Broderick Crawford also won as best actor.

Moulton: 22, 46, 138, 366, 457, 487, 560, 706, 798, 962, 1153, 1200, 1451, 1510, 1607, 1849, 2294. Zanuck: 34, 46, 550, 710, 759, 815, 946, 952, 990, 1201, 1327, 1666, 2286. Peck: 759, 1082, 2101, 2320.

2155 • *20,000 LEAGUES UNDER THE SEA*

WALT DISNEY PRODUCTIONS; BUENA VISTA. 1954.

AWARDS *Color Art Direction—Set Decoration:* John Meehan; Emile Kuri. *Special Effects.* (No individual citation.)

NOMINATION *Film Editing:* Elmo Williams.

James Mason [761 . . .] plays Nemo, the captain of the atomic-powered submarine *Nautilus,* in this adaptation of the Jules Verne fantasy. Kirk Douglas [130], Paul Lukas [2233], and Peter Lorre are the unwilling guests of the mad captain. One of the Disney studio's first ventures into full-scale live-action features. It had previously released some British-made costume adventures—*The Story of Robin Hood* (1952), *The Sword and the Rose* (1953), and *Rob Roy, the Highland Rogue* (1954)—but this was a far more ambitious project, using CinemaScope for the first time on a Disney film. It's also one of the most successful of the live Disney features, thanks to first-rate casting and elaborate special effects. Richard Fleischer directs from a screenplay by Earl Felton.

Meehan and Kuri brilliantly imagined what twentieth-century technology would look like if it were invented in the nineteenth-century: The *Nautilus* has filigree ironwork like a Victorian bridge and is furnished like a gentleman's lodgings. The special effects included matte work and miniatures, animation enhancement of the undersea sequences, and a hydraulically operated giant squid. Although the Academy chose not to cite effects technicians by name, among those responsible are cinematographer Franz Planer [380 . . .], underwater cameraman Till Gabbani, effects photographer Ralph Hammeras [520 . . .], matte artist Peter Ellenshaw [166 . . .], mechanical effects specialist Robert Mattey [4], and animators Ub Iwerks [211], John Hench, and Joshua Meador.

The Oscar for film editing went to Gene Milford for *On the Waterfront.*

Meehan: 894, 1975. Kuri: 4, 166, 363, 629, 894, 1284, 1823. Williams: 912.

2156 • *TWICE IN A LIFETIME*

YORKIN COMPANY PRODUCTIONS; BUD YORKIN PRODUCTIONS. 1985.

NOMINATION *Supporting Actress:* Amy Madigan.

Turning fifty, Gene Hackman [255 . . .] realizes he doesn't love his wife, Ellen Burstyn [41 . . .], anymore, but that he does love Ann-Margret [362 . . .]. Madigan and Ally Sheedy are his daughters, who grow confused and angry at this state of affairs. Well-handled and extremely well-cast character drama that unfortunately has nothing new to say on the subject of midlife angst. (When so much effort is spent on so familiar a topic, one suspects that some of the people who made the film are trying to work out their own problems.) Producer Bud Yorkin also directed; the script is by Colin Welland [386].

Madigan, one of the most interesting and gifted younger actresses, has been seen to good advantage in such films as *Places in the Heart* and *Field of Dreams* but has yet to have a breakthrough role that would make her a star. She lost to Anjelica Huston in *Prizzi's Honor.*

2157 • TWILIGHT OF HONOR

PERLBERG-SEATON PRODUCTION; MGM. 1963.
NOMINATIONS *Supporting Actor:* Nick Adams. *Black-and-White Art Direction—Set Decoration:* George W. Davis and Paul Groesse; Henry Grace and Hugh Hunt.

Young lawyer Richard Chamberlain gets help from a more experienced one, Claude Rains [365 . . .], in defending Adams on a murder rap. Okay courtroom stuff, directed by Boris Sagal from a screenplay by Henry Denker. The cast includes Joey Heatherton, James Gregory, and Pat Buttram.

Adams made his screen debut in 1952 and became a regular supporting juvenile in the fifties in such films as *Picnic, Mister Roberts, Rebel Without a Cause, Teacher's Pet,* and *Pillow Talk.* In the sixties, when he entered his thirties, roles became scarcer. He died of an overdose of prescription drugs in 1968. He owes his sole Oscar nomination to an aggressive self-mounted publicity campaign. The Oscar went to Melvyn Douglas for *Hud.* Gene Callahan won for the art direction for *America, America.*

Davis: 46, 69, 401, 495, 542, 736, 953, 1213, 1335, 1388, 1537, 1552, 1706, 1814, 2184, 2312. Groesse: 87, 1173, 1190, 1232, 1309, 1335, 1385, 1604, 2112, 2320. Grace: 69, 227, 401, 769, 953, 1335, 1388, 1450, 1537, 1552, 2184, 2312. Hunt: 175, 401, 980, 1069, 1232, 1335, 1388, 1567, 1644, 1657, 1673, 2184.

2158 • TWIN SISTERS OF KYOTO

SHOCHIKU COMPANY LTD. (JAPAN). 1963.
NOMINATION *Foreign Language Film.*

A young woman raised in a comfortable mercantile household in Kyoto discovers that she has a twin whom her parents abandoned at birth because of an old superstition that twins are bad luck. Eventually she finds her twin living in poverty and has to come to terms with this knowledge. Subtle, provocative tale, directed by Noboru Nakamura, with Shima Iwashita playing both twins. The Oscar went to *8¹/₂.*

2159 • TWO ARABIAN KNIGHTS

THE CADDO COMPANY; UNITED ARTISTS. 1927–28.
AWARD *Comedy Direction:* Lewis Milestone.

Louis Wolheim and William Boyd (later to be famous as Hopalong Cassidy) play Americans escaping from prison in Arabian garb in this silent comedy, produced by Howard Hughes [734 . . .]. A pre-*Frankenstein* Boris Karloff has a small role. Mary Astor [822], an Arabian princess, is the love interest. Milestone was the sole winner of the comedy direction Oscar, which was discontinued after the first year.

Milestone: 48, 734, 1464.

2160 • TWO FOR THE ROAD

STANLEY DONEN FILMS PRODUCTION; 20TH CENTURY-FOX (U.S./UNITED KINGDOM). 1967.
NOMINATION *Story and Screenplay—Written Directly for the Screen:* Frederic Raphael.

Their marriage of twelve years is coming apart, but as Audrey Hepburn [278 . . .] and Albert Finney [579 . . .] drive through France, scenes of their life together—and the spats and infidelities that drove them apart—come back. Sometimes witty, sometimes annoying comedy directed by Stanley Donen. Hepburn and Finney are a phenomenally attractive pair, though their attempts to play their younger selves are unfortunate, and real insights into the characters are sometimes undercut by sitcom glibness. Eleanor Bron and William Daniels play a bickering American couple with a spoiled child, and the cast includes Claude Dauphin and Jacqueline Bisset. The screenplay Oscar went to William Rose for *Guess Who's Coming to Dinner.*

Raphael: 493.

2161 • TWO FOR THE SEESAW

MIRISCH-ARGYLE-TALBOT PRODUCTION IN ASSOCIATION WITH SEVEN ARTS PRODUCTIONS; UNITED ARTISTS. 1962.
NOMINATIONS *Black-and-White Cinematography:* Ted McCord. *Song:* "Song From *Two for the Seesaw* (Second Chance)," music by André Previn, lyrics by Dory Langdon.

Robert Mitchum [1935] is a straitlaced midwestern lawyer on the verge of divorce, and Shirley MacLaine

[91 . . .] is the kooky New Yorker he becomes involved with. Passable "opening up" of a two-character Broadway dramatic comedy by William Gibson [1326], adapted by Isobel Lennart [1216 . . .]. It's spread very thinly over two hours, though. Directed by Robert Wise [407 . . .]. The Broadway version starred Henry Fonda [815 . . .] and Anne Bancroft [28 . . .]. The cinematography Oscar went to Jean Bourgoin and Walter Wottitz for *The Longest Day.* Henry Mancini and Johnny Mercer's title song for *Days of Wine and Roses* won the song Oscar.

McCord: 1052, 1881. Previn: 172, 609, 769, 1017, 1034, 1044, 1097, 1393, 1550, 1592, 2064, 2077. Langdon: 1550, 1926.

2162 • *TWO GIRLS AND A SAILOR*

MGM. 1944.

NOMINATION *Original Screenplay:* Richard Connell and Gladys Lehman.

June Allyson and Gloria DeHaven run a canteen for servicemen. Both fall for sailor Van Johnson. In the course of things, a bunch of people do musical and comedy turns: Jose Iturbi, Jimmy Durante, Lena Horne, Gracie Allen, and the orchestras of Harry James and Xavier Cugat. Likable, unpretentious musical, directed by Richard Thorpe and photographed by Robert Surtees [130 . . .]. The screenplay Oscar went to Lamar Trotti for *Wilson.*

Connell: 1297.

2163 • *TWO MINUTE WARNING*

FILMWAYS/LARRY PEERCE-EDWARD S. FELDMAN FILM PRODUCTION; UNIVERSAL. 1976.

NOMINATION *Film Editing:* Eve Newman and Walter Hannemann.

A sniper starts picking off the crowd at a football game, and Charlton Heston [175] is the cop who tries to catch him. Lame disaster movie, directed by Larry Peerce from a screenplay by Edward Hume. The all-star victims include John Cassavetes [548 . . .], Martin Balsam [2067], Beau Bridges, David Janssen, Jack Klugman, Gena Rowlands [777 . . .], Walter Pidgeon [1232 . . .], and Brock Peters. The editing

Oscar went to Richard Halsey and Scott Conrad for *Rocky.*

Newman: 2281. Hannemann: 1848.

2164 • *2001: A SPACE ODYSSEY*

POLARIS PRODUCTION; MGM (U.S./UNITED KINGDOM). 1968.

AWARD *Special Visual Effects:* Stanley Kubrick.

NOMINATIONS *Director:* Stanley Kubrick. *Story and Screenplay—Written Directly for the Screen:* Stanley Kubrick and Arthur C. Clarke. *Art Direction—Set Decoration:* Tony Masters, Harry Lange, and Ernie Archer.

A mysterious black monolith that seems to have some connection with humankind's evolutionary leaps makes an appearance to prehistoric ape-men, who then develop the power to use tools (and weapons). Millennia later it appears to an astronaut (Keir Dullea) who undergoes an enigmatic transformation. But any attempt to paraphrase *2001* is doomed to failure. It is what it is: a sometimes dazzling, sometimes boring, epoch-making sci-fi adventure, with touches of wit, satire, and even poetry. It tantalized and infuriated contemporary critics, some of whom complained that the computer HAL was the only fully drawn character in it. The movie's defenders retorted that that was precisely the point. Others suspected that the film's success was generated by the drugs that many in its audience were known to be taking. But like *Bonnie and Clyde, The Graduate,* and *Easy Rider, 2001* was one of the essential movies of the late sixties, sending the medium off into new directions as Hollywood woke up to the fact that audiences were prepared to treat movies as cultural phenomena, not just as an evening's diversion. It also sent Richard Strauss' tone poem "Also Sprach Zarathustra" to the top of the pop charts. The cinematography is by Geoffrey Unsworth [164 . . .] and John Alcott [151].

After such films as *Lolita* and *Dr. Strangelove,* it was no surprise that Kubrick should produce a quirky, original, and influential work, but many find it baffling that his sole Oscar is for special effects and not for writing or directing—particularly many of the special effects technicians, such as Douglas Trumbull

[228 . . .], who executed the effects that Kubrick wanted. A former photographer, Kubrick had made some low-budget self-produced films before breaking into Hollywood with *The Killing* (1956) and *Paths of Glory* (1957), both of which he wrote and directed. The participation of Kirk Douglas on the latter film led to Kubrick's hiring for *Spartacus*. In the quarter century since *2001,* Kubrick has made only four features, but each has generated intense critical debate: *A Clockwork Orange, Barry Lyndon, The Shining* (1980), and *Full Metal Jacket.*

Critics of the Academy were quick to point out that *2001* was far more interesting than any of the films nominated for best picture: *Funny Girl, The Lion in Winter, Rachel, Rachel, Romeo and Juliet,* and the winner, *Oliver!* Kubrick lost the directing Oscar to Carol Reed for *Oliver!,* which also won for art direction. The screenplay award went to Mel Brooks for *The Producers.*

Kubrick: 151, 415, 574, 735. Lange: 614. Archer: 1429.

2165 • 2010

METRO-GOLDWYN-MAYER PRESENTATION OF A PETER HYAMS FILM PRODUCTION; MGM/UNITED ARTISTS. 1984.

NOMINATIONS *Art Direction—Set Decoration:* Albert Brenner; Rick Simpson. *Sound:* Michael J. Kohut, Aaron Rochin, Carlos De Larios, and Gene S. Cantamessa. *Costume Design:* Patricia Norris. *Makeup:* Michael Westmore. *Visual Effects:* Richard Edlund, Neil Krepela, George Jenson, and Mark Stetson.

An American and Soviet (!) joint mission sets out to discover what happened to the *Discovery,* the spacecraft whose mission was stymied by the computer HAL in *2001: A Space Odyssey.* They encounter the aged Keir Dullea as well as the black monolith. Well-produced sequel, with some impressive special effects and some fine performers: Roy Scheider [49 . . .], John Lithgow [2020 . . .], and Helen Mirren [1234.5]. But the script by director Peter Hyams makes the mistake of getting too literal—the enigmatic quality of the first film was its greatest strength. Where *2001* was playful, *2010* is just pretentious. Fans of the original were derisive, and those who

weren't fans didn't much care to check this one out, so it was an expensive box-office flop, wrecking the studio's hopes of becoming a major force in the industry again.

Oscars went to *Amadeus* for art direction, sound, Theodor Pistek's costumes, and Paul LeBlanc and Dick Smith's makeup. *Indiana Jones and the Temple of Doom* took the visual effects award.

Brenner: 159, 332, 1976, 2152. Simpson: 543. Kohut: 641, 1310, 1548, 1711, 2124, 2231. Rochin: 521, 641, 1089, 1310, 1711, 2124, 2231, 2287. De Larios: 1711, 2124, 2231. Cantamessa: 339, 416, 588, 1439, 1914, 2331. Norris: 506, 608, 1974, 2201. Westmore: 409, 1287. Edlund: 45.5, 544, 614, 766, 1589, 1590, 1652, 1684, 1916. Krepela: 413.5.

2166 • TWO TICKETS TO BROADWAY

RKO RADIO. 1951.

NOMINATION *Sound Recording:* John O. Aalberg.

Janet Leigh [1632], Gloria DeHaven, Eddie Bracken, and Tony Martin conspire to get on Bob Crosby's TV show. Lightweight musical, directed by James V. Kern, with enough good music to let you overlook the tediousness of the plot. The sound award went to Douglas Shearer for *The Great Caruso.*

Aalberg: 407, 923, 959, 1033, 1102, 1978, 1991, 2030, 2213.

2167 • TWO WOMEN

CHAMPION-LES FILMS MARCEAU-COCINOR AND SOCIÉTÉ GÉNÉRALE DE CINÉMATOGRAPHIE PRODUCTION; EMBASSY PICTURES CORPORATION (ITALY/FRANCE). 1961.

AWARD *Actress:* Sophia Loren.

Loren and her daughter (Eleanora Brown) flee the bombing of Rome in 1943 and return to their village, where schoolteacher Jean-Paul Belmondo falls in love with Loren, to the dismay of Brown, who loves him. He is forced to guide the retreating Nazis, and Loren and Brown are brutally raped by Moroccan soldiers. The traumatized young woman lashes out at her mother, but they are reconciled when they learn of Belmondo's death. Grim but sometimes touching drama, adapted by Cesare Zavattini [194 . . .] from a novel by Alberto Moravia. Directed by Vittorio De Sica [650].

Loren became the first person to win an acting Oscar for a foreign language role. Born in poverty in Naples, she was pushed by her ambitious mother into beauty contests and modeling jobs that eventually led to her discovery by producer Carlo Ponti [558], whom she would later marry. After numerous Italian films, she came to Hollywood in the late fifties, but except for a few films, such as the comedy *Houseboat,* she was often miscast or exploited for her physical endowments. *Two Women* demonstrated her considerable range as an actress, but she is best known for her work as a comedian, particularly in her films with Marcello Mastroianni, such as *Yesterday, Today and Tomorrow* and *Marriage Italian Style.* She received an honorary award from the Academy at the 1990 awards ceremony as "one of the genuine treasures of world cinema who, in a career rich with memorable performances, has added permanent luster to our art form."

Loren: 1280.

2168 • TYPHOON

PARAMOUNT. 1940.

NOMINATION *Special Effects:* Farciot Edouart and Gordon Jennings, photographic; Loren Ryder, sound.

Sailors Robert Preston [2201] and Lynne Overman discover castaway Dorothy Lamour on a South Sea island. Flimsy but amusing attempt to capitalize on the success of *Hurricane,* which had made Lamour (in her sarong) a star. Louis King directs a cast that includes J. Carrol Naish [1294 . . .] and Jack Carson. The award for special effects went to *The Thief of Bagdad.*

Edouart: 56, 570, 975, 1668, 1855, 1887, 1934, 2175, 2181. Jennings: 56, 570, 975, 1668, 1855, 1887, 1934, 2175, 2181. Ryder: 566, 827, 979, 1452, 1669, 1697, 1703, 1837, 1887, 2012, 2181, 2183, 2230, 2242.

2169 • UGETSU

DAIEI MOTION PICTURE COMPANY; EDWARD HARRISON (JAPAN). 1955.

NOMINATION *Black-and-White Costume Design:* Tadaoto Kainoscho.

A potter (Masayuki Mori) in sixteenth-century Japan travels from his village to Kyoto, where he is seduced by a ghostly woman (Machiko Kyo) into a life of luxury and wealth. Escaping, he returns to his village to find that his wife has died and become a ghost, too. Meanwhile, the potter's neighbor also leaves the village, seeking military glory as a samurai; achieving that by dubious means, he finds his wife has become a prostitute. Extraordinarily beautiful, extraordinarily disturbing film, widely regarded as one of the classics of Japanese cinema. Directed by Kenji Mizoguchi. The cinematography is by Kazuo Miyagawa. The costuming Oscar went to Helen Rose for *I'll Cry Tomorrow.*

2170 • ULYSSES

WALTER READE, JR.-JOSEPH STRICK PRODUCTION; WALTER READE-CONTINENTAL DISTRIBUTING (U.S./UNITED KINGDOM). 1967.

NOMINATION *Screenplay—Based on Material From Another Medium:* Joseph Strick and Fred Haines.

Dubliner Leopold Bloom (Milo O'Shea), whose wife, Molly (Barbara Jefford), is unfaithful to him, wanders through the streets of the city one June day. Meanwhile, young Stephen Dedalus (Maurice Roëves), a penniless poet, is also roaming the streets. The two meet that night in a whorehouse, where Stephen has grown very drunk and obstreperous, and Bloom helps the young man sober up before setting him on his way. This synopsis of James Joyce's great lyrical puzzle of a novel is only slightly less sketchy than the film that producer-writer-director Strick made of it. The movie is an ambitious but low-budget botch, slightly redeemed by some good performers reading some of the most wonderful prose written in this century. Lovers of the book will enjoy the words even as they're wincing at the inadequate images: Unable to re-create the Dublin of June 16, 1904, the novel's "Bloomsday," Strick gave it a contemporary setting. The language in the film, as well as the book's notorious history as the subject of a landmark censorship case, led the producers to give it a limited release at inflated prices—a then-unheard-of five dollars per ticket—designed both to certify its status as an event and to make it too expensive for the prurient and the young to see. Strick subsequently undertook the filming of another scandalous novel, Henry Miller's *Tropic of Cancer* (1970), with somewhat more success, and his 1979 film of Joyce's *Portrait of the Artist as a Young Man* is a respectable attempt. *Ulysses* might make an interesting miniseries if one had an unlimited budget, but this two-hour twenty-minute condensation is hardly even worthy of *Cliff's Notes*. The screenplay Oscar went to Stirling Silliphant for *In the Heat of the Night*.

2171 • UMBERTO D

Rizzoli-De Sica-Amato Production; Harrison & Davidson (Italy). 1956.

Nomination *Motion Picture Story:* Cesare Zavattini.

A lonely but proud old man faces abject poverty, with only his dog as companion and consolation. Enormously moving neorealist classic, directed by Vittorio De Sica [650]. Frequently mentioned on lists of the all-time great films, it elicits tears without resorting to melodramatic sentimentality. The Oscar went to Dalton Trumbo (under his blacklist pseudonym Robert Rich) for *The Brave One*.

Zavattini: 194, 1815.

2172 • UMBRELLAS OF CHERBOURG, THE

Parc-Madeleine-Beta Films; American International Pictures (France). 1965.

Nominations *Story and Screenplay—Written Directly for the Screen:* Jacques Demy. *Song:* "I Will Wait for You," music by Michel Legrand, lyrics by Jacques Demy and Norman Gimbel. *Music Score—Substantially Original:* Michel Legrand and Jacques Demy. *Scoring of Music—Adaptation or Treatment:* Michel Legrand. *Foreign Language Film.* (1964)

Catherine Deneuve [998.5] and Nino Castelnuovo play young lovers who are separated when he is called up for military service. Deneuve, who is pregnant, agrees to marry someone else. The former lovers have a bittersweet meeting years later. Demy, who also directed, was a passionate admirer of the Hollywood musical, but this is very, very French, and very much a matter of taste: Friendships have been wrecked by arguments over this movie. Those who love it relish the sheer romantic folly of the whole thing: It's entirely sung—there's no dialogue—and it's designed in a rainbow of hues, featuring the prettiest gas station ever shown on screen. Even those who hate the movie agree that Deneuve is breathtakingly lovely. As the unusual number of nominations for a foreign language film shows, it had fans among the Academy members, but the Oscars went to Frederic Raphael for the screenplay for *Darling,* to Johnny Mandel and Paul Francis Webster for "The Shadow of Your Smile," from *The Sandpiper,* to Maurice Jarre for the original score for *Doctor Zhivago,* to Irwin Kostal for the adaptation score for *The Sound of Music,* and to *Yesterday, Today and Tomorrow* for best foreign language film. (As sometimes happens, the movie qualified for the foreign language award a year before it met eligibility requirements for the other competitive categories.)

Demy: 2332. Legrand: 179, 867, 1568, 1960, 2063, 2321, 2332. Gimbel: 711, 1448, 1508.

2173 • UNBEARABLE LIGHTNESS OF BEING, THE

Saul Zaentz Company Production; Orion. 1988.

Nominations *Screenplay Based on Material From Another Medium:* Jean-Claude Carrière and Philip Kaufman. *Cinematography:* Sven Nykvist.

Daniel Day-Lewis [992.5 . . .] plays Tomas, a womanizing young Czech physician who has a casually uncomplicated relationship with Sabina, an artist played by Lena Olin [617]. On a trip to the country, he meets and sleeps with Tereza (Juliette Binoche), a young woman who follows him back to Prague and moves in with him. When the Soviets invade Prague in 1968, Tomas and Tereza go to Geneva, where they meet Sabina. Tomas begins sleeping with Sabina again, to Tereza's dismay. Eventually, however, it becomes clear that Tomas and Tereza truly love one another. And just as Tomas can't avoid love, he also can't avoid politics when he and Tereza return to Czechoslovakia. A rich, brilliant, absorbing movie with a trio of exceptional performances. The film's failure to attain more nominations is something of a puzzle, although late-eighties Hollywood had grown nervous about films about sexuality, and *The Unbearable Lightness* is unquestionably erotic—in an honest and adult fashion. Certainly the film merited a best picture nomination more than such nominees as the ploddingly literal *The Accidental Tourist,* the politically muddled *Mississippi Burning,* or the uneven comedy *Working Girl.* And Philip Kaufman's direction is more impressive than that of Charles Crichton, who may have only assisted John Cleese in directing *A Fish Called Wanda* but received a nomination anyway. In the categories in which *Unbearable Lightness* did receive nominations, the Oscars went to Christopher Hampton for the screenplay for *Dangerous Liaisons* and Peter Biziou for the cinematography for *Mississippi Burning.*

Carrière: 549, 2034. Nykvist: 460, 644.

2174 • UNCHAINED

HALL BARTLETT PRODUCTIONS; WARNER BROS. 1955.
NOMINATION *Song:* ''Unchained Melody,'' music by Alex North, lyrics by Hy Zaret.

A low-budget prison drama designed in part to try to make a star of football player Elroy ''Crazylegs'' Hirsch. It didn't. The movie, written and directed by Hall Bartlett, also features Chester Morris [38], Barbara Hale, and Jerry Paris. *Unchained* would be long forgotten if it weren't for the hugely popular song—a perennial that has been recorded by Roy Hamilton, Al Hibbler, the Righteous Brothers, and others, and became a hit again in 1990 when it was used in a Patrick Swayze–Demi Moore makeout scene in *Ghost.* The Oscar went to Sammy Fain and Paul Francis Webster for the title song from *Love Is a Many-Splendored Thing.*

North: 29, 215, 413, 515, 577, 1654, 1727, 1802, 1814, 1886, 1949, 2177, 2212, 2277.

2175 • UNCONQUERED

PARAMOUNT. 1947.
NOMINATION *Special Effects:* Farciot Edouart, Devereux Jennings, Gordon Jennings, Wallace Kelley, and Paul Lerpae, visual; George Dutton, audible.

Paulette Goddard [1855] gets transported to the colonies where she hooks up with Gary Cooper [701 . . .] and fights off Indians in pre-Revolutionary Virginia. Boris Karloff plays an Indian chief, and even George Washington (Richard Gaines) shows up for a while. Like most films directed by Cecil B. DeMille [412 . . .], it's a hoot. The cast also includes Howard da Silva, Cecil Kellaway [843 . . .], Ward Bond, Katherine DeMille, Henry Wilcoxon, C. Aubrey Smith, Porter Hall, Mike Mazurki, Chief Thundercloud, and lots of others. The Technicolor cinematography of Ray Rennahan [235 . . .] makes it look a lot better than it is. The special effects Oscar went to *Green Dolphin Street.*

Edouart: 56, 570, 975, 1668, 1855, 1887, 1934, 2168, 2181. D. Jennings: 1887. G. Jennings: 56, 570, 975, 1668, 1855, 1887, 1934, 2168, 2181. Dutton: 847, 1855, 1934, 2200.

2176 • UNDER FIRE

LIONS GATE FILMS PRODUCTION; ORION. 1983.
NOMINATION *Original Score:* Jerry Goldsmith.

A trio of journalists—photographer Nick Nolte [1612], radio reporter Joanna Cassidy, and war correspondent Gene Hackman [255 . . .]—cover the fall of Somoza in Nicaragua in 1979 and gradually get caught up in the conflict. Superb political thriller with a strong whiff of actuality, greatly helped by the performances of the leads, plus Ed Harris as a chilling mercenary, Jean-Louis Trintignant as a French agent of the CIA, René Enriquez as Somoza, and Richard Masur as an oily American flack for the Somoza regime. Roger Spottiswoode directed from a screenplay by Ron Shelton [310] and Clayton Frohman. The cinematography by John Alcott [151] is also exceptional. The failure of the film to net more nominations may have to do with its poor showing at the box office. Surely it couldn't have anything to do with squeamishness about offending the Reagan administration, which was deeply involved in its own meddling in Nicaragua, now could it? Goldsmith's haunting score lost to Bill Conti's work on *The Right Stuff*.

Goldsmith: 152.5, 268, 395, 727, 939, 1472, 1527, 1537, 1541, 1583, 1589, 1753, 1913, 2287.

2176.5 • *UNDER SIEGE*

NORTHWEST PRODUCTION; WARNER BROS. 1992.

NOMINATIONS *Sound:* Don Mitchell, Frank A. Montaño, Rick Hart, Scott Smith. *Sound Effects Editing:* John Leveque, Bruce Stambler.

A gang masterminded by disaffected CIA op Tommy Lee Jones [734.5 . . .] and bitter navy officer Gary Busey [307] takes over the USS *Missouri*, intending to off-load its nuclear missiles and sell them to the highest bidder. But they didn't count on Steven Seagal being on board—he's the ship's cook, though he's actually a weapons specialist who got in trouble and was allowed to serve out his term because the skipper of the *Missouri* (Patrick O'Neal) is his buddy. Though the hijackers have killed the captain and locked up the crew, Seagal manages to get loose, round up a team that includes a *Playboy* centerfold (Erika Eleniak) who was brought on board by the bad guys as part of their cover, and save the day. Witty action adventure, smashingly directed by Andrew Davis, who would make his name the following year with *The Fugitive*. As in that film, one of the best things about *Under Siege* is Jones, playing a hilarious wacko who's also a real cold-blooded menace. Busey is also terrific as the short-fused commander. Unfortunately *Under Siege* stars Seagal, who has never been better but is still an exceptionally unappealing hero: His facial expressions run the gamut from frown to scowl. The screenplay is by J. F. Lawton. The sound Oscar went to *The Last of the Mohicans*. The award for sound effects editing was won by Tom C. McCarthy and David E. Stone for *Bram Stoker's Dracula*.

Mitchell: 223, 398, 411.5, 507, 734.5, 779, 1525, 1650, 1824, 1825, 2020, 2114. Montaño: 411.5, 734.5. Smith: 734.5. Leveque: 411.5, 734.5. Stambler: 411.5, 734.5.

2177 • *UNDER THE VOLCANO*

ITHACA ENTERPRISES PRODUCTION; UNIVERSAL. 1984.

NOMINATIONS *Actor:* Albert Finney. *Original Score:* Alex North.

Finney plays an alcoholic former British consul living, or rather dying, in Cuernavaca—which is near the volcano Popocatepetl. He's visited there by his ex-wife (Jacqueline Bisset) and his half brother (Anthony Andrews), who have had an affair. Wearying study of a self-destructive personality with little other than Finney's performance and some atmospheric cinematography by Gabriel Figueroa [1432] to sustain it. John Huston [24 . . .] directs this adaptation by Guy Gallo of the novel by Malcolm Lowry. Finney lost to F. Murray Abraham in *Amadeus*. The scoring award went to Maurice Jarre for *A Passage to India*.

Finney: 579, 1378, 2106. North: 29, 215, 413, 515, 577, 1654, 1727, 1802, 1814, 1886, 1949, 2174, 2212, 2277.

2178 • *UNDER WESTERN STARS*

REPUBLIC. 1938.

NOMINATION *Song:* "Dust," music and lyrics by Johnny Marvin.

Roy Rogers gets elected to Congress, where he fights for water for his drought-stricken district, as well as, this being the New Deal/TVA era, public ownership of utilities. He also gets to sing. Rogers' first starring role was directed by Joe Kane, who went on to do an endless series of Rogers programmers. The Oscar went to Ralph Rainger and Leo Robin for "Thanks for the Memory," from *The Big Broadcast of 1938*.

2179 • *UNDERWORLD*

PARAMOUNT FAMOUS LASKY. 1927–28.

AWARD *Original Story:* Ben Hecht.

George Bancroft [2085] plays the gangster Bull Weed, who befriends an alcoholic, disbarred lawyer, played by Clive Brook, whom Bull nicknames Rolls Royce. Unfortunately, Rolls falls in love with Bull's girlfriend, Feathers (Evelyn Brent). The jealous Bull murders a man who flirts with Feathers, and is arrested and sentenced to death. Bull breaks out, determined to take revenge on Rolls and Feathers, whose love he has become aware of. But in a climactic shootout with the cops, Bull learns that Rolls and Feathers had actually tried to free him from jail themselves. When Rolls is killed by the cops, Bull surrenders himself. Very influential silent film, directed by Josef von Sternberg [1358 . . .], that made a star of Bancroft, launched the thirties vogue for gangster movies, and helped establish Hecht's phenomenal career, winning him the first Oscar ever given for an original screenplay.

Hecht began his writing career while in his teens as a Chicago newspaperman; a heavily fictionalized version of his experiences forms the plot of the 1969 movie *Gaily, Gaily.* In 1925 he began his screenwriting career at the suggestion of Herman Mankiewicz [407 . . .], who supposedly summoned Hecht to Hollywood with a telegram saying, "Millions are to be grabbed out here and your only competition is idiots." Hecht became one of the most enormously prolific and sought-after screenwriters, frequently called on by producers such as David O. Selznick [497 . . .] and Samuel Goldwyn [102 . . .] not only for original screenplays but also for script doctoring. Over the course of nearly forty years writing for the movies, Hecht received credits on an estimated seventy films, and may have contributed dialogue to and/or rewritten nearly that many more without receiving screen credit.

Hecht: 78, 1455, 1765, 2211, 2316.

2179.5 • *UNFORGIVEN*

WARNER BROS. PRODUCTION; WARNER BROS. 1992.

AWARDS *Picture:* Clint Eastwood, producer. *Supporting Actor:* Gene Hackman. *Director:* Clint Eastwood. *Film Editing:* Joel Cox.

NOMINATIONS *Actor:* Clint Eastwood. *Original Screenplay:* David Webb Peoples. *Art Direction–Set Decoration:* Henry Bumstead; Janice Blackie-Goodine. *Cinematography:* Jack N. Green. *Sound:* Les Fresholtz, Vern Poore, Dick Alexander, Rob Young.

When a prostitute is mutilated by a brutal cowboy, other prostitutes pool their money and put a bounty on the attacker and the other cowboys who let him get away with it. William Munny (Eastwood), an impoverished former gunfighter, now a widower struggling to raise two children on a farm, hears about the reward from a kid (Jaimz Woolvett) who wants to prove he's a gunfighter. Munny collects an old partner, Ned Logan, played by Morgan Freeman [580 . . .], and the three set off for the town where the attack took place. There they encounter another gunfighter, English Bob, played by Richard Harris [660 . . .], who's also after the reward. But the sheriff of the town, Little Billy Daggett (Hackman), who let the cowboys get off light in the first place, isn't happy about all this action. In the ensuing bloody showdown, Munny demonstrates why he gave up the killing game. Strongly written, tautly directed, finely acted western, with a solid antiviolence message— although, like the year's other important antiviolence film, *Boyz N the Hood, Unforgiven* has to resort to a conventionally cathartic scene of revenge against the bad guys to make its point that revenge is never very sweet. *Unforgiven* is only the third western to receive the best picture Oscar, after *Cimarron* and *Dances With Wolves.*

As a huge critical and commercial success, *Unforgiven* had a solid lead over its competitors—*The Crying Game, A Few Good Men, Howards End,* and *Scent of a Woman*—but it was also a sentimental favorite: Its producer-director-actor, Eastwood, was an old-style Hollywood legend. He was also a man who had amply paid his dues: He began as a Universal contract bit player in a *Francis the Talking Mule* movie in 1955 but failed to advance in his career until he moved over to TV and played Rowdy Yates in the early-sixties series *Rawhide.* Film stardom came from a series of low-budget "spaghetti westerns," filmed in Spain by director Sergio Leone with a polyglot cast. In *A Fistful of Dollars* (1964), *For a Few Dollars More* (1965), and *The Good, the Bad, and the Ugly* (1966), Eastwood played a taciturn "man with no name" gunfighter. Crude but stylish, the movies were a big hit around the world, and Eastwood came back to Hollywood an unexpected star. He didn't become a superstar, however, until 1971 and *Dirty Harry,* an ultraviolent movie about a vigilante cop. The same year, Eastwood also made his debut as a director with *Play Misty for Me,* a well-done thriller that has been likened to the later, slicker *Fatal Attraction.* Even at this new peak of success, however, Eastwood seemed no more likely to win an Oscar than, say, Steven Seagal does today. But hard work and genuine talent will out: Eastwood's Malpaso has been one of the most consistently successful production companies ever founded by an actor, and it has not only allowed him to grow as both actor and director but also earned him the Irving G. Thalberg Award at the 1994 ceremonies. Many of Eastwood's films have been unpleasantly violent—especially the *Dirty Harry* sequels *Magnum Force* (1973) and *Sudden Impact* (1983)—but he has also made some gentler, more reflective films, such as *Bronco Billy* (1980), *Honkytonk Man* (1982), and *Bird. Unforgiven* revealed a man who had perhaps matured late—in his early sixties—as an actor and director, but it was an impressive maturity. And in the year following his Oscar win, Eastwood went from strength to strength, giving perhaps his best performance as the haunted Secret Service agent in *In the Line of Fire* and directing one of his richest films—an unaccountable box-office disappointment, except that it appeared at the end of a year of exceptional movies—*A Perfect World.*

Hackman's win was also greeted with universal approval. In the twenty-one years since his first Oscar, for *The French Connection,* Hackman had been one of the hardest-working actors in Hollywood, often making three or four films a year, when stars of his caliber usually make only one. Not handsome enough for conventional leading roles, Hackman has often taken character parts. His range is wide, from men of action in movies such as *Mississippi Burning* to goofy comic relief in the *Superman* series.

Like many of the other behind-the-scenes nominees, including cinematographer Green, Cox has worked for Eastwood on numerous films over the years.

The best actor Oscar went to Al Pacino for *Scent of a Woman.* Neil Jordan won for the screenplay for *The Crying Game.* Luciana Arrighi and Ian Whittaker took the art direction Oscar for *Howards End.* The award for cinematography went to Philippe Rousselot for *A River Runs Through It. The Last of the Mohicans* won for sound.

Hackman: 255, 724, 971, 1333. Bumstead: 1927, 2102, 2200. Fresholtz: 54, 58, 209, 215, 606, 888, 1127, 1158.5, 1279, 1526, 2113. Poore: 209, 888, 1127, 1158.5. Alexander: 54, 209, 519, 888, 1127, 1158.5, 2113.

2180 • UNINVITED, THE
PARAMOUNT. 1944.

NOMINATION *Black-and-White Cinematography:* Charles Lang.

Brother and sister Ray Milland [1208] and Ruth Hussey [1563] find that the old house they've bought is haunted. One of the ghosts, in fact, is the mother of Gail Russell, with whom Milland is in love. Very effective ghost story, directed by Lewis Allen from a screenplay by Dodie Smith. It helps that Milland and Hussey are sane and skeptical types. The cast includes Donald Crisp [952] and Cornelia Otis Skinner. The cinematography Oscar went to Joseph LaShelle for *Laura.*

Lang: 97, 250, 319, 636, 649, 705, 765, 953, 1480, 1640, 1699, 1738, 1778, 1855, 1860, 1955, 1968.

2181 • UNION PACIFIC
PARAMOUNT. 1939.

NOMINATION *Special Effects:* Farciot Edouart and Gordon Jennings, photographic; Loren Ryder, sound.

Joel McCrea builds the transcontinental railroad while romancing spunky Irishwoman Barbara Stanwyck [138 . . .] and fighting off bad guys Brian Donlevy [161] and Robert Preston [2201]. Director Cecil B. DeMille [412 . . .] rewrites American history again, but it's a lot of fun, thanks to the stars, plus Akim Tamiroff [701 . . .], Lynne Overman, Anthony Quinn [1226 . . .], Evelyn Keyes, Regis Toomey, Fuzzy Knight, and Lon Chaney, Jr., and lots of epic action stuff. The special effects award went to Fred Sersen and E. H. Hansen for *The Rains Came.*

Edouart: 56, 570, 975, 1668, 1855, 1887, 1934, 2168, 2175. Jennings: 56, 570, 975, 1668, 1855, 1887, 1934, 2168, 2175. Ryder: 566, 827, 979,

1452, 1669, 1697, 1703, 1837, 1887, 2012, 2168, 2183, 2230, 2242.

2182 • UNMARRIED WOMAN, AN

20TH CENTURY-FOX PRODUCTION; 20TH CENTURY-FOX. 1978.
NOMINATIONS *Picture:* Paul Mazursky and Tony Ray, producers. *Actress:* Jill Clayburgh. *Screenplay Written Directly for the Screen:* Paul Mazursky.

Clayburgh plays Erica, who has a good job in a Manhattan art gallery and, she thinks, a solid marriage to a broker played by Michael Murphy. Then one day her husband breaks out in tears and tells her that he's fallen in love with a woman he met while shopping at Bloomingdale's. Stunned, Erica walks away, then stops at a street corner and throws up. She spends the rest of the movie trying to put her life back together again, first as an unattached woman, then as a player of the dating game, and then in a blissfully volatile relationship with an artist played by Alan Bates [678]. Witty, sharply observed, with the right blend of poignancy and satire, and a good deal of very lifelike surprises in the performances. Lisa Lucas plays Erica's capable, intelligent, but confused teenage daughter; Cliff Gorman is the slimeball sex machine Erica turns to for physical gratification; and Penelope Russianoff is Erica's therapist. (Russianoff, a real-life shrink, did her profession no favor with the glib compassion her character exhibits and got roundly denounced by other therapists for her work in the movie.) Also in the cast are Pat Quinn, Kelly Bishop, and future *L.A. Law*-yers Michael Tucker and Jill Eikenberry. Mazursky was the only director of a best picture nominee this year not to get a directing nomination; his slot went to Woody Allen for *Interiors.*

The best picture Oscar went to *The Deer Hunter.* Clayburgh lost to Jane Fonda in *Coming Home,* which also won in the writing category for Nancy Dowd's story and Waldo Salt and Robert C. Jones' screenplay.

Mazursky: 250, 617, 875. Clayburgh: 1919.

2183 • UNSEEN, THE

PARAMOUNT. 1945.
NOMINATION *Sound Recording:* Loren L. Ryder.

Governess Gail Russell is spooked by mysterious goings-on in the old dark house next door, and suspects her employer, Joel McCrea, of murder. Dud attempt to recapture the success of *The Uninvited,* which also starred Russell and like this one was directed by Lewis Allen. The screenplay is by Hagar Wilde and Raymond Chandler [242 . . .], but Chandler was better at writing intricate plots with inconclusive endings than at crafting conventional thrillers, which this most definitely is. The cast also includes Herbert Marshall and Norman Lloyd. The award for sound went to Stephen Dunn for *The Bells of St. Mary's.*

Ryder: 566, 827, 979, 1452, 1669, 1697, 1703, 1837, 1887, 2012, 2168, 2181, 2230, 2242.

2184 • UNSINKABLE MOLLY BROWN, THE

MARTEN PRODUCTION; MGM. 1964.
NOMINATIONS *Actress:* Debbie Reynolds. *Color Cinematography:* Daniel L. Fapp. *Color Art Direction—Set Decoration:* George W. Davis and Preston Ames; Henry Grace and Hugh Hunt. *Sound:* Franklin E. Milton, sound director, MGM Studio Sound Department. *Scoring of Music—Adaptation or Treatment:* Robert Armbruster, Leo Arnaud, Jack Elliott, Jack Hayes, Calvin Jackson, and Leo Shuken. *Color Costume Design:* Morton Haack.

Molly (Reynolds) and her miner husband, Johnny (Harve Presnell), strike it rich, so Molly gets her dream, a big, fine house in Denver. When the nouveau riche Browns are snubbed by Denver society, Molly is crushed, but she and Johnny head off to Europe to acquire a veneer of culture. It doesn't take on Johnny, who returns to America and the simpler life, but Molly becomes a big hit in Europe because of her unaffected candor. She not only makes a smash in Denver by presenting an array of European aristocrats to the town's thunderstruck snobs, she also becomes a hero during the sinking of the *Titanic.* But she still has to win Johnny back. This version of the Meredith

Willson [818 . . .] Broadway musical is a bit too eager to please, and Reynolds works so hard it's sometimes exhausting to watch. But the big, bright tunes, including "He's My Friend," "Belly Up to the Bar, Boys," and "I Ain't Down Yet," are enjoyable, and there's some amusing support from Ed Begley [1985], Jack Kruschen [91], Hermione Baddeley [1724], Harvey Lembeck, Martita Hunt, and Audrey Christie, among others. Directed by Charles Walters [1173] from a screenplay by Helen Deutsch [1173] based on Richard Morris' book for the musical.

Reynolds got her start in the movies by winning a California beauty contest, which brought her to the attention of the studios. In 1950 she signed with MGM, and after a few small roles landed a starring part in *Singin' in the Rain*. She was a popular ingenue in both musical and nonmusical films of the fifties but was perhaps more famous for her storybook marriage to singer Eddie Fisher and its scandalous end, when Fisher left her for Elizabeth Taylor [318 . . .]. Reynolds continued her film career through most of the sixties, but as it waned in the seventies, she turned to theater and nightclub appearances. Her daughter, Carrie Fisher, is an actress, screenwriter, and novelist who has written several thinly veiled portraits of Reynolds into her books, most notably in *Postcards From the Edge*. This was Reynolds' sole Oscar nomination, and it was something of a shocker: Most people had expected Audrey Hepburn to be nominated instead for her work in *My Fair Lady*. Reynolds lost to Julie Andrews for *Mary Poppins*.

My Fair Lady got its own back by winning in all the other categories for which *Molly Brown* was nominated: Oscars went to Harry Stradling for cinematography, to Gene Allen, Cecil Beaton, and George James Hopkins for art direction–set decoration, to George R. Groves for sound, to André Previn for scoring, and to Beaton for costumes.

Fapp: 529, 675, 978, 1279, 1492, 2244. Davis: 46, 69, 401, 495, 542, 736, 953, 1213, 1335, 1388, 1537, 1552, 1706, 1814, 2157, 2312. Ames: 31, 66, 290, 591, 769, 1226, 1937. Grace: 69, 227, 401, 769, 953, 1335, 1388, 1450, 1537, 1552, 2157, 2312. Hunt: 175, 401, 980, 1069, 1232, 1335, 1388, 1567, 1644, 1657, 1673, 2157. Milton: 175, 401, 558, 814, 953. Hayes: 423. Shuken: 1901. Haack: 1583, 2252.

2185 • UNTOUCHABLES, THE

Art Linson Production; Paramount. 1987.
Award *Supporting Actor:* Sean Connery.
Nominations *Art Direction–Set Decoration:* Patrizia Von Brandenstein and William A. Elliott; Hal Gausman. *Original Score:* Ennio Morricone. *Costume Design:* Marilyn Vance-Straker.

G-man Eliot Ness, played by Kevin Costner [482], and mob boss Al Capone, played by Robert De Niro [113 . . .], battle it out in thirties Chicago. Well-cast period gangster movie that provides uncomplicated old-fashioned entertainment, but annoyed some critics who found it an indulgence in style for style's sake—particularly the climactic train-station shootout which is, depending on your admiration for director Brian DePalma, either an *hommage* to or a rip-off of the Odessa Steps sequence from Eisenstein's *Potemkin*. Because he's surrounded by showy performances from De Niro and Connery and colorful support from Charles Martin Smith and Andy Garcia [786], Costner does well to underplay his part, suggesting that Ness is the strong silent type. The screenplay is by David Mamet [2198] and the cinematography by Stephen H. Burum [924.5].

Connery plays a tough, honest Chicago cop who takes the greenhorn Ness under his wing and shows him how to play the roughhouse game of Chicago municipal politics. When his character is killed off, the movie loses some of its soul. Few acting Oscars have been more richly deserved than Connery's. The Scottish-born actor was discovered doing TV work in Britain in the late fifties by 20th Century-Fox, and he played a variety of small roles before he was released from the contract. He became world-famous as James Bond, starting with *Dr. No* in 1962, but for years, despite a strong screen presence and great natural acting ability, his non-Bond films were flops. He was seen to best advantage in such action-adventure movies as *The Wind and the Lion, The Man Who Would Be King,* and the 1976 *Robin and Marian.* But from John

Wayne [33 . . .] to Clint Eastwood [2179.5] to Harrison Ford [2296], the Academy has consistently undervalued action performers. Since the Oscar, Connery has given strong performances in numerous films, particularly *Indiana Jones and the Last Crusade, The Hunt for Red October,* and the underrated *The Russia House* (1990).

The Last Emperor took all of the awards for which *The Untouchables* was nominated, winning for art direction, the scoring of Ryuichi Sakamoto, David Byrne, and Cong Su, and the costuming of James Acheson. Some resentment was expressed that Vance-Straker's nomination for costumes excluded the credited contribution to the film of designer Giorgio Armani.

Von Brandenstein: 60, 1651. Gausman: 4, 166, 1022, 1284. Morricone: 308, 506, 1331.

2186 • UP IN ARMS

AVALON PRODUCTIONS; RKO RADIO. 1944.
NOMINATIONS *Song:* "Now I Know," music by Harold Arlen, lyrics by Ted Koehler. *Scoring of a Musical Picture:* Louis Forbes and Ray Heindorf.

Danny Kaye is a hypochondriac elevator operator in love with Constance Dowling, who loves Kaye's friend Dana Andrews. When Kaye and Andrews are drafted, Dowling and her friend Dinah Shore accidentally wind up on the troop ship with them. Still more accidents happen, turning Kaye into a war hero. Kaye's debut film is a silly jumble, but it has some good musical numbers. Directed by Elliott Nugent, with Louis Calhern [1243], Lyle Talbot, Margaret Dumont, and Elisha Cook, Jr. Virginia Mayo, who would be Kaye's costar in later films, is a chorus girl in this one. The song Oscar went to James Van Heusen and Johnny Burke for "Swinging on a Star," from *Going My Way.* Morris Stoloff and Carmen Dragon won the scoring award for *Cover Girl.*

Arlen: 248, 322, 368, 903, 1838, 1910, 1912, 2300. Koehler: 930, 1750. Forbes: 282, 1006, 2057, 2310. Heindorf: 331, 479, 666, 930, 1043, 1204, 1385, 1408, 1430, 1690, 1719, 1750, 1910, 2058, 2243, 2310.

2187 • UP IN MABEL'S ROOM

EDWARD SMALL; UNITED ARTISTS. 1944.
NOMINATION *Scoring of a Dramatic or Comedy Picture:* Edward Paul.

Dennis O'Keefe, a meek professor married to Marjorie Reynolds, is embroiled in circumstances that suggest he's having an affair with old girlfriend Gail Patrick. His attempts to straighten things out only make them worse. Antique farce written originally for the stage and filmed once before as a silent. It's still funny, thanks to performers that include Mischa Auer [1401] and Charlotte Greenwood and the direction of Allan Dwan. The scoring award went to Max Steiner for *Since You Went Away.*

Paul: 855.

2188 • USUAL UNIDENTIFIED THIEVES, THE (A.K.A. BIG DEAL ON MADONNA STREET)

LUX-VIDES-CINECITTA (ITALY). 1958.
NOMINATION *Foreign Language Film.*

A gang of amateur thieves crafts an elaborate plot to break into a pawnshop, but they're undone by circumstances, as well as their own incompetence—with hilarious results. Delightful comedy, directed by Mario Monicelli [367 . . .] and starring Vittorio Gassman, Marcello Mastroianni [490 . . .], Totò, and Claudia Cardinale. The screenplay is by Monicelli, Age [367 . . .], Scarpelli [367 . . .], and Suso Cecchi D'Amico [367]. The original Italian title is *I Soliti Ignoti,* which can be translated as "Persons Unknown," the British title. It received a wide American release under the title *Big Deal on Madonna Street.* The Oscar went to *My Uncle.*

2189 • VACATION FROM MARRIAGE

LONDON FILMS; MGM (UNITED KINGDOM). 1946.
AWARD *Original Story:* Clemence Dane.

A drab British couple, played by Robert Donat [406 . . .] and Deborah Kerr [599 . . .], volunteer for service in World War II. During the three years in which they are separated, each blossoms: Donat finds romance with Ann Todd, Kerr with Roland Culver. When peace comes, they fear the return to the tedium of their prewar life together, and each vows to separate from the other—until they actually meet. Enjoyable romantic drama, directed by Alexander Korda [1620]. Glynis Johns [1969] is particularly good as Kerr's feisty pal. Dane's story was turned into a screenplay with the help of Anthony Pelissier.

2190 • VAGABOND KING, THE

PARAMOUNT PUBLIX. 1929–30.

NOMINATION Interior Decoration: Hans Dreier.

Dennis King plays the swashbuckling poet François Villon in this version of the operetta by Rudolph Friml, directed by Ludwig Berger and costarring Jeanette MacDonald and Lillian Roth. Unfortunately the film seems to be lost. It was remade without music as *If I Were King* in 1938, and with the music under the original title in 1956. Dreier lost to Herman Rosse for *King of Jazz.*

Dreier: 97, 151, 649, 674, 701, 726, 925, 979, 1101, 1120, 1194, 1214, 1217, 1358, 1443, 1452, 1540, 1668, 1748, 1880, 1975, 1994.

2191 • VALIANT, THE

FOX. 1928–29.

NOMINATIONS Actor: Paul Muni. *Writing Achievement:* Tom Barry.

Muni plays a drifter sentenced to death for murder who chooses to conceal his identity to protect his family in this little-seen melodrama directed by William K. Howard. Muni and Barry, like all the runners-up in the 1928–29 Oscar race, were not "official" nominees; only the winners were announced, but the committees of the various branches that actually voted the awards kept lists of the names that were under consideration. Warner Baxter won the acting award for *In Old Arizona,* which had also been written by Barry, who lost to Hans Kräly for *The Patriot.*

Muni: 218.5, 965, 1133, 1169, 1936. Barry: 989.

2192 • VALIANT IS THE WORD FOR CARRIE

PARAMOUNT. 1936.

NOMINATION Actress: Gladys George.

Carrie Snyder (George) prostitutes herself in order to provide for two orphaned children but is forced to surrender them to the authorities. Later, when accused of a crime she didn't commit, she pleads guilty rather than appear in a trial that would reveal the truth to the embarrassment of the now-grown children. Sentimental drama, directed by Wesley Ruggles, with John Howard, Dudley Digges, Harry Carey, Isabel Jewell, and Jackie Moran. George had made a few silent films, but her pre-sound career was largely on the stage. Today she is perhaps best known for the brief role of Iva Archer, Sam Spade's partner's wife, with whom he has apparently been having an affair, in *The Maltese Falcon.* George, who lost the Oscar to Luise Rainer in *The Great Ziegfeld,* died in 1954.

2193 • VALLEY OF DECISION, THE

MGM. 1945.

NOMINATIONS Actress: Greer Garson. *Scoring of a Dramatic or Comedy Picture:* Herbert Stothart.

Garson plays an Irish immigrant who goes to work as a maid for a family that owns the Pennsylvania coal mines in which her own father, Lionel Barrymore [723 . . .], has been crippled. Naturally she falls in love with her employer's son, played by Gregory Peck [759 . . .]. Donald Crisp [952] and Gladys Cooper [1393 . . .] are Peck's parents. When Crisp and Barrymore are killed during strike violence, Garson and Peck are forced apart, and he marries the shrewish Jessica Tandy [580 . . .]. But Cooper leaves Garson her share of the mine in her will, bringing Garson and Peck together again—if only he will leave the wife he has come to hate. Okay romantic melodrama, given several coats of MGM polish. Directed by Tay Garnett, with Preston Foster, Marsha Hunt, Reginald Owen, Dan Duryea, and Dean Stockwell [1281]. John Meehan [271 . . .] and Sonya Levien [1007 . . .] adapted a novel by Marcia Davenport. Garson lost to Joan Crawford in *Mildred Pierce.* The scoring award went to Miklos Rozsa for *Spellbound.*

Garson: 239, 804, 1232, 1371, 1372, 1973. Stothart: 397, 1096, 1232, 1274, 1292, 1387, 1662, 1988, 2068, 2234, 2300.

2194 • VALLEY OF THE DOLLS

RED LION PRODUCTIONS; 20TH CENTURY-FOX. 1967.
NOMINATION *Scoring of Music—Adaptation or Treatment:* John Williams.

Patty Duke [1326], Barbara Parkins, and Sharon Tate play aspiring actresses who find that fame exacts a price. Trash begets trash: The screenplay by Helen Deutsch [1173] and Dorothy Kingsley [1782] is based on the novel by Jacqueline Susann—who gets a cameo as a reporter. Also wallowing about in this mess are Susan Hayward [973 . . .], Martin Milner, and Lee Grant [534 . . .]. There are star cameos by Joey Bishop and George Jessel, which may give you another clue to the film's quality. Directed by Mark Robson [1001 . . .]. The scoring award went to Alfred Newman and Ken Darby for *Camelot.*

Williams: 6, 260, 403, 416, 588, 613, 614, 659, 805, 933, 937, 982, 996, 997, 1041, 1047, 1596, 1652, 1679, 1684, 1701, 1764.65, 1916, 1977, 2107, 2126, 2293, 2322.

2195 • VALMONT

CLAUDE BERRI AND RENN PRODUCTION; ORION. 1989.
NOMINATION *Costume Design:* Theodor Pistek.

Valmont (Colin Firth) and the Marquise de Merteuil, played by Annette Bening [840], amuse themselves by playing games with other people's lives. She sets him the task of spoiling the marriage of an old lover (Jeffrey Jones) by deflowering his innocent bride-to-be (Fairuza Balk), and wagers that Valmont won't be able to seduce the virtuous Madame de Tourvel, played by Meg Tilly [28]. Eventually their sexual games backfire. This version of the Choderlos de Laclos novel *Les Liaisons Dangereuses,* adapted by Jean-Claude Carrière [549 . . .] and directed by Milos Forman [60 . . .], had the misfortune of reaching the screen a year after the version known as *Dangerous Liaisons.* Critics—and the handful of people who made up *Valmont's* audience—were able to make point-to-point comparisons of the two, with results that were damning to *Valmont.* Although Bening was generally thought to be in the same league as Glenn Close, who played the earlier film's Marquise, Firth seemed callow in comparison with John Malkovich's

serpentine Valmont, and Michelle Pfeiffer gave Madame de Tourvel a tragic vulnerability that Tilly's character lacks. Forman's film is generally softer and more romantic than the earlier one, which was directed by Stephen Frears with an eye to the story's wit and irony. But *Valmont* stands on its own, and is by no means a poor film—just an ill-timed one. The cast also includes Henry Thomas, Sian Phillips, and Fabia Drake. The costuming award went to Phyllis Dalton for *Henry V.*

Pistek: 60.

2196 • VARSITY SHOW

WARNER BROS. 1937.
NOMINATION *Dance Direction:* Busby Berkeley.

Old alum Dick Powell puts on a benefit show for his college. Passable excuse for a bunch of musical numbers by Fred Waring and His Pennsylvanians, Buck and Bubbles, Johnny "Scat" Davis, and others. William Keighley directs a cast that includes Priscilla Lane, Rosemary Lane, and Walter Catlett. Nominated for the Finale, Berkeley lost to Hermes Pan for *A Damsel in Distress.*

Berkeley: 791, 792.

2197 • VENGANZA, LA

GUION PRODUCCIONES CINEMATOGRÁFICAS (SPAIN). 1958.
NOMINATION *Foreign Language Film.*

Sworn to vengeance against the man who caused his wrongful imprisonment, Luis (Raf Vallone) is dissuaded when his sister falls in love with his enemy. Written and directed by Juan Antonio Bardem. The Oscar went to *My Uncle.*

2198 • VERDICT, THE

FOX-ZANUCK/BROWN PRODUCTION; 20TH CENTURY-FOX. 1982.
NOMINATIONS *Picture:* Richard D. Zanuck and David Brown, producers. *Actor:* Paul Newman. *Supporting Actor:* James Mason. *Director:* Sidney Lumet. *Screenplay Based on Material From Another Medium:* David Mamet.

Newman plays an aging alcoholic lawyer whose promising career has been sabotaged by his own thirst. But he gets a chance at redemption when he takes on a medical malpractice case involving a comatose woman. The opposition is no less than the Catholic church, which owns the Boston hospital where the woman was given the wrong anesthetic. The archdiocese is represented by a prestigious law firm headed by Mason. Solid courtroom drama that's perhaps undermined by its own prestige packaging—it takes itself a little too seriously and gets glum where it should be tense. The performances—which also include Charlotte Rampling, Jack Warden [890 . . .], Milo O'Shea, and Lindsay Crouse [1580]—are terrific. Bruce Willis can be spotted among the extras.

Gandhi was the year's big spoiler, taking the awards for picture, for Ben Kingsley as best actor, and for Richard Attenborough as best director. Mason lost to Louis Gossett, Jr., in *An Officer and a Gentleman.* The screenplay award went to Costa-Gavras and Donald Stewart for *Missing.*

Zanuck: 580, 1041. Brown: 658.5, 1041. Newman: 3, 372, 422, 443, 956, 964, 1444.5, 1645. Mason: 761, 1910. Lumet: 561, 1424, 1611, 2153.

2199 • VÉRITÉ, LA

HAN PRODUCTIONS (FRANCE). 1960.
NOMINATION *Foreign Language Film.*

Brigitte Bardot goes on trial for murdering her sister's lover, with whom Bardot was also having an affair. Passable blend of courtroom drama and love triangle, directed by Henri-Georges Clouzot. The Oscar went to *The Virgin Spring.*

2200 • VERTIGO

ALFRED J. HITCHCOCK PRODUCTIONS INC.; PARAMOUNT. 1958.
NOMINATIONS *Art Direction—Set Decoration:* Hal Pereira and Henry Bumstead; Sam Comer and Frank McKelvy. *Sound:* George Dutton, sound director, Paramount Studio Sound Department.

Because of a harrowing experience that resulted in the death of his partner, policeman James Stewart [73 . . .] is left with a fear of heights and retires from the force. He takes a job shadowing a friend's wife, played by Kim Novak. Just as he's falling in love with her, she falls to her death—or does she? Soon he meets another woman who looks just like her and is caught in a spiral of obsession. When first released, this Alfred Hitchcock [1171 . . .] psychological drama was thought to be slow, unsuspenseful, and miscast—Novak was accused of sleepwalking through the part, and jokers dubbed her "Kim Novocain" because of her limited expressiveness. Much, too, was made of the twenty-five-year age difference between Stewart and Novak. But as the years passed, *Vertigo* came to be hailed as a masterpiece—the most complete working-out of the director's theme of sexual obsession, with Novak the epitome of the "cool blonde" type embodied in other Hitchcock films by Grace Kelly [450 . . .], Eva Marie Saint [1477], and Tippi Hedren. It's possible now that the critical dialectic has swung back to the center, where the thematic richness can be admired while the film's too-stately pace can be singled out as a flaw. But there will probably never be an end to debates over Hitchcock's work—or to denunciation of the Academy for failing to give him the honor he was due. For even if one grants *Vertigo* its flaws, it's a far more impressive piece of filmmaking than some, if not all, of the year's best picture nominees: *Auntie Mame, Cat on a Hot Tin Roof, The Defiant Ones, Separate Tables,* and the winner, *Gigi.* And Hitchcock surely looks like a better choice for a best director nomination than Mark Robson for *The Inn of the Sixth Happiness.* Other stunning oversights include the cinematography of Robert Burks [1537 . . .] and the score by Bernard Herrmann [50 . . .]. The screenplay is an adaptation by Alec Coppel [354] and Samuel Taylor [1738] of a novel by Pierre Boileau and Thomas Narcejac. The cast also includes Barbara Bel Geddes [972], Ellen Corby [972], Henry Jones, and Lee Patrick.

The Oscar for art direction went to *Gigi.* Fred Hynes won for the sound for *South Pacific.*

Pereira: 278, 357, 363, 426, 450, 736, 956, 1029, 1219, 1504, 1570, 1631, 1674, 1716, 1727, 1738, 1840, 1897, 1959, 2012, 2098, 2208. Bumstead: 1927, 2101, 2179.5. Comer: 278, 357, 426, 450, 726, 736, 925, 956, 1029, 1101, 1214, 1219, 1443, 1570, 1631, 1674, 1727, 1738, 1748, 1959, 1975, 1994, 2012, 2098, 2208. McKelvy: 591, 917, 1450, 1570, 1631, 2047. Dutton: 847, 1855, 1934, 2175.

2201 • *VICTOR/VICTORIA*

METRO-GOLDWYN-MAYER PRODUCTION; MGM/UNITED ARTISTS. 1982.

AWARD *Original Song Score and Its Adaptation or Adaptation Score:* song score by Henry Mancini and Leslie Bricusse; adaptation score by Henry Mancini.

NOMINATIONS *Actress:* Julie Andrews. *Supporting Actor:* Robert Preston. *Supporting Actress:* Lesley Ann Warren. *Screenplay Based on Material From Another Medium:* Blake Edwards. *Art Direction–Set Decoration:* Rodger Maus, Tim Hutchinson, and William Craig Smith; Harry Cordwell. *Costume Design:* Patricia Norris.

Parisian nightclub performer Preston rescues starving singer Andrews and comes up with an ingenious way for her to get the work she needs: She'll pretend to be a man who's a female impersonator—a woman playing a man playing a woman. She becomes a big success, but things get complicated when she catches the eye of a visiting American gangster, played by James Garner [1380], who discovers she's really a woman. The two fall in love, to the confusion of his mistress (Warren) and his bodyguard (Alex Karras). One of the few successful musicals of the last twenty years, though in fact it's not a very good musical: Notice, for instance, that none of the songs by Mancini and Bricusse received a nomination. Perhaps its high point comes when Preston goes on in drag and camps up a number Andrews had done earlier. Only in that scene do we get some of the sense of a performer in love with the sheer joy of performing that we get from the great musicals starring Gene Kelly [74], Fred Astaire [2126], or Judy Garland [1065 . . .]—or for that matter, from Preston's own performance in *The Music Man* twenty years earlier. The movie is, however, an enjoyable farce, if marred by the sniggeriness that afflicts most of director Edwards' comedies. It keeps moving swiftly, so we don't mind that Andrews is not even remotely convincing as a man, or hear too clearly the note of misogyny struck in Warren's character.

This was the fourth of Mancini's four Oscars, and the second of two won by Bricusse. Mancini died in 1994.

Andrews, whose career had sagged badly since *Mary Poppins* and *The Sound of Music* made her a movie star a decade and a half earlier, lost to Meryl Streep for *Sophie's Choice.*

This was the sole nomination for Preston, a durable performer who made his film debut in 1938 and played second leads in major films and leads in B pictures for the next two decades, and became a star only after going to Broadway and winning a Tony for *The Music Man.* His performance in the 1962 film version of that musical was shockingly ignored by the Academy, but he worked steadily in movies for another twenty years. He died in 1987. The Oscar went to Louis Gossett, Jr., for *An Officer and a Gentleman.*

Warren, who made her screen debut in 1967 in *The Happiest Millionaire,* moved from playing ingenues into sexy and sometimes villainous types. Despite strong performances, her career in movies has never made her a star, and she is now more often seen in TV dramas. The supporting actress Oscar went to Jessica Lange for *Tootsie.*

Edwards began as an actor in the early forties and moved into writing and directing in the fifties. He made his reputation with comedies such as *Operation Petticoat* and *Breakfast at Tiffany's* but has occasionally ventured into serious drama, such as *Days of Wine and Roses.* He struck gold in 1964 with *The Pink Panther,* the first of a lucrative series. His films have often featured his wife, Andrews. The screenplay for *Victor/Victoria* was based on a 1933 German film that was also remade in 1936 in England as *First a Girl.* The Oscar went to Costa-Gavras and Donald Stewart for *Missing.*

Gandhi took the awards for art direction and for the costumes of John Mollo and Bhanu Athaiya.

Mancini: 122, 278, 384, 494, 508, 512, 776, 825, 1573, 1574, 1864, 1970, 2011, 2037. Bricusse: 557, 805, 933, 937, 1766, 2037, 2285. Andrews: 1284, 1881. Cordwell: 613. Norris: 506, 608, 1974, 2165.

2202 • *VICTORY THROUGH AIR POWER*

WALT DISNEY PRODUCTIONS; UNITED ARTISTS. 1943.

NOMINATION *Scoring of a Dramatic or Comedy Picture:* Edward H. Plumb, Paul J. Smith, and Oliver G. Wallace.

This propaganda documentary, which blends a Disney animated history of aviation with an illustrated lecture by Maj. Alexander P. de Seversky on strategic uses of airpower to win the war, was actually somewhat controversial at the time: Old-line military strategists had never quite factored in the role of airplanes in warfare, even though the Japanese attack on Pearl Harbor made it pretty clear that they'd have to, and much of the early American rearmament efforts were focused on shipbuilding. De Seversky was unpopular among the brass, but Walt Disney himself was enthralled by the major's 1942 book on the subject and persisted in making the film, without government sponsorship. (The government was deeply involved in other Disney wartime training and propaganda films, however.) It was released as an entertainment feature, not as a documentary, but the public saw through that ruse and the film made only a small profit. Eventually de Seversky would be hailed as a pioneer and a visionary. The film is no longer in general circulation, although its history of aviation section has been seen frequently on Disney TV shows and the studio's cable channel. The scoring award went to Alfred Newman for *The Song of Bernadette.*

Plumb: 140, 1745, 2071. Smith: 402, 1553, 1576, 1745, 1851, 1871, 2071. Wallace: 42, 402, 585, 2273.5.

2203 • *VILLAGE ON THE RIVER, THE*

N.V. Nationale Film Productie Maatschappij (the Netherlands). 1959.

Nomination *Foreign Language Film.*

A country doctor battles village officialdom to serve the people who love him. Low-key debut film of director Fons Rademakers. The Oscar went to *Black Orpheus.*

2204 • *V.I.P.'S, THE*

MGM (United Kingdom). 1963.

Award *Supporting Actress:* Margaret Rutherford.

Fog delays a flight out of London, and various passengers are forced to spend the night at a hotel. They include Elizabeth Taylor [318 . . .], Richard Burton [85 . . .], Maggie Smith [332 . . .], Orson Welles [407 . . .], and Rutherford, who plays a dotty duchess. Their separate and intersecting stories make up this glitzy stuff, written by Terence Rattigan [281 . . .] and directed by Anthony Asquith. It's made tolerable by good performances by a group of people who seldom put this movie on their résumés. Others in it include Louis Jourdan, Elsa Martinelli, Linda Christian, Robert Coote, Michael Hordern, and David Frost.

Rutherford was a much-loved character actress, most famous for four films in which she played Agatha Christie's Miss Marple—or a character by that name, for she resembles not at all the modest, fluffy spinster sleuth of the famous mystery stories. Her best film performances were as Madame Arcati, the medium in *Blithe Spirit,* and as Miss Prism in the splendid 1952 film of *The Importance of Being Earnest.* She died in 1972 at the age of eighty.

2205 • *VIRGIN QUEEN, THE*

20th Century-Fox. 1955.

Nomination *Color Costume Design:* Charles LeMaire and Mary Wills.

Bette Davis [46 . . .] does her second turn at Queen Elizabeth I (the first was in *The Private Lives of Elizabeth and Essex,* sixteen years earlier). This time she's carrying on with Sir Walter Raleigh, played by Richard Todd [878]. Dullish pseudo-historical pageant, though it's amusing to see Joan Collins square off against Davis. (Watch it, Joan—that's not Linda Evans you're dealing with!) Also on hand, directed by Henry Koster [214], Herbert Marshall, Jay Robinson, Dan O'Herlihy [18], and Rod Taylor. LeMaire won the Oscar this time, but it was for *Love Is a Many-Splendored Thing.*

LeMaire: 21, 46, 376, 495, 530, 542, 954, 1213, 1338, 1391, 1601, 1706, 2008, 2043, 2294. Wills: 376, 542, 864, 1534, 2008, 2312.

2206 • *VIRGIN SPRING, THE*

A.B. Svensk Filmindustri Production; Janus Films (Sweden). 1960.

Award *Foreign Language Film.*

Nomination *Black-and-White Costume Design:* Marik Vos.

In a medieval village a young girl (Brigitta Petters-son) is brutally raped and murdered by three itiner-ants. Her father, played by Max von Sydow [1546], takes a terrifying revenge on the killers, and a spring begins to flow from the site of the girl's death. Grim but beautifully made fable directed by Ingmar Berg-man [111 . . .] from a screenplay by Ulla Isaakson. The cinematography is by Sven Nykvist [460], the first in his long collaboration with Bergman. The cos-tuming Oscar went to Edith Head and Edward Ste-venson for *The Facts of Life.*

Vos: 460, 644.

2207 • VISIT, THE

CINECITTA-DEAR FILM-LES FILMS DU SIÈCLE-P.E.C.S. PRODUC-TION; 20TH CENTURY-FOX (U.S./FRANCE/ITALY/WEST GER-MANY). 1964.

NOMINATION *Black-and-White Costume Design:* Rene Hu-bert.

Ingrid Bergman [72 . . .] plays one of the world's richest women, who returns to the village where she grew up and offers a fortune to the towns-people if they will try, find guilty, and execute An-thony Quinn [1226 . . .], who once seduced her. This adaptation of the Friedrich Duerrenmatt play is ultimately betrayed by its star casting—Bergman was unwilling to be portrayed as an old crone. The theat-ricality of the story is also at odds with the realistic treatment it receives from director Bernhard Wicki. The cast also includes Valentina Cortese [501]. The costuming Oscar went to Dorothy Jeakins for *The Night of the Iguana.*

Hubert: 530.

2208 • VISIT TO A SMALL PLANET

HAL WALLIS PRODUCTIONS; PARAMOUNT. 1960.

NOMINATION *Black-and-White Art Direction—Set Decora-tion:* Hal Pereira and Walter Tyler; Sam Comer and Arthur Krams.

Jerry Lewis comes from outer space to observe human ways. What sounds like a studio's high-con-cept premise for an outlandish star is actually a mis-fired slapstick adaptation of a sophisticated satirical Broadway play by Gore Vidal—who has never fully recovered from what Paramount did to it. Some of it is still funny, thanks to supporting players like Fred Clark, Jerome Cowan, Lee Patrick, and Gale Gordon, but Lewis' admirers don't regard it as *le vrai Jerry.* Norman Taurog [271 . . .] directed. The art direction award went to *The Apartment.*

Pereira: 278, 357, 363, 426, 450, 736, 956, 1029, 1219, 1504, 1570, 1631, 1674, 1716, 1727, 1738, 1840, 1897, 1959, 2012, 2098, 2200. Tyler: 357, 1022, 1101, 1716, 1738, 1748, 1959, 2012. Comer: 278, 357, 426, 450, 726, 736, 925, 956, 1029, 1101, 1214, 1219, 1443, 1570, 1631, 1674, 1727, 1738, 1748, 1959, 1975, 1994, 2012, 2098, 2200. Krams: 357, 1173, 1309, 1727, 1937, 1959, 2098.

2209 • VITELLONI, I

PEG FILMS/CITÉ FILMS; API-JANUS FILMS (ITALY/FRANCE). 1957.

NOMINATION *Story and Screenplay—Written Directly for the Screen:* Federico Fellini, Ennio Flaiano, and Tullio Pinelli.

A group of idle young men in an Italian seaside town face the future in various ways: There's the leader of the pack who gets his girlfriend pregnant and finds himself trapped. There's the fat clown and the would-be poet, and then there's the one who finally gets it together and leaves for Rome—just as director Fellini had left his Adriatic hometown of Ri-mini two decades earlier. Wonderful, funny, touch-ing, and extremely influential coming-of-age story, the inspiration for *American Graffiti, Diner,* and *Stand By Me,* among others. The screenplay Oscar went, rather infuriatingly, to George Wells for *Designing Woman.*

Fellini: 61, 562, 603, 657, 658, 1496, 1519, 1938. Flaiano: 562, 603. Pinelli: 562, 603, 1938.

2210 • VIVA ITALIA!

DEAN FILM PRODUCTION (ITALY). 1978.

NOMINATION *Foreign Language Film.*

An anthology film with nine satiric episodes, per-formed by Vittorio Gassman, Ornella Muti, Albert Sordi, Ugo Tognazzi, and others. Directed by Mario Monicelli [367 . . .], Dino Risi [1764], and Ettore

Scola from a screenplay by Age [367 . . .], Scarpelli [367 . . .], Ruggero Maccari [1764], and Bernardino Zapponi [658]. Also known as *I Nuovi Mostri*—''The New Monsters.'' The Oscar went to *Get Out Your Handkerchiefs.*

2211 • *VIVA VILLA!*
MGM. 1934.
AWARD *Assistant Director:* John Waters.
NOMINATIONS *Picture:* David O. Selznick, producer. *Adaptation:* Ben Hecht. *Sound Recording:* Douglas Shearer.

Wallace Beery [202 . . .] plays the Mexican revolutionary as a fun-loving rogue, with Fay Wray as the aristocratic woman who falls for him, Stuart Erwin [1571] as an American journalist involved in creating the Villa legend, and Leo Carrillo, Joseph Schildkraut [1169], Henry B. Walthall, and Katherine DeMille, among throngs of others. Hokum passing as history that's enjoyable but might have been a lot better. Howard Hawks [1779] was hired to direct, but he had small patience with control freaks like Selznick and was replaced by the more docile Jack Conway. Lee Tracy [181], cast in the part played by Erwin, was fired after an incident in which he allegedly urinated on some Mexican cadets from a hotel balcony. The cinematography is by James Wong Howe [1 . . .] and Charles G. Clarke [837 . . .].

Waters was the first to win the short-lived assistant director Oscar in competition with assistant directors from other studios. When the award was given at the 1932–33 ceremonies, a slate of eighteen names was drawn up, representing seven major studios, and one assistant director from each studio was given an award. After Waters' win, the category continued for only three more years.

The best picture Oscar went to *It Happened One Night,* which also won for Robert Riskin's screenplay adaptation. (Hecht came in third after Frances Goodrich and Albert Hackett for *The Thin Man.*) The award for sound went to John Livadary for *One Night of Love.*

Selznick: 497, 798, 1670, 1828, 1890, 1909, 1996. Hecht: 78, 1455, 1765, 2179, 2316. Shearer: 136, 202, 256, 397, 685, 817, 835, 1096, 1232, 1293, 1371, 1419, 1751, 1950, 1988, 2048, 2055, 2300.

2212 • *VIVA ZAPATA!*
20TH CENTURY-FOX. 1952.
AWARD *Supporting Actor:* Anthony Quinn.
NOMINATIONS *Actor:* Marlon Brando. *Story and Screenplay:* John Steinbeck. *Black-and-White Art Direction—Set Decoration:* Lyle Wheeler and Leland Fuller; Thomas Little and Claude Carpenter. *Scoring of a Dramatic or Comedy Picture:* Alex North.

Brando plays the Mexican peasant revolutionary Emiliano Zapata, with Quinn as his brother and Jean Peters as the young woman who becomes Zapata's wife. Elia Kazan's [63 . . .] direction keeps things moving, and the performances are exciting. Kazan had proposed the story to Steinbeck and collaborated on the screenplay, which is too self-consciously arty for its own good. Fox production chief Darryl F. Zanuck [34 . . .] was not impressed with the young Brando, particularly with his infamous ''mumbling,'' and was not happy that Kazan had sent the script to him, preferring Tyrone Power or Quinn for the title role. Kazan also wanted Julie Harris [1302] for the part played by Peters but was forced to accept Peters in order to cast Brando. Also in the cast are Joseph Wiseman, Mildred Dunnock [119 . . .], and Margo.

Quinn had been in films since the mid-thirties, usually in supporting roles as a heavy. He was also frequently cast as an Indian in westerns, such as *They Died With Their Boots On* (1941), in which he plays Chief Crazy Horse. In the late forties he left Hollywood for a while to try his luck on Broadway, where he had a success when he replaced Brando as Stanley Kowalski in *A Streetcar Named Desire*—a fact that Kazan used to advantage when preparing for a big fight scene between Brando and Quinn: He told each actor that the other had been boasting about how much better his own performance as Stanley was. Quinn's Oscar triumph greatly boosted his career, and while his brooding presence never made him a candidate for conventional leading roles, he worked steadily afterward.

This was the second consecutive nomination for

Brando, but it would take him two more tries until his triumph for *On the Waterfront*. This time the Oscar went to Gary Cooper for *High Noon*.

Steinbeck adapted to Hollywood somewhat more easily than other famous American writers, such as F. Scott Fitzgerald and William Faulkner, who had been lured by the studios' big money. Steinbeck's stories, with their broad-brush larger-than-life characters, were comparatively easy to translate to the screen, so that *Of Mice and Men, The Grapes of Wrath,* and *East of Eden* were turned into memorable movies. The dialogue in *Viva Zapata!* is somewhat pretentious and flowery, and the screenplay went through several versions before something filmable was achieved. The Academy preferred the droll story and screenplay by T. E. B. Clarke for *The Lavender Hill Mob*.

The art direction award went to *The Bad and the Beautiful* and the scoring Oscar to Dimitri Tiomkin for *High Noon*.

Quinn: 1226, 2282, 2346. Brando: 583, 784, 1069, 1141, 1477, 1763, 1949. Steinbeck: 1171, 1294. Wheeler: 19, 46, 83, 356, 376, 428, 476, 495, 530, 542, 719, 721, 798, 950, 1062, 1088, 1149, 1153, 1213, 1391, 1475, 1601, 1616, 1670, 1706, 1852, 2008, 2093. Fuller: 530, 719, 1149, 1475, 1601. Little: 46, 83, 235, 428, 495, 719, 721, 746, 950, 952, 1082, 1149, 1153, 1397, 1475, 1666, 1852, 1868, 2055, 2286. Carpenter: 632, 1924. North: 29, 215, 413, 515, 577, 1654, 1727, 1802, 1814, 1886, 1949, 2174, 2177, 2277.

2213 • VIVACIOUS LADY

RKO RADIO. 1938.
NOMINATIONS *Cinematography:* Robert de Grasse. *Sound Recording:* John Aalberg.

College professor James Stewart [73 . . .] and nightclub singer Ginger Rogers [1102] get married, but then they have to tell his parents, played by Beulah Bondi [807 . . .] and Charles Coburn [535 . . .], and find a way for Ginger to settle down in a stuffy little academic community. Fine comedy of manners, directed by George Stevens [542 . . .], with a delightful cast that includes Grady Sutton, Jack Carson, and Franklin Pangborn.

This was the sole nomination for de Grasse, who began in the silent era and became one of RKO's top directors of photography, with credits that include *Alice Adams, Stage Door, Carefree, Bachelor Mother,* and *Kitty Foyle*. He died in 1971. The Oscar went to Joseph Ruttenberg for *The Great Waltz*. The award for sound was won by Thomas Moulton for *The Cowboy and the Lady*.

Aalberg: 407, 923, 959, 1033, 1102, 1978, 1991, 2030, 2166.

2214 • VOGUES OF 1938

WALTER WANGER; UNITED ARTISTS. 1937.
NOMINATIONS *Interior Decoration:* Alexander Toluboff. *Song:* "That Old Feeling," music by Sammy Fain, lyrics by Lew Brown.

Bored rich girl Joan Bennett decides to take a whirl at modeling in this musical whose chief distinction, other than the introduction of a song that became a standard, is that it was made in Technicolor. The cinematography is by Ray Rennahan [235 . . .]. The period fashion shows are amusing, but not much else in the movie is. Directed by Irving Cummings [989], with Warner Baxter [989], Mischa Auer [1401], Alan Mowbray, Jerome Cowan, and Hedda Hopper. The art direction Oscar went to Stephen Goosson for *Lost Horizon*. "Sweet Leilani," by Harry Owens, from *Waikiki Wedding,* took the song Oscar. The movie is also known as *Walter Wanger's Vogues of 1938,* as *All This and Glamour Too,* and sometimes just as *Vogues*.

Toluboff: 36, 1901. Fain: 95, 331, 376, 856, 1213, 1276, 1681, 1925, 2014.

2215 • VOICE IN THE WIND, A

RIPLEY-MONTER; UNITED ARTISTS. 1944.
NOMINATIONS *Sound Recording:* W. M. Dalgliesh, RCA Sound. *Scoring of a Dramatic or Comedy Picture:* Michel Michelet.

Lovers Francis Lederer and Sigrid Gurie, separated in wartime Europe, are reunited in death. Low-budget romantic drama with a lot of atmosphere, but it needed real stars to make any kind of impact. Directed by Arthur Ripley, with J. Carrol Naish

[1294 . . .]. The award for sound went to E. H. Hansen for *Wilson*. Max Steiner won for the score for *Since You Went Away*.

Michelet: 855.

2216 • *VOLVER A EMPEZAR (TO BEGIN AGAIN)*

Nickel Odeon S.A. Production (Spain). 1982.
Award *Foreign Language Film*.

A Nobel Prize—winning writer, exiled from Spain during Franco's lifetime, returns to his hometown and reconciliation with an old lover. Sentimental drama, directed by José Luis Garci, that was Spain's first Oscar winner, and hence something of a landmark in post-Franco filmmaking.

2217 • *VON RYAN'S EXPRESS*

P-R Productions; 20th Century-Fox. 1965.
Nomination *Sound Effects:* Walter A. Rossi.

Frank Sinatra [732 . . .] plays an American POW whose arrogance gets him likened to the Nazis— hence the "Von"—by his fellow prisoners, mostly Brits under the leadership of a major played by Trevor Howard [1875]. But Sinatra wins them over when he masterminds a daring escape plan that involves hijacking a freight train. Good, tense action adventure, though Sinatra's performance occasionally gets a little lazy. Directed by Mark Robson [1001 . . .], with Sergio Fantoni, Raffaella Carra, Brad Dexter, Edward Mulhare, James Brolin, Adolfo Celi, and Vito Scotti. The screenplay, from a novel by Davis Westheimer, is by Wendell Mayes [73] and Joseph Landon. The sound effects award went to Tregoweth Brown for *The Great Race*.

Rossi: 618, 646.

2218 • *VOYAGE OF THE DAMNED*

ITC Entertainment Production; Avco Embassy (United Kingdom). 1976.
Nominations *Supporting Actress:* Lee Grant. *Screenplay —Based on Material From Another Medium:* Steve Shagan and David Butler. *Original Score:* Lalo Schifrin.

German Jews sail for Cuba on a luxury liner in 1939 but are denied permission to land and must return to Germany and extermination. Depressing fictionalization of a true story that's undermined by a melodramatic script and the decision to pack it with an all-star cast, sapping some of the drama while the audience whispers, "Isn't that . . . ?" Max von Sydow [1546] plays the captain, and the passengers include Faye Dunaway [255 . . .], Oskar Werner [1812], Orson Welles [407 . . .], Malcolm McDowell, James Mason [761 . . .], Wendy Hiller [1252 . . .], Jose Ferrer [473 . . .], Katharine Ross [810], Denholm Elliott [1725], Julie Harris [1301], Maria Schell, and Ben Gazzara. Directed by Stuart Rosenberg.

Grant lost to Beatrice Straight in *Network*. The screenplay award went to William Goldman for *All the President's Men*. Jerry Goldsmith won for the score for *The Omen*.

Grant: 534, 1130, 1798. Shagan: 1761. Schifrin: 70, 434, 443, 720, 1928.

2219 • *WABASH AVENUE*

20th Century-Fox. 1950.
Nomination *Song:* "Wilhelmina," music by Josef Myrow, lyrics by Mack Gordon.

Victor Mature discovers Betty Grable at the 1892 World's Fair in Chicago and woos her with big plans for advancing her singing career—to which her boss, Phil Harris, rightly objects. Yet another in Fox's long string of period musicals, a formula it latched onto in the late thirties and stuck with through seemingly endless variations and remakes: Grable is here remaking her earlier film, *Coney Island*. Director Henry Koster [214] keeps things moving nicely. Also on hand are Reginald Gardiner and Margaret Hamilton. The song Oscar went to Ray Evans and Jay Livingston for "Mona Lisa," from *Captain Carey, U.S.A.*

Myrow: 1362. Gordon: 428, 563, 569, 897, 1362, 1501, 1964, 1984.

2220 • *WAIKIKI WEDDING*

Paramount. 1937.
Award *Song:* "Sweet Leilani," music and lyrics by Harry Owens.
Nomination *Dance Direction:* Leroy Prinz.

Publicist Bing Crosby [173 . . .] stages a beauty contest in Honolulu, then finds himself involved with the very reluctant winner, Shirley Ross. Dated nonsense, with too-broad comedy supplied by Bob Burns and Martha Raye, and Hawaiian settings mostly supplied by process shots. Directed by Frank Tuttle, with Leif Erikson, Grady Sutton, and Anthony Quinn [1226 . . .].

Owens was a minor songwriter whose other familiar song, "Blue Hawaii," was also written for *Waikiki Wedding*. "Sweet Leilani" was a huge hit for Crosby —it was his first record to sell more than a million copies—but its Oscar win caused a mini-scandal because it defeated the only song by George and Ira Gershwin ever nominated for an Oscar: "They Can't Take That Away From Me," from *Shall We Dance*. The controversy centered on the voting participation, for the first time in the history of the awards, of all members of the industry guilds and unions, expanding the potential electorate from a handful to twelve thousand people. The enfranchising of so many was partly the idea of Academy president Frank Capra [1025 . . .]. The contentious unionizing of the industry in the earlier thirties, when the actors', directors', and writers' guilds were formed, had nearly destroyed the Academy, which was resented by union members because it had begun, under the leadership of L. B. Mayer and others, as an antiunion organization. Capra oversaw the rewriting of the bylaws which took the Academy out of labor negotiating and arbitrating. But democratizing the Academy Awards was criticized as a potential lowering of standards. The participation of the members of the Screen Extras Guild in particular was blamed for the triumph of the somewhat saccharine "Sweet Leilani" over the sophisticated "They Can't Take That Away From Me." George Gershwin's sudden death in 1937 had also made the song a sentimental favorite for the award. The following year the extras were not allowed to vote for the best song, but their participation in the other awards continued until 1944.

Prinz was nominated for the "Luau" number but lost to Hermes Pan's work on *A Damsel in Distress*. The dance direction award was discontinued after this year.

Prinz: 52, 196.

2221 • WAIT UNTIL DARK
WARNER BROS.-SEVEN ARTS. 1967.
NOMINATION *Actress:* Audrey Hepburn.

Hepburn is a blind woman whose husband, Efrem Zimbalist, Jr., unwittingly comes in possession of a doll filled with heroin. While he's away, Alan Arkin [884 . . .] and Richard Crenna try to get into her apartment to find it—Crenna by posing as a nice guy, Arkin by out-and-out thuggery. Well-made thriller, a bit slick and stagy—it's based on a Broadway hit by Frederick Knott—but splendidly performed: Arkin is a memorable villain and Hepburn a most sympathetic victim. Directed by Terence Young, who stages the movie's big shock moment well. Although it's been imitated so often that it no longer comes as such a shock, at the time audiences shrieked with surprise.

This was Hepburn's last nomination, and it was her last film before a nine-year absence from the screen. She returned in 1976 for *Robin and Marian* but made only three more movies after that, none of them memorable. She died in 1993 and was posthumously awarded the Jean Hersholt Humanitarian Award at the 1992 Oscar ceremonies for her work for UNICEF. She lost the Oscar this time to Katharine Hepburn in *Guess Who's Coming to Dinner*.

Hepburn: 278, 1457, 1716, 1738.

2222 • WAKE ISLAND
PARAMOUNT. 1942.
NOMINATIONS *Picture:* Joseph Sistrom, producer. *Supporting Actor:* William Bendix. *Director:* John Farrow. *Original Screenplay:* W. R. Burnett and Frank Butler.

At the outbreak of World War II, Americans struggle to maintain their hold on the Pacific island. They include Brian Donlevy [161], Macdonald Carey, Robert Preston [2201], Albert Dekker, Walter Abel, and Rod Cameron, as well as Bendix, who plays a character known as Smacksie. Considering that the film was made soon after the events in it took place, it's remarkably convincing stuff. In the Oscar race, however, American heroism in the South Pacific, it seems, couldn't match up to British heroism on the home front: The best picture Oscar went to *Mrs. Miniver,* which also won for its director, William Wyler.

This was the sole nomination for Bendix, a sturdy, sandpaper-voiced character actor in his first year in movies. He worked steadily through the forties, usually in comedy roles but sometimes as heavies, in such films as *Guadalcanal Diary* (1943), *Lifeboat, The Blue Dahlia,* and the title role in *The Babe Ruth Story* (1948). In the fifties he turned to TV, where he became best known for *The Life of Riley,* a sitcom he had starred in on radio, but continued to make occasional film appearances up to his death in 1964. The Oscar went to Van Heflin for *Johnny Eager.*

The screenplay Oscar went to Ring Lardner, Jr., and Michael Kanin for *Woman of the Year.*

Sistrom: 566. Farrow: 101. Butler: 787, 1703.

2223 • WALK ON THE WILD SIDE

FAMOUS ARTISTS PRODUCTIONS; COLUMBIA. 1962.
NOMINATION *Song:* ''Walk on the Wild Side,'' music by Elmer Bernstein, lyrics by Mack David.

Drifter Laurence Harvey [1724] comes to New Orleans in search of old flame Capucine and finds her working in a whorehouse run by Barbara Stanwyck [138 . . .]. Overheated mess whose wildness is all in its title and in Bernstein's score. Directed by Edward Dmytryk [467], with Anne Baxter [46 . . .] and Jane Fonda [394 . . .] in one of her first films. John Fante and Edmund Morris adapted Nelson Algren's novel, but censorship robbed it of its edge and left little more than a hint of the lesbianism of Stanwyck's character. The song—not to be confused with Lou Reed's walk on a much wilder side—lost to Henry Mancini and Johnny Mercer's title song from *Days of Wine and Roses.*

Bernstein: 27.5, 789, 882, 1242, 1264, 1685, 1959, 2064, 2101, 2130, 2147. David: 122, 371, 402, 861, 882, 963, 1032.

2224 • WALL STREET

OAXATAL PRODUCTION; 20TH CENTURY FOX. 1987.
AWARD *Actor:* Michael Douglas.

Douglas plays Gordon Gekko, a Wall Street supertrader who becomes mentor to Bud Fox (Charlie Sheen), a young broker who's going nowhere and is willing to sacrifice all his principles for the fabulous wealth available at the top. For Gekko, however, it's not so much the perks as the thrill of the deal and the scent of the kill that count; he delivers a spellbinding sermon on the virtues of greed that's modeled on the words of insider trader Ivan Boesky. A vivid portrait of high-finance high life that's an important document of the eighties madness embodied in men like Boesky, Michael Milken, and Donald Trump, but like most of the films of writer-director Oliver Stone [260 . . .], it finally gets shrill and tiring. Also in the cast are Daryl Hannah as Fox's interior-decorator girlfriend, Martin Sheen as Fox's working-class father, and Terence Stamp [206], Hal Holbrook, Sean Young, James Spader, and Sylvia Miles [648 . . .].

Before *Wall Street,* Douglas had been more successful as a producer than as an actor. He made an inauspicious debut in a flop antiwar film, *Hail, Hero!,* in 1969, but made more impression as an actor in the early-seventies TV series *The Streets of San Francisco.* Then in 1975 he won his first Oscar as producer of *One Flew Over the Cuckoo's Nest,* a property he had taken over from his father, Kirk Douglas [130 . . .]. He had another hit four years later with *The China Syndrome,* which he not only produced but also played a supporting role in. And the big success of *Romancing the Stone* in 1984 established him not only as a very successful producer but for the first time as a leading man. Douglas began to set aside his producing and concentrate more on acting, developing the persona of a man toughened and somewhat brutalized by experience. The intensity of his performance as Gordon Gekko surprised many critics, who had thought of him as merely a pleasant leading man. The year of *Wall Street* was also the year of *Fatal Attraction,* which was a huge hit, and made Douglas the center of controversy over what many considered the film's antifeminist bias. Douglas did little to dodge controversy, however: In 1992 he appeared in *Basic Instinct,* the following year in *Falling Down,* and in 1994 in *Disclosure*—all movies that were denounced for perceived sexual and/or racial biases.

Douglas: 1481.

2225 • WALLS OF MALAPAGA, THE
FRANCINEX (FRANCE/ITALY). 1950.
AWARD *Special Award:* Voted by the Academy Board of Governors as the most outstanding foreign language film released in the United States during 1950.

Fleeing France, where he has murdered his lover, Jean Gabin arrives in Genoa, where he meets a waitress (Isa Miranda), with whom he spends a few days before the police arrive to arrest him. Plotless, sensitively played neorealist film, directed by René Clément from a script that Jean Aurenche and Pierre Bost rewrote from an earlier one by Cesare Zavattini [194 . . .] and Suso Cecchi D'Amico [367].

2226 • WALTZING REGITZE
NORDISK FILM/DANISH FILM INSTITUTE PRODUCTION (DENMARK). 1989.
NOMINATION *Foreign Language Film.*

A look back at the lives of a couple who met and married during World War II, directed by Kaspar Rostrup, who adapted a Danish best-seller by Martha Christensen. The film has not yet received wide distribution in America. The Oscar went to *Cinema Paradiso.*

2227 • WAR AGAINST MRS. HADLEY, THE
MGM. 1942.
NOMINATION *Original Screenplay:* George Oppenheimer.

Fay Bainter [393 . . .] plays the title role, a dowager who is determined not to let either wartime restrictions or calls to do her part change her life. Naturally she gets her comeuppance and converts to the patriotic cause. Dated and now little-seen propagandrama with a strong cast, including Edward Arnold, Sara Allgood [952], Spring Byington [2325], and Van Johnson. Directed by Harold Bucquet. The

screenplay Oscar went to Ring Lardner, Jr., and Michael Kanin for *Woman of the Year.*

2228 • WAR AND PEACE
PONTI-DE LAURENTIIS PRODUCTION; PARAMOUNT (ITALY/U.S.). 1956.
NOMINATIONS *Director:* King Vidor. *Color Cinematography:* Jack Cardiff. *Color Costume Design:* Marie De Matteis.

Audrey Hepburn [278 . . .] plays the vivacious young Natasha Rostov, who marries the soldier Prince Andrey (Mel Ferrer). Henry Fonda [815 . . .] is Pierre Bezuhov, the awkward, carousing intellectual who loves Natasha from afar. The trio is caught up in the turmoil of the Napoleonic wars. Also in the cast are Vittorio Gassman as the libertine Anatole, who almost ruins Natasha's chances of marrying Andrey; Anita Ekberg as Anatole's beautiful, frivolous sister, Helene, who marries Pierre and almost ruins his life; Herbert Lom as Napoleon; Oscar Homolka [972] as General Kutuzov; John Mills [1737] as Platon; Jeremy Brett as Natasha's brother Nicholas; and the usual epic cast of thousands. Though it's only a brightly colored shadow of the monumental novel by Leo Tolstoy, this three-and-a-half-hour spectacular is just that—spectacular. The casting is problematic: The rail-thin Fonda is all wrong as the rotund Pierre, but he plays his part with intelligence. (A contemporary reviewer noted that he seemed to be the only member of the cast who had read the book.) The ever-bland Ferrer lacks the steely spirit the role demands. And though Hepburn would seem ideal casting, she is often awkwardly directed, and is unable to shade the development of her character from impulsive young girl to saddened and mature woman. The much-reworked screenplay is credited to Bridget Boland [85], Robert Westerby, Vidor, Mario Camerini, Ennio De Concini [554], and Ivo Perilli. The music is by Nino Rota [784 . . .].

The directing Oscar went to George Stevens for *Giant.* Lionel Lindon won for the cinematography for *Around the World in 80 Days.* The costuming award went to Irene Sharaff for *The King and I.*

Vidor: 378, 406, 468, 857. Cardiff: 221, 643, 1875.

2229 • WAR AND PEACE

MOSFILM STUDIOS PRODUCTION; WALTER READE-CONTINENTAL DISTRIBUTING (USSR). 1968.
AWARD *Foreign Language Film.*
NOMINATION *Art Direction–Set Decoration:* Mikhail Bogdanov and Gennady Myasnikov; G. Koshelev and V. Uvarov.

This Soviet version of the Leo Tolstoy novel is one of the most breathtaking films ever made, with aerial photography of the Battle of Borodino that is simply mind-boggling. The central consciousness of the film, in more ways than one, is that of Sergei Bondarchuk, who plays the book's focal character, Pierre, but also directed the film and cowrote it with Vasily Solovyov. Ludmila Savelyeva, a noted ballet dancer, plays Natasha, and Vyacheslav Tikhonov is Andrey. In its original version, the film lasted more than seven hours and was shown in four parts. The version released in the United States was shortened by two and a quarter hours and was shown in two installments with poorly dubbed English. Even so, it was a memorable moviegoing experience, and remains one of the most satisfying literary transcriptions in film history. It was also possibly the most expensive movie ever made, estimated at the time to have cost $100 million—in 1968 dollars.

The art direction Oscar went to *Oliver!*

2230 • WAR OF THE WORLDS

PARAMOUNT. 1953.
AWARD *Special Effects.* (No individual citation.)
NOMINATIONS *Sound Recording:* Loren L. Ryder, sound director, Paramount Sound Department. *Film Editing:* Everett Douglas.

The Martians invade Los Angeles, and the assembled scientists and military find that even the atomic bomb can't stop them. Among the people rushing about in panic are Gene Barry, Ann Robinson, Jack Kruschen [91], and, in a bit part billed as "Bird-Brained Blonde," Carolyn Jones [124]. Cedric Hardwicke does the portentous narration. Huge fun—

one of the classics of fifties sci-fi, and one of the few with impressive production values, including the rich Technicolor cinematography of George Barnes [537 . . .]. (It was his last film.) Unfortunately they skimped on the script—Robinson's many shrieks are more eloquent than any of the dialogue, which was written by Barre Lyndon. The ultimate source is the novel by H. G. Wells, but the famous Halloween 1938 radio show of Orson Welles [407 . . .] is the proximate source. Produced by George Pal and directed by special effects master Byron Haskin [531 . . .]. The special effects team was headed by Gordon Jennings [56 . . .].

The Oscar for sound went to John P. Livadary for *From Here to Eternity,* which also won for William Lyon's editing.

Ryder: 566, 827, 979, 1452, 1669, 1697, 1703, 1837, 1887, 2012, 2168, 2181, 2183, 2242.

2231 • WARGAMES

UNITED ARTISTS PRESENTATION OF A LEONARD GOLDBERG PRODUCTION; MGM/UNITED ARTISTS. 1983.
NOMINATIONS *Screenplay Written Directly for the Screen:* Lawrence Lasker and Walter F. Parkes. *Cinematography:* William A. Fraker. *Sound:* Michael J. Kohut, Carlos de Larios, Aaron Rochin, and Willie D. Burton.

Teenager Matthew Broderick thinks he's playing a computer game called Global Thermonuclear War, but he's actually tapped into a sophisticated computerized weapons system and he's started the real thing. Soon the FBI has tracked him down, but he and his girlfriend (Ally Sheedy) have to persuade the reclusive genius (John Wood) who designed the computer to help them shut the thing off. Entertaining part comedy, part nail-biter that takes itself a little too seriously for its own good—there are a few too many heavy message moments and a few too many caricature figures of authority, like the officious systems specialist played by Dabney Coleman and the blustery general played by Barry Corbin. Directed by John Badham.

The screenplay award went to Horton Foote for *Tender Mercies.* Sven Nykvist won for the cinematography for *Fanny & Alexander. The Right Stuff* took the sound Oscar.

Lasker: 113. Parkes: 113. Fraker: 890, 1205, 1380, 1439. Kohut: 641, 1310, 1548, 1711, 2124, 2165. De Larios: 1711, 2124, 2165. Rochin: 521, 641, 1089, 1310, 1711, 2124, 2165, 2287. Burton: 58, 209, 307, 1802.5.

2232 • *WARTIME ROMANCE*

ODESSA FILM STUDIO PRODUCTION (USSR). 1984.

NOMINATION *Foreign Language Film.*

Alexander, a soldier at the front during World War II, develops a crush on Liuba, a pretty nurse who's having an affair with an officer. Some years later, Alexander, now married, encounters Liuba, now a shabby street vendor in Odessa. The officer was killed, leaving her pregnant, and she lives a drab, hopeless life with her daughter. Alexander's affection gives her new hope, but also arouses the jealousy of his wife. Slight dramatic comedy, written and directed by Pyotr Todorovsky. The Oscar went to *Dangerous Moves.*

2233 • *WATCH ON THE RHINE*

WARNER BROS. 1943.

AWARD *Actor:* Paul Lukas.

NOMINATIONS *Picture:* Hal B. Wallis, producer. *Supporting Actress:* Lucile Watson. *Screenplay:* Dashiell Hammett.

Lukas plays a European Resistance leader who comes to pre–Pearl Harbor Washington with his American wife, played by Bette Davis [46 . . .], and their children. Nazi agents pursue him, however, leading to a dramatic confrontation. Watson plays Davis' bossy mother, and the cast includes Geraldine Fitzgerald [2316], Beulah Bondi [807 . . .], Henry Daniell, and George Coulouris. High-minded melodrama, adapted by Hammett from the Broadway play by Lillian Hellman [1182 . . .]. Lukas, Watson, and Coulouris appeared in it on stage, and Herman Shumlin, the play's director, was also brought to Hollywood for the film, but because of Shumlin's unfamiliarity with the medium, cinematographer Hal Mohr [718 . . .] acted as an uncredited codirector. The

film has lost its timeliness and thus much of its impact, but the Hellman-Hammett dialogue is still good to listen to.

Lukas, born in Hungary, had been a stage and screen star in both that country and Germany. He came to Hollywood in 1927, where he slipped into character roles, often as the foreign-born villain. His most memorable films before *Watch on the Rhine* were *Little Women,* in which he plays Professor Bhaer, *Dodsworth,* and *The Lady Vanishes* (1938). Today he is probably best known for defeating Humphrey Bogart in *Casablanca* in the Oscar race; the other nominees were Gary Cooper for *For Whom the Bell Tolls,* Walter Pidgeon for *Madame Curie,* and Mickey Rooney for *The Human Comedy.* The Oscar failed to boost his career significantly, although Lukas continued to work regularly in films such as *20,000 Leagues Under the Sea* and *Lord Jim* (1965)—not to mention Elvis Presley's *Fun in Acapulco*—through the late sixties. He died in 1971.

The best picture Oscar went to *Casablanca,* which also won for the screenplay by Julius J. Epstein, Philip G. Epstein, and Howard Koch. This was the sole Oscar nomination for Hammett, who worked off and on as a screenwriter starting in 1931 but is best known as the mystery novelist who created both *The Maltese Falcon* and *The Thin Man.* He and Lillian Hellman had a long and sometimes stormy relationship. Hammett himself has been portrayed at least twice on screen—by Jason Robards in *Julia* and by Frederic Forrest [1726] in the 1983 Wim Wenders film *Hammett.*

Watson, a prominent stage actress for the first three decades of the century, entered films in 1934 and typically played imperious dowagers. Her credits include *The Garden of Allah, Three Smart Girls, The Women* (1939), *Waterloo Bridge, The Great Lie, The Razor's Edge, Song of the South,* and the 1949 remake of *Little Women.* She died in 1962. The Oscar went to Katina Paxinou for *For Whom the Bell Tolls.*

Wallis: 17, 55, 85, 164, 343, 365, 676, 689, 712, 965, 1046, 1095, 1162, 1248, 1482, 1727, 1779, 2318.

2234 · WATERLOO BRIDGE

MGM. 1940.

NOMINATIONS *Black-and-White Cinematography:* Joseph Ruttenberg. *Original Score:* Herbert Stothart.

Ballet dancer Vivien Leigh [798 . . .] and soldier Robert Taylor meet in London during World War I, but he's shipped back to the front and reported killed. Down on her luck, Leigh turns to prostitution —though of course under the Production Code censorship, it's a little hard to tell what she's up to: perhaps just depending on the kindness of strangers, as a later Leigh character would put it. Then Taylor turns up alive, finds her, and takes her home to Mama, played by Lucile Watson [2233]. Knowing the truth will out, and that she'll be a blot on his noble family's escutcheon, Leigh runs away to her doom. Slurpy sentimental drama that was Leigh's first film after her triumph in *Gone With the Wind.* She's superb, of course, but though the movie is very watchable, it's also scarcely credible—especially Taylor's casting as a British aristocrat, and the big scene in which Watson guesses the truth and Leigh knows that she knows, etc. Directed by Mervyn LeRoy [1662 . . .] from a screenplay by S. N. Behrman, Hans Rameau, and George Froeschel [1371 . . .] based on a play by Robert E. Sherwood [184 . . .] that had been filmed in 1931—that one has the young Bette Davis [46 . . .] in a supporting role. Also on view are those prime scene-stealers Maria Ouspenskaya [560 . . .] and C. Aubrey Smith. In short, it's not to be missed, though you may hate yourself when it's over.

The cinematography Oscar went to George Barnes for *Rebecca.* The scoring award went to Leigh Harline, Paul J. Smith, and Ned Washington for *Pinocchio.*

Ruttenberg: 318, 573, 749, 769, 828, 1069, 1232, 1371, 1861. Stothart: 397, 1096, 1232, 1274, 1292, 1387, 1662, 1988, 2068, 2193, 2300.

2235 · WAY DOWN SOUTH

SOL LESSER; RKO RADIO. 1939.

NOMINATION *Score:* Victor Young.

There's trouble on the old plantation and the villain threatens to sell young Bobby Breen's slaves. This curious little sentimental musical, which sounds like pure racist tripe, was actually written by black character actor Clarence Muse, who also appears in the film, and the poet Langston Hughes. Also in the cast, directed by Bernard Vorhaus, are Alan Mowbray, Ralph Morgan, Charles Middleton, and the Hall Johnson Choir. The scoring award went to Richard Hageman, Frank Harling, John Leipold, and Leo Shuken for *Stagecoach.*

Young: 97, 98, 100, 101, 280, 489, 612, 693, 701, 794, 846, 925, 1214, 1257, 1396, 1452, 1748, 1823, 1994, 2315.

2236 · WAY OF ALL FLESH, THE

PARAMOUNT FAMOUS LASKY. 1927–28.

AWARD *Actor:* Emil Jannings.

Jannings plays a bank clerk intrusted with some valuable bonds; he's seduced by temptress Phyllis Haver, who steals them. When he causes the death of her accomplice, Jannings switches clothes and identification with the man—who has been conveniently mutilated beyond recognition—to spare his family from disgrace. In the end, like Stella Dallas, he watches his family through the windows of their home. Silent melodrama, based on a novel by Perley Poore Sheehan—not the more respectable novel by Samuel Butler. Directed by Victor Fleming [798]. (Some lists cite *The Way of All Flesh* as a nominee for the best picture Oscar. The Academy's most recent revision of its list of nominees and winners, however, doesn't include it.)

Of the two films for which Jannings was cited by the Academy when they granted him the first best actor award, *The Last Command* is the more celebrated and more frequently seen today. Jannings made his film debut in Germany in 1914 and came to Hollywood in 1927. But though he was the most celebrated of all film actors in Europe, he remained in Hollywood only two years, recognizing that his accent would restrict his American career after the arrival of sound. He returned to Germany in 1929, where he made *The Blue Angel* (1930), the only one of his films that is regularly shown in America today, largely because it launched the career of Marlene Dietrich

[1359]. Jannings' reputation was later damaged because of his support for the Nazis. He died in 1950.

Jannings: 1134.

2237 • WAY OUT WEST

HAL ROACH; MGM. 1937.

NOMINATION Score: Hal Roach Studio Music Department, Marvin Hatley, head; score by Marvin Hatley.

Stan Laurel and Oliver Hardy are waylaid by villain James Finlayson in their attempt to deliver the deed to a gold mine to its rightful owner. Enchanting comedy, the high point of a great team's somewhat spotty feature film career. Their soft-shoe pas de deux is one of the most sweetly lyrical moments on film. Directed by James W. Horne. The scoring award went to Charles Previn for One Hundred Men and a Girl.

Hatley: 234, 2042.

2238 • WAY WE WERE, THE

RASTAR PRODUCTIONS; COLUMBIA. 1973.

AWARDS Song: "The Way We Were," music by Marvin Hamlisch, lyrics by Alan Bergman and Marilyn Bergman. Original Dramatic Score: Marvin Hamlisch. NOMINATIONS Actress: Barbra Streisand. Cinematography: Harry Stradling, Jr. Art Direction—Set Decoration: Stephen Grimes; William Kiernan. Costume Design: Dorothy Jeakins and Moss Mabry.

Katie Morosky (Streisand) is a campus radical in the thirties, and Hubbell Gardiner, played by Robert Redford [1502 . . .], is a Big Man on Campus type, with a sensitive streak under his WASP-jock exterior. But Katie the commie and Hubbell the frat rat get together, first in a creative writing class in which his talent astonishes her, then in New York during the war when they meet and fall in love. But in the fifties their marriage is torn apart when his future as an aspiring screenwriter is threatened by her political past. An old-fashioned romance that was a huge hit, thanks to enormously charismatic leads. Streisand had built her career to this point by playing off her unconventional appearance against handsome leads—Omar Sharif in Funny Girl, Yves Montand in On a Clear Day You Can See Forever (1970), Ryan O'Neal in What's Up, Doc? (1972)—and she snared the prince of Hollywood

when she landed Redford. The movie is a bit of a mess because both stars wanted script rewrites that would show them to the best advantage. And the section dealing with the Hollywood blacklist comes off worst—much of the motivation and characterization seem to have been left in the cutting room. But the movie still delivers solid entertainment. Sydney Pollack [1512 . . .] is the director who had the unenviable task of refereeing off-camera disputes. The screenplay was adapted by Arthur Laurents [2152] from his own novel, which was written with the movies—and Streisand—in mind; many uncredited hands took part in the revisions. Also in the cast are Bradford Dillman as a friend who follows Redford from college to Hollywood, Lois Chiles as Dillman's wife, Viveca Lindfors as a blacklisted screenwriter, James Woods [1746] as one of Streisand's college fellow travelers, and Murray Hamilton, Patrick O'Neal, Allyn Ann McLerie, Herb Edelman, Sally Kirkland [82], and George Gaynes.

This was the year that Hamlisch scored a clean sweep of the music awards, taking not only the Oscars for song and original score but also the one for adaptation score for The Sting. This was the second of the three Oscars won by the Bergmans.

Streisand lost to Glenda Jackson in A Touch of Class. The cinematography Oscar went to Sven Nykvist for Cries and Whispers. The Sting won for art direction and for Edith Head's costumes.

Hamlisch: 398, 977, 1109, 1747, 1813, 1876, 1898, 1927. A. Bergman: 179, 867, 1168, 1568, 1628, 1747, 1813, 1864, 2063, 2113, 2321, 2322. M. Bergman: 179, 867, 1168, 1568, 1628, 1747, 1813, 1864, 2063, 2113, 2321, 2322. Streisand: 737, 1612, 1911. Stradling: 1790. Grimes: 1432, 1512. Kiernan: 1133, 1521, 1550, 1753, 1858. Jeakins: 393, 509, 832, 882, 1048, 1385, 1391, 1432, 1748, 1881, 2012. Mabry: 768, 1355, 2247.

2239 • WEARY RIVER

FIRST NATIONAL. 1928–29.

NOMINATION Director: Frank Lloyd.

Richard Barthelmess [1447 . . .] plays a gangster who becomes a singer while in prison, gaining his release because he's so good. Out-of-circulation early talkie, with Betty Compson [148] and William Holden—but not *the* William Holden [1424 . . .]. Some sources cite Lloyd as having won the Oscar for three films—*Weary River, Drag,* and *The Divine Lady.* The Academy, however, cites him as winner only for *The Divine Lady.* In the official records of the directors branch, which voted the awards but did not release a list of nominees during this second year of Oscars, the other two films are listed as ones for which he was also under consideration.

Lloyd: 374, 552, 575, 1387.

2239.5 • *WEDDING BANQUET, THE*

CENTRAL MOTION PICTURES CORPORATION PRODUCTION (REPUBLIC OF CHINA ON TAIWAN). 1993.

NOMINATION *Foreign Language Film.*

Wai Tung (Winston Chao) lives in New York with his lover, Simon (Mitchell Lichtenstein), and his parents back in Taiwan have no idea that he's gay. To help out a friend, Wei Wei (May Chin), a young artist who's in danger of being deported to China, Wai Tung agrees to marry her. This will solve her problem and his, too—namely, that his parents are always pestering him to get married. But then his parents arrive in New York for the wedding, and a restaurateur friend of theirs prepares the wedding banquet at which the plot finally unravels. Very good-natured comedy, directed by Ang Lee from a screenplay by Lee, Neil Peng, and James Schamus. Much of the film is in English, set in New York, and made with a largely American crew, which only served to point up again one of the foreign language film category's persistent anomalies: In an era of international filmmaking, in which funding comes from various sources and movies are made in a variety of locations, the Academy's stipulation that a film be primarily the work of personnel from the country submitting it for consideration cannot always be fairly enforced. A year earlier, this policy had led to the disqualification of the film *A Place in the World,* which had been submitted by Uruguay, but was withdrawn after the nominations were announced, when the Academy learned it had been produced in Argentina. During the nominating

process for 1993, the Academy disqualified an entry from Poland, *Blue,* whose director, writers, cinematographer, and composer were all Polish, on the grounds that the film was set in France and the dialogue was entirely in French. And *Red,* another film from the same Polish director, Krzysztof Kieslowski, was disqualified by the foreign film committee on the same grounds when the Swiss submitted it for the 1994 awards. *The Wedding Banquet* lost to *Belle Epoque.*

2240 • *WEE WILLIE WINKIE*

20TH CENTURY-FOX. 1937.

NOMINATION *Interior Decoration:* William S. Darling and David Hall.

Shirley Temple stars as the daughter of the regiment. She and her mother, a widow, are living on a British army post in India, where her biggest chum is a sergeant played by Victor McLaglen [999 . . .], but her crabby old grandfather, C. Aubrey Smith, thinks she has no business there. She shows him a thing or two, you can bet. Tolerable nonsense if you have a low Temple threshold. Directed by, of all people, John Ford [815 . . .], with June Lang, Cesar Romero, and Constance Collier. The ostensible source is a story by Rudyard Kipling, but he wouldn't recognize it. Mostly it's the work of screenwriters Ernest Pascal and Julien Josephson. The art direction award went to Stephen Goosson for *Lost Horizon.*

Darling: 83, 374, 1082, 1195, 1655, 1868. Hall: 833.

2241 • *WELL, THE*

HARRY M. POPKIN; UNITED ARTISTS. 1951.

NOMINATIONS *Story and Screenplay:* Clarence Greene and Russell Rouse. *Film Editing:* Chester Schaeffer.

The disappearance of a black child stirs racial animosity in a town, but when it's discovered that she's fallen down a well, the community unites to save her. Okay problem drama, very much of its period but still suspenseful despite the earnest message-delivering. Rouse codirected with Leo Popkin. Harry Morgan—still billed as Henry—is the biggest name in the cast. Alan Jay Lerner won the Oscar for the story and screenplay for *An American in Paris*. The editing award went to William Hornbeck for *A Place in the Sun*.

Greene: 1572. Rouse: 1572.

2242 • *WELLS FARGO*

PARAMOUNT. 1937.

NOMINATION *Sound Recording:* L. L. Ryder.

Joel McCrea stars as the founder of the western delivery service, with Frances Dee as the wife he has to neglect to get his business going. Lively western, with Bob Burns, Lloyd Nolan, Ralph Morgan, John Mack Brown, Porter Hall, Robert Cummings, and Harry Davenport. Directed by Frank Lloyd [374 . . .]. The sound award went to Thomas T. Moulton for *The Hurricane*.

Ryder: 566, 827, 979, 1452, 1669, 1697, 1703, 1837, 1887, 2012, 2168, 2181, 2183, 2230.

2243 • *WEST POINT STORY, THE*

WARNER BROS. 1950.

NOMINATION *Scoring of a Musical Picture:* Ray Heindorf.

James Cagney [79 . . .] is an unemployed Broadway director hired by some West Point cadets to stage their variety show. Though it has songs by Sammy Cahn [74 . . .] and Jule Styne [74 . . .], and the performers include Doris Day [1572], Gordon MacRae, and Gene Nelson, it's a drag. Cagney does his best to bring it to life, and considering how few musicals he made, and how good he was in the ones he did make, it's worth watching for his sake. Directed by Roy Del Ruth.

The scoring Oscar was won by *Annie Get Your Gun*.

Heindorf: 331, 479, 666, 930, 1043, 1204, 1385, 1408, 1430, 1690, 1719, 1750, 1910, 2058, 2186, 2310.

2244 • *WEST SIDE STORY*

MIRISCH PICTURES INC. AND B AND P ENTERPRISES INC.; UNITED ARTISTS. 1961.

AWARDS *Picture:* Robert Wise, producer. *Supporting Actor:* George Chakiris. *Supporting Actress:* Rita Moreno. *Director:* Robert Wise and Jerome Robbins. *Color Cinematography:* Daniel L. Fapp. *Color Art Direction—Set Decoration:* Boris Leven; Victor A. Gangelin.

Sound: Fred Hynes, sound director, Todd-AO Sound Department, and Gordon E. Sawyer, sound director, Goldwyn Studio Sound Department. *Scoring of a Musical Picture:* Saul Chaplin, Johnny Green, Sid Ramin, and Irwin Kostal. *Film Editing:* Thomas Stanford. *Color Costume Design:* Irene Sharaff.

NOMINATION *Screenplay—Based on Material From Another Medium:* Ernest Lehman.

In the slums of Manhattan, a Polish kid named Tony (Richard Beymer) falls in love with a Puerto Rican girl named Maria, played by Natalie Wood [1219 . . .]. But Tony is a member of a gang called the Jets, and Maria's brother, Bernardo (Chakiris), belongs to a gang called the Sharks. As Anita (Moreno), Bernardo's girlfriend, tells Maria: "Stick to your own kind." Tony's attempts to break up a rumble between Sharks and Jets accidentally leads to the deaths of both Bernardo and Tony's friend Riff, played by Russ Tamblyn [1558]. And the vendettas continue . . . Blockbuster filming of a Broadway classic, with music by Leonard Bernstein [1477] and lyrics by Stephen Sondheim [543]. Though it was a huge hit and is some people's favorite film musical, the strengths lie primarily in the score—one of the greatest ever written for a Broadway show—and not in what shows up on screen. Beymer is bland, and Wood is about as convincingly Latina as Janet Leigh was in *Bye, Bye Birdie*. Both are dubbed: Beymer by Jimmy Bryant, Wood by the ubiquitous Marni Nixon. And though the dancing is exciting, it suffers from being performed in a realistic setting—much of the film was shot on location in New York. The Sharks and Jets look like chorus boys warming up outside the theater. Some elements of the transition to film, however, do work: "America" has been restaged from an all-female number to a debate between the Sharks and their girls, and the dancing here, performed on a soundstage rooftop, may be the film's most exciting. The additional lyrics provided for the song, too, have more bite—unlike some of the other songs, such as "Officer Krupke," which have been bowdlerized. The supporting cast is generally good: The Jets include Tucker Smith, Tony Mordente, and Eliot Feld (later the founder of a major ballet company); Simon

Oakland is the police detective in charge of trying to keep order, Ned Glass is Doc, the pharmacist, and John Astin is the social worker called Glad Hand.

Wise began his career as an editor, receiving his first Oscar nomination in that field, for *Citizen Kane.* In 1944 he was drafted into directing by producer Val Lewton, who needed a last-minute replacement on the film *The Curse of the Cat People.* In the years that followed, he amassed some interesting credits, including one of the most memorable sci-fi films of the fifties, *The Day the Earth Stood Still* (1951), as well as *Somebody Up There Likes Me* and *I Want to Live!* He turned to producing in 1959 on the film *Odds Against Tomorrow.*

The wins by Chakiris and Moreno were somewhat controversial. Many had believed that Montgomery Clift and Judy Garland, who had never won Oscars, would take home awards for their performances in *Judgment at Nuremberg.* Chakiris began his film career as a dancer and can be spotted in the production number ensembles for such films as *Gentlemen Prefer Blondes* (1953), *There's No Business Like Show Business,* and *Brigadoon.* Bernardo was his first major film role, but the Oscar he received for it was no career-maker; most of his subsequent films have been minor ones. He can be seen in *Is Paris Burning?* and *The Young Girls of Rochefort,* among about a dozen others, and was a regular on the TV prime-time soap *Dallas.*

Moreno is one of the few people to have won all four major entertainment-industry awards: Oscar, Emmy, Tony, and Grammy. (Helen Hayes [31 . . .] and Richard Rodgers [1921] also won all four. Barbra Streisand [737 . . .] received Oscar, Emmy, and Grammy awards in competition, but her Tony was a special award.) Moreno made her film debut at fourteen in *A Medal for Benny* and appeared in supporting roles in such films as *Singin' in the Rain, The King and I,* and *Summer and Smoke* before her Oscar win. Although her subsequent film career has not been spectacular, she has had better luck than Chakiris in sustaining it, with performances in such movies as *Marlowe* (1969), *Carnal Knowledge,* and *The Four Seasons* (1981) to her credit, as well as frequent television appearances, including a long run on the children's

television show *The Electric Company.* Her singing in *West Side Story* was dubbed by Betty Wand.

Though Wise and Robbins are the only codirecting team to win an Oscar, they were not on the best of terms during the filming, and neither thanked the other during his acceptance speech. The original Broadway show had been based on an idea by Robbins —to contemporize *Romeo and Juliet* for a musical. Robbins began as a dancer in the thirties and moved into choreography in the forties. His ballet *Fancy Free* inspired the musical *On the Town,* which was staged in 1944 and filmed (in a greatly altered version and with different choreography) five years later. Robbins also choreographed such stage hits as *Call Me Madam* and *The King and I.* In 1954 he turned to directing as well as choreographing, with *The Pajama Game,* the start of a string of hits that includes *Bells Are Ringing, West Side Story, Gypsy, A Funny Thing Happened on the Way to the Forum, Funny Girl,* and *Fiddler on the Roof.* The film of *West Side Story* is his only significant film directing credit, although he also choreographed the film of *The King and I,* and his choreography for *Gypsy* and *Fiddler on the Roof* was adapted for the movies. Robbins was the recipient of a special Oscar at the 1961 ceremonies "for his brilliant achievements in the art of choreography on film."

This is the sole Oscar for Fapp, who worked as a technician for Paramount for many years before becoming a cinematographer in the forties. He retired in 1969, after shooting his last film, *Marooned.*

West Side Story's ten Oscars set a record exceeded only by one film, *Ben-Hur,* which won eleven. The sole nominee to go home empty-handed was Lehman, whose screenplay was based on the play by Arthur Laurents [2152]. Lehman lost to Abby Mann for *Judgment at Nuremberg.*

Wise: 407, 973, 1753, 1881. Fapp: 529, 675, 978, 1279, 1492, 2184. Leven: 34, 77, 422, 768, 1753, 1801, 1881, 1907. Gangelin: 1828. Hynes: 33, 413, 1469, 1592, 1881, 1883. Sawyer: 33, 91, 184, 214, 393, 730, 864, 882, 973, 974, 1032, 1511, 1592, 2297, 2310. Chaplin: 66, 914, 1097, 1782. Green: 66, 320, 594, 662, 817, 914, 1298, 1471, 1550, 1657, 2047. Kostal: 166, 1284, 1557, 1881.

Sharaff: 66, 290, 333, 338, 413, 690, 852, 896, 1088, 1507, 1592, 1910, 2000, 2277. Lehman: 896, 1450, 1738, 2277.

2245 • WESTERNER, THE

SAMUEL GOLDWYN PRODUCTIONS; UNITED ARTISTS. 1940.

AWARD *Supporting Actor:* Walter Brennan.

NOMINATIONS *Original Story:* Stuart N. Lake. *Black-and-White Interior Decoration:* James Basevi.

Gary Cooper [701 . . .] plays drifter Cole Harden, who rides into a town run by Judge Roy Bean (Brennan), the self-styled "law west of the Pecos." After talking his way out of being hanged, Harden winds up on the opposite side from the judge in a range war. Entertainingly glossy western that Cooper was reluctant to appear in because he knew Brennan would steal the movie. He was right. William Wyler [175 . . .] directs his first western in more than a decade—he began his Hollywood career churning them out for Universal in the late twenties. The cast includes Forrest Tucker and Dana Andrews in their screen debuts, plus Fred Stone and Chill Wills [33]. The screenplay, credited to Jo Swerling [1607] and Niven Busch [990], was also worked on by Lillian Hellman [1182 . . .] and Oliver La Farge. The cinematography is by Gregg Toland [407 . . .].

Brennan's third Oscar set a record in the acting categories that has been tied only by Ingrid Bergman [72 . . .] and surpassed only by four-time winner Katharine Hepburn [24 . . .]. He would continue as a character player for another thirty years, with memorable performances in *Sergeant York, To Have and Have Not* (1944), *Red River, Bad Day at Black Rock,* and *Rio Bravo* (1959), among scores of others, and achieve TV fame in the late fifties and early sixties on the sitcom *The Real McCoys.* Brennan died in 1974 at the age of eighty.

The award for story went to Benjamin Glazer and John S. Toldy for *Arise, My Love. Pride and Prejudice* won for art direction.

Brennan: 424, 1080, 1779. Basevi: 746, 1082, 1868, 2316.

2245.5 • WET BLANKET POLICY

WALTER LANTZ PRODUCTIONS; UNITED ARTISTS. 1948.

NOMINATION *Song:* "The Woody Woodpecker Song," music and lyrics by Ramey Idriss and George Tibbles.

A Woody Woodpecker animated short subject— the only cartoon short ever to receive a nomination in the song category. Idriss and Tibbles were inspired by the character's signature laugh, which was first heard in the 1940 cartoon "Knock Knock." Woody's creator, Walter Lantz, began using their song as the theme music for the series in 1948. The novelty tune was a big hit for bandleader Kay Kyser, but Mel Blanc, who had created Woody's laugh in 1940, was upset at the song's success, and although he recorded his own version of it, brought suit against Lantz. The suit was finally settled out of court. The Oscar went to Jay Livingston and Ray Evans for "Buttons and Bows," from *The Paleface.*

2246 • WHALES OF AUGUST, THE

ALIVE FILMS PRODUCTION WITH CIRCLE ASSOCIATES; ALIVE FILMS. 1987.

NOMINATION *Supporting Actress:* Ann Sothern.

Lillian Gish [584] and Bette Davis [46 . . .] play sisters making an annual visit to their cottage on the Maine coast, where they delight in watching the migrating whales—although Davis, who is blind, can see them only through the descriptions provided by her sister. There are tensions between the two women, but also a more deeply rooted affection. They are visited during their stay by their rather officious old friend (Sothern), an elderly European former aristocrat now dependent on others for his welfare (Vincent Price), and their longtime handyman (Harry Carey, Jr.). In a flashback to their youth, Gish's character is played by Mary Steenburgen [1300] and Sothern's by the actress' daughter, Tisha Sterling. Gentle, sentimental character drama that's mostly a valedictory for two great screen actresses—this was Gish's last film in a career that spanned seventy-five years, and Davis' next to last. Directed by Lindsay Anderson from a screenplay by David Berry [419].

This was the sole nomination for Sothern, who made her screen debut in 1929 and appeared mostly in B pictures for the next two decades, usually as the wisecracking secretary or sidekick, but sometimes in leads, as in the popular series of *Maisie* pictures made at MGM in the early forties, as well as *Lady Be Good* and *Panama Hattie* (1942). Her most important role was as one of the wives in *A Letter to Three Wives*. She also appeared in some popular TV sitcoms in the fifties. The Oscar went to Olympia Dukakis for *Moonstruck*.

2247 • WHAT A WAY TO GO!

APJAC-ORCHARD PRODUCTION; 20TH CENTURY-FOX. 1964.

NOMINATIONS *Color Art Direction–Set Decoration:* Jack Martin Smith and Ted Haworth; Walter M. Scott and Stuart A. Reiss. *Color Costume Design:* Edith Head and Moss Mabry.

Shirley MacLaine [91 . . .] plays a woman looking for a good man. Trouble is, each time she finds one, he gets rich and then dies. The successive husbands are Dick Van Dyke, Paul Newman [3 . . .], Robert Mitchum [1935], and Gene Kelly [74]. With a bright script by Betty Comden [141 . . .] and Adolph Green [141 . . .] and a fine cast—it also includes Dean Martin, Bob Cummings, Reginald Gardiner, and Margaret Dumont—this parody of the "woman's picture" genre is a lot of fun, though it ought to be better. It's undermined by the poor pacing of director J. Lee Thompson [850] and the garish look that afflicts a lot of mid-sixties color films. The Oscars went to *My Fair Lady* for art direction and Cecil Beaton's costumes.

Smith: 29, 413, 557, 646, 896, 1230, 2008, 2120. Haworth: 1201, 1283, 1550, 1763, 1860. Scott: 46, 376, 413, 476, 530, 542, 557, 646, 896, 1062, 1088, 1213, 1391, 1475, 1706, 1753, 1881, 1907, 2008, 2120. Reiss: 542, 557, 646, 2008, 2093. Head: 31, 32, 46, 305, 357, 363, 612, 636, 675, 736, 832, 894, 945, 1003, 1219, 1261, 1263, 1398, 1427, 1504, 1550, 1579, 1587, 1631, 1716, 1727, 1738, 1748, 1840, 1927, 1986, 2012, 2098, 2298. Mabry: 768, 1355, 2238.

2248 • WHAT EVER HAPPENED TO BABY JANE?

SEVEN ARTS-ASSOCIATES & ALDRICH COMPANY PRODUCTION; WARNER BROS. 1962.

AWARD *Black-and-White Costume Design:* Norma Koch. **NOMINATIONS** *Actress:* Bette Davis. *Supporting Actor:* Victor Buono. *Black-and-White Cinematography:* Ernest Haller. *Sound:* Joseph Kelly, sound director, Glen Glenn Sound Department.

Davis plays the title role, a former child star living with her invalid sister, Blanche, played by Joan Crawford [1319 . . .], also a former movie star, in a gloomy old mansion. Madness and murder ensue. Trash melodrama, and a trashing of two stars whose careers, like those of most film actresses, had faded when they reached their late forties. The film's huge success spawned a series of similar camp horrors, such as *Hush . . . Hush, Sweet Charlotte*. Produced and directed by Robert Aldrich from a screenplay by Lukas Heller based on a novel by Henry Farrell. In addition to Buono, who plays the musical director Davis hires for her planned comeback, the cast includes Davis' daughter, B. D. Merrill, as a neighbor girl. The scenes of Davis and Crawford during their movie careers are from Davis' *Parachute Jumper* (1933) and Crawford's *Sadie McKee* (1934).

The stories of the off-screen rivalry of Crawford and Davis are perhaps more enduring than the movie itself. The contest continued until Oscar night when Crawford managed to upstage nominee Davis by gaining permission from the Academy to accept the award for absentee Anne Bancroft—who was performing in *Mother Courage* on Broadway—if Bancroft should win for *The Miracle Worker*. Crawford lucked out, to Davis' lasting disgust.

Buono, a twenty-five-year-old actor who weighed three hundred pounds, made his film debut in *Baby Jane* and continued his career for several years, with appearances in *Robin and the Seven Hoods, Hush . . . Hush, Sweet Charlotte, The Greatest Story Ever Told,* and *Beneath the Planet of the Apes* (1970), among others. He died in 1982. The Oscar went to Ed Begley for *Sweet Bird of Youth*.

The cinematography award went to Jean Bourgoin

and Walter Wottitz for *The Longest Day.* John Cox won the award for sound for *Lawrence of Arabia.*

Koch: 963, 1126. Davis: 46, 484, 492, 1046, 1162, 1182, 1369, 1456, 1462.5, 1908. Haller: 55, 679, 798, 1046, 1174, 1319.

2249 • WHAT HAPPENED TO SANTIAGO

DIOS LOS CRÍA PRODUCCIONES/PEDRO MUNIZ PRODUCTION (PUERTO RICO). 1989.

NOMINATION *Foreign Language Film.*

A retired accountant has trouble getting along with his children, but his life is changed by a relationship with a woman fifteen years his junior. Slow-moving film directed by Jacobo Morales that was Puerto Rico's first entry in the foreign film Oscar race. It was also released under the title *Santiago, the Story of His New Life.* The Oscar went to *Cinema Paradiso.*

2250 • WHAT NEXT, CORPORAL HARGROVE?

MGM. 1945.

NOMINATION *Original Screenplay:* Harry Kurnitz.

Robert Walker plays the title role, an American soldier in liberated France at the end of World War II. Routine service comedy, a sequel to *See Here, Private Hargrove* (1944), which also starred Walker in an adaptation by Kurnitz of a book by Marion Hargrove. Richard Thorpe directs a cast that includes Keenan Wynn, Jean Porter, Chill Wills [33], and Cameron Mitchell. The year was apparently a lean one for original screenplays; even the winning film in this category, *Marie-Louise,* whose screenplay was by Richard Schweizer, has been long forgotten, as have most of the other nominees: *Dillinger, Music for Millions,* and *Salty O'Rourke.*

2250.3 • WHAT PRICE HOLLYWOOD?

RKO PATHÉ. 1931–32.

NOMINATION *Original Story:* Adela Rogers St. Johns, Jane Murfin.

Hollywood waitress Constance Bennett becomes a star under the tutelage of an alcoholic director (Lowell Sherman), whose own career hits the skids. The obvious source for the three movies called *A Star Is Born,* this one is more satiric and less sentimental, without the romantic involvement of star and mentor that forms the central plot of the later films. Like the first *Star Is Born,* it was produced by David O. Selznick [497 . . .], and like the second it was directed by George Cukor [262 . . .]. It was also Cukor's first film for Selznick at RKO, and it gave a great boost to his career. Gregory Ratoff does a particularly entertaining turn as a producer. Sherman, an actor-director whose own career was ruined by alcohol, is said to have modeled his portrayal on John Barrymore, who was married to Sherman's wife's sister, Dolores Costello. The character is also said to have been based on Marshall (Mickey) Neilan, an important silent film director whose drinking and generally wild behavior cut short his career. The Oscar went to Frances Marion for *The Champ.*

2250.5 • WHAT'S EATING GILBERT GRAPE

MATALON TEPER OHLSSON PRODUCTION; PARAMOUNT. 1993.

NOMINATION *Supporting Actor:* Leonardo DiCaprio.

Gilbert (Johnny Depp) lives in a small town in Iowa, where he clerks in a grocery store and takes care of his retarded brother, Arnie (DiCaprio), and his enormously obese mother (Darlene Cates), as well as his younger sisters. Then one day he falls in love with a young woman, played by Juliette Lewis [342], who is just passing through town. What will happen to the Grapes if Gilbert decides to have his own life? Charmingly eccentric character-based comedy-drama, directed by Lasse Hallström [1400] from a screenplay based by Peter Hedges on his own novel. The fine cast also includes Mary Steenburgen [1300] as a housewife to whom Gilbert delivers more than groceries, and Crispin Glover as Gilbert's creepy friend who works in the local funeral parlor.

DiCaprio had made a well-received debut earlier in the year in *This Boy's Life,* and his performance in *Gilbert Grape* established him as one of the hottest young actors in Hollywood. The Oscar went to Tommy Lee Jones for *The Fugitive.*

2250.7 • *WHAT'S LOVE GOT TO DO WITH IT*

Touchstone Pictures Production; Buena Vista. 1993.
Nominations *Actor:* Laurence Fishburne. *Actress:* Angela Bassett.

Bassett is rocker Tina Turner, with Fishburne as her abusive husband, Ike, in this powerful biopic that shows how Anna Mae Bullock of Nutbush, Tennessee, rose to become a showbiz legend. The movie occasionally succumbs to genre clichés: Tina is a bit too much the naïf who succeeds on the force of talent alone to be entirely credible as a character—the film is based on the autobiography *I, Tina,* written with Kurt Loder. But for the most part it's compelling drama, well scripted by Kate Lanier and directed by Brian Gibson. Terrific musical numbers in which Bassett lip-synchs to Tina's voice also help, but the greatest credit for the film's success should go to the phenomenal performances of Bassett and Fishburne. The latter makes Ike Turner suitably repellent, but we also see clearly what attracted Tina to him.

Fishburne made his screen debut at the age of twelve in *Cornbread, Earl & Me* (1975) and four years later played a member of the crew going upriver in *Apocalypse Now.* Although leading roles for black actors have always been scarce, he made strong impressions in supporting roles in such movies as *The Cotton Club* and *The Color Purple. Boyz N the Hood* provided a breakthrough into more important parts, but he continues to compete with stars such as Denzel Washington [471 . . .], Morgan Freeman [580 . . .], and Wesley Snipes for the few leads open to black actors. The Oscar went to Tom Hanks for *Philadelphia.*

Bassett has more recently arrived in movies, gaining notice for her work as Fishburne's ex-wife in *Boyz N the Hood,* as Betty Shabazz in *Malcolm X,* and as a soap-opera actress in *Passion Fish.* She lost to Holly Hunter in *The Piano.*

2251 • *WHAT'S NEW, PUSSYCAT?*

Famous Artists-Famartists Production; United Artists. 1965.
Nomination *Song:* "What's New, Pussycat?," music by Burt Bacharach, lyrics by Hal David.

Peter O'Toole [164 . . .] plays a fashion magazine editor who is pursued by beautiful women. He goes to psychiatrist Peter Sellers [169 . . .] for help, but Sellers is more interested in finding out the secret of O'Toole's success than in curing him. Fitfully amusing farce, written by Woody Allen [39 . . .] and directed by Clive Donner, who is probably responsible for the herky-jerky pace. As with many films of the mid-sixties, its style and attitudes have dated. Allen reportedly modeled the O'Toole character on Warren Beatty [255 . . .]—the title is said to have been one of his pickup lines—and for a while, Beatty was set to star in it. The Sellers character was written by Allen for himself, but he hadn't achieved stardom, so he was persuaded to take a smaller role. The cast also includes Romy Schneider, Capucine, Paula Prentiss, and Ursula Andress. Richard Burton [85 . . .] has a cameo in a bar scene. The song Oscar went to Johnny Mandel and Paul Francis Webster for "The Shadow of Your Smile," from *The Sandpiper.*

Bacharach: 35, 103, 317, 370. David: 35, 317, 370.

2252 • *WHAT'S THE MATTER WITH HELEN?*

Filmways-Raymax Production; United Artists. 1971.
Nomination *Costume Design:* Morton Haack.

Debbie Reynolds [2184] and Shelley Winters [542 . . .] play two women with a past who start a dance studio in thirties Hollywood. But murder will out . . . Camped-up mystery with good period detail, but the same exploitation of over-the-hill actresses that started with *What Ever Happened to Baby Jane?* Directed by Curtis Harrington, with Dennis Weaver, Agnes Moorehead [963 . . .], and Micheal MacLiammoir. The costuming award went to Yvonne Blake and Antonia Castillo for *Nicholas and Alexandra.*

Haack: 1583, 2184.

2253 • WHEN DINOSAURS RULED THE EARTH

HAMMER FILM PRODUCTION; WARNER BROS. (UNITED KING-DOM). 1971.

NOMINATION *Special Visual Effects:* Jim Danforth and Roger Dicken.

Victoria Vetri and Robin Hawdon star as prehistoric lovers from rival tribes in this British-made action adventure from the Hammer Studios, written and directed by Val Guest. No one takes it seriously, which makes it pretty good fun. The Oscar went to *Bedknobs and Broomsticks.*

Danforth: 1785.

2254 • WHEN FATHER WAS AWAY ON BUSINESS

FORUM FILM PRODUCTION (YUGOSLAVIA). 1985.

NOMINATION *Foreign Language Film.*

Father is actually sent to a labor camp when his mistress gets mad and rats on him to the authorities, claiming he's a Stalinist, in this comedy-drama set in Sarajevo in 1950. The events are seen through the eyes of a six-year-old boy, giving the narrative a fresh and funny spin. Directed by Emir Kusturica. The Oscar went to *The Official Story.*

2255 • WHEN HARRY MET SALLY . . .

CASTLE ROCK PRODUCTION; COLUMBIA. 1989.

NOMINATION *Screenplay Written Directly for the Screen:* Nora Ephron.

College students Harry (Billy Crystal) and Sally (Meg Ryan) share a ride to New York and decide that they have nothing in common. A few years later they meet again and still have nothing in common: She's engaged and he's married. But a few more years later they meet, after his divorce and her breakup with her boyfriend, and decide that they have enough in common to be good friends—nothing more—even though Harry has once pronounced that men and women can't be friends because sex always intervenes. And guess what—it does. Enormously likable romantic comedy, directed by Rob Reiner as an affec-

tionate but sometimes too obvious *hommage* to the early romantic comedies of Woody Allen—particularly *Annie Hall* and *Manhattan.* There's the same scoreful of pop standards—many of them performed by Harry Connick, Jr.—and the same bantering strolls through New York parks and museums, with Sally at one point garbed in *Annie Hall*-ish menswear, and a climactic sprint by Harry through the streets of New York that echoes Allen's similar run in *Manhattan.* Crystal and Ryan are warm and winning performers, and they receive peerless support from Bruno Kirby and Carrie Fisher as their respective confidants. The celebrated delicatessen scene, with a hilarious kicker line spoken by director Reiner's mother, Estelle, is wholly out of character for the reserved Sally, but nobody really minds. The screenplay Oscar went to Tom Schulman for *Dead Poets Society.*

Ephron: 1821, 1839.5.

2256 • WHEN LADIES MEET

MGM. 1932–33.

NOMINATION *Interior Decoration:* Cedric Gibbons

Ann Harding [927] is married to publisher Frank Morgan [22 . . .], who's having an affair with one of his novelists, Myrna Loy. Harding and Loy meet on a weekend at the home of Alice Brady [990 . . .] and become great buddies—until Loy realizes who her new friend is, whereupon she renounces Morgan. Fortunately she has Robert Montgomery [904 . . .] to fall back on. Pleasant but stagy comedy of manners, directed by Harry Beaumont [296] from a screenplay by John Meehan [271 . . .] and Leon Gordon based on a play by Rachel Crothers. Gibbons came in third in the Oscar race, which was won by William S. Darling for *Cavalcade.*

Gibbons: 66, 87, 130, 217, 227, 239, 285, 290, 440, 629, 749, 831, 980, 1069, 1096, 1173, 1190, 1226, 1230, 1232, 1274, 1308, 1309, 1417, 1567, 1604, 1644, 1662, 1673, 1721, 1861, 1937, 2068, 2112, 2257, 2300, 2320, 2330.

2257 • WHEN LADIES MEET

MGM. 1941.

NOMINATION *Black-and-White Interior Decoration:* Cedric Gibbons and Randall Duell, art direction; Edwin B. Willis, set decoration.

Unnecessary, dullish remake of the 1933 comedy, with Greer Garson [239 . . .] as the wronged wife, Herbert Marshall her philandering publisher husband, Joan Crawford [1319 . . .] the other woman, Robert Taylor as Crawford's fallback boyfriend, and Spring Byington [2325] as the hostess of the fateful meeting. This version of the Rachel Crothers play was adapted by S. K. Lauren and Anita Loos and directed by Robert Z. Leonard [555 . . .]. The art direction Oscar went to *How Green Was My Valley.*

Gibbons: 66, 87, 130, 217, 227, 239, 285, 290, 440, 629, 749, 831, 980, 1069, 1096, 1173, 1190, 1226, 1230, 1232, 1274, 1308, 1309, 1417, 1567, 1604, 1644, 1662, 1673, 1721, 1861, 1937, 2068, 2112, 2256, 2300, 2320, 2330. Duell: 227, 1662. Willis: 66, 87, 130, 227, 239, 290, 629, 749, 831, 980, 1069, 1096, 1157, 1173, 1190, 1226, 1230, 1232, 1309, 1417, 1567, 1657, 1662, 1673, 1721, 1861, 1937, 2068, 2112, 2320, 2330.

2258 • WHEN MY BABY SMILES AT ME

20TH CENTURY-FOX. 1948.

NOMINATIONS *Actor:* Dan Dailey. *Scoring of a Musical Picture:* Alfred Newman.

Dailey and Betty Grable are a burlesque team who split up when she gets the chance at the big time. She rescues him after he hits the skids. Average period musical of the kind Fox ground out relentlessly through the forties, directed by Walter Lang [1088], with Jack Oakie [818], June Havoc, Richard Arlen, and James Gleason [904].

A gifted song-and-dance man whose own career had encompassed vaudeville and burlesque, Dailey made his screen debut in 1940, but his career was interrupted after a handful of films by military service. He returned to the screen after the war in the musical *Mother Wore Tights* and made numerous musicals in the late forties and fifties, such as *There's No Business Like Show Business* and *It's Always Fair Weather.*

He also appeared frequently in dramatic roles, most notably as ballplayer Dizzy Dean in *The Pride of St. Louis.* His nomination as best actor, however, was something of a shocker—most people expected Humphrey Bogart to gain a slot on the best actor ballot for his performance in *The Treasure of the Sierra Madre.* The Oscar went to Laurence Olivier for *Hamlet.*

The scoring award went to Johnny Green and Roger Edens for *Easter Parade.*

Newman: 31, 34, 46, 72, 138, 182, 226, 333, 334, 347, 375, 428, 437, 457, 476, 495, 542, 690, 797, 833, 952, 953, 959, 962, 1016, 1082, 1088, 1213, 1278, 1362, 1397, 1475, 1616, 1655, 1849, 1868, 1883, 1921, 2043, 2046, 2091, 2286, 2294, 2316.

2259 • WHEN TIME RAN OUT

WARNER BROS. PRODUCTION; WARNER BROS. 1980.

NOMINATION *Costume Design:* Paul Zastupnevich.

A volcanic eruption on a South Sea island threatens the guests of a luxury resort. Flat, tedious disaster epic—time had run out for the genre, too, after the vogue launched by the success of *The Poseidon Adventure.* Like the others from producer Irwin Allen [2126], this has a big all-star cast, many of whom die horribly: Paul Newman [3 . . .], Jacqueline Bisset, William Holden [1424 . . .], James Franciscus, Edward Albert, Red Buttons [1763], Ernest Borgnine [1283], Burgess Meredith [504 . . .], Valentina Cortese [501], Veronica Hamel, Barbara Carrera, Alex Karras and Noriyuki "Pat" Morita [1077]. Written by two Oscar winners, Carl Foreman [287 . . .] and Stirling Silliphant [992], but you couldn't tell it. Directed by James Goldstone. The costuming award was won by Anthony Powell for *Tess.*

Zastupnevich: 1596, 1983.

2260 • WHEN TOMORROW COMES

UNIVERSAL. 1939.

AWARD *Sound Recording:* Bernard B. Brown.

Waitress Irene Dunne [114 . . .] falls in love with concert pianist Charles Boyer [36 . . .]. Unfortunately he's unhappily married to Barbara O'Neil [55], who is insane. A routine tearjerker, designed primarily to reunite the stars of *Love Affair*. Boyer and O'Neil would follow up this one with *All This and Heaven Too,* in which their relationship is similar. Directed by John M. Stahl [983], from a screenplay by Dwight Taylor based on a story by James M. Cain. *When Tomorrow Comes* was remade twice, in 1957 and 1968, under the title *Interlude.* The win by Brown, longtime head of the Universal sound department, was something of a surprise upset in a category whose nominees included *Gone With the Wind.*

Brown: 93, 96, 269, 919, 1010, 1011, 1125, 1560, 1896, 2028.

2261 • WHEN WILLIE COMES MARCHING HOME

20TH CENTURY-FOX. 1950.
NOMINATION *Motion Picture Story:* Sy Gomberg.

Dan Dailey [2258] stars as a naive soldier who becomes an accidental hero in France during World War II. Very minor comedy from a very major director: John Ford [815 . . .]. Even Fordians have little good to say about it; Andrew Sarris comments that it "seemed to be a Preston Sturges project that Ford directed with undue seriousness." Also in the cast are Corinne Calvet, Colleen Townsend, William Demarest [1058], Evelyn Varden, and Mae Marsh. The writing Oscar went to Edward and Edna Anhalt for *Panic in the Streets.*

2262 • WHEN WORLDS COLLIDE

PARAMOUNT. 1951.
AWARD *Special Effects.* (No individual citation.)
NOMINATION *Color Cinematography:* John F. Seitz and W. Howard Greene.

A planetoid strays from its orbit and heads for earth, so scientists put together a plan to evacuate a saving remnant and head for a new world. Naturally there's a lot of intrigue involving who gets on board —mostly white folks, it seems—and some spectacular scenes of destruction as the gravitational forces of the wandering planet throw the earth's orbit out of whack. New York, for example, gets handsomely flooded. The cornball dialogue detracts from the generally exciting action in this George Pal production directed by Rudolph Maté [455 . . .]. The screenplay is by Sidney Boehm from a novel by Philip Wylie and Edwin Balmer. The cast includes Richard Derr, Barbara Rush, Peter Hanson, and Larry Keating. Like Pal's later and better *War of the Worlds,* this one has exceptional production values for a fifties sci-fi film, especially the fine cinematography, which lost to Alfred Gilks and John Alton's work on *An American in Paris.*

Seitz: 552, 566, 674, 1208, 1714, 1975. Greene: 96, 239, 1070, 1452, 1560, 1621, 1909.

2263 • WHERE LOVE HAS GONE

PARAMOUNT-EMBASSY PICTURES PRODUCTION; PARAMOUNT. 1964.
NOMINATION *Song:* "Where Love Has Gone," music by James Van Heusen, lyrics by Sammy Cahn.

Teenager Joey Heatherton kills her mother's abusive lover in this thinly veiled fictionalization of the Lana Turner [1558]–Joey Stompanato–Cheryl Crane case. Mom is Susan Hayward [973 . . .] and Grandma is Bette Davis [46 . . .], so there's some heavy-duty emoting to be seen. Edward Dmytryk [467] directs from a script by John Michael Hayes [1558 . . .] based on a trashy novel by Harold Robbins. Consider the source, and don't say we didn't warn you. Also in the cast are Michael Connors, Jane Greer, and George Macready. The Oscar went to Richard M. and Robert B. Sherman for "Chim Chim Cher-ee," from *Mary Poppins.*

Van Heusen: 171, 173, 787, 915, 926, 1056, 1524, 1587, 1708, 1859, 1907, 2016, 2064. Cahn: 74, 163, 182, 696, 915, 926, 1031, 1056, 1216, 1524, 1587, 1692, 1708, 1719, 1859, 1907, 2016, 2064, 2072, 2103, 2110, 2125, 2264, 2315, 2343.

2264 • WHIFFS

BRUT PRODUCTIONS; 20TH CENTURY-FOX. 1975.
NOMINATION *Song:* "Now That We're in Love," music by George Barrie, lyrics by Sammy Cahn.

Elliott Gould [250] plays a volunteer in an army experiment who discovers novel ways, both erotic and larcenous, to use the chemicals to which he's exposed. Stupid comedy that deserved all the bad jokes critics made at the expense of its title. Directed by Ted Post, with Eddie Albert [887 . . .], Harry Guardino, Godfrey Cambridge, and Jennifer O'Neill. The Oscar went to Keith Carradine for "I'm Easy," from *Nashville.*

Barrie: 2125. Cahn: 74, 163, 182, 696, 915, 926, 1031, 1056, 1216, 1524, 1587, 1692, 1708, 1719, 1859, 1907, 2016, 2064, 2072, 2103, 2110, 2125, 2263, 2315, 2343.

2265 • *WHISPERERS, THE*
SEVEN PINES PRODUCTIONS LTD.; UNITED ARTISTS (UNITED KINGDOM). 1967.
NOMINATION *Actress:* Edith Evans.

Evans plays an elderly woman, living alone and on the verge of senility, who has paranoid delusions of voices plotting against her. She is taken advantage of by her no-good son (Ronald Fraser) and her estranged husband (Eric Portman). The melodrama, written and directed by Bryan Forbes [81], is thin and depressing, but Evans' brilliance as an actress was never better showcased—the film was written with her in mind. Also in the cast are Avis Bunnage, Gerald Sim, Nanette Newman, and Margaret Tyzack. The score is by John Barry [259 . . .].

This was the third of Evans' three nominations, all unsuccessful. She died in 1976. The Oscar went to Katharine Hepburn for *Guess Who's Coming to Dinner.*

Evans: 377, 2106.

2266 • *WHITE BANNERS*
WARNER BROS.-COSMOPOLITAN. 1938.
NOMINATION *Actress:* Fay Bainter.

Bainter plays a homeless woman who is hired as a cook-housekeeper and takes charge of the disorganized lives of a household headed by Claude Rains [365 . . .], an inventor. Eventually she reveals that she's the real mother of Jackie Cooper [1836], Rains' adopted teenage son. Sentimental drama, now seldom seen, directed by Edmund Goulding from a screenplay by Lenore Coffee [712], Cameron Rogers, and Abem Finkel [1779]. The cast includes Bonita Granville [2044] and James Stephenson [1162]. Bainter be-

came the first person to receive dual nominations in both leading and supporting categories, and while she lost this one to Bette Davis in *Jezebel,* she won for her supporting role in that picture.

Bainter: 393, 1046.

2267 • *WHITE BIM BLACK EAR*
CENTRAL STUDIO OF FILMS FOR CHILDREN AND YOUTH PRODUCTION (USSR). 1978.
NOMINATION *Foreign Language Film.*

Vyacheslav Tikhonov, who played Prince Andrey in *War and Peace,* is an ailing war veteran whose closest companion is a dog that uncovers criminal activities in the neighborhood. Directed by Stanislav Rostotsky. The Oscar went to *Get Out Your Handkerchiefs.*

2268 • *WHITE CHRISTMAS*
PARAMOUNT. 1954.
NOMINATION *Song:* "Count Your Blessings Instead of Sheep," music and lyrics by Irving Berlin.

Bing Crosby [173 . . .] and Danny Kaye are entertainers who teamed up in the army but would rather go their separate ways. Then they're enlisted in an effort to help their former general, played by Dean Jagger [2154], run his winter resort, and meet up with Rosemary Clooney and Vera Ellen. Semi-remake of *Holiday Inn,* which also used the tension between song-and-dance men and a resort setting to string together a bunch of Berlin songs. Fred Astaire [2126] was asked to reteam with Crosby, but declined—Kaye was third choice after Donald O'Connor, who quit because of an injury. Directed by Michael Curtiz [79 . . .] from a screenplay by Norman Krasna [535 . . .], Norman Panama [636 . . .], and Melvin Frank [636 . . .]. It was the first film made in VistaVision, Paramount's answer to CinemaScope. In addition to the title song and "Blue Skies," there were several new songs, among them, "Sisters," "The Best Things Happen While You're Dancing," and the nominee are the standouts. The Oscar went to Jule Styne and Sammy Cahn for the title song from *Three Coins in the Fountain.*

Berlin: 34, 244, 358, 929, 1773, 2115.

2269 • WHITE CLIFFS OF DOVER, THE

MGM. 1944.

Nomination *Black-and-White Cinematography:* George Folsey.

Irene Dunne [114 . . .] plays an American who marries an Englishman (Alan Marshal) and goes to live with his aristocratic family, headed by Gladys Cooper [1393 . . .]. When her husband is killed in World War I, Dunne is distraught, but she pulls herself together for the sake of her son, played by Roddy McDowall. Years pass, and war again looms—this time for her son, now played by Peter Lawford. Dunne does her part during World War II by becoming a nurse—and of course she finds Lawford among the wounded. Long, slow patriotic epic, an attempt by MGM to recapture the spirit of *Mrs. Miniver.* Unfortunately two years of war had passed, and the sentimentality overwhelms the patriotism. Directed by Clarence Brown [84 . . .] from a screenplay by Claudine West [804 . . .], Jan Lustig, and George Froeschel [1371 . . .]. (Froeschel and West had both won Oscars for *Mrs. Miniver,* so the resemblance between the films is hardly accidental.) Also in the cast are Frank Morgan [22 . . .] as Dunne's father, May Whitty [1371 . . .] as a nanny, Elizabeth Taylor [318 . . .] as the neighbor girl who's McDowall's childhood flame, June Lockhart (!) as the same girl grown up, and C. Aubrey Smith, Van Johnson, Jill Esmond, and Norma Varden, among lots of others.

The cinematography Oscar went to Joseph LaShelle for *Laura.*

Folsey: 51, 137, 629, 807, 835, 838, 1124, 1299, 1320, 1500, 1688, 1782, 2068.

2270 • WHITE HEAT

Warner Bros. 1949.

Nomination *Motion Picture Story:* Virginia Kellogg.

James Cagney [79 . . .] plays Cody Jarrett, a gangster with a mother fixation. Mom is Margaret Wycherly [1779], and Edmond O'Brien [146 . . .] plays the G-man who infiltrates Cagney's gang. Strange, fascinatingly Freudian melodrama, exceptionally well directed by Raoul Walsh. The ending, in which Cagney blows up an oil storage tank, and himself with it, is famous, as is the scene in prison when Cagney goes berserk on learning of his mother's death. Cagney certainly deserved a nomination instead of Richard Todd for *The Hasty Heart,* but the film's violence may have been too much for the Academy.

The writing award went to Douglas Morrow for *The Stratton Story.*

Kellogg: 328.

2271 • WHITE NIGHTS

New Visions Production; Columbia. 1985.

Award *Song:* "Say You, Say Me," music and lyrics by Lionel Richie.

Nomination *Song:* "Separate Lives (Love Theme from White Nights)," music and lyrics by Stephen Bishop.

Exiled dancer Mikhail Baryshnikov [2152] is accidentally repatriated when his plane is forced to make an emergency landing in the Soviet Union. While the Americans try to negotiate his return, the KGB lodges him with an American defector, played by Gregory Hines, who chose to come to the Soviet Union to protest racism and the Vietnam War and has married a Russian woman, played by Isabella Rossellini. But Hines has grown weary of his exile and joins Baryshnikov in plotting their escape. Unfortunately, despite a promising idea, the script by James Goldman [1177] and Eric Hughes fails to deliver: There's not enough tension to sustain the movie's two hours and fifteen minutes. Baryshnikov is, however, terrific, giving a performance that's at least the equal of his nominated one in *The Turning Point.* There are several great dance scenes, when the movie comes vividly to life, and Hines makes an impressive partner in a couple of them. Also in the cast, directed by Taylor Hackford, are Polish film director Jerzy Skolimowski as a KGB agent, Helen Mirren [1234.5] as Baryshnikov's old lover, now a Soviet ballet impresario, and Geraldine Page [935 . . .] as Baryshnikov's agent. The choreography is by Twyla Tharp.

Richie founded one of Motown's most successful groups, the Commodores, in the seventies and went solo in 1981. He moved from soul onto the pop charts and became one of the biggest singer-songwriters of the eighties. In recent years, however, his prominence on the music scene has declined.

Richie: 423, 616.

2272 • WHITE PARADE, THE

JESSE L. LASKY; FOX. 1934.

NOMINATIONS *Picture:* Jesse L. Lasky, producer. *Sound Recording:* Fox Studio Sound Department, E. H. Hansen, sound director.

Loretta Young [428 . . .] stars in this docudrama about the experiences of student nurses at a hospital. The film, directed by Irving Cummings [989] from a screenplay by Sonya Levien [1007 . . .] and Ernest Pascal, is not in circulation today. The cast includes Astrid Allwyn, Jane Darwell [815], and Frank Conroy. The Oscar went to *It Happened One Night.*

Lasky: 1779. Hansen: 143, 241, 815, 952, 990, 1655, 1868, 1957, 2027, 2056, 2286, 2317.

2273 • WHITE SHADOWS IN THE SOUTH SEAS

COSMOPOLITAN; MGM. 1928–29.

AWARD *Cinematography:* Clyde de Vinna.

Monte Blue plays an alcoholic doctor who finds paradise and native woman Raquel Torres along with it, but loses both when other white colonials arrive. Picturesque melodrama that began under the codirection of W. S. Van Dyke [1751 . . .] and the great documentarian Robert Flaherty [1211], but Flaherty quit out of frustration with the inanity of the script and the awkwardness of the collaboration. The partial talkie was one of MGM's first ventures into sound—among other things, it's the first movie in which audiences heard Leo roar in the opening credits. Otherwise, it's long forgotten.

De Vinna began his career as a cinematographer in 1915 and became a specialist in outdoor and action photography, working on the 1926 *Ben-Hur,* as well as *Trader Horn* and the first of the MGM Johnny Weissmuller *Tarzan* films. He died in 1953.

2273.5 • WHITE WILDERNESS

WALT DISNEY PRODUCTIONS; BUENA VISTA. 1958.

NOMINATION *Music Score of a Dramatic or Comedy Picture:* Oliver Wallace.

A Disney True-Life Adventure exploring the Arctic, with the usual extraordinary nature footage of polar bears, wolves, and other animals. More solid and straightforward than many in the series, less prone to the cutes, although its simplistic portrayal of the lemmings' supposed headlong rush to self-destruction makes some naturalists want to tear their hair. Eleven photographers worked on the footage, all of which was shot in 16mm and blown up—quite successfully—to 35mm. Directed by James Algar, with the familiar narrative voice of Winston Hibler. The scoring award went to Dimitri Tiomkin for *The Old Man and the Sea.* The film won the Oscar for best documentary feature.

Wallace: 42, 402, 585, 2202.

2274 • WHO FRAMED ROGER RABBIT

AMBLIN ENTERTAINMENT AND TOUCHSTONE PICTURES PRODUCTION; BUENA VISTA. 1988.

AWARDS *Film Editing:* Arthur Schmidt. *Visual Effects:* Ken Ralston, Richard Williams, Edward Jones, and George Gibbs. *Sound Effects Editing:* Charles L. Campbell and Louis L. Edemann. *Special Achievement Award:* Richard Williams for animation direction.

NOMINATIONS *Cinematography:* Dean Cundey. *Art Direction–Set Decoration:* Elliot Scott, art direction; Peter Howitt, set decoration. *Sound:* Robert Knudson, John Boyd, Don Digirolamo, and Tony Dawe.

Bob Hoskins [1343] is a seedy detective in forties L.A., who gets (literally) drawn into a murder investigation involving a cartoon rabbit with a cartoon wife; much of the intrigue hinges on a plot to replace L.A.'s efficient public transportation system with (gasp!) freeways. Ingenious fantasia on the premise that cartoon characters actually lived in a part of L.A. called Toontown, but were considered lower-class citizens by flesh-and-blood types. The result is part *Chinatown,* part Looney Tunes and Merrie Melodies. The truly astonishing blend of live action and animation won a deserved raft of technical Oscars, but the movie is so hyped-up that one comes away from it with a bit of a hangover. Hoskins, Christopher Lloyd, Joanna Cassidy, Stubby Kaye, and the other live actors give impressive performances, considering that they were acting and reacting to thin air and blue screens for much of the time. The speaking voice for the voluptuous Jessica Rabbit is that of Kathleen Turner [1545], but her singing voice belongs to Amy Irving [2321]. The live performers were directed by Robert Zemeckis [127 . . .]. The screenplay is by Jeffrey Price and Peter S. Seaman. The project was made possible by the collaboration of Disney and Amblin, the production company headed by Steven Spielberg [416 . . .]; the collaboration of other license holders allowed the first on-screen appearances of Warner Bros.' Bugs Bunny and Daffy Duck together with Disney's Mickey Mouse and Donald Duck and many other familiar toons. There were, however, some holdouts: The owners of the Popeye copyright refused to have their characters appear.

The cinematography Oscar went to Peter Biziou for *Mississippi Burning. Dangerous Liaisons* took the award for art direction. *Bird* won the Oscar for sound.

Schmidt: 418, 708.5, 1763, 1975. Ralston: 128, 419, 513.5, 577, 708.5, 1684. Gibbs: 45.5, 997. Campbell: 127, 588, 684. Scott: 69, 995. Howitt: 995, 1285, 1651. Knudson: 321, 416, 588, 613, 631, 938, 1439, 1877, 1911. Boyd: 613. Dawe: 613, 996, 1684.

2275 • *WHO IS HARRY KELLERMAN, AND WHY IS HE SAYING THESE TERRIBLE THINGS ABOUT ME?*

WHO IS HARRY KELLERMAN COMPANY PRODUCTION; CINEMA CENTER FILMS PRESENTATION; NATIONAL GENERAL PICTURES. 1971.
NOMINATION *Supporting Actress:* Barbara Harris.

Dustin Hoffman [810 . . .] plays a hugely successful singer-songwriter who develops paranoid delusions. Misfired and confusing satirical drama written by Herb Gardner [2067] and directed by Ulu Grosbard, with Jack Warden [890 . . .], David Burns, Gabriel Dell, and Dom DeLuise. Its chief dis-

tinction is that it has the longest title of any movie nominated for an Oscar—one word longer than *Dr. Strangelove* . . .

Harris plays Hoffman's girlfriend, an aspiring—but awful—singer. An actress of immense charm, she has confined her career for the most part to the Broadway stage. She made her film debut in *A Thousand Clowns,* also written by Gardner, and has been seen in occasional movies, including *Nashville* and the last film directed by Alfred Hitchcock [1171 . . .], *The Family Plot* (1976). She lost the Oscar to Cloris Leachman in *The Last Picture Show*.

2276 • *WHOOPEE!*

SAMUEL GOLDWYN PRODUCTIONS; UNITED ARTISTS. 1930–31.
NOMINATION *Interior Decoration:* Richard Day.

Eddie Cantor plays a hypochondriac who goes West and has a series of farcical adventures in which he winds up an inadvertent hero. Very early movie musical that was a groundbreaker in several important ways. For one thing, it was filmed in Technicolor—the two-color version that looks today like the insipid "colorizing" of black-and-white movies for TV. This necessitated three top-notch cameramen—Lee Garmes [201 . . .], Gregg Toland [407 . . .], and color specialist Ray Rennahan [235 . . .]. It introduced to films one of the essential figures of the movie musical, choreographer Busby Berkeley [791 . . .]. And it was coproduced by Broadway legend Florenz Ziegfeld and Hollywood legend Samuel Goldwyn [102 . . .]—a volatile collaboration to say the least. Ziegfeld had produced the original version of the show on Broadway, where it had been a big hit. He had always steered clear of Hollywood, but having lost his shirt in the stock market crash, he needed the money. Still, the movie, directed by Thornton Freeland, is at best a cultural artifact, and a document of the entertainment phenomenon of Eddie Cantor—who strikes contemporary tastes as very odd indeed.

This was also the first Goldwyn film to be designed by Day, who would be a key member of the producer's team for the next twenty years. The art direction Oscar went to Max Ree for *Cimarron*.

Day: 22, 102, 235, 487, 510, 560, 569, 797, 833,

864, 952, 1048, 1175, 1397, 1477, 1666, 1949, 2056, 2120.

2277 • WHO'S AFRAID OF VIRGINIA WOOLF?

CHENAULT PRODUCTIONS; WARNER BROS. 1966.
AWARDS *Actress:* Elizabeth Taylor. *Supporting Actress:* Sandy Dennis. *Black-and-White Cinematography:* Haskell Wexler. *Black-and-White Art Direction–Set Decoration:* Richard Sylbert; George James Hopkins. *Black-and-White Costume Design:* Irene Sharaff.
NOMINATIONS *Picture:* Ernest Lehman, producer. *Actor:* Richard Burton. *Supporting Actor:* George Segal. *Director:* Mike Nichols. *Screenplay—Based on Material From Another Medium:* Ernest Lehman. *Sound:* George R. Groves, sound director, MGM Studio Sound Department. *Original Music Score:* Alex North. *Film Editing:* Sam O'Steen.

George (Burton) and Martha (Taylor), an academic couple locked in a sadomasochistic relationship, invite a young professor (Segal) and his wife (Dennis) for an evening of alcohol and abuse. Edward Albee's play was brought to the screen with much of its language intact, making 1966 a watershed year in Hollywood censorship: The old Production Code finally collapsed. Today, what's said on screen in *Virginia Woolf* seems tame, but it remains a powerful, corrosive drama, made palatable by its wit and a quartet of superb performances.

Taylor was a surprise choice for the role of Martha, who was supposed to be some fifteen years older and a good deal plainer than the famous violet-eyed beauty. Albee himself is said to have wanted Bette Davis [46 . . .] for the part. But Taylor was at the peak of her celebrity and a top box-office draw, so when her agent, Hugh French, suggested her to Lehman, the producer was intrigued. Those who had doubts about the casting included the director, who reportedly said before filming started that it was "like asking a chocolate milk shake to do the work of a double martini." But in the end, having gained weight—the start of an unfortunate problem for the actress—and submitted to deglamorizing makeup, Taylor gave an extraordinary performance. Her voice,

always on the shrill side, particularly suited Martha's nagging manner. Ironically the second Oscar—the one that she deserved, as opposed to the one she received for *Butterfield 8* after a near-fatal illness—marked the beginning of her career's decline. Most of her subsequent roles have been in substandard films and eccentric roles. Personal problems and poor health have also limited her career in recent years to TV movies and occasional cameos in films such as the 1994 *The Flintstones*. At the Oscar ceremony in 1993, she received the Jean Hersholt Humanitarian Award for her work on behalf of funding AIDS research.

Dennis made her screen debut in 1961 in *Splendor in the Grass* but returned to New York for the next five years, winning two Tony Awards for her work in the plays *A Thousand Clowns* and *Any Wednesday*. Her roles in the film versions of those plays, however, went to Barbara Harris [2275] and Jane Fonda [394 . . .] respectively. The Oscar gave her a new career on screen, most notably as the schoolteacher in *Up the Down Staircase* (1967), but her rather rabbity persona was too eccentric for a steady film career. She died in 1992 at the age of fifty-four.

Wexler had built his career on documentary work, and his earlier films had a street-real quality to them. Burton reportedly objected to him because the actor was self-conscious about the acne scarring on his face and feared a too-realistic cameraman would play up his blemishes. The veteran Harry Stradling [110 . . .] was considered, but Stradling declined to work with a novice film director, Nichols, and was reluctant to deglamorize Taylor. The Oscar established Wexler's career, enabling him to make one of the most remarkable films of the sixties, *Medium Cool* (1969), a blend of documentary footage of the rioting at the 1968 Democratic Convention with a story about a photographer who tries to detach himself from what he's filming. Wexler wrote, directed, produced, and photographed *Medium Cool,* which unaccountably received not a single Oscar nomination.

Sylbert has become one of the most sought-after art directors in the poststudio era. Here he works with set decorator Hopkins, a veteran of the heyday of the studios. Sharaff was Taylor's favorite costumer, and she proves as adept at dressing the star down as she was at dressing her up.

Lehman had been one of Hollywood's most successful screenwriters since the early fifties. With *Virginia Woolf* he moved into producing, but his subsequent films as producer were not distinguished: They include *Hello, Dolly!*, the peculiar attempt to film Philip Roth's *Portnoy's Complaint* (1972)—which he also directed—and the last film of Alfred Hitchcock [1171 . . .], *The Family Plot.* The best picture Oscar went to *A Man for All Seasons.*

At first, Burton had not wanted to play George, feeling the mousy, put-upon spouse was not the image he wanted to project, especially since he had just played another gray little man in *The Spy Who Came in From the Cold.* But he was attracted by the prospect of working with Taylor on a film that would be more serious and prestigious than the trashy melodramas that had previously teamed them—*Cleopatra, The V.I.P.'s, The Sandpiper.* Albee's choice for George was James Mason [761 . . .], and there had been talk of Jack Lemmon [91 . . .], Arthur Hill, and Peter O'Toole [164 . . .] for the part as well. In the end the combined force of the Burtons was irresistible, and it turned out to be one of Burton's strongest roles. He was considered the front-runner for the Oscar, but the high-gloss prestige of a costume drama, *A Man For All Seasons,* carried Paul Scofield to the award.

Segal's career was already on the ascent when he was nominated for *Virginia Woolf.* His somewhat abrasive manner limited his career to character leads, and as he grew older such roles went more frequently to actors like Richard Dreyfuss [803]. The Oscar went to Walter Matthau for *The Fortune Cookie.*

Nichols made his screen directing debut with *Virginia Woolf.* Fred Zinnemann [732 . . .] had been approached about directing the film, but turned it down to direct *A Man for All Seasons,* for which he won the Oscar. Nichols had begun his career as an improvisational actor in a company that included Elaine May [890], Alan Arkin [884 . . .], and Barbara Harris. He formed a stand-up comedy team with May, appearing on Broadway and frequently on television. He

made his directorial debut on Broadway with a smash hit, *Barefoot in the Park,* and directed a string of hits, which brought him to the attention of the Burtons. He has continued to divide his time as director between Broadway and Hollywood.

Lehman's screenplay lost to Robert Bolt's for *A Man for All Seasons.* The sound and editing awards went to *Grand Prix.* The scoring award was won by John Barry for *Born Free.*

Taylor: 318, 372, 1657, 1956. Wexler: 229, 264, 1288, 1481. Sylbert: 395, 448, 543, 1678, 1798. Hopkins: 110, 508, 896, 1003, 1170, 1332, 1385, 1393, 1910, 1949, 1973, 2058. Sharaff: 66, 290, 333, 338, 413, 690, 852, 896, 1088, 1507, 1592, 1910, 2000, 2244. Lehman: 896, 1450, 1738, 2244. Burton: 85, 164, 621, 1391, 1706, 1897. Nichols: 810, 1679.5, 1821, 2313. Groves: 825, 1385, 1393, 1457, 1763, 1869, 1973. North: 29, 215, 413, 515, 577, 1654, 1727, 1802, 1814, 1886, 1949, 2174, 2177, 2212. O'Steen: 395, 1821.

2278 • WHY GIRLS LEAVE HOME

PRC. 1945.

NOMINATIONS *Song:* ''The Cat and the Canary,'' music by Jay Livingston, lyrics by Ray Evans. *Scoring of a Musical Picture:* Walter Greene.

Pamela Blake plays a young woman who runs away from home and gets a job as a nightclub singer but finds herself in trouble when she accidentally learns too much about her shady employers. Low-rent melodrama, directed by William Berke, with Lola Lane, Sheldon Leonard, and Elisha Cook, Jr.

This was the first nomination for the songwriting team of Livingston and Evans, who would go on to win three Oscars, but they owe it primarily to the practice—discontinued after this year—of allowing each studio, including ''poverty row'' PRC (short for Producers Releasing Corporation), to submit its own candidates in certain categories. The Oscar went to a somewhat more established team: Richard Rodgers and Oscar Hammerstein II for ''It Might As Well Be Spring,'' from *State Fair.* The scoring award went to Georgie Stoll for *Anchors Aweigh.*

Livingston: 344, 512, 951, 1260, 1522, 2001. Evans: 344, 512, 951, 1260, 1522, 2001.

2279 • WILD AT HEART

POLYGRAM/PROPAGANDA FILMS PRODUCTION; SAMUEL GOLD-
WYN COMPANY. 1990.

NOMINATION *Supporting Actress:* Diane Ladd.

Nicolas Cage is Sailor Ripley and Laura Dern [1659] is his girlfriend Lula Fortune in this eccentric road movie directed by David Lynch [247 . . .], who also wrote the screenplay, based on a novel by Barry Gifford. The two murderous lovers are on the run from her mother (Ladd), who has hired some goons, including a particularly over-the-top one played by Willem Dafoe [1584], to pursue them. The movie is a surreal grab bag of cultural allusions ranging from *The Wizard of Oz* to Elvis Presley to the films of Kurosawa. The jury at Cannes gave it the Palme d'Or—which was greeted with both cheers and boos. Most American critics panned the film, finding it disjointed and gruesomely silly, and the box office returns were poor. It seems to have damaged Lynch's career rather than advancing it from the cult celebrity he had earned with *Blue Velvet* and the *Twin Peaks* TV series. For those who can stomach its occasional forays into mad violence, *Wild at Heart* has plenty to watch, and a colorful cast including Isabella Rossellini, Harry Dean Stanton, Crispin Glover, Grace Zabriskie, Sherilyn Fenn, and Sheryl Lee. Ladd lost to Whoopi Goldberg in *Ghost.*

Ladd: 41, 1659.

2280 • WILD BUNCH, THE

PHIL FELDMAN PRODUCTION; WARNER BROS.-SEVEN ARTS. 1969.

NOMINATIONS *Story and Screenplay—Based on Material Not Previously Published or Produced:* story by Walon Green and Roy N. Sickner; screenplay by Walon Green and Sam Peckinpah. *Original Score—for a Motion Picture (Not a Musical):* Jerry Fielding.

Four over-the-hill outlaws, played by William Holden [1424 . . .], Ernest Borgnine [1283], Warren Oates, and Ben Johnson [1139], set out on a final adventure in Mexico during the revolution of 1914, pursued by a posse headed by Robert Ryan [467]. Extraordinary western, a genuine classic, that uses extravagantly bloody violence to underscore its portrait of human folly. Directed by Peckinpah, the film was severely cut by the studio before release, which may have harmed its initial critical reception and prevented the Academy from giving it its due. It's certainly far more deserving of a best picture nomination than the dull and stately *Anne of the Thousand Days* or the overstuffed *Hello, Dolly!* A version restored to two hours and twenty-two minutes is now available on video. The movie also made headlines in 1994, when the motion picture ratings board screened a restored print of *The Wild Bunch* and reclassified it from its original R rating to NC-17; the decision was reversed after an appeal. The cinematography is by Lucien Ballard [359]. Also in the cast are Jaime Sanchez, Strother Martin, L. Q. Jones, Albert Dekker, Bo Hopkins, Emilio Fernandez, Dub Taylor, and Alfonso Arau, who would later win acclaim as a director, including the hit *Like Water for Chocolate* (1992).

Peckinpah began as a TV director of westerns and made his first big-screen film, *The Deadly Companions,* in 1961. Many of his subsequent films have become critical or cult favorites, though most received little or no attention from the Academy. They include *Ride the High Country* (1962), *Major Dundee* (1965), *The Ballad of Cable Hogue* (1970), *The Getaway* (1972), *Straw Dogs, Junior Bonner* (1972), and *Pat Garrett and Billy the Kid* (1973). He died in 1984. The story and screenplay Oscar went to William Goldman for *Butch Cassidy and the Sundance Kid,* which also won for Burt Bacharach's score.

Fielding: 1514, 1944.

2281 • WILD IN THE STREETS

AMERICAN INTERNATIONAL PICTURES. 1968.

NOMINATION *Film Editing:* Fred Feitshans and Eve Newman.

Rock star Christopher Jones uses his celebrity (and judicious applications of LSD in the right places) to get himself elected president of the United States, whereupon everyone over thirty is put into concentration camps and kept high on acid. Dated, camp, dumb but funny youth-cult exploitation fantasy that would have worked better if Jones were a more charismatic actor. Shelley Winters [542 . . .] plays his mom, and the cast includes Diane Varsi [1558], Hal

Holbrook, Millie Perkins, Ed Begley [1985], and Richard Pryor. Directed by Barry Shear. The editing Oscar went to Frank P. Keller for *Bullitt*.

Newman: 2163.

2282 • WILD IS THE WIND

HAL WALLIS PRODUCTIONS; PARAMOUNT. 1957.
NOMINATIONS *Actor:* Anthony Quinn. *Actress:* Anna Magnani. *Song:* "Wild Is the Wind," music by Dimitri Tiomkin, lyrics by Ned Washington.

When his wife dies, Nevada rancher Quinn sends for her sister, Magnani, in Italy, but he is disappointed because of her lack of resemblance to his first wife and neglects her. So she and his adopted son, played by Anthony Franciosa [880], fall in love. Tiresome reworking of an old story—part *They Knew What They Wanted,* part *Phaedra*—with an unconvincing happy ending. Quinn, Magnani, and Franciosa, all over-the-top actors, are just barely held in check by director George Cukor [262 . . .], handling material to which he was not particularly suited—he replaced the original director, John Sturges [131]. Written by Arnold Schulman [802 . . .]. The best actor Oscar went to Alec Guinness for *The Bridge on the River Kwai.* Magnani lost to Joanne Woodward in *The Three Faces of Eve.* The song award went to James Van Heusen and Sammy Cahn for "All the Way," from *The Joker Is Wild.*

Quinn: 1226, 2212, 2346. Magnani: 1727. Tiomkin: 33, 286, 380, 446, 638, 663, 730, 768, 850, 911, 912, 1206, 1347, 1370, 1470, 2006, 2127, 2335. Washington: 274, 585, 911, 912, 1329, 1396, 1576, 1745, 2127, 2335.

2283 • WILD STRAWBERRIES

A.B. SVENSK FILMINDUSTRI PRODUCTION; JANUS FILMS (SWEDEN). 1959.
NOMINATION *Story and Screenplay—Written Directly for the Screen:* Ingmar Bergman.

An elderly professor (Victor Sjöström) is on his way by car, driven by his daughter-in-law (Ingrid Thulin), to receive an honor at his university. On the way, they stop at his old family home, where memories and fantasies come flooding in. One of the first films by Bergman to make an international impression, and many regard it as one of his best. The director's style became more spare and grim in later films, but this one is given great warmth by the performance of Sjöström—an important Swedish director who had an impressive brief career in Hollywood, where, as Victor Seastrom, he directed several silent films, including *The Wind* (1928). The Oscar went, believe it or not, to Russell Rouse, Clarance Greene, Stanley Shapiro, and Maurice Richlin for *Pillow Talk.*

Bergman: 111, 460, 634, 644, 2082.

2284 • WILLOW

LUCASFILM PRODUCTION IN ASSOCIATION WITH IMAGINE ENTERTAINMENT; MGM. 1988.
NOMINATIONS *Visual Effects:* Dennis Muren, Michael McAlister, Phil Tippett, and Chris Evans. *Sound Effects Editing:* Ben Burtt and Richard Hymns.

Warwick Davis plays the title role in this fantasy about a little person who finds a baby and discovers that it is the key to breaking the spell cast by a sorceress (Jean Marsh). Willow sets out with the baby, encountering along the way a roguish drifter, Madmartigan (Val Kilmer), who winds up battling the forces marshaled by the sorceress—and winning her beautiful daughter (Joanne Whalley-Kilmer), who turns against her mother. Many critics carped at the derivativeness of this adventure story; there are elements of the Tolkien *Lord of the Rings* saga, bits of *Star Wars,* and borrowings from myth, legend, fairy tale, and of course other movies. And the obvious criticism that followed is that *Willow* isn't as good as most of its sources. But it's a handsomely executed pastiche, with enough special effects wizardry to hold one's interest through most of its slightly overextended length. (Some of the bad guys are given the names of prominent critics: There's a monster called the Siskbert and an enemy general named Kael.) Directed by Ron Howard. The effects awards went to *Who Framed Roger Rabbit.*

Muren: 5, 577, 588, 614, 997, 1002, 1071.5, 1684, 2019, 2339. McAlister: 997. Tippett: 577, 1071.5, 1684. Burtt: 588, 996, 1652, 1684, 1916. Hymns: 129, 996, 1071.5.

2285 • WILLY WONKA AND THE CHOCOLATE FACTORY

WOLPER PICTURES LTD. PRODUCTION; PARAMOUNT. 1971.

NOMINATION *Scoring—Adaptation and Original Song Score:* song score by Leslie Bricusse and Anthony Newley; adaptation score by Walter Scharf.

Gene Wilder [1626 . . .] plays the curious, somewhat sinister candy manufacturer Wonka who holds a contest whose award is a tour of his factory. In the end it's revealed that the contest is really a test of the children's honesty. Offbeat but unpleasantly overwhelming fantasy-musical for children, directed by Mel Stuart from Roald Dahl's adaptation of his own book. The cast includes Jack Albertson [1954] and Roy Kinnear. The set designs by Harper Goff are the main attraction. The Oscar went to John Williams for *Fiddler on the Roof.*

Bricusse: 557, 805, 933, 937, 1766, 2037, 2201. Scharf: 174, 274, 665, 737, 864, 921, 991, 1054, 1305.

2286 • WILSON

20TH CENTURY-FOX. 1944.

AWARDS *Original Screenplay:* Lamar Trotti. *Color Cinematography:* Leon Shamroy. *Color Interior Decoration:* Wiard Ihnen, art direction; Thomas Little, set decoration. *Sound Recording:* E. H. Hansen. *Film Editing:* Barbara McLean.

NOMINATIONS *Picture:* Darryl F. Zanuck, producer. *Actor:* Alexander Knox. *Director:* Henry King. *Scoring of a Dramatic or Comedy Picture:* Alfred Newman. *Special Effects:* Fred Sersen, photographic; Roger Heman, sound.

The life of President Woodrow Wilson, and his disillusioning experience trying to establish the League of Nations. Blockbuster biopic, more than two and a half hours long, and somewhat more entertaining than you might expect. Unfortunately for producer Zanuck, who was as obsessed with the project as Wilson was with the League, contemporary audiences didn't expect it to be entertaining at all, and stayed away. The huge cast includes Charles Coburn [535 . . .], Geraldine Fitzgerald [2316] as Mrs. Wilson, Thomas Mitchell [962 . . .], Cedric Hardwicke

as Henry Cabot Lodge, Vincent Price, Sidney Blackmer, Marcel Dalio as Clemenceau, and Francis X. Bushman as Bernard Baruch. Zanuck's obsession was rewarded with the second of his three Irving G. Thalberg awards, but he was infuriated at the film's failure to win best picture—an award that went to *Going My Way.* When *Gentleman's Agreement* won the best picture Oscar four years later, Zanuck accepted the award with the comment "I should have got this for *Wilson.*"

Trotti, a former newspaper and movie trade magazine publisher, started his career as a screenwriter in 1933 and moved into producing at Fox in the forties. He died in 1952.

This was the second of four Oscars for Shamroy, the first of Ihnen's two Oscars, and the fifth win out of six for Little. Ihnen had studied architecture before turning to design for the movies in 1919 at Famous Players-Lasky, which later became Paramount. He was married to costumer Edith Head [31 . . .].

Hansen and McLean were leading figures in their respective fields. McLean was the mainstay of Fox's editing department, a division that had a great deal of importance under Zanuck, who was notorious for maintaining strict control of the final cut of all films under his supervision. She retired in 1955.

Knox had a career lasting more than fifty years in movies, starting in England in 1931 and continuing into the mid-eighties. Primarily a character player, *Wilson* provided him with one of his few leading roles. He was also a screenwriter and novelist. His films as actor include *The Four Feathers, The Sea Wolf, This Above All, Khartoum,* the James Bond movie *You Only Live Twice* (1967), and *Nicholas and Alexandra.* The Oscar went to Bing Crosby for *Going My Way,* which also won for Leo McCarey's direction. Max Steiner took the scoring Oscar for *Since You Went Away.* The award for special effects went to *Thirty Seconds Over Tokyo.*

Trotti: 1516, 2043, 2337. Shamroy: 29, 226, 356, 413, 495, 569, 602, 1088, 1153, 1213, 1592, 1610, 1706, 1852, 1883, 2013, 2334. Ihnen: 237, 627. Little: 46, 83, 235, 428, 495, 719, 721, 746, 950, 952, 1082, 1149, 1153, 1397, 1475, 1666, 1852, 1868, 2056, 2212. Hansen: 143, 241, 815, 952, 990, 1655, 1868, 1957, 2027, 2056, 2272, 2317.

McLean: 34, 46, 1195, 1327, 1655, 1868. Zanuck: 34, 46, 550, 710, 759, 815, 946, 952, 990, 1201, 1327, 1666, 2154. King: 1868. Newman: 31, 34, 46, 72, 138, 182, 226, 333, 334, 347, 375, 428, 437, 457, 476, 495, 542, 690, 797, 833, 952, 953, 959, 962, 1016, 1082, 1088, 1213, 1278, 1362, 1397, 1475, 1616, 1655, 1849, 1868, 1883, 1921, 2043, 2046, 2091, 2258, 2294, 2316. Sersen: 226, 241, 346, 458, 520, 1655, 2317. Heman: 226, 346, 418, 458, 520, 1041.

2287 • WIND AND THE LION, THE

HERB JAFFE PRODUCTION; MGM. 1975.

NOMINATIONS *Sound:* Harry W. Tetrick, Aaron Rochin, William McCaughey, and Roy Charman. *Original Score:* Jerry Goldsmith.

Berber chieftain Sean Connery [2185] kidnaps an American widow, Candice Bergen [1919], and her children, provoking an international incident in which President Teddy Roosevelt, played by Brian Keith, becomes involved. John Huston [24 . . .] plays Secretary of State John Hay. Very loosely based on an actual incident (the real kidnap victim was a man, and there was no invasion), the script by writer-director John Milius [92] is all over the place. The action scenes are fine, and the romance that (naturally) flares between Connery and Bergen is entertaining. But the attempt to make it all mean something—perhaps something about Vietnam—undermines the whole project. Connery is terrific, and Bergen, who was beginning to emerge from a period of just being a decorative presence in films, is an apt foil. If Keith's role were less of a caricature, his fine playing of it might have had more effect.

Jaws won the Oscars for sound and for John Williams' score.

Tetrick: 1089, 1712. Rochin: 521, 641, 1089, 1310, 1711, 2124, 2165, 2231. McCaughey: 521, 1089, 1310, 1712. Charman: 45, 1652, 1977. Goldsmith: 152.5, 268, 395, 727, 939, 1472, 1527, 1537, 1541, 1583, 1589, 1753, 1913, 2176.

2288 • WINDOW, THE

RKO RADIO. 1949.

NOMINATION *Film Editing:* Frederic Knudtson.

Bobby Driscoll plays the boy who cried "Wolf!" A city kid with a reputation for fibbing, one day he sees a murder being committed across the way but is unable to persuade anyone that he's telling the truth this time. But the murderer knows he's telling the truth . . . Good little thriller, directed by Ted Tetzlaff [1998] from a screenplay by Mel Dinelli based on a story by Cornell Woolrich. The cast includes Barbara Hale, Arthur Kennedy [291 . . .], Paul Stewart, and Ruth Roman. Driscoll, who received an honorary Oscar for his work in this film and the same year's *So Dear to My Heart,* had begun acting in films in 1943, at the age of six. He achieved stardom in *Song of the South* and later appeared in the 1950 Disney version of *Treasure Island* and supplied the voice of the title character in the 1953 animated version of *Peter Pan.* Adolescence put an end to his career: He made his last film appearance in a 1958 exploitation flick about teen gangs, *The Party Crashers,* then descended into the drug culture. His body was discovered in 1968 in an abandoned building in New York City.

The editing Oscar went to Harry Gerstad for *Champion.*

Knudtson: 522, 1000, 1032, 1065, 1474.

2289 • WING AND A PRAYER

20TH CENTURY-FOX. 1944.

NOMINATION *Original Screenplay:* Jerome Cady.

Don Ameche [419] stars as a flight officer aboard an aircraft carrier during World War II, with the climactic action taking place during the Battle of Midway. Solid patriotic action movie with a strong cast: Dana Andrews, Richard Jaeckel [1864], Cedric Hardwicke, Charles Bickford [651 . . .], and Harry (still billed as Henry) Morgan. Directed by Henry Hathaway [1194]. The screenplay Oscar went to Lamar Trotti for *Wilson.*

2290 • WINGS

PARAMOUNT FAMOUS LASKY. 1927–28.

AWARDS *Production:* Lucien Hubbard, producer. *Engineering Effects:* Roy Pomeroy.

Charles "Buddy" Rogers and Richard Arlen play small-town pals who enlist in the flying corps in World War I. Clara Bow is the hometown girl in love with Rogers, who loves another, alas. Bow volunteers as an ambulance driver and is reunited with the guys in France, where she performs an act of self-sacrifice that wins Rogers' love in the end—after he accidentally causes Arlen's death. *Wings,* directed by William A. Wellman [157 . . .] from a screenplay by Hope Loring and Louis D. Lighton [352 . . .] based on a story by John Monk Saunders [498], has survived the mass extinction of the silent film to be one of the few pre-1930 movies still shown with some regularity on TV. The reason is certainly not the cornball romantic melodrama of its story or the sometimes callow performances. It may have something to do with the truly spectacular flying sequences, which were filmed under the supervision of cinematographer Harry Perry [898] near San Antonio by a crew of daredevil pilots, including Rogers and Arlen. (Arlen had been a flier with the Royal Flying Corps; Rogers learned to fly for the film.) It also may have something to do with the appearance of Gary Cooper [701 . . .] in a small but star-making supporting part as a doomed pilot. The cast also includes Jobyna Ralston, El Brendel, Henry B. Walthall, Hedda Hopper, and Roscoe Karns.

The chief reason *Wings* has endured when scores of movies with better performances and more sophisticated stories to tell go unseen—and hundreds more have vanished entirely—is that it's the official first winner of the best picture Academy Award. Like many of the Academy's honors, a bit of controversy dogs this one: Two films were honored as outstanding during the eligibility period; the other one, *Sunrise,* was given an award for "artistic quality of production." The Academy's official records, however, single out only *Wings* as the film that heads up the list of best picture winners. Over the years, *Sunrise* has maintained its aura of prestige, receiving high status in periodic polls of film critics to name the best films

of all time. *Wings* never makes those lists—but then few of the Academy's top-honored films do. So the only question is why the Academy chooses to trace the best picture lineage from *Wings* instead of *Sunrise,* and on this topic the Academy is mum.

Hubbard: 1844, 1917.

2291 • WINGS OVER HONOLULU

UNIVERSAL. 1937.

NOMINATION *Cinematography:* Joseph Valentine.

Ray Milland [1208] plays a navy pilot who gets transferred to Pearl Harbor on his wedding day. His bride, Wendy Barrie, is understandably miffed, and when his flight duties continue to come first, she links up with an old beau, Kent Taylor. Passable romantic drama, directed by H. C. Potter, with William Gargan [2045], Clara Blandick, and Louise Beavers. The Oscar went to Karl Freund for *The Good Earth.*

Valentine: 668, 776, 1048, 1229, 1896.

2292 • WINTERSET

RKO RADIO. 1936.

NOMINATIONS *Interior Decoration:* Perry Ferguson. *Score:* RKO Radio Studio Music Department, Nathaniel Shilkrat, head; score by Nathaniel Shilkrat.

Burgess Meredith [504 . . .] plays a young man whose father, a political radical, was executed for a crime he didn't commit. Meredith seeks out the witness who might have exonerated his father but failed to come forth because he was being bullied by the real culprit, a gangster. Meredith falls in love with the witness' sister (Margo), who persuades him not to betray her brother. In the end both lovers are gunned down by the gangster. Lifeless, tedious filming of a once-celebrated (and now mostly forgotten) verse drama by Maxwell Anderson [48], adapted—ineffectively—for the screen by Anthony Veiller [1085 . . .] and directed by Alfred Santell. The cast includes Eduardo Cinnelli, John Carradine, Myron McCormick, and Mischa Auer [1401]. The art direction Oscar went to Richard Day for *Dodsworth.* Charles Previn won for the scoring for *One Hundred Men and a Girl.*

Ferguson: 366, 407, 1451, 1607.

2293 • WITCHES OF EASTWICK, THE
WARNER BROS. PRODUCTION; WARNER BROS. 1987.

NOMINATIONS *Sound:* Wayne Artman, Tom Beckert, Tom Dahl, and Art Rochester. *Original Score:* John Williams.

In a poshly quaint New England village, three bored and unhappy women—Cher [1351 . . .], Susan Sarandon [107 . . .], and Michelle Pfeiffer [485 . . .]—accidentally summon up the devil, Jack Nicholson [395 . . .]. After each woman has an erotic fling with him, they decide he's much more than they bargained for and have to figure out how to get rid of him. With more star power than any movie has a right to, *Witches* nevertheless winds up something of an unsatisfying mess. The adaptation by Michael Cristofer of a novel by John Updike never quite decides what the movie is going to be: fantasy, satire, horror movie, or comedy of manners. Director George Miller [1205.5] isn't much help, either—the film veers wildly in all directions, held together only by the skill of its performers: Nicholson goes appropriately over the top, Cher is appealingly droll, Sarandon—who switched roles with Cher after the initial casting—brings a terrific sensuality to her part, and Pfeiffer's performance moved her out of minor roles and secondary films into stardom. But Veronica Cartwright gets appallingly misused in the part of the officious neighbor who wants to exorcise Nicholson from the start. The Oscar for sound went to *The Last Emperor,* which also won for the score by Ryuichi Sakamoto, David Byrne, and Cong Su.

Beckert: 519. Rochester: 411.5, 442. Williams: 6, 260, 403, 416, 588, 613, 614, 659, 805, 933, 937, 982, 996, 997, 1041, 1047, 1596, 1652, 1679, 1684, 1701, 1764.65, 1916, 1977, 2107, 2126, 2194, 2322.

2294 • WITH A SONG IN MY HEART
20TH CENTURY-FOX. 1952.

AWARD *Scoring of a Musical Picture:* Alfred Newman.
NOMINATIONS *Actress:* Susan Hayward. *Supporting Actress:* Thelma Ritter. *Sound Recording:* 20th Century-Fox Sound Department, Thomas T. Moulton, sound director. *Color Costume Design:* Charles LeMaire.

Hayward plays Jane Froman, a popular singer who was crippled in a plane crash while entertaining the troops in World War II and struggled to regain the use of her legs and reestablish her career. Standard inspirational biopic, directed by Walter Lang [1088] from a screenplay by Lamar Trotti [1516 . . .], with Ritter as Froman's you-can-do-it nurse, Clancy, plus Rory Calhoun, David Wayne, Una Merkel [1959], Lyle Talbot, and Leif Erickson. Robert Wagner attracted so much fan mail with his small part as a serviceman to whom Froman sings that Fox decided to make him a star. The songs, which are dubbed by Froman, include a string of pop classics: "Blue Moon," "That Old Feeling," "Tea for Two," "I'll Walk Alone," "Give My Regards to Broadway," "I'm Through With Love," "Embraceable You," and many more. Froman had a handsome voice but was a colorless interpreter, so the songs all sound pretty much alike. The film's climax is something of a hoot —a patriotic medley that goes on and on, as Hayward stands there gamely but unconvincingly lip-synching.

This was the fifth of Newman's nine Oscars. The best actress Oscar went to Shirley Booth for *Come Back, Little Sheba.* Ritter lost the third of her six unsuccessful tries at the award to Gloria Grahame in *The Bad and the Beautiful.* The sound award went to *Breaking the Sound Barrier.* Marcel Vertes won for the costumes for *Moulin Rouge.*

Newman: 31, 34, 46, 72, 138, 182, 226, 333, 334, 347, 375, 428, 437, 457, 476, 495, 542, 690, 797, 833, 952, 953, 959, 962, 1016, 1082, 1088, 1213, 1278, 1362, 1397, 1475, 1616, 1655, 1849, 1868, 1883, 1921, 2043, 2046, 2091, 2258, 2286, 2316. Hayward: 973, 980, 1396, 1845. Ritter: 46, 210, 1289, 1564, 1572. Moulton: 22, 46, 138, 366, 457, 487, 560, 706, 798, 962, 1153, 1200, 1451, 1510, 1607, 1849, 2154. LeMaire: 21, 46, 376, 495, 530, 542, 954, 1213, 1338, 1391, 1601, 1706, 2008, 2043, 2205.

2295 • *WITH BYRD AT THE SOUTH POLE*

PARAMOUNT PUBLIX. 1929–30.

AWARD *Cinematography:* Joseph T. Rucker and Willard Van Der Veer.

Absorbing, effective documentary of Adm. Richard E. Byrd's expedition to Antarctica. No director is credited, but the film was edited by Emanuel Cohen. For the first few years of the Academy Awards, documentary or semidocumentary films such as *White Shadows in the South Seas* and *Tabu* dominated the cinematography category. Documentarians, who weren't hindered by the need for synchronized sound, had greater freedom to come up with impressive imagery than did the studio cinematographers struggling to adapt to the arrival of sound. So the cinematography Oscars went to the technical achievement of cameramen like Rucker and Van Der Veer, who had no significant Hollywood careers. As Hollywood camera and sound technology came into sync in the early thirties, the documentarians were shut out of the honors until the establishment of the documentary awards at the 1941 ceremony.

2296 • *WITNESS*

EDWARD S. FELDMAN PRODUCTION; PARAMOUNT. 1985.

AWARDS *Screenplay Written Directly for the Screen:* Earl W. Wallace and William Kelley; story by William Kelley, Pamela Wallace, and Earl W. Wallace. *Film Editing:* Thom Noble.

NOMINATIONS *Picture:* Edward S. Feldman, producer. *Actor:* Harrison Ford. *Director:* Peter Weir. *Cinematography:* John Seale. *Art Direction–Set Decoration:* Stan Jolley; John Anderson. *Original Score:* Maurice Jarre.

On a journey to Philadelphia with his widowed mother (Kelly McGillis), a young Amish boy (Lukas Haas) witnesses a brutal murder. Ford is the detective in charge of the case who has to protect not only the witness but also himself after he discovers that the murder plot originated in the police department hierarchy. He hides out among the Amish and falls in love with the widow. But when the bad guys come in pursuit, he finds the pacifist beliefs of the Amish won't allow them to aid in his fight. This tense, effec-

tive thriller was a big hit, thanks to an ingenious premise and fine performances by Ford, nine-year-old Haas, ballet dancer Alexander Godunov as McGillis' Amish suitor, Danny Glover as one of the bad guys, and Patti LuPone as Ford's sister. Some critics, however, found the production too full of old-style Hollywood clichés. The real Amish were forbidden to have anything to do with the production of the movie.

The director was aware of the script's clichés—it was the work of three novice screenwriters—and was eager to rewrite it. Paramount overruled Weir's desire to excise the Ford-McGillis love story, but he was able to have his way on other elements of the script. Accepting their Oscars, none of the writing team thanked the director.

The best picture Oscar went to *Out of Africa,* which also won for Sydney Pollack's direction, David Watkin's cinematography, Stephen Grimes and Josie MacAvin's art direction, and John Barry's score.

This is the sole nomination for Ford, who has appeared in perhaps more top box-office films than any star in history. Attracted to acting while in college, he had small luck at first in Hollywood, appearing in bit parts in films and TV in the late sixties. While supporting himself as a carpenter, he landed the small part of drag racer Bob Falfa in *American Graffiti,* which brought him to the attention of producer-director George Lucas, who cast him in the epochal *Star Wars.* Though the part of Han Solo in that film meant that he would appear in the sequels, it was by no means a guarantee of stardom— as Mark Hamill would learn to his regret. Ford continued to have major roles in minor films such as *Hanover Street* (1979) and *The Frisco Kid* (1979) until Lucas gave him a second lucky break—the lead in *Raiders of the Lost Ark,* which Tom Selleck was unable to do because he had signed for the TV series *Magnum, P.I. Witness* allowed Ford to demonstrate that he could do characters other than Han Solo and Indiana Jones. His other big moneymakers include *Working Girl, Presumed Innocent* (1990), *Patriot Games* (1992), *The Fugitive,* and *Clear and Present Danger.* The Oscar went to William Hurt in *Kiss of the Spider Woman.*

Noble: 2039. Weir: 511, 834. Seale: 1653. Jarre: 558, 764, 808, 1151, 1168, 1340, 1533, 1967.

2297 • *WITNESS FOR THE PROSECUTION*

EDWARD SMALL-ARTHUR HORNBLOW PRODUCTION; UNITED ARTISTS. 1957.

NOMINATIONS *Picture:* Arthur Hornblow, Jr., producer. *Actor:* Charles Laughton. *Supporting Actress:* Elsa Lanchester. *Director:* Billy Wilder. *Sound:* Gordon Sawyer, sound director, Samuel Goldwyn Studio Sound Department. *Film Editing:* Daniel Mandell.

Tyrone Power, accused of murdering a wealthy widow, is defended in court by Laughton, an aging, ailing barrister, who has agreed to take his case over the strenuous objections of his nurse, Lanchester. During the trial, Power's wife, played by Marlene Dietrich [1359], gives testimony that results in his acquittal, but the plot has several surprise twists yet to come. Engrossing if overlong star vehicle, based on a play by Agatha Christie. Wilder's screenplay, written with Harry Kurnitz [2250], is less smart and cynical than most of his work, though the dialogue often sounds more like Wilder than Christie. Dietrich's performance is one of her best; she was coached by Laughton and Noël Coward [993] in the accent necessary for one key scene, though there were rumors that the scene was eventually dubbed. She pushed hard for an Oscar nomination, but to no avail. This was Power's last film; he died the following year at age forty-four during the filming of *Solomon and Sheba*, which was completed with Yul Brynner [1088] in the lead. *Witness* was remade for TV in 1982 with an interesting cast: Beau Bridges in the Power role, Diana Rigg for Dietrich, Ralph Richardson [839 . . .] for Laughton, and Deborah Kerr [599 . . .] doing the Lanchester part delightfully.

The best picture Oscar went to *The Bridge on the River Kwai*, for which Alec Guinness won as best actor in a role that Laughton passed over in order to direct and perform in a revival of *Major Barbara* on Broadway. Nearing the end of his impressive career, Laughton had two more important film roles ahead of him, in *Spartacus* and 1962's *Advise and Consent*, before his death in 1962.

Lanchester had married Laughton in 1929. They frequently performed together—notably in *The Private Life of Henry VIII*, in which she does a wonderful turn as Anne of Cleves. After his death, she continued to act for many years, always in eccentric character parts. She died in 1986. A pre-Oscar poll had shown Lanchester the favorite in the race, but the award went to Miyoski Umeki for *Sayonara*, which also won for sound.

Wilder later asserted that rewarding the director of a filmed play was like giving the crew that moved Michelangelo's *Pietà* to the New York World's Fair an award for best sculpture. He may have been recognizing that *Witness*, which is essentially a courtroom drama, is more static than the films he wrote himself. The Oscar went to David Lean for *The Bridge on the River Kwai*, which also won for Peter Taylor's editing.

Hornblow: 925, 1732. Laughton: 1387, 1620. Lanchester: 428. Wilder: 91, 138, 198, 566, 705, 709, 925, 1208, 1440, 1738, 1860, 1903, 1975. Sawyer: 33, 91, 184, 214, 393, 730, 864, 882, 973, 974, 1032, 1511, 1592, 2244, 2310. Mandell: 91, 184, 1182, 1607.

2298 • *WIVES AND LOVERS*

HAL WALLIS PRODUCTIONS; PARAMOUNT. 1963.

NOMINATION *Black-and-White Costume Design:* Edith Head.

Having written a best-seller, novelist Van Johnson and his wife, Janet Leigh [1632], move to Connecticut, but when he's called away to the city to adapt the book for the stage, predatory Martha Hyer [1859] tries to steal Van away from Janet. Inconsequential marital comedy adapted by Edward Anhalt [164 . . .] from a play by Jay Presson Allen [321 . . .]. Directed by John Rich, with Shelley Winters [542 . . .] and Ray Walston. The costuming Oscar went to Piero Gherardi for *8¹/₂*.

Head: 31, 32, 46, 305, 357, 363, 612, 636, 675, 736, 832, 894, 945, 1003, 1219, 1261, 1263, 1398, 1427, 1504, 1550, 1579, 1587, 1631, 1716, 1727, 1738, 1748, 1840, 1927, 1986, 2012, 2098, 2247.

2299 • WIZ, THE

MOTOWN/UNIVERSAL PICTURES PRODUCTION; UNIVERSAL. 1978.

NOMINATIONS *Cinematography:* Oswald Morris. *Art Direction–Set Decoration:* Tony Walton and Philip Rosenberg; Edward Stewart and Robert Drumheller. *Original Song Score and Its Adaptation or Adaptation Score:* Quincy Jones. *Costume Design:* Tony Walton.

L. Frank Baum's Dorothy is transformed into a Harlem schoolteacher in her twenties, played by Diana Ross [1126], in this all-black musical, directed by Sidney Lumet [561 . . .] and adapted by Joel Schumacher from the stage version written by William F. Brown. The familiar characters are played by Michael Jackson (the Scarecrow), Nipsey Russell (the Tin Woodman), Ted Ross (the Cowardly Lion), Mabel King (the Wicked Witch), Lena Horne (Glinda, the Good Witch), Theresa Merritt (Aunt Em), and Richard Pryor (the Wizard). Despite elaborate and imaginative staging and some lively songs, mostly by Charlie Smalls from the original Broadway version, plus some new ones supplied by Jones and Smalls, *The Wiz* is an elaborate, expensive flop—another nail in the coffin of the movie musical. Ross has been misdirected into sentimentality and the film is loud when it should be lively.

The cinematography Oscar went to Nestor Almendros for *Days of Heaven.* The art direction award was won by *Heaven Can Wait.* Joe Renzetti took the scoring award for *The Buddy Holly Story.* Anthony Powell won for the costumes for *Death on the Nile.*

Morris: 659, 1471. Walton: 49, 1284, 1378. Rosenberg: 49. Stewart: 49. Jones: 144, 423, 698, 987.

2300 • WIZARD OF OZ, THE

MGM. 1939.

AWARDS *Song:* ''Over the Rainbow,'' music by Harold Arlen, lyrics by E. Y. Harburg. *Original Score:* Herbert Stothart.

NOMINATIONS *Picture:* Mervyn LeRoy, producer. *Color Cinematography:* Hal Rosson. *Interior Decoration:* Cedric Gibbons and William A. Horning. *Special Effects:* A. Arnold Gillespie, photographic; Douglas Shearer, sound.

Dorothy, played by Judy Garland [1065 . . .], is blown by a tornado over the rainbow to Oz, where with her dog, Toto, she joins the Scarecrow (Ray Bolger), the Tin Woodman (Jack Haley), and the Cowardly Lion (Bert Lahr) in a quest for the wonderful Wizard of Oz, played by Frank Morgan [22 . . .], who grants them all their wishes once they have vanquished the Wicked Witch of the West (Margaret Hamilton). The most durable of all Hollywood live-action fantasies, it has entered the consciousness of a nation more profoundly than almost any other movie, particularly since its regular appearances on TV began in 1956. The film had its origins in the desire of Arthur Freed [66 . . .], an MGM lyricist who was just beginning to move into producing, to find a vehicle for Garland, who made her first big impression in *Broadway Melody of 1938.* But when the Oz project was assigned to LeRoy, with Freed as his associate, LeRoy felt it needed an established star —either Shirley Temple, who was under contract to 20th Century-Fox, or Deanna Durbin, contracted to Universal. When neither actress proved available, the part was Garland's. Bolger had a lock on the Scarecrow, but Buddy Ebsen was originally cast as the Tin Woodman. He was replaced by Haley after Ebsen had an allergic reaction to the metallic makeup he had to wear. Lahr was cast at the suggestion of Harburg, who had done two Broadway shows with him. Morgan, under contract to MGM, became the Wizard after W. C. Fields turned down the part. Fanny Brice was considered for the part of the good witch, Glinda, finally played by Billie Burke [1306]. And Edna May Oliver was the first choice for the wicked witch; when she proved unavailable, the role went first to Gale Sondergaard [83 . . .] and finally to Hamilton. The choice of a director proved even more complex. After Norman Taurog [271 . . .] dropped out, the film began under the direction of Richard Thorpe, who proved too heavy-handed. Then George Cukor [262 . . .] took over for a few days, until he was replaced by Victor Fleming [798], who threw out all the footage that had been shot, and worked on the film for several months until he was called to replace Cukor on *Gone With the Wind.* King Vidor [378 . . .]

took over and completed the film, including the opening and closing black-and-white (actually sepia) sequences. Fleming returned, however, to supervise the cutting. In the process of editing, the film lost a number in which a "jitterbug" bites Lahr and Garland sings a song, "The Jitterbug." The movie was a substantial but not spectacular box-office success, although the reviews were lukewarm.

The job of writing songs for the film almost went to Jerome Kern [340 . . .], but Freed recalled a song by Arlen and Harburg, "In the Shade of the New Apple Tree," that seemed to have the spirit he wanted for *Oz*. Arlen, who had been a bandleader and a singer, had gained fame as a songwriter for the Cotton Club in the twenties and first collaborated with Harburg on Broadway in 1935. "Over the Rainbow" emerged from Freed's feeling that a song was needed to introduce the transition from Kansas to Oz. Harburg at first felt the melody Arlen supplied was more suited to Nelson Eddy than to a Kansas farm girl, but he submitted to the task. Still, the song was almost cut from the final-release version of the film—several preview screenings omitted it with inconclusive results. Only Freed's insistence kept it in at last, and it became one of the most beloved songs of all time—particularly after the troubled life of Judy Garland gave Harburg's wistful lines a special poignance. Neither Arlen nor Harburg would ever receive another Oscar, but together and in collaboration with others they are responsible for some of the most memorable songs ever written. Arlen died in 1986, Harburg in 1981.

Stothart was assisted in the preparation of the musical numbers by Roger Edens [87 . . .], who later became a key member of the production unit headed by Freed at MGM.

The awards were dominated by *Gone With the Wind*, which won the Oscars for best picture, for Ernest Haller and Ray Rennahan's cinematography, and for Lyle Wheeler's art direction. The special effects Oscar went to *The Rains Came*.

Arlen: 248, 322, 368, 903, 1838, 1910, 1912, 2186. Harburg: 322, 340. Stothart: 397, 1096, 1232, 1274, 1292, 1387, 1662, 1988, 2068, 2193, 2234.

LeRoy: 1662. Rosson: 105, 133, 256, 747, 2055. Gibbons: 66, 87, 130, 217, 227, 239, 285, 290, 440, 629, 749, 831, 980, 1069, 1096, 1173, 1190, 1226, 1230, 1232, 1274, 1308, 1309, 1417, 1567, 1604, 1644, 1662, 1673, 1721, 1861, 1937, 2068, 2112, 2256, 2257, 2320, 2330. Horning: 175, 440, 769, 1157, 1450, 1644, 1657. Gillespie: 175, 256, 685, 704, 835, 1371, 1388, 1905, 2048, 2055, 2122. Shearer: 136, 202, 256, 397, 685, 817, 835, 1096, 1232, 1293, 1371, 1419, 1751, 1950, 1988, 2048, 2055, 2211.

2301 • WOMAN IN RED, THE

WOMAN IN RED PRODUCTION; ORION. 1984.
AWARD *Song:* "I Just Called to Say I Love You," music and lyrics by Stevie Wonder.

Gene Wilder [1626 . . .] jeopardizes his marriage, his career, and everything else when he becomes obsessed with a beautiful model (Kelly LeBrock). Amusing farce, based on the French film *Pardon Mon Affaire* (original title: *Un Eléphant Ça Trompe Enormement*). Wilder also directed and did the screenplay. The cast includes Gilda Radner, Joseph Bologna, Charles Grodin, and Judith Ivey.

Wonder is apparently the only blind person ever to receive an Oscar. Blind from birth, he had his first hit record in 1962 when he was twelve years old and has continued to be one of the most prolific and successful figures in popular music, as both composer and performer. His hits include "Superstition" and "You Are the Sunshine of My Life."

2302 • WOMAN IN THE DUNES

TESHIGAHARA PRODUCTION; PATHÉ CONTEMPORARY FILMS (JAPAN). 1965.
NOMINATIONS *Director:* Hiroshi Teshigahara. *Foreign Language Film (1964).*

When a scientist, stranded in a remote part of Japan, seeks shelter for the night, the villagers lodge him with a woman living alone in a sand pit. He discovers that he has been trapped there as a replacement for the woman's dead husband, whose task was to continually shovel the shifting sand, which threatens the village. Eerie, haunting erotic fable from a screenplay by Kobo Abe, based on his novel. The cinematography by Hiroshi Segawa is exceptionally fine.

Because of the differing eligibility rules for the foreign language film Oscar and the other competitive awards, Teshigahara was nominated for best director a year after his film had been a contender for foreign film, losing to *Yesterday, Today and Tomorrow.* Teshigahara, who started out as a painter, began making short films and documentaries in the fifties. *Woman in the Dunes* was his second feature, winning a special jury prize at Cannes in 1964. He was also the first Japanese to receive a best director Oscar nomination. (The award went to Robert Wise for *The Sound of Music.*) His subsequent work, except for the 1972 *Summer Soldiers,* about American deserters from the Vietnam War, has been mostly unexceptional. After that film, Teshigahara turned his attention to other arts, including floral design and ceramics, and subsequently has made only one more feature film, *Rikyu* (1989).

2303 • WOMAN IN THE WINDOW, THE

INTERNATIONAL PICTURES; RKO RADIO. 1945.

NOMINATION *Scoring of a Dramatic or Comedy Picture:* Hugo Friedhofer and Arthur Lange.

Edward G. Robinson plays a psychology professor who admires the portrait of a beautiful woman (Joan Bennett) in the window of a gallery and is startled when he meets her in person. Visiting her apartment, he is attacked by an intruder whom he kills in self-defense. He soon finds himself not only being blackmailed but also involved in helping the officials track down the killer. Nifty, tense thriller with a controversial surprise ending. Directed by Fritz Lang from a screenplay by Nunnally Johnson [815 . . .] based on a novel, *Once Off Guard,* by J. H. Wallis. The cast includes Dan Duryea and Raymond Massey [1]. The scoring Oscar went to Miklos Rozsa for *Spellbound.*

Friedhofer: 2, 21, 184, 187, 214, 267, 1048, 2336. Lange: 171, 366, 827, 1123.

2303.5 • WOMAN OF AFFAIRS, A

MGM. 1928–29.

NOMINATION *Writing Achievement:* Bess Meredyth.

Greta Garbo [84 . . .] plays a reckless woman whose life is changed when her husband kills himself because he is caught embezzling. Silly late silent directed by Clarence Brown [84 . . .], with John Gilbert, Lewis Stone [1540], John Mack Brown, and Douglas Fairbanks, Jr. Meredyth's screenplay is based on the once-scandalous novel by Michael Arlen, *The Green Hat,* in which the husband's suicide is caused by the discovery that he has syphilis. The writing award went to Hans Kräly for *The Patriot.*

Meredyth, who began as an actress for D. W. Griffith but soon moved into writing, worked on numerous silent films, including *Ben-Hur* (1926) and *Don Juan* (1926). Her sound films include *The Affairs of Cellini, Folies Bergère,* and *The Mark of Zorro* (1940). She was not an official nominee—the Academy announced only the winners in this second year of the awards—but her name is listed among the contenders being considered by the writers branch for the award. Some sources cite only *Wonder of Women* as the title that put her in contention, but the Academy's list of winners and nominees also includes *A Woman of Affairs.*

Meredyth: 2311.

2304 • WOMAN OF THE TOWN

SHERMAN; UNITED ARTISTS. 1944.

NOMINATION *Scoring of a Dramatic or Comedy Picture:* Miklos Rozsa.

Claire Trevor [510 . . .] is that familiar Hollywood-western euphemism, a "dance hall hostess," whose involvement with Dodge City's new marshal, Bat Masterson (Albert Dekker), threatens to get in the way of his job. Pleasant, unassuming western, directed by George Archainbaud from a script by Aeneas Mackenzie, with Barry Sullivan, Henry Hull, Porter Hall, and Percy Kilbride. The scoring award went to Max Steiner for *Since You Went Away.*

Rozsa: 175, 566, 567, 604, 1035, 1069, 1070, 1085, 1208, 1227, 1644, 1872, 1890, 1968, 2050.

2305 • *WOMAN OF THE YEAR*

MGM. 1942.

AWARD *Original Screenplay:* Michael Kanin and Ring Lardner, Jr.

NOMINATION *Actress:* Katharine Hepburn.

Hepburn is a no-nonsense, sophisticated political journalist and Spencer Tracy [131 . . .] a no-nonsense, rough-edged sportswriter. Opposites attract, they wed, and the nonsense begins. The first of the nine films that Tracy and Hepburn made together is not one of their best, but it was hugely popular at the time. Today the sexist subtext is all too glaring: Because of her devotion to her career, Hepburn is not a "real" woman—as demonstrated in a notorious scene at the end in which she tries to make breakfast and makes a mess instead. Mostly the movie relies on the chemistry between the leads, which continued on and off screen for twenty-five years. Directed by George Stevens [542 . . .], with Fay Bainter [393 . . .], Reginald Owen, Roscoe Karns, and William Bendix [2222] in his film debut.

Kanin, the brother of Garson Kanin [11 . . .], began working as a screenwriter in 1939. He often collaborated with his wife, Fay [2007]. He died in 1969. Lardner, the son of a famous humor writer, began his Hollywood career as a publicist for David O. Selznick [497 . . .] and started his screenwriting career in 1937 with uncredited work on Selznick's *A Star Is Born* and *Nothing Sacred*. His refusal to testify before the House Un-American Activities Committee about his political beliefs led to his imprisonment for contempt of Congress and subsequent blacklisting in Hollywood. During the fifties he worked under various pseudonyms or without credit. He returned to credited screenwriting in 1965 with *The Cincinnati Kid* and won a second Oscar for *MASH*.

Hepburn lost to Greer Garson in *Mrs. Miniver*.

Kanin: 2007. Lardner: 1286. Hepburn: 24, 40, 843, 1177, 1199, 1357, 1473, 1563, 1654, 1956, 1963.

2306 • *WOMAN UNDER THE INFLUENCE, A*

FACES INTERNATIONAL FILMS PRODUCTION. 1974.

NOMINATIONS *Actress:* Gena Rowlands. *Director:* John Cassavetes.

Rowlands is married to Peter Falk [1377 . . .], a working-class guy who can't handle her mental instability and eventually colludes with his mother (Katherine Cassavetes) to have Rowlands institutionalized and subjected to shock therapy. A long—more than two and a half hours—film's journey into night, with a tour de force performance by Rowlands. At the time of its release, the movie was highly praised, and it still has many admirers, but there are also many who find it unwatchable. Although director Cassavetes, who wrote the screenplay, clearly sees the character played by Rowlands as a victim, a free spirit undone by the repressions of society, the movie goes on so long that many viewers begin to side with Falk instead.

Rowlands' work on the Broadway stage in the mid-fifties brought her to Hollywood's attention, but her screen career was never a major one. Her most prominent roles were in the films of her husband, Cassavetes, which include *Faces, Minnie and Moskowitz* (1971), *Opening Night* (1977), and *Gloria*. She lost to Ellen Burstyn in *Alice Doesn't Live Here Anymore*.

Cassavetes had been nominated before as a supporting actor for *The Dirty Dozen* and as a writer for *Faces,* putting him in the company of such triple-threat figures as Charles Chaplin [405 . . .], Woody Allen [39 . . .], Orson Welles [407 . . .], and Warren Beatty [255 . . .]. Fiercely independent, Cassavetes financed his own films, and in the case of *A Woman Under the Influence,* actually handled distribution, booking, and promotion himself. He died at the age of fifty-nine in 1989. The Oscar went to Francis Ford Coppola for *The Godfather, Part II.*

Rowlands: 777. Cassavetes: 548, 635.

2307 • WOMEN IN LOVE

LARRY KRAMER-MARTIN ROSEN PRODUCTION; UNITED ARTISTS (UNITED KINGDOM). 1970.

AWARD *Actress:* Glenda Jackson.

NOMINATIONS *Director:* Ken Russell. *Screenplay—Based on Material From Another Medium:* Larry Kramer. *Cinematography:* Billy Williams.

Jackson plays Gudrun Brangwen, an intense, intellectual young woman living in an English mining town. Jennie Linden is her sister, Ursula. The two women fall in love with, respectively, the mine owner, Gerald Crich, played by Oliver Reed, and a school inspector, Rupert Birkin, played by Alan Bates [678]. The film explores the interplay among the four people, and the destructiveness of the relationship between Gudrun and Gerald that leads to his death. A handsomely filmed and often compellingly acted version of the novel by D. H. Lawrence. Unfortunately it leaves those who know and love the book irritated and dissatisfied, while those who don't may be puzzled about what's going on and why. Lawrence's strength was the analysis of the inner lives of his characters, and neither screenwriter Kramer nor director Russell has found a way to communicate the novel's subtlety. (Russell, who goes for the bold at every opportunity, is probably more at fault.) At the time, the film was perhaps as notorious for a full-frontal-nude wrestling scene between Reed and Bates as for its dramatic or intellectual content. The cast also includes Eleanor Bron, Christopher Gable, and Michael Gough. The art direction was by Luciana Arrighi [954.5 . . .] and the costumes by Shirley Russell [27 . . .].

Jackson first came to fame as a member of the Royal Shakespeare Company in the Peter Brook production of *Marat/Sade,* which was filmed in 1967. *Women in Love,* and the Oscar she won for it, established her as a strikingly unconventional new screen presence, and in the early seventies she was a major figure in both films and TV, winning acclaim in 1972 for the BBC TV series *Elizabeth R,* which was shown on PBS in the States.

Russell got his start as a director with BBC TV, producing an acclaimed and controversial series of biographical films. He made his first theatrical film, *French Dressing,* in 1963, but *Women in Love* was his first major success. He followed it with a series of increasingly eccentric and often excessive films, such as *The Music Lovers* (1971), a highly fictionalized biography of Tchaikovsky; *The Devils* (1971), which drew fire from the censors for its sexual excesses; *Tommy,* a phantasmagoric version of the Who's rock opera; and *Lisztomania* (1975), with the Who's Roger Daltrey as the composer Franz Liszt, visualized as the nineteenth-century equivalent of a rock star, groupies and all. His most recent film, *Whore* (1991), an unpleasant look at prostitution, was rated NC-17, a sign that Russell is still playing the bad boy of British film. In 1990 he also played an amusing character role in *The Russia House.* The directing Oscar went to Franklin J. Schaffner for *Patton.*

Kramer, who also produced the film, subsequently won acclaim for his play about AIDS, *The Normal Heart.* He has become a prominent and outspoken figure in the gay rights movement. Ring Lardner, Jr., took the screenplay award for *MASH.* Freddie Young won for the cinematography of *Ryan's Daughter.*

Jackson: 893, 1966, 2125. Williams: 745, 1473.

2308 • WOMEN IN WAR

REPUBLIC. 1940.

NOMINATION *Special Effects:* Howard J. Lydecker, William Bradford, and Ellis J. Thackery, photographic; Herbert Norsch, sound.

When she gets into scrapes with the law, rich girl Wendy Barrie volunteers as an army nurse to escape jail. Eve-of-war flick with Elsie Janis, Patric Knowles, Mae Clark, and Billy Gilbert, directed by John H. Auer from a screenplay by F. Hugh Herbert and Doris Anderson. The special effects Oscar went to *The Thief of Bagdad.*

Lydecker: 693.

2309 • WOMEN ON THE VERGE OF A NERVOUS BREAKDOWN

EL DESEO/LAURENFILM PRODUCTION (SPAIN). 1988.

NOMINATION *Foreign Language Film.*

Carmen Maura plays a woman whose lover breaks

up their relationship with a message on her answering machine. She spends most of the rest of the film trying to get in touch with him, encountering a variety of eccentrics and odd situations along the way. Very funny screwball farce that was the first big international hit for its director, Pedro Almodóvar, and made a Hollywood heartthrob of one of its stars, Antonio Banderas. The Oscar went to *Pelle the Conqueror.*

2310 • WONDER MAN

BEVERLY PRODUCTIONS; RKO RADIO. 1945.
AWARD *Special Effects:* John Fulton, photographic; A. W. Johns, sound.
NOMINATIONS *Sound Recording:* Gordon Sawyer. *Song:* "So in Love," music by David Rose, lyrics by Leo Robin. *Scoring of a Musical Picture:* Lou Forbes and Ray Heindorf.

Danny Kaye plays twins: a nightclub entertainer and a shy intellectual. When the entertainer is killed by mobsters because he knows too much, he comes back to haunt his brother, forcing him to assume his identity and track down his killer. Amusing musical extravaganza, with Vera-Ellen making her film debut as the entertainer's dance partner, and Virginia Mayo playing the intellectual's librarian girlfriend. Directed by Bruce Humberstone from a screenplay by Don Hartman [753 . . .], Melville Shavelson [951 . . .], and Philip Rapp. The cast includes S. Z. Sakall, Steve Cochran, Otto Kruger, Natalie Schafer, Luis Alberni, Carol Haney, and Huntz Hall.

This was the first of three Oscars for Fulton, a former assistant cameraman who first won acclaim as a visual effects artist with his work on the *Invisible Man* films and other horror movies at Universal. After *Wonder Man,* he moved over to head the effects department at Paramount. He continued his career as an effects specialist up to his death in 1966.

The sound award went to Stephen Dunn for *The Bells of St. Mary's.* Richard Rodgers and Oscar Hammerstein II won for the song "It Might As Well Be Spring," from *State Fair.* Georgie Stoll took the Oscar for scoring *Anchors Aweigh.*

Fulton: 269, 1010, 1011, 1012, 2012. Johns: 798, 1670, 1828. Sawyer: 33, 91, 184, 214, 393, 730, 864, 882, 973, 974, 1032, 1592, 2244, 2297. Rose: 1613. Robin: 104, 197, 368, 846, 1072, 1805, 1843, 2032, 2088. Forbes: 282, 1006, 2057, 2186. Heindorf: 331, 479, 666, 930, 1043, 1204, 1385, 1408, 1430, 1511, 1690, 1719, 1750, 1910, 2058, 2186, 2243, 2318.

2311 • WONDER OF WOMEN

MGM. 1928–29.
NOMINATION *Writing Achievement:* Bess Meredyth.

Concert pianist Lewis Stone [1540] cheats on his wife, Peggy Wood [1881], but learns how valuable she is when she dies. This sentimental drama, based on a novel by Hermann Sudermann and directed by Clarence Brown [84 . . .], is no longer in circulation. Meredyth was an unofficial nominee—one of the people considered by the writers branch for the writing award before it was presented to Hans Kräly for *The Patriot.* Only the winners were announced, but Meredyth's name remained on record at the Academy.

Meredyth: 2303.5.

2312 • WONDERFUL WORLD OF THE BROTHERS GRIMM, THE

METRO-GOLDWYN-MAYER AND CINERAMA; MGM. 1962.
AWARD *Color Costume Design:* Mary Wills.
NOMINATIONS *Color Cinematography:* Paul C. Vogel. *Color Art Direction—Set Decoration:* George W. Davis and Edward Carfagno; Henry Grace and Dick Pefferle. *Scoring of Music—Adaptation or Treatment:* Leigh Harline.

Laurence Harvey [1724] and Karl Boehm are the brothers in this musical fantasy with a bit of pseudo-biography thrown in. The bio part is directed by Henry Levin and features Claire Bloom, Walter Slezak, Barbara Eden, Oscar Homolka [972], Arnold Stang, and Martita Hunt. The three fairy tales are directed by George Pal, who also produced the film. "The Dancing Princess" stars Yvette Mimieux, Russ Tamblyn [1558], Jim Backus, and Beulah Bondi [807 . . .]. "The Cobbler and the Elves" features Harvey as the cobbler and the Puppetoons as the elves. "The Singing Bone" has Terry-Thomas and Buddy Hackett slaying a dragon. The feature was designed for the super-wide-screen Cinerama, so it's a bit overblown, and the songs by Bob Merrill [737] and Charles Beaumont are unmemorable. It's passable kid stuff, however, with some picturesque location shooting in the quaint German towns of Rothenburg and Dinkelsbühl.

Fred A. Young took the cinematography Oscar for *Lawrence of Arabia,* which also won for art direction. The award for adaptation score went to Ray Heindorf for *The Music Man.*

Wills: 376, 542, 864, 1534, 2008, 2205. Vogel: 157. Davis: 46, 69, 401, 495, 542, 736, 953, 1213, 1335, 1388, 1537, 1552, 1706, 1814, 2157, 2184. Carfagno: 130, 175, 629, 917, 1069, 1552, 1644, 1814, 1937. Grace: 69, 227, 401, 769, 953, 1335, 1388, 1450, 1537, 1552, 2157, 2184. Pefferle: 87, 1096, 1157, 1230, 1552. Harline: 1053, 1576, 1607, 1838, 1851, 2327.

2312.5 • WOODSTOCK

WADLEIGH-MAURICE LTD. PRODUCTION; WARNER BROS. 1970. **NOMINATIONS** *Sound:* Dan Wallin and Larry Johnson. *Film Editing:* Thelma Schoonmaker.

Classic documentary of the epoch-making music festival held on Max Yasgur's upstate New York farm one summer weekend in 1969, with performances by Joan Baez, Crosby, Stills and Nash, the Jefferson Airplane, Joe Cocker, Sly and the Family Stone, Santana, Country Joe and the Fish, the Who, Arlo Guthrie, and of course Jimi Hendrix. A much better thing than being there, despite the legendary aura of the event. Directed by Michael Wadleigh and produced by Bob Maurice, the film also received an Oscar for best documentary feature. It's one of the few documentaries in recent years to receive a nomination in the categories usually populated exclusively by fiction films, but it was a well-deserved nomination: The film's use of multiple images is superb. In 1994 the twenty-fifth anniversary of the event, Wadleigh released an expanded, recut version of the film, with footage never before seen. Schoonmaker was assisted in the editing by a former NYU classmate, Martin

Scorsese [27.5 . . .], whose films, starting with *Raging Bull,* she would subsequently edit. The Oscar went to Hugh S. Fowler for *Patton,* which also won for sound.

Wallin: 1911. Schoonmaker: 806, 1650.

2313 • WORKING GIRL

20TH CENTURY FOX PRODUCTION; 20TH CENTURY FOX. 1988. **AWARD** *Song:* "Let the River Run," music and lyrics by Carly Simon.
NOMINATIONS *Picture:* Douglas Wick, producer. *Actress:* Melanie Griffith. *Supporting Actress:* Joan Cusack. *Supporting Actress:* Sigourney Weaver. *Director:* Mike Nichols.

Griffith has, as she puts it, "a head for business and a bod for sin." Unfortunately the fact that she's not a polished B-school grad relegates her to the secretary pool with no hope for advancement. Then she gets assigned to Weaver, who pretends to be her mentor while in fact stealing Griffith's bright ideas. But when Weaver breaks a leg on a skiing weekend, Griffith gets a chance to get even by closing a big deal with the aid of Harrison Ford [2296], who just happens to be Weaver's lover. But then Weaver gets wise and shows up to squelch it. Entertaining comedy, written by Kevin Wade, that's soured a little by the sexist treatment of both Griffith and Weaver, who have gratuitous scenes in their underwear (Griffith even vacuums topless). But Griffith has a charm that she's rarely shown in other films, Ford has an engaging way with light comedy that doesn't get exploited often enough in movies, and Weaver is a tremendously cunning villain. They're well supported by Cusack as one of Griffith's big-haired buddies in the steno pool, Alec Baldwin as Griffith's sleazy boyfriend, and Philip Bosco, Nora Dunn, Oliver Platt, Olympia Dukakis [1351], and Ricki Lake.

Simon is a member of a remarkable family. Her father was one of the founders of the Simon and Schuster publishing house, her uncle Henry is a noted musicologist, and her other uncles, George and Alfred, have also had distinguished music-related careers. Her sister Joanna is an opera singer. Carly rebelled against the family's classical-music tradition by turning in the direction of folk music and rock, and in 1971 won a Grammy as outstanding new artist. Her career as a singer-songwriter flourished in the seventies, but began to wane somewhat in the eighties. Her most famous song, "You're So Vain," is often said to be about a former lover, Warren Beatty [255 . . .].

The best picture Oscar went to *Rain Man,* which also won for its director, Barry Levinson.

Griffith, the daughter of Tippi Hedren, made her film debut at eighteen in *Night Moves* in 1975 but did not achieve stardom until the mid-eighties, in films such as *Body Double* (1984) and *Something Wild* (1986). *Working Girl* advanced her career, but she has had trouble finding roles that would keep her on the A list. The notorious flop *Bonfire of the Vanities* (1990) certainly didn't help. The Oscar went to Jodie Foster for *The Accused.*

Cusack made her film debut in 1980 in *My Bodyguard,* but her breakthrough role came—after a season on TV's *Saturday Night Live*—in *Broadcast News,* in which she plays a frantic production assistant. Although she has played occasional leads, she's best known for character roles in such movies as *Married to the Mob* and *Addams Family Values.* Her brother is actor John Cusack. The supporting actress Oscar went to Geena Davis for *The Accidental Tourist.*

Weaver: 45, 808. Nichols: 810, 1679.5, 1821, 2277.

2314 • *WORLD ACCORDING TO GARP, THE*

WARNER BROS. PRODUCTION; WARNER BROS. 1982.
NOMINATIONS *Supporting Actor:* John Lithgow. *Supporting Actress:* Glenn Close.

Robin Williams [511 . . .] plays T. S. Garp, the son of an unmarried woman, Jenny Fields (Close), who becomes a militant feminist with a bodyguard, Roberta Muldoon (Lithgow), who's a transsexual ex–football player. That's only a taste of this picaresque saga based on the best-selling novel by John Irving. Steve Tesich [279] did the adaptation, after others had tried and failed, and in the hands of director George Roy Hill [317 . . .] it's certainly watchable. But it doesn't make a lot of sense as a film: It's a sometimes mystifying, sometimes infuriating, sometimes entertaining, and sometimes even moving skim through an overstuffed book. The best thing about it are the performances of the nominees, plus the always ingratiating Williams, well supported by Hume Cronyn [1791], Jessica Tandy [580 . . .], Swoosie Kurtz, and Amanda Plummer.

Lithgow, a Harvard graduate who acted in student theater with classmates Stockard Channing [1835.5] and Tommy Lee Jones [734.5 . . .], made one film, *Dealing* (1972), before becoming a Broadway star and winning a Tony for his role in *The Changing Room.* After smallish roles in a handful of films in the late seventies and early eighties, including *All That Jazz,* his standout role in *Garp* established him as a major character actor. The Oscar went to Louis Gossett, Jr., for *An Officer and a Gentleman.*

Close also used a Broadway appearance as a springboard to movies: Hill saw her in the musical *Barnum* and cast her in *Garp,* her first film, which began a string of unsuccessful Oscar nominations. She lost to Jessica Lange in *Tootsie.*

Lithgow: 2020. Close: 199, 485, 653, 1418.

2315 • *WRITTEN ON THE WIND*

UNIVERSAL-INTERNATIONAL. 1956.
AWARD *Supporting Actress:* Dorothy Malone.
NOMINATIONS *Supporting Actor:* Robert Stack. *Song:* "Written on the Wind," music by Victor Young, lyrics by Sammy Cahn.

Lauren Bacall marries rich, weak oilman Stack, who's jealous of his friend, geologist Rock Hudson [768], because he thinks (rightly) that Hudson is in love with Bacall. Meanwhile, Stack's trampy sister, Malone, wants Hudson, and when she can't have him, she gets even by fueling Stack's jealousy. A great trashy candy box full of *Dallas*-style feuding and fussing, directed by Douglas Sirk, whose undeniable if dubious talent was that he took melodramatic chestnuts like this one seriously enough to make them entertaining. He worked the same perverse magic with *Magnificent Obsession, All That Heaven Allows* (1956), *The Tarnished Angels* (1958), and *Imitation of*

Life—some of the quintessential movies of the fifties. The screenplay is by George Zuckerman, from a novel by Robert Wilder.

In 1943 Malone was discovered by an RKO scout in a play at Southern Methodist University and signed to a studio contract, playing minor roles in second features. In 1945 she moved to Warners, where her films improved somewhat—she has a memorable seductive moment with Humphrey Bogart [24 . . .] in *The Big Sleep* (1946)—but stardom still eluded her. After the Oscar, she was cast in a few good roles, playing Lon Chaney's first wife in *The Man of a Thousand Faces* and self-destructive actress Diana Barrymore in *Too Much, Too Soon* (1958). But her film career faded in the sixties, and she turned to TV, with a long run on the *Peyton Place* series. Her most recent screen appearance was a cameo role in *Basic Instinct*.

Stack made his film debut in 1939 in *First Love*, reaping a publicity bonanza because he gave Deanna Durbin her first screen kiss. His other important pre–World War II role was as the flier with whom Carole Lombard keeps a comic liaison in *To Be or Not to Be*. He returned to films after serving in the navy and became a second-string leading man in fifties movies. His most famous role was on TV, as Elliott Ness in the sixties series *The Untouchables*. The Oscar went to Anthony Quinn for *Lust for Life*.

Jay Livingston and Ray Evans won the song Oscar for "Whatever Will Be, Will Be (Que Será, Será)," from *The Man Who Knew Too Much*.

Young: 97, 98, 100, 101, 280, 489, 612, 693, 701, 794, 846, 925, 1214, 1257, 1396, 1452, 1748, 1823, 1994, 2235. Cahn: 74, 163, 182, 696, 915, 926, 1031, 1056, 1216, 1524, 1587, 1692, 1708, 1719, 1859, 1907, 2016, 2064, 2072, 2103, 2110, 2125, 2263, 2264, 2343.

2316 • *WUTHERING HEIGHTS*

SAMUEL GOLDWYN PRODUCTIONS; UNITED ARTISTS. 1939.
AWARD *Black-and-White Cinematography:* Gregg Toland. **NOMINATIONS** *Picture:* Samuel Goldwyn, producer. *Actor:* Laurence Olivier. *Supporting Actress:* Geraldine Fitzgerald. *Director:* William Wyler. *Screenplay:* Ben Hecht and Charles MacArthur. *Interior Decoration:* James Basevi. *Original Score:* Alfred Newman.

Olivier is Heathcliff, the stable boy who falls desperately in love with Catherine Earnshaw, played by Merle Oberon [487], but is prevented by his low birth from marrying her. He leaves for America, and when he returns a wealthy man, he finds that she has married Edgar Linton, played by David Niven [1778]. He gets his revenge by marrying and then neglecting Edgar's sister, Isabella (Fitzgerald), and by leading Catherine's brother, Hindley (Hugh Williams), who had tormented him as a boy, into a life of dissipation. But the long-suppressed love between Heathcliff and Cathy remains to torment them. Though it covers only the first half of Emily Brontë's great mad novel, the film is one of Hollywood's romantic classics, thanks to the incredible beauty of the two leads, Toland's brilliant chiaroscuro photography, and the sure-handed direction of Wyler, greatly aided by editor Daniel Mandell [91 . . .]. The cast includes Donald Crisp [952], Flora Robson [1759], Cecil Kellaway [843 . . .], Leo G. Carroll, and Miles Mander. *Wuthering Heights* began as a spec script by Hecht and MacArthur; they first sold it to Walter Wanger [413 . . .], who wanted it as a vehicle for Charles Boyer [36 . . .] and Sylvia Sidney [1962]. When Wanger decided not to make the film, the writers pressured Goldwyn to buy it. The producer was initially unenthusiastic but was persuaded when he realized it was a vehicle for Oberon, his contract player. Olivier was signed at the suggestion of Hecht and Oberon, but not without difficulty: Olivier felt Oberon was a poor actress and wanted Vivien Leigh [798 . . .] for his costar. Robert Newton and Douglas Fairbanks, Jr., were considered as fallbacks for the role, before Olivier reluctantly agreed to take it. His distaste for Oberon, exacerbated by resentment that Leigh was not playing the role, continued through the filming. Initially Olivier battled with Wyler as well, as the director tried to get him to scale down his stagy performance for the camera. In the end he credited Wyler with teaching him the art of film acting. And Wyler and Goldwyn squabbled, too, over the ending of the film, for which the producer insisted on an upbeat shot of the spirits of Cathy and Heathcliff united in death. Wyler refused to direct it, so Goldwyn hired H. C. Potter to supervise a shot of Olivier and Oberon's doubles, seen from behind, walking away across the heath.

This is the sole Oscar for Toland, one of the most acclaimed cinematographers in Hollywood history, whose career was linked with Goldwyn's—he photographed thirty-seven of the producer's films. He had begun his career as an apprentice to George Barnes [537 . . .] in the late twenties, and at the time of his death in 1948 from a heart attack at the age of forty-four, was the highest paid cameraman in Hollywood. His specialty, deep-focus composition, was used to great effect in *Citizen Kane* and *The Little Foxes*.

Wuthering Heights provided the sole nomination in the career of Fitzgerald, a Dublin-born actress making her American film debut after a few British films in the early thirties. She became a Warner Bros. contract player, usually in supporting parts, in such films as *Dark Victory* and *Watch on the Rhine*. After the late forties, her film roles became fewer, but she has been seen in character parts in such movies as *The Pawnbroker, Rachel, Rachel, Harry and Tonto,* and *Arthur*. The supporting actress Oscar went to Hattie McDaniel in *Gone With the Wind*, which also took the awards for best picture, director Victor Fleming, screenwriter Sidney Howard, and art director Lyle Wheeler.

Olivier lost the first of his record-setting ten nominations to Robert Donat in *Goodbye, Mr. Chips*. The scoring award went to Herbert Stothart for *The Wizard of Oz*.

Toland: 407, 510, 1006, 1200, 1327. Goldwyn: 102, 184, 214, 510, 560, 1182, 1607. Olivier: 268, 619, 858, 901, 1272, 1506, 1670, 1693, 1841. Wyler: 175, 184, 420, 534, 560, 730, 894, 1162, 1182, 1371, 1716. Hecht: 78, 1455, 1765, 2179, 2211. MacArthur: 1664, 1765. Basevi: 746, 1082, 1868, 2245. Newman: 31, 34, 46, 72, 138, 182, 226, 333, 334, 347, 375, 428, 437, 457, 476, 495, 542, 690, 797, 833, 952, 953, 959, 962, 1016, 1082, 1088, 1213, 1278, 1362, 1397, 1475, 1616, 1655, 1849, 1868, 1883, 1921, 2043, 2046, 2091, 2258, 2286, 2294.

2316.5 • *WYATT EARP*

TIG PRODUCTION; WARNER BROS. 1994.

NOMINATION *Cinematography:* Owen Roizman.

Kevin Costner [482] plays the title role in a film that follows the lawman from boyhood through a doomed first marriage and a period of despondency and lawlessness, to the celebrated showdown at the O.K. Corral and its aftermath. Long (three hours), languid attempt at an epic Western that was a huge critical and commercial dud, putting serious blotches on the careers of Costner and director Lawrence Kasdan [6 . . .], who were coproducers of the film along with Jim Wilson [482]. Kasdan was also responsible, along with Dan Gordon, for the screenplay. Poor pacing undermines the effect of some good performances, especially those of Dennis Quaid, who lost nearly forty pounds to play the tubercular Doc Holliday; Gene Hackman [255 . . .] as Wyatt's father; and Michael Madsen as Virgil Earp. Also in the cast are Mare Winningham, Bill Pullman, Jeff Fahey, Mark Harmon, Annabeth Gish, Catherine O'Hara, and Isabella Rossellini. Roizman's cinematography gives the film some visual interest, but many critics of the awards questioned his nomination over the superb black-and-white cinematography of Stefan Czapsky for *Ed Wood*. The Oscar went to John Toll for *Legends of the Fall*.

Roizman: 631, 724, 1424, 2113.

2317 • *YANK IN THE R.A.F., A*

20TH CENTURY-FOX. 1941.

NOMINATION *Special Effects:* Fred Sersen, photographic; E. H. Hansen, sound.

The title character is Tyrone Power, who falls for showgirl Betty Grable, another American expatriate. To impress her, he joins the R.A.F. and eventually wins her with his heroics. Pleasant romance with music and a little pre–Pearl Harbor flag-waving adventure. Directed by Henry King [1868 . . .] from a screenplay by Karl Tunberg [175 . . .] and Darrell Ware [1999] based on a story written by Fox studio head Darryl F. Zanuck [34 . . .] under the pseudonym Melville Crossman. The cast includes John Sutton and Reginald Gardiner. The special effects award went to *I Wanted Wings*.

Sersen: 226, 241, 346, 458, 520, 1655, 2286. Hansen: 143, 241, 815, 952, 990, 1655, 1868, 1957, 2027, 2056, 2272, 2286.

2318 • *YANKEE DOODLE DANDY*

WARNER BROS. 1942.

AWARDS *Actor:* James Cagney. *Sound Recording:* Nathan Levinson. *Scoring of a Musical Picture:* Ray Heindorf and Heinz Roemheld.

NOMINATIONS *Picture:* Jack Warner and Hal B. Wallis, with William Cagney, producers. *Supporting Actor:* Walter Huston. *Director:* Michael Curtiz. *Original Story:* Robert Buckner. *Film Editing:* George Amy.

Cagney is George M. Cohan, the most celebrated member of a vaudeville family: father Huston, mother Rosemary DeCamp (who was fourteen years younger than the man playing her son), sister Jeanne Cagney (James' real sister). Cohan rises, by determination and talent, to become a major songwriter, playwright, and performer. The film, which waves every flag in Hollywood, ends with Cohan's visit to the White House to which he's been summoned by FDR, whom he has just been lampooning in the musical *I'd Rather Be Right*. Like most Hollywood biopics, it sentimentalizes and sanitizes its subject, glossing over, for example, Cohan's acrimonious battle with Actors Equity, which as a rich and powerful producer he tried to block in its struggle to become a Broadway bargaining agent. But thanks to Cagney, who sings, dances, and acts superbly, it's one of the greatest Hollywood musicals, with marvelous re-creations of Cohan's routines. The cinematography is by James Wong Howe [1 . . .], and the cast includes George Tobias, Irene Manning, S. Z. Sakall, Frances Langford, and Eddie Foy, Jr. Cagney called it his favorite film—as well he might, for he dominates it as few performers have ever dominated a movie. He's on screen virtually throughout, blazing with energy. As a boy, he had seen Cohan on stage, and he shared Cohan's Irish roots, modeling his own style as a dancer on Cohan's stiff-legged strut. Cohan himself had proposed the idea of a biopic to Sam Goldwyn [102 . . .], who talked to Fred Astaire [2126] about doing it. Astaire quite sensibly turned it down, so the picture went to Warners, with Cohan's recommendation that Cagney do it. Cagney disliked the screenplay and called on Julius J. Epstein [365 . . .] and Philip G. Epstein [365] for some uncredited polishing.

Cagney began in vaudeville and moved into Broadway theater, playing a lead in *Penny Arcade,* a hit of 1930. He was brought to Hollywood to star in the film of the play, retitled *Sinners' Holiday*. After a handful of films, he became a star in *The Public Enemy* and was soon one of Warners' biggest stars, though he fought bitterly with the studio over the terms of his contract. In 1942 he formed an independent production company with his brother, William, but the venture was not very successful. He retired from movies in 1961 but was persuaded out of retirement in 1981 for an appearance in *Ragtime;* he also made a TV movie, *Terrible Joe Moran,* in 1984, two years before his death.

Yankee Doodle Dandy earned sound man Levinson the sole Oscar out of the more than a score of nominations he racked up in his years as head of Warners' sound department. He also received an honorary award in 1940 for his work in helping the film industry mobilize to produce army training films.

This was the first of three Oscars for Heindorf, the head of Warners' music department. It is the sole award for Roemheld.

For all its flag-waving, *Yankee Doodle Dandy* was outdone at the Oscars by *Mrs. Miniver,* whose heroic Brits seemed to the Academy a more noble embodiment of wartime patriotism. William Wyler also took the directing award for *Mrs. Miniver.* Huston lost to Van Heflin in *Johnny Eager.* The writing Oscar went to Emeric Pressburger for *The Invaders* (also known as *49th Parallel*). Daniel Mandell won for the editing of *The Pride of the Yankees.*

J. Cagney: 79, 1216. Levinson: 16, 30, 343, 385, 531, 689, 710, 712, 790, 930, 965, 1052, 1169, 1621, 1690, 1768, 1769, 1779, 1930, 1949, 2058. Heindorf: 331, 479, 666, 930, 1043, 1204, 1385, 1408, 1430, 1690, 1719, 1750, 1910, 2058, 2186, 2243, 2310. Roemheld: 1945. Warner: 55, 110,

550, 689, 1393. Wallis: 17, 55, 85, 164, 343, 365, 676, 689, 712, 965, 1046, 1095, 1162, 1248, 1482, 1727, 1779, 2233. Huston: 50, 560, 2136. Curtiz: 79, 365, 712. Amy: 30, 1459.

2319 • YEAR OF LIVING DANGEROUSLY, THE

FREDDIE FIELDS PRESENTATION OF A METRO-GOLDWYN-MAYER PRODUCTION; MGM/UNITED ARTISTS (AUSTRALIA). 1983.

AWARD *Supporting Actress:* Linda Hunt.

Mel Gibson plays an Australian journalist in Indonesia in 1965, when the government of Sukarno began to topple. Hunt is Billy Kwan, an Indonesian who worships but comes to be disillusioned by Sukarno, and who loves to indulge in power fantasies involving the people he knows, which include Gibson and Sigourney Weaver [45 . . .], as a British embassy aide. The country's political intrigue, Billy's personal intrigue, and the romantic intrigue of Gibson and Weaver form a potent, and ultimately deadly, brew. Highly entertaining melodrama that's like a sophisticated update of the old MGM movies in which Clark Gable [798 . . .] played a soldier of fortune and fell in love with Jean Harlow or Myrna Loy or Joan Crawford [1319 . . .]. It helped make Gibson a superstar, and Weaver is a splendid match for him, even though her role is somewhat sketchy. Michael Murphy also turns in a fine performance as a dissipated American colleague of Gibson's. Directed by Peter Weir [511 . . .] from a screenplay on which he collaborated with David Williamson and C. J. Koch. It's an adaptation of Koch's novel, though the author was reportedly quite ticked off by some of Weir's alterations. The hypnotic score, augmented by one of Richard Strauss' "Four Last Songs" and some well-chosen rock and roll, is by Maurice Jarre [558 . . .].

Hunt's performance, which won the only Oscar ever given to a performer playing a member of the opposite sex, is more than a tour de force of gender switching. It's a wholly natural and astonishingly skilled creation of a complex character. Primarily known as a stage actress, Hunt made her screen debut in 1980 in *Popeye.* After her Oscar, she has been seen in various character roles in such films as *The Bostonians, Dune, Silverado,* and *Kindergarten Cop* (1990).

2320 • YEARLING, THE

MGM. 1946.

AWARDS *Color Cinematography:* Charles Rosher, Leonard Smith, and Arthur Arling. *Color Interior Decoration:* Cedric Gibbons and Paul Groesse, art direction; Edwin B. Willis, set decoration.

NOMINATIONS *Picture:* Sidney Franklin, producer. *Actor:* Gregory Peck. *Actress:* Jane Wyman. *Director:* Clarence Brown. *Film Editing:* Harold Kress.

Claude Jarman, Jr., plays Jody Baxter, a boy living in the Florida backwoods, who discovers an orphaned fawn and raises it with the encouragement of his father (Peck). But his mother (Wyman), struggling with the poverty in which the family lives, finds the animal just another mouth to feed. And as the deer grows older, it becomes more of a trial to her. A classic "family film" that ranks with MGM's other great forties achievements in that genre, *National Velvet* and *Lassie Come Home.* The screenplay by Paul Osborn [593 . . .] is based on the novel by Marjorie Kinnan Rawlings, and some of the film was shot near her home in Florida, the setting of the later film about Rawlings, *Cross Creek.* Jarman, who made his screen debut in *The Yearling,* received a miniature Oscar as "outstanding child actor of 1946." His only other memorable film, also directed by Brown, was *Intruder in the Dust* (1949). He now lives in San Francisco, where he's active in arts management.

Rosher had received the very first Oscar given for cinematography, for *Sunrise.* In the forties he became a specialist in the lush Technicolor for which MGM films were noted. He retired in 1955 and died in 1974. His son, Charles Rosher, Jr., is also a cinematographer. Arling, who was a cameraman on *Gone With the Wind,* became a director of photography after World War II. These are the sole Oscars for Arling and Smith.

This was the sixth and last nomination for Brown, who began his moviemaking career in 1915 as an assistant to director Maurice Tourneur. Brown became one of the mainstays of MGM, a studio dominated by producers rather than directors, so he never received full credit for the skill and professionalism of his work; he racked up more unsuccessful Oscar nominations than any other director. Among other things, he's known for having nurtured Greta Garbo [84 . . .] into stardom. In the forties he also produced many films for MGM. He retired from movies in 1953 and died in 1987. This time he lost to William Wyler for *The Best Years of Our Lives,* which also won the best picture Oscar and awards for Fredric March as actor and Daniel Mandell as editor. Wyman lost to Olivia de Havilland in *To Each His Own.*

Rosher: 22, 87, 1096, 1818, 1972. Smith: 208, 1132, 1417. Arling: 980. Gibbons: 66, 87, 130, 217, 227, 239, 285, 290, 440, 629, 749, 831, 980, 1069, 1096, 1173, 1190, 1226, 1230, 1232, 1274, 1308, 1309, 1417, 1567, 1604, 1644, 1662, 1673, 1721, 1861, 1937, 2068, 2112, 2256, 2257, 2300, 2330. Groesse: 87, 1173, 1190, 1232, 1309, 1335, 1385, 1604, 2112, 2157. Willis: 66, 87, 130, 227, 239, 290, 629, 749, 831, 980, 1069, 1096, 1157, 1173, 1190, 1226, 1230, 1232, 1309, 1417, 1567, 1657, 1662, 1673, 1721, 1861, 1937, 2068, 2112, 2257, 2330. Franklin: 799, 1232, 1371, 1440, 1662. Peck: 759, 1082, 2101, 2154. Wyman: 246, 1052, 1241. Brown: 84, 723, 957, 1417, 1718. Kress: 573, 953, 1371, 1596, 2126.

2321 • YENTL

UNITED ARTISTS/LADBROKE FEATURE/BARWOOD PRODUCTION; MGM/UNITED ARTISTS. 1983.

AWARD *Original Song Score or Adaptation Score:* Michel Legrand, Alan Bergman, and Marilyn Bergman.
NOMINATIONS *Supporting Actress:* Amy Irving. *Art Direction—Set Decoration:* Roy Walker and Leslie Tomkins; Tessa Davies. *Song:* "Papa, Can You Hear Me?," music by Michel Legrand, lyrics by Alan Bergman and Marilyn Bergman. *Song:* "The Way He Makes Me Feel," music by Michel Legrand, lyrics by Alan Bergman and Marilyn Bergman.

Women are prevented from studying the Torah in nineteenth-century Poland, but Yentl, played by Barbra Streisand [737 . . .], studies under the tutelage of her father (Nehemiah Persoff). When he dies, she disguises herself as a boy and sets out to enroll in a yeshiva in a town where she won't be recognized. On the way, she meets Avigdor (Mandy Patinkin), a yeshiva student who is engaged to the beautiful Hadass (Irving). Yentl, now known as Anshel, becomes a star student, but Hadass has fallen in love with Anshel—just as Anshel/Yentl has fallen in love with Avigdor. This presents even more of a problem when Hadass' father breaks off the engagement, and Avigdor persuades his friend Anshel to marry Hadass instead. The only way out for Yentl is to tell the truth and to set off alone in search of a world in which a woman can be a scholar. The film, produced and directed by Streisand, has passages of beauty and wit and some very nice performances by Streisand, Patinkin, and Irving. But the elaborate, overlong production overwhelms the simple, ironic story by Isaac Bashevis Singer, adapted by Streisand and Jack Rosenthal. For fans of the producer-director-writer-star, *Yentl* is a real treat. For nonfans, it confirms all their worst suspicions about her ego: Since both Patinkin and Irving are accomplished vocalists, why does Streisand get to sing all twelve—count 'em—songs? It has to be admitted that only a huge talent could have accomplished as much as Streisand does with the film, which had been a dream project of hers for years. But unfortunately for her, there seemed to be more nonfans among Academy members, and the failure of her film to receive nominations for best picture, best actress, and best director was widely interpreted as a snub. More than a decade later, in her acclaimed 1994 concert tour, Streisand—after having been passed over for a directing nomination a second time for *The Prince of Tides*—was still making pointed jokes about being punished for being too ambitious.

Legrand and the Bergmans, frequent collaborators, each received the third Oscar in their careers.

After studying acting in San Francisco and London, Irving made her screen debut in 1976 in *Carrie.* Her career in the eighties was sidetracked by motherhood during her marriage to Steven Spielberg [416 . . .], which lasted from 1985 to 1989, and she has had only modest success restarting it. The Oscar went to Linda Hunt for *The Year of Living Dangerously.*

The art direction award was won by Anna Asp for *Fanny & Alexander*. Giorgio Moroder, Keith Forsey, and Irene Cara won for the song "Flashdance . . . What a Feeling," from *Flashdance*.

Legrand: 179, 867, 1568, 1960, 2063, 2172, 2332. A. Bergman: 867, 1168, 1568, 1628, 1747, 1813, 1864, 2063, 2113, 2238, 2322. M. Bergman: 867, 1168, 1568, 1628, 1747, 1813, 1864, 2063, 2113, 2238, 2322. Walker: 151. Tomkins: 1533.

2322 • YES, GIORGIO

METRO-GOLDWYN-MAYER PRODUCTION; MGM/UNITED ARTISTS. 1982.

NOMINATION *Song:* "If We Were in Love," music by John Williams, lyrics by Alan Bergman and Marilyn Bergman.

A tenor (Luciano Pavarotti) falls in love with his throat doctor (Kathryn Harrold). "No, Luciano!" cried both audiences and critics about this romantic comedy directed by Franklin J. Schaffner [1541]. The cast includes Eddie Albert [887 . . .]. The Oscar went to Jack Nitzsche, Buffy Sainte-Marie, and Will Jennings for "Up Where We Belong," from *An Officer and a Gentleman*.

Williams: 6, 260, 403, 416, 588, 613, 614, 659, 805, 933, 937, 982, 996, 997, 1041, 1047, 1596, 1652, 1679, 1684, 1701, 1764.65, 1916, 1977, 2107, 2126, 2194, 2293. A. Bergman: 867, 1168, 1568, 1628, 1747, 1813, 1864, 2063, 2113, 2238, 2321. M. Bergman: 867, 1168, 1568, 1628, 1747, 1813, 1864, 2063, 2113, 2238, 2321.

2323 • YESTERDAY, TODAY AND TOMORROW

C.C. CHAMPION-LES FILMS CONCORDIA PRODUCTION (ITALY). 1964.

AWARD *Foreign Language Film.*

Three stories, all starring Sophia Loren [1280 . . .] and Marcello Mastroianni [490 . . .] and directed by Vittorio de Sica [650]. "Adelina" features Loren as a Neapolitan woman who avoids a jail sentence by invoking a law that prevents a nursing mother from going to prison, so her husband, Mastroianni, has the task of keeping her constantly preg-

nant. In "Anna," Loren is a wealthy woman in Milan who is having an affair with Mastroianni, who is poor. She's infuriated when he swerves to avoid a child and wrecks her car. In "Mara," she's a Roman prostitute who, because she has led a young seminarian astray, takes a vow of chastity—to the dismay of Mastroianni, her boyfriend. Somewhat self-consciously "naughty," but very well acted, and handsomely filmed by Giuseppe Rotunno [49].

2324 • YOJIMBO

TOHO COMPANY LTD. & KUROSAWA PRODUCTION; TOHO COMPANY LTD. (JAPAN). 1961.

NOMINATION *Black-and-White Costume Design:* Yoshiro Muraki.

Toshiro Mifune plays a samurai who wanders into a village where two rival factions are wreaking havoc. He's hired by one side but discovers he's being cheated, so he goes over to the other, then engineers the destruction of both factions. Brilliantly comic action film, directed by Akira Kurosawa [1661], and generally recognized as one of his best, as well as one of his most entertaining. It also served as the source of the "spaghetti western" that made Clint Eastwood [2179.5] a star, *A Fistful of Dollars* (1964). The costuming award went to Piero Gherardi for *La Dolce Vita*.

Muraki: 1074, 1661, 2021.

2325 • YOU CAN'T TAKE IT WITH YOU

COLUMBIA. 1938.

AWARDS *Picture:* Frank Capra, producer. *Director:* Frank Capra.

NOMINATIONS *Supporting Actress:* Spring Byington. *Screenplay:* Robert Riskin. *Cinematography:* Joseph Walker. *Sound Recording:* John Livadary. *Film Editing:* Gene Havlick.

Jean Arthur [1353] plays Alice Sycamore, and James Stewart [73 . . .] is Tony Kirby. The two fall in love, but there's a problem: His family is wealthy and snobbish; hers is freewheeling and eccentric. Her grandfather, played by Lionel Barrymore [723 . . .], dropped out of the rat race years ago. Her mother (Byington) dabbles in painting and sculpture, and started writing when a typewriter was delivered to the house by mistake. Her sister, Essie (Ann Miller), spends her days practicing to be a ballet dancer, coached by a flamboyant Russian played by Mischa Auer [1401]. Meanwhile, Alice's father (Samuel S. Hinds) is in the basement inventing fireworks, while Essie's husband, Ed (Dub Taylor), is printing up leaflets that innocently get the family investigated by the police for subversion. And so on . . . Eventually the head of the Kirby household, played by Edward Arnold, comes to visit Alice's family, and fireworks, both figurative and literal, ensue. This adaptation of the Pulitzer Prize–winning comedy by George S. Kaufman and Moss Hart [297 . . .] tweaks the material into the sentimental populism characteristic of the Capra films, and the result isn't nearly as much fun as the stage play. Barrymore in particular is given some rambling speeches about American ideals that deflate the screwball comedy just when it should be at its most buoyant, and Arnold's caricature capitalist makes a most unlikely about-face at movie's end. But YCTIWY has enough of the play's ebullience left to make it entertaining, and it's certainly well played. It helped make Stewart a star. It was the first of his three films for Capra, though he's remembered more for *Mr. Smith Goes to Washington* and *It's a Wonderful Life* than for this one. Also in the cast are Donald Meek, H. B. Warner [1206], Mary Forbes, Lillian Yarbo, Eddie "Rochester" Anderson, Harry Davenport, and Ward Bond (who plays one of the detectives investigating Alice's family for subversive activities, anticipating the role he would play in real life in the fifties, when he was one of the most outspoken Hollywood right-wingers).

Today, YCTIWY seems one of the less inspired of the Academy's choices for best picture—it's not even prime Capra. Of the nominees, *The Adventures of Robin Hood* and *Jezebel* have worn better, and *Grand Illusion* has been hailed as one of the greatest films of all time. But Capra had served as president of the Academy since 1935, helping build its membership after labor struggles of the early thirties had come close to causing the organization's death. (Members of the newly formed guilds resented the Academy's origins as a sort of company union. Capra was instrumental in eliminating the Academy from all bargaining and mediating activities.) So although he already had two Oscars as director, and one of his films, *It Happened One Night,* had taken the best picture Oscar four years earlier, the Academy remained grateful. These were, however, Capra's last Oscars. He would continue to make films until 1961 and live thirty years beyond that. But of his subsequent work, only *Mr. Smith Goes to Washington* and *It's a Wonderful Life* would receive critical and popular acclaim, and the latter film was not considered a success until repeated showings on TV made it an annual Christmastime event.

Byington is an affectionately remembered character actress who spent her long career playing motherly scatterbrains. After a career of more than thirty years on stage, she made her film debut at the age of forty-seven as Marmee in the 1933 version of *Little Women.* Her numerous films include *Mutiny on the Bounty, Dodsworth, The Charge of the Light Brigade, The Devil and Miss Jones, Meet John Doe,* and the 1943 *Heaven Can Wait,* but she is perhaps best known for her role in the TV sitcom *December Bride.* She died in 1971. The supporting actress Oscar went to Fay Bainter for *Jezebel.*

The screenplay award went to George Bernard Shaw and his adapters, W. P. Lipscomb, Cecil Lewis, and Ian Dalrymple, for *Pygmalion.*

Joseph Ruttenberg won for the cinematography for *The Great Waltz.* The award for sound went to Thomas T. Moulton for *The Cowboy and the Lady.* Ralph Dawson took the editing Oscar for *The Adventures of Robin Hood.*

Capra: 1025, 1033, 1119, 1206, 1366, 1370. Riskin: 905, 1025, 1119, 1366. Walker: 904, 1058, 1494. Livadary: 330, 455, 596, 732, 1058, 1206, 1215, 1303, 1366, 1370, 1488, 1521, 1740, 1872, 2111, 2327. Havlick: 1206, 1370.

2326 • *YOU LIGHT UP MY LIFE*

THE SESSION COMPANY PRODUCTION; COLUMBIA. 1977.
AWARD *Original Song:* "You Light Up My Life," music and lyrics by Joseph Brooks.

Didi Conn, the daughter of a comedian (Joe Silver), wants her own show business career. She's engaged to a tennis coach (Stephen Nathan) but also attracted to a director (Michael Zaslow). Moderately entertaining but overfamiliar story that lacks the star power to make it in any way memorable. It's really a one-man show: In addition to writing the Oscar-winning song, Brooks also produced, directed, scored, and wrote the screenplay for the movie. Debby Boone's recording of the title song was a huge hit that many people are still trying to get out of their heads.

2327 • YOU WERE NEVER LOVELIER

COLUMBIA. 1942.

NOMINATIONS *Sound Recording:* John Livadary. *Song:* "Dearly Beloved," music by Jerome Kern, lyrics by Johnny Mercer. *Scoring of a Musical Picture:* Leigh Harline.

Adolphe Menjou [734] wants to marry off his daughter, Rita Hayworth, but she falls for the penniless Fred Astaire [2126]. Menjou tries to break up their infatuation, but by the time he succeeds in doing so, he has changed his mind about Astaire, so they have to join forces to win her back. The second of Astaire's two teamings with Hayworth is much better than the first, *You'll Never Get Rich*. The plot never gets in the way of the musical numbers, which include a lovely duet to Kern and Mercer's "I'm Old Fashioned" and a lively jitterbug number, "The Shorty George." After Ginger Rogers [1102], Hayworth may have been Astaire's best screen dance partner. Directed by William A. Seiter from a screenplay by Michael Fessier, Ernest Pagano, and Delmer Daves. The supporting cast includes Adele Mara, Larry Parks [1058], and Xavier Cugat and his orchestra. Hayworth's songs are dubbed by Nan Wynn.

Yankee Doodle Dandy won for Nathan Levinson's sound and Ray Heindorf and Heinz Roemheld's scoring. "Dearly Beloved" lost to a song from another Astaire musical, Irving Berlin's "White Christmas," from *Holiday Inn*.

Livadary: 330, 455, 596, 732, 1058, 1206, 1215, 1303, 1366, 1370, 1488, 1521, 1740, 1872, 2111, 2325. Kern: 340, 375, 455, 1117, 1707, 1990. Mercer: 248, 278, 384, 476, 494, 508, 636, 788, 825, 877, 903, 905, 1109, 1772, 1838, 1912, 2328. Harline: 1053, 1576, 1607, 1838, 1851, 2312.

2328 • YOU'LL FIND OUT

RKO RADIO. 1940.

NOMINATION *Song:* "I'd Know You Anywhere," music by Jimmy McHugh, lyrics by Johnny Mercer.

Kay Kyser and his orchestra are hired to play a debutante party at a spooky old house, and Boris Karloff, Peter Lorre, and Bela Lugosi show up as the chief spooks. Silly musical programmer that wastes the talents of its sinister trio. Directed by David Butler and featuring Dennis O'Keefe, Ginny Simms, Helen Parrish, Alma Kruger, Harry Babbitt, and Ish Kabibble. The Oscar went to Leigh Harline and Ned Washington for "When You Wish Upon a Star," from *Pinocchio*.

McHugh: 907, 916, 1707, 2028. Mercer: 248, 278, 384, 476, 494, 508, 636, 788, 825, 877, 903, 905, 1109, 1772, 1838, 1912, 2327.

2329 • YOU'LL NEVER GET RICH

COLUMBIA. 1941.

NOMINATIONS *Song:* "Since I Kissed My Baby Goodbye," music and lyrics by Cole Porter. *Scoring of a Musical Picture:* Morris Stoloff.

Robert Benchley, the producer of a Broadway show that Fred Astaire [2126] is choreographing, is attempting to hide his infatuation with Hayworth from his wife. Embroiled in the plot, which involves a diamond necklace, Astaire falls for Hayworth. Their paths cross again, and the plot snarls, after Astaire is drafted. Released shortly before Pearl Harbor, this attempt at a musical service comedy never quite takes off, partly because its unreality soon became painfully obvious, and partly because Astaire was a bit old to be playing a draftee. It is notable mainly as the first of two teamings of Astaire with Rita Hayworth. (The other is *You Were Never Lovelier*.) Directed by Sidney Lanfield, with Osa Massen, Frieda Inescort, and Guinn Williams. Hayworth's singing voice is dubbed by Nan Wynn.

Porter's song score is not one of his more memorable, though it includes the lovely "So Near and Yet

So Far,'' which may be more familiar today than the nominated song. The Oscar went to Jerome Kern and Oscar Hammerstein's "The Last Time I Saw Paris,'' from *Lady Be Good*. The scoring award went to Frank Churchill and Oliver Wallace for *Dumbo*.

Porter: 261, 914, 1862. Stoloff: 13, 432, 455, 596, 643, 677, 732, 773, 1057, 1058, 1115, 1206, 1862, 1872, 1873, 1998, 2110.

2330 • *YOUNG BESS*

MGM. 1953.

NOMINATIONS *Color Art Direction—Set Decoration:* Cedric Gibbons and Urie McCleary; Edwin B. Willis and Jack D. Moore. *Color Costume Design:* Walter Plunkett.

Jean Simmons [858 . . .] plays the future Queen Elizabeth I in this posh, romantic version of her emergence into womanhood, in which she's romanced by Stewart Granger as Thomas Seymour. Twenty years after winning an Oscar as Henry VIII, Charles Laughton [1387 . . .] plays the part again. Deborah Kerr [599 . . .] is his sixth and final wife, Catharine Parr. George Sidney directs from a screenplay by Arthur Wimperis [1371 . . .] and Jan Lustig, and the cast includes Cecil Kellaway [843 . . .] and Leo G. Carroll. Handsomely filmed by Charles Rosher [22 . . .]. The art direction Oscar went to *The Robe*, for which Charles LeMaire and Emile Santiago also won for costumes.

Gibbons: 66, 87, 130, 217, 227, 239, 285, 290, 440, 629, 749, 831, 980, 1069, 1096, 1173, 1190, 1226, 1230, 1232, 1274, 1308, 1309, 1417, 1567, 1604, 1644, 1662, 1673, 1721, 1861, 1937, 2068, 2112, 2256, 2257, 2300, 2320. McCleary: 239, 1417, 1537, 1541, 1657. Willis: 66, 87, 130, 227, 239, 290, 629, 749, 831, 980, 1069, 1096, 1157, 1173, 1190, 1226, 1230, 1232, 1309, 1417, 1567, 1657, 1662, 1673, 1721, 1861, 1937, 2068, 2112, 2257, 2320. Moore: 31, 1190, 1662, 1937, 1986, 2112. Plunkett: 9, 66, 953, 1087, 1243, 1587, 1657, 1859, 2029.

2331 • *YOUNG FRANKENSTEIN*

GRUSKOFF/VENTURE FILMS-CROSSBOW PRODUCTIONS-JOUER LTD. PRODUCTION; 20TH CENTURY-FOX. 1974.

NOMINATIONS *Screenplay Adapted From Other Material:* Gene Wilder and Mel Brooks. *Sound:* Richard Portman and Gene Cantamessa.

Wilder is Victor Frankenstein, the mad scientist's American grandson, who with his fiancée, played by Madeline Kahn [230 . . .], goes back to Transylvania and becomes involved in more monster-making. Superbly done Brooksian parody, with many screamingly funny moments—and some routine shtick, too, though this is probably writer-producer-director Brooks' best movie. Peter Boyle is the sweetly charming monster, Marty Feldman the hunchbacked Igor, Cloris Leachman [1139] the hatchet-faced housekeeper, Teri Garr [2113] a ditzy villager, and Kenneth Mars the Strangelovian chief of police. The film's high point may be a cameo appearance by a near-unrecognizable Gene Hackman [255 . . .] as a blind man who befriends the monster—a wonderful parody of a scene in *The Bride of Frankenstein*. Or maybe it's when the monster and his creator perform "Puttin' on the Ritz.'' Or . . . The beautiful black-and-white cinematography is by Gerald Hirschfeld, and art director Dale Hennesy [86 . . .] and set decorator Robert de Vestel [1196 . . .] brilliantly re-create the look of the old Universal horror movies.

The screenplay Oscar went to Francis Ford Coppola and Mario Puzo for *The Godfather, Part II*. *Earthquake* took the award for sound.

Wilder: 1626. Brooks: 230, 1626. Portman: 339, 418, 502, 521, 738, 784, 1109, 1473, 1526, 1701. Cantamessa: 339, 416, 588, 1439, 1914, 2165.

2332 • *YOUNG GIRLS OF ROCHEFORT, THE*

MAG BODARD-GILBERT DE GOLDSCHMIDT-PARC FILM-MADELEINE FILMS PRODUCTION; WARNER BROS.-SEVEN ARTS (FRANCE). 1968.

NOMINATION *Score of a Musical Picture—Original or Adaptation:* music and adaptation score by Michel Legrand, lyrics by Jacques Demy.

Catherine Deneuve [998.5] and Françoise Dorléac

are the girls, who go to the fair and find romance. Saccharine attempt to recapture the magic of writer-director Demy's earlier *The Umbrellas of Cherbourg.* It's meant as a tribute to the Hollywood musicals, with guest-star appearances by Gene Kelly [74] and George Chakiris [2244]. Prettily filmed by Ghislain Cloquet [2021]. The scoring Oscar went to John Green for *Oliver!*

Legrand: 179, 867, 1568, 1960, 2063, 2172, 2321. Demy: 2172.

2333 • YOUNG GUNS II

MORGAN CREEK PRODUCTION; 20TH CENTURY FOX. 1990.
NOMINATION *Song:* "Blaze of Glory," music and lyrics by Jon Bon Jovi.

Emilio Estevez plays Billy the Kid, as he did in the 1988 film to which this is a sequel. He's joined by Kiefer Sutherland and Lou Diamond Phillips from the first movie, plus Christian Slater, Alan Ruck, and Balthazar Getty as new members of his gang, as they try to outrun the law, particularly Marshal Pat Garrett (William Petersen). Like the earlier film, it's a tolerable western whose casting is designed to draw a younger audience than the genre normally attracts. But for older admirers of the genre it's nothing special. Directed by Geoff Murphy. The Oscar went to Stephen Sondheim for "Sooner or Later (I Always Get My Man)," from *Dick Tracy.*

2334 • YOUNG IN HEART, THE

SELZNICK INTERNATIONAL PICTURES; UNITED ARTISTS. 1938.
NOMINATIONS *Cinematography:* Leon Shamroy. *Original Score:* Franz Waxman. *Scoring:* Franz Waxman.

Billie Burke [1306] and Roland Young [2117] and their children, Douglas Fairbanks, Jr., and Janet Gaynor [1792 . . .], are a family of con artists, but their latest pigeon, a wealthy old lady played by Minnie Dupree, proves to be more than a match for them. Charming little sentimental comedy, directed by Richard Wallace from a script by Paul Osborn [593 . . .] and Charles Bennett [706]. The cast also includes Paulette Goddard [1855] and Richard Carlson. The cinematography Oscar went to Joseph Ruttenberg for *The Great Waltz.* Waxman received a

double nomination because the Academy, for the first time, divided the scoring awards into categories for composers and arrangers. The division lasted through the 1940 awards, when it was changed to a more sensible division into scores for dramatic films and scores for musicals. In the first category, for composers, Erich Wolfgang Korngold won for *The Adventures of Robin Hood;* in the second, for arrangers, the award went to Alfred Newman for *Alexander's Ragtime Band.*

Shamroy: 29, 226, 356, 413, 495, 569, 602, 1088, 1153, 1213, 1592, 1610, 1706, 1852, 1883, 2013, 2286. Waxman: 573, 958, 1457, 1459, 1579, 1670, 1822, 1975, 1979, 2004.

2335 • YOUNG LAND, THE

C.V. WHITNEY PICTURES INC.; COLUMBIA. 1959.
NOMINATION *Song:* "Strange Are the Ways of Love," music by Dimitri Tiomkin, lyrics by Ned Washington.

Pat Wayne stars as the sheriff in a California town who arrests Dennis Hopper [595 . . .] for the murder of a Mexican and has to contend with the racial unrest stirred up by the trial. Okay message film directed by Ted Tetzlaff from a screenplay by Norman Shannon Hall. The most interesting thing about it may be that it was produced by Patrick Ford, the son of director John Ford [815 . . .], and starred the son of the elder Ford's most famous star, John Wayne [33 . . .]. Also in the cast are Yvonne Craig and Dan O'Herlihy [18]. The Oscar went to James Van Heusen and Sammy Cahn for "High Hopes," from *A Hole in the Head.*

Tiomkin: 33, 286, 380, 446, 638, 663, 730, 768, 850, 911, 912, 1206, 1347, 1370, 1470, 2006, 2127, 2282. Washington: 274, 585, 911, 912, 1329, 1396, 1576, 1745, 2127, 2282.

2336 • YOUNG LIONS, THE

20TH CENTURY-FOX. 1958.
NOMINATIONS *Black-and-White Cinematography:* Joe MacDonald. *Sound:* Carl Faulkner, sound director, 20th Century-Fox Studio Sound Department. *Scoring of a Dramatic or Comedy Picture:* Hugo Friedhofer.

Three young men, German skiing instructor Marlon Brando [583 . . .], American Jew Montgomery Clift [732 . . .], and playboy Dean Martin, meet before World War II and again, tragically, during it, when all three have become soldiers. Brando bleached his hair blond to play a young German who turns Nazi, but has a change of heart when he learns the truth about the extermination camps. Maximilian Schell [1065 . . .] also appears, as a nastier Nazi. Edward Anhalt [164 . . .] adapted Irwin Shaw's novel and Edward Dmytryk [467] directed, but it's loose and overextended, interesting mainly for the chance to see Brando and Clift in the same film. Neither is at his best, however. Clift was still recovering from the disastrous auto accident that had nearly killed him, and was drinking heavily. Brando was forced into the picture because he had walked out on a role in *The Egyptian* four years earlier and was still trying to work off his contractual obligation to Fox. He found the character fascinating and is partly responsible for the change from the novel, in which the character is an unregenerate Nazi, but his performance is mannered and overstated, and director Dmytryk was unable to discipline him. The cast also includes Hope Lange [1558], Barbara Rush, Mai Britt, and Lee Van Cleef.

The cinematography award went to Sam Leavitt for *The Defiant Ones.* Fred Hynes won for the sound for *South Pacific* and Dimitri Tiomkin for the score for *The Old Man and the Sea.*

MacDonald: 1550, 1753. Faulkner: 1062, 1088, 1213. Friedhofer: 2, 21, 184, 187, 214, 267, 1048, 2303.

2337 • *YOUNG MR. LINCOLN*

COSMOPOLITAN; 20TH CENTURY-FOX. 1939.
NOMINATION *Original Story:* Lamar Trotti.

Henry Fonda [815 . . .] plays the title role in this tale of the backwoods lawyer's defense of two young men (Richard Cromwell and Eddie Quillan) accused of murder. Alice Brady [990 . . .] plays the mother of the defendants. Superlative performances by Fonda and Brady and the direction of John Ford [815 . . .], as well as the absorbing courtroom drama, make this a true classic. If it's not as well known as some Ford films, it may be because people expect this kind of historical drama to be stiff and boring. It isn't. Marjorie Weaver is Mary Todd, and Pauline Moore plays Anne Rutledge. The cast also includes Donald Meek, Ward Bond, Milburn Stone, and Francis Ford. The writing Oscar went to Lewis R. Foster for *Mr. Smith Goes to Washington.*

Trotti: 1516, 2043, 2286.

2338 • *YOUNG PHILADELPHIANS, THE*

WARNER BROS. 1959.
NOMINATIONS *Supporting Actor:* Robert Vaughn. *Black-and-White Cinematography:* Harry Stradling, Sr. *Black-and-White Costume Design:* Howard Shoup.

Philadelphia lawyer Paul Newman [3 . . .] was born not only on the wrong side of the tracks but also on the wrong side of the sheets, but he elbows aside the Main Liners—except for potential trophy wife Barbara Rush—on the way to the top. Slick melodrama with some good performers, including Alexis Smith as that staple of the genre, the horny, neglected wife; plus Brian Keith, Billie Burke [1306], Otto Kruger, and Adam West. Directed by Vincent Sherman from a screenplay by James Gunn based on a novel, *The Philadelphian,* by Richard Powell.

Vaughn, who plays a friend of Newman's accused of murder, made his film debut in 1957, and the following year had the title role in *Teenage Cave Man,* a Roger Corman schlocker. Fortunately his career went upward, and through the sixties and seventies he was a regular supporting player, often as a cunning corporate or political villain. His films include *The Magnificent Seven, Bullitt,* and *The Towering Inferno,* but he is best known for his work in TV, particularly as Napoleon Solo in the mid-sixties spy-spoof series *The Man From U.N.C.L.E.* The Oscar went to Hugh Griffith for *Ben-Hur.*

The cinematography Oscar went to William C. Mellor for *The Diary of Anne Frank.* Orry-Kelly won for the costumes for *Some Like It Hot.*

Stradling: 110, 149, 596, 737, 852, 853, 864, 896, 957, 1246, 1393, 1567, 1949. Shoup: 410, 1100, 1649, 1700.

2339 • YOUNG SHERLOCK HOLMES

AMBLIN ENTERTAINMENT PRODUCTION IN ASSOCIATION WITH HENRY WINKLER/ROBERT BIRNBAUM; PARAMOUNT. 1985.

NOMINATION *Visual Effects:* Dennis Muren, Kit West, John Ellis, and David Allen.

Nicholas Rowe is Holmes and Alan Cox is Watson —as teenagers. They team up on their first case, which involves the skulduggery of a mysterious oriental cult. A bright idea badly handled: Though it begins well, with some engaging suppositions about what the detective and his chronicler might have been like as Victorian schoolboys, it trails off into a muddled fantasy replete with special effects that seem to be there only to show off what the effects men could do, such as a duel with an animated stained-glass knight. The plot's killer cult reminded many critics of *Indiana Jones and the Temple of Doom*—not surprising, since the producer was Steven Spielberg [416 . . .]. Directed by Barry Levinson [75 . . .] from a screenplay by Chris Columbus. The cast includes Sophie Ward, Anthony Higgins, Freddie Jones, and Michael Hordern. The fine cinematography and production design are by Stephen Goldblatt [1612] and Norman Reynolds [613 . . .] respectively. The special effects Oscar went to *Cocoon.*

Muren: 5, 577, 588, 614, 997, 1002, 1071.5, 1684, 2019, 2284. West: 1652. Allen: 1775.

2340 • YOUNG WINSTON

OPEN ROAD FILMS LTD. PRODUCTION; COLUMBIA. 1972.

NOMINATIONS *Story and Screenplay—Based on Factual Material or Material Not Previously Published or Produced:* Carl Foreman. *Art Direction–Set Decoration:* Don Ashton, Geoffrey Drake, John Graysmark, and William Hutchinson; Peter James. *Costume Design:* Anthony Mendleson.

Portrait of the politician as a young imperialist: Russell Lewis plays Winston Churchill as a child, then Michael Anderson takes over for his years as a reluctant schoolboy, and finally Simon Ward becomes the dashing young officer in the Sudan, enterprising journalist covering the Boer War, and budding political genius in Parliament. The action scenes help shake off the torpor induced by the historical pageantry, mak-

ing this one of the more successful of the *Masterpiece Theatre*–style movie epics about the fading glory of the British Empire. Foreman, who also produced the film, based his screenplay on Churchill's autobiography, *My Early Life: A Roving Commission.* Churchill himself, before his death in 1965, is said to have urged Foreman to make a film of the book because he admired Foreman's *The Guns of Navarone.* Richard Attenborough [745] directs, and the cast includes Anne Bancroft [28 . . .] as Churchill's beautiful but remote actress mother, Robert Shaw [1252] as his harsh, syphilitic father, John Mills [1737] as Kitchener, Anthony Hopkins [1679.5 . . .] as Lloyd George, and Jack Hawkins, Patrick Magee, Ian Holm [386], Jane Seymour, Edward Woodward, Laurence Naismith, Robert Hardy, Pat Heywood, Colin Blakely, and Maurice Roëves.

The story and screenplay Oscar went to Jeremy Larner for *The Candidate.* The art direction award went to *Cabaret.* Anthony Powell won for the costumes for *Travels With My Aunt.*

Foreman: 287, 380, 850, 912, 1302. Graysmark: 1651. James: 1263. Mendleson: 995.

2341 • YOU'RE A BIG BOY NOW

SEVEN ARTS PRODUCTIONS. 1966.

NOMINATION *Supporting Actress:* Geraldine Page.

Peter Kastner is a shy young New York City librarian trying to break away from his smothering mother, played by Page. Elizabeth Hartman [1537] is the aspiring actress who tries to teach him a thing or two. Amusing sixties-style coming-of-age comedy written and directed by Francis Ford Coppola [65 . . .] as his master's thesis at UCLA. It provided his first mainstream movie success. It's more than a little dated, like a lot of once-hip sixties movies, but it has a terrific supporting cast: Julie Harris [1301], Rip Torn [466], Michael Dunn [1812], Tony Bill [1927], and Karen Black [672].

This was the fourth of seven unsuccessful nominations before Page finally landed an Oscar on her eighth try, for *The Trip to Bountiful.* This time the award went to Sandy Dennis for *Who's Afraid of Virginia Woolf?*

Page: 935, 1005, 1555, 1591, 1959, 1985, 2142.

2342 • YOU'RE A SWEETHEART

UNIVERSAL. 1937.

NOMINATION *Interior Decoration:* Jack Otterson

Producer Ken Murray tries to cook up publicity for a Broadway show starring Alice Faye. George Murphy comes up with a gimmick that saves the day —and wins him Faye's hand. Blah musical comedy with Andy Devine, William Gargan [2045], Charles Winninger, and Donald Meek, directed by David Butler. The title song by Harold Adamson [21 . . .] and Jimmy McHugh [907 . . .] is the only memorable thing about the movie. The art direction Oscar went to Stephen Goosson for *Lost Horizon*.

Otterson: 96, 269, 668, 681, 1229, 1240, 1895.

2343 • YOUTH ON PARADE

REPUBLIC. 1942.

NOMINATION *Song:* "It Seems I've Heard That Song Before," music by Jule Styne, lyrics by Sammy Cahn.

Innocuous college musical about a prank involving a fictitious student. When a professor (John Hubbard) wants to meet her, the pranksters hire an actress (Ruth Terry) to play their creation. The prof, of course, falls in love with her. The nominated song is the only memorable thing about this low-budget programmer directed by Al Rogell. It was Styne's second nomination but his first with Cahn; they would become one of the most important songwriting teams of the forties. The Oscar went to Irving Berlin for "White Christmas," from *Holiday Inn*.

Styne: 74, 696, 737, 920, 921, 1031, 1719, 2072, 2110. Cahn: 74, 163, 182, 696, 915, 926, 1031, 1056, 1216, 1524, 1587, 1692, 1708, 1719, 1859, 1907, 2016, 2064, 2072, 2103, 2110, 2125, 2263, 2264, 2315.

2344 • Z

REGGANE FILMS-O.N.C.I.C. PRODUCTION; CINEMA V DISTRIBUTING (ALGERIA). 1969.

AWARDS *Film Editing:* Françoise Bonnot. *Foreign Language Film*.

NOMINATIONS *Picture:* Jacques Perrin and Hamed Rachedi, producers. *Director:* Costa-Gavras. *Screenplay —Based on Material From Another Medium:* Jorge Semprun and Costa-Gavras.

Yves Montand plays the leader of the opposition party in a Mediterranean country. Following a peace rally, he is hit by a speeding van and dies. An official investigation is mounted, but unfortunately for the ruling party, the magistrate in charge of the investigation, played by Jean-Louis Trintignant, is an honest man who uncovers an intricate government plot. Superb political thriller, one of the best ever, that hasn't dated at all—possibly because world events keep turning up chilling parallels to the film's story. It's based on the murder of Gregorios Lambrakis in Greece in 1965 and the investigation that brought George Papandreou to power—only to be overthrown in 1967 by a military coup that held power in Greece for seven years. *Z* was, of course, banned in Greece, the homeland of Costa-Gavras as well as Irene Papas, who plays Montand's wife. Coscenarist Semprun was also a political exile from his native Spain. The film has music by Mikis Theodorakis, who was under house arrest in Greece at the time it was made. A part of the score was smuggled out of the country; the rest is made up of existing works. Producer Perrin plays a journalist in the film.

Z is the first movie nominated as best foreign language film that also received a nomination for best picture. The Oscar in the latter category went to *Midnight Cowboy*, which also won for director John Schlesinger and screenwriter Waldo Salt.

Because of his father's leftist activities, Costa-Gavras was denied university entrance in Greece and was unable to obtain a visa to the United States during the Red-scared fifties. He studied in Paris, where he began his directing career in 1965 with *The Sleeping Car Murders*, for which he also wrote the screenplay. *Z* made him a much sought-after director, and he has continued to make films with strong antitotalitarian messages, including *Missing* and *Music Box*. Semprun, who was deported from Spain in 1942, joined the French Resistance and was imprisoned at Buchenwald. He has continued his career as a screenwriter in France and directed a 1973 film, *Les Deux Mémoires*.

Costa-Gavras: 1330. Semprun: 842.

2345 • ZELIG

JACK ROLLINS AND CHARLES H. JOFFE PRODUCTION; ORION/
WARNER BROS. THROUGH WARNER BROS. 1983.
NOMINATIONS *Cinematography:* Gordon Willis. *Costume
Design:* Santo Loquasto.

Woody Allen [39 . . .] plays Leonard Zelig, who
has a peculiar disorder: He's so self-effacing that he
blends into his surroundings, automatically taking on
the characteristics of the people he's with. Among
other things, he becomes a black musician, a baseball
player in the batting lineup with Babe Ruth and Lou
Gehrig, and even a Nazi at a rally presided over by
Adolf Hitler. The transformations make him a celebrity, but a reluctant one. Mia Farrow plays the psychiatrist who tries to cure him. (Of course, he becomes
a psychiatrist during the analysis.) Droll little film,
written and directed by Allen, with impressive camera tricks that insert Allen-Zelig into old photos and
newsreels. Clever as it is, it's a one-joke film that
seems overextended even at seventy-nine minutes.

This was the first nomination for Willis, who became the center of controversy when the Academy
passed him over for his magisterial work on such
movies as *Klute, The Godfather, The Godfather, Part II,
All the President's Men, Annie Hall,* and *Manhattan.*
How, the critics asked, could the man who shot three
Academy Award best pictures go unnominated so
long? The cinematographers branch has never come
up with an answer. This time he lost to Sven Nykvist
for *Fanny & Alexander,* which also won for Anna Asp's
art direction.

Willis: 786. Loquasto: 311.5, 1647.

2346 • ZORBA THE GREEK

ROCHLEY LTD. PRODUCTION; INTERNATIONAL CLASSICS (U.S./
GREECE). 1964.
AWARDS *Supporting Actress:* Lila Kedrova. *Black-and-
White Cinematography:* Walter Lassally. *Black-and-White
Art Direction—Set Decoration:* Vassilis Fotopoulos.

NOMINATIONS *Picture:* Michael Cacoyannis, producer.
Actor: Anthony Quinn. *Director:* Michael Cacoyannis.
Screenplay—Based on Material From Another Medium: Mi-
chael Cacoyannis.

Alan Bates [678] plays Basil, a young Englishman
who comes to Crete to write and finds his life being
taken over by the flamboyant Zorba (Quinn), who
wants the buttoned-down Basil to become less English
and more Greek. Kedrova is the dying former prostitute who rents a room to Basil; Irene Papas is the
widow to whom he's attracted, with tragic consequences. Enjoyable if somewhat long-winded adaptation of the novel by Nikos Kazantzakis. It gets more
life from Quinn's performance and the music score by
Mikis Theodorakis than it does from Cacoyannis' direction.

Kedrova was born in Russia but from the age of
ten lived in France, where she began her screen career as a character actress in the fifties. Since the
Oscar, for her first English-language film, she has
been seen in such movies as *Torn Curtain* (1966), *The
Kremlin Letter* (1970), and *Tell Me a Riddle* (1980).

Lassally worked on *A Taste of Honey* (1961), *The
Loneliness of the Long Distance Runner* (1962), and *Tom
Jones,* as well as *Electra* and other films directed by
Cacoyannis, before winning the Oscar. More recently
he has been cinematographer on some films from
the Ismail Merchant [954.5 . . .]–James Ivory
[954.5 . . .] team, *Heat and Dust* and *The Bostonians.*

Cacoyannis, born on Cyprus, was educated in England and began his career as an actor at the Old Vic.
He switched to directing in the early fifties, returning
to Greece to launch his career. In 1961 his version of
the Greek tragedy *Electra* gained him his first international fame. The best picture Oscar went to *My Fair
Lady,* for which Rex Harrison won the acting award
and George Cukor the directing Oscar. Edward Anhalt took the screenplay award for *Becket.*

Quinn: 1226, 2212, 2282.

The following list includes all persons nominated for Oscars for the films included in this book. The numbers following their names correspond to the entry numbers for the films for which they were nominated. Winners, and the entries for the films for which they won, are indicated in **boldface**. The list also includes winners of the Irving G. Thalberg, Jean Hersholt, Gordon E. Sawyer, and special or honorary awards, followed by the years for which they received the awards.

1628, 1747, 1813, 1864, **2063**, 2113, **2238, 2321,** 2322.

Bergman, Ingmar: 111, 460, 634, 644, 2082, 2283. **Thalberg '70.**

Bergman, Ingrid: 72, 111, 173, 701, **749,** 1048, **1378.**

Bergman, Marilyn: 179, 867, 1168, 1568, 1628, 1747, 1813, 1864, **2063,** 2113, **2238, 2321,** 2322.

Bergner, Elisabeth: 622.

Bergren, Eric: 608.

Berkeley, Busby: 791, 792, 2196.

Berkey, Jim: 892.

Berkos, Peter: 917.

Berlin, Irving: 34, 244, 358, **929,** 1773, 2115, 2268.

Berlin, Jeannie: 887.

Berman, Henry: 814.

Berman, Pandro S.: 40, 656, 754, 1035, 1899, 2115. **Thalberg '76.**

Bernard, James: 1784.

Bernari, Carlo: 713.

Bernds, Edward: 913.

Bernstein, Elmer: 27.5, 789, 882, 1242, 1264, 1685, 1959, **2064,** 2101, 2130, 2147, 2223.

Bernstein, Leonard: 1477.

Bernstein, Walter: 733.

Berri, Claude: 2021.

Berry, David: 419.

Bert, Malcolm: 110, 1910.

Bertino, Tom: 1287.5.

Bertolucci, Bernardo: 439, **1136,** 1141.

Bertrand, Robert: 1927.

Bessie, Alvah: 1459.

Best, Marjorie: 15, 768, 833, 1973.

Bettis, John: 786.

Bickel, Moidele: 1640.5.

Bickford, Charles: 651, 1052, 1868.

Biddiscombe, Carl: 743, 2120.

Biddle, Adrian: 2039.

Biedrzycka-Sheppard, Anna: 1764.65.

Bikel, Theodore: 522.

Bill, Tony: 1927.

Binger, R. O.: 1200, 1451, 1607.

Biro, Lajos: 1134.

Biroc, Joseph: 963, 2126.

Bishop, Stephen: 2271.

Biziou, Peter: 1333.

Black, Don: 174, **259,** 789, 1574, 2147.

Black, Karen: 672.

Blackie-Goodine, Janice: 2179.5.

Blackton, Jay: 852, **1469.**

Blair, Betsy: 1283.

Blair, Linda: 631.

Blake, John: 924.5.

Blake, Michael: 482.

Blake, Yvonne: 717, **1429.**

Blakley, Ronee: 1415.

Blalack, Robert: 1916.

Blane, Ralph: 801, 1299.

Blangsted, Folmar: 1960.

Blanke, Henry: 17, 90, 712, 1046, **1169,** 1315, 1457, 1936, 2136.

Blankfort, Michael: 298.

Blatty, William Peter: 631.

Blewitt, David: 434.

Block, Ralph: Honorary '39.

Blondell, Joan: 246.

Bloom, Harold Jack: 1412.

Bloom, John: 398, 725, **745.**

Bloom, Les: 448, 1647.

Bloomberg, Daniel: 274, 680, 693, 991, 1350, 1642, 1756. **Honorary '45.**

Blumenthal, Herman: 413, 896, 1062.

Blumofe, Robert: 264.

Blyth, Ann: 1319.

Boardman, Chris: 423.

Boates, Brent: 544.

Bode, Ralf D.: 418.

Bode, Susan: 311.5.

Boehm, David: 851.

Boehm, Sydney: 108.

Boekelheide, Jay: 1698.

Boekelheide, Todd: 60, 1425.

Boemler, George: 1469.

Boetticher, Budd: 312.

Bogart, Humphrey: 24, 330, 365.

Bogdanov, Mikhail: 2229.

Bogdanovich, Peter: 1139.

Bohanan, Fred: 768.

Boisson, Noëlle: 160.

Boland, Bridget: 85.

Bolger, John: 917.

Bologna, Joseph: 1221.

Bolt, Robert: 558, 1151, **1252.**

Bomba, Ray: 2066.

Bonar, John: 1567.

Bond, Edward: 240.

Bondi, Beulah: 807, 1463.

Bonicelli, Vittorio: 748.

Bon Jovi, Jon: 2333.

Bonner, John A.: Honorary '94.

Bonnot, Françoise: 2344.

Boorman, John: 523, 940.

Booth, Charles G.: 949.

Booth, Margaret: 1387. **Honorary '77.**

Booth, Shirley: 425.

Bor, Milan: 258.

Borders, Gloria S.: 708.5, **2019.**

Boren, Charles S.: Honorary '72.

Borgnine, Ernest: 1283.

Borradaile, Osmond: 715.

Bortnik, Aida: 1466.

Borzage, Frank: 132, 1792.

Botkin, Perry: 231.

Bottin, Rob: 1154, **2124.**

Boulange, Daniel: 2033.

Boulle, Pierre: 287.

Bourgoin, Jean: 1201.

Bourguignon, Serge: 1967.

Bourne, Mel: 671, 1005, 1418.

Boutelje, Phil: 827, 909.

Bowie, Les: 1977.

Box, Betty: 177.

Box, Euel: 177.

Box, John: 558, 1151, 1429, 1471, 1533, 2134.

Box, Muriel: 1793.

Box, Sydney: 1793.

Boxer, Nat: 92.

Boyd, John: 613, 2274.

Boyer, Charles: 36, 440, 643, 749. **Honorary '42.**

Boyer, François: 703.

Boyle, Charles: 74.

Boyle, Edward G.: 91, 393, 709, 743, 1783, 1860, 1866.

Boyle, Richard: 1746.

Boyle, Robert: 659, 743, 1450, 1816.

Bozman, Ron: 1820.

Brabourne, John: 1533, 1722.

Bracco, Lorraine: 806.

Bracht, Frank: 1461.

Brackett, Charles: 705, 925, 1088, **1208,** 1440, **1975, 2093,** 2099. **Honorary '57.**

Bradford, William: 2308.

Brady, Alice: 990, 1401.

Bramall, John: 1737.

Branagh, Kenneth: 902.

Brand, Millen: 1849.

Brandauer, Klaus Maria: 1512.

Brando, Marlon: 583, **784,** 1069, 1141, **1477,** 1763, 1949, 2212.

Brännström, Brasse: 1400.

Bratton, Robert L.: 752, 1193.

Braun, Ewa: 1764.65.

Brecher, Irving: 1299.

Breen, Joseph I.: Honorary '53.

Breen, Richard: 350, 705, **2093.**

Bregman, Martin: 561.

Brendel, Frank: 591.

Brennan, Eileen: 1617.

Brennan, Walter: 424, **1080,** 1779, **2245.**

Brenner, Albert: 159, 332, 1976, 2152, 2165.

Brenner, David: 260.

Brenon, Herbert: 1878.

Breschi, Arrigo: 1029.

Brest, Martin: 1764.5.

Bretherton, David: 321.

Bretton, Raphael: 896, 963, 1596, 2126.

Brevig, Eric: 937, 2124.

Bricusse, Leslie: 557, 805, 933, 937, 1766, 2037, **2201,** 2285.

Bridge, Joan: 1252.

Bridges, James: 394, 1525.

Bridges, Jeff: 1139, 1918, 2086.

Bright, John (costume designer): 263, 954.5, 1290, 1679.5, **1725.**

Bright, John (writer): 1633.

Briley, John: 745.

Brink, Gary: 49.

Brinton, Ralph: 2106.

Bristol, Howard: 690, 852, 864, 1182, 1451, 1607, 1613, 1907, 2064.

Broccoli, Albert S.: Thalberg '81.

Brochu, Don: 734.5.

Brodine, Norbert: 731, 1306, 1464.

Brodney, Oscar: 776.

Brodszky, Nicholas: 163, 1216, 1692, 1843, 2103.

Broidy, Steve: Hersholt '62.

Brooks, Albert: 293.

Brooks, Donald: 356, 494, 1907.

Brooks, Jack: 324, 341, 1867.

Brooks, James L.: 293, 2020.

Brooks, Joseph: 2326.

Brooks, Mel: 230, **1626,** 2331.

Brooks, Richard: 227, 372, **609,** 987, 1627.

Broughton, Bruce: 1825.

Brown, Bernard B.: 93, 96, 269, 919, 1010, 1011, 1125, 1560, 1896, 2028, **2260.**

Brown, Clarence: 84, 723, 957, 1417, 1718, 2320.

Brown, David: 658.5, 1041, 2198. **Thalberg '90.**

Brown, Frederick J.: 1660.

Brown, Harry: 1579, 1756.

Brown, Harry Joe: 34, 343.

Brown, Hilyard: 413.

Brown, John W.: 334.

Brown, Lew: 2214.

Brown, Malcolm: 980, **1861.**

Brown, Rowland: 79, 564.

Brown, Tregoweth: 825.

Browne, Leslie: 2152.

Brun, Joseph C.: 1282.

Bruno, John: 5, 153.5, 413.5, 766, 1590, 2147.5.

Bruns, George: 116, 1709, 1839, 1992.

Bryan, John: 164, 325, **820.**

Brynner, Yul: 1088.

Buchman, Sidney: 904, 1057, 1370, 1998.

Buckner, Robert: 2318.

Buff, Conrad: 2019.

Bujold, Genevieve: 85.

Bullock, Walter: 920, 1829.

Bumstead, Henry: 1927, 2101, 2179.5, 2200.

Buñuel, Luis: 549, 2034.

Buono, Victor: 2248.

Burbridge, Lyle: 1712.

Burgess, Don: 708.5.

Burke, Billie: 1306.

Burke, Edwin: 132.

Burke, Johnny: 171, 173, **787,** 1547, 1691.

Burke, Marcella: 1229.

Burke, Michèle: 272.5, 409, 474, **1641.**

Burks, Robert: 1537, 1669, 1941, **2098.**

Burman, Tom: 1767.

Burnett, W. R.: 2222.

Burns, Allan: 1187.

Burns, Catherine: 1140.

Burns, George: 1976.

Burns, Ralph: 49, 86, **321.**

Burnside, Norman: 571.

Burrill, Timothy: 2021.

Burrow, Milton: 223.

Burstyn, Ellen: 41, 631, 1139, 1682, 1747.

Burton, Bernard W.: 1485.

Burton, Richard: 85, 164, 621, 1391, 1706, 1897, 2277.

Burton, Willie D.: 58, 209, 307, 1802.5, 2231.

Burtt, Ben: 588, 996, **1652,** 1684, **1916,** 2284.

Burum, Stephen H.: 924.5.

Busch, Niven: 990.

Busey, Gary: 307.

Butler, Bill (cinematographer): 1481.

Butler, Bill (editor): 415.

Butler, Chris A.: 382.5.

Butler, David: 2218.

Butler, Frank: 787, 1703, 2222.

Butler, Hugo: 597.

Butler, Lawrence: 1070, 2031, **2050,** 2066.

Buttons, Red: 1763.

Butts, Dale: 681.

Byington, Spring: 2325.

Byrne, David: 1136.

Caan, James: 784.

Cacoyannis, Michael: 2346.

Cady, Jerome: 2289.

Caesar, Adolph: 1857.

Caesar, Arthur: 1268.

Caglione, John, Jr.: 543.

Cagney, James: 79, 1216, **2318.**

Cagney, William: 2318.

Cahn, Sammy: 74, 163, 182, **696,** 915, 926, 1031, **1056,** 1216, **1524,** 1587, 1692, 1708, 1719, 1859, 1907, 2016, 2064, **2072,** 2103, 2110, 2125, 2263, 2264, 2315, 2343.

Caine, Michael: 35, 598, **863,** 1841.

Calandrelli, Jorge: 423.

Calhern, Louis: 1243.

Callahan, Gene: 63, 356, **964,** 1143.

Calley, John: 1679.5.

Cambern, Donn: 1720.

Cameron, John: 2125.

Campanile, Pasquale Festa: *see* Festa Campanile, Pasquale.

Campbell, Alan: 1909.

Fink, Michael: 153.5.

Finkel, Abem: 1779.

Finklehoffe, Fred: 1299.

Finlay, Frank: 1506.

Finney, Albert: 579, 1378, 2106, 2177.

Finston, Nat: 1292, 1387.

Firth, Peter: 621.

Fishburne, Laurence: 2250.7.

Fisher, Steve: 533.

Fisher, Thomas L.: 2147.5.

Fitzgerald, Barry: 787.

Fitzgerald, Geraldine: 2316.

Flagg, Fannie: 728.

Flaherty, Frances: 1211.

Flaherty, Robert: 1211.

Flaiano, Ennio: 562, 603, 2209.

Flannery, William: 1566.

Fleischman, Tom: 1678, 1820.

Fleming, Victor: 798.

Fletcher, Louise: 1481.

Flick, Stephen: 544, 1589, **1711, 1888.5,** 2124.

Flournoy, Richard: 1353.

Flowers, A. D.: 1439, **1596, 2120.**

Foch, Nina: 629.

Folsey, George: 51, 137, 629, 807, 835, 838, 1124, 1299, 1320, 1500, 1688, 1782, 2068, 2269.

Fonda, Henry: 815, **1473,** 2153. **Honorary '80.**

Fonda, Jane: 394, **430,** 1066, **1104,** 1356, 1473, 2047.

Fonda, Peter: 595.

Foner, Naomi: 1735.

Fontaine, Joan: 441, 1670, **1979.**

Fontanne, Lynn: 841.

Foote, Horton: 2015, 2101, 2142.

Forbes, Bryan: 81.

Forbes, Lou: 282, 1006, 2057, 2186, 2310.

Forbstein, Leo: 90, 385, 1169.

Ford, Harrison: 2296.

Ford, John: 815, 952, 999, 1200, **1642,** 1901.

Ford, Michael: 614, **1652,** 1684.

Foreman, Carl: 287, 380, 850, 912, 1302, 2340.

Foreman, John: 317, 1625.

Forman, Milos: 60, 1481.

Forrest, Chet: 694, 1270, 1384.

Forrest, Frederic: 1726.

Forsey, Keith: 189, 682.

Forslund, Bengt: 610.

Fosse, Bob: 49, **321,** 1155.

Foster, David: 251.5, 1078.

Foster, Jodie: 7, 1421.5, **1820,** 2005.

Foster, Lewis R.: 1353, **1370.**

Fotopoulos, Vassilis: 2346.

Fowler, Gene, Jr.: 1032.

Fowler, Hugh S.: 1541.

Fowler, Marjorie: 557.

Fox, Charles: 711, 1508.

Fox, Paul S.: 376, **413,** 428, 476, 495, 530, 721, 950, **1088,** 1601, 1666, **1706,** 1852.

Fox, William: 1792.

Fraisse, Robert: 1219.5.

Fraker, William: 890, 1205, 1380, 1439, 2231.

Franci, Adolfo: 1815.

Franciosa, Anthony: 880.

Franciosa, Massimo: 713.

Francis, Freddie: 779, 1875.

Francis-Bruce, Richard: 1802.5.

Franco, Robert J.: 27.5.

Frank, Frederic M.: 832.

Frank, Harriet, Jr.: 956, 1448.

Frank, Melvin: 636, 1108, 1705, 2125.

Franklin, Richard: 684.

Franklin, Sidney: 799, 1232, **1371,** 1440, 1662, 2320. **Thalberg '42.**

Frankovich, M. J.: Hersholt '83.

Fraser, Ian: 1766.

Frayne, John G.: Honorary '79. Sawyer '83.

Frears, Stephen: 840.

Fredericks, Ellsworth: 1763.

Frederickson, Gray: 92, **785.**

Frederix, Marc: 1020.

Freed, Arthur: 66, 769, 1950. **Honorary '67. Thalberg '51.**

Freed, Ralph: 117.

Freeman, Charles: 1595.

Freeman, Morgan: 580, 1802.5, 1948.

Freeman, Y. Frank: Hersholt '56. Honorary '66.

French, Edward: 1915.

Frend, Charles: 804.

Fresholtz, Les: 54, 58, **209,** 215, 606, 888, 1127, 1158.5, 1279, 1526, 2113, 2179.5.

Freund, Karl: 239, 397, **799.**

Frey, Leonard: 659.

Friberg, Arnold: 2012.

Fricker, Brenda: 1399.

Fried, Gerald: 212.

Friedenberg, Richard: 1701.5.

Friedhofer, Hugo: 2, 21, **184,** 187, 214, 267, 1048, 2303, 2336.

Friedkin, William: 631, **724.**

Friedman, Bruce Jay: 1893.

Friedman, Jud: 251.5.

Friedman, Stephen J.: 1139.

Frigerio, Ezio: 474.

Froeschel, George: 1371, 1662.

Fruchtman, Lisa: 92, 786, **1698.**

Fuchs, Daniel: 1216.

Fuller, Charles: 1857.

Fuller, Leland: 530, 719, 1149, 1475, 1601, 2212.

Fullerton, Carl: 1562.5, 1680.

Fulton, John P.: 269, 1010, 1011, 1012, **2012, 2310.**

Funke, Alex: 2124.

Furness, John: 477.

Furse, Margaret: 85, 164, 1177, 1285, 1374, 1766.

Furse, Roger: 858.

Furst, Anton: 153.

Furthman, Jules: 1387.

Furuya, Osami: 2120.

Gable, Clark: 798, **1025,** 1387.

Gaines, George: 54, 448, 890, **1798.**

Galati, Frank: 6.

Gale, Bob: 127.

Gallico, Paul: 1607.

Galloway, James: 1059.

Gamley, Douglas: 1186.

Gangelin, Victor: 1828, 2244.

Gannon, Kim: 59, 589, 1870.

Ganton, Douglas: 1154.5.

Ganz, Armin: 2148.

Ganz, Lowell: 1893.

Garbo, Greta: 84, 336, 1440, 1718. **Honorary '54.**

Garcia, Andy: 786.

Gardenia, Vincent: 142, 1351.

Gardiner, Lizzy: 16.5.

Gardner, Ava: 1339.

Gardner, Herb: 2067.

Garfield, John: 251, 712.

Garfinkle, Louis: 521.

Gargan, William: 2045.

Garity, William: 645. Honorary '41.

Granville, Bonita: 2044.

Granville, Roy: 253, 505.

Grashin, Mauri: 910.

Grauman, Sid: Honorary '48.

Graves, Ed: 557.

Gray, Maggie: 275.

Gray, Mike: 394.

Gray, William S.: 831.

Graysmark, John: 1651, 2340.

Grazer, Brian: 1893.

Green, Adolph: 141, 1034.

Green, Guy: 820.

Green, Jack N.: 2179.5.

Green, Johnny: 66, 320, **594,** 662,
817, 914, 1298, **1471,** 1550, 1657,
2047, **2244.**

Green, Paul: 1920.

Green, Walon: 2280.

Greenberg, Adam: 2019.

Greenberg, Jerry (also Gerald B.): 92,
724, 1111.

Greenberg, Richard: 1600.

Greenberg, Robert M.: 1600.

Greene, Clarence: 1572, 2241.

Greene, Danford B.: 230, 1286.

Greene, Graham (actor): 482.

Greene, Graham (writer): 639.

Greene, Mort: 1291.

Greene, W. Howard: 96, 239, 747,
1070, 1452, **1560,** 1621, 1909, 2262.
Honorary '36. Honorary '37.

Greene, Walter: 2278.

Greenfeld, Josh: 875.

Greenham, Vivian C.: 850.

Greenhut, Robert: 863.

Greenstreet, Sydney: 1248.

Greenwell, Peter: 265.

Greenwood, Don: 953.

Gregory, Grace: 450, 1219.

Gregory, Robin: 519, 1513.

Gregson, Richard: 81.

Gresham, Gloria: 112.

Grenzbach, Bud: 395, 784, **1584.**

Grey, Joel: 321.

Griffin, Eleanore: 271.

Griffin, James (a.k.a. Arthur James):
1221.

Griffith, Corinne: 552.

Griffith, David Wark: Honorary '35.

Griffith, Hugh: 175, 2106.

Griffith, Melanie: 2313.

Griffith, Raymond: 946.

Griffiths, Mildred: 1417.

Griffiths, Trevor: 1678.

Griggs, Loyal: 833, 988, **1799, 1887,**
2012. **Honorary '38.**

Grignon, Marcel: 1020.

Grillo, Michael: 6.

Grimes, Stephen: 1432, **1512,** 2238.

Groesse, Paul: 87, 1173, **1190,** 1232,
1309, 1335, 1385, **1604,** 2112, 2157,
2320.

Grofé, Ferde: 1322.

Gross, Roland: 1445.

Grot, Anton: 90, 1169, 1621, 1768,
1981.

Groves, George R.: 825, 1385, **1393,**
1457, **1763,** 1869, 1973, 2277.

Gruault, Jean: 1342.

Gruenberg, Louis: 432, 664, 1854.

Grusin, Dave: 379, 633, 667.5, 881,
890, **1318,** 1473, 2113.

Guaraldi, Vince: 266.

Guare, John: 107.

Guerra, Tonino: 61, 240, 367.

Guffey, Burnett: 210, **255, 732,** 870,
1093.

Guffroy, Pierre: 1020, **2021.**

Guidice, Don: 2074.

Guinness, Alec: 287, 941, 1150, 1181,
1916. **Honorary '79.**

Guiol, Fred: 768.

Guthrie, A. B., Jr.: 1799.

Gutteridge, Martin: 1188.

Gwangwa, Jonas: 471.

Gwenn, Edmund: 1325, 1336.

Haack, Morton: 1583, 2184, 2252.

Haas, Robert M.: 1052, 1170.

Hackett, Albert: 25, 656, 1782, 2052.

Hackett, Joan: 1495.

Hackman, Gene: 255, **724,** 971, 1333,
2179.5.

Hadjidakis, Manos: 1426.

Hafenrichter, Oswald: 2053.

Haffenden, Elizabeth: 175, 1252.

Haft, Steven: 511.

Hageman, Richard: 955, 979, 1200,
1801, **1901,** 2062.

Hagen, Earle H.: 1160.

Hagen, Jean: 1831.

Hahn, Don: 162.

Hahn, Edwin C.: 1494.

Haigh, Nancy: 152, **308,** 708.5.

Haines, Fred: 2170.

Hajos, Karl: 1262, 1961.

Hale, Joe: 219.

Hale, John: 85.

Hall, Alexander; 904.

Hall, Allen: 129, **708.5**

Hall, Cecilia: 961, 2114.

Hall, Charles D.: 348, 1306.

Hall, Conrad: 317, 504, 987, 1355,
1627, 1771.5, 2017.

Hall, David: 833, 2240.

Hall, Grayson: 1432.

Hall, John: 1012.

Hallenberger, Harry: 1210.

Haller, Ernest: 55, 679, **798,** 1046,
1174, 1319, 2248.

Hallström, Lasse: 1400.

Halprin, Sol: 346.

Halsey, Richard: 1712.

Ham, Al: 1931.

Hambling, Gerry: 433, 641, 992.5,
1313, 1333.

Hamilton, Arthur: 1235.

Hamlisch, Marvin: 398, 977, 1109,
1747, 1813, 1876, 1898, **1927, 2238.**

Hammeras, Ralph: 520, 1073, 1619.

Hammerstein, Oscar: 375, **1117,**
1122, **1921,** 1951.

Hammett, Dashiell: 2233.

Hammond, Albert: 1271.

Hampton, Christopher: 485.

Hampton, Orville H.: 1490.

Hancock, Herbie: 1729.

Handford, Peter: 808, **1512.**

Haney, Kevin: 580.

Hanks, Tom: 195, **708.5, 1562.5.**

Hannemann, Walter: 1848, 2163.

Hansen, E. H.: 143, 241, 815, 952,
990, **1655,** 1868, 1957, 2027, 2056,
2272, **2286,** 2317.

Hansen, Franklin: 412, **649,** 1194,
1217, 2024.

Harburg, E. Y.: 322, 340, **2300.**

Harding, Ann: 927.

Harding, Jay: 641, 1548.

Hardy, Jonathan: 277.

Harlan, Russell: 204, 227, 825, 879,
882, 2101.

Harline, Leigh: 1053, **1576,** 1607,
1838, 1851, 2312, 2327.

Harling, Franke: 1880, **1901,** 2080.

Harmon, Sidney: 1998.

Kiernan, William R.: 1133, 1521, 1550, 1753, 1858, 2238.

Kieslowski, Krzysztof: 1671.5.

Kilvert, Lilly: 1154.5.

Kimball, David J.: 1650.

King, Henry: 1868, 2286.

King, Paul: 1498.

Kingsley, Ben: 308, 745.

Kingsley, Dorothy: 1782.

Kirk, Mark-Lee: 760, 1394, 1828.

Kirkland, Geoffrey: 1698.

Kirkland, Sally: 82.

Kish, Joseph: 13, 1048, 1062, 1812, 1840.

Kleban, Edward: 398.

Kline, Kevin: 670.

Kline, Richard: 334, 1089.

Kline, Rick: 507, 658.5, 1333, 1825, 2020, 2114.

Klingman, Lynzee: 1481.

Klotz, Florence: 1185.

Knight, Charles: 319.

Knight, Darin: 521.

Knight, Shirley: 488, 1985.

Knowles, Bernard: 1317.

Knox, Alexander: 2286.

Knudson, Robert: 321, 416, **588,** 613, **631,** 938, 1439, 1877, 1911, 2274.

Knudtson, Frederic: 522, 1000, 1032, 1065, 1474, 2288.

Koch, Howard: 365, 1779.

Koch, Howard W.: Hersholt '89.

Koch, Norma: 963, 1126, **2248.**

Koehler, Ted: 930, 1750, 2186.

Koenekamp, Fred: 1023, 1541, **2126.**

Koenekamp, Hans: 30.

Koenig, John: 2058.

Kohlmar, Fred: 1566.

Kohn, John: 420.

Kohner, Frederick: 1229.

Kohner, Susan: 984.

Kohut, Michael: 641, 1310, 1548, 1711, 2124, 2165, 2231.

Kopelson, Arnold: 734.5, 1584.

Korda, Alexander: 1620.

Korda, Vincent: 1070, 1201, 2031, **2050.**

Korjus, Miliza: 828.

Korngold, Erich Wolfgang: 17, 90, 1621, 1768.

Kosa, Emil, Jr.: 413.

Koshelev, G.: 2229.

Kostal, Irwin: 166, 1284, 1557, **1881, 2244.**

Koster, Henry: 214.

Kovic, Ron: 260.

Kozachik, Pete: 1434.5.

Kraft, Robert: 1249.5.

Krainin, Julian: 1643.5.

Kräly, Hans: 1137.5, 1485, **1540.**

Kramer, Larry: 2307.

Kramer, Stanley: 330, 522, 843, 912, 1065, 1812. **Thalberg '61.**

Krams, Arthur: 357, 1173, 1309, **1727,** 1937, 1959, 2098, 2208.

Krasker, Robert: 2053.

Krasna, Norman: 535, 741, **1615,** 1694.

Krasner, Milton: 21, 46, 96, 654, 953, 1219, **2072.**

Krepela, Neil: 413.5, 2165.

Kress, Carl: 2126.

Kress, Harold F.: 573, **953,** 1371, 1596, **2126,** 2320.

Krim, Arthur B.: Hersholt '74.

Kristofferson, Kris: 1874.

Kruschen, Jack: 91.

Kubrick, Stanley: 151, 415, 574, 735, **2164.**

Kudelski, Stefan: Sawyer '90.

Kuljian, Anne: 5.

Kureishi, Hanif: 1389.

Kuri, Emile: 4, 166, 363, 629, **894,** 1284, 1823, **2155.**

Kurland, Gilbert: 283.

Kurland, Jeffrey: 311.5.

Kurnitz, Harry: 2250.

Kurosawa, Akira: 1661. **Honorary '89.**

Kurtz, Gary: 65, 1916.

Kusnick, Harry: 1775.

Kymry, Tylwyth: 120.

La Cava, Gregory: 1401, 1899.

Ladd, Diane: 41, 1659, 2279.

Laden, Bob: 868.

Laemmle, Carl, Jr.: 48.

LaGarde, Jocelyne: 882.

Lagerstrom, Oscar: 1648.

LaGravenese, Richard: 671.

Lahti, Christine: 1989.

Lai, Francis: 1218.

Laing, Bob: 745, 2134.

Lake, Stuart N.: 2245.

Lambert, Gavin: 970, 1875.

Lamont, Peter: 45, 659, 1898.

Lamorisse, Albert: 1672.

L'Amour, Louis: 935.

Lancaster, Burt: 107, 210, **609,** 732.

Lanchester, Elsa: 428, 2297.

Landaker, Gregg: 614, 1047, **1652, 1888.5.**

Landau, Martin: 461, **595.8,** 2148.

Lane, Burton: 117, 1731.

Lang, Charles: 97, 250, 319, 636, **649,** 705, 765, 953, 1480, 1640, 1699, 1738, 1778, 1855, 1860, 1955, 1968, 2180.

Lang, Walter: 1088.

Langdon, Dory (a.k.a. Dory Previn): 1550, 1926, 2161.

Lange, Arthur: 171, 366, 827, 1123, 2303.

Lange, Harry: 614, 2164.

Lange, Hope: 1558.

Lange, Jessica: 244.5, 449, 722, 1381, 1987, **2113.**

Lange, Johnny: 1832.

Lange, Robert John: 1710.

Langlois, Henri: Honorary '73.

Lansbury, Angela: 749, 1265, 1567.

Lansing, Sherry: 653.

Lantieri, Michael: 128, 937, **1071.5.**

Lantz, Walter: Honorary '78.

Lapis, Joseph: 269.

LaPorte, Steve: 167.

Lardner, Ring, Jr.: 1286, 2305.

Larner, Jeremy: 339.

Larsen, Tambi: 892, 956, 1341, **1727,** 1897.

La Rue, Jim: 2144.

LaShelle, Joseph: 91, 357, 428, 709, 953, 1017, **1149,** 1283, 1391.

Lasker, Lawrence: 113, 2231.

Lasky, Jesse L.: 1779, 2272.

Lassally, Walter: 2346.

Laszlo, Ernest: 31, 646, 1000, 1032, 1065, 1196, **1812,** 1907.

Lathrop, Philip: 69, 591.

Laughton, Charles: 1387, **1620,** 2297.

Laurel, Stan: Honorary '60.

Laurents, Arthur: 2152.

Laurie, Piper: 364, 390, 964.

Lavery, Emmett: 453.

Lawrence, Jack: 1978.

Lawrence, Richard J.: 1698.

Newell, Norman: 1344.

Newley, Anthony: 2285.

Newman, Alfred: 31, **34**, 46, 72, 138, 182, 226, **333, 334**, 347, 375, 428, 437, 457, 476, 495, 542, 690, 797, 833, 952, 953, 959, 962, 1016, 1082, **1088, 1213**, 1278, **1362**, 1397, 1475, 1616, 1655, 1849, **1868**, 1883, 1921, 2043, 2046, **2091**, 2258, 2286, **2294**, 2316.

Newman, Charles: 1121.

Newman, Chris: 60, 398, **631**, 641, 724, 784, 1820.

Newman, David: 255.

Newman, Emil: 1964.

Newman, Eve: 2163, 2281.

Newman, Joseph: 497, 1751.

Newman, Lionel: 183, 457, 557, 795, **896**, 981, 1160, 1273, 1585, 1762, 2043.

Newman, Paul: 3, 372, **422**, 443, 956, 964, 1444.5, 1645, 2198. **Hersholt '93. Honorary '85.**

Newman, Randy: 112, 1418, 1524.5, 1530, 1651.

Newman, Thomas: 1190.5, 1802.5.

Newman, Walter: 198, 238, 371.

Ngor, Haing S.: 1086.

Niblo, Fred, Jr.: 463.

Nichols, Dudley: 30, **999**, 1200, 2092.

Nichols, Mike: 810, **1679.5**, 1821, 2277, 2313.

Nicholson, Bill: 1650.

Nicholson, Bruce: 614, 1589, **1652**.

Nicholson, Jack: 395, 595, 658.5, 672, 1019, 1135, **1481**, 1625, 1678, **2020**.

Nicholson, William: 1795.5.

Nikel, Hannes: 258.

Nini, Diane: 1078.

Nitzsche, Jack: 1465, 1481.

Niven, David: 1778.

Niver, Kemp R.: Honorary '54.

Noble, Thom: 2039, **2296**.

Nolte, Nick: 1612.

Nord, Richard: 734.5.

Noremark, Henny: 1237.

Norlind, Lloyd B.: 47.

Norris, Patricia: 506, 608, 1974, 2165, 2201.

Norsch, Herbert: 2308.

North, Alex: 29, 215, 413, 515, 577, 1654, 1727, 1802, 1814, 1886, 1949, 2174, 2177, 2212, 2277. **Honorary '85.**

North, Edmund H.: 1541.

Norton, Rosanna: 2144.

Novarese, Vittorio Nino: 29, **413, 465**, 833, 1610.

Novi, Charles: 527.

Nozaki, Albert: 2012.

Nozik, Michael: 1643.5.

Nugent, Frank S.: 1642.

Nyberg, Mary Ann: 141, 1910.

Nyby, Christian: 1676.

Nykvist, Sven: 460, 644, 2173.

Nyswaner, Ron: 1562.5.

Oakie, Jack: 818.

Oakland, Ben: 1122.

Oberon, Merle: 487.

Oberst, Walter: 1887. Honorary '38.

O'Brien, Edmond: 146, 1783.

O'Brien, Liam: 905.

O'Brien, Margaret: Honorary '44.

O'Brien, Sheila: 1955.

Obzina, Martin: 668, 681.

O'Connell, Arthur: 73, 1566.

O'Connell, Kevin: 223, 507, 586, 658.5, 1825, 2020, 2114.

Odell, Cary: 170, 455, 1783.

Odell, Robert: 161.

O'Donoghue, Robin: 745.

O'Donovan, Edwin: 890.

O'Hara, Karen: 422.

O'Herlihy, Dan: 18.

O'Keefe, Michael: 826.

Okey, Jack: 632, 1743.

Okun, Charles: 6.

Olin, Lena: 617.

Oliver, Edna May: 581.

Oliver, Harry: 1792, 1946.

Olivier, Laurence: 268, 619, **858, 901**, 1272, 1506, 1670, 1693, 1841, 2316. **Honorary '46. Honorary '78.**

Oliviero, Nino: 1344.

Olmos, Edward James: 1904.

Olson, Nancy: 1975.

O'Meara, C. Timothy: 1726.

Ondricek, Miroslav: 60, 1651.

O'Neal, Ryan: 1218.

O'Neal, Tatum: 1526.

O'Neil, Barbara: 55.

Ophüls, Max: 1582, 1723.

Oppenheimer, George: 2227.

Orbom, Eric: 1886.

Orkin, Ruth: 1183.

Orloff, Lee: 5, 761.5, **2019**.

Orry-Kelly: 66, 853, **1157, 1860**.

Ortolani, Riz: 1235, 1344.

Osbiston, Alan: 850.

Osborn, Paul: 593, 1763.

Osborne, John: 2106.

O'Steen, Sam: 395, 1821, 2277.

O'Toole, Peter: 164, 805, 1151, 1177, 1395, 1733, 1953.

Otterson, John: 96, 269, 668, 681, 1229, 1240, 1895, 2342.

Ouspenskaya, Maria: 560, 1212.

Overton, Alfred J.: 215, 540, 544, 606, 1548.

Overton, Richard: 5, 544, 961.

Overton, Tom: 1911.

Owen, Alun: 869.

Owens, Harry: 2220.

Pacino, Al: 75, 543, 561, 775.5, 784, 785, **1764.5**, 1780.

Page, Geraldine: 935, 1005, 1555, 1591, 1959, 1985, **2142**, 2341.

Pagliero, Marcello: 1519.

Pakula, Alan J.: 54, 1876, 2101.

Pal, George: Honorary '43.

Palance, Jack: 408, 1799, 1955.

Palmer, Adele: 182.

Palmer, Ernest: 235, 298, 714, 1946.

Palmer, Patrick: 390, 1351, 1857.

Palminteri, Chazz: 311.5.

Pan, Hermes: 481, 1990, 2115.

Pan, Kant: 472.5.

Panama, Norman: 636, 1108, 1705.

Paquin, Anna: 1563.5.

Parker, Alan: 1313, 1333.

Parker, Arthur Jeph: 394, 1816.

Parker, Daniel: 1285.5.

Parker, David: 1425.

Parker, Dorothy: 1845, 1909.

Parker, Eleanor: 328, 534, 1007.

Parker, Max: 760.

Parker, Ray, Jr.: 766.

Parkes, Walter F.: 113, 2231.

Parks, Larry: 1058.

Parrish, Robert: 53, **251**.

Parrondo, Gil: 1429, 1541, 2134.

Parsons, Estelle: 255, 1645.

Parton, Dolly: 1438.

Puttnam, David: 386, 1086, 1313, 1331.
Puzo, Mario: 784, 785.
Pye, Merrill: 1450.
Pyke, Trevor: 258.

Quaid, Randy: 1135.
Quaranta, Gianni: 300, **1725,** 2135.
Quayle, Anthony: 85.
Quenzer, Arthur: 457, 1306.
Quinn, Anthony: 1226, 2212, 2282, 2346.

Rachedi, Hamed: 2344.
Rachmil, Lewis J.: 1510.
Radnitz, Robert B.: 1882.
Rafelson, Bob: 672.
Raguse, Elmer: 345, 757.5, 1306, 1464, 1487, 2117, 2118.
Raine, Norman Reilly: 1169.
Rainer, Luise: 799, 831.
Rainger, Ralph: 197, 846, 1805.
Rains, Claude: 365, 1369, 1370, 1455.
Raksin, David: 707, 1778.
Ralston, Ken: 128, 419, **513.5,** 577, **708.5, 1684, 2274.**
Rambaldi, Carlo: 44, 588, 1089.
Rambeau, Marjorie: 1609, 2121.
Ramin, Sid: 2244.
Ramsey, Anne: 2083.
Rand, Tom: 725.
Random, Ida: 1653.
Ransford, Maurice: 721, 1153, 2093.
Rapf, Harry: 296, 931.
Raphael, Frederic: 493, 2160.
Raposo, Joe: 824.
Rappeneau, Jean-Paul: 2033.
Rasch, Raymond: 1176.
Rathbone, Basil: 979, 1721.
Rattigan, Terence: 281, 1778.
Raucher, Herman: 1960.
Ravetch, Irving: 956, 1448.
Rawlings, Terry: 386.
Ray, Nicholas: 1671.
Ray, Satyajit: Honorary '91.
Ray, Tony: 2182.
Raye, Don: 306, 899.
Raye, Martha: Hersholt '68.
Rea, Stephen: 472.5.
Reading, Anthony: 1651.
Redeker, Quinn K.: 521.
Redford, Robert: 1502, 1643.5, 1927.

Redgrave, Lynn: 761.
Redgrave, Michael: 1364.
Redgrave, Vanessa: 263, 954.5, 1021, **1066,** 1285, 1354.
Redman, Joyce: 1506, 2106.
Ree, Max: 400.
Reed, Carol: 639, **1471,** 2053.
Reed, Donna: 732.
Reed, Tom: 1433.
Reid, Cliff: 999.
Reid, Kenneth: 636.
Reifsnider, Lyle: 15.
Reiner, Rob: 658.5.
Reinhardt, Betty: 1149.
Reinhardt, Wolfgang: 727.
Reisch, Walter: 435, 749, 1440, **2093.**
Reiss, Stuart A.: 542, 557, **646,** 2008, 2093, 2247.
Reitz, John: 506.
Relph, Michael: 1757.
Remick, Lee: 508.
Renie (a.k.a. Renie Conley): 201, 355, **413,** 1338, 1601.
Rennahan, Ray: 235, 241, 569, 581, 701, **798,** 1120, 1210.
Renoir, Jean: 1884. **Honorary '74.**
Renzetti, Joe: 307.
Revel, Harry: 1291, 1322.
Revere, Anne: 759, **1417,** 1868.
Reynolds, Debbie: 2184.
Reynolds, Norman: 613, 614, 995, **1652,** 1684, **1916.**
Reynolds, William: 643, 784, 896, 1753, **1881, 1927,** 2152.
Rhodes, Leah: 15.
Rice, Charles: 320, 1550.
Rice, Tim: 32.5, 1177.5.
Rich, Allan: 251.5.
Rich, Frederic: 1036, 1900.
Rich, Robert: 273.
Richard, James A.: 992.
Richard, Jean-Louis: 501.
Richards, Beah: 843.
Richards, Dick: 2113.
Richardson, Henry: 1734.
Richardson, John: 45, 413.5.
Richardson, Miranda: 478.5, 2104.5.
Richardson, Ralph: 839, 894.
Richardson, Robert: 260, **1047,** 1584.
Richardson, Tony: 2106.
Richie, Lionel: 423, 616, **2271.**
Richler, Mordecai: 94.

Richlin, Maurice: 1498, **1572.**
Richter, W. D.: 303.
Rickards, Jocelyn: 1354.
Rickman, Tom: 418.
Riddle, Nelson: 338, **821,** 1172, 1518, 1708.
Riedel, Richard H.: 1572.
Ries, Irving: 704.
Riesenfeld, Hugo: 1247.
Ringwood, Bob: 613.
Risi, Dino: 1764.
Riskin, Everett: 114, 904, 1488.
Riskin, Robert: 905, **1025,** 1119, 1366, 2325.
Ritt, Martin: 956.
Ritter, Thelma: 46, 210, 1289, 1564, 1572, 2294.
Riva, J. Michael: 423.
Roach, Hal: Honorary '83.
Roach, Janet: 1625.
Robards, Jason: 54, 1066, 1300.
Robbe-Grillet, Alain: 1145.
Robbins, Ayn: 1681, 1712.
Robbins, Jerome: 2244. Honorary '61.
Robbins, Richard: 954.5, 1679.5.
Robb-King, Peter: 1154.
Robert, Daniel: 1005.
Roberts, Austin: 2015.
Roberts, Ben: 1256.
Roberts, Casey: 353, 760, 1048.
Roberts, Eric: 1734.
Roberts, Irmin: 1887. Honorary '38.
Roberts, Julia: 1603, 1922.
Roberts, Rachel: 2061.
Roberts, Stanley: 330.
Robertson, Cliff: 387.
Robertson, Hugh A.: 1312.
Robertson, Robbie: 1279.
Robin, Leo: 104, **197,** 368, 846, 1072, 1805, 1843, 2032, 2088, 2310.
Robinson, Bruce: 1086.
Robinson, Edward G.: Honorary '72.
Robinson, Edward R.: 1895.
Robinson, Glen: 591, 917, 1089, 1196.
Robinson, Jane: 860.
Robinson, Phil Alden: 661.
Robson, Flora: 1759.
Robson, Mark: 1001, 1558.
Robson, May: 1119.
Rocchetti, Manlio: 580.
Rochester, Arthur: 411.5, 442, 2293.

Rochin, Aaron: 521, 641, 1089, 1310, 1711, 2124, 2165, 2231, 2287.
Rockett, Norman: 833, 2120.
Rode, Fred: 719.
Roder, Milan: 1880.
Rodgers, Richard: 1921.
Roelfs, Jan: 1503.5.
Roelofs, Al: 1022.
Roemheld, Heinz: 1945, **2318.**
Rogers, Aggie Guerard: 423.
Rogers, Charles: 1485, 2081.
Rogers, Charles "Buddy": Hersholt '85.
Rogers, Ginger: 1102.
Rogers, Gregory: 741.5.
Rogers, Richard: 1584.
Rohmer, Eric: 1402.
Roizman, Owen: 631, 724, 1424, 2113, 2316.5.
Rolf, Tom: 1698.
Rolfe, Sam: 1412.
Rollins, Howard E., Jr.: 1651.
Rollmer, Frank: 813.
Romero, Peter: 1698.
Rondi, Brunello: 562, 603.
Ronell, Ann: 1935.
Ronne, David: 1473, 1701, 1825.
Rooney, Mickey: 115, 225, 252, 957. **Honorary '38. Honorary '82.**
Roos, Fred: 92, 442, **785.**
Rose, Alex: 1448.
Rose, David: 1613, 2310.
Rose, Fred: 1696.
Rose, Helen: 130, 578, 629, 755, 817, **980,** 1007, 1309, 1335, 1599.
Rose, Jack: 951, 1786, 2125.
Rose, Kay: 1701.
Rose, Reginald: 2153.
Rose, William: 758, **843,** 1128, 1736.
Rosenbaum, Joel: 423.
Rosenbaum, Stephen: 708.5.
Rosenberg, Aaron: 1388.
Rosenberg, Philip: 49, **2299.**
Rosenblum, Steven: 779.
Rosenman, Leonard: 151, 264, 466, 1914.
Rosenthal, Lawrence: 164, 1259.
Rosher, Charles: 22, 87, 1096, 1818, **1972, 2320.**
Ross, Angelo: 1848.
Ross, Arthur: 303.
Ross, Diana: 1126.

Ross, Frank: 1353, 1706.
Ross, Gary: 195, 494.5.
Ross, Herbert: 2152.
Ross, Katharine: 810.
Rosse, Herman: 1091.
Rossellini, Roberto: 1519.
Rossen, Robert: 53, 964.
Rossi, Walter: 618, 646, 2217.
Rosson, Harold: 105, 133, 256, 747, 2055, 2300. **Honorary '36.**
Rota, Nino: 784, **785.**
Roth, Ann: 1580.
Roth, Eric: 708.5.
Roth, Richard: 1066.
Rotter, Stephen A.: 1698.
Rotunno, Giuseppe: 49.
Rouse, Russell: 1572, 2241.
Rousselot, Philippe: 900, 940, **1701.5.**
Rouxel, Jacques: 474.
Rowe, Bill: 1136.
Rowlands, Gena: 777, 2306.
Royer, Robb (a.k.a. Robb Wilson): **1221.**
Rozhdestvensky, Gennady: 252.5.
Rozsa, Miklos: 175, 566, **567,** 604, 1035, 1069, 1070, 1085, 1208, 1227, 1644, 1872, **1890,** 1968, 2050, 2304.
Rubeo, Bruno: 580.
Rubin, Bruce Joel: 764.
Ruby, Harry: 1951.
Rucker, Joseph T.: 2295.
Ruddy, Albert S.: 784.
Rudloff, Gregg: 779.
Rudloff, Tex: 307.
Ruehl, Mercedes: 671.
Ruggiero, Gene: 101, 1469.
Ruggles, Wesley: 400.
Rush, Richard: 1953.
Russell, Bob: 144, 698.
Russell, Greg P.: 223.
Russell, Harold: 184. Honorary '46.
Russell, John L.: 1632.
Russell, Ken: 2307.
Russell, Larry: 1176.
Russell, Robert: 1353.
Russell, Rosalind: 110, 1364, 1403, 1834. **Hersholt '72.**
Russell, Shirley: 27, 1678.
Russell, Willy: 598.
Rutherford, Margaret: 2204.
Rutledge, Robert: 127.
Ruttenberg, Joseph: 318, 573, 749,

769, 828, 1069, 1232, **1371,** 1861, 2234.
Ryan, Robert: 467.
Ryan, Roderick T.: Honorary '90.
Rydell, Mark: 1473.
Ryder, Loren: 566, 827, 979, 1452, 1669, 1697, 1703, 1837, **1887,** 2012, 2168, 2181, 2183, 2230, 2242. **Honorary '38. Honorary '78.**
Ryder, Winona: 27.5, 1190.5.
Rydstrom, Gary: 129, **1071.5, 2019.**
Ryskind, Morris: 1401, 1899.

Sabbatini, Enrico: 1331.
Sager, Carole Bayer: 103, 166.5, 977, 1071.3, 1898.
Saint, Eva Marie: 1477.
Sainte-Marie, Buffy: 1465.
Saito, Takao: 1661.
Sakamoto, Ryuichi: 1136.
Salinger, Conrad: 1818.
Sallis, Crispian: 45, 580.
Salomon, Mikael: 5, 129.
Salt, Waldo: 430, 1312, 1780.
Salter, Hans: 62, 340, 399, 1030, 1307, 2060.
Salvioni, Giorgio: 367.
Samuels, Lesser: 198, 1444.
Sanders, George: 46.
Sanders, Thomas: 272.5.
Sands, Dennis: 708.5.
Sands, William: 737.
Sanger, Jonathan: 608.
Santiago, Emile: 1706.
Santillo, Frank: 814.
Sarandon, Chris: 561.
Sarandon, Susan: 107, 413.3, 1205.5, 2039.
Sarde, Philippe: 2021.
Sargent, Alvin: 1066, 1502, 1526.
Saroyan, William: 957.
Sartre, Jean-Paul: 1630.
Satoh, Masamichi: 2120.
Saunders, Brian: 808.
Saunders, John Monk: 498.
Saunders, Russ: 1169.
Savage, Norman: 558.
Savalas, Telly: 210.
Savegar, Brian: 1725.
Saville, Victor: 406, 804.
Sawley, George: 532, 1668.
Sawyer, Gordon E.: 33, 91, 184, **214,**

393, 730, 864, 882, 973, 974, 1032, 1511, 1592, **2244**, 2297, 2310. **Honorary '77.**

Saxon, Edward: 1820.

Sayles, John: 1533.5.

Scaccianoce, Luigi: 809.

Scaife, Hugh: 608, 1533, 1898.

Scalia, Pietro: 1047.

Scarfiotti, Ferdinando: 1136, 2127.5.

Scarpelli (Furio Scarpelli): 367, 1503.

Scarwid, Diana: 1004.

Schaeffer, Chester: 2241.

Schaffner, Franklin J.: 1541.

Scharf, Walter: 174, 274, 665, 737, 864, 921, 991, 1054, 1305, 2285.

Schary, Dore: 157, 271, 597.

Scheider, Roy: 49, 724.

Scheinman, Andrew: 658.5.

Schell, Maximilian: 1065, 1066, 1253.

Schenck, Joseph M.: Honorary '52.

Schermer, Jules: 1958.

Schertzinger, Victor: 1488, 1863.

Schiffman, Suzanne: 501.

Schifrin, Lalo: 70, 434, 443, 720, 1928, 2218.

Schildkraut, Joseph: 1169.

Schisgal, Murray: 2113.

Schlesinger, John: 493, 1312, 1966.

Schmidt, Arthur: 418, 708.5, 1763, 1975, **2274.**

Schnee, Charles: 130.

Schoenbaum, Charles: 1190.

Schoenfeld, Bernard: 328.

Schoonmaker, Thelma: 806, 1650, 2312.5.

Schoppe, James: 1684.

Schrader, Leonard: 1099.

Schroeder, Barbet: 1689.

Schulberg, Budd: 1477.

Schulman, Arnold: 802, 1219.

Schulman, Tom: 511.

Schulze, John DuCasse: 1405, 1866.

Schwartz, Arthur: 2026, 2088.

Schwartz, Bernard: 418.

Schwary, Ronald L.: 1502, 1857.

Schweizer, Richard: 1275, 1771.

Scofield, Paul: 1252, 1643.5.

Scognamillo, Gabriel: 1937.

Scorsese, Martin: 27.5, 806, 1142, 1650.

Scott, Adrian: 467.

Scott, Allan: 1855.

Scott, Carolyn: 1234.5.

Scott, Elliot: 69, 995, 2274.

Scott, George C.: 73, 942, 964, 1541.

Scott, Martha: 1510.

Scott, Morton: 680, 922.

Scott, Rey: Honorary '41.

Scott, Ridley: 2039.

Scott, Tom: 60, 1698.

Scott, Walter M.: 46, 376, **413,** 476, 530, **542,** 557, **646, 896,** 1062, **1088,** 1213, 1391, 1475, **1706,** 1753, 1881, 1907, 2008, 2120, 2247.

Seale, John: 1653, 2296.

Seaton, George: 31, **450, 1325,** 1868. **Hersholt '61.**

Seawright, Roy: 1487, 2118, 2119.

Sebastian, B. Tennyson, II: 127.

Segal, Erich: 1218.

Segal, George: 2277.

Segall, Harry: 904.

Seger, Bob: 189.

Seirton, Michael: 745, 1678.

Seitz, John: 552, 566, 674, 1208, 1714, 1975, 2262.

Selig, William N.: Honorary '47.

Sellers, Peter: 169, 574.

Selznick, David O.: 497, **798, 1670,** 1828, 1890, 1909, 1996, 2211. **Thalberg '39.**

Sembello, Michael: 682.

Semenya, Caiphus: 423.

Semler, Dean: 482.

Semprun, Jorge: 842, 2344.

Senior, Anna: 1390.

Sennett, Mack: Honorary '37.

Sersen, Fred: 226, 241, 346, **458,** 520, **1655,** 2286, 2317.

Seymour, Michael: 44.

Seymour, Stephen A.: 1210.

Sforza, Fabrizio: 14.

Shadie, Ken: 464.

Shaffer, Peter: 60, 621.

Shagan, Steve: 1761, 2218.

Shaiman, Marc: 1839.5.

Shamberg, Michael: 199.

Shamroy, Leon: 29, **226,** 356, **413,** 495, 569, 602, 1088, **1153,** 1213, 1592, 1610, 1706, 1852, 1883, 2013, **2286,** 2334.

Shankar, Ravi: 745.

Shanley, John Patrick: 1351.

Shapiro, Stanley: 1220, 1498, **1572,** 2035.

Sharaff, Irene: 66, 290, 333, 338, **413,** 690, 852, 896, **1088,** 1507, 1592, 1910, 2000, **2244, 2277.**

Sharif, Omar: 1151.

Sharpe, Don: 45.

Sharpless, Don: 917.

Sharrock, Ivan: 1136.

Shavelson, Melville: 951, 1786.

Shaw, Ariel Velasco: 1434.5.

Shaw, Artie: 1772.

Shaw, George Bernard: 1637.

Shaw, Irwin: 1998.

Shaw, Robert: 1252.

Shean, Al: 266.

Shearer, Douglas: 136, **202,** 256, 397, 685, **817, 835,** 1096, 1232, 1292, 1371, **1419, 1751, 1950,** 1988, 2048, **2055,** 2211, 2300.

Shearer, Norma: 150, **555,** 723, 1274, 1721, 2038.

Shearman, Russell: 1595.

Sheehan, Winfield: 132, **374,** 592, 989, 1920.

Sheldon, Sidney: 121.

Shelton, Ron: 310.

Shepard, Sam: 1698.

Sheridan, Jim: 992.5, 1399.

Sheriff, Paul: 901, 1363.

Sheriff, R. C.: 804.

Sherman, Richard M.: 166, 396, 1238, **1284,** 1842, 2107.

Sherman, Robert B.: 166, 396, 1238, **1284,** 1842, 2107.

Sherwood, Robert E.: 184, 1670.

Shilkrat, Nathaniel: 2292.

Shingleton, Wilfred: 820.

Shire, David: 1448, 1628.

Shire, Talia: 785, 1712.

Shirley, Anne: 1923.

Shorr, Richard: 544.

Short, Robert: 167.

Shostakovich, Dimitri: 1084.

Shoup, Howard: 410, 1100, 1649, 1700, 2338.

Shuftan, Eugen: 964.

Shuken, Leo: 1901, 2184.

Shyer, Charles: 1617.

Sickner, Roy N.: 2280.

Sidney, Sylvia: 1962.

Siegel, Otto: 401.

Siegel, Sol C.: 1163, 2072.

Signoret, Simone: 1724, 1812.

the annotated academy awards

The following is a list of all Academy Award nominees and winners by year in the categories covered in this book, plus special awards including the Irving G. Thalberg Memorial Award to producers, the Jean Hersholt Award for humanitarian work, the Gordon E. Sawyer Award for outstanding technical achievement, and the honorary awards granted by the Academy. Not listed are the documentary and short film categories or the Academy's annual scientific and technical awards. The winners are listed first, in **boldface,** in each category.

1927–28
Awards presented May 16, 1929.

PRODUCTION[1]
Wings, Paramount Famous Lasky. Produced by Lucien Hubbard.
The Racket, The Caddo Company, Paramount Famous Lasky. Produced by Howard Hughes.
Seventh Heaven, Fox. Produced by William Fox.

UNIQUE AND ARTISTIC PICTURE[2]
Sunrise, Fox.
Chang, Paramount Famous Lasky.
The Crowd, MGM.

ACTOR
Emil Jannings in *The Last Command,* Paramount Famous Lasky, and *The Way of All Flesh,* Paramount Famous Lasky.
Richard Barthelmess in *The Noose,* First National, and *The Patent Leather Kid,* First National.

Charles Chaplin in *The Circus,* Chaplin, United Artists.[3]

ACTRESS
Janet Gaynor in *Seventh Heaven,* Fox; *Street Angel,* Fox; and *Sunrise,* Fox.
Louise Dresser in *A Ship Comes In,* Pathé-RKO Radio.
Gloria Swanson in *Sadie Thompson,* United Artists.

DIRECTION
Frank Borzage for *Seventh Heaven,* Fox.
Herbert Brenon for *Sorrell and Son,* United Artists.
King Vidor for *The Crowd,* MGM.

COMEDY DIRECTION[4]
Lewis Milestone for *Two Arabian Knights,* United Artists.
Charles Chaplin for *The Circus,* Chaplin, United Artists.[5]
Ted Wilde for *Speedy,* Paramount.

WRITING
(Adaptation)
Benjamin Glazer, *Seventh Heaven,* Fox.
Alfred Cohn, *The Jazz Singer,* Warner Bros.
Anthony Coldeway, *Glorious Betsy,* Warner Bros.
(Original Story)
Ben Hecht, *Underworld,* Paramount.
Lajos Biro, *The Last Command,* Paramount.
(Title Writing)[6]
Joseph Farnham, *Telling the World,* MGM; *The Fair Co-ed,* MGM; and *Laugh, Clown, Laugh,* MGM.[7]
Gerald Duffy, *The Private Life of Helen of Troy,* First National.
George Marion, Jr., *Oh Kay!,* First National.[8]

CINEMATOGRAPHY[9]
Charles Rosher and Karl Struss for *Sunrise,* Fox.
George Barnes for *The Devil Dancer,* Goldwyn, United Artists; *The Magic*

---

[1] Through the 1950 awards, the Oscar was presented to the studio or production company responsible for the film. From 1951 onward, it was presented to the producers. We have, however, included the names of the producers for all best picture nominees. Note: Some lists of nominees also include *The Last Command* (Paramount Famous Lasky; produced by J. G. Bachmann, with B. P. Schulberg) and *The Way of All Flesh* (Paramount Famous Lasky; produced by Adolph Zukor and Jesse L. Lasky). The Academy's most recent revision of its nominees and winners list, however, omits them.

[2] Also known as Artistic Quality of Production, discontinued after this year.

[3] Chaplin was originally announced as one of the nominees, but on February 19, 1929, the Academy sent him a letter saying that its Board of Judges had "unanimously decided that your name should be removed from the competitive classes and that a special first award should be conferred upon you for writing, acting, directing and producing *The Circus*. The collective accomplishments thus displayed place you in a class by yourself."

[4] Discontinued after this year.

[5] See note 3.

[6] Discontinued after this year.

[7] Farnham's Oscar, according to the Academy's latest revision of its nominees and winners list, was for cumulative achievement during the eligibility period (August 1, 1927, through July 31, 1928), and not for a single film. Some older lists, however, cite these three films as the works for which he was honored, so they have been included in this book.

[8] Like Farnham, Marion was nominated for cumulative work, but some older lists cite his work on *Oh Kay!,* which has been included.

[9] Because the awards this year could be for either a single film or multiple achievements during the eligibility period, the Academy's records of just who was nominated for what are sometimes confusing. Thus, some lists of nominees cite Struss as a nominee for *Drums of Love,* as well as for the film for which he was honored, *Sunrise,* while others omit *Drums of Love*. We have included it in this book.

Flame, Goldwyn, United Artists; and *Sadie Thompson,* United Artists.

Karl Struss for *Drums of Love,* United Artists.

INTERIOR DIRECTION

William Cameron Menzies, *The Dove,* **United Artists, and** *Tempest,* **United Artists.**

Rochus Gliese, *Sunrise,* Fox.

Harry Oliver, *Seventh Heaven,* Fox.

ENGINEERING EFFECTS[10]

Roy Pomeroy, *Wings,* **Paramount Famous Lasky.**

Ralph Hammeras, *The Private Life of Helen of Troy,* First National.[11]

Nugent Slaughter, *The Jazz Singer,* Warner Bros.

SPECIAL AWARDS[12]

To Warner Bros., for producing *The Jazz Singer,* **the pioneer outstanding talking picture, which has revolutionized the industry.**[13]

To Charles Chaplin, for versatility and genius in writing, acting, directing and producing *The Circus.*

1928–29

Awards presented April 30, 1930.

PRODUCTION[14]

Broadway Melody, **MGM. Produced by Harry Rapf.**

Alibi, Art Cinema, United Artists. Produced by Roland West.

Hollywood Revue, MGM. Produced by Harry Rapf.

In Old Arizona, Fox. Winfield Sheehan, studio head.

The Patriot, Paramount Famous Lasky. Produced by Ernst Lubitsch.

ACTOR

Warner Baxter in *In Old Arizona,* **Fox.**

George Bancroft in *Thunderbolt,* Paramount Famous Lasky.

Chester Morris in *Alibi,* United Artists.

Paul Muni in *The Valiant,* Fox.

Lewis Stone in *The Patriot,* Paramount Famous Lasky.

ACTRESS

Mary Pickford in *Coquette,* **United Artists.**

Ruth Chatterton in *Madame X,* MGM.

Betty Compson in *The Barker,* First National.

Jeanne Eagels[15] in *The Letter,* Paramount.

Corinne Griffith in *The Divine Lady,* First National.

Bessie Love in *Broadway Melody,* MGM.

DIRECTOR

Frank Lloyd for *The Divine Lady,* **First National.**[16]

Lionel Barrymore for *Madame X,* MGM.

Harry Beaumont for *Broadway Melody,* MGM.

Irving Cummings for *In Old Arizona,* Fox.

Frank Lloyd for *Drag,* First National, and *Weary River,* First National.[17]

Ernst Lubitsch for *The Patriot,* Paramount Famous Lasky.

WRITING

Hans Kraly for *The Patriot,* **Paramount Famous Lasky.**

Tom Barry for *In Old Arizona,* Fox, and *The Valiant,* Fox.

Elliott Clawson for *The Cop,* Pathé; *The Leatherneck,* Pathé; *Sal of Singapore,* Pathé; and *Skyscraper,* Pathé.

Hans Kraly for *The Last of Mrs. Cheney,* MGM.

Josephine Lovett for *Our Dancing Daughters,* MGM.

Bess Meredyth for *A Woman of Affairs,* MGM, and *Wonder of Women,* MGM.

CINEMATOGRAPHY

Clyde de Vinna for *White Shadows in the South Seas,* **MGM.**

George Barnes for *Our Dancing Daughters,* MGM.

Arthur Edeson for *In Old Arizona,* Fox.

Ernest Palmer for *Four Devils,* Fox, and *Street Angel,*[18] Fox.

John Seitz for *The Divine Lady,* First National.

INTERIOR DECORATION

Cedric Gibbons for *The Bridge of San Luis Rey,* **MGM, and other pictures.**

Hans Dreier for *The Patriot,* Paramount Famous Lasky.

Mitchell Leisen for *Dynamite,* MGM.

William Cameron Menzies for *Alibi,*

---

[10] Discontinued after this year.

[11] Hammeras and Slaughter were not cited for particular films, but some sources indicate that the former was under consideration for *The Private Life of Helen of Troy,* which has been included in this book. Academy records indicate that Slaughter's work on *The Jazz Singer* put him in contention for the award.

[12] Most recipients of the Academy's honorary awards, which were called Special Awards until the 1950 ceremonies, were given Oscar statuettes. The exceptions have been noted.

[13] The Academy ruled that only silent films would be eligible for the best picture awards.

[14] In all categories this year, the nominees were unofficial: The Academy announced only the winners. However, the films and people traditionally listed as "nominees" were, according to Academy records, under consideration by the various branches voting the awards.

[15] First person to be considered for the award posthumously.

[16] Except for Lewis Milestone, the previous year's winner for direction of a comedy picture, a category that was eliminated after the first year of the awards, Lloyd is the only person to receive a directing Oscar for a film not nominated for best picture.

[17] Some sources list Lloyd as a winner for these films as well as *The Divine Lady,* but the Academy's latest revision of its nominees and winners list cites him only for *The Divine Lady.* Academy records show that he was under consideration for the other two films as well.

[18] Although Janet Gaynor received an Oscar for her performance in this film the previous year, it was ruled eligible for a second year.

United Artists, and *The Awakening,* Goldwyn, United Artists.[19]

Harry Oliver for *Street Angel,* Fox.

1929–30
Awards presented November 5, 1930.

PRODUCTION
All Quiet on the Western Front, Universal. Produced by Carl Laemmle, Jr.

The Big House, Cosmopolitan, MGM. Produced by Irving G. Thalberg.

Disraeli, Warner Bros. Produced by Jack L. Warner, with Darryl F. Zanuck.

The Divorcée, MGM. Produced by Robert Z. Leonard.

The Love Parade, Paramount Famous Lasky. Produced by Ernst Lubitsch.

ACTOR
George Arliss in *Disraeli,* Warner Bros.

George Arliss in *The Green Goddess,* Warner Bros.[20]

Wallace Beery in *The Big House,* MGM.

Maurice Chevalier in *The Big Pond,* Paramount Publix.

Maurice Chevalier in *The Love Parade,* Paramount Famous Lasky.

Ronald Colman in *Bulldog Drummond,* Samuel Goldwyn, United Artists.

Ronald Colman in *Condemned,* Samuel Goldwyn, United Artists.

Lawrence Tibbett in *The Rogue Song,* MGM.

ACTRESS
Norma Shearer in *The Divorcée,* MGM.

Nancy Carroll in *The Devil's Holiday,* Paramount Publix.

Ruth Chatterton in *Sarah and Son,* Paramount Famous Lasky.

Greta Garbo in *Anna Christie,* MGM.

Greta Garbo in *Romance,* MGM.

Norma Shearer in *Their Own Desire,* MGM.[21]

Gloria Swanson in *The Trespasser,* United Artists.

DIRECTOR
Lewis Milestone for *All Quiet on the Western Front,* Universal.

Clarence Brown for *Anna Christie,* MGM, and *Romance,* MGM.

Robert Z. Leonard for *The Divorcée,* MGM.

Ernst Lubitsch for *The Love Parade,* Paramount Famous Lasky.

King Vidor for *Hallelujah,* MGM.

WRITING[22]
Frances Marion[23] for *The Big House,* MGM.

George Abbott, Maxwell Anderson, and Del Andrews for *All Quiet on the Western Front,* Universal.

Howard Estabrook for *Street of Chance,* Paramount Famous Lasky.

Julian Josephson for *Disraeli,* Warner Bros.

John Meehan for *The Divorcée,* MGM.

CINEMATOGRAPHY
Joseph T. Rucker and Willard Van Der Veer for *With Byrd at the South Pole,* Paramount Publix.

William Daniels for *Anna Christie,* MGM.

Arthur Edeson for *All Quiet on the Western Front,* Universal.

Gaetano Gaudio and Harry Perry for *Hell's Angels,* United Artists.

Victor Milner for *The Love Parade,* Paramount Famous Lasky.

INTERIOR DECORATION
Herman Rosse for *King of Jazz,* Universal.

Hans Dreier for *The Love Parade,* Paramount Famous Lasky.

Hans Dreier for *The Vagabond King,* Paramount Publix.

William Cameron Menzies for *Bulldog Drummond,* Goldwyn, United Artists.

Jack Okey for *Sally,* First National.

SOUND RECORDING[24]
Douglas Shearer for *The Big House,* MGM.

George Groves for *Song of the Flame,* First National.

Franklin Hansen for *The Love Parade,* Paramount Famous Lasky.

Oscar Lagerstrom for *Raffles,* Goldwyn, United Artists.

John Tribby for *The Case of Sergeant Grischa,* RKO Radio.

1930–31
Awards presented November 10, 1931.

PRODUCTION
Cimarron, RKO Radio. Produced by William LeBaron.

East Lynne, Fox. Winfield Sheehan, studio head.

The Front Page, The Caddo Company, United Artists. Produced by Howard Hughes.

Skippy, Paramount Publix. Adolph Zukor, studio head.

---

[19] Some lists of Oscar nominees include *The Iron Mask,* United Artists, as one of the films for which Menzies was under consideration. Because the nominations were unofficial, we have also included *The Iron Mask* in this book.

[20] Although the ballot listed both *Disraeli* and *The Green Goddess* after Arliss' name, the award was announced as only for *Disraeli.* The Academy records don't explain why.

[21] Shearer's performances in both *The Divorcée* and *Their Own Desire* were listed together on the ballot, but the award citation was for *The Divorcée* only. As with Arliss' two nominations above, the Academy records offer no explanation.

[22] This year, in this category, as well as Cinematography, Interior Decoration, and Sound Recording, the Academy handed out no certificates of nomination and announced only the titles of the nominated films. We've included the names of the people credited with the work in the various categories.

[23] First woman to win an Oscar for something other than acting.

[24] New category. Until the 1969 awards, the Oscars went to the studio sound department, rather than to the individual technicians actually involved in sound recording. Sound department heads, however, were often mentioned in the citations, so we have given their names when available.

Trader Horn, MGM. Produced by Irving G. Thalberg.

ACTOR

Lionel Barrymore in *A Free Soul*, MGM.

Jackie Cooper in *Skippy*, Paramount Publix.

Richard Dix in *Cimarron*, RKO Radio.

Fredric March in *The Royal Family of Broadway*, Paramount Publix.

Adolphe Menjou in *The Front Page*, Caddo, United Artists.

ACTRESS

Marie Dressler in *Min and Bill*, MGM.

Marlene Dietrich in *Morocco*, Paramount Publix.

Irene Dunne in *Cimarron*, RKO Radio.

Ann Harding in *Holiday*, Pathé.

Norma Shearer in *A Free Soul*, MGM.

DIRECTOR

Norman Taurog for *Skippy*, Paramount Publix.

Clarence Brown for *A Free Soul*, MGM

Lewis Milestone for *The Front Page*, United Artists.

Wesley Ruggles for *Cimarron*, RKO Radio.

Josef Von Sternberg for *Morocco*, Paramount Publix.

WRITING

(Adaptation)

Howard Estabrook for *Cimarron*, RKO Radio.

Francis Faragoh and Robert N. Lee for *Little Caesar*, First National.

Horace Jackson for *Holiday*, Pathé.

Joseph L. Mankiewicz and Sam Mintz for *Skippy*, Paramount Publix.

Seton I. Miller and Fred Niblo, Jr., for *The Criminal Code*, Columbia.

(Original Story)

John Monk Saunders for *The Dawn Patrol*, Warner Bros.-First National.

John Bright and Kubec Glasmon for *The Public Enemy*, First National.

Rowland Brown for *Doorway to Hell*, Warner Bros.

Harry d'Abbadie d'Arrast, Douglas Doty, and Donald Ogden Stewart for *Laughter*, Paramount Publix.

Lucien Hubbard and Joseph Jackson for *Smart Money*, Warner Bros.

CINEMATOGRAPHY

Floyd Crosby for *Tabu*, Paramount Publix.

Edward Cronjager for *Cimarron*, RKO Radio.

Lee Garmes for *Morocco*, Paramount Publix.

Charles Lang for *The Right to Love*, Paramount Publix.

Barney "Chick" McGill for *Svengali*, Warner Bros.

INTERIOR DECORATION

Max Ree for *Cimarron*, RKO Radio.

Richard Day for *Whoopee*, Goldwyn, United Artists.

Hans Dreier for *Morocco*, Paramount Publix.

Stephen Goosson and Ralph Hammeras for *Just Imagine*, Fox.

Anton Grot for *Svengali*, Warner Bros.-First National.

SOUND RECORDING[25]

Paramount Publix Studio Sound Dept.

MGM Studio Sound Dept.

RKO Radio Studio Sound Dept.

Samuel Goldwyn-United Artists Studio Sound Dept.

1931–32

Awards presented November 18, 1932.

PRODUCTION

Grand Hotel, MGM. Produced by Irving Thalberg.[26]

Arrowsmith, Samuel Goldwyn Productions, United Artists. Produced by Samuel Goldwyn.

Bad Girl, Fox. Winfield Sheehan, studio head.

The Champ, MGM. Produced by King Vidor.

Five Star Final, First National. Produced by Hal B. Wallis.

One Hour With You, Paramount Publix. Produced by Ernst Lubitsch.

Shanghai Express, Paramount Publix. Adolph Zukor, studio head.

The Smiling Lieutenant, Paramount Publix. Produced by Ernst Lubitsch.

ACTOR

Tie: Wallace Beery in *The Champ*, MGM, and Fredric March in *Dr. Jekyll and Mr. Hyde*, Paramount Publix.[27]

Alfred Lunt in *The Guardsman*, MGM.

ACTRESS[28]

Helen Hayes in *The Sin of Madelon Claudet*, MGM.

Marie Dressler in *Emma*, MGM.

Lynn Fontanne[29] in *The Guardsman*, MGM.

---

[25] No individual films cited. The award was for collective achievement during the eligibility period: August 1, 1930, through July 31, 1931.

[26] Only best picture winner to receive no other nominations.

[27] To date, the only tie win in best actor category. Katharine Hepburn and Barbra Streisand tied for best actress in 1968. In the balloting, March led Beery by one vote; the rules, which at that time considered a margin of three votes equivalent to a tie, were subsequently changed so that only an identical number of votes would count as a tie.

[28] The first time all nominees in a category were for films from a single studio.

[29] Married to best actor nominee Alfred Lunt, the first time a married couple would receive simultaneous acting nominations. Richard Burton and Elizabeth Taylor were also married when both were nominated for *Who's Afraid of Virginia Woolf?* (1966), as were Charles Laughton and Elsa Lanchester, nominees for *Witness for the Prosecution* (1957). Two other couples had the distinction of receiving simultaneous nominations for separate films: Ava Gardner for *Mogambo* and Frank Sinatra for *From Here to Eternity* (1953), and Rex Harrison for *Cleopatra* and Rachel Roberts for *This Sporting Life* (1963).

DIRECTOR

Frank Borzage for *Bad Girl*, Fox.

King Vidor for *The Champ*, MGM.

Josef Von Sternberg for *Shanghai Express*, Paramount Publix.

WRITING

(Adaptation)

Edwin Burke for *Bad Girl*, Fox.

Percy Heath and Samuel Hoffenstein for *Dr. Jekyll and Mr. Hyde*, Paramount Publix.

Sidney Howard for *Arrowsmith*, Goldwyn, United Artists.

(Original Story)

Frances Marion for *The Champ*, MGM.

Lucien Hubbard for *Star Witness*, Warner Bros.

Grover Jones and William Slavens McNutt for *Lady and Gent*, Paramount Publix.

Adela Rogers St. Johns and Jane Murfin for *What Price Hollywood?*, RKO Pathé.

CINEMATOGRAPHY

Lee Garmes for *Shanghai Express*, Paramount Publix.

Ray June for *Arrowsmith*, Goldwyn, United Artists.

Karl Struss for *Dr. Jekyll and Mr. Hyde*, Paramount Publix.

INTERIOR DECORATION

Gordon Wiles for *Transatlantic*, Fox.

Richard Day for *Arrowsmith*, Goldwyn, United Artists.

Lazare Meerson for *À Nous la Liberté*, Film Sonores-Tobis; Harold Auten (France).[30]

SOUND RECORDING[31]

Paramount Publix Studio Sound Dept.

MGM Studio Sound Dept.

RKO Radio Studio Sound Dept.

Warner Bros.-First National Studio Sound Dept.

SPECIAL AWARD

Walt Disney for the creation of Mickey Mouse.

1932–33[32]

Awards presented March 16, 1934.

PICTURE

***Cavalcade*, Fox. Winfield Sheehan, studio head.**

A Farewell to Arms, Paramount. Adolph Zukor, studio head. (2nd place)

42nd Street, Warner Bros. Produced by Darryl F. Zanuck.

I Am a Fugitive From a Chain Gang, Warner Bros. Produced by Hal. B. Wallis.

Lady for a Day, Columbia. Produced by Frank Capra.

Little Women, RKO Radio. Produced by Merian C. Cooper, with Kenneth MacGowan. (3rd place)

The Private Life of Henry VIII, London Films, United Artists (United Kingdom). Produced by Alexander Korda.[33]

She Done Him Wrong, Paramount. Produced by William LeBaron.

Smilin' Through, MGM. Produced by Irving Thalberg.

State Fair, Fox. Winfield Sheehan, studio head.

ACTOR

Charles Laughton in *The Private Life of Henry VIII*, London Films, United Artists (United Kingdom).

Leslie Howard in *Berkeley Square*, Jesse L. Lasky; Fox. (3rd place)

Paul Muni in *I Am a Fugitive From a Chain Gang*, Warner Bros. (2nd place)

ACTRESS

Katharine Hepburn in *Morning Glory*, RKO Radio.

May Robson in *Lady for a Day*, Columbia. (2nd place)

Diana Wynyard in *Cavalcade*, Fox. (3rd place)

DIRECTOR

Frank Lloyd for *Cavalcade*, Fox.

Frank Capra for *Lady for a Day*, Columbia. (2nd place)

George Cukor for *Little Women*, RKO Radio. (3rd place)

WRITING

(Adaptation)

Victor Heerman and Sarah Y. Mason for *Little Women*, RKO Radio.

Paul Green and Sonya Levien for *State Fair*, Fox. (3rd place)

Robert Riskin for *Lady for a Day*, Columbia. (2nd place)

(Original Story)

Robert Lord for *One Way Passage*, Warner Bros.

Charles MacArthur for *Rasputin and the Empress*, MGM. (3rd place)

Frances Marion for *The Prizefighter and the Lady*, MGM. (2nd place)

CINEMATOGRAPHY

Charles Bryant Lang, Jr., for *A Farewell to Arms*, Paramount.

George J. Folsey for *Reunion in Vienna*, MGM. (2nd place)

Karl Struss for *Sign of the Cross*, Paramount Publix. (3rd place)

INTERIOR DECORATION

William S. Darling for *Cavalcade*, Fox.

Hans Dreier and Roland Anderson for *A Farewell to Arms*, Paramount. (2nd place)

Cedric Gibbons for *When Ladies Meet*, MGM. (3rd place)

---

[30] First foreign language film to receive a nomination in any category.

[31] No individual films cited. The award was for collective achievement during the eligibility period: August 1, 1931, through July 31, 1932.

[32] For the next three years, the Academy announced not only the winners but also the first two runners-up in each category. The 2nd- and 3rd-place finishers are indicated.

[33] First foreign-made film to be nominated for best picture.

SOUND RECORDING

Franklin B. Hansen for *A Farewell to Arms*, Paramount.

Nathan Levinson for *42nd Street*, Warner Bros.

Nathan Levinson for *Gold Diggers of 1933*, Warner Bros. (3rd place)

Nathan Levinson for *I Am a Fugitive From a Chain Gang*, Warner Bros. (2nd place)

ASSISTANT DIRECTOR[34]

Charles Barton, Paramount; Scott Beal, Universal; Charles Dorian, MGM; Fred Fox, United Artists; Gordon Hollingshead, Warner Bros.; Dewey Starkey, RKO Radio; William Tummel, Fox.

Al Alborn, Warner Bros.

Sidney S. Brod, Paramount.

Bunny Dull, MGM.

Percy Ikerd, Fox.

Arthur Jacobson, Paramount.

Eddie Killey, RKO Radio.

Joe McDonough, Universal.

W. J. Reiter, Universal.

Frank X. Shaw, Warner Bros.

Benjamin Silvey, United Artists.

John S. Waters, MGM.

1934

Awards presented February 27, 1935.

PRODUCTION

It Happened One Night, Columbia. Produced by Harry Cohn.[35]

The Barretts of Wimpole Street, MGM. Produced by Irving Thalberg. (2nd place)

Cleopatra, Paramount. Produced by Cecil B. DeMille.

Flirtation Walk, First National. Produced by Jack L. Warner and Hal Wallis, with Robert Lord.

The Gay Divorcée, RKO Radio. Produced by Pandro S. Berman.

Here Comes the Navy, Warner Bros. Produced by Lou Edelman.

The House of Rothschild, 20th Century, United Artists. Produced by Darryl F. Zanuck, with William Goetz and Raymond Griffith. (3rd place)

Imitation of Life, Universal. Produced by John M. Stahl.

One Night of Love, Columbia. Produced by Harry Cohn, with Everett Riskin.

The Thin Man, MGM. Produced by Hunt Stromberg.

Viva Villa!, MGM. Produced by David O. Selznick.

The White Parade, Fox. Produced by Jesse L. Lasky.

ACTOR

Clark Gable in *It Happened One Night*, Columbia.

Frank Morgan in *Affairs of Cellini*, 20th Century, United Artists. (2nd place)

William Powell in *The Thin Man*, MGM. (3rd place)

ACTRESS

Claudette Colbert in *It Happened One Night*, Columbia.

Bette Davis in *Of Human Bondage*, RKO Radio. (3rd place)[36]

Grace Moore in *One Night of Love*, Columbia.

Norma Shearer in *The Barretts of Wimpole Street*, MGM. (2nd place)

DIRECTOR

Frank Capra for *It Happened One Night*, Columbia.

Victor Schertzinger for *One Night of Love*, Columbia. (3rd place)

W. S. Van Dyke for *The Thin Man*, MGM. (2nd place)

WRITING

(Adaptation)

Robert Riskin for *It Happened One Night*, Columbia.

Frances Goodrich and Albert Hackett for *The Thin Man*, MGM. (2nd place)

Ben Hecht for *Viva Villa!*, MGM. (3rd place)

(Original Story)

Arthur Caesar for *Manhattan Melodrama*, MGM.

Mauri Grashin for *Hide-Out*, MGM. (3rd place)

Norman Krasna for *The Richest Girl in the World*, RKO Radio. (2nd place)

CINEMATOGRAPHY

Victor Milner for *Cleopatra*, Paramount.

George Folsey for *Operator 13*, MGM. (2nd place)

Charles Rosher for *Affairs of Cellini*, United Artists. (3rd place)

INTERIOR DECORATION

Cedric Gibbons and Frederic Hope for *The Merry Widow*, MGM.

Richard Day for *Affairs of Cellini*, United Artists. (3rd place)

Van Nest Polglase and Carroll Clark for *The Gay Divorcée*, RKO Radio. (2nd place)

SOUND RECORDING

John Livadary for *One Night of Love*, Columbia.

Carl Dreher for *The Gay Divorcée*, RKO Radio. (3rd place)

E. H. Hansen for *The White Parade*, Fox.

Franklin B. Hansen for *Cleopatra*, Paramount.

Nathan Levinson for *Flirtation Walk*, First National. (2nd place)

Thomas T. Moulton for *Affairs of Cellini*, 20th Century, United Artists.

Douglas Shearer for *Viva Villa*, MGM.

---

[34] New category. For this year only, each studio submitted a slate of assistant director candidates. The Academy gave the award to one from each studio.

[35] First film to win the "top five" Oscars: picture, actor, actress, director, and writer. *One Flew Over the Cuckoo's Nest* (1975) and *The Silence of the Lambs* (1991) also swept the top five.

[36] Write-in candidate—not an official nominee. The outcry over Davis' failure to receive an official nomination led the Academy to permit write-in votes for this year and the following year, after which they were no longer counted. Although there may have been other write-in candidates, the Academy records only the names of those who received enough votes to place 2nd or 3rd.

Theodore Soderberg for *Imitation of Life,* Universal.

ASSISTANT DIRECTOR
John Waters for *Viva Villa!,* MGM.
Scott Beal for *Imitation of Life,* Universal. (3rd place)
Cullen Tate for *Cleopatra,* Paramount. (2nd place)

MUSIC[37]
(Song)
"The Continental" from *The Gay Divorcée,* RKO Radio. Music by Con Conrad, lyrics by Herb Magidson.
"Carioca" from *Flying Down to Rio,* RKO Radio. Music by Vincent Youmans, lyrics by Edward Eliscu and Gus Kahn. (3rd place)
"Love in Bloom" from *She Loves Me Not,* Paramount. Music by Ralph Rainger, lyrics by Leo Robin. (2nd place)
(Score)[38]
One Night of Love, Columbia. Columbia Studio Music Dept., Louis Silvers, head. Thematic music by Victor Schertzinger and Gus Kahn.
The Gay Divorcée, RKO Radio. RKO Radio Studio Music Dept., Max Steiner, head. Score by Kenneth Webb and Samuel Hoffenstein. (2nd place)
The Lost Patrol, RKO Radio. RKO Radio Studio Music Dept., Max Steiner, head. Score by Max Steiner. (3rd place)

FILM EDITING[39]
Conrad Nervig for *Eskimo,* MGM.
Anne Bauchens for *Cleopatra,* Paramount. (3rd place)

Gene Milford for *One Night of Love,* Columbia. (2nd place)

SPECIAL AWARD
Shirley Temple, in grateful recognition of her outstanding contribution to screen entertainment during the year 1934.[40]

1935
Awards presented March 5, 1936.

PRODUCTION
***Mutiny on the Bounty,* MGM. Produced by Irving Thalberg, with Albert Lewin.[41]**
Alice Adams, RKO Radio. Produced by Pandro S. Berman.
Broadway Melody of 1936, MGM. Produced by John W. Considine, Jr.
Captain Blood, Cosmopolitan, First National. Produced by Hal Wallis, with Harry Joe Brown and Gordon Hollingshead. (3rd place)
David Copperfield, MGM. Produced by David O. Selznick.
The Informer, RKO Radio. Produced by Cliff Reid. (2nd place)
Lives of a Bengal Lancer, Paramount. Produced by Louis D. Lighton.
A Midsummer Night's Dream, Warner Bros. Produced by Henry Blanke.
Les Misérables, 20th Century, United Artists. Produced by Darryl F. Zanuck.
Naughty Marietta, MGM. Produced by Hunt Stromberg.
Ruggles of Red Gap, Paramount. Produced by Arthur Hornblow, Jr.
Top Hat, RKO Radio. Produced by Pandro S. Berman.

ACTOR[42]
Victor McLaglen in *The Informer,* RKO Radio.
Clark Gable in *Mutiny on the Bounty,* MGM.
Charles Laughton in *Mutiny on the Bounty,* MGM. (3rd place)
Paul Muni in *Black Fury,* First National. (2nd place)[43]
Franchot Tone in *Mutiny on the Bounty,* MGM.

ACTRESS
Bette Davis in *Dangerous,* Warner Bros.
Elisabeth Bergner in *Escape Me Never,* United Artists (United Kingdom). (3rd place)
Claudette Colbert in *Private Worlds,* Paramount.
Katharine Hepburn in *Alice Adams,* RKO Radio. (2nd place)
Miriam Hopkins in *Becky Sharp,* RKO Radio.
Merle Oberon in *The Dark Angel,* Goldwyn, United Artists.

DIRECTOR
John Ford for *The Informer,* RKO Radio.
Michael Curtiz for *Captain Blood,* First National. (2nd place)[44]
Henry Hathaway for *Lives of a Bengal Lancer,* Paramount. (3rd place)
Frank Lloyd for *Mutiny on the Bounty,* MGM.

WRITING
(Original Story)
Ben Hecht and Charles MacArthur for *The Scoundrel,* Paramount.
Moss Hart for *Broadway Melody of 1936,* MGM. (3rd place)

---

[37] New category.
[38] For the first four years, through the 1937 awards, the scoring Oscar went to the studio music department head, and not to the composer of the score.
[39] New category.
[40] At five, the youngest person to receive an Academy Award. She was given a miniature Oscar. The tradition of giving miniature Oscars for "outstanding juvenile performance" continued, off and on, until the 1960 awards ceremony.
[41] Last winner for best picture to receive no other awards. The others were *Broadway Melody* and *Grand Hotel.*
[42] Although rules called for only three nominees in the acting categories, tie votes resulted in four official nominations for best actor and six for best actress.
[43] Write-in candidate—not an official nominee.
[44] Write-in candidate—not an official nominee.

Don Hartman and Stephen Avery for *The Gay Deception*, Fox.

Gregory Rogers for *"G" Men*, Warner Bros.-First National. (2nd place)[45]

(Screenplay)

Dudley Nichols for *The Informer*, RKO Radio.

Talbot Jennings, Jules Furthman, and Carey Wilson for *Mutiny on the Bounty*, MGM. (2nd place)

Casey Robinson for *Captain Blood*, First National. (3rd place)[46]

Waldemar Young, John L. Balderston, and Achmed Abdullah, screenplay; Grover Jones and William Slavens McNutt, adaptation, for *Lives of a Bengal Lancer*, Paramount.

CINEMATOGRAPHY

Hal Mohr for *A Midsummer Night's Dream*, Warner Bros.[47]

Ray June for *Barbary Coast*, Goldwyn, United Artists.

Victor Milner for *The Crusades*, Paramount. (3rd place)

Gregg Toland for *Les Misérables*, United Artists. (2nd place)

INTERIOR DECORATION

Richard Day for *The Dark Angel*, Goldwyn, United Artists.

Hans Dreier and Roland Anderson for *Lives of a Bengal Lancer*, Paramount. (3rd place)

Van Nest Polglase and Carroll Clark for *Top Hat*, RKO Radio. (2nd place)

SOUND RECORDING

Douglas Shearer for *Naughty Marietta*, MGM.

Carl Dreher for *I Dream Too Much*, RKO Radio.

E. H. Hansen for *Thanks a Million*, 20th Century-Fox.

Franklin B. Hansen for *Lives of a Bengal Lancer*, Paramount. (3rd place)

Gilbert Kurland for *The Bride of Frankenstein*, Universal.

Nathan Levinson for *Captain Blood*, First National. (2nd place)

John Livadary for *Love Me Forever*, Columbia.

Thomas T. Moulton for *The Dark Angel*, Goldwyn, United Artists.

Republic Studio Sound Dept. for *$1,000 a Minute*, Republic.

ASSISTANT DIRECTOR

Clem Beauchamp and Paul Wing for *Lives of a Bengal Lancer*, Paramount.

Joseph Newman for *David Copperfield*, MGM. (3rd place)

Sherry Shourds for *A Midsummer Night's Dream*, Warner Bros. (2nd place)[48]

Eric Stacey for *Les Misérables*, 20th Century, United Artists.

MUSIC

(Song)

"Lullaby of Broadway" from *Gold Diggers of 1935*, First National. Music by Harry Warren, lyrics by Al Dubin.

"Cheek to Cheek" from *Top Hat*, RKO Radio. Music and lyrics by Irving Berlin. (2nd place)

"Lovely to Look At" from *Roberta*, RKO Radio. Music by Jerome Kern, lyrics by Dorothy Fields and Jimmy McHugh. (3rd place)

(Score)

***The Informer*, RKO Radio. RKO Radio Studio Music Dept., Max Steiner, head. Score by Max Steiner.**

Captain Blood, First National. Warner Bros.-First National Studio Music Dept., Leo Forbstein, head. Score by Erich Wolfgang Korngold. (3rd place)[49]

Mutiny on the Bounty, MGM. MGM Studio Music Dept., Nat W. Finston, head. Score by Herbert Stothart. (2nd place)

Peter Ibbetson, Paramount. Paramount Studio Music Dept., Irvin Talbot, head. Score by Ernst Toch.

FILM EDITING

Ralph Dawson, *A Midsummer Night's Dream*, Warner Bros.

Margaret Booth, *Mutiny on the Bounty*, MGM. (2nd place)

George Hively, *The Informer*, RKO Radio. (3rd place)

Ellsworth Hoagland, *Lives of a Bengal Lancer*, Paramount.

Robert J. Kern, *David Copperfield*, MGM.

Barbara McLean, *Les Misérables*, United Artists.

DANCE DIRECTION[50]

Dave Gould for "I've Got a Feeling You're Fooling" number from *Broadway Melody of 1936*, MGM, and "Straw Hat" number from *Folies Bergère*, United Artists.

Busby Berkeley for "Lullaby of Broadway" and "The Words Are in My Heart" numbers from *Gold Diggers of 1935*, First National. (3rd place)

Bobby Connolly for "Latin From Manhattan" number from *Go Into Your Dance*, First National, and "Playboy From Paree" number from *Broadway Hostess*, Warner Bros.-First National.

Sammy Lee for "Lovely Lady" and "Too Good to Be True" numbers from *King of Burlesque*, 20th Century-Fox.

Hermes Pan for "Piccolino" and "Top Hat, White Tie, and Tails" numbers from *Top Hat*, RKO Radio. (2nd place)

LeRoy Prinz for "It's the Animal in Me" number from *Big Broadcast of 1936*, Paramount, and "Viennese Waltz"

---

[45] Write-in candidate—not an official nominee.
[46] Write-in candidate—not an official nominee.
[47] Only award ever given to a write-in candidate.
[48] Write-in candidate—not an official nominee.
[49] Write-in candidate—not an official nominee.
[50] New category.

number from *All the King's Horses*,
Paramount.
Benjamin Zemach for "Hall of Kings"
number from *She*, RKO Radio.

SPECIAL AWARD

**David Wark Griffith, for his
distinguished creative
achievements as director and
producer and his invaluable
initiative and lasting
contributions to the progress of
the motion picture arts.**

1936
Awards presented March 4, 1937.

PRODUCTION

***The Great Ziegfeld*, MGM. Produced
by Hunt Stromberg.**

Anthony Adverse, Warner Bros. Produced
by Henry Blanke.
Dodsworth, Samuel Goldwyn Productions,
United Artists. Produced by Samuel
Goldwyn, with Merritt Hulburd.
Libeled Lady, MGM. Produced by
Lawrence Weingarten.
Mr. Deeds Goes to Town, Columbia.
Produced by Frank Capra.
Romeo and Juliet, MGM. Produced by
Irving Thalberg.
San Francisco, MGM. Produced by John
Emerson and Bernard H. Hyman.
The Story of Louis Pasteur, Cosmopolitan,
Warner Bros.-First National.
Produced by Henry Blanke.
A Tale of Two Cities, MGM. Produced by
David O. Selznick.
Three Smart Girls, Universal. Produced by
Joseph Pasternak, with Charles
Rogers.

ACTOR

**Paul Muni in *The Story of Louis
Pasteur*, Warner Bros.-First
National.**

Gary Cooper in *Mr. Deeds Goes to Town*,
Columbia.

Walter Huston in *Dodsworth*, Goldwyn,
United Artists.
William Powell in *My Man Godfrey*,
Universal.
Spencer Tracy in *San Francisco*, MGM.

ACTRESS

**Luise Rainer in *The Great Ziegfeld*,
MGM.**

Irene Dunne in *Theodora Goes Wild*,
Columbia.
Gladys George in *Valiant Is the Word for
Carrie*, Paramount.
Carole Lombard in *My Man Godfrey*,
Universal.
Norma Shearer in *Romeo and Juliet*,
MGM.

SUPPORTING ACTOR[51]

**Walter Brennan in *Come and Get It*,
Goldwyn, United Artists.**

Mischa Auer in *My Man Godfrey*,
Universal.
Stuart Erwin in *Pigskin Parade*, 20th
Century-Fox.
Basil Rathbone in *Romeo and Juliet*, MGM.
Akim Tamiroff in *The General Died at
Dawn*, Paramount.

SUPPORTING ACTRESS[52]

**Gale Sondergaard in *Anthony
Adverse*, Warner Bros.**

Beulah Bondi in *The Gorgeous Hussy*,
MGM.
Alice Brady in *My Man Godfrey*, Universal.
Bonita Granville in *These Three*, Goldwyn,
United Artists.
Maria Ouspenskaya in *Dodsworth*,
Goldwyn, United Artists.

DIRECTOR

**Frank Capra for *Mr. Deeds Goes to
Town*, Columbia.**

Gregory La Cava for *My Man Godfrey*,
Universal.
Robert Z. Leonard for *The Great Ziegfeld*,
MGM.
W. S. Van Dyke for *San Francisco*, MGM.

William Wyler for *Dodsworth*, Goldwyn,
United Artists.

WRITING

(Original Story)

**Pierre Collings and Sheridan
Gibney for *The Story of Louis
Pasteur*, Warner Bros.-First
National.**

Adele Comandini for *Three Smart Girls*,
Universal.
Robert Hopkins for *San Francisco*, MGM.
Norman Krasna for *Fury*, MGM.
William Anthony McGuire for *The Great
Ziegfeld*, MGM.

(Screenplay)

**Pierre Collings and Sheridan
Gibney for *The Story of Louis
Pasteur*, Warner Bros.-First
National.**

Frances Goodrich and Albert Hackett for
After the Thin Man, MGM.
Eric Hatch and Morris Ryskind for *My
Man Godfrey*, Universal.
Sidney Howard for *Dodsworth*, Goldwyn,
United Artists.
Robert Riskin for *Mr. Deeds Goes to Town*,
Columbia.

CINEMATOGRAPHY

**Gaetano Gaudio for *Anthony Adverse*,
Warner Bros.**

George Folsey for *The Gorgeous Hussy*,
MGM.
Victor Milner for *The General Died at
Dawn*, Paramount.

INTERIOR DECORATION

**Richard Day for *Dodsworth*,
Goldwyn, United Artists.**

Albert S. D'Agostino and Jack Otterson
for *The Magnificent Brute*, Universal.
William S. Darling for *Lloyd's of London*,
20th Century-Fox.
Perry Ferguson for *Winterset*, RKO Radio.
Cedric Gibbons, Frederic Hope, and
Edwin B. Willis for *Romeo and Juliet*,
MGM.

---

[51] New category.
[52] New category.

Cedric Gibbons, Eddie Imazu, and Edwin
B. Willis for *The Great Ziegfeld,* MGM.

Anton Grot for *Anthony Adverse,* Warner
Bros.

SOUND RECORDING

**Douglas Shearer for *San Francisco,*
MGM.**

J. O. Aalberg for *That Girl From Paris,*
RKO Radio.

E. H. Hansen for *Banjo on My Knee,* 20th
Century-Fox.

Franklin B. Hansen for *The Texas Rangers,*
Paramount.

Nathan Levinson for *The Charge of the
Light Brigade,* Warner Bros.

John Livadary for *Mr. Deeds Goes to Town,*
Columbia.

Thomas T. Moulton for *Dodsworth,*
Goldwyn, United Artists.

Elmer A. Raguse for *General Spanky,*
Roach, MGM.

Homer G. Tasker for *Three Smart Girls,*
Universal.

ASSISTANT DIRECTOR

**Jack Sullivan for *The Charge of the
Light Brigade,* Warner Bros.**

Clem Beauchamp for *The Last of the
Mohicans,* United Artists.

William Cannon for *Anthony Adverse,*
Warner Bros.

Joseph Newman for *San Francisco,* MGM.

Eric G. Stacey for *The Garden of Allah,*
Selznick, United Artists.

MUSIC

(Song)

**"The Way You Look Tonight" from
Swing Time, RKO Radio. Music
by Jerome Kern, lyrics by
Dorothy Fields.**

"Did I Remember" from *Suzy,* MGM.
Music by Walter Donaldson, lyrics by
Harold Adamson.

"I've Got You Under My Skin" from
Born to Dance, MGM. Music and lyrics
by Cole Porter.

"A Melody From the Sky" from *Trail of
the Lonesome Pine,* Paramount. Music

by Louis Alter, lyrics by Sidney
Mitchell.

"Pennies From Heaven" from *Pennies
From Heaven,* Columbia. Music by
Arthur Johnston, lyrics by Johnny
Burke.

"When Did You Leave Heaven" from
Sing Baby Sing, 20th Century-Fox.
Music by Richard A. Whiting, lyrics
by Walter Bullock.

(Score)

***Anthony Adverse,* Warner Bros.
Warner Bros. Studio Music
Dept., Leo Forbstein, head. Score
by Erich Wolfgang Korngold.**

The Charge of the Light Brigade, Warner
Bros. Warner Bros. Studio Music
Dept., Leo Forbstein, head. Score by
Max Steiner.

The Garden of Allah, Selznick, United
Artists. Selznick International Pictures
Music Dept., Max Steiner, head.
Score by Max Steiner.

The General Died at Dawn, Paramount.
Paramount Studio Music Dept., Boris
Morros, head. Score by Werner
Janssen.

Winterset, RKO Radio. RKO Radio Studio
Music Dept., Nathaniel Shilkrat, head.
Score by Nathaniel Shilkrat.

FILM EDITING

**Ralph Dawson for *Anthony Adverse,*
Warner Bros.**

Edward Curtiss for *Come and Get It,*
Goldwyn, United Artists.

William S. Gray for *The Great Ziegfeld,*
MGM.

Barbara McLean for *Lloyd's of London,*
20th Century-Fox.

Otto Meyer for *Theodora Goes Wild,*
Columbia.

Conrad A. Nervig for *A Tale of Two Cities,*
MGM.

DANCE DIRECTION

**Seymour Felix for "A Pretty Girl Is
Like a Melody" number from
The Great Ziegfeld, MGM.**

Busby Berkeley for "Love and War"

number from *Gold Diggers of 1937,*
Warner Bros.-First National.

Bobby Connolly for "1000 Love Songs"
number from *Cain and Mabel,* Warner
Bros.-Cosmopolitan.

Dave Gould for "Swingin' the Jinx"
number from *Born to Dance,* MGM.

Jack Haskell for "Skating Ensemble"
number from *One in a Million,* 20th
Century-Fox.

Russell Lewis for "The Finale" number
from *Dancing Pirate,* RKO Radio.

Hermes Pan for "Bojangles of Harlem"
number from *Swing Time,* RKO Radio.

SPECIAL AWARDS

**March of Time for its significance
to motion pictures and for
having revolutionized one of the
most important branches of the
industry—the newsreel.**

**W. Howard Greene and Harold
Rosson for the color
cinematography of the Selznick
International Production, *The
Garden of Allah.*[53]**

1937

Awards presented March 10, 1938.

PICTURE

***The Life of Emile Zola,* Warner Bros.
Produced by Henry Blanke.**

The Awful Truth, Columbia. Produced by
Leo McCarey, with Everett Riskin.

Captains Courageous, MGM. Produced by
Louis D. Lighton.

Dead End, Samuel Goldwyn Productions,
United Artists. Produced by Samuel
Goldwyn, with Merritt Hulburd.

The Good Earth, MGM. Produced by
Irving Thalberg, with Albert Lewin.

In Old Chicago, 20th Century-Fox.
Produced by Darryl F. Zanuck, with
Kenneth MacGowan.

Lost Horizon, Columbia. Produced by
Frank Capra.

One Hundred Men and a Girl, Universal.

---

[53] Greene and Rosson received plaques instead of Oscars.

Produced by Charles R. Rogers, with Joe Pasternak.

Stage Door, RKO Radio. Produced by Pandro S. Berman.

A Star Is Born, Selznick International Pictures, United Artists. Produced by David O. Selznick.

ACTOR

Spencer Tracy in *Captains Courageous*, MGM.

Charles Boyer in *Conquest*, MGM.

Fredric March in *A Star Is Born*, Selznick, United Artists.

Robert Montgomery in *Night Must Fall*, MGM.

Paul Muni in *The Life of Emile Zola*, Warner Bros.

ACTRESS

Luise Rainer in *The Good Earth*, MGM.[54]

Irene Dunne in *The Awful Truth*, Columbia.

Greta Garbo in *Camille*, MGM.

Janet Gaynor in *A Star Is Born*, Selznick, United Artists.

Barbara Stanwyck in *Stella Dallas*, Goldwyn, United Artists.

SUPPORTING ACTOR

Joseph Schildkraut in *The Life of Emile Zola*, Warner Bros.

Ralph Bellamy in *The Awful Truth*, Columbia.

Thomas Mitchell in *The Hurricane*, Goldwyn, United Artists.

H. B. Warner in *Lost Horizon*, Columbia.

Roland Young in *Topper*, Roach, MGM.

SUPPORTING ACTRESS

Alice Brady in *In Old Chicago*, 20th Century-Fox.

Andrea Leeds in *Stage Door*, RKO Radio.

Anne Shirley in *Stella Dallas*, Goldwyn, United Artists.

Claire Trevor in *Dead End*, Goldwyn, United Artists.

May Whitty in *Night Must Fall*, MGM.

DIRECTOR

Leo McCarey for *The Awful Truth*, Columbia.

William Dieterle for *The Life of Emile Zola*, Warner Bros.

Sidney Franklin for *The Good Earth*, MGM.

Gregory La Cava for *Stage Door*, RKO Radio.

William Wellman for *A Star Is Born*, Selznick, United Artists.

WRITING

(Original Story)

William A. Wellman and Robert Carson for *A Star Is Born*, Selznick, United Artists.

Niven Busch for *In Old Chicago*, 20th Century-Fox.

Heinz Herald and Geza Herczeg for *The Life of Emile Zola*, Warner Bros.

Hans Kräly for *One Hundred Men and a Girl*, Universal.

Robert Lord for *Black Legion*, Warner Bros.

(Screenplay)

Norman Reilly Raine, Heinz Herald, and Geza Herczeg for *The Life of Emile Zola*, Warner Bros.

Viña Delmar for *The Awful Truth*, Columbia.

John Lee Mahin, Marc Connelly, and Dale Van Every for *Captains Courageous*, MGM.

Dorothy Parker, Alan Campbell, and Robert Carson for *A Star Is Born*, Selznick, United Artists.

Morris Ryskind and Anthony Veiller for *Stage Door*, RKO Radio.

CINEMATOGRAPHY

Karl Freund for *The Good Earth*, MGM.

Gregg Toland for *Dead End*, Goldwyn, United Artists.

Joseph Valentine for *Wings Over Honolulu*, Universal.

INTERIOR DECORATION

Stephen Goosson for *Lost Horizon*, Columbia.

Carroll Clark for *A Damsel in Distress*, RKO Radio.

William S. Darling and David Hall for *Wee Willie Winkie*, 20th Century-Fox.

Richard Day for *Dead End*, Goldwyn, United Artists.

Hans Dreier and Roland Anderson for *Souls at Sea*, Paramount.

Cedric Gibbons and William Horning for *Conquest*, MGM.

Anton Grot for *The Life of Emile Zola*, Warner Bros.

Wiard Ihnen for *Every Day's a Holiday*, Paramount.

John Victor MacKay for *Manhattan Merry-Go-Round*, Republic.

Jack Otterson for *You're a Sweetheart*, Universal.

Alexander Toluboff for *Vogues of 1938*, Wanger, United Artists.

Lyle Wheeler for *The Prisoner of Zenda*, Selznick, United Artists.

SOUND RECORDING

Thomas T. Moulton for *The Hurricane*, Goldwyn, United Artists.

John Aalberg for *Hitting a New High*, RKO Radio.

E. H. Hansen for *In Old Chicago*, 20th Century-Fox.

A. E. Kaye for *The Girl Said No*, Grand National.

Nathan Levinson for *The Life of Emile Zola*, Warner Bros.

John Livadary for *Lost Horizon*, Columbia.

Elmer Raguse for *Topper*, Roach, MGM.

Loren L. Ryder for *Wells Fargo*, Paramount.

Douglas Shearer for *Maytime*, MGM.

Homer G. Tasker for *One Hundred Men and a Girl*, Universal.

---

[54] First person to win two consecutive Oscars for acting. The others are Spencer Tracy (1937, 1938), Katharine Hepburn (1967, 1968), Jason Robards (1976, 1977), and Tom Hanks (1993, 1994).

ASSISTANT DIRECTOR[55]
Robert Webb for *In Old Chicago*, 20th Century-Fox.

C. C. Coleman, Jr., for *Lost Horizon,* Columbia.

Russ Saunders for *The Life of Emile Zola,* Warner Bros.

Eric Stacey for *A Star Is Born,* Selznick, United Artists.

Hal Walker for *Souls at Sea,* Paramount.

MUSIC
(Song)
"Sweet Leilani" from *Waikiki Wedding,* Paramount. Music and lyrics by Harry Owens.

"Remember Me" from *Mr. Dodd Takes the Air,* Warner Bros.-First National. Music by Harry Warren, lyrics by Al Dubin.

"That Old Feeling" from *Vogues of 1938.* Music by Sammy Fain, lyrics by Lew Brown.

"They Can't Take That Away From Me" from *Shall We Dance,* RKO Radio. Music by George Gershwin, lyrics by Ira Gershwin.

"Whispers in the Dark" from *Artists and Models,* Paramount. Music by Frederick Hollander, lyrics by Leo Robin.

(Score)
***One Hundred Men and a Girl,* Universal. Universal Studio Music Dept., Charles Previn, head. No credited composer.**

The Hurricane, Goldwyn, United Artists. Samuel Goldwyn Studio Music Dept., Alfred Newman, head. Score by Alfred Newman.

In Old Chicago, 20th Century-Fox. 20th Century-Fox Studio Music Dept., Louis Silvers, head. No credited composer.

The Life of Emile Zola, Warner Bros. Warner Bros. Studio Music Dept.,

Leo Forbstein, head. Score by Max Steiner.

Lost Horizon, Columbia. Columbia Studio Music Dept., Morris Stoloff, head. Score by Dimitri Tiomkin.

Make a Wish, RKO Radio. Principal Productions, Hugo Riesenfeld, musical director. Score by Hugo Riesenfeld.

Maytime, MGM. MGM Studio Music Dept., Nat W. Finston, head. Score by Herbert Stothart.

Portia on Trial, Republic. Republic Studio Music Dept., Alberto Colombo, head. Score by Alberto Colombo.

The Prisoner of Zenda, Selznick, United Artists. Selznick International Pictures Music Dept., Alfred Newman, musical director. Score by Alfred Newman.

Quality Street, RKO Radio. RKO Radio Studio Music Dept., Roy Webb, musical director. Score by Roy Webb.

Snow White and the Seven Dwarfs, Disney, RKO Radio. Walt Disney Studio Music Dept., Leigh Harline, head. Score by Frank Churchill, Leigh Harline, and Paul J. Smith.

Something to Sing About, Grand National. Grand National Studio Music Dept., C. Bakaleinikoff, musical director. Score by Victor Schertzinger.

Souls at Sea, Paramount. Paramount Studio Music Dept., Boris Morros, head. Score by W. Franke Harling and Milan Roder.

Way Out West, MGM. Hal Roach Studio Music Dept., Marvin Hatley, head. Score by Marvin Hatley.

FILM EDITING
Gene Havlick and Gene Milford for *Lost Horizon,* Columbia.

Bernard W. Burton for *One Hundred Men and a Girl,* Universal.

Al Clark for *The Awful Truth,* Columbia.

Elmo Vernon for *Captains Courageous,* MGM.

Basil Wrangell for *The Good Earth,* MGM.

DANCE DIRECTION[56]
Hermes Pan for "Fun House" number from *A Damsel in Distress,* RKO Radio.

Busby Berkeley for "The Finale" number from *Varsity Show,* Warner Bros.

Bobby Connolly for "Too Marvelous for Words" number from *Ready, Willing and Able,* Warner Bros.

Dave Gould for "All God's Children Got Rhythm" number from *A Day at the Races,* MGM.

Sammy Lee for "Swing Is Here to Stay" number from *Ali Baba Goes to Town,* 20th Century-Fox.

Harry Losee for "Prince Igor Suite" number from *Thin Ice,* 20th Century-Fox.

LeRoy Prinz for "Luau" number from *Waikiki Wedding,* Paramount.

IRVING G. THALBERG MEMORIAL AWARD[57]
Darryl F. Zanuck.

SPECIAL AWARDS
Mack Sennett: For his lasting contribution to the comedy technique of the screen, the basic principles of which are as important today as when they were first put into practice, the Academy presents a Special Award to that master of fun, discoverer of stars, sympathetic, kindly, understanding comedy genius—Mack Sennett.

Edgar Bergen for his outstanding comedy creation, Charlie McCarthy.[58]

The Museum of Modern Art Film Library for its significant work in collecting films dating from 1895 to the present and for the

---

[55] Discontinued after this year.
[56] Discontinued after this year.
[57] New award.
[58] Bergen received a wooden Oscar with a movable mouth.

first time making available to the public the means of studying the historical and aesthetic development of the motion picture as one of the major arts.[59]

W. Howard Greene for the color photography of *A Star Is Born*.[60]

1938
Awards presented February 23, 1939.

PRODUCTION

***You Can't Take It With You*, Columbia. Produced by Frank Capra.**

The Adventures of Robin Hood, Warner Bros.-First National. Produced by Hal B. Wallis, with Henry Blanke.

Alexander's Ragtime Band, 20th Century-Fox. Produced by Darryl F. Zanuck, with Harry Joe Brown.

Boys Town, MGM. Produced by John W. Considine, Jr.

The Citadel, MGM (United Kingdom). Produced by Victor Saville.

Four Daughters, Warner Bros.-First National. Produced by Hal B. Wallis, with Henry Blanke.

Grand Illusion, Réalization d'Art Cinématographique, World Pictures (France). Produced by Frank Rollmer and Albert Pinkovitch.[61]

Jezebel, Warner Bros. Produced by Hal B. Wallis, with Henry Blanke.

Pygmalion, MGM (United Kingdom). Produced by Gabriel Pascal.

Test Pilot, MGM. Produced by Louis D. Lighton.

ACTOR

Spencer Tracy in *Boys Town*, MGM.

Charles Boyer in *Algiers*, Wanger, United Artists.

James Cagney in *Angels With Dirty Faces*, Warner Bros.-First National.

Robert Donat in *The Citadel*, MGM (United Kingdom).

Leslie Howard in *Pygmalion*, MGM (United Kingdom).

ACTRESS

Bette Davis in *Jezebel*, Warner Bros.

Fay Bainter[62] in *White Banners*, Warner Bros.-Cosmopolitan.

Wendy Hiller in *Pygmalion*, MGM (United Kingdom).

Norma Shearer in *Marie Antoinette*, MGM.

Margaret Sullavan in *Three Comrades*, MGM.

SUPPORTING ACTOR

Walter Brennan in *Kentucky*, 20th Century-Fox.

John Garfield in *Four Daughters*, Warner Bros.-First National.

Gene Lockhart in *Algiers*, Wanger, United Artists.

Robert Morley in *Marie Antoinette*, MGM.

Basil Rathbone in *If I Were King*, Paramount.

SUPPORTING ACTRESS

Fay Bainter in *Jezebel*, Warner Bros.

Beulah Bondi in *Of Human Hearts*, MGM.

Billie Burke in *Merrily We Live*, MGM.

Spring Byington in *You Can't Take It With You*, Columbia.

Miliza Korjus in *The Great Waltz*, MGM.

DIRECTOR

Frank Capra for *You Can't Take It With You*, Columbia.

Michael Curtiz for *Angels With Dirty Faces*, Warner Bros.

Michael Curtiz for *Four Daughters*, Warner Bros.-First National.

Norman Taurog for *Boys Town*, MGM.

King Vidor for *The Citadel*, MGM (United Kingdom).

WRITING

(Original Story)

Dore Schary and Eleanore Griffin for *Boys Town*, MGM.

Irving Berlin for *Alexander's Ragtime Band*, 20th Century-Fox.

Rowland Brown for *Angels With Dirty Faces*, Warner Bros.

Marcella Burke and Frederick Kohner for *Mad About Music*, Universal.

John Howard Lawson for *Blockade*, United Artists.

Frank Wead for *Test Pilot*, MGM.

(Screenplay)

George Bernard Shaw,[63] screenplay and dialogue; W. P. Lipscomb, Ian Dalrymple, and Cecil Lewis, adaptation, for *Pygmalion*, MGM (United Kingdom).

Ian Dalrymple, Frank Wead, and Elizabeth Hill for *The Citadel*, MGM (United Kingdom).

Julius J. Epstein and Lenore Coffee for *Four Daughters*, Warner Bros.

John Meehan and Dore Schary for *Boys Town*, MGM.

Robert Riskin for *You Can't Take It With You*, Columbia.

CINEMATOGRAPHY

Joseph Ruttenberg for *The Great Waltz*, MGM.

Norbert Brodine for *Merrily We Live*, MGM.

Robert de Grasse for *Vivacious Lady*, RKO Radio.

---

[59] The museum was presented a scroll certificate instead of an Oscar.

[60] Greene's award, a plaque, the Academy noted, "was recommended by a committee of leading cinematographers after viewing all the color pictures made during the year." The cinematography award was not divided into black-and-white and color films until 1939.

[61] First foreign language film to be nominated for best picture.

[62] First person to receive simultaneous nominations in both leading and supporting acting categories. The others are Teresa Wright (1942), Barry Fitzgerald (1944), Jessica Lange (1982), Sigourney Weaver (1988), Al Pacino (1992), Holly Hunter (1993), and Emma Thompson (1994).

[63] Only person to win both the Nobel Prize for literature and an Academy Award. Nobel laureate John Steinbeck received three nominations (1944, 1945, 1952), and Jean-Paul Sartre was nominated once (1956), but neither won the award.

Ernest Haller for *Jezebel*, Warner Bros.

James Wong Howe for *Algiers*, United Artists.

Peverell Marley for *Suez*, 20th Century-Fox.

Ernest Miller and Harry Wild for *Army Girl*, Republic.

Victor Milner for *The Buccaneer*, Paramount.

Leon Shamroy for *The Young in Heart*, Selznick, United Artists.

Joseph Valentine for *Mad About Music*, Universal.

Joseph Walker for *You Can't Take It With You*, Columbia.

INTERIOR DECORATION

Carl J. Weyl for *The Adventures of Robin Hood*, Warner Bros.

Richard Day for *The Goldwyn Follies*, Goldwyn, United Artists.

Hans Dreier and John Goodman for *If I Were King*, Paramount.

Cedric Gibbons for *Marie Antoinette*, MGM.

Stephen Goosson and Lionel Banks for *Holiday*, Columbia.

Charles D. Hall for *Merrily We Live*, MGM.

Bernard Herzbrun and Boris Leven for *Alexander's Ragtime Band*, 20th Century-Fox.

Jack Otterson for *Mad About Music*, Universal.

Van Nest Polglase for *Carefree*, RKO Radio.

Alexander Toluboff for *Algiers*, Wanger, United Artists.

Lyle Wheeler for *The Adventures of Tom Sawyer*, Selznick, United Artists.

SOUND RECORDING

Thomas T. Moulton for *The Cowboy and the Lady*, Goldwyn, United Artists.

John Aalberg for *Vivacious Lady*, RKO Radio.

Bernard B. Brown for *That Certain Age*, Universal.

Edmund H. Hansen for *Suez*, 20th Century-Fox.

Nathan Levinson for *Four Daughters*, Warner Bros.-First National.

John Livadary for *You Can't Take It With You*, Columbia.

Charles L. Lootens for *Army Girl*, Republic.

Elmer Raguse for *Merrily We Live*, MGM.

Loren L. Ryder for *If I Were King*, Paramount.

Douglas Shearer for *Sweethearts*, MGM.

MUSIC[64]
(Song)

"Thanks for the Memory" from *The Big Broadcast of 1938*, Paramount. Music by Ralph Rainger, lyrics by Leo Robin.

"Always and Always" from *Mannequin*, MGM. Music by Edward Ward, lyrics by Chet Forrest and Bob Wright.

"Change Partners and Dance With Me" from *Carefree*, RKO Radio. Music and lyrics by Irving Berlin.

"The Cowboy and the Lady" from *The Cowboy and the Lady*, Goldwyn, United Artists. Music by Lionel Newman, lyrics by Arthur Quenzer.

"Dust" from *Under Western Stars*, Republic. Music and lyrics by Johnny Marvin.

"Jeepers Creepers" from *Going Places*, Warner Bros. Music by Harry Warren, lyrics by Johnny Mercer.

"Merrily We Live" from *Merrily We Live*, MGM. Music by Phil Craig, lyrics by Arthur Quenzer.

"A Mist Over the Moon" from *The Lady Objects*, Columbia. Music by Ben Oakland, lyrics by Oscar Hammerstein II.

"My Own" from *That Certain Age*, Universal. Music by Jimmy McHugh, lyrics by Harold Adamson.

"Now It Can Be Told" from *Alexander's Ragtime Band*, 20th Century-Fox. Music and lyrics by Irving Berlin.

(Scoring)

Alfred Newman for *Alexander's Ragtime Band*, 20th Century-Fox.

Victor Baravelle for *Carefree*, RKO Radio.

Cy Feuer for *Storm Over Bengal*, Republic.

Marvin Hatley for *There Goes My Heart*, United Artists.

Boris Morros for *Tropic Holiday*, Paramount.

Alfred Newman for *Goldwyn Follies*, Goldwyn, United Artists.

Charles Previn and Frank Skinner for *Mad About Music*, Universal.

Max Steiner for *Jezebel*, Warner Bros.

Morris Stoloff and Gregory Stone for *Girls School*, Columbia.

Herbert Stothart for *Sweethearts*, MGM.

Franz Waxman for *The Young in Heart*, Selznick, United Artists.

(Original Score)

Erich Wolfgang Korngold for *The Adventures of Robin Hood*, Warner Bros.

Russell Bennett for *Pacific Liner*, RKO Radio.

Richard Hageman for *If I Were King*, Paramount.

Marvin Hatley for *Blockheads*, MGM.

Werner Janssen for *Blockade*, United Artists.

Alfred Newman for *The Cowboy and the Lady*, Goldwyn, United Artists.

Louis Silvers for *Suez*, 20th Century-Fox.

Herbert Stothart for *Marie Antoinette*, MGM.

Franz Waxman for *The Young in Heart*, Selznick, United Artists.

Victor Young for *Army Girl*, Republic.

Victor Young for *Breaking the Ice*, RKO Radio.

FILM EDITING

Ralph Dawson for *The Adventures of Robin Hood*, Warner Bros.

Gene Havlick for *You Can't Take It With You*, Columbia.

Tom Held for *The Great Waltz*, MGM.

Tom Held for *Test Pilot*, MGM.

Barbara McLean for *Alexander's Ragtime Band*, 20th Century-Fox.

---

[64] Awards for scoring divided into "Scoring" (regardless of source) and "Original Score" (compositions specifically for the nominated film).

IRVING G. THALBERG MEMORIAL AWARD[65]

Hal B. Wallis.
Samuel Goldwyn.
Joe Pasternak.
David O. Selznick.
Hunt Stromberg.
Walter Wanger.
Darryl F. Zanuck.

SPECIAL AWARDS

Deanna Durbin and Mickey Rooney for their significant contribution in bringing to the screen the spirit and personification of youth, and as juvenile players setting a high standard of ability and achievement.

Harry M. Warner in recognition of patriotic service in the production of historical short subjects presenting significant episodes in the early struggle of the American people for liberty.[66]

Walt Disney for *Snow White and the Seven Dwarfs*, recognized as a significant screen innovation which has charmed millions and pioneered a great new entertainment field for the motion picture cartoon.[67]

Oliver Marsh and Allen Davey for the color cinematography of the MGM production *Sweethearts*.[68]

For outstanding achievement in creating special photographic and sound effects in the Paramount production *Spawn of the North*: special effects by Gordon Jennings, assisted by Jan Domela, Dev Jennings, Irmin Roberts and Art Smith; transparencies by Farciot Edouart, assisted by Loyal Griggs; sound effects by Loren Ryder, assisted by Harry Mills, Louis H. Mesenkop and Walter Oberst.[69]

J. Arthur Ball for his outstanding contributions to the advancement of color in motion picture photography.[70]

1939
Awards presented February 29, 1940.

PRODUCTION

***Gone With the Wind*, Selznick International Pictures, MGM. Produced by David O. Selznick.**
Dark Victory, Warner Bros.-First National. Produced by David Lewis.
Goodbye, Mr. Chips, MGM (United Kingdom). Produced by Victor Saville.
Love Affair, RKO Radio. Produced by Leo McCarey.
Mr. Smith Goes to Washington, Columbia. Produced by Frank Capra.
Ninotchka, MGM. Produced by Sidney Franklin.
Of Mice and Men, Hal Roach, United Artists. Produced by Lewis Milestone.
Stagecoach, Walter Wanger, United Artists. Produced by Walter Wanger.
The Wizard of Oz, MGM. Produced by Mervyn LeRoy.
Wuthering Heights, Samuel Goldwyn Productions, United Artists. Produced by Samuel Goldwyn.

ACTOR

Robert Donat in *Goodbye, Mr. Chips*, MGM (United Kingdom).
Clark Gable in *Gone With the Wind*, Selznick, MGM.
Laurence Olivier in *Wuthering Heights*, Goldwyn, United Artists.
Mickey Rooney in *Babes in Arms*, MGM.
James Stewart in *Mr. Smith Goes to Washington*, Columbia.

ACTRESS

Vivien Leigh in *Gone With the Wind*, Selznick, MGM.
Bette Davis in *Dark Victory*, Warner Bros.-First National.
Irene Dunne in *Love Affair*, RKO Radio.
Greta Garbo in *Ninotchka*, MGM.
Greer Garson in *Goodbye, Mr. Chips*, MGM (United Kingdom).

SUPPORTING ACTOR

Thomas Mitchell in *Stagecoach*, United Artists.
Brian Aherne in *Juarez*, Warner Bros.
Harry Carey in *Mr. Smith Goes to Washington*, Columbia.
Brian Donlevy in *Beau Geste*, Paramount.
Claude Rains in *Mr. Smith Goes to Washington*, Columbia.

SUPPORTING ACTRESS

Hattie McDaniel[71] in *Gone With the Wind*, Selznick, MGM.
Olivia de Havilland in *Gone With the Wind*, Selznick, MGM.
Geraldine Fitzgerald in *Wuthering Heights*, Goldwyn, United Artists.
Edna May Oliver in *Drums Along the Mohawk*, 20th Century-Fox.
Maria Ouspenskaya in *Love Affair*, RKO Radio.

DIRECTOR

Victor Fleming for *Gone With the Wind*, Selznick, MGM.
Frank Capra for *Mr. Smith Goes to Washington*, Columbia.
John Ford for *Stagecoach*, United Artists.

---

[65] For this year only, the Academy announced the Thalberg Award nominees.
[66] Warner received a scroll.
[67] Disney was given an Oscar surrounded by seven miniature Oscars. The film was eligible in the competitive categories the previous year, but was nominated for only one award, for Score. The *Snow White* phenomenon became apparent during 1938 as the film entered wide release.
[68] Marsh and Davey received plaques.
[69] The studio received a plaque.
[70] Ball was presented a scroll.
[71] First African-American to be nominated for acting.

Sam Wood for *Goodbye, Mr. Chips*, MGM (United Kingdom).

William Wyler for *Wuthering Heights*, Goldwyn, United Artists.

WRITING

(Original Story)

Lewis R. Foster for *Mr. Smith Goes to Washington*, Columbia.

Mildred Cram and Leo McCarey for *Love Affair*, RKO Radio.

Felix Jackson for *Bachelor Mother*, RKO Radio.

Melchior Lengyel for *Ninotchka*, MGM.

Lamar Trotti for *Young Mr. Lincoln*, 20th Century-Fox.

(Screenplay)

Sidney Howard[72] for *Gone With the Wind*, Selznick, MGM.

Charles Brackett, Billy Wilder, and Walter Reisch for *Ninotchka*, MGM.

Sidney Buchman for *Mr. Smith Goes to Washington*, Columbia.

Charles MacArthur and Ben Hecht for *Wuthering Heights*, Goldwyn, United Artists.

R. C. Sherriff, Claudine West, and Eric Maschwitz for *Goodbye, Mr. Chips*, MGM (United Kingdom).

CINEMATOGRAPHY[73]

(Black and White)

Gregg Toland for *Wuthering Heights*, Goldwyn, United Artists.

Bert Glennon for *Stagecoach*, United Artists.

—————

Joseph H. August for *Gunga Din*, RKO Radio.

Norbert Brodine for *Of Mice and Men*, United Artists.

George Folsey for *Lady of the Tropics*, MGM.

Tony Gaudio for *Juarez*, Warner Bros.

Arthur Miller for *The Rains Came*, 20th Century-Fox.

Victor Milner for *The Great Victor Herbert*, Paramount.

Gregg Toland for *Intermezzo: A Love Story*, Selznick, United Artists.

Joseph Valentine for *First Love*, Universal.

Joseph Walker for *Only Angels Have Wings*, Columbia.

(Color)

Ernest Haller and Ray Rennahan for *Gone With the Wind*, Selznick, MGM.

Sol Polito and W. Howard Greene for *The Private Lives of Elizabeth and Essex*, Warner Bros.

—————

Georges Périnal and Osmond Borradaile for *Four Feathers*, United Artists (United Kingdom).

Ray Rennahan and Bert Glennon for *Drums Along the Mohawk*, 20th Century-Fox.

Hal Rosson for *The Wizard of Oz*, MGM.

William V. Skall and Bernard Knowles for *The Mikado*, Universal (United Kingdom).

INTERIOR DECORATION

Lyle Wheeler for *Gone With the Wind*, Selznick, MGM.

Lionel Banks for *Mr. Smith Goes to Washington*, Columbia.

James Basevi for *Wuthering Heights*, Goldwyn, United Artists.

William Darling and George Dudley for *The Rains Came*, 20th Century-Fox.

Hans Dreier and Robert Odell for *Beau Geste*, Paramount.

Cedric Gibbons and William A. Horning for *The Wizard of Oz*, MGM.

Anton Grot for *The Private Lives of Elizabeth and Essex*, Warner Bros.

Charles D. Hall for *Captain Fury*, United Artists.

John Victor Mackay for *Man of Conquest*, Republic.

Jack Otterson and Martin Obzina for *First Love*, Universal.

Van Nest Polglase and Al Herman for *Love Affair*, RKO Radio.

Alexander Toluboff for *Stagecoach*, United Artists.

SOUND RECORDING

Bernard B. Brown for *When Tomorrow Comes*, Universal.

John Aalberg for *The Hunchback of Notre Dame*, RKO Radio.

E. H. Hansen for *The Rains Came*, 20th Century-Fox.

Nathan Levinson for *The Private Lives of Elizabeth and Essex*, Warner Bros.

John Livadary for *Mr. Smith Goes to Washington*, Columbia.

Charles L. Lootens for *Man of Conquest*, Republic.

Thomas T. Moulton for *Gone With the Wind*, Selznick, MGM.

Elmer Raguse for *Of Mice and Men*, United Artists.

Loren L. Ryder for *The Great Victor Herbert*, Paramount.

Douglas Shearer for *Balalaika*, MGM.

A. W. Watkins for *Goodbye, Mr. Chips*, MGM (United Kingdom).

MUSIC

(Song)

"Over the Rainbow" from *The Wizard of Oz*, MGM. Music by Harold Arlen, lyrics by E. Y. Harburg.

"Faithful Forever" from *Gulliver's Travels*, Paramount. Music by Ralph Rainger, lyrics by Leo Robin.

"I Poured My Heart Into a Song" from *Second Fiddle*, 20th Century-Fox. Music and lyrics by Irving Berlin.

"Wishing" from *Love Affair*, RKO Radio. Music and lyrics by Buddy De Sylva.

(Scoring)

Richard Hageman, Frank Harling, John Leipold, and Leo Shuken for *Stagecoach*, Wanger, United Artists.

---

[72] First person to win an Oscar posthumously.

[73] Category divided into black-and-white and color films. This year the Academy also announced a preliminary slate of cinematography nominees, then whittled the candidates down to two for black and white and two for color. The official nominee in each division is listed after the winner. The remaining preliminary nominees are listed below the dotted line.

Phil Boutelje and Arthur Lange for *The Great Victor Herbert*, Paramount.

Aaron Copland for *Of Mice and Men*, United Artists.

Roger Edens and George E. Stoll for *Babes in Arms*, MGM.

Cy Feuer for *She Married a Cop*, Republic.

Lou Forbes for *Intermezzo: A Love Story*, Selznick, United Artists.

Erich Wolfgang Korngold for *The Private Lives of Elizabeth and Essex*, Warner Bros.

Alfred Newman for *The Hunchback of Notre Dame*, RKO Radio.

Alfred Newman for *They Shall Have Music*, Goldwyn, United Artists.

Charles Previn for *First Love*, Universal.

Louis Silvers for *Swanee River*, 20th Century-Fox.

Dimitri Tiomkin for *Mr. Smith Goes to Washington*, Columbia.

Victor Young for *Way Down South*, RKO Radio.

(Original Score)

Herbert Stothart for *The Wizard of Oz*, MGM.

Anthony Collins for *Nurse Edith Cavell*, RKO Radio.

Aaron Copland for *Of Mice and Men*, United Artists.

Lud Gluskin and Lucien Moraweck for *The Man in the Iron Mask*, United Artists.

Werner Janssen for *Eternally Yours*, United Artists.

Alfred Newman for *The Rains Came*, 20th Century-Fox.

Alfred Newman for *Wuthering Heights*, Goldwyn, United Artists.

Max Steiner for *Dark Victory*, Warner Bros.

Max Steiner for *Gone With the Wind*, Selznick, MGM.

Victor Young for *Golden Boy*, Columbia.

Victor Young for *Gulliver's Travels*, Paramount.

Victor Young for *Man of Conquest*, Republic.

FILM EDITING

Hal C. Kern and James E. Newcom for *Gone With the Wind*, Selznick, MGM.

Charles Frend for *Goodbye, Mr. Chips*, MGM (United Kingdom).

Gene Havlick and Al Clark for *Mr. Smith Goes to Washington*, Columbia.

Otho Lovering and Dorothy Spencer for *Stagecoach*, United Artists.

Barbara McLean for *The Rains Came*, 20th Century-Fox.

SPECIAL EFFECTS[74]

***The Rains Came*, 20th Century-Fox. Fred Sersen and E. H. Hansen.**

Gone With the Wind, Selznick, MGM. Photographic: John R. Cosgrove, Fred Albin, and Arthur Johns.

Only Angels Have Wings, Columbia. Roy Davidson and Edwin C. Hahn.

The Private Lives of Elizabeth and Essex, Warner Bros. Byron Haskin and Nathan Levinson.

Topper Takes a Trip, United Artists. Roy Seawright.

Union Pacific, Paramount. Farciot Edouart, Gordon Jennings, and Loren Ryder.

The Wizard of Oz, MGM. Photographic: A. Arnold Gillespie and Douglas Shearer.

IRVING G. THALBERG MEMORIAL AWARD
David O. Selznick.

SPECIAL AWARDS

Douglas Fairbanks (Commemorative Award), recognizing the unique and outstanding contribution of Douglas Fairbanks, first president of the Academy, to the international development of the motion picture.[75]

The Motion Picture Relief Fund, acknowledging the outstanding services to the industry during the past year of the Motion Picture Relief Fund and its progressive leadership. Presented to Jean Hersholt, president; Ralph Morgan, chairman of the executive committee; Ralph Block, first vice-president; and Conrad Nagel.[76]

Judy Garland for her outstanding performance as a screen juvenile during the past year.

William Cameron Menzies for outstanding achievement in the use of color for the enhancement of dramatic mood in the production of *Gone With the Wind*.[77]

The Technicolor Company for its contributions in successfully bringing three-color feature production to the screen.

1940
Awards presented February 27, 1941.

PRODUCTION

***Rebecca*, Selznick International Pictures, United Artists. Produced by David O. Selznick.[78]**

All This, and Heaven Too, Warner Bros. Produced by Jack L. Warner and Hal B. Wallis, with David Lewis.

Foreign Correspondent, Walter Wanger, United Artists. Produced by Walter Wanger.

The Grapes of Wrath, 20th Century-Fox. Produced by Darryl F. Zanuck, with Nunnally Johnson.

The Great Dictator, Charles Chaplin Productions, United Artists. Produced by Charles Chaplin.

---

[74] New category.
[75] A posthumous award: Fairbanks died in December 1939.
[76] The principals received plaques.
[77] Menzies, the film's design director, was given a plaque.
[78] First person to produce two consecutive winners of the best picture Oscar.

Kitty Foyle, RKO Radio. Produced by David Hempstead.

The Letter, Warner Bros. Produced by Hal B. Wallis.

The Long Voyage Home, Argosy-Wanger, United Artists. Produced by John Ford.

Our Town, Sol Lesser, United Artists. Produced by Sol Lesser.

The Philadelphia Story, MGM. Produced by Joseph L. Mankiewicz.

ACTOR

James Stewart in *The Philadelphia Story*, MGM.

Charles Chaplin[79] in *The Great Dictator*, Chaplin, United Artists.

Henry Fonda in *The Grapes of Wrath*, 20th Century-Fox.

Raymond Massey in *Abe Lincoln in Illinois*, RKO Radio.

Laurence Olivier in *Rebecca*, Selznick, United Artists.

ACTRESS

Ginger Rogers in *Kitty Foyle*, RKO Radio.

Bette Davis in *The Letter*, Warner Bros.

Joan Fontaine in *Rebecca*, Selznick, United Artists.

Katharine Hepburn in *The Philadelphia Story*, MGM.

Martha Scott in *Our Town*, United Artists.

SUPPORTING ACTOR

Walter Brennan[80] in *The Westerner*, Goldwyn, United Artists.

Albert Basserman in *Foreign Correspondent*, Wanger, United Artists.

William Gargan in *They Knew What They Wanted*, RKO Radio.

Jack Oakie in *The Great Dictator*, Chaplin, United Artists.

James Stephenson in *The Letter*, Warner Bros.

SUPPORTING ACTRESS

Jane Darwell in *The Grapes of Wrath*, 20th Century-Fox.

Judith Anderson in *Rebecca*, Selznick, United Artists.

Ruth Hussey in *The Philadelphia Story*, MGM.

Barbara O'Neil in *All This, and Heaven Too*, Warner Bros.

Marjorie Rambeau in *Primrose Path*, RKO Radio.

DIRECTOR

John Ford for *The Grapes of Wrath*, 20th Century-Fox.

George Cukor for *The Philadelphia Story*, MGM.

Alfred Hitchcock for *Rebecca*, Selznick, United Artists.

Sam Wood for *Kitty Foyle*, RKO Radio.

William Wyler for *The Letter*, Warner Bros.

WRITING

(Original Screenplay)[81]

Preston Sturges for *The Great McGinty*, Paramount.

Charles Bennett and Joan Harrison for *Foreign Correspondent*, United Artists.

Charles Chaplin for *The Great Dictator*, Chaplin, United Artists.

Ben Hecht for *Angels Over Broadway*, Columbia.

John Huston, Heinz Herald, and Norman Burnside for *Dr. Ehrlich's Magic Bullet*, Warner Bros.

(Original Story)

Benjamin Glazer and John S. Toldy for *Arise, My Love*, Paramount.

Stuart N. Lake for *The Westerner*, Goldwyn, United Artists.

Walter Reisch for *Comrade X*, MGM.

Dore Schary and Hugo Butler for *Edison the Man*, MGM.

Bella Spewack, Samuel Spewack, and Leo McCarey for *My Favorite Wife*, RKO Radio.

(Screenplay)

Donald Ogden Stewart for *The Philadelphia Story*, MGM.

Nunnally Johnson for *The Grapes of Wrath*, 20th Century-Fox.

Dudley Nichols for *The Long Voyage Home*, United Artists.

Robert E. Sherwood and Joan Harrison for *Rebecca*, Selznick, United Artists.

Dalton Trumbo for *Kitty Foyle*, RKO Radio.

CINEMATOGRAPHY

(Black and White)

George Barnes for *Rebecca*, Selznick, United Artists.

Gaetano "Tony" Gaudio for *The Letter*, Warner Bros.

Ernest Haller for *All This, and Heaven Too*, Warner Bros.

James Wong Howe for *Abe Lincoln in Illinois*, RKO Radio.

Charles B. Lang, Jr., for *Arise, My Love*, Paramount.

Rudolph Maté for *Foreign Correspondent*, United Artists.

Harold Rosson for *Boom Town*, MGM.

Joseph Ruttenberg for *Waterloo Bridge*, MGM.

Gregg Toland for *The Long Voyage Home*, United Artists.

Joseph Valentine for *Spring Parade*, Universal.

(Color)

Georges Périnal for *The Thief of Bagdad*, United Artists (United Kingdom/U.S.).

Oliver T. Marsh and Allen Davey for *Bitter Sweet*, MGM.

Arthur Miller and Ray Rennahan for *The Blue Bird*, 20th Century-Fox.

Victor Milner and W. Howard Greene for *North West Mounted Police*, Paramount.

Leon Shamroy and Ray Rennahan for *Down Argentine Way*, 20th Century-Fox.

---

[79] First person to receive simultaneous nominations as producer, actor, and writer. The only others are Orson Welles (1941) and Warren Beatty (1978 and 1981). Unlike Chaplin, Welles and Beatty were also nominated as director.

[80] First person to receive three Oscars for acting. Ingrid Bergman also received three (1944, 1956, 1974). Katharine Hepburn has four (1932–33, 1967, 1968, 1981).

[81] New category.

Sidney Wagner and William V. Skall for *Northwest Passage*, MGM.

INTERIOR DECORATION[82]

(Black and White)

Cedric Gibbons and Paul Groesse for *Pride and Prejudice*, MGM.

Lionel Banks and Robert Peterson for *Arizona*, Columbia.

James Basevi for *The Westerner*, Goldwyn, United Artists.

Richard Day and Joseph C. Wright for *Lillian Russell*, 20th Century-Fox.

Hans Dreier and Robert Usher for *Arise, My Love*, Paramount.

Alexander Golitzen for *Foreign Correspondent*, United Artists.

Anton Grot for *The Sea Hawk*, Warner Bros.

John Victor Mackay for *Dark Command*, Republic.

John Otterson for *The Boys From Syracuse*, Universal.

Van Nest Polglase and Mark-Lee Kirk for *My Favorite Wife*, RKO Radio.

Lewis J. Rachmil for *Our Town*, United Artists.

John DuCasse Schulze for *My Son, My Son*, United Artists.

Lyle Wheeler for *Rebecca*, Selznick, United Artists.

(Color)

Vincent Korda for *The Thief of Bagdad*, United Artists (United Kingdom/U.S.).

Richard Day and Joseph C. Wright for *Down Argentine Way*, 20th Century-Fox.

Hans Dreier and Roland Anderson for *North West Mounted Police*, Paramount.

Cedric Gibbons and John S. Detlie for *Bitter Sweet*, MGM.

SOUND RECORDING

Douglas Shearer for *Strike Up the Band*, MGM.

John Aalberg for *Kitty Foyle*, RKO Radio.

Bernard B. Brown for *Spring Parade*, Universal.

E. H. Hansen for *The Grapes of Wrath*, 20th Century-Fox.

Nathan Levinson for *The Sea Hawk*, Warner Bros.

John Livadary for *Too Many Husbands*, Columbia.

Charles L. Lootens for *Behind the News*, Republic.

Thomas T. Moulton, Samuel Goldwyn Studio Sound Dept., for *Our Town*, United Artists.

Elmer A. Raguse for *Captain Caution*, United Artists.

Loren L. Ryder for *North West Mounted Police*, Paramount.

Jack Whitney, General Service Sound Dept., for *The Howards of Virginia*, Columbia.

MUSIC

(Song)

"When You Wish Upon a Star" from *Pinocchio*, Disney, RKO Radio. Music by Leigh Harline, lyrics by Ned Washington.

"Down Argentine Way" from *Down Argentine Way*, 20th Century-Fox. Music by Harry Warren, lyrics by Mack Gordon.

"I'd Know You Anywhere" from *You'll Find Out*, RKO Radio. Music by Jimmy McHugh, lyrics by Johnny Mercer.

"It's a Blue World" from *Music in My Heart*, Columbia. Music and lyrics by Chet Forrest and Bob Wright.

"Love of My Life" from *Second Chorus*, Paramount. Music by Artie Shaw, lyrics by Johnny Mercer.

"Only Forever" from *Rhythm on the River*, Paramount. Music by James Monaco, lyrics by Johnny Burke.

"Our Love Affair" from *Strike Up the Band*, MGM. Music and lyrics by Roger Edens and Arthur Freed.

"Waltzing in the Clouds" from *Spring Parade*, Universal. Music by Robert Stolz, lyrics by Gus Kahn.

"Who Am I?" from *Hit Parade of 1941*, Republic. Music by Jule Styne, lyrics by Walter Bullock.

(Scoring)

Alfred Newman for *Tin Pan Alley*, 20th Century-Fox.

Anthony Collins for *Irene*, RKO Radio.

Aaron Copland for *Our Town*, United Artists.

Cy Feuer for *Hit Parade of 1941*, Republic.

Erich Wolfgang Korngold for *The Sea Hawk*, Warner Bros.

Charles Previn for *Spring Parade*, Universal.

Artie Shaw for *Second Chorus*, Paramount.

Georgie Stoll and Roger Edens for *Strike Up the Band*, MGM.

Victor Young for *Arise, My Love*, Paramount.

(Original Score)

Leigh Harline, Paul J. Smith, and Ned Washington for *Pinocchio*, Disney, RKO Radio.

Aaron Copland for *Our Town*, United Artists.

Louis Gruenberg for *The Fight for Life*, U.S. Film Service, Columbia.

Richard Hageman for *The Howards of Virginia*, Columbia.

Richard Hageman for *The Long Voyage Home*, United Artists.

Werner Heymann for *One Million B.C.*, United Artists.

Alfred Newman for *The Mark of Zorro*, 20th Century-Fox.

Miklos Rozsa for *The Thief of Bagdad*, United Artists (United Kingdom/U.S.).

Frank Skinner for *The House of Seven Gables*, Universal.

Max Steiner for *The Letter*, Warner Bros.

Herbert Stothart for *Waterloo Bridge*, MGM.

Franz Waxman for *Rebecca*, Selznick, United Artists.

Roy Webb for *My Favorite Wife*, RKO Radio.

Meredith Willson for *The Great Dictator*, Chaplin, United Artists.

Victor Young for *Arizona*, Columbia.

Victor Young for *Dark Command*, Republic.

---

[82] Category divided into black-and-white and color films.

Victor Young for *North West Mounted Police,* Paramount.

FILM EDITING

Anne Bauchens for *North West Mounted Police,* Paramount.

Hal C. Kern for *Rebecca,* Selznick, United Artists.

Warren Low for *The Letter,* Warner Bros.

Robert E. Simpson for *The Grapes of Wrath,* 20th Century-Fox.

Sherman Todd for *The Long Voyage Home,* United Artists.

SPECIAL EFFECTS

***The Thief of Bagdad,* United Artists (United Kingdom/U.S.). Photographic: Lawrence Butler; sound: Jack Whitney.**

The Blue Bird, 20th Century-Fox. Photographic: Fred Sersen; sound: E. H. Hansen.

Boom Town, MGM. Photographic: A. Arnold Gillespie; sound: Douglas Shearer.

The Boys From Syracuse, Universal. Photographic: John P. Fulton; sound: Bernard B. Brown and Joseph Lapis.

Dr. Cyclops, Paramount. Photographic: Farciot Edouart and Gordon Jennings.

Foreign Correspondent, United Artists. Photographic: Paul Eagler; sound: Thomas T. Moulton.

The Invisible Man Returns, Universal. Photographic: John P. Fulton; sound: Bernard B. Brown and William Hedgecock.

The Long Voyage Home, United Artists. Photographic: R. T. Layton and R. O. Binger; sound: Thomas T. Moulton.

One Million B.C., United Artists. Photographic: Roy Seawright; sound: Elmer Raguse.

Rebecca, Selznick, United Artists. Photographic: Jack Cosgrove; sound: Arthur Johns.

The Sea Hawk, Warner Bros. Photographic: Byron Haskin; sound: Nathan Levinson.

Swiss Family Robinson, RKO Radio. Photographic: Vernon L. Walker; sound: John O. Aalberg.

Typhoon, Paramount. Photographic: Farciot Edouart and Gordon Jennings; sound: Loren Ryder.

Women in War, Republic. Photographic: Howard J. Lydecker, William Bradford, and Ellis J. Thackery; sound: Herbert Norsch.

SPECIAL AWARDS

Bob Hope, in recognition of his unselfish services to the motion picture industry.[83]
Col. Nathan Levinson for his outstanding service to the industry and the Army during the past nine years, which has made possible the present efficient mobilization of the motion picture industry facilities for the production of Army training films.

1941
Awards presented February 26, 1942.

PICTURE

***How Green Was My Valley,* 20th Century-Fox. Produced by Darryl F. Zanuck.**

Blossoms in the Dust, MGM. Produced by Irving Asher.

Citizen Kane, Mercury, RKO Radio. Produced by Orson Welles.[84]

Here Comes Mr. Jordan, Columbia. Produced by Everett Riskin.

Hold Back the Dawn, Paramount. Produced by Arthur Hornblow, Jr.

The Little Foxes, Samuel Goldwyn Productions, RKO Radio. Produced by Samuel Goldwyn.

The Maltese Falcon, Warner Bros. Produced by Hal B. Wallis.

One Foot in Heaven, Warner Bros. Produced by Hal B. Wallis.

Sergeant York, Warner Bros. Produced by Jesse L. Lasky and Hal B. Wallis.

Suspicion, RKO Radio. Produced by RKO Radio.

ACTOR

Gary Cooper in *Sergeant York,* Warner Bros.

Cary Grant in *Penny Serenade,* Columbia.

Walter Huston in *All That Money Can Buy* (a.k.a. *The Devil and Daniel Webster),* RKO Radio.

Robert Montgomery in *Here Comes Mr. Jordan,* Columbia.

Orson Welles in *Citizen Kane,* Mercury, RKO Radio.

ACTRESS[85]

Joan Fontaine in *Suspicion,* RKO Radio.

Bette Davis in *The Little Foxes,* Goldwyn, RKO Radio.

Olivia de Havilland in *Hold Back the Dawn,* Paramount.

Greer Garson in *Blossoms in the Dust,* MGM.

Barbara Stanwyck in *Ball of Fire,* Goldwyn, RKO Radio.

SUPPORTING ACTOR

Donald Crisp in *How Green Was My Valley,* 20th Century-Fox.

Walter Brennan in *Sergeant York,* Warner Bros.

Charles Coburn in *The Devil and Miss Jones,* RKO Radio.

James Gleason in *Here Comes Mr. Jordan,* Columbia.

Sydney Greenstreet in *The Maltese Falcon,* Warner Bros.

---

[83] Hope received a silver plaque.

[84] First person to receive simultaneous nominations as producer, actor, director, and writer. The only other one is Warren Beatty (1978, 1981).

[85] Sisters Joan Fontaine and Olivia de Havilland both nominated. Lynn Redgrave and Vanessa Redgrave are the only other sisters to receive simultaneous acting nominations (1966).

SUPPORTING ACTRESS

Mary Astor in *The Great Lie*, Warner Bros.

Sara Allgood in *How Green Was My Valley*, 20th Century-Fox.

Patricia Collinge in *The Little Foxes*, Goldwyn, RKO Radio.

Teresa Wright in *The Little Foxes*, Goldwyn, RKO Radio.

Margaret Wycherly in *Sergeant York*, Warner Bros.

DIRECTOR

John Ford for *How Green Was My Valley*, 20th Century-Fox.

Alexander Hall for *Here Comes Mr. Jordan*, Columbia.

Howard Hawks for *Sergeant York*, Warner Bros.

Orson Welles for *Citizen Kane*, RKO Radio.

William Wyler for *The Little Foxes*, Goldwyn, RKO Radio.

WRITING

(Original Screenplay)

Herman J. Mankiewicz and Orson Welles for *Citizen Kane*, RKO Radio.

Abem Finkel, Harry Chandlee, Howard Koch, and John Huston for *Sergeant York*, Warner Bros.

Paul Jarrico for *Tom, Dick and Harry*, RKO Radio.

Norman Krasna for *The Devil and Miss Jones*, RKO Radio.

Karl Tunberg and Darrell Ware for *Tall, Dark and Handsome*, 20th Century-Fox.

(Original Story)

Harry Segall for *Here Comes Mr. Jordan*, Columbia.

Richard Connell and Robert Presnell for *Meet John Doe*, Warner Bros.

Monckton Hoffe for *The Lady Eve*, Paramount.

Gordon Wellesley for *Night Train*, 20th Century-Fox (United Kingdom).

Billy Wilder and Thomas Monroe for *Ball of Fire*, Goldwyn, RKO Radio.

(Screenplay)

Sidney Buchman and Seton I. Miller for *Here Comes Mr. Jordan*, Columbia.

Charles Brackett and Billy Wilder for *Hold Back the Dawn*, Paramount.

Philip Dunne for *How Green Was My Valley*, 20th Century-Fox.

Lillian Hellman for *The Little Foxes*, Goldwyn, RKO Radio.

John Huston for *The Maltese Falcon*, Warner Bros.

CINEMATOGRAPHY

(Black and White)

Arthur Miller for *How Green Was My Valley*, 20th Century-Fox.

Edward Cronjager for *Sun Valley Serenade*, 20th Century-Fox.

Karl Freund for *The Chocolate Soldier*, MGM.

Charles Lang for *Sundown*, United Artists.

Rudolph Maté for *That Hamilton Woman*, United Artists.

Sol Polito for *Sergeant York*, Warner Bros.

Joseph Ruttenberg for *Dr. Jekyll and Mr. Hyde*, MGM.

Gregg Toland for *Citizen Kane*, RKO Radio.

Leo Tover for *Hold Back the Dawn*, Paramount.

Joseph Walker for *Here Comes Mr. Jordan*, Columbia.

(Color)

Ernest Palmer and Ray Rennahan for *Blood and Sand*, 20th Century-Fox.

Wilfred M. Cline, Karl Struss, and William Snyder for *Aloma of the South Seas*, Paramount.

Karl Freund and W. Howard Greene for *Blossoms in the Dust*, MGM.

Bert Glennon for *Dive Bomber*, Warner Bros.

Harry Hallenberger and Ray Rennahan for *Louisiana Purchase*, Paramount.

William V. Skall and Leonard Smith for *Billy the Kid*, MGM.

INTERIOR DECORATION[86]

(Black and White)

How Green Was My Valley, 20th Century-Fox. **Richard Day, Nathan Juran; Thomas Little.**

Citizen Kane, RKO Radio. Perry Ferguson, Van Nest Polglase; Al Fields, Darrell Silvera.

Flame of New Orleans, Universal. Martin Obzina, Jack Otterson; Russell A. Gausman.

Hold Back the Dawn, Paramount. Hans Dreier, Robert Usher; Sam Comer.

Ladies in Retirement, Columbia. Lionel Banks; George Montgomery.

The Little Foxes, Goldwyn, RKO Radio. Stephen Goosson; Howard Bristol.

Sergeant York, Warner Bros. John Hughes; Fred MacLean.

Son of Monte Cristo, United Artists. John DuCasse Schulze; Edward G. Boyle.

Sundown, United Artists. Alexander Golitzen; Richard Irvine.

That Hamilton Woman, United Artists. Vincent Korda; Julia Heron.

When Ladies Meet, MGM. Cedric Gibbons, Randall Duell; Edwin B. Willis.

(Color)

***Blossoms in the Dust*, MGM. Cedric Gibbons, Urie McCleary; Edwin B. Willis.**

Blood and Sand, 20th Century-Fox. Richard Day, Joseph C. Wright; Thomas Little.

Louisiana Purchase, Paramount. Raoul Pène du Bois; Stephen A. Seymour.

SOUND RECORDING

Jack Whitney, General Service, for *That Hamilton Woman*, United Artists.

John Aalberg for *Citizen Kane*, RKO Radio.

Bernard B. Brown for *Appointment for Love*, Universal.

E. H. Hansen for *How Green Was My Valley*, 20th Century-Fox.

Nathan Levinson for *Sergeant York*, Warner Bros.

---

[86] Set decorators now cited along with art directors.

John Livadary for *The Men in Her Life*, Columbia.

Charles Lootens for *The Devil Pays Off*, Republic.

Thomas T. Moulton for *Ball of Fire*, Goldwyn, RKO Radio.

Elmer Raguse for *Topper Returns*, United Artists.

Loren Ryder for *Skylark*, Paramount.

Douglas Shearer for *The Chocolate Soldier*, MGM.

MUSIC[87]

(Song)

"The Last Time I Saw Paris" from *Lady Be Good*, MGM. Music by Jerome Kern, lyrics by Oscar Hammerstein II.

"Baby Mine" from *Dumbo*, Disney, RKO Radio. Music by Frank Churchill, lyrics by Ned Washington.

"Be Honest With Me" from *Ridin' on a Rainbow*, Republic. Music and lyrics by Gene Autry and Fred Rose.

"Blues in the Night" from *Blues in the Night*, Warner Bros. Music by Harold Arlen, lyrics by Johnny Mercer.

"Boogie Woogie Bugle Boy of Company B" from *Buck Privates*, Universal. Music by Hugh Prince, lyrics by Don Raye.

"Chattanooga Choo Choo" from *Sun Valley Serenade*, 20th Century-Fox. Music by Harry Warren, lyrics by Mack Gordon.

"Dolores" from *Las Vegas Nights*, Paramount. Music by Lou Alter, lyrics by Frank Loesser.

"Out of the Silence" from *All-American Co-ed*, United Artists. Music and lyrics by Lloyd B. Norlind.

"Since I Kissed My Baby Goodbye" from *You'll Never Get Rich*, Columbia. Music and lyrics by Cole Porter.

(Music Score of a Dramatic Picture)

Bernard Herrmann for *All That Money Can Buy*, RKO Radio.

Cy Feuer and Walter Scharf for *Mercy Island*, Republic.

Louis Gruenberg for *So Ends Our Night*, United Artists.

Richard Hageman for *That Woman Is Mine*, Universal.

Bernard Herrmann for *Citizen Kane*, RKO Radio.

Werner Heymann for *That Uncertain Feeling*, Lubitsch, United Artists.

Edward Kay for *King of the Zombies*, Monogram.

Alfred Newman for *Ball of Fire*, Goldwyn, RKO Radio.

Alfred Newman for *How Green Was My Valley*, 20th Century-Fox.

Miklos Rozsa for *Lydia*, United Artists.

Miklos Rozsa for *Sundown*, United Artists.

Frank Skinner for *Back Street*, Universal.

Max Steiner for *Sergeant York*, Warner Bros.

Morris Stoloff and Ernst Toch for *Ladies in Retirement*, Columbia.

Edward Ward for *Cheers for Miss Bishop*, United Artists.

Edward Ward for *Tanks a Million*, Roach, United Artists.

Franz Waxman for *Dr. Jekyll and Mr. Hyde*, MGM.

Franz Waxman for *Suspicion*, RKO Radio.

Meredith Willson for *The Little Foxes*, Goldwyn, RKO Radio.

Victor Young for *Hold Back the Dawn*, Paramount.

(Scoring of a Musical Picture)

Frank Churchill and Oliver Wallace for *Dumbo*, Disney, RKO Radio.

Anthony Collins for *Sunny*, RKO Radio.

Robert Emmett Dolan for *Birth of the Blues*, Paramount.

Cy Feuer for *Ice Capades*, Republic.

Emil Newman for *Sun Valley Serenade*, 20th Century-Fox.

Charles Previn for *Buck Privates*, Universal.

Heinz Roemheld for *The Strawberry Blonde*, Warner Bros.

Morris Stoloff for *You'll Never Get Rich*, Columbia.

Herbert Stothart and Bronislau Kaper for *The Chocolate Soldier*, MGM.

Edward Ward for *All-American Co-ed*, United Artists.

FILM EDITING

William Holmes for *Sergeant York*, Warner Bros.

James B. Clark for *How Green Was My Valley*, 20th Century-Fox.

Harold F. Kress for *Dr. Jekyll and Mr. Hyde*, MGM.

Daniel Mandell for *The Little Foxes*, Goldwyn, RKO Radio.

Robert Wise for *Citizen Kane*, RKO Radio.

SPECIAL EFFECTS

***I Wanted Wings*, Paramount. Farciot Edouart and Gordon Jennings, photographic; Louis Mesenkop, sound.**

Aloma of the South Seas, Paramount. Farciot Edouart and Gordon Jennings, photographic; Louis Mesenkop, sound.

Flight Command, MGM. A. Arnold Gillespie, photographic; Douglas Shearer, sound.

The Invisible Woman, Universal. John Fulton, photographic; John Hall, sound.

The Sea Wolf, Warner Bros. Byron Haskin, photographic; Nathan Levinson, sound.[88]

That Hamilton Woman, United Artists. Lawrence Butler, photographic; William H. Wilmarth, sound.

Topper Returns, United Artists. Roy Seawright, photographic; Elmer Raguse, sound.

A Yank in the R.A.F., 20th Century-Fox. Fred Sersen, photographic; E. H. Hansen, sound.

---

[87] Scoring categories changed to "Music Score of a Dramatic Picture" and "Scoring of a Musical Picture."

[88] *Dive Bomber*, from the same studio and with the same special effects personnel, was originally announced as a nominee in this category, but within a week and a half after the nominations, it was replaced by *The Sea Wolf*. The Academy has no record of why or how this switch took place.

IRVING G. THALBERG MEMORIAL AWARD
Walt Disney.

SPECIAL AWARDS[89]
Rey Scott, for his extraordinary achievement in producing *Kukan*, the film record of China's struggle, including its photography with a 16mm camera under the most difficult and dangerous conditions.
The British Ministry of Information, for its vivid and dramatic presentation of the heroism of the RAF in the documentary film *Target for Tonight*.
Leopold Stokowski and his associates for their unique achievement in the creation of a new form of visualized music in Walt Disney's production *Fantasia*, thereby widening the scope of the motion picture as entertainment and as an art form.
Walt Disney, William Garity, John N. A. Hawkins and the RCA Manufacturing Company for their outstanding contribution to the advancement of the use of sound in motion pictures through the production of *Fantasia*.

1942
Awards presented March 4, 1943.

PICTURE
***Mrs. Miniver*, MGM. Produced by Sidney Franklin.**
The Invaders, Ortus, Columbia (United Kingdom). Produced by Michael Powell.
Kings Row, Warner Bros. Produced by Hal B. Wallis.
The Magnificent Ambersons, Mercury, RKO Radio. Produced by Orson Welles.
The Pied Piper, 20th Century-Fox. Produced by Nunnally Johnson.
The Pride of the Yankees, Samuel Goldwyn Productions, RKO Radio. Produced by Samuel Goldwyn.
Random Harvest, MGM. Produced by Sidney Franklin.
The Talk of the Town, Columbia. Produced by George Stevens.
Wake Island, Paramount. Produced by Joseph Sistrom.
Yankee Doodle Dandy, Warner Bros. Produced by Jack Warner and Hal B. Wallis, with William Cagney.

ACTOR
James Cagney in *Yankee Doodle Dandy*, Warner Bros.
Ronald Colman in *Random Harvest*, MGM.
Gary Cooper in *The Pride of the Yankees*, Goldwyn, RKO Radio.
Walter Pidgeon in *Mrs. Miniver*, MGM.
Monty Woolley in *The Pied Piper*, 20th Century-Fox.

ACTRESS
Greer Garson in *Mrs. Miniver*, MGM.
Bette Davis in *Now, Voyager*, Warner Bros.
Katharine Hepburn in *Woman of the Year*, MGM.
Rosalind Russell in *My Sister Eileen*, Columbia.
Teresa Wright in *The Pride of the Yankees*, Goldwyn, RKO Radio.

SUPPORTING ACTOR
Van Heflin in *Johnny Eager*, MGM.
William Bendix in *Wake Island*, Paramount.
Walter Huston in *Yankee Doodle Dandy*, Warner Bros.
Frank Morgan in *Tortilla Flat*, MGM.
Henry Travers in *Mrs. Miniver*, MGM.

SUPPORTING ACTRESS
Teresa Wright in *Mrs. Miniver*, MGM.
Gladys Cooper in *Now, Voyager*, Warner Bros.
Agnes Moorehead in *The Magnificent Ambersons*, RKO Radio.
Susan Peters in *Random Harvest*, MGM.
May Whitty in *Mrs. Miniver*, MGM.

DIRECTOR
William Wyler for *Mrs. Miniver*, MGM.
Michael Curtiz for *Yankee Doodle Dandy*, Warner Bros.
John Farrow for *Wake Island*, Paramount.
Mervyn LeRoy for *Random Harvest*, MGM.
Sam Wood for *Kings Row*, Warner Bros.

WRITING
(Original Motion Picture Story)
Emeric Pressburger for *The Invaders*, Columbia (United Kingdom).
Irving Berlin for *Holiday Inn*, Paramount.
Robert Buckner for *Yankee Doodle Dandy*, Warner Bros.
Paul Gallico for *The Pride of the Yankees*, Goldwyn, RKO Radio.
Sidney Harmon for *The Talk of the Town*, Columbia.
(Original Screenplay)
Ring Lardner, Jr., and Michael Kanin for *Woman of the Year*, MGM.
W. R. Burnett and Frank Butler for *Wake Island*, Paramount.
Frank Butler and Don Hartman for *The Road to Morocco*, Paramount.
George Oppenheimer for *The War Against Mrs. Hadley*, MGM.
Michael Powell and Emeric Pressburger for *One of Our Aircraft Is Missing*, United Artists (United Kingdom).
(Screenplay)
Arthur Wimperis, George Froeschel, James Hilton, and

[89] At the ceremonies from 1941 through 1944, most recipients of honorary awards were given certificates instead of statuettes, in part because of the shortage of metal for making Oscars. Even winners in the competitive categories received plaster Oscar statuettes, which they were allowed to exchange for metal ones after the war.

Claudine West for Mrs. Miniver, MGM.

Rodney Ackland and Emeric Pressburger for *The Invaders,* Columbia (United Kingdom).

Irwin Shaw and Sidney Buchman for *The Talk of the Town,* Columbia.

Jo Swerling and Herman J. Mankiewicz for *The Pride of the Yankees,* Goldwyn, RKO Radio.

Claudine West, George Froeschel, and Arthur Wimperis for *Random Harvest,* MGM.

CINEMATOGRAPHY
(Black and White)

Joseph Ruttenberg for Mrs. Miniver, MGM.

Charles Clarke for *Moontide,* 20th Century-Fox.

Stanley Cortez for *The Magnificent Ambersons,* RKO Radio.

Edward Cronjager for *The Pied Piper,* 20th Century-Fox.

James Wong Howe for *Kings Row,* Warner Bros.

Rudolph Maté for *The Pride of the Yankees,* RKO Radio.

John Mescall for *Take a Letter, Darling,* Paramount.

Arthur Miller for *This Above All,* 20th Century-Fox.

Leon Shamroy for *Ten Gentlemen From West Point,* 20th Century-Fox.

Ted Tetzlaff for *The Talk of the Town,* Columbia.

(Color)

Leon Shamroy for The Black Swan, 20th Century-Fox.

Edward Cronjager and William V. Skall for *To the Shores of Tripoli,* 20th Century-Fox.

W. Howard Greene for *Jungle Book,* United Artists.

Milton Krasner, William V. Skall, and W. Howard Greene for *Arabian Nights,* Universal.

Victor Milner and William V. Skall for *Reap the Wild Wind,* Paramount.

Sol Polito for *Captains of the Clouds,* Warner Bros.

INTERIOR DECORATION
(Black and White)

This Above All, 20th Century-Fox. Richard Day, Joseph Wright; Thomas Little.

George Washington Slept Here, Warner Bros. Max Parker, Mark-Lee Kirk; Casey Roberts.

The Magnificent Ambersons, RKO Radio. Albert S. D'Agostino; Darrell Silvera, Al Fields.

The Pride of the Yankees, Goldwyn, RKO Radio. Perry Ferguson; Howard Bristol.

Random Harvest, MGM. Cedric Gibbons, Randall Duell; Edwin B. Willis, Jack Moore.

The Shanghai Gesture, United Artists. Boris Leven.

Silver Queen, United Artists. Ralph Berger; Emile Kuri.

The Spoilers, Universal. Jack Otterson, John B. Goodman; Russell A. Gausman, Edward R. Robinson.

Take a Letter, Darling, Paramount. Hans Dreier, Roland Anderson; Sam Comer.

The Talk of the Town, Columbia. Lionel Banks, Rudolph Sternad; Fay Babcock.

(Color)

My Gal Sal, 20th Century-Fox. Richard Day, Joseph Wright; Thomas Little.

Arabian Nights, Universal. Jack Otterson, Alexander Golitzen; Russell A. Gausman, Ira S. Webb.

Captains of the Clouds, Warner Bros. Ted Smith; Casey Roberts.

Jungle Book, United Artists. Vincent Korda; Julia Heron.

Reap the Wild Wind, Paramount. Hans Dreier, Roland Anderson; George Sawley.

SOUND RECORDING

Nathan Levinson for Yankee Doodle Dandy, Warner Bros.

Daniel Bloomberg for *Flying Tigers,* Republic.

Bernard B. Brown for *Arabian Nights,* Universal.

Steve Dunn for *Once Upon a Honeymoon,* RKO Radio.

James Fields, RCA Sound, for *The Gold Rush,* Chaplin, United Artists.[90]

E. H. Hansen for *This Above All,* 20th Century-Fox.

John Livadary for *You Were Never Lovelier,* Columbia.

Thomas T. Moulton for *The Pride of the Yankees,* Goldwyn, RKO Radio.

Loren Ryder for *Road to Morocco,* Paramount.

Douglas Shearer for *Mrs. Miniver,* MGM.

Sam Slyfield for *Bambi,* Disney, RKO Radio.

Jack Whitney, Sound Service Inc., for *Friendly Enemies,* United Artists.

MUSIC
(Song)

"White Christmas" from Holiday Inn, Paramount. Music and lyrics by Irving Berlin.

"Always in My Heart" from *Always in My Heart,* Warner Bros. Music by Ernesto Lecuona, lyrics by Kim Gannon.

"Dearly Beloved" from *You Were Never Lovelier,* Columbia. Music by Jerome Kern, lyrics by Johnny Mercer.

"How About You?" from *Babes on Broadway,* MGM. Music by Burton Lane, lyrics by Ralph Freed.

"It Seems I've Heard That Song Before" from *Youth on Parade,* Republic. Music by Jule Styne, lyrics by Sammy Cahn.

"I've Got a Gal in Kalamazoo" from *Orchestra Wives,* 20th Century-Fox. Music by Harry Warren, lyrics by Mack Gordon.

"Love Is a Song" from *Bambi,* Disney, RKO Radio. Music by Frank Churchill, lyrics by Larry Morey.

---

[90] Originally released in 1925, this film was rereleased in 1942 with narration, sound effects, and music, and was judged eligible for an award in this category.

"Pennies for Peppino" from *Flying With Music,* United Artists. Music by Edward Ward, lyrics by Chet Forrest and Bob Wright.

"Pig Foot Pete" from *Hellzapoppin',* Universal. Music by Gene de Paul, lyrics by Don Raye.[91]

"There's a Breeze on Lake Louise" from *The Mayor of 44th Street,* RKO Radio. Music by Harry Revel, lyrics by Mort Greene.

(Music Score of a Dramatic or Comedy Picture)[92]

Max Steiner for *Now, Voyager,* Warner Bros.

Frank Churchill and Edward Plumb for *Bambi,* Disney, RKO Radio.

Richard Hageman for *The Shanghai Gesture,* United Artists.

Leigh Harline for *The Pride of the Yankees,* Goldwyn, RKO Radio.

Werner Heymann for *To Be or Not to Be,* United Artists.

Frederick Hollander and Morris Stoloff for *The Talk of the Town,* Columbia.

Edward Kay for *Klondike Fury,* Monogram.

Alfred Newman for *The Black Swan,* 20th Century-Fox.

Miklos Rozsa for *Jungle Book,* United Artists.

Frank Skinner for *Arabian Nights,* Universal.

Herbert Stothart for *Random Harvest,* MGM.

Max Terr for *The Gold Rush,* Chaplin, United Artists.

Dimitri Tiomkin for *The Corsican Brothers,* United Artists.

Roy Webb for *I Married a Witch,* United Artists.

Roy Webb for *Joan of Paris,* RKO Radio.

Victor Young for *Flying Tigers,* Republic.

Victor Young for *Silver Queen,* United Artists.

Victor Young for *Take a Letter, Darling,* Paramount.

(Scoring of a Musical Picture)

Ray Heindorf and Heinz Roemheld for *Yankee Doodle Dandy,* Warner Bros.

Robert Emmett Dolan for *Holiday Inn,* Paramount.

Roger Edens and Georgie Stoll for *For Me and My Gal,* MGM.

Leigh Harline for *You Were Never Lovelier,* Columbia.

Alfred Newman for *My Gal Sal,* 20th Century-Fox.

Charles Previn and Hans Salter for *It Started With Eve,* Universal.

Walter Scharf for *Johnny Doughboy,* Republic.

Edward Ward for *Flying With Music,* United Artists.

FILM EDITING

Daniel Mandell for *The Pride of the Yankees,* Goldwyn, RKO Radio.

George Amy for *Yankee Doodle Dandy,* Warner Bros.

Harold F. Kress for *Mrs. Miniver,* MGM.

Otto Meyer for *The Talk of the Town,* Columbia.

Walter Thompson for *This Above All,* 20th Century-Fox.

SPECIAL EFFECTS

***Reap the Wild Wind,* Paramount. Farciot Edouart, Gordon Jennings, and William L. Pereira, photographic; Louis Mesenkop, sound.**

The Black Swan, 20th Century-Fox. Fred Sersen, photographic; Roger Heman and George Leverett, sound.

Desperate Journey, Warner Bros. Byron Haskin, photographic; Nathan Levinson, sound.

Flying Tigers, Republic. Howard Lydecker, photographic; Daniel J. Bloomberg, sound.

Invisible Agent, Universal. John Fulton, photographic; Bernard B. Brown, sound.

Jungle Book, United Artists. Lawrence Butler, photographic; William H. Wilmarth, sound.

Mrs. Miniver, MGM. A. Arnold Gillespie and Warren Newcombe, photographic; Douglas Shearer, sound.

The Navy Comes Through, RKO Radio. Vernon L. Walker, photographic; James G. Stewart, sound.

One of Our Aircraft Is Missing, United Artists (United Kingdom). Ronald Neame, photographic; C. C. Stevens, sound.

The Pride of the Yankees, Goldwyn, RKO Radio. Jack Cosgrove and Ray Binger, photographic; Thomas T. Moulton, sound.

IRVING G. THALBERG MEMORIAL AWARD
Sidney Franklin.

SPECIAL AWARDS

Charles Boyer, for his progressive cultural achievement in establishing the French Research Foundation in Los Angeles as a source of reference for the Hollywood motion picture industry.

Noël Coward, for his outstanding production achievement in *In Which We Serve.*

Metro-Goldwyn-Mayer, for its achievement in representing the American Way of Life in the production of the *Andy Hardy* series of films.

1943
Awards presented March 2, 1944.

PICTURE
***Casablanca,* Warner Bros. Produced by Hal B. Wallis.**

For Whom the Bell Tolls, Paramount. Produced by Sam Wood.

---

[91] Curiously this nominated song doesn't appear in *Hellzapoppin'.* It was introduced by Martha Raye in an Abbott and Costello comedy, *Keep 'Em Flying,* that was released by Universal in 1941, so it would have been ineligible for consideration for a 1942 award. *Hellzapoppin'* was also released by Universal, and both films featured Martha Raye and songs by Gene de Paul and Don Raye, so the mix-up may have occurred when the studio submitted its nomination in this category—as each studio was allowed to do at the time. The Academy has no record of how the mix-up occurred.

[92] Category renamed.

Heaven Can Wait, 20th Century-Fox. Produced by Ernst Lubitsch.

The Human Comedy, MGM. Produced by Clarence Brown.

In Which We Serve, Two Cities, United Artists (United Kingdom). Produced by Noël Coward.[93]

Madame Curie, MGM. Produced by Sidney Franklin.

The More the Merrier, Columbia. Produced by George Stevens.

The Ox-Bow Incident, 20th Century-Fox. Produced by Lamar Trotti.

The Song of Bernadette, 20th Century-Fox. Produced by William Perlberg.

Watch on the Rhine, Warner Bros. Produced by Hal B. Wallis.

ACTOR

Paul Lukas in *Watch on the Rhine*, Warner Bros.

Humphrey Bogart in *Casablanca*, Warner Bros.

Gary Cooper in *For Whom the Bell Tolls*, Paramount.

Walter Pidgeon in *Madame Curie*, MGM.

Mickey Rooney in *The Human Comedy*, MGM.

ACTRESS

Jennifer Jones in *The Song of Bernadette*, 20th Century-Fox.

Jean Arthur in *The More the Merrier*, Columbia.

Ingrid Bergman in *For Whom the Bell Tolls*, Paramount.

Joan Fontaine in *The Constant Nymph*, Warner Bros.

Greer Garson in *Madame Curie*, MGM.

SUPPORTING ACTOR

Charles Coburn in *The More the Merrier*, Columbia.

Charles Bickford in *The Song of Bernadette*, 20th Century-Fox.

J. Carrol Naish in *Sahara*, Columbia.

Claude Rains in *Casablanca*, Warner Bros.

Akim Tamiroff in *For Whom the Bell Tolls*, Paramount.

SUPPORTING ACTRESS

Katina Paxinou in *For Whom the Bell Tolls*, Paramount.

Gladys Cooper in *The Song of Bernadette*, 20th Century-Fox.

Paulette Goddard in *So Proudly We Hail*, Paramount.

Anne Revere in *The Song of Bernadette*, 20th Century-Fox.

Lucile Watson in *Watch on the Rhine*, Warner Bros.

DIRECTOR

Michael Curtiz for *Casablanca*, Warner Bros.

Clarence Brown for *The Human Comedy*, MGM.

Henry King for *The Song of Bernadette*, 20th Century-Fox.

Ernst Lubitsch for *Heaven Can Wait*, 20th Century-Fox.

George Stevens for *The More the Merrier*, Columbia.

WRITING

(Original Motion Picture Story)

William Saroyan for *The Human Comedy*, MGM.

Steve Fisher for *Destination Tokyo*, Warner Bros.

Guy Gilpatric for *Action in the North Atlantic*, Warner Bros.

Gordon McDonell for *Shadow of a Doubt*, Universal.

Robert Russell and Frank Ross for *The More the Merrier*, Columbia.

(Original Screenplay)

Norman Krasna for *Princess O'Rourke*, Warner Bros.

Noël Coward for *In Which We Serve*, United Artists (United Kingdom).

Lillian Hellman for *The North Star*, Goldwyn, RKO Radio.

Dudley Nichols for *Air Force*, Warner Bros.

Allan Scott for *So Proudly We Hail*, Paramount.

(Screenplay)

Julius J. Epstein, Philip G. Epstein, and Howard Koch for *Casablanca*, Warner Bros.

Dashiell Hammett for *Watch on the Rhine*, Warner Bros.

Nunnally Johnson for *Holy Matrimony*, 20th Century-Fox.

Robert Russell, Frank Ross, Richard Flournoy, and Lewis R. Foster for *The More the Merrier*, Columbia.

George Seaton for *The Song of Bernadette*, 20th Century-Fox.

CINEMATOGRAPHY

(Black and White)

Arthur Miller for *The Song of Bernadette*, 20th Century-Fox.

Arthur Edeson for *Casablanca*, Warner Bros.

Tony Gaudio for *Corvette K-225*, Universal.

James Wong Howe, Elmer Dyer, and Charles Marshall for *Air Force*, Warner Bros.

James Wong Howe for *The North Star*, Goldwyn, RKO Radio.

Charles Lang for *So Proudly We Hail*, Paramount.

Rudolph Maté for *Sahara*, Columbia.

Joseph Ruttenberg for *Madame Curie*, MGM.

John Seitz for *Five Graves to Cairo*, Paramount.

Harry Stradling for *The Human Comedy*, MGM.

(Color)

Hal Mohr and W. Howard Greene for *The Phantom of the Opera*, Universal.

Charles G. Clarke and Allen Davey for *Hello, Frisco, Hello*, 20th Century-Fox.

Edward Cronjager for *Heaven Can Wait*, 20th Century-Fox.

George Folsey for *Thousands Cheer*, MGM.

Ray Rennahan for *For Whom the Bell Tolls*, Paramount.

Leonard Smith for *Lassie Come Home*, MGM.

---

[93] Although Coward received an honorary award for this film at the 1942 ceremonies, it did not meet eligibility requirements for the competitive categories until the 1943 awards.

INTERIOR DECORATION
(Black and White)

The Song of Bernadette, 20th Century-Fox. James Basevi, William Darling; Thomas Little.

Five Graves to Cairo, Paramount. Hans Dreier, Ernst Fegte; Bertram Granger.

Flight for Freedom, RKO Radio. Albert S. D'Agostino, Carroll Clark; Darrell Silvera, Harley Miller.

Madame Curie, MGM. Cedric Gibbons, Paul Groesse; Edwin B. Willis, Hugh Hunt.

Mission to Moscow, Warner Bros. Carl Weyl; George J. Hopkins.

The North Star, Goldwyn, RKO Radio. Perry Ferguson; Howard Bristol.

(Color)

The Phantom of the Opera, Universal. John B. Goodman, Alexander Golitzen; Russell A. Gausman, Ira S. Webb.

For Whom the Bell Tolls, Paramount. Hans Dreier, Haldane Douglas; Bertram Granger.

The Gang's All Here, 20th Century-Fox. James Basevi, Joseph C. Wright; Thomas Little.

This Is the Army, Warner Bros. John Hughes, Lt. John Koenig; George J. Hopkins.

Thousands Cheer, MGM. Cedric Gibbons, Daniel Cathcart; Edwin B. Willis, Jacques Mersereau.

SOUND RECORDING

Stephen Dunn for This Land Is Mine, RKO Radio.

Daniel J. Bloomberg for *In Old Oklahoma,* Republic.

Bernard B. Brown for *The Phantom of the Opera,* Universal.

J. L. Fields, RCA Sound, for *So This Is Washington,* RKO Radio.

E. H. Hansen for *The Song of Bernadette,* 20th Century-Fox.

Nathan Levinson for *This Is the Army,* Warner Bros.

John Livadary for *Sahara,* Columbia.

Thomas T. Moulton for *The North Star,* Goldwyn, RKO Radio.

Loren L. Ryder for *Riding High,* Paramount.

Douglas Shearer for *Madame Curie,* MGM.

C. O. Slyfield for *Saludos Amigos,* Disney, RKO Radio.

Jack Whitney, Sound Service Inc., for *Hangmen Also Die,* United Artists.

MUSIC
(Song)

"You'll Never Know" from Hello, Frisco, Hello, 20th Century-Fox. Music by Harry Warren, lyrics by Mack Gordon.

"Change of Heart" from *Hit Parade of 1943,* Republic. Music by Jule Styne, lyrics by Harold Adamson.

"Happiness Is a Thing Called Joe" from *Cabin in the Sky,* MGM. Music by Harold Arlen, lyrics by E. Y. Harburg.

"My Shining Hour" from *The Sky's the Limit,* RKO Radio. Music by Harold Arlen, lyrics by Johnny Mercer.

"Saludos Amigos" from *Saludos Amigos,* Disney, RKO Radio. Music by Charles Wolcott, lyrics by Ned Washington.

"Say a Prayer for the Boys Over There" from *Hers to Hold,* Universal. Music by Jimmy McHugh, lyrics by Herb Magidson.

"That Old Black Magic" from *Star Spangled Rhythm,* Paramount. Music by Harold Arlen, lyrics by Johnny Mercer.

"They're Either Too Young or Too Old" from *Thank Your Lucky Stars,* Warner Bros. Music by Arthur Schwartz, lyrics by Frank Loesser.

"We Mustn't Say Goodbye" from *Stage Door Canteen,* United Artists. Music by James Monaco, lyrics by Al Dubin.

"You'd Be So Nice to Come Home To" from *Something to Shout About,* Columbia. Music and lyrics by Cole Porter.

(Music Score of a Dramatic or Comedy Picture)

Alfred Newman for The Song of Bernadette, 20th Century-Fox.

C. Bakaleinikoff and Roy Webb for *The Fallen Sparrow,* RKO Radio.

Phil Boutelje for *Hi Diddle Diddle,* United Artists.

Gerard Carbonara for *The Kansan,* United Artists.

Aaron Copland for *The North Star,* Goldwyn, United Artists.

Hanns Eisler for *Hangmen Also Die,* United Artists.

Louis Gruenberg and Morris Stoloff for *The Commandos Strike at Dawn,* Columbia.

Leigh Harline for *Johnny Come Lately,* United Artists.

Arthur Lange for *Lady of Burlesque,* United Artists.

Edward H. Plumb, Paul J. Smith, and Oliver G. Wallace for *Victory Through Air Power,* Disney, United Artists.

Hans J. Salter and Frank Skinner for *The Amazing Mrs. Holliday,* Universal.

Walter Scharf for *In Old Oklahoma,* Republic.

Max Steiner for *Casablanca,* Warner Bros.

Herbert Stothart for *Madame Curie,* MGM.

Dimitri Tiomkin for *The Moon and Sixpence,* United Artists.

Victor Young for *For Whom the Bell Tolls,* Paramount.

(Scoring of a Musical Picture)

Ray Heindorf for This Is the Army, Warner Bros.

Robert Emmett Dolan for *Star Spangled Rhythm,* Paramount.

Leigh Harline for *The Sky's the Limit,* RKO Radio.

Alfred Newman for *Coney Island,* 20th Century-Fox.

Edward H. Plumb, Paul J. Smith, and Charles Wolcott for *Saludos Amigos,* Disney, RKO Radio.

Frederic E. Rich for *Stage Door Canteen,* United Artists.

Walter Scharf for *Hit Parade of 1943,* Republic.

Morris Stoloff for *Something to Shout About,* Columbia.

Herbert Stothart for *Thousands Cheer,* MGM.

Edward Ward for *The Phantom of the Opera,* Universal.

FILM EDITING

George Amy for *Air Force,* Warner Bros.

Doane Harrison for *Five Graves to Cairo,* Paramount.

Owen Marks for *Casablanca,* Warner Bros.

Barbara McLean for *The Song of Bernadette,* 20th Century-Fox.

Sherman Todd and John Link for *For Whom the Bell Tolls,* Paramount.

SPECIAL EFFECTS

***Crash Dive,* 20th Century-Fox. Fred Sersen, photographic; Roger Heman, sound.**

Air Force, Warner Bros. Hans Koenekamp and Rex Wimpy, photographic; Nathan Levinson, sound.

Bombardier, RKO Radio. Vernon L. Walker, photographic; James G. Stewart and Roy Granville, sound.

The North Star, Goldwyn, RKO Radio. Clarence Slifer and R. O. Binger, photographic; Thomas T. Moulton, sound.

So Proudly We Hail, Paramount. Farciot Edouart and Gordon Jennings, photographic; George Dutton, sound.

Stand By for Action, MGM. A. Arnold Gillespie and Donald Jahraus, photographic; Michael Steinore, sound.

IRVING G. THALBERG MEMORIAL AWARD

Hal B. Wallis.

SPECIAL AWARD

George Pal, for the development of novel methods and techniques in the production of short subjects known as Puppetoons.[94]

1944

Awards presented March 15, 1945.

PICTURE

***Going My Way,* Paramount. Produced by Leo McCarey.**

Double Indemnity, Paramount. Produced by Joseph Sistrom.

Gaslight, MGM. Produced by Arthur Hornblow, Jr.

Since You Went Away, Selznick International Pictures, United Artists. Produced by David O. Selznick.

Wilson, 20th Century-Fox. Produced by Darryl F. Zanuck.

ACTOR

Bing Crosby in *Going My Way,* Paramount.

Charles Boyer in *Gaslight,* MGM.

Barry Fitzgerald in *Going My Way,* Paramount.

Cary Grant in *None but the Lonely Heart,* RKO Radio.

Alexander Knox in *Wilson,* 20th Century-Fox.

ACTRESS

Ingrid Bergman in *Gaslight,* MGM.

Claudette Colbert in *Since You Went Away,* Selznick, United Artists.

Bette Davis in *Mr. Skeffington,* Warner Bros.

Greer Garson in *Mrs. Parkington,* MGM.

Barbara Stanwyck in *Double Indemnity,* Paramount.

SUPPORTING ACTOR

Barry Fitzgerald[95] in *Going My Way,* Paramount.

Hume Cronyn in *The Seventh Cross,* MGM.

Claude Rains in *Mr. Skeffington,* Warner Bros.

Clifton Webb in *Laura,* 20th Century-Fox.

Monty Woolley in *Since You Went Away,* Selznick, United Artists.

SUPPORTING ACTRESS

Ethel Barrymore[96] in *None but the Lonely Heart,* RKO Radio.

Jennifer Jones in *Since You Went Away,* Selznick, United Artists.

Angela Lansbury in *Gaslight,* MGM.

Aline MacMahon in *Dragon Seed,* MGM.

Agnes Moorehead in *Mrs. Parkington,* MGM.

DIRECTOR

Leo McCarey for *Going My Way,* Paramount.

Alfred Hitchcock for *Lifeboat,* 20th Century-Fox.

Henry King for *Wilson,* 20th Century-Fox.

Otto Preminger for *Laura,* 20th Century-Fox.

Billy Wilder for *Double Indemnity,* Paramount.

WRITING

(Original Motion Picture Story)

Leo McCarey[97] for *Going My Way,* Paramount.

Chandler Sprague and David Boehm for *A Guy Named Joe,* MGM.

Edward Doherty and Jules Schermer for *The Sullivans,* 20th Century-Fox.

Alfred Neumann and Joseph Than for *None Shall Escape,* Columbia.

John Steinbeck for *Lifeboat,* 20th Century-Fox.

(Original Screenplay)

Lamar Trotti for *Wilson,* 20th Century-Fox.

Jerome Cady for *Wing and a Prayer,* 20th Century-Fox.

Richard Connell and Gladys Lehman for *Two Girls and a Sailor,* MGM.

---

[94] Pal received a plaque.

[95] Only person to receive two acting nominations for a single performance. Academy rules were subsequently changed to prevent it from happening again.

[96] Her brother Lionel received an award as best actor (1931–32), making the two Barrymores the only brother and sister to receive acting Oscars. Shirley MacLaine and her brother, Warren Beatty, have both received multiple acting nominations, but while MacLaine has received the Oscar as best actress (1983), Beatty's sole award is for directing (1981).

[97] First person to receive Oscars as producer, director, and writer for a single film. Billy Wilder (1960), Francis Ford Coppola (1974), and James L. Brooks (1983) also achieved this distinction.

Preston Sturges for *Hail the Conquering Hero,* Paramount.

Preston Sturges for *The Miracle of Morgan's Creek,* Paramount.

(Screenplay)

Frank Butler and Frank Cavett for *Going My Way,* Paramount.

Irving Brecher and Fred F. Finkelhoffe for *Meet Me in St. Louis,* MGM.

Jay Dratler, Samuel Hoffenstein, and Betty Reinhardt for *Laura,* 20th Century-Fox.

John Van Druten, Walter Reisch, and John L. Balderston for *Gaslight,* MGM.

Billy Wilder and Raymond Chandler for *Double Indemnity,* Paramount.

CINEMATOGRAPHY

(Black and White)

Joseph LaShelle for *Laura,* 20th Century-Fox.

Stanley Cortez and Lee Garmes for *Since You Went Away,* Selznick, United Artists.

George Folsey for *The White Cliffs of Dover,* MGM.

Charles Lang for *The Uninvited,* Paramount.

Lionel Lindon for *Going My Way,* Paramount.

Glen MacWilliams for *Lifeboat,* 20th Century-Fox.

Joseph Ruttenberg for *Gaslight,* MGM.

John Seitz for *Double Indemnity,* Paramount.

Robert Surtees and Harold Rosson for *Thirty Seconds Over Tokyo,* MGM.

Sidney Wagner for *Dragon Seed,* MGM.

(Color)

Leon Shamroy for *Wilson,* 20th Century-Fox.

Edward Cronjager for *Home in Indiana,* 20th Century-Fox.

George Folsey for *Meet Me in St. Louis,* MGM.

Rudolph Maté and Allen M. Davey for *Cover Girl,* Columbia.

Ray Rennahan for *Lady in the Dark,* Paramount.

Charles Rosher for *Kismet,* MGM.

INTERIOR DECORATION

(Black and White)

Gaslight, MGM. Cedric Gibbons, William Ferrari; Edwin B. Willis, Paul Huldschinsky.

Address Unknown, Columbia. Lionel Banks, Walter Holscher; Joseph Kish.

The Adventures of Mark Twain, Warner Bros. John J. Hughes; Fred MacLean.

Casanova Brown, RKO Radio. Perry Ferguson; Julia Heron.

Laura, 20th Century-Fox. Lyle Wheeler, Leland Fuller; Thomas Little.

No Time for Love, Paramount. Hans Dreier, Robert Usher; Sam Comer.

Since You Went Away, Selznick, United Artists. Mark-Lee Kirk; Victor A. Gangelin.

Step Lively, RKO Radio. Albert S. D'Agostino, Carroll Clark; Darrell Silvera, Claude Carpenter.

(Color)

Wilson, 20th Century-Fox. Wiard Ihnen; Thomas Little.

The Climax, Universal. John B. Goodman, Alexander Golitzen; Russell A. Gausman, Ira S. Webb.

Cover Girl, Columbia. Lionel Banks, Cary Odell; Fay Babcock.

The Desert Song, Warner Bros. Charles Novi; Jack McConaghy.

Kismet, MGM. Cedric Gibbons, Daniel B. Cathcart; Edwin B. Willis, Richard Pefferle.

Lady in the Dark, Paramount. Hans Dreier, Raoul Pène du Bois; Ray Moyer.

The Princess and the Pirate, RKO Radio. Ernst Fegte; Howard Bristol.

SOUND RECORDING

E. H. Hansen for *Wilson,* 20th Century-Fox.

Daniel J. Bloomberg for *Brazil,* Republic.

Bernard B. Brown for *His Butler's Sister,* Universal.

W. M. Dalgliesh, RCA Sound, for *Voice in the Wind,* United Artists.

Stephen Dunn for *Music in Manhattan,* RKO Radio.

Nathan Levinson for *Hollywood Canteen,* Warner Bros.

John Livadary for *Cover Girl,* Columbia.

Thomas T. Moulton, Samuel Goldwyn Studio Sound Dept., for *Casanova Brown,* RKO Radio.

Loren L. Ryder for *Double Indemnity,* Paramount.

Douglas Shearer for *Kismet,* MGM.

Jack Whitney, Sound Service Inc., for *It Happened Tomorrow,* United Artists.

MUSIC

(Song)

"Swinging on a Star" from *Going My Way,* Paramount. Music by James Van Heusen, lyrics by Johnny Burke.

"I Couldn't Sleep a Wink Last Night" from *Higher and Higher,* RKO Radio. Music by Jimmy McHugh, lyrics by Harold Adamson.

"I'll Walk Alone" from *Follow the Boys,* Universal. Music by Jule Styne, lyrics by Sammy Cahn.

"I'm Making Believe" from *Sweet and Lowdown,* 20th Century-Fox. Music by James V. Monaco, lyrics by Mack Gordon.

"Long Ago and Far Away" from *Cover Girl,* Columbia. Music by Jerome Kern, lyrics by Ira Gershwin.

"Now I Know" from *Up in Arms,* RKO Radio. Music by Harold Arlen, lyrics by Ted Koehler.

"Remember Me to Carolina" from *Minstrel Man,* PRC. Music by Harry Revel, lyrics by Paul Webster.

"Rio de Janeiro" from *Brazil,* Republic. Music by Ary Barroso, lyrics by Ned Washington.

"Silver Shadows and Golden Dreams" from *Lady, Let's Dance,* Monogram. Music by Lew Pollack, lyrics by Charles Newman.

"Sweet Dreams Sweetheart" from *Hollywood Canteen,* Warner Bros. Music by M. K. Jerome, lyrics by Ted Koehler.

"Too Much in Love" from *Song of the Open Road,* United Artists. Music by Walter Kent, lyrics by Kim Gannon.

"The Trolley Song" from *Meet Me in St.*

Louis, MGM. Music and lyrics by Ralph Blane and Hugh Martin.

(Music Score of a Dramatic or Comedy Picture)

Max Steiner for *Since You Went Away,* Selznick, United Artists.

C. Bakaleinikoff and Hanns Eisler for *None but the Lonely Heart,* RKO Radio.

Karl Hajos for *Summer Storm,* United Artists.

Franke Harling for *Three Russian Girls,* United Artists.

Arthur Lange for *Casanova Brown,* RKO Radio.

Michel Michelet for *Voice in the Wind,* United Artists.

Michel Michelet and Edward Paul for *The Hairy Ape,* United Artists.

Alfred Newman for *Wilson,* 20th Century-Fox.

Edward Paul for *Up in Mabel's Room,* Small, United Artists.

Frederic Efrem Rich for *Jack London,* United Artists.

David Rose for *The Princess and the Pirate,* RKO Radio.

Miklos Rozsa for *Double Indemnity,* Paramount.

Miklos Rozsa for *Woman of the Town,* United Artists.

H. J. Salter for *Christmas Holiday,* Universal.

Walter Scharf and Roy Webb for *The Fighting Seabees,* Republic.

Max Steiner for *The Adventures of Mark Twain,* Warner Bros.

Morris Stoloff and Ernst Toch for *Address Unknown,* Columbia.

Robert Stolz for *It Happened Tomorrow,* United Artists.

Herbert Stothart for *Kismet,* MGM.

Dimitri Tiomkin for *The Bridge of San Luis Rey,* United Artists.

(Scoring of a Musical Picture)

Carmen Dragon and Morris Stoloff for *Cover Girl,* Columbia.

C. Bakaleinikoff for *Higher and Higher,* RKO Radio.

Robert Emmett Dolan for *Lady in the Dark,* Paramount.

Leo Erody and Ferde Grofé for *Minstrel Man,* PRC.

Louis Forbes and Ray Heindorf for *Up in Arms,* RKO Radio.

Ray Heindorf for *Hollywood Canteen,* Warner Bros.

Werner R. Heymann and Kurt Weill for *Knickerbocker Holiday,* United Artists.

Edward Kay for *Lady Let's Dance,* Monogram.

Mahlon Merrick for *Sensations of 1945,* United Artists.

Alfred Newman for *Irish Eyes Are Smiling,* 20th Century-Fox.

Charles Previn for *Song of the Open Road,* United Artists.

H. J. Salter for *The Merry Monahans,* Universal.

Walter Scharf for *Brazil,* Republic.

Georgie Stoll for *Meet Me in St. Louis,* MGM.

FILM EDITING

Barbara McLean for *Wilson,* 20th Century-Fox.

Roland Gross for *None but the Lonely Heart,* RKO Radio.

Hal C. Kern and James E. Newcom for *Since You Went Away,* Selznick, United Artists.

Owen Marks for *Janie,* Warner Bros.

Leroy Stone for *Going My Way,* Paramount.

SPECIAL EFFECTS

Thirty Seconds Over Tokyo, MGM. A. Arnold Gillespie, Donald Jahraus, and Warren Newcombe, photographic; Douglas Shearer, sound.

The Adventures of Mark Twain, Warner Bros. Paul Detlefsen and John Crouse, photographic; Nathan Levinson, sound.

Days of Glory, RKO Radio. Vernon L. Walker, photographic; James G. Stewart and Roy Granville, sound.

Secret Command, Columbia. David Allen, Ray Cory, and Robert Wright, photographic; Russell Malmgren and Harry Kusnick, sound.

Since You Went Away, Selznick, United Artists. John R. Cosgrove, photographic; Arthur Johns, sound.

The Story of Dr. Wassell, Paramount. Farciot Edouart and Gordon Jennings, photographic; George Dutton, sound.

Wilson, 20th Century-Fox. Fred Sersen, photographic; Roger Heman, sound.

IRVING G. THALBERG MEMORIAL AWARD

Darryl F. Zanuck.

SPECIAL AWARDS

Margaret O'Brien, outstanding child actress of 1944.[98]

Bob Hope, for his many services to the Academy.[99]

1945

Awards presented March 7, 1946.

PICTURE

The Lost Weekend, Paramount. Produced by Charles Brackett.

Anchors Aweigh, MGM. Produced by Joe Pasternak.

The Bells of St. Mary's, Rainbow Productions, RKO Radio. Produced by Leo McCarey.[100]

Mildred Pierce, Warner Bros. Produced by Jerry Wald.

Spellbound, Selznick International Pictures, United Artists. Produced by David O. Selznick.

ACTOR

Ray Milland in *The Lost Weekend,* Paramount.

---

[98] The Academy resumed its practice of honoring child stars with miniature Oscars.
[99] Hope's second honorary award was a life membership in the Academy.
[100] First sequel (to 1944 best picture winner *Going My Way*) to be nominated for best picture.

Bing Crosby in *The Bells of St. Mary's*, RKO Radio.[101]

Gene Kelly in *Anchors Aweigh*, MGM.

Gregory Peck in *The Keys of the Kingdom*, 20th Century-Fox.

Cornel Wilde in *A Song to Remember*, Columbia.

ACTRESS

Joan Crawford in *Mildred Pierce*, Warner Bros.

Ingrid Bergman in *The Bells of St. Mary's*, RKO Radio.

Greer Garson in *The Valley of Decision*, MGM.

Jennifer Jones in *Love Letters*, Paramount.

Gene Tierney in *Leave Her to Heaven*, 20th Century-Fox.

SUPPORTING ACTOR

James Dunn in *A Tree Grows in Brooklyn*, 20th Century-Fox.

Michael Chekhov in *Spellbound*, Selznick, United Artists.

John Dall in *The Corn Is Green*, Warner Bros.

Robert Mitchum in *The Story of G.I. Joe*, United Artists.

J. Carrol Naish in *A Medal for Benny*, Paramount.

SUPPORTING ACTRESS

Anne Revere in *National Velvet*, MGM.

Eve Arden in *Mildred Pierce*, Warner Bros.

Ann Blyth in *Mildred Pierce*, Warner Bros.

Angela Lansbury in *The Picture of Dorian Gray*, MGM.

Joan Lorring in *The Corn Is Green*, Warner Bros.

DIRECTOR

Billy Wilder for *The Lost Weekend*, Paramount.

Clarence Brown for *National Velvet*, MGM.

Alfred Hitchcock for *Spellbound*, Selznick, United Artists.

Leo McCarey for *The Bells of St. Mary's*, RKO Radio.

Jean Renoir for *The Southerner*, United Artists.

WRITING

(Original Motion Picture Story)

Charles G. Booth for *The House on 92nd Street*, 20th Century-Fox.

Alvah Bessie for *Objective, Burma*, Warner Bros.

Ernst Marischka for *A Song to Remember*, Columbia.

Thomas Monroe and Laszlo Gorog for *The Affairs of Susan*, Paramount.

John Steinbeck and Jack Wagner for *A Medal for Benny*, Paramount.

(Original Screenplay)

Richard Schweizer for *Marie-Louise*, Praesens Films (Switzerland).[102]

Myles Connolly for *Music for Millions*, MGM.

Milton Holmes for *Salty O'Rourke*, Paramount.

Harry Kurnitz for *What Next, Corporal Hargrove?*, MGM.

Philip Yordan for *Dillinger*, Monogram.

(Screenplay)

Charles Brackett and Billy Wilder for *The Lost Weekend*, Paramount.

Leopold Atlas, Guy Endore, and Philip Stevenson for *The Story of G.I. Joe*, United Artists.

Albert Maltz for *Pride of the Marines*, Warner Bros.

Ranald MacDougall for *Mildred Pierce*, Warner Bros.

Tess Slesinger and Frank Davis for *A Tree Grows in Brooklyn*, 20th Century-Fox.

CINEMATOGRAPHY

(Black and White)

Harry Stradling for *The Picture of Dorian Gray*, MGM.

George Barnes for *Spellbound*, Selznick, United Artists.

Ernest Haller for *Mildred Pierce*, Warner Bros.

Arthur Miller for *The Keys of the Kingdom*, 20th Century-Fox.

John F. Seitz for *The Lost Weekend*, Paramount.

(Color)

Leon Shamroy for *Leave Her to Heaven*, 20th Century-Fox.

George Barnes for *The Spanish Main*, RKO Radio.

Tony Gaudio and Allen M. Davey for *A Song to Remember*, Columbia.

Robert Planck and Charles Boyle for *Anchors Aweigh*, MGM.

Leonard Smith for *National Velvet*, MGM.

INTERIOR DECORATION

(Black and White)

Blood on the Sun, United Artists. Wiard Ihnen; A. Roland Fields.

Experiment Perilous, RKO Radio. Albert S. D'Agostino, Jack Okey; Darrell Silvera, Claude Carpenter.

The Keys of the Kingdom, 20th Century-Fox. James Basevi, William Darling; Thomas Little, Frank E. Hughes.

Love Letters, Paramount. Hans Dreier, Roland Anderson; Sam Comer, Ray Moyer.

The Picture of Dorian Gray, MGM. Cedric Gibbons, Hans Peters; Edwin B. Willis, Hugh Hunt, John Bonar.

(Color)

Frenchman's Creek, Paramount. Hans Dreier, Ernst Fegte; Sam Comer.

Leave Her to Heaven, 20th Century-Fox. Lyle Wheeler, Maurice Ransford; Thomas Little.

National Velvet, MGM. Cedric Gibbons, Urie McCleary; Edwin B. Willis, Mildred Griffiths.

San Antonio, Warner Bros. Ted Smith; Jack McConaghy.

A Thousand and One Nights, Columbia.

---

[101] First actor to be nominated for playing the same character in two different films. (He won the 1944 best actor Oscar as Father O'Malley in *Going My Way*.) Others who have received nominations for playing the same character twice are Paul Newman as Fast Eddie Felson in *The Hustler* (1961) and *The Color of Money* (1986), Peter O'Toole as Henry II in *Becket* (1964) and *The Lion in Winter* (1968), and Al Pacino as Michael Corleone in *The Godfather* (1972) and *The Godfather, Part II* (1974).

[102] First writing award to go to a foreign language film.

Stephen Goosson, Rudolph Sternad; Frank Tuttle.

SOUND RECORDING

Stephen Dunn for *The Bells of St. Mary's*, RKO Radio.

Daniel J. Bloomberg for *Flame of Barbary Coast*, Republic.

Bernard B. Brown for *Lady on a Train*, Universal.

Nathan Levinson for *Rhapsody in Blue*, Warner Bros.

John Livadary for *A Song to Remember*, Columbia.

Thomas T. Moulton for *Leave Her to Heaven*, 20th Century-Fox.

Loren L. Ryder for *The Unseen*, Paramount.

Gordon Sawyer, Samuel Goldwyn Studio Sound Dept., for *Wonder Man*, RKO Radio.

Douglas Shearer for *They Were Expendable*, MGM.

C. O. Slyfield for *The Three Caballeros*, Disney, RKO Radio.

Jack Whitney, General Service, for *The Southerner*, United Artists.

W. V. Wolfe, RCA Sound, for *Three Is a Family*, United Artists.

MUSIC

(Song)

"It Might As Well Be Spring" from *State Fair*, 20th Century-Fox. Music by Richard Rodgers, lyrics by Oscar Hammerstein II.

"Ac-cent-tchu-ate the Positive" from *Here Come the Waves*, Paramount. Music by Harold Arlen, lyrics by Johnny Mercer.

"Anywhere" from *Tonight and Every Night*, Columbia. Music by Jule Styne, lyrics by Sammy Cahn.

"Aren't You Glad You're You?" from *The Bells of St. Mary's*, RKO Radio. Music by James Van Heusen, lyrics by Johnny Burke.

"The Cat and the Canary" from *Why Girls Leave Home*, PRC. Music by Jay Livingston, lyrics by Ray Evans.

"Endlessly" from *Earl Carroll Vanities*, Republic. Music by Walter Kent, lyrics by Kim Gannon.

"I Fall in Love Too Easily" from *Anchors Aweigh*, MGM. Music by Jule Styne, lyrics by Sammy Cahn.

"I'll Buy That Dream" from *Sing Your Way Home*, RKO Radio. Music by Allie Wrubel, lyrics by Herb Magidson.

"Linda" from *The Story of G.I. Joe*, United Artists. Music and lyrics by Ann Ronell.

"Love Letters" from *Love Letters*, Paramount. Music by Victor Young, lyrics by Edward Heyman.

"More and More" from *Can't Help Singing*, Universal. Music by Jerome Kern, lyrics by E. Y. Harburg.

"Sleighride in July" from *Belle of the Yukon*, RKO Radio. Music by James Van Heusen, lyrics by Johnny Burke.

"So in Love" from *Wonder Man*, RKO Radio. Music by David Rose, lyrics by Leo Robin.

"Some Sunday Morning" from *San Antonio*, Warner Bros. Music by Ray Heindorf and M. K. Jerome, lyrics by Ted Koehler.

(Music Score of a Dramatic or Comedy Picture)

Miklos Rozsa for *Spellbound*, Selznick, United Artists.

Daniele Amfitheatrof for *Guest Wife*, United Artists.

Louis Applebaum and Ann Ronell for *The Story of G.I. Joe*, United Artists.

Dale Butts and Morton Scott for *Flame of the Barbary Coast*, Republic.

Robert Emmett Dolan for *The Bells of St. Mary's*, RKO Radio.

Lou Forbes for *Brewster's Millions*, United Artists.

Hugo Friedhofer and Arthur Lange for *The Woman in the Window*, RKO Radio.

Karl Hajos for *The Man Who Walked Alone*, PRC.

Werner Janssen for *Captain Kidd*, United Artists.

Werner Janssen for *Guest in the House*, United Artists.

Werner Janssen for *The Southerner*, United Artists.

Edward J. Kay for *G.I. Honeymoon*, Monogram.

Alfred Newman for *The Keys of the Kingdom*, 20th Century-Fox.

Miklos Rozsa for *The Lost Weekend*, Paramount.

Miklos Rozsa and Morris Stoloff for *A Song to Remember*, Columbia.

H. J. Salter for *This Love of Ours*, Universal.

Herbert Stothart for *The Valley of Decision*, MGM.

Alexander Tansman for *Paris, Underground*, United Artists.

Franz Waxman for *Objective, Burma*, Warner Bros.

Roy Webb for *The Enchanted Cottage*, RKO Radio.

Victor Young for *Love Letters*, Paramount.

(Scoring of a Musical Picture)

Georgie Stoll for *Anchors Aweigh*, MGM.

Robert Emmett Dolan for *Incendiary Blonde*, Paramount.

Lou Forbes and Ray Heindorf for *Wonder Man*, Goldwyn, RKO Radio.

Walter Greene for *Why Girls Leave Home*, PRC.

Ray Heindorf and Max Steiner for *Rhapsody in Blue*, Warner Bros.

Charles Henderson and Alfred Newman for *State Fair*, 20th Century-Fox.

Edward J. Kay for *Sunbonnet Sue*, Monogram.

Jerome Kern and H. J. Salter for *Can't Help Singing*, Universal.

Arthur Lange for *Belle of the Yukon*, RKO Radio.

Edward Plumb, Paul J. Smith, and Charles Wolcott for *The Three Caballeros*, Disney, RKO Radio.

Morton Scott for *Hitchhike to Happiness*, Republic.

Marlin Skiles and Morris Stoloff for *Tonight and Every Night*, Columbia.

FILM EDITING

Robert J. Kern for *National Velvet*, MGM.

George Amy for *Objective, Burma*, Warner Bros.

Doane Harrison for *The Lost Weekend*, Paramount.

Harry Marker for *The Bells of St. Mary's*, RKO Radio.

Charles Nelson for *A Song to Remember*, Columbia.

SPECIAL EFFECTS

Wonder Man, RKO Radio. John Fulton, photographic; Arthur W. Johns, sound.

Captain Eddie, 20th Century-Fox. Fred Sersen and Sol Halprin, photographic; Roger Heman and Harry Leonard, sound.

Spellbound, Selznick, United Artists. Jack Cosgrove, photographic.

They Were Expendable, MGM. A. Arnold Gillespie, Donald Jahraus, and Robert A. MacDonald, photographic; Michael Steinore, sound.

A Thousand and One Nights, Columbia. L. W. Butler, photographic; Ray Bomba, sound.

SPECIAL AWARDS

Walter Wanger, for his six years service as president of the Academy of Motion Picture Arts and Sciences.[103]

Peggy Ann Garner, outstanding child actress of 1945.

***The House I Live In*, tolerance short subject, produced by Frank Ross and Mervyn LeRoy; directed by Mervyn LeRoy; screenplay by Albert Maltz; song "The House I Live In," music by Earl Robinson, lyrics by Lewis Allen; starring Frank Sinatra; released by RKO Radio.**[104]

Republic Studio, Daniel J. Bloomberg and the Republic Sound Department, for the building of an outstanding musical scoring auditorium which provides optimum recording conditions and combines all elements of acoustic and engineering design.[105]

1946
Awards presented March 13, 1947.

PICTURE

***The Best Years of Our Lives*, Samuel Goldwyn Productions, RKO Radio. Produced by Samuel Goldwyn.**

Henry V, J. Arthur Rank-Two Cities Films, United Artists (United Kingdom). Produced by Laurence Olivier.

It's a Wonderful Life, Liberty Films, RKO Radio. Produced by Frank Capra.

The Razor's Edge, 20th Century-Fox. Produced by Darryl F. Zanuck.

The Yearling, MGM. Produced by Sidney Franklin.

ACTOR

Fredric March in *The Best Years of Our Lives*, Goldwyn, RKO Radio.

Laurence Olivier in *Henry V*, Rank-Two Cities, United Artists (United Kingdom).

Larry Parks in *The Jolson Story*, Columbia.

Gregory Peck in *The Yearling*, MGM.

James Stewart in *It's a Wonderful Life*, RKO Radio.

ACTRESS

Olivia de Havilland in *To Each His Own*, Paramount.

Celia Johnson in *Brief Encounter*, Universal-International (United Kingdom).

Jennifer Jones in *Duel in the Sun*, Selznick Releasing Organization.

Rosalind Russell in *Sister Kenny*, RKO Radio.

Jane Wyman in *The Yearling*, MGM.

SUPPORTING ACTOR

Harold Russell in *The Best Years of Our Lives*, Goldwyn, RKO Radio.

Charles Coburn in *The Green Years*, MGM.

William Demarest in *The Jolson Story*, Columbia.

Claude Rains in *Notorious*, RKO Radio.

Clifton Webb in *The Razor's Edge*, 20th Century-Fox.

SUPPORTING ACTRESS

Anne Baxter in *The Razor's Edge*, 20th Century-Fox.

Ethel Barrymore in *The Spiral Staircase*, RKO Radio.

Lillian Gish in *Duel in the Sun*, Selznick Releasing Organization.

Flora Robson in *Saratoga Trunk*, Warner Bros.

Gale Sondergaard in *Anna and the King of Siam*, 20th Century-Fox.

DIRECTOR

William Wyler for *The Best Years of Our Lives*, Goldwyn, RKO Radio.

Clarence Brown for *The Yearling*, MGM.[106]

Frank Capra for *It's a Wonderful Life*, RKO Radio.

David Lean for *Brief Encounter*, Universal-International (United Kingdom).

Robert Siodmak for *The Killers*, Universal.

WRITING

(Original Motion Picture Story)

Clemence Dane for *Vacation From Marriage*, MGM (United Kingdom).

Charles Brackett for *To Each His Own*, Paramount.

Jack Patrick for *The Strange Love of Martha Ivers*, Paramount.

Vladimir Pozner for *The Dark Mirror*, Universal-International.

Victor Trivas for *The Stranger*, RKO Radio.

(Original Screenplay)

---

[103] Wanger received a plaque.

[104] In this short film, Sinatra deters some bullies from roughing up a foreign kid. Maltz, the screenwriter responsible for this fable about tolerance, was later imprisoned as one of the Hollywood Ten for his refusal to testify about communism in the film industry.

[105] The principals were given certificates.

[106] Brown's sixth nomination without a win sets a record among directors for unsuccessful nominations.

Muriel Box and Sydney Box for *The Seventh Veil*, **Universal (United Kingdom).**

Raymond Chandler for *The Blue Dahlia*, Paramount.

Ben Hecht for *Notorious*, RKO Radio.

Norman Panama and Melvin Frank for *The Road to Utopia*, Paramount.

Jacques Prévert for *Children of Paradise*, Tricolore (France).

(Screenplay)

Robert E. Sherwood for *The Best Years of Our Lives*, **Goldwyn, RKO Radio.**

Sergio Amidei and Federico Fellini for *Open City*, Mayer-Burstyn (Italy).

Talbot Jennings and Sally Benson for *Anna and the King of Siam*, 20th Century-Fox.

David Lean, Anthony Havelock-Allan, and Ronald Neame for *Brief Encounter*, Universal-International (United Kingdom).

Anthony Veiller for *The Killers*, Hellinger, Universal-International.

CINEMATOGRAPHY

(Black and White)

Arthur Miller for *Anna and the King of Siam*, **20th Century-Fox.**

George Folsey for *The Green Years*, MGM.

(Color)

Charles Rosher, Leonard Smith, and Arthur Arling for *The Yearling*, **MGM.**

Joseph Walker for *The Jolson Story*, Columbia.

INTERIOR DECORATION

(Black and White)

Anna and the King of Siam, **20th Century-Fox. Lyle Wheeler, William Darling; Thomas Little, Frank E. Hughes.**

Kitty, Paramount. Hans Dreier, Walter Tyler; Sam Comer, Ray Moyer.

The Razor's Edge, 20th Century-Fox.

Richard Day, Nathan Juran; Thomas Little, Paul S. Fox.

(Color)

The Yearling, **MGM. Cedric Gibbons, Paul Groesse; Edwin B. Willis.**

Caesar and Cleopatra, United Artists (United Kingdom). John Bryan.

Henry V, United Artists (United Kingdom). Paul Sheriff, Carmen Dillon.

SOUND RECORDING

John Livadary, *The Jolson Story*, **Columbia.**

John Aalberg, *It's a Wonderful Life*, RKO Radio.

Gordon Sawyer, *The Best Years of Our Lives*, Goldwyn, RKO Radio.

MUSIC

(Song)

"On the Atchison, Topeka and Santa Fe" from *The Harvey Girls*, **MGM. Music by Harry Warren, lyrics by Johnny Mercer.**

"All Through the Day" from *Centennial Summer*, 20th Century-Fox. Music by Jerome Kern, lyrics by Oscar Hammerstein II.

"I Can't Begin to Tell You" from *The Dolly Sisters*, 20th Century-Fox. Music by James Monaco, lyrics by Mack Gordon.

"Ole Buttermilk Sky" from *Canyon Passage*, Universal. Music by Hoagy Carmichael, lyrics by Jack Brooks.

"You Keep Coming Back Like a Song" from *Blue Skies*, Paramount. Music and lyrics by Irving Berlin.

(Music Score of a Dramatic or Comedy Picture)

Hugo Friedhofer for *The Best Years of Our Lives*, **Goldwyn, RKO Radio.**

Bernard Herrmann for *Anna and the King of Siam*, 20th Century-Fox.

Miklos Rozsa for *The Killers*, Universal.

William Walton for *Henry V*, United Artists (United Kingdom).

Franz Waxman for *Humoresque*, Warner Bros.

(Scoring of a Musical Picture)

Morris Stoloff for *The Jolson Story*, **Columbia.**

Robert Emmett Dolan for *Blue Skies*, Paramount.

Lennie Hayton for *The Harvey Girls*, MGM.

Ray Heindorf and Max Steiner for *Night and Day*, Warner Bros.

Alfred Newman for *Centennial Summer*, 20th Century-Fox.

FILM EDITING

Daniel Mandell for *The Best Years of Our Lives*, **Goldwyn, RKO Radio.**

Arthur Hilton for *The Killers*, Universal.

William Hornbeck for *It's a Wonderful Life*, RKO Radio.

Harold Kress for *The Yearling*, MGM.

William Lyon for *The Jolson Story*, Columbia.

SPECIAL EFFECTS

Blithe Spirit, **United Artists (United Kingdom). Thomas Howard, visual.**

A Stolen Life, Warner Bros. William McGann, visual; Nathan Levinson, audible.

IRVING G. THALBERG MEMORIAL AWARD

Samuel Goldwyn.

SPECIAL AWARDS

Laurence Olivier, for his outstanding achievement as actor, producer and director in bringing *Henry V* **to the screen.**

Harold Russell, for bringing hope and courage to his fellow veterans through his appearance in *The Best Years of Our Lives*.[107]

Ernst Lubitsch, for his distinguished

---

[107] This honorary award made Russell, who also won the competition for supporting actor, the only performer to receive two Oscars for a single role. In 1992 he made news when he sold one of the Oscars to pay his wife's medical expenses.

contributions to the art of the motion picture.[108]

Claude Jarman, Jr., outstanding child actor of 1946.

1947
Awards presented March 20, 1948.

PICTURE

Gentleman's Agreement, 20th Century-Fox. Produced by Darryl F. Zanuck.

The Bishop's Wife, Samuel Goldwyn Productions, RKO Radio. Produced by Samuel Goldwyn.

Crossfire, RKO Radio. Produced by Adrian Scott.

Great Expectations, J. Arthur Rank-Cineguild, Universal-International (United Kingdom). Produced by Ronald Neame.

Miracle on 34th Street, 20th Century-Fox. Produced by William Perlberg.

ACTOR

Ronald Colman in A Double Life, Universal-International.

John Garfield in Body and Soul, United Artists.

Gregory Peck in Gentleman's Agreement, 20th Century-Fox.

William Powell in Life With Father, Warner Bros.

Michael Redgrave in Mourning Becomes Electra, RKO Radio.

ACTRESS

Loretta Young in The Farmer's Daughter, RKO Radio.

Joan Crawford in Possessed, Warner Bros.

Susan Hayward in Smash Up—the Story of a Woman, Universal-International.

Dorothy McGuire in Gentleman's Agreement, 20th Century-Fox.

Rosalind Russell in Mourning Becomes Electra, RKO Radio.

SUPPORTING ACTOR

Edmund Gwenn in Miracle on 34th Street, 20th Century-Fox.

Charles Bickford in The Farmer's Daughter, RKO Radio.

Thomas Gomez in Ride the Pink Horse, Universal-International.

Robert Ryan in Crossfire, RKO Radio.

Richard Widmark in Kiss of Death, 20th Century-Fox.

SUPPORTING ACTRESS

Celeste Holm in Gentleman's Agreement, 20th Century-Fox.

Ethel Barrymore in The Paradine Case, Selznick Releasing Organization.

Gloria Grahame in Crossfire, RKO Radio.

Marjorie Main in The Egg and I, Universal-International.

Anne Revere in Gentleman's Agreement, 20th Century-Fox.

DIRECTOR

Elia Kazan for Gentleman's Agreement, 20th Century-Fox.

George Cukor for A Double Life, Universal-International.

Edward Dmytryk for Crossfire, RKO Radio.

Henry Koster for The Bishop's Wife, Goldwyn, RKO Radio.

David Lean for Great Expectations, Universal-International (United Kingdom).

WRITING

(Motion Picture Story)

Valentine Davies for Miracle on 34th Street, 20th Century-Fox.

Georges Chaperot and René Wheeler for A Cage of Nightingales, Lopert Films (France).

Herbert Clyde Lewis and Frederick Stephani for It Happened on Fifth Avenue, Allied Artists.

Eleazar Lipsky for Kiss of Death, 20th Century-Fox.

Dorothy Parker and Frank Cavett for

Smash Up—the Story of a Woman, Universal-International.

(Original Screenplay)

Sidney Sheldon for The Bachelor and the Bobby-Soxer, RKO Radio.

Sergio Amidei, Adolfo Franci, C. G. Viola, and Cesare Zavattini for Shoeshine, Lopert Films (Italy).

Charles Chaplin for Monsieur Verdoux, Chaplin, United Artists.

Ruth Gordon and Garson Kanin for A Double Life, Universal-International.

Abraham Polonsky for Body and Soul, United Artists.

(Screenplay)

George Seaton for Miracle on 34th Street, 20th Century-Fox.

Moss Hart for Gentleman's Agreement, 20th Century-Fox.

David Lean, Anthony Havelock-Allan, and Ronald Neame for Great Expectations, Universal-International (United Kingdom).

Richard Murphy for Boomerang!, 20th Century-Fox.

John Paxton for Crossfire, RKO Radio.

CINEMATOGRAPHY

(Black and White)

Guy Green for Great Expectations, Universal-International (United Kingdom).

George Folsey for Green Dolphin Street, MGM.

Charles Lang, Jr., for The Ghost and Mrs. Muir, 20th Century-Fox.

(Color)

Jack Cardiff for Black Narcissus, Universal-International (United Kingdom).

Harry Jackson for Mother Wore Tights, 20th Century-Fox.

Peverell Marley and William V. Skall for Life With Father, Warner Bros.

ART DIRECTION—SET DECORATION[109]

(Black and White)

Great Expectations, Universal-

---

[108] Lubitsch received a scroll.
[109] Category renamed.

International (United Kingdom). John Bryan; Wilfred Shingleton.

The Foxes of Harrow, 20th Century-Fox. Lyle Wheeler, Maurice Ransford; Thomas Little, Paul S. Fox.

(Color)

Black Narcissus, Universal-International (United Kingdom). Alfred Junge.

Life With Father, Warner Bros. Robert M. Haas; George James Hopkins.

SOUND RECORDING

Gordon Sawyer for *The Bishop's Wife,* Goldwyn, RKO Radio.

Douglas Shearer for *Green Dolphin Street,* MGM.

Jack R. Whitney, Sound Service Inc., for *T-Men,* Eagle Lion.

MUSIC

(Song)

"Zip-A-Dee-Doo-Dah" from *Song of the South,* Disney, RKO Radio. Music by Allie Wrubel, lyrics by Ray Gilbert.

"A Gal in Calico" from *The Time, the Place and the Girl,* Warner Bros. Music by Arthur Schwartz, lyrics by Leo Robin.

"I Wish I Didn't Love You So" from *The Perils of Pauline,* Paramount. Music and lyrics by Frank Loesser.

"Pass That Peace Pipe" from *Good News,* MGM. Music and lyrics by Ralph Blane, Hugh Martin, and Roger Edens.

"You Do" from *Mother Wore Tights,* 20th Century-Fox. Music by Josef Myrow, lyrics by Mack Gordon.

(Music Score of a Dramatic or Comedy Picture)

Miklos Rozsa for *A Double Life,* Universal-International.

Hugo Friedhofer for *The Bishop's Wife,* Goldwyn, RKO Radio.

Alfred Newman for *Captain From Castile,* 20th Century-Fox.

David Raksin for *Forever Amber,* 20th Century-Fox.

Max Steiner for *Life With Father,* Warner Bros.

(Scoring of a Musical Picture)

Alfred Newman for *Mother Wore Tights,* 20th Century-Fox.

Daniele Amfitheatrof, Paul J. Smith, and Charles Wolcott for *Song of the South,* Disney, RKO Radio.

Robert Emmett Dolan for *Road to Rio,* Paramount.

Johnny Green for *Fiesta,* MGM.

Ray Heindorf and Max Steiner for *My Wild Irish Rose,* Warner Bros.

FILM EDITING

Francis Lyon and Robert Parrish for *Body and Soul,* United Artists.

Monica Collingwood for *The Bishop's Wife,* Goldwyn, RKO Radio.

Harmon Jones for *Gentleman's Agreement,* 20th Century-Fox.

Fergus McDonnell for *Odd Man Out,* Universal-International (United Kingdom).

George White for *Green Dolphin Street,* MGM.

SPECIAL EFFECTS

Green Dolphin Street, MGM. A. Arnold Gillespie and Warren Newcombe, visual; Douglas Shearer and Michael Steinore, audible.

Unconquered, Paramount. Farciot Edouart, Devereux Jennings, Gordon Jennings,

Wallace Kelley, and Paul Lerpae, visual; George Dutton, audible.

SPECIAL AWARDS

James Baskette, for his able and heart-warming characterization of Uncle Remus, friend and storyteller to the children of the world in Walt Disney's *Song of the South.*[110]

Bill and Coo, in which artistry and patience blended in a novel and entertaining use of the medium of motion pictures.[111]

Shoeshine (Italy): The high quality of this motion picture, brought to eloquent life in a country scarred by war, is proof to the world that the creative spirit can triumph over adversity.[112]

Col. William N. Selig, Albert E. Smith, Thomas Armat and George K. Spoor, the small group of pioneers whose belief in a new medium, and whose contributions in its development, blazed the trail along which the motion picture has progressed, in their lifetime, from obscurity to world-wide acclaim.[113]

1948

Awards presented March 24, 1949.

PICTURE

Hamlet, J. Arthur Rank-Two Cities, Universal-International (United Kingdom). Produced by Laurence Olivier.[114]

Johnny Belinda, Warner Bros. Produced by Jerry Wald.

---

[110] Baskette's award was the first ever given to an African-American man for acting.

[111] The filmmakers received a plaque.

[112] The first in a series of honorary awards to foreign language films. The competitive foreign language film category was inaugurated with the 1956 awards.

[113] Selig began exhibiting films in Chicago in 1896; he soon moved into production and in 1909 was the first producer to locate in Hollywood. Smith cofounded the Vitagraph studio in 1896; it became one of the industry's most successful, with stars such as Norma Talmadge, Rudolph Valentino, and Adolphe Menjou, and was sold to the Warner brothers in 1925. Armat was an inventor whose projector was manufactured by Edison and began being sold as the Edison Vitascope in 1896. Spoor was a pioneering exhibitor who cofounded the Essanay production and distribution company in 1907; Wallace Beery was one of the studio's early stars, and Charles Chaplin worked for the company in 1915.

[114] First foreign-made film to win best picture.

The Red Shoes, J. Arthur Rank-Archers, Eagle Lion (United Kingdom). Produced by Michael Powell and Emeric Pressburger.

The Snake Pit, 20th Century-Fox. Produced by Anatole Litvak and Robert Bassler.

The Treasure of the Sierra Madre, Warner Bros. Produced by Henry Blanke.

ACTOR

Laurence Olivier[115] in *Hamlet*, Rank-Two Cities, Universal-International (United Kingdom).

Lew Ayres in *Johnny Belinda*, Warner Bros.

Montgomery Clift in *The Search*, MGM (Switzerland/U.S.).

Dan Dailey in *When My Baby Smiles at Me*, 20th Century-Fox.

Clifton Webb in *Sitting Pretty*, 20th Century-Fox.

ACTRESS

Jane Wyman in *Johnny Belinda*, Warner Bros.

Ingrid Bergman in *Joan of Arc*, RKO Radio.

Olivia de Havilland in *The Snake Pit*, 20th Century-Fox.

Irene Dunne in *I Remember Mama*, RKO Radio.

Barbara Stanwyck in *Sorry, Wrong Number*, Paramount.

SUPPORTING ACTOR

Walter Huston[116] in *The Treasure of the Sierra Madre*, Warner Bros.

Charles Bickford in *Johnny Belinda*, Warner Bros.

Jose Ferrer in *Joan of Arc*, RKO Radio.

Oscar Homolka in *I Remember Mama*, RKO Radio.

Cecil Kellaway in *The Luck of the Irish*, 20th Century-Fox.

SUPPORTING ACTRESS

Claire Trevor in *Key Largo*, Warner Bros.

Barbara Bel Geddes in *I Remember Mama*, RKO Radio.

Ellen Corby in *I Remember Mama*, RKO Radio.

Agnes Moorehead in *Johnny Belinda*, Warner Bros.

Jean Simmons in *Hamlet*, Rank-Two Cities, Universal-International (United Kingdom).

DIRECTOR

John Huston[117] for *The Treasure of the Sierra Madre*, Warner Bros.

Anatole Litvak for *The Snake Pit*, 20th Century-Fox.

Jean Negulesco for *Johnny Belinda*, Warner Bros.

Laurence Olivier for *Hamlet*, Universal-International (United Kingdom).

Fred Zinnemann for *The Search*, MGM (Switzerland/U.S.).

WRITING[118]

(Motion Picture Story)

Richard Schweizer and David Wechsler for *The Search*, MGM (Switzerland/U.S.).

Borden Chase for *Red River*, United Artists.

Frances Flaherty and Robert Flaherty for *The Louisiana Story*, Lopert Films.

Emeric Pressburger for *The Red Shoes*, Eagle Lion (United Kingdom).

Malvin Wald for *The Naked City*, Universal-International.

(Screenplay)

John Huston for *The Treasure of the Sierra Madre*, Warner Bros.

Charles Brackett, Billy Wilder, and Richard L. Breen for *A Foreign Affair*, Paramount.

Frank Partos and Millen Brand for *The Snake Pit*, 20th Century-Fox.

Richard Schweizer and David Wechsler for *The Search*, MGM (Switzerland/U.S.).

Irmgard Von Cube and Allen Vincent for *Johnny Belinda*, Warner Bros.

CINEMATOGRAPHY

(Black and White)

William Daniels for *The Naked City*, Universal-International.

Joseph August for *Portrait of Jennie*, Selznick Releasing Organization.

Charles B. Lang, Jr., for *A Foreign Affair*, Paramount.

Ted McCord for *Johnny Belinda*, Warner Bros.

Nicholas Musuraca for *I Remember Mama*, RKO Radio.

(Color)

Joseph Valentine, William V. Skall, and Winton Hoch for *Joan of Arc*, RKO Radio.

Charles G. Clarke for *Green Grass of Wyoming*, 20th Century-Fox.

Robert Planck for *The Three Musketeers*, MGM.

William Snyder for *The Loves of Carmen*, Columbia.

ART DIRECTION—SET DECORATION

(Black and White)

***Hamlet*, Universal-International (United Kingdom). Roger K. Furse; Carmen Dillon.**

Johnny Belinda, Warner Bros. Robert Haas; William Wallace.

(Color)

***The Red Shoes*, Eagle Lion (United Kingdom). Hein Heckroth; Arthur Lawson.**

Joan of Arc, RKO Radio. Richard Day; Edwin Casey Roberts, Joseph Kish.

SOUND RECORDING

Thomas T. Moulton for *The Snake Pit*, 20th Century-Fox.

Daniel J. Bloomberg for *Moonrise*, Republic.

---

[115] Only person to direct himself in an Oscar-winning role. Others who have directed themselves to nominations are Orson Welles (1941), Woody Allen (1977), Warren Beatty (1978, 1981), Kenneth Branagh (1989), Kevin Costner (1990), and Clint Eastwood (1992).

[116] Only person to be directed in an Oscar-winning role by his own son.

[117] Only person to direct both his father and his child in Oscar-winning roles: Walter Huston (1948) and Anjelica Huston (1985).

[118] Original Screenplay category dropped.

Nathan O. Levinson for *Johnny Belinda,* Warner Bros.

MUSIC

(Song)

"Buttons and Bows" from *The Paleface,* Paramount. Music and lyrics by Jay Livingston and Ray Evans.

"For Every Man There's a Woman" from *Casbah,* Universal-International. Music by Harold Arlen, lyrics by Leo Robin.

"It's Magic" from *Romance on the High Seas,* Warner Bros. Music by Jule Styne, lyrics by Sammy Cahn.

"This Is the Moment" from *That Lady in Ermine,* 20th Century-Fox. Music by Frederick Hollander, lyrics by Leo Robin.

"The Woody Woodpecker Song" from *Wet Blanket Policy,* Lantz, United Artists (cartoon). Music and lyrics by Ramey Idriss and George Tibbles.[119]

(Music Score of a Dramatic or Comedy Picture)

Brian Easdale for *The Red Shoes,* Eagle Lion (United Kingdom).

Hugo Friedhofer for *Joan of Arc,* RKO Radio.

Alfred Newman for *The Snake Pit,* 20th Century-Fox.

Max Steiner for *Johnny Belinda,* Warner Bros.

William Walton for *Hamlet,* Universal-International (United Kingdom).

(Scoring of a Musical Picture)

Johnny Green and Roger Edens for *Easter Parade,* MGM.

Lennie Hayton for *The Pirate,* MGM.

Ray Heindorf for *Romance on the High Seas,* Warner Bros.

Alfred Newman for *When My Baby Smiles at Me,* 20th Century-Fox.

Victor Young for *The Emperor Waltz,* Paramount.

FILM EDITING

Paul Weatherwax for *The Naked City,* Universal-International.

Reginald Mills for *The Red Shoes,* Eagle Lion (United Kingdom).

Christian Nyby for *Red River,* United Artists.

Frank Sullivan for *Joan of Arc,* RKO Radio.

David Weisbart for *Johnny Belinda,* Warner Bros.

COSTUME DESIGN[120]

(Black and White)

Roger K. Furse for *Hamlet,* Universal-International (United Kingdom).

Irene for *B.F.'s Daughter,* MGM.

(Color)

Dorothy Jeakins and Karinska for *Joan of Arc,* RKO Radio.

Edith Head and Gile Steele for *The Emperor Waltz,* Paramount.

SPECIAL EFFECTS

***Portrait of Jennie,* Selznick Releasing Organization. Paul Eagler, J. McMillan Johnson, Russell Shearman, and Clarence Slifer, visual; Charles Freeman and James G. Stewart, audible.**

Deep Waters, 20th Century-Fox. Ralph Hammeras, Fred Sersen, and Edward Snyder, visual; Roger Heman, audible.

IRVING G. THALBERG MEMORIAL AWARD

Jerry Wald.

SPECIAL AWARDS

***Monsieur Vincent* (France). Voted by the Academy Board of Governors as the most outstanding foreign language film released in the United States during 1948.**

Ivan Jandl, for the outstanding juvenile performance of 1948 in *The Search.*

Sid Grauman, master showman, who raised the standard of exhibition of motion pictures.

Adolph Zukor, a man who has been called the father of the feature film in America, for his services to the industry over a period of 40 years.

Walter Wanger, for distinguished service to the industry in adding to its moral stature in the world community by his production of the picture *Joan of Arc.*

1949

Awards presented March 23, 1950.

PICTURE

***All the King's Men,* Robert Rossen Productions, Columbia. Produced by Robert Rossen.**

Battleground, MGM. Produced by Dore Schary.

The Heiress, Paramount. Produced by William Wyler.

A Letter to Three Wives, 20th Century-Fox. Produced by Sol C. Siegel.

Twelve O'Clock High, 20th Century-Fox. Produced by Darryl F. Zanuck.

ACTOR

Broderick Crawford in *All the King's Men,* Columbia.

Kirk Douglas in *Champion,* United Artists.

Gregory Peck in *Twelve O'Clock High,* 20th Century-Fox.

Richard Todd in *The Hasty Heart,* Warner Bros.

John Wayne in *Sands of Iwo Jima,* Republic.

ACTRESS

Olivia de Havilland in *The Heiress,* Paramount.

Jeanne Crain in *Pinky,* 20th Century-Fox.

Susan Hayward in *My Foolish Heart,* Goldwyn, RKO Radio.

Deborah Kerr in *Edward, My Son,* MGM.

---

[119] The only song from a cartoon short to be nominated for an Oscar.
[120] New category.

Loretta Young in *Come to the Stable*, 20th Century-Fox.

SUPPORTING ACTOR

Dean Jagger in *Twelve O'Clock High*, 20th Century-Fox.

John Ireland in *All the King's Men*, Columbia.

Arthur Kennedy in *Champion*, United Artists.

Ralph Richardson in *The Heiress*, Paramount.

James Whitmore in *Battleground*, MGM.

SUPPORTING ACTRESS

Mercedes McCambridge in *All the King's Men*, Columbia.

Ethel Barrymore in *Pinky*, 20th Century-Fox.

Celeste Holm in *Come to the Stable*, 20th Century-Fox.

Elsa Lanchester in *Come to the Stable*, 20th Century-Fox.

Ethel Waters in *Pinky*, 20th Century-Fox.

DIRECTOR

Joseph L. Mankiewicz for *A Letter to Three Wives*, 20th Century-Fox.

Carol Reed for *The Fallen Idol*, Selznick Releasing Organization (United Kingdom).

Robert Rossen for *All the King's Men*, Columbia.

William A. Wellman for *Battleground*, MGM.

William Wyler for *The Heiress*, Paramount.

WRITING

(Motion Picture Story)

Douglas Morrow for *The Stratton Story*, MGM.

Harry Brown for *Sands of Iwo Jima*, Republic.

Virginia Kellogg for *White Heat*, Warner Bros.

Clare Boothe Luce for *Come to the Stable*, 20th Century-Fox.

Shirley W. Smith and Valentine Davies

for *It Happens Every Spring*, 20th Century-Fox.

(Screenplay)

Joseph L. Mankiewicz for *A Letter to Three Wives*, 20th Century-Fox.

Carl Foreman for *Champion*, United Artists.

Graham Greene for *The Fallen Idol*, Selznick Releasing Organization (United Kingdom).

Robert Rossen for *All the King's Men*, Columbia.

Cesare Zavattini for *The Bicycle Thief*, Mayer-Burstyn (Italy).

(Story and Screenplay)[121]

Robert Pirosh for *Battleground*, MGM.

Sidney Buchman for *Jolson Sings Again*, Columbia.

T. E. B. Clarke for *Passport to Pimlico*, Eagle Lion (United Kingdom).

Alfred Hayes, Federico Fellini, Sergio Amidei, Marcello Pagliero, and Roberto Rossellini for *Paisan*, Mayer-Burstyn (Italy).

Helen Levitt, Janice Loeb, and Sidney Meyers for *The Quiet One*, Mayer-Burstyn.

CINEMATOGRAPHY

(Black and White)

Paul C. Vogel for *Battleground*, MGM.

Joseph LaShelle for *Come to the Stable*, 20th Century-Fox.

Frank Planer for *Champion*, United Artists.

Leon Shamroy for *Prince of Foxes*, 20th Century-Fox.

Leo Tover for *The Heiress*, Paramount.

(Color)

Winton Hoch for *She Wore a Yellow Ribbon*, RKO Radio.

Charles G. Clarke for *Sand*, 20th Century-Fox.

Robert Planck and Charles Schoenbaum for *Little Women*, MGM.

William Snyder for *Jolson Sings Again*, Columbia.

Harry Stradling for *The Barkleys of Broadway*, MGM.

ART DIRECTION—SET DECORATION

(Black and White)

***The Heiress*, Paramount. Harry Horner, John Meehan; Emile Kuri.**

Come to the Stable, 20th Century-Fox. Lyle Wheeler, Joseph C. Wright; Thomas Little, Paul S. Fox.

Madame Bovary, MGM. Cedric Gibbons, Jack Martin Smith; Edwin B. Willis, Richard A. Pefferle.

(Color)

***Little Women*, MGM. Cedric Gibbons, Paul Groesse; Edwin B. Willis, Jack D. Moore.**

The Adventures of Don Juan, Warner Bros. Edward Carrere; Lyle Reifsnider.

Saraband, Eagle-Lion (United Kingdom). Jim Morahan, William Kellner, and Michael Relph.

SOUND RECORDING

Thomas T. Moulton for *Twelve O'Clock High*, 20th Century-Fox.

Daniel J. Bloomberg for *Sands of Iwo Jima*, Republic.

Leslie I. Carey for *Once More, My Darling*, Universal-International.

MUSIC

(Song)

"Baby, It's Cold Outside" from *Neptune's Daughter*, MGM. Music and lyrics by Frank Loesser.

"It's a Great Feeling" from *It's a Great Feeling*, Warner Bros. Music by Jule Styne, lyrics by Sammy Cahn.

"Lavender Blue" from *So Dear to My Heart*, Disney, RKO Radio. Music by Eliot Daniel, lyrics by Larry Morey.

"My Foolish Heart" from *My Foolish Heart*, Goldwyn, RKO Radio. Music by Victor Young, lyrics by Ned Washington.

"Through a Long and Sleepless Night" from *Come to the Stable*, 20th Century-

---

[121] Original Screenplay category reinstated under this name.

Fox. Music by Alfred Newman, lyrics by Mack Gordon.

(Music Score of a Dramatic or Comedy Picture)

Aaron Copland for *The Heiress*, Paramount.

Max Steiner for *Beyond the Forest*, Warner Bros.

Dimitri Tiomkin for *Champion*, United Artists.

(Scoring of a Musical Picture)

Roger Edens and Lennie Hayton for *On the Town*, MGM.

Ray Heindorf for *Look for the Silver Lining*, Warner Bros.

Morris Stoloff and George Duning for *Jolson Sings Again*, Columbia.

FILM EDITING

Harry Gerstad for *Champion*, United Artists.

John Dunning for *Battleground*, MGM.

Frederic Knudtson for *The Window*, RKO Radio.

Robert Parrish and Al Clark for *All the King's Men*, Columbia.

Richard L. Van Enger for *Sands of Iwo Jima*, Republic.

COSTUME DESIGN

(Black and White)

Edith Head and Gile Steele for *The Heiress*, Paramount.

Vittorio Nino Novarese for *Prince of Foxes*, 20th Century-Fox.

(Color)

Leah Rhodes, Travilla, and Marjorie Best for *The Adventures of Don Juan*, Warner Bros.

Kay Nelson for *Mother Is a Freshman*, 20th Century-Fox.

SPECIAL EFFECTS[122]

***Mighty Joe Young*, RKO Radio.**

Tulsa, Eagle Lion.

SPECIAL AWARDS

The Bicycle Thief (Italy), voted by the Academy Board of

Governors as the most outstanding foreign language film released in the United States during 1949.

Bobby Driscoll, as the outstanding juvenile actor of 1949.

Fred Astaire, for his unique artistry and his contributions to the technique of motion pictures.

Cecil B. DeMille, distinguished motion picture pioneer, for 37 years of brilliant showmanship.

Jean Hersholt, for distinguished service to the motion picture industry.

1950

Awards presented March 29, 1951.

PICTURE

***All About Eve*,[123] 20th Century-Fox. Produced by Darryl F. Zanuck.[124]**

Born Yesterday, Columbia. Produced by S. Sylvan Simon.

Father of the Bride, MGM. Produced by Pandro S. Berman.

King Solomon's Mines, MGM. Produced by Sam Zimbalist.

Sunset Boulevard, Paramount. Produced by Charles Brackett.

ACTOR

Jose Ferrer in *Cyrano de Bergerac*, United Artists.

Louis Calhern in *The Magnificent Yankee*, MGM.

William Holden in *Sunset Boulevard*, Paramount.

James Stewart in *Harvey*, Universal-International.

Spencer Tracy in *Father of the Bride*, MGM.

ACTRESS

Judy Holliday in *Born Yesterday*, Columbia.

Anne Baxter in *All About Eve*, 20th Century-Fox.

Bette Davis in *All About Eve*, 20th Century-Fox.

Eleanor Parker in *Caged*, Warner Bros.

Gloria Swanson in *Sunset Boulevard*, Paramount.

SUPPORTING ACTOR

George Sanders in *All About Eve*, 20th Century-Fox.

Jeff Chandler in *Broken Arrow*, 20th Century-Fox.

Edmund Gwenn in *Mister 880*, 20th Century-Fox.

Sam Jaffe in *The Asphalt Jungle*, MGM.

Erich von Stroheim in *Sunset Boulevard*, Paramount.

SUPPORTING ACTRESS

Josephine Hull in *Harvey*, Universal-International.

Hope Emerson in *Caged*, Warner Bros.

Celeste Holm in *All About Eve*, 20th Century-Fox.

Nancy Olson in *Sunset Boulevard*, Paramount.

Thelma Ritter in *All About Eve*, 20th Century-Fox.

DIRECTOR

Joseph L. Mankiewicz for *All About Eve*, 20th Century-Fox.

George Cukor for *Born Yesterday*, Columbia.

John Huston for *The Asphalt Jungle*, MGM.

Carol Reed for *The Third Man*, Selznick Releasing Organization (United Kingdom).

Billy Wilder for *Sunset Boulevard*, Paramount.

WRITING

(Motion Picture Story)

Edna Anhalt and Edward Anhalt for *Panic in the Streets*, 20th Century-Fox.

---

[122] No individuals were cited in this category through the 1955 awards.

[123] Received fourteen nominations, more than any other film in the history of the awards.

[124] Zanuck's third film to win best picture, a record for producers equaled only by Sam Spiegel (1954, 1957, 1962).

William Bowers and Andre de Toth for *The Gunfighter*, 20th Century-Fox.

Giuseppe De Santis and Carlo Lizzani for *Bitter Rice*, Lux Films (Italy).

Sy Gomberg for *When Willie Comes Marching Home*, 20th Century-Fox.

Leonard Spiegelgass for *Mystery Street*, MGM.

(Screenplay)

Joseph L. Mankiewicz[125] for All About Eve, 20th Century-Fox.

Michael Blankfort[126] for *Broken Arrow*, 20th Century-Fox.

Frances Goodrich and Albert Hackett for *Father of the Bride*, MGM.

Ben Maddow and John Huston for *The Asphalt Jungle*, MGM.

Albert Mannheimer for *Born Yesterday*, Columbia.

(Story and Screenplay)

Charles Brackett, Billy Wilder, and D. M. Marshman, Jr., for Sunset Boulevard, Paramount.

Carl Foreman for *The Men*, United Artists.

Ruth Gordon and Garson Kanin for *Adam's Rib*, MGM.

Virginia Kellogg and Bernard C. Schoenfeld for *Caged*, Warner Bros.

Joseph L. Mankiewicz and Lesser Samuels for *No Way Out*, 20th Century-Fox.

CINEMATOGRAPHY

(Black and White)

Robert Krasker for The Third Man, Selznick Releasing Organization (United Kingdom).

Milton Krasner for *All About Eve*, 20th Century-Fox.

Victor Milner for *The Furies*, Paramount.

Harold Rosson for *The Asphalt Jungle*, MGM.

John F. Seitz for *Sunset Boulevard*, Paramount.

(Color)

Robert Surtees for King Solomon's Mines, MGM.

George Barnes for *Samson and Delilah*, Paramount.

Ernest Haller for *The Flame and the Arrow*, Warner Bros.

Ernest Palmer for *Broken Arrow*, 20th Century-Fox.

Charles Rosher for *Annie Get Your Gun*, MGM.

ART DIRECTION—SET DECORATION

(Black and White)

Sunset Boulevard, Paramount. Hans Dreier, John Meehan; Sam Comer, Ray Moyer.

All About Eve, 20th Century-Fox. Lyle Wheeler, George Davis; Thomas Little, Walter M. Scott.

The Red Danube, MGM. Cedric Gibbons, Hans Peters; Edwin B. Willis, Hugh Hunt.

(Color)

Samson and Delilah, DeMille, Paramount. Hans Dreier, Walter Tyler; Sam Comer, Ray Moyer.

Annie Get Your Gun, MGM. Cedric Gibbons, Paul Groesse; Edwin B. Willis, Richard A. Pefferle.

Destination Moon, Eagle Lion Classics. Ernst Fegte; George Sawley.

SOUND RECORDING

Thomas T. Moulton for All About Eve, 20th Century-Fox.

Leslie I. Carey for *Louisa*, Universal-International.

Cyril Crowhurst for *Trio*, Paramount (United Kingdom).

Gordon Sawyer for *Our Very Own*, Goldwyn, RKO Radio.

C. O. Slyfield for *Cinderella*, Disney, RKO Radio.

MUSIC

(Song)

"Mona Lisa" from Captain Carey, USA, Paramount. Music and lyrics by Ray Evans and Jay Livingston.

"Be My Love" from *The Toast of New Orleans*, MGM. Music by Nicholas Brodszky, lyrics by Sammy Cahn.

"Bibbidi-Bobbidi-Boo" from *Cinderella*, Disney, RKO Radio. Music and lyrics by Mack David, Al Hoffman, and Jerry Livingston.

"Mule Train" from *Singing Guns*, Republic. Music and lyrics by Fred Glickman, Hy Heath, and Johnny Lange.

"Wilhelmina" from *Wabash Avenue*, 20th Century-Fox. Music by Josef Myrow, lyrics by Mack Gordon.

(Music Score of a Dramatic or Comedy Picture)

Franz Waxman for Sunset Boulevard, Paramount.

George Duning for *No Sad Songs for Me*, Columbia.

Alfred Newman for *All About Eve*, 20th Century-Fox.

Max Steiner for *The Flame and the Arrow*, Warner Bros.

Victor Young for *Samson and Delilah*, Paramount.

(Scoring of a Musical Picture)

Adolph Deutsch and Roger Edens for Annie Get Your Gun, MGM.

Ray Heindorf for *The West Point Story*, Warner Bros.

Lionel Newman for *I'll Get By*, 20th Century-Fox.

André Previn for *Three Little Words*, MGM.

Oliver Wallace and Paul J. Smith for *Cinderella*, Disney, RKO Radio.

FILM EDITING

Ralph E. Winters and Conrad A. Nervig for King Solomon's Mines, MGM.

Oswald Hafenrichter for *The Third Man*, Selznick Releasing Organization (United Kingdom).

---

[125] Mankiewicz, who also received the directing and writing awards the previous year, for *A Letter to Three Wives*, becomes the first person to receive more than one Oscar two years in a row. The only other sequential multiple winner is Alan Menken, who won both scoring and song awards for *Beauty and the Beast* (1991) and *Aladdin* (1992).

[126] Blankfort was actually fronting for Albert Maltz, a blacklisted screenwriter who posthumously received official credit from the Writers Guild of America in 1991.

Barbara McLean for *All About Eve*, 20th Century-Fox.

James E. Newcom for *Annie Get Your Gun*, MGM.

Arthur Schmidt and Doane Harrison for *Sunset Boulevard*, Paramount.

COSTUME DESIGN

(Black and White)

Edith Head and Charles LeMaire for *All About Eve*, 20th Century-Fox.

Jean Louis for *Born Yesterday*, Columbia.

Walter Plunkett for *The Magnificent Yankee*, MGM.

(Color)

Edith Head, Dorothy Jeakins, Elois Jenssen, Gile Steele, and Gwen Wakeling for *Samson and Delilah*, Paramount.

Walter Plunkett and Valles for *That Forsyte Woman*, MGM.

Michael Whittaker for *The Black Rose*, 20th Century-Fox.

SPECIAL EFFECTS

***Destination Moon*, Eagle Lion.**

Samson and Delilah, Paramount.

IRVING G. THALBERG MEMORIAL AWARD

Darryl F. Zanuck.

HONORARY AWARDS[127]

George Murphy, for his services in interpreting the film industry to the country at large.

Louis B. Mayer, for distinguished service to the motion picture industry.

***The Walls of Malapaga* (France/Italy), voted by the Board of Governors as the most outstanding foreign language film released in the United States in 1950.**

1951

Awards presented March 20, 1952.

PICTURE

***An American in Paris*, MGM. Produced by Arthur Freed.**

Decision Before Dawn, 20th Century-Fox. Produced by Anatole Litvak and Frank McCarthy.

A Place in the Sun, Paramount. Produced by George Stevens.

Quo Vadis?, MGM. Produced by Sam Zimbalist.

A Streetcar Named Desire, Charles K. Feldman Group Productions, Warner Bros. Produced by Charles K. Feldman.

ACTOR

Humphrey Bogart in *The African Queen*, United Artists.

Marlon Brando in *A Streetcar Named Desire*, Warner Bros.

Montgomery Clift in *A Place in the Sun*, Paramount.

Arthur Kennedy in *Bright Victory*, Universal-International.

Fredric March in *Death of a Salesman*, Columbia.

ACTRESS

Vivien Leigh in *A Streetcar Named Desire*, Warner Bros.

Katharine Hepburn in *The African Queen*, United Artists.

Eleanor Parker in *Detective Story*, Paramount.

Shelley Winters in *A Place in the Sun*, Paramount.

Jane Wyman in *The Blue Veil*, RKO Radio.

SUPPORTING ACTOR

Karl Malden in *A Streetcar Named Desire*, Warner Bros.

Leo Genn in *Quo Vadis?*, MGM.

Kevin McCarthy in *Death of a Salesman*, Columbia.

Peter Ustinov in *Quo Vadis?*, MGM.

Gig Young in *Come Fill the Cup*, Warner Bros.

SUPPORTING ACTRESS

Kim Hunter in *A Streetcar Named Desire*, Warner Bros.

Joan Blondell in *The Blue Veil*, RKO Radio.

Mildred Dunnock in *Death of a Salesman*, Columbia.

Lee Grant in *Detective Story*, Paramount.

Thelma Ritter in *The Mating Season*, Paramount.

DIRECTOR

George Stevens for *A Place in the Sun*, Paramount.

John Huston for *The African Queen*, United Artists.

Elia Kazan for *A Streetcar Named Desire*, Warner Bros.

Vincente Minnelli for *An American in Paris*, MGM.

William Wyler for *Detective Story*, Paramount.

WRITING

(Motion Picture Story)

Paul Dehn and James Bernard for *Seven Days to Noon*, Mayer-Kingsley-Distinguished Films (United Kingdom).

Budd Boetticher and Ray Nazarro for *The Bullfighter and the Lady*, Republic.

Alfred Hayes and Stewart Stern for *Teresa*, MGM.

Oscar Millard for *The Frogmen*, Warner Bros.

Robert Riskin and Liam O'Brian for *Here Comes the Groom*, Paramount.

(Screenplay)

Michael Wilson and Harry Brown for *A Place in the Sun*, Paramount.

James Agee and John Huston for *The African Queen*, United Artists.

Jacques Natanson and Max Ophuls for *La Ronde*, Commercial Pictures (France).

Tennessee Williams for *A Streetcar Named Desire*, Warner Bros.

Philip Yordan and Robert Wyler for *Detective Story*, Paramount.

(Story and Screenplay)

---

[127] Category renamed (formerly Special Awards).

Alan Jay Lerner for *An American in Paris*, MGM.

Philip Dunne for *David and Bathsheba*, 20th Century-Fox.

Clarence Greene and Russell Rouse for *The Well*, United Artists.

Robert Pirosh for *Go for Broke!*, MGM.

Billy Wilder, Lesser Samuels, and Walter Newman for *The Big Carnival*, Paramount.

CINEMATOGRAPHY
(Black and White)

William C. Mellor for *A Place in the Sun*, Paramount.

Norbert Brodine for *The Frogmen*, 20th Century-Fox.

Robert Burks for *Strangers on a Train*, Warner Bros.

Frank Planer for *Death of a Salesman*, Columbia.

Harry Stradling for *A Streetcar Named Desire*, Warner Bros.

(Color)

Alfred Gilks and John Alton (ballet photography) for *An American in Paris*, MGM.

Charles Rosher for *Show Boat*, MGM.

John F. Seitz and W. Howard Greene for *When Worlds Collide*, Pal, Paramount.

Leon Shamroy for *David and Bathsheba*, 20th Century-Fox.

Robert Surtees and William V. Skall for *Quo Vadis?*, MGM.

ART DIRECTION—SET DECORATION
(Black and White)

***A Streetcar Named Desire*, Warner Bros. Richard Day; George James Hopkins.**

Fourteen Hours, 20th Century-Fox. Lyle Wheeler, Leland Fuller; Thomas Little, Fred J. Rode.

House on Telegraph Hill, 20th Century-Fox. Lyle Wheeler, John DeCuir; Thomas Little, Paul S. Fox.

La Ronde, Commercial Pictures (France). D'Eaubonne.

Too Young to Kiss, MGM. Cedric Gibbons, Paul Groesse; Edwin B. Willis, Jack D. Moore.

(Color)

An American in Paris, MGM. Cedric Gibbons, Preston Ames; Edwin B. Willis, Keogh Gleason.

David and Bathsheba, 20th Century-Fox. Lyle Wheeler, George Davis; Thomas Little, Paul S. Fox.

On the Riviera, 20th Century-Fox. Lyle Wheeler, Leland Fuller, musical settings by Joseph C. Wright; Thomas Little, Walter M. Scott.

Quo Vadis?, MGM. William A. Horning, Cedric Gibbons, Edward Carfagno; Hugh Hunt.

Tales of Hoffman, Lopert (United Kingdom). Hein Heckroth.

SOUND RECORDING

Douglas Shearer for *The Great Caruso*, MGM.

John O. Aalberg for *Two Tickets to Broadway*, RKO Radio.

Leslie I. Carey for *Bright Victory*, Universal-International.

Nathan Levinson for *A Streetcar Named Desire*, Warner Bros.

Gordon Sawyer for *I Want You*, Goldwyn, RKO Radio.

MUSIC
(Song)

"In the Cool, Cool, Cool of the Evening" from *Here Comes the Groom*, Paramount. Music by Hoagy Carmichael, lyrics by Johnny Mercer.

"A Kiss to Build a Dream On" from *The Strip*, MGM. Music and lyrics by Bert Kalmar, Harry Ruby, and Oscar Hammerstein II.

"Never" from *Golden Girl*, 20th Century-Fox. Music by Lionel Newman, lyrics by Eliot Daniel.

"Too Late Now" from *Royal Wedding*, MGM. Music by Burton Lane, lyrics by Alan Jay Lerner.

"Wonder Why" from *Rich, Young and Pretty*, MGM. Music by Nicholas Brodszky, lyrics by Sammy Cahn.

(Music Score of a Dramatic or Comedy Picture)

Franz Waxman for *A Place in the Sun*, Paramount.

Alfred Newman for *David and Bathsheba*, 20th Century-Fox.

Alex North for *Death of a Salesman*, Columbia.

Alex North for *A Streetcar Named Desire*, Warner Bros.

Miklos Rozsa for *Quo Vadis?*, MGM.

(Scoring of a Musical Picture)

Johnny Green and Saul Chaplin for *An American in Paris*, MGM.

Peter Herman Adler and Johnny Green for *The Great Caruso*, MGM.

Adolph Deutsch and Conrad Salinger for *Show Boat*, MGM.

Alfred Newman for *On the Riviera*, 20th Century-Fox.

Oliver Wallace for *Alice in Wonderland*, Disney, RKO Radio.

FILM EDITING

William Hornbeck for *A Place in the Sun*, Paramount.

Adrienne Fazan for *An American in Paris*, MGM.

Chester Schaeffer for *The Well*, United Artists.

Dorothy Spencer for *Decision Before Dawn*, 20th Century-Fox.

Ralph E. Winters for *Quo Vadis?*, MGM.

COSTUME DESIGN
(Black and White)

Edith Head for *A Place in the Sun*, Paramount.

Lucinda Ballard for *A Streetcar Named Desire*, Warner Bros.

Charles LeMaire and Renie for *The Model and the Marriage Broker*, 20th Century-Fox.

Walter Plunkett and Gile Steele for *Kind Lady*, MGM.

Edward Stevenson and Margaret Furse for *The Mudlark*, 20th Century-Fox (United Kingdom).

(Color)

Orry-Kelly, Walter Plunkett, and Irene Sharaff for *An American in Paris*, MGM.

Hein Heckroth for *Tales of Hoffmann*, Lopert (United Kingdom).

Charles LeMaire and Edward Stevenson

for *David and Bathsheba*, 20th Century-Fox.

Herschel McCoy for *Quo Vadis?*, MGM.

Helen Rose and Gile Steele for *The Great Caruso*, MGM.

SPECIAL EFFECTS
When Worlds Collide, Paramount.

IRVING G. THALBERG MEMORIAL AWARD
Arthur Freed.

HONORARY AWARDS
Gene Kelly, in appreciation of his versatility as an actor, singer, director and dancer, and specifically for his brilliant achievements in the art of choreography on film.

Rashomon **(Japan). Voted by the Board of Governors as the most outstanding foreign language film released in the United States during 1951.**

1952
Awards presented March 19, 1953.

PICTURE
The Greatest Show on Earth, Cecil B. DeMille Productions, Paramount. Produced by Cecil B. DeMille.

High Noon, Stanley Kramer Productions, United Artists. Produced by Stanley Kramer.

Ivanhoe, MGM. Produced by Pandro S. Berman.

Moulin Rouge, Romulus Films, Ltd., United Artists. Produced by John Huston.

The Quiet Man, Argosy Pictures, Republic. Produced by John Ford and Merian C. Cooper.

ACTOR
Gary Cooper in *High Noon*, United Artists.

Marlon Brando in *Viva Zapata!*, 20th Century-Fox.

Kirk Douglas in *The Bad and the Beautiful*, MGM.

Jose Ferrer in *Moulin Rouge*, United Artists.

Alec Guinness in *The Lavender Hill Mob*, Rank-Ealing, Universal-International (United Kingdom).

ACTRESS
Shirley Booth[128] in *Come Back, Little Sheba*, Paramount.

Joan Crawford in *Sudden Fear*, RKO Radio.

Bette Davis in *The Star*, 20th Century-Fox.

Julie Harris in *The Member of the Wedding*, Columbia.

Susan Hayward in *With a Song in My Heart*, 20th Century-Fox.

SUPPORTING ACTOR
Anthony Quinn in *Viva Zapata!*, 20th Century-Fox.

Richard Burton in *My Cousin Rachel*, 20th Century-Fox.

Arthur Hunnicutt in *The Big Sky*, RKO Radio.

Victor McLaglen[129] in *The Quiet Man*, Republic.

Jack Palance in *Sudden Fear*, RKO Radio.

SUPPORTING ACTRESS
Gloria Grahame in *The Bad and the Beautiful*, MGM.[130]

Jean Hagen in *Singin' in the Rain*, MGM.

Colette Marchand in *Moulin Rouge*, United Artists.

Terry Moore in *Come Back, Little Sheba*, Paramount.

Thelma Ritter in *With a Song in My Heart*, 20th Century-Fox.

DIRECTOR
John Ford for *The Quiet Man*, Republic.[131]

Cecil B. DeMille for *The Greatest Show on Earth*, Paramount.

John Huston for *Moulin Rouge*, United Artists.

Joseph L. Mankiewicz for *Five Fingers*, 20th Century-Fox.

Fred Zinnemann for *High Noon*, United Artists.

WRITING
(Motion Picture Story)
Frederic M. Frank, Theodore St. John, and Frank Cavett for *The Greatest Show on Earth*, Paramount.

Edna Anhalt and Edward Anhalt for *The Sniper*, Columbia.

Martin Goldsmith and Jack Leonard for *The Narrow Margin*, RKO Radio.

Leo McCarey for *My Son John*, Paramount.

Guy Trosper for *The Pride of St. Louis*, 20th Century-Fox.

(Screenplay)
Charles Schnee for *The Bad and the Beautiful*, MGM.

Carl Foreman for *High Noon*, United Artists.

Roger MacDougall, John Dighton, and Alexander Mackendrick for *The Man in the White Suit*, Universal-International (United Kingdom).

Frank S. Nugent for *The Quiet Man*, Republic.

Michael Wilson for *Five Fingers*, 20th Century-Fox.

(Story and Screenplay)
T. E. B. Clarke for *The Lavender Hill*

---

[128] Apparently the only actress in her fifties to receive the Oscar for a leading role. Most reference works give her birthday as August 30, 1907, which would make her forty-five at the time of the award. But when she died in 1992, it was reported that she was ninety-four, making her some nine years older than previously thought, and fifty-four when she received the Oscar.

[129] First best actor winner to receive a subsequent nomination as a supporting actor.

[130] *The Bad and the Beautiful* won five Oscars, more than any other film not nominated for best picture.

[131] Ford's fourth Oscar makes him the most honored director in the history of the awards. Frank Capra, who won as best director for 1934, 1936, and 1938, and William Wyler, best director for 1942, 1946, and 1959, are tied for second place.

Mob, Universal-International (United Kingdom).

Sydney Boehm for *The Atomic City,* Paramount.

Ruth Gordon and Garson Kanin for *Pat and Mike,* MGM.

Terence Rattigan for *Breaking the Sound Barrier,* United Artists (United Kingdom).

John Steinbeck for *Viva Zapata!,* 20th Century-Fox.

CINEMATOGRAPHY
(Black and White)

Robert Surtees for *The Bad and the Beautiful,* MGM.

Russell Harlan for *The Big Sky,* RKO Radio.

Charles B. Lang, Jr., for *Sudden Fear,* RKO Radio.

Joseph LaShelle for *My Cousin Rachel,* 20th Century-Fox.

Virgil E. Miller for *Navajo,* Lippert.
(Color)

Winton C. Hoch and Archie Stout for *The Quiet Man,* Republic.

George J. Folsey for *Million Dollar Mermaid,* MGM.

Leon Shamroy for *The Snows of Kilimanjaro,* 20th Century-Fox.

Harry Stradling for *Hans Christian Andersen,* Goldwyn, RKO Radio.

F. A. Young for *Ivanhoe,* MGM.

ART DIRECTION—SET DECORATION
(Black and White)

***The Bad and the Beautiful,* MGM. Cedric Gibbons, Edward Carfagno; Edwin B. Willis, Keogh Gleason.**

Carrie, Paramount. Hal Pereira, Roland Anderson; Emile Kuri.

My Cousin Rachel, 20th Century-Fox. Lyle Wheeler, John DeCuir; Walter M. Scott.

Rashomon, RKO Radio (Japan). Matsuyama; H. Motsumoto.

Viva Zapata!, 20th Century-Fox. Lyle Wheeler, Leland Fuller; Thomas Little, Claude Carpenter.
(Color)

Moulin Rouge, **United Artists. Paul Sheriff; Marcel Vertes.**

Hans Christian Andersen, Goldwyn, RKO Radio. Richard Day, Clave; Howard Bristol.

The Merry Widow, MGM. Cedric Gibbons, Paul Groesse; Edwin B. Willis, Arthur Krams.

The Quiet Man, Republic. Frank Hotaling; John McCarthy, Jr., Charles Thompson.

The Snows of Kilimanjaro, 20th Century-Fox. Lyle Wheeler, John DeCuir; Thomas Little, Paul S. Fox.

SOUND RECORDING

London Film Sound Dept. for *Breaking the Sound Barrier,* United Artists (United Kingdom).

Daniel J. Bloomberg for *The Quiet Man,* Republic.

Thomas T. Moulton for *With a Song in My Heart,* 20th Century-Fox.

Pinewood Studios Sound Dept. for *The Promoter,* Universal-International (United Kingdom).

Gordon Sawyer for *Hans Christian Andersen,* Goldwyn, RKO Radio.

MUSIC
(Song)

"High Noon (Do Not Forsake Me, Oh My Darlin')" from *High Noon,* United Artists. Music by Dimitri Tiomkin, lyrics by Ned Washington.

"Am I in Love" from *Son of Paleface,* Paramount. Music and lyrics by Jack Brooks.

"Because You're Mine" from *Because You're Mine,* MGM. Music by Nicholas Brodszky, lyrics by Sammy Cahn.

"Thumbelina" from *Hans Christian Andersen,* Goldwyn, RKO Radio. Music and lyrics by Frank Loesser.

"Zing a Little Zong" from *Just for You,* Paramount. Music by Harry Warren, lyrics by Leo Robin.

(Music Score of a Dramatic or Comedy Picture)

Dimitri Tiomkin for *High Noon,* United Artists.

Herschel Burke Gilbert for *The Thief,* United Artists.

Alex North for *Viva Zapata!,* 20th Century-Fox.

Miklos Rozsa for *Ivanhoe,* MGM.

Max Steiner for *The Miracle of Our Lady of Fatima,* Warner Bros.

(Scoring of a Musical Picture)

Alfred Newman for *With a Song in My Heart,* 20th Century-Fox.

Lennie Hayton for *Singin' in the Rain,* MGM.

Ray Heindorf and Max Steiner for *The Jazz Singer,* Warner Bros.

Gian-Carlo Menotti for *The Medium,* Lopert (Italy).

Walter Scharf for *Hans Christian Andersen,* Goldwyn, RKO Radio.

FILM EDITING

Elmo Williams and Harry Gerstad for *High Noon,* United Artists.

William Austin for *Flat Top,* Monogram.

Anne Bauchens for *The Greatest Show on Earth,* Paramount.

Ralph Kemplen for *Moulin Rouge,* United Artists.

Warren Low for *Come Back, Little Sheba,* Paramount.

COSTUME DESIGN
(Black and White)

Helen Rose for *The Bad and the Beautiful,* MGM.

Edith Head for *Carrie,* Paramount.

Charles LeMaire and Dorothy Jeakins for *My Cousin Rachel,* 20th Century-Fox.

Jean Louis for *Affair in Trinidad,* Columbia.

Sheila O'Brien for *Sudden Fear,* RKO Radio.
(Color)

Marcel Vertes for *Moulin Rouge,* United Artists.

Clave, Mary Wills, and Karinska for *Hans Christian Andersen,* Goldwyn, RKO Radio.

Edith Head, Dorothy Jeakins, and Miles White for *The Greatest Show on Earth,* Paramount.

Charles LeMaire for *With a Song in My Heart,* 20th Century-Fox.

Helen Rose and Gile Steele for *The Merry Widow,* MGM.

SPECIAL EFFECTS

Plymouth Adventure, MGM.

IRVING G. THALBERG MEMORIAL AWARD

Cecil B. DeMille.

HONORARY AWARDS

George Alfred Mitchell, for the design and development of the camera which bears his name and for his continued and dominant presence in the field of cinematography.

Joseph M. Schenck, for long and distinguished service to the motion picture industry.

Merian C. Cooper, for his many innovations and contributions to the art of motion pictures.

Harold Lloyd, master comedian and good citizen.

Bob Hope, for his contribution to the laughter of the world, his service to the motion picture industry, and his devotion to the American premise.[132]

Forbidden Games (France). Best Foreign Language Film first released in the United States during 1952.

1953

Awards presented March 25, 1954.

PICTURE

From Here to Eternity, Columbia. Produced by Buddy Adler.

Julius Caesar, MGM. Produced by John Houseman.

The Robe, 20th Century-Fox. Produced by Frank Ross.

Roman Holiday, Paramount. Produced by William Wyler.

Shane, Paramount. Produced by George Stevens.

ACTOR

William Holden in *Stalag 17,* Paramount.

Marlon Brando in *Julius Caesar,* MGM.

Richard Burton in *The Robe,* 20th Century-Fox.

Montgomery Clift in *From Here to Eternity,* Columbia.

Burt Lancaster in *From Here to Eternity,* Columbia.

ACTRESS

Audrey Hepburn in *Roman Holiday,* Paramount.

Leslie Caron in *Lili,* MGM.

Ava Gardner in *Mogambo,* MGM.

Deborah Kerr in *From Here to Eternity,* Columbia.

Maggie McNamara in *The Moon Is Blue,* United Artists.

SUPPORTING ACTOR

Frank Sinatra in *From Here to Eternity,* Columbia.

Eddie Albert in *Roman Holiday,* Paramount.

Brandon De Wilde in *Shane,* Paramount.

Jack Palance in *Shane,* Paramount.

Robert Strauss in *Stalag 17,* Paramount.

SUPPORTING ACTRESS

Donna Reed in *From Here to Eternity,* Columbia.

Grace Kelly in *Mogambo,* MGM.

Geraldine Page in *Hondo,* Warner Bros.

Marjorie Rambeau in *Torch Song,* MGM.

Thelma Ritter in *Pickup on South Street,* 20th Century-Fox.

DIRECTOR

Fred Zinnemann for *From Here to Eternity,* Columbia.

George Stevens for *Shane,* Paramount.

Charles Walters for *Lili,* MGM.

Billy Wilder for *Stalag 17,* Paramount.

William Wyler for *Roman Holiday,* Paramount.

WRITING

(Motion Picture Story)

Dalton Trumbo[133] **for *Roman Holiday,* Paramount.**

Ray Ashley, Morris Engel, and Ruth Orkin for *Little Fugitive,* Joseph Burstyn Inc.

Alec Coppel for *The Captain's Paradise,* Lopert Films-United Artists (United Kingdom).

Louis L'Amour for *Hondo,* Wayne-Fellows, Warner Bros.[134]

Beirne Lay, Jr., for *Above and Beyond,* MGM.

(Screenplay)

Daniel Taradash for *From Here to Eternity,* Columbia.

Eric Ambler for *The Cruel Sea,* Universal-International (United Kingdom).

Helen Deutsch for *Lili,* MGM.

A. B. Guthrie, Jr., for *Shane,* Paramount.

Ian McLellan Hunter and John Dighton for *Roman Holiday,* Paramount.

(Story and Screenplay)

Charles Brackett, Walter Reisch, and Richard Breen for *Titanic,* 20th Century-Fox.

Betty Comden and Adolph Green for *The Band Wagon,* MGM.

Millard Kaufman for *Take the High Ground,* MGM.

Richard Murphy for *The Desert Rats,* 20th Century-Fox.

Sam Rolfe and Harold Jack Bloom for *The Naked Spur,* MGM.

CINEMATOGRAPHY

(Black and White)

Burnett Guffey for *From Here to Eternity,* Columbia.

---

[132] Hope received an Oscar statuette for his third honorary award, but as emcee of the awards ceremonies he continued to joke about wanting an Oscar.

[133] The award was originally presented to Ian McLellan Hunter, who was fronting for the story's actual author, Trumbo, who was blacklisted. On December 15, 1992, the Academy removed Hunter's name from the records and inserted Trumbo's—posthumously.

[134] This nomination was withdrawn when the producer and the writer revealed that the story had been published in a magazine two years earlier.

Joseph C. Brun for *Martin Luther*, Louis de Rochemont Associates.

Hal Mohr for *The Four Poster*, Columbia.

Frank Planer and Henry Alekan for *Roman Holiday*, Paramount.

Joseph Ruttenberg for *Julius Caesar*, MGM.

(Color)

Loyal Griggs for *Shane*, Paramount.

Edward Cronjager for *Beneath the 12 Mile Reef*, 20th Century-Fox.

George Folsey for *All the Brothers Were Valiant*, MGM.

Robert Planck for *Lili*, MGM.

Leon Shamroy for *The Robe*, 20th Century-Fox.

ART DIRECTION—SET DECORATION

(Black and White)

***Julius Caesar*, MGM. Cedric Gibbons, Edward Carfagno; Edwin B. Willis, Hugh Hunt.**

Martin Luther, Louis de Rochemont Associates. Fritz Maurischat, Paul Markwitz.

The President's Lady, 20th Century-Fox. Lyle Wheeler, Leland Fuller; Paul S. Fox.

Roman Holiday, Paramount. Hal Pereira and Walter Tyler.

Titanic, 20th Century-Fox. Lyle Wheeler, Maurice Ransford; Stuart Reiss.

(Color)

The Robe, 20th Century-Fox. Lyle Wheeler, George W. Davis; Walter M. Scott, Paul S. Fox.

Knights of the Round Table, MGM. Alfred Junge, Hans Peters; John Jarvis.

Lili, MGM. Cedric Gibbons, Paul Groesse; Edwin B. Willis, Arthur Krams.

The Story of Three Loves, MGM. Cedric Gibbons, Preston Ames, Edward Carfagno, Gabriel Scognamillo; Edwin B. Willis, Keogh Gleason, Arthur Krams, Jack D. Moore.

Young Bess, MGM. Cedric Gibbons, Urie McCleary; Edwin B. Willis, Jack D. Moore.

SOUND RECORDING

John P. Livadary for *From Here to Eternity*, Columbia.

Leslie I. Carey for *Mississippi Gambler*, Universal-International.

William A. Mueller for *Calamity Jane*, Warner Bros.

Loren L. Ryder for *War of the Worlds*, Paramount.

A. W. Watkins for *Knights of the Round Table*, MGM.

MUSIC

(Song)

"Secret Love" from *Calamity Jane*, Warner Bros. Music by Sammy Fain, lyrics by Paul Francis Webster.

"The Moon Is Blue" from *The Moon Is Blue*, United Artists. Music by Herschel Burke Gilbert, lyrics by Sylvia Fine.

"My Flaming Heart" from *Small Town Girl*, MGM. Music by Nicholas Brodszky, lyrics by Leo Robin.

"Sadie Thompson's Song (Blue Pacific Blues)" from *Miss Sadie Thompson*, Columbia. Music by Lester Lee, lyrics by Ned Washington.

"That's Amore" from *The Caddy*, Paramount. Music by Harry Warren, lyrics by Jack Brooks.

(Music Score of a Dramatic or Comedy Picture)

Bronislau Kaper for *Lili*, MGM.

Hugo Friedhofer for *Above and Beyond*, MGM.

Louis Forbes for *This Is Cinerama*, Cinerama Productions Corp.

Miklos Rozsa for *Julius Caesar*, MGM.

Morris Stoloff and George Duning for *From Here to Eternity*, Columbia.

(Scoring of a Musical Picture)

Alfred Newman for *Call Me Madam*, 20th Century-Fox.

Adolph Deutsch for *The Band Wagon*, MGM.

Ray Heindorf for *Calamity Jane*, Warner Bros.

Frederick Hollander and Morris Stoloff for *The 5,000 Fingers of Dr. T.*, Columbia.

André Previn and Saul Chaplin for *Kiss Me Kate*, MGM.

FILM EDITING

William Lyon for *From Here to Eternity*, Columbia.

Everett Douglas for *War of the Worlds*, Paramount.

Otto Ludwig for *The Moon Is Blue*, United Artists.

Robert Swink for *Roman Holiday*, Paramount.

Irvine "Cotton" Warburton for *Crazylegs*, Republic.

COSTUME DESIGN

(Black and White)

Edith Head for *Roman Holiday*, Paramount.

Charles LeMaire and Renie for *The President's Lady*, 20th Century-Fox.

Jean Louis for *From Here to Eternity*, Columbia.

Walter Plunkett for *The Actress*, MGM.

Helen Rose and Herschel McCoy for *Dream Wife*, MGM.

(Color)

Charles LeMaire and Emile Santiago for *The Robe*, 20th Century-Fox.

Charles LeMaire and Travilla for *How to Marry a Millionaire*, 20th Century-Fox.

Mary Ann Nyberg for *The Band Wagon*, MGM.

Walter Plunkett for *Young Bess*, MGM.

Irene Sharaff for *Call Me Madam*, 20th Century-Fox.

SPECIAL EFFECTS

War of the Worlds, Paramount.

IRVING G. THALBERG MEMORIAL AWARD

George Stevens.

HONORARY AWARDS

Pete Smith, for his witty and pungent observations on the American scene in his series of "Pete Smith Specialties."

20th Century-Fox Film Corporation, in recognition of their imagination, showmanship and foresight in introducing the

revolutionary process known as CinemaScope.

Joseph I. Breen, for his conscientious, open-minded and dignified management of the Motion Picture Production Code.

The Bell and Howell Company, for their pioneering and basic achievements in the advancement of the motion picture industry.

1954
Awards presented March 30, 1955.

PICTURE

***On the Waterfront*, Horizon-American Corporation, Columbia. Produced by Sam Spiegel.**

The Caine Mutiny, Stanley Kramer Productions, Columbia. Produced by Stanley Kramer.

The Country Girl, Perlberg-Seaton Production, Paramount. Produced by William Perlberg.

Seven Brides for Seven Brothers, MGM. Produced by Jack Cummings.

Three Coins in the Fountain, 20th Century-Fox. Produced by Sol C. Siegel.

ACTOR

Marlon Brando in *On the Waterfront*, Columbia.

Humphrey Bogart in *The Caine Mutiny*, Columbia.

Bing Crosby in *The Country Girl*, Paramount.

James Mason in *A Star Is Born*, Warner Bros.

Dan O'Herlihy in *Adventures of Robinson Crusoe*, United Artists (Mexico).

ACTRESS

Grace Kelly in *The Country Girl*, Paramount.

Dorothy Dandridge[135] in *Carmen Jones*, Preminger, 20th Century-Fox.

Judy Garland in *A Star Is Born*, Warner Bros.

Audrey Hepburn in *Sabrina*, Paramount.

Jane Wyman in *Magnificent Obsession*, Universal-International.

SUPPORTING ACTOR

Edmond O'Brien in *The Barefoot Contessa*, United Artists.

Lee J. Cobb in *On the Waterfront*, Columbia.

Karl Malden in *On the Waterfront*, Columbia.

Rod Steiger in *On the Waterfront*, Columbia.

Tom Tully in *The Caine Mutiny*, Columbia.

SUPPORTING ACTRESS

Eva Marie Saint in *On the Waterfront*, Columbia.

Nina Foch in *Executive Suite*, MGM.

Katy Jurado in *Broken Lance*, 20th Century-Fox.

Jan Sterling in *The High and the Mighty*, Warner Bros.

Claire Trevor in *The High and the Mighty*, Warner Bros.

DIRECTOR

Elia Kazan for *On the Waterfront*, Columbia.

Alfred Hitchcock for *Rear Window*, Paramount.

George Seaton for *The Country Girl*, Paramount.

William Wellman for *The High and the Mighty*, Warner Bros.

Billy Wilder for *Sabrina*, Paramount.

WRITING

(Motion Picture Story)

Philip Yordan for *Broken Lance*, 20th Century-Fox.

François Boyer for *Forbidden Games*, Times Film Corp. (France).

Jed Harris and Tom Reed for *Night People*, 20th Century-Fox.

Ettore Margadonna for *Bread, Love and Dreams*, I.F.E. Releasing Corp. (Italy).

Lamar Trotti for *There's No Business Like Show Business*, 20th Century-Fox.

(Screenplay)

George Seaton for *The Country Girl*, Paramount.

Albert Hackett, Frances Goodrich, and Dorothy Kingsley for *Seven Brides for Seven Brothers*, MGM.

John Michael Hayes for *Rear Window*, Paramount.

Stanley Roberts for *The Caine Mutiny*, Columbia.

Billy Wilder, Samuel Taylor, and Ernest Lehman for *Sabrina*, Paramount.

(Story and Screenplay)

Budd Schulberg for *On the Waterfront*, Columbia.

Valentine Davies and Oscar Brodney for *The Glenn Miller Story*, Universal-International.

Joseph Mankiewicz for *The Barefoot Contessa*, United Artists.

Norman Panama and Melvin Frank for *Knock on Wood*, Paramount.

William Rose for *Genevieve*, Universal-International (United Kingdom).

CINEMATOGRAPHY

(Black and White)

Boris Kaufman for *On the Waterfront*, Columbia.

George Folsey for *Executive Suite*, MGM.

Charles Lang, Jr., for *Sabrina*, Paramount.

John Seitz for *Rogue Cop*, MGM.

John F. Warren for *The Country Girl*, Paramount.

(Color)

Milton Krasner for *Three Coins in the Fountain*, 20th Century-Fox.

Robert Burks for *Rear Window*, Patron Inc., Paramount.

George Folsey for *Seven Brides for Seven Brothers*, MGM.

Leon Shamroy for *The Egyptian*, 20th Century-Fox.

William V. Skall for *The Silver Chalice*, Warner Bros.

---

[135] First African-American performer to be nominated for a leading role.

ART DIRECTION—SET DECORATION

(Black and White)

On the Waterfront, Columbia. Richard Day.

The Country Girl, Paramount. Hal Pereira, Roland Anderson; Sam Comer, Grace Gregory.

Executive Suite, MGM. Cedric Gibbons, Edward Carfagno; Edwin B. Willis, Emile Kuri.

Le Plaisir, Mayer-Kingsley (France). Max Ophuls.

Sabrina, Paramount. Hal Pereira, Walter Tyler; Sam Comer, Ray Moyer.

(Color)

20,000 Leagues Under the Sea, Disney, Buena Vista. John Meehan; Emile Kuri.

Brigadoon, MGM. Cedric Gibbons, Preston Ames; Edwin B. Willis, Keogh Gleason.

Desirée, 20th Century-Fox. Lyle Wheeler, Leland Fuller; Walter M. Scott, Paul S. Fox.

Red Garters, Paramount. Hal Pereira, Roland Anderson; Sam Comer, Ray Moyer.

A Star Is Born, Warner Bros. Malcolm Bert, Gene Allen, Irene Sharaff; George James Hopkins.

SOUND RECORDING

Leslie I. Carey for The Glenn Miller Story, Universal-International.

John O. Aalberg for *Susan Slept Here,* RKO Radio.

John P. Livadary for *The Caine Mutiny,* Columbia.

Wesley C. Miller for *Brigadoon,* MGM.

Loren L. Ryder for *Rear Window,* Paramount.

MUSIC

(Song)

"Three Coins in the Fountain" from Three Coins in the Fountain, 20th
Century-Fox. Music by Jule Styne, lyrics by Sammy Cahn.

"Count Your Blessings Instead of Sheep" from *White Christmas,* Paramount. Music and lyrics by Irving Berlin.

"The High and the Mighty" from *The High and the Mighty,* Warner Bros. Music by Dimitri Tiomkin, lyrics by Ned Washington.

"Hold My Hand" from *Susan Slept Here,* RKO Radio. Music and lyrics by Jack Lawrence and Richard Myers.

"The Man That Got Away" from *A Star Is Born,* Warner Bros. Music by Harold Arlen, lyrics by Ira Gershwin.

(Music Score of a Dramatic or Comedy Picture)

Dimitri Tiomkin for The High and the Mighty, Warner Bros.

Larry Adler[136] for *Genevieve,* Universal-International (United Kingdom).

Leonard Bernstein for *On the Waterfront,* Horizon-American, Columbia.

Max Steiner for *The Caine Mutiny,* Columbia.

Franz Waxman for *The Silver Chalice,* Warner Bros.

(Scoring of a Musical Picture)

Adolph Deutsch and Saul Chaplin for Seven Brides for Seven Brothers, MGM.

Joseph Gershenson and Henry Mancini for *The Glenn Miller Story,* Universal-International.

Herschel Burke Gilbert for *Carmen Jones,* 20th Century-Fox.

Ray Heindorf for *A Star Is Born,* Warner Bros.

Alfred Newman and Lionel Newman for *There's No Business Like Show Business,* 20th Century-Fox.

FILM EDITING

Gene Milford for On the Waterfront, Columbia.

Ralph Dawson for *The High and the Mighty,* Warner Bros.

William A. Lyon and Henry Batista for *The Caine Mutiny,* Columbia.

Elmo Williams for *20,000 Leagues Under the Sea,* Disney, Buena Vista.

Ralph E. Winters for *Seven Brides for Seven Brothers,* MGM.

COSTUME DESIGN

(Black and White)

Edith Head for Sabrina, Paramount.

Georges Annenkov and Rosine Delamare for *The Earrings of Madame De . . .,* Arlan Pictures (France).

Christian Dior for *Indiscretion of an American Wife,* Columbia (U.S./Italy).

Jean Louis for *It Should Happen to You,* Columbia.

Helen Rose for *Executive Suite,* MGM.

(Color)

Sanzo Wada for Gate of Hell, Edward Harrison (Japan).[137]

Charles LeMaire and Rene Hubert for *Desirée,* 20th Century-Fox.

Charles LeMaire, Travilla, and Miles White for *There's No Business Like Show Business,* 20th Century-Fox.

Jean Louis, Mary Ann Nyberg, and Irene Sharaff for *A Star Is Born,* Warner Bros.

Irene Sharaff for *Brigadoon,* MGM.

SPECIAL EFFECTS

20,000 Leagues Under the Sea, Disney, Buena Vista.

Hell and High Water, 20th Century-Fox.

Them! Warner Bros.

HONORARY AWARDS

The Bausch & Lomb Optical Company, for their contributions to the advancement of the motion picture industry.

Kemp R. Niver, for the development of the Renovare Process, which has made possible the restoration of the

---

[136] Adler, the American-born harmonica virtuoso, was blacklisted because of his leftist politics, so he exiled himself to England, where he composed the score for this film. But because of the blacklist, Universal-International removed Adler's name from the credits for the film in the United States, substituting arranger and conductor Muir Mathieson's name. In June 1986 the Academy Board of Governors set the record straight and credited Adler with the nomination.

[137] First Japanese-made film to win a competitive award.

Library of Congress Paper Film Collection.

Greta Garbo, for her unforgettable screen performances.

Danny Kaye, for his unique talents, his service to the Academy, the motion picture industry, and the American people.

Jon Whiteley, for his outstanding juvenile performance in *The Little Kidnappers.*

Vincent Winter, for his outstanding juvenile performance in *The Little Kidnappers*

Gate of Hell (Japan). Best Foreign Language Film first released in the United States during 1954.

1955
Awards presented March 21, 1956.

PICTURE
Marty, Hecht and Lancaster's Steven Productions, United Artists. Produced by Harold Hecht.[138]

Love Is a Many-Splendored Thing, 20th Century-Fox. Produced by Buddy Adler.

Mister Roberts, Orange Productions, Warner Bros. Produced by Leland Hayward.

Picnic, Columbia. Produced by Fred Kohlmar.

The Rose Tattoo, Hal Wallis Productions, Paramount. Produced by Hal Wallis.

ACTOR
Ernest Borgnine in Marty, United Artists.

James Cagney in *Love Me or Leave Me,* MGM.

James Dean in *East of Eden,* Warner Bros.[139]

Frank Sinatra in *The Man With the Golden Arm,* Preminger, United Artists.

Spencer Tracy in *Bad Day at Black Rock,* MGM.

ACTRESS
Anna Magnani in The Rose Tattoo, Paramount.

Susan Hayward in *I'll Cry Tomorrow,* MGM.

Katharine Hepburn in *Summertime,* United Artists (United Kingdom/U.S.).

Jennifer Jones in *Love Is a Many-Splendored Thing,* 20th Century-Fox.

Eleanor Parker in *Interrupted Melody,* MGM.

SUPPORTING ACTOR
Jack Lemmon in Mister Roberts, Warner Bros.

Arthur Kennedy in *Trial,* MGM.

Joe Mantell in *Marty,* United Artists.

Sal Mineo in *Rebel Without a Cause,* Warner Bros.

Arthur O'Connell in *Picnic,* Columbia.

SUPPORTING ACTRESS
Jo Van Fleet in East of Eden, Warner Bros.

Betsy Blair in *Marty,* United Artists.

Peggy Lee in *Pete Kelly's Blues,* Warner Bros.

Marisa Pavan in *The Rose Tattoo,* Paramount.

Natalie Wood in *Rebel Without a Cause,* Warner Bros.

DIRECTOR
Delbert Mann for Marty, United Artists.

Elia Kazan for *East of Eden,* Warner Bros.

David Lean for *Summertime,* United Artists (United Kingdom/U.S.).

Joshua Logan for *Picnic,* Columbia.

John Sturges for *Bad Day at Black Rock,* MGM.

WRITING
(Motion Picture Story)
Daniel Fuchs for Love Me or Leave Me, MGM.

Joe Connelly and Bob Mosher for *The Private War of Major Benson,* Universal-International.

Beirne Lay, Jr., for *Strategic Air Command,* Paramount.

Jean Marsan, Henry Troyat, Jacques Perret, Henri Verneuil, and Raoul Ploquin for *The Sheep Has Four Legs,* U.M.P.O. (France).

Nicholas Ray for *Rebel Without a Cause,* Warner Bros.

(Screenplay)
Paddy Chayefsky for Marty, United Artists.

Richard Brooks for *Blackboard Jungle,* MGM.

Daniel Fuchs and Isobel Lennart for *Love Me or Leave Me,* MGM.

Millard Kaufman for *Bad Day at Black Rock,* MGM.

Paul Osborn for *East of Eden,* Warner Bros.

(Story and Screenplay)
William Ludwig and Sonya Levien for Interrupted Melody, MGM.

Betty Comden and Adolph Green for *It's Always Fair Weather,* MGM.

Melville Shavelson and Jack Rose for *The Seven Little Foys,* Paramount.

Milton Sperling and Emmett Lavery for *The Court-Martial of Billy Mitchell,* Warner Bros.

Jacques Tati and Henri Marquet for *Mr. Hulot's Holiday,* GBD International Releasing Corp. (France).

CINEMATOGRAPHY
(Black and White)
James Wong Howe for The Rose Tattoo, Paramount.

Arthur E. Arling for *I'll Cry Tomorrow,* MGM.

Russell Harlan for *Blackboard Jungle,* MGM.

Charles Lang for *Queen Bee,* Columbia.

Joseph LaShelle for *Marty,* United Artists.

(Color)
Robert Burks for To Catch a Thief, Paramount.

Harold Lipstein for *A Man Called Peter,* 20th Century-Fox.

---

[138] First best picture winner based on a play written for and previously produced on television.

[139] Posthumous nomination.

Leon Shamroy for *Love Is a Many-Splendored Thing,* 20th Century-Fox.

Harry Stradling for *Guys and Dolls,* Goldwyn, MGM.

Robert Surtees for *Oklahoma!,* Magna Theatre Corp.

ART DIRECTION—SET DECORATION

(Black and White)

The Rose Tattoo, Paramount. Hal Pereira, Tambi Larsen; Sam Comer, Arthur Krams.

Blackboard Jungle, MGM. Cedric Gibbons, Randall Duell; Edwin B. Willis, Henry Grace.

I'll Cry Tomorrow, MGM. Cedric Gibbons, Malcolm Brown; Edwin B. Willis, Hugh B. Hunt.

The Man With the Golden Arm, United Artists. Joseph C. Wright; Darrell Silvera.

Marty, United Artists. Edward S. Haworth, Walter Simonds; Robert Priestley.

(Color)

Picnic, Columbia. William Flannery, Jo Mielziner; Robert Priestley.

Daddy Long Legs, 20th Century-Fox. Lyle Wheeler, John DeCuir; Walter M. Scott, Paul S. Fox.

Guys and Dolls, Goldwyn, MGM. Oliver Smith, Joseph C. Wright; Howard Bristol.

Love Is a Many-Splendored Thing, 20th Century-Fox. Lyle Wheeler, George W. Davis; Walter M. Scott, Jack Stubbs.

To Catch a Thief, Paramount. Hal Pereira, Joseph McMillan Johnson; Sam Comer, Arthur Krams.

SOUND RECORDING

Fred Hynes, sound director, Todd-AO Sound Dept., for *Oklahoma!,* Magna Theatre Corp.

Carl W. Faulkner for *Love Is a Many-Splendored Thing,* 20th Century-Fox.

Watson Jones, sound director, RCA Sound Dept., for *Not as a Stranger,* United Artists.

Wesley C. Miller for *Love Me or Leave Me,* MGM.

William A. Mueller for *Mister Roberts,* Warner Bros.

MUSIC

(Song)

"Love Is a Many-Splendored Thing" from *Love Is a Many-Splendored Thing,* 20th Century-Fox. Music by Sammy Fain, lyrics by Paul Francis Webster.

"I'll Never Stop Loving You" from *Love Me or Leave Me,* MGM. Music by Nicholas Brodszky, lyrics by Sammy Cahn.

"Something's Gotta Give" from *Daddy Long Legs,* 20th Century-Fox. Music and lyrics by Johnny Mercer.

"(Love Is) The Tender Trap" from *The Tender Trap,* MGM. Music by James Van Heusen, lyrics by Sammy Cahn.

"Unchained Melody" from *Unchained,* Warner Bros. Music by Alex North, lyrics by Hy Zaret.

(Music Score of a Dramatic or Comedy Picture)

Alfred Newman for *Love Is a Many-Splendored Thing,* 20th Century-Fox.

Elmer Bernstein for *The Man With the Golden Arm,* United Artists.

George Duning for *Picnic,* Columbia.

Alex North for *The Rose Tattoo,* Paramount.

Max Steiner for *Battle Cry,* Warner Bros.

(Scoring of a Musical Picture)

Robert Russell Bennett, Jay Blackton, and Adolph Deutsch for *Oklahoma!,* Magna Theatre Corp.

Jay Blackton and Cyril J. Mockridge for *Guys and Dolls,* Goldwyn, MGM.

Percy Faith and George Stoll for *Love Me or Leave Me,* MGM.

Alfred Newman for *Daddy Long Legs,* 20th Century-Fox.

André Previn for *It's Always Fair Weather,* MGM.

FILM EDITING

Charles Nelson and William A. Lyon for *Picnic,* Columbia.

Warren Low for *The Rose Tattoo,* Paramount.

Alma Macrorie for *The Bridges at Toko-Ri,* Paramount.

Gene Ruggiero and George Boemler for *Oklahoma!,* Magna Theatre Corp.

Ferris Webster for *Blackboard Jungle,* MGM.

COSTUME DESIGN

(Black and White)

Helen Rose for *I'll Cry Tomorrow,* MGM.

Beatrice Dawson for *The Pickwick Papers,* Kingsley International (United Kingdom).

Edith Head for *The Rose Tattoo,* Paramount.

Tadaoto Kainoscho for *Ugetsu,* Edward Harrison (Japan).

Jean Louis for *Queen Bee,* Columbia.

(Color)

Charles LeMaire for *Love Is a Many-Splendored Thing,* 20th Century-Fox.

Edith Head for *To Catch a Thief,* Paramount.

Charles LeMaire and Mary Wills for *The Virgin Queen,* 20th Century-Fox.

Helen Rose for *Interrupted Melody,* MGM.

Irene Sharaff for *Guys and Dolls,* Goldwyn, MGM.

SPECIAL EFFECTS

The Bridges at Toko-Ri, Paramount.

The Dam Busters, Warner Bros. (United Kingdom).

The Rains of Ranchipur, 20th Century-Fox.

HONORARY AWARD

Samurai, The Legend of Musashi (Japan). Best Foreign Language Film first released in the United States during 1955.

1956
Awards presented March 27, 1957.

PICTURE[140]

Around the World in 80 Days, The
Michael Todd Co., Inc., United
Artists. Produced by Michael
Todd.

Friendly Persuasion, Allied Artists.
Produced by William Wyler.

Giant, Giant Production, Warner Bros.
Produced by George Stevens and
Henry Ginsberg.

The King and I, 20th Century-Fox.
Produced by Charles Brackett.

The Ten Commandments, Motion Picture
Associates, Inc., Paramount. Produced
by Cecil B. DeMille.

ACTOR

**Yul Brynner in *The King and I*, 20th
Century-Fox.**

James Dean in *Giant*, Warner Bros.[141]

Kirk Douglas in *Lust for Life*, MGM.

Rock Hudson in *Giant*, Warner Bros.

Laurence Olivier in *Richard III*, London
Films, Lopert Films (United
Kingdom).

ACTRESS

**Ingrid Bergman in *Anastasia*, 20th
Century-Fox.**

Carroll Baker in *Baby Doll*, Warner Bros.

Katharine Hepburn in *The Rainmaker*,
Paramount.

Nancy Kelly in *The Bad Seed*, Warner
Bros.

Deborah Kerr in *The King and I*, 20th
Century-Fox.

SUPPORTING ACTOR

**Anthony Quinn in *Lust for Life*,
MGM.**

Don Murray in *Bus Stop*, 20th Century-
Fox.

Anthony Perkins in *Friendly Persuasion*,
Allied Artists.

Mickey Rooney in *The Bold and the Brave*,
RKO Radio.

Robert Stack in *Written on the Wind*,
Universal-International.

SUPPORTING ACTRESS

**Dorothy Malone in *Written on the
Wind*, Universal-International.**

Mildred Dunnock in *Baby Doll*, Warner
Bros.

Eileen Heckart in *The Bad Seed*, Warner
Bros.

Mercedes McCambridge in *Giant*, Warner
Bros.

Patty McCormack in *The Bad Seed*,
Warner Bros.

DIRECTOR

**George Stevens for *Giant*, Warner
Bros.**

Michael Anderson for *Around the World in
80 Days*, United Artists.

Walter Lang for *The King and I*, 20th
Century-Fox.

King Vidor for *War and Peace*, Paramount
(Italy/U.S.).

William Wyler for *Friendly Persuasion*,
Allied Artists.

WRITING

(Motion Picture Story)

**Dalton Trumbo for *The Brave One*,
King Bros., RKO Radio.[142]**

Edward Bernds and Elwood Ullman for
High Society, Allied Artists.[143]

Leo Katcher for *The Eddy Duchin Story*,
Columbia.

Jean-Paul Sartre for *The Proud and the
Beautiful*, Kingsley International
(France).

Cesare Zavattini for *Umberto D.*, Harrison
& Davidson (Italy).

(Screenplay—Adapted)[144]

**James Poe, John Farrow, and S. J.
Perelman for *Around the World in
80 Days*, United Artists.**

Norman Corwin for *Lust for Life*, MGM.

Fred Guiol and Ivan Moffat for *Giant*,
Warner Bros.

Tennessee Williams for *Baby Doll*, Warner
Bros.

Michael Wilson for *Friendly Persuasion*,
Allied Artists.[145]

(Screenplay—Original)[146]

**Albert Lamorisse for *The Red
Balloon*, Lopert Films (France).**

Federico Fellini and Tullio Pinelli for *La
Strada*, Trans-Lux Distributing Corp.
(Italy).

Robert Lewin for *The Bold and the Brave*,
RKO Radio.

William Rose for *The Ladykillers*,
Continental Distributing (United
Kingdom).

Andrew L. Stone for *Julie*, MGM.

---

[140] For the first time, all the nominees for best picture were filmed in color.

[141] Only person to receive two posthumous nominations for acting. Lyricist Howard Ashman was also nominated posthumously two years in a row (1991, 1992).

[142] The film's credits listed the author as "Robert Rich," and that was the name called out at the awards ceremony. Rich failed to show, however, and it was eventually learned that Rich was the pseudonym of Trumbo, who was blacklisted. The Academy presented the Oscar to Trumbo on May 2, 1975.

[143] Members of the writers branch apparently thought they were voting for the authors of the year's other film called *High Society*, so when Bernds and Ullman learned that they had been nominated for their work on a Bowery Boys movie, they good-naturedly declined the nomination. But how this error happened is one of the Academy's abiding mysteries: John Patrick's screenplay for the MGM musical *High Society* would not have been eligible in this category, since it was based on *The Philadelphia Story* and wasn't an original story.

[144] Category renamed.

[145] In a year of astonishing mix-ups in the writing nominations, Wilson was ruled ineligible for the award because of his refusal to testify about communism in the film industry. His name also did not appear in the credits for the film. At first the Academy said that it would consider the screenplay for the award but not the writer. Finally the nomination was withdrawn from the ballot.

[146] Category renamed.

CINEMATOGRAPHY
(Black and White)
Joseph Ruttenberg for *Somebody Up There Likes Me*, MGM.

Burnett Guffey for *The Harder They Fall*, Columbia.

Boris Kaufman for *Baby Doll*, Warner Bros.

Hal Rosson for *The Bad Seed*, Warner Bros.

Walter Strenge for *Stagecoach to Fury*, 20th Century-Fox.

(Color)
Lionel Lindon for *Around the World in 80 Days*, United Artists.

Jack Cardiff for *War and Peace*, Paramount (Italy/U.S.).

Loyal Griggs for *The Ten Commandments*, Paramount.

Leon Shamroy for *The King and I*, 20th Century-Fox.

Harry Stradling for *The Eddy Duchin Story*, Columbia.

ART DIRECTION—SET DECORATION
(Black and White)
***Somebody Up There Likes Me*, MGM. Cedric Gibbons,[147] Malcolm F. Brown; Edwin B. Willis, F. Keogh Gleason.**

The Proud and the Profane, Paramount. Hal Pereira, A. Earl Hedrick; Samuel M. Comer, Frank R. McKelvy.

Seven Samurai,[148] Kingsley International (Japan). Takashi Matsuyama.

The Solid Gold Cadillac, Columbia. Ross Bellah; William R. Kiernan, Louis Diage.

Teenage Rebel, 20th Century-Fox. Lyle R. Wheeler, Jack Martin Smith; Walter M. Scott, Stuart A. Reiss.

(Color)
***The King and I*, 20th Century-Fox. Lyle R. Wheeler, John DeCuir; Walter M. Scott, Paul S. Fox.**

Around the World in 80 Days, United Artists. James W. Sullivan, Ken Adam; Ross J. Dowd.

Giant, Warner Bros. Boris Leven; Ralph S. Hurst.

Lust for Life, MGM. Cedric Gibbons, Hans Peters, Preston Ames; Edwin B. Willis, F. Keogh Gleason.

The Ten Commandments, Paramount. Hal Pereira, Walter H. Tyler, Albert Nozaki; Sam M. Comer, Ray Moyer.

SOUND RECORDING
Carl Faulkner for *The King and I*, 20th Century-Fox.

Gordon R. Glennan, Westrex Sound Services Inc., and Gordon Sawyer, Samuel Goldwyn Studio Sound Dept., for *Friendly Persuasion*, Allied Artists.

John Livadary for *The Eddy Duchin Story*, Columbia.

John Myers, King Bros. Productions Inc. Sound Dept., for *The Brave One*, RKO Radio.

Loren L. Ryder for *The Ten Commandments*, Paramount.

MUSIC
(Song)
"Whatever Will Be, Will Be (Que Será, Será)" from *The Man Who Knew Too Much*, Paramount. Music and lyrics by Jay Livingston and Ray Evans.

"Friendly Persuasion (Thee I Love)" from *Friendly Persuasion*, Allied Artists. Music by Dimitri Tiomkin, lyrics by Paul Francis Webster.

"Julie" from *Julie*, MGM. Music by Leith Stevens, lyrics by Tom Adair.

"True Love" from *High Society*, MGM. Music and lyrics by Cole Porter.

"Written on the Wind" from *Written on the Wind*, Universal-International. Music by Victor Young, lyrics by Sammy Cahn.

(Music Score of a Dramatic or Comedy Picture)

Victor Young for *Around the World in 80 Days*, United Artists.[149]

Hugo Friedhofer for *Between Heaven and Hell*, 20th Century-Fox.

Alfred Newman for *Anastasia*, 20th Century-Fox.

Alex North for *The Rainmaker*, Paramount.

Dimitri Tiomkin for *Giant*, Warner Bros.

(Scoring of a Musical Picture)
Alfred Newman and Ken Darby for *The King and I*, 20th Century-Fox.

Johnny Green and Saul Chaplin for *High Society*, MGM.

Lionel Newman for *The Best Things in Life Are Free*, 20th Century-Fox.

George Stoll and Johnny Green for *Meet Me in Las Vegas*, MGM.

Morris Stoloff and George Duning for *The Eddy Duchin Story*, Columbia.

FILM EDITING
Gene Ruggiero and Paul Weatherwax for *Around the World in 80 Days*, United Artists.

Albert Akst for *Somebody Up There Likes Me*, MGM.

Anne Bauchens for *The Ten Commandments*, Paramount.

William Hornbeck, Philip W. Anderson, and Fred Bohanan for *Giant*, Warner Bros.

Merrill G. White for *The Brave One*, RKO Radio.

COSTUME DESIGN
(Black and White)
Jean Louis for *The Solid Gold Cadillac*, Columbia.

Kohei Ezaki for *Seven Samurai*, Kingsley International (Japan).

Edith Head for *The Proud and the Profane*, Paramount.

Charles LeMaire and Mary Wills for *Teenage Rebel*, 20th Century-Fox.

---

[147] With his eleventh win, Gibbons sets a record for most Oscars received by an individual other than a producer. Only Walt Disney was cited more often. Gibbons' two nominations this year, his last, bring his career total to forty.
[148] The Academy cited the film under its original American-release title, *The Magnificent Seven*. To avoid confusion with the 1960 American remake, we've used the title by which the Japanese film is now generally known.
[149] Award presented posthumously—after twenty-one unsuccessful nominations.

Helen Rose for *The Power and the Prize*, MGM.

(Color)

Irene Sharaff for *The King and I*, 20th Century-Fox.

Marie De Matteis for *War and Peace*, Paramount (Italy/U.S.).

Edith Head, Ralph Jester, John Jensen, Dorothy Jeakins, and Arnold Friberg for *The Ten Commandments*, Paramount.

Moss Mabry and Marjorie Best for *Giant*, Warner Bros.

Miles White for *Around the World in 80 Days*, United Artists.

SPECIAL EFFECTS

John Fulton for *The Ten Commandments*, Paramount.

A. Arnold Gillespie, Irving Ries, and Wesley C. Miller for *Forbidden Planet*, MGM.

FOREIGN LANGUAGE FILM[150]

***La Strada*, Italy.**

The Captain of Kopenick, Federal Republic of Germany.

Gervais, France.

Harp of Burma, Japan.

Qivitoq, Denmark.

IRVING G. THALBERG MEMORIAL AWARD

Buddy Adler.

JEAN HERSHOLT HUMANITARIAN AWARD[151]

Y. Frank Freeman.

HONORARY AWARD

Eddie Cantor, for distinguished service to the film industry.

1957

Awards presented March 26, 1958.

PICTURE

***The Bridge on the River Kwai*, A Horizon Pictures Productions,**

Columbia (United Kingdom). Produced by Sam Spiegel.

Peyton Place, Jerry Wald Productions, Inc., 20th Century-Fox. Produced by Jerry Wald.

Sayonara, William Goetz Productions, Warner Bros. Produced by William Goetz.

12 Angry Men, Orion-Nova Production, United Artists. Produced by Henry Fonda and Reginald Rose.

Witness for the Prosecution, Edward Small-Arthur Hornblow Production, United Artists. Produced by Arthur Hornblow, Jr.

ACTOR

Alec Guinness in *The Bridge on the River Kwai*, Columbia.

Marlon Brando in *Sayonara*, 20th Century-Fox.

Anthony Franciosa in *A Hatful of Rain*, 20th Century-Fox.

Charles Laughton in *Witness for the Prosecution*, United Artists.

Anthony Quinn in *Wild Is the Wind*, Wallis, Paramount.

ACTRESS

Joanne Woodward in *The Three Faces of Eve*, 20th Century-Fox.

Deborah Kerr in *Heaven Knows, Mr. Allison*, 20th Century-Fox.

Anna Magnani in *Wild Is the Wind*, Paramount.

Elizabeth Taylor in *Raintree County*, MGM.

Lana Turner in *Peyton Place*, 20th Century-Fox.

SUPPORTING ACTOR

Red Buttons in *Sayonara*, Warner Bros.

Vittorio De Sica in *A Farewell to Arms*, Selznick, 20th Century-Fox.

Sessue Hayakawa in *The Bridge on the River Kwai*, Columbia (United Kingdom).

Arthur Kennedy in *Peyton Place*, 20th Century-Fox.

Russ Tamblyn in *Peyton Place*, 20th Century-Fox.

SUPPORTING ACTRESS

Miyoski Umeki in *Sayonara*, Warner Bros.

Carolyn Jones in *The Bachelor Party*, United Artists.

Elsa Lanchester in *Witness for the Prosecution*, United Artists.

Hope Lange in *Peyton Place*, 20th Century-Fox.

Diane Varsi in *Peyton Place*, 20th Century-Fox.

DIRECTOR

David Lean for *The Bridge on the River Kwai*, Columbia (United Kingdom).

Joshua Logan for *Sayonara*, Warner Bros.

Sidney Lumet for *12 Angry Men*, United Artists.

Mark Robson for *Peyton Place*, 20th Century-Fox.

Billy Wilder for *Witness for the Prosecution*, United Artists.

WRITING

(Screenplay—Based on Material From Another Medium)[152]

Pierre Boulle, Michael Wilson, and Carl Foreman[153] for *The Bridge on the River Kwai*, Columbia.

John Michael Hayes for *Peyton Place*, 20th Century-Fox.

John Lee Mahin and John Huston for *Heaven Knows, Mr. Allison*, 20th Century-Fox.

Paul Osborn for *Sayonara*, Warner Bros.

Reginald Rose for *12 Angry Men*, United Artists.

(Story and Screenplay—Written Directly for the Screen)[154]

George Wells for *Designing Woman*, MGM.

Federico Fellini, Ennio Flaiano, and Tullio Pinelli, story; Federico Fellini and

---

[150] New category.
[151] New award.
[152] Category renamed.
[153] The Oscar was originally presented only to Boulle, because Wilson and Foreman, both blacklisted, did not receive screen credit for their adaptation of the novel by Boulle. In December 1984 the Academy altered its records and presented Oscars to Wilson and Foreman posthumously.
[154] Category renamed.

Ennio Flaiano, screenplay, for *I Vitelloni,* API-Janus (Italy/France).

Leonard Gershe for *Funny Face,* Paramount.

Barney Slater and Joel Kane, story; Dudley Nichols, screenplay, for *The Tin Star,* Paramount.

Ralph Wheelwright, story; R. Wright Campbell, Ivan Goff, and Ben Roberts, screenplay, for *Man of a Thousand Faces,* Universal-International.

CINEMATOGRAPHY[155]

Jack Hildyard for *The Bridge on the River Kwai,* Columbia (United Kingdom).

Ellsworth Fredericks for *Sayonara,* Warner Bros.

Ray June for *Funny Face,* Paramount.

Milton Krasner for *An Affair to Remember,* 20th Century-Fox.

William Mellor for *Peyton Place,* 20th Century-Fox.

ART DIRECTION—SET DECORATION

***Sayonara,* Warner Bros. Ted Haworth; Robert Priestley.**

Funny Face, Paramount. Hal Pereira, George W. Davis; Sam Comer, Ray Moyer.

Les Girls, Siegel, MGM. William A. Horning, Gene Allen; Edwin B. Willis, Richard Pefferle.

Pal Joey, Columbia. Walter Holscher; William Kiernan, Louis Diage.

Raintree County, MGM. William A. Horning, Urie McCleary; Edwin B. Willis, Hugh Hunt.

SOUND

George Groves for *Sayonara,* Goetz, Warner Bros.

George Dutton for *Gunfight at the O.K. Corral,* Paramount.

John P. Livadary for *Pal Joey,* Essex-Sidney, Columbia.

Wesley C. Miller for *Les Girls,* MGM.

Gordon Sawyer, Samuel Goldwyn Studio Sound Dept., for *Witness for the Prosecution,* United Artists.

MUSIC
(Song)

"All the Way" from *The Joker Is Wild,* Paramount. Music by James Van Heusen, lyrics by Sammy Cahn.

"An Affair to Remember" from *An Affair to Remember,* 20th Century-Fox. Music by Harry Warren, lyrics by Harold Adamson and Leo McCarey.

"April Love" from *April Love,* 20th Century-Fox. Music by Sammy Fain, lyrics by Paul Francis Webster.

"Tammy" from *Tammy and the Bachelor,* Universal-International. Music and lyrics by Ray Evans and Jay Livingston.

"Wild Is the Wind" from *Wild Is the Wind,* Paramount. Music by Dimitri Tiomkin, lyrics by Ned Washington.

(Score)[156]

Malcolm Arnold for *The Bridge on the River Kwai,* Columbia (United Kingdom).

Hugo Friedhofer for *An Affair to Remember,* 20th Century-Fox.

Hugo Friedhofer for *Boy on a Dolphin,* 20th Century-Fox.

Johnny Green for *Raintree County,* MGM.

Paul Smith for *Perri,* Disney, Buena Vista.

FILM EDITING

Peter Taylor for *The Bridge on the River Kwai,* Columbia (United Kingdom).

Viola Lawrence and Jerome Thoms for *Pal Joey,* Columbia.

Warren Low for *Gunfight at the O.K. Corral,* Paramount.

Daniel Mandell for *Witness for the Prosecution,* United Artists.

Arthur P. Schmidt and Philip W. Anderson for *Sayonara,* Warner Bros.

COSTUME DESIGN

Orry-Kelly for *Les Girls,* MGM.

Edith Head and Hubert de Givenchy for *Funny Face,* Paramount.

Charles LeMaire for *An Affair to Remember,* 20th Century-Fox.

Jean Louis for *Pal Joey,* Columbia.

Walter Plunkett for *Raintree County,* MGM.

SPECIAL EFFECTS

***The Enemy Below,* 20th Century-Fox. Walter Rossi, audible.**

The Spirit of St. Louis, Warner Bros. Louis Lichtenfield, visual.

FOREIGN LANGUAGE FILM

***The Nights of Cabiria,* Italy.**

The Devil Came at Night, Federal Republic of Germany.

Gates of Paris, France.

Mother India, India.

Nine Lives, Norway.

JEAN HERSHOLT HUMANITARIAN AWARD

Samuel Goldwyn.

HONORARY AWARDS

Charles Brackett, for outstanding service to the Academy.

B. B. Kahane, for distinguished service to the motion picture industry.

Gilbert M. ("Broncho Billy") Anderson, motion picture pioneer, for his contributions to the development of motion pictures as entertainment.

The Society of Motion Picture and Television Engineers for their contributions to the advancement of the motion picture industry.

---

[155] Separation of Cinematography, Art Direction, and Costume categories into black and white and color temporarily eliminated.
[156] Division of the category into scores for musicals and scores for nonmusical films temporarily abandoned.

1958
Awards presented April 6, 1959.

PICTURE
Gigi, Arthur Freed Productions, Inc., MGM. Produced by Arthur Freed.

Auntie Mame, Warner Bros. Jack L. Warner, studio head.

Cat on a Hot Tin Roof, Avon Productions, Inc., MGM. Produced by Lawrence Weingarten.

The Defiant Ones, Stanley Kramer Productions, United Artists. Produced by Stanley Kramer.

Separate Tables, Clifton Productions, Inc., United Artists. Produced by Harold Hecht.

ACTOR
David Niven in *Separate Tables,* United Artists.

Tony Curtis in *The Defiant Ones,* United Artists.

Paul Newman in *Cat on a Hot Tin Roof,* MGM.

Sidney Poitier in *The Defiant Ones,* United Artists.

Spencer Tracy in *The Old Man and the Sea,* Warner Bros.

ACTRESS
Susan Hayward in *I Want to Live!,* United Artists.

Deborah Kerr in *Separate Tables,* United Artists.

Shirley MacLaine in *Some Came Running,* MGM.

Rosalind Russell in *Auntie Mame,* Warner Bros.

Elizabeth Taylor in *Cat on a Hot Tin Roof,* Avon, MGM.

SUPPORTING ACTOR
Burl Ives in *The Big Country,* United Artists.

Theodore Bikel in *The Defiant Ones,* Kramer, United Artists.

Lee J. Cobb in *The Brothers Karamazov,* MGM.

Arthur Kennedy in *Some Came Running,* MGM.

Gig Young in *Teacher's Pet,* Paramount.

SUPPORTING ACTRESS
Wendy Hiller in *Separate Tables,* United Artists.

Peggy Cass in *Auntie Mame,* Warner Bros.

Martha Hyer in *Some Came Running,* MGM.

Maureen Stapleton in *Lonelyhearts,* United Artists.

Cara Williams in *The Defiant Ones,* United Artists.

DIRECTOR
Vincente Minnelli for *Gigi,* MGM.

Richard Brooks for *Cat on a Hot Tin Roof,* MGM.

Stanley Kramer for *The Defiant Ones,* United Artists.

Mark Robson for *The Inn of the Sixth Happiness,* 20th Century-Fox.

Robert Wise for *I Want to Live!,* United Artists.

WRITING
(Screenplay—Based on Material From Another Medium)

Alan Jay Lerner for *Gigi,* MGM.

Richard Brooks and James Poe for *Cat on a Hot Tin Roof,* MGM.

Nelson Gidding and Don Mankiewicz for *I Want to Live!,* United Artists.

Alec Guinness for *The Horse's Mouth,* United Artists (United Kingdom).

Terence Rattigan and John Gay for *Separate Tables,* United Artists.

(Story and Screenplay—Written Directly for the Screen)

Nedrick Young[157] and Harold Jacob Smith for *The Defiant Ones,* Kramer, United Artists.

Paddy Chayefsky for *The Goddess,* Columbia.

James Edward Grant, story; William Bowers and James Edward Grant, screenplay, for *The Sheepman,* MGM.

Fay Kanin and Michael Kanin for *Teacher's Pet,* Paramount.

Melville Shavelson and Jack Rose for *Houseboat,* Paramount.

CINEMATOGRAPHY[158]
(Black and White)

Sam Leavitt for *The Defiant Ones,* United Artists.

Daniel L. Fapp for *Desire Under the Elms,* Paramount.

Charles Lang, Jr., for *Separate Tables,* United Artists.

Lionel Lindon for *I Want to Live!,* United Artists.

Joe MacDonald for *The Young Lions,* 20th Century-Fox.

(Color)

Joseph Ruttenberg for *Gigi,* MGM.[159]

William Daniels for *Cat on a Hot Tin Roof,* MGM.

James Wong Howe for *The Old Man and the Sea,* Warner Bros.

Leon Shamroy for *South Pacific,* 20th Century-Fox.

Harry Stradling, Sr., for *Auntie Mame,* Warner Bros.

ART DIRECTION—SET DECORATION
Gigi, Freed, MGM. William A. Horning, Preston Ames; Henry Grace, Keogh Gleason.

Auntie Mame, Warner Bros. Malcolm Bert; George James Hopkins.

Bell, Book and Candle, Columbia. Cary Odell; Louis Diage.

A Certain Smile, 20th Century-Fox. Lyle R. Wheeler, John DeCuir; Walter M. Scott, Paul S. Fox.

Vertigo, Paramount. Hal Pereira, Henry

---

[157] The award was originally presented to Young, who was blacklisted, under his pseudonym, Nathan E. Douglas. The record was corrected posthumously.

[158] Division into black-and-white and color categories reinstated.

[159] With his fourth Oscar, Ruttenberg sets a record for wins in the cinematography category, later tied by Leon Shamroy (1963).

Bumstead; Sam Comer, Frank McKelvy.

SOUND[160]

Fred Hynes, Todd-AO Sound Dept., for *South Pacific*, Magna Theatre Corp.

Leslie I. Carey for *A Time to Love and a Time to Die*, Universal-International.

George Dutton for *Vertigo*, Paramount.

Carl Faulkner for *The Young Lions*, 20th Century-Fox.

Gordon E. Sawyer, Samuel Goldwyn Studio Sound Dept., for *I Want to Live!*, United Artists.

MUSIC
(Song)

"Gigi" from *Gigi*, MGM. Music by Frederick Loewe, lyrics by Alan Jay Lerner.

"Almost in Your Arms (Love Song from *Houseboat*)" from *Houseboat*, Paramount. Music and lyrics by Jay Livingston and Ray Evans.

"A Certain Smile" from *A Certain Smile*, 20th Century-Fox. Music by Sammy Fain, lyrics by Paul Francis Webster.

"To Love and Be Loved" from *Some Came Running*, MGM. Music by James Van Heusen, lyrics by Sammy Cahn.

"A Very Precious Love" from *Marjorie Morningstar*, Warner Bros. Music by Sammy Fain, lyrics by Paul Francis Webster.

(Scoring of a Dramatic or Comedy Picture)[161]

Dimitri Tiomkin for *The Old Man and the Sea*, Warner Bros.

Hugo Friedhofer for *The Young Lions*, 20th Century-Fox.

Jerome Moross for *The Big Country*, United Artists.

David Raksin for *Separate Tables*, United Artists.

Oliver Wallace for *White Wilderness*, Disney, Buena Vista.

(Scoring of a Musical Picture)

André Previn for *Gigi*, Freed, MGM.

Yuri Faier and Gennady Rozhdestvensky for *The Bolshoi Ballet*, Rank Film Distributors of America (United Kingdom).

Ray Heindorf for *Damn Yankees*, Warner Bros.

Alfred Newman and Ken Darby for *South Pacific*, Magna Theatre Corp.

Lionel Newman for *Mardi Gras*, 20th Century-Fox.

FILM EDITING

Adrienne Fazan for *Gigi*, MGM.

William Hornbeck for *I Want to Live!*, United Artists.

Frederick Knudtson for *The Defiant Ones*, United Artists.

William A. Lyon and Al Clark for *Cowboy*, Columbia.

William Ziegler for *Auntie Mame*, Warner Bros.

COSTUME DESIGN
(Black and White or Color)

Cecil Beaton for *Gigi*, MGM.

Ralph Jester, Edith Head, and John Jensen for *The Buccaneer*, Paramount.

Charles LeMaire and Mary Wills for *A Certain Smile*, 20th Century-Fox.

Jean Louis for *Bell, Book and Candle*, Columbia.

Walter Plunkett for *Some Came Running*, MGM.

SPECIAL EFFECTS

***Tom Thumb*, MGM. Tom Howard, visual.**

Torpedo Run, MGM. A. Arnold Gillespie, visual; Harold Humbrock, audible.

FOREIGN LANGUAGE FILM

***My Uncle*, France.**

Arms and the Man, Federal Republic of Germany.

The Road a Year Long, Yugoslavia.

The Usual Unidentified Thieves (a.k.a. *Big Deal on Madonna Street*), Italy.

La Venganza, Spain.

IRVING G. THALBERG MEMORIAL AWARD

Jack L. Warner.

HONORARY AWARD

Maurice Chevalier, for his contributions to the world of entertainment for more than half a century.

1959
Awards presented April 4, 1960.

PICTURE

***Ben-Hur*, MGM.[162] Produced by Sam Zimbalist.**

Anatomy of a Murder, Otto Preminger Productions, Columbia. Produced by Otto Preminger.

The Diary of Anne Frank, 20th Century-Fox. Produced by George Stevens.

The Nun's Story, Warner Bros. Produced by Henry Blanke.

Room at the Top, Romulus Films, Ltd., Production, Continental Distributing Inc. (United Kingdom). Produced by John Woolf and James Woolf.

ACTOR

Charlton Heston in *Ben-Hur*, MGM.

Laurence Harvey in *Room at the Top*, Romulus, Continental (United Kingdom).

Jack Lemmon in *Some Like It Hot*, United Artists.

Paul Muni in *The Last Angry Man*, Columbia.

James Stewart in *Anatomy of a Murder*, Preminger, Columbia.

ACTRESS

Simone Signoret in *Room at the Top*, Romulus, Continental (United Kingdom).

---

[160] Category renamed (formerly Sound Recording).
[161] Division into musical and nonmusical films reinstated.
[162] Winner of eleven Oscars, more than any other picture.

Doris Day in *Pillow Talk*, Universal-International.
Audrey Hepburn in *The Nun's Story*, Warner Bros.
Katharine Hepburn in *Suddenly, Last Summer*, Columbia.
Elizabeth Taylor in *Suddenly, Last Summer*, Columbia.

SUPPORTING ACTOR

Hugh Griffith in *Ben-Hur*, MGM.
Arthur O'Connell in *Anatomy of a Murder*, Columbia.
George C. Scott in *Anatomy of a Murder*, Columbia.
Robert Vaughn in *The Young Philadelphians*, Warner Bros.
Ed Wynn in *The Diary of Anne Frank*, 20th Century-Fox.

SUPPORTING ACTRESS

Shelley Winters in *The Diary of Anne Frank*, 20th Century-Fox.
Hermione Baddeley in *Room at the Top*, Romulus, Continental (United Kingdom).
Susan Kohner in *Imitation of Life*, Universal-International.
Juanita Moore in *Imitation of Life*, Universal-International.
Thelma Ritter in *Pillow Talk*, Universal-International.

DIRECTOR

William Wyler for *Ben-Hur*, MGM.
Jack Clayton for *Room at the Top*, Continental (United Kingdom).
George Stevens for *The Diary of Anne Frank*, 20th Century-Fox.
Billy Wilder for *Some Like It Hot*, United Artists.
Fred Zinnemann for *The Nun's Story*, Warner Bros.

WRITING

(Screenplay—Based on Material From Another Medium)
Neil Paterson for *Room at the Top*, Continental (United Kingdom).

Robert Anderson for *The Nun's Story*, Warner Bros.
Wendell Mayes for *Anatomy of a Murder*, Columbia.
Karl Tunberg for *Ben-Hur*, MGM.
Billy Wilder and I. A. L. Diamond for *Some Like It Hot*, United Artists.

(Story and Screenplay—Written Directly for the Screen)
Russell Rouse and Clarence Greene, story; Stanley Shapiro and Maurice Richlin, screenplay, for *Pillow Talk*, Universal-International.
Ingmar Bergman for *Wild Strawberries*, Janus Films (Sweden).
Paul King and Joseph Stone, story; Stanley Shapiro and Maurice Richlin, screenplay, for *Operation Petticoat*, Universal-International.
Ernest Lehman for *North by Northwest*, MGM.
François Truffaut and Marcel Moussy for *The 400 Blows*, Zenith International (France).

CINEMATOGRAPHY

(Black and White)
William C. Mellor for *The Diary of Anne Frank*, 20th Century-Fox.
Charles Lang, Jr., for *Some Like It Hot*, United Artists.
Joseph LaShelle for *Career*, Paramount.
Sam Leavitt for *Anatomy of a Murder*, Columbia.
Harry Stradling, Sr., for *The Young Philadelphians*, Warner Bros.
(Color)
Robert L. Surtees for *Ben-Hur*, MGM.
Daniel L. Fapp for *The Five Pennies*, Paramount.
Lee Garmes for *The Big Fisherman*, Buena Vista.
Franz Planer for *The Nun's Story*, Warner Bros.
Leon Shamroy for *Porgy and Bess*, Goldwyn, Columbia.

ART DIRECTION—SET DECORATION[163]
(Black and White)
***The Diary of Anne Frank*, 20th Century-Fox. Lyle R. Wheeler, George W. Davis; Walter M. Scott, Stuart A. Reiss.**
Career, Paramount. Hal Pereira, Walter Tyler; Sam Comer, Arthur Krams.
The Last Angry Man, Columbia. Carl Anderson; William Kiernan.
Some Like It Hot, United Artists. Ted Haworth; Edward G. Boyle.
Suddenly, Last Summer, Columbia. Oliver Messel, William Kellner; Scot Slimon.
(Color)
***Ben-Hur*, MGM. William A. Horning, Edward Carfagno; Hugh Hunt.**
The Big Fisherman, Buena Vista. John DeCuir; Julia Heron.
Journey to the Center of the Earth, 20th Century-Fox. Lyle R. Wheeler, Franz Bachelin, Herman A. Blumenthal; Walter M. Scott, Joseph Kish.
North by Northwest, MGM. William A. Horning, Robert Boyle, Merrill Pye; Henry Grace, Frank McKelvy.
Pillow Talk, Universal-International. Richard H. Riedel; Russell A. Gausman, Ruby R. Levitt.

SOUND
Franklin E. Milton for *Ben-Hur*, MGM.
Carl Faulkner for *Journey to the Center of the Earth*, 20th Century-Fox.
George R. Groves for *The Nun's Story*, Warner Bros.
Gordon E. Sawyer, Samuel Goldwyn Studio Sound Dept., and Fred Hynes, Todd-AO Sound Dept., for *Porgy and Bess*, Goldwyn, Columbia.
A. W. Watkins, MGM London Studio Sound Dept., for *Libel!*, MGM (United Kingdom).

MUSIC
(Song)
"High Hopes" from *A Hole in the Head*, United Artists. Music by

---

[163] Division into black-and-white and color categories reinstated.

James Van Heusen, lyrics by Sammy Cahn.

''The Best of Everything'' from *The Best of Everything*, 20th Century-Fox. Music by Alfred Newman, lyrics by Sammy Cahn.

''The Five Pennies'' from *The Five Pennies*, Paramount. Music and lyrics by Sylvia Fine.

''The Hanging Tree'' from *The Hanging Tree*, Warner Bros. Music by Jerry Livingston, lyrics by Mack David.

''Strange Are the Ways of Love'' from *The Young Land*, Columbia. Music by Dimitri Tiomkin, lyrics by Ned Washington.

(Music Score of a Dramatic or Comedy Picture)

Miklos Rozsa for *Ben-Hur*, MGM.

Frank DeVol for *Pillow Talk*, Universal-International.

Ernest Gold for *On the Beach*, United Artists.

Alfred Newman for *The Diary of Anne Frank*, 20th Century-Fox.

Franz Waxman for *The Nun's Story*, Warner Bros.

(Scoring of a Musical Picture)

André Previn and Ken Darby for *Porgy and Bess*, Goldwyn, Columbia.

George Bruns for *Sleeping Beauty*, Disney, Buena Vista.

Lionel Newman for *Say One for Me*, 20th Century-Fox.

Nelson Riddle and Joseph J. Lilley for *Li'l Abner*, Paramount.

Leith Stevens for *The Five Pennies*, Paramount.

FILM EDITING

Ralph E. Winters and John D. Dunning for *Ben-Hur*, MGM.

Frederic Knudtson for *On the Beach*, United Artists.

Louis R. Loeffler for *Anatomy of a Murder*, Columbia.

Walter Thompson for *The Nun's Story*, Warner Bros.

George Tomasini for *North by Northwest*, MGM.

COSTUME DESIGN[164]

(Black and White)

Orry-Kelly for *Some Like It Hot*, United Artists.

Edith Head for *Career*, Paramount.

Charles LeMaire and Mary Wills for *The Diary of Anne Frank*, 20th Century-Fox.

Helen Rose for *The Gazebo*, MGM.

Howard Shoup for *The Young Philadelphians*, Warner Bros.

(Color)

Elizabeth Haffenden for *Ben-Hur*, MGM.

Edith Head for *The Five Pennies*, Paramount.

Adele Palmer for *The Best of Everything*, 20th Century-Fox.

Renie for *The Big Fisherman*, Buena Vista.

Irene Sharaff for *Porgy and Bess*, Goldwyn, Columbia.

SPECIAL EFFECTS

***Ben-Hur*, MGM. A. Arnold Gillespie and Robert MacDonald, visual; Milo Lory, audible.**

Journey to the Center of the Earth, 20th Century-Fox. L. B. Abbott and James B. Gordon, visual; Carl Faulkner, audible.

FOREIGN LANGUAGE FILM

***Black Orpheus*, France.**

The Bridge, Federal Republic of Germany.

The Great War, Italy.

Paw, Denmark.

The Village on the River, the Netherlands.

JEAN HERSHOLT HUMANITARIAN AWARD

Bob Hope.

HONORARY AWARDS

Lee De Forest, for his pioneering inventions which brought sound to the motion picture.

Buster Keaton, for his unique talents, which brought immortal comedies to the screen.

1960
Awards presented April 17, 1961.

PICTURE

***The Apartment*, The Mirisch Company, Inc., United Artists. Produced by Billy Wilder.**

The Alamo, Batjac Production, United Artists. Produced by John Wayne.

Elmer Gantry, Burt Lancaster-Richard Brooks Production, United Artists. Produced by Bernard Smith.

Sons and Lovers, Company of Artists, Inc., 20th Century-Fox. Produced by Jerry Wald.

The Sundowners, Warner Bros. Produced by Fred Zinnemann.

ACTOR

Burt Lancaster in *Elmer Gantry*, United Artists.

Trevor Howard in *Sons and Lovers*, 20th Century-Fox.

Jack Lemmon in *The Apartment*, United Artists.

Laurence Olivier in *The Entertainer*, Woodfall, Continental (United Kingdom).

Spencer Tracy in *Inherit the Wind*, Kramer, United Artists.

ACTRESS

Elizabeth Taylor in *Butterfield 8*, MGM.

Greer Garson in *Sunrise at Campobello*, Warner Bros.

Deborah Kerr in *The Sundowners*, Warner Bros.[165]

---

[164] Division into black-and-white and color categories reinstated.

[165] Kerr's sixth nomination gives her the record among actresses for most nominations without a win. Thelma Ritter will tie the record in 1962. Richard Burton and Peter O'Toole, with seven unsuccessful nominations each, hold the record among actors.

Shirley MacLaine in *The Apartment*, United Artists.

Melina Mercouri in *Never on Sunday*, Melinafilm, Lopert Pictures (Greece).

SUPPORTING ACTOR

Peter Ustinov in *Spartacus*, Universal-International.

Peter Falk in *Murder, Inc.*, 20th Century-Fox.

Jack Kruschen in *The Apartment*, United Artists.

Sal Mineo in *Exodus*, United Artists.

Chill Wills in *The Alamo*, United Artists.

SUPPORTING ACTRESS

Shirley Jones in *Elmer Gantry*, United Artists.

Glynis Johns in *The Sundowners*, Warner Bros.

Shirley Knight in *The Dark at the Top of the Stairs*, Warner Bros.

Janet Leigh in *Psycho*, Paramount.

Mary Ure in *Sons and Lovers*, 20th Century-Fox.

DIRECTOR

Billy Wilder for *The Apartment*, United Artists.

Jack Cardiff for *Sons and Lovers*, 20th Century-Fox.

Jules Dassin for *Never on Sunday*, Lopert Pictures (Greece).

Alfred Hitchcock for *Psycho*, Paramount.

Fred Zinnemann for *The Sundowners*, Warner Bros.

WRITING

(Screenplay—Based on Material From Another Medium)

Richard Brooks for *Elmer Gantry*, United Artists.

Nedrick Young[166] and Harold Jacob Smith for *Inherit the Wind*, United Artists.

James Kennaway for *Tunes of Glory*, Lopert Pictures (United Kingdom).

Gavin Lambert and T. E. B. Clarke for *Sons and Lovers*, 20th Century-Fox.

Isobel Lennart for *The Sundowners*, Warner Bros.

(Story and Screenplay—Written Directly for the Screen)

Billy Wilder and I. A. L. Diamond for *The Apartment*, United Artists.

Jules Dassin for *Never on Sunday*, Lopert Pictures (Greece).

Marguérite Duras for *Hiroshima, Mon Amour*, Zenith International (France/Japan).

Richard Gregson and Michael Craig, story; Bryan Forbes, screenplay, for *The Angry Silence*, Joseph Harris-Sig Shore (United Kingdom).

Norman Panama and Melvin Frank for *The Facts of Life*, United Artists.

CINEMATOGRAPHY

(Black and White)

Freddie Francis for *Sons and Lovers*, 20th Century-Fox.

Charles B. Lang, Jr., for *The Facts of Life*, United Artists.

Joseph LaShelle for *The Apartment*, United Artists.

Ernest Laszlo for *Inherit the Wind*, United Artists.

John L. Russell for *Psycho*, Paramount.

(Color)

Russell Metty for *Spartacus*, Universal-International.

William H. Clothier for *The Alamo*, United Artists.

Sam Leavitt for *Exodus*, United Artists.

Joe MacDonald for *Pepe*, Columbia.

Joseph Ruttenberg and Charles Harten for *Butterfield 8*, MGM.

ART DIRECTION—SET DECORATION

(Black and White)

The Apartment, United Artists. Alexander Trauner; Edward G. Boyle.

The Facts of Life, United Artists. Joseph McMillan Johnson, Kenneth A. Reid; Ross Dowd.

Psycho, Paramount. Joseph Hurley, Robert Clatworthy; George Milo.

Sons and Lovers, 20th Century-Fox. Tom Morahan; Lionel Couch.

Visit to a Small Planet, Paramount. Hal Pereira, Walter Tyler; Sam Comer, Arthur Krams.

(Color)

Spartacus, Universal-International. Alexander Golitzen, Eric Orbom; Russell A. Gausman, Julia Heron.

Cimarron, MGM. George W. Davis, Addison Hehr; Henry Grace, Hugh Hunt, Otto Siegel.

It Started in Naples, Paramount. Hal Pereira, Roland Anderson; Sam Comer, Arrigo Breschi.

Pepe, Columbia. Ted Haworth; William Kiernan.

Sunrise at Campobello, Warner Bros. Edward Carrere; George James Hopkins.

SOUND

Gordon E. Sawyer, Samuel Goldwyn Studio Sound Dept., and Fred Hynes, Todd-AO Sound Dept., for *The Alamo*, United Artists.

George R. Groves for *Sunrise at Campobello*, Warner Bros.

Franklin E. Milton for *Cimarron*, MGM.

Charles Rice for *Pepe*, Columbia.

Gordon E. Sawyer for *The Apartment*, United Artists.

MUSIC

(Song)

"Never on Sunday" from *Never on Sunday*, Lopert Pictures (Greece). Music and lyrics by Manos Hadjidakis.[167]

"The Facts of Life" from *The Facts of Life*, United Artists. Music and lyrics by Johnny Mercer.

"Faraway Part of Town" from *Pepe*, Columbia. Music by André Previn, lyrics by Dory Langdon.

"The Green Leaves of Summer" from *The Alamo*, United Artists. Music by

---

[166] Young, who was blacklisted, was nominated under his pseudonym, Nathan E. Douglas. The record was corrected posthumously.

[167] First song from a foreign-made film to win the Oscar.

Dimitri Tiomkin, lyrics by Paul
Francis Webster.

''The Second Time Around'' from *High
Time,* 20th Century-Fox. Music by
James Van Heusen, lyrics by Sammy
Cahn.

(Music Score of a Dramatic or Comedy
Picture)

**Ernest Gold for *Exodus,* United
Artists.**

Elmer Bernstein for *The Magnificent Seven,*
United Artists.

Alex North for *Spartacus,* Universal-
International.

André Previn for *Elmer Gantry,* United
Artists.

Dimitri Tiomkin for *The Alamo,* United
Artists.

(Scoring of a Musical Picture)

**Morris Stoloff and Harry Sukman
for *Song Without End,* Columbia.**

Johnny Green for *Pepe,* Columbia.

Lionel Newman and Earle H. Hagen for
Let's Make Love, 20th Century-Fox.

André Previn for *Bells Are Ringing,* MGM.

Nelson Riddle for *Can-Can,* 20th
Century-Fox.

FILM EDITING

**Daniel Mandell for *The Apartment,*
United Artists.**

Stuart Gilmore for *The Alamo,* United
Artists.

Frederic Knudtson for *Inherit the Wind,*
United Artists.

Robert Lawrence for *Spartacus,* Universal-
International.

Viola Lawrence and Al Clark for *Pepe,*
Columbia.

COSTUME DESIGN

(Black and White)

**Edith Head and Edward Stevenson
for *The Facts of Life,* United
Artists.**

Howard Shoup for *The Rise and Fall of
Legs Diamond,* Warner Bros.

Bill Thomas for *Seven Thieves,* 20th
Century-Fox.

Deni Vachlioti for *Never on Sunday,* Lopert
Pictures (Greece).

Marik Vos for *The Virgin Spring,* Janus
Films (Sweden).

(Color)

**Valles and Bill Thomas for
Spartacus, Universal-
International.**

Marjorie Best for *Sunrise at Campobello,*
Warner Bros.

Edith Head for *Pepe,* Columbia.

Irene for *Midnight Lace,* Universal-
International.

Irene Sharaff for *Can-Can,* 20th Century-
Fox.

SPECIAL EFFECTS

**The Time Machine, MGM. Gene
Warren and Tim Baar, visual.**

The Last Voyage, MGM. A. J. Lohman,
visual.

FOREIGN LANGUAGE FILM

The Virgin Spring, Sweden.

Kapo, Italy.

Macario, Mexico.

The Ninth Circle, Yugoslavia.

La Vérité, France.

JEAN HERSHOLT HUMANITARIAN AWARD

Sol Lesser.

HONORARY AWARDS

**Gary Cooper, for his many
memorable screen performances
and the international
recognition he, as an individual,
has gained for the motion
picture industry.**

**Stan Laurel, for his creative
pioneering in the field of cinema
comedy.**

**Hayley Mills, for *Pollyanna,* the
most outstanding juvenile
performance during 1960.[168]**

1961

Awards presented April 9, 1962.

PICTURE

**West Side Story, Mirisch Pictures,
Inc., and B and P Enterprises,
Inc., United Artists. Produced
by Robert Wise.**

Fanny, Mansfield Production, Warner
Bros. Produced by Joshua Logan.

The Guns of Navarone, Carl Foreman
Production, Columbia (U.S./United
Kingdom). Produced by Carl
Foreman.

The Hustler, Robert Rossen Productions,
20th Century-Fox. Produced by
Robert Rossen.

Judgment at Nuremberg, Stanley Kramer
Productions, United Artists. Produced
by Stanley Kramer.

ACTOR

**Maximilian Schell in *Judgment at
Nuremberg,* United Artists.**

Charles Boyer in *Fanny,* Warner Bros.

Paul Newman in *The Hustler,* 20th
Century-Fox.

Spencer Tracy in *Judgment at Nuremberg,*
United Artists.

Stuart Whitman in *The Mark,* Continental
(United Kingdom).

ACTRESS

**Sophia Loren[169] in *Two Women,*
Ponti, Embassy (Italy/France).**

Audrey Hepburn in *Breakfast at Tiffany's,*
Paramount.

Piper Laurie in *The Hustler,* 20th
Century-Fox.

Geraldine Page in *Summer and Smoke,*
Paramount.

Natalie Wood in *Splendor in the Grass,*
Warner Bros.

SUPPORTING ACTOR

**George Chakiris in *West Side Story,*
United Artists.**

---

[168] Mills is the last child star to receive a miniature Oscar. Henceforth, the Academy let child actors prove themselves in the competitive awards
categories.
[169] Only person to win an acting Oscar in a foreign language film.

Montgomery Clift in *Judgment at Nuremberg*, United Artists.

Peter Falk in *Pocketful of Miracles*, United Artists.

Jackie Gleason in *The Hustler*, 20th Century-Fox.

George C. Scott in *The Hustler*, 20th Century-Fox.

SUPPORTING ACTRESS

Rita Moreno in *West Side Story*, United Artists.

Fay Bainter in *The Children's Hour*, United Artists.

Judy Garland in *Judgment at Nuremberg*, United Artists.

Lotte Lenya in *The Roman Spring of Mrs. Stone*, Warner Bros. (U.S./United Kingdom).

Una Merkel in *Summer and Smoke*, Paramount.

DIRECTOR

Robert Wise and Jerome Robbins[170] for *West Side Story*, United Artists.

Federico Fellini for *La Dolce Vita*, Astor Pictures (Italy).

Stanley Kramer for *Judgment at Nuremberg*, United Artists.

J. Lee Thompson for *The Guns of Navarone*, Columbia (U.S./United Kingdom).

Robert Rossen for *The Hustler*, 20th Century-Fox.

WRITING

(Screenplay—Based on Material From Another Medium)

Abby Mann for *Judgment at Nuremberg*, United Artists.

George Axelrod for *Breakfast at Tiffany's*, Paramount.

Sidney Carroll and Robert Rossen for *The Hustler*, 20th Century-Fox.

Carl Foreman for *The Guns of Navarone*, Columbia (U.S./United Kingdom).

Ernest Lehman for *West Side Story*, United Artists.

(Story and Screenplay—Written Directly for the Screen)

William Inge for *Splendor in the Grass*, Warner Bros.

Sergio Amidei, Diego Fabbri, and Indro Montanelli for *General Della Rovere*, Continental Distributing (Italy).

Federico Fellini, Tullio Pinelli, Ennio Flaiano, and Brunello Rondi for *La Dolce Vita*, Astor Pictures (Italy).

Stanley Shapiro and Paul Henning for *Lover Come Back*, Universal-International.

Valentin Yoshov and Grigori Chukhrai for *Ballad of a Soldier*, Kingsley International-M.J.P (USSR).

CINEMATOGRAPHY

(Black and White)

Eugen Shuftan for *The Hustler*, 20th Century-Fox.

Edward Colman for *The Absent-Minded Professor*, Disney, Buena Vista.

Daniel L. Fapp for *One, Two, Three*, United Artists.

Ernest Laszlo for *Judgment at Nuremberg*, United Artists.

Franz F. Planer for *The Children's Hour*, United Artists.

(Color)

Daniel L. Fapp for *West Side Story*, United Artists.

Jack Cardiff for *Fanny*, Warner Bros.

Charles Lang, Jr., for *One-Eyed Jacks*, Paramount.

Russell Metty for *Flower Drum Song*, Universal-International.

Harry Stradling, Sr., for *A Majority of One*, Warner Bros.

ART DIRECTION—SET DECORATION

(Black and White)

The Hustler, 20th Century-Fox. Harry Horner; Gene Callahan.

The Absent-Minded Professor, Disney, Buena Vista. Carroll Clark; Emile Kuri, Hal Gausman.

The Children's Hour, United Artists. Fernando Carrere; Edward G. Boyle.

Judgment at Nuremberg, United Artists. Rudolph Sternad; George Milo.

La Dolce Vita, Astor Pictures (Italy). Piero Gherardi.

(Color)

West Side Story, United Artists. Boris Leven; Victor A. Gangelin.

Breakfast at Tiffany's, Paramount. Hal Pereira, Roland Anderson; Sam Comer, Ray Moyer.

El Cid, Allied Artists. Veniero Colasanti, John Moore.

Flower Drum Song, Universal-International. Alexander Golitzen, Joseph Wright; Howard Bristol.

Summer and Smoke, Paramount. Hal Pereira, Walter Tyler; Sam Comer, Arthur Krams.

SOUND

Fred Hynes, Todd-AO Sound Dept., and Gordon E. Sawyer, Samuel Goldwyn Studio Sound Dept., for *West Side Story*, United Artists.

Robert O. Cook, Walt Disney Studio Sound Dept., for *The Parent Trap*, Disney, Buena Vista.

John Cox, Shepperton Studio Sound Dept., for *The Guns of Navarone*, Columbia (U.S./United Kingdom).

Gordon E. Sawyer, Samuel Goldwyn Studio Sound Dept., for *The Children's Hour*, United Artists.

Waldon O. Watson, Revue Studio Sound Dept., for *Flower Drum Song*, Universal-International.

MUSIC

(Song)

"Moon River" from *Breakfast at Tiffany's*, Paramount. Music by Henry Mancini, lyrics by Johnny Mercer.

"Bachelor in Paradise" from *Bachelor in Paradise*, MGM. Music by Henry Mancini, lyrics by Mack David.

"Love Theme From *El Cid* (The Falcon and the Dove)" from *El Cid*, Allied

---

[170] Only codirectors to win the directing Oscar. The only other codirecting team to be nominated is Warren Beatty and Buck Henry for *Heaven Can Wait* (1978).

Artists (U.S./Italy). Music by Miklos Rozsa, lyrics by Paul Francis Webster.

"Pocketful of Miracles" from *Pocketful of Miracles,* United Artists. Music by James Van Heusen, lyrics by Sammy Cahn.

"Town Without Pity" from *Town Without Pity,* United Artists (U.S./Switzerland/West Germany). Music by Dimitri Tiomkin, lyrics by Ned Washington.

(Music Score of a Dramatic or Comedy Picture)

Henry Mancini for *Breakfast at Tiffany's,* Paramount.

Elmer Bernstein for *Summer and Smoke,* Paramount.

Miklos Rozsa for *El Cid,* Allied Artists (U.S./Italy).

Morris Stoloff and Harry Sukman for *Fanny,* Warner Bros.

Dimitri Tiomkin for *The Guns of Navarone,* Columbia (U.S./United Kingdom).

(Scoring of a Musical Picture)

Saul Chaplin, Johnny Green, Sid Ramin, and Irwin Kostal for *West Side Story,* United Artists.

George Bruns for *Babes in Toyland,* Disney, Buena Vista.

Duke Ellington for *Paris Blues,* United Artists.

Alfred Newman and Ken Darby for *Flower Drum Song,* Universal-International.

Dimitri Shostakovich for *Khovanshchina,* Artkino (USSR).

FILM EDITING

Thomas Stanford for *West Side Story,* United Artists.

Philip W. Anderson for *The Parent Trap,* Disney, Buena Vista.

Frederic Knudtson for *Judgment at Nuremberg,* United Artists.

Alan Osbiston for *The Guns of Navarone,* Columbia.

William H. Reynolds for *Fanny,* Warner Bros.

COSTUME DESIGN

(Black and White)

Piero Gherardi for *La Dolce Vita,* Astor Pictures (Italy).

Dorothy Jeakins for *The Children's Hour,* United Artists.

Jean Louis for *Judgment at Nuremberg,* United Artists.

Yoshiro Muraki for *Yojimbo,* Toho Company (Japan).

Howard Shoup for *Claudelle Inglish,* Warner Bros.

(Color)

Irene Sharaff for *West Side Story,* United Artists.

Edith Head and Walter Plunkett for *Pocketful of Miracles,* United Artists.

Jean Louis for *Back Street,* Universal-International.

Irene Sharaff for *Flower Drum Song,* Universal-International.

Bill Thomas for *Babes in Toyland,* Disney, Buena Vista.

SPECIAL EFFECTS

***The Guns of Navarone,* Columbia (U.S./United Kingdom). Bill Warrington, visual; Vivian C. Greenham, audible.**

The Absent-Minded Professor, Disney, Buena Vista. Robert A. Mattey and Eustace Lycett, visual.

FOREIGN LANGUAGE FILMS

***Through a Glass Darkly,* Sweden.**

Harry and the Butler, Denmark.

Immortal Love, Japan.

The Important Man, Mexico.

Plácido, Spain.

IRVING G. THALBERG MEMORIAL AWARD

Stanley Kramer.

JEAN HERSHOLT HUMANITARIAN AWARD

George Seaton.

HONORARY AWARDS

William Hendricks, for his outstanding patriotic service in the conception, writing and production of the Marine Corps

film, *A Force in Readiness,* which has brought honor to the Academy and the motion picture industry.

Fred L. Metzler, for his dedication and outstanding service to the Academy of Motion Picture Arts and Sciences.

Jerome Robbins, for his brilliant achievements in the art of choreography on film.

1962
Awards presented April 8, 1963.

PICTURE

Lawrence of Arabia, Horizon Pictures (G.B.), Ltd.-Sam Spiegel-David Lean Production, Columbia (United Kingdom). Produced by Sam Spiegel.[171]

The Longest Day, Darryl F. Zanuck Productions, 20th Century-Fox. Produced by Darryl F. Zanuck.

The Music Man, Warner Bros. Produced by Morton Da Costa.

Mutiny on the Bounty, Arcola Production, MGM. Produced by Aaron Rosenberg.

To Kill a Mockingbird, Universal-International-Pakula-Mulligan-Brentwood Production, Universal-International. Produced by Alan J. Pakula.

ACTOR

Gregory Peck in *To Kill a Mockingbird,* Universal-International.

Burt Lancaster in *Birdman of Alcatraz,* United Artists.

Jack Lemmon in *Days of Wine and Roses,* Warner Bros.

Marcello Mastroianni in *Divorce—Italian Style,* Lux-Vides-Galatea, Embassy Pictures (Italy).

Peter O'Toole in *Lawrence of Arabia,* Horizon (G.B.)-Spiegel-Lean, Columbia (United Kingdom).

[171] Spiegel's third best picture win ties the record set by Darryl Zanuck in 1950.

ACTRESS

Anne Bancroft in *The Miracle Worker*, United Artists.

Bette Davis in *What Ever Happened to Baby Jane?*, Warner Bros.[172]

Katharine Hepburn in *Long Day's Journey Into Night*, Embassy.

Geraldine Page in *Sweet Bird of Youth*, MGM.

Lee Remick in *Days of Wine and Roses*, Warner Bros.

SUPPORTING ACTOR

Ed Begley in *Sweet Bird of Youth*, MGM.

Victor Buono in *What Ever Happened to Baby Jane?*, Warner Bros.

Telly Savalas in *Birdman of Alcatraz*, United Artists.

Omar Sharif in *Lawrence of Arabia*, Horizon (G.B.)-Spiegel-Lean, Columbia (United Kingdom).

Terence Stamp in *Billy Budd*, Harvest, Allied Artists (United Kingdom).

SUPPORTING ACTRESS

Patty Duke in *The Miracle Worker*, United Artists.

Mary Badham in *To Kill a Mockingbird*, Universal-International.

Shirley Knight in *Sweet Bird of Youth*, MGM.

Angela Lansbury in *The Manchurian Candidate*, United Artists.

Thelma Ritter in *Birdman of Alcatraz*, United Artists.[173]

DIRECTOR

David Lean for *Lawrence of Arabia*, Columbia (United Kingdom).

Pietro Germi for *Divorce—Italian Style*, Embassy Pictures (Italy).

Robert Mulligan for *To Kill a Mockingbird*, Universal-International.

Arthur Penn for *The Miracle Worker*, United Artists.

Frank Perry for *David and Lisa*, Continental.

WRITING

(Screenplay—Based on Material From Another Medium)

Horton Foote for *To Kill a Mockingbird*, Universal-International.

Robert Bolt for *Lawrence of Arabia*, Columbia (United Kingdom).

William Gibson for *The Miracle Worker*, United Artists.

Vladimir Nabokov for *Lolita*, MGM (U.S./United Kingdom).

Eleanor Perry for *David and Lisa*, Continental.

(Story and Screenplay—Written Directly for the Screen)

Ennio de Concini, Alfred Giannetti, and Pietro Germi for *Divorce—Italian Style*, Embassy Pictures (Italy).

Ingmar Bergman for *Through a Glass Darkly*, Janus Films (Sweden).

Charles Kaufman, story; Charles Kaufman and Wolfgang Reinhardt, screenplay, for *Freud*, Universal-International.

Alain Robbe-Grillet for *Last Year at Marienbad*, Astor Pictures (France).

Stanley Shapiro and Nate Monaster for *That Touch of Mink*, Universal-International.

CINEMATOGRAPHY

(Black and White)

Jean Bourgoin and Walter Wottitz[174] for *The Longest Day*, 20th Century-Fox.

Burnett Guffey for *Birdman of Alcatraz*, United Artists.

Ernest Haller for *What Ever Happened to Baby Jane?*, Warner Bros.

Russell Harlan for *To Kill a Mockingbird*, Universal-International.

Ted McCord for *Two for the Seesaw*, United Artists.

(Color)

Fred A. Young for *Lawrence of Arabia*, Columbia (United Kingdom).

Russell Harlan for *Hatari!*, Paramount.

Harry Stradling, Sr., for *Gypsy*, Warner Bros.

Robert L. Surtees for *Mutiny on the Bounty*, MGM.

Paul C. Vogel for *The Wonderful World of the Brothers Grimm*, MGM.

ART DIRECTION—SET DECORATION

(Black and White)

***To Kill a Mockingbird*, Universal-International. Alexander Golitzen, Henry Bumstead; Oliver Emert.**

Days of Wine and Roses, Warner Bros. Joseph Wright; George James Hopkins.

The Longest Day, 20th Century-Fox. Ted Haworth, Leon Barsacq, Vincent Korda; Gabriel Bechir.

Period of Adjustment, MGM. George W. Davis, Edward Carfagno; Henry Grace, Dick Pefferle.

The Pigeon That Took Rome, Paramount. Hal Pereira, Roland Anderson; Sam Comer, Frank R. McKelvy.

(Color)

***Lawrence of Arabia*, Columbia. John Box, John Stoll; Dario Simoni.**

The Music Man, Warner Bros. Paul Groesse; George James Hopkins.

Mutiny on the Bounty, MGM. George W. Davis, J. McMillan Johnson; Henry Grace, Hugh Hunt.

That Touch of Mink, Universal-International. Alexander Golitzen, Robert Clatworthy; George Milo.

The Wonderful World of the Brothers Grimm, MGM. George W. Davis, Edward

---

[172] Davis' tenth nomination, a number subsequently tied by Laurence Olivier (1978) and Jack Nicholson (1992). It was a record for acting nominations that Katharine Hepburn tied in 1967, then broke in 1968; Hepburn set the current record of twelve nominations in 1981.

[173] Ritter ties Deborah Kerr's record among actresses of six nominations without a win.

[174] Henri Persin was also originally listed as a nominee for the cinematography for *The Longest Day*—and in fact, the film's credits list a fourth cinematographer, Pierre Levent. But Levent was never cited as a nominee, and at some point Persin's name was dropped. The Academy has no recorded explanation for the omissions.

Carfagno; Henry Grace, Dick
Pefferle.

SOUND

**John Cox, Shepperton Studio
Sound Dept., for *Lawrence of
Arabia*, Columbia (United
Kingdom).**

Robert O. Cook, Walt Disney Studio
Sound Dept., for *Bon Voyage*, Disney,
Buena Vista.

George R. Groves for *The Music Man*,
Warner Bros.

Joseph Kelly, Glen Glenn Sound Dept.,
for *What Ever Happened to Baby Jane?*,
Warner Bros.

Waldon O. Watson for *That Touch of
Mink*, Universal-International.

MUSIC

(Song)

**"Days of Wine and Roses" from
Days of Wine and Roses, Warner
Bros. Music by Henry Mancini,
lyrics by Johnny Mercer.**

"Love Song from *Mutiny on the Bounty*
(Follow Me)" from *Mutiny on the
Bounty*, MGM. Music by Bronislau
Kaper, lyrics by Paul Francis Webster.

"Song from *Two for the Seesaw* (Second
Chance)" from *Two for the Seesaw*,
United Artists. Music by André
Previn, lyrics by Dory Langdon.

"Tender Is the Night" from *Tender Is the
Night*, 20th Century-Fox. Music by
Sammy Fain, lyrics by Paul Francis
Webster.

"Walk on the Wild Side" from *Walk on
the Wild Side*, Columbia. Music by
Elmer Bernstein, lyrics by Mack
David.

(Music Score—Substantially Original)[175]

**Maurice Jarre for *Lawrence of
Arabia*, Columbia (United
Kingdom).**

Elmer Bernstein for *To Kill a Mockingbird*,
Universal-International.

Jerry Goldsmith for *Freud*, Universal-
International.

Bronislau Kaper for *Mutiny on the Bounty*,
MGM.

Franz Waxman for *Taras Bulba*, United
Artists.

(Scoring of Music—Adaptation or
Treatment)

**Ray Heindorf for *The Music Man*,
Warner Bros.**

Leigh Harline for *The Wonderful World of
the Brothers Grimm*, MGM.

Michel Magne for *Gigot*, 20th Century-
Fox.

Frank Perkins for *Gypsy*, Warner Bros.

George Stoll for *Billy Rose's Jumbo*, MGM.

FILM EDITING

**Anne Coates for *Lawrence of Arabia*,
Columbia (United Kingdom).**

Samuel E. Beetley for *The Longest Day*,
20th Century-Fox.

John McSweeney, Jr., for *Mutiny on the
Bounty*, MGM.

Ferris Webster for *The Manchurian
Candidate*, United Artists.

William Ziegler for *The Music Man*,
Warner Bros.

COSTUME DESIGN

(Black and White)

**Norma Koch for *What Ever
Happened to Baby Jane?*, Warner
Bros.**

Don Feld for *Days of Wine and Roses*,
Warner Bros.

Edith Head for *The Man Who Shot Liberty
Valance*, Paramount.

Ruth Morley for *The Miracle Worker*,
United Artists.

Denny Vachlioti for *Phaedra*, Lopert
Pictures (U.S./Greece).

(Color)

**Mary Wills for *The Wonderful World
of the Brothers Grimm*, MGM.**

Edith Head for *My Geisha*, Paramount.

Dorothy Jeakins for *The Music Man*,
Warner Bros.

Orry-Kelly for *Gypsy*, Warner Bros.

Bill Thomas for *Bon Voyage*, Disney, Buena
Vista.

SPECIAL EFFECTS

***The Longest Day*, 20th Century-Fox.
Robert MacDonald, visual;
Jacques Maumont, audible.**

Mutiny on the Bounty, MGM. A. Arnold
Gillespie, visual; Milo Lory, audible.

FOREIGN LANGUAGE FILM

***Sundays and Cybèle*, France.**

Electra, Greece.

The Four Days of Naples, Italy.

The Keeper of Promises (The Given Word),
Brazil.

Tlayucan, Mexico.

JEAN HERSHOLT HUMANITARIAN AWARD

Steve Broidy.

1963
Awards presented April 13, 1964.

PICTURE

***Tom Jones*, Woodfall Production,
United Artists-Lopert Pictures
(United Kingdom). Produced by
Tony Richardson.**

America, America, Athena Enterprises
Production, Warner Bros. Produced
by Elia Kazan.

Cleopatra, 20th Century-Fox, Ltd.-MCL
Films S.A.-WALWA Films S.A.
Production, 20th Century-Fox.
Produced by Walter Wanger.

How the West Was Won, Metro-Goldwyn-
Mayer & Cinerama, MGM. Produced
by Bernard Smith.

Lilies of the Field, Rainbow Productions,
United Artists. Produced by Ralph
Nelson.

ACTOR

**Sidney Poitier[176] in *Lilies of the
Field*, United Artists.**

Albert Finney in *Tom Jones*, Woodfall,
United Artists-Lopert (United
Kingdom).

Richard Harris in *This Sporting Life*,

---

[175] Scoring categories renamed, eliminating division into musical and nonmusical films.
[176] Only African-American performer to win an Oscar for a leading role.

Wintle-Parkyn, Reade-Sterling-Continental (United Kingdom).

Rex Harrison in *Cleopatra,* 20th Century-Fox.

Paul Newman in *Hud,* Paramount.

ACTRESS

Patricia Neal in *Hud,* Paramount.

Leslie Caron in *The L-Shaped Room,* Romulus, Columbia (United Kingdom).

Shirley MacLaine in *Irma la Douce,* United Artists.

Rachel Roberts in *This Sporting Life,* Wintle-Parkyn, Reade-Sterling-Continental (United Kingdom).

Natalie Wood in *Love With the Proper Stranger,* Paramount.

SUPPORTING ACTOR

Melvyn Douglas in *Hud,* Paramount.

Nick Adams in *Twilight of Honor,* MGM.

Bobby Darin in *Captain Newman, M.D.,* Universal.

Hugh Griffith in *Tom Jones,* Woodfall, United Artists-Lopert (United Kingdom).

John Huston in *The Cardinal,* Columbia.

SUPPORTING ACTRESS

Margaret Rutherford in *The V.I.P.'s,* MGM.

Diane Cilento in *Tom Jones,* United Artists-Lopert (United Kingdom).

Edith Evans in *Tom Jones,* United Artists-Lopert (United Kingdom).

Joyce Redman in *Tom Jones,* United Artists-Lopert (United Kingdom).

Lilia Skala in *Lilies of the Field,* United Artists.

DIRECTOR

Tony Richardson for *Tom Jones,* United Artists-Lopert (United Kingdom).

Federico Fellini for *8½,* Embassy Pictures (Italy).

Elia Kazan for *America, America,* Warner Bros.

Otto Preminger for *The Cardinal,* Columbia.

Martin Ritt for *Hud,* Paramount.

WRITING

(Screenplay—Based on Material From Another Medium)

John Osborne for *Tom Jones,* United Artists-Lopert (United Kingdom).

Serge Bourguigon and Antoine Tudal for *Sundays and Cybèle,* Columbia (France).[177]

Richard L. Breen, Phoebe Ephron, and Henry Ephron for *Captain Newman, M.D.,* Universal.

James Poe for *Lilies of the Field,* United Artists.

Irving Ravetch and Harriet Frank, Jr., for *Hud,* Paramount.

(Story and Screenplay—Written Directly for the Screen)

James R. Webb for *How the West Was Won,* MGM.

Pasquale Festa Campanile, Massimo Franciosa, Nanni Loy, and Vasco Pratolini, story; Carlo Bernari, Pasquale Festa Campanile, Massimo Franciosa, and Nanni Loy, screenplay, for *The Four Days of Naples,* MGM (Italy).

Federico Fellini, Ennio Flaiano, Tullio Pinelli, and Brunello Rondi for *8½,* Embassy Pictures (Italy).

Elia Kazan for *America, America,* Warner Bros.

Arnold Schulman for *Love With the Proper Stranger,* Paramount.

CINEMATOGRAPHY

(Black and White)

James Wong Howe for *Hud,* Paramount.

Lucien Ballard for *The Caretakers,* United Artists.

George Folsey for *The Balcony,* Reade-Sterling-Continental Distributing (United Kingdom).

Ernest Haller for *Lilies of the Field,* United Artists.

Milton Krasner for *Love With the Proper Stranger,* Paramount.

(Color)

Leon Shamroy for *Cleopatra,* 20th Century-Fox.[178]

William H. Daniels, Milton Krasner, Charles Lang, Jr., and Joseph LaShelle for *How the West Was Won,* MGM.

Joseph LaShelle for *Irma la Douce,* United Artists.

Ernest Laszlo for *It's a Mad, Mad, Mad, Mad World,* United Artists.

Leon Shamroy for *The Cardinal,* Columbia.

ART DIRECTION—SET DECORATION

(Black and White)

***America, America,* Warner Bros. Gene Callahan.**

8½, Embassy Pictures (Italy). Piero Gherardi.

Hud, Paramount. Hal Pereira, Tambi Larsen; Sam Comer, Robert Benton.

Love With the Proper Stranger, Paramount. Hal Pereira, Roland Anderson; Sam Comer, Grace Gregory.

Twilight of Honor, MGM. George W. Davis, Paul Groesse; Henry Grace, Hugh Hunt.

(Color)

***Cleopatra,* 20th Century-Fox. John DeCuir, Jack Martin Smith, Hilyard Brown, Herman Blumenthal, Elven Webb, Maurice Pelling, Boris Juraga; Walter M. Scott, Paul S. Fox, Ray Moyer.**

The Cardinal, Columbia. Lyle Wheeler; Gene Callahan.

Come Blow Your Horn, Paramount. Hal Pereira, Roland Anderson;[179] Sam Comer, James Payne.

How the West Was Won, MGM. George W. Davis, William Ferrari, Addison Hehr; Henry Grace, Don Greenwood, Jr., Jack Mills.

Tom Jones, United Artists-Lopert (United Kingdom). Ralph Brinton, Ted

---

[177] Although it won the foreign language film Oscar for 1963, this film was not eligible for other competitive awards until the 1964 ceremonies.

[178] Shamroy's fourth Oscar ties Joseph Ruttenberg's record (set 1958) for cinematographers. He also shares with Charles B. Lang the record for most nominations (eighteen) for cinematography.

[179] Anderson's fifteenth unsuccessful nomination is an Academy record tied only by composer Alex North (1984). North, however, received an honorary award from the Academy at the 1985 ceremonies, while Anderson was never honored.

Marshall, Jocelyn Herbert; Josie MacAvin.

SOUND
Franklin E. Milton for *How the West Was Won*, MGM.

James P. Corcoran, 20th Century-Fox Studio Sound Dept., and Fred Hynes, Todd-AO Sound Dept., for *Cleopatra*, 20th Century-Fox.

Charles Rice for *Bye Bye Birdie*, Columbia.

Gordon E. Sawyer, Samuel Goldwyn Studio Sound Dept., for *It's a Mad, Mad, Mad, Mad World*, United Artists.

Waldon O. Watson for *Captain Newman, M.D.*, Universal.

MUSIC
(Song)
"Call Me Irresponsible" from *Papa's Delicate Condition*, Paramount. Music by James Van Heusen, lyrics by Sammy Cahn.

"Charade" from *Charade*, Universal. Music by Henry Mancini, lyrics by Johnny Mercer.

"It's a Mad, Mad, Mad, Mad World" from *It's a Mad, Mad, Mad, Mad World*, United Artists. Music by Ernest Gold, lyrics by Mack David.

"More" from *Mondo Cane*, Times Film (Italy). Music by Riz Ortolani and Nino Oliviero, lyrics by Norman Newell.

"So Little Time" from *55 Days at Peking*, Allied Artists. Music by Dimitri Tiomkin, lyrics by Paul Francis Webster.

(Music Score—Substantially Original)
John Addison for *Tom Jones*, United Artists-Lopert (United Kingdom).

Ernest Gold for *It's a Mad, Mad, Mad, Mad World*, United Artists.

Alfred Newman and Ken Darby for *How the West Was Won*, MGM.

Alex North for *Cleopatra*, 20th Century-Fox.

Dimitri Tiomkin for *55 Days at Peking*, Allied Artists.

(Scoring of Music—Adaptation or Treatment)
André Previn for *Irma la Douce*, United Artists.

George Bruns for *The Sword in the Stone*, Disney, Buena Vista.

John Green for *Bye Bye Birdie*, Columbia.

Maurice Jarre for *Sundays and Cybèle*, Columbia (France).

Leith Stevens for *A New Kind of Love*, Paramount.

FILM EDITING
Harold F. Kress for *How the West Was Won*, MGM.

Frederic Knudtson, Robert C. Jones, and Gene Fowler, Jr., for *It's a Mad, Mad, Mad, Mad World*, United Artists.

Louis R. Loeffler for *The Cardinal*, Columbia.

Dorothy Spencer for *Cleopatra*, 20th Century-Fox.

Ferris Webster for *The Great Escape*, United Artists.

COSTUME DESIGN
(Black and White)
Piero Gherardi for *8¹/₂*, Embassy Pictures (Italy).

Edith Head for *Love With the Proper Stranger*, Paramount.

Edith Head for *Wives and Lovers*, Paramount.

Bill Thomas for *Toys in the Attic*, United Artists.

Travilla for *The Stripper*, 20th Century-Fox.

(Color)
Irene Sharaff, Vittorio Nino Novarese, and Renie for *Cleopatra*, 20th Century-Fox.

Donald Brooks for *The Cardinal*, Columbia.

Edith Head for *A New Kind of Love*, Paramount.

Walter Plunkett for *How the West Was Won*, MGM.

Piero Tosi for *The Leopard*, 20th Century-Fox (Italy/U.S.).

SPECIAL EFFECTS[180]
Emil Kosa, Jr., for *Cleopatra*, 20th Century-Fox.

Ub Iwerks for *The Birds*, Paramount.

SOUND EFFECTS
Walter G. Elliott for *It's a Mad, Mad, Mad, Mad World*, United Artists.

Robert L. Bratton for *A Gathering of Eagles*, Universal.

FOREIGN LANGUAGE FILM
8¹/₂, Italy.

Knife in the Water, Poland.
The Red Lanterns, Greece.
Los Tarantos, Spain.
Twin Sisters of Kyoto, Japan.

IRVING G. THALBERG MEMORIAL AWARD
Sam Spiegel.

1964
Awards presented April 5, 1965.

PICTURE
***My Fair Lady*, Warner Bros. Produced by Jack L. Warner.**

Becket, Hal Wallis Productions, Paramount (U.S./United Kingdom). Produced by Hal B. Wallis.

Dr. Strangelove or: How I Learned to Stop Worrying and Love the Bomb, Hawk Films, Ltd., Production, Columbia (United Kingdom). Produced by Stanley Kubrick.

Mary Poppins, Walt Disney Productions, Buena Vista. Produced by Walt Disney and Bill Walsh.

Zorba the Greek, Rochley, Ltd., Production, International Classics (U.S./Greece). Produced by Michael Cacoyannis.

ACTOR
Rex Harrison in *My Fair Lady*, Warner Bros.

Richard Burton in *Becket*, Paramount (U.S./United Kingdom).

---

[180] Special Effects category divided into visual and sound effects awards.

Peter O'Toole in *Becket,* Paramount (U.S./United Kingdom).

Anthony Quinn in *Zorba the Greek,* Rochley, International Classics (U.S./Greece).

Peter Sellers in *Dr. Strangelove or: How I Learned to Stop Worrying and Love the Bomb,* Columbia (United Kingdom).

ACTRESS

Julie Andrews in *Mary Poppins,* Disney, Buena Vista.

Anne Bancroft in *The Pumpkin Eater,* Romulus, Royal Films International (United Kingdom).

Sophia Loren in *Marriage Italian Style,* Embassy (France/Italy).

Debbie Reynolds in *The Unsinkable Molly Brown,* MGM.

Kim Stanley in *Séance on a Wet Afternoon,* Attenborough-Forbes, Artixo (United Kingdom).

SUPPORTING ACTOR

Peter Ustinov in *Topkapi,* United Artists.

John Gielgud in *Becket,* Paramount (U.S./United Kingdom).

Stanley Holloway in *My Fair Lady,* Warner Bros.

Edmond O'Brien in *Seven Days in May,* Paramount.

Lee Tracy in *The Best Man,* United Artists.

SUPPORTING ACTRESS

Lila Kedrova in *Zorba the Greek,* Rochley, International Classics (U.S/Greece).

Gladys Cooper in *My Fair Lady,* Warner Bros.

Edith Evans in *The Chalk Garden,* Universal.

Grayson Hall in *The Night of the Iguana,* MGM.

Agnes Moorehead in *Hush . . . Hush, Sweet Charlotte,* 20th Century-Fox.

DIRECTOR

George Cukor[181] for *My Fair Lady,* Warner Bros.

Michael Cacoyannis for *Zorba the Greek,* International Classics (U.S./Greece).

Peter Glenville for *Becket,* Paramount (U.S./United Kingdom).

Stanley Kubrick for *Dr. Strangelove or: How I Learned to Stop Worrying and Love the Bomb,* Columbia (United Kingdom).

Robert Stevenson for *Mary Poppins,* Disney, Buena Vista.

WRITING

(Screenplay—Based on Material From Another Medium)

Edward Anhalt for *Becket,* Paramount (U.S./United Kingdom).

Michael Cacoyannis for *Zorba the Greek,* International Classics (U.S./Greece).

Stanley Kubrick, Peter George, and Terry Southern for *Dr. Strangelove or: How I Learned to Stop Worrying and Love the Bomb,* Columbia (United Kingdom).

Alan Jay Lerner for *My Fair Lady,* Warner Bros.

Bill Walsh and Don DaGradi for *Mary Poppins,* Disney, Buena Vista.

(Story and Screenplay—Written Directly for the Screen)

S. H. Barnett, story; Peter Stone and Frank Tarloff, screenplay, for *Father Goose,* Universal.

Age, Scarpelli, and Mario Monicelli for *The Organizer,* Reade-Sterling-Continental (France/Italy/Yugoslavia).

Orville H. Hampton, story; Raphael Hayes and Orville H. Hampton, screenplay, for *One Potato, Two Potato,* Cinema V.

Alan Owen for *A Hard Day's Night,* United Artists (United Kingdom).

Jean-Paul Rappenau, Ariane Mnouchkine, Daniel Boulanger, and Philippe de Broca for *That Man From Rio,* Lopert (France/Italy).

CINEMATOGRAPHY

(Black and White)

Walter Lassally for *Zorba the Greek,* International Classics (U.S./Greece).

Joseph Biroc for *Hush . . . Hush, Sweet Charlotte,* 20th Century-Fox.

Gabriel Figueroa for *The Night of the Iguana,* MGM.

Milton Krasner for *Fate Is the Hunter,* 20th Century-Fox.

Philip H. Lathrop for *The Americanization of Emily,* MGM.

(Color)

Harry Stradling for *My Fair Lady,* Warner Bros.

William H. Clothier for *Cheyenne Autumn,* Warner Bros.

Edward Colman for *Mary Poppins,* Disney, Buena Vista.

Daniel L. Fapp for *The Unsinkable Molly Brown,* MGM.

Geoffrey Unsworth for *Becket,* Paramount (U.S./United Kingdom).

ART DIRECTION—SET DECORATION

(Black and White)

***Zorba the Greek,* International Classics (U.S./Greece). Vassilis Fotopoulos.**

The Americanization of Emily, MGM. George W. Davis, Hans Peters, Elliot Scott; Henry Grace, Robert R. Benton.

Hush . . . Hush, Sweet Charlotte, 20th Century-Fox. William Glasgow; Raphael Bretton.

The Night of the Iguana, MGM. Stephen Grimes.

Seven Days in May, Paramount. Cary Odell; Edward G. Boyle.

(Color)

***My Fair Lady,* Warner Bros. Gene Allen, Cecil Beaton; George James Hopkins.**

Becket, Paramount. John Bryan, Maurice Carter; Patrick McLoughlin, Robert Cartwright.

Mary Poppins, Disney, Buena Vista. Carroll

---

[181] Cukor, sixty-five, is the oldest winner of the directing Oscar.

Clark, William H. Tuntke; Emile
Kuri, Hal Gausman.

The Unsinkable Molly Brown, MGM.
George W. Davis, Preston Ames;
Henry Grace, Hugh Hunt.

What a Way to Go!, 20th Century-Fox.
Jack Martin Smith, Ted Haworth;
Walter M. Scott, Stuart A. Reiss.

SOUND

**George R. Groves for *My Fair Lady,*
Warner Bros.**

Robert O. Cook for *Mary Poppins,*
Disney, Buena Vista.

John Cox, Shepperton Studio Sound
Dept., for *Becket,* Paramount (U.S./
United Kingdom).

Franklin E. Milton for *The Unsinkable
Molly Brown,* MGM.

Waldon O. Watson for *Father Goose,*
Universal.

MUSIC

(Song)

**"Chim Chim Cher-ee" from *Mary
Poppins,* Disney, Buena Vista.
Music and lyrics by Richard M.
Sherman and Robert B.
Sherman.**

"Dear Heart" from *Dear Heart,* Warner
Bros. Music by Henry Mancini, lyrics
by Jay Livingston and Ray Evans.

"Hush . . . Hush, Sweet Charlotte"
from *Hush . . . Hush, Sweet Charlotte,*
20th Century-Fox. Music by Frank
DeVol, lyrics by Mack David.

"My Kind of Town" from *Robin and the
7 Hoods,* Warner Bros. Music by
James Van Heusen, lyrics by Sammy
Cahn.

"Where Love Has Gone" from *Where
Love Has Gone,* Embassy, Paramount.
Music by James Van Heusen, lyrics by
Sammy Cahn.

(Music Score—Substantially Original)

**Richard M. Sherman and Robert B.
Sherman for *Mary Poppins,*
Disney, Buena Vista.**

Frank DeVol for *Hush . . . Hush, Sweet
Charlotte,* 20th Century-Fox.

Henry Mancini for *The Pink Panther,*
United Artists.

Laurence Rosenthal for *Becket,* Paramount
(U.S./United Kingdom).

Dimitri Tiomkin for *The Fall of the Roman
Empire,* Paramount.

(Scoring of Music—Adaptation or
Treatment)

**André Previn for *My Fair Lady,*
Warner Bros.**

Robert Armbruster, Leo Arnaud, Jack
Elliott, Jack Hayes, Calvin Jackson,
and Leo Shuken for *The Unsinkable
Molly Brown,* MGM.

Irwin Kostal for *Mary Poppins,* Disney,
Buena Vista.

George Martin for *A Hard Day's Night,*
United Artists (United Kingdom).

Nelson Riddle for *Robin and the 7 Hoods,*
Warner Bros.

FILM EDITING

**Cotton Warburton for *Mary Poppins,*
Disney, Buena Vista.**

Anne Coates for *Becket,* Paramount (U.S./
United Kingdom).

Ted J. Kent for *Father Goose,* Universal.

Michael Luciano for *Hush . . . Hush,
Sweet Charlotte,* 20th Century-Fox.

William Ziegler for *My Fair Lady,* Warner
Bros.

COSTUME DESIGN

(Black and White)

**Dorothy Jeakins for *The Night of the
Iguana,* MGM.**

Edith Head for *A House Is Not a Home,*
Embassy Pictures.

René Hubert for *The Visit,* 20th Century-
Fox (U.S./France/Italy/West
Germany).

Norma Koch for *Hush . . . Hush, Sweet
Charlotte,* 20th Century-Fox.

Howard Shoup for *Kisses for My President,*
Warner Bros.

(Color)

**Cecil Beaton for *My Fair Lady,*
Warner Bros.**

Margaret Furse for *Becket,* Paramount
(U.S./United Kingdom).

Morton Haack for *The Unsinkable Molly
Brown,* MGM.

Edith Head and Moss Mabry for *What a
Way to Go,* 20th Century-Fox.

Tony Walton for *Mary Poppins,* Disney,
Buena Vista.

SPECIAL VISUAL EFFECTS

**Peter Ellenshaw, Hamilton Luske,
and Eustace Lycett for *Mary
Poppins,* Disney, Buena Vista.**

Jim Danforth for *7 Faces of Dr. Lao,*
MGM.

SOUND EFFECTS

**Norman Wanstall for *Goldfinger,*
United Artists (United
Kingdom).**

Robert L. Bratton for *The Lively Set,*
Universal.

FOREIGN LANGUAGE FILM

***Yesterday, Today and Tomorrow,* Italy.**

Raven's End, Sweden.

Sallah, Israel.

The Umbrellas of Cherbourg, France.

Woman in the Dunes, Japan.

HONORARY AWARD

**William Tuttle for his outstanding
makeup achievement for *7 Faces
of Dr. Lao.*[182]**

1965

Awards presented April 18, 1966.

PICTURE

***The Sound of Music,* Argyle
Enterprises Production, 20th
Century-Fox. Produced by
Robert Wise.**

Darling, Anglo-Amalgamated, Ltd.,
Production, Embassy Pictures
Corporation (United Kingdom).
Produced by Joseph Janni.

Doctor Zhivago, Sostar S.A.-Metro-
Goldwyn-Mayer British Studios, Ltd.,
Production, MGM. Produced by
Carlo Ponti.

---

[182] First person to be recognized by the Academy for makeup, which did not become a competitive category until the 1981 awards.

Ship of Fools, Columbia. Produced by Stanley Kramer.

A Thousand Clowns, Harrell Production, United Artists. Produced by Fred Coe.

ACTOR

Lee Marvin in *Cat Ballou*, Columbia.

Richard Burton in *The Spy Who Came in From the Cold,* Paramount (United Kingdom).

Laurence Olivier in *Othello,* Warner Bros. (United Kingdom).

Rod Steiger in *The Pawnbroker,* American International.

Oskar Werner in *Ship of Fools,* Columbia.

ACTRESS

Julie Christie in *Darling*, Embassy (United Kingdom).

Julie Andrews in *The Sound of Music,* 20th Century-Fox.

Samantha Eggar in *The Collector,* Columbia.

Elizabeth Hartman in *A Patch of Blue,* MGM.

Simone Signoret in *Ship of Fools,* Columbia.

SUPPORTING ACTOR

Martin Balsam in *A Thousand Clowns*, United Artists.

Ian Bannen in *The Flight of the Phoenix,* 20th Century-Fox.

Tom Courtenay in *Doctor Zhivago,* MGM.

Michael Dunn in *Ship of Fools,* Columbia.

Frank Finlay in *Othello,* Warner Bros. (United Kingdom).

SUPPORTING ACTRESS

Shelley Winters in *A Patch of Blue*, MGM.

Ruth Gordon in *Inside Daisy Clover,* Warner Bros.

Joyce Redman in *Othello,* Warner Bros. (United Kingdom).

Maggie Smith in *Othello,* Warner Bros. (United Kingdom).

Peggy Wood in *The Sound of Music,* 20th Century-Fox.

DIRECTOR

Robert Wise for *The Sound of Music*, 20th Century-Fox.

David Lean for *Doctor Zhivago,* MGM.

John Schlesinger for *Darling,* Embassy (United Kingdom).

Hiroshi Teshigahara for *Woman in the Dunes,* Pathé Contemporary Films (Japan).

William Wyler[183] for *The Collector,* Columbia (U.S./United Kingdom).

WRITING

(Screenplay—Based on Material From Another Medium)

Robert Bolt for *Doctor Zhivago*, MGM.

Herb Gardner for *A Thousand Clowns,* United Artists.

Abby Mann for *Ship of Fools,* Columbia.

Stanley Mann and John Kohn for *The Collector,* Columbia (U.S./United Kingdom).

Walter Newman and Frank R. Pierson for *Cat Ballou,* Columbia.

(Story and Screenplay—Written Directly for the Screen)

Frederic Raphael for *Darling*, Embassy (United Kingdom).

Age, Scarpelli, Mario Monicelli, Tonino Guerra, Giorgio Salvioni, and Suso Cecchi D'Amico for *Casanova '70,* Embassy (France/Italy).

Franklin Coen and Frank Davis for *The Train,* United Artists (U.S./France/Italy).

Jack Davies and Ken Annakin for *Those Magnificent Men in Their Flying Machines,* 20th Century-Fox.

Jacques Demy for *The Umbrellas of Cherbourg,* American International (France).

CINEMATOGRAPHY

(Black and White)

Ernest Laszlo for *Ship of Fools*, Columbia.

Robert Burks for *A Patch of Blue,* MGM.

Loyal Griggs for *In Harm's Way,* Paramount.

Burnett Guffey for *King Rat,* Columbia.

Conrad Hall for *Morituri,* 20th Century-Fox.

(Color)

Freddie Young for *Doctor Zhivago*, MGM.

Russell Harlan for *The Great Race,* Warner Bros.

Ted McCord for *The Sound of Music,* 20th Century-Fox.

William C. Mellor and Loyal Griggs for *The Greatest Story Ever Told,* United Artists.

Leon Shamroy for *The Agony and the Ecstasy,* 20th Century-Fox.

ART DIRECTION—SET DECORATION

(Black and White)

***Ship of Fools*, Columbia. Robert Clatworthy; Joseph Kish.**

King Rat, Columbia. Robert Emmet Smith; Frank Tuttle.

A Patch of Blue, MGM. George W. Davis, Urie McCleary; Henry Grace, Charles S. Thompson.

The Slender Thread, Paramount. Hal Pereira, Jack Poplin; Robert Benton, Joseph Kish.

The Spy Who Came in From the Cold, Paramount (United Kingdom). Hal Pereira, Tambi Larsen, Edward Marshall; Josie McAvin.

(Color)

***Doctor Zhivago*, MGM. John Box, Terry Marsh; Dario Simoni.**

The Agony and the Ecstasy, 20th Century-Fox. John DeCuir, Jack Martin Smith; Dario Simoni.

The Greatest Story Ever Told, United Artists. Richard Day, William Creber, David Hall; Ray Moyer, Fred MacLean, Norman Rockett.

---

[183] Wyler's twelfth nomination is a record for directors. He won three Oscars, a number tied by Frank Capra and exceeded only by John Ford, who won four.

Inside Daisy Clover, Warner Bros. Robert Clatworthy; George James Hopkins.

The Sound of Music, 20th Century-Fox. Boris Leven; Walter M. Scott, Ruby Levitt.

SOUND

James P. Corcoran, 20th Century-Fox Studio Sound Dept., and Fred Hynes, Todd-AO Sound Dept., for *The Sound of Music*, 20th Century-Fox.

James P. Corcoran for *The Agony and the Ecstasy*, 20th Century-Fox.

George R. Groves for *The Great Race*, Warner Bros.

A. W. Watkins, MGM British Studio Sound Dept., and Franklin E. Milton, MGM Studio Sound Dept., for *Doctor Zhivago*, MGM.

Waldon O. Watson for *Shenandoah*, Universal.

MUSIC

(Song)

"The Shadow of Your Smile" from *The Sandpiper*, MGM. Music by Johnny Mandel, lyrics by Paul Francis Webster.

"The Ballad of Cat Ballou" from *Cat Ballou*, Columbia. Music by Jerry Livingston, lyrics by Mack David.

"I Will Wait for You" from *The Umbrellas of Cherbourg*, American International (France). Music by Michel Legrand, lyrics by Jacques Demy, English lyrics by Norman Gimbel.

"The Sweetheart Tree" from *The Great Race*, Warner Bros. Music by Henry Mancini, lyrics by Johnny Mercer.

"What's New Pussycat?" from *What's New Pussycat?*, United Artists. Music by Burt Bacharach, lyrics by Hal David.

(Music Score—Substantially Original)

Maurice Jarre for *Doctor Zhivago*, MGM.

Jerry Goldsmith for *A Patch of Blue*, MGM.

Michel Legrand and Jacques Demy for *The Umbrellas of Cherbourg*, American International (France).

Alfred Newman for *The Greatest Story Ever Told*, United Artists.

Alex North for *The Agony and the Ecstasy*, 20th Century-Fox.

(Scoring of Music—Adaptation or Treatment)

Irwin Kostal for *The Sound of Music*, 20th Century-Fox.

DeVol for *Cat Ballou*, Columbia.

Michel Legrand for *The Umbrellas of Cherbourg*, American International (France).

Lionel Newman and Alexander Courage for *The Pleasure Seekers*, 20th Century-Fox.

Don Walker for *A Thousand Clowns*, United Artists.

FILM EDITING

William Reynolds for *The Sound of Music*, 20th Century-Fox.

Michael Luciano for *The Flight of the Phoenix*, 20th Century-Fox.

Charles Nelson for *Cat Ballou*, Columbia.

Norman Savage for *Doctor Zhivago*, MGM.

Ralph E. Winters for *The Great Race*, Warner Bros.

COSTUME DESIGN

(Black and White)

Julie Harris for *Darling*, Embassy (United Kingdom).

Edith Head for *The Slender Thread*, Paramount.

Moss Mabry for *Morituri*, 20th Century-Fox.

Howard Shoup for *A Rage to Live*, United Artists.

Bill Thomas and Jean Louis for *Ship of Fools*, Columbia.

(Color)

Phyllis Dalton for *Doctor Zhivago*, MGM.

Edith Head and Bill Thomas for *Inside Daisy Clover*, Warner Bros.

Dorothy Jeakins for *The Sound of Music*, 20th Century-Fox.

Vittorio Nino Novarese for *The Agony and the Ecstasy*, 20th Century-Fox.

Vittorio Nino Novarese and Marjorie Best for *The Greatest Story Ever Told*, United Artists.

SPECIAL VISUAL EFFECTS

John Stears for *Thunderball*, United Artists (United Kingdom).

J. McMillan Johnson for *The Greatest Story Ever Told*, United Artists.

SOUND EFFECTS

Tregoweth Brown for *The Great Race*, Warner Bros.

Walter A. Rossi for *Von Ryan's Express*, 20th Century-Fox.

FOREIGN LANGUAGE FILM

***The Shop on Main Street*, Czechoslovakia.**

Blood on the Land, Greece.

Dear John, Sweden.

Kwaidan, Japan.

Marriage Italian Style, Italy.

IRVING G. THALBERG MEMORIAL AWARD

William Wyler.

JEAN HERSHOLT HUMANITARIAN AWARD

Edmond L. DePatie.

HONORARY AWARD

Bob Hope, for unique and distinguished service to our industry and the Academy.[184]

1966

Awards presented April 10, 1967.

PICTURE

A Man for All Seasons, Highland Films, Ltd., Production,

---

[184] The gold medal presented to Hope was his fifth honorary award, including the Jean Hersholt Humanitarian Award, making him the most honored performer in the history of the Oscars.

Columbia (United Kingdom). Produced by Fred Zinnemann.

Alfie, Sheldrake Films, Ltd., Production, Paramount (United Kingdom). Produced by Lewis Gilbert.

The Russians Are Coming, the Russians Are Coming, Mirisch Corporation of Delaware Production, United Artists. Produced by Norman Jewison.

The Sand Pebbles, Argyle-Solar Production, 20th Century-Fox. Produced by Robert Wise.

Who's Afraid of Virginia Woolf?, Chenault Productions, Warner Bros. Produced by Ernest Lehman.

ACTOR

Paul Scofield in *A Man for All Seasons*, Columbia (United Kingdom).

Alan Arkin in *The Russians Are Coming, the Russians Are Coming*, United Artists.

Richard Burton in *Who's Afraid of Virginia Woolf?*, Warner Bros.

Michael Caine in *Alfie*, Paramount (United Kingdom).

Steve McQueen in *The Sand Pebbles*, 20th Century-Fox.

ACTRESS[185]

Elizabeth Taylor in *Who's Afraid of Virginia Woolf?*, Warner Bros.

Anouk Aimée in *A Man and a Woman*, Allied Artists (France).

Ida Kaminska in *The Shop on Main Street*, Prominent Films (Czechoslovakia).

Lynn Redgrave in *Georgy Girl*, Columbia (United Kingdom).

Vanessa Redgrave in *Morgan!*, Cinema V (United Kingdom).

SUPPORTING ACTOR

Walter Matthau in *The Fortune Cookie*, United Artists.

Mako in *The Sand Pebbles*, 20th Century-Fox.

James Mason in *Georgy Girl*, Columbia (United Kingdom).

George Segal in *Who's Afraid of Virginia Woolf?*, Warner Bros.

Robert Shaw in *A Man for All Seasons*, Columbia (United Kingdom).

SUPPORTING ACTRESS

Sandy Dennis in *Who's Afraid of Virginia Woolf?*, Warner Bros.

Wendy Hiller in *A Man for All Seasons*, Columbia (United Kingdom).

Jocelyn Lagarde in *Hawaii*, United Artists.

Vivien Merchant in *Alfie*, Paramount (United Kingdom).

Geraldine Page in *You're a Big Boy Now*, Seven Arts.

DIRECTOR

Fred Zinnemann for *A Man for All Seasons*, Columbia (United Kingdom).

Michelangelo Antonioni for *Blowup*, Premier Productions (United Kingdom/Italy).

Richard Brooks for *The Professionals*, Columbia.

Claude Lelouch for *A Man and a Woman*, Allied Artists (France).

Mike Nichols for *Who's Afraid of Virginia Woolf?*, Warner Bros.

WRITING

(Screenplay—Based on Material From Another Medium)

Robert Bolt for *A Man for All Seasons*, Columbia (United Kingdom).

Richard Brooks for *The Professionals*, Columbia.

Ernest Lehman for *Who's Afraid of Virginia Woolf?*, Warner Bros.

Bill Naughton for *Alfie*, Paramount (United Kingdom).

William Rose for *The Russians Are Coming, the Russians Are Coming*, United Artists.

(Story and Screenplay—Written Directly for the Screen)

Claude Lelouch and Pierre Uytterhoeven for *A Man and a Woman*, Allied Artists (France).

Michelangelo Antonioni, story; Michelangelo Antonioni, Tonino Guerra, and Edward Bond, screenplay, for *Blowup*, Premier Productions (United Kingdom/Italy).

Robert Ardrey for *Khartoum*, United Artists (United Kingdom).

Clint Johnston and Don Peters for *The Naked Prey*, Paramount (U.S./South Africa).

Billy Wilder and I. A. L. Diamond for *The Fortune Cookie*, United Artists.

CINEMATOGRAPHY

(Black and White)

Haskell Wexler for *Who's Afraid of Virginia Woolf?*, Warner Bros.

Marcel Grignon for *Is Paris Burning?*, Paramount (U.S./France).

Ken Higgins for *Georgy Girl*, Columbia (United Kingdom).

James Wong Howe for *Seconds*, Paramount.

Joseph LaShelle for *The Fortune Cookie*, United Artists.

(Color)

Ted Moore for *A Man for All Seasons*, Columbia (United Kingdom).

Conrad Hall for *The Professionals*, Columbia.

Russell Harlan for *Hawaii*, United Artists.

Ernest Laszlo for *Fantastic Voyage*, 20th Century-Fox.

Joseph MacDonald for *The Sand Pebbles*, 20th Century-Fox.

ART DIRECTION—SET DECORATION

(Black and White)

Who's Afraid of Virginia Woolf?, Warner Bros. Richard Sylbert; George James Hopkins.

The Fortune Cookie, United Artists. Robert Luthardt; Edward G. Boyle.

The Gospel According to St. Matthew, Reade-Continental (France/Italy). Luigi Scaccianoce.

Is Paris Burning?, Paramount (U.S./

---

[185] Lynn and Vanessa Redgrave are the only sisters to receive simultaneous nominations in the acting categories other than Joan Fontaine and Olivia de Havilland, who were competitors at the 1941 awards.

France). Willy Holt; Marc Frederix, Pierre Guffroy.

Mister Buddwing, MGM. George W. Davis, Paul Groesse; Henry Grace, Hugh Hunt.

(Color)

Fantastic Voyage, 20th Century-Fox. Jack Martin Smith, Dale Hennesy; Walter M. Scott, Stuart A. Reiss.

Gambit, Universal. Alexander Golitzen, George C. Webb; John McCarthy, John Austin.

Juliet of the Spirits, Rizzoli Films (Italy). Piero Gherardi.

The Oscar, Embassy. Hal Pereira, Arthur Longergan; Robert Benton, James Payne.

The Sand Pebbles, 20th Century-Fox. Boris Leven; Walter M. Scott, John Sturtevant, William Kiernan.

SOUND

Franklin E. Milton for *Grand Prix*, MGM.

James P. Corcoran for *The Sand Pebbles*, 20th Century-Fox.

George R. Groves for *Who's Afraid of Virginia Woolf?*, Warner Bros.

Gordon E. Sawyer, Samuel Goldwyn Studio Sound Dept., for *Hawaii*, United Artists.

Waldon O. Watson for *Gambit*, Universal.

MUSIC

(Song)

"Born Free" from *Born Free*, Columbia (United Kingdom). Music by John Barry, lyrics by Don Black.

"Alfie" from *Alfie*, Paramount (United Kingdom). Music by Burt Bacharach, lyrics by Hal David.

"Georgy Girl" from *Georgy Girl*, Columbia (United Kingdom). Music by Tom Springfield, lyrics by Jim Dale.

"My Wishing Doll" from *Hawaii*, United Artists. Music by Elmer Bernstein, lyrics by Mack David.

"A Time for Love" from *An American Dream*, Warner Bros. Music by Johnny Mandel, lyrics by Paul Francis Webster.

(Original Music Score)[186]

John Barry for *Born Free*, Columbia (United Kingdom).

Elmer Bernstein for *Hawaii*, United Artists.

Jerry Goldsmith for *The Sand Pebbles*, 20th Century-Fox.

Toshiro Mayazumi for *The Bible*, 20th Century-Fox (U.S./Italy).

Alex North for *Who's Afraid of Virginia Woolf?*, Warner Bros.

(Scoring of Music—Adaptation or Treatment)

Ken Thorne for *A Funny Thing Happened on the Way to the Forum*, United Artists.

Luis Enrique Bacalov for *The Gospel According to St. Matthew*, Reade-Continental (France/Italy).

Elmer Bernstein for *Return of the Seven*, United Artists (U.S./Spain).

Al Ham for *Stop the World—I Want to Get Off*, Warner Bros. (United Kingdom).

Harry Sukman for *The Singing Nun*, MGM.

FILM EDITING

Fredric Steinkamp, Henry Berman, Stewart Linder, and Frank Santillo for *Grand Prix*, MGM.

Hal Ashby and J. Terry Williams for *The Russians Are Coming, the Russians Are Coming*, United Artists.

William B. Murphy for *Fantastic Voyage*, 20th Century-Fox.

Sam O'Steen for *Who's Afraid of Virginia Woolf?*, Warner Bros.

William Reynolds for *The Sand Pebbles*, 20th Century-Fox.

COSTUME DESIGN

(Black and White)

Irene Sharaff for *Who's Afraid of Virginia Woolf?*, Warner Bros.

Danilo Donati for *The Gospel According to St. Matthew*, Reade-Continental (France/Italy).

Danilo Donati for *Mandragola*, Europix-Consolidated (France/Italy).

Jocelyn Rickards for *Morgan!*, Cinema V (United Kingdom).

Helen Rose for *Mister Buddwing*, MGM.

(Color)

Elizabeth Haffenden and Joan Bridge for *A Man for All Seasons*, Columbia.

Piero Gherardi for *Juliet of the Spirits*, Rizzoli Films (France/Italy/West Germany).

Edith Head for *The Oscar*, Embassy.

Dorothy Jeakins for *Hawaii*, United Artists.

Jean Louis for *Gambit*, Universal.

SPECIAL VISUAL EFFECTS

Art Cruickshank for *Fantastic Voyage*, 20th Century-Fox.

Linwood G. Dunn for *Hawaii*, United Artists.

SOUND EFFECTS

Gordon Daniel for *Grand Prix*, MGM.

Walter Rossi for *Fantastic Voyage*, 20th Century-Fox.

FOREIGN LANGUAGE FILM

A Man and a Woman, France.
The Battle of Algiers, Italy.
Loves of a Blonde, Czechoslovakia.
Pharaoh, Poland.
Three, Yugoslavia.

IRVING G. THALBERG MEMORIAL AWARD
Robert Wise.

JEAN HERSHOLT HUMANITARIAN AWARD
George Bagnall.

HONORARY AWARDS
Y. Frank Freeman, for unusual and outstanding service to the Academy during his 30 years in Hollywood.

Yakima Canutt, for achievements as

---

[186] Name of category changed.

a stunt man and for developing safety devices to protect stunt men everywhere.

1967
Awards presented April 10, 1968.

PICTURE
In the Heat of the Night, Mirisch Corporation Production, United Artists. Produced by Walter Mirisch.

Bonnie and Clyde, Tatira-Hiller Production, Warner Bros.-Seven Arts. Produced by Warren Beatty.

Doctor Dolittle, Apjac Productions, 20th Century-Fox. Produced by Arthur P. Jacobs.

The Graduate, Mike Nichols-Lawrence Turman Production, Embassy Pictures Corporation. Produced by Lawrence Turman.

Guess Who's Coming to Dinner, Columbia. Produced by Stanley Kramer.

ACTOR
Rod Steiger in *In the Heat of the Night,* United Artists.

Warren Beatty in *Bonnie and Clyde,* Warner Bros.-Seven Arts.

Dustin Hoffman in *The Graduate,* Embassy.

Paul Newman in *Cool Hand Luke,* Warner Bros.-Seven Arts.

Spencer Tracy in *Guess Who's Coming to Dinner,* Columbia.

ACTRESS
Katharine Hepburn in *Guess Who's Coming to Dinner,* Columbia.

Anne Bancroft in *The Graduate,* Embassy.

Faye Dunaway in *Bonnie and Clyde,* Warner Bros.-Seven Arts.

Edith Evans in *The Whisperers,* United Artists (United Kingdom).

Audrey Hepburn in *Wait Until Dark,* Warner Bros.-Seven Arts.

SUPPORTING ACTOR
George Kennedy in *Cool Hand Luke,* Warner Bros.-Seven Arts.

John Cassavetes in *The Dirty Dozen,* MGM (U.S./United Kingdom).

Gene Hackman in *Bonnie and Clyde,* Warner Bros.-Seven Arts.

Cecil Kellaway in *Guess Who's Coming to Dinner,* Columbia.

Michael J. Pollard in *Bonnie and Clyde,* Warner Bros.-Seven Arts.

SUPPORTING ACTRESS
Estelle Parsons in *Bonnie and Clyde,* Warner Bros.-Seven Arts.

Carol Channing in *Thoroughly Modern Millie,* Universal.

Mildred Natwick in *Barefoot in the Park,* Paramount.

Beah Richards in *Guess Who's Coming to Dinner,* Columbia.

Katharine Ross in *The Graduate,* Embassy.

DIRECTOR
Mike Nichols for *The Graduate,* Embassy.

Richard Brooks for *In Cold Blood,* Columbia.

Norman Jewison for *In the Heat of the Night,* United Artists.

Stanley Kramer for *Guess Who's Coming to Dinner,* Columbia.

Arthur Penn for *Bonnie and Clyde,* Warner Bros.-Seven Arts.

WRITING
(Screenplay—Based on Material From Another Medium)

Stirling Silliphant for *In the Heat of the Night,* United Artists.

Richard Brooks for *In Cold Blood,* Columbia.

Donn Pearce and Frank R. Pierson for *Cool Hand Luke,* Warner Bros.-Seven Arts.

Joseph Strick and Fred Haines for *Ulysses,* Walter Reade-Continental Distributing (U.S./United Kingdom).

Calder Willingham and Buck Henry for *The Graduate,* Embassy.

(Story and Screenplay—Written Directly for the Screen)

William Rose for *Guess Who's Coming to Dinner,* Columbia.

Robert Kaufman, story; Norman Lear, screenplay, for *Divorce American Style,* Columbia.

David Newman and Robert Benton for *Bonnie and Clyde,* Warner Bros.-Seven Arts.

Frederic Raphael for *Two for the Road,* 20th Century-Fox (U.S./United Kingdom).

Jorge Semprun for *La Guerre Est Finie,* Brandon Films (France/Sweden).

CINEMATOGRAPHY[187]
Burnett Guffey for *Bonnie and Clyde,* Warner Bros.-Seven Arts.

Conrad Hall for *In Cold Blood,* Columbia.

Richard H. Kline for *Camelot,* Warner Bros.-Seven Arts.

Robert Surtees for *Doctor Dolittle,* 20th Century-Fox.

Robert Surtees for *The Graduate,* Embassy.

ART DIRECTION—SET DECORATION
Camelot, Warner Bros.-Seven Arts. John Truscott, Edward Carrere; John W. Brown.

Doctor Dolittle, 20th Century-Fox. Mario Chiari, Jack Martin Smith, Ed Graves; Walter M. Scott, Stuart A. Reiss.

Guess Who's Coming to Dinner, Columbia. Robert Clatworthy; Frank Tuttle.

The Taming of the Shrew, Columbia (U.S./Italy). Renzo Mongiardino, John DeCuir, Elven Webb, Giuseppe Mariani; Dario Simoni, Luigi Gervasi.

Thoroughly Modern Millie, Universal. Alexander Golitzen, George C. Webb; Howard Bristol.

SOUND
In the Heat of the Night, United Artists. Samuel Goldwyn Studio Sound Dept.

Camelot, Warner Bros.-Seven Arts. Seven Arts Studio Sound Dept.

---

[187] Division of cinematography, art direction, and costume awards into black-and-white and color categories eliminated.

The Dirty Dozen, MGM (U.S./United Kingdom). MGM Studio Sound Dept.
Doctor Dolittle, 20th Century-Fox. 20th Century-Fox Studio Sound Dept.
Thoroughly Modern Millie, Universal. Universal City Studio Sound Dept.

MUSIC
(Song)
"Talk to the Animals" from *Doctor Dolittle,* 20th Century-Fox. Music and lyrics by Leslie Bricusse.
"The Bare Necessities" from *The Jungle Book,* Disney, Buena Vista. Music and lyrics by Terry Gilkyson.
"The Eyes of Love" from *Banning,* Universal. Music by Quincy Jones, lyrics by Bob Russell.
"The Look of Love" from *Casino Royale,* Columbia (United Kingdom). Music by Burt Bacharach, lyrics by Hal David.
"Thoroughly Modern Millie" from *Thoroughly Modern Millie,* Universal. Music and lyrics by James Van Heusen and Sammy Cahn.

(Original Music Score)
Elmer Bernstein for *Thoroughly Modern Millie,* Universal.
Richard Rodney Bennett for *Far From the Madding Crowd,* MGM (United Kingdom).
Leslie Bricusse for *Doctor Dolittle,* 20th Century-Fox.
Quincy Jones for *In Cold Blood,* Columbia.
Lalo Schifrin for *Cool Hand Luke,* Warner Bros.-Seven Arts.

(Scoring of Music—Adaptation or Treatment)
Alfred Newman and Ken Darby for *Camelot,* Warner Bros.-Seven Arts.
DeVol for *Guess Who's Coming to Dinner,* Columbia.
Lionel Newman and Alexander Courage for *Doctor Dolittle,* 20th Century-Fox.
André Previn and Joseph Gershenson for *Thoroughly Modern Millie,* Universal.

John Williams for *Valley of the Dolls,* 20th Century-Fox.

FILM EDITING
Hal Ashby for *In the Heat of the Night,* United Artists.
Samuel E. Beetley and Marjorie Fowler for *Doctor Dolittle,* 20th Century-Fox.
Robert C. Jones for *Guess Who's Coming to Dinner,* Columbia.
Frank P. Keller for *Beach Red,* United Artists.
Michael Luciano for *The Dirty Dozen,* MGM (U.S./United Kingdom).

COSTUME DESIGN[188]
John Truscott for *Camelot,* Warner Bros.-Seven Arts.
Jean Louis for *Thoroughly Modern Millie,* Universal.
Irene Sharaff and Danilo Donati for *The Taming of the Shrew,* Columbia (U.S./Italy).
Bill Thomas for *The Happiest Millionaire,* Disney, Buena Vista.
Theadora Van Runkle for *Bonnie and Clyde,* Warner Bros.-Seven Arts.

SPECIAL VISUAL EFFECTS
L. B. Abbott for *Doctor Dolittle,* 20th Century-Fox.
Howard A. Anderson, Jr., and Albert Whitlock for *Tobruk,* Universal.

SOUND EFFECTS
John Poyner for *The Dirty Dozen,* MGM (U.S./United Kingdom).
James A. Richard for *In the Heat of the Night,* United Artists.

FOREIGN LANGUAGE FILM
***Closely Watched Trains,* Czechoslovakia.**
El Amor Brujo, Spain.
I Even Met Happy Gypsies, Yugoslavia.
Live for Life, France.
Portrait of Chieko, Japan.

IRVING G. THALBERG MEMORIAL AWARD
Alfred Hitchcock.

JEAN HERSHOLT HUMANITARIAN AWARD
Gregory Peck.

HONORARY AWARD
Arthur Freed, for distinguished service to the Academy and the production of six top-rated Awards telecasts.

1968
Awards presented April 14, 1969.

PICTURE
***Oliver!,* Romulus Films, Ltd., Production, Columbia (United Kingdom). Produced by John Woolf.**
Funny Girl, Rastar Productions, Columbia. Produced by Ray Stark.
The Lion in Winter, Haworth Productions Ltd., Avco Embassy (United Kingdom). Produced by Martin Poll.
Rachel, Rachel, Kayos Production, Warner Bros.-Seven Arts. Produced by Paul Newman.
Romeo and Juliet, B.H.E. Film-Verona Production-Dino de Laurentiis Cinematografica S.p.A. Production, Paramount (United Kingdom/Italy). Produced by Anthony Havelock-Allan and John Brabourne.

ACTOR
Cliff Robertson in *Charly,* Cinerama.
Alan Arkin in *The Heart Is a Lonely Hunter,* Warner Bros.-Seven Arts.
Alan Bates in *The Fixer,* MGM.
Ron Moody in *Oliver!,* Columbia (United Kingdom).
Peter O'Toole in *The Lion in Winter,* Avco Embassy (United Kingdom).

---

[188] For the first time since the costume awards were created in 1948, Edith Head is not a nominee.

ACTRESS

Tie: Katharine Hepburn[189] in *The Lion in Winter*, Avco Embassy, and Barbra Streisand in *Funny Girl*, Columbia.[190]

Patricia Neal in *The Subject Was Roses*, MGM.

Vanessa Redgrave in *Isadora*, Universal.

Joanne Woodward in *Rachel, Rachel*, Warner Bros.-Seven Arts.

SUPPORTING ACTOR

Jack Albertson in *The Subject Was Roses*, MGM.

Seymour Cassel in *Faces*, Cassavetes, Reade-Continental.

Daniel Massey in *Star!*, 20th Century-Fox.

Jack Wild in *Oliver!*, Columbia (United Kingdom).

Gene Wilder in *The Producers*, Avco Embassy.

SUPPORTING ACTRESS

Ruth Gordon in *Rosemary's Baby*, Paramount.

Lynn Carlin in *Faces*, Reade-Continental.

Sondra Locke in *The Heart Is a Lonely Hunter*, Warner Bros.-Seven Arts.

Kay Medford in *Funny Girl*, Columbia.

Estelle Parsons in *Rachel, Rachel*, Warner Bros.-Seven Arts.

DIRECTOR

Carol Reed for *Oliver!*, Columbia (United Kingdom).

Anthony Harvey for *The Lion in Winter*, Avco Embassy (United Kingdom).

Stanley Kubrick for *2001: A Space Odyssey*, MGM (U.S./United Kingdom).

Gillo Pontecorvo for *The Battle of Algiers*, Allied Artists (Italy).

Franco Zeffirelli for *Romeo and Juliet*, Paramount (United Kingdom/Italy).

WRITING

(Screenplay—Based on Material From Another Medium)

James Goldman for *The Lion in Winter*, Avco Embassy (United Kingdom).

Vernon Harris for *Oliver!*, Columbia (United Kingdom).

Roman Polanski for *Rosemary's Baby*, Paramount.

Neil Simon for *The Odd Couple*, Paramount.

Stewart Stern for *Rachel, Rachel*, Warner Bros.-Seven Arts.

(Story and Screenplay—Written Directly for the Screen)

Mel Brooks for *The Producers*, Avco Embassy.

John Cassavetes for *Faces*, Walter Reade-Continental.

Stanley Kubrick and Arthur C. Clarke for *2001: A Space Odyssey*, MGM (U.S./United Kingdom).

Franco Solinas and Gillo Pontecorvo for *The Battle of Algiers*, Allied Artists (Italy).

Ira Wallach and Peter Ustinov for *Hot Millions*, MGM (United Kingdom).

CINEMATOGRAPHY

Pasqualino De Santis for *Romeo and Juliet*, Paramount (United Kingdom/Italy).

Daniel L. Fapp for *Ice Station Zebra*, MGM.

Ernest Laszlo for *Star!*, 20th Century-Fox.

Oswald Morris for *Oliver!*, Columbia (United Kingdom).

Harry Stradling for *Funny Girl*, Columbia.

ART DIRECTION—SET DECORATION

Oliver!, Columbia (United Kingdom). John Box, Terence Marsh; Vernon Dixon, Ken Muggleston.

The Shoes of the Fisherman, MGM. George W. Davis and Edward Carfagno.

Star!, 20th Century-Fox. Boris Leven; Walter M. Scott, Howard Bristol.

2001: A Space Odyssey, MGM (U.S./United Kingdom). Tony Masters, Harry Lange, Ernie Archer.

War and Peace, Reade-Continental (USSR). Mikhail Bogdanov, Gennady Myasnikov; G. Koshelev, V. Uvarov.

SOUND

Oliver!, Columbia (United Kingdom). Shepperton Studio Sound Dept.

Bullitt, Warner Bros.-Seven Arts. Warner Bros.-Seven Arts Studio Sound Dept.

Finian's Rainbow, Warner Bros.-Seven Arts. Warner Bros.-Seven Arts Studio Sound Dept.

Funny Girl, Columbia. Columbia Studio Sound Dept.

Star!, 20th Century-Fox. 20th Century-Fox Studio Sound Dept.

MUSIC

(Song)

"The Windmills of Your Mind" from *The Thomas Crown Affair*, United Artists. Music by Michel Legrand, lyrics by Alan Bergman and Marilyn Bergman.

"Chitty Chitty Bang Bang" from *Chitty Chitty Bang Bang*, United Artists (United Kingdom). Music and lyrics by Richard M. Sherman and Robert B. Sherman.

"For Love of Ivy" from *For Love of Ivy*, Cinerama. Music by Quincy Jones, lyrics by Bob Russell.

"Funny Girl" from *Funny Girl*, Columbia. Music by Jule Styne, lyrics by Bob Merrill.

"Star!" from *Star!*, 20th Century-Fox. Music by Jimmy Van Heusen, lyrics by Sammy Cahn.

---

[189] Only person to win three Oscars in a leading-role category. (She subsequently won a fourth.) Walter Brennan won three as a supporting performer—1936, 1938, and 1940. Ingrid Bergman won two for leading roles, 1944 and 1956, and one as a supporting player, 1974. Hepburn is also the third person to win back-to-back awards for acting. The others are Luise Rainer (1936, 1937), Spencer Tracy (1937, 1938), Jason Robards (1976, 1977), and Tom Hanks (1993, 1994).

[190] Second tie in an acting category, and the only actual one. The other tie, between Fredric March and Wallace Beery at the 1931–32 awards, was an "official" tie—March led by one vote. Hepburn and Streisand received identical numbers of votes.

(Original Score—for a Motion Picture [Not a Musical])[191]

John Barry for *The Lion in Winter*, Avco Embassy (United Kingdom).

Jerry Goldsmith for *Planet of the Apes*, 20th Century-Fox.

Michel Legrand for *The Thomas Crown Affair*, United Artists.

Alex North for *The Shoes of the Fisherman*, MGM.

Lalo Schifrin for *The Fox*, Claridge Pictures.

(Score of a Musical Picture—Original or Adaptation)

John Green for the adaptation score for *Oliver!*, Columbia (United Kingdom).

Lennie Hayton for the adaptation score for *Star!*, 20th Century-Fox.

Ray Heindorf for the adaptation score for *Finian's Rainbow*, Warner Bros.-Seven Arts.

Michel Legrand for the music and adaptation score and Jacques Demy for the lyrics for *The Young Girls of Rochefort*, Warner Bros.-Seven Arts (France).

Walter Scharf for the adaptation score for *Funny Girl*, Columbia.

FILM EDITING

Frank P. Keller for *Bullitt*, Warner Bros.-Seven Arts.

Frank Bracht for *The Odd Couple*, Paramount.

Fred Feitshans and Eve Newman for *Wild in the Streets*, American International.

Ralph Kemplen for *Oliver!*, Columbia (United Kingdom).

Robert Swink, Maury Winetrobe, and William Sands for *Funny Girl*, Columbia.

COSTUME DESIGN

Danilo Donati for *Romeo and Juliet*, Paramount (United Kingdom/Italy).

Donald Brooks for *Star!*, 20th Century-Fox.

Phyllis Dalton for *Oliver!*, Columbia (United Kingdom).

Margaret Furse for *The Lion in Winter*, Avco Embassy (United Kingdom).

Morton Haack for *Planet of the Apes*, 20th Century-Fox.

SPECIAL VISUAL EFFECTS[192]

Stanley Kubrick for *2001: A Space Odyssey*, MGM (U.S./United Kingdom).

Hal Millar and J. McMillan Johnson for *Ice Station Zebra*, MGM.

FOREIGN LANGUAGE FILM

***War and Peace*, USSR.**

The Boys of Paul Street, Hungary.
The Fireman's Ball, Czechoslovakia.
The Girl With the Pistol, Italy.
Stolen Kisses, France.

JEAN HERSHOLT HUMANITARIAN AWARD

Martha Raye.

HONORARY AWARDS

John Chambers, for his outstanding makeup achievement for *Planet of the Apes*.

Onna White, for her outstanding choreography achievement for *Oliver!*

1969
Awards presented April 7, 1970.

PICTURE

***Midnight Cowboy*, Jerome Hellman-John Schlesinger Production,**

United Artists. Produced by Jerome Hellman.[193]

Anne of the Thousand Days, Hal B. Wallis-Universal Pictures, Ltd. Production, Universal (United Kingdom). Produced by Hal B. Wallis.[194]

Butch Cassidy and the Sundance Kid, George Roy Hill-Paul Monash Production, 20th Century-Fox. Produced by John Foreman.

Hello, Dolly! Chenault Productions, 20th Century-Fox. Produced by Ernest Lehman.

Z, Reggane Films-O.N.C.I.C. Production, Cinema V Distributing (Algeria). Produced by Jacques Perrin and Hamed Rachedi.

ACTOR

John Wayne in *True Grit*, Wallis, Paramount.

Richard Burton in *Anne of the Thousand Days*, Wallis, Universal (United Kingdom).[195]

Dustin Hoffman in *Midnight Cowboy*, United Artists.

Peter O'Toole in *Goodbye, Mr. Chips*, MGM (U.S./United Kingdom).

Jon Voight in *Midnight Cowboy*, United Artists.

ACTRESS

Maggie Smith in *The Prime of Miss Jean Brodie*, 20th Century-Fox (United Kingdom).

Genevieve Bujold in *Anne of the Thousand Days*, Universal (United Kingdom).

Jane Fonda in *They Shoot Horses, Don't They?*, Cinerama.

Liza Minnelli in *The Sterile Cuckoo*, Paramount.

Jean Simmons in *The Happy Ending*, United Artists.

---

[191] Categories renamed to indicate a division of scoring awards into musical and nonmusical pictures once again.
[192] Award for sound effects eliminated.
[193] Only X-rated film to receive a best picture Oscar. The film was subsequently rerated R.
[194] This is the nineteenth film produced by Wallis to be nominated for best picture—an Academy record. But only one of his films, *Casablanca* (1943), received the best picture Oscar.
[195] More people have been nominated for playing Henry VIII than for any other character, historic or fictional. Burton is the third, after Charles Laughton for *The Private Life of Henry VIII* (1932–33) and Robert Shaw for *A Man for All Seasons* (1966).

SUPPORTING ACTOR

Gig Young in *They Shoot Horses, Don't They?*, Cinerama.

Rupert Crosse in *The Reivers,* National General.

Elliott Gould in *Bob & Carol & Ted & Alice,* Columbia.

Jack Nicholson in *Easy Rider,* Columbia.

Anthony Quayle in *Anne of the Thousand Days,* Wallis, Universal (United Kingdom).

SUPPORTING ACTRESS

Goldie Hawn in *Cactus Flower,* Columbia.

Catherine Burns in *Last Summer,* Allied Artists.

Dyan Cannon in *Bob & Carol & Ted & Alice,* Columbia.

Sylvia Miles in *Midnight Cowboy,* United Artists.

Susannah York in *They Shoot Horses, Don't They?,* Cinerama.

DIRECTOR

John Schlesinger for *Midnight Cowboy,* United Artists.

Costa-Gavras for *Z,* Cinema V (Algeria).

George Roy Hill for *Butch Cassidy and the Sundance Kid,* 20th Century-Fox.

Arthur Penn for *Alice's Restaurant,* United Artists.

Sydney Pollack for *They Shoot Horses, Don't They?,* Cinerama.

WRITING

(Screenplay—Based on Material From Another Medium)

Waldo Salt for *Midnight Cowboy,* United Artists.

John Hale and Bridget Boland, screenplay; Richard Sokolove, adaptation, for *Anne of the Thousand Days,* Universal (United Kingdom).

James Poe and Robert E. Thompson for *They Shoot Horses, Don't They?,* Cinerama.

Arnold Schulman for *Goodbye, Columbus,* Paramount.

Jorge Semprun and Costa-Gavras for *Z,* Cinema V (Algeria).

(Story and Screenplay—Based on Material Not Previously Published or Produced)

William Goldman for *Butch Cassidy and the Sundance Kid,* 20th Century-Fox.

Nicola Badalucco, story; Nicola Badalucco, Enrico Medioli, and Luchino Visconti, screenplay, for *The Damned,* Warner Bros. (Italy/West Germany).

Peter Fonda, Dennis Hopper, and Terry Southern for *Easy Rider,* Columbia.

Walon Green and Roy N. Sicker, story; Walon Green and Sam Peckinpah, screenplay, for *The Wild Bunch,* Warner Bros.-Seven Arts.

Paul Mazursky and Larry Tucker for *Bob & Carol & Ted & Alice,* Columbia.

CINEMATOGRAPHY

Conrad Hall for *Butch Cassidy and the Sundance Kid,* 20th Century-Fox.

Daniel Fapp for *Marooned,* Columbia.

Arthur Ibbetson for *Anne of the Thousand Days,* Universal.

Charles B. Lang for *Bob & Carol & Ted & Alice,* Columbia.

Harry Stradling for *Hello, Dolly!,* 20th Century-Fox.

ART DIRECTION—SET DECORATION

Hello, Dolly!, 20th Century-Fox. John DeCuir, Jack Martin Smith, Herman Blumenthal; Walter M. Scott, George Hopkins, Raphael Bretton.

Anne of the Thousand Days, Universal (United Kingdom). Maurice Carter, Lionel Couch; Patrick McLoughlin.

Gaily, Gaily, United Artists. Robert Boyle, George B. Chan; Edward Boyle, Carl Biddiscombe.

Sweet Charity, Universal. Alexander Golitzen, George C. Webb; Jack D. Moore.

They Shoot Horses, Don't They?, Cinerama. Harry Horner; Frank McKelvy.

SOUND[196]

Hello, Dolly!, 20th Century-Fox. Jack Solomon and Murray Spivack.

Anne of the Thousand Days, Universal (United Kingdom). John Aldred.

Butch Cassidy and the Sundance Kid, 20th Century-Fox. William Edmundson and David Dockendorf.

Gaily, Gaily, United Artists. Robert Martin and Clem Portman.

Marooned, Columbia. Les Fresholtz and Arthur Piantadosi.

MUSIC

(Song)

"Raindrops Keep Fallin' on My Head" from *Butch Cassidy and the Sundance Kid,* 20th Century-Fox. Music by Burt Bacharach, lyrics by Hal David.

"Come Saturday Morning" from *The Sterile Cuckoo,* Paramount. Music by Fred Karlin, lyrics by Dory Previn.

"Jean" from *The Prime of Miss Jean Brodie,* 20th Century-Fox (United Kingdom). Music and lyrics by Rod McKuen.

"True Grit" from *True Grit,* Paramount. Music by Elmer Bernstein, lyrics by Don Black.

"What Are You Doing the Rest of Your Life?" from *The Happy Ending,* United Artists. Music by Michel Legrand, lyrics by Alan Bergman and Marilyn Bergman.

(Original Score—for a Motion Picture [Not a Musical])

Burt Bacharach for *Butch Cassidy and the Sundance Kid,* 20th Century-Fox.

Georges Delerue for *Anne of the Thousand Days,* Universal (United Kingdom).

Jerry Fielding for *The Wild Bunch,* Warner Bros.

Ernest Gold for *The Secret of Santa Vittoria,* United Artists.

John Williams for *The Reivers,* National General.

---

[196] From now on, Oscars are presented to individual sound technicians rather than to their sound departments.

(Score of a Musical Picture—[Original or Adaptation])

Lennie Hayton and Lionel Newman for the adaptation score for *Hello, Dolly!*, 20th Century-Fox.

Leslie Bricusse for music and lyrics and John Williams for the adaptation score for *Goodbye, Mr. Chips*, MGM (U.S./United Kingdom).

Cy Coleman for the adaptation score for *Sweet Charity*, Universal.

John Green and Albert Woodbury for the adaptation score for *They Shoot Horses, Don't They?*, Cinerama.

Nelson Riddle for the adaptation score for *Paint Your Wagon*, Paramount.

FILM EDITING

Françoise Bonnot for *Z*, Cinema V (Algeria).

William Lyon and Earle Herdan for *The Secret of Santa Vittoria*, United Artists.

William Reynolds for *Hello, Dolly!*, 20th Century-Fox.

Hugh A. Robertson for *Midnight Cowboy*, United Artists.

Fredric Steinkamp for *They Shoot Horses, Don't They?*, Cinerama.

COSTUME DESIGN

Margaret Furse for *Anne of the Thousand Days*, Universal (United Kingdom).

Ray Aghayan for *Gaily, Gaily*, United Artists.

Donfeld for *They Shoot Horses, Don't They?*, Cinerama.

Edith Head for *Sweet Charity*, Universal.

Irene Sharaff for *Hello, Dolly!*, 20th Century-Fox.

SPECIAL VISUAL EFFECTS

Robbie Robertson for *Marooned*, Columbia.

Eugene Lourie and Alex Weldon for *Krakatoa, East of Java*, Cinerama.

FOREIGN LANGUAGE FILM

Z, Algeria.[197]

Adalen '31, Sweden.

The Battle of Neretva, Yugoslavia.

The Brothers Karamazov, USSR.

My Night With Maud, France.

JEAN HERSHOLT HUMANITARIAN AWARD

George Jessel.

HONORARY AWARD

Cary Grant, for his unique mastery of the art of screen acting with the respect and affection of his colleagues.

1970

Awards presented April 15, 1971.

PICTURE

***Patton*, 20th Century-Fox. Produced by Frank McCarthy.**

Airport, Ross Hunter-Universal Production, Universal. Produced by Ross Hunter.

Five Easy Pieces, BBS Productions, Columbia. Produced by Bob Rafelson and Richard Wechsler.

Love Story, The Love Story Company Production, Paramount. Produced by Howard G. Minsky.

MASH, Aspen Productions, 20th Century-Fox. Produced by Ingo Preminger.

ACTOR

George C. Scott in *Patton*, 20th Century-Fox.[198]

Melvyn Douglas in *I Never Sang for My Father*, Columbia.

James Earl Jones in *The Great White Hope*, 20th Century-Fox.

Jack Nicholson in *Five Easy Pieces*, Columbia.

Ryan O'Neal in *Love Story*, Paramount.

ACTRESS

Glenda Jackson in *Women in Love*, United Artists (United Kingdom).

Jane Alexander in *The Great White Hope*, 20th Century-Fox.

Ali MacGraw in *Love Story*, Paramount.

Sarah Miles in *Ryan's Daughter*, MGM (United Kingdom).

Carrie Snodgress in *Diary of a Mad Housewife*, Universal.

SUPPORTING ACTOR

John Mills in *Ryan's Daughter*, MGM (United Kingdom).

Richard Castellano in *Lovers and Other Strangers*, Cinerama.

Chief Dan George in *Little Big Man*, National General.

Gene Hackman in *I Never Sang for My Father*, Columbia.

John Marley in *Love Story*, Paramount.

SUPPORTING ACTRESS

Helen Hayes[199] in *Airport*, Universal.

Karen Black in *Five Easy Pieces*, Columbia.

Lee Grant in *The Landlord*, United Artists.

Sally Kellerman in *MASH*, 20th Century-Fox.

Maureen Stapleton in *Airport*, Universal.

DIRECTOR

Franklin J. Schaffner for *Patton*, 20th Century-Fox.

Robert Altman for *MASH*, 20th Century-Fox.

Federico Fellini for *Fellini Satyricon*, United Artists (France/Italy).

Arthur Hiller for *Love Story*, Paramount.

---

[197] First film to be nominated in both the best picture and foreign language film categories.

[198] Declined the award.

[199] First person to receive an Oscar for a supporting performance after previously winning in a leading role (1931–32). Subsequently, Ingrid Bergman (1974), Maggie Smith (1978), Jack Nicholson (1983), and Gene Hackman (1992) also won supporting performance Oscars after prior wins for leading roles. The thirty-eight-year hiatus between Hayes' acting nominations was the longest on record. It has subsequently been tied by Jack Palance, who was nominated in 1952 and 1953, but not again until his win at the 1991 awards. But the record was set by Henry Fonda, nominated in 1940 and 1981—although he received an interim nomination as producer of *12 Angry Men* (1957).

Ken Russell for *Women in Love,* United Artists (United Kingdom).

WRITING

(Screenplay—Based on Material From Another Medium)

Ring Lardner, Jr., for *MASH,* 20th Century-Fox.

Robert Anderson for *I Never Sang for My Father,* Columbia.

Larry Kramer for *Women in Love,* United Artists (United Kingdom).

George Seaton for *Airport,* Universal.

Renee Taylor, Joseph Bologna, and David Zelag Goodman for *Lovers and Other Strangers,* Cinerama.

(Story and Screenplay—Based on Factual Material or Material Not Previously Published or Produced)[200]

Francis Ford Coppola and Edmund H. North for *Patton,* 20th Century-Fox.

Bob Rafelson and Adrien Joyce, story; Adrien Joyce, screenplay, for *Five Easy Pieces,* Columbia.

Eric Rohmer for *My Night at Maud's,* Pathé Contemporary (France).

Erich Segal for *Love Story,* Paramount.

CINEMATOGRAPHY

Freddie Young for *Ryan's Daughter,* MGM (United Kingdom).

Fred Koenekamp for *Patton,* 20th Century-Fox.

Ernest Laszlo for *Airport,* Universal.

Charles F. Wheeler, Osami Furuya, Sinsaku Himeda, and Masamichi Satoh for *Tora! Tora! Tora!,* 20th Century-Fox (U.S./Japan).

Billy Williams for *Women in Love,* United Artists (United Kingdom).

ART DIRECTION—SET DECORATION

***Patton,* 20th Century-Fox. Urie McCleary, Gil Parrondo;**

Antonio Mateos, Pierre-Louis Thevenet.

Airport, Universal. Alexander Golitzen, E. Preston Ames; Jack D. Moore, Mickey S. Michaels.

The Molly Maguires, Paramount. Tambi Larsen; Darrell Silvera.

Scrooge, National General (United Kingdom). Terry Marsh, Bob Cartwright; Pamela Cornell.

Tora! Tora! Tora!, 20th Century-Fox (U.S./Japan). Jack Martin Smith, Yoshiro Muraki, Richard Day, Taizoh Kawashima; Walter M. Scott, Norman Rockett, Carl Biddiscombe.

SOUND

***Patton,* 20th Century-Fox. Douglas Williams and Don Bassman.**

Airport, Universal. Ronald Pierce and David Moriarty.

Ryan's Daughter, MGM (United Kingdom). Gordon K. McCallum and John Bramall.

Tora! Tora! Tora!, 20th Century-Fox (U.S./Japan). Murray Spivack and Herman Lewis.

Woodstock, Warner Bros. Dan Wallin and Larry Johnson.

MUSIC[201]

(Song)

"For All We Know" from *Lovers and Other Strangers,* Cinerama. Music by Fred Karlin, lyrics by Robb Royer and James Griffin (a.k.a. Robb Wilson and Arthur James).

"Pieces of Dreams" from *Pieces of Dreams,* United Artists. Music by Michel Legrand, lyrics by Alan Bergman and Marilyn Bergman.

"Thank You Very Much" from *Scrooge,* National General (United Kingdom). Music and lyrics by Leslie Bricusse.

"Till Love Touches Your Life" from *Madron,* Four Star-Excelsior Releasing.

Music by Riz Ortolani, lyrics by Arthur Hamilton.

"Whistling Away the Dark" from *Darling Lili,* Paramount. Music by Henry Mancini, lyrics by Johnny Mercer.

(Original Score)

Francis Lai for *Love Story,* Paramount.

Frank Cordell for *Cromwell,* Columbia (United Kingdom).

Jerry Goldsmith for *Patton,* 20th Century-Fox.

Henry Mancini for *Sunflower,* Avco Embassy (France/Italy).

Alfred Newman[202] for *Airport,* Universal.

(Original Song Score)

The Beatles for music and lyrics for *Let It Be,* United Artists (United Kingdom).

Leslie Bricusse for music and lyrics and Ian Fraser and Herbert W. Spencer for adaptation score for *Scrooge,* National General (United Kingdom).

Fred Karlin for music and Tylwyth Kymry for lyrics for *The Baby Maker,* National General.

Henry Mancini for music and Johnny Mercer for lyrics for *Darling Lili,* Paramount.

Rod McKuen and John Scott Trotter for music, McKuen, Bill Melendez, and Al Shean for lyrics, and Vince Guaraldi for adaptation score for *A Boy Named Charlie Brown,* National General.

FILM EDITING

Hugh S. Fowler for *Patton,* 20th Century-Fox.

Stuart Gilmore for *Airport,* Universal.

Danford B. Greene for *MASH,* 20th Century-Fox.

James E. Newcom, Pembroke J. Herring, and Inoue Chikaya for *Tora! Tora! Tora!,* 20th Century-Fox (U.S./Japan).

---

[200] Category renamed.
[201] Scoring categories renamed.
[202] Newman's forty-fifth nomination, his last, is an Academy record. He also won nine Oscars, a number exceeded only by art director Cedric Gibbons, who won eleven. Both Newman and Gibbons were heads of their respective departments at 20th Century-Fox and MGM, so the number of their nominations reflects their administrative roles as much as their creative contributions. Walt Disney is sometimes cited as the person who received the most Oscars, largely a consequence of his position as head of production for his studio.

Thelma Schoonmaker for *Woodstock,* Warner Bros.

COSTUME DESIGN

Nino Novarese for *Cromwell,* Columbia (United Kingdom).

Donald Brooks and Jack Bear for *Darling Lili,* Paramount.

Margaret Furse for *Scrooge,* National General (United Kingdom).

Edith Head for *Airport,* Universal.

Bill Thomas for *The Hawaiians,* United Artists.

SPECIAL VISUAL EFFECTS

A. D. Flowers and L. B. Abbott for *Tora! Tora! Tora!,* 20th Century-Fox.

Alex Weldon for *Patton,* 20th Century-Fox.

FOREIGN LANGUAGE FILM

***Investigation of a Citizen Above Suspicion,* Italy.**

First Love, Switzerland.

Hoa-Binh, France.

Paix sur les Champs, Belgium.

Tristana, Spain.

IRVING G. THALBERG MEMORIAL AWARD

Ingmar Bergman.

JEAN HERSHOLT HUMANITARIAN AWARD

Frank Sinatra.

HONORARY AWARDS

Lillian Gish, for superlative artistry and for distinguished contribution to the progress of motion pictures.

Orson Welles, for superlative artistry and versatility in the creation of motion pictures.

1971

Awards presented April 10, 1972.

PICTURE

***The French Connection,* Philip D'Antoni Production in association with Schine-Moore**

Productions, 20th Century-Fox. Produced by Philip D'Antoni.

A Clockwork Orange, Hawk Films, Ltd., Production, Warner Bros. (United Kingdom). Produced by Stanley Kubrick.

Fiddler on the Roof, Mirisch-Cartier Productions, United Artists. Produced by Norman Jewison.

The Last Picture Show, BBS Productions, Columbia. Produced by Stephen J. Friedman.

Nicholas and Alexandra, A Horizon Pictures Production, Columbia (United Kingdom). Produced by Sam Spiegel.

ACTOR

Gene Hackman in *The French Connection,* 20th Century-Fox.

Peter Finch in *Sunday, Bloody Sunday,* United Artists (United Kingdom).

Walter Matthau in *Kotch,* Cinerama.

George C. Scott in *The Hospital,* United Artists.

Topol in *Fiddler on the Roof,* United Artists.

ACTRESS

Jane Fonda in *Klute,* Warner Bros.

Julie Christie in *McCabe and Mrs. Miller,* Warner Bros.

Glenda Jackson in *Sunday, Bloody Sunday,* United Artists (United Kingdom).

Vanessa Redgrave in *Mary, Queen of Scots,* Universal (United Kingdom).

Janet Suzman in *Nicholas and Alexandra,* Columbia (United Kingdom).

SUPPORTING ACTOR

Ben Johnson in *The Last Picture Show,* Columbia.

Jeff Bridges in *The Last Picture Show,* Columbia.

Leonard Frey in *Fiddler on the Roof,* United Artists.

Richard Jaeckel in *Sometimes a Great Notion,* Universal.

Roy Scheider in *The French Connection,* 20th Century-Fox.

SUPPORTING ACTRESS

Cloris Leachman in *The Last Picture Show,* Columbia.

Ann-Margret in *Carnal Knowledge,* Avco Embassy.

Ellen Burstyn in *The Last Picture Show,* Columbia.

Barbara Harris in *Who Is Harry Kellerman, and Why Is He Saying Those Terrible Things About Me?,* National General.

Margaret Leighton in *The Go-Between,* Columbia (United Kingdom).

DIRECTOR

William Friedkin for *The French Connection,* 20th Century-Fox.

Peter Bogdanovich for *The Last Picture Show,* Columbia.

Norman Jewison for *Fiddler on the Roof,* United Artists.

Stanley Kubrick for *A Clockwork Orange,* Warner Bros. (United Kingdom).

John Schlesinger for *Sunday, Bloody Sunday,* United Artists (United Kingdom).

WRITING

(Screenplay—Based on Material From Another Medium)

Ernest Tidyman for *The French Connection,* 20th Century-Fox.

Bernardo Bertolucci for *The Conformist,* Paramount (Italy/France).

Stanley Kubrick for *A Clockwork Orange,* Warner Bros. (United Kingdom).

Larry McMurtry and Peter Bogdanovich for *The Last Picture Show,* Columbia.

Ugo Pirro and Vittorio Bonicelli for *The Garden of the Finzi-Continis,* Cinema 5, Ltd. (Italy).

(Story and Screenplay—Based on Factual Material or Material Not Previously Published or Produced)

Paddy Chayefsky for *The Hospital,* United Artists.

Penelope Gilliatt for *Sunday, Bloody Sunday,* United Artists (United Kingdom).

Andy Lewis and Dave Lewis for *Klute,* Warner Bros.

Elio Petri and Ugo Pirro for *Investigation*

of a Citizen Above Suspicion, Columbia (Italy).

Herman Raucher for *Summer of '42*, Warner Bros.

CINEMATOGRAPHY

Oswald Morris for *Fiddler on the Roof*, United Artists.

Owen Roizman for *The French Connection*, 20th Century-Fox.

Robert Surtees for *The Last Picture Show*, Columbia.

Robert Surtees for *Summer of '42*, Warner Bros.

Freddie Young for *Nicholas and Alexandra*, Columbia (United Kingdom).

ART DIRECTION—SET DECORATION

***Nicholas and Alexandra*, Columbia (United Kingdom). John Box, Ernest Archer, Jack Maxsted, Gil Parrondo; Vernon Dixon.**

The Andromeda Strain, Universal. Boris Leven, William Tuntke; Ruby Levitt.

Bedknobs and Broomsticks, Disney, Buena Vista. John B. Mansbridge, Peter Ellenshaw; Emile Kuri, Hal Gausman.

Fiddler on the Roof, United Artists. Robert Boyle, Michael Stringer; Peter Lamont.

Mary, Queen of Scots, Universal (United Kingdom). Terence Marsh, Robert Cartwright; Peter Howitt.

SOUND

***Fiddler on the Roof*, United Artists. Gordon K. McCallum and David Hildyard.**

Diamonds Are Forever, United Artists. Gordon K. McCallum, John Mitchell, and Alfred J. Overton.

The French Connection, 20th Century-Fox. Theodore Soderberg and Christopher Newman.

Kotch, Cinerama. Richard Portman and Jack Solomon.

Mary, Queen of Scots, Universal (United Kingdom). Bob Jones and John Aldred.

MUSIC[203]

(Song)

"Theme from *Shaft*" from *Shaft*, MGM. Music and lyrics by Isaac Hayes.

"The Age of Not Believing" from *Bedknobs and Broomsticks*, Disney, Buena Vista. Music and lyrics by Richard M. Sherman and Robert B. Sherman.

"All His Children" from *Sometimes a Great Notion*, Universal. Music by Henry Mancini, lyrics by Alan Bergman and Marilyn Bergman.

"Bless the Beasts and Children" from *Bless the Beasts and Children*, Columbia. Music and lyrics by Barry DeVorzon and Perry Botkin, Jr.

"Life Is What You Make It" from *Kotch*, Cinerama. Music by Marvin Hamlisch, lyrics by Johnny Mercer.

(Original Dramatic Score)

Michel Legrand for *Summer of '42*, Warner Bros.

John Barry for *Mary, Queen of Scots*, Universal (United Kingdom).

Richard Rodney Bennett for *Nicholas and Alexandra*, Columbia (United Kingdom).

Jerry Fielding for *Straw Dogs*, Cinerama (United Kingdom).

Isaac Hayes for *Shaft*, MGM.

(Scoring: Adaptation and Original Song Score)

John Williams for the adaptation score for *Fiddler on the Roof*, United Artists.

Leslie Bricusse and Anthony Newley for the song score and Walter Scharf for the adaptation score for *Willie Wonka and the Chocolate Factory*, Paramount.

Peter Maxwell Davies and Peter Greenwell for the adaptation score for *The Boy Friend*, MGM (United Kingdom).

Richard M. Sherman and Robert B. Sherman for the song score and Irwin Kostal for the adaptation score for *Bedknobs and Broomsticks*, Disney, Buena Vista.

Dimitri Tiomkin for the adaptation score for *Tchaikovsky*, Dimitri Tiomkin-Mosfilm Studios (USSR).

FILM EDITING

Jerry Greenberg for *The French Connection*, 20th Century-Fox.

Folmar Blangsted for *Summer of '42*, Warner Bros.

Bill Butler for *A Clockwork Orange*, Warner Bros. (United Kingdom).

Stuart Gilmore and John W. Holmes for *The Andromeda Strain*, Universal.

Ralph E. Winters for *Kotch*, Cinerama.

COSTUME DESIGN

Yvonne Blake and Antonia Castillo for *Nicholas and Alexandra*, Columbia (United Kingdom).

Margaret Furse for *Mary, Queen of Scots*, Universal (United Kingdom).

Morton Haack for *What's the Matter With Helen?*, United Artists.

Bill Thomas for *Bedknobs and Broomsticks*, Disney, Buena Vista.

Piero Tosi for *Death in Venice*, Warner Bros. (Italy/France).

SPECIAL VISUAL EFFECTS

Alan Maley, Eustace Lycett, and Danny Lee for *Bedknobs and Broomsticks*, Disney, Buena Vista.

Jim Danforth and Roger Dicken for *When Dinosaurs Ruled the Earth*, Warner Bros. (United Kingdom).

FOREIGN LANGUAGE FILM

***The Garden of the Finzi-Continis*, Italy.**

Dodes'ka-den, Japan.

The Emigrants, Sweden.

The Policeman, Israel.

Tchaikovsky, USSR.

HONORARY AWARD

Charles Chaplin, for the incalculable effect he has had in making motion pictures the art form of this century.

[203] Scoring awards renamed.

1972
Awards presented March 27, 1973.

PICTURE

The Godfather, Albert S. Ruddy Production, Paramount. Produced by Albert S. Ruddy.

Cabaret, ABC Pictures Production, Allied Artists. Produced by Cy Feuer.[204]

Deliverance, Warner Bros. Produced by John Boorman.

The Emigrants, A.B. Svensk Filmindustri Production, Warner Bros. (Sweden). Produced by Bengt Forslund.[205]

Sounder, Radnitz/Mattel Productions, 20th Century-Fox. Produced by Robert B. Radnitz.

ACTOR

Marlon Brando in The Godfather, Paramount.

Michael Caine in *Sleuth*, 20th Century-Fox (United Kingdom).

Laurence Olivier in *Sleuth*, 20th Century-Fox (United Kingdom).

Peter O'Toole in *The Ruling Class*, Avco Embassy (United Kingdom).

Paul Winfield in *Sounder*, 20th Century-Fox.

ACTRESS

Liza Minnelli[206] in Cabaret, Allied Artists.

Diana Ross in *Lady Sings the Blues*, Paramount.

Maggie Smith in *Travels With My Aunt*, MGM (United Kingdom).

Cicely Tyson in *Sounder*, 20th Century-Fox.

Liv Ullmann in *The Emigrants*, Warner Bros. (Sweden).

SUPPORTING ACTOR

Joel Grey in Cabaret, Allied Artists.

Eddie Albert in *The Heartbreak Kid*, 20th Century-Fox.

James Caan in *The Godfather*, Paramount.

Robert Duvall in *The Godfather*, Paramount.

Al Pacino in *The Godfather*, Paramount.

SUPPORTING ACTRESS

Eileen Heckart in Butterflies Are Free, Columbia.

Jeannie Berlin in *The Heartbreak Kid*, 20th Century-Fox.

Geraldine Page in *Pete 'n' Tillie*, Universal.

Susan Tyrrell in *Fat City*, Columbia.

Shelley Winters in *The Poseidon Adventure*, 20th Century-Fox.

DIRECTOR

Bob Fosse for Cabaret, Allied Artists.

John Boorman for *Deliverance*, Warner Bros.

Francis Ford Coppola for *The Godfather*, Paramount.

Joseph L. Mankiewicz for *Sleuth*, 20th Century-Fox (United Kingdom).

Jan Troell for *The Emigrants*, Warner Bros. (Sweden).

WRITING

(Screenplay—Based on Material From Another Medium)

Mario Puzo and Francis Ford Coppola for The Godfather, Paramount.

Jay Allen for *Cabaret*, Allied Artists.

Lonne Elder III for *Sounder*, 20th Century-Fox.

Julius J. Epstein for *Pete 'n' Tillie*, Universal.

Jan Troell and Bengt Forslund for *The Emigrants*, Warner Bros. (Sweden).

(Story and Screenplay—Based on Factual Material or Material Not Previously Published or Produced)

Jeremy Larner for The Candidate, Warner Bros.

Luis Buñuel in collaboration with Jean-Claude Carrière for *The Discreet Charm of the Bourgeoisie*, 20th Century-Fox (France).

Carl Foreman for *Young Winston*, Columbia (United Kingdom).

Louis Malle for *Murmur of the Heart*, Continental Distributing (France).

Terence McCloy, Chris Clark, and Suzanne de Passe for *Lady Sings the Blues*, Paramount.

CINEMATOGRAPHY

Geoffrey Unsworth for Cabaret, Allied Artists.

Charles B. Lang for *Butterflies Are Free*, Columbia.[207]

Douglas Slocombe for *Travels With My Aunt*, MGM (United Kingdom).

Harold E. Stine for *The Poseidon Adventure*, 20th Century-Fox.

Harry Stradling, Jr., for *"1776,"* Columbia.

ART DIRECTION—SET DECORATION

Cabaret, Allied Artists. Rolf Zehetbauer, Jurgen Kiebach; Herbert Strabel.

Lady Sings the Blues, Paramount. Carl Anderson; Reg Allen.

The Poseidon Adventure, 20th Century-Fox. William Creber; Raphael Bretton.

Travels With My Aunt, MGM (United Kingdom). John Box, Gil Parrondo, Robert W. Laing.

Young Winston, Columbia (United Kingdom). Geoffrey Drake, Don Ashton, John Graysmark, William Hutchinson; Peter James.

SOUND

Cabaret, Allied Artists. Robert Knudson and David Hildyard.

Butterflies Are Free, Columbia. Arthur Piantadosi and Charles Knight.

The Candidate, Warner Bros. Richard Portman and Gene Cantamessa.

The Godfather, Paramount. Bud

---

[204] *Cabaret* received eight Oscars, more than any other film not named best picture.

[205] Although a nominee for foreign language film in 1971, *The Emigrants* did not become eligible for other competitive categories until its release in 1972.

[206] Only Oscar winner whose parents both received Oscars: Vincente Minnelli, 1958, and Judy Garland, who received an honorary award, 1939.

[207] Although Lang received only one Oscar (1932–33), he is tied with four-time winner Leon Shamroy for the most nominations for cinematography: eighteen.

Grenzbach, Richard Portman, and Christopher Newman.

The Poseidon Adventure, 20th Century-Fox. Theodore Soderberg and Herman Lewis.

MUSIC

(Song)
"The Morning After" from *The Poseidon Adventure,* 20th Century-Fox. Music and lyrics by Al Kasha and Joel Hirschhorn.

"Ben" from *Ben,* Cinerama. Music by Walter Scharf, lyrics by Don Black.

"Come Follow, Follow Me" from *The Little Ark,* National General. Music by Fred Karlin, lyrics by Marsha Karlin.

"Marmalade, Molasses & Honey" from *The Life and Times of Judge Roy Bean,* National General. Music by Maurice Jarre, lyrics by Marilyn Bergman and Alan Bergman.

"Strange Are the Ways of Love" from *The Stepmother,* Crown International. Music by Sammy Fain, lyrics by Paul Francis Webster.

(Original Dramatic Score)
Charles Chaplin, Raymond Rasch, and Larry Russell for *Limelight,* Chaplin, Columbia.[208]

John Addison for *Sleuth,* 20th Century-Fox (United Kingdom).[209]

Buddy Baker for *Napoleon and Samantha,* Disney, Buena Vista.

John Williams for *Images,* Columbia (U.S./Ireland).

John Williams for *The Poseidon Adventure,* 20th Century-Fox.

(Scoring: Adaptation and Original Song Score)
Ralph Burns for the adaptation score for *Cabaret,* Allied Artists.

Gil Askey for the adaptation score for *Lady Sings the Blues,* Paramount.

Laurence Rosenthal for the adaptation

score for *Man of La Mancha,* United Artists (Italy).

FILM EDITING
David Bretherton for *Cabaret,* Allied Artists.

Frank P. Keller and Fred W. Berger for *The Hot Rock,* 20th Century-Fox.

Harold F. Kress for *The Poseidon Adventure,* 20th Century-Fox.

Tom Priestley for *Deliverance,* Warner Bros.

William Reynolds and Peter Zinner for *The Godfather,* Paramount.

COSTUME DESIGN
Anthony Powell for *Travels With My Aunt,* MGM (United Kingdom).

Anna Hill Johnstone for *The Godfather,* Paramount.

Bob Mackie, Ray Aghayan, and Norma Koch for *Lady Sings the Blues,* Paramount.

Anthony Mendleson for *Young Winston,* Columbia (United Kingdom).

Paul Zastupnevich for *The Poseidon Adventure,* 20th Century-Fox.

FOREIGN LANGUAGE FILM
The Discreet Charm of the Bourgeoisie, France.

The Dawns Here Are Quiet, USSR.

I Love You Rosa, Israel.

My Dearest Señorita, Spain.

The New Land, Sweden.

JEAN HERSHOLT HUMANITARIAN AWARD
Rosalind Russell.

HONORARY AWARDS
Charles S. Boren, leader for 38 years of the industry's enlightened labor relations and architect of its policy of non-discrimination. With the respect

and affection of all who work in films.
Edward G. Robinson, who achieved greatness as a player, a patron of the arts and a dedicated citizen . . . in sum, a Renaissance man. From his friends in the industry he loves.

SPECIAL ACHIEVEMENT AWARD
Visual Effects: L. B. Abbott and A. D. Flowers for *The Poseidon Adventure,* 20th Century-Fox.

1973
Awards presented April 2, 1974.

PICTURE
***The Sting,* Universal-Bill/Phillips-George Roy Hill Film Production, Zanuck/Brown Presentation, Universal. Tony Bill, Michael Phillips, and Julia Phillips, producers.**

American Graffiti, Universal-Lucasfilm, Ltd./Coppola Company Production, Universal. Francis Ford Coppola, producer; Gary Kurtz, coproducer.

Cries and Whispers, Svenska Filminstitutet-Cinematograph AB Production, New World Pictures (Sweden). Ingmar Bergman, producer.

The Exorcist, Hoya Productions, Warner Bros. William Peter Blatty, producer.

A Touch of Class, Brut Productions, Avco Embassy (United Kingdom). Melvin Frank, producer.

ACTOR
Jack Lemmon[210] **in *Save the Tiger,* Paramount.**

Marlon Brando in *Last Tango in Paris,* United Artists (Italy/France).

Jack Nicholson in *The Last Detail,* Columbia.

---

[208] Although made in 1952, *Limelight* did not qualify for Oscar competition until its rerelease in 1972.

[209] Addison's score for *Sleuth* was not among the nominees originally announced, but Nino Rota's score for *The Godfather* was. Then it was pointed out that some of the score for *The Godfather* had been composed by Rota for a 1958 film, *Fortunella,* and it was disqualified. The music branch was allowed to take another vote to come up with a fifth nominee.

[210] First person to win an Oscar for a leading role after previously winning in the supporting performance category (1955). Subsequently Robert De Niro (1974, 1980), Meryl Streep (1979, 1982), and Jessica Lange (1982, 1994) also won for leading roles after supporting performance wins.

Al Pacino in *Serpico*, Paramount.

Robert Redford in *The Sting*, Universal.

ACTRESS

Glenda Jackson in *A Touch of Class*, Avco Embassy (United Kingdom).

Ellen Burstyn in *The Exorcist*, Warner Bros.

Marsha Mason in *Cinderella Liberty*, 20th Century-Fox.

Barbra Streisand in *The Way We Were*, Columbia.

Joanne Woodward in *Summer Wishes, Winter Dreams*, Columbia.

SUPPORTING ACTOR

John Houseman in *The Paper Chase*, 20th Century-Fox.

Vincent Gardenia in *Bang the Drum Slowly*, Paramount.

Jack Gilford in *Save the Tiger*, Paramount.

Jason Miller in *The Exorcist*, Warner Bros.

Randy Quaid in *The Last Detail*, Columbia.

SUPPORTING ACTRESS

Tatum O'Neal[211] in *Paper Moon*, Paramount.

Linda Blair in *The Exorcist*, Warner Bros.

Candy Clark in *American Graffiti*, Universal.

Madeline Kahn in *Paper Moon*, Paramount.

Sylvia Sidney in *Summer Wishes, Winter Dreams*, Columbia.

DIRECTOR

George Roy Hill for *The Sting*, Universal.

Ingmar Bergman for *Cries and Whispers*, New World Pictures (Sweden).

Bernardo Bertolucci for *Last Tango in Paris*, United Artists (Italy/France).

William Friedkin for *The Exorcist*, Warner Bros.

George Lucas for *American Graffiti*, Universal.

WRITING

(Screenplay—Based on Material From Another Medium)

William Peter Blatty for *The Exorcist*, Warner Bros.

James Bridges for *The Paper Chase*, 20th Century-Fox.

Waldo Salt and Norman Wexler for *Serpico*, Paramount.

Alvin Sargent for *Paper Moon*, Paramount.

Robert Towne for *The Last Detail*, Columbia.

(Story and Screenplay—Based on Factual Material or Material Not Previously Published or Produced)

David S. Ward for *The Sting*, Universal.

Ingmar Bergman for *Cries and Whispers*, New World Pictures (Sweden).

Melvin Frank and Jack Rose for *A Touch of Class*, Avco Embassy (United Kingdom).

George Lucas, Gloria Katz, and Willard Huyck for *American Graffiti*, Universal.

Steve Shagan for *Save the Tiger*, Paramount.

CINEMATOGRAPHY

Sven Nykvist for *Cries and Whispers*, New World Pictures (Sweden).

Jack Couffer for *Jonathan Livingston Seagull*, Paramount.

Owen Roizman for *The Exorcist*, Warner Bros.

Harry Stradling, Jr., for *The Way We Were*, Columbia.

Robert Surtees for *The Sting*, Universal.

ART DIRECTION—SET DECORATION

***The Sting*, Universal. Henry Bumstead; James Payne.**

Brother Sun, Sister Moon, Paramount (Italy/United Kingdom). Lorenzo Mongiardino, Gianni Quaranta; Carmelo Patrono.

The Exorcist, Warner Bros. Bill Malley; Jerry Wunderlich.

Tom Sawyer, United Artists. Philip Jefferies; Robert de Vestel.

The Way We Were, Columbia. Stephen Grimes; William Kiernan.

SOUND

***The Exorcist*, Warner Bros. Robert Knudson and Chris Newman.**

The Day of the Dolphin, Avco Embassy. Richard Portman and Lawrence O. Jost.

The Paper Chase, 20th Century-Fox. Donald O. Mitchell and Lawrence O. Jost.

Paper Moon, Paramount. Richard Portman and Les Fresholtz.

The Sting, Universal. Ronald K. Pierce and Robert Bertrand.

MUSIC

(Song)

"The Way We Were" from *The Way We Were*, Columbia. Music by Marvin Hamlisch, lyrics by Alan Bergman and Marilyn Bergman.

"All That Love Went to Waste" from *A Touch of Class*, Avco Embassy (United Kingdom). Music by George Barrie, lyrics by Sammy Cahn.

"Live and Let Die" from *Live and Let Die*, United Artists (United Kingdom). Music and lyrics by Paul McCartney and Linda McCartney.

"Love" from *Robin Hood*, Disney, Buena Vista. Music by George Bruns, lyrics by Floyd Huddleston.

"You're So Nice to Be Around" from *Cinderella Liberty*, 20th Century-Fox. Music by John Williams, lyrics by Paul Williams.

(Original Dramatic Score)

Marvin Hamlisch for *The Way We Were*, Columbia.

John Cameron for *A Touch of Class*, Avco Embassy (United Kingdom).

Georges Delerue for *The Day of the Dolphin*, Avco Embassy.

Jerry Goldsmith for *Papillon*, Allied Artists.

John Williams for *Cinderella Liberty*, 20th Century-Fox.

---

[211] At age ten, the youngest person ever to win an Oscar in competition.

(Scoring: Original Song Score and Adaptation, or Scoring: Adaptation)[212]

Marvin Hamlisch[213] for the adaptation score for *The Sting*, Universal.

André Previn, Herbert Spencer, and Andrew Lloyd Webber for the adaptation score for *Jesus Christ Superstar*, Universal.

Richard M. Sherman and Robert B. Sherman for the song score and John Williams for the adaptation score for *Tom Sawyer*, United Artists.

FILM EDITING

William Reynolds for *The Sting*, Universal.

Verna Fields and Marcia Lucas for *American Graffiti*, Universal.

Frank P. Keller and James Galloway for *Jonathan Livingston Seagull*, Paramount.

Ralph Kemplen for *The Day of the Jackal*, Universal (United Kingdom/France).

Jordan Leondopoulos, Bud Smith, Evan Lottman, and Norman Gay for *The Exorcist*, Warner Bros.

COSTUME DESIGN

Edith Head[214] for *The Sting*, Universal.

Donfeld for *Tom Sawyer*, United Artists.

Dorothy Jeakins and Moss Mabry for *The Way We Were*, Columbia.

Piero Tosi for *Ludwig*, MGM (Italy/France/West Germany).

Marik Vos for *Cries and Whispers*, New World Pictures (Sweden).

FOREIGN LANGUAGE FILM

***Day for Night*, France.**

The House on Chelouche Street, Israel.

L'Invitation, Switzerland.

The Pedestrian, Federal Republic of Germany.

Turkish Delight, the Netherlands.

IRVING G. THALBERG MEMORIAL AWARD

Lawrence Weingarten.

JEAN HERSHOLT HUMANITARIAN AWARD

Lew Wasserman.

HONORARY AWARDS

Henri Langlois, for his devotion to the art of film, his massive contributions in preserving its past and his unswerving faith in its future.

Groucho Marx, in recognition of his brilliant creativity and for the unequaled achievements of the Marx Brothers in the art of motion picture comedy.

1974
Awards presented April 8, 1975.

PICTURE

***The Godfather, Part II*, Coppola Company Production, Paramount. Produced by Francis Ford Coppola; Gray Frederickson and Fred Roos, coproducers.[215]**

Chinatown, Robert Evans Production,

Paramount. Produced by Robert Evans.

The Conversation, A Directors Company Production, Paramount. Produced by Francis Ford Coppola; Fred Roos, coproducer.

Lenny, Marvin Worth Production, United Artists. Produced by Marvin Worth.

The Towering Inferno, Irwin Allen Production, 20th Century-Fox/Warner Bros. Produced by Irwin Allen.

ACTOR

Art Carney in *Harry and Tonto*, 20th Century-Fox.

Albert Finney in *Murder on the Orient Express*, Paramount (United Kingdom).

Dustin Hoffman in *Lenny*, United Artists.

Jack Nicholson in *Chinatown*, Paramount.

Al Pacino in *The Godfather, Part II*, Coppola Co., Paramount.

ACTRESS

Ellen Burstyn in *Alice Doesn't Live Here Anymore*, Warner Bros.

Diahann Carroll in *Claudine*, 20th Century-Fox.

Faye Dunaway in *Chinatown*, Paramount.

Valerie Perrine in *Lenny*, United Artists.

Gena Rowlands in *A Woman Under the Influence*, Faces International.

SUPPORTING ACTOR

Robert De Niro[216] in *The Godfather, Part II*, Paramount.

Fred Astaire in *The Towering Inferno*, 20th Century-Fox/Warner Bros.

---

[212] The Academy wrestled with the problem of creating a music category that would include musicals if enough were produced, but which might be filled out with other films that used music adapted from other sources, rather than an original score, such as *The Sting*'s Scott Joplin–based score. The attempts to create a category flexible enough to cover all possibilities were sometimes awkward, as this renaming of the adapted score category demonstrates.

[213] The only person to sweep all three music categories.

[214] Her eighth and final award, making Head the most honored woman in Oscar history. The only people to receive more awards are 20th Century-Fox music director Alfred Newman, who won nine, MGM art department head Cedric Gibbons, who won eleven, and studio head Walt Disney, who collected Oscars for twelve cartoons and ten live-action shorts and documentary features, plus honorary awards for the creation of Mickey Mouse and for *Snow White and the Seven Dwarfs* and *Fantasia*, as well as the Irving G. Thalberg Award. Because Gibbons, Newman, and Disney were often nominated by virtue of their administrative roles, Head's achievement may be the most impressive.

[215] Only sequel to win the Oscar for best picture, although some would count *The Silence of the Lambs* (1991) as a sequel because a 1986 film, *Manhunter*, was based on a novel by Thomas Harris, *Red Dragon*, that introduced the character of Hannibal Lecter. Unlike the *Godfather* films, however, the two Lecter movies were made by different producers and directors, featured different actors in the Lecter role, and no attempt was made to suggest a connection between the two films.

[216] Only person to win an Oscar for playing a character for which someone else—in this case Marlon Brando (1972)—also won an Oscar.

Jeff Bridges in *Thunderbolt and Lightfoot,*
United Artists.

Michael V. Gazzo in *The Godfather, Part II,*
Paramount.

Lee Strasberg in *The Godfather, Part II,*
Paramount.

SUPPORTING ACTRESS

**Ingrid Bergman in *Murder on the
Orient Express,* Paramount
(United Kingdom).**

Valentina Cortese in *Day for Night,*
Warner Bros. (France).

Madeline Kahn in *Blazing Saddles,* Warner
Bros.

Diane Ladd in *Alice Doesn't Live Here
Anymore,* Warner Bros.

Talia Shire in *The Godfather, Part II,*
Paramount.

DIRECTOR

**Francis Ford Coppola for *The
Godfather, Part II,* Paramount.**

John Cassavetes for *A Woman Under the
Influence,* Faces International.

Bob Fosse for *Lenny,* United Artists.

Roman Polanski for *Chinatown,*
Paramount.

François Truffaut for *Day for Night,*
Warner Bros. (France).

WRITING[217]

(Original Screenplay)

**Robert Towne for *Chinatown,*
Paramount.**

Francis Ford Coppola for *The Conversation,*
Paramount.

Robert Getchell for *Alice Doesn't Live Here
Anymore,* Warner Bros.

Paul Mazursky and Josh Greenfeld for
Harry and Tonto, 20th Century-Fox.

François Truffaut, Jean-Louis Richard,
and Suzanne Schiffman for *Day for
Night,* Warner Bros. (France).

(Screenplay Adapted From Other
Material)

**Francis Ford Coppola and Mario
Puzo for *The Godfather, Part II,*
Paramount.**

Julian Barry for *Lenny,* United Artists.

Paul Dehn for *Murder on the Orient Express,*
Paramount (United Kingdom).

Mordecai Richler, screenplay; Lionel
Chetwynd, adaptation, for *The
Apprenticeship of Duddy Kravitz,*
Paramount (Canada).

Gene Wilder and Mel Brooks for *Young
Frankenstein,* 20th Century-Fox.

CINEMATOGRAPHY

**Fred Koenekamp and Joseph Biroc
for *The Towering Inferno,* 20th
Century-Fox/Warner Bros.**

John A. Alonzo for *Chinatown,*
Paramount.

Philip Lathrop for *Earthquake,* Universal.

Bruce Surtees for *Lenny,* United Artists.

Geoffrey Unsworth for *Murder on the
Orient Express,* Paramount (United
Kingdom).

ART DIRECTION—SET DECORATION

**The Godfather, Part II, Paramount.
Dean Tavoularis, Angelo
Graham; George R. Nelson.**

Chinatown, Paramount. Richard Sylbert,
W. Stewart Campbell; Ruby Levitt.

Earthquake, Universal. Alexander
Golitzen, E. Preston Ames; Frank
McKelvy.

The Island at the Top of the World, Disney,
Buena Vista. Peter Ellenshaw, John B.
Mansbridge, Walter Tyler, Al Roelofs;
Hal Gausman.

The Towering Inferno, 20th Century-Fox/
Warner Bros. William Creber, Ward
Preston; Raphael Bretton.

SOUND

**Earthquake, Universal. Ronald
Pierce and Melvin Metcalfe, Sr.**

Chinatown, Paramount. Bud Grenzbach
and Larry Jost.

The Conversation, Paramount. Walter
Murch and Arthur Rochester.

Young Frankenstein, 20th Century-Fox.
Richard Portman and Gene
Cantamessa.

The Towering Inferno, 20th Century-Fox/

Warner Bros. Theodore Soderberg
and Herman Lewis.

MUSIC

(Song)

**"We May Never Love Like This
Again" from *The Towering
Inferno,* 20th Century-Fox/
Warner Bros. Music and lyrics
by Al Kasha and Joel
Hirschhorn.**

"Benji's Theme (I Feel Love)" from
Benji, Mulberry Square. Music by Euel
Box, lyrics by Betty Box.

"Blazing Saddles" from *Blazing Saddles,*
Warner Bros. Music by John Morris,
lyrics by Mel Brooks.

"Little Prince" from *The Little Prince,*
Paramount (United Kingdom). Music
by Frederick Loewe, lyrics by Alan
Jay Lerner.

"Wherever Love Takes Me" from *Gold,*
Allied Artists. Music by Elmer
Bernstein, lyrics by Don Black.

(Original Dramatic Score)

**Nino Rota and Carmine Coppola
for *The Godfather, Part II,*
Paramount.**

Richard Rodney Bennett for *Murder on the
Orient Express,* Paramount (United
Kingdom).

Jerry Goldsmith for *Chinatown,*
Paramount.

Alex North for *Shanks,* Paramount.

John Williams for *The Towering Inferno,*
20th Century-Fox/Warner Bros.

(Scoring: Original Song Score and
Adaptation, or Scoring: Adaptation)

**Nelson Riddle for the adaptation
score for *The Great Gatsby,*
Merrick, Paramount.**

Alan Jay Lerner and Frederick Loewe for
the song score and Angela Morley and
Douglas Gamley for the adaptation
score for *The Little Prince,* Paramount
(United Kingdom).

Paul Williams for the song score and
Williams and George Aliceson Tipton
for the adaptation score for *Phantom of
the Paradise,* 20th Century-Fox.

___

[217] Categories renamed.

FILM EDITING

Harold F. Kress and Carl Kress for
The Towering Inferno, 20th
Century-Fox / Warner Bros.
John C. Howard and Danford Greene for
Blazing Saddles, Warner Bros.
Michael Luciano for _The Longest Yard,_
Paramount.
Sam O'Steen for _Chinatown,_ Paramount.
Dorothy Spencer for _Earthquake,_
Universal.

COSTUME DESIGN[218]

Theoni V. Aldredge for _The Great_
Gatsby, Paramount.
John Furness for _Daisy Miller,_ Paramount.
Anthea Sylbert for _Chinatown,_ Paramount.
Theadora Van Runkle for _The Godfather,_
Part II, Paramount.
Tony Walton for _Murder on the Orient_
Express, Paramount (United Kingdom).

FOREIGN LANGUAGE FILM

Amarcord, Italy.
Cats' Play, Hungary.
The Deluge, Poland.
Lacombe, Lucien, France.
The Truce, Argentina.

JEAN HERSHOLT MEMORIAL AWARD

Arthur B. Krim.

HONORARY AWARDS

Howard Hawks, a master American
filmmaker whose creative efforts
hold a distinguished place in
world cinema.
Jean Renoir, a genius who, with
grace, responsibility and
enviable devotion through silent
film, sound film, feature,
documentary and television, has
won the world's admiration.

SPECIAL ACHIEVEMENT AWARD

Visual Effects: Frank Brendel, Glen
Robinson and Albert Whitlock
for _Earthquake,_ Universal.

1975
Awards presented March 29, 1976.

PICTURE

One Flew Over the Cuckoo's Nest,
Fantasy Films Production,
United Artists. Produced by Saul
Zaentz and Michael Douglas.[219]
Barry Lyndon, Hawk Films, Ltd.,
Production, Warner Bros. (United
Kingdom). Produced by Stanley
Kubrick.
Dog Day Afternoon, Warner Bros.
Produced by Martin Bregman and
Marin Elfand.
Jaws, Universal-Zanuck / Brown
Production, Universal. Produced by
Richard D. Zanuck and David Brown.
Nashville, ABC Entertainment-Jerry
Weintraub-Robert Altman Production,
Paramount. Produced by Robert
Altman.

ACTOR

Jack Nicholson in _One Flew Over the_
Cuckoo's Nest, United Artists.
Walter Matthau in _The Sunshine Boys,_
MGM.
Al Pacino in _Dog Day Afternoon,_ Warner
Bros.
Maximilian Schell in _The Man in the Glass_
Booth, AFT Distributing.
James Whitmore in _Give 'Em Hell, Harry!_
Theatrovision, Avco Embassy.

ACTRESS

Louise Fletcher in _One Flew Over the_
Cuckoo's Nest, United Artists.
Isabelle Adjani in _The Story of Adele H.,_
New World Pictures (France).

Ann-Margret in _Tommy,_ Columbia (United
Kingdom).
Glenda Jackson in _Hedda,_ Brut
Productions (United Kingdom).
Carol Kane in _Hester Street,_ Midwest Film.

SUPPORTING ACTOR

George Burns[220] in _The Sunshine_
Boys, MGM.
Brad Dourif in _One Flew Over the Cuckoo's_
Nest, United Artists.
Burgess Meredith in _The Day of the Locust,_
Paramount.
Chris Sarandon in _Dog Day Afternoon,_
Warner Bros.
Jack Warden in _Shampoo,_ Columbia.

SUPPORTING ACTRESS

Lee Grant in _Shampoo,_ Columbia.
Ronee Blakley in _Nashville,_ Paramount.
Sylvia Miles in _Farewell, My Lovely,_ Avco
Embassy.
Lily Tomlin in _Nashville,_ Paramount.
Brenda Vaccaro in _Jacqueline Susann's Once_
Is Not Enough, Paramount.

DIRECTOR

Milos Forman for _One Flew Over the_
Cuckoo's Nest, United Artists.
Robert Altman for _Nashville,_ ABC
Entertainment-Weintraub-Altman,
Paramount.
Federico Fellini for _Amarcord,_ New World
Pictures (Italy).
Stanley Kubrick for _Barry Lyndon,_ Warner
Bros. (United Kingdom).
Sidney Lumet for _Dog Day Afternoon,_
Warner Bros.

WRITING

(Original Screenplay)
Frank Pierson for _Dog Day_
Afternoon, Warner Bros.
Ted Allan for _Lies My Father Told Me,_
Columbia (Canada).

---

[218] First time since the 1931–32 awards that all nominees in a category have been from the films released by a single studio. In the earlier instance, the three best actress nominees were from MGM films.
[219] First film since _It Happened One Night_ (1934) to win the awards for picture, actor, actress, director, and writing. The only other one is _The Silence of the Lambs_ (1991).
[220] At age eighty, the oldest actor to win the Oscar. Jessica Tandy, who was a few months shy of eighty-one when she received the Oscar for _Driving Miss Daisy_ (1989), is the oldest winner.

Federico Fellini and Tonino Guerra for *Amarcord,* New World Pictures (Italy).

Claude Lelouch and Pierre Uytterhoeven for *And Now My Love,* Avco Embassy (France).

Robert Towne and Warren Beatty for *Shampoo,* Columbia.

(Screenplay Adapted From Other Material)

Laurence Hauben and Bo Goldman for *One Flew Over the Cuckoo's Nest,* United Artists.

John Huston and Gladys Hill for *The Man Who Would Be King,* Allied Artists.

Stanley Kubrick for *Barry Lyndon,* Warner Bros.

Ruggero Maccari and Dino Risi for *Scent of a Woman,* 20th Century-Fox (Italy).

Neil Simon for *The Sunshine Boys,* MGM.

CINEMATOGRAPHY

John Alcott for *Barry Lyndon,* Warner Bros. (United Kingdom).

Conrad Hall for *The Day of the Locust,* Paramount.

James Wong Howe for *Funny Lady,* Columbia.

Robert Surtees for *The Hindenburg,* Universal.

Haskell Wexler and Bill Butler for *One Flew Over the Cuckoo's Nest,* United Artists.

ART DIRECTION—SET DECORATION

***Barry Lyndon,* Warner Bros. (United Kingdom). Ken Adam, Roy Walker; Vernon Dixon.**

The Hindenburg, Universal. Edward Carfagno; Frank McKelvy.

The Man Who Would Be King, Allied Artists. Alexander Trauner, Tony Inglis; Peter James.

Shampoo, Columbia. Richard Sylbert, W. Stewart Campbell; George Gaines.

The Sunshine Boys, MGM. Albert Brenner; Marvin March.

SOUND

***Jaws,* Universal. Robert L. Hoyt, Roger Heman, Earl Madery, and John Carter.**

Bite the Bullet, Columbia. Arthur Piantadosi, Les Fresholtz, Richard Tyler, and Al Overton, Jr.

Funny Lady, Columbia. Richard Portman, Don MacDougall, Curly Thirlwell, and Jack Solomon.

The Hindenburg, Universal. Leonard Peterson, John A. Bolger, Jr., John Mack, and Don K. Sharpless.

The Wind and the Lion, MGM. Harry W. Tetrick, Aaron Rochin, William McCaughey, and Roy Charman.

MUSIC

(Original Song)[221]

"I'm Easy" from *Nashville,* Paramount. Music and lyrics by Keith Carradine.

"How Lucky Can You Get" from *Funny Lady,* Columbia. Music and lyrics by Fred Ebb and John Kander.

"Now That We're in Love" from *Whiffs,* 20th Century-Fox. Music by George Barrie, lyrics by Sammy Cahn.

"Richard's Window" from *The Other Side of the Mountain,* Universal. Music by Charles Fox, lyrics by Norman Gimbel.

"Theme from *Mahogany* (Do You Know Where You're Going To)" from *Mahogany,* Paramount. Music by Michael Masser, lyrics by Gerry Goffin.

(Original Score)[222]

John Williams for *Jaws,* Universal.

Gerald Fried for *Birds Do It, Bees Do It,* Columbia.

Jerry Goldsmith for *The Wind and the Lion,* MGM.

Jack Nitzsche for *One Flew Over the Cuckoo's Nest,* United Artists.

Alex North for *Bite the Bullet,* Columbia.

(Scoring: Original Song Score and Adaptation, or Scoring: Adaptation)

Leonard Rosenman for the

adaptation score for *Barry Lyndon,* Warner Bros. (United Kingdom).**

Peter Matz for the adaptation score for *Funny Lady,* Columbia.

Peter Townshend for the adaptation score for *Tommy,* Columbia (United Kingdom).

FILM EDITING

Verna Fields for *Jaws,* Universal.

Dede Allen for *Dog Day Afternoon,* Warner Bros.

Richard Chew, Lynzee Klingman, and Sheldon Kahn for *One Flew Over the Cuckoo's Nest,* United Artists.

Russell Lloyd for *The Man Who Would Be King,* Allied Artists.

Frederic Steinkamp and Don Guidice for *Three Days of the Condor,* Paramount.

COSTUME DESIGN

Ulla-Britt Soderlund and Milena Canonero for *Barry Lyndon,* Warner Bros. (United Kingdom).

Ray Aghayan and Bob Mackie for *Funny Lady,* Columbia.

Yvonne Blake and Ron Talsky for *The Four Musketeers,* 20th Century-Fox.

Edith Head for *The Man Who Would Be King,* Allied Artists.

Henny Noremark and Karin Erskine for *The Magic Flute,* Surrogate Releasing (Sweden).

FOREIGN LANGUAGE FILM

***Dersu Uzala,* USSR.**

Land of Promise, Poland.

Letters From Marusia, Mexico.

Sandakan No. 8, Japan.

Scent of a Woman, Italy.

IRVING G. THALBERG MEMORIAL AWARD

Mervyn LeRoy.

JEAN HERSHOLT HUMANITARIAN AWARD

Jules C. Stein.

---

[221] Category renamed.
[222] Category renamed.

HONORARY AWARD

Mary Pickford, in recognition of her unique contributions to the film industry and the development of film as an artistic medium.

SPECIAL ACHIEVEMENT AWARDS

Sound Effects: Peter Berkos for *The Hindenburg,* **Universal.**

Visual Effects: Albert Whitlock and Glen Robinson for *The Hindenburg,* **Universal.**

1976
Awards presented March 29, 1977.

PICTURE

Rocky, **Robert Chartoff-Irwin Winkler Production, United Artists. Produced by Irwin Winkler and Robert Chartoff.**

All the President's Men, Wildwood Enterprises Inc. Production, Warner Bros. Produced by Walter Coblenz.

Bound for Glory, The Bound for Glory Company Production; United Artists. Produced by Robert F. Blumofe and Harold Leventhal.

Network, Howard Gottfried-Paddy Chayefsky Production, MGM/United Artists. Produced by Howard Gottfried.

Taxi Driver, Bill/Phillips Production of a Martin Scorsese Film, Columbia. Produced by Michael Phillips and Julia Phillips.

ACTOR

Peter Finch[223] in *Network,* **MGM/ United Artists.**

Robert De Niro in *Taxi Driver,* Columbia.

Giancarlo Giannini in *Seven Beauties,* Medusa Distribuzione, Cinema 5 (Italy).

William Holden in *Network,* MGM/ United Artists.

Sylvester Stallone in *Rocky,* United Artists.

ACTRESS

Faye Dunaway in *Network,* **MGM/ United Artists.**

Marie-Christine Barrault in *Cousin, Cousine,* Northal Film Distributors (France).

Talia Shire in *Rocky,* United Artists.

Sissy Spacek in *Carrie,* United Artists.

Liv Ullmann in *Face to Face,* Cinematograph A.B., Paramount (Sweden).

SUPPORTING ACTOR

Jason Robards in *All the President's Men,* **Warner Bros.**

Ned Beatty in *Network,* MGM/United Artists.

Burgess Meredith in *Rocky,* United Artists.

Laurence Olivier in *Marathon Man,* Paramount.

Burt Young in *Rocky,* United Artists.

SUPPORTING ACTRESS

Beatrice Straight in *Network,* **MGM/ United Artists.**

Jane Alexander in *All the President's Men,* Warner Bros.

Jodie Foster in *Taxi Driver,* Columbia.

Lee Grant in *Voyage of the Damned,* Avco Embassy (United Kingdom).

Piper Laurie in *Carrie,* United Artists.

DIRECTOR

John G. Avildsen for *Rocky,* **United Artists.**

Ingmar Bergman for *Face to Face,* Paramount (Sweden).

Sidney Lumet for *Network,* MGM/United Artists.

Alan J. Pakula for *All the President's Men,* Warner Bros.

Lina Wertmüller[224] for *Seven Beauties,* Cinema 5 (Italy).

WRITING[225]

(Screenplay—Based on Material From Another Medium)

William Goldman for *All the President's Men,* **Warner Bros.**

Federico Fellini and Bernadino Zapponi for *Fellini's Casanova,* Universal (Italy).

Robert Getchell for *Bound for Glory,* United Artists.

Nicholas Meyer for *The Seven-Per-Cent Solution,* Universal (United Kingdom).

Steve Shagan and David Butler for *Voyage of the Damned,* Avco Embassy (United Kingdom).

(Screenplay Written Directly for the Screen—Based on Factual Material or on Story Material not Previously Published or Produced)

Paddy Chayefsky for *Network,* **MGM/United Artists.**

Walter Bernstein for *The Front,* Columbia.

Sylvester Stallone for *Rocky,* United Artists.

Jean-Charles Tacchella, story and screenplay; Daniele Thompson, adaptation, for *Cousin, Cousine,* Northal Film Distributors (France).

Lina Wertmüller for *Seven Beauties,* Cinema 5 (Italy).

CINEMATOGRAPHY

Haskell Wexler for *Bound for Glory,* **United Artists.**

Richard H. Kline for *King Kong,* Paramount.

Ernest Laszlo for *Logan's Run,* MGM.

Owen Roizman for *Network,* MGM/ United Artists.

Robert Surtees for *A Star Is Born,* Warner Bros.

ART DIRECTION—SET DECORATION

All the President's Men, **Warner Bros. George Jenkins; George Gaines.**

The Incredible Sarah, Seymour Borde & Associates (United Kingdom). Elliot Scott, Norman Reynolds; Peter Howitt.

---

[223] Only person to receive an acting Oscar posthumously.

[224] First woman to be nominated for directing.

[225] Categories renamed.

The Last Tycoon, Paramount. Gene Callahan, Jack Collis; Jerry Wunderlich.

Logan's Run, MGM. Dale Hennesy; Robert de Vestel.

The Shootist, Paramount. Robert F. Boyle; Arthur Jeph Parker.

SOUND

All the President's Men, Warner Bros. Arthur Piantadosi, Les Fresholtz, Dick Alexander, and Jim Webb.

King Kong, Paramount. Harry Warren Tetrick, William McCaughey, Aaron Rochin, and Jack Solomon.

Rocky, United Artists. Harry Warren Tetrick, William McCaughey, Lyle Burbridge, and Bud Alper.

Silver Streak, 20th Century-Fox. Donald Mitchell, Douglas Williams, Richard Tyler, and Hal Etherington.

A Star Is Born, Warner Bros. Robert Knudson, Dan Wallin, Robert Glass, and Tom Overton.

MUSIC

(Original Song)

"Evergreen (Love Theme From *A Star Is Born*)" from *A Star Is Born*, Warner Bros. Music by Barbra Streisand,[226] lyrics by Paul Williams.

"Ave Satani" from *The Omen*, 20th Century-Fox. Music and lyrics by Jerry Goldsmith.

"Come to Me" from *The Pink Panther Strikes Again*, United Artists. Music by Henry Mancini, lyrics by Don Black.

"Gonna Fly Now" from *Rocky*, United Artists. Music by Bill Conti, lyrics by Carol Connors and Ayn Robbins.

"A World That Never Was" from *Half a House*, First American Films. Music by Sammy Fain, lyrics by Paul Francis Webster.

(Original Score)

Jerry Goldsmith for *The Omen*, 20th Century-Fox.

Jerry Fielding for *The Outlaw Josey Wales*, Warner Bros.

Bernard Herrmann for *Obsession*, Columbia.

Bernard Herrmann for *Taxi Driver*, Columbia.

Lalo Schifrin for *Voyage of the Damned*, Avco Embassy (United Kingdom).

(Original Song Score and Its Adaptation or Adaptation Score)[227]

Leonard Rosenman for the adaptation score for *Bound for Glory*, United Artists.

Roger Kellaway for the adaptation score for *A Star Is Born*, Warner Bros.

Paul Williams for the song score and adaptation score for *Bugsy Malone*, Paramount.

FILM EDITING

Richard Halsey and Scott Conrad for *Rocky*, United Artists.

Alan Heim for *Network*, MGM/United Artists.

Robert Jones and Pembroke J. Herring for *Bound for Glory*, United Artists.

Eve Newman and Walter Hannemann for *Two-Minute Warning*, Universal.

Robert L. Wolfe for *All the President's Men*, Warner Bros.

COSTUME DESIGN

Danilo Donati for *Fellini's Casanova*, Universal (Italy).

Alan Barrett for *The Seven-Per-Cent Solution*, Universal (United Kingdom).

Anthony Mendleson for *The Incredible Sarah*, Seymour Borde & Associates (United Kingdom).

William Theiss for *Bound for Glory*, United Artists.

Mary Wills for *The Passover Plot*, Atlas Films (U.S./Israel).

FOREIGN LANGUAGE FILM[228]

Black and White in Color, Ivory Coast.

Cousin, Cousine, France.

Jacob, the Liar, German Democratic Republic.

Nights and Days, Poland.

Seven Beauties, Italy.

IRVING G. THALBERG MEMORIAL AWARD

Pandro S. Berman.

SPECIAL ACHIEVEMENT AWARDS

Visual Effects: Carlo Rambaldi, Glen Robinson and Frank Van der Veer for *King Kong*, Paramount.

Visual Effects: L. B. Abbott, Glen Robinson and Matthew Yuricich for *Logan's Run*, MGM.

1977

Awards presented March 29, 1978.

PICTURE

Annie Hall, **Jack Rollins and Charles H. Joffe Production, United Artists. Produced by Charles H. Joffe.**

The Goodbye Girl, Ray Stark Production, MGM/Warner Bros. Produced by Ray Stark.

Julia, 20th Century-Fox. Produced by Richard Roth.

Star Wars, Lucasfilm, Ltd., Production; 20th Century-Fox. Produced by Gary Kurtz.

The Turning Point, Hera Productions, 20th Century-Fox. Produced by Herbert Ross and Arthur Laurents.[229]

ACTOR

Richard Dreyfuss[230] in *The Goodbye Girl*, MGM/Warner Bros.

---

[226] Only winner for acting to receive an Oscar for songwriting.

[227] Category renamed.

[228] A rules change restricts voting in the foreign language film category to active members of the Academy who have seen all five nominated films. Previously all active members could vote.

[229] The film with the most nominations (eleven) without winning an Oscar. Later tied by *The Color Purple* (1985).

[230] At thirty, the youngest person to win the Oscar as best actor.

Woody Allen[231] in *Annie Hall*, United Artists.

Richard Burton[232] in *Equus*, United Artists.

Marcello Mastroianni in *A Special Day*, Canafox Films, Cinema 5 (Italy/Canada).

John Travolta in *Saturday Night Fever*, Paramount.

ACTRESS

Diane Keaton in *Annie Hall*, United Artists.

Anne Bancroft in *The Turning Point*, 20th Century-Fox.

Jane Fonda in *Julia*, 20th Century-Fox.

Shirley MacLaine in *The Turning Point*, 20th Century-Fox.

Marsha Mason in *The Goodbye Girl*, MGM/Warner Bros.

SUPPORTING ACTOR

Jason Robards[233] in *Julia*, 20th Century-Fox.

Mikhail Baryshnikov in *The Turning Point*, 20th Century-Fox.

Peter Firth in *Equus*, United Artists.

Alec Guinness in *Star Wars*, Lucasfilm, 20th Century-Fox.

Maximilian Schell in *Julia*, 20th Century-Fox.

SUPPORTING ACTRESS

Vanessa Redgrave in *Julia*, 20th Century-Fox.

Leslie Browne in *The Turning Point*, 20th Century-Fox.

Quinn Cummings in *The Goodbye Girl*, MGM/Warner Bros.

Melinda Dillon in *Close Encounters of the Third Kind*, Columbia.

Tuesday Weld in *Looking for Mr. Goodbar*, Paramount.

DIRECTOR

Woody Allen for *Annie Hall*, United Artists.

George Lucas for *Star Wars*, 20th Century-Fox.

Herbert Ross for *The Turning Point*, 20th Century-Fox.

Steven Spielberg for *Close Encounters of the Third Kind*, Columbia.

Fred Zinnemann for *Julia*, 20th Century-Fox.

WRITING

(Screenplay—Based on Material From Another Medium)

Alvin Sargent for *Julia*, 20th Century-Fox.

Luis Buñuel and Jean-Claude Carrière for *That Obscure Object of Desire*, First Artists (Spain).

Larry Gelbart for *Oh, God!*, Warner Bros.

Gavin Lambert and Lewis John Carlino for *I Never Promised You a Rose Garden*, New World Pictures.

Peter Shaffer for *Equus*, United Artists.

(Screenplay Written Directly for the Screen—Based on Factual Material or on Story Material not Previously Published or Produced)

Woody Allen and Marshall Brickman for *Annie Hall*, United Artists.

Robert Benton for *The Late Show*, Warner Bros.

Arthur Laurents for *The Turning Point*, 20th Century-Fox.

George Lucas for *Star Wars*, 20th Century-Fox.

Neil Simon for *The Goodbye Girl*, MGM/Warner Bros.

CINEMATOGRAPHY

Vilmos Zsigmond for *Close Encounters of the Third Kind*, Columbia.

William A. Fraker for *Looking for Mr. Goodbar*, Paramount.

Fred J. Koenekamp for *Islands in the Stream*, Paramount.

Douglas Slocombe for *Julia*, 20th Century-Fox.

Robert Surtees for *The Turning Point*, 20th Century-Fox.

ART DIRECTION—SET DECORATION

Star Wars, 20th Century-Fox. John Barry, Norman Reynolds, Leslie Dilley; Roger Christian.

Airport '77, Universal. George C. Webb; Mickey S. Michaels.

Close Encounters of the Third Kind, Columbia. Joe Alves, Dan Lomino; Phil Abramson.

The Spy Who Loved Me, United Artists (United Kingdom). Ken Adam, Peter Lamont; Hugh Scaife.

The Turning Point, 20th Century-Fox. Albert Brenner; Marvin March.

SOUND

Star Wars, 20th Century-Fox. Don MacDougall, Ray West, Bob Minkler, and Derek Ball.

Close Encounters of the Third Kind, Columbia. Robert Knudson, Robert J. Glass, Don MacDougall, and Gene S. Cantamessa.

The Deep, Columbia. Walter Goss, Dick Alexander, Tom Beckert, and Robin Gregory.

Sorcerer, Paramount/Universal. Robert Knudson, Robert J. Glass, Richard Tyler, and Jean-Louis Ducarme.

The Turning Point, 20th Century-Fox. Theodore Soderberg, Paul Wells, Douglas O. Williams, and Jerry Jost.

MUSIC

(Original Song)

"You Light Up My Life" from *You Light Up My Life*, Columbia. Music and lyrics by Joseph Brooks.

"Candle on the Water" from *Pete's Dragon*, Disney, Buena Vista. Music

---

[231] First person nominated for acting, directing, and writing since Orson Welles (1941). The only other person to receive simultaneous nominations in those three categories is Warren Beatty (1978, 1981). Unlike Allen, Welles and Beatty were also nominated as producer.

[232] With his seventh unsuccessful nomination, Burton sets a record for most nominations without a win that will be tied by Peter O'Toole (1982).

[233] Fourth person to win two consecutive Oscars for acting. The others are Luise Rainer (1936, 1937), Spencer Tracy (1937, 1938), Katharine Hepburn (1967, 1968), and Tom Hanks (1993, 1994).

and lyrics by Al Kasha and Joel Hirschhorn.

"Nobody Does It Better" from *The Spy Who Loved Me*, United Artists. Music by Marvin Hamlisch, lyrics by Carole Bayer Sager.

"The Slipper and the Rose Waltz (He Danced With Me/She Danced With Me)" from *The Slipper and the Rose— the Story of Cinderella*, Universal (United Kingdom). Music and lyrics by Richard M. Sherman and Robert B. Sherman.

"Someone's Waiting for You" from *The Rescuers*, Disney, Buena Vista. Music by Sammy Fain, lyrics by Carol Connors and Ayn Robbins.

(Original Score)

John Williams for *Star Wars*, 20th Century-Fox.

Georges Delerue for *Julia*, 20th Century-Fox.

Marvin Hamlisch for *The Spy Who Loved Me*, United Artists (United Kingdom).

Maurice Jarre for *Mohammad—Messenger of God*, Yablans (United Kingdom).

John Williams for *Close Encounters of the Third Kind*, Columbia.

(Original Song Score and Its Adaptation or Adaptation Score)

Jonathan Tunick for the adaptation score for *A Little Night Music*, New World Pictures (Austria/ West Germany).

Al Kasha and Joel Hirschhorn for the song score and Irwin Kostal for the adaptation score for *Pete's Dragon*, Disney, Buena Vista.

Richard M. Sherman and Robert B. Sherman for the song score and Angela Morley for the adaptation score for *The Slipper and the Rose—the Story of Cinderella*, Universal (United Kingdom).

FILM EDITING

Paul Hirsch, Marcia Lucas, and Richard Chew for *Star Wars*, 20th Century-Fox.

Walter Hannemann and Angelo Ross for *Smokey and the Bandit*, Universal.

Michael Kahn for *Close Encounters of the Third Kind*, Columbia.

Walter Murch for *Julia*, 20th Century-Fox.

William Reynolds for *The Turning Point*, 20th Century-Fox.

COSTUME DESIGN

John Mollo for *Star Wars*, 20th Century-Fox.

Edith Head and Burton Miller for *Airport '77*, Universal.

Florence Klotz for *A Little Night Music*, New World Pictures (Austria/West Germany).

Irene Sharaff for *The Other Side of Midnight*, 20th Century-Fox.

Anthea Sylbert for *Julia*, 20th Century-Fox.

VISUAL EFFECTS

***Star Wars*, 20th Century-Fox. John Stears, John Dykstra, Richard Edlund, Grant McCune, and Robert Blalack.**

Close Encounters of the Third Kind, Columbia. Roy Arbogast, Douglas Trumbull, Matthew Yuricich, Gregory Jein, and Richard Yuricich.

FOREIGN LANGUAGE FILM

***Madame Rosa*, France.**

Iphigenia, Greece.

Operation Thunderbolt, Israel.

A Special Day, Italy.

That Obscure Object of Desire, Spain.

IRVING G. THALBERG MEMORIAL AWARD

Walter Mirisch.

JEAN HERSHOLT HUMANITARIAN AWARD

Charlton Heston.

HONORARY AWARDS

Margaret Booth, for her exceptional contribution to the art of film editing in the motion picture industry.

Gordon E. Sawyer and Sidney P. Solow, in appreciation for outstanding service and dedication in upholding the high standards of the Academy of Motion Picture Arts and Sciences.[234]

SPECIAL ACHIEVEMENT AWARDS

Sound Effects Editing: Frank E. Warner for *Close Encounters of the Third Kind*, Columbia.

Benjamin Burtt, Jr., for the creation of the alien, creature and robot voices in *Star Wars*, 20th Century-Fox.

1978
Awards presented April 9, 1979.

PICTURE

***The Deer Hunter*, EMI Films/ Michael Cimino Film Production, Universal. Produced by Barry Spikings, Michael Deeley, Michael Cimino, and John Peverall.**

Coming Home, Jerome Hellman Enterprises Production, United Artists. Produced by Jerome Hellman.

Heaven Can Wait, Dogwood Productions, Paramount. Produced by Warren Beatty.[235]

Midnight Express, Casablanca Filmworks Production, Columbia (United Kingdom). Produced by Alan Marshall and David Puttnam.

An Unmarried Woman, 20th Century-Fox. Produced by Paul Mazursky and Tony Ray.

---

[234] Starting with Sawyer and Solow, the Academy presented a series of medals of commendation to technicians. These continued through the 1980 awards and were replaced with the Gordon E. Sawyer Award at the 1981 ceremonies.

[235] Only person other than Orson Welles (1941) to receive simultaneous nominations as producer, actor, director, and writer.

ACTOR

Jon Voight in *Coming Home*, United Artists.

Warren Beatty in *Heaven Can Wait*, Paramount.

Gary Busey in *The Buddy Holly Story*, Columbia.

Robert De Niro in *The Deer Hunter*, Universal.

Laurence Olivier in *The Boys From Brazil*, 20th Century-Fox.[236]

ACTRESS

Jane Fonda in *Coming Home*, United Artists.

Ingrid Bergman in *Autumn Sonata*, New World Pictures (Sweden).

Ellen Burstyn in *Same Time, Next Year*, Universal.

Jill Clayburgh in *An Unmarried Woman*, 20th Century-Fox.

Geraldine Page in *Interiors*, United Artists.

SUPPORTING ACTOR

Christopher Walken in *The Deer Hunter*, Universal.

Bruce Dern in *Coming Home*, United Artists.

Richard Farnsworth in *Comes a Horseman*, United Artists.

John Hurt in *Midnight Express*, Columbia (United Kingdom).

Jack Warden in *Heaven Can Wait*, Paramount.

SUPPORTING ACTRESS

Maggie Smith in *California Suite*, Columbia.

Dyan Cannon in *Heaven Can Wait*, Paramount.

Penelope Milford in *Coming Home*, United Artists.

Maureen Stapleton in *Interiors*, United Artists.

Meryl Streep in *The Deer Hunter*, Universal.

DIRECTOR

Michael Cimino for *The Deer Hunter*, Universal.

Woody Allen for *Interiors*, United Artists.

Hal Ashby for *Coming Home*, United Artists.

Warren Beatty and Buck Henry for *Heaven Can Wait*, Paramount.

Alan Parker for *Midnight Express*, Columbia (United Kingdom).

WRITING

(Screenplay Based on Material From Another Medium)

Oliver Stone for *Midnight Express*, Columbia.

Elaine May and Warren Beatty for *Heaven Can Wait*, Paramount.

Walter Newman for *Bloodbrothers*, Warner Bros.

Neil Simon for *California Suite*, Columbia.

Bernard Slade for *Same Time, Next Year*, Universal.

(Screenplay Written Directly for the Screen)

Nancy Dowd, story; Waldo Salt and Robert C. Jones, screenplay, for *Coming Home*, United Artists.

Woody Allen for *Interiors*, United Artists.

Ingmar Bergman for *Autumn Sonata*, New World Pictures (Sweden).

Michael Cimino, Deric Washburn, Louis Garfinkle, and Quinn K. Redeker, story; Deric Washburn, screenplay, for *The Deer Hunter*, Universal.

Paul Mazursky for *An Unmarried Woman*, 20th Century-Fox.

CINEMATOGRAPHY

Nestor Almendros for *Days of Heaven*, Paramount.

William A. Fraker for *Heaven Can Wait*, Paramount.

Oswald Morris for *The Wiz*, Universal.

Robert Surtees for *Same Time, Next Year*, Universal.

Vilmos Zsigmond for *The Deer Hunter*, Universal.

ART DIRECTION—SET DECORATION

***Heaven Can Wait*, Paramount. Paul Sylbert, Edwin O'Donovan; George Gaines.**

The Brink's Job, Universal. Dean Tavoularis, Angelo Graham; George R. Nelson, Bruce Kay.

California Suite, Columbia. Albert Brenner; Marvin March.

Interiors, United Artists. Mel Bourne; Daniel Robert.

The Wiz, Universal. Tony Walton, Philip Rosenberg; Edward Stewart, Robert Drumheller.

SOUND

***The Deer Hunter*, Universal. Richard Portman, William McCaughey, Aaron Rochin, and Darin Knight.**

The Buddy Holly Story, Columbia. Tex Rudloff, Joel Fein, Curly Thirlwell, and Willie Burton.

Days of Heaven, Paramount. John K. Wilkinson, Robert W. Glass, Jr., John T. Reitz, and Barry Thomas.

Hooper, Warner Bros. Robert Knudson, Robert J. Glass, Don MacDougall, and Jack Solomon.

Superman, Warner Bros. (United Kingdom). Gordon K. McCallum, Graham Hartstone, Nicolas Le Messurier, and Roy Charman.

MUSIC

(Original Song)

"Last Dance" from *Thank God It's Friday*, Columbia. Music and lyrics by Paul Jabara.

"Hopelessly Devoted to You" from *Grease*, Paramount. Music and lyrics by John Farrar.

"The Last Time I Felt Like This" from *Same Time, Next Year*, Universal. Music by Marvin Hamlisch, lyrics by Alan Bergman and Marilyn Bergman.

"Ready to Take a Chance Again" from *Foul Play*, Paramount. Music by

---

[236] Olivier's tenth nomination puts him in a tie for number of nominations with Bette Davis. Jack Nicholson subsequently also achieved ten nominations (1992). Katharine Hepburn holds the record with twelve nominations.

Charles Fox, lyrics by Norman Gimbel.

"When You're Loved" from *The Magic of Lassie*, The International Picture Show Company. Music and lyrics by Richard M. Sherman and Robert B. Sherman.

(Original Score)
Giorgio Moroder for *Midnight Express*, Columbia (United Kingdom).

Jerry Goldsmith for *The Boys From Brazil*, 20th Century-Fox.

Dave Grusin for *Heaven Can Wait*, Paramount.

Ennio Morricone for *Days of Heaven*, Paramount.

John Williams for *Superman*, Warner Bros. (United Kingdom).

(Adaptation Score)[237]
Joe Renzetti for *The Buddy Holly Story*, Columbia.

Quincy Jones for *The Wiz*, Universal.

Jerry Wexler for *Pretty Baby*, Paramount (U.S./France).

FILM EDITING
Peter Zinner for *The Deer Hunter*, Universal.

Stuart Baird for *Superman*, Warner Bros. (United Kingdom).

Gerry Hambling for *Midnight Express*, Columbia (United Kingdom).

Robert E. Swink for *The Boys From Brazil*, 20th Century-Fox.

Don Zimmerman for *Coming Home*, United Artists.

COSTUME DESIGN
Anthony Powell for *Death on the Nile*, Paramount (United Kingdom).

Renie Conley for *Caravans*, Universal (U.S./Iran).

Patricia Norris for *Days of Heaven*, Paramount.

Tony Walton for *The Wiz*, Universal.

Paul Zastupnevich for *The Swarm*, Warner Bros.

FOREIGN LANGUAGE FILM
Get Out Your Handkerchiefs, France.
The Glass Cell, Federal Republic of Germany.
Hungarians, Hungary.
Viva Italia! Italy.
White Bim Black Ear, USSR.

JEAN HERSHOLT HUMANITARIAN AWARD
Leo Jaffe.

HONORARY AWARDS
Walter Lantz, for bringing joy and laughter to every part of the world through his unique animated motion pictures.
Laurence Olivier, for the full body of his work, for the unique achievements of his entire career and his lifetime of contribution to the art of film.
King Vidor, for his incomparable achievements as a cinematic creator and innovator.
The Museum of Modern Art Department of Film for the contribution it has made to the public's perception of movies as an art form.
Linwood G. Dunn, Loren L. Ryder and Waldon O. Watson, in appreciation for outstanding service and dedication in upholding the high standards of the Academy of Motion Picture Arts and Sciences.[238]

SPECIAL ACHIEVEMENT AWARDS
Visual Effects: Les Bowie, Colin Chilvers, Denys Coop, Roy Field, Derek Meddings and Zoran Perisic for *Superman*, Warner Bros. (United Kingdom).

1979
Awards presented April 14, 1980.

PICTURE
Kramer vs. Kramer, Stanley Jaffe Productions, Columbia. Produced by Stanley R. Jaffe.

All That Jazz, Columbia/20th Century-Fox Production, 20th Century-Fox. Produced by Robert Alan Aurthur.

Apocalypse Now, Omni Zoetrope Production, United Artists. Produced by Francis Coppola, coproduced by Fred Roos, Gray Frederickson, and Tom Sternberg.

Breaking Away, 20th Century-Fox. Produced by Peter Yates.

Norma Rae, 20th Century-Fox. Produced by Tamara Asseyev and Alex Rose.

ACTOR
Dustin Hoffman in *Kramer vs. Kramer*, Columbia.

Jack Lemmon in *The China Syndrome*, Columbia.

Al Pacino in . . . *And Justice for All*, Columbia.

Roy Scheider in *All That Jazz*, Columbia/20th Century-Fox.

Peter Sellers in *Being There*, United Artists (U.S./Germany).

ACTRESS
Sally Field in *Norma Rae*, 20th Century-Fox.

Jill Clayburgh in *Starting Over*, Paramount.

Jane Fonda in *The China Syndrome*, Columbia.

Marsha Mason in *Chapter Two*, Columbia.

Bette Midler in *The Rose*, 20th Century-Fox.

SUPPORTING ACTOR
Melvyn Douglas in *Being There*, United Artists (U.S./Germany).

Robert Duvall in *Apocalypse Now*, United Artists.

Frederic Forrest in *The Rose*, 20th Century-Fox.

---

[237] Category renamed.
[238] Medals of commendation.

Justin Henry[239] in *Kramer vs. Kramer*, Columbia.

Mickey Rooney in *The Black Stallion*, United Artists.

SUPPORTING ACTRESS

Meryl Streep in *Kramer vs. Kramer*, Columbia.

Jane Alexander in *Kramer vs. Kramer*, Columbia.

Barbara Barrie in *Breaking Away*, 20th Century-Fox.

Candice Bergen in *Starting Over*, Paramount.

Mariel Hemingway in *Manhattan*, United Artists.

DIRECTOR

Robert Benton for *Kramer vs. Kramer*, Columbia.

Francis Coppola for *Apocalypse Now*, United Artists.

Bob Fosse for *All That Jazz*, 20th Century-Fox.

Edouard Molinaro for *La Cage aux Folles*, United Artists (France).

Peter Yates for *Breaking Away*, 20th Century-Fox.

WRITING

(Screenplay Based on Material From Another Medium)

Robert Benton for *Kramer vs. Kramer*, Columbia.

Allan Burns for *A Little Romance*, Orion.

John Milius and Francis Coppola for *Apocalypse Now*, United Artists.

Irving Ravetch and Harriet Frank, Jr., for *Norma Rae*, 20th Century-Fox.

Francis Veber, Edouard Molinaro, Marcello Danon, and Jean Poiret for *La Cage aux Folles*, United Artists (France).

(Screenplay Written Directly for the Screen)

Steve Tesich for *Breaking Away*, 20th Century-Fox.

Woody Allen and Marshall Brickman for *Manhattan*, United Artists.

Robert Alan Aurthur and Bob Fosse for *All That Jazz*, 20th Century-Fox.

Valerie Curtin and Barry Levinson for *. . . And Justice for All*, Columbia.

Mike Gray, T. S. Cook, and James Bridges for *The China Syndrome*, Columbia.

CINEMATOGRAPHY

Vittorio Storaro for *Apocalypse Now*, United Artists.

Nestor Almendros for *Kramer vs. Kramer*, Columbia.

William A. Fraker for *1941*, Universal.

Frank Phillips for *The Black Hole*, Disney, Buena Vista.

Giuseppe Rotunno for *All That Jazz*, 20th Century-Fox.

ART DIRECTION—SET DECORATION

***All That Jazz*, 20th Century-Fox. Philip Rosenberg, Tony Walton; Edward Stewart, Gary Brink.**

Alien, 20th Century-Fox. Michael Seymour, Les Dilley, Roger Christian; Ian Whittaker.

Apocalypse Now, United Artists. Dean Tavoularis, Angelo Graham; George R. Nelson.

The China Syndrome, Columbia. George Jenkins; Arthur Jeph Parker.

Star Trek—the Motion Picture, Paramount. Harold Michelson, Joe Jennings, Leon Harris, John Vallone; Linda DeScenna.

SOUND

***Apocalypse Now*, United Artists. Walter Murch, Mark Berger, Richard Beggs, and Nat Boxer.**

The Electric Horseman, Columbia. Arthur Piantadosi, Les Fresholtz, Michael Minkler, and Al Overton.

Meteor, American International. William McCaughey, Aaron Rochin, Michael J. Kohut, and Jack Solomon.

1941, Universal. Robert Knudson, Robert J. Glass, Don MacDougall, and Gene S. Cantamessa.

The Rose, 20th Century-Fox. Theodore

Soderberg, Douglas Williams, Paul Wells, and Jim Webb.

MUSIC

(Original Song)

"It Goes Like It Goes" from *Norma Rae*, 20th Century-Fox. Music by David Shire, lyrics by Norman Gimbel.

"The Rainbow Connection" from *The Muppet Movie*, AFD. Music and lyrics by Paul Williams and Kenny Ascher.

"Song From *10* (It's Easy to Say)" from *10*, Orion. Music by Henry Mancini, lyrics by Robert Wells.

"Theme From *Ice Castles* (Through the Eyes of Love)" from *Ice Castles*, Columbia. Music by Marvin Hamlisch, lyrics by Carole Bayer Sager.

"Theme From *The Promise* (I'll Never Say 'Goodbye')" from *The Promise*, Universal. Music by David Shire, lyrics by Alan Bergman and Marilyn Bergman.

(Original Score)

Georges Delerue for *A Little Romance*, Orion.

Jerry Goldsmith for *Star Trek—the Motion Picture*, Paramount.

Dave Grusin for *The Champ*, MGM.

Henry Mancini for *10*, Orion.

Lalo Schifrin for *The Amityville Horror*, American International.

(Original Song Score and Its Adaptation, or Adaptation Score)[240]

Ralph Burns for the adaptation score for *All That Jazz*, 20th Century-Fox.

Patrick Williams for the adaptation score for *Breaking Away*, 20th Century-Fox.

Paul Williams and Kenny Ascher for the song score and Williams for the adaptation score for *The Muppet Movie*, AFD.

FILM EDITING

Alan Heim for *All That Jazz*, 20th Century-Fox.

---

[239] At age nine, the youngest person to be nominated for an Oscar.
[240] Category reverts to an old name.

Robert Dalva for *The Black Stallion,* United Artists.

Jerry Greenberg for *Kramer vs. Kramer,* Columbia.

Richard Marks, Walter Murch, Gerald B. Greenberg, and Lisa Fruchtman for *Apocalypse Now,* United Artists.

Robert L. Wolfe and C. Timothy O'Meara for *The Rose,* 20th Century-Fox.

COSTUME DESIGN

Albert Wolsky for *All That Jazz,* 20th Century-Fox.

Judy Moorcroft for *The Europeans,* Merchant Ivory, Levitt-Pickman (United Kingdom).

Shirley Russell for *Agatha,* Warner Bros.

William Ware Theiss for *Butch and Sundance: The Early Days,* 20th Century-Fox.

Piero Tosi and Ambra Danon for *La Cage aux Folles,* United Artists (France).

VISUAL EFFECTS[241]

***Alien,* 20th Century-Fox. H. R. Giger, Carlo Rambaldi, Brian Johnson, Nick Allder, and Denys Ayling.**

The Black Hole, Disney, Buena Vista. Peter Ellenshaw, Art Cruickshank, Eustace Lycett, Danny Lee, Harrison Ellenshaw, and Joe Hale.

Moonraker, United Artists. Derek Meddings, Paul Wilson, and John Evans.

1941, Universal. William A. Fraker, A. D. Flowers, and Gregory Jein.

Star Trek—the Motion Picture, Paramount. Douglas Trumbull, John Dykstra, Richard Yuricich, Robert Swarthe, Dave Stewart, and Grant McCune.

FOREIGN LANGUAGE FILM

***The Tin Drum,* Federal Republic of Germany.**

The Maids of Wilko, Poland.

Mama Turns a Hundred, Spain.

A Simple Story, France.

To Forget Venice, Italy.

IRVING G. THALBERG MEMORIAL AWARD

Ray Stark.

JEAN HERSHOLT HUMANITARIAN AWARD

Robert Benjamin.

HONORARY AWARDS

Hal Elias, for his dedication and distinguished service to the Academy of Motion Picture Arts and Sciences.

Alec Guinness, for advancing the art of screen acting through a host of memorable and distinguished performances.

John O. Aalberg, Charles G. Clarke and John G. Frayne, in appreciation for outstanding service and dedication in upholding the high standards of the Academy of Motion Picture Arts and Sciences.[242]

SPECIAL ACHIEVEMENT AWARD

Sound Editing: Alan Splet for *The Black Stallion,* United Artists.

1980
Awards presented March 31, 1981.

PICTURE

***Ordinary People,* Wildwood Enterprises Inc. Production, Paramount. Produced by Ronald L. Schwary.**

Coal Miner's Daughter, Bernard Schwartz-Universal Pictures Production, Universal. Produced by Bernard Schwartz.

The Elephant Man, Brooksfilms, Ltd., Production, Paramount. Produced by Jonathan Sanger.

Raging Bull, Robert Chartoff-Irwin Winkler Production, United Artists.

Produced by Irwin Winkler and Robert Chartoff.

Tess, Renn-Burrill Co-production with the participation of the Société Française de Production (S.F.P.), Columbia (France/United Kingdom). Produced by Claude Berri, coproducer Timothy Burrill.

ACTOR

Robert De Niro in *Raging Bull,* United Artists.

Robert Duvall in *The Great Santini,* Orion.

John Hurt in *The Elephant Man,* Paramount.

Jack Lemmon in *Tribute,* 20th Century-Fox (Canada/U.S.).

Peter O'Toole in *The Stunt Man,* 20th Century-Fox.

ACTRESS

Sissy Spacek in *Coal Miner's Daughter,* Universal.

Ellen Burstyn in *Resurrection,* Universal.

Goldie Hawn in *Private Benjamin,* Warner Bros.

Mary Tyler Moore in *Ordinary People,* Paramount.

Gena Rowlands in *Gloria,* Columbia.

SUPPORTING ACTOR

Timothy Hutton[243] in *Ordinary People,* Paramount.

Judd Hirsch in *Ordinary People,* Paramount.

Michael O'Keefe in *The Great Santini,* Orion.

Joe Pesci in *Raging Bull,* United Artists.

Jason Robards in *Melvin and Howard,* Universal.

SUPPORTING ACTRESS

Mary Steenburgen in *Melvin and Howard,* Universal.

Eileen Brennan in *Private Benjamin,* Warner Bros.

---

[241] After being treated as a "special" award since 1972, visual special effects becomes a competitive award once more.

[242] Medals of commendation.

[243] At age nineteen, the youngest male to win an acting Oscar.

Eva Le Gallienne in *Resurrection,*
Universal.

Cathy Moriarty in *Raging Bull,* United
Artists.

Diana Scarwid in *Inside Moves,* Associated
Film Distribution.

DIRECTOR

**Robert Redford[244] for *Ordinary
People,* Paramount.**

David Lynch for *The Elephant Man,*
Paramount.

Roman Polanski for *Tess,* Columbia
(France/United Kingdom).

Richard Rush for *The Stunt Man,* 20th
Century-Fox.

Martin Scorsese for *Raging Bull,* United
Artists.

WRITING

(Screenplay Based on Material From
Another Medium)

**Alvin Sargent for *Ordinary People,*
Paramount.**

Christopher Devore, Eric Bergren, and
David Lynch for *The Elephant Man,*
Paramount.

Jonathan Hardy, David Stevens, and
Bruce Beresford for *Breaker Morant,*
New World Pictures/Quartet/Films
Incorporated (Australia).

Lawrence B. Marcus, screenplay; Richard
Rush, adaptation, for *The Stunt Man,*
20th Century-Fox.

Tom Rickman for *Coal Miner's Daughter,*
Universal.

(Screenplay Written Directly for the
Screen)

**Bo Goldman for *Melvin and Howard,*
Universal.**

Christopher Gore for *Fame,* MGM.

Jean Gruault for *Mon Oncle d'Amérique,*
New World Pictures (France).

Nancy Meyers, Charles Shyer, and
Harvey Miller for *Private Benjamin,*
Warner Bros.

W. D. Richter, screenplay; Richter and
Arthur Ross, story, for *Brubaker,* 20th
Century-Fox.

CINEMATOGRAPHY

**Geoffrey Unsworth and Ghislain
Cloquet for *Tess,* Columbia
(France/United Kingdom).**

Nestor Almendros for *The Blue Lagoon,*
Columbia.

Ralf D. Bode for *Coal Miner's Daughter,*
Universal.

Michael Chapman for *Raging Bull,* United
Artists.

James Crabe for *The Formula,* MGM.

ART DIRECTION—SET DECORATION

***Tess,* Columbia (France/United
Kingdom). Pierre Guffroy, Jack
Stephens.**

Coal Miner's Daughter, Universal. John W.
Corso; John M. Dwyer.

The Elephant Man, Paramount. Stuart
Craig, Bob Cartwright; Hugh Scaife.

The Empire Strikes Back, 20th Century-Fox.
Norman Reynolds, Leslie Dilley,
Harry Lange, and Alan Tomkins;
Michael Ford.

Kagemusha (The Shadow Warrior), 20th
Century-Fox (Japan). Yoshiro Muraki.

SOUND

***The Empire Strikes Back,* 20th
Century-Fox. Bill Varney, Steve
Maslow, Gregg Landaker, and
Peter Sutton.**

Altered States, Warner Bros. Arthur
Piantadosi, Les Fresholtz, Michael
Minkler, and Willie D. Burton.

Coal Miner's Daughter, Universal. Richard
Portman, Roger Heman, and Jim
Alexander.

Fame, MGM. Michael J. Kohut, Aaron
Rochin, Jay M. Harding, and Chris
Newman.

Raging Bull, United Artists. Donald O.
Mitchell, Bill Nicholson, David J.
Kimball, and Les Lazarowitz.

MUSIC

(Original Song)

**"Fame" from *Fame,* MGM. Music by
Michael Gore, lyrics by Dean
Pitchford.**

"9 to 5" from *9 to 5,* 20th Century-Fox.
Music and lyrics by Dolly Parton.

"On the Road Again" from *Honeysuckle
Rose,* Warner Bros. Music and lyrics
by Willie Nelson.

"Out Here on My Own" from *Fame,*
MGM. Music by Michael Gore, lyrics
by Lesley Gore.

"People Alone" from *The Competition,*
Columbia. Music by Lalo Schifrin,
lyrics by Wilbur Jennings.

(Original Score)[245]

Michael Gore for *Fame,* MGM.

John Corigliano for *Altered States,* Warner
Bros.

John Morris for *The Elephant Man,*
Paramount.

Philippe Sarde for *Tess,* Columbia
(France/United Kingdom).

John Williams for *The Empire Strikes Back,*
20th Century-Fox.

FILM EDITING

**Thelma Schoonmaker for *Raging
Bull,* United Artists.**

David Blewitt for *The Competition,*
Columbia.

Anne V. Coates for *The Elephant Man,*
Paramount.

Gerry Hambling for *Fame,* MGM.

Arthur Schmidt for *Coal Miner's Daughter,*
Universal.

COSTUME DESIGN

**Anthony Powell for *Tess,* Columbia
(France/United Kingdom).**

Jean-Pierre Dorleac for *Somewhere in Time,*
Universal.

Patricia Norris for *The Elephant Man,*
Paramount.

Anna Senior for *My Brilliant Career,*
Analysis Film Releasing (Australia).

Paul Zastupnevich for *When Time Ran Out,*
Warner Bros.

---

[244] Only person previously nominated for acting to receive an award as director of a film in which he did not appear.

[245] For the first time since the 1937 awards, there is only one category for musical scores.

FOREIGN LANGUAGE FILM

Moscow Does Not Believe in Tears,
   USSR.
Confidence, Hungary.
Kagemusha (The Shadow Warrior), Japan.
The Last Metro, France.
The Nest, Spain.

SPECIAL ACHIEVEMENT AWARD[246]

**Visual Effects: Brian Johnson,
   Richard Edlund, Dennis Muren
   and Bruce Nicholson for *The
   Empire Strikes Back,* 20th
   Century-Fox.**

HONORARY AWARDS

**Henry Fonda, the consummate
   actor, in recognition of his
   brilliant accomplishments and
   enduring contribution to the art
   of motion pictures.**

**Fred Hynes, in appreciation of
   outstanding service and
   dedication in upholding the
   high standards of the Academy
   of Motion Picture Arts and
   Sciences.[247]**

1981
Awards presented March 29, 1982.

PICTURE

***Chariots of Fire,* Enigma
   Productions, Ltd., The Ladd
   Company/Warner Bros. (United
   Kingdom). Produced by David
   Puttnam.**
Atlantic City, International Cinema
   Corporation Production, Paramount
   (U.S./France/Canada). Produced by
   Denis Heroux and John Kemeny.
On Golden Pond, ITC Films/IPC Films

Production, Universal. Produced by
   Bruce Gilbert.
Raiders of the Lost Ark, Lucasfilm, Ltd.,
   Production, Paramount. Produced by
   Frank Marshall.
Reds, J.R.S. Production, Paramount.
   Produced by Warren Beatty.[248]

ACTOR

**Henry Fonda[249] in *On Golden Pond,*
   Universal.**
Warren Beatty in *Reds,* Paramount.
Burt Lancaster in *Atlantic City,* Paramount
   (U.S./France/Canada).
Dudley Moore in *Arthur,* Orion.
Paul Newman in *Absence of Malice,*
   Columbia.

ACTRESS

**Katharine Hepburn[250] in *On Golden
   Pond,* Universal.**
Diane Keaton in *Reds,* Paramount.
Marsha Mason in *Only When I Laugh,*
   Columbia.
Susan Sarandon in *Atlantic City,*
   Paramount (U.S./France/Canada).
Meryl Streep in *The French Lieutenant's
   Woman,* United Artists (United
   Kingdom).

SUPPORTING ACTOR

John Gielgud in *Arthur,* Orion.
James Coco in *Only When I Laugh,*
   Columbia.
Ian Holm in *Chariots of Fire,* The Ladd
   Company/Warner Bros. (United
   Kingdom).
Jack Nicholson in *Reds,* Paramount.
Howard E. Rollins, Jr., in *Ragtime,*
   Paramount.

SUPPORTING ACTRESS

**Maureen Stapleton in *Reds,*
   Paramount.**

Melinda Dillon in *Absence of Malice,*
   Columbia.
Jane Fonda in *On Golden Pond,* Universal.
Joan Hackett in *Only When I Laugh,*
   Columbia.
Elizabeth McGovern in *Ragtime,*
   Paramount.

DIRECTOR

Warren Beatty for *Reds,* Paramount.
Hugh Hudson for *Chariots of Fire,* The
   Ladd Company/Warner Bros. (United
   Kingdom).
Louis Malle for *Atlantic City,* Paramount
   (U.S./France/Canada).
Mark Rydell for *On Golden Pond,*
   Universal.
Steven Spielberg for *Raiders of the Lost
   Ark,* Paramount.

WRITING

(Screenplay Based on Material From
   Another Medium)
**Ernest Thompson for *On Golden
   Pond,* Universal.**
Jay Presson Allen and Sidney Lumet for
   Prince of the City, Orion/Warner Bros.
Harold Pinter for *The French Lieutenant's
   Woman,* United Artists (United
   Kingdom).
Dennis Potter for *Pennies From Heaven,*
   MGM.
Michael Weller for *Ragtime,* Paramount.
(Screenplay Written Directly for the
   Screen)
**Colin Welland for *Chariots of Fire,*
   The Ladd Company/Warner
   Bros. (United Kingdom).**
Warren Beatty and Trevor Griffiths for
   Reds, Paramount.
Steve Gordon for *Arthur,* Orion.
John Guare for *Atlantic City,* Paramount
   (U.S./France/Canada).

---

[246] After one year as a competitive award, visual effects returns to noncompetitive status.
[247] Medal of commendation.
[248] For the second time (the first was the 1978 awards), Beatty is nominated as producer, actor, director, and writer—the only person to be so honored twice, and only the second person in Academy history (the first was Orson Welles, 1941) to be nominated simultaneously in all four categories.
[249] At age seventy-six Fonda is the oldest person to win the best actor Oscar. He is also the person who went the longest between acting nominations. It was forty-one years since his nomination for *The Grapes of Wrath.* He did, however, receive a nomination as producer of *12 Angry Men,* 1957, and an honorary award at the 1980 ceremonies.
[250] Hepburn's fourth Oscar and twelfth nomination make her the person most honored in the acting categories.

Kurt Luedtke for *Absence of Malice,* Columbia.

CINEMATOGRAPHY
Vittorio Storaro for *Reds,*. Paramount.
Miroslav Ondricek for *Ragtime,* Paramount.
Douglas Slocombe for *Raiders of the Lost Ark,* Paramount.
Alex Thomson for *Excalibur,* Orion.
Billy Williams for *On Golden Pond,* Universal.

ART DIRECTION—SET DECORATION
***Raiders of the Lost Ark,* Paramount. Norman Reynolds, Leslie Dilley; Michael Ford.**
The French Lieutenant's Woman, United Artists (United Kingdom). Assheton Gorton; Ann Mollo.
Heaven's Gate, United Artists. Tambi Larsen; Jim Berkey.
Ragtime, Paramount. John Graysmark, Patrizia Von Brandenstein, Anthony Reading; George De Titta, Sr., George De Titta, Jr., Peter Howitt.
Reds, Paramount. Richard Sylbert; Michael Seirton.

SOUND
***Raiders of the Lost Ark,* Paramount. Bill Varney, Steve Maslow, Gregg Landaker, and Roy Charman.**
On Golden Pond, Universal. Richard Portman and David Ronne.
Outland, The Ladd Company. John K. Wilkinson, Robert W. Glass, Jr., Robert M. Thirlwell, and Robin Gregory.
Pennies From Heaven, MGM. Michael J. Kohut, Jay M. Harding, Richard Tyler, and Al Overton.
Reds, Paramount. Dick Vorisek, Tom Fleischman, and Simon Kaye.

MUSIC
(Original Song)
"Arthur's Theme (Best That You Can Do)" from *Arthur,* Orion. Music and lyrics by Burt Bacharach, Carole Bayer Sager, Christopher Cross, and Peter Allen.
"Endless Love" from *Endless Love,* Universal. Music and lyrics by Lionel Richie.
"The First Time It Happens" from *The Great Muppet Caper,* Universal (United Kingdom). Music and lyrics by Joe Raposo.
"For Your Eyes Only" from *For Your Eyes Only,* United Artists (United Kingdom). Music by Bill Conti, lyrics by Mick Leeson.
"One More Hour" from *Ragtime,* Paramount. Music and lyrics by Randy Newman.
(Original Score)
Vangelis for *Chariots of Fire,* The Ladd Company/Warner Bros. (United Kingdom).
Dave Grusin for *On Golden Pond,* Universal.
Randy Newman for *Ragtime,* Paramount.
Alex North for *Dragonslayer,* Paramount.
John Williams for *Raiders of the Lost Ark,* Paramount.

FILM EDITING
Michael Kahn for *Raiders of the Lost Ark,* Paramount.
Dede Allen and Craig McKay for *Reds,* Paramount.
John Bloom for *The French Lieutenant's Woman,* United Artists (United Kingdom).
Terry Rawlings for *Chariots of Fire,* The Ladd Company/Warner Bros. (United Kingdom).
Robert L. Wolfe for *On Golden Pond,* Universal.

COSTUME DESIGN
Milena Canonero for *Chariots of Fire,* The Ladd Company/Warner Bros. (United Kingdom).
Anna Hill Johnstone for *Ragtime,* Paramount.
Bob Mackie for *Pennies From Heaven,* MGM.
Tom Rand for *The French Lieutenant's Woman,* United Artists (United Kingdom).
Shirley Russell for *Reds,* Paramount.

MAKEUP[251]
Rick Baker for *An American Werewolf in London,* Universal.
Stan Winston for *Heartbeeps,* Universal.

VISUAL EFFECTS
***Raiders of the Lost Ark,* Paramount. Richard Edlund, Kit West, Bruce Nicholson, and Joe Johnston.**
Dragonslayer, Paramount. Dennis Muren, Phil Tippett, Ken Ralston, and Brian Johnson.

FOREIGN LANGUAGE FILM
***Mephisto,* Hungary.**
The Boat Is Full, Switzerland.
Man of Iron, Poland.
Muddy River, Japan.
Three Brothers, Italy.

IRVING G. THALBERG MEMORIAL AWARD
Albert R. "Cubby" Broccoli.

JEAN HERSHOLT HUMANITARIAN AWARD
Danny Kaye.

GORDON E. SAWYER AWARD[252]
Joseph B. Walker.

HONORARY AWARD
Barbara Stanwyck, for superlative creativity and unique contribution to the art of screen acting.

SPECIAL ACHIEVEMENT AWARD
Sound Effects Editing: Ben Burtt and Richard L. Anderson for *Raiders of the Lost Ark,* Paramount.

---

[251] New category.
[252] New award, honoring scientific or technical achievement.

1982

Awards presented April 11, 1983.

PICTURE

Gandhi, Indo-British Film Production, Columbia (United Kingdom). Produced by Richard Attenborough.

E.T. The Extra-Terrestrial, Universal. Produced by Steven Spielberg and Kathleen Kennedy.

Missing, Universal Pictures/Polygram Pictures Presentation of an Edward Lewis Production, Universal. Produced by Edward Lewis and Mildred Lewis.

Tootsie, Mirage/Punch Production, Columbia. Produced by Sydney Pollack and Dick Richards.

The Verdict, Fox-Zanuck/Brown Production, 20th Century-Fox. Produced by Richard D. Zanuck and David Brown.

ACTOR

Ben Kingsley in *Gandhi,* Columbia (United Kingdom).

Dustin Hoffman in *Tootsie,* Columbia.

Jack Lemmon in *Missing,* Universal.

Paul Newman in *The Verdict,* 20th Century-Fox.

Peter O'Toole in *My Favorite Year,* MGM/United Artists.[253]

ACTRESS

Meryl Streep in *Sophie's Choice,* Universal/AFD.

Julie Andrews in *Victor/Victoria,* MGM/United Artists.

Jessica Lange in *Frances,* Universal/AFD.

Sissy Spacek in *Missing,* Universal.

Debra Winger in *An Officer and a Gentleman,* Paramount.

SUPPORTING ACTOR

Louis Gossett, Jr., in *An Officer and a Gentleman,* Paramount.

Charles Durning in *The Best Little Whorehouse in Texas,* Universal.

John Lithgow in *The World According to Garp,* Warner Bros.

James Mason in *The Verdict,* 20th Century-Fox.

Robert Preston in *Victor/Victoria,* MGM/United Artists.

SUPPORTING ACTRESS

Jessica Lange in *Tootsie,* Columbia.

Glenn Close in *The World According to Garp,* Warner Bros.

Teri Garr in *Tootsie,* Columbia.

Kim Stanley in *Frances,* Universal/AFD.

Lesley Ann Warren in *Victor/Victoria,* MGM/United Artists.

DIRECTOR

Richard Attenborough for *Gandhi,* Columbia (United Kingdom).

Sidney Lumet for *The Verdict,* 20th Century-Fox.

Wolfgang Petersen for *Das Boot,* Columbia (Federal Republic of Germany).[254]

Sydney Pollack for *Tootsie,* Columbia.

Steven Spielberg for *E.T. The Extra-Terrestrial,* Universal.

WRITING

(Screenplay Based on Material From Another Medium)

Costa-Gavras and Donald Stewart for *Missing,* Universal.

Blake Edwards for *Victor/Victoria,* MGM/United Artists.

David Mamet for *The Verdict,* 20th Century-Fox.

Wolfgang Petersen for *Das Boot,* Columbia/PSO (Federal Republic of Germany).

Alan J. Pakula for *Sophie's Choice,* Universal/AFD.

(Screenplay Written Directly for the Screen)

John Briley for *Gandhi,* Columbia (United Kingdom).

Larry Gelbart and Murray Schisgal,

screenplay; Don McGuire and Larry Gelbart, story, for *Tootsie,* Columbia.

Barry Levinson for *Diner,* MGM/United Artists.

Melissa Mathison for *E.T. The Extra-Terrestrial,* Universal.

Douglas Day Stewart for *An Officer and a Gentleman,* Paramount.

CINEMATOGRAPHY

Billy Williams and Ronnie Taylor for *Gandhi,* Columbia (United Kingdom).

Nestor Almendros for *Sophie's Choice,* Universal/AFD.

Allen Daviau for *E.T. The Extra-Terrestrial,* Universal.

Owen Roizman for *Tootsie,* Columbia.

Jost Vacano for *Das Boot,* Columbia/PSO (Federal Republic of Germany).

ART DIRECTION—SET DECORATION

Gandhi, Columbia (United Kingdom). Stuart Craig, Bob Laing; Michael Seirton.

Annie, Columbia. Dale Hennesy; Marvin March.

Blade Runner, The Ladd Company/Sir Run Run Shaw. Lawrence G. Paull, David Snyder; Linda DeScenna.

La Traviata, Universal Classics (Italy/France). Franco Zeffirelli; Gianni Quaranta.

Victor/Victoria, MGM/United Artists. Rodger Maus, Tim Hutchinson, William Craig Smith; Harry Cordwell.

SOUND

E.T. The Extra-Terrestrial, Universal. Buzz Knudson, Robert Glass, Don Digirolamo, and Gene Cantamessa.

Das Boot, Columbia (Federal Republic of Germany). Milan Bor, Trevor Pyke, and Mike Le-Mare.

Gandhi, Columbia (United Kingdom). Gerry Humphreys, Robin

---

[253] O'Toole's seventh nomination puts him in a tie with Richard Burton for most acting nominations without a win.

[254] With six nominations, *Das Boot* sets a record for nominations for a foreign language film. The record will be tied the following year by *Fanny & Alexander.*

O'Donoghue, Jonathan Bates, and Simon Kaye.

Tootsie, Columbia. Arthur Piantadosi, Les Fresholtz, Dick Alexander, and Les Lazarowitz.

Tron, Disney, Buena Vista. Michael Minkler, Bob Minkler, Lee Minkler, and Jim La Rue.

MUSIC

(Song)

"Up Where We Belong" from *An Officer and a Gentleman,* Paramount. Music by Jack Nitzsche and Buffy Sainte-Marie, lyrics by Will Jennings.

"Eye of the Tiger" from *Rocky III,* MGM/United Artists. Music and lyrics by Jim Peterik and Frankie Sullivan III.

"How Do You Keep the Music Playing?" from *Best Friends,* Warner Bros. Music by Michel Legrand, lyrics by Alan Bergman and Marilyn Bergman.

"If We Were in Love" from *Yes, Giorgio,* MGM/United Artists. Music by John Williams, lyrics by Alan Bergman and Marilyn Bergman.

"It Might Be You" from *Tootsie,* Columbia. Music by Dave Grusin, lyrics by Alan Bergman and Marilyn Bergman.

(Original Score)

John Williams for *E.T. The Extra-Terrestrial,* Universal.

Jerry Goldsmith for *Poltergeist,* MGM/United Artists.

Marvin Hamlisch for *Sophie's Choice,* Universal/AFD.

Jack Nitzsche for *An Officer and a Gentleman,* Paramount.

Ravi Shankar and George Fenton for *Gandhi,* Columbia (United Kingdom).

(Original Song Score and Its Adaptation, or Adaptation Score)[255]

Henry Mancini and Leslie Bricusse for song score and Mancini for

adaptation score for *Victor/Victoria,* **MGM/United Artists.**

Ralph Burns for adaptation score for *Annie,* Columbia.

Tom Waits for song score for *One From the Heart,* Columbia.

FILM EDITING

John Bloom for *Gandhi,* Columbia (United Kingdom).

Carol Littleton for *E.T. The Extra-Terrestrial,* Universal.

Hannes Nikel for *Das Boot,* Columbia/PSO (West Germany).

Fredric Steinkamp and William Steinkamp for *Tootsie,* Columbia.

Peter Zinner for *An Officer and a Gentleman,* Paramount.

COSTUME DESIGN

John Mollo and Bhanu Athaiya for *Gandhi,* Columbia (United Kingdom).

Elois Jenssen and Rosanna Norton for *Tron,* Disney, Buena Vista.

Patricia Norris for *Victor/Victoria,* MGM/United Artists.

Piero Tosi for *La Traviata,* Universal Classics (Italy/France).

Albert Wolsky for *Sophie's Choice,* Universal/AFD.

MAKEUP

Sarah Monzani and Michèle Burke for *Quest for Fire,* 20th Century-Fox (France/Canada).

Tom Smith for *Gandhi,* Columbia (United Kingdom).

VISUAL EFFECTS

E.T. The Extra-Terrestrial, Universal. Carlo Rambaldi, Dennis Muren, and Kenneth F. Smith.

Blade Runner, The Ladd Company/Sir Run Run Shaw. Douglas Trumbull, Richard Yuricich, and David Dryer.

Poltergeist, MGM/United Artists. Richard

Edlund, Michael Wood, and Bruce Nicholson.

SOUND EFFECTS EDITING[256]

E.T. The Extra-Terrestrial, Universal. Charles L. Campbell and Ben Burtt.

Das Boot, Columbia/PSO (Federal Republic of Germany). Mike Le-Mare.

Poltergeist, MGM/United Artists. Stephen Hunter Flick and Richard L. Anderson.

FOREIGN LANGUAGE FILM

Volver a Empezar (To Begin Again), Spain.

Alsino and the Condor, Nicaragua.

Coup de Torchon (Clean Slate), France.

The Flight of the Eagle, Sweden.

Private Life, USSR.

JEAN HERSHOLT HUMANITARIAN AWARD

Walter Mirisch.

GORDON E. SAWYER AWARD

John O. Aalberg.

HONORARY AWARD

Mickey Rooney, for 50 years of versatility in a variety of memorable film performances.

1983

Awards presented April 9, 1984.

PICTURE

Terms of Endearment, James L. Brooks Production, Paramount. Produced by James L. Brooks.[257]

The Big Chill, Carson Productions Group Production, Columbia. Produced by Michael Shamberg.

The Dresser, Goldcrest Films/Television Limited/World Film Services

---

[255] Category reintroduced.
[256] New category.
[257] Brooks is the fourth person to win Oscars as producer, director, and writer on a single film. Leo McCarey for *Going My Way* (1944), Billy Wilder for *The Apartment* (1960), and Francis Ford Coppola for *The Godfather, Part II* (1974) also won three in those categories.

Production, Columbia (U.S./United Kingdom). Produced by Peter Yates.

The Right Stuff, Robert Chartoff-Irwin Winkler Production, The Ladd Company through Warner Bros. Produced by Irwin Winkler and Robert Chartoff.

Tender Mercies, EMI Presentation of an Antron Media Production, Universal/AFD. Produced by Philip S. Hobel.

ACTOR

Robert Duvall in *Tender Mercies*, Universal/AFD.

Michael Caine in *Educating Rita*, Columbia (United Kingdom).

Tom Conti in *Reuben, Reuben*, 20th Century-Fox International Classics.

Tom Courtenay in *The Dresser*, Columbia (U.S./United Kingdom).

Albert Finney in *The Dresser*, Columbia (U.S./United Kingdom).

ACTRESS

Shirley MacLaine in *Terms of Endearment*, Paramount.

Jane Alexander in *Testament*, Paramount.

Meryl Streep in *Silkwood*, 20th Century-Fox.

Julie Walters in *Educating Rita*, Columbia (United Kingdom).

Debra Winger in *Terms of Endearment*, Paramount.

SUPPORTING ACTOR

Jack Nicholson in *Terms of Endearment*, Paramount.

Charles Durning in *To Be or Not to Be*, 20th Century-Fox.

John Lithgow in *Terms of Endearment*, Paramount.

Sam Shepard in *The Right Stuff*, Warner Bros.

Rip Torn in *Cross Creek*, Universal.

SUPPORTING ACTRESS

Linda Hunt[258] in *The Year of Living Dangerously*, MGM/United Artists (Australia).

Cher in *Silkwood*, 20th Century-Fox.

Glenn Close in *The Big Chill*, Columbia.

Amy Irving in *Yentl*, MGM/United Artists.

Alfre Woodard in *Cross Creek*, Universal.

DIRECTOR

James L. Brooks for *Terms of Endearment*, Paramount.

Bruce Beresford for *Tender Mercies*, Universal/AFD.

Ingmar Bergman for *Fanny & Alexander*, Embassy (Sweden).

Mike Nichols for *Silkwood*, 20th Century-Fox.

Peter Yates for *The Dresser*, Columbia (U.S./United Kingdom).

WRITING

(Screenplay Based on Material From Another Medium)

James L. Brooks for *Terms of Endearment*, Paramount.

Julius J. Epstein for *Reuben, Reuben*, 20th Century-Fox International Classics.

Ronald Harwood for *The Dresser*, Columbia (U.S./United Kingdom).

Harold Pinter for *Betrayal*, 20th Century-Fox International Classics (United Kingdom).

Willy Russell for *Educating Rita*, Columbia (United Kingdom).

(Screenplay Written Directly for the Screen)

Horton Foote for *Tender Mercies*, Universal/AFD.

Ingmar Bergman for *Fanny & Alexander*, Embassy (Sweden).

Nora Ephron and Alice Arlen for *Silkwood*, 20th Century-Fox.

Lawrence Kasdan and Barbara Benedek for *The Big Chill*, Columbia.

Lawrence Lasker and Walter F. Parkes for *WarGames*, MGM/United Artists.

CINEMATOGRAPHY

Sven Nykvist for *Fanny & Alexander*, Embassy (Sweden).

Caleb Deschanel for *The Right Stuff*, The Ladd Company through Warner Bros.

William A. Fraker for *WarGames*, MGM/United Artists.

Don Peterman for *Flashdance*, Paramount.

Gordon Willis for *Zelig*, Orion/Warner Bros. through Warner Bros.

ART DIRECTION—SET DECORATION

Fanny & Alexander, Embassy (Sweden). Anna Asp.

Return of the Jedi, 20th Century-Fox. Norman Reynolds, Fred Hole, James Schoppe; Michael Ford.

The Right Stuff, The Ladd Company through Warner Bros. Geoffrey Kirkland, Richard J. Lawrence, W. Stewart Campbell, Peter Romero; Pat Pending, George R. Nelson.

Terms of Endearment, Paramount. Polly Platt, Harold Michelson; Tom Pedigo, Anthony Mondello.

Yentl, MGM/United Artists. Roy Walker, Leslie Tomkins; Tessa Davies.

SOUND

The Right Stuff, The Ladd Company through Warner Bros. Mark Berger, Tom Scott, Randy Thom, and David MacMillan.

Never Cry Wolf, Disney, Buena Vista. Alan R. Splet, Todd Boekelheide, Randy Thom, and David Parker.

Return of the Jedi, 20th Century-Fox. Ben Burtt, Gary Summers, Randy Thom, and Tony Dawe.

Terms of Endearment, Paramount. Donald O. Mitchell, Rick Kline, Kevin O'Connell, and Jim Alexander.

WarGames, MGM/United Artists. Michael J. Kohut, Carlos de Larios, Aaron Rochin, and Willie D. Burton.

MUSIC

(Song)

"Flashdance . . . What a Feeling" from *Flashdance*, Paramount. Music by Giorgio Moroder, lyrics by Keith Forsey and Irene Cara.

"Maniac" from *Flashdance*, Paramount.

---

[258] Only person to win an Oscar for playing a member of the opposite sex.

Music and lyrics by Michael Sembello and Dennis Matkosky.

"Over You" from *Tender Mercies*, Universal/AFD. Music and lyrics by Austin Roberts and Bobby Hart.

"Papa, Can You Hear Me?" from *Yentl*, MGM/United Artists. Music by Michel Legrand, lyrics by Alan Bergman and Marilyn Bergman.

"The Way He Makes Me Feel" from *Yentl*, MGM/United Artists. Music by Michel Legrand, lyrics by Alan Bergman and Marilyn Bergman.

(Original Score)

Bill Conti for *The Right Stuff*, The Ladd Company through Warner Bros.

Jerry Goldsmith for *Under Fire*, Orion.

Michael Gore for *Terms of Endearment*, Paramount.

Leonard Rosenman for *Cross Creek*, Universal.

John Williams for *Return of the Jedi*, 20th Century-Fox.

(Original Song Score or Adaptation Score)[259]

Michel Legrand, Alan Bergman, and Marilyn Bergman for song score for *Yentl*, MGM/United Artists.

Elmer Bernstein for adaptation score for *Trading Places*, Paramount.

Lalo Schifrin for adaptation score for *The Sting II*, Universal.

FILM EDITING

Glenn Farr, Lisa Fruchtman, Stephen A. Rotter, Douglas Stewart, and Tom Rolf for *The Right Stuff*, The Ladd Company through Warner Bros.

Richard Marks for *Terms of Endearment*, Paramount.

Frank Morriss and Edward Abroms for *Blue Thunder*, Columbia.

Sam O'Steen for *Silkwood*, 20th Century-Fox.

Bud Smith and Walt Mulconery for *Flashdance*, Paramount.

COSTUME DESIGN

Marik Vos for *Fanny & Alexander*, Embassy (Sweden).

Santo Loquasto for *Zelig*, Orion/Warner Bros. through Warner Bros.

Anne-Marie Marchand for *The Return of Martin Guerre*, European International Distribution (France).

William Ware Theiss for *Heart Like a Wheel*, 20th Century-Fox.

Joe I. Tompkins for *Cross Creek*, Universal.

SOUND EFFECTS EDITING

Jay Boekelheide for *The Right Stuff*, The Ladd Company through Warner Bros.

Ben Burtt for *Return of the Jedi*, 20th Century-Fox.

FOREIGN LANGUAGE FILM

***Fanny & Alexander*, Sweden.**[260]

Carmen, Spain.

Entre Nous, France.

Job's Revolt, Hungary.

Le Bal, Algeria.

JEAN HERSHOLT HUMANITARIAN AWARD

M. J. "Mike" Frankovich.

GORDON E. SAWYER AWARD

John G. Frayne.

HONORARY AWARD

Hal Roach, in recognition of his unparalleled record of distinguished contributions to the motion picture art form.

SPECIAL ACHIEVEMENT AWARD

Visual Effects: Richard Edlund, Dennis Muren, Ken Ralston, and Phil Tippett for *Return of the Jedi*, 20th Century-Fox.

1984
Awards presented March 25, 1985.

PICTURE

***Amadeus*, Saul Zaentz Company Production, Orion. Produced by Saul Zaentz.**

The Killing Fields, Enigma Productions, Ltd., Warner Bros. (United Kingdom). Produced by David Puttnam.

A Passage to India, G.W. Films, Ltd., Production, Columbia (United Kingdom). Produced by John Brabourne and Richard Goodwin.

Places in the Heart, Tri-Star. Produced by Arlene Donovan.

A Soldier's Story, Caldix Films Production, Columbia. Produced by Norman Jewison, Ronald L. Schwary, and Patrick Palmer.

ACTOR

F. Murray Abraham in *Amadeus*, Orion.

Jeff Bridges in *Starman*, Columbia.

Albert Finney in *Under the Volcano*, Universal.

Tom Hulce in *Amadeus*, Orion.

Sam Waterston in *The Killing Fields*, Warner Bros.

ACTRESS

Sally Field in *Places in the Heart*, Tri-Star.

Judy Davis in *A Passage to India*, Columbia (United Kingdom).

Jessica Lange in *Country*, Touchstone, Buena Vista.

Vanessa Redgrave in *The Bostonians*, Merchant Ivory, Almi (United Kingdom).

Sissy Spacek in *The River*, Universal.

SUPPORTING ACTOR

Haing S. Ngor in *The Killing Fields*, Warner Bros.

Adolph Caesar in *A Soldier's Story*, Caldix, Columbia.

---

[259] Category renamed.
[260] With four Oscars, the most honored foreign language film.

John Malkovich in *Places in the Heart*, Tri-Star.

Noriyuki "Pat" Morita in *The Karate Kid*, Columbia.

Ralph Richardson in *Greystoke: The Legend of Tarzan, Lord of the Apes*, Warner Bros. (United Kingdom).

SUPPORTING ACTRESS

Peggy Ashcroft in *A Passage to India*, Columbia (United Kingdom).

Glenn Close in *The Natural*, Tri-Star.

Lindsay Crouse in *Places in the Heart*, Tri-Star.

Christine Lahti in *Swing Shift*, Warner Bros.

Geraldine Page in *The Pope of Greenwich Village*, MGM/United Artists.

DIRECTOR

Milos Forman for *Amadeus*, Orion.

Woody Allen for *Broadway Danny Rose*, Orion.

Robert Benton for *Places in the Heart*, Tri-Star.

Roland Joffé for *The Killing Fields*, Warner Bros. (United Kingdom).

David Lean for *A Passage to India*, Columbia (United Kingdom).

WRITING

(Screenplay Based on Material From Another Medium)

Peter Shaffer for *Amadeus*, Orion.

Charles Fuller for *A Soldier's Story*, Columbia.

David Lean for *A Passage to India*, Columbia (United Kingdom).

Bruce Robinson for *The Killing Fields*, Warner Bros. (United Kingdom).

P. H. Vazak[261] and Michael Austin for *Greystoke: The Legend of Tarzan, Lord of the Apes*, Warner Bros. (United Kingdom).

(Screenplay Written Directly for the Screen)

Robert Benton for *Places in the Heart*, Tri-Star.

Woody Allen for *Broadway Danny Rose*, Orion.

Lowell Ganz, Babaloo Mandel, and Bruce Jay Friedman, screenplay; Bruce Jay Friedman, screen story; based on a story by Brian Grazer, for *Splash*, Touchstone, Buena Vista.

Gregory Nava and Anna Thomas for *El Norte*, Cinecom International/Island Alive.

Daniel Petrie, Jr., screenplay; Danilo Bach and Daniel Petrie, Jr., story, for *Beverly Hills Cop*, Paramount.

CINEMATOGRAPHY

Chris Menges for *The Killing Fields*, Warner Bros. (United Kingdom).

Ernest Day for *A Passage to India*, Columbia (United Kingdom).

Caleb Deschanel for *The Natural*, Tri-Star.

Miroslav Ondricek for *Amadeus*, Orion.

Vilmos Zsigmond for *The River*, Universal.

ART DIRECTION—SET DECORATION

Amadeus, Orion. Patrizia Von Brandenstein; Karel Cerny.

The Cotton Club, Orion. Richard Sylbert; George Gaines, Les Bloom.

The Natural, Tri-Star. Angelo Graham, Mel Bourne, James J. Murakami, Speed Hopkins; Bruce Weintraub.

A Passage to India, Columbia (United Kingdom). John Box, Leslie Tomkins; Hugh Scaife.

2010, MGM/United Artists. Albert Brenner; Rick Simpson.

SOUND

Amadeus, Orion. Mark Berger, Tom Scott, Todd Boekelheide, and Chris Newman.

Dune, Universal. Bill Varney, Steve Maslow, Kevin O'Connell, and Nelson Stoll.

A Passage to India, Columbia (United Kingdom). Graham V. Hartstone, Nicolas Le Messurier, Michael A. Carter, and John Mitchell.

The River, Universal. Nick Alphin, Robert Thirlwell, Richard Portman, and David Ronne.

2010, MGM/United Artists. Michael J. Kohut, Aaron Rochin, Carlos De Larios, and Gene S. Cantamessa.

MUSIC

(Song)

"I Just Called to Say I Love You" from *The Woman in Red*, Orion. Music and lyrics by Stevie Wonder.

"Against All Odds (Take a Look at Me Now)" from *Against All Odds*, Columbia. Music and lyrics by Phil Collins.

"Footloose" from *Footloose*, Paramount. Music and lyrics by Kenny Loggins and Dean Pitchford.

"Ghostbusters" from *Ghostbusters*, Columbia. Music and lyrics by Ray Parker, Jr.

"Let's Hear It for the Boy" from *Footloose*, Paramount. Music and lyrics by Dean Pitchford and Tom Snow.

(Original Score)

Maurice Jarre for *A Passage to India*, Columbia (United Kingdom).

Randy Newman for *The Natural*, Tri-Star.

Alex North for *Under the Volcano*, Universal.[262]

John Williams for *Indiana Jones and the Temple of Doom*, Paramount.

John Williams for *The River*, Universal.

(Original Song Score)[263]

Prince for *Purple Rain*, Warner Bros.

Kris Kristofferson for *Songwriter*, Tri-Star.

Jeff Moss for *The Muppets Take Manhattan*, Tri-Star.

---

[261] Pseudonym of Robert Towne, who so disliked the changes made in his screenplay that he accepted credit only in the name of his dog.
[262] North's fifteenth unsuccessful nomination ties the record set by art director Roland Anderson at the 1963 awards. North, however, will receive an honorary award at the 1985 ceremonies, while Anderson remained unhonored.
[263] Category renamed.

FILM EDITING

Jim Clark for *The Killing Fields*, Warner Bros. (United Kingdom).

Donn Cambern and Frank Morriss for *Romancing the Stone*, 20th Century-Fox.

Nena Danevic and Michael Chandler for *Amadeus*, Orion.

David Lean for *A Passage to India*, Columbia (United Kingdom).

Barry Malkin and Robert Q. Lovett for *The Cotton Club*, Orion.

COSTUME DESIGN

Theodor Pistek for *Amadeus*, Orion.

Jenny Beavan and John Bright for *The Bostonians*, Merchant Ivory, Almi (United Kingdom).

Judy Moorcroft for *A Passage to India*, Columbia (United Kingdom).

Patricia Norris for *2010*, MGM/United Artists.

Ann Roth for *Places in the Heart*, Tri-Star.

MAKEUP

Paul LeBlanc and Dick Smith for *Amadeus*, Orion.

Rick Baker and Paul Engelen for *Greystoke: The Legend of Tarzan, Lord of the Apes*, Warner Bros. (United Kingdom).

Michael Westmore for *2010*, MGM/United Artists.

VISUAL EFFECTS

***Indiana Jones and the Temple of Doom*, Paramount. Dennis Muren, Michael McAlister, Lorne Peterson, and George Gibbs.**

Ghostbusters, Columbia. Richard Edlund, John Bruno, Mark Vargo, and Chuck Gasper.

2010, MGM/United Artists. Richard Edlund, Neil Krepela, George Jenson, and Mark Stetson.

FOREIGN LANGUAGE FILM

***Dangerous Moves*, Switzerland.**

Beyond the Walls, Israel.

Camila, Argentina.

Double Feature, Spain.

Wartime Romance, USSR.

JEAN HERSHOLT HUMANITARIAN AWARD

David L. Wolper.

GORDON E. SAWYER AWARD

Linwood G. Dunn.

HONORARY AWARDS

The National Endowment of the Arts, in recognition of its 20th anniversary and its dedicated commitment to fostering artistic and creative activity and excellence in every area of the arts.

James Stewart, for his 50 years of meaningful performances, for his high ideals, both on and off the screen, with the respect and affection of his colleagues.

SPECIAL ACHIEVEMENT AWARD

Sound Effects Editing: Kay Rose for *The River*, Universal.

1985
Awards presented March 24, 1986.

PICTURE

***Out of Africa*, Universal. Produced by Sydney Pollack.**

The Color Purple, Warner Bros. Produced by Steven Spielberg, Kathleen Kennedy, Frank Marshall, and Quincy Jones.[264]

Kiss of the Spider Woman, H.B. Filmes Production in association with Sugarloaf Films, Island Alive (Brazil). Produced by David Weisman.

Prizzi's Honor, ABC Motion Pictures Production, 20th Century Fox. Produced by John Foreman.

Witness, Edward S. Feldman Production, Paramount. Produced by Edward S. Feldman.

ACTOR[265]

William Hurt in *Kiss of the Spider Woman*, Island Alive (Brazil).

Harrison Ford in *Witness*, Paramount.

James Garner in *Murphy's Romance*, Columbia.

Jack Nicholson in *Prizzi's Honor*, 20th Century Fox.

Jon Voight in *Runaway Train*, Cannon.

ACTRESS

Geraldine Page in *The Trip to Bountiful*, Island.[266]

Anne Bancroft in *Agnes of God*, Columbia.

Whoopi Goldberg in *The Color Purple*, Warner Bros.

Jessica Lange in *Sweet Dreams*, Tri-Star.

Meryl Streep in *Out of Africa*, Universal.

SUPPORTING ACTOR

Don Ameche in *Cocoon*, 20th Century Fox.

Klaus Maria Brandauer in *Out of Africa*, Universal.

William Hickey in *Prizzi's Honor*, 20th Century Fox.

Robert Loggia in *Jagged Edge*, Columbia.

Eric Roberts in *Runaway Train*, Cannon.

SUPPORTING ACTRESS

Anjelica Huston[267] in *Prizzi's Honor*, 20th Century Fox.

Margaret Avery in *The Color Purple*, Warner Bros.

Amy Madigan in *Twice in a Lifetime*, Bud Yorkin Productions.

Meg Tilly in *Agnes of God*, Columbia.

Oprah Winfrey in *The Color Purple*, Warner Bros.

---

[264] Ties with *The Turning Point*, 1977, for the most nominations (eleven) without winning any Oscars.

[265] Only time in the history of the Oscars that all ten nominees in the leading-role categories have been American-born.

[266] First person to win an acting Oscar after seven previously unsuccessful nominations. Richard Burton and Peter O'Toole are tied for the most unsuccessful nominations, seven. Deborah Kerr and Thelma Ritter had six each.

[267] First person to be directed to an Oscar by her own father, John Huston. First Oscar winner whose father and grandfather (Walter Huston) are also Oscar winners.

DIRECTOR

Sydney Pollack for *Out of Africa*, Universal.

Hector Babenco for *Kiss of the Spider Woman*, Island Alive (Brazil).

John Huston[268] for *Prizzi's Honor*, 20th Century Fox.

Akira Kurosawa for *Ran*, Orion Classics (Japan).

Peter Weir for *Witness*, Paramount.

WRITING

(Screenplay Based on Material From Another Medium)

Kurt Luedtke for *Out of Africa*, Universal.

Richard Condon and Janet Roach for *Prizzi's Honor*, 20th Century Fox.

Horton Foote for *The Trip to Bountiful*, Island.

Menno Meyjes for *The Color Purple*, Warner Bros.

Leonard Schrader for *Kiss of the Spider Woman*, Island Alive (Brazil).

(Screenplay Written Directly for the Screen)

Earl W. Wallace and William Kelley, screenplay; William Kelley, Pamela Wallace, and Earl W. Wallace, story, for *Witness*, Paramount.

Woody Allen for *The Purple Rose of Cairo*, Orion.

Terry Gilliam, Tom Stoppard, and Charles McKeown for *Brazil*, Universal (United Kingdom).

Luis Puenzo and Aida Bortnik for *The Official Story*, Almi (Argentina).

Robert Zemeckis and Bob Gale for *Back to the Future*, Universal.

CINEMATOGRAPHY

David Watkin for *Out of Africa*, Universal.

Allen Daviau for *The Color Purple*, Warner Bros.

William A. Fraker for *Murphy's Romance*, Columbia.

Takao Saito, Masaharu Ueda, and Asakazu Nakai for *Ran*, Orion Classics (Japan).

John Seale for *Witness*, Paramount.

ART DIRECTION—SET DECORATION

***Out of Africa*, Universal. Stephen Grimes; Josie MacAvin.**

Brazil, Universal (United Kingdom). Norman Garwood; Maggie Gray.

The Color Purple, Warner Bros. J. Michael Riva, Robert W. Welch; Linda De Scenna.

Ran, Orion Classics (Japan). Yoshiro Muraki and Shinobu Muraki.

Witness, Paramount. Stan Jolley; John Anderson.

SOUND

***Out of Africa*, Universal. Chris Jenkins, Gary Alexander, Larry Stensvold, and Peter Handford.**

Back to the Future, Universal. Bill Varney, B. Tennyson Sebastian II, Robert Thirlwell, and William B. Kaplan.

A Chorus Line, Columbia. Donald O. Mitchell, Michael Minkler, Gerry Humphreys, and Chris Newman.

Ladyhawke, Warner Bros. Les Fresholtz, Dick Alexander, Vern Poore, and Bud Alper.

Silverado, Columbia. Donald O. Mitchell, Rick Kline, Kevin O'Connell, and David Ronne.

MUSIC

(Song)

"Say You, Say Me" from *White Nights*, Columbia. Music and lyrics by Lionel Richie.

"Miss Celie's Blues (Sister)" from *The Color Purple*, Warner Bros. Music by Quincy Jones and Rod Temperton, lyrics by Quincy Jones, Rod Temperton, and Lionel Richie.

"Power of Love" from *Back to the Future*, Universal. Music by Chris Hayes and Johnny Colla, lyrics by Huey Lewis.

"Separate Lives" (Love Theme from *White Nights*)" from *White Nights*, Columbia. Music and lyrics by Stephen Bishop.

"Surprise, Surprise" from *A Chorus Line*, Columbia. Music by Marvin Hamlisch, lyrics by Edward Kleban.

(Original Score)[269]

John Barry for *Out of Africa*, Universal.

Bruce Broughton for *Silverado*, Columbia.

Georges Delerue for *Agnes of God*, Columbia.

Maurice Jarre for *Witness*, Paramount.

Quincy Jones, Jeremy Lubbock, Rod Temperton, Caiphus Semenya, Andrae Crouch, Chris Boardman, Jorge Calandrelli, Joel Rosenbaum, Fred Steiner, Jack Hayes, Jerry Hey, and Randy Kerber for *The Color Purple*, Warner Bros.[270]

FILM EDITING

Thom Noble for *Witness*, Paramount.

John Bloom for *A Chorus Line*, Columbia.

Rudi Fehr and Kaja Fehr for *Prizzi's Honor*, 20th Century Fox.

Henry Richardson for *Runaway Train*, Cannon.

Fredric Steinkamp, William Steinkamp, Pembroke Herring, and Sheldon Kahn for *Out of Africa*, Universal.

COSTUME DESIGN

Emi Wada for *Ran*, Orion Classics (Japan).

Milena Canonero for *Out of Africa*, Universal.

Donfeld for *Prizzi's Honor*, 20th Century Fox.

Aggie Guerard Rodgers for *The Color Purple*, Warner Bros.

Albert Wolsky for *The Journey of Natty Gann*, Disney, Buena Vista.

MAKEUP

Michael Westmore and Zoltan Elek for *Mask*, Universal.

---

[268] At age seventy-nine, the oldest person ever nominated for a directing Oscar.

[269] Henceforth, there is only one scoring category.

[270] Most people ever nominated for a single film in any category.

Ken Chase for *The Color Purple,* Warner Bros.

Carl Fullerton for *Remo Williams: The Adventure Begins,* Orion.

VISUAL EFFECTS

Cocoon, 20th Century Fox. Ken Ralston, Ralph McQuarrie, Scott Farrar, and David Berry.

Return to Oz, Disney, Buena Vista. Will Vinton, Ian Wingrove, Zoran Perisic, and Michael Lloyd.

Young Sherlock Holmes, Paramount. Dennis Muren, Kit West, John Ellis, and David Allen.

SOUND EFFECTS EDITING

Back to the Future, Universal. Charles L. Campbell and Robert Rutledge.

Ladyhawke, Warner Bros. Bob Henderson and Alan Murray.

Rambo: First Blood Part II, Tri-Star. Frederick J. Brown.

FOREIGN LANGUAGE FILM

The Official Story, Argentina.

Angry Harvest, Federal Republic of Germany.

Colonel Redl, Hungary.

Three Men and a Cradle, France.

When Father Was Away on Business, Yugoslavia.

JEAN HERSHOLT HUMANITARIAN AWARD

Charles "Buddy" Rogers.

HONORARY AWARDS

Paul Newman, in recognition of his many memorable and compelling screen performances and for his personal integrity and dedication to his craft.

Alex North, in recognition of his brilliant artistry in the creation of memorable music for a host of distinguished motion pictures.

John H. Whitney, Sr., for cinematic pioneering.[271]

1986
Awards presented March 30, 1987.

PICTURE

Platoon, Hemdale Film Production, Orion. Produced by Arnold Kopelson.

Children of a Lesser God, Burt Sugarman Production, Paramount. Produced by Burt Sugarman and Patrick Palmer.[272]

Hannah and Her Sisters, Jack Rollins and Charles H. Joffe Production, Orion. Produced by Robert Greenhut.

The Mission, Warner Bros./Goldcrest and Kingsmere Production, Warner Bros. Produced by Fernando Ghia and David Puttnam.

A Room With a View, Merchant Ivory Production for Goldcrest and Cinecom, Cinecom Pictures (United Kingdom). Produced by Ismail Merchant.

ACTOR

Paul Newman in The Color of Money, Touchstone, Buena Vista.

Dexter Gordon in *'Round Midnight,* Warner Bros.

Bob Hoskins in *Mona Lisa,* Island.

William Hurt in *Children of a Lesser God,* Paramount.

James Woods in *Salvador,* Hemdale.

ACTRESS

Marlee Matlin[273] **in Children of a Lesser God, Paramount.**

Jane Fonda in *The Morning After,* 20th Century Fox.

Sissy Spacek in *Crimes of the Heart,* De Laurentiis Entertainment Group.

Kathleen Turner in *Peggy Sue Got Married,* Tri-Star.

Sigourney Weaver in *Aliens,* 20th Century Fox.

SUPPORTING ACTOR

Michael Caine in Hannah and Her Sisters, Orion.

Tom Berenger in *Platoon,* Orion.

Willem Dafoe in *Platoon,* Orion.

Denholm Elliott in *A Room With a View,* Merchant Ivory, Cinecom.

Dennis Hopper in *Hoosiers,* Orion.

SUPPORTING ACTRESS

Dianne Wiest in Hannah and Her Sisters, Orion.

Tess Harper in *Crimes of the Heart,* De Laurentiis Entertainment Group.

Piper Laurie in *Children of a Lesser God,* Paramount.

Mary Elizabeth Mastrantonio in *The Color of Money,* Touchstone, Buena Vista.

Maggie Smith in *A Room With a View,* Merchant Ivory, Cinecom (United Kingdom).

DIRECTOR

Oliver Stone for Platoon, Orion.

Woody Allen for *Hannah and Her Sisters,* Orion.

James Ivory for *A Room With a View,* Merchant Ivory, Cinecom.

Roland Joffe for *The Mission,* Warner Bros.

David Lynch for *Blue Velvet,* De Laurentiis Entertainment Group.

WRITING

(Screenplay Based on Material From Another Medium)

Ruth Prawer Jhabvala for A Room With a View, Merchant Ivory, Cinecom (United Kingdom).

Hesper Anderson and Mark Medoff for *Children of a Lesser God,* Paramount.

Raynold Gideon and Bruce A. Evans for *Stand By Me,* Columbia.

---

[271] Medal of commendation.

[272] First film directed by a woman to be nominated for best picture. Director Randa Haines, however, was not nominated—nor were the next two women who directed best picture nominees, Penny Marshall for *Awakenings* (1990) and Barbra Streisand for *The Prince of Tides* (1991). Not until Jane Campion was nominated as director of best picture nominee *The Piano* (1993) did a film directed by a woman receive nominations in both categories.

[273] At age twenty-one, the youngest person to win an Oscar in a leading role.

Beth Henley for *Crimes of the Heart,* De Laurentiis Entertainment Group.

Richard Price for *The Color of Money,* Touchstone, Buena Vista.

(Screenplay Written Directly for the Screen)

Woody Allen for *Hannah and Her Sisters,* Orion.

Paul Hogan, Ken Shadie, and John Cornell, screenplay; Paul Hogan, story, for *"Crocodile" Dundee,* Paramount (Australia).

Hanif Kureishi for *My Beautiful Laundrette,* Orion Classics (United Kingdom).

Oliver Stone for *Platoon,* Orion.

Oliver Stone and Richard Boyle for *Salvador,* Hemdale Releasing.

CINEMATOGRAPHY

Chris Menges for *The Mission,* Warner Bros.

Jordan Cronenweth for *Peggy Sue Got Married,* Tri-Star.

Don Peterman for *Star Trek IV: The Voyage Home,* Paramount.

Tony Pierce-Roberts for *A Room With a View,* Merchant Ivory, Cinecom (United Artists).

Robert Richardson for *Platoon,* Orion.

ART DIRECTION—SET DECORATION

***A Room With a View,* Merchant Ivory, Cinecom (United Kingdom). Gianni Quaranta, Brian Ackland-Snow; Brian Savegar, Elio Altamura.**

Aliens, 20th Century Fox. Peter Lamont; Crispian Sallis.

The Color of Money, Touchstone, Buena Vista. Boris Leven; Karen A. O'Hara.

Hannah and Her Sisters, Orion. Stuart Wurtzel; Carol Joffe.

The Mission, Warner Bros. Stuart Craig; Jack Stephens.

SOUND

***Platoon,* Orion. John K. Wilkinson, Richard Rogers, Charles "Bud" Grenzbach, and Simon Kaye.**

Aliens, 20th Century Fox. Graham V. Hartstone, Nicolas Le Messurier,

Michael A. Carter, and Roy Charman.

Heartbreak Ridge, Warner Bros. Les Fresholtz, Dick Alexander, Vern Poore, and William Nelson.

Star Trek IV: The Voyage Home, Paramount. Terry Porter, Dave Hudson, Mel Metcalfe, and Gene S. Cantamessa.

Top Gun, Paramount. Donald O. Mitchell, Kevin O'Connell, Rick Kline, and William B. Kaplan.

MUSIC

(Song)

"Take My Breath Away" from *Top Gun,* Paramount. Music by Giorgio Moroder, lyrics by Tom Whitlock.

"Glory of Love" from *The Karate Kid II,* Columbia. Music by Peter Cetera and David Foster, lyrics by Peter Cetera and Diane Nini.

"Life in a Looking Glass" from *That's Life!,* Columbia. Music by Henry Mancini, lyrics by Leslie Bricusse.

"Mean Green Mother From Outer Space" from *Little Shop of Horrors,* Geffen Company through Warner Bros. Music by Alan Menken, lyrics by Howard Ashman.

"Somewhere Out There" from *An American Tail,* Universal. Music by James Horner and Barry Mann, lyrics by Cynthia Weil.

(Original Score)

Herbie Hancock for *'Round Midnight,* Warner Bros.

Jerry Goldsmith for *Hoosiers,* Orion.

James Horner for *Aliens,* 20th Century Fox.

Ennio Morricone for *The Mission,* Warner Bros.

Leonard Rosenman for *Star Trek IV: The Voyage Home,* Paramount.

FILM EDITING

Claire Simpson for *Platoon,* Orion.

Jim Clark for *The Mission,* Warner Bros.

Ray Lovejoy for *Aliens,* 20th Century Fox.

Susan E. Morse for *Hannah and Her Sisters,* Orion.

Billy Weber and Chris Lebenzon for *Top Gun,* Paramount.

COSTUME DESIGN

Jenny Beavan and John Bright for *A Room With a View,* Merchant Ivory, Cinecom (United Kingdom).

Anna Anni and Maurizio Millenotti for *Otello,* Cannon (Italy).

Anthony Powell for *Pirates,* Cannon.

Enrico Sabatini for *The Mission,* Warner Bros.

Theadora Van Runkle for *Peggy Sue Got Married,* Tri-Star.

MAKEUP

Chris Walas and Stephan Dupuis for *The Fly,* 20th Century Fox.

Rob Bottin and Peter Robb-King for *Legend,* Universal.

Michael G. Westmore and Michèle Burke for *The Clan of the Cave Bear,* Warner Bros.

VISUAL EFFECTS

***Aliens,* 20th Century Fox. Robert Skotak, Stan Winston, John Richardson, and Suzanne Benson.**

Little Shop of Horrors, Geffen Company through Warner Bros. Lyle Conway, Bran Ferren, and Martin Gutteridge.

Poltergeist II: The Other Side, MGM. Richard Edlund, John Bruno, Garry Waller, and William Neil.

SOUND EFFECTS EDITING

***Aliens,* 20th Century Fox. Don Sharpe.**

Star Trek IV: The Voyage Home, Paramount. Mark Mangini.

Top Gun, Paramount. Cecelia Hall and George Watters II.

FOREIGN LANGUAGE FILM

***The Assault,* the Netherlands.**

Betty Blue, France.

The Decline of the American Empire, Canada.

My Sweet Little Village, Czechoslovakia.

"38," Austria.

IRVING G. THALBERG MEMORIAL AWARD
Steven Spielberg.

HONORARY AWARDS
**Ralph Bellamy, for his unique
artistry and his distinguished
service to the profession of
acting.
E. M. "Al" Lewis, in appreciation
for outstanding service in
upholding the high standards of
the Academy of Motion Picture
Arts and Sciences.**[274]

1987
Awards presented April 11, 1988.

PICTURE
The Last Emperor, **Hemdale Film
Production, Columbia (United
Kingdom). Produced by Jeremy
Thomas.**
Broadcast News, 20th Century Fox.
Produced by James L. Brooks.
Fatal Attraction, Jaffe/Lansing Production,
Paramount. Produced by Stanley R.
Jaffe and Sherry Lansing.
Hope and Glory, Davros Production
Services, Ltd., Production, Columbia
(United Kingdom). Produced by John
Boorman.
Moonstruck, Patrick Palmer & Norman
Jewison Production, MGM. Produced
by Patrick Palmer and Norman
Jewison.

ACTOR
**Michael Douglas in *Wall Street,* 20th
Century Fox.**
William Hurt in *Broadcast News,* 20th
Century Fox.
Marcello Mastroianni in *Dark Eyes,* Island
(Italy).
Jack Nicholson in *Ironweed,* Tri-Star.
Robin Williams in *Good Morning, Vietnam,*
Touchstone, Buena Vista.

ACTRESS
Cher in *Moonstruck,* MGM.
Glenn Close in *Fatal Attraction,*
Paramount.
Holly Hunter in *Broadcast News,* 20th
Century Fox.
Sally Kirkland in *Anna,* Vestron.
Meryl Streep in *Ironweed,* Tri-Star.

SUPPORTING ACTOR
**Sean Connery in *The Untouchables,*
Paramount.**
Albert Brooks in *Broadcast News,* 20th
Century Fox.
Morgan Freeman in *Street Smart,* Cannon.
Vincent Gardenia in *Moonstruck,* MGM.
Denzel Washington in *Cry Freedom,*
Universal.

SUPPORTING ACTRESS
**Olympia Dukakis in *Moonstruck,*
MGM.**
Norma Aleandro in *Gaby—a True Story,*
Tri-Star.
Anne Archer in *Fatal Attraction,*
Paramount.
Anne Ramsey in *Throw Momma From the
Train,* Orion.
Ann Sothern in *The Whales of August,*
Alive.

DIRECTOR
**Bernardo Bertolucci for *The Last
Emperor,* Columbia (United
Kingdom).**
John Boorman for *Hope and Glory,*
Columbia (United Kingdom).
Lasse Hallström for *My Life as a Dog,*
Skouras (Sweden).
Norman Jewison for *Moonstruck,* MGM.
Adrian Lyne for *Fatal Attraction,*
Paramount.

WRITING
(Screenplay Based on Material From
Another Medium)
**Mark Peploe and Bernardo
Bertolucci for *The Last Emperor,*
Columbia (United Kingdom).**

James Dearden for *Fatal Attraction,*
Paramount.
Lasse Hallström, Reidar Jönsson, Brasse
Brännström, and Per Berglund for *My
Life as a Dog,* Skouras Pictures
(Sweden).
Tony Huston for *The Dead,* Vestron.
Stanley Kubrick, Michael Herr, and
Gustav Hasford for *Full Metal Jacket,*
Warner Bros.
(Screenplay Written Directly for the
Screen)
**John Patrick Shanley for *Moonstruck,*
MGM.**
Woody Allen for *Radio Days,* Orion.
John Boorman for *Hope and Glory,*
Columbia (United Kingdom).
James L. Brooks for *Broadcast News,* 20th
Century Fox.
Louis Malle for *Au Revoir, les Enfants,*
Orion Classics (France).

CINEMATOGRAPHY
**Vittorio Storaro for *The Last
Emperor,* Columbia (United
Kingdom).**
Michael Ballhaus for *Broadcast News,* 20th
Century Fox.
Allen Daviau for *Empire of the Sun,*
Warner Bros.
Philippe Rousselot for *Hope and Glory,*
Columbia (United Kingdom).
Haskell Wexler for *Matewan,* Cinecom.

ART DIRECTION—SET DECORATION
The Last Emperor, **Columbia (United
Kingdom). Ferdinando Scarfiotti;
Bruno Cesari, Osvaldo Desideri.**
Empire of the Sun, Warner Bros. Norman
Reynolds; Harry Cordwell.
Hope and Glory, Columbia (United
Kingdom). Anthony Pratt; Joan
Woolard.
Radio Days, Orion. Santo Loquasto; Carol
Joffe, Les Bloom, George De Titta,
Jr.
The Untouchables, Paramount. Patrizia Von
Brandenstein, William A. Elliott; Hal
Gausman.

---

[274] Medal of commendation.

Frank J. Urioste and John F. Link for *Die Hard*, 20th Century Fox.

COSTUME DESIGN

James Acheson for *Dangerous Liaisons*, Warner Bros.

Milena Canonero for *Tucker: The Man and His Dream*, Paramount.

Deborah Nadoolman for *Coming to America*, Paramount.

Patricia Norris for *Sunset*, Tri-Star.

Jane Robinson for *A Handful of Dust*, New Line.

MAKEUP

Ve Neill, Steve LaPorte, and Robert Short for *Beetlejuice*, Geffen/Warner Bros.

Rick Baker for *Coming to America*, Paramount.

Tom Burman and Bari Dreiband-Burman for *Scrooged*, Paramount.

VISUAL EFFECTS

***Who Framed Roger Rabbit*, Amblin and Touchstone, Buena Vista. Ken Ralston, Richard Williams, Edward Jones, and George Gibbs.**

Die Hard, 20th Century Fox. Richard Edlund, Al DiSarro, Brent Boates, and Thaine Morris.

Willow, MGM. Dennis Muren, Michael McAlister, Phil Tippett, and Chris Evans.

SOUND EFFECTS EDITING

***Who Framed Roger Rabbit*, Amblin and Touchstone, Buena Vista. Charles L. Campbell and Louis L. Edemann.**

Die Hard, 20th Century Fox. Stephen H. Flick and Richard Shorr.

Willow, MGM. Ben Burtt and Richard Hymns.

FOREIGN LANGUAGE FILM

***Pelle the Conqueror*, Denmark.**

Hanussen, Hungary.

The Music Teacher, Belgium.

Salaam Bombay! India.

Women on the Verge of a Nervous Breakdown, Spain.

GORDON E. SAWYER AWARD

Gordon Henry Cook.

HONORARY AWARDS

The National Film Board of Canada, in recognition of its 50th anniversary and its dedicated commitment to originate artistic, creative and technological activity and excellence in every area of film making.

Eastman Kodak Company, in recognition of the company's fundamental contributions to the art of motion pictures during the first century of film history.

SPECIAL ACHIEVEMENT AWARD

Richard Williams for the animation direction of *Who Framed Roger Rabbit*, Amblin and Touchstone, Buena Vista.

1989

Awards presented March 26, 1990.

PICTURE

***Driving Miss Daisy*, Zanuck Company Production, Warner Bros. Produced by Richard D. Zanuck and Lili Fini Zanuck.[276]**

Born on the Fourth of July, A. Kitman Ho & Ixtlan Production, Universal. Produced by A. Kitman Ho and Oliver Stone.

Dead Poets Society, Touchstone Pictures Production in association with Silver Screen Partners IV, Buena Vista. Produced by Steven Haft, Paul Junger Witt, and Tony Thomas.

Field of Dreams, Gordon Company Production, Universal. Produced by Lawrence Gordon and Charles Gordon.

My Left Foot, Ferndale/Granada Production, Miramax (Ireland). Produced by Noel Pearson.

ACTOR

Daniel Day-Lewis in *My Left Foot*, Miramax (Ireland).

Kenneth Branagh in *Henry V*, Renaissance Films in association with BBC, Samuel Goldwyn (United Kingdom).

Tom Cruise in *Born on the Fourth of July*, Universal.

Morgan Freeman in *Driving Miss Daisy*, Warner Bros.

Robin Williams in *Dead Poets Society*, Touchstone, Buena Vista.

ACTRESS

Jessica Tandy[277] in *Driving Miss Daisy*, Warner Bros.

Isabelle Adjani in *Camille Claudel*, Orion Classics (France).

Pauline Collins in *Shirley Valentine*, Paramount (United Kingdom).

Jessica Lange in *Music Box*, Tri-Star.

Michelle Pfeiffer in *The Fabulous Baker Boys*, 20th Century Fox.

SUPPORTING ACTOR

Denzel Washington in *Glory*, Tri-Star.

Danny Aiello in *Do the Right Thing*, Universal.

Dan Aykroyd in *Driving Miss Daisy*, Warner Bros.

Marlon Brando in *A Dry White Season*, MGM.

Martin Landau in *Crimes and Misdemeanors*, Orion.

SUPPORTING ACTRESS

Brenda Fricker in *My Left Foot*, Miramax (Ireland).

Anjelica Huston in *Enemies, a Love Story*, 20th Century Fox.

---

[276] First film since *Grand Hotel*, 1931–32, to win best picture without a nomination for its director (Bruce Beresford).

[277] Less than three months before her eighty-first birthday—she was born June 7, 1909—Tandy becomes the oldest person to win an acting Oscar.

Lena Olin in *Enemies, a Love Story*, 20th Century Fox.

Julia Roberts in *Steel Magnolias*, Tri-Star.

Dianne Wiest in *Parenthood*, Universal.

DIRECTOR

Oliver Stone for *Born on the Fourth of July*, Universal.

Woody Allen for *Crimes and Misdemeanors*, Orion.

Kenneth Branagh for *Henry V*, Samuel Goldwyn.

Jim Sheridan for *My Left Foot*, Miramax (Ireland).

Peter Weir for *Dead Poets Society*, Touchstone, Buena Vista.

WRITING

(Screenplay Based on Material From Another Medium)

Alfred Uhry for *Driving Miss Daisy*, Warner Bros.

Phil Alden Robinson for *Field of Dreams*, Universal.

Jim Sheridan and Shane Connaughton for *My Left Foot*, Miramax (Ireland).

Roger L. Simon and Paul Mazursky for *Enemies, a Love Story*, 20th Century Fox.

Oliver Stone and Ron Kovic for *Born on the Fourth of July*, Universal.

(Screenplay Written Directly for the Screen)

Tom Schulman for *Dead Poets Society*, Touchstone, Buena Vista.

Woody Allen for *Crimes and Misdemeanors*, Orion.

Nora Ephron for *When Harry Met Sally . . .* , Columbia.

Spike Lee for *Do the Right Thing*, Universal.

Steven Soderbergh for *sex, lies, and videotape*, Miramax.

CINEMATOGRAPHY

Freddie Francis for *Glory*, Tri-Star.

Michael Ballhaus for *The Fabulous Baker Boys*, 20th Century Fox.

Robert Richardson for *Born on the Fourth of July*, Universal.

Mikael Solomon for *The Abyss*, 20th Century Fox.

Haskell Wexler for *Blaze*, Touchstone, Buena Vista.

ART DIRECTION—SET DECORATION

***Batman*, Warner Bros. Anton Furst; Peter Young.**

The Abyss, 20th Century Fox. Leslie Dilley; Anne Kuljian.

The Adventures of Baron Munchausen, Columbia (United Kingdom). Dante Ferretti; Francesca Lo Schiavo.

Driving Miss Daisy, Warner Bros. Bruno Rubeo; Crispian Sallis.

Glory, Tri-Star. Norman Garwood; Garrett Lewis.

SOUND

***Glory*, Tri-Star. Donald O. Mitchell, Gregg C. Rudloff, Elliot Tyson, and Russell Williams II.**

The Abyss, 20th Century Fox. Don Bassman, Kevin F. Cleary, Richard Overton, and Lee Orloff.

Black Rain, Paramount. Donald O. Mitchell, Kevin O'Connell, Greg P. Russell, and Keith A. Wester.

Born on the Fourth of July, Universal. Michael Minkler, Gregory H. Watkins, Wylie Stateman, and Tod A. Maitland.

Indiana Jones and the Last Crusade, Paramount. Ben Burtt, Gary Summers, Shawn Murphy, and Tony Dawe.

MUSIC

(Song)

"Under the Sea" from *The Little Mermaid*, Disney, Buena Vista. Music by Alan Menken, lyrics by Howard Ashman.

"After All" from *Chances Are*, Tri-Star. Music by Tom Snow, lyrics by Dean Pitchford.

"The Girl Who Used to Be Me" from *Shirley Valentine*, Paramount (United Kingdom). Music by Marvin Hamlisch, lyrics by Alan Bergman and Marilyn Bergman.

"I Love to See You Smile" from *Parenthood*, Universal. Music and lyrics by Randy Newman.

"Kiss the Girl" from *The Little Mermaid*,

Disney, Buena Vista. Music by Alan Menken, lyrics by Howard Ashman.

(Original Score)

Alan Menken for *The Little Mermaid*, Disney, Buena Vista.

David Grusin for *The Fabulous Baker Boys*, 20th Century Fox.

James Horner for *Field of Dreams*, Universal.

John Williams for *Born on the Fourth of July*, Universal.

John Williams for *Indiana Jones and the Last Crusade*, Paramount.

FILM EDITING

David Brenner and Joe Hutshing for *Born on the Fourth of July*, Universal.

Noëlle Boisson for *The Bear*, Tri-Star (France).

Steven Rosenblum for *Glory*, Tri-Star.

William Steinkamp for *The Fabulous Baker Boys*, 20th Century Fox.

Mark Warner for *Driving Miss Daisy*, Warner Bros.

COSTUME DESIGN

Phyllis Dalton for *Henry V*, Samuel Goldwyn.

Elizabeth McBride for *Driving Miss Daisy*, Warner Bros.

Gabriella Pescucci for *The Adventures of Baron Munchausen*, Columbia (United Kingdom).

Theodor Pistek for *Valmont*, Orion.

Joe I. Tompkins for *Harlem Nights*, Paramount.

MAKEUP

Manlio Rocchetti, Lynn Barber, and Kevin Haney for *Driving Miss Daisy*, Warner Bros.

Dick Smith, Ken Diaz, and Greg Nelson for *Dad*, Universal.

Maggie Weston and Fabrizio Sforza for *The Adventures of Baron Munchausen*, Columbia (United Kingdom).

VISUAL EFFECTS

***The Abyss*, 20th Century Fox. John Bruno, Dennis Muren, Hoyt Yeatman, and Dennis Skotak.**

The Adventures of Baron Munchausen,

Columbia (United Kingdom). Richard Conway and Kent Houston.

Back to the Future Part II, Universal. Ken Ralston, Michael Lantieri, John Bell, and Steve Gawley.

SOUND EFFECTS EDITING
Indiana Jones and the Last Crusade, Paramount. Ben Burtt and Richard Hymns.

Black Rain, Paramount. Milton C. Burrow and William L. Manger.

Lethal Weapon 2, Warner Bros. Robert Henderson and Alan Robert Murray.

FOREIGN LANGUAGE FILM
Cinema Paradiso, Italy.
Camille Claudel, France.
Jesus of Montreal, Canada.
Waltzing Regitze, Denmark.
What Happened to Santiago, Puerto Rico.

JEAN HERSHOLT HUMANITARIAN AWARD
Howard W. Koch.

GORDON E. SAWYER AWARD
Pierre Angenieux.

HONORARY AWARDS
Akira Kurosawa, for accomplishments that have inspired, delighted, enriched and entertained audiences and influenced filmmakers throughout the world.

The members of the engineering committees of the Society of Motion Picture and Television Engineers (SMPTE). By establishing industry standards, they have greatly contributed to making film a primary form of international communication.[278]

1990
Awards presented March 25, 1991.

PICTURE
Dances With Wolves, Tig Production, Orion. Produced by Jim Wilson and Kevin Costner.

Awakenings, Columbia. Produced by Walter F. Parkes and Lawrence Lasker.

Ghost, Howard W. Koch Production, Paramount. Produced by Lisa Weinstein.

The Godfather, Part III, Zoetrope Studios Production, Paramount. Produced by Francis Ford Coppola.

GoodFellas, Warner Bros. Produced by Irwin Winkler.

ACTOR
Jeremy Irons in *Reversal of Fortune,* Warner Bros.

Kevin Costner in *Dances With Wolves,* Orion.

Robert De Niro in *Awakenings,* Columbia.

Gérard Depardieu in *Cyrano de Bergerac,* Orion Classics (France).

Richard Harris in *The Field,* Avenue Pictures (Ireland).

ACTRESS
Kathy Bates in *Misery,* Columbia.

Anjelica Huston in *The Grifters,* Miramax.

Julia Roberts in *Pretty Woman,* Touchstone, Buena Vista.

Meryl Streep in *Postcards From the Edge,* Columbia.

Joanne Woodward in *Mr. & Mrs. Bridge,* Merchant Ivory, Miramax.

SUPPORTING ACTOR
Joe Pesci in *GoodFellas,* Warner Bros.

Bruce Davison in *Longtime Companion,* American Playhouse, Samuel Goldwyn.

Andy Garcia in *The Godfather, Part III,* Paramount.

Graham Greene in *Dances With Wolves,* Orion.

Al Pacino in *Dick Tracy,* Touchstone, Buena Vista.

SUPPORTING ACTRESS
Whoopi Goldberg[279] in *Ghost,* Paramount.

Annette Bening in *The Grifters,* Miramax.

Lorraine Bracco in *GoodFellas,* Warner Bros.

Diane Ladd in *Wild at Heart,* Samuel Goldwyn.

Mary McDonnell in *Dances With Wolves,* Orion.

DIRECTOR
Kevin Costner for *Dances With Wolves,* Orion.

Francis Ford Coppola for *The Godfather, Part III,* Paramount.

Stephen Frears for *The Grifters,* Miramax.

Barbet Schroeder for *Reversal of Fortune,* Warner Bros.

Martin Scorsese for *GoodFellas,* Warner Bros.

WRITING
(Screenplay Based on Material From Another Medium)
Michael Blake for *Dances With Wolves,* Orion.

Nicholas Kazan for *Reversal of Fortune,* Warner Bros.

Nicholas Pileggi and Martin Scorsese for *GoodFellas,* Warner Bros.

Donald E. Westlake for *The Grifters,* Miramax.

Steven Zaillian for *Awakenings,* Columbia.

(Screenplay Written Directly for the Screen)
Bruce Joel Rubin for *Ghost,* Paramount.

Woody Allen for *Alice,* Orion.

Barry Levinson for *Avalon,* Tri-Star.

Whit Stillman for *Metropolitan,* New Line.

Peter Weir for *Green Card,* Buena Vista.

CINEMATOGRAPHY
Dean Semler for *Dances With Wolves,* Orion.

Allen Daviau for *Avalon,* Tri-Star.

Philippe Rousselot for *Henry & June,* Universal.

---

[278] Special commendation.
[279] First African-American woman to win an acting Oscar since Hattie McDaniel, 1939.

Vittorio Storaro for *Dick Tracy*, Touchstone, Buena Vista.

Gordon Willis for *The Godfather, Part III*, Paramount.

ART DIRECTION—SET DECORATION

Dick Tracy, Touchstone, Buena Vista. Richard Sylbert; Rick Simpson.

Cyrano de Bergerac, Orion Classics (France). Ezio Frigerio; Jacques Rouxel.

Dances With Wolves, Orion. Jeffrey Beecroft; Lisa Dean.

The Godfather, Part III, Paramount. Dean Tavoularis; Gary Fettis.

Hamlet, Warner Bros. Dante Ferretti, Francesca Lo Schiavo.

SOUND

Dances With Wolves, Orion. Jeffrey Perkins, Bill W. Benton, Greg Watkins, and Russell Williams II.

Days of Thunder, Paramount. Donald O. Mitchell, Rick Kline, Kevin O'Connell, and Charles Wilborn.

Dick Tracy, Touchstone, Buena Vista. Chris Jenkins, David E. Campbell, D. M. Hemphill, and Thomas Causey.

The Hunt for Red October, Paramount. Don Bassman, Richard Overton, Kevin F. Cleary, and Richard Bryce Goodman.

Total Recall, Tri-Star. Michael J. Kohut, Carlos de Larios, Aaron Rochin, and Nelson Stoll.

MUSIC

(Song)

"Sooner or Later (I Always Get My Man)" from Dick Tracy, Touchstone, Buena Vista. Music and lyrics by Stephen Sondheim.

"Blaze of Glory" from *Young Guns II*, 20th Century Fox. Music and lyrics by Jon Bon Jovi.

"I'm Checkin' Out" from *Postcards From the Edge*, Columbia. Music and lyrics by Shel Silverstein.

"Promise Me You'll Remember" from

The Godfather, Part III, Paramount. Music by Carmine Coppola, lyrics by John Bettis.

"Somewhere in My Memory" from *Home Alone*, 20th Century Fox. Music by John Williams, lyrics by Leslie Bricusse.

(Original Score)

John Barry for Dances With Wolves, Orion.

David Grusin for *Havana*, Universal.

Maurice Jarre for *Ghost*, Paramount.

Randy Newman for *Avalon*, Tri-Star.

John Williams for *Home Alone*, 20th Century Fox.

FILM EDITING

Neil Travis for Dances With Wolves, Orion.

Barry Malkin, Lisa Fruchtman, and Walter Murch for *The Godfather, Part III*, Paramount.

Walter Murch for *Ghost*, Paramount.

Thelma Schoonmaker for *GoodFellas*, Warner Bros.

Dennis Virkler and John Wright for *The Hunt for Red October*, Paramount.

COSTUME DESIGN

Franca Squarciapino for Cyrano de Bergerac, Orion Classics (France).

Milena Canonero for *Dick Tracy*, Touchstone, Buena Vista.

Gloria Gresham for *Avalon*, Tri-Star.

Maurizio Millenotti for *Hamlet*, Warner Bros.

Elsa Zamparelli for *Dances With Wolves*, Orion.

MAKEUP

John Caglione, Jr., and Doug Drexler for Dick Tracy, Touchstone, Buena Vista.

Michèle Burke and Jean-Pierre Eychenne for *Cyrano de Bergerac*, Orion Classics (France).

Ve Neill and Stan Winston for *Edward Scissorhands*, 20th Century Fox.

SOUND EFFECTS EDITING

The Hunt for Red October, Paramount. Cecelia Hall and George Watters II.

Flatliners, Columbia. Charles L. Campbell and Richard Franklin.

Total Recall, Tri-Star. Stephen H. Flick.

FOREIGN LANGUAGE FILM

Journey of Hope, Switzerland.

Cyrano de Bergerac, France.

Ju Dou, China.

The Nasty Girl, Germany.

Open Doors, Italy.

IRVING G. THALBERG MEMORIAL AWARD

Richard D. Zanuck and David Brown.

GORDON E. SAWYER AWARD

Stefan Kudelski.

HONORARY AWARDS

Sophia Loren, one of the genuine treasures of world cinema who, in a career rich with memorable performances, has added permanent luster to our art form.

Myrna Loy, in recognition of her extraordinary qualities both on screen and off, with appreciation for a lifetime's worth of indelible performances.

Roderick T. Ryan, Don Trumbull, and Geoffrey H. Williamson, in appreciation for outstanding service and dedication in upholding the high standards of the Academy of Motion Picture Arts and Sciences.[280]

SPECIAL ACHIEVEMENT AWARD

Eric Brevig, Rob Bottin, Tim McGovern, and Alex Funke for Visual Effects for Total Recall, Tri-Star.

---

[280] Medals of commendation.

1991
Awards presented March 30, 1992.

PICTURE
***The Silence of the Lambs*, Strong Heart/Demme Production, Orion. Edward Saxon, Kenneth Utt, and Ron Bozman.**[281]

Beauty and the Beast, Walt Disney Pictures Production, Buena Vista. Produced by Don Hahn.[282]

Bugsy, TriStar. Produced by Mark Johnson, Barry Levinson, and Warren Beatty.

JFK, Camelot Production, Warner Bros. Produced by A. Kitman Ho and Oliver Stone.

The Prince of Tides, Barwood/Longfellow Production, Columbia. Produced by Barbra Streisand and Andrew Karsch.

ACTOR
Anthony Hopkins in *The Silence of the Lambs,* Orion.

Warren Beatty in *Bugsy,* TriStar.
Robert De Niro in *Cape Fear,* Universal.
Nick Nolte in *The Prince of Tides,* Columbia.
Robin Williams in *The Fisher King,* TriStar.

ACTRESS
Jodie Foster[283] in *The Silence of the Lambs,* Orion.

Geena Davis in *Thelma & Louise,* MGM.
Laura Dern[284] in *Rambling Rose,* Seven Arts.
Bette Midler in *For the Boys,* 20th Century Fox.
Susan Sarandon in *Thelma & Louise,* MGM.

SUPPORTING ACTOR
Jack Palance[285] in *City Slickers,* Columbia.

Tommy Lee Jones in *JFK,* Warner Bros.
Harvey Keitel in *Bugsy,* TriStar.
Ben Kingsley in *Bugsy,* TriStar.
Michael Lerner in *Barton Fink,* 20th Century Fox.

SUPPORTING ACTRESS
Mercedes Ruehl in *The Fisher King,* TriStar.

Diane Ladd in *Rambling Rose,* Seven Arts.
Juliette Lewis in *Cape Fear,* Universal.
Kate Nelligan in *The Prince of Tides,* Columbia.
Jessica Tandy[286] in *Fried Green Tomatoes,* Universal.

DIRECTOR
Jonathan Demme for *The Silence of the Lambs,* Orion.

Barry Levinson for *Bugsy,* TriStar.
Ridley Scott for *Thelma & Louise,* MGM.
John Singleton[287] for *Boyz N the Hood,* Columbia.
Oliver Stone for *JFK,* Warner Bros.

WRITING
(Screenplay Based on Material Previously Produced or Published)
Ted Tally for *The Silence of the Lambs,* Orion.

Pat Conroy and Becky Johnston for *The Prince of Tides,* Columbia.
Fannie Flagg and Carol Sobieski for *Fried Green Tomatoes,* Universal.
Agnieszka Holland for *Europa Europa,* Orion Classics (West Germany/ France/Poland).
Oliver Stone and Zachary Sklar for *JFK,* Warner Bros.

(Screenplay Written Directly for the Screen)
Callie Khouri for *Thelma & Louise,* MGM.

Lawrence Kasdan and Meg Kasdan for *Grand Canyon,* 20th Century Fox.
Richard LaGravenese for *The Fisher King,* TriStar.
John Singleton for *Boyz N the Hood,* Columbia.
James Toback for *Bugsy,* TriStar.

CINEMATOGRAPHY
Robert Richardson for *JFK,* Warner Bros.

Adrian Biddle for *Thelma & Louise,* MGM.
Allen Daviau for *Bugsy,* TriStar.
Stephen Goldblatt for *The Prince of Tides,* Columbia.
Adam Greenberg for *Terminator 2: Judgment Day,* TriStar.

ART DIRECTION—SET DECORATION
***Bugsy,* TriStar. Dennis Gassner; Nancy Haigh.**

Barton Fink, 20th Century Fox. Dennis Gassner; Nancy Haigh.
The Fisher King, TriStar. Mel Bourne; Cindy Carr.
Hook, TriStar. Norman Garwood; Garrett Lewis.
The Prince of Tides, Columbia. Paul Sylbert; Caryl Heller.

SOUND
***Terminator 2: Judgment Day,* TriStar. Tom Johnson, Gary Rydstrom, Gary Summers, and Lee Orloff.**

Backdraft, Universal. Gary Summers, Randy Thom, Gary Rydstrom, and Glenn Williams.
Beauty and the Beast, Disney, Buena Vista.

---

[281] Third film to win the picture, actor, actress, director, and writing awards. The others are *It Happened One Night* (1934) and *One Flew Over the Cuckoo's Nest* (1975).

[282] Only completely animated feature to be nominated for best picture.

[283] Foster and Luise Rainer (1936, 1937) are the only performers to win two acting Oscars while still under thirty.

[284] Dern's mother, Diane Ladd, is nominated for supporting actress, the only time a mother and daughter have received simultaneous acting nominations.

[285] Palance's previous nomination was in 1953, giving him a tie with Helen Hayes (1931–32, 1970) as the actors who went the longest between nominations. Henry Fonda (1940, 1981) actually went longer but received an interim nomination as producer of *12 Angry Men* (1957).

[286] At eighty-two, the oldest person to be nominated for acting.

[287] At twenty-three, the youngest person (as well as the only African-American) to be nominated for directing.

Terry Porter, Mel Metcalfe, David J. Hudson, and Doc Kane.

JFK, Warner Bros. Michael Minkler, Gregg Landaker, and Tod A. Maitland.

The Silence of the Lambs, Orion. Tom Fleischman and Christopher Newman.

MUSIC

(Song)

"Beauty and the Beast" from *Beauty and the Beast,* Disney, Buena Vista. Music by Alan Menken, lyrics by Howard Ashman.[288]

"Be Our Guest" from *Beauty and the Beast,* Disney, Buena Vista. Music by Alan Menken, lyrics by Howard Ashman.

"Belle" from *Beauty and the Beast,* Disney, Buena Vista. Music by Alan Menken, lyrics by Howard Ashman.

"(Everything I Do) I Do It for You" from *Robin Hood: Prince of Thieves,* Warner Bros. Music by Michael Kamen, lyrics by Bryan Adams and Robert John Lange.

"When You're Alone" from *Hook,* TriStar. Music by John Williams, lyrics by Leslie Bricusse.

(Original Score)

Alan Menken for *Beauty and the Beast,* Disney, Buena Vista.

George Fenton for *The Fisher King,* TriStar.

James Newton Howard for *The Prince of Tides,* Columbia.

Ennio Morricone for *Bugsy,* TriStar.

John Williams for *JFK,* Warner Bros.

FILM EDITING

Joe Hutshing and Pietro Scalia for *JFK,* Warner Bros.

Conrad Buff, Mark Goldblatt, and Richard A. Harris for *Terminator 2: Judgment Day,* TriStar.

Gerry Hambling for *The Commitments,* 20th Century Fox (United Kingdom).

Craig McKay for *The Silence of the Lambs,* Orion.

Thom Noble for *Thelma & Louise,* MGM.

COSTUME DESIGN

Albert Wolsky for *Bugsy,* TriStar.

Richard Hornung for *Barton Fink,* 20th Century Fox.

Corinne Jorry for *Madame Bovary,* Samuel Goldwyn (France).

Ruth Myers for *The Addams Family,* Paramount.

Anthony Powell for *Hook,* TriStar.

MAKEUP

Stan Winston and Jeff Dawn for *Terminator 2: Judgment Day,* TriStar.

Michael Mills, Edward French, and Richard Snell for *Star Trek VI: The Undiscovered Country,* Paramount.

Christina Smith, Monty Westmore, and Greg Cannom for *Hook,* TriStar.

VISUAL EFFECTS

Terminator 2: Judgment Day, TriStar. Dennis Muren, Stan Winston, Gene Warren, Jr., and Robert Skotak.

Backdraft, Universal. Mikael Salomon, Allen Hall, Clay Pinney, and Scott Farrar.

Hook, TriStar. Eric Brevig, Harley Jessup, Mark Sullivan, and Michael Lantieri.

SOUND EFFECTS EDITING

Terminator 2: Judgment Day, TriStar. Gary Rydstrom and Gloria S. Borders.

Backdraft, Universal. Gary Rydstrom and Richard Hymns.

Star Trek VI: The Undiscovered Country, Paramount. George Watters II and F. Hudson Miller.

FOREIGN LANGUAGE FILM

Mediterraneo, Italy.

Children of Nature, Iceland.

The Elementary School, Czechoslovakia.

The Ox, Sweden.

Raise the Red Lantern, Hong Kong.

IRVING G. THALBERG MEMORIAL AWARD

George Lucas.

GORDON E. SAWYER AWARD

Ray Harryhausen.

HONORARY AWARDS

Satyajit Ray, in recognition of his rare mastery of the art of motion pictures, and of his profound humanitarian outlook, which has had an indelible influence on filmmakers and audiences throughout the world.

Pete Comandini, Richard T. Dayton, Donald Hagans, and Richart T. Ryan of YCM Laboratories for the creation and development of a motion picture film restoration process using liquid gate and registration correction on a contact printer.[289]

Richard J. Stumpf and Joseph Westheimer for outstanding service and dedication in upholding the high standards of the Academy of Motion Picture Arts and Sciences.[290]

1992

Awards presented March 29, 1993.

PICTURE

Unforgiven, Warner Bros. Produced by Clint Eastwood.

The Crying Game, Palace Pictures Production, Miramax (United Kingdom). Produced by Stephen Woolley.

A Few Good Men, Castle Rock Entertainment Production, Columbia. Produced by David Brown, Rob Reiner, and Andrew Scheinman.

---

[288] The award to Ashman was presented posthumously.
[289] They received a special plaque.
[290] Medals of commendation.

Howards End, Merchant Ivory Productions, Sony Pictures Classics (United Kingdom/U.S.). Produced by Ismail Merchant.

Scent of a Woman, Universal Release/City Light Films Production, Universal. Produced by Martin Brest.

ACTOR

Al Pacino[291] in *Scent of a Woman*, Universal.

Robert Downey, Jr., in *Chaplin*, TriStar.

Clint Eastwood in *Unforgiven*, Warner Bros.

Stephen Rea in *The Crying Game*, Palace Pictures, Miramax (United Kingdom).

Denzel Washington in *Malcolm X*, Warner Bros.

ACTRESS

Emma Thompson in *Howards End*, Merchant Ivory, Sony Pictures Classics (United Kingdom/U.S.).

Catherine Deneuve in *Indochine*, Sony Pictures Classics (France).

Mary McDonnell in *Passion Fish*, Miramax.

Michelle Pfeiffer in *Love Field*, Orion.

Susan Sarandon in *Lorenzo's Oil*, Universal (Australia).

SUPPORTING ACTOR

Gene Hackman in *Unforgiven*, Warner Bros.

Jaye Davidson in *The Crying Game*, Palace Pictures, Miramax (United Kingdom).

Jack Nicholson[292] in *A Few Good Men*, Columbia.

Al Pacino in *Glengarry Glen Ross*, New Line.

David Paymer in *Mr. Saturday Night*, Columbia.

SUPPORTING ACTRESS

Marisa Tomei in *My Cousin Vinny*, 20th Century Fox.

Judy Davis in *Husbands and Wives*, TriStar.

Joan Plowright in *Enchanted April*, Miramax (United Kingdom).

Vanessa Redgrave in *Howards End*, Merchant Ivory, Sony Pictures Classics (United Kingdom/U.S.).

Miranda Richardson in *Damage*, New Line (United Kingdom/France).

DIRECTOR

Clint Eastwood for *Unforgiven*, Warner Bros.

Robert Altman for *The Player*, Fine Line.

Martin Brest for *Scent of a Woman*, Universal.

James Ivory for *Howards End*, Merchant Ivory, Sony Pictures Classics (United Kingdom/U.S.).

Neil Jordan for *The Crying Game*, Miramax (United Kingdom).

WRITING

(Screenplay Based on Material Previously Produced or Published)

Ruth Prawer Jhabvala for *Howards End*, Merchant Ivory, Sony Pictures Classics (United Kingdom/U.S.).

Peter Barnes for *Enchanted April*, Miramax (United Kingdom).

Richard Friedenberg for *A River Runs Through It*, Columbia.

Bo Goldman for *Scent of a Woman*, Universal.

Michael Tolkin for *The Player*, Fine Line.

(Screenplay Written Directly for the Screen)

Neil Jordan for *The Crying Game*, Miramax (United Kingdom).

Woody Allen for *Husbands and Wives*, TriStar.

George Miller and Nick Enright for *Lorenzo's Oil*, Universal (Australia).

David Webb Peoples for *Unforgiven*, Warner Bros.

John Sayles for *Passion Fish*, Miramax.

CINEMATOGRAPHY

Philippe Rousselot for *A River Runs Through It*, Columbia.

Stephen H. Burum for *Hoffa*, 20th Century Fox.

Robert Fraisse for *The Lover*, MGM/United Artists (United Kingdom/France).

Jack N. Green for *Unforgiven*, Warner Bros.

Tony Pierce-Roberts for *Howards End*, Merchant Ivory, Sony Pictures Classics (United Kingdom/U.S.).

ART DIRECTION—SET DECORATION

***Howards End*, Merchant Ivory, Sony Pictures Classics (United Kingdom/U.S.). Luciana Arrighi; Ian Whittaker.**

Bram Stoker's Dracula, Columbia. Thomas Sanders; Garrett Lewis.

Chaplin, TriStar. Stuart Craig; Chris A. Butler.

Toys, 20th Century Fox. Ferdinando Scarfiotti; Linda DeScenna.

Unforgiven, Warner Bros. Henry Bumstead; Janice Blackie-Goodine.

SOUND

***The Last of the Mohicans*, 20th Century Fox. Chris Jenkins, Doug Hemphill, Mark Smith, and Simon Kaye.**

Aladdin, Disney, Buena Vista. Terry Porter, Mel Metcalfe, David J. Hudson, and Doc Kane.

A Few Good Men, Columbia. Kevin O'Connell, Rick Kline, and Bob Eber.

Under Siege, Warner Bros. Don Mitchell, Frank A. Montano, Rick Hart, and Scott Smith.

Unforgiven, Warner Bros. Les Fresholtz, Vern Poore, Dick Alexander, and Rob Young.

---

[291] First person to receive simultaneous nominations for both a leading and a supporting role and to win the Oscar for the leading role. All previous simultaneous nominees won for supporting performances: Fay Bainter (1938), Teresa Wright (1942), Barry Fitzgerald (1944), and Jessica Lange (1982). Holly Hunter (1993) subsequently also won for a leading role while also nominated for a supporting performance.

[292] With his tenth nomination, Nicholson ties Bette Davis and Laurence Olivier in number of acting nominations. Only Katharine Hepburn, with twelve nominations, has more.

MUSIC

(Song)

"A Whole New World" from *Aladdin*, Disney, Buena Vista. Music by Alan Menken, lyrics by Tim Rice.

"Beautiful Maria of My Soul" from *The Mambo Kings*, Warner Bros. Music by Robert Kraft, lyrics by Arne Glimcher.

"Friend Like Me" from *Aladdin*, Disney, Buena Vista. Music by Alan Menken, lyrics by Howard Ashman.

"I Have Nothing" from *The Bodyguard*, Warner Bros. Music by David Foster, lyrics by Linda Thompson.

"Run to You" from *The Bodyguard*, Warner Bros. Music by Jud Friedman, lyrics by Allan Rich.

(Original Score)

Alan Menken[293] for *Aladdin*, Disney, Buena Vista.

John Barry for *Chaplin*, TriStar.

Jerry Goldsmith for *Basic Instinct*, TriStar.

Mark Isham for *A River Runs Through It*, Columbia.

Richard Robbins for *Howards End*, Merchant Ivory, Sony Pictures Classics (United Kingdom/U.S.).

FILM EDITING

Joel Cox for *Unforgiven*, Warner Bros.

Robert Leighton for *A Few Good Men*, Columbia.

Kant Pan for *The Crying Game*, Miramax (United Kingdom).

Geraldine Peroni for *The Player*, Fine Line.

Frank J. Urioste for *Basic Instinct*, TriStar.

COSTUME DESIGN

Eiko Ishioka for *Bram Stoker's Dracula*, Columbia.

Jenny Beavan and John Bright for *Howards End*, Merchant Ivory, Sony Pictures Classics (United Kingdom/U.S.).

Ruth Carter for *Malcolm X*, Warner Bros.

Sheena Napier for *Enchanted April*, Miramax (United Kingdom).

Albert Wolsky for *Toys*, 20th Century Fox.

MAKEUP

Greg Cannom, Michèle Burke, and Matthew W. Mungle for *Bram Stoker's Dracula*, Columbia.

Ve Neill, Greg Cannom, and John Blake for *Hoffa*, 20th Century Fox.

Ve Neill, Ronnie Specter, and Stan Winston for *Batman Returns*, Warner Bros.

VISUAL EFFECTS

***Death Becomes Her*, Universal. Ken Ralston, Doug Chiang, Doug Smythe, and Tom Woodruff, Jr.**

Alien³, 20th Century Fox. Richard Edlund, Alec Gillis, Tom Woodruff, Jr., and George Gibbs.

Batman Returns, Warner Bros. Michael Fink, Crag Barron, John Bruno, and Dennis Skotak.

SOUND EFFECTS EDITING

***Bram Stoker's Dracula*, Columbia. Tom C. McCarthy and David E. Stone.**

Aladdin, Disney, Buena Vista. Mark Mangini.

Under Siege, Warner Bros. John Leveque and Bruce Stambler.

FOREIGN LANGUAGE FILM[294]

***Indochine*, France.**

Close to Eden, Russia.

Daens, Belgium.

Schtonk, Germany.

JEAN HERSHOLT HUMANITARIAN AWARD[295]

Audrey Hepburn.

Elizabeth Taylor.

GORDON E. SAWYER AWARD

Erich Kaestner.

HONORARY AWARDS

Federico Fellini, in recognition of his place as one of the screen's master storytellers.

Petro Vlahos, in appreciation for outstanding service and dedication in upholding the high standards of the Academy of Motion Picture Arts and Sciences.[296]

1993

Awards presented March 21, 1994.

PICTURE

***Schindler's List*, Universal Pictures/ Amblin Entertainment Production, Universal. Produced by Steven Spielberg, Gerald R. Molen, and Branko Lustig.**

The Fugitive, Warner Bros. Produced by Arnold Kopelson.

In the Name of the Father, Hell's Kitchen/ Gabriel Byrne Production; Universal (Ireland). Produced by Jim Sheridan.

The Piano, Jan Chapman & CIBY 2000 Production, Miramax (Australia/ France). Produced by Jan Chapman.

The Remains of the Day, Mike Nichols/ John Calley/Merchant Ivory Production, Columbia. Produced by Mike Nichols, John Calley, and Ismail Merchant.

---

[293] Menken, who also received the scoring and song awards the previous year, for *Beauty and the Beast*, becomes only the second person in Oscar history to receive more than one Oscar two years in a row. The first sequential multiple winner was Joseph L. Mankiewicz, who won both directing and writing awards for *A Letter to Three Wives* (1949) and *All About Eve* (1950).

[294] *A Place in the World*, Uruguay, originally announced as a nominee, was disqualified when it was discovered that the film was not actually produced in Uruguay.

[295] The only time two Hersholt awards have been given in a single year. Hepburn's, the first Hersholt award to be presented posthumously, honored her work with UNICEF. Taylor's was for her work raising funds for AIDS research.

[296] Medal of commendation.

ACTOR

Tom Hanks in *Philadelphia*, TriStar.

Daniel Day-Lewis in *In the Name of the Father*, Universal (Ireland).

Laurence Fishburne in *What's Love Got to Do With It*, Touchstone, Buena Vista.

Anthony Hopkins in *The Remains of the Day*, Columbia (United Kingdom).

Liam Neeson in *Schindler's List*, Universal.

ACTRESS

Holly Hunter in *The Piano*, Miramax (Australia/France).[297]

Angela Bassett in *What's Love Got to Do With It*, Touchstone, Buena Vista.

Stockard Channing in *Six Degrees of Separation*, MGM/United Artists.

Emma Thompson[298] in *The Remains of the Day*, Columbia (United Kingdom).

Debra Winger in *Shadowlands*, Savoy (United Kingdom).

SUPPORTING ACTOR

Tommy Lee Jones in *The Fugitive*, Warner Bros.

Leonardo DiCaprio in *What's Eating Gilbert Grape*, Paramount.

Ralph Fiennes in *Schindler's List*, Universal.

John Malkovich in *In the Line of Fire*, Columbia.

Pete Postlethwaite in *In the Name of the Father*, Universal (Ireland).

SUPPORTING ACTRESS

Anna Paquin in *The Piano*, Miramax (Australia/France).

Holly Hunter in *The Firm*, Paramount.

Rosie Perez in *Fearless*, Warner Bros.

Winona Ryder in *The Age of Innocence*, Columbia.

Emma Thompson in *In the Name of the Father*, Universal (Ireland).

DIRECTOR

Steven Spielberg for *Schindler's List*, Universal.

Robert Altman for *Short Cuts*, Fine Line.

Jane Campion for *The Piano*, Miramax (Australia/France).[299]

James Ivory for *The Remains of the Day*, Columbia (United Kingdom).

Jim Sheridan for *In the Name of the Father*, Universal (Ireland).

WRITING

(Screenplay Based on Material Previously Produced or Published)

Steven Zaillian for *Schindler's List*, Universal.

Jay Cocks and Martin Scorsese for *The Age of Innocence*, Columbia.

Terry George and Jim Sheridan for *In the Name of the Father*, Universal (Ireland).

Ruth Prawer Jhabvala for *The Remains of the Day*, Columbia (United Kingdom).

William Nicholson for *Shadowlands*, Savoy (United Kingdom).

(Screenplay Written Directly for the Screen)

Jane Campion for *The Piano*, Miramax (Australia/France).

Nora Ephron, David S. Ward, and Jeff Arch, screenplay; Jeff Arch, story, for *Sleepless in Seattle*, TriStar.

Jeff Maguire for *In the Line of Fire*, Columbia.

Ron Nyswaner for *Philadelphia*, TriStar.

Gary Ross for *Dave*, Warner Bros.

CINEMATOGRAPHY

Janusz Kaminski for *Schindler's List*, Universal.

Gu Changwei for *Farewell My Concubine*, Miramax (Hong Kong).

Michael Chapman for *The Fugitive*, Warner Bros.

Stuart Dryburgh for *The Piano*, Miramax (Australia/France).

Conrad L. Hall for *Searching for Bobby Fischer*, Paramount.

ART DIRECTION—SET DECORATION

***Schindler's List*, Universal. Allan Starski; Ewa Braun.**

Addams Family Values, Paramount. Ken Adam; Marvin March.

The Age of Innocence, Columbia. Dante Ferretti; Robert J. Franco.

Orlando, Sony Pictures Classics (United Kingdom). Ben Van Os, Jan Roelfs.

The Remains of the Day, Columbia (United Kingdom). Luciana Arrighi; Ian Whittaker.

SOUND

***Jurassic Park*, Universal. Gary Summers, Gary Rydstrom, Shawn Murphy, and Ron Judkins.**

Cliffhanger, TriStar. Michael Minkler, Bob Beemer, and Tim Cooney.

The Fugitive, Warner Bros. Donald O. Mitchell, Michael Herbick, Frank A. Montaño, and Scott D. Smith.

Geronimo: An American Legend, Columbia. Chris Carpenter, D. M. Hemphill, Bill W. Benton, and Lee Orloff.

Schindler's List, Universal. Andy Nelson, Steve Pederson, Scott Millan, and Ron Judkins.

MUSIC

(Song)

"Streets of Philadelphia" from *Philadelphia*, TriStar. Music and lyrics by Bruce Springsteen.

"Again" from *Poetic Justice*, Columbia. Music and lyrics by Janet Jackson, James Harris III, and Terry Lewis.

"The Day I Fall in Love" from *Beethoven's 2nd*, Universal. Music and lyrics by Carole Bayer Sager, James Ingram, and Clif Magness.

"Philadelphia" from *Philadelphia*, TriStar. Music and lyrics by Neil Young.

---

[297] First woman to be simultaneously nominated in both leading-role and supporting performance categories and to win for a leading role. Al Pacino (1992) was the first man to do so.

[298] The first time two performers—Thompson and Holly Hunter—received simultaneous nominations in leading-role and supporting performance categories in a single year. Thompson is the second person to receive simultaneous nominations and to lose in both categories; Sigourney Weaver (1988) was the first.

[299] The second woman to receive a nomination for directing. The first was Lina Wertmüller, 1976.

"A Wink and a Smile" from *Sleepless in Seattle,* TriStar. Music by Marc Shaiman, lyrics by Ramsey McLean. (Original Score)

John Williams for *Schindler's List,* Universal.

Elmer Bernstein for *The Age of Innocence,* Columbia.

Dave Grusin for *The Firm,* Paramount.

James Newton Howard for *The Fugitive,* Warner Bros.

Richard Robbins for *The Remains of the Day,* Columbia (United Kingdom).

FILM EDITING

Michael Kahn for *Schindler's List,* Universal.

Anne V. Coates for *In the Line of Fire,* Columbia.

Gerry Hambling for *In the Name of the Father,* Universal (Ireland).

Veronika Jenet for *The Piano,* Miramax (Australia/France).

Dennis Virkler, David Finfer, Dean Goodhill, Don Brochu, Richard Nord, and Dov Hoenig for *The Fugitive,* Warner Bros.

COSTUME DESIGN

Gabriella Pescucci for *The Age of Innocence,* Columbia.

Jenny Beavan and John Bright for *The Remains of the Day,* Columbia (United Kingdom).

Anna Biedrzycka-Sheppard for *Schindler's List,* Universal.

Janet Patterson for *The Piano,* Miramax (Australia/France).

Sandy Powell for *Orlando,* Sony Pictures Classics (United Kingdom).

MAKEUP

Greg Cannom, Ve Neill, and Yolanda Toussieng for *Mrs. Doubtfire,* 20th Century Fox.

Carl Fullerton and Alan D'Angerio for *Philadelphia,* TriStar.

Christina Smith, Matthew Mungle, and Judy Alexander Cory for *Schindler's List,* Universal.

VISUAL EFFECTS

Jurassic Park, Universal. Dennis Muren, Stan Winston, Phil Tippett, and Michael Lantieri.

Cliffhanger, TriStar. Neil Krepela, John Richardson, John Bruno, and Pamela Easley.

The Nightmare Before Christmas, Touchstone, Buena Vista. Pete Kozachik, Eric Leighton, Ariel Velasco Shaw, and Gordon Baker.

SOUND EFFECTS EDITING

Jurassic Park, Universal. Gary Rdystrom and Richard Hymns.

Cliffhanger, TriStar. Wylie Stateman and Gregg Baxter.

The Fugitive, Warner Bros. John Leveque and Bruce Stambler.

FOREIGN LANGUAGE FILM

Belle Epoque, Spain.

Farewell My Concubine, Hong Kong.

Hedd Wyn, United Kingdom.[300]

The Scent of Green Papaya, Vietnam.

The Wedding Banquet, Republic of China on Taiwan.

JEAN HERSHOLT HUMANITARIAN AWARD

Paul Newman.

GORDON E. SAWYER AWARD

Petro Vlahos.

HONORARY AWARD

Deborah Kerr, in appreciation for a full career's worth of elegant and beautifully crafted performances.

1994

Awards presented March 27, 1995.

PICTURE

***Forrest Gump,* Steve Tisch/Wendy Finerman Production, Paramount. Produced by Wendy Finerman, Steve Tisch, and Steve Starkey.**

Four Weddings and a Funeral, Working Title Production, Gramercy Pictures (United Kingdom). Produced by Duncan Kenworthy.

Pulp Fiction, Band Apart/Jersey Films Production, Miramax. Produced by Lawrence Bender.

Quiz Show, Hollywood Pictures Presentation of a Wildwood Enterprises/Baltimore Pictures Production, Buena Vista. Produced by Robert Redford, Michael Jacobs, Julian Krainin and Michael Nozik.

The Shawshank Redemption, Castle Rock Entertainment Production, Columbia. Produced by Niki Marvin.

ACTOR[301]

Tom Hanks in *Forrest Gump,* Paramount.[302]

Morgan Freeman in *The Shawshank Redemption,* Columbia.

Nigel Hawthorne in *The Madness of King George,* Samuel Goldwyn Company in association with Channel Four (United Kingdom).

Paul Newman in *Nobody's Fool,* Paramount in association with Capella International.

John Travolta in *Pulp Fiction,* Miramax.

ACTRESS

Jessica Lange in *Blue Sky,* Orion.[303]

Jodie Foster in *Nell,* 20th Century Fox.

Miranda Richardson in *Tom & Viv,* Miramax.

Winona Ryder in *Little Women,* Columbia.

---

[300] The first film in the Welsh language to receive a nomination.

[301] First time since the 1938 awards that three of the four Oscars for acting went to previous Oscar winners.

[302] Hanks joins Spencer Tracy (1937, 1938) as the only winners of two consecutive Oscars as best actor. Jason Robards (1976, 1977) won two consecutive supporting actor Oscars. Luise Rainer (1936, 1937) and Katharine Hepburn (1967, 1968) won consecutive best actress awards.

[303] Lange, who won as supporting actress for 1982, joins Meryl Streep (1979, 1982) as the only women to win best actress Oscars after a prior win as supporting actress.

Susan Sarandon in *The Client*, Warner Bros.

SUPPORTING ACTOR

Martin Landau in *Ed Wood*, Buena Vista.

Samuel L. Jackson in *Pulp Fiction*, Miramax.

Chazz Palminteri in *Bullets Over Broadway*, Miramax.

Paul Scofield in *Quiz Show*, Buena Vista.

Gary Sinise in *Forrest Gump*, Paramount.

SUPPORTING ACTRESS

Dianne Wiest in *Bullets Over Broadway*, Miramax.[304]

Rosemary Harris in *Tom & Viv*, Miramax.

Helen Mirren in *The Madness of King George*, Samuel Goldwyn Company in association with Channel Four (United Kingdom).

Uma Thurman in *Pulp Fiction*, Miramax.

Jennifer Tilly in *Bullets Over Broadway*, Miramax.

DIRECTOR

Robert Zemeckis for *Forrest Gump*, Paramount.

Woody Allen for *Bullets Over Broadway*, Miramax.

Krzysztof Kieslowski for *Red*, Miramax (Switzerland/France/Poland).

Robert Redford for *Quiz Show*, Buena Vista.

Quentin Tarantino for *Pulp Fiction*, Miramax.

WRITING

(Screenplay Based on Material Previously Produced or Published)

Eric Roth for *Forrest Gump*, Paramount.

Paul Attanasio for *Quiz Show*, Buena Vista.

Alan Bennett for *The Madness of King George*, Samuel Goldwyn Company in association with Channel Four (United Kingdom).

Robert Benton for *Nobody's Fool*, Paramount in association with Capella International.

Frank Darabont for *The Shawshank Redemption*, Columbia.

(Screenplay Written Directly for the Screen)

Quentin Tarantino, screenplay; Quentin Tarantino and Roger Avary, stories, for *Pulp Fiction*, Miramax.

Woody Allen and Douglas McGrath for *Bullets Over Broadway*, Miramax.

Richard Curtis for *Four Weddings and a Funeral*, Gramercy Pictures (United Kingdom).

Krzysztof Piesiewicz and Krzysztof Kieslowski for *Red*, Miramax (Switzerland/France/Poland).

Frances Walsh and Peter Jackson for *Heavenly Creatures*, Miramax (New Zealand).

CINEMATOGRAPHY

John Toll for *Legends of the Fall*, TriStar.

Don Burgess for *Forrest Gump*, Paramount.

Roger Deakins for *The Shawshank Redemption*, Columbia.

Owen Roizman for *Wyatt Earp*, Warner Bros.

Piotr Sobocinski for *Red*, Miramax (Switzerland/France/Poland).

ART DIRECTION—SET DECORATION

The Madness of King George, Samuel Goldwyn Company in association with Channel Four (United Kingdom). Ken Adam; Carolyn Scott.

Bullets Over Broadway, Miramax. Santo Loquasto; Susan Bode.

Forrest Gump, Paramount. Rick Carter; Nancy Haigh.

Interview With the Vampire, Geffen Pictures through Warner Bros. Dante Ferretti; Francesca Lo Schiavo.

Legends of the Fall, TriStar. Lilly Kilvert; Dorree Cooper.

SOUND

Speed, 20th Century Fox. Gregg Landaker, Steve Maslow, Bob Beemer, and David R. B. MacMillan.

Clear and Present Danger, Paramount. Donald O. Mitchell, Michael Herbick, Frank A. Montaño, and Arthur Rochester.

Forrest Gump, Paramount. Randy Thom, Tom Johnson, Dennis Sands, and William B. Kaplan.

Legends of the Fall, TriStar. Paul Massey, David Campbell, Christopher David, and Douglas Ganton.

The Shawshank Redemption, Columbia. Robert J. Litt, Elliot Tyson, Michael Herbick, and Willie Burton.

MUSIC

(Song)

"Can You Feel the Love Tonight" from *The Lion King*, Buena Vista. Music by Elton John, lyrics by Tim Rice.

"Circle of Life" from *The Lion King*, Buena Vista. Music by Elton John, lyrics by Tim Rice.

"Hakuna Matata" from *The Lion King*, Buena Vista. Music by Elton John, lyrics by Tim Rice.

"Look What Love Has Done" from *Junior*, Universal. Music and lyrics by Carole Bayer Sager, James Newton Howard, James Ingram, and Patty Smyth.

"Make Up Your Mind" from *The Paper*, Universal. Music and lyrics by Randy Newman.

(Original Score)

Hans Zimmer for *The Lion King*, Buena Vista.

Elliot Goldenthal for *Interview With the Vampire*, Geffen Pictures through Warner Bros.

---

[304] Wiest becomes the only woman other than Shelley Winters (1959, 1965) to win two supporting actress Oscars. Her prior win was for *Hannah and Her Sisters* (1986), which like *Bullets Over Broadway* was directed by Woody Allen, making her the only performer to win two acting Oscars under the direction of one person.

Alan Silvestri for *Forrest Gump*, Paramount.

Thomas Newman for *Little Women*, Columbia.

Thomas Newman for *The Shawshank Redemption*, Columbia.

FILM EDITING

Arthur Schmidt for *Forrest Gump*, Paramount.

Richard Francis-Bruce for *The Shawshank Redemption*, Columbia.

Frederick Marx, Steve James, and Bill Haugse for *Hoop Dreams*, Fine Line Features.

Sally Menke for *Pulp Fiction*, Miramax.

John Wright for *Speed*, 20th Century Fox.

COSTUME DESIGN

Lizzy Gardiner and Tim Chappel for *The Adventures of Priscilla, Queen of the Desert*, Gramercy Pictures (Australia).

Colleen Atwood for *Little Women*, Columbia.

Moidele Bickel for *Queen Margot*, Miramax (France).

April Ferry for *Maverick*, Warner Bros.

Jeffrey Kurland for *Bullets Over Broadway*, Miramax.

MAKEUP

Rick Baker, Ve Neill, and Yolanda Toussieng for *Ed Wood*, Buena Vista.

Daniel Parker, Paul Engelen, and Carol Hemming for *Mary Shelley's Frankenstein*, TriStar.

Daniel C. Striepeke, Hallie D'Amore, and Judith A. Cory for *Forrest Gump*, Paramount.

VISUAL EFFECTS

***Forrest Gump*, Paramount. Ken Ralston, George Murphy, Stephen Rosenbaum, and Allen Hall.**

The Mask, New Line. Scott Squires, Steve Williams, Tom Bertino, and John Farhat.

True Lies, 20th Century Fox. John Bruno, Thomas L. Fisher, Jacques Stroweis, and Patrick McClung.

SOUND EFFECTS EDITING

***Speed*, 20th Century Fox. Stephen Hunter Flick.**

Clear and Present Danger, Paramount. Bruce Stambler and John Leveque.

Forrest Gump, Paramount. Gloria S. Borders and Randy Thom.

FOREIGN LANGUAGE FILM

***Burnt by the Sun*, Russia.**

Before the Rain, Former Yugoslav Republic of Macedonia.

Eat Drink Man Woman, Taiwan.

Farinelli: Il Castrato, Belgium.

Strawberry and Chocolate, Cuba.

JEAN HERSHOLT HUMANITARIAN AWARD

Quincy Jones.

IRVING G. THALBERG MEMORIAL AWARD

Clint Eastwood.

HONORARY AWARDS

Michelangelo Antonioni, in recognition of his place as one of the cinema's master visual stylists.

John A. Bonner, in appreciation for outstanding service and dedication in upholding the high standards of the Academy of Motion Picture Arts and Sciences.[305]

---

[305] Medals of Commendation.